The Norton Anthology of English Literature

FIFTH EDITION

THE MAJOR AUTHORS

E. Talbot Donaldson
LATE OF INDIANA UNIVERSITY

Alfred David
PROFESSOR OF ENGLISH, INDIANA UNIVERSITY

Hallett Smith
SENIOR RESEARCH FELLOW, HUNTINGTON LIBRARY

Barbara K. Lewalski
WILLIAM R. KENAN PROFESSOR OF ENGLISH AND OF HISTORY
AND LITERATURE, HARVARD UNIVERSITY

Robert M. Adams
PROFESSOR OF ENGLISH EMERITUS,
UNIVERSITY OF CALIFORNIA AT LOS ANGELES

George M. Logan
PROFESSOR OF ENGLISH, QUEEN'S UNIVERSITY

Samuel Holt Monk
LATE OF THE UNIVERSITY OF MINNESOTA

Lawrence Lipking
PROFESSOR OF ENGLISH AND CHESTER D. TRIPP PROFESSOR OF THE
HUMANITIES, NORTHWESTERN UNIVERSITY

Jack Stillinger
PROFESSOR OF ENGLISH, UNIVERSITY OF ILLINOIS

George H. Ford
JOSEPH H. GILMORE PROFESSOR OF ENGLISH EMERITUS,
UNIVERSITY OF ROCHESTER

Carol T. Christ
PROFESSOR OF ENGLISH, UNIVERSITY OF CALIFORNIA AT BERKELEY

David Daiches
DIRECTOR OF THE INSTITUTE FOR ADVANCED STUDIES,
UNIVERSITY OF EDINBURGH

Jon Stallworthy
ANDERSON PROFESSOR OF ENGLISH, CORNELL UNIVERSITY

The Norton Anthology
of English Literature

FIFTH EDITION

THE MAJOR AUTHORS

M. H. Abrams, *General Editor*

CLASS OF 1916 PROFESSOR OF ENGLISH EMERITUS,
CORNELL UNIVERSITY

W · W · NORTON & COMPANY · *New York* · *London*

Printed in the United States of America

Fifth Edition

The text of this book is composed in Electra, with display type set in Bernhard Modern. Composition by Vail-Ballou. Manufacturing by R. R. Donnelley. Book design by Antonina Krass.

Library of Congress Cataloging-in-Publication Data

The Norton anthology of English literature. The major authors.

A selection of writings of 34 authors from the 5th ed. of the 2-vol. Norton anthology of English literature, c1986
Bibliography: p.
Includes index.
1. English literature.   I. Abrams, M. H. (Meyer Howard), 1912-
II. Norton anthology of English literature.
PR1109.N64   1987   820'.8   86-23646

ISBN 0-393-95562-1

ISBN 0-393-95563-X PBK.

W. W. Norton & Company Inc., 500 Fifth Avenue, New York, N.Y. 10110
W. W. Norton & Company Ltd., 10 Coptic Street, London WC1A 1PU

1 2 3 4 5 6 7 8 9 0

Contents

The Sixteenth Century (1485–1603)   239

BEN JONSON (1572–1637)   623

The Restoration and the Eighteenth
Century (1660–1798)

WILLIAM WORDSWORTH (1770–1850)   1367

The Twentieth Century   2195

Preface

This anthology is a selection of the best and most characteristic writings of thirty-four major authors, reprinted (with a few exceptions noted below) from the fifth edition of the two-volume *Norton Anthology of English Literature*. It also includes a biographical and critical headnote for each author, as well as an introduction to each literary period which sets out the historical and social context and clarifies the relations of individual authors to earlier writings and to the literary and intellectual events of their own era.

The anthology has from its origins been based on the experience of its editors in actually teaching an introduction to English literature, and each edition has been tested by them in the classroom. They continue to be guided by the principles established for the first edition. These are: (1) that the selections make possible a study in some depth of the major British writers in verse and prose (exceptions are novelists and some dramatists whose major works are too long for inclusion); (2) that as many works as space allows be reprinted in their entirety, and that the representation be abundant enough to permit instructors to select from the total those authors and works that each one prefers to teach; (3) that the student be given the most reliable texts available, edited so as to make them readily accessible, and printed in a format that is easy to the hand and inviting to the eye; (4) that the introductions and glosses be adequate to free the student from dependence on reference books, so that the anthology may be read anywhere—in one's room, in a coffee lounge, on a bus, or under a tree; (5) that the anthology be comfortably portable, for if students won't bring the book to class, lectures are hindered and discussions made profitless.

A vital literary culture, however, is always on the move. The policy, accordingly, has been to provide periodic revisions designed to take advantage of improved texts, as well as to stay current with new developments in criticism, the changing interests of readers, and evolving cultural and intellectual concerns. It is now more than a decade since the last Major Authors edition, and two developments have made this an especially propitious time for a revision. First, the original editorial staff has been enlarged with a younger generation of women and men who have worked closely with the founding editors in preparing the present volume. In addition, the two parent volumes of the anthology have been redesigned and reset in a more readable type, thereby making it feasible to introduce extensive changes in the texts. As a result of these developments, the choice of selections has been carefully reconsidered, and the introductions, headnotes, and footnotes have been revised and in some instances totally rewritten.

In revising the Major Authors edition, we have benefited from a steady flow of suggestions by teachers and students, as well as from opinions about the works hitherto included, and proposals for additions or replacements, that were solicited from scores of teachers who use the anthology in their courses. The present volume is thus the product of an ongoing collaboration among editors, teachers, and students, in a way that ensures the inclusion of texts that instructors want to teach, and not simply those the editors have chosen for them. The anthology has reached the limit of pages possible in a single volume. Some selections which, as our canvass revealed, were assigned infrequently or not at all have therefore had to be dropped, in order to make space for widely requested additions, or else for supplementing or completing works hitherto represented by more limited excerpts. An overview here of the more important innovations may help the instructor to appraise the opportunities that this new version provides.

One author who was little assigned, Thomas Carlyle, has been dropped, but has been replaced by four new authors, often requested, who greatly expand the range of voices, forms, and subjects contained in the anthology: Christopher Marlow (represented by *Dr. Faustus*), Elizabeth Barrett Browning (including extensive selections from *Aurora Leigh*, her equivalent of Wordsworth's *Prelude*), Virginia Woolf (three short stories, a critical essay, a selection from her trailblazing *A Room of One's Own*, and an essential memoir), and Dylan Thomas. Some writings by E. B. Browning and Woolf, not in the two parent volumes, have been added to this Major Authors edition.

The prose translation of the complete *Beowulf* by E. Talbot Donaldson, acclaimed for its accuracy and verve, has been supplemented by a translation in verse by Alfred David of the poignant "Last Survivor's Speech," side by side with the Old English text, to give the student a sense of the strong beat and emphatic alliteration of the original versification. Spenser's "Mutabilitie Cantos," which most teachers found too demanding for use in an introductory course, have been dropped; but the first Book of *The Faerie Queene* remains complete; October in *The Shepheardes Calendar* has been replaced by the more interesting *Aprill*; and the sonnets from *Amoretti* have been reselected and expanded. In response to numerous requests, Shakespeare's *King Lear* has been replaced by *Henry IV, Part 1* (if supplementary plays are wanted, reliable texts are readily available in low-priced paperbacks), and some of Shakespeare's finest sonnets have been added, to make a total of twenty-nine. Donne and Jonson are better represented by revised and (especially for Jonson) expanded selections. Milton's *Samson Agonistes*, very rarely assigned, has been omitted, but *Paradise Lost* is now represented not only by the complete Books 1, 2, and 9, but also by the addition to our earlier selections of almost 900 lines from Books 4, 5, and 8 to fill out the narrative of Adam and Eve before and after the.Fall.

An addition to the earlier selections from Book 3 of *Gulliver's Travels*, "A Voyage to Laputa," together with all of the other three books, now makes this masterpiece virtually complete. Pope's *Eloisa to Abelard* has been replaced by Part 3 of his *Essay on Criticism*, to supplement Parts 1 and 2. Samuel Johnson's eminently teachable *Rasselas*, we are glad to announce, is now entire, and Johnson's other writings have been supplemented by selections from the preface to his *Dictionary of the English Language* and a short anthology of its most celebrated definitions, as well as by two *Rambler* essays on literary subjects. The selections from Blake have been strengthened, and the short excerpts from *Jerusalem* have been replaced by the whole of his earlier "prophetic book," *Visions of the Daughters of Albion*, with its radical presentation, fascinating to students, of the parallels between black slavery and the sexual and social oppression of women. When in the last edition of this anthology we included Wordsworth's *Two-Part Prelude* of 1799, it was not available elsewhere; its ready accessibility now has made it possible to replace it by the addition of 1,400 lines to the author's final version of *The Prelude* in 1850. Books 1, 2, and 12 are now complete (it should be noted that the first and second books, together with the passage on "spots of time" in Book 12, incorporate almost all of the original *Two-Part Prelude*). The other books have also been supplemented, both to include Wordsworth's superlative passages—readily locatable, for selective assignment, by the invented subtitles that have been added to the table of contents—and to bring out more adequately the overall design of Wordsworth's autobiography of imaginative crisis, recovery, and the discovery of his poetic vocation. Also added is the remarkable *Nutting*, originally planned to be incorporated in *The Prelude*. We have omitted Keats's fragmentary *Fall of Hyperion*, since it was almost never assigned, but have added two more of the remarkable letters that illuminate his life and his intellectual and poetic development.

The selections from Tennyson's *In Memoriam* have been improved, and *Maud* has been considerably augmented; the representation of Browning's dramatic monologues has been made more inclusive by the addition of *A Woman's Last Word* and *Karshish*; the selections from Hopkins have been strengthened, shifted back to their chronological position among the Victorians, and furnished with a new introduction. Hardy, Lawrence, and Auden have, we think, been improved. At the urgent request of many instructors we reprint, in place of shorter and lesser stories, the undisputed masterworks, Conrad's *Heart of Darkness* and Joyce's *The Dead*. We have also replaced fragmented selections from Samuel Beckett with a complete and characteristic drama, *Happy Days*. At the end of the volume, we have added two visual aids that will be useful to students—exterior and interior views of a London playhouse of Shakespeare's time, drawn especially for us by C. Walter Hodges, author of *The Globe Restored*, and a schematic drawing of the Ptolemaic universe. Finally, a new supplementary section, "Poems in Process," includes exact transcriptions of working drafts, letters, and early printed versions, to show the different ways in which ten poets, from Milton to Yeats and Lawrence, have worked their initial sketches into a final text. Such drafts, of great interest to students, may be used either in special sections of a course, or else referred to when teaching a poem in its final form; to facilitate the latter procedure, there is a footnote reference under each of the eleven poems in the body of the anthology for which earlier versions are made available.

In accord with the policy that students deserve the most accurate texts available, we continue to introduce improved versions of the works we reprint—in this volume, Wordsworth's *Ruined Cottage* and *The Prelude* from the Cornell Wordsworth; Shelley's texts from *Shelley's Poetry and Prose*, edited by Donald H. Reiman and Sharon B. Powers (Norton Critical Edition, 1977); Keats's poems from the edition by Jack Stillinger (Harvard University Press, 1978); and the poems of Gerard Manley Hopkins from the fourth edition edited by W. H. Gardner and N. H. MacKenzie (Oxford University Press). To ease a student's access to all the other texts, we have normalized spelling and capitalization according to modern usage. There are, however, two large-scale exceptions: (1) Texts are left in the original spelling if modernizing them would alter the meaning or meter, or would obscure distinctive features of the original. Thus the verse of Spenser and Hopkins and the prose of Keats's letters and of Joyce have been reproduced exactly, and only minor changes in his erratic punctuation have been made in the writings etched by Blake. Chaucer is reprinted in the original language; each word, however, has been spelled consistently in that form of its scribal variants that is closest to modern English. (2) We also leave unchanged the texts we have introduced from new or specially prepared editions: Wordsworth's *Ruined Cottage* and *Prelude*, and the verse and prose of Shelley and Keats.

The paired editors for each period have revised, and sometimes entirely rewritten, the introductory essays, headnotes, and footnotes, to take advantage of recent scholarship as well as to make the editorial materials as tersely and clearly informative as possible. We have minimized commentary that is interpretive rather than, in a very narrow sense, explanatory. It has, however, seemed unwise, in the instance of an especially problematic work or passage, to eliminate any guidance whatever to the student, on the ground that most teachers assign texts which there is not time to discuss adequately—or sometimes to discuss at all—in class. What we undertake, in especially difficult instances, is to suggest possibilities in a way that does not foreclose independent judgment and that provides no more than a point of departure for lectures or dialogue in the classroom.

We retain other procedures that have proved useful in earlier editions. The various introductions, although succinct, eliminate any immediate need for supplementary books on the literary, political, and cultural history of England, or on the lives of individual authors. At the beginning of each introduction we list a few crucial dates by way of preliminary orientation to the student. After each work we cite (when known) the date of composition on the left and that of first publication on the right; in some instances the latter is followed by the date of a revised reprinting. The texts of Chaucer and Spenser, with their large proportion of archaic words, are glossed in the margin so that readers may assimilate the meanings without repeated interruptions to the flow of the reading. In the occasional instances when parts of a work have had to be omitted, that fact is indicated by the word *From* before the title, and the place of the omission is indicated in the text by three asterisks. If the omitted section is important for following the plot or argument, we provide a brief summary of its content, sometimes within the text but usually in a footnote; where the material makes it feasible, we also provide invented titles (bracketed in the text, and also listed in the table of contents) to identify the subject matter of the passages that have been included. Bibliographical guides at the end of the volume, arranged alphabetically, are provided for each author in the anthology. They have been revised and brought up to date, and are kept short, but include brief comments, so that students may know what writings are particularly adapted to their needs, whether for independent reading or as initial references for assigned essays.

The editors are deeply grateful to the hundreds of teachers, both in North America and on other continents, who helped us improve the parent volumes of the fifth edition; we cannot name them all, but each will recognize changes, in the major authors here represented, that he or she suggested. A separate acknowledgments page names (1) those instructors who told us specifically what they like to teach in their major-authors courses; and (2) special critics of the parent volumes. Two of the contributing editors would like to thank their assistants, Jacqueline Doyle and Patsy Griffin, while the publishers gratefully acknowledge the valuable help of Nina Bouis, Sue Crooks, Ruth Dworkin, Diane O'Connor, Nancy Palmquist, Antonina Krass, and Carol Stiles. Our greatest debt is to two members of W. W. Norton and Company, Inc.—George P. Brockway, who first conceived this anthology and greatly aided its accomplishment, and John Benedict, who has been a superb editor and indispensable collaborator in all editions of this work. They have helped greatly to mitigate the chronic dilemmas in trying to represent, in a single volume, the major authors in the incomparably rich and diverse heritage of English literature.

M. H. ABRAMS

Acknowledgments

The following instructors were of especial help in telling us what they teach in their major-authors courses: Nathaniel B. Atwater (Southeastern Massachusetts University); Christopher Baker (Lamar University); R. M. Bedell (Virginia Military Institute); Kenneth Bleeth (Connecticut College); Harry Boardmore (University College of Cape Breton); Kristin Brady (University of Western Ontario); Matthew C. Brennan (Indiana State University); Ursula Carfague (Montgomery County Community College); Janice Carlisle (Washington University); Charles W. Carter (Shepherd College); Howard Cole (University of Illinois); Richard J. Dircks (St. John's University); Roman Dubinski (University of Waterloo); Anthony Farrow (St. Bonaventure University); W. Craig Ferguson (Queen's University); Susan Fox (Queens College); John L. Gaunt (West Chester University); Allan J. Gedalof (University of Western Ontario); Thomas B. Gentry (Virginia Military Institute); Marilyn Georgas (Lamar University); Carolyn Hample (University of Winnipeg); John Mark Heumann (Lamar University); Claude Hunsberger (West Chester University); Glenn James (Florida Southern College); Emily Jensen (Lycoming College); Wayne R. Kime (Fairmont State College); Elaine Kleiner (Indiana State University); Raymond Lott (Florida Southern College); M. MacDonald (Mount Allison University); H. R. MacGallum (University of Toronto); R. G. MacGregor (Dalhousie University); Richard Matlak (College of the Holy Cross); Philip Milner (St. Francis Xavier University); Anne B. Morgan (Fairmont State College); Louise Murdy (Winthrop College); David Nelson (Bates College); Steven Olson (University of Illinois); Dorothy Parker (University of Toronto); A. H. de Quehen (University of Toronto); Stanley Rich (University of South Carolina at Aiken); Michael Shea (Southern Connecticut State University); Michael Shelden (Indiana State University); William W. E. Slights (University of Saskatchewan); Charles H. Vivian (Bentley College); David Ward (University of Pittsburgh at Johnston); Mallory Young (Tarleton State University); Gwendolyn Ziemann (Florida Southern College).

Among our many critics, advisers, and friends, the following were of especial help in providing critiques of particular periods or of the anthology as a whole, or assisted in preparing texts and editorial matter: Paul Alpers (University of California, Berkeley); Lisa Miller Barnes (Queen's University); W. J. Barnes (Queen's University); Stephen A. Barney (University of California, Irvine); David Bevington (University of Chicago); Mary Carruthers (University of Illinois at Chicago); Paul Christianson (Queen's University); R. W. Crump (Louisiana State University); Eugene R. Cunnar (New Mexico State University); Seamus Deane (University College, Dublin); Hubert English, Jr. (University of Michigan); Robert Essick (University of California, Riverside); Barbara C. Ewell (University of Mississippi); Robert D. Fulk (Indiana University); Paul Gabriner (University of Amsterdam); Nancy M. Goslee (University of Tennessee); Donald J. Gray (Indiana University); A. C. Hamilton (Queen's University); Carolyn C. Heilbrun (Columbia University); James R. Kincaid (University of Colorado, Boulder); Hugh Maclean (State University of New York at Albany); Kevin J. McManus (College of William and Mary); Juliet McMaster (University of Alberta); Phillip L. Marcus (Cornell University); Ruth Perry (Massachusetts Institute of Technology); Jonathan Post (University of California, Los Angeles); Stephen Prickett (The Australian National University); John R. Reed (Wayne State University); David G. Riede (University of Rochester); James Rieger (University of Rochester); Sue Sandera Rummel (State University of New York at Canton); Harry Rusche (Emory University); Peter Sabor (Queen's University); Daniel Schwarz (Cornell University); Ronald A. Sharp (Kenyon College); Elain Showalter (Rutgers University); Sandra Siegel (Cornell University); Pincus Silverman (El Centro College); John Tinkler (University of Sydney); and Joseph Viscomi (University of North Carolina at Chapel Hill).

The Middle Ages

to ca. 1485

ca. 450:   Anglo-Saxon Conquest.
597:          St. Augustine arrives in Kent; beginning of Anglo-
              Saxon conversion to Christianity.
871–899:   Reign of King Alfred.
1066:   Norman Conquest.
ca. 1200:   Beginnings of Middle English literature.
1360–1400:   The summit of Middle English literature: Geoffrey
              Chaucer; *Piers Plowman*; *Sir Gawain and the Green
              Knight*.
1485:   William Caxton's printing of Sir Thomas Malory's
              Morte Darthur, one of the first books printed in
              England.

The medieval period in English literature extends for more than 800 years, from Cædmon's *Hymn* at the end of the seventh century to *Everyman* at the beginning of the sixteenth. The date 1485 with the accession of Henry VII to the throne of England is an arbitrary but convenient one to mark the "end" of the Middle Ages. Historians used to divide this period into two parts, unfairly calling the earlier centuries the Dark Ages in order to distinguish them from the later centuries, when European culture attained one of the summits of its history. While the term is misleading—for the Dark Ages were only relatively dark—it is nevertheless true that the English Middle Ages embraced two quite different periods of literary history, the Old English (or Anglo-Saxon) and the Middle English, sharply divided from each other by the Norman duke William's conquest of the island in 1066. Both English culture and the English language changed radically in the years following this event, and English literature developed a new spirit.

Because it is impossible to read the Old English language without a great deal of study, we give *Beowulf* in translation. Chaucer's Middle English text, written in a dialect which is the ancestor of Modern Standard English, appears in the original, but has been spelled in a way that it is hoped will aid the reader. *Sir Gawain and the Green Knight*, written in a more difficult regional Middle English dialect, is given in translation. Analyses of the sounds and grammar of Middle English, and of Old and Middle English prosody, appear at the end of this introduction.

THE OLD ENGLISH PERIOD

THE ANGLO-SAXONS AND THE HEROIC IDEAL

The Anglo-Saxon invasion of the island of Britain which began in the first half of the fifth century was a phase of a great folk migration that had started some centuries earlier and was to continue for several more—the movement of the Germanic tribes from the northeast of Europe into the areas of the Roman Empire to the west, south, and southeast. The so-called Anglo-Saxon invaders of Britain actually consisted of three tribes, the Angles, the Saxons, and the Jutes. Although each was independent, through their common Germanic heritage these tribes were closely allied with one another and with the many other tribes that already had or would in the future overrun much of the old Roman Empire. They shared the same prehistoric ancestors; even in historical times their individual tongues amounted to little other than variant dialects of a common language, while the customs of one tribe differed little from those of another.

In its earliest period Germanic society had been organized by families: the head of the family was the chief of his close kinsmen, and the family formed an independent political entity. With the passing of time, the unit of society tended to grow larger as a number of families united under a single superior chieftain or "king," to use the word derived from the Old Germanic name for chief. But the unit grew to be very large only rarely, when some particularly successful king attracted others to him in order to perform some specific exploit; and such larger unions rarely endured long after the completion of the venture for which they had been formed. The normal order of society was made up of a number of small bands, which, while they did not always live at peace with one another, still shared a sense of community and kinship, especially in the face of a common enemy such as the people whose lands they were invading; but when they had conquered, their natural political divisiveness reasserted itself. Thus long after the Anglo-Saxons had become settled in Britain, the island was still broken up into a bewildering number of kingdoms, some of them very short-lived, and a coherent union of all England was not achieved until after the Norman conquest.

The same general organization of many kings coexisting within a common culture had been characteristic of that other migratory people, the Greeks (or, more accurately, Achaeans), who centuries earlier had overrun the region of the eastern Mediterranean. And both to the Achaeans and to the Germanic peoples the ideal of kingly behavior was enormously important—indeed, it was perhaps the chief spiritual force behind the civilizations they both developed, the creative power that, in their earliest periods, shaped their history and their literature. It is generally called the heroic ideal; and put most simply, the heroic ideal was excellence. The hero-king strove to do better than anyone else the things that an essentially migratory life demanded: to sail a ship through a storm, to swim a river or a bay, to tame a horse, to choose a campsite and set firm defenses, in times of peace even to plow a field or build a hall, but always and above all, to fight. Skill and courage were the primary qualities of a king who should successfully lead his people in battle and sustain them during peace.

In its oldest form, the ideal was appropriate only to kings, but because society was so closely knit, all the more important male members of the tribe tended to imitate it. (Germanic society was wholly dominated by males: women are rarely mentioned in the surviving records of it, and only if they are the wives or daughters of kings.) In general, of course, the heroic ideal of conduct was aristocratic, restricted to the king and his immediate retainers, though without that quality of unreality and remoteness from daily life that we associate with later medieval aristocracy. The king was the active leader of a small number of fellow warriors who, as members of his household, beheld all that he did. A successful king won from his retainers complete loyalty. It was their duty to defend him in battle, to give up their own lives while defending or avenging his. In return the king gave his retainers gifts from the spoil that had been accumulated in warfare. Royal generosity was one of the most important aspects of heroic behavior, for it symbolized the excellence of the king's rule, implying on the one hand that the retainers deserved what they were given because of their loyalty to him, and, on the other, showing that he himself was worthy of such loyalty. The heroic ideal had a very practical bearing on the life of the people whom the king ruled.

While the heroic ideal would win practical success for a king, it had also another, perhaps more important end—enduring fame. In cultures whose religion, unlike Christianity, offers no promise of an afterlife, a name that will live on after one's death serves as the closest substitute for immortality. From this arises the heroic paradox, still latent in our own civilization, that by dying gloriously one may achieve immortality. The poet who could sing the story of his heroic life was, of course, the agent upon whom the hero depended for his fame, and a good poet—or bard, to use the customary term for the poet of heroic life—was a valued member of a primitive court. Alexander is said to have expressed envy of Achilles because he had had a Homer to celebrate his deeds. The poetic form which primitive bards evolved for their heroic narratives is called "epic"; it is characterized by a solemn dignity of tone and elevation of style. Their poems were not written down, but recited aloud from memory, and hence most of them have been lost: in Greek there have survived Homer's two epics, the *Iliad* and the *Odyssey*, while from Germanic culture the chief survivor is the Old English *Beowulf*. But enough has been preserved to show the enduring popularity of heroic stories throughout the migratory phase of the two peoples, who never tired of hearing the deeds of their folk heroes. Thus the immortality that the old heroes had sought was achieved through poetry, and poetry in turn gave inspiration to later men in leading their own lives.

CHRISTIANITY AND OLD ENGLISH CULTURE

Whatever literary materials the Anglo-Saxons brought with them when they came to Britain existed only in their memories, for the making of written records was something they learned only when they were converted to Christianity. The Celtic inhabitants whose land they were seizing were Christians, as had been the Romans whose forces had occupied the island since the first century and whose withdrawal at the beginning of the fifth had opened the way to the Anglo-Saxons; but for one hundred fifty years after the beginning of the invasion Christianity was maintained only in the remoter regions where the Anglo-Saxons failed to penetrate. In the year 597, however, St. Augustine was sent by Pope Gregory as a missionary to King Ethelbert of Kent, one of the most southerly of the kingdoms into which England was divided, and about the same time missionaries from Ireland began to preach Christianity in the north. Within seventy-five years the island was once more predominantly Christian. Ethelbert himself was one of the first Christian converts, and it is indicative of the relationship between

Christianity and writing that the first written specimen of the Old English (Anglo-Saxon) language is a code of laws promulgated by the first English Christian king.

In the centuries that followed up till the Norman Conquest England produced a large number of distinguished, highly literate churchmen. One of the earliest of these was Bede, whose *Ecclesiastical History of the English People*, written in Latin, was completed in 731; this remains our most important source of knowledge about the Anglo-Saxon period. In the next generation Alcuin, a man of wide culture, became the friend and advisor of the Frankish Emperor Charlemagne, whom he assisted in making the Frankish court a great center of learning: thus by the year 800 English culture had developed so richly that it overflowed its insular boundaries. But the greatest impetus on English culture came from a man who was not of the clergy: Alfred, king of the West Saxons from 871 to 899, who for a time united all the kingdoms of southern England and beat off those new Germanic invaders, the Vikings. This most active king was an enthusiastic patron of literature. He himself translated various works from Latin, the most important of which was Boethius' *Consolation of Philosophy*, the early sixth-century Roman work whose heroic stoicism has proved continuingly congenial to the English temperament. Apparently under Alfred's direction Bede's *History* was also translated into Old English, and the *Anglo-Saxon Chronicle* was begun: this year-by-year record of important events in England was maintained until the middle of the twelfth century. Furthermore, the preservation of many of the surviving earlier English works, including *Beowulf*, is due to the fact that copies of them were made in the West Saxon dialect because, in large part, of the impetus Alfred gave to literary studies. Though the political stability that Alfred achieved was not long-lived, the culture he nourished so lovingly was maintained at a high level until the very end of the Old English period.

OLD ENGLISH POETRY

The genius for heroic poetry the Anglo-Saxons brought with them when they came to Britain, as they probably also brought with them the alliterative form (see the section on "Old and Middle English Prosody") in which all the Old English poetry that has survived was composed. Since they wrote nothing down until they had become Christianized, and since in many respects Christian ideals and heroic ideals are difficult to reconcile, it is natural that very little poetry has survived that is surely pre-Christian in composition. But *Beowulf*, the greatest of Germanic epics, contains much evidently pre-Christian material, even though the author of the particular form of the poem that has come down to us was a Christian who refers to events of the Old (but not of the New) Testament. Several other short pieces or fragments also seem to reflect the pagan period without Christian coloring. Yet the vast bulk of Old English poetry is specifically Christian, devoted to religious subjects. Interestingly enough, however, it is almost all in the heroic mode: while the Anglo-Saxons adapted themselves readily to the ideals of Christianity, they did not do so without adapting Christianity to their own heroic ideal. In order to make the alien world of the Bible intelligible to their hearers, Old English poets (almost all of whom are nameless) infused it with many of the values that they had inherited from their own history. Thus Moses and St. Andrew, Christ and God the Father share the attributes of a Beowulf, are represented as heroes who performed famous deeds. In the *Dream of the Rood*, the Cross speaks of Christ as "the young hero, . . .

strong and stouthearted," whose crucifixion is less a passion—a suffering— than a heroic action. In Cædmon's *Hymn* the creation of heaven and earth is seen as a mighty deed, an "establishment of wonders" not altogether unlike Hrothgar's building of the hall Heorot in *Beowulf*. The sad consciousness of the transience of all earthly good combined with the compulsion to go on striving—so characteristic of the heroic spirit—appears most poignantly in two Christian laments, the *Wanderer* and the *Seafarer*. That the heroic ideal held its value down to the end of the Old English period is shown by the *Battle of Maldon*, in which the defeat of English defenders by a band of marauding Vikings is described in the highest tradition of Germanic heroism. Against doom, there is only courage.

The world of Old English poetry is a dark one, and to a modern reader it may also seem a narrow one with narrow laws that exclude all but sardonic laughter. Men in the mead-hall are said to be cheerful, but even there they think of struggle in war, of possible triumph but more possible failure. Romantic love—one of the principal topics of later literature—appears hardly at all. Men seem seldom to relax: clothed in their armor, they are always preparing to test their courage against fate. (They are, indeed, so habitually seen as warriors that in the earlier poetry the words for "man" and "warrior" are often interchangeable.) Depressing as this world may seem, it is recreated in Old English poetry with extraordinary intensity, with high spiritual excitement. This excitement is achieved in part by the frequent use of ironic understatement. Actions and things are spoken of as less than they really are because, apparently, the speaker wishes to suggest that they are more—or perhaps other—than they are. "They cared not for battle," says the author of the *Battle of Maldon* about those cowardly Englishmen who fled the fight. Even the "kenning," that highly formalized compound metaphor common to Old Germanic poetry, often seems to suggest potentials ironically—"whale's road" or "swan's path" for a sea so perilous for men lacking the physical equipment of whales and swans. The dignity the Anglo-Saxons assigned to poetry—which was the repository of the ancient traditions by which they lived—apparently prevented the humor latent in ironic understatement from reaching any expression more overt than a grim smile. Yet despite its somberness, Old English poetry goes about its business of depicting harsh reality with an extraordinary subtlety and intensity.

THE MIDDLE ENGLISH PERIOD

THE NORMAN CONQUEST AND ITS EFFECTS

In the year 1066 England was once more invaded and conquered by a Germanic people, though one whose culture was widely different from the Anglo-Saxons. The Normans—the name is actually a form of "Norsemen"—were the descendants of Scandinavian adventurers who at the beginning of the tenth century had seized a wide part of northern France. A highly adaptable nation, they had adopted the language of the land they had settled in and had set up a powerful state; while its ruler was technically a duke subject to the king of France, Normandy was actually an independent political entity. The invasion of England was led by the energetic Duke William. The English were divided and irresolute; at the decisive Battle of Hastings they were defeated by the Normans and their leader Harold was killed. Thereafter William's forces overran much of England, and the Norman duke became its king and insured the succession to his descendants. But, kings of England though they were, he and his followers were not as much interested in the country he had won (though they were constantly fighting the Welsh, the Scots, and their own barons for control of parts or the whole of it) as they were in their continental possessions. The first seven English kings were mostly absentee rulers—and their presence within the kingdom was seldom less troublesome for it than their absence from it. It was not, indeed, until the thirteenth century, with the reign of Henry III (1216–72) that England became the principal concern of its kings. And it was not until the very end of the Middle Ages that English monarchs finally gave up trying to make good their continental claims and became, perforce, purely English.

The immediate effect of the Norman Conquest upon English literature was to remove it from the care of the aristocracy—the spiritual if not actual descendants of the Anglo-Saxon kings and their retainers—and to deprive it of that cohesive spirit that it had previously possessed. The great aristocratic households, which were the centers of pre-Conquest cultural activity, were broken up or parceled out to the Conqueror's Norman barons, and the English aristocracy was either displaced or forced into service with the invaders. For a considerable time, even the English language seems to have fallen into disuse as a vehicle for written literature, for very little survives of English between the Conquest and the year 1200. Initially, educated people who continued to produce literary works wrote either in Latin or in Anglo-Norman, the dialect of French that was spoken by the new rulers of England. While the practical Normans were less preoccupied with culture than the English, the literature in Anglo-Norman contains several works of distinction, but it was not very long enduring, hardly surviving the reign of Edward I (1272–1307). Latin, which had always been and continued to be the language of the international church, produced a fairly rich literature in England during this period—especially in the twelfth century. But throughout the Middle Ages, Latin literature remained essentially conservative and remote, not much dealing with the subjects that are of importance in the development of vernacular literature. Thus for more than a century the twin snobberies—social on the part of Anglo-Norman, intellectual on the part of Latin—probably preempted the energies of educated authors who might at an earlier or a later time have written in English.

But even if the educated were writing literature in other languages, the uneducated were undoubtedly continuing to compose—if not to write—in English. When written English literature begins to reappear at the end of the twelfth century, the larger part of it carries the stamp of popular or at least semipopular origin; indeed, considered in its bulk, Middle English literature is a popular literature. Its origin in the orders of society below the top provides its most striking contrast with Old English literature: most of the latter seems to be uttered by a single aristocratic voice, grave, decorous, responsible, speaking in terms of high communal aspirations. Middle English literature, on the other hand, is uttered by a medley of different voices, dealing with a wide range of topics in a great diversity of styles and tones and genres. Because its writers addressed themselves to a popular audience, they achieved a greater immediacy, a greater recognizability; a modern reader experiences little difficulty in understanding the world they are talking about. The change is perhaps most obvious in the narrative of adventure, where the idealized hero of Old English yields place to the more sympathetic if less admirable protagonist who not only fights and fights again, but also laughs and cries, plays games, and above all, falls in and out of love—the nonaristocrat was the readier to supplant the epic hero because a mature Christianity places as much value on an ordinary human soul as it does on an epic hero's. In dealing with this new kind of hero the imaginative perspective of popular writers was broadened as much, perhaps, as their ability to see deeply was decreased. And the perspective now included women, who became, finally, recognized as half of the human race. True, they appear ordinarily as stereotypes, whether in romance and love lyric or in antifeminist satire—that enormous body of literature that had its foundation in the monastic culture that dominated so much of European thought in the Middle Ages. But woman's place in society was, in any case, recognized in literature, and this recognition undoubtedly reflects a changing attitude in history itself. There are no arch-feminists in literature before Chaucer's Wife of Bath, but she could never have been invented, even by a Chaucer, unless she had had recognizable forebears, with independent minds and incomes, in Bath and elsewhere before Chaucer's time.

While the portrayal of life in Middle English literature is sometimes shallow, it is nevertheless a life in which we find much that evokes our sympathy. Sometimes, when it is portrayed as lively and gay, colorful, full of surprise, its attractiveness earns our active appreciation, and even when some austere moralist reduces human experience to mere wretchedness we may experience amid the overlying gloom the sudden charm of poignancy. Middle English literature gives an accurate presentation of the details of life that is pleasing and sometimes moving. And humor—the chief virtue of Middle English literature—is apt to flash anywhere, even in the most solemn and foreboding of moralizations.

The conventional character of much Middle English literature is partly due to the attempt by many writers, both religious and secular, to make their works reflect the unchanging principles of medieval Christian doctrine. Until almost the end of the fourteenth century Christian teaching was primarily concerned with the issue of personal salvation, putting more emphasis on the moral and spiritual responsibilities of the individual than it did on his ethical or social responsibilities. Medieval religious idealism characteristically looked to the world to come for the only answer to people's troubles and considered the reformation of this world neither possible nor especially desirable. So constant is the attitude that life in this world is only a waiting period before we enter something better (or worse) that the modern reader is apt to get the impression that the Middle Ages was a period of intellectual and social stasis, a period in which time was standing still. And the fact is that not only in specifically moral and doctrinal literature, whose premises are timeless, but also in ephemeral literature designed merely to provide entertainment one senses this unchangingness: a romance written at the beginning of the thirteenth century differs little from one written in the fifteenth (with which it shares its plot), and at the very end of the period Malory is still peopling with his knights a never-never land of chivalry that had its origin in twelfth-century France.

It is clear enough that between 1066 and 1485 England underwent large political and social changes—in the developments in feudalism, the gradual evolution of Parliament, the growth of cities and of the middle class along with the increase in foreign trade, and in many other similar phenomena. But apparently the changes occurred too slowly to produce much intellectual awareness of them on the part of writers. The great exception—to this and to all other generalizations—is Chaucer, whose pages are informed, especially in his handling of the bourgeois, by an excited sense of the novelty of social life in his own times. Langland's *Piers Plowman* also possesses something of this quality—though without Chaucer's tone of approval. But in an age where most people were born in the same village where their grandparents had been born and lived virtually the same lives, doing the same work with the same tools, enjoying the same sports and the same festivals, large slow-moving change is probably bound to be imperceptible to all but the most acute observers—imperceptible and, if perceived, disapproved.

But if in a broad historical sense change was imperceptible, in the daily lives of medieval people it was all too visible. Indeed, the inevitability of change—for the worse, even in the lives of people already apparently wholly wretched—is one of the most insistently repetitive themes of Middle English literature. Nor is this theme to be thought of merely as another expression of the world-hating doctrine. Rather, the theme and the world-hating doctrine itself are both results of the violence of life in the Middle Ages, a violence not matched again in western history until our own times. Famine, war, pestilence, and death—these are the riders who passed through the streets of medieval cities and villages by night and by day. The fact that eight of the eighteen kings who ruled England between 1066 and 1485 died deaths of violence or deaths resulting from violent activity is characteristic of the era. Men hardly less august were also constantly meeting death in battles, or by murder, or by accident, or, not infrequently, on the scaffold before a fascinated populace. The chroniclers who record these events say little of the lower orders of society, but constant warfare against enemies at home and abroad, the depredations of the powerful in supplying themselves from the fruits of the toil of the poor, the fearful severity of the laws combined with the failure to enforce them against the strong, and, especially after the middle of the fourteenth century, recurrent pestilence compounded by famine—all these explain why change for the worse seems to have been the unchanging expectation of medieval people. And, even in the temporary absence of these events, the coldness and darkness of an English winter for people living in badly insulated dwellings with only minimal heat and light might well seem to make life a bleak perpetual twilight.

In view of the violence prevalent during most of the period, it is perhaps extraordinary that so much literature was produced. But even in the worst of times things are not always and everywhere at their worst; spring does come, and some people get through life almost untouched by disasters that seem historically to be omnipresent. And the fact is that, except in its most ruthlessly world-hating forms, Middle English literature is often permeated by a curious normality, and is, indeed, less preoccupied with its age's violence than we are with ours, probably because people then never conceived of a time when violence was not a fact of life. Despite being constantly warned to expect change for the worse, people in the Middle Ages seem, in their daily lives, to have pursued the same pleasures that we pursue today—pursued them with rather more relish because they were rarer: this is clear from the accounts both of those who approved of the pursuit and of those who did not. People took tremendous pleasure in color, in dress, in ritual, in parades, in spectacles, in elaborate food and drink (when they could get them), in all those aspects of life that children especially love, and most adults do not scorn. Medieval people were subject to emotional extremes—they wept more quickly than we do, went more quickly from weeping to laughter and back again, were headstrong and hasty, quick to sin zestily and to repent heartily and then to sin and repent again. Their life was physically more limited than ours, without our comforts, our mobility, our communications; it was even more precarious, more uncertain; but as it is reflected in the best writers, they lived their life very richly and perhaps with greater awareness and greater savor than we do ours.

MIDDLE ENGLISH LITERATURE

It has been said earlier that from the century and a half after the Conquest very little English literature has survived, and it is probable that in that period very little was written. But that literature was still being composed, if not written down, during the period is suggested by the first considerable Middle English poem to have come down to us: this is Layamon's *Brut*, written about 1205 in an alliterative prosody that is clearly directly descended from the Old English poetic measure, though the subtleties of the older measure have disappeared. Apparently, at least for oral purposes, alliterative poetry never ceased to be composed, as is further suggested by its reappearance later in written form in the so-called alliterative revival of the fourteenth century, which culminated in *Piers Plowman* and *Sir Gawain and the Green Knight*. Layamon's *Brut* is also interesting because it contains the first treatment in English of the Arthurian legend, the story that was to catch the imagination of so many English writers of later times. Layamon's source was a Norman work by the poet Wace, which was in turn based on the Englishman Geoffrey of Monmouth's Latin *History of the Kings of Britain*. According to the old tradition, England had been founded by one Brutus who was a descendant of the Trojan Aeneas, the founder of Rome, and after whom *Brit*ain was named (hence the title *Brut*). Of Brutus' descendants the most distinguished was Arthur, who according to the legend freed Britain from the Roman yoke and successfully defended it from the Anglo-Saxon invaders. It is a double curiosity about the Arthurian legend that not only did the British (Celtic) Arthur become in later centuries the great legendary hero of the English—whose ancestors he was presumably successful in beating off the island—but also that the Arthurian legend itself reached its fullest development in France, whither it may have been brought by Celts crossing the channel to Brittany—some of them perhaps fleeing from the Anglo-Saxons.

Both the poet of *Beowulf* and the creators of the Arthurian saga dealt with legendary materials which they thought of as history. The latter's treatment, however, is different from (and far less impressive than) the epic mode of *Beowulf*: it moves toward the genre, so characteristic of the later Middle Ages, known as "romance." The romance has certain typical features: it generally concerns knights and involves a large amount of fighting as well as a number of miscellaneous adventures; it makes liberal use of the improbable, often of the supernatural; it is often—though not always—involved with romantic love; characterization is standardized, so that heroes, heroines, and wicked stewards could easily move from one romance to another without causing any disturbance in the narrative; the plots generally consist of a great number of events, and the same event is apt to occur several times within the same romance; and the style is apt to be easy and colloquial—not infrequently loose and repetitious.

Although it was enormously popular in medieval England—it makes up a large fraction of the total of preserved Middle English literature—Middle

English romance is apt to disappoint the modern reader. Unfortunately, very few accomplished poets—the *Gawain*-poet and Chaucer are two of the principal exceptions—turned their hand to romance; it was apparently left largely to minstrels and other uncultivated versifiers addressing a semiliterate audience, often in dog-trot verse full of windy clichés. The great age of medieval romance had been the twelfth and early thirteenth centuries, and its chief breeding ground had been aristocratic society in France, where such poets as Chrétien de Troyes spun their marvelously sophisticated tales. The Middle English purveyors of romance, functioning before nonaristocratic audiences in the second half of the thirteenth and in the fourteenth century, introduced the French romances into English (the majority of the surviving English romances are either proved or suspected adaptations from the French). The result of the lag in time and change in audience is artistically unfortunate, though often unintentionally amusing. Aristocratic ideals of behavior of a different era and an alien society were replaced by patterns of behavior that could be easily comprehended by bourgeois and lower-class English folk. Heroes who have all the accouterments of the most chivalrous of knights are apt to behave in the crudest fashion, whether they are fighting, eating, or making love: they act as a petty bourgeois might if suddenly given an opportunity to enjoy the high scale of living of chivalric aristocracy with no education in how such a life should be conducted. Nevertheless, it is often agreeable to watch the blunt Englishman who replaced the aristocratic hero react with practical common sense to the extravagant situations in which the poem has placed him. These popular romances tend to be lengthy, rambling, and episodic yarns almost impossible to represent in a brief selection.

By far the larger proportion of surviving Middle English literature is religious, though it is not necessarily true that an equal proportion of the literature actually composed in Middle English was religious. The church had a virtual monopoly on literacy during much of the Middle Ages, for the average person who had learned to read and write probably had done so because he had signified his intention (not always fulfilled) of becoming a cleric—that is, an ecclesiast, performing one of the many functions of the church: otherwise, he would probably not have received any but the most elementary kind of education. Furthermore, the church not only had this direct claim upon the services of the majority of literate men but also was itself a large producer of books in the physical sense (books were actually handwritten manuscripts) as well as a maintainer (especially in monasteries) of libraries. Therefore it is quite natural that religious literature should bulk large. But the literature that has been lost probably contained a very large number of secular items. Professional storytellers such as minstrels committed to memory tales that they had heard others recite or had composed themselves and did not trouble to write down—if, indeed, they could write. Their stories depended for survival on some literate hearer who thought them worth recording—and perhaps few clerics would take the trouble. And even secular literature that had been recorded might sometimes be lost because of the low esteem in which it was held by austere churchmen who would enforce St. Paul's precept that everything that is written ought to express specific Christian doctrine: when library shelves became crowded, it was probably the secular works that were removed to make room for books more beneficial to the spirit.

Unfortunately, good doctrine is not necessarily good literature, and the larger part of Middle English religious writing is literature at all only in the broadest sense of that word: sermons, homilies, saints' lives, penitential tracts, manuals for priests, mystical writings, lyric poems, moral allegories, stories of miracles—all the possible genres of religious writing are represented profusely, though not, in quality, richly. An occasional individual work distinguishes itself strikingly from the surrounding drabness—for instance, the very early *Ancrene Riwle*, or "Rule for Anchoresses" (female religious recluses), or a late lyric like *I Sing of a Maiden*. But the brilliant exceptions are few and far between: few minds were able to sustain originality amid the oppressive conventionality of doctrine and response to doctrine. And few educated people before the time of Chaucer seem to have had the temerity to venture into the secular. We are fortunate that the work of one such person, the author of the early *Owl and the Nightingale*, has survived, for this humorous debate between birds is the most original and Chaucer-like poem before Chaucer himself.

During the last quarter of the fourteenth century Middle English literature flowered suddenly in three great poets, writing at almost the same time and giving supreme artistic expression to almost all the characteristic genres of Middle English. The author of *Sir Gawain and the Green Knight* not only produced the best romance of the entire period, but also wrote some of its best religious poetry; his Biblical narrative in alliterative verse, *Patience*, the story of Jonah, is rivaled only by certain Old English poems. In the *Pearl* he combined elegy with theology to produce the most moving religious poem— and the most finely wrought poem—of the English later Middle Ages. William Langland's achievement in *Piers Plowman* is important both in literature and in history, since he faced squarely the great religious and social issues of his day—and these became the great issues of the following century and a half: imitations of *Piers Plowman* which borrow both Piers himself and Langland's anti-ecclesiastical satire played an important part in bringing on the reformation of the church which Langland prophesied but would have deplored. Needless to say, no imitator approaches Langland in the extraordinary originality of his weaving together of all sorts of genres of religious literature, from the most menacing sermon to the most dazzling lyric. Geoffrey Chaucer's achievement was greatest of all. The new perspective which English literature after the Conquest had attained had revealed broader horizons, but they were too broad and too clouded with distractions to enable the average writer to bring everything into clear focus. It takes a powerfully disciplined mind to comprehend infinite variety in a single artistic vision. Such a mind was Chaucer's. While he was entirely rooted in the soil of the Middle Ages and tried his hand at a large number of medieval genres, his art is so fully realized as to carry him out of the Middle Ages and make him one of the two or three greatest poets in English.

This sudden florescence in the *Gawain*-poet, Langland, and Chaucer may have been partly due to patronage of literature by the well-to-do. Chaucer was a "court" poet who seems to have been encouraged not only by John of Gaunt but perhaps also by Gaunt's father, Edward III (died 1377), as well as by his nephew Richard II (deposed 1399), and, in the last year of the poet's life, by Gaunt's son, Henry IV. Within the broad category of the "court," one must also include members of the lower nobility and the middle class who, like Chaucer himself, constituted both a new bureaucracy for the management of England's increasingly complex affairs and a new kind of literary audience. The *Gawain*-poet probably wrote for a provincial aristocratic court, remote from London but no less interested in literary art.

Even William Langland seems to have enjoyed patronage, but from what source it is hard to be sure; it is probable that at one time or another he was sheltered by monasteries, and it is not unlikely that he ended his life in one. In any case English literature is fortunate that these three great contemporary poets all found encouragement from one source or another.

But patronage does not assure great poetry. Chaucer's friend, the poet John Gower, also enjoyed royal patronage, but he has not proved much of a threat to Chaucer's reputation. He seems a far more typically medieval writer than Chaucer: he wrote three works which, linguistically at least, summarized the English Middle Ages: one in Latin, one in Norman French, and one, *Confessio Amantis* ("The Lover's Confession"), in English. Were it not for its proximity to Chaucer, this last would probably be rated somewhat higher than it has been, for it is a work of considerable skill and interest. And it is certainly infinitely superior to anything produced by the English poets of the next century, some of whom enjoyed patronage but all of whom seem, after Chaucer, to represent regression into the worst vices of medieval literature. The most Chaucerian of Chaucer's followers are, indeed, Scotsmen, and the best of them, Robert Henryson and William Dunbar, who often reflect Chaucer's satirical spirit and his liveliness, belong not to the medieval period but to the Renaissance.

Yet if the fifteenth century in England lacks great names (Thomas Malory alone enjoys a high reputation as a literary artist), it is nevertheless a period in which popular literature flourished. Some of the best lyrics, religious and secular, date from this time; and this was also the century in which many of the ballads were composed. It was also the period of much activity in drama. The mystery plays, which had probably become established in the previous century, continued to be performed widely, and the cycles of these religious dramas that have been preserved from York, Chester, and Wakefield date from the fifteenth century. The same century saw the development of the morality play, culminating in *Everyman*. The authors of the plays, ballads, and lyrics of the century are nameless; aside from the plays, manuscripts of which were kept only by the towns in which the performances were given, these anonymous works were probably transmitted orally and only haphazardly written down. Fortunately for the future history of English literature, Malory's *Morte Darthur*, written during its author's long sojourn in prison, did not have to depend on the chance survival of a manuscript; it was printed in 1485 by William Caxton, who had introduced printing by movable type to England less than ten years earlier. Malory's is the last great medieval work of literature. Using mostly French sources, Malory put together a history of King Arthur and his knights which, while wholly fictional, has received much the same honor from later centuries that the Anglo-Saxons accorded *Beowulf*.

MEDIEVAL ENGLISH

The medieval works in this book were composed in two different states of our language: Old English, the language which took shape among the Germanic settlers of England and preserved its integrity until the Norman Conquest radically altered English civilization; and Middle English, the earliest records of which date from the early twelfth century and which gave way to Modern English shortly after the introduction of printing at the end of the fifteenth century. Old English is a very heavily inflected language (that is, the words change form to indicate changes in usage, such as person, number, tense, case, mood, etc. Most languages have some inflection—for example, the personal pronouns in Modern English have different forms when used as objects—but a "heavily inflected" language is one in which almost all classes of words undergo elaborate patterns of change). Its vocabulary is almost entirely Germanic. In Middle English, the inflectional system was weakened; and a large number of words were introduced into it from France, so that many of the older native words disappeared. Because of the difficulty of Old English, all selections from it in this book have been given in translation. In order that the reader may see an example of the language, a passage from *Beowulf* has been printed in the original, together with a verse translation. The present discussion, then, is concerned only with Middle English.

The chief difficulty with Middle English for the modern reader is caused not by its inflections so much as by its spelling, which may be described as a rough-and-ready phonetic system, and by the fact that it is not a single standardized language, but consists of a number of regional dialects each with its own peculiarities of sound and its own systems for representing sounds in writing. The Midland dialect—the dialect of London and of Chaucer, and the ancestor of our own standard speech—differs greatly from the dialect spoken in the west of England (the original dialect of *Piers Plowman*), and from that of the northwest *(Sir Gawain and the Green Knight)*, and from that of the north *(The Second Shepherds' Play)*, and these dialects differ from one another. In this book, *Sir Gawain and the Green Knight* has been translated; the text of Chaucer appears in the original, but has been respelled in a way that it is hoped will aid the reader. The remarks which follow apply to Chaucer's Midland English.

I. THE SOUNDS OF MIDDLE ENGLISH: GENERAL RULES

The following general analysis of the sounds of Middle English will enable the reader who has not time for detailed study to read Middle English aloud so as to preserve some of its most essential characteristics, without, however, giving heed to many important details. Section II, Detailed Analysis, is designed for the reader who wishes to go more deeply into the pronunciation of Middle English.

Middle English differs from Modern English in three principal respects: 1. the pronunciation of the long vowels *a, e, i* (or *y*), *o,* and *u* (spelled *ou, ow*); 2. the fact that Middle English final *e* is often sounded; 3. the fact that all Middle English consonants are sounded.

1. Long Vowels

Middle English vowels are long when they are doubled *(aa, ee, oo)* or when they are terminal *(he, to, holy)*; *a, e,* and *o* are long when followed by a single consonant plus a vowel *(name, mete, note)*. Middle English vowels are short when they are followed by two consonants.

Long *a* is sounded like the *a* in Modern English "father": *maken, maad.*

Long *e* may be sounded like the *a* in Modern English "name" (ignoring the distinction between the close and open vowel): *be, sweete.*

Long *i* (or *y*) is sounded like the *i* in Modern English "machine": *lif, whit; myn, holy.*

Long *o* may be sounded like the *o* in Modern English "note" (again ignoring the distinction between the close and open vowel): *do, soone.*

Long *u* (spelled *ou, ow*) is sounded like the *oo* in Modern English "goose": *hous, flowr.*

Note that in general Middle English long vowels are pronounced like long vowels in modern languages other than English. Short vowels and diphthongs, however, may be pronounced as in Modern English.

2. *Final e*

In Middle English syllabic verse, final *e* is sounded like the *a* in "sofa" to provide a needed unstressed syllable: *Another Nonnë with hire haddë she.* But (cf. *hire* in the example) final *e* is suppressed when not needed for the meter. It is commonly silent before words beginning with a vowel or *h*.

3. *Consonants*

Middle English consonants are pronounced separately in all combinations—*gnat*: *g-nat*; *knave*: *k-nave*; *write*: *w-rite*; *folk*: *fol-k*. In a simplified system of pronunciation the combination *gh* as in *night* or *thought* may be treated as if it were silent.

II. THE SOUNDS OF MIDDLE ENGLISH: DETAILED ANALYSIS

1. *Simple Vowels*

Sound	Pronunciation	Example
long *a* (spelled *a, aa*)	*a* in "father"	*maken, maad*
short *a*	*o* in "hot"	*cappe*
long *e* close (spelled *e, ee*)	*a* in "name"	*be, sweete*
long *e* open (spelled *e, ee*)	*e* in "there"	*mete, heeth*
short *e*	*e* in "set"	*setten*
final *e*	*a* in "sofa"	*large*
long *i* (spelled *i, y*)	*i* in "machine"	*lif, myn*
short *i*	*i* in "wit"	*wit*
long *o* close (spelled *o, oo*)	*o* in "note"	*do, soone*
long *o* open (spelled *o, oo*)	*oa* in "broad"	*go, goon*
short *o*	*o* in "oft"	*pot*
long *u* when spelled *ou, ow*	*oo* in "goose"	*hous, flowr*
long *u* when spelled *u*	*u* in "pure"	*vertu*
short *u* (spelled *u, o*)	*u* in "full"	*ful, love*

Doubled vowels and terminal vowels are always long, while single vowels before two consonants other than *th, ch* are always short. The vowels *a, e,* and *o* are long before a single consonant followed by a vowel: *nāmë, sēkë* (sick), *hōly.* In general, words that have descended into Modern English reflect their original Middle English quantity: *līven* (to live), but *līf* (life).

The close and open sounds of long *e* and long *o* may often be identified by the Modern English spellings of the words in which they appear. Original long close *e* is generally represented in Modern English by *ee*: "sweet," "knee," "teeth," "see" have close *e* in Middle English, but so does "be"; original long open *e* is generally represented in Modern English by *ea*: "meat," "heath," "sea," "great," "breath" have open *e* in Middle English. Similarly, original long close *o* is now generally represented by *oo*: "soon," "food," "good," but also "do," "to"; original long open *o* is represented either by *oa* or by *o*: "coat," "boat," "moan," but also "go," "bone," "foe," "home." Notice that original close *o* is now almost always pronounced like the *oo* in "goose," but that original open *o* is almost never so pronounced; thus it is often possible to identify the Middle English vowels through Modern English sounds.

The nonphonetic Middle English spelling of *o* for short *u* has been preserved in a number of Modern English words ("love," "son," "come"), but in others *u* has been restored: "sun" *(sonne)*, "run" *(ronne)*.

For the treatment of final *e*, see above, General Rules, section 2.

2. Diphthongs

Sound	Pronunciation	Example
ai, ay, ei, ay	between *ai* in "aisle" and *ay* in "day"	*saide, day, veine, preye*
au, aw	*ou* in "out"	*chaunge, bawdy*
eu, ew	*ew* in "few"	*newe*
oi, oy	*oy* in "joy"	*joye, point*
ou, ow	*ou* in "thought"	*thought, lowe*

Note that in words with *ou, ow* which in Modern English are sounded with the *ou* of "about," the combination indicates not the diphthong but the simple vowel long *u* (see above, Simple Vowels).

3. Consonants

In general, all consonants except *h* were always sounded in Middle English, including consonants that have become silent in Modern English, such as the *g* in *gnaw*, the *k* in *knight*, the *l* in *folk*, and the *w* in *write*. In noninitial *gn*, however, the *g* was silent as in Modern English "sign." Initial *h* was silent in short common English words and in words borrowed from French, and may have been almost silent in all words. The combination *gh* as in *night* or *thought* was sounded like the *ch* of German *ich* or *nach*. Note that Middle English *gg* represents both the hard sound of "dagger" and the soft sound of "bridge."

III. PARTS OF SPEECH AND GRAMMAR

1. Nouns

The plural and possessive of nouns end in *es*, formed by adding *s* or *es* to the singular: *knight, knightes; roote, rootes*; a final consonant is frequently doubled before *es*: *bed, beddes*. A common irregular plural is *yën*, from *yë*, eye.

2. Pronouns

The chief differences from Modern English are as follows:

Modern English	Middle English
I	*I, ich* (*ik* is a northern form)
you (singular)	*thou* (subjective); *thee* (objective)
her	*hir(e), her(e)*
its	*his*
you (plural)	*ye* (subjective); *you* (objective)
their	*hir*
them	*hem*

In formal speech, the second person plural is often used for the singular. The possessive adjectives *my, thy* take *n* before a word beginning with a vowel or *h*: *thyn yë, myn host*.

3. Adjectives

Adjectives ending in a consonant add final *e* when they stand before the noun they modify and after another modifying word such as *the, this, that*, or nouns or pronouns in the possessive: *a good hors*, but *the (this, my, the kinges) goode hors*. They also generally add *e* when standing before and modifying a plural noun, a noun in the vocative, or any proper noun: *goode men, oh goode man, faire* Venus.

Adjectives are compared by adding *er(e)* for the comparative, *est(e)* for the superlative. Sometimes the stem vowel is shortened or altered in the process: *sweete, swettere, swettest; long, lenger, lengest.*

4. Adverbs

Adverbs are formed from adjectives by adding *e, ly,* or *liche*; the adjective *fair* thus yields *faire, fairly, fairliche.*

5. Verbs

Middle English verbs, like Modern English verbs, are either "weak" or "strong." Weak verbs form their preterites and past participles with a *t* or *d* suffix and preserve the same stem vowel throughout their systems, though it is sometimes shortened in the preterite and past participle: *love, loved; bend, bent; hear, heard; meet, met.* Strong verbs do not use the *t* or *d* suffix, but vary their stem vowel in the preterite and past participle: *take, took, taken; begin, began, begun; find, found, found.*

The inflectional endings are the same for Middle English strong verbs and weak verbs except in the preterite singular and the imperative singular. In the following paradigms, the weak verbs *loven* (to love) and *heeren* (to hear), and the strong verbs *taken* (to take) and *ginnen* (to begin) serve as models.

	Present Indicative	Preterite Indicative
I	love, heere	loved(e), herde
	take, ginne	took, gan
thou	lovest, heerest	lovedest, herdest
	takest, ginnest	tooke, gonne
he, she, it	loveth, heereth	loved(e), herde
	taketh, ginneth	took, gan
we, ye, they	love(n) (th), heere(n) (th)	loved(e) (en), herde(n)
	take(n) (th), ginne(n) (th)	tooke(n), gonne(n)

The present plural ending *eth* is southern, while the *e(n)* ending is Midland and characteristic of Chaucer. In the north, *s* may appear as the ending of all persons of the present. In the weak preterite, when the ending *e* gave a verb three or more syllables, it was frequently dropped. Note that in certain strong verbs like *ginnen* there are two distinct stem vowels in the preterite: even in Chaucer's time, however, one of these had begun to replace the other, and Chaucer occasionally writes *gan* for all persons of the preterite.

	Present Subjunctive	Preterite Subjunctive
Singular	love, heere	lovede, herde
	take, ginne	tooke, gonne
Plural	love(n), heere(n)	lovede(n), herde(n)
	take(n), ginne(n)	tooke(n), gonne(n)

In verbs like *ginnen*, which have two stem vowels in the indicative preterite, it is the vowel of the plural and of the second person singular that is used for the preterite subjunctive.

The imperative singular of most weak verbs is *e: (thou) love*, but of some weak verbs and all strong verbs, the imperative singular is without termination: *(thou) heer, taak, gin.* The imperative plural of all verbs is either *e* or *eth: (ye) love(th), heere(th), take(th), ginne(th).*

The infinitive of verbs is *e* or *en*: *love(n)*, *heere(n)*, *take(n)*, *ginne(n)*.

The past participle of weak verbs is the same as the preterite without inflectional ending: *loved*, *herd*. In strong verbs the ending is either *e* or *en*: *take(n)*, *gonne(n)*. The prefix *y* often appears on past participles: *yloved*, *yherd*, *ytake(n)*.

OLD AND MIDDLE ENGLISH PROSODY

All the poetry of Old English is in the same verse form. The verse unit is the single line, since rhyme was not used to link one line to another, except very occasionally in late Old English. The organizing device of the line is alliteration, the beginning of several words with the same sound ("Foemen fled"). The Old English alliterative line contains four principal stresses, and is divided into two half-lines of two stresses each by a strong medial caesura, or pause. These two half-lines are linked to each other by the alliteration: at least one of the two stressed words in the first half-line, and often both of them, begin with the same sound as the first stressed word of the second half-line (the second stressed word is generally nonalliterative). The fourth line of *Beowulf* is an example (*sc* has the value of modern *sh*; *þ* is a runic symbol with the value of modern *th*):

> Oft Scyld Scefing   sceaþena þreatum.

For further examples, see the passage from *Beowulf*, printed below. It will be noticed that any vowel alliterates with any other vowel. In addition to the alliteration, the length of the unstressed syllables and their number and pattern are governed by a highly complex set of rules. When sung or intoned—as it was—to the rhythmic strumming of a harp, Old English poetry must have been wonderfully impressive in the dignified, highly formalized way which aptly fits both its subject matter and tone.

The majority of Middle English verse is either in alternately stressed rhyming verse, adapted from French after the Conquest, or in alliterative verse that is descended from Old English. The latter preserves the caesura of Old English and in its purest form the same alliterative system, the two stressed words of the first half-line (or at least one of them) alliterating with the first stressed word in the second half-line. But most of the alliterative poets allowed themselves a number of deviations from the norm. All four stressed words may alliterate, as in the first line of *Piers Plowman*:

> In a summer season   when soft was the sun.

Or the line may contain five, six, or even more stressed words, of which all or only the basic minimum may alliterate:

> A *fair field full* of *folk*   *found* I therebetween.

There is no rule determining the number of unstressed syllables, and at times some poets seem to ignore alliteration entirely. As in Old English, any vowel may alliterate with any other vowel; furthermore, since initial *h* was silent or lightly pronounced in Middle English, words beginning with *h* are treated as though they began with the following vowel.

There are two general types of stressed verse with rhyme. In the more common, stressed and unstressed syllables alternate regularly: x X x X x X; or, with two unstressed syllables intervening: x x X x x X x x X; or a combination of the two: x x X x X x x X (of the reverse patterns, only X x X x X x is common in English). There is also a line which can only be defined as containing a predetermined number of stressed syllables but an irregular number and pattern of unstressed syllables. Much Middle English verse has to be read without expectation of regularity: some of this was evidently composed in the irregular meter, but some was probably originally composed according to a strict metrical system which has been obliterated by scribes careless of fine points. One receives the impression that many of the lyrics— as well as the *Second Shepherds' Play*—were at least composed with regular syllabic alternation. In the ballads, on the other hand, and in the play *Everyman*, only the number of stresses is predetermined (and perhaps not even this in *Everyman*), but not the number or placement of unstressed syllables.

In pre-Chaucerian verse the number of stresses, whether regularly or irregularly alternated, was most often four, though sometimes the number was three, and rose in some poems to seven. Rhyme in Middle English as in Modern English may be either between adjacent or alternate lines, or may occur in more complex patterns. The *Canterbury Tales* are in rhymed couplets, the line containing five stresses with regular alternation—technically known as iambic pentameter, the standard English poetic line, perhaps introduced into English by Chaucer. In reading Chaucer and much pre-Chaucerian verse one must remember that the final *e*, which is silent in Modern English, was pronounced at any time in order to provide a needed unstressed syllable. Evidence seems to indicate that it was also pronounced at the end of the line, even though it thus produced a line with eleven syllables. Although he was a very regular metricist, Chaucer used various conventional devices which are apt to make the reader stumble until he understands them. Final *e* is often not pronounced before a word beginning with a vowel or *h*, and may be suppressed whenever metrically convenient. The same medial and terminal syllables that are slurred in Modern English are apt to be suppressed in Chaucer's English: *Canterb'ry* for *Canterbury*; *ev'r* (perhaps *e'er*) for *evere*. The plural in *es* may either be syllabic or reduced to *s* as in Modern English. Despite these seeming irregularities, Chaucer's verse is not difficult to read if one constantly bears in mind the basic pattern of the iambic pentameter line.

BEOWULF

Beowulf, the oldest of the great long poems written in English, may have been composed more than twelve hundred years ago, in the first half of the eighth century, though some scholars would place it as late as the tenth century. Its author may have been a native of what was then West Mercia, the West Midlands of England today, though the late tenth-century manuscript, which alone preserves the poem, originated in the south in the kingdom of the West Saxons. In 1731, before any modern transcription of the text had been made, the manuscript was seriously damaged in the fire that destroyed the building in London which housed the extraordinary collection of medieval English manuscripts made by Sir Robert Bruce Cotton (1571–1631). As a result of the fire and of subsequent deterioration of the manuscript, a number of lines and words have been lost from the poem, but even if the manuscript had not been damaged, the poem would still have been difficult, because the poetic Old English (or Anglo-Saxon) in which it was written is itself hard, the style is allusive, the ideas often seem remote and strange to modern perceptions, and because the text was inevitably corrupted during the transcriptions which must have intervened between the poem's composition and the copying of the extant manuscript. Yet despite its difficulty, the somber grandeur of *Beowulf* is still capable of stirring the hearts of readers, and because of its excellence as well as its antiquity, the poem merits the high position that it is generally assigned in the study of English poetry.

While the poem itself is English in language and origin, it deals not with native Englishmen, but with their Germanic forebears, especially with two south Scandinavian tribes, the Danes and the Geats, who lived on the Danish island of Zealand and in southern Sweden, respectively. Thus, the historical period it concerns—insofar as it may be said to refer to history at all—is some centuries before the poem was written; that is, it concerns a time following the initial invasion of England by Germanic tribes in 449, but before the Anglo-Saxon migration was completed, and perhaps before the arrival of the ancestors of the audience to whom the poem was sung: this audience may have considered itself to be of the same Geatish stock as the hero, Beowulf. The one datable fact of history mentioned in the poem is a raid on the Franks made by Hygelac, the king of the Geats at the time Beowulf was a young man, and this raid occurred in the year 520. Yet despite their antiquity, the poet's materials must have been very much alive to his audience, for the elliptical way in which he alludes to events not directly concerned with his plot demands of the listener a wide knowledge of traditional Germanic history. This knowledge was probably kept alive by other heroic poetry, of which little has been preserved in English, though much must once have existed. As it stands, *Beowulf* is not only unique as an example of the Old English epic, but is also the greatest of the surviving epics composed by the Germanic peoples.

It is generally agreed that the poet who put the old materials into their present form was a Christian, and that his poem reflects a Christian tradition: the conversion of the Germanic settlers in England had largely been completed during the centuries preceding the one in which the poet wrote.

But there is little general agreement as to how clearly *Beowulf* reflects a Christian tradition or, conversely, the actual nature of the Christian tradition that it is held to reflect. Many specifically Christian references occur, especially to the Old Testament: God is said to be the Creator of all things and His will seems recognized (sporadically if not systematically) as being identical with Fate (*wyrd*); Grendel is described as a descendant of Cain, and the sword that Beowulf finds in Grendel's mother's lair has engraved on it the story of the race of giants and their destruction by flood; the dead await God's judgment, and Hell and the Devil are ready to receive the souls of Grendel and his mother, while believers will find the Father's embrace; Hrothgar's speech of advice to Beowulf (pp. 50–51) seems to reflect patristic doctrine in its emphasis on conscience and the Devil's lying in wait for the unwary. Yet there is no reference to the New Testament—to Christ and His Sacrifice which are the real bases of Christianity in any intelligible sense of the term. Furthermore, readers may well feel that the poem achieves rather little of its emotional power through any direct invocation of Christian values or of values that are consonant with Christian doctrine as we know it. Perhaps the sense of tragic waste which pervades the Finnsburg episode (pp. 40–42) springs from a Christian perception of the insane futility of the primitive Germanic thirst for vengeance; and the facts that Beowulf's chief adversaries are not men but monsters and that before his death he is able to boast that as king of the Geats he did not seek wars with neighboring tribes may reflect a Christian's appreciation for peace among men. But while admitting such values, the poet also invokes many others of a very different order, values that seem to belong to an ancient, pagan, warrior society of the kind described by the Roman historian Tacitus at the end of the first century. It should be noted that even Hrothgar's speech about conscience is directed more toward making Beowulf a good Germanic leader of men than a good Christian. One must, indeed, draw the conclusion from the poem itself that while Christian is a correct term for the religion of the poet and of his audience, it was a Christianity that had not yet by any means succeeded in obliterating an older pagan tradition, which still called forth powerful responses from the hearts of men and women, despite the fact that many aspects of this tradition must be abhorrent to a sophisticated Christian. In this connection it is well to recall that the missionaries from Rome who initiated the conversion of the English proceeded in a conciliatory manner, not so much uprooting paganism in order to plant Christianity as planting Christianity in the faith that it would ultimately choke out the weeds of paganism. And the English clung long to some of their ancient traditions: for instance, the legal principle of the payment of *wergild* (defined below) remained in force until the Norman Conquest, four centuries after the conversion of the English.

In the warrior society whose values the poem constantly invokes, the most important of human relationships was that which existed between the warrior—the thane—and his lord, a relationship based less on subordination of one man's will to another's than on mutual trust and respect. When a warrior vowed loyalty to his lord, he became not so much his servant as his voluntary companion, one who would take pride in defending him and fighting in his wars. In return, the lord was expected to take affectionate care of his thanes and to reward them richly for their valor: a good king, one like Hrothgar or Beowulf, is referred to by such poetic epithets as "protector of warriors" and "dispenser of treasure" or "ring-giver," and the failure of bad kings is ascribed to their ill-temper and avarice, both of which alienate them from their retainers. The material benefit of this arrangement between lord and thane is obvious, yet under a good king the relationship seems to have had a significance more spiritual than material. Thus the treasure that an ideal Germanic king seizes from his enemies and rewards his retainers with is regarded as something more than mere wealth that will serve the well-being of its possessor; rather, it is a kind of visible proof that all parties are realizing themselves to the full in a spiritual sense—that the men of this band are congenially and successfully united with one another. The symbolic importance of treasure is illustrated by the poet's remark that the gift Beowulf gave the Danish coast guard brought the latter honor among his companions, and even more by the fact that although Beowulf dies while obtaining a great treasure for his people, such objects as are removed from the dragon's hoard are actually buried with him as a fitting sign of his ultimate achievement.

The relationship between kinsmen was also of deep significance to this society and provides another emotional value for Old English heroic poetry. If one of his kinsmen had been slain, a man had the special duty of either killing the slayer or exacting from him the payment of *wergild* ("manprice"): each rank of society was evaluated at a definite price, which had to be paid to the dead man's kinsmen by the killer who wished to avoid their vengeance—even if the killing had been accidental. Again, the money itself had less significance as wealth than as a proof that the kinsmen had done what was right. Relatives who failed either to exact *wergild* or to take vengeance could never be happy, having found no practical way of satisfying their grief for their kinsman's death. "It is better for a man to avenge his friend than much mourn," Beowulf says to the old Hrothgar, who is bewailing Aeschere's killing by Grendel's mother. And one of the most poignant passages in the poem describes the sorrow of King Hrethel after one of his sons had accidentally killed another: by the code of kinship Hrethel was forbidden to kill or to exact compensation from a kinsman, yet by the same code he was required to do one or the other in order to avenge the dead. Caught in this curious dilemma, Hrethel became so disconsolate that he could no longer face life.

It is evident that the need to take vengeance would create never-ending feuds, which the practice of marrying royal princesses to the kings or princes of hostile tribes did little to mitigate, though the purpose of such marriages was to replace hostility by alliance. Hrothgar wishes to make peace with the Heatho-Bards by marrying his daughter to their king, Ingeld, whose father was killed by the Danes; but as Beowulf predicts, sooner or later the Heatho-Bards' desire for vengeance on the Danes will erupt, and there will be more bloodshed. And the Danish princess Hildeburh, married to Finn of the Jutes, will see her son and her brother both killed while fighting on opposite sides in a battle at her own home, and ultimately will see her husband killed by the Danes in revenge for her brother's death. Beowulf himself is, for a Germanic hero, curiously free of involvement in feuds of this sort, though he does boast that he avenged the death of his king, Heardred, on his slayer Onela. Yet the potentiality—or inevitability—of sudden attack, sudden change, swift death is omnipresent in *Beowulf*: men seem to be caught in a vast web of reprisals and counterreprisals from which there is little hope of escape. This is the aspect of the poem which is apt to make the most powerful impression on the reader—its strong sense of doom.

Beowulf himself is chiefly concerned not with tribal feuds but with fatal evil both less and more complex. Grendel and the dragon are threats to the security of the lands they infest just as human enemies would be, but they are not part of the social order and presumably have no one to avenge their deaths (that Grendel's mother appeared as an avenger seems to have been a surprise both to Beowulf and to the Danes). On the other hand, because they are outside the normal order of things, they require of their conqueror something greater than normal warfare requires. In each case, it is the clear duty of the king and his companions to put down the evil. But the Danish Hrothgar is old and his companions unenterprising, and excellent though Hrothgar has been in the kingship, he nevertheless lacks the quality that later impels the old Beowulf to fight the dragon that threatens his people. The poem makes no criticism of Hrothgar for this lack; he merely seems not to be the kind of man—one might almost say he was not fated—to develop his human potential to the fullest extent that Fate would permit: that is Beowulf's role. In undertaking to slay Grendel, and later Grendel's mother, Beowulf is testing his relationship with unknowable destiny. At any time, as he is fully aware, his luck may abandon him and he may be killed, as, indeed, he is in the otherwise successful encounter with the dragon. But whether he lives or dies, he will have done all that any man could do to develop his character heroically. It is this consciousness of testing Fate that probably explains the boasting that modern readers of heroic poetry often find offensive. When he boasts, Beowulf is not only demonstrating that he has chosen the heroic way of life, but is also choosing it, for when he invokes his former courage as pledge of his future courage, his boast becomes a vow; the hero has put himself in a position from which he cannot withdraw.

Courage is the instrument by which the hero realizes himself. "Fate often saves an undoomed man when his courage is good," says Beowulf in his account of his swimming match: that is, if Fate has not entirely doomed a man in advance, courage is the quality that can perhaps influence Fate against its natural tendency to doom him now. It is this complex statement (in which it is hard to read the will of God for Fate) that Beowulf's life explores: he will use his great strength in the most courageous way by going alone, even unarmed, against monsters. Doom, of course, ultimately claims him, but not until he has fulfilled to its limits the pagan ideal of a heroic life. And despite the desire he often shows to Christianize pagan virtues, the Christian poet remains true to the older tradition when, at the end of his poem, he leaves us with the impression that Beowulf's chief reward is pagan immortality: the memory in the minds of later generations of a hero's heroic actions. The poem itself is, indeed, a noble expression of that immortality.

TRIBES AND GENEALOGIES

1. The Danes (Bright-, Half-, Ring-, Spear-, North-, East-, South-, West-Danes; Scyldings, Honor-, Victor-, War-Scyldings; Ing's friends).

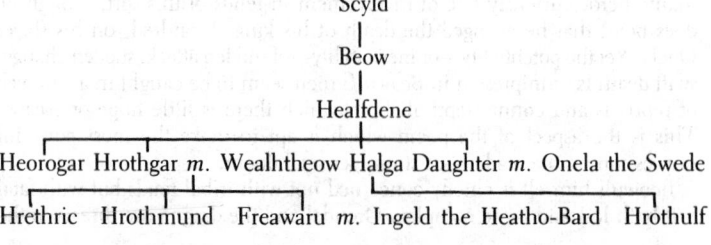

2. The Geats (Sea-, War-, Weather-Geats)

Hrethel

Herebeald Haethcyn Hygelac *m.* Hygd Daughter *m.* Ecgtheow

Heardred Daughter† *m.* Eofor Beowulf the Geat

3. The Swedes.

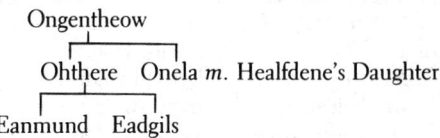

Ongentheow

Ohthere Onela *m.* Healfdene's Daughter

Eanmund Eadgils

4. Miscellaneous.

A. The Half-Danes (also called Scyldings) involved in the fight at Finnsburg may represent a different tribe from the Danes of paragraph 1, above. Their king Hoc had a son, Hnaef, who succeeded him, and a daughter Hildeburh, who married Finn, king of the Jutes.

B. The Jutes or Frisians are represented as enemies of the Danes in the fight at Finnsburg and as allies of the Franks or Hugas at the time Hygelac the Geat made the attack in which he lost his life and from which Beowulf swam home. Also allied with the Franks at this time were the Hetware.

C. The Heatho-Bards (i.e., "Battle-Bards") are represented as inveterate enemies of the Danes. Their king Froda had been killed in an attack on the Danes, and Hrothgar's attempt to make peace with them by marrying his daughter Freawaru to Froda's son Ingeld failed when the latter attacked Heorot. The attack was repulsed, though Heorot was burned.

The Last Survivor's Speech in Old English with Verse Translation

In order to give the reader a sample of the language, style, and texture of *Beowulf* we print the following passage in the original followed by a verse translation that attempts to convey the terseness and strong beat of the alliterative measure, though to observe the strict rules of classical Old English alliterative verse is hardly possible in modern idiom. The famous passage comes late in the poem (lines 2247–66, p. 58). It tells the history of the dragon's hoard for which Beowulf, now an old king who has ruled the Geats for fifty years, sacrifices his life. The treasure is the accumulated inheritance of a noble race of warriors, now extinct except for the last nameless "hringa hyrde" (shepherd of rings) who, himself at the point of death, carries it into a barrow and utters this speech on the transitoriness of all earthly things.

† The; daughter of Hygelac who was given to Eofor may have been born to him by a former wife, older than Hygd.

[The Last Survivor's Speech][1]

"Heald þu nu, hruse,   nu hæleð ne mostan,
eorla æhte!   Hwæt, hyt ær on ðe
gode begeaton.   Gu-deað fornam,
feorh-bealo frecne   fyra gehwylcne   2250
leoda minra,   þara ðe þis lif ofgeaf,
gesawon sele-dreamas.   Nah hwa sweord wege
oððe feormie   fæted wæge,
drync fæt deore;   duguð ellor scoc.
Sceal se hearda helm   hyrsted golde   2255
fætum befeallen;   feormynd swefað,
þa ðe beado-griman   bywan sceoldon;
ge swylce seo here-pad,   sio æt hilde gebad
ofer borda gebræc   bite irena,
brosnað æfter beorne;   ne mæg byrnan hring   2260
æfter wig-fruman   wide feran
hæleðum be healfe.   Næs hearpan wyn
gomen gleo-beames,   ne god hafoc
geond sæl swingeð,   ne se swifta mearh
burh-stede beateð.   Bealo-cwealm hafað   2265
fela feorh-cynna   forð onsended!"

"Hold them now, Earth,   now hand of man cannot,
A great tribe's treasures.   Truly, from you
Brave men first got them;   battle-death has taken,
Murderous fighting,   the men, one and all,   2250
Peers of my people: they have passed from this life,
Rest from hall-joys.   None remains with me
To bear the sword,   burnish the rich goblet,
Costly drinking-cup;   the company has gone elsewhere.
Now the hard helmet,   hammered with gold,   2255
Must be stripped of its plating;   the polishers sleep
Who once made bright   those grim battle-masks;
Also the armor,   which endured in battle,
Mid breaking of shields,   the bite of swords,
Rots with the warrior.   The ringed-corselet   2260
May not wander far   on the war-chief's path,
At the soldiers' side.   The harp is silent,
No glad music sounds,   nor any good hawk
Sweeps through the hall,   nor swift hoofbeats
Drum in the courtyard.   Death-qualm has sent   2265
Full many a folk   forth on their way."

---

1. The verse translation is by the junior editor.

Beowulf[1]

[Prologue: The Earlier History of the Danes]

Yes, we have heard of the glory of the Spear-Danes' kings in the old days—how the princes of that people did brave deeds.

Often Scyld Scefing[2] took mead-benches away from enemy bands, from many tribes, terrified their nobles—after the time that he was first found destitute. He lived to find comfort for that, became great under the skies, prospered in honors until every one of those who lived about him, across the whale-road, had to obey him, pay him tribute. That was a good king.

Afterwards a son was born to him, a young boy in his house, whom God sent to comfort the people: He had seen the sore need they had suffered during the long time they lacked a king. Therefore the Lord of Life, the Ruler of Heaven, gave him honor in the world: Beow[3] was famous, the glory of the son of Scyld spread widely in the Northlands. In this way a young man ought by his good deeds, by giving splendid gifts while still in his father's house, to make sure that later in life beloved companions will stand by him, that people will serve him when war comes. Through deeds that bring praise, a man shall prosper in every country.

Then at the fated time Scyld the courageous went away into the protection of the Lord. His dear companions carried him down to the sea-currents, just as he himself had bidden them do when, as protector of the Scyldings,[4] he had ruled them with his words—long had the beloved prince governed the land. There in the harbor stood the ring-prowed ship, ice-covered and ready to sail, a prince's vessel. Then they laid down the ruler they had loved, the ring-giver, in the hollow of the ship, the glorious man beside the mast. There was brought great store of treasure, wealth from lands far away. I have not heard of a ship more splendidly furnished with war-weapons and battle-dress, swords and mail-shirts. On his breast lay a great many treasures that should voyage with him far out into the sea's possession. They provided him with no lesser gifts, treasure of the people, than those had done who at his beginning first sent him forth on the waves, a child alone.[5] Then also they set a golden standard high over his head, let the water take him, gave him to the sea. Sad was their spirit, mournful their mind. Men cannot truthfully say

---

1. The translation into modern English, by the senior editor (1966), is based on F. Klaeber's 3rd ed. of the poem (1950); in general, the emendations suggested by J. C. Pope, *The Rhythm of Beowulf*, 2nd ed. (1966), have been adopted.
2. The meaning is probably "son of Sceaf," although Scyld's origins are mysterious.
3. Although the manuscript reads "Beowulf," most

scholars now agree that it should read "Beow." Beow was the grandfather of the Danish king Hrothgar.
4. I.e., the Danes ("descendants of Scyld").
5. In view of the fact that Scyld was said to have arrived destitute, this statement should probably be taken as a kind of curious understatement emphasizing the reversal in Scyld's fortunes.

who received that cargo, neither counsellors in the hall nor warriors under the skies.

Then in the cities was Beow of the Scyldings beloved king of the people, long famous among nations (his father had gone elsewhere, the king from his land), until later great Healfdene was born to him. As long as he lived, old and fierce in battle, he upheld the glorious Scyldings. To him all told were four children born into the world, to the leader of the armies: Heorogar and Hrothgar and the good Halga. I have heard tell that [. . . was On]ela's queen,[6] beloved bed-companion of the Battle-Scylfing.

[Beowulf and Grendel]

[THE HALL HEOROT IS ATTACKED BY GRENDEL]

Then Hrothgar was given success in warfare, glory in battle, so that his retainers gladly obeyed him and their company grew into a great band of warriors. It came to his mind that he would command men to construct a hall, a great mead-building that the children of men should hear of forever, and therein he would give to young and old all that God had given him, except for common land and men's bodies.[7] Then I have heard that the work was laid upon many nations, wide through this middle-earth, that they should adorn the folk-hall. In time it came to pass—quickly, as men count it—that it was finished, the largest of hall-dwellings. He gave it the name of Heorot,[8] he who ruled wide with his words. He did not forget his promise: at the feast he gave out rings, treasure. The hall stood tall, high and wide-gabled: it would wait for the fierce flames of vengeful fire;[9] the time was not yet at hand for sword-hate between son-in-law and father-in-law to awaken after murderous rage.

Then the fierce spirit[1] painfully endured hardship for a time, he who dwelt in the darkness, for every day he heard loud mirth in the hall; there was the sound of the harp, the clear song of the scop.[2] There he spoke who could relate the beginning of men far back in time, said that the Almighty made earth, a bright field fair in the water that surrounds it, set up in triumph the lights of the sun and the moon to lighten land-dwellers, and adorned the surfaces of the earth with branches and leaves, created also life for each of the kinds that move and breathe.—Thus these warriors lived in joy, blessed, until one began to do evil deeds, a hellish enemy. The grim spirit was called Grendel, known as a rover of the borders, one who held the moors, fen and fastness. Unhappy creature, he lived for a time in the home of the monsters' race, after God

6. The text is faulty, so that the name of Healf-dene's daughter has been lost; her husband Onela was a Swedish (Scylfing) king.
7. Or "men's lives." Apparently slaves, along with public land, were not in the king's power to give away.
8. I.e., "Hart."
9. The destruction by fire of Heorot occurred at a later time than that of the poem's action, probably during the otherwise unsuccessful attack of the Heatho-Bard Ingeld on his father-in-law, Hrothgar, mentioned in the next clause.
1. I.e., Grendel.
2. The "scop" was the Anglo-Saxon minstrel, who recited poetic stories to the accompaniment of a harp.

had condemned them as kin of Cain. The Eternal Lord avenged the murder in which he slew Abel. Cain had no pleasure in that feud, but He banished him far from mankind, the Ruler, for that misdeed. From him sprang all bad breeds, trolls and elves and monsters—likewise the giants who for a long time strove with God: He paid them their reward for that.

Then, after night came, Grendel went to survey the tall house—how, after their beer-drinking, the Ring-Danes had disposed themselves in it. Then he found therein a band of nobles asleep after the feast: they felt no sorrow, no misery of men. The creature of evil, grim and fierce, was quickly ready, savage and cruel, and seized from their rest thirty thanes. From there he turned to go back to his home, proud of his plunder, sought his dwelling with that store of slaughter.

Then in the first light of dawning day Grendel's war-strength was revealed to men: then after the feast weeping arose, great cry in the morning. The famous king, hero of old days, sat joyless; the mighty one suffered, felt sorrow for his thanes, when they saw the track of the foe, of the cursed spirit: that hardship was too strong, too loathsome and long-lasting. Nor was there a longer interval, but after one night Grendel again did greater slaughter—and had no remorse for it—vengeful acts and wicked: he was too intent on them. Thereafter it was easy to find the man who sought rest for himself elsewhere, farther away, a bed among the outlying buildings—after it was made clear to him, told by clear proof, the hatred of him who now controlled the hall.[3] Whoever escaped the foe held himself afterwards farther off and more safely. Thus Grendel held sway and fought against right, one against all, until the best of houses stood empty. It was a long time, the length of twelve winters, that the lord of the Scyldings suffered grief, all woes, great sorrows. Therefore, sadly in songs, it became well-known to the children of men that Grendel had fought a long time with Hrothgar, for many half-years maintained mortal spite, feud, and enmity—constant war. He wanted no peace with any of the men of the Danish host, would not withdraw his deadly rancor, or pay compensation: no counselor there had any reason to expect splendid repayment at the hands of the slayer.[4] For the monster was relentless, the dark death-shadow, against warriors old and young, lay in wait and ambushed them. In the perpetual darkness he held to the misty moors: men do not know where hell-demons direct their footsteps.

Thus many crimes the enemy of mankind committed, the terrible walker-alone, cruel injuries one after another. In the dark nights he dwelt in Heorot, the richly adorned hall. He might not approach the throne, [receive] treasure, because of the Lord; He had no love for him.[5]

This was great misery to the lord of the Scyldings, a breaking of spirit.

3. I.e., Grendel.
4. According to old Germanic law, a slayer could achieve peace with his victim's kinsmen only by paying them *wergild*, i.e., compensation for the life of the slain man.

5. Behind this obscure passage seems to lie the idea that Grendel, unlike Hrothgar's thanes, could not approach the throne to receive gifts from the king, having been condemned by God as an outlaw.

Many a noble sat often in council, sought a plan, what would be best for strong-hearted men to do against the awful attacks. At times they vowed sacrifices at heathen temples, with their words prayed that the soul-slayer[6] would give help for the distress of the people. Such was their custom, the hope of heathens; in their spirits they thought of Hell, they knew not the Ruler, the Judge of Deeds, they recognized not the Lord God, nor indeed did they know how to praise the Protector of Heaven, the glorious King. Woe is him who in terrible trouble must thrust his soul into the fire's embrace, hope for no comfort, not expect change. Well is the man who after his death-day may seek the Lord and find peace in the embrace of the Father.

[THE COMING OF BEOWULF TO HEOROT]

So in the cares of his times the son of Healfdene constantly brooded, nor might the wise warrior set aside his woe. Too harsh, hateful and long-lasting was the hardship that had come upon the people, distress dire and inexorable, worst of night-horrors.

A thane of Hygelac,[7] a good man among the Geats, heard in his homeland of Grendel's deeds: of mankind he was the strongest of might in the time of this life, noble and great. He bade that a good ship be made ready for him, said he would seek the war-king over the swan's road, the famous prince, since he had need of men. Very little did wise men blame him for that adventure, though he was dear to them; they urged the brave one on, examined the omens. From the folk of the Geats the good man had chosen warriors of the bravest that he could find; one of fifteen he led the way, the warrior sought the wooden ship, the sea-skilled one the land's edge. The time had come: the ship was on the waves, the boat under the cliff. The warriors eagerly climbed on the prow—the sea-currents eddied, sea against sand; men bore bright weapons into the ship's bosom, splendid armor. Men pushed the well-braced ship from shore, warriors on a well-wished voyage. Then over the sea-waves, blown by the wind, the foam-necked boat traveled, most like a bird, until at good time on the second day the curved prow had come to where the seafarers could see land, the sea-cliffs shine, towering hills, great headlands. Then was the sea crossed, the journey at end. Then quickly the men of the Geats climbed upon the shore, moored the wooden ship; mail-shirts rattled, dress for battle. They thanked God that the wave-way had been easy for them.

Then from the wall the Scyldings' guard who should watch over the sea-cliffs saw bright shields borne over the gangway, armor ready for battle; strong desire stirred him in mind to learn what the men were. He went riding on his horse to the shore, thane of Hrothgar, forcefully brandished a great spear in his hands, with formal words questioned them: "What are you, bearers of armor, dressed in mail-coats, who thus have

---

6. I.e., the Devil. It was believed that pagan deities were actually devils.

7. I.e., Beowulf the Geat, whose king was Hygelac.

come bringing a tall ship over the sea-road, over the water to this place? Lo, for a long time I have been guard of the coast, held watch by the sea so that no foe with a force of ships might work harm on the Danes' land: never have shieldbearers more openly undertaken to come ashore here; nor did you know for sure of a word of leave from our warriors, consent from my kinsmen. I have never seen a mightier warrior on earth than is one of you, a man in battle-dress. That is no retainer made to seem good by his weapons—may his appearance, his unequalled form, never belie him. Now I must learn your lineage before you go any farther from here, spies on the Danes' land. Now you far-dwellers, sea-voyagers, hear what I think: you must straightway say where you have come from."

To him replied the leader, the chief of the band unlocked his word-hoard: "We are men of the Geatish nation and Hygelac's hearth-companions. My father was well-known among the tribes, a noble leader named Ecgtheow. He lived many winters before he went on his way, an old man, from men's dwellings. Every wise man wide over the earth readily remembers him. Through friendly heart we have come to seek your lord, the son of Healfdene, protector of the people. Be good to us and tell us what to do: we have a great errand to the famous one, the king of the Danes. And I too do not think that anything ought to be kept secret: you know whether it is so, as we have indeed heard, that among the Scyldings I know not what foe, what dark doer of hateful deeds in the black nights, shows in terrible manner strange malice, injury and slaughter. In openness of heart I may teach Hrothgar remedy for that, how he, wise and good, shall overpower the foe—if change is ever to come to him, relief from evil's distress—and how his surging cares may be made to cool. Or else ever after he will suffer tribulations, constraint, while the best of houses remains there on its high place."

The guard spoke from where he sat on his horse, brave officer: "A sharp-witted shield-warrior who thinks well must be able to judge each of the two things, words and works. I understand this: that here is a troop friendly to the Scyldings' king. Go forward, bearing weapons and war-gear. I will show you the way; I shall also bid my fellow-thanes honorably to hold your boat against all enemies, your new-tarred ship on the sand, until again over the sea-streams it bears its beloved men to the Geatish shore, the wooden vessel with curved prow. May it be granted by fate that one who behaves so bravely pass whole through the battle-storm."

Then they set off. The boat lay fixed, rested on the rope, the deep-bosomed ship, fast at anchor. Boar-images[8] shone over cheek-guards gold-adorned, gleaming and fire-hardened—the war-minded boar held guard over fierce men. The warriors hastened, marched together until they might see the timbered hall, stately and shining with gold; for earth-dwellers under the skies that was the most famous of buildings in which

8. Carved images of boars (sometimes represented as clothed like human warriors) were placed on helmets in the belief that they would protect the wearer in battle.

the mighty one waited—its light gleamed over many lands. The battle-brave guide pointed out to them the shining house of the brave ones so that they might go straight to it. Warrior-like he turned his horse, then spoke words: "It is time for me to go back. The All-Wielding Father in His grace keep you safe in your undertakings. I shall go back to the sea to keep watch against hostile hosts."

The road was stone-paved, the path showed the way to the men in ranks. War-corselet shone, hard and hand-wrought, bright iron rings sang on their armor when they first came walking to the hall in their grim gear. Sea-weary they set down their broad shields, marvelously strong protections, against the wall of the building. Then they sat down on the bench—mail-shirts, warrior's clothing, rang out. Spears stood together, seamen's weapons, ash steel-gray at the top. The armed band was worthy of its weapons.

Then a proud-spirited man[9] asked the warriors there about their lineage: "Where do you bring those gold-covered shields from, gray mail-shirts and visored helmets, this multitude of battle-shafts? I am Hrothgar's herald and officer. I have not seen strangers—so many men—more bold. I think that it is for daring—not for refuge, but for greatness of heart—that you have sought Hrothgar." The man known for his courage replied to him; the proud man of the Geats, hardy under helmet, spoke words in return: "We are Hygelac's table-companions. Beowulf is my name. I will tell my errand to Healfdene's son, the great prince your lord, if, good as he is, he will grant that we might address him." Wulfgar spoke—he was a man of the Wendels, his bold spirit known to many, his valor and wisdom: "I will ask the lord of the Danes about this, the Scyldings' king, the ring-giver, just as you request—will ask the glorious ruler about your voyage, and will quickly make known to you the answer the good man thinks best to give me."

He returned at once to where Hrothgar sat, old and hoary, with his company of earls. The man known for his valor went forward till he stood squarely before the Danes' king: he knew the custom of tried retainers. Wulfgar spoke to his lord and friend: "Here have journeyed men of the Geats, come far over the sea's expanse. The warriors call their chief Beowulf. They ask that they, my prince, might exchange words with you. Do not refuse them your answer, gracious Hrothgar. From their wargear they seem worthy of earls' esteem. Strong indeed is the chief who has led the warriors here."

Hrothgar spoke, protector of the Scyldings: "I knew him when he was a boy. His father was called Ecgtheow: Hrethel of the Geats[1] gave him his only daughter for his home. Now has his hardy offspring come here, sought a fast friend. Then, too, seafarers who took gifts there to please the Geats used to say that he has in his handgrip the strength of thirty men, a man famous in battle. Holy God of His grace has sent him to us West-Danes, as I hope, against the terror of Grendel. I shall offer the

---

9. Identified below as Wulfgar.
1. Hrethel was the father of Hygelac and Beowulf's grandfather and guardian.

good man treasures for his daring. Now make haste, bid them come in together to see my company of kinsmen. In your speech say to them also that they are welcome to the Danish people."

Then Wulfgar went to the hall's door, gave the message from within: "The lord of the East-Danes, my victorious prince, has bidden me say to you that he knows your noble ancestry, and that you brave-hearted men are welcome to him over the sea-swells. Now you may come in your war-dress, under your battle helmets, to see Hrothgar. Let your war-shields, your wooden spears, await here the outcome of the talk."

Then the mighty one rose, many a warrior about him, a company of strong thanes. Some waited there, kept watch over the weapons as the brave one bade them. Together they hastened, as the warrior directed them, under Heorot's roof. The war-leader, hardy under helmet, advanced till he stood on the hearth. Beowulf spoke, his mail-shirt glistened, armor-net woven by the blacksmith's skill: "Hail, Hrothgar! I am kinsman and thane of Hygelac. In my youth I have set about many brave deeds. The affair of Grendel was made known to me on my native soil: sea-travelers say that this hall, best of buildings, stands empty and useless to all warriors after the evening-light becomes hidden beneath the cover of the sky. Therefore my people, the best wise earls, advised me thus, lord Hrothgar, that I should seek you because they know what my strength can accomplish. They themselves looked on when, bloody from my foes, I came from the fight where I had bound five, destroyed a family of giants, and at night in the waves slain water-monsters, suffered great pain, avenged an affliction of the Weather-Geats on those who had asked for trouble—ground enemies to bits. And now alone I shall settle affairs with Grendel, the monster, the demon. Therefore, lord of the Bright-Danes, protector of the Scyldings, I will make a request of you, refuge of warriors, fair friend of nations, that you refuse me not, now that I have come so far, that alone with my company of earls, this band of hardy men, I may cleanse Heorot. I have also heard say that the monster in his recklessness cares not for weapons. Therefore, so that my liege lord Hygelac may be glad of me in his heart, I scorn to bear sword or broad shield, yellow wood, to the battle, but with my grasp I shall grapple with the enemy and fight for life, foe against foe. The one whom death takes can trust the Lord's judgment. I think that if he may accomplish it, unafraid he will feed on the folk of the Geats in the war-hall as he has often done on the flower of men. You will not need to hide my head[2] if death takes me, for he will have me blood-smeared; he will bear away my bloody flesh meaning to savor it, he will eat ruthlessly, the walker alone, will stain his retreat in the moor; no longer will you need trouble yourself to take care of my body. If battle takes me, send to Hygelac the best of war-clothes that protects my breast, finest of mail-shirts. It is a legacy of Hrethel, the work of Weland.[3] Fate always goes as it must."

2. I.e., "bury my body."   3. The blacksmith of the Norse gods.

Hrothgar spoke, protector of the Scyldings: "For deeds done, my friend Beowulf, and for past favors you have sought us. A fight of your father's brought on the greatest of feuds. With his own hands he became the slayer of Heatholaf among the Wylfings. After that the country of the Weather-Geats might not keep him, for fear of war. From there he sought the folk of the South-Danes, the Honor-Scyldings, over the sea-swell. At that time I was first ruling the Danish people and, still in my youth, held the wide kingdom, hoard-city of heroes. Heorogar had died then, gone from life, my older brother, son of Healfdene—he was better than I. Afterwards I paid blood-money to end the feud; over the sea's back I sent to the Wylfings old treasures; he[4] swore oaths to me.

"It is a sorrow to me in spirit to say to any man what Grendel has brought me with his hatred—humiliation in Heorot, terrible violence. My hall-troop, warrior-band, has shrunk; fate has swept them away into Grendel's horror. (God may easily put an end to the wild ravager's deeds!) Full often over the ale-cups warriors made bold with beer have boasted that they would await with grim swords Grendel's attack in the beer-hall. Then in the morning this mead-hall was a hall shining with blood, when the day lightened, all the bench-floor blood-wet, a gore-hall. I had fewer faithful men, beloved retainers, for death had destroyed them. Now sit down to the feast and unbind your thoughts, your famous victories, as heart inclines."

[THE FEAST AT HEOROT]

Then was a bench cleared in the beer-hall for the men of the Geats all together. Then the stout-hearted ones went to sit down, proud in their might. A thane did his work who bore in his hands an embellished ale-cup, poured the bright drink. At times a scop sang, clear-voiced in Heorot. There was joy of brave men, no little company of Danes and Weather-Geats.

Unferth spoke, son of Ecglaf, who sat at the feet of the king of the Scyldings, unbound words of contention—to him was Beowulf's undertaking, the brave seafarer, a great vexation, for he would not allow that any other man of middle-earth should ever achieve more glory under the heavens than himself: "Are you that Beowulf who contended with Breca, competed in swimming on the broad sea, where for pride you explored the water, and for foolish boast ventured your lives in the deep? Nor might any man, friend nor enemy, keep you from the perilous venture of swimming in the sea. There you embraced the sea-streams with your arms, measured the sea-ways, flung forward your hands, glided over the ocean; the sea boiled with waves, with winter's swell. Seven nights you toiled in the water's power. He overcame you at swimming, had more strength. Then in the morning the sea bore him up among the Heathoraemas; from there he sought his own home, dear to his people, the land of the Brondings, the fair stronghold, where he had

---

4. Ecgtheow, whose feud with the Wylfings Hrothgar had settled.

folk, castle, and treasures. All his boast against you the son of Beanstan carried out in deed. Therefore I expect the worse results for you—though you have prevailed everywhere in battles, in grim war—if you dare wait near Grendel a night-long space."

Beowulf spoke, the son of Ecgtheow: "Well, my friend Unferth, drunk with beer you have spoken a great many things about Breca—told about his adventures. I maintain the truth that I had more strength in the sea, hardship on the waves, than any other man. Like boys we agreed together and boasted—we were both in our first youth—that we would risk our lives in the salt sea, and that we did even so. We had naked swords, strong in our hands, when we went swimming; we thought to guard ourselves against whale-fishes. He could not swim at all far from me in the flood-waves, be quicker in the water, nor would I move away from him. Thus we were together on the sea for the time of five nights until the flood drove us apart, the swelling sea, coldest of weathers, darkening night, and the north wind battle-grim turned against us: rough were the waves. The anger of the sea-fishes was roused. Then my body-mail, hard and hand-linked, gave me help against my foes; the woven war-garment, gold-adorned, covered my breast. A fierce cruel attacker dragged me to the bottom, held me grim in his grasp, but it was granted me to reach the monster with my sword-point, my battle-blade. The war-stroke destroyed the mighty sea-beast—through my hand.

"Thus often loathsome assailants pressed me hard. I served them with my good sword, as the right was. They had no joy at all of the feast, the malice-workers, that they should eat me, sit around a banquet near the sea-bottom. But in the morning, sword-wounded they lay on the shore, left behind by the waves, put to sleep by the blade, so that thereafter they would never hinder the passage of sea-voyagers over the deep water. Light came from the east, bright signal of God, the sea became still so that I might see the headlands, the windy walls of the sea. Fate often saves an undoomed man when his courage is good. In any case it befell me that I slew with my sword nine sea-monsters. I have not heard tell of a harder fight by night under heaven's arch, nor of a man more hard-pressed in the sea-streams. Yet I came out of the enemies' grasp alive, weary of my adventure. Then the sea bore me onto the lands of the Finns, the flood with its current, the surging waters.

"I have not heard say of you any such hard matching of might, such sword-terror. Breca never yet in the games of war—neither he nor you—achieved so bold a deed with bright swords (I do not much boast of it), though you became your brothers' slayer, your close kin; for that you will suffer punishment in hell, even though your wit is keen. I tell you truly, son of Ecglaf, that Grendel, awful monster, would never have performed so many terrible deeds against your chief, humiliation in Heorot, if your spirit, your heart, were so fierce in fight as you claim. But he has noticed that he need not much fear the hostility, not much dread the terrible sword-storm of your people, the Victory-Scyldings. He exacts forced levy, shows mercy to none of the Danish people; but he is glad, kills, carves for feasting, expects no fight from the Spear-Danes. But I shall show him soon now the strength and courage of the Geats, their warfare. Afterwards he will walk who may, glad to the mead, when the morning light of another day, the bright-clothed sun, shines from the south on the children of men."

Then was the giver of treasure in gladness, gray-haired and battle-brave. The lord of the Bright-Danes could count on help. The folk's guardian had heard from Beowulf a fast-resolved thought.

There was laughter of warriors, voices rang pleasant, words were cheerful. Wealhtheow came forth, Hrothgar's queen, mindful of customs, gold-adorned, greeted the men in the hall; and the noble woman offered the cup first to the keeper of the land of the East-Danes, bade him be glad at the beer-drinking, beloved of the people. In joy he partook of feast and hall-cup, king famous for victories. Then the woman of the Helmings went about to each one of the retainers, young and old, offered them the costly cup, until the time came that she brought the mead-bowl to Beowulf, the ring-adorned queen, mature of mind. Sure of speech she greeted the man of the Geats, thanked God that her wish was fulfilled, that she might trust in some man for help against deadly deeds. He took the cup, the warrior fierce in battle, from Wealhtheow, and then spoke, one ready for fight—Beowulf spoke, the son of Ecgtheow: "I resolved, when I set out on the sea, sat down in the sea-boat with my band of men, that I should altogether fulfill the will of your people or else fall in slaughter, fast in the foe's grasp. I shall achieve a deed of manly courage or else have lived to see in this mead-hall my ending day." These words were well-pleasing to the woman, the boast of the Geat. Gold-adorned, the noble folk-queen went to sit by her lord.

Then there were again as at first strong words spoken in the hall, the people in gladness, the sound of a victorious folk, until, in a little while, the son of Healfdene wished to seek his evening rest. He knew of the battle in the high hall that had been plotted by the monster, plotted from the time that they might see the light of the sun until the night, growing dark over all things, the shadowy shapes of darkness, should come gliding, black under the clouds. The company all arose. Then they saluted each other, Hrothgar and Beowulf, and Hrothgar wished him good luck, control of the wine-hall, and spoke these words: "Never before, since I could raise hand and shield, have I entrusted to any man the great hall of the Danes, except now to you. Hold now and guard the best of houses: remember your fame, show your great courage, keep watch against the fierce foe. You will not lack what you wish if you survive that deed of valor."

[THE FIGHT WITH GRENDEL]

Then Hrothgar went out of the hall with his company of warriors, the protector of the Scyldings. The war-chief would seek the bed of Wealhtheow the queen. The King of Glory—as men had learned—had appointed a hall-guard against Grendel; he had a special mission to the prince of the Danes: he kept watch against monsters.

And the man of the Geats had sure trust in his great might, the favor of the Ruler. Then he took off his shirt of armor, the helmet from his head, handed his embellished sword, best of irons, to an attendant, bade him keep guard over his war-gear. Then the good warrior spoke some boast-words before he went to his bed, Beowulf of the Geats: "I claim myself no poorer in war-strength, war works, than Grendel claims himself. Therefore I will not put him to sleep with a sword, so take away his life, though surely I might. He knows no good tools with which he might strike against me, cut my shield in pieces, though he is strong in fight. But we shall forgo the sword in the night—if he dare seek war without weapon—and then may wise God, Holy Lord, assign glory on whichever hand seems good to Him."

The battle-brave one laid himself down, the pillow received the earl's head, and about him many a brave seaman lay down to hall-rest. None of them thought that he would ever again seek from there his dear home, people or town where he had been brought up; for they knew that bloody death had carried off far too many men in the wine-hall, folk of the Danes. But the Lord granted to weave for them good fortune in war, for the folk of the Weather-Geats, comfort and help that they should quite overcome their foe through the might of one man, through his sole strength: the truth has been made known that mighty God has always ruled mankind.

There came gliding in the black night the walker in darkness. The warriors slept who should hold the horned house—all but one. It was known to men that when the Ruler did not wish it the hostile creature might not drag them away beneath the shadows. But he, lying awake for the fierce foe, with heart swollen in anger awaited the outcome of the fight.

Then from the moor under the mist-hills Grendel came walking, wearing God's anger. The foul ravager thought to catch some one of mankind there in the high hall. Under the clouds he moved until he could see most clearly the wine-hall, treasure-house of men, shining with gold. That was not the first time that he had sought Hrothgar's home. Never before or since in his life-days did he find harder luck, hardier hall-thanes. The creature deprived of joy came walking to the hall. Quickly the door gave way, fastened with fire-forged bands, when he touched it with his hands. Driven by evil desire, swollen with rage, he tore it open, the hall's mouth. After that the foe at once stepped onto the shining floor, advanced angrily. From his eyes came a light not fair, most like a flame. He saw many men in the hall, a band of kinsmen all asleep together, a company of war-men. Then his heart laughed: dreadful monster, he thought that before the day came he would divide the life from the body of every one of them, for there had come to him a hope of full-feasting. It was not his fate that when that night was over he should feast on more of mankind.

The kinsman of Hygelac, mighty man, watched how the evil-doer would make his quick onslaught. Nor did the monster mean to delay it, but, starting his work, he suddenly seized a sleeping man, tore at him ravenously, bit into his bone-locks, drank the blood from his veins, swallowed huge morsels; quickly he had eaten all of the lifeless one, feet and hands. He stepped closer, then felt with his arm for the brave-hearted man on the bed, reached out towards him, the foe with his hand; at once in fierce response Beowulf seized it and sat up, leaning on his own arm. Straightway the fosterer of crimes knew that he had not encountered on middle-earth, anywhere in this world, a harder hand-grip from another man. In mind he became frightened, in his spirit: not for that might he escape the sooner. His heart was eager to get away, he would flee to his hiding-place, seek his rabble of devils. What he met there was not such as he had ever before met in the days of his life. Then the kinsman of Hygelac, the good man, thought of his evening's speech, stood upright and laid firm hold on him: his fingers cracked. The giant was pulling away, the earl stepped forward. The notorious one thought to move farther away, wherever he could, and flee his way from there to his fen-retreat; he knew his fingers' power to be in a hateful grip. That was a painful journey that the loathsome despoiler had made to Heorot. The retainers' hall rang with the noise—terrible drink[5] for all the Danes, the house-dwellers, every brave man, the earls. Both were enraged, fury-filled, the two who meant to control the hall. The building resounded. Then was it much wonder that the wine-hall withstood them joined in fierce fight, that it did not fall to the ground, the fair earth-dwelling; but it was so firmly made fast with iron bands, both inside and outside, joined by skillful smith-craft. There started from the floor—as I have heard say—many a mead-bench, gold-adorned, when the furious ones fought. No wise men of the Scyldings ever before thought that any men in any manner might break it down, splendid with bright horns, have skill to destroy it, unless flame should embrace it, swallow it in fire. Noise rose up, sound strange enough. Horrible fear came upon the North-Danes, upon every one of those who heard the weeping from the wall, God's enemy sing his terrible song, song without triumph—the hell-slave bewail his pain. There held him fast he who of men was strongest of might in the days of this life.

Not for anything would the protector of warriors let the murderous guest go off alive: he did not consider his life-days of use to any of the nations. There more than enough of Beowulf's earls drew swords, old heirlooms, wished to protect the life of their dear lord, famous prince, however they might. They did not know when they entered the fight, hardy-spirited warriors, and when they thought to hew him on every side, to seek his soul, that not any of the best of irons on earth, no war-sword, would touch the evil-doer: for with a charm he had made victory-weapons useless, every sword-edge. His departure to death from the time

---

5. The metaphor reflects the idea that the chief purpose of a hall such as Heorot was as a place for men to feast in.

of this life was to be wretched; and the alien spirit was to travel far off into the power of fiends. Then he who before had brought trouble of heart to mankind, committed many crimes—he was at war with God— found that his body would do him no good, for the great-hearted kinsman of Hygelac had him by the hand. Each was hateful to the other alive. The awful monster had lived to feel pain in his body, a huge wound in his shoulder was exposed, his sinews sprang apart, his bonelocks broke. Glory in battle was given to Beowulf. Grendel must flee from there, mortally sick, seek his joyless home in the fen-slopes. He knew the more surely that his life's end had come, the full number of his days. For all the Danes was their wish fulfilled after the bloody fight. Thus he who had lately come from far off, wise and stout-hearted, had purged Heorot, saved Hrothgar's house from affliction. He rejoiced in his night's work, a deed to make famous his courage. The man of the Geats had fulfilled his boast to the East-Danes; so too he had remedied all the grief, the malice-caused sorrow that they had endured before, and had had to suffer from harsh necessity, no small distress. That was clearly proved when the battle-brave man set the hand up under the curved roof—the arm and the shoulder: there all together was Grendel's grasp.

[CELEBRATION AT HEOROT]

Then in the morning, as I have heard, there was many a warrior about the gift-hall. Folk-chiefs came from far and near over the wide-stretching ways to look on the wonder, the footprints of the foe. Nor did his going from life seem sad to any of the men who saw the tracks of the one without glory—how, weary-hearted, overcome with injuries, he moved on his way from there to the mere[6] of the water-monsters with life-failing footsteps, death-doomed and in flight. There the water was boiling with blood, the horrid surge of waves swirling, all mixed with hot gore, sword-blood. Doomed to die he had hidden, then, bereft of joys, had laid down his life in his fen-refuge, his heathen soul: there hell took him.

From there old retainers—and many a young man, too—turned back in their glad journey to ride from the mere, high-spirited on horseback, warriors on steeds. There was Beowulf's fame spoken of; many a man said—and not only once—that, south nor north, between the seas, over the wide earth, no other man under the sky's expanse was better of those who bear shields, more worthy of ruling. Yet they found no fault with their own dear lord, gracious Hrothgar, for he was a good king. At times battle-famed men let their brown horses gallop, let them race where the paths seemed fair, known for their excellence. At times a thane of the king, a man skilled at telling adventures, songs stored in his memory, who could recall many of the stories of the old days, wrought a new tale

6. Lake.

in well-joined words; this man undertook with his art to recite in turn
Beowulf's exploit, and skillfully to tell an apt tale, to lend words to it.

He spoke everything that he had heard tell of Sigemund's valorous
deeds, many a strange thing, the strife of Waels's son,[7] his far journeys,
feuds and crimes, of which the children of men knew nothing—except
for Fitela with him, to whom he would tell everything, the uncle to his
nephew, for they were always friends in need in every fight. Many were
the tribes of giants that they had laid low with their swords. For Sigemund there sprang up after his death-day no little glory—after he, hardy
in war, had killed the dragon, keeper of the treasure-hoard: under the
hoary stone the prince's son had ventured alone, a daring deed, nor was
Fitela with him. Yet it turned out well for him, so that his sword went
through the gleaming worm and stood fixed in the wall, splendid weapon:
the dragon lay dead of the murdering stroke. Through his courage the
great warrior had brought it about that he might at his own wish enjoy
the ring-hoard. He loaded the sea-boat, bore into the ship's bosom the
bright treasure, offspring of Waels. The hot dragon melted.

He was adventurer most famous, far and wide through the nations,
for deeds of courage—he had prospered from that before, the protector
of warriors—after the war-making of Heremod had come to an end, his
strength and his courage.[8] Among the Jutes Heremod came into the
power of his enemies, was betrayed, quickly dispatched. Surging sorrows
had oppressed him too long: he had become a great care to his people,
to all his princes; for many a wise man in former times had bewailed the
journey of the fierce-hearted one—people who had counted on him as
a relief from affliction—that that king's son should prosper, take the rank
of his father, keep guard over the folk, the treasure and stronghold, the
kingdom of heroes, the home of the Scyldings. The kinsman of Hygelac
became dearer to his friends, to all mankind: crime took possession of
Heremod.

Sometimes racing their horses they passed over the sand-covered ways.
By then the morning light was far advanced, hastening on. Many a
stout-hearted warrior went to the high hall to see the strange wonder.
The king himself walked forth from the women's apartment, the guardian of the ring-hoards, secure in his fame, known for his excellence,
with much company; and his queen with him passed over the path to
the mead-hall with a troop of attendant women.

Hrothgar spoke—he had gone to the hall, taken his stand on the steps,
looked at the high roof shining with gold, and at Grendel's hand: "For
this sight may thanks be made quickly to the Almighty: I endured much
from the foe, many griefs from Grendel: God may always work wonder
upon wonder, the Guardian of Heaven. It was not long ago that I did
not expect ever to live to see relief from any of my woes—when the best

---

7. Waels was Sigemund's father.
8. Heremod was an unsuccessful king of the Danes,
one who began brilliantly but became cruel and
avaricious, ultimately having to take refuge among
the Jutes, who put him to death. His reputation
was thus overshadowed by that of Sigemund.

of houses stood shining with blood, stained with slaughter, a far-reaching woe for each of my counselors, for every one, since none thought he could ever defend the people's stronghold from its enemies, from demons and evil spirits. Now through the Lord's might a warrior has accomplished the deed that all of us with our skill could not perform. Yes, she may say, whatever woman brought forth this son among mankind—if she still lives—that the God of Old was kind to her in her childbearing. Now, Beowulf, best of men, in my heart I will love you as a son: keep well this new kinship. To you will there be no lack of the good things of the world that I have in my possession. Full often I have made reward for less, done honor with gifts to a lesser warrior, weaker in fighting. With your deeds you yourself have made sure that your glory will be ever alive. May the Almighty reward you with good—as just now he has done."

Beowulf spoke, the son of Ecgtheow: "With much good will we have achieved this work of courage, that fight, have ventured boldly against the strength of the unknown one. I should have wished rather that you might have seen him, your enemy brought low among your furnishings. I thought quickly to bind him on his deathbed with hard grasp, so that because of my hand-grip he should lie struggling for life—unless his body should escape. I could not stop his going, since the Lord did not wish it, nor did I hold him firmly enough for that, my life-enemy: he was too strong, the foe in his going. Yet to save his life he has left his hand behind to show that he was here—his arm and shoulder; nor by that has the wretched creature bought any comfort; none the longer will the loathsome ravager live, hard-pressed by his crimes, for a wound has clutched him hard in its strong grip, in deadly bonds. There, like a man outlawed for guilt, he shall await the great judgment, how the bright Lord will decree for him."

Then was the warrior more silent in boasting speech of warlike deeds, the son of Ecglaf,[9] after the nobles had looked at the hand, now high on the roof through the strength of a man, the foe's fingers. The end of each one, each of the nail-places, was most like steel; the hand-spurs of the heathen warrior were monstrous spikes. Everyone said that no hard thing would hurt him, no iron good from old times would harm the bloody battle-hand of the monster.

Then it was ordered that Heorot be within quickly adorned by hands. Many there were, both men and women, who made ready the wine-hall, the guest-building. The hangings on the walls shone with gold, many a wondrous sight for each man who looks on such things. That bright building was much damaged, though made fast within by iron bonds, and its door-hinges sprung; the roof alone came through unharmed when the monster, outlawed for his crimes, turned in flight, in despair of his life. That is not easy to flee from—let him try it who will—but

9. I.e., Unferth, who had taunted Beowulf the night before.

driven by need one must seek the place prepared for earth-dwellers, soul-bearers, the sons of men, the place where, after its feasting, one's body will sleep fast in its death-bed.

Then had the proper time come that Healfdene's son should go to the hall; the king himself would share in the feast. I have never heard that a people in a larger company bore themselves better about their treasurer-giver. Men who were known for courage sat at the benches, rejoiced in the feast. Their kinsmen, stout-hearted Hrothgar and Hrothulf, partook fairly of many a mead-cup in the high hall. Heorot within was filled with friends: the Scylding-people had not then known treason's web.[1]

Then the son of Healfdene gave Beowulf a golden standard to reward his victory—a decorated battle-banner—a helmet and mail-shirt: many saw the glorious, costly sword borne before the warrior. Beowulf drank of the cup in the mead-hall. He had no need to be ashamed before fighting men of those rich gifts. I have not heard of many men who gave four precious, gold-adorned things to another on the ale-bench in a more friendly way. The rim around the helmet's crown had a head-protection, wound of wire, so that no battle-hard sharp sword might badly hurt him when the shield-warrior should go against his foe. Then the people's protector commanded eight horses with golden bridles to be led into the hall, within the walls. The saddle of one of them stood shining with hand-ornaments, adorned with jewels: that had been the war-seat of the high king when the son of Healfdene would join sword-play: never did the warfare of the wide-known one fail when men died in battle. And then the prince of Ing's friends[2] yielded possession of both, horses and weapons, to Beowulf: he bade him use them well. So generously the famous prince, guardian of the hoard, repaid the war-rior's battle-deeds with horses and treasure that no man will ever find fault with them—not he that will speak truth according to what is right.

Then further the lord gave treasure to each of the men on the mead-bench who had made the sea-voyage with Beowulf, gave heirlooms; and he commanded that gold be paid for the one whom in his malice Gren-del had killed—as he would have killed more if wise God and the man's courage had not forestalled that fate. The Lord guided all the race of men then, as he does now. Yet is discernment everywhere best, fore-thought of mind. Many a thing dear and loath he shall live to see who here in the days of trouble long makes use of the world.

There was song and music together before Healfdene's battle-leader, the wooden harp touched, tale oft told, when Hrothgar's scop should speak hall-pastime among the mead-benches . . . [of] Finn's retainers when the sudden disaster fell upon them. . . .[3]

The hero of the Half-Danes, Hnaef of the Scyldings, was fated to fall

1. A reference to the later history of the Danes, when, after Hrothgar's death, his nephew Hro-thulf apparently drove his son and successor Hrethric from the throne.

2. Ing was a Germanic deity, and his "friends" are the Danes.

3. The lines introducing the scop's song seem faulty. The story itself is recounted in a highly allusive way, and many of its details are obscure, though some help is offered by an independent version of the story given in a fragmentary Old English lay called The Fight at Finnsburg.

on Frisian battlefield. And no need had Hildeburh[4] to praise the good faith of the Jutes: blameless she was deprived of her dear ones at the shield-play, of son and brother; wounded by spears they fell to their fate. That was a mournful woman. Not without cause did Hoc's daughter lament the decree of destiny when morning came and she might see, under the sky, the slaughter of kinsmen—where before she had the greatest of world's joy. The fight took away all Finn's thanes except for only a few, so that he could in no way continue the battle on the field against Hengest, nor protect the survivors by fighting against the prince's thane. But they offered them peace-terms,[5] that they should clear another building for them, hall and high sea, that they might have control of half of it with the sons of the Jutes; and at givings of treasure the son of Folcwalda[6] should honor the Danes each day, should give Hengest's company rings, such gold-plated treasure as that with which he would cheer the Frisians' kin in the high hall. Then on both sides they confirmed the fast peace-compact. Finn declared to Hengest, with oaths deep-sworn, unfeigned, that he would hold those who were left from the battle in honor in accordance with the judgment of his counselors, so that by words or by works no man should break the treaty nor because of malice should ever mention that, princeless, the Danes followed the slayer of their own ring-giver, since necessity forced them. If with rash speech any of the Frisians should insist upon calling to mind the cause of murderous hate, then the sword's edge should settle it.

The funeral pyre was made ready and gold brought up from the hoard. The best of the warriors of the War-Scyldings[7] was ready on the pyre. At the fire it was easy to see many a blood-stained battle-shirt, boar-image all golden—iron-hard swine—many a noble destroyed by wounds: more than one had died in battle. Then Hildeburh bade give her own son to the flames on Hnaef's pyre, burn his body, put him in the fire at the shoulder of his uncle. The woman mourned, sang her lament. The warrior took his place.[8] The greatest of death-fires wound to the skies, roared before the barrow. Heads melted as blood sprang out—wounds opened wide, hate-bites of the body. Fire swallowed them—greediest of spirits—all of those whom war had taken away from both peoples: their strength had departed.

Then warriors went to seek their dwellings, bereft of friends, to behold Friesland, their homes and high city.[9] Yet Hengest stayed on with Finn

---

4. Hildeburh, daughter of the former Danish king Hoc and sister of the ruling Danish king Hnaef, was married to Finn, king of the Jutes (Frisians). Hnaef with a party of Danes made what was presumably a friendly visit to Hildeburh and Finn at their home Finnsburg, but during a feast a quarrel broke out between the Jutes and the Danes (since the scop's sympathies are with the Danes, he ascribes the cause to the bad faith of the Jutes), and in the ensuing fight Hnaef and his nephew, the son of Finn and Hildeburh, were killed, along with many other Danes and Jutes.
5. It is not clear who proposed the peace terms,

but in view of the teller's Danish sympathies, it was probably the Jutes that sought the uneasy truce from Hengest, who became the Danes' leader after Hnaef's death. The truce imposed upon Hengest and the Danes the intolerable condition of having to dwell in peace with the Jutish king who was responsible for the death of their own king.
6. I.e., Finn.
7. I.e., Hnaef.
8. The line is obscure, but it perhaps means that the body of Hildeburh's son was placed on the pyre.
9. This seems to refer to the few survivors on the Jutish side.

for a winter darkened with the thought of slaughter, all desolate. He thought of his land, though he might not drive his ring-prowed ship over the water—the sea boiled with storms, strove with the wind, winter locked the waves in ice-bonds—until another year came to men's dwellings, just as it does still, glorious bright weather always watching for its time. Then winter was gone, earth's lap fair, the exile was eager to go, the guest from the dwelling: [yet] more he thought of revenge for his wrongs than of the sea-journey—if he might bring about a fight where he could take account of the sons of the Jutes with his iron. So he made no refusal of the world's custom when the son of Hunlaf[1] placed on his lap Battle-Bright, best of swords: its edges were known to the Jutes. Thus also to war-minded Finn in his turn cruel sword-evil came in his own home, after Guthlaf and Oslaf complained of the grim attack, the injury after the sea-journey, assigned blame for their lot of woes: breast might not contain the restless heart. Then was the hall reddened from foes' bodies, and thus Finn slain, the king in his company, and the queen taken. The warriors of the Scyldings bore to ship all the hall-furnishings of the land's king, whatever of necklaces, skillfully wrought treasures, they might find at Finn's home. They brought the noble woman on the sea-journey to the Danes, led her to her people.

The lay was sung to the end, the song of the scop. Joy mounted again, bench-noise brightened, cup-bearers poured wine from wonderful vessels. Then Wealhtheow came forth to walk under gold crown to where all good men sat, nephew and uncle: their friendship was then still unbroken, each true to the other.[2] There too Unferth the spokesman sat at the feet of the prince of the Scyldings: each of them trusted his spirit, that he had much courage, though he was not honorable to his kinsmen at sword-play. Then the woman of the Scyldings spoke:

"Take this cup, my noble lord, giver of treasure. Be glad, gold-friend of warriors, and speak to the Geats with mild words, as a man ought to do. Be gracious to the Geats, mindful of gifts [which][3] you now have from near and far. They have told me that you would have the warrior for your son. Heorot is purged, the bright ring-hall. Enjoy while you may many rewards, and leave to your kinsmen folk and kingdom when you must go forth to look on the Ruler's decree. I know my gracious Hrothulf, that he will hold the young warriors in honor if you, friend of the Scyldings, leave the world before him. I think he will repay our sons with good if he remembers all the favors we did to his pleasure and honor when he was a child."

Then she turned to the bench where her sons were, Hrethric and

---

1. The text is open to various interpretations. The one adopted here assumes that the Dane Hunlaf, brother of Guthlaf and Oslaf, had been killed in the fight, and that ultimately Hunlaf's son demanded vengeance by the symbolical act of placing his father's sword in Hengest's lap, while at the same time Guthlaf and Oslaf reminded Hengest of the Jutes' treachery. It is not clear whether the subsequent fight in which Finn was killed was waged by the Danish survivors alone, or whether the party first went back to Denmark and then returned to Finnsburg with reinforcements.

2. See note 1, above.

3. The text seems corrupt.

Hrothmund, and the sons of the warriors, young men together. There sat the good man Beowulf of the Geats beside the two brothers.

The cup was borne to him and welcome offered in friendly words to him, and twisted gold courteously bestowed on him, two arm-ornaments, a mail-shirt and rings, the largest of necklaces of those that I have heard spoken of on earth. I have heard of no better hoard-treasure under the heavens since Hama carried away to his bright city the necklace of the Brosings,[4] chain and rich setting: he fled the treacherous hatred of Eormenric, got eternal favor. This ring Hygelac of the Geats,[5] grandson of Swerting, had on his last venture, when beneath his battle-banner he defended his treasure, protected the spoils of war: fate took him when for pride he sought trouble, feud with the Frisians. Over the cup of the waves the mighty prince wore that treasure, precious stone. He fell beneath his shield; the body of the king came into the grasp of the Franks, his breast-armor and the neck-ring together. Lesser warriors plundered the fallen after the war-harvest: people of the Geats held the place of corpses.

The hall was filled with noise. Wealhtheow spoke, before the company she said to him: "Wear this ring, beloved Beowulf, young man, with good luck, and make use of this mail-shirt from the people's treasure, and prosper well; make yourself known with your might, and be kind of counsel to these boys: I shall remember to reward you for that. You have brought it about that, far and near, for a long time all men shall praise you, as wide as the sea surrounds the shores, home of the winds. While you live, prince, be prosperous. I wish you well of your treasure. Much favored one, be kind of deeds to my son. Here is each earl true to other, mild of heart, loyal to his lord; the thanes are at one, the people obedient, the retainers cheered with drink do as I bid."

Then she walked to her seat. There was the best of feasts, men drank wine. They did not know the fate, the grim decree made long before, as it came to pass to many of the earls after evening had come and Hrothgar had gone to his chambers, the noble one to his rest. A great number of men remained in the hall, just as they had often done before. They cleared the benches from the floor. It was spread over with beds and pillows. One of the beer-drinkers, ripe and fated to die, lay down to his hall-rest. They set at their heads their battle-shields, bright wood; there on the bench it was easy to see above each man his helmet that towered in battle, his ringed mail-shirt, his great spear-wood. It was their custom to be always ready for war whether at home or in the field, in any case at any time that need should befall their liege lord: that was a good nation.

4. The Brisings' (Brosings') necklace had been worn by the goddess Freya. Nothing more is known of this story of Hama, who seems to have stolen the necklace from the famous Gothic king Eormenric. 5. Beowulf is later said to have presented the neck-lace to Hygelac's queen, Hygd, though here Hygelac is said to have been wearing it on his ill-fated expedition against the Franks and Frisians, into whose hands it fell at his death.

[GRENDEL'S MOTHER'S ATTACK]

Then they sank to sleep. One paid sorely for his evening rest, just as
had often befallen them when Grendel guarded the gold-hall, wrought
wrong until the end came, death after misdeeds. It came to be seen,
wide-known to men, that after the bitter battle an avenger still lived for
an evil space: Grendel's mother, woman, monster-wife, was mindful of
her misery, she who had to dwell in the terrible water, the cold currents,
after Cain became sword-slayer of his only brother, his own father's son.
Then Cain went as an outlaw to flee the cheerful life of men, marked
for his murder, held to the wasteland. From him sprang many a devil
sent by fate. Grendel was one of them, hateful outcast who at Heorot
found a waking man waiting his warfare. There the monster had laid
hold upon him, but he was mindful of the great strength, the large gift
God had given him, and relied on the Almighty for favor, comfort and
help. By that he overcame the foe, subdued the hell-spirit. Then he
went off wretched, bereft of joy, to seek his dying-place, enemy of mankind. And his mother, still greedy and gallows-grim, would go on a
sorrowful venture, avenge her son's death.

Then she came to Heorot where the Ring-Danes slept throughout the
hall. Then change came quickly to the earls there, when Grendel's mother
made her way in. The attack was the less terrible by just so much as is
the strength of women, the war-terror of a wife, less than an armed
man's when a hard blade, forge-hammered, a sword shining with blood,
good of its edges, cuts the stout boar on a helmet opposite. Then in the
hall was hard-edged sword raised from the seat, many a broad shield
lifted firmly in hand: none thought of helmet, of wide mail-shirt, when
the terror seized him. She was in haste, would be gone out from there,
protect her life after she was discovered. Swiftly she had taken fast hold
on one of the nobles, then she went to the fen. He was one of the men
between the seas most beloved of Hrothgar in the rank of retainer, a
noble shield-warrior whom she destroyed at his rest, a man of great repute.
Beowulf was not there, for earlier, after the treasure-giving, another lodging
had been appointed for the renowned Geat. Outcry arose in Heorot: she
had taken, in its gore, the famed hand. Care was renewed, come again
on the dwelling. That was not a good bargain, that on both sides they
had to pay with the lives of friends.

Then was the old king, the hoary warrior, of bitter mind when he
learned that his chief thane was lifeless, his dearest man dead. Quickly
Beowulf was fetched to the bed-chamber, man happy in victory. At daybreak together with his earls he went, the noble champion himself with
his retainers, to where the wise one was, waiting to know whether after
tidings of woe the All-Wielder would ever bring about change for him.
The worthy warrior walked over the floor with his retainers—hall-wood
resounded—that he might address words to the wise prince of Ing's friends,
asked if the night had been pleasant according to his desires.

Hrothgar spoke, protector of the Scyldings: "Ask not about pleasure.

Sorrow is renewed to the people of the Danes: Aeschere is dead, Yrmen-laf's elder brother, my speaker of wisdom and my bearer of counsel, my shoulder-companion when we used to defend our heads in battle, when troops clashed, beat on boar-images. Whatever an earl should be, a man good from old times, such was Aeschere. Now a wandering mur-derous spirit has slain him with its hands in Heorot. I do not know by what way the awful creature, glorying in its prey, has made its retreat, gladdened by its feast. She has avenged the feud—that last night you killed Grendel with hard hand-grips, savagely, because too long he had diminished and destroyed my people. He fell in the fight, his life for-feited, and now the other has come, a mighty worker of wrong, would avenge her kinsman, and has carried far her revenge—as many a thane may think who weeps in his spirit for his treasure-giver, bitter sorrow in heart. Now the hand lies lifeless that was strong in support of all your desires.

"I have heard landsmen, my people, hall-counselors, say this, that they have seen two such huge walkers in the wasteland holding to the moors, alien spirits. One of them, so far as they could clearly discern, was the likeness of a woman. The other wretched shape trod the tracks of exile in the form of a man, except that he was bigger than any other man. Land-dwellers in the old days named him Grendel. They know of no father, whether in earlier times any was begotten for them among the dark spirits. They hold to the secret land, the wolf-slopes, the windy headlands, the dangerous fen-paths where the mountain stream goes down under the darkness of the hills, the flood under the earth. It is not far from here, measured in miles, that the mere stands; over it hang frost-covered woods, trees fast of root close over the water. There each night may be seen fire on the flood, a fearful wonder. Of the sons of men there lives none, old of wisdom, who knows the bottom. Though the heath-stalker, the strong-horned hart, harassed by hounds makes for the forest after long flight, rather will he give his life, his being, on the bank than save his head by entering. That is no pleasant place. From it the surging waves rise up black to the heavens when the wind stirs up awful storms, until the air becomes gloomy, the skies weep. Now once again is the cure in you alone. You do not yet know the land, the per-ilous place, where you might find the seldom-seen creature: seek if you dare. I will give you wealth for the feud, old treasure, as I did before, twisted gold—if you come away."

Beowulf spoke, the son of Ecgtheow: "Sorrow not, wise warrior. It is better for a man to avenge his friend than much mourn. Each of us must await his end of the world's life. Let him who may get glory before death: that is best for the warrior after he has gone from life. Arise, guardian of the kingdom, let us go at once to look on the track of Gren-del's kin. I promise you this: she will not be lost under cover, not in the earth's bosom nor in the mountain woods nor at the bottom of the sea, go where she will. This day have patience in every woe—as I expect you to."

Then the old man leapt up, thanked God, the mighty Lord, that the man had so spoken. Then was a horse bridled for Hrothgar, a curly-maned mount. The wise king moved in state; the band of shield-bearers marched on foot. The tracks were seen wide over the wood-paths where she had gone on the ground, made her way forward over the dark moor, borne lifeless the best of retainers of those who watched over their home with Hrothgar. The son of noble forebears[6] moved over the steep rocky slopes, narrow paths where only one could go at a time, an unfamiliar trail, steep hills, many a lair of water-monsters. He went before with a few wise men to spy out the country, until suddenly he found mountain trees leaning out over hoary stone, a joyless wood: water lay beneath, bloody and troubled. It was pain of heart for all the Danes to suffer, for the friends of the Scyldings, for many a thane, grief to each earl when on the cliff over the water they came upon Aeschere's head. The flood boiled with blood—the men looked upon it—with hot gore. Again and again the horn sang its urgent war-song. The whole troop sat down to rest. Then they saw on the water many a snake-shape, strong sea-serpents exploring the mere, and water-monsters lying on the slopes of the shore such as those that in the morning often attend a perilous journey on the paths of the sea, serpents and wild beasts.

These fell away from the shore, fierce and rage-swollen: they had heard the bright sound, the war-horn sing. One of them a man of the Geats with his bow cut off from his life, his water-warring, after the hard war-arrow stuck in his heart: he was weaker in swimming the lake when death took him. Straightway he was hard beset on the waves with barbed boar-spears, strongly surrounded, pulled up on the shore, strange spawn of the waves. The men looked on the terrible alien thing.

Beowulf put on his warrior's dress, had no fear for his life. His war-shirt, hand-fashioned, broad and well-worked, was to explore the mere: it knew how to cover his body-cave so that foe's grip might not harm his heart, or grasp of angry enemy his life. But the bright helmet guarded his head, one which was to stir up the lake-bottom, seek out the troubled water—made rich with gold, surrounded with splendid bands, as the weapon-smith had made it in far-off days, fashioned it wonderfully, set it about with boar-images so that thereafter no sword or battle-blade might bite into it. And of his strong supports that was not the least which Hrothgar's spokesman[7] lent to his need: Hrunting was the name of the hilted sword; it was one of the oldest of ancient treasures; its edge was iron, decorated with poison-stripes, hardened with battle-sweat. Never had it failed in war any man of those who grasped it in their hands, who dared enter on dangerous enterprises, onto the common meeting place of foes: this was not the first time that it should do work of courage. Surely the son of Ecglaf, great of strength, did not have in mind what, drunk with wine, he had spoken, when he lent that weapon to a better swordfighter. He did not himself dare to risk his life under the warring

6. I.e. Hrothgar.   7. I.e., Unferth.

waves, to engage his courage: there he lost his glory, his name for valor. It was not so with the other when he had armed himself for battle.

[BEOWULF ATTACKS GRENDEL'S MOTHER]

Beowulf spoke, the son of Ecgtheow: "Think now, renowned son of Healfdene, wise king, now that I am ready for the venture, gold-friend of warriors, of what we said before, that, if at your need I should go from life, you would always be in a father's place for me when I am gone: be guardian of my young retainers, my companions, if battle should take me. The treasure you gave me, beloved Hrothgar, send to Hygelac. The lord of the Geats may know from the gold, the son of Hrethel may see when he looks on that wealth, that I found a ring-giver good in his gifts, enjoyed him while I might. And let Unferth have the old heirloom, the wide-known man my splendid-waved sword, hard-edged: with Hrunting I shall get glory, or death will take me."

After these words the man of the Weather-Geats turned away boldly, would wait for no answer: the surging water took the warrior. Then was it a part of a day before he might see the bottom's floor. Straightway that which had held the flood's tract a hundred half-years, ravenous for prey, grim and greedy, saw that some man from above was exploring the dwelling of monsters. Then she groped toward him, took the warrior in her awful grip. Yet not the more for that did she hurt his hale body within: his ring-armor shielded him about on the outside so that she could not pierce the war-dress, the linked body-mail, with hateful fingers. Then as she came to the bottom the sea-wolf bore the ring-prince to her house so that—no matter how brave he was—he might not wield weapons; but many monsters attacked him in the water, many a sea-beast tore at his mail-shirt with war-tusks, strange creatures afflicted him. Then the earl saw that he was in some hostile hall where no water harmed him at all, and the flood's onrush might not touch him because of the hall-roof. He saw firelight, a clear blaze shine bright.

Then the good man saw the accursed dweller in the deep, the mighty mere-woman. He gave a great thrust to his sword—his hand did not withhold the stroke—so that the etched blade sang at her head a fierce war-song. Then the stranger found that the battle-lightning would not bite, harm her life, but the edge failed the prince in his need: many a hand-battle had it endured before, often sheared helmet, war-coat of man fated to die: this was the first time for the rare treasure that its glory had failed.

But still he was resolute, not slow of his courage, mindful of fame, the kinsman of Hygelac. Then, angry warrior, he threw away the sword, wavy-patterned, bound with ornaments, so that it lay on the ground, hard and steel-edged: he trusted in his strength, his mighty hand-grip. So ought a man to do when he thinks to get long-lasting praise in battle: he cares not for his life. Then he seized by the hair Grendel's mother— the man of the War-Geats did not shrink from the fight. Battle-hard-

ened, now swollen with rage, he pulled his deadly foe so that she fell to
the floor. Quickly in her turn she repaid him his gift with her grim claws
and clutched at him: then weary-hearted, the strongest of warriors, of
foot-soldiers, stumbled so that he fell. Then she sat upon the hall-guest
and drew her knife, broad and bright-edged. She would avenge her child,
her only son. The woven breast-armor lay on his shoulder: that protected
his life, withstood entry of point or of edge. Then the son of Ecgtheow
would have fared amiss under the wide ground, the champion of the
Geats, if the battle-shirt had not brought help, the hard war-net—and
holy God brought about victory in war; the wise Lord, Ruler of the
Heavens, decided it with right, easily, when Beowulf had stood up again.

   Then he saw among the armor a victory-blessed blade, an old sword
made by the giants, strong of its edges, glory of warriors: it was the best
of weapons, except that it was larger than any other man might bear to
war-sport, good and adorned, the work of giants. He seized the linked
hilt, he who fought for the Scyldings, savage and slaughter-bent, drew
the patterned-blade; desperate of life, he struck angrily so that it bit her
hard on the neck, broke the bone-rings. The blade went through all the
doomed body. She fell to the floor, the sword was sweating, the man
rejoiced in his work.

   The blaze brightened, light shone within, just as from the sky heaven's
candle shines clear. He looked about the building; then he moved
along the wall, raised his weapon hard by the hilt, Hygelac's thane,
angry and resolute: the edge was not useless to the warrior, for he would
quickly repay Grendel for the many attacks he had made on the West-
Danes—many more than the one time when he slew in their sleep fifteen hearth-companions of Hrothgar, devoured men of the Danish people while they slept, and another such number bore away, a hateful
prey. He had paid him his reward for that, the fierce champion, for there
he saw Grendel, weary of war, lying at rest, lifeless with the wounds he
had got in the fight at Heorot. The body bounded wide when it suffered
the blow after death, the hard sword-swing; and thus he cut off his head.

   At once the wise men who were watching the water with Hrothgar
saw that the surging waves were troubled, the lake stained with blood.
Gray-haired, old, they spoke together of the good warrior, that they did
not again expect of the chief that he would come victorious to seek their
great king; for many agreed on it, that the sea-wolf had destroyed him.

   Then came the ninth hour of the day. The brave Scyldings left the
hill. The gold-friend of warriors went back to his home. The strangers
sat sick at heart and stared at the mere. They wished—and did not expect—
that they would see their beloved lord himself.

   Then the blade began to waste away from the battle-sweat, the war-
sword into battle-icicles. That was a wondrous thing, that it should all
melt, most like the ice when the Father loosens the frost's fetters, undoes
the water-bonds—He Who has power over seasons and times: He is the
true Ruler. Beowulf did not take from the dwelling, the man of the
Weather-Geats, more treasures—though he saw many there—but only

the head and the hilt, bright with jewels. The sword itself had already melted, its patterned blade burned away: the blood was too hot for it, the spirit that had died there too poisonous. Quickly he was swimming, he who had lived to see the fall of his foes; he plunged up through the water. The currents were all cleansed, the great tracts of the water, when the dire spirit left her life-days and this loaned world.

Then the protector of seafarers came toward the land, swimming stout-hearted; he had joy of his sea-booty, the great burden he had with him. They went to meet him, thanked God, the strong band of thanes, rejoiced in their chief that they might see him again sound. Then the helmet and war-shirt of the mighty one were quickly loosened. The lake drowsed, the water beneath the skies, stained with blood. They went forth on the foot-tracks, glad in their hearts, measured the path back, the known ways, men bold as kings. They bore the head from the mere's cliff, toilsomely for each of the great-hearted ones: four of them had trouble in carrying Grendel's head on spear-shafts to the gold-hall—until at last they came striding to the hall, fourteen bold warriors of the Geats; their lord, high-spirited, walked in their company over the fields to the mead-hall.

Then the chief of the thanes, man daring in deeds, enriched by new glory, warrior dear to battle, came in to greet Hrothgar. Then Grendel's head was dragged by the hair over the floor to where men drank, a terrible thing to the earls and the woman with them, an awful sight: the men looked upon it.

[FURTHER CELEBRATION AT HEOROT]

Beowulf spoke, the son of Ecgtheow: "Yes, we have brought you this sea-booty, son of Healfdene, man of the Scyldings, gladly, as evidence of glory—what you look on here. Not easily did I come through it with my life, the war under water, not without trouble carried out the task. The fight would have been ended straightway if God had not guarded me. With Hrunting I might not do anything in the fight, though that is a good weapon. But the Wielder of Men granted me that I should see hanging on the wall a fair, ancient great-sword—most often He has guided the man without friends—that I should wield the weapon. Then in the fight when the time became right for me I hewed the house-guardians. Then that war-sword, wavy-patterned, burnt away as their blood sprang forth, hottest of battle-sweats. I have brought the hilt away from the foes. I have avenged the evil deeds, the slaughter of Danes, as it was right to do. I promise you that you may sleep in Heorot without care with your band of retainers, and that for none of the thanes of your people, old or young, need you have fear, prince of the Scyldings—for no life-injury to your men on that account, as you did before."

Then the golden hilt was given into the hand of the old man, the hoary war-chief—the ancient work of giants. There came into the possession of the prince of the Danes, after the fall of devils, the work of wonder-smiths. And when the hostile-hearted creature, God's enemy, guilty of murder, gave up this world, and his mother too, it passed into the control of the best of worldly kings between the seas, of those who gave treasure in the Northlands.

Hrothgar spoke—he looked on the hilt, the old heirloom, on which was written the origin of ancient strife, when the flood, rushing water, slew the race of giants—they suffered terribly: that was a people alien to the Everlasting Lord. The Ruler made them a last payment through water's welling. On the sword-guard of bright gold there was also rightly marked through rune-staves, set down and told, for whom that sword, best of irons, had first been made, its hilt twisted and ornamented with snakes. Then the wise man spoke, the son of Healfdene—all were silent: "Lo, this may one say who works truth and right for the folk, recalls all things far distant, an old guardian of the land: that this earl was born the better man. Glory is raised up over the far ways—your glory over every people, Beowulf my friend. All of it, all your strength, you govern steadily in the wisdom of your heart. I shall fulfill my friendship to you, just as we spoke before. You shall become a comfort, whole and long-lasting, to your people, a help to warriors.

"So was not Heremod to the sons of Ecgwela, the Honor-Scyldings. He grew great not for their joy, but for their slaughter, for the destruction of Danish people. With swollen heart he killed his table-companions, shoulder-comrades, until he turned away from the joys of men, alone, notorious king, although mighty God had raised him in power, in the joys of strength, had set him up over all men. Yet in his breast his heart's thought grew blood-thirsty: no rings did he give to the Danes for glory. He lived joyless to suffer the pain of that strife, the long-lasting harm of the people. Teach yourself by him, be mindful of munificence. Old of winters, I tell this tale for you.

"It is a wonder to say how in His great spirit mighty God gives wisdom to mankind, land and earlship—He possesses power over all things. At times He lets the thought of a man of high lineage move in delight, gives him joy of earth in his homeland, a stronghold of men to rule over, makes regions of the world so subject to him, wide kingdoms, that in his unwisdom he may not himself have mind of his end. He lives in plenty; illness and age in no way grieve him, neither does dread care darken his heart, nor does enmity bare sword-hate, for the whole world turns to his will—he knows nothing worse—until his portion of pride increases and flourishes within him; then the watcher sleeps, the soul's guardian; that sleep is too sound, bound in its own cares, and the slayer most near whose bow shoots treacherously. Then is he hit in the heart, beneath his armor, with the bitter arrow—he cannot protect himself— with the crooked dark commands of the accursed spirit. What he has long held seems to him too little, angry-hearted he covets, no plated rings does he give in men's honor, and then he forgets and regards not his destiny because of what God, Wielder of Heaven, has given him before, his portion of glories. In the end it happens in turn that the loaned body weakens, falls doomed; another takes the earl's ancient treasure, one who recklessly gives precious gifts, does not fearfully guard them.

"Keep yourself against that wickedness, beloved Beowulf, best of men, and choose better—eternal gains. Have no care for pride, great warrior. Now for a time there is glory in your might: yet soon it shall be that sickness or sword will diminish your strength, or fire's fangs, or flood's surge, or sword's swing, or spear's flight, or appalling age; brightness of eyes will fail and grow dark; then it shall be that death will overcome you, warrior.

"Thus I ruled the Ring-Danes for a hundred half-years under the skies, and protected them in war with spear and sword against many nations over middle-earth, so that I counted no one as my adversary underneath the sky's expanse. Well, disproof of that came to me in my own land, grief after my joys, when Grendel, ancient adversary, came to invade my home. Great sorrow of heart I have always suffered for his persecution. Thanks be to the Ruler, the Eternal Lord, that after old strife I have come to see in my lifetime, with my own eyes, his blood-stained head. Go now to your seat, have joy of the glad feast, made famous in battle. Many of our treasures will be shared when morning comes."

The Geat was glad at heart, went at once to seek his seat as the wise one bade. Then was a feast fairly served again, for a second time, just as before, for those famed for courage, sitting about the hall.

Night's cover lowered, dark over the warriors. The retainers all arose. The gray-haired one would seek his bed, the old Scylding. It pleased the Geat, the brave shield-warrior, immensely that he should have rest. Straightway a hall-thane led the way on for the weary one, come from far country, and showed every courtesy to the thane's need, such as in those days seafarers might expect as their due.

Then the great-hearted one rested; the hall stood high, vaulted and gold-adorned; the guest slept within until the black raven, blithe-hearted, announced heaven's joy. Then the bright light came passing over the shadows. The warriors hastened, the nobles were eager to set out again for their people. Bold of spirit, the visitor would seek his ship far thence.

Then the hardy one bade that Hrunting be brought to the son of Ecglaf,[8] that he take back his sword, precious iron. He spoke thanks for that loan, said that he accounted it a good war-friend, strong in battle; in his words he found no fault at all with the sword's edge; he was a thoughtful man. And then they were eager to depart, the warriors ready in their armor. The prince who had earned honor of the Danes went to the high seat where the other was: the man dear to war greeted Hrothgar.

8. I.e., Unferth.

[Beowulf Returns Home]

Beowulf spoke, the son of Ecgtheow: "Now we sea-travelers come
from afar wish to say that we desire to seek Hygelac. Here we have been
entertained splendidly according to our desire: you have dealt well with
us. If on earth I might in any way earn more of your heart's love, prince
of warriors, than I have done before with warlike deeds, I should be
ready at once. If beyond the sea's expanse I hear that men dwelling near
threaten you with terrors, as those who hated you did before, I shall
bring you a thousand thanes, warriors to your aid. I know of Hygelac,
lord of the Geats, though he is young as a guardian of the people, that
he will further me with words and works so that I may do you honor and
bring spears to help you, strong support where you have need of men. If
Hrethric, king's son, decides to come to the court of the Geats, he can
find many friends there; far countries are well sought by him who is
himself strong."

Hrothgar spoke to him in answer: "The All-Knowing Lord sent those
words into your mind: I have not heard a man of so young age speak
more wisely. You are great of strength, mature of mind, wise of words.
I think it likely if the spear, sword-grim war, takes the son of Hrethel,
sickness or weapon your prince, the people's ruler, and you have your
life, that the Sea-Geats will not have a better to choose as their king, as
guardian of their treasure, if you wish to hold the kingdom of your kinsmen. So well your heart's temper has long pleased me, beloved Beowulf.
You have brought it about that peace shall be shared by the peoples, the
folk of the Geats and the Spear-Danes, and enmity shall sleep, acts of
malice which they practiced before; and there shall be, as long as I rule
the wide kingdom, sharing of treasures, many a man shall greet his fellow with good gifts over the sea-bird's baths; the ring-prowed ship will
bring gifts and tokens of friendship over the sea. I know your people,
blameless in every respect, set firm after the old way both as to foe and
to friend."

Then the protector of earls, the kinsman of Healfdene, gave him there
in the hall twelve precious things; he bade him with these gifts seek his
own dear people in safety, quickly come back. Then the king noble of
race, the prince of the Scyldings, kissed the best of thanes and took him
by his neck: tears fell from the gray-haired one. He had two thoughts of
the future, the old and wise man, one more strongly than the other—
that they would not see each other again, bold men at council. The
man was so dear to him that he might not restrain his breast's welling,
for fixed in his heartstrings a deep-felt longing for the beloved man burned
in his blood. Away from him Beowulf, warrior glorious with gold, walked
over the grassy ground, proud of his treasure. The sea-goer awaited its
owner, riding at anchor. Then on the journey the gift of Hrothgar was
oft-praised: that was a king blameless in all things until age took from
him the joys of his strength—old age that has often harmed many.

There came to the flood the band of brave-hearted ones, of young men. They wore mail-coats, locked limb-shirts. The guard of the coast saw the coming of the earls, just as he had done before. He did not greet the guests with taunts from the cliff's top, but rode to meet them, said that the return of the warriors in bright armor in their ship would be welcome to the people of the Weather-Geats. There on the sand the broad sea-boat was loaded with armor, the ring-prowed ship with horses and rich things. The mast stood high over Hrothgar's hoard-gifts. He gave the boat-guard a sword wound with gold, so that thereafter on the mead-bench he was held the worthier for the treasure, the heirloom. The boat moved out to furrow the deep water, left the land of the Danes. Then on the mast a sea-cloth, a sail, was made fast by a rope. The boat's beams creaked: wind did not keep the sea-floater from its way over the waves. The sea-goer moved, foamy-necked floated forth over the swell, the ship with bound prow over the sea-currents until they might see the cliffs of the Geats, the well-known headlands. The ship pressed ahead, borne by the wind, stood still at the land. Quickly the harbor-guard was at the sea-side, he who had gazed for a long time far out over the currents, eager to see the beloved men. He[9] moored the deep ship in the sand, fast by its anchor ropes, lest the force of the waves should drive away the fair wooden vessel. Then he bade that the prince's wealth be borne ashore, armor and plated gold. It was not far for them to seek the giver of treasure, Hygelac son of Hrethel, where he dwelt at home near the sea-wall, himself with his retainers.

The building was splendid, its king most valiant, set high in the hall, Hygd[1] most youthful, wise and well-taught, though she had lived within the castle walls few winters, daughter of Haereth. For she was not niggardly, nor too sparing of gifts to the men of the Geats, of treasures. Modthryth,[2] good folk-queen, did dreadful deeds [in her youth]: no bold one among her retainers dared venture—except her great lord—to set his eyes on her in daylight, but [if he did] he should reckon deadly bonds prepared for him, arresting hands: that straightway after his seizure the sword awaited him, that the patterned blade must settle it, make known its death-evil. Such is no queenly custom for a woman to practice, though she is peerless—that one who weaves peace[3] should take away the life of a beloved man after pretended injury. However the kinsman of Hemming stopped that:[4] ale-drinkers gave another account, said that she did less harm to the people, fewer injuries, after she was given, gold-adorned, to the young warrior, the beloved noble, when by her father's teaching

9. Beowulf.

1. Hygd is Hygelac's young queen. The suddenness of her introduction here is perhaps due to a faulty text.

2. A transitional passage introducing the contrast between Hygd's good behavior and Modthryth's bad behavior as young women of royal blood seems to have been lost. Modthryth's practice of having those who looked into her face put to death may reflect the folk-motif of the princess whose unsuccessful suitors are executed, though the text does not say

that Modthryth's victims were suitors. Modthryth's "great lord" was probably her father.

3. Daughters of kings were frequently given in marriage to the king of a hostile nation in order to bring about peace; hence Modthryth may be called "one who weaves peace."

4. I.e., Offa I, a legendary king of the Angles, and presumably the ancestor of his namesake Offa II who ruled Mercia from 757–796; who Hemming was—besides being Offa's forebear—is not known.

she sought Offa's hall in a voyage over the pale sea. There on the throne she was afterwards famous for generosity, while living made use of her life, held high love toward the lord of warriors, [who was] of all mankind the best, as I have heard, between the seas of the races of men. Since Offa was a man brave of wars and gifts, wide-honored, he held his native land in wisdom. From him sprang Eomer to the help of warriors, kinsman of Hemming, grandson of Garmund, strong in battle.[5]

Then the hardy one came walking with his troop over the sand on the sea-plain, the wide shores. The world-candle shone, the sun moved quickly from the south. They made their way, strode swiftly to where they heard that the protector of earls, the slayer of Ongentheow,[6] the good young war-king, was dispensing rings in the stronghold. The coming of Beowulf was straightway made known to Hygelac, that there in his home the defender of warriors, his comrade in battle, came walking alive to the court, sound from the battle-play. Quickly the way within was made clear for the foot-guests, as the mighty one bade.

Then he sat down with him, he who had come safe through the fight, kinsman with kinsman, after he had greeted his liege lord with formal speech, loyal, with vigorous words. Haereth's daughter moved through the hall-building with mead-cups, cared lovingly for the people, bore the cup of strong drink to the hands of the warriors. Hygelac began fairly to question his companion in the high hall, curiosity pressed him, what the adventures of the Sea-Geats had been. "How did you fare on your journey, beloved Beowulf, when you suddenly resolved to seek distant combat over the salt water, battle in Heorot? Did you at all help the wide-known woes of Hrothgar, the famous prince? Because of you I burned with seething sorrows, care of heart—had no trust in the venture of my beloved man. I entreated you long that you should in no way approach the murderous spirit, should let the South-Danes themselves settle the war with Grendel. I say thanks to God that I may see you sound."

Beowulf spoke, the son of Ecgtheow: "To many among men it is not hidden, lord Hygelac, the great encounter—what a fight we had, Grendel and I, in the place where he made many sorrows for the Victory-Scyldings, constant misery. All that I avenged, so that none of Grendel's kin over the earth need boast of that clash at night—whoever lives longest of the loathsome kind, wrapped in malice. There I went forth to the ring-hall to greet Hrothgar. At once the famous son of Healfdene, when he knew my purpose, gave me a seat with his own sons. The company was in joy: I have not seen in the time of my life under heaven's arch more mead-mirth of hall-sitters. At times the famous queen, peace-pledge of the people, went through all the hall, cheered the young men; often

5. Stories about Offa, who provides the only English connection in this English poem, and the names of his father Garmund and son Eomer would presumably have been familiar to the poet's audience. The passage has been seen as a compliment to the royal house of Mercia.

6. Ongentheow was a Scylfing (Swedish) king, whose story is fully told below. In fact Hygelac was not his slayer, but is called so because he led the attack on the Scylfings in which Ongentheow was killed.

she would give a man a ring-band before she went to her seat. At times Hrothgar's daughter bore the ale-cup to the retainers, to the earls throughout the hall. I heard hall-sitters name her Freawaru when she offered the studded cup to warriors. Young and gold-adorned, she is promised to the fair son of Froda.[7] That has seemed good to the lord of the Scyldings, the guardian of the kingdom, and he believes of this plan that he may, with this woman, settle their portion of deadly feuds, of quarrels.[8] Yet most often after the fall of a prince in any nation the deadly spear rests but a little while, even though the bride is good.

"It may displease the lord of the Heatho-Bards and each thane of that people when he goes in the hall with the woman, [that while] the noble sons of the Danes, her retainers, [are] feasted,[9] the heirlooms of their ancestors will be shining on them[1]—the hard and wave-adorned treasure of the Heatho-Bards, [which was theirs] so long as they might wield those weapons, until they led to the shield-play, to destruction, their dear companions and their own lives. Then at the beer he[2] who sees the treasure, an old ash-warrior who remembers it all, the spear-death of warriors—grim is his heart—begins, sad of mind, to tempt a young fighter in the thoughts of his spirit, to awaken war-evil, and speaks this word:

" 'Can you, my friend, recognize that sword, the rare iron-blade, that your father, beloved man, bore to battle his last time in armor, where the Danes slew him, the fierce Scyldings, got possession of the battle-field, when Withergeld[3] lay dead, after the fall of warriors? Now here some son of his murderers walks in the hall, proud of the weapon, boasts of the murder, and wears the treasure that you should rightly possess.' So he will provoke and remind at every chance with wounding words until that moment comes that the woman's thane,[4] forfeiting life, shall lie dead, blood-smeared from the sword-bite, for his father's deeds. The other escapes with his life, knows the land well. Then on both sides the oath of the earls will be broken; then deadly hate will well up in Ingeld, and his wife-love after the surging of sorrows will become cooler. Therefore I do not think the loyalty of the Heatho-Bards, their part in the alliance with the Danes, to be without deceit—do not think their friendship fast.

"I shall speak still more of Grendel, that you may readily know, giver of treasure, what the hand-fight of warriors came to in the end. After heaven's jewel had glided over the earth, the angry spirit came, awful in the evening, to visit us where, unharmed, we watched over the hall. There the fight was fatal to Hondscioh, deadly to one who was doomed. He was dead first of all, armed warrior. Grendel came to devour him,

7. I.e., Ingeld, who succeeded his father as king of the Heatho-Bards.
8. I.e., the feud between the Danes and Heatho-Bards.
9. The text is faulty here.
1. I.e., the weapons and armor which had once belonged to the Heatho-Bards and were captured by the Danes will be worn by the Danish atten-dants of Hrothgar's daughter Freawaru when she goes to the Heatho-Bards to marry king Ingeld.
2. I.e., some old Heatho-Bard warrior.
3. Apparently a leader of the Heatho-Bards in their unsuccessful war with the Danes.
4. I.e., the Danish attendant of Freawaru who is wearing the sword of his Heatho-Bard attacker's father.

good young retainer, swallowed all the body of the beloved man. Yet not for this would the bloody-toothed slayer, bent on destruction, go from the gold-hall empty-handed; but, strong of might, he made trial of me, grasped me with eager hand. His glove[5] hung huge and wonderful, made fast with cunning clasps: it had been made all with craft; with devil's devices and dragon's skins. The fell doer of evils would put me therein, guiltless, one of many. He might not do so after I had stood up in anger. It is too long to tell how I repaid the people's foe his due for every crime. My prince, there with my deeds I did honor to your people. He slipped away, for a little while had use of life's joy. Yet his right hand remained as his spoor in Heorot, and he went from there abject, mournful of heart sank to the mere's bottom.

"The lord of the Scyldings repaid me for that bloody combat with much plated gold, many treasures, after morning came and we sat down to the feast. There was song and mirth. The old Scylding, who has learned many things, spoke of times far-off. At times a brave one in battle touched the glad wood, the harp's joy; at times he told tales, true and sad; at times he related strange stories according to right custom; at times, again, the great-hearted king, bound with age, the old warrior, would begin to speak of his youth, his battle-strength. His heart welled within when, old and wise, he thought of his many winters. Thus we took pleasure there the livelong day until another night came to men.

"Then in her turn Grendel's mother swiftly made ready to take revenge for his injuries, made a sorrowful journey. Death had taken her son, war-hate of the Weather-Geats. The direful woman avenged her son, fiercely killed a warrior: there the life of Aeschere departed, a wise old counselor. And when morning came the folk of the Danes might not burn him, death-weary, in the fire, nor place him on the pyre, beloved man: she had borne his body away in fiend's embrace beneath the mountain stream. That was the bitterest of Hrothgar's sorrows, of those that had long come upon the people's prince. Then the king, sore-hearted, implored me by your life[6] that I should do a man's work in the tumult of the waters, venture my life, finish a glorious deed. He promised me reward. Then I found the guardian of the deep pool, the grim horror, as is now known wide. For a time there we were locked hand in hand. Then the flood boiled with blood, and in the war-hall I cut off the head of Grendel's mother with a mighty sword. Not without trouble I came from there with my life. I was not fated to die then, but the protector of earls again gave me many treasures, the son of Healfdene.

"Thus the king of that people lived with good customs. I had lost none of the rewards, the meed of my might, but he gave me treasures, the son of Healfdene, at my own choice. I will bring these to you, great king, show my good will. On your kindnesses all still depends: I have few close kinsmen besides you, Hygelac."

Then he bade bring in the boar-banner—the head-sign—the helmet

5. Apparently a large glove that could be used as a pouch.   6. I.e., "in your name."

towering in battle, the gray battle-shirt, the splendid sword—afterwards spoke words: "Hrothgar, wise king, gave me this armor; in his words he bade that I should first tell you about his gift: he said that king Heoro-gar,[7] lord of the Scyldings, had had it for a long time; not for that would he give it, the breast-armor, to his son, bold Heoroweard, though he was loyal to him. Use it all well!"

I have heard that four horses, swift and alike, followed that treasure, fallow as apples. He gave him the gift of both horses and treasure. So ought kinsmen do, not weave malice-nets for each other with secret craft, prepare death for comrades. To Hygelac his nephew was most true in hard fights, and each one mindful of helping the other. I have heard that he gave Hygd the neck-ring, the wonderfully wrought treasure, that Wealhtheow had given him—gave to the king's daughter as well three horses, supple and saddle-bright. After the gift of the necklace, her breast was adorned with it.

Thus Beowulf showed himself brave, a man known in battles, of good deeds, bore himself according to discretion. Drunk, he slew no hearth-companions. His heart was not savage, but he held the great gift that God had given him, the most strength of all mankind, like one brave in battle. He had long been despised,[8] so that the sons of the Geats did not reckon him brave, nor would the lord of the Weather-Geats do him much gift-honor on the mead-bench. They strongly suspected that he was slack, a young man unbold. Change came to the famous man for each of his troubles.

Then the protector of earls bade fetch in the heirloom of Hrethel,[9] king famed in battle, adorned with gold. There was not then among the Geats a better treasure in sword's kind. He laid that in Beowulf's lap, and gave him seven thousand [hides of land], a hall and a throne. To both of them alike land had been left in the nation, home and native soil: to the other more especially wide was the realm, to him who was higher in rank.

[Beowulf and the Dragon]

Afterwards it happened, in later days, in the crashes of battle, when Hygelac lay dead and war-swords came to slay Heardred[1] behind the shield-cover, when the Battle-Scylfings, hard fighters, sought him among his victorious nation, attacked bitterly the nephew of Hereric—then the broad kingdom came into Beowulf's hand. He held it well fifty win-ters—he was a wise king, an old guardian of the land—until in the dark nights a certain one, a dragon, began to hold sway, which on the high heath kept watch over a hoard, a steep stone-barrow. Beneath lay a path

---

7. Hrothgar's elder brother, whom Hrothgar suc-ceeded as king.
8. Beowulf's poor reputation as a young man is mentioned only here.
9. Hygelac's father.

1. Hygelac's son Heardred, who succeeded Hyge-lac as king, was killed by the Swedes (Battle-Scylf-ings) in his own land, as is explained more fully below, p. 60. His uncle Hereric was perhaps Hygd's brother.

unknown to men. By this there went inside a certain man [who made his way near to the heathen hoard; his hand took a cup, large, a shining treasure. The dragon did not afterwards conceal it though in his sleep he was tricked by the craft of the thief. That the people discovered, the neighboring folk—that he was swollen with rage].[2]

Not of his own accord did he who had sorely harmed him[3] break into the worm's hoard, not by his own desire, but for hard constraint; the slave of some son of men fled hostile blows, lacking a shelter, and came there, a man guilty of wrong-doing. As soon as he saw him,[4] great horror arose in the stranger; [yet the wretched fugitive escaped the terrible worm . . . When the sudden shock came upon him, he carried off a precious cup.][5] There were many such ancient treasures in the earth-house, as in the old days some one of mankind had prudently hidden there the huge legacy of a noble race, rare treasures. Death had taken them all in earlier times, and the only one of the nation of people who still survived, who walked there longest, a guardian mourning his friends, supposed the same of himself as of them—that he might little while enjoy the long-got treasure. A barrow stood all ready on the shore near the sea-waves, newly placed on the headland, made fast by having its entrances skill-fully hidden. The keeper of the rings carried in the part of his riches worthy of hoarding, plated gold; he spoke few words:

"Hold now, you earth, now that men may not, the possession of earls. What, from you good men got it first! War-death has taken each man of my people, evil dreadful and deadly, each of those who has given up this life, the hall-joys of men. I have none who wears sword or cleans the plated cup, rich drinking vessel. The company of retainers has gone elsewhere. The hard helmet must be stripped of its fair-wrought gold, of its plating. The polishers are asleep who should make the war-mask shine. And even so the coat of mail, which withstood the bite of swords after the crashing of the shields, decays like its warrior. Nor may the ring-mail travel wide on the war-chief beside his warriors. There is no harp-delight, no mirth of the singing wood, no good hawk flies through the hall, no swift horse stamps in the castle court. Baleful death has sent away many races of men."

So, sad of mind, he spoke his sorrow, alone of them all, moved joyless through day and night until death's flood reached his heart. The ancient night-ravager found the hoard-joy standing open, he who burning seeks barrows, the smooth hateful dragon who flies at night wrapped in flame. Earth-dwellers much dread him. He it is who must seek a hoard in the earth where he will guard heathen gold, wise for his winters: he is none the better for it.

So for three hundred winters the harmer of folk held in the earth one of its treasure-houses, huge and mighty, until one man angered his heart. He bore to his master a plated cup, asked his lord for a compact of peace:

2. This part of the manuscript is badly damaged, and the text within brackets is highly conjectural.
3. The dragon.
4. The dragon.
5. Several lines of the text have been lost.

thus was the hoard searched, the store of treasures diminished. His requests were granted the wretched man: the lord for the first time looked on the ancient work of men. Then the worm woke; cause of strife was renewed: for then he moved over the stones, hard-hearted beheld his foe's foot-prints—with secret stealth he had stepped forth too near the dragon's head. (So may an undoomed man who holds favor from the Ruler easily come through his woes and misery.) The hoard-guard sought him eagerly over the ground, would find the man who had done him injury while he slept. Hot and fierce-hearted, often he moved all about the outside of the barrow. No man at all was in the emptiness. Yet he took joy in the thought of war, in the work of fighting. At times he turned back into the barrow, sought his rich cup. Straightway he found that some man had tampered with his gold, his splendid treasure. The hoard-guard waited restless until evening came; then the barrow-keeper was in rage: he would requite that precious drinking cup with vengeful fire. Then the day was gone—to the joy of the worm. He would not wait long on the sea-wall, but set out with fire, ready with flame. The beginning was terrible to the folk on the land, as the ending was soon to be sore to their giver of treasure.

Then the evil spirit began to vomit flames, burn bright dwellings; blaze of fire rose, to the horror of men; there the deadly flying thing would leave nothing alive. The worm's warfare was wide-seen, his cruel malice, near and far—how the destroyer hated and hurt the people of the Geats. He winged back to the hoard, his hidden hall, before the time of day. He had circled the land-dwellers with flame, with fire and burning. He had trust in his barrow, in his war and his wall: his expectation deceived him.

Then the terror was made known to Beowulf, quickly in its truth, that his own home, best of buildings, had melted in surging flames, the throne-seat of the Geats. That was anguish of spirit to the good man, the greatest of heart-sorrows. The wise one supposed that he had bitterly offended the Ruler, the Eternal Lord, against old law. His breast within boiled with dark thoughts—as was not for him customary. The fiery dragon with his flames had destroyed the people's stronghold, the land along the sea, the heart of the country. Because of that the war-king, the lord of the Weather-Geats, devised punishment for him. The protector of fighting men, lord of earls, commanded that a wonderful battle-shield be made all of iron. Well he knew that the wood of the forest might not help him—linden against flame. The prince good from old times was to come to the end of the days that had been lent him, life in the world, and the worm with him, though he had long held the hoarded wealth. Then the ring-prince scorned to seek the far-flier with a troop, a large army. He had no fear for himself of the combat, nor did he think the worm's war-power anything great, his strength and his courage, because he himself had come through many battles before, dared perilous straits, clashes of war, after he had purged Hrothgar's hall, victorious warrior, and in combat crushed to death Grendel's kin, loathsome race.

Nor was that the least of his hand-combats where Hygelac was slain,
when the king of the Geats, the noble lord of the people, the son of
Hrethel, died of sword-strokes in the war-storm among the Frisians, laid
low by the blade. From there Beowulf came away by means of his own
strength, performed a feat of swimming; he had on his arm the armor of
thirty earls when he turned back to the sea. There was no need for the
Hetware[6] to exult in the foot-battle when they bore their shields against
him: few came again from that warrior to seek their homes. Then the
son of Ecgtheow swam over the water's expanse, forlorn and alone, back
to his people. There Hygd offered him hoard and kingdom, rings and a
prince's throne. She had no trust in her son, that he could hold his
native throne against foreigners now that Hygelac was dead. By no means
the sooner might the lordless ones get consent from the noble that he
would become lord of Heardred or that he would accept royal power.[7]
Yet he held him up among the people by friendly counsel, kindly with
honor, until he became older,[8] ruled the Weather-Geats.

Outcasts from over the sea sought him, sons of Ohthere.[9] They had
rebelled against the protector of the Scylfings, the best of the sea-kings
of those who gave treasure in Sweden, a famous lord. For Heardred that
became his life's limit: because of his hospitality there the son of Hygelac
got his life's wound from the strokes of a sword. And the son of Ongentheow went back to seek his home after Heardred lay dead, let Beowulf
hold the royal throne, rule the Geats: that was a good king.

In later days he was mindful of repaying the prince's fall, became the
friend of the destitute Eadgils;[1] with folk he supported the son of Ohthere
over the wide sea, with warriors and weapons. Afterwards he got vengeance by forays that brought with them cold care: he took the king's
life.

Thus he had survived every combat, every dangerous battle, every
deed of courage, the son of Ecgtheow, until that one day when he should
fight with the worm. Then, one of twelve, the lord of the Geats, swollen
with anger, went to look on the dragon. He had learned then from what
the feud arose, the fierce malice to men: the glorious cup had come to
his possession from the hand of the finder: he was the thirteenth of that
company, the man who had brought on the beginning of the war, the
sad-hearted slave—wretched, he must direct them to the place. Against
his will he went to where he knew of an earth-hall, a barrow beneath
the ground close to the sea-surge, to the struggling waves: within, it was
full of ornaments and gold chains. The terrible guardian, ready for com-

---

6. I.e., a tribe, with whom the Frisians were allied.
7. I.e., Beowulf refused to take the throne from
the rightful heir Heardred.
8. I.e., Beowulf supported the young Heardred.
9. Ohthere succeeded his father Ongentheow as
king of the Scylfings (Swedes), but after his death
his brother Onela seized the throne, driving out
Ohthere's sons Eanmund and Eadgils. They were

given refuge at the Geatish court by Heardred,
whom Onela attacked for this act of hospitality. In
the fight Eanmund and Heardred were killed, and
Onela left the kingdom in Beowulf's charge.
1. The surviving son of Ohthere was befriended by
Beowulf, who supported him in his successful
attempt to gain the Swedish throne and who killed
the usurper Onela.

bat, held the gold treasure, old under the earth. It was no easy bargain for any man to obtain. Then the king, hardy in fight, sat down on the headland; there he saluted his hearth-companions, gold-friend of the Geats. His mind was mournful, restless and ripe for death: very close was the fate which should come to the old man, seek his soul's hoard, divide life from his body; not for long then was the life of the noble one wound in his flesh.

Beowulf spoke, the son of Ecgtheow: "In youth I lived through many battle-storms; times of war. I remember all that. I was seven winters old when the lord of treasure, the beloved king of the folk, received me from my father: King Hrethel had me and kept me, gave me treasure and feast, mindful of kinship. During his life I was no more hated by him as a man in his castle than any of his own sons, Herebeald and Haethcyn, or my own Hygelac. For the eldest a murder-bed was wrongfully spread through the deed of a kinsman, when Haethcyn struck him down with an arrow from his horned bow—his friend and his lord—missed the mark and shot his kinsman dead, one brother the other, with the bloody arrowhead. That was a fatal fight, without hope of recompense, a deed wrongly done, baffling to the heart; yet it had happened that a prince had to lose life unavenged.

"So it is sad for an old man to endure that his son should ride young on the gallows. Then he may speak a story, a sorrowful song, when his son hangs for the joy of the raven, and, old in years and knowing, he can find no help for him. Always with every morning he is reminded of his son's journey elsewhere. He cares not to wait for another heir in his hall, when the first through death's force has come to the end of his deeds. Sorrowful he sees in his son's dwelling the empty wine-hall, the windy resting place without joy—the riders sleep, the warriors in the grave. There is no sound of the harp, no joy in the dwelling, as there was of old. Then he goes to his couch, sings a song of sorrow, one alone for one gone. To him all too wide has seemed the land and the dwelling.

"So the protector of the Weather-Geats bore in his heart swelling sorrow for Herebeald. In no way could he settle his feud with the life-slayer; not the sooner could he wound the warrior with deeds of hatred, though he was not dear to him. Then for the sorrow that had too bitterly befallen him he gave up the joys of men, chose God's light. To his sons he left—as a happy man does—his land and his town when he went from life.

"Then there was battle and strife of Swedes and Geats, over the wide water a quarrel shared, hatred between hardy ones, after Hrethel died. And the sons of Ongentheow[2] were bold and active in war, wanted to have no peace over the seas, but about Hreosnabeorh often devised awful slaughter. That my friends and kinsmen avenged, both the feud and the crime, as is well-known, though one of them bought it with his life, a

2. I.e., the Swedes Onela and Ohthere: the reference is, of course, to a time earlier than that referred to on p. 60, note 9.

hard bargain: the war was mortal to Haethcyn, lord of the Geats.[3] Then in the morning, I have heard, one kinsman avenged the other on his slayer with the sword's edge, when Ongentheow attacked Eofor: the war-helm split, the old Scylfing fell mortally wounded: his hand remembered feuds enough, did not withstand the life-blow.

"I repaid in war the treasures that he[4] gave me—with my bright sword, as was granted me by fate: he had given me land, a pleasant dwelling. There was not any need for him, any reason, that he should have to seek among the Gifthas or the Spear-Danes or in Sweden in order to buy with treasure a worse warrior. I would always go before him in the troop, alone in the front. And so all my life I shall wage battle while this sword endures that has served me early and late ever since I became Daeghrefn's slayer in the press—the warrior of the Hugas.[5] He could not bring armor to the king of the Frisians, breast ornament, but fell in the fight, keeper of the standard, a noble man. Nor was my sword's edge his slayer, but my warlike grip broke open his heart-streams, his bone-house. Now shall the sword's edge, the hand and hard blade, fight for the hoard."

[BEOWULF ATTACKS THE DRAGON]

Beowulf spoke, for the last time spoke words in boast: "In my youth I engaged in many wars. Old guardian of the people, I shall still seek battle, perform a deed of fame, if the evil-doer will come to me out of the earth-hall."

Then he saluted each of the warriors, the bold helmet-bearers, for the last time—his own dear companions. "I would not bear sword, weapon, to the worm, if I knew how else according to my boast I might grapple with the monster, as I did of old with Grendel. But I expect here hot battle-fire, steam and poison. Therefore I have on me shield and mail-shirt. I will not flee a foot-step from the barrow-ward, but it shall be with us at the wall as fate allots, the ruler of every man. I am confident in heart, so I forgo help against the war-flier. Wait on the barrow, safe in your mail-shirts, men in armor—which of us two may better bear wounds after our bloody meeting. This is not your venture, nor is it right for any man except me alone that he should spend his strength against the monster, do this man's deed. By my courage I shall get gold, or war will take your king, dire life-evil."

Then the brave warrior arose by his shield; hardy under helmet he went in his mail-shirt beneath the stone-cliffs, had trust in his strength—that of one man: such is not the way of the cowardly. Then he saw by the wall—he who had come through many wars, good in his great-heartedness, many clashes in battle when troops meet together—a stone

3. Haethcyn had succeeded his father Hrethel as king of the Geats after his accidental killing of his brother Herebeald. When Haethcyn was killed while attacking the Swedes, he was succeeded by Hygelac, who, as the next sentence relates, avenged Haethcyn's death on Ongentheow. The death of Ongentheow is described below.
4. Hygelac.
5. I.e., the Franks. The battle is the one in which Hygelac was slain.

arch standing, through it a stream bursting out of the barrow: there was welling of a current hot with killing fires, and he might not endure any while unburnt by the dragon's flame the hollow near the hoard. Then the man of the Weather-Geats, enraged as he was, let a word break from his breast. Stout-hearted he shouted; his voice went roaring, clear in battle, in under the gray stone. Hate was stirred up, the hoard's guard knew the voice of a man. No more time was there to ask for peace. First the monster's breath came out of the stone, the hot war-steam. The earth resounded. The man below the barrow, the lord of the Geats, swung his shield against the dreadful visitor. Then the heart of the coiled thing was aroused to seek combat. The good war-king had drawn his sword, the old heirloom, not blunt of edge. To each of them as they threatened destruction there was terror of the other. Firm-hearted he stood with his shield high, the lord of friends, while quickly the worm coiled itself; he waited in his armor. Then, coiling in flames, he came gliding on, hastening to his fate. The good shield protected the life and body of the famous prince, but for a shorter while than his wish was. There for the first time, the first day in his life, he might not prevail, since fate did not assign him such glory in battle. The lord of the Geats raised his hand, struck the shining horror so with his forged blade that the edge failed, bright on the bone, bit less surely than its folk-king had need, hard-pressed in perils. Then because of the battle-stroke the barrow-ward's heart was savage, he exhaled death-fire—the war-flames sprang wide. The gold-friend of the Geats boasted of no great victories: the war blade had failed, naked at need, as it ought not to have done, iron good from old times. That was no pleasant journey, not one on which the famous son of Ecgtheow would wish to leave his land; against his will he must take up a dwelling-place elsewhere—as every man must give up the days that are lent him.

It was not long until they came together again, dreadful foes. The hoard-guard took heart, once more his breast swelled with his breathing. Encircled with flames, he who before had ruled a folk felt harsh pain. Nor did his companions, sons of nobles, take up their stand in a troop about him with the courage of fighting men, but they crept to the wood, protected their lives. In only one of them the heart surged with sorrows: nothing can ever set aside kinship in him who means well.

He was called Wiglaf, son of Weohstan, a rare shield-warrior, a man of the Scylfings,[6] kinsman of Aelfhere. He saw his liege lord under his war-mask suffer the heat. Then he was mindful of the honors he had given him before, the rich dwelling-place of the Waegmundings, every folk-right such as his father possessed. He might not then hold back, his hand seized his shield, the yellow linden-wood; he drew his ancient

6. Though in the next sentence Wiglaf is said to belong to the family of the Waegmundings, the Geatish family to which Beowulf belonged, he is here called a Scylfing (Swede), and immediately below his father Weohstan is represented as having fought for the Swede Onela in his attack on the Geats. But for a man to change his nation was not unusual, and Weohstan, who may have had both Swedish and Geatish blood, had evidently become a Geat long enough before to have brought up his son Wiglaf as one. The identity of Aelfhere is not known.

sword. Among men it was the heirloom of Eanmund, the son of Ohth-ere:[7] Weohstan had become his slayer in battle with sword's edge—an exile without friends; and he bore off to his kin the bright-shining hel-met, the ringed mail-armor, the old sword made by giants that Onela had given him,[8] his kinsman's war-armor, ready battle-gear: he did not speak of the feud, though he had killed his brother's son.[9] He[1] held the armor many half-years, the blade and the battle-dress, until his son might do manly deeds like his old father. Then he gave him among the Geats war-armor of every kind, numberless, when, old, he went forth on the way from life. For the young warrior this was the first time that he should enter the war-storm with his dear lord. His heart's courage did not slacken, nor did the heirloom of his kinsman fail in the battle. That the worm found when they had come together.

Wiglaf spoke, said many fit words to his companions—his mind was mournful: "I remember that time we drank mead, when we promised our lord in the beer-hall—him who gave us these rings—that we would repay him for the war-arms if a need like this befell him—the helmets and the hard swords. Of his own will he chose us among the host for this venture, thought us worthy of fame—and gave me these treasures—because he counted us good war-makers, brave helm-bearers, though our lord intended to do this work of courage alone, as keeper of the folk, because among men he had performed the greatest deeds of glory, daring actions. Now the day has come that our liege lord has need of the strength of good fighters. Let us go to him, help our war-chief while the grim terrible fire persists. God knows of me that I should rather that the flame enfold my body with my gold-giver. It does not seem right to me for us to bear our shields home again unless we can first fell the foe, defend the life of the prince of the Weather-Geats. I know well that it would be no recompense for past deeds that he alone of the company of the Geats should suffer pain, fall in the fight. For us both shall there be a part in the work of sword and helmet, of battle-shirt and war-clothing."

Then he waded through the deadly smoke, bore his war-helmet to the aid of his king, spoke in few words: "Beloved Beowulf, do all well, for, long since in your youth, you said that you would not let your glory fail while you lived. Now, great-spirited noble, brave of deeds, you must protect your life with all your might. I shall help you."

After these words, the worm came on, angry, the terrible malice-filled foe, shining with surging flames, to seek for the second time his ene-mies, hated men. Fire advanced in waves; shield burned to the boss; mail-shirt might give no help to the young spear-warrior; but the young

7. See above, p. 60, note 9. Not only did Weoh-stan support Onela's attack on the Geat king Heardred, but actually killed Eanmund whom Heardred was supporting, and it is Eanmund's sword that Wiglaf is now wielding.

8. The spoils of war belonged to the victorious king, who apportioned them among his fighters: thus Onela gave Weohstan the armor of Eanmund,

whom Weohstan had killed.

9. This ironic remark points out that Onela did not claim *wergild* or seek vengeance from Weohs-tan, as in other circumstances he ought to have done inasmuch as Weohstan had killed Onela's close kinsman, his nephew Eanmund: but Onela was himself trying to kill Eanmund.

1. Weohstan.

man went quickly under his kinsman's shield when his own was consumed with flames. Then the war-king was again mindful of fame, struck
with his war-sword with great strength so that it stuck in the head-bone,
driven with force: Naegling broke, the sword of Beowulf failed in the
fight, old and steel-gray. It was not ordained for him that iron edges
might help in the combat. Too strong was the hand that I have heard
strained every sword with its stroke, when he bore wound-hardened
weapon to battle: he was none the better for it.

Then for the third time the folk-harmer, the fearful fire-dragon, was
mindful of feuds, set upon the brave one when the chance came, hot
and battle-grim seized all his neck with his sharp fangs: he was smeared
with life-blood, gore welled out in waves.

Then, I have heard, at the need of the folk-king the earl at his side
made his courage known, his might and his keenness—as was natural to
him. He took no heed for that head,[2] but the hand of the brave man
was burned as he helped his kinsman, as the man in armor struck the
hateful foe a little lower down, so that the sword sank in, shining and
engraved; and then the fire began to subside. The king himself then still
controlled his senses, drew the battle-knife, biting and war-sharp, that
he wore on his mail-shirt: the protector of the Weather-Geats cut the
worm through the middle. They felled the foe, courage drove his life
out, and they had destroyed him together, the two noble kinsmen. So
ought a man be, a thane at need. To the prince that was the last moment
of victory for his own deeds, of work in the world.

Then the wound that the earth-dragon had caused began to burn and
to swell; at once he felt dire evil boil in his breast, poison within him.
Then the prince, wise of thought, went to where he might sit on a seat
near the wall. He looked on the work of giants, how the timeless earth-
hall held within it stone-arches fast on pillars. Then with his hands the
thane, good without limit, washed him with water, blood-besmeared,
the famous prince, his beloved lord, sated with battle; and he unfastened
his helmet.

Beowulf spoke—despite his wounds spoke, his mortal hurts. He knew
well he had lived out his days' time, joy on earth; all passed was the
number of his days, death very near. "Now I would wish to give my son
my war-clothing, if any heir after me, part of my flesh, were granted. I
held this people fifty winters. There was no folk-king of those dwelling
about who dared approach me with swords, threaten me with fears. In
my land I awaited what fate brought me, held my own well, sought no
treacherous quarrels, nor did I swear many oaths unrightfully. Sick with
life-wounds, I may have joy of all this, for the Ruler of Men need not
blame me for the slaughter of kinsmen when life goes from my body.
Now quickly go to look at the hoard under the gray stone, beloved Wiglaf, now that the worm lies sleeping from sore wounds, bereft of his
treasure. Be quick now, so that I may see the ancient wealth, the golden

2. I.e., the dragon's flame-breathing head.

things, may clearly look on the bright curious gems, so that for that, because of the treasure's richness, I may the more easily leave life and nation I have long held."

Then I have heard that the son of Weohstan straightway obeyed his lord, sick with battle-wounds, according to the words he had spoken, went wearing his ring-armor, woven battle-shirt, under the barrow's roof. Then he saw, as he went by the seat, the brave young retainer, triumphant in heart, many precious jewels, glittering gold lying on the ground, wonders on the wall, and the worm's lair, the old night-flier's—cups standing there, vessels of men of old, with none to polish them, stripped of their ornaments. There was many a helmet old and rusty, many an arm-ring skillfully twisted. (Easily may treasure, gold in the ground, betray each one of the race of men, hide it who will.) Also he saw a standard all gold hang high over the hoard, the greatest of hand-wonders, linked with fingers' skill. From it came a light so that he might see the ground, look on the works of craft. There was no trace of the worm, for the blade had taken him. Then I have heard that one man in the mound pillaged the hoard, the old work of giants, loaded in his bosom cups and plates at his own desire. He took also the standard, brightest of banners. The sword of the old lord—its edge was iron—had already wounded the one who for a long time had been guardian of the treasure, waged his fire-terror, hot for the hoard, rising up fiercely at midnight, till he died in the slaughter.

The messenger was in haste, eager to return, urged on by the treasures. Curiosity tormented him, whether eagerly seeking he should find the lord of the Weather-Geats, strength gone, alive in the place where he had left him before. Then with the treasures he found the great prince, his lord, bleeding, at the end of his life. Again he began to sprinkle him with water until this word's point broke through his breast-hoard—he spoke, the king, old man in sorrow, looked on the gold: "I speak with my words thanks to the Lord of All for these treasures, to the King of Glory, Eternal Prince, for what I gaze on here, that I might get such for my people before my death-day. Now that I have bought the hoard of treasures with my old life, you attend to the people's needs hereafter: I can be here no longer. Bid the battle-renowned make a mound, bright after the funeral fire, on the sea's cape. It shall stand high on Hronesness as a reminder to my people, so that sea-travelers later will call it Beowulf's barrow, when they drive their ships far over the darkness of the seas."

He took off his neck the golden necklace, bold-hearted prince, gave it to the thane, to the young spear-warrior—gold-gleaming helmet, ring, and mail-shirt, bade him use them well. "You are the last left of our race, of the Waegmundings. Fate has swept away all my kinsmen, earls in their strength, to destined death. I have to go after." That was the last word of the old man, of the thoughts of his heart, before he should taste the funeral pyre, hot hostile flames. The soul went from his breast to seek the doom of those fast in truth.

[*Beowulf's Funeral*]

Then sorrow came to the young man that he saw him whom he most loved on the earth, at the end of his life, suffering piteously. His slayer likewise lay dead, the awful earth-dragon bereft of life, overtaken by evil. No longer should the coiled worm rule the ring-hoard, for iron edges had taken him, hard and battle-sharp work of the hammers, so that the wide-flier, stilled by wounds, had fallen on the earth near the treasure-house. He did not go flying through the air at midnight, proud of his property, showing his aspect, but he fell to earth through the work of the chief's hands. Yet I have heard of no man of might on land, though he was bold of every deed, whom it should prosper to rush against the breath of the venomous foe or disturb with hands the ring-hall, if he found the guard awake who lived in the barrow. The share of the rich treasures became Beowulf's, paid for by death: each of the two had journeyed to the end of life's loan.

Then it was not long before the battle-slack ones left the woods, ten weak troth-breakers together, who had not dared fight with their spears in their liege lord's great need. But they bore their shields, ashamed, their war-clothes, to where the old man lay, looked on Wiglaf. He sat wearied, the foot-soldier near the shoulders of his lord, would waken him with water: it gained him nothing. He might not, though he much wished it, hold life in his chieftain on earth nor change anything of the Ruler's: the judgment of God would control the deeds of every man, just as it still does now. Then it was easy to get from the young man a grim answer to him who before had lost courage. Wiglaf spoke, the son of Weohstan, a man sad at heart, looked on the unloved ones:

"Yes, he who will speak truth may say that the liege lord who gave you treasure, the war-gear that you stand in there, when he used often to hand out to hall-sitters on the ale-benches, a prince to his thanes, helmets and war-shirts such as he could find mightiest anywhere, both far and near—that he quite threw away the war-gear, to his distress when war came upon him. The folk-king had no need to boast of his war-comrades. Yet God, Ruler of Victories, granted him that he might avenge himself, alone with his sword, when there was need for his courage. I was able to give him little life-protection in the fight, and yet beyond my power I did begin to help my kinsman. The deadly foe was ever the weaker after I struck him with my sword, fire poured less strongly from his head. Too few defenders thronged about the prince when the hard time came upon him. Now there shall cease for your race the receiving of treasure and the giving of swords, all enjoyment of pleasant homes, comfort. Each man of your kindred must go deprived of his land-right when nobles from afar learn of your flight, your inglorious deed. Death is better for any earl than a life of blame."

Then he bade that the battle-deed be announced in the city, up over the cliff-edge, where the band of warriors sat the whole morning of the day, sad-hearted, shield-bearers in doubt whether it was the beloved man's last day or whether he would come again. Little did he fail to speak of new tidings, he who rode up the hill, but spoke to them all truthfully: "Now the joy-giver of the people of the Weathers, the lord of the Geats, is fast on his death-bed, lies on his slaughter-couch through deeds of the worm. Beside him lies his life-enemy, struck down with dagger-wounds— with his sword he might not work wounds of any kind on the monster. Wiglaf son of Weohstan sits over Beowulf, one earl by the lifeless other, in weariness of heart holds death-watch over the loved and the hated.

"Now may the people expect a time of war, when the king's fall becomes wide-known to the Franks and the Frisians. A harsh quarrel was begun with the Hugas when Hygelac came traveling with his sea-army to the land of the Frisians, where the Hetware assailed him in battle, quickly, with stronger forces, made the mailed warrior bow; he fell in the ranks: that chief gave no treasure to his retainers. Ever since then the good will of the Merewioing king has been denied us.

"Nor do I expect any peace or trust from the Swedish people, for it is wide-known that Ongentheow took the life of Haethcyn, Hrethel's son, near Ravenswood when in their over-pride the people of the Geats first went against the War-Scylfings. Straightway the wary father of Oht-here,[3] old and terrible, gave a blow in return, cut down the sea-king,[4] rescued his wife, old woman of times past, bereft of her gold, mother of Onela and Ohthere, and then he followed his life-foes until they escaped, lordless, painfully, to Ravenswood. Then with a great army he besieged those whom the sword had left, weary with wounds, often vowed woes to the wretched band the livelong night, said that in the morning he would cut them apart with sword-blades, [hang] some on gallows-trees as sport for birds. Relief came in turn to the sorry-hearted together with dawn when they heard Hygelac's horn and trumpet, his sound as the good man came on their track with a body of retainers. Wide-seen was the bloody track of Swedes and Geats, the slaughter-strife of men, how the peoples stirred up the feud between them. Then the good man went with his kinsmen, old and much-mourning, to seek his stronghold: the earl Ongentheow moved further away. He had heard of the warring of Hygelac, of the war-power of the proud one. He did not trust in resis-tance, that he might fight off the sea-men, defend his hoard against the war-sailors, his children and wife. Instead he drew back, the old man behind his earth-wall.

"Then pursuit was offered to the people of the Swedes, the standards of Hygelac overran the stronghold as Hrethel's people pressed forward to the citadel. There Ongentheow the gray-haired was brought to bay by sword-blades, and the people's king had to submit to the judgment of Eofor alone. Wulf[5] son of Wonred had struck him angrily with his weapon

3. I.e., Ongentheow.
4. I.e., Haethcyn, king of the Geats. Haethcyn's brother Hygelac, who succeeded him, was not present at this battle, but arrived after the death of Haethcyn with reinforcements to relieve the sur-vivors and to pursue Ongentheow in his retreat to

his city.
5. The two sons of Wonred, Wulf and Eofor, attacked Ongentheow in turn. Wulf was struck down but not killed by the old Swedish king, who was then slain by Eofor.

so that for the blow the blood sprang forth in streams beneath his hair. Yet not for that was he afraid, the old Scylfing, but he quickly repaid the assault with worse exchange, the folk-king, when he turned toward him. The strong son of Wonred could not give the old man a return blow, for Ongentheow had first cut through the helmet of his head so that he had to sink down, smeared with blood—fell on the earth: he was not yet doomed, for he recovered, though the wound hurt him. The hardy thane of Hygelac,[6] when his brother lay low, let his broad sword, old blade made by giants, break the great helmet across the shield-wall; then the king bowed, the keeper of the folk was hit to the quick.

"Then there were many who bound up the brother, quickly raised him up after it was granted them to control the battle-field. Then one warrior stripped the other, took from Ongentheow his iron-mail, hard-hilted sword, and his helmet, too; he bore the arms of the hoary one to Hygelac. He accepted that treasure and fairly promised him rewards among the people, and he stood by it thus: the lord of the Geats, the son of Hrethel, when he came home, repaid Wulf and Eofor for their battle-assault with much treasure, gave each of them a hundred thousand [units] of land and linked rings: there was no need for any man on middle-earth to blame him for the rewards, since they had performed great deeds. And then he gave Eofor his only daughter as a pledge of friendship—a fair thing for his home.

"That is the feud and the enmity, the death-hatred of men, for which I expect that the people of the Swedes, bold shield-warriors after the fall of princes, will set upon us after they learn that our prince has gone from life, he who before held hoard and kingdom against our enemies, did good to the people, and further still, did what a man should. Now haste is best, that we look on the people's king there and bring him who gave us rings on his way to the funeral pyre. Nor shall only a small share melt with the great-hearted one, but there is a hoard of treasure, gold uncounted, grimly purchased, and rings bought at the last now with his own life. These shall the fire devour, flames enfold—no earl to wear ornament in remembrance, nor any bright maiden add to her beauty with neck-ring; but mournful-hearted, stripped of gold, they shall walk, often, not once, in strange countries—now that the army-leader has laid aside laughter, his game and his mirth. Therefore many a spear, cold in the morning, shall be grasped with fingers, raised by hands; no sound of harp shall waken the warriors, but the dark raven, low over the doomed, shall tell many tales, say to the eagle how he fared at the feast when with the wolf he spoiled the slain bodies."

Thus the bold man was a speaker of hateful news, nor did he much lie in his words or his prophecies. The company all arose. Without joy they went below Earnaness[7] to look on the wonder with welling tears. Then they found on the sand, soulless, keeping his bed of rest, him who in former times had given them rings. Then the last day of the good

6. I.e., Eofor.
7. The headland near where Beowulf had fought the dragon.

man had come, when the war-king, prince of the Weather-Geats, died a wonderful death. First they saw the stranger creature, the worm lying loathsome, opposite him in the place. The fire-dragon was grimly terrible with his many colors, burned by the flames; he was fifty feet long in the place where he lay. Once he had joy of the air at night, came back down to seek his den. Then he was made fast by death, had made use of the last of his earth-caves. Beside him stood cups and pitchers, plates and rich swords lay eaten through by rust, just as they had been there in the bosom of the earth for a thousand winters. Then that huge heritage, gold of men of old, was wound in a spell, so that no one of men must touch the ring-hall unless God himself, the True King of Victories—He is men's protection—should grant to whom He wished to open the hoard—whatever man seemed fit to Him.

Then it was seen that the act did not profit him who wrongly kept hidden the handiworks under the wall. The keeper had first slain a man like few others, then the feud had been fiercely avenged. It is a wonder where an earl famed for courage may reach the end of his allotted life—then may dwell no longer in the mead-hall, man with his kin. So it was with Beowulf when he sought quarrels, the barrow's ward: he himself did not then know in what way his parting with the world should come. The great princes who had put it[8] there had laid on it so deep a curse until doomsday that the man who should plunder the place should be guilty of sins, imprisoned in idol-shrines, fixed with hell-bonds, punished with evils—unless the Possessor's favor were first shown the more clearly to him who desired the gold.

Wiglaf spoke, the son of Weohstan: "Often many a man must suffer distress for the will of one man, as has happened to us. We might by no counsel persuade our dear prince, keeper of the kingdom, not to approach the gold-guardian, let him lie where he long was, live in his dwelling to the world's end. He held to his high destiny. The hoard has been made visible, grimly got. What drove the folk-king thither was too powerfully fated. I have been therein and looked at it all, the rare things of the chamber, when it was granted me—not at all friendly was the journey that I was permitted beneath the earth-wall. In haste I seized with my hands a huge burden of hoard-treasures, of great size, bore it out here to my king. He was then still alive, sound-minded and aware. He spoke many things, old man in sorrow, and bade greet you, commanded that for your lord's deeds you make a high barrow in the place of his pyre, large and conspicuous, since he was of men the worthiest warrior through the wide earth, while he might enjoy wealth in his castle.

"Let us now hasten to see and visit for the second time the heap of precious jewels, the wonder under the walls. I shall direct you so that you may look on enough of them from near at hand—rings and broad gold. Let the bier be made ready, speedily prepared, when we come out,

8. The treasure.

and then let us carry our prince, beloved man, where he shall long dwell in the Ruler's protection."

Then the son of Weohstan, man brave in battle, bade command many warriors, men who owned houses, leaders of the people, that they carry wood from afar for the pyre for the good man. "Now shall flame eat the chief of warriors—the fire shall grow dark—who often survived the iron-shower when the storm of arrows driven from bow-strings passed over the shield-wall—the shaft did its task, made eager by feather-gear served the arrowhead."

And then the wise son of Weohstan summoned from the host thanes of the king, seven together, the best; one of eight warriors, he went beneath the evil roof. One who walked before bore a torch in his hands. Then there was no lot to decide who should plunder that hoard, since the men could see that every part of it rested in the hall without guard-ian, lay wasting. Little did any man mourn that hastily they should bear out the rare treasure. Also they pushed the dragon, the worm, over the cliff-wall, let the wave take him, the flood enfold the keeper of the treas-ure. Then twisted gold was loaded on a wagon, an uncounted number of things, and the prince, hoary warrior, borne to Hronesness.

Then the people of the Geats made ready for him a funeral pyre on the earth, no small one, hung with helmets, battle-shields, bright mail-shirts, just as he had asked. Then in the midst they laid the great prince, lamenting their hero, their beloved lord. Then warriors began to awaken on the barrow the greatest of funeral-fires; the wood-smoke climbed, black over the fire; the roaring flame mixed with weeping—the wind-surge died down—until it had broken the bone-house, hot at its heart. Sad in spirit they lamented their heart-care, the death of their liege lord. [And the Geatish woman, wavy-haired, sang a sorrowful song about Beowulf, said][9] again and again that she sorely feared for herself inva-sions of armies, many slaughters, terror of troops, humiliation, and cap-tivity. Heaven swallowed the smoke.

Then the people of the Weather-Geats built a mound on the promon-tory, one that was high and broad, wide-seen by seafarers, and in ten days completed a monument for the bold in battle, surrounded the remains of the fire with a wall, the most splendid that men most skilled might devise. In the barrow they placed rings and jewels, all such ornaments as troubled men had earlier taken from the hoard. They let the earth hold the wealth of earls, gold in the ground, where now it still dwells, as useless to men as it was before. Then the brave in battle rode round the mound, children of nobles, twelve in all, would bewail their sorrow and mourn their king, recite dirges and speak of the man. They praised his great deeds and his acts of courage, judged well of his prowess. So it is fitting that man honor his liege lord with words, love him in heart when he must be led forth from the body. Thus the people of the Geats,

---

9. The manuscript is badly damaged and the interpretation conjectural.

his hearth-companions, lamented the death of their lord. They said that he was of world-kings the mildest of men and the gentlest, kindest to his people, and most eager for fame.

GEOFFREY CHAUCER

ca. 1343–1400

1372: First Italian journey: contact with Italian literature.
1385: *Troilus and Criseide.*
1386: *Canterbury Tales* begun.

Social thought in the Middle Ages lagged far behind social realities. Medieval England did not recognize the existence of any class between the aristocracy, a relatively small group that attained its position by birth alone, and the commons, which included everyone not of high birth. There was, theoretically, no way by which one might advance from the commons to the aristocracy. But in actual fact there existed a large and increasingly important middle class that was constantly infiltrating the aristocracy, and it was into this middle class that Chaucer was born. He was the son of a well-to-do wine merchant, and probably spent his boyhood in the down-to-earth atmosphere of London's Vintry, the wine merchandising area; here, despite the privileges, especially in the way of education, that his father's wealth secured for him, he must have mixed daily with other commoners of all sorts. He might well have passed his whole life there, counting casks and money; but in his early teens he was sent to serve as a page in one of the great aristocratic households of England, that of Lionel of Antwerp, a son of the reigning monarch, Edward III. The rest of his life Chaucer spent in close association with the ruling nobility of the kingdom, not only with Lionel, but with his more powerful brother, John of Gaunt; with their father King Edward; with their nephew, Richard II, who succeeded to the throne in 1377; and finally with John's son, Henry IV, who deposed his cousin and became king in 1399. Chaucer's wife, Philippa, was a member of the households of Edward's queen and of John of Gaunt's second wife, Constance of Castile, and she was doubtless of higher birth than the poet. A Thomas Chaucer, who was probably their son, was an eminent man in the next generation, and an Alice Chaucer, quite possibly Chaucer's granddaughter, was sufficiently important in her day to have been married successively to the Earl of Salisbury and the Duke of Norfolk. The theoretically unbridgeable gap between the commons and the aristocracy was thus ably bridged by the poet.

In order to accomplish this, Chaucer must have been able in other ways than as a poet, though doubtless his extraordinary poetic ability was of great service to his advancement. Yet if one were to rely merely on the preserved historical records, one would have little reason to suspect that the Geoffrey Chaucer they keep mentioning ever wrote a line of verse. We catch glimpses of him serving as a page in Lionel's household (1357); as a soldier getting himself captured by the French in one of Edward III's many sallies to the

continent (1359); of his being the well-beloved *vallectus* of Edward III (1367)—
despite the term, which means "valet," Chaucer's duties were hardly menial—and the well-beloved servant of John of Gaunt (1374), and of receiving
substantial rewards for his services; of his being sent to Italy to assist in arranging
a trade agreement with the Genoese (1372), and to France, perhaps to assist
in getting a royal bride for young Prince Richard (1377); of his receiving a
rent-free house on the city wall of London (1374); of his keeping, "in his
own hand," the accounts for which he was responsible as Controller of the
Customs and Subsidies on Wool for the port of London (1374–86)—and
the wool trade was England's largest trade; of other trips abroad on official
business; of his becoming Justice of the Peace and Knight of the Shire (Member
of Parliament) for the county of Kent (1385–86); of his erecting grandstands,
inventorying pots and pans, and getting himself robbed as Clerk of the King's
Works (1389–91); of his being appointed deputy forester of one of the royal
preserves in Somerset (1391); and—throughout his life—of his receiving grants
and annuities, or having them confirmed by royal act when a new king took
the throne, or asking that butts of wine given him by the crown be transformed into cash, or merely asking for money or more money. We last
glimpse him, in the final months of his life, renting a house in the garden
of Westminster Abbey, within a stone's throw of Westminster Hall, the ancient
seat of English government.

It might seem that a man so busy would have had little time to write
poetry, but Chaucer seems to have been an assiduous versifier all his adult
life. Unfortunately, few of his poems can be precisely dated, and some have
not been preserved. Probably among his earliest works was a translation of
the *Roman de la Rose*, a thirteenth-century French poem that exercised a
profound influence on Chaucer's work. The first part of the *Roman* is an
allegory, written by Guillaume de Lorris, which tells, in the form of a dream,
the progress of a youthful love affair. Guillaume left the poem unfinished,
but an enormous sequel was added to it after Guillaume's death by Jean de
Meun: in this sequel the young courtier finally wins his lady (the rose), but
not until Jean has discussed at great length many of the issues considered
important by medieval intellectuals. The poem is a mixture of highly diverse
elements, and it is characteristic of Chaucer's love of variety that he was able
to assimilate into his own work both the courtly emotionalism of Guillaume
and the philosophical, often satiric, detachment of Jean. Of a fourteenth-
century English translation of the French poem only a fragment has come
down to us, and that without any mention of the translator's name; scholars
are generally agreed that the first 1700 lines of this fragment are Chaucer's.

Chaucer's work on the *Roman* is thought to have been done during the
sixties. During this decade he probably made other translations from the
French, and kept on sharpening his rhetorical tools. At the end of the decade
he produced his first major work (and the only one of his poems that can be
accurately dated): the *Book of the Duchess*, probably completed in early 1369,
an elegy for John of Gaunt's first wife, the lovely Blanche of Lancaster, who
died in 1368. This is at once one of Chaucer's most derivative and most
original poems: many of its octosyllabic lines are translated directly from
various works by Jean Froissart, a French poet contemporary with Chaucer,
and from his countryman Guillaume de Machaut as well as from other
Frenchmen; yet the plan of the work is imaginative and daring, and as a
whole the elegy is on a level of excellence never attained by the poets from

whom Chaucer is borrowing. It is also interesting to observe how that tact which was later to earn Chaucer his status as a minor diplomat controls the direction of the poem and gives it artistic form.

In the first period of his literary activity Chaucer's specific poetic models were French, but a knowledge of writings in Latin lies behind virtually everything he wrote—although the Latin writers Chaucer read were not the same as those whom we should study today. He probably had a more than adequate knowledge of the *Aeneid* and of Ovid in the original, but it is likely that he knew the other classical authors mostly through French translations and paraphrases. He was directly familiar with a number of (to us) cumbersome medieval Latin poems. Certainly his favorite Latin writer was Boethius, the sixth-century Roman whose *Consolation of Philosophy*, written while its author was in prison awaiting his execution, became one of the most valued of books for the whole Middle Ages, which never failed to find inspiration and comfort in its nobly stoic doctrine. Chaucer's own philosophical attitude, that of living wholeheartedly in the world while remaining spiritually detached from it, is at least partially a legacy from Boethius. His wooden but painstaking prose translation of the *Consolation*, probably made during the seventies, is only one of innumerable indications of Chaucer's reverence for the Roman writer.

The journey that Chaucer made to Italy in 1372 was in all likelihood a milestone in his literary development. Hitherto the influences upon him had been largely French and Latin, and while he may have read Italian before, it is likely that it was his Italian journey that immersed him in the works of Dante, Petrarch, and Boccaccio—the last two still alive at the time of Chaucer's visit, though he probably did not meet them. Between Chaucer and the greatest of the Italian writers, Dante, there was a large dissimilarity of temperament; yet if Chaucer could not assimilate *The Divine Comedy*, he nevertheless appreciated its austere moral grandeur, and his work shows its influences in subtle, oblique ways. Moreover, one of his funniest poems, the *House of Fame*, written sometime while he was in the customs (1374–86), may be read as a lighthearted imitation of the *Comedy*, though not a wholly successful one. From the works of Petrarch, also a writer of alien temperament, Chaucer obtained less, though he accords him respect on the several occasions when he mentions him. It was Boccaccio, whose cast of mind was far more congenial to Chaucer than the more sober Dante and Petrarch, who was to provide the source for some of Chaucer's finest poems— though his name is never mentioned in Chaucer's works. Many of the *Canterbury Tales* are indebted to one or another of Boccaccio's works, as is his lovely, cryptic love vision, the *Parliament of Fowls* (between 1375 and 1385). And his longest poem, *Troilus and Criseide*, probably completed about 1385, is an adaptation of Boccaccio's *Il Filostrato* ("The Love-Stricken"). The Italian work is one of considerable stature, which Chaucer reworked into one of the greatest love poems in any language. Even if he had never written the *Canterbury Tales*, *Troilus* would have secured Chaucer a place among the great English poets.

Chaucer probably began work on the *Canterbury Tales* in 1386, and this was his chief literary interest until his death. The old tripartite division of Chaucer's literary career which assigns him a French period (to 1372), and an Italian period (1372–85), calls this last period of his life "English." But it was not English in the same sense as the earlier periods were French and Italian (i.e., dominated by French and Italian models), for the fact is that

Chaucer from the beginning to the end stands apart from the mainstream of English literature. In the Tale of Sir Thopas, which he assigns himself in the *Canterbury Tales*, the wonderful fun he makes of popular Middle English romances shows his intimate knowledge of them; and undoubtedly he had read much English writing of all kinds. Yet his notion of literary art seems to have excluded many of the common characteristics—and the characteristic vices—of what had been and was being written in English, so that it is difficult to relate his work to that of his fellow English writers. His friend John Gower is a case in point: like Chaucer, he wrote a collection of English narrative poems in his *Confessio Amantis* ("The Lover's Confession"), and Chaucer tells some of the same stories in the *Canterbury Tales* and in the *Legend of Good Women*. The last, which may have interrupted Chaucer's work on the *Canterbury Tales* in the late 1380s, was apparently assigned him by some eminent person; in order to make amends for his portrait of the unfaithful Criseide, he had to write a series of short poems celebrating famous faithful women. To make each story prove exactly the same point and nothing more is something that the conventional Gower had no trouble in doing. Yet Chaucer was able to complete the tales of only nine solemnly steadfast ladies before giving up in something like despair, and the most amusing thing about his narratives is his evident exasperation with having to make everything accord to a single formula. He could not bring himself to use the simple moralistic technique of conventional English poetry, and what Gower treats seriously appears in Chaucer often to be bordering on burlesque. Every comparison between Chaucer and run-of-the-mill English poetry either so exalts him as to make the act of comparison ludicrous or else, when Chaucer is trying to behave conventionally, shows him writing with his left hand. Chaucer had no really "English" period; English poetry had little to teach the first great English poet.

The extraordinary variety of the *Canterbury Tales* as well as their number might well have demanded their author's full energy and attention during the last fourteen years of his life, but while he was at work on them he continued, almost to the end, to perform what seem to have been full-time jobs having nothing to do with literature. Doubtless this practical business prevented him from achieving more than the twenty-two tales he finished; and it probably made him search his old papers for tales that he could work in without substantial revision. Yet if it reduced his literary output—which, even so, is enormous—this lifelong involvement with the practical is one of the chief reasons for his greatness as a poet. From his birth to his death he dealt continually with all sorts of people, the highest and the lowest, and his wonderfully observant mind made the most of this ever-present opportunity. His wide reading gave him plots and ideas, but his experience gave him people. As a commoner himself he had a sympathy with and understanding of the lower classes that few people who attained his ultimate station might boast of—and the lower classes must have accepted him. Similarly, he seems to have won full acceptance from the proud and important personages with whom he associated at court, and this he could not have won if he had not understood them perfectly. He understands both the high and the low, but he remains curiously detached from both, and it is detachment, perfectly balanced in his poetry by sympathy, which distinguishes Chaucer's art. Although he was born a commoner, he did not live as a commoner; and although he was accepted by the aristocracy, he must always have been conscious of the fact that he did not really belong to that society of which birth alone could make one a true member. Medieval aristocratic society arrogated to itself all idealism, and Chaucer characteristically regards life in terms of aristocratic ideals; but he never lost the ability, which for the poorer class was also a positive necessity, of regarding life as a purely practical matter. The art of being at once involved in and detached from a given situation is peculiarly Chaucer's.

In the physical realm, double vision results in a blurred image, but not so in Chaucer's poetic world, where images have often an extraordinary clarity, as if reality itself were made more real. His Prioress in the *Canterbury Tales* is an example of the basic human paradox which places what people are in opposition to what they think they are or pretend to be: Chaucer shows us clearly her inability to be what she professes to be, a nun; shows also the inadequacy of what she thinks a nun ought to be, a lady; and shows the great human charm of what she is, a woman. The elements of the portrait are divided between the critical and the admiring: a heavily satiric poet might well enhance the critical comment, so that our ultimate impression would be of the Prioress' weakness, while a sentimental one might enhance her amiable side so as to make that the aspect which we should remember. But in Chaucer's handling the reality comprehends both sides of the Prioress, expresses the paradox without attempting to resolve it. He appears to have been a man who had no illusions about the world or its inhabitants, but was nevertheless deeply fond of them both, and thought it worth while to keep the world spinning as well as possible, either by telling stories of high artistic truth or by counting pots and pans.

The text given here is from the senior editor's *Chaucer's Poetry: An Anthology for the Modern Reader* (1958, 1975). For the *Canterbury Tales* the Hengwrt Manuscript has provided the textual basis. The spelling has been altered to improve consistency and has been modernized in so far as is possible without distorting the phonological values of the Middle English. Discussions of Middle English pronunciation, grammar, and prosody will be found in the introduction to the period.

The Canterbury Tales

Chaucer's original plan for the *Canterbury Tales* projected about one hundred twenty stories, two for each pilgrim to tell on the way to Canterbury and two more on the way back. Chaucer actually completed only twenty-two, though two more exist in fragments; a modification of the original plan is seen in the assignment of one of the completed tales to a pilgrim who was not a member of the group that assembled at Southwark. The work was probably first conceived in 1386, when Chaucer was living in Greenwich, some miles east of London. From his house he might have been able to see the pilgrim road that led toward the shrine of the famous English saint, Thomas à Becket, the Archbishop of Canterbury who was murdered in his cathedral in 1170. Medieval pilgrims were notorious tale tellers (liars, according to the austere Langland), and the sight and sound of the bands riding toward Canterbury may well have suggested to Chaucer the idea of using a fictitious pilgrimage as a "framing" device for a number of stories. Collections of stories linked by such a device were common in the later Middle Ages. Chaucer's contemporary John Gower had used one in his *Confessio Amantis*; earlier in the century Boccaccio had placed the hundred tales of his *Decameron* in the mouths of ten characters, each of whom told a tale a day for ten days; and another Italian, Giovanni Sercambi, had placed a series of stories in the mouth of the leader of a group of persons journeying on horseback. Even if, as seems likely, Chaucer was unaware of the Italian precedents, the device of the framing fiction was in the air.

Chaucer's artistic exploitation of the device is, however, altogether his own. In Gower and Sercambi, one speaker relates all the stories; and in Boccaccio, the relationship between any one of the ten speakers and the stories they tell is haphazard, so that reassignment of all the stories to different speakers would not materially change the effect. But in the best of the *Canterbury Tales* there is a fascinating accord between the narrators and their stories, so that the story takes on rich overtones from what we have learned of its teller in the General Prologue and elsewhere, and the character itself grows and is revealed by the story. Chaucer conducts two fictions simultaneously—that of the individual tale and that of the pilgrim to whom he has assigned it. He develops the second fiction not only through the General Prologue but also through the "links," the interchanges among the pilgrims between stories. These interchanges sometimes lead to animosities. Thus the Miller's Tale offends the Reeve, who, formerly a carpenter, sees himself slandered in the figure of the Miller's silly, cuckolded carpenter; and the Reeve replies with a story that scores a miller who seems very like the pilgrim Miller. Similarly the Friar and the Summoner quarrel at the end of the Wife of Bath's Prologue, so that when the Friar is called upon he tells a tale most offensive to the Summoner, who in turn retaliates with an even more offensive story about a friar. The effect of each of these tales is enhanced by the animus of its teller, while the description of the animus in the links is exciting in itself: we are given at once a story and a drama. Furthermore, the Wife of Bath's aggressive feminism sets up resonances that are felt through all the succeeding tales. Indeed, so powerful are these resonances that some see in them a thematic unifying device: the question of marriage that the Wife introduces is further treated from two opposing points of view by the Clerk and the Merchant, and is finally settled by the common sense of the Franklin. In addition to such artistic stratagems as these, the personality and mind of the reporter—a half-burlesque version of Chaucer himself—permeate the poem and enrich its meaning.

The composition of none of the tales can be accurately dated; most of them were written during the last fourteen years of Chaucer's life, though some that fail to fit their tellers may be much earlier. The popularity of the poem in late medieval England is attested by the number of surviving manuscripts: more than eighty, none from Chaucer's lifetime. It was also twice printed by Caxton, and often reprinted by Caxton's early successors. The manuscripts reflect the unfinished state of the poem—the fact that when he died Chaucer had not made up his mind about a number of details, and hence left many inconsistencies. The poem appears in the manuscripts as nine or ten "fragments" or blocks of tales; the order of the poems within each fragment is generally the same, but the order of the fragments themselves varies widely. The fragment containing the General Prologue, the Knight's, Miller's and Reeve's Tales, and the Cook's unfinished tale, always comes first, and the fragment consisting of the Parson's Tale and the Retraction always comes last; but the others, such as that containing the Wife of Bath, the Friar, and the Summoner, or that consisting of the Physician and Pardoner, or the longest fragment consisting of six tales concluding with the

Nun's Priest's, are by no means stable in relation to one another. The order followed here is one of the two that seem most nearly satisfactory.

THE GENERAL PROLOGUE

Chaucer did not need to make a pilgrimage himself in order to meet the types of people that his fictitious pilgrimage includes, for most of them had long inhabited literature as well as life: the ideal Knight, who had fought against the pagans in all the great battles of the last half-century; his son the Squire, a lover out of any love poem; the Prioress without a vocation but with the dogs and jewelry that satirical literature was always condemning nuns for; the hunting Monk and flattering Friar, chief butts of medieval satirists; the too-busy and too-rich Sergeant of the Law; the prosperous Franklin; the fraudulent Doctor; the Wife—or Archwife—of Bath; the austere Parson; and so on down through the lower orders to that flamboyant hypocrite, the Pardoner, a living vice. One meets all these types in medieval literature, and, since literature imitates life, one might have met them also in medieval society, as Chaucer, with his wide experience, undoubtedly did. Indeed, it has been argued that in some of his portraits he is drawing real people; but the appearance of doing so is actually a function of his art, which is able to endow types with a reality we generally associate only with people we know. Chaucer achieves this effect largely by persuading us that his own interest lies only in the visible, in what actually met his eye on the pilgrimage. He pretends to let the salient features of each pilgrim leap out directly at the reader, and does not seem to mind if some of his descriptions are from top to toe, others all toe and no top. This imitation of the way our minds actually perceive reality may make us fail to notice the care with which Chaucer has selected his details in order to give an integrated sketch of the person being described. While they are generally not full-blown literary symbols, most of these details give something more than mere verisimilitude to the description; actually, they mediate between the world of types and the world of real people. Independent bourgeois women of the time were often makers of cloth, so that the Wife of Bath's proficiency at the trade is, in one way, merely part of her historical reality; yet the first weaver of cloth was the unparadised Eve, and her descendant is an unregenerate member of her sex. The Franklin's red face and white beard are in the same way merely individualizing factors in the portrait; yet the red face and white beard seem always to associate themselves with a man of good will who likes good living, and since Chaucer's time they have become the distinguishing marks of a kind of mythic Franklin, Santa Claus.

The rich suggestiveness of the details is what makes the portraits worth reading again and again. One may begin by enjoying the bright if flat photographic image of reality that the reporter creates, but one will find that the initial appearance of flatness is deceptive, and that the more one rereads the more complex and significant the portraits become. Here, as elsewhere in his work, Chaucer shows himself to be a rival to Shakespeare in the art of providing entertainment on the most primitive level, and at the same time, of significantly increasing the reader's ability to comprehend reality.

From THE CANTERBURY TALES

The General Prologue

Whan that April with his° showres soote°	*its / sweet*
The droughte of March hath perced to the roote,	
And bathed every veine[1] in swich° licour,°	*such / liquid*
Of which vertu[2] engendred is the flowr;	
5 Whan Zephyrus[3] eek° with his sweete breeth	*also*
Inspired hath in every holt° and heeth°	*grove / field*
The tendre croppes,° and the yonge sonne[4]	*shoots*
Hath in the Ram his halve cours yronne,	
And smale fowles maken melodye	
10 That sleepen al the night with open yë°—	*eye*
So priketh hem° Nature in hir corages[5]—	*them*
Thanne longen folk to goon° on pilgrimages,	*go*
And palmeres[6] for to seeken straunge strondes, *All walks of life*	
To ferne halwes, couthe° in sondry londes;	*known*
15 And specially from every shires ende	
Of Engelond to Canterbury they wende,	
The holy blisful martyr[7] for to seeke	
That hem hath holpen° whan that they were seke.°	*helped / sick*
Bifel that in that seson on a day,	
20 In Southwerk[8] at the Tabard as I lay,	
Redy to wenden on my pilgrimage	
To Canterbury with ful° devout corage,	*very*
At night was come into that hostelrye	
Wel nine and twenty in a compaignye	
25 Of sondry folk, by aventure° yfalle	*chance*
In felaweshipe, and pilgrimes were they alle	
That toward Canterbury wolden° ride.	*would*
The chambres and the stables weren wide,	
And wel we weren esed° at the beste.[9]	*accommodated*
30 And shortly, whan the sonne was to reste,[1]	
So hadde I spoken with hem everichoon°	*every one*
That I was of hir felaweshipe anoon,°	*at once*
And made forward[2] erly for to rise,	
To take oure way ther as[3] I you devise.°	*describe*
35 But nathelees,° whil I have time and space,[4]	*nevertheless*
Er° that I ferther in this tale pace,°	*before / pass*

1. I.e., in plants.
2. By the power of which.
3. The west wind.
4. The sun is young because it has run only halfway through its course in Aries, the Ram—the first sign of the zodiac in the solar year.
5. Their hearts.
6. Palmers, wide-ranging pilgrims—especially those who sought out the "straunge strondes" (foreign shores) of the Holy Land. "Ferne halwes": far-off

shrines.
7. St. Thomas à Becket, murdered in Canterbury Cathedral in 1170.
8. Southwark, site of the Tabard Inn, was then a suburb of London, south of the Thames River.
9. In the best possible way.
1. Had set.
2. I.e., (we) made an agreement.
3. "Ther as": where.
4. I.e., opportunity.

Me thinketh it accordant to resoun[5]
To telle you al the condicioun
Of eech of hem, so as it seemed me,
40   And whiche they were, and of what degree,
And eek in what array that they were inne:
And at a knight thanne° wol I first biginne.   *then*
A Knight ther was, and that a worthy man,
That fro the time that he first bigan
45   To riden out, he loved chivalrye,
Trouthe[6] and honour, freedom and curteisye.
Ful worthy was he in his lordes werre,°   *war*
And therto hadde he riden, no man ferre,°   *further*
As wel in Cristendom as hethenesse,°   *heathen lands*
50   And[7] evere honoured for his worthinesse.
At Alisandre[8] he was whan it was wonne;
Ful ofte time he hadde the boord bigonne[9]
Aboven alle nacions in Pruce;
In Lettou had he reised,° and in Ruce,   *campaigned*
55   No Cristen man so ofte of his degree;
In Gernade at the sege eek hadde he be
Of Algezir, and riden in Belmarye;
At Lyeis was he, and at Satalye,
Whan they were wonne; and in the Grete See[1]
60   At many a noble arivee° hadde he be.   *military landing*
At mortal batailes[2] hadde he been fifteene,
And foughten for oure faith at Tramissene
In listes[3] thries,° and ay° slain his fo.   *thrice / always*
This ilke° worthy Knight hadde been also   *same*
65   Sometime with the lord of Palatye[4]
Again° another hethen in Turkye;   *against*
And everemore he hadde a soverein pris.°   *reputation*
And though that he were worthy,[5] he was wis,
And of his port° as meeke as is a maide.   *demeanor*
70   He nevere yit no vilainye° ne saide   *rudeness*
In al his lif unto no manere wight:[6]
He was a verray,° parfit,° gentil knight.   *true / perfect*
But for to tellen you of his array,
His hors° were goode, but he was nat gay.   *horses*
75   Of fustian° he wered° a gipoun[7]   *thick cloth / wore*

5. It seems to me according to reason.
6. Integrity. "Freedom" is here generosity of spirit, while "curteisye" is courtesy.
7. I.e., and he was.
8. The Knight has taken part in campaigns fought against all three groups of pagans who threatened Europe during the 14th century: the Moslems in the Near East, from whom Alexandria was seized after a famous siege; the northern barbarians in Prussia, Lithuania, and Russia; and the Moors in North Africa. The place names in the following lines refer to battlegrounds in these continuing wars.
9. Sat in the seat of honor at military feasts.

1. The Mediterranean.
2. Tournaments fought to the death.
3. Lists, tournament grounds.
4. "The lord of Palatye" was a pagan: alliances of convenience were often made during the Crusades between Christians and pagans.
5. I.e., a valiant knight.
6. "No manere wight": any sort of person. In Middle English, negatives are multiplied for emphasis: as in these two lines: "nevere," "no," "ne," "no."
7. Tunic worn underneath the coat of mail.

Al bismotered with his haubergeoun,[8]
For he was late° come from his viage,°   *lately / expedition*
And wente for to doon his pilgrimage.
   With him ther was his sone, a yong <u>Squier</u>,[9]
80 A lovere and a lusty bacheler,
With lokkes crulle° as° they were laid in presse.   *curly / as if*
Of twenty yeer of age he was, I gesse.
Of his stature he was of evene° lengthe,   *moderate*
And wonderly delivere,° and of greet° strengthe.   *agile / great*
85 And he hadde been som time in chivachye[1]
In Flandres, in Artois, and Picardye,
And born him wel as of so litel space,[2]
In hope to stonden in his lady° grace.   *lady's*
   Embrouded° was he as it were a mede,[3]   *embroidered*
90 Al ful of fresshe flowres, white and rede;°   *red*
Singing he was, or floiting,° al the day: *whistling*
He was as fressh as is the month of May.
Short was his gowne, with sleeves longe and wide.
Wel coude he sitte on hors, and faire ride;
95 He coude songes make, and wel endite,°   *compose verse*
Juste[4] and eek daunce, and wel portraye° and write.   *sketch*
So hote° he loved that by nightertale[5]   *hotly*
He slepte namore than dooth a nightingale.
Curteis he was, lowely,° and servisable,   *humble*
100 And carf biforn his fader at the table.[6]
   A <u>Yeman</u>[7] hadde he and servants namo°   *no more*
At that time, for him liste[8] ride so;
And he[9] was clad in cote and hood of greene.
A sheef of pecok arwes,° bright and keene,   *arrows*
105 Under his belt he bar° ful thriftily;°   *bore / properly*
Wel coude he dresse° his takel° yemanly:[1]   *tend to / gear*
His arwes drouped nought with fetheres lowe.
And in his hand he bar a mighty bowe.
A not-heed° hadde he with a brown visage.   *close-cut head*
110 Of wodecraft wel coude° he al the usage.   *knew*
Upon his arm he bar a gay bracer,[2]
And by his side a swerd° and a bokeler,[3]   *sword*
And on that other side a gay daggere,
Harneised° wel and sharp as point of spere;   *mounted*
115 A Cristophre[4] on his brest of silver sheene;°   *bright*

---

8. All rust-stained from his hauberk (coat of mail).
9. The vague term "Squier" (Squire) here seems
to be the equivalent of "bacheler," a young knight
still in the service of an older one.
1. On cavalry expeditions. The places in the next
line are sites of skirmishes in the constant warfare
between the English and the French.
2. I.e., considering the little time he had been in
service.
3. Mead, meadow.
4. Joust, fight in a tournament.

5. At night.
6. It was a squire's duty to carve his lord's meat.
7. The "Yeman" (Yeoman) is an independent
commoner who acts as the Knight's military servant; "he" is the Knight.
8. "Him liste": it pleased him to.
9. I.e., the Yeoman.
1. In a workmanlike way.
2. Wristguard for archers.
3. Buckler (a small shield).
4. St. Christopher medal.

An horn he bar, the baudrik[5] was of greene.
A forster° was he soothly,° as I gesse.   *forester / truly*
    Ther was also a Nonne, a Prioresse,[6]
That of hir smiling was ful simple and coy.
120   Hir gretteste ooth was but by sainte Loy!°   *Eloi*
And she was cleped° Madame Eglantine.   *named*
Ful wel she soong° the service divine,   *sang*
Entuned° in hir nose ful semely;[7]   *chanted*
And Frenssh she spak ful faire and fetisly,°   *elegantly*
125   After the scole° of Stratford at the Bowe[8]—   *school*
For Frenssh of Paris was to hire unknowe.
At mete° wel ytaught was she withalle:°   *meals / besides*
She leet° no morsel from hir lippes falle,   *let*
Ne wette hir fingres in hir sauce deepe;
130   Wel coude she carye a morsel, and wel keepe°   *take care*
That no drope ne fille° upon hir brest.   *should fall*
In curteisye was set ful muchel hir lest.[9]
Hir over-lippe wiped she so clene
That in hir coppe° ther was no ferthing° seene   *cup / bit*
135   Of grece,° whan she dronken hadde hir draughte;   *grease*
Ful semely after hir mete she raughte.°   *reached*
And sikerly° she was of greet disport,[1]   *certainly*
And ful plesant, and amiable of port,°   *mien*
And pained hire to countrefete cheere[2]
140   Of court, and to been statlich° of manere,   *dignified*
And to been holden digne[3] of reverence.
But, for to speken of hir conscience,
She was so charitable and so pitous°   *merciful*
She wolde weepe if that she saw a mous
145   Caught in a trappe, if it were deed° or bledde.   *dead*
Of[4] smale houndes hadde she that she fedde
With rosted flessh, or milk and wastelbreed;°   *fine white bread*
But sore wepte she if oon of hem were deed,
Or if men smoot it with a yerde smerte;[5]
150   And al was conscience and tendre herte.
Ful semely hir wimpel° pinched° was,   *headdress / pleated*
Hir nose tretis,° hir yën° greye as glas,   *well-formed / eyes*
Hir mouth ful smal, and therto° softe and reed,°   *moreover / red*
But sikerly° she hadde a fair forheed: *certainly*
155   It was almost a spanne brood,[6] I trowe,°   *believe*
For hardily,° she was nat undergrowe.   *assuredly*
Ful fetis° was hir cloke, as I was war;°   *becoming / aware*
Of smal° coral aboute hir arm she bar   *dainty*

---

5. Baldric (a supporting strap).
6. The Prioress is the mother superior of her nunnery. "Simple and coy": sincere and mild.
7. In a seemly manner.
8. The French learned in a convent school in Stratford-at-the-Bow, a suburb of London, was evidently not up to the Parisian standard.

9. I.e., her chief delight lay in good manners.
1. Of great good cheer.
2. And took pains to imitate the behavior.
3. And to be considered worthy.
4. I.e., some.
5. If someone struck it with a rod sharply.
6. A handsbreadth wide.

A paire[7] of bedes, gauded all with greene,
160 And theron heeng° a brooch of gold ful sheene,°   *hung / bright*
On which ther was first writen a crowned A,[8]
And after, *Amor vincit omnia.*[9]
    Another Nonne with hire hadde she
That was hir chapelaine,° and preestes three.[1]   *secretary*
165   A Monk ther was, a fair for the maistrye,[2]
An outridere[3] that loved venerye,°   *hunting*
A manly man, to been an abbot able.°   *worthy*
Ful many a daintee° hors hadde he in stable,   *fine*
And whan he rood,° men mighte his bridel heere   *rode*
170 Ginglen° in a whistling wind as clere   *jingle*
And eek as loude as dooth the chapel belle
Ther as this lord was kepere of the celle.[4]
The rule of Saint Maure or of Saint Beneit,[5]
By cause that it was old and somdeel strait—
175 This ilke Monk leet olde thinges pace,°   *pass away*
And heeld° after the newe world the space.[6]   *held*
He yaf nought of that text a pulled hen[7]
That saith that hunteres been° nought holy men,   *are*
Ne that a monk, whan he is recchelees,[8]
180 Is likned til° a fissh that is waterlees—   *to*
This is to sayn, a monk out of his cloistre;
But thilke° text heeld he nat worth an oystre.   *that same*
And I saide his opinion was good:
What° sholde he studye and make himselven wood°   *why / crazy*
185 Upon a book in cloistre alway to poure,
Or swinke° with his handes and laboure,   *work*
As Austin bit?[9] How shal the world be served?
Lat Austin have his swink to him reserved!
Therefore he was a prikasour° aright.   *hard rider*
190 Grehoundes he hadde as swift as fowl in flight.
Of priking° and of hunting for the hare   *riding*
Was al his lust,° for no cost wolde he spare.   *pleasure*
I sawgh his sleeves purfiled° at the hand   *fur-lined*
With gris,° and that the fineste of a land;   *gray fur*
195 And for to festne his hood under his chin
He hadde of gold wrought a ful curious[1] pin:
A love-knotte in the grettere° ende ther was.   *greater*
His heed was balled,° that shoon as any glas,   *bald*
And eek his face, as he hadde been anoint:

---

7. String (i.e., a rosary). "Gauded al with greene": provided with green beads to mark certain prayers.
8. An A with an ornamental crown on it.
9. A Latin motto meaning "Love conquers all."
1. Although he here awards this charming lady three priests, Chaucer later reduces the number to one.
2. I.e., a superlatively fine one.
3. A monk charged with supervising property distant from the monastery.

4. Keeper of an outlying cell (branch) of the monastery.
5. St. Maurus and St. Benedict, authors of monastic rules. "Somdeel strait": somewhat strict.
6. I.e., in his own lifetime (?).
7. He didn't give a plucked hen for that text.
8. Reckless, careless of rule.
9. I.e., as St. Augustine bids. St. Augustine had written that monks should perform manual labor.
1. Of careful workmanship.

200 He was a lord ful fat and in good point;[2]
    His yën steepe,° and rolling in his heed,   *protruding*
    That stemed as a furnais of a leed,[3]
    His bootes souple,° his hors in greet estat°—   *supple / condition*
    Now certainly he was a fair prelat.[4]
205 He was nat pale as a forpined° gost: *wasted away*
    A fat swan loved he best of any rost.
    His palfrey° was as brown as is a berye.   *saddle horse*
        A Frere[5] ther was, a wantoune and a merye,
    A limitour, a ful solempne° man.   *pompous*
210 In alle the ordres foure is noon that can°   *knows*
    So muche of daliaunce° and fair langage: *flirtation*
    He hadde maad ful many a mariage
    Of yonge wommen at his owene cost;
    Unto his ordre he was a noble post.[6]
215 Ful wel biloved and familier was he
    With frankelains over al[7] in his contree,
    And with worthy wommen of the town—
    For he hadde power of confessioun,
    As saide himself, more than a curat,°   *parish priest*
220 For of° his ordre he was licenciat.[8]   *by*
    Ful swetely herde he confessioun,
    And plesant was his absolucioun.
    He was an esy man to yive penaunce
    Ther as he wiste to have[9] a good pitaunce;°   *donation*
225 For unto a poore ordre for to yive
    Is signe that a man is wel yshrive,[1]
    For if he yaf, he dorste make avaunt°   *boast*
    He wiste that a man was repentaunt;
    For many a man so hard is of his herte
230 He may nat weepe though him sore smerte:[2]
    Therfore, in stede of weeping and prayeres,
    Men mote° yive silver to the poore freres.[3]   *may*
        His tipet° was ay farsed° ful of knives   *scarf / packed*
    And pinnes, for to yiven faire wives;
235 And certainly he hadde a merye note;
    Wel coude he singe and playen on a rote;°   *fiddle*
    Of yeddinges he bar outrely the pris.[4]
    His nekke whit was as the flowr-de-lis;°   *lily*
    Therto he strong was as a champioun.

2. In good shape, plump.
3. That glowed like a furnace with a pot in it.
4. Prelate (an important churchman).
5. The "Frere" (Friar) is a member of one of the four religious orders whose members live by begging; as a "limitour" (line 209) he has been granted by his order exclusive begging rights within a certain limited area.
6. I.e., pillar.
7. I.e., with franklins everywhere. Franklins were well-to-do country men.

8. I.e., licensed to hear confessions.
9. Where he knew he would have.
1. Shriven, absolved.
2. Though he is sorely grieved.
3. Before granting absolution, the confessor must be sure the sinner is contrite; moreover, the absolution is contingent upon the sinner's performance of an act of satisfaction. In the case of Chaucer's Friar, a liberal contribution served both as proof of contrition and as satisfaction.
4. He absolutely took the prize for ballads.

240　He knew the tavernes wel in every town,
　　　And every hostiler° and tappestere,° .... *innkeeper / barmaid*
　　　Bet° than a lazar[5] or a beggestere. .... *better*
　　　For unto swich a worthy man as he
　　　Accorded nat, as by his facultee,[6]
245　To have with sike° lazars aquaintaunce: .... *sick*
　　　It is nat honeste,° it may nought avaunce,° .... *dignified / profit*
　　　For to delen with no swich poraile,[7]
　　　But al with riche, and selleres of vitaile;° .... *foodstuffs*
　　　And over al ther as profit sholde arise.
250　Curteis he was, and lowely of servise.
　　　Ther was no man nowher so vertuous:° .... *efficient*
　　　He was the beste beggere in his hous.° .... *friary*
　　　And yaf a certain ferme for the graunt:[8]
　　　Noon of his bretheren cam ther in his haunt.[9]
255　For though a widwe° hadde nought a sho,° .... *widow / shoe*
　　　So plesant was his *In principio*[1]
　　　Yit wolde he have a ferthing° er he wente; .... *small coin*
　　　His purchas was wel bettre than his rente.[2]
　　　And rage he coude as it were right a whelpe;[3]
260　In love-dayes[4] ther coude he muchel° helpe, ... *much*
　　　For ther he was nat lik a cloisterer,
　　　With a thredbare cope, as is a poore scoler,
　　　But he was lik a maister[5] or a pope.
　　　Of double worstede was his semicope,° .... *short robe*
265　And rounded as a belle out of the presse.° .... *bell-mold*
　　　Somwhat he lipsed° for his wantounesse° .... *lisped / affectation*
　　　To make his Englissh sweete upon his tonge;
　　　And in his harping, whan he hadde songe,° .... *sung*
　　　His yën twinkled in his heed aright
270　As doon the sterres° in the frosty night. .... *stars*
　　　This worthy limitour was cleped Huberd.
　　　　A Marchant was ther with a forked beerd,
　　　In motelee,[6] and hye on hors he sat,
　　　Upon his heed a Flandrissh° bevere hat, ... *Flemish*
275　His bootes clasped faire and fetisly.° .... *elegantly*
　　　His resons° he spak ful solempnely, ... *opinions*
　　　Souning° alway th' encrees of his winning. .... *sounding*
　　　He wolde the see were kept for any thing[7]

5. Leper. "Beggestere": female beggar.
6. It was not suitable because of his position.
7. I.e., poor people. The oldest order of friars had been founded by St. Francis to administer to the spiritual needs of precisely those classes the Friar avoids.
8. And he paid a certain rent for the privilege of begging.
9. Assigned territory.
1. A friar's usual salutation: "In the beginning [was the Word]" (John 1.1).
2. I.e., the money he got through such activity

was more than his regular income.
3. And he could flirt wantonly, as if he were a puppy.
4. Days appointed for the settlement of lawsuits out of court.
5. A man of recognized learning.
6. Motley, a cloth of mixed color.
7. I.e., he wished the sea to be guarded at all costs. The sea route between Middelburgh (in the Netherlands) and Orwell (in Suffolk) was vital to the Merchant's export and import of wool—the basis of England's chief trade at the time.

Bitwixen Middelburgh and Orewelle.
280 Wel coude he in eschaunge sheeldes[8] selle.
This worthy man ful wel his wit bisette:°   *employed*
Ther wiste° no wight that he was in dette,   *knew*
So statly° was he of his governaunce,[9]   *dignified*
With his bargaines,[1] and with his chevissaunce.
285 Forsoothe he was a worthy man withalle;
But, sooth to sayn, I noot° how men him calle.   *don't know*
    A Clerk[2] ther was of Oxenforde also
That unto logik hadde longe ygo.[3]
As lene was his hors as is a rake,
290 And he was nought right fat, I undertake,
But looked holwe,° and therto sobrely.   *hollow*
Ful thredbare was his overeste courtepy,[4]
For he hadde geten him yit no benefice,
Ne was so worldly for to have office.°   *secular employment*
295 For him was levere[5] have at his beddes heed
Twenty bookes, clad in blak or reed,
Of Aristotle and his philosophye,
Than robes riche, or fithele,° or gay sautrye.[6]   *fiddle*
But al be that he was a philosophre[7]
300 Yit hadde he but litel gold in cofre;°   *coffer*
But al that he mighte of his freendes hente,°   *take*
On bookes and on lerning he it spente,
And bisily gan for the soules praye
Of hem that yaf him wherwith to scoleye.°   *study*
305 Of studye took he most cure° and most heede.   *care*
Nought oo° word spak he more than was neede,   *one*
And that was said in forme[8] and reverence,
And short and quik,° and ful of heigh sentence:[9]   *lively*
Souning° in moral vertu was his speeche,   *resounding*
310 And gladly wolde he lerne, and gladly teche.
    A Sergeant of the Lawe,[1] war and wis,
That often hadde been at the Parvis[2]
Ther was also, ful riche of excellence.
Discreet he was, and of greet reverence—
315 He seemed swich, his wordes weren so wise.
Justice he was ful often in assise°   *circuit courts*
By patente[3] and by plein° commissioun.   *full*

8. Shields, *ecus* (French coins): he made a profit trading on international credit and exchange rates.
9. The management of his affairs.
1. Bargainings. "Chevissaunce": borrowing.
2. The Clerk is a student at Oxford; in order to become a student, he would have had to signify his intention of becoming a cleric, but he was not bound to proceed to a position of responsibility in the church.
3. Who had long since matriculated in philosophy.
4. Outer cloak. "Benefice": ecclesiastical living,

such as the income a parish priest receives.
5. He would rather.
6. Psaltery (a kind of harp).
7. The word may also mean "alchemist."
8. With decorum.
9. Elevated thought.
1. The Sergeant is not only a practicing lawyer, but one of the high justices of the nation. "War and wis": wary and wise.
2. The "Paradise," a meeting place for lawyers and their clients.
3. Royal warrant.

For his science° and for his heigh renown   *knowledge*
Of fees and robes hadde he many oon.
320   So greet a purchasour° was nowher noon;   *speculator in land*
Al was fee simple[4] to him in effect—
His purchasing mighte nat been infect.[5]
Nowher so bisy a man as he ther nas;°   *was not*
And yit he seemed bisier than he was.
325   In termes[6] hadde he caas and doomes alle
That from the time of King William[7] were falle.
Therto he coude endite and make a thing,[8]
Ther coude no wight pinchen° at his writing;   *cavil*
And every statut coude° he plein° by rote.[9]   *knew / entire*
330   He rood but hoomly° in a medlee cote,[1]   *unpretentiously*
Girt with a ceint of silk, with barres smale.
Of his array telle I no lenger tale.
      A Frankelain[2] was in his compaignye:
Whit was his beerd as is the dayesye;°   *daisy*
335   Of his complexion he was sanguin.[3]
Wel loved he by the morwe a sop in win.[4]
To liven in delit° was evere his wone,°   *sensual delight / wont*
For he was Epicurus[5] owene sone,
That heeld opinion that plein° delit   *full*
340   Was verray felicitee parfit.
An housholdere and that a greet was he:
Saint Julian[6] he was in his contree.
His breed, his ale, was always after oon;[7]
A bettre envined° man was nevere noon.   *wine-stocked*
345   Withouten bake mete was nevere his hous,
Of fissh and flessh, and that so plentevous°   *plenteous*
It snewed° in his hous of mete and drinke,   *snowed*
Of alle daintees that men coude thinke.
After° the sondry sesons of the yeer   *according to*
350   So chaunged he his mete[8] and his soper.
Ful many a fat partrich hadde he in mewe,°   *cage*
And many a breem,° and many a luce° in stewe.[9]   *carp / pike*
Wo was his cook but if his sauce were
Poinant° and sharp, and redy all his gere.   *pungent*
355   His table dormant in his halle alway

4. "Fee simple": owned outright without legal impediments.
5. Invalidated on a legal technicality.
6. I.e., by heart. "Caas and doomes": lawcases and decisions.
7. I.e., the Conqueror (reigned 1066–87).
8. Compose and draw up a deed.
9. By heart.
1. A coat of mixed color. "Ceint": belt. "Barres": transverse stripes.
2. The "Frankelain" (Franklin) is a prosperous country man, whose lower-class ancestry is no impediment to the importance he has attained in his county.
3. A reference to the fact that the Franklin's temperament is dominated by blood as well as to his red face.
4. I.e., in the morning he was very fond of a piece of bread soaked in wine.
5. The Greek philosopher whose teaching is popularly believed to make pleasure the chief goal of life.
6. The patron saint of hospitality.
7. Always of the same high quality.
8. Dinner. "Soper": supper.
9. Fishpond.

Stood redy covered all the longe day.[1]
At sessions[2] ther was he lord and sire.
Ful ofte time he was Knight of the Shire.
An anlaas° and a gipser° al of silk   *dagger / purse*
360   Heeng at his girdel,[3] whit as morne° milk.   *morning*
A shirreve° hadde he been, and countour.[4]   *sheriff*
Was nowhere swich a worthy vavasour.[5]
    An Haberdasshere and a Carpenter,
A Webbe,° a Dyere, and a Tapicer°—   *weaver / tapestry-maker*
365   And they were clothed alle in oo liveree[6]
Of a solempne and greet fraternitee.
Ful fresshe and newe hir gere apiked° was;   *polished*
Hir knives were chaped° nought with bras,   *mounted*
But al with silver; wrought ful clene and weel
370   Hir girdles and hir pouches everydeel.°   *altogether*
Wel seemed eech of hem a fair burgeis°   *burgher*
To sitten in a yeldehalle° on a dais.   *guildhall*
Everich, for the wisdom that he can,[7]
Was shaply° for to been an alderman.   *suitable*
375   For catel° hadde they ynough and rente,°   *property / income*
And eek hir wives wolde it wel assente—
And elles certain were they to blame:
It is ful fair to been ycleped "Madame,"
And goon to vigilies[8] all bifore,
380   And have a mantel royalliche ybore.[9]
    A Cook they hadde with hem for the nones,[1]
To boile the chiknes with the marybones,°   *marrowbones*
And powdre-marchant tart and galingale.[2]
Wel coude he knowe° a draughte of London ale.   *recognize*
385   He coude roste, and seethe,° and broile, and frye,   *boil*
Maken mortreux,° and wel bake a pie.   *stews*
But greet harm was it, as it thoughte° me,   *seemed to*
That on his shine a mormal° hadde he,   *ulcer*
For blankmanger,[3] that made he with the beste.
390   A Shipman was ther, woning° fer by weste—   *dwelling*
For ought I woot,° he was of Dertemouthe.[4]   *know*
He rood upon a rouncy° as he couthe,[5]   *large nag*
In a gowne of falding° to the knee.   *heavy wool*
A daggere hanging on a laas° hadde he   *strap*

1. Tables were usually dismounted when not in use, but the Franklin kept his mounted and set ("covered"), hence "dormant."
2. I.e., sessions of the justices of the peace. "Knight of the Shire": county representative in Parliament.
3. Hung at his belt.
4. Auditor of county finances.
5. Member of an upper, but not an aristocratic, feudal class.
6. In one livery, i.e., the uniform of their "fraternitee" or guild, a partly religious, partly social organization.
7. Was capable of.
8. Feasts held on the eve of saints' days. "Al bifore": i.e., at the head of the procession.
9. Royally carried.
1. For the occasion.
2. "Powdre-marchant" and "galingale" are flavoring materials.
3. An elaborate stew.
4. Dartmouth, a port in the southwest of England.
5. As best he could.

color

395 Aboute his nekke, under his arm adown.
    The hote somer hadde maad his hewe° al brown;   *color*
    And certainly he was a good felawe.
    Ful many a draughte of win hadde he drawe[6]
    Fro Burdeuxward,[7] whil that the chapman sleep:
400 Of nice° conscience took he no keep;°   *fastidious / heed*
    If that he faught and hadde the hyer hand,
    By water he sente hem hoom to every land.[8]
    But of his craft, to rekene wel his tides,
    His stremes° and his daungers° him bisides,[9]   *currents / hazards*
405 His herberwe° and his moone, his lodemenage,[1]   *anchorage*
    There was noon swich from Hulle to Cartage.[2]
    Hardy he was and wis to undertake;
    With many a tempest hadde his beerd been shake;
    He knew alle the havenes° as they were   *harbors*
410 Fro Gotlond to the Cape of Finistere,[3]
    And every crike° in Britaine° and in Spaine.   *inlet / Brittany*
    His barge ycleped was the Maudelaine.°   *Magdalene*
        With us ther was a Doctour of Physik:°   *medicine*
    In al this world ne was ther noon him lik
415 To speken of physik and of surgerye.
    For° he was grounded in astronomye,°   *because / astrology*
    He kepte° his pacient a ful greet deel[4]   *tended to*
    In houres[5] by his magik naturel.
    Wel coude he fortunen the ascendent
420 Of his images[6] for his pacient.
    He knew the cause of every maladye,
    Were it of hoot or cold or moiste or drye,
    And where engendred and of what humour:[7]
    He was a verray parfit praktisour.[8]
425 The cause yknowe,° and of his harm the roote,   *known*
    Anoon he yaf the sike man his boote.°   *remedy*
        Ful redy hadde he his apothecaries
    To senden him drogges° and his letuaries,°   *drugs / medicines*
    For eech of hem made other for to winne:

6. Drawn, i.e., stolen.
7. From Bordeaux; i.e., while carrying wine from Bordeaux (the wine center of France). "Chapman sleep": merchant slept.
8. He drowned his prisoners.
9. Around him.
1. Pilotage.
2. From Hull (in northern England) to Cartagena (in Spain).
3. From Gotland (an island in the Baltic) to Finisterre (the westernmost point in Spain).
4. Closely.
5. I.e., the astrologically important hours (when conjunctions of the planets might help his recovery). "Magik naturel": natural—as opposed to black—magic.

6. Assign the propitious time, according to the position of stars, for using talismanic images. Such images, representing either the patient himself or points in the zodiac, were thought to be influential on the course of the disease.
7. Diseases were thought to be caused by a disturbance of one or another of the four bodily "humors," each of which, like the four elements, was a compound of two of the elementary qualities mentioned in line 422: the melancholy humor, seated in the black bile, was cold and dry (like earth); the sanguine, seated in the blood, hot and moist (like air); the choleric, seated in the yellow bile, hot and dry (like fire); the phlegmatic, seated in the phlegm, cold and moist (like water).
8. True perfect practitioner.

430 Hir frendshipe was nought newe to biginne.
    Wel knew he the olde Esculapius,[9]
    And Deiscorides and eek Rufus,
    Olde Ipocras, Hali, and Galien,
    Serapion, Razis, and Avicen,
435 Averrois, Damascien, and Constantin,
    Bernard, and Gatesden, and Gilbertin.
    Of his diete mesurable° was he,   *moderate*
    For it was of no superfluitee,
    But of greet norissing° and digestible.   *nourishment*
440 His studye was but litel on the Bible.
    In sanguin° and in pers° he clad was al,   *blood-red / blue*
    Lined with taffata and with sendal;°   *silk*
    And yit he was but esy of dispence;°   *expenditure*
    He kepte that he wan in pestilence.[1]
445 For° gold in physik is a cordial,[2]   *because*
    Therfore he loved gold in special.
      A good Wif was ther of biside Bathe,
    But she was somdeel deef, and that was scathe.° *a pity*
    Of cloth-making she hadde swich an haunt,°   *practice*
450 She passed° hem of Ypres and of Gaunt.[3]   *surpassed*
    In al the parissh wif ne was ther noon
    That to the offring[4] bifore hire sholde goon,
    And if ther dide, certain so wroth° was she   *angry*
    That she was out of alle charitee.
455 Hir coverchiefs ful fine were of ground°—   *texture*
    I dorste° swere they weyeden° ten pound *dare / weighed*
    That on a Sonday weren° upon hir heed.   *were*
    Hir hosen weren of fin scarlet reed,°   *red*
    Ful straite yteyd,[5] and shoes ful moiste° and newe. *unworn*
460 Bold was hir face and fair and reed of hewe.
    She was a worthy womman al hir live:
    Housbondes at chirche dore[6] she hadde five,
    Withouten other compaignye in youthe—
    But therof needeth nought to speke as nouthe.°   *now*
465 And thries hadde she been at Jerusalem;
    She hadde passed many a straunge° streem;   *foreign*
    At Rome she hadde been, and at Boloigne,
    In Galice at Saint Jame, and at Coloigne:[7]

---

9. The Doctor is familiar with the treatises that the Middle Ages attributed to the "great names" of medical history, whom Chaucer names in lines 431–36: the purely legendary Greek demigod Aesculapius; the Greeks Dioscorides, Rufus, Hippocrates, Galen, and Serapion; the Persians Hali and Rhazes; the Arabians Avicenna and Averroës; the early Christians John (?) of Damascus and Constantine Afer; the Scotsman Bernard Gordon; the Englishmen John of Gatesden and Gilbert, the former an early contemporary of Chaucer.
1. He saved the money he made during the plague time.

2. A stimulant. Gold was thought to have some medicinal properties.
3. Ypres and Ghent ("Gaunt") were Flemish cloth-making centers.
4. The offering in church, when the congregation brought its gifts forward.
5. Tightly laced.
6. In medieval times, weddings were performed at the church door.
7. Rome; Boulogne (in France); St. James (of Compostella) in Galicia (Spain); Cologne (in Germany): all sites of shrines much visited by pilgrims.

| | She coude° muchel of wandring by the waye: | *knew* |

She coude° muchel of wandring by the waye: *knew*
470 Gat-toothed[8] was she, soothly for to saye.
Upon an amblere[9] esily she sat,
Ywimpled° wel, and on hir heed an hat   *veiled*
As brood as is a bokeler or a targe,[1]
A foot-mantel° aboute hir hipes large,   *riding skirt*
475 And on hir feet a paire of spores° sharpe.   *spurs*
In felaweshipe wel coude she laughe and carpe:°   *talk*
Of remedies of love she knew parchaunce,°   *as it happened*
For she coude of that art the olde daunce.[2]
    A good man was ther of religioun,
480 And was a poore Person° of a town,   *parson*
But riche he was of holy thought and werk.
He was also a lerned man, a clerk,
That Cristes gospel trewely° wolde preche;   *faithfully*
His parisshens° devoutly wolde he teche.   *parishioners*
485 Benigne he was, and wonder° diligent,   *wonderfully*
And in adversitee ful pacient,
And swich he was preved° ofte sithes.°   *proved / times*
Ful loth were him to cursen for his tithes,[3]
But rather wolde he yiven, out of doute,[4]
490 Unto his poore parisshens aboute
Of his offring[5] and eek of his substaunce:°   *property*
He coude in litel thing have suffisaunce.°   *sufficiency*
Wid was his parissh, and houses fer asonder,
But he ne lafte° nought for rain ne thonder,   *neglected*
495 In siknesse nor in meschief,° to visite   *misfortune*
The ferreste° in his parissh, muche and lite,[6]   *farthest*
Upon his feet, and in his hand a staf.
This noble ensample° to his sheep he yaf   *example*
That first he wroughte,[7] and afterward he taughte.
500 Out of the Gospel he tho° wordes caughte,°   *those / took*
And this figure he added eek therto:
That if gold ruste, what shal iren do?
For if a preest be foul, on whom we truste,
No wonder is a lewed° man to ruste.   *uneducated*
505 And shame it is, if a preest take keep,°   *heed*
A shiten° shepherde and a clene sheep.   *befouled*
Wel oughte a preest ensample for to yive
By his clennesse how that his sheep sholde live.
He sette nought his benefice[8] to hire
510 And leet° his sheep encombred in the mire   *left*

8. Gap-toothed, considered to be a sign of amorousness.
9. Horse with an easy gait.
1. "Bokeler" and "targe": small shields.
2. I.e., she knew all the tricks of that trade.
3. He would be most reluctant to invoke excommunication in order to collect his tithes.
4. Without doubt.

5. The offering made by the congregation of his
church was at the Parson's disposal.
6. Great and small.
7. I.e., he practiced what he preached.
8. I.e., his parish. A priest might rent his parish
to another and take a more profitable position.
"Leet": i.e., he did not leave.

And ran to London, unto Sainte Poules,[9]
To seeken him a chaunterye[1] for soules,
Or with a bretherhede to been withholde,[2]
But dwelte at hoom and kepte wel his folde,
515 So that the wolf ne made it nought miscarye:
He was a shepherde and nought a mercenarye.
And though he holy were and vertuous,
He was to sinful men nought despitous,°   *scornful*
Ne of his speeche daungerous° ne digne,°   *disdainful / haughty*
520 But in his teching discreet and benigne,
To drawen folk to hevene by fairnesse
By good ensample—this was his bisinesse.
But it° were any persone obstinat,   *if there*
What so he were, of heigh or lowe estat,
525 Him wolde he snibben° sharply for the nones:[3]   *scold*
A bettre preest I trowe° ther nowher noon is.   *believe*
He waited after[4] no pompe and reverence,
Ne maked him a spiced conscience,[5]
But Cristes lore° and his Apostles twelve   *teaching*
530 He taughte, but first he folwed it himselve.
    With him ther was a Plowman, was his brother,
That hadde ylad° of dong° ful many a fother.[6]   *carried / dung*
A trewe swinkere° and a good was he,   *worker*
Living in pees° and parfit charitee.   *peace*
535 God loved he best with al his hoole° herte   *whole*
At alle times, though him gamed or smerte,[7]
And thanne his neighebor right as himselve.
He wolde thresshe, and therto dike° and delve,   *dig ditches*
For Cristes sake, for every poore wight,
540 Withouten hire, if it laye in his might.
His tithes payed he ful faire and wel,
Bothe of his propre swink[8] and his catel.°   *property*
In a tabard° he rood upon a mere.°   *short coat / mare*
    Ther was also a Reeve° and a Millere,   *estate manager*
545 A Somnour, and a Pardoner[9] also,
A Manciple,° and myself—ther were namo.   *steward*
    The Millere was a stout carl° for the nones.   *fellow*
Ful big he was of brawn° and eek of bones—   *muscle*
That preved[1] wel, for overal ther he cam
550 At wrastling he wolde have alway the ram.[2]

9. St. Paul's Cathedral.
1. Chantry, i.e., a foundation that employed priests for the sole duty of saying masses for the souls of certain persons. St. Paul's had many of them.
2. Or to be employed by a brotherhood; i.e., to take a lucrative and fairly easy position as chaplain with a parish guild.
3. On any occasion.
4. I.e., expected.
5. Nor did he assume an overfastidious conscience.

6. Load.
7. Whether he was pleased or grieved.
8. His own work.
9. "Somnour" (Summoner): server of summonses to the ecclesiastical court; Pardoner: dispenser of papal pardons. See lines 625 and 671, and notes, below.
1. Proved, i.e., was evident.
2. A ram was frequently offered as the prize in wrestling.

He was short-shuldred, brood,[3] a thikke knarre.
Ther was no dore that he nolde heve of harre,[4]
Or breke it at a renning° with his heed.°   *running / head*
His beerd as any sowe or fox was reed,°   *red*
555 And therto brood, as though it were a spade;
Upon the cop right[5] of his nose he hade
A werte,° and theron stood a tuft of heres,   *wart*
Rede as the bristles of a sowes eres;
His nosethirles° blake were and wide.   *nostrils*
560 A swerd and a bokeler° bar° he by his side.   *shield / bore*
His mouth as greet was as a greet furnais.°   *furnace*
He was a janglere° and a Goliardais,[6]   *chatterer*
And that was most of sinne and harlotries.°   *obscenities*
Wel coude he stelen corn and tollen thries[7]—
565 And yit he hadde a thombe[8] of gold, pardee.°   *by heaven*
A whit cote and a blew hood wered° he.   *wore*
A baggepipe wel coude he blowe and soune,°   *sound*
And therwithal° he broughte us out of towne.   *therewith*
     A gentil Manciple[9] was ther of a temple,
570 Of which achatours° mighte take exemple   *buyers of food*
For to been wise in bying of vitaile;°   *victuals*
For wheither that he paide or took by taile,[1]
Algate he waited so in his achat[2]
That he was ay biforn[3] and in good stat.
575   Now is nat that of God a ful fair grace
That swich a lewed° mannes wit shal pace°   *ignorant / surpass*
The wisdom of an heep of lerned men?
Of maistres° hadde he mo than thries ten   *masters*
That weren of lawe expert and curious,°   *cunning*
580 Of whiche ther were a dozeine in that hous
Worthy to been stiwardes of rente° and lond   *income*
Of any lord that is in Engelond,
To make him live by his propre good[4]
In honour dettelees but if[5] he were wood,°   *insane*
585 Or live as scarsly° as him list° desire,   *sparely / it pleases*
And able for to helpen al a shire
In any caas° that mighte falle° or happe,   *event / befall*
And yit this Manciple sette hir aller cappe![6]
     The Reeve[7] was a sclendre° colerik man;   *slender*
590 His beerd was shave as neigh° as evere he can;   *close*

---

3. Broad. "Knarre": sturdy fellow.
4. He would not heave off (its) hinge.
5. Right on the tip.
6. Goliard, teller of ribald stories.
7. Take toll thrice—i.e., deduct from the grain far
more than the lawful percentage.
8. Thumb. The narrator seems to be questioning
the validity of the adage that (only) an honest miller
has a golden thumb.
9. The Manciple is the steward of a community
of lawyers in London (a "temple").

1. By talley, i.e., on credit.
2. Always he was on the watch in his purchasing.
3. I.e., ahead of the game. "Stat": financial condition.
4. His own money.
5. Out of debt unless.
6. This Manciple made fools of them all.
7. The Reeve is the superintendent of a large
farming estate; "colerik" (choleric) describes a man
whose dominant humor is yellow bile (choler)—
i.e., a hot-tempered man.

His heer was by his eres ful round yshorn;
His top was dokked[8] lik a preest biforn;
Ful longe were his legges and ful lene,
Ylik a staf, ther was no calf yseene.°   *visible*
595 Wel coude he keepe° a gerner° and a binne—   *guard / granary*
Ther was noon auditour coude on him winne.[9]
Wel wiste° he by the droughte and by the rain   *knew*
The yeelding of his seed and of his grain.
His lordes sheep, his neet,° his dayerye,   *cattle*
600 His swin, his hors, his stoor,° and his pultrye   *stock*
Was hoolly° in this Reeves governinge,   *wholly*
And by his covenant yaf[1] the rekeninge,
Sin° that his lord was twenty-yeer of age.   *since*
There coude no man bringe him in arrerage.[2]
605 Ther nas baillif, hierde, nor other hine,
That he ne knew his sleighte and his covine[3]—
They were adrad° of him as of the deeth.°   *afraid / plague*
His woning° was ful faire upon an heeth;°   *dwelling / meadow*
With greene trees shadwed was his place.
610 He coude bettre than his lord purchace.°   *acquire goods*
Ful riche he was astored° prively.°   *stocked / secretly*
His lord wel coude he plesen subtilly,
To yive and lene° him of his owene good,°   *lend / property*
And have a thank, and yit a cote and hood.
615 In youthe he hadde lerned a good mister:°   *occupation*
He was a wel good wrighte, a carpenter.
This Reeve sat upon a ful good stot°   *stallion*
That was a pomely° grey and highte° Scot.   *dapple / was named*
A long surcote° of pers° upon he hade,[4]   *overcoat / blue*
620 And by his side he bar° a rusty blade.   *bore*
Of Northfolk was this Reeve of which I telle,
Biside a town men clepen Baldeswelle.°   *Bawdswell*
Tukked[5] he was as is a frere aboute,
And evere he rood the hindreste of oure route.[6]
625   A Somnour[7] was ther with us in that place
That hadde a fir-reed° cherubinnes[8] face,   *fire-red*
For saucefleem° he was, with yën narwe,   *pimply*
And hoot° he was, and lecherous as a sparwe,°   *hot / sparrow*
With scaled° browes blake and piled[9] beerd: *scabby*
630 Of his visage children were aferd.°   *afraid*

---

8. Cut short: the clergy wore the head partially shaved.
9. I.e., find him in default.
1. And according to his contract he gave.
2. Convict him of being in arrears financially.
3. There was no bailiff (i.e., foreman), shepherd, nor other farm laborer whose craftiness and plots he didn't know.
4. "Upon he hade": he had on.
5. With clothing tucked up.
6. Hindmost of our group.

7. The "Somnour" (Summoner) is an employee of the ecclesiastical court, whose defined duty is to bring to court persons whom the archdeacon—the justice of the court—suspects of offenses against canon law. By this time, however, summoners had generally transformed themselves into corrupt detectives who spied out offenders and blackmailed them by threats of summonses.
8. Cherub's, often depicted in art with a red face.
9. Uneven, partly hairless.

Ther nas quiksilver, litarge, ne brimstoon,
Boras, ceruce, ne oile of tartre noon,[1]
Ne oinement that wolde clense and bite,
That him mighte helpen of his whelkes° white,   *blotches*
635 Nor of the knobbes° sitting on his cheekes.   *lumps*
Wel loved he garlek, oinons, and eek leekes,
And for to drinke strong win reed as blood.
Thanne wolde he speke and crye as he were wood;°   *mad*
And whan that he wel dronken hadde the win,
640 Thanne wolde he speke no word but Latin:
A fewe termes hadde he, two or three,
That he hadde lerned out of som decree;
No wonder is—he herde it al the day,
And eek ye knowe wel how that a jay°   *parrot*
645 Can clepen "Watte"[2] as wel as can the Pope—
But whoso coude in other thing him grope,°   *examine*
Thanne hadde he spent all his philosophye;[3]
Ay *Questio quid juris*[4] wolde he crye.
     He was a gentil harlot° and a kinde;   *rascal*
650 A bettre felawe sholde men nought finde:
He wolde suffre,° for a quart of win,   *permit*
A good felawe to have his concubin
A twelfmonth, and excusen him at the fulle;[5]
Ful prively a finch eek coude he pulle.[6]
655 And if he foond° owher° a good felawe   *found / anywhere*
He wolde techen him to have noon awe
In swich caas of the Ercedekenes curs,[7]
But if[8] a mannes soule were in his purs,
For in his purs he sholde ypunisshed be.
660 "Purs is the Ercedekenes helle," saide he.
     But wel I woot he lied right in deede:
Of cursing° oughte eech gilty man him drede,   *excommunication*
For curs wol slee° right as assoiling° savith—   *slay / absolution*
And also war him of a *significavit*.[9]
665 In daunger[1] hadde he at his owene gise°   *disposal*
The yonge girles of the diocise,
And knew hir conseil,° and was al hir reed.[2]   *secrets*
A gerland hadde he set upon his heed
As greet as it were for an ale-stake,[3]

1. These are all ointments for diseases affecting
the skin, probably diseases of venereal origin.
2. Call out: "Walter"—like modern parrots'
"Polly."
3. I.e., learning.
4. "What point of law does this investigation
involve?": a phrase frequently used in ecclesiastical courts.
5. "At the fulle": fully. Ecclesiastical courts had
jurisdiction over many offenses which today would
come under civil law, including sexual offenses.
6. "To pull a finch" is to have carnal dealings with
a woman.
7. Archdeacon's sentence of excommunication.
8. "But if": unless.
9. And also one should be careful of a *significavit*
(the writ which transferred the guilty offender from
the ecclesiastical to the civil arm for punishment).
1. Under his domination.
2. Was their chief source of advice.
3. A tavern was signalized by a pole ("ale-stake"),
rather like a modern flagpole, projecting from its
front wall; on this hung a garland, or "bush."

670 A bokeler hadde he maad him of a cake.
        With him ther rood a gentil Pardoner[4]
     Of Rouncival, his freend and his compeer,°   comrade
     That straight was comen fro the Court of Rome.
     Ful loude he soong,° "Com hider, love, to me."   sang
675 This Somnour bar to him a stif burdoun:[5]
     Was nevere trompe° of half so greet a soun.   trumpet
        This Pardoner hadde heer as yelow as wex,
     But smoothe it heeng° as dooth a strike° of flex;° hung / hank / flax
     By ounces[6] heenge his lokkes that he hadde,
680 And therwith he his shuldres overspradde,°   overspread
     But thinne it lay, by colpons,° oon by oon;   strands
     But hood for jolitee° wered° he noon,   nonchalance / wore
     For it was trussed up in his walet:°   pack
     Him thoughte he rood al of the newe jet.°   fashion
685 Dischevelee° save his cappe he rood al bare.   with hair down
     Swiche glaring yën hadde he as an hare.
     A vernicle[7] hadde he sowed upon his cappe,
     His walet biforn him in his lappe,
     Bretful° of pardon, come from Rome al hoot.°   brimful / hot
690 A vois he hadde as smal° as hath a goot;°   fine / goat
     No beerd hadde he, ne nevere sholde have;
     As smoothe it was as it were late yshave:
     I trowe° he were a gelding or a mare.   believe
     But of his craft, fro Berwik into Ware,[8]
695 Ne was ther swich another pardoner;
     For in his male° he hadde a pilwe-beer°   bag / pillowcase
     Which that he saide was Oure Lady veil;
     He saide he hadde a gobet° of the sail   piece
     That Sainte Peter hadde whan that he wente
700 Upon the see, til Jesu Crist him hente.°   seized
     He hadde a crois° of laton,° ful of stones,   cross / brassy metal
     And in a glas he hadde pigges bones,
     But with thise relikes[9] whan that he foond°   found
     A poore person° dwelling upon lond,[1]   parson
705 Upon° a day he gat° him more moneye   in / got
     Than that the person gat in monthes twaye;
     And thus with feined° flaterye and japes°   false / tricks
     He made the person and the peple his apes.°   dupes
     But trewely to tellen at the laste,
710 He was in chirche a noble ecclesiaste;
     Wel coude he rede a lesson and a storye,°   liturgical narrative

4. A Pardoner dispensed papal pardon for sins to
those who contributed to the charitable institution
that he was licensed to represent; this Pardoner
purported to be collecting for the hospital of Roncesvalles ("Rouncival") in Spain, which had a
London branch.
5. I.e., provided him with a strong vocal accompaniment.

6. I.e., thin strands.
7. Portrait of Christ's face as it was said to have
been impressed on St. Veronica's handkerchief.
8. Probably towns south and north of London.
9. Relics—i.e., the pigs' bones which the Pardoner represented as saints' bones.
1. "Upon lond": upcountry.

But alderbest° he soong an offertorye,   *best of all*
For wel he wiste° whan that song was songe,   *knew*
He moste° preche and wel affile° his tonge   *must / sharpen*
715 To winne silver, as he ful wel coude—
Therefore he soong the merierly° and loude.   *more merrily*
    Now have I told you soothly in a clause[2]
Th'estaat, th'array, the nombre, and eek the cause
Why that assembled was this compaignye
720 In Southwerk at this gentil hostelrye
That highte the Tabard, faste° by the Belle;[3]   *close*
But now is time to you for to telle
How that we baren us[4] that ilke° night   *same*
Whan we were in that hostelrye alight;
725 And after wol I telle of oure viage,°   *trip*
And al the remenant of oure pilgrimage.
But first I praye you of youre curteisye
That ye n'arette it nought my vilainye[5]
Though that I plainly speke in this matere
730 To telle you hir wordes and hir cheere,°   *behavior*
Ne though I speke hir wordes proprely;°   *accurately*
For this ye knowen also wel as I:
Who so shal telle a tale after a man
He moot° reherce,° as neigh as evere he can, *must / repeat*
735 Everich a word, if it be in his charge,°   *responsibility*
Al speke he[6] nevere so rudeliche and large,°   *broadly*
Or elles he moot telle his tale untrewe,
Or feine° thing, or finde° wordes newe;   *falsify / devise*
He may nought spare[7] although he were his brother:
740 He moot as wel saye oo word as another.
Crist spak himself ful brode° in Holy Writ,   *broadly*
And wel ye woot no vilainye is it;
Eek Plato saith, who so can him rede,
The wordes mote be cosin to the deede.
745   Also I praye you to foryive it me
Al° have I nat set folk in hir degree   *although*
Here in this tale as that they sholde stonde:
My wit is short, ye may wel understonde.
    Greet cheere made oure Host[8] us everichoon,
750 And to the soper sette he us anoon.°   *at once*
He served us with vitaile° at the beste.   *food*
Strong was the win, and wel to drinke us leste.° *it pleased*
A semely man oure Hoste was withalle
For to been a marchal[9] in an halle;
755 A large man he was, with yën steepe,°   *prominent*
A fairer burgeis° was ther noon in Chepe[1]—   *burgher*

---

2. I.e., in a short space.
3. Another tavern in Southwark.
4. Bore ourselves.
5. That you do not charge it to my lack of decorum.
6. Although he speak.
7. I.e., spare anyone.
8. The Host is the landlord of the Tabard Inn.
9. Marshal, one who was in charge of feasts.
1. Cheapside, bourgeois center of London.

Bold of his speeche, and wis, and wel ytaught,
And of manhood him lakkede right naught.
Eek therto he was right a merye man,
760   And after soper playen he bigan,
And spak of mirthe amonges othere thinges—
Whan that we hadde maad oure rekeninges[2]—
And saide thus, "Now, lordinges, trewely,
Ye been to me right welcome, hertely.°   *heartily*
765   For by my trouthe, if that I shal nat lie,
I sawgh nat this yeer so merye a compaignye
At ones in this herberwe° as is now.   *inn*
Fain° wolde I doon you mirthe, wiste I[3] how.   *gladly*
And of a mirthe I am right now bithought,
770   To doon you ese, and it shal coste nought.
      "Ye goon to Canterbury—God you speede;
The blisful martyr quite you youre meede.[4]
And wel I woot as ye goon by the waye
Ye shapen you[5] to talen° and to playe,   *converse*
775   For trewely, confort ne mirthe is noon
To ride by the waye domb as stoon;°   *stone*
And therefore wol I maken you disport
As I saide erst,° and doon you som confort;   *before*
And if you liketh alle, by oon assent,
780   For to stonden at[6] my juggement,
And for to werken as I shall you saye,
Tomorwe whan ye riden by the waye—
Now by my fader° soule that is deed,   *father's*
But° ye be merye I wol yive you myn heed!°   *unless / head*
785   Holde up youre handes withouten more speeche."
      Oure counseil was nat longe for to seeche;°   *seek*
Us thought it was not worth to make it wis,[7]
And graunted him withouten more avis,°   *deliberation*
And bade him saye his voirdit° as him leste.[8]   *verdict*
790   "Lordinges," quod he, "now herkneth for the beste;
But taketh it nought, I praye you, in desdain.
This is the point, to speken short and plain,
That eech of you, to shorte with oure waye
In this viage, shal tellen tales twaye°—   *two*
795   To Canterburyward, I mene it so,
And hoomward he shal tellen othere two,
Of aventures that whilom° have bifalle;   *once upon a time*
And which of you that bereth him best of alle—
That is to sayn, that telleth in this cas
800   Tales of best sentence° and most solas°—   *purport / delight*
Shal have a soper at oure aller cost,[9]

---

2. Had paid our bills.
3. If I knew.
4. Pay you your reward.
5. "Shapen you": intend.
6. Abide by.

7. We didn't think it worthwhile to make an issue
of it.
8. It pleased.
9. At the cost of us all.

Here in this place, sitting by this post,
Whan that we come again fro Canterbury.
And for to make you the more mury°   *merry*
805 I wol myself goodly° with you ride—   *gladly*
Right at myn owene cost—and be youre gide.
And who so wol my juggement withsaye°   *contradict*
Shal paye al that we spende by the waye.
And if ye vouche sauf that it be so,
810 Telle me anoon, withouten wordes mo,°   *more*
And I wol erly shape me[1] therefore."
    This thing was graunted and oure othes swore
With ful glad herte, and prayden[2] him also
That he wolde vouche sauf for to do so,
815 And that he wolde been oure governour,
And of oure tales juge and reportour,°   *accountant*
And sette a soper at a certain pris,°   *price*
And we wol ruled been at his devis,°   *disposal*
In heigh and lowe; and thus by oon assent
820 We been accorded to his juggement.
And therupon the win was fet° anoon;   *fetched*
We dronken and to reste wente eechoon
Withouten any lenger° taryinge.   *longer*
    Amorwe° whan that day bigan to springe *in the morning*
825 Up roos oure Host and was oure aller cok,[3]
And gadred us togidres in a flok,
And forth we riden, a litel more than pas,°   *a step*
Unto the watering of Saint Thomas;[4]
And ther oure Host bigan his hors arreste,°   *halt*
830 And saide, "Lordes, herkneth if you leste:° *it please*
    Ye woot youre forward° and it you recorde:[5] *agreement*
If evensong and morwesong° accorde,° *morningsong / agree*
Lat see now who shal telle the firste tale.
As evere mote I drinken win or ale,
835 Who so be rebel to my juggement
Shal paye for al that by the way is spent.
Now draweth cut[6] er that we ferrer twinne:
He which that hath the shorteste shal biginne.
    "Sire Knight," quod he, "my maister and my lord,
840 Now draweth cut, for that is myn accord.°   *will*
Cometh neer," quod he, "my lady Prioresse,
And ye, sire Clerk, lat be youre shamefastnesse°— *modesty*
Ne studieth nought. Lay hand to, every man!"
    Anoon to drawen every wight bigan,
845 And shortly for to tellen as it was
Were it by aventure, or sort, or cas,[7]

---

1. Prepare myself.
2. I.e., we prayed.
3. Was rooster for us all.
4. A watering place near Southwark.
5. You recall it.
6. I.e., draw straws. "Ferrer twinne": go farther.
7. Whether it was luck, fate, or chance.

The soothe° is this, the cut fil° to the Knight;   *truth / fell*
Of which ful blithe and glad was every wight,
And telle he moste° his tale, as was resoun,   *must*
850 By forward and by composicioun,[8]
As ye han herd. What needeth wordes mo?
And whan this goode man sawgh that it was so,
As he that wis was and obedient
To keepe his forward by his free assent,
855 He saide, "Sin I shal biginne the game,
What, welcome be the cut, in Goddes name!
Now lat us ride, and herkneth what I saye."
And with that word we riden forth oure waye,
And he bigan with right a merye cheere°   *countenance*
860 His tale anoon, and saide as ye may heere.

The Miller's Tale[1]

The Introduction

Whan that the Knight hadde thus his tale ytold,[2]
In al the route° nas ther yong ne old   *group*
That he ne saide it was a noble storye,
And worthy for to drawen° to memorye,   *recall*
5   And namely° the gentils everichoon.   *especially*
Oure Hoste lough° and swoor, "So mote I goon,[3]   *laughed*
This gooth aright: unbokeled is the male.°   *pouch*
Lat see now who shal telle another tale.
For trewely the game is wel bigonne.
10   Now telleth ye, sire Monk, if that ye conne,°   *can*
Somwhat to quite° with the Knightes tale."   *repay*
The Millere, that for dronken[4] was al pale,
So that unnethe° upon his hors he sat,   *with difficulty*
He nolde avalen° neither hood ne hat,   *doff*
15   Ne abiden no man for his curteisye,
But in Pilates vois[5] he gan to crye,
And swoor, "By armes[6] and by blood and bones,
I can° a noble tale for the nones,   *know*
With which I wol now quite the Knightes tale."
20   Oure Hoste sawgh that he was dronke of ale,
And saide, "Abide, Robin, leve° brother,   *dear*

---

8. By agreement and compact.
1. The Miller's Tale belongs to the literary genre known as the "fabliau," a short story in verse that generally involves bourgeois or lower-class characters in an outrageous, often obscene plot, which is, however, realistically handled by the narrator. The fabliau is peculiarly French, and aside from the three or four examples in Chaucer there are few representatives of it in English. Yet Chaucer was supreme in this kind of tale as in many others,

and the Miller's Tale is generally considered the best-told fabliau in any language.
2. The Knight's Tale is actually the first one told on the Canterbury pilgrimage, immediately following the General Prologue.
3. So might I walk, an oath
4. I.e., drunkenness.
5. The harsh voice usually associated with the character of Pontius Pilate in the mystery plays.
6. I.e., by God's arms, a blasphemous oath.

Som bettre man shal telle us first another.
Abide, and lat us werken thriftily."°   *with propriety*
    "By Goddes soule," quod he, "that wol nat I,
25 For I wol speke or elles go my way."
    Oure Host answerde, "Tel on, a devele way![7]
Thou art a fool; thy wit is overcome."
    "Now herkneth," quod the Millere, "alle and some.[8]
But first I make a protestacioun°   *public affirmation*
30 That I am dronke: I knowe it by my soun.°   *tone of voice*
And therfore if that I mis° speke or saye,   *amiss*
Wite it[9] the ale of Southwerk, I you praye;
For I wol telle a legende and a lif
Bothe of a carpenter and of his wif,
35 How that a clerk hath set the wrightes cappe."[1]
    The Reeve answerde and saide, "Stint thy clappe![2]
Lat be thy lewed° dronken harlotrye.°   *ignorant / obscenity*
It is a sinne and eek° a greet folye   *also*
To apairen° any man or him defame,   *injure*
40 And eek to bringen wives in swich fame.°   *report*
Thou maist ynough of othere thinges sayn."
    This dronken Millere spak ful soone again,
And saide, "Leve° brother Osewold,   *dear*
Who hath no wif, he is no cokewold.°   *cuckold*
45 But I saye nat therfore that thou art oon.
Ther ben ful goode wives many oon,°   *a one*
And evere a thousand goode ayains oon badde.
That knowestou wel thyself but if thou madde.°   *rave*
Why artou angry with my tale now?
50 I have a wif, pardee, as wel as thou,
Yit nolde° I, for the oxen in my plough,   *would not*
Take upon me more than ynough
As deemen of myself that I were oon:
I wol bileve wel that I am noon.
55 An housbonde shal nought been inquisitif
Of Goddes privetee,° nor of his wif.   *secrets*
So[3] he may finde Goddes foison° there,   *plenty*
Of the remenant° needeth nought enquere."°   *rest / inquire*
    What sholde I more sayn but this Millere
60 He nolde his wordes for no man forbere,
But tolde his cherles tale in his manere.
M'athinketh° that I shal reherce° it here,   *I regret / repeat*
And therefore every gentil wight I praye,
Deemeth nought, for Goddes love, that I saye
65 Of yvel entente, but for ° I moot reherse   *because*
Hir tales alle, be they bet° or werse,   *better*
Or elles falsen° som of my matere.   *falsify*

---

7. I.e., in the devil's name.   1. I.e., how a clerk made a fool of a carpenter.
8. Each and every one.   2. Stop your chatter.
9. Blame it on.   3. Provided that.

And therfore, whoso list it nought yheere
Turne over the leef, and chese° another tale,   *choose*
70 For he shal finde ynowe,° grete and smale,   *enough*
Of storial[4] thing that toucheth gentilesse,°   *gentility*
And eek moralitee and holinesse:
Blameth nought me if that ye chese amis.
The Millere is a cherl, ye knowe wel this,
75 So was the Reeve eek, and othere mo,
And harlotrye° they tolden bothe two.   *ribaldry*
Aviseth you,[5] and putte me out of blame:
And eek men shal nought maken ernest of game.

The Tale

Whilom° ther was dwelling at Oxenforde   *once upon a time*
80 A riche gnof° that gestes heeld to boorde,[6]   *boor*
And of his craft he was a carpenter.
With him ther was dwelling a poore scoler,
Hadde lerned art,[7] but al his fantasye°   *interest*
Was turned for to lere° astrologye,   *learn*
85 And coude a certain of conclusiouns,
To deemen by interrogaciouns,[8]
If that men axed° him in certain houres   *asked*
Whan that men sholde have droughte or elles showres,
Or if men axed him what shal bifalle
90 Of every thing—I may nat rekene hem alle.
    This clerk was cleped° hende[9] Nicholas.   *called*
Of derne love he coude, and of solas,[1]
And therto he was sly and ful privee,°   *secretive*
And lik a maide meeke for to see.
95 A chambre hadde he in that hostelrye
Allone, withouten any compaignye,
Ful fetisly ydight[2] with herbes swoote,°   *sweet*
And he himself as sweete as is the roote
Of licoris or any setewale.[3]
100 His *Almageste*[4] and bookes grete and smale,
His astrelabye,[5] longing for his art,
His augrim stones,[6] layen faire apart
On shelves couched° at his beddes heed;   *set*
His presse° ycovered with a falding reed;[7]   *storage chest*
105 And al above ther lay a gay sautrye,°   *psaltery*

4. Historical, i.e., true.
5. Take heed.
6. I.e., took in boarders.
7. Who had completed the first stage of university education (the trivium).
8. I.e., and he knew a number of propositions on which to base astrological analyses (which would reveal the matters in ll. 87–90).
9. Handy, sly, attractive.
1. I.e., he knew about secret love and pleasurable practices.
2. Elegantly furnished.
3. Setwall, a spice.
4. The 2nd-century treatise by Ptolemy, still the standard astronomy textbook.
5. Astrolabe, an astronomical instrument. "Longing for": belonging to.
6. Counters used in arithmetic.
7. Red coarse wool.

On which he made a-nightes melodye
So swetely that al the chambre roong,°   *rang*
And *Angelus ad Virginem*[8] he soong,
And after that he soong the *Kinges Note:*
110 Ful often blessed was his merye throte.
And thus this sweete clerk his time spente
After his freendes finding and his rente.[9]
    This carpenter hadde wedded newe° a wif   *lately*
Which that he loved more than his lif.
115 Of eighteteene yeer she was of age;
Jalous he was, and heeld hire narwe in cage,
For she was wilde and yong, and he was old,
And deemed himself been lik a cokewold.[1]
He knew nat Caton,[2] for his wit was rude,
120 That bad men sholde wedde his similitude:[3]
Men sholde wedden after hir estat,[4]
For youthe and elde° is often at debat.   *age*
But sith that he was fallen in the snare,
He moste endure, as other folk, his care.
125   Fair was this yonge wif, and therwithal
As any wesele° hir body gent and smal.[5]   *weasel*
A ceint she wered, barred[6] al of silk;
A barmcloth° as whit as morne milk   *apron*
Upon hir lendes,° ful of many a gore;°   *loins / strip of cloth*
130 Whit was hir smok,° and broiden[7] al bifore   *undergarment*
And eek bihinde, on hir coler° aboute,   *collar*
Of° col-blak silk, withinne and eek withoute;   *with*
The tapes° of hir white voluper°   *ribbons / cap*
Were of the same suite of[8] hir coler;
135 Hir filet° brood° of silk and set ful hye;   *headband / broad*
And sikerly° she hadde a likerous° yë;   *certainly / wanton*
Ful smale ypulled[9] were hir browes two,
And tho were bent,° and blake as any slo.°   *arching / sloeberry*
She was ful more blisful on to see
140 Than is the newe perejonette° tree,   *pear*
And softer than the wolle° is of a wether;°   *wool / ram*
And by hir girdel° heeng° a purs of lether,   *belt / hung*
Tasseled with silk and perled with latoun.[1]
In al this world, to seeken up and down,
145 Ther nis no man so wis that coude thenche°   *imagine*
So gay a popelote° or swich° a wenche.   *doll / such*
Ful brighter was the shining of hir hewe

8. "The Angel's Address to the Virgin," a hymn;
"*Kinges Note*": probably a popular song of the time.
9. In accordance with his friends' provision and
his own income.
1. I.e., suspected of himself that he was like a
cuckold.
2. Dionysius Cato, the supposed author of a book
of maxims used in elementary education.
3. Commanded that one should wed his equal.

4. Men should marry according to their condition.
5. Slender and delicate.
6. A belt she wore, with transverse stripes.
7. Embroidered.
8. I.e., the same pattern as.
9. Delicately plucked.
1. I.e., with brassy spangles on it.

Than in the Towr[2] the noble° yforged newe.   *gold coin*
But of hir song, it was as loud and yerne°   *lively*
150 As any swalwe sitting on a berne.°   *barn*
Therto she coude skippe and make game[3]
As any kide or calf folwing his dame.°   *mother*
Hir mouth was sweete as bragot or the meeth,[4]
Or hoord of apples laid in hay or heeth.°   *heather*
155 Winsing° she was as is a joly° colt,   *skittish / high-spirited*
Long as a mast, and upright° as a bolt.°   *straight / arrow*
A brooch she bar upon hir lowe coler
As brood as is the boos° of a bokeler;°   *boss / shield*
Hir shoes were laced on hir legges hye.
160 She was a primerole,° a piggesnye,[5]   *cowslip*
For any lord to leggen° in his bedde,   *lay*
Or yit for any good yeman to wedde.
   Now sire, and eft° sire, so bifel the cas   *again*
That on a day this hende Nicholas
165 Fil° with this yonge wif to rage° and playe,   *happened / flirt*
Whil that hir housbonde was at Oseneye[6]
(As clerkes been ful subtil and ful quainte),°   *clever*
And prively he caughte hire by the queinte,°   *pudendum*
And saide, "Ywis, but if ich° have my wille,   *I*
170 For derne° love of thee, lemman, I spille,"°   *secret / die*
And heeld hire harde by the haunche-bones,
And saide, "Lemman,° love me al atones,[7]   *mistress*
Or I wol dien, also° God me save."   *so*
And she sproong° as a colt dooth in a trave,[8]   *sprang*
175 And with hir heed she wried° faste away;   *twisted*
She saide, "I wol nat kisse thee, by my fay.°   *faith*
Why, lat be," quod she, "lat be, Nicholas!
Or I wol crye 'Out, harrow,° and allas!'   *help*
Do way youre handes, for your curteisye!"
180   This Nicholas gan mercy for to crye,
And spak so faire, and profred him so faste,[9]
That she hir love him graunted atte laste,
And swoor hir ooth by Saint Thomas of Kent[1]
That she wolde been at his comandement,
185 Whan that she may hir leiser[2] wel espye.
"Myn housbonde is so ful of jalousye
That but ye waite° wel and been privee   *be on guard*
I woot right wel I nam but deed," quod she.
"Ye moste been ful derne as in this cas."
190   "Nay, therof care thee nought," quod Nicholas.
"A clerk hadde litherly biset his while,[3]

---

2. The Tower of London, the Mint.   8. Frame for a restive horse.
3. Play.   9. I.e., pushed himself so vigorously.
4. "Bragot" and "meeth" are honey drinks.   1. Thomas à Becket.
5. A pig's eye, a name for a common flower.   2. I.e., opportunity.
6. A town near Oxford.   3. Poorly employed his time.
7. Right now.

But if he coude a carpenter bigile."
And thus they been accorded and ysworn
To waite° a time, as I have told biforn.   *watch for*
195 Whan Nicholas hadde doon this everydeel,
And thakked° hire upon the lendes° weel,   *patted / loins*
He kiste hire sweete, and taketh his sautrye,
And playeth faste, and maketh melodye.
     Thanne fil° it thus, that to the parissh chirche,   *befell*
200 Cristes owene werkes for to wirche,°   *perform*
This goode wif wente on an haliday:°   *holy day*
Hir forheed shoon as bright as any day,
So was it wasshen whan she leet° hir werk.   *left*
     Now was ther of that chirche a parissh clerk,
205 The which that was ycleped° Absolon: *called*
Crul° was his heer, and as the gold it shoon,   *curly*
And strouted° as a fanne⁴ large and brode;   *spread out*
Ful straight and evene lay his joly shode.⁵
His rode° was reed, his yën greye as goos.°   *complexion / goose*
210 With Poules window corven⁶ on his shoos,
In hoses° rede he wente fetisly.°   *stockings / elegantly*
Yclad he was ful smale° and proprely,   *finely*
Al in a kirtel° of a light waget°—   *tunic / blue*
Ful faire and thikke been the pointes⁷ set—
215 And therupon he hadde a gay surplis,°   *surplice*
As whit as is the blosme upon the ris.°   *bough*
A merye child° he was, so God me save.   *lad*
Wel coude he laten° blood, and clippe, and shave,   *let*
And maken a chartre of land, or acquitaunce;⁸
220 In twenty manere° coude he trippe and daunce   *ways*
After the scole of Oxenforde tho,
And with his legges casten° to and fro,   *prance*
And playen songes on smal rubible;°   *fiddle*
Therto he soong somtime a loud quinible,⁹
225 And as wel coude he playe on a giterne:°   *guitar*
In al the town nas brewhous ne taverne
That he ne visited with his solas,°   *entertainment*
Ther any gailard tappestere¹ was.
But sooth to sayn, he was somdeel squaimous°   *squeamish*
230 Of farting, and of speeche daungerous.°   *fastidious*
     This Absolon, that joly° was and gay,   *pretty, amorous*
Gooth with a cencer° on the haliday,   *incense-burner*
Cencing the wives of the parissh faste,
And many a lovely look on hem he caste,
235 And namely° on this carpenteres wif: *especially*

4. Wide-mouthed basket for separating grain from chaff.
5. Parting of the hair.
6. Carved with intricate designs, like the tracery in the windows of St. Paul's.
7. Laces for fastening the tunic and holding up the hose.
8. Legal release.
9. Part requiring a very high voice.
1. Gay barmaid.

To looke on hire him thoughte a merye lif.
She was so propre° and sweete and likerous,[2]   *neat*
I dar wel sayn, if she hadde been a mous,
And he a cat, he wolde hire hente° anoon.   *pounce on*
240   This parissh clerk, this joly Absolon,
Hath in his herte swich a love-longinge°   *lovesickness*
That of no wif ne took he noon offringe—
For curteisye he saide he wolde noon.
The moone, whan it was night, ful brighte shoon,°   *shone*
245   And Absolon his giterne° hath ytake—   *guitar*
For paramours° he thoughte for to wake—   *love*
And forth he gooth, jolif° and amorous,   *pretty*
Til he cam to the carpenteres hous,
A litel after cokkes hadde ycrowe,
250   And dressed him up by a shot-windowe[3]
That was upon the carpenteres wal.
He singeth in his vois gentil and smal,°   *dainty*
"Now dere lady, if thy wille be,
I praye you that ye wol rewe° on me,"   *have pity*
255   Ful wel accordant to his giterninge.[4]
This carpenter awook and herde him singe,
And spak unto his wif, and saide anoon,
"What, Alison, heerestou nought Absolon
That chaunteth thus under oure bowres° wal?"   *bedroom's*
260   And she answerde hir housbonde therwithal,
"Yis, God woot, John, I heere it everydeel."
    This passeth forth. What wol ye bet than weel?[5]
Fro day to day this joly Absolon
So woweth° hire that him is wo-bigoon: *woos*
265   He waketh° al the night and al the day;   *stays awake*
He kembed° his lokkes brode[6] and made him gay;   *combed*
He woweth hire by menes and brocage,[7]
And swoor he wolde been hir owene page;°   *personal servant*
He singeth, brokking° as a nightingale;   *trilling*
270   He sente hire piment,[8] meeth, and spiced ale,
And wafres° piping hoot out of the gleede;°   *pastries / coals*
And for she was of towne,[9] he profred meede°—   *bribe*
For som folk wol be wonnen for richesse,
And som for strokes,° and som for gentilesse.   *blows*
275   Somtime to shewe his lightnesse and maistrye,[1]
He playeth Herodes[2] upon a scaffold° hye.   *platform, stage*
But what availeth him as in this cas?
She loveth so this hende Nicholas

2. Wanton, appetizing.
3. Took his position by a hinged window.
4. In harmony with his guitar playing.
5. Better than well.
6. I.e., wide-spreading.
7. By intermediaries and mediation.

8. Spiced wine. "Meeth": mead.
9. Since she was a town woman.
1. Facility and virtuosity.
2. Herod, a role traditionally played as a bully in the mystery plays.

That Absolon may blowe the bukkes horn;[3]
280 He ne hadde for his labour but a scorn.
And thus she maketh Absolon hir ape,[4]
And al his ernest turneth til a jape.°   *joke*
Ful sooth is this proverbe, it is no lie;
Men saith right thus: "Alway the nye slye
285 Maketh the ferre leve to be loth."[5]
For though that Absolon be wood° or wroth,   *furious*
By cause that he fer was from hir sighte,
This nye° Nicholas stood in his lighte.   *nearby*
    Now beer° thee wel, thou hende Nicholas,   *bear*
290 For Absolon may waile and singe allas.
    And so bifel it on a Saterday
This carpenter was goon til Oseney,
And hende Nicholas and Alisoun
Accorded been to this conclusioun,
295 That Nicholas shal shapen° hem a wile°   *arrange / trick*
This sely[6] jalous housbonde to bigile,
And if so be this game wente aright,
She sholden sleepen in his arm al night—
For this was his desir and hire° also.   *hers*
300 And right anoon, withouten wordes mo,
This Nicholas no lenger wolde tarye,
But dooth ful softe unto his chambre carye
Bothe mete and drinke for a day or twaye,
And to hir housbonde bad hire for to saye,
305 If that he axed after Nicholas,
She sholde saye she niste° wher he was—   *didn't know*
Of al that day she sawgh him nought with yë:
She trowed° that he was in maladye,   *believed*
For for no cry hir maide coude him calle,
310 He nolde answere for no thing that mighte falle.°   *happen*
    This passeth forth al thilke° Saterday   *this*
That Nicholas stille in his chambre lay,
And eet,° and sleep,° or dide what him leste,[7]   *ate / slept*
Til Sonday that the sonne gooth to reste.
315 This sely carpenter hath greet mervaile
Of Nicholas, or what thing mighte him aile,
And saide, "I am adrad,° by Saint Thomas,   *afraid*
It stondeth nat aright with Nicholas.
God shilde° that he deide sodeinly!   *forbid*
320 This world is now ful tikel,° sikerly: *changeable*
I sawgh today a corps yborn to chirche
That now a° Monday last I sawgh him wirche.°   *on / work*
Go up," quod he unto his knave° anoon,   *manservant*

3. Blow the buck's horn, i.e., go without reward.   dear one hated.
4. I.e., thus she makes a fool of Absolon.   6. "Poor innocent."
5. Always the sly man at hand makes the distant   7. He wanted.

"Clepe° at his dore or knokke with a stoon.°   *call / stone*
325 Looke how it is and tel me boldely."
      This knave gooth him up ful sturdily,
And at the chambre dore whil that he stood
He cride and knokked as that he were wood,°   *mad*
"What? How? What do ye, maister Nicholay?
330 How may ye sleepen al the longe day?"
But al for nought: he herde nat a word.
An hole he foond ful lowe upon a boord,
Ther as the cat was wont in for to creepe,
And at that hole he looked in ful deepe,
335 And atte laste he hadde of him a sighte.
      This Nicholas sat evere caping° uprighte   *gaping*
As he hadde kiked° on the newe moone.   *gazed*
Adown he gooth and tolde his maister soone
In what array° he saw this ilke° man.   *condition / same*
340   This carpenter to blessen him[8] bigan,
And saide, "Help us, Sainte Frideswide!
A man woot litel what him shal bitide.
This man is falle, with his astromye,[9]
In som woodnesse° or in som agonye.   *madness*
345 I thoughte ay° wel how that it sholde be: *always*
Men sholde nought knowe of Goddes privetee.
Ye, blessed be alway a lewed° man   *ignorant*
That nought but only his bileve° can.°   *creed / knows*
So ferde° another clerk with astromye: *fared*
350 He walked in the feeldes for to prye
Upon the sterres,° what ther sholde bifallé,   *stars*
Til he was in a marle-pit[1] yfalle—
He saw nat that. But yit, by Saint Thomas,
Me reweth sore[2] for hende Nicholas.
355 He shal be rated of[3] his studying,
If that I may, by Jesus, hevene king!
Get me a staf that I may underspore,°   *pry up*
Whil that thou, Robin, hevest° up the dore.   *heave*
He shal[4] out of his studying, as I gesse."
360 And to the chambre dore he gan him dresse.[5]
His knave was a strong carl° for the nones,°   *fellow / purpose*
And by the haspe he haaf° it up atones: *heaved*
Into° the floor the dore fil° anoon.   *on / fell*
This Nicholas sat ay as stille as stoon,
365 And evere caped up into the air.
This carpenter wende° he were in despair,   *thought*
And hente° him by the shuldres mightily,   *seized*
And shook him harde, and cride spitously,°   *roughly*

---

8. Cross himself.   3. Scolded for.
9. Illiterate form of "astronomye." 4. I.e., shall come.
1. Pit from which a fertilizing clay is dug.   5. Took his stand.
2. I sorely pity.

"What, Nicholay, what, how! What! Looke adown!
370 Awaak and thenk on Cristes passioun![6]
I crouche[7] thee from elves and fro wightes."
Therwith the nightspel saide he anoonrightes[8]
On foure halves° of the hous aboute,   *sides*
And on the thresshfold° on the dore withoute: *threshold*
375 "Jesu Crist and Sainte Benedight,°   *Benedict*
Blesse this hous from every wikked wight!
For nightes nerye the White Pater Noster.[9]
Where wentestou, thou Sainte Petres soster?°   *sister*
And at the laste this hende Nicholas
380 Gan for to sike° sore, and saide, "Allas,   *sigh*
Shal al the world be lost eftsoones° now?"   *again*
This carpenter answerde, "What saistou?
What, thenk on God as we doon, men that swinke."[1]
This Nicholas answerde, "Fecche me drinke,
385 And after wol I speke in privetee
Of certain thing that toucheth me and thee.
I wol telle it noon other man, certain."
This carpenter gooth down and comth again,
And broughte of mighty ale a large quart,
390 And when that eech of hem hadde dronke his part,
This Nicholas his dore faste shette,°   *shut*
And down the carpenter by him he sette,
And saide, "John, myn hoste lief° and dere,   *beloved*
Thou shalt upon thy trouthe° swere me here   *word of honor*
395 That to no wight thou shalt this conseil° wraye;°   *secret / disclose*
For it is Cristes conseil that I saye,
And if thou telle it man,[2] thou art forlore,°   *lost*
For this vengeance thou shalt have therfore,
That if thou wraye me, thou shalt be wood."[3]
400   "Nay, Crist forbede it, for his holy blood,"
Quod tho this sely° man. "I nam no labbe,[4]   *innocent*
And though I saye, I nam nat lief to gabbe.[5]
Say what thou wilt, I shal it nevere telle
To child ne wif, by him that harwed helle."[6]
405   "Now John," quod Nicholas, "I wol nought lie.
I have yfounde in myn astrologye,
As I have looked in the moone bright,
That now a Monday next, at quarter night,[7]
Shal falle a rain, and that so wilde and wood,°   *furious*
410 That half so greet was nevere Noees° flood.   *Noah's*

---

6. I.e., the Crucifixion.
7. Make the sign of the cross on. "Wightes": wicked creatures.
8. The night-charm he said right away.
9. I.e., the White Lord's Prayer defend (us). This personification was considered a powerful beneficent spirit.
1. Work.

2. To anyone.
3. Go mad.
4. Blabbermouth.
5. And though I say it myself, I don't like to gossip.
6. By Him that despoiled hell—i.e., Christ.
7. I.e., shortly before dawn.

This world," he saide, "in lasse° than an hour　　　　　　　*less*
Shal al be dreint,° so hidous is the showr.　　　　　　　*drowned*
Thus shal mankinde drenche° and lese° hir lif."　　　　*drown / lose*
　　This carpenter answerde, "Allas, my wif!
415　And shal she drenche? Allas, myn Alisoun!"
For sorwe of this he fil almost[8] adown,
And saide, "Is there no remedye in this cas?"
　　"Why yis, for[9] Gode," quod hende Nicholas,
"If thou wolt werken after lore and reed[1]—
420　Thou maist nought werken after thyn owene heed;°　　*head*
For thus saith Salomon that was ful trewe,
'Werk al by conseil and thou shalt nought rewe.'°　　*be sorry*
And if thou werken wolt by good conseil,
I undertake, withouten mast or sail,
425　Yit shal I save hire and thee and me.
Hastou nat herd how saved was Noee
Whan that oure Lord hadde warned him biforn
That al the world with water sholde be lorn?"°　　　　*lost*
　　"Yis," quod this carpenter, "ful yore ago."
430　　"Hastou nat herd," quod Nicholas, "also
The sorwe of Noee with his felaweshipe?
Er that he mighte gete his wif to shipe,
Him hadde levere,[2] I dar wel undertake,
At thilke time than alle his wetheres blake
435　That she hadde had a ship hirself allone.[3]
And therfore woostou° what is best to doone?　　　*do you know*
This axeth° haste, and of an hastif° thing　　　*requires / urgent*
Men may nought preche or maken tarying.
Anoon go gete us faste into this in°　　　　　　　　　*lodging*
440　A kneeding trough or elles a kimelin°　　　　　　*brewing tub*
For eech of us, but looke that they be large,°　　　　*wide*
In whiche we mowen swimme as in a barge,[4]
And han therinne vitaile suffisaunt[5]
But for a day—fy° on the remenaunt!　　　　　　　　　*fie*
445　The water shal aslake° and goon away　　　　　　　*diminish*
Aboute prime[6] upon the nexte day.
But Robin may nat wite° of this, thy knave,　　　　　*know*
Ne eek thy maide Gille I may nat save.
Axe nought why, for though thou axe me,
450　I wol nought tellen Goddes privetee.°　　　　　　　*secrets*
Suffiseth thee, but if thy wittes madde,°　　　　　　*go mad*
To han° as greet a grace as Noee hadde.　　　　　　　*have*
Thy wif shal I wel saven, out of doute.
Go now thy way, and speed thee heraboute.
455　But whan thou hast for hire° and thee and me　　　*her*

---

8. Almost fell.　　　　　　　　　　　3. The reluctance of Noah's wife to board the ark
9. I.e., by.　　　　　　　　　　　　　is a traditional comic theme in the mystery plays.
1. Act according to learning and advice.　　4. In which we can float as in a vessel.
2. He had rather. "Wetheres": rams. I.e., he'd have　5. Sufficient food.
given all the rams he had.　　　　　　6. 9 A.M.

Ygeten us thise kneeding-tubbes three,
Thanne shaltou hangen hem in the roof ful hye,
That no man of oure purveyance° espye.   *foresight*
And whan thou thus hast doon as I have said,
460 And hast oure vitaile faire in hem ylaid,
And eek an ax to smite the corde atwo,
Whan that the water comth that we may go,
And broke an hole an heigh[7] upon the gable
Unto the gardinward,[8] over the stable,
465 That we may freely passen forth oure way,
Whan that the grete showr is goon away,
Thanne shaltou swimme as merye, I undertake,
As dooth the white doke° after hir drake.   *duck*
Thanne wol I clepe,° 'How, Alison? How, John?   *call*
470 Be merye, for the flood wol passe anoon.'
And thou wolt sayn, 'Hail, maister Nicholay!
Good morwe, I see thee wel, for it is day!'
And thanne shal we be lordes al oure lif
Of al the world, as Noee and his wif.
475 But of oo thing I warne thee ful right:
Be wel avised on that ilke night
That we been entred into shippes boord
That noon of us ne speke nought a word,
Ne clepe, ne crye, but been in his prayere,
480 For it is Goddes owene heeste dere.[9]
Thy wif and thou mote hange fer atwinne,[1]
For that bitwixe you shal be no sinne—
Namore in looking than ther shal in deede.
This ordinance is said: go, God thee speede.
485 Tomorwe at night whan men been alle asleepe,
Into oure kneeding-tubbes wol we creepe,
And sitten there, abiding Goddes grace.
Go now thy way, I have no lenger space°   *time*
To make of this no lenger sermoning.
490 Men sayn thus: 'Send the wise and say no thing.'
Thou art so wis it needeth thee nat teche:
Go save oure lif, and that I thee biseeche."
    This sely carpenter gooth forth his way:
Ful ofte he saide allas and wailaway,
495 And to his wif he tolde his privetee,
And she was war,° and knew it bet° than he,   *aware / better*
What al this quainte cast° was for to saye.°   *trick / mean*
But nathelees she ferde° as she wolde deye,   *acted*
And saide, "Allas, go forth thy way anoon.
500 Help us to scape,° or we been dede eechoon.   *escape*
I am thy trewe verray wedded wif:
Go, dere spouse, and help to save oure lif."

7. On high.   9. Precious commandment.
8. Toward the garden.   1. Far apart.

Lo, which a greet thing is affeccioun!°   *emotion*
Men may dien of imaginacioun,
505 So deepe° may impression be take.   *deeply*
This sely carpenter biginneth quake;
Him thinketh verrailiche° that he may see   *truly*
Noees flood come walwing° as the see   *rolling*
To drenchen° Alison, his hony dere.   *drown*
510 He weepeth, waileth, maketh sory cheere;
He siketh° with ful many a sory swough,°   *sighs / breath*
And gooth and geteth him a kneeding-trough,
And after a tubbe and a kimelin,
And prively he sente hem to his in,°   *dwelling*
515 And heeng° hem in the roof in privetee;   *hung*
His° owene hand he made laddres three,   *with his*
To climben by the ronges° and the stalkes°   *rungs / uprights*
Unto the tubbes hanging in the balkes,°   *rafters*
And hem vitailed,° bothe trough and tubbe,   *victualed*
520 With breed and cheese and good ale in a jubbe,°   *jug*
Suffising right ynough as for a day.
But er that he hadde maad al this array,
He sente his knave, and eek his wenche also,
Upon his neede[2] to London for to go.
525 And on the Monday whan it drow to[3] nighte,
He shette° his dore withouten candel-lighte,   *shut*
And dressed° alle thing as it sholde be,   *arranged*
And shortly up they clomben° alle three.   *climbed*
They seten° stille wel a furlong way.[4]   *sat*
530 "Now, Pater Noster, clum,"[5] saide Nicholay,
And "Clum" quod John, and "Clum" saide Alisoun.
This carpenter saide his devocioun,
And stille he sit° and biddeth his prayere,   *sits*
Awaiting on the rain, if he it heere.°   *might hear*
535   The dede sleep, for wery bisinesse,
Fil° on this carpenter right as I gesse   *fell*
Aboute corfew time,[6] or litel more.
For travailing of his gost[7] he groneth sore,
And eft° he routeth,° for his heed mislay.[8]   *then / snores*
540   Down of the laddre stalketh Nicholay,
And Alison ful softe adown she spedde:
Withouten wordes mo they goon to bedde
Ther as the carpenter is wont to lie.
Ther was the revel and the melodye,
545 And thus lith° Alison and Nicholas   *lies*
In bisinesse of mirthe and of solas,°   *pleasure*
Til that the belle of Laudes[9] gan to ringe,

---

2. On an errand for him.
3. Drew toward.
4. The time it takes to go a furlong (i.e., a few minutes).
5. Hush (?).

6. Probably about 8 P.M.
7. Affliction of his spirit.
8. Lay in the wrong position.
9. The first church service of the day.

And freres in the chauncel° gonne singe.   *chancel*
   This parissh clerk, this amorous Absolon,
550 That is for love alway so wo-bigoon,
Upon the Monday was at Oseneye,
With compaignye him to disporte and playe,
And axed upon caas[1] a cloisterer
Ful prively after John the carpenter;
555 And he drow him apart out of the chirche,
And saide, "I noot:[2] I sawgh him here nought wirche
Sith Saterday. I trowe that he be went
For timber ther oure abbot hath him sent.
For he is wont for timber for to go,
560 And dwellen atte grange[3] a day or two.
Or elles he is at his hous, certain.
Where that he be I can nought soothly sayn."
   This Absolon ful jolif was and light,[4]
And thoughte, "Now is time to wake al night,
565 For sikerly,° I sawgh him nought stiringe   *certainly*
Aboute his dore sin day bigan to springe.
So mote° I thrive, I shal at cokkes crowe   *may*
Ful prively knokken at his windowe
That stant° ful lowe upon his bowres[5] wal.   *stands*
570 To Alison now wol I tellen al
My love-longing,° for yet I shal nat misse   *lovesickness*
That at the leeste way[6] I shal hire kisse.
Som manere confort shal I have, parfay.°   *in faith*
My mouth hath icched al this longe day:
575 That is a signe of kissing at the leeste.
Al night me mette[7] eek I was at a feeste.
Therfore I wol go sleepe an hour or twaye,
And al the night thanne wol I wake and playe."
   Whan that the firste cok hath crowe, anoon
580 Up rist° this joly lovere Absolon,   *rises*
And him arrayeth gay at point devis.[8]
But first he cheweth grain[9] and licoris,
To smellen sweete, er he hadde kembd° his heer.   *combed*
Under his tonge a trewe-love[1] he beer,°   *bore*
585 For therby wende° he to be gracious.°   *supposed / pleasing*
He rometh° to the carpenteres hous,   *strolls*
And stille he stant° under the shot-windowe—   *stands*
Unto his brest it raughte,° it was so lowe—   *reached*
And ofte he cougheth with a semisoun.°   *small sound*
590 "What do ye, hony-comb, sweete Alisoun,
My faire brid,[2] my sweete cinamome?

---

1. By chance. "Cloisterer": here, a member of the
religious order of Osney Abbey.
2. Don't know. "Wirche": work.
3. The outlying farm belonging to the abbey.
4. Was very amorous and gay.
5. Bower's, bedroom's.

6. I.e., at least.
7. I dreamed.
8. To perfection.
9. Grain of paradise (a spice).
1. Sprig of a clover-like plant.
2. Bird or bride.

Awaketh, lemman° myn, and speketh to me.   *mistress*
Wel litel thinken ye upon my wo
That for your love I swete° ther I go.   *sweat*
595 No wonder is though that I swelte° and swete: *melt*
I moorne as doth a lamb after the tete.°   *teat*
Ywis, lemman, I have swich love-longinge,
That lik a turtle° trewe is my moorninge: *dove*
I may nat ete namore than a maide."
600   "Go fro the windowe, Jakke fool," she saide.
"As help me God, it wol nat be com-pa-me.°   *come-kiss-me*
I love another, and elles I were to blame,
Wel bet° than thee, by Jesu, Absolon.   *better*
Go forth thy way or I wol caste a stoon,
605 And lat me sleepe, a twenty devele way."[3]
     "Allas," quod Absolon, "and wailaway,
That trewe love was evere so yvele biset.[4]
Thanne kis me, sin that it may be no bet,
For Jesus love and for the love of me."
610   "Woltou thanne go thy way therwith?" quod she.
"Ye, certes, lemman," quod this Absolon.
"Thanne maak thee redy," quod she. "I come anoon."
And unto Nicholas she saide stille,°   *quietly*
"Now hust,° and thou shalt laughen al thy fille."   *hush*
615   This Absolon down sette him on his knees,
And said, "I am a lord at alle degrees,[5]
For after this I hope ther cometh more.
Lemman, thy grace, and sweete brid, thyn ore!"°   *mercy*
The windowe she undooth, and that in haste.
620 "Have do," quod she, "come of and speed thee faste,
Lest that oure neighebores thee espye."
     This Absolon gan wipe his mouth ful drye:
Derk was the night as pich or as the cole,
And at the windowe out she putte hir hole,
625 And Absolon, him fil no bet ne wers,[6]
But with his mouth he kiste hir naked ers,
Ful savourly,° er he were war of this.   *with relish*
Abak he sterte,° and thoughte it was amis,   *started*
For wel he wiste a womman hath no beerd.
630 He felte a thing al rough and longe yherd,°   *haired*
And saide, "Fy, allas, what have I do?"
     "Teehee," quod she, and clapte the windowe to.
And Absolon gooth forth a sory pas.[7]
     "A beerd, a beerd!" quod hende Nicholas,
635 "By Goddes corpus,° this gooth faire and weel."   *body*
     This sely Absolon herde everydeel,
And on his lippe he gan for anger bite,

---

3. In the name of twenty devils.   6. It befell him neither better nor worse.
4. Ill-used.   7. I.e., walking sadly.
5. In every way.

And to himself he saide, "I shal thee quite."°   *repay*
   Who rubbeth now, who froteth° now his lippes   *wipes*
640 With dust, with sond,[8] with straw, with cloth, with chippes,
But Absolon, that saith ful ofte allas?
"My soule bitake° I unto Satanas,°   *commit / Satan*
But me were levere[9] than all this town," quod he,
"Of this despit° awroken° for to be.   *insult / avenged*
645 Allas," quod he, "allas I ne hadde ybleint!"°   *turned aside*
His hote love was cold and al yqueint,°   *quenched*
For fro that time that he hadde kist hir ers
Of paramours he sette nought a kers,[1]
For he was heled° of his maladye.   *cured*
650 Ful ofte paramours he gan defye,°   *renounce*
And weep° as dooth a child that is ybete.   *wept*
A softe paas[2] he wente over the streete
Until° a smith men clepen daun Gervais,[3]   *to*
That in his forge smithed plough harneis:°   *equipment*
655 He sharpeth shaar and cultour[4] bisily.
This Absolon knokketh al esily,°   *quietly*
And saide, "Undo, Gervais, and that anoon."°   *at once*
   "What, who artou?" "It am I, Absolon."
"What, Absolon? What, Cristes sweete tree!
660 Why rise ye so rathe?° Ey, benedicite,°   *early / bless me*
What aileth you? Som gay girl, God it woot,
Hath brought you thus upon the viritoot.[5]
By Sainte Note, ye woot wel what I mene."
   This Absolon ne roughte nat a bene[6]
665 Of al his play. No word again he yaf:
He hadde more tow on his distaf[7]
Than Gervais knew, and saide, "Freend so dere,
This hote cultour in the chimenee° here,   *fireplace*
As lene[8] it me: I have therwith to doone.
670 I wol bringe it thee again ful soone."
   Gervais answerde, "Certes, were it gold,
Or in a poke nobles alle untold,[9]
Thou sholdest have, as I am trewe smith.
Ey, Cristes fo,[1] what wol ye do therwith?"
675   "Therof," quod Absolon, "be as be may.
I shal wel telle it thee another day."
And caughte the cultour by the colde stele.°   *handle*
Ful softe out at the dore he gan to stele,
And wente unto the carpenteres wal:
680 He cougheth first and knokketh therwithal

8. Sand.
9. I had rather.
1. He didn't care a piece of cress for woman's love.
2. I.e., quiet walk.
3. Master Gervais.
4. He sharpens plowshare and coulter (the turf-cutter on a plow).

5. I.e., on the prowl.
6. Didn't care a bean.
7. I.e., more on his mind.
8. I.e., please lend.
9. Or gold coins all uncounted in a bag.
1. Foe, i.e., Satan.

Upon the windowe, right as he dide er.°   *before*
    This Alison answerde, "Who is ther
That knokketh so? I warante[2] it a thief."
    "Why, nay," quod he, "God woot, my sweete lief,°   *dear*
685 I am thyn Absolon, my dereling.
Of gold," quod he, "I have thee brought a ring—
My moder yaf it me, so God me save;
Ful fin it is and therto wel ygrave:°   *engraved*
This wol I yiven thee if thou me kisse."
690   This Nicholas was risen for to pisse,
And thoughte he wolde amenden[3] al the jape:°   *joke*
He sholde kisse his ers er that he scape.
And up the windowe dide he hastily,
And out his ers he putteth prively,
695 Over the buttok to the haunche-boon.
    And therwith spak this clerk, this Absolon,
"Speek, sweete brid, I noot nought wher thou art."
This Nicholas anoon leet flee[4] a fart
As greet as it hadde been a thonder-dent°   *thunderbolt*
700 That with the strook he was almost yblent,°   *blinded*
And he was redy with his iren hoot,°   *hot*
And Nicholas amidde the ers he smoot:°   *smote*
Of gooth the skin an hande-brede° aboute;   *handsbreadth*
The hote cultour brende so his toute°   *buttocks*
705 That for the smert he wende for to[5] die;
As he were wood° for wo he gan to crye,   *crazy*
"Help! Water! Water! Help, for Goddes herte!"
    This carpenter out of his slomber sterte,
And herde oon cryen "Water!" as he were wood,
710 And thoughte, "Allas, now cometh Noweles[6] flood!"
He sette him up withoute wordes mo,
And with his ax he smoot the corde atwo,
And down gooth al: he foond neither to selle
Ne breed ne ale til he cam to the celle,[7]
715 Upon the floor, and ther aswoune° he lay.   *in a faint*
    Up sterte hire[8] Alison and Nicholay,
And criden "Out" and "Harrow" in the streete.
The neighebores, bothe smale and grete,
In ronnen for to gauren° on this man   *gape*
720 That aswoune lay bothe pale and wan,
For with the fal he brosten° hadde his arm;   *broken*
But stonde he moste° unto his owene harm,   *must*
For whan he spak he was anoon bore down[9]
With° hende Nicholas and Alisoun: *by*
725 They tolden every man that he was wood—

2. I.e., wager.
3. Improve on.
4. Let fly.
5. Thought he would.
6. The carpenter is confusing Noah and Noel

(Christmas).
7. He found time to sell neither bread nor ale until
he arrived at the foundation.
8. Started.
9. Refuted.

He was agast so of Noweles flood,
Thurgh fantasye, that of his vanitee°   *folly*
He hadde ybought him kneeding-tubbes three,
And hadde hem hanged in the roof above,

730 And that he prayed hem, for Goddes love,
To sitten in the roof, *par compaignye.*[1]
   The folk gan laughen at his fantasye.
Into the roof they kiken° and they cape,°   *peer / gape*
And turned al his harm unto a jape,°   *joke*

735 For what so that this carpenter answerde,
It was for nought: no man his reson° herde;   *argument*
With othes grete he was so sworn adown,
That he was holden° wood in al the town,   *considered*
For every clerk anoonright heeld with other:

740 They saide, "The man was wood, my leve brother,"
And every wight gan laughen at this strif.°   *fuss*
Thus swived° was the carpenteres wif   *slept with*
For al his keeping° and his jalousye,   *guarding*
And Absolon hath kist hir nether° yë,   *lower*

745 And Nicholas is scalded in the toute:
This tale is doon, and God save al the route!°   *company*

The Wife of Bath's Prologue and Tale

The Prologue[1]

Experience, though noon auctoritee
Were in this world, is right ynough for me

1. For company's sake.

1. The Wife of Bath is the remarkable culmination of many centuries of an antifeminism that was particularly nurtured by the medieval church. In their eagerness to exalt the spiritual ideal of chastity, certain theologians developed an idea of womankind that was nothing less than monstrous. According to these, insatiable lecherousness and indomitable shrewishness (plus a host of attendant vices) were characteristic of women. This notion was given most eloquent expression by St. Jerome in his attack (written about A.D. 400) on the monk Jovinian, who had uttered some good words for matrimony, and it is Jerome that the Wife of Bath comes forward not, curiously enough, to refute, but to confirm. The first part of her Prologue is a mass of quotations from that part of Jerome's tract where he is appealing to St. Paul's Epistle (1 Corinthians 7) for antimatrimonial authority. On the narrow issue of her right to remarry, to be sure, the Wife finds fault—rather mildly—with Jerome, but on the more central issue of why she wishes to marry and remarry she expresses no disagreement with him. Yet in the failure to defend herself and refute the saint, she somehow manages to make the latter's point of view look a good deal sillier than she looks herself; and instead of embodying the satire on womanhood that one would expect because of her origins in antifeminist literature, she becomes instead a satirist of the grotesquely woman-hating men who had first defined her personality.

More important, because of the extraordinary vitality that Chaucer has imparted to her, the Wife of Bath by the end of her Prologue comes to bear a less significant relation to satire than she does to reality itself. Making the best of the world in which they have arbitrarily been placed is the occupation of both the Wife of Bath and the reader, and it is in doing this that the Wife ceases to be a monstrosity of fiction and becomes alive—wonderfully alive, both to the potentialities of which she and her world are capable and to the limitations that even in her world time and age place upon her. It is especially in the attitude with which she regards these limitations that her fiction becomes most true to life, since they are also the limitations imposed by the real world. Despite the loss of youth and beauty, her best weapons, she faces her future not only with a woman's ability to endure and enjoy what she cannot reshape, but also with a zest for life on its own terms that is almost more than human.

To speke of wo that is in mariage:
For lordinges,° sith I twelf yeer was of age—   *gentlemen*
5   Thanked be God that is eterne on live—
Housbondes at chirche dore[2] I have had five
(If I so ofte mighte han wedded be),
And alle were worthy men in hir degree.
But me was told, certain, nat longe agoon is,
10 That sith that Crist ne wente nevere but ones
To wedding in the Cane[3] of Galilee,
That by the same ensample° taughte he me   *example*
That I ne sholde wedded be but ones.
Herke eek,° lo, which° a sharp word for the nones,[4]   *also / what*
15 Biside a welle, Jesus, God and man,
Spak in repreve° of the Samaritan: *reproof*
"Thou hast yhad five housbondes," quod he,
"And that ilke° man that now hath thee   *same*
Is nat thyn housbonde." Thus saide he certain.
20 What that he mente therby I can nat sayn,
But that I axe° why the fifthe man   *ask*
Was noon housbonde to the Samaritan?[5]
How manye mighte she han in mariage?
Yit herde I nevere tellen in myn age
25 Upon this nombre diffinicioun.°   *definition*
Men may divine° and glosen° up and down,   *guess / interpret*
But wel I woot,° expres,° withouten lie,   *know / expressly*
God bad us for to wexe[6] and multiplye:
That gentil text can I wel understonde.
30   Eek wel I woot° he saide that myn housbonde   *know*
Sholde lete° fader and moder and take to me,[7]   *leave*
But of no nombre mencion made he—
Of bigamye or of octogamye:[8]
Why sholde men thanne speke of it vilainye?
35   Lo, here the wise king daun° Salomon: *master*
I trowe° he hadde wives many oon,[9]   *believe*
As wolde God it leveful° were to me   *permissible*
To be refresshed half so ofte as he.
Which yifte[1] of God hadde he for alle his wives!
40 No man hath swich that in this world alive is.
God woot this noble king, as to my wit,°   *knowledge*
The firste night hadde many a merye fit°   *bout*
With eech of hem, so wel was him on live.[2]
Blessed be God that I have wedded five,

---

2. The actual wedding ceremony was celebrated
at the church door, not in the chancel.
3. Cana (see John 2.1).
4. To the purpose.
5. Christ was actually referring to a sixth man who
was not married to the Samaritan woman (cf. John
4.6 ff.).
6. I.e., increase. See Genesis 1.28.

7. See Matthew 19.5.
8. I.e., of two or even eight marriages. The Wife
is referring to successive, rather than simultaneous
marriages.
9. Solomon had 700 wives and 300 concubines (1
Kings 11.3).
1. What a gift.
2. I.e., so pleasant a life he had.

45 Of whiche I have piked out the beste,[3]
   Bothe of hir nether° purs and of hir cheste.°   *lower / moneybox*
   Diverse scoles maken parfit° clerkes,   *perfect*
   And diverse practikes[4] in sondry werkes
   Maken the werkman parfit sikerly:°   *certainly*
50 Of five housbondes scoleying° am I.   *schooling*
   Welcome the sixte whan that evere he shal![5]
   For sith I wol nat kepe me chast in al,
   Whan my housbonde is fro the world agoon,
   Som Cristen man shal wedde me anoon.°   *right away*
55 For thanne th'Apostle[6] saith that I am free
   To wedde, a Goddes half,[7] where it liketh me.
   He saide that to be wedded is no sinne:
   Bet° is to be wedded than to brinne.°   *better / burn*
   What rekketh me[8] though folk saye vilainye
60 Of shrewed° Lamech[9] and his bigamye?   *cursed*
   I woot wel Abraham was an holy man,
   And Jacob eek, as fer as evere I can,°   *know*
   And eech of hem hadde wives mo than two,
   And many another holy man also.

65   Where can ye saye in any manere age
   That hye God defended° mariage   *prohibited*
   By expres word? I praye you, telleth me.
   Or where comanded he virginitee?
   I woot as wel as ye, it is no drede,°   *doubt*
70 Th'Apostle, whan he speketh of maidenhede,°   *maidenhood*
   He saide that precept therof hadde he noon:
   Men may conseile a womman to be oon,°   *single*
   But conseiling nis no comandement.
   He putte it in oure owene juggement.
75 For hadde God comanded maidenhede,
   Thanne hadde he dampned° wedding with the   *condemned*
        deede;[1]
   And certes, if there were no seed ysowe,
   Virginitee, thanne wherof sholde it growe?
   Paul dorste nat comanden at the leeste
80 A thing of which his maister yaf° no heeste.°   *gave / command*
   The dart[2] is set up for virginitee:
   Cacche whoso may, who renneth° best lat see.   *runs*
   But this word is nought take of[3] every wight,
   But ther as[4] God list° yive it of his might.   *it pleases*
85 I woot wel that th'Apostle was a maide,°   *virgin*
   But nathelees, though that he wroot and saide

---

3. Whom I have cleaned out of everything worthwhile.
4. Practical experiences.
5. I.e., shall come along.
6. St. Paul.
7. On God's behalf. "It liketh me": I please.
8. What do I care.

9. The first man whom the Bible mentions as
having two wives (Genesis 4.19–24).
1. I.e., at the same time.
2. I.e., prize in a race.
3. Understood for, i.e., applicable to.
4. Where.

He wolde that every wight were swich° as he,   *such*
Al nis but conseil to virginitee;
And for to been a wif he yaf me leve
90   Of indulgence; so nis it no repreve°   *disgrace*
To wedde me[5] if that my make° die,   *mate*
Withouten excepcion of bigamye[6]—
Al° were it good no womman for to touche   *although*
(He mente as in his bed or in his couche,
95   For peril is bothe fir° and tow° t'assemble—   *fire / flax*
Ye knowe what this ensample may resemble).[7]
This al and som,[8] he heeld virginitee
More parfit than wedding in freletee.°   *frailty*
(Freletee clepe I but if[9] that he and she
100 Wolde leden al hir lif in chastitee.)
I graunte it wel, I have noon envye
Though maidenhede preferre° bigamye:°   *excel / remarriage*
It liketh hem to be clene in body and gost.°   *spirit*
Of myn estaat ne wol I make no boost;
105 For wel ye knowe, a lord in his houshold
Ne hath nat every vessel al of gold:
Some been of tree,° and doon hir lord servise.   *wood*
God clepeth folk to him in sondry wise,
And everich hath of God a propre[1] yifte,
110 Som this, som that, as him liketh shifte.°   *ordain*
Virginitee is greet perfeccioun,
And continence eek with devocioun,
But Crist, that of perfeccion is welle,°   *source*
Bad nat every wight he sholde go selle
115 Al that he hadde and yive it to the poore,
And in swich wise folwe him and his fore:[2]
He spak to hem that wolde live parfitly°—   *perfectly*
And lordinges, by youre leve, that am nat I.
I wol bistowe the flour of al myn age
120 In th'actes and in fruit of mariage.
     Telle me also, to what conclusioun°   *end*
Were membres maad of generacioun
And of so parfit wis a wrighte ywrought?[3]
Trusteth right wel, they were nat maad for nought.
125 Glose° whoso wol, and saye bothe up and down   *interpret*
That they were maked for purgacioun
Of urine, and oure bothe thinges smale
Was eek to knowe a femele from a male,
And for noon other cause—saye ye no?
130 Th'experience woot it is nought so.

---

5. For me to marry.
6. I.e., without there being any legal objection on
the score of remarriage.
7. I.e., what this metaphor may apply to.
8. This is all there is to it.

9. Frailty I call it unless.
1. I.e., his own.
2. Matthew 19.21. "Fore": footsteps.
3. And wrought by so perfectly wise a maker.

So that the clerkes be nat with me wrothe,
I saye this, that they been maad for bothe—
That is to sayn, for office° and for ese   *excretion*
Of engendrure, ther we nat God displese.
135 Why sholde men elles in hir bookes sette
That man shal yeelde[4] to his wif hir dette?
Now wherwith sholde he make his payement
If he ne used his sely° instrument?   *innocent*
Thanne were they maad upon a creature
140 To purge urine, and eek for engendrure.
      But I saye nought that every wight is holde,°   *bound*
That hath swich harneis° as I to you tolde,   *equipment*
To goon and usen hem in engendrure:
Thanne sholde men take of chastitee no cure.°   *heed*
145 Crist was a maide° and shapen as a man,   *virgin*
And many a saint sith that the world bigan,
Yit lived they evere in parfit chastitee.
I nil envye no virginitee:
Lat hem be breed° of pured° whete seed,   *bread / refined*
150 And lat us wives hote° barly breed—   *be called*
And yit with barly breed, Mark telle can,
Oure Lord Jesu refresshed many a man.[5]
In swich estaat as God hath cleped us
I wol persevere: I nam nat precious.°   *fastidious*
155 In wifhood wol I use myn instrument
As freely° as my Makere hath it sent.   *generously*
If I be daungerous,° God yive me sorwe: *stand-offish*
Myn housbonde shal it han both eve and morwe,°   *morning*
Whan that him list[6] come forth and paye his dette.
160 An housbonde wol I have, I wol nat lette,[7]
Which shal be bothe my dettour° and my thral,°   *debtor / slave*
And have his tribulacion withal
Upon his flessh whil that I am his wif.
I have the power during al my lif
165 Upon his propre° body, and nat he: *own*
Right thus th'Apostle tolde it unto me,
And bad oure housbondes for to love us weel.
Al this sentence° me liketh everydeel.°   *purport / entirely*

[AN INTERLUDE]

    Up sterte° the Pardoner and that anoon: *started*
170 "Now dame," quod he, "by God and by Saint John,
Ye been a noble prechour in this cas.
I was aboute to wedde a wif: allas,
What° sholde I bye° it on my flessh so dere?   *why / purchase*

---

4. I.e., pay.
5. In the descriptions of the miracle of the loaves
and fishes, it is actually John, not Mark, who

mentions barley bread (6.9).
6. When he wishes to.
7. I will make no difficulty.

Yit hadde I levere wedde no wif toyere."°   *this year*
175   "Abid," quod she, "my tale is nat bigonne.
Nay, thou shalt drinken of another tonne,°   *tun*
Er that I go, shal savoure wors than ale.
And whan that I have told thee forth my tale
Of tribulacion in mariage,
180   Of which I am expert in al myn age—
This is to saye, myself hath been the whippe—
Thanne maistou chese° wheither thou wolt sippe   *choose*
Of thilke° tonne that I shal abroche;°   *this same / broach*
Be war of it, er thou come too neigh approche,
185   For I shal telle ensamples mo than ten.
'Whoso that nile° be war by othere men,   *will not*
By him shal othere men corrected be.'
Thise same wordes writeth Ptolomee:
Rede in his *Almageste* and take it there."[8]
190   "Dame, I wolde praye you if youre wil it were,"
Saide this Pardoner, "as ye bigan,
Telle forth youre tale; spareth for no man,
And teche us yonge men of youre practike."°   *mode of operation*
"Gladly," quod she, "sith it may you like;°   *please*
195   But that I praye to al this compaignye,
If that I speke after my fantasye,[9]
As taketh nat agrief° of that I saye,   *amiss*
For myn entente nis but for to playe."

[THE WIFE CONTINUES]

Now sire, thanne wol I telle you forth my tale.
200   As evere mote I drinke win or ale,
I shal saye sooth: tho° housbondes that I hadde,   *those*
As three of hem were goode, and two were badde.
The three men were goode, and riche, and olde;
Unnethe° mighte they the statut holde   *with difficulty*
205   In which they were bounden unto me—
Ye woot wel what I mene of this, pardee.
As help me God, I laughe whan I thinke
How pitously anight I made hem swinke;°   *work*
And by my fay,° I tolde of it no stoor:[1]   *faith*
210   They hadde me yiven hir land and hir tresor;
Me needed nat do lenger diligence
To winne hir love or doon hem reverence.
They loved me so wel, by God above,
That I ne tolde no daintee of[2] hir love.
215   A wis womman wol bisye hire evere in oon[3]

8. The *Almagest*, an astronomical work by the Greek astronomer and mathematician Ptolemy (2nd century A.D.), contains no such aphorism. The aphorism does, however, appear in a collection ascribed to him.
9. If I speak according to my whim.
1. I set no store by it.
2. Set no value on.
3. Busy herself constantly.

To gete hire love, ye, ther as she hath noon.
But sith I hadde hem hoolly in myn hand,
And sith that they hadde yiven me al hir land,
What° sholde I take keep° hem for to plese,   *why / care*
220   But it were for my profit and myn ese?
I sette hem so awerke,° by my fay,   *awork*
That many a night they songen° wailaway.   *sang*
The bacon was nat fet° for hem, I trowe,   *brought back*
That some men han in Essexe at Dunmowe.[4]
225   I governed hem so wel after° my lawe   *according to*
That eech of hem ful blisful was and fawe°   *glad*
To bringe me gaye thinges fro the faire;
They were ful glade whan I spak hem faire,
For God it woot, I chidde° hem spitously.°   *chided / cruelly*
230   Now herkneth how I bar me[5] proprely:
Ye wise wives, that conne understonde,
Thus sholde ye speke and bere him wrong on honde[6]—
For half so boldely can ther no man
Swere and lie as a woman can.
235   I saye nat this by wives that been wise,
But if it be whan they hem misavise.[7]
A wis wif, if that she can hir good,[8]
Shal bere him on hande the cow is wood,[9]
And take witnesse of hir owene maide
240   Of hir assent.[1] But herkneth how I saide:
    "Sire olde cainard,° is this thyn array?[2]   *sluggard*
Why is my neighebores wif so gay?
She is honoured overal ther she gooth:
I sitte at hoom; I have no thrifty° cloth.   *decent*
245   What doostou at my neighebores hous?
Is she so fair? Artou so amorous?
What roune° ye with oure maide, benedicite?[3]   *whisper*
Sire olde lechour, lat thy japes° be.   *tricks, intrigues*
And if I have a gossib° or a freend,   *confidant*
250   Withouten gilt ye chiden as a feend,
If that I walke or playe unto his hous.
Thou comest hoom as dronken as a mous,
And prechest on thy bench, with yvel preef.[4]
Thou saist to me, it is a greet meschief°   *misfortune*
255   To wedde a poore womman for costage.[5]
And if that she be riche, of heigh parage,°   *descent*
Thanne saistou that it is a tormentrye

4. The Dunmow flitch was awarded to the couple
who after a year of marriage could claim no quarrels, no regrets, and the desire, if freed, to remarry
one another.
5. Bore myself, behaved.
6. Accuse him falsely.
7. When they make a mistake.
8. If she knows what's good for her.
9. Shall persuade him the chough has gone crazy.

The chough, or jackdaw, was popularly supposed
to tell husbands of their wives' infidelity.
1. And call as a witness her maid, who is on her
side.
2. I.e., is this how you behave?
3. Bless me.
4. I.e., (may you have) bad luck.
5. Because of the expense.

To suffre hir pride and hir malencolye.
And if that she be fair, thou verray knave,
260   Thou saist that every holour° wol hire have: *whoremonger*
She may no while in chastitee abide
That is assailed upon eech a side.
      "Thou saist som folk desiren us for richesse,
Som[6] for oure shap, and som for oure fairnesse,
265   And som for she can outher° singe or daunce,   *either*
And som for gentilesse and daliaunce,°   *flirtatiousness*
Som for hir handes and hir armes smale°—   *slender*
Thus gooth al to the devel by thy tale![7]
Thou saist men may nat keepe[8] a castel wal,
270   It may so longe assailed been overal.°   *everywhere*
And if that she be foul, thou saist that she
Coveiteth° every man that she may see;   *desires*
For as a spaniel she wol on him lepe,
Til that she finde som man hire to chepe.°   *buy*
275   Ne noon so grey goos gooth ther in the lake,
As, saistou, wol be withoute make;°   *mate*
And saist it is an hard thing for to weelde°   *possess*
A thing that no man wol, his thankes, heelde.[9]
Thus saistou, lorel,° whan thou goost to bedde,   *loafer*
280   And that no wis man needeth for to wedde,
Ne no man that entendeth° unto hevene—   *aims*
With wilde thonder-dint[1] and firy levene
Mote thy welked nekke be tobroke![2]
Thou saist that dropping° houses and eek smoke   *leaking*
285   And chiding wives maken men to flee
Out of hir owene hous: a, benedicite,
What aileth swich an old man for to chide?
Thou saist we wives wil oure vices hide
Til we be fast,[3] and thanne we wol hem shewe—
290   Wel may that be a proverbe of a shrewe!°   *villain*
Thou saist that oxen, asses, hors,° and houndes,   *horses*
They been assayed at diverse stoundes;°   *times*
Bacins, lavours,° er that men hem bye,   *washbowls*
Spoones, stooles, and al swich housbondrye,°   *household goods*
295   And so be° pottes, clothes, and array°—   *are / clothing*
But folk of wives maken noon assay
Til they be wedded—olde dotard shrewe!
And thanne, saistou, we wil oure vices shewe.
Thou saist also that it displeseth me
300   But if that thou wolt praise my beautee,
And but thou poure alway upon my face,
And clepe me 'Faire Dame' in every place,

---

6. "Som," in this and the following lines, means "one."
7. I.e., according to your story.
8. I.e., keep safe.

9. No man would willingly hold.
1. Thunderbolt. "Levene": lightning.
2. May thy withered neck be broken!
3. I.e., married.

And but thou make a feeste on thilke day
That I was born, and make me fressh and gay,
305 And but thou do to my norice° honour,   *nurse*
And to my chamberere within my bowr,[4]
And to my fadres folk, and his allies[5]—
Thus saistou, olde barel-ful of lies.
And yit of our apprentice Janekin,
310 For his crispe° heer, shining as gold so fin,   *curly*
And for he squiereth me bothe up and down,
Yit hastou caught a fals suspecioun;
I wil° him nat though thou were deed° tomorwe.   *want / dead*
    "But tel me this, why hidestou with sorwe[6]
315 The keyes of thy cheste away fro me?
It is my good° as wel as thyn, pardee.   *property*
What, weenestou° make an idiot of oure dame?   *do you think to*
Now by that lord that called is Saint Jame,
Thou shalt nought bothe, though thou were wood,°   *furious*
320 Be maister of my body and of my good:
That oon thou shalt forgo, maugree thine yën.[7]
    "What helpeth it of me enquere° and spyen?   *inquire*
I trowe thou woldest loke° me in thy cheste.   *lock*
Thou sholdest saye, 'Wif, go wher thee leste.°   *it may please*
325 Taak youre disport. I nil leve° no tales.   *believe*
I knowe you for a trewe wif, dame Alis.'
We love no man that taketh keep or charge[8]
Wher that we goon: we wol been at oure large.[9]
Of alle men yblessed mote he be
330 The wise astrologen° daun Ptolomee,   *astronomer*
That saith this proverbe in his *Almageste*:
'Of alle men his wisdom is the hyeste
That rekketh° nat who hath the world in honde.'   *cares*
By this proverbe thou shalt understonde,
335 Have thou[1] ynough, what thar° thee rekke or care   *need*
How merily that othere folkes fare?
For certes, olde dotard, by youre leve,
Ye shal han queinte° right ynough at eve: *pudendum*
He is too greet a nigard that wil werne°   *refuse*
340 A man to lighte a candle at his lanterne;
He shal han nevere the lasse° lighte, pardee.   *less*
Have thou ynough, thee thar nat plaine thee.[2]
    "Thou saist also that if we make us gay
With clothing and with precious array,
345 That it is peril of oure chastitee,
And yit with sorwe thou moste enforce thee,[3]

---

4. And to my chambermaid within my bedroom.
5. Relatives by marriage.
6. I.e., with sorrow to you.
7. Despite your eyes—i.e., despite anything you can do about it.
8. Notice or interest.
9. I.e., liberty.
1. If you have.
2. I.e., you need not complain.
3. Strengthen your position.

And saye thise wordes in th' Apostles name:
'In habit° maad with chastitee and shame   *clothing*
Ye wommen shal apparaile you,' quod he,
350   'And nat in tressed heer[4] and gay perree,°   *jewelry*
As perles ne with gold ne clothes riche.'[5]
After thy text, ne after thy rubriche,[6]
I wol nat werke as muchel as a gnat.
Thou saidest this, that I was lik a cat:
355   For whoso wolde senge° a cattes skin,   *singe*
Thanne wolde the cat wel dwellen in his in;°   *lodging*
And if the cattes skin be slik° and gay,   *sleek*
She wol nat dwelle in house half a day,
But forth she wol, er any day be dawed,[7]
360   To shewe her skin and goon a-caterwawed.°   *caterwauling*
This is to saye, if I be gay, sire shrewe,
I wol renne° out, my borel° for to shewe.   *run / clothing*
Sir olde fool, what helpeth[8] thee t'espyen?
Though thou praye Argus with his hundred yën
365   To be my wardecors,° as he can best,   *bodyguard*
In faith, he shal nat keepe° me but me lest:[9]   *guard*
Yit coude I make his beerd,[1] so mote I thee.°   *thrive*
"Thou saidest eek that ther been thinges three,
The whiche thinges troublen al this erthe,
370   And that no wight may endure the ferthe.°   *fourth*
O leve° sire shrewe, Jesu shorte° thy lif!   *dear / shorten*
Yit prechestou and saist an hateful wif
Yrekened is for oon of thise meschaunces.
Been ther nat none othere resemblaunces
375   That ye may likne youre parables to,[2]
But if[3] a sely° wif be oon of tho?   *innocent*
"Thou liknest eek wommanes love to helle,
To bareine° land ther water may nat dwelle;   *barren*
Thou liknest it also to wilde fir—
380   The more it brenneth,° the more it hath desir   *burns*
To consumen every thing that brent° wol be;   *burned*
Thou saist right° as wormes shende° a tree,   *just / destroy*
Right so a wif destroyeth hir housbonde—
This knowen they that been to wives bonde."°   *bound*
385   Lordinges, right thus, as ye han understonde,
Bar I stifly mine olde housbondes on honde[4]
That thus they saiden in hir dronkenesse—
And al was fals, but that I took witnesse
On Janekin and on my nece also.
390   O Lord, the paine I dide hem and the wo,

---

4. I.e., elaborate hairdo.
5. See 1. Timothy 2.9.
6. Rubric, i.e., direction.
7. Has dawned.
8. What does it help.
9. Unless I please.

1. I.e., deceive him.
2. Isn't there something else appropriate to which you can apply your metaphors?
3. Unless.
4. I rigorously accused my old husbands.

Ful giltelees, by Goddes sweete pine!°   *suffering*
For as an hors I coude bite and whine;°   *whinny*
I coude plaine° and° I was in the gilt,   *complain / if*
Or elles often time I hadde been spilt.°   *ruined*
395   Whoso that first to mille comth first grint.°   *grinds*
I plained first: so was oure werre stint.[5]
They were ful glade to excusen hem ful blive°   *quickly*
Of thing of which they nevere agilte hir live.[6]
Of wenches wolde I beren hem on honde,
400   Whan that for sik[7] they mighte unnethe° stonde,   *scarcely*
Yit tikled I his herte for that he
Wende° I hadde had of him so greet cheertee.[8]   *thought*
I swoor that al my walking out by nighte
Was for to espye wenches that he dighte.[9]
405   Under that colour[1] hadde I many a mirthe.
For al swich wit is yiven us in oure birthe:
Deceite, weeping, spinning God hath yive
To wommen kindely° whil they may live.   *naturally*
And thus of oo thing I avaunte me:[2]
410   At ende I hadde the bet° in eech degree,   *better*
By sleighte or force, or by som manere thing,
As by continuel murmur° or grucching;°   *complaint / grumbling*
Namely° abedde hadden they meschaunce: *especially*
Ther wolde I chide and do hem no plesaunce;[3]
415   I wolde no lenger in the bed abide
If that I felte his arm over my side,
Til he hadde maad his raunson° unto me;   *ransom*
Thanne wolde I suffre him do his nicetee.°   *lust*
And therfore every man this tale I telle:
420   Winne whoso may, for al is for to selle;
With empty hand men may no hawkes lure.
For winning° wolde I al his lust endure,   *profit*
And make me a feined appetit—
And yit in bacon[4] hadde I nevere delit.
425   That made me that evere I wolde hem chide;
For though the Pope hadde seten° hem biside,   *sat*
I wolde nought spare hem at hir owene boord.
For by my trouthe, I quitte° hem word for word.   *repaid*
As help me verray God omnipotent,
430   Though I right now sholde make my testament,
I ne owe hem nat a word that it nis quit.
I broughte it so aboute by my wit
That they moste yive it up as for the beste,
Or elles hadde we nevere been in reste;

5. Our war brought to an end.   9. Had intercourse with.
6. Of a thing in which they never offended in their   1. I.e., excuse.
lives.   2. Boast.
7. I.e., sickness.   3. Show them no affection.
8. Affection.   4. I.e., old meat.

435 For though he looked as a wood° leoun, *furious*
Yit sholde he faile of his conclusioun.° *object*
    Thanne wolde I saye, "Goodelief, taak keep,[5]
How mekely looketh Wilekin, oure sheep!
Com neer my spouse, lat me ba° thy cheeke— *kiss*
440 Ye sholden be al pacient and meeke,
And han a sweete-spiced[6] conscience,
Sith ye so preche of Jobes pacience;
Suffreth alway, sin ye so wel can preche;
And but ye do, certain, we shal you teche
445 That it is fair to han a wif in pees.
Oon of us two moste bowen, doutelees,
And sith a man is more resonable
Than womman is, ye mosten been suffrable.° *patient*
What aileth you to grucche° thus and grone? *grumble*
450 Is it for ye wolde have my queinte° allone? *pudendum*
Why, taak it al—lo, have it everydeel.° *altogether*
Peter, I shrewe° you but ye love it weel. *curse*
For if I wolde selle my bele chose,[7]
I coude walke as fressh as is a rose;
455 But I wol keepe it for youre owene tooth.° *taste*
Ye be to blame. By God, I saye you sooth!"
Swiche manere° wordes hadde we on honde. *kind of*
Now wol I speke of my ferthe° housbonde. *fourth*
    My ferthe housbonde was a revelour—
460 This is to sayn, he hadde a paramour°— *mistress*
And I was yong and ful of ragerye,° *wantonness*
Stibourne° and strong and joly as a pie:° *untamable / magpie*
How coude I daunce to an harpe smale,° *gracefully*
And singe, ywis,° as any nightingale, *indeed*
465 Whan I hadde dronke a draughte of sweete win.
Metellius, the foule cherl, the swin,
That with a staf birafte° his wif hir lif *deprived*
For° she drank win, though I hadde been his wif, *because*
Ne sholde nat han daunted me fro drinke;
470 And after win on Venus moste° I thinke, *must*
For also siker° as cold engendreth hail, *sure*
A likerous° mouth moste han a likerous° tail: *greedy / lecherous*
In womman vinolent° is no defence— *bibulous*
This knowen lechours by experience.
475   But Lord Crist, whan that it remembreth me[8]
Upon my youthe and on my jolitee,
It tikleth me aboute myn herte roote—
Unto this day it dooth myn herte boote° *good*
That I have had my world as in my time.
480 But age, allas, that al wol envenime,° *poison*

---

5. Good friend, take notice.   7. Fair thing.
6. I.e., delicate.   8. When I look back.

Hath me biraft[9] my beautee and my pith—
Lat go, farewel, the devel go therwith!
The flour is goon, ther is namore to telle:
The bren° as I best can now moste I selle;   *bran*
485   But yit to be right merye wol I fonde.°   *strive*
Now wol I tellen of my ferthe housbonde.
      I saye I hadde in herte greet despit
That he of any other hadde delit,
But he was quit,° by God and by Saint Joce: *paid back*
490   I made him of the same wode a croce[1]—
Nat of my body in no foul manere—
But, certainly, I made folk swich cheere
That in his owene grece I made him frye,
For angre and for verray jalousye.
495   By God, in erthe I was his purgatorye,
For which I hope his soule be in glorye.
For God it woot, he sat ful ofte and soong°   *sang*
Whan that his sho ful bitterly him wroong.°   *pinched*
Ther was no wight save God and he that wiste°   *knew*
500   In many wise how sore I him twiste.
He deide whan I cam fro Jerusalem,
And lith ygrave under the roode-beem,[2]
Al° is his tombe nought so curious[3]   *although*
As was the sepulcre of him Darius,
505   Which that Apelles wroughte subtilly:[4]
It nis but wast to burye him preciously.°   *expensively*
Lat him fare wel, God yive his soule reste;
He is now in his grave and in his cheste.
      Now of my fifthe housbonde wol I telle—
510   God lete his soule nevere come in helle—
And yit he was to me the moste shrewe:[5]
That feele I on my ribbes al by rewe,[6]
And evere shal unto myn ending day.
But in oure bed he was so fressh and gay,
515   And therwithal so wel coulde he me glose°   *wheedle*
Whan that he wolde han my bele chose,
That though he hadde me bet° on every boon,°   *beaten / bone*
He coude winne again my love anoon.°   *immediately*
I trowe I loved him best for that he
520   Was of his love daungerous[7] to me.
We wommen han, if that I shal nat lie,
In this matere a quainte fantasye:

9. Has taken away from me.
1. I made him a cross of the same wood. The proverb has much the same sense as the one quoted in line 493.
2. And lies buried under the rood beam (the crucifix beam running between nave and chancel).
3. Carefully wrought.

4. Accordingly to medieval legend, the artist Apelles decorated the tomb of Darius, king of the Persians.
5. Worst rascal.
6. In a row.
7. I.e., he played hard to get.

Waite what[8] thing we may nat lightly° have,   *easily*
Therafter wol we crye al day and crave;
525   Forbede us thing, and that desiren we;
Preesse on us faste, and thanne wol we flee.
With daunger oute we al oure chaffare:[9]
Greet prees° at market maketh dere° ware,   *crowd / expensive*
And too greet chepe is holden at litel pris.[1]
530   This knoweth every womman that is wis.
      My fifthe housbonde—God his soule blesse!—
Which that I took for love and no richesse,
He somtime was a clerk at Oxenforde,
And hadde laft° scole and wente at hoom to boorde   *left*
535   With my gossib,° dwelling in oure town—   *confidante*
God have hir soule!—hir name was Alisoun;
She knew myn herte and eek my privetee°   *secrets*
Bet° than oure parissh preest, as mote I thee.°   *better / thrive*
To hire biwrayed° I my conseil° al,   *disclosed / secrets*
540   For hadde myn housbonde pissed on a wal,
Or doon a thing that sholde han cost his lif,
To hire,° and to another worthy wif,   *her*
And to my nece which I loved weel,
I wolde han told his conseil everydeel;°   *entirely*
545   And so I dide ful often, God it woot,
That made his face often reed° and hoot°   *red / hot*
For verray shame, and blamed himself for he
Hadde told to me so greet a privetee.
      And so bifel that ones in a Lente—
550   So often times I to my gossib wente,
For evere yit I loved to be gay,
And for to walke in March, Averil, and May,
From hous to hous, to heere sondry tales—
That Janekin clerk and my gossib dame Alis
555   And I myself into the feeldes wente.
Myn housbonde was at London al that Lente:
I hadde the better leiser for to playe,
And for to see, and eek for to be seye°   *seen*
Of lusty folk—what wiste I wher my grace°   *luck*
560   Was shapen° for to be, or in what place?   *destined*
Therfore I made my visitaciouns
To vigilies[2] and to processiouns,
To preching eek, and to thise pilgrimages,
To playes of miracles and to mariages,
565   And wered upon[3] my gaye scarlet gites°—   *dress*
Thise wormes ne thise motthes ne thise mites,
Upon my peril, frete° hem neveradeel: *ate*
And woostou why? For they were used weel.

Now wol I tellen forth what happed me.
570 I saye that in the feeldes walked we,
Til trewely we hadde swich daliaunce,°   *flirtation*
This clerk and I, that of my purveyaunce°   *foresight*
I spak to him and saide him how that he,
If I were widwe, sholde wedde me.
575 For certainly, I saye for no bobaunce,°   *boast*
Yit was I nevere withouten purveyaunce
Of mariage n'of othere thinges eek:
I holde a mouses herte nought worth a leek
That hath but oon hole for to sterte° to,   *run*
580 And if that faile thanne is al ydo.[4]
I bar him on hand[5] he hadde enchaunted me
(My dame taughte me that subtiltee);
And eek I saide I mette° of him al night: *dreamed*
He wolde han slain me as I lay upright,°   *supine*
585 And al my bed was ful of verray blood—
"But yit I hope that ye shul do me good;
For blood bitokeneth gold, as me was taught."
And al was fals, I dremed of it right naught,
But as I folwed ay my dames° lore°   *mother's / teaching*
590 As wel of that as othere thinges more.
But now sire—lat me see, what shal I sayn?
Aha, by God, I have my tale again.
Whan that my ferthe housbonde was on beere,°   *bier*
I weep,° algate,° and made sory cheere,   *wept / anyhow*
595 As wives moten,° for it is usage,°   *must / custom*
And with my coverchief covered my visage;
But for I was purveyed° of a make.°   *provided / mate*
I wepte but smale, and that I undertake.°   *guarantee*
To chirche was myn housbonde born amorwe[6]
600 With neighebores that for him maden sorwe,
And Janekin oure clerk was oon of tho.
As help me God, whan that I saw him go
After the beere, me thoughte he hadde a paire
Of legges and of feet so clene[7] and faire,
605 That al myn herte I yaf unto his hold.°   *possession*
He was, I trowe,° twenty winter old,   *believe*
And I was fourty, if I shal saye sooth—
But yit I hadde alway a coltes tooth:[8]
Gat-toothed was I, and that bicam me weel;
610 I hadde the prente[9] of Sainte Venus seel.
As help me God, I was a lusty oon,
And fair and riche and yong and wel-bigoon,°   *well-situated*
And trewely, as mine housbondes tolde me,

4. I.e., the game is up.
5. I pretended to him.
6. In the morning.
7. I.e., neat.

8. I.e., youthful appetites. "Gat-toothed": gap-toothed women were considered to be amorous.
9. Print, i.e., a birthmark. "Seel": seal.

      I hadde the beste quoniam° mighte be.   *pudendum*

615 For certes I am al Venerien[1]

      In feeling, and myn herte is Marcien:

      Venus me yaf my lust, my likerousnesse,°   *lecherousness*

      And Mars yaf me my sturdy hardinesse.

      Myn ascendent was Taur[2] and Mars therinne—

620 Allas, allas, that evere love was sinne!

      I folwed ay° my inclinacioun   *ever*

      By vertu of my constellacioun;[3]

      That made me I coude nought withdrawe

      My chambre of Venus from a good felawe.

625 Yit have I Martes° merk upon my face,   *Mars'*

      And also in another privee place.

      For God so wis° be my savacioun,°   *surely / salvation*

      I loved nevere by no discrecioun,

      But evere folwede myn appetit,

630 Al were he short or long or blak or whit;

      I took no keep,° so that he liked° me,   *heed / pleased*

      How poore he was, ne eek of what degree.

         What sholde I saye but at the monthes ende

      This joly clerk Janekin that was so hende°   *nice*

635 Hath wedded me with greet solempnitee,°   *splendor*

      And to him yaf I al the land and fee°   *property*

      That evere was me yiven therbifore—

      But afterward repented me ful sore:

      He nolde suffre no thing of my list.°   *pleasure*

640 By God, he smoot° me ones on the list°   *struck / ear*

      For that I rente° out of his book a leef,   *tore*

      That of the strook° myn ere weex° al deef.   *blow / grew*

      Stibourne° I was as is a leonesse,   *stubborn*

      And of my tonge a verray jangleresse,°   *blabbermouth*

645 And walke I wolde, as I hadde doon biforn,

      From hous to hous, although he hadde it[4] sworn;

      For which he often times wolde preche,

      And me of olde Romain geestes° teche,   *stories*

      How he Simplicius Gallus lafte° his wif,   *left*

650 And hire forsook for terme of al his lif,

      Nought but for open-heveded he hire sey[5]

      Looking out at his dore upon a day.

         Another Romain tolde he me by name

      That, for his wif was at a someres° game   *summer's*

655 Withouten his witing,° he forsook hire eke;   *knowledge*

      And thanne wolde he upon his Bible seeke

      That ilke proverbe of Ecclesiaste[6]

      Where he comandeth and forbedeth faste°   *strictly*

---

1. Astrologically influenced by Venus. "Mar-
cien": influenced by Mars.
2. My birth sign was the constellation Taurus.
3. I.e., horoscope.

4. I.e., the contrary.
5. Just because he saw her bareheaded.
6. Ecclesiasticus (25.25).

Man shal nat suffre his wif go roule° aboute;   roam
660 Thanne wolde he saye right thus withouten doute:
"Whoso that buildeth his hous al of salwes,°   willow sticks
And priketh° his blinde hors over the falwes,[7]   rides
And suffreth his wif to go seeken halwes,°   shrines
Is worthy to be hanged on the galwes.'"°   gallows
665 But al for nought—I sette nought an hawe[8]
Of his proverbes n'of his olde sawe;
N' I wolde nat of him corrected be:
I hate him that my vices telleth me,
And so doon mo, God woot, of us than I.
670 This made him with me wood al outrely:[9]
I nolde nought forbere° him in no cas.   submit to
    Now wol I saye you sooth, by Saint Thomas,
Why that I rente° out of his book a leef,   tore
For which he smoot me so that I was deef.
675 He hadde a book that gladly night and day
For his disport he wolde rede alway.
He cleped it Valerie[1] and Theofraste,
At which book he lough° alway ful faste;   laughed
And eek ther was somtime a clerk at Rome,
680 A cardinal, that highte Saint Jerome,
That made a book[2] again Jovinian;
In which book eek ther was Tertulan,[3]
Crysippus, Trotula, and Helouis,
That was abbesse nat fer fro Paris;
685 And eek the Parables of Salomon,[4]
Ovides Art, and bookes many oon—
And alle thise were bounden in oo volume.
And every night and day was his custume,
Whan he hadde leiser and vacacioun
690 From other worldly occupacioun,
To reden in this book of wikked wives.
He knew of hem mo legendes and lives
Than been of goode wives in the Bible.
For trusteth wel, it is an impossible°   impossibility
695 That any clerk wol speke good of wives,
But if it be of holy saintes lives,
N'of noon other womman nevere the mo—
Who painted the leon, tel me who?[5]

7. Plowed land.
8. I did not rate at the value of a hawthorn berry.
9. Entirely.
1. I.e., the Letter of Valerius Concerning Not Marrying, by Walter Map; "Theofraste": Theophrastus's Book Concerning Marriage. Medieval manuscripts often contained a number of different works, sometimes, as here, dealing with the same subject.
2. St. Jerome's antifeminist Reply to Jovinian. "Again": against.
3. Tertullian, author of treatises on sexual mod-

esty. Crysippus (or Chrysippus), in the next line, is mentioned by Jerome as an antifeminist; Trotula was a female doctor whose presence here is unexplained; "Helouis" is Eloise, whose love affair with the great scholar Abelard was a medieval scandal.
4. The Biblical Book of Proverbs. "Ovides Art": Ovid's Art of Love.
5. In one of Aesop's fables, the lion, shown a picture of a man killing a lion, asked who painted the picture. Had a lion been the artist, of course, the roles would have been reversed.

　　　By God, if wommen hadden writen stories,
700　As clerkes han within hir oratories,
　　　They wolde han writen of men more wikkednesse
　　　Than al the merk[6] of Adam may redresse.
　　　The children of Mercurye and Venus[7]
　　　Been in hir werking° ful contrarious:°　　　　　　operation / opposed
705　Mercurye loveth wisdom and science,
　　　And Venus loveth riot° and dispence;°　　　　　　parties / expenditures
　　　And for hir diverse disposicioun
　　　Each falleth in otheres exaltacioun,[8]
　　　And thus, God woot, Mercurye is desolat
710　In Pisces wher Venus is exaltat,[9]
　　　And Venus falleth ther Mercurye is raised:
　　　Therfore no womman of no clerk is praised.
　　　The clerk, whan he is old and may nought do
　　　Of Venus werkes worth his olde sho,°　　　　　　　shoe
715　Thanne sit° he down and writ° in his dotage　　　sits / writes
　　　That wommen can nat keepe hir mariage.
　　　　　But now to purpose why I tolde thee
　　　That I was beten for a book, pardee:
　　　Upon a night Janekin, that was our sire,[1]
720　Redde on his book as he sat by the fire
　　　Of Eva first, that for hir wikkednesse
　　　Was al mankinde brought to wrecchednesse,
　　　For which that Jesu Crist himself was slain
　　　That boughte° us with his herte blood again—　　redeemed
725　Lo, heer expres of wommen may ye finde
　　　That womman was the los° of al mankinde.[2]　　　ruin
　　　　　Tho° redde he me how Sampson loste his heres:　then
　　　Sleeping his lemman° kitte° it with hir sheres,　mistress / cut
　　　Thurgh which treson loste he both his yën.
730　　Tho redde he me, if that I shal nat lien,
　　　Of Ercules and of his Dianire,[3]
　　　That caused him to sette himself afire.
　　　　　No thing forgat he the sorwe and wo
　　　That Socrates hadde with his wives two—
735　How Xantippa caste pisse upon his heed:
　　　This sely° man sat stille as he were deed;　　　　silly
　　　He wiped his heed, namore dorste he sayn
　　　But "Er that thonder stinte,° comth a rain."　　　stops
　　　　　Of Pasipha[4] that was the queene of Crete—
740　For shrewednesse° him thoughte the tale sweete—　malice

6. Mark, sex.
7. I.e., clerks and women, astrologically ruled by Mercury and Venus respectively.
8. Because of their contrary positions (as planets), each one descends (in the belt of the zodiac) as the other rises; hence one loses its power as the other becomes dominant.
9. I.e., Mercury is deprived of power in Pisces (the sign of the Fish), where Venus is most powerful.
1. My husband.
2. The stories of wicked women Chaucer drew mainly from St. Jerome and Walter Map.
3. Dejanira unwittingly gave Hercules a poisoned shirt, which hurt him so much that he committed suicide by fire.
4. Pasiphaë, who fell in love with a bull.

Fy, speek namore, it is a grisly thing
Of hir horrible lust and hir liking.°   *pleasure*
   Of Clytermistra[5] for hir lecherye
That falsly made hir housbonde for to die,
745 He redde it with ful good devocioun.
   He tolde me eek for what occasioun
Amphiorax[6] at Thebes loste his lif:
Myn housbonde hadde a legende of his wif
Eriphylem, that for an ouche° of gold   *trinket*
750 Hath prively unto the Greekes told
Wher that hir housbonde hidde him in a place,
For which he hadde at Thebes sory grace.
   Of Livia[7] tolde he me and of Lucie:
They bothe made hir housbondes for to die,
755 That oon for love, that other was for hate;
Livia hir housbonde on an even late
Empoisoned hath for that she was his fo;
Lucia likerous° loved hir housbonde so   *lecherous*
That for° he sholde alway upon hire thinke,   *in order that*
760 She yaf him swich a manere love-drinke
That he was deed er it were by the morwe.[8]
And thus algates° housbondes han sorwe.   *constantly*
   Thanne tolde he me how oon Latumius
Complained unto his felawe Arrius
765 That in his garden growed swich a tree,
On which he saide how that his wives three
Hanged hemself for herte despitous.[9]
   "O leve° brother," quod this Arrius,   *dear*
"Yif me a plante of thilke blessed tree,
770 And in my gardin planted shal it be."
   Of latter date of wives hath he red
That some han slain hir housbondes in hir bed
And lete hir lechour dighte[1] hire al the night,
Whan that the cors° lay in the floor upright;°   *corpse / supine*
775 And some han driven nailes in hir brain
Whil that they sleepe, and thus they han hem slain;
Some han hem yiven poison in hir drinke.
He spak more harm than herte may bithinke,°   *imagine*
And therwithal he knew of mo proverbes
780 Than in this world ther growen gras or herbes:
"Bet is," quod he, "thyn habitacioun
Be with a leon or a foul dragoun
Than with a womman using° for to chide."   *accustomed*
"Bet is," quod he, "hye in the roof abide

---

5. Clytemnestra, who, with her lover Aegisthus, slew her husband Agamemnon.
6. Amphiaraus, betrayed by his wife Eriphyle and forced to go to the war against Thebes.
7. Livia murdered her husband in behalf of her lover Sejanus. "Lucie": Lucilla, who was said to

have poisoned her husband, the poet Lucretius, with a potion designed to keep him faithful.
8. He was dead before it was near morning.
9. For malice of heart.
1. Have intercourse with.

785   Than with an angry wif down in the hous:
They been so wikked° and contrarious,   *perverse*
They haten that hir housbondes loveth ay."
He saide, "A womman cast° hir shame away   *casts*
When she cast of° hir smok,"[2] and ferthermo,   *off*
790   "A fair womman, but she be chast also,
Is like a gold ring in a sowes nose."
Who wolde weene,° or who wolde suppose   *think*
The wo that in myn herte was and pine?°   *suffering*
    And whan I sawgh he wolde nevere fine°   *end*
795   To reden on this cursed book al night,
Al sodeinly three leves have I plight°   *snatched*
Out of his book right as he redde, and eke
I with my fist so took[3] him on the cheeke
That in oure fir he fil° bakward adown.   *fell*
800   And up he sterte as dooth a wood° leoun,   *raging*
And with his fist he smoot me on the heed°   *head*
That in the floor I lay as I were deed.
And whan he sawgh how stille that I lay,
He was agast, and wolde have fled his way,
805   Til atte laste out of my swough° I braide:° *swoon / started*
"O hastou slain me, false thief?" I saide,
"And for my land thus hastou mordred° me?   *murdered*
Er I be deed° yit wol I kisse thee."   *dead*
And neer he cam and kneeled faire adown,
810   And saide, "Dere suster Alisoun,
As help me God, I shal thee nevere smite.
That I have doon, it is thyself to wite.°   *blame*
Foryif it me, and that I thee biseeke."
And yit eftsoones° I hitte him on the cheeke, *again*
815   And saide, "Thief, thus muchel am I wreke.° *avenged*
Now wol I die: I may no lenger speke."
    But at the laste with muchel care and wo
We fille[4] accorded by us selven two.
He yaf me al the bridel° in myn hand,   *bridle*
820   To han the governance of hous and land,
And of his tonge and his hand also;
And made[5] him brenne° his book anoonright tho. *burn*
And whan that I hadde geten unto me
By maistrye° al the sovereinetee,°   *skill / dominion*
825   And that he saide, "Myn owene trewe wif,
Do as thee lust° the terme of al thy lif;   *it pleases*
Keep thyn honour, and keep eek myn estat,"
After that day we hadde nevere debat.
God help me so, I was to him as kinde
830   As any wif from Denmark unto Inde,
And also trewe, and so was he to me.

---

2. Undergarment.   4. I.e., became.
3. I.e., hit.   5. I.e., I made.

I praye to God that sit° in majestee,   *sits*
So blesse his soule for his mercy dere.
Now wol I saye my tale if ye wol heere.

[ANOTHER INTERRUPTION]

835   The Frere lough° whan he hadde herd all this: *laughed*
      "Now dame," quod he, "so have I joye or blis,
      This is a long preamble of a tale."
      And whan the Somnour herde the Frere gale,°   *exclaim*
      "Lo," quod the Somnour, "Goddes armes two,
840   A frere wol entremette him[6] everemo!
      Lo, goode men, a flye and eek a frere
      Wol falle in every dissh and eek matere.
      What spekestou of preambulacioun?
      What, amble or trotte or pisse or go sitte down!
845   Thou lettest° oure disport in this manere."   *hinder*
         "Ye, woltou so, sire Somnour?" quod the Frere.
      "Now by my faith, I shal er that I go
      Telle of a somnour swich a tale or two
      That al the folk shal laughen in this place."
850   "Now elles, Frere, I wol bishrewe° thy face,"   *curse*
      Quod this Somnour, "and I bishrewe me,
      But if I telle tales two or three
      Of freres, er I come to Sidingborne,[7]
      That I shal make thyn herte for to moorne—
855   For wel I woot thy pacience is goon."
         Oure Hoste cride, "Pees, and that anoon!"
      And saide, "Lat the womman telle hir tale:
      Ye fare as folk that dronken been of ale.
      Do, dame, tel forth youre tale, and that is best."
860   "Al redy, sire," quod she, "right as you lest°—   *it pleases*
      If I have licence of this worthy Frere."
      "Yis, dame," quod he, "tel forth and I wol heere."

The Tale[1]

In th'olde dayes of the King Arthour,
Of which that Britouns° speken greet honour,   *Bretons*

6. Intrude himself.
7. Sittingbourne (a town 40 miles from London).
1. The story of the knight who fully realizes what women most desire only after having been told it in a number of ways was popular in Chaucer's time and a natural one for him to assign to the Wife of Bath, whose well-loved fifth husband had also been slow to learn. But Chaucer reshaped the tale in such a way as to make it fit the Wife and her thesis even more closely. In the other medieval versions of the story the knight is guiltless of any offense to womanhood, and in several of them he is Sir Gawain, traditional model of chivalric courtesy,

who weds the hideous hag to save not his own life but that of his lord, King Arthur. Chaucer has made the knight a most ill-behaved and ill-mannered man who needs to learn what women most desire as much in order to redeem his disagreeably virile character as to save his neck. Because within her story he is the sole male in a world of women, Dame Alice is able not only to prove conclusively the value of woman's sovereignty, but also to pay her respects to a world of men that had preached antifeminism, a world here represented by a single rapist.

The story is suited to the Wife's own character

865   Al was this land fulfild of faïrye:[2]
     The elf-queene with hir joly compaignye
     Daunced ful ofte in many a greene mede°—   *meadow*
     This was the olde opinion as I rede;
     I speke of many hundred yeres ago.
870   But now can no man see none elves mo,
     For now the grete charitee and prayeres
     Of limitours,[3] and othere holy freres,
     That serchen every land and every streem,
     As thikke as motes in the sonne-beem,
875   Blessing halles, chambres, kichenes, bowres,
     Citees, burghes,° castels, hye towres,   *townships*
     Thropes, bernes, shipnes,[4] dayeries—
     This maketh that ther been no faïries.
     For ther as wont to walken was an elf
880   Ther walketh now the limitour himself,
     In undermeles° and in morweninges,°   *afternoons / mornings*
     And saith his Matins and his holy thinges,
     As he gooth in his limitacioun.[5]
     Wommen may go saufly° up and down: *safely*
885   In every bussh or under every tree
     Ther is noon other incubus[6] but he,
     And he ne wol doon hem but dishonour.
       And so bifel it that this King Arthour
     Hadde in his hous a lusty bacheler,
890   That on a day cam riding fro river,[7]
     And happed° that, allone as he was born,   *it happened*
     He sawgh a maide walking him biforn;
     Of which maide anoon, maugree hir heed,[8]
     By verray force he rafte° hir maidenheed;   *deprived her of*
895   For which oppression° was swich clamour,   *rape*
     And swich pursuite° unto the King Arthour,   *petitioning*
     That dampned was this knight for to be deed[9]
     By cours of lawe, and sholde han lost his heed—
     Paraventure° swich was the statut tho—   *perchance*
900   But that the queene and othere ladies mo
     So longe prayeden the king of grace,
     Til he his lif him graunted in the place,
     And yaf him to the queene, al at hir wille,
     To chese° wheither she wolde him save or spille.[1]   *choose*

---

psychologically as well as dramatically, for she, like the old hag, had wedded a young man—though unlike the hag she could not restore her former beauty. But if there is a touch of melancholy in the incompleteness of this similarity, it is sharply dispelled by the Wife's final comments, which reassert the sturdy fighting spirit that permeates her Prologue.

2. I.e., filled full of supernatural creatures.
3. Friars licensed to beg in a certain territory.
4. Thorps (villages), barns, stables.

5. I.e., the friar's assigned area. His "holy thinges" are prayers.
6. A spirit that lies with mortal women. "Ne . . . but" in the next line means "only."
7. Hawking, usually carried out on the banks of a stream.
8. Despite her head, i.e., despite anything she could do.
9. This knight was condemned to death.
1. Put to death.

905 The queene thanked the king with al hir might,
     And after this thus spak she to the knight,
     Whan that she saw hir time upon a day:
     "Thou standest yit," quod she, "in swich array°   condition
     That of thy lif yit hastou no suretee.°   guarantee
910 I graunte thee lif if thou canst tellen me
     What thing it is that wommen most desiren:
     Be war and keep thy nekke boon° from iren.   bone
     And if thou canst nat tellen me anoon,
     Yit wol I yive thee leve for to goon
915 A twelfmonth and a day to seeche° and lere°   search / learn
     An answere suffisant° in this matere,   satisfactory
     And suretee wol I han er that thou pace,°   pass
     Thy body for to yeelden in this place."
        Wo was this knight, and sorwefully he siketh.°   sighs
920 But what, he may nat doon al as him liketh,
     And atte laste he chees° him for to wende,   chose
     And come again right at the yeres ende,
     With swich answere as God wolde him purveye,°   provide
     And taketh his leve and wendeth forth his waye.
925 He seeketh every hous and every place
     Wher as he hopeth for to finde grace,
     To lerne what thing wommen love most.
     But he ne coude arriven in no coost[2]
     Wher as he mighte finde in this matere
930 Two creatures according in fere.[3]
        Some saiden wommen loven best richesse;
     Some saide honour, some saide jolinesse;°   wantonness
     Some riche array, some saiden lust° abedde,   pleasure
     And ofte time to be widwe and wedde.
935 Some saide that oure herte is most esed
     Whan that we been yflatered and yplesed—
     He gooth ful neigh the soothe, I wol nat lie:
     A man shal winne us best with flaterye,
     And with attendance and with bisinesse°   assiduousness
940 Been we ylimed,° bothe more and lesse.   ensnared
        And some sayen that we loven best
     For to be free, and do right as us lest,°   it pleases
     And that no man repreve° us of oure vice,   reprove
     But saye that we be wise and no thing nice.°   foolish
945 For trewely, ther is noon of us alle,
     If any wight wol clawe us on the galle,°   sore spot
     That we nil kike° for° he saith us sooth: kick / because
     Assaye and he shal finde it that so dooth.
     For be we nevere so vicious withinne,
950 We wol be holden° wise and clene of sinne.   considered
        And some sayn that greet delit han we

---

2. I.e., country.   3. Agreeing together.

For to be holden stable and eek secree,[4]
And in oo purpos stedefastly to dwelle,
And nat biwraye° thing that men us telle—   *disclose*
955   But that tale is nat worth a rake-stele.°   *rake handle*
Pardee, we wommen conne no thing hele:°   *conceal*
Witnesse on Mida.° Wol ye heere the tale?   *Midas*
      Ovide, amonges othere thinges smale,
Saide Mida hadde under his longe heres,
960   Growing upon his heed, two asses eres,
The whiche vice° he hidde as he best mighte   *defect*
Ful subtilly from every mannes sighte,
That save his wif ther wiste° of it namo.   *knew*
He loved hire most and trusted hire also.
965   He prayed hire that to no creature
She sholde tellen of his disfigure.°   *deformity*
      She swoor him nay, for al this world to winne,
She nolde do that vilainye or sinne
To make hir housbonde han so foul a name:
970   She nolde nat telle it for hir owene shame.
But nathelees, hir thoughte that she dyde°   *would die*
That she so longe sholde a conseil° hide;   *secret*
Hire thoughte it swal° so sore about hir herte   *swelled*
That nedely som word hire moste asterte,[5]
975   And sith she dorste nat telle it to no man,
Down to a mareis° faste° by she ran—   *marsh / close*
Til she cam there hir herte was afire—
And as a bitore[6] bombleth in the mire,
She laide hir mouth unto the water down:
980   "Biwray° me nat, thou water, with thy soun,"°   *betray / sound*
Quod she. "To thee I telle it and namo:°   *to no one else*
Myn housbonde hath longe asses eres two.
Now is myn herte al hool,[7] now is it oute.
I mighte no lenger keep it, out of doute."
985   Here may ye see, though we a time abide,
Yit oute it moot:° we can no conseil hide.   *must*
The remenant of the tale if ye wol heere,
Redeth Ovide, and ther ye may it lere.[8]
      This knight of which my tale is specially,
990   Whan that he sawgh he mighte nat come thereby—
This is to saye what wommen loven most—
Within his brest ful sorweful was his gost,°   *spirit*
But hoom he gooth, he mighte nat sojourne:°   *delay*
The day was come that hoomward moste° he turne.   *must*
995   And in his way it happed him to ride
In al this care under a forest side,

---

4. Reliable and also close-mouthed.
5. Of necessity some word must escape her.
6. Bittern, a heron. "Bombleth": makes a boom-ing noise.

7. I.e., sound.
8. Learn. The reeds disclosed the secret by whis-pering "*aures aselli*" (ass's ears).

Wher as he sawgh upon a daunce go
Of ladies foure and twenty and yit mo;
Toward the whiche daunce he drow ful yerne,[9]
1000   In hope that som wisdom sholde he lerne.
But certainly, er he cam fully there,
Vanisshed was this daunce, he niste° where.   *knew not*
No creature sawgh he that bar° lif,   *bore*
Save on the greene he sawgh sitting a wif—
1005   A fouler wight ther may no man devise.°   *imagine*
Again[1] the knight this olde wif gan rise,
And saide, "Sire knight, heer forth lith° no way.°   *lies / road*
Telle me what ye seeken, by youre fay.°   *faith*
Paraventure it may the better be:
1010   Thise olde folk conne° muchel thing," quod she.   *know*
    "My leve moder,"° quod this knight, "certain,   *mother*
I nam but deed but if that I can sayn
What thing it is that wommen most desire.
Coude ye me wisse,° I wolde wel quite youre hire."[2]   *teach*
1015   "Plight me thy trouthe here in myn hand," quod she,
"The nexte thing that I requere° thee,   *require of*
Thou shalt it do, if it lie in thy might,
And I wol telle it you er it be night."
    "Have heer my trouthe," quod the knight. "I graunte."
1020   "Thanne," quod she, "I dar me wel avaunte°   *boast*
Thy lif is sauf,° for I wol stande therby.   *safe*
Upon my lif the queene wol saye as I.
Lat see which is the pruddeste° of hem alle   *proudest*
That wereth on[3] a coverchief or a calle°   *headdress*
1025   That dar saye nay of that I shal thee teche.
Lat us go forth withouten lenger speeche."
Tho rouned° she a pistel° in his ere,   *whispered / sentence*
And bad him to be glad and have no fere.
    Whan they be comen to the court, this knight
1030   Saide he hadde holde his day as he hadde hight,°   *promised*
And redy was his answere, as he saide.
Ful many a noble wif, and many a maide,
And many a widwe—for that they been wise—
The queene hirself sitting as justise,
1035   Assembled been this answere for to heere,
And afterward this knight was bode° appere.   *bidden to*
To every wight comanded was silence,
And that the knight sholde telle in audience°   *open hearing*
What thing that worldly wommen loven best.
1040   This knight ne stood nat stille as dooth a best,°   *beast*
But to his question anoon answerde
With manly vois that al the court it herde.
    "My lige° lady, generally," quod he,   *liege*

9. Drew very quickly.   2. Repay your trouble.
1. I.e., to meet.   3. That wears.

"Wommen desire to have sovereinetee°   *dominion*
1045 As wel over hir housbonde as hir love,
And for to been in maistrye him above.
This is youre moste desir though ye me kille.
Dooth as you list:° I am here at youre wille."   *please*
In al the court ne was ther wif ne maide
1050 Ne widwe that contraried° that he saide,   *contradicted*
But saiden he was worthy han° his lif.   *to have*
And with that word up sterte° that olde wif,   *started*
Which that the knight sawgh sitting on the greene;
"Mercy," quod she, "my soverein lady queene,
1055 Er that youre court departe, do me right.
I taughte this answere unto the knight,
For which he plighte me his trouthe there
The firste thing I wolde him requere°   *require*
He wolde it do, if it laye in his might.
1060 Bifore the court thanne praye I thee, sire knight,"
Quod she, "that thou me take unto thy wif,
For wel thou woost that I have kept° thy lif.   *saved*
If I saye fals, say nay, upon thy fay."
This knight answerde, "Allas and wailaway,
1065 I woot right wel that swich was my biheeste.°   *promise*
For Goddes love, as chees° a newe requeste: *choose*
Taak al my good and lat my body go."
"Nay thanne," quod she, "I shrewe° us bothe two.   *curse*
For though that I be foul and old and poore,
1070 I nolde for al the metal ne for ore
That under erthe is grave° or lith° above,   *buried / lies*
But if thy wif I were and eek thy love."
"My love," quod he. "Nay, my dampnacioun!°   *damnation*
Allas, that any of my nacioun[4]
1075 Sholde evere so foule disparaged° be."   *disgraced*
But al for nought, th'ende is this, that he
Constrained was: he needes moste hire wedde,
And taketh his olde wif and gooth to bedde.
Now wolden some men saye, paraventure,
1080 That for my necligence I do no cure[5]
To tellen you the joye and al th'array
That at the feeste was that ilke day.
To which thing shortly answere I shal:
I saye ther nas no joye ne feeste at al;
1085 Ther nas but hevinesse and muche sorwe.
For prively he wedded hire on morwe,[6]
And al day after hidde him as an owle,
So wo was him, his wif looked so foule.
Greet was the wo the knight hadde in his thought:
1090 Whan he was with his wif abedde brought,

4. I.e., family.   6. In the morning.
5. I do not take the trouble.

He walweth° and he turneth to and fro.   *tosses*
His olde wif lay smiling everemo,
And saide, "O dere housbonde, benedicite,°   *bless me*
Fareth° every knight thus with his wif as ye?   *behaves*
1095   Is this the lawe of King Arthures hous?
Is every knight of his thus daungerous?°   *stand-offish*
I am youre owene love and youre wif;
I am she which that saved hath youre lif;
And certes yit ne dide I you nevere unright.
1100   Why fare ye thus with me this firste night?
Ye faren like a man hadde lost his wit.
What is my gilt? For Goddes love, telle it,
And it shal been amended if I may."
        "Amended!" quod this knight. "Allas, nay, nay,
1105   It wol nat been amended neveremo.
Thou art so lothly° and so old also,   *loathsome*
And therto comen of so lowe a kinde,°   *race*
That litel wonder is though I walwe and winde.°   *turn*
So wolde God myn herte wolde breste!"°   *break*
1110   "Is this," quod she, "the cause of youre unreste?"
"Ye, certainly," quod he. "No wonder is."
        "Now sire," quod she, "I coude amende al this,
If that me liste, er it were dayes three,
So° wel ye mighte bere you⁷ unto me.   *provided that*
1115   "But for ye speken of swich gentilesse
As is descended out of old richesse—
That therfore sholden ye be gentilmen—
Swich arrogance is nat worth an hen.
Looke who that is most vertuous alway,
1120   Privee and apert,⁸ and most entendeth ay
To do the gentil deedes that he can,
Taak him for the gretteste° gentilman.   *greatest*
Crist wol° we claime of him oure gentilesse,   *desires that*
Nat of oure eldres for hir 'old richesse.'⁹
1125   For though they yive us al hir heritage,
For which we claime to been of heigh parage,°   *descent*
Yit may they nat biquethe for no thing
To noon of us hir vertuous living,
That made hem gentilmen ycalled be,
1130   And bad¹ us folwen hem in swich degree.
        "Wel can the wise poete of Florence,
That highte Dant,² speken in this sentence;°   *topic*
Lo, in swich manere rym is Dantes tale:
'Ful selde° up riseth by his braunches³ smale   *seldom*
1135   Prowesse° of man, for God of his prowesse   *excellence*
Wol that of him we claime oure gentilesse.'

7. Behave.   1. I.e., they bade.
8. Privately and publicly.   2. Dante; see his *Convivio*.
9. See Chaucer's *Gentilesse*, line 16.   3. I.e., by its own efforts.

For of oure eldres may we no thing claime
But temporel thing that man may hurte and maime.
Eek every wight woot this as wel as I,
1140 If gentilesse were planted natureelly
Unto a certain linage down the line,
Privee and apert, thanne wolde they nevere fine°   cease
To doon of gentilesse the faire office°—   function
They mighte do no vilainye or vice.
1145 "Taak fir and beer° it in the derkeste hous   bear
Bitwixe this and the Mount of Caucasus,
And lat men shette° the dores and go thenne,°   shut / thence
Yit wol the fir as faire lie[4] and brenne°   burn
As twenty thousand men mighte it biholde:
1150 His° office natureel ay wol it holde,   its
Up° peril of my lif, til that it die.   upon
Heer may ye see wel how that genterye°   gentility
Is nat annexed° to possessioun,[5]   related
Sith folk ne doon hir operacioun
1155 Alway, as dooth the fir, lo, in his kinde.°   nature
For God it woot, men may wel often finde
A lordes sone do shame and vilainye;
And he that wol han pris of his gentrye,[6]
For he was boren° of a gentil hous,   born
1160 And hadde his eldres noble and vertuous,
And nil himselven do no gentil deedes,
Ne folwen his gentil auncestre that deed° is,   dead
He nis nat gentil, be he duc or erl—
For vilaines sinful deedes maken a cherl.
1165 Thy gentilesse[7] nis but renomee°   renown
Of thine auncestres for hir heigh bountee,°   magnanimity
Which is a straunge° thing for thy persone.   alien
For gentilesse[8] cometh fro God allone.
Thanne comth oure verray gentilesse of grace:
1170 It was no thing biquethe us with oure place.
Thenketh how noble, as saith Valerius,[9]
Was thilke Tullius Hostilius
That out of poverte° roos to heigh noblesse.   poverty
Redeth Senek° and redeth eek Boece:°   Seneca / Boethius
1175 Ther shul ye seen expres that no drede° is   doubt
That he is gentil that dooth gentil deedes.
And therfore, leve housbonde, I thus conclude:
Al were it that mine auncestres weren rude,[1]
Yit may the hye God—and so hope I—
1180 Graunte me grace to liven vertuously.
Thanne am I gentil whan that I biginne

4. I.e., remain.   8. I.e., true gentility.
5. I.e., inheritable property.   9. A Roman historian.
6. Have credit for his noble birth.   1. I.e., low born.
7. I.e., the gentility you claim.

To liven vertuously and waive° sinne.   *avoid*
    "And ther as ye of poverte me repreve,°   *reprove*
The hye God, on whom that we bileve,
1185 In wilful° poverte chees° to live his lif;   *voluntary / chose*
And certes every man, maiden, or wif
May understonde that Jesus, hevene king,
Ne wolde nat chese° a vicious living.   *choose*
Glad poverte is an honeste° thing, certain;   *honorable*
1190 This wol Senek and othere clerkes sayn.
Whoso that halt him paid of[2] his poverte,
I holde him riche al hadde he nat a sherte.°   *shirt*
He that coveiteth[3] is a poore wight,
For he wolde han that is nat in his might;
1195 But he that nought hath, ne coveiteth° have,   *desires to*
Is riche, although we holde him but a knave.
Verray poverte it singeth proprely.°   *appropriately*
Juvenal saith of poverte, 'Merily
The poore man, whan he gooth by the waye,
1200 Biforn the theves he may singe and playe.'
Poverte is hateful good, and as I gesse,
A ful greet bringere out of bisinesse;[4]
A greet amendere eek of sapience
To him that taketh it in pacience;
1205 Poverte is thing, although it seeme elenge,°   *wretched*
Possession that no wight wol chalenge;[5]
Poverte ful often, whan a man is lowe,
Maketh[6] his God and eek himself to knowe;
Poverte a spectacle° is, as thinketh me,   *pair of spectacles*
1210 Thurgh which he may his verray freendes see.
And therfore, sire, sin that I nought you greve,
Of my poverte namore ye me repreve.°   *reproach*
    "Now sire, of elde° ye repreve me: *old age*
And certes sire, though noon auctoritee
1215 Were in no book, ye gentils of honour
Sayn that men sholde an old wight doon favour,
And clepe him fader for youre gentilesse—
And auctours[7] shal I finde, as I gesse.
    "Now ther ye saye that I am foul and old:
1220 Thanne drede you nought to been a cokewold,°   *cuckold*
For filthe and elde, also mote I thee,[8]
Been grete wardeins° upon chastitee.   *guardians*
But nathelees, sin I knowe your delit,
I shal fulfille youre worldly appetit.
1225   "Chees now," quod she, "oon of thise thinges twaye:
To han me foul and old til that I deye

---

2. Considers himself satisfied with.   6. I.e., makes him.
3. I.e., suffers desires.   7. I.e., authorities.
4. I.e., cares.   8. So may I thrive.
5. Claim as his property.

And be to you a trewe humble wif,
And nevere you displese in al my lif,
Or elles ye wol han me yong and fair,
1230   And take youre aventure° of the repair[9]   chance
That shal be to youre hous by cause of me—
Or in some other place, wel may be.
Now chees youreselven wheither° that you liketh."   whichever
  This knight aviseth him[1] and sore siketh;°   sighs
1235   But atte laste he saide in this manere:
"My lady and my love, and wif so dere,
I putte me in youre wise governaunce:
Cheseth° youreself which may be most plesaunce[2]   choose
And most honour to you and me also.
1240   I do no fors the wheither[3] of the two,
For as you liketh it suffiseth° me."   satisfies
  "Thanne have I gete° of you maistrye," quod she,   got
"Sin I may chese and governe as me lest?"°   it pleases
  "Ye, certes, wif," quod he. "I holde it best."
1245   "Kisse me," quod she. "We be no lenger wrothe.
For by my trouthe, I wol be to you bothe—
This is to sayn, ye, bothe fair and good.
I praye to God that I mote sterven wood,[4]
But° I to you be al so good and trewe   unless
1250   As evere was wif sin that the world was newe.
And but I be tomorn° as fair to seene   tomorrow morning
As any lady, emperisse, or queene,
That is bitwixe the eest and eek the west,
Do with my lif and deeth right as you lest:
1255   Caste up the curtin,[5] looke how that it is."
  And whan the knight sawgh verraily al this,
That she so fair was and so yong therto,
For joye he hente° hire in his armes two;   took
His herte bathed in a bath of blisse;
1260   A thousand time arewe° he gan hire kisse,   in a row
And she obeyed him in every thing
That mighte do him plesance or liking.°   pleasure
And thus they live unto hir lives ende
In parfit° joye. And Jesu Crist us sende   perfect
1265   Housbondes meeke, yonge, and fresshe abedde—
And grace t'overbide° hem that we wedde.   outlive
And eek I praye Jesu shorte° hir lives   shorten
That nought wol be governed by hir wives,
And olde and angry nigardes of dispence°—   expenditure
1270   God sende hem soone a verray° pestilence!   veritable

---

9. I.e., visits.   3. I do not care whichever.
1. Considers.   4. Die mad.
2. Pleasure.   5. The curtain around the bed.

The Pardoner's Prologue and Tale[1]

The Introduction

 Oure Hoste gan to swere as he were wood;°   *insane*
"Harrow,"° quod he, "by nailes[2] and by blood,   *help*
This was a fals cherl and a fals justise.[3]
As shameful deeth as herte may devise
5 Come to thise juges and hir advocats.
Algate° this sely° maide is slain, allas!   *at any rate / innocent*
Allas, too dere boughte she beautee!
Wherfore I saye alday° that men may see   *always*

1. The Pardoner is the chief actor in a grim comedy which shows how a clever hypocrite exploits Christian principles in order to enrich himself— and which, in the Epilogue, suggests that the exploiter of Christian principles is not immune to their operation. The medieval pardoner's function was to collect money for charitable enterprises supported by branches of the church and to act as the Pope's agent in rewarding donors with some temporal remission of their sins. According to theological doctrine, St. Peter—and through him his papal successors—received from Christ the power to make a gift of mercy from God's infinite treasury to those of the faithful that had earned special favor, such as contributors to charity. The charitable enterprises themselves—generally hospitals—hired pardoners to raise money, but the pardoners had also to be licensed by the Pope to pass on to contributors the papal indulgence. By canon law pardoners were permitted to work only in a prescribed area; within that area they might visit churches during Sunday service, briefly explain their mission, receive contributions, and, in the Pope's name, issue indulgence, which was considered not a sale, but a free gift made in return for a free gift. In actual fact pardoners seem seldom to have behaved as the law required them. Since a parish priest was forbidden to exclude properly licensed pardoners, they made their way into churches at will, and once there did not confine themselves to a mere statement of their business, but rather, in order to make the congregation free of its gifts, preached highly emotive sermons and boasted of the extraordinary efficacy of their own particular pardon, claiming for it powers that not even the Pope could have invested it with. An honest pardoner, if such existed, was entitled to a percentage of his collections; dishonest pardoners took more than their share, and some took everything; indeed, some were complete frauds, bearing forged credentials which, in an age when even clerical illiteracy was common, were no less impressive than if they had been real.

 While Chaucer's Pardoner belongs, as he boastfully tells us, to the most dishonest class of fundgatherers, he is an extremely able one. His text is always the same: *Radix malorum est cupiditas*, "The love of money is the root of all evil," and he uses it most effectively in order to frighten his hearers

into a generosity that will fulfill his own cupidity. The Pardoner's audacious description of his behavior in a parish church is followed by a sample sermon on his invariable text. Aware that his audience is more interested in narrative than in the moralization one expects of a sermon he first introduces the three dissolute young men of his *exemplum*, that is, of the story which is to illustrate concretely the sermon's point. Having titillated his hearers with the promise of a lurid story, he proceeds to the moralization; curiously enough, this does not concern the sin of avarice, but drunkenness, gluttony, lechery, gambling, and cursing. Yet the apparent lack of logic serves the Pardoner's deeper purpose, for these are the sins people find it exciting to hear about. When his audience has thus been emotionally prepared by a discussion of the debauchees' more flamboyant sins, the Pardoner tells his *exemplum* of the destructiveness of avarice, shutting it off at the moment of highest interest, and concluding with a demand to the congregation for money in return for his pardon.

 The story of the young men who seek Death only to find him in a treasure that had made them forget him is a masterpiece of irony, and indeed the Pardoner is in all ways a master ironist. So highly developed is his own sense of irony that it enables him to feel superior not only to other men but to God, for he dares to exempt himself from the effect of his Christian text. Yet the brief Epilogue seems to show that God's irony, like His other attributes, is supreme. The one fact that the Pardoner's candid confession has concealed—that it was perhaps spoken in order to conceal—is that he is a eunuch. When in the Epilogue his proud avarice leads him to see if he can get money from the pilgrims to whom he has revealed his hypocrisy, the Pardoner's secret is revealed by the Host's coarse response, and the verbal facility by which he maintains his superiority fails him.

2. I.e., God's nails.

3. The Host has been affected by the Physician's sad tale of the Roman maiden Virginia, whose great beauty caused a judge to attempt to obtain her person by means of a trumped-up lawsuit in which he connived with a "churl" who claimed her as his slave; in order to preserve her chastity, her father killed her.

The yiftes of Fortune and of Nature
10 Been cause of deeth to many a creature.
As bothe yiftes that I speke of now,
Men han ful ofte more for harm than prow.°   *benefit*
    "But trewely, myn owene maister dere,
This is a pitous tale for to heere.
15 But nathelees, passe over, is no fors:[4]
I praye to God to save thy gentil cors,°   *body*
And eek thine urinals and thy jurdones,[5]
Thyn ipocras[6] and eek thy galiones,
And every boiste° ful of thy letuarye°—   *box / medicine*
20 God blesse hem, and oure lady Sainte Marye.
So mote I theen,[7] thou art a propre man,
And lik a prelat, by Saint Ronian![8]
Saide I nat wel? I can nat speke in terme.[9]
But wel I woot, thou doost° myn herte to erme°   *make / grieve*
25 That I almost have caught a cardinacle.[1]
By corpus bones,[2] but if I have triacle,°   *medicine*
Or elles a draughte of moiste° and corny° ale,   *fresh / malty*
Or but I here anoon° a merye tale,   *at once*
Myn herte is lost for pitee of this maide.
30 "Thou bel ami,[3] thou Pardoner," he saide,
"Tel us som mirthe or japes° right anoon."   *joke*
    "It shal be doon," quod he, "by Saint Ronion.
But first," quod he, "here at this ale-stake[4]
I wol bothe drinke and eten of a cake."
35   And right anoon thise gentils gan to crye,
"Nay, lat him telle us of no ribaudye.°   *ribaldry*
Tel us som moral thing that we may lere,°   *learn*
Som wit,[5] and thanne wol we gladly heere."
    "I graunte, ywis," quod he, "but I moot thinke
40 Upon som honeste° thing whil that I drinke."   *decent*

The Prologue

Lordinges—quod he—in chirches whan I preche,
I paine me[6] to han an hautein° speeche,   *loud*
And ringe it out as round as gooth a belle,
For I can al by rote[7] that I telle.
45 My theme is alway oon,[8] and evere was:

4. I.e., never mind.
5. Jordans (chamber pots): the Host is somewhat confused in his endeavor to use technical medical terms.
6. A medicinal drink named after Hippocrates. "Galiones": a medicine, probably invented on the spot by the Host, named after Galen.
7. So might I thrive.
8. St. Ronan or St. Ninian, with a possible play on "runnion" (sexual organ).
9. Speak in technical idiom.

1. Apparently a cardiac condition, confused in the Host's mind with a cardinal.
2. An illiterate oath, mixing "God's bones" with *corpus dei*. "But if": unless.
3. Fair friend.
4. Sign of a tavern.
5. I.e., something with significance.
6. Take pains.
7. I know all by heart.
8. I.e., the same.

Radix malorum est cupiditas.[9]

<table>
<tr><td></td><td>First I pronounce whennes° that I come,</td><td style="text-align:right">*whence*</td></tr>
<tr><td></td><td>And thanne my bulles[1] shewe I alle and some:</td><td></td></tr>
<tr><td></td><td>Oure lige lordes seel on my patente,[2]</td><td></td></tr>
<tr><td>50</td><td>That shewe I first, my body to warente,°</td><td style="text-align:right">*keep safe*</td></tr>
<tr><td></td><td>That no man be so bold, ne preest ne clerk,</td><td></td></tr>
<tr><td></td><td>Me to destourbe of Cristes holy werk.</td><td></td></tr>
<tr><td></td><td>And after that thanne telle I forth my tales[3]—</td><td></td></tr>
<tr><td></td><td>Bulles of popes and of cardinales,</td><td></td></tr>
<tr><td>55</td><td>Of patriarkes and bisshopes I shewe,</td><td></td></tr>
<tr><td></td><td>And in Latin I speke a wordes fewe,</td><td></td></tr>
<tr><td></td><td>To saffron with[4] my predicacioun,°</td><td style="text-align:right">*preaching*</td></tr>
<tr><td></td><td>And for to stire hem to devocioun.</td><td></td></tr>
<tr><td></td><td>Thanne shewe I forth my longe crystal stones,°</td><td style="text-align:right">*jars*</td></tr>
<tr><td>60</td><td>Ycrammed ful of cloutes° and of bones—</td><td style="text-align:right">*rags*</td></tr>
<tr><td></td><td>Relikes been they, as weenen° they eechoon.</td><td style="text-align:right">*suppose*</td></tr>
<tr><td></td><td>Thanne have I in laton° a shulder-boon</td><td style="text-align:right">*zinc*</td></tr>
<tr><td></td><td>Which that was of an holy Jewes sheep.</td><td></td></tr>
<tr><td></td><td>"Goode men," I saye, "take of my wordes keep:°</td><td style="text-align:right">*notice*</td></tr>
<tr><td>65</td><td>If that this boon be wasshe in any welle,</td><td></td></tr>
<tr><td></td><td>If cow, or calf, or sheep, or oxe swelle,</td><td></td></tr>
<tr><td></td><td>That any worm hath ete or worm ystonge,[5]</td><td></td></tr>
<tr><td></td><td>Take water of that welle and wassh his tonge,</td><td></td></tr>
<tr><td></td><td>And it is hool[6] anoon. And ferthermoor,</td><td></td></tr>
<tr><td>70</td><td>Of pokkes° and of scabbe and every soor°</td><td style="text-align:right">*pox / sore*</td></tr>
<tr><td></td><td>Shal every sheep be hool that of this welle</td><td></td></tr>
<tr><td></td><td>Drinketh a draughte. Take keep eek° that I telle:</td><td style="text-align:right">*also*</td></tr>
<tr><td></td><td>If that the goode man that the beestes oweth°</td><td style="text-align:right">*owns*</td></tr>
<tr><td></td><td>Wol every wike,° er that the cok him croweth,</td><td style="text-align:right">*week*</td></tr>
<tr><td>75</td><td>Fasting drinken of this welle a draughte—</td><td></td></tr>
<tr><td></td><td>As thilke° holy Jew oure eldres taughte—</td><td style="text-align:right">*that same*</td></tr>
<tr><td></td><td>His beestes and his stoor° shal multiplye.</td><td style="text-align:right">*stock*</td></tr>
<tr><td></td><td>"And sire, also it heleth jalousye:</td><td></td></tr>
<tr><td></td><td>For though a man be falle in jalous rage,</td><td></td></tr>
<tr><td>80</td><td>Lat maken with this water his potage,°</td><td style="text-align:right">*soup*</td></tr>
<tr><td></td><td>And nevere shal he more his wif mistriste,°</td><td style="text-align:right">*mistrust*</td></tr>
<tr><td></td><td>Though he the soothe of hir defaute wiste,[7]</td><td></td></tr>
<tr><td></td><td>Al hadde she[8] taken preestes two or three.</td><td></td></tr>
<tr><td></td><td>"Here is a mitein° eek that ye may see:</td><td style="text-align:right">*mitten*</td></tr>
<tr><td>85</td><td>He that his hand wol putte in this mitein</td><td></td></tr>
<tr><td></td><td>He shal have multiplying of his grain,</td><td></td></tr>
<tr><td></td><td>Whan he hath sowen, be it whete or otes—</td><td></td></tr>
<tr><td></td><td>So that he offre pens or elles grotes.[9]</td><td></td></tr>
<tr><td></td><td>"Goode men and wommen, oo thing warne I you:</td><td></td></tr>
</table>

9. Avarice is the root of evil (1 Timothy 6.10).
1. Episcopal mandates. "Alle and some": each and every one.
2. I.e., the Pope's seal on my papal license.
3. I go on with my yarn.
4. To add spice to.

5. That has eaten any worm or been bitten by any snake.
6. I.e., sound.
7. Knew the truth of her infidelity.
8. Even if she had.
9. Pennies, groats, coins.

90 If any wight be in this chirche now
That hath doon sinne horrible, that he
Dar nat for shame of it yshriven° be,   *absolved*
Or any womman, be she yong or old,
That hath ymaked hir housbonde cokewold,°   *cuckold*
95 Swich folk shal have no power ne no grace
To offren to[1] my relikes in this place;
And whoso findeth him out of swich blame,
He wol come up and offre in Goddes name,
And I assoile° him by the auctoritee   *absolve*
100 Which that by bulle ygraunted was to me."
    By this gaude° have I wonne, yeer by yeer,   *trick*
An hundred mark[2] sith° I was pardoner.   *since*
I stonde lik a clerk in my pulpet,
And whan the lewed° peple is down yset,   *ignorant*
105 I preche so as ye han herd bifore,
And telle an hundred false japes° more.   *tricks*
Thanne paine I me[3] to strecche forth the nekke,
And eest and west upon the peple I bekke[4]
As dooth a douve,° sitting on a berne;°   *dove / barn*
110 Mine handes and my tonge goon so yerne°   *fast*
That it is joye to see my bisinesse.
Of avarice and of swich cursednesse°   *sin*
Is al my preching, for to make hem free°   *generous*
To yiven hir pens, and namely° unto me,   *especially*
115 For myn entente is nat but for to winne,[5]
And no thing for correccion of sinne:
I rekke° nevere whan that they been beried°   *care / buried*
Though that hir soules goon a-blakeberied.[6]
For certes, many a predicacioun°   *sermon*
120 Comth ofte time of yvel entencioun:
Som for plesance of folk and flaterye,
To been avaunced° by ypocrisye,   *promoted*
And som for vaine glorye, and som for hate;
For whan I dar noon otherways debate,°   *fight*
125 Thanne wol I stinge him with my tonge smerte
In preching, so that he shal nat asterte°   *escape*
To been defamed falsly, if that he
Hath trespassed to my bretheren[7] or to me.
For though I telle nought his propre name,
130 Men shal wel knowe that it is the same
By signes and by othere circumstaunces.
Thus quite° I folk that doon us displesaunces;[8]   *pay back*
Thus spete° I out my venim under hewe°   *spit / color*
Of holinesse, to seeme holy and trewe.

---

1. To make gifts in reverence of.   5. Only to gain.
2. Marks (pecuniary units).   6. Go blackberrying, i.e., go to hell.
3. I take pains.   7. Injured my fellow-pardoners.
4. I.e., I shake my head.   8. Do us discourtesies.

135 But shortly myn entente I wol devise:°   *describe*
     I preche of no thing but for coveitise;
     Therfore my theme is yit and evere was
     Radix malorum est cupiditas.
         Thus can I preche again that same vice
140 Which that I use, and that is avarice.
     But though myself be gilty in that sinne,
     Yit can I make other folk to twinne°   *separate*
     From avarice, and sore to repente—
     But that is nat my principal entente:
145 I preche no thing but for coveitise.
     Of this matere it oughte ynough suffise.
         Thanne telle I hem ensamples⁹ many oon
     Of olde stories longe time agoon,
     For lewed° peple loven tales olde—   *ignorant*
150 Swiche thinges can they wel reporte and holde.¹
     What, trowe° ye that whiles I may preche,   *believe*
     And winne gold and silver for° I teche,   *because*
     That I wol live in poverte wilfully?
     Nay, nay, I thoughte° it nevere, trewely,   *intended*
155 For I wol preche and begge in sondry landes;
     I wol nat do no labour with mine handes,
     Ne make baskettes and live therby,
     By cause I wol nat beggen idelly.²
     I wol none of the Apostles countrefete:°   *imitate*
160 I wol have moneye, wolle,° cheese, and whete,   *wool*
     Al were it³ yiven of the pooreste page,
     Or of the pooreste widwe in a village—
     Al sholde hir children sterve⁴ for famine.
     Nay, I wol drinke licour of the vine
165 And have a joly wenche in every town.
     But herkneth, lordinges, in conclusioun,
     Youre liking° is that I shal telle a tale: *pleasure*
     Now have I dronke a draughte of corny ale,
     By God, I hope I shal you telle a thing
170 That shal by reson been at youre liking;
     For though myself be a ful vicious man,
     A moral tale yit I you telle can,
     Which I am wont to preche for to winne.
     Now holde youre pees, my tale I wol biginne.

The Tale

175   In Flandres whilom° was a compaignye   *once*
     Of yonge folk that haunteden° folye—   *practiced*
     As riot, hasard, stewes,⁵ and tavernes,

---

9. *Exempla* (stories illustrating moral principles).   3. Even though it were.
1. Repeat and remember.   4. Even though her children should die.
2. I.e., without profit.   5. Wild parties, gambling, brothels.

Wher as with harpes, lutes, and giternes°   *guitars*
They daunce and playen at dees° bothe day and night,   *dice*
180 And ete also and drinke over hir might,[6]
Thurgh which they doon the devel sacrifise
Within that develes temple in cursed wise
By superfluitee° abhominable.   *overindulgence*
Hir othes been so grete and so dampnable
185 That it is grisly for to heere hem swere:
Oure blessed Lordes body they totere[7]—
Hem thoughte that Jewes rente° him nought ynough.   *tore*
And eech of hem at otheres sinne lough.°   *laughed*
And right anoon thanne comen tombesteres,°   *dancing girls*
190 Fetis° and smale,° and yonge frutesteres,[8]   *shapely / neat*
Singeres with harpes, bawdes,° wafereres[9]—   *pimps*
Whiche been the verray develes officeres,
To kindle and blowe the fir of lecherye
That is annexed unto glotonye:[1]
195 The Holy Writ take I to my witnesse
That luxure° is in win and dronkenesse.   *lechery*
Lo, how that dronken Lot[2] unkindely°   *unnaturally*
Lay by his doughtres two unwitingly:
So dronke he was he niste° what he wroughte.   *didn't know*
200 Herodes, who so wel the stories soughte,[3]
Whan he of win was repleet at his feeste,
Right at his owene table he yaf his heeste°   *command*
To sleen° the Baptist John, ful giltelees.   *slay*
Senek[4] saith a good word doutelees:
205 He saith he can no difference finde
Bitwixe a man that is out of his minde
And a man which that is dronkelewe,°   *drunken*
But that woodnesse, yfallen in a shrewe,[5]
Persevereth lenger than dooth dronkenesse.
210 O glotonye, ful of cursednesse!°   *wickedness*
O cause first of oure confusioun!°   *downfall*
O original of oure dampnacioun,°   *damnation*
Til Crist hadde bought° us with his blood again!   *redeemed*
Lo, how dere, shortly for to sayn,
215 Abought° was thilke° cursed vilainye;   *paid for / that same*
Corrupt was al this world for glotonye:
Adam oure fader and his wif also
Fro Paradis to labour and to wo
Were driven for that vice, it is no drede.°   *doubt*
220 For whil that Adam fasted, as I rede,

---

6. Beyond their capacity.
7. Tear apart (a reference to oaths sworn by parts of His body, such as "God's bones!" or "God's teeth!").
8. Fruit-selling girls.
9. Girl cake-vendors.
1. I.e., closely related to gluttony.

2. For Lot, see Genesis 19.30–36.
3. For the story of Herod and St. John the Baptist, see Mark 6.17–29. "Who so . . . soughte": i.e., whoever looked it up in the Gospel would find.
4. Seneca, the Roman Stoic philosopher.
5. But that madness, occurring in a wicked man.

He was in Paradis; and whan that he
Eet° of the fruit defended° on a tree,   *ate / forbidden*
Anoon he was out cast to wo and paine.
O glotonye, on thee wel oughte us plaine!°   *complain*
225   O, wiste a man[6] how manye maladies
Folwen of excesse and of glotonies,
He wolde been the more mesurable°   *moderate*
Of his diete, sitting at his table.
Allas, the shorte throte, the tendre mouth,
230   Maketh that eest and west and north and south,
In erthe, in air, in water, men to swinke,°   *work*
To gete a gloton daintee mete and drinke.
Of this matere, O Paul, wel canstou trete:
"Mete unto wombe,° and wombe eek unto mete,   *belly*
235   Shal God destroyen bothe," as Paulus saith.[7]
Allas, a foul thing is it, by my faith,
To saye this word, and fouler is the deede
Whan man so drinketh of the white and rede[8]
That of his throte he maketh his privee°   *privy*
240   Thurgh thilke cursed superfluitee.°   *overindulgence*
    The Apostle[9] weeping saith ful pitously,
"Ther walken manye of which you told have I—
I saye it now weeping with pitous vois—
They been enemies of Cristes crois,°   *cross*
245   Of whiche the ende is deeth—wombe is hir god!"[1]
O wombe, O bely, O stinking cod,°   *bag*
Fulfilled° of dong° and of corrupcioun!   *filled full / dung*
At either ende of thee foul is the soun.°   *sound*
How greet labour and cost is thee to finde!°   *provide for*
250   Thise cookes, how they stampe[2] and straine and grinde,
And turnen substance into accident[3]
To fulfillen al thy likerous° talent!°   *dainty / appetite*
Out of the harde bones knokke they
The mary,° for they caste nought away   *marrow*
255   That may go thurgh the golet[4] softe and soote.°   *sweetly*
Of spicerye° of leef and bark and roote   *spices*
Shal been his sauce ymaked by delit,
To make him yit a newer appetit.
But certes, he that haunteth swiche delices°   *pleasures*
260   Is deed° whil that he liveth in tho° vices.   *dead / those*
    A lecherous thing is win, and dronkenesse
Is ful of striving° and of wrecchednesse.   *quarreling*
O dronke man, disfigured is thy face!
Sour is thy breeth, foul artou to embrace!
265   And thurgh thy dronke nose seemeth the soun

6. If a man knew.
7. See 1 Corinthians 6.13.
8. I.e., white and red wines.
9. I.e., St. Paul.
1. See Philippians 3.18.

2. Pound.
3. A philosophic joke, depending on the distinction between inner reality (substance) and outward appearance (accident).
4. Through the gullet.

As though thou saidest ay,° "Sampsoun, Sampsoun." *always*
And yit, God woot,° Sampson drank nevere win.[5] *knows*
Thou fallest as it were a stiked swin;[6]
Thy tonge is lost, and al thyn honeste cure,
270 For dronkenesse is verray sepulture° *burial*
Of mannes wit° and his discrecioun. *intelligence*
In whom that drinke hath dominacioun
He can no conseil° keepe, it is no drede.° *secrets / doubt*
Now keepe you fro the white and fro the rede—
275 And namely° fro the white win of Lepe[7] *particularly*
That is to selle in Fisshstreete or in Chepe:[8]
The win of Spaine creepeth subtilly
In othere wines growing faste° by, *close*
Of which ther riseth swich fumositee° *heady fumes*
280 That whan a man hath dronken draughtes three
And weeneth° that he be at hoom in Chepe, *supposes*
He is in Spaine, right at the town of Lepe,
Nat at The Rochele ne at Burdeux town;[9]
And thanne wol he sayn, "Sampsoun, Sampsoun."
285 But herkneth, lordinges, oo° word I you praye, *one*
That alle the soverein actes,[1] dar I saye,
Of victories in the Olde Testament,
Thurgh verray God that is omnipotent,
Were doon in abstinence and in prayere:
290 Looketh° the Bible and ther ye may it lere.° *behold / learn*
  Looke Attila, the grete conquerour,[2]
Deide° in his sleep with shame and dishonour, *died*
Bleeding at his nose in dronkenesse:
A capitain sholde live in sobrenesse.
295 And overal this, aviseth you[3] right wel
What was comanded unto Lamuel[4]—
Nat Samuel, but Lamuel, saye I—
Redeth the Bible and finde it expresly,
Of win-yiving° to hem that han[5] justise: *wine-serving*
300 Namore of this, for it may wel suffise.
  And now that I have spoken of glotonye,
Now wol I you defende° hasardrye:° *prohibit / gambling*
Hasard is verray moder° of lesinges,° *mother / lies*
And of deceite and cursed forsweringes,
305 Blaspheme of Crist, manslaughtre, and wast° also *waste*
Of catel° and of time; and ferthermo, *property*
It is repreve° and contrarye of honour *disgrace*

5. Before Samson's birth an angel told his mother
that he would be a Nazarite throughout his life;
members of this sect took no strong drink.
6. Stuck pig. "Honeste cure": care for self-respect.
7. A town in Spain.
8. Fishstreet and Cheapside in the London market district.
9. The Pardoner is joking about the illegal custom
of adulterating fine wines of Bordeaux and La

Rochelle with strong Spanish wine.
1. Distinguished deeds.
2. Attila was the leader of the Huns who captured
Rome in the 5th century.
3. Consider.
4. Lemuel's mother told him that kings should not
drink (Proverbs 31.4–5).
5. I.e., administer.

For to been holden a commune hasardour,°   *gambler*
And evere the hyer he is of estat
310 The more is he holden desolat.[6]
If that a prince useth hasardrye,
In alle governance and policye
He is, as by commune opinioun,
Yholde the lasse° in reputacioun.   *less*
315   Stilbon, that was a wis embassadour,
Was sent to Corinthe in ful greet honour
Fro Lacedomye° to make hir alliaunce,   *Sparta*
And whan he cam him happede° parchaunce   *it happened*
That alle the gretteste° that were of that lond   *greatest*
320 Playing at the hasard he hem foond,°   *found*
For which as soone as it mighte be
He stal him[7] hoom again to his contree,
And saide, "Ther wol I nat lese° my name,   *lose*
N'I wol nat take on me so greet defame°   *dishonor*
325 You to allye unto none hasardours:
Sendeth othere wise embassadours,
For by my trouthe, me were levere[8] die
Than I you sholde to hasardours allye.
For ye that been so glorious in honours
330 Shal nat allye you with hasardours
As by my wil, ne as by my tretee."°   *treaty*
This wise philosophre, thus saide he.
    Looke eek that to the king Demetrius
The King of Parthes,° as the book[9] saith us,   *Parthians*
335 Sente him a paire of dees° of gold in scorn,   *dice*
For he hadde used hasard therbiforn,
For which he heeld his glorye or his renown
At no value or reputacioun.
Lordes may finden other manere play
340 Honeste° ynough to drive the day away.   *honorable*
    Now wol I speke of othes false and grete
A word or two, as olde bookes trete:
    Greet swering is a thing abhominable,
And fals swering is yit more reprevable.°   *reprehensible*
345 The hye God forbad swering at al—
Witnesse on Mathew.[1] But in special
Of swering saith the holy Jeremie,[2]
"Thou shalt swere sooth thine othes and nat lie,
And swere in doom[3] and eek in rightwisnesse,
350 But idel swering is a cursednesse."°   *wickedness*
    Biholde and see that in the firste Table[4]

---

6. I.e. dissolute.
7. He stole away.
8. I had rather.
9. The book that relates this and the previous incident is the *Policraticus* of the 12th-century Latin writer, John of Salisbury.

1. "But I say unto you, Swear not at all" (Matthew 5.34).
2. Jeremiah 4.2.
3. Equity. "Rightwisnesse": righteousness.
4. I.e., the first 4 of the Ten Commandments.

Of hye Goddes heestes° honorable　　　　　　　*commandments*
How that the seconde heeste of him is this:
"Take nat my name in idel or amis."
355　Lo, rather° he forbedeth swich swering　　　　*sooner*
Than homicide, or many a cursed thing.
I saye that as by ordre thus it stondeth—
This knoweth that[5] his heestes understondeth
How that the seconde heeste of God is that.
360　And fertherover,° I wol thee telle al plat°　　*moreover / flat*
That vengeance shal nat parten° from his hous　　*depart*
That of his othes is too outrageous.
"By Goddes precious herte!" and "By his nailes!"°　*fingernails*
And "By the blood of Crist that is in Hailes,[6]
365　Sevene is my chaunce, and thyn is cink and traye!"[7]
"By Goddes armes, if thou falsly playe
This daggere shal thurghout thyn herte go!"
This fruit cometh of the bicche bones[8] two—
Forswering, ire, falsnesse, homicide.
370　Now for the love of Crist that for us dyde,
Lete° youre othes bothe grete and smale.　　　　*leave*
But sires, now wol I telle forth my tale.
　　Thise riotoures° three of whiche I telle,　　*revelers*
Longe erst er prime[9] ronge of any belle,
375　Were set hem in a taverne to drinke,
And as they sat they herde a belle clinke
Biforn a cors° was caried to his grave.　　　　*corpse*
That oon of hem gan callen to his knave:°　　　*servant*
Go bet,"[1] quod he, "and axe° redily°　　　　*ask / promptly*
380　What cors is this that passeth heer forby,
And looke° that thou reporte his name weel."°　*be sure / well*
　　"Sire," quod this boy, "it needeth neveradeel:[2]
It was me told er ye cam heer two houres.
He was, pardee, an old felawe of youres,
385　And sodeinly he was yslain tonight,°　　　　*last night*
Fordronke° as he sat on his bench upright;　　　*very drunk*
Ther cam a privee° thief men clepeth° Deeth,　*stealthy / call*
That in this contree al the peple sleeth,°　　　*slays*
And with his spere he smoot his herte atwo,
390　And wente his way withouten wordes mo.
He hath a thousand slain this° pestilence.　　　*during this*
And maister, er ye come in his presence,
Me thinketh that it were necessarye
For to be war of swich an adversarye;
395　Beeth redy for to meete him everemore:
Thus taughte me my dame.° I saye namore."　　*mother*

5. I.e., he that.
6. An abbey in Gloucestershire supposed to possess some of Christ's blood.
7. Five and three.

8. I.e., damned dice.
9. Long before 9 A.M.
1. Better, i.e., quick.
2. It isn't a bit necessary.

"By Sainte Marye," saide this taverner,
"The child saith sooth, for he hath slain this yeer,
Henne° over a mile, within a greet village,   *hence*
400 Bothe man and womman, child and hine³ and page.
I trowe° his habitacion be there.   *believe*
To been avised° greet wisdom it were   *wary*
Er that he dide a man a dishonour."
        "Ye, Goddes armes," quod this riotour,
405 "Is it swich peril with him for to meete?
I shal him seeke by way and eek by streete,⁴
I make avow to Goddes digne° bones.   *worthy*
Herkneth, felawes, we three been alle ones:°   *of one mind*
Lat eech of us holde up his hand to other
410 And eech of us bicome otheres brother,
And we wol sleen this false traitour Deeth.
He shal be slain, he that so manye sleeth,
By Goddes dignitee, er it be night."
        Togidres han thise three hir trouthes plight⁵
415 To live and dien eech of hem with other,
As though he were his owene ybore° brother.   *born*
And up they sterte,° al dronken in this rage,   *started*
And forth they goon towardes that village
Of which the taverner hadde spoke biforn,.
420 And many a grisly ooth thanne han they sworn,
And Cristes blessed body they torente:°   *tore apart*
Deeth shal be deed° if that they may him hente.°   *dead / catch*
        Whan they han goon nat fully half a mile,
Right as they wolde han treden° over a stile,   *stepped*
425 An old man and a poore with hem mette;
This olde man ful mekely hem grette,°   *greeted*
And saide thus, "Now lordes, God you see."⁶
        The pruddeste° of thise riotoures three   *proudest*
Answerde again, "What, carl° with sory grace,   *churl*
430 Why artou al forwrapped save thy face?
Why livestou so longe in so greet age?"
        This olde man gan looke in his visage,
And saide thus, "For° I ne can nat finde   *because*
A man, though that I walked into Inde,
435 Neither in citee ne in no village,
That wolde chaunge his youthe for myn age;
And therefore moot I han myn age stille,
As longe time as it is Goddes wille.
        "Ne Deeth, allas, ne wol nat have my lif.
440 Thus walke I lik a restelees caitif,°   *captive*
And on the ground which is my modres° gate   *mother's*
I knokke with my staf bothe erly and late,
And saye, 'Leve° moder, leet me in: *dear*

---

3. Farm laborer.   5. Pledged their words of honor.
4. By highway and byway.   6. May God protect you.

Lo, how I vanisshe, flessh and blood and skin.
445 Allas, whan shal my bones been at reste?
Moder, with you wolde I chaunge° my cheste[7]   *exchange*
That in my chambre longe time hath be,
Ye, for an haire-clout[8] to wrappe me.'
But yit to me she wol nat do that grace,
450 For which ful pale and welked° is my face.   *withered*
But sires, to you it is no curteisye
To speken to an old man vilainye,°   *rudeness*
But° he trespasse° in word or elles in deede.   *unless / offend*
In Holy Writ ye may yourself wel rede,
455 'Agains[9] an old man, hoor° upon his heed,   *hoar*
Ye shall arise.'[1] Wherfore I yive you reed,°   *advice*
Ne dooth unto an old man noon harm now,
Namore than that ye wolde men dide to you
In age, if that ye so longe abide.
460 And God be with you wher ye go° or ride: *walk*
I moot go thider as I have to go."
     "Nay, olde cherl, by God thou shalt nat so,"
Saide this other hasardour anoon.
"Thou partest nat so lightly,° by Saint John!   *easily*
465 Thou speke° right now of thilke traitour Deeth,   *spoke*
That in this contree alle oure freendes sleeth:
Have here my trouthe, as thou art his espye,°   *spy*
Tel wher he is, or thou shalt it abye,°   *pay for*
By God and by the holy sacrament!
470 For soothly thou art oon of his assent[2]
To sleen us yonge folk, thou false thief."
     "Now sires," quod he, "if that ye be so lief°   *anxious*
To finde Deeth, turne up this crooked way,
For in that grove I lafte° him, by my fay,°   *left / faith*
475 Under a tree, and ther he wol abide:
Nat for youre boost° he wol him no thing hide.   *boast*
See ye that ook?° Right ther ye shal him finde.   *oak*
God save you, that boughte again[3] mankinde,
And you amende." Thus saide this olde man.
480   And everich of thise riotoures ran
Til he cam to that tree, and ther they founde
Of florins° fine of gold ycoined rounde   *coins*
Wel neigh an eighte busshels as hem thoughte—
Ne lenger thanne after Deeth they soughte,
485 But eech of hem so glad was of the sighte,
For that the florins been so faire and brighte,
That down they sette hem by this precious hoord.
The worste of hem he spak the firste word:

---

7. Chest for one's belongings, used here as the
symbol for life—or perhaps a coffin.
8. Haircloth, for a winding sheet.
9. In the presence of.

1. Cf. Leviticus 19.32.
2. I.e., one of his party.
3. Redeemed.

"Bretheren," quod he, "take keep° what that I saye: *heed*
490 My wit is greet though that I bourde° and playe.   *joke*
This tresor hath Fortune unto us yiven
In mirthe and jolitee oure lif to liven,
And lightly° as it cometh so wol we spende.   *easily*
Ey, Goddes precious dignitee, who wende[4]
495 Today that we sholde han so fair a grace?
But mighte this gold be caried fro this place
Hoom to myn hous—or elles unto youres—
For wel ye woot that al this gold is oures—
Thanne were we in heigh felicitee.
500 But trewely, by daye it mighte nat be:
Men wolde sayn that we were theves stronge,°   *flagrant*
And for oure owene tresor doon us honge.[5]
This tresor moste ycaried be by nighte,
As wisely and as slyly as it mighte.
505 Therefore I rede° that cut° amonges us alle   *advise / lots*
Be drawe, and lat see wher the cut wol falle;
And he that hath the cut with herte blithe
Shal renne° to the town, and that ful swithe,°   *run / quickly*
And bringe us breed and win ful prively;
510 And two of us shal keepen° subtilly   *guard*
This tresor wel, and if he wol nat tarye,
Whan it is night we wol this tresor carye
By oon assent wher as us thinketh best."
That oon of hem the cut broughte in his fest°   *fist*
515 And bad hem drawe and looke wher it wol falle;
And it fil° on the yongeste of hem alle,   *fell*
And forth toward the town he wente anoon.
And also° soone as that he was agoon,°   *as / gone away*
That oon of hem spak thus unto that other:
520 "Thou knowest wel thou art my sworen brother;
Thy profit wol I telle thee anoon:
Thou woost wel that oure felawe is agoon,
And here is gold, and that ful greet plentee,
That shall departed° been among us three.   *divided*
525 But nathelees, if I can shape° it so   *arrange*
That it departed were among us two,
Hadde I nat doon a freendes turn to thee?"
That other answerde, "I noot[6] how that may be:
He woot that the gold is with us twaye.
530 What shal we doon? What shal we to him saye?"
"Shal it be conseil?"[7] saide the firste shrewe.°   *villain*
"And I shal telle in a wordes fewe
What we shul doon, and bringe it wel aboute."
"I graunte," quod that other, "out of doute,
535 That by my trouthe I wol thee nat biwraye."°   *expose*

4. Who would have supposed.   6. Don't know.
5. Have us hanged.   7. A secret.

"Now," quod the firste, "thou woost wel we be twaye,
And two of us shal strenger° be than oon: *stronger*
Looke whan that he is set that right anoon
Aris as though thou woldest with him playe,
540   And I shal rive° him thurgh the sides twaye,   *pierce*
Whil that thou strugelest with him as in game,
And with thy daggere looke thou do the same;
And thanne shal al this gold departed be,
My dere freend, bitwixe thee and me.
545   Thanne we may bothe oure lustes° al fulfille,   *desires*
And playe at dees° right at oure owene wille."   *dice*
And thus accorded been thise shrewes twaye
To sleen the thridde, as ye han herd me saye.
     This yongeste, which that wente to the town,
550   Ful ofte in herte he rolleth up and down
The beautee of thise florins newe and brighte.
"O Lord," quod he, "if so were that I mighte
Have al this tresor to myself allone,
Ther is no man that liveth under the trone°   *throne*
555   Of God that sholde live so merye as I."
And at the laste the feend oure enemy
Putte in his thought that he sholde poison beye,°   *buy*
With which he mighte sleen his felawes twaye—
Forwhy° the feend foond him in swich livinge   *because*
560   That he hadde leve° him to sorwe bringe:[8]   *permission*
For this was outrely° his fulle entente,   *plainly*
To sleen hem bothe, and nevere to repente.
     And forth he gooth—no lenger wolde he tarye—
Into the town unto a pothecarye,°   *apothecary*
565   And prayed him that he him wolde selle
Som poison that he mighte his rattes quelle,°   *kill*
And eek ther was a polcat[9] in his hawe°   *yard*
That, as he saide, his capons hadde yslawe,°   *slain*
And fain he wolde wreke him[1] if he mighte
570   On vermin that destroyed him[2] by nighte.
     The pothecarye answerde, "And thou shalt have
A thing that, also° God my soule save,   *as*
In al this world there is no creature
That ete or dronke hath of this confiture°—   *mixture*
575   Nat but the mountance° of a corn° of whete—   *amount / grain*
That he ne shal his lif anoon forlete.°   *lose*
Ye, sterve° he shal, and that in lasse° while   *die / less*
Than thou wolt goon a paas[3] nat but a mile,
The poison is so strong and violent."
580   This cursed man hath in his hand yhent°   *taken*
This poison in a box and sith° he ran   *then*

---

8. Christian doctrine teaches that the devil may
not tempt men except with God's permission.
9. A weasellike animal.

1. He would gladly avenge himself.
2. I.e., were ruining his farming.
3. Take a walk.

Into the nexte streete unto a man
And borwed of him large botels three,
And in the two his poison poured he—
585   The thridde he kepte clene for his drinke,
For al the night he shoop him[4] for to swinke°   *work*
In carying of the gold out of that place.
And whan this riotour with sory grace
Hadde filled with win his grete botels three,
590   To his felawes again repaireth he.
     What needeth it to sermone of it more?
For right as they had cast° his deeth bifore,   *plotted*
Right so they han him slain, and that anoon.
And whan that this was doon, thus spak that oon:
595   "Now lat us sitte and drinke and make us merye,
And afterward we wol his body berye."°   *bury*
And with that word it happed him par cas[5]
To take the botel ther the poison was,
And drank, and yaf his felawe drinke also,
600   For which anoon they storven° bothe two.   *died*
     But certes I suppose that Avicen
Wroot nevere in no canon ne in no *fen*[6]
Mo wonder signes[7] of empoisoning
Than hadde thise wrecches two er hir ending:
605   Thus ended been thise homicides two,
And eek the false empoisonere also.
     O cursed sinne of alle cursednesse!
O traitours homicide, O wikkednesse!
O glotonye, luxure,° and hasardrye!   *lechery*
610   Thou blasphemour of Crist with vilainye
And othes grete of usage° and of pride!   *habit*
Allas, mankinde, how may it bitide
That to thy Creatour which that thee wroughte,
And with his precious herte blood thee boughte,°   *redeemed*
615   Thou art so fals and so unkinde,° allas?   *unnatural*
     Now goode men, God foryive you youre trespas,
And ware° you fro the sinne of avarice: *guard*
Myn holy pardon may you alle warice°—   *save*
So that ye offre nobles or sterlinges,[8]
620   Or elles silver brooches, spoones, ringes.
Boweth your heed under this holy bulle!
Cometh up, ye wives, offreth of youre wolle!°   *wool*
Youre name I entre here in my rolle: anoon
Into the blisse of hevene shul ye goon.
625   I you assoile° by myn heigh power—   *absolve*
Ye that wol offre—as clene and eek as cleer

---

4. He was preparing.
5. By chance.
6. The *Canon of Medicine*, by Avicenna, an 11th-century Arabic philosopher, was divided into sections called "fens."
7. More wonderful symptoms.
8. "Nobles" and "sterlinges" were valuable coins.

As ye were born.—And lo, sires, thus I preche.
And Jesu Crist that is oure soules leeche°   *physician*
So graunte you his pardon to receive,
630 For that is best—I wol you nat deceive.

The Epilogue

"But sires, oo word forgat I in my tale:
I have relikes and pardon in my male°   *bag*
As faire as any man in Engelond,
Whiche were me yiven by the Popes hond.
635 If any of you wol of devocioun
Offren and han myn absolucioun,
Come forth anoon, and kneeleth here adown,
And mekely receiveth my pardoun,
Or elles taketh pardon as ye wende,
640 Al newe and fressh at every miles ende—
So that ye offre alway newe and newe⁹
Nobles or pens whiche that be goode and trewe.
It is an honour to everich that is heer
That ye have a suffisant° pardoner   *competent*
645 T'assoile you in contrees as ye ride,
For aventures whiche that may bitide:
Paraventure ther may falle oon or two
Down of his hors and breke his nekke atwo;
Looke which a suretee° is it to you alle   *safeguard*
650 That I am in youre felaweshipe yfalle
That may assoile you, bothe more and lasse,¹
Whan that the soule shal fro the body passe.
I rede° that oure Hoste shal biginne,   *advise*
For he is most envoluped° in sinne.   *involved*
655 Com forth, sire Host, and offre first anoon,
And thou shalt kisse the relikes everichoon,°   *each one*
Ye, for a grote: unbokele° anoon thy purs."   *unbuckle*
    "Nay, nay," quod he, "thanne have I Cristes curs!
Lat be," quod he, "it shal nat be, so theech!°   *may I thrive*
660 Thou woldest make me kisse thyn olde breech°   *breeches*
And swere it were a relik of a saint,
Though it were with thy fundament depeint.°   *stained*
But, by the crois which that Sainte Elaine foond,²
I wolde I hadde thy coilons° in myn hond,   *testicles*
665 In stede of relikes or of saintuarye.°   *relic-box*
Lat cutte hem of: I wol thee helpe hem carye.
They shal be shrined in an hogges tord."°   *turd*
    This Pardoner answerde nat a word:
So wroth he was no word ne wolde he saye.

---

9. Over and over.
1. Both high and low (i.e., everybody).
2. I.e., by the cross that St. Helena found. Helena, mother of Constantine the Great, was reputed
to have found the True Cross.

670   "Now," quod oure Host, "I wol no lenger playe
    With thee, ne with noon other angry man."
       But right anoon the worthy Knight bigan,
    Whan that he sawgh that al the peple lough,°   *laughed*
    "Namore of this, for it is right ynough.
675   Sire Pardoner, be glad and merye of cheere,
    And ye, sire Host that been to me so dere,
    I praye you that ye kisse the Pardoner,
    And Pardoner, I praye thee, draw thee neer,
    And as we diden lat us laughe and playe."
680   Anoon they kiste and riden forth hir waye.

The Nun's Priest's Tale[1]

    A poore widwe somdeel stape° in age   *advanced*
    Was whilom° dwelling in a narwe[2] cotage,   *once upon a time*
    Biside a grove, stonding in a dale:
    This widwe of which I telle you my tale,
5   Sin thilke° day that she was last a wif,   *that same*
    In pacience ladde° a ful simple lif.   *led*
    For litel was hir catel° and hir rente,°   *property / income*
    By housbondrye° of swich as God hire sente   *economy*
    She foond° hirself and eek hir doughtren two.   *provided for*
10   Three large sowes hadde she and namo,
    Three kin,° and eek a sheep that highte° Malle. *cows / was called*
    Ful sooty was hir bowr° and eek hir halle.   *bedroom*
    In which she eet ful many a sclendre° meel;   *scanty*
    Of poinant° sauce hire needed neveradeel: *pungent*
15   No daintee morsel passed thurgh hir throte—
    Hir diete was accordant to hir cote.°   *cottage*
    Repleccioun° ne made hire nevere sik: *overeating*

1. The Nun's Priest's Tale is an example of the literary genre known as the "beast fable," in which animals behave like human beings. The beast fable is inevitably injurious to man's dignity, since to pretend that animals behave like men is to suggest that men behave like animals, for a pig cannot look like a man unless a man in some way looks like a pig. In the Nun's Priest's tale, as in its French source, the history of Reynard the Fox, the beast fable is combined with the mock heroic, and the result is doubly injurious to man's dignity. The elevated language of true heroic poetry means to enhance the splendid deeds of men of great stature, while the elevated language of mock heroic, by treating the trivial as if it were sublime, reveals man's lack of dignity in the awful gulf that separates the idealized language from the petty action it describes; and when the petty action is carried on not even by men, but by animals masquerading as men (that is, by men reduced to the status of animals), the loss of human dignity is even greater.

    The nominal hero of the Tale is Chauntecleer, a fowl of courtly bearing, profound learning, and superior crowing. This rooster is, like Achilles or Aeneas, made the center of a "great" action—which, however, takes up a relatively small portion of the total number of lines in the poem. The hero of the larger portion, and the real hero of the poem, is rhetoric, which is responsible for all Chauntecleer's importance, though it almost drowns his story in its vast tumid flow. Rhetoric as employed by the Nun's Priest includes not only elevated speech, but proverbs, saws, conventional similes—all the clichés of formal language and thought. Epic mannerisms abound; proverbs fly thick and fast and contradict one another with impunity; sententious generalizations about the tragic inevitability of certain events, the bad counsel given by women, and the folly of heeding flattery are successively used to account for Chauntecleer's near-fall; and throughout the tale learned pedantry invokes rhetorical tradition to footnote the least original of ideas. All rhetoric's ordering devices achieve a fine disorder.

2. I.e., small.

Attempre° diete was al hir physik,°   *moderate / medicine*
And exercise and hertes suffisaunce.°   *contentment*
20 The goute lette hire nothing for to daunce,[3]
N'apoplexye shente° nat hir heed.°   *hurt / head*
No win ne drank she, neither whit ne reed:°   *red*
Hir boord° was served most with whit and blak,[4]   *table*
Milk and brown breed, in which she foond no lak;[5]
25 Seind bacon, and somtime an ey° or twaye,   *egg*
For she was as it were a manere daye.[6]
A yeerd° she hadde, enclosed al withoute   *yard*
With stikkes, and a drye dich aboute,
In which she hadde a cok heet° Chauntecleer: *named*
30 In al the land of crowing nas° his peer.   *was not*
His vois was merier than the merye orgon
On massedayes that in the chirche goon;[7]
Wel sikerer[8] was his crowing in his logge°   *dwelling*
Than is a clok or an abbeye orlogge;°   *timepiece*
35 By nature he knew eech ascensioun
Of th'equinoxial[9] in thilke town:
For whan degrees fifteene were ascended,
Thanne crew[1] he that it mighte nat been amended.
His comb was redder than the fin coral,
40 And batailed° as it were a castel wal;   *battlemented*
His bile° was blak, and as the jeet° it shoon;   *bill / jet*
Like asure[2] were his legges and his toon;°   *toes*
His nailes whitter° than the lilye flowr,   *whiter*
And lik the burned° gold was his colour.   *burnished*
45 This gentil cok hadde in his governaunce
Sevene hennes for to doon al his plesaunce,°   *pleasure*
Whiche were his sustres and his paramours,[3]
And wonder like to him as of colours;
Of whiche the faireste hewed° on hir throte   *colored*
50 Was cleped faire damoisele Pertelote:
Curteis she was, discreet, and debonaire,°   *meek*
And compaignable,[4] and bar° hirself so faire,   *bore*
Sin thilke day that she was seven night old,
That trewely she hath the herte in hold
55 Of Chauntecleer, loken° in every lith.°   *locked / limb*
He loved hire so that wel was him therwith.[5]
But swich a joye was it to heere hem singe,
Whan that the brighte sonne gan to springe,

---

3. The gout didn't hinder her at all from dancing.
4. I.e., milk and bread.
5. Found no fault. "Seind": scorched (i.e., broiled).
6. I.e., a kind of dairymaid.
7. I.e., is played.
8. More reliable.
9. I.e., he knew by instinct each step in the progression of the celestial equator. The celestial equator was thought to make a 360-degree rotation

around the earth every 24 hours; therefore a progression of 15 degrees would be equal to the passage of an hour (line 37).
1. Crowed. "Amended": improved.
2. Lapis lazuli.
3. His sisters and his mistresses.
4. Companionable.
5. That he was well contented.

In sweete accord *My Lief is Faren in Londe*[6]—
60　For thilke time, as I have understonde,
　　Beestes and briddes couden speke and singe.
　　　And so bifel that in a daweninge,
　　As Chauntecleer among his wives alle
　　Sat on his perche that was in the halle,
65　And next him sat this faire Pertelote,
　　This Chauntecleer gan gronen in his throte,
　　As man that in his dreem is drecched° sore.　　　　troubled
　　　And whan that Pertelote thus herde him rore,
　　She was agast, and saide, "Herte dere,
70　What aileth you to grone in this manere?
　　Ye been a verray slepere,[7] fy, for shame!"
　　　And he answerde and saide thus, "Madame,
　　I praye you that ye take it nat agrief.°　　　　amiss
　　By God, me mette I was in swich meschief[8]
75　Right now, that yit myn herte is sore afright.
　　Now God," quod he, "my swevene recche aright,[9]
　　And keepe my body out of foul prisoun!
　　Me mette how that I romed up and down
　　Within oure yeerd, wher as I sawgh a beest,
80　Was lik an hound and wolde han maad arrest[1]
　　Upon my body, and han had me deed.[2]
　　His colour was bitwixe yelow and reed,
　　And tipped was his tail and bothe his eres
　　With blak, unlik the remenant° of his heres;°　　　rest / hairs
85　His snoute smal, with glowing yën twaye.
　　Yit of his look for fere almost I deye:°　　　die
　　This caused me my groning, doutelees."
　　　"Avoi,"° quod she, "fy on you, hertelees!°　　　fie / coward
　　Allas," quod she, "for by that God above,
90　Now han ye lost myn herte and al my love!
　　I can nat love a coward, by my faith.
　　For certes, what so any womman saith,
　　We alle desiren, if it mighte be,
　　To han housbondes hardy, wise, and free,°　　　generous
95　And secree,° and no nigard, ne no fool,　　　discreet
　　Ne him that is agast of every tool,°　　　weapon
　　Ne noon avauntour.° By that God above,　　　boaster
　　How dorste ye sayn for shame unto youre love
　　That any thing mighte make you aferd?
100　Have ye no mannes herte and han a beerd?
　　Allas, and conne° ye been agast of swevenes?°　　　can / dreams
　　No thing, God woot, but vanitee[3] in swevene is!

---

6. A popular song of the time.
7. Sound sleeper.
8. I dreamed that I was in such misfortune.
9. Interpret my dream correctly (i.e., in an auspi-

cious manner).
1. Would have laid hold.
2. I.e., killed me.
3. I.e., empty illusion.

Swevenes engendren of replexiouns,[4]
And ofte of fume° and of complexiouns,°   gas / bodily humors
105 Whan humours been too habundant in a wight.[5]
Certes, this dreem which ye han met° tonight   dreamed
Comth of the grete superfluitee
Of youre rede colera,[6] pardee,
Which causeth folk to dreden° in hir dremes   fear
110 Of arwes,° and of fir with rede lemes,°   arrows / flames
Of rede beestes, that they wol hem bite,
Of contek,° and of whelpes grete and lite[7]—   strife
Right° as the humour of malencolye[8]   just
Causeth ful many a man in sleep to crye
115 For fere of blake beres° or boles° blake,   bears / bulls
Or elles blake develes wol hem take.
Of othere humours coude I tell also
That werken many a man in sleep ful wo,
But I wol passe as lightly° as I can.   quickly
120 Lo, Caton,[9] which that was so wis a man,
Saide he nat thus? 'Ne do no fors of[1] dremes.'
Now, sire," quod she, "whan we flee fro the bemes,[2]
For Goddes love, as take som laxatif.
Up° peril of my soule and of my lif,   upon
125 I conseile you the beste, I wol nat lie,
That bothe of colere and of malencolye
Ye purge you; and for° ye shal nat tarye,   in order that
Though in this town is noon apothecarye,
I shal myself to herbes techen you,
130 That shal been for youre hele[3] and for youre prow,
And in oure yeerd tho herbes shal I finde,
The whiche han of hir propretee by kinde°   nature
To purge you binethe and eek above.
Foryet° nat this, for Goddes owene love.   forget
135 Ye been ful colerik° of complexioun;   bilious
Ware° the sonne in his ascencioun   beware that
Ne finde you nat repleet° of humours hote;°   filled / hot
And if it do, I dar wel laye° a grote   bet
That ye shul have a fevere terciane,[4]
140 Or an agu that may be youre bane.°   death
A day or two ye shul han digestives
Of wormes, er ye take youre laxatives
Of lauriol, centaure, and fumetere,[5]

---

4. Dreams have their origin in overeating.
5. I.e., when humors are too abundant in a person. Pertelote's diagnosis is based on the familiar
concept that an overabundance of one of the bodily humors in a person affected his temperament.
6. Red bile.
7. And of big and little dogs.
8. I.e., black bile.
9. Dionysius Cato, supposed author of a book of

maxims used in elementary education.
1. Pay no attention to.
2. Fly down from the rafters.
3. Health. "Prow": benefit.
4. Tertian (recurring every other day).
5. Of laureole, centaury, and fumitory. These, and
the herbs mentioned in the next lines, were all
common medieval medicines used as cathartics.

Or elles of ellebor° that groweth there,   *hellebore*
145 Of catapuce, or of gaitres beries,[6]
Of herb-ive° growing in oure yeerd ther merye is[7]   *herb ivy*
Pekke hem right up as they growe and ete hem in.
Be merye, housbonde, for youre fader kin!
Dredeth no dreem: I can saye you namore."
150   "Madame," quod he, "graunt mercy of youre lore,[8]
But nathelees, as touching daun° Catoun,   *master*
That hath of wisdom swich a greet renown,
Though that he bad no dremes for to drede,
By God, men may in olde bookes rede
155 Of many a man more of auctoritee°   *authority*
Than evere Caton was, so mote I thee,°   *thrive*
That al the revers sayn of his sentence,°   *opinion*
And han wel founden by experience
That dremes been significaciouns
160 As wel of joye as tribulaciouns
That folk enduren in this lif present.
Ther needeth make of this noon argument:
The verray preve[9] sheweth it in deede.
        "Oon of the gretteste auctour[1] that men rede
165 Saith thus, that whilom two felawes wente
On pilgrimage in a ful good entente,
And happed so they comen in a town,
Wher as ther was swich congregacioun
Of peple, and eek so strait of herbergage,[2]
170 That they ne founde as muche as oo cotage
In which they bothe mighte ylogged° be;   *lodged*
Wherfore they mosten° of necessitee   *must*
As for that night departe° compaignye.   *part*
And eech of hem gooth to his hostelrye,
175 And took his logging as it wolde falle.°   *befall*
That oon of hem was logged in a stalle,
Fer° in a yeerd, with oxen of the plough;   *far away*
That other man was logged wel ynough,
As was his aventure° or his fortune,   *lot*
180 That us governeth alle as in commune.
And so bifel that longe er it were day,
This man mette° in his bed, ther as he lay,   *dreamed*
How that his felawe gan upon him calle,
And saide, 'Allas, for in an oxes stalle
185 This night I shal be mordred° ther I lie!   *murdered*
Now help me, dere brother, or I die!
In alle haste com to me,' he saide.
        "This man out of his sleep for fere abraide,°   *started up*

---

6. Of caper berry or of gaiter berry.
7. Where it is pleasant.
8. Many thanks for your instruction.
9. Actual experience.

1. I.e., one of the greatest authors (perhaps Cicero or Valerius Maximus).
2. And also such a shortage of lodging.

But whan that he was wakened of his sleep,
190   He turned him and took of this no keep:°   *heed*
Him thoughte his dreem nas but a vanitee.
Thus twies in his sleeping dremed he,
And atte thridde time yit his felawe
Cam, as him thoughte, and saide, 'I am now slawe:°   *slain*
195   Bihold my bloody woundes deepe and wide.
Aris up erly in the morwe tide[3]
And atte west gate of the town,' quod he,
'A carte ful of dong° ther shaltou see,   *dung*
In which my body is hid ful prively:
200   Do thilke carte arresten boldely.[4]
My gold caused my mordre, sooth to sayn'
—And tolde him every point how he was slain,
With a ful pitous face, pale of hewe.
And truste wel, his dreem he foond° ful trewe,   *found*
205   For on the morwe° as soone as it was day,   *morning*
To his felawes in° he took the way,   *lodging*
And whan that he cam to this oxes stalle,
After his felawe he bigan to calle.
    "The hostiler° answerde him anoon,   *innkeeper*
210   And saide, 'Sire, youre felawe is agoon:°   *gone away*
As soone as day he wente out of the town.'
    "This man gan fallen in suspecioun,
Remembring on his dremes that he mette;°   *dreamed*
And forth he gooth, no lenger wolde he lette,°   *tarry*
215   Unto the west gate of the town, and foond
A dong carte, wente as it were to donge° lond, *put manure on*
That was arrayed in that same wise
As ye han herd the dede° man devise;   *dead*
And with an hardy herte he gan to crye,
220   'Vengeance and justice of this felonye!
My felawe mordred is this same night,
And in this carte he lith° gaping upright!°   *lies / supine*
I crye out on the ministres,' quod he,
'That sholde keepe and rulen this citee.
225   Harrow,° allas, here lith my felawe slain!'   *help*
What sholde I more unto this tale sayn?
The peple up sterte° and caste the carte to grounde, *started*
And in the middel of the dong they founde
The dede man that mordred was al newe.[5]
230   "O blisful God that art so just and trewe,
Lo, how that thou biwrayest° mordre alway!   *disclose*
Mordre wol out, that see we day by day:
Mordre is so wlatsom° and abhominable   *loathsome*
To God that is so just and resonable,
235   That he ne wol nat suffre it heled° be,   *concealed*

---

3. In the morning.   5. Recently.
4. Boldly have this same cart stopped.

Though it abide a yeer or two or three.
Mordre wol out: this my conclusioun.
And right anoon ministres of that town
Han hent° the cartere and so sore him pined,[6]   *seized*
240 And eek the hostiler so sore engined,°   *racked*
That they biknewe° hir wikkednesse anoon,   *confessed*
And were anhanged° by the nekke boon.   *hanged*
Here may men seen that dremes been to drede.[7]
    "And certes, in the same book I rede—
245 Right in the nexte chapitre after this—
I gabbe° nat, so have I joye or blis—   *lie*
Two men that wolde han passed over see
For certain cause into a fer contree,
If that the wind ne hadde been contrarye
250 That made hem in a citee for to tarye,
That stood ful merye upon an haven° side—   *harbor's*
But on a day again° the even tide   *toward*
The wind gan chaunge, and blewe right as hem leste:[8]
Jolif° and glad they wenten unto reste,   *merry*
255 And casten[9] hem ful erly for to saile.
    "But to that oo man fil° a greet mervaile;   *befell*
That oon of hem, in sleeping as he lay,
Him mette[1] a wonder dreem again the day:
Him thoughte a man stood by his beddes side,
260 And him comanded that he sholde abide,
And saide him thus, 'If thou tomorwe wende,
Thou shalt be dreint:° my tale is at an ende.'   *drowned*
    "He wook and tolde his felawe what he mette,
And prayed him his viage° to lette;°   *voyage / delay*
265 As for that day he prayed him to bide.
    "His felawe that lay by his beddes side
Gan for to laughe, and scorned him ful faste.°   *hard*
'No dreem,' quod he, 'may so myn herte agaste°   *terrify*
That I wol lette° for to do my thinges.°   *delay / business*
270 I sette nat a straw by thy dreminges,[2]
For swevenes been but vanitees and japes:[3]
Men dreme alday° of owles or of apes,[4]   *constantly*
And of many a maze° therwithal—   *delusion*
Men dreme of thing that nevere was ne shal.[5]
275 But sith I see that thou wolt here abide,
And thus forsleuthen° wilfully thy tide,°   *waste / time*
Good woot, it reweth me;[6] and have good day.'
And thus he took his leve and wente his way.
But er that he hadde half his cours ysailed—

---

6. Tortured.
7. Worthy of being feared.
8. Just as they wished.
9. Determined.
1. He dreamed.

2. I don't care a straw for your dreamings.
3. Dreams are but illusions and frauds.
4. I.e., of absurdities.
5. I.e., shall be.
6. I'm sorry.

280 Noot I nat why ne what meschaunce it ailed—
But casuelly the shippes botme rente,[7]
And ship and man under the water wente,
In sighte of othere shippes it biside,
That with hem sailed at the same tide.

285 And therfore, faire Pertelote so dere,
By swiche ensamples olde maistou lere°   *learn*
That no man sholde been too recchelees°   *careless*
Of dremes, for I saye thee douteles
That many a dreem ful sore is for to drede.

290   "Lo, in the lif of Saint Kenelm[8] I rede—
That was Kenulphus sone, the noble king
Or Mercenrike°—how Kenelm mette a thing   *Mercia*
A lite° er he was mordred on a day.   *little*
His mordre in his avision° he sey.°   *dream / saw*
295 His norice° him expounded everydeel° *nurse / entirely*
His swevene, and bad him for to keepe him[9] weel
For traison, but he nas but seven yeer old,
And therfore litel tale hath he told
Of any dreem,[1] so holy was his herte.
300 By God, I hadde levere than my sherte[2]
That ye hadde rad° his legende as have I.   *read*
   "Dame Pertelote, I saye you trewely,
Macrobeus,[3] that writ the *Avisioun*
In Affrike of the worthy Scipioun,
305 Affermeth° dremes, and saith that they been   *confirms*
Warning of thinges that men after seen.
   "And ferthermore, I praye you looketh wel
In the Olde Testament of Daniel,
If he heeld° dremes any vanitee.[4]   *considered*
310   "Rede eek of Joseph[5] and ther shul ye see
Wher° dremes be somtime—I saye nat alle—   *whether*
Warning of thinges that shul after falle.
   "Looke of Egypte the king daun Pharao,
His bakere and his botelere° also,   *butler*
315 Wher they ne felte noon effect in dremes.[6]
Whoso wol seeke actes of sondry remes°   *realms*
May rede of dremes many a wonder thing.
   "Lo Cresus, which that was of Lyde° king,   *Lydia*
Mette° he nat that he sat upon a tree,   *dreamed*
320 Which signified he sholde anhanged° be?   *hanged*
   "Lo here Andromacha, Ectores° wif,   *Hector's*
That day that Ector sholde lese° his lif,   *lose*

---

7. I don't know why nor what was the trouble with it—but accidentally the ship's bottom split.
8. Kenelm succeeded his father as king of Mercia at the age of 7, but was slain by his aunt (in 821).
9. Guard himself.
1. Therefore he has set little store by any dream.
2. I.e., I'd give my shirt.

3. Macrobius wrote a famous commentary on Cicero's account in *De Republica* of the dream of Scipio Africanus Minor; the commentary came to be regarded as a standard authority on dream lore.
4. See Daniel 7.
5. See Genesis 37.
6. See Genesis 39–41.

> She dremed on the same night biforn
> How that the lif of Ector sholde be lorn,°   *lost*
325 If thilke° day he wente into bataile;   *that same*
> She warned him, but it mighte nat availe:°   *do any good*
> He wente for to fighte nathelees,
> But he was slain anoon° of Achilles.   *right away*
> But thilke tale is al too long to telle,
330 And eek it is neigh day, I may nat dwelle.
> Shortly I saye, as for conclusioun,
> That I shal han of this avisioun[7]
> Adversitee, and I saye ferthermoor
> That I ne telle of[8] laxatives no stoor,
335 For they been venimes,° I woot it weel: *poisons*
> I hem defye, I love hem neveradeel.°   *not a bit*
>   "Now lat us speke of mirthe and stinte° al this.   *stop*
> Madame Pertelote, so have I blis,
> Of oo thing God hath sente me large grace:
340 For whan I see the beautee of youre face—
> Ye been so scarlet reed° aboute youre yën—   *red*
> It maketh al my drede for to dien.
> For also siker° as *In principio*,[9]   *certain*
> *Mulier est hominis confusio.*[1]
345 Madame, the sentence° of this Latin is,   *meaning*
> 'Womman is mannes joye and al his blis.'
> For whan I feele anight youre softe side—
> Al be it that I may nat on you ride,
> For that oure perche is maad so narwe, allas—
350 I am so ful of joye and of solas°   *delight*
> That I defye bothe swevene and dreem."
> And with that word he fleigh° down fro the beem,   *flew*
> For it was day, and eek his hennes alle,
> And with a "chuk" he gan hem for to calle,
355 For he hadde founde a corn lay in the yeerd.
> Real° he was, he was namore aferd:°   *regal / afraid*
> He fethered[2] Pertelote twenty time,
> And trad[3] hire as ofte er it was prime.
> He looketh as it were a grim leoun,
360 And on his toes he rometh up and down:
> Him deined[4] nat to sette his foot to grounde.
> He chukketh whan he hath a corn yfounde,
> And to him rennen° thanne his wives alle.   *run*
> Thus royal, as a prince is in his halle,
365 Leve I this Chauntecleer in his pasture,
> And after wol I telle his aventure.
>   Whan that the month in which the world bigan,

7. Divinely inspired dream (as opposed to the more ordinary "swevene" or "dreem").
8. Set by.
9. A tag from the Gospel of St. John which gives the essential premises of Christianity: "In the beginning was the Word."
1. Woman is man's ruination.
2. I.e., embraced.
3. Trod, copulated with. "Prime": 9 A.M.
4. He deigned.

That highte March, whan God first maked man,
Was compleet, and passed were also,
370 Sin March biran, thritty days and two,[5]
Bifel that Chauntecleer in al his pride,
His sevene wives walking him biside,
Caste up his yën to the brighte sonne,
That in the signe of Taurus hadde yronne
375 Twenty degrees and oon and somwhat more,
And knew by kinde,° and by noon other lore,   *nature*
That it was prime, and crew with blisful stevene.°   *voice*
"The sonne," he saide, "is clomben[6] up on hevene
Fourty degrees and oon and more, ywis.
380 Madame Pertelote, my worldes blis,
Herkneth thise blisful briddes° how they singe,   *birds*
And see the fresshe flowers how they springe:
Ful is myn herte of revel and solas."
But sodeinly him fil° a sorweful cas,°   *befell / chance*
385 For evere the latter ende of joye is wo—
God woot that worldly joye is soone ago,
And if a rethor° coude faire endite,   *rhetorician*
He in a cronicle saufly° mighte it write,   *safely*
As for a soverein notabilitee.[7]
390 Now every wis man lat him herkne me:
This storye is also° trewe, I undertake,   *as*
As is the book of *Launcelot de Lake*,[8]
That wommen holde in ful greet reverence.
Now wol I turne again to my sentence.°   *main point*
395   A colfox[9] ful of sly iniquitee,
That in the grove hadde woned° yeres three,   *dwelled*
By heigh imaginacion forncast,[1]
The same night thurghout the hegges° brast°   *hedges / burst*
Into the yeerd ther Chauntecleer the faire
400 Was wont, and eek his wives, to repaire;
And in a bed of wortes° stille he lay   *cabbages*
Til it was passed undren° of the day,   *midmorning*
Waiting his time on Chauntecleer to falle,
As gladly doon thise homicides alle,
405 That in await liggen to mordre[2] men.
O false mordrour, lurking in thy den!
O newe Scariot![3] Newe Geniloun!
False dissimilour!° O Greek Sinoun,[4]   *dissembler*
That broughtest Troye al outrely° to sorwe!   *utterly*

---

5. The rhetorical time telling yields the date
May 3. "Biran": passed by.
6. Has climbed.
7. Indisputable fact.
8. Romances of the courteous knight Lancelot of
the Lake were very popular.
9. Fox with black markings.
1. Predestined by divine planning.

2. That lie in ambush to murder.
3. Judas Iscariot. "Geniloun" is Ganelon, who
betrayed Roland to the Saracens (in the medieval
French epic *The Song of Roland*).
4. Sinon, who persuaded the Trojans to take the
Greeks' wooden horse into their city—with, of
course, the result that the city was destroyed.

410 O Chauntecleer, accursed be that morwe°   *morning*
That thou into the yeerd flaugh° fro the bemes!   *flew*
Thou were ful wel ywarned by thy dremes
That thilke day was perilous to thee;
But what that God forwoot° moot° needes be,   *foreknows / must*
415 After° the opinion of certain clerkes: *according to*
Witnesse on him that any parfit° clerk is   *perfect*
That in scole is greet altercacioun
In this matere, and greet disputisoun,°   *disputation*
And hath been of an hundred thousand men.
420 But I ne can nat bulte° it to the bren,°   *sift / husks*
As can the holy doctour Augustin,
Or Boece, or the bisshop Bradwardin[5]—
Wheither that Goddes worthy forwiting°   *foreknowledge*
Straineth me nedely[6] for to doon a thing
425 ("Nedely" clepe I simple necessitee),
Or elles if free chois be graunted me
To do that same thing or do it naught,
Though God forwoot° it er that I was wrought;   *foreknew*
Or if his witing° straineth neveradeel,   *knowledge*
430 But by necessitee condicionel[7]—
I wol nat han to do of swich matere:
My tale is of a cok, as ye may heere,
That took his conseil of his wif with sorwe,
To walken in the yeerd upon that morwe
435 That he hadde met° the dreem that I you tolde.   *dreamed*
Wommenes conseils been ful ofte colde,[8]
Wommanes conseil broughte us first to wo,
And made Adam fro Paradis to go,
Ther as he was ful merye and wel at ese.
440 But for I noot° to whom it mighte displese   *don't know*
If I conseil of wommen wolde blame,
Passe over, for I saide it in my game°—   *sport*
Rede auctours where they trete of swich matere,
And what they sayn of wommen ye may heere—
445 Thise been the cokkes wordes and nat mine:
I can noon harm of no womman divine.°   *guess*
   Faire in the sond° to bathe hire merily   *sand*
Lith° Pertelote, and alle hir sustres by,   *lies*
Again° the sonne, and Chauntecleer so free°   *in / noble*
450 Soong° merier than the mermaide in the see—   *sang*
For Physiologus[9] saith sikerly
How that they singen wel and merily.

---

5. St. Augustine, Boethius (6th-century Roman philosopher, whose *Consolation of Philosophy* was translated by Chaucer), and Thomas Bradwardine (archbishop of Canterbury, d. 1349) were all concerned with the interrelationship between man's free will and God's foreknowledge.
6. Constrains me necessarily.

7. Boethius' "conditional necessity" permitted a large measure of free will.
8. I.e., baneful.
9. Supposed author of a bestiary, a book of moralized zoology describing both natural and supernatural animals (including mermaids).

And so bifel that as he caste his yë
Among the wortes on a boterflye,°   *butterfly*
455   He was war of this fox that lay ful lowe.
No thing ne liste him[1] thanne for to crowe,
But cride anoon "Cok cok!" and up he sterte,°   *started*
As man that[2] was affrayed in his herte—
For naturelly a beest desireth flee
460   Fro his contrarye[3] if he may it see,
Though he nevere erst° hadde seen it with his yë.   *before*
This Chauntecleer, whan he gan him espye,
He wolde han fled, but that the fox anoon
Saide, "Gentil sire, allas, wher wol ye goon?
465   Be ye afraid of me that am youre freend?
Now certes, I were worse than a feend
If I to you wolde° harm or vilainye.   *meant*
I am nat come youre conseil° for t'espye,   *secrets*
But trewely the cause of my cominge
470   Was only for to herkne how ye singe:
For trewely, ye han as merye a stevene°   *voice*
As any angel hath that is in hevene.
Therwith ye han in musik more feelinge
Than hadde Boece,[4] or any that can singe.
475   My lord your fader—God his soule blesse!—
And eek youre moder, of hir gentilesse,°   *gentility*
Han in myn hous ybeen, to my grete ese.
And certes sire, ful fain° wolde I you plese.   *gladly*
"But for men speke of singing, I wol saye,
480   So mote I brouke[5] wel mine yën twaye,
Save ye, I herde nevere man to singe
As dide youre fader in the morweninge.
Certes, it was of herte[6] al that he soong.°   *sang*
And for to make his vois the more strong,
485   He wolde so paine him[7] that with bothe his yën
He moste winke,[8] so loude wolde he cryen;
And stonden on his tiptoon therwithal,
And strecche forth his nekke long and smal;
And eek he was of swich discrecioun
490   That ther nas no man in no regioun
That him in song or wisdom mighte passe.
I have wel rad° in *Daun Burnel the Asse*[9]   *read*
Among his vers how that ther was a cok,
For a preestes sone yaf him a knok[1]
495   Upon his leg whil he was yong and nice,°   *foolish*

---

1. He wished.
2. Like one who.
3. I.e., his natural enemy.
4. Boethius also wrote a treatise on music.
5. So might I enjoy the use of.
6. Heartfelt.

7. Take pains.
8. He had to shut his eyes.
9. Master Brunellus, a discontented donkey, was the hero of a 12th-century satirical poem by Nigel Wireker.
1. Because a priest's son gave him a knock.

He made him for to lese° his benefice. [2]   lose
But certain, ther nis no comparisoun
Bitwixe the wisdom and discrecioun
Of youre fader and of his subtiltee.
500 Now singeth, sire, for sainte° charitee!   holy
Lat see, conne° ye youre fader countrefete?"°   can / imitate
       This Chauntecleer his winges gan to bete,
As man that coude his traison nat espye,
So was he ravisshed with his flaterye.
505   Allas, ye lordes, many a fals flatour°   flatterer
Is in youre court, and many a losengeour°   deceiver
That plesen you wel more, by my faith,
Than he that soothfastnesse° unto you saith!   truth
Redeth Ecclesiaste[3] of flaterye.
510 Beeth war, ye lordes, of hir trecherye.
       This Chauntecleer stood hye upon his toos,
Strecching his nekke, and heeld his yën cloos,
And gan to crowe loude for the nones;°   occasion
And daun Russel the fox sterte° up atones,   jumped
515 And by the gargat° hente° Chauntecleer,   throat / seized
And on his bak toward the wode him beer,°   bore
For yit ne was ther no man that him sued.°   followed
       O destinee that maist nat been eschued!°   eschewed
Allas that Chauntecleer fleigh° fro the bemes!   flew
520 Allas his wif ne roughte nat of[4] dremes!
And on a Friday fil° al this meschaunce!   befell
       O Venus that art goddesse of plesaunce,
Sin that thy servant was this Chauntecleer,
And in thy service dide al his power—
525 More for delit than world[5] to multiplye—
Why woldestou suffre him on thy day[6] to die?
       O Gaufred,[7] dere maister soverein,
That, whan thy worthy king Richard was slain
With shot,[8] complainedest his deeth so sore,
530 Why ne hadde I now thy sentence and thy lore,[9]
The Friday for to chide as diden ye?
For on a Friday soothly slain was he.
Thanne wolde I shewe you how that I coude plaine[1]
For Chauntecleres drede and for his paine.
535   Certes, swich cry ne lamentacioun
Was nevere of ladies maad when Ilioun°   Ilium, Troy

---

2. The offended cock neglected to crow so that his
master, now grown to manhood, overslept, missing his ordination and losing his benefice.
3. The Book of Ecclesiasticus, in the Apocrypha.
4. Didn't care for.
5. I.e., population.
6. Friday is Venus's day.

7. Geoffrey of Vinsauf, a famous medieval rhetorician, who wrote a lament on the death of Richard I in which he scolded Friday, the day on which
the king died.
8. I.e., a missile.
9. Thy wisdom and thy learning.
1. Lament.

Was wonne, and Pyrrus[2] with his straite swerd,
Whan he hadde hent° King Priam by the beerd   *seized*
And slain him, as saith us *Eneidos*,[3]
540   As maden alle the hennes in the cloos,°   *yard*
Whan they hadde seen of Chauntecleer the sighte.
But sovereinly[4] Dame Pertelote shrighte°   *shrieked*
Ful louder than dide Hasdrubales[5] wif
Whan that hir housbonde hadde lost his lif,
545   And that the Romains hadden brend° Cartage: *burned*
She was so ful of torment and of rage°   *madness*
That wilfully unto the fir she sterte,°   *jumped*
And brende hirselven with a stedefast herte.
    O woful hennes, right so criden ye
550   As, whan that Nero brende the citee
Of Rome, criden senatoures wives
For that hir housbondes losten alle hir lives:[6]
Withouten gilt this Nero hath hem slain.
Now wol I turne to my tale again.
555   The sely° widwe and eek hir doughtres two   *innocent*
Herden thise hennes crye and maken wo,
And out at dores sterten° they anoon,   *leaped*
And sien° the fox toward the grove goon,   *saw*
And bar upon his bak the cok away,
560   And criden, "Out, harrow,° and wailaway,   *help*
Ha, ha, the fox," and after him they ran,
And eek with staves many another man;
Ran Colle oure dogge, and Talbot and Gerland,[7]
And Malkin with a distaf in hir hand,
565   Ran cow and calf, and eek the verray hogges,
Sore aferd° for berking of the dogges   *frightened*
And shouting of the men and wommen eke.
They ronne° so hem thoughte hir herte breke;[8]   *ran*
They yelleden as feendes doon in helle;
570   The dokes° criden as men wolde hem quelle;°   *ducks / kill*
The gees for fere flowen° over the trees;   *flew*
Out of the hive cam the swarm of bees;
So hidous was the noise, a, benedicite,°   *bless me*
Certes, he Jakke Straw[9] and his meinee°   *company*
575   Ne made nevere shoutes half so shrille
Whan that they wolden any Fleming kille,
As thilke day was maad upon the fox:
Of bras they broughten bemes° and of box,°   *trumpets / boxwood*

---

2. Pyrrhus was the Greek who slew Priam, king of Troy. "Straite": rigorous, unsparing.
3. As the *Aeneid* tells us.
4. Splendidly.
5. Hasdrubal was king of Carthage when it was destroyed by the Romans.
6. According to the legend, Nero not only set fire to Rome (in A.D 64) but also put many senators to death.
7. Two other dogs.
8. Would break.
9. One of the leaders of the Peasants' Revolt in 1381, which was partially directed against the Flemings living in London.

Of horn, of boon,° in whiche they blewe and pouped,[1]   *bone*
580 And therwithal they skriked[2] and they houped—
It seemed as that hevene sholde falle.
          Now goode men, I praye you herkneth alle:
Lo, how Fortune turneth° sodeinly   *reverses, overturns*
The hope and pride eek of hir enemy.
585 This cok that lay upon the foxes bak,
In al his drede unto the fox he spak,
And saide, "Sire, if that I were as ye,
Yit sholde I sayn, as wis° God helpe me,   *surely*
'Turneth ayain, ye proude cherles alle!
590 A verray pestilence upon you falle!
Now am I come unto this wodes side,
Maugree your heed,[3] the cok shal here abide.
I wol him ete, in faith, and that anoon.' "
          The fox answerde, "In faith, it shal be doon."
595 And as he spak that word, al sodeinly
The cok brak from his mouth deliverly,°   *nimbly*
And hye upon a tree he fleigh° anoon.   *flew*
          And whan the fox sawgh that he was agoon,
"Allas," quod he, "O Chauntecleer, allas!
600 I have to you," quod he, "ydoon trespas,
In as muche as I maked you aferd
Whan I you hente° and broughte out of the yeerd.   *seized*
But sire, I dide it in no wikke° entente: *wicked*
Come down, and I shal telle you what I mente.
605 I shal saye sooth to you, God help me so."
          "Nay thanne," quod he, "I shrewe° us bothe two: *curse*
But first I shrewe myself, bothe blood and bones,
If thou bigile me ofter than ones;
Thou shalt namore thurgh thy flaterye
610 Do° me to singe and winken with myn yë.   *cause*
For he that winketh whan he sholde see,
Al wilfully, God lat him nevere thee."°   *thrive*
          "Nay," quod the fox, "but God yive him meschaunce
That is so undiscreet of governaunce°   *self-control*
615 That jangleth° whan he sholde holde his pees."   *chatters*
          Lo, swich it is for to be reccheless°   *careless*
And necligent and truste on flaterye.
But ye that holden this tale a folye
As of a fox, or of a cok and hen,
620 Taketh the moralitee, goode men.
For Saint Paul saith that al that writen is
To oure doctrine it is ywrit, ywis:[4]
Taketh the fruit, and lat the chaf be stille.

---

1. Tooted.
2. Shrieked. "Houped": whooped.
3. Despite your head—i.e., despite anything you
can do.
4. See Romans 15.4.

Now goode God, if that it be thy wille,
625 As saith my lord, so make us alle goode men,
And bringe us to his hye blisse. Amen.

From The Parson's Tale[1]

The Introduction

By that[2] the Manciple hadde his tale al ended,
The sonne fro the south line[3] was descended
So lowe, that he has nat to my sighte
Degrees nine and twenty as in highte.
5 Four of the clokke it was, so as I gesse,
For elevene foot, or litel more or lesse,
My shadwe was at thilke time as there,
Of swich feet as° my lengthe parted° were   *as if / divided*
In sixe feet equal of proporcioun.[4]
10 Therwith the moones exaltacioun[5]—
I mene Libra—always gan ascende,
As we were entring at a thropes° ende.   *village's*
For which oure Host, as he was wont to gie°   *lead*
As in this caas oure joly compaignye,
15 Saide in this wise, "Lordinges everichoon,
Now lakketh us no tales mo than oon:
Fulfild is my sentence° and my decree;   *purpose*
I trowe° that we han herd of ech degree;   *believe*

1. Among the moral writers of the later Middle Ages the pilgrimage was so commonly treated as an allegory of man's life that Chaucer's audience must have been surprised to find the *Canterbury Tales* so little allegorical. At the end of his life, however, and at the end of his work, Chaucer seems to have been caught up in the venerable allegory. Some 10 months before his death he rented a house in the garden of Westminster Abbey, and it is possible that during these months—perhaps when he felt his death approaching—he fell under the influence of the monks of Westminster. In any case, in the Parson's Tale, and in its short Introduction and in the Retraction that follows it, Chaucer seems to be making an end for two pilgrimages that had become one, that of his fiction and that of his life.

In the Introduction to the tale we find the 29 pilgrims moving through a nameless little village as the sun sinks to within 29 degrees of the horizon. The atmosphere contains something of both the chill and the urgency of a late autumn afternoon, and we are surprised to find that the pilgrimage is almost over, that there is need for haste in order to make that "good end" that every medieval Christian hoped for. This delicately suggestive passage, rich with allegorical overtones, introduces an extremely long sermon on penitence and the deadly sins, probably translated by Chaucer from French or Latin some years earlier, before he had begun the *Canterbury Tales*.

The sermon is at times not without animation, but in general Chaucer provides no exception to the statement that Middle English prose is inferior to Middle English verse. But then the intent of the sermon is didactic, not artistic, and according to the more rigorous theologians of the time, didactic intent is infinitely more important than artistic expression.

It is to this doctrine that Chaucer yielded at the end of his life. The Retraction which follows and concludes the Parson's Tale offers Chaucer's apology for having written all the works on which his reputation as a great poet depends, not only such stories as the Miller's Tale, but also his loveliest and seemingly most harmless poems. Yet a readiness to deny his own reality before the reality of his God is implicit in many of Chaucer's works, and the placement of the Retraction within the artistic structure of the *Canterbury Tales* suggests that while Chaucer denied his art, he seems to have recognized that he and it were inseparable.

2. By the time that.
3. I.e., the line that runs some 28 degrees to the south of the celestial equator and parallel to it.
4. This detailed analysis merely says that the shadows are lengthening.
5. I.e., the astrological sign in which the moon's influence was dominant. "Libra": the constellation of the Scales.

Almost fulfild is al myn ordinaunce.
20 I praye to God, so yive him right good chaunce
That telleth this tale to us lustily.
Sire preest," quod he, "artou a vicary,°   *vicar*
Or arte a Person? Say sooth, by thy fay.°   *faith*
Be what thou be, ne breek° thou nat oure play,   *break*
25 For every man save thou hath told his tale.
Unbokele and shew us what is in thy male!°   *bag*
For trewely, me thinketh by thy cheere°   *expression*
Thou sholdest knitte up wel a greet matere.
Tel us a fable anoon, for cokkes bones!"
30   This Person answerde al atones,[6]
"Thou getest fable noon ytold for me,
For Paul, that writeth unto Timothee,
Repreveth° hem that waiven soothfastnesse,[7]   *reproves*
And tellen fables and swich wrecchednesse.
35 Why sholde I sowen draf° out of my fest,°   *chaff / fist*
Whan I may sowen whete if that me lest?[8]
For which I saye that if you list to heere
Moralitee and vertuous matere,
And thanne that ye wol yive me audience,
40 I wol ful fain,° at Cristes reverence,   *gladly*
Do you plesance leveful° as I can.   *lawful*
But trusteth wel, I am a southren man:
I can nat geeste Rum-Ram-Ruf by lettre[9]—
Ne, God woot, rym holde° I but litel bettre.   *consider*
45 And therfore, if you list, I wol nat glose;[1]
I wol you telle a merye tale in prose,
To knitte up al this feeste and make an ende.
And Jesu for his grace wit me sende
To shewe you the way in this viage°   *journey*
50 Of thilke parfit glorious pilgrimage
That highte Jerusalem celestial.
And if ye vouche sauf, anoon I shal
Biginne upon my tale, for which I praye
Telle youre avis:° I can no bettre saye.   *opinion*
55 But nathelees, this meditacioun
I putte it ay under correccioun
Of clerkes, for I am nat textuel:[2]
I take but the sentence,° trusteth wel.   *meaning*
Therefore I make protestacioun°   *public acknowledgment*
60 That I wol stonde to correccioun."
    Upon this word we han assented soone,
For, as it seemed, it was for to doone
To enden in som vertuous sentence,°   *doctrine*

---

6. Immediately.
7. Depart from truth. See 1 Timothy 1.4.
8. It pleases me.
9. I.e., I cannot tell stories in the alliterative mea-

sure (without rhyme): this form of poetry was not
common in southeastern England.
1. I.e., speak in order to please.
2. Literal, faithful to the letter.

And for to yive him space and audience;
65   And bede³ oure Host he sholde to him saye
That alle we to telle his tale him praye.
    Oure Hoste hadde the wordes for us alle:
"Sire preest," quod he, "now faire you bifalle:
Telleth," quod he, "youre meditacioun.
70   But hasteth you; the sonne wol adown.
Beeth fructuous,° and that in litel space,°   *fruitful / time*
And to do wel God sende you his grace.
Saye what you list, and we wol gladly heere."
And with that word he saide in this manere.

Chaucer's Retraction

Now praye I to hem alle that herkne this litel tretis¹ or rede, that if ther be any thing in it that liketh² hem, that therof they thanken oure Lord Jesu Crist, of whom proceedeth al wit³ and al goodnesse. And if ther be any thing that displese hem, I praye hem also that they arrette it to the defaute of myn unconning,⁴ and nat to my wil, that wolde ful fain have said bettre if I hadde had conning. For oure book saith, "Al that is writen is writen for oure doctrine,"⁵ and that is myn entente. Wherfore I biseeke⁶ you mekely, for the mercy of God, that ye praye for me that Crist have mercy on me and foryive me my giltes, and namely⁷ of my translacions and enditinges of worldly vanitees, the whiche I revoke in my retraccions: as is the *Book of Troilus*; the Book also of *Fame*; the *Book of the Five and Twenty Ladies*;⁸ the *Book of the Duchesse*; the *Book of Saint Valentines Day of the Parlement of Briddes*; the *Tales of Canterbury*, thilke that sounen into⁹ sinne; the *Book of the Leon*;¹ and many another book, if they were in my remembrance, and many a song and many a leccherous lay: that Crist for his grete mercy foryive me the sinne. But of the translacion of Boece² *De Consolatione*, and othere bookes of legendes of saintes, and omelies,³ and moralitee, and devocion, that thanke I oure Lord Jesu Crist and his blisful Moder and alle the saintes of hevene, biseeking hem that they from hennes⁴ forth unto my lives ende sende me grace to biwaile my giltes and to studye to the salvacion of my soule, and graunte me grace of verray penitence, confession, and satisfaccion to doon in this present lif, thurgh the benigne grace of him that is king of kinges and preest over alle preestes, that boughte⁵ us with the precious blood of his herte, so that I may been oon

3. I.e., we bade.
1. Hear this little treatise.
2. Pleases.
3. Understanding.
4. Ascribe it to the defect of my lack of skill.
5. Romans 15.4.
6. Beseech.
7. Especially. "Enditinges": compositions.

8. I.e., the *Legend of Good Women*.
9. Those that tend toward.
1. The *Book of the Lion* has not been preserved.
2. Boethius.
3. Homilies.
4. Hence.
5. Redeemed.

of hem at the day of doom that shulle be saved. *Qui cum patre et Spiritu Sancto vivis et regnas Deus per omnia saecula.*[6] *Amen.*

1386–1400

6. Who with the Father and the Holy Spirit livest and reignest God forever.

SIR GAWAIN AND THE GREEN KNIGHT
ca. 1375–1400

Nothing is known about the author of *Sir Gawain and the Green Knight* except that he probably wrote the three religious poems—*Pearl, Patience,* and *Purity*—that are preserved in the same manuscript as *Sir Gawain* (no other copies of any of the poems have come to light); and he may also have written a fifth poem, which, like the others, is alliterative, but is preserved in a different manuscript—a charming legend of St. Erkenwald. The dialect of *Sir Gawain* points to an origin in provincial England, about 150 miles northwest of the capital: thus of the three great poets of late medieval England, two, the authors of *Sir Gawain* and *Piers Plowman,* were representatives of cultural centers remote from the royal court at London where Chaucer spent his life. We know almost nothing about these provincial centers, but the works that emanated from them demonstrate a high level of culture. The poet of *Sir Gawain,* indeed, was a most sophisticated and urbane writer, and even though his language (a dialect most difficult for us today and probably difficult for Londoners in his own time) and his alliterative measure would have been considered barbaric by Chaucer's London audience, the subtlety of his perceptions and the delicacy with which he handles his narrative is not unworthy of Chaucer himself. And although it is impossible to date the poem with any accuracy, its author must have been an almost exact contemporary of Chaucer.

Sir *Gawain* ingeniously combines two plots, common in folklore and romance, though not found together elsewhere: the beheading contest, in which two parties agree to an exchange of blows with a sword or ax, and the temptation, an attempted seduction of the hero by a lady. The motif of the green man's decapitation originates in very ancient folklore, probably in a vegetation myth in which the beheading would have been a ritual death that insured the return of spring to the earth and the regrowth of the crops. But this primitive theme has been entirely rationalized by the late medieval poet, who sees in his inherited plot an opportunity to study how successfully Gawain, as a man wholly dedicated to Christian ideals, maintains those ideals when he is subjected to unusual pressures. The poem is a rare combination: at once a comedy—even a satire—of manners and a profoundly Christian view of character and its destiny. The court of King Arthur is presented, in the most grandiose and laudatory of language, as the place where the ideal of chivalry has reached its zenith, where all is courtesy and martial prowess in defense of the right. The praise bestowed by the poet upon this court may seem excessive, and indeed the sequel suggests that the author made it so intentionally. For when the court is invaded by the Green Knight, arrogant, monstrous, and yet exasperatingly reasonable, it suddenly seems to become slightly unreal, as if, the Green Knight insultingly implies, its reputation were founded more on fiction than on fact—as if the poets that celebrated it had been working harder to enhance its glory than the knights themselves. In any case, the court is to receive a testing, which is naturally entrusted to the most courteous and valiant knight of the Round Table (in this most English of Arthurian romances Gawain has not been replaced as the best of knights by the continental-born Lancelot).

Sir Gawain's coat of arms, displayed on his shield, is the five-pointed star called the pentangle, which the poet tells us is a symbol of truth—the first of the chivalric virtues also loved by Chaucer's Knight. Truth is the quality, even more than martial courage, that is put to the test in Gawain's quest to seek out the Green Chapel where he will presumably die under the Green Knight's return blow. It is also tested, however, in the bedroom of a magical castle in the wilderness in ways that are by no means obvious to the hero— or to the reader—until the final encounter with the Green Knight.

Sir Gawain is one of the latest and certainly the best of the Middle English romances; yet its greatness lies in the fact that, without ever ceasing to be a romance, a fiction full of the most exquisite comic touches, it is something much larger, one of the really significant literary achievements of the Middle Ages.

Sir Gawain belongs to the so-called Alliterative Revival, a sudden emergence of a body of poems in the alliterative meter of Old English verse. Actually the alliterative tradition must have continued almost without interruption, but only a handful of alliterative poems survives to testify to it from the eleventh century until the Revival in the latter half of the fourteenth. Although the Middle English alliterative line preserves the essential feature of Old English verse—the binding of the two halves of the line together through alliteration—it is longer and does not observe all the rules governing alliteration and stress in Old English. For details, see the section on Old and Middle English Prosody in the general introduction. *Sir Gawain* is written in a unique stanza combining alliteration and rhyme. A group of long alliterative lines (the number of lines varies) concludes with a word or phrase of two syllables—the "bob"—followed by a quatrain—the "wheel"— rhyming *ababa* with the bob. The opening stanza is given below in Middle English with a literal interlinear translation. The alliterating sounds, which should be stressed in reading, have been italicized.

Sithen the *sege* and the *assaut* was *sesed* at Troye,
After the siege and the assault was ceased at Troy,

The *borgh brittened* and *brent* to *brondes* and askes,
The city crumbled and burned to brands and ashes,

The *tulk* that the *trammes* of *tresoun* ther wroght
The man who the plots of treason there wrought

Was tried for his *tricherie*, the *trewest* on erthe.
Was tried for his treachery, the truest on earth.

Hit was Ennias the *athel* and his *highe* kynde,
It was Aeneas the noble and his high race,

That sithen depreced provinces, and patrounes bicome
Who after subjugated provinces, and lords became

Welneghe of al the wele in the west iles.
Wellnigh of all the wealth in the west isles.

Fro riche Romulus to Rome ricchis hym swythe,
Then noble Romulus to Rome proceeds quickly,

Wellnigh of all the wealth in the west isles.

With gret bobbaunce that burghe he biges upon fyrst
With great pride that city he builds at first

And nevenes hit his aune nome, as hit now hat;
And names it his own name, as it now is called;

Ticius to Tuskan and teldes bigynnes,
Ticius (goes) to Tuscany and houses begins,

Langaberde in Lumbardie lyftes up homes,
Longbeard in Lombardy raises up homes,

And fer over the French flod, Felix Brutus
And far over the English Channel, Felix Brutus

On mony bonkkes ful brode Bretayn he settes
On many banks very broad Brittain he sets

                    Wyth wynne,
                      With joy,

Where werre and wrake and wonder
Where war and revenge and wondrous happenings

Bi sythes has wont therinne,
On occasions have dwelled therein

And oft bothe blysse and blunder
And often both joy and strife

Ful skete has skyfted synne.
Very swiftly have alternated since.

Sir Gawain and the Green Knight[1]

Part 1

Since the siege and the assault was ceased at Troy,
The walls breached and burnt down to brands and ashes,
The knight that had knotted the nets of deceit
Was impeached for his perfidy, proven most true,[2]
It was high-born Aeneas and his haughty race   5

---

1. The Modern English translation is by Marie Borroff (1967), who has reproduced the alliterative meter of the original as well as the "bob and wheel," the five-line rhyming group that concludes each of the long irregular stanzas.

2. The treacherous knight is Aeneas who was a traitor to his city, Troy, according to medieval tradition, but Aeneas was actually tried ("impeached") by the Greeks for his refusal to hand over to them his sister Polyxena.

That since prevailed over provinces, and proudly reigned
Over well-nigh all the wealth of the West Isles.[3]
Great Romulus[4] to Rome repairs in haste;
With boast and with bravery builds he that city
And names it with his own name, that it now bears.　　10
Ticius[5] to Tuscany, and towers raises,
Langobard in Lombardy lays out homes,
And far over the French Sea, Felix Brutus[6]
On many broad hills and high Britain he sets,
　　　　　　　　most fair.　　15
　　　　Where war and wrack and wonder
　　　　By shifts have sojourned there,
　　　　And bliss by turns with blunder
　　　　In that land's lot had share.

And since this Britain was built by this baron great,　　20
Bold boys bred there, in broils delighting,
That did in their day many a deed most dire.
More marvels have happened in this merry land
Than in any other I know, since that olden time,
But of those that here built, of British kings,　　25
King Arthur was counted most courteous of all,
Wherefore an adventure I aim to unfold,
That a marvel of might some men think it,
And one unmatched among Arthur's wonders.
If you will listen to my lay but a little while,　　30
As I heard it in hall, I shall hasten to tell
　　　　　　　　anew.
　　　　As it was fashioned featly
　　　　In tale of derring-do,
　　　　And linked in measures meetly　　35
　　　　By letters tried and true.

This king lay at Camelot[7] at Christmastide;
Many good knights and gay his guests were there,
Arrayed of the Round Table[8] rightful brothers,
With feasting and fellowship and carefree mirth.　　40
There true men contended in tournaments many,
Joined there in jousting these gentle knights,
Then came to the court for carol-dancing,
For the feast was in force full fifteen days,
With all the meat and the mirth that men could devise,　　45
Such gaiety and glee, glorious to hear,

---

3. Perhaps Western Europe.
4. The legendary founder of Rome is here given Trojan ancestry, like Aeneas.
5. Not otherwise known. "Langobard" was the reputed founder of Lombardy.
6. Great-grandson of Aeneas and legendary founder of Britain; not elsewhere given the name Felix

(Latin "happy").
7. Capital of Arthur's kingdom, presumably located in southwest England or southern Wales.
8. According to legend, Merlin made the Round Table after a dispute broke out among Arthur's knights about precedence: it seated 100 knights. The table described in the poem is not round.

Brave din by day, dancing by night.
High were their hearts in halls and chambers,
These lords and these ladies, for life was sweet.
In peerless pleasures passed they their days,   50
The most noble knights known under Christ,
And the loveliest ladies that lived on earth ever,
And he the comeliest king, that that court holds,
For all this fair folk in their first age
                  were still.   55
        Happiest of mortal kind,
        King noblest famed of will;
        You would now go far to find
        So hardy a host on hill.

While the New Year was new, but yesternight come,   60
This fair folk at feast two-fold was served,
When the king and his company were come in together,
The chanting in chapel achieved and ended.
Clerics and all the court acclaimed the glad season,
Cried Noel anew, good news to men;   65
Then gallants gather gaily, hand-gifts to make,
Called them out clearly, claimed them by hand,
Bickered long and busily about those gifts.
Ladies laughed aloud, though losers they were,
And he that won was not angered, as well you will know. [9]   70
All this mirth they made until meat was served;
When they had washed them worthily, they went to their seats,
The best seated above, as best it beseemed,
Guenevere the goodly queen gay in the midst
On a dais well-decked and duly arrayed   75
With costly silk curtains, a canopy over,
Of Toulouse and Turkestan tapestries rich,
All broidered and bordered with the best gems
Ever brought into Britain, with bright pennies
                  to pay.   80
        Fair queen, without a flaw,
        She glanced with eyes of grey.
        A seemlier that once he saw,
        In truth, no man could say.

But Arthur would not eat till all were served;   85
So light was his lordly heart, and a little boyish;
His life he liked lively—the less he cared
To be lying for long, or long to sit,
So busy his young blood, his brain so wild.
And also a point of pride pricked him in heart,   90
For he nobly had willed, he would never eat

---

9. The dispensing of New Year's gifts seems to have involved kissing.

On so high a holiday, till he had heard first
Of some fair feat or fray some far-borne tale,
Of some marvel of might, that he might trust,
By champions of chivalry achieved in arms,   95
Or some suppliant came seeking some single knight
To join with him in jousting, in jeopardy each
To lay life for life, and leave it to fortune
To afford him on field fair hap or other.
Such is the king's custom, when his court he holds   100
At each far-famed feast amid his fair host
so dear.
The stout king stands in state
Till a wonder shall appear;
He leads, with heart elate,   105
High mirth in the New Year.

So he stands there in state, the stout young king,
Talking before the high table[1] of trifles fair.
There Gawain the good knight by Guenevere sits,
With Agravain à la dure main on her other side,   110
Both knights of renown, and nephews of the king.
Bishop Baldwin above begins the table,
And Yvain, son of Urien, ate with him there.
These few with the fair queen were fittingly served;
At the side-tables sat many stalwart knights.   115
Then the first course comes, with clamor of trumpets
That were bravely bedecked with bannerets bright,
With noise of new drums and the noble pipes.
Wild were the warbles that wakened that day
In strains that stirred many strong men's hearts.   120
There dainties were dealt out, dishes rare,
Choice fare to choose, on chargers so many
That scarce was there space to set before the people
The service of silver, with sundry meats,
on cloth.   125
Each fair guest freely there
Partakes, and nothing loth;
Twelve dishes before each pair;
Good beer and bright wine both.

Of the service itself I need say no more,   130
For well you will know no tittle was wanting.
Another noise and a new was well-nigh at hand,
That the lord might have leave his life to nourish;
For scarce were the sweet strains still in the hall,
And the first course come to that company fair,   135
There hurtles in at the hall-door an unknown rider,

---

1. The high table is on a dais; the side tables (line   at a right angle with the high table.
115) are on the main floor and run along the walls

One the greatest on ground in growth of his frame:
From broad neck to buttocks so bulky and thick,
And his loins and his legs so long and so great,
Half a giant on earth I hold him to be,   140
But believe him no less than the largest of men,
And that the seemliest in his stature to see, as he rides,
For in back and in breast though his body was grim,
His waist in its width was worthily small,
And formed with every feature in fair accord   145
                             was he.
                    Great wonder grew in hall
                    At his hue most strange to see,
                    For man and gear and all
                    Were green as green could be.   150

And in guise all of green, the gear and the man:
A coat cut close, that clung to his sides,
And a mantle to match, made with a lining
Of furs cut and fitted—the fabric was noble,
Embellished all with ermine, and his hood beside,   155
That was loosed from his locks, and laid on his shoulders.
With trim hose and tight, the same tint of green,
His great calves were girt, and gold spurs under
He bore on silk bands that embellished his heels,
And footgear well-fashioned, for riding most fit.   160
And all his vesture verily was verdant green;
Both the bosses on his belt and other bright gems
That were richly ranged on his raiment noble
About himself and his saddle, set upon silk,
That to tell half the trifles would tax my wits,   165
The butterflies and birds embroidered thereon
In green of the gayest, with many a gold thread.
The pendants of the breast-band, the princely crupper,
And the bars of the bit were brightly enameled;
The stout stirrups were green, that steadied his feet,   170
And the bows of the saddle and the side-panels both,
That gleamed all and glinted with green gems about.
The steed he bestrides of that same green
                             so bright.
                    A green horse great and thick;   175
                    A headstrong steed of might;
                    In broidered bridle quick,
                    Mount matched man aright.

Gay was this goodly man in guise all of green,
And the hair of his head to his horse suited;   180
Fair flowing tresses enfold his shoulders;
A beard big as a bush on his breast hangs,
That with his heavy hair, that from his head falls,

Was evened all about above both his elbows,
That half his arms thereunder were hid in the fashion   185
Of a king's cap-à-dos,[2] that covers his throat.
The mane of that mighty horse much to it like,
Well curled and becombed, and cunningly knotted
With filaments of fine gold amid the fair green,
Here a strand of the hair, here one of gold;   190
His tail and his foretop twin in their hue,
And bound both with a band of a bright green
That was decked adown the dock with dazzling stones
And tied tight at the top with a triple knot
Where many bells well burnished rang bright and clear.   195
Such a mount in his might, nor man on him riding,
None had seen, I dare swear, with sight in that hall
                            so grand.
            As lightning quick and light
            He looked to all at hand;   200
            It seemed that no man might
            His deadly dints withstand.

Yet had he no helm, nor hauberk neither,
Nor plate, nor appurtenance appending to arms,
Nor shaft pointed sharp, nor shield for defense,   205
But in his one hand he had a holly bob
That is goodliest in green when groves are bare,
And an ax in his other, a huge and immense,
A wicked piece of work in words to expound:
The head on its haft was an ell long;   210
The spike of green steel, resplendent with gold;
The blade burnished bright, with a broad edge,
As well shaped to shear as a sharp razor;
Stout was the stave in the strong man's gripe,
That was wound all with iron to the weapon's end,   215
With engravings in green of goodliest work.
A lace lightly about, that led to a knot,
Was looped in by lengths along the fair haft,
And tassels thereto attached in a row,
With buttons of bright green, brave to behold.   220
This horseman hurtles in, and the hall enters;
Riding to the high dais, recked he no danger;
Not a greeting he gave as the guests he o'erlooked,
Nor wasted his words, but "Where is," he said,
"The captain of this crowd? Keenly I wish   225
To see that sire with sight, and to himself say
                            my say."

2. The word *capados* occurs in this form in Middle English only in *Gawain*, here and in line 572. The translator has interpreted it, as the poet apparently did also, as *cap-à-dos*—i.e., a garment covering its wearer "from head to back," on the model of *cap-à-pie*, "from head to foot," referring to armor.

He swaggered all about
To scan the host so gay;
He halted, as if in doubt   230
Who in that hall held sway.

There were stares on all sides as the stranger spoke,
For much did they marvel what it might mean
That a horseman and a horse should have such a hue,
Grow green as the grass, and greener, it seemed,   235
Than green fused on gold more glorious by far.
All the onlookers eyed him, and edged nearer,
And awaited in wonder what he would do,
For many sights had they seen, but such a one never,
So that phantom and faerie the folk there deemed it,   240
Therefore chary of answer was many a champion bold,
And stunned at his strong words stone-still they sat
In a swooning silence in the stately hall.
As all were slipped into sleep, so slackened their speech
                                    apace.   245
            Not all, I think, for dread,
            But some of courteous grace
            Let him who was their head
            Be spokesman in that place.

Then Arthur before the high dais that entrance beholds,   250
And hailed him, as behooved, for he had no fear,
And said "Fellow, in faith you have found fair welcome;
The head of this hostelry Arthur am I;
Leap lightly down, and linger, I pray,
And the tale of your intent you shall tell us after."   255
"Nay, so help me," said the other, "He that on high sits,
To tarry here any time, 'twas not mine errand;
But as the praise of you, prince, is puffed up so high,
And your court and your company are counted the best,
Stoutest under steel-gear on steeds to ride,   260
Worthiest of their works the wide world over,
And peerless to prove in passages of arms,
And courtesy here is carried to its height,
And so at this season I have sought you out.
You may be certain by the branch that I bear in hand   265
That I pass here in peace, and would part friends,
For had I come to this court on combat bent,
I have a hauberk at home, and a helm beside,
A shield and a sharp spear, shining bright,
And other weapons to wield, I ween well, to boot,   270
But as I willed no war, I wore no metal.
But if you be so bold as all men believe,
You will graciously grant the game that I ask
                                    by right."

Arthur answer gave   275
And said, "Sir courteous knight,
If contest bare you crave,
You shall not fail to fight."

"Nay, to fight, in good faith, is far from my thought;
There are about on these benches but beardless children,   280
Were I here in full arms on a haughty steed,
For measured against mine, their might is puny.
And so I call in this court for a Christmas game,
For 'tis Yule and New Year, and many young bloods about;
If any in this house such hardihood claims,   285
Be so bold in his blood, his brain so wild,
As stoutly to strike one stroke for another,
I shall give him as my gift this gisarme noble,
This ax, that is heavy enough, to handle as he likes,
And I shall bide the first blow, as bare as I sit.   290
If there be one so wilful my words to assay,
Let him leap hither lightly, lay hold of this weapon;
I quitclaim it forever, keep it as his own,
And I shall stand him a stroke, steady on this floor,
So you grant me the guerdon to give him another,   295
               sans blame.
        In a twelvemonth and a day
        He shall have of me the same;
        Now be it seen straightway
        Who dares take up the game."   300

If he astonished them at first, stiller were then
All that household in hall, the high and the low;
The stranger on his green steed stirred in the saddle,
And roisterously his red eyes he rolled all about,
Bent his bristling brows, that were bright green,   305
Wagged his beard as he watched who would arise.
When the court kept its counsel he coughed aloud,
And cleared his throat coolly, the clearer to speak:
"What, is this Arthur's house," said that horseman then,
"Whose fame is so fair in far realms and wide?   310
Where is now your arrogance and your awesome deeds,
Your valor and your victories and your vaunting words?
Now are the revel and renown of the Round Table
Overwhelmed with a word of one man's speech,
For all cower and quake, and no cut felt!"   315
With this he laughs so loud that the lord grieved;
The blood for sheer shame shot to his face,
             and pride.
        With rage his face flushed red,
        And so did all beside.   320

Then the king as bold man bred
Toward the stranger took a stride.

And said "Sir, now we see you will say but folly,
Which whoso has sought, it suits that he find.
No guest here is aghast of your great words.   325
Give to me your gisarme, in God's own name,
And the boon you have begged shall straight be granted."
He leaps to him lightly, lays hold of his weapon;
The green fellow on foot fiercely alights.
Now has Arthur his ax, and the haft grips,   330
And sternly stirs it about, on striking bent.
The stranger before him stood there erect,
Higher than any in the house by a head and more;
With stern look as he stood, he stroked his beard,
And with undaunted countenance drew down his coat,   335
No more moved nor dismayed for his mighty dints
Than any bold man on bench had brought him a drink
              of wine.
        Gawain by Guenevere
        Toward the king doth now incline: 340
        "I beseech, before all here,
        That this melee may be mine."

"Would you grant me the grace," said Gawain to the king,
"To be gone from this bench and stand by you there,
If I without discourtesy might quit this board,   345
And if my liege lady misliked it not,
I would come to your counsel before your court noble.
For I find it not fit, as in faith it is known,
When such a boon is begged before all these knights,
Though you be tempted thereto, to take it on yourself   350
While so bold men about upon benches sit,
That no host under heaven is hardier of will,
Nor better brothers-in-arms where battle is joined;
I am the weakest, well I know, and of wit feeblest;
And the loss of my life would be least of any;   355
That I have you for uncle is my only praise;
My body, but for your blood, is barren of worth;
And for that this folly befits not a king,
And 'tis I that have asked it, it ought to be mine,
And if my claim be not comely let all this court judge,   360
              in sight."
        The court assays the claim,
        And in counsel all unite
        To give Gawain the game
        And release the king outright.   365

Then the king called the knight to come to his side,
And he rose up readily, and reached him with speed,
Bows low to his lord, lays hold of the weapon,
And he releases it lightly, and lifts up his hand,
And gives him God's blessing, and graciously prays   370
That his heart and his hand may be hardy both.
"Keep, cousin," said the king, "what you cut with this day,
And if you rule it aright, then readily, I know,
You shall stand the stroke it will strike after."
Gawain goes to the guest with gisarme in hand,   375
And boldly he bides there, abashed not a whit.
Then hails he Sir Gawain, the horseman in green:
"Recount we our contract, ere you come further.
First I ask and adjure you, how you are called
That you tell me true, so that trust it I may."   380
"In good faith," said the good knight, "Gawain am I
Whose buffet befalls you, what'er betide after,
And at this time twelvemonth take from you another
With what weapon you will, and with no man else
                    alive."   385
              The other nods assent:
              "Sir Gawain, as I may thrive,
              I am wondrous well content
              That you this dint shall drive."

"Sir Gawain," said the Green Knight, "By God, I rejoice   390
That your fist shall fetch this favor I seek,
And you have readily rehearsed, and in right terms,
Each clause of my covenant with the king your lord,
Save that you shall assure me, sir, upon oath,
That you shall seek me yourself, wheresoever you deem   395
My lodgings may lie, and look for such wages
As you have offered me here before all this host."
"What is the way there?" said Gawain. "Where do you dwell?
I heard never of your house, by him that made me,
Nor I know you not, knight, your name nor your court.   400
But tell me truly thereof, and teach me your name,
And I shall fare forth to find you, so far as I may,
And this I say in good certain, and swear upon oath."
"That is enough in New Year, you need say no more,"
Said the knight in the green to Gawain the noble,   405
"If I tell you true, when I have taken your knock,
And if you handily have hit, you shall hear straightway
Of my house and my home and my own name;
Then follow in my footsteps by faithful accord.
And if I spend no speech, you shall speed the better: 410
You can feast with your friends, nor further trace
                    my tracks.

> Now hold your grim tool steady
> And show us how it hacks."
> "Gladly, sir; all ready,"   415
> Says Gawain; he strokes the ax.

The Green Knight upon ground girds him with care:
Bows a bit with his head, and bares his flesh:
His long lovely locks he laid over his crown,
Let the naked nape for the need be shown.   420
Gawain grips to his ax and gathers it aloft—
The left foot on the floor before him he set—
Brought it down deftly upon the bare neck,
That the shock of the sharp blow shivered the bones
And cut the flesh cleanly and clove it in twain,   425
That the blade of bright steel bit into the ground.
The head was hewn off and fell to the floor;
Many found it at their feet, as forth it rolled;
The blood gushed from the body, bright on the green,
Yet fell not the fellow, nor faltered a whit,   430
But stoutly he starts forth upon stiff shanks,
And as all stood staring he stretched forth his hand,
Laid hold of his head and heaved it aloft,
Then goes to the green steed, grasps the bridle,
Steps into the stirrup, bestrides his mount,   435
And his head by the hair in his hand holds,
And as steady he sits in the stately saddle
As he had met with no mishap, nor missing were
> his head.
> His bulk about he haled,   440
> That fearsome body that bled;
> There were many in the court that quailed
> Before all his say was said.

For the head in his hand he holds right up;
Toward the first on the dais directs he the face, ·   445
And it lifted up its lids, and looked with wide eyes,
And said as much with its mouth as now you may hear:
"Sir Gawain, forget not to go as agreed,
And cease not to seek till me, sir, you find,
As you promised in the presence of these proud knights.   450
To the Green Chapel come, I charge you, to take
Such a dint as you have dealt—you have well deserved
That your neck should have a knock on New Year's morn.
The Knight of the Green Chapel I am well-known to many,
Wherefore you cannot fail to find me at last;   455
Therefore come, or be counted a recreant knight."
With a roisterous rush he flings round the reins,
Hurtles out at the hall-door, his head in his hand,

That the flint-fire flew from the flashing hooves.
Which way he went, not one of them knew   460
Nor whence he was come in the wide world
                        so fair.
            The king and Gawain gay
            Make game of the Green Knight there,
            Yet all who saw it say   465
            'Twas a wonder past compare.

Though high-born Arthur at heart had wonder,
He let no sign be seen, but said aloud
To the comely queen, with courteous speech,
"Dear dame, on this day dismay you no whit;   470
Such crafts are becoming at Christmastide,
Laughing at interludes, light songs and mirth,
Amid dancing of damsels with doughty knights.
Nevertheless of my meat now let me partake,
For I have met with a marvel, I may not deny."   475
He glanced at Sir Gawain, and gaily he said,
"Now, sir, hang up your ax,³ that has hewn enough,"
And over the high dais it was hung on the wall
That men in amazement might on it look,
And tell in true terms the tale of the wonder.   480
Then they turned toward the table, these two together,
The good king and Gawain, and made great feast,
With all dainties double, dishes rare,
With all manner of meat and minstrelsy both,
Such happiness wholly had they that day   485
                    in hold.
            Now take care, Sir Gawain,
            That your courage wax not cold
            When you must turn again
            To your enterprise foretold.   490

Part 2

This adventure had Arthur of handsels⁴ first
When young was the year, for he yearned to hear tales;
Though they wanted for words when they went to sup,
Now are fierce deeds to follow, their fists stuffed full.
Gawain was glad to begin those games in hall,   495
But if the end be harsher, hold it no wonder,
For though men are merry in mind after much drink,
A year passes apace, and proves ever new:
First things and final conform but seldom.
And so this Yule to the young year yielded place,   500
And each season ensued at its set time;

3. A colloquial expression equivalent to "bury the   also.
hatchet," but here with an appropriate literal sense   4. New Year's presents.

After Christmas there came the cold cheer of Lent,
When with fish and plainer fare our flesh we reprove;
But then the world's weather with winter contends:
The keen cold lessens, the low clouds lift;   505
Fresh falls the rain in fostering showers
On the face of the fields; flowers appear.
The ground and the groves wear gowns of green;
Birds build their nests, and blithely sing
That solace of all sorrow with summer comes   510
                            ere long.
                    And blossoms day by day
                    Bloom rich and rife in throng;
                    Then every grove so gay
                    Of the greenwood rings with song.   515

And then the season of summer with the soft winds,
When Zephyr sighs low over seeds and shoots;
Glad is the green plant growing abroad,
When the dew at dawn drops from the leaves,
To get a gracious glance from the golden sun.   520
But harvest with harsher winds follows hard after,
Warns him to ripen well ere winter comes;
Drives forth the dust in the droughty season,
From the face of the fields to fly high in air.
Wroth winds in the welkin wrestle with the sun,   525
The leaves launch from the linden and light on the ground,
And the grass turns to gray, that once grew green.
Then all ripens and rots that rose up at first,
And so the year moves on in yesterdays many,
And winter once more, by the world's law,   530
                            draws nigh.
                    At Michaelmas[5] the moon
                    Hangs wintry pale in sky;
                    Sir Gawain girds him soon
                    For travails yet to try.   535

Till All-Hallows' Day[6] with Arthur he dwells,
And he held a high feast to honor that knight
With great revels and rich, of the Round Table.
Then ladies lovely and lords debonair
With sorrow for Sir Gawain were sore at heart;   540
Yet they covered their care with countenance glad:
Many a mournful man made mirth for his sake.
So after supper soberly he speaks to his uncle
Of the hard hour at hand, and openly says,
"Now, liege lord of my life, my leave I take;   545
The terms of this task too well you know—

5. September 29.   6. All Saints' Day, November 1.

To count the cost over concerns me nothing.
But I am bound forth betimes to bear a stroke
From the grim man in green, as God may direct."
Then the first and foremost came forth in throng: 550
Yvain and Eric and others of note,
Sir Dodinal le Sauvage, the Duke of Clarence,
Lionel and Lancelot and Lucan the good,
Sir Bors and Sir Bedivere, big men both,
And many manly knights more, with Mador de la Porte.   555
All this courtly company comes to the king
To counsel their comrade, with care in their hearts;
There was much secret sorrow suffered that day
That one so good as Gawain must go in such wise
To bear a bitter blow, and his bright sword   560
                  lay by.
          He said, "Why should I tarry?"
          And smiled with tranquil eye;
          "In destinies sad or merry,
          True men can but try."   565

He dwelt there all that day, and dressed in the morning;
Asked early for his arms, and all were brought.
First a carpet of rare cost was cast on the floor
Where much goodly gear gleamed golden bright;
He takes his place promptly and picks up the steel,   570
Attired in a tight coat of Turkestan silk
And a kingly cap-à-dos, closed at the throat,
That was lavishly lined with a lustrous fur.
Then they set the steel shoes on his sturdy feet
And clad his calves about with comely greaves,   575
And plate well-polished protected his knees,
Affixed with fastenings of the finest gold.
Fair cuisses enclosed, that were cunningly wrought,
His thick-thewed thighs, with thongs bound fast,
And massy chain-mail of many a steel ring   580
He bore on his body, above the best cloth,
With brace burnished bright upon both his arms,
Good couters and gay, and gloves of plate,
And all the goodly gear to grace him well
                  that tide.   585
          His surcoat blazoned bold;
          Sharp spurs to prick with pride;
          And a brave silk band to hold
          The broadsword at his side.

When he had on his arms, his harness was rich,   590
The least latchet or loop laden with gold;
So armored as he was, he heard a mass,
Honored God humbly at the high altar.

Then he comes to the king and his comrades-in-arms,
Takes his leave at last of lords and ladies,   595
And they clasped and kissed him, commending him to Christ.
By then Gringolet was girt with a great saddle
That was gaily agleam with fine gilt fringe,
New-furbished for the need with nail-heads bright;
The bridle and the bars bedecked all with gold;   600
The breast-plate, the saddlebow, the side-panels both,
The caparison and the crupper accorded in hue,
And all ranged on the red the resplendent studs
That glittered and glowed like the glorious sun.
His helm now he holds up and hastily kisses,   605
Well-closed with iron clinches, and cushioned within;
It was high on his head, with a hasp behind,
And a covering of cloth to encase the visor,
All bound and embroidered with the best gems
On broad bands of silk, and bordered with birds,   610
Parrots and popinjays preening their wings,
Lovebirds and love-knots as lavishly wrought
As many women had worked seven winters thereon,
                              entire.
          The diadem costlier yet   615
          That crowned that comely sire,
          With diamonds richly set,
          That flashed as if on fire.

Then they showed forth the shield, that shone all red,
With the pentangle[7] portrayed in purest gold.   620
About his broad neck by the baldric he casts it,
That was meet for the man, and matched him well.
And why the pentangle is proper to that peerless prince
I intend now to tell, though detain me it must.
It is a sign by Solomon sagely devised   625
To be a token of truth, by its title of old,
For it is a figure formed of five points,
And each line is linked and locked with the next
For ever and ever, and hence it is called
In all England, as I hear, the endless knot.   630
And well may he wear it on his worthy arms,
For ever faithful five-fold in five-fold fashion
Was Gawain in good works, as gold unalloyed,
Devoid of all villainy, with virtues adorned
                              in sight.   635
          On shield and coat in view
          He bore that emblem bright,
          As to his word most true
          And in speech most courteous knight.

---

7. A five-pointed star, formed by five lines which are drawn without lifting the pencil from the paper, supposed to have mystical significance; as Solomon's sign (line 625) it was enclosed in a circle.

And first, he was faultless in his five senses,   640
Nor found ever to fail in his five fingers,
And all his fealty was fixed upon the five wounds
That Christ got on the cross, as the creed tells;
And wherever this man in melee took part,
His one thought was of this, past all things else,   645
That all his force was founded on the five joys[8]
That the high Queen of heaven had in her child.
And therefore, as I find, he fittingly had
On the inner part of his shield her image portrayed,
That when his look on it lighted, he never lost heart.   650
The fifth of the five fives followed by this knight
Were beneficence boundless and brotherly love
And pure mind and manners, that none might impeach,
And compassion most precious—these peerless five
Were forged and made fast in him, foremost of men.   655
Now all these five fives were confirmed in this knight,
And each linked in other, that end there was none,
And fixed to five points, whose force never failed,
Nor assembled all on a side, nor asunder either,
Nor anywhere at an end, but whole and entire   660
However the pattern proceeded or played out its course.
And so on his shining shield shaped was the knot
Royally in red gold against red gules,
That is the peerless pentangle, prized of old
                                        in lore.   665
                    Now armed is Gawain gay,
                    And bears his lance before,
                    And soberly said good day,
                    He thought forevermore.

He struck his steed with the spurs and sped on his way   670
So fast that the flint-fire flashed from the stones.
When they saw him set forth they were sore aggrieved,
And all sighed softly, and said to each other,
Fearing for their fellow, "Ill fortune it is
That you, man, must be marred, that most are worthy!   675
His equal on this earth can hardly be found;
To have dealt more discreetly had done less harm,
And have dubbed him a duke, with all due honor.
A great leader of lords he was like to become,
And better so to have been than battered to bits,   680
Beheaded by an elf-man,[9] for empty pride!
Who would credit that a king could be counseled so,
And caught in a cavil in a Christmas game?"
Many were the warm tears they wept from their eyes

8. The Annunciation, Nativity, Resurrection, Ascension, and Assumption.
9. Supernatural being.

When goodly Sir Gawain was gone from the court   685
                    that day.
                    No longer he abode,
                    But speedily went his way
                    Over many a wandering road,
                    As I heard my author say.   690

Now he rides in his array through the realm of Logres,[1]
Sir Gawain, God knows, though it gave him small joy!
All alone must he lodge through many a long night
Where the food that he fancied was far from his plate;
He had no mate but his mount, over mountain and plain,   695
Nor man to say his mind to but almighty God,
Till he had wandered well-nigh into North Wales.
All the islands of Anglesey he holds on his left,
And follows, as he fares, the fords by the coast,
Comes over at Holy Head, and enters next   700
The Wilderness of Wirral[2]—few were within
That had great good will toward God or man.
And earnestly he asked of each mortal he met
If he had ever heard aught of a knight all green,
Or of a Green Chapel, on ground thereabouts,   705
And all said the same, and solemnly swore
They saw no such knight all solely green
                    in hue.
                    Over country wild and strange
                    The knight sets off anew;   710
                    Often his course must change
                    Ere the Chapel comes in view.

Many a cliff must he climb in country wild;
Far off from all his friends, forlorn must he ride;
At each strand or stream where the stalwart passed   715
'Twere a marvel if he met not some monstrous foe,
And that so fierce and forbidding that fight he must.
So many were the wonders he wandered among
That to tell but the tenth part would tax my wits.
Now with serpents he wars, now with savage wolves,   720
Now with wild men of the woods, that watched from the rocks,
Both with bulls and with bears, and with boars besides,
And giants that came gibbering from the jagged steeps.
Had he not borne himself bravely, and been on God's side,
He had met with many mishaps and mortal harms.   725
And if the wars were unwelcome, the winter was worse,
When the cold clear rains rushed from the clouds

1. One of the names for Arthur's kingdom.   sey; there he turned east across the Dee to the forest
2. Gawain went from Camelot north to the north-   of Wirral in Cheshire.
ern coast of Wales, opposite the islands of Angle-

And froze before they could fall to the frosty earth.
Near slain by the sleet he sleeps in his irons
More nights than enough, among naked rocks,   730
Where clattering from the crest the cold stream ran
And hung in hard icicles high overhead.
Thus in peril and pain and predicaments dire
He rides across country till Christmas Eve,
                    our knight.   735
            And at that holy tide
            He prays with all his might
            That Mary may be his guide
            Till a dwelling comes in sight.

By a mountain next morning he makes his way   740
Into a forest fastness, fearsome and wild;
High hills on either hand, with hoar woods below,
Oaks old and huge by the hundred together.
The hazel and the hawthorn were all intertwined
With rough raveled moss, that raggedly hung,   745
With many birds unblithe upon bare twigs
That peeped most piteously for pain of the cold.
The good knight on Gringolet glides thereunder
Through many a marsh and mire, a man all alone;
He feared for his default, should he fail to see   750
The service of that Sire that on that same night
Was born of a bright maid, to bring us his peace.
And therefore sighing he said, "I beseech of Thee, Lord,
And Mary, thou mildest mother so dear,
Some harborage where haply I might hear mass   755
And Thy matins tomorrow—meekly I ask it,
And thereto proffer and pray my pater and ave
                    and creed."
            He said his prayer with sighs,
            Lamenting his misdeed;   760
            He crosses himself, and cries
            On Christ in his great need.

No sooner had Sir Gawain signed himself thrice
Than he was ware, in the wood, of a wondrous dwelling,
Within a moat, on a mound, bright amid boughs   765
Of many a tree great of girth that grew by the water—
A castle as comely as a knight could own,
On grounds fair and green, in a goodly park
With a palisade of palings planted about
For two miles and more, round many a fair tree.   770
The stout knight stared at that stronghold great
As it shimmered and shone amid shining leaves,
Then with helmet in hand he offers his thanks

To Jesus and Saint Julian,[3] that are gentle both,
That in courteous accord had inclined to his prayer;   775
"Now fair harbor," said he, "I humbly beseech!"
Then he pricks his proud steed with the plated spurs,
And by chance he has chosen the chief path
That brought the bold knight to the bridge's end
                              in haste.   780
                    The bridge hung high in air;
                    The gates were bolted fast;
                    The walls well-framed to bear
                    The fury of the blast.

The man on his mount remained on the bank   785
Of the deep double moat that defended the place.
The wall went in the water wondrous deep,
And a long way aloft it loomed overhead.
It was built of stone blocks to the battlements' height,
With corbels under cornices in comeliest style;   790
Watch-towers trusty protected the gate,
With many a lean loophole, to look from within:
A better-made barbican the knight beheld never.
And behind it there hoved a great hall and fair:
Turrets rising in tiers, with tines[4] at their tops,   795
Spires set beside them, splendidly long,
With finials[5] well-fashioned, as filigree fine.
Chalk-white chimneys over chambers high
Gleamed in gay array upon gables and roofs;
The pinnacles in panoply, pointing in air,   800
So vied there for his view that verily it seemed
A castle cut of paper for a king's feast.[6]
The good knight on Gringolet thought it great luck
If he could but contrive to come there within
To keep the Christmas feast in that castle fair   805
                              and bright.
                    There answered to his call
                    A porter most polite;
                    From his station on the wall
                    He greets the errant knight.   810

"Good sir," said Gawain, "Wouldst go to inquire
If your lord would allow me to lodge here a space?"
"Peter!" said the porter, "For my part, I think
So noble a knight will not want for a welcome!"
Then he bustles off briskly, and comes back straight,   815
And many servants beside, to receive him the better.
They let down the drawbridge and duly went forth

3. Patron saint of hospitality.   5. Gable ornaments.
4. Spikes.   6. A common table decoration at feasts.

And kneeled down on their knees on the naked earth
To welcome this warrior as best they were able.
They proffered him passage—the portals stood wide—   820
And he beckoned them to rise, and rode over the bridge.
Men steadied his saddle as he stepped to the ground,
And there stabled his steed many stalwart folk.
Now come the knights and the noble squires
To bring him with bliss into the bright hall.   825
When his high helm was off, there hied forth a throng
Of attendants to take it, and see to its care;
They bore away his brand[7] and his blazoned shield;
Then graciously he greeted those gallants each one,
And many a noble drew near, to do the knight honor.   830
All in his armor into hall he was led,
Where fire on a fair hearth fiercely blazed.
And soon the lord himself descends from his chamber
To meet with good manners the man on his floor.
He said, "To this house you are heartily welcome: 835
What is here is wholly yours, to have in your power
                    and sway."
                "Many thanks," said Sir Gawain;
                "May Christ your pains repay!"
                The two embrace amain   840
                As men well met that day.

Gawain gazed on the host that greeted him there,
And a lusty fellow he looked, the lord of that place:
A man of massive mold, and of middle age;
Broad, bright was his beard, of a beaver's hue,   845
Strong, steady his stance, upon stalwart shanks,
His face fierce as fire, fair-spoken withal,
And well-suited he seemed in Sir Gawain's sight
To be a master of men in a mighty keep.
They pass into a parlor, where promptly the host   850
Has a servant assigned him to see to his needs,
And there came upon his call many courteous folk
That brought him to a bower where bedding was noble,
With heavy silk hangings hemmed all in gold,
Coverlets and counterpanes curiously wrought,   855
A canopy over the couch, clad all with fur,
Curtains running on cords, caught to gold rings,
Woven rugs on the walls of eastern work,
And the floor, under foot, well-furnished with the same.
Amid light talk and laughter they loosed from him then   860
His war-dress of weight and his worthy clothes.
Robes richly wrought they brought him right soon,
To change there in chamber and choose what he would.

7. Sword.

When he had found one he fancied, and flung it about,
Well-fashioned for his frame, with flowing skirts,   865
His face fair and fresh as the flowers of spring,
All the good folk agreed, that gazed on him then,
His limbs arrayed royally in radiant hues,
That so comely a mortal never Christ made
                         as he.   870
             Whatever his place of birth,
             It seemed he well might be
             Without a peer on earth
             In martial rivalry.

A couch before the fire, where fresh coals burned,   875
They spread for Sir Gawain splendidly now
With quilts quaintly stitched, and cushions beside,
And then a costly cloak they cast on his shoulders
Of bright silk, embroidered on borders and hems,
With furs of the finest well-furnished within,   880
And bound about with ermine, both mantle and hood;
And he sat at that fireside in sumptuous estate
And warmed himself well, and soon he waxed merry.
Then attendants set a table upon trestles broad,
And lustrous white linen they laid thereupon,   885
A saltcellar of silver, spoons of the same.
He washed himself well and went to his place,
Men set his fare before him in fashion most fit.
There were soups of all sorts, seasoned with skill,
Double-sized servings, and sundry fish,   890
Some baked, some breaded, some broiled on the coals,
Some simmered, some in stews, steaming with spice,
And with sauces to sup that suited his taste.
He confesses it a feast with free words and fair;
They requite him as kindly with courteous jests,   895
                    well-sped.
             "Tonight you fast[8] and pray;
             Tomorrow we'll see you fed."
             The knight grows wondrous gay
             As the wine goes to his head.   900

Then at times and by turns, as at table he sat,
They questioned him quietly, with queries discreet,
And he courteously confessed that he comes from the court,
And owns him of the brotherhood of high-famed Arthur,
The right royal ruler of the Round Table,   905
And the guest by their fireside is Gawain himself,
Who has happened on their house at that holy feast.
When the name of the knight was made known to the lord,

8. Gawain is said to be "fasting" because the meal, though elaborate, consisted only of fish dishes,
appropriate to a fasting day.

Then loudly he laughed, so elated he was,
And the men in that household made haste with joy   910
To appear in his presence promptly that day,
That of courage ever-constant, and customs pure,
Is pattern and paragon, and praised without end:
Of all knights on earth most honored is he.
Each said solemnly aside to his brother,   915
"Now displays of deportment shall dazzle our eyes
And the polished pearls of impeccable speech;
The high art of eloquence is ours to pursue
Since the father of fine manners is found in our midst.
Great is God's grace, and goodly indeed,   920
That a guest such as Gawain he guides to us here
When men sit and sing of their Savior's birth
     in view.
    With command of manners pure
    He shall each heart imbue;   925
    Who shares his converse, sure,
    Shall learn love's language true."

When the knight had done dining and duly arose,
The dark was drawing on; the day nigh ended.
Chaplains in chapels and churches about   930
Rang the bells aright, reminding all men
Of the holy evensong of the high feast.
The lord attends alone: his fair lady sits
In a comely closet, secluded from sight.
Gawain in gay attire goes thither soon;   935
The lord catches his coat, and calls him by name,
And has him sit beside him, and says in good faith
No guest on God's earth would he gladlier greet.
For that Gawain thanked him; the two then embraced
And sat together soberly the service through.   940
Then the lady, that longed to look on the knight,
Came forth from her closet with her comely maids.
The fair hues of her flesh, her face and her hair
And her body and her bearing were beyond praise,
And excelled the queen herself, as Sir Gawain thought.   945
He goes forth to greet her with gracious intent;
Another lady led her by the left hand
That was older than she—an ancient, it seemed,
And held in high honor by all men about.
But unlike to look upon, those ladies were,   950
For if the one was fresh, the other was faded:
Bedecked in bright red was the body of one;
Flesh hung in folds on the face of the other;
On one a high headdress, hung all with pearls;
Her bright throat and bosom fair to behold,   955
Fresh as the first snow fallen upon hills;

A wimple the other one wore round her throat;
Her swart chin well swaddled, swathed all in white;
Her forehead enfolded in flounces of silk
That framed a fair fillet, of fashion ornate,   960
And nothing bare beneath save the black brows,
The two eyes and the nose, the naked lips,
And they unsightly to see, and sorrily bleared.
A beldame, by God, she may well be deemed,
                              of pride!   965
          She was short and thick of waist,
          Her buttocks round and wide;
          More toothsome, to his taste,
          Was the beauty by her side.

When Gawain had gazed on that gay lady,   970
With leave of her lord, he politely approached;
To the elder in homage he humbly bows;
The lovelier he salutes with a light embrace.
He claims a comely kiss, and courteously he speaks;
They welcome him warmly, and straightway he asks   975
To be received as their servant, if they so desire.
They take him between them; with talking they bring him
Beside a bright fire; bade then that spices
Be freely fetched forth, to refresh them the better,
And the good wine therewith, to warm their hearts.   980
The lord leaps about in light-hearted mood;
Contrives entertainments and timely sports;
Takes his hood from his head and hangs it on a spear,
And offers him openly the honor thereof
Who should promote the most mirth at that Christmas feast;   985
"And I shall try for it, trust me—contend with the best,
Ere I go without my headgear by grace of my friends!"
Thus with light talk and laughter the lord makes merry
To gladden the guest he had greeted in hall
                              that day.   990
          At the last he called for light
          The company to convey;
          Gawain says goodnight
          And retires to bed straightway.

On the morn when each man is mindful in heart   995
That God's son was sent down to suffer our death,
No household but is blithe for his blessed sake;
So was it there on that day, with many delights.
Both at larger meals and less they were lavishly served
By doughty lads on dais, with delicate fare;   1000
The old ancient lady, highest she sits;
The lord at her left hand leaned, as I hear;
Sir Gawain in the center, beside the gay lady,

Where the food was brought first to that festive board,
And thence throughout the hall, as they held most fit,   1005
To each man was offered in order of rank.
There was meat, there was mirth, there was much joy,
That to tell all the tale would tax my wits,
Though I pained me, perchance, to paint it with care;
But yet I know that our knight and the noble lady   1010
Were accorded so closely in company there,
With the seemly solace of their secret words,
With speeches well-sped, spotless and pure,
That each prince's pastime their pleasures far
                                        outshone.   1015
                    Sweet pipes beguile their cares,
                    And the trumpet of martial tone;
                    Each tends his affairs
                    And those two tend their own.

That day and all the next, their disport was noble,   1020
And the third day, I think, pleased them no less;
The joys of St. John's Day[9] were justly praised,
And were the last of their like for those lords and ladies;
Then guests were to go in the gray morning,
Wherefore they whiled the night away with wine and with mirth, 1025
Moved to the measures of many a blithe carol;
At last, when it was late, took leave of each other,
Each one of those worthies, to wend his way.
Gawain bids goodbye to his goodly host
Who brings him to his chamber, the chimney beside,   1030
And detains him in talk, and tenders his thanks
And holds it an honor to him and his people
That he has harbored in his house at that holy time
And embellished his abode with his inborn grace.
"As long as I may live, my luck is the better   1035
That Gawain was my guest at God's own feast!"
"Noble sir," said the knight, "I cannot but think
All the honor is your own—may heaven requite it!
And your man to command I account myself here
As I am bound and beholden, and shall be, come   1040
                                        what may."
                    The lord with all his might
                    Entreats his guest to stay;
                    Brief answer makes the knight:
                    Next morning he must away.   1045

Then the lord of that land politely inquired
What dire affair had forced him, at that festive time,
So far from the king's court to fare forth alone

9. December 27.

Ere the holidays wholly had ended in hall.
"In good faith," said Gawain, "you have guessed the truth: 1050
On a high errand and urgent I hastened away,
For I am summoned by myself to seek for a place—
I would I knew whither, or where it might be!
Far rather would I find it before the New Year
Than own the land of Logres, so help me our Lord!   1055
Wherefore, sir, in friendship this favor I ask,
That you say in sober earnest, if something you know
Of the Green Chapel, on ground far or near,
Or the lone knight that lives there, of like hue of green.
A certain day was set by assent of us both   1060
To meet at that landmark, if I might last,
And from now to the New Year is nothing too long,
And I would greet the Green Knight there, would God but allow,
More gladly, by God's Son, than gain the world's wealth!
And I must set forth to search, as soon as I may;   1065
To be about the business I have but three days
And would as soon sink down dead as desist from my errand."
Then smiling said the lord, "Your search, sir, is done,
For we shall see you to that site by the set time.
Let Gawain grieve no more over the Green Chapel;   1070
You shall be in your own bed, in blissful ease,
All the forenoon, and fare forth the first of the year,
And make the goal by midmorn, to mind your affairs,
no fear!
Tarry till the fourth day   1075
And ride on the first of the year.
We shall set you on your way;
It is not two miles from here."

The Gawain was glad, and gleefully he laughed:
"Now I thank you for this, past all things else!   1080
Now my goal is here at hand! With a glad heart I shall
Both tarry, and undertake any task you devise."
Then the host seized his arm and seated him there;
Let the ladies be brought, to delight them the better,
And in fellowship fair by the fireside they sit;   1085
So gay waxed the good host, so giddy his words,
All waited in wonder what next he would say.
Then he stares on the stout knight, and sternly he speaks:
"You have bound yourself boldly my bidding to do—
Will you stand by that boast, and obey me this once?"   1090
"I shall do so indeed," said the doughty knight;
"While I lie in your lodging, your laws will I follow."
"As you have had," said the host, "many hardships abroad
And little sleep of late, you are lacking, I judge,
Both in nourishment needful and nightly rest;   1095
You shall lie abed late in your lofty chamber

Tomorrow until mass, and meet then to dine
When you will, with my wife, who will sit by your side
And talk with you at table, the better to cheer
                           our guest.   1100
              A-hunting I will go
              While you lie late and rest."
              The knight, inclining low,
              Assents to each behest.

"And Gawain," said the good host, "agree now to this: 1105
Whatever I win in the woods I will give you at eve,
And all you have earned you must offer to me;
Swear now, sweet friend, to swap as I say,
Whether hands, in the end, be empty or better."
"By God," said Sir Gawain, "I grant it forthwith!   1110
If you find the game good, I shall gladly take part."
"Let the bright wine be brought, and our bargain is done,"
Said the lord of that land—the two laughed together.
Then they drank and they dallied and doffed all constraint,
These lords and these ladies, as late as they chose,   1115
And then with gaiety and gallantries and graceful adieux
They talked in low tones, and tarried at parting.
With compliments comely they kiss at the last;
There were brisk lads about with blazing torches
To see them safe to bed, for soft repose   1120
                           long due.
              Their covenants, yet awhile,
              They repeat, and pledge anew;
              That lord could well beguile
              Men's hearts, with mirth in view.   1125

Part 3

Long before daylight they left their beds;
Guests that wished to go gave word to their grooms,
And they set about briskly to bind on saddles,
Tend to their tackle, tie up trunks.
The proud lords appear, appareled to ride,   1130
Leap lightly astride, lay hold of their bridles,
Each one on his way to his worthy house.
The liege lord of the land was not the last
Arrayed there to ride, with retainers many;
He had a bite to eat when he had heard mass;   1135
With horn to the hills he hastens amain.
By the dawn of that day over the dim earth,
Master and men were mounted and ready.
Then they harnessed in couples the keen-scented hounds,
Cast wide the kennel-door and called them forth,   1140
Blew upon their bugles bold blasts three;

The dogs began to bay with a deafening din,
And they quieted them quickly and called them to heel,
A hundred brave huntsmen, as I have heard tell,
                    together.   1145
          Men at stations meet;
          From the hounds they slip the tether;
          The echoing horns repeat,
          Clear in the merry weather.

At the clamor of the quest, the quarry trembled;   1150
Deer dashed through the dale, dazed with dread;
Hastened to the high ground, only to be
Turned back by the beaters, who boldly shouted.
They harmed not the harts, with their high heads,
Let the bucks go by, with their broad antlers,   1155
For it was counted a crime, in the close season,
If a man of that demesne should molest the male deer.
The hinds were headed up, with "Hey!" and "Ware!"
The does with great din were driven to the valleys.
Then you were ware, as they went, of the whistling of arrows;   1160
At each bend under boughs the bright shafts flew
That tore the tawny hide with their tapered heads.
Ah! they bray and they bleed, on banks they die,
And ever the pack pell-mell comes panting behind;
Hunters with shrill horns hot on their heels—   1165
Like the cracking of cliffs their cries resounded.
What game got away from the gallant archers
Was promptly picked off at the posts below
When they were harried on the heights and herded to the streams:
The watchers were so wary at the waiting-stations,   1170
And the greyhounds so huge, that eagerly snatched,
And finished them off as fast as folk could see
                    with sight.
          The lord, now here, now there,
          Spurs forth in sheer delight.   1175
          And drives, with pleasures rare,
          The day to the dark night.

So the lord in the linden-wood leads the hunt
And Gawain the good knight in gay bed lies,
Lingered late alone, till daylight gleamed,   1180
Under coverlet costly, curtained about.
And as he slips into slumber, slyly there comes
A little din at his door, and the latch lifted,
And he holds up his heavy head out of the clothes;
A corner of the curtain he caught back a little   1185
And waited there warily, to see what befell.
Lo! it was the lady, loveliest to behold,
That drew the door behind her deftly and still

And was bound for his bed—abashed was the knight,
And laid his head low again in likeness of sleep;   1190
And she stepped stealthily, and stole to his bed,
Cast aside the curtain and came within,
And set herself softly on the bedside there,
And lingered at her leisure, to look on his waking.
The fair knight lay feigning for a long while,   1195
Conning in his conscience what his case might
Mean or amount to—a marvel he thought it.
But yet he said within himself, "More seemly it were
To try her intent by talking a little."
So he started and stretched, as startled from sleep,   1200
Lifts wide his lids in likeness of wonder,
And signs himself swiftly, as safer to be,
                                        with art.
                    Sweetly does she speak
                    And kindling glances dart,
                    Blent white and red on cheek   1205
                    And laughing lips apart.

"Good morning, Sir Gawain," said that gay lady,
"A slack sleeper you are, to let one slip in!
Now you are taken in a trice—a truce we must make;   1210
Or I shall bind you in your bed, of that be assured."
Thus laughing lightly that lady jested.
"Good morning, good lady," said Gawain the blithe,
"Be it with me as you will; I am well content!
For I surrender myself, and sue for your grace,   1215
And that is best, I believe, and behooves me now."
Thus jested in answer that gentle knight.
"But if, lovely lady, you misliked it not,
And were pleased to permit your prisoner to rise,
I should quit this couch and accoutre me better,   1220
And be clad in more comfort for converse here."
"Nay, not so, sweet sir," said the smiling lady;
"You shall not rise from your bed; I direct you better:
I shall hem and hold you on either hand,
And keep company awhile with my captive knight.   1225
For as certain as I sit here, Sir Gawain you are,
Whom all the world worships, whereso you ride;
Your honor, your courtesy are highest acclaimed
By lords and by ladies, by all living men;
And lo! we are alone here, and left to ourselves: 1230
My lord and his liegemen are long departed,
The household asleep, my handmaids too,
The door drawn, and held by a well-driven bolt,
And since I have in this house him whom all love,
I shall while the time away with mirthful speech   1235
                    at will.

My body is here at hand,
Your each wish to fulfill;
Your servant to command
I am, and shall be still."   1240

"In good faith," said Gawain, "my gain is the greater,
Though I am not he of whom you have heard;
To arrive at such reverence as you recount here
I am one all unworthy, and well do I know it.
By heaven, I would hold me the happiest of men   1245
If by word or by work I once might aspire
To the prize of your praise—'twere a pure joy!"
"In good faith, Sir Gawain," said that gay lady,
"The well-proven prowess that pleases all others,
Did I scant or scout it, 'twere scarce becoming.   1250
But there are ladies, believe me, that had liefer far
Have thee here in their hold, as I have today,
To pass an hour in pastime with pleasant words,
Assuage all their sorrows and solace their hearts,
Than much of the goodly gems and gold they possess.   1255
But laud be to the Lord of the lofty skies,
For here in my hands all hearts' desire
               doth lie."
        Great welcome got he there
        From the lady who sat him by;   1260
        With fitting speech and fair
        The good knight makes reply.

"Madame," said the merry man, "Mary reward you!
For in good faith, I find your beneficence noble.
And the fame of fair deeds runs far and wide,   1265
But the praise you report pertains not to me,
But comes of your courtesy and kindness of heart."
"By the high Queen of heaven" (said she) "I count it not so,
For were I worth all the women in this world alive,
And all wealth and all worship were in my hands,   1270
And I should hunt high and low, a husband to take,
For the nurture I have noted in thee, knight, here,
The comeliness and courtesies and courtly mirth—
And so I had ever heard, and now hold it true—
No other on this earth should have me for wife."   1275
"You are bound to a better man," the bold knight said,
"Yet I prize the praise you have proffered me here,
And soberly your servant, my sovereign I hold you,
And acknowledge me your knight, in the name of Christ."
So they talked of this and that until 'twas nigh noon,   1280
And ever the lady languishing in likeness of love.
With feat words and fair he framed his defense,
For were she never so winsome, the warrior had

The less will to woo, for the wound that his bane
must be.   1285
He must bear the blinding blow,
For such is fate's decree:
The lady asks leave to go;
He grants it full and free.

Then she gaily said goodbye, and glanced at him, laughing,   1290
And as she stood, she astonished him with a stern speech:
"Now may the Giver of all good words these glad hours repay!
But our guest is not Gawain—forgot is that thought."
"How so?" said the other, and asks in some haste,
For he feared he had been at fault in the forms of his speech.   1295
But she held up her hand, and made answer thus:
"So good a knight as Gawain is given out to be,
And the model of fair demeanor and manners pure,
Had he lain so long at a lady's side,
Would have claimed a kiss, by his courtesy,   1300
Through some touch or trick of phrase at some tale's end."
Said Gawain, "Good lady, I grant it at once!
I shall kiss at your command, as becomes a knight,
And more, lest you mislike, so let be, I pray."
With that she turns toward him, takes him in her arms,   1305
Leans down her lovely head, and lo! he is kissed.
They commend each other to Christ with comely words,
He sees her forth safely, in silence they part,
And then he lies no later in his lofty bed,
But calls to his chamberlain, chooses his clothes,   1310
Goes in those garments gladly to mass,
Then takes his way to table, where attendants wait,
And made merry all day, till the moon rose
in view
Was never knight beset   1315
'Twixt worthier ladies two:
The crone and the coquette;
Fair pastimes they pursue.

And the lord of the land rides late and long,
Hunting the barren hind over the broad heath.   1320
He had slain such a sum, when the sun sank low,
Of does and other deer, as would dizzy one's wits.
Then they trooped in together in triumph at last,
And the count of the quarry quickly they take.
The lords lent a hand with their liegemen many,   1325
Picked out the plumpest and put them together
And duly dressed the deer, as the deed requires.
Some were assigned the assay of the fat:
Two fingers' width fully they found on the leanest.
Then they slit the slot open and searched out the paunch,   1330

Trimmed it with trencher-knives and tied it up tight.
They flayed the fair hide from the legs and trunk,
Then broke open the belly and laid bare the bowels,
Deftly detaching and drawing them forth.
And next at the neck they neatly parted   1335
The weasand[1] from the windpipe, and cast away the guts.
At the shoulders with sharp blades they showed their skill,
Boning them from beneath, lest the sides be marred;
They breached the broad breast and broke it in twain,
And again at the gullet they begin with their knives,   1340
Cleave down the carcass clear to the breach;
Two tender morsels they take from the throat,
Then round the inner ribs they rid off a layer
And carve out the kidney-fat, close to the spine,
Hewing down to the haunch, that all hung together,   1345
And held it up whole, and hacked it free,
And this they named the numbles,[2] that knew such terms
                    of art.
        They divide the crotch in two,
        And straightway then they start   1350
        To cut the backbone through
        And cleave the trunk apart.

With hard strokes they hewed off the head and the neck,
Then swiftly from the sides they severed the chine,
And the corbie's bone[3] they cast on a branch.   1355
Then they pierced the plump sides, impaled either one
With the hock of the hind foot, and hung it aloft,
To each person his portion most proper and fit.
On a hide of a hind the hounds they fed
With the liver and the lights,[4] the leathery paunches,   1360
And bread soaked in blood well blended therewith.
High horns and shrill set hounds a-baying,
Then merrily with their meat they make their way home,
Blowing on their bugles many a brave blast.
Ere dark had descended, that doughty band   1365
Was come within the walls where Gawain waits
                    at leisure.
        Bliss and hearth-fire bright
        Await the master's pleasure;
        When the two men met that night,   1370
        Joy surpassed all measure.

Then the host in the hall his household assembles,
With the dames of high degree and their damsels fair.

1. Esophagus.
2. The other internal organs.
3. A bit of gristle assigned to the ravens

("corbies").
4. Lungs.

In the presence of the people, a party he sends
To convey him his venison in view of the knight.   1375
And in high good-humor he hails him then,
Counts over the kill, the cuts on the tallies,
Holds high the hewn ribs, heavy with fat.
"What think you, sir, of this? Have I thriven well?
Have I won with my woodcraft a worthy prize?"   1380
"In good earnest," said Gawain, "this game is the finest
I have seen in seven years in the season of winter."
"And I give it to you, Gawain," said the goodly host,
"For according to our convenant, you claim it as your own."
"That is so," said Sir Gawain, "the same say I: 1385
What I worthily have won within these fair walls,
Herewith I as willingly award it to you."
He embraces his broad neck with both his arms,
And confers on him a kiss in the comeliest style.
"Have here my profit, it proved no better;   1390
Ungrudging do I grant it, were it greater far."
"Such a gift," said the good host, "I gladly accept—
Yet it might be all the better, would you but say
Where you won this same award, by your wits alone."
"That was no part of the pact; press me no further,   1395
For you have had what behooves; all other claims
                              forbear."
                    With jest and compliment
                    They conversed, and cast off care;
                    To the table soon they went;   1400
                    Fresh dainties wait them there.

And then by the chimney-side they chat at their ease;
The best wine was brought them, and bounteously served;
And after in their jesting they jointly accord
To do on the second day the deeds of the first: 1405
That the two men should trade, betide as it may,
What each had taken in, at eve when they met.
They seal the pact solemnly in sight of the court;
Their cups were filled afresh to confirm the jest;
Then at last they took their leave, for late was the hour,   1410
Each to his own bed hastening away.
Before the barnyard cock had crowed but thrice
The lord had leapt from his rest, his liegemen as well.
Both of mass and their meal they made short work:
By the dim light of dawn they were deep in the woods   1415
                              away.
                    With huntsmen and with horns
                    Over plains they pass that day;
                    They release, amid the thorns,
                    Swift hounds that run and bay.   1420

Soon some were on a scent by the side of a marsh;
When the hounds opened cry, the head of the hunt
Rallied them with rough words, raised a great noise.
The hounds that had heard it came hurrying straight
And followed along with their fellows, forty together.   1425
Then such a clamor and cry of coursing hounds
Arose, that the rocks resounded again.
Hunters exhorted them with horn and with voice;
Then all in a body bore off together
Between a mere in the marsh and a menacing crag,   1430
To a rise where the rock stood rugged and steep,
And boulders lay about, that blocked their approach.
Then the company in consort closed on their prey:
They surrounded the rise and the rocks both,
For well they were aware that it waited within,   1435
The beast that the bloodhounds boldly proclaimed.
Then they beat on the bushes and bade him appear,
And he made a murderous rush in the midst of them all;
The best of all boars broke from his cover,
That had ranged long unrivaled, a renegade old,   1440
For of tough-brawned boars he was biggest far,
Most grim when he grunted—then grieved were many,
For three at the first thrust he threw to the earth,
And dashed away at once without more damage.
With "Hi!" "Hi!" and "Hey!" "Hey!" the others followed,   1445
Had horns at their lips, blew high and clear.
Merry was the music of men and of hounds
That were bound after this boar, his bloodthirsty heart
                            to quell.
                  Often he stands at bay,   1450
                  Then scatters the pack pell-mell;
                  He hurts the hounds, and they
                  Most dolefully yowl and yell.

Men then with mighty bows moved in to shoot,
Aimed at him with their arrows and often hit,   1455
But the points had no power to pierce through his hide,
And the barbs were brushed aside by his bristly brow;
Though the shank of the shaft shivered in pieces,
The head hopped away, wheresoever it struck.
But when their stubborn strokes had stung him at last,   1460
Then, foaming in his frenzy, fiercely he charges,
Hies at them headlong that hindered his flight,
And many feared for their lives, and fell back a little.
But the lord on a lively horse leads the chase;
As a high-mettled huntsman his horn he blows;   1465
He sounds the assembly and sweeps through the brush,
Pursuing this wild swine till the sunlight slanted.

All day with this deed they drive forth the time
While our lone knight so lovesome lies in his bed,
Sir Gawain safe at home, in silken bower   1470
                 so gay.
        The lady, with guile in heart,
        Came early where he lay;
        She was at him with all her art
        To turn his mind her way.   1475

She comes to the curtain and coyly peeps in;
Gawain thought it good to greet her at once,
And she richly repays him with her ready words,
Settles softly at his side, and suddenly she laughs,
And with a gracious glance, she begins on him thus: 1480
"Sir, if you be Gawain, it seems a great wonder—
A man so well-meaning, and mannerly disposed,
And cannot act in company as courtesy bids,
And if one takes the trouble to teach him, 'tis all in vain.
That lesson learned lately is lightly forgot,   1485
Though I painted it as plain as my poor wit allowed."
"What lesson, dear lady?" he asked all alarmed;
"I have been much to blame, if your story be true."
"Yet my counsel was of kissing," came her answer then,
"Where favor has been found, freely to claim   1490
As accords with the conduct of courteous knights."
"My dear," said the doughty man, "dismiss that thought;
Such freedom, I fear, might offend you much;
It were rude to request if the right were denied."
"But none can deny you," said the noble dame,   1495
"You are stout enough to constrain with strength, if you choose,
Were any so ungracious as to grudge you aught."
"By heaven," said he, "you have answered well,
But threats never throve among those of my land,
Nor any gift not freely given, good though it be.   1500
I am yours to command, to kiss when you please;
You may lay on as you like, and leave off at will.
              With this,
        The lady lightly bends
        And graciously gives him a kiss;   1505
        The two converse as friends
        Of true love's trials and bliss.

"I should like, by your leave," said the lovely lady,
"If it did not annoy you, to know for what cause
So brisk and so bold a young blood as you,   1510
And acclaimed for all courtesies becoming a knight—
And name what knight you will, they are noblest esteemed
For loyal faith in love, in life as in story;
For to tell the tribulations of these true hearts,

Why, 'tis the very title and text of their deeds,   1515
How bold knights for beauty have braved many a foe,
Suffered heavy sorrows out of secret love,
And then valorously avenged them on villainous churls
And made happy ever after the hearts of their ladies.
And you are the noblest knight known in your time;   1520
No household under heaven but has heard of your fame,
And here by your side I have sat for two days
Yet never has a fair phrase fallen from your lips
Of the language of love, not one little word!
And you, that with sweet vows sway women's hearts,   1525
Should show your winsome ways, and woo a young thing,
And teach by some tokens the craft of true love.
How! are you artless, whom all men praise?
Or do you deem me so dull, or deaf to such words?
     Fie! Fie!   1530
   In hope of pastimes new
   I have come where none can spy;
   Instruct me a little, do,
   While my husband is not nearby."

"God love you, gracious lady!" said Gawain then;   1535
"It is a pleasure surpassing, and a peerless joy,
That one so worthy as you would willingly come
And take the time and trouble to talk with your knight
And content you with his company—it comforts my heart.
But to take to myself the task of telling of love,   1540
And touch upon its texts, and treat of its themes
To one that, I know well, wields more power
In that art, by a half, than a hundred such
As I am where I live, or am like to become,
It were folly, fair dame, in the first degree!   1545
In all that I am able, my aim is to please,
As in honor behooves me, and am evermore
Your servant heart and soul, so save me our Lord!"
Thus she tested his temper and tried many a time,
Whatever her true intent, to entice him to sin,   1550
But so fair was his defense that no fault appeared,
Nor evil on either hand, but only bliss
     they knew.
   They linger and laugh awhile;
   She kisses the knight so true,   1555
   Takes leave in comeliest style
   And departs without more ado.

Then he rose from his rest and made ready for mass,
And then a meal was set and served, in sumptuous style;
He dallied at home all day with the dear ladies,   1560
But the lord lingered late at his lusty sport;

Pursued his sorry swine, that swerved as he fled,
And bit asunder the backs of the best of his hounds
When they brought him to bay, till the bowmen appeared
And soon forced him forth, though he fought for dear life,   1565
So sharp were the shafts they shot at him there.
But yet the boldest drew back from his battering head,
Till at last he was so tired he could travel no more,
But in as much haste as he might, he makes his retreat
To a rise on rocky ground, by a rushing stream.   1570
With the bank at his back he scrapes the bare earth,
The froth foams at his jaws, frightful to see.
He whets his white tusks—then weary were all
Those hunters so hardy that hoved round about
Of aiming from afar, but ever they mistrust   1575
                    his mood.
          He had hurt so many by then
          That none had hardihood
          To be torn by his tusks again,
          That was brainsick, and out for blood.   1580

Till the lord came at last on his lofty steed,
Beheld him there at bay before all his folk;
Lightly he leaps down, leaves his courser,
Bares his bright sword, and boldly advances;
Straight into the stream he strides towards his foe.   1585
The wild thing was wary of weapon and man;
His hackles rose high; so hotly he snorts
That many watched with alarm, lest the worst befall.
The boar makes for the man with a mighty bound
So that he and his hunter came headlong together   1590
Where the water ran wildest—the worse for the beast,
For the man, when they first met, marked him with care,
Sights well the slot, slips in the blade,
Shoves it home to the hilt, and the heart shattered,
And he falls in his fury and floats down the water,   1595
                    ill-sped.
          Hounds hasten by the score
          To maul him, hide and head;
          Men drag him in to shore
          And dogs pronounce him dead.   1600

With many a brave blast they boast of their prize,
All hallooed in high glee, that had their wind;
The hounds bayed their best, as the bold men bade
That were charged with chief rank in that chase of renown.
Then one wise in woodcraft, and worthily skilled,   1605
Began to dress the boar in becoming style:
He severs the savage head and sets it aloft,
Then rends the body roughly right down the spine;

Takes the bowels from the belly, broils them on coals,
Blends them well with bread to bestow on the hounds.   1610
Then he breaks out the brawn in fair broad flitches,
And the innards to be eaten in order he takes.
The two sides, attached to each other all whole,
He suspended from a spar that was springy and tough;
And so with this swine they set out for home;   1615
The boar's head was borne before the same man
That had stabbed him in the stream with his strong arm,
                    right through.
          He thought it long indeed
          Till he had the knight in view;   1620
          At his call, he comes with speed
          To claim his payment due.

The lord laughed aloud, with many a light word,
When he greeted Sir Gawain—with good cheer he speaks.
They fetch the fair dames and the folk of the house;   1625
He brings forth the brawn, and begins the tale
Of the great length and girth, the grim rage as well,
Of the battle of the boar they beset in the wood.
The other man meetly commended his deeds
And praised well the prize of his princely sport,   1630
For the brawn of that boar, the bold knight said,
And the sides of that swine surpassed all others.
Then they handled the huge head; he owns it a wonder,
And eyes it with abhorrence, to heighten his praise.
"Now, Gawain," said the good man, "this game becomes yours   1635
By those fair terms we fixed, as you know full well."
"That is true," returned the knight, "and trust me, fair friend,
All my gains, as agreed, I shall give you forthwith."
He clasps him and kisses him in courteous style,
Then serves him with the same fare a second time.   1640
"Now we are even," said he, "at this evening feast,
And clear is every claim incurred here to date,
                    and debt."
          "By Saint Giles!" the host replies,
          "You're the best I ever met!   1645
          If your profits are all this size,
          We'll see you wealthy yet!"

Then attendants set tables on trestles about,
And laid them with linen; light shone forth,
Wakened along the walls in waxen torches.   1650
The service was set and the supper brought;
Royal were the revels that rose then in hall
At that feast by the fire, with many fair sports:
Amid the meal and after, melody sweet,
Carol-dances comely and Christmas songs,   1655

With all the mannerly mirth my tongue may describe.
And ever our gallant knight beside the gay lady;
So uncommonly kind and complaisant was she,
With sweet stolen glances, that stirred his stout heart,
That he was at his wits' end, and wondrous vexed;   1660
But he could not rebuff her, for courtesy forbade,
Yet took pains to please her, though the plan might
                go wrong.
         When they to heart's delight
         Had reveled there in throng,   1665
         To his chamber he calls the knight,
         And thither they go along.

And there they dallied and drank, and deemed it good sport
To enact their play anew on New Year's Eve,
But Gawain asked again to go on the morrow,   1670
For the time until his tryst was not two days.
The host hindered that, and urged him to stay,
And said, "On my honor, my oath here I take
That you shall get to the Green Chapel to begin your chores
By dawn on New Year's Day, if you so desire.   1675
Wherefore lie at your leisure in your lofty bed,
And I shall hunt hereabouts, and hold to our terms,
And we shall trade winnings when once more we meet,
For I have tested you twice, and true have I found you;
Now think this tomorrow: the third pays for all;   1680
Be we merry while we may, and mindful of joy,
For heaviness of heart can be had for the asking."
This is gravely agreed on and Gawain will stay.
They drink a last draught and with torches depart
                to rest.   1685
         To bed Sir Gawain went:
         His sleep was of the best;
         The lord, on his craft intent,
         Was early up and dressed.

After mass, with his men, a morsel he takes;   1690
Clear and crisp the morning; he calls for his mount;
The folk that were to follow him afield that day
Were high astride their horses before the hall gates.
Wondrous fair were the fields, for the frost was light;
The sun rises red amid radiant clouds,   1695
Sails into the sky, and sends forth his beams.
They let loose the hounds by a leafy wood;
The rocks all around re-echo to their horns;
Soon some have set off in pursuit of the fox,
Cast about with craft for a clearer scent;   1700
A young dog yaps, and is yelled at in turn;
His fellows fall to sniffing, and follow his lead,

Running in a rabble on the right track,
And he scampers all before; they discover him soon,
And when they see him with sight they pursue him the faster,   1705
Railing at him rudely with a wrathful din.
Often he reverses over rough terrain,
Or loops back to listen in the lee of a hedge;
At last, by a little ditch, he leaps over the brush,
Comes into a clearing at a cautious pace,   1710
Then he thought through his wiles to have thrown off the hounds
Till he was ware, as he went, of a waiting-station
Where three athwart his path threatened him at once,
                          all gray.
                    Quick as a flash he wheels   1715
                    And darts off in dismay;
                    With hard luck at his heels
                    He is off to the wood away.

Then it was heaven on earth to hark to the hounds
When they had come on their quarry, coursing together!   1720
Such harsh cries and howls they hurled at his head
As all the cliffs with a crash had come down at once.
Here he was hailed, when huntsmen met him;
Yonder they yelled at him, yapping and snarling;
There they cried "Thief!" and threatened his life,   1725
And ever the harriers at his heels, that he had no rest.
Often he was menaced when he made for the open,
And often rushed in again, for Reynard was wily;
And so he leads them a merry chase, the lord and his men,
In this manner on the mountains, till midday or near,   1730
While our hero lies at home in wholesome sleep
Within the comely curtains on the cold morning.
But the lady, as love would allow her no rest,
And pursuing ever the purpose that pricked her heart,
Was awake with the dawn, and went to his chamber   1735
In a fair flowing mantle that fell to the earth,
All edged and embellished with ermines fine;
No hood on her head, but heavy with gems
Were her fillet and the fret[5] that confined her tresses;
Her face and her fair throat freely displayed;   1740
Her bosom all but bare, and her back as well.
She comes in at the chamber-door, and closes it with care,
Throws wide a window—then waits no longer,
But hails him thus airily with her artful words,
                          with cheer: 1745
                    "Ah, man, how can you sleep?
                    The morning is so clear!"
                    Though dreams have drowned him deep,
                    He cannot choose but hear.

5. Ornamental net.

Deep in his dreams he darkly mutters　　　　　　　　　　1750
As a man may that mourns, with many grim thoughts
Of that day when destiny shall deal him his doom
When he greets his grim host at the Green Chapel
And must bow to his buffet, bating all strife.
But when he sees her at his side he summons his wits,　　1755
Breaks from the black dreams, and blithely answers.
That lovely lady comes laughing sweet,
Sinks down at his side, and salutes him with a kiss.
He accords her fair welcome in courtliest style;
He sees her so glorious, so gaily attired,　　　　　　　　1760
So faultless her features, so fair and so bright,
His heart swelled swiftly with surging joys.
They melt into mirth with many a fond smile,
Nor was fair language lacking, to further that hour's
　　　　　　　　　　　　　delight.　　　　　　　　　　1765
　　　　　　　　Good were their words of greeting;
　　　　　　　　Each joyed in other's sight;
　　　　　　　　Great peril attends that meeting
　　　　　　　　Should Mary forget her knight.

For that high-born beauty so hemmed him about,　　　　1770
Made so plain her meaning, the man must needs
Either take her tendered love or distastefully refuse.
His courtesy concerned him, lest crass he appear,
But more his soul's mischief, should he commit sin
And belie his loyal oath to the lord of that house.　　　　1775
"God forbid!" said the bold knight, "That shall not befall!"
With a little fond laughter he lightly let pass
All the words of special weight that were sped his way;
"I find you much at fault," the fair one said,
"Who can be cold toward a creature so close by your side,　1780
Of all women in this world most wounded in heart,
Unless you have a sweetheart, one you hold dearer,
And allegiance to that lady so loyally knit
That you will never love another, as now I believe.
And, sir, if it be so, then say it, I beg you;　　　　　　　1785
By all your heart holds dear, hide it no longer
　　　　　　　　　　with guile."
　　　　　　　　"Lady, by Saint John,"
　　　　　　　　He answers with a smile,
　　　　　　　　"Lover have I none,　　　　　　　　　　1790
　　　　　　　　Nor will have, yet awhile."

"Those words," said the woman, "are the worst of all,
But I have had my answer, and hard do I find it!
Kiss me now kindly: I can but go hence
To lament my life long like a maid lovelorn."　　　　　　1795

She inclines her head quickly and kisses the knight,
Then straightens with a sigh, and says as she stands,
"Now, dear, ere I depart, do me this pleasure:
Give me some little gift, your glove or the like,
That I may think on you, man, and mourn the less."   1800
"Now by heavens," said he, "I wish I had here
My most precious possession, to put it in your hands,
For your deeds, beyond doubt, have often deserved
A repayment far passing my power to bestow.
But a love-token, lady, were of little avail;   1805
It is not to your honor to have at this time
A glove as a guerdon from Gawain's hand,
And I am here on an errand in unknown realms
And have no bearers with baggage with becoming gifts,
Which distresses me, madame, for your dear sake.   1810
A man must keep within his compass: account it neither grief
                              nor slight."
                    "Nay, noblest knight alive,"
                    Said that beauty of body white,
                    "Though you be loath to give,   1815
                    Yet you shall take, by right."

She reached out a rich ring, wrought all of gold,
With a splendid stone displayed on the band
That flashed before his eyes like a fiery sun;
It was worth a king's wealth, you may well believe.   1820
But he waved it away with these ready words:
"Before God, good lady, I forgo all gifts;
None have I to offer, nor any will I take."
And she urged it on him eagerly, and ever he refused,
And vowed in very earnest, prevail she would not.   1825
And she sad to find it so, and said to him then,
"If my ring is refused for its rich cost—
You would not be my debtor for so dear a thing—
I shall give you my girdle; you gain less thereby."
She released a knot lightly, and loosened a belt   1830
That was caught about her kirtle, the bright cloak beneath,
Of a gay green silk, with gold overwrought,
And the borders all bound with embroidery fine,
And this she presses upon him, and pleads with a smile,
Unworthy though it were, that it would not be scorned.   1835
But the man still maintains that he means to accept
Neither gold nor any gift, till by God's grace
The fate that lay before him was fully achieved.
"And be not offended, fair lady, I beg,
And give over your offer, for ever I must   1840
                              decline.
                    I am grateful for favor shown
                    Past all deserts of mine,

And ever shall be your own
True servant, rain or shine."   1845

"Now does my present displease you," she promptly inquired,
"Because it seems in your sight so simple a thing?
And belike, as it is little, it is less to praise,
But if the virtue that invests it were verily known,
It would be held, I hope, in higher esteem.   1850
For the man that possesses this piece of silk,
If he bore it on his body, belted about,
There is no hand under heaven that could hew him down,
For he could not be killed by any craft on earth."
Then the man began to muse, and mainly he thought   1855
It was a pearl for his plight, the peril to come
When he gains the Green Chapel to get his reward:
Could he escape unscathed, the scheme were noble!
Then he bore with her words and withstood them no more,
And she repeated her petition and pleaded anew,
And he granted it, and gladly she gave him the belt,   1860
And besought him for her sake to conceal it well,
Lest the noble lord should know—and, the knight agrees
That not a soul save themselves shall see it thenceforth
                              with sight.
                    He thanked her with fervent heart,   1865
                    As often as ever he might;
                    Three times, before they part,
                    She has kissed the stalwart knight.

Then the lady took her leave, and left him there,   1870
For more mirth with that man she might not have.
When she was gone, Sir Gawain got from his bed,
Arose and arrayed him in his rich attire;
Tucked away the token the temptress had left,
Laid it reliably where he looked for it after.   1875
And then with good cheer to the chapel he goes,
Approached a priest in private, and prayed to be taught
To lead a better life and lift up his mind,
Lest he be among the lost when he must leave this world.
And shamefaced at shrift he showed his misdeeds   1880
From the largest to the least, and asked the Lord's mercy,
And called on his confessor to cleanse his soul,
And he absolved him of his sins as safe and as clean
As if the dread Day of Doom were to dawn on the morrow.
And then he made merry amid the fine ladies   1885
With deft-footed dances and dalliance light,
As never until now, while the afternoon wore
                              away.
                    He delighted all around him,
                    And all agreed, that day,   1890

They never before had found him
So gracious and so gay.

Now peaceful be his pasture, and love play him fair!
The host is on horseback, hunting afield;
He has finished off this fox that he followed so long: 1895
As he leapt a low hedge to look for the villain
Where he heard all the hounds in hot pursuit,
Reynard comes racing out of a rough thicket,
And all the rabble in a rush, right at his heels.
The man beholds the beast, and bides his time,   1900
And bares his bright sword, and brings it down hard,
And he blenches from the blade, and backward he starts;
A hound hurries up and hinders that move,
And before the horse's feet they fell on him at once
And ripped the rascal's throat with a wrathful din.   1905
The lord soon alighted and lifted him free,
Swiftly snatched him up from the snapping jaws,
Holds him over his head, halloos with a will,
And the dogs bayed the dirge, that had done him to death.
Hunters hastened thither with horns at their lips,   1910
Sounding the assembly till they saw him at last.
When that comely company was come in together,
All that bore bugles blew them at once,
And the others all hallooed, that had no horns.
It was the merriest medley that ever a man heard,   1915
The racket that they raised for Sir Reynard's soul
                      that died.
            Their hounds they praised and fed,
            Fondling their heads with pride,
            And they took Reynard the Red   1920
            And stripped away his hide.

And then they headed homeward, for evening had come,
Blowing many a blast on their bugles bright.
The lord at long last alights at his house,
Finds fire on the hearth where the fair knight waits,   1925
Sir Gawain the good, that was glad in heart.
With the ladies, that loved him, he lingered at ease;
He wore a rich robe of blue, that reached to the earth
And a surcoat lined softly with sumptuous furs;
A hood of the same hue hung on his shoulders;   1930
With bands of bright ermine embellished were both.
He comes to meet the man amid all the folk,
And greets him good-humoredly, and gaily he says,
"I shall follow forthwith the form of our pledge
That we framed to good effect amid fresh-filled cups."   1935
He clasps him accordingly and kisses him thrice,
As amiably and as earnestly as ever he could.

"By heaven," said the host, "you have had some luck
Since you took up this trade, if the terms were good."
"Never trouble about the terms," he returned at once,   1940
"Since all that I owe here is openly paid."
"Marry!" said the other man, "mine is much less,
For I have hunted all day, and nought have I got
But this foul fox pelt, the fiend take the goods!
Which but poorly repays such precious things   1945
That you have cordially conferred, such kisses three
                    so good."
                    "Enough!" said Sir Gawain;
                    "I thank you, by the rood!"
                    And how the fox was slain   1950
                    He told him, as they stood.

With minstrelsy and mirth, with all manner of meats,
They made as much merriment as any men might
(Amid laughing of ladies and light hearted girls;
So gay grew Sir Gawain and the goodly host)   1955
Unless they had been besotted, or brainless fools.
The knight joined in jesting with that joyous folk,
Until at last it was late; ere long they must part,
And be off to their beds, as behooved them each one.
Then politely his leave of the lord of the house   1960
Our noble knight takes, and renews his thanks:
"The courtesies countless accorded me here,
Your kindness at this Christmas, may heaven's King repay!
Henceforth, if you will have me, I hold you my liege,
And so, as I have said, I must set forth tomorrow,   1965
If I may take some trusty man to teach, as you promised,
The way to the Green Chapel, that as God allows
I shall see my fate fulfilled on the first of the year."
"In good faith," said the good man, "with a good will
Every promise on my part shall be fully performed."   1970
He assigns him a servant to set him on the path,
To see him safe and sound over the snowy hills,
To follow the fastest way through forest green
                    and grove.
                    Gawain thanks him again,   1975
                    So kind his favors prove,
                    And of the ladies then
                    He takes his leave, with love.

Courteously he kissed them, with care in his heart,
And often wished them well, with warmest thanks,   1980
Which they for their part were prompt to repay.
They commend him to Christ with disconsolate sighs;
And then in that hall with the household he parts—
Each man that he met, he remembered to thank

For his deeds of devotion and diligent pains,   1985
And the trouble he had taken to tend to his needs;
And each one as woeful, that watched him depart,
As he had lived with him loyally all his life long.
By lads bearing lights he was led to his chamber
And blithely brought to his bed, to be at his rest.   1990
How soundly he slept, I presume not to say,
For there were matters of moment his thoughts might well
                             pursue.
              Let him lie and wait;
              He has little more to do,   1995
              Then listen, while I relate
              How they kept their rendezvous.

Part 4

Now the New Year draws near, and the night passes,
The day dispels the dark, by the Lord's decree;
But wild weather awoke in the world without: 2000
The clouds in the cold sky cast down their snow
With great gusts from the north, grievous to bear.
Sleet showered aslant upon shivering beasts;
The wind warbled wild as it whipped from aloft,
And drove the drifts deep in the dales below.   2005
Long and well he listens, that lies in his bed;
Though he lifts not his eyelids, little he sleeps;
Each crow of the cock he counts without fail.
Readily from his rest he rose before dawn,
For a lamp had been left him, that lighted his chamber.   2010
He called to his chamberlain, who quickly appeared,
And bade him get him his gear, and gird his good steed,
And he sets about briskly to bring in his arms,
And makes ready his master in manner most fit.
First he clad him in his clothes, to keep out the cold,   2015
And then his other harness, made handsome anew,
His plate-armor of proof, polished with pains,
The rings of his rich mail rid of their rust,
And all was fresh as at first, and for this he gave thanks
                             indeed.   2020
              With pride he wears each piece,
              New-furbished for his need:
              No gayer from here to Greece;
              He bids them bring his steed.

In his richest raiment he robed himself then: 2025
His crested coat-armor, close-stitched with craft,
With stones of strange virtue on silk velvet set;
All bound with embroidery on borders and seams
And lined warmly and well with furs of the best.

Yet he left not his love-gift, the lady's girdle;   2030
Gawain, for his own good, forgot not that:
When the bright sword was belted and bound on his haunches,
Then twice with that token he twined him about.
Sweetly did he swathe him in that swatch of silk,
That girdle of green so goodly to see,   2035
That against the gay red showed gorgeous bright.
Yet he wore not for its wealth that wondrous girdle,
Nor pride in its pendants, though polished they were,
Though glittering gold gleamed at the tips,
But to keep himself safe when consent he must   2040
To endure a deadly dint, and all defense
                                    denied.
                    And now the bold knight came
                    Into the courtyard wide;
                    That folk of worthy fame   2045
                    He thanks on every side.

Then was Gringolet girt, that was great and huge,
And had sojourned safe and sound, and savored his fare;
He pawed the earth in his pride, that princely steed.
The good knight draws near him and notes well his look,   2050
And says sagely to himself, and soberly swears,
"Here is a household in hall that upholds the right!
The man that maintains it, may happiness be his!
Likewise the dear lady, may love betide her!
If thus they in charity cherish a guest   2055
That are honored here on earth, may they have his reward
That reigns high in heaven—and also you all;
And might I live in this land but a little while,
I should willingly reward you, and well, if I might."
Then he steps into the stirrup and bestrides his mount;   2060
His shield is shown forth; on his shoulder he casts it;
Strikes the side of his steed with his steel spurs,
And he starts across the stones, nor stands any longer
                                    to prance.
                    On horseback was the swain   2065
                    That bore his spear and lance;
                    "May Christ this house maintain
                    And guard it from mischance!"

The bridge was brought down, and the road gates
Unbarred and carried back upon both sides;
He commended him to Christ, and crossed over the planks;   2070
Praised the noble porter, who prayed on his knees
That God save Sir Gawain, and bade him good day,
And went on his way alone with the man
That was to lead him ere long to that luckless place   2075
Where the dolorous dint must be dealt him at last.

Under bare boughs they ride, where steep banks rise,
Over high cliffs they climb, where cold snow clings;
The heavens held aloof, but heavy thereunder
Mist mantled the moors, moved on the slopes.   2080
Each hill had a hat, a huge cape of cloud;
Brooks bubbled and broke over broken rocks,
Flashing in freshets that waterfalls fed.
Roundabout was the road that ran through the wood
Till the sun at that season was soon to rise,   2085
                    that day.
          They were on a hilltop high;
          The white snow round them lay;
          The man that rode nearby
          Now bade his master stay.   2090

"For I have seen you here safe at the set time,
And now you are not far from that notable place
That you have sought for so long with such special pains.
But this I say for certain, since I know you, sir knight,
And have your good at heart, and hold you dear—   2095
Would you heed well my words, it were worth your while—
You are rushing into risks that you reck not of:
There is a villain in yon valley, the veriest on earth,
For he is rugged and rude, and ready with his fists,
And most immense in his mold of mortals alive,   2100
And his body bigger than the best four
That are in Arthur's house, Hector[6] or any.
He gets his grim way at the Green Chapel;
None passes by that place so proud in his arms
That he does not dash him down with his deadly blows,   2105
For he is heartless wholly, and heedless of right,
For be it chaplain or churl that by the Chapel rides,
Monk or mass-priest or any man else,
He would as soon strike him dead as stand on two feet.
Wherefore I say, just as certain as you sit there astride,   2110
You cannot but be killed, if his counsel holds,
For he would trounce you in a trice, had you twenty lives
                    for sale.
          He has lived long in this land
          And dealt out deadly bale;   2115
          Against his heavy hand
          Your power cannot prevail.

"And so, good Sir Gawain, let the grim man be;
Go off by some other road, in God's own name!
Leave by some other land, for the love of Christ,   2120
And I shall get me home again, and give you my word."

---

6. Either the Trojan hero or one of Arthur's knights.

That I shall swear by God's self and the saints above,
By heaven and by my halidom[7] and other oaths more,
To conceal this day's deed, nor say to a soul
That ever you fled for fear from any that I knew."   2125
"Many thanks!" said the other man—and demurring he speaks—
"Fair fortune befall you for your friendly words!
And conceal this day's deed I doubt not you would,
But though you never told the tale, if I turned back now,
Forsook this place for fear, and fled, as you say,   2130
I were a caitiff coward; I could not be excused.
But I must to the Chapel to chance my luck
And say to that same man such words as I please,
Befall what may befall through Fortune's will
                    or whim.   2135
           Though he be a quarrelsome knave
           With a cudgel great and grim,
           The Lord is strong to save:
           His servants trust in him."

"Marry," said the man, "since you tell me so much,   2140
And I see you are set to seek your own harm,
If you crave a quick death, let me keep you no longer!
Put your helm on your head, your hand on your lance,
And ride the narrow road down yon rocky slope
Till it brings you to the bottom of the broad valley.   2145
Then look a little ahead, on your left hand,
And you will soon see before you that self-same Chapel,
And the man of great might that is master there.
Now goodbye in God's name, Gawain the noble!
For all the world's wealth I would not stay here,   2150
Or go with you in this wood one footstep further!"
He tarried no more to talk, but turned his bridle,
Hit his horse with his heels as hard as he might,
Leaves the knight alone, and off like the wind
                    goes leaping.   2155
           "By God," said Gawain then,
           "I shall not give way to weeping;
           God's will be done, amen!
           I commend me to his keeping."

He puts his heels to his horse, and picks up the path;   2160
Goes in beside a grove where the ground is steep,
Rides down the rough slope right to the valley;
And then he looked a little about him—the landscape was wild,
And not a soul to be seen, nor sign of a dwelling,
But high banks on either hand hemmed it about,   2165

---

7. Holiness or, more likely, patron saints.

With many a ragged rock and rough-hewn crag;
The skies seemed scored by the scowling peaks.
Then he halted his horse, and hoved there a space,
And sought on every side for a sight of the Chapel,
But no such place appeared, which puzzled him sore,   2170
Yet he saw some way off what seemed like a mound,
A hillock high and broad, hard by the water,
Where the stream fell in foam down the face of the steep
And bubbled as if it boiled on its bed below.
The knight urges his horse, and heads for the knoll;   2175
Leaps lightly to earth; loops well the rein
Of his steed to a stout branch, and stations him there.
He strides straight to the mound, and strolls all about,
Much wondering what it was, but no whit the wiser;
It had a hole at one end, and on either side,   2180
And was covered with coarse grass in clumps all without,
And hollow all within, like some old cave,
Or a crevice of an old crag—he could not discern
           aright.
       "Can this be the Chapel Green?   2185
       Alack!" said the man, "here might
       The devil himself be seen
       Saying matins at black midnight!"

"Now by heaven," said he, "it is bleak hereabouts;
This prayer-house is hideous, half-covered with grass!   2190
Well may the grim man mantled in green
Hold here his orisons, in hell's own style!
Now I feel it is the Fiend, in my five wits,
That has tempted me to this tryst, to take my life;
This is a Chapel of mischance, may the mischief take it!   2195
As accursed a country church as I came upon ever!"
With his helm on his head, his lance in his hand,
He stalks toward the steep wall of that strange house.
Then he heard, on the hill, behind a hard rock,
Beyond the brook, from the bank, a most barbarous din: 2200
Lord! it clattered in the cliff fit to cleave it in two,
As one upon a grindstone ground a great scythe!
Lord! it whirred like a mill-wheel whirling about!
Lord! it echoed loud and long, lamentable to hear!
Then "By heaven," said the bold knight, "that business
      up there   2205
Is arranged for my arrival, or else I am much
          misled.
       Let God work! Ah me!
       All hope of help has fled!
       Forfeit my life may be   2210
       But noise I do not dread."

Then he listened no longer, but loudly he called,
"Who has power in this place, high parley to hold?
For none greets Sir Gawain, or gives him good day;
If any would a word with him, let him walk forth   2215
And speak now or never, to speed his affairs."
"Abide," said one on the bank above over his head,
"And what I promised you once shall straightway be given."
Yet he stayed not his grindstone, nor stinted its noise,
But worked awhile at his whetting before he would rest,   2220
And then he comes around a crag, from a cave in the rocks,
Hurtling out of hiding with a hateful weapon,
A Danish[8] ax devised for that day's deed,
With a broad blade and bright, bent in a curve,
Filed to a fine edge—four feet it measured   2225
By the length of the lace that was looped round the haft.
And in form as at first, the fellow all green,
His lordly face and his legs, his locks and his beard,
Save that firm upon two feet forward he strides,
Sets a hand on the ax-head, the haft to the earth;   2230
When he came to the cold stream, and cared not to wade,
He vaults over on his ax, and advances amain
On a broad bank of snow, overbearing and brisk
                          of mood.
              Little did the knight incline   2235
              When face to face they stood;
              Said the other man, "Friend mine,
              It seems your word holds good!"

"God love you, Sir Gawain!" said the Green Knight then,
"And well met this morning, man, at my place!   2240
And you have followed me faithfully and found me betimes,
And on the business between us we both are agreed:
Twelve months ago today you took what was yours,
And you at this New Year must yield me the same.
And we have met in these mountains, remote from all eyes: 2245
There is none here to halt us or hinder our sport;
Unhasp your high helm, and have here your wages;
Make no more demur than I did myself
When you hacked off my head with one hard blow."
"No, by God," said Sir Gawain, "that granted me life,   2250
I shall grudge not the guerdon, grim though it prove;
Bestow but one stroke, and I shall stand still,
And you may lay on as you like till the last of my part
                          be paid."
              He proffered, with good grace,   2255
              His bare neck to the blade,

8. I.e., long-bladed.

And feigned a cheerful face:
He scorned to seem afraid.

Then the grim man in green gathers his strength,
Heaves high the heavy ax to hit him the blow.   2260
With all the force in his frame he fetches it aloft,
With a grimace as grim as he would grind him to bits;
Had the blow he bestowed been as big as he threatened,
A good knight and gallant had gone to his grave.
But Gawain at the great ax glanced up aside.   2265
As down it descended with death-dealing force,
And his shoulders shrank a little from the sharp iron.
Abruptly the brawny man breaks off the stroke,
And then reproved with proud words that prince among knights.
"You are not Gawain the glorious," the green man said,   2270
"That never fell back on field in the face of the foe,
And now you flee for fear, and have felt no harm:
Such news of that knight I never heard yet!
I moved not a muscle when you made to strike,
Nor caviled at the cut in King Arthur's house;   2275
My head fell to my feet, yet steadfast I stood,
And you, all unharmed, are wholly dismayed—
Wherefore the better man I, by all odds,
                    must be."
              Said Gawain, "Strike once more;   2280
              I shall neither flinch nor flee;
              But if my head falls to the floor
              There is no mending me!"

"But go on, man, in God's name, and get to the point!
Deliver me my destiny, and do it out of hand,   2285
For I shall stand to the stroke and stir not an inch
Till your ax has hit home—on my honor I swear it!"
"Have at thee then!" said the other, and heaves it aloft,
And glares down as grimly as he had gone mad.
He made a mighty feint, but marred not his hide;   2290
Withdrew the ax adroitly before it did damage.
Gawain gave no ground, nor glanced up aside,
But stood still as a stone, or else a stout stump
That is held in hard earth by a hundred roots.
Then merrily does he mock him, the man all in green: 2295
"So now you have your nerve again, I needs must strike;
Uphold the high knighthood that Arthur bestowed,
And keep your neck-bone clear, if this cut allows!"
Then was Gawain gripped with rage, and grimly he said,
"Why, thrash away, tyrant, I tire of your threats;   2300
You make such a scene, you must frighten yourself."
Said the green fellow, "In faith, so fiercely you speak

That I shall finish this affair, nor further grace
                    allow."
                He stands prepared to strike   2305
                And scowls with both lip and brow;
                No marvel if the man mislike
                Who can hope no rescue now.

He gathered up the grim ax and guided it well:
Let the barb at the blade's end brush the bare throat;   2310
He hammered down hard, yet harmed him no whit
Save a scratch on one side, that severed the skin;
The end of the hooked edge entered the flesh,
And a little blood lightly leapt to the earth.
And when the man beheld his own blood bright on the snow, 2315
He sprang a spear's length with feet spread wide,
Seized his high helm, and set it on his head,
Shoved before his shoulders the shield at his back,
Bares his trusty blade, and boldly he speaks—
Not since he was a babe born of his mother   2320
Was he once in this world one-half so blithe—
"Have done with your hacking—harry me no more!
I have borne, as behooved, one blow in this place;
If you make another move I shall meet it midway
And promptly, I promise you, pay back each blow   2325
                    with brand.
                One stroke acquits me here;
                So did our covenant stand
                In Arthur's court last year—
                Wherefore, sir, hold your hand!"   2330

He lowers the long ax and leans on it there,
Sets his arms on the head, the haft on the earth,
And beholds the bold knight that bides there afoot,
How he faces him fearless, fierce in full arms,
And plies him with proud words—it pleases him well.   2335
Then once again gaily to Gawain he calls,
And in a loud voice and lusty, delivers these words:
"Bold fellow, on this field your anger forbear!
No man has made demands here in manner uncouth,
Nor done, save as duly determined at court.   2340
I owed you a hit and you have it; be happy therewith!
The rest of my rights here I freely resign.
Had I been a bit busier, a buffet, perhaps,
I could have dealt more directly, and done you some harm.
First I flourished with a feint, in frolicsome mood,   2345
And left your hide unhurt—and here I did well
By the fair terms we fixed on the first night;
And fully and faithfully you followed accord:
Gave over all your gains as a good man should.

A second feint, sir, I assigned for the morning   2350
You kissed my comely wife—each kiss you restored.
For both of these there behooved two feigned blows
                    by right.
          True men pay what they owe;
          No danger then in sight.   2355
          You failed at the third throw,
          So take my tap, sir knight.

"For that is my belt about you, that same braided girdle,
My wife it was that wore it; I know well the tale,
And the count of your kisses and your conduct too,   2360
And the wooing of my wife—it was all my scheme!
She made trial of a man most faultless by far
Of all that ever walked over the wide earth;
As pearls to white peas, more precious and prized,
So is Gawain, in good faith, to other gay knights.   2365
Yet you lacked, sir, a little in loyalty there,
But the cause was not cunning, nor courtship either,
But that you loved your own life; the less, then, to blame."
The other stout knight in a study stood a long while,
So gripped with grim rage that his great heart shook.   2370
All the blood of his body burned in his face
As he shrank back in shame from the man's sharp speech.
The first words that fell from the fair knight's lips:
"Accursed be a cowardly and covetous heart!
In you is villainy and vice, and virtue laid low!"   2375
Then he grasps the green girdle and lets go the knot,
Hands it over in haste, and hotly he says:
"Behold there my falsehood, ill hap betide it!
Your cut taught me cowardice, care for my life,
And coveting came after, contrary both   2380
To largesse and loyalty belonging to knights.
Now am I faulty and false, that fearful was ever
Of disloyalty and lies, bad luck to them both!
                    and greed.
          I confess, knight, in this place,   2385
          Most dire is my misdeed;
          Let me gain back your good grace,
          And thereafter I shall take heed."

Then the other laughed aloud, and lightly he said,
"Such harm as I have had, I hold it quite healed.   2390
You are so fully confessed, your failings made known,
And bear the plain penance of the point of my blade,
I hold you polished as a pearl, as pure and as bright
As you had lived free of fault since first you were born.
And I give you, sir, this girdle that is gold-hemmed   2395
And green as my garments, that, Gawain, you may

Be mindful of this meeting when you mingle in throng
With nobles of renown—and known by this token
How it chanced at the Green Chapel, to chivalrous knights.
And you shall in this New Year come yet again   2400
And we shall finish out our feast in my fair hall,
     with cheer."
    He urged the knight to stay,
    And said, "With my wife so dear
    We shall see you friends this day,   2405
    Whose enmity touched you near."

"Indeed," said the doughty knight, and doffed his high helm,
And held it in his hands as he offered his thanks,
"I have lingered long enough—may good luck be yours,
And he reward you well that all worship bestows!   2410
And commend me to that comely one, your courteous wife,
Both herself and that other, my honoured ladies,
That have trapped their true knight in their trammels so quaint.
But if a dullard should dote, deem it no wonder,
And through the wiles of a woman be wooed into sorrow,   2415
For so was Adam by one, when the world began,
And Solomon by many more, and Samson the mighty—
Delilah was his doom, and David thereafter
Was beguiled by Bathsheba, and bore much distress;
Now these were vexed by their devices—'twere a very joy   2420
Could one but learn to love, and believe them not.
For these were proud princes, most prosperous of old,
Past all lovers lucky, that languished under heaven,
     bemused.
    And one and all fell prey   2425
    To women that they had used;
    If I be led astray,
    Methinks I may be excused.

"But your girdle. God love you! I gladly shall take
And be pleased to possess, not for the pure gold,   2430
Nor the bright belt itself, nor the beauteous pendants,
Nor for wealth, nor worldly state, nor workmanship fine,
But a sign of excess it shall seem oftentimes
When I ride in renown, and remember with shame
The faults and the frailty of the flesh perverse,   2435
How its tenderness entices the foul taint of sin;
And so when praise and high prowess have pleased my heart,
A look at this love-lace will lower my pride.
But one thing would I learn, if you were not loath,
Since you are lord of yonder land where I have long sojourned   2440
With honor in your house—may you have His reward
That upholds all the heavens, highest on throne!
How runs your right name?—and let the rest go."

"That shall I give you gladly," said the Green Knight then;
"Bercilak de Hautdesert this barony I hold,   2445
Through the might of Morgan le Faye,[9] that lodges at my house,
By subtleties of science and sorcerers' arts,
The mistress of Merlin,[1] she has caught many a man,
For sweet love in secret she shared sometime
With that wizard, that knows well each one of your knights   2450
                    and you.
                    Morgan the Goddess, she,
                    So styled by title true;
                    None holds so high degree
                    That her arts cannot subdue.   2455

"She guided me in this guise to your glorious hall,
To assay, if such it were, the surfeit of pride
That is rumored of the retinue of the Round Table.
She put this shape upon me to puzzle your wits,
To afflict the fair queen, and frighten her to death   2460
With awe of that elvish man that eerily spoke
With his head in his hand before the high table.
She was with my wife at home, that old withered lady,
Your own aunt[2] is she, Arthur's half-sister,
The Duchess' daughter of Tintagel, that dear King Uther   2465
Got Arthur on after, that honored is now.
And therefore, good friend, come feast with your aunt;
Make merry in my house; my men hold you dear,
And I wish you as well, sir, with all my heart,
As any man God ever made, for your great good faith."   2470
But the knight said him nay, that he might by no means.
They clasped then and kissed, and commended each other
To the Prince of Paradise, and parted with one
                    assent.
                    Gawain sets out anew;   2475
                    Toward the court his course is bent;
                    And the knight all green in hue,
                    Wheresoever he wished, he went.

Wild ways in the world our worthy knight rides
On Gringolet, that by grace had been granted his life.   2480
He harbored often in houses, and often abroad,
And with many valiant adventures verily he met
That I shall not take time to tell in this story.
The hurt was whole that he had had in his neck,
And the bright green belt on his body he bore,   2485
Oblique, like a baldric, bound at his side,

9. Arthur's half-sister, an enchantress who sometimes abetted him, sometimes made trouble for
him.
1. The wise magician who had helped Arthur
become king.

2. Morgan was the daughter of Igraine, Duchess
of Tintagel, and her husband the Duke; Igraine
conceived Arthur when his father Uther lay with
her through one of Merlin's trickeries.

Below his left shoulder, laced in a knot,
In betokening of the blame he had borne for his fault;
And so to court in due course he comes safe and sound.
Bliss abounded in hall when the high-born heard   2490
That good Gawain was come; glad tidings they thought it.
The king kisses the knight, and the queen as well,
And many a comrade came to clasp him in arms,
And eagerly they asked, and awesomely he told,
Confessed all his cares and discomfitures many,   2495
How it chanced at the Chapel, what cheer made the knight,
The love of the lady, the green lace at last.
The nick on his neck he naked displayed
That he got in his disgrace at the Green Knight's hands,
           alone.   2500
        With rage in heart he speaks,
        And grieves with many a groan;
        The blood burns in his cheeks
        For shame at what must be shown.

"Behold, sir," said he, and handles the belt,   2505
"This is the blazon of the blemish that I bear on my neck;
This is the sign of sore loss that I have suffered there
For the cowardice and coveting that I came to there;
This is the badge of false faith that I was found in there,
And I must bear it on my body till I breathe my last.   2510
For one may keep a deed dark, but undo it no whit,
For where a fault is made fast, it is fixed evermore."
The king comforts the knight, and the court all together
Agree with gay laughter and gracious intent
That the lords and the ladies belonging to the Table,   2515
Each brother of that band, a baldric should have,
A belt borne oblique, of a bright green,
To be worn with one accord for that worthy's sake.
So that was taken as a token by the Table Round,
And he honored that had it, evermore after,   2520
As the best book of knighthood bids it be known.
In the old days of Arthur this happening befell;
The books of Brutus' deeds bear witness thereto
Since Brutus, the bold knight, embarked for this land
After the siege ceased at Troy and the city fared   2525
           amiss.
        Many such, ere we were born,
        Have befallen here, ere this.
        May He that was crowned with thorn
        Bring all men to His bliss! Amen.   2530

Hony Soyt Qui Mal Pense[3]

---

3. "Shame be to the man who has evil in his mind." This is the motto of the Order of the Garter, founded ca. 1350: apparently a copyist of the poem associated this order with the one founded to honor Gawain.

The Sixteenth Century
1485-1603

1485: Accession of Henry VII, inaugurates age of the Tudor sovereigns.

1509: Accession of Henry VIII.

1517: Martin Luther's Wittenberg Theses; beginning of the Reformation.

1534: Henry VIII acknowledged "Supreme Head on Earth" of the English church.

1557: Publication of *Tottel's Miscellany*, containing poems by Sir Thomas Wyatt, Henry Howard Earl of Surrey, and others.

1558: Accession of Queen Elizabeth I.

1576: Building of The Theatre, the first permanent structure in England for the presentation of plays.

1588: Defeat of the Spanish Armada.

1603: Death of Elizabeth I; accession of James I, the first Stuart king.

ENGLAND UNDER HENRY VII

The sixteenth century in England is the age of the Tudor sovereigns. Three generations of Tudors ruled England from 1485 to 1603. The earl of Richmond became Henry VII, the first Tudor monarch: he won his crown by defeating Richard III at Bosworth field, ending the dynastic strife that had raged for more than thirty years between the noble houses of York and Lancaster. Henry VII was Lancastrian, but he married Elizabeth of the house of York, niece of the Yorkist king Richard III. The barons, impoverished and divided by the dynastic wars, could not effectively oppose the power of the crown, and the church also generally supported the royal power. So Henry VII was able to counter the multiple and competing power structures characteristic of feudal society and to impose a much stronger central authority and order upon the nation.

Seven years after Henry VII became king, Columbus discovered America, and a few years later Vasco da Gama reached India by sailing around the Cape of Good Hope. The English were not pioneers in the discovery and exploration of the western hemisphere, but the discoveries affected their place in the world profoundly, for in the next century they became great colonizers and merchant adventurers.

Significant changes in trade and in the arts of war also marked the early years of the Tudor regime. Henry VII made commercial treaties with European countries; England, which had always been a sheep-raising country, was by now manufacturing and exporting significant amounts of cloth. As lands were enclosed to permit grazing on a larger scale, people were driven off the land to the cities, and London grew into a metropolitan market, with sophisticated commercial institutions. At the same time the feudal order continued its decline, partly because the introduction of firearms made armored knights on horseback obsolete, as well as the English bowmen who had won famous victories in France under King Henry V. The "new men" who supported the Tudors and profited from their favor could adapt themselves more easily to a changed society than could the descendants of the great families of the feudal fifteenth century.

About a decade before Henry VII won his throne, the art of printing from movable type, a German invention, was introduced into England by William Caxton (ca. 1422–1491), who had learned and practiced it in the Low Countries. Literacy increased during the fifteenth century, so that many more people could read than in Chaucer's time; it is estimated that some 30 percent of the people could read English in the early fifteenth century and some 60 percent by 1530. Printing made books cheaper and more plentiful, providing more opportunity to read, and more incentive to learn.

Yet it would be a mistake to imagine these changes as sudden and dramatic. Although Caxton introduced printed books, and was an author and translator as well as a printer, his publications consisted of long prose romances translated from the French, collections of moral sayings, and other works—such as Malory's *Morte Darthur*—that were medieval rather than modern. Also, jousts and tournaments continued at court for a century, and the approved code of behavior was the traditional code of chivalry. As often in an age of spectacular novelty, people dreamed of an idealized past instead of looking forward to an uncertain future. The best writers of the time of Henry VII were imitators of Chaucer, who had died about a century before. They were Scottish rather than English: William Dunbar (ca. 1460–1530), Gavin Douglas (1475–1522), and Sir David Lindsay (1485–1555). English writers also looked back, for example, Stephen Hawes (1474–1523), who imitated not Chaucer but John Lydgate, monk of Bury.

HUMANISM

During the fifteenth century a few English clerics and government officials had journeyed to Italy and had seen something of the extraordinary cultural and intellectual movement flourishing in the city-states there. That movement, generally known as the Renaissance, involved a rebirth of letters and arts stimulated by the recovery and study of texts from classical antiquity, and the development of new aesthetic norms based on classical models. It also unleashed new ideas and new social, political, and economic forces that displaced the otherworldly and communal values of the Middle Ages, emphasizing instead the dignity and potential of the individual and the worth of life in this world. These Renaissance ideals were variously reflected in the poetry of Petrarch, the philosophy of Pico della Mirandola, the art of Leonardo da Vinci, and the statecraft of Lorenzo di Medici. But it was not until Henry VII's reign brought some measure of political stability to England that the Renaissance could take root there, and it was not until the accession of Henry VIII that it began to flower.

Humanism was a fundamental intellectual current in the Renaissance, whose first major exponents in England were Sir Thomas More and Desiderius Erasmus of Rotterdam. More rose to become lord chancellor to Henry

VIII: his masterpiece, *Utopia*, written in Latin, was a critique of European social, political, and religious institutions and practices, from the vantage point of an imaginary society based on reason. His English writings were chiefly controversial tracts against Luther and the Protestants, but he also wrote a vivid and impressive history of Richard III. More's friend Erasmus spent some time in England, but his influence was spread also through his scripture translations and commentaries, and his writings on rhetoric and education.

Education—of the Christian prince, of the courtier, of the Christian gentleman—was a prime concern of the English humanists. John Colet (founder of St. Paul's School), Roger Ascham (tutor to Princess Elizabeth), and Sir Thomas Elyot, among others, wrote treatises on education to promote the kind of learning they regarded as the most suitable preparation for public service. That education—conducted by tutors in the great families or in grammar schools—was ordered according to the subjects of the medieval *trivium* (grammar, logic, and rhetoric) and the *quadrivium* (arithmetic, geometry, astronomy, and music), but with new emphasis on rhetoric and classical texts. The grammar studied was Latin grammar, and the rhetoric was a rigorous discipline in all the stylistic devices used by classical authors. The purpose was to train the sons of the nobility and gentry to speak and write good Latin, the language of diplomacy, of the professions, and of all higher learning. (Their sisters were always educated at home, in modern languages, religion, music, and art, but most often they did not receive the firm grounding in Latin and classical literature so central to Renaissance culture.) Elizabethan schoolmasters might use the system of double translation, from English into Latin and then from Latin back into English, to develop facility and rhetorical elegance. But the books read and studied rhetorically were not considered mere exhibitions of literary style: from the *Sententiae Pueriles* (Childish Maxims) for beginners, on up through the dramatist Terence, the poets Virgil and Horace, and the orator Cicero, the classics were also studied for the moral, political, and philosophical truth they contained, and as a means to inculcate moral values.

From the outset, English Humanism was vitally concerned with Christianity as well as with classical learning. The second generation of humanists—men like Roger Ascham (1515–1568), Sir John Cheke (1514–1557), professor of Greek at Cambridge, and Thomas Wilson (1525–1581), rhetorician and translator—combined an earnest Protestantism with their classical learning, and Ascham vigorously opposed the more secular, pagan humanism that was coming out of Italy. These men had a profound influence on the University of Cambridge, and Cambridge, in turn, educated many of the greatest writers of the age—including Spenser and Milton, who are also in this special English sense, Christian humanists.

For humanists committed to classical learning, the question of whether to write one's own works in Latin or in English became an issue of great seriousness. Sir Thomas More turned naturally to Latin in writing his *Utopia*. And to many other learned men, influenced both by the Humanist exaltation of the classical languages and by the characteristic Renaissance desire for eternal fame, the vernacular languages seemed relatively new and unstable. But at the same time, a revolt was being mounted in Italy, France, and England against the slavish imitation, in Latin, of Cicero and other classical writers. In his *Défense et Illustration de la Langue Française* (1549), Joachim Du Bellay argued that the value of a language is dependent upon the great works written in it, and urged scholars and poets to refine and improve the native tongue by writing ambitious works in it, thereby promoting a sense of national identity. In his book on archery, *Toxophilus*, dedicated to Henry VIII, Roger Ascham defended using the vernacular, though he said he found it easier to write in Latin or Greek. Later, Richard Mulcaster (ca. 1530–1611), principal of the Merchant Taylors' School and teacher of Edmund Spenser, waxed much more eloquent in praise of English:

> Is it not indeed a marvelous bondage, to become servants to one tongue for learning's sake the most of our time, with loss of most time, whereas we may have the very same treasure in our own tongue, with the gain of more time? our own bearing the joyful title of our liberty and freedom, the Latin tongue remembering us of our thralldom and bondage? I love Rome, but London better; I favor Italy, but England more; I honor the Latin, but I worship the English.

These two impulses—Humanist reverence for the classics and English pride in the vernacular language—gave rise to many distinguished translations throughout the century: Virgil's *Aeneid* by the Earl of Surrey; Homer's *Iliad* and *Odyssey* by George Chapman; Plutarch's *Lives of the Noble Grecians and Romans* by Sir Thomas North; and Ovid's *Metamorphoses* by Arthur Golding. Translators also sought to make available in English the most notable literary works in the modern languages: Castiglione's *Il Cortegiano* ("The Courtier") by Sir Thomas Hoby, Ariosto's *Orlando Furioso* ("Orlando Mad") by Sir John Harington, Tasso's *Gerusalemme Liberata* ("Jerusalem Delivered") by Edward Fairfax. At the midcentury, Ralph Robynson put into English the Latin *Utopia* of that notable English humanist, Sir Thomas More.

THE REFORMATION

Humanists like Erasmus advocated and engaged in a scholarly and critical study of the Scriptures; Humanists like More satirized the corrupt and ignorant clergy, and such abuses as the sale of papal indulgences and pardons. But neither Erasmus nor More followed the course which led to the Protestant Reformation: for both, the unity of Christendom was an overriding value. Nor did Martin Luther at first intend schism: when he nailed his famous ninety-five theses to the church door in Wittenberg on the first of November 1517, he thought he was simply opening up some topics for academic discussion. But his ideas soon sparked a mass revolution.

What was the Reformation? From the point of view of those who supported it, it was a return to pure Christianity—cleansing the church of all the corruption and idolatry that had accumulated over the centuries. From the point of view of the Catholic Church it was, of course, damnable heresy. From the perspective of later ages, it can be recognized as a major factor in the break-up of Western Christendom, the secularization of society, the establishment of princely ascendancy over the church and, consequently, the identification of religion and nationalism.

For medieval people, the Roman Catholic Church was a universal, infallible, omnicompetent guide to the conduct of life from cradle to grave. They walked hand in hand with it, instructed by its teachings, corrected by its discipline, sustained by its sacraments, comforted by its promises. A vast system of confession, pardons, penance, absolution, indulgences, sacred relics, and ceremonies gave the hierarchy great power over their largely illiterate flock. The Bible, the order of the Mass, and most of the theological discussions were in Latin, which lay people could not understand; however, religious doctrine and spirituality were mediated to them by priests and hierarchy, by church art and music, and by the liturgical ceremonies of daily life—festivals, holy days, baptisms, marriages, funerals.

When Luther revolted against the ancient church, was cast out by it, and founded his own church, he did so in the name of individual conscience enlightened by a personal reading of the Scriptures. The common watchwords of the Reformation were these: only the Scriptures (not the Church or Tradition) have authority in matters of religion; only God's grace and personal faith (not good works or religious practices) can effect a Christian's salvation; and only the enlightened individual conscience (not priests or ministers or hierarchies) can determine what an individual must believe and do. Despite differences in many matters of doctrine and church order, these principles were common to Lutherans in Germany, Calvinists at Geneva, and other Protestant groups throughout Europe.

In England, however, the Reformation did not begin with ideological controversy. In the time of Chaucer, John Wycliffe and the Lollard movement had mounted a grass-roots challenge to some practices and doctrines of the church, elements of which lasted into the sixteenth century. But the split with the Church of Rome was caused by a man who considered himself a Catholic champion against Luther and his opinions: Henry VIII, who received from Pope Leo X the title "Defender of the Faith" for writing a book against Luther. Henry's motives for the break with Rome were dynastic, not religious: he needed a legitimate son; his queen, Catherine of Aragon, could not give him one; and he was unable after long negotiations to obtain permission from Rome to divorce her. He then declared himself Supreme Head of the English church and required oaths of allegiance affirming his right to that role. His lord chancellor, Sir Thomas More, resigned and was at length executed for refusing to sign that oath. Thomas Cromwell, Henry's powerful secretary of state, dissolved the monasteries and distributed their property to his courtiers, thereby binding them firmly to his cause. In his earlier role as Defender of the (Roman Catholic) Faith, Henry had caused the great English translator of the Bible, William Tyndale, to be persecuted, driven out of England, and finally martyred in 1536. But after his break with Rome, Henry authorized a vernacular translation (The Great Bible), making the Bible available in English to anyone who could read.

Henry's son (by his third wife, Lady Jane Seymour) was the boy king Edward VI (1537–1553). In his brief reign (1547–53) the English Reformation acquired a strong doctrinal basis and spiritual energy, as Lutheran and Calvinist theologians from the continent swarmed into England. The Book of Common Prayer was published in 1549 and 1552, and by 1553 the beliefs of the English Church were officially defined in forty-two articles, thoroughly Protestant in formulation.

The successor to the young Protestant king was his older sister, Mary Tudor, the half-Spanish and devoutly Catholic daughter of Henry and Catherine of Aragon, who married her cousin Philip II of Spain. In her reign the leading Protestants either fled to the Continent or were burned at the stake as heretics. Mary tried to reverse the doctrinal changes of the Reformation, but some of its practical consequences, like the distribution of monastery lands, were irreversible. A Spaniard on the throne of England was not popular, and Mary dared not press her people too far: her accession had been opposed by the Privy Council, which proclaimed Lady Jane Grey queen, and she was also challenged by a rebellion led by Sir Thomas Wyatt the Younger, son of the poet. She maintained her Roman allegiance, she burned many Protestants at the stake, but she could not undo the work of her father and brother. Had she been able to produce an heir she might have done so, but failing that, her death in 1558 brought the Protestants back to power. The Protestant exiles returned from the continent to become a potent force in English society during the long reign of Mary's half sister, Elizabeth Tudor, daughter of Henry's second wife, Anne Boleyn.

Queen Elizabeth established the English Church in terms acceptable to the vast majority of her subjects. She imposed a form of service (retaining much of the old Roman ritual), and while she compelled her subjects to attend it she left their consciences to themselves. The Elizabethan manifesto of faith, the Thirty-Nine Articles, formulated the chief matters of doctrinal controversy in somewhat ambiguous terms; and Elizabeth made every effort to eliminate controversial preaching from the pulpits. That compromise satisfied neither Roman Catholics, who sought to return to Rome, nor the Puritans, who pressed for more radical reform. But it accommodated most of the populace, who now looked neither to Rome nor Geneva as the prime source of authority in religion, but to their own sovereign.

NATIONALISM—ELIZABETH I

Queen Elizabeth I, who ascended the throne in 1558 and ruled until 1603, was one of the most remarkable political geniuses England has ever produced. Vain, difficult, and headstrong, she nevertheless had a very shrewd instinct about her country's strengths and weaknesses, and she identified herself with England as no previous ruler had done. Although she was susceptible to the flattery of courtiers and favorites, she entrusted the power of state to solid men such as William Cecil (Lord Burleigh) and Francis Walsingham. Cecil (1520–1598) was her chief and most trusted secretary. With unswerving loyalty he devoted his great talents to the service of the queen in domestic affairs, as well as in the complex relations with the governments of Europe. He sought also, with limited success, to raise money from Parliament to pay for the increasing cost of government. Walsingham (ca. 1530–1590) was a radical Protestant, who tried to promote a more ideologically committed foreign policy than the queen and Cecil were prepared to support.

England's strength lay in its power to sway the balance of power in Europe: it could throw its weight either way in the ongoing power struggle between Spain and France; and it could support or fail to support the Protestant uprisings against Spain in the Low Countries. Moreover, Elizabeth made adroit use of her situation as an unmarried monarch generally expected to marry so as to provide a legitimate heir to the throne. She kept all Europe guessing as to her intentions, skillfully playing her several suitors off against one another—and at length insisted that England alone was her spouse. By the time it was too late for her to marry and bear children, England was strong and united.

Ironically, the papal bull (decree) of 1570, excommunicating Elizabeth and relieving her subjects of their loyalty to her, contributed greatly to that unity. This bull was intended to bring to the throne Mary Stuart, Queen of Scots, who was Catholic by faith and French by culture—an insupportable thought. The English rallied to their queen, and she became a symbol of Englishness and nationalism. The adulation of her, in the face of trouble on the Scottish border, near-chaos in Ireland, and continued threats from the Continent, took on religious intensity. Her reputation for beauty (which was exaggerated) and for wisdom (which was not) became articles of faith. In 1588 God himself seemed to testify to her divine mission to guide England: Philip II of Spain sent out the mightiest invasion fleet ever mounted against England, but that Spanish Armada was almost wholly destroyed by a violent storm, which seemed an act of God.

Despite the Elizabethan settlement of the English Church, Elizabeth's reign continued to be plagued by politico-religious unrest. Catholics who adhered to the pro-Spanish faction of the previous reign continued their plots to put Mary Stuart on the throne (causing Elizabeth at length to concur in her execution). And the Protestant exiles whose sojourn on the Continent had sharpened their zeal for more radical reforms coalesced into a strong and vocal Puritan movement. But most English people, remembering the civil conflicts of the previous century, placed a high value on order in church and state; and for them Elizabeth became, in her person and her policy, a symbol of national unity.

The desire for commercial profit also strengthened nationalistic feelings. In 1493 the Pope had divided the new world between the Spanish and the Portuguese by drawing a line from pole to pole (hence Brazil speaks Portuguese today, and the rest of Latin America speaks Spanish): the English were not in the picture. But by the end of Edward VI's reign the Company of Merchant Adventurers was founded, and Englishmen began to explore Asia and North America. Some of these adventurers turned to piracy, preying on Spanish ships which were returning laden with wealth from the New World. This business soon became a private undeclared war, with the queen and her courtiers investing in these raids privately but accepting no responsibility for them. The greatest of many dazzling exploits was the voyage of Francis Drake in 1577–80: he sailed through the Straits of Magellan, pillaged Spanish towns on the Pacific, reached as far north as San Francisco, crossed to the Philippines, and returned around the Cape of Good Hope; he came back with one million pounds in treasure, and his investors earned a dividend of 5,000 percent. Queen Elizabeth knighted him on the deck of his ship, *The Golden Hind*.

The mere survival of Elizabeth for so long provided the opportunity for nationalistic consciousness to become firmly established. When she came to the throne in 1558 she was only twenty-five years old, and she remained queen for almost forty-five years. It is wholly appropriate therefore that the second half of the sixteenth century bear her name, the Elizabethan Age.

PATRONS, WRITERS, AND PUBLISHERS

During Elizabeth's reign patronage was a social institution of the first importance, a major force in transforming the great nobles and gentry from independently powerful local magnates into courtiers dependent upon the monarch. The queen's chief ministers and favorites (Cecil, Leicester, Essex) were the primary channels through which patronage was dispensed to courtiers who wanted offices in the court, the government bureaucracies, the royal household, the army, the Church, the universities, or who sought titles, grants of land, leases, or similar favors. In their turn, successful courtiers could dispense benefits to their petitioners. Men like Sir Christopher

Hatton and Sir Walter Ralegh leapt from obscurity to great power and prominence as a result of their success as courtiers, which owed as much to their gallantry and their dancing as to their more solid abilities. And some noble women also wielded considerable power and influence as patrons, notably Mary Herbert, Countess of Pembroke, Margaret Clifford, Countess of Cumberland, Anne Dudley, Countess of Warwick, and Lucy (Harington) Russell, Countess of Bedford.

The great guide and conduct book for the courtier was Castiglione's *Il Cortegiano* (1528, translated into English by Sir Thomas Hoby in 1561). That book declared that the chief function of the courtier is to give good and honest advice to the prince, but courtiers who followed that honorable course were very likely to provoke a monarch's resentment, as Sir Philip Sidney found out when he tried to advise Queen Elizabeth against a proposed French marriage. Literary men of lower rank who were not in a position to be real courtiers might still look to the court for livelihood, notice, and encouragement, but that prospect was often discouraging. "A thousand hopes, but all nothing," wailed John Lyly, alluding to his long wait for the office of Master of the Revels; "a hundred promises, but yet nothing." Spenser's bitter disappointment in failing to win court patronage (reflected in *Mother Hubberds Tale* and *Colin Clouts Come Home Againe*) was dispelled only toward the end of his life when Queen Elizabeth awarded him a pension of fifty pounds. Indeed, a pervasive sense of court life as precarious, superficial, and hypocritical gave rise to works in the vein of the poems of Horace praising the retired country life far from corruptions of the court: early examples are Sir Thomas Wyatt's verse epistles to Sir Francis Bryan and John Poins, and the motif remained prominent to the time of Ralegh—and beyond.

Literary patronage was part of the interlocking patronage system whereby grants, offices, and honors were exchanged for service and praise. We must recognize that the career of a professional man or woman of letters did not exist: literature was regarded as an adjunct activity, not a primary occupation, and there were comparatively few readers, purchasers, and publishers of books. Elizabethan writers of higher rank, like Sir Philip Sidney, thought of themselves as courtiers, statesmen, landowners; they considered poetry a social grace and a courtly pastime. Writers of lower rank like Samuel Daniel or Michael Drayton sought careers as civil servants, secretaries, tutors, and divines; they might take up more or less permanent residence in a noble household, or, more casually, they might offer their literary work to actual or prospective patrons, amid lavish praises, in the hope of support, career advancement, or financial reward. Even Ben Jonson, who more than most of his contemporaries claimed the role of poet and managed to live tolerably well by it, summed up the situation in these words:

> Poetry in this latter age hath proved but a mean mistress to such as have wholly addicted themselves to her, or given their names up to her family. Those who have but saluted her on the way, and now and then tendered their visits, she hath done much for, and advanced in the way of their own professions (both the law and the gospel) beyond all they could have hoped or done for themselves without her favor.

Financial rewards for writing prose or poetry came mostly in the form of gifts from patrons, who sought to enhance their status and flatter their vanity through the service and lavish praises of many clients. But we hear constant complaints about patrons who do not reward authors for dedications (the usual reward was two or three pounds for a pamphlet or small volume of verse). Shakespeare's relations with his patron, the Earl of Southampton, little as we know about them, were apparently satisfactory, as the dedication to *The Rape of Lucrece* (1594) attests. But the experience of Robert Greene is perhaps more typical: the fact that he had sixteen different patrons for seventeen books suggests that he did not find much favor or support from any one of them. Indeed, a fraudulent practice grew up of printing off several dedications to be inserted into particular copies of a book, so that an impecunious author could deceive several patrons each into thinking that he was the one to be honored by the volume. However, some Elizabethan patrons were well-educated humanists motivated by genuine literary interests, and with them, patronage extended beyond financial support to the creation of literary and intellectual circles. Several writers (among them Samuel Daniel, Fulke Greville, Spenser) enjoyed long- or short-term hospitality and stimulation as members of the circles of the Sidneys at Penshurst or the Pembrokes at Wilton.

In addition to the court and the great families as dispensers of patronage, the two universities and the City of London were also major influences on the literary production of this period. Before Elizabeth's time, the universities were mainly devoted to educating the clergy, and that remained an important part of their function. But in the second half of the century the sons of the gentry and the aristocracy were going in increasing numbers to the universities and the Inns of Court (law schools), though often they did not take degrees or get called to the bar. Their residence in these places was simply an educational preparation for public service or managing their estates. A group of graduates, the so-called "university wits," associated themselves with the literary scene in London; these men (among them Thomas Nashe, Christopher Marlowe, Robert Greene, and George Peele) gave to the Elizabethan drama some of the classical form it needed and contributed to the great outpouring of literature in the 1590s. But their lives testify to the difficulties they found trying to sustain themselves by writing. The diary of Philip Henslowe, a leading theatrical manager, has entry after entry showing university graduates in prison or in debt, or at best eking out a miserable existence patching plays.

The City of London itself had a major impact on the literature of Elizabeth's reign. In Chaucer's time London had a population of about 50,000; in 1563 it had around 93,250, and nearly 225,000 in 1605. It was by far the most important city in the realm, and the political history of the seventeenth century is incomprehensible unless one recognizes the great power the City had, even as against the Crown. The printing presses were located in London, the printers and booksellers were in London, and the mass of the middle-class population that set the style for literature written for ordinary people was also in London. And although Thomas Nashe scornfully rejected the claim of the bourgeoisie to have any literary taste at all, or any ability to produce literature, that class had its own writers, like Thomas Deloney, and it knew what it liked—books of instruction, romances, religious tracts, conduct books for men and women, and sensational ballads. The London populace also found among the university men some writers who catered to them: Thomas Heywood is a good example. Whether the aristocrats admitted it or not, the standards and tastes of the middle class affected all publishing and literary success. The customers who frequented the stalls of St. Pauls

Churchyard—the center of the book trade—were more often members of the middle class than of the court circle. Louis B. Wright has shown (in his *Middle-Class Culture in Elizabethan England*) how extensive and profound was the influence of the citizenry upon the writing and publication of books, and how bourgeois standards of edification and utility dictated to most of the authors of the time.

The sixteenth century was the first century of the printed book, and the Elizabethan age was an extremely prolific one in writing and publishing. The *Short Title Catalogue* of the Bibliographical Society, which lists works and editions published in England between 1475 and 1640, includes over 26,000 items, and that is an incomplete list. But the rewards for having books published were nothing like they are today. There was no such thing as copyright, and no such thing, in the ordinary way, as royalties paid to an author according to the sale of the book. Authors sold their manuscripts to the printer or bookseller outright, for what now seems like a ridiculously low price—for a pamphlet or small book of poetry, usually forty shillings.

Nor did the author's troubles end with that sale. Writers as well as their publishers had to abide by stringent regulations governing the publication of books, and might be punished for failure to do so by several political and ecclesiastical authorities. The regulations provided that the number of printers (not booksellers) be strictly limited; that nothing could be printed except in the City of London and at the universities of Oxford and Cambridge; that everything printed must receive the imprimatur of the archbishop of Canterbury and the bishop of London or their representatives; and that everything published in London must be entered on the registers of the Stationers' Company—a regulation that protected the property rights of the publisher and printer rather than the author. The enforcing authorities included the Privy Council, the highest political authority in the realm below the queen; the Court of Star Chamber, which punished breaches of censorship; the Court of High Commission, the supreme ecclesiastical authority; and the Stationers' Company.

An extreme example of the dangers besetting authors is provided by the history of John Stubbs, who protested against Elizabeth's projected French marriage in a pamphlet called *The Discovery of a Gaping Gulf* (1579). For writing this pamphlet, Stubbs had his right hand cut off with one stroke of a butcher's cleaver—after which he took up his hat with his left hand and cried, "God save the queen." Indeed, almost every writer of the period got into some sort of trouble for publishing a book. It might be prison, it might be merely a reprimand, it might be an investigation by the Star Chamber. It was dangerous to put pen to paper and so unprofitable that it is a wonder any original writing was published at all.

However, to suppose that poetry, or even prose, circulated only in printed form would be a mistake. The older way of passing works around in manuscript lingered on into the seventeenth century, and was especially the practice of poets of gentle or noble rank. Sidney is the most prominent example. Sir John Harington, in his translation of Ariosto's *Orlando Furioso* in 1591, mentions a sonnet of Sidney's "which many I am sure have read;" but that sonnet was not published until seven years later. This was certainly the practice of some noblewomen: we have a few manuscript poems by Queen Elizabeth and the Countess of Pembroke, but those of other women reputed to have written poetry have been lost. Many people kept commonplace books in which they copied down poems from borrowed manuscript copies.

Professional scribes made a living by copying manuscripts for authors and for readers. There were even complaints by printers that literary manuscripts were being hoarded by "their grand possessors." Difference of audience clearly affected the kinds of literature produced—on the one hand by professional writers intending to publish, and on the other, by gentle or noble poets who passed their work about among their cultivated friends.

ART AND NATURE: ELIZABETHAN AESTHETICS

We can read Elizabethan literature with more comprehension if we recognize the differences between the aesthetic principles of the sixteenth century and those of our own day. At the root of the matter is a different conception of art, and of the relation between art and nature. The Romantic movement (which still profoundly affects our aesthetics) glorified nature and valued art that seems "natural," personal, sincere, uncontrived; it also valued the artist for originality, and often ascribed that quality to a special, mysterious inspiration. Such views would have seemed strange indeed to the Elizabethans. They recognized of course that nature is the basis of art, but had no uneasiness about a possible conflict between art and nature. The term "artificial" had for them good rather than dubious meanings, referring to the proper use of human ingenuity to enhance nature, to enable it to outdo itself. The point is underscored in Shakespeare's *Winter's Tale*, in an amusing exchange about horticulture. Perdita exclaims that she will have no streaked carnations or gillyflowers in her garden because the art that produces them seems to challenge "great creating nature," but Polixenes replies that such art is itself a part of nature:

> Yet Nature is made better by no mean
> But Nature makes that mean; so over that art
> Which you say adds to Nature, is an art
> That Nature makes. You see, sweet maid, we marry
> A gentler scion to the wildest stock,
> And make conceive a bark of baser kind
> By bud of nobler race. This is an art
> Which does mend Nature—change it rather; but
> The art itself is Nature.

Such concern with the improvement by device, by arrangement, by human ingenuity, by art of something naturally beautiful extended to all aspects of life, so that there was no great gulf between the art or craft of writing and the techniques of other crafts—hawking, archery, building, cookery, managing a great horse in a tournament, sailing, planting a garden. And intricacy of design, elaborateness of pattern were especially valued. The Elizabethan garden was designed as a square, filled with elaborate and intricate, but perfectly regular, design. Some Elizabethans had their houses built in the shape of an E, out of honor to the queen, and one man, John Thorpe, designed his house in the form of his own initials. The several Elizabethan dances—pavans, galliards, almains, sarabands—also presented elaborate, highly patterned designs. Contrapuntal music (composed of several independent melodies joined together) was very intricate, with its elaborate patterns and complex harmonies. The composer Thomas Morley (ca. 1557–1603) praises the madrigal for displaying just such qualities:

As for the music it is, next unto the motet, the most artificial and to men of understanding most delightful. If therefore you will compose in this kind . . . you must in your music be wavering like the wind, sometime wanton, sometime grave and staid, otherwise effeminate; you may maintain points and revert them, use triplaes [triplets] and show the very uttermost of your variety, and the more variety you show the better shall you please.

But a rigid form was to control all of this extravagance, and the fusion of such complexity with such order was often seen, as in Sir John Davies's poem, *Orchestra, or, a Poem on Dancing,* as an emblem of concord and harmony in the universe.

Another vital principal of Elizabethan aesthetics was the concern with models, with conventions, with the literary tradition as the very vehicle for artistic expression. Renaissance writers were in their own way profoundly original, but they did not think of originality as involving opposition to or revolt against literary traditions or artistic conventions. But neither were they slavish imitators. Rather, they looked to classical (and continental) works as models to learn from, emulate, transform, and if possible surpass. The chief models were Homer and Virgil for epic, Theocritus and Virgil for pastoral, Cicero for rhetoric and prose style, Plautus and Terence for comedy, Seneca for tragedy, Petrarch for the sonnet, Ariosto and Tasso for the romantic epic, Ovid for love poetry and erotic mythological narratives.

Sidney's *Defence of Poesy* is the only major work of literary criticism in sixteenth-century England, a period during which Italy and France produced large numbers of critical treatises, heavily influenced by Aristotle's *Poetics.* By contrast, Sidney's engaging tract is highly eclectic, drawing together aesthetic precepts from several traditions and underscoring those which are of primary importance to the Elizabethans: ideal imitation, moral teaching, decorum. Looking back to Aristotle, Sidney defines poetry as an imitation of nature, but links that imitation to his view of the poet as maker, whose activity reflects that of the Divine Creator. The poet imitates not the real, fallen nature we see, but "lifted up with the vigor of his own invention" he imitates an ideal nature: "her world is brazen, the Poets only deliver a golden." Sidney also makes large claims for the didactic role of poetry: he invokes Horace's formula that poetry teaches by delighting, but (staunch Protestant that he is) he emphasizes even more its rhetorical power to move us to be virtuous. He also highlights the importance of suiting subject to genre and style—the idea of literary decorum that Milton was later to term "the grand masterpiece to observe."

From Sidney, from Puttenham's *Art of English Poesy,* and from numerous Elizabethan treatises on rhetoric that define and illustrate literally hundreds of rhetorical and poetic figures of speech, we can infer some other aesthetic principles: the delight in *copia* or "abundance" of words, poetic figures, ornament; the close relation of poetry and rhetoric; the concern with levels of style (high, middle, and low); and the continuing importance of allegory as a means to teach moral truths, and also to suggest the mysterious analogies and symbolic relationships that permeate and order God's universe. Among such symbolic relationships are those suggested by the pervasive macrocosm–microcosm analogy, according to which everything in the vast universe may be found, replicated in little, in the human body; and also those suggested by the image of the Great Chain of Being, according to which all orders of being, from speck of dust to highest angel, are ranged hierarchically in their divinely ordered stations.

POETIC CONVENTIONS, MODES, AND GENRES

Literary conventions are patterns that have become habitual, and arouse certain expectations in the reader. They are by no means stale and lifeless, but are charged with values and associations: for example, we all recognize the conventions in a patriotic song or a religious hymn pertaining to subject, topics, tone, and expected responses. Literary conventions challenged Elizabethan poets to find fit forms for their experiences, to show their learning and virtuosity by the ingenious elaboration of these well-known patterns, and to create from these patterns something fresh and new. Because such conventions are shared cultural codes, they enable poets to elicit particular responses from readers and to relate both poets and readers to other times, other languages, other cultures.

Clusters of such literary conventions—pertaining to subject matter, attitude, tone, values, and some set topics—identify several important literary modes (or "kinds" as Sidney terms them) in the period, including pastoral, heroic, lyric, satiric, elegiac, tragic, and comic. Other conventions—pertaining not only to subject matter and attitude but also to formal structure, meter, style, size, occasion, and the like—identify such important Elizabethan genres or particular literary forms as epic, tragedy, sonnet, verse epistle, epigram, hymn, masque, funeral elegy, and many more. Though Aristotle considered tragedy the noblest form, Elizabethans commonly placed epic at the pinnacle of their genre system, and pastoral poems at the base. Accordingly, Renaissance poets of lofty ambition, like Spenser and Milton, consciously followed the course of poetic development set by Virgil, beginning with pastoral and rising to epic. It is important to remember, however, that such genres and modes are not simply a cluster of conventions and patterns: they carry with them a whole range of culturally defined assumptions and values relating to man and woman, nature, language, heroism, virtue, pleasure, work, and love.

The conventions of the pastoral mode (or kind) present a simple and idealized world inhabited by shepherds and shepherdesses who are chiefly concerned to tend their flocks, fall in love, engage in friendly poetry contests. The values of this mode are defined by *otium* (leisure and humble contentment)—which is at the opposite pole from pride, ambition, the pursuit of fame and fortune. Pastoral exalts the simple country life over the city and its business, the military camp and its warfare, the court and its burdens of rule. The conventions of the pastoral mode could be assimilated to several different genres. Pastoral songs commonly expressed the joys of the shepherd's life, or disappointment in love. Pastoral eclogues were dialogues between shepherds, which might stage a simple poetry contest or might conceal serious, satiric comment on abuses in the great world under the guise of homely, local concerns. There were also pastoral funeral elegies, pastoral dramas, pastoral romances (prose fiction), and even pastoral episodes within epics.

Poems in the satirical mode were also placed among the "low" kinds, plain in matter and style. The genres for satire were less well fixed in the sixteenth century than they were later, but there is a good deal of satirical verse. Some early examples belong to a medieval tradition coming down from *Piers Plowman*, while others, notably Wyatt's epistolary satires, are related to the classical satirists Horace and Juvenal. In the 1590s verse satires, chiefly in rhymed iambic pentameter couplets and closely modeled upon Horace, Juvenal, and Persius, were published by Joseph Hall and John Marston; at the same time, the young John Donne was circulating satires in manuscript that were published only after his death (in 1631). These satires hold up to ridicule and scorn a society (usually a city society) peopled by fops and fools, venal lawyers, toadying courtiers, money-grubbing merchants, self-deluded lovers, and all their ilk. The brief, pointed epigram in the tradition of Martial (often with a surprise ending or "sting" in the tail) was probably the most important of the Elizabethan satiric genres, but throughout the sixteenth and seventeenth centuries epigrams were still often written in Latin. The most notable English achievement in this kind is Ben Jonson's *Epigrams*, first published in 1616. (It is worth noting, however, that some epigrams were lyric in mode, sometimes in the form of words for a madrigal: *The Silver Swan* is an example.)

Poems in the lyric mode were comparatively brief, and usually concerned with praises of various kinds, with love in its various moods, or with celebrations of nature, the good life, or other such matters. The noblest lyric genres were thought to be hymns (praises of God or the gods) and odes (celebrating worthy men and women, and notable occasions); such poems were conventionally exalted in tone, elevated in language, charged with feeling; they often had complex stanzaic patterns and frequent apostrophes. An important variety of ode in the sixteenth century was the epithalamium, a poem in praise of marriage, conventionally following the course of the wedding day—and night. The most famous example is Spenser's *Epithalamion*, whose long stanzas (varying from 17 to 19 lines) display an astonishing metrical complexity, fairly illustrating the height of Elizabethan craft in verse. Notable classical models were Horace, Catullus, Pindar, and Callimachus, and notable biblical models were the Book of Psalms and the Song of Songs.

Often, Elizabethan lyrics retained something of the original association of this mode with song (the lyre). There were dance songs with their definite rhythms and refrains, and many well-known tunes provided the formula by which poet after poet composed new words. There were also many varieties of song, written to fixed formal specifications: the popular ballad with its simple four-line stanza, of anonymous or perhaps composite authorship; the polyphonic madrigal for two or more voices in counterpoint, which had to be short and simple both in language and ideas; the stanzaic "air" for single voice and lute, its more complex thought carried by the recurrent melody.

A most important lyric genre in the sixteenth century was the sonnet, which reached the height of its vogue in the 1590s. Its conventions were established by Petrarch (1304–1374), carried on by his numerous imitators in Italy and France, and introduced into England by Wyatt and Surrey in the reign of Henry VIII. The Petrarchan sonnet sequence is a series of fourteen-line sonnets (with songs interspersed) exploring the contrary states of feeling a lover experiences as he desires and idolizes an unattainable lady: some conventional themes concern the lady's great beauty, her power over him, her cruelty to him, his sleeplessness, the fire of his love and the ice of her chastity, the pain of absence, the renunciation of love, the eternity and originality of his poems. One late sequence by Lady Mary Wroth (*Pamphilia to Amphilanthus*, 1621) reverses the conventional situation, presenting a female speaker who explores her various emotions, conflicts, and experiences in love. The purposes of the love sonneteers differed, of course, but they chiefly sought to celebrate the dignity and power of love by the elaborate rhetorical and stylistic devices available in the Petrarchan tradition.

All love sonnets were not Petrarchan, nor were all sonnets, or sonnet sequences, devoted to love: some sequences treated religious devotion, and occasional sonnets might address a wide variety of topics. More than most genres the sonnet has come to be identified by its formal structure, a fourteen-line poem in iambic pentameter, in three principal rhyming patterns. The most common Italian form, which Wyatt, Sidney, and others imitated, was divided structurally into an octave (first eight lines, rhymed *abba abba*) and a sestet (last six, typically rhymed *cdecde* or some variant thereof). The so-called English sonnet, introduced by Surrey and practiced by Shakespeare, is divided structurally into three quatrains and a couplet, rhymed *abab cdcd efef gg*. Spenser, the most experimental and gifted prosodist of the century, preferred a form that is harder to write and richer in rhymes: *abab bcbc cdcd ee*. Yet sonnets were not so rigidly defined in the sixteenth century: Elizabethans often called them "quatorzains," and often used the term "sonnet" quite loosely, to refer to any short poem.

There were also poems (as well as dramas) in the tragic mode. A principal genre was the complaint, developed especially by the Italian Boccaccio and his English imitators, Lydgate and the authors of *The Mirror for Magistrates*. The chief convention of the complaint is that the ghost of someone who fell from high place bemoans his fate and warns others; the warning carries a moral lesson. If the ghost is a woman like Daniel's Rosamond, her fall was caused by the frailty of her sex. A related kind of poem is the heroical epistle, in which the complaint is written as a letter, usually by a wronged woman to the man who abandoned or betrayed her. Drayton was the chief Elizabethan writer in this kind, which harks back to Ovid.

Another set of conventions defined a mythological-erotic mode, derived mainly from the *Metamorphoses* of Ovid but influenced also by his Italian imitators. The medieval disposition to allegorize and moralize Ovid's poetry continued into the seventeenth century (as did the habit of allegorizing the erotic love songs in the Song of Solomon in the Old Testament). But in the late sixteenth century the Ovidian erotic mode was revived: its values and conventions of lush and elaborate descriptions of physical beauty, of delight in the pleasures of the senses, and of frank eroticism appealed to a courtly taste. In this vein were several poems in the genre of the epyllion, or short mythological narrative, among them Shakespeare's *Venus and Adonis* and Marlowe's *Hero and Leander*.

Finally of course, there was the heroic mode, with its values of honor, battle courage, loyalty, leadership, endurance, glorification of nation or people. The chief genre was the epic, conventionally a long, exalted poem in the high style, based on a heroic story from the nation's distant history and imitating Homer and Virgil in structure and specific topics. Renaissance poets throughout Europe undertook to honor their nations and their vernacular languages by writing this highest kind of poetry. In sixteenth-century England the only real success in epic is Spenser's *Faerie Queene*, which is, properly speaking, a romantic epic, in that it draws more heavily upon the conventions of the romantic Italian epics of Ariosto and Tasso (with their interwoven plots, their exotic adventures and marvels, and their fundamental concern with love as well as war) than upon the classical epics. Spenser points to that genre explicitly when he declares, "Fierce warres and faithfull loves shall moralize my song." By convention, epics had to achieve an elevated, high style, and Spenser devised an elaborate nine-line stanza (called after him the "Spenserian stanza") to serve his special narrative and descriptive needs. It consisted of eight lines of iambic pentameter (rhymed *ababbcbc*), concluding with a line of twelve syllables, an Alexandrine, which rhymes with the preceding line and provides firm closure for each stanza.

We should remember that genres and modes were often mixed in Renaissance England, and that large poems like *The Faerie Queene* contained elements of many kinds. Some new, mixed kinds—like tragicomedy—attracted considerable criticism, but flourished nonetheless. Some others, like Sidney's *Arcadia*, are obviously experimental—a prose romance incorporating both pastoral and heroic elements. The Elizabethans did not approach genre with the rigidity and purism of the Italian or French neoclassicists, but in the spirit of Sidney's inclusivism: "if severed they be good, the conjunction cannot be hurtful."

Also worth noting are some distinctive verse patterns that came to be associated, conventionally, with certain kinds of poems. Henry Howard, earl of Surrey, introduced blank verse (unrhymed iambic pentameter) into England, in his translation of Virgil; this became the conventional meter for Elizabethan tragedy (and later for Milton's epics.) The most common verse form in the 1560s and 1570s was an iambic couplet in which the first line had twelve syllables and the second fourteen, called "poulter's measure" (because a poultryman typically gave twelve eggs in the first dozen and fourteen in the second). An example is:

> The young man eke that feels his bones with pains oppressed,
> How he would be a rich old man, to live and lie at rest.

The dreary monotony of this meter is matched only by the "fourteener" couplet of fourteen syllables to a line. But both were taken into the Elizabethan hymnbooks and survive there: when each line of poulter's measure is printed as two lines it is called "short meter"; when fourteeners are so divided it is called "common meter." Also, some Chaucerian verse forms survive, to be used by Shakespeare in his narrative poems: the six-line pentameter stanza (a quatrain and a couplet, rhymed *ababcc*) in *Venus and Adonis*; and the rhyme royal stanza (seven iambic pentameter lines, rhymed *ababbcc*) in *The Rape of Lucrece*.

DRAMATIC LITERATURE AND THE THEATER

If the morality play *Everyman* at the end of the fifteenth century marks the end of medieval drama, some new beginnings are in evidence at the same time in the household of John Morton, archbishop of Canterbury and chancellor of England under Henry VII, where young Thomas More served as a page. There at Christmastime, plays or revels were put on, and the story goes that young More would sometimes improvise a part and step in with the players. Cardinal Morton even maintained a chaplain on his staff, Henry Medwall, to write plays for his entertainment; two of them survive, called *Nature* and *Fulgens and Lucrece*. These plays were short, given in the great hall at Lambeth Palace, and were called "interludes." Some interludes, especially those by John Heywood, are heavily dependent upon French farce.

Interludes and morality plays continued to be popular down to Shakespeare's lifetime, but the development of drama into a sophisticated art form required another influence, the classics. In the middle of the century a schoolmaster, Nicholas Udall, wrote a classical comedy in English, based upon the Latin comedies his students had been reading; he called it *Ralph Roister Doister*. At about the same time another comedy, putting vivid, native English material into classical form, was amusing the students at Cambridge. It was called *Gammar Gurton's Needle*. In the development of comedy as a genre the great classical models were the Latin comic playwrights Plautus and Terence, from whom English dramatists derived some elements of structure and content: intrigue plots, a structure of acts and scenes, and type characters such as the rascally servant and the *miles gloriosus* (cowardly braggart soldier). The latter type appears in *Ralph Roister Doister* and is a remote ancestor of Shakespeare's Sir John Falstaff in *1 Henry IV*. Comedy was generally taken to be a lower genre than tragedy, and the style often mixed prose and verse: middle and lower class characters especially tended to speak prose.

Many varieties of comedy developed during the Elizabethan and Jacobean age, influenced by classical models and also Italian and French examples. The conventions of romantic comedy call for noble characters and a central love plot (as in Shakespeare's *As You Like It* and *Twelfth Night*). Domestic comedy, as the name implies, has a domestic situation at the center of the plot (as in Thomas Dekker's *Shoemaker's Holiday*). City comedy typically has bourgeois characters, a London setting, and much satire (as in Thomas Middleton's *A Chaste Maid in Cheapside*). Humor comedy (such as Ben Jonson's *Every Man in his Humour*) has type characters created on the theory that the predominance of a particular fluid, or humor, in the body creates a specific temperament (melancholic, choleric, splenetic, phlegmatic). Jonson also wrote classical intrigue comedy in *The Alchemist* and *Volpone*, with their complex, fast-paced plots and discoveries, their characters based on classical types, their witty dialogue. Tragicomedy was a mixed kind, in which evils and problems which seem destined to end tragically are brought to sudden, happy resolution (as in Shakespeare's *Measure for Measure* and, in different mood, *The Winter's Tale*.)

Elizabethan tragedy also began with a fusion of medieval and classical elements. The precarious position of men in high estate formed the basis for medieval notions of tragedy; it owed much to the Latin tragedies of Seneca (known throughout the Middle Ages) which portray the Roman Goddess Fortuna turning her wheel, and thereby bringing low those that were high. This is the tragic vision of the narrative tales in Boccaccio's *Falls of Illustrious Men*, in Chaucer's *Monk's Tale*, and Lydgate's *Falls of Princes*; it is also the conception of tragedy in the collection of tales and complaints about the falls of princes called *The Mirror for Magistrates*, first published in 1559 and reprinted with additions in 1563, 1587, and 1610). A "mirror" in this sense is a warning, something to see oneself in and learn from; a "magistrate" is anyone in a position of power or authority.

When tragedies began to be dramatized, they took over very different elements from Seneca: violent and bloody plots, resounding rhetorical speeches, the frequent use of ghosts among the cast of characters, and sometimes the five-act structure. The first regular English tragedy using some of these elements was called *Gorboduc or Ferrex and Porrex*; it was written by two lawyers, Thomas Sackville and Thomas Norton, was first produced at the Inner Temple (a law school) in 1561, and was later acted before the queen. Significantly, *Gorboduc* was written in blank verse rather than in one of the awkward verse forms characteristic of much midcentury writing; its use here begins the establishment of blank verse as the accepted medium for English tragedy. In due course it evolved into "Marlowe's mighty line" and Shakespeare's wonderfully flexible and expressive poetry.

While Aristotle's *Poetics* did not provide rigid norms for tragedy in England as it did on the continent, it did influence the conception of the genre. Particularly important were the Aristotelian principles that the tragic fall should be caused by some error or moral weakness in the protagonist; that the plot should involve a fall from eminent success into misery, marked by reversals and discoveries; that the characters should be persons of high estate, "better than we"; and that the tragedy should evoke pity and fear in the viewers, working at last to achieve a purgation (catharsis) of those emotions. Some of Shakespeare's great tragedies (e.g., *Othello*, *King Lear*) can be analyzed in such terms, though, like most other Elizabethan tragedies, they are far from classical in their use of subplots and comic relief, their violations of the unities of time and place, their sheer expansiveness.

Several distinct varieties of tragedy developed during the Elizabethan period. The Senecan influence remained pervasive, giving rise to a subgenre of revenge tragedy, in which a wronged protagonist plots and executes revenge, destroying himself (or herself) in the process. An early, highly influential example is Thomas Kyd's *Spanish Tragedy* (1592); and for all its psychological complexity Shakespeare's *Hamlet* is also of this kind. A related but distinct kind (which Aristotle considered untragic) is the villain tragedy in which the protagonist is blatantly evil, as in Shakespeare's *Richard III* and *Macbeth*. Still another sort is the heroic tragedy, in which the hero is larger than life, continually challenging the limits of human possibility: Marlowe's "overreaching" heroes (Tamberlaine and Dr. Faustus) are of this kind, as are the two protagonists of Shakespeare's *Antony and Cleopatra*.

This exuberant era also gave rise to dramatic kinds that fall quite outside the generic boundaries of comedy and tragedy. The festival beginnings of drama in entertainments presented by the servants of a lord in the hall of his castle (often at winter and midsummer holidays and festivals) find some continuity in the several dramatic entertainments provided for Queen Elizabeth when she made progresses through her realm, visiting her nobles in their great houses. Another offshoot was the masque, an entertainment at court combining dance, song, dialogue, and spectacle; there were masques at the courts of Henry VIII and Queen Elizabeth, but the form was especially fostered by the Stuart monarchs in the next century—at which time it took on its characteristic qualities of extravagant display in costume and scenery. Yet another Elizabethan kind is the history play: taking its subjects from English history, it was especially suited to reflect the nationalistic sentiment, the sense of epic destiny, and the moral complexities of gaining and holding on to sovereign power. Shakespeare offers the prime example in his two cycles of history plays. His *1 Henry IV* is perhaps his supreme achievement in that kind.

This flowering of English drama depended centrally upon professional actors, a theater, and an audience. The earliest English drama had been acted by members of the clergy in the church; and medieval miracle and mystery plays had been acted by amateurs—members of the local trade guilds—ordinarily on wagons in the streets of the towns. Moralities and interludes were produced by the servants of a lord in the hall of his castle, or by semi-professional groups who traveled about, giving their performances wherever they could. Such actors did not have respectable status; they tended to be classified with jugglers, acrobats, mountebanks, and other persons of dubious character. In 1545 they were classified by statute as idle rogues and vagabonds, and as such were subject to arrest.

Some noblemen, however, maintained a company of actors as personal servants; since they wore the livery and badge of their master they were exempt from the statute and could travel when not needed by their master and practice their craft where they would. This practice explains why the professional acting companies of Shakespeare's time, including Shakespeare's own, attached themselves to a nobleman and were technically his servants (the Lord Chamberlain's men, the Lord Admiral's men), even though virtually all their time was devoted to, and their income came from, the public. The rise in social status of actors during Shakespeare's lifetime is illustrated by the fact that he and his fellows were made officers of the royal household when James came to the throne and became known as the King's Men. However, the earliest successful acting companies, if success is measured by acceptance at court, were companies of boys. Richard Edwards, master of the children of the Chapel Royal in the 1560s, wrote plays for them, and for almost twenty years the rival company, the Children of Paul's (the choir school of St. Paul's cathedral) regularly presented plays at court.

At first, the adult companies played in various places—great houses, the hall of an Inn of Court, on makeshift stages, or in London inn-yards. In 1576 James Burbage, one of the earl of Leicester's players, built a structure to house their performances and called it The Theatre. It was in Shoreditch, outside the limits of the City of London, and accordingly beyond the jurisdiction of the city authorities who were generally hostile to dramatic spectacles. Soon, other public theaters were erected, which could accommodate some 2,000 spectators: they were usually oval in shape, with an unroofed yard in the center where the groundlings (apprentices, servants, men of the lower classes) stood, and covered seats in three rising tiers around the yard for the spectators of higher social status. A large platform stage jutted out into the yard, surrounded on three sides by spectators—who sometimes also sat on the stage. (See the drawing of a typical London playhouse on p. 2617).

Plays were acted at high speed, without the act-and-scene breaks we are used to; there was no scenery and few props, but costumes were usually sumptuous and elaborate. Performances were given in the afternoon, and were subject to cancelation by bad weather or by epidemics of plague that periodically ravaged the city. Before long there were also enclosed private theaters, secured under conditions that would also allow them freedom from municipal control; they were indoors, artificially lighted, and patronized by a more select audience. After 1608 Shakespeare's company had its regular public theater, the Globe, and a private theater, the Blackfriars.

The companies of players were what would now be called "repertory companies"—that is, they filled the roles of each play from members of their own group, not employing outsiders. They performed a number of different plays on consecutive days, and the principal actors were shareholders in the profits of the company. Boys were apprenticed to actors just as they had been apprenticed to master craftsmen in the guilds; they took the women's parts in plays until their voices changed. The plays might be bought for the company from hack writers, or as in Shakespeare's company, the group might include an actor-playwright who could supply it with some (but by no means all) of its plays. The text remained the property of the company, but a popular play was eagerly sought by the printers, and the company sometimes had trouble achieving effective control over its rights to the play. The editors of the first collected edition of Shakespeare's plays, the First Folio (1623) alluded to the prior publication of "divers stolen and surreptitious copies" of his plays, "maimed and deformed by the frauds and stealths of injurious imposters."

ELIZABETHAN ATTITUDES

The English Renaissance made no sharp break with the past. Attitudes characteristic of the fourteenth or fifteenth centuries persisted well into the era of Humanism and Reformation. George Gascoigne, the leading poet of the 1570s, has in many ways a medieval point of view, as well as a notably plain style, and that flamboyant and "modern" Elizabethan Sir Walter Ralegh also dwells on the vanity and transitoriness of all earthly ambitions and achievements. The Dance of Death and related images were still living symbols to the Elizabethans, as Shakespeare's *Richard II* (3.2.155–70) indicates:

> For God's sake let us sit upon the ground
> And tell sad stories of the death of kings:
> How some have been depos'd; some slain in war,
> Some haunted by the ghosts they have deposed,
> Some poisoned by their wives, some sleeping killed,
> All murthered—for within the hollow crown
> That rounds the mortal temples of a king
> Keeps Death his court, and there the antic sits,
> Scoffing his state and grinning at his pomp,
> Allowing him a breath, a little scene,
> To monarchize, be feared, and kill with looks,
> Infusing him with self and vain conceit,
> As if this flesh which walls about our life
> Were brass impregnable, and humor'd thus,
> Comes at the last and with a little pin
> Bores through the castle wall, and farewell king!

Yet there was at the same time a spirit of joy and gaity, of innocence and lightheartedness, which welds the love of the English for their countryside to the mood of pastoral—quiet contentment and reflective leisure. Marlowe's *Passionate Shepherd to His Love* embodies this spirit, as do also many songs from Shakespeare's plays:

> When daisies pied, and violets blue,
> And lady-smocks all silver-white,
> And cookoo-buds of yellow hue
> Do paint the meadows with delight.

But the Elizabethans also manifest the opposite mood: the burning desire for conquest, for achievement, for surmounting all obstacles. The great poet of this "aspiring mind" is Christopher Marlowe, whose several heroes fling themselves into the lust for gold—"Infinite riches in a little room"; or into the pursuit of power—"Is it not passing brave to be a king / And ride in triumph through Persepolis?"; or into the search for knowledge—"All things that move between the quiet poles / Shall be at my command. . . . / [For]

. . . his dominion that excels in this / Stretches as far as doth the mind of man." Marlowe's heroes are defeated finally, all of them, but their fiery striving spirit endures long after they are gone.

The Elizabethan spirit has been described as "sensuous, comprehensive, extravagant, disorderly, thirsty for beauty, abounding in the zest for life." But we need also to remember Ben Jonson, with his classical principles of structure and decorum, his ideal of the centered self and the balanced moral life, his emphasis upon learning, and his reconciliation of classical and native English elements in his poetry and drama. Even more centrally, there is Sidney, the very embodiment of the Elizabethan Renaissance man—courtier, soldier, humanist scholar, Petrarchan sonneteer, literary critic, and earnest supporter of Protestant reform at home and abroad.

If the beginning of the Tudor era showed more links with the past than with the future, the end of Elizabeth's reign prefigured the conflict and uncertainty of the next age. In 1599, the year of Spenser's death, the headstrong Earl of Essex returned from Ireland, and at length mounted a rebellion that led to his execution in 1601. Elizabeth was old, a peaceful succession was by no means assured, and the rifts (religious and social, and political) which were to lead to civil war in the mid-seventeenth century were already in evidence. An outbreak of satire and epigrams in the 1590s was thought to be dangerous and was repressed by the authorities. Some of the cynical undercurrents in Shakespeare's *Hamlet* and *Troilus and Cressida* reflect the general disenchantment and disillusionment. In 1603, Elizabeth, the last of the Tudors, died, and, to the immense relief of anxious Englishmen, the succession that brought in the Stuart kings took place peacefully. The new monarch was the Protestant James VI of Scotland, who became James I of England.

EDMUND SPENSER
1552–1599

1579: Publication of *The Shepheardes Calender*.
1580: In Ireland, where he remains for the rest of his life.
1590: Publication of *The Faerie Queene*, books 1–3; 1596, books 1–6.

The greatest nondramatic poet of the English Renaissance, Edmund Spenser, was born in London, probably in 1552, and attended the Merchant Taylors' School under its famous headmaster Richard Mulcaster. In 1569 he went to Cambridge as a "sizar" or poor scholar. In the Puritan environment of Cambridge, where the popular preacher Thomas Cartwright was beginning to make the authorities uneasy, Spenser began as a poet by translating some poems for a volume of anti-Catholic propaganda. He also began his friendship with Gabriel Harvey, an eccentric Cambridge don, humanist, and pamphleteer. Their correspondence shows that both men were interested in theories of poetry and in experiments in quantitative versification in English; it also shows that Spenser had ambitious plans as a poet.

After receiving the degree of A. B. in 1573 and A. M. in 1576, Spenser served as personal secretary and aide to several prominent men, including Dr. John Young, bishop of Rochester, and the earl of Leicester, the queen's favorite. During his employment in Leicester's household he came to know Sir Philip Sidney and his friend Sir Edward Dyer, courtiers who sought to promote a new English poetry. Spenser's contribution to the movement is *The Shepheardes Calender*, published in 1579 and dedicated to Sidney.

In the *Shepheardes Calender* Spenser used a deliberately archaic language, partly out of homage to Chaucer, whom he identified as Tityrus, "Who taught me homely, as I can, to make"; but Spenser also used this language to achieve a rustic effect. Sidney did not approve; in his *Defence of Poesy* he wrote, "*The Shepheardes Calender* hath much poetry in his Eclogues, indeed worthy the reading, if I be not deceived. That same framing of his style to an old rustic language I dare not allow, since neither Theocritus in Greek, Virgil in Latin, nor Sannazaro in Italian did affect it." Another classical purist, Ben Jonson, growled that Spenser "writ no language," but that he would have him read nevertheless for his matter. Now, however, we can recognize that Spenser's skillful use of many verse forms and his extraordinary musical effects did much to inaugurate the "new poetry" of the Elizabethan age.

There are thirteen different meters in *The Shepheardes Calender*. Some of these Spenser invented, some he adapted, but most of them were novel; only three or four were at all common in 1579. Spenser was a prolific experimenter who went on to make further innovations in his later poems: the special rhyme scheme of the Spenserian sonnet, the remarkably beautiful adaptation of the Italian *canzone* forms for the *Epithalamion* and *Prothalamion*, and the nine-line stanza of *The Faerie Queene*, with its extraordinary six-foot line at the end, are the best known. Spenser is sometimes called the "poet's poet" because so many later English poets learned the art of versification from him. In the nineteenth century alone his influence may be seen in Shelley's *Revolt of Islam*, Byron's *Childe Harold's Pilgrimage*, Keats's *Eve of St. Agnes*, and Tennyson's *The Lotos-Eaters*.

The year after the publication of *The Shepheardes Calender* Spenser went to Ireland as secretary and aide to Lord Grey of Wilton, Lord Deputy of Ireland. He spent the rest of his life there holding various minor government posts, except for two visits to England. He was at work on his great romantic epic, *The Faerie Queene*, when Sir Walter Ralegh visited him at Kilcolman Castle; the result was a trip to England and the publication, in 1590, of the first three books of *The Faerie Queene*. Soon after, he published a volume of poems called *Complaints*; a pastoral called *Colin Clouts Come Home Againe* (1595), commenting on the courtiers and ladies at the center of English court life at the time of his visit in 1590; the sonnet cycle *Amoretti*; and two marriage poems, *Epithalamion* and *Prothalamion*. But he completed only six of his projected twelve books of *The Faerie Queene*. The six-book *Faerie Queene* was published in 1596, with some revisions in the first part and a changed ending to book 3, to provide a bridge to the added books; the so-called "Mutability Cantos" first appeared in the edition of 1609.

In the second half of the decade, Ireland was torn by revolt and civil war; Spenser's castle was destroyed, and the poet was sent to England with messages from the besieged garrison in Ireland. He died in Westminster on January 13, 1599, and was buried near his beloved Chaucer in what is now called the Poets' Corner of Westminster Abbey.

Spenser is a complex genius who cannot be put into neatly labeled categories. He was strongly influenced by Renaissance Neoplatonism, but was also earthy and practical. He is a lover and celebrator of physical beauty yet also sternly moral. His is not a repressive morality, however, but an attitude based upon his understanding of right action and of the temptations that entrap people as they try to achieve such action. Spenser was strongly influenced by Puritanism in his early days, remained a thoroughgoing Protestant all his life, and portrayed the Roman Catholic Church as a villain in *The Faerie Queene*; yet his understanding of faith and of sin owes much to the great Catholic thinkers. He is profoundly English and patriotic; in him nationality and religion were inextricably joined. He is in some ways a backward-looking poet who paid homage to Chaucer, used archaic language, and compared his own age unfavorably to the antique world. Yet as Christian humanist, British epic poet, and poet-prophet he points to the future directions of poetry, especially the poetry of Milton—who himself paid homage to Spenser as "a better teacher than Scotus or Aquinas."

Since it was a deliberate choice on Spenser's part that his language should seem antique, Spenser's poetry is here printed in the original spelling and punctuation; a few of the most confusing punctuation marks have however been altered in the present text, Spenser also spells words in such a way as to suggest rhymes to the eye, or to suggest etymologies (often incorrect ones). This inconsistency in his spelling is typical of his time; in the sixteenth century people even, from time to time, varied the spelling of their own names.

The Shepheardes Calender   The twelve eclogues of the *Shepheardes Calender* are titled for the months of the year. Each is prefaced by

an illustrative woodcut representing the characters or theme of the poem and picturing the appropriate sign of the zodiac for that month in the clouds above. The eclogue was a classical form practiced by Virgil and others; it presents, usually in dialogue between shepherds, the moods and feelings and attitudes of the simple, rural life. But often the eclogue criticizes the world as it is by measuring it against the idealized pastoral world, so that, in Spenser as in other Renaissance poets, the eclogue at times becomes a didactic or satirical comment on contemporary affairs. The eclogues of the *Calender* are divided by its commentator, "E. K.," into three groups—plaintive, recreative, and moral. *Aprill* is the finest of the recreative eclogues: it includes Hobbinol's rendering of Colin's elegantly artful pastoral song praising Elisa, Queen of Shepherds (Queen Elizabeth).

From The Shepheardes Calender

To His Booke

Goe little booke:[1] thy selfe present,
As child whose parent is unkent:°   *unknown*
To him that is the president°   *pattern*
Of noblesse and of chevalree,
5   And if that Envie barke at thee,
As sure it will, for succoure flee
    Under the shadow of his wing,[2]
And askèd, who thee forth did bring,
A shepheards swaine saye did thee sing,
10   All as his straying flocke he fedde:
And when his honor has thee redde,°   *seen*
Crave pardon for my hardyhedde.°   *boldness*
    But if that any aske thy name,
Say thou wert base° begot with blame: *lowly*
15   For thy[3] thereof thou takest shame.
And when thou art past jeopardee,
Come tell me, what was sayd of mee:
And I will send more after thee.
           IMMERITO.[4]

---

1. A deliberate echo of Chaucer's line, "Go, litel bok, go litel myn tragedye" (*Troilus and Criseyde* 5.1786).

2. I.e., the protective sponsorship of Sir Philip Sidney.

3. Therefore.

4. Unworthy.

Aprill[1]

Aegloga Quarta[2]

ARGUMENT

This Aeglogue is purposely intended to the honor and prayse of our most gracious sovereigne, Queene Elizabeth. The speakers herein be Hobbinoll and Thenot, two shepheardes: the which Hobbinoll being before mentioned, greatly to have loved Colin, is here set forth more largely, complayning him of that boyes great misadventure in Love, whereby his mynd was alienate and with drawen not onely from him, who moste loved him, but also from all former delightes and studies, aswell in pleasaunt pyping, as conning[3] ryming and singing, and other his laudable exercises. Whereby he taketh occasion, for proofe of his more excellencie and skill in poetrie, to recorde a songe, which the sayd Colin sometime made in honor of her Majestie, whom abruptely[4] he termeth Elysa.

THENOT	HOBBINOLL

Tell me good Hobbinoll, what garres thee greete?[5]
What? hath some Wolfe thy tender Lambes ytorne?

1. When *The Shepheardes Calender* was published in 1579, each of the 12 eclogues was followed by a "Glosse," which contained explications of difficult or archaic words, together with learned discussions of—and disagreements with—Spenser's ideas, imagery, and poetics. The glosses are by one "E. K.," whom some scholars identify with one of Spenser's friends, others with Spenser himself. E. K.'s editorial apparatus is usually published along with the poems. In these notes, the editors have incorporated the glosses that are especially useful to the modern reader; they are marked [E. K.]. The original spelling is retained.
2. Fourth Eclogue. An eclogue ("aeglogue") is a short pastoral poem in the form of a dialogue or soliloquy. Spenser's spelling is based on a false etymology (*aix*-goat + *logos*-speech), satisfying, according to E. K., "Goteheards tales." The illustration portrays Colin Clout (the Shepherd persona assumed by Spenser) piping a song of Elizabeth, shown with the ladies of her court. The shepherds Thenot and Hobbinol are in the background, and the astrological sign for April, Taurus the bull, is at the top of the picture.
3. Learning.
4. With a sudden change.
5. "Causeth thee weepe and complain" [E. K.]

Or is thy Bagpype broke, that soundes so sweete?
Or art thou of thy lovèd lasse forlorne°?   *forsaken*

5 Or bene thine eyes attempred to the yeare,[6]
Quenching the gasping furrowes thirst with rayne?
Like April shoure, so stremes the trickling teares
Adowne thy cheeke, to quenche thy thirstye° payne.   *thirsty*

HOBBINOLL

Nor thys, nor that, so muche doeth make me mourne,
10 But for the ladde,[7] whome long I lovd so deare,
Nowe loves a lasse,[8] that all his love doth scorne:
He plongd in payne, his tressèd° locks dooth teare.   *curled*

Shepheards delights he dooth them all forsweare,
Hys pleasaunt Pipe, whych made us meriment,
15 He wylfully hath broke, and doth forbeare
His wonted songs, wherein he all outwent.[9]

THENOT

What is he for a Ladde,[1] you so lament?
Ys love such pinching payne to them, that prove?
And hath he skill to make[2] so excellent,
20 Yet hath so little skill to brydle love?

HOBBINOLL

Colin thou kenst,° the Southerne shepheardes boye: *knowest*
Him Love hath wounded with a deadly darte.
Whilome° on him was all my care and joye,   *once*
Forcing° with gyfts to winne his wanton heart.   *striving*

25 But now from me hys madding° mynd is   *foolish*
      starte,°   *broken away*
And woes the Widdowes daughter of the glenne:[3]
So nowe fayre Rosalind hath bredde° hys smart,   *caused*
So now his frend is chaungèd for a frenne.°   *stranger*

THENOT

But if hys ditties bene so trimly dight,[4]
30 I pray thee Hobbinoll, recorde° some one: *sing*

6. "Agreeable to the season of the yeare, that is Aprill, which moneth is most bent to shoures and seasonable rayne: to quench . . . the drought" [E. K.]. "Bene": are.
7. "Colin Clout" [E. K.]; "for": that.
8. "Rosalinda" [E. K.].
9. His usual songs, which surpassed those of all others.
1. "What maner of Ladde is he?" [E. K.].

2. "To rime and versifye" [E. K.]. "Maker" is the Greek word for "poet."
3. "He calleth Rosalind the Widowes daughter of the glenne, that is, of a country Hamlet or borough, which I thinke is rather sayde to conceale the person, then simply spoken. For it is well knowen . . . that shee is a Gentle woman of no meane house" [E. K.]. "Woes": woos.
4. "Adorned" [E. K.].

The whiles our flockes doe graze about in sight,
And we close shrowded in thys shade alone.

HOBBINOLL

Contented I: then will I singe his laye°   *song*
Of fayre Elisa, Queene of shepheardes all:[5]
35 Which once he made, as by a spring he laye,
And tunèd it unto the Waters fall.

"Ye dayntye Nymphs, that in this blessèd Brooke
doe bathe your brest,
For sake your watry bowres, and hether looke,
40   at my request:
And eke you Virgins, that on Parnasse dwell,
Whence floweth Helicon the learnèd well,[6]
      Helpe me to blaze[7]
      Her worthy praise,
45 Which in her sexe doth all excell.

"Of fayre Elisa be your silver song,
      that blessèd wight:°   *being*
The flowre of Virgins, may shee florish long,
      In princely plight.°   *condition*
50 For shee is Syrinx daughter without spotte,
Which *Pan* the shepheards God of her begot:[8]
      So sprong° her grace   *sprung*
      Of heavenly race,
No mortall blemishe may her blotte.

55 "See, where she sits upon the grassie greene,
      (O seemely° sight)   *pleasing*
Yclad in Scarlot like a mayden Queene,
      And Ermines white.
Upon her head a Cremosin° coronet,   *crimson*
60 With Damaske roses and Daffadillies set:
      Bayleaves betweene,
      And Primroses greene
Embellish[9] the sweete Violet.

---

5. "In all this songe is not to be respected, what
the worthinesse of her Majestie deserveth, nor what
to the highnes of a Prince is agreeable, but what is
moste comely for the meanesse of a shepheards
witte, or to conceive, or to utter" [E. K.].
6. "The nine Muses, daughters of Apollo and
Memorie, whose abode the Poets faine to be on
Parnassus, a hill in Grece" [E. K.]. According to
Spenser and E. K., Helicon is a well or spring at
the foot of Parnassus, but in fact it is a mountain
itself sacred to the Muses.

7. A blason was a poem cataloguing and praising
a lady's various physical features.
8. "Syrinx is the name of a Nymphe of Arcadie,
whom when Pan being in love pursued. . . . By
Pan is here meant the most famous and victorious
King, her highnesse Father, late of worthy memorye K. Henry the eyght" [E. K.]. "Without spotte"
qualifies Syrinx, not daughter, a covert repudiation of the scandals surrounding Anne Boleyn.
9. "Beautifye and set out" [E. K.], i.e., by contrast of colors.

"Tell me, have ye seene her angelick face,
65   Like Phoebe fayre?[1]
Her heavenly haveour,° her princely grace   *bearing*
        can you well compare?
The Redde rose medled with the White yfere,[2]
In either cheeke depeincten° lively chere.   *depict*
70   Her modest eye,
        Her Majestie,
Where have you seene the like, but there?

"I sawe Phoebus thrust out his golden hedde,
        upon her to gaze:
75   But when he sawe, how broade her beames did spredde,
        it did him amaze.
He blusht to see another Sunne belowe,
Ne durst againe his fyrye face out showe:[3]
        Let him, if he dare,
80   His brightnesse compare
With hers, to have the overthrowe.[4]

"Shewe thy selfe Cynthia[5] with thy silver rayes,
        and be not abasht:
When shee the beames of her beauty displayes,
85   O how art thou dasht?
But I will not match her with *Latonaes* seede,
Such follie great sorow to Niobe did breede.[6]
        Now she is a stone,
        And makes dayly mone,
90   Warning all other to take heede.

"Pan may be proud, that ever he begot
        such a Bellibone,[7]
And Syrinx rejoyse, that ever was her lot
        to beare such an one.
95   Soone as my younglings cryen for the dam,
To her will I offer a milkwhite Lamb:
        Shee is my goddesse plaine,°   *absolute*
        And I her shepherds swayne,°   *servant*
Albee forswonck and forswatt I am.[8]

---

1. "The Moone, whom the Poets faine to be sister
unto Phoebus, that is the Sunne" [E. K.].
2. "Together" [E. K.]. "Medled": mingled. Elizabeth, like her father Henry VIII, descends from
both the houses of Lancaster and of York (symbolized, respectively, by the red and the white rose),
whose conflicting claims to the throne caused the
Hundred Years' War.
3. Show abroad.
4. Be overthrown.

5. "The Moone" [E. K.].
6. When Niobe vaunted herself above Latona by
reason of her seven sons and seven daughters, the
goddess caused her two children, Apollo and Diana,
to slay Niobe's entire progeny, after which her sorrow transformed her to stone.
7. A *belle bonne:* "homely spoken for a fayre mayde
or Bonilasse" [E. K.].
8. "Overlaboured and sunneburnt" [E. K.].

100 "I see Calliope[9] speede her to the place,
　　　　where my Goddesse shines:
　　And after her the other Muses trace,°　　　　　　　　　*step*
　　　　with their Violines.
　　Bene° they not Bay braunches,[1] which they doe beare,　　*are*
105 All for Elisa in her hand to weare?
　　　　So sweetely they play,
　　　　And sing all the way,
　　That it a heaven is to heare.

　　"Lo how finely the graces[2] can it foote
110　　　to the Instrument:
　　They dauncen deffly,° and singen soote,°　　　*nimbly/sweet*
　　　　in their meriment.
　　Wants not a fourth grace, to make the daunce even?
　　Let that rowme° to my Lady be yeven:°　　　*place/given*
115　　　She shalbe a grace,
　　　　To fyll the fourth place,
　　And reigne with the rest in heaven.

　　"And whither rennes° this bevie° of Ladies bright,　*runs/company*
　　　　raungèd in a rowe?
120　They bene all Ladyes of the lake[3] behight,
　　　　that unto her goe.
　　Chloris,[4] that is the chiefest Nymph of al,
　　Of Olive braunches beares a Coronall:°　　　*crown*
　　　　Olives bene° for peace,　　　　　　　*are*
125　　　When wars doe surcease:
　　Such for a Princesse bene principall.°　　　*princely*

　　"Ye shepheards daughters, that dwell on the greene,
　　　　hye° you there apace:°　　　　　*come/quickly*
　　Let none come there, but that Virgins bene,
130　　　to adorne her grace.
　　And when you come, whereas shee is in place,
　　See, that your rudenesse doe not you disgrace:
　　　　Binde your fillets° faste,　　　　*hair ribbons*
　　　　And gird in your waste,°　　　　　*waist*
135　For more finesse, with a tawdrie lace.[5]

---

9. The muse of epic poetry.
1. "Be the signe of honor and victory . . . and eke [also] of famous Poets" [E. K.].
2. "Be three sisters, the daughters of Jupiter, whose names are Aglaia, Thalia, Euphrosyne . . . whom the Poetes feyned to be Goddesses of al bountie and comelines" [E. K.]. "Foote": dance.
3. Nymphs. E. K. records the ancient view that every spring and fountain had a goddess as its sovereign. "Behight": called.
4. According to E. K., the nymph of flowers and green herbs; her name signifies greenness.
5. I.e., to present a finer appearance, with a band of lace bought at the fair of St. Audrey (Etheldreda).

"Bring hether the Pincke and purple Cullambine,
    With Gelliflowres:
Bring Coronations, and Sops in wine,
    worne of Paramoures.°   *lovers*
140 Strowe me the ground with Daffadowndillies,
And Cowslips, and Kingcups, and lovèd Lillies:
    The pretie° Pawnce,   *pretty*
    And the Chevisaunce,[6]
Shall match with the fayre flowre Delice.

145 "Now ryse up Elisa,[7] deckèd as thou art,
    in royall aray:
And now ye daintie Damsells may depart
    echeone° her way.   *each one*
I feare, I have troubled your troupes to° longe: *too*
150 Let dame Eliza thanke you for her song.
    And if you come hether,
    When Damsines° I gether,   *plums*
I will part them all you among."[8]

THENOT

And was thilk° same song of Colins owne making?   *this*
155 Ah foolish boy, that is with love yblent:°   *blinded*
Great pittie is, he be in such taking,°   *plight*
For naught caren, that bene so lewdly bent.[9]

HOBBINOLL

Sicker° I hold him, for a greater fon,°   *surely/fool*
That loves the thing, he cannot purchase.
160 But let us homeward: for night draweth on,
And twincling starres the daylight hence chase.

        Thenots Embleme[1]
      O quam te memorem virgo?
      Hobbinolls Embleme
        O dea certe.

              1597

---

6. All these are names of flowers common in pastoral poetry. "Coronations" are carnations; "sops in wine" are clove pinks; "paunce," the pansy; "daffadowndillies," daffodils; "flowre Delice (fleur de lis)," a kind of iris; "chevisaunce" may be a species of wallflower.
7. "Is the conclusion. For having so decked her with prayses and comparisons, he returneth all the thanck of hys laboure to the excellencie of her Majestie" [E. K.].
8. Among you all.

9. I.e., for they that are so foolishly inclined are heedless of everything.
1. An "embleme" is a motto or relevant quotation. Both emblems are from *Aeneid* 1.327–8, in which Aeneas is overwhelmed by the appearance of Venus in the guise of one of Diana's maidens and cries out: "By what name should I call thee, O maiden? . . . O goddess surely." E. K. notes that Hobbinoll and Thenot are similarly struck with amazement by the "divine" Elizabeth.

The Faerie Queene   Spenser's exuberant, multifaceted poem is
peculiarly characteristic of its age. In some respects it is a "courtesy book,"
like Castiglione's *Courtier*, intended to "fashion a gentleman or noble person" by exhibiting the qualities such a person should have. The six books
which Spenser completed (of the projected twelve) exhibit the virtues of
Holiness, Temperance, Chastity, Friendship, Justice, and Courtesy. A fragment of another book, the cantos on Mutability (the principle of constant
change in nature), also survives.

In other respects *The Faerie Queene* is a romantic epic, like Ariosto's
Orlando Furioso ("Orlando Mad," 1516), full of adventures and marvels,
dragons, witches, enchanted trees, giants, jousting knights, and castles. As
such it fulfills the expectation that a romance will produce wonder, that it
will enthrall us with its intricate plots, amazing episodes, heroic characters,
elaborate descriptions. It also fulfills the common Elizabethan expectation
that poetry should teach by delighting.

The poem is also an allegory like Tasso's *Gerusalemme Liberata* ("Jerusalem Delivered," 1575), as Spenser's preliminary letter to Sir Walter Ralegh indicates. That letter invites us to interpret the characters and adventures
in the several books in terms of particular virtues and vices: e.g., the Redcrosse Knight in book 1 is the knight of Holiness (and also St. George, the
patron saint of England); Sir Guyon in book 2 is the knight of Temperance;
and the female knight Britomart in book 3 is the knight of Chastity (in her,
chaste love leading toward marriage). However, far from being static embodiments of their respective virtues, each advances in the understanding and
practice of the virtue in question in the course of his or her book. By the
same token the meaning of the various characters, episodes, and places is
dense and complex, and is revealed to us only by degrees as we read and
interpret the poem. In addition, persistent allusions to many personages and
events in Spenser's own England lead us to recognize that the poem incorporates historical allegory. The poem may be enjoyed as a fascinating story
with multiple meanings. It works on several levels at once, inviting the reader
to move as the story moves, taking the meaning at whatever level seems most
viable at the moment.

The introductory lines of the poem are intended to remind the reader of
Virgil, who began his poetic career with pastoral poetry and moved on to
the epic, as Spenser did in moving from the *Shepheardes Calender* to the
Faerie Queene. The organization of each book into twelve cantos also imitates the twelve books of Virgil's *Aeneid*. But Spenser replaces Virgil's theme
of epic heroism, "Arms and the man," with something more romantic—
"Fierce warres and faithfull loves." The scenery too is romantic: plains and
forests and caves and castles and magical trees and springs, where one meets
dwarfs and giants and lions and pilgrims and magicians and Saracens or
"paynims" (with French names). In Spenser's Faerie Land, if you are going
somewhere you just start out, and after many adventures, get there. A clear,
pleasant stream may be dangerous to drink because it produces loss of strength.
Any stranger you meet may well be a villain and may be in disguise. Houses,
castles, and gardens are often places of education or of especially dense allegorical significance, affording special keys to the meaning of the books in
which they appear.

The Faerie Queene's subjects in Faeryland are called Faeries or Elves.
They are human beings, and undergo the trials and tribulations people undergo

in the ordinary world. But Faerie Land is also inhabited by knights who are not Faeries but Britons—Redcrosse, Britomart, and Prince Arthur (who loves and seeks for the Faerie Queene throughout the poem). The bad creatures, people and monsters, represent various vices, evils, and temptations. Spenser's characters, both good and evil, may be initially identified to the reader by their names or by the short verse summaries at the beginning of each canto, but their natures are revealed progressively, in the course of the narrative. Some of Spenser's characters are identified by conventional symbols and attributes which would be obvious to every reader of his time. For example, such a reader would know immediately that a woman who wears a miter and scarlet clothes, and who dwells near the river Tiber, represents (in one sense at least) the Roman Catholic Church, which had often been identified by Protestant preachers with the Whore of Babylon in the Book of Revelation.

The various books are composed on different structural principles. Book 1 is almost entirely self-contained: it has been called a miniature epic in itself, centering upon the adventures of one principal hero, Redcrosse, who at length achieves the quest he undertakes at Una's behest—killing the dragon who has imprisoned her parents, and winning her as his bride. The spiritual allegory is similarly self-contained: it presents the Christian struggling heroically against many evils—error, hypocrisy, the seven deadly sins, despair—but succumbing to some of them, shows him separated from the one true faith and, aided by many interventions of divine grace, at length reunited with it once more; and treats his purgation from sin, his education in the House of Holiness, and his final salvation. By contrast, the structure of book 3 is romance-like, with its many heroines and heroes.

The Faerie Queene draws constantly upon the riches of literary and pictorial traditions. Entire episodes are adopted from the Italian romantic epics of Ariosto and Tasso, and either through them or independently, from Homer, Virgil, or Ovid. (In the Renaissance, borrowing from and reworking older materials was praiseworthy in a poet.) Places, such as Lucifera's castle; individual attributes, such as Una's lamb or Speranza's anchor; and even certain names and colors come to Spenser from the classics, from theologians, from liturgical tradition, from folk tales and pageants, from tapestries, paintings, and emblem books. Our notes point to some of these sources—but more important is the understanding that these were living traditions for Spenser and his readers. They flow together, separate, and recombine to produce the uniquely Spenserian delights of the *Faerie Queene*.

From THE FAERIE QUEENE

A Letter of the Authors

EXPOUNDING HIS WHOLE INTENTION IN THE COURSE OF THIS WORKE: WHICH FOR THAT IT GIVETH GREAT LIGHT TO THE READER, FOR THE BETTER UNDERSTANDING IS HEREUNTO ANNEXED

To the Right noble, and Valorous, Sir Walter Raleigh knight, Lo. Wardein of the Stanneryes, and her Majesties liefetenaunt of the County of Cornewayll

Sir knowing how doubtfully all Allegories may be construed, and this booke of mine, which I have entituled the *Faery Queene*, being a continued Allegory, or darke conceit,[1] I have thought good as well for avoyding of gealous opinions and misconstructions, as also for your better light in reading thereof, (being so by you commanded,) to discover unto you the general intention and meaning, which in the whole course thereof I have fashioned, without expressing of any particular purposes or by-accidents[2] therein occasioned. The generall end therefore of all the booke is to fashion[3] a gentleman or noble person in vertuous and gentle[4] discipline: Which for that I conceived shoulde be most plausible and pleasing, being coloured with an historicall fiction, the which the most part of men delight to read, rather for variety of matter, then for profite of the ensample:[5] I chose the historye of King Arthure, as most fitte for the excellency of his person, being made famous by many mens former workes, and also furthest from the daunger of envy, and suspition of present time.[6] In which I have followed all the antique Poets historicall, first Homere, who in the Persons of Agamemnon and Ulysses hath ensampled a good governour and a vertuous man, the one in his *Ilias*, the other in his *Odysseis*: then Virgil, whose like intention was to doe in the person of Aeneas: after him Ariosto comprised them both in his *Orlando*: and lately Tasso dissevered them againe, and formed both parts in two persons, namely that part which they in Philosophy call Ethice, or vertues of a private man, coloured in his Rinaldo: The other named Politice in his Godfredo.[7] By ensample of which excellente Poets, I labour to pourtraict in Arthure, before he was king, the image of a brave knight, perfected in the twelve private morall vertues, as Aristotle hath devised,[8] the which is the purpose of these first twelve bookes: which if I finde to be well accepted, I may be perhaps encouraged, to frame the other part of polliticke vertues in his person, after that hee came to be king. To some I know this Methode will seeme displeasaunt, which had rather have good discipline delivered plainly in way of precepts, or sermoned at large, as they use, then thus clowdily enwrapped in Allegoricall devises. But such, me seeme, should be satisfide with the use of these dayes, seeing all things accounted by their showes,[9] and nothing esteemed of, that is not delightfull and pleasing to commune sence.[1] For this cause is Xenophon preferred before Plato, for that the one in the exquisite depth of his judgment, formed a Commune welth[2] such as it should be, but the other in the person of Cyrus and the Persians fashioned a gov-

---

1. Poetic figure.
2. Secondary matters.
3. I.e., to represent, to educate.
4. Pertaining to a gentleman.
5. Example.
6. I.e., free from current political controversy.
7. Lodovico Ariosto (1474–1533) was author of the epic-romance *Orlando Furioso*, first published in complete form in 1532. Torquato Tasso (1544–1595) published his chivalric romance *Rinaldo* in 1562 and the epic *Gerusalemme Liberata* (centered on the heroic figure of Count Godfredo) in

1581.
8. Aristotle did not devise 12 private moral virtues: Spenser was in fact relying upon more modern philosophers—his friend Lodowick Bryskett and the Italian Piccolomini. That Spenser actually planned a poem 4 times as long as the 6 books we now have rather staggers the imagination.
9. Appearances.
1. The notions of the many.
2. The allusion is to Plato's *Republic* and Xenophon's *Cyropaedia*.

ernement such as might best be: So much more profitable and gratious
is doctrine by ensample, then by rule. So have I laboured to doe in the
person of Arthure: whome I conceive after his long education by Timon,
to whom he was by Merlin delivered to be brought up, so soone as he
was borne of the Lady Igrayne, to have seene in a dream or vision the
Faery Queen, with whose excellent beauty ravished, he awaking resolved
to seeke her out, and so being by Merlin armed, and by Timon throughly
instructed, he went to seeke her forth in Faerye land. In that Faery
Queene I meane glory in my generall intention, but in my particular I
conceive the most excellent and glorious person of our soveraine the
Queene, and her kingdome in Faery land. And yet in some places els, I
doe otherwise shadow[3] her. For considering she beareth two persons,
the one of a most royall Queene or Empresse, the other of a most vertuous and beautifull Lady, this latter part in some places I doe express
in Belphoebe, fashioning her name according to your owne excellent
conceipt of Cynthia,[4] (Phoebe and Cynthia being both names of Diana.)
So in the person of Prince Arthure I sette forth magnificence in particular, which vertue for that (according to Aristotle and the rest) it is the
perfection of all the rest, and conteineth in it them all, therefore in the
whole course I mention the deedes of Arthure applyable to that vertue,
which I write of in that booke. But of the xii. other vertues, I make xii.
other knights the patrones, for the more variety of the history. Of which
these three bookes contayn three, The first of the knight of the Redcrosse, in whome I express Holynes: The seconde of Sir Guyon, in
whome I sette forth Temperaunce: The third of Britomartis a Lady knight,
in whome I picture Chastity. But because the beginning of the whole
worke seemeth abrupte and as depending upon other antecedents, it
needs that ye know the occasion of these three knights severall adventures. For the Methode of a Poet historical is not such, as of an Historiographer.[5] For an Historiographer discourseth of affayres orderly as
they were donne, accounting as well the times as the actions, but a Poet
thrusteth into the middest, even where it most concerneth him, and
there recoursing to the thinges forepaste,[6] and divining of thinges to
come, maketh a pleasing Analysis of all. The beginning therefore of my
history, if it were to be told by an Historiographer, should be the twelfth
booke, which is the last, where I devise that the Faery Queene kept her
Annuall feaste xii. dayes, upon which xii. severall dayes, the occasions
of the xii. severall adventures hapned, which being undertaken by xii.
severall knights, are in these xii books severally handled and discoursed.
The first was this. In the beginning of the feaste, there presented him
selfe a tall clownishe[7] younge man, who falling before the Queen of
Faeries desired a boone (as the manner then was) which during that feast
she might not refuse: which was that hee might have the atchievement
of any adventure, which during that feaste should happen, that being

3. Picture, portray.
4. Ralegh's poem *Cynthia* praised Queen Elizabeth.
5. Historian.
6. Past.
7. Rustic-looking.

graunted, he rested him on the floore, unfitte through his rusticity for a better place. Soone after entred a faire Ladye in mourning weedes, riding on a white Asse, with a dwarfe behind her leading a warlike steed, that bore the Armes of a knight, and his speare in the dwarfes hand. Shee falling before the Queene of Faeries, complayned that her father and mother an ancient King and Queene, had bene by an huge dragon many years shut up in a brasen Castle, who thence suffred them not to yssew:[8] and therefore besought the Faery Queene to assygne her some one of her knights to take on him that exployt. Presently that clownish person upstarting, desired that adventure: whereat the Queene much wondering, and the Lady much gainesaying, yet he earnestly importuned his desire. In the end the Lady told him that unlesse that armour which she brought, would serve him (that is the armour of a Christian man specified by Saint Paul v. Ephes.[9]) that he could not succeed in that enterprise, which being forthwith put upon him with dewe furnitures[1] thereunto, he seemed the goodliest man in al that company, and was well liked of the Lady. And eftesoones taking on him knighthood, and mounting on that straunge Courser, he went forth with her on that adventure: where beginneth the first booke, vz.

A gentle knight was pricking on the playne. &c.

The second day ther came in a Palmer bearing an Infant with bloody hands, whose Parents he complained to have bene slayn by an Enchaunteresse called Acrasia: and therfore craved of the Faery Queene, to appoint him some knight, to performe that adventure, which being assigned to Sir Guyon, he presently went forth with that same Palmer: which is the beginning of the second booke and the whole subject thereof. The third day there came in, a Groome who complained before the Faery Queene, that a vile Enchaunter called Busirane had in hand a most faire Lady called Amoretta, whom he kept in most grievous torment, because she would not yield him the pleasure of her body. Whereupon Sir Scudamour the lover of that Lady presently tooke on him that adventure. But being unable to performe it by reason of the hard Enchauntments, after long sorrow, in the end met with Britomartis, who succoured him, and reskewed his love.

But by occasion hereof, many other adventures are intermedled, but rather as Accidents, then intendments.[2] As the love of Britomart, the overthrow of Marinell, the misery of Florimell, the vertuousnes of Belphoebe, the lasciviousnes of Hellenora, and many the like.

Thus much Sir, I have briefly overronne to direct your understanding to the wel-head of the History, that from thence gathering the whole intention of the conceit,[3] ye may as in a handfull gripe al the discourse,

---

8. Come forth.

9. Ephesians 6.13–17 itemizes the "whole armor of God" as follows: loins girt about with truth; breastplate of righteousness; feet shod with the gospel of peace; shield of faith "wherewith ye shall be able to quench all the fiery darts of the wicked"; helmet of salvation; and "sword of the Spirit, which is the word of God."

1. Suitable equipment.

2. I.e., there are episodes that are not part of these principal stories.

3. Conception.

which otherwise may happily[4] seeme tedious and confused. So humbly craving the continuaunce of your honorable favour towards me, and th' eternall establishment of your happines, I humbly take leave.

23. January, 1589
Yours most humbly affectionate.
ED. SPENSER.

The First Booke of the Faerie Queene

Contayning
The Legende of the
Knight of the Red Crosse,
or
of Holinesse

1

Lo I the man, whose Muse whilome did maske,
　　As time her taught, in lowly Shepheards weeds,[1]
　　Am now enforst a far unfitter taske,
　　For trumpets sterne to chaunge mine Oaten reeds,[2]
5　　And sing of Knights and Ladies gentle° deeds;　　　　noble
　　Whose prayses having slept in silence long,[3]
　　Me, all too meane, the sacred Muse areeds°　　　　appoints
　　To blazon° broad emongst her learned throng:　　　　proclaim
Fierce warres and faithfull loves shall moralize my song.

2

10　Helpe then, O holy Virgin chiefe of nine,[4]
　　Thy weaker Novice to performe thy will,
　　Lay forth out of thine everlasting scryne[5]
　　The antique rolles, which there lye hidden still,
　　Of Faerie knights and fairest Tanaquill,[6]
15　Whom that most noble Briton Prince[7] so long
　　Sought through the world, and suffered so much ill,
　　That I must rue his undeservèd wrong:
O helpe thou my weake wit, and sharpen my dull tong.

3

And thou most dreaded impe[8] of highest Jove,
20　　Faire Venus sonne, that with thy cruell dart
　　At that good knight so cunningly didst rove,°　　　　shoot
　　That glorious fire it kindled in his hart,

---

4. By chance.
1. I.e., behold me, the poet who appropriately appeared before ("whilome") as a writer of humble pastoral (i.e., *The Shepheardes Calender*). These lines are imitated from the verses prefixed to Renaissance editions of Virgil's *Aeneid*. "Weeds:" garb.
2. To write heroic poetry, of which the trumpet is a symbol, instead of pastoral poetry symbolized by the humble shepherd's pipe ("Oaten reeds").
3. Lines 5 and 6 are imitated from the opening lines of Ariosto's *Orlando Furioso*.
4. Clio, the muse of history. "Weaker": too weak.
5. A chest for papers.
6. I.e., Gloriana.
7. I.e., Arthur, named in canto 9, line 50.
8. Child, i.e., Cupid.

Lay now thy deadly Heben° bow apart,   *ebony*
    And with thy mother milde come to mine ayde:
25   Come both, and with you bring triumphant Mart,[9]
    In loves and gentle jollities arrayd,
After his murdrous spoiles and bloudy rage allayd.

4

And with them eke,° O Goddesse heavenly bright,   *also*
    Mirrour of grace and Majestie divine,
30   Great Lady of the greatest Isle, whose light
    Like Phoebus lampe throughout the world doth shine,
    Shed thy faire beames into my feeble eyne,
    And raise my thoughts too humble and too vile,°   *lowly*
    To thinke of that true glorious type[1] of thine,
35   The argument of mine afflicted stile:
The which to heare, vouchsafe, O dearest dred[2] a-while.

Canto 1

The Patron of true Holinesse,
    Foule Errour doth defeate:
Hypocrisie him to entrappe,
    Doth to his home entreate.

1

A Gentle Knight was pricking° on the plaine,   *cantering*
    Ycladd in mightie armes and silver shielde,
    Wherein old dints of deepe wounds did remaine,
    The cruell markes of many a bloudy fielde;
5   Yet armes till that time did he never wield:[3]
    His angry steede did chide his foming bitt,
    As much disdayning to the curbe to yield:
    Full jolly° knight he seemd, and faire did sitt,   *gallant*
As one for knightly giusts° and fierce encounters   *tourneys, jousts*
    fitt.

2

10   But on his brest a bloudie Crosse he bore,
    The deare remembrance of his dying Lord,
    For whose sweete sake that glorious badge he wore,
    And dead as living ever him adored:
    Upon his shield the like was also scored,
15   For soveraine[4] hope, which in his helpe he had:
    Right faithfull true[5] he was in deede and word,

---

9. Mars, god of war and lover of Venus.
1. I.e., Gloriana is the "type" (foreshadowing) of
Queen Elizabeth.
2. Object of awe.
3. Redcrosse wears the armor of the Christian man,
as Spenser explained in the letter to Ralegh: "put
on the whole armor of God, that ye may be able
to stand against the wiles of the devil" (Ephesians

6.10–22). The armor bears the dents of every
Christian's fight against evil; Redcrosse himself is
as yet untried.
4. Having greatest power (often applied to medical
remedies).
5. An echo of Revelation 19.11: "And I saw heaven
opened; and behold a white horse; and he that sat
upon him was called Faithful and True. . . ."

But of his cheere[6] did seeme too solemne sad;°   *grave*
Yet nothing did he dread, but ever was ydrad.°   *dreaded, feared*

3

Upon a great adventure he was bond,
20   That greatest Gloriana to him gave,
That greatest Glorious Queene of Faerie Lond,
To winne him worship,° and her grace to have,   *honor*
Which of all earthly things he most did crave;
And ever as he rode, his hart did earne°   *yearn*
25   To prove his puissance in battell brave
Upon his foe, and his new force to learne;
Upon his foe, a Dragon horrible and stearne.

4

A lovely Ladie rode him faire beside,
Upon a lowly Asse more white then snow,
30   Yet she much whiter, but the same did hide
Under a vele, that wimpled° was full low,   *lying in folds*
And over all a blacke stole she did throw,
As one that inly mournd: so was she sad,
And heavie sat upon her palfrey slow:
35   Seemèd in heart some hidden care she had,
And by her in a line a milke white lambe she lad.

5

So pure an innocent, as that same lambe,
She was in life and every vertuous lore,
And by descent from Royall lynage came
40   Of ancient Kings and Queenes, that had of yore
Their scepters stretcht from East to Westerne shore,
And all the world in their subjection held;
Till that infernall feend with foule uprore
Forwasted° all their land, and them expeld: *laid waste*
45 Whom to avenge, she had this Knight from far compeld.°   *summoned*

6

Behind her farre away a Dwarfe did lag,
That lasie seemd in being ever last,
Or wearied with bearing of her bag
Of needments at his backe. Thus as they past,
50   The day with cloudes was suddeine overcast,
And angry Jove an hideous storme of raine
Did poure into his Lemans[7] lap so fast,
That every wight° to shrowd° it did constrain,   *creature/cover*
And this faire couple eke° to shroud themselves were fain.° *also/forced*

7

55 Enforst to seeke some covert nigh at hand,
A shadie grove not far away they spide,
That promist ayde the tempest to withstand:
Whose loftie trees yclad with sommers pride,

---

6. Facial expression, mood.   7. His lover, i.e., the earth.

Did spred so broad, that heavens light did hide,
60   Not perceable° with power of any starre: *penetrable*
        And all within were pathes and alleies wide,
        With footing worne, and leading inward farre:
Faire harbour that them seemes; so in they entred arre.

8

And foorth they passe, with pleasure forward led,
65   Joying to heare the birdes sweete harmony,
        Which therein shrouded from the tempest dred,°   *fearful*
        Seemd in their song to scorne the cruell sky.
        Much can° they prayse the trees, so straight and hy,   *did*
        The sayling Pine, the Cedar proud and tall,
70   The vine-prop Elme, the Poplar never dry,
        The builder Oake, sole king of forrests all,
The Aspine good for staves, the Cypresse funerall.

9

The Laurell, meed° of mightie Conquerours   *reward*
        And Poets sage, the Firre that weepeth still,
75   The Willow worne of forlorne Paramours,
        The Eugh° obedient to the benders will,   *yew*
        The Birch for shaftes, the Sallow° for the mill,   *willow*
        The Mirrhe sweete bleeding in the bitter wound,
        The warlike Beech, the Ash for nothing ill,
80   The fruitfull Olive, and the Platane° round,   *plane-tree*
The carver Holme, the Maple seeldom inward sound. [8]

10

Led with delight, they thus beguile the way,
        Untill the blustring storme is overblowne;
        When weening° to returne, whence they did stray,   *supposing*
85   They cannot finde that path, which first was showne,
        But wander too and fro in wayes unknowne,
        Furthest from end then, when they neerest weene,
        That makes them doubt, their wits be not their owne:
        So many pathes, so many turnings seene,
90 That which of them to take, in diverse doubt they been.

11

At last resolving forward still to fare,
        Till that some end they finde or° in or out,   *either*
        That path they take, that beaten seemed most bare,
        Which when by tract[9] they hunted had throughout,
95   And like to lead the labyrinth about;°   *out of*
        At length it brought them to a hollow cave,
        Amid the thickest woods. The Champion stout
        Eftsoones° dismounted from his courser brave,   *forthwith*
And to the Dwarfe a while his needlesse spere[1] he gave.

---

8. In these lines, Spenser has been imitating Chaucer's catalogue of trees in the *Parliament of Fowls*; the convention goes back to Ovid. The oak is used in building; the cypress is used to dress graves; the holly ("holm") is suitable for carving.
9. By following the track.
1. "Needlesse" because the spear is used only on horseback.

12

100 "Be well aware,"° quoth then that Ladie milde,   *watchful*
     "Least suddaine mischiefe° ye too rash provoke: *misfortune*
     The danger hid, the place unknowne and wilde,
     Breedes dreadfull doubts: Oft fire is without smoke,
     And perill without show: therefore your stroke
105 Sir knight with-hold, till further triall made."
     "Ah Ladie," said he, "shame were to revoke°   *draw back*
     The forward footing for° an hidden shade: *because of*
Vertue gives her selfe light, through darkenesse for to wade."

13

"Yea but," quoth she, "the perill of this place
110 I better wot then[2] you, though now too late
     To wish you backe returne with foule disgrace,
     Yet wisedome warnes, whilest foot is in the gate,
     To stay the stepe, ere forcèd to retrate.
     This is the wandring wood, this Errours den,
115 A monster vile, whom God and man does hate:
     Therefore I read° beware." "Fly fly," quoth then   *advise*
The fearefull Dwarfe: "this is no place for living men."

14

But full of fire and greedy hardiment,°   *boldness*
     The youthfull knight could not for ought° be staide,   *anything*
120 But forth unto the darksome hole he went,
     And lookèd in: his glistring° armor made   *shining*
     A litle glooming light, much like a shade,
     By which he saw the ugly monster plaine,
     Halfe like a serpent horribly displaide,[3]
125 But th' other halfe did womans shape retaine,
Most lothsom, filthie, foule, and full of vile
        disdaine.°   *loathsomeness*

15

And as she lay upon the durtie ground,
     Her huge long taile her den all overspred,
     Yet was in knots and many boughtes° upwound,   *coils*
130 Pointed with mortall sting. Of her there bred
     A thousand yong ones, which she dayly fed,
     Sucking upon her poisonous dugs, eachone
     Of sundry shapes, yet all ill favorèd:
     Soone as that uncouth° light upon them shone,   *unfamiliar*
135 Into her mouth they crept, and suddain all were gone.

16

Their dam upstart, out of her den effraide,°   *alarmed*
     And rushèd forth, hurling her hideous taile
     About her cursèd head, whose folds displaid°   *extended*

---

2. Know than.
3. That Errour (or doctrinal heresy) is half serpent reminds us of the primal error in Eden, which the serpent instigated. The description echoes both classical and biblical monsters (cf. Revelation 9.7–10).

Were stretcht now forth at length without
140   entraile.°   *winding, coiling*
She lookt about, and seeing one in mayle
Armèd to point,[4] sought backe to turne againe;
For light she hated as the deadly bale,°   *evil*
Ay wont in desert darknesse to remain,
145 Where plaine none might her see, nor she see any plaine.

17

Which when the valiant Elfe[5] perceived, he lept
As Lyon fierce upon the flying pray,
And with his trenchand° blade her boldly kept   *cutting*
From turning backe, and forcèd her to stay:
150 Therewith enraged she loudly gan to bray,
And turning fierce, her speckled taile advaunst,
Threatning her angry sting, him to dismay:°   *defeat*
Who nough° aghast, his mightie hand enhaunst:° *now/lifted up*
The stroke down from her head unto her shoulder glaunst.

18

Much daunted with that dint,° her sence was dazd,   *blow*
155 Yet kindling rage, her selfe she gathered round,
And all attonce her beastly body raizd
With doubled forces high above the ground:
Tho° wrapping up her wrethèd sterne arownd,   *then*
Lept fierce upon his shield, and her huge traine°   *tail*
160 All suddenly about his body wound,
That hand or foot to stirre he strove in vaine:
God helpe the man so wrapt in Errours endlesse traine.

19

His Lady sad to see his sore constraint,°   *fettered state*
Cride out, "Now now Sir knight, shew what ye bee,
165 Add faith unto your force, and be not faint:
Strangle her, else she sure will strangle thee."
That when he heard, in great perplexitie,°   *entangled state*
His gall did grate for griefe° and high disdaine,   *wrath*
And knitting all his force got one hand free,
170 Wherewith he grypt her gorge° with so great paine,   *neck*
That soone to loose her wicked bands did her constraine.

20

Therewith she spewd out of her filthy maw
A floud of poyson horrible and blacke,
Full of great lumpes of flesh and gobbets raw,
175 Which stunck so vildly, that it forst him slacke
His grasping hold, and from her turne him backe:
Her vomit full of bookes and papers was,[6]
With loathly frogs and toades, which eyes did lacke,

4. I.e., completely.
5. Knight of Faerie Land.
6. This alludes to books and pamphlets of Catholic propaganda, notably attacks on Queen Elizabeth in 1588.

And creeping sought way in the weedy gras:
180 Her filthy parbreake° all the place defilèd has.[7]   *vomit*

21

As when old father Nilus gins to swell
  With timely° pride above the Aegyptian vale,   *in season*
  His fattie° waves do fertile slime outwell,   *rich*
  And overflow each plaine and lowly dale:
185 But when his later spring gins to avale,°   *subside*
  Huge heapes of mudd he leaves, wherein there breed
  Ten thousand kindes of creatures, partly male
  And partly female of his fruitfull seed;
Such ugly monstrous shapes elswhere may no man reed.°   *see*

22

190 The same so sore annoyèd has the knight,
  That welnigh chokèd with the deadly stinke,
  His forces faile, ne can no longer fight.
  Whose corage when the feend perceived to shrinke,
  She pourèd forth out of her hellish sinke
195 Her fruitfull cursèd spawne of serpents small,
  Deformèd monsters, fowle, and blacke as inke,
  Which swarming all about his legs did crall,
And him encombred sore, but could not hurt at all.

23

As gentle Shepheard in sweete even-tide,
200 When ruddy Phoebus gins to welke° in west,   *sink*
  High on an hill, his flocke to vewen wide,
  Markes° which do byte their hasty supper best;   *observes*
  A cloud of combrous° gnattes do him molest,   *encumbering*
  All striving to infixe their feeble stings,
205 That from their noyance he no where can rest,
  But with his clownish° hands their tender wings   *rustic*
He brusheth oft, and oft doth mar their murmurings.

24

Thus ill bestedd,° and fearful more of shame,   *situated*
  Then of the certaine perill he stood in,
210 Halfe furious unto his foe he came,
  Resolved in minde all suddenly to win,
  Or soone to lose, before he once would lin;°   *cease, stop*
  And strooke at her with more then manly force,
  That from her body full of filthie sin
215 He raft° her hatefull head without remorse;   *cut away*
A streame of cole black bloud forth gushèd from her corse.

25

Her scattred brood, soone as their Parent deare
  They saw so rudely° falling to the ground,   *with great force*
  Groning full deadly, all with troublous feare,

---

7. Revelation 16.13: "And I saw three unclean spirits like frogs come out of the mouth of the dragon, and out of the mouth of the beast, and out of the mouth of the false prophet."

220 Gathred themselves about her body round,
   Weening° their wonted entrance to have found   *thinking*
   At her wide mouth: but being there withstood
   They flockèd all about her bleeding wound,
   And suckèd up their dying mothers blood,
225 Making her death their life, and eke her hurt their good.   *also*

26

That detestable sight him much amazde,°   *stunned*
   To see th' unkindly Impes[8] of heaven accurst,
   Devoure their dam; on whom while so he gazd,
   Having all satisfide their bloudy thurst,
230 Their bellies swolne he saw with fulnesse burst,
   And bowels gushing forth: well worthy end
   Of such as drunke her life, the which them nurst;
   Now needeth him no lenger labour spend,
His foes have slaine themselves, with whom he should contend.

27

235 His Ladie seeing all, that chaunst, from farre
   Approcht in hast to greet° his victorie,   *congratulate*
   And said, "Faire knight, borne under happy starre,
   Who see your vanquisht foes before you lye;
   Well worthy be you of that Armorie,[9]
240 Wherein ye have great glory wonne this day,
   And prooved your strength on a strong enimie,
   Your first adventure: many such I pray,
And henceforth ever wish, that like succeed it may."

28

Then mounted he upon his Steede againe,
245 And with the Lady backward sought to wend;°   *go*
   That path he kept, which beaten was most plaine,
   Ne ever would to any by-way bend,
   But still did follow one unto the end,
   The which at last out of the wood them brought.
250 So forward on his way (with God to frend[1])
   He passèd forth, and new adventure sought;
Long way he travelèd, before he heard of ought.

29

At length they chaunst to meet upon the way
   An aged Sire, in long blacke weedes yclad,[2]
255 His feete all bare, his beard all hoarie gray,
   And by his belt his booke he hanging had;
   Sober he seemde, and very sagely sad,°   *pensive*
   And to the ground his eyes were lowly bent,
   Simple in shew, and voyde of malice bad,
260 And all the way he prayèd, as he went,
And often knockt his brest, as one that did repent.

8. Unnatural offspring.
9. I.e., Christian armor.

1. With God as friend.
2. Dressed in long black garments.

30

He faire the knight saluted, louting° low,	*bowing*
Who faire him quited,° as that courteous was:	*answered*

And after askèd him, if he did know
265   Of straunge adventures, which abroad did pas.
"Ah my deare Sonne," quoth he, "how should, alas,
Silly° old man, that lives in hidden cell,   *simple*
Bidding° his beades all day for his trespas,   *telling*
Tydings of warre and worldly trouble tell?
270 With holy father sits not with such things to mell.[3]

31

"But if of daunger which hereby doth dwell,
And homebred evill ye desire to heare,
Of a straunge man I can you tidings tell,
That wasteth all this countrey farre and neare."
275   "Of such," said he, "I chiefly do inquere,
And shall you well reward to shew the place,
In which that wicked wight his dayes doth weare.°   *spend*
For to all knighthood it is foule disgrace,
That such a cursed creature lives so long a space."

32

280 "Far hence," quoth he, "in wastfull° wildernesse   *desolate*
His dwelling is, by which no living wight
May ever passe, but thorough great distresse."
"Now," sayd the Lady, "draweth toward night,
And well I wote, that of your later° fight   *recent*
285   Ye all forwearied be: for what so strong,
But wanting rest will also want of might?
The Sunne that measures heaven all day long,
At night doth baite° his steedes the Ocean waves emong.   *feed, refresh*

33

"Then with the Sunne take Sir, your timely rest,
290   And with new day new worke at once begin:
Untroubled night they say gives counsell best."
"Right well Sir knight ye have advisèd bin,"
Quoth then that aged man; "the way to win
Is wisely to advise:° now day is spent;   *take thought*
295   Therefore with me ye may take up your In°   *lodging*
For this same night." The knight was well content.
So with that godly father to his home they went.

34

A little lowly Hermitage it was,
Downe in a dale, hard by a forests side,
300   Far from resort of people, that did pas
In travell to and froe: a little wyde°   *apart*
There was an holy Chappell edifyde,°   *built*

---

3. I.e., it is not fitting for a holy hermit to meddle ("mell") with such things.

Wherein the Hermite dewly wont° to say   *was wont*
   His holy things° each morne and eventyde: *prayers*
305   Thereby a Christall streame did gently play,
Which from a sacred fountaine wellèd forth alway.

35

Arrivèd there, the little house they fill,
   Ne looke for entertainement, where none was:
   Rest is their feast, and all things at their will;
310   The noblest mind the best contentment has.
   With faire discourse the evening so they pas:
   For that old man of pleasing wordes had store,
   And well could file° his tongue as smooth as glas;   *polish*
   He told of Saintes and Popes, and evermore
315 He strowd an *Ave-Mary* after and before.

36

The drouping Night thus creepeth on them fast,
   And the sad humour[4] loading their eye liddes,
   As messenger of Morpheus[5] on them cast
   Sweet slombring deaw, the which to sleepe them biddes.
320   Unto their lodgings then his guestes he riddes:°   *leads*
   Where when all drownd in deadly sleepe[6] he findes,
   He to his study goes, and there amiddes
   His Magick bookes and artes of sundry kindes,
He seekes out mighty charmes, to trouble sleepy mindes.

37

325 Then choosing out few wordes most horrible
   (Let none them read), thereof did verses frame,
   With which and other spelles like terrible,
   He bade awake blacke Plutoes griesly Dame,[7]
   And cursèd heaven, and spake reprochfull shame
330   Of highest God, the Lord of life and light;
   A bold bad man, that dared to call by name
   Great Gorgon[8], Prince of darknesse and dead night,
At which Cocytus quakes, and Styx is put to flight.

38

And forth he cald out of deepe darknesse dred
335   Legions of Sprights, the which like little flyes[9]
   Fluttring about his ever damnèd hed,
   A-waite whereto their service he applyes,
   To aide his friends, or fray° his enimies: *frighten*
   Of those he chose out two, the falsest twoo,
340   And fittest for to forge true-seeming lyes;
   The one of them he gave a message too,
The other by him selfe staide other worke to doo.

4. Heavy moisture.
5. The god of sleep.
6. Sleep like death.
7. I.e., Proserpine, as patron of witchcraft.
8. Demogorgon, in some myths the progenitor of

all the gods, so powerful that the mention of his
name causes hell's rivers (Styx and Cocytus) to
tremble.
9. The simile associates him with Beelzebub (Lord
of Flies).

39

He making speedy way through spersèd° ayre,   *dispersed*
  And through the world of waters wide and deepe,
345 To Morpheus house doth hastily repaire.
  Amid the bowels of the earth full steepe,
  And low, where dawning day doth never peepe,
  His dwelling is; there Tethys[1] his wet bed
  Doth ever wash, and Cynthia[2] still doth steepe
350 In silver deaw his ever-drouping hed,
Whiles sad° Night over him her mantle black doth spred.   *sober*

40

Whose double gates he findeth lockèd fast,
  The one faire framed of burnisht Yvory,
  The other all with silver overcast;
355 And wakefull dogges before them farre do lye,
  Watching to banish Care their enimy,
  Who oft is wont° to trouble gentle Sleepe.   *accustomed to*
  By them the Sprite doth passe in quietly,
  And unto Morpheus comes, whom drownèd deepe
360 In drowsie fit he findes: of nothing he takes keepe.°   *notice*

41

And more, to lulle him in his slumber soft,
  A trickling streame from high rocke tumbling downe
  And ever-drizling raine upon the loft,
  Mixt with a murmuring winde, much like the sowne°   *sound*
365 Of swarming Bees, did cast him in a swowne:°   *faint*
  No other noyse, nor peoples troublous cryes,
  As still° are wont t'annoy the wallèd towne,   *always*
  Might there be heard: but carelesse° Quiet lyes,   *free from care*
Wrapt in eternall silence farre from enemyes.[3]

42

370 The messenger approching to him spake,
  But his wast° wordes returnd to him in vaine: *wasted*
  So sound he slept, that nought mought° him awake.   *might*
  Then rudely he him thrust, and pusht with paine,°   *effort*
  Whereat he gan to stretch: but he againe
375 Shooke him so hard, that forced him to speake.
  As one then in a dreame, whose dryer braine[4]
  Is tost with troubled sights and fancies° weake,   *fantasies*
He mumbled soft, but would not all his silence breake.

43

The Sprite then gan more boldly him to wake,
380 And threatned unto him the dreaded name
  Of Hecate:[5] whereat he gan to quake,

---

1. The wife of Ocean.
2. I.e., Diana, the goddess of the moon. "Still": continually.
3. Spenser is imitating descriptions of the house of Morpheus in Chaucer, Ovid, and other ancient writers.
4. According to the old physiology, old people and other light sleepers had too little moisture in the brain.
5. Queen of Hades.

And lifting up his lumpish head, with blame
Halfe angry askèd him, for what[6] he came.
"Hither," quoth he, "me Archimago[7] sent,
385 He that the stubborne Sprites can wisely tame,
He bids thee to him send for his intent
A fit false dreame, that can delude the sleepers sent."°   *senses*

44

The God obayde, and calling forth straight way
A diverse° dreame out of his prison darke,   *misleading*
390 Delivered it to him, and downe did lay
His heavie head, devoide of carefull carke,[8]
Whose sences all were straight benumbd and starke.
He backe returning by the Yvorie dore,[9]
Remounted up as light as chearefull Larke,
395 And on his litle winges the dreame he bore
In hast unto his Lord, where he him left afore.

45

Who all this while with charmes and hidden artes,
Had made a Lady of that other Spright,
And framed of liquid ayre her tender partes
400 So lively,° and so like in all mens sight,   *lifelike*
That weaker° sence it could have ravisht quight   *too weak*
The maker selfe for all his wondrous witt,
Was nigh beguilèd with so goodly sight:
Her all in white he clad, and over it
405 Cast a blacke stole, most like to seeme for Una[1] fit.

46

Now when that ydle dreame was to him brought
Unto that Elfin knight he bad him fly,
Where he slept soundly void of evill thought
And with false shewes abuse his fantasy,°   *imagination*
410 In sort as[2] he him schoolèd privily:
And that new creature borne without her dew[3]
Full of the makers guile, with usage sly
He taught to imitate that Lady trew,
Whose semblance she did carrie under feignèd hew.°   *form*

47

415 Thus well instructed, to their worke they hast
And comming where the knight in slomber lay
The one upon his hardy head him plast,°   *placed*
And made him dreame of loves and lustfull play
That nigh his manly hart did melt away,
420 Bathèd in wanton blis and wicked joy:

6. Why.
7. Archmagician or chief deceiver; also, *arch-imago*, architect of images.
8. Anxious concerns.
9. False dreams came through the ivory door, true dreams through the gate of horn (Homer, *Odyssey* 19.562–67: Virgil, *Aeneid* 6.893–96).

1. Her name means "one, unity." Elizabethan readers would know the Latin *Una Vera Fides* (one true faith) and also the proverb, "Truth is one." She is named now, when her false double is introduced.
2. In the way.
3. Unnaturally.

Then seemèd him his Lady by him lay,
  And to him playnd,° how that false wingèd boy[4]   *complained*
Her chast hart had subdewd, to learne Dame pleasures toy.

                        48
And she her selfe of beautie soveraigne Queene
425   Faire Venus seemde unto his bed to bring
        Her, whom he waking evermore did weene°   *think*
        To be the chastest flowre, that ay° did spring   *ever*
        On earthly braunch, the daughter of a king,
        Now a loose Leman° to vile service bound: *paramour*
430   And eke the Graces seemèd all to sing,
        Hymen iô Hymen, dauncing all around,
Whilst freshest Flora her with Yvie girlond crownd.[5]

                        49
In this great passion of unwonted° lust,   *unaccustomed*
  Or wonted feare of doing ought amis,
435   He started up, as seeming to mistrust°   *suspect*
        Some secret ill, or hidden foe of his:
        Lo there before his face his Lady is,
        Under blake stole hyding her bayted hooke,
        And as halfe blushing offred him to kis,
440   With gentle blandishment and lovely° looke,   *loving*
Most like that virgin true, which for her knight him took.

                        50
All cleane dismayd to see so uncouth° sight,   *unseemly*
  And halfe enragèd at her shamelesse guise,
        He thought have slaine her in his fierce despight:°   *indignation*
445   But hasty heat tempring with sufferance wise,
        He stayde his hand, and gan himselfe advise
        To prove his sense, and tempt° her faignèd truth.   *test*
        Wringing her hands in wemens pitteous wise,
        Tho can she[6] weepe, to stirre up gentle ruth,°   *pity*
450   Both for her noble bloud, and for her tender youth.

                        51
And said, "Ah Sir, my liege Lord and my love,
  Shall I accuse the hidden cruell fate,
        And mightie causes wrought in heaven above,
        Or the blind God, that doth me thus amate,°   *dismay*
455   For° hopèd love to winne me certaine hate?   *instead of*
        Yet thus perforce° he bids me do, or die.   *forcibly*
        Die is my dew[7]: yet rew my wretched state
        You, whom my hard avenging destinie
Hath made judge of my life or death indifferently.

---

4. Cupid.
5. The three graces of classical mythology were
personifications of grace and beauty; here they sing
a call to the pleasures of the marriage bed (Hymen
was god of marriage). On Flora, cf. E. K.'s gloss

to the March eclogue: "the Goddesse of flowres,
but indede (as saith Tacitus) a famous harlot."
6. Then she began to.
7. I.e., I deserve to die.

52

460 "Your owne deare sake forst me at first to leave
    My Fathers kingdome," There she stopt with teares;
    Her swollen hart her speach seemd to bereave,
    And then againe begun, "My weaker yeares
    Captived to fortune and frayle worldly feares,
465 Fly to your faith for succour and sure ayde:
    Let me not dye in languor° and long teares.   *sorrow*
    "Why Dame," quoth he, "what hath ye thus dismayd?
    What frayes° ye, that were wont to comfort me affrayd?"   *frightens*

53

    "Love of your selfe," she said, "and deare° constraint   *dire*
470 Lets me not sleepe, but wast the wearie night
    In secret anguish and unpittied plaint,
    Whiles you in carelesse sleepe are drownèd quight."
    Her doubtfull words made that redoubted[8] knight
    Suspect her truth: yet since no untruth he knew,
475 Her fawning love with foule disdainefull spight
    He would not shend,° but said, "Deare dame I rew,°   *reject/pity*
    That for my sake unknowne such griefe unto you grew.

54

    "Assure your selfe, it fell not all to ground;
    For all so deare as life is to my hart,
480 I deeme your love, and hold me to you bound;
    Ne let vaine feares procure your needlesse smart,
    Where cause is none, but to your rest depart."
    Not all content, yet seemd she to appease°   *cease*
    Her mournefull plaintes, beguiléd° of her art,   *foiled*
485 And fed with words, that could not chuse but please,
    So slyding softly forth, she turnd° as to her ease.   *returned*

55

    Long after lay he musing at her mood,
    Much grieved to thinke that gentle Dame so light,
    For whose defence he was to shed his blood.
490 At last dull wearinesse of former fight
    Having yrockt a sleepe his irkesome spright,°   *spirit*
    That troublous dreame gan freshly tosse his braine,
    With bowres and beds, and Ladies deare delight:
    But when he[9] saw his labour all was vaine,
495 With that misformèd spright he backe returnd againe.

Canto 2

The guilefull great Enchaunter parts
The Redcrosse Knight from Truth:
Into whose stead faire falshood steps,
And workes him wofull ruth.

---

8. Dreaded, also, doubting again. "Doubtfull":   9. I.e., Archimago.
fearful, also questionable.

1

By this the Northerne wagoner had set
    His seven fold teame behind the stedfast starre,[1]
    That was in Ocean waves yet never wet,
    But firme is fixt, and sendeth light from farre
5   To all, that in the wide deepe wandring arre.
    And chearefull Chaunticlere with his note shrill
    Had warnèd once, that Phoebus fiery carre[2]
    In hast was climbing up the Easterne hill,
Full envious that night so long his roome did fill.

2

10 When those accursèd messengers of hell,
    That feigning dreame, and that faire-forgèd Spright
    Came to their wicked maister, and gan tell
    Their bootelesse° paines, and ill succeeding night: *useless*
    Who all in rage to see his skilfull might
15   Deluded so, gan threaten hellish paine
    And sad Prosèrpines wrath, them to affright.
    But when he saw his threatning was but vaine,
He cast about, and searcht his balefull° of bookes againe.   *deadly*

3

Eftsoones° he tooke that miscreated faire,   *soon after*
20   And that false other Spright, on whom he spred
    A seeming body of the subtile° aire,   *rarefied*
    Like a young Squire, in loves and lusty-hed
    His wanton dayes that ever loosely led,
    Without regard of armes and dreaded fight:
25   Those two he tooke, and in a secret bed,
    Covered with darknesse and misdeeming° night,   *misleading*
Them both together laid, to joy in vaine delight.

4

Forthwith he runnes with feignèd faithfull hast
    Unto his guest, who after troublous sights
30   And dreames, gan now to take more sound repast,°   *rest*
    Whom suddenly he wakes with fearefull frights,
    As one aghast with feends or damnèd sprights,
    And to him cals, "Rise rise unhappy Swaine,
    That here wex° old in sleepe, whiles wicked wights   *grows*
35   Have knit themselves in Venus shamefull chaine;
Come see, where your false Lady doth her honour staine."

5

All in amaze he suddenly up start
    With sword in hand, and with the old man went;
    Who soone him brought into a secret part,
40   Where that false couple were full closely ment°   *mingled*
    In wanton lust and lewd embracèment:
    Which when he saw, he burnt with gealous fire,

---

1. I.e., by this time the Big Dipper had set behind   2. The chariot of the sun.
the North Star.

The eye of reason was with rage yblent,°   *blinded*
And would have slaine them in his furious ire,
45 But hardly° was restreinèd of that aged sire.   *with difficulty*

6

Returning to his bed in torment great,
    And bitter anguish of his guiltie sight,
    He could not rest, but did his stout heart eat,
    And wast his inward gall with deepe despight,°   *malice*
50 Yrkesome° of life, and too long lingring night.   *tired*
    At last faire Hesperus³ in highest skie
    Had spent his lampe, and brought forth dawning light
Then up he rose, and clad him hastily;
The Dwarfe him brought his steed: so both away do fly.

7

55 Now when the rosy-fingred Morning faire,
    Weary of aged Tithones⁴ saffron bed,
    Had spred her purple robe through deawy aire,
    And the high hils Titan° discoverèd,°   *the sun/revealed*
    The royall virgin shooke off drowsy-hed,
60 And rising forth out of her baser° bowre,   *humbler*
    Lookt for her knight, who far away was fled,
    And for her Dwarfe, that wont to wait each houre:
Then gan she waile and weepe, to see that woefull stowre.° *affliction*

8

And after him she rode with so much speede
65 As her slow beast could make; but all in vaine:
    For him so far had borne his light-foot steede,
    Prickéd with wrath and fiery fierce disdaine,°   *indignation*
    That him to follow was but fruitlesse paine;
    Yet she her weary limbes would never rest,
70 But every hill and dale, each wood and plaine
    Did search, sore grievèd in her gentle brest,
He so ungently left her, whom she lovèd best.

9

But subtill° Archimago, when his guests   *cunning*
    He saw divided into double parts,
75 And Una wandring in woods and forrests,
    Th' end of his drift,° he praisd his divelish arts   *plot*
    That had such might over true meaning harts;
    Yet rests not so, but other meanes doth make,
    How he may worke unto her further smarts:
80 For her he hated as the hissing snake,
And in her many troubles did most pleasure take.

10

He then devisde himselfe how to disguise;
    For by his mightie science° he could take   *knowledge*
    As many formes and shapes in seeming wise,°   *in appearance*

3. The evening star.   4. The husband of Aurora, goddess of the dawn.

85   As ever Proteus to himselfe could make:
      Sometime a fowle, sometime a fish in lake,
      Now like a foxe, now like a dragon fell,°   *fierce*
      That of himselfe he oft for feare would quake,
      And oft would flie away. O who can tell
90 The hidden power of herbes, and might of Magicke spell?

11

      But now seemde best, the person to put on
      Of that good knight, his late beguilèd guest:
      In mighty armes he was yclad anon,
      And silver shield: upon his coward brest
95 A bloudy crosse, and on his craven crest
      A bounch of haires discolourd diversly:°   *variously colored*
      Full jolly° knight he seemde, and well addrest,°   *gallant/armed*
      And when he sate upon his courser free,
  Saint George himself ye would have deemèd him to be.

12

100 But he the knight, whose semblaunt° he did beare,   *likeness*
      The true Saint George was wandred far away,
      Still flying from° his thoughts and gealous feare;   *because of*
      Will was his guide,[5] and griefe led him astray.
      At last him chaunst to meete upon the way
105 A faithlesse Sarazin° all armed to point,   *Saracen*
      In whose great shield was writ with letters gay
      Sans foy:[6] full large of limbe and every joint
  He was, and carèd not for God or man a point.[7]

13

      He had a faire companion of his way,
110 A goodly Lady clad in scarlot red,
      Purfled with gold and pearle of rich assay,[8]
      And like a Persian mitre on her hed
      She wore, with crownes and owches° garnishèd,   *brooches*
      The which her lavish lovers to her gave;[9]
115 Her wanton° palfrey all was overspred   *unruly*
      With tinsell trappings, woven like a wave,
  Whose bridle rung with golden bels and bosses brave.[1]

14

      With faire disport° and courting dalliaunce   *diversion*
      She intertainde her lover all the way:
120 But when she saw the knight his speare advaunce,
      She soone left off her mirth and wanton play,
      And bad her knight addresse him to the fray:

---

5. Will should not be the guide, but should itself
be under the guidance of intelligence or truth.
6. Literally, without faith, faithless.
7. At all.
8. Proven valuable by analysis. "Purfled": decorated.
9. The lady's garb associates her with the Whore of Babylon (Revelation 17.3–4): "And I saw a woman sit upon a scarlet colored beast, full of names of blasphemy, having seven heads and ten horns. And the woman was arrayed in purple and scarlet color, and decked with gold and precious stones and pearls, having a golden cup in her hand full of abominations and filthiness of her fornication."
1. Handsome metal knobs.

His foe was nigh at hand. He prickt° with pride *pranced*
 And hope to winne his Ladies heart that day,
125 Forth spurrèd fast: adowne his coursers side
The red bloud trickling staind the way, as he did ride.

15

The knight of the Redcrosse when him he spide,
 Spurring so hote with rage dispiteous,°   *cruel*
 Gan fairely couch° his speare, and towards ride: *lower*
130 Soone meete they both, both fell and furious,
 That daunted with their forces hideous,
 Their steeds do stagger, and amazèd stand,
 And eke° themselves too rudely rigorous,° *also/violent*
 Astonied° with the stroke of their owne hand, *stunned*
135 Do backe rebut,° and each to other yeeldeth land. *recoil*

16

As when two rams stird with ambitious pride,
 Fight for the rule of the rich fleecèd flocke,
 Their hornèd fronts so fierce on either side
 Do meete, that with the terrour of the shocke
140 Astonied both, stand sencelesse as a blocke,° *inanimate object*
 Forgetfull of the hanging[2] victory:
 So stood these twaine, unmovèd as a rocke,
 Both staring fierce, and holding idely
The broken reliques of their former cruelty.

17

145 The Sarazin sore daunted with the buffe
 Snatcheth his sword, and fiercely to him flies;
 Who well it wards, and quyteth° cuff with cuff: *requites*
 Each others equall puissaunce envies,
 And through their iron sides with cruell spies° *looks*
150 Does seeke to perce: repining courage yields
 No foote to foe. The flashing fier flies
 As from a forge out of their burning shields,
And streames of purple bloud new dies the verdant fields.

18

"Curse on that Crosse," quoth then the Sarazin,
155 "That keepes thy body from the bitter fit;° *stroke*
 Dead long ygoe I wote° thou haddest bin, *thought*
 Had not that charme from thee forwarnéd° it: *prevented*
 But yet I warne thee now assurèd° sitt, *securely*
 And hide thy head." Therewith upon his crest
160 With rigour° so outrageous he smitt, *violence*
 That a large share it hewd out of the rest,
And glauncing downe his shield, from blame him fairely blest.[3]

19

Who thereat wondrous wroth, the sleeping spark
 Of native vertue° gan eftsoones revive, *strength*

---

2. In the balance.   3. Preserved him from harm.

165 And at his haughtie helmet making mark,
     So hugely° stroke, that it the steele did rive,   *mightily*
     And cleft his head. He tumbling downe alive,
     With bloudy mouth his mother earth did kis
     Greeting his grave: his grudging° ghost did strive   *complaining*
170 With the fraile flesh; at last it flitted is,
     Whither the soules do fly of men, that live amis.

                   20

The Lady when she saw her champion fall,
     Like the old ruines of a broken towre,
     Staid not to waile his woefull funerall,°   *death*
175 But from him fled away with all her powre;
     Who after her as hastily gan scowre,°   *scurry*
     Bidding the Dwarfe with him to bring away
     The Sarazins shield, signe of the conqueroure.
     Her soone he overtooke, and bad to stay,
180 For present cause was none of dread her to dismay.

                   21

She turning backe with ruefull countenaunce,
     Cride, "Mercy mercy Sir vouchsafe to show
     On silly° Dame, subject to hard mischaunce,   *helpless*
     And to your mighty will." Her humblesse low
185 In so ritch weedes and seeming glorious show,
     Did much emmove his stout heroicke heart,
     And said, "Deare dame, your suddein overthrow
     Much rueth° me; but now put feare apart,   *grieves*
     And tell, both who ye be, and who that tooke your part."

                   22

190 Melting in teares, then gan she thus lament;
     "The wretched woman, whom unhappy howre
     Hath now made thrall° to your commandèment,   *slave*
     Before that angry heavens list to lowre,°   *frown*
     And fortune false betraide me to your powre
195 Was (O what now availeth that I was!)
     Borne the sole daughter of an Emperour,
     He that the wide West under his rule has,
     And high hath set his throne, where Tiberis doth pas.[4]

                   23

     "He in the first flowre of my freshest age,
200 Betrothèd me unto the onely haire°   *heir*
     Of a most mighty king, most rich and sage;
     Was never Prince so faithfull and so faire,
         Was never Prince so meeke and debonaire;°   *gracious*
     But ere my hopèd day of spousall shone,
205 My dearest Lord fell from high honours staire,

---

4. The Tiber River runs through Rome. The lady is the daughter of Rome (and hence is associated with the Roman Catholic Church). Her father, she says, is ruler of the West—but Una's father had the rule of both East *and* West (canto 1, line 41): on the historical plane, the true church once embraced east and west whereas the false rules only the west.

Into the hands of his accursed fone,°   foes
And cruelly was slaine, that shall I ever mone.[5]

24

'His blessed body spoild of lively breath,
  Was afterward, I know not how, convaid°   carried away
210 And fro me hid: of whose most innocent death
  When tidings came to me unhappy maid,
  O how great sorrow my sad soule assaid.°   afflicted
  Then forth I went his woefull corse to find,
  And many yeares throughout the world I straid,
215 A virgin widow, whose deepe wounded mind
With love, long time did languish as the striken hind.°   deer

25

"At last it chauncèd this proud Sarazin
  To meete me wandring, who perforce° me led   by violence
  With him away, but yet could never win
220 The fort, that Ladies hold in soveraigne dread.
  There lies he now with foule dishonour dead,
  Who whiles he livde, was callèd proud Sans foy,
  The eldest of three brethren, all three bred
  Of one bad sire, whose youngest is Sans joy,
225 And twixt them both was borne the bloudy bold Sans loy.[6]

26

"In this sad plight, friendlesse, unfortunate,
  Now miserable I Fidessa[7] dwell,
  Craving of you in pitty of my state,
  To do none° ill, if please ye not do well."   no
230 He in great passion all this while did dwell,°   continue
  More busying his quicke eyes, her face to view,
  Then his dull eares, to heare what she did tell;
  And said, "Faire Lady hart of flint would rew
The undeservèd woes and sorrowes, which ye shew.

27

235 "Henceforth in safe assuraunce may ye rest,
  Having both found a new friend you to aid,
  And lost an old foe, that did you molest:
  Better new friend than an old foe is[8] said."
  With chaunge of cheare the seeming simple maid
240 Let fall her eyen, as shamefast[9] to the earth,
  And yeelding soft, in that she nought gain-said,
  So forth they rode, he feining° seemely merth,   simulating
And she coy lookes: so dainty they say maketh derth.[1]

28

Long time they thus together traveilèd,
245 Till weary of their way, they came at last,

---

5. The lady claims to be betrothed to Christ,   8. I.e., it is.
bridegroom of the Church.   9. As if modestly.
6. Literally, "without law." Sans joy means   1. Proverbial: "what's dear is rare." Here, "coy-
"without joy."   ness creates unsatisfied desire."
7. Faith.

Where grew two goodly trees, that faire did spred
   Their armes abroad, with gray mosse overcast,
   And their greene leaves trembling with every blast,°   *breeze*
   Made a calme shadow far in compasse round:
250   The fearefull Shepheard often there aghast
   Under them never sat, ne wont[2] there sound
His mery oaten pipe, but shund th' unlucky ground.

29

But this good knight soone as he them can° spie,   *did*
   For the coole shade him thither hastly got:
255   For golden Phoebus now ymounted hie,
   From fiery wheeles of his faire chariot
   Hurlèd his beame so scorching cruell hot,
   That living creature mote° it not abide;   *might*
   And his new Lady it endurèd not.
260   There they alight, in hope themselves to hide
From the fierce heat, and rest their weary limbs a tide.°   *time*

30

Faire seemely pleasaunce° each to other makes,   *courtesy*
   With goodly purposes there as they sit:
   And in his falsèd° fancy he her takes   *deceived*
265   To be the fairest wight that livèd yit;
   Which to expresse, he bends his gentle wit,
   And thinking of those braunches greene to frame
   A girlond for her dainty forehead fit,
   He pluckt a bough; out of whose rift there came
270 Small drops of gory bloud, that trickled downe the same.

31

Therewith a piteous yelling voyce was heard,
   Crying, "O spare with guilty hands to teare
   My tender sides in this rough rynd embard,°   *imprisoned*
   But fly, ah fly far hence away, for feare
275   Least to you hap, that happened to me heare,
   And to this wretched Lady, my deare love,
   O too deare love, love bought with death too deare."
   Astond he stood, and up his haire did hove°   *heave, raise*
And with that suddein horror could no member move.

32

280 At last whenas the dreadfull passion
   Was overpast, and manhood well awake,
   Yet musing at the straunge occasion,
   And doubting much his sence, he thus bespake;
   "What voyce of damnèd Ghost from Limbo[3] lake,
285   Or guilefull spright wandring in empty aire,
   Both which fraile men do oftentimes mistake,°   *mislead*
   Sends to my doubtfull eares these speaches rare,
And ruefull plaints, me bidding guiltlesse bloud to spare?"

---

2. Nor was accustomed to.   unbaptized.
3. A region of Hell, traditionally the abode of the

33

Then groning deepe, "Nor damned Ghost," quoth he,
290   "Nor guilefull sprite to thee these wordes doth speake,
       But once a man Fradubio,[4] now a tree,
       Wretched man, wretched tree; whose nature weake,
       A cruell witch her cursèd will to wreake,
       Hath thus transformed, and plast in open plaines,
295   Where Boreas° doth blow full bitter bleake,   *the North Wind*
       And scorching Sunne does dry my secret vaines:
For though a tree I seeme, yet cold and heat me paines."

34

       "Say on Fradubio then, or° man, or tree,"   *whether*
       Quoth then the knight, "by whose mischievous arts
300   Art thou misshapèd thus, as now I see?
       He oft finds med'cine, who his griefe imparts;
       But double griefs afflict concealing harts,
       As raging flames who striveth to suppresse."
       "The author then," said he, "of all my smarts,
       Is one Duessa[5] a false sorceresse,
That many errant° knights hath brought to wretchednesse. *wandering*

35

       "In prime of youthly yeares, when corage hot
       The fire of love and joy of chevalree
       First kindled in my brest, it was my lot
310   To love this gentle Lady, whom ye see,
       Now not a Lady, but a seeming tree;
       With whom as once I rode accompanyde,
       Me chauncèd of a knight encountred bee,
       That had a like faire Lady by his syde,
315 Like a faire Lady, but did fowle Duessa hyde.

36

       "Whose forgèd beauty he did take in hand,[6]
       All other Dames to have exceeded farre,
       I in defence of mine did likewise stand,
       Mine, that did then shine as the Morning starre:
320   So both to battell fierce arraungèd arre,
       In which his harder fortune was to fall
       Under my speare: such is the dye° of warre: *hazard*
       His Lady left as a prise martiall,[7]
Did yield her comely person, to be at my call.

37

325   "So doubly loved of Ladies unlike° faire,   *diversely*
       Th' one seeming such, the other such indeede,
       One day in doubt I cast° for to compare,   *determined*
       Whether° in beauties glorie did exceede;   *which one (of two)*

---

4. *Fra* (Italian in, or brother) + *dubbio* (doubt).
The motif of a man imprisoned in a tree derives
from Virgil (*Aeneid* 3.27–42) and is used by Ariosto
(*Orlando Furioso* 6.26–53).

5. Duessa means "double being." *Due* (Italian two)
+ *esse* (Latin, being).
6. He maintained.
7. Spoil of battle.

A Rosy girlond was the victors meede:°   *reward*
330   Both seemde to win, and both seemde won to bee,
So hard the discord was to be agreede.
Fraelissa[8] was as faire, as faire mote bee,
And ever false Duessa seemde as faire as shee.

38

"The wicked witch now seeing all this while
335   The doubtfull ballaunce equally to sway,
What not by right, she cast to win by guile,
And by her hellish science° raisd streight way   *magic*
A foggy mist, that overcast the day,
And a dull blast, that breathing on her face,
340   Dimmed her former beauties shining ray,
And with foule ugly forme did her disgrace:
Then was she[9] faire alone, when none was faire in place.

39

"Then cride she out, 'Fye, fye, deformèd wight,
Whose borrowed beautie now appeareth plaine
345   To have before bewitchèd all mens sight;
O leave her soone, or let her soone be slaine.'
Her lothly visage viewing with disdaine,
Eftsoones° I thought her such, as she me told,   *before*
And would have kild her; but with faignèd paine,
350   The false witch did my wrathfull hand withhold;
So left her, where she now is turnd to trëen mould.[1]

40

"Thens forth I tooke Duessa for my Dame,
And in the witch unweeting° joyd long time,   *unknowingly*
Ne ever wist, but that she was the same,
355   Till on a day (that day is every Prime,[2]
When Witches wont do penance for their crime)
I chaunst to see her in her proper hew,[3]
Bathing her selfe in origane and thyme:[4]
A filthy foule old woman I did vew,
360   That ever to have toucht her, I did deadly rew.°   *regret*

41

"Her neather partes misshapen, monstruous,
Were hidd in water, that I could not see,
But they did seeme more foule and hideous,
Then womans shape man would beleeve to bee.
365   Thens forth from her most beastly companie
I gan refraine, in minde to slip away,
Soone as appeard safe opportunitie:

---

8. Frailty (Italian *Fralezza*).
9. Duessa. "In place": when nobody else was fair.
1. The form of a tree.
2. The first appearance of the new moon.

3. In her own shape.
4. Oregano and thyme were used to cure scabs and itching.

For danger great, if not assured decay°   *destruction*
I saw before mine eyes, if I were knowne to stray.

42

370 "The divelish hag by chaunges of my cheare°   *countenance*
Perceived my thought, and drownd in sleepie night,
With wicked herbes and ointments did besmeare
My bodie all, through charmes and magicke might,
That all my senses were bereavèd quight:°   *quite*
375 Then brought she me into this desert waste,
And by my wretched lovers side me pight,°   *planted*
Where now enclosd in wooden wals full faste,[5]
Banisht from living wights,° our wearie dayes we waste."   *persons*

43

"But how long time," said then the Elfin knight,
380 "Are you in this misformèd house to dwell?"
"We may not chaunge," quoth he, "this evil plight,
Till we be bathèd in a living well;[6]
That is the terme prescribèd by the spell."
"O how," said he, "mote° I that well out find,   *might*
385 That may restore you to your wonted well?"°   *well-being*
"Time and suffisèd fates to former kynd
Shall us restore,[7] none else from hence may us unbynd."

44

The false Duessa, now Fidessa hight,°   *called*
Heard how in vaine Fradubio did lament,
390 And knew well all was true. But the good knight
Full of sad feare and ghastly dreriment,°   *gloom*
When all this speech the living tree had spent,
The bleeding bough did thrust into the ground,
That from the bloud he might be innocent,
395 And with fresh clay did close the wooden wound:
Then turning to his Lady, dead with feare her found.

45

Her seeming dead he found with feignèd feare,
As all unweeting of that well she knew,[8]
And paynd himselfe with busie care to reare
400 Her out of carelesse° swowne. Her eylids blew   *unconscious*
And dimmèd sight with pale and deadly hew[9]
At last she up gan lift: with trembling cheare°   *demeanor*
Her up he tooke, too simple and too trew,
And oft her kist. At length all passèd feare,[1]
405 He set her on her steede, and forward forth did beare.

---

5. I.e., imprisoned within the trees.
6. With allusion to 1 John 4.14, the "well of water, springing up into eternal life."
7. I.e., time and the satisfaction of the fates alone can restore us to our former human nature.

8. I.e., pretending ignorance of what she knew well.
9. Deathlike appearance.
1. I.e., having overcome all fear.

Canto 3

Forsaken Truth long seekes her love,
And makes the Lyon mylde,
Marres° blind Devotions mart,° and fals   *spoils/business*
In hand of leachour° vylde.   *lecher*

1

Nought is there under heav'ns wide hollownesse,°   *concavity*
  That moves more deare compassion of mind,
  Then beautie brought t' unworthy° wretchednesse   *undeserved*
  Through envies snares or fortunes freakes° unkind: *sudden changes*
5 I, whether lately through her brightnesse blind,
  Or through alleageance and fast fealtie,
  Which I do owe unto all woman kind,
  Feele my heart perst° with so great agonie,   *pierced*
When such I see, that all for pittie I could die.

2

10 And now it is empassionèd° so deepe,   *moved*
  For fairest Unas sake, of whom I sing,
  That my fraile eyes these lines with teares do steepe,
  To thinke how she through guilefull handeling,°   *treatment*
  Though true as touch,° though daughter of a king,   *touchstone*
15 Though faire as ever living wight was faire,
  Though nor in word nor deede ill meriting,
  Is from her knight divorcèd° in despaire   *separated*
And her due loves derived° to that vile witches share.   *diverted*

3

Yet she most faithfull Ladie all this while
20 Forsaken, wofull, solitarie mayd
  Farre from all peoples prease,° as in exile,   *press, crowd*
  In wildernesse and wastfull° deserts strayd,   *desolate*
  To seeke her knight; who subtilly betrayd
  Through that late vision, which th' Enchaunter wrought,
25 Had her abandond. She of nought affrayd,
  Through woods and wastnesse° wide him daily sought;   *wilderness*
Yet wishèd tydings more of him unto her brought.

4

One day nigh wearie of the yrkesome way,
  From her unhastie° beast she did alight,   *slow*
30 And on the grasse her daintie limbes did lay
  In secret shadow,° farre from all mens sight: *shade*
  From her faire head her fillet she undight,[1]
  And laid her stole aside. Her angels face
  As the great eye of heaven shynèd bright,
35 And made a sunshine in the shadie place;
Did never mortall eye behold such a heavenly grace.

---

1. She took off her headband.

5

It fortunèd out of the thickest wood   *chanced*
   A ramping° Lyon rushèd suddainly,   *raging*
   Hunting full greedie after salvage blood;[2]
40 Soone as the royall virgin he did spy,
   With gaping mouth at her ran greedily,
   To have attonce devoured her tender corse;°   *body*
   But to the pray when as he drew more ny,
   His bloudie rage asswagèd with remorse,
45 And with the sight amazd, forgat his furious forse.

6

In stead thereof he kist her wearie feet,
   And lickt her lilly hands with fawning tong,
   As he her wrongèd innocence did weet.[3]
   O how can beautie maister the most strong,
50 And simple truth subdue avenging wrong?
   Whose yeelded pride and proud submission,
   Still dreading death, when she had markèd long,
   Her hart gan melt in great compassion,
And drizling teares did shed for pure affection.

7

55 "The Lyon Lord of everie beast in field,"
   Quoth she, "his princely puissance° doth abate   *power*
   And mightie proud to humble weake does yield,
   Forgetfull of the hungry rage, which late
   Him prickt, in pittie of my sad estate:°   *condition*
60 But he my Lyon, and my noble Lord,
   How does he find in cruell hart to hate
   Her that him loved, and ever most adord,
As the God of my life? why hath he me abhord?"

8

Redounding° teares did choke th' end of her plaint,   *overflowing*
65 Which softly ecchoed from the neighbour wood;
   And sad to see her sorrowfull constraint°   *affliction*
   The kingly beast upon her gazing stood;
   With pittie calmd, downe fell his angry mood.
   At last in close hart shutting up her paine,
70 Arose the virgin borne of heavenly brood,°   *parentage*
   And to her snowy Palfrey got againe,
To seeke her strayèd Champion, if she might attaine.°   *overtake*

9

The Lyon would not leave her desolate,
   But with her went along, as a strong gard
75 Of her chast person, and a faithfull mate
   Of her sad troubles and misfortunes hard:
   Still° when she slept, he kept both watch and ward,   *always*

2. Wild game.
3. As though he understood ("did weet") her innocence.

And when she wakt, he waited diligent,
  With humble service to her will prepard:
80   From her faire eyes he tooke commaundement,
  And ever by her lookes conceivèd her intent.[4]

10

Long she thus traveilèd through deserts wyde,
  By which she thought her wandring knight shold pas,
  Yet never shew of living wight espyde;
85   Till that at length she found the troden gras,
  In which the tract° of peoples footing was,   *track*
  Under the steepe foot of a mountaine hore:°   *gray*
  The same she followes, till at last she has
  A damzell spyde slow footing her before,[5]
90 That on her shoulders sad° a pot of water bore.   *heavy*

11

To whom approching she to her gan call,
  To weet, if dwelling place were nigh at hand;
  But the rude° wench her answered nought at all,   *ignorant*
  She could not heare, nor speake, nor understand;[6]
95   Till seeing by her side the Lyon stand,
  With suddaine feare her pitcher downe she threw,
  And fled away: for never in that land
  Face of faire Ladie she before did vew,
And that dread Lyons looke her cast in deadly° hew.   *deathlike*

12

100 Full fast she fled, ne ever lookt behynd,
  As if her life upon the wager lay,[7]
  And home she came, whereas her mother blynd
  Sate in eternall night: nought could she say,
  But suddaine catching hold, did her dismay
105   With quaking hands, and other signes of feare:
  Who full of ghastly fright and cold affray,°   *terror*
  Gan shut the dore. By this arrived there
Dame Una, wearie Dame, and entrance did requere.°   *request*

13

Which when none yeelded, her unruly Page
110   With his rude° clawes the wicket° open rent,   *rough/door*
  And let her in; where of his cruell rage
  Nigh dead with feare, and faint astonishment,[8]
  She found them both in darkesome corner pent;°   *huddled*
  Where that old woman day and night did pray
115 Upon her beades° devoutly penitent;   *rosary*

---

4. Lions have long been associated with the British crown.
5. I.e., walking slowly in front of her.
6. Cf. Mark 4.11–12: ". . . unto them that are without, all these things are done in parables: / That seeing they may see, and not perceive; and hearing they may hear, and not understand."
7. Were at stake.
8. I.e., fainting with amazement.

Nine hundred *Pater nosters* every day,
And thrise nine hundred *Aves* she was wont to say.[9]

14

And to augment her painefull pennance more,
   Thrise every weeke in ashes she did sit,
120   And next her wrinkled skin rough sackcloth wore,[1]
   And thrise three times did fast from any bit:°   *food*
But now for feare her beads she did forget.
Whose needlesse dread for to remove away,
Faire Una framèd words and count'nance fit:
125 Which hardly° doen, at length she gan them pray,   *with difficulty*
That in their cotage small, that night she rest her may.[2]

15

The day is spent, and commeth drowsie night,
   When every creature shrowded is in sleepe;
   Sad Una downe her laies in wearie plight,
130   And at her feet the Lyon watch doth keepe:
   In stead of rest, she does lament, and weepe
For the late° losse of her deare lovèd knight,   *recent*
And sighes, and grones, and evermore does steepe
Her tender brest in bitter teares all night,
135 All night she thinks too long, and often lookes for light.

16

Now when Aldeboran was mounted hie
   Above the shynie Cassiopeias chaire,[3]
   And all in deadly sleepe did drownèd lie,
   One knockèd at the dore, and in would fare;°   *come*
140   He knockèd fast,° and often curst, and sware,   *insistently*
That readie entrance was not at his call:
For on his backe a heavy load he bare
Of nightly stelths and pillage severall,[4]
Which he had got abroad by purchase° criminall.   *acquisition*

17

145 He was to weete[5] a stout and sturdie thiefe,
   Wont to robbe Churches of their ornaments,
   And poore mens boxes[6] of their due reliefe,
   Which given was to them for good intents;
   The holy Saints of their rich vestiments
150   He did disrobe, when all men carelesse slept,
   And spoild the Priests of their habiliments,°   *vestments*
Whiles none the holy things in safety kept;
Then he by cunning sleights in at the window crept.

---

9. Her prayers are the Lord's Prayer ("Our Father") and the "Hail Mary."
1. Sackcloth and ashes are symbols of penitence.
2. I.e., that she might rest herself.
3. The star Aldebaran, in the constellation Tau-

rus, mounts over the constellation Cassiopeia.
4. I.e., he carried the booty gained from nightly thefts and various kinds of pillage.
5. In fact.
6. A box for alms for the poor.

18

    And all that he by right or wrong could find,
155   Unto this house he brought, and did bestow
      Upon the daughter of this woman blind,
      Abessa daughter of Corceca[7] slow,
      With whom he whoredome usd, that few did know,
      And fed her fat with feast of offerings,
160   And plentie, which in all the land did grow;
      Ne sparèd he to give her gold and rings:
    And now he to her brought part of his stolen things.

19

    Thus long the dore with rage and threats he bet,°   *beat*
      Yet of those fearefull women none durst rize,
165   The Lyon frayèd them, him in to let:[8]
      He would no longer stay him to advize,°   *consider*
      But open breakes the dore in furious wize,
      And entring is; when that disdainfull° beast   *indignant*
      Encountring fierce, him suddaine doth surprize,
170   And seizing° cruell clawes on trembling brest,   *fastening*
    Under his Lordly foot him proudly hath supprest.

20

    Him booteth not resist,[9] nor succour call,
      His bleeding hart is in the vengers hand,
      Who streight him rent in thousand peeces small,
175   And quite dismembred hath: the thirstie land
      Drunke up his life; his corse left on the strand.°   *ground*
      His fearefull friends weare out the wofull night,
      Ne dare to weepe, nor seeme to understand
      The heavie hap,° which on them is alight,°   *lot/fallen*
180   Affraid, least to themselves the like mishappen might.[1]

21

    Now when broad day the world discovered° has,   *revealed*
      Up Una rose, up rose the Lyon eke,
      And on their former journey forward pas,
      In wayes unknowne, her wandring knight to seeke,
185   With paines farre passing that long wandring Greeke,
      That for his love refusèd deitie;[2]
      Such were the labours of this Lady meeke,
      Still seeking him, that from her still did flie,
    Then furthest from her hope, when most she weenèd nie.[3]

22

190   Soone as she parted thence, the fearefull twaine,
      That blind old woman and her daughter deare
      Came forth, and finding Kirkrapine° there slaine,   *church robber*

---

7. Corceca means "blind heart"; her daughter Abessa's name comes from "abbess." Also *ab* + *esse* (Latin), away from being.
8. I.e., neither of the women dared rise to let him in because the lion terrified ("frayed") them.
9. It does no good to resist.

1. I.e., lest the same thing might happen amiss ("mishappen") to them.
2. Odysseus, who renounced immortality and the love of the nymph Calypso for his wife Penelope.
3. Believed near.

For anguish great they gan to rend their heare,
And beat their brests, and naked flesh to teare.
195   And when they both had wept and wayld their fill,
Then forth they ranne like two amazèd deare,
Halfe mad through malice, and revenging will,[4]
To follow her, that was the causer of their ill.

23

Whom overtaking, they gan loudly bray,
200   With hollow howling, and lamenting cry,
Shamefully at her rayling all the way,
And her accusing of dishonesty,°   *unchastity*
That was the flowre of faith and chastity;
And still amidst her rayling, she[5] did pray,
That plagues, and mischiefs, and long misery
Might fall on her, and follow all the way,
And that in endlesse error° she might ever stray.   *wandering*

24

But when she saw her prayers nought prevaile,
She backe returnèd with some labour lost;
210   And in the way as she did weepe and waile
A knight her met in mighty armes embost,°   *encased*
Yet knight was not for all his bragging bost,°   *boast*
But subtill Archimag, that Una sought
By traynes° into new troubles to have tost: *tricks*
215   Of that old woman tydings he besought,
If that of such a Ladie she could tellen ought.[6]

25

Therewith she gan her passion to renew,
And cry, and curse, and raile, and rend her heare,°   *hair*
Saying, that harlot she too lately knew,
220   That causd her shed so many a bitter teare,
And so forth told the story of her feare:
Much seemèd he to mone her haplesse chaunce,
And after for that Ladie did inquere;
Which being taught, he forward gan advaunce
225   His fair enchaunted steed, and eke his charmèd launce.

26

Ere long he came, where Una traveild slow,
And that wilde Champion wayting° her besyde,   *attending*
Whom seeing such, for dread he durst not show
Himselfe too nigh at hand, but turnèd wyde
230   Unto an hill; from whence when she him spyde,
By his like seeming shield, her knight by name
She weend it was, and towards him gan ryde:
Approching nigh, she wist° it was the same,   *believed*
And with faire fearefull humblesse° towards him shee   *humility*
    came.

---

4. Desire of revenge.
5. I.e., Corceca.

6. I.e., if she could tell anything ("ought") about
such a lady.

27

235 And weeping said, "Ah my long lackèd Lord,
     Where have ye bene thus long out of my sight?
     Much fearèd I to have bene quite abhord,
     Or ought° have done, that ye displeasen might,   *aught*
     That should as death unto my deare hart light:[7]
240   For since mine eye your joyous sight did mis,
     My chearefull day is turnd to chearelesse night,
     And eke my night of death the shadow is;
But welcome now my light, and shining lampe of blis."

28

He thereto meeting[8] said, "My dearest Dame,
245   Farre be it from your thought, and fro my will,
     To thinke that knighthood I so much should shame,
     As you to leave, that have me lovèd still.
     And chose in Faery court of meere° goodwill,   *pure*
     Where noblest knights were to be found on earth:
250   The earth shall sooner leave her kindly° skill   *natural*
     To bring forth fruit, and make eternall derth,°   *desert*
Then I leave you, my liefe,° yborne of heavenly berth.   *beloved*

29

"And sooth to say, why I left you so long,
     Was for to seeke adventure in strange place,
255   Where Archimago said a felon strong
     To many knights did daily worke disgrace;
     But knight he now shall never more deface:°   *discredit*
     Good cause of mine excuse; that mote° ye please   *may*
     Well to accept, and evermore embrace
260   My faithfull service, that by land and seas
Have vowd you to defend, now then your plaint appease."°   *cease*

30

His lovely° words her seemd due recompence   *loving*
     Of all her passèd paines: one loving howre
     For many yeares of sorrow can dispence:°   *make amends*
265   A dram of sweet is worth a pound of sowre:
     She has forgot, how many a wofull stowre°   *trouble*
     For him she late endured; she speakes no more
     Of past: true is, that true love hath no powre
     To looken backe; his eyes be fixt before.
270 Before her stands her knight, for whom she toyld so sore.

31

Much like, as when the beaten marinere,
     That long hath wandred in the Ocean wide,
     Oft soust° in swelling Tethys[9] saltish teare,   *soaked*
     And long time having tand his tawney hide
275   With blustring breath of heaven, that none can bide,

---

7. I.e., be as a death blow to my sad heart.   9. The wife of Ocean; here, the Ocean.
8. Answering in like manner.

And scorching flames of fierce Orions hound,[1]
Soone as the port from farre he has espide,
His chearefull whistle merrily doth sound,
And Nereus crownes with cups;[2] his mates him
    pledg° around.   *toast*

32

280   Such joy made Una, when her knight she found;
And eke th' enchaunter joyous seemd no lesse,
Then the glad marchant, that does vew from ground
His ship farre come from watrie wildernesse,
He hurles out vowes, and Neptune oft doth blesse:
285   So forth they past, and all the way they spent
Discoursing of her dreadfull late distresse,
In which he askt her, what the Lyon ment:
Who told her all that fell° in journey as she went.[3]   *befell*

33

They had not ridden farre, when they might see
290   One pricking° towards them with hastie heat,   *riding*
Full strongly armd, and on a courser free,
That through his fiercenesse fomed all with sweat,
And the sharpe yron° did for anger eat,   *bit*
When his hot ryder spurd his chauffèd° side;   *heated*
295   His looke was sterne, and seemèd still to threat
Cruell revenge, which he in hart did hyde,
And on his shield Sans loy in bloudie lines was dyde.

34

When nigh he drew unto this gentle payre
And saw the Red-crosse, which the knight did beare,
300   He burnt in fire, and gan eftsoones prepare
Himselfe to battell with his couchèd speare.
Loth was that other, and did faint through feare,
To taste th' untryed dint° of deadly steele;   *blow*
But yet his Lady did so well him cheare,
305   That hope of new good hap he gan to feele;
So bent° his speare, and spurnd his horse with yron heele.   *lowered*

35

But that proud Paynim° forward came so fierce,   *pagan*
And full of wrath, that with his sharp-head speare
Through vainely crossèd shield[4] he quite did pierce,
310   And had his staggering steede not shrunke for feare,
Through shield and bodie eke° he should him beare:°   *also/thrust*
Yet so great was the puissance of his push,
That from his saddle quite he did him beare:
He tombling rudely° downe to ground did rush,   *violently*
315   And from his gorèd wound a well of bloud did gush.

---

1. Sirius, the dog star, symbolizing hot weather
(the "dog days").
2. Nereus is god of the Mediterranean, to whom
the mariner in gratitude makes libations.

3. I.e., she told all that befell ("fell") her.
4. The cross on Archimago's shield was false and
did not give him the protection the Redcrosse knight
received in his fight with Sans Foy; see 1.2.18.

36

Dismounting lightly from his loftie steed,
 He to him lept, in mind to reave° his life,   *take*
 And proudly said, "Lo there the worthie meed°   *recompense*
 Of him, that slew Sans foy with bloudie knife;
320 Henceforth his ghost freed from repining strife,
 In peace may passen over Lethe[5] lake,
 When mourning altars purgd° with enemies life,   *cleansed*
 The blacke infernall Furies[6] doen aslake:
Life from Sans foy thou tookst, Sans loy shall from thee take."

37

325 Therewith in haste his helmet gan unlace,
 Till Una cride, "O hold that heavie hand,
 Deare Sir, what ever that thou be in place:[7]
 Enough is, that thy foe doth vanquisht stand
 Now at thy mercy: Mercie not withstand:
330 For he is one the truest knight alive,[8]
 Though conquered now he lie on lowly land,[9]
 And whilest him fortune favourd, faire did thrive
In bloudie field: therefore of life him not deprive."

38

Her piteous words might not abate his rage,
335 But rudely rending up his helmet, would
 Have slaine him straight: but when he sees his age,
 And hoarie head of Archimago old,
 His hastie hand he doth amazèd hold,
 And halfe ashamèd, wondred at the sight:
340 For the old man well knew he, though untold,
 In charmes and magicke to have wondrous might,
Ne ever wont in field, ne in round lists[1] to fight.

39

And said, "Why Archimago, lucklesse syre,
 What doe I see? what hard mishap is this,
345 That hath thee hither brought to taste mine yre?
 Or thine the fault, or mine the error is,
 In stead of foe to wound my friend amis?"
 He answered nought, but in a traunce still lay,
 And on those guilefull dazèd eyes of his
350 The cloud of death did sit. Which doen away,[2]
He left him lying so, ne would no lenger stay.

40

But to the virgin comes, who all this while
 Amasèd stands, her selfe so mockt° to see   *deceived*
 By him, who has the guerdon° of his guile,   *reward*

---

5. The river of forgetfulness in Hades.
6. Spirits of discord and revenge. "Aslake": appease.
7. Whoever you are.
8. I.e., do not withhold mercy, for he is the one

truest knight.
9. I.e., low on the ground.
1. Enclosures for fighting tournaments.
2. When the swoon passed.

355 For so misfeigning her true knight to bee:
　　Yet is she now in more perplexitie,°   *trouble*
　　Left in the hand of that same Paynim bold,
　　From whom her booteth not³ at all to flie;
　　Who by her cleanly° garment catching hold,   *pure*
360 Her from her Palfrey pluckt, her visage to behold.

41

　　But her fierce servant full of kingly awe
　　And high disdaine,° whenas his soveraine Dame   *indignation*
　　So rudely handled by her foe he sawe,
　　With gaping jawes full greedy at him came,
365 And ramping on his shield, did weene° the same   *intend*
　　Have reft away with his sharpe rending clawes
　　But he was stout, and lust did now inflame
　　His corage more, that from his griping pawes
　　He hath his shield redeemed,° and foorth his swerd he *recovered*
　　　drawes.

42

370 O then too weake and feeble was the forse
　　Of salvage beast, his puissance to withstand:
　　For he was strong, and of so mightie corse,
　　As ever wielded speare in warlike hand,
　　And feates of armes did wisely° understand.   *skilfully*
375 Eftsoones he percèd through his chaufèd chest
　　With thrilling point of deadly yron brand,⁴
　　And launcht° his Lordly hart: with death opprest   *pierced*
　　He roared aloud, whiles life forsooke his stubborne brest.

43

　　Who now is left to keepe the forlorne maid
380 From raging spoile of lawlesse victors will?
　　Her faithfull gard removed, her hope dismaid,
　　Her selfe a yeelded pray to save or spill.°   *destroy*
　　He now Lord of the field, his pride to fill,
　　With foule reproches, and disdainfull spight
385 Her vildly entertaines, and will or nill,
　　Beares her away upon his courser light:⁵
　　Her prayers nought prevaile; his rage is more of might.

44

　　And all the way, with great lamenting paine,
　　And piteous plaints she filleth his dull° eares,   *deaf*
390 That stony hart could riven have in twaine,
　　And all the way she wets with flowing teares:
　　But he enraged with rancor, nothing heares.
　　Her servile beast yet would not leave her so,

---

3. Was of no use.
4. I.e., afterwards he pierced through the lion's angry ("chaufed") chest with the penetrating ("thrilling") point of his sword.
5. I.e., he treats her basely ("vildly") and willingly or not bears her away quickly ("light") upon his horse.

But followes her farre off, ne ought he feares,
395   To be partaker of her wandring woe,
More mild in beastly kind,° then that her beastly foe.   *nature*

Canto 4

To sinfull house of Pride, Duessa
guides the faithfull knight,
Where brothers death to wreak° Sansjoy   *avenge*
doth chalenge him to fight.

1

Young knight, what ever that dost armes professe,
And through long labours huntest after fame,
Beware of fraud, beware of ficklenesse,
In choice, and change of thy deare lovèd Dame,
5   Least thou of her beleeve too lightly blame,
And rash misweening° doe thy hart remove: *misjudgment*
For unto knight there is no greater shame,
Then lightnesse and inconstancie in love;
That doth this Redcrosse knights ensample° plainly prove.   *example*

2

10   Who after that he had faire Una lorne,°   *forsaken*
Through light misdeeming° of her loialtie,   *misjudging*
And false Duessa in her sted had borne,[1]
Called Fidess', and so supposd to bee;
Long with her traveild, till at last they see
15   A goodly building, bravely garnishèd,°   *adorned*
The house of mightie Prince it seemd to bee:
And towards it a broad high way[2] that led,
All bare through peoples feet, which thither traveilèd.

3

Great troupes of people traveild thitherward
20   Both day and night, of each degree and place,°   *rank*
But few returnèd, having scapèd hard,°   *with difficulty*
With balefull° beggerie, or foule disgrace,   *wretched*
Which ever after in most wretched case,
Like loathsome lazars,° by the hedges lay.   *lepers*
25   Thither Duessa bad him bend his pace:[3]
For she is wearie of the toilesome way,
And also nigh consumèd is the lingring day.

4

A stately Pallace built of squarèd bricke,
Which cunningly was without morter laid,
30   Whose wals were high, but nothing strong, nor thick,
And golden foile[4] all over them displaid,
That purest skye with brightnesse they dismaid°:   *outdid*

---

1. Taken as companion.
2. "Broad is the way that leadeth to destruction"
(Matthew 7.13).
3. Direct his steps.
4. Thin layer of gold.

High lifted up were many loftie towres,
And goodly galleries farre over laid,[5]
35 Full of faire windowes, and delightfull bowres;
And on the top a Diall told the timely howres.[6]

5

It was a goodly heape° for to behould,   *building*
    And spake the praises of the workmans wit;°   *skill*
    But full great pittie, that so faire a mould°   *structure*
40 Did on so weake foundation ever sit:
    For on a sandie hill,[7] that still did flit,
    And fall away, it mounted was full hie,
    That every breath of heaven shakèd it:
    And all the hinder parts, that few could spie,
45 Were ruinous and old, but painted cunningly.

6

Arrivèd there they passèd in forth right;
    For still to all the gates stood open wide,
    Yet charge of them was to a Porter hight°   *committed*
    Cald Malvenù,[8] who entrance none denide:
50 Thence to the hall, which was on every side
    With rich array and costly arras dight:[9]
    Infinite sorts of people did abide
    There waiting long, to win the wishèd sight
Of her, that was the Lady of that Pallace bright.

7

55 By them they passe, all gazing on them round,
    And to the Presence[1] mount; whose glorious vew
    Their frayle amazèd senses did confound:
    In living Princes court none ever knew
    Such endlesse richesse, and so sumptuous shew;
60 Ne Persia selfe, the nourse of pompous pride
    Like ever saw. And there a noble crew
    Of Lordes and Ladies stood on every side,
Which with their presence faire, the place much beautifide.

8

High above all a cloth of State[2] was spred,
65 And a rich throne, as bright as sunny day,
    On which there sate most brave embellishèd[3]
    With royall robes and gorgeous array,
    A mayden Queene, that shone as Titans° ray,   *the sun's*
    In glistring gold, and peerelesse pretious stone:
70 Yet her bright blazing beautie did assay°   *attempt*

---

5. Placed above.
6. A sundial measured the hours of the day.
7. Matthew 7.26–7: "A foolish man . . . built his
house upon the sand:/ And the rain descended,
and the floods came, and the winds blew, and beat
upon that house; and it fell; and great was the fall
of it." "Flit": shift.
8. The name means "unwelcome." In courtly love

allegories, the porter is often called "Bienvenu" or
"Bel-accueil" ("welcome").
9. Decorated with costly wall hangings.
1. Presence chamber, where a sovereign receives
guests.
2. Canopy.
3. Handsomely clad.

To dim the brightnesse of her glorious throne,
As envying her selfe, that too exceeding shone.

9

Exceeding shone, like Phoebus fairest childe,
  That did presume his fathers firie wayne,°   *chariot*
75 And flaming mouthes of steedes unwonted° wilde   *unusually*
  Through highest heaven with weaker° hand to rayne; *too weak*
  Proud of such glory and advancement vaine,
  While flashing beames do daze his feeble eyen,
  He leaves the welkin° way most beaten plaine,   *skyey*
80 And rapt° with whirling wheeles, inflames the skyen, *carried away*
With fire not made to burne, but fairely for to shyne.[4]

10

So proud she shynèd in her Princely state,°   *throne*
  Looking to heaven; for earth she did disdayne,
  And sitting high; for lowly° she did hate: *lowliness*
85 Lo underneath her scornefull feete, was layne
  A dreadfull Dragon with an hideous trayne,°   *tail*
  And in her hand she held a mirrhour bright,[5]
  Wherein her face she often vewèd fayne,°   *with pleasure*
  And in her selfe-loved semblance tooke delight;
90 For she was wondrous faire, as any living wight.

11

Of griesly° Pluto she the daughter was,   *horrid*
  And sad Proserpina the Queene of hell;
  Yet did she thinke her pearelesse worth to pas° *surpass*
  That parentage, with pride so did she swell,
95 And thundring Jove, that high in heaven doth dwell,
  And wield° the world, she claymèd for her syre, *govern*
  Or if that any else did Jove excell:
  For to the highest she did still aspyre,
Or if ought° higher were then that, did it desyre. *anything*

12

100 And proud Lucifera men did her call,
  That made her selfe a Queene, and crownd to be,
  Yet rightfull kingdome she had none at all,
  Ne heritage of native soveraintie,
  But did usurpe with wrong and tyrannie
105 Upon the scepter, which she now did hold:
  Ne ruld her Realmes with lawes, but pollicie,° *political cunning*
  And strong advizement of six wisards old,
That with their counsels bad her kingdome did uphold.

13

Soone as the Elfin knight in presence came,
110 And false Duessa seeming Lady faire,

---

4. Phaëton tried to drive the chariot of Phoebus, his father, but set the skies on fire and fell.
5. Pride, and figures associated with her in Renaissance literature and art, often hold a mirror, emblematic of self-love.

A gentle Husher,° Vanitie by name   *usher*
Made rowme, and passage for them did prepaire:
So goodly° brought them to the lowest staire   *graciously*
Of her high throne, where they on humble knee
115   Making obeyssance,° did the cause declare,   *submission*
Why they were come, her royall state to see,
To prove° the wide report of her great Majestee.   *verify*

14

With loftie eyes, halfe loth to looke so low,
She thankèd them in her disdainefull wise,
120   Ne other grace vouchsafèd them to show
Of Princesse worthy, scarse them bad arise.
Her Lordes and Ladies all this while devise°   *make ready*
Themselves to setten forth to straungers sight:
Some frounce° their curlèd haire in courtly guise,   *frizzle*
125   Some prancke° their ruffes, and others trimly dight°   *pleat/arrange*
Their gay attire: each others greater pride does spight.

15

Goodly they all that knight do entertaine,
Right glad with him to have increast their crew:
But to Duess' each one himselfe did paine
130   All kindnesse and faire courtesie to shew;
For in that court whylome° her well they knew: *formerly*
Yet the stout Faerie mongst the middest° crowd   *thickest*
Thought all their glorie vaine in knightly vew,
And that great Princesse too exceeding prowd,
135   That to strange° knight no better countenance° allowd.   *stranger / favor*

16

Suddein upriseth from her stately place
The royall Dame, and for her coche doth call:
All hurtlen° forth and she with Princely pace,   *rush*
As faire Aurora in her purple pall,[6]
140   Out of the East the dawning day doth call:
So forth she comes: her brightnesse brode° doth blaze;   *abroad*
The heapes of people thronging in the hall,
Do ride° each other, upon her to gaze: *climb up*
Her glorious glitterand° light doth all mens eyes amaze.   *glittering*

17

145   So forth she comes, and to her coche does clyme,
Adornèd all with gold, and girlonds gay,
That seemd as fresh as Flora in her prime,
And strove to match, in royall rich array,
Great Junos golden chaire,° the which they say   *chariot*
150   The Gods stand gazing on, when she does ride
To Joves high house through heavens bras-pavèd way

6. Goddess of dawn, in her crimson robe ("purple pall").

    Drawne of by faire Pecocks, that excell in pride,
    And full of Argus eyes their tailes dispredden wide.[7]

18

    But this was drawne of six unequall beasts,
155   On which her six sage Counsellours did ryde,
      Taught to obay their bestiall beheasts,
      With like conditions to their kinds applyde:[8]
      Of which the first, that all the rest did guyde,
      Was sluggish Idlenesse the nourse of sin;
160   Upon a slouthfull Asse he chose to ryde,
      Arayd in habit blacke, and amis thin,[9]
    Like to an holy Monck, the service to begin.

19

    And in his hand his Portesse° still he bare,   *breviary*
    That much was worne, but therein little red,
165   For of devotion he had little care,
      Still drownd in sleepe, and most of his dayes ded;
      Scarse could he once uphold his heavie hed,
      To looken, whether it were night or day:
      May seeme the wayne° was very evill led,   *chariot*
170   When such an one had guiding of the way,
    That knew not, whether right he went, or else astray.

20

    From worldly cares himselfe he did esloyne,°   *withdraw*
    And greatly shunnèd manly exercise,
    From every worke he chalengèd essoyne,[1]
175   For contemplation sake: yet otherwise,
      His life he led in lawlesse riotise;°   *riotous conduct*
      By which he grew to grievous malady;
      For in his lustlesse° limbs through evill guise°   *feeble/living*
      A shaking fever raignd continually:
180   Such one was Idlenesse, first of this company

21

    And by his side rode loathsome Gluttony,
    Deformèd creature, on a filthie swyne,
    His belly was up-blowne with luxury.[2]
    And eke with fatnesse swollen were his eyne,
185   And like a Crane his necke was long and fyne,[3]
      With which he swallowd up excessive feast,
      For want whereof poore people oft did pyne;°   *starve*

---

7. Peacocks, with their tails outspread ("dispredden wide") are a symbol of pride. The hundred-eyed monster Argus was set by Juno to watch Io, Jupiter's love. When Mercury killed Argus, his eyes were put in the peacock's tail feathers.
8. It is not clear whether the "sage Counsellors" command their beasts or are guided by them; since riders and their mounts are alike bestial, the same conditions pertain (are "applyed") to both natures ("kinds"). This procession of the seven deadly sins— of which Pride is queen—had a long tradition in medieval art and literature. See also Marlowe's *Doctor Faustus* (2.2.111–164).
9. Idleness wears the garb ("habit") and hood or amice ("amis") of a monk. Traditionally, Idleness led the procession of the deadly sins.
1. Claimed exemption.
2. Indulgence (in rich food).
3. The crane is a common symbol of gluttony because its long and thin ("fyne") neck allows more pleasure in swallowing.

And all the way, most like a brutish beast,
He spuèd up his gorge,[4] that all did him deteast.

22

190 In greene vine leaves he was right fitly clad;
      For other clothes he could not weare for heat,
      And on his head an yvie girland had,[5]
      From under which fast trickled downe the sweat:
      Still as he rode, he somewhat° still did eat,   *something*
195 And in his hand did beare a bouzing° can,   *drinking*
      Of which he supt so oft, that on his seat
      His dronken corse° he scarse upholden can,   *body*
      In shape and life more like a monster, then a man.

23

      Unfit he was for any worldly thing,
200 And eke unhable once° to stirre or go,°   *at all/walk*
      Not meet to be of counsell to a king,
      Whose mind in meat and drinke was drownèd so,
      That from his friend he seldome knew his fo:
      Full of diseases was his carcas blew,
205 And a dry dropsie through his flesh did flow:
      Which by misdiet daily greater grew:
      Such one was Gluttony, the second of that crew.

24

      And next° to him rode lustfull Lechery,   *just after*
      Upon a bearded Goat,[6] whose rugged haire,
210 And whally° eyes (the signe of gelosy,)   *glaring*
      Was like the person selfe, whom he did beare:
      Who rough, and blacke, and filthy did appeare,
      Unseemely man to please faire Ladies eye;
      Yet he of Ladies oft was lovèd deare,
215 When fairer faces were bid standen by:°   *away*
      O who does know the bent of womens fantasy?

25

      In a greene gowne he clothèd was full faire,
      Which underneath did hide his filthinesse,
      And in his hand a burning hart he bare,
220 Full of vaine follies, and new fangleness:°   *fickleness*
      For he was false, and fraught with ficklenesse,
      And learnèd had to love with secret lookes,
      And well could daunce, and sing with ruefulnesse,°   *pity*
      And fortunes tell, and read in loving° bookes,   *erotic*
225 And thousand other wayes, to bait his fleshly hookes.

26

      Inconstant man, that lovèd all he saw,
      And lusted after all, that he did love,
      Ne would his looser life be tide to law,

4. Vomited.   Bacchus.
5. He resembles the drunken satyr Silenus, foster   6. Traditional symbol of Lust.
father of Bacchus, god of wine; ivy is sacred to

But joyd weake wemens hearts to tempt and prove°   *try*
230   If from their loyall loves he might them move;
Which lewdnesse fild him with reprochfull paine
Of that fowle evill, which all men reprove,
That rots the marrow, and consumes the braine:[7]
Such one was Lecherie, the third of all this traine.

27

235   And greedy Avarice by him did ride,
Upon a Camell loaden all with gold;[8]
Two iron coffers hong on either side,
With precious mettall full, as they might hold,
And in his lap an heape of coine he told;°   *counted*
240   For of his wicked pelfe° his God he made,   *money*
And unto hell him selfe for money sold;
Accursèd usurie was all his trade,
And right and wrong ylike in equall ballaunce waide.[9]

28

His life was nigh unto deaths doore yplast,
245   And thread-bare cote, and cobled shoes he ware,
Ne scarse good morsell all his life did tast,
But both from backe and belly still did spare,
To fill his bags, and richesse to compare;°   *acquire*
Yet chylde ne kinsman living had he none
250   To leave them to; but thorough daily care
To get, and nightly feare to lose his owne,
He led a wretched life unto him selfe unknowne.

29

Most wretched wight, whom nothing might suffise,
Whose greedy lust did lacke in greatest store,°   *plenty*
255   Whose need had end, but no end covetise,
Whose wealth was want, whose plenty made him pore,
Who had enough, yet wishèd ever more;
A vile disease, and eke in foote and hand
A grievous gout tormented him full sore,
260   That well he could not touch, not go,° nor stand: *walk*
Such one was Avarice, the fourth of this faire band.

30

And next to him malicious Envie rode,
Upon a ravenous wolfe,[1] and still did chaw
Betweene his cankred° teeth a venemous tode,   *ulcerated*
265   That all the poison ran about his chaw;°   *jaw*
But inwardly he chawèd his owne maw°   *entrails*
At neighbours wealth, that made him ever sad;
For death it was, when any good he saw,

---

7. I.e., syphilis.
8. The camel as a symbol of avarice is based on
Matthew 19.24: "It is easier for a camel to go
through the eye of a needle, than for a rich man
to enter into the kingdom of God."

9. I.e., he made no distinction between right and
wrong.
1. Traditional attribute of Envy. "Still": continually.

And wept, that cause of weeping none he had,
270   But when he heard of harme, he wexèd wondrous glad.

31

All in a kirtle of discolourd say[2]
    He clothèd was, ypainted full of eyes;
    And in his bosome secretly there lay
    An hatefull Snake,[3] the which his taile uptyes
275   In many folds, and mortall sting implyes.°   *enfolds*
    Still as he rode, he gnasht his teeth, to see
    Those heapes of gold with griple° Covetyse,   *grasping*
    And grudgèd at the great felicitie
Of proud Lucifera, and his owne companie.

32

280   He hated all good workes and vertuous deeds,
    And him no lesse, that any like did use,°   *perform*
    And who with gracious bread the hungry feeds,
    His almes for want of faith he doth accuse;
    So every good to bad he doth abuse:°   *twist*
285   And eke° the verse of famous Poets witt
    He does backebite, and spightfull poison spues
    From leprous mouth on all, that ever writt:
Such one vile Envie was, that fifte in row did sitt.

33

And him beside rides fierce revenging Wrath,
290   Upon a Lion,[4] loth for to be led;
    And in his hand a burning brond° he hath,   *sword*
    The which he brandisheth about his hed;
    His eyes did hurle forth sparkles fiery red,
    And starèd sterne on all, that him beheld,
295   As ashes pale of hew and seeming ded;
    And on his dagger still his hand he held,
Trembling through hasty rage, when choler° in him sweld.   *anger*

34

His ruffin° raiment all was staind with blood,   *disorderly*
    Which he had spilt, and all to rags yrent,°   *torn*
300   Through unadvisèd rashnesse woxen wood,[5]
    For of his hands he had no governement,°   *control*
    He cared for bloud in his avengement:
    But when the furious fit was overpast,
    His cruell facts° he often would repent;   *actions*
305   Yet wilfull man he never would forecast,
How many mischieves should ensue his heedlesse hast.[6]

35

Full many mischiefes follow cruell Wrath;
    Abhorrèd bloudshed, and tumultuous strife,

2. Jacket of many-colored wool.
3. The traditional attribute of Envy.
4. The lion is the symbol of Wrath.
5. Grown insane.
6. I.e., he never would foresee ("forecast") the calamities his "heedless haste" caused.

Unmanly murder, and unthrifty scath,[7]
310   Bitter despight,° with rancours rusty knife,   *malice*
   And fretting griefe the enemy of life;
   All these, and many evils moe° haunt ire,°   *more/anger*
   The swelling Splene,[8] and Frenzy raging rife,
   The shaking Palsey, and Saint Fraunces fire:[9]
315 Such one was Wrath, the last of this ungoldly tire.°   *train*

                36

And after all, upon the wagon beame
   Rode Sathan, with a smarting whip in hand,
   With which he forward lasht the laesie teme,
   So oft as Slowth[1] still in the mire did stand.
320   Huge routs° of people did about them band,   *crowds*
   Showting for joy, and still before their way
   A foggy mist had covered all the land;
   And underneath their feet, all scattered lay
Dead sculs and bones of men, whose life had gone astray.

                37

325 So forth they marchen in this goodly sort,
   To take the solace° of the open aire,   *recreation*
   And in fresh flowring fields themselves to sport;
   Emongst the rest rode that false Lady faire,
   The fowle Duessa, next unto the chaire
330   Of proud Lucifera, as one of the traine:
   But that good knight would not so nigh repaire,°   *approach*
   Him selfe estraunging from their joyaunce° vaine,   *festivity*
Whose fellowship seemd far unfit for warlike swaine.

                38

So having solacèd themselves a space
335   With pleasaunce of the breathing° fields yfed,   *emitting fragrance*
   They backe returnèd to the Princely Place;
   Whereas an errant knight in armes ycled,°   *clad*
   And heathnish shield, wherein with letters red
   Was writ Sans joy,[2] they new arrivèd find:
340   Enflamed with fury and fiers hardy-hed,°   *boldness*
   He seemd in hart to harbour thoughts unkind,
And nourish bloudy vengeaunce in his bitter mind.

                39

Who when the shamèd shield[3] of slaine Sans foy
   He spied with that same Faery champions page,
345   Bewraying° him, that did of late destroy   *revealing*
   His eldest brother, burning all with rage
He to him leapt, and that same envious gage[4]

---

7. I.e., inhuman murder and destructive harm ("unthrifty scath").
8. Organ associated with anger in Renaissance physiology.
9. St. Anthony's fire, erysipelas, or the flaming itch; appropriate to Wrath.

1. I.e., Idleness (stanzas 18–20).
2. Sans Joy ("without joy"), darkness of spirit.
3. Carrying a shield upside down, with the heraldic arms reversed, was a great insult. See below, line 369.
4. Envied prize.

Of victors glory from him snatcht away:
But th 'Elfin knight, which ought that warlike wage,[5]
350   Disdaind to loose the meed he wonne in fray,°   *battle*
And him rencountring fierce, reskewd the noble pray.

40

Therewith they gan to hurtlen° greedily,   *rush together*
Redoubted battaile ready to darrayne,°   *contest*
And clash their shields, and shake their swords on hy,
355   That with their sturre° they troubled all the traine;   *tumult*
Till that great Queene upon eternall paine
Of high displeasure, that ensewen° might,   *ensue*
Commaunded them their fury to refraine,
And if that either to that shield had right,
360   In equall lists[6] they should the morrow next it fight.

41

"Ah dearest Dame," quoth then the Paynim bold,
"Pardon the errour of enragèd wight,
Whom great griefe made forget the raines to hold
Of reasons rule, to see this recreant° knight,   *cowardly*
365   No knight, but treachour° full of false despight° *deceiver/disdain*
And shamefull treason, who through guile hath slayn
The prowest° knight, that ever field did fight,   *bravest*
Even stout Sans foy (O who can then refrayn?)
Whose shield he beares renverst, the more to heape disdayn.

42

370   "And to augment the glorie of his guile,
His dearest love[7] the faire Fidessa loe
Is there possessed of° the traytour vile,   *by*
Who reapes the harvest sowen by his foe,
Sowen in bloudy field, and bought with woe:
375   That[8] brothers hand shall dearely well requight
So be, O Queene, you equall favour showe."[9]
Him litle answerd th 'angry Elfin knight:
He never meant with words, but swords to plead his right.

43

But threw his gauntlet as a sacred pledge,
380   His cause in combat the next day to try:
So been they parted both, with harts on edge,
To be avenged each on his enimy.
That night they pas in joy and jollity,
Feasting and courting both in bowre and hall;
385   For Steward was excessive Gluttonie,
That of his plenty pourèd forth to all;
Which doen, the Chamberlain[1] Slowth did to rest them call.

5. The knight (Redcrosse) who owned ("ought")
that spoil of war ("warlike wage").
6. Impartial formal combat.
7. I.e., Sans Foy's.
8. I.e., that act.

9. I.e., if, O Queen, you show impartiality ("equall
favour").
1. The court attendant in charge of the bedcham-
bers. "Doen": done.

44

Now whenas darkesome night had all displayd
　　Her coleblacke curtein over brightest skye,
390　The warlike youthes on dayntie° couches layd,　　　　　　*fine*
　　Did chace away sweet sleepe from sluggish eye,
　　To muse on meanes of hopèd victory.
　　But whenas Morpheus[2] had with leaden mace
　　Arrested all that courtly company,
395　Up-rose Duessa from her resting place,
And to the Paynims° lodging comes with silent pace.　　　*pagan*

45

Whom broad awake she finds, in troublous fit,[3]
　　Forecasting, how his foe he might annoy,°　　　　　*injure*
　　And him amoves° with speaches seeming fit:　　　　*arouses*
400　"Ah deare Sans joy, next dearest to Sans foy,
　　Cause of my new griefe, cause of my new joy,
　　Joyous, to see his ymage in mine eye,
　　And greeved, to thinke how foe did him destroy,
　　That was the flowre of grace and chevalrye;
405　Lo his Fidessa to thy secret faith I flye."

46

With gentle wordes he can° her fairely° greet,　　　*did/courteously*
　　And bad say on the secret of her hart.
　　Then sighing soft, "I learne that litle sweet
　　Oft tempred is," quoth she, "with muchell° smart:　　　*much*
410　For since my brest was launcht with lovely dart[4]
　　Of deare Sans foy, I never joyèd howre,
　　But in eternall woes my weaker hart
　　Have wasted, loving him with all my powre,
And for his sake have felt full many an heavie stowre.°　　　*grief*

47

415　"At last when perils all I weenèd past,
　　And hoped to reape the crop of all my care,
　　Into new woes unweeting° I was cast,　　　　　*unknowing*
　　By this false faytor,° who unworthy ware°　　*deceiver/wore*
　　His worthy shield, whom he with guilefull snare
420　Entrappèd slew, and brought to shamefull grave.
　　Me silly° maid away with him he bare,　　　　　*helpless*
　　And ever since hath kept in darksome cave,
For that I would not yeeld, that° to Sans foy I gave.　　　*what*

48

"But since faire Sunne hath sperst° that lowring clowd,　　*dispersed*
425　And to my loathèd life now shewes some light,
　　Under your beames I will me safely shrowd,°　　*take shelter*
　　From dreaded storme of his disdainfull spight:
　　To you th' inheritance belongs by right
　　Of brothers prayse, to you eke longs° his love.　　　*belongs*

---

2. The god of sleep.　　　　　　　4. I.e., since my breast was pierced with the dart
3. Troubled mood.　　　　　　　　of love.

430   Let not his love, let not his restlesse spright°   *ghost*
       Be unrevenged, that calles to you above
    From wandring Stygian[5] shores, where it doth endlesse move."
                              49
    Thereto said he, "Faire Dame be nought dismaid
       For sorrowes past; their griefe is with them gone:
435   Ne yet of present perill be affraid;
       For needlesse feare did never vantage° none,   *aid*
       And helplesse hap it booteth not to mone.[6]
       Dead is Sans-foy, his vitall° paines are past,   *living*
       Though greevèd ghost for vengeance deepe do grone:
440   He lives, that shall him pay his dewties° last,   *rites*
    And guiltie Elfin bloud shall sacrifice in hast."
                              50
    "O but I feare the fickle freakes,"[7] quoth shee,
       "Of fortune false, and oddes of armes[8] in field."
       "Why dame," quoth he, "what oddes can ever bee,
445   Where both do fight alike, to win or yield?"
       "Yea but," quoth she, "he beares a charmèd shield,
       And eke enchaunted armes, that none can perce,
       Ne none can wound the man, that does them wield."
       "Charmd or enchaunted," answerd he then ferce,°   *fiercely*
450   "I no whit reck,[9] ne you the like need to reherce.°   *recount*
                              51
    "But faire Fidessa, sithens° fortunes guile,   *since*
       Or enimies powre hath now captivèd you,
       Returne from whence ye came, and rest a while
       Till morrow next, that I the Elfe subdew,
455   And with Sans foyes dead dowry you endew."[1]
       "Ay me, that is a double death," she said,
       "With proud foes sight my sorrow to renew:
       Where ever yet I be, my secrete aid
    Shall follow you." So passing forth she him obaid.

                              Canto 5

                  The faithfull knight in equall field
                  subdewes his faithlesse foe,
                  Whom false Duessa saves, and for
                  his cure to hell does goe.
                              1
       The noble hart, that harbours vertuous thought,
          And is with child of glorious great intent,
          Can never rest, untill it forth have brought

5. I.e., from wandering on the banks of the Styx
river, in Hades.
6. I.e., it does not help to moan over that which
is beyond help ("helplesse hap").
7. Unpredictable tricks.

8. Advantage of superior arms.
9. I do not care at all. "Reherce": recount.
1. I.e., endow you with the legacy of the dead
Sans Joy.

Th' eternall brood of glorie excellent:[1]
5　　Such restlesse passion did all night torment
　　The flaming corage of that Faery knight,
　　Devizing, how that doughtie° turnament　　　　　　*worthy*
　　With greatest honour he atchieven might;
Still did he wake, and still did watch for dawning light.

2

10　At last the golden Orientall gate
　　Of greatest heaven gan to open faire,
　　And Phoebus[2] fresh, as bridegrome to his mate,
　　Came dauncing forth, shaking his deawie haire:
　　And hurld his glistring beames through gloomy aire.
15　　Which when the wakeful Elfe perceived, streight way
　　He started up, and did him selfe prepaire,
　　In sun-bright armes, and battailous° array:　　　　*warlike*
For with that Pagan proud he combat will that day.

3

　　And forth he comes into the commune hall,
20　　Where earely waite him many a gazing eye,
　　To weet what end to straunger knights may fall.
　　There many Minstrales maken melody,
　　To drive away the dull melancholy,
　　And many Bardes, that to the trembling chord
25　　Can tune their timely° voyces cunningly,　　　　*measured*
　　And many Chroniclers, that can record
Old loves, and warres for ladies doen by many a Lord.[3]

4

　　Soone after comes the cruell Sarazin,
　　In woven maile all armèd warily,
30　　And sternly lookes at him, who not a pin
　　Does care for looke of living creatures eye.
　　They bring them wines of Greece and Araby,
　　And daintie spices fetcht from furthest Ynd,°　　　*India*
　　To kindle heat of courage privily:°　　　　　　　*within*
35　　And in the wine a solemne oth they bynd
T'observe the sacred lawes of armes, that are assynd.

5

　　At last forth comes that far renowmèd Queene,
　　With royall pomp and Princely majestie;
　　She is ybrought unto a palèd° greene,　　　　　　*fenced*
40　　And placèd under stately canapee,°　　　　　　　*canopy*
　　The warlike feates of both those knights to see.
　　On th' other side in all mens open vew
　　Duessa placèd is, and on a tree

---

1. That good is manifested only in action, not in
mere intent, is an important Renaissance commonplace.
2. The sun. Cf. Psalm 19.4–5: "In them hath he
sat a Tabernacle for the sun, / Which is as a bridegroom coming out of his chamber."
3. Minstrels play the music on their instruments,
Bards sing the words, Chroniclers—historians, epic
poets—write of love and war.

Sans-foy his shield is hangd with bloudy hew:
45 Both those the lawrell girlonds[4] to the victor dew.

6

A shrilling trompet sownded from on hye,
    And unto battaill bad them selves addresse:
    Their shining shieldes about their wrestes° they tye,   *wrists*
    And burning blades about their heads do blesse,°   *brandish*
50 The instruments of wrath and heavinesse:°   *rage*
    With greedy force each other doth assayle,
    And strike so fiercely, that they do impresse
    Deepe dinted furrowes in the battred mayle;
The yron walles to ward their blowes are weake and fraile.[5]

7

55 The Sarazin was stout,° and wondrous strong,   *fierce*
    And heapèd blowes like yron hammers great:
    For after bloud and vengeance he did long.
    The knight was fiers,° and full of youthly heat: *high-spirited*
    And doubled strokes, like dreaded thunders threat:
60 For all for prayse and honour he did fight.
    Both stricken strike, and beaten both do beat,
    That from their shields forth flyeth firie light,
And helmets hewen deepe, shew marks of eithers might.

8

So th' one for wrong, the other strives for right:
65 As when a Gryfon[6] seizèd of his pray,
    A Dragon fiers encountreth in his flight,
    Through widest ayre making his ydle° way,   *casual*
    That would his rightfull ravine° rend away;   *plunder*
    With hideous horrour both together smight,
70 And souce° so sore, that they the heavens affray: *strike*
    The wise Southsayer° seeing so sad sight,   *soothsayer*
Th' amazèd vulgar tels of warres and mortall fight.

9

So th' one for wrong, the other strives for right,
    And each to deadly shame would drive his foe:
75 The cruell steele so greedily doth bight
    In tender flesh, that streames of bloud down flow,
    With which the armes, that earst so bright did show,
    Into a pure vermillion now are dyde:
    Great ruth° in all the gazers harts did grow,   *pity*
80 Seeing the gorèd woundes to gape so wyde,
That victory they dare not wish to either side.

10

At last the Paynim chaunst to cast his eye,
    His suddein° eye, flaming with wrathfull fyre,   *darting*
    Upon his brothers shield, which hong thereby:

---

4. Garlands of victory.
5. I.e., their armor is too frail to withstand such blows.

6. A legendary monster, half eagle, half lion. "Seized": in possession.

85   Therewith redoubled was his raging yre,°   *anger*
         And said, "Ah wretched sonne of wofull syre,
         Doest thou sit wayling by black Stygian lake
         Whilest here thy shield is hangd for victors hyre,°   *reward*
         And sluggish german[7] doest thy forces slake,
90   To after-send his foe, that him may overtake?

                              11

         "Goe caytive° Elfe, him quickly overtake,   *miserable*
         And soone redeeme from his long wandring woe;
         Goe guiltie ghost, to him my message make,
         That I his shield have quit° from dying foe."   *rescued*
95   Therewith upon his crest he stroke him so,
         That twise he reelèd, readie twise to fall;
         End of the doubtfull battell deemèd tho
         The lookers on,[8] and lowd to him gan call
         The false Duessa, "Thine the shield, and I, and all."[9]

                              12

100 Soone as the Faerie heard his Ladie speake,
         Out of his swowning dreame he gan awake,
         And quickning° faith, that earst was woxen weake,   *life-restoring*
         The creeping deadly cold away did shake:
         Tho moved with wrath, and shame, and Ladies sake,°   *cause*
105   Of all attonce he cast° avengd to bee,   *determined*
         And with so'exceeding furie at him strake,
         That forcèd him to stoupe upon his knee;
         Had he not stoupèd so, he should have cloven bee,

                              13

         And to him said, "Goe now proud Miscreant,°   *misbeliever*
110   Thy selfe thy message doe° to german deare,   *give*
         Alone he wandring thee too long doth want:
         Goe say, his foe thy shield with his doth beare."
         Therewith his heavie hand he high gan reare,
         Him to have slaine; when loe a darkesome clowd
115   Upon him fell: he no where doth appeare,
         But vanisht is. The Elfe him cals alowd,
         But answer none receives: the darknes him does shrowd.[1]

                              14

         In haste Duessa from her place arose,
         And to him running said, "O prowest° knight,   *bravest*
120   That ever Ladie to her love did chose,
         Let now abate the terror of your might,
         And quench the flame of furious despight,°   *anger*
         And bloudie vengeance; lo th' infernall powres
         Covering your foe with cloud of deadly night,

---

7. Kinsman, here, brother. "Slake": slacken.
8. I.e., the onlookers then ("tho") thought this would end the battle, heretofore in doubt ("doubt-full").
9. Duessa is, of course, calling to Sans Joy, but

Redcrosse (lines 100 ff.) hears her as "Fidessa."
1. The device of a god rescuing a hero in danger by hiding him in a cloud has parallels in *Iliad* 3.380, *Aeneid* 5.810–12, and *Gerusalemme Liberata* 7.44–45.

125   Have borne him hence to Plutoes balefull bowres.[2]
        The conquest yours, I yours, the shield, and glory yours."

                                15
        Not all so satisfide, with greedie eye
            He sought all round about, his thirstie blade
            To bath in bloud of faithlesse enemy;
130   Who all that while lay hid in secret shade:
            He standes amazèd, how he thence should fade.
            At last the trumpets Triumph sound on hie,
            And running Heralds humble homage made,
            Greeting him goodly with new victorie,
135   And to him brought the shield, the cause of enmitie.

                                16
        Wherewith he goeth to that soveraine Queene,
            And falling her before on lowly knee,
            To her makes present of his service seene;°   proved
            Which she accepts, with thankes, and goodly gree,°   favor
140   Greatly advancing° his gay chevalree.   extolling
            So marcheth home, and by her takes the knight,
            Whom all the people follow with great glee,
            Shouting, and clapping all their hands on hight,[3]
            That all the aire it fils, and flyes to heaven bright.

                                17
145   Home is he brought, and laid in sumptuous bed:
            Where many skilfull leaches° him abide,°   doctors / attend
            To salve° his hurts, that yet still freshly bled.   annoint
            In wine and oyle they wash his woundes wide,
            And softly can embalme[4] on every side.
150   And all the while, most heavenly melody
            About the bed sweet musicke did divide,[5]
            Him to beguile of griefe and agony:
            And all the while Duessa wept full bitterly.

                                18
        As when a wearie traveller that strayes
155   By muddy shore of broad seven-mouthèd Nile,
            Unweeting of the perillous wandring wayes,
            Doth meet a cruell craftie Crocodile,
            Which in false griefe hyding his harmefull guile,
            Doth weepe full sore, and sheddeth tender teares:
160   The foolish man, that pitties all this while
            His mournefull plight, is swallowed up unwares,°   unexpectedly
            Forgetfull of his owne, that mindes anothers cares.

                                19
        So wept Duessa untill eventide,
            That shyning lampes in Joves high house were light:[6]
165   Then forth she rose, ne lenger would abide,

But comes unto the place, where th' Hethen knight
In slombring swownd nigh voyd of vitall spright,[7]
Lay covered with inchaunted cloud all day:
Whom when she found, as she him left in plight,[8]
170   To wayle his woefull case she would not stay,
But to the easterne coast of heaven makes speedy way.

20

Where griesly° Night, with visage deadly sad,   *grim, horrible*
That Phoebus chearefull face durst never vew,
And in a foule blacke pitchie mantle clad,
175   She findes forth comming from her darkesome mew,°   *den*
Where she all day did hide her hated hew.°   *shape, color*
Before the dore her yron charet stood,
Alreadie harness**è**d for journey new;
And cole blacke steedes yborne of hellish brood,
180   That on their rustie bits did champ, as they were wood.°   *mad*

21

Who when she saw Duessa sunny bright,
Adorned with gold and jewels shining cleare,°   *brightly*
She greatly grew amaz**è**d at the sight,
And th' unacquainted° light began to feare: *unfamiliar*
185   For never did such brightnesse there appeare,
And would have backe retyred to her cave,
Untill the witches speech she gan to heare,
Saying, "Yet O thou dreaded Dame, I crave
Abide,° till I have told the message, which I have."   *stay*

22

190 She stayd, and foorth Duessa gan proceede,
"O thou most auncient Grandmother of all,[9]
More old then Jove, whom thou at first didst breede,
Or that great house of Gods caelestiall,
Which wast begot in Daemogorgons hall,
195   And sawst the secrets of the world unmade,[1]
Why suffredst thou thy Nephewes° deare to rall   *grandsons*
With Elfin sword, most shamefully betrade?
Lo where the stout Sans joy doth sleepe in deadly shade.

23

"And him before, I saw with bitter eyes
200   The bold Sans foy shrinke underneath his speare;
And now the pray of fowles in field he lyes,
Nor wayld of friends, nor laid on groning beare,[2]
That whylome was to me too dearely deare.
O what of Gods then boots it[3] to be borne,
205   If old Aveugles sonnes so evill heare?[4]

---

7. Nearly ("nigh") devoid of life.
8. I.e., in the same desperate state she left him.
9. By tradition Night was eldest of the gods, existing before the world was formed and the Olympian gods were begotten in the hall of Demogorgon (Chaos).

1. Before it was made.
2. Bier attended by mourners ("groning").
3. What is it worth ("boots it").
4. I.e., are so badly thought of. "Aveugle" means "blind"; he is the son of Night and father of Sans Foy, Sans Joy, and Sans Loy.

Or who shall not great Nightes children scorne,
When two of three her Nephews are so fowle forlorne. [5]

24

"Up then, up dreary Dame, of darknesse Queene,
Go gather up the reliques of thy race,
210 Or else goe them avenge, and let be seene,
That dreaded Night in brightest day hath place,
And can the children of faire light deface."°   destroy
Her feeling speeches some compassion moved
In hart, and chaunge in that great mothers face:
215 Yet pittie in her hart was never proved°   known
Till then: for evermore she hated, never loved.

25

And said, "Deare daughter rightly may I rew
The fall of famous children borne of mee,
And good successes, which their foes ensew:°   attend
220 But who can turne the streame of destinee,
Or breake the chayne of strong necessitee,
Which fast is tyde to Joves eternall seat?[6]
The sonnes of Day he favoureth, I see,
And by my ruines thinkes to make them great:
225 To make one great by others losse, is bad excheat.°   exchange

26

"Yet shall they not escape so freely all;
For some shall pay the price of others guilt:
And he the man that made Sans foy to fall,
Shall with his owne bloud price that[7] he hath spilt.
230 But what art thou, that telst of Nephews kilt?"
"I that do seeme not I, Duessa am,"
Quoth she, "how ever now in garments gilt,
And gorgeous gold arayd I to thee came:
Duessa I, the daughter of Deceipt and Shame."

27

235 Then bowing downe her agèd backe, she kist
The wicked witch, saying; "In that faire face
The false resemblance of Deceipt, I wist
Did closely° lurke; yet so true-seeming grace   secretly
It carried, that I scarse in darkesome place
240 Could it discerne, though I the mother bee
Of falshood, and root of Duessaes race.
O welcome child, whom I have longd to see,
And now have seene unwares.° Lo now I go with thee."unexpectedly

28

Then to her yron wagon she betakes,
245 And with her beares the fowle welfavourd witch:
Through mirkesome° aire her readie way she makes. murky, dense

---

5. Wretchedly lost.   8.18–27).
6. The golden chain that binds the entire uni-   7. I.e., pay for what.
verse; the image goes back as far as Homer (*Iliad*

Her twyfold° Teme, of which two blacke as pitch,   *twofold*
And two were browne, yet each to each unlich,°   *unlike*
Did softly swim away, ne ever stampe,
250   Unlesse she chaunst their stubborne mouths to twitch;
Then forming tarre,[8] their bridles they would champe,
And trampling the fine element,[9] would fiercely rampe.

                    29

So well they sped, that they be come at length
Unto the place, whereas the Paynim lay,
255   Devoid of outward sense, and native strength,
Coverd with charmèd cloud from vew of day,
And sight of men, since his late luckelesse fray.
His cruell wounds with cruddy° bloud congealed,   *clotted*
They binden up so wisely,° as they may,   *skillfully*
260   And handle softly, till they can be healed:
So lay him in her charet, close in night concealed.

                    30

And all the while she stood upon the ground,
The wakefull dogs did never cease to bay,
As giving warning of th' unwonted° sound,   *unusual*
265   With which her yron wheeles did them affray,
And her darke griesly° looke them much dismay;   *horrid*
The messenger of death, the ghastly Owle
With drearie shriekes did also her bewray;°   *reveal*
And hungry Wolves continually did howle,
270   At her abhorrèd face, so filthy and so fowle.

                    31

Thence turning backe in silence soft they stole,
And brought the heavie corse with easie pace
To yawning gulfe of deepe Avernus hole.[1]
By that same hole an entrance darke and bace
275   With smoake and sulphure hiding all the place,
Descends to hell: there creature never past,
That backe returnèd without heavenly grace;
But dreadfull Furies, which their chaines have brast,°   *burst*
And damnèd sprights sent forth to make ill° men aghast.   *evil*

                    32

280   By that same way the direfull dames doe drive
Their mournefull charet, fild° with rusty blood,   *defiled*
And downe to Plutoes house are come bilive:°   *quickly, alive*
Which passing through, on every side them stood
The trembling ghosts with sad amazèd mood,
285   Chattring their yron teeth, and staring wide
With stonie eyes; and all the hellish brood

8. Black froth.
9. The air. "Rampe": rear up.
1. In classical mythology, Avernus is Hell, where
Pluto reigns (line 282). Acheron (line 289) and

Phlegeton (line 291) are rivers in Hell. Cerberus
(line 298), the three-headed dog, is guardian there.
Stanzas 31–35 recall Aeneas's descent into Hell
(Virgil, *Aeneid* 6.200, 239–40).

Of feends infernall flockt on every side,
To gaze on earthly wight, that with the Night durst ride.

33

They pas the bitter waves of Acheron,
290   Where many soules sit wailing woefully,
And come to fiery flood of Phlegeton,
Whereas the damnèd ghosts in torments fry,
And with sharpe shrilling shriekes doe bootlesse° cry,   *without avail*
Cursing high Jove, the which them thither sent.
295   The house of endlesse paine is built thereby,
In which ten thousand sorts of punishment
The cursèd creatures doe eternally torment.

34

Before the threshold dreadfull Cerberus
His three deformèd heads did lay along,°   *at full length*
300   Curled with thousands adders venemous,
And lillèd° forth his bloudie flaming tong: *lolled*
At them he gan to reare his bristles strong,
And felly gnarre,[2] untill dayes enemy
Did him appease; then downe his taile he hong
305   And suffered them to passen quietly:
For she in hell and heaven had power equally.

35

There was Ixion turnèd on a wheele,
For daring tempt the Queene of heaven to sin;
And Sisyphus an huge round stone did reele°   *roll*
310   Against an hill, ne° might from labour lin;°   *nor/cease*
There thirstie Tantalus hong by the chin;
And Tityus fed a vulture on his maw;°   *liver*
Typhoeus joynts were stretchèd on a gin,°   *rack*
Theseus condemned to endlesse slouth° by law,   *sloth*
315 And fifty sisters water in leake vessels draw.[3]

36

They all beholding worldly° wights in place,°   *mortal/there*
Leave off their worke, unmindfull of their smart,
To gaze on them; who forth by them doe pace,
Till they be come unto the furthest part:
320   Where was a Cave ywrought by wondrous art,
Deepe, darke, uneasie,° dolefull, comfortlesse,   *lacking ease*
In which sad Aesculapius farre a part
Emprisond was in chaines remedilesse,°   *beyond any remedy*
For that Hippolytus rent corse he did redresse.[4]

---

2. Savagely snarl.
3. Ixion was being punished for attempting to seduce Juno; Sisyphus for refusing to pray to the gods; Tantalus for stealing the gods' nectar; Tityus for having tried to seduce Apollo's mother; the monster Typhoeus for creating destructive winds; Theseus for stealing Persephone from Hades; and the daughters of King Danaus for having killed their husbands on their wedding night. Tantalus stood chin-deep in water which receded whenever he tried to drink—hence he is "thirstie." Ovid, Virgil, and Homer are Spenser's sources here.
4. Aesculapius was god of medicine. "Redresse": cure.

37

325   Hippolytus a jolly° huntsman was,   *gallant*
      That wont° in charet chace the foming Bore;   *used to*
      He all his Peeres in beautie did surpas,
      But Ladies love as losse of time forbore:
      His wanton stepdame[5] lovèd him the more,
330   But when she saw her offred sweets refused
      Her love she turnd to hate, and him before
      His father fierce of treason false accused,
  And with her gealous° termes his open eares
         abused.   *arousing jealousy*

38

  Who all in rage his Sea-god syre[6] besought,
335   Some cursèd vengeance on his sonne to cast:
      From surging gulf two monsters straight were brought,
      With dread whereof his chasing steedes aghast,
      Both charet swift and huntsman overcast.
      His goodly corps on ragged cliffs yrent,
340   Was quite dismembred, and his members chast
      Scattered on every mountaine, as he went,
  That of Hippolytus was left no moniment.[7]

39

  His cruell stepdame seeing what was donne,
      Her wicked dayes with wretched knife did end,
345   In death avowing th' innocence of her sonne.
      Which hearing his rash Syre, began to rend
      His haire, and hastie tongue, that did offend:
      Tho gathering up the relicks of his smart[8]
      By Dianes meanes, who was Hippolyts frend,
350   Them brought to Aesculape, that by his art
  Did heale them all againe, and joynèd every part.

40

  Such wondrous science in mans wit to raine
      When Jove avizd,° that could the dead revive,   *discovered*
      And fates expirèd[9] could renew againe,
355   Of endlesse life he might him not deprive,
      But unto hell did thrust him downe alive,
      With flashing thunderbolt ywounded sore:
      Where long remaining, he did alwaies strive
      Himselfe with salves to health for to restore,
360   And slake the heavenly fire, that raged evermore.

41

  There auncient Night arriving, did alight
      From her nigh wearie waine,[1] and in her armes
      To Aesculapius brought the wounded knight:

---

5. Phaedra, the wife of his father, Theseus.   "Tho": then.
6. Poseidon (Neptune).   9. The completed term of life as fixed by the Fates.
7. I.e., no trace of identity.   1. I.e., the horses of Night's chariot are nearly
8. I.e., his son's remains, that caused his grief.   exhausted.

Whom having softly disarayd of armes,
365   Tho gan to him discover all his harmes,
    Beseeching him with prayer, and with praise,
    If either salves, or oyles, or herbes, or charmes
    A fordonne° wight from dore of death mote raise,   *undone*
    He would at her request prolong her nephews daies.

42

370 "Ah Dame," quoth he, "thou temptest me in vaine,
    To dare the thing, which daily yet I rew,
    And the old cause of my continued paine
    With like attempt to like end to renew.
    Is not enough, that thrust from heaven dew[2]
375   Here endlesse penance for one fault I pay,
    But that redoubled crime with vengeance new
    Thou biddest me to eeke?° Can Night defray°   *increase/appease*
    The wrath of thundring Jove, that rules both night and day?"

43

"Not so," quoth she; "but sith that heavens king
380   From hope of heaven hath thee excluded quight,
    Why fearest thou, that canst not hope for thing,°   *anything*
    And fearest not, that more thee hurten might,
    Now in the powre of everlasting Night?
    Goe to them, O thou farre renowmèd sonne
385   Of great Apollo, shew thy famous might
    In medicine, that else° hath to thee wonne   *already*
    Great paines, and greater praise, both never to be donne."°   *ended*

44

Her words prevaild: And then the learnèd leach°   *doctor*
    His cunning hand gan to his wounds to lay,
390   And all things else, the which his art did teach:
    Which having seene, from thence arose away
    The mother of dread darknesse, and let stay
    Aveugles sonne there in the leaches cure,°   *care*
    And backe returning tooke her wonted way,
395   To runne her timely race,[3] whilst Phoebus pure
    In westerne waves his wearie wagon did recure.°   *refresh*

45

The false Duessa leaving noyous° Night,   *harmful*
    Returnd to stately pallace of dame Pride;
    Where when she came, she found the Faery knight
400   Departed thence, albe° his woundes wide   *although*
    Not throughly heald, unreadie were to ride.
    Good cause he had to hasten thence away;
    For on a day his wary Dwarfe had spide,
    Where in a dongeon deepe huge numbers lay
405   Of caytive° wretched thrals,° that waylèd night   *captive/slaves*
    and day.

---

2. The proper ("due") place for a god.   3. Her nightly journey.

46

A ruefull sight, as could be seene with eie;
Of whom he learnèd had in secret wise
The hidden cause of their captivitie,
How mortgaging their lives to Covetise,
410   Through wastfull° Pride, and wanton Riotise,   *causing desolation*
They were by law of that proud Tyrannesse[4]
Provokt with Wrath, and Envies false surmise,
Condemnèd to that Dongeon mercilesse,
Where they should live in woe, and die in wretchednesse.

47

415 There was that great proud king of Babylon[5]
That would compell all nations to adore,
And him as onely God to call upon,
Till through celestiall doome° throwne out of dore,   *judgment*
Into an Oxe he was transformed of yore:
420   There also was king Croesus,[6] that enhaunst°   *exalted*
His heart too high through his great riches store;
And proud Antiochus,[7] the which advaunst
His cursèd hand gainst God, and on his altars daunst.°   *danced*

48

And them long time before, great Nimrod[8] was,
425   That first the world with sword and fire warrayd;°   *ravaged*
And after him old Ninus farre did pas°   *surpass*
In princely pompe, of all the world obayd;
There also was that mightie Monarch layd
Low under all, yet above all in pride,
430   That name of native° syre did fowle upbrayd,   *natural*
And would as Ammons sonne[9] be magnifide,
Till scornd of God and man a shamefull death he dide.

49

All these together in one heape were throwne,
Like carkases of beasts in butchers stall.
435 And in another corner wide were strowne
The antique ruines of the Romaines fall:
Great Romulus[1] the Grandsyre of them all,
Proud Tarquin, and too lordly Lentulus,
Stout Scipio, and stubborne Hanniball,
440   Ambitious Sylla, and sterne Marius,
High Caesar, great Pompey, and fierce Antonius.

---

4. Lucifera. The noble sinners named in stanzas 47–50 exemplify a theme common in Renaissance morality, the fall of princes.
5. Nebuchadnezzar (Daniel 3–4).
6. King of Lydia, famous for his riches.
7. King of Syria, who desecrated the Jewish temple of Jerusalem (1 Maccabees 1.20–24).
8. Nimrod, identified as the first tyrant, caused the Tower of Babel to be built in defiance of God (Genesis 10.9). Ninus was founder of Ninevah,

archetype of the wicked city (See the Book of Jonah).
9. Alexander the Great, occasionally worshiped as the son of Jupiter Ammon.
1. Romulus, founder of Rome; Tarquin, Roman tyrant; Lentulus, a conspirator with Catiline; Scipio, Roman general, conqueror of Carthage; Hannibal, Carthaginian general; Sulla, Roman civil war general; Marius, Sulla's rival; Julius Caesar; Pompey the Great; and Mark Anthony. All are memorialized in Plutarch's *Lives*.

50

Amongst these mighty men were wemen mixt,
   Proud wemen, vaine, forgetfull of their yoke:°   *duty*
   The bold Semiramis,[2] whose sides transfixt
445   With sonnes owne blade, her fowle reproches spoke;
   Faire Sthenoboea,[3] that her selfe did choke
   With wilfull cord, for wanting° of her will;   *lacking*
   High minded Cleopatra, that with stroke
   Of Aspes sting her selfe did stoutly kill:
450 And thousands moe the like, that did that dongeon fill.

51

Besides the endlesse routs° of wretched thralles,   *crowds*
   Which thither were assembled day by day,
   From all the world after their wofull falles,
   Through wicked pride, and wasted wealthes decay.
455   But most of all, which in that Dongeon lay
   Fell from high Princes courts, or Ladies bowres,
   Where they in idle pompe, or wanton play,
   Consumèd had their goods, and thriftlesse howres,
And lastly throwne themselves into these heavy stowres.°   *disasters*

52

460 Whose case wheneas the carefull° Dwarfe had tould,   *anxious*
   And made ensample of their mournefull sight
   Unto his maister, he no lenger would
   There dwell in perill of like painefull plight,
   But early rose, and ere that dawning light
465   Discovered had the world to heaven wyde,
   He by a privie Posterne° tooke his flight,   *gate*
   That of no envious eyes he mote be spyde:
For doubtlesse death ensewd, if any him descryde.

53

Scarse could he footing find in that fowle way,
470   For many corses, like a great Lay-stall°   *rubbish heap*
   Of murdred men which therein strowèd lay,
   Without remorse, or decent funerall:
   Which all through that great Princesse pride did fall
   And came to shamefull end. And them beside
475   Forth ryding underneath the castell wall,
   A donghill of dead carkases he spide,
The dreadfull spectacle of that sad house of Pride.[4]

Canto 6

*From lawlesse lust by wondrous grace
fayre Una is releast:*

---

2. Wife of Ninus.
3. Queen of King Proteus of Argos, who lusted after her brother-in-law Bellerophon.

4. Named now, after we have been shown what the name means. "Spectacle": example.

> Whom salvage° nation does adore,   *wild, of the woods*
> and learnes her wise beheast.°   *bidding*

1

As when a ship, that flyes faire under saile,
    An hidden rocke escapèd hath unwares,°   *unexpectedly*
    That lay in waite her wrack for to bewaile,[1]
    The Marriner yet halfe amazèd stares
5   At perill past, and yet in doubt ne dares
    To joy at his foole-happie oversight:[2]
    So doubly is distrest twixt joy and cares
    The dreadlesse° courage of this Elfin knight,   *fearless*
Having escapt so sad ensamples in his sight.

2

10 Yet sad he was that his too hastie speed
    The faire Duess' had forst him leave behind;
    And yet more sad, that Una his deare dreed°   *object of reverence*
    Her truth had staind with treason so unkind;
    Yet crime in her could never creature find,
15   But for his love, and for her owne selfe sake,
    She wandred had from one to other Ynd,[3]
    Him for to seeke, ne ever would forsake,
Till her unwares the fierce Sansloy did overtake.

3

Who after Archimagoes fowle defeat,
20   Led her away into a forrest wilde,
    And turning wrathfull fire to lustfull heat,
    With beastly sin thought her to have defilde,
    And made the vassall of his pleasures vilde.°   *vile*
    Yet first he cast by treatie,° and by traynes,°   *persuasion/tricks*
25   Her to perswade, that stubborne fort to yilde:
    For greater conquest of hard love he gaynes,
That workes it to his will, then he that it constraines.°   *forces*

4

With fawning wordes he courted her a while,
    And looking lovely,° and oft sighing sore,   *lovingly*
30   Her constant hart did tempt with diverse guile:
    But wordes, and lookes, and sighes she did abhore,
    As rocke of Diamond stedfast evermore.[4]
    Yet for to feed his fyrie lustfull eye,
    He snatcht the vele, that hong her face before;
35   Then gan her beautie shine, as brightest skye,
And burnt his beastly hart t' efforce° her chastitye.   *violate*

5

So when he saw his flatt'ring arts to fayle,
    And subtile engines bet from batteree,[5]

---

1. I.e., cause the shipwreck and thereby cause it
to be bewailed.
2. Lucky ignorance.
3. I.e., she would have wandered from the East
to the West Indies.

4. The diamond, because of its hardness, was an
emblem of fidelity.
5. I.e., beaten ("bet") from their fruitless assault
("batteree") upon her unmovable virtue.

With greedy force he gan the fort assayle,
40   Whereof he weend° possessèd soone to bee,   *thought*
  And win rich spoile of ransackt chastetee.
  Ah heavens, that do this hideous act behold,
  And heavenly virgin thus outragèd see,
  How can ye vengeance just so long withhold,
45 And hurle not flashing flames upon that Paynim bold?

6

The pitteous maden carefull° comfortlesse,   *full of cares*
  Does throw out thrilling° shriekes, and shrieking cryes,   *piercing*
  The last vaine helpe of womens great distresse,
  And with loud plaints importuneth the skyes,
50 That molten starres do drop like weeping eyes;
  And Phoebus flying so most shamefull sight,
  His blushing face in foggy cloud implyes,[6]
  And hides for shame. What wit of mortall wight
Can now devise to quit a thrall[7] from such a plight?

7

55 Eternall providence exceeding° thought,   *transcending*
  Where none appeares can make her selfe a way:
  A wondrous way it for this Lady wrought,
  From Lyons clawes to pluck the gripèd pray.
  Her shrill outcryes and shriekes so loud did bray,
60 That all the woodes and forestes did resownd;
  A troupe of Faunes and Satyres[8] far away
  Within the wood were dauncing in a rownd,
Whiles old Sylvanus slept in shady arber sownd.

8

Who when they heard that pitteous strainèd voice,
65 In hast forsooke their rurall meriment,
  And ran towards the far rebownded° noyce,   *re-echoed*
  To weet, what wight so loudly did lament.
  Unto the place they come incontinent:°   *immediately*
  Whom when the raging Sarazin espide,
70 A rude, misshapen, monstrous rablement,
  Whose like he never saw, he durst not bide,
But got his ready steed, and fast away gan ride.

9

The wyld woodgods arrivèd in the place,
  There find the virgin dolefull desolate,
75 With ruffled rayments, and faire blubbred° face,   *flooded with tears*
  As her outrageous foe had left her late,
  And trembling yet through feare of former hate;
  All stand amazèd at so uncouth° sight,   *strange*
  And gin to pittie her unhappie state,

---

6. The sun is overcast by clouds. "Implyes": buries.
7. Release a victim.
8. Woodland deities with men's bodies above the waist and goats' bodies below, noted for their sensuality. Sylvanus, Roman god of the woods, is traditionally associated with fauns.

80   All stand astonied° at her beautie bright,   *stupified*
      In their rude° eyes unworthie° of so wofull plight. *rustic/undeserving*

                              10

      She more amazed, in double dread doth dwell;
          And every tender part for feare does shake:
          As when a greedie Wolfe through hunger fell
85   A seely° Lambe farre from the flocke does take,   *innocent*
          Of whom he meanes his bloudie feast to make,
          A Lyon spyes fast running towards him,
          The innocent pray in hast he does forsake,
          Which quit from death yet quakes in every lim
90   With chaunge of feare, to see the Lyon looke so grim.°   *savage*

                              11

      Such fearefull fit assaid° her trembling hart,   *assailed*
          Ne word to speake, ne joynt to move she had:
          The salvage nation feele her secret smart,
          And read her sorrow in her count'nance sad;
95   Their frowning forheads with rough hornes yclad,
          And rusticke horror° all a side doe lay,   *roughness*
          And gently grenning, shew a semblance glad
          To comfort her, and feare to put away,
      Their backward bent knees teach her humbly to obay.[9]

                              12

100   The doubtfull Damzell dare not yet commit
          Her single person to their barbarous truth,[1]
          But still twixt feare and hope amazd does sit,
          Late learnd° what harme to hastie trust ensu'th,   *taught*
          They in compassion of her tender youth,
105   And wonder of her beautie soveraine,
          Are wonne with pitty and unwonted ruth,°   *pity*
          And all prostrate upon the lowly plaine,
      Do kisse her feete, and fawne on her with count'nance faine.° *glad*

                              13

      Their harts she ghesseth by their humble guise,°   *appearance*
110   And yieldes her to extremitie of time;[2]
          So from the ground she fearelesse doth arise,
          And walketh forth without suspect° of crime: *suspicion*
          They all as glad, as birdes of joyous Prime,°   *springtime*
          Thence lead her forth, about her dauncing round,
115   Shouting, and singing all a shepheards ryme,
          And with greene braunches strowing all the ground,
      Do worship her, as Queene, with olive girlond cround.

                              14

      And all the way their merry pipes they sound,
          That all the woods with doubled Eccho ring,
120   And with their hornèd feet do weare the ground,

---

9. I.e., teach their knees, bent backwards like a   ("barbarous truth").
goat's, to obey her.   2. I.e., necessity of the time.
1. I.e., her solitary self to their wild allegiance

Leaping like wanton kids in pleasant Spring.
So towards old Sylvanus they her bring;
Who with the noyse awakèd, commeth out,
To weet° the cause, his weake steps governing   *learn*
125   And agèd limbs on Cypresse stadle° stout,   *staff*
And with an yvie twyne his wast is girt about.

                              15
Far off he wonders, what them makes so glad,
Or Bacchus merry fruit they did invent,[3]
Or Cybeles franticke rites[4] have made them mad;
130   They drawing nigh, unto their God present
That flowre of faith and beautie excellent.
The God himselfe vewing that mirrhour rare,
Stood long amazd, and burnt in his intent;[5]
His owne faire Dryope now he thinkes not faire,
135   And Pholoe fowle, when her to this he doth compaire.[6]

                              16
The woodborne people fall before her flat,
And worship her as Goddesse of the wood;
And old Sylvanus selfe bethinkes not,[7] what
To thinke of wight so faire, but gazing stood,
140   In doubt to deeme her borne of earthly brood;
Sometimes Dame Venus selfe he seemes to see,
But Venus never had so sober mood;
Sometimes Diana he her takes to bee,
But misseth bow, and shaftes, and buskins° to her knee.   *soft boots*

                              17
145   By vew of her he ginneth to revive
His ancient love, and dearest Cyparisse,[8]
And calles to mind his pourtraiture alive,[9]
How faire he was, and yet not faire to this,
And how he slew with glauncing dart amisse
150   A gentle Hynd, the which the lovely boy
Did love as life, above all worldly blisse;
For griefe whereof the lad n'ould° after joy,   *would not*
But pynd away in anguish and selfe-wild annoy.°   *suffering*

                              18
The wooddy Nymphes, faire Hamadryades[1]
155   Her to behold do thither runne apace,
And all the troupe of light-foot Naiades,[2]
Flocke all about to see her lovely face:
But when they vewèd have her heavenly grace,

3. I.e., whether ("or") they did find ("invent") wine
grapes.
4. Orgiastic dances in worship of Cybele, goddess
of the powers of Nature.
5. Glowed with intense concentration. Una is a
"mirrhour rare" in that she reflects heavenly beauty.
6. Dryope and Pholoe were nymphs loved by
Faunus and Pan; for Spenser, the names "Faunus,"
"Pan," and "Sylvanus" were apparently interchangeable.
7. Cannot decide.
8. A fair youth, beloved of Sylvanus, turned into
a cypress tree.
9. I.e., his appearance when alive.
1. Spirits of trees whose lives ended when the tree
they inhabited died.
2. Water nymphs.

> They envie her in their malitious mind,
160 And fly away for feare of fowle disgrace:
> But all the Satyres scorne their woody kind,[3]
> And henceforth nothing faire, but her on earth they find.

19

> Glad of such lucke, the luckelesse lucky maid,
> Did her content to please their feeble eyes,
165 And long time with that salvage people staid,
> To gather breath in many miseries.
> During which time her gentle wit she plyes,
> To teach them truth, which worshipt her in vaine,
> And made her th' Image of Idolatryes;[4]
170 But when their bootlesse zeale she did restraine
> From her own worship, they her Asse would worship fayn.°   *willingly*

20

> It fortunèd a noble warlike knight
> By just occasion to that forrest came,
> To seeke his kindred, and the lignage right,°   *true*
175 From whence he tooke his well deservèd name:
> He had in armes abroad wonne muchell° fame,   *great*
> And fild far landes with glorie of his might,
> Plaine, faithfull, true, and enimy of shame,
> And ever loved to fight for Ladies right,
180 But in vaine glorious frayes he litle did delight.

21

> A Satyres sonne yborne in forrest wyld,
> By straunge adventure as it did betyde,°   *happen*
> And there begotten of a Lady myld,
> Faire Thyamis the daughter of Labryde,
185 That was in sacred bands of wedlocke tyde
> To Therion, a loose unruly swayne;[5]
> Who had more joy to raunge the forrest wyde,
> And chase the salvage beast with busie payne,[6]
> Then serve his Ladies love, and wast° in pleasures vayne.   *live idly*

22

190 The forlorne mayd did with loves longing burne,
> And could not lacke° her lovers company,   *be without*
> But to the wood she goes, to serve her turne,
> And seeke her spouse, that from her still does fly,
> And followes other game and venery:[7]
195 A Satyre chaunst her wandring for to find,
> And kindling coles of lust in brutish eye,
> The loyall links of wedlocke did unbind,
> And made her person thrall unto his beastly kind.

---

3. Forest inhabitants.
4. The idol of their idolatries.
5. "Thyamis" means passion; "Labryde," turbulent; "Therion," wild beast.

6. Painstaking care.
7. The word means both "hunting" and "sexual play."

23

So long in secret cabin there he held
200 Her captive to his sensuall desire,
     Till that with timely fruit her belly sweld,
     And bore a boy unto that salvage sire:
     Then home he suffred her for to retire,°   return
     For ransome leaving him the late borne childe;
205 Whom till to ryper yeares he gan aspire,°   grow up
     He noursled° up in life and manners wilde,   reared
Emongst wild beasts and woods, from lawes of men exilde.

24

For all he taught the tender ymp,° was but   child
     To banish cowardize and bastard° feare;   base
210 His trembling hand he would him force to put
     Upon the Lyon and the rugged Beare,
     And from the she Beares teats her whelps to teare;
     And eke wyld roring Buls he would him make
     To tame, and ryde their backes not made to beare;
215 And the Robuckes[8] in flight to overtake,
That every beast for feare of him did fly and quake.

25

Thereby so fearelesse, and so fell° he grew,   fierce
     That his owne sire and maister of his guise[9]
     Did often tremble at his horrid vew,[1]
220 And oft for dread of hurt would him advise,
     The angry beasts not rashly to despise,
     Nor too much to provoke; for he would learne°   teach
     The Lyon stoup to him in lowly wise,
     (A lesson hard) and make the Libbard° sterne   leopard
225 Leave roaring, when in rage he for revenge did earne.°   yearn

26

And for to make his powre approvèd° more,   demonstrated
     Wyld beasts in yron yokes he would compell;
     The spotted Panther, and the tuskèd Bore,
     The Pardale° swift, and the Tigre cruell;   female leopard
230 The Antelope, and Wolfe both fierce and fell;°   savage
     And them constraine in equall teme[2] to draw.
     Such joy he had, their stubborne harts to quell,
     And sturdie courage tame with dreadfull aw,
That his beheast they fearèd, as a tyrans law.

27

235 His loving mother came upon a day
     Unto the woods, to see her little sonne;
     And chaunst unwares° to meet him in the way,   unexpectedly
     After his sportes, and cruell pastime donne,
     When after him a Lyonesse did runne,

8. Deer, especially noted for their speed.   1. Rough appearance.
9. Teacher of his behavior.   2. Side by side, yoked together in a team.

240   That roaring all with rage, did lowd requere°   *demand*
      Her children deare, whom he away had wonne:°   *seized*
      The Lyon whelpes she saw how he did beare,
   And lull in rugged armes, withouten childish feare.

28

   The fearefull Dame all quakèd at the sight,
245   And turning backe, gan fast to fly away,
      Untill with love revokt° from vaine affright,   *recalled*
      She hardly° yet perswaded was to stay,   *with difficulty*
      And then to him these womanish words gan say;
      "Ah Satyrane, my dearling, and my joy,
250   For love of me leave off this dreadfull play;
      To dally thus with death, is no fit toy,
   Go find some other play-fellowes, mine own sweet boy."

29

   In these and like delights of bloudy game
      He traynèd was, till ryper yeares he raught,°   *reached*
255   And there abode, whilst any beast of name
      Walkt in that forest, whom he had not taught
      To feare his force: and then his courage haught°   *high*
      Desird of forreine foemen to be knowne;
      And far abroad for straunge adventures sought:
260   In which his might was never overthrowne,
   But through all Faery lond his famous worth was blown.°   *spread*

30

   Yet evermore it was his manner faire,
      After long labours and adventures spent,
      Unto those native woods for to repaire,°   *return*
265   To see his sire and ofspring° auncient.   *origin*
      And now he thither came for like intent;
      Where he unwares the fairest Una found,
      Straunge Lady, in so straunge habiliment,°   *attire*
      Teaching the Satyres, which her sat around,
270   Trew sacred lore, which from her sweet lips did redound.°   *flow*

31

   He wondred at her wisedome heavenly rare,
      Whose like in womens wit he never knew;
      And when her curteous deeds he did compare,
      Gan her admire, and her sad sorrowes rew,°   *pity*
275   Blaming of Fortune, which such troubles threw,
      And joyd to make proofe of her crueltie
      On gentle Dame, so hurtlesse,° and so trew: *harmless*
      Thenceforth he kept her goodly company,
   And learnd her discipline° of faith and veritie.   *teachings*

32

280   But she all vowd[3] unto the Redcrosse knight,
      His wandring perill closely° did lament,   *secretly*

---

3. Entirely promised.

Ne in this new acquaintaunce could delight,
But her deare° heart with anguish did torment,   *loving*
And all her wit in secret counsels spent,
285   How to escape. At last in privie wise[4]
To Satyrane she shewèd her intent;
Who glad to gain such favour, gan devise,
How with that pensive Maid he best might thence arise.°   *depart*

33

So on a day when Satyres all were gone,
290   To do their service to Sylvanus old,
The gentle virgin left behind alone
He led away with courage stout and bold.
Too late it was, to Satyres to be told,
Or ever hope recover her againe:
295   In vaine he seekes that having cannot hold.
So fast he carried her with carefull paine,[5]
That they the woods are past, and come now to the plaine.

34

The better part now of the lingring day,
They traveild had, when as they farre espide
300   A wearie wight forwandring° by the way,   *wandering far and wide*
And towards him they gan in hast to ride,
To weet of newes, that did abroad betide,
Or tydings of her knight of the Redcrosse.
But he them spying, gan to turne aside,
305   For feare as seemid, or for some fieignèd losse;[6]
More greedy they of newes, fast towards him do crosse.

35

A silly° man, in simple weedes forworne,°   *simple/worn out*
And soild with dust of the long dried way;
His sandales were with toilesome travell torne,
310   And face all tand with scorching sunny ray,
As he had traveild many a sommers day,
Through boyling sands of Arabie and Ynde;°   *India*
And in his hand a Jacobs staffe,[7] to stay
His wearie limbes upon: and eke behind,
315 His scrip° did hang, in which his needments he did bind.   *bag*

36

The knight approching nigh, of him inquerd
Tydings of warre, and of adventures new;
But warres, nor new adventures none he herd.
Then Una gan to aske, if ought he knew,
320   Or heard abroad of that her champion trew,
That in his armour bare a croslet° red.   *small cross*
"Aye me, Deare dame," quoth he, "well may I rew

---

4. Privately.
5. Painstaking care.

6. Pretended harm.
7. I.e., pilgrim's staff.

To tell the sad sight, which mine eies have red:°   *beheld*
These eyes did see that knight both living and eke ded."

37

325 That cruell word her tender hart so thrild,°   *pierced*
    That suddein cold did runne through every vaine,
    And stony horrour all her sences fild
    With dying fit,[8] that downe she fell for paine.
    The knight her lightly° rearèd up againe,   *quickly*
330 And comforted with curteous kind reliefe:
    Then wonne from death, she bad him tellen plaine
    The further processe° of her hidden griefe;   *account*
The lesser pangs can beare, who hath endured the chiefe.

38

Then gan the Pilgrim thus, "I chaunst this day,
335 This fatall day, that shall I ever rew,
    To see two knights in travell on my way
    (A sory° sight) arraunged in battell new,   *grievous*
    Both breathing vengeaunce, both of wrathfull hew:
    My fearefull flesh did tremble at their strife,
340 To see their blades so greedily imbrew,[9]
    That drunke with bloud, yet thristed after life:
What more? the Redcrosse knight was slaine with Paynim knife."

39

"Ah dearest Lord," quoth she, "how might that bee,
    And he the stoutest knight, that ever wonne?"°   *lived*
345 "Ah dearest dame," quoth he, "how might I see
    The thing, that might not be, and yet was donne?"
    "Where is," said Satyrane, "that Paynims sonne,
    That him of life, and us of joy hath reft?"
    "Not far away," quoth he, "he hence doth wonne°   *stay*
350 Foreby° a fountaine, where I late him left   *close by*
Washing his bloudy wounds, that through° the steele were cleft."   *by*

40

Therewith the knight thence marchèd forth in hast,
    Whiles Una with huge heavinesse° opprest,   *grief*
    Could not for sorrow follow him so fast;
355 And soone he came, as he the place had ghest,
    Whereas that Pagan proud him selfe did rest,
    In secret shadow by a fountaine side:
    Even he it was, that earst would have supprest°   *violated*
    Faire Una: whom when Satyrane espide,
360 With fowle reprochfull words he boldly him defide.

41

And said, "Arise thou cursèd Miscreaunt,°   *infidel*
    That hast with knightlesse° guile and trecherous   *unknightly*
      train°   *deceit*

---

8. Deathlike swoon.   9. Soak themselves in blood.

Faire knighthood fowly shamed, and doest vaunt
That good knight of the Redcrosse to have slain:
365 Arise, and with like treason now maintain°   *defend*
Thy guilty wrong, or else thee guilty yield."
The Sarazin this hearing, rose amain,°   *at once*
And catching up in hast his three square[1] shield,
And shining helmet, soone him buckled to the field.

42

370 And drawing nigh him said, "Ah misborne Elfe,[2]
In evill houre thy foes thee hither sent,
Anothers wrongs to wreake upon thy selfe:
Yet ill thou blamest me, for having blent°   *stained*
My name with guile and traiterous intent;
375 That Redcrosse knight, perdie, I never slew,
But had he beene, where earst° his armes were lent,   *before*
Th' enchaunter vaine his errour should not rew:
But thou his errour shalt, I hope now proven trew."[3]

43

Therewith they gan, both furious and fell,°   *fierce*
380 To thunder blowes, and fiersly to assaile
Each other bent° his enimy to quell,°   *determined/kill*
That with their force they perst° both plate and maile, *pierced*
And made wide furrowes in their fleshes fraile,
That it would pitty° any living eie.   *bring pity to*
385 Large floods of bloud adowne their sides did raile:°   *flow*
But floods of bloud could not them satisfie:
Both hungred after death: both chose to win, or die.

44

So long they fight, and fell revenge pursue,
That fainting each, themselves to breathen let,
390 And oft refreshèd, battell oft renue:
As when two Bores with rancling malice met,
Their gory sides fresh bleeding fiercely fret,°   *tear*
Til breathlesse both them selves aside retire,
Where foming wrath, their cruell tuskes they whet,
395 And trample th' earth, the whiles they may respire
Then backe to fight againe, new breathèd and entire.°   *fresh*

45

So fiersly, when these knights had breathèd once,
They gan to fight returne, increasing more
Their puissant force, and cruell rage attonce,
400 With heapèd strokes more hugely, then before,
That with their drerie° wounds and bloudy gore   *gory*
They both deformèd,° scarsely could be known.   *disfigured*

---

1. Triangular.
2. Base-born knight of Faerie Land ("Elfe").
3. I.e., had Redcrosse been wearing his arms the enchanter Archimago would not have to regret his error in fighting me. But you will now repeat his error in fighting me and demonstrate what an error it is.

By this sad Una fraught with anguish sore,
Led with their noise, which through the aire was thrown,
405   Arrived, where they in erth their fruitles bloud had sown.

46

Whom all so soone as that proud Sarazin
Espide, he gan revive the memory
Of his lewd lusts, and late attempted sin,
And left the doubtfull° battell hastily,   *undecided*
410   To catch her, newly offred to his eie:
But Satyrane with strokes him turning, staid,
And sternely bad him other businesse plie,
Then hunt the steps of pure unspotted Maid:
Wherewith he all enraged, these bitter speaches said.

47

415   "O foolish faeries sonne, what furie mad
Hath thee incenst, to hast thy dolefull fate?
Were it not better, I that Lady had,
Then that thou hadst repented it too late?
Most sencelesse man he, that himselfe doth hate,
420   To love another. Lo then for thine ayd
Here take thy lovers token on thy pate."
So they to fight; the whiles the royall Mayd
Fled farre away, of that proud Paynim sore afrayd.

48

But that false Pilgrim, which that leasing° told,   *lie*
425   Being in deed old Archimage, did stay
In secret shadow, all this to behold,
And much rejoycèd in their bloudy fray:
But when he saw the Damsell passe away
He left his stond,° and her pursewd apace,   *place*
430   In hope to bring her to her last decay.°   *death*
But for to tell her lamentable cace,
And eke this battels end, will need another place.

Canto 7

*The Redcrosse knight is captive made
By Gyaunt proud opprest,°*   *overwhelmed*
*Prince Arthur meets with Una great-
ly with those newes distrest.*

1

What man so wise, what earthly wit so ware,°   *wary*
As to descry° the crafty cunning traine,°   *perceive/guile*
By which deceipt doth maske in visour° faire,   *a mask*
And cast her colours dyèd deepe in graine,[1]

---

1. I.e., Deceit disposes her colors, thoroughly dyed, so as to seem like Truth.

5   To seeme like Truth, whose shape she well can faine,
     And fitting gestures to her purpose frame,
     The guiltlesse man with guile to entertaine?°   *receive*
     Great maistresse of her art was that false Dame,
The false Duessa, clokèd with Fidessaes name.

2

10   Who when returning from the drery° Night,   *dismal*
     She fownd not in that perilous house of Pryde,
     Where she had left, the noble Redcrosse knight,
     Her hopèd pray, she would no lenger bide,
     But forth she went, to seeke him far and wide.
15   Ere long she fownd, whereas° he wearie sate,   *where*
     To rest him selfe, foreby° a fountaine side,   *beside*
     Disarmèd all of yron-coted Plate,
And by his side his steed the grassy forage ate.

3

     He feedes upon the cooling shade, and bayes[2]
20   His sweatie forehead in the breathing wind,
     Which through the trembling leaves full gently playes
     Wherein the cherefull birds of sundry kind
     Do chaunt sweet musick, to delight his mind:
     The Witch approaching gan him fairely° greet,   *courteously*
25   And with reproch of carelesnesse unkind
     Upbrayd, for leaving her in place unmeet,°   *unfitting*
With fowle words tempring faire, soure gall with hony sweet.

4

     Unkindnesse past, they gan of solace treat,°   *speak*
     And bathe in pleasaunce of the joyous shade,
30   Which shielded them against the boyling heat,
     And with greene boughes decking a gloomy glade,
     About the fountaine like a girlond made;
     Whose bubbling wave did ever freshly well,
     Ne ever would through fervent° sommer fade:°   *hot/dry up*
35   The sacred Nymph, which therein wont to dwell,
Was out of Dianes favour, as it then befell.

5

     The cause was this: one day when Phoebe[3] fayre
     With all her band was following the chace,
     This Nymph, quite tyred with heat of scorching ayre
40   Sat downe to rest in middest of the race:
     The goddesse wroth gan fowly her disgrace,
     And bad the waters, which from her did flow,
     Be such as she her selfe was then in place.[4]
     Thenceforth her waters waxèd dull and slow,
45   And all that drunke thereof, did faint and feeble grow.

---

2. Bathes. "Feedes upon": enjoys.
3. I.e., Diana, goddess of the moon and of chastity.
4. I.e., in that place.

6

Hereof this gentle knight unweeting° was,   *ignorant*
   And lying downe upon the sandie graile,°   *gravel*
   Drunke of the streame, as cleare as cristall glas;
   Eftsoones his manly forces gan to faile,
50   And mightie strong was turnd to feeble fraile.
   His chaunged powres at first themselves not felt,
   Till crudled° cold his corage° gan assaile,   *congealing/vigor*
   And chearefull° bloud in faintnesse chill did melt,   *lively*
Which like a fever fit through all his body swelt.°   *raged*

7

55 Yet goodly court he made still to his Dame,
   Pourd out in loosnesse[5] on the grassy grownd,
   Both carelesse of his health, and of his fame:
   Till at the last he heard a dreadfull sownd,
   Which through the wood loud bellowing, did rebownd,
60   That all the earth for terrour seemed to shake,
   And trees did tremble. Th' Elfe therewith astownd,°   *amazed*
   Upstarted lightly from his looser make,[6]
And his unready weapons gan in hand to take.

8

But ere he could his armour on him dight,
65   Or get his shield, his monstrous enimy
   With sturdie steps came stalking in his sight,
   An hideous Geant horrible and hye,
   That with his talnesse seemd to threat the skye,
   The ground eke groned under him for dreed;
70   His living like saw never living eye,
   Ne durst behold: his stature did exceed
The hight of three the tallest sonnes of mortall seed.

9

The greatest Earth his uncouth mother was,
   And blustring Aeolus his boasted sire,[7]
75   Who with his breath, which through the world doth pas,
   Her hollow womb did secretly inspire,°   *breathe into*
   And fild her hidden caves with stormie yre,
   That she conceived; and trebling the dew time,
   In which the wombes of women do expire,°   *bring forth*
80   Brought forth this monstrous masse of earthly slime,
Puft up with emptie wind, and fild with sinfull crime.

10

So growen great through arrogant delight
   Of th' high descent, whereof he was yborne,
   And through presumption of his matchlesse might,
85   All other powres and knighthood he did scorne.

---

5. Stretched out and indulging in amorous play ("loosnesse").
6. More licentious ("looser") companion. "Lightly": quickly.

7. Aeolus was keeper of the winds. The giant's descent from Earth and Wind links him to earth-quakes.

Such now he marcheth to this man forlorne,°   *abandoned*
And left to losse:° his stalking steps are stayde   *destruction*
Upon a snaggy Oke,[8] which he had torne
Out of his mothers bowelles, and it made
90 His mortall mace, wherewith his foemen he dismayde.[9]

11

That when the knight he spide, he gan advance
    With huge force and insupportable mayne,[1]
    And towardes him with dreadfull fury praunce;
    Who haplesse, and eke hopelesse, all in vaine
95 Did to him pace, sad battaile to darrayne,°   *engage*
    Disarmd, disgrast, and inwardly dismayde,
    And eke so faint in every joynt and vaine,
    Through that fraile° fountaine, which him feeble made, *enfeebling*
That scarsely could he weeld his bootlesse° single blade.   *useless*

12

100 The Geaunt strooke so maynly° mercilesse,   *mightily*
    That could have overthrowne a stony towre,
    And were not heavenly grace, that him did blesse,
    He had beene pouldred° all, as thin as flowre: *powdered*
    But he was wary of that deadly stowre,°   *peril*
105 And lightly° lept from underneath the blow: *quickly*
    Yet so exceeding was the villeins powre,
    That with the wind it did him overthrow,
And all his sences stound,° that still he lay full low.   *stunned*

13

As when that divelish yron Engin[2] wrought
110 In deepest Hell, and framd by Furies skill,
    With windy Nitre and quick Sulphur fraught,[3]
    And ramd with bullet round, ordaind to kill,
    Conceiveth fire, the heavens it doth fill
    With thundring noyse, and all the ayre doth choke,
115 That none can breath, nor see, nor heare at will,
    Through smouldry cloud of duskish stincking smoke,
That th' onely breath[4] him daunts, who hath escapt the stroke.

14

So daunted when the Geaunt saw the knight,
    His heavie hand he heavèd up on hye,
120 And him to dust thought to have battred quight,
    Untill Duessa loud to him gan crye;
    "O great Orgoglio,[5] greatest under skye,
    O hold thy mortall hand for Ladies sake,
    Hold for my sake, and do him not to dye,[6]

---

8. I.e., he uses as walking stick a knotty ("snaggy") oak tree.
9. Dis-made, dissolved (also in line 96). "Mortall": death-dealing.
1. Irresistible power.
2. I.e., cannon.
3. Filled ("fraught") with gunpowder ("Nitre" and "Sulphur").
4. I.e., the blast or smell alone ("onely") overcomes him.
5. Orgoglio is Italian for "pride," haughtiness, disdain.
6. Do not cause him to die.

125   But vanquisht thine eternall bondslave make,
        And me thy worthy meed unto thy Leman take."7

15

        He hearknd, and did stay° from further harmes,   refrain
            To gayne so goodly guerdon,° as she spake: reward
        So willingly she came into his armes,
130   Who her as willingly to grace° did take,   favor
        And was possessèd of his new found make.°   mate
        Then up he tooke the slombred° sencelesse corse,   unconscious
        And ere he could out of his swowne awake,
        Him to his castle brought with hastie forse,
135 And in a Dongeon deepe him threw without remorse.

16

        From that day forth Duessa was his deare,
            And highly honourd in his haughtie eye,
        He gave her gold and purple pall8 to weare,
        And triple crowne set on her head full hye,9
140   And her endowd with royall majestye:
        Then for to make her dreaded more of men,
        And peoples harts with awfull terrour tye,°   enthrall
        A monstrous beast ybred in filthy fen
        He chose, which he had kept long time in darksome den.

17

145 Such one it was, as that renowmèd Snake
            Which great Alcides in Stremona slew,
        Long fostred in the filth of Lerna lake,
        Whose many heads out budding ever new,
        Did breed° him endlesse labour to subdew: cause
150   But this same Monster much more ugly was;1
        For seven great heads out of his body grew,
        An yron brest, and backe of scaly bras,
        And all embrewd° in bloud, his eyes did shine as glas.   stained

18

        His tayle was stretchèd out in wondrous length,
155   That to the house of heavenly gods it raught,°   reached
        And with extorted powre, and borrowed strength,
        The ever-burning lamps° from thence it brought,   stars
        And prowdly threw to ground, as things of nought;
        And underneath his filthy feet did tread
160   The sacred things, and holy heasts foretaught.2

---

7. I.e., take me, your worthy reward, as your mistress.
8. Crimson robe of royalty.
9. Duessa is attired like the Whore of Babylon in Revelation 17.3–4; the triple crown is that of the papacy. See canto 2, stanzas 13 and 22, and notes.
1. The nine-headed Lernean hydra slain by Hercules (Alcides). The seven-headed monster is the red dragon of Revelation: "behold a great red dragon, having seven heads and ten horns, and seven crowns upon his heads . . . [whose] tail drew the third part of the stars of heaven, and did cast them to the earth . . . [he is] that old serpent, called the Devil, and Satan, which deceiveth the whole world" (12.3–4,9). Many Protestants associated the Beast with the Roman church.
2. Doctrines ("holy heasts") previously taught.

Upon this dreadfull Beast with sevenfold head
He set the false Duessa, for more aw and dread.

19

The wofull Dwarfe, which saw his maisters fall,
    Whiles he had keeping of his grasing steed,
165   And valiant knight become a caytive° thrall,   *captive*
    When all was past, tooke up his forlorne weed,[3]
    His mightie armour, missing most at need;
    His silver shield, now idle maisterlesse;
    His poynant° speare, that many made to bleed,   *sharp*
170   The ruefull moniments° of heavinesse,°   *memorials/grief*
And with them all departes, to tell his great distresse.

20

He had not travaild long, when on the way
    He wofull Ladie, wofull Una met,
    Fast flying from the Paynims greedy pray,°   *clutch*
175   Whilest Satyrane him from pursuit did let:°   *prevent*
    Who when her eyes she on the Dwarfe had set,
    And saw the signes, that deadly tydings spake,
    She fell to ground for sorrowfull regret,°   *grief*
    And lively breath her sad brest did forsake,
180 Yet might her pitteous hart be seene to pant and quake.

21

The messenger of so unhappie newes
    Would faine have dyde: dead was his hart within,
    Yet outwardly some little comfort shewes:
    At last recovering hart, he does begin
185   To rub her temples, and to chaufe her chin,
    And every tender part does tosse and turne:
    So hardly he the flitted life does win,
    Unto her native prison to retourne:[4]
Then gins her grievèd ghost° thus to lament and mourne.   *spirit*

22

190 "Ye dreary instruments of dolefull sight,
    That doe this deadly spectacle behold,
    Why do ye lenger feed on loathèd light,
    Or liking find to gaze on earthly mould,[5]
    Sith cruell fates the carefull° threeds unfould,   *sad*
195   The which my life and love together tyde?
    Now let the stony dart of senselesse cold[6]
    Perce to my hart, and pas through every side,
And let eternall night so sad sight fro me hide.

---

3. Abandoned garment.
4. I.e., with such difficulty ("so hardly") he per-
suades ("does win") the life back to her body ("native
prison").

5. I.e., or find it pleasure to gaze on earthly forms
("mould").
6. I.e., death.

23

"O lightsome day, the lampe of highest Jove,
200   First made by him,[7] mens wandring wayes to guyde,
When darknesse he in deepest dongeon drove,
Henceforth thy hated face for ever hyde,
And shut up heavens windowes shyning wyde:
For earthly sight can nought but sorrow breed,
205   And late° repentance, which shall long abyde.   *too late*
Mine eyes no more on vanitie shall feed,
But seelèd up with death, shall have their deadly meed."[8]

24

Then downe againe she fell unto the ground;
But he her quickly rearèd up againe:
210   Thrise did she sinke adowne in deadly swownd,
And thrise he her revived with busie paine:°   *care*
At last when life recovered had the raine,°   *rein*
And over-wrestled his strong enemie,
With foltring° tong, and trembling every vaine,   *faltering*
215   "Tell on," quoth she, "the wofull Tragedie,
The which these reliques sad present unto mine eie.

25

"Tempestuous fortune hath spent all her spight,
And thrilling° sorrow throwne his utmost dart;   *piercing*
Thy sad tongue cannot tell more heavy plight,
220   Then that I feele, and harbour in mine hart:
Who hath endured the whole, can beare each part.
If death it be, it is not the first wound,
That launchèd° hath my brest with bleeding smart.   *pierced*
Begin, and end the bitter balefull stound;°   *blow*
225   If lesse, then that I feare, more favour I have found."

26

Then gan the Dwarfe the whole discourse° declare,   *story*
The subtill traines° of Archimago old;   *wiles*
The wanton loves of false Fidessa faire,
Bought with the bloud of vanquisht Paynim bold:
230   The wretched payre transformed to treen mould;[9]
The house of Pride, and perils round about;
The combat, which he with Sans joy did hould;
The lucklesse conflict with the Gyant stout,
Wherein captived, of life or death he stood in doubt.

27

235 She heard with patience all unto the end,
And strove to maister sorrowfull assay,°   *affliction*
Which greater grew, the more she did contend,
And almost rent her tender hart in tway°   *two*
And love fresh coles unto her fire did lay:
240 For greater love, the greater is the losse.

---

7. An allusion to Genesis 1.3: "And God said, Let there be light: and there was light."   8. Reward of death.
    9. Shape of a tree.

Was never Ladie lovèd dearer day,[1]
Then she did love the knight of the Redcrosse;
For whose deare sake so many troubles her did tosse.

28

At last when fervent sorrow slakèd was,
245   She up arose, resolving him to find
Alive or dead: and forward forth doth pas,
All° as the Dwarfe the way to her assynd:°   *just/showed*
And evermore in constant carefull mind
She fed her wound with fresh renewèd bale;°   *anguish*
250   Long tost with stormes, and bet° with bitter wind,   *beaten*
High over hils, and low adowne the dale,
She wandred many a wood, and measurd many a vale.

29

At last she chauncèd by good hap to meet
A goodly knight, faire marching by the way
255   Together with his Squire, arayèd meet:°   *properly*
His glitterand° armour shinéd farre away,   *glittering*
Like glauncing° light of Phoebus brightest ray;   *flashing*
From top to toe no place appearèd bare,
That deadly dint° of steele endanger may: *stroke*
260   Athwart his brest a bauldrick[2] brave he ware,
That shynd, like twinkling stars, with stons most pretious rare.

30

And in the midst thereof one pretious stone
Of wondrous worth, and eke of wondrous mights,°   *powers*
Shapt like a Ladies head, exceeding shone,
265   Like Hesperus° emongst the lesser lights,°   *evening star/stars*
And strove for to amaze the weaker sights;
Thereby his mortall blade full comely hong
In yvory sheath, ycarved with curious slights;°   *designs*
Whose hilts were burnisht gold, and handle strong
270   Of mother pearle, and buckled with a golden tong.°   *pin*

31

His haughtie helmet, horrid° all with gold,   *bristling*
Both glorious brightnesse, and great terrour bred;
For all the crest a Dragon did enfold
With greedie pawes, and over all did spred
275   His golden wings: his dreadfull hideous hed
Close couchèd on the bever,° seemed to throw   *visor*
From flaming mouth bright sparkles fierie red,
That suddeine horror to faint harts did show;
And scaly tayle was stretcht adowne his backe full low.

32

280   Upon the top of all his loftie crest,°   *top of helmet*
A bunch of haires discolourd° diversly,   *dyed*
With sprincled pearle, and gold full richly drest,

---

1. I.e., there was never a lady who loved life ("day") more dearly than she loved Redcrosse.   2. Sash worn over the shoulder to support the sword.

Did shake, and seemed to daunce for jollity,
　　Like to an Almond tree ymounted hye
285　On top of greene Selinis[3] all alone,
　　With blossomes brave bedeckèd daintily;
　　Whose tender locks do tremble every one
At every little breath, that under heaven is blowne.

33

His warlike shield all closely covered was,
290　Ne might of mortall eye be ever seene;
　　Not made of steele, nor of enduring bras,
　　Such earthly mettals soone consumèd bene:
　　But all of Diamond perfect pure and cleene°　　　　　*clear*
　　It framèd was, one massie entire mould,[4]
295　Hewen out of Adamant rocke with engines keene,
　　That point of speare it never percen could,
Ne dint of direfull sword divide the substance would.

34

The same to wight° he never wont disclose,　　　　　*creature*
　　But° when as monsters huge he would dismay,　　*except*
300　Or daunt unequall armies of his foes,
　　Or when the flying heavens he would affray;[5]
　　For so exceeding shone his glistring ray,
　　That Phoebus golden face it did attaint,°　　　　*make dim*
　　As when a cloud his beames doth over-lay;
305　And silver Cynthia° wexèd pale and faint,　　　*the moon*
As when her face is staynd with magicke arts constraint.[6]

35

No magicke arts hereof had any might,
　　Nor bloudie wordes of bold Enchaunters call,
　　But all that was not such, as seemd in sight,
310　Before that shield did fade, and suddeine fall:
　　And when him list the raskall routes[7] appall,
　　Men into stones therewith he could transmew,°　　*change*
　　And stones to dust, and dust to nought at all;
　　And when him list the prouder lookes subdew,
315　He would them gazing blind, or turne to other hew.°　*form*

36

Ne let it seeme, that credence this exceedes,
　　For he that made the same, was knowne right well
　　To have done much more admirable° deedes.　　*marvelous*
　　It Merlin was, which whylome° did excell　　　*formerly*
320　All living wightes in might of magicke spell:
　　Both shield, and sword, and armour all he wrought
　　For this young Prince, when first to armes he fell;°　*came*

3. Town associated with the palm awarded to victors (Virgil, *Aeneid* 3.705).
4. The shield was made of one solid piece of Diamond, whose qualities—unflawed, unpierceable,
translucent—point to this knight's significance and
role.
5. I.e., when he would frighten ("affray") the
revolving constellations.
6. Magicians were believed to be able to cause an
eclipse of the moon.
7. Unruly mobs.

But when he dyde, the Faerie Queene it brought
To Faerie lond, where yet it may be seene, if sought.[8]

37

325 A gentle youth, his dearely lovèd Squire
His speare of heben° wood behind him bare,   *ebony*
Whose harmefull head, thrice heated in the fire,
Had riven many a brest with pikehead square;
A goodly person, and could menage° faire   *control*
330 His stubborne steed with curbèd canon bit,[9]
Who under him did trample as the aire,
And chauft,° that any on his backe should sit;   *fretted*
The yron rowels° into frothy fome he bit.   *ends of the bit*

38

When as this knight nigh to the Ladie drew,
335 With lovely° court he gan her entertaine;   *kind*
But when he heard her answers loth, he knew
Some secret sorrow did her heart distraine:°   *afflict*
Which to allay, and calme her storming paine,
Faire feeling words he wisely gan display,°   *pour forth*
340 And for her humour fitting purpose faine,[1]
To tempt the cause it selfe for to bewray;°   *reveal*
Wherewith emmoved, these bleeding words she gan to say.

39

"What worlds delight, or joy of living speach
Can heart, so plunged in sea of sorrowes deepe,
345 And heapèd with so huge misfortunes, reach?
The carefull° cold beginneth for to creepe,   *afflicting*
And in my heart his yron arrow steepe,
Soone as I thinke upon my bitter bale:°   *grief*
Such helplesse harmes yts better hidden keepe,
350 Then rip up griefe, where it may not availe,
My last left comfort is, my woes to weepe and waile."

40

"Ah Ladie deare," quoth then the gentle knight,
"Well may I weene, your griefe is wondrous great;
For wondrous great griefe groneth in my spright,°   *spirit*
355 Whiles thus I heare you of your sorrowes treat.
But wofull Ladie let me you intrete,
For to unfold the anguish of your hart:
Mishaps are maistred by advice discrete,
And counsell mittigates the greatest smart;
360 Found never helpe, who never would his hurts impart."[2]

---

8. I.e., Arthur's virtues may be seen still in Queen
Elizabeth's England. By the references to Merlin
and the Faerie Queene, we now know that this
knight is Arthur, identified in the *Letter to Ralegh*
with "magnificence," understood as the perfection
of all the virtues and containing them all. The *Letter*
also states that in each book the deeds of Arthur
are applicable to the particular virtue treated in that
book.
9. Cannon-bit; a smooth, round bit.
1. I.e., suited his manner to her mood.
2. I.e., he never found help who would not tell
his sorrows.

41

"O but," quoth she, "great griefe will not be tould,
And can more easily be thought, then said."
"Right so"; quoth he, "but he, that never would,
Could never: will to might gives greatest aid."[3]
365   "But grief," quoth she, "does greater grow displaid,
If then it find not helpe, and breedes despaire."
"Despaire breedes not," quoth he, "where faith is staid."°   *firm*
"No faith so fast," quoth she, "but flesh does paire."°   *impair*
"Flesh may empaire," quoth he, "but reason can repaire."

42

370   His goodly reason, and well guided speach
     So deepe did settle in her gratious thought,
     That her perswaded to disclose the breach,
     Which love and fortune in her heart had wrought,
     And said; "Faire Sir, I hope good hap hath brought
375   You to inquire the secrets of my griefe,
     Or° that your wisedome will direct my thought,   *either*
     Or that your prowesse can me yield reliefe:
Then heare the storie sad, which I shall tell you briefe.

43

"The forlorne° Maiden, whom your eyes have seene   *forsaken*
380   The laughing stocke of fortunes mockeries,
     Am th' only daughter of a King and Queene,
     Whose parents deare, whilest equall destinies
     Did runne about,[4] and their felicities
     The favourable heavens did not envy,
385   Did spread their rule through all the territories,
     Which Phison and Euphrates floweth by,
And Gehons golden waves doe wash continually.[5]

44

"Till that their cruell cursèd enemy,
     An huge great Dragon horrible in sight,
390   Bred in the loathly lakes of Tartary,°   *Tartarus (Hell)*
     With murdrous ravine,° and devouring might   *destruction*
     Their kingdome spoild, and countrey wasted quight:
     Themselves, for feare into his jawes to fall,
     He forst to castle strong to take their flight,
395   Where fast embard° in mightie brasen wall,   *imprisoned*
He has them now foure yeres besiegd to make them thrall.

45

"Full many knights adventurous and stout
     Have enterprizd that Monster to subdew;
     From every coast° that heaven walks about,   *land*
400   Have thither come the noble Martiall crew,

---

3. I.e., he that fails to will something cannot do
it: willing gives the greatest help to one's power
("might").
4. I.e., while the impartial fates ran their course.

5. Since these three rivers flow in the Garden of
Eden (Genesis 2.11–14), we know that Eden is
the country of Una's parents.

That famous hard atchievements still pursew,
Yet never any could that girlond win,
But all still shronke,° and still he greater grew: *quailed*
All they for want of faith, or guilt of sin,
405   The pitteous pray of his fierce crueltie have bin.

46

"At last yledd° with farre reported praise,   *led*
Which flying fame throughout the world had spread,
Of doughtie° knights, whom Faery land did raise,   *brave*
That noble order hight of Maidenhed,[6]
410   Forthwith to court of Gloriane I sped,
Of Gloriane great Queene of glory bright,
Whose kingdomes seat Cleopolis is red,[7]
There to obtaine some such redoubted knight,
That Parents deare from tyrants powre deliver might.

47

415   "It was my chance (my chance was faire and good)
There for to find a fresh unprovèd° knight,   *untried*
Whose manly hands imbrewed in guiltie blood
Had never bene,[8] ne ever by his might
Had throwne to ground the unregarded° right: *unrespected*
420   Yet of his prowesse proofe he since hath made
(I witnesse am) in many a cruell fight;
The groning ghosts of many one dismaide°   *defeated*
Have felt the bitter dint of his avenging blade.

48

"And ye the forlorne reliques of his powre,
425   His byting sword, and his devouring speare,
Which have endurèd many a dreadfull stowre,°   *conflict*
Can speake his prowesse, that did earst° you beare,   *before*
And well could rule: now he hath left you heare,
To be the record of his ruefull losse,
430   And of my dolefull disaventurous deare:[9]
O heavie record of the good Redcrosse,
Where have you left your Lord, that could so well you tosse?°*handle*

49

"Well hopèd I, and faire beginnings had,
That he my captive langour should redeeme,[1]
435   Till all unweeting,° an Enchaunter bad   *unknowing*
His sence abusd, and made him to misdeeme°   *misjudge*
My loyalty, not such as it did seeme;
That rather death desire, then such despight.[2]
Be judge ye heavens, that all things right esteeme,
440   How I him loved, and love with all my might,
So thought I eke of him, and thinke I thought aright.

6. The type or analogue of the Order of the Garter. Its emblem shows St. George killing the dragon and its star is the Red Cross. "Hight": called.
7. Named. "Cleopolis" means "famous city."
8. I.e., his strong hands had never been guiltily stained ("imbrewed") with blood.
9. Sad unfortunate dear one.
1. I.e., relieve my state, captive to sadness.
2. I.e., I, who prefer death to such treachery ("despight").

50

"Thenceforth me desolate he quite forsooke,
   To wander, where wilde fortune would me lead,
   And other bywaies he himselfe betooke,
445   Where never foot of living wight did tread,
   That brought not backe the balefull body dead;[3]
   In which him chauncèd false Duessa meete,
   Mine onely foe, mine onely deadly dread,[4]
   Who with her witchcraft and misseeming° sweete,   *false appearance*
450 Inveigled him to follow her desires unmeete.°   *improper*

51

"At last by subtill sleights she him betraid
   Unto his foe, a Gyant huge and tall,
   Who him disarmèd, dissolute,° dismaid,   *enfeebled*
   Unwares surprisèd and with mightie mall°   *club*
455   The monster mercilesse him made to fall,
   Whose fall did never foe before behold;
   And now in darkesome dungeon, wretched thrall,
   Remedilesse, for aie[5] he doth him hold;
This is my cause of griefe, more great, then may be told."

52

460 Ere she had ended all, she gan to faint:
   But he her comforted and faire bespake,
   "Certes, Madame, ye have great cause of plaint,
   That stoutest heart, I weene, could cause to quake.
   But be of cheare, and comfort to you take:
465   For till I have acquit° your captive knight,   *freed*
   Assure your selfe, I will you not forsake."
   His chearefull words revived her chearelesse spright,
So forth they went, the Dwarfe them guiding ever right.

Canto 8

Faire virgin to redeeme her deare
   brings Arthur to the fight:
Who slayes the Gyant, wounds the beast,
   and strips Duessa quight.

1

Ay me, how many perils doe enfold
   The righteous man, to make him daily fall?
   Were not, that heavenly grace doth him uphold,
   And stedfast truth acquite° him out of all.   *deliver*
5   Her love is firme, her care continuall,
   So oft as he through his owne foolish pride,
   Or weaknesse is to sinfull bands° made thrall: *bonds*
   Else should this Redcrosse knight in bands have dyde,
For whose deliverance she this Prince doth thither guide.

---

3. I.e., who returned alive.
4. I.e., the only object of my mortal fear.

5. I.e., forever ("for aie") without hope of rescue ("remedilesse").

2

10 They sadly traveild thus, untill they came
  Nigh to a castle builded strong and hie:
  Then cryde the Dwarfe, "lo yonder is the same;
  In which my Lord my liege doth lucklesse lie,
  Thrall to that Gyants hatefull tyrannie:
15 Therefore, deare Sir, your mightie powres assay."°   *put to trial*
  The noble knight alighted by and by[1]
  From loftie steede, and bad the Ladie stay,
  To see what end of fight should him befall that day.

3

  So with the Squire, th' admirer of his might,
20 He marchèd forth towards that castle wall;
  Whose gates he found fast shut, ne living wight
  To ward° the same, nor answere commers call.   *guard*
  Then tooke that Squire an horne of bugle small,[2]
  Which hong adowne his side in twisted gold,
25 And tassels gay. Wyde wonders over all[3]
  Of that same hornes great vertues weren told,
  Which had approvèd° bene in uses manifold.   *demonstrated*

4

  Was never wight, that heard that shrilling sound,
  But trembling feare did feele in every vaine;°   *vein*
30 Three miles it might be easie heard around,
  And Ecchoes three answered it selfe againe:
  No false enchauntment, nor deceiptfull traine°   *snare*
  Might once abide the terror of that blast,
  But presently° was voide and wholly vaine: *at once*
35 No gate so strong, no locke so firme and fast,
  But with that percing noise flew open quite, or brast.°   *burst*

5

  The same before the Geants gate he blew,
  That all the castle quakèd from the ground,
  And every dore of freewill open flew.
40 The Gyant selfe dismaièd with that sownd,
  Where he with his Duessa dalliance° fownd,   *amorous play*
  In hast came rushing forth from inner bowre,
  With staring° countenance sterne, as one astownd,   *glaring*
  And staggering steps, to weet, what suddein stowre°   *disturbance*
45 Had wrought that horror strange, and dared his dreaded powre.

6

  And after him the proud Duessa came,
  High mounted on her manyheaded beast,
  And every head with fyrie tongue did flame,
  And every head was crownèd on his creast,

---

1. Immediately.
2. A "bugle" is a wild ox; the "wide wonders" (marvelous tales) told of the horn connect it with the horn of Roland and the ram's horn of Joshua, with which he razed the walls of Jericho (Joshua 6.5). See also Romans 10.18, referring to the word of God as the horn of salvation.
3. Everywhere.

50   And bloudie mouthèd with late cruell feast.
      That when the knight beheld, his mightie shild
      Upon his manly arme he soone addrest,°   *made ready*
      And at him fiercely flew, with courage fild,
   And eger greedinesse[4] through every member thrild.

7

55 And lifting up his dreadfull club on hight,
   Therewith the Gyant buckled him to fight,
      Inflamed with scornefull wrath and high disdaine,°   *indignation*
      And lifting up his dreadfull club on hight,
      All armed with ragged snubbes° and knottie graine,   *snags*
      Him thought at first encounter to have slaine.
60   But wise and warie was that noble Pere,°   *peer*
      And lightly leaping from so monstrous maine,°   *force*
      Did faire° avoide the violence him nere;   *quite*
   It booted nought, to thinke, such thunderbolts to beare.[5]

8

   Ne shame he thought to shunne so hideous might:
65   The idle° stroke, enforcing furious way,   *useless*
      Missing the marke of his misaymèd sight
      Did fall to ground, and with his° heavie sway°   *its/force*
      So deepely dinted in the driven clay,
      That three yardes deepe a furrow up did throw:
70   The sad earth wounded with so sore assay,°   *assault*
      Did grone full grievous underneath the blow,
   And trembling with strange feare, did like an earthquake show.

9

   As when almightie Jove in wrathfull mood,
      To wreake° the guilt of mortall sins is bent,   *punish*
75   Hurles forth his thundring dart with deadly food,[6]
      Enrold in flames, and smouldring dreriment,°   *horror*
      Through riven cloudes and molten firmament;
      The fierce threeforkèd engin° making way,   *weapon*
      Both loftie towres and highest trees hath rent,
80   And all that might his angrie passage stay,
   And shooting in the earth, casts up a mount of clay.

10

   His boystrous° club, so buried in the ground,   *massive*
      He could not rearen up againe so light,°   *easily*
      But that the knight him at avantage found,
85   And whiles he strove his combred° clubbe to   *encumbered*
         quight°   *release*
      Out of the earth, with blade all burning bright
      He smote off his left arme, which like a blocke
      Did fall to ground, deprived of native might;

---

4. Intense eagerness for battle.
5. I.e., it is useless to think to withstand such blows. This battle alludes to the struggle of the Protestant against the Roman church, as well as to the struggle of divine grace against evil, the Antichrist.
6. Hatred (feud).

Large streames of bloud out of the trunckèd stocke
90   Forth gushèd, like fresh water streame from riven rocke.[7]

11

Dismaièd with so desperate deadly wound,
    And eke impatient of unwonted paine,[8]
    He loudly brayd with beastly yelling sound,
    That all the fields rebellowèd againe;
95   As great a noyse, as when in Cymbrian[9] plaine
    An heard of Bulles, whom kindly° rage doth sting,   *natural*
    Do for the milkie mothers want complaine,[1]
    And fill the fields with troublous bellowing,
The neighbour woods around with hollow murmur ring.

12

100 That when his deare Duessa heard, and saw
    The evill stownd, that daungerd her estate,[2]
    Unto his aide she hastily did draw
    Her dreadfull beast, who swolne with bloud of late
    Came ramping° forth with proud presumpteous gate,°   *rearing/gait*
105   And threatned all his heads like flaming brands.°   *torches*
    But him the Squire made quickly to retrate,
    Encountring fierce with single° sword in hand,   *only*
And twixt him and his Lord did like a bulwarke stand,

13

The proud Duessa full of wrathfull spight,
110   And fierce disdaine, to be affronted so,
    Enforst her purple beast with all her might
    That stop° out of the way to overthroe,   *obstacle*
    Scorning the let° of so unequall foe: *hindrance*
    But nathemore° would that courageous swayne   *never the more*
115   To her yeeld passage, gainst his Lord to goe,
    But with outrageous° strokes did him restraine,   *exceedingly fierce*
And with his bodie bard the way atwixt them twaine.

14

Then tooke the angrie witch her golden cup,
    Which still she bore, replete with magick artes;[3]
120   Death and despeyre did many thereof sup,
    And secret poyson through their inner parts,
    Th' eternall bale° of heavie wounded harts;   *woe*
    Which after charmes and some enchauntments said,
    She lightly sprinkled on his weaker° parts;   *too weak*
125   Therewith his sturdie courage soone was quayd,°   *quelled*
And all his senses were with suddeine dread dismayd.

---

7. Cf. Exodus 17.6, where Moses smites the rock
and water flows forth.
8. I.e., unable to bear ("impatient of") this unfamiliar ("unwonted") pain.
9. Probably Wales.
1. I.e., mourn the cows' absence.
2. I.e., the peril ("stownd") that endangered her

state.
3. Cf. the golden cup of the woman in Revelation, which is "full of abominations and filthiness
of her fornications" (17.4), the chalice of the Roman
church, and the cup of Circe, the sorceress who
turned men into beasts (in *Odyssey* 10).

15

So downe he fell before the cruell beast,
  Who on his necke his bloudie clawes did seize,
  That life nigh crusht out of his panting brest:
130 No powre he had to stirre, nor will to rize.
  That when the carefull° knight gan well avise,°   *watchful/observe*
  He lightly° left the foe, with whom he fought,   *quickly*
  And to the beast gan turne his enterprise;
  For wondrous anguish in his hart it wrought,
135 To see his lovèd Squire into such thraldome° brought.   *slavery*

16

And high advauncing° his bloud-thirstie blade,   *lifting up*
  Stroke one of those deformèd heads so sore,[4]
  That of his puissance proud ensample made;
  His monstrous scalpe° downe to his teeth it tore   *skull*
140 And that misformèd shape mis-shapèd more:
  A sea of bloud gusht from the gaping wound,
  That her gay garments staynd with filthy gore,
  And overflowèd all the field around;
  That over shoes in bloud he waded on the ground.

17

145 Thereat he roarèd for exceeding paine,
  That to have heard, great horror would have bred,°   *produced*
  And scourging th' emptie ayre with his long traine,°   *tail*
  Through great impatience of his grievèd hed[5]
  His gorgeous ryder from her loftie sted°   *place*
150 Would have cast downe, and trod in durtie myre,
  Had not the Gyant soone her succourèd;
  Who all enraged with smart° and franticke yre,°   *pain/anger*
  Came hurtling in full fierce, and forst the knight retyre.

18

The force, which wont in two to be disperst,
155 In one alone left hand[6] he now unites,
  Which is through rage more strong then both were erst;°   *before*
  With which his hideous club aloft he dites,°   *raises*
  And at his foe with furious rigour° smites,   *violence*
  That strongest Oake might seeme to overthrow:
160 The stroke upon his shield so heavie lites,
  That to the ground it doubleth him full low:
  What mortall wight could ever beare so monstrous blow?

19

And in his fall his shield, that covered was,
  Did loose his vele[7] by chaunce, and open flew:
165 The light whereof, that heavens light did pas,°   *surpass*
  Such blazing brightnesse through the aier threw,
  That eye mote not the same endure to vew.

---

4. "I saw one of [the beast's] heads as it were wounded to death" (Revelation 13.3).
5. I.e., through inability to endure ("impatience")
his afflicted ("grieved") head.
6. I.e., in the one hand left to him.
7. Its covering.

Which when the Gyaunt spyde with staring° eye,   *awed*
He downe let fall his arme, and soft withdrew
170   His weapon huge, that heavèd was on hye
For to have slaine the man, that on the ground did lye.

20

And eke the fruitfull-headed° beast, amazed   *many-headed*
At flashing beames of that sunshiny shield,
Became starke blind, and all his senses dazed,
175   That downe he tumbled on the durtie field,
And seemed himselfe as conquerèd to yield.
Whom when his maistresse proud perceived to fall,
Whiles yet his feeble feet for faintnesse reeld,
Unto the Gyant loudly she gan call,
180   "O helpe Orgoglio, helpe, or else we perish all."

21

At her so pitteous cry was much amooved
Her champion stout, and for to ayde his frend,°   *lover*
Againe his wonted angry weapon prooved:°   *tried*
But all in vaine: for he has read his end
185   In that bright shield, and all their forces spend
Themselves in vaine: for since that glauncing° sight,   *flashing*
He hath no powre to hurt, nor to defend;
As where th' Almighties lightning brond does light,
It dimmes the dazèd eyen, and daunts the senses quight.

22

190   Whom when the Prince, to battell new addrest,
And threatning high his dreadfull stroke did see,
His sparkling blade about his head he blest,°   *brandished*
And smote off quite his right leg by the knee,
That downe he tombled; as an aged tree,
195   High growing on the top of rocky clift,
Whose hartstrings with keene steele nigh hewen be,
The mightie trunck halfe rent, with ragged rift°   *split*
Doth roll adowne the rocks, and fall with fearefull drift.°   *impact*

23

Or as a Castle rearèd high and round,
200   By subtile engins and malitious slight[8]
Is underminèd from the lowest ground,
And her foundation forst,° and feebled quight,   *shattered*
At last downe falles, and with her heapèd hight
Her hastie ruine does more heavie make,
205   And yields it selfe unto the victours might;
Such was this Gyaunts fall, that seemed to shake
The stedfast globe of earth, as it for feare did quake.

24

The knight then lightly° leaping to the pray,   *quickly*
With mortall steele him smot againe so sore,

---

8. Clever machines of war ("engins") and evil strategy.

210   That headlesse his unweldy bodie lay,
        All wallowd in his owne fowle bloudy gore,
        Which flowèd from his wounds in wondrous store.
        But soone as breath out of his breast did pas,
        That huge great body, which the Gyaunt bore,
215   Was vanisht quite, and of that monstrous mas
  Was nothing left, but like an emptie bladder was.

             25

  Whose grievous fall, when false Duessa spide,
        Her golden cup she cast unto the ground,
        And crownèd mitre[9] rudely threw aside;
220   Such percing griefe her stubborne hart did wound,
        That she could not endure that dolefull stound,°   *sorrow*
        But leaving all behind her, fled away:
        The light-foot Squire her quickly turned around,
        And by hard meanes enforcing her to stay,
225 So brought unto his Lord, as his deservèd pray.

             26

  The royall Virgin, which beheld from farre,
        In pensive° plight, and sad perplexitie,   *anxious*
        The whole atchievement of this doubtfull warre,[1]
        Came running fast to greet his victorie,
230   With sober gladnesse, and myld modestie,
        And with sweet joyous cheare him thus bespake;
        "Faire braunch of noblesse, flowre of chevalrie,
        That with your worth the world amazèd make,
  How shall I quite° the paines, ye suffer for my sake?   *requite*

             27

235 "And you[2] fresh bud of vertue springing fast,
        Whom these sad eyes saw nigh unto deaths dore,
        What hath poore Virgin for such perill past,
        Wherewith you to reward? Accept therefore
        My simple selfe, and service evermore;
240   And he that high does sit, and all things see
        With equall° eyes, their merites to restore,°   *impartial/reward*
        Behold what ye this day have done for mee,
  And what I cannot quite, requite with usuree.°   *interest*

             28

  "But sith the heavens, and your faire handeling°   *conduct*
245   Have made you maister of the field this day,
        Your fortune maister eke with governing,[3]
        And well begun end all so well, I pray,
        Ne let that wicked woman scape away;
        For she it is, that did my Lord bethrall,
250   My dearest Lord, and deepe in dongeon lay,

---

9. An allusion to the pope's triple tiara. "Rudely":
violently.
1. I.e., the final outcome, long in doubt ("doubtfull") of this battle.

2. I.e., the Squire.
3. Secure your good fortune also by prudent management.

Where he his better dayes hath wasted all.[4]
O heare, how piteous he to you for ayd does call."

29

Forthwith he gave in charge unto his Squire,
That scarlot whore to keepen carefully;
255   Whiles he himselfe with greedie° great desire   *eager*
Into the Castle entred forcibly,
Where living creature none he did espye;
Then gan he lowdly through the house to call:
But no man cared to answere to his crye.
260   There raignd a solemne silence over all,
Nor voice was heard, nor wight was seene in bowre or hall.

30

At last with creeping crooked pace forth came
An old old man, with beard as white as snow,
That on a staffe his feeble steps did frame,°   *support*
265   And guide his wearie gate° both too and fro: *gait*
For his eye sight him failèd long ygo,
And on his arme a bounch of keyes he bore,
The which unusèd rust did overgrow:
Those were the keyes of every inner dore,
270   But he could not them use, but kept them still in store.

31

But very uncouth° sight was to behold,   *strange*
How he did fashion his untoward° pace,   *awkward*
For as he forward mooved his footing old,
So backward still was turned his wrincled face,
275   Unlike to men, who ever as they trace,°   *walk*
Both feet and face one way are wont to lead.
This was the auncient keeper of that place,
And foster father of the Gyant dead;
His name Ignaro did his nature right aread.[5]

32

280   His reverend haires and holy gravitie
The knight much honord, as beseemèd well,[6]
And gently askt, where all the people bee,
Which in that stately building wont to dwell.
Who answerd him full soft, he could not tell.
285   Againe he askt, where that same knight was layd,
Whom great Orgoglio with his puissaunce fell
Had made his caytive° thrall; againe he sayde,   *captive*
He could not tell: ne ever other answere made.

33

Then askèd he, which way he in might pas:
290   He could not tell, againe he answerèd.
Thereat the curteous knight displeasèd was,

4. I.e., he has consumed ("wasted") here his best
days.
5. His name Ignaro makes clear ("did aread") that

his nature is Ignorance, fit servant for Pride and
the false church.
6. Seemed proper.

And said, "Old sire, it seemes thou hast not red°   *recognized*
How ill it sits with[7] that same silver hed
In vaine to mocke, or mockt in vaine to bee:
295   But if thou be, as thou art pourtrahèd
With natures pen, in ages grave degree,[8]
Aread° in graver wise, what I demaund of thee."   *answer*

34

His answere likewise was, he could not tell.
Whose sencelesse speach, and doted° ignorance   *foolish*
300   When as the noble Prince had markèd well,
He ghest his nature by his countenance,
And calmd his wrath with goodly temperance.
Then to him stepping, from his arme did reach
Those keyes, and made himselfe free enterance.
305   Each dore he openèd without any breach;°   *forcing*
There was no barre to stop, nor foe him to empeach.°   *hinder*

35

There all within full rich arayd he found,
With royal arras° and resplendent gold.   *tapestry*
And did with store of every thing abound,
310   That greatest Princes presence° might behold.   *person*
But all the floore (too filthy to be told)
With bloud of guiltlesse babes, and innocents trew,[9]
Which there were slaine, as sheepe out of the fold,
Defilèd was, that dreadfull was to vew,
315   And sacred ashes over it was strowèd new.

36

And there beside of marble stone was built
An Altare, carved with cunning imagery,°   *images*
On which true Christians bloud was often spilt,
And holy Martyrs often doen to dye,[1]
320   With cruell malice and strong tyranny:
Whose blessed sprites from underneath the stone
To God for vengeance cryde continually,[2]
And with great griefe were often heard to grone,
That hardest heart would bleede, to heare their piteous mone.

37

325   Through every rowme he sought, and every bowr,
But no where could he find that wofull thrall:
At last he came unto an yron doore,
That fast was lockt, but key found not at all
Emongst that bounch, to open it withall;
330   But in the same a little grate was pight,°   *placed*

---

7. I.e., suits.
8. I.e., dignity.
9. Probably a reference to Herod's massacre of the Innocents (Matthew 2.16), traditionally viewed as the first martyrs for Christ.
1. Put to death.
2. "And when he had opened the fifth seal, I saw

under the altar the souls of them that were slain for the word of God, and for the testimony which they held: And they cried with a loud voice, saying, How long, O Lord, holy and true, dost thou not judge and avenge our blood on them that dwell on the earth?" (Revelation 6.9.10).

Through which he sent his voyce, and lowd did call
With all his powre, to weet, if living wight
Were housèd therewithin, whom he enlargen° might.   *set free*

38

Therewith an hollow, dreary, murmuring voyce
335   These piteous plaints and dolours° did resound;   *laments*
"O who is that, which brings me happy choyce°   *chance*
Of death, that here lye dying every stound,°   *moment*
Yet live perforce in balefull° darkenesse bound?   *evil*
For now three Moones have changèd thrice their hew,°   *shape*
340   And have beene thrice hid underneath the ground,
Since I the heavens chearefull face did vew,
O welcome thou, that doest of death bring tydings trew."

39

Which when that Champion heard, with percing point
Of pitty deare° his hart was thrillèd sore,   *extreme*
345   And trembling horrour ran through every joynt,
For ruth of gentle knight so fowle forlore:[3]
Which shaking off, he rent that yron dore,
With furious force, and indignation fell;°   *fierce*
Where entred in, his foot could find no flore,
350   But all a deepe descent, as darke as hell,
That breathèd ever forth a filthie banefull smell.

40

But neither darkenesse fowle, nor filthy bands,
Nor noyous° smell his purpose could withhold,   *noxious*
(Entire affection hateth nicer° hands)   *too fastidious*
355   But that with constant zeale, and courage bold,
After long paines and labours manifold,
He found the meanes that Prisoner up to reare;
Whose feeble thighes, unhable to uphold
His pinèd° corse, him scarse to light could beare,   *wasted*
360   A ruefull spectacle of deathe and ghastly drere.°   *wretchedness*

41

His sad dull eyes deepe sunck in hollow pits,
Could not endure th' unwonted sunne to view;
His bare thin cheekes for want of better bits,°   *food*
And empty sides deceivèd° of their dew,   *cheated*
365   Could make a stony hart his hap to rew;
His rawbone armes, whose mighty brawnèd bowrs[4]
Were wont to rive steele plates, and helmets hew,
Were cleane consumed, and all his vitall powres
Decayd, and all his flesh shronk up like withered flowres.

42

370   Whom when his Lady saw, to him she ran
With hasty joy: to see him made her glad,
And sad to view his visage pale and wan,

---

3. Foully forsaken.   4. Brawny muscles.

Who earst in flowres of freshest youth was clad.
Tho when her well of teares she wasted had,
375   She said, "Ah dearest Lord, what evill starre
On you hath frownd, and pourd his influence bad,
That of your selfe ye thus berobbèd arre,
And this misseeming hew[5] your manly looks doth marre?

43

"But welcome now my Lord, in wele or woe,
380   Whose presence I have lackt to long a day;
And fie on Fortune mine avowèd foe,
Whose wrathfull wreakes° them selves do now alay.   *punishments*
And for these wrongs shall treble penaunce pay
Of treble good: good growes of evils priefe."[6]
385   The chearelesse man, whom sorrow did dismay,°   *unnerve*
Had no delight to treaten° of his griefe;   *speak*
His long endurèd famine needed more reliefe.

44

"Faire Lady," then said that victorious knight,[7]
"The things, that grievous were to do, or beare,
390   Them to renew,° I wote,° breeds no delight;   *recall/know*
Best musicke breeds delight in loathing eare
But th' onely good, that growes of passèd feare,
Is to be wise, and ware° of like agein.   *wary*
This dayes ensample hath this lesson deare
395   Deepe written in my heart with yron pen,
That blisse may not abide in state of mortall men.

45

"Henceforth sir knight, take to you wonted strength,
And maister these mishaps with patient might;
Loe where your foe lyes stretcht in monstrous length,
400   And loe that wicked woman in your sight,
The roote of all your care, and wretched plight,
Now in your powre, to let her live, or dye."
"To do her dye," quoth Una, "were despight,[8]
And shame t' avenge so weake an enimy;
405   But spoile° her of her scarlot robe, and let her fly."   *despoil*

46

So as she bad, that witch they disaraid,
And robd of royall robes, and purple pall,°   *cloak*
And ornaments that richly were displaid;
Ne sparèd they to strip her naked all.
410   Then when they had despoild her tire° and call,°   *robe/headdress*
Such as she was, their eyes might her behold,
That her misshapèd parts did them appall,
A loathly, wrinckled hag, ill favoured, old,
Whose secret filth good manners biddeth not be told.

---

5. Unseemly shape.
6. I.e., Fortune will now make amends for his
wrongs with triple benefits, as good comes from

evils endured ("priefe").
7. I.e., Arthur.
8. I.e., to cause her to die would be despicable.

47

415　Her craftie head was altogether bald,
　　　And as in hate of honorable eld,°　　　　　　　　*age*
　　　Was overgrowne with scurfe and filthy scald;[9]
　　　Her teeth out of her rotten gummes were feld,°　　*fallen*
　　　And her sowre breath abhominably smeld;
420　Her dried dugs, like bladders lacking wind,
　　　Hong downe, and filthy matter from them weld;°　*welled*
　　　Her wrizled° skin as rough, as maple rind,　　　*wrinkled*
　　So scabby was, that would have loathd all womankind.

48

　　Her neather parts, the shame of all her kind,[1]
425　My chaster Muse for shame doth blush to write;
　　　But at her rompe she growing had behind
　　　A foxes taile, with dong all fowly dight;°　　　*covered*
　　　And eke her feete most monstrous were in sight;
　　　For one of them was like an Eagles claw,
430　With griping talaunts armd to greedy fight,
　　　The other like a Beares uneven° paw:　　　　　*rough*
　　More ugly shape yet never living creature saw.[2]

49

　　Which when the knights beheld, amazd they were,
　　　And wondred at so fowle deformèd wight.
435　"Such their," said Una, "as she seemeth here,
　　　Such is the face of falshood, such the sight
　　　Of fowle Duessa, when her borrowed light
　　　Is laid away, and counterfesaunce° knowne."　*deceit*
　　　Thus when they had the witch disrobèd quight,
440　And all her filthy feature° open showne,　　　*form*
　　They let her goe at will, and wander wayes unknowne.

50

　　She flying fast from heavens hated face,
　　　And from the world that her discovered wide,
　　　Fled to the wastfull° wildernesse apace,　　　*desolate*
445　From living eyes her open shame to hide,
　　　And lurkt in rocks and caves long unespide.
　　　But that faire crew° of knights, and Una faire　*company*
　　　Did in that castle afterwards abide,
　　　To rest them selves, and weary powres repaire,
450　Where store they found of all, that dainty° was and rare.　*precious*

Canto 9

His loves and lignage Arthur tells:
The knights knit friendly bands:°　　　　　*bonds*

---

9. A scabby disease of the scalp. "Scurfe": scabs.
1. I.e., womankind.
2. An allusion to Revelation 17.16: "these shall hate the whore, and shall make her desolate and naked." Foxes (cf. line 427) were emblems of cunning; eagles and bears (lines 429, 431) of rapacity, of cruelty, and brutality.

Sir Trevisan flies from Despayre,
Whom Redcrosse knight withstands.

1

O goodly golden chaine,[1] wherewith yfere°   *together*
    The vertues linkèd are in lovely wize:
    And noble minds of yore allyèd were,
    In brave poursuit of chevalrous emprize,°   *adventure*
5   That none did others safety despize,°   *disregard*
    Nor aid envy° to him, in need that stands,   *begrudge*
    But friendly each did others prayse devize
    How to advaunce with favourable hands,
As this good Prince redeemd the Redcrosse knight from bands.

2

10 Who when their powres, empaird through labour long,
    With dew repast they had recurèd° well,   *restored*
    And that weake captive wight now wexèd strong,
    Them list no lenger there at leasure dwell,
    But forward fare, as their adventures fell,
15   But ere they parted, Una faire besought
    That straunger knight his name and nation tell;
    Least so great good, as he for her had wrought,
Should die unknown, and buried be in thanklesse thought.

3

"Faire virgin," said the Prince, "ye me require
20   A thing without the compas[2] of my wit:
    For both the lignage and the certain Sire,
    From which I sprong, from me are hidden yit.
    For all so soone as life did me admit
    Into this world, and shewèd heavens light,
25   From mothers pap I taken was unfit:[3]
    And streight delivered to a Faery knight,
To be upbrought in gentle thewes° and martiall might.   *manners*

4

"Unto old Timon[4] he me brought bylive,
    Old Timon, who in youthly yeares hath beene
30   In warlike feates th' expertest man alive,
    And is the wisest now on earth I weene;
    His dwelling is low in a valley greene,
    Under the foot of Rauran mossy hore,°   *gray*
    From whence the river Dee as silver cleene°   *pure*
35   His tombling billowes rolls with gentle rore:[5]
There all my dayes he traind me up in vertuous lore.

---

1. The golden chain of love or concord which binds the world and the human race together (cf. canto 5, stanza 25, and note).
2. I.e., beyond the reach of.
3. I.e., not yet weened.
4. The name means "Honor." "Bylive": immediately.

5. The hill Rauran is in Wales; the river Dee also flows in, and forms part of, the boundary of Wales. The Tudors (Queen Elizabeth's family) were orginally Welsh, and the legends of Arthur had their beginnings in the Celtic mythology of early Wales.

5

"Thither the great Magicien Merlin came,
　　As was his use, ofttimes to visit me:
　　For he had charge my discipline° to frame,   *education*
40　　And Tutours nouriture° to oversee.   *upbringing*
　　Him oft and oft I askt in privitie,
　　Of what loines and what lignage I did spring:
　　Whose aunswere bad me still assurèd bee,
　　That I was sonne and heire unto a king,
45　As time in her just terme[6] the truth to light should bring."

6

"Well worthy impe,"° said then the Lady gent,°   *offspring/gentle*
　　"And Pupill fit for such a Tutours hand.
　　But what adventure, or what high intent
　　Hath brought you hither into Faery land,
50　　Aread Prince Arthur,[7] crowne of Martiall band?"
　　"Full hard it is," quoth he, "to read° aright   *discern*
　　The course of heavenly cause, or understand
　　The secret meaning of th' eternall might,
That rules mens wayes, and rules the thoughts of living wight.

7

55　"For whither he through fatall deepe foresight[8]
　　Me hither sent, for cause to me unghest,
　　Or that fresh bleeding wound, which day and night
　　Whilome° doth rancle in my riven brest,   *all the while*
　　With forcèd fury following his° behest,   *its*
60　　Me hither brought by wayes yet never found,
　　You to have helpt I hold my selfe yet blest."
　　"Ah curteous knight," quoth she, "what secret wound
Could ever find,° to grieve the gentlest hart on ground?"   *succeed*

8

"Deare Dame," quoth he, "you sleeping sparkes awake,
65　　Which trubled once, into huge flames will grow,
　　Ne ever will their fervent fury slake
　　Till living moysture into smoke do flow,
　　And wasted° life do lye in ashes low.   *consumed*
　　Yet sithens° silence lesseneth not my fire,   *since*
70　　But told it flames, and hidden it does glow,
　　I will revele, what ye so much desire:
Ah Love, lay downe thy bow, the whiles I may respire.°   *breathe*

9

"It was in freshest flowre of youthly yeares,
　　When courage first does creepe in manly chest,
75　　Then first the coale of kindly° heat appeares   *natural*
　　To kindle love in every living brest;
　　But me had warnd old Timons wise behest,

6. Due course.
7. Arthur is named here for the first time. "Aread":
declare.

8. I.e., whether he (God—"eternal might") sent
me here through foresight ordained by fate ("fatall").

Those creeping flames by reason to subdew,
   Before their rage grew to so great unrest,
80   As miserable lovers use to rew,
Which still wex° old in woe, whiles woe still wexeth new.   *grow*

10

"That idle name of love, and lovers life,
   As losse of time, and vertues enimy
   I ever scornd, and joyd to stirre up strife,
85   In middest of their mournfull Tragedy,
   Ay wont to laugh, when them I heard to cry,
   And blow the fire, which them to ashes brent:°   *burned*
   Their God himselfe, grieved at my libertie,
   Shot many a dart at me with fiers intent,
90   But I them warded all with wary government.[9]

11

"But all in vaine: no fort can be so strong,
   Ne fleshly brest can armèd be so sound,
   But will at last be wonne with battrie° long,   *siege*
   Or unawares at disavantage found;
95   Nothing is sure, that growes on earthly ground:
   And who most trustes in arme of fleshly might,
   And boasts, in beauties chaine not to be bound,
   Doth soonest fall in disaventrous° fight.   *disastrous*
And yeeldes his caytive neck to victours most° despight.   *greatest*

12

100 "Ensample make of him your haplesse joy,
   And of my selfe now mated,° as ye see;   *overcome*
   Whose prouder° vaunt that proud avenging boy   *too proud*
   Did soone pluck downe, and curbd my libertie.
   For on a day prickt° forth with jollitie   *spurred*
105   Of looser life, and heat of hardiment,°   *boldness*
   Raunging the forest wide on courser free,
   The fields, the floods, the heavens with one consent
Did seeme to laugh° on me, and favour mine intent.   *smile*

13

"For-wearied° with my sports, I did alight   *utterly wearied*
110 From loftie steed, and downe to sleepe me layd;
   The verdant° gras my couch did goodly dight,°   *green/make*
   And pillow was my helmet faire displayd:
   Whiles every sence the humour sweet embayd,[1]
   And slombring soft my hart did steale away,
115   Me seemèd, by my side a royall Mayd
   Her daintie limbes full softly down did lay:
So faire a creature yet saw never sunny day.

---

9. I.e., self-control. The descriptions here of
Cupid's archery and of the siege of the castle of
chastity (in the next stanza) have many echoes from
the courtly-love traditions.
1. I.e., While the dew of sleep ("humour") pervaded ("embayd") every sense.

14

"Most goodly glee° and lovely blandishment°   *entertainment/compli-*
 She to me made, and bad me love here deare,   *ment*
120 For dearely sure her love was to me bent,
 As when just time expirèd² should appeare.
 But whether dreames delude, or true it were,
 Was never hart so ravisht with delight,
 Ne living man like words did ever heare,
125 As she to me delivered all that night;
And at her parting said, She Queene of Faeries hight.³

15

"When I awoke, and found her place devoyd,°   *empty*
 And nought but pressèd gras, where she had lyen,
 I sorrowed all so much, as earst I joyd,
130 And washèd all her place with watry eyen.
 From that day forth I loved that face divine;
 From that day forth I cast in carefull° mind,   *care-filled*
 To seeke her out with labour, and long tyne,°   *hardship*
 And never vow to rest, till her I find,
135 Nine monethes I seeke in vaine yet ni'll° that vow unbind." *will not*

16

Thus as he spake, his visage wexèd pale,
 And chaunge of hew great passion did bewray;°   *reveal*
 Yet still he strove to cloke his inward bale,°   *grief*
 And hide the smoke, that did his fire display,
140 Till gentle Una thus to him gan say;
 "Oh happy Queene of Faeries, that hast found
 Mongst many, one that with his prowesse may
 Defend thine honour, and thy foes confound:
True Loves are often sown, but seldom grow on ground."

17

145 "Thine, O then," said the gentle Redcrosse knight,
 "Next to that Ladies love, shalbe the place,
 O fairest virgin, full of heavenly light,
 Whose wondrous faith, exceeding earthly race,
 Was firmest fixt in mine extremest case.°   *plight*
150 And you, my Lord, the Patrone° of my life,   *protector*
 Of that great Queene may well gaine worthy grace:
 For onely worthy you through prowes priefe⁴
Yf living man mote° worthy be, to be her liefe."°   *may/love*

18

So diversly discoursing of their loves,
155 The golden Sunne his glistring head gan shew,

---

2. A fitting length of time having passed.
3. Was called. This is one of the passages where
the "faery" nature of *The Faerie Queene* makes itself
strongly felt. In the background are many folktales
and ballads of a hero bewitched by the Queen of

Faery. Spenser's *Letter to Ralegh* identifies Gloriana allegorically with glory and with Queen
Elizabeth.
4. Demonstration of prowess.

And sad remembraunce now the Prince amoves,
With fresh desire his voyage to pursew:
Als° Una earnd° her traveill to renew.　　　　　　　*so/yearned*
Then those two knights, fast friendship for to bynd,
160　　And love establish each to other trew,
　　　Gave goodly gifts, the signes of gratefull mynd,
And eke as pledges firme, right hands together joynd.

19

Prince Arthur gave a boxe of Diamond sure,°　　　　*true*
　　　Embowd° with gold and gorgeous ornament,　　　*bound*
165　　Wherein were closd few drops of liquor pure,
　　　Of wondrous worth, and vertue excellent,
　　　That any wound could heale incontinent:°　　　*immediately*
　　　Which to requite, the Redcrosse knight him gave
　　　A booke, wherein his Saveours testament
170　　Was writ with golden letters rich and brave;°　　*splendid*
A worke of wondrous grace, and able soules to save.[5]

20

Thus beene they parted, Arthur on his way
　　　To seeke his love, and th' other for to fight
　　　With Unas foe, that all her realme did pray.°　　*prey upon*
175　　But she now weighing the decayèd plight,
　　　And shrunken synewes of her chosen knight,
　　　Would not a while her forward course pursew,
　　　Ne bring him forth in face of dreadfull fight,
　　　Till he recovered had his former hew:°　　　　*appearance*
180　For him to be yet weake and wearie well she knew.

21

So as they traveild, lo they gan espy
　　　An armèd knight towards them gallop fast,
　　　That seemèd from some fearèd foe to fly,
　　　Or other griesly thing, that him agast.°　　　*terrified*
185　　Still as he fled, his eye was backward cast,
　　　As if his feare still followed him behind;
　　　Als flew his steed, as he his bands had brast,°　　*broken*
　　　And with his wingèd heeles did tread the wind,
As he had beene a fole of Pegasus his kind.[6]

22

190　Nigh as he drew, they might perceive his head
　　　To be unarmd, and curld uncombèd heares
　　　Upstaring° stiffe, dismayd with uncouth° dread;　*bristling/unknown*
　　　Nor drop of bloud in all his face appeares
　　　Nor life in limbe: and to increase his feares,
195　　In fowle reproch° of knighthoods faire degree,°　*disgrace/condition*
　　　About his neck an hempen rope he weares,

---

5. Medieval romances mention such healing balms, but here the "drops of liquor pure" represent grace, perhaps in the Eucharist; Redcrosse gives Arthur the New Testament.
6. I.e., as if he had been a foal of a horse like Pegasus (a flying horse).

That with his glistring armes does ill agree;
But he of rope or armes has now no memoree.

23

The Redcrosse knight toward him crossèd fast,
200   To weet, what mister° wight was so dismayd: *kind of*
There him he finds all sencelesse and aghast,
That of him selfe he seemd to be afrayd;
Whom hardly he from flying forward stayd,
Till he these wordes to him deliver might;
205   "Sir knight, aread° who hath ye thus arayd,   *declare*
And eke° from whom make ye this hasty flight: *also*
For never knight I saw in such misseeming° plight."   *unseemly*

24

He answerd nought at all, but adding new
Feare to his first amazment, staring wide
210   With stony eyes, and hartlesse hollow hew,[7]
Astonisht stood, as one that had aspide
Infernall furies, with their chaines untide.
Him yet againe, and yet againe bespake
The gentle knight; who nought to him replide,
215   But trembling every joynt did inly quake,
And foltring tongue at last these words seemd forth to shake.

25

"For Gods deare love, Sir knight, do me not stay;
For loe he comes, he comes fast after mee."
Eft° looking backe would faine have runne away;   *again*
220   But he him forst to stay, and tellen free
The secret cause of his perplexitie:°   *distress*
Yet nathemore° by his bold hartie speach,   *not at all*
Could his bloud-frosen hart emboldned bee,
But through his boldnesse rather feare did reach,
225 Yet forst, at last he made through silence suddein breach.

26

"And am I now in safetie sure," quoth he,
"From him, that would have forcèd me to dye?
And is the point of death now turnd fro mee,
That I may tell this haplesse history?"
230   "Feare nought:" quoth he, "no daunger now is nye."
"Then shall I you recount a ruefull cace,"°   *event*
Said he, "the which with this unlucky eye
I late beheld, and had not greater grace
Me reft from it, had bene partaker of the place.[8]

27

235 "I lately chaunst (Would I had never chaunst)
With a faire knight to keepen companee,
Sir Terwin hight, that well himselfe advaunst

---

7. I.e., with blanched, bloodless countenance.   8. I.e., shared the same fate; "reft": carried from.

In all affaires, and was both bold and free,
But not so happie as mote happie bee:
240   He loved, as was his lot, a Ladie gent,°   *noble*
That him againe° loved in the least degree: *in return*
For she was proud, and of too high intent,°   *spirit*
And joyd to see her lover languish and lament.

                              28

"From whom returning sad and comfortlesse,°   *desolate*
245   As on the way together we did fare,
We met that villen (God from him me blesse°)   *defend*
That cursèd wight, from whom I scapt why leare,[9]
A man of hell, that cals himselfe Despaire;[1]
Who first us greets, and after faire areedes°   *tells*
250   Of tydings strange, and of adventures rare:
So creeping close, as Snake in hidden weedes,
Inquireth of our states, and of our knightly deedes.

                              29

"Which when he knew, and felt our feeble harts
Embost° with bale,° and bitter byting griefe,   *exhausted/sorrow*
255   Which love had launchèd° with his deadly darts,   *pierced*
With wounding words and termes of foule repriefe°   *insult*
He pluckt from us all hope of due reliefe,
That earst us held in love of lingring life;
Then hopelesse hartlesse, gan the cunning thiefe
260   Perswade us die, to stint° all further strife: *end*
To me he lent this rope, to him a rustie knife.

                              30

"With which sad instrument of hastie death,
That wofull lover, loathing lenger° light,   *longer*
A wide way made to let forth living breath.
265   But I more fearefull, or more luckie wight,
Dismayd with that deformèd dismall sight,
Fled fast away, halfe dead with dying feare:[2]
Ne yet assured of life by you, Sir knight,
Whose like infirmitie like chaunce may beare:
270   But God you never let his charmèd speeches heare."[3]

                              31

"How may a man," said he, "with idle speach
Be wonne, to spoyle° the Castle of his health?"   *destroy*
"I wote," quoth he, "whom triall° late did teach,   *experience*
That like would not[4] for all this worldes wealth:
275   His subtill tongue, like dropping honny, mealt'th°   *melts*
Into the hart, and searcheth every vaine,
That ere one be aware, by secret stealth

---

9. A while before.   2. Fear of death.
1. Despair is the ultimate Christian sin, denying   3. I.e., may God never let you hear his mesmer-
the possibility of Divine mercy and grace. Dr.   izing ("charmed") speeches.
Faustus at the end of Marlowe's play is in a state   4. I.e., would not do the like again.
of despair (see pp. 482–83).

His powre is reft, and weaknesse doth remaine.
O never Sir desire to try° his guilefull traine."°   *test/treachery*

32

280   "Certes,"° said he, "hence shall I never rest,   *surely*
    Till I that treachours art have heard and tride;
    And you Sir knight, whose name mote° I request,   *might*
    Of grace° do me unto his cabin° guide."   *favor/cave*
    "I that hight Trevisan,"⁵ quoth he, "will ride
285   Against my liking backe, to doe you grace:
    But nor for gold nor glee⁶ will I abide
    By you, when ye arrive in that same place;
For lever° had I die, then see his deadly face."   *rather*

33

Ere long they come, where that same wicked wight
290   His dwelling has, low in an hollow cave,
    Farre underneath a craggie clift ypight,°   *placed*
    Darke, dolefull, drearie, like a greedie grave,
    That still for carrion carcases doth crave:
    On top whereof aye dwelt the ghastly Owle,⁷
295   Shrieking his balefull note, which ever drave
    Farre from that haunt all other chearefull fowle;
And all about it wandring ghostes did waile and howle.

34

And all about old stockes° and stubs of trees,   *stumps*
    Whereon nor fruit, nor leafe was ever seene,
300   Did hang upon the ragged rocky knees;°   *crags*
    On which had many wretches hangèd beene,
    Whose carcases were scattered on the greene,
    And throwne about the cliffs. Arrivèd there,
    That bare-head knight for dread and dolefull teene,°   *grief*
305   Would faine° have fled, ne durst approachen neare,   *gladly*
But th' other forst him stay, and comforted in feare.

35

That darkesome cave they enter, where they find
    That cursèd man, low sitting on the ground,
    Musing full sadly in his sullein° mind;   *morose*
310   His griesie° lockes, long growen, and unbound,   *gray*
    Disordred hong about his shoulders round,
    And hid his face; through which his hollow eyne
    Lookt deadly dull, and starèd as astound;
    His raw-bone cheekes through penurie and pine,°   *starvation*
315   Were shronke into his jawes, as° he did never dine.   *as if*

36

His garment nought but many ragged clouts,°   *rags*
    With thornes together pind and patchèd was,
    The which his naked sides he wrapt abouts;

---

5. His name may connote weariness, fatigue ("terwyn"); "hight": am called.

6. Song; i.e., anything you can say to me.

7. Traditionally a messenger of death.

And him beside there lay upon the gras
320   A drearie° corse, whose life away did pas,   *bloody*
       All wallowd in his owne yet luke-warme blood,
       That from his wound yet wellèd fresh alas;
       In which a rustie° knife fast fixèd stood,   *bloodstained*
And made an open passage for the gushing flood.

37

325 Which piteous spectacle, approving° trew   *confirming*
     The wofull tale that Trevisan had told,
     When as the gentle Redcrosse knight did vew,
     With firie zeale he burnt in courage bold,
     Him to avenge, before his bloud were cold,
330 And to the villein said, "Thou damnèd wight,
     The author of this fact,° we here behold,   *deed*
     What justice can but judge against thee right,
With thine owne bloud to price° his bloud, here   *pay for*
       shed in sight?"

38

     "What franticke fit," quoth he,[8] "hath thus distraught
335   Thee, foolish man, so rash a doome° to give?   *judgment*
       What justice ever other judgement taught,
       But he should die, who merites not to live?
       None else to death this man despayring drive,°   *drove*
       But his owne guiltie mind deserving death.
340   Is then unjust to each his due to give?
       Or let him die, that loatheth living breath?
Or let him die at ease, that liveth here uneath°?   *in unease*

39

     "Who travels by the wearie wandring way,
       To come unto his wishèd home in haste,
345   And meetes a flood, that doth his passage stay,
       Is not great grace to helpe him over past,
       Or free his feet, that in the myre sticke fast?
       Most envious man, that grieves at neighbours good,
       And fond,° that joyest in the woe thou hast,   *foolish*
350   Why wilt not let him passe, that long hath stood
Upon the banke, yet wilt thy selfe not passe the flood?

40

     "He there does now enjoy eternall rest
       And happie ease, which thou doest want and crave,
       And further from it daily wanderest:
355   What if some litle paine the passage have,
       That makes fraile flesh to feare the bitter wave?
       Is not short paine well borne, that brings long ease,
       And layes the soule to sleepe in quiet grave?

---

8. I.e., Despaire.

Sleepe after toyle, port after stormie seas,
360 Ease after warre, death after life does greatly please."[9]

41

The knight much wondred at his suddeine wit,[1]
And said, "The terme of life is limited,
Ne may a man prolong, nor shorten it;
The souldier may not move from watchfull sted,[2]
365 Nor leave his stand, untill his Captaine bed."°   *commands*
"Who life did limit by almightie doome,"
Quoth he,[3] "knowes best the termes establishèd;
And he, that points the Centonell his roome,°   *station*
Doth license him depart at sound of morning droome.[4]

42

370 "Is not his deed, what ever thing is donne,
In heaven and earth? did not he all create
To die againe? all ends that was begonne.
Their times in his eternall booke of fate
Are written sure, and have their certaine° date.   *fixed*
375 Who then can strive with strong necessitie,
That holds the world in his still chaunging state,
Or shunne the death ordaynd by destinie?
When houre of death is come, let none aske whence, nor why.

43

"The lenger life, I wote° the greater sin,   *know°*
380 The greater sin, the greater punishment:
All those great battels, which thou boasts to win,
Through strife, and bloud-shed, and avengement,
Now praysd, hereafter deare° thou shalt repent: *bitterly*
For life must life, and bloud must bloud repay.[5]
385 Is not enough thy evill life forespent?
For he, that once hath missèd the right way,
The further he doth goe, the further he doth stray.

44

"Then do no further goe, no further stray,
But here lie downe, and to thy rest betake,
390 Th' ill to prevent, that life ensewen may.[6]
For what hath life, that may it lovèd make,
And gives not rather cause it to forsake?
Feare, sicknesse, age, losse, labour, sorrow, strife,
Paine, hunger, cold, that makes the hart to quake;

---

9. Despaire's arguments on behalf of suicide as against a painful life are derived, like those of Hamlet in his third soliloquy (*Hamlet* 3.1.56–88), principally from Seneca, Marcus Aurelius, and the ancient Stoics, and from Old Testament utterings on divine justice. His speech is devised according to classical rules of rhetoric.
1. Quick intelligence.

2. The sentry post assigned him.
3. I.e., Despaire.
4. Drum, with a pun on doom.
5. An echo of Genesis 9.6: "Whoso sheddeth man's blood, by man shall his blood be shed."
6. I.e., to prevent the evil that will ensue in the rest of your life.

395   And ever fickle fortune rageth rife,
     All which, and thousands mo° do make a loathsome life.   *more*

              45

     "Thou wretched man, of death hast greatest need,
        If in true ballance thou wilt weigh thy state:
        For never knight, that darèd warlike deede,
400   More lucklesse disaventures° did amate:°   *misfortunes/appall*
        Witnesse the dongeon deepe, wherein of late
        Thy life shut up, for death so oft did call;
        And though good lucke prolongèd hath thy date,°   *span of life*
        Yet death then, would the like mishaps forestall,
405   Into the which hereafter thou maiest happen fall.[7]

              46

     "Why then doest thou, O man of sin, desire
        To draw thy dayes forth to their last degree?
        Is not the measure of thy sinfull hire[8]
        High heapèd up with huge iniquitie,
410   Against the day of wrath,[9] to burden thee?
        Is not enough that to this Ladie milde
        Thou falsèd° hast thy faith with perjurie,   *betrayed*
        And sold thy selfe to serve Duessa vilde,°   *vile*
     With whom in all abuse thou hast thy selfe defilde?

              47

415 "Is not he just, that all this doth behold
        From highest heaven, and beares an equall° eye?   *impartial*
        Shall he thy sins up in his knowledge fold,
        And guiltie be of thine impietie?
        Is not his law, Let every sinner die:[1]
420   Die shall all flesh? what then must needs be donne,
        Is it not better to doe willinglie,
        Then linger, till the glasse° be all out ronne?   *hourglass*
     Death is the end of woes: die soone, O faeries sonne."

              48

     The knight was much enmovèd with his speach,
425   That as a swords point through his hart did perse,
        And in his conscience made a secret breach,
        Well knowing true all, that he did reherse°   *recount*
        And to his fresh remembrance did reverse°   *bring back*
        The ugly vew of his deformèd crimes,
430   That all his manly powres it did disperse,
        As he were charmèd with inchaunted rimes,
     That oftentimes he quakt, and fainted oftentimes.

              49

     In which amazement, when the Miscreant°   *wretch*
        Perceivèd him to waver weake and fraile,
435   Whiles trembling horror did his conscience dant,°   *daunt*

7. Happen to fall.
8. Service to sin.
9. Judgment Day.
1. Despaire cites only half of the scripture verse:

"The wages of sin is death; but the gift of God is eternal life through Jesus Christ our Lord" (Romans 6.23).

And hellish anguish² did his soule assaile,
To drive him to despaire, and quite to quaile,°   *be dismayed*
He shewed him painted in a table° plaine,   *picture*
The damnèd ghosts, that doe in torments waile,
440   And thousand feends that doe them endlesse paine
With fire and brimstone, which for ever shall remaine.

50

The sight whereof so throughly him dismaid,
That nought but death before his eyes he saw,
And ever burning wrath before him laid,
445   By righteous sentence of th' Almighties law:
Then gan the villein him to overcraw,°   *exult over*
And brought unto him swords, ropes, poison, fire,
And all that might him to perdition draw;
And bad him choose, what death he would desire:
450   For death was due to him, that had provokt Gods ire.

51

But when as none of them he saw him take,
He to him raught° a dagger sharpe and keene,   *reached*
And gave it him in hand: his hand did quake,
And tremble like a leafe of Aspin greene,
455   And troubled bloud through his pale face was seene
To come, and goe with tydings from the hart,
As it a running messenger had beene.
At last resolved to worke his finall smart,
He lifted up his hand, that backe againe did start.

52

460   Which when as Una saw, through every vaine
The crudled° cold ran to her well of life,°   *congealing/heart*
As in a swowne: but soone relived° againe,   *revived*
Out of his hand she snatcht the cursèd knife,
And threw it to the ground, enragèd rife,°   *deeply*
465   And to him said, "Fie, fie, faint harted knight,
What meanest thou by this reprochfull° strife?   *deserving reproach*
Is this the battell, which thou vauntst to fight
With the fire-mouthèd Dragon, horrible and bright?

53

"Come, come away, fraile, feeble, fleshly wight,
470   Ne let vaine words bewitch thy manly hart,
Ne divelish thoughts dismay thy constant spright.
In heavenly mercies hast thou not a part?
Why shouldst thou then despeire, that chosen art?
Where justice growes, there grows eke° greater grace,   *also*
475   The which doth quench the brond of hellish smart,
And that accurst hand-writing³ doth deface.°   *blot out*
Arise, Sir knight arise, and leave this cursèd place."

---

2. I.e., fear of hell.
3. An echo of Colossians 2.14: "Blotting out the handwriting that was against us, which was con- trary to us [The Old Testament Law], and took it out of the way, nailing it to his cross."

54

So up he rose, and thence amounted[4] streight.
Which when the carle° beheld, and saw his guest   *churl*
480 Would safe depart, for° all his subtill sleight,   *in spite of*
He chose an halter from among the rest,
And with it hung himselfe, unbid° unblest.   *unprayed for*
But death he could not worke himselfe thereby;
For thousand times he so himselfe had drest,°   *made ready*
485 Yet nathelesse it could not doe him die,
Till he should die his last, that is eternally.

Canto 10

Her faithfull knight faire Una brings
to house of Holinesse,
Where he is taught repentance, and
the way to heavenly blesse.°   *bliss*

1

What man is he, that boasts of fleshly might,
And vaine assurance of mortality,°   *mortal life*
Which all so soone, as it doth come to fight,
Against spirituall foes, yeelds by and by,[1]
5 Or from the field most cowardly doth fly?
Ne let the man ascribe it to his skill,
That thorough grace hath gainèd victory.
If any strength we have, it is to ill,
But all the good is Gods, both power and eke will.[2]

2

10 By that, which lately hapned, Una saw,
That this her knight was feeble, and too faint;
And all his sinews woxen weake and raw,°   *unready*
Through long enprisonment, and hard constraint,°   *affliction*
Which he endurèd in his late restraint,
15 That yet he was unfit for bloudie fight:
Therefore to cherish him with diets daint,°   *choice*
She cast to bring him, where he chearen° might,   *be cheered*
Till he recovered had his[3] late decayèd plight.

3

There was an auntient house not farre away,
20 Renowmd throughout the world for sacred lore,
And pure unspotted life: so well they say
It governd was, and guided evermore,
Through wisedome of a matrone grave and hore;°   *venerable*
Whose onely joy was to relieve the needes

---

4. Mounted his horse.
1. Immediately.
2. "For by grace ye saved through faith; and that not of yourselves: it is the gift of God: Not of

works, lest any men should boast" (Ephesians 2.8–9). "Eke": also.
3. I.e., from his.

25 Of wretched soules, and helpe the helpelesse pore:
    All night she spent in bidding of her bedes,[4]
And all the day in doing good and godly deedes.

4

    Dame Caelia[5] men did her call, as thought
      From heaven to come, or thither to arise,
30 The mother of three daughters, well upbrought
      In goodly thewes,° and godly exercise: *habits*
    The eldest two most sober, chast, and wise,
    Fidelia and Speranza virgins were,
    Though spousd,° yet wanting wedlocks solemnize;   *bethrothed*
35 But faire Charissa to a lovely fere[6]
Was linckèd, and by him had many pledges dere.[7]

5

    Arrivèd there, the dore they find fast lockt;
      For it was warely watchèd night and day,
    For feare of many foes: but when they knockt,
40 The Porter opened unto them streight way:
      He was an agèd syre, all hory gray,
    With lookes full lowly cast, and gate full slow,
    Wont on a staffe his feeble steps to stay,
    Hight° Humilta.° They passe in stouping low; *called/humility*
45 For streight and narrow was the way, which he did show.[8]

6

Each goodly thing is hardest to begin,
    But entred in a spacious court they see,
    Both plaine, and pleasant to be walkèd in,
    Where them does meete a francklin° faire and free,   *freeholder*
50 And entertaines with comely courteous glee,
      His name was Zele,° that him right well became,   *zeal*
    For in his speeches and behaviour hee
    Did labour lively to expresse the same,
And gladly did them guide, till to the Hall they came.

7

55 There fairely them receives a gentle Squire,
    Of milde demeanure, and rare courtesie,
    Right cleanly clad in comely sad° attire;   *sober*
    In word and deede that shewed great modestie,
    And knew his good° to all of each degree,   *proper respect*
60 Hight Reverence. He them with speeches meet
    Does faire entreat; no courting nicetie,[9]

---

4. Saying prayers.
5. The name means "heavenly."
6. Loving mate.
7. I.e., many children. The daughters' names mean "faith," "hope," and "charity." Cf. with them the three Saracens, Sans Foy, Sans Joy, and Sans Loy. This canto draws heavily on scriptural references, especially 1 Corinthians 13.13. "And now abideth faith, hope, charity, these three; but the greatest of these is charity." Many aspects of the House of Holiness oppose their counterparts in the House of Pride (canto 4).
8. See note 3, p. 380.
9. He treats them courteously ("faire"); no courtly affectation ("nicetie").

But simple true, and eke° unfainèd sweet,   *also*
  As might become a Squire so great persons to greet.

8

And afterwards them to his Dame he leades,
65   That agèd Dame, the Ladie of the place:
  Who all this while was busie at her beades:
  Which doen, she up arose with seemely grace,
  And toward them full matronely¹ did pace.
  Where when that farest Una she beheld,
70   Whom well she knew to spring from heavenly race,
  Her hart with joy unwonted inly sweld,°   *swelled*
  As feeling wondrous comfort in her weaker eld.°   *older age*

9

And her embracing said, "O happie earth,
  Whereon thy innocent feet doe ever tread,
75   Most vertuous virgin borne of heavenly berth,
  That to redeeme thy woefull parents head,
  From tyrans rage, and ever-dying dread,²
  Hast wandred through the world now long a day;
  Yet ceasest not thy wearie soles to lead,
80   What grace hath thee now hither brought this way?
  Or doen thy feeble feet unweeting° hither stray?   *unknowing*

10

"Strange thing it is an errant° knight to see   *wandering*
  Here in this place, or any other wight,
  That hither turnes his steps. So few there bee,
85   That chose the narrow path, or seeke the right:
  All keepe the broad high way, and take delight
  With many rather for to go astray,
  And be partakers of their evill plight,
  Then with a few to walke the rightest way;³
90 O foolish men, why haste ye to your owne decay?"

11

"Thy selfe to see, and tyred limbs to rest,
  O matrone sage," quoth she, "I hither came,
  And this good knight his way with me addrest,°   *directed*
  Led with thy prayses and broad-blazèd fame,
95   That up to heaven is blowne."⁴ The auncient Dame
  Him goodly greeted in her modest guise,
  And entertaynd them both, as best became,
  With all the court'sies,° that she could devise,   *courtesies*
Ne wanted ought, to shew her bounteous or wise.

---

1. Like a matron, i.e., a woman in charge of an establishment.
2. Continuing fear of death; "long a day": many a long day.
3. An echo of Matthew 7.13–4: "Broad is the way that leadeth to destruction, and many there be which go in thereat: / . . . strait is the gate and narrow is the way, which leadeth unto life, and few there be that find it."
4. I.e., your praises and fame are widely celebrated ("blazed"), reaching ("blowne") up to heaven.

12

100 Thus as they gan of sundry things devise,°   *talk*
    Loe two most goodly virgins came in place,
    Ylinkèd arme in arme in lovely° wise,   *loving*
    With countenance demure, and modest grace,
    They numbred even steps and equall pace:
105   Of which the eldest, that Fidelia hight,
    Like sunny beames threw from her Christall face,
    That could have dazd° the rash beholders sight,   *dazzled*
And round about her head did shine like heavens light.

13

    She was araièd° all in lilly white,   *arrayed*
110   And in her right hand bore a cup of gold,
    With wine and water fild up to the hight,
    In which a Serpent did himselfe enfold,
    That horrour made to all, that did behold;
    But she no whit did chaunge her constant mood:[5]
115   And in her other hand she fast did hold
    A booke, that was both signd and seald with blood,
Wherein darke things were writ, hard to be understood.[6]

14

    Her younger sister, that Speranza hight,
    Was clad in blew, that her beseemèd well;
120   Not all so chearefull seemèd she of sight,[7]
    As was her sister; whether dread° did dwell,   *fear*
    Or anguish in her hart, is hard to tell:
    Upon her arme a silver anchor[8] lay,
    Whereon she leanèd ever, as befell:
125   And ever up to heaven, as she did pray,
Her stedfast eyes were bent, ne swarvèd other way.

15

    They seeing Una, towards her gan wend,°   *walk*
    Who them encounters° with like courtesie;   *meets*
    Many kind speeches they betwene them spend,
130   And greatly joy each other well to see:
    Then to the knight with shamefast° modestie   *humble*
    They turne themselves, at Unas meeke request,
    And him salute with well beseeming glee:[9]
    Who faire them quites,° as him beseeméd best,   *returns the salute*
135 And goodly gan discourse of many a noble gest.°   *deed*

16

    Then Una thus; "But she your sister deare;
    The deare Charissa where is she become?°   *gone to*

5. Expression. The cup of wine and water signifies the sacrament of Communion: the serpent is a symbol of the crucified Christ (of whom the serpent lifted up by Moses, Numbers 21.9, is a recognized type).

6. The New Testament. See 2 Peter 3.16: "in which are some things hard to be understood."

7. In appearance.

8. The iconographic symbol of hope.

9. Appropriate joy.

Or wants she health, or busie is elsewhere?"
"Ah no," said they, "but forth she may not come:
140 For she of late is lightned of her wombe,
And hath encreast the world with one sonne more,[1]
That her to see should be but troublesome."
"Indeede," quoth she, "that should her trouble sore,
But thankt be God, that her encrease so evermore."[2]

17

145 Then said the aged Caelia, "Deare dame,
And you good Sir, I wote that of your toyle,
And labours long, through which ye hither came,
Ye both forwearied° be: therefore a whyle   *utterly weary*
I read you rest, and to your bowres recoyle."[3]
150 Then callèd she a Groome, that forth him led
Into a goodly lodge, and gan despoile°   *disrobe*
Of puissant armes, and laid in easie bed;
His name was meeke Obedience rightfully aréd.° *understood*

18

Now when their wearie limbes with kindly° rest, *natural*
155 And bodies were refresht with due repast,
Faire Una gan Fidelia faire request,
To have her knight into her schoolehouse plaste,
That of her heavenly learning he might taste,
And heare the wisedome of her words divine.
160 She graunted, and that knight so much agraste,° *favored*
That she him taught celestiall discipline,
And opened his dull eyes, that light mote in them shine.

19

And that her sacred Booke, with bloud[4] ywrit,
That none could read, except she did them teach,
165 She unto him disclosèd every whit,
And heavenly documents° thereout did preach, *doctrines*
That weaker wit of man could never reach,
Of God, of grace, of justice, of free will,
That wonder was to heare her goodly speach:
170 For she was able, with her words to kill,
And raise againe to life the hart, that she did thrill.° *pierce*

20

And when she list poure out her larger spright,[5]
She would commaund the hastie Sunne to stay,
Or backward turne his course from heavens hight;
175 Sometimes great hostes of men she could dismay,
Dry-shod to passe, she parts the flouds in tway;
And eke huge mountaines from their native seat
She would commaund, themselves to beare away,

---

1. Charity, the fruitful virtue, is often depicted pictorially as a mother with many children.
2. I.e., God be thanked, who continually increases her thus.
3. Retire to your rooms. "Read": counsel.
4. I.e., the blood of Christ.
5. Full spiritual power.

And throw in raging sea with roaring threat.
180 Almightie God her gave such powre, and puissance great.[6]

21

The faithfull knight now grew in litle space,°   *time*
  By hearing her, and by her sisters lore,
  To such perfection of all heavenly grace,
  That wretched world he gan for to abhore,[7]
185 And mortall life gan loath, as thing forelore,°   *doomed*
  Greeved with remembrance of his wicked wayes,
  And prickt with anguish of his sinnes so sore,
  That he desirde to end his wretched dayes:
So much the dart of sinfull guilt the soule dismayes.

22

190 But wise Speranza gave him comfort sweet,
  And taught him how to take assurèd hold
  Upon her silver anchor, as was meet;
  Else had his sinnes so great, and manifold
  Made him forget all that Fidelia told.
195 In this distressèd doubtfull° agonie,   *fearful*
  When him his dearest Una did behold,
  Disdeining life, desiring leave to die,
She found her selfe assayld with great perplexitie.°   *distress*

23

And came to Caelia to declare her smart,
200 Who well acquainted with that commune° plight,   *common*
  Which sinfull horror[8] workes in wounded hart,
  Her wisely comforted all that she might,
  With goodly counsell and advisement right;
  And streightway sent with carefull diligence,
205 To fetch a Leach,° the which had great insight   *doctor*
  In that disease of grievèd° conscience,   *distressed*
And well could cure the same; His name was Patience.

24

Who comming to that soule-diseasèd knight,
  Could hardly° him intreat, to tell his griefe: *with difficulty*
210 Which knowne, and all that noyd° his heavie spright   *troubled*
  Well searcht,° eftsoones° he gan apply reliefe   *probed/soon after*
  Of salves and med'cines, which had passing priefe,[9]
  And thereto added words of wondrous might:
  By which to ease he him recurèd briefe,[1]
215 And much asswaged the passion° of his plight,   *suffering*
That he his paine endured, as seeming now more light.

---

6. Joshua made the sun stand still (Joshua 10.12);
Hezekiah made it turn backwards (2 Kings 20.10);
Gideon was victorious over the Midianite hosts
(Judges 7.7); Moses led the Israelites through the
parted waters of the Red Sea (Exodus 14.21–31);
faith, said Christ, can move mountains (Matthew
21.21). All these are miracles of faith.

7. I.e., he began to abhor the world.
8. Horror of sin.
9. Which had extraordinary power.
1. I.e., he spoke words of spiritual consolation to
ease the knight he had quickly cured of sin (by
grace).

25

But yet the cause and root of all his ill,
   Inward corruption, and infected sin,[2]
   Not purged nor heald, behind remainéd still,
220   And festring sore did rankle yet within,
   Close° creeping twixt the marrow and the skin.   *secretly*
   Which to extirpe,° he laid him privily   *extirpate*
   Downe in a darkesome lowly place farre in,
   Whereas he meant his corrosives to apply,
225 And with streight° diet tame his stubborne malady.   *strict*

26

In ashes and sackcloth he did array
   His daintie corse, proud humors[3] to abate,
   And dieted with fasting every day,
   The swelling of his wounds to mitigate,
230   And made him pray both earely and eke late:
   And ever as superfluous flesh did rot
   Amendment readie still at hand did wayt,
   To pluck it out with pincers firie whot,°   *hot*
That soone in him was left no one corrupted jot.

27

235 And bitter Penance with an yron whip,
   Was wont him once to disple° every day: *discipline*
   And sharpe Remorse his hart did pricke and nip,
   That drops of bloud thence like a well did play;
   And sad Repentance uséd to embay°   *bathe*
240   His bodie in salt water smarting sore,
   The filthy blots of sinne to wash away.[4]
   So in short space they did to health restore
The man that would not live, but earst° lay at deathes dore.   *formerly*

28

In which his torment often was so great,
245   That like a Lyon he would cry and rore,
   And rend his flesh, and his owne synewes eat.
   His own deare Una hearing evermore
   His ruefull shriekes and gronings, often tore
   Her guiltlesse garments, and her golden heare,
250   For pitty of his paine and anguish sore;
   Yet all with patience wisely she did beare;
For well she wist, his crime could else be never cleare.°   *cleansed*

29

Whom thus recovered by wise Patience,
   And trew Repentance they to Una brought:
255   Who joyous of his curéd conscience,
   Him dearely kist, and fairely° eke besought   *courteously*
   Himselfe to chearish,° and consuming thought   *cheer, cherish*

---

2. I.e., the effects of original sin.
3. Whatever is conducive to pride.

4. "Wash me throughly from mine iniquity, and cleanse me from my sin" (Psalms 51.2).

To put away out of his carefull° brest.   *care-full*
By this⁵ Charissa, late in child-bed brought,
260   Was woxen strong, and left her fruitfull nest;
To her faire Una brought this unacquainted guest.

                              30
She was a woman in her freshest age,
   Of wondrous beauty, and of bountie° rare,   *goodness*
   With goodly grace and comely personage,°   *appearance*
265   That was on earth not easie to compare;°   *rival*
   Full of great love, but Cupids wanton snare
   As hell she hated, chast in worke and will;
   Her necke and breasts were ever open bare,
   That ay thereof her babes might sucke their fill;
270   The rest was all in yellow robes arayèd still.⁶

                              31
A multitude of babes about her hong,
   Playing their sports, that joyd her to behold,
   Whom still she fed, whiles they were weake and young,
   But thrust them forth still, as they wexèd old:
275   And on her head she wore a tyre° of gold,   *headdress*
   Adornd with gemmes and owches° wondrous faire,   *jewels*
   Whose passing° price uneath° was to be told;   *surpassing/scarcely*
   And by her side there sate a gentle paire
Of turtle doves,⁷ she sitting in an yvorie chaire.

                              32
280   The knight and Una entring, faire her greet,
   And bid her joy of that her happie brood;
   Who them requites with court'sies seeming meet,°   *appropriate*
   And entertaines with friendly chearefull mood.
   Then Una her besought, to be so good,
285   As in her vertuous rules to schoole her knight,
   Now after all his torment well withstood,
   In that sad° house of Penaunce, where his spright   *solemn*
Had past° the paines of hell, and long enduring night. *passed through*

                              33
She was right joyous of her just request,
290   And taking by the hand that Faeries sonne,
   Gan him instruct in every good behest,°   *command*
   Of love, and righteousness, and well to donne,⁸
   And wrath, and hatred warely° to shonne,   *warily*
   That drew on men Gods hatred, and his wrath,
295   And many soules in dolours° had fordonne:°   *misery/destroyed*
   In which when him she well instructed hath,
From thence to heaven she teacheth him the ready° path.   *direct*

---

5. By this time.
6. Her yellow (saffron) robe is the color of marriage, fertility, and maternity. Her chaste, fruitful love (Christian *agape*) is opposed to "Cupid's wanton snare" *(eros)*.
7. Emblem of true love and faithful marriage.
8. I.e., right action.

34

Wherein his weaker° wandring steps to guide,   *too weak*
An auncient matrone she to her does call,
300   Whose sober lookes her wisedome well descride:°   *made known*
Her name was Mercie, well knowne over all,
To be both gratious, and eke° liberall: *also*
To whom the carefull charge of him she gave,
To lead aright, that he should never fall
305   In all his wayes through this wide worldès wave,°   *expanse*
That Mercy in the end his righteous soule might save.

35

The godly Matrone by the hand him beares°   *leads*
Forth from her[9] presence, by a narrow way,
Scattred with bushy thornes, and ragged breares,°   *briers*
310   Which still before him she removed away,
That nothing might his ready passage stay:
And ever when his feet encombred were,
Or gan to shrinke, or from the right to stray,
She held him fast, and firmely did upbeare,
315   As carefull Nourse her child from falling oft does reare.

36

Eftsoones unto an holy Hospitall,[1]
That was fore° by the way, she did him bring,   *close*
In which seven Bead-men[2] that had vowèd all
Their life to service of high heavens king
320   Did spend their dayes in doing godly thing:
Their gates to all were open evermore,
That by the wearie way were traveiling,
And one sate wayting ever them before,
To call in commers-by, that needy were and pore.[3]

37

325   The first of them that eldest was, and best,°   *chief*
Of all the house had charge and governement,
As Guardian and Steward of the rest:
His office was to give entertainement
And lodging, unto all that came, and went:
330   Not unto such, as could him feast againe,°   *in return*
And double quite,° for that he on them spent,   *repay*
But such, as want of harbour° did constraine:°   *shelter/afflict*
Those for Gods sake his dewty was to entertaine.

38

The second was as Almner[4] of the place,
335   His office was, the hungry for to feed,
And thristy give to drinke, a worke of grace:
He feard not once him selfe to be in need,

---

9. I.e., Charissa's.
1. House of rest for pilgrims and travelers.
2. Men of prayer.

3. I.e., one beadsman sat in front of the gates, to
call in needy wayfarers.
4. An almoner distributed charity to the poor.

Ne cared to hoord for those, whom he did breede:[5]
The grace of God he layd up still in store,
340 Which as a stocke° he left unto his seede;°   *resource/children*
He had enough, what need him care for more?
And had he lesse, yet some he would give to the pore.

                          39

The third had of their wardrobe custodie,
In which were not rich tyres,° nor garments gay,   *robes*
345 The plumes of pride, and wings of vanitie,
But clothes meet to keepe keene could° away,   *cold*
And naked nature seemely° to aray;   *decently*
With which bare wretched wights he dayly clad,
The images of God in earthly clay;
350 And if that no spare clothes to give he had,
His owne coate he would cut, and it distribute glad.

                          40

The fourth appointed by his office was,
Poore prisoners to relieve with gratious ayd,
And captives to redeeme with price of bras,[6]
355 From Turkes and Sarazins, which them had stayd;°   *held captive*
And though they faultie were, yet well he wayd,
That God to us forgiveth every howre
Much more then that, why° they in bands were layd,   *for which*
And he that harrowd hell[7] with heavie stowre,
360 The faultie° soules from thence brought to his heavenly   *sinful*
    bowre.

                          41

The fift had charge sicke persons to attend,
And comfort those, in point of death which lay;
For them most needeth comfort in the end,
When sin, and hell, and death do most dismay
365 The feeble soule departing hence away.
All is but lost, that living we bestow,°   *store up*
If not well ended at our dying day.
O man have mind of that last bitter throw;°   *throes of death*
For as the tree does fall, so lyes it ever low.

                          42

370 The sixt had charge of them now being dead,
In seemely sort their courses to engrave,[8]
And deck with dainty flowres their bridall bed,
That to their heavenly spouse both sweet and brave°   *fair*
They might appeare, when he their soules shall save.
375 The wondrous workemanship of Gods owne mould,[9]

5. I.e., his children.
6. Payment of money.
7. I.e., Christ, who journeyed to hell to deliver those good people who lived before his time, according to a popular story in the Middle Ages. It originated in the apocryphal gospel of Nicodemus.

"Stowre": assault.
8. Bodies ("courses," i.e., corpses) to bury.
9. The human body is God's own image ("mould") and a "mould" of God's making. See Genesis 1.26–30, 2.7.

Whose face he made, all beasts to feare, and gave
All in his hand, even dead we honour should.
Ah dearest God me graunt, I dead be not defould.°   *defiled*

43

The seventh now after death and buriall done,
380   Had charge the tender Orphans of the dead
And widowes ayd, least they should be undone:
In face of judgement[1] he their right would plead,
Ne ought[2] the powre of mighty men did dread
In their defence, nor would for gold or fee°   *bribe*
385   Be wonne their rightfull causes downe to tread:
And when they stood in most necessitee,
He did supply their want, and gave them ever free.[3]

44

There when the Elfin knight arrivèd was,
The first and chiefest of the seven, whose care
390   Was guests to welcome, towardes him did pas:
Where seeing Mercie, that his steps up bare,[4]
And alwayes led, to her with reverence rare
He humbly louted° in meeke lowlinesse,   *bowed*
And seemely welcome for her did prepare:
395   For of their order she was Patronesse,
Albe° Charissa were their chiefest founderesse.   *although*

45

There she awhile him stayes, him selfe to rest,
That to the rest more able he might bee:
During which time, in every good behest°   *command*
400   And godly worke of Almes and charitee
She him instructed with great industree;
Shortly therein so perfect he became,
That from the first unto the last degree,
His mortall life he learnèd had to frame,
405   In holy righteousnesse, without rebuke or blame.

46

Thence forward by that painfull way they pas,
Forth to an hill, that was both steepe and hy;
On top whereof a sacred chappell was,
And eke° a litle Hermitage thereby,   *also*
410   Wherein an agèd holy man did lye,°   *live*
That day and night said his devotion,
Ne other worldly busines did apply;[5]
His name was heavenly Contemplation;
Of God and goodnesse was his meditation.

---

1. I.e., in court.
2. Neither at all.
3. Always freely. The seven beadsmen here correspond to, and perform, the seven works of charity, or corporal mercy: lodging the homeless, feeding
the hungry, clothing the naked, redeeming the
captive, comforting the sick, burying the dead, and
succoring the orphan.
4. Supported.
5. I.e., he did not attend to any worldly activities.

47

415 Great grace that old man to him given had;
    For God he often saw from heavens hight,
    All° were his earthly eyen both blunt° and bad,   *although/dim*
    And through great age had lost their kindly° sight,   *natural*
    Yet wondrous quick and persant° was his spright,°   *piercing/spirit*
420 As Eagles eye, that can behold the Sunne:
    That hill they scale with all their powre and might,
    That his frayle thighes nigh wearie and fordonne°   *exhausted*
Gan faile, but by her helpe the top at last he wonne.

48

There they do finde that godly agèd Sire,
425   With snowy lockes adowne his shoulders shed,
    As hoarie frost with spangles doth attire
    The mossy braunches of an Oke halfe ded.
    Each bone might through his body well be red,°   *observed*
    And every sinew seene through° his long fast: *because of*
430 For nought he cared his carcas long unfed;
    His mind was full of spirituall repast,
And pynèd° his flesh, to keepe his body low° and chast.   *starved / thin*

49

Who when these two approching he aspide,
    At their first presence grew agrievèd sore,[6]
435 That forst him lay his heavenly thoughts aside;
    And had he not that Dame respected more,°   *greatly*
    Whom highly he did reverence and adore,
    He would not once have movèd for the knight.
    They him saluted standing far afore;°   *away*
440 Who well them greeting, humbly did requight,°   *respond*
And asked, to what end they clomb° that tedious height.   *had climbed*

50

"What end," quoth she, "should cause us take such paine,
    But that same end, which every living wight
    Should make his marke,° high heaven to attaine?   *goal*
445 Is not from hence the way, that leadeth right
    To that most glorious house, that glistreth bright
    With burning starres, and everliving fire,
    Whereof the keyes are to thy hand behight°   *entrusted*
    By wise Fidelia? she doth thee require,
450 To shew it to this knight, according his desire."

51

"Thrise happy man," said then the father grave,
    "Whose staggering steps thy[7] steady hand doth lead,
    And shewes the way, his sinfull soule to save.
    Who better can the way to heaven aread°   *direct*
455 Then thou thy selfe, that was both borne and bred

6. I.e., he was at first sorely grieved at their arrival.   7. I.e., Mercy's.

In heavenly throne, where thousand Angels shine?
Thou doest the prayers of the righteous sead°   seed
Present before the majestie divine,
And his avenging wrath to clemencie incline.

52

460 "Yet since thou bidst, thy pleasure shalbe donne.
Then come thou man of earth,[8] and see the way,
That never yet was seene of Faeries sonne,
That never leads the traveiler astray,
But after labours long, and sad delay,
465 Brings them to joyous rest and endlesse blis.
But first thou must a season fast and pray,
Till from her bands the spright assoilèd° is,   released
And have her strength recured° from fraile infirmitis."   recovered

53

That done, he leads him to the highest Mount;
470 Such one, as that same mighty man of God,
That bloud-red billowes like a wallèd front
On either side disparted° with his rod,   parted asunder
Till that his army dry-foot through them yod,°   went
Dwelt fortie dayes upon; where writ in stone
475 With bloudy letters by the hand of God,
The bitter doome of death and balefull mone[9]
He did receive, whiles flashing fire about him shone.

54

Or like that sacred hill, whose head full hie,
Adornd with fruitfull Olives all arownd,
480 Is, as it were for endlesse memory
Of that deare Lord, who oft thereon was fownd,
For ever with a flowring girlond crownd:
Or like that pleasaunt Mount, that is for ay
Through famous Poets verse each where° renownd,   everywhere
485 On which the thrise three learned Ladies play
Their heavenly notes, and make full many a lovely lay.[1]

55

From thence, far off he unto him did shew
A litle path, that was both steepe and long,
Which to a goodly Citie led his vew;
490 Whose wals and towres were builded high and strong
Of perle and precious stone, that earthly tong
Cannot describe, nor wit of man can tell;
Too high a ditty° for my simple song;   subject

8. An allusion to humankind's formation from the dust of the earth (Genesis 2.7) and also to the knight's name. See 66.5–6 and note.
9. I.e., the ten commandments ("bloudy letters") carried with them the judgment ("doome") of death and pain (causing sorrowful moans—"balefull mone").

1. Song. The mountain is successively compared to Mt. Sinai (lines 469–77), where Moses, after parting the "bloud-red billowes" of the Red Sea, received the tablets of the ten commandments; to the Mount of Olives (lines 478–82), associated with Christ; and to Mount Parnassus (lines 483–86), where dwelled the nine muses of art and poetry.

The Citie of the great king hight it well,
495 Wherein eternall peace and happinesse doth dwell.

56

As he thereon stood gazing, he might see
The blessed Angels to and fro descend
From highest heaven, in gladsome companee,
And with great joy into that Citie wend,
500 As commonly as friend does with his frend.[2]
Whereat he wondred much, and gan enquere,
What stately building durst so high extend
Her loftie towres unto the starry sphere,
And what unknowen nation there empeopled were.

57

505 "Faire knight," quoth he, "Hierusalem that is,
The new Hierusalem, that God has built
For those to dwell in, that are chosen his,
His chosen people purged from sinfull guilt,
With pretious bloud, which cruelly was spilt
510 On cursèd tree, of that unspotted lam,[3]
That for the sinnes of all the world was kilt:
Now are they Saints all in that Citie sam,°   together
More deare unto their God, then younglings to their dam."[4]

58

"Till now," said then the knight, "I weenèd well,
515 That great Cleopolis,[5] where I have beene,
In which that fairest Faerie Queene doth dwell,
The fairest Citie was, that might be seene;
And that bright towre all built of christall cleene,°   clear
Panthea,[6] seemd the brightest thing, that was:
520 But now by proofe all otherwise I weene;
For this great Citie[7] that does far surpas,
And this bright Angels towre quite dims that towre of glas."

59

"Most trew," then said the holy aged man;
"Yet is Cleopolis for earthly frame,°   structure
525 The fairest peece,° that eye beholden can: masterpiece
And well beseemes° all knights of noble name,   becomes
That covet in th' immortall booke of fame
To be eternizèd, that same to haunt,°   frequent
And doen their service to that soveraigne Dame,
530 That glorie does to them for guerdon° graunt: reward
For she is heavenly borne, and heaven may justly vaunt.°   claim

---

2. Cf. Jacob's ladder, which "reached to heaven; and behold the angels of God ascending and descending on it" (Genesis 28.12). "Commonly": familiarly.
3. Lamb; a reference to Christ (the lamb of God) whose death on the cross ("cursed tree") purged the guilt of sin from those "chosen his."
4. The New Jerusalem is described in Revelation 21–22; "the nations of them which are saved shall walk in the light of it" (21.24).
5. London, Camelot—the earthly counterpart of the Heavenly Kingdom.
6. Reminiscent of the temple of glass in Chaucer's *Hous of Fame*; perhaps intended to represent Richmond Palace or Westminster Abbey.
7. I.e., The New Jerusalem far surpasses Cleopolis ("that").

60

"And thou faire ymp,° sprong out from English race,   *youth*
   How ever now accompted° Elfins sonne,   *accounted*
   Well worthy doest thy service for her grace,°   *favor*
535 To aide a virgin desolate foredonne.°   *undone*
   But when thou famous victorie hast wonne,
   And high emongst all knights has hong thy shield,
   Thenceforth the suit° of earthly conquest shonne,   *pursuit*
   And wash thy hands from guilt of bloudy field:
540 For bloud can nought but sin, and wars but sorrowes yield.

61

"Then seeke this path, that I to thee presage,°   *point out prophetically*
   Which after all to heaven shall thee send;
   Then peaceably thy painefull° pilgrimage   *laborious*
   To yonder same Hierusalem do bend,
545 Where is for thee ordaind a blessed end:
   For thou emongst those Saints, whom thou doest see,
   Shalt be a Saint, and thine owne nations frend
   And Patrone: thou Saint George shalt callèd bee,
Saint George of mery England, the signe of victoree."[8]

62

550 "Unworthy wretch," quoth he, "of so great grace,
   How dare I thinke such glory to attaine?"
   "These that have it attaind, were in like cace,"
   Quoth he, "as wretched, and lived in like paine."
   "But deeds of armes must I at last be faine,°   *content to leave*
555 And Ladies love to leave so dearely bought?"
   "What need of armes, where peace doth ay remaine,"
   Said he, "and battailes none are to be fought?
As for loose loves are[9] vaine, and vanish into nought."

63

"O let me not," quoth he, "then turne againe
560 Backe to the world, whose joyes so fruitlesse are;
   But let me here for aye in peace remaine,
   Or streight way on that last long voyage fare,
   That nothing may my present hope empare."°   *impair*
   "That may not be," said he, "ne maist thou yit
565 Forgo that royall maides bequeathèd care,°   *charge*
   Who did her cause into thy hand commit,
Till from her cursèd foe thou have her freely quit."°   *released*

64

"Then shall I soone," quoth he, "so God me grace,
   Abet° that virgins cause disconsolate,   *maintain*
570 And shortly backe returne unto this place
   To walke this way in Pilgrims poore estate.

---

8. Spenser's conception of St. George, patron saint   pageants, and folklore.
of England, draws on the *Legenda Aurea* (trans-   9. I.e., they are.
lated by Caxton in 1487); on pictures, tapestries,

But now aread,° old father, why of late   declare
Didst thou behight° me borne of English blood,   call
Whom all a Faeries sonne doen nominate?"°   name
575 "That word shall I," said he, "avouchen° good,   prove
Sith to thee is unknowne the cradle of thy brood.

                                    65
"For well I wote,° thou springst from ancient race   know
Of Saxon kings, that have with mightie hand
And many bloudie battailes fought in place°   there
580 High reard their royall throne in Britane land,
And vanquisht them, unable to withstand:
From thence a Faerie thee unweeting reft,[1]
There as thou slepst in tender swadling band,
And her base Elfin brood there for thee left.
585 Such men do Chaungelings call, so chaungd by Faeries theft.

                                    66
"Thence she thee brought into this Faerie lond,
And in an heapèd furrow did thee hyde,
Where thee a Ploughman all unweeting° fond,   unknowing
As he his toylesome teme° that way did guyde,   team of oxen
590 And brought thee up in ploughmans state to byde,
Whereof Georgos he thee gave to name;[2]
Till prickt° with courage, and thy forces pryde,   spurred
To Faery court thou cam'st to seeke for fame,
And prove thy puissaunt armes, as seemes thee best became."[3]

                                    67
595 "O holy Sire," quoth he, "how shall I quight°   repay
The many favours I with thee have found,
That has my name and nation red aright,
And taught the way that does to heaven bound?"°   go
This said, adowne he lookèd to the ground,
600 To have returnd, but dazèd° were his eyne,   dazzled
Through passing° brightnesse, which did   surpassing
     quite confound
His feeble sence, and too exceeding shyne.
So darke are earthly things compard to things divine.

                                    68
At last whenas himselfe he gan to find,°   recover
605 To Una back he cast him to retire;
Who him awaited still with pensive° mind.   anxious
Great thankes and goodly meed° to that good syre,   gift
He thence departing gave for his paines hyre.°   reward
So came to Una, who him joyd to see,
610 And after litle rest, gan him desire,
Of her adventure mindfull for to bee.
So leave they take of Caelia, and her daughters three.

---

1. Secretly stole.   (cf. Virgil's *Georgics*, on farming).
2. I.e., as a name. *Georgos* is Greek for "farmer"   3. As best suited you.

Canto 11

The knight with that old Dragon fights
two dayes incessantly:
The third him overthrowes, and gayns
most glorious victory.

1

High time now gan it wex° for Una faire,   grow
   To thinke of those her captive Parents deare,
   And their forwasted kingdome to repaire:[1]
   Whereto whenas they now approachèd neare,
5   With hartie° words her knight she gan to cheare,   bold
   And in her modest manner thus bespake;
   "Deare knight, as deare, as ever knight was deare,
   That all these sorrowes suffer for my sake,
High heaven behold the tedious toyle, ye for me take.

2

10 "Now are we come unto my native soyle,
   And to the place, where all our perils dwell;
   Here haunts that feend, and does his dayly spoyle,
   Therefore henceforth be at your keeping well,[2]
   And ever ready for your foeman fell.
15   The sparke of noble courage now awake,
   And strive your excellent selfe to excell;
   That shall ye evermore renowmèd make,
Above all knights on earth, that batteill undertake."

3

And pointing forth, "lo yonder is," said she,
20 "The brasen towre in which my parents deare
   For dread of that huge feend emprisond be,
   Whom I from far see on the walles appeare,
   Whose sight my feeble° soule doth greatly cheare: doleful
   And on the top of all I do espye
25   The watchman wayting tydings glad to heare,
   That O my parents might I happily
Unto you bring, to ease you of your misery."

4

With that they heard a roaring hideous sound,
   That all the ayre with terrour fillèd wide,
30   And seemd uneath° to shake the stedfast ground.   almost
   Eftsoones° that dreadfull Dragon they espide,   soon after
   Where stretcht he lay upon the sunny side
   Of a great hill, himselfe like a great hill.
   But all so soone, as he from far descride
35   Those glistring armes, that heaven with light díd fill,
He rousd himselfe full blith,° and hastned them   joyfully
    untill.°   toward

---

1. I.e., to restore their kingdom, laid waste (by the   2. I.e., be well on your guard.
dragon).

5

Then bad the knight his Lady yede° aloofe,   *step*
  And to an hill her selfe withdraw aside,
  From whence she might behold that battailles proof°   *outcome*
40 And eke be safe from daunger far descryde:
  She him obayd, and turnd a little wyde.°   *aside*
  Now O thou sacred Muse,[3] most learned Dame,
  Faire ympe of Phoebus, and his aged bride,[4]
  The Nourse of time, and everlasting fame,
45 That warlike hands ennoblest with immortall name;

6

O gently come into my feeble brest,
  Come gently, but not with that mighty rage,
  Wherewith the martiall troupes thou doest infest,°   *arouse*
  And harts of great Heroës doest enrage,
50 That nought their kindled courage may aswage,
  Soone as thy dreadfull trompe° begins to sownd;   *trumpet*
  The God of warre with his fiers equipage
  Thou doest awake, sleepe never he so sownd,°   *sound*
  And scarèd nations doest with horrour sterne astown.°   *appall*

7

55 Faire Goddesse lay that furious fit° aside,   *strain*
  Till I of warres and bloudy Mars do sing[5]
  And Briton fields with Sarazin bloud bedyde,
  Twixt that great faery Queene and Paynim king,
  That with their horrour heaven and earth did ring,
60 A worke of labour long, and endlesse prayse:
  But now a while let downe that haughtie string,
  And to my tunes thy second tenor rayse,[6]
  That I this man of God his godly armes may blaze.°   *describe*

8

  By this the dreadfull Beast drew nigh to hand,
65 Halfe flying, and halfe footing° in his hast,   *walking*
  That with his largenesse measurèd much land,
  And made wide shadow under his huge wast;°   *girth*
  As mountaine doth the valley overcast.
  Approching nigh, he rearèd high afore
70 His body monstrous, horrible, and vast,
  Which to increase his wondrous greatnesse more,
  Was swolne with wrath, and poyson, and with bloudy gore.

9

  And over, all with brasen scales was armd,
  Like plated coate of steele, so couchèd neare,[7]
75 That nought mote perce,[8] ne might his corse be harmd

---

3. Calliope, muse of epic poetry, or Clio, muse
of history.
4. I.e., Mnemosyne (memory). "Impe": child.
5. Apparently a reference to a projected but
unwritten book of *The Faerie Queene*.

6. The "haughtie" (high-pitched) mode would be
appropriate to a large-scale epic war; the "second
tenor" (lower in pitch) to this present battle.
7. Closely overlaid.
8. Nothing might pierce ("perce"). "Corse": body.

With dint of sword, nor push of pointed speare;
Which as an Eagle, seeing pray appeare,
His acry Plumes doth rouze, full rudely dight,[9]
So shakèd he, that horrour was to heare,
80 For as the clashing of an Armour bright,
Such noyse his rouzèd scales did send unto the knight.

10

His flaggy° wings when forth he did display,   *drooping*
Were like two sayles, in which the hollow wynd
Is gathered full, and worketh speedy way:
85 And eke the pennes,° that did his pineons bynd,   *quills*
Were like mayne-yards, with flying canvas lynd,
With which whenas him list the ayre to beat,
And there by force unwonted° passage find,   *unaccustomed*
The cloudes before him fled for terrour great,
90 And all the heavens stood still amazèd with his threat.

11

His huge long tayle wound up in hundred foldes,
Does overspred his long bras-scaly backe,
Whose wreathèd boughts° when ever he unfoldes,   *coils*
And thicke entangled knots adown does slacke,
95 Bespotted as with shields° of red and blacke,   *scales*
It sweepeth all the land behind him farre,
And of three furlongs does but litle lacke;
And at the point two stings in-fixèd arre,
Both deadly sharpe, that sharpest steele exceeden farre.

12

100 But stings and sharpest steele did far exceed[1]
The sharpnesse of his cruell rending clawes;
Dead was it sure, as sure as death in deed,[2]
What ever thing does touch his ravenous pawes,
Or what within his reach he ever drawes.
105 But his most hideous head my toung to tell
Does tremble: for his deepe devouring jawes
Wide gapèd, like the griesly° mouth of hell,   *horrid*
Through which into his darke abisse all ravin° fell.   *prey, booty*

13

And that° more wondrous was, in either jaw   *what*
110 Threeranckes of yron teeth enraungèd were,
In which yet trickling bloud and gobbets raw[3]
Of late devourèd bodies did appeare,
That sight thereof bred cold congealèd feare:
Which to increase, and all at once to kill,
115 A cloud of smoothering smoke and sulphur seare°   *burning*
Out of his stinking gorge° forth steemèd still,   *maw*
That all the ayre about with smoke and stench did fill.

---

9. Ruggedly arrayed. "Rouze": shake.   2. In its effect.
1. I.e., were far exceeded by.   3. Chunks of undigested food.

14

His blazing eyes, like two bright shining shields,
  Did burne with wrath, and sparkled living fyre;
120 As two broad Beacons, set in open fields,
  Send forth their flames farre off to every shyre,°   *shire*
  And warning give, that enemies conspyre,
  With fire and sword the region to invade;
  So flamed his eyne° with rage and rancorous yre:°   *eyes/anger*
125 But farre within, as in a hollow glade,
Those glaring lampes were set, that made a dreadfull shade.

15

So dreadfully he towards him did pas,
  Forelifting up aloft his speckled brest,
  And often bounding on the brusèd gras,
130 As for great joyance of his newcome guest.
  Eftsoones he gan advance his haughtie crest,
  As chauffèd° Bore his bristles doth upreare,   *vexed*
  And shoke his scales to battell readie drest;°   *prepared*
  That made the Redcrosse knight nigh quake for feare,
135 As bidding bold defiance to his foeman neare.

16

The knight gan fairely couch° his steadie speare,   *rest, aim*
  And fiercely ran at him with rigorous° might: *violent*
  The pointed steele arriving rudely° theare,   *roughly*
  His harder hide would neither perce, nor bight,
140 But glauncing by forth passèd forward right;
  Yet sore amovèd with so puissant push,
  The wrathfull beast about him turnèd light,°   *quickly*
  And him so rudely passing by, did brush
With his long tayle, that horse and man to ground did rush.

17

145 Both horse and man up lightly rose againe,
  And fresh encounter towards him addrest:
  But th' idle stroke yet backe recoyld in vaine,
  And found no place his° deadly point to rest.   *its*
  Exceeding rage enflamed the furious beast,
150 To be avengèd of so great despight;°   *outrage*
  For never felt his imperceable brest
  So wondrous force, from hand of living wight;
Yet had he provèd° the powre of many a puissant knight. *tested*

18

Then with his waving wings displayèd wyde,
155 Himselfe up high he lifted from the ground,
  And with strong flight did forcibly divide
  The yielding aire, which nigh too feeble found
  Her flitting° partes, and element unsound,°   *moving/weak*
  To beare so great a weight: he cutting way
160 With his broad sayles, about him soarèd round:

At last low stouping with unweldie sway,[4]
Snatcht up both horse and man, to beare them quite away.

                              19
Long he them bore above the subject plaine,[5]
    So farre as Ewghen[6] bow a shaft may send,
165   Till struggling strong did him at last constraine,
    To let them downe before his flightès end:
    As hagard° hauke presuming to contend   *untamed*
    With hardie fowle, above his hable might,[7]
    His wearie pounces° all in vaine doth spend,   *claws*
170   To trusse° the pray too heavie for his flight;   *seize*
Which comming downe to ground, does free it selfe by fight.

                              20
He so disseizèd of his gryping grosse,[8]
    The knight his thrilant° speare againe assayd   *piercing*
    In his bras-plated body to embosse,°   *plunge*
175   And three mens strength unto the stroke he layd;
    Wherewith the stiffe beame quakèd, as affrayd,
    And glauncing from his scaly necke, did glyde
    Close under his left wing, then broad displayd.
    The percing steele there wrought a wound full wyde,
180 That with the uncouth° smart the Monster lowdly cryde.   *unusual*

                              21
He cryde, as raging seas are wont to rore,
    When wintry storme his wrathfull wreck does threat,
    The rolling billowes beat the ragged shore,
    As they the earth would shoulder from her seat,
185   And greedie gulfe[9] does gape, as he would eat
    His neighbour element[1] in his revenge:
    Then gin the blustring brethren[2] boldly threat,
    To move the world from off his stedfast henge,°   *axis*
And boystrous battell make, each other to avenge.

                              22
190 The steely head stucke fast still in his flesh,
    Till with his cruell clawes he snatcht the wood,
    And quite a sunder broke. Forth flowèd fresh
    A gushing river of blacke goarie° blood,   *clotted*
    That drownèd all the land, whereon he stood;
195   The stream thereof would drive a water-mill.
    Trebly augmented was his furious mood
    With bitter sense of his deepe rooted ill,°   *injury*
That flames of fire he threw forth from his large noséthrill.

                              23
His hideous tayle then hurlèd he about,
200   And therewith all enwrapt the nimble thyes°   *thighs*

---

4. Ponderous force.   8. Freed from his formidable grip.
5. I.e., the ground below.   9. I.e., the sea.
6. Yewen, of yew.   1. I.e., earth.
7. Able power.   2. I.e., the winds.

Of his froth-fomy steed, whose courage stout
Striving to loose the knot, that fast him tyes,
Himselfe in streighter bandes too rash implyes,[3]
That to the ground he is perforce constraynd
205   To throw his rider: who can° quickly ryse   *began to*
From off the earth, with durty bloud distaynd,°   *defiled*
For that reprochfull fall right fowly he disdaynd.

24

And fiercely tooke his trenchand° blade in hand,   *sharp*
With which he stroke so furious and so fell,
210   That nothing seemd the puissance could withstand:
Upon his crest the hardned yron fell,
But his more hardned crest was armd so well,
That deeper dint therein it would not make;[4]
Yet so extremely did the buffe° him quell,°   *blow/dismay*
215   That from thenceforth he shund the like to take,
But when he saw them come, he did them still forsake.°   *avoid*

25

The knight was wrath to see his stroke beguyld,°   *foiled*
And smote againe with more outrageous might;
But backe againe the sparckling steele recoyld,
220   And left not any marke, where it did light;
As if in Adamant rocke it had bene pight.°   *struck against*
The beast impatient of his smarting wound,
And of so fierce and forcible despight,[5]
Thought with his wings to stye° above the ground;   *mount*
225   But his late wounded wing unserviceable found.

26

Then full of griefe and anguish vehement,
He lowdly brayd, that like was never heard,
And from his wide devouring oven sent
A flake° of fire, that flashing in his beard,   *flash*
230   Him all amazd, and almost made affeard;
The scorching flame sore swingèd° all his face,   *singed*
And through his armour all his bodie seard,
That he could not endure so cruell cace,°   *plight*
But thought his armes to leave, and helmet to unlace.

27

235 Not that great Champion of the antique world,
Whom famous Poetes verse so much doth vaunt,
And hath for twelve huge labours high extold,
So many furies and sharpe fits did haunt,
When him the poysoned garment did enchaunt
240   With Centaures bloud, and bloudie verses charmed,
As did this knight twelve thousand dolours° daunt,   *sufferings*

---

3. I.e., too suddenly entangles. "Streighter": tigh-   4. I.e., it could not make a deep gash there.
ter.   5. Powerful injury.

Whom fyrie steele now burnt, that earst° him armed,   *formerly*
That erst him goodly armed, now most of all him harmed.[6]

28

Faint, wearie, sore, emboylèd, grievèd, brent°   *burned*
245   With heat, toyle, wounds, armes, smart, and inward fire
That never man such mischiefes° did torment;   *misfortunes*
Death better were, death did he oft desire,
But death will never come, when needes require.
Whom so dismayd when that his foe beheld,
250   He cast to suffer him no more respire,°   *rest*
But gan his sturdie sterne° about to weld,°   *tail/lash*
And him so strongly stroke, that to the ground him feld.

29

It fortunèd (as faire it then befell)
Behind his backe unweeting,° where he stood,   *unnoticed*
255   Of auncient time there was a springing well,
From which fast trickled forth a silver flood,
Full of great vertues, and for med'cine good.
Whylome,° before that cursèd Dragon got   *formerly*
That happie land, and all with innocent blood
260   Defyld those sacred waves, it rightly hot°   *was called*
The Well of Life,[7] ne yet his vertues had forgot.

30

For unto life the dead it could restore,
And guilt of sinfull crimes cleane wash away,
Those that with sicknesse were infected sore,
265   It could recure, and aged long decay
Renew, as one were borne that very day.
Both Silo this, and Jordan did excell,
And th' English Bath, and eke the german Spau,
Ne can Cephise, nor Hebrus match this well:
270   Into the same the knight backe overthrowen, fell.[8]

31

Now gan the golden Phoebus for to steepe
His fierie face in billowes of the west,
And his faint steedes watred in Ocean deepe,
Whiles from their journall° labours they did rest,   *daily*
275   When that infernall Monster, having kest°   *cast*
His wearie foe into that living well,
Can° high advaunce his broad discoloured brest,   *did*
Above his wonted pitch,° with countenance fell,°   *height/sinister*
And clapt his yron wings, as victor he did dwell.°   *remain*

6. Redcrosse's fire-baptism is compared to the burning shirt of Nessus, which killed Hercules, "that great Champion of the antique world" (line 235). His "twelve huge labours" are replicated in the knight's "twelve thousand dolours."
7. An allusion to Revelation 22.1–2: "And he showed me a pure river of water of life, clear as crystal, proceeding out of the throne of God, and of the Lamb. In the midst of the street of it, and on either side of the river, was the tree of life which bore twelve manner of fruits and gave fruit every month, and the leaves of the tree served to heal the nation with."
8. The Well of Life, with its powers of renewal, is successively compared to waters of the Bible, of England and Europe, and of classical antiquity. In Siloam (Silo) a blind man was cured by Christ (John

32

280 Which when his pensive Ladie saw from farre,
     Great woe and sorrow did her soule assay,°   *attack*
     As weening that the sad end of the warre,
     And gan to highest God entirely° pray,   *earnestly*
     That fearèd chaunce° from her to turne away;   *fate*
285 With folded hands and knees full lowly bent
     All night she watcht, ne once adowne would lay
     Her daintie limbs in her sad dreriment,[9]
   But praying still did wake, and waking did lament.

33

   The morrow next gan early to appeare,
290 That Titan[1] rose to runne his daily race;
     But early ere the morrow next gan reare
     Out of the sea faire Titans deawy face,
     Up rose the gentle virgin from her place,
     And lookèd all about, if she might spy
295 Her loved knight to move his manly pace:
     For she had great doubt of his safety,
   Since late she saw him fall before his enemy.

34

   At last she saw, where he upstarted brave
     Out of the well, wherein he drenchèd lay;
300 As Eagle fresh out of the Ocean wave,
     Where he hath left his plumes all hoary gray,
     And deckt himselfe with feathers youthly gay,
     Like Eyas° hauke up mounts unto the skies,   *young*
     His newly budded pineons to assay,
305 And marveiles at himselfe, still as he flies:
   So new this new-borne knight to battell new did rise.[2]

35

   Whom when the damnèd feend so fresh did spy,
     No wonder if he wondred at the sight,
     And doubted, whether his late enemy
310 It were, or other new supplièd knight.
     He, now to prove his late renewèd might,
     High brandishing his bright deaw-burning blade,
     Upon his crested scalpe so sore did smite,
     That to the scull a yawning wound it made:
315 The deadly dint° his dullèd senses all dismaid.   *blow*

36

   I wote° not, whether the revenging steele   *know*
     Were hardnèd with that holy water dew,
     Wherein he fell, or sharper edge did feele,
     Or his baptizèd hands now greater° grew;   *stronger*

9.7); the crossing of the river Jordan saved the Jews
(Deuteronomy 27.2–9), and Christ was baptized
therein (Matthew 3.16); "Bath" and "Spau" (Spa)
were famed for their medicinal waters; "Cephise"
and "Hebrus" in Greece were noted for purifying
and healing powers.
9. Dismal condition.
1. When the sun.
2. Legend had it that the eagle could renew its
youth by bathing in a spring.

320 Or other secret vertue did ensew;
    Else never could the force of fleshly arme,
    Ne molten mettall in his bloud embrew:°   *plunge*
    For till that stownd° could never wight him harme, *stunning blow*
By subtilty, nor slight,° nor might, nor mighty charme.   *trickery*

37

325 The cruell wound enragèd him so sore,
    That loud he yellèd for exceeding paine;
    As hundred ramping Lyons seemed to rore,
    Whom ravenous hunger did there to constraine:
    Then gan he tosse aloft his stretchèd traine,°   *tail*
330 And therewith scourge the buxome° aire so sore,   *yielding*
    That to his force to yeelden it was faine;°   *obliged*
    Ne ought his sturdie strokes might stand afore,[3]
That high trees overthrew, and rocks in peeces tore.

38

The same advauncing high above his head,
335 With sharpe intended° sting so rude° him smot,   *extended/roughly*
    That to the earth him drove, as stricken dead,
    Ne living wight would have him life behot:[4]
    The mortall sting his angry needle shot
    Quite through his shield, and in his shoulder seasd,
340 Where fast it stucke, ne would there out be got:
    The griefe° thereof him wondrous sore diseasd,°   *pain/afflicted*
Ne might his ranckling paine with patience be appeasd.

39

But yet more mindfull of his honour deare,
    Then of the grievous smart, which him did wring,°   *torment*
345 From loathèd soile he can° him lightly reare,   *began to*
    And strove to loose the farre infixèd sting:
    Which when in vaine he tryde with struggeling,
    Inflamed with wrath, his raging blade he heft,°   *heaved*
    And strooke so strongly, that the knotty string
350 Of his huge taile he quite a sunder cleft,
Five joynts thereof he hewd, and but the stump him left.

40

Hart cannot thinke, what outrage,° and what cryes,   *violent clamor*
    With foule enfouldred[5] smoake and flashing fire,
    The hell-bred beast threw forth unto the skyes,
355 That all was coverèd with darknesse dire:
    Then fraught with rancour, and engorgèd° ire,   *choking*
    He cast at once him to avenge for all,
    And gathering up himselfe out of the mire,
    With his uneven wings did fiercely fall
360 Upon his sunne-bright shield, and gript it fast withall.

---

3. I.e., neither could anything ("ought") stand   called) him alive.
before his violent ("sturdie") strokes.   5. Black as a thunderbolt.
4. I.e., no one would have thought ("behot"—

41

Much was the man encombred with his hold,
   In feare to lose his weapon in his paw,
   Ne wist yet, how his talents° to unfold;   *talons*
   Nor harder was from Cerberus[6] greedie jaw
365 To plucke a bone, then from his cruell claw
   To reave° by strength the gripéd gage° away: *seize/prize*
   Thrise he assayd it from his foot to draw,
   And thrise in vaine to draw it did assay,
It booted nought to thinke, to robbe him of his pray.

42

370 Tho° when he saw no power might prevaile,   *then*
   His trustie sword he cald to his last aid,
   Wherewith he fiercely did his foe assaile,
   And double blowes about him stoutly laid,
   That glauncing fire out of the yron plaid;
375 As sparckles from the Andvile° use to fly,   *anvil*
   When heavie hammers on the wedge are swaid;° *struck*
   Therewith at last he forst him to unty°   *loosen*
One of his grasping feete, him to defend thereby.

43

The other foot, fast fixèd on his shield,
380 Whenas no strength, nor stroks mote° him constraine *might*
   To loose, ne yet the warlike pledge to yield,
   He smot thereat with all his might and maine,
   That nought so wondrous puissance might sustaine;
   Upon the joynt the lucky steele did light,
385 And made such way, that hewd it quite in twaine;
   The paw yet missèd not his minisht° might,   *lessened*
But hong still on the shield, as it at first was pight.° *placed*

44

For griefe thereof, and divelish despight,
   From his infernall fournace forth he threw
390 Huge flames, that dimmèd all the heavens light,
   Enrold in duskish smoke and brimstone blew;
   As burning Aetna from his boyling stew°   *cauldron*
   Doth belch out flames, and rockes in peeces broke,
   And ragged ribs of mountaines molten new
395 Enwrapt in coleblacke clouds and filthy smoke,
That all the land with stench, and heaven with horror choke.

45

The heate whereof, and harmefull pestilence
   So sore him noyd,° that forst him to retire   *troubled*
   A little backward for his best defence,
400 To save his bodie from the scorching fire,
   Which he from hellish entrailes did expire.° *breathe out*

6. The dog that guards the mouth of Hell.

It chaunst (eternall God that chaunce did guide)
    As he recoylèd backward, in the mire
    His nigh forwearied feeble feet did slide,
405   And downe he fell, with dread of shame sore terrifide.

46

There grew a goodly tree him faire beside,
    Loaden with fruit and apples rosie red,
    As they in pure vermilion had beene dide,
    Whereof great vertues over all were red:°   *declared*
410   For happie life to all, which thereon fed,
    And life eke everlasting did befall:
    Great God it planted in that blessed sted°   *place*
    With his almightie hand, and did it call
The Tree of Life, the crime of our first fathers fall.[7]

47

415 In all the world like was not to be found,
    Save in that soile, where all good things did grow,
    And freely sprong out of the fruitfull ground,
    As incorrupted Nature did them sow,
    Till that dread Dragon all did overthrow.
420   Another like faire tree eke grew thereby,
    Whereof who so did eat, eftsoones did know
    Both good and ill: O mornefull memory:
That tree through one mans fault hath doen us all to dy.[8]

48

From that first tree forth flowd, as from a well,
425   A trickling streame of Balme, most soveraine°   *powerful for cures*
    And daintie deare,[9] which on the ground still fell,
    And overflowèd all the fertill plaine,
    As it had deawèd bene with timely° raine: *seasonable*
    Life and long health that gratious° ointment gave,   *full of grace*
430   And deadly woundes could heale, and reare° againe   *raise*
    The senselesse corse appointed° for the grave.   *made ready*
Into that same he fell: which did from death him save.[1]

49

For nigh thereto the ever damnèd beast
    Durst not approch, for he was deadly made,[2]
435   And all that life preservèd, did detest:
    Yet he it oft adventured° to invade.   *attempted*
    By this the drouping day-light gan to fade,
    And yeeld his roome to sad succeeding night,
    Who with her sable mantle gan to shade

---

7. Genesis 2.9 describes the Tree of Life and also the Tree of Knowledge of Good and Evil, both of which God planted in the Garden of Eden. The "crime of our first fathers fall" is that Adam, in eating of the second and being banished from Eden, separated himself—and us—from the first. The Tree of Life appears again in the New Jerusalem (Revelation 22.2).
8. I.e., killed us.
9. Precious.
1. The healing balm flowing from the Tree of Life is understood to be Christ's blood, shed to redeem mankind from eternal damnation.
2. I.e., a child of death.

440   The face of earth, and wayes of living wight,
       And high her burning torch set up in heaven bright.

                        50

       When gentle Una saw the second fall
           Of her deare knight, who wearie of long fight,
           And faint through losse of bloud, moved not at all,
445   But lay as in a dreame of deepe delight,
           Besmeard with pretious Balme, whose vertuous might
           Did heale his wounds, and scorching heat alay,[3]
           Againe she stricken was with sore affright,
           And for his safetie gan devoutly pray;
450   And watch the noyous° night, and wait for joyous day.   *afflicting*

                        51

       The joyous day gan early to appeare,
           And faire Aurora from the deawy bed
           Of aged Tithone gan her selfe to reare,[4]
           With rosie cheekes, for shame as blushing red;
455   Her golden lockes for haste were loosely shed
           About her eares, when Una her did marke
           Clymbe to her charet, all with flowers spred,
           From heaven high to chase the chearelesse darke;
       With merry note her loud salutes the mounting larke.

                        52

460   Then freshly up arose the doughtie knight,
           All healèd of his hurts and woundès wide,
           And did himselfe to battell readie dight;°   *prepare*
           Whose early foe awaiting him beside
           To have devourd, so soone as day he spyde,
465   When now he saw himselfe so freshly reare,
           As if late fight had nought him damnifyde,°   *injured*
           He woxe° dismayd, and garr his fate to feare;   *grew*
       Nathlesse° with wonted rage he him advauncèd neare.   *nevertheless*

                        53

       And in his first encounter, gaping wide,
470   He thought attonce him to have swallowed quight,
           And rusht upon him with outragious pride;
           Who him r'encountring fierce, as hauke in flight,
           Perforce rebutted° backe. The weapon bright   *drove*
           Taking advantage of his open jaw,
475   Ran through his mouth with so importune° might,   *violent*
           That deepe emperst his darksome hollow maw,
       And back retyrd,[5] his life bloud forth with all did draw.

                        54

       So downe he fell, and forth his life did breath,
           That vanisht into smoke and cloudès swift;

---

3. Cf. Revelation 2.7,11: "To him that overcometh will I give to eat of the tree of life;" "He that
overcometh shall not be hurt of the second death."
4. Aurora is goddess of the dawn, Tithones her
husband ("aged" because he was granted everlasting life without everlasting youth).
5. On being drawn back.

480   So downe he fell, that th' earth him underneath
      Did grone, as feeble so great load to lift;
      So downe he fell, as an huge rockie clift,
      Whose false° foundation waves have washt away,   *insecure*
      With dreadfull poyse° is from the mayneland   *falling weight*
         rift,°   *split*
485   And rolling downe, great Neptune doth dismay;
      So downe he fell, and like an heapèd mountaine lay.

55

      The knight himselfe even trembled at his fall,
      So huge and horrible a masse it seemed;
      And his deare Ladie, that beheld it all,
490   Durst not approch for dread, which she misdeemed,°   *misjudged*
      But yet at last, when as the direfull feend
      She saw not stirre, off-shaking vaine affright,
      She nigher drew, and saw that joyous end:
      Then God she praysd, and thankt her faithfull knight,
495   That had atchieved so great a conquest by his might.

Canto 12

Faire Una to the Redcrosse knight
betrouthéd is with joy:
Though false Duessa it to barre
her false sleights doe imploy.

1

      Behold I see the haven nigh at hand,
      To which I meane my wearie course to bend;
      Vere the maine shete, and beare up with the land,[1]
      The which afore is fairely to be kend,°   *recognized*
5   And seemeth safe from stormes, that may offend;
      There this faire virgin wearie of her way
      Must landed be, now at her journeyes end:
      There eke my feeble barke° a while may stay,   *ship*
    Till merry° wind and weather call her thence away.   *favorable*

2

10   Scarsely had Phoebus in the glooming East[2]
      Yet harnessèd his firie-footed teeme,
      Ne reard above the earth his flaming creast,°   *crest*
      When the last deadly smoke aloft did steeme,
      That signe of last outbreathèd life did seeme
15   Unto the watchman on the castle wall;
      Who thereby dead that balefull° Beast did deeme,   *evil*
      And to his Lord and Ladie lowd gan call,
    To tell, how he had seene the Dragons fatall fall.

---

1. Release the mainsail line and sail toward the   (2.1–7).
land. The nautical metaphor echoes many classi-   2. I.e., dawn.
cal authors and Chaucer's *Troilus and Criseyde*

3

Uprose with hastie joy, and feeble speed
20   That aged Sire, the Lord of all that land,
      And lookèd forth, to weet, if true indeede
      Those tydings were, as he did understand,
      Which whenas true by tryall he out fond,
      He bad to open wyde his brazen gate,
25   Which long time had bene shut, and out of hond[3]
      Proclaymèd joy and peace through all his state;
For dead now was their foe, which them forrayèd late.[4]

4

Then gan triumphant Trompets sound on hie,
      That sent to heaven the ecchoèd report
30   Of their new joy, and happie victorie
      Gainst him, that had them long opprest with tort,°   *wrong*
      And fast imprisonèd in siegèd fort.
      Then all the people, as in solemne feast,
      To him assembled with one full consort,[5]
35   Rejoycing at the fall of that great beast,
From whose eternall bondage now they were releast.

5

Forth came that auncient Lord and aged Queene,
      Arayd in antique robes downe to the ground,
      And sad habiliments right well beseene;[6]
40   A noble crew about them waited round
      Of sage and sober Peres,° all gravely gownd;   *peers*
      Whom farre before did march a goodly band
      Of tall young men, all hable armes to sownd,[7]
      But now they laurell braunches bore in hand;
45 Glad signe of victorie and peace in all their land.

6

Unto that doughtie Conquerour they came,
      And him before themselves prostrating low,
      Their Lord and Patrone° loud did him proclame,   *defender*
      And at his feet their laurell boughes did throw.
50   Soone after them all dauncing on a row
      The comely virgins came, with girlands dight,°   *adorned*
      As fresh as flowres in medow greene do grow,
      When morning deaw upon their leaves doth light:
And in their hands sweet Timbrels° all upheld   *tambourines*
          on hight.

7

55 And them before, the fry° of children young   *crowd*
      Their wanton° sports and childish mirth did play,   *playful*
      And to the Maydens sounding tymbrels sung

---

3. Straightway.
4. Had recently ravaged.
5. All together.

6. I.e., their sober, appropriate ("right well beseene") attire.
7. Able to fight with weapons.

In well attunèd notes, a joyous lay,
And made delightfull musicke all the way,
60   Untill they came, where that faire virgin stood;
As faire Diana[8] in fresh sommers day
Beholds her Nymphes, enraungèd° in shadie wood,   *ranged*
Some wrestle, some do run, some bathe in christall flood.

8

So she beheld those maydens meriment
65   With chearefull vew; who when to her they came,
Themselves to ground with gratious humblesse° bent,   *humility*
And her adored by honorable name,[9]
Lifting to heaven her everlasting fame:
Then on her head they set a girland greene,
70   And crownèd her twixt earnest and twixt game:[1]
Who in her selfe-resemblance well beseene,[2]
Did seeme such, as she was, a goodly maiden Queene.

9

And after all, the raskall many ran,
Heapèd together in rude rablement,[3]   *confusion*
75   To see the face of that victorious man:
Whom all admired,° as from heaven sent,   *wondered at*
And gazd upon with gaping wonderment.
But when they came, where that dead Dragon lay,
Stretcht on the ground in monstrous large extent,
80   The sight with idle° feare did them dismay,   *baseless*
Ne durst approch him nigh, to touch, or once assay.

10

Some feard, and fled; some feard and well it faynd;°   *concealed*
One that would wiser seeme, then all the rest,
Warnd him not touch, for yet perhaps remaynd
85   Some lingring life within his hollow brest,
Or in his wombe might lurke some hidden nest
Of many Dragonets,° his fruitfull seed;   *young dragons*
Another said, that in his eyes did rest
Yet sparckling fire, and bad thereof take heed;
90   Another said, he saw him move his eyes indeed.

11

One mother, when as her foolehardie chyld
Did come too neare, and with his talants° play,   *talons*
Halfe dead through feare, her litle babe revyld,°   *scolded*
And to her gossips° gan in counsell° say;   *women friends/private*
95   "How can I tell, but that his talants may
Yet scratch my sonne, or rend his tender hand?"
So diversly themselves in vaine they fray;°   *scare*
Whiles some more bold, to measure him nigh stand,
To prove° how many acres he did spread of land.   *determine*

---

8. Goddess of the hunt.   2. I.e., looking appropriately like herself.
9. With titles of honor.   3. Discordant confusion. "Raskall many": rabble
1. I.e., half in fun.   throng.

12

100 Thus flockèd all the folke him round about,
  The whiles that hoarie° king, with all his traine,   *gray-haired*
  Being arrivèd, where that champion stout
  After his foes defeasance° did remaine,   *defeat*
  Him goodly greetes, and faire does entertaine,
105 With princely gifts of yvorie and gold,
  And thousand thankes him yeelds for all his paine.
  Then when his daughter deare he does behold,
Her dearely doth imbrace, and kisseth manifold.°   *many times*

13

And after to his Pallace he them brings,
110 With shaumes,[4] and trompets, and with Clarions sweet;
  And all the way the joyous people sings,
  And with their garments strowes the pavèd street:
  Whence mounting up, they find purveyance° meet   *provisions*
  Of all, that royall Princes court became,°   *suited*
115 And all the floore was underneath their feet
  Bespred with costly scarlot of great name,[5]
On which they lowly sit, and fitting purpose frame.

14

What needs me tell their feast and goodly guize,°   *behavior*
  In which was nothing riotous nor vaine?
120 What needs of daintie dishes to devize,°   *talk*
  Of comely services, or courtly trayne?
  My narrow leaves cannot in them containe
  The large discourse[6] of royall Princes state.
  Yet was their manner then but bare and plaine:
125 For th' antique world excesse and pride did hate,
Such proud luxurious pompe is swollen up but late.[7]

15

Then when with meates and drinkes of every kinde
  Their fervent appetites they quenchèd had,
  That auncient Lord gan fit occasion finde,
130 Of straunge adventures, and of perils sad,°   *grave*
  Which in his travell him befallen had,
  For to demaund of his renowmèd guest:
  Who then with utt'rance grave, and count'nance sad,
  From point to point, as is before exprest,
135 Discourst his voyage long, according° his request.   *granting*

16

Great pleasure mixt with pittifull° regard,   *sympathetic*
  That godly King and Queene did passionate,[8]
  Whiles they his pittifull° adventures heard,   *deserving pity*
  That oft they did lament his lucklesse state,
140 And often blame the too importune° fate,   *severe*

4. Ancient wind instrument like an oboe.   7. Just recently.
5. I.e., famous scarlet cloth.   8. I.e., did feel and express.
6. I.e., full description.

That heapd on him so many wrathfull wreakes:[9]
For never gentle knight, as he of late,
So tossèd was in fortunes cruell freakes,°   whims
And all the while salt teares bedeawd the hearers cheaks.

17

145 Then said that royall Pere in sober wise:
"Deare Sonne, great beene the evils, which ye bore
From first to last in your late enterprise,
That I note,° whether prayse, or pitty more: know not
For never living man, I weene, so sore
150 In sea of deadly daungers was distrest;
But since now safe ye seisèd° have the shore,   reached
And well arrivèd are (high God be blest),
Let us devize° of ease and everlasting rest."   think

18

"Ah dearest Lord," said then that doughty knight,
155 "Of ease or rest I may not yet devize;
For by the faith, which I to armes have plight,°   pledged
I bounden am streight after this emprize,°   enterprise
As that your daughter can ye well advize,
Backe to returne to that great Faerie Queene,
160 And her to serve six yeares in warlike wize,
Gainst that proud Paynim king, that workes her teene:°   sorrow
Therefore I ought crave pardon, till I there have beene."[1]

19

"Unhappie falles that hard necessitie,"
Quoth he, "the troubler of my happie peace,
165 And vowèd foe of my felicitie;
Ne° I against the same can justly preace:°   Neither/press
But since that band° ye cannot now release,   obligation
Nor doen undo (for vowes may not be vaine),[2]
Soone as the terme of those six yeares shall cease,
170 Ye then shall hither backe returne againe,
The marriage to accomplish vowd betwixt you twain.

20

"Which for my part I covet to performe,
In sort as through the world I did proclame,
That who so kild that monster most deforme,
175 And him in hardy battaile overcame,
Should have mine onely daughter to his Dame,°   wife
And of my kingdome heire apparaunt bee:
Therefore since now to thee perteines° the same,   belongs
By dew desert of noble chevalree,
180 Both daughter and eke° kingdome, lo I yield to thee."   also

9. Vengeful injuries.
1. The final Christian triumph, the marriage of
Christ and the true church, will be achieved only
at the end of time, the Day of Judgment. Mean-

while, the struggle against evil (and the Roman
Church) continues. "Ought": must.
2. I.e., you cannot undo what is done ("doen"),
for vows may not be (made) vain.

21

Then forth he callèd that his daughter faire,
  The fairest Un' his onely daughter deare,
  His onely daughter, and his onely heyre;
  Who forth proceeding with sad° sober cheare,°   *grave/countenance*
185 As bright as doth the morning starre appeare
  Out of the East, with flaming lockes bedight,°   *bedecked*
  To tell that dawning day is drawing neare,
  And to the world does bring long wishèd light;
So faire and fresh that Lady shewd her selfe in sight.

22

190 So faire and fresh, as freshest flowre in May;
  For she had layd her mournefull stole aside,
  And widow-like sad wimple° throwne away,   *veil*
  Wherewith her heavenly beautie she did hide,
  Whiles on her wearie journey she did ride;
195 And on her now a garment she did weare,
  All lilly white, withoutten spot, or pride,°   *ornament*
  That seemed like silke and silver woven neare,°   *tightly*
But neither silke nor silver therein did appeare.[3]

23

The blazing brightnesse of her beauties beame,
200 And glorious light of her sunshyny face[4]
  To tell, were as to strive against the streame.
  My ragged rimes are all too rude and bace,
  Her heavenly lineaments for to enchace.°   *adorn*
  Ne wonder; for her owne deare lovèd knight,
205 All° were she dayly with himselfe in place,   *although*
  Did wonder much at her celestiall sight:
Oft had he seene her faire, but never so faire dight.

24

So fairely dight, when she in presence came,
  She to her Sire made humble reverence,
210 And bowèd low, that her right well became,
  And added grace unto her excellence:
  Who with great wisdome, and grave eloquence
  Thus gan to say. But eare° he thus had said,   *ere*
  With flying speede, and seeming great pretence,°   *purpose*
215 Came running in, much like a man dismaid,
A Messenger with letters, which his message said.

25

All in the open hall amazèd stood,
  At suddeinnesse of that unwarie° sight,   *unexpected*
  And wondred at his breathlesse hastie mood.

---

3. "The marriage of the Lamb is come, and his wife hath made herself ready. And to her was granted that she should be arrayed in fine linen, clean and white: for the fine linen is the righteous- ness of saints" (Revelation 19.7–8).
4. Revelation 21.9,11 describes the New Jerusa- lem as "the bride, the Lamb's wife . . . her light was like unto a stone most precious."

220 But he for nought would stay his passage right°   *direct*
Till fast° before the king he did alight;   *close*
Where falling flat, great humblesse he did make,
And kist the ground, whereon his foot was pight;°   *placed*
Then to his hands that writ° he did betake,°   *document/deliver*
225 Which he disclosing, red thus, as the paper spake.

26

"To thee, most mighty king of Eden faire,
Her greeting sends in these sad lines addrest,
The wofull daughter, and forsaken heire
Of that great Emperour of all the West;
230 And bids thee be advizèd for the best,
Ere thou thy daughter linck in holy band
Of wedlocke to that new unknowen guest:
For he already plighted his right hand
Unto another love, and to another land.

27

235 "To me sad mayd, or rather widow sad,
He was affiauncèd long time before,
And sacred pledges he both gave, and had,
False erraunt knight, infamous, and forswore:
Witnesse the burning Altars, which° he swore,   *by which*
240 And guiltie heavens of⁵ his bold perjury,
Which though he hath polluted oft of yore,
Yet I to them for judgement just do fly,
And them conjure° t' avenge this shamefull injury.   *implore*

28

"Therefore since mine he is, or° free or bond,°   *whether/bound*
245 Or false or trew, or living or else dead,
Withhold, O soveraine Prince, your hasty hond
From knitting league with him, I you aread;°   *advise*
Ne wene° my right with strength adowne to tread,   *think*
Through weakenesse of my widowhed, or woe:
250 For truth is strong, her rightfull cause to plead,
And shall find friends, if need requireth soe,
So bids thee well to fare, Thy neither friend, nor foe, Fidessa."

29

When he these bitter byting words had red,
The tydings straunge did him abashèd make,
255 That still he sate long time astonishèd
As in great muse,° ne word to creature spake.   *amazement*
At last his solemne silence thus he brake,
With doubtfull eyes fast fixèd on his guest:
"Redoubted knight, that for mine onely sake⁶
260 Thy life and honour late adventurest,
Let nought be hid from me, that ought to be exprest.

---

5. I.e., and heavens polluted by.   6. For my sake alone. "Redoubted": honored.

30

"What meane these bloudy vowes, and idle threats,
  Throwne out from womanish impatient mind?
  What heavens? what altars? what enragèd heates
265 Here heapèd up with termes of love unkind,°   *unnatural*
  My conscience cleare with guilty bands⁷ would bind?
  High God be witnesse, that I guiltlesse ame.
  But if your selfe, Sir knight, ye faultie° find,   *guilty*
  Or wrappèd be in loves of former Dame,
270 With crime do not it cover, but disclose the same."

31

To whom the Redcrosse knight this answere sent,
  "My Lord, my King, be nought hereat dismayd,
  Till well ye wote by grave intendiment,⁸
  What woman, and wherefore doth me upbrayd
275 With breach of love, and loyalty betrayd.
  It was in my mishaps, as hitherward
  I lately traveild, that unwares I strayd
  Out of my way, through perils straunge and hard;
That day should faile me, ere I had them all declard.

32

280 "There did I find, or rather I was found
  Of this false woman, that Fidessa hight,
  Fidessa hight the falsest Dame on ground,
  Most false Duessa, royall richly dight,
  That easie was t' invegle° weaker sight: *deceive*
285 Who by her wicked arts, and wylie skill,
  Too false and strong for earthly skill or might,
  Unwares me wrought unto her wicked will,
And to my foe betrayd, when least I fearèd ill."

33

Then steppèd forth the goodly royall Mayd,
290 And on the ground her selfe prostrating low,
  With sober countenaunce thus to him sayd:
  "O pardon me, my soveraigne Lord, to show
  The secret treasons, which of late I know
  To have bene wroght by that false sorceresse.
295 She onely she it is, that earst did throw
  This gentle knight into so great distresse,
That death him did awaite in dayly wretchednesse.

34

"And now it seemes, that she subornèd hath
  This craftie messenger with letters vaine,
300 To worke new woe and improvided scath,⁹
  By breaking of the band betwixt us twaine;
  Wherein she usèd hath the practicke paine¹

---

7. I.e., bonds of guilt.   9. Unexpected harm.
8. I.e., serious investigation.   1. Treacherous skill.

    Of this false footman, clokt with simplenesse,
    Whom if ye please for to discover plaine,
305   Ye shall him Archimago find, I ghesse,
    The falsest man alive; who tries shall find no lesse."

35

    The king was greatly movèd at her speach,
    And all with suddein indignation fraight,°   *filled*
    Bad° on that Messenger rude hands to reach.   *bade*
310   Eftsoones° the Gard, which on his state did wait,
    Attacht that faitor° false, and bound him strait: *impostor*
    Who seeming sorely chauffèd° at his band,   *angered*
    As chainèd Beare, whom cruell dogs do bait,
    With idle force did faine them to withstand,
315 And often semblaunce made to scape out of their hand.

36

    But they him layd full low in dungeon deepe,
    And bound him hand and foote with yron chains.
    And with continuall watch did warely° keepe;   *vigilantly*
    Who then would thinke, that by his subtile trains
320   He could escape fowle death or deadly paines?[2]
    Thus when that Princes wrath was pacifide,
    He gan renew the late forbidden banes,[3]
    And to the knight his daughter deare he tyde,
    With sacred rites and vowes for ever to abyde.

37

325 His owne two hands the holy knots did knit,
    That none but death for ever can devide;
    His owne two hands, for such a turne° most fit,   *act*
    The housling° fire did kindle and provide,   *sacramental*
    And holy water thereon sprinckled wide;[4]
330   At which the bushy Teade° a groome did light,   *marriage torch*
    And sacred lampe in secret chamber hide,
    Where it should not be quenchèd day nor night,
    For feare of evill fates, but burnen ever bright.

38

    Then gan they sprinckle all the posts with wine,
335   And made great feast to solemnize that day;
    They all perfumde with frankencense divine,
    And precious odours fetcht from far away,
    That all the house did sweat with great aray:
    And all the while sweete Musicke did apply
340   Her curious° skill, the warbling notes to play,   *intricate*

---

2. "And he laid hold on the dragon, that old serpent, which is the Devil, and Satan, and bound him a thousand years, And cast him into the bottomless pit, and shut him up, and set a seal upon him, that he should deceive the nations no more, till the thousand years should be fulfilled: and after that he must be loosed a little season" (Revelation 20.2–3).
3. Banns, i.e., announcements of marriage.
4. Marriages in ancient times were solemnized with sacramental fire and water.

To drive away the dull Melancholy;
The whiles one sung a song of love and jollity.

39

During the which there was an heavenly noise
Heard sound through all the Pallace pleasantly,
345 Like as it had bene many an Angels voice,
Singing before th' eternall majesty,
In their trinall triplicities[5] on hye;
Yet wist no creature, whence that heavenly sweet°   *delight*
Proceeded, yet each one felt secretly°   *inwardly*
350 Himselfe thereby reft of his sences meet,°   *proper*
And ravishèd with rare impression in his sprite.[6]

40

Great joy was made that day of young and old,
And solemne feast proclaimd throughout the land,
That their exceeding merth may not be told:
355 Suffice it heare by signes to understand
The usuall joyes at knitting of loves band.
Thrise happy man the knight himselfe did hold,
Possessèd of his Ladies hart and hand,
And ever, when his eye did her behold,
360 His heart did seeme to melt in pleasures manifold.

41

Her joyous presence and sweet company
In full content he there did long enjoy,
Ne wicked envie, ne vile gealosy
His deare delights were able to annoy:
365 Yet swimming in that sea of blisfull joy,
He nought forgot, how he whilome had sworne,
In case he could that monstrous beast destroy,
Unto his Faerie Queene backe to returne:
The which he shortly did, and Una left to mourne.

42

370 Now strike your sailes ye jolly Mariners,
For we be come unto a quiet rode,°   *harbor*
Where we must land some of our passengers,
And light this wearie vessell of her lode.
Here she a while may make her safe abode,
375 Till she repairèd have her tackles spent,°   *worn out*
And wants supplide. And then againe abroad
On the long voyage whereto she is bent:
Well may she speede and fairely finish her intent.

1590, 1596

---

5. The "trinall triplicities" are the 9 angelic orders, divided into 3 groups of 3, the whole hierarchy corresponding to the 9 spheres of the universe. The music heard in this stanza is the music of the spheres, not audible on earth since the Fall.

6. Spirit. "Let us be glad and rejoice, and give honor to him: for the marriage of the Lamb is come" (Revelation 9.6). In Revelation, the marriage of Christ and the New Jerusalem signals the general redemption.

From Amoretti[1]

Sonnet 1

Happy ye leaves when as those lilly hands,
Which hold my life in their dead doing[2] might,
Shall handle you and hold in loves soft bands,
Lyke captives trembling at the victors sight.
5   And happy lines, on which with starry light,
Those lamping° eyes will deigne sometimes to look   *flashing*
And reade the sorrowes of my dying spright,°   *spirit*
Written with teares in harts close° bleeding book.   *secret*
And happy rymes bathed in the sacred brooke,
10   Of Helicon[3] whence she derivèd is,
When ye behold that Angels blessed looke,
My soules long lackèd foode, my heavens blis.
Leaves, lines, and rymes, seeke her to please alone,
Whom if ye please, I care for other none.

Sonnet 34

Lyke as a ship that through the ocean wyde,
By conduct of some star doth make her way,
Whenas a storme hath dimd her trusty guyde,
Out of her course doth wander far astray.
5   So I whose star, that wont with her bright ray,
Me to direct, with cloudes is overcast,
Doe wander now in darknesse and dismay,
Through hidden perils round about me plast.°   *placed*
Yet hope I well, that when this storme is past
10   My Helice[4] the lodestar of my lyfe
Will shine again, and looke on me at last,
With lovely light to cleare my cloudy grief.
Till then I wander carefull° comfortlesse,   *full of cares*
In secret sorow and sad pensivenesse.

Sonnet 37

What guyle is this, that those her golden tresses,
She doth attyre under a net of gold:
And with sly° skill so cunningly them dresses,   *clever*

---

1. I.e., "little loves" or "little love poems." They are sonnets to a woman named Elizabeth—probably Elizabeth Boyle, who became Spenser's second wife. The sequence, or cycle, tells of a courtship (*Epithalamion*, with which they were published, is a song for a wedding). The *Amoretti* draws, like other sonnet cycles, upon characteristic and conventional themes and conceits; what is characteristically Spenserian about them is his yoking of the spirit and the flesh. The rhyme scheme is *abab bcbc cdcd ee*, a difficult pattern requiring 4 words for 2 of the rhymes.
2. I.e., killing.
3. The "sacred brooke" is the Hippocrene, which flows from Mount Helicon, the mountain sacred to the Muses.
4. The Big Dipper or North Star.

That which is gold or heare,° may scarse be told?   *hair*
5 Is it that mens frayle eyes, which gaze too bold,
She may entangle in that golden snare:
And being caught may craftily enfold,
Theyr weaker harts, which are not wel aware?
Take heed therefore, myne eyes, how ye doe stare
10 Henceforth too rashly on that guilefull net,
In which if ever ye entrappèd are,
Out of her bands ye by no means shall get.
Fondnesse° it were for any being free,   *foolishness*
To covet fetters, though they golden bee.

Sonnet 54

Of this worlds theatre in which we stay,
My love like the spectator ydly sits
Beholding me that all the pageants° play,   *roles*
Disguysing diversly my troubled wits.
5 Sometimes I joy when glad occasion fits,
And mask in myrth lyke to a comedy:
Soone after when my joy to sorrow flits,
I waile and make my woes a tragedy.
Yet she, beholding me with constant eye,
10 Delights not in my merth nor rues my smart:
But when I laugh she mocks, and when I cry
She laughs and hardens evermore her heart.
What then can move her? if nor merth nor mone,°   *moan*
She is no woman, but a sencelesse stone.

Sonnet 64[5]

Comming to kisse her lyps (such grace I found)
Me seemd I smelt a gardin of sweet flowres
That dainty odours from them threw around
For damzels fit to decke their lovers bowres.
5 Her lips did smell lyke unto gillyflowers,°   *carnations*
Her ruddy cheeks like unto roses red;
Her snowy browes lyke budded bellamoures,°   *bellflowers*
Her lovely eyes like pincks but newly spred,
Her goodly bosome lyke a strawberry bed,
10 Her neck lyke to a bounch of cullambynes;
Her brest lyke lillyes ere theyr leaves be shed,
Her nipples lyke yong blossomd jessemynes.°   *jasmines*
Such fragrant flowres doe give most odorous smell,
But her sweet odour did them all excell.

5. Much of the imagery of this sonnet is imitated from the Song of Solomon 4.10–16.

Sonnet 65

The doubt which ye misdeeme, fayre love, is vaine,
That fondly feare to loose your liberty,
When loosing one, two liberties ye gayne,
And make him bond that bondage earst° dyd fly.   *formerly*
5 Sweet be the bands, the which true love doth tye,
Without constraynt or dread of any ill:
The gentle birde feels no captivity
Within her cage, but singes and feeds her fill.
There pride dare not approch, nor discord spill°   *destroy*
10 The league twixt them, that loyal love hath bound;
But simple truth and mutuall good will,
Seekes with sweet peace to salve each others wound.
There fayth doth fearlesse dwell in brasen towre,
And spotlesse pleasure builds her sacred bowre.

Sonnet 67[6]

Lyke as a huntsman after weary chace,
Seeing the game from him escapt away,
Sits downe to rest him in some shady place,
With panting hounds beguiled of their pray,
So after long pursuit and vaine assay,
When I all weary had the chace forsooke,
The gentle deare returnd the selfe-same way,
Thinking to quench her thirst at the next brooke.
There she beholding me with mylder looke,
Sought not to fly, but fearelesse still did bide,
Till I in hand her yet halfe trembling tooke,
And with her owne goodwill hir fyrmely tyde.
Strange thing me seemd to see a beast so wyld,
So goodly wonne with her owne will beguyld.°   *entangled*

Sonnet 68

Most glorious Lord of lyfe, that on this day,[7]
Didst make thy triumph over death and sin:
And having harrowed hell,[8] didst bring away
Captivity thence captive us to win:
5 This joyous day, deare Lord, with joy begin,
And grant that we for whom thou diddest dye
Being with thy deare blood clene washt from sin,
May live for ever in felicity.
And that thy love we weighing worthily,

---

6. An imitation of Petrarch's sonnet 190, *Una candida cerva*, but with a very different ending.
7. Easter Day.
8. In the apocryphal gospels, Christ descended into hell and led out those who had lived before his time that deserved to be saved. "Captivity thence captive" is a biblical phrase, as in Judges 5.12 and Ephesians 4.8.

10 May likewise love thee for the same againe:
    And for thy sake that all lyke deare didst buy,
    With love may one another entertayne.
    So let us love, deare love, lyke as we ought,
    Love is the lesson which the Lord us taught.[9]

Sonnet 74

    Most happy letters framed by skilfull trade,°   *practice*
    With which that happy name was first desynd:
    The which three times thrise happy hath me made,
    With guifts of body, fortune and of mind.
5   The first my being to me gave by kind,°   *nature*
    From mothers womb derived by dew descent,
    The second is my sovereigne Queene most kind,
    That honour and large richesse to me lent.
    The third my love, my lives last ornament,
10 By whom my spirit out of dust was raysed:
    To speake her prayse and glory excellent,
    Of all alive most worthy to be praysed.
    Ye three Elizabeths for ever live,
    That three such graces did unto me give.

Sonnet 75

    One day I wrote her name upon the strand,°   *beach*
    But came the waves and washèd it away:
    Agayne I wrote it with a second hand,
    But came the tyde, and made my paynes his pray.°   *prey*
5   "Vayne man," sayd she, "that doest in vaine assay,° *attempt*
    A mortall thing so to immortalize,
    For I my selve shall lyke to this decay,
    And eek° my name bee wypèd out lykewize."   *also*
    "Not so," quod° I, "let baser things devize,°   *quoth/contrive*
10 To dy in dust, but you shall live by fame:
    My verse your vertues rare shall eternize,
    And in the heavens wryte your glorious name.
    Where whenas death shall all the world subdew,
    Our love shall live, and later life renew."

Sonnet 79

    Men call you fayre, and you doe credit° it,   *believe*
    For that your selfe ye dayly such doe see:
    But the trew fayre,° that is the gentle wit,   *beauty*
    And vertuous mind, is much more praysd of me.
5   For all the rest, how ever fayre it be,

9. Cf. John 15.12: "This is my commandment, That ye love one another, as I have loved you."

Shall turne to nought and loose that glorious hew:°   *form*
But onely that is permanent and free
From frayle corruption, that doth flesh ensew.°   *outlast*
That is true beautie: that doth argue you
10   To be divine and borne of heavenly seed:
Derived from that fayre Spirit,[1] from whom al true
And perfect beauty did at first proceed.
He onely fayre, and what he fayre hath made:
All other fayre, lyke flowres, untymely fade.

1595

Epithalamion

Epithalamion   An epithalamion is a wedding song or poem; its Greek name conveys that it was sung on the threshold of the bridal chamber. The genre was widely practiced by the Latin poets, particularly Catullus. Common elements are the invocation to the Muses, the bringing home of the bride, the singing and dancing at the wedding party, and the preparations for the wedding night. The poem's merit is not in its "originality" but in its evocative commingling of the conventions, with which Spenser blends his own Irish setting and native folklore.

The *Epithalamion* has a complex structure. First there is an introductory stanza, then two 10-stanza sections on each side of the two central stanzas about the church ceremony itself. Each of the 10-stanza sections is divided into units of 3-4-3. As A. Kent Hieatt has pointed out in his book, *Short Time's Endless Monument* (1960), the poem also has a numerical structure that reinforces the motif of the passage of time. For example, the poem has exactly 365 long lines (composed of 5 or more metrical feet) matching the number of days in the year. There are 24 stanzas, counting the envoy, matching the hours of one day and night. Of these stanzas, the first 16 describe the course of the day, in which the woods echo the various sounds; the last 8 describe the night, a time of silence in which the woods no longer echo. At the summer solstice (cf. line 266 and note) in the latitude of Ireland, night falls after 16 hours of daylight.

The subtle time structure serves to reinforce the idea implicit throughout the poem that this marriage has reference to all marriages. It emphasizes the endless cycle of time, measured by the passing of the hours and the years— as against which marriage, as a Christian sacrament, stands firm, "eterne in mutabilitie."

Epithalamion

Ye learned sisters which have oftentimes
Beene to me ayding, others to adorne:[1]
Whom ye thought worthy of your gracefull rymes,
That even the greatest did not greatly scorne
5   To heare theyr names sung in your simple layes,

---

1. I.e., God.
1. I.e., to write poems in praise of others. The   "learned sisters" are the Muses.

But joyèd in theyr prayse.
And when ye list your owne mishaps to mourne,
Which death, or love, or fortunes wreck did rayse,
Your string could soone to sadder tenor° turne,   *mood*
10 And teach the woods and waters to lament
Your dolefull dreriment.°   *sorrow*
Now lay those sorrowfull complaints aside,
And having all your heads with girland crownd,
Helpe me mine owne loves prayses to resound,
15 Ne let the same of° any be envide: *by*
So Orpheus did for his owne bride,[2]
So I unto my selfe alone will sing,
The woods shall to me answer and my Eccho ring.

Early before the worlds light giving lampe,
20 His golden beame upon the hils doth spred,
Having disperst the nights unchearefull dampe,
Doe ye awake, and with fresh lustyhed°   *vigor*
Go to the bowre° of my belovèd love,   *bedchamber*
My truest turtle dove,
25 Bid her awake; for Hymen[3] is awake,
And long since ready forth his maske to move,
With his bright Tead[4] that flames with many a flake,°   *spark*
And many a bachelor to waite on him,
In theyr fresh garments trim.
30 Bid her awake therefore and soone her dight,°   *dress*
For lo the wishèd day is come at last,
That shall for al the paynes and sorrowes past,
Pay to her usury° of long delight: *interest*
And whylest she doth her dight,
35 Doe ye to her of joy and solace sing,
That all the woods may answer and your Eccho ring.

Bring with you all the Nymphes that you can heare[5]
Both of the rivers and the forrests greene:
And of the sea that neighbours to her neare,
40 Al with gay girlands goodly wel beseene.[6]
And let them also with them bring in hand,
Another gay girland
For my fayre love of lillyes and of roses,
Bound truelove wize[7] with a blew silke riband.
45 And let them make great store of bridale poses,°   *posies*
And let them eeke° bring store of other flowers   *also*
To deck the bridale bowers.

---

2. Orpheus, archetype of the poet in classical antiquity, was equally famous for his love for his wife Eurydice.
3. The god of marriage, who leads a "maske" or procession at weddings.
4. A ceremonial torch, associated with marriages since classical times.
5. I.e., that can hear you.
6. I.e., beautified.
7. I.e., in a love knot.

And let the ground whereas her foot shall tread,
For feare the stones her tender foot should wrong
50   Be strewed with fragrant flowers all along,
And diapred lyke the discolored mead.[8]
Which done, doe at her chamber dore awayt,
For she will waken strayt,°   straightway
The whiles doe ye this song unto her sing,
55   The woods shall to you answer and your Eccho ring.

Ye Nymphes of Mulla[9] which with careful heed,
The silver scaly trouts doe tend full well,
And greedy pikes which use therein to feed,
(Those trouts and pikes all others doo excell)
60   And ye likewise, which keepe the rushy lake,
Where none doo fishes take,
Bynd up the locks the which hang scatterd light,
And in his waters which your mirror make,
Behold your faces as the christall bright,
65   That when you come whereas° my love doth lie,   where
No blemish she may spie.
And eke ye lightfoot mayds which keepe the deere,[1]
That on the hoary mountayne use to towre,
And the wylde wolves which seeke them to devoure,
70   With your steele darts doo chace from comming neer
Be also present heere,
To helpe to decke her and to help to sing,
That all the woods may answer and your Eccho ring.

Wake, now my love, awake; for it is time,
75   The Rosy Morne long since left Tithones bed,[2]
All ready to her silver coche° to clyme,   coach
And Phoebus gins to shew his glorious hed.
Hark how the cheerefull birds do chaunt theyr laies
And carroll of loves praise.
80   The merry Larke hir mattins° sings aloft,   morning prayers
The thrush replyes, the Mavis descant[3] playes,
The Ouzell shrills, the Ruddock warbles soft,
So goodly all agree with sweet consent,
To this dayes merriment.
85   Ah my deere love why doe ye sleepe thus long,
When meeter° were that ye should now awake,   more fitting

---

8. I.e., ornamented like the many-colored meadow.
9. The vale of Mulla, near Spenser's home in Ireland.
1. I.e., all wild animals, kept by the forest nymphs. To "towre" (a falconry term) is to occupy heights.
2. See Song of Songs 2.10–13: "Rise up, my love, my fair one, and come away. For, lo, the winter is past, the rain is over and gone; the flowers appear on the earth; the time of the singing of birds is come. . . ." In myth, Tithones is the aged husband of Aurora, the dawn.
3. A melody or counterpoint written above a musical theme—a soprano obbligato. The "Mavis" is the thrush. The "Ouzell" is the blackbird (which sings in England); the "Ruddock," the European robin. The birds' concert is a convention of medieval love poetry.

T' awayt the comming of your joyous make,°   *mate*
And hearken to the birds lovelearnèd song,
The deawy leaves among.
90   For they of joy and pleasance to you sing,
That all the woods them answer and theyr Eccho ring.

My love is now awake out of her dreame,
And her fayre eyes like stars that dimmèd were
With darksome cloud, now shew theyr goodly beams
95   More bright then Hesperus° his head doth rere.   *evening star*
Come now ye damzels, daughters of delight,
Helpe quickly her to dight,°   *adorn*
But first come ye fayre houres which were begot
In Joves sweet paradice, of Day and Night,
100   Which doe the seasons of the yeare allot,
And al that ever in this world is fayre
Doe make and still repayre.°   *continuously*
And ye three handmayds of the Cyprian Queene,[4]
The which doe still adorne her beauties pride,
105   Helpe to addorne my beautifullest bride:
And as ye her array, still throw betweene°   *now and then*
Some graces to be seene,
And as ye use to Venus, to her sing,
The whiles the woods shal answer and your Eccho ring.

110   Now is my love all ready forth to come,
Let all the virgins therefore well awayt,
And ye fresh boyes that tend upon her groome
Prepare your selves; for he is comming strayt.
Set all your things in seemely good aray°   *order*
115   Fit for so joyfull day,
The joyfulst day that ever sunne did see.
Faire Sun, shew forth thy favourable ray,
And let thy lifull° heat not fervent be   *lifegiving*
For feare of burning her sunshyny face,
120   Her beauty to disgrace.
O fayrest Phoebus, father of the Muse,[5]
If ever I did honour thee aright,
Or sing the thing, that mote° thy mind delight,   *might*
Doe not thy servants simple boone° refuse,   *request*
125   But let this day let this one day be myne,
Let all the rest be thine.
Then I thy soverayne prayses loud wil sing,
That all the woods shal answer and theyr Eccho ring.

Harke how the Minstrels gin° to shrill aloud   *begin*
130   Their merry Musick that resounds from far,

---

4. The Graces attending on Venus ("Cyprian Queene"), representing brightness, joy, and bloom.   5. Phoebus (Apollo), god of the sun, was also father of the 9 muses.

The pipe, the tabor, and the trembling Croud,[6]
That well agree withouten breach or jar.°   *discord*
But most of all the Damzels doe delite,
When they their tymbrels° smyte,   *tambourines*
135 And thereunto doe daunce and carrol sweet,
That all the sences they doe ravish quite,
The whyles the boyes run up and downe the street,
Crying aloud with strong confusèd noyce,
As if it were one voyce.
140 *Hymen iô Hymen, Hymen*[7] they do shout,
That even to the heavens theyr shouting shrill
Doth reach, and all the firmament doth fill,
To which the people standing all about,
As in approvance doe thereto applaud
145 And loud advaunce her laud,°   *praise*
And evermore they *Hymen Hymen* sing,
That all the woods them answer and theyr Eccho ring.

Loe where she comes along with portly° pace   *stately*
Lyke Phoebe from her chamber of the East,
150 Arysing forth to run her mighty race,[8]
Clad all in white, that seemes° a virgin best.   *suits*
So well it her beseems that ye would weene
Some angell she had beene.
Her long loose yellow locks lyke golden wyre,
155 Sprinckled with perle, and perling° flowres a tweene,   *winding*
Doe lyke a golden mantle her attyre,
And being crownèd with a girland greene,
Seeme lyke some mayden Queene.
Her modest eyes abashèd to behold
160 So many gazers, as on her do stare,
Upon the lowly ground affixèd are.
Ne dare lift up her countenance too bold,
But blush to heare her prayses sung so loud,
So farre from being proud.
165 Nathlesse doe ye still loud her prayses sing.
That all the woods may answer and your Eccho ring.

Tell me ye merchants daughters did ye see
So fayre a creature in your towne before,
So sweet, so lovely, and so mild as she,
170 Adornd with beautyes grace and vertues store,
Her goodly eyes lyke Saphyres shining bright,
Her forehead yvory white,
Her cheekes lyke apples which the sun hath rudded,°   *made red*

---

6. Primitive fiddle; the "tabor" is a small drum. Spenser here designates Irish, not classical, instruments and music for the classical masque or ballet.
7. The name of the god of marriage, used as a conventional exclamation at weddings.
8. Phoebe is the moon, a virgin like the bride; the reference to her anticipates the night.

Her lips lyke cherryes charming men to byte,
175 Her brest like to a bowle of creame uncrudded,°   *uncurdled*
Her paps lyke lyllies budded,
Her snowie necke lyke to a marble towre,
And all her body like a pallace fayre,
Ascending uppe with many a stately stayre,
180 To honors seat and chastities sweet bowre.[9]
Why stand ye still ye virgins in amaze,
Upon her so to gaze,
Whiles ye forget your former lay to sing,
To which the woods did answer and your Eccho ring.

185 But if ye saw that which no eyes can see,
The inward beauty of her lively spright,°   *soul*
Garnisht with heavenly guifts of high degree,
Much more then would ye wonder at that sight,
And stand astonisht lyke to those which red°   *saw*
190 Medusaes mazeful hed.[1]
There dwels sweet love and constant chastity,
Unspotted fayth and comely womanhood,
Regard of honour and mild modesty,
There vertue raynes as Queene in royal throne,
195 And giveth lawes alone.
The which the base° affections doe obay,   *lower*
And yeeld theyr services unto her will,
Ne thought of thing uncomely ever may
Thereto approch to tempt her mind to ill.
200 Had ye once seene these her celestial threasures,
And unrevealèd pleasures,
Then would ye wonder and her prayses sing,
That all the woods should answer and your Eccho ring.

Open the temple gates unto my love,
205 Open them wide that she may enter in,[2]
And all the postes adorne as doth behove,[3]
And all the pillours deck with girlands trim,
For to recyve this Saynt with honour dew,
That commeth in to you.
210 With trembling steps and humble reverence,
She commeth in, before th' almighties vew,
Of her ye virgins learne obedience,
When so ye come into those holy places,
To humble your proud faces:

---

9. The head, where the higher faculties are. The catalogue of qualities is a convention in love poetry. Cf. also The Song of Solomon 4–8.
1. Medusa, one of the Gorgons, had serpents instead of hair (hence a "mazeful hed"): the effect on a beholder was to turn him to stone.
2. Cf. Psalm 24.7: "Lift up your heads, O ye gates; and be ye lift up, ye everlasting doors; and the King of glory shall come in."
3. As is proper. The doorposts were trimmed for weddings in classical times, and the custom was often referred to in classical and medieval love poetry.

215 Bring her up to th' high altar, that she may
    The sacred ceremonies there partake,
    The which do endless matrimony make,
    And let the roring Organs loudly play
    The praises of the Lord in lively notes,
220 The whiles with hollow throates
    The Choristers the joyous Antheme sing,
    That all the woods may answere and theyr Eccho ring.

    Behold whiles she before the altar stands
    Hearing the holy priest that to her speakes
225 And blesseth her with his two happy hands,
    How the red roses flush up in her cheekes,
    And the pure snow with goodly vermill° stayne,   *vermilion*
    Like crimsin dyde in grayne,°   *fast color*
    That even th' Angels which continually,
230 About the sacred Altare doe remaine,
    Forget their service and about her fly,
    Ofte peeping in her face that seemes more fayre,
    The more they on it stare.
    But her sad° eyes still fastened on the ground,   *modest*
235 Are governèd with goodly modesty,
    That suffers not one looke to glaunce awry,
    Which may let in a little thought unsownd.
    Why blush ye love to give to me your hand,
    The pledge of all our band?°   *bond, tie*
240 Sing ye sweet Angels, Alleluya sing,
    That all the woods may answere and your Eccho ring.

    Now al is done; bring home the bride againe,
    Bring home the triumph of our victory,
    Bring home with you the glory of her gaine,[4]
245 With joyance bring her and with jollity.
    Never had man more joyfull day then this,
    Whom heaven would heape with blis.
    Make feast therefore now all this live long day,
    This day for ever to me holy is,
250 Poure out the wine without restraint or stay,
    Poure not by cups, but by the belly full,
    Poure out to all that wull,°   *want it*
    And sprinkle all the postes and wals with wine,
    That they may sweat, and drunken be withall.
255 Crowne ye God Bacchus[5] with a coronall,°   *flower garland*
    And Hymen also crowne with wreathes of vine,
    And let the Graces daunce unto the rest;
    For they can doo it best:

---

4. I.e., the glory of gaining her.   5. God of wine.

The whiles the maydens doe theyr carroll sing,
260 To which the woods shall answer and theyr Eccho ring.

Ring ye the bels, ye young men of the towne,
And leave your wonted° labors for this day: *usual*
This day is holy; doe ye write it downe,
That ye for ever it remember may.
265 This day the sunne is in his chiefest hight,
With Barnaby the bright,[6]
From whence declining daily by degrees,
He somewhat loseth of his heat and light,
When once the Crab[7] behind his back he sees.
270 But for this time it ill ordainèd was,
To chose the longest day in all the yeare,
And shortest night, when longest fitter weare:
Yet never day so long, but late° would passe.   *at last*
Ring ye the bels, to make it weare away,
275 And bonefiers make all day,
And daunce about them, and about them sing:
That all the woods may answer, and your Eccho ring.

Ah when will this long weary day have end,
And lende me leave to come unto my love?
280 How slowly do the houres theyr numbers spend?
How slowly does sad Time his feathers move?
Hast thee O fayrest Planet to thy home
Within the Westerne fome:
Thy tyred steedes long since have need of rest.[8]
285 Long though it be, at last I see it gloome,
And the bright evening star[9] with golden creast
Appeare out of the East.
Fayre childe of beauty, glorious lampe of love
That all the host of heaven in rankes doost lead,
290 And guydest lovers through the nightès dread,
How chearefully thou lookest from above,
And seemst to laugh atweene thy twinkling light
As joying in the sight
Of these glad many which for joy doe sing,
295 That all the woods them answer and theyr Eccho ring.

Now ceasse ye damsels your delights forepast;
Enough is it, that all the day was youres:
Now day is doen, and night is nighing fast:
Now bring the Bryde into the brydall boures.

---

6. St. Barnabas' Day, at the time of the summer solstice.
7. The constellation Cancer between Gemini and Leo. The sun, passing through the zodiac, leaves the Crab behind toward the end of July.
8. The sun's chariot completes its daily course in the western sea.
9. Hesperus

300 Now night is come, now soone her disaray,
And in her bed her lay;
Lay her in lillies and in violets,
And silken courteins over her display,°   *spread*
And odourd sheetes, and Arras° coverlets.   *tapestry*
305 Behold how goodly my faire love does ly
In proud humility;
Like unto Maia,[1] when as Jove her tooke,
In Tempe, lying on the flowry gras,
Twixt sleepe and wake, after she weary was,
310 With bathing in the Acidalian brooke.
Now it is night, ye damsels may be gon,
And leave my love alone,
And leave likewise your former lay to sing:
The woods no more shall answere, nor your Eccho ring.

315 Now welcome night, thou night so long expected,
That long daies labour doest at last defray,°   *pay*
And all my cares, which cruell love collected,
Hast sumd in one, and cancellèd for aye:
Spread thy broad wing over my love and me,
320 That no man may us see,
And in thy sable mantle us enwrap,
From feare of perrill and foule horror free.
Let no false treason seeke us to entrap,
Nor any dread disquiet once annoy
325 The safety of our joy:
But let the night be calme and quietsome,
Without tempestuous storms or sad afray:
Lyke as when Jove with fayre Alcmena[2] lay,
When he begot the great Tirynthian groome:
330 Or lyke as when he with thy selfe[3] did lie,
And begot Majesty.
And let the mayds and yongmen cease to sing:
Ne let the woods them answer, nor theyr Eccho ring.

Let no lamenting cryes, nor dolefull teares,
335 Be heard all night within nor yet without.
Ne let false whispers, breeding hidden feares,
Breake gentle sleepe with misconceivèd dout.°   *fear*
Let no deluding dreames, nor dreadful sights
Make sudden sad affrights;
340 Ne let housefyres, nor lightnings helpelesse harmes,
Ne let the Pouke,[4] nor other evill sprights,
Ne let mischivous witches with theyr charmes,

1. The eldest and most beautiful of the Pleiades.
2. The mother of Hercules ("the great Tirynthian groome"). Jove made that one night last as long as three.
3. I.e., night. This is Spenser's own myth.
4. Puck, Robin Goodfellow—here more powerful and evil than Shakespeare made him.

Ne let hob Goblins, names whose sence we see not,
Fray° us with things that be not.   *terrify*
345 Let not the shriech Oule, nor the Storke be heard:
Nor the night Raven that still° deadly yels,[5]   *continuously*
Nor damnèd ghosts cald up with mighty spels,
Nor griesly° vultures make us once affeard: *horrid*
Ne let th' unpleasant Quyre of Frogs still croking
350 Make us to wish theyr choking.
Let none of these theyr drery accents sing;
Ne let the woods them answer, nor theyr Eccho ring.

But let stil Silence trew night watches keepe,
That sacred peace may in assurance rayne,
355 And tymely sleep, when it is tyme to sleepe,
May poure his limbs forth on your pleasant playne,
The whiles an hundred little wingèd loves,[6]
Like divers fethered doves,
Shall fly and flutter round about your bed,
360 And in the secret darke, that none reproves,
Their prety stealthes shal worke, and snares shal spread
To filch away sweet snatches of delight,
Conceald through covert night.
Ye sonnes of Venus, play your sports at will,
365 For greedy pleasure, carelesse of your toyes,°   *amorous dallying*
Thinks more upon her paradise of joyes,
Then what ye do, albe it good or ill.
All night therefore attend your merry play,
For it will soone be day:
370 Now none doth hinder you, that say or sing,
Ne will the woods now answer, nor your Eccho ring.

Who is the same, which at my window peepes?
Or whose is that faire face, that shines so bright,
Is it not Cinthia,[7] she that never sleepes,
375 But walkes about high heaven al the night?
O fayrest goddesse, do thou not envy
My love with me to spy:
For thou likewise didst love, though now unthought,° *unsuspected*
And for a fleece of woll,° which privily,   *wool*
380 The Latmian shephard[8] once unto thee brought,
His pleasures with thee wrought,
Therefore to us be favorable now;
And sith of wemens labours thou hast charge,[9]
And generation goodly dost enlarge,

5. The owl and the night raven were birds of ill
omen; the stork, in Chaucer's *Parliament of Fowls*,
is called an avenger of adultery. "Still": always.
6. Cupids (or amoretti).
7. I.e., the moon.
8. Endymion, beloved by the moon. The "fleece

of woll," however, comes from another story—that
of Pan's enticement of the moon.
9. Diana (the moon, "Cinthia") is, as Lucina,
patroness of births; the "labours" are, of course,
those of childbirth.

385 Encline thy will t' effect our wishfull vow,
     And the chast wombe informe° with timely seed,   *give life to*
     That may our comfort breed:
     Till which we cease our hopefull hap[1] to sing,
     Ne let the woods us answer, nor our Eccho ring.

390 And thou great Juno, which with awful might
     The lawes of wedlock still dost patronize,
     And the religion° of the faith first plight   *sanctity*
     With sacred rites hast taught to solemnize:
     And eeke° for comfort often callèd art   *also*
395 Of women in their smart,°   *labor*
     Eternally bind thou this lovely band,
     And all thy blessings unto us impart.
     And thou glad Genius,[2] in whose gentle hand,
     The bridale bowre and geniall bed remaine,
400 Without blemish or staine,
     And the sweet pleasures of theyr loves delight
     With secret ayde doest succour and supply,
     Till they bring forth the fruitfull progeny,
     Send us the timely fruit of this same night.
405 And thou fayre Hebe,[3] and thou Hymen free,
     Grant that it may so be.
     Til which we cease your further prayse to sing,
     Ne any woods shall answer, nor your Eccho ring.

     And ye high heavens, the temple of the gods,
410 In which a thousand torches flaming bright
     Doe burne, that to us wretched earthly clods,
     In dreadful darknesse lend desirèd light;
     And all ye powers which in the same remayne,
     More than we men can fayne,°   *imagine*
415 Poure out your blessing on us plentiously,
     And happy influence upon us raine,
     That we may raise a large posterity,
     Which from the earth, which they may long possesse,
     With lasting happinesse,
420 Up to your haughty pallaces may mount,
     And for the guerdon° of theyr glorious merit   *reward*
     May heavenly tabernacles there inherit,
     Of blessed Saints for to increase the count.
     So let us rest, sweet love, in hope of this,
425 And cease till then our tymely joyes to sing,
     The woods no more us answer, nor our Eccho ring.

     Song made in lieu of many ornaments,
     With which my love should duly have bene dect,°   *adorned*

---

1. The fortune we hope for.   3. Patron of youth and freedom.
2. Patron of sex, pregnancy, reproduction.

Which cutting off through hasty accidents,
430 Ye would not stay your dew time to expect,°   *await*
But promist both to recompens,
Be unto her a goodly ornament,
And for short time an endlesse moniment.[4]

1595

4. The envoy is traditionally apologetic in tone: the poem is offered as a substitute for wedding presents ("ornaments") that did not arrive in time for the wedding. But this elaborate poem is itself a "goodly ornament," for it stands as a timeless monument of art to the passing day which it celebrates.

CHRISTOPHER MARLOWE
1564–1593

ca. 1587:   *Tamburlaine* produced, introducing blank verse, "Marlowe's mighty line," to the stage.
ca. 1592–93:   *Dr. Faustus, Hero and Leander.*

Christopher Marlowe was born two months before William Shakespeare. He was the son of a Canterbury shoemaker; in 1580 he went to Corpus Christi College, Cambridge, on a scholarship which was ordinarily awarded to students preparing for the ministry. He held the scholarship for the maximum time, six years, but did not take holy orders. Instead, he began to write plays. When he came to supplicate for his Master of Arts degree in 1587, the university was about to deny it to him on the grounds that he intended to go abroad to Reims, the center of Catholic intrigue and propaganda against Elizabeth, and remain there. But the Privy Council intervened and requested that, since Marlowe had done the queen good service, he be granted his degree at the next commencement "because it is not Her Majesty's pleasure that anyone employed as he had been in matters touching the benefit of his country should be defamed by those that are ignorant in the affairs he went about." Although much sensational information about Marlowe has been discovered in modern times, we are still "ignorant in the affairs he went about."

Before he left Cambridge, he had certainly written his tremendously successful play *Tamburlaine* and perhaps also, in collaboration with his younger Cambridge contemporary, Thomas Nashe, the tragedy of *Dido, Queen of Carthage. Tamburlaine*, which soon was followed by a sequel (*Tamburlaine*, part 2), dramatizes the exploits of a fourteenth-century Scythian shepherd who conquered much of the known world, as Alexander had before him. In some sixteenth-century narratives Tamburlaine is represented as the type of modern (i.e., Renaissance) man, and in others he is portrayed as God's Scourge. In Marlowe's play he is the vehicle for the expression of boundless energy and ambition, the impulse to strive constantly upward to absolute power. When one of his victims accuses him of bloody cruelty,

Tamburlaine answers that ambition to rule is embedded in the laws of nature and in basic human psychology:

> Nature, that framed us of four elements
> Warring within our breasts for regiment,
> Doth teach us all to have aspiring minds;
> Our souls, whose faculties can comprehend
> The wondrous architecture of the world
> And measure every planet's wandering course,
> Still climbing after knowledge infinite,
> And always moving as the restless spheres,
> Wills us to wear ourselves and never rest
> Until we reach the ripest fruit of all,
> That perfect bliss and sole felicity,
> The sweet fruition of an earthly crown.

The English theater had heard nothing like this before. Here is a resonant, rhetorical blank verse, eminently suited to projection from the stage, and appropriate also, as it turned out, for the robust talents of the actor Edward Alleyn who happily appeared in time to portray Marlowe's heroes.

From the time of his first great success, when he was twenty-three, Marlowe had only six years to live. They were not calm years. In 1589 he was involved in a brawl with one William Bradley, in which the poet Thomas Watson intervened and killed Bradley. Both poets were jailed, but Watson got off on a plea of self-defense and Marlowe was released. In 1591 Marlowe was living in London with the playwright Thomas Kyd, who later gave information to the Privy Council accusing Marlowe of atheism and treason. On May 30, 1593, at the inn of the Widow Bull in Deptford, Marlowe was killed by a dagger thrust in an argument over the bill. In these six violent years, Marlowe composed five more plays: his sequel to *Tamburlaine; The Massacre at Paris*; two major tragedies, *The Jew of Malta* and *Dr. Faustus*; and a chronicle history play, *Edward II*.

The major tragedies all portray a hero who passionately seeks power—the power of rule, the power of money, and the power of knowledge, respectively. Each of the heroes is an "overreacher," striving beyond the bounds of human capacity, or at least the limits imposed upon human achievement.

Unlike Tamburlaine, whose aim and goal is "the sweet fruition of an earthly crown," and Barabas, the Jew of Malta, who lusts for "infinte riches in a little room," Faustus seeks the power that comes from knowledge, no matter at what cost that knowledge is acquired. To get this power Faustus must make (or chooses to make) a bargain with the devil. Such a situation is an old folklore motif, but it would have been taken seriously in a time when everyone believed in the reality of devils. Faustus on his part is in search of the power that comes from black magic, but the devil on his side exacts a fearful price in exchange—the eternal damnation of Faustus's soul. This, like the reality of devils, would have been taken literally by an Elizabethan audience. Faustus aspires to be more than a man—a demigod, a deity. His fall is caused by the same pride and ambition that caused the fall of the angels in heaven, and of humanity in the Garden of Eden. So to aspire is to incur inevitable defeat, but it is characteristic of Marlowe that he makes those aspirations nonetheless magnificent.

The immediate source of the play is a German narrative called, in its English translation, *The History of the Damnable Life and Deserved Death of Doctor John Faustus.* It contains those scenes of horseplay and low practical joking which, in the drama, contrast so markedly with the passages of grand aspiration. It is quite possible that these low scenes are the work of a collaborator, and the early records from the theater and the early editions of the play (1604 and 1616, both long after Marlowe's death) show that the true text of the play is difficult to establish. What does seem clear is that no other Elizabethan could have written the first scene (which projects the insatiable aspiring mind of the hero), the famous address to Helen of Troy, or the final scene of Faustus's last hour.

The Tragical History
of the Life and Death of Doctor Faustus

Dramatis Personae

CHORUS
DR. JOHN FAUSTUS, *of the University of Wittenberg*
WAGNER, *his servant*
GOOD ANGEL *and* BAD ANGEL
VALDES *and* CORNELIUS, *magicians and friends of* FAUSTUS
THREE SCHOLARS, *students at the university*
LUCIFER, MEPHISTOPHILIS, *and* BELZEBUB, *devils*
ROBIN *and* DICK, *rustic clowns*
THE SEVEN DEADLY SINS
POPE ADRIAN
RAYMOND, *King of Hungary*
BRUNO, *a rival Pope, appointed by the* EMPEROR
CARDINALS OF FRANCE *and* PADUA
ARCHBISHOP OF RHEIMS
MARTINO, FREDERICK, *and* BENVOLIO, *gentlemen at the* EMPEROR's *court*
CAROLUS (CHARLES) THE FIFTH, EMPEROR
DUKE OF SAXONY
DUKE *and* DUCHESS OF VANHOLT
HORSE-COURSER
CARTER
HOSTESS *of a tavern*
OLD MAN
SPIRITS *of* DARIUS, ALEXANDER *and his* PARAMOUR, *and* HELEN OF TROY
ATTENDANTS, MONKS *and* FRIARS, SOLDIERS, PIPER, *two* CUPIDS

Act 1

[*Enter* CHORUS.[1]]

CHO. Not marching in the fields of Trasimene[2]
    Where Mars did mate the warlike Carthagens,

---

1. A single actor who recited a prologue to an act or a whole play, and occasionally delivered an epilogue.

2. The battle of Lake Trasimene (217 B.C.) was one of the Carthaginian leader Hannibal's great victories. "Mate": join with.

Nor sporting in the dalliance of love
In courts of kings where state[3] is overturned,
Nor in the pomp of proud audacious deeds   5
Intends our Muse to vaunt his heavenly verse:
Only this, gentles, we must now perform
The form of Faustus' fortunes good or bad.
And so to patient judgments we appeal
And speak for Faustus in his infancy.   10
Now is he born, his parents base of stock,
In Germany within a town called Rhode;[4]
At riper years to Wittenberg he went
Whereas his kinsmen chiefly brought him up;
So much he profits in divinity,   15
The fruitful plot of scholarism graced,[5]
That shortly he was graced with Doctor's name,
Excelling all whose sweet delight disputes[6]
In th' heavenly matters of theology,
Till, swollen with cunning,[7] of a self-conceit,   20
His waxen wings did mount above his reach
And melting, heavens conspired his overthrow.[8]
For, falling to a devilish exercise
And glutted more with learning's golden gifts,
He surfeits upon cursèd necromancy;[9]   25
Nothing so sweet as magic is to him,
Which he prefers before his chiefest bliss[1]—
And this the man that in his study sits.

[*Draws the curtain[2] and exit.*]

SCENE 1

[FAUSTUS *in his study.*]

FAUST. Settle thy studies, Faustus, and begin
To sound the depth of that thou wilt profess.
Having commenced,[3] be a divine in show,
Yet level at the end of every art
And live and die in Aristotle's works: 5
Sweet Analytics,[4] 'tis thou hast ravished me!   [*Reads.*]
Bene disserere est finis logicis—
Is to dispute well logic's chiefest end?
Affords this art no greater miracle?

3. Political power.
4. Roda. Wittenberg, in the next line, was the famous university where Martin Luther studied, as did Shakespeare's Hamlet and Horatio; "whereas": where.
5. Grazed. In line 17 "graced" refers to the Cambridge word for permission to proceed to a degree.
6. The usual academic exercises were disputations, which took the place of examinations.
7. Learning.
8. The reference is to the Greek myth of Icarus, who flew too near the sun on wings of feathers and wax made by his father Daedalus. The wax melted and he fell into the sea and was drowned.
9. Black magic.
1. The salvation of his soul.
2. A curtain to the enclosed space at the rear of the stage.
3. "Commenced": graduated, i.e., received the doctor's degree; "in show": in external appearance; "level": aim.
4. The title of a treatise on logic by Aristotle. The Latin means, "To carry on a disputation well is the end or purpose of logic."

Then read no more; thou hast attained that end.   10
A greater subject fitteth Faustus' wit:
Bid on kaì mē on[5] farewell, Galen come,
Seeing *ubi desinit philosophus, ibi incipit medicus;*[6]
Be a physician, Faustus, heap up gold
And be eternized for some wondrous cure.   [*Reads.*] 15
Summum bonum medicinae sanitas[7]—
The end of physic is our bodies' health:
Why, Faustus, hast thou not attained that end?
Is not thy common talk sound aphorisms?[8]
Are not thy bills hung up as monuments   20
Whereby whole cities have escaped the plague
And thousand desperate maladies been eased?
Yet art thou still but Faustus, and a man.
Couldst thou make men to live eternally
Or, being dead, raise them to life again,   25
Then this profession were to be esteemed.
Physic, farewell. Where is Justinian?[9]   [*Reads.*]
Si una eademque res legatur duobus,
Alter rem, alter valorem rei, etc.[1]—
A pretty case of paltry legacies!   30
Exhaereditare filium non potest pater nisi—
Such is the subject of the Institute
And universal body of the law.
This study fits a mercenary drudge
Who aims at nothing but external trash,   35
Too servile and illiberal for me.
When all is done, divinity is best.
Jerome's Bible,[2] Faustus, view it well: [*Reads.*]
Stipendium peccati mors est—Ha! *Stipendium, etc.*
The reward of sin is death? That's hard.   40
Si pecasse negamus, fallimur, et nulla est in nobis veritas[3]—
If we say that we have no sin
We deceive ourselves, and there's no truth in us.
Why then belike
We must sin and so consequently die,   45
Aye, we must die an everlasting death.
What doctrine call you this, *Che sera, sera:*[4]
What will be, shall be? Divinity, adieu!
These metaphysics[5] of magicians
And necromantic books are heavenly: 50
Lines, circles, signs, letters, and characters—

---

5. "Being and not being," i.e., philosophy. Galen: the ancient authority on medicine (2nd century A.D.).
6. "Where the philosopher leaves off the physician begins."
7. "Good health is the object of medicine" (or "physic").
8. I.e., reliable medical pronouncements. "Bills": prescriptions.
9. Roman emperor and authority on law (483–565), author of the *Institutes*.

1. "If something is bequeathed to two persons, one shall have the thing itself, the other something of equal value." The next Latin phrase means: "A father cannot disinherit his son unless."
2. The Latin translation, or "Vulgate," of St. Jerome (ca. 340–420). The Latin (Romans vi.23) is translated in line 40.
3. 1 John i.8, translated in the next 2 lines.
4. Translated in the first half of the next line.
5. Basic principles.

Aye, these are those that Faustus most desires.
O what a world of profit and delight,
Of power, of honor, of omnipotence,
Is promised to the studious artisan![6]   55
All things that move between the quiet[7] poles
Shall be at my command. Emperors and kings
Are but obeyed in their several provinces,
Nor can they raise the wind or rend the clouds;
But his dominion that exceeds in this   60
Stretcheth as far as doth the mind of man.
A sound magician is a demigod:
Here tire my brains to gain a deity!
Wagner!

      [*Enter* WAGNER.]

Commend me to my dearest friends,   65
The German Valdes and Cornelius;
Request them earnestly to visit me.
WAG. I will, sir.   [*Exit.*]
FAUST. Their conference will be a greater help to me
Than all my labors, plod I ne'er so fast.   70

      [*Enter the* GOOD ANGEL *and the* BAD ANGEL.]

G. ANG. O Faustus, lay that damnèd book aside
And gaze not on it, lest it tempt thy soul
And heap God's heavy wrath upon thy head.
Read, read the Scriptures! That is blasphemy.
B. ANG. Go forward, Faustus, in that famous art   75
Wherein all nature's treasury is contained:
Be thou on earth, as Jove[8] is in the sky,
Lord and commander of these elements.

      [*Exeunt* ANGELS.]

FAUST. How am I glutted with conceit[9] of this!
Shall I make spirits fetch me what I please,   80
Resolve me of all ambiguities,
Perform what desperate enterprise I will?
I'll have them fly to India[1] for gold,
Ransack the ocean for orient pearl,
And search all corners of the new-found world[2]   85
For pleasant fruits and princely delicates;
I'll have them read me strange philosophy
And tell the secrets of all foreign kings;
I'll have them wall all Germany with brass
And make swift Rhine circle fair Wittenberg;   90
I'll have them fill the public schools[3] with silk
Wherewith the students shall be bravely clad;
I'll levy soldiers with the coin they bring,

---

6. I.e., a master of the occult arts, such as necromancy.
7. Unmoving.
8. God (a common substitution in Elizabethan
drama).

9. Filled with the idea.
1. "India" could mean the West Indies, America,
or Ophir (in the east).
2. The western hemisphere.
3. The university lecture rooms.

And chase the Prince of Parma[4] from our land
And reign sole king of all our provinces; 95
Yea, stranger engines for the brunt of war
Than was the fiery keel[5] at Antwerp's bridge
I'll make my servile spirits to invent!

[*Enter* VALDES *and* CORNELIUS.]

Come, German Valdes and Cornelius,
And make me blest with your sage conference. 100
Valdes, sweet Valdes and Cornelius,
Know that your words have won me at the last
To practice magic and concealèd arts;
Yet not your words only, but mine own fantasy
That will receive no object,[6] for my head 105
But ruminates on necromantic skill.
Philosophy is odious and obscure,
Both law and physic are for petty wits,
Divinity is basest of the three,
Unpleasant, harsh, contemptible, and vile; 110
'Tis magic, magic, that hath ravished me!
Then, gentle friends, aid me in this attempt,
And I, that have with concise syllogisms
Graveled[7] the pastors of the German church,
And made the flowering pride of Wittenberg 115
Swarm to my problems[8] as the infernal spirits
On sweet Musaeus when he came to hell,
Will be as cunning as Agrippa[9] was
Whose shadows made all Europe honor him.
VALD. Faustus, these books, thy wit, and our experience 120
Shall make all nations to canonize us.
As Indian Moors[1] obey their Spanish lords
So shall the spirits of every element
Be always serviceable to us three:
Like lions shall they guard us when we please. 125
Like Almain rutters[2] with their horsemen's staves,
Or Lapland giants trotting by our sides;
Sometimes like women, or unwedded maids,
Shadowing[3] more beauty in their airy brows
Than in the white breasts of the queen of love; 130
From Venice shall they drag huge argosies
And from America the golden fleece
That yearly stuffs old Philip's[4] treasury,
If learned Faustus will be resolute.

4. The duke of Parma was the Spanish governor general of the Low Countries from 1579 to 1592.
5. A reference to the burning ship sent by the Netherlanders in 1585 against the barrier on the river Scheldt which Parma had built as a part of the blockade of Antwerp.
6. That will pay no attention to physical reality.
7. Confounded.
8. Lectures in logic and mathematics. Musaeus was a mythical singer, son of Orpheus; it was, however, the latter who charmed the denizens of hell with his music.
9. Cornelius Agrippa, German author of *The Vanity and Uncertainty of Arts and Sciences*, popularly supposed to have the power of calling up shades ("shadows") of the dead.
1. I.e., dark-skinned American Indians.
2. German horsemen.
3. Harboring.
4. Philip II, king of Spain.

FAUST. Valdes, as resolute am I in this   135
   As thou to live; therefore object it not.[5]
CORN. The miracles that magic will perform
   Will make thee vow to study nothing else.
   He that is grounded in astrology,
   Enriched with tongues, well seen[6] in minerals,   140
   Hath all the principles magic doth require.
   Then doubt not, Faustus, but to be renowned
   And more frequented for this mystery[7]
   Than heretofore the Delphian oracle.
   The spirits tell me they can dry the sea   145
   And fetch the treasure of all foreign wrecks—
   Aye, all the wealth that our forefathers hid
   Within the massy[8] entrails of the earth.
   Then tell me, Faustus, what shall we three want?
FAUST. Nothing, Cornelius. O this cheers my soul!   150
   Come, show me some demonstrations magical
   That I may conjure in some lusty[9] grove
   And have these joys in full possession.
VALD. Then haste thee to some solitary grove
   And bear wise Bacon's[1] and Abanus' works,   155
   The Hebrew Psalter and New Testament;
   And whatsoever else is requisite
   We will inform thee ere our conference cease.
CORN. Valdes, first let him know the words of art,
   And then, all other ceremonies learned,   160
   Faustus may try his cunning by himself.
VALD. First I'll instruct thee in the rudiments,
   And then wilt thou be perfecter than I.
FAUST. Then come and dine with me, and after meat
   We'll canvass every quiddity[2] thereof;   165
   For ere I sleep I'll try what I can do:
   This night I'll conjure[3] though I die therefore.   [*Exeunt.*]

SCENE 2

[*Enter two* SCHOLARS.]

1 SCH. I wonder what's become of Faustus, that was wont to make
   our schools ring with *sic probo*.[4]
2 SCH. That shall we presently know; here comes his boy.[5]

[*Enter* WAGNER *carrying wine*.]

1 SCH. How now, sirrah; where's thy master?
WAG. God in heaven knows.   5
2 SCH. Why, dost not thou know then?

5. I.e., don't make it a condition.
6. Expert.
7. Craft. The "Delphian oracle" was the oracle of
Apollo at Delphi, much frequented in antiquity.
8. Massive.
9. Flourishing, beautiful.
1. Roger Bacon, the medieval friar and scientist,
popularly thought a magician. "Abanus" is Pietro
d'Abano, 13th-century alchemist.
2. Essential feature.
3. Call up spirits.
4. "Thus I prove," a phrase in scholastic disputation.
5. Poor student earning his keep.

WAG. Yes, I know; but that follows not.

1 SCH. Go to, sirrah; leave your jesting and tell us where he is.

WAG. That follows not by force of argument, which you, being licentiate,[6] should stand upon; therefore acknowledge your error and be attentive.   10

2 SCH. Then you will not tell us?

WAG. You are deceived, for I will tell you. Yet if you were not dunces you would never ask me such a question, for is he not *corpus naturale*, and is not that *mobile?*[7] Then wherefore should you ask me such a question? But that I am by nature phlegmatic,[8] slow to wrath and prone to lechery (to love, I would say), it were not for you to come within forty foot of the place of execution,[9] although I do not doubt to see you both hanged the next sessions. Thus having triumphed over you, I will set my countenance like a precisian,[1] and begin to speak thus: Truly, my dear brethren, my master is within at dinner with Valdes and Cornelius, as this wine, if it could speak, would inform your worships; and so the Lord bless you, preserve you, and keep you, my dear brethren.   25

[*Exit.*]

1 SCH. O Faustus, then I fear that which I have long suspected,
That thou art fallen into that damnèd art
For which they two are infamous through the world.

2 SCH. Were he a stranger, not allied to me,
The danger of his soul would make me mourn.   30
But come, let us go and inform the Rector,[2]
It may be his grave counsel may reclaim him.

1 SCH. I fear me nothing will reclaim him now.

2 SCH. Yet let us see what we can do.   [*Exeunt.*]

SCENE 3

[*Enter* FAUSTUS *to conjure.*]

FAUST. Now that the gloomy shadow of the night,
Longing to view Orion's drizzling look,[3]
Leaps from the antarctic world unto the sky
And dims the welkin[4] with her pitchy breath,
Faustus, begin thine incantations   5
And try if devils will obey thy hest,
Seeing thou hast prayed and sacrificed to them.
Within this circle is Jehovah's name

[*He draws the circle[5] on the ground.*]

---

6. I.e., graduate students.

7. *Corpus naturale et mobile* (natural, movable matter) was a scholastic definition of the subject matter of physics. Wagner is here parodying the language of learning he hears around the university.

8. Dominated by the phlegm, one of the 4 humors of medieval medicine and psychology.

9. I.e., the dining room.

1. A Puritan. The rest of his speech is in the style of the Puritans.

2. The head of a German university.

3. Orion appears at the beginning of winter. The phrase is a reminiscence of Virgil.

4. Sky.

5. I.e., the magic circle on the ground within which the spirits rise.

Forward and backward anagrammatized,
The breviated names of holy saints,   10
Figures of every adjunct[6] to the heavens
And characters of signs and erring stars,
By which the spirits are enforced to rise.
Then fear not, Faustus, but be resolute
And try the uttermost magic can perform.   [*Thunder.*]   15
Sint mihi dei Acherontis propitii! Valeat numen triplex Iehovae!
Ignei aerii aquatici terreni spiritus, salvete! Orientis princeps Lucifer
Belzebub, inferni ardentis monarcha, et Demogorgon, propitia-
mus vos, ut appareat et surgat Mephistophilis![7]

     [FAUSTUS *pauses. Thunder still.*]

Quid tu moraris?[8] *Per Iehovam, Gehennam et consecratam aquam*
quam nunc spargo, signumque crucis quod nunc facio, et per vota
nostra, ipse nunc surgat nobis dicatus Mephistophilis!

     [*Enter* MEPHISTOPHILIS *in the shape of a dragon.*]

I charge thee to return and change thy shape;   25
Thou art too ugly to attend on me.
Go, and return an old Franciscan friar;
That holy shape becomes a devil best.   [*Exit* MEPH.]
I see there's virtue in my heavenly words:
Who would not be proficient in this art?   30
How pliant is this Mephistophilis,
Full of obedience and humility!
Such is the force of magic and my spells.
Now, Faustus, thou art conjurer laureate
That canst command great Mephistophilis: 35
Quin redis, Mephistophilis, fratris imagine![9]

     [*Re-enter* MEPHISTOPHILIS *like a Friar.*]

MEPH. Now, Faustus, what wouldst thou have me do?
FAUST. I charge thee wait upon me whilst I live
     To do whatever Faustus shall command,
     Be it be make the moon drop from her sphere   40
     Or the ocean to overwhelm the world.
MEPH. I am a servant to great Lucifer
     And may not follow thee without his leave:
     No more than he commands must we perform.
FAUST. Did not he charge thee to appear to me?   45
MEPH. No, I came now hither of my own accord.
FAUST. Did not my conjuring speeches raise thee?
     Speak!

6. Heavenly body, thought to be joined to the solid firmament. "Characters of signs" are signs of the zodiac and the planets; "erring": wandering.
7. This first part of the incantation means: "May the gods of the lower regions favor me! Goodbye to the Trinity! Hail, spirits of fire, air, water, and earth! Prince of the East, Belzebub, monarch of burning hell, and Demogorgon, we pray to you that Mephistophilis may appear and rise."
8. Nothing has happened, so Faustus asks, "What are you waiting for?" and continues to conjure: "By Jehovah, Gehenna, and the holy water which I now sprinkle, and the sign of the cross which I now make, and by our vows, may Mephistophilis himself now rise to serve us."
9. "Return, Mephistophilis, in the shape of a friar."

MEPH. That was the cause, but yet *per accidens*,[1]
   For when we hear one rack[2] the name of God,   50
   Abjure the Scriptures and his Saviour Christ,
   We fly in hope to get his glorious soul;
   Nor will we come unless he use such means
   Whereby he is in danger to be damned;
   Therefore the shortest cut for conjuring   55
   Is stoutly to abjure the Trinity
   And pray devoutly to the prince of hell.
FAUST. So I have done, and hold this principle,
   There is no chief but only Belzebub
   To whom Faustus doth dedicate himself.   60
   This word "damnation" terrifies not me
   For I confound hell in Elysium;
   My ghost be with the old philosophers![3]
   But leaving these vain trifles of men's souls—
   Tell me, what is that Lucifer thy lord?   65
MEPH. Arch-regent and commander of all spirits.
FAUST. Was not that Lucifer an angel once?
MEPH. Yes, Faustus, and most dearly loved of God.
FAUST. How comes it, then, that he is prince of devils?   70
MEPH. O, by aspiring pride and insolence,
   For which God threw him from the face of heaven.
FAUST. And what are you that live with Lucifer?
MEPH. Unhappy spirits that fell with Lucifer,
   Conspired against our God with Lucifer,   75
   And are forever damned with Lucifer.
FAUST. Where are you damned?
MEPH. In hell.
FAUST. How comes it, then, that thou art out of hell?
MEPH. Why, this is hell, nor am I out of it: 80
   Thinkst thou that I who saw the face of God
   And tasted the eternal joys of heaven
   Am not tormented with ten thousand hells
   In being deprived of everlasting bliss?[4]
   O Faustus, leave these frivolous demands   85
   Which strike a terror to my fainting soul!
FAUST. What, is great Mephistophilis so passionate
   For being deprivèd of the joys of heaven?
   Learn thou of Faustus manly fortitude
   And scorn those joys thou never shalt possess.   90
   Go, bear these tidings to great Lucifer:
   Seeing Faustus hath incurred eternal death
   By desperate thoughts against Jove's deity,
   Say he surrenders up to him his soul
   So he will spare him four and twenty years,   95
   Letting him live in all voluptuousness,

---

1. By the immediate, not ultimate, cause.
2. Torture (by anagrammatizing).
3. I.e., I consider the true hell to be the classical Elysium, where philosophy is discussed, not the

Christian place of punishment for sinners.
4. This is the *poena damni*, or punishment of loss, supposed to constitute the greatest spiritual suffering.

Having thee ever to attend on me:
To give me whatsoever I shall ask,
To tell me whatsoever I demand,
To slay mine enemies and aid my friends,   100
And always be obedient to my will.
Go, and return to mighty Lucifer,
And meet me in my study at midnight
And then resolve me of thy master's mind.[5]
MEPH. I will, Faustus.   [*Exit.*]   105
FAUST. Had I as many souls as there be stars
I'd give them all for Mephistophilis!
By him I'll be great emperor of the world,
And make a bridge thorough the moving air
To pass the ocean with a band of men;   110
I'll join the hills that bind the Afric shore
And make that country continent to Spain,
And both contributory to my crown;
The Emperor[6] shall not live but by my leave,
Nor any potentate of Germany.   115
Now that I have obtained what I desire
I'll live in speculation[7] of this art
Till Mephistophilis return again.   [*Exit.*]

SCENE 4

[*Enter* WAGNER *and the* CLOWN ⟨ROBIN.⟩[8]]

WAG. Come hither, sirrah boy.
CLOWN. Boy! O disgrace to my person! Zounds, boy in your face!
    You have seen many boys with such pickadevaunts, I am sure.[9]
WAG. Sirrah, hast thou no comings in?[1]
CLOWN. Yes, and goings out too; you may see, sir.   5
WAG. Alas, poor slave. See how poverty jests in his nakedness: the
    villain's out of service, and so hungry that I know he would give
    his soul to the devil for a shoulder of mutton, though it were
    blood-raw.
CLOWN. Not so, neither; I had need to have it well-roasted, and   10
    good sauce to it, if I pay so dear, I can tell you.
WAG. Sirrah, wilt thou be my man and wait on me? And I will
    make thee go like *Qui mihi discipulus.*[2]
CLOWN. What, in verse?
WAG. No, slave, in beaten silk and staves-acre.[3]   15
CLOWN. Staves-acre! that's good to kill vermin. Then, belike, if I
    serve you I shall be lousy.

5. Give me his decision.
6. The Holy Roman Emperor.
7. Contemplation.
8. Not a court jester (as in some of Shakespeare's
plays), but the older-fashioned stock character, a
rustic buffoon. The name "Robin" has been interpolated by later editors of the text; all such inter-
polations, introduced for clarity of understanding,
are indicated by the special brackets used here.
9. The point of the Clown's retort is that he is a

man and wears a beard ("pickadevaunt"). "Zounds":
an oath ("God's wounds").
1. Income, but the Clown then puns on the literal
meaning.
2. "You who are my pupil" (the opening phrase
of a poem on how students should behave, from
Lily's *Latin Grammar*). Wagner means, 'like a
proper servant of a learned man."
3. A kind of delphinium used for killing vermin.

WAG. Why, so thou shalt be, whether thou dost it or no; for, sirrah, if thou dost not presently bind thyself to me for seven years, I'll turn all the lice about thee into familiars[4] and make them tear thee in pieces.   20

CLOWN. Nay, sir, you may save yourself a labor, for they are as familiar with me as if they paid for their meat and drink, I can tell you.

WAG. Well, sirrah, leave your jesting and take these guilders.[5]   25

CLOWN. Yes, marry, sir, and I thank you, too.

WAG. So, now thou art to be at an hour's warning whenever and wheresoever the devil shall fetch thee.

CLOWN. Here, take your guilders again, I'll none of 'em.

WAG. Not I, thou art pressed;[6] prepare thyself, for I will presently   30
raise up two devils to carry thee away. Banio! Belcher!

CLOWN. Belcher? And Belcher come here I'll belch him. I am not afraid of a devil.

[*Enter two* DEVILS, *and the* CLOWN *runs up and down crying.*]

WAG. How now, sir! Will you serve me now?

CLOWN. Aye, good Wagner, take away the devil then.   35

WAG. Spirits, away!   [DEVILS *exeunt.*]
          Now, sirrah, follow me.

CLOWN. I will, sir. But hark you, master, will you teach me this conjuring occupation?

WAG. Aye, sirrah, I'll teach thee to turn thyself to a dog, or a cat,   40
or a mouse, or a rat, or anything.

CLOWN. A dog, or a cat, or a mouse, or a rat! O brave[7] Wagner!

WAG. Villain, call me Master Wagner; and see that you walk attentively, and let your right eye be always diametrally[8] fixed upon my left heel, that thou mayst *quasi vestigiis nostris insistere.*[9]   45

CLOWN. Well, sir, I warrant you.   [*Exeunt.*]

Act 2

SCENE 1

[*Enter* FAUSTUS *in his study.*]

FAUST. Now, Faustus, must thou needs be damned,
          And canst thou not be saved.
          What boots[1] it, then, to think of God or heaven?
          Away with such vain fancies, and despair—
          Despair in God and trust in Belzebub.   5
          Now go not backward, no, be resolute!
          Why waverest thou? O something soundeth in mine ears:
          "Abjure this magic, turn to God again!"
          Aye, and Faustus will turn to God again.

4. Familiar spirits, demons.   8. Diametrically.
5. Money.   9. A pedantic way of saying "follow my footsteps."
6. Impressed, i.e., hired.   1. Avails.
7. Marvelous, wonderful.

To God? He loves thee not;   10
The God thou servest is thine own appetite,
Wherein is fixed the love of Belzebub.
To him I'll build an altar and a church
And offer lukewarm blood of newborn babes.

[*Enter* GOOD ANGEL *and* BAD ANGEL.]

G. ANG. Sweet Faustus, leave that execrable art.   15
B. ANG. Go forward, Faustus, in that famous art.
FAUST. Contrition, prayer, repentance—what of them?
G. ANG. O they are means to bring thee unto heaven!
B. ANG. Rather illusions, fruits of lunacy,
    That makes men foolish that do use them most.   20
G. ANG. Sweet Faustus, think of heaven and heavenly things.
B. ANG. No, Faustus, think of honor and of wealth.

[⟨*Exeunt* ANGELS.⟩]

FAUST. Of wealth!
    Why, the signiory of Emden² shall be mine.
    When Mephistophilis shall stand by me   25
    What power can hurt me? Faustus, thou art safe;
    Cast no more doubts. Come, Mephistophilis,
    And bring glad tidings from great Lucifer.
    Is 't not midnight? Come, Mephistophilis!
    *Veni, veni, Mephistophile!*³   30

[*Enter* MEPHISTOPHILIS.]

    Now tell me what saith Lucifer, thy lord?
MEPH. That I shall wait on Faustus whilst I live,
    So he will buy my service with his soul.
FAUST. Already Faustus hath hazarded that for thee.
MEPH. But, Faustus, thou must bequeath it solemnly   35
    And write a deed of gift with thine own blood,
    For that security craves Lucifer.
    If thou deny it, I must back to hell.
FAUST. Stay, Mephistophilis, and tell me what good
    Will my soul do thy lord?
MEPH.   Enlarge his kingdom.   40
FAUST. Is that the reason why he tempts us thus?
MEPH. *Solamen miseris socios habuisse doloris.*⁴
FAUST. Why, have you any pain that tortures others?
MEPH. As great as have the human souls of men.
    But tell me, Faustus, shall I have thy soul?   45
    And I will be thy slave, and wait on thee,
    And give thee more than thou hast wit to ask.
FAUST. Aye, Mephistophilis, I'll give it him.
MEPH. Then, Faustus, stab thine arm courageously,
    And bind thy soul that at some certain day   50

---

2. A wealthy German trade center.   4. "Misery loves company."
3. "Come, come, Mephistophilis!"

Great Lucifer may claim it as his own,
And then be thou as great as Lucifer.
FAUST. Lo, Mephistophilis, for love of thee

[*Stabbing his arm.*]

Faustus hath cut his arm, and with his proper[5] blood
Assures his soul to be great Lucifer's.   55
Chief lord and regent of perpetual night,
View here the blood that trickles from mine arm
And let it be propitious for my wish!
MEPH. But, Faustus,
Write it in manner of a deed of gift.   60
FAUST. Aye, so I do. [*Writes.*] But, Mephistophilis,
My blood congeals and I can write no more.
MEPH. I'll fetch thee fire to dissolve it straight.   [*Exit.*]
FAUST. What might the staying of my blood portend?
Is it unwilling I should write this bill?[6]   65
Why streams it not, that I may write afresh?
"Faustus gives to thee his soul"—ah, there it stayed.
Why shouldst thou not? Is not thy soul thine own?
Then write again: "Faustus gives to thee his soul."

[*Enter* MEPHISTOPHILIS *with a chafer*[7] *of fire.*]

MEPH. See, Faustus, here is fire; set it on.   70
FAUST. So: now the blood begins to clear again;
Now will I make an end immediately.   [⟨*Writes.*⟩]
MEPH. [*aside*] What will not I do to obtain his soul!
FAUST. *Consummatum est*[8]—this bill is ended;
And Faustus hath bequeathed his soul to Lucifer.   75
But what is this inscription on mine arm?
"*Homo, fuge!*"[9] Whither should I fly?
If unto God, he'll throw me down to hell.
My senses are deceived; here's nothing writ.
O yes, I see it plain: even here is writ   80
"*Homo, fuge!*" Yet shall not Faustus fly.
MEPH. I'll fetch him somewhat to delight his mind.   [*Exit.*]

[*Re-enter* MEPHISTOPHILIS *with* DEVILS, *giving crowns and
rich apparel to* FAUSTUS, *and dance, and then depart.*]

FAUST. What means this show?
Speak, Mephistophilis.
MEPH. Nothing, Faustus, but to delight thy mind   85
And let thee see what magic can perform.
FAUST. But may I raise such spirits when I please?
MEPH. Aye, Faustus, and do greater things than these.
FAUST. Then, Mephistophilis, receive this scroll,
A deed of gift of body and of soul;   90

5. Own.   8. "It is finished." A blasphemy, as these are the
6. Contract.   words of Christ on the Cross (see John 19.30).
7. A portable grate.   9. "O man, fly!"

But yet conditionally that thou perform
All covenant-articles between us both.
MEPH. Faustus, I swear by hell and Lucifer
To effect all promises between us made.
FAUST. Then hear me read it, Mephistophilis.   [⟨Reads.⟩]   95
"On these conditions following:
First, that Faustus may be a spirit in form and substance.
Secondly, that Mephistophilis shall be his servant and at his
command.
Thirdly, that Mephistophilis shall do for him, and bring him   100
whatsoever.
Fourthly, that he shall be in his chamber or house invisible.
Lastly, that he shall appear to the said John Faustus at all times,
in what form or shape soever he please.
I, John Faustus of Wittenberg, Doctor, by these presents do give   105
both body and soul to Lucifer, Prince of the East, and his min-
ister Mephistophilis, and furthermore grant unto them, that four
and twenty years being expired, the articles above written invio-
late, full power to fetch or carry the said John Faustus, body and
soul, flesh, blood, or goods, into their habitation wheresoever.   110
                    By me John Faustus."
MEPH. Speak, Faustus, do you deliver this as your deed?
FAUST. Aye, take it, and the devil give thee good of it.
MEPH. Now, Faustus, ask what thou wilt.
FAUST. First will I question with thee about hell.   115
   Tell me, where is the place that men call hell?
MEPH. Under the heavens.
FAUST. Aye, so are all things else, but whereabout?
MEPH. Within the bowels of these elements,
   Where we are tortured and remain forever.   120
   Hell hath no limits, nor is circumscribed
   In one self place, for where we are is hell,
   And where hell is there must we ever be;
   And, to be short, when all the world dissolves
   And every creature shall be purified,   125
   All places shall be hell that is not heaven.
FAUST. I think hell's a fable.
MEPH. Aye, think so still, till experience change thy mind.
FAUST. Why, thinkst thou that Faustus shall be damned?
MEPH. Aye, of necessity, for here's the scroll   130
   In which thou hast given thy soul to Lucifer.
FAUST. Aye, and body too; but what of that?
   Thinkst thou that Faustus is so fond[1] to imagine
   That after this life there is any pain?
   Tush, no, these are trifles and mere old wives' tales.   135
MEPH. But I am an instance to prove the contrary,
   For I tell thee I am damned and now in hell.
FAUST. Nay, and this be hell I'll willingly be damned.

---

1. Foolish.

What, sleeping, eating, walking, and disputing?
But leaving off this, let me have a wife,   140
The fairest maid in Germany,
For I am wanton and lascivious
And cannot live without a wife.
MEPH. I prithee, Faustus, talk not of a wife.[2]
FAUST. Nay, sweet Mephistophilis, fetch me one, for I will have   145
one.
MEPH. Well, thou shalt have a wife. Sit there till I come. [⟨Exit.⟩]

[Re-enter MEPHISTOPHILIS with a DEVIL dressed like a woman,
with fireworks.]

FAUST. What sight is this?
MEPH. Now, Faustus, how dost thou like thy wife?
FAUST. Here's a hot whore indeed! No, I'll no wife.   150
MEPH. Marriage is but a ceremonial toy,
And if thou lovest me, think no more of it.
I'll cull thee out the fairest courtesans
And bring them every morning to thy bed;
She whom thine eye shall like thy heart shall have,   155
Were she as chaste as was Penelope,[3]
As wise as Saba, or as beautiful
As was bright Lucifer before his fall.
Hold, take this book: peruse it thoroughly.
The iterating[4] of these lines brings gold,   160
The framing[5] of this circle on the ground
Brings whirlwinds, tempests, thunder, and lightning;
Pronounce this thrice devoutly to thyself
And men in harness[6] shall appear to thee,
Ready to execute what thou desirest.   165
FAUST. Thanks, Mephistophilis, yet fain would I have a book wherein
I might behold all spells and incantations, that I might raise up
spirits when I please.
MEPH. Here they are in this book.   [There turn to them.]
FAUST. Now would I have a book where I might see all characters   170
and planets of the heavens, that I might know their motions and
dispositions.
MEPH. Here they are too.   [Turn to them.]
FAUST. Nay, let me have one book more, and then I have done,
wherein I might see all plants, herbs, and trees that grow upon   175
the earth.
MEPH. Here they be.
FAUST. O thou art deceived!
MEPH. Tut, I warrant thee.   [Turn to them.]

     [⟨Exeunt.⟩][7]

---

2. Mephistophilis cannot produce a wife for Faustus because marriage is a sacrament.
3. The wife of Ulysses, famed for chastity and fidelity. "Saba": the Queen of Sheba.
4. Repeating.
5. Drawing.

6. Armor.
7. After this a comic scene has been lost from the text. In it, apparently the Clown, Robin, stole one of Faustus's conjuring books and left Wagner's service. He then became an hostler at an inn.

SCENE 2

[*Enter* FAUSTUS *in his study and* MEPHISTOPHILIS.]

FAUST. When I behold the heavens then I repent
  And curse thee, wicked Mephistophilis,
  Because thou hast deprived me of those joys.
MEPH. 'Twas thine own seeking, Faustus, thank thyself.
  But thinkest thou heaven is such a glorious thing?   5
  I tell thee, Faustus, it is not half so fair
  As thou or any man that breathes on earth.
FAUST. How provest thou that?
MEPH. 'Twas made for man; then he's more excellent.
FAUST. If heaven was made for man 'twas made for me.   10
  I will renounce this magic and repent.

[Enter GOOD ANGEL and BAD ANGEL.]

G. ANG. Faustus, repent; yet God will pity thee.
B. ANG. Thou art a spirit; God cannot pity thee.
FAUST. Who buzzeth in mine ears I am a spirit?[8]
  Be I a devil, yet God may pity me.   15
  Yea, God will pity me, if I repent.
B. ANG. Aye, but Faustus never shall repent.

[Exeunt ANGELS.]

FAUST. My heart is hardened; I cannot repent.
  Scarce can I name salvation, faith, or heaven,
  But fearful echoes thunder in mine ears: 20
  "Faustus, thou are damned!" Then guns and knives,
  Swords, poison, halters, and envenomed steel
  Are laid before me to dispatch myself,
  And long ere this I should have done the deed
  Had not sweet pleasure conquered deep despair.   25
  Have I not made blind Homer sing to me
  Of Alexander's love and Oenon's death,[9]
  And hath not he that built the walls of Thebes
  With ravishing sound of his melodious harp[1]
  Made music with my Mephistophilis?   30
  Why should I die, then, or basely despair?
  I am resolved Faustus shall not repent.
  Come, Mephistophilis, let us dispute again
  And reason of divine astrology.
  Speak, are there many spheres above the moon?   35
  Are all celestial bodies but one globe
  As is the substance of this centric earth?[2]

---

8. Evil spirit, devil.
9. Alexander is another name for Paris, the lover of Oenone; later he deserted her and abducted Helen, causing the Trojan War. Oenone refused to heal the wounds Paris received in battle, and when he died of them she killed herself in remorse.
1. I.e., the legendary musician Amphion.
2. "Faustus asks whether all the apparently different heavenly bodies form really one globe, like the earth. Mephistophilis answers that like the elements, which are separate but combined, the heavenly bodies are separate, though their spheres are infolded, and they move on one axletree. Hence we are not in error in giving individual names to Saturn, Mars, or Jupiter; they are separate planets" (F. S. Boas). The "empyreal orb," or outermost sphere, was also called the empyrean.

MEPH. As are the elements, such are the heavens,
   Even from the moon unto the empyreal orb,
   Mutually folded in each other's spheres,   40
   And jointly move upon one axletree
   Whose termine[3] is termed the world's wide pole;
   Nor are the names of Saturn, Mars, or Jupiter
   Feigned, but are erring stars.
FAUST. But tell me, have they all one motion, both *situ et tem-*   45
   pore?[4]
MEPH. All move from east to west in four and twenty hours upon
   the poles of the world, but differ in their motions upon the poles
   of the zodiac.[5]
FAUST. These slender questions Wagner can decide.   50
   Hath Mephistophilis no greater skill?
   Who knows not the double motion of the planets?
   That the first is finished in a natural day;
   The second thus, Saturn in thirty years, Jupiter in twelve, Mars
   in four, the Sun, Venus, and Mercury in a year, the Moon in   55
   twenty-eight days. These are freshmen's suppositions. But tell
   me, hath every sphere a dominion or *intelligentia?*[6]
MEPH. Aye.
FAUST. How many heavens or spheres are there?
MEPH. Nine: the seven planets, the firmament, and the empyreal   60
   heaven.
FAUST. But is there not *coelum igneum, et crystallinum?*[7]
MEPH. No, Faustus, they be but fables.
FAUST. Resolve me then in this one question: why are not conjunc-
   tions, oppositions, aspects, eclipses, all at one time, but in some   65
   years we have more, in some less?
MEPH. *Per inequalem motum respectu totius.*[8]
FAUST. Well, I am answered. Tell me, who made the world?
MEPH. I will not.
FAUST. Sweet Mephistophilis, tell me.   70
MEPH. Move[9] me not, Faustus.
FAUST. Villain, have I not bound thee to tell me anything?
MEPH. Aye, that is not against our kingdom; this is.
   Thou art damned; think thou of hell.
FAUST. Think, Faustus, upon God that made the world!   75
MEPH. Remember this!   [*Exit.*]
FAUST. Aye, go, accursèd spirit, to ugly hell;
   'Tis thou has damned distressed Faustus' soul.
   Is 't not too late?

      [*Enter* GOOD ANGEL *and* BAD ANGEL.]

B. ANG. Too late.   80
G. ANG. Never too late, if Faustus will repent.

3. End.
4. In position and time.
5. I.e., the common axletree on which all the spheres revolve.
6. I.e., an angel or intelligence (thought to be the source of motion in each sphere).
7. The "heaven of fire" and the "crystalline sphere," introduced by some of the old authorities to explain the precession of the equinoxes.
8. "Because of their unequal velocities within the system."
9. Anger.

B. ANG. If thou repent, devils will tear thee in pieces.

G. ANG. Repent, and they shall never raze[1] thy skin.

[*Exeunt* ANGELS.]

FAUST. O Christ, my Saviour! my Saviour!
　　Help to save distressèd Faustus' soul.   85

[*Enter* LUCIFER, BELZEBUB, *and* MEPHISTOPHILIS.]

LUC. Christ cannot save thy soul, for he is just;
　　There's none but I have interest in the same.

FAUST. O what art thou that lookst so terrible?

LUC. I am Lucifer,
　　And this is my companion prince in hell.   90

FAUST. O Faustus, they are come to fetch thy soul!

BEL. We are come to tell thee thou dost injure us.

LUC. Thou call'st on Christ, contrary to thy promise.

BEL. Thou shouldst not think on God.

LUC. Think on the devil.   95

BEL. And his dam too.[2]

FAUST. Nor will I henceforth. Pardon me in this,
　　And Faustus vows never to look to heaven,
　　Never to name God or pray to him,
　　To burn his Scriptures, slay his ministers,   100
　　And make my spirits pull his churches down.

LUC. So shalt thou show thyself an obedient servant, and we will
　　highly gratify thee for it.

BEL. Faustus, we are come from hell in person to show thee some
　　pastime. Sit down, and thou shalt behold the Seven Deadly Sins   105
　　appear to thee in their own proper shapes and likeness.

FAUST. That sight will be as pleasant to me as Paradise was to Adam,
　　the first day of his creation.

LUC. Talk not of Paradise or Creation, but mark the show. Go,
　　Mephistophilis, fetch them in.   110

[*Enter the* SEVEN DEADLY SINS,[3] *led by a piper.*]

Now, Faustus, question them of their names and dispositions.

FAUST. That shall I soon. What art thou, the first?

PRIDE. I am Pride. I disdain to have any parents. I am like to Ovid's
　　flea:[4] I can creep into every corner of a wench; sometimes like a
　　periwig I sit upon her brow; next like a necklace I hang about her   115
　　neck; then like a fan of feathers I kiss her lips; and then turning
　　myself to a wrought smock[5] do what I list. But fie, what a smell
　　is here! I'll not speak another word except the ground be per-
　　fumed and covered with cloth of arras.[6]

---

1. Scratch.

2. "The devil and his dam" was a common colloquial expression.

3. The Seven Deadly Sins are pride, avarice, gluttony, lust, sloth, envy, and anger. (They are deadly
because other sins grow out of them.) They were
frequently represented in medieval plays, sometimes in the rather grimly comic tone used here;
in the old morality plays all the characters, not
merely the sins, were abstractions.

4. A salacious medieval poem *Carmen de Pulice*
("The Flea") was attributed to Ovid.

5. A decorated or ornamented petticoat.

6. Arras in Flanders exported fine cloth used for
tapestry hangings.

FAUST. Thou art a proud knave indeed. What art thou, the second?   120
COVET. I am Covetousness, begotten of an old churl in a leather
    bag; and, might I now obtain my wish, this house, you and all,
    should turn to gold, that I might lock you safe into my chest. O
    my sweet gold!
FAUST. And what art thou, the third?   125
ENVY. I am Envy, begotten of a chimney-sweeper and an oyster-
    wife. I cannot read, and therefore wish all books were burned. I
    am lean with seeing others eat. O that there would come a fam-
    ine over all the world, that all might die, and I live alone; then
    thou shouldst see how fat I'd be! But must thou sit and I stand?   130
    Come down, with a vengeance!
FAUST. Out, envious wretch! But what art thou, the fourth?
WRATH. I am Wrath. I had neither father nor mother; I leapt out of
    a lion's mouth when I was scarce an hour old, and ever since
    have run up and down the world with these case of rapiers,   135
    wounding myself when I could get none to fight withal. I was
    born in hell; and look to it, for some of you shall be my father.
FAUST. And what art thou, the fifth?
GLUT. I am Gluttony. My parents are all dead, and the devil a
    penny they have left me but a small pension, and that buys me   140
    thirty meals a day and ten bevers[7]—a small trifle to suffice nature.
    I come of a royal pedigree: my father was a gammon[8] of bacon,
    and my mother was a hogshead of claret wine. My godfathers
    were these: Peter Pickle-herring and Martin Martlemas-beef. But
    my godmother, O, she was a jolly gentlewoman, and well beloved   145
    in every good town and city: her name was mistress Margery
    March-beer. Now, Faustus, thou hast heard all my progeny;[9]
    wilt thou bid me to supper?
FAUST. Not I. Thou wilt eat up all my victuals.
GLUT. Then the devil choke thee!   150
FAUST. Choke thyself, glutton. What art thou, the sixth?
SLOTH. Heigh ho! I am Sloth. I was begotten on a sunny bank,
    where I have lain ever since, and you have done me great injury
    to bring me from thence; let me be carried thither again by Glut-
    tony and Lechery. Heigh ho! I'll not speak word more for a king's   155
    ransom.
FAUST. And what are you, mistress minx, the seventh and last?
LECHERY. Who, I, sir? I am one that loves an inch of raw mutton[1]
    better than an ell of fried stockfish, and the first letter of my name
    begins with Lechery.   160
LUC. Away, to hell, away! On, piper![2]

            [*Exeunt the* SINS.]

FAUST. O how this sight doth delight my soul!
LUC. Tut, Faustus, in hell is all manner of delight.

---

7. Snacks.
8. The lower side of pork, including the leg.
9. Ancestry, lineage.
1. Frequently a word of indecent meaning in
Elizabethan English; here it means the penis. "Ell":

45 inches; "stockfish": dried cod.
2. The command to the piper who led the procession of the Deadly Sins onto the stage to strike up
a tune for their exit.

FAUST. O might I see hell and return again safe, how happy were I
then!   165
LUC. Faustus, thou shalt. At midnight I will send for thee. In mean-
time peruse this book, and view it throughly, and thou shalt turn
thyself into what shape thou wilt.
FAUST. Thanks, mighty Lucifer; this will I keep as chary[3] as my life.
LUC. Now Faustus, farewell.   170
FAUST. Farewell, great Lucifer. Come, Mephistophilis.

[*Exeunt* OMNES.]

SCENE 3

[*Enter the* CLOWN (ROBIN).]
ROBIN. What, Dick, look to the horses there till I come again. I
have gotten one of Dr. Faustus' conjuring books, and now we'll
have such knavery as 't passes.

[*Enter* DICK.]

DICK. What, Robin, you must come away and walk the horses.
ROBIN. I walk the horses! I scorn 't, faith: I have other matters in   5
hand; let the horses walk themselves and they will. "A *per se*[4] a;
t, h, e, the; o *per se* o; deny orgon, gorgon." Keep further from
me, O thou illiterate and unlearned hostler.
DICK. 'Snails,[5] what has thou got there? a book? Why, thou canst
not tell ne'er a word on 't.   10
ROBIN. That thou shalt see presently. Keep out of the circle, I say,
lest I send you into the ostry[6] with a vengeance.
DICK. That's like, faith! You had best leave your foolery, for an my
master come, he'll conjure you, faith.
ROBIN. My master conjure me! I'll tell thee what; an my master   15
come here, I'll clap as fair a pair of horns on 's head as e'er thou
sawest in thy life.[7]
DICK. Thou needst not do that, for my mistress hath done it.
ROBIN. Aye, there be of us here have waded as deep into matters as
other men, if they were disposed to talk.   20
DICK. A plague take you! I thought you did not sneak up and down
after her for nothing. But I prithee tell me in good sadness, Robin,
is that a conjuring book?
ROBIN. Do but speak what thou 't have me do, and I'll do 't. If thou
't dance naked, put off thy clothes, and I'll conjure thee about   25
presently. Or if thou 't but to the tavern with me, I'll give thee
white wine, red wine, claret wine, sack, muscadine, malmesey,
and whippincrust,[8] hold-belly-hold, and we'll not pay one penny
for it.

3. Carefully.
4. "A by itself," a method of reading the letters of
the alphabet taught to children. Robin's semiliter-
acy is being satirized. "Deny orgon, gorgon" is a
parody of Faustus' invocation of Demogorgon in
1.3.
5. I.e., God's nails (on the Cross).

6. Hostelry, inn.
7. A wife's infidelity was supposed in legend, and
in the standard Elizabethan joke, to cause her husband to grow horns.
8. Robin's pronunciation of "hippocras," a spiced
wine; "hold-belly-hold": as much as we can drink.

DICK. O brave! Prithee let's to it presently, for I am as dry as a dog.   30
ROBIN. Come then, let's away.   [*Exeunt.*]

Act 3

[*Enter* CHORUS.]

CHO. Learned Faustus,
    To find the secrets of astronomy
    Graven in the book of Jove's high firmament,
    Did mount himself to scale Olympus' top.
    Where sitting in a chariot burning bright   5
    Drawn by the strength of yokèd dragons' necks,
    He views the clouds, the planets, and the stars,
    The tropics, zones, and quarters of the sky
    From the bright circle of the hornèd moon
    Even to the height of *Primum Mobile;*[9]   10
    And whirling round with this circumference
    Within the concave compass of the pole,
    From east to west his dragons swiftly glide
    And in eight days did bring him home again.
    Not long he stayed within his quiet house   15
    To rest his bones after his weary toil
    But new exploits do hale him out again;
    And mounted then upon a dragon's back
    That with his wings did part the subtle air,
    He now is gone to prove cosmography[1]   20
    That measures coasts and kingdoms of the earth:
    And, as I guess, will first arrive at Rome
    To see the Pope and manner of his court
    And take some part of holy Peter's feast,
    The which this day is highly solemnized.   25

    [*Exit.*]

SCENE 1

[*Enter* FAUSTUS *and* MEPHISTOPHILIS.]

FAUST. Having now, my good Mephistophilis,
    Passed with delight the stately town of Trier[2]
    Environed round with airy mountain tops,
    With walls of flint and deep-entrenchèd lakes,[3]
    Not to be won by any conquering prince;   5
    From Paris next coasting the realm of France,
    We saw the river Main fall into Rhine,
    Whose banks are set with groves of fruitful vines;
    Then up to Naples, rich Campania,
    With buildings fair and gorgeous to the eye,   10

---

9. The outermost sphere, the empyrean.   2. Treves (in Prussia).
1. I.e., to test the accuracy of maps.   3. Moats.

Whose streets straight forth and paved with finest brick
Quarter the town in four equivalents.
There saw we learned Maro's[4] golden tomb,
The way he cut, an English mile in length,
Thorough a rock of stone in one night's space.   15
From thence to Venice, Padua, and the rest,
In midst of which a sumptuous temple[5] stands
That threats the stars with her aspiring top,
Whose frame is paved with sundry colored stones
And roofed aloft with curious work in gold.   20
Thus hitherto hath Faustus spent his time.
But tell me now, what resting place is this?
Hast thou, as erst I did command,
Conducted me within the walls of Rome?
MEPH. I have, my Faustus, and for proof thereof   25
   This is the goodly palace of the Pope,
   And 'cause we are no common guests
   I choose his privy chamber for our use.
FAUST. I hope his Holiness will bid us welcome.
MEPH. All's one, for we'll be bold with his venison.   30
   But now, my Faustus, that thou mayst perceive
   What Rome contains for to delight thine eyes,
   Know that this city stands upon seven hills
   That underprop the groundwork of the same;
   Just through the midst runs flowing Tiber's stream,   35
   With winding banks that cut it in two parts
   Over the which four stately bridges lean
   That make safe passage to each part of Rome.
   Upon the bridge called Ponte Angelo
   Erected is a castle passing strong,   40
   Where thou shalt see such store of ordnance
   As that the double cannons forged of brass
   Do match the number of the days contained
   Within the compass of one complete year;
   Besides the gates and high pyramides[6]   45
   That Julius Caesar brought from Africa.
FAUST. Now by the kingdoms of infernal rule,
   Of Styx, Acheron, and the fiery lake
   Of ever-burning Phlegethon,[7] I swear
   That I do long to see the monuments   50
   And situation of bright-splendent Rome.
   Come, therefore, let's away.
MEPH. Nay, stay, my Faustus; I know you'd see the Pope
   And take some part of holy Peter's feast,
   The which in state and high solemnity   55

---

4. Virgil's. In medieval legend the Roman poet
Virgil was considered a magician, and a tunnel
("way") on the promontory of Posilippo at Naples,
near his tomb, was accredited to his magical powers.
5. I.e., St. Mark's in Venice.

6. *Py-rám-i-des*, a singular noun, meaning an
obelisk.
7. Classical names for rivers of the underworld;
symbolic of hell, they are appropriate as oaths for
Faustus.

This day is held through Rome and Italy
In honor of the Pope's triumphant victory.
FAUST. Sweet Mephistophilis, thou pleasest me;
    Whilst I am here on earth let me be cloyed
    With all things that delight the heart of man.   60
    My four and twenty years of liberty
    I'll spend in pleasure and in dalliance,
    That Faustus' name, whilst this bright frame doth stand,
    May be admirèd through the furthest land.
MEPH. 'Tis well said, Faustus; come then, stand by me   65
    And thou shalt see them come immediately.
FAUST. Nay, stay, my gentle Mephistophilis,
    And grant me my request, and then I go.
    Thou knowst, within the compass of eight days
    We viewed the face of heaven, of earth, of hell;   70
    So high our dragons soared into the air
    That, looking down, the earth appeared to me
    No bigger than my hand in quantity.
    There did we view the kingdoms of the world,
    And what might please mine eye I there beheld.   75
    Then in this show let me an actor be,
    That this proud Pope may Faustus' cunning see.
MEPH. Let it be so, my Faustus, but first stay
    And view their triumphs[8] as they pass this way,
    And then devise what best contents thy mind,   80
    By cunning of thine art to cross the Pope
    Or dash the pride of this solemnity,
    To make his monks and abbots stand like apes
    And point like antics[9] at his triple crown,
    To beat the beads about the friars' pates   85
    Or clap huge horns upon the cardinals' heads,
    Or any villainy thou canst devise,
    And I'll perform it, Faustus. Hark, they come!
    This day shall make thee be admired in Rome.

    [*Enter the* CARDINALS *and* BISHOPS, *some bearing crosiers,*
    some the pillars; MONKS *and* FRIARS *singing their procession;*
    then the POPE *and* RAYMOND, *King of Hungary, with* BRUNO
    led in chains.][1]

POPE. Cast down our footstool.
RAY.   Saxon Bruno, stoop,   90
    Whilst on thy back his Holiness ascends
    St. Peter's chair and state pontifical.
BRUNO. Proud Lucifer, that state belongs to me;
    But thus I fall, to Peter, not to thee.
POPE. To me and Peter shalt thou groveling lie   95

---

8. Parades.
9. Grotesque figures.
1. "Crosiers": crosses borne before prelates; "the pillars" (of silver), however, are known to have been used by only two English cardinals, Wolsey and De la Pole. "Raymond, King of Hungary" is unknown to history. "Bruno" is likewise fictitious; he is the German pretender to the papal throne over whom the Pope has just triumphed (line 57).

And crouch before the papal dignity.
Sound trumpets, then, for thus St. Peter's heir
From Bruno's back ascends St. Peter's chair.

[A *flourish while he ascends.*]

Thus as the gods creep on with feet of wool
Long ere with iron hands they punish men,   100
So shall our sleeping vengeance now arise
And smite with death thy hated enterprise.
Lord Cardinals of France and Padua,
Go forthwith to our holy consistory
And read among the statutes decretal   105
What, by the holy council held at Trent,[2]
The sacred synod hath decreed for him
That doth assume the papal government
Without election and a true consent.
Away and bring us word with speed.   110
1 CARD. We go, my lord.   [*Exeunt* CARDINALS.]
POPE. Lord Raymond—
FAUST. Go, haste thee, gentle Mephistophilis,
    Follow the cardinals to the consistory,
    And as they turn their superstitious books,   115
    Strike them with sloth and drowsy idleness
    And make them sleep so sound that in their shapes
    Thyself and I may parley with this Pope,
    This proud confronter of the Emperor,[3]
    And in despite of all his holiness   120
    Restore this Bruno to his liberty
    And bear him to the states of Germany.
MEPH. Faustus, I go.
FAUST.   Dispatch it soon.
    The Pope shall curse that Faustus came to Rome.

    [*Exeunt* FAUSTUS *and* MEPHISTOPHILIS.]

BRUNO. Pope Adrian, let me have some right of law;   125
    I was elected by the Emperor.
POPE. We will depose the Emperor for that deed
    And curse the people that submit to him;
    Both he and thou shalt stand excommunicate
    And interdict from church's privilege   130
    And all society of holy men.
    He grows too proud in his authority,
    Lifting his lofty head above the clouds,
    And like a steeple overpeers the church,
    But we'll pull down his haughty insolence.   135
    And as Pope Alexander,[4] our progenitor,
    Trod on the neck of German Frederick,

---

2. The famous council of the Catholic Church which lasted from 1545 to 1563.
3. Holy Roman Emperor. Faustus refers to the conflict between the Pope and the Emperor; the former was victorious and captured the Emperor's choice for Pope, "Saxon Bruno."
4. Pope Alexander III (1159–81) compelled the Emperor Frederick Barbarossa to submit to him.

Adding this golden sentence to our praise,
That Peter's heirs should tread on emperors
And walk upon the dreadful adder's back,   140
Treading the lion and the dragon down,
And fearless spurn the killing basilisk;[5]
So will we quell that haughty schismatic,
And by authority apostolical
Depose him from his regal government.   145
BRUNO. Pope Julius swore to princely Sigismond,
    For him and the succeeding popes of Rome,
    To hold the emperors their lawful lords.
POPE. Pope Julius did abuse the church's rights,
    And therefore none of his decrees can stand.   150
    Is not all power on earth bestowed on us?
    And therefore though we would we cannot err.
    Behold this silver belt, whereto is fixed
    Seven golden keys fast sealed with seven seals
    In token of our sevenfold power from heaven,   155
    To bind or loose, lock fast, condemn, or judge,
    Resign or seal, or whatso pleaseth us.
    Then he and thou and all the world shall stoop,
    Or be assurèd of our dreadful curse
    To light as heavy as the pains of hell.   160

[*Enter* FAUSTUS *and* MEPHISTOPHILIS *like cardinals.*]

MEPH. Now tell me, Faustus, are we not fitted well?
FAUST. Yes, Mephistophilis, and two such cardinals
    Ne'er served a holy pope as we shall do.
    But whilst they sleep within the consistory
    Let us salute his reverend Fatherhood.   165
RAY. Behold, my lord, the cardinals are returned.
POPE. Welcome, grave fathers, answer presently;[6]
    What have our holy council there decreed
    Concerning Bruno and the Emperor
    In quittance of their late conspiracy   170
    Against our state and papal dignity?
FAUST. Most sacred patron of the church of Rome,
    By full consent of all the synod
    Of priests and prelates it is thus decreed:
    That Bruno and the German Emperor   175
    Be held as lollards[7] and bold schismatics
    And proud disturbers of the church's peace.
    And if that Bruno by his own assent,
    Without enforcement of the German peers,
    Did seek to wear the triple diadem   180
    And by your death to climb St. Peter's chair,
    The statutes decretal have thus decreed:

5. A mythical monster capable of killing by a look.
6. Immediately.

7. Protestants, usually English followers of
Wycliffe, the 14th-century religious reformer.

He shall be straight condemned of heresy
And on a pile of fagots burned to death.
POPE. It is enough. Here, take him to your charge   185
And bear him straight to Ponte Angelo,
And in the strongest tower enclose him fast.
Tomorrow, sitting in our consistory
With all our college of grave cardinals,
We will determine of his life or death.   190
Here, take his triple crown along with you
And leave it in the church's treasury.
Make haste again, my good lord cardinals,
And take our blessing apostolical.
MEPH. So, so. Was never devil thus blessed before!   195
FAUST. Away, sweet Mephistophilis, be gone;
The cardinals will be plagued for this anon.

> [*Exeunt* FAUSTUS *and* MEPHISTOPHILIS *with* BRUNO.]

POPE. Go presently and bring a banquet forth,
That we may solemnize St. Peter's feast
And with Lord Raymond, King of Hungary,   200
Drink to our late and happy victory.   [*Exeunt.*]

SCENE 2

> [*The banquet is brought in, and then enter* FAUSTUS *and*
> MEPHISTOPHILIS *in their own shapes.*]

MEPH. Now Faustus, come prepare thyself for mirth;
The sleepy cardinals are hard at hand
To censure Bruno, that is posted hence
And on a proud-paced steed as swift as thought
Flies o'er the Alps to fruitful Germany,   5
There to salute the woeful Emperor.
FAUST. The Pope will curse them for their sloth today
That slept both Bruno and his crown away.
But now, that Faustus may delight his mind
And by their folly make some merriment,   10
Sweet Mephistophilis, so charm me here
That I may walk invisible to all
And do whate'er I please unseen of any.
MEPH. Faustus, thou shalt; then kneel down presently,
Whilst on thy head I lay my hand   15
And charm thee with this magic wand.
First wear this girdle, then appear
Invisible to all are here.
The planets seven, the gloomy air,
Hell, and the Furies' forkèd hair,   20
Pluto's blue fire and Hecate's[8] tree

8. The goddess of magic and witchcraft, whose name the Elizabethans pronounced *Héc-at*. She is not known to have any special "tree"; the word may be a mistake for "three," since she was often represented as a triple goddess—of heaven, earth, and hell.

With magic spells so compass thee
That no eye may thy body see.
So, Faustus, now, for all their holiness,
Do what thou wilt thou shalt not be discerned.   25
FAUST. Thanks, Mephistophilis. Now friars, take heed
Lest Faustus make your shaven crowns to bleed.
MEPH. Faustus, no more; see where the cardinals come.

> [*Enter* POPE *and all the lords, with* KING RAYMOND *and the*
> ARCHBISHOP OF RHEIMS. *Enter the two* CARDINALS *with a*
> book.]

POPE. Welcome, lord cardinals; come, sit down.
Lord Raymond, take your seat. Friars, attend,   30
And see that all things be in readiness
As best beseems this solemn festival.
1 CARD. First may it please your sacred holiness
To view the sentence of the reverend synod
Concerning Bruno and the Emperor.   35
POPE. What needs this question? Did I not tell you
Tomorrow we would sit i' th' consistory
And there determine of his punishment?
You brought us word, even now, it was decreed
That Bruno and the cursèd Emperor   40
Were by the holy council both condemned
For loathèd lollards and base schismatics;
Then wherefore would you have me view that book?
1 CARD. Your Grace mistakes; you gave us no such charge.
RAY. Deny it not; we all are witnesses   45
That Bruno here was late delivered you,
With his rich triple crown to be reserved
And put into the church's treasury.
BOTH CARD. By holy Paul we saw them not.
POPE. By Peter, you shall die   50
Unless you bring them forth immediately.
Hale them to prison! Lade their limbs with gyves![9]
False prelates, for this hateful treachery,
Cursed be your souls to hellish misery.   [*Exeunt* CARDINALS.]
FAUST. So they are safe. Now, Faustus, to the feast;   55
The Pope had never such a frolic guest.
POPE. Lord Archbishop of Rheims, sit down with us.
ARCH. I thank your Holiness.
FAUST. Fall to! The devil choke you an you spare!
POPE. Who's that spoke? Friars, look about.   60
Lord Raymond, pray fall to. I am beholden
To the Bishop of Milan for this so rare a present.
FAUST. I thank you, sir.

> [FAUSTUS *snatches the meat from the* POPE.]

POPE. How now! Who snatched the meat from me? Villains, why
speak you not?   65

9. I.e., load their limbs with prisoners' shackles.

FRIAR. Here's nobody, if it like your Holiness.
POPE. My good Lord Archbishop, here's a most dainty dish
    Was sent me from a cardinal in France.
FAUST. I'll have that, too.

      [FAUSTUS *snatches the dish from the* POPE.]

POPE. What lollards do attend our Holiness   70
    That we receive such great indignity?
    Fetch me some wine.
FAUST. Aye, pray do, for Faustus is adry.
POPE. Lord Raymond, I drink unto your Grace.
FAUST. I pledge your Grace.   75

      [FAUSTUS *snatches the cup from the* POPE.]

POPE. My wine gone, too? Ye lubbers, look about
    And find the man that doth this villainy,
    Or by my sanctitude you all shall die.
    I pray, my lords, have patience at this troublesome banquet.
ARCH. Please your Holiness, I think it be some ghost crept out of   80
    purgatory and now is come unto your Holiness for his pardon.
POPE. It may be so;
    Go then, command our priests to sing a dirge
    To lay the fury of this same troublesome ghost.
    Once again, my lord, fall to.   85

      [*The* POPE *crosses himself.*]

FAUST. How now!
    Must every bit be spicèd with a cross?
    Well, use that trick no more, I would advise you.

      [*The* POPE *crosses himself.*]

Well, there's the second time; aware the third;
I give you fair warning.   90

      [*The* POPE *crosses himself again.*]

Nay then, take that!

      [FAUSTUS *hits the* POPE *a box on the ear.*]

POPE. O, I am slain! Help me, my lords!
    O come and help to bear my body hence!
    Damned be his soul forever for this deed.

      [*Exeunt the* POPE *and his train.*]

MEPH. Now Faustus, what will you do now? For I can tell you   95
    you'll be cursed with bell, book, and candle.[1]
FAUST. Bell, book, and candle; candle, book, and bell
    Forward and backward, to curse Faustus to hell!

      [*Enter all the* FRIARS *with bell, book, and candle to sing the*
      dirge.]

---

1. The traditional paraphernalia for cursing and excommunication.

FRIAR. Come, brethren, let's about our business with good devotion.

[ALL *sing this:*]

Cursèd be he that stole away his Holiness' meat from the table— 100
maledicat dominus![2]
Cursèd be he that struck his Holiness a blow on the face—*maledicat dominus!*
Cursèd be he that took Friar Sandelo a blow on the face—*maledicat dominus!* 105
Cursèd be he that disturbeth our holy dirge—*maledicat dominus!*
Cursèd be he that took away his Holiness' wine—*maledicat dominus! Et omnes sancti!*[3] Amen.

[FAUSTUS *and* MEPHISTOPHILIS *beat the* FRIARS, *and fling fireworks among them, and so exeunt.*]

SCENE 3

[*Enter* CLOWN (ROBIN) *and* DICK *with a cup.*]

DICK. Sirrah Robin, we were best look that your devil can answer the stealing of this same cup, for the vintner's boy follows us at the hard heels.

ROBIN. 'Tis no matter, let him come! An he follow us I'll so conjure him as he was never conjured in his life, I warrant him. Let me 5
see the cup.

[*Enter* VINTNER.]

DICK. Here 'tis. Yonder he comes. Now, Robin, now or never show thy cunning.

VINT. O, are you here? I am glad I have found you. You are a couple of fine companions! Pray, where's the cup you stole from 10
the tavern?

ROBIN. How, how? We steal a cup? Take heed what you say! We look not like cup-stealers, I can tell you.

VINT. Never deny it, for I know you have it, and I'll search you.

ROBIN. Search me? Aye, and spare not. Hold the cup, Dick! Come, 15
come; search me, search me.

VINT. Come on, sirrah, let me search you now.

DICK. Aye, aye, do; do. Hold the cup, Robin, I fear not your searching. We scorn to steal your cups, I can tell you.

VINT. Never outface me for the matter, for sure the cup is between 20
you two.

ROBIN. Nay, there you lie. 'Tis beyond us both.

VINT. A plague take you! I thought 'twas your knavery to take it away. Come, give it me again.

ROBIN. Aye, much! When, can you tell?[4] Dick, make me a circle, 25
and stand close at my back and stir not for thy life. Vintner, you

---

2. "May the Lord curse him!"
3. And all saints (also curse him).

4. A common Elizabethan scornful retort.

shall have your cup anon. Say nothing, Dick. O *per se* O; Demogorgon, Belcher and Mephistophilis!

[*Enter* MEPHISTOPHILIS.]

MEPH. Monarch of hell, under whose black survey
  Great potentates do kneel with awful fear,   30
  Upon whose altars thousand souls do lie,
  How am I vexèd with these villains' charms!
  From Constantinople am I hither brought
  Only for pleasure of these damnèd slaves.   [*Exit* VINTNER.]

ROBIN. By Lady, sir, you have had a shrewd journey of it; will it   35
  please you to take a shoulder of mutton to supper and a tester[5] in
  your purse, and go back again?

DICK. Aye, I pray you heartily, sir; for we called you but in jest, I
  promise you.

MEPH. To purge the rashness of this cursèd deed,   40
  First be thou turnèd to this ugly shape:
  For apish deeds transformèd to an ape.

ROBIN. O brave! an ape! I pray, sir, let me have the carrying of him
  about to show some tricks.

MEPH. And so thou shalt. Be thou transformed to a dog and carry   45
  him upon thy back. Away! Be gone!

ROBIN. A dog! That's excellent! Let the maids look well to their
  porridge pots, for I'll into the kitchen presently. Come, Dick,
  come.

[*Exeunt* ROBIN *and* DICK.]

MEPH. Now with the flames of ever-burning fire   50
  I'll wing myself and forthwith fly amain
  Unto my Faustus, to the Great Turk's court.   [*Exit.*]

Act 4

[*Enter* CHORUS.]

CHO. When Faustus had with pleasure ta'en the view
  Of rarest things and royal courts of kings,
  He stayed his course and so returnèd home,
  Where such as bear his absence but with grief,
  I mean his friends and nearest companións,   5
  Did gratulate his safety with kind words,
  And in their conference of what befell
  Touching his journey through the world and air,
  They put forth questions of astrology
  Which Faustus answered with such learned skill   10
  As they admired and wondered at his wit.
  Now is his fame spread forth in every land:
  Amongst the rest the Emperor is one,
  Carolus the Fifth,[6] at whose palace now
  Faustus is feasted 'mongst his noblemen.   15

5. Sixpence.   6. I.e., Emperor Charles V (1519–56).

What there he did in trial of his art
I leave untold, your eyes shall see performed.   [*Exit.*]

SCENE 1

[*Enter* MARTINO *and* FREDERICK *at several doors.*[7]]

MART. What ho! Officers, gentlemen!
    Hie to the presence to attend the Emperor.
    Good Frederick, see the rooms be voided straight;
    His Majesty is coming to the hall.
    Go back, and see the state in readiness.   5
FRED. But where is Bruno, our elected Pope,
    That on a fury's back came post from Rome?
    Will not his Grace consort[8] the Emperor?
MART. O yes, and with him comes the German conjurer,
    The learned Faustus, fame of Wittenberg,   10
    The wonder of the world for magic art;
    And he intends to show great Carolus
    The race of all his stout progenitors
    And bring in presence of his majesty
    The royal shapes and warlike semblances   15
    Of Alexander and his beauteous paramour.[9]
FRED. Where is Benvolio?
MART. Fast asleep, I warrant you;
    He took his rouse with stoups[1] of Rhenish wine
    So kindly yesternight to Bruno's health   20
    That all this day the sluggard keeps his bed.
FRED. See, see; his window's ope; we'll call to him.
MART. What ho, Benvolio!

[*Enter* BENVOLIO *above at a window, in his nightcap, but-*
toning.]

BENV. What a devil ail you two?
MART. Speak softly, sir, lest the devil hear you;   25
    For Faustus at the court is late arrived
    And at his heels a thousand furies wait
    To accomplish whatsoever the Doctor please.
BENV. What of this?
MART. Come, leave thy chamber first and thou shalt see   30
    This conjurer perform such rare exploits
    Before the Pope[2] and royal Emperor
    As never yet was seen in Germany.
BENV. Has not the Pope enough of conjuring yet?
    He was upon the devil's back late enough,   35
    And if he be so far in love with him
    I would he would post home to Rome with him again.
FRED. Speak, wilt thou come and see this sport?

---

7. I.e., at different entrances.   1. Drank many full glasses.
8. Accompany.   2. Bruno.
9. Alexander the Great and his mistress Thaïs.

BENV. Not I.

MART. Wilt thou stand in thy window and see it, then?   40

BENV. Aye, an, I fall not asleep i' th' meantime.

MART. The Emperor is at hand, who comes to see
   What wonders by black spells may compassed be.

BENV. Well, go you attend the Emperor. I am content for this once
   to thrust my head out a window, for they say if a man be drunk   45
   overnight the devil cannot hurt him in the morning. If that be
   true, I have a charm in my head shall control him as well as the
   conjurer, I warrant you.

   [*Exit* MARTINO *and* FREDERICK.]

                          SCENE 2

   [*A sennet.*[3] *Enter* CHARLES THE GERMAN EMPEROR, BRUNO,
   the DUKE OF SAXONY, FAUSTUS, MEPHISTOPHILIS, FREDER-
   ICK, MARTINO *and* ATTENDANTS. BENVOLIO *remains at his
   window.*]

EMP. Wonder of men, renowned magician,
   Thrice-learned Faustus, welcome to our court.
   This deed of thine, in setting Bruno free
   From his and our professèd enemy,
   Shall add more excellence unto thine art   5
   Than if by powerful necromantic spells
   Thou couldst command the world's obedience.
   Forever be beloved of Carolus;
   And if this Bruno thou hast late redeemed
   In peace possess the triple diadem   10
   And sit in Peter's chair despite of chance,
   Thou shalt be famous through all Italy
   And honored of the German Emperor.

FAUST. These gracious words, most royal Carolus,
   Shall make poor Faustus to his utmost power   15
   Both love and serve the German Emperor
   And lay his life at holy Bruno's feet.
   For proof whereof, if so your Grace be pleased,
   The Doctor stands prepared by power of art
   To cast his magic charms that shall pierce through   20
   The ebon gates of ever-burning hell
   And hale the stubborn furies from their caves
   To compass whatsoe'er your Grace commands.

BENV. [*aside*] Blood! He speaks terribly, but for all that I do not
   greatly believe him. He looks as like a conjurer as the Pope to a   25
   costermonger.[4]

EMP. Then Faustus, as thou late didst promise us,
   We would behold that famous conqueror,
   Great Alexander and his paramour,

---

3. A trumpet signal.   4. Fruitseller.

In their true shapes and state majestical,   30
That we may wonder at their excellence.

FAUST. Your Majesty shall see them presently.
Mephistophilis, away!
And with a solemn noise of trumpets' sound
Present before this royal Emperor   35
Great Alexander and his beauteous paramour.

MEPH. Faustus, I will.   [*Exit.*]

BENV. [*aside*] Well, master Doctor, an your devils come not away
quickly, you shall have me asleep presently. Zounds, I could eat
myself for anger to think I have been such an ass all this while to   40
stand gaping after the devil's governor, and can see nothing.

FAUST. [*aside*] I'll make you feel something anon if my art fail me
not.—
My lord, I must forewarn your Majesty
That when my spirits present the royal shapes   45
Of Alexander and his paramour,
Your Grace demand no questions of the King,
But in dumb silence let them come and go.

EMP. Be it as Faustus please; we are content.

BENV. [*aside*] Aye, Aye, and I am content, too. And thou bring   50
Alexander and his paramour before the Emperor, I'll be Actaeon[5]
and turn myself into a stag.

FAUST. [*aside*] And I'll play Diana and send you the horns presently.

[*Sennet. Enter at one door the emperor* ALEXANDER, *at the
other* DARIUS. *They meet;* DARIUS *is thrown down;* ALEXAN-
DER *kills him, takes off his crown and, offering to go out,
his* PARAMOUR *meets him; he embraceth her and sets* DARIUS'
crown upon her head and, coming back, both salute the
EMPEROR, *who, leaving his state,[6] offers to embrace them,
which* FAUSTUS *seeing, suddenly stays him. Then trumpets
cease and music sounds.*]

FAUST. My gracious lord, you do forget yourself;   55
These are but shadows, not substantial.

EMP. O pardon me; my thoughts are ravished so
With sight of this renownèd Emperor
That in mine arms I would have compassed him.
But Faustus, since I may not speak to them   60
To satisfy my longing thoughts at full,
Let me this tell thee: I have heard it said
That this fair lady, whilst she lived on earth,
Had on her neck a little wart or mole.
How may I prove that saying to be true?   65

FAUST. Your Majesty may boldly go and see.

EMP. Faustus, I see it plain;

5. The hunter of classical legend who happened   hounds.
to see the goddess Diana bathing. In punishment   6. Throne.
he was changed into a stag and pursued by his own

And in this sight thou better pleasest me
Than if I gained another monarchy.

FAUST. Away, be gone!   [*Exit* SHOW.]   70
See, see, my gracious lord, what strange beast is yon, that thrusts
its head out at the window!

EMP. O wondrous sight! See, Duke of Saxony, two spreading horns
most strangely fastened upon the head of young Benvolio.

SAX. What, is he asleep, or dead?   75

FAUST. He sleeps, my lord, but dreams not of his horns.

EMP. This sport is excellent. We'll call and wake him. What ho!
Benvolio!

BENV. A plague upon you! Let me sleep a while

EMP. I blame thee not to sleep, much, having such a head of thine   80
own.

SAX. Look up, Benvolio. 'Tis the Emperor calls.

BENV. The Emperor! Where? O zounds, my head!

EMP. Nay, and thy horns hold 'tis no matter for thy head, for that's
armed sufficiently.   85

FAUST. Why, how now, sir knight! What, hanged by the horns?
This is most horrible. Fie, fie! Pull in your head, for shame! Let
not all the world wonder at you.

BENV. Zounds, Doctor, is this your villainy?

FAUST. O, say not so, sir. The Doctor has no skill,   90
No art, no cunning to present these lords
Or bring before this royal Emperor
The mighty monarch, warlike Alexander?
If Faustus do it, you are straight resolved
In bold Actaeon's shape to turn a stag?   95
And therefore, my lord, so please your Majesty,
I'll raise a kennel of hounds shall hunt him so
As all his footmanship shall scarce prevail
To keep his carcass from their bloody fangs.
Ho, Belimote, Argiron, Asterote!   100

BENV. Hold, hold! Zounds, he'll raise up a kennel of devils, I think,
anon. Good my lord, entreat for me. 'Sblood, I am never able
to endure these torments.

EMP. Then good master Doctor,
Let me entreat you to remove his horns;   105
He has done penance now sufficiently.

FAUST. My gracious lord, not so much for injury done to me, as to
delight your Majesty with some mirth, hath Faustus justly requited
this injurious knight; which, being all I desire, I am content to
remove his horns.—Mephistophilis, transform him.—And here-   110
after, sir, look you speak well of scholars.

BENV. [*aside*] Speak well of ye! 'Sblood, and scholars be such cuck-
oldmakers to clap horns of honest men's heads o' this order, I'll
ne'er trust smooth faces and small ruffs[7] more. But an I be not

___

7. I.e., scholars, who were often smooth-shaven   tiers. But Faustus has a beard; see the next scene.
and did not wear the large "ruffs" (collars) of cour-

revenged for this, would I might be turned to a gaping oyster and   115
drink nothing but salt water!

EMP. Come, Faustus. While the Emperor lives,
  In recompense of this thy high desert,
  Thou shalt command the state of Germany
  And live beloved of mighty Carolus.   [*Exeunt* OMNES.]   120

SCENE 3

[*Enter* BENVOLIO, MARTINO, FREDERICK, *and* SOLDIERS.]

MART. Nay, sweet Benvolio, let us sway thy thoughts
  From this attempt against the conjurer.
BENV. Away! You love me not to urge me thus.
  Shall I let slip so great an injury
  When every servile groom jests at my wrongs   5
  And in their rustic gambols proudly say,
  "Benvolio's head was graced with horns today"?
  O, may these eyelids never close again
  Till with my sword I have that conjurer slain.
  If you will aid me in this enterprise,   10
  Then draw your weapons and be resolute;
  If not, depart. Here will Benvolio die,
  But Faustus' death shall quit[8] my infamy.
FRED. Nay, we will stay with thee, betide what may,
  And kill that Doctor if he come this way.   15
BENV. Then gentle Frederick, hie thee to the grove
  And place our servants and our followers
  Close in an ambush there behind the trees.
  By this I know the conjurer is near;
  I saw him kneel and kiss the Emperor's hand   20
  And take his leave laden with rich rewards.
  Then, soldiers, boldly fight. If Faustus die,
  Take you the wealth, leave us the victory.
FRED. Come, soldiers, follow me unto the grove;
  Who kills him shall have gold and endless love.   25

[*Exit* FREDERICK *with the* SOLDIERS.]

BENV. My head is lighter than it was by th' horns,
  But yet my heart's more ponderous than my head
  And pants until I see that conjurer dead.
MART. Where shall we place ourselves, Benvolio?
BENV. Here will we stay to bide the first assault.   30
  O, were that damnèd hell-hound but in place
  Thou soon shouldst see me quit my foul disgrace.

[*Enter* FREDERICK.]

FRED. Close, close! The hated conjurer is at hand
  And all alone comes walking in his gown;

8. Avenge.

Be ready then and strike the peasant down.   35
BENV. Mine be that honor then. Now, sword, strike home!
  For horns he gave I'll have his head anon.

  [*Enter* FAUSTUS *wearing a false head.*]

MART. See, see, he comes.
BENV.   No words; this blow ends all;
  Hell take his soul, his body thus must fall.
FAUST. O!   40
FRED. Groan you, master Doctor?
BENV. Break may his heart with groans. Dear Frederick, see
  Thus will I end his griefs immediately.

  [*Cuts off the false head.*]

MART. Strike with a willing hand! His head is off.
BENV. The devil's dead; the furies now may laugh.   45
FRED. Was this that stern aspect, that awful frown,
  Made the grim monarch of infernal spirits
  Tremble and quake at his commanding charms?
MART. Was this that damnèd head whose art conspired
  Benvolio's shame before the Emperor?   50
BENV. Aye, that's the head, and here the body lies
  Justly rewarded for his villainies.
FRED. Come, let's devise how we may add more shame
  To the black scandal of his hated name.
BENV. First, on his head, in quittance of my wrongs,   55
  I'll nail huge forkèd horns and let them hang
  Within the window where he yoked me first,
  That all the world may see my just revenge.
MART. What use shall we put his beard to?
BENV. We'll sell it to a chimney-sweeper; it will wear out ten birchen 60
  brooms, I warrant you.
FRED. What shall his eyes do?
BENV. We'll put out his eyes, and they shall serve for buttons to his
  lips to keep his tongue from catching cold.
MART. An excellent policy. And now, sirs, having divided him,   65
  what shall the body do?

  [FAUSTUS *rises.*]

BENV. Zounds, the devil's alive again!
FRED. Give him his head, for God's sake!
FAUST. Nay, keep it. Faustus will have heads and hands,
  Aye, all your hearts, to recompense this deed.   70
  Knew you not, traitors, I was limited
  For four and twenty years to breathe on earth?
  And had you cut my body with your swords
  Or hewed this flesh and bones as small as sand,
  Yet in a minute had my spirit returned   75
  And I had breathed a man made free from harm.
  But wherefore do I dally my revenge?
  Asteroth, Belimoth, Mephistophilis!

[*Enter* MEPHISTOPHILIS *and other* DEVILS.]

Go, horse these traitors on your fiery backs
And mount aloft with them as high as heaven,   80
Then pitch them headlong to the lowest hell.
Yet stay, the world shall see their misery,
And hell shall after plague their treachery.
Go, Belimoth, and take this caitiff[9] hence
And hurl him in some lake of mud and dirt;   85
Take thou this other, drag him through the woods
Amongst the pricking thorns and sharpest briars,
Whilst with my gentle Mephistophilis
This traitor flies unto some steepy rock
That rolling down may break the villain's bones   90
As he intended to dismember me.
Fly hence, dispatch my charge immediately.
FRED. Pity us, gentle Faustus; save our lives!
FAUST. Away!
FRED. He must needs go that the devil drives.   95

[*Exeunt* SPIRITS *with the* KNIGHTS.]
[*Enter the ambushed* SOLDIERS.]

1 SOLD. Come, sirs, prepare yourselves in readiness;
    Make haste to help these noble gentlemen;
    I heard them parley with the conjurer.
2 SOLD. See where he comes; dispatch, and kill the slave!
FAUST. What's here? An ambush to betray my life?   100
    Then, Faustus, try thy skill. Base peasants, stand!
    For lo, these trees remove at my command
    And stand as bulwarks 'twixt yourselves and me
    To shield me from your hated treachery;
    Yet to encounter this, your weak attempt,   105
    Behold an army comes incontinent.[1]

[FAUSTUS *strikes the door, and enter a* DEVIL *playing on a
drum; after him another bearing an ensign, and divers with
weapons;* MEPHISTOPHILIS *with fireworks. They set upon the*
SOLDIERS *and drive them out. Exeunt.*]

SCENE 4

[*Enter at several doors* BENVOLIO, FREDERICK, *and* MAR-
TINO, *their heads and faces bloody and besmeared with mud
and dirt, all having horns on their heads.*]

MART. What ho, Benvolio!
BENV. Here! What, Frederick, ho!
FRED. O help me, gentle friend. Where is Martino?
MART. Dear Frederick, here—
    Half smothered in a lake of mud and dirt   5
    Through which the furies dragged me by the heels.

9. Wretch.   1. Immediately.

FRED. Martino, see! Benvolio's horns again.
MART. O misery! How now, Benvolio!
BENV. Defend me, heaven! Shall I be haunted still?
MART. Nay, fear not, man; we have no power to kill.   10
BENV. My friends transformèd thus! O hellish spite!
 Your heads are all set with horns.
FRED. You hit it right;
 It is your own you mean; feel on your head.
BENV. Zounds, horns again!   15
MART. Nay, chafe not, man; we are all sped.[2]
BENV. What devil attends this damned magician
 That spite of spite our wrongs are doublèd?
FRED. What may we do that we may hide our shames?
BENV. If we should follow him to work revenge,   20
 He'd join long asses' ears to those huge horns
 And make us laughingstocks to all the world.
MART. What shall we then do, dear Benvolio?
BENV. I have a castle joining near these woods,
 And thither we'll repair and live obscure   25
 Till time shall alter this our brutish shapes.
 Sith black disgrace hath thus eclipsed our fame,
 We'll rather die with grief than live with shame.

          [*Exeunt* OMNES.]

SCENE 5

[*Enter* FAUSTUS *and the* HORSE-COURSER.[3]]

HOR. I beseech your Worship, accept of these forty dollars.[4]
FAUST. Friend, thou canst not buy so good a horse for so small a
 price. I have no great need to sell him, but if thou likest him for
 ten dollars more, take him, because I see thou hast a good mind
 to him.   5
HOR. I beseech you, sir, accept of this; I am a very poor man and
 have lost very much of late by horseflesh, and this bargain will
 set me up again.
FAUST. Well, I will not stand with thee; give me the money. Now,
 sirrah, I must tell you that you may ride him o'er hedge and ditch   10
 and spare him not; but—do you hear?—in any case ride him not
 into the water.
HOR. How, sir, not into the water? Why, will he not drink of all
 waters?
FAUST. Yes, he will drink of all waters, but ride him not into the   15
 water; o'er hedge and ditch or where thou wilt, but not into the
 water. Go bid the hostler deliver him unto you, and remember
 what I say.
HOR. I warrant you, sir. O joyful day! Now am I a made man forever.   20

---

2. Don't fret, man, we are all done for.
3. Horse trader, traditionally a sharp bargainer or
cheat.

4. Common German coins; the word originally
comes from the German *Joachimsthaler*.

[*Exit.*]

FAUST. What art thou, Faustus, but a man condemned to die?
　Thy fatal time draws to a final end;
　Despair doth drive distrust into my thoughts.
　Confound these passions with a quiet sleep.
　Tush, Christ did call the thief upon the cross;[5]   25
　Then rest thee, Faustus, quiet in conceit.

　　　　　　　　　　　　　[*He sits to sleep in his chair.*]
　　　　　[*Enter the* HORSE-COURSER *wet.*]

HOR. O, what a cozening Doctor was this! I riding my horse into
　the water, thinking some hidden mystery had been in the horse,
　I had nothing under me but a little straw, and had much ado to
　escape drowning. Well, I'll go rouse him and make him give me   30
　my forty dollars again. Ho! sirrah Doctor, you cozening scab!
　Master Doctor, awake and rise, and give me my money again,
　for your horse is turned to a bottle[6] of hay. Master Doctor—

　　　　　[*He pulls off his leg.*]

　Alas, I am undone! What shall I do? I have pulled off his leg.
FAUST. O help! Help! The villain hath murdered me!   35
HOR. Murder or not murder, now he has but one leg I'll outrun
　him and cast this leg into some ditch or other.

　　　　　[*Exit.*]

FAUST. Stop him, stop him, stop him! Ha ha ha! Faustus hath his
　leg again, and the horse-courser a bundle of hay for his forty
　dollars.   40

　　　　　[*Enter* WAGNER.]

FAUST. How now, Wagner! What news with thee?
WAG. If it please you, the Duke of Vanholt doth earnestly entreat
　your company and hath sent some of his men to attend you with
　provision fit for your journey.
FAUST. The Duke of Vanholt's an honorable gentleman, and one   45
　to whom I must be no niggard of my cunning. Come, away!

　　　　　[*Exeunt* OMNES.]

SCENE 6

　　　[*Enter* ROBIN, DICK, HORSE-COURSER, *and a* CARTER.]

CART. Come, my masters, I'll bring you to the best beer in Europe—
　What ho, Hostess!—Where be these whores?[7]

　　　　　[*Enter* HOSTESS.]

HOST. How now! What lack you? What, my old guests, welcome.
ROBIN. Sirrah Dick, dost thou know why I stand so mute?

---

5. In Luke 23.39–43 one of the two thieves crucified with Jesus is promised Paradise. "In conceit": in mind.

6. Bundle.
7. I.e., the hostess and maids of the inn.

DICK. No, Robin, why is 't?   5

ROBIN. I am eighteen pence on the score,[8] but say nothing; see if
she have forgotten me.

HOST. Who's this that stands so solemnly by himself? What, my
old guest!

ROBIN. O, hostess, how do you do? I hope my score stands still.   10

HOST. Aye, there's no doubt of that, for methinks you make no
haste to wipe it out.

DICK. Why, hostess, I say, fetch us some beer.

HOST. You shall presently; look up into th' hall. There, ho!

　　　　[Exit.]

DICK. Come, sirs; what shall we do now till mine hostess comes?   15

CART. Marry, sir, I'll tell you the bravest tale how a conjurer served
me. You know Dr. Faustus?

HOR. Aye, a plague take him! Here's some on 's have cause to know
him. Did he conjure thee too?

CART. I'll tell you how he served me. As I was going to Wittenberg   20
t' other day, he met me and asked me what he should give me
for as much hay as he could eat. Now, sir, I, thinking that a little
would serve his turn, bade him take as much as he would for
three farthings. So he presently gave me my money and fell to
eating; and, as I am a cursen[9] man, he never left eating till he   25
had eat up all my load of hay.

ALL. O monstrous; eat a whole load of hay!

ROBIN. Yes, yes; that may be, for I have heard of one that has eat a
load of logs.[1]

HOR. Now, sirs, you shall hear how villainously he served me. I   30
went to him yesterday to buy a horse of him, and he would by
no means sell him under forty dollars. So, sir, because I knew
him to be such a horse as would run over hedge and ditch and
never tire, I gave him my money. So, when I had my horse, Dr.
Faustus bade me ride him night and day and spare him no time;   35
"But," quoth he, "in any case ride him not into the water." Now
sir, I thinking the horse had had some quality that he would not
have me know of, what did I but ride him into a great river, and
when I came just in the midst my horse vanished away and I sat
straddling upon a bottle of hay.   40

ALL. O brave Doctor!

HOR. But you shall hear how bravely I served him for it. I went me
home to his house, and there I found him asleep; I kept a hallowing and whooping in his ears, but all could not wake him. I
seeing that, took him by the leg and never rested pulling till I   45
had pulled me his leg quite off, and now 'tis at home in mine
hostry.

DICK. And has the Doctor but one leg then? That's excellent, for
one of his devils turned me into the likeness of an ape's face.

CART. Some more drink, hostess!   50

8. Charged, not paid for.　　　　　　　　　1. Comic expression for being drunk—to carry a
9. Mispronunciation of "Christian."　　　　jag (or load) of logs.

ROBIN. Hark you, we'll into another room and drink awhile, and then we'll go seek out the Doctor.

[*Exeunt* OMNES.]

SCENE 7

[*Enter the* DUKE OF VANHOLT, *his* DUCHESS, FAUSTUS, *and* MEPHISTOPHILIS.]

DUKE. Thanks, master Doctor, for these pleasant sights; nor know I how sufficiently to recompense your great deserts in erecting that enchanted castle in the air, the sight whereof so delighted me as nothing in the world could please me more.

FAUST. I do think myself, my good lord, highly recompensed that   5
it pleaseth your Grace to think but well of that which Faustus hath performed. But gracious lady, it may be that you have taken no pleasure in those sights; therefore I pray you tell me what is the thing you most desire to have; be it in the world it shall be yours. I have heard that great-bellied women do long for things   10
that are rare and dainty.

DUCH. True, master Doctor, and since I find you so kind, I will make known unto you what my heart desires to have; and were it now summer, as it is January, a dead time of winter, I would request no better meat than a dish of ripe grapes.   15

FAUST. This is but a small matter.—Go, Mephistophilis, away!—

[*Exit* MEPHISTOPHILIS.]

Madam, I will do more than this for your content.

[*Enter* MEPHISTOPHILIS *again with the grapes.*]

Here, now taste ye these; they should be good, for they come from a far country, I can tell you.

DUKE. This makes me wonder more than all the rest, that at this   20
time of year, when every tree is barren of his fruit, from whence you had these ripe grapes.

FAUST. Please it your Grace, the year is divided into two circles over the whole world, so that when it is winter with us, in the contrary circle it is likewise summer with them, as in India, Saba,[2] and   25
such countries that lie far east, where they have fruit twice a year. From whence, by means of a swift spirit that I have, I had these grapes brought as you see.

DUCH. And trust me they are the sweetest grapes that e'er I tasted.

[*The* CLOWNS *bounce*[3] *at the gate within.*]

DUKE. What rude disturbers have we at the gate?   30
Go pacify their fury, set it ope,
And then demand of them what they would have.

[*They knock again and call out to talk with* FAUSTUS.]

2. Sheba.   3. Bang.

A SERVANT. Why, how now, masters, what a coil[4] is there!
  What is the reason you disturb the Duke?
DICK. We have no reason for it, therefore a fig[5] for him!   35
SERV. Why, saucy varlets! Dare you be so bold?
HOR. I hope, sir, we have wit enough to be more bold than wel-
  come.
SERV. It appears so; Pray be bold elsewhere
  And trouble not the Duke.   40
DUKE. What would they have?
SERV. They all cry out to speak with Dr. Faustus.
CART. Aye, and we will speak with him.
DUKE. Will you, sir? Commit[6] the rascals!
DICK. Commit with us? He were as good commit with his father as
  commit with us.   45
FAUST. I do beseech your Grace, let them come in;
  They are good subject for a merriment.
DUKE. Do as thou wilt, Faustus; I give thee leave.
FAUST. I thank your Grace.

          [*Enter* ROBIN, DICK, CARTER, *and* HORSE-COURSER.]

                    Why, how now, my good friends?   50
  'Faith you are too outrageous; but come near,
  I have procured your pardons. Welcome all!
ROBIN. Nay, sir, we will be welcome for our money, and we will
  pay for what we take. What ho! Give 's half a dozen of beer here,
  and be hanged.   55
FAUST. Nay, hark you, can you tell me where you are?[7]
CART. Aye, marry, can I; we are under heaven.
SERV. Aye, but, sir saucebox, know you in what place?
HOR. Aye, aye, the house is good enough to drink in. Zounds, fill
  us some beer, or we'll break all the barrels in the house and dash 60
  out all your brains with your bottles.
FAUST. Be not so furious; come, you shall have beer.
  My lord, beseech you give me leave awhile;
  I'll gage my credit 'twill content your Grace.
DUKE. With all my heart, kind Doctor, please thyself;   65
  Our servants and our court's at thy command.
FAUST. I humbly thank your Grace. Then fetch some beer.
HOR. Aye, marry, there spake a doctor indeed; and, faith, I'll drink
  a health to thy wooden leg for that word.
FAUST. My wooden leg! What dost thou mean by that?   70
CART. Ha ha ha, dost hear him, Dick? He has forgot his leg.
HOR. Aye, he does not stand much upon that.
FAUST. No, faith, not much upon a wooden leg.
CART. Good lord, that flesh and blood should be so frail with your

---

4. Disturbance.
5. An obscene gesture, implying contempt.
6. Put in jail. Dick puns on its other meaning ("commit adultery"), from the Ten Command-ments.

7. At the end of 4.6, the clowns thought they were stepping into another room, but Faustus has had them transported to the court of the Duke of Vanholt.

worship! Do you not remember a horse-courser you sold a horse   75
to?

FAUST. Yes, I remember I sold one a horse.

CART. And do you remember you bid he should not ride him into
the water?

FAUST. Yes, I do very well remember that.   80

CART. And do you remember nothing of your leg?

FAUST. No, in good sooth.

CART. Then I pray remember your courtesy.

FAUST. I thank you, sir.

CART. 'Tis not so much worth. I pray you tell me one thing.   85

FAUST. What's that?

CART. Be both of your legs bedfellows every night together?

FAUST. Wouldst thou make a colossus[8] of me, that thou askest me
such questions?

CART. No, truly, sir, I would make nothing of you, but I would fain   90
know that.

[*Enter* HOSTESS *with drink.*]

FAUST. Then I assure thee certainly they are.

CART. I thank you; I am fully satisfied.

FAUST. But wherefore dost thou ask?

CART. For nothing, sir; but methinks you should have a wooden   95
bedfellow to one of 'em.

HOR. Why, do you hear, sir, did not I pull off one of your legs
when you were asleep?

FAUST. But I have it again now I am awake; look you here, sir.

ALL. O horrible! Had the doctor three legs?   100

CART. Do you remember, sir, how you cozened me and eat up my
load of——

[FAUSTUS *charms him dumb.*]

DICK. Do you remember how you made me wear an ape's——

HOR. You whoreson conjuring scab, do you remember how you
cozened me of a ho——   105

ROBIN. Ha' you forgotten me? You think to carry it away with your
hey-pass and your re-pass;[9] do you remember the dog's fa——

[*Exeunt* CLOWNS.]

HOST. Who pays for the ale? Hear you, master Doctor, now you
have sent away my guests, I pray who shall pay me for my a——

[*Exit* HOSTESS.]

DUCH. My lord,   110
We are much beholding to this learned man.

DUKE. So are we, madam, which we will recompense
With all the love and kindness that we may;
His artful sport drives all sad thoughts away.   [*Exeunt.*]

8. The huge statue which stood at the entrance to   making his legs as important.
the harbor at Rhodes; boats sailed between its legs,   9. Traditional exclamations of a conjurer.
and Dr. Faustus is suggesting that the clowns are

CHRISTOPHER MARLOWE

Act 5

SCENE 1

[*Thunder and lightning. Enter* DEVILS *with covered dishes;* MEPHISTOPHILIS *leads them into* FAUSTUS' *study. Then enter* WAGNER.]

WAG. I think my master means to die shortly;
   He has made his will and given me his wealth,
   His house, his goods, and store of golden plate,
   Besides two thousand ducats ready coined.
   And yet I wonder, for if death were nigh   5
   He would not banquet and carouse and swill
   Amongst the students as even now he doth,
   Who are at supper with such belly-cheer
   As Wagner ne'er beheld in all his life.
   See where they come; belike the feast is ended.   [*Exit.*]   10

[*Enter* FAUSTUS *and* MEPHISTOPHILIS *with two or three* SCHOLARS.]

1 SCH. Master Doctor Faustus, since our conference about fair ladies, which was the beautifullest in all the world, we have determined with ourselves that Helen of Greece was the admirablest lady that ever lived. Therefore, master Doctor, if you will do us that favor as to let us see that peerless dame of Greece whom all the world   15 admires for majesty, we should think ourselves much beholding unto you.

FAUST. Gentlemen,
   For that I know your friendship is unfeigned,
   And Faustus' custom is not to deny   20
   The just requests of those that wish him well,
   You shall behold that peerless dame of Greece,
   No otherways for pomp and majesty
   Than when Sir Paris crossed the seas with her
   And brought the spoils to rich Dardania.[1]   25
   Be silent, then, for danger is in words.

[*Music sounds.* MEPHISTOPHILIS *brings in* HELEN; *she passeth over the stage.*]

2 SCH. Too simple is my wit to tell her praise
   Whom all the world admires for majesty.
3 SCH. No marvel though the angry Greeks pursued
   With ten years' war the rape of such a queen   30
   Whose heavenly beauty passeth all compare.
1 SCH. Since we have seen the pride of Nature's works
   And only paragon of excellence,
   Let us depart, and for this glorious deed
   Happy and blest be Faustus evermore.   35
FAUST. Gentlemen, farewell; the same I wish to you.

---

1. Troy.

[*Exeunt* SCHOLARS.]

[*Enter an* OLD MAN.]

OLD MAN. O gentle Faustus, leave this damnèd art,
   This magic, that will charm thy soul to hell
   And quite bereave[2] thee of salvation.
   Though thou hast now offended like a man,   40
   Do not persèver in it like a devil.
   Yet, yet, thou hast an amiable soul
   If sin by custom grow not into nature;
   Then, Faustus, will repentance come too late;
   Then thou art banished from the sight of heaven.   45
   No mortal can express the pains of hell.
   It may be this my exhortation
   Seems harsh and all unpleasant; let it not;
   For, gentle son, I speak it not in wrath
   Or envy of thee, but in tender love   50
   And pity of thy future misery,
   And so have hope that this my kind rebuke,
   Checking thy body, may amend thy soul.
FAUST. Where art thou, Faustus? Wretch, what hast thou done?
   Damned art thou, Faustus, damned! Despair and die.   55

      [MEPHISTOPHILIS *gives him a dagger.*]

   Hell claims his right, and with a roaring voice
   Says, "Faustus, come; thine hour is almost come!"
   And Faustus now will come to do thee right.
OLD MAN. O stay, good Faustus, stay thy desperate steps!
   I see an angel hovers o'er thy head   60
   And with a vial full of precious grace
   Offers to pour the same into thy soul:
   Then call for mercy and avoid despair.
FAUST. Ah my sweet friend, I feel thy words
   To comfort my distressèd soul.   65
   Leave me awhile to ponder on my sins.
OLD MAN. Faustus, I leave thee, but with grief of heart,
   Fearing the ruin of thy hapless soul.   [*Exit.*]
FAUST. Accursèd Faustus, where is mercy now?
   I do repent and yet I do despair: 70
   Hell strives with grace for conquest in my breast.
   What shall I do to shun the snares of death?
MEPH. Thou traitor, Faustus, I arrest thy soul
   For disobedience to my sovereign lord.
   Revolt, or I'll in piecemeal tear thy flesh.   75
FAUST. I do repent I e'er offended him.
   Sweet Mephistophilis, entreat thy lord
   To pardon my unjust presumption,
   And with my blood again I will confirm
   The former vow I made to Lucifer.   80

2. Deprive.

MEPH. Do it then, Faustus, with unfeignèd heart
    Lest greater danger do attend thy drift.
FAUST. Torment, sweet friend, that base and aged man
    That durst dissuade me from thy Lucifer,
    With greatest torments that our hell affords.   85
MEPH. His faith is great; I cannot touch his soul;
    But what I may afflict his body with
    I will attempt, which is but little worth.
FAUST. One thing, good servant, let me crave of thee
    To glut the longing of my heart's desire: 90
    That I might have unto my paramour
    That heavenly Helen which I saw of late,
    Whose sweet embracings may extinguish clear
    These thoughts that do dissuade me from my vow,
    And keep mine oath I made to Lucifer.   95
MEPH. This, or what else my Faustus shall desire
    Shall be performed in twinkling of an eye.

      [Enter HELEN again, passing over between two CUPIDS.]

FAUST. Was this the face that launched a thousand ships
    And burnt the topless[3] towers of Ilium?
    Sweet Helen, make me immortal with a kiss.   100
    Her lips suck forth my soul—see where it flies!
    Come, Helen, come, give me my soul again.
    Here will I dwell, for heaven is in these lips
    And all is dross that is not Helena.

      [Enter OLD MAN and stands watching FAUSTUS.]

    I will be Paris, and for love of thee   105
    Instead of Troy shall Wittenberg be sacked,
    And I will combat with weak Menelaus
    And wear thy colors on my plumèd crest;
    Yea, I will wound Achilles in the heel
    And then return to Helen for a kiss.   110
    O thou art fairer than the evening air
    Clad in the beauty of a thousand stars!
    Brighter art thou than flaming Jupiter
    When he appeared to hapless Semele,[4]
    More lovely than the monarch of the sky   115
    In wanton Arethusa's azured arms,[5]
    And none but thou shalt be my paramour!

      [Exeunt ALL except the OLD MAN.]

OLD MAN. Accursèd Faustus, miserable man,
    That from thy soul exclud'st the grace of heaven
    And fliest the throne of his tribunal seat.   120

---

3. So high they seemed to have no tops.
4. A Theban girl, loved by Jupiter and destroyed by the fire of his lightning when he appeared to her in his full splendor.

5. Arethusa was the nymph of a fountain, as well as the fountain itself; no classical myth, however, records her love affair with Jupiter, the "monarch of the sky."

[*Enter the* DEVILS *to torment him.*]

Satan begins to sift me with his pride.[6]
As in this furnace God shall try my faith,
My faith, vile hell, shall triumph over thee!
Ambitious fiends, see how the heavens smiles
At your repulse, and laughs your state to scorn.   125
Hence, hell! for hence I fly unto my God.   [*Exeunt.*]

SCENE 2

[*Thunder. Enter* LUCIFER, BELZEBUB, *and* MEPHISTOPHILIS.]

LUC. Thus from infernal Dis[7] do we ascend
    To view the subjects of our monarchy,
    Those souls which sin seals the black sons of hell.
    'Mong which as chief, Faustus, we come to thee,
    Bringing with us lasting damnation   5
    To wait upon thy soul; the time is come
    Which makes it forfeit.
MEPH.   And this gloomy night
    Here in this room will wretched Faustus be.
BEL. And here we'll stay
    To mark him how he doth demean himself.   10
MEPH. How should he but with desperate lunacy?
    Fond worldling, now his heart-blood dries with grief,
    His conscience kills it, and his laboring brain
    Begets a world of idle fantasies
    To overreach the devil, but all in vain.   15
    His store of pleasure must be sauced with pain.
    He and his servant Wagner are at hand;
    Both come from drawing Faustus' latest will.
    See where they come!

        [*Enter* FAUSTUS *and* WAGNER.]

FAUST. Say, Wagner, thou has perused my will;   20
    How dost thou like it?
WAG.   Sir, so wondrous well
    As in all humble duty I do yield
    My life and lasting service for your love.

        [*Enter the* SCHOLARS.]

FAUST. Gramercies, Wagner.—Welcome, gentlemen.
1 SCH. Now, worthy Faustus, methinks your looks are changed.   25
FAUST. Ah, gentlemen!
2 SCH. What ails Faustus?
FAUST. Ah, my sweet chamber-fellow, had I lived with thee, then
    had I lived still, but now must die eternally. Look, sirs! Comes
    he not? Comes he not?   30
1 SCH. O my dear Faustus, what imports this fear?
2 SCH. Is all our pleasure turned to melancholy?

6. I.e., to test me with his strength.   7. The underworld.

3 SCH. He is not well with being over-solitary.

2 SCH. If it be so, we'll have physicians, and Faustus shall be cured.

3 SCH. 'Tis but a surfeit,[8] sir; fear nothing.   35

FAUST. A surfeit of deadly sin that hath damned both body and soul.

2 SCH. Yet, Faustus, look up to heaven: remember God's mercies
are infinite.

FAUST. But Faustus' offense can ne'er be pardoned; the Serpent that
tempted Eve may be saved, but not Faustus. Ah, gentlemen,   40
hear me with patience, and tremble not at my speeches. Though
my heart pants and quivers to remember that I have been a student here these thirty years, O would I had never seen Wittenberg, never read book! And what wonders I have done all Germany
can witness, yea all the world, for which Faustus hath lost both   45
Germany and the world, yea heaven itself—heaven the seat of
God, the throne of the blessed, the kingdom of joy, and must
remain in hell forever, hell, ah hell, forever! Sweet friends, what
shall become of Faustus, being in hell forever?

3 SCH. Yet, Faustus, call on God.   50

FAUST. On God, whom Faustus hath abjured? on God, whom
Faustus hath blasphemed? Ah, my God, I would weep, but the
devil draws in my tears! Gush forth, blood, instead of tears, yea
life and soul! O he stays my tongue; I would lift up my hands
but, see, they hold 'em, they hold 'em!   55

ALL. Who, Faustus?

FAUST. Why, Lucifer and Mephistophilis.
Ah gentlemen, I gave them my soul for my cunning.

ALL. God forbid!

FAUST. God forbade it indeed, but Faustus hath done it: for the vain   60
pleasure of four and twenty years hath Faustus lost eternal joy
and felicity. I writ them a bill with mine own blood; the date is
expired, this is the time, and he will fetch me.

1 SCH. Why did not Faustus tell us of this before, that divines might
have prayed for thee?   65

FAUST. Oft have I thought to have done so, but the devil threatened
to tear me in pieces if I named God, to fetch both body and soul
if I once gave ear to divinity; and now 'tis too late. Gentlemen,
away, lest you perish with me!

2 SCH. O what may we do to save Faustus?   70

FAUST. Talk not of me, but save yourselves and depart.

3 SCH. God will strengthen me: I will stay with Faustus.

1 SCH. Tempt not God, sweet friend, but let us into the next room,
and there pray for him.

FAUST. Aye, pray for me, pray for me! And what noise soever ye   75
hear, come not unto me, for nothing can rescue me.

2 SCH. Pray thou, and we will pray that God may have mercy upon
thee.

FAUST. Gentlemen, farewell. If I live till morning I'll visit you; if
not, Faustus is gone to hell.   80

ALL. Faustus, farewell.   [*Exeunt* SCHOLARS.]

---

8. Indigestion; the effects of overindulgence.

MEPH. Aye, Faustus, now thou hast no hope of heaven;
    Therefore despair, think only upon hell,
    For that must be thy mansion, there to dwell.
FAUST. O thou bewitching fiend, 'twas thy temptation   85
    Hath robbed me of eternal happiness.
MEPH. I do confess it, Faustus, and rejoice.
    'Twas I, that when thou wert i' the way to heaven
    Damned up thy passage; when thou tookest the book
    To view the scriptures, then I turned the leaves   90
    And led thine eye.
    What, weepst thou? 'tis too late. Despair, farewell!
    Fools that will laugh on earth must weep in hell.   [*Exit.*]

[*Enter the* GOOD ANGEL *and the* BAD ANGEL *at several doors.*]

G. ANG. Ah Faustus, if thou hadst given ear to me,
    Innumerable joys had followed thee,   95
    But thou didst love the world.
B. ANG.   Gave ear to me
    And now must taste hell's pains perpetually.
G. ANG. O what will all thy riches, pleasures, pomps
    Avail thee now?
B. ANG.   Nothing but vex thee more,
    To want in hell, that had on earth such store.   100

[*Music while the throne descends.*[9]]

G. ANG. O, thou hast lost celestial happiness,
    Pleasures unspeakable, bliss without end.
    Hadst thou affected sweet divinity
    Hell or the devil had had no power on thee.
    Hadst thou kept on that way, Faustus, behold   105
    In what resplendent glory thou hadst sit
    In yonder throne, like those bright shining saints,
    And triumphed over hell; that hast thou lost.
    And now, poor soul, must thy good angel leave thee;
    The jaws of hell are open to receive thee.   110

[*Exit. Hell is discovered.*]

B. ANG. Now Faustus, let thine eyes with horror stare
    Into that vast perpetual torture-house.
    There are the furies, tossing damnèd souls
    On burning forks; their bodies boil in lead.
    There are live quarters[1] broiling on the coals   115
    That ne'er can die; this ever-burning chair
    Is for o'ertortured souls to rest them in;
    These that are fed with sops of flaming fire
    Were gluttons and loved only delicates
    And laughed to see the poor starve at their gates.   120

---

9. A throne suspended by ropes descended to the
stage near the end of many Elizabethan plays and
was an expected theatrical display. Here the throne
clearly symbolizes heaven, as the next speech shows.
1. Bodies.

But yet all these are nothing; thou shalt see
Ten thousand tortures that more horrid be.
FAUST. O, I have seen enough to torture me.
B. ANG. Nay, thou must feel them, taste the smart of all;
He that loves pleasure must for pleasure fall.   125
And so I leave thee, Faustus, till anon;
Then wilt thou tumble in confusìon.[2]

[*Exit. The clock strikes eleven.*]

FAUST. Ah, Faustus,
Now hast thou but one bare hour to live
And then thou must be damned perpetually!   130
Stand still, you ever-moving spheres of heaven,
That time may cease and midnight never come;
Fair Nature's eye, rise, rise again, and make
Perpetual day; or let this hour be but
A year, a month, a week, a natural day,   135
That Faustus may repent and save his soul!
O *lente lente currite noctis equi.*[3]
The stars move still, time runs, the clock will strike,
The devil will come, and Faustus must be damned.
O, I'll leap up to my God! Who pulls me down?   140
See, see, where Christ's blood streams in the firmament!—
One drop would save my soul—half a drop! ah, my Christ!
Rend not my heart for naming of my Christ;
Yet will I call on him—O, spare me, Lucifer!
Where is it now? 'Tis gone; and see where God   145
Stretcheth out his arm and bends his ireful brows.
Mountains and hills, come, come and fall on me
And hide me from the heavy wrath of God,
No, no?
Then will I headlong run into the earth: 150
Earth, gape! O no, it will not harbor me.
You stars that reigned at my nativity,
Whose influence hath allotted death and hell,
Now draw up Faustus like a foggy mist
Into the entrails of yon laboring cloud   155
That when you vomit forth into the air,
My limbs may issue from your smoky mouths,
So that my soul may but ascend to heaven.[4]

[*The watch strikes.*]

Ah, half the hour is past; 'twill all be past anon.
O God,   160
If thou wilt not have mercy on my soul,
Yet for Christ's sake whose blood hath ransomed me
Impose some end to my incessant pain:

---

2. Destruction, perdition.
3. "Slowly, slowly run, O horses of the night,"
adapted from a line in Ovid's *Amores.*
4. Faustus begs his natal stars to draw him up into the cloud, where his body may be compacted into a thunderstone and fall to earth, so that his soul, thus purified, may ascend to heaven.

Let Faustus live in hell a thousand years,
A hundred thousand, and at last be saved!   165
O, no end is limited to damnèd souls!
Why wert thou not a creature wanting soul?
Or why is this immortal that thou hast?
Ah, Pythagoras' *metempsychosis*[5]—were that true,
This soul should fly from me, and I be changed   170
Unto some brutish beast. All beasts are happy,
For when they die
Their souls are soon dissolved in elements,
But mine must live still[6] to be plagued in hell.
Cursed be the parents that engendered me!   175
No, Faustus, curse thyself, curse Lucifer
That hath deprived thee of the joys of heaven.

> [*The clock strikes twelve.*]

It strikes, it strikes! Now, body, turn to air
Or Lucifer will bear thee quick[7] to hell!

> [*Thunder and lightning.*]

O soul, be changed to little water drops   180
And fall into the ocean, ne'er be found.
My God, my God, look not so fierce on me!

> [*Enter* DEVILS.]

Adders and serpents, let me breathe awhile!
Ugly hell, gape not—come not, Lucifer—
I'll burn my books—ah, Mephistophilis!   185

> [*Exeunt* DEVILS *with* FAUSTUS.]

SCENE 3

> [*Enter the* SCHOLARS.]

1 SCH. Come, gentlemen, let us go visit Faustus,
     For such a dreadful night was never seen
     Since first the world's creation did begin,
     Such fearful shrieks and cries were never heard.
     Pray heaven the Doctor have escaped the danger.   5
2 SCH. O, help us heaven! See, here are Faustus' limbs
     All torn asunder by the hand of death.
3 SCH. The devils whom Faustus served have torn him thus;
     For 'twixt the hours of twelve and one, methought
     I heard him shriek and call aloud for help.   10
     At which self[8] time the house seemed all on fire
     With dreadful horror of these damnèd fiends.
2 SCH. Well, gentlemen, though Faustus' end be such
     As every Christian heart laments to think on,

---

5. Pythagoras' doctrine of the transmigration of   7. Alive.
souls.   8. Same, exact.
6. Always.

Yet for he was a scholar once admired   15
For wondrous knowledge in our German schools,
We'll give his mangled limbs due burial;
And all the students, clothed in mourning black,
Shall wait upon his heavy[9] funeral.   [*Exeunt.*]

    [*Enter* CHORUS.]

CHO. Cut is the branch that might have grown full straight,   20
And burnèd is Apollo's laurel bough[1]
That sometime grew within this learnèd man.
Faustus is gone: regard his hellish fall,
Whose fiendful fortune may exhort the wise
Only to wonder at[2] unlawful things   25
Whose deepness doth entice such forward wits
To practice more than heavenly power permits.   [*Exit.*]

1604, 1616

9. Tragic, sorrowful.
1. Laurel is a symbol of wisdom and learning;
Apollo was the god of divination, one of whose
shrines was the oracle at Delphi. The image, though

it sounds classical, is really Marlowe's.
2. I.e., to be content with observing with awe.
"Fiendful fortune": devilish fate.

WILLIAM SHAKESPEARE
1564–1616

  ca. 1588–92: In London as actor and playwright.
  ca. 1592–98: Devotes himself mainly to chronicle histories and
               comedies.
  ca. 1601–9: Period of the great tragedies and romantic come-
               dies.
  ca. 1610: Retires to Stratford.

William Shakespeare was born in Stratford-on-Avon in April (probably April 23), 1564. His father was a citizen of some prominence who became an alderman and bailiff, but who later suffered financial reverses. Shakespeare presumably attended the Stratford grammar school, where he could have acquired a respectable knowledge of Latin, but he did not proceed to Oxford or Cambridge. There are legends about Shakespeare's youth but no documented facts. The first record we have of his life after his christening is that of his marriage in 1582 to Anne Hathaway. A daughter was born to the young Shakespeares in 1583 and twins, a boy and a girl, in 1585. We possess no information about his activities for the next seven years, but by 1592 he was in London as an actor and apparently well known as a playwright, for Robert Greene refers to him resentfully in A *Groatsworth of Wit* as "an upstart crow, beautified with our feathers," who, "being an absolute *Johannes Factotum*, is in his own conceit the only Shake-scene in a country."

At this time, there were several companies of actors in London and in the provinces. What connection Shakespeare had with one or more of them before 1592 is conjectural, but we do know of his long and fruitful connection with the most successful troupe, the Lord Chamberlain's Men, who later, when James I came to the throne, became the King's Men. Shakespeare not only acted with this company, but eventually became a leading shareholder and the principal playwright. The company included some of the most famous actors of the day, such as Richard Burbage, who no doubt created the roles of Hamlet, Lear, and Othello, and Will Kempe and Robert Armin, who acted Shakespeare's clowns and fools. In 1599 the Chamberlain's Men built and occupied that best known of Elizabethan theaters, the Globe.

Shakespeare did not, in his early years, confine himself to the theater. In 1593 he published a mythological-erotic poem, *Venus and Adonis*, dedicated to the earl of Southampton; in the next year he dedicated a "graver labor," *The Rape of Lucrece*, to the same noble patron. By 1597 Shakespeare had so prospered that he was able to purchase New Place, a handsome house in Stratford; he could now call himself a gentleman, as his father had been granted a coat of arms in the previous year.

Our first record of the playwright's actual work occurs in Francis Meres' *Palladis Tamia: Wit's Treasury* (1598), in which Meres compared English poets with the ancients; of Shakespeare he says, "As Plautus and Seneca are accounted the best for Comedy and Tragedy among the Latins, so Shakespeare among the English is the most excellent in both kinds for the stage." He goes on to list *Richard II, Richard III, Henry IV, King John, Titus Andronicus*, and *Romeo and Juliet* for tragedy and *Two Gentlemen of Verona, The Comedy of Errors, A Midsummer Night's Dream, The Merchant of Venice, Love's Labor's Lost,* and the unknown (or perhaps retitled) *Love's Labor's Won* as comedy. All of the plays Meres lists as tragedy (except for *Romeo and Juliet* and the very early *Titus Andronicus*) we would call chronicle history plays, a popular kind of drama based upon history books like Raphael Holinshed's *Chronicle* and presenting dramatically the events in the reigns of various English kings. About the turn of the century Shakespeare wrote his great romantic comedies, *As You Like It, Twelfth Night,* and *Much Ado About Nothing,* and his concluding history play in the Prince Hal series, *Henry V.* The next decade was the period of the great tragedies: *Hamlet, Macbeth, Othello, King Lear,* and *Antony and Cleopatra.*

About 1610 Shakespeare apparently retired to Stratford, though he continued to write, both by himself (*The Tempest*) and in collaboration (*Henry VIII*). This is the period of the "romances" or "tragicomedies," which include, besides *The Tempest, Cymbeline* and *The Winter's Tale.* Aside from his two early nondramatic poems, Shakespeare devoted his genius primarily to the stage. Meres mentioned in 1598, however, that he was known for "his sugared sonnets among his private friends"; the sonnets were published in 1609. The publisher, Thomas Thorpe, included a strange dedication "To the only begetter of these ensuing sonnets, Master W. H." that has puzzled Shakespeare scholars ever since.

The sonnets are Shakespeare's contribution to a popular vogue, but his cycle is quite unlike the other sonnet sequences of his day. Shakespeare's cycle suggests a story, though the details are vague, and there is doubt even whether the sonnets as published in 1609 are in the correct order. Certain motifs are clear: a series celebrating the beauty of a young man and urging him to marry; some sonnets to a lady; some sonnets (like *144*) about a strange triangle of love involving two men and a woman; sonnets on the destructive power of time and the permanence of poetry; sonnets about a rival poet; and incidental sonnets of moral insight, like 129 and 146. The biographical background of the sonnets has aroused much speculation, but very little of it is convincing. The poems themselves are what is important. Though the vocabulary is often simple, the metaphorical style of the sonnets is rich. "Shall I compare thee to a summer's day" is a question which might lead to a very ordinary conceit; instead it introduces a profound meditation on time, change, and beauty.

The structure of the sonnet frequently reinforces the power of the metaphors; each quatrain in 73 develops an image of lateness, of approaching extinction—of a season, of a day, and of a fire, but they also apply to a life. The three quatrains may be equally and successively at work preparing for the conclusion in the couplet, or the first eight lines may contain a catalogue and the last six turn in quite a different direction, as in sonnet 29. The rhetorical strategy of the sonnets is also worth careful attention. Some begin with a purported reminiscence; some are imperative; others make an almost proverbial statement, then elaborate it. The imagery comes from a wide variety of sources: gardening, navigation, law, farming, business, pictorial art, astrology, domestic affairs. The moods are also not confined to what the Renaissance thought were those of the despairing Petrarchan lover; they include delight, pride, melancholy, shame, disgust, fear. It is evident that the poet of the sonnets is also the author of the great plays.

The plays contain some of the finest songs ever written. They are of various types: the aubade, or morning song, the gay pastoral invitation, love songs of various kinds, the ballad sung by wandering minstrels, and the funeral dirge. They illustrate many sides of Shakespeare's genius—his incomparable lyric gift, his ready humor, and his marvelous sensitivity to the sights and sounds of English life, especially the life of the country.

When Shakespeare died, in Stratford in 1616, no collected edition of his plays had been published. Some of them had been printed in separate editions ("quartos") without his editorial supervision, sometimes from his manuscripts, sometimes from playhouse prompt books, sometimes from pirated texts secured by shorthand reports of a performance or from reconstruction from memory by an actor or spectator.

In 1623, two members of Shakespeare's company, John Heminges and Henry Condell, published the great collection of all the plays they considered authentic; it is called the First Folio. They printed the best texts they had, according to their lights. The Folio contains an epistle "to the great variety of readers" which urges us to read Shakespeare again and again; if we do not like him, say Heminges and Condell, it is evident that we do not understand him. Another preliminary document in the First Folio is a poem by Shakespeare's great rival, critic, and opposite, Ben Jonson. In it he asserts the superiority of Shakespeare not only to other English playwrights but to the Greek and Latin masters. Jonson first states what has come to be a universal opinion:

> Triumph, my Britain, thou hast one to show
> To whom all scenes of Europe homage owe.
> He was not of an age, but for all time!

Songs from the Plays
Under the Greenwood Tree[1]

Under the greenwood tree
Who loves to lie with me,
And turn his merry note
Unto the sweet bird's throat,[2]
Come hither, come hither, come hither:
    Here shall he see   5
      No enemy
But winter and rough weather.

Who doth ambition shun
And loves to live i' th' sun,
Seeking the food he eats,   10
And pleased with what he gets,
Come hither, come hither, come hither!
    Here shall he see
      No enemy
But winter and rough weather.   15

Blow, Blow, Thou Winter Wind[1]

Blow, blow, thou winter wind,
Thou art not so unkind
    As man's ingratitude;
Thy tooth is not so keen,
Because thou art not seen,   5
    Although thy breath be rude.
Heigh-ho! sing, heigh-ho! unto the green holly:
Most friendship is feigning, most loving mere folly:
    Then, heigh-ho, the holly!
      This life is most jolly.   10

Freeze, freeze, thou bitter sky,
That dost not bite so nigh
    As benefits forgot:
Though thou the waters warp,[2]

---

1. *As You Like It* (1599–1600) 2.5.1 ff.; this song provides a comment on the happy existence of the banished Duke and his followers in the Forest of Arden, where life is "more sweet / Than that of painted pomp."
2. I.e., improvise his song in harmony with the bird's.

1. From *As You Like It* 2.7. 174 ff. The contrast here between nature and man's willful behavior is one of the continuing themes of the play.
2. I.e., roughen by freezing.

Thy sting is not so sharp   15
    As friend remembered not.
Heigh-ho! sing, etc.

It Was a Lover and His Lass[1]

It was a lover and his lass,
    With a hey, and a ho, and a hey nonino,
That o'er the green corn-field[2] did pass,
    In spring time, the only pretty ring
        time,[3]
When birds do sing, hey ding a ding, ding,   5
Sweet lovers love the spring.

Between the acres of the rye,[4]
    With a hey, and a ho, and a hey nonino,
These pretty country folks would lie,
    In spring time, etc.   10

This carol they began that hour,
    With a hey, and a ho, and a hey nonino,
How that a life was but a flower,
    In spring time, etc.

And therefore take[5] the present time,   15
    With a hey, and a ho, and a hey nonino,
For love is crownèd with the prime,[6]
    In spring time, etc.

Oh Mistress Mine[1]

Oh mistress mine! where are you roaming?
O, stay and hear; your true love's coming,
    That can sing both high and low.
Trip no further, pretty sweeting;
Journeys end in lovers meeting,
    Every wise man's son doth know.   5

What is love? 'tis not hereafter;
Present mirth hath present laughter;
    What's to come is still unsure:

---

1. Sung by two pages to the clown Touchstone and his "country wench," Audrey, in *As You Like It* 5.3.16 ff. This *carpe diem* ("seize the time") song anticipates the happy marriages that will conclude the play.
2. Wheat field.

3. I.e., marriage season.
4. I.e., on unplowed ground separating the planted fields.
5. Seize.
6. Springtime.
1. *Twelfth Night* (1601–2) 2.3. 40 ff.

In delay there lies no plenty; 10
Then come kiss me, sweet and twenty,
Youth's a stuff will not endure.

Fear No More the Heat o' the Sun[1]

Fear no more the heat o' the sun,
Nor the furious winter's rages;
Thou thy worldly task hast done,
Home art gone, and ta'en thy wages.
Golden lads and girls all must, 5
As[2] chimney-sweepers, come to dust.

Fear no more the frown o' the great;
Thou art past the tyrant's stroke;
Care no more to clothe and eat;
To thee the reed is as the oak: 10
The scepter, learning, physic,[3] must
All follow this, and come to dust.

Fear no more the lightning flash,
Nor the all-dreaded thunder stone;[4]
Fear not slander, censure rash; 15
Thou hast finished joy and moan:
All lovers young, all lovers must
Consign to thee, and come to dust.

No exorciser harm thee!
Nor no witchcraft charm thee! 20
Ghost unlaid forbear thee!
Nothing ill come near thee!
Quiet consummation have;
And renownèd be thy grave!

Full Fathom Five[1]

Full fathom five thy father lies;
Of his bones are coral made;
Those are pearls that were his eyes:
Nothing of him that doth fade,
But doth suffer a sea change 5

1. A lament for the supposedly dead Imogen, sung in *Cymbeline* 4.2.258 ff.
2. Like.
3. Medical science.
4. The sound of thunder was commonly thought to be caused by the falling of stones or meteorites.

1. *The Tempest* (1611–12) 1.2.396 ff. Ariel, the airy spirit of the enchanted isle, sings this song to Ferdinand, prince of Naples. Ferdinand wonders at it: "The ditty does remember my drowned father. / This is no mortal business, nor no sound/ That the earth owes [owns]."

Into something rich and strange.
Sea nymphs hourly ring his knell:
   Ding-dong.
Hark! now I hear them—Ding-dong, bell.

Where the Bee Sucks, There Suck I[1]

Where the bee sucks, there suck I:
In a cowslip's bell I lie;
There I couch when owls do cry.
On the bat's back I do fly
After summer merrily.   5
Merrily, merrily shall I live now
Under the blossom that hangs on the bough.

SONNETS

3

Look in thy glass and tell the face thou viewest
Now is the time that face should form another,
Whose fresh repair if now thou not renewest,
Thou dost beguile the world, unbless some mother.
For where is she so fair whose uneared[1] womb   5
Disdains the tillage of thy husbandry?
Or who is he so fond[2] will be the tomb
Of his self-love, to stop posterity?
Thou art thy mother's glass,[3] and she in thee
Calls back the lovely April of her prime;   10
So thou through windows of thine age shalt see,
Despite of wrinkles, this thy golden time.
   But if thou live rememb'red not to be,
   Die single, and thine image dies with thee.

1609

12

When I do count the clock that tells the time
And see the brave[1] day sunk in hideous night,
When I behold the violet past prime

---

1. Also from *The Tempest* 5.1.88 ff.: Ariel is happily anticipating the freedom of his future life.
1. Unplowed.

2. Foolish.
3. Mirror.
1. Splendid.

And sable curls all silvered o'er with white,
When lofty trees I see barren of leaves,   5
Which erst[2] from heat did canopy the herd
And summer's green all girded up in sheaves
Borne on the bier with white and bristly beard:
Then of thy beauty do I question make
That thou among the wastes of time must go,   10
Since sweets and beauties do themselves forsake,
And die as fast as they see others grow,
    And nothing 'gainst Time's scythe can make defense
    Save breed,[3] to brave him when he takes thee hence.

                                                    1609

15

When I consider every thing that grows
Holds[1] in perfection but a little moment;
That this huge stage presenteth naught but shows
Whereon the stars in secret influence comment;[2]
When I perceive that men as plants increase,   5
Cheerèd and checked[3] even by the selfsame sky,
Vaunt[4] in their youthful sap, at height decrease,
And wear their brave state out of memory;[5]
Then the conceit[6] of this inconstant stay
Sets you most rich in youth before my sight,   10
Where wasteful Time debateth[7] with Decay
To change your day of youth to sullied[8] night,
    And all in war with Time for love of you,
    As he takes from you, I ingraft[9] you new.

                                                    1609

18

Shall I compare thee to a summer's day?
Thou art more lovely and more temperate:
Rough winds do shake the darling buds of May,
And summer's lease hath all too short a date:
Sometime too hot the eye of heaven shines   5
And often is his gold complexion dimmed;

---

2. Formerly.
3. Offspring; "to brave": to defy.
1. Remains.
2. The stars in an occult way affect human actions.
"Shows": (1) appearances (2) performances.
3. Encouraged and reproached or stopped.
4. Exult, display themselves.

5. Wear their showy splendor out and are forgotten.
6. Conception.
7. Discusses.
8. Soiled, blackened.
9. Renew by grafting, implant beauty again (by my verse).

And every fair from fair sometimes declines,
By chance or nature's changing course untrimmed;[1]
But thy eternal summer shall not fade,
Nor lose possession of that fair thou ow'st;[2]   10
Nor shall death brag thou wander'st in his shade,
When in eternal lines to time thou grow'st:[3]
   So long as men can breathe, or eyes can see,
   So long lives this, and this gives life to thee.[4]

1609

19

Devouring Time, blunt thou the lion's paws,
And make the earth devour her own sweet brood;
Pluck the keen teeth from the fierce tiger's jaws,
And burn the long-lived phoenix in her blood;[1]
Make glad and sorry seasons as thou fleet'st,   5
And do what e'er thou wilt, swift-footed Time,
To the wide world and all her fading sweets:
But I forbid thee one most heinous crime,
O carve not with thy hours my love's fair brow,
Nor draw no lines there with thine antique[2] pen;   10
Him in thy course untainted[3] do allow,
For beauty's pattern to succeeding men.
   Yet do thy worst, old Time: despite thy wrong,
   My love shall in my verse ever live young.

1609

20

A woman's face with Nature's own hand painted[1]
Hast thou, the master mistress of my passion;[2]
A woman's gentle heart but not acquainted
With shifting change as is false women's fashion;
An eye more bright than theirs, less false in rolling,[3]   5
Gilding the object whereupon it gazeth;
A man in hue all hues in his controlling,
Which steals men's eyes and women's souls amazeth.

1. Stripped of gay apparel.
2. Ownest.
3. When in [this] immortal poetry you become even with time.
4. The boast of immortality for one's verse was a Renaissance convention and goes back to the classics. It implies, not egotism on the part of the poet, but a faith in the permanence of poetry.
1. In full vigor of life (a hunting term). The phoenix was a mythical bird that lived five hundred years, then died in flames, to rise again from its ashes.
2. (1) Old, (2) fantastic.
3. (1) Undefiled, (2) untouched by a weapon (a term from tilting).
1. I.e., not made up with cosmetics.
2. (1) Strong feeling, (2) poem.
3. Roving.

And for a woman wert thou first created,
Till Nature as she wrought thee fell a-doting,[4]   10
And by addition me of thee defeated,
By adding one thing to my purpose nothing.
　　But since she pricked thee out for women's pleasure,[5]
　　Mine be thy love, and thy love's use their treasure.[6]

　　　　　　　　　　　　　　　　　　　　　　1609

29

When, in disgrace[1] with Fortune and men's eyes,
I all alone beweep my outcast state,
And trouble deaf heaven with my bootless[2] cries,
And look upon myself and curse my fate,
Wishing me like to one more rich in hope,   5
Featured like him, like him with friends possessed,
Desiring this man's art and that man's scope,
With what I most enjoy contented least;
Yet in these thoughts myself almost despising,
Haply I think on thee, and then my state[3]   10
(Like to the lark at break of day arising
From sullen earth) sings hymns at heaven's gate;
　　For thy sweet love remembered such wealth brings
　　That then I scorn to change my state with kings.

　　　　　　　　　　　　　　　　　　　　　　1609

30

When to the sessions[1] of sweet silent thought
I summon up remembrance of things past,
I sigh the lack of many a thing I sought,
And with old woes new wail[2] my dear time's waste:
Then can I drown an eye (unused to flow)   5
For precious friends hid in death's dateless[3] night,
And weep afresh love's long since canceled woe,
And moan th' expense[4] of many a vanished sight:
Then can I grieve at grievances foregone,[5]
And heavily from woe to woe tell o'er   10
The sad account of fore-bemoanèd moan,

---

4. (1) Crazy, (2) infatuated.
5. Marked, with obvious sexual pun.
6. (1) Sexual enjoyment, (2) interest (as in usury).
1. Out of favor.
2. Futile.
3. Condition, state of mind; but in line 14 there is a pun on "state" meaning chair of state, throne.

1. Sittings of court; "summon up" (line 2) continues the metaphor.
2. Bewail anew.
3. Endless.
4. Loss.
5. Old subjects for grief. "Tell": count.

Which I new pay as if not paid before.
But if the while I think on thee, dear friend,
All losses are restored and sorrows end.

1609

35

No more be grieved at that which thou hast done:
Roses have thorns, and silver fountains mud.
Clouds and eclipses stain[1] both moon and sun,
And loathsome canker[2] lives in sweetest bud.
All men make faults, and even I in this,   5
Authorizing thy trespass with compare,
Myself corrupting, salving thy amiss,
Excusing thy sins more than thy sins are;
For to thy sensual fault I bring in sense[3]—
Thy adverse party is thy advocate—   10
And 'gainst myself a lawful plea commence.
Such civil war is in my love and hate,
    That I an accessary needs must be
    To that sweet thief which sourly robs from me.

1609

55

Not marble, nor the gilded monuments
Of princes, shall outlive this powerful rhyme;
But you shall shine more bright in these contents
Than unswept stone, besmeared with sluttish time.[1]
When wasteful war shall statues overturn,   5
And broils root out the work of masonry,
Nor Mars his[2] sword nor war's quick fire shall burn
The living record of your memory.
'Gainst death and all-oblivious enmity[3]
Shall you pace forth; your praise shall still find room   10
Even in the eyes of all posterity
That wear this world out to the ending doom.[4]
    So, till the judgment that yourself arise,
    You live in this, and dwell in lovers' eyes.

1609

1. Dim.
2. Rose worm.
3. Reason.
1. I.e., than in a stone tomb or effigy which time
wears away and covers with dust.

2. Mars's.
3. The enmity of oblivion, of being forgotten.
4. Judgment Day. The next line is paraphrased,
"Until you rise from the dead on Judgment Day."

60

Like as the waves make towards the pibbled[1] shore,
So do our minutes hasten to their end;
Each changing place with that which goes before,
In sequent toil all forwards do contend.[2]
Nativity, once in the main[3] of light,   5
Crawls to maturity, wherewith being crowned,
Crooked eclipses 'gainst his glory fight,
And Time that gave doth now his gift confound.
Time doth transfix the flourish[4] set on youth
And delves the parallels in beauty's brow,   10
Feeds on the rarities of nature's truth,
And nothing stands but for his scythe to mow.
   And yet to times in hope[5] my verse shall stand,
   Praising thy worth, despite his cruel hand.

1609

65

Since[1] brass, nor stone, nor earth, nor boundless sea,
But sad mortality o'ersways their power,
How with this rage[2] shall beauty hold a plea,
Whose action is no stronger than a flower?
O how shall summer's honey breath hold out   5
Against the wrackful[3] siege of batt'ring days,
When rocks impregnable are not so stout,
Nor gates of steel so strong, but Time decays?
O fearful meditation! where, alack,
Shall Time's best jewel from Time's chest lie hid?[4]   10
Or what strong hand can hold his swift foot back?
Or who his spoil[5] of beauty can forbid?
   O none, unless this miracle have might,
   That in black ink my love may still shine bright.

1609

71

No longer mourn for me when I am dead
Than you shall hear the surly sullen bell[1]

1. Pebbled.
2. Toiling and following each other, the waves struggle to press forward.
3. Broad expanse.
4. Remove the embellishment. "Delves the parallels": digs the parallel furrows (wrinkles). To "flourish" is also to blossom.
5. Future times.
1. I.e., since there is neither.

2. Destructive power.
3. Destructive.
4. Time, like any wealthy person, keeps his jewels in a chest. Once it is taken out, where can his best jewel be hidden from destructive forces?
5. Ravaging.
1. The bell was tolled to announce the death of a member of the parish—one stroke for each year of his life.

Give warning to the world that I am fled
From this vile world, with vilest worms to dwell:
Nay, if you read this line, remember not   5
The hand that writ it; for I love you so,
That I in your sweet thoughts would be forgot,
If thinking on me then should make you woe.
Oh, if, (I say,) you look upon this verse
When I (perhaps) compounded am with clay,   10
Do not so much as my poor name rehearse,
But let your love even with my life decay;
     Lest the wise world should look into your moan,
     And mock you with me after I am gone.

1609

73

That time of year thou mayst in me behold
When yellow leaves, or none, or few, do hang
Upon those boughs which shake against the cold,
Bare ruined choirs, where late the sweet birds sang.
In me thou seest the twilight of such day   5
As after sunset fadeth in the west;
Which by and by black night doth take away,
Death's second self that seals up all in rest.
In me thou seest the glowing of such fire,
That on the ashes of his youth doth lie,   10
As the deathbed whereon it must expire,
Consumed with that which it was nourished by.[1]
     This thou perceiv'st, which makes thy love more strong,
     To love that well, which thou must leave ere long.

1609

87

Farewell: thou art too dear[1] for my possessing,
And like enough thou know'st thy estimate.[2]
The charter[3] of thy worth gives thee releasing;
My bonds in thee are all determinate.[4]
For how do I hold thee but by thy granting,   5
And for that riches where is my deserving?
The cause of this fair gift in me is wanting,
And so my patent[5] back again is swerving.

1. Choked by the ashes of that which once nourished its flame.
1. Expensive, beloved.
2. Value.

3. Deed, contract for property.
4. Expired.
5. Title.

Thy self thou gav'st, thy own worth then not knowing,
Or me, to whom thou gav'st it, else mistaking;   10
So thy great gift, upon misprision[6] growing,
Comes home again, on better judgment making.
 Thus have I had thee as a dream doth flatter,
 In sleep a king, but waking no such matter.

1609

94

They that have power to hurt and will do none,
That do not do the thing they most do show,[1]
Who, moving others, are themselves as stone,
Unmovèd, cold, and to temptation slow;
They rightly do inherit heaven's graces   5
And husband nature's riches from expense;[2]
They are the lords and owners of their faces,
Others but stewards of their excellence.
The summer's flower is to the summer sweet,
Though to itself it only live and die,   10
But if that flower with base infection meet,
The basest weed outbraves[3] his dignity:
 For sweetest things turn sourest by their deeds;
 Lilies that fester smell far worse than weeds.[4]

1609

97

How like a winter hath my absence been
From thee, the pleasure of the fleeting year!
What freezings have I felt, what dark days seen!
What old December's bareness everywhere!
And yet this time removed was summer's time,   5
The teeming autumn, big with rich increase,
Bearing the wanton burthen of the prime,[1]
Like widowed wombs after their lords' decease;
Yet this abundant issue seemed to me
But hope of orphans and unfathered fruit;   10
For summer and his pleasures wait on thee,
And, thou away, the very birds are mute;

---

6. Mistake, oversight.
1. Seem to do.
2. I.e., they do not squander nature's gifts.
3. Surpasses. Gerard's *Herbal* (1597) says "the lilies of the field outbraved him."

4. This line appears in *Edward III* (2.1.451), an apocryphal Shakespearean play licensed Dec. 1, 1595.
1. Spring, which has engendered the lavish crop ("wanton burthen") that autumn is now left to bear.

Or, if they sing, 'tis with so dull a cheer[2]
That leaves look pale, dreading the winter's near.

1609

106

When in the chronicle of wasted[1] time
I see descriptions of the fairest wights,[2]
And beauty making beautiful old rhyme
In praise of ladies dead and lovely knights,
Then, in the blazon[3] of sweet beauty's best,   5
Of hand, of foot, of lip, of eye, of brow,
I see their antique pen would have expressed
Even such a beauty as you master now.
So all their praises are but prophecies
Of this our time, all you prefiguring;   10
And, for they looked but with divining eyes,[4]
They had not skill enough your worth to sing:
   For we, which now behold these present days,
   Have eyes to wonder, but lack tongues to praise.

1609

107

Not mine own fears, nor the prophetic soul
Of the wide world dreaming on things to come,[1]
Can yet the lease of my true love control,
Supposed as forfeit to a confinèd doom.[2]
The mortal moon hath her eclipse endured,   5
And the sad augurs mock their own presage;[3]
Incertainties now crown themselves assured,
And peace[4] proclaims olives of endless age.
Now with the drops of this most balmy time
My love looks fresh, and death to me subscribes,[5]   10
Since, spite of him, I'll live in this poor rhyme,
While he insults o'er dull and speechless tribes:

---

2. Disposition.
1. Past.
2. Persons.
3. Display.
4. Because ("for") they were able *only* ("but") to foresee prophetically.
1. This sonnet refers to contemporary events and the prophecies, common in Elizabethan almanacs, of disaster.
2. I.e., can yet put an end to my love, which I thought doomed to early forfeiture.

3. The "mortal moon" is Queen Elizabeth; her "eclipse" is probably her climacteric year, her 63rd (thought meaningful because the product of two "significant" numbers, 7 and 9), which ended in September 1596. The sober astrologers ("sad augurs") now ridicule their own predictions ("presage") of catastrophe, since they turned out to be false.
4. Probably an agreement between Henry IV of France and Elizabeth.
5. Submits.

And thou in this shalt find thy monument,
When tyrants' crests and tombs of brass are spent.[6]

1609

116

Let me not to the marriage of true minds
Admit impediments;[1] love is not love
Which alters when it alteration finds,
Or bends with the remover to remove:
O, no, it is an ever-fixèd mark,[2]   5
That looks on tempests and is never shaken;
It is the star to every wand'ring bark,
Whose worth's unknown, although his highth[3] be taken.
Love's not Time's fool,[4] though rosy lips and cheeks
Within his[5] bending sickle's compass come;   10
Love alters not with his brief hours and weeks,
But bears it out even to the edge of doom.[6]
   If this be error and upon me proved,
   I never writ, nor no man ever loved.

1609

126

O thou, my lovely boy, who in thy power
Dost hold Time's fickle glass,[1] his sickle, hour;
Who hast by waning grown and therein show'st
Thy lovers withering as thy sweet self grow'st;
If Nature (sovereign mistress over wrack)[2]   5
As thou goest onwards still will pluck thee back,
She keeps thee to this purpose, that her skill
May Time disgrace and wretched minutes kill.
Yet fear her, O thou minion[3] of her pleasure,
She may detain, but not still[4] keep, her treasure!   10
Her audit[5] (though delayed) answered must be,
And her quietus is to render[6] thee.

1609

6. Wasted away.
1. From the Marriage Service: "If any of you know cause or just impediment why these persons should not be joined together . . ."
2. Sea-mark (cf. "landmark").
3. The star's value is not known, though the star's "highth" (altitude) may be known and used for practical investigation.
4. I.e., slave or victim.
5. I.e., Time's (as also in line 11).

6. Brink of the Last Judgment.
1. (1) Mirror, fickle because as the subject ages the mirror reflects a changed image, (2) an hour glass.
2. Destruction, ruin.
3. Darling.
4. Always, forever.
5. Accounting.
6. Surrender; "quietus": settlement.

128

How oft when thou, my music, music play'st
Upon that blessèd wood[1] whose motion sounds
With thy sweet fingers when thou gently sway'st[2]
The wiry concord that mine ear confounds,[3]
Do I envý those jacks[4] that nimble leap   5
To kiss the tender inward of thy hand,
Whilst my poor lips, which should that harvest reap,
At the wood's boldness by thee blushing stand.
To be so tickled they would change their state
And situation[5] with those dancing chips,   10
O'er whom thy fingers walk with gentle gait,
Making dead wood more blessed than living lips.
    Since saucy jacks[6] so happy are in this,
    Give them thy fingers, me thy lips to kiss.

1609

129

Th' expense of spirit in a waste of shame
Is lust in action;[1] and till action, lust
Is perjured, murd'rous, bloody, full of blame,
Savage, extreme, rude, cruel, not to trust;
Enjoyed no sooner but despisèd straight: 5
Past reason hunted; and no sooner had,
Past reason hated, as a swallowed bait,
On purpose laid to make the taker mad:
Mad in pursuit, and in possession so;
Had, having, and in quest to have, extreme;   10
A bliss in proof[2] and proved, a very woe;
Before, a joy proposed; behind, a dream.
    All this the world well knows; yet none knows well
    To shun the heaven that leads men to this hell.

1609

130

My mistress' eyes are nothing like the sun;[1]
Coral is far more red than her lips' red;

---

1. Keys of the spinet or virginal.
2. Governest.
3. The harmony from the strings which overcomes my ear with delight.
4. I.e., keys (actually, "jacks" are the plectra which pluck the strings when activated by the keys).
5. Physical location; "state": place in the order of things.
6. With a quibble on the sense "impertinent fellows."

1. The word order here is inverted and slightly obscures the meaning. Lust, when put into action, expends "spirit" (life, vitality) in a "waste" (desert, with a possible pun on "waist," also) of shame.
2. A bliss during the experience.
1. An anti-Petrarchan sonnet. All of the details commonly attributed by other Elizabethan sonneteers to their ladies are here denied to the poet's mistress.

If snow be white, why then her breasts are dun;
If hairs be wires, black wires grow on her head.
I have seen roses damasked,[2] red and white,   5
But no such roses see I in her cheeks;
And in some perfumes is there more delight
Than in the breath that from my mistress reeks.
I love to hear her speak, yet well I know
That music hath a far more pleasing sound;   10
I grant I never saw a goddess go;[3]
My mistress, when she walks, treads on the ground.
    And yet, by heaven, I think my love as rare[4]
    As any she belied[5] with false compare.

                                                        1609

135

Whoever hath her wish, thou hast thy *Will*,[1]
And *Will* to boot, and *Will* in overplus;
More than enough am I that vex thee still,
To thy sweet will making addition thus.
Wilt thou, whose will is large and spacious,   5
Not once vouchsafe to hide my will in thine?
Shall will in others seem right gracious,
And in my will no fair acceptance shine?
The sea, all water, yet receives rain still,
And in abundance addeth to his store,[2]   10
So thou being rich in *Will* add to thy *Will*
One will of mine to make thy large Will more.
    Let no unkind, no fair beseechers kill;[3]
    Think all but one, and me in that one *Will*.

                                                        1609

138

When my love swears that she is made of truth,
I do believe her, though I know she lies,
That she might think me some untutored youth,
Unlearnèd in the world's false subtleties.
Thus vainly thinking that she thinks me young,   5
Although she knows my days are past the best,[1]

2. Variegated. The damask rose (supposedly from
Damascus, originally) is pink.
3. Walk.
4. Admirable, extraordinary.
5. Misrepresented.
1. (1) Wishes, (2) carnal desire, (3) the male and
female sexual organs, (4) one or more persons
named Will. This is one of 3, possibly 4, sonnets

punning on the word.
2. Plenty.
3. I.e., do not kill with unkindness any of your
wooers.
1. Shakespeare was 35 or younger when he wrote
this sonnet (it first appeared in *The Passionate Pilgrim*, 1599). "Simply": like a simpleton.

Simply I credit her false-speaking tongue:
On both sides thus is simple truth suppressed.
But wherefore says she not she is unjust?[2]
And wherefore say not I that I am old?   10
Oh, love's best habit[3] is in seeming trust,
And age in love loves not to have years told.
    Therefore I lie with her and she with me,
    And in our faults by lies we flattered be.

                                  1599, 1609

144

Two loves I have of comfort and despair,
Which like two spirits do suggest me still:[1]
The better angel is a man right fair,
The worser spirit a woman, colored ill.[2]
To win me soon to hell, my female evil   5
Tempteth my better angel from my side,
And would corrupt my saint to be a devil,
Wooing his purity with her foul pride.
And whether that my angel be turned fiend
Suspect I may, yet not directly tell;   10
But being both from[3] me, both to each friend,
I guess one angel in another's hell.
    Yet this shall I ne'er know, but live in doubt,
    Till my bad angel fire[4] my good one out.

                                  1599, 1609

146

Poor soul, the center of my sinful earth,
Lord of[1] these rebel powers that thee array,[2]
Why dost thou pine within and suffer dearth,
Painting thy outward walls so costly gay?
Why so large cost, having so short a lease,   5
Dost thou upon thy fading mansion spend?
Shall worms, inheritors of this excess,
Eat up thy charge? Is this thy body's end?
Then, soul, live thou upon thy servant's loss,
And let that pine to aggravate thy store;[3]   10

2. Unfaithful.
3. Appearance, deportment.
1. Tempt me constantly.
2. Dark.
3. Away from; "each": each other.
4. Drive out by fire.
1. An emendation. The Quarto repeats the last 3

words of line 1. Other suggestions are "Thrall to,"
"Starved by," "Pressed by," and leaving the repetition but dropping "that thee" in line 2.
2. Dress out, often used in a military sense.
3. Let "that" (i.e., the body) deteriorate to increase
("aggravate") the soul's riches ("thy store").

Buy terms[4] divine in selling hours of dross;
Within be fed, without be rich no more.
    So shalt thou feed on death, that feeds on men,
    And death once dead, there's no more dying then.

1609

147

My love is as a fever, longing still[1]
For that which longer nurseth[2] the disease,
Feeding on that which doth preserve the ill,[3]
Th' uncertain sickly appetite[4] to please.
My reason, the physician to my love,   5
Angry that his prescriptions are not kept,
Hath left me, and I desperate now approve
Desire is death, which physic did except.[5]
Past cure I am, now reason is past care,[6]
And frantic mad with evermore unrest;   10
My thoughts and my discourse as madmen's are,
At random from the truth vainly expressed;[7]
    For I have sworn thee fair, and thought thee bright,
    Who art as black as hell, as dark as night.

1609

1 Henry IV   The title page of the first quarto edition of Shakespeare's
1 Henry IV, published in 1598, reads: "THE HISTORY OF HENRIE THE FOURTH;
With the battell at Shrewsburie, *betweene the King and Lord* Henry Percy,
surnamed Henrie Hotspur of the North. *With the humorous conceits of Sir*
John Falstalffe." It had been performed on the stage and at court before
publication, and from that time to this it has remained one of Shakespeare's
most popular plays.

Shakespeare had already inaugurated a new dramatic type by writing four
plays dealing with fairly recent English history, and had then gone back to
a period two centuries earlier to portray, in *Richard II*, the downfall of the
weak, effeminate, and poetic young King Richard ("that sweet lovely rose,"
as he is called in this play) at the hands of the hard, efficient Bullingbrook,
who came to the throne as Henry IV. Before this seizure of the crown there
had been a prophecy, put by Shakespeare into the mouth of the bishop of
Carlisle in *Richard II* (4.1.136–44), of the dire consequences to follow:

        And if you crown him, let me prophesy,
        The blood of English shall manure the ground

---

4. Long periods; "dross": refuse, rubbish.
1. Continually.
2. (1) Nourishes, (2) takes care of.
3. Maintain the illness.
4. (1) Desire for food, (2) lust.

5. I.e., learn by experience, that desire, which
medicine forbade, is death.
6. I.e., medical care (of me). The line is a version
of the proverb "past cure, past care."
7. Wide of the mark and senselessly uttered.

And future ages groan for this foul act;
Peace shall go sleep with Turks and infidels,
And in this seat of peace tumultuous wars
Shall kin with kin and kind with kind confound;
Disorder, horror, fear, and mutiny
Shall here inhabit, and this land be called
The field of Golgotha and dead men's skulls.

Shakespeare drew his historical material from the prose chronicle histories, specifically Raphael Holinshed's *Chronicles of England, Scotland, and Ireland*, Samuel Daniel's historical poem *Civil Wars*, and an earlier play, either the popular farcical piece called *The Famous Victories of Henry V* or a lost play which was its source. His sources gave him the portrait of a madcap and reckless Prince of Wales and his roistering companions. Chief of these was a fat knight, Sir John Oldcastle; Shakespeare at first used this name, but later, because of protests from the descendants of that Protestant martyr, changed the name to Sir John Falstaff. This character, whose "humorous conceits" are advertised on the title page, is one of the greatest comic creations in all literature. Shakespeare continued to exploit his inexhaustible exuberance through a sequel, *The Second Part of Henry IV*, and a comedy of middle-class life, supposed to have been written at Queen Elizabeth's command, *The Merry Wives of Windsor*.

The ominous wars of Carlisle's prophecy could thus be mixed with hilarious fooling, but *1 Henry IV* succeeds, not only as a comedy, but as a serious play about character and history. The real hero is not King Henry IV, nor the fat Falstaff, but Prince Hal, the handsome playboy who in time of crisis reforms and saves his father's throne. He is the prince who later became Henry V, the English national hero who reconquered France.

Shakespeare's theme in all his history plays is the importance of order and degree, of the disruptive effects of civil strife and rebellion. But as he matured as a dramatist (and *1 Henry IV* stands at the beginning of his great period of maturity), he found character to be more interesting than the philosophy or events of history. How to demonstrate the kind of character that would make the English national hero was his problem, and he solved it by a method of comparison and contrast, utilizing four men of different types. At one extreme is Falstaff, who loves to eat, drink, joke, and dramatize himself, and to whom anything as intangible as honor is a mere word, a breath of air. Opposite in every way is Hotspur, fiery and impatient, completely ambitious for honor and fame, scornful of the soft, civilized arts of poetry and music, a hardheaded fanatic. A third type is the wild Welshman Glendower, a believer in magic and a practitioner of it, an accomplished poet yet a valiant, if superstitious, warrior, and an egotist like his ally Hotspur. Finally there is Prince Hal, whose sense of humor rivals Falstaff's, but who turns out to be the match for Hotspur in valor and his superior in knightly courtesy. It is worth noting that Shakespeare changed history in order to make this dramatic contrast: in Holinshed's *Chronicle* Hotspur is older than Prince Hal's father, but Shakespeare makes Hal and Hotspur contemporaries. It is in the excesses of the other three that we see the merits of the Prince's character illuminated. The four characters represent not only men but ways of life. And these ways of life are all relevant to fundamental questions about social and political responsibility, honor, and loyalty to a cause.

Some background in fifteenth-century English history, as Shakespeare understood it, is needed if we are to respond readily to the play. Henry Hereford, called Bullingbrook, was in exile in France when his father, John of Gaunt, died. He returned to England to claim his inheritance, and profited from the aid of the Percy family, powerful nobles in the north. The two brothers, Henry Percy, earl of Northumberland, and Thomas Percy, earl of Worcester, together with Northumberland's son Henry (called Hotspur) received Bullingbrook's oath at Doncaster (see 5.1.32–58) to seize only his inheritance. But King Richard II was in Ireland fighting, having named Edmund Mortimer, earl of March, his successor if he did not return. In the confused situation in England, Bullingbrook was able to collect enough power so that on Richard's return he could force him to abdicate and then have him killed in prison. Various troubles on the borders made the throne of the new king (Henry IV) insecure. Hotspur managed to defeat the Scots under Douglas at Holmedon (see 1.1.62–75) and took many important prisoners. But Mortimer, in fighting against Glendower in Wales, was taken captive and married Glendower's daughter. Henry IV refused to ransom Mortimer, and the indignation of Mortimer's brother-in-law, Hotspur, led him to refuse to turn over his prisoners to the king. So came the conspiracy into being— and such a formidable opposition as that of the Percies, Douglas, Glendower, and certain disaffected churchmen like the archbishop of York meant a critical danger to Henry's throne. The Battle of Shrewsbury, the climax of this play, decides the conflict.

Much critical comment has been devoted to the character of Falstaff. He has certain resemblances to the traditional *miles gloriosus* (braggart soldier) of Latin comedy, but he far transcends the type; he sometimes resembles the Vice, a comic character in the old morality plays, who is usually an allegorical personification of extreme self-indulgence or of a particular sin; and he often uses, or parodies, the language of the Puritans. Critics differ on whether Falstaff is really a coward or not, and on the question of how much he expects his lies to be believed. But everyone agrees about his inexhaustible vitality and resilience. It is not surprising that he, like other immortal characters in literature, remains something of a mystery.

The First Part of
King Henry the Fourth

Dramatis Personae

KING HENRY THE FOURTH
HENRY, *Prince of Wales*
PRINCE JOHN OF LANCASTER } *Sons to the* KING
EARL OF WESTMORELAND
SIR WALTER BLUNT
THOMAS PERCY, *Earl of Worcester*
HENRY PERCY, *Earl of Northumberland*
HENRY PERCY, *surnamed* HOTSPUR, *his son*
EDMUND MORTIMER, *Earl of March*
RICHARD SCROOP, *Archbishop of York*
ARCHIBALD, *Earl of Douglas*
OWEN GLENDOWER

SIR RICHARD VERNON
SIR MICHAEL, *a friend to the* ARCHBISHOP OF YORK
SIR JOHN FALSTAFF
POINS
GADSHILL
PETO
BARDOLPH
LADY PERCY, *wife to* HOTSPUR, *and sister to* MORTIMER
LADY MORTIMER, *daughter to* GLENDOWER, *and wife to* MORTIMER
MISTRESS QUICKLY, *hostess of a tavern in Eastcheap*
LORDS, OFFICERS, SHERIFF, VINTNER, CHAMBERLAIN, DRAWERS, *two* CAR-
RIERS, TRAVELERS, *and* ATTENDANTS

Act 1

SCENE 1

[*Enter the* KING, PRINCE JOHN OF LANCASTER, THE EARL OF WEST-
MORELAND, SIR WALTER BLUNT, *with others.*]

KING. So shaken as we are, so wan with care,
Find we a time for frighted peace to pant,[1]
And breathe short-winded accents of new broils[2]
To be commenced in stronds afar remote.
No more the thirsty entrance[3] of this soil   5
Shall daub her lips with her own children's blood;
No more shall trenching war channel her fields,
Nor bruise her flow'rets with the armèd hoofs
Of hostile paces:[4] those opposèd eyes,
Which, like the meteors of a troubled heaven,   10
All of one nature, of one substance bred,
Did lately meet in the intestine shock[5]
And furious close of civil butchery,
Shall now, in mutual well-beseeming ranks,
March all one way and be no more opposed   15
Against acquaintance, kindred, and allies.
The edge of war, like an ill-sheathèd knife,
No more shall cut his master: Therefore, friends,
As far as to the sepulchre of Christ,—
Whose soldier now, under whose blessèd cross   20
We are impressèd and engaged to fight,
Forthwith a power[6] of English shall we levy,
Whose arms were molded in their mother's womb
To chase these pagans in those holy fields
Over whose acres walked those blessèd feet   25
Which fourteen hundred years ago were nailed
For our advantage on the bitter cross.
But this our purpose now is twelve month old,

1. I.e., let us allow peace to catch her breath.
2. I.e., news of new wars; "stronds": strands,
regions.
3. Surface.

4. The tread of war horses.
5. Internal violence; "close": encounter.
6. Army. He is planning a crusade, in expiation
of his guilt for the death of Richard II.

And bootless[7] 'tis to tell you we will go.
Therefore we meet not now.[8] Then let me hear   30
Of you, my gentle cousin Westmoreland,
What yesternight our Council did decree
In forwarding this dear expedience.[9]

WEST. My liege, this haste was hot in question,[1]
And many limits of the charge set down   35
But yesternight, when all athwart[2] there came
A post from Wales loaden with heavy news,
Whose worst was that the noble Mortimer,
Leading the men of Herefordshire to fight
Against the irregular[3] and wild Glendower,   40
Was by the rude hands of that Welshman taken,
A thousand of his people butcherèd,
Upon whose dead corpse[4] there was such misuse,
Such beastly shameless transformatiòn,
By those Welshwomen done as may not be   45
Without much shame retold or spoken of.

KING. It seems then that the tidings of this broil
Brake off our business for the Holy Land.

WEST. This matched with other did, my gracious lord,
For more uneven and unwelcome news   50
Came from the north, and thus it did import:
On Holyrood Day[5] the gallant Hotspur there,
Young Harry Percy, and brave Archibald,
That ever-valiant and approvèd Scot,
At Holmedon met,   55
Where they did spend a sad and bloody hour;
As by discharge of their artillery,
And shape of likelihood,[6] the news was told;
For he that brought them[7] in the very heat
And pride of their contention did take horse,   60
Uncertain of the issue any way.

KING. Here is a dear, a true industrious friend,
Sir Walter Blunt, new lighted from his horse,
Stained with the variation of each soil
Betwixt that Holmedon and this seat of ours;   65
And he hath brought us smooth and welcome news.
The Earl of Douglas is discomfited;
Ten thousand bold Scots, two and twenty knights
Balked[8] in their own blood did Sir Walter see
On Holmedon's plains. Of prisoners Hotspur took   70
Mordake Earl of Fife, and eldest son
To beaten Douglas, and the Earl of Athol,

---

7. Useless.
8. I.e., that is not the reason for our present meeting. "Cousin": kinsman.
9. Important, urgent matter.
1. Actively discussed. "Limits of the charge": assignment of commands.
2. Interrupting, crossing our purpose. "Post": messenger.

3. Guerrilla.
4. Bodies.
5. Holy Cross Day (September 14).
6. Probable inference. "As": since.
7. I.e., the news (usually a plural in Shakespeare). "Pride": height; literally, the top of a falcon's flight.
8. Heaped.

Of Murray, Angus, and Menteith;
And is not this an honorable spoil,
A gallant prize? Ha, cousin, is it not?   75
WEST. In faith,
    It is a conquest for a prince to boast of.
KING. Yea, there thou mak'st me sad and mak'st me sin
    In envy that my Lord Northumberland
    Should be the father to so blest a son,   80
    A son who is the theme of honor's tongue,
    Amongst a grove the very straightest plant,
    Who is sweet Fortune's minion[9] and her pride;
    Whilst I, by looking on the praise of him,
    See riot and dishonor stain the brow   85
    Of my young Harry. O that it could be proved
    That some night-tripping fairy had exchanged
    In cradle-clothes our children where they lay,
    And called mine Percy, his Plantagenet!
    Then would I have his Harry, and he mine.   90
    But let him from my thoughts. What think you, coz,
    Of this young Percy's pride? The prisoners
    Which he in this adventure hath surprised
    To his own use he keeps, and sends me word
    I shall have none but Mordake Earl of Fife.   95
WEST. This is his uncle's teaching, this is Worcester,
    Malevolent to you in all aspects,[1]
    Which makes him prune himself,[2] and bristle up
    The crest of youth against your dignity.
KING. But I have sent for him to answer this;   100
    And for this cause awhile we must neglect
    Our holy purpose to Jerusalem.
    Cousin, on Wednesday next our council we
    Will hold at Windsor, so inform the lords;
    But come yourself with speed to us again,   105
    For more is to be said and to be done
    Than out of anger can be utterèd.
WEST. I will, my liege.   [Exeunt.]

SCENE 2

[Enter HENRY, PRINCE OF WALES, and SIR JOHN FALSTAFF.]

FAL. Now Hal, what time of day is it, lad?
PRINCE. Thou art so fat-witted with drinking of old sack,[3] and
    unbuttoning thee after supper, and sleeping upon benches after
    noon, that thou hast forgotten to demand that truly which thou
    wouldst truly know. What a devil hast thou to do with the time   5
    of the day? Unless hours were cups of sack, and minutes capons,
    and clocks the tongues of bawds, and dials the signs of leaping-

---

9. Favorite.
1. Hostile in every way. The figure is from astrology.

2. Plume himself. "Bristle up" and "crest" continue the image, which is that of a fighting cock.
3. Sherry.

houses,[4] and the blessed sun himself a fair hot wench in flame-
colored taffeta, I see no reason why thou shouldst be so superfluous to demand the time of the day.   10

FAL. Indeed you come near me now, Hal, for we that take purses
go by the moon and the seven stars, and not by Phoebus,[5] he,
"that wandering knight so fair." And I prithee, sweet wag, when
thou art king, as, God save thy grace—majesty I should say, for
grace[6] thou wilt have none—   15

PRINCE. What, none?

FAL. No, by my troth, not so much as will serve to be prologue to
an egg and butter.

PRINCE. Well, how then? come, roundly, roundly.[7]

FAL. Marry then, sweet wag, when thou art king, let not us that are   20
squires of the night's body[8] be called thieves of the day's beauty;
let us be Diana's foresters, gentlemen of the shade, minions of
the moon; and let men say we be men of good government,
being governed as the sea is, by our noble and chaste mistress the
moon, under whose countenance we steal.   25

PRINCE. Thou sayest well, and it holds well too, for the fortune of
us that are the moon's men doth ebb and flow like the sea, being
governed as the sea is by the moon. As for proof now: a purse of
gold most resolutely snatched on Monday night and most disso-
lutely spent on Tuesday morning, got with swearing "Lay by"   30
and spent with crying "Bring in," now in as low an ebb as the
foot of the ladder and by and by in as high a flow as the ridge of
the gallows.[9]

FAL. By the Lord thou sayest true, lad. And is not my hostess of the
tavern a most sweet wench?   35

PRINCE. As the honey of Hybla,[1] my old lad of the castle. And is
not a buff jerkin a most sweet robe of durance?[2]

FAL. How now, how now, mad wag! what, in thy quips and thy
quiddities?[3] what a plague have I to do with a buff jerkin?

PRINCE. Why, what a pox have I to do with my hostess of the tav-   40
ern?

FAL. Well, thou hast called her to a reckoning many a time and oft.

PRINCE. Did I ever call for thee to pay thy part?

FAL. No, I'll give thee thy due, thou hast paid all there.

PRINCE. Yea, and elsewhere, so far as my coin would stretch, and   45
where it would not I have used my credit.

FAL. Yea, and so used it that were it not here apparent that thou art

---

4. Whorehouses.

5. The sun. Falstaff then quotes from a popular
ballad.

6. A triple pun: (1) "your Grace," the correct
manner of addressing a prince or duke; (2) the divine
influence which produces sanctity; and (3) a short
prayer before a meal—hence Falstaff's allusion to
"egg and butter," a common hasty breakfast.

7. Plainly.

8. Two puns are involved: a "squire of the body"
was an attendant on a knight, and "body" would
be pronounced *bawdy*. "Beauty" also puns with
"booty" (which thieves take); Diana is, of course,

the moon goddess.

9. "Lay by": i.e., hand over (a robber's command
to his victim); "bring in": a customer's command
for more drink at a tavern. The "foot of the ladder"
is at the bottom of the gallows (robbery was a hanging offense); the "ridge" is the crosspiece at the top.

1. A town in Sicily, famous for honey; "old lad of
the castle" is a reference to Falstaff's original name,
Oldcastle.

2. A "buff jerkin" was the leather jacket worn by
a sheriff's sergeant; "durance" is a pun: (1) lasting
quality and (2) imprisonment.

3. Quibbles.

heir apparent[4]—but I prithee, sweet wag, shall there be gallows standing in England when thou art king? and resolution thus fobbed as it is with the rusty curb of old father antic the law?[5] Do   50
not thou, when thou art king, hang a thief.

PRINCE. No, thou shalt.

FAL. Shall I? O rare! By the Lord, I'll be a brave judge.

PRINCE. Thou judgest false already; I mean thou shalt have the hanging of the thieves and so become a rare hangman.   55

FAL. Well, Hal, well; and in some sort it jumps with my humor[6] as well as waiting in the court, I can tell you.

PRINCE. For obtaining of suits?[7]

FAL. Yea, for obtaining of suits, whereof the hangman hath no lean wardrobe. 'Sblood,[8] I am as melancholy as a gib cat or a lugged   60
bear.

PRINCE. Or an old lion, or a lover's lute.

FAL. Yea, or the drone of a Lincolnshire bagpipe.

PRINCE. What sayest thou to a hare, or the melancholy of Moorditch?[9]   65

FAL. Thou hast the most unsavory similes and art indeed the most comparative,[1] rascalliest, sweet young prince. But Hal, I prithee, trouble me no more with vanity. I would to God thou and I knew where a commodity of good names were to be bought. An old lord of the council rated[2] me the other day in the street about   70
you, sir, but I marked him not; and yet he talked very wisely, but I regarded him not; and yet he talked wisely, and in the street too.

PRINCE. Thou didst well, for wisdom cries out in the streets and no man regards it.[3]   75

FAL. O, thou hast damnable iteration[4] and art indeed able to corrupt a saint. Thou hast done much harm upon me, Hal, God forgive thee for it! Before I knew thee, Hal, I knew nothing, and now am I, if a man should speak truly, little better than one of the wicked. I must give over this life, and I will give it over; by   80
the Lord, an[5] I do not, I am a villain; I'll be damned for never a king's son in Christendom.

PRINCE. Where shall we take a purse tomorrow, Jack?

FAL. Zounds, where thou wilt, lad; I'll make one; an I do not, call me villain and baffle[6] me.   85

PRINCE. I see a good amendment of life in thee—from praying to purse-taking.

---

4. "Here" and "heir" would pun in Elizabethan pronunciation.
5. "Resolution": bravery; "fobbed": cheated; "antic": a clown.
6. I.e., agrees with my disposition.
7. Special favors, but "clothing" in the next line. The hangman was given the clothes of his victims.
8. God's blood, a common oath. "Gib cat": tomcat; "lugged": baited (in the bear-baiting pits a bear was attacked by dogs as a public amusement).
9. The "hare" was traditionally associated with melancholy; Moorditch was a foul-smelling ditch

on the outskirts of London.
1. Affecting wit, dealing in comparisons.
2. Scolded, berated.
3. Prince Hal is quoting Proverbs 1.20 and 24.
4. Repetition, especially of sacred texts.
5. If.
6. A knight in the days of chivalry was "baffled" or disgraced by having his shield hung upside down. Falstaff may mean "hang me up by the heels." "Zounds": a common oath, a contraction of "by God's wounds" (i.e., Jesus's wounds on the Cross).

FAL. Why, Hal, 'tis my vocation,[7] Hal; 'tis no sin for a man to labor in his vocation.

[*Enter* POINS.]

Poins! Now shall we know if Gadshill[8] have set a match. O, if men were to be saved by merit, what hole in hell were hot enough for him? This is the most omnipotent villain that ever cried "stand" to a true man.   90

PRINCE. Good morrow, Ned.

POINS. Good morrow, sweet Hal. What says Monsieur Remorse? what says Sir John Sack and Sugar? Jack! how agrees the devil and thee about thy soul, that thou soldest him on Good Friday last for a cup of Madeira and a cold capon's leg?   95

PRINCE. Sir John stands to his word; the devil shall have his bargain, for he was never yet a breaker of proverbs; he will give the devil his due.   100

POINS. Then art thou damned for keeping thy word with the devil.

PRINCE. Else he had been damned for cozening[9] the devil.

POINS. But my lads, my lads, tomorrow morning by four o'clock, early at Gadshill, there are pilgrims going to Canterbury with rich offerings, and traders riding to London with fat purses. I have vizards[1] for you all, you have horses for yourselves; Gadshill lies tonight in Rochester; I have bespoke supper tomorrow night in Eastcheap; we may do it as secure as sleep. If you will go, I will stuff your purses full of crowns; if you will not, tarry at home and be hanged.   105   110

FAL. Hear ye, Yedward, if I tarry at home and go not, I'll hang you for going.

POINS. You will, chops?[2]

FAL. Hal, wilt thou make one?   115

PRINCE. Who, I rob? I a thief? not I, by my faith.

FAL. There's neither honesty, manhood, nor good fellowship in thee, nor thou camest not of the blood royal,[3] if thou darest not stand for ten shillings.

PRINCE. Well then, once in my days I'll be a madcap.   120

FAL. Why, that's well said.

PRINCE. Well, come what will, I'll tarry at home.

FAL. By the Lord, I'll be a traitor then, when thou art king.

PRINCE. I care not.

POINS. Sir John, I prithee leave the prince and me alone; I will lay him down such reasons for this adventure that he shall go.   125

FAL. Well, God give thee the spirit of persuasion and him the ears of profiting, that what thou speakest may move and what he hears may be believed, that the true prince may (for recreation sake)

---

7. Falstaff is here making fun of the Puritan doctrine of "calling" or vocation, based on the parable of the talents (see Matthew 25.25 ff.).
8. Gadshill is both a man and a place: the place is a hill 27 miles from London on the road to Rochester; it was notorious for robberies. The man, so called from the place, is the thieves' "setter," who arranges when and where the robbery will occur.
9. Cheating.
1. Masks.
2. Fat face.
3. A pun: the coin called a "royal" was worth 10 shillings. "Stand for" also puns: it means both "represent" and "fight for."

prove a false thief; for the poor abuses of the time want counte-   130
nance.[4] Farewell; you shall find me in Eastcheap.
PRINCE. Farewell, thou latter spring, farewell, Allhallown summer![5]

    [⟨*Exit* FALSTAFF.⟩][6]

POINS. Now, my good sweet honey lord, ride with us tomorrow; I
have a jest to execute that I cannot manage alone. Falstaff, Bar-   135
dolph, Peto, and Gadshill shall rob those men that we have already
waylaid;[7] yourself and I will not be there, and when they have
the booty, if you and I do not rob them, cut this head off from
my shoulders.
PRINCE. How shall we part with them in setting forth?   140
POINS. Why, we will set forth before or after them, and appoint
them a place of meeting, wherein it is at our pleasure to fail, and
then will they adventure upon the exploit themselves, which they
shall have no sooner achieved but we'll set upon them.
PRINCE. Yea, but 'tis like that they will know us by our horses,   145
by our habits,[8] and by every other appointment to be ourselves.
POINS. Tut, our horses they shall not see—I'll tie them in the wood;
our vizards we will change after we leave them: and, sirrah, I
have cases of buckram for the nonce,[9] to immask our noted outward garments.   150
PRINCE. Yea, but I doubt[1] they will be too hard for us.
POINS. Well, for two of them, I know them to be as true-bred cowards as ever turned back; and for the third, if he fight longer than
he sees reason, I'll forswear arms. The virtue of this jest will be
the incomprehensible lies that this same fat rogue will tell us   155
when we meet at supper: how thirty at least he fought with; what
wards,[2] what blows, what extremities he endured; and in the
reproof[3] of this lies the jest.
PRINCE. Well, I'll go with thee. Provide us all things necessary and
meet me tomorrow night[4] in Eastcheap; there I'll sup. Farewell.   160
POINS. Farewell, my lord.   [*Exit* POINS.]
PRINCE. I know you all, and will awhile uphold
    The unyoked humor[5] of your idleness;
    Yet herein will I imitate the sun,

---

4. A satirical reference to the common complaint that the nobility did not properly give "counte-nance" to (i.e., encourage) good causes, and to the Puritan habit of attacking the "abuses of the time." This entire speech parodies the language of the Puritans.
5. I.e., Indian summer. The 2 epithets are intended to suggest how unseasonable it is for Falstaff, an old man, to be engaged in youthful, hoodlum exploits.
6. This stage direction, like some others in the play, does not appear in the earliest editions; it was added by a later editor. All such interpolated directions are indicated in our text by the special brackets used here.
7. Set an ambush for.
8. Clothes.

9. I.e., outer clothes (of a coarse, stiff cloth) for the occasion.
1. Suspect.
2. Guards in fencing.
3. Disproof.
4. Either the text should read "tonight" (before the robbery) or else Shakespeare intends to show Prince Hal's mind intent, not on the robbery, but on its aftermath. The soliloquy of the Prince that follows has provoked much critical discussion. Read psychologically, it makes Hal seem like a prig and a self-conscious schemer, but this surely was not Shakespeare's intention. Rather, the speech belongs to the old dramatic convention in which the speaker steps out of character for a moment to deliver a message from the playwright to the audience.
5. Undisciplined whim.

Who doth permit the base contagious clouds   165
To smother up his beauty from the world,
That, when he please again to be himself,
Being wanted, he may be more wondered at
By breaking through the foul and ugly mists
Of vapors that did seem to strangle him.   170
If all the year were playing holidays,
To sport would be as tedious as to work;
But when they seldom come, they wished for come,
And nothing pleaseth but rare accidents.
So, when this loose behavior I throw off   175
And pay the debt I never promisèd,
By how much better than my word I am,
By so much shall I falsify men's hopes,
And like bright metal on a sullen ground,[6]
My reformation, glitt'ring o'er my fault,   180
Shall show more goodly and attract more eyes
Than that which hath no foil[7] to set it off.
I'll so offend to make offense a skill,[8]
Redeeming time when men think least I will.   [*Exit.*]

SCENE 3

[*Enter the* KING, NORTHUMBERLAND, WORCESTER, HOTSPUR,
SIR WALTER BLUNT, *with others.*]

KING. My blood hath been too cold and temperate,
    Unapt to stir at these indignities,
    And you have found me,[9] for accordingly
    You tread upon my patience; but be sure
    I will from henceforth rather be myself,   5
    Mighty and to be feared, than my condition,[1]
    Which hath been smooth as oil, soft as young down,
    And therefore lost that title of respect
    Which the proud soul ne'er pays but to the proud.
WOR. Our house, my sovereign liege, little deserves   10
    The scourge of greatness to be used on it,
    And that same greatness too which our own hands
    Have holp[2] to make so portly.
NORTH. My lord—
KING. Worcester, get thee gone, for I do see   15
    Danger and disobedience in thine eye;
    O, sir, your presence is too bold and peremptory,
    And majesty might never yet endure
    The moody frontier of a servant brow.[3]

6. Dull background.
7. I.e., contrast.
8. Piece of good policy. "Redeeming time": making good use of time, following the advice given to Christians in a non-Christian world. See Ephesians 5.16.

9. Discovered this to be true.
1. Disposition.
2. Helped; "portly": stately.
3. I.e., a servant's brow showing defiance, like a fortification ("frontier").

You have good leave to leave us; when we need   20
Your use and counsel we shall send for you.   [*Exit* WOR.]
You were about to speak.   [⟨*to* NORTH.⟩]
NORTH.   Yea, my good lord.
  Those prisoners in your highness' name demanded,
  Which Harry Percy here at Holmedon took,
  Were, as he says, not with such strength denied   25
  As is delivered to your majesty.
  Either envy therefore or misprisiòn[4]
  Is guilty of this fault, and not my son.
HOT. My liege, I did deny no prisoners.
  But I remember, when the fight was done,   30
  When I was dry with rage and extreme toil,
  Breathless and faint, leaning upon my sword,
  Came there a certain lord, neat and trimly dressed,
  Fresh as a bridegroom, and his chin new reaped
  Showed like a stubble-land at harvest-home;   35
  He was perfumèd like a milliner,[5]
  And 'twixt his finger and his thumb he held
  A pouncet box,[6] which ever and anon
  He gave his nose and took 't away again;
  Who therewith angry, when it next came there,   40
  Took it in snuff;[7] and still he smiled and talked,
  And as the soldiers bore dead bodies by,
  He called them untaught knaves, unmannerly,
  To bring a slovenly[8] unhandsome corse
  Betwixt the wind and his nobility.   45
  With many holiday and lady terms[9]
  He questioned me; amongst the rest, demanded
  My prisoners in your majesty's behalf.
  I then, all smarting with my wounds being cold,
  To be so pestered with a popinjay,[1]   50
  Out of my grief and my impatience
  Answered neglectingly I know not what,
  He should, or he should not—for he made me mad
  To see him shine so brisk and smell so sweet
  And talk so like a waiting-gentlewoman   55
  Of guns and drums and wounds, God save the mark!
  And telling me the sovereign'st thing on earth
  Was parmaceti[2] for an inward bruise,
  And that it was great pity, so it was,
  This villanous saltpeter[3] should be digged   60
  Out of the bowels of the harmless earth,
  Which many a good tall[4] fellow had destroyed
  So cowardly, and but for these vile guns

---

4. "Envy": malice; "misprision": mistake.
5. Not a maker of hats, but a dealer in perfumes, women's gloves, etc.
6. Perfume box.
7. I.e., was annoyed at it, with a pun on "snuffing it up."
8. Nasty, disgusting; "corse": corpse, body.

9. Affected and effeminate language (not "everyday" English).
1. Parrot.
2. Spermaceti, whale oil used as an ointment.
3. Used in gunpowder.
4. Brave.

He would himself have been a soldier.
This bald[5] unjointed chat of his, my lord,   65
I answered indirectly as I said,
And I beseech you, let not his report
Come current[6] for an accusation
Betwixt my love and your high majesty.

BLUNT. The circumstance considered, good my lord,   70
  Whate'er Lord Harry Percy then had said
  To such a person and in such a place,
  At such a time, with all the rest retold,
  May reasonably die and never rise
  To do him wrong or any way impeach   75
  What then he said, so he unsay it now.

KING. Why, yet[7] he doth deny his prisoners,
  But with proviso and exceptiòn,
  That we at our own charge shall ransom straight
  His brother-in-law, the foolish Mortimer,   80
  Who, on my soul, hath willfully betrayed
  The lives of those that he did lead to fight
  Against that great magician, damned Glendower,
  Whose daughter, as we hear, the Earl of March
  Hath lately married. Shall our coffers then   85
  Be emptied to redeem a traitor home?
  Shall we buy treason? and indent with fears,[8]
  When they have lost and forfeited themselves?
  No, on the barren mountains let him starve;
  For I shall never hold that man my friend   90
  Whose tongue shall ask me for one penny cost
  To ransom home revolted Mortimer.

HOT. Revolted Mortimer!
  He never did fall off, my sovereign liege,
  But by the chance of war. To prove that true   95
  Needs no more but one tongue for all those wounds,
  Those mouthèd wounds[9] which valiantly he took
  When on the gentle Severn's sedgy bank
  In single opposition, hand to hand,
  He did confound the best part of an hour   100
  In changing hardiment[1] with great Glendower;
  Three times they breathed[2] and three times did they drink
  Upon agreement of swift Severn's flood,
  Who then, affrighted with their bloody looks,
  Ran fearfully among the trembling reeds,   105
  And hid his crisp[3] head in the hollow bank
  Bloodstainèd with these valiant combatants.

5. Trivial. "Indirectly": negligently.
6. Be considered valid.
7. I.e., even after all this (the strong use of "yet"). "But": except. "Straight": immediately.
8. Enter into a contract with cowards.
9. Wounds are often likened to mouths in Shakespeare. The image may derive from their appear-ance and from the idea that they could speak as witnesses to what caused them. Cf. *Julius Caesar* 3.2.229–31 and *Richard III* 1.2.55–56.
1. Testing prowess and exchanging blows. "Confound": spend.
2. Paused for breath.
3. I.e., curly (because of the waves).

Never did bare and rotten policy[4]
Color her working with such deadly wounds,
Nor never could the noble Mortimer   110
Receive so many, and all willingly;
Then let not him be slandered with revolt.
KING. Thou dost belie him, Percy, thou dost belie him;
He never did encounter with Glendower.
I tell thee,   115
He durst as well have met the devil alone
As Owen Glendower for an enemy.
Art thou not ashamed? But, sirrah,[5] henceforth
Let me not hear you speak of Mortimer;
Send me your prisoners with the speediest means,   120
Or you shall hear in such a kind from me
As will displease you. My Lord Northumberland,
We license your departure with your son.
Send us your prisoners, or you will hear of it.

      [*Exeunt* KING, ⟨BLUNT, *and train.*⟩]

HOT. An if the devil come and roar for them   125
I will not send them; I will after straight
And tell him so, for I will ease my heart
Albeit I make a hazard of my head.
NORTH. What, drunk with choler?[6] stay and pause awhile.
Here comes your uncle.

      [*Enter* WORCESTER.]

HOT.   Speak of Mortimer!   130
Zounds, I will speak of him, and let my soul
Want mercy if I do not join with him;
Yea, on his part[7] I'll empty all these veins,
And shed my dear blood drop by drop in the dust,
But I will lift the downtrod Mortimer   135
As high in the air as this unthankful king,
As this ingrate and cankered[8] Bullingbrook.
NORTH. Brother, the king hath made your nephew mad.
WOR. Who struck this heat up after I was gone?
HOT. He will, forsooth, have all my prisoners;   140
And when I urged the ransom once again
Of my wife's brother, then his cheek looked pale,
And on my face he turned an eye of death,
Trembling even at the name of Mortimer.
WOR. I cannot blame him; was not he proclaimed   145
By Richard, that dead is, the next of blood?
NORTH. He was—I heard the proclamatiòn;
And then it was when the unhappy king

---

4. Craftiness or conspiracy; "color": disguise.
5. A form of "sir," but used familiarly, and sometimes, as here, with a tone of contempt. "Speak of": i.e., even mention (an emphatic sense of "speak").
6. Anger.
7. Behalf.
8. Ungrateful and malignant.

(Whose wrongs in us God pardon![9]) did set forth
  Upon his Irish expedition;   150
    From whence he intercepted did return
    To be deposed and shortly murderèd.
WOR. And for whose death we in the world's wide mouth
    Live scandalized and foully spoken of.
HOT. But soft, I pray you; did King Richard then   155
    Proclaim my brother[1] Edmund Mortimer
    Heir to the crown?
NORTH.   He did; myself did hear it.
HOT. Nay, then I cannot blame his cousin king
    That wished him on the barren mountains starve.
    But shall it be that you, that set the crown   160
    Upon the head of this forgetful man
    And for his sake wear the detested blot
    Of murderous subornation[2]—shall it be
    That you a world of curses undergo,
    Being the agents, or base second means,[3]   165
    The cords, the ladder, or the hangman rather?
    O pardon me that I descend so low
    To show the line and the predicament
    Wherein you range[4] under this subtle king!
    Shall it for shame be spoken in these days,   170
    Or fill up chronicles in time to come,
    That men of your nobility and power
    Did gage[5] them both in an unjust behalf,
    As both of you—God pardon it!—have done,
    To put down Richard, that sweet lovely rose,   175
    And plant this thorn, this canker,[6] Bullingbrook?
    And shall it in more shame be further spoken,
    That you are fooled, discarded, and shook off
    By him for whom these shames ye underwent?
    No; yet time serves wherein you may redeem   180
    Your banished honors and restore yourselves
    Into the good thoughts of the world again,
    Revenge the jeering and disdained[7] contempt
    Of this proud king, who studies day and night
    To answer all the debt he owes to you   185
    Even with the bloody payment of your deaths:
    Therefore, I say—
WOR.   Peace, cousin, say no more;
    And now I will unclasp a secret book,
    And to your quick-conceiving discontents
    I'll read you matter deep and dangerous,   190
    As full of peril and adventurous spirit
    As to o'er-walk a current roaring loud

9. I.e., God pardon in us the wrongs we did to
him.
1. Brother-in-law.
2. I.e., the stain of aiding and abetting murder.
3. Tools, helpers.
4. I.e., to show the position and the category (or
class) in which you are placed.
5. Pledge; "behalf": cause.
6. "Canker" meant not only a wild rose but also a
diseased spot in a nose.
7. Disdainful.

On the unsteadfast footing of a spear.[8]

HOT. If he fall in, good night, or sink or swim;
Send danger from the east unto the west,   195
So[9] honor cross it from the north to south,
And let them grapple; O, the blood more stirs
To rouse a lion than to start[1] a hare!

NORTH. Imagination of some great exploit
Drives him beyond the bounds of patience.   200

HOT. By heaven, methinks it were an easy leap
To pluck bright honor from the pale-faced moon,
Or dive into the bottom of the deep,
Where fathom line could never touch the ground,
And pluck up drownèd honor by the locks,   205
So he that doth redeem her thence might wear
Without corrival[2] all her dignities;
But out upon this half-faced fellowship![3]

WOR. He apprehends a world of figures[4] here,
But not the form of what he should attend.   210
Good cousin, give me audience for a while.

HOT. I cry you mercy.[5]

WOR.   Those same noble Scots
That are your prisoners—

HOT.   I'll keep them all;
By God, he shall not have a Scot of them;
No, if a Scot would save his soul he shall not.   215
I'll keep them, by his hand.

WOR.   You start away
And lend no ear unto my purposes.
Those prisoners you shall keep.

HOT.   Nay, I will; that's flat.
He said he would not ransom Mortimer,
Forbade my tongue to speak of Mortimer,   220
But I will find him when he lies asleep,
And in his ear I'll holla "Mortimer!"
Nay,
I'll have a starling shall be taught to speak[6]
Nothing but "Mortimer," and give it him   225
To keep his anger still in motion.

WOR. Hear you, cousin, a word.

HOT. All studies here I solemnly defy,
Save how to gall[7] and pinch this Bullingbrook,
And that same sword-and-buckler[8] Prince of Wales,   230
But that I think his father loves him not
And would be glad he met with some mischance,
I would have him poisoned with a pot of ale.[9]

---

8. A spear laid down as a foot-bridge.
9. Provided that.
1. Arouse, in hunting.
2. Rival.
3. Miserable sharing (of honor) with someone else.
4. Rhetorical figures of speech.
5. Beg your pardon.

6. Starlings used to be taught to speak, as parrots are now.
7. Irritate.
8. Weapons used not by gentlemen but by servants or rustic clowns.
9. The drink of the lower classes.

WOR. Farewell, kinsman; I'll talk to you
  When you are better tempered to attend.   235
NORTH. Why, what a wasp-stung and impatient fool
  Art thou to break into this woman's mood,
  Tying thine ear to no tongue but thine own!
HOT. Why, look you, I am whipped and scourged with rods,
  Nettled and stung with pismires,[1] when I hear   240
  Of this vile politician Bullingbrook.
  In Richard's time—what do you call the place?—
  A plague upon it, it is in Gloucestershire—
  'Twas where the madcap duke his uncle kept,[2]
  His uncle York, where I first bow'd my knee   245
  Unto this king of smiles, this Bullingbrook
  'Sblood!—
  When you and he came back from Ravenspurgh.
NORTH. At Berkeley castle.
HOT. You say true.   250
  Why, what a candy deal of courtesy
  This fawning greyhound[3] then did proffer me!
  "Look when his infant fortune came to age,"
  And "gentle Harry Percy," and "kind cousin";
  O, the devil take such cozeners![4] God forgive me!   255
  Good uncle, tell your tale; I have done.
WOR. Nay, if you have not, to it again;
  We will stay your leisure.
HOT.   I have done, i' faith.
WOR. Then once more to your Scottish prisoners.
  Deliver them up without their ransom straight,   260
  And make the Douglas' son your only mean
  For powers in Scotland, which, for divers reasons
  Which I shall send you written, be assured
  Will easily be granted. You, my lord, [⟨*to* NORTHUMBERLAND⟩]
  Your son in Scotland being thus employed,   265
  Shall secretly into the bosom creep
  Of that same noble prelate well beloved,
  The archbishop.
HOT. Of York, is it not?
WOR. True; who bears hard   270
  His brother's death at Bristol, the Lord Scroop.
  I speak not this in estimation,[5]
  As what I think might be, but what I know
  Is ruminated, plotted, and set down,
  And only stays but to behold the face   275
  Of that occasion that shall bring it on.
HOT. I smell it; upon my life, it will do well.

---

1. Ants.
2. Lived.
3. A complex image which occurs in Shakespeare several times (cf. *Hamlet* 3.2.1.65–67 and *Antony and Cleopatra* 4.12.20–23). The idea of fawning or flattery called up to Shakespeare's mind the image of a dog begging for sweetmeats ("candy").
4. Cheaters, with of course a pun on the word "cousin."
5. I.e., guessing.

NORTH. Before the game is afoot, thou still let'st slip.[6]
HOT. Why, it cannot choose but be a noble plot;
   And then the power of Scotland and of York   280
   To join with Mortimer, ha?
WOR.   And so they shall.
HOT. In faith, it is exceedingly well aimed.
WOR. And 'tis no little reason bids us speed,
   To save our heads by raising of a head;[7]
   For, bear ourselves as even as we can,   285
   The king will always think him in our debt,
   And think we think ourselves unsatisfied,
   Till he hath found a time to pay us home;
   And see already how he doth begin
   To make us strangers to his looks of love.   290
HOT. He does, he does; we'll be revenged on him.
WOR. Cousin, farewell. No further go in this
   Than I by letters shall direct your course.
   When time is ripe, which will be suddenly,
   I'll steal to Glendower and Lord Mortimer,   295
   Where you and Douglas and our powers at once,
   As I will fashion it, shall happily meet,
   To bear our fortunes in our own strong arms,
   Which now we hold at much uncertainty.
NORTH. Farewell, good brother; we shall thrive, I trust.   300
HOT. Uncle, adieu; O, let the hours be short
   Till fields and blows and groans applaud our sport! [*Exeunt.*]

Act 2

SCENE 1

[*Enter a* CARRIER *with a lantern in his hand.*]

FIRST CAR. Heigh-ho! an it be not four by the day, I'll be hanged;
   Charles' wain[1] is over the new chimney, and yet our horse not
   packed. What, ostler!
OST. [*within*] Anon, anon.
FIRST CAR. I prithee, Tom, beat Cut's saddle,[2] put a few flocks in   5
   the point; poor jade, is wrung in the withers out of all cess.[3]

   [*Enter another* CARRIER.]

SEC. CAR. Peas and beans are as dank here as a dog, and that is the
   next way to give poor jades the bots;[4] this house is turned upside
   down since Robin Ostler died.

---

6. An image from hunting. The meaning is: "You always ('still') release the dogs before we are ready to pursue the game."
7. Raising an army.
1. The constellation of the Great Bear or Big Dipper.
2. The saddle was beaten to make it soft; "Cut" is a name for a horse with a docked tail. "Flocks in the point": pieces of wool under the point of the saddle.
3. I.e., is sore in the shoulders excessively.
4. I.e., that is the easiest way to give poor nags worms in the stomach.

FIRST CAR. Poor fellow, never joyed since the price of oats rose; it   10
was the death of him.
SEC. CAR. I think this be the most villainous house in all London
road for fleas; I am stung like a tench.[5]
FIRST CAR. Like a tench! by the mass, there is ne'er a king christen[6]
could be better bit than I have been since the first cock.   15
SEC. CAR. Why, they will allow us ne'er a jordan, and then we leak
in your chimney, and your chamber-lye breeds fleas like a loach.[7]
FIRST CAR. What, ostler! come away and be hanged, come away!
SEC. CAR. I have a gammon[8] of bacon and two razes of ginger, to
be delivered as far as Charing Cross.   20
FIRST CAR. God's body! the turkeys in my pannier[9] are quite starved.
What, ostler! A plague on thee, hast thou never an eye in thy
head? canst not hear? An 'twere not as good deed as drink to
break the pate on thee, I am a very villain. Come and be hanged!
hast no faith in thee?   25

[*Enter* GADSHILL.]

GADS. Good morrow, carriers. What's o'clock?
FIRST CAR. I think it be two o'clock.
GADS. I prithee lend me thy lantern to see my gelding in the stable.
FIRST CAR. Nay, by God, soft; I know a trick worth two of that, i'
faith.   30
GADS. I pray thee lend me thine.
SEC. CAR. Aye, when? canst tell?[1] Lend me thy lantern, quoth he?
marry, I'll see thee hanged first.
GADS. Sirrah carrier, what time do you mean to come to London?
SEC. CAR. Time enough to go to bed with a candle, I warrant thee.   35
Come, neighbor Mugs, we'll call up the gentlemen; they will
along with company, for they have great charge.[2]

[*Exeunt* ⟨CARRIERS.⟩]

GADS. What ho! chamberlain!

[*Enter* CHAMBERLAIN.]

CHAM. At hand, quoth pickpurse.
GADS. That's even as fair as At hand, quoth the chamberlain, for   40
thou variest no more from picking of purses than giving direction[3]
doth from laboring; thou layest the plot how.
CHAM. Good morrow, Master Gadshill. It holds current[4] that I told
you yesternight; there's a franklin[5] in the weald of Kent hath
brought three hundred marks with him in gold—I heard him tell   45
it to one of his company last night at supper—a kind of auditor,[6]

5. A fish covered with red spots, like fleabites.
6. Christian king.
7. "Jordan": chamber pot; "chamber-lye": urine.
The "loach" is a fish which breeds prolifically.
8. Haunch; "razes": roots.
9. Basket.
1. A colloquial expression of contemptuous refusal.
2. Valuable cargo.
3. A pun: "giving direction" means supervising,

as contrasted with "laboring," but it was also the
name for informing thieves about the journeys of
prospective victims (laying "the plot how").
4. Remains true.
5. A freeholder, just below a gentleman in rank.
"Weald of Kent": a section of that county, formerly wooded.
6. Revenue officer; "abundance of charge": considerable property.

one that hath abundance of charge too, God knows what. They
are up already and call for eggs and butter; they will away presently.[7]

GADS. Sirrah, if they meet not with Saint Nicholas' clerks,[8] I'll give   50
thee this neck.

CHAM. No, I'll none of it; I pray thee, keep that for the hangman,
for I know thou worshipest Saint Nicholas as truly as a man of
falsehood may.

GADS. What talkest thou to me of the hangman? if I hang, I'll make   55
a fat pair of gallows; for if I hang, old Sir John hangs with me,
and thou knowest he is no starveling. Tut! there are other Trojans[9]
that thou dream'st not of, the which for sport sake are content to
do the profession some grace, that would, if matters should be
looked into, for their own credit sake make all whole. I am joined   60
with no foot land-rakers,[1] no long-staff sixpenny strikers, none of
these mad mustachio purple-hued maltworms,[2] but with nobility
and tranquility, burgomasters and great oneyers, such as can hold
in, such as will strike sooner than speak, and speak sooner than
drink, and drink sooner than pray; and yet, zounds, I lie, for they   65
pray continually to their saint, the commonwealth, or rather, not
pray to her but prey on her, for they ride up and down on her
and make her their boots.[3]

CHAM. What, the commonwealth their boots? will she hold out
water in foul way?   70

GADS. She will, she will; justice hath liquored her. We steal as in a
castle, cocksure; we have the receipt of fern seed,[4] we walk invisible.

CHAM. Nay, by my faith, I think you are more beholding to the
night than to fern seed for your walking invisible.   75

GADS. Give me thy hand; thou shalt have a share in our purchase,[5]
as I am a true man.

CHAM. Nay, rather let me have it, as you are a false thief.

GADS. Go to; *homo* is a common name to all men. Bid the ostler
bring my gelding out of the stable. Farewell, you muddy[6] knave.   80

[*Exeunt.*]

SCENE 2

[*Enter* PRINCE *and* POINS.]

POINS. Come shelter, shelter; I have removed Falstaff's horse, and
he frets like a gummed velvet.[7]

PRINCE. Stand close.

[*Enter* FALSTAFF.]

---

7. At once.
8. Highwaymen.
9. Roisterers, good fellows.
1. Footpads; "sixpenny strikers": small-time thieves.
2. Flushed, swaggering barflies. "Oneyers": dignitaries; "hold in": keep secret.
3. Booty.

4. I.e., we have the recipe for fern seed (supposed to make one invisible). "Liquored": greased.
5. Takings.
6. Muddle-headed.
7. Cheap velvet was treated with gum to make the pile stiff; as a result it soon fretted or wore away. "Stand close": hide.

FAL. Poins! Poins, and be hanged! Poins!

PRINCE. Peace, ye fat-kidneyed rascal! what a brawling dost thou   5
keep!

FAL. Where's Poins, Hal?

PRINCE. He is walked up to the top of the hill; I'll go seek him.

[⟨*He pretends to go, but hides onstage with* POINS.⟩]

FAL. I am accursed to rob in that thief's company; the rascal hath
removed my horse, and tied him I know not where. If I travel   10
but four foot by the squier[8] further afoot, I shall break my wind.
Well, I doubt not but to die a fair death for all this, if I 'scape
hanging for killing that rogue. I have forsworn his company hourly
any time this two and twenty years, and yet I am bewitched with
the rogue's company. If the rascal have not given me medicines   15
to make me love him, I'll be hanged; it could not be else; I have
drunk medicines. Poins! Hal! a plague upon you both! Bardolph!
Peto! I'll starve ere I'll rob a foot further. An 'twere not as good a
deed as drink to turn true man and to leave these rogues, I am
the veriest varlet that ever chewed with a tooth. Eight yards of   20
uneven ground is threescore and ten miles afoot with me, and
the stony-hearted villains know it well enough; a plague upon it
when thieves cannot be true one to another! [*They whistle.*] Whew!
A plague upon you all! Give me my horse, you rogues; give me
my horse, and be hanged!   25

PRINCE. Peace, ye fat-guts! lie down; lay thine ear close to the ground
and list if thou canst hear the tread of travelers.

FAL. Have you any levers to lift me up again, being down? 'Sblood,
I'll not bear my own flesh so far afoot again for all the coin in
thy father's exchequer. What a plague mean ye to colt[9] me thus?   30

PRINCE. Thou liest; thou art not colted, thou art uncolted.

FAL. I prithee, good Prince, Hal, help me to my horse, good king's
son.

PRINCE. Out, ye rogue! shall I be your ostler?

FAL. Go hang thyself in thine own heir-apparent garters![1] If I be   35
ta'en, I'll peach for this. An I have not ballads made on you all
and sung to filthy tunes, let a cup of sack be my poison; when a
jest is so forward, and afoot too! I hate it.

[*Enter* GADSHILL.]

GADS. Stand.

FAL. So I do, against my will.   40

POINS. [*Coming forward with* BARDOLPH *and* PETO] O, 'tis our setter;
I know his voice. Bardolph, what news?

BARD. Case[2] ye, case ye, on with your vizards; there's money of the
king's coming down the hill; 'tis going to the king's exchequer.

FAL. You lie, you rogue; 'tis going to the king's tavern.   45

GADS. There's enough to make us all.

FAL. To be hanged.

8. Ruler, yardstick.
9. Trick.
1. As heir apparent to the throne, Hal would of

course be a knight of the Order of the Garter.
2. Mask.

PRINCE. Sirs, you four shall front them in the narrow lane; Ned
Poins and I will walk lower; if they 'scape from your encounter,
then they light on us.   50
PETO. How many be there of them?
GADS. Some eight or ten.
FAL. Zounds, will they not rob us?
PRINCE. What, a coward, Sir John Paunch?
FAL. Indeed, I am not John of Gaunt, your grandfather, but yet no   55
coward, Hal.
PRINCE. Well, we leave that to the proof.
POINS. Sirrah Jack, thy horse stands behind the hedge; when thou
need'st him, there thou shalt find him. Farewell, and stand fast.
FAL. Now cannot I strike him, if I should be hanged.   60
PRINCE. [⟨*aside to* POINS⟩] Ned, where are our disguises?
POINS. [⟨*aside*⟩] Here, hard by; stand close.

[⟨*Exeunt* PRINCE *and* POINS.⟩]

FAL. Now, my masters, happy man be his dole,[3] say I; every man
to his business.

[*Enter the* TRAVELERS.]

FIRST TRAV. Come, neighbor, the boy shall lead our horses down   65
the hill; we'll walk afoot awhile, and ease our legs.
THIEVES. Stand!
TRAVELERS. Jesus bless us!
FAL. Strike; down with them; cut the villains' throats. Ah, whoreson
caterpillars,[4] bacon-fed knaves, they hate us youth! Down with   70
them, fleece them.
TRAVELERS. O, we are undone, both we and ours forever!
FAL. Hang ye, gorbellied[5] knaves, are ye undone? No, ye fat chuffs,
I would your store were here! On, bacons, on! What, ye knaves,
young men must live! You are grand jurors, are ye? we'll jure ye,   75
faith.

[*Here they rob them and bind them. Exeunt.*]
[*Enter the* PRINCE *and* POINS *in buckram.*]

PRINCE. The thieves have bound the true men. Now could thou
and I rob the thieves and go merrily to London; it would be
argument[6] for a week, laughter for a month, and a good jest
forever.   80
POINS. Stand close; I hear them coming.

[*Enter the* THIEVES *again.*]

FAL. Come, my masters, let us share, and then to horse before day.
An the Prince and Poins be not two arrant cowards, there's no
equity stirring;[7] there's no more valor in that Poins than in a wild
duck.   85

---

3. I.e., good luck!
4. "Caterpillars of the commonwealth" was a
common phrase, referring to rogues. Falstaff here
applies ridiculously inappropriate terms to the

travelers and to himself (e.g., "youth").
5. Fat; "chuffs": misers.
6. Subject of stories.
7. There's no justice.

PRINCE. Your money!
POINS. Villains!

> [*As they are sharing, the* PRINCE *and* POINS *set upon them;
> they all run away; and* FALSTAFF, *after a blow or two, runs
> away too, leaving the booty behind them.*]

PRINCE. Got with much ease. Now merrily to horse;
The thieves are all scattered and possessed with fear
So strongly that they dare not meet each other;   90
Each takes his fellow for an officer.
Away, good Ned. Falstaff sweats to death,
And lards the lean earth as he walks along;
Were't not for laughing, I should pity him.
POINS. How the fat rogue roared!   [*Exeunt.*]   95

SCENE 3

> [*Enter* HOTSPUR, *alone, reading a letter.*]

HOT. "But for mine own part, my lord, I could be well contented
to be there, in respect of the love I bear your house." He could
be contented; why is he not, then? In respect of the love he bears
our house, he shows in this, he loves his own barn better than
he loves our house. Let me see some more. "The purpose you   5
undertake is dangerous." Why, that's certain. 'Tis dangerous to
take a cold, to sleep, to drink; but I tell you, my lord fool, out of
this nettle, danger, we pluck this flower, safety.[8] "The purpose
you undertake is dangerous, the friends you have named uncertain, the time itself unsorted,[9] and your whole plot too light for   10
the counterpoise of so great an opposition." Say you so, say you
so? I say unto you again, you are a shallow cowardly hind,[1] and
you lie. What a lackbrain is this! By the Lord, our plot is a good
plot as ever was laid, our friends true and constant; a good plot,
good friends, and full of expectation; an excellent plot, very good   15
friends. What a frosty-spirited rogue is this! Why, my lord of
York[2] commends the plot and the general course of the action.
Zounds, an I were now by this rascal I could brain him with his
lady's fan. Is there not my father, my uncle, and myself? Lord
Edmund Mortimer, my lord of York, and Owen Glendower? is   20
there not besides the Douglas? have I not all their letters to meet
me in arms by the ninth of the next month, and are they not
some of them set forward already? What a pagan rascal is this,
an infidel! Ha! you shall see now in very sincerity of fear and
cold heart, will he to the king and lay open all our proceedings.   25
O, I could divide myself and go to buffets,[3] for moving such a
dish of skim milk with so honorable an action! Hang him! let
him tell the king. We are prepared; I will set forward tonight.

---

8. The nettle if touched tenderly will sting; if
grasped firmly, will not.
9. Unsuitable.
1. Peasant.

2. The archbishop of York.
3. Split myself in two and let the parts fight each
other; "moving": urging.

[Enter his LADY.*]*

How now, Kate! I must leave you within these two hours.

LADY. O, my good lord, why are you thus alone?   30
For what offense have I this fortnight been
A banished woman from my Harry's bed?
Tell me, sweet lord, what is 't that takes from thee
Thy stomach,[4] pleasure, and thy golden sleep?
Why dost thou bend thine eyes upon the earth,   35
And start so often when thou sit'st alone?
Why hast thou lost the fresh blood in thy cheeks,
And given my treasures and my rights of thee
To thick-eyed musing and cursed melancholy?
In thy faint slumbers I by thee have watched   40
And heard thee murmur tales of iron wars,
Speak terms of manage[5] to thy bounding steed,
Cry "Courage! to the field!" And thou hast talked
Of sallies and retires, of trenches, tents,
Of palisadoes, frontiers, parapets,   45
Of basilisks, of cannon, culverin,[6]
Of prisoners' ransom and of soldiers slain,
And all the currents of a heady fight.
Thy spirit within thee hath been so at war
And thus hath so bestirred thee in thy sleep   50
That beads of sweat have stood upon thy brow
Like bubbles in a late-disturbèd stream,
And in thy face strange motions have appeared
Such as we see when men restrain their breath
On some great sudden hest.[7] O, what portents are these?   55
Some heavy business hath my lord in hand
And I must know it, else he loves me not.

HOT. What, ho!

[⟨Enter SERVANT.⟩*]*

Is Gilliams with the packet gone?

SERV. He is, my lord, an hour ago.   60

HOT. Hath Butler brought those horses from the sheriff?

SERV. One horse, my lord, he brought even now.

HOT. What horse? a roan, a crop-ear, is it not?

SERV. It is, my lord.

HOT.   That roan shall be my throne.
Well, I will back[8] him straight; O Esperance![9]   65
Bid Butler lead him forth into the park.   *[⟨Exit* SERVANT.⟩*]*

LADY. But hear you, my lord.

HOT. What say'st thou, my lady?

LADY. What is it carries you away?

HOT. Why, my horse, my love, my horse.   70

LADY. Out, you mad-headed ape!

---

4. Appetite.
5. Horsemanship.
6. Three kinds of artillery (named here in decreas-
ing order of weight).

7. Command.
8. Mount.
9. The battle cry of the Percies: "Hope!"

A weasel hath not such a deal of spleen[1]
As you are tossed with. In faith
I'll know your business, Harry, that I will.
I fear my brother Mortimer doth stir   75
About his title, and hath sent for you
To line his enterprise; but if you go[2]—
HOT. So far afoot, I shall be weary, love.
LADY. Come, come, you paraquito, answer me
Directly unto this question that I ask;   80
In faith, I'll break thy little finger, Harry,
An if thou wilt not tell me all things true.
HOT. Away,
Away, you trifler! Love! I love thee not,
I care not for thee, Kate; this is no world   85
To play with mammets and to tilt with lips;
We must have bloody noses and cracked crowns,[3]
And pass them current too. God's me, my horse!
What say'st thou, Kate? what wouldst thou have with me?
LADY. Do you not love me? do you not, indeed?   90
Well, do not then, for since you love me not
I will not love myself. Do you not love me?
Nay, tell me if you speak in jest or no.
HOT. Come, wilt thou see me ride?
And when I am o' horseback, I will swear   95
I love thee infinitely. But hark you, Kate,
I must not have you henceforth question me
Whither I go, nor reason whereabout;
Whither I must, I must; and, to conclude,
This evening must I leave you, gentle Kate.   100
I know you wise, but yet no farther wise
Than Harry Percy's wife; constant you are,
But yet a woman, and for secrecy
No lady closer; for I well believe
Thou wilt not utter what thou dost not know,   105
And so far will I trust thee, gentle Kate.
LADY. How! so far?
HOT. Not an inch further. But hark you, Kate,
Whither I go, thither shall you go too;
Today will I set forth, tomorrow you.   110
Will this content you, Kate?
LADY.   It must of force.[4]   [*Exeunt.*]

SCENE 4

[*Enter the* PRINCE *and* POINS.]

PRINCE. Ned, prithee come out of that fat[5] room, and lend me thy
hand to laugh a little.

1. The spleen was supposed to be the source of sudden and violent emotions; the weasel was considered a very impetuous animal.
2. Besides its ordinary sense, which Lady Percy uses, "go" also meant "walk," the sense in which Hotspur takes it. "Line": support.
3. Broken heads, with a pun on "crowns" as coins. "Mammets": dolls.
4. Of necessity.
5. Vat. This establishes that the scene is a tavern.

POINS. Where hast been, Hal?

PRINCE. With three or four loggerheads[6] amongst three or four-score
hogsheads. I have sounded the very bass string of humility. Sir-   5
rah, I am sworn brother to a leash of drawers,[7] and can call them
all by their christen names, as Tom, Dick, and Francis. They
take it already upon their salvation, that though I be but Prince
of Wales, yet I am the king of courtesy, and tell me flatly I am
no proud Jack, like Falstaff, but a Corinthian,[8] a lad of mettle, a   10
good boy—by the Lord, so they call me—and when I am king of
England I shall command all the good lads in Eastcheap. They
call drinking deep, dyeing scarlet, and when you breathe in your
watering[9] they cry "hem!" and bid you play it off. To conclude,
I am so good a proficient in one quarter of an hour that I can   15
drink with any tinker in his own language during my life. I tell
thee, Ned, thou hast lost much honor, that thou wert not with
me in this action. But, sweet Ned—to sweeten which name of
Ned, I give thee this pennyworth of sugar, clapped even now into
my hand by an underskinker,[1] one that never spake other English   20
in his life than "Eight shillings and sixpence," and "You are
welcome," with this shrill addition, "Anon, anon, sir! Score a
pint of bastard in the Half-Moon,"[2] or so. But, Ned, to drive
away the time till Falstaff come, I prithee do thou stand in some
by-room, while I question my puny drawer to what end he gave   25
me the sugar, and do thou never leave calling "Francis," that his
tale to me may be nothing but "Anon." Step aside, and I'll show
thee a precedent.

POINS. Francis!

PRINCE. Thou art perfect.   30

POINS. Francis!   [⟨Exit POINS.⟩]

        [Enter DRAWER.]

FRAN. Anon, anon, sir. Look down into the Pomgarnet,[3] Ralph.

PRINCE. Come hither, Francis.

FRAN. My lord?

PRINCE. How long hast thou to serve,[4] Francis?   35

FRAN. Forsooth, five years, and as much as to—

POINS. [Within] Francis!

FRAN. Anon, anon, sir.

PRINCE. Five year! by 'r Lady, a long lease for the clinking of pewter. But, Francis, darest thou be so valiant as to play the coward   40
with thy indenture and show it a fair pair of heels and run from it?

FRAN. O Lord, sir, I'll be sworn upon all the books[5] in England, I
could find in my heart—

POINS. [within] Francis!

FRAN. Anon, sir.   45

6. Blockheads.
7. Group of tapsters, waiters.
8. Good fellow.
9. Drinking.
1. Assistant waiter.
2. I.e., charge a pint of "bastard" (a sweet Spanish
wine) to a customer in the room called "Half-

Moon." "Anon": immediately (the reply of a servant when called, equivalent to "Coming!").
3. Pomegranate (another room in the tavern).
4. I.e., to finish out his apprenticeship, usually a
seven-year period under an "indenture" or agreement.
5. I.e., Bibles.

PRINCE. How old art thou, Francis?

FRAN. Let me see— about Michaelmas[6] next I shall be—

POINS. [within] Francis!

FRAN. Anon, sir. Pray stay a little, my lord.

PRINCE. Nay, but hark you, Francis: for the sugar thou gavest me, 'twas a pennyworth, was't not?   50

FRAN. O Lord, I would it had been two!

PRINCE. I will give thee for it a thousand pound; ask me when thou wilt, and thou shalt have it.

POINS. [within] Francis!   55

FRAN. Anon, anon.

PRINCE. Anon, Francis? No, Francis, but tomorrow, Francis; or Francis, o' Thursday, or indeed, Francis, when thou wilt. But, Francis!

FRAN. My lord?   60

PRINCE. Wilt thou rob this leathern-jerkin,[7] crystal-button, not-pated, agate-ring, puke-stocking, caddis-garter, smooth-tongue, Spanish-pouch—

FRAN. O Lord, sir, who do you mean?

PRINCE. Why, then, your brown bastard is your only drink, for look you, Francis, your white canvas doublet will sully. In Barbary, sir, it cannot come to so much.[8]   65

FRAN. What, sir?

POINS. [within] Francis!

PRINCE. Away, you rogue, dost thou not hear them call?   70

> [Here they both call him; the drawer stands amazed, not knowing which way to go.]
> [Enter VINTNER.]

VINT. What, stand'st thou still, and hear'st such a calling? Look to the guests within. [Exit FRANCIS.] My lord, old Sir John with half-a-dozen more are at the door; shall I let them in?

PRINCE. Let them alone awhile, and then open the door. [Exit VINTNER.] Poins!   75

> [Enter POINS.]

POINS. Anon, anon, sir.

PRINCE. Sirrah, Falstaff and the rest of the thieves are at the door; shall we be merry?

POINS. As merry as crickets, my lad. But hark ye, what cunning match have you made with this jest of the drawer? come, what's the issue?   80

PRINCE. I am now of all humors[9] that have showed themselves humors since the old days of goodman Adam to the pupil[1] age of this present twelve o'clock at midnight.

> [⟨Enter FRANCIS.⟩]

---

6. September 29.

7. Leather-jacketed; "not-pated": with short hair; "puke": dark gray; "caddis": worsted tape.

8. Deliberate nonsense to confuse Francis, and one

of the first instances of doubletalk in English literature.

9. Temperaments, dispositions.

1. Youthful.

What's o'clock, Francis?   85
FRAN. Anon, anon, sir.   [⟨*Exit.*⟩]
PRINCE. That ever this fellow should have fewer words than a par-
    rot, and yet the son of a woman! His industry is upstairs and
    downstairs, his eloquence the parcel[2] of a reckoning. I am not
    yet of Percy's mind, the Hotspur of the north, he that kills me   90
    some six or seven dozen of Scots at a breakfast, washes his hands,
    and says to his wife "Fie upon this quiet life! I want work." "O
    my sweet Harry," says she, "how many hast thou killed today?"
    "Give my roan horse a drench," says he, and answers "Some
    fourteen," an hour after, "a trifle, a trifle." I prithee, call in   95
    Falstaff; I'll play Percy, and that damned brawn shall play Dame
    Mortimer his wife. "Rivo!"[3] says the drunkard. Call in ribs, call
    in tallow.

        [*Enter* FALSTAFF, ⟨GADSHILL, BARDOLPH, *and* PETO, FRAN-
        CIS *following with wine.*⟩]

POINS. Welcome, Jack; where hast thou been?
FAL. A plague of all cowards, I say, and a vengeance too, marry   100
    and amen! Give me a cup of sack, boy. Ere I lead this life long,
    I'll sew nether stocks[4] and mend them and foot them too. A
    plague of all cowards! Give me a cup of sack, rogue. Is there no
    virtue extant?   [*He drinks.*]
PRINCE. Didst thou ever see Titan[5] kiss a dish of butter, pitiful-   105
    hearted butter that melted at the sweet tale of the sun's? If thou
    didst, then behold that compound.
FAL. You rogue, here's lime in this sack too;[6] there is nothing but
    roguery to be found in villainous man, yet a coward is worse than
    a cup of sack with lime in it. A villainous coward! Go thy ways,   110
    old Jack, die when thou wilt; if manhood, good manhood, be
    not forgot upon the face of the earth, then am I a shotten her-
    ring.[7] There lives not three good men unhanged in England, and
    one of them is fat and grows old. God help the while; a bad
    world, I say. I would I were a weaver; I could sing psalms[8] or   115
    anything. A plague of all cowards, I say still.
PRINCE. How now, woolsack, what mutter you?
FAL. A king's son! If I do not beat thee out of thy kingdom with a
    dagger of lath,[9] and drive all thy subjects afore thee like a flock
    of wild geese, I'll never wear hair on my face more. You Prince   120
    of Wales!
PRINCE. Why, you whoreson round man, what's the matter?
FAL. Are not you a coward? answer me to that; and Poins there?
POINS. Zounds, ye fat paunch, an ye call me coward, by the Lord
    I'll stab thee.   125
FAL. I call thee coward! I'll see thee damned ere I call thee coward;
    but I would give a thousand pound I could run as fast as thou
    canst. You are straight enough in the shoulders, you care not

2. Item.
3. Drink up!
4. Stockings.
5. The sun.
6. Lime was used to make wine sparkle.

7. A herring that has cast its spawn and is lean.
8. Protestant weavers from Flanders were noto-
    rious for singing psalms.
9. A stick used by Vice in the old morality plays.

who sees your back; call you that backing of your friends? A
plague upon such backing! give me them that will face me.   130
Give me a cup of sack; I am a rogue if I drunk today.

PRINCE. O villain! thy lips are scarce wiped since thou drunk'st last.

FAL. All's one for that. [*He drinks.*] A plague of all cowards, still say
I.

PRINCE. What's the matter?   135

FAL. What's the matter! there be four of us here have ta'en a thousand pound this day morning.

PRINCE. Where is it, Jack? where is it?

FAL. Where is it? taken from us it is—a hundred upon poor four of
us.   140

PRINCE. What, a hundred, man?

FAL. I am a rogue if I were not at half-sword[1] with a dozen of them
two hours together. I have 'scaped by miracle. I am eight times
thrust through the doublet, four through the hose,[2] my buckler
cut through and through, my sword hacked like a handsaw—*ecce*   145
signum![3] I never dealt better since I was a man; all would not do.
A plague of all cowards! Let them speak; if they speak more or
less than truth, they are villains and the sons of darkness.

PRINCE. Speak, sirs; how was it?

GADS. We four set upon some dozen—   150

FAL. Sixteen at least, my lord.

GADS. And bound them.

PETO. No, no, they were not bound.

FAL. You rogue, they were bound, every man of them, or I am a
Jew else, an Ebrew Jew.   155

GADS. As we were sharing, some six or seven fresh men set upon
us—

FAL. And unbound the rest, and then come in the other.

PRINCE. What, fought you with them all?

FAL. All! I know not what you call all, but if I fought not with fifty   160
of them, I am a bunch of radish; if there were not two or three
and fifty upon poor old Jack, then am I no two-legged creature.

PRINCE. Pray God you have not murdered some of them.

FAL. Nay, that's past praying for; I have peppered two of them. Two
I am sure I have paid, two rogues in buckram suits. I tell thee   165
what, Hal, if I tell thee a lie, spit in my face, call me horse.
Thou knowest my old ward;[4] here I lay, and thus I bore my
point. Four rogues in buckram let drive at me—

PRINCE. What, four? thou saidst but two even now.

FAL. Four, Hal; I told thee four.   170

POINS. Aye, aye, he said four.

FAL. These four came all a-front, and mainly[5] thrust at me. I made
me no more ado but took all their seven points in my target,[6]
thus.

PRINCE. Seven? why, there were but four even now.   175

FAL. In buckram?

---

1. At half a sword's length.
2. Breeches.
3. Here's the proof!

4. Defense; "here I lay": this was my stance.
5. Strongly.
6. Shield.

POINS. Aye, four, in buckram suits.

FAL. Seven, by these hilts, or I am a villain else.

PRINCE. Prithee, let him alone; we shall have more anon.

FAL. Dost thou hear me, Hal?   180

PRINCE. Aye, and mark thee too, Jack.

FAL. Do so, for it is worth the listening to. These nine in buckram
that I told thee of—

PRINCE. So, two more already.

FAL. Their points being broken—   185

POINS. Down fell their hose.[7]

FAL. Began to give me ground; but I followed me close, came in
foot and hand, and with a thought[8] seven of the eleven I paid.

PRINCE. O monstrous! eleven buckram men grown out of two!

FAL. But, as the devil would have it, three misbegotten knaves in   190
Kendal green came at my back and let drive at me, for it was so
dark, Hal, that thou couldst not see thy hand.

PRINCE. These lies are like their father that begets them—gross as a
mountain, open, palpable. Why, thou clay-brained guts, thou
knotty-pated fool, thou whoreson, obscene, greasy tallow-catch[9]—   195

FAL. What, art thou mad? art thou mad? is not the truth the truth?

PRINCE. Why, how couldst thou know these men in Kendal green,
when it was so dark thou couldst not see thy hand? come, tell us
your reason. What sayest thou to this?

POINS. Come, your reason, Jack, your reason.   200

FAL. What, upon compulsion? Zounds, an I were at the strappado,[1]
or all the racks in the world, I would not tell you on compulsion.
Give you a reason on compulsion! if reasons[2] were as plentiful
as blackberries, I would give no man a reason upon compulsion,
I.   205

PRINCE. I'll be no longer guilty of this sin; this sanguine coward,
this bed-presser, this horseback-breaker, this huge hill of flesh—

FAL. 'Sblood, you starveling, you eelskin, you dried neat's tongue,
you bull's pizzle, you stockfish![3] O for breath to utter what is like
thee! you tailor's yard, you sheath, you bow case, you vile stand-   210
ing-tuck[4]

PRINCE. Well, breathe awhile, and then to it again; and when thou
hast tired thyself in base comparisons, hear me speak but this.

POINS. Mark, Jack.

PRINCE. We two saw you four set on four and bound them, and   215
were masters of their wealth. Mark now, how a plain tale shall
put you down. Then did we two set on you four; and, with a
word, outfaced you from your prize, and have it, yea, and can
show it you here in the house; and, Falstaff, you carried your
guts away as nimbly, with as quick dexterity, and roared for mercy   220
and still run and roared, as ever I heard bullcalf. What a slave

---

7. Poins puns on the other meaning of "points":
the laces used to tie up trousers ("hose").

8. As quick as thought.

9. Piece of tallow from which chandlers made
candles.

1. A method of torture; "racks": another method.

2. A pun on the word "raisin," which was spelled
and pronounced like "reason" in Elizabethan
England.

3. I.e., you ox tongue, you bull's penis, you dried
cod!

4. Stiff rapier.

art thou, to hack thy sword as thou hast done, and then say it
was in fight! What trick, what device, what starting-hole,[5] canst
thou now find out to hide thee from this open and apparent
shame?   225
POINS. Come, let's hear, Jack; what trick hast thou now?
FAL. By the Lord, I knew ye as well as he that made ye. Why, hear
you, my masters: was it for me to kill the heir apparent? should I
turn upon the true prince? why, thou knowest I am as valiant as
Hercules; but beware instinct; the lion will not touch the true   230
prince.[6] Instinct is a great matter; I was now a coward on instinct.
I shall think the better of myself and thee during my life; I for a
valiant lion, and thou for a true prince. But, by the Lord, lads, I
am glad you have the money. Hostess, clap to the doors; watch[7]
tonight, pray tomorrow. Gallants, lads, boys, hearts of gold, all   235
the titles of good fellowship come to you! What, shall we be
merry? shall we have a play extempore?
PRINCE. Content; and the argument[8] shall be thy running away.
FAL. Ah, no more of that, Hal, an thou lovest me!

    [Enter HOSTESS.]

HOST. O Jesu, my lord the prince!   240
PRINCE. How now, my lady the hostess! what sayest thou to me?
HOST. Marry, my lord, there is a nobleman of the court at door
    would speak with you; he says he comes from your father.
PRINCE. Give him as much as will make him a royal[9] man, and
    send him back again to my mother.   245
FAL. What manner of man is he?
HOST. An old man.
FAL. What doth gravity out of his bed at midnight? Shall I give him
    his answer?
PRINCE. Prithee, do, Jack.   250
FAL. Faith, and I'll send him packing.   [Exit.]
PRINCE. Now, sirs. By 'r Lady, you fought fair; so did you, Peto; so
    did you, Bardolph; you are lions too, you ran away upon instinct,
    you will not touch the true prince; no, fie!
BARD. Faith, I ran when I saw others run.   255
PRINCE. Faith, tell me now in earnest, how came Falstaff's sword
    so hacked?
PETO. Why, he hacked it with his dagger, and said he would swear
    truth out of England but he would make you believe it was done
    in fight, and persuaded us to do the like.   260
BARD. Yea, and to tickle our noses with speargrass to make them
    bleed, and then to beslubber our garments with it and swear it
    was the blood of true men. I did that I did not this seven year
    before, I blushed to hear his monstrous devices.
PRINCE. O villain, thou stolest a cup of sack eighteen years ago, and 265
    wert taken with the manner,[1] and ever since thou hast blushed

5. Evasion.
6. In many medieval romances the lion, as king
of beasts, shows respect for royalty.
7. Stay up.
8. Plot or story.
9. A "royal" was half of a pound sterling, a "noble"
was a third.
1. In the act.

extempore. Thou hadst fire[2] and sword on thy side, and yet thou
ran'st away; what instinct hadst thou for it?

BARD. My lord, do you see these meteors? do you behold these
exhalations?   270

PRINCE. I do.

BARD. What think you they portend?

PRINCE. Hot livers and cold purses.[3]

BARD. Choler, my lord, if rightly taken.

PRINCE. No, if rightly taken, halter.   275

[*Enter* FALSTAFF.]

Here comes lean Jack, here comes bare-bone. How now, my
sweet creature of bombast,[4] how long is 't ago, Jack, since thou
sawest thine own knee?

FAL. My own knee! when I was about thy years, Hal, I was not an
eagle's talon in the waist; I could have crept into any alderman's   280
thumb ring. A plague of sighing and grief—it blows a man up
like a bladder. There's villainous news abroad; here was Sir John
Bracy from your father; you must to the court in the morning.
That same mad fellow of the north, Percy, and he of Wales, that
gave Amamon[5] the bastinado and made Lucifer cuckold and swore   285
the devil his true liegeman upon the cross of a Welsh hook[6]—
what a plague call you him?

POINS. O, Glendower.

FAL. Owen, Owen, the same; and his son-in-law Mortimer, and
old Northumberland, and that sprightly Scot of Scots, Douglas,   290
that runs o' horseback up a hill perpendicular—

PRINCE. He that rides at high speed and with his pistol kills a sparrow flying.

FAL. You have hit it.

PRINCE. So did he never the sparrow.   295

FAL. Well, that rascal hath good mettle in him; he will not run.

PRINCE. Why, what a rascal art thou then, to praise him so for
running!

FAL. O' horseback, ye cuckoo; but afoot he will not budge a foot.

PRINCE. Yes, Jack, upon instinct.   300

FAL. I grant ye, upon instinct. Well, he is there too, and one Mordake, and a thousand blue-caps[7] more. Worcester is stolen away
tonight; thy father's beard is turned white with the news; you may
buy land now as cheap as stinking mackerel.

PRINCE. Why then, it is like, if there come a hot June, and this civil   305
buffeting hold, we shall buy maidenheads as they buy hobnails,
by the hundreds.

FAL. By the mass, lad, thou sayest true; it is like we shall have good
trading that way. But tell me, Hal, art not thou horrible afeard?
thou being heir apparent, could the world pick thee out three   310
such enemies again as that fiend Douglas, that spirit Percy, and

2. "Fire" and the allusions to "meteors" and
"exhalations" (shooting stars) refer to Bardolph's red
nose.
3. I.e., drunkenness and poverty.

4. Padding, stuffing.
5. A devil. "Bastinado": a beating, cudgelling.
6. A long spear with a hook on it.
7. Scots.

that devil Glendower? Art thou not horribly afraid? doth not thy
blood thrill at it?

PRINCE. Not a whit, i' faith; I lack some of thy instinct.

FAL. Well, thou wilt be horribly chid tomorrow when thou comest   315
to thy father; if thou love me, practice an answer.

PRINCE. Do thou stand for[8] my father and examine me upon the
particulars of my life.

FAL. Shall I? Content. This chair shall be my state,[9] this dagger my
scepter, and this cushion my crown.   320

PRINCE. Thy state is taken for a joint-stool,[1] thy golden scepter for
a leaden dagger, and thy precious rich crown for a pitiful bald
crown!

FAL. Well, an the fire of grace be not quite out of thee, now shalt
thou be moved. Give me a cup of sack to make my eyes look   325
red, that it may be thought I have wept, for I must speak in
passion, and I will do it in King Cambyses'[2] vein.

PRINCE. Well, here is my leg.[3]

FAL. And here is my speech. Stand aside, nobility.

HOST. O Jesu, this is excellent sport, i' faith!   330

FAL. Weep not, sweet queen, for trickling tears are vain.

HOST. O, the father, how he holds his countenance!

FAL. For God's sake, lords, convey my tristful queen,
For tears do stop the floodgates of her eyes.[4]

HOST. O Jesu, he doth it as like one of these harlotry players as ever   335
I see!

FAL. Peace, good pint pot, peace, good ticklebrain. Harry, I do not
only marvel where thou spendest thy time, but also how thou art
accompanied, for though the camomile,[5] the more it is trodden
on the faster it grows, so youth, the more it is wasted the sooner   340
it wears. That thou art my son, I have partly thy mother's word,
partly my own opinion, but chiefly a villainous trick of thine eye
and a foolish hanging of thy nether lip that doth warrant[6] me. If
then thou be son to me, here lies the point; why, being son to
me, art thou so pointed at? Shall the blessed sun of heaven prove   345
a micher[7] and eat blackberries? a question not to be asked. Shall
the son of England prove a thief and take purses? a question to
be asked. There is a thing, Harry, which thou hast often heard
of and it is known to many in our land by the name of pitch.
This pitch, as ancient writers do report, doth defile; so doth the   350
company thou keepest: for, Harry, now I do not speak to thee in
drink but in tears, not in pleasure but in passion, not in words
only, but in woes also: and yet there is a virtuous man whom I
have often noted in thy company, but I know not his name.

PRINCE. What manner of man, an it like your majesty?   355

FAL. A goodly portly man, i' faith, and a corpulent; of a cheerful

8. Represent.
9. Throne.
1. An ordinary stool, made by a joiner (cabinet maker).
2. Like the bombastic hero of the old play *Cambyses*.
3. I.e., he bows, makes an obeisance.

4. Falstaff's blank verse lines parody the old-fashioned tragedies of the 1570s and 80s.
5. An aromatic herb. The style in this speech is a parody of Euphuism, the ornate, elaborate, balanced style made popular by Lyly's *Euphues*.
6. Assure.
7. Truant.

look, a pleasing eye and a most noble carriage, and, as I think, his age some fifty, or, by 'r Lady, inclining to threescore; and now I remember me, his name is Falstaff. If that man should be lewdly given, he deceiveth me, for, Harry, I see virtue in his   360 looks. If then the tree may be known by the fruit, as the fruit by the tree, then, peremptorily I speak it, there is virtue in that Falstaff; him keep with, the rest banish. And tell me now, thou naughty varlet, tell me, where hast thou been this month?

PRINCE. Dost thou speak like a king? Do thou stand for me, and I'll   365 play my father.

FAL. Depose me? if thou dost it half so gravely, so majestically, both in word and matter, hang me up by the heels for a rabbit-sucker[8] or a poulter's hare.

PRINCE. Well, here I am set.[9]   370

FAL. And here I stand; judge, my masters.

PRINCE. Now, Harry, whence come you?

FAL. My noble lord, from Eastcheap.

PRINCE. The complaints I hear of thee are grievous.

FAL. 'Sblood, my lord, they are false: nay, I'll tickle ye for a young   375 prince, i' faith.

PRINCE. Swearest thou, ungracious boy? Henceforth ne'er look on me. Thou art violently carried away from grace; there is a devil haunts thee in the likeness of an old fat man; a tun[1] of man is thy companion. Why dost thou converse with that trunk of   380 humors, that bolting-hutch[2] of beastliness, that swollen parcel of dropsies, that huge bombard of sack, that stuffed cloak-bag of guts, that roasted Manningtree[3] ox with the pudding in his belly, that reverend vice, that gray iniquity, that father ruffian, that vanity in years? Wherein is he good, but to taste sack and drink   385 it? wherein neat and cleanly, but to carve a capon and eat it? wherein cunning, but in craft? wherein crafty, but in villainy? wherein villainous, but in all things? wherein worthy, but in nothing?

FAL. I would your grace would take me with you; whom means   390 your grace?

PRINCE. That villainous abominable misleader of youth, Falstaff, that old white-bearded Satan.

FAL. My lord, the man I know.

PRINCE. I know thou dost.   395

FAL. But to say I know more harm in him than in myself were to say more than I know. That he is old the more the pity, his white hairs do witness it; but that he is, saving your reverence, a whore-master, that I utterly deny. If sack and sugar be a fault, God help the wicked! if to be old and merry be a sin, then many an   400 old host that I know is damned; if to be fat be to be hated, then Pharaoh's lean kine[4] are to be loved. No, my good lord, banish Peto, banish Bardolph, banish Poins, but for sweet Jack Falstaff,

---

8. Suckling rabbit.
9. Seated.
1. Large barrel.
2. Trough; "bombard": leather wine vessel.
3. Town in Essex, noted for barbecues; "pud-

ding": sausage. The "vice" was a comic character in the old morality plays. Falstaff is in some respects a descendant of this type-character.
4. In the dream Joseph interpreted. See Genesis 41.19–21.

kind Jack Falstaff, true Jack Falstaff, valiant Jack Falstaff, and
therefore more valiant, being as he is old Jack Falstaff, banish   405
not him thy Harry's company, banish not him thy Harry's company; banish plump Jack, and banish all the world.
PRINCE. I do, I will.   [⟨A knocking heard.⟩]

[⟨Exeunt HOSTESS and BARDOLPH.⟩]
[Enter BARDOLPH, running.]

BARD. O, my lord, my lord, the sheriff with a most monstrous watch
is at the door.   410
FAL. Out, ye rogue! Play out the play; I have much to say in the
behalf of that Falstaff.

[Enter the HOSTESS.]

HOST. O Jesu, my lord, my lord!
FAL. Heigh, heigh! the devil rides upon a fiddlestick;[5] what's the   415
matter?
HOST. The sheriff and all the watch are at the door; they are come
to search the house. Shall I let them in?
FAL. Dost thou hear, Hal? never call a true piece of gold a counter-
feit; thou art essentially mad, without seeming so.[6]
PRINCE. And thou a natural coward, without instinct.   420
FAL. I deny your major;[7] if you will deny the sheriff, so; if not, let
him enter. If I become not a cart as well as another man, a
plague on my bringing up! I hope I shall as soon be strangled
with a halter as another.[8]
PRINCE. Go hide thee behind the arras;[9] the rest walk up above.   425
Now, my masters, for a true face and good conscience.
FAL. Both which I have had; but their date is out,[1] and therefore I'll
hide me.
PRINCE. Call in the sheriff.

[Exeunt ⟨all except the PRINCE and POINS.⟩]
[Enter SHERIFF and the CARRIER.]

Now, master sheriff, what is your will with me?   430
SHER. First pardon me, my lord. A hue and cry
Hath followed certain men unto this house.
PRINCE. What men?
SHER. One of them is well known, my gracious lord,
A gross fat man.
CAR.   As fat as butter.   435
PRINCE. The man, I do assure you, is not here,
For I myself at this time have employed him,
And, sheriff, I will engage my word to thee

5. I.e., there's a commotion.
6. I.e., don't give a true man (me, Falstaff) away
as a thief. He goes on to accuse the prince, in his
reversal of values in the play scene, of being out of
his mind, though he appears rational.
7. Your major premise (that I, Falstaff, am a coward).

8. I.e., I hope my fat neck will not make the process of strangling on the gallows longer for me than
for the rest of you. The "cart" is the wagon on
which criminals were taken to be hanged.
9. The hangings or draperies which covered the
walls. "Up above": on the balcony.
1. Lease has expired.

That I will by tomorrow dinnertime
Send him to answer thee or any man   440
For anything he shall be charged withal;
And so let me entreat you leave the house.
SHER. I will, my lord. There are two gentlemen
    Have in this robbery lost three hundred marks.
PRINCE. It may be so; if he have robbed these men   445
    He shall be answerable; and so farewell.
SHER. Good night, my noble lord.
PRINCE. I think it is good morrow, is it not?
SHER. Indeed, my lord, I think it be two o'clock.

    [*Exeunt* ⟨SHERIFF *and* CARRIER.⟩]

PRINCE. This oily rascal is known as well as Paul's.[2] Go call him   450
    forth.
POINS. Falstaff!—Fast asleep behind the arras, and snorting like a
    horse.
PRINCE. Hark, how hard he fetches breath. Search his pockets. [*He
    searcheth his pockets, and findeth certain papers.*] What hast thou   455
    found?
POINS. Nothing but papers, my lord.
PRINCE. Let's see what they be: read them.
POINS. [*reads*] "Item, a capon. . . . 2*s.* 2*d.*
          Item, sauce. . . . .   4*d.*
          Item, sack, two gallons. . 5*s.* 8*d.*
          Item, anchovies and sack
            after supper. . . . 2*s.* 6*d.*
          Item, bread. . . . .   ob."[3]

PRINCE. O monstrous! but one halfpennyworth of bread to this   465
    intolerable deal of sack! What there is else, keep close; we'll read
    it at more advantage; there let him sleep till day. I'll to the court
    in the morning. We must all to the wars, and thy place shall be
    honorable. I'll procure this fat rogue a charge of foot,[4] and I
    know his death will be a march of twelvescore. The money shall   470
    be paid back again with advantage. Be with me betimes[5] in the
    morning, and so good morrow, Poins.
POINS. Good morrow, good my lord.   [*Exeunt.*]

Act 3

SCENE 1

    [*Enter* HOTSPUR, WORCESTER, LORD MORTIMER, *and* OWEN
GLENDOWER.]

MORT. These promises are fair, the parties sure,
    And our induction[1] full of prosperous hope.

---

2. St. Paul's Cathedral.
3. Oble, a halfpenny.
4. Company of infantry. "Twelvescore": i.e., 240   yards.
5. Early.
1. Initial step.

HOT. Lord Mortimer, and cousin Glendower,
  Will you sit down?
  And uncle Worcester; a plague upon it,   5
  I have forgot the map.
GLEND.   No, here it is.
  Sit, cousin Percy, sit, good cousin Hotspur,
  For by that name as oft as Lancaster[2]
  Doth speak of you, his cheek looks pale and with
  A rising sigh he wisheth you in heaven.   10
HOT. And you in hell as often as he hears Owen Glendower spoke
  of.
GLEND. I cannot blame him; at my nativity
  The front[3] of heaven was full of fiery shapes,
  Of burning cressets, and at my birth   15
  The frame and huge foundation of the earth
  Shaked like a coward.
HOT. Why, so it would have done at the same season if your moth-
  er's cat had but kittened, though yourself had never been born.
GLEND. I say the earth did shake when I was born.   20
HOT. And I say the earth was not of my mind,
  If you suppose as fearing you it shook.
GLEND. The heavens were all on fire, the earth did tremble.
HOT. O then the earth shook to see the heavens on fire,
  And not in fear of your nativity.   25
  Diseasèd nature oftentimes breaks forth
  In strange eruptions; oft the teeming earth
  Is with a kind of colic pinched and vexed
  By the imprisoning of unruly wind
  Within her womb, which for enlargement striving   30
  Shakes the old beldam[4] earth and topples down
  Steeples and moss-grown towers. At your birth
  Our grandam earth, having this distemperature,[5]
  In passion shook.
GLEND.   Cousin, of many men
  I do not bear these crossings. Give me leave   35
  To tell you once again that at my birth
  The front of heaven was full of fiery shapes,
  The goats ran from the mountains, and the herds
  Were strangely clamorous to the frighted fields.
  These signs have marked me extraordinary,   40
  And all the courses of my life do show
  I am not in the roll of common men.
  Where is he living, clipped in with[6] the sea
  That chides the banks of England, Scotland, Wales,
  Which calls me pupil or hath read to me?   45
  And bring him out that is but woman's son

---

2. I.e., King Henry IV. To call him by his lesser   4. Old woman.
title is insulting.   5. Ailment.
3. The forehead. "Cressets": lamps.   6. Within the limits of.

Can trace me in the tedious ways of art[7]
And hold me pace in deep experiments.
HOT. I think there's no man speaks better Welsh. I'll to dinner.
MORT. Peace, cousin Percy; you will make him mad.   50
GLEND. I can call spirits from the vasty deep.
HOT. Why, so can I, or so can any man;
    But will they come when you do call for them?
GLEND. Why, I can teach you, cousin, to command
    The devil.   55
HOT. And I can teach thee, coz, to shame the devil
    By telling truth; tell truth and shame the devil.[8]
    If thou have power to raise him, bring him hither,
    And I'll be sworn I have power to shame him hence.
    O, while you live, tell truth and shame the devil!   60
MORT. Come, come, no more of this unprofitable chat.
GLEND. Three times hath Henry Bullingbrook made head
    Against my power, thrice from the banks of Wye
    And sandy-bottomed Severn have I sent him
    Bootless[9] home and weather-beaten back.   65
HOT. Home without boots, and in foul weather too!
    How 'scapes he agues,[1] in the devil's name?
GLEND. Come, here is the map; shall we divide our right
    According to our threefold order ta'en?[2]
MORT. The archdeacon hath divided it   70
    Into three limits very equally:
    England, from Trent and Severn hitherto,
    By south and east is to my part assigned;
    All westward, Wales beyond the Severn shore,
    And all the fertile land within that bound,   75
    To Owen Glendower; and, dear coz, to you
    The remnant northward lying off from Trent;
    And our indentures tripartite are drawn,
    Which being sealèd interchangeably,
    A business that this night may execute,   80
    Tomorrow, cousin Percy, you and I
    And my good Lord of Worcester will set forth
    To meet your father and the Scottish power,
    As is appointed us, at Shrewsbury.
    My father[3] Glendower is not ready yet,   85
    Nor shall we need his help these fourteen days.
    Within that space you may have drawn together
    Your tenants, friends, and neighboring gentlemen.
GLEND. A shorter time shall send me to you, lords,
    And in my conduct shall your ladies come,   90
    From whom you now must steal and take no leave,

---

7. Follow me in practicing difficult magic.
8. A proverb.
9. Unsuccessful; but Hotspur takes it in the other
sense.

1. Fevers and chills.
2. Divide our property according to the arrangement for division into 3 parts.
3. Father-in-law.

For there will be a world of water shed
Upon the parting of your wives and you.
HOT. Methinks my moiety,[4] north from Burton here,
In quantity equals not one of yours;   95
See how this river comes me cranking[5] in,
And cuts me from the best of all my land
A huge half-moon, a monstrous cantle[6] out.
I'll have the current in this place dammed up;
And here the smug[7] and silver Trent shall run   100
In a new channel, fair and evenly;
It shall not wind with such a deep indent
To rob me of so rich a bottom[8] here.
GLEND. Not wind? it shall, it must; you see it doth.
MORT. Yea, but   105
Mark how he bears his course, and runs me up
With like advantage on the other side;
Gelding the opposèd continent[9] as much
As on the other side it takes from you.
WOR. Yea, but a little charge will trench him here   110
And on this north side win this cape of land,
And then he runs straight and even.
HOT. I'll have it so; a little charge will do it.
GLEND. I'll not have it altered.
HOT.   Will not you?
GLEND. No, nor you shall not.
HOT.   Who shall say me nay?   115
GLEND. Why, that will I.
HOT. Let me not understand you then; speak it in Welsh.
GLEND. I can speak English, lord, as well as you,
For I was trained up in the English court,
Where, being but young, I framèd to the harp   120
Many an English ditty lovely well
And gave the tongue a helpful ornament,
A virtue that was never seen in you.
HOT. Marry,
And I am glad of it with all my heart;   125
I had rather be a kitten and cry mew
Than one of these same meter ballad-mongers;
I had rather hear a brazen canstick turned,[1]
Or a dry wheel grate on the axletree,
And that would set my teeth nothing on edge,   130
Nothing so much as mincing[2] poetry;
'Tis like the forced gait of a shuffling nag.
GLEND. Come, you shall have Trent turned.
HOT. I do not care; I'll give thrice so much land

---

4. Part, share.
5. Curving.
6. Corner.
7. Smooth.

8. Valley.
9. I.e., cutting off from the opposite side.
1. A brass candlestick turned on a lathe.
2. Affected. "Shuffling": hobbled.

To any well-deserving friend;   135
But in the way of bargain, mark ye me,
I'll cavil[3] on the ninth part of a hair.
Are the indentures drawn? shall we be gone?
GLEND. The moon shines fair; you may be away by night.
   I'll haste the writer, and withal   140
   Break with[4] your wives of your departure hence.
   I am afraid my daughter will run mad,
   So much she doteth on her Mortimer.   [*Exit.*]
MORT. Fie, cousin Percy, how you cross my father!
HOT. I cannot choose; sometime he angers me   145
   With telling me of the moldwarp[5] and the ant,
   Of the dreamer Merlin and his prophecies,
   And of a dragon and a finless fish,
   A clip-winged griffin and a molten raven,
   A couching lion and a ramping[6] cat,   150
   And such a deal of skimble-skamble stuff
   As puts me from my faith. I tell you what;
   He held me last night at least nine hours
   In reckoning up the several devils' names
   That were his lackeys. I cried "hum" and "well, go to,"   155
   But marked him not a word. O, he is as tedious
   As a tired horse, a railing[7] wife,
   Worse than a smoky house. I had rather live
   With cheese and garlic in a windmill,[8] far,
   Than feed on cates and have him talk to me   160
   In any summer house in Christendom.
MORT. In faith, he is a worthy gentleman,
   Exceedingly well read, and profited
   In strange concealments,[9] valiant as a lion
   And wondrous affable and as bountiful   165
   As mines of India. Shall I tell you, cousin?
   He holds your temper[1] in a high respect
   And curbs himself even of his natural scope
   When you come 'cross his humor; faith, he does.
   I warrant you that man is not alive   170
   Might so have tempted him as you have done
   Without the taste of danger and reproof;
   But do not use it oft, let me entreat you.
WOR. In faith, my lord, you are too willful-blame,
   And since your coming hither have done enough   175
   To put him quite beside his patience.

---

3. Quibble.
4. Inform.
5. Mole. According to the chronicler Holinshed there were prophecies in which Henry IV was referred to as "a moldwarp, cursed of God." Merlin was the famous prophet of King Arthur's court; many later prophecies were attributed to him.
6. "Couching" and "ramping" are Hotspur's ver-

sions of the heraldic terms "couchant" (lying down) and "rampant" (erect, on hind feet).
7. Nagging.
8. Cheese and garlic would be smelly, and the living quarters in a mill would be noisy. "Cates": delicacies.
9. Experienced in secret mysteries.
1. Character.

You must needs learn, lord, to amend this fault.
Though sometimes it show greatness, courage, blood[2]—
And that's the dearest grace it renders you—
Yet oftentimes it doth present harsh rage,   180
Defect of manners, want of government,[3]
Pride, haughtiness, opinion, and disdain;
The least of which haunting a nobleman
Loseth men's hearts and leaves behind a stain
Upon the beauty of all parts besides,   185
Beguiling them of commendation.
HOT. Well, I am schooled; good manners be your speed!
Here come our wives, and let us take our leave.

    [*Enter* GLENDOWER *with the ladies.*]

MORT. This is the deadly spite that angers me;
My wife can speak no English, I no Welsh.   190
GLEND. My daughter weeps; she will not part with you,
She'll be a soldier too, she'll to the wars.
MORT. Good father, tell her that she and my aunt Percy
Shall follow in your conduct speedily.

    [GLENDOWER *speaks to her in Welsh, and she answers him
in the same.*]

GLEND. She is desperate here; a peevish self-willed harlotry,[4] one   195
that no persuasion can do good upon.

    [*The lady speaks in Welsh.*]

MORT. I understand thy looks; that pretty Welsh
Which thou pour'st down from these swelling heavens[5]
I am too perfect in; and, but for shame,
In such a parley should I answer thee.   200

    [*The lady speaks again in Welsh.*]

I understand thy kisses and thou mine,
And that's a feeling disputation,
But I will never be a truant, love,
Till I have learned thy language, for thy tongue
Makes Welsh as sweet as ditties highly penned,   205
Sung by a fair queen in a summer's bower,
With ravishing division,[6] to her lute.
GLEND. Nay, if you melt, then will she run mad.

    [*The lady speaks again in Welsh.*]

MORT. O, I am ignorance itself in this!
GLEND. She bids you on the wanton rushes[7] lay you down   210
And rest your gentle head upon her lap,

---

2. Breeding, blood-lines.
3. Self-control. "Opinion": arrogance.
4. Wench; used affectionately, not seriously (Juliet's father applies the same phrase to her in *Romeo and Juliet*).
5. I.e., tears from her eyes. "Answer thee": cry likewise.
6. Musical variation.
7. The dry reeds used as a floor covering in Elizabethan England.

And she will sing the song that pleaseth you
And on your eyelids crown the god of sleep,
Charming your blood with pleasing heaviness,[8]
Making such difference 'twixt wake and sleep   215
As is the difference betwixt day and night
The hour before the heavenly-harnessed team[9]
Begins his golden progress in the east.
MORT. With all my heart I'll sit and hear her sing;
By that time will our book,[1] think, be drawn.   220
GLEND. Do so:
And those musicians that shall play to you
Hang in the air a thousand leagues from hence,
And straight they shall be here; sit, and attend.
HOT. Come, Kate, thou art perfect in lying down; come, quick,   225
quick, that I may lay my head in thy lap.
LADY P. Go, ye giddy goose.

[The music plays.]

HOT. Now I perceive the devil understands Welsh,
And 'tis no marvel, he is so humorous.[2]
By 'r Lady, he is a good musician.   230
LADY P. Then should you be nothing but musical, for you are alto-
gether governed by humors. Lie still, ye thief, and hear the lady
sing in Welsh.
HOT. I had rather hear Lady, my brach,[3] howl in Irish.
LADY P. Wouldst thou have thy head broken?   235
HOT. No.
LADY P. Then be still.
HOT. Neither; 'tis a woman's fault.[4]
LADY P. Now God help thee.
HOT. To the Welsh lady's bed.   240
LADY P. What's that?
HOT. Peace! she sings.

[Here the lady sings a Welsh song.]

HOT. Come, Kate, I'll have your song too.
LADY P. Not mine, in good sooth.[5]
HOT. Not yours, in good sooth! Heart! you swear like a comfitmaker's[6]   245
wife. "Not you, in good sooth," and "as true as I live," and "as
God shall mend me," and "as sure as day,"
And givest such sarcenet[7] surety for thy oaths
As if thou never walk'st further than Finsbury.
Swear me, Kate, like a lady as thou art,   250
A good mouth-filling oath, and leave "in sooth,"

8. Drowsiness.
9. The horses of the sun.
1. The indenture.
2. Capricious, governed by humors.
3. My bitch hound, Lady.
4. Hotspur sarcastically reverses the usual saying

about women and talkativeness.
5. Truth.
6. Confectioner's.
7. Thin silk. Finsbury: a recreation ground outside London, frequented by citizens and their wives
on Sundays, but not by ladies of Lady Percy's class.

And such protest of pepper-gingerbread,[8]
To velvet-guards and Sunday citizens.
Come, sing.
LADY P. I will not sing.   255
HOT. 'Tis the next way to turn tailor, or be redbreast teacher.[9] An
   the indentures be drawn, I'll away within these two hours; and
   so, come in when ye will.   [*Exit.*]
GLEND. Come, come, Lord Mortimer, you are as slow
   As hot Lord Percy is on fire to go.   260
   By this our book is drawn; we will but seal,
   And then to horse immediately.
MORT.   With all my heart.   [*Exeunt.*]

SCENE 2

[*Enter the* KING, PRINCE OF WALES, *and others.*]

KING. Lords, give us leave; the Prince of Wales and I
   Must have some private conference; but be near at hand,
   For we shall presently have need of you.   [*Exeunt* LORDS.]
   I know not whether God will have it so
   For some displeasing service I have done,   5
   That, in his secret doom, out of my blood[1]
   He'll breed revengement and a scourge for me;
   But thou dost in thy passages[2] of life
   Make me believe that thou art only marked
   For the hot vengeance and the rod of heaven   10
   To punish my mistreadings.[3] Tell me else,
   Could such inordinate and low desires,
   Such poor, such bare, such lewd,[4] such mean attempts,
   Such barren pleasures, rude society
   As thou art matched withal and grafted to   15
   Accompany the greatness of thy blood
   And hold their level with thy princely heart?
PRINCE. So please your majesty, I would I could
   Quit[5] all offenses with as clear excuse
   As well as I am doubtless I can purge   20
   Myself of many I am charged withal;
   Yet such extenuation let me beg,
   As, in reproof of many tales devised
   (Which oft the ear of greatness needs must hear)
   By smiling pickthanks[6] and base newsmongers,   25
   I may, for some things true, wherein my youth

---

8. I.e., such tame oaths, as crumbly and unsubstantial as gingerbread. "Velvet-guards": respectable people of the middle class, who wore velvet stripes on their clothes; "Sunday citizens": city folk out for a stroll on Sunday.
9. I.e., it is the easiest way to become a tailor (supposedly tailors sang at their work) or a person who teaches birds to sing. Hotspur is equally

scornful of music and of people who work for a living.
1. Unknown judgment, through my son.
2. Actions.
3. False steps, misdeeds.
4. Low.
5. Acquit myself of. "Doubtless": sure.
6. Flatterers; "newsmongers": tattletales.

Hath faulty wandered and irregular,
Find pardon on my true submissiòn.
KING. God pardon thee; yet let me wonder, Harry,
  At thy affections, which doth hold a wing   30
  Quite from the flight of all thy ancestors.
  Thy place in council thou hast rudely lost,
  Which by thy younger brother is supplied,
  And art almost an alien to the hearts
  Of all the court and princes of my blood.   35
  The hope and expectation of thy time[7]
  Is ruined, and the soul of every man
  Prophetically do forethink thy fall.
  Had I so lavish of my presence been,
  So common-hackneyed[8] in the eyes of men,   40
  So stale and cheap to vulgar company,
  Opinion,[9] that did help me to the crown,
  Had still kept loyal to possessiòn
  And left me in reputeless banishment,
  A fellow of no mark nor likelihood.   45
  By being seldom seen, I could not stir
  But like a comet I was wondered at,
  That men would tell their children "This is he";
  Others would say "Where, which is Bullingbrook?"
  And then I stole all courtesy from heaven,   50
  And dressed myself in such humility.
  That I did pluck allegiance from men's hearts,
  Loud shouts and salutations from their mouths,
  Even in the presence of the crownèd king.
  Thus did I keep my person fresh and new,   55
  My presence like a robe pontifical,
  Ne'er seen but wondered at; and so my state,[1]
  Seldom but sumptuous, showed like a feast
  And wan[2] by rareness such solemnity.
  The skipping king, he ambled up and down   60
  With shallow jesters and rash bavin wits,[3]
  Soon kindled and soon burnt, carded his state,
  Mingled his royalty with cap'ring fools,
  Had his great name profanèd with their scorns
  And gave his countenance[4] against his name   65
  To laugh at gibing boys and stand the push
  Of every beardless vain comparative,[5]
  Grew a companion to the common streets,
  Enfeoffed himself to popularity,[6]

---

7. Lifetime.
8. Cheapened, vulgarized.
9. Popularity, public opinion.
1. Public ceremonial appearances.
2. Won. "Such solemnity": i.e., the greatest possible majestic effect (an intensive use of "such"). King Henry's theory of public relations is of course not based upon the assumption of a democratic society.

3. "Rash": quick; "bavin": brushwood; the image is explained in the next line. "Carded his state": degraded his royal dignity; "card" also means "to adulterate wine."
4. Authority; "name": reputation.
5. Shallow satirical pretender to wit.
6. Made himself the common property of the public.

That, being daily swallowed by men's eyes,   70
They surfeited with honey and began
To loathe the taste of sweetness, whereof a little
More than a little is by much too much.
So when he had occasion to be seen
He was but as the cuckoo is in June,[7]   75
Heard, not regarded, seen, but with such eyes
As, sick and blunted with community,[8]
Afford no extraordinary gaze
Such as is bent on sunlike majesty
When it shines seldom in admiring eyes,   80
But rather drowsed and hung their eyelids down,
Slept in his face[9] and rendered such aspèct
As cloudy men use to their adversaries,
Being with his presence glutted, gorged, and full.
And in that very line, Harry, standest thou,   85
For thou hast lost thy princely privilege
With vile participation.[1] Not an eye
But is a-weary of thy common sight,
Save mine, which hath desired to see thee more,
Which now doth that I would not have it do,   90
Make blind itself with foolish tenderness.
PRINCE. I shall hereafter, my thrice gracious lord,
    Be more myself.
KING.   For all the world
    As thou art to this hour was Richard then
    When I from France set foot at Ravenspurgh,   95
    And even as I was then is Percy now.
    Now, by my scepter and my soul to boot,
    He hath more worthy interest to the state
    Than thou the shadow of successiòn;[2]
    For of no right, nor color like to right,   100
    He doth fill fields with harness in the realm,
    Turns head against the lion's armèd jaws,[3]
    And, being no more in debt to years than thou,
    Leads ancient lords and reverend bishops on
    To bloody battles and to bruising arms.   105
    What never-dying honor hath he got
    Against renownèd Douglas! whose high deeds,
    Whose hot incursions and great name in arms
    Holds from all soldiers chief majority
    And military title capital[4]   110
    Through all the kingdoms that acknowledge Christ.

---

7. The cuckoo is noticed in April, when its song is first heard; by June it is commonplace.
8. Commonness.
9. I.e., yawned in his face. "Aspect": looks; "cloudy": sullen.
1. Association with vile companions.
2. I.e., Hotspur's claim to the throne is more solid,
because of his achievements, than is Hal's, which rests only on shadowy rights of succession by birth. "Color": false pretense.
3. I.e., takes military action against the king's army. "Harness": armor.
4. Has the greatest reputation among soldiers. "Incursions": raids; "majority": superiority.

Thrice hath this Hotspur, Mars in swaddling clothes,
This infant warrior, in his enterprises
Discomfited great Douglas, ta'en him once,
Enlargèd[5] him and made a friend of him,   115
To fill the mouth of deep defiance up[6]
And shake the peace and safety of our throne.
And what say you to this? Percy, Northumberland,
The Archbishop's grace of York, Douglas, Mortimer,
Capitulate[7] against us and are up.   120
But wherefore do I tell these news to thee?
Why, Harry, do I tell thee of my foes,
Which art my nearest and dearest enemy?
Thou that art like enough through vassal fear,
Base inclinatìon and the start of spleen,[8]   125
To fight against me under Percy's pay,
To dog his heels and curtsy at his frowns,
To show how much thou art degenerate.
PRINCE. Do not think so; you shall not find it so;
      And God forgive them that so much have swayed   130
Your majesty's good thoughts away from me.
I will redeem all this on Percy's head
And in the closing of some glorious day
Be bold to tell you that I am your son,
When I will wear a garment all of blood   135
And stain my favors[9] in a bloody mask,
Which, washed away, shall scour my shame with it;
And that shall be the day, whene'er it lights,
That this same child of honor and renown,
This gallant Hotspur, this all-praisèd knight,   140
And your unthought-of Harry chance to meet.
For every honor sitting on his helm—
Would they were multitudes, and on my head
My shames redoubled!—for the time will come
That I shall make this northern youth exchange   145
His glorious deeds for my indignities.
Percy is but my factor,[1] good my lord,
To engross up glorious deeds on my behalf,
And I will call him to so strict account,
That he shall render every glory up,   150
Yea, even the slightest worship[2] of his time,
Or I will tear the reckoning from his heart.
This in the name of God I promise here,
The which if He be pleased I shall perform,
I do beseech your majesty, may salve   155
The long-grown wounds of my intemperance;

5. Freed.
6. I.e., to make the voice of defiance full in volume.
7. Raise a head, revolt.

8. Unreasoning impulse.
9. Features.
1. Agent; "engross up": collect, acquire.
2. Honor.

If not, the end of life cancels all bands,[3]
And I will die a hundred thousand deaths
Ere break the smallest parcel of this vow.

KING. A hundred thousand rebels die in this;   160
    Thou shalt have charge and sovereign trust herein.

[*Enter* BLUNT.]

How now, good Blunt? thy looks are full of speed.

BLUNT. So hath the business that I come to speak of.
    Lord Mortimer of Scotland hath sent word
    That Douglas and the English rebels met   165
    The eleventh of this month at Shrewsbury;
    A mighty and a fearful head[4] they are,
    If promises be kept on every hand,
    As ever offered foul play in a state.

KING. The Earl of Westmoreland set forth today,   170
    With him my son, Lord John of Lancaster,
    For this advertisement[5] is five days old.
    On Wednesday next, Harry, you shall set forward;
    On Thursday we ourselves will march. Our meeting
    Is Bridgenorth and, Harry, you shall march   175
    Through Gloucestershire, by which account,[6]
    Our business valued, some twelve days hence
    Our general forces at Bridgenorth shall meet.
    Our hands are full of business: let's away;
    Advantage feeds him fat while men delay.[7]   [*Exeunt.*] 180

SCENE 3

[*Enter* FALSTAFF *and* BARDOLPH.]

FAL. Bardolph, am I not fall'n away vilely since this last action?[8] do
    I not bate? do I not dwindle? Why, my skin hangs about me like
    an old lady's loose gown; I am withered like an old applejohn.[9]
    Well, I'll repent, and that suddenly, while I am in some liking;
    I shall be out of heart shortly, and then I shall have no strength   5
    to repent. An I have not forgotten what the inside of a church is
    made of, I am a peppercorn, a brewer's horse. The inside of a
    church! Company, villainous company, hath been the spoil of
    me.

BARD. Sir John, you are so fretful you cannot live long.   10

FAL. Why, there is it; come sing me a bawdy song, make me merry.
    I was as virtuously given as a gentleman need to be: virtuous
    enough: swore little; diced not above seven times a week; went to
    a bawdyhouse not above once in a quarter—of an hour; paid
    money that I borrowed three or four times; lived well and in good   15

---

3. Bonds, debts.
4. Power.
5. News.
6. Method. "Our business valued": according to estimates.

7. I.e., the rebels' "advantage" (opportunity) grows as the king's men delay.
8. I.e., the Gadshill robbery; "bate": lose weight.
9. A keeping apple with a wrinkled skin. "In some liking": in good condition, in the mood.

compass; and now I live out of all order, out of all compass.

BARD. Why, you are so fat, Sir John, that you must needs be out of all compass, out of all reasonable compass, Sir John.

FAL. Do thou amend thy face, and I'll amend my life; thou art our admiral,[1] thou bearest the lantern in the poop, but 'tis in the nose of thee; thou art the Knight of the Burning Lamp. 20

BARD. Why, Sir John, my face does you no harm.

FAL. No, I'll be sworn; I make as good use of it as many a man doth of a death's-head or a *memento mori*.[2] I never see thy face but I think upon hell-fire and Dives[3] that lived in purple, for there he is in his robes, burning, burning. If thou wert any way given to virtue, I would swear by thy face; my oath should be "By this fire, that's God's angel"; but thou art altogether given over, and wert indeed, but for the light in thy face, the son of utter darkness. When thou ran'st up Gadshill in the night to catch my horse, if I did not think thou hadst been an *ignis fatuus*[4] or a ball of wildfire, there's no purchase in money. O, thou art a perpetual triumph,[5] an everlasting bonfire light! Thou hast saved me a thousand marks in links[6] and torches, walking with thee in the night betwixt tavern and tavern, but the sack that thou hast drunk me would have bought me lights as good cheap at the dearest chandler's[7] in Europe. I have maintained that salamander of yours with fire any time this two and thirty years, God reward me for it. 25 30 35

BARD. 'Sblood, I would my face were in your belly! 40

FAL. God-a-mercy! so should I be sure to be heartburnt.

[*Enter* HOSTESS.]

How now, Dame Partlet[8] the hen! have you inquired yet who picked my pocket?

HOST. Why, Sir John, what do you think, Sir John? do you think I keep thieves in my house? I have searched, I have inquired, so has my husband, man by man, boy by boy, servant by servant; the tithe[9] of a hair was never lost in my house before. 45

FAL. Ye lie, hostess; Bardolph was shaved and lost many a hair, and I'll be sworn my pocket was picked. Go to, you are a woman, go. 50

HOST. Who, I? no, I defy thee; God's light, I was never called so in mine own house before.

FAL. Go to, I know you well enough.

HOST. No, Sir John; you do not know me, Sir John. I know you, Sir John; you owe me money, Sir John, and now you pick a quarrel to beguile me of it; I bought you a dozen of shirts to your back. 55

---

1. Flagship.
2. I.e., a skull or some other reminder of death.
3. The rich man who would not give food to Lazarus and was punished in hell for it. See Luke 16.19–31.
4. Will-o'-the-wisp; "wildfire": a firework used for military purposes.
5. Illumination at a public festival.
6. Small torches carried at night.
7. Candlemaker's. "Salamanders" were lizards that supposedly lived in fire and ate it.
8. A nickname from the hen in Chaucer's Nun's Priest's Tale; in Shakespeare's time a conventional name for a scolding woman.
9. Tenth part.

FAL. Dowlas,[1] filthy dowlas; I have given them away to bakers' wives, and they have made bolters of them.

HOST. Now, as I am a true woman, holland[2] of eight shillings an ell. You owe money here besides, Sir John, for your diet and by-drinkings,[3] and money lent you, four and twenty pound.   60

FAL. He had his part of it; let him pay.

HOST. He? alas, he is poor; he hath nothing.

FAL. How! poor? look upon his face; what call you rich? let them coin his nose, let them coin his cheeks; I'll not pay a denier.[4] What, will you make a younker of me? shall I not take mine ease in mine inn but I shall have my pocket picked? I have lost a seal ring of my grandfather's worth forty mark.[5]   65

HOST. O Jesu, I have heard the prince tell him I know not how oft that that ring was copper.   70

FAL. How! the prince is a Jack,[6] a sneak-up; 'sblood, an he were here, I would cudgel him like a dog if he would say so.

[Enter the PRINCE ⟨and POINS⟩, marching, and FALSTAFF meets them playing upon his truncheon like a fife.]

How now, lad, is the wind in that door, i' faith? must we all march?   75

BARD. Yea, two and two, Newgate fashion.[7]

HOST. My lord, I pray you hear me.

PRINCE. What say'st thou, Mistress Quickly? How doth thy husband? I love him well; he is an honest man.

HOST. Good my lord, hear me.   80

FAL. Prithee let her alone, and list to me.

PRINCE. What say'st thou, Jack?

FAL. The other night I fell asleep here behind the arras and had my pocket picked; this house is turned bawdyhouse, they pick pockets.   85

PRINCE. What didst thou lose, Jack?

FAL. Wilt thou believe me, Hal? three or four bonds of forty pound apiece, and a seal ring of my grandfather's.

PRINCE. A trifle, some eightpenny matter.

HOST. So I told him, my lord, and I said I heard your grace say so; and, my lord, he speaks most vilely of you, like a foulmouthed man as he is, and said he would cudgel you.   90

PRINCE. What, he did not?

HOST. There's neither faith, truth, nor womanhood in me else.

FAL. There's no more faith in thee than in a stewed prune,[8] nor no more truth in thee than in a drawn fox, and for womanhood Maid Marian may be the deputy's wife of the ward to thee.[9] Go, you thing, go.   95

---

1. A coarse cloth. "Bolters": sieves for flour.
2. Fine linen; "ell": 45 inches.
3. Drinks between meals.
4. French penny, worth a tenth of an English penny. "Younker": youngster, novice.
5. A mark was worth two thirds of a pound.
6. Rascal; "sneak-up": a sneak.
7. Chained together, like prisoners at Newgate.

8. Stewed prunes were commonly served in bawdyhouses, as a supposed protection against venereal disease. "Drawn": hunted.
9. "Maid Marian" was a female character of low morals in the popular Robin Hood plays; a "deputy's wife of the ward" would be a respectable woman.

HOST. Say, what thing, what thing?

FAL. What thing! why, a thing to thank God on.   100

HOST. I am no thing to thank God on, I would thou shouldst know
it; I am an honest man's wife, and, setting thy knighthood aside,[1]
thou art a knave to call me so.

FAL. Setting thy womanhood aside, thou art a beast to say otherwise.   105

HOST. Say, what beast, thou knave, thou?

FAL. What beast? why, an otter.

PRINCE. An otter, Sir John, why an otter?

FAL. Why, she's neither fish nor flesh, a man knows not where to
have her.[2]   110

HOST. Thou art an unjust man in saying so; thou or any man knows
where to have me, thou knave, thou!

PRINCE. Thou sayest true, hostess, and he slanders thee most grossly.

HOST. So he doth you, my lord, and said this other day you ought[3]
him a thousand pound.   115

PRINCE. Sirrah, do I owe you a thousand pound?

FAL. A thousand pound, Hal! A million. Thy love is worth a million; thou owest me thy love.

HOST. Nay, my lord, he called you Jack, and said he would cudgel
you.   120

FAL. Did I, Bardolph?

BARD. Indeed, Sir John, you said so.

FAL. Yea, if he said my ring was copper.

PRINCE. I say 'tis copper; darest thou be as good as thy word now?

FAL. Why, Hal, thou knowest, as thou art but man, I dare; but as   125
thou art prince, I fear thee as I fear the roaring of the lion's
whelp.

PRINCE. And why not as the lion?

FAL. The king himself is to be feared as the lion; dost thou think I'll
fear thee as I fear thy father? Nay, an I do, I pray God my girdle[4]   130
break.

PRINCE. O, if it should, how would thy guts fall about thy knees!
But, sirrah, there's no room for faith, truth, nor honesty in this
bosom of thine; it is all filled up with guts and midriff. Charge
an honest woman with picking thy pocket! Why, thou whoreson,   135
impudent, embossed rascal[5] if there were anything in thy pocket
but tavern-reckonings, memorandums of bawdyhouses, and one
poor pennyworth of sugar candy to make thee long-winded, if
thy pocket were enriched with any other injuries but these, I am
a villain. And yet you will stand to it, you will not pocket up   140
wrong; art thou not ashamed?

FAL. Dost thou hear, Hal? thou knowest in the state of innocency
Adam fell, and what should poor Jack Falstaff do in the days of
villainy? Thou seest I have more flesh than another man, and

---

1. I.e., ignoring, or intending no disrespect to, the
rank of knighthood. Falstaff intentionally misun-
derstands the phrase.
2. I.e., how to understand her. But the Hostess'
retort is, unconsciously, equivalent to saying that
she is completely promiscuous.

3. Owed.
4. Belt.
5. Swollen rascal; "embossed" was also a technical term in hunting, applied to a deer which was
exhausted and foaming at the mouth.

therefore more frailty. You confess then, you picked my pocket?   145
PRINCE. It appears so by the story.
FAL. Hostess, I forgive thee; go make ready breakfast, love thy hus-
band, look to thy servants, cherish thy guests; thou shalt find me
tractable to any honest reason; thou seest I am pacified still. Nay,
prithee begone. [*Exit* HOSTESS.] Now, Hal, to the news at court;   150
for the robbery, lad, how is that answered?
PRINCE. O, my sweet beef, I must still be good angel to thee; the
money is paid back again.
FAL. O, I do not like that paying back; 'tis a double labor.
PRINCE. I am good friends with my father and may do anything.   155
FAL. Rob me the exchequer the first thing thou doest, and do it
with unwashed hands too.
BARD. Do, my lord.
PRINCE. I have procured thee, Jack, a charge of foot.[6]
FAL. I would it had been of horse. Where shall I find one that can   160
steal well? O for a fine thief, of the age of two and twenty or
thereabouts! I am heinously unprovided. Well, God be thanked
for these rebels, they offend none but the virtuous; I laud them,
I praise them.
PRINCE. Bardolph!   165
BARD. My lord?
PRINCE. Go bear this letter to Lord John of Lancaster, to my brother
John; this to my Lord of Westmoreland. [*Exit* BARDOLPH.] Go,
Poins, to horse, to horse; for thou and I have thirty miles to ride
yet ere dinnertime. [*Exit* POINS.] Jack, meet me tomorrow in the   170
Temple Hall at two o'clock in the afternoon.
There shalt thou know thy charge, and there receive
Money and order for their furniture.[7]
The land is burning, Percy stands on high,
And either we or they must lower lie.   [⟨*Exit.*⟩]   175
FAL. Rare words, brave world! Hostess, my breakfast, come.
O, I could wish this tavern were my drum![8]   *Exit.*]

Act 4

SCENE 1

[*Enter* HOTSPUR, WORCESTER, *and* DOUGLAS.]

HOT. Well said, my noble Scot. If speaking truth
In this fine age were not thought flattery,
Such attribution should the Douglas have
As not a soldier of this season's stamp
Should go so general current[1] through the world.   5
By God, I cannot flatter; I do defy
The tongues of soothers,[2] but a braver place

---

6. Command of a company of foot-soldiers.
"Horse": cavalry.
7. Furnishings, equipment.
8. Headquarters.

1. I.e., that not a soldier of this year's coinage
should achieve such currency. "Attribution": praise.
2. Flatterers; "braver": more distinguished.

In my heart's love hath no man than yourself;
Nay, task me to my word,[3] approve me, lord.
DOUG. Thou art the king of honor;   10
No man so potent breathes upon the ground
But I will beard him.[4]
HOT.   Do so, and 'tis well.

[*Enter a* MESSENGER *with letters.*]

What letters hast thou there?—I can but thank you.
MESS. These letters come from your father.
HOT. Letters from him! why comes he not himself?   15
MESS. He cannot come, my lord; he is grievous sick.
HOT. Zounds! how has he the leisure to be sick
In such a justling[5] time? Who leads his power?
Under whose government come they along?
MESS. His letters bears his mind, not I, my lord.   20
WOR. I prithee tell me, doth he keep his bed?
MESS. He did, my lord, four days ere I set forth,
And at the time of my departure thence
He was much feared by[6] his physiciáns.
WOR. I would the state of time had first been whole   25
Ere he by sickness had been visited;
His health was never worth than now.
HOT. Sick now! droop now! this sickness doth infect
The very lifeblood of our enterprise;
'Tis catching hither, even to our camp.   30
He writes me here that inward sickness—
And that his friends by deputation could not
So soon be drawn,[7] nor did he think it meet
To lay so dangerous and dear a trust
On any soul removed but on his own.   35
Yet doth he give us bold advertisement
That with our small conjunction[8] we should on
To see how fortune is disposed to us;
For, as he writes, there is no quailing now,
Because the king is certainly possessed[9]   40
Of all our purposes. What say you to it?
WOR. Your father's sickness is a maim to us.
HOT. A perilous gash, a very limb lopped off;
And yet in faith it is not; his present want[1]
Seems more than we shall find it. Were it good   45
To set the exact wealth of all our states
All at one cast, to set so rich a main[2]
On the nice hazard of one doubtful hour?
It were not good, for therein should we read

3. Compare my actions with my speech. "Approve": prove, test.
4. I.e., I will take on anybody, however powerful.
5. Turbulent.
6. Feared for by. "State of time": public affairs.
7. Could not quickly be organized under a deputy. "Soul removed": other person.
8. Unified forces.
9. Informed.
1. Our present awareness of his absence.
2. Stake, in betting; "nice hazard": risky chance.

The very bottom and the soul of hope,[3]   50
The very list, the very utmost bound
Of all our fortunes.
DOUG.   Faith, and so we should,
Where now remains a sweet reversiòn.[4]
We may boldly spend upon the hope of what
Is to come in;   55
A comfort of retirement[5] lives in this.
HOT. A rendezvous, a home to fly unto,
If that the devil and mischance look big
Upon the maidenhead of our affairs.[6]
WOR. But yet I would your father had been here.   60
The quality and hair[7] of our attempt
Brooks no division; it will be thought
By some that know not why he is away
That wisdom, loyalty, and mere dislike
Of our proceedings kept the earl from hence.   65
And think how such an apprehensiòn
May turn the tide of fearful factiòn[8]
And breed a kind of question in our cause,
For well you know we of the off'ring[9] side
Must keep aloof from strict arbitrement,   70
And stop all sight-holes, every loop[1] from whence
The eye of reason may pry in upon us.
This absence of your father's draws a curtain,
That shows the ignorant a kind of fear
Before not dreamt of.
HOT.   You strain too far.   75
I rather of his absence make this use:
It lends a luster and more great opinion,
A larger dare to our great enterprise,
Than if the earl were here, for men must think,
If we without his help can make a head   80
To push against a kingdom, with his help
We shall o'erturn it topsy-turvy down.
Yet all goes well, yet all our joints are whole.
DOUG. As heart can think; there is not such a word
Spoke of in Scotland as this term of fear.   85

          [*Enter* SIR RICHARD VERNON.]

HOT. My cousin Vernon, welcome, by my soul!
VER. Pray God my news be worth a welcome, lord.
The Earl of Westmoreland, seven thousand strong,
Is marching hitherwards; with him Prince John.
HOT. No harm; what more?   And further I have learned   90
VER.

---

3. Foundation and essence of our expectations.
"List": limit.
4. A fund to be inherited in the future.
5. Sustaining place to fall back on.
6. I.e., threaten the beginning of our affairs.

7. Character; "brooks": allows.
8. Conspiracy.
9. Challenging. "Arbitrement": investigation.
1. Loophole.

The king himself in person is set forth,
Or hitherwards intended speedily,
With strong and mighty preparatiòn.
HOT. He shall be welcome too. Where is his son,
  The nimble-footed madcap Prince of Wales,   95
  And his comrades that daft[2] the world aside
  And bid it pass?
VER.   All furnished, all in arms,
  All plumed like estridges that with the wind
  Bated, like eagles having lately bathed,[3]
  Glittering in golden coats like images,   100
  As full of spirit as the month of May,
  And gorgeous as the sun at midsummer,
  Wanton as youthful goats, wild as young bulls.
  I saw young Harry, with his beaver[4] on,
  His cushes on his thighs, gallantly armed,   105
  Rise from the ground like feathered Mercury,
  And vaulted with such ease into his seat,
  As if an angel dropped down from the clouds,
  To turn and wind[5] a fiery Pegasus
  And witch the world with noble horsemanship.   110
HOT. No more, no more. Worse than the sun in March
  This praise doth nourish agues.[6] Let them come;
  They come like sacrifices in their trim,
  And to the fire-eyed maid of smoky war[7]
  All hot and bleeding will we offer them;   115
  The mailèd Mars shall on his altar sit
  Up to the ears in blood. I am on fire
  To hear this rich reprisal[8] is so nigh
  And yet not ours. Come, let me taste my horse,
  Who is to bear me like a thunderbolt   120
  Against the bosom of the Prince of Wales;
  Harry to Harry shall, hot horse to horse,
  Meet and ne'er part till one drop down a corse.
  O that Glendower were come!
VER.   There is more news;
  I learned in Worcester, as I rode along,   125
  He cannot draw his power[9] this fourteen days.
DOUG. That's the worst tidings that I hear of yet.
WOR. Aye, by my faith, that bears a frosty sound.
HOT. What may the king's whole battle[1] reach unto?
VER. To thirty thousand.
HOT.   Forty let it be;   130
  My father and Glendower being both away,
  The powers of us may serve so great a day.

---

2. Push.
3. Eagles were supposed to renew their youth by bathing in the ocean. "Estridges": ostriches; "bated": fluttering their wings.
4. Helmet. "Cushes": cuisses, armor for the thighs.
5. Direct. "Pegasus": winged horse.
6. Fevers. Malaria was thought to be caused by

vapors from the marshes, drawn up by the sun in spring.
7. Bellona, goddess of war.
8. Prize.
9. Assemble his forces.
1. Army.

Come, let us take a muster speedily;
Doomsday is near; die all, die merrily.
DOUG. Talk not of dying; I am out of fear   135
Of death or death's hand for this one-half year.   [*Exeunt.*]

SCENE 2

[*Enter* FALSTAFF *and* BARDOLPH.]

FAL. Bardolph, get thee before to Coventry; fill me a bottle of sack,
   our soldiers shall march through. We'll to Sutton Co'fil'[2] tonight.
BARD. Will you give me money, captain?
FAL. Lay out, lay out.
BARD. This bottle makes an angel.[3]   5
FAL. An if it do, take it for thy labor; and if it make twenty, take
   them all; I'll answer the coinage. Bid my lieutenant Peto meet
   me at town's end.
BARD. I will, captain; farewell.   [*Exit.*]
FAL. If I be not ashamed of my soldiers, I am a soused gurnet.[4] I   10
   have misused the king's press damnably. I have got in exchange
   of a hundred and fifty soldiers three hundred and odd pounds. I
   press me none but good householders, yeomen's sons, inquire
   me out contracted bachelors, such as had been asked twice on
   the banns,[5] such a commodity[6] of warm slaves as had as lieve   15
   hear the devil as a drum, such as fear the report of a caliver worse
   than a struck fowl or a hurt wild duck. I pressed me none but
   such toasts-and-butter[7] with hearts in their bellies no bigger than
   pins' heads, and they have bought out their services, and now
   my whole charge consists of ancients,[8] corporals, lieutenants,   20
   gentlemen of companies, slaves as ragged as Lazarus in the painted
   cloth where the glutton's dogs licked his sores, and such as indeed
   were never soldiers, but discarded unjust serving-men, younger
   sons to younger brothers, revolted tapsters and ostlers trade-fall'n,[9]
   the cankers of a calm world and a long peace, ten times more   25
   dishonorable ragged than an old-fac'd ancient,[1] and such have I
   to fill up the rooms of them that have bought out their services,
   that you would think that I had a hundred and fifty tattered prod-
   igals lately come from swine-keeping, from eating draff[2] and husks.
   A mad fellow met me on the way and told me I had unloaded   30
   all the gibbets and pressed the dead bodies. No eye hath seen
   such scarecrows. I'll not march through Coventry with them,
   that's flat; nay, and the villains march wide betwixt the legs, as if
   they had gyves[3] on, for indeed I had the most of them out of
   prison. There's but a shirt and a half in all my company, and the   35

---

2. Sutton Coldfield, about 25 miles from Coventry.
3. Ten shillings' worth.
4. Pickled anchovy. "Press": the draft or impressment of soldiers into service.
5. Notice of approaching marriage, announced three times publicly in church before the marriage could take place.
6. "Commodity": collection; "warm": well-to-do;

"caliver": musket.
7. Sissies.
8. Ensigns.
9. Hostlers out of work; "cankers": canker worms.
1. Frayed flag.
2. Garbage. The prodigal son, in the Bible, fed on husks before returning to the paternal board.
3. Leg-irons.

half shirt is two napkins tacked together and thrown over the
shoulders like a herald's coat without sleeves, and the shirt, to
say the truth, stolen from my host at Saint Alban's, or the red-
nose innkeeper of Daventry. But that's all one; they'll find linen
enough on every hedge.[4]   40

[*Enter the* PRINCE *and the* LORD OF WESTMORELAND.]

PRINCE. How now, blown Jack! how now, quilt![5]
FAL. What, Hal, how now, mad wag! what a devil dost thou in
    Warwickshire? My good Lord of Westmoreland, I cry you mercy;
    I thought your honor had already been at Shrewsbury.
WEST. Faith, Sir John, 'tis more than time that I were there, and   45
    you too; but my powers are there already. The king, I can tell
    you, looks for us all; we must away all night.
FAL. Tut, never fear me; I am as vigilant as a cat to steal cream.
PRINCE. I think, to steal cream indeed, for thy theft hath already
    made thee butter. But tell me, Jack, whose fellows are these that   50
    come after?
FAL. Mine, Hal, mine.
PRINCE. I did never see such pitiful rascals.
FAL. Tut, tut, good enough to toss,[6] food for powder, food for pow-
    der; they'll fill a pit as well as better; tush, man, mortal men,   55
    mortal men.
WEST. Aye, but, Sir John, methinks they are exceeding poor and
    bare, too beggarly.
FAL. Faith, for their poverty I know not where they had that, and
    for their bareness I am sure they never learned that of me.   60
PRINCE. No, I'll be sworn, unless you call three fingers[7] on the ribs
    bare. But, sirrah, make haste; Percy is already in the field.
FAL. What, is the king encamped?
WEST. He is, Sir John; I fear we shall stay too long.
FAL. Well,   65
    To the latter end of a fray and the beginning of a feast
    Fits a dull fighter and a keen guest.   [*Exeunt.*]

SCENE 3

[*Enter* HOTSPUR, WORCESTER, DOUGLAS, *and* VERNON.]

HOT. We'll fight with him tonight.
WOR.   It may not be.
DOUG. You give him then advantage.
VER.   Not a whit.
HOT. Why say you so? looks he not for supply?
VER. So do we.
HOT.   His is certain, ours is doubtful.
WOR. Good cousin, be advised; stir not tonight.   5
VER. Do not, my lord.
DOUG.   You do not counsel well;
    You speak it out of fear and cold heart.

---

4. Laundry was customarily hung on hedges to dry.   6. I.e., on a pike, or long spear.
5. Padded material, a substitute for armor.   7. Layers of fat. A finger was ¾ of an inch.

VER. Do me no slander, Douglas; by my life,
    And I dare well maintain it with my life,
    If well-respected honor[8] bid me on,   10
    I hold as little counsel with weak fear
    As you, my lord, or any Scot that this day lives.
    Let it be seen tomorrow in the battle
    Which of us fears.
DOUG.   Yea, or tonight.
VER.   Content.
HOT. Tonight, say I.   15
VER. Come, come, it may not be. I wonder much,
    Being men of such great leading as you are,
    That you foresee not what impediments
    Drag back our expedition;[9] certain horse
    Of my cousin Vernon's are not yet come up,   20
    Your uncle Worcester's horse came but today,
    And now their pride and mettle is asleep,
    Their courage with hard labor tame and dull,
    That not a horse is half the half of himself.
HOT. So are the horses of the enemy   25
    In general, journey-bated[1] and brought low;
    The better part of ours are full of rest.
WOR. The number of the king exceedeth ours;
    For God's sake, cousin, stay till all come in.

    [*The trumpet sounds a parley. Enter* SIR WALTER BLUNT.]

BLUNT. I come with gracious offers from the king,   30
    If you vouchsafe me hearing and respect.
HOT. Welcome, Sir Walter Blunt; and would to God
    You were of our determinatiòn!
    Some of us love you well, and even those some
    Envy your great deservings and good name   35
    Because you are not of our quality,[2]
    But stand against us like an enemy.
BLUNT. And God defend[3] but still I should stand so,
    So long as out of limit and true rule
    You stand against anointed majesty.   40
    But to my charge. The king hath sent to know
    The nature of your griefs, and whereupon
    You conjure from the breast of civil peace
    Such bold hostility, teaching his duteous land
    Audacious cruelty. If that the king   45
    Have any way your good deserts forgot,
    Which he confesseth to be manifold,
    He bids you name your griefs, and with all speed
    You shall have your desires with interest
    And pardon absolute for yourself and these   50
    Herein misled by your suggestiòn.[4]

---

8. Well-considered (not rash, like Hotspur's).   2. Fellowship, party.
9. Retard our speed.   3. Forbid; "still": always.
1. Tired from travel.   4. Temptation.

HOT. The king is kind, and well we know the king
  Knows at what time to promise, when to pay.
  My father and my uncle and myself
  Did give him that same royalty he wears;   55
  And when he was not six and twenty strong,
  Sick in the world's regard, wretched and low,
  A poor unminded outlaw sneaking home,
  My father gave him welcome to the shore;
  And when he heard him swear and vow to God   60
  He came but to be Duke of Lancaster,
  To sue his livery[5] and beg his peace,
  With tears of innocency and terms of zeal,
  My father, in kind heart and pity moved,
  Swore him assistance and performed it too.   65
  Now when the lords and barons of the realm
  Perceived Northumberland did lean to him,
  The more and less came in with cap and knee,[6]
  Met him in boroughs, cities, villages,
  Attended him on bridges, stood in lanes,   70
  Laid gifts before him, proffered him their oaths,
  Gave him their heirs as pages, followed him
  Even at the heels in golden multitudes.
  He presently, as greatness knows itself,
  Steps me a little higher than his vow,   75
  Made to my father while his blood was poor
  Upon the naked shore at Ravenspurgh,
  And now, forsooth, takes on him to reform
  Some certain edicts and some strait[7] decrees
  That lie too heavy on the commonwealth,   80
  Cries out upon abuses, seems to weep
  Over his country's wrongs, and by this face,[8]
  This seeming brow of justice, did he win
  The hearts of all that he did angle for;
  Proceeded further, cut me off the heads   85
  Of all the favorites that the absent king
  In deputation left behind him here,
  When he was personal[9] in the Irish war.
BLUNT. Tut, I came not to hear this.
HOT.   Then to the point.
  In short time after he deposed the king,   90
  Soon after that deprived him of his life,
  And in the neck of that tasked[1] the whole state;
  To make that worse, suffered his kinsman March
  (Who is, if every owner were well placed,
  Indeed his king) to be engaged[2] in Wales,   95
  There without ransom to lie forfeited;
  Disgraced[3] me in my happy victories,

---

5. I.e., claim title to his late father's lands (held by King Richard II).
6. Cap in hand and on bended knee; i.e., offering homage.
7. Strict.
8. Pretense.
9. Actively participating in person.
1. I.e., immediately after that, (he) taxed.
2. Pawned as a hostage.
3. I.e., did not favor.

Sought to entrap me by intelligence,[4]
Rated mine uncle from the council board,
In rage dismissed my father from the court,   100
Broke oath on oath, committed wrong on wrong,
And in conclusion drove us to seek out
This head of safety,[5] and withal to pry
Into his title, the which we find
Too indirect for long continuance.   105
BLUNT. Shall I return this answer to the king?
HOT. Not so, Sir Walter; we'll withdraw awhile.
Go to the king, and let there be impawned[6]
Some surety for a safe return again,
And in the morning early shall mine uncle   110
Bring him our purposes; and so farewell.
BLUNT. I would you would accept of grace and love.
HOT. And may be so we shall.
BLUNT.   Pray God you do.   [*Exeunt.*]

SCENE 4

[*Enter the* ARCHBISHOP OF YORK *and* SIR MICHAEL.]

ARCH. Hie, good Sir Michael; bear this sealèd brief[7]
With wingèd haste to the lord marshal,
This to my cousin Scroop, and all the rest
To whom they are directed. If you knew
How much they do import you would make haste.   5
SIR M. My good lord,
I guess their tenor.
ARCH.   Like enough you do.
Tomorrow, good Sir Michael, is a day
Wherein the fortune of ten thousand men
Must bide the touch;[8] for, sir, at Shrewsbury,   10
As I am truly given to understand,
The king with mighty and quick-raisèd power
Meets with Lord Harry; and I fear, Sir Michael,
What with the sickness of Northumberland,
Whose power was in the first proportiòn,[9]   15
And what with Owen Glendower's absence thence,
Who with them was a rated[1] sinew too
And comes not in, o'er-ruled by prophecies—
I fear the power of Percy is too weak
To wage an instant trial with the king.   20
SIR M. Why, my good lord, you need not fear;
There is Douglas and Lord Mortimer.
ARCH. No, Mortimer is not there.
SIR M. But there is Mordake, Vernon, Lord Harry Percy,

4. Spying; "rated": angrily dismissed.
5. Army for our safety.
6. Pledged; "surety": guarantee.
7. Letter.

8. Stand the test.
9. The largest part.
1. Highly regarded.

And there is my Lord of Worcester and a head   25
Of gallant warriors, noble gentlemen.
ARCH. And so there is; but yet the king hath drawn
   The special head[2] of all the land together:
   The Prince of Wales, Lord John of Lancaster,
   The noble Westmoreland, and warlike Blunt,   30
   And many more corrivals[3] and dear men
   Of estimation and command in arms.
SIR M. Doubt not, my lord, they shall be well opposed.
ARCH. I hope no less, yet needful 'tis to fear,
   And to prevent[4] the worst, Sir Michael, speed;   35
   For if Lord Percy thrive not, ere the king
   Dismiss his power, he means to visit[5] us,
   For he hath heard of our confederacy,
   And 'tis but wisdom to make strong against him;
   Therefore make haste. I must go write again   40
   To other friends; and so farewell, Sir Michael.   [*Exeunt.*]

Act 5

SCENE 1

[*Enter the* KING, PRINCE OF WALES, PRINCE JOHN OF LAN-
CASTER, SIR WALTER BLUNT, *and* FALSTAFF.]

KING. How bloodily the sun begins to peer
   Above yon busky[1] hill! The day looks pale
   At his distemp'rature.[2]
PRINCE.   The southern wind
   Doth play the trumpet to his purposes,[3]
   And by his hollow whistling in the leaves   5
   Foretells a tempest and a blustering day.
KING. Then with the losers let it sympathize,
   For nothing can seem foul to those that win.

[*The trumpet sounds. Enter* WORCESTER ⟨*and* VERNON.⟩]

How now, my lord of Worcester! 'Tis not well
That you and I should meet upon such terms   10
As now we meet. You have deceived our trust
And made us doff our easy robes of peace,
To crush[4] our old limbs in ungentle steel;
This is not well, my lord, this is not well.
What say you to it? will you again unknit   15
This churlish knot of all-abhorrèd war
And move in that obedient orb[5] again
Where you did give a fair and natural light,
And be no more an exhaled meteor,[6]

2. Principal army.
3. Associates; "dear": noble.
4. Forestall.
5. Attack.
1. Wooded.
2. I.e., the sun's illness or malevolence.
3. I.e., the sun's intentions; the southern wind
supports them.
4. Enfold, cramp.
5. Regular orbit, as of a planet.
6. Meteors were thought to be made of gas exhaled
by a planet and were commonly associated with
civil commotion.

A prodigy of fear and a portent   20
Of broachèd mischief to the unborn times?[7]
WOR. Hear me, my liege:
For mine own part I could be well content
To entertain the lag end of my life
With quiet hours, for I do protest   25
I have not sought the day of this dislike.
KING. You have not sought it! how comes it then?
FAL. Rebellion lay in his way, and he found it.
PRINCE. Peace, chewet,[8] peace!
WOR. It pleased your majesty to turn your looks   30
Of favor from myself and all our house,
And yet I must remember[9] you, my lord,
We were the first and dearest of your friends.
For you my staff of office did I break
In Richard's time, and posted day and night   35
To meet you on the way and kiss your hand
When yet you were in place and in account
Nothing so strong and fortunate as I.
It was myself, my brother, and his son
That brought you home and boldly did outdare   40
The dangers of the time. You swore to us,
And you did swear that oath at Doncaster,
That you did nothing purpose 'gainst the state
Nor claim no further than your new-fall'n[1] right,
The seat of Gaunt, dukedom of Lancaster.   45
To this we swore our aid. But in short space
It rained down fortune showering on your head
And such a flood of greatness fell on you,
What with our help, what with the absent king,
What with the injuries of a wanton time,   50
The seeming sufferances[2] that you had borne,
And the contrarious winds that held the king
So long in his unlucky Irish wars
That all in England did repute him dead;
And from this swarm of fair advantages   55
You took occasion to be quickly wooed
To gripe the general sway[3] into your hand,
Forgot your oath to us at Doncaster,
And being fed by us you used us so
As that ungentle gull[4] the cuckoo's bird   60
Useth the sparrow, did oppress our nest,
Grew by our feeding to so great a bulk
That even our love durst not come near your sight
For fear of swallowing;[5] but with nimble wing
We were enforced for safety sake to fly   65

---

7. I.e., of harm or disaster opened up ("broached")
to plague the future. Note that "mischief" conveyed a stronger meaning to Shakespeare than it
does to us.
8. Chattering bird.
9. Remind.

1. Recently inherited.
2. Sufferings.
3. Seize power over the whole state.
4. Rude nestling; the cuckoo hatches its young in
other birds' nests.
5. Being swallowed.

Out of your sight and raise this present head,
Whereby we stand opposèd by such means
As you yourself have forged against yourself
By unkind usage, dangerous countenance,[6]
And violation of all faith and troth   70
Sworn to us in your younger enterprise.
KING. These things indeed you have articulate,[7]
Proclaimed at market crosses, read in churches,
To face[8] the garment of rebelliòn
With some fine color that may please the eye   75
Of fickle changelings and poor discontents,
Which gape and rub the elbow at the news
Of hurlyburly innovatiòn;
And never yet did insurrection want
Such water colors to impaint his cause,   80
Nor moody beggars starving for a time
Of pellmell havoc and confusiòn.
PRINCE. In both our armies there is many a soul
Shall pay full dearly for this encounter,
If once they join in trial. Tell your nephew   85
The Prince of Wales doth join with all the world
In praise of Henry Percy; by my hopes,
This present enterprise set off his head,[9]
I do not think a braver gentleman,
More active-valiant or more valiant-young,   90
More daring or more bold, is now alive
To grace this latter age with noble deeds.
For my part, I may speak it to my shame,
I have a truant been to chivalry—
And so I hear he doth account me too—   95
Yet this before my father's majesty:
I am content that he shall take the odds
Of his great name and estimatiòn,
And will, to save the blood on either side,
Try fortune with him in a single fight.   100
KING. And, Prince of Wales, so dare we venture thee,
Albeit considerations infinite
Do make[1] against it. No, good Worcester, no,
We love our people well; even those we love
That are misled upon your cousin's part;   105
And, will they take the offer of our grace,
Both he and they and you, yea, every man
Shall be my friend again and I'll be his.
So tell your cousin, and bring me word
What he will do; but if he will not yield,   110
Rebuke and dread correction wait on[2] us

6. Threatening looks.   9. Deducted from his account.
7. Drawn up in detail.   1. Weigh.
8. Decorate.   2. Accompany.

And they shall do their office. So, be gone;
We will not now be troubled with reply.
We offer fair; take it advisedly.

[*Exit* WORCESTER ⟨*and* VERNON.⟩]

PRINCE. It will not be accepted, on my life;   115
  The Douglas and the Hotspur both together
  Are confident against the world in arms.
KING. Hence, therefore, every leader to his charge,
  For on their answer will we set on them,
  And God befriend us, as our cause is just!   120

[*Exeunt all but the* PRINCE *and* FALSTAFF.]

FAL. Hal, if thou see me down in the battle and bestride me, so; 'tis
  a point of friendship.
PRINCE. Nothing but a colossus can do thee that friendship. Say thy
  prayers, and farewell.
FAL. I would 'twere bedtime, Hal, and all well.   125
PRINCE. Why, thou owest God a death.   [⟨*Exit.*⟩]
FAL. 'Tis not due yet; I would be loath to pay him before his day.
  What need I be so forward with him that calls not on me? Well,
  'tis no matter; honor pricks me on. Yea, but how if honor prick
  me off when I come on? How then? can honor set to a leg? No. 130
  Or an arm? No. Or take away the grief[3] of a wound? No. Honor
  hath no skill in surgery, then? No. What is honor? A word. What
  is in that word honor? what is that honor? Air. A trim reckoning![4]
  Who hath it? He that died o' Wednesday. Doth he feel it? No.
  Doth he hear it? No. 'Tis insensible,[5] then? Yea, to the dead. 135
  But will it not live with the living? No. Why? Detraction will not
  suffer it. Therefore I'll none of it; Honor is a mere scutcheon.[6]
  And so ends my catechism.   [*Exit.*]

SCENE 2

[*Enter* WORCESTER *and* SIR RICHARD VERNON.]

WOR. O no, my nephew must not know, Sir Richard,
  The liberal and kind offer of the king.
VER. 'Twere best he did.
WOR.   Then are we all undone.
  It is not possible, it cannot be,
  The king should keep his word in loving us;   5
  He will suspect us still and find a time
  To punish this offense in other faults.
  Suspicion all our lives shall be stuck full of eyes,
  For treason is but trusted like the fox
  Who, ne'er so tame, so cherished and locked up,   10
  Will have a wild trick of his ancestors;
  Look how we can, or sad or merrily,

3. Pain.   5. Not capable of being felt.
4. A fine totaling of the bill.   6. A coat of arms, as often put on a tombstone.

Interpretation will misquote[7] our looks,
And we shall feed like oxen at a stall,
The better cherished, still the nearer death.   15
My nephew's trespass may be well forgot;
It hath the excuse of youth and heat of blood
And an adopted name of privilege,[8]
A harebrained Hotspur, governed by a spleen.
All his offenses live upon my head   20
And on his father's; we did train him on,
And, his corruption being ta'en from us,[9]
We, as the spring of all, shall pay for all.
Therefore, good cousin, let not Harry know
In any case the offer of the king.   25
VER. Deliver what you will; I'll say 'tis so.
Here comes your cousin.

          [*Enter* HOTSPUR ⟨*and* DOUGLAS.⟩]

HOT. My uncle is returned;
Deliver up my Lord of Westmoreland.
Uncle, what news?   30
WOR. The king will bid you battle presently.[1]
DOUG. Defy him by the Lord of Westmoreland.
HOT. Lord Douglas, go you and tell him so.
DOUG. Marry, and shall, and very willingly.   [*Exit.*]
WOR. There is no seeming mercy in the king.   35
HOT. Did you beg any? God forbid!
WOR. I told him gently of our grievances,
Of his oath-breaking, which he mended thus,
By now forswearing[2] that he is forsworn;
He calls us rebels, traitors, and will scourge   40
With haughty arms this hateful name in us.

          [*Enter* DOUGLAS.]

DOUG. Arm, gentlemen, to arms! for I have thrown
A brave defiance in King Henry's teeth,
And Westmoreland, that was engaged,[3] did hear it,
Which cannot choose but bring him quickly on.   45
WOR. The Prince of Wales stepped forth before the king,
And, nephew, challenged you to single fight.
HOT. O, would the quarrel lay upon our heads,
And that no man might draw short breath today
But I and Harry Monmouth! Tell me, tell me,   50
How showed his tasking?[4] seemed it in contempt?
VER. No, by my soul; I never in my life
Did hear a challenge urged more modestly,
Unless a brother should a brother dare
To gentle exercise and proof of arms.   55

---

7. Misinterpret.
8. A nickname which gives him privileges.
"Spleen": impetuous temperament.
9. Being attributed to. "Train": entice.

1. Immediately.
2. Swearing falsely.
3. Held as a hostage.
4. Challenge.

He gave you all the duties[5] of a man,
Trimmed up your praises with a princely tongue,
Spoke your deservings like a chronicle,
Making you ever better than his praise
By still dispraising praise valued with[6] you;   60
And, which became him like a prince indeed,
He made a blushing cital[7] of himself,
And chid his truant youth with such a grace
As if he mastered there a double spirit
Of teaching and of learning instantly.   65
There did he pause; but let me tell the world,
If he outlive the envy[8] of this day,
England did never owe[9] so sweet a hope,
So much miscònstrued in his wantonness.[1]

HOT. Cousin, I think thou art enamoured   70
On his follies; never did I hear
Of any prince so wild a liberty.[2]
But be he as he will, yet once ere night
I will embrace him with a soldier's arm,
That he shall shrink under my courtesy.   75
Arm, arm with speed; and, fellows, soldiers, friends,
Better consider what you have to do
Than I, that have not well the gift of tongue,
Can lift your blood up with persuasiòn.

        [*Enter a* MESSENGER.]

MESS. My lord, here are letters for you.   80
HOT. I cannot read them now.
O gentlemen, the time of life is short!
To spend that shortness basely were too long,
If life did ride upon a dial's point,[3]
Still ending at the arrival of an hour;   85
And if we live, we live to tread on kings,
If die, brave death when princes die with us!
Now, for our consciences, the arms are fair,
When the intent of bearing them is just.

        [*Enter another* MESSENGER.]

MESS. My lord, prepare; the king comes on apace.   90
HOT. I thank him that he cuts me from my tale,
For I profess not talking; only this—
Let each man do his best; and here draw I
A sword whose temper I intend to stain
With the best blood that I can meet withal   95
In the adventure of this perilous day.
Now, *Esperance! Percy!*[4] and set on.

---

5. Good qualities.
6. Compared to.
7. Mention, recital.
8. Malice.
9. Own.
1. Frivolity.

2. Reckless dissipation.
3. Hand of a clock; "still": always. Hotspur's meaning (in lines 83–85) is that a base life would be too long even if it lasted only an hour.
4. Hope, Percy! (the family motto).

Sound all the lofty instruments of war,
And by that music let us all embrace;
For, heaven to earth,[5] some of us never shall   100
A second time do such a courtesy.

[*The trumpets sound. They embrace and exeunt.*]

SCENE 3

[*The* KING *enters with his power. Alarum*[6] *to the battle.
Then enter* DOUGLAS *and* SIR WALTER BLUNT.]

BLUNT. What is thy name, that in the battle thus
　Thou crossest me? what honor dost thou seek
　Upon my head?
DOUG. 　　　　　Know then, my name is Douglas,
　And I do haunt thee in the battle thus
　Because some tell me that thou art a king.[7]   5
BLUNT. They tell thee true.
DOUG. The Lord of Stafford dear[8] today hath bought
　Thy likeness, for instead of thee, King Harry,
　This sword hath ended him; so shall it thee,
　Unless thou yield thee as my prisoner.   10
BLUNT. I was not born a yielder, thou proud Scot,
　And thou shalt find a king that will revenge
　Lord Stafford's death.　　　[*They fight.* DOUGLAS *kills* BLUNT.]

　　　　[*Enter* HOTSPUR.]

HOT. O Douglas, hadst thou fought at Holmedon thus,
　I never had triumphed upon a Scot.   15
DOUG. All's done, all's won; here breathless lies the king.
HOT. Where?
DOUG. Here.
HOT. This, Douglas? No, I know this face full well;
　A gallant knight he was, his name was Blunt;   20
　Semblably furnished like the king himself.
DOUG. Ah fool, go with thy soul whither it goes!
　A borrowed title hast thou bought too dear;
　Why didst thou tell me that thou wert a king?
HOT. The king hath many marching in his coats.   25
DOUG. Now, by my sword, I will kill all his coats;
　I'll murder all his wardrobe, piece by piece,
　Until I meet the king.
HOT. 　　　　　　　Up and away!
　Our soldiers stand full fairly for the day.　　　　　[*Exeunt.*]

　　　[*Alarum. Enter* FALSTAFF *alone.*]

FAL. Though I could 'scape shot-free[9] at London, I fear the shot   30
　here; here's no scoring but upon the pate. Soft, who are you? Sir

---

5. I.e., the odds are heaven to earth that.
6. Trumpet signal.
7. Blunt and others are dressed to look like the king.

8. Expensively.
9. Scot-free, without paying the bill at a tavern; "scoring" continues the pun; it means (1) marking up a charge, (2) cutting with a sword.

Walter Blunt; there's honor for you, here's no vanity! I am as hot
as molten lead, and as heavy too; God keep lead out of me! I
need no more weight than mine own bowels. I have led my
ragamuffins where they are peppered; there's not three of my   35
hundred and fifty left alive, and they are for the town's end, to
beg during life. But who comes here?

[*Enter the* PRINCE.]

PRINCE. What, stand'st thou idle here? lend me thy sword;
    Many a nobleman lies stark and stiff
    Under the hoofs of vaunting enemies,   40
    Whose deaths are yet unrevenged; I prithee, lend me thy sword.
FAL. O Hal, I prithee give me leave to breathe awhile. Turk Gregory[1]
    never did such deeds in arms as I have done this day. I have paid
    Percy, I have made him sure.
PRINCE. He is indeed, and living to kill thee. I prithee, lend me thy   45
    sword.
FAL. Nay, before God, Hal, if Percy be alive, thou get'st not my
    sword; but take my pistol if thou wilt.
PRINCE. Give it me; what, is it in the case?
FAL. Aye, Hal; 'tis hot, 'tis hot; there's that will sack a city.   50

[*The* PRINCE *draws it out, and finds it to be a bottle of sack.*]

PRINCE. What, is it a time to jest and dally now?

[*He throws the bottle at him. Exit.*]

FAL. Well, if Percy be alive, I'll pierce him. If he do come in my
    way, so; if he do not, if I come in his willingly, let him make a
    carbonado[2] of me. I like not such grinning honor as Sir Walter
    hath; give me life, which if I can save, so; if not, honor comes   55
    unlooked for, and there's an end.   [*Exit.*]

SCENE 4

[*Alarum. Excursions.*[3] *Enter the* KING, *the* PRINCE, PRINCE
JOHN OF LANCASTER, *and* EARL OF WESTMORELAND.]

KING. I prithee,
    Harry, withdraw thyself; thou bleed'st too much.
    Lord John of Lancaster, go you with him.
LAN. Not I, my lord, unless I did bleed too.
PRINCE. I beseech your majesty, make up,[4]   5
    Lest your retirement do amaze your friends.
KING. I will do so.
    My Lord of Westmoreland, lead him to his tent.
WEST. Come, my lord, I'll lead you to your tent.
PRINCE. Lead me, my lord? I do not need your help,   10
    And God forbid a shallow scratch should drive
    The Prince of Wales from such a field as this,

---

1. Falstaff combines Pope Gregory VII, of whom   2. A cubed steak.
fantastic stories were told, with "Turk" (the Turks   3. Brief appearances and exits of soldiers fighting.
were noted for ferocity).   4. Advance; "amaze": dismay.

Where stained nobility lies trodden on,
And rebels' arms triumph in massacres!
LAN. We breathe too long; come, cousin Westmoreland,　　　15
Our duty this way lies; for God's sake, come.

> [⟨*Exeunt* PRINCE JOHN *and* WESTMORELAND.⟩]

PRINCE. By God, thou hast deceived me, Lancaster;
I did not think thee lord of such a spirit.
Before, I loved thee as a brother, John,
But now I do respect thee as my soul.　　　20
KING. I saw him hold Lord Percy at the point
With lustier maintenance than I did look for
Of such an ungrown warrior.
PRINCE.　　　　　　　　　　O, this boy
Lends mettle to us all!　　　　　　　　　[*Exit.*]

> [*Enter* DOUGLAS.]

DOUG. Another king! they grow like Hydra's heads.[5]　　　25
I am the Douglas, fatal to all those
That wear those colors on them; what art thou,
That counterfeit'st the person of a king?
KING. The king himself, who, Douglas, grieves at heart
So many of his shadows[6] thou hast met　　　30
And not the very king. I have two boys
Seek Percy and thyself about the field,
But seeing thou fall'st on me so luckily
I will assay thee; so defend thyself.
DOUG. I fear thou art another counterfeit,　　　35
And yet, in faith, thou bearest thee like a king;
But mine I am sure thou art, whoe'er thou be.
And thus I win thee.

> [*They fight; the* KING *being in danger, enter* PRINCE OF WALES.]

PRINCE. Hold up thy head, vile Scot, or thou art like
Never to hold it up again! the spirits　　　40
Of valiant Shirley, Stafford, Blunt, are in my arms;
It is the Prince of Wales that threatens thee,
Who never promiseth but he means to pay.

> [*They fight;* DOUGLAS *flieth.*]

Cheerly, my lord; how fares your grace?
Sir Nicholas Gawsey hath for succor sent,　　　45
And so hath Clifton; I'll to Clifton straight.
KING. Stay, and breathe awhile.
Thou hast redeemed thy lost opiniòn,
And showed thou makest some tender of[7] my life
In this fair rescue thou hast brought to me.　　　50

---

5. The heads of this fabulous monster grew back
faster than they could be cut off.
6. Likenesses.

7. I.e., you have some concern for. "Opinion":
reputation.

PRINCE. O God, they did me too much injury
 That ever said I hearkened for your death.
 If it were so, I might have let alone
 The insulting hand of Douglas over you,
 Which would have been as speedy in your end   55
 As all the poisonous potions in the world
 And saved the treacherous labor of your son.
KING. Make up to Clifton; I'll to Sir Nicholas Gawsey. [*Exit.*]

  [*Enter* HOTSPUR.]

HOT. If I mistake not, thou art Harry Monmouth.
PRINCE. Thou speak'st as if I would deny my name.   60
HOT. My name is Harry Percy.
PRINCE.   Why then I see
 A very valiant rebel of the name.
 I am the Prince of Wales, and think not, Percy,
 To share with me in glory any more:
 Two stars keep not their motion in one sphere,[8]   65
 Nor can one England brook a double reign
 Of Harry Percy and the Prince of Wales.
HOT. Nor shall it, Harry, for the hour is come
 To end the one of us; and would to God
 Thy name in arms were now as great as mine!   70
PRINCE. I'll make it greater ere I part from thee,
 And all the budding honors on thy crest
 I'll crop to make a garland for my head.
HOT. I can no longer brook thy vanities.   [*They fight.*]

  [*Enter* FALSTAFF.]

FAL. Well said, Hal, to it, Hal! Nay, you shall find no boy's play 75
here, I can tell you.

  [*Enter* DOUGLAS; *he fighteth with* FALSTAFF, *who falls down
  as if he were dead.* ⟨*Exit* DOUGLAS.⟩ *The* PRINCE *killeth*
  PERCY.]

HOT. O Harry, thou hast robbed me of my youth!
 I better brook the loss of brittle life
 Than those proud titles thou hast won of me;
 They wound my thoughts worse than thy sword my flesh; 80
 But thought's the slave of life, and life time's fool,
 And time, that takes survey of all the world,
 Must have a stop. O, I could prophesy,
 But that the earthy and cold hand of death
 Lies on my tongue; no, Percy, thou art dust,   85
 And food for—   [⟨*Dies.*⟩]
PRINCE. For worms, brave Percy; fare thee well, great heart!
 Ill-weaved ambition, how much art thou shrunk!
 When that this body did contain a spirit
 A kingdom for it was too small a bound,   90

8. Orbit. "Brook": endure.

But now two paces of the vilest earth
Is room enough; this earth that bears thee dead
Bears not alive so stout[9] gentleman.
If thou wert sensible of courtesy,
I should not make so dear[1] show of zeal;   95
But let my favors hide thy mangled face[2]
And, even in thy behalf, I'll thank myself
For doing these fair rites of tenderness.
Adieu, and take thy praise with thee to heaven;
Thy ignominy sleep with thee in the grave,   100
But not remembered in thy epitaph!

     [*He spieth* FALSTAFF *on the ground.*]

What, old acquaintance, could not all this flesh
Keep in a little life? Poor Jack, farewell!
I could have better spared a better man.
O, I should have a heavy miss of thee,   105
If I were much in love with vanity![3]
Death hath not struck so fat a deer today,
Though many dearer,[4] in this bloody fray.
Emboweled will I see thee by and by;
Till then in blood by noble Percy lie.   [*Exit.*]   110

FAL. [*rising up*] Emboweled! if thou embowel me today, I'll give
you leave to powder[5] me and eat me tomorrow. 'Sblood, 'twas
time to counterfeit, or that hot termagant[6] Scot had paid me scot
and lot too. Counterfeit? I lie, I am no counterfeit; to die is to be
a counterfeit, for he is but the counterfeit of a man who hath not   115
the life of a man; but to counterfeit dying when a man thereby
liveth is to be no counterfeit, but the true and perfect image of
life indeed. The better part[7] of valor is discretion, in the which
better part I have saved my life. Zounds, I am afraid of this gunpowder Percy, though he be dead; how if he should counterfeit   120
too and rise? By my faith, I am afraid he would prove the better
counterfeit. Therefore I'll make him sure; yea, and I'll swear I
killed him. Why may not he rise as well as I? Nothing confutes
me but eyes, and nobody sees me. Therefore, sirrah [*stabbing
him*], with a new wound in your thigh, come you along with   125
me.

     [*He takes up* HOTSPUR *on his back.*]
    [*Enter the* PRINCE *and* JOHN OF LANCASTER.]

PRINCE. Come, brother John, full bravely hast thou fleshed[8]
  Thy maiden sword.
LAN.   But soft, whom have we here?
  Did you not tell me this fat man was dead?
PRINCE. I did; I saw him dead,   130
  Breathless and bleeding on the ground. Art thou alive?

9. Valiant.
1. Open.
2. Prince Hal here covers Hotspur's face with a scarf.
3. Frivolity.

4. Nobler. "Emboweled": embalmed.
5. Pickle.
6. Violent; "scot and lot": completely.
7. Quality, not "portion."
8. Initiated.

Or is it fantasy[9] that plays upon our eyesight?
I prithee speak; we will not trust our eyes
Without our ears; thou art not what thou seem'st.

FAL. No, that's certain, I am not a double man; but if I be not Jack   135
Falstaff, then am I a Jack.[1] There is Percy [*throwing the body
down*]; if your father will do me any honor, so; if not, let him kill
the next Percy himself. I look to be either earl or duke, I can
assure you.

PRINCE. Why, Percy I killed myself and saw thee dead.   140

FAL. Didst thou? Lord, Lord, how this world is given to lying! I
grant you I was down and out of breath, and so was he; but we
rose both at an instant and fought a long hour by Shrewsbury
clock. If I may be believed, so; if not, let them that should reward
valor bear the sin upon their own heads. I'll take it upon my   145
death, I gave him this wound in the thigh; if the man were alive
and would deny it, zounds, I would make him eat a piece of my
sword.

LAN. This is the strangest tale that ever I heard.

PRINCE. This is the strangest fellow, brother John.   150
Come, bring your luggage nobly on your back;
For my part, if a lie may do thee grace,
I'll gild it with the happiest terms I have.

[*A retreat is sounded.*]

The trumpet sounds retreat;[2] the day is ours.
Come, brother, let us to the highest[3] of the field,   155
To see what friends are living, who are dead.

[*Exeunt* (PRINCE OF WALES *and* LANCASTER.)]

FAL. I'll follow, as they say, for reward. He that rewards me, God
reward him! If I do grow great,[4] I'll grow less, for I'll purge and
leave sack, and live cleanly as a nobleman should do. [*Exit.*]

SCENE 5

[*The trumpets sound. Enter the* KING, PRINCE OF WALES,
PRINCE JOHN OF LANCASTER, EARL OF WESTMORELAND, *with*
WORCESTER *and* VERNON *prisoners.*]

KING. Thus ever did rebellion find rebuke.
Ill-spirited Worcester, did not we send grace,
Pardon, and terms of love to all of you?
And wouldst thou turn our offers contrary,
Misuse the tenor of thy kinsman's trust?   5
Three knights upon our party slain today,
A noble earl and many a creature else
Had been alive this hour,
If like a Christian thou hadst truly borne
Betwixt our armies true intelligence.   10

9. Illusion.
1. I.e., a worthless fellow.
2. The signal to stop pursuit of the defeated enemy.

3. Highest part.
4. I.e., become "either earl or duke." "Purge": take
cleansing medicines.

WOR. What I have done my safety urged me to,
And I embrace this fortune patiently,
Since not to be avoided it falls on me.
KING. Bear Worcester to the death and Vernon too;
Other offenders we will pause upon.   15

[*Exeunt* WORCESTER *and* VERNON ⟨*guarded.*⟩]

How goes the field?
PRINCE. The noble Scot, Lord Douglas, when he saw
The fortune of the day quite turned from him,
The noble Percy slain, and all his men
Upon the foot of fear,[5] fled with the rest,   20
And falling from a hill he was so bruised
That the pursuers took him. At my tent
The Douglas is, and I beseech your grace
I may dispose of him.
KING.   With all my heart.
PRINCE. Then, brother John of Lancaster, to you   25
This honorable bounty shall belong;
Go to the Douglas and deliver him
Up to his pleasure, ransomless and free;
His valor shown upon our crests today
Hath taught us how to cherish such high deeds   30
Even in the bosom of our adversaries.
LAN. I thank your grace for this high courtesy,
Which I shall give away immediately.
KING. Then this remains, that we divide our power.
You, son John and my cousin Westmoreland,   35
Towards York shall bend you with your dearest[6] speed
To meet Northumberland and the prelate Scroop,
Who, as we hear, are busily in arms;
Myself and you, son Harry, will towards Wales
To fight with Glendower and the Earl of March.   40
Rebellion in this land shall lose his sway,
Meeting the check[7] of such another day;
And since this business so fair is done,
Let us not leave till all our own be won.   [*Exeunt.*]

1598

5. Fleeing in panic.   7. (1) Hindrance, (2) rebuke.
6. Greatest.

The Early
Seventeenth Century
1603-1660

1603: Death of Elizabeth Tudor, accession of James I, first Stuart king of England.

1605: The Gunpowder Plot, a failed effort by Catholic extremists to blow up Parliament and the King. Responsible for prolonged and bitter anti-Catholic feeling: "Guy Fawkes Day" (November 5) still preserves the memory of one of the conspirators.

1620: Arrival of the Pilgrim Fathers in the New World.

1625: Death of James I, accession of Charles I.

1642: Outbreak of civil war: theaters closed.

1649: Execution of Charles I, beginning of Commonwealth and Protectorate, known inclusively as the Interregnum (1649–1660).

1660: End of the Protectorate, Restoration of Charles II.

In its narrowest definition, the "early seventeenth century" extends from the accession of the first Stuart king (James I) in 1603 to the coronation of the third (Charles II) in 1660. But the events of those years are historically meaningful only if seen in a pattern extending from 1588 to 1688. Between these two outer dates occurred those massive social events which, in their cumulative effect, bridge the gap between the Tudor "tyranny-by-consent" of the sixteenth century and the equally ill-defined but equally functional constitutional monarchy of the eighteenth century. At the center of the period lies the Puritan Revolution of 1640–1660. The quarrels and controversies that culminated in this upheaval began to reach an inflammatory stage shortly after 1588; its tremors and aftershocks largely subsided after 1688. In more senses than one, the Revolution was the central event of the century.

Armada year, 1588, marked a decisive turning point in the reign of Elizabeth. Like most of her subjects, she had expected the nation's supreme triumph over a long-awaited, much-hated invader to release a tide of patriotic good feeling. Nothing of the sort happened: quite the contrary. Social problems that had long lain suppressed in the interests of national unity suddenly surfaced when the nation was secure. They gave rise to bitter and divisive quarrels, fought out for the most part between the aging queen and her successive parliaments, but also in local encounters throughout the land. Wherever a stiff-necked parson encountered a strong-willed bishop, a grumbling consumer confronted an unjust monopoly, or a truculent House-of-Commons man complained that his freedom of speech was being abridged, the frictions of society built up. Individually, perhaps, they were minor grievances, but, being neglected, they festered, tending over the years to reinforce one another. The queen's traditional measures of cajolery and grandiose rhetoric failed to placate the malcontents; and the peaceful accession of James, first English monarch of the Stuart family, did nothing to mollify them. By pleas and remonstrations, and by voting to withhold taxes from the royal administration, Parliament sought redress, but to little avail. Agitation against the authoritarian episcopal church continued, mostly subsurface, but flaring up occasionally in acts of fierce despair, as when the Pilgrim Fathers left their native land forever, rather than submit to episcopal rule. (They went to Amsterdam in 1608 and then in 1620 to the wilderness of Plymouth, Massachusetts.) Under the increasingly strict rule of James's son, Charles, discontents spread more widely if even less openly; they expanded from Puritan preachers and their relatively small congregations to the merchant classes, the lawyers, the Parliament-men, and the gentry—to Scotland, to the mercantile towns, through the cloth-making countryside of East Anglia. By the late 1630s tempers were strained, and in 1637 an episode in Edinburgh led to the first of two half-hearted wars between England and Scotland. But domestic peace was an ingrained habit in most of England, and it was not till 1642, after five years of muted struggle and negotiation, that open conflict broke out.

In the wars that followed, the forces of insurrection (the Parliamentary, Puritan, or Roundhead armies) were successful in one of their aims: they rendered Charles powerless, brought him to trial, and executed him (1649). But they failed to set up a stable government of their own, free from the faults of the one they had destroyed, and they failed to set up a new national church, to replace the episcopacy that they had long criticized. The military dictatorship (1649–1660) established first by Oliver Cromwell under the name of Commonwealth and then maintained as a Protectorate, even after his death in 1658, was no more than a makeshift effort to contain a political instability that had got out of hand. When Charles II was recalled from exile (1660) and put back on his father's throne but without his father's powers, it became clear that England was bound to have, in religion and politics, some sort of organization looser than anyone had anticipated, looser than anyone really wanted. But its exact form was subject to constant pulling and hauling among the parties, and no solid settlement was reached till 1688, when Charles's brother and successor, James II, was ejected from the throne and sent into exile. After 1688, its social problems compromised if not solved, the country settled down to a long constitutional nap under a series of monarchs who made little trouble for their parliaments and therefore had little trouble with their thrones. The crisis was over.

Though infinitely complex in details, the main social problems that exercised the seventeenth century can be broadly stated, with their solutions, in two sentences. In the religious sphere, the basic issue was: How far should the reformation of the Protestant church be carried? and the solution accomplished in 1688 was, "As far as each individual self-defined religious group wants." In the sphere of constitutional politics, the basic issue was: How much authority should the monarch have independent of Parliament? and the solution accomplished in 1688 was, "Almost none."

BEFORE AND AFTER THE PURITAN REVOLT

To visualize the immense changes wrought by the crisis years of the Puritan Revolt, and their relation to the quality of English literature, it may be useful to anatomize very roughly the value structure of English society before and after the event. Oversimplifications are inevitable but necessary, to point up a set of broad changes which actually took place; and definitions are possible because the Revolution was preceded and followed by periods of relative order and tranquility. Under Elizabeth Tudor the court was the undisputed center of national authority, influence, power, reward, and intellectual inspiration. Careers were made and fortunes established through court connections. London was the center of the kingdom, and the court was the unchallenged center of London. Particularly was this true in matters of the intellect, of literature and the arts. The characteristic forms of literature under Elizabeth were courtly. Courtiers patronized the theater by attending plays (of which the middle class generally disapproved) and by lending the prestige of their names to different acting companies. The sonnet sequence, the pastoral romance (Sidney's *Arcadia*), the chivalric allegory (Spenser's *Faerie Queene*), the learned sermon, the erotic idyll *(Hero and Leander* or *Venus and Adonis)*, the masque, the epic—all these were courtly forms, implying courtly readers and writers who were either courtiers themselves or concerned to please courtiers. For patronage flowed, when it flowed at all, from courtly donors; and, apart from the precarious rewards of the theater, patronage was almost the only way for the writer to live by writing. The same pattern continued under the first two Stuarts, James I and Charles I. Whether in his sermons or in his poems, a man like Donne wrote primarily for courtiers. Versatile and various as he was, Ben Jonson channeled almost all his energies into writing for court and courtiers. Carew, Suckling, Lovelace, and a host of lesser writers were themselves courtiers, simply in the sense that they spent much of their time at court. A man like George Herbert was much remarked because he could have been a courtier and chose not to be. There were exceptions, of course; country doctors and rural parsons sometimes exercised themselves in literature. But the court influence was predominant, and so far as a literary society existed, it took its tone from the court. Because court circles were narrow, a poet did not have to wait for publication in order to be widely known among his fellow poets. Manuscript collections of poems by one author, or by several, circulated through the court; a poem could become popular, be set to music several times over, and yet never appear in print. The books that were printed generally appeared in small editions, and, being destined for a particular audience, could take a good deal for granted in the way of special background and training. A court preacher like Lancelot Andrewes assumed in his hearers acquaintance with at least the rudiments of three ancient languages; Sir Philip Sidney in the *Arcadia* assumed familiarity not only with the codes of learned pastoralism, but with the traditions and conventions of courtly behavior. For court society had many characteristic and distinctive values. It implied a belief in hierarchical order within a strict framework of uniformity, involving obedience to the national church, loyalty to the national monarch. Within that framework, it tended to produce intricate, allusive, and highly decorative writing. Courtiers generally valued the heroic passions—love (but not necessarily marriage), warfare (largely free of a political context), and devotional piety (quite apart from practical morality). The controlling principle behind all these distinctions was an emphasis upon honor as the supreme principle in life, not to be estimated in any way by criteria of mere prudence. Literature written within this framework and primarily for readers who accepted it tended generally to reflect its arrangement of values.

After 1660, and even more strikingly after 1688, the pattern of values was quite different. For one thing, the court was no longer an unchallenged center of intellectual and literary influence. It did not have the power, social and financial, to be anything of the sort. For now money and influence no longer flowed exclusively from the court. London City (a network of banks and merchants, jobbers, financiers, brokers, tradesmen, and credit-managers) was one rival source of power and influence; Parliament itself, which in 1688 would assert decisive power over the throne by expelling James II and appointing a Dutchman to be his successor as William III, was another. Instead of standing above interest as the sole fountain of honor, the court thus became in effect one of several competing interests. The relatively conservative "landed interest" tended toward the court, as the more innovative "money interest" found its chief support in the City; and Parliament-men, ranking themselves under the deliberately meaningless nicknames of "Tory" and "Whig," sided with either interest as they chose or with both as they found the occasion proper. One's connection with an interest was not through the inflexible principle of honor, but through the flexible one of . . . interest.

In precisely the same way, the established church, which had once claimed to be sole guardian of men's spiritual welfare and therefore of their worldly behavior—the authoritative voice disciplining every Englishman's private interests—became after 1660 simply one of many possible religious communities. (It was the most powerful, the most socially acceptable, and for the moment the largest one; but it was not, and could not be made, the only one.) The Puritan sects, originally factions within the English church, had been freed to multiply and develop their independence during the Interregnum; after the Restoration, they could not be got back into the episcopal (Anglican) church by force or persuasion. When several sects exist side by side in open competition, they are all voluntary. Each interprets Scripture after its own fashion, each follows its own moral code, each tries to attract proselytes, all agree in not trying to persecute one another. But that creates problems of discipline; if a member does not like the social code of his sect, he transfers to a more understanding sect, or out of them all. When neither monarch nor church could control social and economic behavior, most of it passed out of control altogether. For morality in a social or business sense applies mainly to people, considered as responsible economic agents; and the new forms of economic organization involved either artificial personalities or legal fictions to which moral laws do not apply. Corporations and joint-stock companies, cartels and syndicates, mutual-aid societies and credit unions, banks and bankers' combines (a whole gamut of anonymous voluntary associations) began to develop England piecemeal, amorphously, after the fashion of a modern capitalist nation. New money brought to the fore new men, enterprising and respectable, but with few pretensions to courtly manners or intellectual sophistication. The literature that appealed to them was less dogmatic and moralistic than the old hell-and-damnation puritanism; it was more serious than the frankly bawdy wit of the Restoration stage. Observing these and other divergencies of taste, enterprising publishers began to aim their products at a particular market, in which they specialized. Before long, they were hiring writers to turn out titles on order. The "booksellers," as they were called, thus began to replace the older courtly patrons as makers of public taste. Authors who wrote to order at the bidding of publishers became known collectively, from the cheap lodgings where they congregated, as Grub Street authors. For them, at least, the change from a society organized around honor to one organized around interest was very palpable indeed.

Around the broad social changes sketched above there took place a set of intellectual and spiritual changes, no less striking and significant. The Elizabethan monarchy and church had been hierarchical in organization because that was thought to be the inevitable structure of things, the natural pattern of the world. Every creature had his place in the great order of divine appointments; and the different families of being were bound together by a chain of universal analogy. The king was to his subjects as Michael was to the other archangels, as the bishop was to his pastors, as the lion was to other beasts, as the eagle was to other birds, as the diamond was to other stones, as gold was to other metals. The head ruled the other parts of the body because, as the seat of reason, it was nobler. Reason, which ruled in man, made him natural head of the family because passion was thought to rule in woman. The king was head of the body politic; in him, reason ruled as it ought, over the passionate and tumultuous multitude. And all this ruling was necessary because of Adam's fall, as a result of which not only human psychology but the whole structure of the universe had been disordered. Though they differed over the form of the rule and the name of the ruler, almost all the contestants in the civil wars agreed that the people needed strict discipline of some sort, because in themselves they were radically imperfect. While the various leaders were disputing over details, the people, simply as a result of slow experience (by living under an "illegitimate" authority, without any sort of religious conformity), demonstrated that they were less imperfect, and needed less rigid discipline, than had been supposed.

One universal truth emerged from the revolution and civil wars—that no one universal truth was to be had, whether by sword, by prayer, or by study. Nor was it really needed. Individuals, it seemed, could hold differing views about foreign policy, the nature of Christ's presence in the sacrament, or the lawfulness of infant baptism, without necessarily precipitating social chaos. A single true belief in these matters, and in many, many others, was evidently unnecessary. And thus the whole notion of human beings as radically fallen creatures, who needed a special saving truth and a dose of stiff discipline to redeem their faults, began fading toward obsolescence. A reasonable person (one who behaved sensibly and didn't bother his or her neighbor) seemed to be almost as good as need be. In a long list of controversies, over which people had once been willing to slit throats, it turned out that nobody was right and nobody was wrong. And thus the English community changed from one founded on the concepts of hierarchy, uniformity, and personal relatedness, to one founded on the concepts of multiplicity, disparity, and toleration. In less than a hundred years the nation had passed from a strict authoritarian regime legitimated (in its own eyes) by eternal divine constitutions—to a vigorous, materialistic community of competing pressure groups within an accepted framework of political, religious, and social differences. Slowly the notion that a critic of the government must be a heretic and a traitor gave way to a gentler formula which in the nineteenth century became classic: one could be "a member of His Majesty's loyal opposition."

LITERARY CROSSCURRENTS

With the obvious and immensely important exception of Milton (and perhaps his friend Marvell), hardly any of the high literature of the early seventeenth century was the work of Puritans or men sympathetic to the Puritan cause. The great Puritan art forms of the age were the sermon and the religious tract. This is not just the joke it seems; Puritan sermons, of which there were many thousands, explored in intimate detail the psychology of the Christian trying to be sure of his own salvation, and Puritan tracts developed dramatic new ways of exciting the zeal of their readers. Yet on the whole the Puritans mistrusted *belles-lettres*, on the same principle that they mistrusted graven idols (statues, stained-glass windows, or paintings), music, and religious rituals. These were all allurements and enticements of the sensual world; they threatened to contaminate and diffuse the pure spiritual energy of divinely infused faith. The Puritans, therefore, did not directly compete with the old courtly forms of literature; they subjected those who did follow the old forms to heavy moral and social pressure. A sense of deep disquiet, of ancient traditions under challenge, is felt everywhere in the early seventeenth century; and it can hardly be accounted for except as a response to the growing discontents that ultimately erupted in the Revolt.

One may well think of Metaphysical poets who followed Donne (such as Herbert, Crashaw, Vaughan, Cowley) as trying to deepen the traditional lyric forms of love and devotion by stretching them to comprehend new and extreme intellectual energies. In the other direction, Jonson and his "sons" the Cavalier poets (Herrick, Suckling, Lovelace, Waller, Denham) generally tried to compress and limit their poems, giving them a high finish and a strong sense of easy domination at the expense (occasionally) of their explicit intellectual content. Though these alternate "schools" do not by any means represent watertight compartments (Donne wrote some poems that sound like Jonson, Jonson some in the manner of Donne), the common contrast of "Cavalier" with "Metaphysical" does describe two major poetic alternatives of the early century. Yet both styles were wholly inadequate containers for the sort of gigantic energy that Milton, for example, was trying to express.

For Milton, with his deep sense of moral imperative, his heroic ambitions for poetry, and his proud Englishness, the fashionable verses of his contemporaries must have seemed unbearably constricting. Like any great artist, Milton was capable of profiting from the study of craftsmen whom he had no intention of imitating; and in different ways, he did profit by a study of Donne and Jonson, we may be sure. But for his central inspiration Milton reached back beyond both Metaphysicals and Jonsonians to the figure of Spenser. In youth particularly his mind ran to Spenserian projects—chivalric romances based on Arthurian themes or sometimes on scriptural stories. Milton's style was fully formed by the late 1630s—it is usual to say that he found his voice in *Lycidas* (1637); and he might well have proceeded to complete one or more of these semi-Spenserian projects. But it is not altogether a loss that the civil war intervened, and prevented him for twenty years from putting his mind full-time to poetic work.

Agonizing as they were, the wars did not involve constant bloodshed;

rather, they were intervals of fighting separated by periods of negotiation and argument, and accompanied by a constant, deep-seated turmoil of popular agitation. Especially on the parliamentary side, enthusiasts for a wide array of causes, political, social, and religious, began appealing for public support in the only way available to them, through the printing press. Most of their pamphlets, broadsheets, and newsletters were not literary at all; but many achieved a direct and forceful prose style and a few attained not only a high level of eloquence, but some distinction of thought. The pamphlet wars, in which over twenty thousand verbal shots were fired off, wrought a mighty change in English public life. They accustomed thousands of Englishmen, whose mental life had previously been guarded by strict censorship, to free reading and open argumentation; they created something close to what we now call public opinion. And the experience of Puritanism gave to English life a strong steady moral tone, never so widely or deeply established before.

Thus, when Milton returned to his epic ambitions after 1660, neither he nor his potential audience was anything like what they had been before the war. Chivalric romance was out of the question; the issue on Milton's mind, and the nation's, was whether God maintained, behind the chaotic reversals of history, a sustaining plan for his favored people. That theme could not be addressed through the favorite metaphors of Spenser, jousting knights, lovely ladies, dark enchanters, and hospitals for sick souls. It had to be approached through the central and very simple narrative of mainline Christianity. As the work of Milton's fifties, *Paradise Lost* was deeper, larger, more evangelical than anything he might have written in his thirties; it was well suited to appeal to a nation which had just passed through a massive spiritual crisis. Its author could not have risen so confidently above the twin temptations of pride and despair, had he himself not experienced both in full measure.

But *Paradise Lost* was also, and could not help being, the product of Milton's surpassingly thorough classical education. It is thus a major monument—one of the last perhaps, certainly one of the most impressive—of the Renaissance tradition of Christian humanism. This is the assurance, shared by many writers of the period, that the classical virtues, such as justice, magnanimity, and temperance, when joined in the service of the Christian faith, strengthen both it and themselves. Gathering together in a grasp of unparalleled amplitude these major strands of European culture, and forming them into a poised and balanced structure of epic dimensions, Milton forged a poem that would remain for centuries to come a supreme literary achievement.

During the twenty years of Puritan rule at mid-century, most of the theaters were closed and hardly anything was written for the stage; during this period, most of the old actors and playwrights died, and the revival of the English stage after 1660 depended very largely on the work of one man, Sir William Davenant, and on the example of the French stage, then at its height. Shakespeare's emulators and successors under the first two Stuarts had been much influenced by the melancholy then so largely prevalent; the dark, oppressive mood is almost unbroken in the work of tragic writers such as Webster, Ford, Tourneur, and Middleton. But alongside this somber and sometimes morbid tragedy, and serving as relief from it, flourished a great variety of tragicomic spectacles, romantic comedies, and pastoral fantasies. Very often these plays were influenced by the masques so popular at court— that is, they included a great deal in the way of spectacle, display, pageant, music, and sometimes fantasy. Though Shakespeare was long dead, though Jonson was in his dotage, and though none of the successors to these two men quite met their measure, the stage continued vigorously active right up to the civil war. But then the theaters were shut, abruptly and apparently forever. When they reopened in 1660, they were forced at first to rely on a backlog of twenty-year-old plays. But gradually they built up a repertoire of comedies (generally bawdy) and tragedies in the rhetorical, declamatory manner which gave them, and the couplets in which they were cast, the name of "heroic." Both these fashions, like so much else in the Restoration, were extreme and temporary. Dryden, who practiced both modes, lived to see them both at an end—the heroic tragedies under the weight of their own pomposity, the bawdy comedies under the attack of an infuriated clergyman, Jeremy Collier.

Beyond, perhaps outside, literature as such lies a change in the intellectual tone of the century which cannot be ignored, hard as it is to describe. The great minds of the early century were lawyers and theologians. Coke, Bacon, Selden, and Spelman among the lawyers, Laud, Andrewes, Cudworth, Ussher, and Chillingworth among the theologians were men famous in their generation. Among the lawyers, some are still consulted as authorities to this day—Coke is a name to conjure with in English law, and Selden's treatise on *Titles of Honor* is obsolete only because the subject itself is. As for the theologians, their work too has ceased to be "relevant"; but a brief browsing expedition through the *Library of Anglo-Catholic Theology* cannot fail to convince the student that they were men who worked—in their chosen trade—to very high standards of precise and authoritative scholarship. And yet, as the century's intellectual weather changed, these disciplines ceased to be at the center of things. There were great lawyers after 1660, but they were not the makers and shakers of society; there were famous clergymen, but they were not the builders of society's central codes of belief. Starting about mid-century, the great names belong to other disciplines—they are scientists like the astronomers Hooke and Halley, the physicist Robert Boyle, Locke the physician-philosopher, John Wallis and Sir Isaac Newton the mathematicians, William Harvey the anatomist. Few of them set out consciously to reconstruct an entire view of the cosmos, and Sir Isaac, who did so most successfully, retained to the end streaks and patches of the old beliefs. (He wrote a commentary on the Book of Revelation that has rather baffled those who admire his scientific work.) But the coming of a secular, materialist world view was in the air; even before the Puritans were forced to give up their dream of a community of saints, the tide had set and was ebbing rapidly another way.

BIRTH AND DEATH OF LITERARY FORMS

The stress and strain of a revolutionary age can thus be read at large in the century's literature, from the somber, sluggish melancholy of the early decades, through the hoarse, incoherent warfare of the middle years, to the slow firming up of new standards of decorum and correctness after 1660. Still another mark of violent change is provided by the number of literary forms which perished or dropped from favor in the course of the century, even as others were being born.

Sonnets, for example, were all the rage in the last years of Elizabeth, the first years of James. Almost always they dealt with erotic themes, often they were linked together in sequences to suggest, if not tell, a story. Donne turned the sonnet primarily to religious themes; Milton's sonnets are mostly on religion and politics. And thereafter sonnets largely faded from the poetic repertory; like epic poetry in our own day, they practically disappeared. Allegory suffered an even more curious fate. It was of course the essential method of Spenser's *Faerie Queene*, and the figures of Sin and Death in the midst of *Paradise Lost* testify to its survival. But when Dryden used allegory (exceptionally, as in *The Hind and the Panther*), there was a kind of grotesque comedy about it, as if the form were fundamentally a joke. Serious allegory had slid far down the social scale; it was now the natural mode for an inspired primitive like Bunyan.

Blighted by the frosts of Puritan disapproval, the masque and madrigal both perished. The one was a courtly, the other a popular form; but both were suspect as vain, sensual, and worldly. Madrigals, as a blend of folk- and art-songs, were particularly to be regretted. For many years they had been sung in the yeoman's home or merchant's parlor, to the accompaniment of lutes, viols, and recorders. Many developed complex polyphonic harmonies; many had been composed by distinguished musicians. But they faded away, with other folk arts and folk customs—rounds and carols and morris-dancing, Maypoles, and rural pageants, and country games—to make way for psalm singing and sermon listening. For the gentry, indigenous music was replaced by oratorios and operas, many of them imported from Italy, Germany, or France.

As the many intricate stanzaic forms of the early century lost favor, rhymed couplets came to the fore. They are a superb meter for verse argumentation; they can combine the stinging effect of epigrams with the impetus of cumulative rhythms that build into splendid verse paragraphs. Whether coincidentally or as a consequence, the rise of strict and regular couplets accompanied a perceptible decline of the lyric impulse. Elizabethan and Jacobean lyrics make up (in the ancient phrase) a paradise of dainty devices; Restoration lyrics, though occasionally elegant and sometimes magnificently obscene, are far less numerous as well as less expressive.

Formal verse satire, which had been a self-conscious novelty at the start of the century, was a well-established mode of poetry by the end. Under the molding of many hands, satire grew subtler and more various; the satirist recognized his responsibility to divert his reader as well as to insult his antagonist. Indeed, a whole new mode of gentlemanly discourse grew up after the Restoration; it went sometimes by the name of "raillery," sometimes "banter," and amounted to nothing more than light irony. But serious things could be said in it, about which nonetheless a gentleman might not want to show himself too earnest. Below satire, burlesque was another literary mode which the seventeenth century nurtured, with the aid of France. After the unrelieved earnestness of the Puritans, derision and buffoonery became the order of the day; and with the advent of burlesque, we find ourselves on the very threshold of the modern novel, one vein of which reaches as far back as *Don Quixote*.

Alongside perishing forms, new ones sprang up, many involving prose rather than verse, and reaching out toward a popular readership. As the century passed, preachers found that they could no longer entertain audiences with intricate similitudes and microscopic, word-by-word explication of texts; ranting and raving (known more politely as "zeal") were equally out of fashion. Instead, they turned increasingly to plainly phrased, commonsense discussions of practical morality, and found that such discourses pleased their audiences about as well as anything. Prose in general grew simpler and less artful; as it did so, its applications multiplied. In Walton we have the first intimate English biographer, in Clarendon the first large-scale political historian. The diarists Pepys and Evelyn, the scandalmongers Wood and Aubrey, the "character-writers" Overbury and Earle, professed psychologists like Robert Burton, and quizzical self-explorers like Sir Thomas Browne all contribute liberally and originally to the arts of human personality. Less than a hundred years elapsed between the early publications of Francis Bacon, England's first secular philosopher, and those of John Locke, one of her greatest. For better or worse, the first English newspapers sprang up during the civil wars; under the familiar rubric of "A Letter to a Friend in the Country," political commentators made themselves heard. Abraham Cowley, better as a writer of prose than a poet, produced a series of personal essays, more relaxed than those of Bacon, and soon to be followed by many others. The second great age of English translation began in 1660; it introduced Englishmen not only to the classics, and to works written in French or Italian, but to works of their own past—as when Dryden "translated" into modern English some of Chaucer's *Canterbury Tales*.

All these developments were predicated on a reading audience responsive, alert, and eager to be informed; not necessarily instructed in foreign tongues or trained in courtly conventions, but ready to follow a sustained discourse in unrhetorical, commonsense English. Such an audience, so tuned and so motivated, not expecting too much from its reading, but responsive to acute arguments or vivid touches of the imagination, is a first premise of modern literature. We are apt to think it as normal and natural a phenomenon as the air we breathe, but it is not. In fact, it had to be created slowly, hesitantly, without much conscious direction on anyone's part, by a process of gradual accretion and expansion. Its existence is the foundation of the new age, and the culminating achievement of the early seventeenth century.

Being diverse out of harsh necessity and tolerant only reluctantly, the later seventeenth century was often halting and unsteady in its taste. It was forging new standards, not accepting the guidance of old ones; its hallmark is a widening eclecticism. Women, freed by the civil wars to assume previously unfamiliar roles, struggled to find a voice of their own; despite striking many false notes at first, they made their presence felt, and the age to come would speak out more assuredly because of them. Science also advanced gropingly through a series of corrected errors and inspired guesses. The same age saw Sir Kenelm Digby's solemn proposal that one could cure wounds by medicating the sword that caused them, and William Harvey's proclamation of the circulation of the blood. Though much of Inigo Jones's work in architecture was destroyed, some of his actual structures and more of his important translations of Italian books on architecture survived, to provide a lead for neoclassical building in England and North America during the eighteenth century. Though the Puritan commonwealth went to smash as a political organization, many of the ideas expressed during those hectic mid-century years maintained an underground existence, and blossomed at the time of the American Revolution, more than a century later.

Thus the early seventeenth century brought to its culmination much that had been characteristic from the beginning of the English Renaissance, and at the same time advanced boldly across the threshold of the next age, whatever one prefers to call it. Though its elapsed time is relatively brief, the period changed not only the tone of literature, but the very definition of what literature could be. Like all great cultural shifts, this one was too complex to be captured in a single phrase or attributed to a single cause. It had neither a fixed beginning nor a precise end. But in the seamless web of history we can hardly fail to notice new colors and textures which, over the short course of the early seventeenth century, enter into the warp and woof of the nation's literary as of its social life, to make it look and feel like a whole new piece of cloth.

JOHN DONNE
1572–1631

1601: Secret marriage to Ann More.
1615: Becomes an Anglican priest.
1621: Appointed dean of St. Paul's Cathedral.
1633: First publication of *Poems*.

Donne himself originated an observation about his life and character which, though only partly accurate, has become commonplace. In a private letter, he distinguished Jack Donne, an adventurous young spark who wrote bawdy and cynical verses to an assortment of mistresses, from the grave and eloquent divine, Doctor Donne, the dean of St. Paul's. The contrast is striking, but the key to both characters is the same; it is a restless, searching energy that scorns the easy platitude and the smooth, vacant phrase; that is vivid, immediate, troubling. Whether he is flaunting his pleasure at chasing every girl in sight (as in *The Indifferent*), or voicing total repentance and devotion to God (as in the *Holy Sonnets*), Donne's poetry demands imaginative effort of the reader, and absorbs him in a tense, complex experience.

Donne was born into an old Roman Catholic family, at a time when anti-Catholic feeling in England was near its height and Catholics were subject to constant harassment by the Elizabethan secret police. His faith barred him from many of the usual avenues of success, and his point of view was always that of an insecure outsider. Though he attended both Oxford and Cambridge Universities, as well as Lincoln's Inn (where lawyers got their training), he never took any academic degrees and never practiced law. After quietly abandoning Catholicism some time during the 1590s, he had scruples about becoming an Anglican. He had no gift for commerce, and though he inherited money from his father (who died when Donne was only four), it was far from enough to render him independent. Hence he had to make his way in the world indirectly—by wit, charm, learning, valor, and above all, favor. Partly from sheer intellectual curiosity, he read enormously in divinity, medicine, law, and the classics; he wrote to display his learning and wit. He traveled on the Continent, especially, it would seem, to Spain; even in later years, he did a good deal of moving around. With Ralegh and Essex he took part in two hit-and-run expeditions against Cadiz and the Azores. He put himself in the way of court employment, danced attendance on great court ladies, and generally lived the life of a brilliant young man hopeful of preferment.

When in 1598 Donne was appointed private secretary to Sir Thomas Egerton, one of the highest officials in the queen's court, his prospects for worldly advancement seemed good. He sat in Elizabeth's last Parliament; he cultivated those who wielded power and had patronage to dispense. But in 1601 he secretly married Lady Egerton's niece, seventeen-year-old Ann More, and thereby ruined his own worldly hopes. The marriage turned out happily, but Donne's bad faith to his employer was neither forgotten nor forgiven. Sir George More had Donne imprisoned and dismissed from his post; and for the next dozen years the poet had to struggle at a series of makeshift employments to support his growing family. In his middle thirties, Donne was far from the brilliant young gallant of the 1590s; sick, poor, and unhappy, he wrote, but dared not publish, a treatise of the lawfulness of suicide (*Biathanatos*). As he approached forty, he published two anti-Catholic polemics (*Pseudo-Martyr*, 1610; *Ignatius his Conclave*, 1611); they sealed publicly his renunciation of the Catholic faith. In return for patronage from Sir Robert Drury, he wrote in 1611 and 1612 a pair of long poems, the *Anniversaries*, on the death of Sir Robert's daughter Elizabeth. None of these activities represented a full employment of Donne's pent-up intellectual energy. To be sure, his social position should not be painted too blackly. He still had friends among courtiers, politicians, poets, and the great ladies around court, like Lucy Countess of Bedford and Magdalen Herbert with her two poet-sons, George and Edward. Donne was never quite without resources; yet, broadly speaking, the middle years of his life were a period of uncertainty and discontent.

Though Donne had flatly refused in 1607 to take Anglican orders, King James was certain that he would some day make a great Anglican preacher. Hence he declared that Donne could have no preferment or employment from him, except in the church. Finally, in 1615, Donne overcame his scruples, not the least of which was the fear of seeming ambitious, and entered the ministry. He was in due course appointed Reader in Divinity at Lincoln's Inn. In the seventeenth century, among court circles and at the Inns of Court where lawyers congregated, preaching was at once a form of spiritual devotion, an intellectual exercise, and a dramatic entertainment. Donne's metaphorical style, bold erudition, and dramatic wit at once established him as a great preacher in an age of great preachers. Fully one hundred sixty of his sermons survive. In 1621 he was made dean of St. Paul's, where he preached to great congregations of "City" lawyers, courtiers, merchants, and tradesmen. In addition, his private devotions were published in 1624, and he continued to write sacred poetry till within a few years of his death. Obsessed with the idea of death, Donne preached what was called his own funeral sermon just a few weeks before he died. It is a terrifyingly personal meditation on dissolution, as befits a man who arranged for a final portrait of himself to be painted, dressed in his shroud.

The poetry of Donne represents a sharp break with that written by his predecessors and most of his contemporaries. Much Elizabethan verse is decorative and flowery. Its images adorn, its rhythm is mellifluous. Its frequent "conceits" (elaborately sustained metaphors) are often variations on comparisons passed down through generations of poets in a line from Petrarch in the fourteenth century. But Donne, taking his cue from recent Continental poets who had freshened the Petrarchan tradition by developing a more intellectualized form of conceit, created highly concentrated images which involve a major element of dramatic contrast or of intellectual strain. The clichés of earlier love poetry—bleeding hearts, cheeks like roses, lips like cherries, Cupid shooting the arrows of love—appear in Donne's poetry only to be mocked, or in some ingenious transmutation. The tears which flow in *A Valediction: of Weeping* are different from, and more complex than, the ordinary saline fluid of unhappy lovers; they are ciphers, naughts, symbols of the world's emptiness without the beloved; or else, suddenly reflecting her image, they are globes, worlds, they contain the sum of things. By using such conceits, the poet not only displays his own ingenuity; he may express a deep vision of the world and the strands of analogy that seem to hold it together. Donne's conceits leap continually in a restless orbit from the personal to the cosmic and back again.

Donne likes to twist and distort not only images and ideas, but traditional rhythmic and stanzaic patterns. His speech patterns are colloquial and various. Ben Jonson expressed the shock of some contemporaries by saying that "Donne, for not keeping of accent [i.e., metrical uniformity], deserved hanging"—though he also said that Donne was "the first poet in the world in some things." While Donne sometimes uses traditional verse forms, and indeed very simple ones, he is also fond of inventing elaborate and intricate stanzas. His penchant for compressed and elliptical expression often produces difficulty for the reader. In the satires, which Renaissance writers understood to be "harsh" and "crabbed" as a genre, Donne's distortions often threaten to choke off the stream of expression entirely. But in the lyrics (both those which are worldly and those which are religious in theme), as in the elegies and sonnets, the verse repeatedly achieves a complex and memorable melody. Donne had an unusual gift, rather like that of a modern poet, T. S. Eliot, for striking off phrases which ring in the mind like a silver coin. They are two masters of the colloquial style, removed alike from the dignified, weighty manner of Milton and the sugared sweetness of the Elizabethans.

Donne and his followers are known to literary history as the "Metaphysical school" of poets. Strictly speaking, this is a misnomer. There was no organized group of poets who imitated Donne, and if there had been, they would not have called themselves "Metaphysical" poets. That term was invented by John Dryden and Samuel Johnson. But the influence of Donne's poetic style was widely felt, especially by men whose taste was formed before 1660. George Herbert, Richard Crashaw, Henry Vaughan, Andrew Marvell, and Abraham Cowley are only the best known of those in whom this influence is recognizable. The great change of taste which took place in 1660 threw Donne and the "conceited" style out of fashion; during the eighteenth and nineteenth centuries both he and his followers were rarely read and still more rarely appreciated. Finally, in the late nineteenth and early twentieth centuries, three new editions of Donne appeared, of which Sir H. J. C. Grierson's, published in 1912, was quickly accepted as standard. By clarifying and purifying the often-garbled text, Grierson did a great deal to make Donne's poetry more available to the modern reader. Almost at once it started to exert an influence on modern poetic practice, the modern poets being hungry for a "tough" style which would free them from the worn-out rhetoric of late nineteenth-century Romanticism. And Donne's status among the English poets quickly climbed from that of a curiosity to that of an acknowledged master.

No more than a couple of the poems on which Donne's modern reputation is built were published during his lifetime, though most of them were widely circulated through court and literary circles in handwritten copies. There were practical reasons for this halfway state of affairs. Many of the poems would have constituted black marks on Donne's reputation as an earnest and godly divine; and because they were difficult and allusive, only a few people wanted to read them. Thus Donne was known, outside the relatively limited circles which had access to manuscript collections, primarily as a preacher and devotional writer. His collected poems were first published in 1633; in the second edition (1635), the poems were divided into nine generic groups (one of which includes only a single long poem,

The Progress of the Soul). The *Songs and Sonnets*, which open the volume, are generally amorous in theme; the *Divine Poems*, which close it, are described by their title. In between fall groups of epigrams, love elegies, epithalamia (wedding songs), satires, verse letters, and funeral elegies. For convenience, our selections, like those of most other editors, follow the order of the 1635 edition, though this is distinctly *not* the order in which Donne wrote the poems. Indeed, a detailed chronology is impossible to construct. The basic text for most of the poems, though, is that of the first, 1633, edition, sometimes supplemented and corrected by reference to other early editions and to manuscript materials. Recent editions, especially those by Helen Gardner and W. Milgate, have also been consulted.

The Good-Morrow[1]

I wonder, by my troth, what thou and I
Did, till we loved? Were we not weaned till then,
But sucked on country pleasures, childishly?
Or snorted we in the seven sleepers' den?[2]
'Twas so; but this, all pleasures fancies be.   5
If ever any beauty I did see,
Which I desired, and got, 'twas but a dream of thee.

And now good morrow to our waking souls,
Which watch not one another out of fear;
For love all love of other sights controls,   10
And makes one little room an everywhere.
Let sea-discoverers to new worlds have gone,
Let maps to others, worlds on worlds have shown:[3]
Let us possess one world; each hath one, and is one.

My face in thine eye, thine in mine appears,   15
And true plain hearts do in the faces rest;
Where can we find two better hemispheres,
Without sharp North, without declining West?
Whatever dies was not mixed equally;[4]
If our two loves be one, or thou and I   20
Love so alike that none do slacken, none can die.

1633

---

1. This is the first poem of the *Songs and Sonnets* in the 1635 edition. Confusingly, the group doesn't include any sonnets in our sense: in Donne's time, the term often meant simply "love lyric." Though precise dating is impossible, it is safe to suppose that Donne wrote all, or almost all, of the 53 poems in the 1590s and the first decade of the 17th century.

2. Many ancient authors recite the legend of 7 youths of Ephesus who hid in a cave from their pagan persecutors and slept there for 187 years,

awakening to find, amazedly, that the world had become Christian while they slept. "But" (line 5): except for.

3. I.e., let us concede that maps (or charts of the heavens) have shown to other investigators, etc. In line 14 an alternative reading is "Let us possess *our* world."

4. Scholastic philosophy taught that when the elements were imperfectly ("not equally") mixed, matter was mutable and mortal, but when they were perfectly mixed, it was unchanging and undying.

Song

Go and catch a falling star,
 Get with child a mandrake root,[1]
Tell me where all past years are,
 Or who cleft the Devil's foot,
Teach me to hear mermaids[2] singing,   5
Or to keep off envy's stinging,
  And find
  What wind
Serves to advance an honest mind.

If thou beest born to strange sights,   10
 Things invisible to see,
Ride ten thousand days and nights,
 Till age snow white hairs on thee,
Thou, when thou return'st, wilt tell me
All strange wonders that befell thee,   15
  And swear
  No where
Lives a woman true, and fair.

If thou find'st one, let me know,
 Such a pilgrimage were sweet;   20
Yet do not, I would not go,
 Though at next door we might meet;
Though she were true when you met her,
And last till you write your letter,
  Yet she   25
  Will be
False, ere I come, to two, or three.

          1633

The Undertaking

I have done one braver thing
 Than all the Worthies[1] did,
And yet a braver thence doth spring,
 Which is, to keep that hid.

---

1. The mandrake root, or mandragora, is often forked like the lower part of the male body. Legend has it that when pulled from the ground, the root is castrated and shrieks in agony; its shriek is death to hear. Getting such a vegetable with child presents obvious difficulties.
2. Identified with the sirens, whose song only the wily Odysseus survived.

1. According to medieval legend, the Nine Worthies, or supreme heroes of history, included three Jews (Joshua, David, Judas Maccabeus), three pagans (Hector, Alexander, Julius Caesar), and three Christians (Arthur, Charlemagne, Godfrey of Bouillon).

It were but madness now t' impart   5
    The skill of specular stone,[2]
When he which can have learned the art
    To cut it, can find none.

So, if I now should utter this,
    Others (because no more   10
Such stuff to work upon, there is)
    Would love but as before.

But he who loveliness within
    Hath found, all outward loathes,
For he who color loves, and skin,   15
    Loves but their[3] oldest clothes.

If, as I have, you also do
    Virtue attired in woman see,
And dare love that, and say so too,
    And forget the He and She;   20

And if this love, though placèd so,
    From profane men you hide,
Which will no faith on this bestow,
    Or, if they do, deride;

Then you have done a braver thing   25
    Than all the Worthies did;
And a braver thence will spring,
    Which is, to keep that hid.

                                          1633

The Sun Rising

Busy old fool, unruly sun,
    Why dost thou thus,
Through windows and through curtains call on us?
Must to thy motions lovers' seasons run?
    Saucy pedantic wretch, go chide   5
    Late schoolboys and sour prentices,
Go tell court huntsmen that the King will ride,[1]
    Call country ants to harvest offices;
Love, all alike, no season knows nor clime,
Nor hours, days, months, which are the rags of time.   10

2. A transparent or translucent material, reputed to have been used in antiquity for windows, but no longer known.
3. I.e., women's.

1. King James was addicted to hunting. "Harvest offices": autumn chores. The "country ants" may imply an allusion to the old fable of the ant and the grasshopper.

Thy beams, so reverend and strong
  Why shouldst thou think?
I could eclipse and cloud them with a wink,
But that I would not lose her sight so long;
    If her eyes have not blinded thine,   15
      Look, and tomorrow late, tell me,
    Whether both th' Indias of spice and mine[2]
    Be where thou leftst them, or lie here with me.
Ask for those kings whom thou saw'st yesterday,
And thou shalt hear, All here in one bed lay.   20

    She is all states,[3] and all princes I,
      Nothing else is.
Princes do but play us; compared to this,
All honor's mimic, all wealth alchemy.[4]
    Thou, sun, art half as happy as we,   25
      In that the world's contracted thus;
  Thine age asks ease, and since thy duties be
  To warm the world, that's done in warming us.
Shine here to us, and thou art everywhere;
This bed thy center is,[5] these walls thy sphere.   30

                                                  1633

The Indifferent

I can love both fair and brown,[1]
Her whom abundance melts, and her whom want betrays,[2]
Her who loves loneness best, and her who masks and plays,
Her whom the country formed, and whom the town,
Her who believes, and her who tries,   5
Her who still weeps with spongy eyes,
And her who is dry cork, and never cries;
I can love her, and her, and you, and you,
I can love any, so she be not true.

Will no other vice content you?   10
Will it not serve your turn to do as did your mothers?
Or have you all old vices spent, and now would find out others?
Or doth a fear that men are true torment you?
O we are not, be not you so;
Let me, and do you, twenty know.   15

2. The India of "spice" is East India, that of "mine" (gold) the West Indies.
3. All the nations of the world.
4. I.e., fraudulent.
5. As the earth was the center of the sun's orbit (according to the old Ptolemaic astronomy), so the bed will be the new center of the sun's activities, and the walls of the bedroom will outline its motion.
1. Both blonde and brunette.
2. The girl with lots of lovers, the girl with none at all; also, perhaps, the plump girl and the thin girl.

Rob me, but bind me not, and let me go.
Must I, who came to travail[3] thorough you,
Grow your fixed subject, because you are true?

Venus heard me sigh this song,
And by love's sweetest part, variety, she swore,   20
She heard not this till now; and that it should be so no more.
She went, examined, and returned ere long,
And said, Alas, some two or three
Poor heretics in love there be,
Which think to 'stablish dangerous constancy.   25
But I have told them, Since you will be true,
You shall be true to them who are false to you.

1633

The Canonization

For God's sake hold your tongue, and let me love,
    Or chide my palsy, or my gout,
My five gray hairs, or ruined fortune, flout,
        With wealth your state, your mind with arts improve
            Take you a course, get you a place,[1]   5
                Observe His Honor, or His Grace,
        Or the King's real, or his stampèd face[2]
                Contemplate; what you will, approve,[3]
            So you will let me love.

Alas, alas, who's injured by my love?   10
    What merchant's ships have my sighs drowned?
Who says my tears have overflowed his ground?
        When did my colds a forward spring remove?[4]
            When did the heats which my veins fill
                Add one man to the plaguy bill?[5]   15
        Soldiers find wars, and lawyers find out still
            Litigious men, which quarrels move,
                Though she and I do love.

Call us what you will, we are made such by love;
    Call her one, me another fly,   20
    We're tapers too, and at our own cost die,[6]

3. "Grief, sorrow," but also "journey, travel."
1. "Take you a course": in the general sense of "settle yourself in life." A "place" is an appointment, at court or elsewhere.
2. On coins.
3. Put to proof, find by experience.
4. Petrarchan lovers traditionally sigh, weep, and are frozen by their mistresses' neglect. The "for-ward spring" is either a fountain or a season.
5. Deaths from the hot-weather plague were recorded, by parish, in weekly bills.
6. We're both fly (the ephemeral moth) and the self-consuming candle that attracts it. Donne hints here at the old superstition that intercourse short-ens life. (To "die" in the punning terminology of the 17th century was to experience orgasm.)

And we in us find the eagle and the dove.[7]
    The phoenix riddle hath more wit
    By us:[8] we two being one, are it.
So, to one neutral thing both sexes fit.   25
    We die and rise the same, and prove
    Mysterious by this love.

We can die by it, if not live by love,
    And if unfit for tombs and hearse
Our legend be, it will be fit for verse;   30
    And if no piece of chronicle we prove,
      We'll build in sonnets pretty rooms;[9]
      As well a well-wrought urn becomes
The greatest ashes, as half-acre tombs,
    And by these hymns,[1] all shall approve   35
    Us canonized for love:

And thus invoke us: You whom reverend love
    Made one another's hermitage;
You, to whom love was peace, that now is rage;
    Who did the whole world's soul contract,[2] and
        drove   40
      Into the glasses of your eyes
      (So made such mirrors, and such spies,
That they did all to you epitomize)
    Countries, towns, courts: Beg from above
A pattern of your love![3]   45

                       1633

Air and Angels

Twice or thrice had I loved thee,
Before I knew thy face or name;
So in a voice, so in a shapeless flame,
Angels affect us oft, and worshipped be;
    Still when, to where thou wert, I came,   5

7. The eagle signifies such qualities as strength and vision; the dove, meekness and mercy. The phoenix was a fabulous Arabian bird, only one of which existed at any one time. After living 500 years, it lit its nest of spices, jumped in, and sang its funeral song as it was consumed—then rose triumphantly from its ashes, a new bird. Thus it was a symbol of immortality, and was sometimes associated with Christ. "Eagle" and "dove" are also alchemical terms for processes leading to the rise of "phoenix," a stage in the transmutation of metals.
8. I.e., the story of the phoenix seems more plausible, now that we've shown how male and female can fuse.
9. The "rooms" (punning on the Italian meaning of "stanza") will hold the ashes—i.e., record their exploits—as prose history records great deeds in other spheres. "Becomes": befits.
1. The lover's own poems, which become hymns for a new love religion. "All" (posterity) shall "approve" (confirm) us as love's saints.
2. An alternative reading is "extract."
3. The poet and his mistress, turned to saints, are implored by the rest of the population to get from heaven ("above") a pattern of their love for general distribution. "Countries, towns, courts" are objects of the verb "drove"; the notion that eyes both see and reflect the outside world, and so "contain" it doubly, was very delightful to Donne.

Some lovely glorious nothing I did see.
    But since my soul, whose child love is,
Takes limbs of flesh, and else could nothing do,[1]
    More subtle than the parent is
Love must not be, but take a body too;   10
    And therefore what thou wert, and who,
        I bid love ask, and now
That it assume thy body I allow,
And fix itself in thy lip, eye, and brow.

Whilst thus to ballast love I thought,   15
And so more steadily to have gone,
With wares which would sink admiration,
I saw I had love's pinnace overfraught;[2]
    Every thy hair for love to work upon
Is much too much, some fitter must be sought;   20
    For, nor in nothing, nor in things
Extreme and scatt'ring[3] bright, can love inhere.
    Then as an angel, face and wings
Of air, not pure as it, yet pure doth wear,
    So thy love may be my love's sphere;   25
        Just such disparity
As is 'twixt air and angels' purity,
'Twixt women's love and men's will ever be.[4]

1633

Break of Day[1]

'Tis true, 'tis day; what though it be?
O wilt thou therefore rise from me?
Why should we rise because 'tis light?
Did we lie down because 'twas night?
Love, which in spite of darkness brought us hither,   5
Should in despite of light keep us together.

Light hath no tongue, but is all eye;
If it could speak as well as spy,
This were the worst that it could say,
That being well, I fain would stay,   10

1. As my soul could not function unless it were in a body, so love, which is the soul's child, must also be corporeal.
2. Her physical beauty (his "wares") would sink admiration—i.e., overwhelm wonder itself. This is too much ballast for love's "pinnace" (a small boat).
3. Diffused, dazzling.
4. Some Scholastic philosophers held that angels, when they appeared to humans, assumed a body of air. Such a body, though pure, was less so than the angel's spiritual being. Similarly, women's love, which Donne assumes to be *less* pure than that of men, may serve as the "sphere" within which the love of men moves as a governing angel. It is not unusual for a Donne poem to reverse itself in this way.
1. Recalling the Provençal aubade or song of the lovers' parting at dawn, this poem is a departure for Donne in that it assumes a feminine point of view.

And that I loved my heart and honor so
That I would not from him, that had them, go.

Must business thee from hence remove?
O, that's the worst disease of love.
The poor, the foul, the false, love can   15
Admit, but not the busied man.
He which hath business, and makes love, doth do
Such wrong, as when a married man doth woo.

                                                                1633

A Valediction: Of Weeping

              Let me pour forth
My tears before thy face whilst I stay here,
For thy face coins them,[1] and thy stamp they bear,
And by this mintage they are something worth,
              For thus they be   5
              Pregnant of thee;
Fruits of much grief they are, emblems of more—
When a tear falls, that Thou falls which it bore,
So thou and I are nothing then, when on a diverse shore.[2]

              On a round ball   10
A workman that hath copies by can lay
An Europe, Afric, and an Asia,
And quickly make that, which was nothing, all;[3]
              So doth each tear
              Which thee doth wear,   15
A globe, yea world, by that impression grow,
Till thy tears mixed with mine do overflow
This world; by waters sent from thee, my heaven dissolvèd so.

              O more than moon,
Draw not up seas to drown me in thy sphere;   20
Weep me not dead in thine arms, but forbear
To teach the sea what it may do too soon.
              Let not the wind
              Example find
To do me more harm than it purposeth;   25
Since thou and I sigh one another's breath,
Whoe'er sighs most is cruelest, and hastes the other's death.

                                                                1633

1. I.e., they reflect her face.
2. The extinction of the lovers in their separation
is prefigured in the fall of a tear that contains the
image of the mistress.

3. I.e., on a blank globe an artist can paste maps
of the continents, and so convert a cipher, the image
of nothingness, to the whole world. "Thee doth
wear": bears your image.

Love's Alchemy

Some that have deeper digged love's mine than I,
Say where his centric happiness doth lie:
    I have loved, and got, and told,
But should I love, get, tell, till I were old,
I should not find that hidden mystery;   5
    O, 'tis imposture all:
And as no chemic yet the elixir got,[1]
    But glorifies his pregnant pot[2]
    If by the way to him befall
Some odoriferous thing, or medicinal;   10
    So lovers dream a rich and long delight,
    But get a winter-seeming summer's night.[3]

Our ease, our thrift, our honor, and our day,
Shall we for this vain bubble's shadow pay?
    Ends love in this, that my man   15
Can be as happy as I can, if he can
Endure the short scorn of a bridegroom's play?
    That loving wretch that swears
'Tis not the bodies marry, but the minds,
    Which he in her angelic finds,   20
    Would swear as justly that he hears,
In that day's rude hoarse minstrelsy, the spheres.[4]
    Hope not for mind in women; at their best
    Sweetness and wit they are but mummy possessed.[5]

1633

The Flea

Mark but this flea, and mark in this,
How little that which thou deniest me is;
Me it sucked first, and now sucks thee,
And in this flea our two bloods mingled be;
Thou know'st that this cannot be said   5
A sin, or shame, or loss of maidenhead,
    Yet this enjoys before it woo,

---

1. "Chemic": alchemist. "The elixir": a magic medicine sought by alchemists and reputed to heal all ills.
2. Praises his fertile (and womb-shaped) retort.
3. A night cold as in winter and short as in summer.
4. The perfect harmony of the planets, moving in concentric crystalline spheres, is contrasted with the charivari, a boisterous serenade for pots, pans, and trumpets, performed on the wedding night.

5. The syntax of the last two lines is very dark; the last line in particular may be read with a comma after "wit," after "are," or after "mummy." The final word may modify "mummy," to signify "mummy with a demon in it," or "they," to signify "women who when you have possessed them." A comma after "best" would change the whole balance of the ending. Some sort of mysogyny is almost certainly expressed.

And pampered swells with one blood made of two,
And this, alas, is more than we would do.[1]

Oh stay, three lives in one flea spare,   10
Where we almost, nay more than married are.
This flea is you and I, and this
Our marriage bed and marriage temple is;
Though parents grudge, and you, we are met,
And cloistered in these living walls of jet.   15
 Though use[2] make you apt to kill me
 Let not to that, self-murder added be,
 And sacrilege, three sins in killing three.

Cruel and sudden, hast thou since
Purpled thy nail in blood of innocence?[3]   20
Wherein could this flea guilty be,
Except in that drop which it sucked from thee?
Yet thou triumph'st, and say'st that thou
Find'st not thy self nor me the weaker now;
 'Tis true; then learn how false fears be: 25
 Just so much honor, when thou yield'st to me,
 Will waste, as this flea's death took life from thee.

           1633

A Nocturnal upon Saint Lucy's Day, Being the Shortest Day[1]

'Tis the year's midnight and it is the day's,
Lucy's, who scarce seven hours herself unmasks;
 The sun is spent, and now his flasks
 Send forth light squibs,[2] no constant rays.
  The world's whole sap is sunk;   5
The general balm th' hydroptic[3] earth hath drunk,
Whither, as to the bed's feet, life is shrunk,
Dead and interred; yet all these seem to laugh,
Compared with me, who am their epitaph.

---

1. I.e., we, alas, don't dare hope for this consummation of our love, which the flea freely accepts. The idea of swelling suggests pregnancy.
2. Habit.
3. Like Herod, Donne's mistress has slaughtered the innocents and is now clothed in imperial purple.
1. A "nocturnal" seems to suggest a dreamy, meditative poem about dark thoughts; but the more common 17th-century usage alluded to a kind of astrolabe for finding one's latitude or telling the time at night. Donne probably wanted both mean-

ings. St. Lucy's Day falls on December 13, which under the old calendar was very close to the winter solstice (December 21 under our modern calendar). At this time of year the sun rises after eight in the latitude of London, and sets well before four.
2. The sun is compared to a gun shooting powder from powder flasks, but in small "squibs" like firecrackers.
3. Dropsical, thus insatiably thirsty. "General balm": the supposed life-preserving essence of all things.

Study me, then, you who shall lovers be   10
At the next world, that is, at the next spring;
   For I am every dead thing
    In whom love wrought new alchemy.
     For his art did express[4]
A quintessence even from nothingness,   15
From dull privations and lean emptiness.
He ruined me, and I am re-begot
Of absence, darkness, death: things which are not.

All others from all things draw all that's good,
Life, soul, form, spirit, whence they being have;   20
   I, by love's limbeck,[5] am the grave
    Of all that's nothing. Oft a flood
     Have we two wept, and so
Drowned the whole world, us two; oft did we grow
To be two chaoses when we did show   25
Care to aught else; and often absences
Withdrew our souls, and made us carcasses.

But I am by her death (which word wrongs her)[6]
Of the first nothing the elixir grown;[7]
   Were I a man, that I were one   30
    I needs must know; I should prefer,
     If I were any beast,
Some ends, some means; yea plants, yea stones detest
And love.[8] All, all some properties invest.
If I an ordinary nothing were,   35
As shadow, a light and body must be here.

But I am none; nor will my sun renew.
You lovers, for whose sake the lesser sun
   At this time to the Goat[9] is run
    To fetch new lust and give it you,   40
     Enjoy your summer all.
Since she enjoys her long night's festival,
Let me prepare towards her, and let me call
This hour her vigil and her eve, since this
Both the year's and the day's deep midnight is.   45

1633

4. Squeeze out.
5. Alembic, retort; a vessel used in distilling.
6. To speak of her death "wrongs" her by implying that she is not now among the immortals, a
saint.
7. He is now "grown" (become) the "elixir of the
first nothing," i.e., the quintessence of that absolute nothingness that existed before the creation.
8. Beasts have intentions, plants instincts, even
stones (like loadstones) attractions and antipathies.
9. The sign of Capricorn, which the sun enters at
the winter solstice; the goat is an emblem of sexual
vigor. The "lesser sun" is the real, everyday sun;
"my sun" is the dead mistress.

The Apparition

When by thy scorn, O murderess, I am dead,
And that thou thinkst thee free
From all solicitation from me,
Then shall my ghost come to thy bed,
And thee, feigned vestal,[1] in worse arms shall see;   5
Then thy sick taper will begin to wink,
And he whose thou art then, being tired before,
Will, if thou stir, or pinch to wake him, think
    Thou call'st for more,
And in false sleep will from thee shrink,   10
And then, poor aspen wretch,[2] neglected thou
Bathed in a cold quicksilver sweat[3] wilt lie
    A verier ghost than I;
What I will say, I will not tell thee now,
Lest that preserve thee; and since my love is spent,   15
I had rather thou shouldst painfully repent,
Than by my threatenings rest still innocent.

1633

A Valediction: Forbidding Mourning[1]

As virtuous men pass mildly away,
   And whisper to their souls to go,
Whilst some of their sad friends do say
   The breath goes now, and some say, No;

So let us melt, and make no noise,   5
   No tear-floods, nor sigh-tempests move,
'Twere profanation of our joys
   To tell the laity our love.

Moving of th' earth brings harms and fears,
   Men reckon what it did and meant;   10
But trepidation of the spheres,
   Though greater far, is innocent.[2]

1. In Roman history the "vestals" were sacred virgins. "Wink": flicker (from the presence of a ghost).
2. Aspen leaves flutter in the slightest breeze.
3. Sweating in terror; quicksilver (mercury) was a
stock prescription for venereal disease, and sweating was part of the cure.
1. The particularly serious and steady tone of this
poem may be due to the circumstances of its composition. Izaak Walton tells us it was addressed to
Donne's wife on the occasion of his trip to the
Continent in 1611. Donne had many forebodings
of misfortune, which were verified when his wife
gave birth to a stillborn child during his absence.
Still, Walton's linkage of these events with this poem
is only a speculation.
2. Earthquakes cause damage, and were thought
portentous. "Trepidation" (in the Ptolemaic cosmology, an oscillation of the ninth or "crystalline"
sphere, imparted to all the inner spheres), though
a vastly greater motion than an earthquake, is neither destructive nor sinister.

Dull sublunary[3] lovers' love
    (Whose soul[4] is sense) cannot admit
Absence, because it doth remove   15
    Those things which elemented[5] it.

But we, by a love so much refined
    That our selves know not what it is,
Inter-assurèd of the mind,
    Care less, eyes, lips, and hands to miss.   20

Our two souls therefore, which are one,
    Though I must go, endure not yet
A breach, but an expansion,
    Like gold to airy thinness beat.

If they be two, they are two so   25
    As stiff twin compasses[6] are two;
Thy soul, the fixed foot, makes no show
    To move, but doth, if th' other do.

And though it in the center sit,
    Yet when the other far doth roam,   30
It leans and hearkens after it,
    And grows erect, as that comes home.

Such wilt thou be to me, who must
    Like th' other foot, obliquely run;
Thy firmness makes my circle just,   35
    And makes me end where I begun.

                    1633

The Ecstasy[1]

Where, like a pillow on a bed,
    A pregnant bank swelled up to rest
The violet's reclining head,
    Sat we two, one another's best.

Our hands were firmly cemented   5
    With a fast balm[2] which thence did spring,

---

3. Beneath the moon, therefore mundane and subject to change.
4. Essence.
5. Composed.
6. I.e., drawing compasses—an emblem of constancy in change, as the circle they produce signifies perfection. This simile is the most famous example of the "metaphysical conceit" (see "Poetic Forms," below).
1. For Donne's readers the word "ecstasy" implied, not wild delight, as it commonly does nowadays, but a standing apart, a movement of the soul outside of the body.
2. I.e., perspiration. "Fast": strong.

Our eye-beams twisted, and did thread
  Our eyes upon one double string;[3]

So to intergraft our hands, as yet
  Was all our means to make us one,   10
And pictures in our eyes[4] to get
  Was all our propagation.

As 'twixt two equal armies Fate
  Suspends uncertain victory,
Our souls (which to advance their state   15
  Were gone out) hung 'twixt her and me;

And whilst our souls negotiate there,
  We like sepulchral statues lay;
All day the same our postures were,
  And we said nothing all the day.   20

If any, so by love refined
  That he soul's language understood,
And by good love were grown all mind,[5]
  Within convenient distance stood,

He (though he know not which soul spake,   25
  Because both meant, both spake the same)
Might thence a new concoction[6] take,
  And part far purer than he came.

This ecstasy doth unperplex,
  We said, and tell us what we love;   30
We see by this it was not sex;
  We see we saw not what did move;[7]

But as all several souls contain
  Mixture of things, they know not what,
Love these mixed souls doth mix again,   35
  And makes both one, each this and that.

A single violet transplant,
  The strength, the color, and the size
(All which before was poor and scant)
  Redoubles still, and multiplies.   40

---

3. Joining hands and eyes is the only intercourse of the lovers: "eyebeams" are invisible shafts of light, thought of as going out of the eyes and so enabling one to see things.
4. I.e., reflections of each other, often called "babies." "Get": beget.
5. I.e., the Neoplatonic idea of love: the soul's yearning after beauty.
6. Literally, ingredients "cooked together"; the word has alchemical overtones.
7. I.e., we see that we did not understand before what motivated ("did move") us. "Several": separate.

When love with one another so
   Interinanimates two souls,
That abler soul, which thence doth flow,
   Defects of loneliness controls.[8]

We then, who are this new soul, know   45
   Of what we are composed and made,
For, th' atomies[9] of which we grow
   Are souls, whom no change can invade.

But O alas, so long, so far
   Our bodies why do we forbear?   50
They are ours, though they are not we; we are
   The intelligences, they the sphere.[1]

We owe them thanks because they thus
   Did us to us at first convey,
Yielded their forces, sense, to us,   55
   Nor are dross to us, but allay.[2]

On man heaven's influence works not so
   But that it first imprints the air:[3]
So soul into the soul may flow,
   Though it to body first repair.   60

As our blood labors to beget
   Spirits as like souls as it can,[4]
Because such fingers need to knit
   That subtle knot which makes us man,

So must pure lovers' souls descend   65
   T' affections, and to faculties
Which sense may reach and apprehend;
   Else a great Prince in prison lies.

To our bodies turn we then, that so
   Weak men on love revealed may look;   70
Love's mysteries in souls do grow,
   But yet the body is his book.[5]

---

8. The "abler soul" which derives from the union of two lesser ones can eliminate the defects with which each of the component souls is afflicted.

9. Units.

1. In Ptolemaic astronomy, each planet, set in a transparent globe ("sphere") that revolved and so carried it round the earth, was inhabited by a controlling angelic "intelligence." Similarly, Donne says, our bodies are guided and controlled by our souls.

2. "Dross" is an impurity that weakens metal, "allay" (alloy) an impurity that strengthens it. Our bodies contribute sensation ("sense") to the soul, and so reinforce it.

3. Astrological influences were thought to work on mankind through the surrounding air.

4. "Spirits" were subtle substances thought to be begotten by the blood to serve as intermediaries between body and soul. "Need": are needed.

5. I.e., Love puts forth in the body a book where his mysteries may be read (as God's mysteries may be read in the book of Nature and the book of Scripture).

And if some lover, such as we,
　　Have heard this dialogue of one,[6]
Let him still mark us; he shall see   75
　　Small change when we are to bodies gone.

　　　　　　　　　　　　　　　　　1633

The Funeral

Whoever comes to shroud me, do not harm
　　Nor question much
That subtle wreath of hair which crowns my arm;
The mystery, the sign you must not touch,
　　For 'tis my outward soul,   5
Viceroy to that, which then to heaven being gone,
　　Will leave this to control,
And keep these limbs, her[1] provinces, from dissolution.

For if the sinewy thread[2] my brain lets fall
　　Through every part   10
Can tie those parts and make me one of all;
These hairs which upward grew, and strength and art
　　Have from a better brain,
Can better do it; except she meant that I
　　By this should know my pain,   15
As prisoners then are manacled, when they're condemned to die.

Whate'er she meant by it, bury it with me,
　　For since I am
Love's martyr, it might breed idolatry,
If into others' hands these relics came: 20
　　As 'twas humility[3]
To afford to it all that a soul can do,
　　So 'tis some bravery,
That since you would save none of me, I bury some of you.

　　　　　　　　　　　　　　　　　1633

The Blossom

Little think'st thou, poor flower,
　　Whom I have watched six or seven days,

---

6. "Dialogue of one" because "both meant, both spake the same" (line 26).
1. The soul's, but also the mistress's; compare "she," below, line 14.
2. The spinal cord and nervous system.

3. It was humility to grant, in the first part of the poem, that her hair could act as a soul; it is also "bravery" (defiance) to bury a part of the mistress in revenge for her cruelty.

And seen thy birth, and seen what every hour
Gave to thy growth, thee to this height to raise,
And now dost laugh and triumph on this bough,   5
    Little think'st thou
That it will freeze anon, and that I shall
Tomorrow find thee fall'n, or not at all.

    Little think'st thou, poor heart,
      That labor'st yet to nestle thee   10
And think'st by hovering here to get a part
In a forbidden or forbidding tree,[1]
And hop'st her stiffness by long siege to bow,
    Little think'st thou
That thou tomorrow, ere that sun[2] doth wake,   15
Must with this sun and me a journey take.

    But thou, which lov'st to be
      Subtle to plague thyself, wilt say,
Alas, if you must go, what's that to me?
Here lies my business, and here I will stay: 20
You go to friends whose love and means present
      Various content
To your eyes, ears, and tongue, and every part.
If then your body go, what need you a heart?

    Well, then, stay here; but know,   25
      When thou hast stayed and done thy most,
A naked thinking heart that makes no show
Is to a woman but a kind of ghost.
How shall she know my heart; or, having none,
      Know thee for one?   30
Practice may make her know some other part,
But take my word, she doth not know a heart.

    Meet me at London, then,
      Twenty days hence, and thou shalt see
Me fresher and more fat by being with men[3]   35
Than if I had stayed still with her and thee.
For God's sake, if you can, be you so too:
    I would give you
There to another friend, whom we shall find
As glad to have my body as my mind.   40

1633

---

1. The fruit of this tree is "forbidden" (presumably
because the woman is married) or "forbidding"
(because she is unwilling).

2. I.e., the woman.
3. I.e., with people (not necessarily just males).

The Relic

When my grave is broke up again
Some second guest to entertain
(For graves have learned that woman-head[1]
To be to more than one a bed),
    And he that digs it, spies   5
A bracelet of bright hair about the bone,
    Will he not let us alone,
And think that there a loving couple lies,
Who thought that this device might be some way
To make their souls, at the last busy day,[2]   10
Meet at this grave, and make a little stay?

    If this fall in a time, or land,
    Where mis-devotion[3] doth command,
    Then he that digs us up, will bring
    Us to the Bishop and the King,   15
        To make us relics; then
Thou shalt be a Mary Magdalen, and I
    A something else[4] thereby;
All women shall adore us, and some men;
And since at such times, miracles are sought,   20
I would have that age by this paper taught
What miracles we harmless lovers wrought.

    First, we loved well and faithfully,
    Yet knew not what we loved, nor why,
    Difference of sex no more we knew,   25
    Than our guardian angels do;
        Coming and going, we
Perchance might kiss, but not between those meals;[5]
    Our hands ne'er touched the seals
Which nature, injured by late law, sets free:[6]
These miracles we did: but now, alas,
All measure and all language I should pass,
Should I tell what a miracle she was.

1633

---

1. I.e., characteristic of women. Graves were often used to inter successive corpses, the bones of previous occupants being deposited in charnel houses.
2. Judgment Day.
3. False devotion, superstition. Donne seems to have in mind Roman Catholicism.
4. What the indefinite subterfuge "something else" stands for, Donne leaves deliberately unclear; the reader may—and indeed, must—speculate.
5. The kiss of salutation and parting was, in the 17th century, a peculiarly English custom.
6. "Late": recent (comparatively speaking). Human law forbids the free love permitted by nature.

A Lecture Upon the Shadow

Stand still, and I will read to thee
A lecture, Love, in love's philosophy.
   These three hours that we have spent
   Walking here, two shadows went
Along with us, which we ourselves produced;   5
But, now the sun is just above our head,
   We do those shadows tread
   And to brave clearness all things are reduced.
So, whilst our infant loves did grow,
Disguises did and shadows flow   10
From us and our care;[1] but now, 'tis not so.

That love hath not attained the high'st degree
Which is still diligent lest others see.

Except[2] our loves at this noon stay,
We shall new shadows make the other way.   15
   As the first were made to blind
   Others, these which come behind
Will work upon ourselves, and blind our eyes.
If our loves faint and westwardly decline,
   To me thou falsely thine   20
   And I to thee mine actions shall disguise.
The morning shadows wear away,
But these grow longer all the day,
But, oh, love's day is short if love decay.

Love is a growing or full constant light,   25
And his first minute after noon is night.

1635

Elegy 16.[1] On His Mistress

By our first strange and fatal interview,
By all desires which thereof did ensue,

---

1. Metaphorically, morning shadows were the disguises with which they anxiously concealed their love from outsiders.
2. Unless.
1. In Latin poetry, an elegy is not necessarily a funeral lament, but may be simply a discursive or reflective poem written in "elegiacs" (unrhymed couplets of alternating dactylic hexameters and pentameters). In fact the subject matter primarily associated with this meter was not death but sex, the most famous collection of elegies being Ovid's *Amores*. Donne's elegies—some 15 poems, almost all written in the 1590s—take Ovid as their principal model, and resemble him in ingenious wit and, for the most part, in frank and unapologetic eroticism. Elegy 16 is uncharacteristically tender. (We retain Grierson's numbering, though he included among the elegies some poems that are probably not Donne's.)

By our long starving hopes, by that remorse
Which my words' masculine persuasive force
Begot in thee, and by the memory   5
Of hurts which spies and rivals threatened me,
I calmly beg; but by thy father's wrath,
By all pains which want and divorcement hath,
I conjure thee: and all the oaths which I
And thou have sworn to seal joint constancy   10
Here I unswear and overswear them thus:
Thou shalt not love by ways so dangerous.
Temper, oh fair love, love's impetuous rage;
Be my true mistress still, not my feigned page. [2]
I'll go, and, by thy kind leave, leave behind   15
Thee, only worthy to nurse in my mind
Thirst to come back. Oh, if thou die before,
My soul from other lands to thee shall soar.
Thy (else almighty) beauty cannot move
Rage from the seas, nor thy love teach them love,   20
Nor tame wild Boreas' harshness. [3] Thou hast read
How roughly he in pieces shiverèd
Fair Orithea, whom he swore he loved.
Fall ill or good, 'tis madness to have proved [4]
Dangers unurged; feed on this flattery,   25
That absent lovers one in th' other be.
Dissemble nothing, not a boy, nor change
Thy body's habit, nor mind's; be not strange
To thyself only; all will spy in thy face
A blushing womanly discovering grace.   30
Richly clothed apes are called apes, and as soon
Eclipsed as bright we call the moon the moon. [5]
Men of France, changeable chameleons,
Spitals [6] of diseases, shops of fashions,
Love's fuellers and the rightest company   35
Of players which upon the world's stage be,
Will quickly know thee, and know thee; and alas!
Th' indifferent Italian, as we pass
His warm land, well content to think thee page,
Will hunt [7] thee with such lust and hideous rage   40
As Lot's fair guests were vexed. [8] But none of these
Nor spongy, hydroptic [9] Dutch shall thee displease
If thou stay here. O stay here, for, for thee,

2. Evidently Donne's mistress (nothing positively identifies her with Ann More, who became his wife) wanted to accompany him abroad, disguised as a page boy. Such escapades occasionally took place in real life; in 1605, Elizabeth Southwell, disguised as a page, went abroad with the scapegrace Sir Robert Dudley.
3. Boreas is god of the north wind; Ovid in the 6th book of the *Metamorphoses* describes his boisterous abduction of Orithea.
4. Sought out.
5. I.e., we recognize the moon as easily when it's in eclipse as when it's not.
6. Hospitals.
7. An alternative reading is "haunt."
8. The inhabitants of Sodom brought destruction on themselves when they tried to rape two angels who visited Lot (Genesis 19.1–11).
9. Dropsical, thus insatiably thirsty ("spongy").

England is only a worthy gallery
To walk in expectation, till from thence   45
Our greatest king call thee to his presence.[1]
When I am gone, dream me some happiness,
Nor let thy looks our long-hid love confess;
Nor praise nor dispraise me, bless nor curse
Openly love's force, nor in bed fright thy nurse   50
With midnight's startings, crying out "Oh, oh!
Nurse, oh my love is slain, I saw him go
O'er the white Alps alone; I saw him, I,
Assailed, fight, taken, stabbed, bleed, fall, and die."
Augur me better chance, except dread Jove   55
Think it enough for me t' have had thy love.

                                                                          1635

Elegy 19. Going to Bed

Come, Madam, come, all rest my powers defy,
Until I labor, I in labor lie.[1]
The foe oft-times, having the foe in sight,
Is tired with standing though he never fight.
Off with that girdle, like heaven's zone[2] glistering,   5
But a far fairer world encompassing.
Unpin that spangled breastplate which you wear
That th' eyes of busy fools may be stopped there.
Unlace yourself, for that harmonious chime
Tells me from you that now it is bed-time.   10
Off with that happy busk,[3] which I envy,
That still can be and still can stand so nigh.
Your gown going off, such beauteous state reveals
As when from flowery meads th' hill's shadow steals.
Off with that wiry coronet and show   15
The hairy diadem which on you doth grow;
Now off with those shoes, and then safely tread
In this love's hallowed temple, this soft bed.
In such white robes, heaven's angels used to be
Received by men; thou, angel, bring'st with thee   20
A heaven like Mahomet's paradise;[4] and though
Ill spirits walk in white, we easily know
By this these angels from an evil sprite,
Those set our hairs, but these our flesh upright.
    License my roving hands, and let them go   25
Before, behind, between, above, below.

---

1. Throne rooms commonly had antechambers
(galleries) where visitors waited until the monarch
was ready to see them. The world itself is such a
gallery for the greatest king of all, God.
1. "Labor" is the sense of "get to work" and in the
sense of "distress."
2. The zodiac.
3. Bodice.
4. Populated by seductive houris, for the delectation of the faithful.

O my America! my new-found-land,
My kingdom, safeliest when with one man manned,
My mine of precious stones, my empery,
How blest am I in this discovering thee!   30
To enter in these bonds is to be free;
There where my hand is set, my seal shall be. [5]
   Full nakedness! All joys are due to thee,
As souls unbodied, bodies unclothed must be,
To taste whole joys. Gems which you women use   35
Are like Atalanta's balls, [6] cast in men's views,
That when a fool's eye lighteth on a gem,
His earthly soul may covet theirs, not them.
Like pictures, or like books' gay coverings, made
For laymen, are all women thus arrayed;   40
Themselves are mystic books, which only we
(Whom their imputed grace will dignify)
Must see revealed. [7] Then since that I may know,
As liberally as to a midwife show
Thyself: cast all, yea, this white linen hence,   45
There is no penance due to innocence. [8]
   To teach thee, I am naked first; why then
What need'st thou have more covering than a man?

                                           1669

Satire 3, Religion

Like his elegies, Donne's five satires were written in his twenties, and follow, though remotely, in classical footsteps. The essence of satire is an attitude: the author holds his subject up to laughter or scorn. Elements of such an attitude appear in many works of prose and poetry that are not, as a whole, satiric—in Chaucer, in Langland, as early as the figure of Thersites in Homer's *Iliad*. But the great examples of formal satiric writing in classical times were the Roman poets Horace and Juvenal, models respectively of the urbanely jocose and the indignant satire. During the sixteenth century their satires were imitated on the continent by the Italian poet Ariosto and some of his contemporaries. Even in England, Sir Thomas Wyatt felt through an Italian intermediary the influence of Juvenal: see, for example, *Mine Own John Poins*, pp. 471–473. Yet satiric poems as such remained rare in English till the 1590s; their sudden appearance at that time evidently grew out of moods of skepticism, discontent, and melancholy that marked the last years of the sixteenth and the first years of the seventeenth century.

   Donne's third satire is not conventional, in terms of the genre, because it does not assume a position of derisive superiority to its victim—indeed, it

---

5. The jokes mingle law with sex; having signed the document with his hand, he will now seal it, and in the bonds of her arms he will find freedom.
6. Atalanta, running a race against her suitor Hippomenes, was beaten when he dropped golden balls (apples) for her to pick up. Donne reverses the story.
7. By granting favors to their lovers, women impute to them grace which they don't deserve, as God imputes grace to undeserving sinners. Laymen can only look at the covers of mystic books (women); but "we" who have saving grace can read them.
8. An alternative reading is "Here is no penance, much less innocence."

does not have a proper victim. It is a strenuous, inconclusive discussion of an acute theological problem: How may a man recognize the true Christian church among the many competing sects? Its theme was of paramount importance to Donne as an ex-Catholic, and to the men of his age, for whom religious polemic was a passion. The poem offers no easy answer to the problem it raises; the point it makes most forcefully is the folly of not thinking about the matter. Its language and meter are harsh and rough, as was traditional in the genre, its concentration is complete; it is a powerful piece of wrought-iron work in poetry.

Satire 3, Religion

Kind pity chokes my spleen;[1] brave scorn forbids
Those tears to issue which swell my eyelids;
I must not laugh,[2] nor weep sins, and be wise:
Can railing then cure these worn maladies?
Is not our mistress, fair Religion,   5
As worthy of all our souls' devotion
As virtue was to the first blinded age?[3]
Are not heaven's joys as valiant to assuage
Lusts, as earth's honor was to them?[4] Alas,
As we do them in means, shall they surpass   10
Us in the end, and shall thy father's spirit
Meet blind philosophers in heaven, whose merit
Of strict life may be imputed faith,[5] and hear
Thee, whom he taught so easy ways and near
To follow, damned? O, if thou dar'st, fear this;   15
This fear great courage and high valor is.
Dar'st thou aid mutinous Dutch,[6] and dar'st thou lay
Thee in ships, wooden sepulchers, a prey
To leaders' rage, to storms, to shot, to dearth?
Dar'st thou dive seas and dungeons of the earth?   20
Hast thou courageous fire to thaw the ice
Of frozen North discoveries? and thrice
Colder than salamanders,[7] like divine
Children in the oven, fires of Spain, and the line,
Whose countries limbecks to our bodies be,   25
Canst thou for gain bear?[8] And must every he
Which cries not, "Goddess!" to thy mistress, draw,[9]

1. The seat of bile, hence scorn and ridicule.
2. Mock.
3. The age of paganism, blind to Christianity but capable of natural morality ("virtue").
4. I.e., hope of heaven should be as strong ("valiant") against our lusts as earthly honor was against theirs, the pagans'.
5. Specially virtuous pagans, it was felt, might achieve heaven by behavior so good that it virtually implied faith.
6. English volunteers took frequent part with the Dutch in their wars against Spain. Donne himself had sailed in two raiding expeditions against the Spanish.
7. The salamander was traditionally so cold-blooded that it could live even in a fire. The "divine children in the oven" are Shadrach, Meshach, and Abednego, rescued from the fiery furnace in Daniel 3.
8. The object of "bear" is "fires of Spain, and the line"—Inquisitorial and equatorial heats, which roast men as chemists heat materials in "limbecks" (alembics, or retorts for distilling).
9. I.e., fight a duel.

Or eat thy poisonous words? Courage of straw!
O desperate coward, wilt thou seem bold, and
To thy foes and his[1] (who made thee to stand   30
Sentinel in his world's garrison) thus yield,
And for forbidden wars leave th' appointed field?
Know thy foes: The foul Devil (whom thou
Strivest to please) for hate, not love, would allow
Thee fain his whole realm to be quit;[2] and as   35
The world's all parts wither away and pass,[3]
So the world's self, thy other loved foe, is
In her decrepit wane, and thou, loving this,
Dost love a withered and worn strumpet; last,
Flesh (itself's death) and joys which flesh can taste   40
Thou lovest; and thy fair goodly soul, which doth
Give this flesh power to taste joy, thou dost loathe.
Seek true religion. O, where? Mirreus,[4]
Thinking her unhoused here, and fled from us,
Seeks her at Rome; there, because he doth know   45
That she was there a thousand years ago.
He loves her rags so, as we here obey
The statecloth[5] where the Prince sat yesterday.
Crantz to such brave loves will not be enthralled,
But loves her only, who at Geneva is called   50
Religion—plain, simple, sullen, young,
Contemptuous, yet unhandsome; as among
Lecherous humors,[6] there is one that judges
No wenches wholesome but coarse country drudges.
Graius stays still at home here, and because   55
Some preachers, vile ambitious bawds, and laws
Still new, like fashions, bid him think that she
Which dwells with us is only perfect, he
Embraceth her whom his godfathers will
Tender to him, being tender, as wards still   60
Take such wives as their guardians offer, or
Pay values.[7] Careless Phrygius doth abhor
All, because all cannot be good, as one
Knowing some women whores, dares marry none.
Graccus loves all as one, and thinks that so   65
As women do in divers countries go
In divers habits, yet are still one kind,
So doth, so is religion; and this blind-
ness too much light breeds; but unmoved thou

---

1. God's.
2. I.e., the Devil would gladly give you a free hand with his whole kingdom.
3. It was a common belief in the 17th century that the world was getting old and decrepit.
4. The imaginary characters in this passage represent different creeds. "Mirreus" is a Roman Catholic, "Crantz" a Geneva Presbyterian, "Graius" an Erastian (i.e., believing in any religion sponsored by the state), "Phrygius" a skeptic, and "Graccus" a Universalist.
5. The royal canopy, a symbol of kingly power.
6. Tempers, temperaments.
7. Young men (of "tender" years) might reject the wives offered ("tendered") them by their guardians; but, if they did so, had to pay "values," i.e., fines.

Of force must one, and forced but one allow;   70
And the right;[8] ask thy father which is she,
Let him ask his; though truth and falsehood be
Near twins, yet truth a little elder is;[9]
Be busy to seek her, believe me this,
He's not of none, nor worst, that seeks the best.[1]   75
To adore, or scorn an image, or protest,
May all be bad; doubt wisely; in strange way
To stand inquiring right, is not to stray;
To sleep, or run wrong, is. On a huge hill,
Cragged and steep, Truth stands, and he that will   80
Reach her, about must, and about must go,
And what the hill's suddenness resists, win so;
Yet strive so, that before age, death's twilight,
Thy soul rest, for none can work in that night.
To will[2] implies delay, therefore now do.   85
Hard deeds, the body's pains; hard knowledge too
The mind's endeavors reach,[3] and mysteries
Are like the sun, dazzling, yet plain to all eyes.
Keep the truth which thou hast found; men do not stand
In so ill case here, that God hath with his hand   90
Signed kings' blank charters to kill whom they hate,
Nor are they vicars, but hangmen to fate.[4]
Fool and wretch, wilt thou let thy soul be tied
To man's laws, by which she shall not be tried
At the last day? O, will it then boot thee   95
To say a Philip, or a Gregory,
A Harry, or a Martin taught thee this?[5]
Is not this excuse for mere contraries
Equally strong? Cannot both sides say so?
That thou mayest rightly obey power, her bounds know;   100
Those passed, her nature and name is changed; to be
Then humble to her is idolatry.
As streams are, power is; those blest flowers that dwell
At the rough stream's calm head, thrive and prove well,
But having left their roots, and themselves given   105
To the stream's tyrannous rage, alas, are driven
Through mills, and rocks, and woods, and at last, almost
Consumed in going, in the sea are lost:

8. I.e., being blind to the differences between religions, Graccus has too much light to see anything (lines 68–69). But the poet insists that without being swayed by human pressures, we must find just one true religion, "the right" true religion.
9. I.e., the true church is the one most like the primitive church.
1. The man who seeks the best church is neither an unbeliever nor the worst sort of believer.
2. To intend a future action.
3. I.e., the body's pains achieve ("reach") hard deeds; the mind's endeavors will reach hard knowledge.
4. Human authority does not represent divine justice on earth; men are not God's vicars on earth (the hit here is at both the Pope and the secular monarch), but his hangmen at best—agents through whom his justice is fulfilled without carte blanche ("blank charters") to use their own judgments.
5. "Philip" is Philip II of Spain, and "Gregory" any one of several Pope Gregories (VII, XIII, XIV); "Harry" is England's Henry VIII, and "Martin" is Martin Luther. Laymen and clergy, Protestants and Catholics, all are covered. "Boot": profit.

So perish souls, which more choose men's unjust
Power from God claimed, than God himself to trust.   110

                                                              1633

From Holy Sonnets[1]

1

Thou hast made me, and shall thy work decay?
Repair me now, for now mine end doth haste;
I run to death, and death meets me as fast,
And all my pleasures are like yesterday.
I dare not move my dim eyes any way,   5
Despair behind, and death before doth cast
Such terror, and my feeble flesh doth waste
By sin in it, which it towards hell doth weigh.
Only thou art above, and when towards thee
By thy leave I can look, I rise again;   10
But our old subtle foe so tempteth me
That not one hour myself I can sustain.
Thy grace may wing me to prevent his art,
And thou like adamant draw mine iron heart.[2]

                                                              1635

5

I am a little world made cunningly
Of elements, and an angelic sprite;[1]
But black sin hath betrayed to endless night
My world's both parts, and O, both parts must die.
You which beyond that heaven which was most high   5
Have found new spheres, and of new lands can write,[2]
Pour new seas in mine eyes, that so I might
Drown my world with my weeping earnestly,
Or wash it if it must be drowned no more.[3]
But O, it must be burnt! Alas, the fire   10
Of lust and envy have burnt it heretofore,

---

1. Donne's religious poetry is collectively known
as the *Divine Poems.* Among these, the largest group
is that of the 19 *Holy Sonnets.* Like others of
Donne's poems, these sonnets reflect his interest
in the formal meditative exercises of the Jesuits—
though Donne began writing them around 1609,
at least a decade after leaving the Catholic church.
   Our selections are numbered as in Sir Herbert
Grierson's influential edition (1912), since it is his
numbers that the sonnets usually go by; but there
is no reason to suppose that this is the order Donne

intended.
2. "Wing": give wings to. "Prevent": forestall.
"Adamant": loadstone.
1. Both body and soul—the former made of elements, the latter an "angelic sprite" (spirit).
2. Astronomers and explorers are to find new
oceans for tears to weep or waters to wash away the
poet's sins.
3. After Noah's experience, God promised (Genesis 9.11) never to flood the earth again.

And made it fouler; let their flames retire,
And burn me, O Lord, with a fiery zeal
Of thee and thy house, which doth in eating heal.[4]

1635

7

At the round earth's imagined corners,[1] blow
Your trumpets, angels; and arise, arise
From death, you numberless infinities
Of souls, and to your scattered bodies go:
All whom the flood did, and fire shall, o'erthrow,   5
All whom war, dearth, age, agues, tyrannies,
Despair, law, chance hath slain, and you whose eyes
Shall behold God, and never taste death's woe.[2]
But let them sleep, Lord, and me mourn a space;
For, if above all these, my sins abound,   10
'Tis late to ask abundance of thy grace
When we are there. Here on this lowly ground,
Teach me how to repent; for that's as good
As if thou hadst sealed my pardon with thy blood.

1633

9

If poisonous minerals, and if that tree
Whose fruit threw death on else-immortal us,
If lecherous goats, if serpents envious
Cannot be damned, alas! why should I be?
Why should intent or reason, born in me,   5
Make sins, else equal, in me more heinous?
And, mercy being easy and glorious
To God, in his stern wrath why threatens he?
But who am I that dare dispute with thee
O God? Oh,[1] of thine only worthy blood   10
And my tears, make a heavenly Lethean[2] flood,
And drown in it my sin's black memory.
That thou remember them some claim as debt;
I think it mercy if thou wilt forget.

1633

---

4. See Psalm 69.9: "For the zeal of thine house
hath eaten me up." The passage involves three sorts
of flame—those of the Last Judgment; those of lust
and envy; and those of zeal, which alone save.
1. Compare Revelation 7.1: "I saw four angels
standing on the four corners of the earth. . . ."

2. I.e., those who will be alive at the Second
Coming.
1. The 1st edition punctuates as follows: "thee? /
O God, oh!"
2. In classical mythology, the waters of the river
Lethe in the underworld caused total forgetfulness.

10

Death, be not proud, though some have callèd thee
Mighty and dreadful, for thou art not so;
For those whom thou think'st thou dost overthrow
Die not, poor Death, nor yet canst thou kill me.
From rest and sleep, which but thy pictures be,   5
Much pleasure; then from thee much more must flow,
And soonest our best men with thee do go,
Rest of their bones, and soul's delivery.[1]
Thou art slave to fate, chance, kings, and desperate men,
And dost with poison, war, and sickness dwell,   10
And poppy[2] or charms can make us sleep as well
And better than thy stroke; why swell'st thou then?[3]
One short sleep past, we wake eternally
And death shall be no more; Death, thou shalt die.

                                                  1633

13

What if this present were the world's last night?
Mark in my heart, O soul, where thou dost dwell,
The picture of Christ crucified, and tell
Whether that countenance can thee affright.
Tears in his eyes quench the amazing light,   5
Blood fills his frowns, which from his pierced head fell;
And can that tongue adjudge thee unto hell
Which prayed forgiveness for his foes' fierce spite?
No, no; but as in my idolatry
I said to all my profane[1] mistresses,   10
Beauty of pity, foulness only is
A sign of rigor:[2] so I say to thee,
To wicked spirits are horrid shapes assigned,
This beauteous form assures a piteous mind.

                                                  1633

14

Batter my heart, three-personed God; for you
As yet but knock, breathe, shine, and seek to mend;
That I may rise and stand, o'erthrow me, and bend
Your force to break, blow, burn, and make me new.
I, like an usurped town, to another due,   5
Labor to admit you, but O, to no end;
Reason, your viceroy in me, me should defend,

---

1. I.e., to find rest for their bones and freedom
("delivery") for their souls.
2. Opium.
3. Why do you puff with pride?

1. Worldly.
2. Beautiful features are a sign of a gentle disposition, ugliness of the contrary.

But is captived, and proves weak or untrue.
Yet dearly I love you, and would be loved fain,
But am betrothed unto your enemy.   10
Divorce me, untie or break that knot again;
Take me to you, imprison me, for I,
Except you enthrall me, never shall be free,
Nor ever chaste, except you ravish me.

                                        1633

                    17

Since she whom I loved hath paid her last debt
To Nature, and to hers, and my good is dead,[1]
And her soul early into heaven ravishèd,
Wholly on heavenly things my mind is set.
Here the admiring her my mind did whet   5
To seek thee, God; so streams do show the head;
But though I have found thee, and thou my thirst hast fed,
A holy thirsty dropsy melts me yet.
But why should I beg more love, whenas thou
Dost woo my soul, for hers offering all thine: 10
And dost not only fear lest I allow
My love to saints and angels, things divine,
But in thy tender jealousy dost doubt
Lest the world, flesh, yea, devil put thee out.[2]

                                        1899

                    18

Show me, dear Christ, thy spouse so bright and clear.[1]
What! is it she which on the other shore
Goes richly painted? or which, robbed and tore,
Laments and mourns in Germany and here?[2]
Sleeps she a thousand, then peeps up one year?   5
Is she self-truth, and errs? now new, now outwore?
Doth she, and did she, and shall she evermore
On one, on seven, or on no hill appear?[3]

1. Donne's wife died in 1617 at the age of 33, having just borne her 12th child. This rough and very personal sonnet, and the following one, survive in a single manuscript, which came to light only in 1892.
2. Donne seems to imply that God took away Ann More in order to have a monopoly of John Donne's love. The last lines even suggest that the bereaved husband saw his wife as having been a temptation to deadly sin.
1. This sonnet embodies Donne's lifelong distress at the fragmentation of the church ("the bride of Christ"). Whether it also embodies doubts as to the superiority of the Anglican church has been a subject of dispute.
2. I.e., neither the painted woman (the Church of Rome) nor the ravished virgin (the Protestant churches) seems very like a bride. "Robbed and tore" may allude to a military defeat suffered by German Protestants in 1620.
3. The church on seven hills is, inescapably, that of Rome; that "on no hill" could be either the presbyterian church of Geneva or the episcopal church of England, with its head at Canterbury. But what then is the church on one hill that could conceivably be the bride of Christ? It is a crux, not easy of solution.

Dwells she with us, or like adventuring knights
First travel we to seek, and then make love?   10
Betray, kind husband, thy spouse to our sights,
And let mine amorous soul court thy mild dove,
Who is most true and pleasing to thee then
When she is embraced and open to most men.[4]

                                                                        1899

Good Friday, 1613. Riding Westward

Let man's soul be a sphere, and then, in this,
The intelligence that moves, devotion is,[1]
And as the other spheres, by being grown
Subject to foreign motions, lose their own,
And being by others hurried every day,   5
Scarce in a year their natural form[2] obey;
Pleasure or business, so, our souls admit
For their first mover, and are whirled by it.[3]
Hence is 't, that I am carried towards the West
This day, when my soul's form bends toward the East.   10
There I should see a Sun,[4] by rising, set,
And by that setting endless day beget:
But that Christ on this cross did rise and fall,
Sin had eternally benighted all.
Yet dare I almost be glad I do not see   15
That spectacle, of too much weight for me.
Who sees God's face, that is self-life, must die;[5]
What a death were it then to see God die?
It made his own lieutenant, Nature, shrink;
It made his footstool crack, and the sun wink.[6]   20
Could I behold those hands which span the poles,
And tune[7] all spheres at once, pierced with those holes?
Could I behold that endless height which is
Zenith to us, and t'our antipodes,[8]
Humbled below us? Or that blood which is   25
The seat[9] of all our souls, if not of his,
Make dirt of dust, or that flesh which was worn
By God for his apparel, ragg'd and torn?

4. The final lines echo the Song of Solomon (5.2), which was often interpreted as the song of love between Christ and the church: "Open to me, my sister, my love, my dove, my undefiled."
1. As angelic intelligences guide the celestial spheres, so devotion is or should be the guiding principle of man's life.
2. Moving principle.
3. I.e., spheres are deflected from their true orbits by outside influences; so our souls are deflected by business or pleasure.
4. The sun-Son pun was an ancient one. Christ, the Son of God, set when he rose on the Cross, and his setting (death) gave rise to the Christian era, with the hope of ultimate immortality.
5. God told Moses, "Thou canst not see my face: for there shall no man see me, and live" (Exodus 33.20).
6. An earthquake and eclipse supposedly accompanied the Crucifixion.
7. Some manuscripts read "turn."
8. "Zenith" is the highest reach of heaven; the "antipodes" are the opposite side of the earth.
9. Center (as of magnetic attraction).

If on these things I durst not look, durst I
Upon his miserable mother cast mine eye,   30
Who was God's partner here, and furnished thus
Half of that sacrifice which ransomed us?
Though these things, as I ride, be from mine eye,
They are present yet unto my memory,
For that looks towards them; and thou look'st towards me,   35
O Savior, as thou hang'st upon the tree.
I turn my back to thee but to receive
Corrections, till thy mercies bid thee leave.[1]
O think me worth thine anger; punish me;
Burn off my rusts and my deformity;   40
Restore thine image so much, by thy grace,
That thou may'st know me, and I'll turn my face.

1633

A Hymn to Christ, at the Author's Last Going into Germany[1]

In what torn ship soever I embark,
That ship shall be my emblem of thy ark;
What sea soever swallow me, that flood
Shall be to me an emblem of thy blood;
Though thou with clouds of anger do disguise   5
    Thy face, yet through that mask I know those eyes,
        Which, though they turn away sometimes, they never
            will despise.[2]

I sacrifice this island unto thee,
And all whom I loved there, and who loved me;
When I have put our seas twixt them and me,   10
Put thou thy sea[3] betwixt my sins and thee.
As the tree's sap doth seek the root below
In winter, in my winter now I go
    Where none but thee, th' eternal root of true love, I
        may know.

Nor thou nor thy religion dost control   15
The amorousness of an harmonious soul,
But thou wouldst have that love thyself; as thou
Art jealous, Lord, so I am jealous now.

1. Cease.
1. Donne went to Germany in 1619 as chaplain to the Earl of Doncaster. The mission was a diplomatic one, to the king and queen of Bohemia, King James's son-in-law and daughter, who at that time were mainstays of the Protestant cause on the Continent.

2. Printed texts break in two parts (an unrhymed tetrameter and a trimeter) the long last line of each stanza. Unrhymed lines would be unique in Donne's poetry, and the manuscripts are unanimous for the "fourteeners" as we print them.
3. An alternate reading is "blood," reemphasizing the metaphor of lines 3 and 4.

Thou lov'st not, till from loving more[4] thou free
My soul; whoever gives, takes liberty;   20
   Oh, if thou car'st not whom I love, alas, thou lov'st not
     me.

Seal then this bill of my divorce to all
On whom those fainter beams of love did fall;
Marry those loves which in youth scattered be
On fame, wit, hopes (false mistresses) to thee.   25
Churches are best for prayer that have least light:
To see God only, I go out of sight,
   And to 'scape stormy days, I choose an everlasting night.

1633

Hymn to God My God, in My Sickness[1]

Since I am coming to that holy room
   Where, with thy choir of saints for evermore,
I shall be made thy music; as I come
    I tune the instrument here at the door,
    And what I must do then, think now before.   5

Whilst my physicians by their love are grown
   Cosmographers, and I their map, who lie
Flat on this bed, that by them may be shown
    That this is my southwest discovery[2]
    Per fretum febris,[3] by these straits to die,   10

I joy, that in these straits, I see my West;[4]
   For, though their currents yield return to none,
What shall my West hurt me? As West and East
    In all flat maps (and I am one) are one,
    So death doth touch the resurrection.   15

Is the Pacific Sea my home? Or are
   The Eastern riches? Is Jerusalem?
Anyan,[5] and Magellan, and Gibraltar,
    All straits, and none but straits, are ways to them,
    Whether where Japhet dwelt, or Cham, or Shem.[6]   20

4. From loving elsewhere. The idea is, "To give me true love, you must take away my freedom to love anyone else."
1. Though Izaak Walton, Donne's pious biographer, assigns this poem to the last days of his life, it was probably written in December 1623.
2. The Strait of Magellan, or something spiritual that is analogous to it.
3. I.e., through the strait of fever.
4. Where the sun sets, hence where life ends.

5. The Bering Strait. Behind these anxious questions lie many ancient speculations about the location of Paradise—which is analogous to Heaven, as the various straits are to death.
6. Japhet, Cham (Ham), and Shem were the three sons of Noah by whom the world was repopulated after the Flood (Genesis 10). The descendants of Japhet were thought to inhabit Europe, those of Ham Africa, and those of Shem Asia.

We think that Paradise and Calvary,
   Christ's cross and Adam's tree, stood in one place;
Look, Lord and find both Adams[7] met in me;
   As the first Adam's sweat surrounds my face,
   May the last Adam's blood my soul embrace.   25

So, in his purple wrapped,[8] receive me, Lord;
   By these his thorns give me his other crown;
And, as to others' souls I preached thy word,
   Be this my text, my sermon to mine own:
   Therefore that he may raise the Lord throws down.   30

                             1635

A Hymn to God the Father[1]

Wilt thou forgive that sin where I begun,
   Which is my sin, though it were done before?[2]
Wilt thou forgive that sin through which I run,
   And do run still, though still I do deplore?
      When thou hast done, thou hast not done,   5
      For I have more.

Wilt thou forgive that sin by which I have won
   Others to sin? and made my sin their door?
Wilt thou forgive that sin which I did shun
   A year or two, but wallowed in a score?   10
      When thou hast done, thou hast not done,
      For I have more.

I have a sin of fear, that when I have spun
   My last thread, I shall perish on the shore;
Swear by thy self, that at my death thy Son   15
   Shall shine as he shines now and heretofore;
      And, having done that, thou hast done,
      I fear[3] no more.

                             1633

7. I.e., Adam and Christ.
8. The purple of Christ is his blood.
1. Izaak Walton tells us that this short hymn was written during Donne's illness of 1623. Donne had it set to music and frequently performed by the choir and organist of St. Paul's Cathedral.
2. I.e., through his parents he inherits the original sin of Adam and Eve.
3. An alternative reading is "have."

From Devotions upon Emergent Occasions[1]

Meditation 17

Nunc lento sonitu dicunt, morieris.
Now this bell tolling softly for another, says to me, Thou must die.[2]

Perchance he for whom this bell[3] tolls may be so ill as that he knows
not it tolls for him; and perchance I may think myself so much better
than I am, as that they who are about me and see my state may have
caused it to toll for me, and I know not that. The church is catholic,
universal, so are all her actions; all that she does belongs to all. When
she baptizes a child, that action concerns me; for that child is thereby
connected to that head which is my head too, and ingrafted into that
body[4] whereof I am a member. And when she buries a man, that action
concerns me: all mankind is of one author and is one volume; when one
man dies, one chapter is not torn out of the book, but translated[5] into a
better language; and every chapter must be so translated. God employs
several translators; some pieces are translated by age, some by sickness,
some by war, some by justice; but God's hand is in every translation,
and his hand shall bind up all our scattered leaves again for that library
where every book shall lie open to one another. As therefore the bell
that rings to a sermon calls not upon the preacher only, but upon the
congregation to come, so this bell calls us all; but how much more me,
who am brought so near the door by this sickness. There was a contention as far as a suit[6] (in which piety and dignity, religion and estimation,
were mingled) which of the religious orders should ring to prayers first
in the morning; and it was determined that they should ring first that
rose earliest. If we understand aright the dignity of this bell that tolls for
our evening prayer, we would be glad to make it ours by rising early, in
that application, that it might be ours as well as his whose indeed it is.
The bell doth toll for him that thinks it doth; and though it intermit
again, yet from that minute that that occasion wrought upon him, he is
united to God. Who casts not up his eye to the sun when it rises? but
who takes off his eye from a comet when that breaks out? Who bends
not his ear to any bell which upon any occasion rings? but who can
remove it from that bell which is passing a piece of himself out of this

---

1. Donne's *Devotions* were written in the aftermath of a serious illness in the winter of 1623—
though Donne characteristically writes as if the
events of the illness were happening at the moment
he describes them. The *Devotions* recount the stages
of his disease and recovery; each stage comprises a
"meditation upon our human condition," an
"expostulation and debatement with God," and a
prayer to Him. The book was published almost
immediately it was written, and to great effect—
the blend of private feeling and public moralizing
rendering it particularly accessible to 17th-century
readers. And its eloquent, richly metaphorical

sentences have provided a title for at least one major
modern novel (see Meditation 17).
   "Emergent" occasions are those which arise
casually or unexpectedly.
2. Donne's Latin epigraphs are followed by his
English translations, some of them very free ones
indeed.
3. The "passing bell" for the dying.
4. The church.
5. Punning on the literal sense, "carried across."
6. Controversy which went as far as a lawsuit.
"Estimation": self-esteem.

world? No man is an island, entire of itself; every man is a piece of the continent, a part of the main.[7] If a clod be washed away by the sea, Europe is the less, as well as if a promontory were, as well as if a manor of thy friend's or of thine own were. Any man's death diminishes me, because I am involved in mankind; and therefore never send to know for whom the bell tolls; it tolls for thee. Neither can we call this a begging of misery or a borrowing of misery, as though we were not miserable enough of ourselves but must fetch in more from the next house, in taking upon us the misery of our neighbors. Truly it were an excusable covetousness if we did; for affliction is a treasure, and scarce any man hath enough of it. No man hath affliction enough that is not matured and ripened by it, and made fit for God by that affliction. If a man carry treasure in bullion, or in a wedge of gold, and have none coined into current moneys, his treasure will not defray him as he travels. Tribulation is treasure in the nature of it, but it is not current money in the use of it, except we get nearer and nearer our home, heaven, by it. Another man may be sick too, and sick to death, and this affliction may lie in his bowels as gold in a mine and be of no use to him; but this bell that tells me of his affliction digs out and applies that gold to me, if by this consideration of another's danger I take mine own into contemplation and so secure myself by making my recourse to my God, who is our only security.

1623   1624

7. Mainland.

BEN JONSON
1572–1637

1598:   *Every Man in His Humor*, Jonson's first published play.
1606:   *Volpone*.
1616:   Jonson appointed poet laureate; publishes his *Works*.
1629:   Decisive failure of *The New Inn*.

Ben Jonson did so many different things in the literary world of the early seventeenth century, and made use of so many different styles to do them, that he is difficult to see as a whole person. Actor, playwright, poet and poet laureate, scholar, critic, translator, man of letters, and head, for the first time in English, of a literary "school," the so-called "sons of Ben," he was a giant of a man. Yet we cannot easily take a perspective of him.

Jonson's life was tough and turbulent. The posthumous child of a clergyman, he was stepson to a master bricklayer of Westminster. He was educated at Westminster School by the great classical scholar and antiquarian William Camden, worked briefly at his stepfather's trade, and then entered the army. In Flanders, where the Dutch with English help were warring against the Spaniards, he fought single-handed with one of the enemy before the massed armies, and killed his man. Returning to England about 1594, he began to work as an actor and playwright but was drawn from one storm center to another. He killed a fellow-actor in a duel, and escaped the gallows only by pleading "benefit of clergy" (i.e., by proving he could read and write, which entitled him to plead before a more lenient ecclesiastical court). He was jailed for insulting the Scottish nation at a time when King James was newly arrived from Scotland. He took furious part in an intricate set of literary wars with his fellow-playwrights. Having converted to Catholicism, he was the object of deep suspicion after the Gunpowder Plot of Guy Fawkes (1605), when the phobia against his religion reached its height. Yet he rode out all these troubles, growing mellower as he grew older (and re-converting to Anglicanism); in his latter years he became the unofficial literary dictator of London, the king's pensioned poet, a favorite around the court, and the good friend of men like Shakespeare, Donne, Francis Beaumont, John Selden, Francis Bacon, dukes, diplomats, and distinguished folk generally. In addition, he engaged the affection of younger men (poets like Robert Herrick, Thomas Carew, and Sir John Suckling, speculative thinkers like Lord Falkland and Sir Kenelm Digby), who delighted to christen themselves "sons of Ben." Sons of Ben provided the nucleus of the entire "Cavalier school" of English poets.

The first of Jonson's great plays was *Every Man in His Humor*, in which Shakespeare acted a leading role. It was also the first of the so-called "comedies of humors," in which the prevailing eccentricities and ruling passions of men (i.e., their "humors") were exposed to satiric deflation. Though Jonson's classical tragedy *Sejanus* (1603) has not been much liked (it is gloomy in mood, static in action, and weighty with antiquarian lore), *Volpone* (1606) and *The Alchemist* (1610) are two supreme satiric comedies of the English stage. Both have been repeatedly "adapted" and "modernized," but even now the original texts are likely to seem more lively and vital than the doctored versions. Meanwhile, starting in 1605, Jonson began writing for the court a series of masques—elaborate semitheatrical displays involving spectacle, allegory, and compliment to the king or queen. Thus he became closely involved with the life of the court, a connection which was formalized in 1616, when he was appointed poet laureate with a substantial pension. In the same year, he published in a splendid volume his collected *Works*, a body of poetry to which he kept adding in the years before his death. Though his later plays were not very successful, he turned out many occasional poems, verse letters, translations, complimentary verses before other poets' volumes—finding in all these different forms a grave, incisive pattern of formal speech through which the reverberations of his immense classical learning make themselves heard.

The bulk of Jonson's poetry falls, without undue strain, into five groups, based mostly on stylistic qualities. He wrote a number of poems of festive ceremony, poems which celebrate those qualities of ordered richness and dignified delight which represent his image of the good life. A poem like *To Penshurst* turns a physical building and its surrounding countryside into an emblem of modest yet noble opulence; the poem *Inviting a Friend to Supper* is an imitation of Horace, yet its tonality is thoroughly English, and the "modest little supper" to which he invites his friend would scandalize a modern weight-watcher. Quite a different side of Jonson's talent is represented by his elegies and epitaphs; they are brief, full, simple poems, such as one could imagine being carved on a marble slab—direct, impersonal, inevitable. Allied to these are his compliments and tributes; often prefixed to his friends' books, but sometimes simple tributes of friendship and admiration, they summarize warmly yet judiciously a man's character and achievement. Jonson the pure poet finds expression in his songs, sometimes occurring in the plays and masques but sometimes standing alone, often intended for musical accompaniment, but generally beautifully melodic, even without it. Finally, Jonson wrote (in imitation of the Roman poet Martial) a great number of epigrams, sometimes lewd, sometimes nasty, occasionally funny. We have largely lost the taste for this sort of thing today, but epigrams were a vital Renaissance genre, and Jonson's profane epigrams can usefully be compared to Crashaw's sacred ones.

Jonson took his calling as a poet with the greatest seriousness, asserting the dignity of the profession with (sometimes) a kind of pedantry and emphasis that contrasts with Shakespeare's extraordinary anonymity. When Jonson published in 1616 his collected works—*The Works of Benjamin Jonson*—it was the first time an English author had been so presumptuous. Yet he succeeded in making the fact of professional authorship somehow respectable; an author like John Dryden, who owed so much to Jonson on stylistic grounds, owed him a social debt as well. His career stood on foundations which Ben, with his pedantry and his pugnacity, was the first to lay down.

To My Book[1]

It will be looked for, book, when some but see
  Thy title, *Epigrams*, and named of me,
Thou should'st be bold, licentious, full of gall,
  Wormwood and sulphur, sharp and toothed[2] withal,
Become a petulant thing, hurl ink and wit   5
  As madmen stones, not caring whom they hit.
Deceive their malice who could wish it so,
  And by thy wiser temper let men know
Thou art not covetous of least self-fame
  Made from the hazard of another's shame—   10
Much less with lewd, profane, and beastly phrase
  To catch the world's loose laughter or vain gaze.
He that departs[3] with his own honesty
  For vulgar praise, doth it too dearly buy.

1616

1. Epigrams are commonly thought of as short, incisive poems of personal invective; but when Jonson included in his collected *Works* of 1616 a separate section headed "Epigrams (Book 1)," he was using the word in a more liberal sense. His "epigrams" included (besides some sharp and sarcastic verses) several poems of compliment and courtesy, some memorial epitaphs, and a verse letter, *Inviting a Friend to Supper*. In our anthology, *To My Book* and the next several poems (through *Epitaph on Elizabeth, L. H.*) come from this section. The "Book 1" of Jonson's title implied at least the promise of a "Book 2," and there are, scattered through his later poetry, a number of verses that might have entered into such a book. But, for whatever reason, Jonson never assembled them under any such title.
2. The distinction between toothed (biting) and toothless (general) satires, originally made by Joseph Hall, who claimed to be the first English satirist, was a commonplace of Jonson's age.
3. I.e., parts.

On Something, That Walks Somewhere

At court I met it, in clothes brave[1] enough
   To be a courtier, and looks grave enough
To seem a statesman: as I near it came,
   It made me a great face. I asked the name.
"A lord," it cried, "buried in flesh and blood,   5
   And such from whom let no man hope least good,
For I will do none; and as little ill,
   For I will dare none." Good lord, walk dead still.

                                         1616

To William Camden[1]

Camden, most reverend head, to whom I owe
   All that I am in arts, all that I know
(How nothing's that!), to whom my country owes
   The great renown and name wherewith she goes;[2]
Than thee the age sees not that thing more grave,   5
   More high, more holy, that she more would crave.
What name, what skill, what faith hast thou in things!
   What sight in searching the most antique springs!
What weight and what authority in thy speech!
   Man scarce can make that doubt, but thou canst teach.[3]   10
Pardon free truth and let thy modesty,
   Which conquers all, be once o'ercome by thee.
Many of thine[4] this better could than I;
   But for their powers, accept my piety.

                                         1616

On My First Daughter

Here lies, to each her parents' ruth,[1]
Mary, the daughter of their youth;
Yet all heaven's gifts being heaven's due,
It makes the father less to rue.
At six months' end she parted hence   5

---

1. Fine.
1. Though first printed among the *Epigrams*, this affectionate tribute to a distinguished scholar and Jonson's old teacher has few of the qualities of an epigram, except brevity. It is just the size (though not the shape) of a sonnet.
2. Camden's antiquarian studies of his native land in *Britannia* (1586) and *Remains of a Greater Work*
Concerning Britain (1605) ran into several editions and were translated abroad.
3. I.e., man can scarcely ask a question to which you don't know the answer.
4. I.e., your pupils. "But for": but in lieu of.
1. Grief. There is no positive date of composition for this poem.

With safety of her innocence;
Whose soul heaven's queen, whose name she bears,
In comfort of her mother's tears,
Hath placed amongst her virgin-train:
Where, while that severed doth remain,   10
This grave partakes the fleshly birth;
Which cover lightly, gentle earth!

1616

On My First Son

Farewell, thou child of my right hand,[1] and joy;
My sin was too much hope of thee, loved boy:
Seven years thou wert lent to me, and I thee pay,
Exacted by thy fate, on the just day.
O could I lose all father[2] now! For why   5
Will man lament the state he should envy,
To have so soon 'scaped world's and flesh's rage,
And, if no other misery, yet age?
Rest in soft peace, and asked, say, "Here doth lie
Ben Jonson his best piece of poetry."   10
For whose sake henceforth all his vows be such
As what he loves may never like too much.[3]

1616

To John Donne

Donne, the delight of Phoebus and each Muse,
Who, to thy one, all other brains refuse;[1]
Whose every work, of thy most early wit,
Came forth example and remains so yet;
Longer a-knowing than most wits do live,   5
And which no affection praise enough can give.
To it[2] thy language, letters, arts, best life,
Which might with half mankind maintain a strife.
All which I meant to praise, and yet I would,
But leave, because I cannot as I should.   10

1616

---

1. "Child of the right hand" is a literal translation of the Hebrew name "Benjamin," which implies the meanings "dexterous," or "fortunate." The boy was born in 1596 and died on his birthday in 1603.
2. Relinquish all fatherly thoughts.
3. The obscure grammar of the last lines seems to recapitulate the feeling in line 2, that too much affection is fatal to the loved one. "Whose sake" is the boy's; "like" may carry the sense of "please."
1. I.e., the muses shower their favors exclusively on you.
2. The verb "add" is understood.

On Don Surly

Don Surly,[1] to aspire the glorious name
  Of a great man, and to be thought the same,
Makes serious use of all great trade[2] he knows.
    He speaks to men with a Rhinocerotes' nose,[3]
Which he thinks great; and so reads verses too,   5
  And that is done as he saw great men do.
He has timpanies[4] of business in his face,
  And can forget men's names with a great grace.
He will both argue and discourse in oaths,
  Both which are great; and laugh at ill-made clothes—   10
That's greater yet—to cry his own up neat.
  He doth, at meals, alone his pheasant eat,
Which is main greatness; and at his still board[5]
  He drinks to no man; that's, too, like a lord.
He keeps another's wife, which is a spice[6]   15
  Of solemn greatness. And he dares, at dice,
Blaspheme God greatly, or some poor hind[7] beat
  That breathes in his dog's way; and this is great.
Nay more, for greatness' sake, he will be one
  May hear my epigrams, but like of none.   20
Surly, use other arts; these only can
  Style thee a most great fool, but no great man.

1616

On Giles and Joan

Who says that Giles and Joan at discord be?
  Th' observing neighbors no such mood can see.
Indeed, poor Giles repents he married ever,
  But that his Joan doth too. And Giles would never
By his free will be in Joan's company;   5
  No more would Joan he should. Giles riseth early,
And having got him out of doors is glad;
  The like is Joan. But turning home is sad,
And so is Joan. Ofttimes, when Giles doth find
  Harsh sights at home, Giles wisheth he were blind: 10
All this doth Joan. Or that his long-yearned[1] life
  Were quite outspun. The like wish hath his wife.
The children that he keeps Giles swears are none

---

1. "Don" is a Spanish title, and the Spanish were
thought to have pompous manners. "Aspire": attain.
2. Tricks.
3. I.e., looking down his nose like a rhinoceros.
4. Figuratively, a kettle-drum; fullness, emptiness, and hollow noises are implied.

5. I.e., his lonely dinner-table.
6. Species, kind.
7. Yokel.
1. Spun from long skeins of yarn, but with the
extra implication of long and futile yearning.

Of his begetting; and so swears his Joan.
In all affections she concurreth still.   15
    If now, with man and wife, to will and nill[2]
The self-same things a note of concord be,
    I know no couple better can agree.

                                                            1616

To Lucy, Countess of Bedford, with Mr. Donne's Satires[1]

Lucy, you brightness of our sphere, who are
    Life of the Muses' day, their morning star!
If works, not th' authors, their own grace should look,
    Whose poems would not wish to be your book?
But these, desired by you, the maker's ends   5
    Crown with their own. Rare poems ask rare friends.
Yet satires, since the most of mankind be
    Their unavoided subject, fewest see:
For none e'er took that pleasure in sin's sense,
    But, when they heard it taxed, took more offense.   10
They then that, living where the matter is bred,
    Dare for these poems yet both ask and read
And like them too, must needfully, though few,
    Be of the best: and 'mongst those, best are you;
Lucy, you brightness of our sphere, who are   15
    The Muses' evening, as their morning star.

                                                            1616

Inviting a Friend to Supper

Tonight, grave sir, both my poor house and I
    Do equally desire your company:
Not that we think us worthy such a guest,
    But that your worth will dignify our feast
With those that come; whose grace may make that seem   5
    Something, which else could hope for no esteem.
It is the fair acceptance, Sir, creates
    The entertainment perfect: not the cates.[1]
Yet shall you have, to rectify your palate,
    An olive, capers, or some better salad   10
Ushering the mutton; with a short-legged hen,
    If we can get her, full of eggs, and then

---

2. To desire and reject; cf. modern "willy-nilly."
1. The Countess of Bedford was a famous patroness of the age, to whom both Jonson and Donne
addressed poems of compliment. With this poem,
Jonson was not offering a printed volume of Donne's

Satires, but simply a manuscript collection, such
as commonly passed from hand to hand in court
circles.
1. Dishes.

Lemons and wine for sauce; to these, a coney[2]
　　Is not to be despaired of for our money;
And though fowl now be scarce, yet there are clerks,[3]
　　The sky not falling, think we may have larks.
I'll tell you of more, and lie, so you will come:
　　Of partridge, pheasant, woodcock, of which some
May yet be there; and godwit if we can,
　　Knot, rail, and ruff, too.[4] Howsoe'er, my man　　　　　20
Shall read a piece of Virgil, Tacitus,
　　Livy, or of some better book to us,
Of which we'll speak our minds amidst our meat;
　　And I'll profess[5] no verses to repeat:
To this, if aught appear which I not know of,　　　　　25
　　That will the pastry, not my paper, show off.[6]
Digestive cheese and fruit there sure will be;
　　But that which most doth take my muse and me
Is a pure cup of rich Canary wine,
　　Which is the Mermaid's[7] now, but shall be mine;　　　30
Of which, had Horace or Anacreon tasted,
　　Their lives, as do their lines, till now had lasted.
Tobacco, Nectar, or the Thespian spring
　　Are all but Luther's beer to this I sing.[8]
Of this we will sup free but moderately,　　　　　35
　　And we will have no Pooly or Parrot[9] by;
Nor shall our cups make any guilty men,
　　But at our parting we will be as when
We innocently met. No simple word
　　That shall be uttered at our mirthful board　　　　40
Shall make us sad next morning; or affright
　　The liberty that we'll enjoy tonight.

　　　　　　　　　　　　　　　　　　　1616

Epitaph on Salomon Pavy, a Child of Queen Elizabeth's Chapel[1]

Weep with me, all you that read
　　This little story;

2. Rabbit.
3. Scholars (pronounced "clarks").
4. The treat of the feast will be these various game birds.
5. Promise.
6. I.e., papers may appear, but they will be under pies (to keep them from sticking to the pan), not for declamation. "To this": add to this.
7. The Mermaid tavern, favorite haunt of the poets; sweet wine from the Canary Islands was popular in England. Horace and Anacreon (one in Latin, the other in Greek) wrote many poems in praise of wine.
8. One of two springs on Mount Helicon near the village of Thespiae, both reputed to be sources of poetic inspiration. Compared to Canary, all these other intoxicants are no better than Luther's beer, i.e., weak stuff.
9. Pooly and Parrot were government spies, though their conjunction also suggests a talkative bird, Poll Parrot. While a Roman Catholic and even after he formally left that communion, Jonson had reason to be wary of undercover agents.
1. Salomon Pavy, a boy actor in the troupe known as the Children of Queen Elizabeth's Chapel, had appeared in several of Jonson's plays; he died in 1602.

And know for whom a tear you shed,
    Death's self is sorry.
'Twas a child that so did thrive   5
    In grace and feature,
As Heaven and Nature seemed to strive
    Which owned the creature.
Years he numbered scarce thirteen
    When Fates turned cruel,   10
Yet three filled zodiacs[2] had he been
    The stage's jewel;
And did act (what now we moan)
    Old men so duly,
As, sooth, the Parcae[3] thought him one,   15
    He played so truly.
So, by error, to his fate
    They all consented;
But, viewing him since (alas, too late),
    They have repented,   20
And have sought (to give new birth)
    In baths[4] to steep him;
But, being so much too good for earth,
    Heaven vows to keep him.

1616

Epitaph on Elizabeth, L. H.[1]

Wouldst thou hear what man can say
    In a little? Reader, stay.
Underneath this stone doth lie
    As much beauty as could die;
Which in life did harbor give   5
    To more virtue than doth live.
If at all she had a fault,
    Leave it buried in this vault.
One name was Elizabeth;
    Th' other, let it sleep with death: 10
Fitter, where it died, to tell,
    Than that it lived at all. Farewell!

1616

2. I.e., had been on the stage for three seasons.
3. The Fates, one of whose functions was to determine the length of lives.
4. Jonson may have had in mind such magic baths as that of Medea, which restored old Aeson, Jason's

father, to his first youth (Ovid, *Metamorphoses* 7).
1. The subject of this epitaph has not been identified; her full name (though we can guess that the L. probably stood for "Lady") has slept with death.

To Penshurst[1]

Thou art not, Penshurst, built to envious show,
   Of touch[2] or marble; nor canst boast a row
Of polished pillars, or a roof of gold;
   Thou hast no lantern[3] whereof tales are told,
Or stair, or courts; but stand'st an ancient pile,   5
   And, these grudged at,[4] art reverenced the while.
Thou joy'st in better marks, of soil, of air,
   Of wood, of water; therein thou art fair.
Thou hast thy walks for health, as well as sport;
   Thy mount, to which the dryads[5] do resort,   10
Where Pan and Bacchus their high feasts have made,
   Beneath the broad beech and the chestnut shade;
That taller tree, which of a nut was set
   At his great birth where all the Muses met.[6]
There in the writhèd bark are cut the names   15
   Of many a sylvan, taken with his flames;[7]
And thence the ruddy satyrs oft provoke
   The lighter fauns to reach thy Lady's Oak.[8]
Thy copse too, named of Gamage,[9] thou hast there,
   That never fails to serve thee seasoned deer   20
When thou wouldst feast or exercise thy friends.
   The lower land, that to the river bends,
Thy sheep, thy bullocks, kine, and calves do feed;
   The middle grounds thy mares and horses breed.
Each bank doth yield thee conies;[1] and the tops,   25
   Fertile of wood, Ashore and Sidney's copse,[2]
To crown thy open table, doth provide
   The purpled pheasant with the speckled side;
The painted partridge lies in every field,
   And for thy mess is willing to be killed.   30
And if the high-swollen Medway[3] fail thy dish,
   Thou hast thy ponds, that pay thee tribute fish:
Fat aged carps that run into thy net,

1. The country seat of the Sidney family (famous for Sir Philip) in Kent. Jonson's is one of the first English poems celebrating a specific place. Later examples are *Cooper's Hill* by Sir John Denham and *Windsor Forest* by Alexander Pope; some modern poets have celebrated their favorite subway stations or particularly atrocious (but fondly remembered) bits of suburbia.
   In the 1616 *Works*, Jonson grouped some of his non-epigrammatic poems under the heading *The Forest*. This was a translation of the term *Silvae*, used by the late Latin poet Statius to designate a poetical miscellany. *To Penshurst* and the two following poems are from that grouping.
2. Touchstone, a fine black (and expensive) variety of basalt.
3. Cupola.

4. More pretentious houses attract criticism.
5. Wood nymphs.
6. Sir Philip Sidney was born at Penshurst; an oak tree, planted the day of his birth, is still shown as "Sidney's oak."
7. Woodsman, in love because of reading Sidney's poems. "His flames" are the fires of love.
8. Lady Leicester's oak, named after a lady of the house who once entered into labor under its branches. "Provoke": challenge to a race.
9. Lady Barbara Gamage gave her name to a grove near the park entrance.
1. Rabbits.
2. Little woods and thickets of the estate, still surviving under their ancient names.
3. The local river.

And pikes, now weary their own kind to eat,
As loath the second draught or cast to stay,   35
   Officiously at first themselves betray;
Bright eels that emulate them, and leap on land
   Before the fisher, or into his hand.
Then hath thy orchard fruit, thy garden flowers,
   Fresh as the air, and new as are the hours.   40
The early cherry, with the later plum,
   Fig, grape, and quince, each in his time doth come;
The blushing apricot and woolly peach
   Hang on thy walls, that every child may reach.
And though thy walls be of the country stone,   45
   They are reared with no man's ruin, no man's groan;
There's none that dwell about them wish them down;
   But all come in, the farmer and the clown,[4]
And no one empty-handed, to salute
   Thy lord and lady, though they have no suit.   50
Some bring a capon, some a rural cake,
   Some nuts, some apples; some that think they make
The better cheeses bring them, or else send
   By their ripe daughters, whom they would commend
This way to husbands, and whose baskets bear   55
   An emblem of themselves in plum or pear.
But what can this (more than express their love)
   Add to thy free provisions, far above
The need of such? whose liberal board doth flow
   With all that hospitality doth know;   60
Where comes no guest but is allowed to eat,
   Without his fear, and of thy lord's own meat;
Where the same beer and bread, and selfsame wine,
   That is his lordship's shall be also mine,
And I not fain to sit (as some this day   65
   At great men's tables), and yet dine away.[5]
Here no man tells[6] my cups; nor, standing by,
   A waiter doth my gluttony envy,
But gives me what I call, and lets me eat;
   He knows below he shall find plenty of meat.   70
Thy tables hoard not up for the next day;
   Nor, when I take my lodging, need I pray
For fire, or lights, or livery;[7] all is there,
   As if thou then wert mine, or I reigned here:
There's nothing I can wish, for which I stay.[8]   75
   That found King James when, hunting late this way
With his brave son, the Prince, they saw thy fires
   Shine bright on every hearth, as the desires

4. Yokel.
5. When tables were large, different courses might
be served at the two ends; hence one could sit at a
man's table and dine away, eating different food
entirely.
6. Counts.
7. In the old sense, provisions, food.
8. Wait.

Of thy Penates[9] had been set on flame
   To entertain them; or the country came   80
With all their zeal to warm their welcome here.
   What (great I will not say, but) sudden cheer
Didst thou then make 'em! and what praise was heaped
   On thy good lady then, who therein reaped
The just reward of her high housewifery;   85
   To have her linen, plate, and all things nigh,
When she was far; and not a room but dressed
   As if it had expected such a guest!
These, Penshurst, are thy praise, and yet not all.
   Thy lady's noble, fruitful, chaste withal.   90
His children thy great lord may call his own,
   A fortune in this age but rarely known.
They are, and have been, taught religion; thence
   Their gentler spirits have sucked innocence.
Each morn and even they are taught to pray,   95
   With the whole household, and may, every day,
Read in their virtuous parents' noble parts
   The mysteries of manners, arms, and arts.
Now, Penshurst, they that will proportion[1] thee
   With other edifices, when they see   100
Those proud, ambitious heaps, and nothing else,
   May say, their lords have built, but thy lord dwells.

                           1616

Song: To Celia[1]

   Drink to me only with thine eyes,
      And I will pledge with mine;
   Or leave a kiss but in the cup,
      And I'll not look for wine.
   The thirst that from the soul doth rise   5
      Doth ask a drink divine:
   But might I of Jove's nectar sup,
      I would not change for thine.

   I sent thee late a rosy wreath,
      Not so much honoring thee,   10
   As giving it a hope that there
      It could not withered be.
   But thou thereon did'st only breathe,
      And sent'st it back to me;

9. Roman household gods. A room in the house
is still known as "King James's room."
1. Compare.
1. These famous lines are a patchwork of five separate prose passages by Philostratus, a Greek sophist (3rd century A.D.). Jonson very carefully reworded
the phrases (there are several manuscript versions
of the poem) into this classic lyric. The music which
has made it a barroom favorite is by an anonymous
18th-century composer.

Since when it grows and smells, I swear,   15
    Not of itself, but thee.

                                                            1616

To Heaven

Good and great God, can I not think of thee
    But it must straight my melancholy be?
Is it interpreted in me disease
    That, laden with my sins, I seek for ease?
Oh, be thou witness, that the reins[1] dost know   5
    And hearts of all, if I be sad for show,
And judge me after, if I dare pretend
    To aught but grace, or aim at other end.
As thou art all, so be thou all to me,
    First, midst, and last, converted[2] one and three,   10
My faith, my hope, my love; and in this state,
    My judge, my witness, and my advocate.
Where have I been this while exiled from thee,
    And whither rapt, now thou but stoop'st[3] to me?
Dwell, dwell here still: Oh, being everywhere,   15
    How can I doubt to find thee ever here?
I know my state, both full of shame and scorn,
    Conceived in sin and unto labor born,
Standing with fear, and must with horror fall,
    And destined unto judgment after all.   20
I feel my griefs too, and there scarce is ground
    Upon my flesh to inflict another wound.
Yet dare I not complain or wish for death
    With holy Paul,[4] lest it be thought the breath
Of discontent; or that these prayers be   25
    For weariness of life, not love of thee.

                                                            1616

In the Person of Womankind[1]
(In Defense of Their Inconstancy)

Hang up those dull and envious fools
    That talk abroad of woman's change;

---

1. Literally, kidneys, but also the seat of the affections, with a further glance at Psalm 7.9: "the righteous God trieth the hearts and reins."
2. Interchanging.
3. Falcons stoop (i.e., dive from the heavens) to snatch their quarry.
4. In Romans 7.24, Paul cries out despairingly,

"Who shall deliver me from the body of this death?"
1. Preparing a second edition of his Works (published posthumously in 1640–41), Jonson added a third section of poems, The Underwood, "out of the analogy they hold to The Forest in my former book." Of its 89 poems we reprint just 3, this and the following two.

We were not bred to sit on stools,
    Our proper virtue is to range:
        Take that away, you take our lives,   5
        We are no women then, but wives.

Such as in valor would excel
    Do change, though man, and often fight,
Which we in love must do as well
    If ever we will love aright.   10
        The frequent varying of the deed
        Is that which doth perfection breed.

Nor is 't inconstancy to change
    For what is better, or to make
(By searching) what before was strange   15
    Familiar for the use's sake.
        The good from bad is not descried
        But as 'tis often vexed[2] and tried.

And this profession of a store[3]
    In love doth not alone help forth   20
Our pleasure, but preserves us more
    From being forsaken than doth worth:
        For were the worthiest woman cursed
        To love one man, he'd leave her first.

                                            1640–41

My Picture Left in Scotland[1]

I now think Love is rather deaf than blind,
        For else it could not be
                That she
Whom I adore so much should so slight me
    And cast my love behind;   5
I'm sure my language to her was as sweet,
        And every close[2] did meet
        In sentence of as subtle feet,
                As hath the youngest he
        That sits in shadow of Apollo's tree.   10

---

2. Examined severely.
3. Abundance.
1. After his walking tour of Scotland in 1618–19,
Jonson sent a manuscript version of this poem to
William Drummond, with whom he had stayed.

No one knows who the woman of the poem was,
or if she existed at all.
2. Cadence. "Sentence": judgment or opinion.
Jonson claims his words to the lady were as eloquent and profound as any younger poet's.

O, but my conscious fears
    That fly my thoughts between,
    Tell me that she hath seen
    My hundreds of gray hairs,
    Told seven and forty years,   15
  Read so much waste[3] as she cannot embrace
  My mountain belly and my rocky face;
And all these through her eyes have stopped her ears.

1619   1640–41

The Ode on Cary and Morison

The ode was originally a classical form, and was therefore always in English a learned and slightly artificial one. It is defined as a serious lyric poem, dignified by its theme, its occasion, or the person to whom it is addressed. The Greek poet Pindar wrote many odes for winners of the Olympic games; because of their exalted style, they are known as "Great Odes." Later, the Latin poet Horace wrote more modest poems that he actually called Carmina (Songs), but which everyone has agreed to call by the equivalent Greek word, Odes—though Horace's are called "Lesser Odes" to distinguish them from those of Pindar.

The Renaissance brought odes into the modern European languages through the agency of Petrarch in Italian and Ronsard in French; but in England the formal ode was slow to appear. Michael Drayton referred to some of his poems as "odes," but they are more like ballads. Jonson's ode to Cary and Morison is the first Great Ode in English; its relation to Pindar is most apparent in the matter of formal structure.

Pindar's odes were designed to be sung by a chorus, and like other Greek choral odes, they often follow a three-part scheme of strophe, antistrophe, and epode: the chorus moved in one direction while chanting the strophe, reversed direction for the antistrophe, and stood still for the epode. This pattern Jonson imitates with his triple division of turn, counterturn, and stand—the terms more or less literally translated from the original Greek. All Jonson's stanzas follow a fixed pattern, the turns and counterturns rhyming in couplets, line lengths varying in all stanzas according to a fixed and uniform schema. The twelve-line stands follow a more complex but equally strict design. Later in the century, under the influence of Abraham Cowley, who thought he was imitating the essential Pindar, odes became more vehement in tone and more irregular in form. But modern opinion views this lawless and extravagant quality as a misunderstanding of the Greek original. So, equally, would be any indulgence in personal details concerning the two central figures; Jonson's emphasis falls, as Pindar's in like circumstances would have, on moral generalizations and dignified, impersonal consolatories. His poem thus rises nearer to the lofty vein of the "Great Ode" than any other in the language.

3. "Waist" is understood behind "waste," and may have been the primary meaning.

To the Immortal Memory and Friendship of That Noble Pair, Sir Lucius Cary and Sir H. Morison[1]

The Turn

Brave infant of Saguntum, clear[2]
Thy coming forth in that great year
When the prodigious Hannibal did crown
His rage, with razing your immortal town.
Thou, looking then about   5
Ere thou wert half got out,
Wise child, didst hastily return
And mad'st thy mother's womb thine urn.
How summed a circle[3] didst thou leave mankind
Of deepest lore, could we the center find!   10

The Counter-Turn

Did wiser nature draw thee back
From out the horror of that sack,
Where shame, faith, honor, and regard of right
Lay trampled on?—the deeds of death and night
Urged, hurried forth, and hurled   15
Upon th' affrighted world?
Sword, fire, and famine, with fell fury met,
And all on utmost ruin set:
As, could they but life's miseries foresee,
No doubt all infants would return like thee.   20

The Stand

For what is life if measured by the space,
Not by the act?
Or maskèd man, if valued by his face,
Above his fact?[4]
Here's one outlived his peers   25
And told forth fourscore years:
He vexèd time, and busied the whole state,
Troubled both foes and friends,
But ever to no ends:
What did this stirrer but die late?   30
How well at twenty had he fall'n or stood!
For three of his four score, he did no good.

---

1. Henry Morison died in 1629 at the age of only
20; his good friend Lucius Cary was a year or two
younger. He lived on, as Jonson could not foresee,
to die bravely and perhaps deliberately, fighting for
his king in the first years of the civil war.
2. Explain, describe. Pliny tells the story of the
infant born while Sagunto, in Spain, was being
assaulted by Hannibal; he dived back into his
mother's womb (setting a record for brevity), and
was buried there.
3. How complete a lesson.
4. Deeds.

The Turn

He[5] entered well, by virtuous parts,
Got up and thrived with honest arts:
He purchased friends and fame and honors then,   35
And had his noble name advanced with men;
But, weary of that flight,
He stooped in all men's sight
To sordid flatteries, acts of strife,
And sunk in that dead sea of life   40
So deep, as he did then death's waters sup;
But that the cork of title buoyed him up.

The Counter-Turn

Alas, but Morison fell young;—
He never fell, thou fall'st,[6] my tongue.
He stood, a soldier, to the last right end,   45
A perfect patriot and a noble friend,
But most a virtuous son.
All offices[7] were done
By him, so ample, full, and round
In weight, in measure, number, sound,   50
As, though his age imperfect might appear,
His life was of humanity the sphere.

The Stand

Go now, and tell out[8] days summed up with fears,
And make them years;
Produce thy mass of miseries on the stage   55
To swell thine age;
Repeat of things a throng,
To show thou hast been long,
Not lived; for life doth her great actions spell,
By what was done and wrought   60
In season, and so brought
To light: her measures are, how well
Each syllab'e answered, and was formed how fair;
These make the lines of life, and that's her air.[9]

The Turn

It is not growing like a tree   65
In bulk, doth make man better be,

---

5. I.e., another man, a separate example.
6. Slip, with a latent pun on Latin *fallo,* "to make a mistake."
7. Duties of life.

8. Count, number.
9. Life is a poem set to music, the music of its meaning. Life's "measures" are its metrical patterns, as well as the standards by which it is judged.

Or standing long an oak, three hundred year,
To fall a log at last, dry, bald, and sere:
A lily of a day
Is fairer far in May   70
Although it fall and die that night;
It was the plant and flower of light.
In small proportions we just beauties see,
And in short measures life may perfect be.

The Counter-Turn

Call, noble Lucius, then for wine,   75
And let thy looks with gladness shine:
Accept this garland, plant it on thy head,
And think, nay, know, thy Morison's not dead.
He leaped the present age,
Possessed with holy rage,   80
To see that bright eternal day,
Of which we priests and poets say
Such truths as we expect for happy men,
And there he lives with memory: and Ben

The Stand

Jonson, who sung this of him ere he went   85
Himself to rest,
Or taste a part of that full joy he meant
To have expressed
In this bright asterism:[1]
Where it were friendship's schism   90
(Were not his Lucius long with us to tarry)
To separate these twi-
Lights, the Dioscuri;[2]
And keep the one half from his Harry.
But fate doth so alternate the design,   95
Whilst that in heaven, this light on earth must shine.

The Turn

And shine as you exalted are,
Two names of friendship, but one star,
Of hearts the union. And those not by chance
Made, or indentured,[3] or leased out t' advance   100
The profits for a time.
No pleasures vain did chime
Of rhymes or riots at your feasts,

---

1. Constellation.   twins.
2. Castor and Pollux, the Dioscuri, are the prin-   3. Contracted for.
cipal stars of the constellation of Gemini, or the

Orgies of drink, or feigned protests;
But simple love of greatness and of good   105
That knits brave minds and manners, more than blood.

The Counter-Turn

This made you first to know the Why
You liked, then after to apply
That liking; and approach so one the tother,
Till either grew a portion of the other;   110
Each stylèd by his end,
The copy of his friend.
You lived to be the great surnames
And titles by which all made claims
Unto the virtue. Nothing perfect done,   115
But as a Cary or a Morison.

The Stand

And such a force the fair example had,
As they that saw
The good and durst not practice it, were glad
That such a law   120
Was left yet to mankind;
Where they might read and find
Friendship in deed was written, not in words.
And with the heart, not pen,
Of two so early[4] men,   125
Whose lives her rolls were, and records,
Who, ere the first down bloomèd on the chin
Had sowed these fruits, and got the harvest in.

1629   1640–41

Slow, Slow, Fresh Fount[1]

Slow, slow, fresh fount, keep time with my salt tears;
Yet slower, yet, O faintly, gentle springs!
List to the heavy part the music bears,
Woe weeps out her division,[2] when she sings.
    Droop herbs and flowers;   5
    Fall grief in showers;
    Our beauties are not ours.
      O, I could still,

---

4. Youthful.
1. From the satiric comedy *Cynthia's Revels*. The play deals with the sin of self-love, and this lyric is a lament sung by Echo for Narcissus, who was entranced by his own reflection and ultimately transformed into a flower.
2. Grief at parting, but also a rapid melodic passage of music.

Like melting snow upon some craggy hill,
    Drop, drop, drop, drop,   10
Since nature's pride is now a withered daffodil.

1600

Queen and Huntress[1]

Queen and huntress, chaste and fair,
Now the sun is laid to sleep,
Seated in thy silver chair,
State in wonted manner keep;
Hesperus entreats thy light,   5
Goddess excellently bright.

Earth, let not thy envious shade
Dare itself to interpose;
Cynthia's shining orb was made
Heaven to clear, when day did close.   10
Bless us then with wishèd sight,
Goddess excellently bright.

Lay thy bow of pearl apart,
And thy crystal-shining quiver;   15
Give unto the flying hart
Space to breathe, how short soever.
Thou that mak'st a day of night,
Goddess excellently bright.

1600

Still to Be Neat[1]

Still to be neat, still to be dressed
As you were going to a feast,
Still to be powdered, still perfumed;
Lady, it is to be presumed,
Though art's hid causes are not found,   5
All is not sweet, all is not sound.

Give me a look, give me a face
That makes simplicity a grace;
Robes loosely flowing, hair as free—

1. Also from *Cynthia's Revels*, this song is sung by Hesperus, the evening star, to Cynthia or Diana, goddess of chastity and the moon—with whom Queen Elizabeth was, almost automatically, equated.

1. This song is sung in the play *Epicoene* at the request of Clerimont, supposed to be its composer; he is irked at the Lady Haughty, who, he says, overdoes the art of makeup.

Such sweet neglect more taketh me   10
Than all the adulteries of art.
They strike mine eyes, but not my heart.

1609

Though I Am Young[1]

Though I am young and cannot tell
 Either what Death or Love is well,
Yet I have heard they both bear darts,
 And both do aim at human hearts.
And then again, I have been told   5
 Love wounds with heat, as Death with cold;
So that I fear they do but bring
 Extremes to touch, and mean one thing.

As in a ruin we it call
 One thing to be blown up or fall;   10
Or to our end like way may have
 By a flash of lightning or a wave;
So Love's inflamèd shaft or brand
 May kill as soon as Death's cold hand;
Except[2] Love's fires the virtue have   15
 To fright the frost out of the grave.

1640–41

To the Memory of My Beloved, The Author, Mr. William Shakespeare, and What He Hath Left Us[1]

To draw no envy, Shakespeare, on thy name
 Am I thus ample to thy book and fame,
While I confess thy writings to be such
 As neither man nor Muse can praise too much.
'Tis true, and all men's suffrage.[2] But these ways   5
 Were not the paths I meant unto thy praise;
For silliest[3] ignorance on these may light,
 Which, when it sounds at best, but echoes right;
Or blind affection,[4] which doth ne'er advance
 The truth, but gropes, and urgeth all by chance;   10
Or crafty malice might pretend this praise,
 And think to ruin where it seemed to raise.

1. This song is sung in *The Sad Shepherd* by Karo-
lin; the pastoral simplicity of his character is caught
in the naive monosyllables of the poem.
2. Unless.
1. This poem was prefixed to the first folio of

Shakespeare's plays, published in 1623.
2. Consent.
3. Emptiest.
4. Prejudice.

These are as some infamous bawd or whore
   Should praise a matron. What could hurt her more?
But thou art proof against them, and, indeed,   15
   Above th' ill fortune of them, or the need.
I therefore will begin. Soul of the age!
   The applause! delight! the wonder of our stage!
My Shakespeare, rise; I will not lodge thee by
   Chaucer or Spenser, or bid Beaumont lie   20
A little further to make thee a room:[5]
   Thou art a monument without a tomb,
And art alive still while thy book doth live,
   And we have wits to read and praise to give.
That I not mix thee so, my brain excuses,   25
   I mean with great, but disproportioned[6] Muses;
For, if I thought my judgment were of years,
   I should commit thee surely with thy peers,
And tell how far thou didst our Lyly outshine,
   Or sporting Kyd, or Marlowe's mighty line.[7]   30
And though thou hadst small Latin and less Greek,[8]
   From thence to honor thee I would not seek
For names, but call forth thund'ring Aeschylus,
   Euripides, and Sophocles to us,
Pacuvius, Accius, him of Cordova dead,[9]   35
   To life again, to hear thy buskin[1] tread
And shake a stage; or, when thy socks were on,
   Leave thee alone for the comparison
Of all that insolent Greece or haughty Rome
   Sent forth, or since did from their ashes come.   40
Triumph, my Britain; thou hast one to show
   To whom all scenes[2] of Europe homage owe.
He was not of an age, but for all time!
   And all the Muses still were in their prime
When like Apollo he came forth to warm   45
   Our ears, or like a Mercury to charm.
Nature herself was proud of his designs,
   And joyed to wear the dressing of his lines,
Which were so richly spun, and woven so fit,
   As, since, she will vouchsafe no other wit: 50
The merry Greek, tart Aristophanes,

---

5. Chaucer, Spenser, and Francis Beaumont were buried in Westminster Abbey; Shakespeare, of course, in Stratford. Jonson endorses the separation; Shakespeare should not be crowded.
6. Not comparable.
7. John Lyly, Thomas Kyd, and Christopher Marlowe, Elizabethan dramatists put in the shade by Shakespeare.
8. Shakespeare had, by modern standards, a very adequate command of Latin; Jonson is speaking from the lofty height of his own remarkable scholarship. Shakespeare's French and Italian (he was

competent in both tongues) Jonson does not think worthy of mention. "Seek": be short of, lacking in.
9. Marcus Pacuvius and Lucius Accius (2nd century B.C.) and "him of Cordova," Seneca the Younger (1st century A.D.), the greatest of the Latin tragedians. Only fragments survive of the plays of Pacuvius and Accius; Jonson's comparisons are more pedantic, in these instances, than relevant.
1. The symbol of tragedy, as contrasted with "socks" (in the next line), symbols of comedy.
2. Stages.

Neat Terence, witty Plautus[3] now not please,
But antiquated and deserted lie,
 As they were not of Nature's family.
Yet must I not give Nature all; thy Art,   55
 My gentle Shakespeare, must enjoy a part.
For though the poet's matter Nature be,
 His Art doth give the fashion;[4] and that he
Who casts to write a living line must sweat
 (Such as thine are) and strike the second heat   60
Upon the muses' anvil; turn the same,
 And himself with it, that he thinks to frame,
Or for the laurel he may gain a scorn;
 For a good poet's made as well as born.
And such wert thou! Look how the father's face   65
 Lives in his issue; even so the race
Of Shakespeare's mind and manners brightly shines
 In his well-turned and true-filed lines,
In each of which he seems to shake a lance,[5]
 As brandished at the eyes of ignorance.   70
Sweet swan of Avon, what a sight it were
 To see thee in our waters yet appear,
And make those flights upon the banks of Thames
 That so did take Eliza and our James![6]
But stay; I see thee in the hemisphere   75
 Advanced and made a constellation there![7]
Shine forth, thou star of poets, and with rage
 Or influence[8] chide or cheer the drooping stage,
Which, since thy flight from hence, hath mourned like night,
 And despairs day, but for thy volume's light.   80

                                1623

Ode to Himself[1]

 Come, leave the loathèd stage,
  And the more loathsome age,
Where pride and impudence, in faction knit,
  Usurp the chair of wit,
Indicting and arraigning every day   5
  Something they call a play.
 Let their fastidious, vain
 Commission of the brain

---

3. Aristophanes, the Greek satirist and comic writer;
Terence and Plautus (2nd and 3rd centuries B.C.),
Roman writers of comedy.
4. Form, style. "Casts": undertakes.
5. Pun on Shake-speare.
6. Queen Elizabeth and King James.
7. Heroes and demigods were typically exalted after

death to a place among the stars.
8. "Rage" and "influence" describe the supposed
effects of the planets on earthly affairs. "Rage" also
implies poetic inspiration.
1. The failure of Jonson's *The New Inn* (1629)
inspired this assault on criticism and the public taste.

Run on and rage, sweat, censure, and condemn:
They were not made for thee, less thou for them.   10

    Say that thou pour'st them wheat,
      And they will acorns eat;
'Twere simple fury still thyself to waste
      On such as have no taste!
To offer them a surfeit of pure bread,   15
      Whose appetites are dead!
    No, give them grains their fill,
      Husks, draff to drink and swill:[2]
If they love lees, and leave the lusty wine,
Envy them not; their palate's with the swine.   20

    No doubt some moldy tale
      Like *Pericles*,[3] and stale
As the shrieve's crusts, and nasty as his fish—
      Scraps, out of every dish
Thrown forth and raked into the common tub,   25
      May keep up the Play-club:
    There, sweepings do as well
      As the best-ordered meal;
For who the relish of these guests will fit
Needs set them but the alms basket of wit.   30

    And much good do 't you then:
      Brave plush and velvet men
Can feed on orts;[4] and, safe in your stage clothes,
      Dare quit,[5] upon your oaths,
The stagers and the stage-wrights[6] too, your peers,   35
      Of larding your large ears
    With their foul comic socks,[7]
      Wrought upon twenty blocks;
Which, if they're torn, and turned, and patched enough,
The gamesters share your guilt, and you their stuff.   40

    Leave things so prostitute
      And take th' Alcaic lute;[8]
Or thine own Horace, or Anacreon's lyre;
      Warm thee by Pindar's fire:
And though thy nerves be shrunk, and blood be cold,   45
      Ere years have made thee old,

2. Jonson gets into one line three words suggestive
of pig-food.
3. Shakespeare's play, at least in part (printed 1609).
"Shrieve": sheriff. The basket left outside the jail
to receive food for the poor was called the sheriff's
tub.
4. Scraps. Actors often wore on the stage clothes
cast off by the gentry; these parasites, Jonson seems
to be saying, wear clothes cast off by actors (cf. line

40, "you [share] their stuff").
5. Acquit.
6. "Stagers": actors (also "gamesters," below).
"Stage-wrights": playwrights.
7. Socks were the traditional footwear of comic
actors, buskins of tragedians.
8. That of Alcaeus, who lived ca. 600 B.C., and
became famous, along with Horace, Anacreon, and
Pindar, among the greatest lyric poets.

Strike that disdainful heat
Throughout, to their defeat,
As curious fools, and envious of thy strain,
May, blushing, swear no palsy's in thy brain.   50

But when they hear thee sing
The glories of thy king,
His zeal to God and his just awe o'er men,
They may, blood-shaken then,
Feel such a flesh-quake to possess their powers   55
As they shall cry, "Like ours,
In sound of peace or wars,
No harp e'er hit the stars
In tuning forth the acts of his sweet reign,
And raising Charles his chariot 'bove his Wain."9   60

1629   1631, 1640–41

9. Jonson's poetry will elevate the chariot of Charles   (Wagon)—the seven bright stars of Ursa Major.
I (symbol of his royal power) above Charles's Wain

JOHN MILTON
1608–1674

1637:   *Lycidas.*
1640–1660:   The pamphlet wars.
1651:   Blindness.
1667:   *Paradise Lost.*

The life of John Milton falls conveniently into three divisions. There is a period of youthful education and apprenticeship, which culminates in the writing of *Lycidas* (1637) and Milton's foreign travels (1638–39). There is a period of prose and controversy (1640–60), when almost all his verse was the by-product of events public or private, and when his major preoccupations were political and social; and finally, there are the last fourteen years of his life, when he returned to literature, a mature and somewhat embittered figure, to publish his three major poems, *Paradise Lost* (1667), *Paradise Regained* (1671), and *Samson Agonistes* (1671).

Milton was born in Bread Street, Cheapside, the elder son of a self-made businessman, who, under the title of scrivener, drew up contracts, lent money at interest, and dealt in real estate. From the beginning, young Milton showed prodigious gifts as a student of languages. At St. Paul's School he mastered Latin and Greek, and before long he was adept in most modern European tongues, as well as Hebrew. Sent to Christ's College, Cambridge, he graduated A. B. in 1629 and A. M. in 1632, meanwhile continuing to read voraciously and writing (too infrequently for his own satisfaction) an occasional poem. In the normal course of events, a career like this would have culminated in ordination to the ministry and a career in the church. But after his A. M., Milton, who disliked the trend of religious and civil affairs in England, did not take orders; leaving the university, first for London, then for his father's country house at Horton in Buckinghamshire, he read, day and night, under his own direction, for six more years. It seems likely that Milton in his time read just about everything of importance written in English, Latin, Greek, and Italian. (Of course, he had the Bible by heart.) In 1634 he wrote, at the invitation of a noble family in Shropshire, the masque known as *Comus*; and in 1637 he contributed to a volume memorializing a college classmate the elegy *Lycidas*. Finally, in 1638, his most indulgent father sent this most avid of students abroad, to put the finishing touches on an already splendid education. For a little over a year Milton traveled on the Continent, visiting famous literary figures and scenes; then, hearing rumors of impending troubles in England, he returned home.

Of Milton's complex and troubled career in controversy, we need not say much. It too is divided into three major phases. He began by publishing antiprelatical tracts, against government of the church by bishops. These are rough, knockabout, name-calling tracts in the style of the times, which take a popular position on a relatively popular issue. In 1644, responding to a book by a German exile in England named Samuel Hartlib, he wrote a short essay *Of Education*; later in the same year, responding to a severe if ineffectual parliamentary ordinance to regulate printing, he published his defense of a free press, *Areopagitica*. But in the meanwhile his personal circumstances had led to a second series of pamphlets that earned Milton a reputation as a radical. In May or June 1642, he had married Mary Powell, daughter of a royalist country squire. The bride was just seventeen years old, half her husband's age. Within a few weeks she left him, to return to her parents' house; and from 1643 to 1645, Milton published a series of pamphlets arguing that divorce should be granted on grounds of incompatibility. Respectable Englishmen, already disturbed by the social troubles of the time, took a dim view of what they called "divorce at pleasure"; it looked like the end of all social order. In fact, Milton's position appears moderate today, and is accepted practice in many modern societies; but it was scandalous in his time, and Milton was much embittered by ridicule of his ideas. After the execution of Charles I in 1649, he published a third set of pamphlets; they were Latin disputations against Continental critics of the Cromwell regime, and they explicitly defended the execution of Charles. In the middle of this work he went blind, as a result of eyestrain continued over many years. With the help of assistants, however, he was able to fulfill his duties as Latin Secretary to Cromwell's Council of State, and to contribute very substantially to the diplomatic dignity of the new government.

Meanwhile, his wife had returned to him in 1645, and having borne him three daughters, died in 1652. In 1656 Milton married Katherine Woodcock, who died in childbirth in 1658. Finally, in 1660, the whole political movement for which Milton had sacrificed so much went to smash. Though Milton boldly published pamphlets in its support to the very last minute, the Good Old Cause was defeated, and Charles II recalled from his travels. For a time under the Restoration, Milton was imprisoned and in danger of his life; but friends intervened (among them, Andrew Marvell), and he escaped with a fine and the loss of most of his property.

In 1663 Milton married his third wife, Elizabeth Minshull; and in blindness, poverty, defeat, and relative isolation, he set about completing a poem "justifying the ways of God to men," which he had first envisaged many years before. It was published in 1667, as *Paradise Lost*; and despite the many difficulties which it presented, despite its unfamiliar meter (blank verse was rare outside drama), despite the unpopularity of its attitudes and Milton's reputation as a dangerous man, it was recognized at once as a supreme epic achievement. In 1671 Milton published *Paradise Regained*, an epic poem in four books describing Christ's temptation in the wilderness, and *Samson Agonistes*, a "closet" tragedy (i.e., not intended for the stage). He died, of complications arising from gout, in 1674.

In the writings of Milton, the work of two tremendous intellectual and social movements comes to a head. The Renaissance is responsible for the rich and complex texture of Milton's style, the multiplicity of its classical references, its wealth of ornament and decoration. *Paradise Lost*, being an epic, not only challenges comparison with Homer and Virgil, it undertakes to encompass the whole life of mankind—war, love, religion, Hell, Heaven, the cosmos. It is a poem vastly capacious of worldly experience. On the other hand, the Reformation speaks with equal, if not greater, authority in Milton's earnest and individually minded Christianity. The great epic, which resounds with the grandeur and multiplicity of the world, is also a poem whose central actions take place inwardly, at the core of man's conscience. Adam's fate culminates in an act of passive suffering, not of active heroism. He does not kill Hector or Turnus, much less Satan, he picks up the burden of worldly existence, and triumphs over his guilt by admitting it and repenting of it.

These two contrasting aspects of Milton's life and thought place him within the long tradition of Renaissance Christian humanism. His literary art places him in the small circle of great epic writers.

On Shakespeare[1]

What needs my Shakespeare for his honored bones
The labor of an age in pilèd stones,
Or that his hallowed relics should be hid
Under a star-ypointing pyramid?[2]
Dear son of memory, great heir of fame,   5
What need'st thou such weak witness of thy name?
Thou in our wonder and astonishment
Hast built thyself a livelong monument.
For whilst to th' shame of slow-endeavoring art
Thy easy numbers flow, and that each heart   10
Hath from the leaves of thy unvalued book[3]
Those Delphic lines with deep impression took,
Then thou, our fancy of itself bereaving,

---

1. Milton's tribute to Shakespeare appeared in the Second Folio of the plays.
2. "Star-ypointing" uses one of Spenser's archaic "y-" prefixes to eke out the meter. (Note also the interpolated "that" in line 10, serving the same purpose.) Milton's poem begins by answering the common complaint of the day, that Shakespeare should have been buried in some place more splendid than Stratford. Shakespeare is described as the "son of memory" because that makes him a brother of the muses, daughters of Mnemosyne (four syllables; the word means "memory") by Zeus.
3. Beyond all value, invaluable book.

Dost make us marble with too much conceiving;[4]
And so sepùlchered in such pomp dost lie,   15
That kings for such a tomb would wish to die.

1630   1632

L'Allegro[1]

Hence loathèd Melancholy,
  Of Cerberus[2] and blackest midnight born,
In Stygian[3] cave forlorn
'Mongst horrid shapes, and shrieks, and sights unholy,
  Find out some uncouth cell,   5
    Where brooding Darkness spreads his jealous wings,
And the night-raven sings;
    There under ebon shades and low-browed rocks,
As ragged as thy locks,
  In dark Cimmerian[4] desert ever dwell.   10
But come thou goddess fair and free,
In heaven yclept Euphrosyne,[5]
  And by men, heart-easing Mirth,
Whom lovely Venus at a birth
With two sister Graces more   15
  To ivy-crownèd Bacchus bore;[6]
Or whether (as some sager sing)[7]
The frolic wind that breathes the spring,
Zephyr with Aurora playing,
As he met her once a-Maying,   20
  There on beds of violets blue,
  And fresh-blown[8] roses washed in dew,
Filled her with thee a daughter fair,
So buxom,[9] blithe, and debonair.

4. The monuments of Shakespeare's tomb are all the enchanted and motionless readers of his book.

1. *L'Allegro* and *Il Penseroso* are companion poems, written in those dancing tetrameter couplets which are so hard to keep from sinking into singsong, so delightful when controlled. Milton's handling of this difficult meter may be compared with other virtuoso performances like Marvell's *To His Coy Mistress*, Keats's *Lines on the Mermaid Tavern*, and Housman's *Terence, This Is Stupid Stuff*.

The titles are almost untranslatable. Within the framework of two contrasted yet parallel days we see the cheerful, social man and the melancholy, contemplative man in their typical postures. Milton's interest in the typical accounts for the striking generality of the pictures; they are in effect "characters" in verse. Melancholy has been much analyzed; in addition to Burton's famous *Anatomy*, it is discussed in Erwin Panofsky's *Albrecht Dürer* (1945), where it arises in connection with Dürer's magnificent engraving *Melencolia*, as well as in the immense study by Saxl, Panofsky, and Klibansky,

Saturn and Melancholy (1964). There is a history of literary cheerfulness too—*The Happy Man*, by Maren Sofie Røstvig (1954).

2. The three-headed hell hound of classical mythology.

3. I.e., near the river Styx, in the underworld.

4. The Cimmerians, who gave their name to Crimea, were supposed to live on the outer edge of the world, in perpetual twilight.

5. Euphrosyne, Aglaia, and Thalia (four syllables, three, and two) were the Graces, goddesses of beauty and delight; antiquity assigned them a variety of parents, though they were most often regarded as products as Zeus' leisure hours.

6. Bacchus is god of wine.

7. The "sager" poets who describe the Graces as born of Zephyr (the west wind) and Aurora (the dawn) are in fact John Milton himself; the story is his invention.

8. Newly opened.

9. Lively.

Haste thee nymph, and bring with thee   25
Jest and youthful Jollity,
Quips and Cranks,[1] and wanton Wiles,
Nods, and Becks, and wreathèd Smiles,
Such as hang on Hebe's[2] cheek,
And love to live in dimple sleek;   30
Sport that wrinkled Care derides,
And Laughter holding both his sides.
Come, and trip it as ye go
On the light fantastic toe,
And in thy right hand lead with thee   35
The mountain nymph, sweet Liberty;
And if I give thee honor due,
Mirth, admit me of thy crew
To live with her and live with thee,
In unreprovèd pleasures free;   40
To hear the lark begin his flight,
And, singing, startle the dull night,
From his watch-tower in the skies,
Till the dappled dawn doth rise;
Then to come[3] in spite of sorrow,   45
And at my window bid good morrow,
Through the sweetbriar or the vine,
Or the twisted eglantine.
While the cock with lively din
Scatters the rear of darkness thin,   50
And to the stack or the barn door,
Stoutly struts his dames before;
Oft listening how the hounds and horn
Cheerly rouse the slumbering morn,
From the side of some hoar hill,   55
Through the high wood echoing shrill.
Sometime walking not unseen
By hedgerow elms, on hillocks green,
Right against the eastern gate,
Where the great sun begins his state,[4]   60
Robed in flames and amber light,
The clouds in thousand liveries dight;[5]
While the plowman near at hand
Whistles o'er the furrowed land,
And the milkmaid singeth blithe,   65
And the mower whets his scythe,
And every shepherd tells his tale
Under the hawthorn in the dale.
Straight mine eye hath caught new pleasures
Whilst the landscape round it measures,   70

1. Jokes.
2. Goddess of youth and cupbearer to the other
gods. Pronounced *Hee-bee*.
3. I.e., then admit me to come.
4. Procession.
5. Dressed.

Russet lawns and fallows gray,
Where the nibbling flocks do stray,
Mountains on whose barren breast
The laboring clouds do often rest;
Meadows trim with daisies pied,[6]   75
Shallow brooks, and rivers wide.
Towers and battlements it sees
Bosomed high in tufted trees,
Where perhaps some beauty lies,
The cynosure[7] of neighboring eyes.   80
Hard by, a cottage chimney smokes
From betwixt two agèd oaks,
Where Corydon and Thyrsis[8] met
Are at their savory dinner set
Of herbs and other country messes,   85
Which the neat-handed Phyllis dresses;
And then in haste her bower she leaves,
With Thestylis to bind the sheaves;
Or if the earlier season lead
To the tanned haycock in the mead.   90
Sometimes with secure delight
The upland hamlets will invite,
When the merry bells ring round
And the jocund rebecks[9] sound
To many a youth and many a maid,   95
Dancing in the checkered shade;
And young and old come forth to play
On a sunshine holiday,
Till the livelong daylight fail;
Then to the spicy nut-brown ale,   100
With stories told of many a feat,
How fairy Mab[1] the junkets eat;
She was pinched and pulled, she said,
And he, by friar's lantern led,
Tells how the drudging goblin[2] sweat   105
To earn his cream-bowl duly set,
When in one night, ere glimpse of morn,
His shadowy flail hath threshed the corn
That ten day-laborers could not end;
Then lies him down the lubber fiend,[3]   110
And stretched out all the chimney's length,
Basks at the fire his hairy strength;

---

6. Dappled.
7. Literally, the bright polestar, by which mariners steer; here, a splendid, eminent object, much gazed at.
8. Since the days of Theocritus, "Corydon," "Thyrsis," "Phyllis," and "Thestylis" have been traditional shepherds' names.
9. A rebeck is a small three-stringed fiddle;

"jocund" implies a festive occasion.
1. Queen Mab, wife of Oberon, the fairy king. "She" and "he" in the next two lines are country folk, telling of their experiences with the fairies. "Junkets": sweetmeats, especially with cream.
2. Robin Goodfellow, alias Puck, Pook, or Hobgoblin. "Friar's lantern": will-o'-the-wisp.
3. Drudging spirit.

And crop-full out of doors he flings
Ere the first cock his matin rings.
Thus done the tales, to bed they creep,   115
By whispering winds soon lulled asleep.
Towered cities please us then,
And the busy hum of men,
Where throngs of knights and barons bold
In weeds[4] of peace high triumphs hold,   120
With store of ladies, whose bright eyes
Rain influence,[5] and judge the prize
Of wit or arms, while both contend
To win her grace, whom all commend.
There let Hymen[6] oft appear   125
In saffron robe, with taper clear,
And pomp and feast and revelry,
With masque and antique pageantry;
Such sights as youthful poets dream
On summer eves by haunted stream.   130
Then to the well-trod stage anon,
If Jonson's learnèd sock[7] be on,
Or sweetest Shakespeare, fancy's child,
Warble his native wood-notes wild.
And ever against eating cares[8]   135
Lap me in soft Lydian airs,[9]
Married to immortal verse
Such as the meeting soul may pierce
In notes with many a winding bout[1]
Of linkèd sweetness long drawn out,   140
With wanton heed and giddy cunning,
The melting voice through mazes running;
Untwisting all the chains that tie
The hidden soul of harmony;
That Orpheus' self[2] may heave his head   145
From golden slumber on a bed
Of heaped Elysian flowers, and hear
Such strains as would have won the ear
Of Pluto, to have quite set free
His half-regained Eurydice.   150

4. Garments. "Triumphs": festive ceremonies.
5. The ladies' eyes are stars, and so have astrological influence over the men.
6. Roman god of marriage, wearing an orange-yellow ("saffron") robe.
7. A low-heeled slipper, worn by actors in classical comedy, and often contrasted with the buskin (high-heeled boot) appropriate to tragedy. The contrast of Jonson as a "learned" poet with Shakespeare as a "natural" one was conventional.
8. "Eating cares" is but one of many classical phrases in the poem; it is from Horace, *Odes* 2.11.18 (*curas edaces*).

9. "Lydian" airs in music would be soft, languishing, sensual—unlike those in the chaste Dorian and brisk Ionian modes.
1. Turn, involution.
2. Orpheus went to the underworld to regain his wife Eurydice (four syllables, accent on the second) and by his music dissolved the guardians of Hades in tears. But as they left, he violated the condition of her release by looking back at her, and so lost her again. Milton uses the Orpheus story again in *Il Penseroso*, *Lycidas*, and *Paradise Lost* 7.32 ff.

These delights if thou canst give,
Mirth, with thee I mean to live.

ca. 1631   1645

Il Penseroso

Hence vain deluding Joys,
   The brood of Folly without father bred,
How little you bestead,[1]
   Or fill the fixèd mind with all your toys;[2]
Dwell in some idle brain,   5
   And fancies fond[3] with gaudy shapes possess,
As thick and numberless
   As the gay motes that people the sunbeams,
Or likest hovering dreams,
   The fickle pensioners[4] of Morpheus' train.   10
But hail thou Goddess sage and holy,
Hail, divinest Melancholy,
Whose saintly visage is too bright
To hit[5] the sense of human sight,
And therefore to our weaker view,   15
O'erlaid with black, staid Wisdom's hue;
Black, but such as in esteem,
Prince Memnon's sister[6] might beseem,
Or that starred Ethiope queen[7] that strove
To set her beauty's praise above   20
The sea nymphs, and their powers offended.
Yet thou art higher far descended;
Thee bright-haired Vesta long of yore
To solitary Saturn bore;[8]
His daughter she (in Saturn's reign   25
Such mixture was not held a stain).
Oft in glimmering bowers and glades
He met her, and in secret shades
Of woody Ida's inmost grove,
While yet there was no fear of Jove.   30
Come pensive nun, devout and pure,
Sober, steadfast, and demure,

1. Avail, help.
2. Trifles.
3. Foolish.
4. Followers. Morpheus is the god of sleep; the melancholy man feels the cheerful man lives in a dream.
5. Suit, agree with.
6. Memnon in *Odyssey* 11 was a handsome Ethiopian prince who fought for Troy; his sister, not mentioned by Homer but by later commentators, was Himera.
7. Cassiopeia was turned into a constellation ("starred") for bragging that her daughter Andromeda or she herself (Milton follows this second version) was more beautiful than the sea-nymphs.
8. Vesta was goddess of the household, and virgin, as were her priestesses; Milton invented the story of her connection with Saturn on Mt. Ida in Crete, and of her giving birth to Melancholy. But Saturn helps out the poem because he was a primitive deity (hence melancholy is "natural"), and because a saturnine complexion is said to evidence a dark and melancholy disposition.

All in a robe of darkest grain,[9]
Flowing with majestic train,
And sable stole of cypress lawn[1]   35
Over thy decent shoulders drawn.
Come, but keep thy wonted state,
With even step and musing gait,
And looks commercing with the skies,
Thy rapt soul sitting in thine eyes: 40
There held in holy passion still,
Forget thyself to marble, till
With a sad leaden downward cast
Thou fix them on the earth as fast.
And join with thee calm Peace and Quiet,   45
Spare Fast, that oft with gods doth diet,
And hears the Muses in a ring
Aye round about Jove's altar sing.
And add to these retired Leisure,
That in trim gardens takes his pleasure;   50
But first, and chiefest, with thee bring
Him that yon soars on golden wing,
Guiding the fiery-wheelèd throne,
The cherub Contemplatiòn;[2]
And the mute Silence hist[3] along,   55
'Less Philomel[4] will deign a song,
In her sweetest, saddest plight,
Smoothing the rugged brow of night,
While Cynthia[5] checks her dragon yoke
Gently o'er th' accustomed oak;   60
Sweet bird that shunn'st the noise of folly,
Most musical, most melancholy!
Thee chantress oft the woods among
I woo to hear thy evensong;
And missing thee, I walk unseen   65
On the dry smooth-shaven green,
To behold the wandering moon,
Riding near her highest noon,
Like one that had been led astray
Through the heaven's wide pathless way;   70
And oft as if her head she bowed,
Stooping through a fleecy cloud.
Oft on a plat[6] of rising ground,
I hear the far-off curfew sound
Over some wide-watered shore,   75

---

9. Color.
1. "Cypress lawn": a delicate cloth (originally
Cyprus, from the island; but the cypress is also the
tree of death). "Decent": comely, proper.
2. The special function of cherubim is contemplation; the fiery-wheeled throne recalls the Biblical vision of Ezekiel.

3. Summon.
4. The nightingale, whose song is traditionally one
of grief.
5. Goddess of the moon and of the underworld as
well, she drives a pair of sleepless dragons.
6. Plot, open space.

Swinging slow with sullen roar;
Or if the air will not permit,
Some still removèd place will fit,
Where glowing embers through the room
Teach light to counterfeit a gloom, 80
Far from all resort of mirth,
Save the cricket on the hearth,
Or the bellman's[7] drowsy charm,
To bless the doors from nightly harm;
Or let my lamp at midnight hour 85
Be seen in some high lonely tower,
Where I may oft outwatch the Bear,[8]
With thrice-great Hermes,[9] or unsphere
The spirit of Plato to unfold
What worlds or what vast regions hold 90
The immortal mind that hath forsook
Her mansion in this fleshly nook;
And of those demons[1] that are found
In fire, air, flood, or under ground,
Whose power hath a true consent[2] 95
With planet, or with element.
Sometime let gorgeous Tragedy
In sceptered pall[3] come sweeping by,
Presenting Thebes, or Pelops' line,
Or the tale of Troy divine,[4] 100
Or what (though rare) of later age
Ennobled hath the buskined[5] stage.
But, O sad virgin, that thy power
Might raise Musaeus[6] from his bower,
Or bid the soul of Orpheus[7] sing 105
Such notes as, warbled to the string,
Drew iron tears down Pluto's cheek,
And made Hell grant what Love did seek.
Or call up him[8] that left half told
The story of Cambuscan bold, 110
Of Camball and of Algarsife,
And who had Canacee to wife,

---

7. The night watchman in towns rang a bell to mark the hours.
8. Since the Great Bear never sets, outwatching it is a major enterprise.
9. The Egyptian god Thoth or Hermes, to whom were attributed various esoteric books of the 3rd and 4th centuries; under the name Hermes Trismegistus ("thrice-great"), he later became a patron of magicians and alchemists. To "unsphere" Plato is to bring him magically back to earth from the sphere he now inhabits.
1. Not devils but halfway beings, between gods and men. There are four sorts of demons, corresponding with the four elements.
2. Sympathetic agreement.

3. Royal robe (from Latin *palla*, the robe of tragic actors).
4. Tragedies about Thebes would include Sophocles' Oedipus cycle; those about the line of Pelops, Aeschylus' *Oresteia*; and those about Troy, Euripides' *Trojan Women*.
5. The buskin of tragedy, contrasted with the sock of comedy.
6. A mythical poet-priest of the pre-Homeric age, supposedly son or pupil of the equally mythical Orpheus.
7. For the story of Orpheus, see *L'Allegro*, line 145, and note.
8. I.e., Chaucer, who in the Squire's Tale left the tale of Cambuscan unfinished.

That owned the virtuous[9] ring and glass,
And of the wondrous horse of brass,
On which the Tartar king did ride;   115
And if aught else great bards beside
In sage and solemn tunes have sung,
Of tourneys and of trophies hung,
Of forests and enchantments drear,
Where more is meant than meets the ear.[1]   120
Thus, Night, oft see me in thy pale career,
Till civil-suited Morn appear,[2]
Not tricked and frounced as she was wont
With the Attic boy to hunt,
But kerchiefed in a comely cloud,   125
While rocking winds are piping loud,
Or ushered with a shower still,
When the gust hath blown his fill,
Ending on the rustling leaves,
With minute drops from off the eaves.   130
And when the sun begins to fling
His flaring beams, me, Goddess, bring
To archèd walks of twilight groves,
And shadows brown that Sylvan[3] loves
Of pine or monumental oak,   135
Where the rude ax with heavèd stroke
Was never heard the nymphs to daunt,
Or fright them from their hallowed haunt.
There in close covert by some brook,
Where no profaner eye may look,   140
Hide me from day's garish eye,
While the bee with honeyed thigh,
That at her flowery work doth sing,
And the waters murmuring
With such consort[4] as they keep,   145
Entice the dewy-feathered sleep;
And let some strange mysterious dream
Wave at his wings in airy stream
Of lively portraiture displayed
Softly on my eyelids laid.[5]   150
And as I wake, sweet music breathe
Above, about, or underneath,
Sent by some spirit to mortals good,
Or th' unseen genius[6] of the wood.
But let my due feet never fail   155

9. Having special power.
1. A capsule description of allegory.
2. The goddess Aurora, who once fell in love with
Cephalus ("the Attic boy," line 124), and used to
go hunting with him. "Tricked and frounced":
adorned and frizzled.
3. Roman god of the woodlands.

4. Accompaniment.
5. Milton's syntax gets loose and dreamy too, here.
He means, "Let some strange dream wave at the
wings of sleep, while a stream of vivid pictures passes
softly over my eyelids."
6. Guardian deity.

To walk the studious cloister's pale,[7]
And love the high embowèd roof,
With antic[8] pillars massy proof,
And storied windows[9] richly dight,
Casting a dim religious light.   160
There let the pealing organ blow
To the full-voiced choir below,
In service high and anthems clear,
As may with sweetness, through mine ear,
Dissolve me into ecstasies,   165
And bring all heaven before mine eyes.
And may at last my weary age
Find out the peaceful hermitage,
The hairy gown and mossy cell,
Where I may sit and rightly spell[1]   170
Of every star that heaven doth shew,
And every herb that sips the dew,
Till old experience do attain
To something like prophetic strain.
These pleasures, Melancholy, give,   175
And I with thee will choose to live.

ca. 1631   1645

Lycidas   This poem is a pastoral elegy; that is, it uses the sometimes
artificial imagery supplied by an idyllic shepherd's existence to bewail the
loss of a friend. Among its many predecessors in the Renaissance and in
classical antiquity are poems by Spenser, Ronsard, Castiglione, Mantuan,
Petrarch, Virgil, Theocritus, Moschus, and Bion; its successors include poems
like *Adonais* by Shelley and *Thyrsis* by Matthew Arnold. T. P. Harrison and
H. J. Leon have collected in *The Pastoral Elegy* (1939) a selection of poems
from the tradition.

   All pastoral poems enjoy the privilege of saying something about the world
as a whole while seeming to talk simply of an artificial play-society; they are
irresistibly allegorical. They have certain conventions—the swain (i.e., the
shepherd) is ignorant but unspoiled, naturally virtuous, inherently poetic;
life is pleasant and easy, yet just for this reason the basic human preoccupations stand out. The pastoral elegy has a further list of conventions—a
history of past friendship, a questioning of destiny, a procession of mourners,
a laying-on of flowers, a consolation, and usually a refrain. Milton adapted
all but the last of these to *Lycidas*.

   Edward King, who was the occasion of the poem if not its subject, was a
junior contemporary of Milton's at Cambridge. He had written a few short
Latin poems, and intended to enter the ministry. On his way to visit family
in his native Ireland, he was drowned, in 1637; and Milton joined with his

---

7. Enclosure.
8. I.e., covered with quaint, grotesque, or antic
carvings; but "antique," which derives from the
same Latin root, was not excluded from the sense.
"Massy proof": massive and strong.

9. I.e., with stories told by stained-glass images.
"Dight": dressed.
1. Study. The melancholy man wants to think his
way into the cosmos until he becomes a prophet.

school fellows the following year to produce a little memorial volume. *Justa Edouardo King (For Edward King)* includes thirty-six poems, twenty in Latin, three in Greek, the rest in English; only *Lycidas* is of literary consequence.

It is written in a flowing, extended manner, with many run-on lines and great impetus, predominantly in pentameter but with a number of trimeter lines mixed in, and an irregular rhyme scheme, including ten unrhymed lines and two perfectly formed stanzas of ottava rima. Many of these technical qualities are reminiscent of the Italian *canzone* or song, already domesticated in English by poems like Spenser's *Epithalamion*.

There are usually taken to be three explicit climaxes in *Lycidas*, each having to do with an aspect of the shepherd's life and with a problem which Milton wished to pose regarding the meaning of existence. Apollo answers his first question about the reward of poetry; St. Peter answers a second question, about the spiritual shepherd who betrays his flock; and finally Lycidas is translated into the Christian Paradise, to be at one with the Lamb of God, the Good Shepherd, the supreme giver of poetic fame, and the proper subject of all song.

For some of the author's revisions while composing *Lycidas*, see "Poems in Process," below.

Lycidas

IN THIS MONODY[1] THE AUTHOR BEWAILS A LEARNED FRIEND,
UNFORTUNATELY DROWNED IN HIS PASSAGE FROM CHESTER ON THE
IRISH SEAS, 1637. AND BY OCCASION FORETELLS THE RUIN OF OUR
CORRUPTED CLERGY, THEN IN THEIR HEIGHT.

Yet once more, O ye laurels, and once more
Ye myrtles brown, with ivy never sere,[2]
I come to pluck your berries harsh and crude,[3]
And with forced fingers rude,
Shatter your leaves before the mellowing year.   5
Bitter constraint, and sad occasion dear,[4]
Compels me to disturb your season due;
For Lycidas is dead, dead ere his prime,
Young Lycidas, and hath not left his peer.
Who would not sing for Lycidas? He knew   10
Himself to sing, and build the lofty rhyme.
He must not float upon his watery bier
Unwept, and welter to the parching wind,
Without the meed[5] of some melodious tear.
    Begin then, sisters of the sacred well[6]   15
That from beneath the seat of Jove doth spring,

1. A dirge sung by a single voice. This Miltonic headnote was added in the edition of 1645.
2. "Laurels" for the crown of poetry given by Apollo; "myrtles" for the undying love granted by Venus; "ivy," the plant of Bacchus, also the reward of learning. All three plants are evergreens associated with poetic inspiration.
3. Unripe.
4. Heartfelt, profoundly moving; but also, in the 17th century, with overtones of "dire."
5. Reward.
6. The nine sister Muses were reported to dwell by various springs or "wells"; most likely Milton had in mind that of Aganippe near Mt. Helicon.

Begin, and somewhat loudly sweep the string.
Hence with denial vain, and coy excuse;
So may some gentle Muse
With lucky words favor my destined urn,[7]   20
And as he passes turn,
And bid fair peace be to my sable shroud.
For we were nursed upon the selfsame hill,
Fed the same flock, by fountain, shade, and rill.
    Together both, ere the high lawns[8] appeared   25
Under the opening eyelids of the morn,
We drove afield, and both together heard
What time the grayfly winds her sultry horn,[9]
Battening our flocks with the fresh dews of night,
Oft till the star that rose at evening bright   30
Toward heaven's descent had sloped his westering wheel.
Meanwhile the rural ditties were not mute,
Tempered to th' oaten flute,[1]
Rough satyrs danced, and fauns with cloven heel
From the glad sound would not be absent long,   35
And old Damoetas[2] loved to hear our song.
    But O the heavy change, now thou art gone,
Now thou art gone, and never must return!
Thee, shepherd, thee the woods and desert caves,
With wild thyme and the gadding[3] vine o'ergrown,   40
And all their echoes mourn.
The willows and the hazel copses green
Shall now no more be seen,
Fanning their joyous leaves to thy soft lays.
As killing as the canker[4] to the rose,   45
Or taint-worm to the weanling herds that graze,
Or frost to flowers that their gay wardrobe wear
When first the white-thorn blows;[5]
Such, Lycidas, thy loss to shepherd's ear.
    Where were ye, nymphs,[6] when the remorseless deep   50
Closed o'er the head of your loved Lycidas?
For neither were ye playing on the steep
Where your old bards, the famous Druids,[7] lie,
Nor on the shaggy top of Mona high,[8]
Nor yet where Deva spreads her wizard stream: 55

7. The speaker suggests that if he sings for Lycidas, "some gentle Muse" (i.e., poet) may some day
sing for him.
8. Upland pastures.
9. I.e., heard the grayfly when she buzzes ("winds
her sultry horn"). "Battening": feeding.
1. Traditional Panpipes, played by shepherds.
2. A type name from pastoral poetry, possibly
referring to some specific tutor at Cambridge.
3. Straggling.
4. Cankerworm.
5. Blossoms (as in the surviving expression, "full-

blown").
6. Nature deities.
7. The Druids, priestly poet-kings of Celtic Britain, worshiped the forces of nature. They lie dead
in their burying ground on the mountain ("steep")
Kerig-y-Druidion in Wales.
8. "Mona" is the island of Anglesey. "Deva" is
the river Dee in Cheshire. The Dee was magic
("wizard") because the size and position of its shifting stream foretold prosperity or dearth for the land.
All the places mentioned in lines 52–55 are in the
West Country, near where King drowned.

Ay me! I fondly dream—
Had ye been there—for what could that have done?
What could the Muse[9] herself that Orpheus bore,
The Muse herself, for her inchanting[1] son
Whom universal Nature did lament,   60
When by the rout[2] that made the hideous roar
His gory visage down the stream was sent,
Down the swift Hebrus to the Lesbian shore?
    Alas! What boots[3] it with incessant care
To tend the homely slighted shepherd's trade,   65
And strictly meditate the thankless Muse?[4]
Were it not better done as others use,
To sport with Amaryllis in the shade,
Or with the tangles of Neaera's hair?[5]
Fame is the spur that the clear spirit doth raise   70
(That last infirmity of noble mind)
To scorn delights, and live laborious days;
But the fair guerdon[6] when we hope to find,
And think to burst out into sudden blaze,
Comes the blind Fury[7] with th' abhorrèd shears,   75
And slits the thin-spun life. "But not the praise,"
Phoebus[8] replied, and touched my trembling ears;
"Fame is no plant that grows on mortal soil,
Nor in the glistering foil[9]
Set off to th' world, nor in broad rumor lies,   80
But lives and spreads aloft by those pure eyes,
And perfect witness of all-judging Jove;
As he pronounces lastly on each deed,
Of so much fame in heaven expect thy meed."
    O fountain Arethuse,[1] and thou honored flood,   85
Smooth-sliding Mincius, crowned with vocal reeds,
That strain I heard was of a higher mood.
But now my oat[2] proceeds,
And listens to the herald of the sea[3]

9. Calliope, Muse of epic poetry, was the mother of Orpheus.
1. "Inchanting" implies both song and magic; the root word survives as "incantation."
2. Orpheus was torn to pieces by a mob ("rout") of screaming Thracian women (Bacchantes), who threw his gory head into the river Hebrus, down which it floated, still singing, and out to Lesbos in the Aegean. The fate of Orpheus and the Druids suggests that nature everywhere is indifferent to the destruction of the priest-poet.
3. Profits.
4. Study to write poetry (the phrase is Virgil's).
5. "Amaryllis" and "Neaera" (Nee-eye-ra), conventional names for pretty shepherdesses, a passing hour's diversion for idle shepherds.
6. Reward.
7. Atropos, one of the three Fates, bearing scissors with which she cuts the thread of human life. Milton, to suggest the bitterness of death, makes her

an avenging Fury.
8. Phoebus Apollo, god of poetic inspiration. Touching the ears of one's hearers was a traditional Roman way of asking them to remember something that had been said.
9. Flashy metal, used to add glitter to gems.
1. Arethusa was a fountain in Sicily, Mincius a river in Lombardy, the former associated with the pastorals of Theocritus, the latter with those of Virgil. Arethusa was originally a nymph who went bathing in the river Alpheus, in Arcadian Greece. The river god grew enamored, and gave chase; she dove into the ocean and fled undersea to Sicily, where she came up as a fountain. Milton plays here with the idea of his pastoral going underground while the "strain of a higher mood" (line 87) is heard.
2. Pipe, hence song.
3. Neptune's "herald" is Triton, pleading his master's innocence in the death of Lycidas.

That came in Neptune's plea.   90
He asked the waves, and asked the felon winds,
"What hard mishap hath doomed this gentle swain?"
And questioned every gust of rugged wings
That blows from off each beakèd promontory;
They knew not of his story,   95
And sage Hippotades[4] their answer brings,
That not a blast was from his dungeon strayed;
The air was calm, and on the level brine,
Sleek Panope[5] with all her sisters played.
It was that fatal and perfidious bark,   100
Built in th' eclipse,[6] and rigged with curses dark,
That sunk so low that sacred head of thine.
   Next Camus,[7] reverend sire, went footing slow,
His mantle hairy, and his bonnet sedge,
Inwrought with figures dim, and on the edge   105
Like to that sanguine flower inscribed with woe.[8]
"Ah! who hath reft," quoth he, "my dearest pledge?"
Last came and last did go
The pilot of the Galilean lake;[9]
Two massy keys he bore of metals twain   110
(The golden opes, the iron shuts amain).[1]
He shook his mitered locks,[2] and stern bespake:
"How well could I have spared for thee, young swain,
Enow[3] of such as for their bellies' sake
Creep and intrude and climb into the fold!   115
Of other care they little reckoning make,
Than how to scramble at the shearers' feast,
And shove away the worthy bidden guest.
Blind mouths![4] that scarce themselves know how to hold
A sheep-hook,[5] or have learned aught else the least   120
That to the faithful herdsman's art belongs!
What recks it them?[6] What need they? They are sped;
And when they list,[7] their lean and flashy songs
Grate on their scrannel[8] pipes of wretched straw.

---

4. Aeolus, god of winds, and son of Hippotas.
5. The chief Nereid or sea nymph.
6. I.e., time of the worst possible luck.
7. God of the river Cam (properly, Granta), representing the ancient University of Cambridge, but slow and shaggy like the stream.
8. The bonnet and mantle of Camus have marks of woe on the edge like the AI AI supposedly found on the hyacinth, a "sanguine flower" sprung from the blood of a youth killed accidentally by Apollo.
9. St. Peter, originally a fisherman on Lake Tiberias (the Sea of Galilee), was first founder and bishop of the Christian church; his keys open and shut the gates to heaven.
1. Literally, "in full force," "exceedingly"; in this context, "for good," "once and for all."
2. He wears the bishop's miter.
3. An old plural form of "enough," used here with

contemptuous intensification, as if to say, "enough and more than enough."
4. This audacious metaphor, as of tapeworms, takes on new depth when one notes that the word *episcopus* (bishop) originally meant "over-seer" and that a "pastor" is properly one who feeds his flock.
5. The bishop's staff, or crozier, is made in the form of a shepherd's crook.
6. What do they care? "They are sped": i.e., they have prospered in a worldly sense; but also, "their doom is sealed."
7. Choose (that is, choose to play on their pipes, as shepherds should); but with the secondary meaning of "listen."
8. Harsh, meager. Milton's is the first recorded literary use of the word in English; it existed previously only in a North Country dialect.

The hungry sheep look up, and are not fed,   125
But swoln with wind, and the rank mist they draw,
Rot inwardly, and foul contagion spread,
Besides what the grim wolf with privy paw[9]
Daily devours apace, and nothing said.
But that two-handed engine at the door[1]   130
Stands ready to smite once, and smite no more."
    Return, Alpheus,[2] the dread voice is past,
That shrunk thy streams; return, Sicilian muse,
And call the vales, and bid them hither cast
Their bells and flowerets of a thousand hues.   135
Ye valleys low where the mild whispers use,[3]
Of shades and wanton winds, and gushing brooks,
On whose fresh lap the swart star[4] sparely looks,
Throw hither all your quaint enameled eyes,
That on the green turf suck the honeyed showers,   140
And purple all the ground with vernal flowers.
Bring the rathe[5] primrose that forsaken dies,
The tufted crow-toe, and pale jessamine,
The white pink, and the pansy freaked[6] with jet,
The glowing violet,   145
The musk-rose, and the well-attired woodbine,
With cowslips wan that hang the pensive head,
And every flower that sad embroidery wears:
Bid amaranthus[7] all his beauty shed,
And daffadillies fill their cups with tears,   150
To strew the laureate hearse[8] where Lycid lies.
For so to interpose a little ease,
Let our frail thoughts dally with false surmise.[9]
Ay me! whilst thee the shores and sounding seas
Wash far away, where'er thy bones are hurled,   155
Whether beyond the stormy Hebrides,[1]
Where thou perhaps under the whelming tide
Visit'st the bottom of the monstrous world;
Or whether thou, to our moist vows denied,
Sleep'st by the fable of Bellerus old,[2]   160
Where the great vision of the guarded mount

---

9. I.e., Roman Catholicism, whose agents operated in secret.
1. Many guesses as to the specific meaning of the
"two-handed engine" are on record; it may be St.
Peter's keys, the two houses of Parliament, or a big
sword, but there is no harm in letting it remain an
indistinct, apocalyptic instrument of revenge.
2. With the return of Alpheus, the pastoral mode
of the poem revives (see lines 85–87), and
a catalogue of flowers serves, as in Castiglione's
Alcon, to "interpose a little ease."
3. I.e., are used or accustomed to be heard.
4. The Dog Star, Sirius, associated with the heats
of late summer, looks but "sparely" (gently) on the
shady valleys. It may not be irrelevant that Edward

King drowned on August 10.
5. Early.
6. Flecked (the early verb survives in our word
"freckle").
7. The amaranth is an imaginary flower that never
fades; but for Lycidas it will.
8. Bier decked with laurels (see line 1).
9. The "false surmise" is that the body of Lycidas
has been recovered and can receive Christian burial.
1. Islands off the coast of Scotland, representing
the northern terminus of the Irish Sea.
2. The fabulous giant Bellerus is supposed to lie
buried on Land's End in Cornwall.

Looks toward Namancos and Bayona's hold;[3]
Look homeward angel now, and melt with ruth:[4]
And, O ye dolphins,[5] waft the hapless youth.

Weep no more, woeful shepherds, weep no more,   165
For Lycidas your sorrow is not dead,
Sunk though he be beneath the wat'ry floor;
So sinks the day-star[6] in the ocean bed,
And yet anon repairs his drooping head,
And tricks[7] his beams, and with new-spangled ore   170
Flames in the forehead of the morning sky:
So Lycidas sunk low, but mounted high,
Through the dear might of him that walked the waves,
Where, other groves and other streams along,
With nectar pure his oozy locks he laves,   175
And hears the unexpressive nuptial song,[8]
In the blest kingdoms meek of joy and love.
There entertain him all the saints above,
In solemn troops and sweet societies
That sing, and singing in their glory move,   180
And wipe the tears forever from his eyes.
Now, Lycidas, the shepherds weep no more;
Henceforth thou art the genius[9] of the shore,
In thy large recompense, and shalt be good
To all that wander in that perilous flood.   185

Thus sang the uncouth swain[1] to th' oaks and rills,
While the still morn went out with sandals gray;
He touched the tender stops of various quills,[2]
With eager thought warbling his Doric[3] lay:
And now the sun had stretched out all the hills,   190
And now was dropped into the western bay;
At last he rose, and twitched his mantle blue:
Tomorrow to fresh woods, and pastures new.

November 1637   1638

Areopagitica   This pamphlet appeared on November 24, 1644. The title, which Milton took from a famous oration delivered by Isocrates in 355 B.C., means "things to be said before the Areopagus." The Areopagus was an ancient, powerful, and much-respected tribunal in Athens, and Milton's

3. St. Michael's Mount, in Cornwall, from which the archangel is envisioned as looking south, over miles of open Atlantic, across the Bay of Biscay, to Bayona (not far from Vigo) and the district of Nemancos, near Cape Finisterre in northern Spain, where the historical Catholic enemy of Protestant England lay entrenched.

4. Michael is implored to look homeward, relaxing his stern guard for a moment of grief and pity ("ruth").

5. Dolphins, admirable sea beasts, brought the Greek poet Arion safely ashore for love of his verses, and also wafted the dead body of Melicertes to land, where he was promptly transformed to a sea god, Palaemon.

6. The sun.

7. Dresses.

8. Inexpressible hymn of joy, sung at "the marriage supper of the Lamb" (Revelation 19).

9. Protective deity.

1. Unknown, unlettered shepherd (a stock convention of this supremely literary form).

2. The oaten stalks of Panpipes.

3. Rustic, simple.

title thus implies a comparison between the Greek institution and the English Parliament, and between Isocrates' role and his own. These comparisons may be thought to validate the florid, oratorical tone of the tract—which was, in fact, subtitled "A Speech," and is structured in accordance with the precepts of classical rhetoric.

Areopagitica is a plea for the liberty of unlicensed printing; its occasion was a severe ordinance for the control of printing which had been passed by Parliament on June 14, 1643. This ordinance, however disagreeable at the moment, was no striking novelty in English history. On the contrary, control of the press had been actively exercised by all the Tudors and both the early Stuarts. The aim of this government regulation was traditionally defined as the preservation of order and uniformity in church and state; but it also had an economic motive. Unlicensed printers threatened a monopoly enjoyed by the twenty licensed printers of London. Thus the censorship laws familiar to Englishmen had generally been strictly defined and had bristled with penalties. But to enforce them was another matter entirely. Tudor and Stuart police forces being what they were, few printers or authors had to worry about the consequences of going to print without a license. As a matter of fact, *Areopagitica* was itself unlicensed, Milton's third unlicensed pamphlet since the passage of the Ordinance for Printing only seventeen months before.

Thus the practical effects of the Ordinance for Printing were less important (particularly, we may be sure, in Milton's eyes) than the principle involved. Having taken the lead in destroying the licensing system of the Stuarts, Parliament was now setting up a censorship of its own. Milton's first effort was to show, through a condensed history of censorship, that the institution was only fit for, and only used by, degenerate cultures. His next argument is still more general, that censorship is evil and un-Christian in itself. As God left man free to choose among the many physical foods of this world, urging only temperance, so (Milton argues) he left man free to pick and choose for himself among ideas.

From Areopagitica

* * * Good and evil we know in the field of this world grow up together almost inseparably; and the knowledge of good is so involved and interwoven with the knowledge of evil, and in so many cunning resemblances hardly to be discerned, that those confused seeds which were imposed on Psyche as an incessant labor to cull out and sort asunder,[1] were not more intermixed. It was from out the rind of one apple tasted, that the knowledge of good and evil, as two twins cleaving together, leaped forth into the world. And perhaps this is that doom which Adam fell into of knowing good and evil, that is to say of knowing good by evil.

As therefore the state of man now is, what wisdom can there be to choose, what continence to forbear, without the knowledge of evil? He that can apprehend and consider vice with all her baits and seeming pleasures, and yet abstain, and yet distinguish, and yet prefer that which

---

1. Angry at her son Cupid's love for Psyche, Venus set Psyche to sorting out a vast mound of mixed seeds; but the ants took pity on her, and did the work. See Apuleius, *The Golden Ass.*

is truly better, he is the true wayfaring[2] Christian. I cannot praise a fugitive and cloistered virtue, unexercised and unbreathed, that never sallies out and sees her adversary, but slinks out of the race where that immortal garland[3] is to be run for, not without dust and heat. Assuredly we bring not innocence into the world, we bring impurity much rather; that which purifies us is trial, and trial is by what is contrary. That virtue therefore which is but a youngling in the contemplation of evil, and knows not the utmost that vice promises to her followers, and rejects it, is but a blank virtue, not a pure; her whiteness is but an excremental[4] whiteness; which was the reason why our sage and serious poet Spenser (whom I dare be known to think a better teacher than Scotus or Aquinas),[5] describing true temperance under the person of Guyon, brings him in with his palmer through the cave of Mammon and the bower of earthly bliss, that he might see and know, and yet abstain.

Since therefore the knowledge and survey of vice is in this world so necessary to the constituting of human virtue, and the scanning of error to the confirmation of truth, how can we more safely, and with less danger, scout into the regions of sin and falsity than by reading all manner of tractates and hearing all manner of reason? And this is the benefit which may be had of books promiscuously read.

But of the harm that may result hence, three kinds are usually reckoned. First is feared the infection that may spread; but then all human learning and controversy in religious points must remove out of the world, yea, the Bible itself; for that ofttimes relates blasphemy not nicely,[6] it describes the carnal sense of wicked men not unelegantly, it brings in holiest men passionately murmuring against providence through all the arguments of Epicurus;[7] in other great disputes it answers dubiously and darkly to the common reader; and ask a Talmudist what ails the modesty of his marginal Keri, that Moses and all the prophets cannot persuade him to pronounce the textual Chetiv.[8] For these causes we all know the Bible itself put by the papist into the first rank of prohibited books. The ancientest Fathers must be next removed, as Clement of Alexandria, and that Eusebian book of evangelic preparation, transmitting our ears through a hoard of heathenish obscenities to receive the Gospel.[9] Who finds not that Irenaeus, Epiphanius, Jerome, and others discover[1] more

---

2. There has been debate whether this word should be "wayfaring" or "warfaring," but in the image of Christian life as a pilgrimage, a crusade, the two ideas are united.
3. The crown of righteousness, the garland of virtue.
4. Exterior (like a whited sepulcher, covering corruption within).
5. Duns Scotus and Thomas Aquinas, taken as types of the Scholastic theologian. The Cave of Mammon is described in *The Faerie Queene* 2.7, the Bower of Bliss in 2.12.
6. Daintily.

7. See the Book of Ecclesiastes.
8. "Keri" are the marginal comments of rabbinical scholars on the "Chetiv" of the Bible, the text itself. When the text was too free-spoken for later commentators, Keri was sometimes read in place of Chetiv.
9. Eusebius' *Preparatio Evangelica*, like many early Christian books of polemic, describes heathen wickedness in fascinating detail, as an encouragement to Christian faith. St. Irenaeus, St. Jerome, and even that ancient and edifying convert, Clement of Alexandria, are all subject to this charge.
1. Describe (and so preserve, report).

heresies than they well confute, and that oft for heresy which is the truer opinion?[2] * * *

* * *

Impunity and remissness, for certain, are the bane of a commonwealth; but here the great art lies, to discern in what the law is to bid restraint and punishment, and in what things persuasion only is to work. If every action which is good or evil in man at ripe years were to be under pittance[3] and prescription and compulsion, what were virtue but a name, what praise could be then due to well-doing, what gramercy[4] to be sober, just, or continent?

Many there be that complain of divine providence for suffering Adam to transgress; foolish tongues! when God gave him reason, he gave him freedom to choose, for reason is but choosing; he had been else a mere artificial Adam, such an Adam as he is in the motions.[5] We ourselves esteem not of that obedience, or love, or gift, which is of force: God therefore left him free, set before him a provoking object, ever almost in his eyes; herein consisted his merit, herein the right of his reward, the praise of his abstinence. Wherefore did he create passions within us, pleasures round about us, but that these rightly tempered are the very ingredients of virtue? They are not skillful considerers of human things, who imagine to remove sin by removing the matter of sin; for, besides that it is a huge heap increasing under the very act of diminishing, though some part of it may for a time be withdrawn from some persons, it cannot from all, in such a universal thing as books are; and when this is done, yet the sin remains entire. Though ye take from a covetous man all his treasure, he has yet one jewel left: ye cannot bereave him of his covetousness. Banish all objects of lust, shut up all youth into the severest discipline that can be exercised in any hermitage, ye cannot make them chaste that came not thither so: such great care and wisdom is required to the right managing of this point.

Suppose we could expel sin by this means; look how much we thus expel of sin, so much we expel of virtue: for the matter of them both is the same; remove that, and ye remove them both alike. This justifies the high providence of God, who, though he commands us temperance, justice, continence, yet pours out before us, even to a profuseness, all desirable things, and gives us minds that can wander beyond all limit and satiety. Why should we then affect a rigor contrary to the manner of God and of nature, by abridging or scanting those means, which

2. Milton now argues that books cannot pervert men unless they are given force and vitality by a teacher, who, if he is a good teacher, needs no books. A fool, he urges, can find material for his folly in the best books, and a wise man material for his wisdom in the worst. Plato, indeed, recommended censorship in his *Laws*; but in real life one cannot censor books without censoring ballads, fiddlers, clothing, conversation, and social life as a whole.

3. Rationing.

4. Reward, thanks.

5. Puppet shows.

books freely permitted are, both to the trial of virtue and the exercise of truth?[6] * * *

* * *

Well knows he who uses to consider, that our faith and knowledge thrives by exercise, as well as our limbs and complexion.[7] Truth is compared in Scripture to a streaming fountain; if her waters flow not in a perpetual progression, they sicken into a muddy pool of conformity and tradition. A man may be a heretic in the truth; and if he believe things only because his pastor says so, or the Assembly so determines, without knowing other reason, though his belief be true, yet the very truth he holds becomes his heresy. There is not any burden that some would gladlier post off to another than the charge and care of their religion. There be, who knows not that there be, of Protestants and professors[8] who live and die in as arrant an implicit faith as any lay papist of Loretto.[9] A wealthy man, addicted to his pleasure and to his profits, finds religion to be a traffic so entangled, and of so many piddling accounts, that of all mysteries he cannot skill[1] to keep a stock going upon that trade. What should he do? Fain he would have the name to be religious, fain he would bear up with his neighbors in that. What does he therefore, but resolves to give over toiling, and to find himself out some factor,[2] to whose care and credit he may commit the whole managing of his religious affairs; some divine of note and estimation that must be. To him he adheres, resigns the whole warehouse of his religion, with all the locks and keys, into his custody; and indeed makes the very person of that man his religion; esteems his associating with him a sufficient evidence and commendatory of his own piety. So that a man may say his religion is now no more within himself, but is become a dividual[3] movable, and goes and comes near him, according as that good man frequents the house. He entertains him, gives him gifts, feasts him, lodges him; his religion comes home at night, prays, is liberally supped, and sumptuously laid to sleep, rises, is saluted, and after the malmsey, or some well-spiced brewage, and better breakfasted than He whose morning appetite would have gladly fed on green figs between Bethany and Jerusalem,[4] his religion walks abroad at eight, and leaves his kind entertainer in the shop trading all day without his religion.

Another sort there be who, when they hear that all things shall be ordered, all things regulated and settled, nothing written but what passes

---

6. Censorship, Milton urges, is a vulgar, mechanical job; no man of intelligence will undertake it, and a dunderhead will make serious blunders. Besides, putting stupid men in authority over intelligent ones will discourage the pursuit of learning on every hand, except so far as censorship, by giving authority to banned books, will encourage men to seek out and cling to perverse opinions.

7. Constitution, regarded as the proper mingling of certain qualities in one's body.

8. "Professors" in this context are people professing the Protestant faith.

9. A famous Catholic shrine.

1. In no way can he manage.

2. Agent.

3. I.e., separate or separable. Milton is describing the common institution of the household chaplain.

4. Mark 11.12–13. Jesus, hungry, found nothing but leaves on the fig tree, for the time of the figs was not yet.

through the custom-house of certain publicans that have the tonnaging and poundaging[5] of all free-spoken truth, will straight give themselves up into your hands, make 'em and cut 'em out what religion ye please: there be delights, there be recreations and jolly pastimes that will fetch the day about from sun to sun, and rock the tedious year as in a delightful dream. What need they torture their heads with that which others have taken so strictly and so unalterably into their own purveying? These are the fruits which a dull ease and cessation of our knowledge will bring forth among the people. How goodly and how to be wished were such an obedient unanimity as this, what a fine conformity would it starch us all into! Doubtless a staunch and solid piece of framework, as any January could freeze together.[6] * * *

* * *

Truth indeed came once into the world with her Divine Master, and was a perfect shape most glorious to look on: but when he ascended, and his apostles after him were laid asleep, then straight arose a wicked race of deceivers, who, as that story goes of the Egyptian Typhon with his conspirators, how they dealt with the good Osiris,[7] took the virgin Truth, hewed her lovely form into a thousand pieces, and scattered them to the four winds. From that time ever since, the sad friends of Truth, such as durst appear, imitating the careful search that Isis made for the mangled body of Osiris, went up and down gathering up limb by limb, still as they could find them. We have not yet found them all, Lords and Commons, nor ever shall do, till her Master's second coming; he shall bring together every joint and member, and shall mold them into an immortal feature of loveliness and perfection. Suffer not these licensing prohibitions to stand at every place of opportunity, forbidding and disturbing them that continue seeking, that continue to do our obsequies to the torn body of our martyred saint.

We boast our light; but if we look not wisely on the sun itself, it smites us into darkness. Who can discern those planets that are oft combust,[8] and those stars of brightest magnitude that rise and set with the sun, until the opposite motion of their orbs bring them to such a place in the firmament where they may be seen evening or morning? The light which we have gained was given us, not to be ever staring on, but by it to discover onward things more remote from our knowledge. It is not the unfrocking of a priest, the unmitering of a bishop, and the removing him from off the Presbyterian shoulders, that will make us a happy nation. No, if other things as great in the church, and in the rule of life both economical[9] and political, be not looked into and reformed, we have

---

5. "Publicans": tax collectors. Tonnage and poundage were excise taxes levied illegally by the king before 1641, and therefore specially odious to Milton's readers.
6. To set barriers in the way of fresh truths implies that a nation has all the truth it needs; but this, Milton argues, is far from the case. England has no grounds for smugness; the nation needs every

bit of truth it can discover.
7. Plutarch tells, in his *Isis and Osiris*, of Typhon's scattering the fragments of his brother Osiris, and of Isis' efforts to recover them.
8. Literally, burned up; in astrology, so close to the sun as not to be visible.
9. Domestic.

looked so long upon the blaze that Zwinglius[1] and Calvin hath beaconed up to us, that we are stark blind.

There be who perpetually complain of schisms and sects, and make it such a calamity that any man dissents from their maxims. 'Tis their own pride and ignorance which causes the disturbing, who neither will hear with meekness, nor can convince; yet all must be suppressed which is not found in their syntagma.[2] They are the troublers, they are the dividers of unity, who neglect and permit not others to unite those dissevered pieces which are yet wanting to the body of Truth. To be still searching what we know not by what we know, still closing up truth to truth as we find it (for all her body is homogeneal and proportional), this is the golden rule in theology as well as in arithmetic, and makes up the best harmony in a church; not the forced and outward union of cold and neutral and inwardly divided minds.

Lords and Commons of England, consider what nation it is whereof ye are, and whereof ye are the governors: a nation not slow and dull, but of a quick, ingenious, and piercing spirit, acute to invent, subtle and sinewy to discourse, not beneath the reach of any point the highest that human capacity can soar to. Therefore the studies of learning in her deepest sciences have been so ancient and so eminent among us, that writers of good antiquity and ablest judgment have been persuaded that even the school of Pythagoras and the Persian wisdom took beginning from the old philosophy of this island.[3] And that wise and civil Roman, Julius Agricola, who governed once here for Caesar, preferred the natural wits of Britain before the labored studies of the French. Nor is it for nothing that the grave and frugal Transylvanian sends out yearly from as far as the mountainous borders of Russia, and beyond the Hercynian wilderness, not their youth, but their staid men, to learn our language and our theologic arts.

Yet that which is above all this, the favor and the love of heaven we have great argument[4] to think in a peculiar manner propitious and propending towards us. Why else was this nation chosen before any other, that out of her, as out of Zion,[5] should be proclaimed and sounded forth the first tidings and trumpet of Reformation to all Europe? And had it not been the obstinate perverseness of our prelates against the divine and admirable spirit of Wycliffe to suppress him as a schismatic and innovator, perhaps neither the Bohemian Huss and Jerome,[6] no, nor the name of Luther or of Calvin, had been ever known: the glory of reforming all our neighbors had been completely ours. But now, as our obdu-

---

1. Zwingli and Calvin, both radical Swiss reformers, were mainstays of the Presbyterian cause, which Milton was already feeling to be a little narrow.
2. Compilation of beliefs, creed.
3. So far as it concerns Pythagoras and the Persians, this sentence is better patriotism than it is intellectual history. Agricola's opinion of the British intellect (referred to next) is found in Tacitus' *Life of Agricola*; "civil" means "cultured, civi-

lized." The Transylvanians, being Protestants, did sometimes come to England from "beyond the Hercynian wilderness" (the Harz mountains) to study.
4. Reason. "Propending": inclining, favorable.
5. Mt. Zion, in Jerusalem, the site of the temple, the holy of holies.
6. Jerome of Prague (martyred in 1416) was a follower of Huss and so of Wycliffe.

rate clergy have with violence demeaned[7] the matter, we are become hitherto the latest and the backwardest scholars of whom God offered to have made us the teachers.

Now once again by all concurrence of signs, and by the general instinct of holy and devout men, as they daily and solemnly express their thoughts, God is decreeing to begin some new and great period in his church, even to the reforming of Reformation itself; what does he then but reveal himself to his servants, and as his manner is, first to his Englishmen? I say, as his manner is, first to us, though we mark not the method of his counsels, and are unworthy. Behold now this vast city: a city of refuge, the mansion house of liberty, encompassed and surrounded with his protection; the shop of war hath not there more anvils and hammers waking, to fashion out the plates[8] and instruments of armed justice in defense of beleaguered truth, than there be pens and heads there, sitting by their studious lamps, musing, searching, revolving new notions and ideas wherewith to present, as with their homage and their fealty, the approaching Reformation: others as fast reading, trying all things, assenting to the force of reason and convincement.

What could a man require more from a nation so pliant and so prone to seek after knowledge? What wants there to such a towardly[9] and pregnant soil, but wise and faithful laborers, to make a knowing people, a nation of prophets, of sages, and of worthies? We reckon more than five months yet to harvest; there need not be five weeks; had we but eyes to lift up, the fields are white already.[1] Where there is much desire to learn, there of necessity will be much arguing, much writing, many opinions; for opinion in good men is but knowledge in the making. Under these fantastic terrors of sect and schism we wrong the earnest and zealous thirst after knowledge and understanding which God hath stirred up in this city.

What some lament of, we rather should rejoice at, should rather praise this pious forwardness among men, to reassume the ill-deputed care of their religion into their own hands again. A little generous prudence, a little forbearance of one another, and some grain of charity might win all these diligences to join, and unite into one general and brotherly search after truth; could we but forego this prelatical tradition of crowding free consciences and Christian liberties into canons and precepts of men. I doubt not, if some great and worthy stranger should come among us, wise to discern the mold and temper of a people, and how to govern it, observing the high hopes and aims, the diligent alacrity of our extended thoughts and reasonings in the pursuance of truth and freedom, but that he would cry out as Pyrrhus did, admiring the Roman docility and courage: "If such were my Epirots, I would not despair the greatest design that could be attempted, to make a church or kingdom happy."[2] Yet

---

7. Conducted.
8. Plate mail, armor plate.
9. Favorable.
1. Milton is paraphrasing Christ's words to the disciples (John 4.35).
2. Though King Pyrrhus of Epirus beat the Roman armies at Heraclea in 280 B.C., he was much impressed by their discipline.

these are the men cried out against for schismatics and sectaries;[3] as if, while the temple of the Lord was building, some cutting, some squaring the marble, others hewing the cedars, there should be a sort of irrational men, who could not consider there must be many schisms and many dissections[4] made in the quarry and in the timber, ere the house of God can be built. And when every stone is laid artfully together, it cannot be united into a continuity, it can but be contiguous in this world; neither can every piece of the building be of one form; nay rather the perfection consists in this, that out of many moderate varieties and brotherly dissimilitudes that are not vastly disproportional, arises the goodly and the graceful symmetry that commends the whole pile and structure. Let us therefore be more considerate builders, more wise in spiritual architecture, when great reformation is expected. For now the time seems come, wherein Moses the great prophet may sit in heaven rejoicing to see that memorable and glorious wish of his fulfilled, when not only our seventy elders, but all the Lord's people, are become prophets.[5]

* * *

Methinks I see in my mind a noble and puissant nation rousing herself like a strong man after sleep, and shaking her invincible locks: methinks I see her as an eagle mewing[6] her mighty youth, and kindling her undazzled eyes at the full midday beam; purging and unscaling her long-abused sight at the fountain itself of heavenly radiance; while the whole noise of timorous and flocking birds, with those also that love the twilight, flutter about, amazed at what she means, and in their envious gabble would prognosticate a year of sects and schisms.

What should ye do then, should ye suppress all this flowery crop of knowledge and new light sprung up and yet springing daily in this city? Should ye set an oligarchy of twenty engrossers[7] over it, to bring a famine upon our minds again, when we shall know nothing but what is measured to us by their bushel? Believe it, Lords and Commons, they who counsel ye to such a suppressing do as good as bid ye suppress yourselves; and I will soon show how.[8]

* * *

And now the time in special is by privilege to write and speak what may help to the further discussing of matters in agitation. The temple of Janus with his two controversial faces might now not unsignificantly be set open.[9] And though all the winds of doctrine were let loose to play

---

3. Sectarians, dividers of the church.

4. Literally, cuttings-up, figuratively dissensions and divisions.

5. In Numbers 11.29 Moses expresses the wish that not only the Sanhedrin, or council of seventy, but the whole people of Israel should be prophets.

6. Molting, shaking off. Or the word may be "newing," i.e., renewing.

7. Engrossers, much hated in the English countryside, bought great quantities of grain and held it for times of famine and consequent high prices.

8. By its liberal and enlightened policies, Milton argues, Parliament has actually created the vigorous and enquiring minds that censorship seeks to suppress. For Parliament to destroy its own creation would be like a father killing his own children.

9. Janus, who gives us our month of January, had two faces looking in opposite directions, because he was god of beginnings and endings. A special door in Rome, dedicated to him, was kept open in times of war, closed in times of peace.

upon the earth, so Truth be in the field, we do injuriously by licensing and prohibiting to misdoubt her strength. Let her and Falsehood grapple; who ever knew Truth put to the worse in a free and open encounter? Her confuting is the best and surest suppressing. He who hears what praying there is for light and clearer knowledge to be sent down among us would think of other matters to be constituted beyond the discipline of Geneva framed and fabricked already to our hands.[1]

Yet when the new light which we beg for shines in upon us, there be who envy and oppose if it come not first in at their casements. What a collusion is this, whenas we are exhorted by the wise man to use diligence, to seek for wisdom as for hidden treasures early and late,[2] that another order shall enjoin us to know nothing but by statute. When a man hath been laboring the hardest labor in the deep mines of knowledge, hath furnished out his findings in all their equipage, drawn forth his reasons as it were a battle[3] ranged, scattered and defeated all objections in his way, calls out his adversary into the plain, offers him the advantage of wind and sun if he please, only that he may try the matter by dint of argument; for his opponents then to skulk, to lay ambushments, to keep a narrow bridge of licensing where the challenger should pass, though it be valor enough in soldiership, is but weakness and cowardice in the wars of Truth.

For who knows not that Truth is strong, next to the Almighty? She needs no policies nor stratagems nor licensings to make her victorious—those are the shifts and the defenses that error uses against her power. Give her but room, and do not bind her when she sleeps, for then she speaks not true, as the old Proteus[4] did, who spake oracles only when he was caught and bound, but then rather she turns herself into all shapes except her own, and perhaps tunes her voice according to the time, as Micaiah did before Ahab,[5] until she be adjured into her own likeness.

Yet it is not impossible that she may have more shapes than one. What else is all that rank of things indifferent, wherein Truth may be on this side or on the other without being unlike herself? What but a vain shadow else is the abolition of those ordinances, that handwriting nailed to the cross?[6] what great purchase is this Christian liberty which Paul so often boasts of? His doctrine is that he who eats or eats not, regards a day or regards it not, may do either to the Lord.[7] How many other things might be tolerated in peace and left to conscience, had we but charity, and were it not the chief stronghold of our hypocrisy to be ever judging one another? I fear yet this iron yoke of outward conformity

1. Milton's Calvinism, a major ingredient of which was hostility to English bishops, was fading fast in 1644, since bishops had been abolished.
2. Solomon was the wise man; the allusion is to Proverbs 8.11.
3. Line of battle, array, Wind and sun were significant advantages in a fight with swords.
4. The old man of the sea, who tried to escape capture by changing shapes, in *Odyssey* 4.

5. The story of Micaiah, who tried to disguise an unpleasant prophecy from King Ahab, is in 1 Kings 22.
6. The locution, from Colossians 2.14, implies that the crucifixion canceled out all the rules and penalties of Mosaic law. Paul's doctrine is expressed in Galatians 5.
7. In the Lord's service.

hath left a slavish print upon our necks; the ghost of a linen decency[8] yet haunts us. We stumble and are impatient at the least dividing of one visible congregation from another, though it be not in fundamentals; and through our forwardness to suppress and our backwardness to recover any enthralled piece of truth out of the gripe of custom, we care not[9] to keep truth separated from truth, which is the fiercest rent and disunion of all. We do not see that while we still affect by all means a rigid and external formality, we may as soon fall again into a gross conforming stupidity, a stark and dead congealment of "wood and hay and stubble,"[1] forced and frozen together, which is more to the sudden degenerating of a church than many sub-dichotomies of petty schisms.

Not that I can think well of every light separation, or that all in a church is to be expected "gold and silver and precious stones." It is not possible for man to sever the wheat from the tares, the good fish from the other fry; that must be the angels' ministry at the end of mortal things.[2] Yet if all cannot be of one mind—as who looks they should be?—this doubtless is more wholesome, more prudent, and more Christian, that many be tolerated rather than all compelled. I mean not tolerated popery and open superstition, which, as it extirpates all religions and civil supremacies, so itself should be extirpate, provided first that all charitable and compassionate means be used to win and regain the weak and the misled; that also which is impious or evil absolutely, either against faith or manners, no law can possibly permit that intends not to unlaw itself; but those neighboring differences or rather indifferences are what I speak of, whether in some point of doctrine or of discipline, which though they may be many yet need not interrupt "the unity of spirit," if we could but find among us the "bond of peace."[3]

In the meanwhile, if anyone would write and bring his helpful hand to the slow-moving reformation which we labor under, if truth have spoken to him before others, or but seemed at least to speak, who hath so bejesuited us that we should trouble that man with asking license to do so worthy a deed? And not consider this, that if it come to prohibiting, there is not aught more likely to be prohibited than truth itself; whose first appearance to our eyes bleared and dimmed with prejudice and custom is more unsightly and unplausible than many errors, even as the person is of many a great man slight and contemptible to see to. And what do they tell us vainly of new opinions, when this very opinion of theirs, that none must be heard but whom they like, is the worst and newest opinion of all others, and is the chief cause why sects and schisms do so much abound, and true knowledge is kept at distance from us; besides yet a greater danger which is in it. For when God shakes a kingdom with strong and healthful commotions to a general reforming, it is

---

8. Strips of white linen at neck and wrist were worn by many men in the 17th century, especially (under the name of "bands") by clergymen. Milton uses them as emblems of formal purity.
9. Scruple not.
1. The contrast between "wood, hay, stubble" and

"gold, silver, precious stones" is from 1 Corinthians 3.12.
2. This is the parable of the wheat and the tares (weeds) in Matthew 13.24–30, 36–43.
3. The phrases are from Paul's letter to the Ephesians.

not untrue that many sectaries and false teachers are then busiest in seducing; but yet more true it is that God then raises to his own work men of rare abilities and more than common industry, not only to look back and revise what hath been taught heretofore, but to gain further and go on some new enlightened steps in the discovery of truth.[4]

✳   ✳   ✳

1644

Sonnets   Between 1630 and 1658 Milton wrote twenty-four sonnets. Five he wrote in Italian, no doubt partly as linguistic exercises, the rest in English, on a variety of occasions, both public and private. Unlike the sonnets of Sidney, Spenser, and Shakespeare, those of Milton do not form any sort of sequence, and they lay very little emphasis on erotic themes. Neither are they devotional like the *Holy Sonnets* of Donne. They are more often public and political than simply personal. Yet, whatever their theme, they speak with a massive and authoritative voice like none other in English.

The form of the sonnets is Petrarchan rather than Shakespearean (see the appendix on poetic forms); and one is a "tailed" sonnet, with two little extra units, each consisting of a half line and a couplet. A special feature of Milton's later sonnets is the way he runs on the sense from line to line, deliberately avoiding end-stopped lines (see particularly that *On the Late Massacre in Piedmont*). In this as in other respects, Milton was following the example of an Italian sonneteer, Giovanni Della Casa, who broke sharply with the Petrarchan tradition of metrical regularity. Milton's break with his English predecessors was just as sharp.

<h2 style="text-align:center">Sonnets</h2>

<h1 style="text-align:center">How Soon Hath Time</h1>

How soon hath Time, the subtle thief of youth,
　Stol'n on his wing my three and twentieth year!
　My hasting days fly on with full career,
　But my late spring no bud or blossom show'th.
Perhaps my semblance might deceive the truth,　　　5
　That I to manhood am arrived so near,
　And inward ripeness doth much less appear,

4. After a few final thoughts, *Areopagitica* ends with an exhortation to Parliament. In practical terms, the argument was unsuccessful; the ordinance against which Milton protested was not repealed, though it was never effectively enforced. In time, Milton himself became for a while a licenser of news sheets under Cromwell, commissioned to give editorial supervision to a small, progovernment paper. But this biographical fact need not be taken as a retraction of the position assumed in *Areopagitica*, which moves throughout on a lofty plane of policy far above mundane details of politics.

That some more timely-happy spirits endu'th.[1]
Yet be it less or more, or soon or slow,
  It shall be still in strictest measure even[2]   10
  To that same lot, however mean or high,
Toward which Time leads me, and the will of Heaven;
  All is, if I have grace to use it so,
  As ever in my great Taskmaster's eye.[3]

1632?   1645

When I Consider How My Light Is Spent[1]

When I consider how my light is spent,
  Ere half my days, in this dark world and wide,
  And that one talent which is death to hide,[2]
  Lodged with me useless, though my soul more bent
To serve therewith my Maker, and present   5
  My true account, lest he returning chide;
  "Doth God exact day-labor, light denied?"
  I fondly[3] ask; but Patience to prevent
That murmur, soon replies, "God doth not need
  Either man's work or his own gifts; who best   10
  Bear his mild yoke, they serve him best. His state
Is kingly. Thousands at his bidding speed
  And post o'er land and ocean without rest:
  They also serve who only stand and wait."

1652?   1673

On the Late Massacre in Piedmont[1]

Avenge, O Lord, thy slaughtered saints, whose bones
  Lie scattered on the Alpine mountains cold;
  Even them who kept thy truth so pure of old

1. Endoweth.
2. Equal, adequate. Whenever it appears and
however much it amounts to, Milton's inner growth
will be adequate to the destiny that time and heaven
are preparing.
3. I.e., nothing has been lost in God's eyes—if
only I can see ("use") it that way.
1. Milton's sonnet on his blindness is close in
theme to *How Soon Hath Time*; but his affliction
(fresh at the time of writing) represents a far more
severe test.
2. The parable of the talents (Matthew 25) loomed
large in Puritan minds, and particularly in Milton's. The servants who put their master's money
(talents of gold and silver) out to earn interest while
he was away were called "good and faithful"; the
one who simply returned what he had been given
was deprived of everything and cast into outer

darkness. Usury, which under Catholic theology
had been a deadly sin, changed its meaning for the
Puritans; it became a metaphor, and sometimes
more than a metaphor, for "working out one's salvation."
3. Foolishly. "Prevent": forestall.
1. The Waldenses were a heretical sect, probably
of Eastern origin by way of Venice: they lived in
the valleys of northern Italy ("the Piedmont") and
southern France, professing a creed which was
particularly akin to Protestantism in its avoidance
of graven images ("stocks and stones"). The understanding which had allowed them freedom of worship was terminated in 1655, and the massacre
which ensued was widely protested by the Protestant powers of Europe. Milton, as Latin secretary
to Cromwell, wrote several indignant letters.

When all our fathers worshipped stocks and stones,
Forget not: in thy book record their groans   5
    Who were thy sheep and in their ancient fold
    Slain by the bloody Piemontese that rolled
    Mother with infant down the rocks. Their moans
The vales redoubled to the hills, and they
    To heaven. Their martyred blood and ashes sow   10
    O'er all th' Italian fields, where still doth sway
The triple tyrant:[2] that from these may grow
    A hundredfold, who having learnt thy way
    Early may fly the Babylonian woe.[3]

1655   1673

Methought I Saw My Late Espousèd Saint

Methought I saw my late espousèd saint
    Brought to me like Alcestis[1] from the grave,
    Whom Jove's great son to her glad husband gave,
    Rescued from death by force though pale and faint.
Mine, as whom washed from spot of childbed taint,   5
    Purification in the old law did save,[2]
    And such, as yet once more I trust to have
Full sight of her in heaven without restraint,
    Came vested all in white, pure as her mind.
    Her face was veiled, yet to my fancied sight   10
    Love, sweetness, goodness, in her person shined
So clear, as in no face with more delight.
    But O, as to embrace me she inclined,
    I waked, she fled, and day brought back my night.

1658   1673

Paradise Lost   Milton's epic begins with a rush. Carried along by the
impetus of Satan's tremendous adventures, readers are apt to forget there is
any other part to the poem. Indeed, while we are getting acclimated to the
Miltonic world, there is no reason to hold back our sympathy with Satan,
our admiration for his heroic energy. It is energy in a bad cause, clearly; but
it is energy, it is heroically exercised, and there is as yet no source of virtuous
power to oppose or offset it. With the appearance of Christ the Son, at the
opening of Book 3, we begin to see in heavenly Love the counterpoise of
Satan's hellish Hate; and in Book 4, as we are introduced not only to Adam

2. I.e., the Pope, wearing his tiara with three
crowns.
3. Protestants in Milton's day frequently identified
the Roman Church with the "whore of Babylon"
(Revelation 17, 18).
1. Alcestis, wife of Admetus, was rescued from the
underworld by Hercules ("Jove's great son").

2. The Mosaic law prescribing periods for the
purification of women after childbirth is found in
Leviticus 12. Line 5 is very compressed; expanded,
it would read, "My wife, like the woman whom,
when washed from spot of childbed taint," etc.
Milton's second wife died after childbirth.

and Eve but to Paradise, our sympathies gradually shift. Satan is no longer a glamorous underdog, fighting his adventurous way through the universe against enormous odds; he is a menacing vulture, a cormorant, a toad, a snake. He is not only dangerous, he is dull; whatever richness and variety he discovers in the universe serve only to produce in him envious hatred and destructiveness. His sin is incestuous, as the allegory of Sin and Death points out; it breeds out of itself ever fresh occasions of sin. Adam and Eve, who are weaker, less active, and less spectacular in every way, finally outweigh Satan in our interest and sympathy simply because they can respond to life, and to the terrifying experience of guilt, more vigorously than Satan can.

Seen overall—from above, as it were—*Paradise Lost* is a vast but delicately balanced structure. Its first half rises from Hell through Chaos to Heaven, and takes place mostly in these cosmic locales; its second half opens with the word "Descend," and is largely confined to earth, ending with Adam and Eve's descent from the Mount of Paradise to the "subjected plain" of our world. The adventure of the fallen Satan in the opening books balances the history of fallen mankind in the closing ones. Book 4, the entry of Satan (and the reader) into Paradise, balances Book 9, describing the loss of Paradise. Books 5 and 10 provide contrasting views of life in Eden before and after the Fall. At the center of the poem, balanced as on a fulcrum, are the account of the destructive war in Heaven (Book 6), and that of the Creation (Book 7).

Within the poem's larger structure, there are all sorts of secondary balances which readers will recognize for themselves. The consult in Hell (Book 2) is paralleled by a consult in Heaven (Book 3); Eve is generated from Adam as Sin is generated from Satan; Satan's fall parallels Adam's fall, and the parallel is prolonged into that extended series of falls and recoveries which is the history of mankind. Moloch contrasts with Mammon; the Son's mercy with the Father's justice; Raphael's affability with Michael's severity; and so on, almost without limit.

The structure of the poem is at once massive and delicate; its language is also both rich and strong. Milton's range of classical reference and gift for epithet are undoubtedly staggering at first view, and his long, complexly subordinated sentences are sometimes hard to follow. Footnotes, alas, provide the only proper solution to this problem. But one need not equal, or even follow, all Milton's learning in order to appreciate his poem, especially at a first reading. The poem progresses as through a garden of metaphor and reference which stretches away on either side of one, as far as the eye can see; on a first tour, it is enough to get the general prospect clear, without learning the name of each particular blossom. Ultimately, the reader who is experienced in the poem comes to appreciate its details—epic similes like Leviathan the seabeast (1.201), no less than the one-eyed Arimaspians and the gryphon (2.943); its epithets and circumlocutions like Mulciber (1.740), who is Vulcan, and Amram's son (1.339) who is Moses—without sense of strain or strangeness. Milton himself moved securely through the literatures of half a dozen languages and as many cultures; it is one of the supreme rewards of literary study to be able to follow him with an equivalent security.

Paradise Lost is at once a deeply traditional and a boldly original poem. Milton takes pains to fulfill the traditional prescriptions of the epic form; he gives us love, war, supernatural characters, a descent into Hell, a catalogue of warriors, all the conventional items of epic machinery. Yet no poem in which the climax of the central action is a woman eating a piece of fruit can be a conventional epic. Similarly, Milton himself defined his moral purpose as being to "justify the ways of God to men." This seems no more than conventionally meek. Yet we cannot even think of equating the message of Milton's poem with Pope's injunction to "submit" because "whatever is is right." The way of life which Adam and Eve take up as the poem ends is that of the Christian pilgrimage through this world. Expelled from Eden, our first "grand parents" pick up the burdens of humanity as we know them, sustained by a faith which we also know, and go forth to seek a blessing that we do not know yet. They are to become wayfaring, warfaring Christians, like John Milton; and in this condition, with its weaknesses and strivings and inevitable defeats, there is a glory that no devil can ever understand. Thus Milton strikes, humanly as well as artistically, a grand resolving chord. It is the careful, triumphant balancing and tempering of this conclusion which completes the noble architecture of Milton's poem; and which makes of the end a richer, if not a more exciting, experience than the beginning.

From PARADISE LOST

Book 1

The Argument[1]

    This first book proposes, first in brief, the whole subject, man's disobedience, and the loss thereupon of Paradise, wherein he was placed: then touches the prime cause of his fall, the serpent, or rather Satan in the serpent; who, revolting from God, and drawing to his side many legions of angels, was, by the command of God, driven out of Heaven with all his crew, into the great deep. Which action passed over, the poem hastes into the midst of things;[2] presenting Satan, with his angels, now fallen into Hell—described here not in the center (for heaven and earth may be supposed as yet not made, certainly not yet accursed), but in a place of utter darkness, fitliest called Chaos. Here Satan with his angels lying on the burning lake, thunderstruck and astonished, after a certain space recovers, as from confusion; calls up him who, next in order and dignity, lay by him; they confer of their miserable fall. Satan awakens all his legions, who lay till then in the same manner confounded. They rise: their numbers; array of battle; their chief leaders named, according to the idols known afterwards in Canaan and the countries adjoining. To these Satan directs his speech; comforts them with hope yet of regaining Heaven; but tells them, lastly, of a new world and new kind of creature to be created, according to an ancient prophecy

---

1. *Paradise Lost* appeared originally without any sort of prose aid to the reader; but, since many readers found the poem hard going, the printer asked Milton for some prose "Arguments" or summary explanations of the action in the various books,

and prefixed them to later issues of the poem. We reprint those for the first two books and the ninth.
2. Adapted from Horace's prescription that the epic poet should start *"in medias res."*

or report in Heaven; for that angels were long before this visible creation was the opinion of many ancient fathers.[3] To find out the truth of this prophecy, and what to determine[4] thereon, he refers to a full council. What his associates thence attempt. Pandemonium, the palace of Satan, rises, suddenly built out of the deep: the infernal peers there sit in council.

Of man's first disobedience, and the fruit[5]
Of that forbidden tree whose mortal[6] taste
Brought death into the world, and all our woe,
With loss of Eden, till one greater Man[7]
Restore us, and regain the blissful seat,   5
Sing, Heavenly Muse,[8] that on the secret top
Of Oreb, or of Sinai, didst inspire
That shepherd who first taught the chosen seed
In the beginning how the heavens and earth
Rose out of Chaos: or, if Sion hill[9]   10
Delight thee more, and Siloa's brook that flowed
Fast[1] by the oracle of God, I thence
Invoke thy aid to my adventurous song,
That with no middle flight intends to soar
Above th' Aonian mount,[2] while it pursues   15
Things unattempted yet in prose or rhyme.
And chiefly thou, O Spirit,[3] that dost prefer
Before all temples th' upright heart and pure,
Instruct me, for thou know'st; thou from the first
Wast present, and, with mighty wings outspread,   20
Dovelike sat'st brooding[4] on the vast abyss,
And mad'st it pregnant: what in me is dark
Illumine; what is low, raise and support;
That to the height of this great argument[5]

3. I.e., Church Fathers, the Christian writers of the first few centuries of the church.
4. I.e., what action to take upon their information.
5. Eve's apple, of course; but also all the consequences of eating it.
6. Deadly; but also "to mortals" (i.e., human beings).
7. Christ, the second Adam.
8. In Greek mythology, Urania, Muse of astronomy; but here identified, by references to Oreb and Sinai, with the Holy Spirit of the Bible, which inspired Moses ("that shepherd") to write Genesis and the other four books of the Pentateuch for the instruction of the Jews ("the chosen seed").
9. The hill of Sion and the brook of Siloa are two features of the landscape around Jerusalem likely to appeal to a Muse whose natural haunts are springs and mountains (see Lycidas, line 15). Milton's aim is to show that poetry is everywhere recognized as an inspiration close to that of religion.
1. Close.

2. Helicon, home of the classical Muses; Milton is deliberately courting comparison with Homer and Virgil. In the very line ("Things unattempted yet in prose or rhyme") where he vaunts his originality, Milton is translating a line in the invocation of Ariosto's Orlando Furioso—thus acknowledging, and challenging, another of his predecessors.
3. The Spirit is an impulse or voice of God, by which the Hebrew prophets were directly inspired.
4. A composite of phrases and ideas from Genesis 1.2 ("And the earth was without form, and void; and darkness was upon the face of the deep. And the Spirit of God moved upon the face of the waters"); Matthew 3.16 ("and he saw the Spirit of God descending like a dove, and lighting upon him"); and Luke 3.22 ("and the Holy Ghost descended in a bodily shape like a dove upon him"). Milton's mind as he wrote was impregnated with expressions from the King James Bible, only a few of which can be indicated in the notes.
5. Theme.

I may assert Eternal Providence,   25
And justify the ways of God to men.
   Say first (for Heaven hides nothing from thy view,
Nor the deep tract of Hell), say first what cause
Moved our grand[6] parents, in that happy state,
Favored of Heaven so highly, to fall off   30
From their Creator, and transgress his will
For[7] one restraint, lords of the world besides?[8]
Who first seduced them to that foul revolt?
   Th' infernal serpent; he it was, whose guile,
Stirred up with envy and revenge, deceived   35
The mother of mankind, what time[9] his pride
Had cast him out from Heaven, with all his host
Of rebel angels, by whose aid aspiring
To set himself in glory above his peers,[1]
He trusted to have equaled the Most High,   40
If he opposed; and with ambitious aim
Against the throne and monarchy of God
Raised impious war in Heaven and battle proud,
With vain attempt. Him the Almighty Power
Hurled headlong flaming from th' ethereal sky   45
With hideous ruin and combustion down
To bottomless perdition, there to dwell
In adamantine chains and penal fire,
Who durst defy th' Omnipotent to arms.
   Nine times the space that measures day and night   50
To mortal men, he with his horrid crew
Lay vanquished, rolling in the fiery gulf
Confounded though immortal. But his doom
Reserved him to more wrath; for now the thought
Both of lost happiness and lasting pain   55
Torments him; round he throws his baleful[2] eyes,
That witnessed huge affliction and dismay,
Mixed with obdùrate pride and steadfast hate.
At once, as far as angels ken,[3] he views
The dismal situation waste and wild: 60
A dungeon horrible, on all sides round
As one great furnace flamed; yet from those flames
No light,[4] but rather darkness visible
Served only to discover sights of woe,
Regions of sorrow, doleful shades, where peace   65

---

6. First in importance; by implication, in time also.
7. Because of.
8. In every other respect.
9. I.e., at the time when.
1. His equals. The sentence mimics Satan's action, piling clause loosely upon clause, and building ever higher, till "with vain attempt" (line 44) brings the whole structure crashing down. It is a dramatic entry

into "the midst of things," where epics begin. Book 6 will recount more largely the war in Heaven, in the full narrative form which Aeneas used to tell Dido of the last days of Troy (*Aeneid* 2).
2. Malignant, as well as suffering.
3. As far as angels can see.
4. Omitting the verb conveys abruptly the paradox: fire-without-light.

And rest can never dwell, hope never comes
That comes to all,[5] but torture without end
Still urges,[6] and a fiery deluge, fed
With ever-burning sulphur unconsumed:
Such place Eternal Justice had prepared   70
For those rebellious; here their prison ordained
In utter[7] darkness and their portion set
As far removed from God and light of Heaven
As from the center[8] thrice to th' utmost pole.
O how unlike the place from whence they fell!   75
There the companions of his fall, o'erwhelmed
With floods and whirlwinds of tempestuous fire,
He soon discerns; and, weltering by his side,
One next himself in power, and next in crime,
Long after known in Palestine, and named   80
Beëlzebub.[9] To whom th' arch-enemy,
And thence in Heaven called Satan,[1] with bold words
Breaking the horrid silence thus began:
    "If thou beëst he—but O how fallen! how changed
From him who in the happy realms of light   85
Clothed with transcendent brightness didst outshine
Myriads, though bright! if he whom mutual league,
United thoughts and counsels, equal hope
And hazard in the glorious enterprise,
Joined with me once, now misery hath joined   90
In equal ruin; into what pit thou seest[2]
From what height fallen, so much the stronger proved
He with his thunder:[3] and till then who knew
The force of those dire arms? Yet not for those,
Nor what the potent Victor in his rage   95
Can else inflict, do I repent or change,
Though changed in outward luster, that fixed mind
And high disdain, from sense of injured merit,
That with the Mightiest raised me to contend,
And to the fierce contention brought along   100
Innumerable force of spirits armed,
That durst dislike his reign, and me preferring,

5. The phrase echoes an expression in Dante ("All hope abandon, ye who enter here"), but Milton expresses it as a logical absurdity. Hope comes to "all" but not to Helldwellers; they are not included in "all."
6. Afflicts.
7. "Complete" but also "outer."
8. The earth. Milton makes use in *Paradise Lost* of two images of the cosmos: (1) the earth is the center of the *created* (Ptolemaic) cosmos of ten concentric spheres; but (2) the earth and the whole created cosmos are a mere appendage, hanging from Heaven by a golden chain, in the larger, aboriginal, and less shapely cosmos. In the present passage, the fall from Heaven to Hell (through the aboriginal universe) is described as thrice as far as

the distance (in the created universe) from the center (earth) to the outermost sphere.
9. A Phoenician deity, or Baal (the name means "Lord of flies"); traditionally, a prince of devils and enemy of Jehovah. The Phoenician Baal, a sun god, had many aspects and so many names; most Baals were nature deities. But in the poem's time scheme all this lies in the future; Beelzebub's angelic name, whatever it was, has been erased from the Book of Life, and as he has not yet got another one, he must be called by the name he will have later on.
1. In Hebrew, the name means "Adversary."
2. Satan's syntax, like that of a man recovering from a stunning blow, is not of the clearest.
3. God with his thunderbolts.

His utmost power with adverse power opposed
In dubious battle on the plains of Heaven,
And shook his throne. What though the field be lost?   105
All is not lost: the unconquerable will,
And study[4] of revenge, immortal hate,
And courage never to submit or yield:
And what is else not to be overcome?[5]
That glory never shall his wrath or might   110
Extort from me. To bow and sue for grace
With suppliant knee, and deify his power[6]
Who from the terror of this arm so late
Doubted[7] his empire—that were low indeed;
That were an ignominy and shame beneath   115
This downfall; since, by fate, the strength of gods[8]
And this empyreal substance cannot fail;
Since, through experience of this great event,
In arms not worse, in foresight much advanced,
We may with more successful hope resolve   120
To wage by force or guile eternal war,
Irreconcilable to our grand Foe,
Who now triùmphs, and in th' excess of joy
Sole reigning holds the tyranny[9] of Heaven."
    So spake th' apostate angel, though in pain,   125
Vaunting aloud, but racked with deep despair;
And him thus answered soon his bold compeer:[1]
    "O prince, O chief of many thronèd powers,
That led th' embattled seraphim[2] to war
Under thy conduct, and in dreadful deeds   130
Fearless, endangered Heaven's perpetual King,
And put to proof his high supremacy,
Whether upheld by strength, or chance, or fate![3]
Too well I see and rue the dire event[4]
That with sad overthrow and foul defeat   135
Hath lost us Heaven, and all this mighty host
In horrible destruction laid thus low,
As far as gods and heavenly essences
Can perish: for the mind and spirit remains

---

4. Pursuit.

5. I.e., what else does it mean not to be beaten? "That glory" is the glory of hearing Satan confess himself overcome.

6. I.e., deify the power of him who. Milton sometimes writes English as if it were an inflected language.

7. Feared for. In the next line, "ignominy" is pronounced "ignomy."

8. The essence of Satan's fault is his claim to the position of a god, subject to fate but to nothing else. His substance is "empyreal" (heavenly, from the empyrean), and cannot be destroyed; but, as he learns in the poem, it can be confounded by God's greater power and weakened by its own cor-

ruption and self-contradictions. "Fail": cease to exist.

9. The accusation is bold, but one of the aims of the poem is to show that Satan is a tyrant and God is not.

1. Comrade and equal

2. According to tradition, there were nine orders of angels—seraphim, cherubim, thrones, dominions, virtues, powers, principalities, archangels, and angels; but Milton does not use these systematic categories systematically.

3. The devils can conceive of any reason for God's continuing rule, except goodness and justice.

4. Outcome.

Invincible, and vigor soon returns,   140
Though all our glory extinct, and happy state
Here swallowed up in endless misery.
But what if he our Conqueror (whom I now
Of force[5] believe almighty, since no less
Than such could have o'erpowered such force as ours)   145
Have left us this our spirit and strength entire,
Strongly to suffer and support our pains,
That we may so suffice[6] his vengeful ire,
Or do him mightier service as his thralls
By right of war, whate'er his business be,   150
Here in the heart of Hell to work in fire,
Or do his errands in the gloomy deep?
What can it then avail though yet we feel
Strength undiminished, or eternal being
To undergo eternal punishment?"   155
    Whereto with speedy words th' arch-fiend[7] replied:
"Fallen cherub, to be weak is miserable,
Doing or suffering:[8] but of this be sure,
To do aught good never will be our task,
But ever to do ill our sole delight,   160
As being the contrary to his high will
Whom we resist. If then his providence
Out of our evil seek to bring forth good,
Our labor must be to pervert that end,
And out of good still to find means of evil;   165
Which ofttimes may succeed, so as perhaps
Shall grieve him, if I fail not,[9] and disturb
His inmost counsels from their destined aim.
But see! the angry Victor hath recalled
His ministers of vengeance and pursuit   170
Back to the gates of Heaven; the sulphurous hail,
Shot after us in storm, o'erblown hath laid
The fiery surge that from the precipice
Of Heaven received us falling; and the thunder,
Winged with red lightning and impetuous rage,   175
Perhaps hath spent his shafts, and ceases now
To bellow through the vast and boundless deep.
Let us not slip[1] th' occasion, whether scorn
Or satiate fury yield it from our Foe.
Seest thou yon dreary plain, forlorn and wild,   180
The seat of desolation, void of light,
Save what the glimmering of these livid flames
Casts pale and dreadful? Thither let us tend

---

5. Perforce, necessarily.
6. Satisfy.
7. A fiend is an enemy, one who hates; the word
is an antonym of "friend."

8. Whether one is active or passive.
9. "Unless I'm mistaken" (direct from the Latin,
nisi fallor).
1. I.e., let slip.

From off the tossing of these fiery waves;
There rest, if any rest can harbor there;   185
And reassembling our afflicted powers,[2]
Consult how we may henceforth most offend
Our enemy, our own loss how repair,
How overcome this dire calamity,
What reinforcement we may gain from hope,   190
If not, what resolution from despair."[3]
    Thus Satan talking to his nearest mate
With head uplift above the wave, and eyes
That sparkling blazed; his other parts besides
Prone on the flood, extended long and large   195
Lay floating many a rood,[4] in bulk as huge
As whom[5] the fables name of monstrous size,
Titanian or Earth-born, that warred on Jove,
Briareos or Typhon,[6] whom the den
By ancient Tarsus held, or that sea beast   200
Leviathan,[7] which God of all his works
Created hugest that swim th' ocean-stream.
Him, haply, slumbering on the Norway foam,
The pilot of some small night-foundered[8] skiff,
Deeming some island, oft, as seamen tell,   205
With fixèd anchor in his scaly rind
Moors by his side under the lee, while night
Invests[9] the sea, and wishèd morn delays:
So stretched out huge in length the arch-fiend lay,
Chained on the burning lake; nor ever thence   210
Had risen or heaved his head, but that the will
And high permission of all ruling Heaven
Left him at large to his own dark designs,
That with reiterated crimes he might
Heap on himself damnation, while he sought   215
Evil to others, and enraged might see
How all his malice served but to bring forth
Infinite goodness, grace, and mercy shown
On man by him seduced, but on himself
Treble confusion, wrath, and vengeance poured.   220
    Forthwith upright he rears from off the pool

2. Stricken armies.
3. Of the last nine lines of Satan's speech, no fewer than five rhyme. Milton may have felt the need for something like the couplet with which blank-verse dramatists cut off their scenes.
4. An old unit of measure, between six and eight yards.
5. I.e., as those whom.
6. Both the Titans, led by Briareos, and the earth-born Giants, represented by Typhon (who lived in Cilicia near Tarsus), fought with Jove. Briareos was said to have a hundred hands, and Typhon a hundred heads; and both were said, by different

authors, to have been punished for their rebellion (like Satan for his) by being thrown into the underworld. Briareos and Typhon are still heard grumbling from time to time under Mt. Etna.
7. The great sea monster of Isaiah 27.1 or Job 41; for Milton and us, simply a whale, but scaly (line 206).
8. Overtaken by darkness.
9. Wraps, covers. The story of sailors mooring to whales was an old one, but the reference to Norway suggests that Milton was thinking of a 16th-century version by Olaus Magnus, the Swedish historian.

His mighty stature; on each hand the flames
Driven backward slope their pointing spires,[1] and rolled
In billows, leave i' th' midst a horrid[2] vale.
Then with expanded wings he steers his flight   225
Aloft, incumbent on[3] the dusky air,
That felt unusual weight; till on dry land
He lights, if it were land that ever burned
With solid, as the lake with liquid fire,
And such appeared in hue; as when the force   230
Of subterranean wind transports a hill
Torn from Pelorus[4] or the shattered side
Of thundering Etna, whose combustible
And fuelèd entrails thence conceiving fire,
Sublimed[5] with mineral fury, aid the winds,   235
And leave a singèd bottom all involved[6]
With stench and smoke: such resting found the sole
Of unblest feet. Him followed his next mate,
Both glorying to have 'scaped the Stygian[7] flood
As gods, and by their own recovered strength,   240
Not by the sufferance[8] of supernal power.
     "Is this the region, this the soil, the clime,"
Said then the lost archangel, "this the seat
That we must change for Heaven? this mournful gloom
For that celestial light? Be it so, since he   245
Who now is sovereign can dispose and bid
What shall be right: farthest from him is best,
Whom reason hath equaled, force hath made supreme
Above his equals.[9] Farewell, happy fields,
Where joy forever dwells! Hail, horrors! hail,   250
Infernal world! and thou, profoundest Hell,
Receive thy new possessor, one who brings
A mind not to be changed by place or time.
The mind is its own place, and in itself
Can make a Heaven of Hell, a Hell of Heaven.[1]   255
What matter where, if I be still the same,
And what I should be, all but less[2] than he
Whom thunder hath made greater? Here at least
We shall be free; th' Almighty hath not built
Here for his envy, will not drive us hence.   260

---

1. Points of flame.
2. Not simply "ghastly," but in the Latin sense, "bristling."
3. Resting upon.
4. Pelorus and Etna are volcanic mountains in Sicily, which Milton pictures as exploding under pressure of underground winds.
5. Vaporized.
6. Wrapped.
7. Of the river Styx, i.e., demonic, hellish.
8. Permission.
9. Satan likes to think that by "reason" he is God's equal; this only shows how far he is from "right reason," that is, reason directed and corrected by a proper sense of religious values.

1. Satan's heroic resolution here, where he fancies he can convert Hell into a kind of plastic Heaven, takes another turn when in Book 4 we find him bringing the Hell of his own mind into Paradise.
2. Second only to. The expression "all but less than" telescopes "all but equal to" and "only less than."

Here we may reign secure; and in my choice
To reign is worth ambition, though in Hell:
Better to reign in Hell than serve in Heaven.
But wherefore let we then our faithful friends,
Th' associates and copartners of our loss,   265
Lie thus astonished[3] on th' oblivious pool,
And call them not to share with us their part
In this unhappy mansion, or once more
With rallied arms to try what may be yet
Regained in Heaven, or what more lost in Hell?"   270
   So Satan spake: and him Beëlzebub
Thus answered: "Leader of those armies bright,
Which but th' Omnipotent none could have foiled!
If once they hear that voice, their liveliest pledge
Of hope in fears and dangers, heard so oft   275
In worst extremes, and on the perilous edge[4]
Of battle when it raged, in all assaults
Their surest signal, they will soon resume
New courage and revive, though now they lie
Groveling and prostrate on yon lake of fire,   280
As we erewhile, astounded and amazed;
No wonder, fallen such a pernicious height!"
   He scarce had ceased when the superior fiend
Was moving toward the shore; his ponderous shield,
Ethereal temper,[5] massy, large, and round,   285
Behind him cast; the broad circumference
Hung on his shoulders like the moon, whose orb
Through optic glass the Tuscan artist[6] views
At evening, from the top of Fesolè,
Or in Valdarno, to descry new lands,   290
Rivers, or mountains in her spotty globe.
His spear, to equal which the tallest pine
Hewn on Norwegian hills, to be the mast
Of some great admiral,[7] were but a wand,
He walked with, to support uneasy steps   295
Over the burning marl,[8] not like those steps
On Heaven's azure; and the torrid clime
Smote on him sore besides, vaulted with fire.
Nathless[9] he so endured, till on the beach
Of that inflamèd[1] sea he stood, and called   300
His legions, angel forms, who lay entranced,
Thick as autumnal leaves that strow the brooks

---

3. Stunned. The epithet "oblivious" is transferred from the fallen angels to the pool in which they have fallen.
4. Not the fringe of battle but the front line (Latin *acies*).
5. Tempered in celestial fire.
6. Galileo, who looked through a telescope ("optic glass") from the hill town of Fiesole outside Flor-

ence in the Val d'Arno, is the only contemporary mentioned by Milton in *Paradise Lost*.
7. Not the naval commander, but his flagship, usually the biggest of the fleet.
8. Soil.
9. A compressed, archaic form of "nonetheless."
1. Flaming, of course, but also fevered.

In Vallombrosa,[2] where th' Etrurian shades
High over-arched embower;[3] or scattered sedge
Afloat, when with fierce winds Orion armed   305
Hath vexed the Red-Sea coast, whose waves o'erthrew
Busiris and his Memphian chivalry,
While with perfidious hatred they pursued
The sojourners of Goshen, who beheld
From the safe shore their floating carcasses   310
And broken chariot wheels;[4] so thick bestrown,
Abject and lost, lay these, covering the flood,
Under amazement of their hideous change.
He called so loud that all the hollow deep
Of Hell resounded: "Princes, potentates,   315
Warriors, the flower of Heaven, once yours, now lost,
If such astonishment as this can seize
Eternal spirits! or have ye chosen this place
After the toil of battle to repose
Your wearied virtue,[5] for the ease you find   320
To slumber here, as in the vales of Heaven?
Or in this abject posture have ye sworn
To adore the Conqueror, who now beholds
Cherub and seraph rolling in the flood
With scattered arms and ensigns,[6] till anon   325
His swift pursuers from Heaven-gates discern
Th' advantage, and descending tread us down
Thus drooping, or with linkèd thunderbolts
Transfix us to the bottom of this gulf?
Awake, arise, or be forever fallen!"   330
    They heard, and were abashed, and up they sprung
Upon the wing, as when men wont to watch
On duty, sleeping found by whom they dread,
Rouse and bestir themselves ere well awake.
Nor did they not perceive[7] the evil plight   335
In which they were, or the fierce pains not feel;
Yet to their general's voice they soon obeyed
Innumerable. As when the potent rod
Of Amram's son[8] in Egypt's evil day
Waved round the coast, up called a pitchy cloud   340

2. "Shady Valley," high in the Apennines about
twenty miles from Florence, "Etruria" is Etruscan
land, i.e., Tuscany.
3. I.e., form bowers by enclosing space.
4. Orion is a constellation, whose rising near sunset in late summer and autumn was associated with
storms; in the Red Sea, where sedge grows thick,
these storms result in much floating seaweed. This
reminds Milton of how the sea must have looked
after the Israelites ("sojourners of Goshen") passed
through it while escaping from Egypt, when it was
covered with the littered corpses of Pharaoh
("Busiris") and his pursuing horsemen ("Mem-

phian chivalry").
5. Strength, but Satan's sarcasm makes use of the
other connotation too.
6. Standards, battle flags.
7. The double negatives make a positive: they did
indeed perceive both plight and pains. (Latin, *neque
non*, "nor . . . not," "and.")
8. Moses, who drew down a plague of locusts on
Egypt (Exodus 10.12–15). Milton's learned locution is designed to keep Moses out of Hell, as well
as from appearing too often in the poem (compare
above, 307–11).

Of locusts, warping[9] on the eastern wind,
That o'er the realm of impious Pharaoh hung
Like night, and darkened all the land of Nile;
So numberless were those bad angels seen
Hovering on wing under the cope[1] of Hell   345
'Twixt upper, nether, and surrounding fires;
Till, as a signal given, th' uplifted spear
Of their great sultan[2] waving to direct
Their course, in even balance down they light
On the firm brimstone, and fill all the plain;   350
A multitude like which the populous North[3]
Poured never from her frozen loins to pass
Rhene or the Danaw, when her barbarous sons
Came like a deluge on the South, and spread
Beneath Gibraltar to the Libyan sands.   355
    Forthwith from every squadron and each band
The heads and leaders thither haste where stood
Their great commander; godlike shapes and forms
Excelling human; princely dignities,
And powers that erst in Heaven sat on thrones,   360
Though of their names in Heavenly records now
Be no memorial, blotted out and rased[4]
By their rebellion from the Books of Life.
Nor had they yet among the sons of Eve
Got them new names, till, wandering o'er the earth,   365
Through God's high sufferance for the trial of man,
By falsities and lies the greatest part
Of mankind they corrupted to forsake
God their Creator, and th' invisible
Glory of him that made them to transform   370
Oft to the image of a brute, adorned
With gay religions[5] full of pomp and gold,
And devils to adore for deities:
Then were they known to men by various names,
And various idols through the heathen world.   375
    Say, Muse, their names then known, who first, who last,[6]
Roused from the slumber on that fiery couch,
At their great emperor's call, as next in worth
Came singly[7] where he stood on the bare strand,
While the promiscuous crowd stood yet aloof.   380

9. Floating.
1. Roof.
2. A first use of the image, which will be reinforced later, of Satan as an Oriental despot.
3. The barbarian invasions of falling Rome began
with crossings of the Rhine ("Rhene") and Danube ("Danaw") Rivers, and spread across Spain,
via Gibraltar, to North Africa.
4. Erased. See above, line 81. Though reluctant

to state the view strongly, Milton believed all the
pagan deities had been devils in disguise.
5. Ceremonies.
6. The catalogue of gods here is an epic convention; Homer catalogues ships, Virgil warriors.
7. One at a time. The diabolical aristocrats rally
round Satan, while the "promiscuous crowd," the
vulgar devils, stand apart.

The chief were those who, from the pit of Hell
Roaming to seek their prey on Earth, durst fix
Their seats, long after, next the seat of God,[8]
Their altars by his altar, gods adored
Among the nations round, and durst abide   385
Jehovah thundering out of Sion, throned
Between the cherubim; yea, often placed
Within his sanctuary itself their shrines,
Abominations; and with cursèd things
His holy rites and solemn feasts profaned,   390
And with their darkness durst affront his light.
First Moloch,[9] horrid king, besmeared with blood
Of human sacrifice, and parents' tears;
Though, for the noise of drums and timbrels loud,
Their children's cries unheard, that passed through fire   395
To his grim idol. Him the Ammonite[1]
Worshiped in Rabba and her watery plain,
In Argob and in Basan, to the stream
Of utmost Arnon. Nor content with such
Audacious neighborhood, the wisest heart   400
Of Solomon he led by fraud to build
His temple right against the temple of God
On that opprobrious hill,[2] and made his grove
The pleasant valley of Hinnom, Tophet thence
And black Gehenna called, the type of Hell.   405
Next Chemos,[3] th' obscene dread of Moab's sons,
From Aroar to Nebo and the wild
Of southmost Abarim; in Hesebon
And Horonaim, Seon's realm, beyond
The flowery dale of Sibma clad with vines,   410
And Elealè to th' asphaltic pool:
Peor[4] his other name, when he enticed
Israel in Sittim, on their march from Nile,
To do him wanton rites, which cost them woe.
Yet thence his lustful orgies he enlarged   415
Even to that hill of scandal, by the grove
Of Moloch homicide,[5] lust hard by hate,

8. The first group of devils come from the Near East, close neighbors and intimate enemies of Jehovah at Jerusalem.
9. A sun god, sometimes represented as a roaring bull or with a calf's head, within whose brazen image living children might be burned as sacrifices (for a lurid fictional account, see Flaubert's *Salammbô*). "Timbrels": tambourines.
1. The Ammonites lived east of the Jordan, and Milton uses uncouth place names ("Rabba," "Argob," "Basan," "utmost Arnon") to suggest wildness.
2. The rites of Moloch on "that opprobrious hill" (the Mount of Olives) right opposite the Jewish temple, and in the valley of Hinnom, so polluted these places that they were turned into the refuse

dump of Jerusalem. Thus they became "types" (analogies) of Hell, under the names "Tophet" and "Gehenna."
3. Chemos or Chemosh was another name for Moloch, used in Moab, a nation lying south and east of the Dead Sea ("th' asphaltic pool"). Many of the geographical names clustered here come from Isaiah 15–16.
4. For the story of how Peor seduced "Israel in Sittim," see Numbers 25.
5. An epithet was often joined to a god's name as a surname (e.g., *Jupiter Tonans*, Jove the Thunderer); Milton's epithet involves almost a parody, Moloch the Mankiller. The story of "good Josiah" and his campaign against pagan gods is told in 2 Kings 23 and in 2 Chronicles 34.

Till good Josiah drove them thence to Hell.
With these came they who, from the bordering flood
Of old Euphrates to the brook that parts   420
Egypt from Syrian ground,[6] had general names
Of Baalim and Ashtaroth, those male,
These feminine.[7] For spirits when they please
Can either sex assume, or both; so soft
And uncompounded is their essence pure,   425
Not tied or manacled with joint or limb,
Nor founded on the brittle strength of bones,
Like cumbrous flesh; but in what shape they choose,
Dilated or condensed, bright or obscure,
Can execute their airy purposes,   430
And works of love or enmity fulfill.
For those the race of Israel oft forsook
Their Living Strength,[8] and unfrequented left
His righteous altar, bowing lowly down
To bestial gods; for which their heads as low   435
Bowed down in battle, sunk before the spear
Of despicable foes. With these in troop
Came Astoreth, whom the Phoenicians called
Astartè, queen of heaven, with crescent horns;
To whose bright image nightly by the moon   440
Sidonian virgins[9] paid their vows and songs;
In Sion also not unsung, where stood
Her temple on th' offensive mountain,[1] built
By that uxorious king[2] whose heart, though large,
Beguiled by fair idolatresses, fell   445
To idols foul. Thammuz[3] came next behind,
Whose annual wound in Lebanon allured
The Syrian damsels to lament his fate
In amorous ditties all a summer's day,
While smooth Adonis[4] from his native rock   450
Ran purple to the sea, supposed with blood
Of Thammuz yearly wounded: the love-tale
Infected Sion's daughters with like heat,
Whose wanton passions in the sacred porch
Ezekiel[5] saw, when, by the vision led,   455
His eye surveyed the dark idolatries

---

6. Palestine lies between the Euphrates and "the
brook Besor" (1 Samuel 30.10).
7. I.e., plural forms, masculine and feminine
respectively, for Baal and Astarte. As Baals were
aspects of the sun god, Astartes (Ishtars) were manifestations of the moon goddess.
8. The Jews lost battles, Milton says, when they
neglected Jehovah.
9. Sidon and Tyre were the chief cities of Phoeni-
cia.
1. The Mount of Olives again (see above, lines
403 and 416).

2. Solomon, who "loved many strange women"
(2 Kings 11.1–8).
3. A Syrian god, who was supposed to have been
killed by a boar in Lebanon; annual festivals
mourned his death and celebrated his revival, imitating the cycle of vegetable life. In his Greek form
he was Adonis, god of the solar year.
4. A Lebanese river, named after the deity because
every spring it turned blood-red with sedimentary
mud.
5. Ezekiel complained that the Jewish women of
his day were worshiping Thammuz (Ezekiel 8.14).

Of alienated Judah. Next came one
Who mourned in earnest, when the captive ark
Maimed his brute image, head and hands lopped off
In his own temple, on the grunsel-edge,[6]   460
Where he fell flat, and shamed his worshipers:
Dagon his name, sea monster, upward man
And downward fish; yet had his temple high
Reared in Azotus, dreaded through the coast
Of Palestine, in Gath and Ascalon,   465
And Accaron and Gaza's frontier bounds.[7]
Him followed Rimmon, whose delightful seat
Was fair Damascus, on the fertile banks
Of Abbana and Pharphar, lucid streams.
He also 'gainst the house of God was bold: 470
A leper once he lost, and gained a king,
Ahaz,[8] his sottish conqueror, whom he drew
God's altar to disparage and displace
For one of Syrian mode, whereon to burn
His odious offerings, and adore the gods   475
Whom he had vanquished. After these appeared
A crew who, under names of old renown,
Osiris, Isis, Orus,[9] and their train,
With monstrous shapes[1] and sorceries abused
Fanatic Egypt and her priests to seek   480
Their wandering gods disguised in brutish forms
Rather than human. Nor did Israel 'scape
Th' infection, when their borrowed gold composed
The calf in Oreb;[2] and the rebel king
Doubled that sin in Bethel and in Dan,   485
Likening his Maker to the grazèd ox[3]—
Jehovah, who in one night when he passed
From Egypt marching, equaled[4] with one stroke
Both her first-born and all her bleating gods.
Belial[5] came last; than whom a spirit more lewd   490
Fell not from Heaven, or more gross to love
Vice for itself. To him no temple stood

---

6. When the Philistines stole the ark of God, they
tried to store it in the temple of their sea god, Dagon;
but in the morning the mutilated statue of Dagon
was found on the threshold ("grunsel-edge"). See
1 Samuel 5.1–5.
7. Milton names the five chief cities of the Philistines as places where Dagon was worshiped.
8. A Syrian general, Naaman, was cured of leprosy and converted from worship of Rimmon by
the waters of the Jordan (2 Kings 5). King Ahaz,
on the other hand, an Israelite monarch who conquered Damascus, was converted there to worship
of Rimmon (2 Kings 16).
9. The second group of devils includes those from
Egypt, driven in terror from heaven by the revolt
of the giants (so Ovid tells us in *Metamorphoses* 5),
and forced to wander through Egypt in animal dis-

guises.
1. Monstrous, because often represented with
animals' heads.
2. Aaron made a golden calf in the wilderness
(Exodus 32); Milton thought it an idol of the Egyptian god Apis because the gold of which it was made
had been borrowed from the Egyptians.
3. Jeroboam, "the rebel king," doubled Aaron's
sin by making *two* golden calves (1 Kings 12.28–
30).
4. Leveled. See Exodus 12.12 for Jehovah's vengeance on the first-born of Egypt and their gods.
5. Belial was never worshiped as a god; his name
was originally an abstract noun meaning "wickedness"; hence used mainly in set phrases like "sons
of Belial." He comes last, because weak and slothful.

Or altar smoked; yet who more oft than he
In temples and at altars, when the priest
Turns atheist, as did Eli's sons,[6] who filled   495
With lust and violence the house of God?
In courts and palaces he also reigns,
And in luxurious cities, where the noise
Of riot ascends above their loftiest towers,
And injury and outrage; and when night   500
Darkens the streets, then wander forth the sons
Of Belial, flown[7] with insolence and wine.
Witness the streets of Sodom,[8] and that night
In Gibeah, when the hospitable door
Exposed a matron, to avoid worse rape.   505
  These were the prime in order and in might;
The rest were long to tell, though far renowned,
Th' Ionian gods, of Javan's issue held
Gods, yet confessed later than Heaven and Earth,
Their boasted parents;[9] Titan, Heaven's first-born,   510
With his enormous brood, and birthright seized
By younger Saturn; he from mightier Jove,
His own and Rhea's son, like measure found;
So Jove usurping reigned.[1] These, first in Crete
And Ida known, thence on the snowy top   515
Of cold Olympus ruled the middle air,
Their highest heaven; or on the Delphian cliff,
Or in Dodona, and through all the bounds
Of Doric land; or who with Saturn old
Fled over Adria to th' Hesperian fields,   520
And o'er the Celtic roamed the utmost isles.
  All these and more came flocking; but with looks
Downcast and damp,[2] yet such wherein appeared
Obscure some glimpse of joy, to have found their chief
Not in despair, to have found themselves not lost   525
In loss itself; which on his countenance cast
Like doubtful hue.[3] But he, his wonted pride
Soon recollecting, with high words that bore

6. The misdeeds of Eli's sons, and the epithet "sons of Belial" applied to them, will be found in 1 Samuel 2.12–17.
7. Flushed. Puritans liked to call their enemies sons of Belial; this passage, with its present tense verbs, may reflect Milton's view of Restoration London.
8. In Sodom and Gibeah ancient outrages befell, described in Genesis 19 and Judges 19.
9. The Titans were regarded as gods by the Greeks ("Javan's issue," i.e., offspring of Javan, son of Japhet, son of Noah), but were admittedly created later than Heaven and Earth (Uranus and Ge), whose children they were said to be. Milton's Christian humanism naturally led him, wherever possible, to use classic myths as analogues (parallels or reflections) of Christian history.

1. Cronos or Saturn, one of the Titans, deposed his elder brother, married his sister Rhea, and ruled until Zeus, who had been reared in secret on Mt. Ida in Crete, overthrew his own father and came to rule on Mt. Olympus. The Olympic gods, headed by Zeus, were also worshiped in Delphi, Dodona, and throughout the "Doric (Grecian) land." Meanwhile Saturn (lines 519–21), after his downfall, fled across the Adriatic Sea ("Adria") to Italy ("th' Hesperian fields"), crossed "the Celtic" (fields) of France, and finally reached Britain ("the utmost isles").
2. Depressed.
3. Their comfort is the chilly one of finding themselves not completely annihilated; and at first it is reflected in Satan's face.

Semblance of worth, not substance, gently raised
Their fainting courage, and dispelled their fears: 530
Then straight commands that at the warlike sound
Of trumpets loud and clarions[4] be upreared
His mighty standard. That proud honor claimed
Azazel[5] as his right, a cherub tall:
Who forthwith from the glittering staff unfurled   535
Th' imperial ensign; which, full high advanced,
Shone like a meteor streaming to the wind,
With gems and golden luster rich emblazed,
Seraphic arms and trophies; all the while
Sonorous metal[6] blowing martial sounds: 540
At which the universal host up sent
A shout that tore Hell's concave,[7] and beyond
Frighted the reign of Chaos and old Night.[8]
All in a moment through the gloom were seen
Ten thousand banners rise into the air,   545
With orient[9] colors waving: with them rose
A forest huge of spears; and thronging helms
Appeared, and serried[1] shields in thick array
Of depth immeasurable. Anon they move
In perfect phalanx to the Dorian[2] mood   550
Of flutes and soft recorders; such as raised
To height of noblest temper heroes old
Arming to battle, and instead of rage
Deliberate valor breathed, firm and unmoved
With dread of death to flight or foul retreat;   555
Nor wanting power to mitigate and swage[3]
With solemn touches troubled thoughts, and chase
Anguish and doubt and fear and sorrow and pain
From mortal or immortal minds. Thus they,
Breathing united force with fixèd thought,   560
Moved on in silence to soft pipes that charmed
Their painful steps o'er the burnt soil. And now
Advanced in view they stand, a horrid[4] front
Of dreadful length and dazzling arms, in guise
Of warriors old with ordered spear and shield,   565
Awaiting what command their mighty chief
Had to impose. He through the armèd files
Darts his experienced eye, and soon traverse[5]
The whole battalion views, their order due,

---

4. Small, shrill, treble trumpets.
5. Among the historians of angels and devils, a traditional diabolic leader.
6. Reverberant trumpets.
7. Vault.
8. Disorder and darkness, the first materials of the cosmos, still maintain a kingdom between Heaven and Hell.
9. Lustrous, like the colors of a pearl.

1. Locked together.
2. Severe, simple. The shrill trumpet, which first roused the courage of the devils, now gives way to firm, martial tones, played on instruments of softer timbre, in the Spartan manner.
3. Assuage.
4. Bristling.
5. Across. Satan glances, like a reviewing officer, down the files and columns.

Their visages and stature as of gods;   570
Their number last he sums. And now his heart
Distends with pride, and hardening in his strength
Glories: for never, since created man,[6]
Met such embodied force as named with these
Could merit more than that small infantry   575
Warred on by cranes:[7] though all the giant brood
Of Phlegra with th' heroic race were joined
That fought at Thebes and Ilium, on each side
Mixed with auxiliar[8] gods; and what resounds
In fable or romance of Uther's son,   580
Begirt with British and Armoric knights;
And all who since, baptized or infidel,
Jousted in Aspramont or Montalban,
Damasco, or Marocco, or Trebisond;
Or whom Biserta sent from Afric shore   585
When Charlemagne with all his peerage fell
By Fontarabbia.[9] Thus far these beyond
Compare of mortal prowess, yet observed[1]
Their dread commander. He above the rest
In shape and gesture proudly eminent   590
Stood like a tower. His form had yet not lost
All her[2] original brightness, nor appeared
Less than archangel ruined, and th' excess
Of glory obscured: as when the sun new-risen
Looks through the horizontal[3] misty air   595
Shorn of his beams, or from behind the moon
In dim eclipse[4] disastrous twilight sheds
On half the nations, and with fear of change
Perplexes monarchs. Darkened so, yet shone
Above them all th' archangel; but his face   600
Deep scars of thunder had intrenched, and care
Sat on his faded cheek, but under brows
Of dauntless courage, and considerate[5] pride
Waiting revenge. Cruel his eye, but cast
Signs of remorse and passion[6] to behold   605
The fellows of his crime, the followers rather

6. I.e., since the creation of man.
7. The pygmies had periodic fights with the cranes, which (according to Pliny) they won by riding to battle on pigs and goats. This would make them cavalry; but Milton wanted the pun on "infants." His idea is that, compared with the devils, all other armies that ever were would look puny.
8. Allied.
9. The Giants of Greek mythology were born at Phlegra (line 577); Milton imagines them joined with the Seven who fought against Thebes, and the whole Greek host that besieged Troy ("Ilium"), plus the various gods who helped on both sides. He even adds the knights "British or Armoric" (from Brittany) who fought with King Arthur ("Uther's

son"), and includes a list of proper names taken from the cycles of romance and suggesting vast, remote armies. Fontarabbia, the best known, was reputed to be the scene of Roland's last stand in the *Chanson de Roland*; Milton thus mingles the fall of Charlemagne with that of his best-known knight.
1. Obeyed.
2. *Forma*, in Latin, is feminine; hence "her."
3. The rays of the sun as it first rises are almost horizontal.
4. Time of ill omen. "Disastrous": threatening disaster.
5. Thoughtful, conscious.
6. Compassion.

(Far other once beheld in bliss), condemned
Forever now to have their lot in pain;
Millions of spirits for his fault amerced[7]
Of Heaven, and from eternal splendors flung   610
For his revolt; yet faithful how they stood,
Their glory withered; as when Heaven's fire
Hath scathed the forest oaks or mountain pines,
With singèd top their stately growth, though bare,
Stands on the blasted heath. He now prepared   615
To speak; whereat their doubled ranks they bend
From wing to wing, and half enclose him round
With all his peers: attention held them mute.
Thrice he essayed, and thrice, in spite of scorn,
Tears such as angels weep burst forth; at last   620
Words interwove with sighs found out their way:
    "O myriads of immortal spirits! O powers
Matchless, but with th' Almighty!—and that strife
Was not inglorious, though th' event[8] was dire,
As this place testifies, and this dire change,   625
Hateful to utter. But what power of mind,
Foreseeing or presaging, from the depth
Of knowledge past or present, could have feared
How such united force of gods, how such
As stood like these, could ever know repulse?   630
For who can yet believe, though after loss,
That all these puissant[9] legions, whose exile
Hath emptied Heaven, shall fail to reascend,
Self-raised, and repossess their native seat?
For me, be witness all the host of Heaven,   635
If counsels different,[1] or danger shunned
By me, have lost our hopes. But he who reigns
Monarch in Heaven, till then as one secure
Sat on his throne, upheld by old repute,
Consent or custom, and his regal state   640
Put forth at full, but still his strength concealed,
Which tempted our attempt,[2] and wrought our fall.
Henceforth his might we know, and know our own,
So as not either to provoke or dread
New war provoked: our better part remains   645
To work in close design,[3] by fraud or guile,
What force effected not; that he no less
At length from us may find, who overcomes
By force hath overcome but half his foe.
Space may produce new worlds; whereof so rife   650

7. Deprived.
8. Outcome, result.
9. Potent, powerful.
1. Contradictory or even selfish, but also, in an
obsolete sense, delaying.

2. Satan is an inveterate punster and player on
words.
3. I.e., our best choice is to achieve by secret
schemes.

There went a fame[4] in Heaven that he ere long
Intended to create, and therein plant
A generation whom his choice regard
Should favor equal to the sons of Heaven.
Thither, if but to pry, shall be perhaps   655
Our first eruption—thither, or elsewhere;
For this infernal pit shall never hold
Celestial spirits in bondage, nor th' abyss
Long under darkness cover. But these thoughts
Full counsel must mature. Peace is despaired,   660
For who can think submission? War, then, war
Open or understood,[5] must be resolved."
    He spake; and, to confirm his words, out flew
Millions of flaming swords, drawn from the thighs
Of mighty cherubim; the sudden blaze   665
Far round illumined Hell. Highly they raged
Against the Highest, and fierce with graspèd arms,
Clashed on their sounding shields the din of war,[6]
Hurling defiance toward the vault of Heaven.
    There stood a hill not far, whose grisly[7] top   670
Belched fire and rolling smoke; the rest entire
Shone with a glossy scurf,[8] undoubted sign
That in his womb was hid metallic ore,
The work of sulphur.[9] Thither, winged with speed,
A numerous brìgade hastened: as when bands   675
Of pioneers[1] with spade and pickax armed
Forerun the royal camp, to trench a field
Or cast a rampart. Mammon led them on,
Mammon, the least erected[2] spirit that fell
From Heaven; for even in Heaven his looks and thoughts   680
Were always downward bent, admiring more
The riches of Heaven's pavement, trodden gold,
Than aught divine or holy else enjoyed
In vision beatific. By him first
Men also, and by his suggestion taught,   685
Ransacked the center, and with impious hands
Rifled the bowels of their mother Earth
For treasures better hid. Soon had his crew
Opened into the hill a spacious wound
And digged out ribs[3] of gold. Let none admire   690
That riches grow in Hell; that soil may best
Deserve the precious bane. And here let those
Who boast in mortal things, and wondering tell

4. Rumor. "Rife": common.
5. Agreed-upon, tacit, hence secret.
6. Like Roman legionaries, the fallen angels applaud by beating swords on shields.
7. Horrible.
8. Crust.
9. Suphur and mercury were considered the basic substances of all metals.
1. Sappers, engineers.
2. Elevated. Mammon is not a god but an abstract word meaning "wealth"; cf. Belial.
3. Bars, of course, but also suggesting golden-haired Eve, who was a "precious bane" (sweet poison) dug out of Adam's side. "Admire": wonder.

Of Babel, and the works of Memphian kings,
Learn how their greatest monuments of fame   695
And strength and art are easily outdone
By spirits reprobate,[4] and in an hour
What in an age they with incessant toil
And hands innumerable scarce perform.
Nigh on the plain, in many cells prepared,   700
That underneath had veins of liquid fire
Sluiced from the lake, a second multitude
With wondrous art founded the massy ore,
Severing each kind, and scummed the bullion-dross.
A third as soon had formed within the ground   705
A various mold, and from the boiling cells
By strange conveyance filled each hollow nook:[5]
As in an organ, from one blast of wind
To many a row of pipes the soundboard breathes.
Anon out of the earth a fabric huge   710
Rose like an exhalation, with the sound
Of dulcet symphonies and voices sweet,
Built like a temple, where pilasters[6] round
Were set, and Doric pillars[7] overlaid
With golden architrave; nor did there want   715
Cornice or frieze, with bossy[8] sculptures graven;
The roof was fretted[9] gold. Not Babylon
Nor great Alcairo such magnificence
Equaled in all their glories,[1] to enshrine
Belus or Serapis their gods, or seat   720
Their kings, when Egypt with Assyria strove
In wealth and luxury. Th' ascending pile
Stood fixed[2] her stately height; and straight the doors
Opening their brazen folds discover, wide
Within, her ample spaces o'er the smooth   725
And level pavement: from the archèd roof,
Pendent by subtle magic, many a row
Of starry lamps and blazing cressets[3] fed
With naphtha and asphaltus yielded light
As from a sky. The hasty multitude   730
Admiring entered; and the work some praise,
And some the architect. His hand was known
In Heaven by many a towered structure high,
Where sceptered angels held their residence,
And sat as princes, whom the sùpreme King   735

4. The tower of Babel and the Pyramids of Egypt
("works of Memphian kings") are easily outdone
by the devils ("spirits reprobate").
5. After melting the gold with fire from the lake
and pouring it into molds, the devils cause their
building to rise by a sort of spiritual-musical magic.
6. Columns set in a wall.
7. Doric pillars are severe and plain.
8. Embossed.

9. Patterned.
1. At Babylon in Assyria there were temples to
"Belus" or Baal; at Alcairo (modern Cairo, ancient
Memphis) in Egypt, they were to Osiris, one of
whose names was Serapis (here, but not ordinarily, accented on the first syllable).
2. Complete. "Straight": straightway.
3. Basketlike lamps, hung from the ceiling.

Exalted to such power, and gave to rule,
Each in his hierarchy, the orders bright.
Nor was his name unheard or unadored
In ancient Greece; and in Ausonian land
Men called him Mulciber;[4] and how he fell   740
From Heaven they fabled, thrown by angry Jove
Sheer o'er the crystal battlements: from morn
To noon he fell, from noon to dewy eve,
A summer's day, and with the setting sun
Dropped from the zenith like a falling star,   745
On Lemnos th' Aegean isle. Thus they relate,
Erring;[5] for he with this rebellious rout
Fell long before; nor aught availed him now
To have built in Heaven high towers; nor did he 'scape
By all his engines, but was headlong sent   750
With his industrious crew to build in Hell.
    Meanwhile the wingèd heralds, by command
Of sovereign power, with awful ceremony
And trumpet's sound, throughout the host proclaim
A solemn council forthwith to be held   755
At Pandemonium,[6] the high capital
Of Satan and his peers.[7] Their summons called
From every band and squarèd regiment
By place or choice the worthiest; they anon
With hundreds and with thousands trooping came   760
Attended.[8] All access was thronged, the gates
And porches wide, but chief the spacious hall
(Though like a covered field, where champions bold
Wont ride in armed, and at the soldan's[9] chair
Defied the best of paynim chivalry   765
To mortal combat, or career with lance)
Thick swarmed, both on the ground and in the air,
Brushed with the hiss of rustling wings. As bees
In springtime, when the sun with Taurus[1] rides,
Pour forth their populous youth about the hive   770
In clusters; they among fresh dews and flowers
Fly to and fro, or on the smoothèd plank,
The suburb of their straw-built citadel,
New rubbed with balm, expatiate, and confer[2]
Their state-affairs: so thick the airy crowd   775
Swarmed and were straitened; till, the signal given,

---

4. Hephaestus, or Vulcan, was sometimes known in "Ausonian land" (Italy) by the secondary epithet of "Mulciber." The story of Jove's tossing him out of Heaven is told, to the accompaniment of much Homeric laughter, in *Iliad* 1.
5. Milton tells the story, and gives it six lines of splendid poetry (740–46), but in the end condemns it as a corrupt version of the Biblical truth.
6. "Pandemonium" (a Miltonic coinage) means literally "All-Demons"; an inversion of Pantheon, "All-Gods."
7. Nobility.
8. I.e., each with his bodyguards.
9. Sultan's. "Paynim": pagan.
1. The sun is in the Zodiacal sign of Taurus from about April 19 to May 20.
2. Spread out and discuss, bring together. The simile of bees prepares for the sudden contraction of the devils' size; they can shrink or dilate at will.

Behold a wonder! They but now who seemed
In bigness to surpass Earth's giant sons,
Now less than smallest dwarfs, in narrow room
Throng numberless—like that pygmean race   780
Beyond the Indian mount;[3] or fairy elves,
Whose midnight revels by a forest side
Or fountain some belated peasant sees,
Or dreams he sees, while overhead the Moon
Sits arbitress,[4] and nearer to the Earth   785
Wheels her pale course; they, on their mirth and dance
Intent, with jocund[5] music charm his ear;
At once with joy and fear his heart rebounds.
Thus incorporeal spirits to smallest forms
Reduced their shapes immense, and were at large,   790
Though without number still, amidst the hall
Of that infernal court. But far within,
And in their own dimensions like themselves,
The great seraphic lords and cherubim
In close recess and secret conclave sat,   795
A thousand demigods on golden seats,
Frequent and full.[6] After short silence then,
And summons read, the great consult began.

Book 2

The Argument

The consultation begun, Satan debates whether another battle be to
be hazarded for the recovery of Heaven: some advise it, others dissuade.
A third proposal is preferred, mentioned before by Satan—to search the
truth of that prophecy or tradition in Heaven concerning another world,
and another kind of creature, equal or not much inferior to themselves,
about this time to be created. Their doubt who shall be sent on this
difficult search; Satan, their chief, undertakes alone the voyage; is honored and applauded. The council thus ended, the rest betake them several ways and to several employments, as their inclinations lead them,
to entertain[1] the time till Satan return. He passes on his journey to Hell-
gates; finds them shut, and who sat there to guard them; by whom at
length they are opened, and discover[2] to him the great gulf between Hell
and Heaven; with what difficulty he passes through, directed by Chaos,
the power of that place, to the sight of this new world which he sought.

High on a throne of royal state, which far
Outshone the wealth of Ormus[3] and of Ind,

---

3. The pygmies were supposed to live beyond the
Himalayas, "the Indian mount."
4. Witness.
5. Merry.
6. Crowded ("frequent") and in full complement

("full"); all present and accounted for.
1. Pass.
2. Disclose.
3. An island in the Persian Gulf, modern Hor-
muz, famous for pearls. "Ind": India.

Or where the gorgeous East with richest hand
Showers on her kings barbaric pearl and gold,
Satan exalted sat, by merit raised   5
To that bad eminence; and from despair
Thus high uplifted beyond hope, aspires
Beyond thus high, insatiate to pursue
Vain war with Heaven; and by success[4] untaught,
His proud imaginations thus displayed: 10
    "Powers and dominions, deities of Heaven!
For since no deep within her gulf can hold
Immortal vigor, though oppressed and fallen,
I give not Heaven for lost: from this descent
Celestial virtues rising will appear   15
More glorious and more dread than from no fall,
And trust themselves to fear no second fate.
Me though just right and the fixed laws of Heaven
Did first create your leader, next, free choice,
With what besides, in council or in fight,   20
Hath been achieved of merit, yet this loss
Thus far at least recovered, hath much more
Established in a safe unenvied throne
Yielded with full consent.[5] The happier state
In Heaven, which follows dignity, might draw   25
Envy from each inferior; but who here
Will envy whom the highest place exposes
Foremost to stand against the Thunderer's aim,
Your bulwark, and condemns to greatest share
Of endless pain? Where there is then no good   30
For which to strive, no strife can grow up there
From faction; for none sure will claim in Hell
Precèdence, none, whose portion is so small
Of present pain, that with ambitious mind
Will covet more. With this advantage then   35
To union and firm faith and firm accord,
More than can be in Heaven, we now return
To claim our just inheritance of old,
Surer to prosper than prosperity
Could have assured us;[6] and by what best way,   40
Whether of open war or covert guile,
We now debate; who can advise, may speak."
    He ceased, and next him Moloch, sceptered king,
Stood up, the strongest and the fiercest spirit
That fought in Heaven, now fiercer by despair.   45
His trust was with th' Eternal to be deemed

4. Outcome, result; experience of either sort, good
or bad.
5. He lays claim to the throne by just right, fixed
laws, free choice—and the fact that no one else
will want such a dangerous job.

6. Note the play on "sure—prosper—prosperity—
assured." An Elizabethan critic famous for his picturesque terminology, George Puttenham, calls this
figure "*epanalepsis*, or the echo sound, otherwise
the slow return." It is a favorite device of Milton's.

Equal in strength, and rather than be less
Cared not to be at all; with that care lost
Went all his fear: of God, or Hell, or worse
He recked[7] not, and these words thereafter spake: 50
    "My sentence[8] is for open war: of wiles,
More unexpert,[9] I boast not: them let those
Contrive who need, or when they need, not now.
For while they sit contriving, shall the rest,
Millions that stand in arms and longing wait   55
The signal to ascend, sit lingering here
Heaven's fugitives, and for their dwelling place
Accept this dark opprobrious den of shame,
The prison of his tyranny who reigns
By our delay? No! let us rather choose,   60
Armed with Hell-flames and fury, all at once
O'er Heaven's high towers to force resistless way,
Turning our tortures into horrid arms
Against the Torturer; when to meet the noise
Of his almighty engine[1] he shall hear   65
Infernal thunder, and for lightning see
Black fire and horror shot with equal rage
Among his angels, and his throne itself
Mixed with Tartarean[2] sulphur and strange fire,
His own invented torments. But perhaps   70
The way seems difficult and steep to scale
With upright wing against a higher foe.
Let such bethink them, if the sleepy drench[3]
Of that forgetful lake benumb not still,
That in our proper motion[4] we ascend   75
Up to our native seat; descent and fall
To us is adverse. Who but felt of late,
When the fierce foe hung on our broken rear
Insulting,[5] and pursued us through the deep,
With what compulsion and laborious flight   80
We sunk thus low? Th' ascent is easy then;
Th' event[6] is feared: should we again provoke
Our stronger,[7] some worse way his wrath may find
To our destruction; if there be in Hell
Fear to be worse destroyed! What can be worse   85
Than to dwell here, driven out from bliss, condemned
In this abhorrèd deep to utter woe;
Where pain of unextinguishable fire
Must exercise us without hope of end,

---

7. Cared.
8. Judgment.
9. Inexperienced. Moloch never had to be clever, and is proud of it.
1. The thunderbolt.
2. Tartarus is a classical name for Hell.
3. A draught of physic, as for animals; hence, used contemptuously here.
4. Natural impulse.
5. With the Latin sense of stamping or dancing on.
6. Outcome.
7. The word "enemy" is understood.

The vassals[8] of his anger, when the scourge   90
Inexorably, and the torturing hour,
Calls us to penance? More destroyed than thus,
We should be quite abolished, and expire.
What fear we then? What[9] doubt we to incense
His utmost ire? Which, to the height enraged,   95
Will either quite consume us, and reduce
To nothing this essential,[1] happier far
Than miserable to have eternal being!
Or if our substance be indeed divine,
And cannot cease to be, we are at worst   100
On this side nothing;[2] and by proof we feel
Our power sufficient to disturb his Heaven,
And with perpetual inroads to alarm,
Though inaccessible, his fatal throne:
Which, if not victory, is yet revenge."   105
        He ended frowning, and his look denounced
Desperate revenge, and battle dangerous
To less than gods.[3] On th' other side up rose
Belial, in act more graceful and humane;
A fairer person lost not Heaven; he seemed   110
For dignity composed, and high exploit.
But all was false and hollow; though his tongue
Dropped manna,[4] and could make the worse appear
The better reason, to perplex and dash
Maturest counsels: for his thoughts were low,   115
To vice industrious, but to nobler deeds
Timorous and slothful: yet he pleased the ear,
And with persuasive accent thus began:
        "I should be much for open war, O peers,
As not behind in hate, if what was urged   120
Main reason to persuade immediate war
Did not dissuade me most, and seem to cast
Ominous conjecture on the whole success;[5]
When he who most excels in fact of arms,
In what he counsels and in what excels   125
Mistrustful, grounds his courage on despair
And utter dissolution, as the scope
Of all his aim, after some dire revenge.
First, what revenge? The towers of Heaven are filled
With armèd watch, that render all access   130
Impregnable; oft on the bordering deep
Encamp their legions, or with òbscure wing
Scout far and wide into the realm of Night,

---

8. Servants, underlings; but perhaps also—or
alternatively—"vessels."
9. Why.
1. Essence.
2. I.e., we are now as badly off as we can be without being nothing, and so need have no fear.

3. Only gods could have withstood Moloch.
4. His tongue was honeyed. To "make the worse
appear / The better reason" was characteristic of
Sophists—mercenary logic-choppers of ancient
Greece. "Dash": confuse.
5. As above, line 9, outcome. "Fact": feat.

Scorning surprise. Or could we break our way
By force, and at our heels all Hell should rise   135
With blackest insurrection, to confound
Heaven's purest light, yet our great enemy
All incorruptible would on his throne
Sit unpolluted, and th' ethereal mold[6]
Incapable of stain would soon expel   140
Her mischief, and purge off the baser fire,
Victorious. Thus repulsed, our final hope
Is flat despair: we must exasperate
Th' almighty Victor to spend all his rage,
And that must end us, that must be our cure,   145
To be no more. Sad cure! for who would lose,
Though full of pain, this intellectual being,
Those thoughts that wander through eternity,
To perish rather, swallowed up and lost
In the wide womb of uncreated Night,   150
Devoid of sense and motion? And who knows,
Let this be good,[7] whether our angry Foe
Can give it, or will ever? How he can
Is doubtful; that he never will is sure.
Will he, so wise, let loose at once his ire,   155
Belike[8] through impotence, or unaware,
To give his enemies their wish, and end
Them in his anger, whom his anger saves
To punish endless? 'Wherefore cease we then?'
Say they who counsel war, 'we are decreed,   160
Reserved and destined to eternal woe;
Whatever doing, what can we suffer more,
What can we suffer worse?' Is this then worst,
Thus sitting, thus consulting, thus in arms?
What when we fled amain,[9] pursued and strook   165
With Heaven's afflicting thunder, and besought
The deep to shelter us? this Hell then seemed
A refuge from those wounds. Or when we lay
Chained on the burning lake? that sure was worse.
What if the breath that kindled those grim fires,   170
Awaked, should blow them into sevenfold rage
And plunge us in the flames? or from above
Should intermitted[1] vengeance arm again
His red right hand to plague us? What if all
Her[2] stores were opened, and this firmament   175
Of Hell should spout her cataracts of fire,
Impendent[3] horrors, threatening hideous fall

---

6. Substance. "Ethereal" substance, derived from
"ether," the fifth and purest element, is thought to
be incorruptible.
7. I.e., suppose it is good to be destroyed.
8. Ironically, in the sense of "I dare say."

9. Headlong. "Strook": struck.
1. Momentarily suspended.
2. Those of Hell.
3. In the Latin sense, hanging down, threatening.

One day upon our heads; while we perhaps
Designing or exhorting glorious war,
Caught in a fiery tempest shall be hurled,   180
Each on his rock transfixed, the sport and prey
Of racking whirlwinds, or forever sunk
Under yon boiling ocean, wrapped in chains;
There to converse with everlasting groans,
Unrespited, unpitied, unreprieved,   185
Ages of hopeless end! This would be worse.
War therefore, open or concealed, alike
My voice dissuades; for what can force or guile[4]
With him, or who deceive his mind, whose eye
Views all things at one view? He from Heaven's height   190
All these our motions[5] vain sees and derides,
Not more almighty to resist our might
Than wise to frustrate all our plots and wiles.
Shall we then live thus vile, the race of Heaven
Thus trampled, thus expelled to suffer here   195
Chains and these torments? Better these than worse,
By my advice; since fate inevitable
Subdues us, and omnipotent decree,
The Victor's will. To suffer, as to do,
Our strength is equal,[6] nor the law unjust   200
That so ordains: this was at first resolved,
If we were wise, against so great a foe
Contending, and so doubtful what might fall.
I laugh when those who at the spear are bold
And venturous, if that fail them, shrink and fear   205
What yet they know must follow, to endure
Exile, or ignominy, or bonds, or pain,
The sentence of their Conqueror. This is now
Our doom; which if we can sustain and bear,
Our sùpreme Foe in time may much remit   210
His anger, and perhaps, thus far removed,
Not mind us not offending, satisfied
With what is punished;[7] whence these raging fires
Will slacken, if his breath stir not their flames.
Our purer essence then will overcome   215
Their noxious vapor, or inured[8] not feel,
Or changed at length, and to the place conformed
In temper and in nature, will receive
Familiar the fierce heat, and void of pain;
This horror will grow mild, this darkness light;   220
Besides what hope the never-ending flight

4. The verb "accomplish" or "achieve" is understood.
5. Proposals, plots.
6. I.e., passive endurance and active energy are both in the devils' power. Belial points out, with dangerous good sense, that they must have known from the beginning that they might have to exercise both (lines 201–3).
7. A Latinism, *quod punitum est;* God will be satisfied with the punishment that has been inflicted.
8. Accustomed.

Of future days may bring, what chance, what change
Worth waiting, since our present lot appears
For happy though but ill, for ill not worst,[9]
If we procure not to ourselves more woe."   225
   Thus Belial, with words clothed in reason's garb,
Counseled ignoble ease and peaceful sloth,
Not peace; and after him thus Mammon spake:
   "Either to disenthrone the King of Heaven
We war, if war be best, or to regain   230
Our own right lost: him to unthrone we then
May hope, when everlasting Fate shall yield
To fickle Chance, and Chaos judge the strife.
The former, vain to hope, argues[1] as vain
The latter; for what place can be for us   235
Within Heaven's bound, unless Heaven's Lord supreme
We overpower? Suppose he should relent
And publish grace to all, on promise made
Of new subjection; with what eyes could we
Stand in his presence humble, and receive   240
Strict laws imposed, to celebrate his throne
With warbled hymns, and to his Godhead sing
Forced Halleluiahs; while he lordly sits
Our envied Sovereign, and his altar breathes
Ambrosial odors and ambrosial flowers,   245
Our servile offerings? This must be our task
In Heaven, this our delight; how wearisome
Eternity so spent in worship paid
To whom we hate! Let us not then pursue,
By force impossible, by leave obtained   250
Unàcceptable, though in Heaven, our state
Of spendid vassalage;[2] but rather seek
Our own good from ourselves, and from our own
Live to ourselves, though in this vast recess,
Free, and to none accountable, preferring   255
Hard liberty before the easy yoke
Of servile pomp. Our greatness will appear
Then most conspicuous, when great things of small,
Useful of hurtful, prosperous of adverse,
We can create, and in what place soe'er   260
Thrive under evil, and work ease out of pain
Through labor and endurance. This deep world
Of darkness do we dread? How oft amidst
Thick clouds and dark doth Heaven's all-ruling Sire
Choose to reside, his glory unobscured,   265
And with the majesty of darkness round
Covers his throne; from whence deep thunders roar,

9. I.e., from the point of view of happiness, the   1. Proves.
devils are but ill off; from the point of view of evil, 2. Servitude.
they could be worse. This is diabolic relativism.

Mustering their rage, and Heaven resembles Hell!
As he our darkness, cannot we his light
Imitate when we please? This desert soil 270
Wants[3] not her hidden luster, gems and gold;
Nor want we skill or art, from whence to raise
Magnificence; and what can Heaven show more?
Our torments also may in length of time
Become our elements, these piercing fires 275
As soft as now severe, our temper charged
Into their temper; which must needs remove
The sensible of pain.[4] All things invite
To peaceful counsels, and the settled state
Of order, how in safety best we may 280
Compose our present evils, with regard
Of what we are and where, dismissing quite
All thoughts of war. Ye have what I advise."
    He scarce had finished, when such murmur filled
Th' assembly, as when hollow rocks retain 285
The sound of blustering winds, which all night long
Had roused the sea, now with hoarse cadence lull
Seafaring men o'erwatched,[5] whose bark by chance,
Or pinnace, anchors in a craggy bay
After the tempest: such applause was heard 290
As Mammon ended, and his sentence pleased,
Advising peace; for such another field
They dreaded worse than Hell; so much the fear
Of thunder and the sword of Michaël[6]
Wrought still within them; and no less desire 295
To found this nether empire, which might rise
By policy, and long process of time,
In emulation opposite to Heaven.
Which when Beëlzebub perceived, than whom,
Satan except, none higher sat, with grave 300
Aspect he rose, and in his rising seemed
A pillar of state; deep on his front[7] engraven
Deliberation sat and public care;
And princely counsel in his face yet shone,
Majestic though in ruin. Sage he stood 305
With Atlantean[8] shoulders fit to bear
The weight of mightiest monarchies; his look
Drew audience and attention still as night
Or summer's noontide air, while thus he spake:
    "Thrones and imperial powers, offspring of Heaven, 310
Ethereal virtues; or these titles now

3. Lacks. Mammon proposes a tawdry imitation-
Heaven in Hell; this is the ultimate in diabolic
degradation.
4. The aspect of pain that is apprehended by the
senses; physical pain.
5. Tired out with watching.

6. The warrior angel, chief stay of the angelic
armies.
7. Forehead, brow.
8. Worthy of Atlas, one of the Titans, who as a
punishment for rebellion was condemned to stand
in North Africa and hold up the heavens.

Must we renounce, and, changing style, be called
Princes of Hell? For so the popular vote
Inclines, here to continue, and build up here
A growing empire—Doubtless! while we dream,   315
And know not that the King of Heaven hath doomed
This place our dungeon, not our safe retreat
Beyond his potent arm, to live exempt
From Heaven's high jurisdiction, in new league
Banded against his throne, but to remain   320
In strictest bondage, though thus far removed,
Under th' inevitable curb, reserved
His captive multitude. For he, be sure,
In height or depth, still first and last will reign
Sole King, and of his kingdom lose no part   325
By our revolt, but over Hell extend
His empire, and with iron scepter rule
Us here, as with his golden those in Heaven.
What[9] sit we then projecting peace and war?
War hath determined us,[1] and foiled with loss   330
Irreparable; terms of peace yet none
Vouchsafed or sought; for what peace will be given
To us enslaved, but custody severe,
And stripes, and arbitrary punishment
Inflicted? and what peace can we return,   335
But, to our power,[2] hostility and hate,
Untamed reluctance,[3] and revenge, though slow,
Yet ever plotting how the Conqueror least
May reap his conquest, and may least rejoice
In doing what we most in suffering feel?[4]   340
Nor will occasion want, nor shall we need
With dangerous expedition to invade
Heaven, whose high walls fear no assault or siege,
Or ambush from the deep. What if we find
Some easier enterprise? There is a place   345
(If ancient and prophetic fame[5] in Heaven
Err not), another world, the happy seat
Of some new race called *Man*, about this time
To be created like to us,[6] though less
In power and excellence, but favored more   350
Of him who rules above; so was his will
Pronounced among the gods, and by an oath,
That shook Heaven's whole circumference, confirmed.
Thither let us bend all our thoughts, to learn
What creatures there inhabit, of what mold   355

9. Why.
1. I.e., war has decided the question for (but also,
limited) us.
2. I.e., to the best of our power.
3. Resistance (in the Latin sense, struggling back).
4. How God may get least pleasure from our pain—

a devil's view of the deity.
5. Report, rumor.
6. The created (Ptolemaic) cosmos came into
existence only after the fall of Satan, and the fallen
angels, being otherwise occupied, could not know
of it.

Or substance, how endued,[7] and what their power,
And where their weakness, how attempted[8] best,
By force or subtlety. Though Heaven be shut,
And Heaven's high Arbitrator sit secure
In his own strength, this place may lie exposed,   360
The utmost border of his kingdom, left
To their defense who hold it;[9] here perhaps
Some advantageous act may be achieved
By sudden onset: either with Hell-fire
To waste[1] his whole creation, or possess   365
All as our own, and drive, as we were driven,
The puny habitants; or if not drive,
Seduce them to our party, that their God
May prove their foe, and with repenting hand
Abolish his own works. This would surpass   370
Common revenge, and interrupt his joy
In our confusion, and our joy upraise
In his disturbance; when his darling sons,
Hurled headlong to partake with us, shall curse
Their frail original,[2] and faded bliss,   375
Faded so soon! Advise if this be worth
Attempting, or to sit in darkness here
Hatching vain empires." Thus Beëlzebub
Pleaded his devilish counsel, first devised
By Satan, and in part proposed; for whence   380
But from the author of all ill could spring
So deep a malice, to confound[3] the race
Of mankind in one root, and Earth with Hell
To mingle and involve, done all to spite
The great Creator? But their spite still serves   385
His glory to augment. The bold design
Pleased highly those infernal states,[4] and joy
Sparkled in all their eyes; with full assent
They vote: whereat his speech he thus renews:
    "Well have ye judged, well ended long debate,   390
Synod of gods, and, like to what ye are,
Great things resolved; which from the lowest deep
Will once more lift us up, in spite of Fate,
Nearer our ancient seat; perhaps in view
Of those bright confines, whence with neighboring arms   395
And opportune excursion we may chance
Re-enter Heaven; or else in some mild zone
Dwell not unvisited of Heaven's fair light,
Secure, and at the brightening orient beam
Purge off this gloom; the soft delicious air,   400

7. Endowed.
8. Attacked, but also "tempted."
9. To be defended by the occupants.
1. Lay waste.
2. Originator, parent; or, perhaps, "their original

condition."
3. Destroy, ruin. Adam, the first man, is the "root"
of mankind.
4. Estates, territorial dignitaries of Hell.

To heal the scar of these corrosive fires,
Shall breathe her balm. But first, whom shall we send
In search of this new world? whom shall we find
Sufficient? who shall tempt[5] with wandering feet
The dark unbottomed infinite abyss,   405
And through the palpable obscure find out
His uncouth[6] way, or spread his airy flight
Upborne with indefatigable wings
Over the vast abrupt,[7] ere he arrive
The happy isle?[8] What strength, what art, can then   410
Suffice, or what evasion bear him safe
Through the strict senteries[9] and stations thick
Of angels watching round? Here he had need
All circumspection, and we now no less
Choice in our suffrage;[1] for on whom we send   415
The weight of all, and our last hope, relies."

    This said, he sat; and expectation held
His look suspense,[2] awaiting who appeared
To second, or oppose, or undertake
The perilous attempt; but all sat mute,   420
Pondering the danger with deep thoughts; and each
In others' countenance read his own dismay,
Astonished. None among the choice and prime
Of those Heaven-warring champions could be found
So hardy as to proffer or accept   425
Alone the dreadful voyage; till at last
Satan, whom now transcendent glory raised
Above his fellows, with monarchal pride
Conscious of highest worth, unmoved thus spake:
    "O progeny of Heaven, empyreal thrones!   430
With reason hath deep silence and demur[3]
Seized us, though undismayed. Long is the way
And hard, that out of Hell leads up to light;
Our prison strong, this huge convex[4] of fire,
Outrageous to devour, immures us round   435
Ninefold,[5] and gates of burning adamant
Barred over us prohibit all egress.
These passed, if any pass, the void profound
Of unessential[6] Night receives him next,
Wide gaping, and with utter loss of being   440
Threatens him, plunged in that abortive gulf.

---

5. Attempt, venture upon (from Latin *temptare*).
The "palpable obscure" is darkness so thick it can
be felt.
6. Unknown.
7. Chaos; a striking example of sound imitating
sense.
8. Wherever man is (for the fallen angels do not
yet know of Earth).
9. Old spelling of *sentries*, necessary here for the
meter.

1. Care in our voting.
2. I.e., everyone sat waiting in suspense.
3. Delay.
4. Vault.
5. Walls us in with nine thicknesses. See below,
lines 645 ff.
6. Without real being, darkness being merely the
absence of light. The "abortive gulf" expresses again
this completely negative quality of Chaos and Night.

If thence he 'scape into whatever world,
Or unknown region, what remains him less[7]
Than unknown dangers and as hard escape?
But I should ill become this throne, O peers,   445
And this imperial sovereignty, adorned
With splendor, armed with power, if aught proposed
And judged of public moment,[8] in the shape
Of difficulty or danger, could deter
Me from attempting. Wherefore do I assume   450
These royalties,[9] and not refuse to reign,
Refusing to accept as great a share
Of hazard as of honor, due alike
To him who reigns, and so much to him due
Of hazard more, as he above the rest   455
High honored sits?[1] Go therefore, mighty powers,
Terror of Heaven, though fallen; intend[2] at home,
While here shall be our home, what best may ease
The present misery, and render Hell
More tolerable; if there be cure or charm   460
To respite or deceive or slack the pain
Of this ill mansion; intermit no watch
Against a wakeful foe, while I abroad
Through all the coasts of dark destruction seek
Deliverance for us all: this enterprise   465
None shall partake with me." Thus saying rose
The monarch, and prevented[3] all reply;
Prudent, lest, from his resolution raised,[4]
Others among the chief might offer now
(Certain to be refused) what erst they feared,   470
And so refused might in opinion stand
His rivals, winning cheap the high repute
Which he through hazard huge must earn. But they
Dreaded not more th' adventure than his voice
Forbidding; and at once with him they rose;   475
Their rising all at once was as the sound
Of thunder heard remote. Towards him they bend
With awful[5] reverence prone; and as a god
Extol him equal to the highest in Heaven.
Nor failed they to express how much they praised,   480
That for the general safety he despised
His own; for neither do the spirits damned
Lose all their virtue; lest bad men should boast
Their specious deeds on Earth, which glory excites,

---

7. I.e., what awaits him except.
8. Importance.
9. Insignia of royalty. "Refusing": i.e., if I refuse.
1. Satan's argument, simple though entangled in
rhetoric, is that rulers must share in the dangers as
well as the rewards of an enterprise.

2. Consider.
3. Forestalled, anticipated.
4. After their courage had been raised by his resolution.
5. Full of respect and awe.

Or close ambition varnished o'er with zeal.[6]   485
    Thus they their doubtful consultations dark
Ended, rejoicing in their matchless chief:
As when from mountain tops the dusky clouds
Ascending, while the north wind sleeps, o'erspread
Heaven's cheerful face, the lowering element   490
Scowls o'er the darkened landscape snow or shower;
If chance the radiant sun with farewell sweet
Extend his evening beam, the fields revive,
The birds their notes renew, and bleating herds
Attest their joy, that hill and valley rings.   495
O shame to men! Devil with devil damned
Firm concord holds, men only disagree
Of creatures rational, though under hope
Of heavenly grace; and, God proclaiming peace,[7]
Yet live in hatred, enmity, and strife   500
Among themselves, and levy cruel wars,
Wasting the earth, each other to destroy:
As if (which might induce us to accord)
Man had not hellish foes enow[8] besides,
That day and night for his destruction wait!   505
    The Stygian council thus dissolved; and forth
In order came the grand infernal peers.
Midst came their mighty paramount,[9] and seemed
Alone th' antagonist of Heaven, nor less
Than Hell's dread emperor, with pomp supreme   510
And godlike imitated state; him round
A globe[1] of fiery seraphim enclosed
With bright emblazonry[2] and horrent arms.
Then of their session ended they bid cry
With trumpets' regal sound the great result: 515
Toward the four winds four speedy cherubim
Put to their mouths the sounding alchemy[3]
By herald's voice explained; the hollow abyss
Heard far and wide, and all the host of Hell
With deafening shout returned them loud acclaim.   520
Thence more at ease their minds and somewhat raised
By false presumptuous hope, the rangèd[4] powers
Disband; and wandering, each his several way
Pursues, as inclination or sad choice
Leads him perplexed where he may likeliest find   525
Truce to his restless thoughts, and entertain
The irksome hours, till his great chief return.

---

6. The sense is that damned spirits still retain some
virtues; lest bad men boast of good deeds they have
done out of glory and ambition, Milton has shown
us that devils do just as much. "Specious": pretending virtue. "Close": secret.
7. I.e., though God proclaims peace.
8. I.e., enough; the old plural emphatic form.

9. Champion, chief.
1. Band or crowd.
2. Decorated shields. "Horrent": bristling.
3. I.e., resonant trumpets (made of the alloy brass
by a marriage of metals which Milton associates
with alchemy).
4. Arrayed in ranks.

Part on the plain, or in the air sublime[5]
Upon the wing, or in swift race contend,
As at th' Olympian games or Pythian fields;[6]   530
Part curb their fiery steeds, or shun the goal
With rapid wheels, or fronted brìgades form.
As when to warn proud cities war appears
Waged in the troubled sky, and armies rush
To battle in the clouds;[7] before each van   535
Prick forth the airy knights, and couch their spears
Till thickest legions close; with feats of arms
From either end of Heaven the welkin[8] burns.
Others with vast Typhoean[9] rage more fell
Rend up both rocks and hills, and ride the air   540
In whirlwind; Hell scarce holds the wild uproar;
As when Alcides, from Oechalia crowned
With conquest, felt th' envenomed robe, and tore
Through pain up by the roots Thessalian pines,
And Lichas from the top of Oeta threw   545
Into th' Euboic sea.[1] Others more mild,
Retreated in a silent valley, sing
With notes angelical to many a harp
Their own heroic deeds and hapless fall
By doom of battle; and complain that Fate   550
Free Virtue should enthrall to Force or Chance.
Their song was partial,[2] but the harmony
(What could it less when spirits immortal sing?)
Suspended[3] Hell, and took with ravishment
The thronging audience. In discourse more sweet   555
(For eloquence the soul, song charms the sense)
Others apart sat on a hill retired,
In thoughts more elevate, and reasoned high
Of providence, foreknowledge, will, and fate,
Fixed fate, free will, foreknowledge absolute,   560
And found no end, in wandering mazes lost.
Of good and evil much they argued then,
Of happiness and final misery,
Passion and apathy,[4] and glory and shame,
Vain wisdom all, and false philosophy![5]   565
Yet with a pleasing sorcery could charm
Pain for a while or anguish, and excite

5. Aloft, uplifted (the adjective modifies the flyer, not the air).
6. The Olympic games were held at Olympia, the Pythian games at Delphi. To "shun the goal" is to drive a chariot as close as possible around a column without hitting it.
7. Warfare in the skies, portending trouble on earth. "Van": vanguard. "Prick": spur.
8. Sky.
9. Like that of Typhon, the hundred-headed Titan. See above 1.199.
1. Poisoned by the malicious centaur Nessus,

Hercules in his dying agonies threw his beloved companion Lichas, along with a good part of Mount Oeta, into the sea of Euboea, near Thermopylae.
2. Prejudiced.
3. Held in suspense.
4. Feeling and lack of feeling; the angels are dabbling in Stoicism.
5. Milton means, not that the subjects themselves are vain (he himself, in the present poem, has a good deal to say on these topics), but that the very premises with which devils start are bound to land them in error.

Fallacious hope, or arm th' obdurèd[6] breast
With stubborn patience as with triple steel.
Another part, in squadrons and gross[7] bands,   570
On bold adventure to discover wide
That dismal world, if any clime perhaps
Might yield them easier habitation, bend
Four ways their flying march, along the banks
Of four infernal rivers that disgorge   575
Into the burning lake their baleful streams:[8]
Abhorrèd Styx, the flood of deadly hate;
Sad Acheron of sorrow, black and deep;
Cocytus, named of lamentation loud
Heard on the rueful stream; fierce Phlegethon   580
Whose waves of torrent fire inflame with rage.
Far off from these a slow and silent stream,
Lethe, the river of oblivion, rolls
Her watery labyrinth, whereof who drinks
Forthwith his former state and being forgets,   585
Forgets both joy and grief, pleasure and pain.
Beyond this flood a frozen continent
Lies dark and wild, beat with perpetual storms
Of whirlwind and dire hail, which on firm land
Thaws not, but gathers heap,[9] and ruin seems   590
Of ancient pile; all else deep snow and ice,
A gulf profound as that Serbonian bog[1]
Betwixt Damiata and Mount Casius old,
Where armies whole have sunk: the parching air
Burns frore,[2] and cold performs th' effect of fire.   595
Thither by harpy-footed[3] Furies haled,
At certain revolutions[4] all the damned
Are brought; and feel by turns the bitter change
Of fierce extremes, extremes by change more fierce,
From beds of raging fire to starve[5] in ice   600
Their soft ethereal warmth, and there to pine
Immovable, infixed, and frozen round
Periods of time; thence hurried back to fire.
They ferry over this Lethean sound
Both to and fro, their sorrow to augment,   605
And wish and struggle, as they pass, to reach
The tempting stream, with one small drop to lose
In sweet forgetfulness all pain and woe,

---

6. Hardened.
7. Solid, dense.
8. The four rivers are traditional in hellish geography; Milton takes pains to distinguish them by the original meanings of their Greek names (Styx means "hateful," Acheron "woeful," etc.). Lethe is "far off" and very different from the others, oblivion being relatively a blessed state in hell.
9. In a heap, so that it looks like the ruin of an old

building ("ancient pile").
1. Lake Serbonis, once famous for its quicksands but today dried up, used to lie on the coast of Egypt, just east of the Nile, between Damiata and Mt. Cassius.
2. Frosty.
3. With hooked claws.
4. I.e., of time.
5. Benumb.

All in one moment, and so near the brink;
But Fate withstands, and to oppose th' attempt   610
Medusa[6] with Gorgonian terror guards
The ford, and of itself the water flies
All taste of living wight, as once it fled
The lips of Tantalus.[7] Thus roving on
In cònfused march forlorn, th' adventurous bands   615
With shuddering horror pale, and eyes aghast
Viewed first their lamentable lot, and found
No rest. Through many a dark and dreary vale
They passed, and many a region dolorous,
O'er many a frozen, many a fiery alp,[8]   620
Rocks, caves, lakes, fens, bogs, dens, and shades of death,
A universe of death, which God by curse
Created evil, for evil only good,
Where all life dies, death lives, and Nature breeds,
Perverse, all monstrous, all prodigious things,   625
Abominable, unutterable, and worse
Than fables yet have feigned, or fear conceived,
Gorgons, and Hydras, and Chimeras[9] dire.
    Meanwhile the adversary of God and man,
Satan with thoughts inflamed of highest design,   630
Puts on swift wings,[1] and toward the gates of Hell
Explores his solitary flight; sometimes
He scours the right-hand coast, sometimes the left;
Now shaves with level wing the deep, then soars
Up to the fiery concave[2] towering high.   635
As when far off at sea a fleet descried
Hangs in the clouds, by equinoctial winds
Close sailing from Bengala,[3] or the isles
Of Ternate and Tidore,[4] whence merchants bring
Their spicy drugs; they on the trading flood   640
Through the wide Ethiopian[5] to the Cape
Ply stemming nightly toward the pole: so seemed
Far off the flying fiend. At last appear
Hell bounds, high reaching to the horrid roof,
And thrice threefold the gates; three folds were brass,   645
Three iron, three of adamantine rock,
Impenetrable, impaled with circling fire,
Yet unconsumed. Before the gates there sat

---

6. One of the three Gorgons, women with snaky hair, scaly bodies, and boar's tusks, the very sight of whose faces changed men to stone.
7. Tantalus, afflicted with a raging thirst, stood in the middle of a lake, the water of which always receded when he tried to drink it (hence, "tantalize").
8. A "fiery alp" is a volcano.
9. The Hydra was a serpent with nine heads, slain by Hercules; the Chimera was a fire-breathing creature, part lion, part dragon, part goat. They exemplify abominations of nature.
1. Satan does not fasten on his wings; he takes swiftly to wing.
2. Vault.
3. An old form of "Bengal."
4. Two of the Molucca or "Spice" Islands, modern Indonesia.
5. The Indian Ocean, east of Africa. "The Cape" is of course the Cape of Good Hope; "the pole," the South Pole.

On either side a formidable shape;[6]
The one seemed woman to the waist, and fair,   650
But ended foul in many a scaly fold
Voluminous and vast, a serpent armed
With mortal sting. About her middle round
A cry[7] of Hellhounds never ceasing barked
With wide Cerberean[8] mouths full loud, and rung   655
A hideous peal; yet, when they list, would creep,
If aught disturbed their noise, into her womb,
And kennel there, yet there still barked and howled
Within unseen. Far less abhorred than these
Vexed Scylla,[9] bathing in the sea that parts   660
Calabria from the hoarse Trinacrian shore;
Nor uglier follow the night-hag,[1] when, called
In secret, riding through the air she comes,
Lured with the smell of infant blood, to dance
With Lapland witches, while the laboring moon   665
Eclipses at their charms.[2] The other shape,
If shape it might be called that shape had none
Distinguishable in member, joint, or limb,
Or substance might be called that shadow seemed,
For each seemed either; black it stood as night,   670
Fierce as ten Furies, terrible as Hell,
And shook a dreadful dart; what seemed his head
The likeness of a kingly crown had on.
Satan was now at hand, and from his seat
The monster moving onward came as fast,   675
With horrid strides; Hell trembled as he strode.
Th' undaunted fiend what this might be admired,[3]
Admired, not feared; God and his Son except,
Created thing naught valued he nor shunned;
And with disdainful look thus first began: 680
    "Whence and what art thou, execrable shape,
That dar'st, though grim and terrible, advance
Thy miscreated front[4] athwart my way
To yonder gates? Through them I mean to pass,
That be assured, without leave asked of thee.   685
Retire, or taste thy folly, and learn by proof,
Hell-born, not to contend with spirits of Heaven."

---

6. The allegorical figures of Sin and Death are founded on James 1.15: "Then when lust hath conceived, it bringeth forth sin: and sin, when it is finished, bringeth forth death." But the incestuous relations of Sin and Death are Milton's own invention. Physically, Sin is modeled on Virgil's or Ovid's Scylla, with some touches adopted from Spenser's Error; Death is a traditional figure, vague and vast.
7. Pack.
8. Like Cerberus, the traditional hound of Hell.
9. Circe out of jealousy threw poison into the water where Scylla bathed, in the straits between Calabria and Sicily ("Trinacria"); as a result of the poison, Scylla developed a ring of barking, snapping dogs around her waist.
1. Hecate (three syllables), goddess of sorcery. She attends the orgies of witches in the home of all witchcraft, Lapland, whither she is drawn by the blood of babies sacrificed for the occasion.
2. Magic formulas, not allurements.
3. Wondered.
4. Misshapen forehead, or face.

To whom the goblin full of wrath replied:
"Art thou that traitor angel, art thou he,
Who first broke peace in Heaven, and faith, till then   690
Unbroken, and in proud rebellious arms
Drew after him the third part of Heaven's sons
Conjured[5] against the Highest, for which both thou
And they, outcast from God, are here condemned
To waste eternal days in woe and pain?   695
And reckon'st thou thyself with spirits of Heaven,
Hell-doomed, and breath'st defiance here and scorn,
Where I reign king, and, to enrage thee more,
Thy king and lord? Back to thy punishment,
False fugitive, and to thy speed add wings,   700
Lest with a whip of scorpions I pursue
Thy ling'ring, or with one stroke of this dart
Strange horror seize thee, and pangs unfelt before."
     So spake the grisly terror, and in shape,
So speaking and so threatening, grew tenfold   705
More dreadful and deform. On th' other side,
Incensed with indignation Satan stood
Unterrified, and like a comet burned
That fires the length of Ophiucus[6] huge
In th' arctic sky, and from his horrid hair   710
Shakes pestilence and war. Each at the head
Leveled his deadly aim; their fatal hands
No second stroke intend,[7] and such a frown
Each cast at th' other, as when two black clouds,
With Heaven's artillery fraught,[8] come rattling on   715
Over the Caspian,[9] then stand front to front
Hovering a space, till winds the signal blow
To join their dark encounter in mid-air:
So frowned the mighty combatants, that Hell
Grew darker at their frown; so matched they stood;   720
For never but once more was either like
To meet so great a foe.[1] And now great deeds
Had been achieved, whereof all Hell had rung,
Had not the snaky sorceress that sat
Fast by Hell-gate, and kept the fatal key,   725
Ris'n, and with hideous outcry rushed between.
     "O father, what intends thy hand," she cried,
"Against thy only son?[2] What fury, O son,
Possesses thee to bend that mortal dart
Against thy father's head? and know'st for whom?   730
For Him who sits above and laughs the while

5. Sworn together by an oath.
6. A vast Northern constellation, "The Serpent-Holder" (also called "Serpentarius"). Satan will soon appear as a snake; and, like a comet, he portends "pestilence and war."
7. I.e., the first stroke will do the business.

8. Loaded with thunderbolts.
9. The Caspian is a particularly stormy area.
1. I.e., the Son of God.
2. Sin, Death, and Satan, in their various interrelations, parody obscenely the relations between God and the Son, Adam and Eve.

At thee ordained his drudge, to execute
Whate'er his wrath, which he calls Justice, bids;
His wrath which one day will destroy ye both!"
    She spake, and at her words the hellish pest   735
Forbore; then these to her Satan returned:
    "So strange thy outcry, and thy words so strange
Thou interposest, that my sudden hand
Prevented[3] spares to tell thee yet by deeds
What it intends, till first I know of thee,   740
What thing thou art, thus double-formed, and why,
In this infernal vale first met, thou call'st
Me father, and that phantasm call'st my son?
I know thee not, nor ever saw till now
Sight more detestable than him and thee."   745
    T' whom thus the portress of Hell-gate replied:
"Hast thou forgot me then, and do I seem
Now in thine eye so foul? once deemed so fair
In Heaven, when at th' assembly, and in sight
Of all the seraphim with thee combined   750
In bold conspiracy against Heaven's King,
All on a sudden miserable pain
Surprised thee; dim thine eyes, and dizzy swum
In darkness, while thy head flames thick and fast
Threw forth, till on the left side opening wide,   755
Likest to thee in shape and countenance bright,
Then shining heavenly fair, a goddess armed
Out of thy head I sprung.[4] Amazement seized
All th' host of Heaven; back they recoiled afraid
At first, and called me *Sin*, and for a sign   760
Portentous held me; but, familiar grown,
I pleased, and with attractive graces won
The most averse, thee chiefly, who full oft
Thyself in me thy perfect image viewing
Becam'st enamored;[5] and such joy thou took'st   765
With me in secret, that my womb conceived
A growing burden. Meanwhile war arose,
And fields were fought in Heaven; wherein remained
(For what could else?) to our almighty foe
Clear victory, to our part loss and rout   770
Through all the empyrean. Down they fell,
Driven headlong from the pitch[6] of Heaven, down
Into this deep, and in the general fall
I also; at which time this powerful key
Into my hand was given, with charge to keep   775
These gates forever shut, which none can pass

3. Forestalled.
4. As Athena sprang full-grown from the head of
Zeus.
5. Sin looks attractive at first, being a lovely woman

at the top of her body; but she is a serpent below,
and ends in a "mortal sting," i.e., death.
6. Height.

Without my opening. Pensive here I sat
Alone, but long I sat not, till my womb
Pregnant by thee, and now excessive grown,
Prodigious motion felt and rueful throes.   780
At last this odious offspring whom thou seest,
Thine own begotten, breaking violent way
Tore through my entrails, that with fear and pain
Distorted, all my nether shape thus grew
Transformed; but he, my inbred enemy,   785
Forth issued, brandishing his fatal dart,
Made to destroy. I fled, and cried out *Death!*
Hell trembled at the hideous name, and sighed
From all her caves, and back resounded *Death!*
I fled; but he pursued (though more, it seems,   790
Inflamed with lust than rage) and swifter far,
Me overtook, his mother, all dismayed,
And in embraces forcible and foul
Engendering with me, of that rape begot
These yelling monsters that with ceaseless cry   795
Surround me, as thou sawest, hourly conceived
And hourly born, with sorrow infinite
To me; for when they list, into the womb
That bred them they return, and howl and gnaw
My bowels, their repast; then bursting forth   800
Afresh, with conscious terrors vex me round,
That rest or intermission none I find.
Before mine eyes in opposition sits
Grim Death, my son and foe, who sets them on,
And me his parent would full soon devour   805
For want of other prey, but that he knows
His end with mine involved; and knows that I
Should prove a bitter morsel, and his bane,
Whenever that shall be; so Fate pronounced.
But thou, O father, I forewarn thee, shun   810
His deadly arrow; neither vainly hope
To be invulnerable in those bright arms,
Though tempered heavenly; for that mortal dint,
Save he who reigns above, none can resist."[7]
     She finished, and the subtle fiend his lore   815
Soon learned, now milder, and thus answered smooth:
"Dear daughter, since thou claimest me for thy sire,
And my fair son here show'st me, the dear pledge
Of dalliance had with thee in Heaven, and joys
Then sweet, now sad to mention, through dire change   820
Befallen us unforeseen, unthought of; know
I come no enemy, but to set free
From out this dark and dismal house of pain,

---

7. I.e., only God is immune to death.

Both him and thee, and all the heavenly host
Of spirits that, in our just pretenses[8] armed,   825
Fell with us from on high. From them I go
This uncouth errand sole,[9] and one for all
Myself expose, with lonely steps to tread
Th' unfounded[1] deep, and through the void immense
To search with wandering quest a place foretold   830
Should be, and, by concurring signs, ere now
Created vast and round, a place of bliss
In the purlieus[2] of Heaven, and therein placed
A race of upstart creatures, to supply
Perhaps our vacant room, though more removed,   835
Lest Heaven surcharged[3] with potent multitude
Might hap to move new broils. Be this or aught
Than this more secret now designed, I haste
To know; and this once known, shall soon return,
And bring ye to the place where thou and Death   840
Shall dwell at ease, and up and down unseen
Wing silently the buxom[4] air, embalmed
With odors: there ye shall be fed and filled
Immeasurably; all things shall be your prey."
He ceased, for both seemed highly pleased, and Death   845
Grinned horrible a ghastly smile, to hear
His famine[5] should be filled, and blessed his maw
Destined to that good hour. No less rejoiced
His mother bad, and thus bespake her sire:
    "The key of this infernal pit by due   850
And by command of Heaven's all-powerful King
I keep, by him forbidden to unlock
These adamantine gates; against all force
Death ready stands to interpose his dart,
Fearless to be o'ermatched by living might.   855
But what owe I to his commands above
Who hates me, and hath hither thrust me down
Into this gloom of Tartarus profound,
To sit in hateful office here confined,
Inhabitant of Heaven and heavenly-born,   860
Here in perpetual agony and pain,
With terrors and with clamors compassed round
Of mine own brood that on my bowels feed?
Thou art my father, thou my author, thou
My being gav'st me; whom should I obey   865
But thee? whom follow? Thou wilt bring me soon
To that new world of light and bliss, among
The gods who live at ease, where I shall reign

8. Pretensions, claims.
9. Alone on a desolate journey.
1. Bottomless.
2. Outskirts, suburbs.

3. Too full. "Broils": controversies.
4. Yielding. "Embalmed": made fragrant, but also
with a thought of the process associated with death.
5. Hunger, belly.

At thy right hand voluptuous,[6] as beseems
Thy daughter and thy darling, without end."   870
    Thus saying, from her side the fatal key,
Sad instrument of all our woe, she took;
And towards the gate rolling her bestial train,[7]
Forthwith the huge portcullis high up-drew,
Which but herself not all the Stygian powers[8]   875
Could once have moved; then in the keyhole turns
Th' intricate wards, and every bolt and bar
Of massy iron or solid rock with ease
Unfastens: on a sudden open fly
With impetuous recoil and jarring sound   880
Th' infernal doors, and on their hinges grate
Harsh thunder, that the lowest bottom shook
Of Erebus.[9] She opened, but to shut
Excelled[1] her power; the gates wide open stood,
That with extended wings a bannered host,   885
Under spread ensigns[2] marching, might pass through
With horse and chariots ranked in loose array;
So wide they stood, and like a furnace-mouth
Cast forth redounding[3] smoke and ruddy flame.
Before their eyes in sudden view appear   890
The secrets of the hoary deep, a dark
Illimitable ocean without bound,
Without dimension; where length, breadth, and height,
And time and place are lost; where eldest Night
And Chaos, ancestors of Nature, hold   895
Eternal anarchy, amidst the noise
Of endless wars, and by confusion stand.
For Hot, Cold, Moist, and Dry, four champions fierce,
Strive here for mastery, and to battle bring
Their embryon atoms;[4] they around the flag   900
Of each his faction, in their several clans,
Light-armed or heavy, sharp, smooth, swift, or slow,
Swarm populous, unnumbered as the sands
Of Barca or Cyrene's torrid soil,[5]
Levied to side with warring winds, and poise[6]   905
Their lighter wings. To whom these most adhere,
He rules a moment; Chaos[7] umpire sits,
And by decision more embroils the fray
By which he reigns: next him, high arbiter,
Chance governs all. Into this wild abyss—   910

6. As the Son sits at God's right hand, Sin will at Satan's; a blasphemous parody of the Creed.
7. I.e., accompanied by her yelping offspring.
8. The powers of Hell.
9. Another classical name for Hell.
1. Exceeded.
2. Standards, flags.
3. Billowing.

4. The four elements, fire, earth, water, and air, struggle endlessly in Chaos. "Embryon": embryo, unformed.
5. Barca and Cyrene were cities built on the shifting sands of North Africa.
6. Give weight to.
7. Chaos is both the place where confusion reigns and personified confusion itself.

The womb of Nature and perhaps her grave,
Of neither sea, nor shore, nor air, nor fire,
But all these in their pregnant causes[8] mixed
Confusedly, and which thus must ever fight,
Unless th' Almighty Maker them ordain   915
His dark materials to create more worlds[9]—
Into this wild abyss the wary fiend
Stood on the brink of Hell and looked awhile,
Pondering his voyage; for no narrow frith[1]
He had to cross. Nor was his ear less pealed[2]   920
With noises loud and ruinous (to compare
Great things with small) than when Bellona[3] storms,
With all her battering engines bent to raze
Some capital city; or less than if this frame
Of Heaven were falling, and these elements   925
In mutiny had from her axle torn
The steadfast earth. At last his sail-broad vans[4]
He spreads for flight, and in the surging smoke
Uplifted spurns the ground; thence many a league,
As in a cloudy chair ascending, rides   930
Audacious; but that seat soon failing, meets
A vast vacuity: all unawares,
Fluttering his pennons[5] vain, plumb down he drops
Ten thousand fathom deep, and to this hour
Down had been falling, had not by ill chance   935
The strong rebuff[6] of some tumultuous cloud
Instinct[7] with fire and niter hurried him
As many miles aloft; that fury stayed,
Quenched in a boggy Syrtis,[8] neither sea,
Nor good dry land, nigh foundered on he fares,   940
Treading the crude consistence, half on foot,
Half flying; behoves[9] him now both oar and sail.
As when a gryphon through the wilderness
With wingèd course o'er hill or moory dale
Pursues the Arimaspian, who by stealth   945
Had from his wakeful custody purloined
The guarded gold:[1] so eagerly the fiend
O'er bog or steep, through strait, rough, dense, or rare,
With head, hands, wings, or feet pursues his way,
And swims, or sinks, or wades, or creeps, or flies.   950

8. Chaos is not organized to the point of being
matter; it is the seeds of all forms of matter.
9. God must impose order on Chaos to create
worlds from it.
1. Channel, firth.
2. Rung.
3. Goddess of war.
4. Wings.
5. Pinions, from Latin *pennae*, "wings."
6. Puff or blast.
7. Filled. "Niter": saltpeter.

8. Quicksand, from the North African gulfs,
famous for their shifting sandbars.
9. Befits.
1. Gryphons, fabulous creatures, half eagle, half
lion, lived in northern Europe, and were said to
hoard gold. When it was stolen from them by the
one-eyed Arimaspians, they pursued these curious
malefactors, hopping, flapping, and squawking. The
story is a piece of moralized natural history, directed
against the love of money.

At length a universal hubbub wild
Of stunning sounds and voices all confused
Borne through the hollow dark assaults his ear
With loudest vehemence. Thither he plies
Undaunted, to meet there whatever power   955
Or spirit of the nethermost abyss
Might in that noise reside, of whom to ask
Which way the nearest coast of darkness lies
Bordering on light; when straight behold the throne
Of Chaos, and his dark pavilion spread   960
Wide on the wasteful deep! With him enthroned
Sat sable-vested Night, eldest of things,
The consort of his reign; and by them stood
Orcus and Ades,[2] and the dreaded name
Of Demogorgon;[3] Rumor next and Chance,   965
And Tumult and Confusion all embroiled,
And Discord with a thousand various mouths.
    T' whom Satan turning boldly, thus: "Ye powers
And spirits of this nethermost abyss,
Chaos and ancient Night, I come no spy,   970
With purpose to explore or to disturb
The secrets of your realm; but by constraint
Wandering this darksome desert, as my way
Lies through your spacious empire up to light,
Alone and without guide, half lost, I seek   975
What readiest path leads where your gloomy bounds
Confine with[4] Heaven; or if some other place
From your dominion won, th' Ethereal King
Possesses lately, thither to arrive
I travel this profound.[5] Direct my course: 980
Directed, no mean recompense it brings
To your behoof,[6] if I that region lost,
All usurpation thence expelled, reduce
To her original darkness and your sway
(Which is my present journey),[7] and once more   985
Erect the standard there of ancient Night.
Yours be th' advantage all, mine the revenge!"
    Thus Satan; and him thus the anarch[8] old,
With faltering speech and visage incomposed,[9]
Answered: "I know thee, stranger, who thou art,   990
That mighty leading angel, who of late
Made head against Heaven's King, though overthrown.
I saw and heard; for such a numerous host
Fled not in silence through the frighted deep

2. Latin and Greek names of Pluto, god of Hell.   6. On your behalf.
3. A mysterious subdeity, stronger than Fate itself,   7. I.e., the purpose of my present journey.
publicized by Boccaccio.   8. Chaos is not "monarch" of his realm, but
4. Border on.   "anarch," i.e., nonruler.
5. Deep pit.   9. Disturbed.

With ruin upon ruin, rout on rout,   995
Confusion worse confounded; and Heaven-gates
Poured out by millions her victorious bands
Pursuing. I upon my frontiers here
Keep residence; if all I can will serve
That little which is left so to defend,   1000
Encroached on still through our intestine broils[1]
Weakening the scepter of old Night: first Hell,
Your dungeon, stretching far and wide beneath;
Now lately Heaven and Earth,[2] another world
Hung o'er my realm, linked in a golden chain   1005
To that side Heaven from whence your legions fell.
If that way be your walk, you have not far;
So much the nearer danger. Go, and speed!
Havoc and spoil and ruin are my gain."
    He ceased; and Satan stayed not to reply,   1010
But glad that now his sea should find a shore,
With fresh alacrity and force renewed
Springs upward like a pyramid of fire
Into the wild expanse, and through the shock
Of fighting elements, on all sides round   1015
Environed, wins his way; harder beset
And more endangered than when Argo[3] passed
Through Bosporus betwixt the jostling rocks;
Or when Ulysses on the larboard shunned
Charybdis, and by th' other whirlpool steered: 1020
So he with difficulty and labor hard
Moved on, with difficulty and labor he;
But, he once past, soon after when man fell,
Strange alteration! Sin and Death amain,[4]
Following his track (such was the will of Heaven),   1025
Paved after him a broad and beaten way
Over the dark abyss, whose boiling gulf
Tamely endured a bridge of wondrous length
From Hell continued reaching th' utmost orb[5]
Of this frail world; by which the spirits perverse   1030
With easy intercourse pass to and fro
To tempt or punish mortals, except whom
God and good angels guard by special grace.

---

1. I.e., the territory of Chaos is continually shrinking because of our civil wars ("intestine broils"). Without textual authority, but with a certain logical force, some students have proposed to amend "our" to "your."
2. Our human cosmos, recently carved out of Chaos, and having a little heaven of its own, as distinguished from "Heaven," as used in line 1006 to mean the eternal empyrean, the abode of the deity and his angels.
3. Jason and his fifty Argonauts, sailing through the Bosporus to the Black Sea in pursuit of the Golden Fleece, had to pass through the Symplegades, or clashing rocks. Ulysses also had a tight squeeze to pass between Scylla and Charybdis, where Italy almost touches Sicily. Charybdis was a whirlpool, but Scylla, the dog-monster who ate alive six of Ulysses' best men, is called by Milton "th' other whirlpool."
4. At full speed, vigorously.
5. The world is surrounded by ten spheres, the whole concentric construction making up the created universe. The bridge built by Sin and Death ends on the outermost of these spheres.

But now at last the sacred influence
Of light appears, and from the walls of Heaven   1035
Shoots far into the bosom of dim Night
A glimmering dawn. Here Nature first begins
Her farthest verge,[6] and Chaos to retire,
As from her outmost works a broken foe
With tumult less and with less hostile din;   1040
That[7] Satan with less toil and now with ease
Wafts on the calmer wave by dubious light,
And like a weather-beaten vessel holds[8]
Gladly the port, though shrouds and tackle torn;
Or in the emptier waste, resembling air,   1045
Weighs his spread wings, at leisure to behold
Far off th' empyreal Heaven, extended wide
In circuit, undetermined[9] square or round,
With opal towers and battlements adorned
Of living sapphire, once his native seat;   1050
And fast by, hanging in a golden chain,
This pendant world,[1] in bigness as a star
Of smallest magnitude close by the moon.
Thither, full fraught with mischievous revenge,
Accursed, and in a cursèd hour, he hies.   1055

From Book 3

[The Invocation, the Council in Heaven, and the Conclusion of Satan's Journey]

Hail, holy Light, offspring of Heaven first-born!
Or of th' Eternal coeternal beam,
May I express thee unblamed?[1] since God is light,
And never but in unapproachèd light
Dwelt from eternity, dwelt then in thee,   5
Bright effluence of bright essence increate![2]
Or hear'st thou rather[3] pure ethereal stream,
Whose fountain who shall tell? Before the sun,
Before the heavens, thou wert, and at the voice
Of God, as with a mantle didst invest[4]   10
The rising world of waters dark and deep,
Won from the void and formless infinite.

---

6. Threshold. The end of Chaos is the beginning of (created) Nature.
7. So that.
8. Makes for.
9. Heaven is so vast that simply by looking at it one cannot tell its shape.
1. Homer first imagined the world as hanging from Heaven by a golden chain (*Iliad* 8). As Milton uses the image, it has a symbolic meaning as well; earth is dependent on Heaven. The world which hangs from Heaven is not just our earth, but earth and all its ten spheres.
1. Milton feels some hesitation at calling Light coeternal with God himself; his reasons for doing so follow.
2. Uncreated, i.e., eternal.
3. I.e., would you rather be called. The construction is a Latinism.
4. Cover, wrap.

Thee I revisit now with bolder wing,
Escaped the Stygian pool, though long detained
In that obscure sojourn, while in my flight,   15
Through utter and through middle darkness[5] borne,
With other notes than to th' Orphean lyre[6]
I sung of Chaos and eternal Night;
Taught by the Heavenly Muse[7] to venture down
The dark descent, and up to reascend,   20
Though hard and rare. Thee I revisit safe,
And feel thy sovereign vital lamp; but thou
Revisit'st not these eyes, that roll in vain
To find thy piercing ray, and find no dawn;
So thick a drop serene[8] hath quenched their orbs,   25
Or dim suffusion veiled. Yet not the more
Cease I to wander where the Muses haunt
Clear spring, or shady grove, or sunny hill,
Smit with the love of sacred song;[9] but chief
Thee, Sion,[1] and the flowery brooks beneath,   30
That wash thy hallowed feet, and warbling flow,
Nightly I visit: nor sometimes forget[2]
Those other two equaled with me in fate,[3]
So were I equaled with them in renown,
Blind Thamyris and blind Maeonides,   35
And Tiresias and Phineus, prophets old:[4]
Then feed on thoughts that voluntary move
Harmonious numbers; as the wakeful bird[5]
Sings darkling, and in shadiest covert hid
Tunes her nocturnal note. Thus with the year   40
Seasons return; but not to me returns
Day, or the sweet approach of even or morn,
Or sight of vernal bloom, or summer's rose,
Or flocks, or herds, or human face divine;
But cloud instead and ever-during dark   45
Surrounds me, from the cheerful ways of men
Cut off, and for the book of knowledge fair
Presented with a universal blank
Of Nature's works to me expunged and rased,[6]
And wisdom at one entrance quite shut out.   50

5. Hell and Chaos.
6. One of the so-called Orphic Hymns is *To Night*, and Orpheus himself visited the underworld. But Milton's song, being Christian, is of a different kind.
7. Urania. The following lines echo *Aeneid* 6. 126–29, where the Sybil tells Aeneas that the descent to hell is easy: getting back is the hard part.
8. *Gutta serena* was the medical term for the kind of blindness from which Milton suffered. "Dim suffusion" was cataract—*suffusio nigra*.
9. Again the phrase is Virgilian, "[*Musarum*] *ingenti percussus amore* (*Georgics* 2. 476); but the adjective "sacred" is Milton's own reservation.
1. The mountain of Scriptural inspiration, with

its brooks Siloa and Kidron.
2. I.e., and never forget: therefore always remember.
3. Blind like me.
4. Thamyris was a blind Thracian poet, who lived before Homer. "Maeonides" is an epithet of Homer, either as a son of Maeon or as a native of Maeonia. Tiresias was the blind prophet of Thebes; Phineus was a blind king and seer (*Aeneid* 3). For Milton poetry and prophecy were intimately joined; blindness of the outer eye rendered more acute the sight of the inner eye.
5. The nightingale. "Darkling": in the dark.
6. Shaved off (like a Roman tablet), erased.

So much the rather thou, Celestial Light,
Shine inward, and the mind through all her powers
Irradiate; there plant eyes; all mist from thence
Purge and disperse, that I may see and tell
Of things invisible to mortal sight.   55
   Now had th' Almighty Father from above,
From the pure empyrean where he sits
High throned above all height, bent down his eye,
His own works and their works at once to view:
About him all the sanctities of Heaven   60
Stood thick as stars, and from his sight[7] received
Beatitude past utterance; on his right
The radiant image of his glory sat,
His only Son. On Earth he first beheld
Our two first parents, yet the only two   65
Of mankind, in the happy garden placed,
Reaping immortal fruits of joy and love,
Uninterrupted joy, unrivaled love,
In blissful solitude. He then surveyed
Hell and the gulf between, and Satan there   70
Coasting the wall of Heaven on this side Night,
In the dun air sublime,[8] and ready now
To stoop, with wearied wings and willing feet,
On the bare outside of this world, that seemed
Firm land embosomed without firmament,   75
Uncertain which, in ocean or in air.
Him God beholding from his prospect high,
Wherein past, present, future he beholds,
Thus to his only Son foreseeing spake:
   "Only begotten Son, seest thou what rage   80
Transports our adversary? whom no bounds
Prescribed, no bars of Hell, nor all the chains
Heaped on him there, nor yet the main abyss
Wide interrupt,[9] can hold; so bent he seems
On desperate revenge, that shall redound   85
Upon his own rebellious head. And now
Through all restraint broke loose he wings his way
Not far off Heaven, in the precincts of light,
Directly towards the new-created world,
And man there placed, with purpose to essay   90
If him by force he can destroy, or worse,
By some false guile pervert: and shall pervert;
For man will hearken to his glozing[1] lies,
And easily transgress the sole command,
Sole pledge of his obedience; so will fall   95

7. From sight of him.
8. From the aspect of God's radiance the air is "dun," i.e., dusky; Satan is literally "sublime" in it, i.e., lifted up, aloft. But from where Satan hangs, outside the world's outer shell, he cannot be sure the world and its ten concentric spheres are not a single solid (line 75). The points of view are precisely distinguished.
9. Dividing, in between.
1. Flattering.

He and his faithless progeny. Whose fault?
Whose but his own? Ingrate, he had of me
All he could have; I made him just and right,
Sufficient to have stood, though free to fall.
Such I created all th' ethereal powers   100
And spirits, both them who stood and them who failed:
Freely they stood who stood, and fell who fell.
Not free, what proof could they have given sincere[2]
Of true allegiance, constant faith, or love,
Where only what they needs must do appeared,   105
Not what they would? What praise could they receive,
What pleasure I, from such obedience paid,
When Will and Reason (Reason also is Choice),
Useless and vain, of freedom both despoiled,
Made passive both, had served Necessity,   110
Not me? They therefore as to right belonged,
So were created, nor can justly accuse
Their Maker or their making or their fate,
As if predestination overruled
Their will, disposed by absolute decree   115
Or high foreknowledge. They themselves decreed
Their own revolt, not I. If I foreknew,
Foreknowledge had no influence on their fault,
Which had no less proved certain unforeknown.[3]
So without least impulse or shadow of fate,   120
Or aught by me immutably foreseen,
They trespass, authors to themselves in all,
Both what they judge and what they choose; for so
I formed them free, and free they must remain
Till they enthrall themselves: I else must change   125
Their nature, and revoke the high decree
Unchangeable, eternal, which ordained
Their freedom; they themselves ordained their fall.
The first sort[4] by their own suggestion fell,
Self-tempted, self-depraved; man falls, deceived   130
By the other first: man therefore shall find grace;
The other, none. In mercy and justice both,[5]
Through Heaven and Earth, so shall my glory excel;
But mercy, first and last, shall brightest shine."
    Thus while God spake ambrosial fragrance filled   135
All Heaven, and in the blessèd spirits elect
Sense of new joy ineffable diffused.
Beyond compare the Son of God was seen
Most glorious; in him all his Father shone

---

2. The delayed modifier is a favorite stylistic device
of Milton's. "Sincere" goes with "proof."
3. I.e., if I had not foreknown it.
4. The bad angels, Satan and his crew.
5. Mercy and justice are key terms in the poem.

Their personifications here are separate: God is
justice (he claims to be merciful, but his speech
does not have this tone at all), the Son is mercy;
but by Book 12 Milton intends to show their identity.

Substantially expressed; and in his face   140
Divine compassion visibly appeared,
Love without end, and without measure grace;
Which uttering, thus he to his Father spake:
    "O Father, gracious was that word which closed
Thy sovereign sentence, that man should find grace;   145
For which both Heaven and Earth shall high extol
Thy praises, with th' innumerable sound
Of hymns and sacred songs, wherewith thy throne
Encompassed shall resound thee ever blest.
For should man finally be lost, should man   150
Thy creature late so loved, thy youngest son,
Fall circumvented thus by fraud, though joined
With his own folly? That be from thee far,
That far be from thee, Father, who art judge
Of all things made, and judgest only right!   155
Or shall the adversary[6] thus obtain
His end, and frustrate thine? Shall he fulfill
His malice, and thy goodness bring to naught,
Or proud return, though to his heavier doom,
Yet with revenge accomplished, and to Hell   160
Draw after him the whole race of mankind,
By him corrupted? Or wilt thou thyself
Abolish thy creation, and unmake
For him, what for thy glory thou hast made?
So should thy goodness and thy greatness both   165
Be questioned and blasphemed without defense."[7]
    To whom the great Creator thus replied:
"O Son, in whom my soul hath chief delight,
Son of my bosom, Son who art alone
My word, my wisdom, and effectual might,   170
All hast thou spoken as my thoughts are, all
As my eternal purpose hath decreed.[8]
Man shall not quite be lost, but saved who will;
Yet not of will in him, but grace in me
Freely vouchsafed. Once more I will renew   175
His lapsèd powers, though forfeit, and enthralled
By sin to foul exorbitant desires:
Upheld by me, yet once more he shall stand
On even ground against his mortal foe,
By me upheld,[9] that he may know how frail   180
His fallen condition is, and to me owe
All his deliverance, and to none but me.
Some I have chosen of peculiar grace,

---

6. "Satan" in Hebrew means "adversary."
7. The Son correctly intuits the motives overtly
expressed by Beëlzebub in the great consult.
8. The Lord's speech is notably rhythmic, even
rhymed.

9. Note the ambiguity: the second "by me upheld"
(line 180) may modify either "he" (line 178) or
"his mortal foe" (line 179). Both divine and hellish
energy are ultimately divine.

Elect above the rest; so is my will:
The rest shall hear me call, and oft be warned   185
Their sinful state,[1] and to appease betimes
Th' incensèd Deity, while offered grace
Invites; for I will clear their senses dark
What may suffice,[2] and soften stony hearts
To pray, repent, and bring obedience due.   190
To prayer, repentance, and obedience due,
Though but endeavored with sincere intent,
Mine ear shall not be slow, mine eye not shut.
And I will place within them as a guide
My umpire Conscience; whom if they will hear,   195
Light after light well used they shall attain,[3]
And to the end persisting, safe arrive.
This my long sufferance and my day of grace
They who neglect and scorn shall never taste;
But hard be hardened, blind be blinded more,   200
That they may stumble on, and deeper fall;
And none but such from mercy I exclude.
    But yet all is not done. Man, disobeying,
Disloyal breaks his fealty, and sins
Against the high supremacy of Heaven,   205
Affecting[4] godhead, and so losing all,
To expiate his treason hath naught left,
But to destruction sacred and devote,
He with his whole posterity must die;
Die he or Justice must; unless for him   210
Some other, able and as willing,[5] pay
The rigid satisfaction, death for death.
Say, heavenly powers, where shall we find such love?
Which of ye will be mortal to redeem
Man's mortal crime,[6] and just th' unjust to save?   215
Dwells in all Heaven charity so dear?"
    He asked, but all the heavenly choir stood mute,[7]
And silence was in Heaven: on man's behalf
Patron or intercessor none appeared,
Much less that durst upon his own head draw   220
The deadly forfeiture and ransom set.
And now without redemption all mankind
Must have been lost, adjudged to Death and Hell
By doom severe, had not the Son of God,
In whom the fullness dwells of love divine,   225
His dearest mediation[8] thus renewed:

---

1. I.e., warned about their sinful state.
2. I.e., as much as need be.
3. By using light well, they will reach even more
light, and, in the end, salvation.
4. Pretending to. "Devote": dedicated, given up
to.
5. I.e., able to pay, and as willing as he is able.

6. Note that "mortal" means "human" (line 214)
but "deadly" (line 215).
7. The silence of the good angels in face of a difficult task parallels that of the devils in the great
consult (2.420–26).
8. Intercession.

"Father, thy word is passed, man shall find grace;
And shall Grace not find means, that finds her way,
The speediest of thy wingèd messengers,
To visit all thy creatures, and to all   230
Comes unprevented,[9] unimplored, unsought?
Happy for man, so coming! He her aid
Can never seek, once dead in sins and lost;
Atonement for himself, or offering meet,
Indebted and undone, hath none to bring.   235
Behold me, then: me for him, life for life,
I offer; on me let thine anger fall;
Account me man: I for his sake will leave
Thy bosom, and this glory next to thee
Freely put off, and for him lastly die   240
Well pleased; on me let Death wreak all his rage;
Under his gloomy power I shall not long
Lie vanquished. Thou hast given me to possess
Life in myself forever; by thee I live;
Though now to Death I yield, and am his due,   245
All that of me can die, yet that debt paid,
Thou wilt not leave me in the loathsome grave
His prey, nor suffer my unspotted soul
Forever with corruption there to dwell;
But I shall rise victorious, and subdue   250
My vanquisher, spoiled of his vaunted spoil.
Death his death's wound shall then receive, and stoop[1]
Inglorious, of his mortal sting disarmed;
I through the ample air in triumph high
Shall lead Hell captive maugre[2] Hell, and show   255
The powers of darkness bound. Thou at the sight
Pleased, out of Heaven shalt look down and smile,
While, by thee raised, I ruin[3] all my foes,
Death last, and with his carcass glut the grave;
Then with the multitude of my redeemed   260
Shall enter Heaven, long absent, and return,
Father, to see thy face, wherein no cloud
Of anger shall remain, but peace assured
And reconcilement: wrath shall be no more
Thenceforth, but in thy presence joy entire."   265
    His words here ended, but his meek aspèct
Silent yet spake, and breathed immortal love
To mortal men, above which only shone
Filial obedience: as a sacrifice
Glad to be offered, he attends the will   270
Of his great Father. Admiration[4] seized

---

9. Unanticipated.
1. Be humbled, fall.
2. In spite of (French, *malgré*). The Son's triumph
is represented in a series of fantastic paradoxes—a

vanquisher vanquished, a spoiler spoiled, death
dead, Hell captured in all Hell's despite.
3. In the Latin sense, throw down.
4. Wonder, curiosity.

All Heaven, what this might mean, and whither tend,
Wondering; but soon th' Almighty thus replied:
    "O thou in Heaven and Earth the only peace
Found out for mankind under wrath,[5] O thou   275
My sole complacence![6] well thou know'st how dear
To me are all my works; nor man the least,
Though last created, that for him I spare
Thee from my bosom and right hand, to save,
By losing thee a while, the whole race lost!   280
Thou, therefore, whom thou only canst redeem,
Their nature also to thy nature join,[7]
And be thyself man among men on Earth,
Made flesh, when time shall be, of virgin seed
By wondrous birth; be thou in Adam's room[8]   285
The head of all mankind, though Adam's son.[9]
As in him perish all men, so in thee,
As from a second root, shall be restored
As many as are restored; without thee, none.
His crime makes guilty all his sons; thy merit   290
Imputed shall absolve them who renounce
Their own both righteous and unrighteous deeds,[1]
And live in thee transplanted, and from thee
Receive new life. So man, as is most just,
Shall satisfy for man, be judged and die,   295
And dying rise, and rising with him raise
His brethren, ransomed with his own dear life.
So heavenly love shall outdo hellish hate,
Giving to death, and dying to redeem,
So dearly to redeem, what hellish hate   300
So easily destroyed, and still destroys
In those who, when they may, accept not grace.
Nor shalt thou, by descending to assume
Man's nature, lessen or degrade thine own.
Because thou hast, though throned in highest bliss   305
Equal to God, and equally enjoying
Godlike fruition,[2] quitted all to save
A world from utter loss, and hast been found
By merit more than birthright Son of God,[3]
Found worthiest to be so by being good,   310

5. The Lord is looking to the future, when mankind will be under his wrath.
6. Contentment.
7. I.e., join the nature of those people (mankind) whom you alone can save to your own nature; in other words, "Become a man and suffer the pains of mortality." The antecedent of "whom" is, loosely construed, the "their" which follows it.
8. Place.
9. Adam is, properly, the "Old Adam"; Christ is the Second Adam (there was an old tradition that the Forbidden Tree and the Cross of Christ stood on the same spot). The Son of God, who long antedates the creation of Adam, and who is actually the first created being (3.383), is historical Jesus Christ in one sense, an eternal spiritual principle in another.
1. I.e., the merit of Christ, imputed to men, frees from original sin those who renounce their own deeds both good and bad and hope to be saved by faith.
2. Godlike pleasures, rewards.
3. An audacious doctrine, that Christ was Son of God by merit. Satan, one notes, was sultan of Hell on the same principle. (See above, 2.5).

Far more than great or high; because in thee
Love hath abounded more than glory abounds;
Therefore thy humiliation shall exalt
With thee thy manhood also to this throne:
Here shalt thou sit incarnate, here shalt reign   315
Both God and man, Son both of God and man,
Anointed[4] universal King. All power
I give thee; reign forever, and assume
Thy merits; under thee, as Head Supreme,
Thrones, princedoms, powers, dominions, I reduce: 320
All knees to thee shall bow of them that bide
In Heaven, or Earth, or under Earth in Hell.
When thou, attended gloriously from Heaven,
Shalt in the sky appear, and from thee send
The summoning archangels to proclaim   325
Thy dread tribunal, forthwith from all winds[5]
The living, and forthwith the cited dead
Of all past ages, to the general doom
Shall hasten; such a peal shall rouse their sleep.
Then, all thy saints assembled, thou shalt judge   330
Bad men and angels; they arraigned shall sink
Beneath thy sentence; Hell, her numbers full,
Thenceforth shall be forever shut. Meanwhile
The world shall burn, and from her ashes spring
New Heaven and Earth, wherein the just shall dwell,[6]   335
And after all their tribulations long
See golden days, fruitful of golden deeds,
With Joy and Love triùmphing, and fair Truth.
Then thou thy regal scepter shalt lay by;
For regal scepter then no more shall need;[7]   340
God shall be all in all. But all ye gods,[8]
Adore him who, to compass all this, dies;
Adore the Son, and honor him as me."
   No sooner had th' Almighty ceased, but all
The multitude of angels with a shout   345
Loud as from numbers without number, sweet
As from blest voices, uttering joy, Heaven rung[9]
With jubilee, and loud hosannas filled
Th' eternal regions. Lowly reverent
Towards either throne[1] they bow, and to the ground   350
With solemn adoration down they cast
Their crowns inwove with amarant[2] and gold;

4. "The Anointed," in Hebrew, is the Messiah.
5. From all directions. "Cited": summoned.
6. The burning of the earth is based on 2 Peter
3.12, 13.
7. Be needed.
8. In addressing the angels as gods, the Lord is
merely indicating their share in his divinity; the
word is not literal.

9. "Multitude" (line 345) is subject of the sentence, "rung" the verb, and "Heaven" the object.
1. Those of God and the Son.
2. Or "amaranth"; in Greek, "unwithering"—an
unfading flower and hence a type of immortality,
which could not continue on earth after man
became subject to death.

Immortal amarant, a flower which once
In Paradise, fast by the Tree of Life,
Began to bloom, but soon for man's offense   355
To Heaven removed, where first it grew, there grows
And flowers aloft, shading the Fount of Life,
And where the River of Bliss through midst of Heaven
Rolls o'er Elysian[3] flowers her amber stream.
With these, that never fade, the spirits elect   360
Bind their resplendent locks enwreathed with beams;
Now in loose garlands thick thrown off, the bright
Pavement, that like a sea of jasper shone,
Empurpled with celestial roses smiled.
Then, crowned again, their golden harps they took,   365
Harps ever tuned, that glittering by their side
Like quivers hung; and with preamble sweet
Of charming symphony they introduce
Their sacred song, and waken raptures high:
No voice exempt,[4] no voice but well could join   370
Melodious part; such concord is in Heaven.
    Thee, Father, first they sung, Omnipotent,
Immutable, Immortal, Infinite,[5]
Eternal King; thee, Author of all being,
Fountain of light, thyself invisible   375
Amidst the glorious brightness where thou sitt'st
Throned inaccessible, but when thou shad'st
The full blaze of thy beams, and through a cloud
Drawn round about thee like a radiant shrine
Dark with excessive bright thy skirts appear,[6]   380
Yet dazzle Heaven, that brightest seraphim
Approach not, but with both wings veil their eyes.
Thee next they sang, of all creation first,
Begotten Son, divine similitude,
In whose conspicuous countenance, without cloud   385
Made visible, th' Almighty Father shines,
Whom else[7] no creature can behold: on thee
Impressed th' effulgence of his glory abides;
Transfused on thee his ample spirit rests.
He Heaven of Heavens, and all the powers therein,   390
By thee created; and by thee threw down
Th' aspiring dominations.[8] Thou that day
Thy Father's dreadful thunder didst not spare,
Nor stop thy flaming chariot wheels that shook

3. Milton draws freely, and with no sense of incongruity, on pagan properties for his Christian Heaven. "Amber": not "yellow," but "clear." Milton's epithets are not always visually strong.
4. Abstaining.
5. Joshua Sylvester, in translating the long, pedestrian poem of Du Bartas on the creation, makes use of this line. It is the only example, and not a very striking one, of Milton's paralleling an English predecessor for ten consecutive syllables.
6. In this hymn, for the first time, we get a sense of the majesty and mystery of the Godhead; hitherto, he has seemed rather querulous and legalistic.
7. Except for whom (if it were not for the Son, no creature could see God).
8. I.e., the rebel angels.

Heaven's everlasting frame, while o'er the necks   395
Thou drov'st of warring angels disarrayed.
Back from pursuit, thy powers with loud acclaim
Thee only extolled, Son of thy Father's might,
To execute fierce vengeance on his foes.
Not so on man: him through their malice fallen,   400
Father of mercy and grace, thou didst not doom
So strictly, but much more to pity incline.
No sooner did thy dear and only Son
Perceive thee purposed not to doom frail man
So strictly, but much more to pity inclined,[9]   405
He, to appease thy wrath, and end the strife
Of mercy and justice in thy face discerned,
Regardless of the bliss wherein he sat
Second to thee, offered himself to die
For man's offense. O unexampled love!   410
Love nowhere to be found less than divine!
Hail, Son of God, Savior of men! Thy name
Shall be the copious matter of my[1] song
Henceforth, and never shall my harp thy praise
Forget, nor from thy Father's praise disjoin!   415
    Thus they in Heaven, above the starry sphere,
Their happy hours in joy and hymning spent.
Meanwhile, upon the firm opacous globe
Of this round world, whose first convex divides
The luminous inferior orbs, enclosed   420
From chaos and th' inroad of darkness old,
Satan alighted walks.[2] A globe far off
It seemed; now seems a boundless continent,
Dark, waste, and wild, under the frown of night
Starless exposed, and ever-threatening storms   425
Of chaos blustering round, inclement sky,
Save on that side which from the wall of Heaven,
Though distant far, some small reflection gains
Of glimmering air less vexed with tempest loud.
Here walked the fiend at large in spacious field.   430
As when a vulture on Imaus bred,
Whose snowy ridge the roving Tartar bounds,[3]
Dislodging from a region scarce of prey
To gorge the flesh of lambs or yeanling[4] kids
On hills where flocks are fed, flies toward the springs   435

9. A "than" or "but" is understood at the end of line 405. The repetition (lines 402, 405) suggests the choral nature of the psalm. Note in 407 the re-emphasis on a conflict of mercy and justice.
1. Either the angels are singing as a single chorus, or Milton wishes to associate himself with them; possibly both. The change of pronoun is deliberate and striking.
2. Satan is not on the earth's surface but on the outermost of the ten concentric spheres that make up the created cosmos. This sphere is "opacous" (opaque) by contrast with the inner nine (containing the planets and the fixed stars), which are crystalline and transparent.
3. Imaus, a ridge of mountains beyond the modern Himalayas, is described by Pliny (Natural History 6.17), and shown in Mercator's Atlas, as running north through Asia from modern Afghanistan to the Arctic Circle.
4. Newborn.

Of Ganges or Hydaspes, Indian streams,
But in his way lights on the barren plains
Of Sericana, where Chineses drive
With sails and wind their cany wagons light;[5]
So, on this windy sea of land, the fiend   440
Walked up and down alone, bent on his prey:
Alone, for other creature in this place,
Living or lifeless, to be found was none;—
None yet; but store hereafter from the earth
Up hither like aërial vapors flew   445
Of all things transitory and vain, when sin
With vanity had filled the works of men:
Both all things vain, and all who in vain things
Built their fond hopes of glory or lasting fame,
Or happiness in this or th' other life.[6]   450
All who have their reward on earth, the fruits
Of painful superstition and blind zeal,
Naught seeking but the praise of men, here find
Fit retribution, empty as their deeds;
All th' unaccomplished works of nature's hand,   455
Abortive, monstrous, or unkindly[7] mixed,
Dissolved on earth, fleet hither, and in vain,
Till final dissolution, wander here—
Not in the neighboring moon, as some have dreamed:
Those argent fields more likely habitants,[8]   460
Translated saints, or middle spirits hold,
Betwixt th' angelical and human kind.
Hither, of ill-joined sons and daughters born,
First from the ancient world those giants came,
With many a vain exploit, though then renowned:[9]   465
The builders next of Babel on the plain
Of Sennaar,[1] and still with vain design
New Babels, had they wherewithal, would build;
Others came single; he who, to be deemed
A god, leaped fondly into Etna flames,   470
Empedocles, and he who, to enjoy
Plato's Elysium, leaped into the sea,
Cleombrotus;[2] and many more, too long,

---

5. Both the Ganges and Hydaspes (a tributary of the river Indus) rise from the mountains of northern India; Sericana is an area in what is now Sinkiang province, in China.

6. Milton's Paradise of Fools (named in line 496) was probably inspired by Ariosto's equivalent valley on the moon (*Orlando Furioso*, canto 34; see below, line 459); it serves much the same function as Dante's Limbo, to dispose of those who deserve neither salvation nor damnation. But, instead of indifferents, Milton's region is reserved for deluded victims of misplaced devotion, chiefly Roman Catholics.

7. Against "kind," against their own natures.

8. Argent: silver. The moon Milton imagines, though only briefly, as a kind of middle Paradise.

9. The "giants in the earth," born of unnatural marriages between the "sons of God" and the daughters of men, are creatures "unkindly mixed," therefore sent to the Paradise of Fools, "though then renowned," as Genesis 6.4 tells us.

1. Shinär, the plain of Babel, as in Genesis 11.2–9. Babel for Milton is an emblem of human pride and folly.

2. Both Empedocles and Cleombrotus carried piety to the point of folly and suicide. Hell is reserved for the wilfully malicious, the Paradise of Fools for the merely misguided.

Embryos and idiots, eremites and friars,
White, black, and gray, with all their trumpery.[3]   475
Here pilgrims roam, that strayed so far to seek
In Golgotha him dead who lives in Heaven;
And they who to be sure of paradise,
Dying put on the weeds of Dominic,
Or in Franciscan think to pass disguised.[4]   480
They pass the planets seven, and pass the fixed,
And that crystàlline sphere whose balance weighs
The trepidation talked, and that first moved;[5]
And now Saint Peter at Heaven's wicket seems
To wait them with his keys, and now at foot   485
Of Heaven's ascent they lift their feet, when, lo!
A violent cross wind from either coast
Blows them transverse ten thousand leagues awry
Into the devious air. Then might ye see
Cowls, hoods, and habits, with their wearers, tossed   490
And fluttered into rags; then relics, beads,
Indulgences, dispenses, pardons, bulls,[6]
The sport of winds: all these upwhirled aloft
Fly o'er the backside of the world far off
Into a limbo large and broad, since called   495
The Paradise of Fools; to few unknown
Long after, now unpeopled and untrod.
    All this dark globe the fiend found as he passed;
And long he wandered, till at last a gleam
Of dawning light turned thitherward in haste   500
His traveled steps. Far distant he descries,
Ascending by degrees magnificent
Up to the wall of Heaven, a structure high;
At top whereof, but far more rich, appeared
The work as of a kingly palace-gate,   505
With frontispiece[7] of diamond and gold
Embellished; thick with sparkling orient gems
The portal shone, inimitable on earth
By model, or by shading pencil drawn.
The stairs were such as whereon Jacob saw   510
Angels ascending and descending, bands

3. Unnatural mixtures produce embryos and idiots; Milton adds to them hermits and friars (the white are Carmelites, the black Dominicans, and the gray Franciscans); he thinks they exemplify unnatural piety, frustrated by its very nature.
4. Pilgrims also are unnatural in their piety, since they worship the relic and forget the spirit. So are those who try to trick God into granting them salvation by wearing religious garb on their deathbeds. The traveler Thomas Coryat reported (1619), with severe Protestant disapproval, that Venetians often buried sinners in the cowls of Franciscan friars, hoping thus to slip them into heaven.
5. Milton follows their souls through the spheres

of the moon and sun and the five then-known planets, that of the fixed stars, and the sphere responsible for what astronomers call "the trepidation," a periodic corrective shudder of the cosmos. This brings them to the outermost sphere, the prime mover, or *primum mobile*—the next step seems to be the empyrean itself.
6. All that Milton considered the "trumpery," that is, the exterior and legal manifestations of ecclesiasticism, is here cast aside as vanity. Milton certainly means "backside" (line 494) to have its vulgar connotation.
7. Portico.

Of guardians bright, when he from Esau fled
To Padan-Aram, in the field of Luz
Dreaming by night under the open sky,
And waking cried, *This is the gate of Heaven*.   515
Each stair mysteriously was meant, nor stood
There always, but drawn up to Heaven sometimes
Viewless;[8] and underneath a bright sea flowed
Of jasper, or of liquid pearl, whereon
Who after came from earth sailing arrived   520
Wafted by angels, or flew o'er the lake
Rapt in a chariot drawn by fiery steeds.
The stairs were then let down, whether to dare
The fiend by easy ascent, or aggravate
His sad exclusion from the doors of bliss.[9]   525
Direct against which opened from beneath,
Just o'er the blissful seat of Paradise,
A passage down to th' earth—a passage wide,
Wider by far than that of after-times
Over Mount Sion, and, though that were large,   530
Over the Promised Land to God so dear,
By which, to visit oft those happy tribes,
On high behests his angels to and fro
Passed frequent,[1] and his eye with choice regard
From Paneas, the fount of Jordan's flood,   535
To Beërsaba, where the Holy Land
Borders on Egypt and the Arabian shore.[2]
So wide the opening seemed, where bounds were set
To darkness, such as bound the ocean wave.
Satan from hence, now on the lower stair   540
That scaled by steps of gold to Heaven-gate,
Looks down with wonder at the sudden view
Of all this world at once. As when a scout,
Through dark and desert ways with peril gone
All night, at last by break of cheerful dawn   545
Obtains the brow of some high-climbing hill,
Which to his eye discovers unaware
The goodly prospect of some foreign land
First seen, or some renowned metropolis
With glistering spires and pinnacles adorned,   550
Which now the rising sun gilds with his beams;
Such wonder seized, though after Heaven seen,
The spirit malign, but much more envy seized,

---

8. Invisible. The story of Jacob's vision is summarized from Genesis 28.1–19. The stairs of the
ladder were meant "mysteriously"—each represented a stage of spiritual growth.
9. In either case, Milton implies, heavenly
authorities were aware of Satan's approach.
1. The crystalline spheres would be impenetrable
if there weren't passages, or holes, in them, through

which heavenly—and, alas, diabolic—spirits could
make their way. The visiting angels (act as) his eye
(in maintaining) a choice regard over the chosen
people.
2. From Paneas (or Dan) in northern Palestine to
Beersaba, or Beersheba, near the Egyptian border—the whole land.

At sight of all this world beheld so fair.
Round he surveys (and well might, where he stood   555
So high above the circling canopy
Of night's extended shade) from eastern point
Of Libra to the fleecy star that bears
Andromeda far off Atlantic seas[3]
Beyond th' horizon; then from pole to pole   560
He views in breadth—and, without longer pause,
Down right into the world's first region throws
His flight precipitant, and winds with ease
Through the pure marble air his oblique way[4]
Amongst innumerable stars, that shone   565
Stars distant, but nigh-hand seemed other worlds.
Or other worlds they seemed, or happy isles,
Like those Hesperian gardens famed of old,
Fortunate fields, and groves, and flowery vales;[5]
Thrice happy isles! But who dwelt happy there   570
He stayed not to inquire: above them all
The golden sun, in splendor likest Heaven,
Allured his eye. Thither his course he bends,
Through the calm firmament (but up or down,
By center or eccentric, hard to tell,   575
Or longitude),[6] where the great luminary,
Aloof the vulgar constellations thick,
That from his lordly eye keep distance due,
Dispenses light from far; they, as they move
Their starry dance in numbers that compute   580
Days, months, and years, towards his all-cheering lamp
Turn swift their various motions, or are turned
By his magnetic beam, that gently warms
The universe, and to each inward part
With gentle penetration, though unseen,   585
Shoots invisible virtue even to the deep;[7]
So wondrously was set his station bright.

Summary   Landing on the bright orb of the sun, Satan disguises himself as a youthful cherub, and approaches the solar guardian, the archangel Uriel. Pretending interest in the new great works of God, he gets directions toward earth and Adam's bower, then spirals down and lands on Mount Niphates (in modern Iran) overlooking the site of Paradise.

3. In the Zodiac, Libra or the Scales are diametrically opposite the Ram ("the fleecy star"), which seems to carry the constellation Andromeda on its back.
4. "Marble" derives from the Greek word for "shining," but there's also a sense of solidity in the adjective to contrast with Satan's "oblique" approach.

5. The gardens of the Hesperides and the "fortunate isles" of Greek mythology lay far out in the Atlantic, almost like separate miniature worlds.
6. Milton is cautious about saying whether the sun or the earth is at the center of the created cosmos.
7. "Virtue" in the sense of "influence," "strength." For example, gold was thought to grow in the depths of the earth as a result of solar influence.

From Book 4

[Satan's Entry into Paradise; Adam and Eve in their Bower of Bliss]

O for that warning voice which he who saw
Th' Apocalypse heard cry in Heaven aloud,
Then when the dragon, put to second rout,
Came furious down to be revenged on men,
Woe to the inhabitants on Earth![1] that now,   5
While time was, our first parents had been warned
The coming of their secret foe, and scaped,
Haply so scaped, his mortal snare![2] For now
Satan, now first inflamed with rage, came down,
The tempter ere th' accuser of mankind,   10
To wreak on innocent frail man his loss
Of that first battle, and his flight to Hell.
Yet not rejoicing in his speed though bold
Far off and fearless, nor with cause to boast,
Begins his dire attempt; which nigh the birth   15
Now rolling, boils in his tumultuous breast,
And like a devilish engine back recoils
Upon himself. Horror and doubt distract
His troubled thoughts, and from the bottom stir
The Hell within him; for within him Hell   20
He brings, and round about him, nor from Hell
One step no more than from himself can fly
By change of place.[3] Now conscience wakes despair
That slumbered, wakes the bitter memory
Of what he was, what is, and what must be   25
Worse; of worse deeds worse sufferings must ensue.
Sometimes towards Eden, which now in his view
Lay pleasant, his grieved look he fixes sad;
Sometimes towards heaven and the full-blazing sun,
Which now sat high in his meridian tower;[4]   30
Then, much revolving, thus in sighs began:
   "O thou that with surpassing glory crowned
Look'st from thy sole dominion like the god
Of this new world—at whose sight all the stars
Hide their diminished heads—to thee I call,   35
But with no friendly voice, and add thy name,

---

1. John of Patmos, in Revelation 12, describes a war in heaven between dragon and angels, in the course of which a voice cries from heaven, "Woe to the inhabitants of the earth and of the sea!"
2. "Haply": by good luck, happily. "Mortal": deadly. The reiterated "first" 's in lines 6, 9, and 12 refer back to "second" in line 3; Milton wants us to remember that his story was the first of all the Bible stories, and is, as it were, their root.
3. Satan's proud statement that "the mind is its own place" (1.254) finds here its bitter ironic echo.
4. Midday, the height of noon. Milton's nephew Edward Phillips tells us that the speech which follows was the first part of the poem that existed, when Milton still thought of making it into the drama of "Adam Unparadised."

O sun, to tell thee how I hate thy beams,
That bring to my remembrance from what state
I fell, how glorious once above thy sphere,
Till pride and worse ambition threw me down,   40
Warring in Heaven against Heaven's matchless King!
Ah, wherefore? He deserved no such return
From me, whom he created what I was
In that bright eminence, and with his good
Upbraided none;[5] nor was his service hard.   45
What could be less than to afford him praise,
The easiest recompense, and pay him thanks,
How due! Yet all his good proved ill in me,
And wrought but malice. Lifted up so high,
I 'sdained[6] subjection, and thought one step higher   50
Would set me highest, and in a moment quit
The debt immense of endless gratitude,
So burdensome, still paying, still to owe,
Forgetful what from him I still received;
And understood not that a grateful mind   55
By owing owes not, but still pays, at once
Indebted and discharged—what burden then?
Oh, had his powerful destiny ordained
Me some inferior angel, I had stood
Then happy; no unbounded hope had raised   60
Ambition. Yet why not? Some other power
As great might have aspired, and me, though mean,
Drawn to his part. But other powers as great
Fell not, but stand unshaken, from within
Or from without to all temptations armed!   65
Hadst thou[7] the same free will and power to stand?
Thou hadst. Whom hast thou then, or what, to accuse,
But Heaven's free love dealt equally to all?
Be then his love accursed, since, love or hate,
To me alike it deals eternal woe.   70
Nay, cursed be thou; since against his thy will
Chose freely what it now so justly rues.
Me miserable![8] which way shall I fly
Infinite wrath and infinite despair?
Which way I fly is Hell; myself am Hell;   75
And in the lowest deep a lower deep
Still threatening to devour me opens wide,
To which the Hell I suffer seems a Heaven.
O then at last relent! Is there no place
Left for repentance, none for pardon left?   80
None left but by submission; and that word

---

5. Demanded no return for his benefits; the phrase echoes James 1.5.
6. Disdained. "Quit": acquit, pay off.
7. Satan addresses himself directly, as Adam will do under parallel circumstances in Book 10, line 758 ff.
8. "Me miserable!": an exact Latinism, *"me miserum!"*

Disdain forbids me, and my dread of shame
Among the spirits beneath, whom I seduced
With other promises and other vaunts
Than to submit, boasting I could subdue   85
Th' omnipotent. Ay me! they little know
How dearly I abide that boast so vain,
Under what torments inwardly I groan.
While they adore me on the throne of Hell,
With diadem and scepter high advanced,   90
The lower still I fall, only supreme
In misery: such joy ambition finds!
But say I could repent and could obtain
By act of grace[9] my former state, how soon
Would height recall high thoughts, how soon unsay   95
What feigned submission swore! Ease would recant
Vows made in pain, as violent and void.
For never can true reconcilement grow
Where wounds of deadly hate have pierced so deep;
Which would but lead me to a worse relapse   100
And heavier fall: so should I purchase dear
Short intermission, bought with double smart.
This knows my punisher; therefore as far
From granting he, as I from begging, peace.
All hope excluded thus, behold, instead   105
Of us outcast, exiled, his new delight,
Mankind created, and for him this world!
So farewell hope, and with hope farewell fear,
Farewell remorse! All good to me is lost;
Evil, be thou my good: by thee at least   110
Divided empire with Heaven's king I hold,
By thee, and more than half perhaps will reign;
As man ere long, and this new world, shall know."
    Thus while he spake, each passion dimmed his face,
Thrice changed with pale—ire, envy, and despair;   115
Which marred his borrowed visage, and betrayed
Him counterfeit, if any eye beheld:
For heavenly minds from such distempers foul
Are ever clear. Whereof he soon aware
Each perturbation smoothed with outward calm,   120
Artificer of fraud; and was the first
That practiced falsehood under saintly show,
Deep malice to conceal, couched with revenge:
Yet not enough had practiced to deceive
Uriel, once warned; whose eye pursued him down   125
The way he went, and on th' Assyrian mount
Saw him disfigured, more than could befall
Spirit of happy sort: his gestures fierce

---

9. The correct technical term for a formal pardon is an "act of grace."

He marked and mad demeanor, then alone,
As he supposed, all unobserved, unseen.   130
    So on he fares, and to the border comes
Of Eden, where delicious Paradise,
Now nearer, crowns with her enclosure green
As with a rural mound the champaign[1] head
Of a steep wilderness, whose hairy sides   135
With thicket overgrown, grotesque[2] and wild,
Access denied; and overhead up grew
Insuperable height of loftiest shade,
Cedar, and pine, and fir, and branching palm,
A sylvan scene, and as the ranks ascend   140
Shade above shade, a woody theater[3]
Of stateliest view. Yet higher than their tops
The verdurous wall of Paradise up sprung;
Which to our general sire[4] gave prospect large
Into his nether empire neighboring round.   145
And higher than that wall a circling row
Of goodliest trees loaden with fairest fruit,
Blossoms and fruits at once of golden hue,
Appeared, with gay enameled colors mixed;
On which the sun more glad impressed his beams   150
Than in fair evening cloud, or humid bow,[5]
When God hath showered the earth: so lovely seemed
That landscape. And of pure now purer air[6]
Meets his approach, and to the heart inspires
Vernal delight and joy, able to drive[7]   155
All sadness but despair. Now gentle gales,
Fanning their odoriferous wings, dispense
Native perfumes, and whisper whence they stole
Those balmy spoils. As when to them who sail
Beyond the Cape of Hope, and now are past   160
Mozambic, off at sea northeast winds blow
Sabean odors from the spicy shore
Of Araby the Blest,[8] with such delay
Well pleased they slack their course, and many a league
Cheered with the grateful smell old Ocean smiles;   165
So entertained those odorous sweets the fiend
Who came their bane, though with them better pleased

---

1. From French *champs*, open countryside. Paradise is an open garden on top of a hill straddling a river in the east of Eden.
2. One of the earliest uses of the word in English to mean "romantic" or "picturesque."
3. As if in a Greek amphitheater, the trees are set row on row.
4. Adam.
5. The rainbow. There is a thick wall of trees around Paradise, which "access denied"; then above them, the shaggy sides of Paradise itself ("the verdurous wall"), and above it the garden of fruit trees.

6. After breathing pure air, Satan now breathes even purer.
7. Scatter.
8. Coasting up East Africa after doubling the Cape of Good Hope, Milton supposes off "Mozambic" (Mozambique) one might meet "Sabean" (i.e., as from Sheba) odors coming from "Araby the Blest" (Arabia Felix). This is the fantasy of a man who learned his geography from medieval atlases and Diodorus Siculus, for the distance between Mozambique and Arabia is close to 2,000 miles.

Than Asmodëus with the fishy fume
That drove him, though enamored, from the spouse
Of Tobit's son,[9] and with a vengeance sent   170
From Media post to Egypt, there fast bound.
   Now to th' ascent of that steep savage[1] hill
Satan had journeyed on, pensive and slow;
But further way found none; so thick entwined,
As one continued brake, the undergrowth   175
Of shrubs and tangling bushes had perplexed
All path of man or beast that passed that way.
One gate there only was, and that looked east
On th' other side; which when th' arch-felon saw,
Due entrance he disdained, and in contempt   180
At one slight bound high overleaped all bound[2]
Of hill or highest wall, and sheer within
Lights on his feet. As when a prowling wolf,
Whom hunger drives to seek new haunt for prey,
Watching where shepherds pen their flocks at eve   185
In hurdled cotes[3] amid the field secure,
Leaps o'er the fence with ease into the fold;
Or as a thief, bent to unhoard the cash
Of some rich burgher, whose substantial doors,
Cross-barred and bolted fast, fear no assault,   190
In at the window climbs, or o'er the tiles;
So clomb[4] this first grand thief into God's fold:
So since into his church lewd hirelings[5] climb.
Thence up he flew, and on the Tree of Life,
The middle tree and highest there that grew,   195
Sat like a cormorant; yet not true life
Thereby regained, but sat devising death
To them who lived; nor on the virtue thought
Of that life-giving plant, but only used
For prospect,[6] what, well used, had been the pledge   200
Of immortality. So little knows
Any, but God alone, to value right
The good before him, but perverts best things
To worst abuse, or to their meanest use.
   Beneath him with new wonder now he views   205
To all delight of human sense exposed

---

9. Milton retells briefly here the story of Tobias, Tobit's son, who married Sara and was saved from the fate of her seven previous husbands by the advice of Raphael, who showed him how to make a fishy smell that would drive away the devil Asmodeus. See the Book of Tobit among the Apocrypha.
1. Wooded, entangled (from Latin, *silvaticus*, through Italian *selvaggio*, and French *sauvage*).
2. Satan enters Paradise, not only illegally, but with a contemptuous pun.
3. Pens made of woven reeds.

4. Old past tense of "climb," but used with a special feeling of ungainly energy. The whole metaphor, of God as a rich citizen hoarding Adam and Eve from Satan the second-story-man, is instinct with comic feeling. On the devil as a thief, see John 10.1.
5. Base men interested only in money; Milton felt strongly that churchmen should be unsalaried to insure the purity of their motives.
6. Perspective, lookout.

In narrow room Nature's whole wealth; yea more,
A Heaven on Earth; for blissful Paradise
Of God the garden was, by him in the east
Of Eden planted. Eden stretched her line   210
From Auran eastward to the royal towers
Of great Seleucia, built by Grecian kings,
Or where the sons of Eden long before
Dwelt in Telassar.[7] In this pleasant soil
His far more pleasant garden God ordained.   215
Out of the fertile ground he caused to grow
All trees of noblest kind for sight, smell, taste;
And all amid them stood the Tree of Life,
High eminent, blooming ambrosial fruit
Of vegetable gold; and next to life,   220
Our death, the Tree of Knowledge, grew fast by—
Knowledge of good bought dear by knowing ill.
Southward through Eden went a river large,
Nor changed his course, but through the shaggy hill
Passed underneath engulfed; for God had thrown   225
That mountain, as his garden-mold,[8] high raised
Upon the rapid current, which, through veins
Of porous earth with kindly[9] thirst up drawn,
Rose a fresh fountain, and with many a rill
Watered the garden; thence united fell   230
Down the steep glade, and met the nether flood,
Which from his darksome passage now appears,
And now, divided into four main streams,
Runs diverse, wandering many a famous realm
And country, whereof here needs no account;[1]   235
But rather to tell how, if art could tell,
How from that sapphire fount the crispèd[2] brooks,
Rolling on orient pearl and sands of gold,
With mazy error[3] under pendant shades
Ran nectar, visiting each plant, and fed   240
Flowers worthy of Paradise; which not nice[4] art
In beds and curious knots, but Nature boon[5]
Poured forth profuse on hill and dale and plain,
Both where the morning sun first warmly smote
The open field, and where the unpierced shade   245

7. By suggesting alternate boundaries of Eden, Milton invokes a hazy sense of the richness, vastness, and antiquity of the Middle East. "Auran" is an area in Syria, to the south of Damascus; "Seleucia," a powerful city founded by one of Alexander's generals (hence, "built by Grecian kings"), lies near modern Bagdad; and "Telassar" is another Near Eastern kingdom, this one probably on the east bank of the Euphrates.
8. The mountain is God's topsoil, out of which grows Paradise. The river (identified as the Tigris in Book 9, line 71) flowed under the hill.
9. Natural.
1. Milton has in mind Genesis 2.10; but the expression "whereof here needs no account" dodges many questions about the correct translation of this passage.
2. Wavy, ruffled.
3. From Latin errare, "wandering."
4. Particular, careful.
5. Liberal, bounteous.

Embrowned[6] the noontide bowers. Thus was this place,
A happy rural seat of various view:[7]
Groves whose rich trees wept odorous gums and balm;
Others whose fruit, burnished with golden rind,
Hung amiable[8]—Hesperian fables true,   250
If true, here only—and of delicious taste.
Betwixt them lawns, or level downs, and flocks
Grazing the tender herb, were interposed,
Or palmy hillock; or the flowery lap
Of some irriguous[9] valley spread her store,   255
Flowers of all hue, and without thorn the rose.[1]
Another side, umbrageous[2] grots and caves
Of cool recess, o'er which the mantling vine
Lays forth her purple grape, and gently creeps
Luxuriant; meanwhile murmuring waters fall   260
Down the slope hills dispersed, or in a lake,
That to the fringèd bank with myrtle crowned
Her crystal mirror holds, unite their streams.
The birds their choir apply;[3] airs, vernal airs,
Breathing the smell of field and grove, attune   265
The trembling leaves, while universal Pan,[4]
Knit with the Graces and the Hours in dance,
Led on th' eternal spring.[5] Not that fair field
Of Enna, where Proserpin gathering flowers,
Herself a fairer flower, by gloomy Dis   270
Was gathered, which cost Ceres all that pain
To seek her through the world; nor that sweet grove
Of Daphne,[6] by Orontes and th' inspired
Castalian spring, might with this Paradise
Of Eden strive; nor that Nyseian isle,   275
Girt with the river Triton, where old Cham,
Whom Gentiles Ammon call and Libyan Jove,
Hid Amalthea and her florid son
Young Bacchus from his stepdame Rhea's eye;[7]
Nor where Abassin kings their issue guard   280

6. Darkened.
7. Aspect.
8. Lovely. These were real golden apples like those
said to have existed in the Hesperides, fabulous
islands of the Western Ocean; Paradise was the only
place where the fable of the Hesperides was literally true.
9. Well-watered.
1. Figuratively and literally, there was no need for
thorns in Paradise.
2. Shady.
3. Practice their song. "Airs" may be either
"breezes" or "melodies," and probably are both.
4. The god of all nature. "Pan" in Greek means
"all," but it is also the name of the goat-legged
nature god.
5. The god of nature dances with the Graces and
Hours, an image of perfect harmony.

6. Milton is comparing Paradise with the famous
beauty spots of antiquity. Enna in Sicily was a lovely
meadow from which "Proserpin" was kidnapped
by "gloomy Dis" (i.e., Pluto); her mother Ceres
sought her throughout the world. The grove of
Daphne, near Antioch and the Orontes river in
the Near East, had a spring called "Castalia" in
imitation of the Muses' fountain near Delphi.
7. The isle of Nysa in the river Triton in Tunisia
was where Ammon hid Bacchus, his bastard child
by Amalthea, from the eye of his wife Rhea.
"Florid" (wine-flushed) Bacchus, when he grew up,
received the name of Dionysus in honor of his
birthplace. The identification of the Egyptian god
Ammon or Hammon with Cham or Ham, the son
of Noah, is a piece of comparative anthropology
like that in 10.580 ff.

Mount Amara[8] (though this by some supposed
True Paradise) under the Ethiop line
By Nilus' head, enclosed with shining rock,
A whole day's journey high, but wide remote
From this Assyrian garden, where the fiend   285
Saw undelighted all delight, all kind
Of living creatures, new to sight and strange.
Two of far nobler shape, erect and tall,
Godlike erect,[9] with native honor clad
In naked majesty, seemed lords of all,   290
And worthy seemed; for in their looks divine,
The image of their glorious Maker, shone
Truth, wisdom, sanctitude severe and pure—
Severe, but in true filial freedom[1] placed,
Whence true authority in men; though both   295
Not equal, as their sex not equal seemed;
For contemplation he and valor formed,
For softness she and sweet attractive grace;
He for God only, she for God in him.[2]
His fair large front[3] and eye sublime declared   300
Absolute rule; and hyacinthine[4] locks
Round from his parted forelock manly hung
Clustering, but not beneath his shoulders broad:
She, as a veil down to the slender waist,
Her unadorned golden tresses wore   305
Disheveled, but in wanton ringlets waved
As the vine curls her tendrils,[5] which implied
Subjection, but required with gentle sway,
And by her yielded, by him best received,
Yielded with coy[6] submission, modest pride,   310
And sweet, reluctant, amorous delay.
Nor those mysterious parts were then concealed;
Then was not guilty shame. Dishonest shame
Of Nature's works, honor dishonorable,
Sin-bred, how have ye troubled all mankind   315
With shows instead, mere shows of seeming pure,
And banished from man's life his happiest life,
Simplicity and spotless innocence!

---

8. Finally, Paradise ("this Assyrian garden," line 285) is finer than the royal residences atop Mt. Amara, where the "Abassin" (Abyssinian) kings had a splendid palace. Milton's authority for this exotic scene was Peter Heylyn (*Cosmographie* 4.64), from whom he took several phrases direct. His passage then had a continuing influence on the names and phrasings of Coleridge's *Kubla Khan*.
9. By emphasizing the word "erect," Milton means to distinguish man from the beasts of the field, who went "prone."
1. Though almost a paradox, the phrase suggests Milton's idea that true freedom always involves respect for authority and hierarchy. Cf. Eve's fool-

ish question, "For, inferior, who is free?" (9.825)
2. Milton's ideas on the relations between the sexes were the strict ones of his time, and of Christian tradition: "The head of every man is Christ; and the head of the woman is the man" (1 Corinthians 11.3).
3. Forehead.
4. A classical metaphor, often applied to hair, and implying "dark" or perhaps "flowing," but actually not very definite in its import.
5. Eve's hair is curly, abundant, uncontrolled; like the vegetation in Paradise, it clings seductively about a severe and masculine virtue.
6. Shy.

So passed they naked on, nor shunned the sight
Of God or angel; for they thought no ill;   320
So hand in hand they passed, the loveliest pair
That ever since in love's embraces met:
Adam the goodliest man of men since born
His sons; the fairest of her daughters Eve.[7]
Under a tuft of shade that on a green   325
Stood whispering soft, by a fresh fountain-side,
They sat them down; and after no more toil
Of their sweet gardening labor than sufficed
To recommend cool Zephyr,[8] and made ease
More easy, wholesome thirst and appetite   330
More grateful, to their supper fruits they fell,
Nectarine fruits which the compliant boughs
Yielded them, sidelong as they sat recline
On the soft downy bank damasked with flowers.
The savory pulp they chew, and in the rind   335
Still as they thirsted scoop the brimming stream;
Nor gentle purpose,[9] nor endearing smiles
Wanted, nor youthful dalliance, as beseems
Fair couple linked in happy nuptial league,
Alone as they. About them frisking played   340
All beasts of th' earth, since wild, and of all chase[1]
In wood or wilderness, forest or den.
Sporting the lion ramped,[2] and in his paw
Dandled the kid; bears, tigers, ounces, pards,[3]
Gamboled before them; th' unwieldy elephant   345
To make them mirth used all his might, and wreathed
His lithe proboscis; close the serpent sly,
Insinuating,[4] wove with Gordian twine
His braided train,[5] and of his fatal guile
Gave proof unheeded. Others on the grass   350
Couched and now filled with pasture, gazing sat,
Or bedward ruminating;[6] for the sun,
Declined, was hasting now with prone career
To th' ocean isles,[7] and in th' ascending scale
Of heaven the stars that usher evening rose: 355
When Satan, still in gaze as first he stood,
Scarce thus at length failed speech recovered sad:[8]
        "O Hell! what do mine eyes with grief behold?
Into our room of bliss thus high advanced

---

7. Logically these constructions are absurd; Adam
was not born since his day, Eve was not one of her
own daughters. Milton combines comparative with
superlative forms for emphatic effect.
8. I.e., to make a cool breeze welcome.
9. Conversation. "Wanted": lacked.
1. Who lurk in every sort of cover.
2. Reared up.
3. Lynxes and leopards.
4. Writhing and twisting, but with a glance at the

Tempter's rhetorical techniques.
5. Checkered body. "Gordian twine": knots, like
the Gordian knot, cut by Alexander the Great.
6. The animals are chewing their cuds before
bedtime; in Paradise, where the animal kingdom
is not yet subject to death, they are perforce vege-
tarians.
7. The Azores.
8. The choked, laborious line mirrors Satan's
heavy, congested mind.

Creatures of other mold, Earth-born perhaps,   360
Not spirits, yet to heavenly spirits bright
Little inferior; whom my thoughts pursue
With wonder, and could love; so lively shines
In them divine resemblance, and such grace
The hand that formed them on their shape hath poured.[9]   365
Ah! gentle pair, ye little think how nigh
Your change approaches, when all these delights
Will vanish, and deliver ye to woe,
More woe, the more your taste is now of joy:
Happy, but for so happy[1] ill secured   370
Long to continue, and this high seat, your Heaven,
Ill fenced for Heaven to keep out such a foe
As now is entered; yet no purposed foe
To you, whom I could pity thus forlorn,
Though I unpitied. League with you I seek,   375
And mutual amity so strait, so close,
That I with you must dwell, or you with me,
Henceforth.[2] My dwelling, haply, may not please,
Like this fair Paradise, your sense; yet such
Accept your Maker's work; he gave it me,   380
Which I as freely give. Hell shall unfold,
To entertain you two, her widest gates,
And send forth all her kings; there will be room,
Not like these narrow limits, to receive
Your numerous offspring; if no better place,   385
Thank him who puts me, loath, to this revenge
On you, who wrong me not, for him who wronged.[3]
And should I at your harmless innocence
Melt, as I do, yet public reason just—
Honor and empire with revenge enlarged   390
By conquering this new world—compels me now
To do what else, though damned, I should abhor."[4]
    So spake the fiend, and with necessity,
The tyrant's plea, excused his devilish deeds.
Then from his lofty stand on that high tree   395
Down he alights among the sportful herd
Of those four-footed kinds, himself now one,
Now other, as their shape served best his end
Nearer to view his prey, and unespied,
To mark what of their state he more might learn   400
By word or action marked. About them round
A lion now he stalks with fiery glare;

9. Though Satan's moral values are topsy-turvy ("Evil, be thou my good," he has said in the first part of Book 4), his aesthetic values are strictly orthodox.
1. Such happiness.
2. Though it starts in simple admiration, Satan's friendship for mankind is, at the end, grisly and sardonic. The turning point seems to be "though I unpitied" (line 375).
3. I.e., it is not my fault; Satan's favorite evasion.
4. Satan's final reason for destroying Adam and Eve is thoroughly Satanic; it is *ragione di stato*, reason of state, the public interest.

Then as a tiger, who by chance hath spied
In some purlieu[5] two gentle fawns at play,
Straight couches close; then, rising, changes oft   405
His couchant watch, as one who chose his ground,
Whence rushing he might surest seize them both
Gripped in each paw; when Adam first of men
To first of women Eve thus moving speech,
Turned him all ear to hear new utterance flow.   410
    "Sole partner and sole part of all these joys,[6]
Dearer thyself than all; needs must the power
That made us, and for us this ample world,
Be infinitely good, and of his good
As liberal and free as infinite,   415
That raised us from the dust and placed us here
In all this happiness, who at his hand
Have nothing merited, nor can perform
Aught of which he hath need; he who requires
From us no other service than to keep   420
This one, this easy charge, of all the trees
In Paradise that bear delicious fruit
So various, not to taste that only Tree
Of Knowledge, planted by the Tree of Life,
So near grows death to life, whate'er death is,   425
Some dreadful thing, no doubt; for well thou know'st
God hath pronounced it death to taste that tree,
The only sign of our obedience left
Among so many signs of power and rule
Conferred upon us, and dominion given   430
Over all other creatures that possess
Earth, air, and sea. Then let us not think hard
One easy prohibition, who enjoy
Free leave so large to all things else, and choice
Unlimited of manifold delights;   435
But let us ever praise him, and extol
His bounty, following our delightful task
To prune these growing plants and tend these flowers,
Which were it toilsome, yet with thee were sweet."
    To whom thus Eve replied: "O thou for whom   440
And from whom I was formed flesh of thy flesh,
And without whom am to no end, my guide
And head, what thou hast said is just and right.
For we to him indeed all praises owe
And daily thanks, I chiefly who enjoy   445
So far the happier lot, enjoying thee
Preeminent by so much odds, while thou
Like consort to thyself canst nowhere find.

5. The outskirt of a forest. Note that Satan can
and does enter any animal he wants; it is only for
the special purposes of the temptation that he finds
the serpent specially convenient.
6. Eve shares Adam's joys, and is herself the principal part of them.

That day I oft remember, when from sleep
I first awaked, and found myself reposed   450
Under a shade on flowers, much wondering where
And what I was, whence thither brought, and how.
Not distant far from thence a murmuring sound
Of waters issued from a cave and spread
Into a liquid plain, then stood unmoved,   455
Pure as th' expanse of heaven; I thither went
With unexperienced thought, and laid me down
On the green bank, to look into the clear
Smooth lake that to me seemed another sky.
As I bent down to look, just opposite,   460
A shape within the wat'ry gleam appeared,
Bending to look on me. I started back,
It started back; but pleased I soon returned,
Pleased it returned as soon with answering looks
Of sympathy and love. There I had fixed   465
Mine eyes till now, and pined with vain desire,[7]
Had not a voice thus warned me: 'What thou seest,
What there thou seest, fair creature, is thyself;
With thee it came and goes. But follow me,
And I will bring thee where no shadow stays   470
Thy coming, and thy soft embraces, he
Whose image thou art, him thou shalt enjoy
Inseparably thine, to him shalt bear
Multitudes like thyself, and thence be called
Mother of human race.' What could I do   475
But follow straight, invisibly thus led?
Till I espied thee, fair indeed and tall
Under a platan,[8] yet methought less fair,
Less winning soft, less amiably mild
Than that smooth wat'ry image. Back I turned;   480
Thou following cried'st aloud, 'Return, fair Eve,
Whom fli'st thou? whom thou fli'st, of him thou art,
His flesh, his bone; to give thee being I lent
Out of my side to thee, nearest my heart,
Substantial life, to have thee by my side   485
Henceforth an individual solace dear.
Part of my soul I seek thee, and thee claim
My other half.' With that, thy gentle hand
Seized mine, I yielded, and from that time see
How beauty is excelled by manly grace   490
And wisdom, which alone is truly fair."
     So spake our general mother, and with eyes
Of conjugal attraction unreproved

---

7. The fate of Narcissus, who fell in love with his own reflection, is hinted at. Like most men of his day, Milton followed the apostle Peter in thinking woman "the weaker vessel," and the attitude pervades his treatment of Eve.
8. Plane tree, with broad leaves and spreading branches.

And meek surrender, half embracing leaned
On our first father; half her swelling breast   495
Naked met his under the flowing gold
Of her loose tresses hid. He in delight
Both of her beauty and submissive charms
Smiled with superior love, as Jupiter
On Juno smiles, when he impregns the clouds   500
That shed May flowers, and pressed her matron lip
With kisses pure. Aside the Devil turned
For envy, yet with jealous leer malign
Eyed them askance, and to himself thus plained:[9]
     "Sight hateful, sight tormenting! thus these two   505
Imparadised in one another's arms,
The happier Eden, shall enjoy their fill
Of bliss on bliss, while I to Hell am thrust,
Where neither joy nor love, but fierce desire,
Among our other torments not the least,   510
Still unfulfilled with pain of longing pines.
Yet let me not forget what I have gained
From their own mouths: all is not theirs, it seems.
One fatal tree there stands, of knowledge called,
Forbidden them to taste. Knowledge forbidden?   515
Suspicious, reasonless. Why should their lord
Envy them that? Can it be sin to know,
Can it be death? and do they only stand
By ignorance, is that their happy state,
The proof of their obedience and their faith?   520
O fair foundation laid whereon to build
Their ruin! Hence I will excite their minds
With more desire to know, and to reject
Envious commands, invented with design
To keep them low whom knowledge might exalt   525
Equal with gods. Aspiring to be such,
They taste and die; what likelier can ensue?
But first with narrow search I must walk round
This garden, and no corner leave unspied;
A chance but chance[1] may lead where I may meet   530
Some wandering spirit of heaven, by fountain side
Or in thick shade retired, from him to draw
What further would be learnt. Live while ye may,
Yet happy pair; enjoy, till I return,
Short pleasures, for long woes are to succeed."   535
     So saying, his proud step he scornful turned,
But with sly circumspection, and began
Through wood, through waste, o'er hill, o'er dale his roam.
Meanwhile, in utmost longitude, where heaven
With earth and ocean meets, the setting sun   540

9. Complained.   1. An opportunity, even if only an accident.

Slowly descended, and with right aspèct
Against the eastern gate of Paradise
Levelled his evening rays.[2] It was a rock
Of alabaster piled up to the clouds,
Conspicuous far, winding with one ascent   545
Accessible from earth, one entrance high;
The rest was craggy cliff that overhung
Still as it rose, impossible to climb.
Betwixt these rocky pillars Gabriel sat,
Chief of th' angelic guards, awaiting night;   550
About him exercised heroic games
Th' unarmèd youth of Heaven, but nigh at hand
Celestial armory, shields, helms, and spears,
Hung high with diamond flaming and with gold.
Thither came Uriel, gliding through the even   555
On a sunbeam, swift as a shooting star
In autumn thwarts[3] the night when vapors fired
Impress the air, and shows the mariner
From what point of his compass to beware
Impetuous winds.[4] He thus began in haste: 560
    "Gabriel, to thee thy course by lot hath given
Charge and strict watch that to this happy place
No evil thing approach or enter in.
This day at height of noon came to my sphere
A spirit, zealous (as he seemed) to know   565
More of th' Almighty's works and chiefly man,
God's latest image. I described his way
Bent all on speed, and marked his airy gait;[5]
But in the mount that lies from Eden north,
Where he first lighted, soon discerned his looks   570
Alien from Heaven, with passions foul obscured.
Mine eye pursued him still, but under shade
Lost sight of him. One of the banished crew
I fear hath ventured from the deep to raise
New troubles; him thy care must be to find."   575
    To whom the wingèd warrior thus returned:
"Uriel, no wonder if thy perfect sight
Amid the sun's bright circle where thou sitst
See far and wide. In at this gate none pass
The vigilance here placed, but such as come   580
Well known from Heaven; and since meridian hour[6]
No creature thence. If spirit of other sort
So minded have o'erleaped these earthy bounds
On purpose, hard thou know'st it to exclude
Spiritual substance with corporeal bar.   585

2. Setting in the west, the sun can strike the eastern gate only from the inside. "Right aspèct": direct
view.
3. Flies across. "Vapors fired": heat lightning.

4. Meteors were thought to indicate by the direction of their fall the source of oncoming storms.
5. Course. "Described": descried.
6. Noon.

But if within the circuit of these walks
In whatsoever shape he lurk of whom
Thou tell'st, by morrow dawning I shall know."
    So promised he, and Uriel to his charge
Returned on that bright beam, whose point now raised   590
Bore him slope downward to the sun now fallen
Beneath th' Azores, whether the prime orb,
Incredible how swift had thither rolled
Diurnal, or this less volùble earth
By shorter flight to th' east,[7] had left him there   595
Arraying with reflected purple and gold
The clouds that on his western throne attend.
Now came still evening on, and twilight gray
Had in her sober livery all things clad.
Silence accompanied, for beast and bird,   600
They to their grassy couch, these to their nests,
Were slunk, all but the wakeful nightingale;
She all night long her amorous descant[8] sung.
Silence was pleased; now glowed the firmament
With living sapphires; Hesperus that led   605
The starry host rode brightest, till the moon,
Rising in clouded majesty, at length
Apparent queen unveiled her peerless light
And o'er the dark her silver mantle threw.
    When Adam thus to Eve: "Fair consort, th' hour   610
Of night and all things now retired to rest
Mind us of like repose, since God hath set
Labor and rest as day and night to men
Successive, and the timely dew of sleep
Now falling with soft slumbrous weight inclines   615
Our eyelids. Other creatures all day long
Rove idle unemployed, and less need rest;
Man hath his daily work of body or mind
Appointed, which declares his dignity
And the regard of Heaven on all his ways,   620
While other animals unactive range,
And of their doings God takes no account.
Tomorrow ere fresh morning streak the east
With first approach of light, we must be risen
And at our pleasant labor, to reform   625
Yon flow'ry arbors, yonder alleys green,
Our walk at noon, with branches overgrown
That mock our scant manuring,[9] and require
More hands than ours to lop their wanton growth.

7. Again Milton avoids the question whether sun
moves around earth or vice versa; he clearly enjoys
Uriel's trick of sliding down a sunbeam to reach
the earth, and then (relative positions having
changed) down the same beam back to his sunny
post. "Volùble": swift-turning.
8. Melody. ("Descant" has more technical meanings as well, but not here.)
9. Cultivating.

Those blossoms also and those dropping gums   630
That lie bestrown unsightly and unsmooth
Ask riddance, if we mean to tread with ease;
Meanwhile, as nature wills, night bids us rest."
    To whom thus Eve with perfect beauty adorned:
"My author and disposer, what thou bidd'st   635
Unargued I obey; so God ordains.
God is thy law, thou mine; to know no more
Is woman's happiest knowledge and her praise.
With thee conversing I forget all time,
All seasons and their change, all please alike.[1]   640
Sweet is the breath of morn, her rising sweet,
With charm of earliest birds; pleasant the sun
When first on this delightful land he spreads
His orient beams on herb, tree, fruit, and flower
Glistering with dew; fragrant the fertile earth   645
After soft showers; and sweet the coming on
Of grateful evening mild, then silent night
With this her solemn bird and this fair moon
And these the gems of heaven, her starry train:
But neither breath of morn when she ascends   650
With charm of earliest birds, nor rising sun
On this delightful land, nor herb, fruit, flower
Glistering with dew, nor fragrance after showers,
Nor grateful evening mild, nor silent night
With this her solemn bird, nor walk by moon   655
Or glittering starlight without thee is sweet.
But wherefore all night long shine these, for whom
This glorious sight, when sleep hath shut all eyes?"
    To whom our general ancestor replied:
"Daughter of God and Man, accomplished Eve,   660
Those have their course to finish round the earth
By morrow evening, and from land to land
In order, though to nations yet unborn,
Minist'ring light prepared, they set and rise,
Lest total darkness should by night regain   665
Her old possession, and extinguish life
In nature and all things, which these soft fires
Not only enlighten, but with kindly heat
Of various influence foment[2] and warm,
Temper or nourish, or in part shed down   670
Their stellar virtue on all kinds that grow
On earth, made hereby apter to receive
Perfection from the sun's more potent ray.[3]
These, then, though unbeheld in deep of night,

---

1. As there are no seasons in Paradise, Eve must mean the times of day. Her incantatory repetitions echo similar effects in the Song of Solomon.
2. Cherish, nurture.

3. The stars were thought to have their own occult influence and also to modulate that of the sun. Before the Fall, all these influences were "kindly" (benign).

Shine not in vain; nor think, though men were none,   675
That heaven would want spectators, God want praise.
Millions of spiritual creatures walk the earth
Unseen, both when we wake and when we sleep;
All these with ceaseless praise his works behold
Both day and night. How often from the steep   680
Of echoing hill or thicket have we heard
Celestial voices to the midnight air
Sole or responsive each to other's note,
Singing their great Creator: oft in bands
While they keep watch or nightly rounding walk,   685
With heavenly touch of instrumental sounds
In full harmonic number joined, their songs
Divide the night and lift our thoughts to Heaven."
    Thus talking, hand in hand alone they passed
On to their blissful bower. It was a place   690
Chos'n by the sovereign planter when he framed
All things to man's delightful use; the roof
Of thickest covert was inwoven shade,
Laurel and myrtle, and what higher grew
Of firm and fragrant leaf; on either side,   695
Acanthus and each odorous bushy shrub
Fenced up the verdant wall. Each beauteous flower,
Iris all hues, roses, and jessamine
Reared high their flourished heads between, and wrought
Mosaic; underfoot the violet,   700
Crocus, and hyacinth with rich inlay
Broidered the ground, more colored than with stone
Of costliest emblem.[4] Other creature here,
Beast, bird, insect, or worm durst enter none,
Such was their awe of man. In shadier bower,   705
More sacred and sequestered, though but feigned,
Pan or Silvanus never slept, nor Nymph
Nor Faunus haunted.[5] Here in close recess
With flowers, garlands, and sweet-smelling herbs
Espousèd Eve decked first her nuptial bed,   710
And heavenly choirs the hymenaean[6] sung,
What day the genial angel to our sire
Brought her in naked beauty more adorned,
More lovely than Pandora, whom the gods
Endowed with all their gifts, and O too like   715
In sad event, when to th' unwiser son
Of Japhet brought by Hermes, she ensnared
Mankind with her fair looks, to be avenged
On him who had stole Jove's authentic fire.[7]

---

4. Inlaid work.
5. Forest-and-field divinities of classical mythology.

6. Marriage hymn.
7. Pandora was a lovely girl, bestowed by the gods on Epimetheus, brother of Prometheus. ("Epime-

Thus at their shady lodge arrived, both stood,   720
Both turned, and under open sky adored
The god that made both sky, air, earth, and heaven
Which they beheld, the moon's resplendent globe
And starry pole: "Thou also mad'st the night,
Maker omnipotent, and thou the day,   725
Which we in our appointed work employed
Have finished happy in our mutual help
And mutual love, the crown of all our bliss
Ordained by thee, and this delicious place
For us too large, where thy abundance wants   730
Partakers, and uncropped falls to the ground.
But thou hast promised from us two a race
To fill the earth, who shall with us extol
Thy goodness infinite, both when we wake
And when we seek, as now, thy gift of sleep."   735
    This said unanimous, and other rites
Observing none but adoration pure
Which God likes best,[8] into their inmost bower
Handed they went; and, eased the putting off
Those troublesome disguises which we wear,   740
Straight side by side were laid. Nor turned, I ween,
Adam from his fair spouse, nor Eve the rites
Mysterious of connubial love refused—
Whatever hypocrites austerely talk
Of purity and place and innocence,   745
Defaming as impure what God declares
Pure and commands to some, leaves free to all.
Our Maker bids increase,[9] who bids abstain
But our destroyer, foe to God and man?
Hail wedded love, mysterious law, true source   750
Of human offspring, sole propriety[1]
In Paradise of all things common else.
By thee adulterous lust was driven from men
Among the bestial herds to range, by thee
Founded in reason, loyal, just, and pure,   755
Relations dear and all the charities[2]
Of father, son, and brother first were known.
Far be 't that I should write thee sin or blame,
Or think thee unbefitting holiest place,
Perpetual fountain of domestic sweets,   760

---

theus" means "hind-sighted," "Prometheus" means "fore-sighted," "Pandora" means "All-Gifts.") The brothers were sons of Iapetos, whom Milton identifies with Japhet, Noah's third son. Pandora's dowry consisted of a closed box, which foolish Epimetheus opened; all the ills of the human race flew out, leaving only hope behind. The Eve-Pandora parallel was often used by learned misogynists.

8. Like many Puritans, Milton hated set forms of prayer. Adam and Eve pray spontaneously, hence (we are to think) sincerely. "Handed": hand in hand; "eased": spared. (As they wore no clothes, they did not have to undress.)
9. Genesis 1.28.
1. Property, specifically private property.
2. Affections.

Whose bed is undefiled and chaste pronounced,
Present or past, as saints and patriarchs used.[3]
Here Love his golden shafts employs, here lights
His constant lamp and waves his purple wings,
Reigns here and revels; not in the bought smile   765
Of harlots, loveless, joyless, unindeared,
Casual fruition, nor in court amours,
Mixed dance or wanton masque or midnight ball
Or serenade, which the starved lover sings
To his proud fair, best quitted with disdain.   770
These, lulled by nightingales, embracing slept,
And on their naked limbs the flowery roof
Showered roses, which the morn repaired.[4] Sleep on,
Blest pair; and O yet happiest if ye seek
No happier state, and know to know no more.[5]   775

Summary   Fulfilling his promise to Uriel, Gabriel divides his night watch into search parties, assigning Ithuriel and Zephon to guard closely the bower of Adam and Eve. They find Satan in the bower, whispering in the ear of the sleeping Eve, and bring him before Gabriel. A battle impends, but is averted by a heavenly signal, and Satan flees out of Paradise.

From Book 5

[Eve's Dream: Trouble in Paradise]

Now Morn her rosy steps in th' eastern clime
Advancing, sowed the earth with orient pearl,
When Adam waked, so customed, for his sleep
Was airy light, from pure digestion bred
And temperate vapors bland, which the only sound   5
Of leaves and fuming rills, Aurora's fan,[1]
Lightly dispersed, and the shrill matin song
Of birds on every bough; so much the more
His wonder was to find unwakened Eve
With tresses discomposed and glowing cheek   10
As through unquiet rest; he on his side
Leaning half-raised with looks of cordial love
Hung over her enamored, and beheld
Beauty which whether waking or asleep
Shot forth peculiar[2] graces; then with voice   15
Mild as when Zephyrus on Flora breathes,

3. Throughout history ("present or past"), Milton says, matrimony has been an honorable estate. The "golden shafts" (arrows) of Cupid produce true love.
4. Replaced.
5. I.e., know enough to be content with what you know.

1. The fan of Aurora (goddess of dawn) is the rustling leaves, as the "orient pearl" of line 2 is dewdrops. "Matin": morning.
2. Distinctive. Zephyrus is god of the gentle west wind, Flora goddess of flowers.

Her soft hand touching, whispered thus. "Awake,
My fairest, my espoused, my latest found,
Heaven's last best gift, my ever new delight,
Awake, the morning shines, and the fresh field   20
Calls us: we lose the prime, to mark how spring
Our tended plants, how blows the citron grove,
What drops the myrrh and what the balmy reed,
How nature paints her colors, how the bee
Sits on the bloom extracting liquid sweet."[3]   25
     Such whispering waked her, but with startled eye
On Adam, whom embracing, thus she spake:
     "Oh sole in whom my thoughts find all repose,
My glory, my perfection, glad I see
Thy face, and morn returned, for I this night—   30
Such night till this I never passed—have dreamed,
If dreamed, not as I oft am wont, of thee,
Works of day past or morrow's next design,
But of offense and trouble, which my mind
Knew never till this irksome night. Methought   35
Close at mine ear one called me forth to walk
With gentle voice; I thought it thine; it said,
'Why sleepest thou, Eve? Now is the pleasant time,
The cool, the silent, save where silence yields
To the night-warbling bird, that now awake   40
Tunes sweetest his love-labored song; now reigns
Full-orbed the moon, and with more pleasing light
Shadowy sets off the face of things—in vain
If none regard. Heaven wakes with all his eyes,[4]
Whom to behold but thee, nature's desire,   45
In whose sight all things joy with ravishment
Attracted by thy beauty still to gaze.'
I rose as at thy call, but found thee not;
To find thee I directed then my walk;
And on, methought, alone I passed through ways   50
That brought me on a sudden to the tree
Of interdicted knowledge: fair it seemed,
Much fairer to my fancy than by day;
And as I wondering looked, beside it stood
One shaped and winged like one of those from Heaven   55
By us oft seen. His dewy locks distilled
Ambrosia;[5] on that tree he also gazed:
And 'Oh, fair plant,' said he, 'with fruit surcharged,
Deigns none to ease thy load and taste thy sweet,
Nor god nor man? is knowledge so despised?   60
Or envy or what reserve forbids to taste?[6]

---

3. Adam's good morning to Eve is phrased after the Song of Solomon.
4. The stars.
5. Technically, the food of the gods; used here of perfume.
6. I.e., does either envy or some other barrier ("reserve") forbid to taste?

Forbid who will, none shall from me withhold
Longer thy offered good, why else set here?'
This said, he paused not, but with venturous arm
He plucked, he tasted; me damp horror chilled   65
At such bold words vouched with a deed so bold.
But he thus overjoyed: 'Oh fruit divine,
Sweet of thyself, but much more sweet thus cropped,
Forbidden here, it seems, as only fit
For gods, yet able to make gods of men: 70
And why not gods of men, since good, the more
Communicated, more abundant grows,
The author not impaired, but honored more?
Here, happy creature, fair angelic Eve,
Partake thou also; happy though thou art,   75
Happier thou may'st be, worthier canst not be.
Taste this, and be henceforth among the gods
Thyself a goddess, not to earth confined,
But sometimes in the air, as we, sometimes
Ascend to heaven, by merit thine, and see   80
What life the gods live there, and such live thou.'
So saying, he drew nigh, and to me held,
Even to my mouth of that same fruit held part
Which he had plucked; the pleasant savory smell
So quickened appetite that I, methought,   85
Could not but taste. Forthwith up to the clouds
With him I flew, and underneath beheld
The earth outstretched immense, a prospect wide
And various: wondering at my flight and change
To this high exaltation, suddenly   90
My guide was gone, and I, methought, sunk down
And fell asleep. But Oh how glad I waked
To find this but a dream!" Thus Eve her night
Related, and thus Adam answered sad:[7]
    "Best image of myself and dearer half,   95
The trouble of thy thoughts this night in sleep
Affects me equally; nor can I like
This uncouth dream, of evil sprung, I fear;
Yet evil whence? In thee can harbor none,
Created pure. But know that in the soul   100
Are many lesser faculties that serve
Reason as chief; among these fancy next
Her office holds. Of all external things
Which the five watchful senses represent
She forms imaginations, airy shapes   105
Which reason, joining or disjoining, frames
All what we affirm or what deny, and call
Our knowledge or opinion; then retires

7. Grave, serious.

Into her private cell when nature rests.
Oft in her absence mimic fancy wakes   110
To imitate her; but, misjoining shapes,
Wild work produces oft, and most in dreams,
Ill matching words and deeds long past or late.
Some such resemblances methinks I find
Of our last evening's talk in this thy dream,[8]   115
But with addition strange. Yet be not sad,
Evil into the mind of god[9] or man
May come and go, so unapproved, and leave
No spot or blame behind; which gives me hope
That what in sleep thou didst abhor to dream,   120
Waking thou never wilt consent to do.
Be not disheartened then, nor cloud those looks
That wont to be more cheerful and serene
Than when fair morning first smiles on the world;
And let us to our fresh employments rise   125
Among the groves, the fountains, and the flowers
That open now their choicest bosomed smells
Reserved from night, and kept for thee in store."
    So cheered he his fair spouse, and she was cheered,
But silently a gentle tear let fall   130
From either eye, and wiped them with her hair;
Two other precious drops that ready stood,
Each in their crystal sluice, he ere they fell
Kissed as the gracious signs of sweet remorse
And pious awe that feared to have offended.   135

Summary Before going to work at their rural tasks, Adam and Eve
recite their spontaneous morning prayers. God, seeing and pitying their
unprotected innocence, dispatches Raphael to warn them of approaching
dangers. The affable archangel enters the bower just about noontime and is
promptly invited to join the midday meal, an invitation which he gladly
accepts.

[A Visit with the Angel: The Scale of Nature]

        * * * So to the sylvan lodge
They came, that like Pomona's arbor[1] smiled
With flowerets decked and fragrant smells; but Eve,
Undecked save with herself, more lovely fair   380
Than wood nymph or the fairest goddess feigned
Of three that on Mount Ida naked strove,[2]

8. Adam recalls his own words in 4.411–39.
9. Probably "angel," as elsewhere; but perhaps also
"God," whose omniscience must encompass evil
as well as good.
1. Pomona, Roman goddess of fruit trees and gardens, dwelt in an orchard.

2. Aphrodite, Hera, and Athena were judged for
their beauty on Mount Ida by Paris, son of Priam.
Milton reminds us that the goddesses were only
"feigned," i.e., not true in the sense that the
Christian god is true.

Stood t' entertain her guest from Heaven; no veil
She needed, virtue-proof, no thought infirm
Altered her cheek. On whom the Angel "Hail"   385
Bestowed, the holy salutation used
Long after to blessed Mary, second Eve.
   "Hail mother of mankind, whose fruitful womb
Shall fill the world more numerous with thy sons
Than with these various fruits the trees of God   390
Have heaped this table." Raised of grassy turf
Their table was, and mossy seats had round,
And on her ample square from side to side
All autumn piled, though spring and autumn here
Danced hand in hand. A while discourse they hold—   395
No fear lest dinner cool—when thus began
Our author.[3] "Heavenly stranger, please to taste
These bounties which our nourisher, from whom
All perfect good, unmeasured-out, descends,
To us for food and for delight hath caused   400
The earth to yield;[4] unsavory food perhaps
To spiritual natures; only this I know,
That one celestial Father gives to all."
   To whom the Angel: "Therefore what he gives
(Whose praise be ever sung) to man in part   405
Spiritual, may of purest spirits be found
No ungrateful food;[5] and food alike those pure
Intelligential substances require
As doth your rational; and both contain
Within them every lower faculty   410
Of sense, whereby they hear, see, smell, touch, taste,
Tasting concoct,[6] digest, assimilate,
And corporeal to incorporeal turn.
For know, whatever was created needs
To be sustained and fed; of elements   415
The grosser feeds the purer, earth the sea,
Earth and the sea feed air, the air those fires
Ethereal, and as lowest first the moon—
Whence in her visage round those spots, unpurged
Vapors not yet into her substance turned.[7]   420
Nor doth the moon no nourishment exhale
From her moist continent to higher orbs.
The sun, that light imparts to all, receives
From all his alimental recompense

---

3. Our creator (i.e., Adam).
4. I.e., please to taste these bounties which God
("our nourisher") has caused the earth to yield to
us for food and for delight.
5. I.e., food that is proper for man, who is partly
spiritual, will be proper also for the very purest
spirits. The idea that within the hierarchical universe higher powers include and comprehend lower
powers is the key to the entire passage that follows.

6. Make ready by heat, warm up.
7. Raphael voices an archaic theory of lunar spots
as still-undigested vapors, drawn up as food from
the inferior planet, earth. This theory fits with
Raphael's exposition of the universal hierarchy, but
Milton knew better: he had referred to Galileo's
correct explanation of the spots—as landscape features—in 1.287–91.

In humid exhalations, and at even   425
Sups with the ocean.[8] Though in Heaven the trees
Of life ambrosial[9] fruitage bear, and vines
Yield nectar, though from off the boughs each morn
We brush mellifluous dews, and find the ground
Covered with pearly grain, yet God hath here   430
Varied his bounty so with new delights
As may compare with Heaven; and to taste
Think not I shall be nice."[1] So down they sat,
And to their viands fell, nor seemingly
The Angel, nor in mist (the common gloss   435
Of theologians),[2] but with keen dispatch
Of real hunger and concoctive heat
To transubstantiate;[3] what redounds, transpires
Through spirits with ease: nor wonder: if by fire
Of sooty coal the empiric alchemist   440
Can turn, or holds it possible to turn,
Metals of drossiest ore to perfect gold
As from the mine. Meanwhile at table Eve
Ministered naked, and their flowing cups
With pleasant liquors crowned. O innocence   445
Deserving Paradise! if ever, then,
Then had the sons of God excuse t' have been
Enamored at that sight; but in those hearts
Love unlibidinous reigned, nor jealousy
Was understood, the injured lover's hell.   450
    Thus when with meats and drinks they had sufficed,
Not burdened nature, sudden mind arose
In Adam, not to let th' occasion pass
Giv'n him by this great conference to know
Of things above his world, and of their being   455
Who dwell in Heaven, whose excellence he saw
Transcend his own so far, whose radiant forms
Divine effulgence,[4] whose high power so far
Exceeded human, and his wary speech
Thus to th' empyreal[5] minister he framed: 460
    "Inhabitant with God, now know I well
Thy favor in this honor done to man,
Under whose lowly roof thou hast vouchsafed

8. The phenomenon of evaporation Milton interprets as the sun dining off the moisture exhaled
from oceans.
9. Ambrosia and nectar are the traditional diet of
angelic creatures.
1. Scrupulous, finicky.
2. Theologians intent on maintaining the pure
spirituality of angels say they experience only the
likeness of eating or loving—seemingly, or in a mist;
Milton will have none of this evasion: the angel
ate with real hunger.
3. In common theological use, transubstantiation
is the Roman Catholic doctrine that the bread and

wine of the eucharist really become the body and
blood of Christ; Milton would vigorously have
denied that doctrine as it applied to the sacrament,
but says that here, by transforming material food
to spiritual substance, the angel performed an act
of true transubstantiation. The excess ("what
redounds") is exhaled through spiritual pores.
4. A verb to the general effect of "diffused" or
"radiated" is omitted.
5. A minister from the empyrean, the highest or
fiery level of heaven; with a perhaps accidental
touch on "imperial," as well.

To enter and these earthly fruits to taste,
Food not of angels, yet accepted so   465
As that more willingly thou couldst not seem
At Heav'n's high feasts t' have fed: yet what compare?"
      To whom the wingèd hierarch replied:
"O Adam, one Almighty is, from whom
All things proceed and up to him return,   470
If not depraved from good, created all
Such to perfection, one first matter all,
Endued with various forms, various degrees
Of substance, and in things that live, of life;[6]
But more refined, more spiritous, and pure,   475
As nearer to him placed or nearer tending,
Each in their several active spheres assigned,
Till body up to spirit work, in bounds
Proportioned to each kind. So from the root
Springs lighter the green stalk, from thence the leaves   480
More airy, last the bright consummate flower
Spirits odorous breathes:[7] flowers and their fruit,
Man's nourishment, by gradual scale sublimed,[8]
To vital spirits aspire, to animal,
To intellectual[9]—give both life and sense,   485
Fancy[1] and understanding, whence the soul
Reason receives, and reason is her being,
Discursive or intuitive;[2] discourse
Is oftest yours, the latter most is ours,
Differing but in degree, of kind the same.   490
Wonder not then, what God for you saw good
If I refuse not,[3] but convert, as you,
To proper substance; time may come when men
With angels may participate, and find
No inconvenient diet, nor too light fare;   495
And from these corporal nutriments perhaps
Your bodies may at last turn all to spirit,
Improved by tract of time, and winged ascend
Ethereal as we,[4] or may at choice
Here or in heavenly paradises dwell;   500
If ye be found obedient, and retain

---

6. Behind Raphael's speech lies the traditional division of natural things into inanimate objects, vegetable, animal, human, and angelic natures; they all derive from one matter, created by God, but are differentiated by Him into distinct levels of purity.
7. As the flower is the consummation of a plant's existence, its odors are efflorescences analogous to man's spiritual life, the consummation of *his* existence.
8. Purified.
9. Man was thought to have three "souls"—vegetative, sensitive, and rational—each of which

worked through subtle fluids called spirits.
1. Imagination.
2. For Milton, discursive reason, which must be learned by rules and study, is quite different from the intuitive reason that especially characterizes angels.
3. I.e., don't be surprised if I accept ("refuse not") what God thought would be good for you.
4. Raphael is talking to unfallen man, who might in time very well turn all spirit; Milton's view of fallen man, strongly idealistic in an early poem like *Comus*, darkened with time and experience.

Unalterably firm his love entire
Whose progeny you are. Meanwhile, enjoy
Your fill what happiness this happy state
Can comprehend, incapable of more."   505
    To whom the patriarch of mankind replied:
"O favorable spirit, propitious guest,
Well hast thou taught the way that might direct
Our knowledge, and the scale of nature set
From center to circumference, whereon   510
In contemplation of created things
By steps we may ascend to God. * * *"

Summary   After this mingled explanation and warning, Raphael, by way of emphasizing the danger that threatens Adam and Eve, enters upon the story of Satan's revolt and fall. Satan, pretending that God's exaltation of the Son was an offense to angelic dignity, persuaded a host of his fellow angels to withdraw their allegiance to God and set up a camp in the north of Heaven. When open war on God was declared, however, one of these angels was able to repent. The seraph Abdiel, though scorned by his fellow rebels, denounced the rebellion, and returned, heroically alone, to the ranks of God's followers.

Book 6. Summary   Continuing the story of the war in Heaven, Raphael describes the assembling of the armies and a first skirmish in which Satan is both insulted and wounded by Abdiel. After the first day's battle, the evil angels retire discomfited; but overnight Satan invents cannon with which, on the second day, the good angels are put to some disorder. In the fury of the fight, however, they pull up mountains by the roots and bury the cannon beneath them; thus the issue remains inconclusive. On the third day, God withdraws all his armies and sends the Son alone into battle; the Son drives his enemies irresistibly over the wall of Heaven, and after falling nine days through Chaos they are swallowed up in Hell.

From Book 7

[*The Invocation*]

Descend from Heaven, Urania,[1] by that name
If rightly thou art called,[2] whose voice divine
Following, above th' Olympian hill I soar,

---

1. To start the second half of his poem, Milton must counterbalance the destruction of the war in Heaven with the creation by God of a new universe, centering on the Earth. Book 7 is devoted to this topic; and to approach so vast a subject, Milton once more invokes his Muse.

2. Milton has only the names of classical Muses with which to invoke the spiritual principles of Christian theology. Properly the Muse of astronomy, Urania is also the symbol of heavenly love and of divine wisdom.

Above the flight of Pegasean wing![3]
The meaning, not the name I call: for thou   5
Nor of the Muses nine, nor on the top
Of old Olympus dwell'st, but heavenly born,
Before the hills appeared, or fountain flowed,
Thou with eternal Wisdom didst converse,
Wisdom thy sister, and with her didst play   10
In presence of th' Almighty Father,[4] pleased
With thy celestial song. Up led by thee
Into the Heaven of Heavens I have presumed,
An earthly guest, and drawn empyreal air,
Thy tempering;[5] with like safety guided down,   15
Return me to my native element:
Lest from this flying steed unreined (as once
Bellerophon,[6] though from a lower clime),
Dismounted, on th' Aleian field I fall,
Erroneous[7] there to wander and forlorn.   20
Half yet remains unsung, but narrower bound
Within the visible diurnal sphere;
Standing on earth, not rapt above the pole,
More safe I sing with mortal voice, unchanged
To hoarse or mute, though fall'n on evil days,   25
On evil days though fall'n, and evil tongues,
In darkness, and with dangers compassed round,
And solitude; yet not alone, while thou
Visit'st my slumbers nightly, or when morn
Purples the east:[8] still govern thou my song,   30
Urania, and fit audience find, though few.
But drive far off the barbarous dissonance
Of Bacchus and his revelers, the race
Of that wild rout that tore the Thracian bard[9]
In Rhodope, where woods and rocks had ears   35
To rapture, till the savage clamor drowned
Both harp and voice; nor could the Muse defend
Her son. So fail not thou, who thee implores:
For thou art heavenly, she an empty dream.

---

3. Pegasus, the flying horse of poetry, suggests (in connection with Bellerophon, line 18) Milton's sense of his own perilous audacity in writing so vast a poem.
4. In Proverbs 8.30, Wisdom is made to speak of "playing always before God," previous even to the Creation. Milton makes his Muse coeval with divine wisdom.
5. Tempered (i.e., mixed and softened) by thee.
6. Bellerophon tried to explore the stars astride Pegasus the flying horse; but Zeus sent a gadfly to sting Pegasus, and his rider, after falling onto the

Aleian plain in Lycia, wandered about there till he died.
7. From Latin *errare*, "to wander," as well as "to be mistaken."
8. Milton composed mostly at night or very early in the morning.
9. The Thracian Bacchantes, female worshipers of Bacchus, tore Orpheus to pieces in Rhodope, though even the rocks and trees were so impressed with his music that they refused to be used against the poet. See *Lycidas*, lines 58–63. Orpheus was son of Calliope, the epic Muse.

Summary   At Adam's request, Raphael continues his narration and describes how God, to replace the fallen angels, created the world, its creatures, and finally man, in the course of six days; the story of the creation concludes, on the seventh day, with a chorus of thanksgiving by the angels.

From Book 8

Summary   Adam, to prolong his visit with Raphael, asks why so many and such splendid stars seem to be at the service of the earth, which appears smaller and less noble than they. At this point Eve discreetly takes her leave. In answer to Adam's question, Raphael proposes various astronomical possibilities, but gives no conclusive answer, advising Adam to concern himself with matters closer to home. The angel, on the other hand, is much interested to hear the story, which Adam proposes to tell, of his own creation.

[*Adam Describes His Own Creation and That of Eve; Having Repeated His Warning, the Angel Departs*]

So spake the godlike power, and thus our sire:
"For man to tell how human life began   250
Is hard; for who himself beginning knew?
Desire with thee still longer to converse
Induced me. As new waked from soundest sleep,
Soft on the flowery herb I found me laid
In balmy sweat, which with his beams the sun   255
Soon dried, and on the reeking moisture fed.
Straight toward heaven my wondering eyes I turned,
And gazed a while the ample sky, till raised
By quick instinctive motion up I sprung
As thitherward endeavoring, and upright   260
Stood on my feet; about me round I saw
Hill, dale, and shady woods, and sunny plains
And liquid lapse of murmuring streams; by these,
Creatures that lived and moved, and walked or flew,
Birds on the branches warbling. All things smiled,   265
With fragrance and with joy my heart o'erflowed.
Myself I then perused,[1] and limb by limb
Surveyed, and sometimes went and sometimes ran
With supple joints as lively vigor led:
But who I was, or where, or from what cause,   270
Knew not. To speak I tried, and forthwith spake,
My tongue obeyed, and readily could name
Whate'er I saw. 'Thou sun,' said I, 'fair light,
And thou enlightened earth, so fresh and gay,
Ye hills and dales, ye rivers, woods, and plains,   275

---

1. Inspected.

And ye that live and move, fair creatures, tell,
Tell, if ye saw, how came I thus, how here?
Not of myself; by some great maker, then,
In goodness and in power preëminent.
Tell me how may I know him, how adore,   280
From whom I have that thus I move and live,
And feel that I am happier than I know.'
    "While thus I called, and strayed I knew not whither
From where I first drew air and first beheld
This happy light, when answer none returned,   285
On a green shady bank profuse of flowers
Pensive I sat me down; there gentle sleep
First found me and with soft oppression seized
My drowsèd sense—untroubled, though I thought
I then was passing to my former state   290
Insensible, and forthwith to dissolve;
When suddenly stood at my head a dream,
Whose inward apparition gently moved
My fancy to believe I yet had being
And lived. One came, methought, of shape divine,   295
And said, 'Thy mansion² wants thee, Adam, rise,
First man, of men innumerable ordained
First father; called by thee I come thy guide
To the garden of bliss, thy seat prepared.'
So saying, by the hand he took me raised,   300
And over fields and waters, as in air
Smooth sliding without step, last led me up
A woody mountain whose high top was plain,
A circuit wide, enclosed, with goodliest trees
Planted, with walks and bowers, that what I saw   305
Of earth before scarce pleasant seemed. Each tree
Loaden with fairest fruit that hung to the eye
Tempting, stirred in me sudden appetite
To pluck and eat; whereat I waked, and found
Before mine eyes all real, as the dream   310
Had lively shadowed. Here had new begun
My wandering, had not he who was my guide
Up hither, from among the trees appeared,
Presence divine. Rejoicing, but with awe,
In adoration at his feet I fell   315
Submiss: he reared me, and, 'Whom thou soughtest I am,'
Said mildly, 'author of all this thou seest
Above or round about thee or beneath.
This Paradise I give thee, count it thine
To till and keep, and of the fruit to eat.   320
Of every tree that in the garden grows
Eat freely with glad heart; fear here no dearth.

---

2. Habitation.

But of the tree whose operation brings
Knowledge of good and ill, which I have set
The pledge of thy obedience and thy faith   325
Amid the garden by the Tree of Life,
Remember what I warn thee, shun to taste
And shun the bitter consequence: for know
The day thou eat'st thereof, my sole command
Transgressed, inevitably thou shalt die,   330
From that day mortal, and this happy state
Shalt lose, expelled from hence into a world
Of woe and sorrow.' Sternly he pronounced
The rigid interdiction, which resounds
Yet dreadful in mine ear, though in my choice   335
Not to incur; but soon his clear aspèct
Returned, and gracious purpose[3] thus renewed:
'Not only these fair bounds, but all the Earth
To thee and to thy race I give; as lords
Possess it, and all things that therein live,   340
Or live in sea or air, beast, fish, and fowl.
In sign whereof each bird and beast behold
After their kinds; I bring them to receive
From thee their names, and pay thee fealty
With low subjection; understand the same   345
Of fish within their watery residence,
Not hither summoned, since they cannot change
Their element to draw the thinner air.'
As thus he spake, each bird and beast behold
Approaching two and two, these[4] cowering low   350
With blandishment, each bird stooped on his wing.
I named them as they passed, and understood
Their nature, with such knowledge God endued
My sudden apprehension. But in these
I found not what methought I wanted still,   355
And to the heavenly vision thus presumed:
    " 'Oh by what name, for thou above all these,
Above mankind, or aught than mankind higher,
Surpassest far my naming, how may I
Adore thee, author of this universe   360
And all this good to man, for whose well-being
So amply and with hands so liberal
Thou hast provided all things? But with me
I see not who partakes. In solitude
What happiness? Who can enjoy alone,   365
Or all enjoying, what contentment find?'
Thus I presumptuous; and the vision bright,
As with a smile more brightened, thus replied:
    " 'What callest thou solitude? Is not the earth

---

3. Speech.   4. I.e., the beasts.

With various living creatures, and the air,   370
Replenished, and all these at thy command
To come and play before thee? Knowest thou not
Their language and their ways?[5] They also know
And reason not contemptibly; with these
Find pastime and bear rule; thy realm is large.'   375
So spake the universal lord, and seemed
So ordering. I with leave of speech implored
And humble deprecation, thus replied:
" 'Let not my words offend thee, heavenly power,
My maker; be propitious while I speak.   380
Hast thou not made me here thy substitute,
And these inferior far beneath me set?
Among unequals what society
Can sort,[6] what harmony or true delight?
Which must be mutual, in proportion due   385
Given and received. But in disparity,
The one intense, the other still remiss,[7]
Cannot well suit with either, but soon prove
Tedious alike. Of fellowship I speak
Such as I seek, fit to participate   390
All rational delight, wherein the brute
Cannot be human consort. They rejoice
Each with their kind, lion with lioness,
So fitly them in pairs thou hast combined;
Much less can bird with beast, or fish with fowl   395
So well converse, nor with the ox the ape;
Worse then can man with beast, and least of all.'
     "Whereto the Almighty answered, not displeased:
'A nice[8] and subtle happiness I see
Thou to thyself proposest, in the choice   400
Of thy associates, Adam, and wilt taste
No pleasure, though in pleasure, solitary.
What thinkest thou then of me and this my state?
Seem I to thee sufficiently possessed
Of happiness or not? who am alone   405
From all eternity, for none I know
Second to me or like, equal much less.
How have I then with whom to hold converse
Save with the creatures which I made, and those
To me inferior, infinite descents   410
Beneath what other creatures are to thee?'
     "He ceased, I lowly answered: 'To attain
The height and depth of thy eternal ways

---

5. Adam in the state of innocence knows instinctively, not only the earliest language (for Milton
and his age, that was Hebrew), but also the languages of all the creatures.
6. Agree.

7. "Intense . . . remiss": taut . . . slack, continuing the musical metaphor begun with "harmony"
(line 384).
8. Delicate, discriminating—with perhaps an
overtone of the sense "finicky."

All human thoughts come short, supreme of things.
Thou in thyself art perfect, and in thee 415
Is no deficience found; not so is man,
But in degree, the cause of his desire[9]
By conversation with his like to help
Or solace his defects. No need that thou
Shouldst propagate, already infinite, 420
And through all numbers absolute, though one.[1]
But man by number is to manifest
His single imperfection,[2] and beget
Like of his like, his image multiplied,
In unity defective, which requires 425
Collateral love and dearest amity.
Thou in thy secrecy although alone,
Best with thyself accompanied, seekest not
Social communication; yet, so pleased,
Canst raise thy creature to what height thou wilt 430
Of union or communion, deified;
I by conversing cannot these erect
From prone, nor in their ways complacence find.'
Thus I emboldened spake, and freedom used
Permissive, and acceptance found, which gained 435
This answer from the gracious voice divine:
   " 'Thus far to try thee, Adam, I was pleased,
And find thee knowing, not of beasts alone
Which thou hast rightly named, but of thyself,
Expressing well the spirit within thee free, 440
My image, not imparted to the brute,
Whose fellowship, therefore unmeet for thee,
Good reason was thou freely shouldst dislike;
And be so minded still. I, ere thou spak'st,
Knew it not good for man to be alone, 445
And no such company as then thou sawest
Intended thee, for trial only brought,
To see how thou couldst judge of fit and meet.
What next I bring shall please thee, be assured:
Thy likeness, thy fit help, thy other self, 450
Thy wish exactly to thy heart's desire.'
   "He ended, or I heard no more, for now,
My earthly by his heavenly overpowered
Which it had long stood under, strained to the height
In that celestial colloquy sublime, 455
As with an object that excels[3] the sense
Dazzled and spent, sunk down and sought repair
Of sleep, which instantly fell on me, called

---

9. Though perfect "in degree" (i.e., for his sort of
creature), man is far from God's perfection, (which
is) the cause of his desire, etc.
1. God, as infinity, contains all numbers, though

he is also and especially one.
2. Imperfection in being single.
3. Exceeds.

By nature as in aid, and closed mine eyes.
Mine eyes he closed, but open left the cell   460
Of fancy, my internal sight, by which
Abstract as in a trance methought I saw,
Though sleeping, where I lay, and saw the shape
Still glorious before whom awake I stood;
Who stooping opened my left side, and took   465
From thence a rib, with cordial[4] spirits warm
And life-blood streaming fresh. Wide was the wound,
But suddenly with flesh filled up and healed.
The rib he formed and fashioned with his hands;
Under his forming hands a creature grew,   470
Manlike, but different sex, so lovely fair
That what seemed fair in all the world seemed now
Mean, or in her summed up, in her contained,
And in her looks, which from that time infused
Sweetness into my heart, unfelt before,   475
And into all things from her air inspired
The spirit of love and amorous delight.
She disappeared, and left me dark; I waked
To find her or forever to deplore
Her loss, and other pleasures all abjure;   480
When out of hope, behold her, not far off,
Such as I saw her in my dream, adorned
With what all earth or heaven could bestow
To make her amiable. On she came,
Led by her heavenly maker, though unseen,   485
And guided by his voice, nor uninformed
Of nuptial sanctity and marriage rites.
Grace was in all her steps, heaven in her eye,
In every gesture dignity and love.
I overjoyed could not forbear aloud: 490
   " 'This turn hath made amends; thou hast fulfilled
Thy words, Creator bounteous and benign,
Giver of all things fair, but fairest this
Of all thy gifts; nor enviest.[5] I now see
Bone of my bone, flesh of my flesh, my self   495
Before me; woman is her name, of man
Extracted; for this cause he shall forego
Father and mother, and to his wife adhere,
And they shall be one flesh, one heart, one soul.'[6]
   "She heard me thus, and though divinely brought, 500
Yet innocence and virgin modesty,
Her virtue and the conscience[7] of her worth
That would be wooed and not unsought be won,

---

4. "Cordial": from the heart.
5. Unlike some other gods (Jove, for example),
Milton's deity does not lust after the females he
bestows on men.
6. Adam's speech to Eve is largely an expansion

of Genesis 2.23–24.
7. Consciousness. Note that Adam cannot find a
verb for what Eve does in consequence of her
innocence and virgin modesty. The poet's touch
at this juncture is delicate in the extreme.

Not obvious, not obtrusive, but retired,
The more desirable—or, to say all,   505
Nature herself, though pure of sinful thought,
Wrought in her so that, seeing me, she turned.
I followed her; she what was honor knew,
And with obsequious[8] majesty approved
My pleaded reason. To the nuptial bower   510
I led her blushing like the morn. All heaven
And happy constellations on that hour
Shed their selectest influence; the earth
Gave sign of gratulation, and each hill;
Joyous the birds; fresh gales and gentle airs   515
Whispered it to the woods, and from their wings
Flung rose, flung odors from the spicy shrub,
Disporting, till the amorous bird of night[9]
Sung spousal, and bid haste the evening star
On his hill-top, to light the bridal lamp.   520
    "Thus have I told thee all my state, and brought
My story to the sum of earthly bliss
Which I enjoy, and must confess to find
In all things else delight indeed, but such
As, used or not, works in the mind no change,   525
Nor vehement desire—these delicacies
I mean of taste, sight, smell, herbs, fruits, and flowers,
Walks and the melody of birds. But here,
Far otherwise, transported I behold,
Transported touch; here passion first I felt,   530
Commotion strange, in all enjoyments else
Superior and unmoved, here only weak
Against the charm of beauty's powerful glance.
Or[1] nature failed in me and left some part
Not proof enough such object to sustain,   535
Or from my side subducting[2] took perhaps
More than enough; at least on her bestowed
Too much of ornament, in outward show
Elaborate, of inward less exact.
For well I understand in the prime end   540
Of nature her th' inferior, in the mind
And inward faculties which most excel,
In outward also her resembling less
His image who made both, and less expressing
The character of that dominion given   545
O'er other creatures. Yet when I approach
Her loveliness, so absolute she seems
And in herself complete, so well to know
Her own, that what she wills to do or say

8. Compliant.
9. The nightingale, present on this auspicious
occasion, as he was in the more doubtful scene of

Eve's tempting dream (5.40).
1. Either.
2. Subtracting.

Seems wisest, virtuousest, discreetest, best.   550
All higher knowledge in her presence falls
Degraded; wisdom in discourse with her
Loses discountenanced, and like folly shows;
Authority and reason on her wait
As one intended first, not after made   555
Occasionally;[3] and to consummate all,
Greatness of mind and nobleness their seat
Build in her loveliest, and create an awe
About her as a guard angelic placed."
   To whom the Angel with contracted brow: 560
"Accuse not nature, she hath done her part;
Do thou but thine, and be not diffident[4]
Of wisdom; she deserts thee not if thou
Dismiss not her when most thou need'st her nigh
By àttributing overmuch to things   565
Less excellent, as thou thyself perceiv'st.
For what admir'st thou, what transports thee so?
An outside? Fair no doubt, and worthy well
Thy cherishing, thy honoring, and thy love;
Not thy subjection. Weigh her with thyself,   570
Then value. Ofttimes nothing profits more
Then self-esteem, grounded on just and right
Well managed. Of that skill the more thou know'st,
The more she will acknowledge thee her head,
And to realities yield all her shows—   575
Made so adorn for thy delight the more,
So aweful[5] that with honor thou may'st love
Thy mate, who sees when thou art seen least wise.
But if the sense of touch whereby mankind
Is propagated seem such dear delight   580
Beyond all other, think the same vouchsafed
To cattle and each beast; which would not be
To them made common and divulged if aught
Therein enjoyed were worthy to subdue
The soul of man, or passion in him move.   585
What higher in her society thou find'st
Attractive, human, rational—love still;
In loving thou dost well, in passion not,
Wherein true love consists not. Love refines
The thoughts, and heart enlarges, hath his seat   590
In reason, and is judicious, is the scale[6]
By which to heavenly love thou may'st ascend,
Not sunk in carnal pleasure, for which cause
Among the beasts no mate for thee was found."

3. Incidentally.
4. Mistrustful, without faith.
5. Awe-inspiring.
6. The scale of nature, as in 5.509 above, but with an important overtone from Latin or Italian *scala*, meaning "ladder." The ladder of love was a Neoplatonic metaphor.

To whom thus half abashed Adam replied: 595
"Neither her outside formed so fair, nor aught
In procreation common to all kinds
(Though higher of the genial[7] bed by far
And with mysterious reverence I deem)
So much delights me as those graceful acts,   600
Those thousand decencies that daily flow
From all her words and actions, mixed with love
And sweet compliance, which declare unfeigned
Union of mind or in us both one soul,
Harmony to behold in wedded pair   605
More grateful than harmonious sound to the ear.
Yet these subject not; I to thee disclose
What inward thence I feel, not therefore foiled,
Who meet with various objects from the sense
Variously representing; yet still free   610
Approve the best, and follow what I approve.[8]
    "To love thou blam'st me not, for love thou say'st
Leads up to heaven, is both the way and guide;
Bear with me then, if lawful what I ask:
Love not the heavenly spirits, and how their love   615
Express they, by looks only, or do they mix
Irradiance, virtual or immediate touch?"
    To whom the Angel with a smile that glowed
Celestial rosy red, love's proper hue,
Answered: "Let it suffice thee that thou know'st   620
Us happy, and without love no happiness.
Whatever pure thou in the body enjoy'st
(And pure thou wert created), we enjoy
In eminence, and obstacle find none
Of membrane, joint, or limb, exclusive bars.   625
Easier than air with air, if spirits embrace,
Total they mix, union of pure with pure
Desiring; nor restrained conveyance need
As flesh to mix with flesh or soul with soul.
But I can now no more; the parting sun   630
Beyond the earth's green cape and verdant isles[9]
Hesperian sets, my signal to depart.
Be strong, live happy, and love, but first of all
Him whom to love is to obey, and keep
His great command; take heed lest passion sway   635
Thy judgment to do aught which else free will
Would not admit; thine and of all thy sons
The weal or woe in thee is placed: beware.
I in thy persevering shall rejoice,

---

7. Procreative, progenitive.
8. The sense of these last few lines is not quite clear; Milton seems to be miming Adam's embarrassment, from which he escapes with an acute question for the angel.
9. Cape Verde near Dakar and the Islas Verdes off that coast are the westernmost ("Hesperian") points of Africa, and so of the Old World as a whole.

And all the blest. Stand fast; to stand or fall   640
Free in thine own arbitrement it lies.
Perfect within, no outward aid require;
And all temptation to transgress repel."[1]
   So saying, he arose; whom Adam thus
Followed with benediction: "Since to part,   645
Go, heavenly guest, ethereal messenger,
Sent from whose[2] sovereign goodness I adore.
Gentle to me and affable hath been
Thy condescension, and shall be honored ever
With grateful memory. Thou to mankind   650
Be good and friendly still, and oft return."
   So parted they, the Angel up to Heaven
From the thick shade, and Adam to his bower.

Book 9

The Argument

   Satan, having compassed the Earth, with meditated guile returns as a mist by night into Paradise; enters into the serpent sleeping. Adam and Eve in the morning go forth to their labors, which Eve proposes to divide in several places, each laboring apart: Adam consents not, alleging the danger lest that enemy of whom they were forewarned should attempt her found alone. Eve, loath to be thought not circumspect or firm enough, urges her going apart, the rather desirous to make trial of her strength; Adam at last yields. The serpent finds her alone: his subtle approach, first gazing, then speaking, with much flattery extolling Eve above all other creatures. Eve, wondering to hear the serpent speak, asks how he attained to human speech and such understanding not till now; the serpent answers that by tasting of a certain tree in the garden he attained both to speech and reason, till then void of both. Eve requires him to bring her to that tree, and finds it to be the Tree of Knowledge forbidden: the serpent, now grown bolder, with many wiles and arguments induces her at length to eat. She, pleased with the taste, deliberates a while whether to impart thereof to Adam or not; at last brings him of the fruit; relates what persuaded her to eat thereof. Adam, at first amazed, but perceiving her lost, resolves, through vehemence of love, to perish with her, and, extenuating[1] the trespass, eats also of the fruit. The effects thereof in them both; they seek to cover their nakedness; then fall to variance and accusation of one another.

---

1. "Require" (i.e., look for, depend on) and "repel" are the two strong imperative verbs with which the angel concludes his mission. *Don't* look for help from outsiders; *do* repel temptation on your own. It is a curious touch that Eve, though she overhears, at least in part, this most forceful of divine

warnings (9.276), is not present to be addressed directly by the admonitory angel.
2. I.e., from Him whose goodness I adore.
1. Not "diminishing" or "excusing" as in customary English usage, but carrying further, drawing out.

No more of talk where God[2] or angel guest
With man, as with his friend, familiar used
To sit indulgent, and with him partake
Rural repast, permitting him the while
Venial[3] discourse unblamed. I now must change   5
Those notes to tragic; foul distrust and breach
Disloyal on the part of man, revolt
And disobedience; on the part of Heaven
Now alienated, distance and distaste,
Anger and just rebuke, and judgment given,   10
That brought into this world a world of woe,
Sin and her shadow Death, and Misery,
Death's harbinger. Sad task! yet argument
Not less but more heroic than the wrath
Of stern Achilles on his foe pursued   15
Thrice fugitive about Troy wall; or rage
Of Turnus for Lavinia disespoused;
Or Neptune's ire, or Juno's, that so long
Perplexed the Greek and Cytherea's son:[4]
If answerable style I can obtain   20
Of my celestial Patroness,[5] who deigns
Her nightly visitation unimplored,
And dictates to me slumbering, or inspires
Easy my unpremeditated verse,[6]
Since first this subject for heroic song   25
Pleased me, long choosing and beginning late,[7]
Not sedulous by nature to indite
Wars, hitherto the only argument
Heroic deemed, chief mastery to dissect[8]
With long and tedious havoc fabled knights   30
In battles feigned (the better fortitude
Of patience and heroic martyrdom
Unsung), or to describe races and games,
Or tilting furniture,[9] emblazoned shields,
Impresses quaint, caparisons and steeds,   35
Bases and tinsel trappings, gorgeous knights

---

2. God, of course, has not been lunching with Adam; but since man is about to fall, the age is now over when such an occasion could be contemplated.

3. Permissible.

4. In the *Iliad* (22), Achilles pursues Hector three times around Troy wall before catching him. In the *Aeneid*, Aeneas must fight with Turnus for the hand of Lavinia. Neptune (or Poseidon) was unfriendly to Odysseus (the Greek); Juno (or Hera) to Aeneas, who was Cytherea's, i.e., Aphrodite's, son by Anchises.

5. The Muse, Urania.

6. Milton, we are told by his nephew Edward Phillips, used to wake up in the morning with lines of poetry full-formed in his head; he would then dictate them to an amanuensis.

7. Milton's early plans for epics, preserved in manuscript, did center on national heroes; his choice of a sacred subject, though not wholly without precedent, was a relative novelty. "Sedulous": eager.

8. I.e., in describing wars one's chief task is to dissect; dissect, in its strict Latin sense of "cut apart," but perhaps also with a comic overtone from the anatomy table.

9. The equipment of tournaments; "impresses quaint": elaborate devices on shields; "bases": trappings for horses.

At joust and tournament; then marshaled feast
Served up in hall with sewers and seneschals:[1]
The skill of artifice or office mean;
Not that which justly gives heroic name   40
To person or to poem. Me of these
Nor skilled nor studious, higher argument
Remains,[2] sufficient of itself to raise
That name,[3] unless an age too late, or cold
Climate, or years, damp my intended wing   45
Depressed; and much they may if all be mine,
Not hers who brings it nightly to my ear.
　　The sun was sunk, and after him the star
Of Hesperus, whose office is to bring
Twilight upon the Earth, short arbiter   50
'Twixt day and night, and now from end to end
Night's hemisphere had veiled the horizon round,
When Satan, who late fled before the threats
Of Gabriel out of Eden,[4] now improved
In meditated fraud and malice, bent   55
On man's destruction, maugre what might hap
Of heavier on himself,[5] fearless returned.
By night he fled, and at midnight returned
From compassing the Earth—cautious of day
Since Uriel, regent of the sun, descried   60
His entrance, and forewarned the cherubim
That kept their watch.[6] Thence, full of anguish, driven,
The space of seven continued nights he rode
With darkness; thrice the equinoctial line[7]
He circled, four times crossed the car of Night   65
From pole to pole, traversing each colure;
On the eighth returned, and on the coast averse
From entrance or cherubic watch by stealth
Found unsuspected way. There was a place
(Now not, though sin, not time, first wrought the change)   70
Where Tigris at the foot of Paradise
Into a gulf shot under ground, till part
Rose up a fountain by the Tree of Life.
In with the river sunk and with it rose
Satan, involved in rising mist; then sought   75
Where to lie hid. Sea he had searched and land
From Eden over Pontus, and the pool

---

1. Waiters and stewards, who also dissect.
2. I.e., for me, when these things are set aside
which I neither can nor want to do, there remains
a higher argument.
3. I.e., the name of heroic poet. "Age too late":
not Milton's age, but the age of the world. Milton
felt a "cold climate" was inimical to epic poetry.
"Damp": stupefy, benumb.
4. At the end of Book 4.
5. Despite the peril of heavier (punishments).

6. In Book 4. These connections with Book 4 not
only bridge the intervening narration, but emphasize a balancing of the whole epic; see the headnote.
7. The equator. The colures are the two great circles of the celestial sphere which intersect at the
poles. By circling the globe, either from east to
west or over the north and south poles, Satan can
remain continually hidden in darkness.

Maeotis, up beyond the river Ob;[8]
Downward as far antarctic; and, in length,
West from Orontes to the ocean barred   80
At Darien, thence to the land where flows
Ganges and Indus.[9] Thus the orb he roamed
With narrow search, and with inspection deep
Considered every creature, which of all
Most opportune might serve his wiles, and found   85
The serpent subtlest beast of all the field.[1]
Him, after long debate, irresolute
Of thoughts revolved,[2] his final sentence chose
Fit vessel, fittest imp[3] of fraud, in whom
To enter, and his dark suggestions hide   90
From sharpest sight; for in the wily snake
Whatever sleights none would suspicious mark,
As from his wit and native subtlety
Proceeding, which, in other beasts observed,
Doubt[4] might beget of diabolic power   95
Active within beyond the sense of brute.
Thus he resolved, but first from inward grief
His bursting passion into plaints thus poured:
    "O Earth, how like to Heaven, if not preferred
More justly, seat worthier of gods, as built   100
With second thoughts, reforming what was old!
For what god, after better, worse would build?
Terrestrial heaven, danced round by other heavens
That shine, yet bear their bright officious lamps,
Light above light, for thee alone, as seems,   105
In thee concent'ring all their precious beams
Of sacred influence![5] As God in Heaven
Is center, yet extends to all, so thou
Cent'ring receiv'st from all those orbs; in thee,
Not in themselves, all their known virtue appears,   110
Productive in herb, plant, and nobler birth
Of creatures animate with gradual life
Of growth, sense, reason,[6] all summed up in man.
With what delight could I have walked thee round,
If I could joy in aught; sweet interchange   115
Of hill and valley, rivers, woods, and plains,
Now land, now sea, and shores with forest crowned,
Rocks, dens, and caves! But I in none of these

---

8. Pontus is the Black Sea, the pool Maeotis the swamps of the Sea of Azov; the river Ob flows north through Siberia into the Arctic Ocean.
9. Flying west from Orontes in Syria, Satan crossed the Atlantic to the Isthmus of Panama (Darien), then the Pacific and southeast Asia to India.
1. Genesis 3.1 so describes the serpent.
2. I.e., unable to decide among his revolving thoughts. "Sentence": decision.
3. Graft, offshoot.

4. Suspicion.
5. Satan, like Adam in Book 8, is impressed that so many heavenly bodies center on (and "serve") the earth—as the old Ptolemaic astronomy taught that they did. "Officious": dutiful.
6. Life on earth is gradual, or graduated, from the herb which merely grows, to the animal which grows and feels, to man, who grows, feels, and thinks.

Find place or refuge; and the more I see
Pleasures about me, so much more I feel   120
Torment within me, as from the hateful siege[7]
Of contraries; all good to me becomes
Bane,[8] and in Heaven much worse would be my state.
But neither here seek I, no, nor in Heaven,
To dwell, unless by mastering Heaven's Supreme;   125
Nor hope to be myself less miserable
By what I seek, but others to make such
As I, though thereby worse to me redound.
For only in destroying I find ease
To my relentless thoughts, and him[9] destroyed,   130
Or won to what may work his utter loss,
For whom all this was made, all this[1] will soon
Follow, as to him linked in weal or woe:
In woe then, that destruction wide may range!
To me shall be the glory sole among   135
The infernal powers, in one day to have marred
What he, Almighty styled, six nights and days
Continued making, and who knows how long
Before had been contriving? though perhaps
Not longer than since I in one night freed   140
From servitude inglorious well-nigh half
Th' angelic name, and thinner left the throng
Of his adorers. He to be avenged,
And to repair his numbers thus impaired,
Whether such virtue,[2] spent of old, now failed   145
More angels to create (if they at least
Are his created),[3] or to spite us more,
Determined to advance into our room
A creature formed of earth, and him endow,
Exalted from so base original,   150
With heavenly spoils, our spoils. What he decreed
He effected; man he made, and for him built
Magnificent this world, and Earth his seat,
Him lord pronounced, and, O indignity!
Subjected to his service angel-wings   155
And flaming ministers, to watch and tend
Their earthy charge. Of these the vigilance
I dread, and to elude, thus wrapped in mist
Of midnight vapor glide obscure, and pry
In every bush and brake, where hap may find   160
The serpent sleeping in whose mazy folds
To hide me, and the dark intent I bring.
O foul descent! that I, who erst contended

---

7. Conflict.
8. Poison. This is exactly what he willed in 4.110, just reversed.
9. I.e., man.
1. I.e., the created cosmos.

2. Strength, energy.
3. Satan never likes to admit that the angels were created by God: he faces the fact squarely only once, in his soliloquy at the beginning of Book 4 (line 43).

With gods to sit the highest, am now constrained
Into a beast, and mixed with bestial slime, 165
This essence to incarnate and imbrute,[4]
That to the height of deity aspired!
But what will not ambition and revenge
Descend to? Who aspires must down as low
As high he soared, obnoxious[5] first or last 170
To basest things. Revenge, at first though sweet,
Bitter ere long back on itself recoils.
Let it; I reck not, so it light well aimed,
Since higher I fall short, on him who next
Provokes my envy, this new favorite 175
Of Heaven, this man of clay, son of despite,
Whom, us the more to spite,[6] his Maker raised
From dust: spite then with spite is best repaid."
    So saying, through each thicket dank or dry,
Like a black mist low-creeping, he held on 180
His midnight search, where soonest he might find
The serpent. Him fast sleeping soon he found
In labyrinth of many a round self-rolled,
His head the midst, well stored with subtle wiles:
Not yet in horrid shade or dismal den, 185
Nor nocent[7] yet, but on the grassy herb,
Fearless, unfeared, he slept. In at his mouth
The devil entered, and his brutal sense,
In heart or head possessing, soon inspired
With act intelligential; but his sleep 190
Disturbed not, waiting close[8] th' approach of morn.
    Now whenas sacred light began to dawn
In Eden on the humid flowers, that breathed
Their morning incense, when all things that breathe
From th' Earth's great altar send up silent praise 195
To the Creator, and his nostrils fill
With grateful smell, forth came the human pair
And joined their vocal worship to the choir
Of creatures wanting voice; that done, partake
The season,[9] prime for sweetest scents and airs; 200
Then còmmune how that day they best may ply
Their growing work; for much their work outgrew
The hands' dispatch of two gardening so wide:
And Eve first to her husband thus began:
    "Adam, well may we labor still[1] to dress 205
This garden, still to tend plant, herb, and flower,
Our pleasant task enjoined; but till more hands
Aid us, the work under our labor grows,

---

4. Satan's incarnation in a snake is a grotesque
parody of the Son of God's incarnation in Christ.
5. Subject to.
6. Satan sees God in his own image, as a spiteful
creature.

7. Harmful.
8. In secret.
9. I.e., go forth into the morning air. "Prime":
the best.
1. Continually.

Luxurious by restraint: what we by day
Lop overgrown, or prune, or prop, or bind,   210
One night or two with wanton growth derides,
Tending to wild. Thou, therefore, now advise,
Or hear what to my mind first thoughts present.
Let us divide our labors; thou where choice
Leads thee, or where most needs, whether to wind   215
The woodbine round this arbor, or direct
The clasping ivy where to climb; while I
In yonder spring[2] of roses intermixed
With myrtle find what to redress till noon.
For while so near each other thus all day   220
Our task we choose, what wonder if so near
Looks intervene and smiles, or object new
Casual discourse draw on, which intermits
Our day's work, brought to little, though begun
Early, and th' hour of supper comes unearned!"   225
        To whom mild answer Adam thus returned:
"Sole Eve, associate sole, to me beyond
Compare above all living creatures dear!
Well hast thou motioned,[3] well thy thoughts employed
How we might best fulfil the work which here   230
God hath assigned us, nor of me shalt pass
Unpraised; for nothing lovelier can be found
In woman than to study household good,
And good works in her husband to promote.[4]
Yet not so strictly hath our Lord imposed   235
Labor as to debar us when we need
Refreshment, whether food or talk between,
Food of the mind, or this sweet intercourse
Of looks and smiles; for smiles from reason flow,
To brute denied, and are of love the food,   240
Love, not the lowest end of human life.
For not to irksome toil, but to delight
He made us, and delight to reason joined.
These paths and bowers doubt not but our joint hands
Will keep from wilderness with ease, as wide   245
As we need walk, till younger hands ere long
Assist us. But if much convèrse perhaps
Thee satiate, to short absence I could yield;
For solitude sometimes is best society,
And short retirement urges sweet return.   250
But other doubt possesses me, lest harm
Befall thee, severed from me; for thou know'st
What hath been warned us, what malicious foe,
Envying our happiness, and of his own
Despairing, seeks to work us woe and shame   255

2. Growth.
3. Suggested.

4. Proverbs 31 is devoted to the praise of a good
wife, and Milton doubtless had it in mind here.

By sly assault; and somewhere nigh at hand
Watches, no doubt, with greedy hope to find
His wish and best advantage, us asunder,[5]
Hopeless to circumvent us joined, where each
To other speedy aid might lend at need.   260
Whether his first design be to withdraw
Our fealty from God, or to disturb
Conjugal love, than which perhaps no bliss
Enjoyed by us excites his envy more;
Or this, or worse,[6] leave not the faithful side   265
That gave thee being, still shades thee and protects.
The wife, where danger or dishonor lurks,
Safest and seemliest by her husband stays,
Who guards her, or with her the worst endures."
    To whom the virgin[7] majesty of Eve,   270
As one who loves, and some unkindness meets,
With sweet austere composure thus replied:
    "Offspring of Heaven and Earth, and all Earth's lord!
That such an enemy we have, who seeks
Our ruin, both by thee informed I learn,   275
And from the parting angel overheard
As in a shady nook I stood behind,
Just then returned at shut of evening flowers.
But that thou shouldst my firmness therefore doubt
To God or thee, because we have a foe   280
May tempt it, I expected not to hear.
His violence thou fear'st not, being such
As we, not capable of death or pain,
Can either not receive, or can repel.
His fraud is, then, thy fear; which plain infers   285
Thy equal fear that my firm faith and love
Can by his fraud be shaken or seduced:
Thoughts, which how found they harbor in thy breast,
Adam, misthought of her to thee so dear?"[8]
    To whom with healing words Adam replied: 290
"Daughter of God and man, immortal Eve,
For such thou art, from sin and blame entire;[9]
Not diffident of thee do I dissuade
Thy absence from my sight, but to avoid
Th' attempt itself, intended by our foe.   295
For he who tempts, though in vain, at least asperses[1]
The tempted with dishonor foul, supposed
Not incorruptible of faith, not proof

---

5. I.e., to find us apart, which will answer his wishes and serve his advantage.
6. I.e., whether this or something worse be his intent.
7. Unspotted.
8. I.e., these thoughts were misthought of (misapplied to) her to thee so dear (me).

9. "Entire" is from Latin *integer*, untouched. "Diffident": the usual English meaning is "shy," "timid"; Milton emphasizes the Latin roots, *dis* + *fides* = mistrustful.
1. The word is from Latin *spargere*, to sprinkle, with overtones from English "aspersion," an ugly insinuation.

Against temptation. Thou thyself with scorn
And anger wouldst resent the offered wrong   300
Though ineffectual found; misdeem not, then,
If such affront I labor to avert
From thee alone, which on us both at once
The enemy, though bold, will hardly dare;
Or, daring, first on me th' assault shall light.   305
Nor thou his malice and false guile contemn—
Subtle he needs must be who could seduce
Angels—nor think superfluous others' aid.
I from the influence of thy looks receive
Access[2] in every virtue; in thy sight   310
More wise, more watchful, stronger, if need were
Of outward strength; while shame, thou looking on,
Shame to be overcome or overreached,[3]
Would utmost vigor raise, and raised unite.
Why shouldst not thou like sense within thee feel   315
When I am present, and thy trial choose
With me, best witness of thy virtue tried?"
     So spake domestic Adam in his care
And matrimonial love; but Eve, who thought
Less[4] attributed to her faith sincere,   320
Thus her reply with accent sweet renewed:
     "If this be our condition, thus to dwell
In narrow circuit straitened by a foe,
Subtle or violent, we not endued
Single with like defense wherever met,   325
How are we happy, still in fear of harm?
But harm precedes not sin: only our foe
Tempting affronts us with his foul esteem
Of our integrity: his foul esteem
Sticks no dishonor on our front,[5] but turns   330
Foul on himself; then wherefore shunned or feared
By us, who rather double honor gain
From his surmise proved false, find peace within,
Favor from Heaven, our witness, from th' event?
And what is faith, love, virtue, unassayed   335
Alone, without exterior help sustained?
Let us not then suspect our happy state
Left so imperfect by the Maker wise
As not secure to single or combined.
Frail is our happiness, if this be so;   340
And Eden were no Eden, thus exposed."
     To whom thus Adam fervently replied:
"O woman, best are all things as the will
Of God ordained them; his creating hand
Nothing imperfect or deficient left   345

2. Extra strength.   4. Too little.
3. Overpowered or outwitted.   5. Forehead.

Of all that he created, much less man,
Or aught that might his happy state secure,
Secure from outward force. Within himself
The danger lies, yet lies within his power;
Against his will he can receive no harm.   350
But God left free the will; for what obeys
Reason is free; and reason he made right,
But bid her well beware, and still erect,[6]
Lest by some fair appearing good surprised,
She dictate false, and misinform the will   355
To do what God expressly hath forbid.
Not then mistrust, but tender love, enjoins
That I should mind[7] thee oft; and mind thou me.
Firm we subsist, yet possible to swerve,
Since reason not impossibly may meet   360
Some specious object by the foe suborned,
And fall into deception unaware,
Not keeping strictest watch, as she was warned.
Seek not temptation, then, which to avoid
Were better, and most likely if from me   365
Thou sever not: trial will come unsought.
Wouldst thou approve thy constancy, approve[8]
First thy obedience; th' other who can know,
Not seeing thee attempted, who attest?
But if thou think trial unsought may find   370
Us both securer[9] than thus warned thou seem'st,
Go; for thy stay, not free, absents thee more.
Go in thy native innocence; rely
On what thou hast of virtue; summon all;
For God towards thee hath done his part: do thine."   375
    So spake the patriarch of mankind; but Eve
Persisted; yet submiss, though last, replied:
    "With thy permission,[1] then, and thus forewarned,
Chiefly by what thy own last reasoning words
Touched only, that our trial, when least sought,   380
May find us both perhaps far less prepared,
The willinger I go, nor much expect
A foe so proud will first the weaker seek;
So bent, the more shall shame him his repulse."
Thus saying, from her husband's hand her hand   385
Soft she withdrew, and like a wood nymph light,
Oread or dryad, or of Delia's train,[2]
Betook her to the groves, but Delia's self

6. Remain alert.
7. Remind; in the next phrase, "mind" means "pay heed to."
8. Prove, give evidence of.
9. The Latin word *securus* can mean either "free from care" or "careless." Adam's warning is at once reassuring and ominous.

1. Eve takes a reluctant and extorted permission as free leave to do what she wants. Though apparently submissive, she gets the last word.
2. An "oread" is a nymph of the mountain, a "dryad" one of the wood. "Delia" is Diana or Artemis, goddess of the chase, who when she hunted was accompanied by a train of nymphs.

In gait surpassed and goddesslike deport,
Though not as she with bow and quiver armed,   390
But with such gardening tools as art yet rude,
Guiltless of fire[3] had formed, or angels brought.
To Pales, or Pomona, thus adorned,
Likest she seemed, Pomona when she fled
Vertumnus, or to Ceres in her prime,   395
Yet virgin of Proserpina from Jove.[4]
Her long with ardent look his eye pursued
Delighted, but desiring more her stay.
Oft he to her his charge of quick return
Repeated; she to him as oft engaged   400
To be returned by noon amid the bower,
And all things in best order to invite
Noontide repast, or afternoon's repose.
O much deceived, much failing, hapless Eve,
Of thy presumed return![5] Event perverse!   405
Thou never from that hour in Paradise
Found'st either sweet repast, or sound repose;
Such ambush hid among sweet flowers and shades
Waited with hellish rancor imminent[6]
To intercept thy way, or send thee back   410
Despoiled of innocence, of faith, of bliss.
For now, and since first break of dawn, the fiend,
Mere serpent in appearance, forth was come,
And on his quest, where likeliest he might find
The only two of mankind, but in them   415
The whole included race, his purposed prey.
In bower and field he sought, where any tuft
Of grove or garden-plot more pleasant lay,
Their tendance[7] or plantation for delight;
By fountain or by shady rivulet   420
He sought them both, but wished his hap might find
Eve separate; he wished, but not with hope
Of what so seldom chanced; when to his wish,
Beyond his hope, Eve separate he spies,
Veiled in a cloud of fragrance, where she stood,   425
Half spied, so thick the roses bushing round
About her glowed, oft stooping to support
Each flower of slender stalk, whose head though gay
Carnation, purple, azure, or specked with gold,
Hung drooping unsustained; them she upstays   430

3. There was no need of fire in Paradise; but that fire is a possession which renders one "guilty" suggests an overtone of the Prometheus myth.
4. Pales is a Roman goddess of flocks, Pomona a Roman divinity of fruits and orchards. Pomona was wooed by Vertumnus, god of the turning year, who assumed all sorts of shapes to win her. Ceres, the Mother Nature of the ancients (hence, the word "cereal"), bore Proserpina to Jupiter. All three goddesses are patronesses of agriculture, like Eve.
5. "Much deceived" carries over; Eve was "much deceived of" (about) her "presumed return."
6. Threatening.
7. Object of their tending.

Gently with myrtle band, mindless[8] the while
Herself, though fairest unsupported flower,
From her best prop so far, and storm so nigh.
Nearer he drew, and many a walk traversed
Of stateliest covert, cedar, pine, or palm;   435
Then voluble[9] and bold, now hid, now seen
Among thick-woven arborets[1] and flowers
Embordered on each bank, the hand of Eve:
Spot more delicious than those gardens feigned
Or of revived Adonis,[2] or renowned   440
Alcinous, host of old Laertes' son,
Or that, not mystic, where the sapient king[3]
Held dalliance with his fair Egyptian spouse.
Much he the place admired, the person more.
As one who long in populous city pent,   445
Where houses thick and sewers annoy[4] the air,
Forth issuing on a summer's morn to breathe
Among the pleasant villages and farms
Adjoined, from each thing met conceives delight,
The smell of grain, or tedded[5] grass, or kine,   450
Or dairy, each rural sight, each rural sound:
If chance with nymphlike step fair virgin pass,[6]
What pleasing seemed, for her now pleases more,
She most, and in her look sums all delight.[7]
Such pleasure took the serpent to behold   455
This flowery plat,[8] the sweet recess of Eve
Thus early, thus alone; her heavenly form
Angelic, but more soft and feminine,
Her graceful innocence, her every air
Of gesture or least action overawed   460
His malice, and with rapine[9] sweet bereaved
His fierceness of the fierce intent it brought:
That space the evil one abstracted stood
From his own evil, and for the time remained
Stupidly good,[1] of enmity disarmed,   465
Of guile, of hate, of envy, of revenge.

---

8. Heedless. The conceit of the flower gatherer who is herself gathered is repeated here from 4.270, where it was applied to Proserpina.

9. Rolling; with a hint from the second sense of "glib, fluent."

1. Bushes. "Hand": handiwork.

2. The garden of Adonis was a heavenly bower where Venus' lover was supposed still to lie in secret, recovering from his wound received on earth (Venus would not allow him to die). Alcinous was king of the Phaeacians. His garden, visited by Odysseus ("old Laertes' son"), is described in *Odyssey* 7.

3. Solomon; his "fair Egyptian spouse" is Pharaoh's daughter: Milton is referring to the Song of Solomon 6.2. The fact that it is "not mystic" (i.e.,

not mythical) distinguishes the Scriptural garden from the "feigned" (line 439) ones of classical legend.

4. Make noisome, befoul.

5. Tossed and drying in the sun. "Kine": cows.

6. I.e., if by chance with nymphlike step a fair virgin should pass.

7. I.e., in her look epitomizes all delight.

8. Meadow.

9. It is a deliberate paradox that her sweetness can ravish his malice; the word "rapine" is deliberately overviolent.

1. I.e., he is momentarily stunned into a kind of vacant goodness.

But the hot Hell that always in him burns,
Though in mid Heaven, soon ended his delight,
And tortures him now more, the more he sees
Of pleasure not for him ordained: then soon   470
Fierce hate he recollects, and all his thoughts
Of mischief, gratulating,[2] thus excites:
    "Thoughts, whither have ye led me? with what sweet
Compulsion thus transported to forget
What hither brought us? hate, not love, nor hope   475
Of Paradise for Hell, hope here to taste[3]
Of pleasure, but all pleasure to destroy,
Save what is in destroying; other joy
To me is lost. Then let me not let pass
Occasion which now smiles: behold alone   480
The woman, opportune to all attempts,
Her husband, for I view far round, not nigh,
Whose higher intellectual more I shun,
And strength, of courage haughty, and of limb
Heroic built, though of terrestrial mold;[4]   485
Foe not informidable, exempt from wound,[5]
I not; so much hath Hell debased and pain
Enfeebled me to what I was in Heaven.
She fair, divinely fair, fit love for gods,
Not terrible, though terror be in love   490
And beauty, not approached by stronger hate,
Hate stronger, under show of love well feigned,
The way which to her ruin now I tend."[6]
    So spake the enemy of mankind, enclosed
In serpent, inmate bad, and toward Eve   495
Addressed his way, not with indented wave,
Prone on the ground, as since, but on his rear,
Circular base of rising folds, that towered
Fold above fold a surging maze; his head
Crested aloft, and carbuncle[7] his eyes;   500
With burnished neck of verdant gold, erect
Amidst his circling spires,[8] that on the grass
Floated redundant. Pleasing was his shape,
And lovely; never since of serpent kind
Lovelier, not those that in Illyria changed   505
Hermione and Cadmus,[9] or the god
In Epidaurus;[1] nor to which transformed
Ammonian Jove, or Capitoline was seen,

---

2. Exulting.
3. A "nor" is understood before "hope," carried over from the negatives of the previous line.
4. Made of earth.
5. Adam in the state of innocence is invulnerable.
6. I.e., love and beauty are terrible unless counteracted by hate—as they are being counteracted in Satan, to the ruin of Eve.
7. Deep red, inflamed.

8. Coils. "Redundant": abundantly, to excess.
9. Ovid tells how Cadmus and Harmonia (Milton's "Hermione") were changed to serpents after they retired (in despair at the misfortunes of their children) to Illyria.
1. Aesculapius, god of medicine, had a temple at Epidaurus, from which he sometimes emerged in the form of a serpent.

He with Olympias, this with her who bore
Scipio, the height of Rome.[2] With tract oblique 510
At first, as one who sought accèss, but feared
To interrupt, sidelong he works his way.
As when a ship by skillful steersman wrought
Nigh river's mouth or foreland, where the wind
Veers oft, as oft so steers and shifts her sail: 515
So varied he, and of his tortuous train
Curled many a wanton wreath in sight of Eve,
To lure her eye: she busied heard the sound
Of rustling leaves, but minded not, as used
To such disport before her through the field, 520
From every beast, more duteous at her call
Than at Circean call the herd disguised.[3]
He bolder now, uncalled before her stood:
But as in gaze admiring; oft he bowed
His turret crest, and sleek enameled neck, 525
Fawning, and licked the ground whereon she trod.
His gentle dumb expression turned at length
The eye of Eve to mark his play: he, glad
Of her attention gained, with serpent tongue
Organic, or impulse of vocal air,[4] 530
His fraudulent temptation thus began:
    "Wonder not, sovereign mistress, if perhaps
Thou canst, who art sole wonder; much less arm
Thy looks, the heaven of mildness, with disdain,
Displeased that I approach thee thus, and gaze 535
Insatiate, I thus single, nor have feared
Thy awful brow, more awful thus retired.
Fairest resemblance of thy Maker fair,
Thee all things living gaze on, all things thine
By gift, and thy celestial beauty adore 540
With ravishment beheld, there best beheld
Where universally admired: but here
In this enclosure wild, these beasts among,
Beholders rude and shallow to discern
Half what in thee is fair, one man except, 545
Who sees thee?[5] (and what is one?) who shouldst be seen
A goddess among gods, adored and served
By angels numberless, thy daily train."
    So glozed[6] the tempter, and his proem tuned;
Into the heart of Eve his words made way, 550

---

2. Jupiter Ammon ("Ammonian Jove"), in the form
of a snake, was said to have consorted with Olympias to beget Alexander the Great; and in the same
way, the Jupiter of the Roman capitol (Jove "Capitoline") was thought to have begotten Scipio Africanus, the savior and greatest leader ("height") of
Rome.
3. Circe, who enchanted men into the shape of
beasts, was attended by an obedient herd in the

Odyssey.
4. I.e., Satan either used the actual tongue of the
serpent or himself impressed the air with speech.
5. The beasts cannot see the beauty of Eve's soul,
only Adam can, Satan's entire speech is couched
in the extravagant phrases of the Petrarchan love
convention.
6. Flattered. "Proem": introduction.

Though at the voice much marveling: at length,
Not unamazed, she thus in answer spake:
"What may this mean? Language of man pronounced
By tongue of brute, and human sense expressed?
The first at least of these I thought denied   555
To beasts, whom God on their creation-day
Created mute to all articulate sound;
The latter I demur,[7] for in their looks
Much reason, and in their actions oft appears.
Thee, serpent, subtlest beast of all the field   560
I knew, but not with human voice endued:[8]
Redouble then this miracle, and say,
How cam'st thou speakable of mute,[9] and how
To me so friendly grown above the rest
Of brutal kind, that daily are in sight?   565
Say, for such wonder claims attention due."
   To whom the guileful tempter thus replied:
"Empress of this fair world, resplendent Eve!
Easy to me it is to tell thee all
What thou command'st and right thou shouldst be obeyed: 570
I was at first as other beasts that graze
The trodden herb, of abject thoughts and low,
As was my food, nor aught but food discerned
Or sex, and apprehended nothing high:
Till on a day, roving the field, I chanced   575
A goodly tree far distant to behold
Loaden with fruit of fairest colors mixed,
Ruddy and gold; I nearer drew to gaze;
When from the boughs a savory odor blown,
Grateful to appetite, more pleased my sense   580
Than smell of sweetest fennel,[1] or the teats
Of ewe or goat dropping with milk at even,
Unsucked of lamb or kid, that tend their play.
To satisfy the sharp desire I had
Of tasting those fair apples, I resolved   585
Not to defer: hunger and thirst at once,
Powerful persuaders, quickened at the scent
Of that alluring fruit, urged me so keen.
About the mossy trunk I wound me soon,
For, high from ground, the branches would require   590
Thy utmost reach, or Adam's: round the tree
All other beasts that saw, with like desire
Longing and envying stood, but could not reach.
Amid the tree now got, where plenty hung
Tempting so nigh, to pluck and eat my fill   595

7. I.e., as to whether rational sense was denied to
brutes, I am doubtful.
8. Endowed.
9. To have speech after being dumb.

1. Milton learned, probably from Pliny, the natural historian, that serpents were fond of fennel;
popular superstition had it that they drank the milk
of sheep and goats.

I spared not;[2] for such pleasure till that hour
At feed or fountain never had I found.
Sated at length, ere long I might perceive
Strange alteration in me, to degree
Of reason in my inward powers, and speech   600
Wanted not long, though to this shape retained.[3]
Thenceforth to speculations high or deep
I turned my thoughts, and with capacious mind
Considered all things visible in Heaven,
Or Earth, or middle, all things fair and good: 605
But all that fair and good in thy divine
Semblance, and in thy beauty's heavenly ray
United I beheld: no fair[4] to thine
Equivalent or second, which compelled
Me thus, though importune perhaps, to come   610
And gaze, and worship thee of right declared
Sovereign of creatures, universal dame."
      So talked the spirited[5] sly snake: and Eve
Yet more amazed, unwary thus replied:
      "Serpent, thy overpraising leaves in doubt   615
The virtue of that fruit, in thee first proved.
But say, where grows the tree, from hence how far?
For many are the trees of God that grow
In Paradise, and various, yet unknown
To us; in such abundance lies our choice,   620
As leaves a greater store of fruit untouched,
Still hanging incorruptible, till men
Grow up to their provision, and more hands
Help to disburden Nature of her bearth."[6]
      To whom the wily adder, blithe and glad: 625
"Empress, the way is ready, and not long,
Beyond a row of myrtles, on a flat,
Fast by a fountain, one small thicket past
Of blowing[7] myrrh and balm: if thou accept
My conduct, I can bring thee thither soon."   630
      "Lead then," said Eve. He leading swiftly rolled
In tangles, and made intricate seem straight,
To mischief swift.[8] Hope elevates, and joy
Brightens his crest; as when a wandering fire
Compact of unctuous vapor,[9] which the night   635
Condenses, and the cold environs round,
Kindled through agitation to a flame
(Which oft, they say, some evil spirit attends),

2. Refrained not.
3. His inward powers, his mental constitution and gift of speech, were changed; but he retained his exterior shape as before.
4. Beauty.
5. Possessed by a spirit, inspired.
6. So spelled to pun on the idea of trees bearing fruit and thus in a way giving birth to young.
7. Blooming.
8. Milton's physical descriptions of the serpent often have distinct moral overtones, as here.
9. Composed of oily vapor; Milton's theory of the *ignis fatuus*, or will-o'-the-wisp, is strikingly material and "scientific."

Hovering and blazing with delusive light,
Misleads th' amazed night-wanderer from his way   640
To bogs and mires, and oft through pond or pool,
There swallowed up and lost, from succor far:
So glistered the dire snake, and into fraud
Led Eve our credulous mother, to the tree
Of prohibition,[1] root of all our woe: 645
Which when she saw, thus to her guide she spake:
    "Serpent, we might have spared our coming hither,
Fruitless to me, though fruit be here to excess,
The credit of whose virtue rest with thee;[2]
Wondrous indeed, if cause of such effects!   650
But of this tree we may not taste nor touch:
God so commanded, and left that command
Sole daughter of his voice;[3] the rest, we live
Law to ourselves; our reason is our law."
    To whom the tempter guilefully replied: 655
"Indeed? Hath God then said that of the fruit
Of all these garden trees ye shall not eat,
Yet lords declared of all in earth or air?"
    To whom thus Eve, yet sinless: "Of the fruit
Of each tree in the garden we may eat,   660
But of the fruit of this fair tree amidst
The garden, God hath said, 'Ye shall not eat
Thereof, nor shall ye touch it, lest ye die.' "
    She scarce had said, though brief, when now more bold
The tempter, but with show of zeal and love   665
To man, and indignation at his wrong,
New part puts on, and as to passion moved,
Fluctuates disturbed, yet comely, and in act
Raised,[4] as of some great matter to begin.
As when of old some orator renowned   670
In Athens or free Rome, where eloquence
Flourished, since mute, to some great cause addressed,
Stood in himself collected, while each part,
Motion, each act, won audience ere the tongue,
Sometimes in height began, as no delay   675
Of preface brooking,[5] through his zeal of right.
So standing, moving, or to height upgrown
The tempter all impassioned thus began:
    "O sacred, wise, and wisdom-giving plant,
Mother of science![6] now I feel thy power   680
Within me clear, not only to discern
Things in their causes, but to trace the ways
Of highest agents, deemed however wise.

1. Prohibited tree (a Hebraism).
2. I.e., you must remain the only evidence of the fruit's power.
3. His one injunction (a Hebraism). "The rest": in everything else.
4. Poised in posture.
5. The orator, as if too much moved to be bothered with a preface, bursts into the middle of his speech.
6. Knowledge.

Queen of this universe! do not believe
Those rigid threats of death. Ye shall not die; 685
How should ye? by the fruit? it gives you life
To knowledge;[7] by the Threatener? look on me,
Me who have touched and tasted, yet both live,
And life more perfect have attained than Fate
Meant me, by venturing higher than my lot. 690
Shall that be shut to man, which to the beast
Is open? Or will God incense his ire
For such a petty trespass, and not praise
Rather your dauntless virtue, whom the pain
Of death denounced, whatever thing death be, 695
Deterred not from achieving what might lead
To happier life, knowledge of good and evil?
Of good, how just![8] Of evil, if what is evil
Be real, why not known, since easier shunned?
God therefore cannot hurt ye, and be just; 700
Not just, not God; not feared then, nor obeyed:
Your fear itself of death removes the fear.[9]
Why then was this forbid? Why but to awe,
Why but to keep ye low and ignorant,
His worshipers? He knows that in the day 705
Ye eat thereof, your eyes that seem so clear,
Yet are but dim, shall perfectly be then
Opened and cleared, and ye shall be as gods,
Knowing both good and evil, as they know.
That ye should be as gods, since I as man, 710
Internal man,[1] is but proportion meet,
I, of brute, human; ye, of human, gods.
So ye shall die perhaps, by putting off
Human, to put on gods:[2] death to be wished,
Though threatened, which no worse than this can bring. 715
And what are gods that man may not become
As they, participating godlike food?
The gods are first, and that advantage use
On our belief, that all from them proceeds.
I question it; for this fair Earth I see, 720
Warmed by the sun, producing every kind,
Them nothing: if they all things,[3] who enclosed
Knowledge of good and evil in this tree,
That whoso eats thereof forthwith attains
Wisdom without their leave? And wherein lies 725
Th' offense, that man should thus attain to know?

---

7. Life in addition to knowledge; or, life with which to enlarge your knowledge.
8. I.e., how just to have knowledge of good!
9. I.e., your fear of death removes your fear of God; since if God inflicts death, he will not be just and hence not God. The serpent's sophism is visible.

1. Man in intellectual powers.
2. The devil can quote Scripture to his purpose, and here he is perverting Saint Paul, who told the Colossians (3.9–10) to put off the old man and put on the new. "Participating" (line 717): sharing.
3. The verb "produced" is understood. Satan is talking now, not about "God," but "the gods."

What can your knowledge hurt him, or this tree
Impart against his will, if all be his?
Or is it envy, and can envy dwell
In heavenly breasts?[4] These, these, and many more   730
Causes import your need of this fair fruit.
Goddess humane,[5] reach then, and freely taste!"
    He ended, and his words, replete with guile,
Into her heart too easy entrance won:
Fixed on the fruit she gazed, which to behold   735
Might tempt alone, and in her ears the sound
Yet rung of his persuasive words, impregned[6]
With reason, to her seeming, and with truth;
Meanwhile the hour of noon drew on, and waked
An eager appetite, raised by the smell   740
So savory of that fruit, which with desire,
Inclinable now grown to touch or taste,
Solicited her longing eye;[7] yet first
Pausing a while, thus to herself she mused:
    "Great are thy virtues, doubtless, best of fruits,   745
Though kept from man, and worthy to be admired,
Whose taste, too long forborne, at first essay
Gave elocution to the mute, and taught
The tongue not made for speech to speak thy praise:
Thy praise he also who forbids thy use   750
Conceals not from us,[8] naming thee the Tree
Of Knowledge, knowledge both of good and evil;
Forbids us then to taste; but his forbidding
Commends thee more, while it infers the good
By thee communicated, and our want: 755
For good unknown, sure is not had, or had
And yet unknown, is as not had at all.[9]
In plain then, what forbids he but to know?
Forbids us good, forbids us to be wise!
Such prohibitions bind not. But if death   760
Bind us with after-bands, what profits then
Our inward freedom? In the day we eat
Of this fair fruit, our doom is, we shall die.
How dies the serpent? He hath eaten and lives,
And knows, and speaks, and reasons, and discerns,   765
Irrational till then. For us alone
Was death invented? Or to us denied
This intellectual food, for beasts reserved?
For beasts it seems: yet that one beast which first
Hath tasted, envies not, but brings with joy   770

---

4. Adapted from Virgil, *Aeneid* 1.15. "Import":
imply, suggest.
5. Not so much "human goddess" (a Satanic paradox) as "kindly," "gracious" goddess.
6. Impregnated.
7. The five senses of Eve—sight, hearing, smell,

taste, and touch—are all solicited by the fruit.
8. God himself, by naming it, has called attention
to the tree's magic powers.
9. An unknown good is like no good at all. "In
plain": i.e., in plain language.

The good befallen him, author unsuspect,[1]
Friendly to man, far from deceit or guile.
What fear I then, rather what know to fear[2]
Under this ignorance of good and evil,
Of God or death, of law or penalty?   775
Here grows the cure of all, this fruit divine,
Fair to the eye, inviting to the taste,
Of virtue[3] to make wise: what hinders then
To reach and feed at once both body and mind?"
   So saying, her rash hand in evil hour   780
Forth reaching to the fruit, she plucked, she eat.[4]
Earth felt the wound, and nature from her seat[5]
Sighing through all her works gave signs of woe,
That all was lost. Back to the thicket slunk
The guilty serpent, and well might, for Eve,   785
Intent now wholly on her taste, naught else
Regarded; such delight till then, as seemed,
In fruit she never tasted, whether true
Or fancied so, through expectation high
Of knowledge; nor was godhead from her thought.[6]   790
Greedily she engorged without restraint,
And knew not eating death:[7] satiate at length,
And heightened as with wine, jocund and boon,[8]
Thus to herself she pleasingly began:
   "O sovereign, virtuous, precious of all trees   795
In Paradise! of operation blest
To sapience,[9] hitherto obscured, infamed,
And thy fair fruit let hang, as to no end
Created; but henceforth my early care,
Not without song each morning, and due praise   800
Shall tend thee, and the fertile burden ease
Of thy full branches offered free to all;
Till dieted by thee I grow mature
In knowledge, as the gods who all things know;
Though others[1] envy what they cannot give: 805
For had the gift been theirs, it had not here
Thus grown. Experience, next to thee I owe,
Best guide; not following thee I had remained
In ignorance; thou open'st Wisdom's way,
And giv'st accèss, though secret she retire.   810
And I perhaps am secret; Heaven is high,

---

1. A witness beyond suspicion.
2. In her ignorance, Eve does not really know what to fear and what not to fear—at least, so she says.
3. Power.
4. In the 17th century, an accepted past tense of "eat."
5. Wherever Nature is hidden, in the heart of things, she sighs.
6. She expected to achieve godhead immediately.
7. A grim pun. She is eating death and does not

know it; but death is eating her too. Compare "eating cares" (*L'Allegro*, line 135).
8. Joyous and liberal.
9. To wisdom, for the wise and those of good taste. (Latin *sapere*, to be wise, has its root in the verb "to taste.") "Infamed": defamed, i.e., maligned.
1. The gods, i.e., other gods. In saying that God did not give the tree, Eve is merely echoing a lesson learned from the serpent.

High and remote to see from thence distinct
Each thing on Earth; and other care perhaps
May have diverted from continual watch
Our great Forbidder,[2] safe with all his spies   815
About him. But to Adam in what sort[3]
Shall I appear? Shall I to him make known
As yet my change, and give him to partake
Full happiness with me, or rather not,
But keep the odds[4] of knowledge in my power   820
Without copartner? so to add what wants
In female sex, the more to draw his love,
And render me more equal, and perhaps,
A thing not undesirable, sometime
Superior: for, inferior, who is free?[5]   825
This may be well: but what if God have seen
And death ensue? Then I shall be no more,
And Adam, wedded to another Eve,
Shall live with her enjoying, I extinct;
A death to think. Confirmed then I resolve,   830
Adam shall share with me in bliss or woe:
So dear I love him, that with him all deaths
I could endure, without him live no life."[6]
    So saying, from the tree her step she turned,
But first low reverence done,[7] as to the power   835
That dwelt within, whose presence had infused
Into the plant sciential[8] sap, derived
From nectar, drink of gods. Adam the while
Waiting desirous her return, had wove
Of choicest flowers a garland to adorn   840
Her tresses, and her rural labors crown,
As reapers oft are wont their harvest queen.
Great joy he promised to his thoughts, and new
Solace in her return, so long delayed:
Yet oft his heart, divine[9] of something ill,   845
Misgave him; he the faltering measure[1] felt;
And forth to meet her went, the way she took
That morn when first they parted. By the Tree
Of Knowledge he must pass; there he her met,
Scarce from the tree returning; in her hand   850
A bough of fairest fruit that downy smiled,
New gathered, and ambrosial smell diffused.
To him she hasted, in her face excuse

2. Now that Eve has fallen, God is a "great Forbidder," and all his gifts in Paradise are forgotten.
3. Guise.
4. Balance.
5. Eve's fatal foolishness implies that the only person in the world who can ever be free is an absolute tyrant.
6. Her affection is not unlike Satan's (4.374–85)

in its destructiveness. In reality, there is no chance
of her living "without him," since she is already
under sentence of death.
7. Eve's first physical act after falling is idolatry.
8. Knowledge-giving.
9. Foreboding, suspicious.
1. I.e., of his pulse.

Came prologue, and apology to prompt,[2]
Which with bland words at will she thus addressed: 855
    "Hast thou not wondered, Adam, at my stay?
Thee I have missed, and thought it long, deprived
Thy presence, agony of love till now
Not felt, nor shall be twice; for never more
Mean I to try what rash untried I sought,   860
The pain of absence from thy sight. But strange
Hath been the cause, and wonderful to hear:
This tree is not as we are told, a tree
Of danger tasted,[3] nor to evil unknown
Opening the way, but of divine effect   865
To open eyes, and make them gods who taste;
And hath been tasted such. The serpent wise,
Or not restrained as we, or not obeying,
Hath eaten of the fruit, and is become,
Not dead, as we are threatened, but thenceforth   870
Endued with human voice and human sense,
Reasoning to admiration,[4] and with me
Persuasively hath so prevailed, that I
Have also tasted, and have also found
Th' effects to correspond, opener mine eyes   875
Dim erst, dilated spirits, ampler heart,
And growing up to godhead;[5] which for thee
Chiefly I sought, without thee can despise.
For bliss, as thou hast part, to me is bliss;
Tedious, unshared with thee, and odious soon.   880
Thou therefore also taste, that equal lot
May join us, equal joy, as equal love;
Lest, thou not tasting, different degree[6]
Disjoin us, and I then too late renounce
Deity for thee, when Fate will not permit."[7]   885
    Thus Eve with countenance blithe her story told;
But in her cheek distemper[8] flushing glowed.
On th' other side, Adam, soon as he heard
The fatal trespass done by Eve, amazed,
Astonied[9] stood and blank, while horror chill   890
Ran through his veins, and all his joints relaxed;
From his slack hand the garland wreathed for Eve
Down dropped, and all the faded roses shed.
Speechless he stood and pale, till thus at length
First to himself he inward silence broke: 895
    "O fairest of creation, last and best

2. Her face had an excuse in it, as prologue to an
apology which followed after.
3. If tasted.
4. Admirably. "Persuasively": by persuasion.
5. Everything that Eve says she feels is what Satan
has told her she will feel.
6. Differing rank in the hierarchy of creatures.

7. Contrast Eve's logic when she is alone (lines
817–25).
8. The proportion of Eve's humors—which, in the
state of innocence, gave her perfect health—has
been disturbed, and she is running a fever.
9. Astonished, "petrified." "Blank": empty of mind.

Of all God's works, creature in whom excelled
Whatever can to sight or thought be formed,
Holy, divine, good, amiable, or sweet!
How art thou lost, how on a sudden lost,   900
Defaced, deflowered, and now to death devote?[1]
Rather how hast thou yielded to transgress
The strict forbiddance, how to violate
The sacred fruit forbidden! Some cursèd fraud
Of enemy hath beguiled thee, yet unknown,[2]   905
And me with thee hath ruined, for with thee
Certain my resolution is to die.
How can I live without thee, how forego
Thy sweet converse and love so dearly joined,
To live again in these wild woods forlorn?[3]   910
Should God create another Eve, and I
Another rib afford, yet loss of thee
Would never from my heart; no, no! I feel
The link of nature draw me: flesh of flesh,
Bone of my bone thou art, and from thy state   915
Mine never shall be parted, bliss or woe."
    So having said, as one from sad dismay
Recomforted, and after thoughts disturbed
Submitting to what seemed remediless,
Thus in calm mood his words to Eve he turned: 920
    "Bold deed thou hast presumed, adventurous Eve,
And peril great provoked, who thus hath dared
Had it been only coveting to eye
That sacred fruit, sacred[4] to abstinence,
Much more to taste it, under ban to touch.   925
But past who can recall, or done undo?
Not God omnipotent, nor Fate! Yet so
Perhaps thou shalt not die, perhaps the fact[5]
Is not so heinous now, foretasted fruit,
Profaned first by the serpent, by him first   930
Made common and unhallowed ere our taste,
Nor yet on him found deadly; he yet lives,
Lives, as thou saidst, and gains to live as man
Higher degree of life: inducement strong
To us, as likely tasting to attain   935
Proportional ascent, which cannot be
But to be gods, or angels, demigods.[6]
Nor can I think that God, Creator wise,
Though threatening, will in earnest so destroy
Us his prime creatures, dignified so high,   940

---

1. Doomed.
2. "Yet unknown" modifies "enemy."
3. Without Eve, Paradise itself would be a wilderness.
4. Devoted.

5. Act.
6. Note how Adam agrees first in Eve's harmless errors about the serpent, then in her sinful ambition to achieve a higher form of life.

Set over all his works, which in our fall,
For us created, needs with us must fail,
Dependent made; so God shall uncreate,
Be frustrate, do, undo, and labor lose;
Not well conceived of God,[7] who, though his power   945
Creation could repeat, yet would be loath
Us to abolish, lest the adversary
Triùmph and say: 'Fickle their state whom God
Most favors; who can please him long? Me first
He ruined, now mankind; whom will he next?'   950
Matter of scorn, not to be given the foe.
However, I with thee have fixed my lot,
Certain to undergo like doom: if death
Consort with thee, death is to me as life;
So forcible within my heart I feel   955
The bond of nature draw me to my own,
My own in thee, for what thou art is mine;
Our state cannot be severed; we are one,
One flesh; to lose thee were to lose myself."
    So Adam, and thus Eve to him replied: 960
"O glorious trial of exceeding love,
Illustrious evidence, example high!
Engaging me to emulate; but short
Of thy perfection, how shall I attain,
Adam? from whose dear side I boast me sprung,   965
And gladly of our union hear thee speak,
One heart, one soul in both; whereof good proof
This day affords, declaring thee resolved,
Rather than death or aught than death more dread
Shall separate us, linked in love so dear,   970
To undergo with me one guilt, one crime,
If any be, of tasting this fair fruit;
Whose virtue (for of good still good proceeds,
Direct, or by occasion)[8] hath presented
This happy trial of thy love, which else   975
So eminently never had been known.
Were it I thought death menaced would ensue[9]
This my attempt, I would sustain alone
The worst, and not persuade thee, rather die
Deserted, than oblige[1] thee with a fact   980
Pernicious to thy peace, chiefly assured
Remarkably so late of thy so true,
So faithful love unequaled;[2] but I feel
Far otherwise th' event;[3] not death, but life

---

7. I.e., not a proper conception of God (as making his actions dependent on those of an inferior).
8. Indirectly.
9. Result from.
1. Render liable, involve.

2. Touched by Adam's devotion, Eve feels a little belated remorse at the damage she may have inflicted on him.
3. Result (of eating the apple).

Augmented, opened eyes, new hopes, new joys,   985
Taste so divine, that what of sweet before
Hath touched my sense, flat seems to this, and harsh.
On my experience, Adam, freely taste,
And fear of death deliver to the winds."
    So saying, she embraced him, and for joy   990
Tenderly wept, much won that he his love
Had so ennobled, as of choice to incur
Divine displeasure for her sake, or death.
In recompense (for such compliance bad
Such recompense best merits), from the bough   995
She gave him of that fair enticing fruit
With liberal hand; he scrupled not to eat,
Against his better knowledge, not deceived,
But fondly overcome with female charm.[4]
Earth trembled from her entrails, as again   1000
In pangs, and Nature gave a second groan,
Sky lowered, and muttering thunder, some sad drops
Wept at completing of the mortal sin
Original; while Adam took no thought,
Eating his fill, nor Eve to iterate   1005
Her former trespass feared, the more to soothe
Him with her loved society; that now
As with new wine intoxicated both,
They swim in mirth, and fancy that they feel
Divinity within them breeding wings   1010
Wherewith to scorn the earth. But that false fruit
Far other operation first displayed,
Carnal desire inflaming; he on Eve
Began to cast lascivious eyes, she him
As wantonly repaid; in lust they burn,   1015
Till Adam thus 'gan Eve to dalliance move:
    "Eve, now I see thou art exact[5] of taste,
And elegant, of sapience no small part,
Since to each meaning savor we apply,
And palate call judicious. I the praise   1020
Yield thee, so well this day thou hast purveyed.[6]
Much pleasure we have lost while we abstained
From this delightful fruit, nor known till now
True relish, tasting; if such pleasure be
In things to us forbidden, it might be wished   1025
For this one tree had been forbidden ten.
But come; so well refreshed, now let us play,
As meet is, after such delicious fare;

---

4. See 1 Timothy 2.14: "And Adam was not deceived, but the woman being deceived was in the transgression."
5. Exacting, demanding. "Sapience" means wisdom, but the word comes from Latin *sapere*, "to taste," which gives rise, via another etymology, to the word "savor." Adam's sentence plays rather heavily on these two meanings of *sapere*.
6. Provided for us, provisioned us.

For never did thy beauty since the day
I saw thee first and wedded thee, adorned   1030
With all perfections, so enflame my sense
With ardor to enjoy thee, fairer now
Than ever, bounty of this virtuous tree."
    So said he, and forbore not glance or toy[7]
Of amorous intent, well understood   1035
Of[8] Eve, whose eye darted contagious fire.
Her hand he seized, and to a shady bank,
Thick overhead with verdant roof embowered
He led her, nothing loath; flowers were the couch,
Pansies, and violets, and asphodel,   1040
And hyacinth, Earth's freshest, softest lap.
There they their fill of love and love's disport
Took largely, of their mutual guilt the seal,
The solace of their sin, till dewy sleep
Oppressed them, wearied with their amorous play.   1045
    Soon as the force of that fallacious fruit,
That with exhilarating vapor bland
About their spirits had played, and inmost powers
Made err, was now exhaled, and grosser sleep
Bred of unkindly fumes,[9] with conscious dreams   1050
Encumbered, now had left them, up they rose
As from unrest, and each the other viewing,
Soon found their eyes how opened, and their minds
How darkened. Innocence, that as a veil
Had shadowed them from knowing ill, was gone;   1055
Just confidence, and native righteousness,
And honor from about them, naked left
To guilty Shame; he covered, but his robe
Uncovered more.[1] So rose the Danite strong,
Herculean Samson, from the harlot-lap   1060
Of Philistean Dalilah, and waked
Shorn of his strength;[2] they destitute and bare
Of all their virtue. Silent, and in face
Confounded, long they sat, as strucken mute;
Till Adam, though not less than Eve abashed,   1065
At length gave utterance to these words constrained:
    "O Eve, in evil hour[3] thou didst give ear
To that false worm,[4] of whomsoever taught
To counterfeit man's voice, true in our fall,
False in our promised rising; since our eyes   1070
Opened we find indeed, and find we know
Both good and evil, good lost and evil got:

7. Caress.
8. By.
9. Unnatural vapors.
1. They were covered with shame, which made
them conscious of their nakedness as they had never
been before.

2. See the story of Samson and Delilah, Judges
16.4–20.
3. Even in his misery, Adam cannot resist the word
play on Eve-evil.
4. Serpent, with a connotation of disgust. "Of":
by.

Bad fruit of knowledge, if this be to know,
Which leaves us naked thus, of honor void,
Of innocence, of faith, of purity,   1075
Our wonted ornaments now soiled and stained,
And in our faces evident the signs
Of foul concupiscence; whence evil store,[5]
Even shame, the last of evils; of the first
Be sure then.[6] How shall I behold the face   1080
Henceforth of God or angel, erst with joy
And rapture so oft beheld? Those heavenly shapes
Will dazzle now this earthly[7] with their blaze
Insufferably bright. O might I here
In solitude live savage, in some glade   1085
Obscured, where highest woods, impenetrable
To star or sunlight, spread their umbrage broad,
And brown[8] as evening! Cover me, ye pines,
Ye cedars, with innumerable boughs
Hide me, where I may never see them more![9]   1090
But let us now, as in bad plight, devise
What best may for the present serve to hide
The parts of each from other that seem most
To shame obnoxious,[1] and unseemliest seen;
Some tree whose broad smooth leaves together sewed,   1095
And girded on our loins, may cover round
Those middle parts, that this newcomer, Shame,
There sit not, and reproach us as unclean."
  So counseled he, and both together went
Into the thickest wood; there soon they chose   1100
The figtree,[2] not that kind for fruit renowned,
But such as at this day, to Indians known,
In Malabar or Deccan[3] spreads her arms
Branching so broad and long, that in the ground
The bended twigs take root, and daughters grow   1105
About the mother tree, a pillared shade
High overarched, and echoing walks between;
There oft the Indian herdsman, shunning heat,
Shelters in cool, and tends his pasturing herds
At loopholes cut through thickest shade. Those leaves   1110
They gathered, broad as Amazonian targe,[4]
And with what skill they had, together sewed,
To gird their waist; vain covering, if to hide
Their guilt and dreaded shame! O how unlike

---

5. A store of evil.
6. I.e., since we now feel shame, the last of evils,
we shall soon experience the first ones.
7. A noun such as "vision" is understood.
8. Dark.
9. Cf. Revelation 6.16: "And said to the mountains and rocks, Fall on us, and hide us from the face of him that sitteth on the throne, and from the wrath of the Lamb."

1. Vulnerable, liable.
2. The banyan, or Indian fig. It has, in fact, small leaves, but Milton's knowledge of it came from Gerard's *Herball*, where all the details of lines 1104–11 may be found.
3. Sections of southern India.
4. Shield. The Amazons, mythical female warriors, carried large crescent-shaped shields.

To that first naked glory! Such of late 1115
Columbus found th' American so girt
With feathered cincture,[5] naked else and wild
Among the trees on isles and woody shores.
Thus fenced, and, as they thought, their shame in part
Covered, but not at rest or ease of mind, 1120
They sat them down to weep; nor only tears
Rained at their eyes, but high winds worse within
Began to rise, high passions, anger, hate,
Mistrust, suspicion, discord, and shook sore
Their inward state of mind, calm region once 1125
And full of peace, now tossed and turbulent:
For Understanding ruled not, and the Will
Heard not her lore, both in subjection now
To sensual Appetite, who from beneath
Usurping over sovereign Reason claimed 1130
Superior sway.[6] From thus distempered breast,
Adam, estranged in look and altered style,
Speech intermitted thus to Eve renewed:
    "Would thou hadst hearkened to my words, and stayed
With me, as I besought thee, when that strange 1135
Desire of wandering, this unhappy morn,
I know not whence possessed thee! we had then
Remained still happy, not as now, despoiled
Of all our good, shamed, naked, miserable.
Let none henceforth seek needless cause to approve[7] 1140
The faith they owe; when earnestly they seek
Such proof, conclude they then begin to fail."
    To whom, soon moved with touch of blame, thus Eve:
"What words have passed thy lips, Adam severe?
Imput'st thou that to my default or will 1145
Of wandering, as thou call'st it, which who knows
But might as ill have happened, thou being by,
Or to thyself perhaps? Hadst thou been there,
Or here th' attempt, thou couldst not have discerned
Fraud in the serpent, speaking as he spake; 1150
No ground of enmity between us known,
Why he should mean me ill, or seek to harm?
Was I to have never parted from thy side?
As good have grown there still, a lifeless rib.
Being as I am, why didst not thou, the head,[8] 1155
Command me absolutely not to go,
Going into such danger, as thou saidst?
Too facile[9] then, thou didst not much gainsay,

---

5. Belt.
6. The psychology of the Fall is made explicit here. The higher faculties of reason are in subjection to the lower faculties of appetite. Moreover, Adam has lost his superiority over Eve.
7. Test, prove. "Owe": own.
8. Head of the family, but also the rational director, as the head is to the rest of the body. Cf. 1 Corinthians 11.3, "the head of the woman is the man."
9. Easy, permissive.

Nay, didst permit, approve, and fair dismiss.
Hadst thou been firm and fixed in thy dissent,   1160
Neither had I transgressed, nor thou with me."
   To whom, then first incensed, Adam replied:
"Is this the love, is this the recompense
Of mine to thee, ingrateful Eve, expressed
Immutable[1] when thou were lost, not I,   1165
Who might have lived and joyed immortal bliss,
Yet willingly chose rather death with thee?
And am I now upbraided as the cause
Of thy transgressing? not enough severe,
It seems, in thy restraint? What could I more?   1170
I warned thee, I admonished thee, foretold
The danger, and the lurking enemy
That lay in wait; beyond this had been force,
And force upon free will hath here no place.
But confidence then bore thee on, secure   1175
Either to meet no danger, or to find
Matter of glorious trial; and perhaps
I also erred in overmuch admiring
What seemed in thee so perfect, that I thought
No evil durst attempt thee! but I rue   1180
That error now, which is become my crime,
And thou th' accuser. Thus it shall befall
Him who, to worth in women overtrusting,
Lets her will rule; restraint she will not brook,[2]
And, left to herself, if evil thence ensue,   1185
She first his weak indulgence will accuse."
   Thus they in mutual accusation spent
The fruitless hours, but neither self-condemning;[3]
And of their vain contèst appeared no end.

From Book 10

Summary   When it is known in Heaven that man has fallen, God sends
his Son to pass judgment on the sinners. Having found them in the garden,
he hears their confession and passes instant sentence, cursing the serpent,
condemning Eve to the pains of childbirth and Adam to those of daily toil;
but in mercy he clothes the human couple both outwardly with the skins of
beasts and inwardly with his righteousness. Meanwhile Sin and Death, sitting by Hell-gate, feel new strength, and pass across Chaos, leaving a great
bridge behind them. On their way they meet with their parent, Satan, learn
of his success on earth, and press eagerly forward in hopes of destroying man
altogether. Satan, on the other hand, continues his flight back toward Hell,
where he is to report to his constituents.

---

1. Shown to be unchangeable.
2. Accept.
3. Sterile recrimination is an early fruit of the forbidden tree; only self-condemnation can turn the
Fall from a mind-closing to a mind-opening event.

[Consequences of the Fall]

* * * Th' other way Satan went down
The causey[1] to Hell-gate; on either side   415
Disparted Chaos overbuilt exclaimed,
And with rebounding surge the bars assailed,
That scorned his indignation.[2] Through the gate,
Wide open and unguarded, Satan passed,
And all about found desolate; for those   420
Appointed to sit there[3] had left their charge,
Flown to the upper world; the rest were all
Far to the inland retired, about the walls
Of Pandemonium, city and proud seat
Of Lucifer, so by allusion called   425
Of that bright star to Satan paragoned.[4]
There kept their watch the legions, while the Grand
In council sat, solicitous what chance
Might intercept their emperor sent; so he
Departing gave command, and they observed.   430
As when the Tartar from his Russian foe,
By Astracan, over the snowy plains
Retires, or Bactrian Sophi, from the horns
Of Turkish crescent, leaves all waste beyond
The realm of Aladule, in his retreat   435
To Tauris or Casbeen;[5] so these, the late
Heaven-banished host, left desert utmost Hell
Many a dark league, reduced in careful watch
Round their metropolis, and now expecting
Each hour their great adventurer from the search   440
Of foreign worlds. He through the midst unmarked,
In show plebeian angel militant[6]
Of lowest order, passed, and from the door
Of that Plutonian hall, invisible
Ascended his high throne, which, under state[7]   445
Of richest texture spread, at th' upper end
Was placed in regal luster. Down a while
He sat, and round about him saw, unseen.
At last, as from a cloud, his fulgent[8] head
And shape star-bright appeared, or brighter, clad   450
With what permissive glory since his fall

1. Causeway.
2. Chaos, as the instinctive enemy of order, is hostile to the bridge built across its gulf by Sin and Death, even though it means an increase in the kingdom of Chaos itself.
3. I.e., Sin and Death.
4. Satan is called Lucifer, the light-bringer, because bright as the morning star (before he fell). The Grand (line 427) are the superior devils, Hell's aristocracy.
5. The comparison is with Tartars retreating before attacking Russians, and Persians before predatory Turks. "Bactrian": Persian; "Tauris": Tabriz; "Casbeen": Kazvin. Milton wants his simile to convey a mingled sense of barbaric oriental splendor, cruelty, and desolation in hell.
6. Literally, an angelic footsoldier or private, but with an ironic overtone from the phrase "church militant."
7. Canopy.
8. Glittering, refulgent.

Was left him, or false glitter. All amazed
At that so sudden blaze, the Stygian throng
Bent their aspèct, and whom they wished beheld,
Their mighty chief returned: loud was th' acclaim.   455
Forth rushed in haste the great consulting peers,
Raised from their dark divan,[9] and with like joy
Congratulant approached him, who with hand
Silence, and with these words attention, won:
    "Thrones, Dominations, Princedoms, Virtues, Powers!   460
For in possession such, not only of right,[1]
I call ye and declare ye now, returned
Successful beyond hope, to lead ye forth
Triumphant out of this infernal pit
Abominable, accursed, the house of woe,   465
And dungeon of our tyrant! Now possess,
As lords, a spacious world, to our native Heaven
Little inferior, by my adventure hard
With peril great achieved. Long were to tell
What I have done, what suffered, with what pain   470
Voyaged th' unreal, vast, unbounded deep
Of horrible confusion, over which
By Sin and Death a broad way now is paved
To expedite your glorious march; but I
Toiled out my uncouth passage, forced to ride   475
Th' untractable abyss, plunged in the womb
Of unoriginal[2] Night and Chaos wild,
That, jealous of their secrets, fiercely opposed
My journey strange, with clamorous uproar
Protesting Fate supreme; thence how I found   480
The new-created world, which fame in Heaven
Long had foretold, a fabric wonderful
Of absolute perfection; therein man
Placed in a paradise, by our exile
Made happy. Him by fraud I have seduced   485
From his creator, and, the more to increase
Your wonder, with an apple! He[3] thereat
Offended—worth your laughter!—hath given up
Both his belovèd man and all his world
To Sin and Death a prey, and so to us,   490
Without our hazard, labor, or alarm,
To range in, and to dwell, and over man
To rule, as over all he should have ruled.
True is, me also he hath judged; or rather
Me not, but the brute serpent in whose shape   495

9. The Turkish council of state; the oriental theme
continues.
1. Satan makes a distinction much in men's minds
since the days of Cromwell and Charles I; a kingdom could be claimed either by right (in law, *de
jure*) or in act (by possession, *de facto*). The devils

now have both claims to their titles. "Returned"
(line 462) modifies "I" at the beginning of the line:
"now that I have returned."
2. Without source or origin, primeval.
3. God.

Man I deceived. That which to me belongs
Is enmity, which he will put between
Me and mankind: I am to bruise his heel;
His seed (when, is not set) shall bruise my head.[4]
A world who would not purchase with a bruise,   500
Or much more grievous pain? Ye have th' account
Of my performance; what remains, ye gods,
But up and enter now into full bliss?"
    So having said, a while he stood, expecting
Their universal shout and high applause   505
To fill his ear; when, contrary, he hears,
On all sides from innumerable tongues
A dismal universal hiss, the sound
Of public scorn. He wondered, but not long
Had leisure, wondering at himself now more.   510
His visage drawn he felt to sharp and spare,
His arms clung to his ribs, his legs entwining
Each other, till, supplanted,[5] down he fell
A monstrous serpent on his belly prone,
Reluctant,[6] but in vain; a greater power   515
Now ruled him, punished in the shape he sinned,
According to his doom. He would have spoke,
But hiss for hiss returned with forkèd tongue
To forkèd tongue; for now were all transformed
Alike, to serpents all, as accessories   520
To his bold riot.[7] Dreadful was the din
Of hissing through the hall, thick-swarming now
With complicated monsters, head and tail—
Scorpion, and asp, and amphisbaena dire,[8]
Cerastes horned, hydrus, and ellops drear,   525
And dipsas (not so thick swarmed once the soil
Bedropped with blood of Gorgon, or the isle
Ophiusa); but still greatest he the midst,
Now dragon grown, larger than whom the sun
Engendered in the Pythian vale on slime,   530
Huge Python;[9] and his power no less he seemed
Above the rest still to retain. They all
Him followed, issuing forth to th' open field,

---

4. Satan seems to have overheard or understood the curse pronounced by God on the serpent, even though he was not present at the time.
5. The word is used with its Latin force of "tripped up by the heels." Ovid (*Metamorphoses* 4.576 ff.), Lucan (*Pharsalia* 9.700 ff.), and Dante (*Inferno* 25) had made set pieces about people being transformed into serpents. Whether Milton's editorial hand does not intervene against Satan too directly in this scene has been the subject of considerable critical debate.
6. The Latin sense is felt again, "struggling against the change."
7. Revolt.

8. "Complicated": again a Latinism, meaning "twined together." The "amphisbaena" was alleged to have a head at each end of its body; "cerastes" was a horned snake, "hydrus" a water-snake, "ellops" perhaps the swordfish, and "dipsas" a snake whose bite was supposed to create outrageous thirst. When Perseus flew over Libya with the head of the snaky-haired Gorgon, the drops of her blood fell to the ground and became serpents. The "isle Ophiusa" is Snake Island, in the Balearics.
9. Python was a gigantic mythological serpent engendered by Apollo, the sun god, from the slime left by Deucalion's flood, and slain by Apollo in a great contest.

Where all yet left of that revolted rout,
Heaven-fallen, in station or just array,   535
Sublime[1] with expectation when to see
In triumph issuing forth their glorious chief.
They saw, but other sight instead, a crowd
Of ugly serpents. Horror on them fell,
And horrid sympathy; for what they saw   540
They felt themselves now changing. Down their arms,
Down fell both spear and shield; down they as fast,
And the dire hiss renewed, and the dire form
Catched by contagion, like in punishment
As in their crime. Thus was th' applause they meant   545
Turned to exploding hiss, triumph to shame
Cast on themselves from their own mouths. There stood
A grove hard by, sprung up with this their change,
His will who reigns above,[2] to aggravate
Their penance, laden with fair fruit, like that   550
Which grew in Paradise, the bait of Eve
Used by the tempter. On that prospect strange
Their earnest eyes they fixed, imagining
For one forbidden tree a multitude
Now risen, to work them further woe or shame;[3]   555
Yet, parched with scalding thirst and hunger fierce,
Though to delude them sent, could not abstain,
But on they rolled in heaps, and up the trees
Climbing, sat thicker than the snaky locks
That curled Megaera.[4] Greedily they plucked   560
The fruitage fair to sight, like that which grew
Near that bituminous lake where Sodom flamed;[5]
This more delusive, not the touch, but taste
Deceived; they fondly[6] thinking to allay
Their appetite with gust, instead of fruit   565
Chewed bitter ashes, which th' offended taste
With spattering noise rejected. Oft they assayed,
Hunger and thirst constraining: drugged as oft,
With hatefulest disrelish writhed their jaws
With soot and cinders filled: so oft they fell   570
Into the same illusion, not as man
Whom they triùmphed once lapsed.[7] Thus were they plagued,
And worn with famine long and ceaseless hiss,
Till their lost shape, permitted, they resumed—
Yearly enjoined, some say, to undergo   575

---

1. On tiptoes. The ordinary devils are standing in
ranks outside Pandemonium, trying to catch a
glimpse of Satan.
2. "By the will of him who reigns above."
3. The punishment of the devils not only fits the
crime, it is the crime (the eating of forbidden fruit)
repeated again and again, in disgust and loathing.
4. Megaera, like her sister Furies, had snakes
instead of hair on her head.
5. Sodom apples grew (legend had it) on the spot
where that accursed city once stood; though good
to look at, they dissolved into ashes when plucked.
6. Foolishly. "Gust": taste.
7. They fell again and again into delusion, though
they had felt superior to man, who fell just once.

This annual humbling certain numbered days,
To dash their pride, and joy for man seduced.[8]
However, some tradition they dispersed
Among the heathen of their purchase got,
And fabled how the serpent, whom they called   580
Ophion, with Eurynome (the wide-
Encroaching Eve perhaps),[9] had first the rule
Of high Olympus, thence by Saturn driven
And Ops, ere yet Dictaean[1] Jove was born.

Summary   Sin and Death proceed without further interruption to the earth, and enter into possession of it. God sees their arrival and declines to interfere, but prophesies that their triumph will be only temporary; in due course they will be forced back to hell again, and forever. Meanwhile, the angels are ordered to twist the earth on its axis, disorder the planets so their influence will in future be bad as well as good, and rearrange the cosmos generally. In consequence, the temperate climate of Paradise at once gives way to extremes of heat and cold, and furious winds begin to blow across the ruined planet.

[*Adam, Eve, and the First Steps to Redemption*]

          * * * Thus began
Outrage from lifeless things; but Discord first,
Daughter of Sin, among th' irrational
Death introduced through fierce antipathy:[1]
Beast now with beast 'gan war, and fowl with fowl,   710
And fish with fish:[2] to graze the herb all leaving,
Devoured each other; nor stood much in awe
Of man, but fled him, or with countenance grim
Glared on him passing. These were from without
The growing miseries, which Adam saw   715
Already in part, though hid in gloomiest shade,
To sorrow abandoned, but worse felt within,
And in a troubled sea of passion tossed,
Thus to disburden sought with sad complaint:
   "O miserable of happy![3] Is this the end   720
Of this new glorious world, and me so late
The glory of that glory? who now, become
Accursed of blessèd, hide me from the face

---

8. There are many folktales about fairies, devils, incubi, and the like, who are forced periodically to take on the shape of some loathsome creature.
9. There is a mythological story about the Titan Ophion (the name means "snake") and his wife Eurynome ("the wide-reacher"), who ruled Olympus till Saturn and his wife Rhea (or Ops) drove them away. Milton feels this story may be a vague, pagan reminiscence of the real truth, the fall of Satan. But there is an unresolved suggestion here that Eve fell with Satan, becoming a kind of Proserpina to his role as Pluto, King of Hell.
1. Zeus was raised in a cave on Mount Dicte, in Crete; hence, "Dictaean Jove."
1. "Discord" is the subject of the sentence, "Death" the object. "Th' irrational" are the beasts.
2. Grass.
3. I.e., change, to misery from happiness.

Of God, whom to behold was then my height
Of happiness! Yet well, if here would end   725
The misery; I deserved it, and would bear
My own deservings; but this will not serve.
All that I eat or drink, or shall beget,
Is propagated curse.[4] O voice, once heard
Delightfully, 'Increase and multiply,'   730
Now death to hear! for what can I increase
Or multiply, but curses on my head?
Who of all ages to succeed, but, feeling
The evil on him brought by me, will curse
My head: 'Ill fare our ancestor impure!   735
For this we may thank Adam!' but his thanks
Shall be the execration;[5] so besides
Mine own that bide upon me, all from me
Shall with a fierce reflux on me redound,
On me, as on their natural center, light   740
Heavy, though in their place.[6] O fleeting joys
Of Paradise, dear bought with lasting woes!
Did I request thee, Maker, from my clay
To mold me man? Did I solicit thee
From darkness to promote me, or here place   745
In this delicious garden? As my will
Concurred not to my being, it were but right
And equal[7] to reduce me to my dust,
Desirous to resign and render back
All I received, unable to perform   750
Thy terms too hard, by which I was to hold
The good I sought not. To the loss of that,
Sufficient penalty, why hast thou added
The sense of endless woes? Inexplicable
Thy justice seems; yet to say truth, too late   755
I thus contèst; then should have been refused
Those terms whatever, when they were proposed.
Thou[8] didst accept them; wilt thou enjoy the good,
Then cavil the conditions? And though God
Made thee without thy leave, what if thy son   760
Prove disobedient, and reproved, retort,
'Wherefore didst thou beget me? I sought it not.'
Wouldst thou admit for his contempt of thee
That proud excuse? Yet him not thy election,[9]
But natural necessity begot.   765
God made thee of choice his own, and of his own

---

4. Whatever prolongs life extends the curse.
5. The only thanks for Adam will be mankind's curses.
6. Adam plays with the notion that natural objects have weight only as long as they are above their "natural" positions; so all curses will flow naturally to him, but they will still be heavy when they have

lighted.
7. Just.
8. "Thou," which referred to God in lines 753 and 755 ("Thy"), here shifts as Adam suddenly addresses himself.
9. Choice.

To serve him; thy reward was of his grace;
Thy punishment then justly is at his will.
Be it so, for I submit; his doom is fair,
That dust I am and shall to dust return.   770
O welcome hour whenever! Why delays
His hand to execute what his decree
Fixed on this day? Why do I overlive?
Why am I mocked with death, and lengthened out
To deathless pain? How gladly would I meet   775
Mortality, my sentence, and be earth
Insensible! how glad would lay me down
As in my mother's lap![1] There I should rest
And sleep secure; his dreadful voice no more
Would thunder in my ears; no fear of worse   780
To me and to my offspring would torment me
With cruel expectation. Yet one doubt
Pursues me still, lest all I cannot die;[2]
Lest that pure breath of life, the spirit of man
Which God inspired, cannot together perish   785
With this corporeal clod; then in the grave,
Or in some other dismal place, who knows
But I shall die a living death? O thought
Horrid, if true! Yet why? It was but breath
Of life that sinned; what dies but what had life   790
And sin? the body properly hath neither.
All of me then shall die: let this appease
The doubt, since human reach no further knows.[3]
For though the Lord of all be infinite,
Is his wrath also? Be it, man is not so,   795
But mortal doomed. How can he exercise
Wrath without end on man whom death must end?
Can he make deathless death? That were to make
Strange contradiction, which to God himself
Impossible is held, as argument   800
Of weakness, not of power.[4] Will he draw out,
For anger's sake, finite to infinite
In punished man, to satisfy his rigor
Satisfied never? That were to extend
His sentence beyond dust and nature's law,   805
By which all causes else according still
To the reception of their matter act,
Not to th' extent of their own sphere.[5] But say
That death be not one stroke, as I supposed,

---

1. Adam's lamentations owe a good deal to the Book of Job 3.
2. Direct from Horace, *Odes* 3.30.6: *non omnis moriar*.
3. Adam convinces himself, as Milton was convinced, that both soul and body die at death; the corollary is that they are resurrected together.

4. For a man in a state of nature, Adam displays a fine command of theological argument. He holds that if God contradicts himself, it is a sign of weakness.
5. An axiom of traditional philosophy: all agents act according to the capacity of the object, not to the extent of their inherent powers.

Bereaving[6] sense, but endless misery   810
From this day onward, which I feel begun
Both in me and without me, and so last
To perpetuity—Ay me! that fear
Comes thundering back with dreadful revolution
On my defenseless head! Both death and I   815
Am found eternal, and incorporate[7] both:
Nor I on my part single; in me all
Posterity stands cursed. Fair patrimony
That I must leave ye, sons! O, were I able
To waste it all myself, and leave ye none!   820
So disinherited, how would ye bless
Me, now your curse! Ah, why should all mankind
For one man's fault thus guiltless be condemned,
If guiltless? But from me what can proceed,
But all corrupt, both mind and will depraved,   825
Not to do only, but to will the same
With me?[8] How can they then acquitted stand
In sight of God? Him, after all disputes,
Forced[9] I absolve. All my evasions vain
And reasonings, though through mazes, lead me still   830
But to my own conviction: first and last
On me, me only, as the source and spring
Of all corruption, all the blame lights due;[1]
So might the wrath! Fond[2] wish! Couldst thou support
That burden, heavier than the earth to bear;   835
Than all the world much heavier, though divided
With that bad woman? Thus, what thou desir'st,
And what thou fear'st, alike destroys all hope
Of refuge, and concludes thee miserable[3]
Beyond all past example and future;   840
To Satan only like, both crime and doom.
O Conscience! into what abyss of fears
And horrors hast thou driven me; out of which
I find no way, from deep to deeper plunged!"
    Thus Adam to himself lamented loud   845
Through the still night, not now, as ere man fell,
Wholesome and cool and mild, but with black air
Accompanied, with damps and dreadful gloom;
Which to his evil conscience represented
All things with double terror. On the ground   850
Outstretched he lay, on the cold ground, and oft
Cursed his creation; Death as oft accused

---

6. Taking away.
7. In the same body. Adam is appalled to find that
he has become death incarnate; the grammar ("both
death and I / Am") displays his shock.
8. Not only will men repeat Adam's sin; their will
is corrupted and they will *want* to be fallen like
Adam.

9. Perforce.
1. In this discovery that he alone must accept the
guilt of mankind, Adam has chosen crucially to be
like Christ and unlike Satan—at the very moment
when he feels exactly the opposite.
2. Foolish.
3. Shows thee to be miserable.

Of tardy execution, since denounced
The day of his offense. "Why comes not Death,"
Said he, "with one thrice-acceptable stroke   855
To end me? Shall Truth fail to keep her word,
Justice divine not hasten to be just?
But Death comes not at call; Justice divine
Mends not her slowest pace for prayers or cries.
O woods, O fountains, hillocks, dales, and bowers!   860
With other echo late I taught your shades
To answer, and resound far other song."
Whom thus afflicted when sad Eve beheld,
Desolate where she sat, approaching nigh,
Soft words to his fierce passion she essayed;   865
But her with stern regard he thus repelled:
    "Out of my sight, thou serpent! that name best
Befits thee, with him leagued, thyself as false
And hateful: nothing wants, but that thy shape,
Like his, and color serpentine, may show   870
Thy inward fraud, to warn all creatures from thee
Henceforth; lest that too heavenly form, pretended[4]
To hellish falsehood, snare them. But for thee
I had persisted happy, had not thy pride
And wandering vanity, when least was safe,   875
Rejected my forewarning, and disdained
Not to be trusted, longing to be seen
Though by the devil himself, him overweening[5]
To overreach, but, with the serpent meeting,
Fooled and beguiled; by him thou, I by thee,   880
To trust thee from my side, imagined wise,
Constant, mature, proof against all assaults;
And understood not all was but a show
Rather than solid virtue, all but a rib
Crooked by nature—bent, as now appears,   885
More to the part sinìster[6]—from me drawn;
Well if thrown out, as supernumerary
To my just number found![7] Oh, why did God,
Creator wise, that peopled highest Heaven
With spirits masculine, create at last   890
This novelty on earth, this fair defect
Of nature, and not fill the world at once
With men, as angels, without feminine;
Or find some other way to generate
Mankind?[8] This mischief had not then befallen,   895
And more that shall befall—innumerable

---

4. Serving as a mask; literally, "held out before."
5. Overconfident.
6. "On the left hand," as in Latin; also "unlucky."
7. Since men visibly have twelve ribs on both sides, it was supposed that Adam originally had thirteen ribs on his left side, so that he could give up one and still have twelve, the proper ("just") number.
8. Ancient traditions of antifeminist thought lie behind these ungenerous questions.

Disturbances on earth through female snares,
And strait conjunction[9] with this sex. For either
He never shall find out fit mate, but such
As some misfortune brings him, or mistake;   900
Or whom he wishes most shall seldom gain,
Through her perverseness, but shall see her gained
By a far worse, or, if she love, withheld
By parents, or his happiest choice too late
Shall meet, already linked and wedlock-bound   905
To a fell[1] adversary, his hate or shame:
Which infinite calamity shall cause
To human life, and household peace confound."

   He added not, and from her turned; but Eve,
Not so repulsed, with tears that ceased not flowing,   910
And tresses all disordered, at his feet
Fell humble, and embracing them besought
His peace, and thus proceeded in her plaint:
   "Forsake me not thus, Adam! witness Heaven
What love sincere and reverence in my heart   915
I bear thee, and unweeting[2] have offended,
Unhappily deceived! Thy suppliant[3]
I beg, and clasp thy knees; bereave me not,
Whereon I live, thy gentle looks, thy aid,
Thy counsel in this uttermost distress,   920
My only strength and stay: forlorn of thee,
Whither shall I betake me, where subsist?
While yet we live, scarce one short hour perhaps,
Between us two let there be peace; both joining,
As joined in injuries, one enmity   925
Against a foe by doom express assigned us,
That cruel serpent. On me exercise not
Thy hatred for this misery befallen;
On me already lost, me than thyself
More miserable. Both have sinned, but thou   930
Against God only; I against God and thee,
And to the place of judgment will return,
There with my cries importune Heaven, that all
The sentence, from thy head removed, may light
On me, sole cause to thee of all this woe,   935
Me, me only, just object of his ire."[4]

   She ended weeping; and her lowly plight,
Immovable till peace obtained from fault
Acknowledged and deplored,[5] in Adam wrought
Commiseration. Soon his heart relented   940

---

9. Close connections, i.e., matrimony.
1. Bitter.
2. Unintentionally.
3. As a suppliant to thee.
4. Eve too now offers to accept the blame for the Fall; and the moral regeneration of man is hence-

forth possible.
5. Her suppliant posture ("lowly plight") would not be changed till she obtained forgiveness ("peace") from his admission of her fault and repentance for it.

Towards her, his life so late and sole delight,
Now at his feet submissive in distress,
Creature so fair his reconcilement seeking,
His counsel, whom she had displeased, his aid;
As one disarmed, his anger all he lost,   945
And thus with peaceful words upraised her soon:
   "Unwary, and too desirous, as before,
So now, of what thou know'st not,[6] who desir'st
The punishment all on thyself! Alas!
Bear thine own first, ill able to sustain   950
His full wrath, whose thou feel'st as yet least part,[7]
And my displeasure bear'st so ill. If prayers
Could alter high decrees, I to that place
Would speed before thee, and be louder heard,
That on my head all might be visited,   955
Thy frailty and infirmer sex forgiven,
To me committed, and by me exposed.
But rise; let us no more contend, nor blame
Each other, blamed enough elsewhere, but strive
In offices of love, how we may lighten   960
Each other's burden in our share of woe;
Since this day's death denounced, if aught I see,
Will prove no sudden, but a slow-paced evil,
A long day's dying to augment our pain,
And to our seed (O hapless seed!) derived."[8]   965
   To whom thus Eve, recovering heart, replied:
"Adam, by sad experiment I know
How little weight my words with thee can find,
Found so erroneous, thence by just event
Found so unfortunate; nevertheless,   970
Restored by thee, vile as I am, to place
Of new acceptance, hopeful to regain
Thy love, the sole contentment of my heart
Living or dying, from thee I will not hide
What thoughts in my unquiet breast are risen,   975
Tending to some relief of our extremes,
Or end, though sharp and sad, yet tolerable,
As in our evils,[9] and of easier choice.
If care of our descent perplex us most,
Which must be born to certain woe, devoured   980
By Death at last—and miserable it is
To be to others cause of misery,
Our own begotten, and of our loins to bring
Into this cursèd world a woeful race

---

6. Adam's remark is rueful but affectionate; Eve is still looking for more trouble than she knows how to handle.
7. I.e., ill able to sustain the full wrath of God— of whose wrath, so far, you have felt only the least part.
8. Handed down.
9. A Latinism. The English meaning is something like "given the evil plight in which we find ourselves."

That after wretched life must be at last   985
Food for so foul a monster—in thy power
It lies yet ere conception to prevent[1]
The race unblessed, to being yet unbegot.
Childless thou art, childless remain: so Death
Shall be deceived his glut, and with us two   990
Be forced to satisfy his ravenous maw.
But if thou judge it hard and difficult,
Conversing, looking, loving, to abstain
From love's due rites, nuptial embraces sweet,
And with desire to languish without hope   995
Before the present object[2] languishing
With like desire, which would be misery
And torment less than none of what we dread,
Then both our selves and seed at once to free
From what we fear for both, let us make short;   1000
Let us seek Death, or he not found, supply
With our own hands his office on ourselves.
Why stand we longer shivering under fears
That show no end but Death, and[3] have the power,
Of many ways to die the shortest choosing,   1005
Destruction with destruction to destroy?"
    She ended here, or vehement despair
Broke off the rest; so much of death her thoughts
Had entertained as dyed her cheeks with pale.
But Adam, with such counsel nothing swayed,   1010
To better hopes his more attentive mind
Laboring had raised, and thus to Eve replied:
    "Eve, thy contempt of life and pleasure seems
To argue in thee something more sublime
And excellent than what thy mind contemns;[4]   1015
But self-destruction therefore[5] sought refutes
That excellence thought in thee, and implies,
Not thy contempt, but anguish and regret
For loss of life and pleasure overloved.
Or if thou covet death as utmost end   1020
Of misery, so thinking to evade
The penalty pronounced, doubt not but God
Hath wiselier armed his vengeful ire than so
To be forestalled; much more I fear lest death
So snatched will not exempt us from the pain   1025
We are by doom to pay; rather such acts
Of contumacy[6] will provoke the Highest

1. Literally, in the Latin root, come before, forestall.
2. The present object is of course Eve herself,
referring to herself obliquely because she is ashamed
to admit that she would pine for Adam, as he for

her.
3. I.e., when we.
4. Despises.
5. For this motive.
6. Contempt.

To make death in us live. Then let us seek
Some safer resolution, which methinks
I have in view, calling to mind with heed   1030
Part of our sentence, that thy seed shall bruise
The serpent's head; piteous amends, unless
Be meant, whom I conjecture, our grand foe
Satan, who in the serpent hath contrived
Against us this deceit. To crush his head   1035
Would be revenge indeed, which will be lost
By death brought on ourselves or childless days
Resolved, as thou proposest; so our foe
Shall 'scape his punishment ordained, and we
Instead shall double ours upon our heads.   1040
No more be mentioned then of violence
Against ourselves and willful barrenness
That cuts us off from hope, and savors only
Rancor and pride, impatience and despite,
Reluctance[7] against God and his just yoke   1045
Laid on our necks. Remember with what mild
And gracious temper he both heard and judged,
Without wrath or reviling; we expected
Immediate dissolution, which we thought
Was meant by death that day, when lo, to thee   1050
Pains only in childbearing were foretold,
And bringing forth, soon recompensed with joy,
Fruit of thy womb. On me the curse aslope
Glanced on the ground:[8] with labor I must earn
My bread. What harm? Idleness had been worse.   1055
My labor will sustain me; and lest cold
Or heat should injure us, his timely care
Hath unbesought provided, and his hands
Clothed us unworthy, pitying while he judged.
How much more, if we pray him, will his ear   1060
Be open and his heart to pity incline,
And teach us further by what means to shun
Th' inclement seasons, rain, ice, hail, and snow,
Which now the sky with various face begins
To show us in this mountain, while the winds   1065
Blow moist and keen, shattering the graceful locks
Of these fair spreading trees—which bids us seek
Some better shroud, some better warmth to cherish
Our limbs benumbed, ere this diurnal star[9]
Leave cold the night, how we his gathered beams,   1070
Reflected, may with matter sere foment,
Or by collision of two bodies grind

7. From Latin *luctare*, to struggle; here, to oppose (the will of God).
8. The curse, like a spear that almost missed its target, glanced aside and stuck in the ground.
9. The sun.

The air attrite to fire,[1] as late the clouds,
Justling or pushed with winds rude in their shock,
Tine[2] the slant lightning, whose thwart flame driven down   1075
Kindles the gummy bark of fir or pine,
And sends a comfortable heat from far,
Which might supply[3] the sun. Such fire to use,
And what may else be remedy or cure
To evils which our own misdeeds have wrought,   1080
He will instruct us praying, and of grace
Beseeching him, so as we need not fear
To pass commodiously this life, sustained
By him with many comforts, till we end
In dust, our final rest and native home.   1085
    "What better can we do than to the place
Repairing where he judged us, prostrate fall
Before him reverent, and there confess
Humbly our faults, and pardon beg, with tears
Watering the ground, and with our sighs the air   1090
Frequenting,[4] sent from hearts contrite, in sign
Of sorrow unfeigned, and humiliation meek?
Undoubtedly he will relent and turn
From his displeasure; in whose look serene,
When angry most he seemed and most severe,   1095
What else but favor, grace, and mercy shone?"
    So spake our father penitent, nor Eve
Felt less remorse: they forthwith to the place
Repairing where he judged them, prostrate fell
Before him reverent, and both confessed   1100
Humbly their faults, and pardon begged, with tears
Watering the ground, and with their sighs the air
Frequenting, sent from hearts contrite, in sign
Of sorrow unfeigned, and humiliation meek.[5]

Book 11. Summary   The prayers of Adam and Eve prove acceptable
to God. But while man may now hope for ultimate redemption, he may no
longer dwell in Paradise; and Michael, the warrior archangel, is dispatched
to explain the sentence, offer some hope for the future, and dismiss mankind
from the happy garden. Adam is at first overcome with grief; but the angel
encourages him, and while Eve is put in a trance, Adam is raised to the
peak of a high hill and shown in a vision the future of the human race as far
as the flood of Noah.

---

1. Adam is inventing the burning glass ("matter
sere" is dry leaves, twigs, etc.) and the use of flint
and steel to start fires. "Attrite": rubbed or worn
down; in this sense, the word is more Latin than
English.
2. Kindle, light.
3. Take the place of.

4. Filling.
5. The deliberate repetition of six consecutive lines,
almost word for word, with only six lines in
between, is a very strong mark of closure. Adam
and Eve have reached most of the major decisions
which will separate their fate from that of Satan.

From Book 12

Summary Continuing his instruction of Adam, Michael relates the history of the world from the time of Noah through the coming of Christ, whose ascent into Heaven and triumph over Death after the Crucifixion he describes.

[The Departure from Eden]

  So spake th' archangel Michaël; then paused,
As at the world's great period;[1] and our sire,
Replete with joy and wonder, thus replied:
  "O goodness infinite, goodness immense!
That all this good of evil shall produce,   470
And evil turn to good; more wonderful
Than that which by creation first brought forth
Light out of darkness! Full of doubt I stand,
Whether I should repent me now of sin
By me done and occasioned, or rejoice   475
Much more that much more good thereof shall spring;
To God more glory, more good will to men
From God, and over wrath grace shall abound.
But say, if our Deliverer up to Heaven
Must reascend, what will betide the few,   480
His faithful, left among th' unfaithful herd,
The enemies of truth? Who then shall guide
His people, who defend? Will they not deal
Worse with his followers than with him they dealt?"
  "Be sure they will," said th' angel; "but from Heaven   485
He to his own a Comforter will send,
The promise of the Father, who shall dwell,
His Spirit, within them, and the law of faith,
Working through love, upon their hearts shall write,
To guide them in all truth, and also arm   490
With spiritual armor, able to resist
Satan's assaults, and quench his fiery darts,
What[2] man can do against them, not afraid,
Though to the death; against such cruelties
With inward consolations recompensed,   495
And oft supported so as shall amaze
Their proudest persecutors.[3] For the Spirit,
Poured first on his apostles, whom he sends
To evangelize the nations, then on all
Baptized, shall them with wondrous gifts endue[4]   500

---

1. Conclusion. Michael has just given a brief prophetic glimpse of the Second Coming and the Last Judgment.
2. As much as.

3. Milton briefly summarizes here the story of the Christian martyrs.
4. Endow.

To speak all tongues, and do all miracles,
As did their Lord before them. Thus they win
Great numbers of each nation to receive
With joy the tidings brought from Heaven: at length,
Their ministry performed, and race well run,   505
Their doctrine and their story written left,
They die; but in their room, as they forewarn,
Wolves shall succeed for teachers, grievous wolves,[5]
Who all the sacred mysteries of Heaven
To their own vile advantages shall turn   510
Of lucre and ambition, and the truth
With superstitions and traditions taint,
Left only in those written records pure,
Though not but by the Spirit understood.
Then shall they seek to avail themselves of names,   515
Places, and titles,[6] and with these to join
Secular power, though feigning still to act
By spiritual; to themselves appropriating
The Spirit of God, promised alike and given
To all believers; and, from that pretense,   520
Spiritual laws by carnal[7] power shall force
On every conscience, laws which none shall find
Left them enrolled, or what the Spirit within
Shall on the heart engrave.[8] What will they then,
But force the Spirit of Grace itself, and bind   525
His consort, Liberty? what but unbuild
His living temples,[9] built by faith to stand,
Their own faith, not another's? for, on Earth,
Who against faith and conscience can be heard
Infallible? Yet many will presume: 530
Whence heavy persecution shall arise
On all who in the worship persevere
Of Spirit and Truth; the rest, far greater part,
Will deem in outward rites and specious[1] forms
Religion satisfied; Truth shall retire   535
Bestuck with slanderous darts, and works of faith
Rarely be found. So shall the world go on,
To good malignant, to bad men benign,
Under her own weight groaning,[2] till the day
Appear of respiration[3] to the just   540
And vengeance to the wicked, at return

---

5. To profit by religion was for Milton the lowest
of crimes. In addition, he regularly uses the wolf
as an emblem of the Papacy; see *Lycidas*, line 128.
6. The name "Catholic," the place of court
preacher, and the title of "bishop," for example.
7. Fleshly, i.e., secular, of this world.
8. I.e., the wolves will enforce laws which have
no ancient authority or appeal to the conscience.
9. Individual believers. Milton's strict Protestant
individualism speaks throughout this passage of

protest against persecution.
1. Fair-seeming.
2. This passage, which in isolation appears to offer
some justification for viewing the end of the poem
as essentially pessimistic, should be set against
Adam's earlier statement (lines 470–78) that the
Fall was really a fortunate event, and gave rise to
more good than evil.
3. Relief, refreshment.

Of Him so lately promised to thy aid,
The Woman's Seed,[4] obscurely then foretold,
Now amplier known thy Savior and thy Lord;
Last in the clouds from Heaven to be revealed   545
In glory of the Father, to dissolve
Satan with his perverted world; then raise
From the conflagrant mass,[5] purged and refined,
New Heavens, new Earth, ages of endless date
Founded in righteousness and peace and love,   550
To bring forth fruits, joy and eternal bliss."
  He ended, and thus Adam last replied:
"How soon hath thy prediction, seer blest,
Measured this transient world, the race of Time,
Till Time stand fixed! Beyond is all abyss,   555
Eternity, whose end no eye can reach.
Greatly instructed I shall hence depart,
Greatly in peace of thought, and have my fill
Of knowledge, what[6] this vessel can contain,
Beyond which was my folly to aspire.   560
Henceforth I learn that to obey is best,
And love with fear the only God, to walk
As in his presence, ever to observe
His providence, and on him sole depend,
Merciful over all his works, with good   565
Still overcoming evil, and by small
Accomplishing great things, by things deemed weak
Subverting worldly-strong, and worldly-wise
By simply meek; that suffering for truth's sake
Is fortitude to highest victory,   570
And to the faithful, death the gate of life;
Taught this by his example whom I now
Acknowledge my Redeemer ever blest."
  To whom thus also th' angel last replied:
"This having learned, thou hast attained the sum[7]   575
Of wisdom; hope no higher, though all the stars
Thou knew'st by name,[8] and all th' ethereal powers,
All secrets of the deep, all Nature's works,
Or works of God in heaven, air, earth, or sea,
And all the riches of this world enjoy'dst,   580
And all the rule, one empire. Only add
Deeds to thy knowledge answerable;[9] add faith,
Add virtue, patience, temperance; add love,
By name to come called charity, the soul
Of all the rest: then wilt thou not be loath   585

---

4. Christ, whose Second Coming is here foreseen.
5. The burning world.
6. As much as.
7. Total.

8. Michael glances back at Raphael's cool warning (in Book 8) that Adam should concern himself with matters closer to home than the stars.
9. Corresponding.

To leave this Paradise, but shalt possess
A Paradise within thee, happier far.
Let us descend now, therefore, from this top
Of speculation;[1] for the hour precise
Exacts[2] our parting hence; and, see! the guards,   590
By me encamped on yonder hill, expect
Their motion,[3] at whose front a flaming sword,
In signal of remove, waves fiercely round.
We may no longer stay. Go, waken Eve;
Her also I with gentle dreams have calmed,   595
Portending good, and all her spirits composed
To meek submission: thou, at season fit,
Let her with thee partake what thou hast heard;
Chiefly what may concern her faith to know,
The great deliverance by her seed to come   600
(For by the Woman's Seed)[4] on all mankind;
That ye may live, which will be many days,[5]
Both in one faith unanimous; though sad
With cause for evils past, yet much more cheered
With meditation on the happy end."   605
    He ended, and they both descend the hill;
Descended, Adam to the bower where Eve
Lay sleeping ran before, but found her waked;
And thus with words not sad she him received:
    "Whence thou return'st and whither went'st, I know;   610
For God is also in sleep, and dreams advise,
Which he hath sent propitious, some great good
Presaging, since with sorrow and heart's distress
Wearied I fell asleep. But now lead on;
In me is no delay; with thee to go   615
Is to stay here; without thee here to stay
Is to go hence unwilling; thou to me
Art all things under Heaven, all places thou,[6]
Who for my willful crime art banished hence.
This further consolation yet secure   620
I carry hence: though all by me is lost,
Such favor I unworthy am vouchsafed,
By me the Promised Seed shall all restore."
    So spake our mother Eve; and Adam heard
Well pleased, but answered not; for now too nigh   625
Th' archangel stood, and from the other hill
To their fixed station, all in bright array
The cherubim descended; on the ground
Gliding meteorous, as evening mist

1. Hill of vision.
2. Requires.
3. Await their order to move. "At whose front":
before whom.
4. The parenthesis seems incomplete; perhaps
something like "deliverance was foretold" is

understood.
5. Adam lived to be 930 (Genesis 5.5).
6. Once more, "The mind is its own place . . ."
(1.254). Eve's resolution may also owe something
to the book of Ruth 1.16.

Risen from a river o'er the marish[7] glides,   630
And gathers ground fast at the laborer's heel
Homeward returning. High in front advanced,
The brandished sword of God before them blazed,
Fierce as a comet; which with torrid heat,
And vapor as the Libyan air adust,[8]   635
Began to parch that temperate clime; whereat
In either hand the hastening angel caught
Our lingering parents, and to th' eastern gate
Led them direct, and down the cliff as fast
To the subjected[9] plain; then disappeared.   640
They, looking back, all th' eastern side beheld
Of Paradise, so late their happy seat,[1]
Waved over by that flaming brand;[2] the gate
With dreadful faces thronged and fiery arms.
Some natural tears they dropped, but wiped them soon;   645
The world was all before them, where to choose
Their place of rest, and Providence their guide.
They, hand in hand, with wandering steps and slow,
Through Eden took their solitary way.

1667, 1674

7. Marsh (an old form).
8. The scorched climate of Libya, in North Africa, was proverbial.
9. Low-lying.
1. Home.
2. "Sword," with the extra overtone of "burning."

The Restoration and the Eighteenth Century
1660-1798

1660:   Charles II restored to the English throne.
1688–89:   The Glorious Revolution: deposition of James II and accession of William of Orange.
1700:   Death of John Dryden.
1707:   Act of Union unites Scotland and England, which thus become "Great Britain."
1714:   Rule by house of Hanover begins with accession of George I.
1744–45:   Deaths of Pope and Swift.
1784:   Death of Samuel Johnson.
1789:   The French Revolution begins.

The England to which Charles Stuart returned in 1660 was a nation divided against itself, exhausted by twenty years of civil war and revolution. Early in Charles's reign, the people were visited by two frightful calamities that seemed to the superstitious to be the work of a divine Providence outraged by rebellion and regicide: the plague of 1665, ravaging the country, carried off over 70,000 souls in London alone; and in September 1666, a fire which raged for four days destroyed a large part of the City (more than 13,000 houses), leaving about two thirds of the population homeless. Yet the nation rose from its ashes, in the century that followed, to become an empire. Within two decades of the king's return, the Royal Navy had defeated the navy of Holland, England's greatest maritime and commercial rival; and, in a series of wars fought between 1689 and 1763 against France, the British acquired dominions that stretched around the world, from Canada in the west to India in the east. Internally, moreover, the nation became whole again. The Glorious Revolution of 1689 established a rule of law, and the Act of Union of 1707 a political alliance, under which England was transformed into Great Britain in fact as well as name—a larger country to which people of widely differing backgrounds and origins felt they owed allegiance. Many of the great British writers of the eighteenth century, like Swift, Burke, Sheridan, and Goldsmith, came from Ireland; many, like Thomson, Boswell, and Hume, came from Scotland. Strengthened from without and from within, Great Britain was able to endure the loss of her thirteen American colonies and to enter the final struggle with Revolutionary and Napoleonic France as a world power.

RELIGION AND POLITICS

Charles came home to the almost universal satisfaction of his subjects, for after the abdication of Richard Cromwell in 1659 the country had seemed at the brink of chaos, and Britons were eager to believe that the king would bring order, peace, freedom under law, and a spirit of mildness back into the national life. But no political settlement could be stable until the religious issues of the age had been resolved. The restoration of the monarchy meant, inevitably, the restoration of the Established Church; and though Charles had promised mildness toward all but a few of his late father's enemies, the bishops and Anglican clergy felt anything but Christian charity toward their Dissenting brothers. In 1662 Parliament reimposed the Book of Common Prayer on all ministers and congregations, and in 1664 religious meetings in which the forms of the Established Church were not followed were declared illegal. Thousands of clergymen resigned their livings, and the jails were filled with Nonconformist preachers who, like John Bunyan, refused to be silenced. In 1673 the triumph of the Establishment was completed by the Test Act, which required all holders of civil and military offices to receive the sacrament according to the Anglican rite and to declare their disbelief in transubstantiation. Thus the two adversaries of the Anglican Church, Protestant Dissenters and Roman Catholics, were alike excluded from public life, though the practice of occasional conformity (i.e., receiving the sacrament in an Anglican church at rare intervals) enabled many Dissenters to comply with the law. Throughout the closing decades of the 17th century, Anglicans associated Nonconformity with revolution, regicide, republicanism, and the rule of the Puritan Saints—hence, with subversion; and with excessive zeal, "enthusiasm" (i.e., belief in private revelation), and irrationality—hence, with absurdity. The scorn and detestation in which Dissenters were held may be measured by the delight that readers took in Samuel Butler's caricature of Presbyterians and Independents in *Hudibras* (1663), an attitude that persisted unchanged for the rest of the century, as Jonathan Swift's *Tale of a Tub*, written about 1697, makes clear. As for the English Catholics, they appeared always as potential traitors of whom anything evil could be believed. Few doubted, for example, that the Great Fire of 1666 had been set by Catholics.

Although ecclesiastical problems seemed to have been quickly and effectively solved, the constitutional issues which had divided Charles I and Parliament were not so readily settled. Charles II had promised to govern through Parliament, but like other members of his family he held strong views on the power and prerogatives of the Crown. Nevertheless, he was content to avoid crises whenever he could, and since he was an astute politician he frequently could. He concealed from his subjects his Catholic sympathies (on his deathbed he received the last rites of the Roman Church), for he had no wish "to go on his travels" again. The one great religious and constitutional crisis of his reign was the Popish Plot and its political consequences (1678–81)—the unsuccessful attempt of a faction in Parliament to force Charles to accept a bill excluding his Catholic brother, James, Duke of York, from the succession. Except in this instance, where he was successful because of his courage, duplicity, and political skill, Charles allowed no opportunity for a test of strength between Crown and Parliament.

One important result of the political and religious turmoils of the decade following the Popish Plot was the emergence of two clearly defined political parties, Whig and Tory. The party of the court, which supported the king in 1681, came to be called Tories; the king's opponents, Whigs. By the end of the century the two parties had developed opposed attitudes on other important issues. The Tories drew their strength largely from the landed gentry and the country clergy. They were the conservatives of the period: strong supporters of the Crown and of the Established Church as the two great sources of political and social stability, they bitterly (though futilely) opposed toleration of Dissenters and successfully supported the Test Act. They were hostile to the new moneyed interests, whether among the newer nobility or the increasingly well-to-do middle class, for they held that landed wealth is the only responsible wealth. The Whigs were a less homogeneous group: many powerful nobles, jealous of the powers of the Crown, the merchants and financiers of London, a number of bishops and Low Church clergymen, and the Dissenters; these varied groups were united by their policies of toleration and support of commerce.

After James II came to the throne in 1685, determined to advance the cause of the Roman Church in England, an atmosphere of crisis rapidly developed. Claiming the right to set aside laws and to overrule Parliament, he issued in 1687 a Declaration of Indulgence, suspending the Tests and penal laws against both Catholics and Dissenters, and he began to fill the army and government—not to mention the universities—with his coreligionists. Matters came to a crisis in the summer of 1688, when a son was born to the queen and the prospect of a succession of Catholic monarchs confronted the nation. Secret negotiations paved the way for the arrival in England of the Dutchman William of Orange at the head of a small armed force. He was the leading champion of Protestantism on the Continent and the husband of James's Protestant daughter Mary. Finding resistance to his hostile subjects impossible, James, after sending his wife and the infant prince out of the country, fled to France on December 11. There he was cordially received by Louis XIV, granted a subsidy, and established with his court at St. Germain. For over half a century the possibility of invasion and the forcible restoration first of James, later of his son "the Old Pretender," and finally of his grandson Prince Charles Edward, was a source of anxiety to the English government. Many of the English and a great many more Scots remained loyal to the house of Stuart until there was nothing left of their cause (called Jacobite from the Latin *Jacobus*, James) but a pleasant sentiment. Two serious Jacobite rebellions actually occurred: in 1715, when the Old Pretender arrived in Scotland to support an uprising against the newly crowned Hanoverian, George I, and more threateningly in 1745, when Prince Charles Edward (the "Bonnie Prince Charlie" of romantic story) came dangerously close to success in his invasion of England, an event which affects the fortunes of the hero in Henry Fielding's novel *Tom Jones*.

It was only with the flight of James that England could begin to bury the past and to turn toward her destiny in the next age. The coming in of William and Mary and the settlement achieved in 1689 were known as the Glorious or Bloodless Revolution, all the more glorious for being bloodless. A more tolerant era was opening, as was made apparent in important acts passed by Parliament in the first year of the new reign. In 1689 the Bill of Rights limited the powers of the Crown, reaffirmed the supremacy of Parliament, and guaranteed important legal rights to individuals. Moreover, the

Toleration Act, although it did not repeal the Test, did grant freedom of worship to Dissenters. A number of the conflicting elements in the national life were thus reconciled through what proved to be a workable compromise; and with the passage of the Act of Settlement in 1701, settling the succession to the throne upon Sophia, Electress of Hanover, and her descendants (as the granddaughter of James I, she was the closest Protestant relative of the Princess Anne, James II's younger daughter, whose sole surviving child died in that year), the difficult problems that had so long divided England seemed resolved. The principles established in 1689 endured unaltered in essentials until the Reform Bill of 1832.

During the reign of Anne, the last Stuart monarch (1702–14), a renewal of tension embittered the political atmosphere. On the Continent England led her allies, Holland, Austria, and Bavaria, to victory in the War of the Spanish Succession against France and Spain (1702–13). The hero of the war was the brilliant Captain-General John Churchill, duke of Marlborough, who, with his duchess, dominated the queen until 1710. The war was a Whig war, supported by powerful Whig lords and the Whig merchants of London, who grew increasingly rich on war profits and who stood to gain by any weakening of the power of France and Spain. The Whigs were anxious to reward the Dissenters for their loyalty by removing the Test. Unfortunately for them, Anne was especially devoted to the church, and when, in 1710, they were made to appear to threaten the health of the Establishment, she dismissed her Whig ministers and called in Robert Harley as Lord Treasurer and the brilliant young Henry St. John as Secretary of State (in charge of foreign relations) to form the Tory ministry which governed England during the last four years of her reign. The Marlboroughs were dismissed, the duke even losing his command in 1711, but not before the royal favor and a grateful nation had made him immensely rich and had given him the land on which he built his famous palace, Blenheim (pronounced *Blen'm*) in memory of the most brilliant victory (pronounced *Blén-hime*) of the war.

It was these Tory ministers whom Defoe and Swift served in their different ways; it was for them that Matthew Prior negotiated the Peace of Utrecht, ratified in 1713. To Swift's despair, a bitter rivalry developed between Harley (then earl of Oxford) and St. John (then Viscount Bolingbroke) during 1713–14, and as the queen's life faded in the summer of 1714, Bolingbroke succeeded in ousting Oxford, only to have his own ambitions thwarted by the death of Anne and the return to power of the vindictive Whigs with the accession of George I, son of the late Sophia, Electress of Hanover. For a moment it seemed as if this event might not occur without bloodshed, but the crisis quickly passed, the Protestant succession was not immediately opposed by Jacobites, and the Whigs turned happily to investigating the conduct of the former ministers. Harley was imprisoned in the Tower of London (where he remained until 1717), and Bolingbroke, charged with treasonable correspondence with the Pretender, fled to France, where he actually became, for a while, secretary of state to the Jacobite court. Pardoned in 1723, but denied his seat in the House of Lords, he returned to England and directed the opposition to Robert Walpole, while seeing much of Pope and playing the gentleman-farmer-philosopher at Dawley Farm.

The three Georges who occupied the throne during the rest of the century presided over a nation that grew increasingly prosperous through war trade, and the beginnings of industrialism. George I (reigned 1714–27) and George II (reigned 1727–60) spoke broken English and had little interest in the affairs of the country. In their hearts they remained petty German princelings even when they were kings of Great Britain, spending as much time as possible in Hanover. Under such circumstances it was inevitable that ministers should become more important and more independent of the Crown than they had been under stronger and more intelligent monarchs. Through the indifference of two kings and the ambition and great abilities of the Whig prime minister Sir Robert Walpole, the modern system of ministerial government began to develop. This was the last important contribution of the age to British political institutions. Walpole's long ascendency (1721–42) brought a period of peace and prosperity and of capable government based, paradoxically, on flagrant political corruption. Although Walpole strengthened the importance of the House of Commons in British politics, he nonetheless continued, if he did not increase, the corruption of its members through bribery. He was a practical man and cared little for literature, preferring to spend money on useful journalists and voting Members of Parliament rather than on poets. Thus with two kings who knew nothing of literature and a prime minister who was indifferent to it, English writers could not expect the shower of offices and government sinecures that had made the age of Anne the great age of patronage: Congreve, Steele, Addison, Prior, Swift had expected and obtained such rewards both for their literary eminence and for their service to party. But after 1715, as patronage declined, authors found that they must turn to the publishers, who could pay them well because of the growing reading public. Indeed, Johnson was accustomed to declare that the booksellers of the midcentury had become the patrons of literature.

The long reign of George III (1760–1820) was dominated by two great concerns: the emergence of Britain as a colonial power and the cry for a new social order based on liberty and radical reform. In 1763 the Peace of Paris consolidated British rule over Canada and India, and not even the loss of the American colonies could stem the rise of the Empire. Great Britain was no longer an isolated island but a nation with interests and responsibilities around the world. At home, however, there was discontent. The wealth brought to England by industrialism and foreign trade did not spread to the working classes. In 1780 the Gordon Riots temporarily put London under mob rule. The king, the first Hanoverian monarch born in England, was popular with his subjects, and tried to take government into his own hands. Meanwhile reformers such as John Wilkes and Richard Price called for a new political democracy. Fear of their radicalism contributed to the British reaction against the French Revolution after 1789. In the last decades of the century British authors were torn between two opposing attitudes: loyalty to the old traditions of subordination and local self-sufficiency, and yearning for a new dispensation on principles of liberty, the rule of reason, and human rights. These conflicts within the nation were not easy to resolve, but they were submerged by the long war with France that broke out in 1793.

INTELLECTUAL BACKGROUND

The political turbulence of the seventeenth century subsided only gradually during the last decades of the century, and during the Restoration period (1660–1700) literature also reflected a conflict of values. Milton's major poems, a culmination of Renaissance art, appeared at the same time that John Dryden was establishing himself as the laureate of a new age of elegance. Bunyan's *Pilgrim's Progress* expressed the Nonconformist conscience at the same time that such court wits as Rochester and Sedley expressed a libertine creed. The town and the country followed different ideas about art and the conduct of life. The Restoration is best known as a period dominated by a fun-loving, dissolute court, whose style of life was reflected in rakish comedies. But the ordinary life of the nation did not radically change. Rural manners remained conservative and old-fashioned. The London citizens, middle class and respectable, cherishing much of the independence and piety of Dissent, were scandalized by the behavior of upper-class rakes who regarded them with contempt and considered their wives and daughters fair game. Even good royalists like John Evelyn and Samuel Pepys often speak anxiously in their diaries of the moral laxity of the court and the danger to the country of the king's example.

Charles himself was easy going, pleasure loving, and amorous, more fond of the society of boon companions—and mistresses—than he was of state business. But he also had serious intellectual interests and was a patron of the arts. He dabbled in chemistry and was interested in the progress of science. A characteristic act was his chartering in 1662 the Royal Society of London for the Improving of Natural Knowledge, thus giving official approval to the scientific movement that Francis Bacon had initiated early in the century and that was just then coming to maturity. The king's love of music and painting led him to import from the Continent composers, musicians, new musical instruments, the French and Italian opera, and painting and painters largely from the Low Countries. His interest in the theater was demonstrated by the chartering of two companies of actors in 1660, both under royal patronage, the King's Players, and the Duke's—the duke being James, duke of York.

It is natural, therefore, that the most characteristic art of the period reflected the interests and tastes of those who supported it. Artists addressed themselves to court and "town," the western suburbs which were the center of fashion. The middle-class tradespeople, who lodged over their shops in the City (i.e., that part of greater London which was once within the city walls and which was then thickly populated), were scorned as tasteless barbarians. Except in the theater, literature was not in itself a gainful profession (as it was to become in the eighteenth century), and writers looked for patronage from the court and the great nobles. Milton, for example, received only £10 for the first edition of *Paradise Lost*. By the end of the century, however, thanks to the enterprise of the bookseller Jacob Tonson and the new device of publishing books through subscription (i.e., soliciting payment in advance for deluxe copies of a work, in addition to publishing a regular trade edition), Dryden was able to earn between £1000 and £1200 by his translation of the works of Virgil (1697). And Pope's Homer, similarly published between 1715 and 1726, was to prove even more profitable.

Perhaps the most important aspect of the Restoration period is the increasing challenge of various forms of secular thought to the old religious orthodoxies which had been matters of life and death since the Reformation. As the contentious voices of Roman, Anglican, and Dissenter grew more and more subdued, other interests attracted adventurous minds. Thomas Hobbes, in *Leviathan* (1651), had taught a philosophic materialism and advocated an absolute government as the most efficacious check to human nature, which he described as wholly driven by egoistic and predatory passions. Detested by the church and attacked on all sides, these ideas nonetheless played their role in the lives and writings of some of the more advanced young people, and they provoked by way of reaction in the next century an optimistic insistence on the natural goodness of humanity. A soberer and more ancient tradition was philosophic skepticism. Originating in ancient Greece, skepticism had found its most persuasive recent statement in the essays of the Frenchman Michel de Montaigne (1533–1592), whose influence was widespread throughout seventeenth-century Europe. The skeptic argued that all our knowledge is derived from our senses, but that our senses do not report the world around us accurately, and that therefore reliable knowledge is an impossibility. The safest course is to affirm nothing as absolutely true, to remember that most beliefs are mere opinions, and, where possible, to be guided by the traditional in matters intellectual, political, and ethical. Butler, Dryden, and Rochester, among others, more or less adhered to this doctrine. But though skeptics remained in doubt about the results of human reasoning, they were not precluded from religious beliefs, for they could assert (as did Dryden after his conversion to Catholicism) that faith alone is necessary for accepting the mysteries of the Christian religion.

The new science, advanced by members of the Royal Society, was rapidly altering views of nature. Science in the seventeenth century was principally concerned with the physical sciences—with astronomy, physics, and, to a lesser degree, chemistry; and the discoveries in these sciences were reassuring in their evidence of universal and immutable law and order, clear proof of the wisdom and goodness of God in His creation. Such laws of nature as Boyle's law of the behavior of gases under pressure or Newton's law of gravitation seemed obviously to support the idea that a beneficent, divine intelligence created and directs the universe. The truest truths proved to be the clearest, the simplest, the most general. Such truths seemed to promise a time, not remote, when mystery would be banished entirely from religion as well as from nature. Indeed, Deism or Natural Religion, which had an increasingly wide appeal to "enlightened" minds, deduced its simple rationalistic creed from the Book of Nature, God's first and, to many in the eighteenth century, only valid revelation. The Deists deduced the existence of a Supreme Being or First Cause from the existence of the universe: a creature presupposes a Creator. The laws of nature sufficiently proved the reasonableness, goodness, and wisdom of this Creator. Him we can and must revere; but, good though He is, it is demonstrable that He does not punish vice and reward virtue in this life; and therefore, being good and just, He must do so in some future life: hence, we must believe in immortality. Meanwhile, here on earth, it is our duty to cooperate with Nature and the Deity, cultivating as best we can wisdom, virtue, and benevolence. This creed is as simple and as rational as one of Newton's laws; but its omission of the "second revelation" of the Scriptures, the scheme of salvation in which Christ died to redeem our sins, made it unacceptable to many Christians, although many others found it possible to accept both Natural Religion and revealed Christianity.

As the seventeenth century drew to a close, its temper became more secular, tolerant, and moderate. The new age was willing to settle for the possible within the limits of human intelligence and of the material world. Its temper was expressed by its most influential philosopher, John Locke (1632–1704), in his *Essay Concerning Human Understanding* (1690):

> If by this inquiry into the nature of the understanding, I can discover the powers thereof; how far they reach; to what things they are in any

degree proportionate; and where they fail us, I suppose it may be of use to prevail with the busy mind of man to be more cautious in meddling with things exceeding its comprehension; to stop when it is at the utmost extent of its tether; and to sit down in a quiet ignorance of those things which, upon examination, are found to be beyond the reach of our capacities. . . . Our business here is not to know all things, but those which concern our conduct.

These words might be taken as the creed of eighteenth-century England. Such a position is Swift's, when he inveighs against metaphysics, abstract logical deductions, and theoretical science; it is similar to Pope's in the *Essay on Man*; it prompts Samuel Johnson to talk of "the business of living"; it helps to account for the emphasis that the Anglican clergy put on good works, rather than faith, as the way to salvation, and for their dislike of emotion and "enthusiasm" in religion.

But if the eighteenth century brought a recognition of human limitations, it also took an optimistic view of human nature. Rejecting Hobbes, some eighteenth-century philosophers asserted that human beings are naturally good and find their highest happiness in the exercise of virtue and benevolence. Such a view of human nature we describe as "sentimental." It found the source of virtue in instinctive and social impulses rather than in a code of conduct sanctioned by divine law. And people began to feel—or to fancy that they felt—exquisite pleasure in the exercise of benevolent impulses. Sentimentalism fostered a benevolence that led to social reforms seldom envisioned in earlier times—to the improvement of jails, to the relief of imprisoned debtors, to the establishment of foundling hospitals and of homes for penitent prostitutes, and ultimately to the abolition of the slave trade; but it also encouraged a ready flow of feeling and tears and a capacity to respond to the joys and sorrows of others. The doctrine of natural goodness seemed to many to suggest that it is civilization which corrupts us and that "noble savages," those who live in a state of nature, might be models of innocence and virtue. Such notions encouraged an interest in primitive societies and even helped to prepare, late in the century, for the warm reception given the peasant poet Robert Burns, an "original genius," as well as for William Wordsworth's interest in children and in simple, rural people.

As the wave of sentimentalism mounted, a parallel rise of religious feeling occurred after about 1740. The great religious revival known as Methodism was led by John Wesley (1703–1791), his brother Charles (1707–1788), and George Whitefield (1714–1770), all Oxford graduates. The Methodists took their gospel to the common people, preaching the necessity of a conviction of sin, and of conversion, and the joy of the "blessed assurance" of being saved. Often denied the privilege of preaching in village churches, they preached to thousands in the open fields and in barns. The somnolent Anglican Church and the self-assured upper classes were repelled by the emotionalism aroused by Methodist preachers among the lower orders. It seemed as if the irrationality, zeal, and enthusiasm of the Puritan sects were being revived. But the religious awakening persisted, and affected many clergymen and laymen within the Establishment, who, as "Evangelicals," reanimated the church and promoted unworldliness and piety. And yet the insistence of Methodists on faith over works as the way to salvation did not prevent them or their Anglican counterparts from playing important roles in many of the social reforms of the time, especially in helping to abolish slavery and the slave trade.

LITERARY THEORY

The literature of the period between 1660 and 1785 can conveniently, though perhaps too schematically, be considered as falling into three lesser periods of about forty years each: the first, extending to the death of Dryden in 1700, may be thought of as the period in which English "neoclassical" literature came into being and its critical principles were formulated; the second, ending with the death of Pope in 1744 and of Swift in 1745, brought to its culmination the literary movement initiated by Dryden and his generation; the third, concluding with the death of Johnson in 1784 and the publication of William Cowper's *The Task* in 1785, was a period in which the old principles were confronted by new ideas which contained within themselves the origins of the Romantic movement of the late eighteenth and early nineteenth centuries.

Apparently a sudden change of taste took place about 1660; but the change was not so sudden as it appears. Like the English Renaissance, it was part of a general movement in European culture, seen perhaps at its most impressive in seventeenth-century France. Described most simply, it was a reaction against the intricacy and occasional obscurity, boldness, and extravagance of European literature of the late Renaissance, in favor of greater simplicity, clarity, restraint, regularity,and good sense. This tendency is most readily to be observed in the preference of Dryden and his contemporaries for "easy, natural" wit, which aims to surprise rather than to shock. It accompanied, though it was not necessarily caused by, the development of certain rationalistic philosophies and the rise of experimental science, as well as a desire for peace and order after an era of violent extremism.

This movement produced in France the impressive body of classical literature that distinguished the age of Louis XIV. In England it produced a literature often termed "neoclassical," or "Augustan," because it was strongly influenced by the writers of the reign of the first Roman emperor, Augustus Caesar, just before the beginning of the Christian era. Rome's Augustan Age was a period of stability and peace after the civil war that followed the death of Julius Caesar. Its chief poets, Virgil, Horace, and Ovid, addressed their polished works to a sophisticated aristocracy, among whom they found generous patrons. Dryden's generation was aware of an analogy between the situations of post–Civil War England and Augustan Rome. Later generations would be suspicious of that analogy; after 1700 most writers stressed that Augustus had been a tyrant who thought himself greater than the law. But in 1660 there was hope that Charles would be a better Augustus, bringing to England the civilized virtues of an Augustan age without its vices.

Charles and his followers inevitably brought back from France an admiration of contemporary French literature as well as of French fashions and elegance. The theories of such writers as Pierre Corneille, René Rapin, and Nicolas Boileau also came into vogue. But English literature remained stubbornly English: English writers took what they required from France, but used it for their own ends. It was not Dryden's aim merely to imitate the French poets or for that matter the Latin, but to produce in England works that would be worthy to stand beside theirs. He knew that this could be done only if English literature remained true to its living tradition: Chaucer, Spenser,

Shakespeare, Jonson, Donne entered into his literary consciousness as well as Virgil, Horace, Longinus, or Corneille.

It is likely that, had Charles never lived abroad, English literature would still have turned toward an ideal of simplicity and elegance. Ben Jonson's poems and criticism had brought the classicizing tendencies of the English Renaissance to a focus. His closed heroic couplets are the model for those of Edmund Waller and Sir John Denham, whom Dryden considered the principal "refiners" of English metrics. One of the lesser "Sons of Ben," Sir John Beaumont, at least as early as 1625—and incidentally in couplets that might have been the very pattern of those of Dryden and Pope—proposed critical standards that became dominant after 1660:

> Pure phrase, fit epithets, a sober care
> Of metaphors, descriptions clear, yet rare,
> Similitudes contracted, smooth and round,
> Not vexed by learning, but with Nature crowned:
> Strong figures drawn from deep inventions, springs,
> Consisting less in words, and more in things:
> A language not affecting ancient times,
> Nor Latin shreds, by which the pedant climbs.
> [*To His Late Majesty, Concerning the True Form
> of English Poetry*]

Such standards, alien to the poetry of Donne, Crashaw, or Milton, prefigure the poetry of the Augustans, and suggest that a native "classicism" existed side by side with metaphysical poetry. The emphasis on the correct ("pure"), the appropriate ("fit"), restraint and discipline ("sober care"), clarity, the fresh and surprising ("rare"), Nature, strength, freedom from pedantry—these indicate exactly the direction English literature was to take after the Restoration.

Above all, the new simplicity of style aimed to give pleasure to the common reader—to write about passions that everyone could recognize in language that everyone could understand. From Dryden to Johnson, English critics value poetry according to its power to affect an audience. Readers, in turn, were supposed to cooperate with authors through the exercise of their own imaginations, creating pictures in the mind. Much poetry of the period comes alive only when it is visualized. A phrase from Horace's *Art of Poetry*, *ut pictura poesis* (as in painting, so in poetry), was interpreted to mean that poetry ought to be a visual as well as a verbal art. Eighteenth-century readers tended to be extremely skilled at translating words into pictures; and a modern reader who wants to appreciate eighteenth-century poems as more than dead words on a page must learn to *see* their images in the mind's eye.

What poets tried to see and represent was "Nature"—a word of many meanings. The Augustans were especially conscious of one meaning: Nature as the universal, permanent, and representative elements in human experience. External nature—the landscape—both as a source of aesthetic pleasure and as an object of scientific inquiry or religious contemplation attracted attention throughout the eighteenth century. But Pope's injunction to the critic, "First follow Nature," has primarily *human* nature and *human* experience in view. Nature is truth in the sense that it includes the enduring, general truths that have been, are, and will be true for everyone in all times, everywhere. Johnson, in chapter 10 of *Rasselas*, says that the poet is to examine "not the individual, but the species; to remark general properties and large appearances . . . to exhibit in his portraits of nature such prominent and striking features as recall the original to every mind." Historians during this period studied the particulars of history in order to observe the universal human nature which those particulars reveal; and scientists formulated, after experiment and observation of particulars, universal and permanent laws of nature. Indeed, Sir Isaac Newton's *Principia* (1687) did much to reinforce scientifically the idea of Nature as order, which underlies such a typical eighteenth-century work as Pope's *Essay on Man*.

But it would be wrong to assume that this emphasis on the general and the representative excluded the particular from the arts. If human nature was held to be uniform, human beings were known to be infinitely varied; and the task of the artist was so to treat the particular as to render it representative. Thus Pope, after praising the characters of Shakespeare because they are "Nature herself," continued: "But every single character in Shakespeare is as much an individual as those in life itself; it is . . . impossible to find any two alike." And Johnson praised the poet James Thomson because he looked on external nature "with a mind that at once comprehends the vast, and attends to the minute."

To study Nature was also to study the ancients—the great artists and thinkers of Greece and imperial Rome. They had expressed the enduring forms of life. Homer and Nature, according to Pope, were the same; and both Pope and his readers found Horace's satires on Roman society thoroughly applicable to their own world, for Horace had followed Nature, "one clear, unchanged, and universal light." Moreover, modern poets could also learn from the ancients how to practice their craft. If a poem is an object to be made, the *poet* (a word derived from a Greek word meaning "maker") must follow sound principles or botch the job. The ancients—for instance, Aristotle in his *Poetics* and Horace in his *Art of Poetry*—had deduced such principles from the practice of early masters like Homer and Sophocles, and during the sixteenth and seventeenth centuries Italian and French critics codified those "rules" and invented new rules of their own. The rules directed poets to plan their works in one of the literary "kinds" or genres: epic, tragedy, comedy, pastoral, satire, ode; to choose a language appropriate to that genre; to select the right style and tone and rhetorical figures. Such rules could serve as a short cut to Nature, for as Pope said, they "are Nature methodized."

In England, however, the rules were followed in rather a casual way. Almost everyone acknowledged that Shakespeare had written the greatest body of drama in modern literature without obeying the formulas of ancients or moderns. He had followed Nature directly, impelled by his wit. "Wit," like "Nature," is a complicated word of many meanings. Here it implies quickness and liveliness of mind, inventiveness, a readiness to perceive resemblances between things apparently unlike and so to enliven literary discourse with appropriate images, similes, and metaphors. This faculty was often identified with "fancy" or "imagination," and was thought to be irregular, wayward, extravagant, unless curbed and disciplined by another and soberer faculty, "judgment." Many poets sought to tame what seemed the wildness of metaphysical wit into a sense of "decorum" or the appropriate. Hence Dryden defined wit as "a propriety of thoughts and words; or, in other terms, thoughts and words elegantly adapted to the subject." Similarly, Pope insists in the *Essay on Criticism*, lines 80–83, on the necessity of a harmonious union of judgment and fancy (which he calls "wit") in a work of literature. Though judgment was to tame, it was not to suppress passion, energy, or originality, but to make them more effective through discipline: "The winged courser, like a generous horse, / Shows most true mettle when you check his course."

The test of mettle in a poet is language. When Wordsworth, in the Preface to *Lyrical Ballads* (1800), declared that the poems were written "in a selection of the language really used by men," he went on to attack eighteenth-century poets for their use of an artificial and stock "diction." Many poets did employ a special language. It is characterized by personification, representing a thing or abstraction in a human form, as when an "Ace of Hearts steps forth" or "Melancholy frowns"; by periphrasis (a roundabout and elegant way of avoiding homely words: "finny tribe" for "fish," or "household feathery people" for "chickens"); frequently used stock phrases, such as "shining sword," "verdant mead," "bounding main," "checkered shade"; words used in their original Latin sense, such as "genial," "gelid," "horrid"; and a fondness for adjectives ending in *y*. This language originated in the attempt of Renaissance poets all over Europe to rival the elegant and golden diction of Virgil and other Roman writers. Milton depended on it to help him obtain "answerable style" for the lofty theme of *Paradise Lost*. Used with discretion it could be both subtle and expressive; but when it became a mannerism, or a dead and conventional language used mechanically, as it did with scores of mere versifiers, it properly became an object of contempt. "Hay and straw were burned in the fields of Thessaly," for instance, was translated into poetic diction:

> There at his words devouring Vulcan feasts
> On all the tribute which Thessalian meads
> Yield to the scythe, and riots on the heaps
> Of Ceres, emptied of the ripened grain.
> [Glover's *Leonidas*, 1737]

But such extremes of mannerism are seldom to be found in the works of the good poets of the century.

Versification also tests the poet's skill. The prevailing form was the "closed" heroic couplet—i.e., a pentameter couplet which more often than not contains within itself a complete statement and so is closed by a semicolon, period, question mark, or exclamation point. Within these two lines it was possible to attain certain rhetorical or witty effects by the use of parallelism, balance, or antithesis within the couplet as a whole or the individual line. The second line of the couplet might be made closely parallel in structure and meaning to the first, or the two could be played off against each other in antithesis; taking advantage of the fact that normally a pentameter line of English verse contains at some point a slight pause called a "caesura," one part of a line so divided can be made parallel with or antithetical to the other or even to one of the two parts of the following line. This can be illustrated by a passage from Sir John Denham's *Cooper Hill* (1642), which was quoted and parodied for many years. The poem addresses the Thames and builds up a witty comparison between the flow of a river and the flow of verse (italics are ours, to illustrate the rhetorical effects):

O could I flow like thee, || and make thy stream
Parallelism: *My great example,* || as it is *my theme!*
Double balance: Though *deep,* yet *clear,* || though *gentle,* yet not *dull,*
Double balance: *Strong* without *rage,* || without *o'erflowing, full.*

It only remained for Dryden and Pope to bind such passages more tightly together with alliteration and assonance, and the typical metrical-rhetorical wit of the new age had been perfected.

Shortly after the beginning of the eighteenth century began the vogue of blank verse—the other metrical form most favored by the age. Philosophical poems, descriptive poems, meditative poems, and original or translated epics employed blank verse of one sort or another from Thomson's *Seasons* (1726–30) to Cowper's *The Task* (1785); and the tradition determined Wordsworth's use of the form in *Tintern Abbey* and *The Prelude.* The two chief patterns of blank verse available to the age were the blank verse of Milton in *Paradise Lost* and the dramatic blank verse of Dryden and other Restoration tragic poets. The influence of Milton is easily detected, not by the success with which his manner was imitated, but by the amateur performance of most of those who try to play on his instrument. The dramatic blank verse of the Restoration too often led in eighteenth-century poetry to mannerism or bombast. But gradually a more lyrical blank verse developed, of which William Cowper is the master; and this more plastic metrical line had a formative influence on the blank verse of William Wordsworth.

RESTORATION LITERATURE, 1660–1700

The period between 1660 and 1700 was remarkably varied and vigorous. Dryden was the dominant figure, writing in all the important contemporary forms—occasional verse, comedy, tragedy, heroic play, ode, satire, translation, and critical essay—and both his example and his precepts had great influence. He gave to the England of his day a *modern* literature, cosmopolitan but possessing the richness and variety that he admired in the Elizabethans, the "God's plenty" that he praised in Chaucer's *Canterbury Tales.*

The prose of the Restoration is a clear indication of the direction in which literature was moving. The styles of Donne's sermons, of Milton's pamphlets, or of Sir Thomas Browne's writings had come to seem too elaborate, too involved, too insistently musical, or too wittily rhetorical and pointed for mere exposition or social intercourse. The Royal Society decreed that its members must employ only a plain, concise, and utilitarian prose style suitable to the clear communication of scientific truths. Metaphors, similes, and rhetorical flourishes were disapproved because they engaged the emotions, not the reason, and though they were tolerable in poetry, they had no place in rational discourse. In polite literature, thanks to the example of such writers as Abraham Cowley, Dryden, and Sir William Temple, the ideal of good prose came to be a clear, simple, and natural style which has the ease and poise of well-bred urbane conversation. This is a social prose, designed for a social age. Later, it was available to the writers of periodical essays, such as Addison or Steele, to the novelists of the eighteenth century, and to the many practitioners of the delightful art of letter-writing, one of the minor literary achievements of the eighteenth century; the brilliant but intimate letters of Lady Mary Wortley Montagu, Horace Walpole, Thomas Gray, and William Cowper have never been surpassed. This movement toward clarity and simplicity in prose accompanied a similar movement away from the intricacies of metaphysical wit in verse, which found an early statement in Dryden's *Essay of Dramatic Poesy*.

But if prose was simplified and wit was tamed, the Restoration did not break wholly with the immediate past. It retained the Renaissance admiration for the typically aristocratic heroic ideal. Most Restoration readers associated the "heroic poem" or epic with "fierce wars and faithful loves" and expected it to offer patterns of ideal virtue for the emulation of princes and generals. But the romantic idealism of the heroic mode was most characteristically expressed during the Restoration not in the heroic poem but in the heroic play, which Dryden, its foremost practitioner, defined as "a heroic poem in little." The theme of these plays (their vogue lasted from about 1664 to about 1675) was the conflict between love and honor in the hearts of impossibly valorous heroes and impossibly high-minded and attractive ladies.

Dryden's one undoubted masterpiece in serious drama is his blank verse tragedy *All for Love* (produced 1677), based on the story of Antony and Cleopatra. Instead of Shakespeare's world-wide panorama, his rapid shifts of scene and complex characters, we have the last hours of the tragic lovers presented according to the unities of action, place, and time, in a neatly symmetrical plot. The two other eminent tragic poets of the period were Nathaniel Lee (ca. 1649–1692), known for violent plots, the wild emotions of his characters, and the extravagance of his rhetoric; and Thomas Otway (1652–1685), who excelled in pathos. Not one enduring tragedy was written during the eighteenth century. Addison's *Cato* (produced in 1713) is a museum piece, illustrating the frigidity of "correct" and rule-bound tragedy. George Lillo's *London Merchant* (produced in 1731), dealing with commonplace characters in mercantile life, took a feeble step in the direction of the sort of realistic, middle-class drama with which we are familiar today.

The real distinction of Restoration drama was comedy. The best plays of Sir George Etherege (ca. 1635–1691), William Wycherley (ca. 1640–1716), William Congreve, and the less accomplished but witty Sir John Vanbrugh (pronounced *Vánbroo* or *Vanbróok*, 1664–1726) and George Farquhar (ca. 1677–1707) still hold the stage today. These writers excelled in representing—and critically evaluating—the social behavior of the fashionable upper classes of the town. This sort of comedy—brilliantly witty, cynical in its view of human nature, which it shows to be sensual, egoistic, and predatory—is known as "the comedy of manners," since its concern is to bring the moral and social behavior of its characters to the test of comic laughter. The male hero lives not for military glory but for pleasure and the conquests that he can achieve in his amorous campaigns. The object of his very practical game of sexual intrigue is a beautiful, witty, pleasure-loving, and emancipated lady, every bit his equal in the strategies of love. The two are distinguished not for virtue, but for the true wit and well-bred grace with which they conduct the often complicated intrigue that makes up the plot. The best examples of the comedy of manners before William Congreve's *The Way of the World* (produced in 1700) are Etherege's *The Man of Mode* (produced in 1676), William Wycherley's *The Country Wife* (produced ca. 1672–74), and Congreve's earlier *Love for Love* (produced in 1695).

During the 1690s a considerable demand arose for moral reform in both literature and daily life, partly because of the nature of Restoration comedy. "Societies for the Reformation of Manners" were founded with the support of the soberer Anglicans and the resurgent Nonconformists. Their members served not only as propagandists of moral respectability, but also as spies and informers who brought offenders to trial for blasphemy, obscenity, and sexual immorality. The most effective attack on the indecencies of language and situation in comedy was made by the Anglican clergyman Jeremy Collier, whose *Short View of the Immorality and Profaneness of the English Stage* (1698) bore hard on Dryden and Congreve, among others. Collier spoke for the outraged moral sense of the godly middle classes as well as for the church, and his attack helped to discredit "wit" and the wits as subversive of religion and morals. One of the tasks that Steele and Addison undertook in the *Tatler* and *Spectator* and Pope in his *Essay on Criticism*, early in the next century, was to rehabilitate "wit" by making it the servant of social and moral decorum. When Dryden died, a more respectable (if not actually more virtuous) society was coming into being.

Decorum was also enforced by the clubs where literary people tended to gather. From 1652 and increasingly during the first half of the eighteenth century, the coffee houses of London served as informal meeting places. There men could smoke, drink chocolate or coffee, read the newspapers, write and receive letters, exchange news, gossip, and opinions, and observe the oddities of character that the English have always been happy to cultivate. Eventually clubs not unlike Addison's imaginary Spectator Club came to preside over literary life. The groups who frequented them helped to determine the tone of literature, the critical reputation of writers, the success or failure of plays, and the character of such periodicals as the *Tatler* and the *Spectator*. At first women were excluded. Around 1750, however, some intellectual women known as bluestockings because of their informal dress (not black silk hose but blue worsted) established clubs of their own under the leadership of the wealthy Mrs. Elizabeth Montague, and gradually men began to join them for literary conversation.

EIGHTEENTH-CENTURY LITERATURE, 1700–45

During the forty-five years between the deaths of Dryden and Swift, the literature that Dryden and his contemporaries had created attained full maturity. A new and brilliant group of writers took the stage: Swift, with *A Tale of a Tub* (1704–10); Addison, with his popular poetic celebration of Marlborough's victory at Blenheim, *The Campaign* (1705); Prior, with *Poems on Several Occasions* (1707); Steele, with the *Tatler* (1709); and the youthful Pope, in the same year, with his *Pastorals*. On the whole, the literature of this period is chiefly a literature of wit, concerned with civilization and social relationships; and consequently it is critical and in some degree moral or satiric. It preserves the earlier period's interest in the heroic, but apart from Pope's translations of Homer, no writer succeeded in heroic poetry. On the other hand some of the finest works of the period are mock-heroic (individual passages in Swift's *Battle of the Books* and *A Description of a City Shower* and Pope's *Rape of the Lock* and *The Dunciad*) or humorous burlesques of serious classic or modern modes (John Gay's delightful town mock-Georgic, *Trivia, or the Art of Walking the Streets of London*, 1716, or his burlesque of the heroics of Italian opera, *The Beggar's Opera*, produced in 1728). Such literature is addressed to highly sophisticated and cultivated readers, and it reminds us that earlier eighteenth-century literature retained the aristocratic bias that had marked the literature of the seventeenth century.

Nevertheless a body of writing that reached a wider audience was coming into being. The reading public expanded steadily throughout the eighteenth century, and its new recruits were upper-class women and the increasingly numerous rich and leisured people of both sexes in the trading middle class. The popular press flourished, producing a succession of newspapers, literary periodicals in the manner of the *Tatler*, miscellanies of various sorts, and finally, in 1731, the first magazine in the modern sense, the *Gentleman's Magazine*, which was to be followed not only by imitations but also by the appearance of such successful literary reviews as the *Monthly Review* (1749) and the *Critical Review* (1756). The new journalism satisfied a hunger for all sorts of information about politics, science, philosophy, literature, as well as for scandal and gossip. It also created a demand for writers—not necessarily for geniuses—who began to subsist, often on harsh terms, as hacks and compilers in a milieu that came to be called Grub Street, from the name of an actual street. To such authors as Pope and Swift, Grub Street with all its denizens (it was to gain the services of both Johnson and Oliver Goldsmith) represented a serious threat to humanistic learning, urbane enlightenment, and good taste. But literature became in this period of expanding publication and increasingly numerous readers a gainful profession. The novel as we know it—a long prose narrative concerned with the actual world and the men and women who inhabit it—very probably could not have come into existence had not these new readers existed. The eighteenth-century novel supplied the place in the life of the common reader that the heroic poem had occupied in the life of the courtly reader of the past.

During this period new literary kinds took the place of the old. The lyric, one of the glories of the Elizabethan age and the first half of the seventeenth century, had become in the Restoration a minor and graceful mode, appropriate to a song or a "paper of verses" addressed to a mistress. The wits of Charles II's court could turn out accomplished, conventional poems of this sort which do not lack distinction; and Matthew Prior was their counterpart in the time of William of Orange and Queen Anne. But between 1700 and 1740 lyric poetry declined, and comedy too lost its edge. The moral reform of the 1690s, together with the increasingly optimistic and flattering view of human nature, made the rakes of Restoration comedy seem distasteful libels on humanity. The old comedy of manners was replaced by a new kind, called "sentimental" not only because of its faith in the triumph of a good heart over vice, but also because its dialogue deals in high moral sentiments rather than wit, and because its virtuous heroines and virtuous (or penitent) heroes suffer misfortunes which move the audience not to laughter but to tears. One of the pleasures invented in eighteenth-century Europe was the delicious pleasure of weeping, and sentimental comedy (or, as the French phrased it, *la comédie larmoyante*, "weeping comedy") brought that pleasure to playgoers through many decades. As tragedy froze into rhetoric, comedy dissolved in tears. And the successes enjoyed by John Gay's comic ballad opera *The Beggar's Opera* (1728), or the laughing comedies of Goldsmith and Sheridan later in the century, could not eradicate the taste for sentimentality. Although during the eighteenth century the *theater* prospered and the stage was adorned by a succession of great actors and actresses (such as David Garrick and Sarah Siddons) the authors of *drama* lapsed into obscurity.

On the other hand satire flourished, its most distinguished practitioners being Pope and Swift, though they are only two among many effective writers. Satirists are usually conservative, using their weapons against those deviations from norms of conduct which threaten to undermine traditional and socially approved behavior. Both Pope and Swift wrote their major satires as Tories, at a time when Britain was dominated by the Whig party. The Tories resisted, but resisted futilely, the social and economic changes which were taking place as England grew from an island kingdom into a world power, and transformed its agrarian into a mercantile economy. They looked with gloomy forebodings on the rising tide of popular taste, on what they considered the invasion and debasement of the polite world by the barbarians from the middle classes and the idle rich, and on the increase of corruption in public life. The satire of both Swift and Pope is great because it was animated by moral urgency and heightened by a tragic sense of doom. Pope saw the issue as a struggle between Darkness and Light, Chaos and Order, Barbarism and Civilization: a vision which he expressed in his greatest work, *The Dunciad*. For Swift the issue was one between "right reason" and "madness"—not clinical insanity, of course, but a blindness to anything but one's own private illusions, which is an abandonment of practical reality.

But the great age of satire also produced a wholly different sort of poetry from that which Pope was writing in the 1730s. After 1726, when James Thomson published the first of his nature poems, *Winter*, the poetry of natural description flourished and the characteristic eighteenth-century English taste for natural and picturesque beauty found expression—not only in poetry, but also in that typical Georgian art, landscape gardening, and finally in the beginning of the art of landscape in water color or oils, which has been England's principal achievement in painting. A love of external nature inspired many eighteenth-century poets, and Wordsworth was their heir. *Tintern Abbey* (1798) not only was written *within* the century, but in most respects is very much a poem *of* the century.

In the course of the century, Britons not only admired tamed and ordered nature, in large landscape gardens or cultivated fields, but also early learned to enjoy the more thrilling, emotional pleasure which they began to feel in the presence of what they called "the sublime" in nature: vast spaces, mountainous country, wild and untamed landscape. Whether enthusiasts of nature went to landscape for evidence of the presence of the Deity or merely to enjoy natural beauty, they inevitably learned to feel emotions in the presence of external nature and to examine the quality of their feelings. Before the death of Pope and Swift, in the poetry of Thomson and others, a literature of feeling had come into existence alongside the dominant literature of wit. The development of such a literature of sentiment is perhaps the crucial fact in the literary history of the century after the deaths of Pope and Swift.

THE EMERGENCE OF NEW LITERARY THEMES AND MODES, 1740–85

When Matthew Arnold, speaking for Victorian taste, called the eighteenth century an "Age of Prose," he meant to cast doubt upon its poetry; but the later part of the century might indeed be honored as an age of prose. Never before nor since have so many great writers of prose flourished at once, nor so many kinds of intellectual prose been perfected: literary criticism, with Samuel Johnson; biography, James Boswell; philosophy, David Hume; politics, Edmund Burke; history, Edward Gibbon; aesthetics, Sir Joshua Reynolds; economics, Adam Smith; natural history, Gilbert White. Each of these authors is a master stylist, whose effort to express himself clearly and fully creates an art as difficult to achieve, and as precise, as poetry. Indeed, the prose style of the period often seems to build upon the principles of neoclassical verse: its elaborately balanced use of parallels and antitheses, its elegant allusions to a classical literature, its public, rhetorical manner, its craving for generality. At its best, however, such prose depends less on formal virtues than on its weight of thought. Unlike the earlier masters of simplicity in prose—Addison, Swift, Defoe—the authors of the Age of Johnson have little confidence in plain speaking. Readers will not be convinced of the truth, they suspect, merely by having the facts laid before them; they must be offered scientific demonstration or passionate eloquence. Some comments by Johnson on the prose of Swift make the point by example as well as precept:

> His style was well suited to his thoughts, which are never subtilized by nice disquisitions, decorated by sparkling conceit, elevated by ambitious sentences, or variegated by far-sought learning. He pays no court to the passions, he excites neither surprise nor admiration; he always understands himself, and his readers always understand him. . . . This easy and safe conveyance of meaning it was Swift's desire to attain, and for having attained he deserves praise, though perhaps not the highest praise. For purposes merely didactic, when something is to be told that was not known before, it is the best mode; but against that inattention by which known truths are suffered to lie neglected, it makes no provision; it instructs, but does not persuade.

Johnson's prose bristles with long words, qualifications of thought, and "ambitious sentences" that are the very opposite of the style he describes; he attempts not merely to be understood, not merely to instruct, but to persuade. And similar ambitions motivate many of the authors of his time. An unprecedented effort to formulate the first principles of philosophy, history, psychology, and art required a whole new language of persuasion, more subtle, logical, and accurate than English had ever been before.

An age of great prose, however, can put a burden on its poets. Many of the generation of talented young poets who emerged about the time of Pope's death, a group that includes William Collins, Thomas Gray, Mark Akenside, and the brothers Joseph and Thomas Warton, are haunted by the fear that the spirit of poetry may have passed away—driven out by the spirit of prose, by an ideal of mere "correctness," by the end of superstitions that had once peopled the landscape with fairies and demons, the stuff of poetry. In an age barren of magic, they ask, where is poetry to be found? That question becomes obsessive in many poems of the period, suffusing them with melancholy. Indeed, more and more poetry itself was associated with melancholy, a sweet sadness, a yearning for another time and place. The prototype of the mid-eighteenth-century melancholy poet was Milton's *Il Penseroso*, a night-loving solitary, who sucks pensive sadness from the "far-off curfew" or the swelling organ in the twilight of a Gothic church. Such a figure is most unlike the Augustan poet, a social being, living in a crowded world and little given to the impropriety of the public confession of private feelings. The idea of the poet was changing from that of a maker to that of an introspective, brooding confessor; the materials of poetry were becoming rather the inner life and private vision of the poet than public, social affairs.

Poets who brood in silence are never far from thoughts of death; and an often morbid fascination with death, suicide, and the grave preoccupies the poets of midcentury. The clergyman Edward Young (1683–1765) wrote an immensely long and popular poem in blank verse, *The Complaint: or Night Thoughts on Life, Death, and Immortality* (1742–46), to supplement the Christian optimism of Pope's *Essay on Man* with a darker view of Christianity based on fear of the life to come. But the "graveyard school" is less concerned with religion than with horror and decay. Within an elaborate stage setting of medieval ruins and fleshless bodies, the soul of the graveyard poet self-consciously acts out its secret fears. The revival of Gothic architectural styles, most famously Horace Walpole's tiny and precious pseudo-Gothic castle, Strawberry Hill, helped influence literary styles as well. The Gothic vogue, like a similar vogue for Chinese decor, seemed to suggest that old-fashioned canons of taste—proportion, balance, simplicity, and harmony—might count for less in art than the pleasures of fancy and extravagance—intricacy, asymmetry, a willful excess. Poets began to cultivate archaic language and antique literary forms; especially, after Thomas Percy's edition of *Reliques of Ancient English Poetry* (1765), the ballad. Thus Thomas Chatterton (1752–1770), whom the Romantics later idolized for his precocious genius and his tragic early death, composed sham medieval ballads he pretended to have found in an old manuscript. The most remarkable literary consequence of such medievalizing, however, was the invention of the Gothic romance. Horace Walpole's *Castle of Otranto* (1765), a dreamlike tale of terror inspired by the physical appearance of Strawberry Hill, created a mode of fiction that retains its popularity to the present day. In the typical Gothic romance, set amidst the glooms and intricacies of a medieval castle, the laws of nightmare replace the laws of probability. Forbidden themes—incest, murder, necrophilia, atheism, the torments of sexual desire—are allowed free play; repressed feelings, morbid fears rise to the surface of the narrative. Although most such romances, like William Beckford's *Vathek* (1786) and Matthew Lewis's *The Monk* (1796), depend on sensationalism and the grotesque, Gothicism also resulted in works, like Anne Radcliffe's, that temper romance with reality, as well as in serious novels of social purpose, like William Godwin's *Caleb Williams* (1794); and Godwin's daughter, Mary Shelley, eventually composed a romantic nightmare, *Frankenstein* (1816), that continues to haunt our dreams.

Ultimately, it was not to a medieval revival that poets looked for a renewal of poetry, but to their own imaginations and feelings. In his *Ode to Fancy* (1746), Joseph Warton associated "fancy" with the natural, the wild and spontaneous, with solitude, and with enthusiasm and the passions. Such a concept of the fancy or imagination emphasizes not rules and crafts of the maker, but original genius, the poet as the seer or nature's priest. True poets, Warton suggests, should not be conversationalists or orators but singers. "The public has seen all that art can do," William Shenstone wrote in 1761, welcoming James Macpherson's bardic *Ossian*, "and they want the more striking efforts of wild, original, enthusiastic genius." But genius is easier to call for than to recognize; when it does come, people are apt to call it madness. Many of the best poets of the period—Collins, Christopher Smart, later William Cowper—suffered from mental illness, and others, like Chatterton, were scorned by society. Nor did many readers so much as notice the extraordinary work of Smart, or later of William Blake. The apocalyptic strain of poetry, bursting the bonds of logical transition, of grammar, and even of the natural world, proved difficult to approach. Cowper, the most popular poet of the latter part of the century, won his readers with a more modest, intimate kind of verse, never departing far from the accents of friendly conversation. Nevertheless, it was to visionary poetry, and to genius, that the future belonged. "The road of excess," Blake notes in a Proverb of Hell, "leads to the palace of wisdom." As the eighteenth century drew to an end amid revolutions in society and thought, poets began to travel that road.

THE BEGINNING OF THE NOVEL

To say that the modern novel came into existence in the eighteenth century is not to say that there was no prose fiction before 1700. There were the ancient Greek romances and their modern European imitators; the courtly *Arcadia* of Sidney and the humbler fiction of Deloney and Nashe and other Elizabethans; the interminable French romances of the seventeenth century and their English translations and imitations, loosely constructed, blending aristocratic refinement, chivalric adventure, and courtly love; the tales of the adventures of rogues and the careers of famous criminals; and, in a world apart, Bunyan's vivid allegories of the spiritual adventures of wayfaring and militant Christians and their adversaries. But it remains true that, if we except Daniel Defoe, the creator of the modern novel was Samuel Richardson (1689–1761). Both Defoe and Richardson belonged to the middle class and expressed in their works middle-class interests and attitudes. They also wrote about and for women. To a large extent, the development of the novel is identical with the attempt to interest the growing number of female readers by shaping their lives into literature. Defoe simply ignored the sentimental and aristocratic refinements of the earlier romances and was content to show his readers not a world as it might be, a heroic world, but their world as it was, populated with believable people who were motivated by the practical concerns that dominate our daily lives. He did not seek—and except through *Robinson Crusoe* (1719) did not often find—readers among the upper classes. He was content to interest shopkeepers, apprentices, and servants, who were already avid readers of tales of crime and adventure, usually heavily laced with pious moral observations.

Richardson, however, caught the attention of all literate Europe, and once for all established the novel as we know it, a solid and enduring object in the literary landscape. His three novels were strikingly new in their minute and subtle analysis of emotions and states of mind. It was while he was compiling a little book of model letters that he conceived the idea of *Pamela*, or *Virtue Rewarded* (1740), a story told in a series of letters, in which a virtuous servant girl who resists her master's base designs on her virtue eventually wins him as her husband. Richardson's masterpiece, *Clarissa* (1747–48), carries the same epistolary method, moral instruction, and sexual titillation to new heights. In the conflict between the libertine Lovelace, an attractive and diabolical aristocrat, and the angelic Clarissa, the perfection of middle-class values, Richardson created a fiction that embodied the ideals and the tensions of his society. No earlier author had involved his readers so fully in the thoughts and emotions of his characters; nor had any author paid such close attention to the pressures on women. Such later novelists as Fanny Burney (1752–1840) and Jane Austen would profit from his example. Richardson's final novel, *Sir Charles Grandison* (1753–54), turns to a model of male perfection with less success.

Henry Fielding (1707–1754), who loved virtue as much as Richardson did, but to whom goodness was a matter of spontaneity and fellow feeling, not of conformity to a code, considered *Pamela* a misleading image of virtue;

therefore, in 1742, he published *Joseph Andrews*, which begins as an hilarious burlesque of *Pamela* by describing the staunch resistance offered to the lewd advances of Lady Booby by her servant, the virtuous Joseph, brother of Pamela. Expelled for his chastity from Lady Booby's household, he takes to the road, joining the guileless Parson Adams, who is walking to London to try to sell a bundle of his sermons to a publisher. Their adventures make up what Fielding called "a comic epic in prose." His great novel is *The History of Tom Jones, A Foundling* (1749). The protagonist became the pattern of the good-natured hero of the age: a young man of manly virtues, generous, high-spirited, loyal, and courageous, but impulsive, wanting prudence, full of animal spirits and sensuality. The novel is crowded with incident and with varied types of men and women; and critics have agreed with Coleridge's praise of its brilliantly constructed plot. Fielding's other important novel, *Amelia* (1751), having as its heroine a long-suffering woman, almost wholly passive, is an example of pathos rather than of Fielding's comic vigor and gusto.

The picaresque tradition was continued by Tobias Smollett (1721–1771) in *Roderick Random* (1748), *Peregrine Pickle* (1751), and *Ferdinand, Count Fathom* (1753). Smollett delighted to depict the grotesque side of eighteenth-century life, its brutality, coarse practical jokes, and strong odors. His masterpiece is *Humphrey Clinker* (1771), which recounts, through letters written by several members of a traveling party, the comic incidents of a journey through England and Scotland. But the most original novelist of the period was Laurence Sterne (1713–1768), an unclerical clergyman, a humorist, a sentimentalist, and an author who reminds us that one of the roots of the novel is the word "novelty." *The Life and Opinions of Tristram Shandy*, produced between 1760 and 1767, deliberately frustrated all the stock expectations of its readers. The plot has not the logical order of a beginning, a middle, and an end; instead it abandons clock time for psychological time, interrupts scenes in order to digress or to recount past or future events, follows whimsically any apparently chance association, digresses for several chapters—in fact, it is designed as an elaborate joke at the reader's expense. And yet the method gets us inside the consciousness of the narrator and the other characters, and into a world peopled by the most engaging of comic characters.

Fielding, Smollett, and Sterne gave to English literature not only vivid scenes from the life of their times, but a gallery of eccentric and original characters that illustrate the interest of the age not only in the ideal and the general, but also in the individual and the unique. The novels of Dickens and of Thackeray in the nineteenth century owe much to their forerunners in the eighteenth.

THE CONTINUITY OF THE AUGUSTAN TRADITION

Despite the emergence of new literary forms, materials, and methods after the death of Pope and Swift, the Augustan line continued vigorously throughout the last half of the eighteenth and even into the nineteenth century. If the years between 1745 and 1784 were years of change and experiment, they were also the period of Samuel Johnson's greatest achievement and influence. A conservative in literature as in politics and religion, Johnson defended in conversation and in his critical writings the principles that he had inherited from the older generation. His two major poems, *London* (1738) and *The Vanity of Human Wishes* (1749), are satirical and ethical and show little influence of the new sensibility of the midcentury. He was loyal to the heroic couplet and to the use of generalized diction. His *Dictionary* (1755) was designed not to fix our language permanently but certainly to retard the process of change and to censure words which he considered superfluous. His critical writings sufficiently reveal his devotion to the standards of Dryden and Pope. But his conservatism was saved from pedantry by the empirical bent of his mind and his broad and humanistic learning.

If Johnson speaks for his age, the reason is partly that he shares a faith, with many of his contemporaries, in common sense and the common reader. "By the common sense of readers uncorrupted with literary prejudices," he wrote in the last of his great *Lives of the Poets* (1780), "must be finally decided all claim to poetical honors." A similar respect for common sense, and for standards of taste and behavior based upon responses that all of us share, marks many of the grandest achievements of the century; for instance, the political writings of Edmund Burke, the great Whig statesman and orator, or the *Discourses on Art* (1769–90) of Sir Joshua Reynolds, who drew the best aesthetic theory of his day into an elegant whole. Moreover, the poets whom everyone read relied less upon apocalyptic visions than upon a verse that could do justice to the ordinary feelings of ordinary people. Gray's *Elegy*, Goldsmith's *The Deserted Village*, Crabbe's *The Village*, and the lyrics of Robert Burns are only a few of the poems that strive to make poetry from and for the lives of the common man. Nor did Goldsmith, Crabbe, and Burns, for all their attachment to the growing wave of sentimentalism, desert the verse forms—the careful craftsmanship, the rhyming couplets— developed by the earlier Augustan masters. Even Cowper's *The Task* (1785), which brings us to the threshold of the Romantic movement, belongs most definitely in the eighteenth century. Indeed, the Augustan age did not die on that day in 1798 when a small and unsuccessful volume of poems, *Lyrical Ballads*, was published by Wordsworth and Coleridge. We hear the accents of that age from time to time in the poems of both Wordsworth and Coleridge, in many of the poems of Byron, and in Byron's ardent defense of Pope and Dryden, when the new age finally brought those masters to judgment. And we hear its old verities expressed in its own vocabulary in the criticism of that arch-enemy of the Romantic movement, Francis Jeffrey, editor of the *Edinburgh Review*, as when, for example, in a review (1808) of a volume of poems by George Crabbe, he paused to rebuke the (as he believed) affectedly eccentric poet Wordsworth for having written *The Thorn* and one of the Lucy poems:

> Now we leave it to any reader of common candor and discernment
> to say whether these representations of character and sentiment are drawn
> from the eternal and universal standard of truth and nature, which
> every one is knowing enough to recognize, and no one great enough to
> depart from with impunity; or whether they are not formed . . . upon
> certain fantastic and affected peculiarities in the mind or fancy of the
> author, into which it is most improbable that many of his readers will
> enter, and which cannot, in some cases, be comprehended without
> much effort and explanation.

JOHN DRYDEN
1631–1700

1668:   Made poet laureate.
1681:   *Absalom and Achitophel.*
ca. 1686: Conversion to Catholicism.
1689:   Loss of court offices upon accession
          of William and Mary.
1697:   Translation of Virgil.

Although John Dryden's parents seem to have sided with Parliament against the king, there is no evidence that the poet grew up in a strict Puritan family. His father, a country gentleman of moderate fortune, gave his son a gentleman's education at Westminster School, under the renowned Dr. Richard Busby, who used the rod as a pedagogical aid in imparting a sound knowledge of the learned languages and literatures to his charges (among others John Locke and Matthew Prior). From Westminster, Dryden went to Trinity College, Cambridge, where he took his A.B. in 1654. His first important and impressive poem, *Heroic Stanzas* (1659), was written to commemorate the death of Cromwell. The next year, however, in *Astraea Redux*, Dryden joined his countrymen in celebrating the return of Charles II to his throne. During the rest of his life Dryden was to remain entirely loyal to Charles and to his successor James II.

Dryden is the commanding literary figure of the last four decades of the seventeenth century. He is that rare phenomenon, the man of letters in whose work the image of an age can be discerned. Every important aspect of the life of his times—political, religious, philosophical, artistic—finds expression somewhere in his writings. Dryden is the least personal of our poets. He is not at all the solitary, subjective poet listening to the murmur of his own voice and preoccupied with his own personal view of experience, but rather a citizen of the world commenting publicly on matters of public concern.

From the beginning to the end of his literary career, Dryden's original nondramatic poems are most typically occasional poems, which celebrate particular events of a public character—a coronation, a military victory, a death, a political crisis. Such poems are social and ceremonial, written not for the self but the nation. Dryden's principal achievements in this form are the two poems on the king's return and his coronation; *Annus Mirabilis* (1667), which celebrates the English naval victory over the Dutch and the fortitude of the people of London and the king during the Great Fire, both events of that "wonderful year," 1666; the political poems; the lines on the death of Oldham (1684); and the odes.

Between 1664 and 1681, however, Dryden was mainly a playwright. The newly chartered theaters needed a modern repertory, and he set out to supply the need. Dryden wrote his plays, as he frankly confessed, to please his audiences, which were not heterogeneous, like Shakespeare's, but were largely drawn from the court and from people of fashion. In the style of the time, he produced rhymed heroic plays, in which incredibly noble heroes and heroines face incredibly difficult choices between love and honor; comedies, in which male and female rakes engage in intrigue and bright repartee; and, later, libretti for the newly introduced dramatic form, the opera. His one great tragedy, *All for Love* (1677), in blank verse, adapts Shakespeare's *Antony and Cleopatra* to the unities of time, place, and action. As his *Essay of Dramatic Poesy* (1668) shows, Dryden had studied the works of the great playwrights of Greece and Rome, of the English Renaissance, and of contemporary France, seeking sound theoretical principles on which to construct the new drama that the age demanded. Indeed his fine critical intelligence always supported his creative powers, and because he took literature seriously and enjoyed discussing it, he became, it appears almost casually, what Samuel Johnson called him: "the father of English criticism." His abilities as both poet and dramatist brought him to the attention of the king, who in 1668 made him poet laureate. Two years later the post of Historiographer Royal was added to the laureateship at a combined stipend of £200, enough money to live on.

Between 1678 and 1681, when he was nearing fifty, Dryden discovered his great gift for writing formal verse satire. A quarrel with Thomas Shadwell, a playwright of some talent, prompted the mock-heroic episode *Mac Flecknoe*, which was probably written about 1678 but which was not published until 1682. Out of the stresses occasioned by the Popish Plot (1678) and its political aftermath came his major political satires, *Absalom and Achitophel* (1681), and *The Medal* (1682), his final attack on the villain of *Absalom and Achitophel*, the earl of Shaftesbury. Twenty years' experience as poet and playwright had prepared him technically for the triumph of *Absalom and Achitophel*. He had completely mastered the heroic couplet, having fashioned it into an instrument suitable in his hands for every sort of discourse from the thrust and parry of quick logical argument, to lyric feeling, rapid narrative, or forensic declamation. Thanks to this long discipline, he was able in one stride to assume his proper place beside the masters of verse satire: Horace, Juvenal, Persius, in ancient Rome, and Boileau, his French contemporary.

The consideration of religious and political questions that the events of 1678–81 forced on Dryden brought a new seriousness to his mind and works. In 1682 he published *Religio Laici*, a poem in which he examined the grounds of his religious faith and defended the middle way of the Anglican Church against the rationalism of Deism on the one hand and the authoritarianism of Rome on the other. But he had moved closer to Rome than he perhaps realized when he wrote the poem. Charles II died in 1685 and was succeeded by his Catholic brother, James II. Within less than a year Dryden and his two sons were converted to Catholicism. Though his enemies accused him of opportunism, he proved his sincerity by his steadfast loyalty to the Roman Church after James abdicated and the Protestant William and Mary came in; as a result he was to lose his offices and their much-needed stipends. From his new position as a Roman Catholic, Dryden wrote in 1687 *The Hind and the Panther*, in which a milk-white Hind (the Roman Church) and a spotted Panther (the Anglican Church) eloquently debate theology. The Hind has the better of the argument; but Dryden already knew that James's policies were failing, and with them the Catholic cause in England.

Dryden was now nearing sixty, with a family to support on a much-diminished income. To earn a living, he resumed writing plays and turned to translations. In 1693 appeared his versions of Juvenal and Persius, with the long dedicatory epistle on satire; and in 1697, his greatest achievement in this mode, the works of Virgil. At the very end, two months before his death, came the *Fables Ancient and Modern*, prefaced by one of the finest of his critical essays and made up of translations from Ovid, Boccaccio, and Chaucer.

What was the nature of Dryden's achievement? His drama, by and large, belongs entirely to his age, though its influence persisted into the next century. His critical writings established canons of taste and theoretical principles that determined the character of neoclassic literature in the next century. He helped establish a new sort of prose—easy, lucid, plain, and shaped to the cadences of natural speech. This is the prose that we like to think of as "modern." Johnson praised it for its informality and apparent artlessness: "every word seems to drop by chance, though it falls into its proper place. Nothing is cold or languid; the whole is airy, animated, and vigorous . . . though all is easy, nothing is feeble; though all seems careless, there is nothing harsh." His satire, as vital today as it was three hundred years ago, exerted a fruitful influence on the most brilliant verse satirist of the next century, Alexander Pope. The vigor and variety of his metrics made inevitable the long-enduring vogue of the heroic couplet among his successors. At the same time, he created a poetic language that remained the basic language of poetry until the early nineteenth century and that even the Romantic movement did not wholly destroy. His poems represent the superbly civilized language of the Augustan style at its best: dignified, unaffected, precise and always musical—a noble instrument of public speech. Johnson's final estimate remains valid: "By him we were taught *sapere et fari*, to think naturally and express forcibly. . . . What was said of Rome, adorned by Augustus, may be applied by an easy metaphor to English poetry embellished by Dryden, *lateritiam invenit, marmoream reliquit*, he found it brick, and he left it marble."

Song from *Marriage à la Mode*

1

Why should a foolish marriage vow,
   Which long ago was made,
Oblige us to each other now,
   When passion is decayed?
We loved, and we loved, as long as we could,   5
   Till our love was loved out in us both;
But our marriage is dead when the pleasure is fled:
   'Twas pleasure first made it an oath.

2

If I have pleasures for a friend,
   And farther love in store,   10
What wrong has he whose joys did end,
   And who could give no more?
'Tis a madness that he should be jealous of me,
   Or that I should bar him of another:

For all we can gain is to give ourselves pain,   15
When neither can hinder the other.

ca. 1672   1673

Absalom and Achitophel   In 1678 a dangerous crisis, both religious and political, threatened to undo the Restoration settlement and to
precipitate England once again into civil war. The Popish Plot and its aftermath not only whipped up extreme anti-Catholic passions, but led between
1679 and 1681 to a bitter political struggle between Charles II (whose adherents came to be called Tories) and the earl of Shaftesbury (whose followers
were termed Whigs). The issues were nothing less than the prerogatives of
the Crown and the possible exclusion of the king's Catholic brother, James,
duke of York, from his rightful position as heir-presumptive to the throne.
Charles's cool courage and brilliant, if unscrupulous, political genius saved
the throne for his brother and gave at least temporary peace to his people.

Charles was a Catholic at heart—he received the last rites of that church
on his deathbed—and was eager to do what he could do discreetly for the
relief of his Catholic subjects, who suffered severe civil and religious disabilities imposed by their numerically superior Protestant countrymen. James
openly professed the Catholic religion, an awkward fact politically, for he
was next in line of succession since Charles had no legitimate children. The
household of the duke, as well as that of Charles's neglected queen, Catherine of Braganza, inevitably became the center of Catholic life and intrigue
at court and consequently of Protestant prejudice and suspicion.

No one understood, however, that the situation was explosive until 1678,
when Titus Oates (a renegade Catholic convert and a man of the most infamous character) offered sworn testimony of the existence of a Jesuit plot to
assassinate the king, burn London, massacre Protestants, and reestablish the
Roman Church.

The country might have kept its head and come to realize (what no historian has doubted) that Oates and his confederates were perjured rascals, as
Charles himself quickly perceived. But panic was created by the discovery
of the murdered body of a prominent London justice of the peace, Sir Edmund
Berry Godfrey, who a few days before had received for safekeeping a copy of
Oates's testimony. The crime, immediately ascribed to the Catholics, has
never been solved. Fear and indignation reached a hysterical pitch when the
seizure of the papers of the duke of York's secretary revealed that he had
been in correspondence with the confessor of Louis XIV regarding the re-
establishment of the Roman Church in England. Before the terror subsided
many innocent men were executed on the increasingly bold and always false
evidence of Oates and his fellows.

The earl of Shaftesbury, the duke of Buckingham, and others quickly took
advantage of the situation. With the support of the Commons and the City
of London, they moved to exclude the duke of York from the succession.
Between 1679 and 1681 Charles and Shaftesbury were engaged in a mighty
struggle. The Whigs found a candidate of their own in the king's favorite
illegitimate son, the handsome and engaging duke of Monmouth, whom
they advanced as a proper successor to his father. They urged Charles to
legitimize him, and when he refused they whispered that there was proof

that the king had secretly married Monmouth's mother. The young man allowed himself to be used against his father. He was sent on a triumphant progress through western England, where he was enthusiastically received. Twice an Exclusion Bill nearly passed both houses. But by early 1681 Charles had secured his own position by secretly accepting from Louis XIV a three-year subsidy that made him independent of Parliament, which had tried to force his hand by refusing to vote him funds. He summoned Parliament to meet at Oxford in the spring of 1681, and, a few moments after the Commons had passed the Exclusion Bill, in a bold stroke he abruptly dissolved Parliament, which never met again during his reign. Already, as Charles was aware, a reaction had set in against the violence of the Whigs. In mid-summer, when he felt it safe to move against his enemies, Shaftesbury was sent to the Tower, charged with high treason. In November the grand jury, packed with Whigs, threw out the indictment, and the earl was free; but his power was broken, and he lived only two more years.

Shortly before the grand jury acted, Dryden published anonymously the first part of *Absalom and Achitophel*, apparently hoping to influence their verdict. It is worthy of the occasion which produced it. The issues in question were grave; the chief actors, the most important men in the realm. Dryden, therefore, could not use burlesque and caricature as had Butler, or the mock-heroic as he himself had done in *Mac Flecknoe*. Only a heroic style and manner were appropriate to his weighty material, and the poem is most original in its blending of the heroic and the satiric. Dryden's task called for all his tact and literary skill; he had to mention, but to gloss over, the king's faults: his indolence and love of pleasure; his neglect of his wife and his devotion to his mistresses—conduct which had left him with many children, but no heir except his Catholic brother. He had to deal gently with Monmouth, whom Charles still loved. And he had to present, or appear to present, the king's case objectively.

The remarkable parallels between the rebellion of Absalom against his father King David (2 Samuel 13–18) had already been remarked in sermons, satires, and pamphlets. Dryden took the hint and gave contemporary events a due distance and additional dignity by approaching them indirectly through their biblical analogues. The poem is famous for its brilliant portraits of the king's enemies and friends; but equally admirable are the temptation scene (which, like other passages, is indebted to *Paradise Lost*) and the remarkably astute analysis of the Popish Plot itself.

A second part of *Absalom and Achitophel* appeared in 1682. Most of it is the work of Nahum Tate, but lines 310–509, which include the devastating portraits of Doeg and Og (two Whig poets, Elkanah Settle and Thomas Shadwell) are certainly by Dryden.

Absalom and Achitophel: A Poem

> In pious times, ere priestcraft did begin,
> Before polygamy was made a sin;
> When man on many multiplied his kind,
> Ere one to one was cursedly confined;
> When nature prompted and no law denied   5
> Promiscuous use of concubine and bride;

Then Israel's monarch after Heaven's own heart,[1]
His vigorous warmth did variously impart
To wives and slaves; and, wide as his command,
Scattered his Maker's image through the land.   10
Michal,[2] of royal blood, the crown did wear,
A soil ungrateful to the tiller's care:
Not so the rest; for several mothers bore
To godlike David several sons before.
But since like slaves his bed they did ascend,   15
No true succession could their seed attend.
Of all this numerous progeny was none
So beautiful, so brave, as Absalom:[3]
Whether, inspired by some diviner lust,
His father got him with a greater gust,[4]   20
Or that his conscious destiny made way,
By manly beauty, to imperial sway.
Early in foreign fields he won renown,
With kings and states allied to Israel's crown:[5]
In peace the thoughts of war he could remove,   25
And seemed as he were only born for love.
Whate'er he did, was done with so much ease,
In him alone 'twas natural to please;
His motions all accompanied with grace;
And paradise was opened in his face.   30
With secret joy indulgent David viewed
His youthful image in his son renewed·
To all his wishes nothing he denied;
And made the charming Annabel[6] his bride.
What faults he had (for who from faults is free?)   35
His father could not, or he would not see.
Some warm excesses which the law forbore,
Were cònstrued youth that purged by boiling o'er:
And Amnon's murther,[7] by a specious name,
Was called a just revenge for injured fame.   40
Thus praised and loved the noble youth remained,
While David, undisturbed, in Sion[8] reigned.
But life can never be sincerely[9] blest;
Heaven punishes the bad, and proves[1] the best.
The Jews,[2] a headstrong, moody, murmuring race,   45

---

1. David ("a man after [God's] own heart," according to 1 Samuel 13.14) represents Charles II.
2. "Michal," one of David's wives, represents the childless queen, Catherine of Braganza.
3. James Scott, duke of Monmouth (1649–1685).
4. Relish, pleasure.
5. Monmouth had won repute as a soldier fighting for France against Holland and for Holland against France.
6. Anne Scott, duchess of Buccleuch (pro-

nounced *Bue-cloo*), a beauty and a great heiress.
7. Absalom killed his half-brother Amnon, who had raped Absalom's sister Tamar (2 Samuel 13.28–29). The parallel with Monmouth is vague. He is known to have committed acts of violence in his youth, but certainly not fratricide.
8. London.
9. Wholly.
1. Tests.
2. The English.

As ever tried the extent and stretch of grace;
God's pampered people, whom, debauched with ease,
No king could govern, nor no God could please
(Gods they had tried of every shape and size
That god-smiths could produce, or priests devise);[3]   50
These Adam-wits,[4] too fortunately free,
Began to dream they wanted liberty;
And when no rule, no precedent was found,
Of men by laws less circumscribed and bound,
They led their wild desires to woods and caves,   55
And thought that all but savages were slaves.
They who, when Saul[5] was dead, without a blow,
Made foolish Ishbosheth the crown forgo;
Who banished David did from Hebron[6] bring,
And with a general shout proclaimed him king: 60
Those very Jews, who, at their very best,
Their humor[7] more than loyalty expressed,
Now wondered why so long they had obeyed
An idol monarch, which their hands had made;
Thought they might ruin him they could create,   65
Or melt him to that golden calf,[8] a state.
But these were random bolts;[9] no formed design
Nor interest made the factious crowd to join:
The sober part of Israel, free from stain,
Well knew the value of a peaceful reign;   70
And, looking backward with a wise affright,
Saw seams of wounds, dishonest[1] to the sight:
In contemplation of whose ugly scars
They cursed the memory of civil wars.
The moderate sort of men, thus qualified,[2]   75
Inclined the balance to the better side;
And David's mildness managed it so well,
The bad found no occasion to rebel.
But when to sin our biased[3] nature leans,
The careful Devil is still at hand with means;   80
And providently pimps for ill desires:
The Good Old Cause[4] revived, a plot requires.
Plots, true or false, are necessary things,
To raise up commonwealths and ruin kings.

3. Dryden recalls the political and religious controversies which, since the Reformation, had divided
England and finally caused civil war.
4. Adam rebelled because he felt that he lacked
("wanted") liberty, since he was forbidden to eat
the fruit of one tree.
5. Oliver Cromwell. "Ishbosheth": Saul's son; he
stands for Richard Cromwell, who succeeded his
father as Lord Protector.
6. Where David reigned over Judah after the death
of Saul and before he became king of Israel (2
Samuel 1–5). Charles had been crowned in Scot-

land in 1651.
7. Caprice.
8. The image worshiped by the Children of Israel
during the period that Moses spent on Mt. Sinai,
receiving the law from God. "A state": a republic.
9. Shots.
1. Disgraceful.
2. Assuaged.
3. Inclined. Cf. *Mac Flecknoe*, line 189 and note.
4. The Commonwealth. Dryden stigmatizes the
Whigs by associating them with subversion.

The inhabitants of old Jerusalem   85
Were Jebusites;[5] the town so called from them;
And theirs the native right.
But when the chosen people[6] grew more strong,
The rightful cause at length became the wrong;
And every loss the men of Jebus bore,   90
They still were thought God's enemies the more.
Thus worn and weakened, well or ill content,
Submit they must to David's government:
Impoverished and deprived of all command,
Their taxes doubled as they lost their land;   95
And, what was harder yet to flesh and blood,
Their gods disgraced, and burnt like common wood.[7]
This set the heathen priesthood[8] in a flame;
For priests of all religions are the same:
Of whatsoe'er descent their godhead be,   100
Stock, stone, or other homely pedigree,
In his defense his servants are as bold,
As if he had been born of beaten gold.
The Jewish rabbins,[9] though their enemies,
In this conclude them honest men and wise: 105
For 'twas their duty, all the learned think,
To espouse his cause, by whom they eat and drink.
From hence began that Plot, the nation's curse,
Bad in itself, but represented worse;
Raised in extremes, and in extremes decried;   110
With oaths affirmed, with dying vows denied;
Not weighed or winnowed by the multitude;
But swallowed in the mass, unchewed and crude.
Some truth there was, but dashed[1] and brewed with lies,
To please the fools, and puzzle all the wise.   115
Succeeding times did equal folly call,
Believing nothing, or believing all.
The Egyptian[2] rites the Jebusites embraced,
Where gods were recommended by their taste.
Such savory deities must needs be good,   120
As served at once for worship and for food.
By force they could not introduce these gods,
For ten to one in former days was odds;
So fraud was used (the sacrificer's trade):
Fools are more hard to conquer than persuade.   125
Their busy teachers mingled with the Jews,
And raked for converts even the court and stews:[3]
Which Hebrew priests the more unkindly took,

---

5. Roman Catholics. The original name of Jerusalem (here, London) was Jebus.
6. Protestants.
7. Such oppressive laws against Roman Catholics
date from the time of Elizabeth I.
8. Roman Catholic clergy.

9. Anglican clergy.
1. Adulterated.
2. French, therefore Catholic. In the next line
Dryden sneers at the doctrine of transubstantiation.
3. Brothels.

Because the fleece accompanies the flock.[4]
Some thought they God's anointed[5] meant to slay   130
By guns, invented since full many a day:
Our author swears it not; but who can know
How far the Devil and Jebusites may go?
This Plot, which failed for want of common sense,
Had yet a deep and dangerous consequence: 135
For, as when raging fevers boil the blood,
The standing lake soon floats into a flood,
And every hostile humor, which before
Slept quiet in its channels, bubbles o'er;
So several factions from this first ferment   140
Work up to foam, and threat the government.
Some by their friends, more by themselves thought wise,
Opposed the power to which they could not rise.
Some had in courts been great, and thrown from thence,
Like fiends were hardened in impenitence;   145
Some, by their monarch's fatal mercy, grown
From pardoned rebels kinsmen to the throne,
Were raised in power and public office high;
Strong bands, if bands ungrateful men could tie.
      Of these the false Achitophel[6] was first;   150
A name to all succeeding ages cursed:
For close designs, and crooked counsels fit;
Sagacious, bold, and turbulent of wit;[7]
Restless, unfixed in principles and place;
In power unpleased, impatient of disgrace: 155
A fiery soul, which, working out its way, ⎱
Fretted the pygmy body to decay,   ⎰
And o'er-informed the tenement of clay.[8] ⎰
A daring pilot in extremity;
Pleased with the danger, when the waves went high,   160
He sought the storms; but, for a calm unfit,
Would steer too nigh the sands, to boast his wit.
Great wits[9] are sure to madness near allied,
And thin partitions do their bounds divide;
Else why should he, with wealth and honor blest,   165
Refuse his age the needful hours of rest?
Punish a body which he could not please;
Bankrupt of life, yet prodigal of ease?

4. Dryden charges that the Anglican clergy ("Hebrew priests") resented proselytizing by Catholics chiefly because they stood to lose their tithes ("fleece").
5. The King.
6. Anthony Ashley Cooper, 1st earl of Shaftesbury (1621–1683). He had served in the parliamentary army and been a member of Cromwell's Council of State. He later helped bring back Charles, and in 1670 was made a member of the notorious Cabal Ministry, which formed an alliance with Louis XIV in which England betrayed her ally, Holland, and joined France in war against that country. In 1672 he became lord chancellor, but with the dissolution of the Cabal in 1673 he was removed from office. Lines 146–49 apply perfectly to him.
7. Unruly imagination.
8. The soul is thought of as the animating principle, the force that puts the body in motion. Shaftesbury's body seemed too small to house his fiery, energetic soul.
9. Men of genius. That genius and madness are akin is a very old idea.

And all to leave what with his toil he won,
To that unfeathered two-legged thing,[1] a son;   170
Got, while his soul did huddled[2] notions try;
And born a shapeless lump, like anarchy.
In friendship false, implacable in hate,
Resolved to ruin or to rule the state.
To compass this the triple bond[3] he broke,   175
The pillars of the public safety shook,
And fitted Israel for a foreign yoke;
Then seized with fear, yet still affecting fame,
Usurped a patriot's all-atoning name.
So easy still it proves in factious times,   180
With public zeal to cancel private crimes.
How safe is treason, and how sacred ill,
Where none can sin against the people's will!
Where crowds can wink, and no offense be known,
Since in another's guilt they find their own!   185
Yet fame deserved, no enemy can grudge;
The statesman we abhor, but praise the judge.
In Israel's courts ne'er sat an Abbethdin[4]
With more discerning eyes, or hands more clean;
Unbribed, unsought, the wretched to redress;   190
Swift of dispatch, and easy of access.
Oh, had he been content to serve the crown,
With virtues only proper to the gown;
Or had the rankness of the soil been freed
From cockle, that oppressed the noble seed;   195
David for him his tuneful harp had strung,
And Heaven had wanted one immortal song.[5]
But wild Ambition loves to slide, not stand,
And Fortune's ice prefers to Virtue's land.
Achitophel, grown weary to possess   200
A lawful fame, and lazy happiness,
Disdained the golden fruit to gather free,
And lent the crowd his arm to shake the tree.
Now, manifest of[6] crimes contrived long since,
He stood at bold defiance with his prince;   205
Held up the buckler of the people's cause
Against the crown, and skulked behind the laws.
The wished occasion of the Plot he takes;
Some circumstances finds, but more he makes.
By buzzing emissaries fills the ears   210

---

1. Cf. Plato's definition of man: "a featherless biped."
2. Confused, hurried.
3. The Triple Alliance of England, Sweden, and Holland against France, 1668. Shaftesbury helped to bring about the war against Holland in 1672.
4. The chief of the seventy elders who composed the Jewish supreme court. The allusion is to Shaftesbury's serving as Lord Chancellor in 1672–

73. Dryden's praise of Shaftesbury's integrity in this office, by suggesting a balanced judgment, makes his condemnation of the statesman more effective than it might otherwise have been.
5. I.e., David would have had occasion to write one less song of praise to Heaven. The reference may be to 2 Samuel 22 or to Psalm 4.
6. Detected in.

Of listening crowds with jealousies[7] and fears
Of arbitrary counsels brought to light,
And proves the king himself a Jebusite.
Weak arguments! which yet he knew full well
Were strong with people easy to rebel.   215
For, governed by the moon, the giddy Jews
Tread the same track when she the prime renews;[8]
And once in twenty years, their scribes record,
By natural instinct they change their lord.
Achitophel still wants a chief, and none   220
Was found so fit as warlike Absalom:
Not that he wished his greatness to create
(For politicians neither love nor hate),
But, for he knew his title not allowed,
Would keep him still depending on the crowd,   225
That kingly power, thus ebbing out, might be
Drawn to the dregs of a democracy.[9]
Him he attempts with studied arts to please,
And sheds his venom in such words as these:
    "Auspicious prince, at whose nativity   230
Some royal planet[1] ruled the southern sky;
Thy longing country's darling and desire;
Their cloudy pillar and their guardian fire:[2]
Their second Moses, whose extended wand
Divides the seas, and shows the promised land;   235
Whose dawning day in every distant age
Has exercised the sacred prophet's rage:
The people's prayer, the glad diviners' theme,
The young men's vision, and the old men's dream![3]
Thee, savior, thee, the nation's vows[4] confess,   240
And, never satisfied with seeing, bless:
Swift unbespoken pomps thy steps proclaim,
And stammering babes are taught to lisp thy name.
How long wilt thou the general joy detain,
Starve and defraud the people of thy reign?   245
Content ingloriously to pass thy days
Like one of Virtue's fools that feeds on praise;
Till thy fresh glories, which now shine so bright,
Grow stale and tarnish with our daily sight.
Believe me, royal youth, thy fruit must be   250

7. Suspicions.
8. The moon "renews her prime" when her several phases recur on the same day of the solar calendar—i.e., complete a cycle—as happens approximately every 20 years. The crisis between Charles I and Parliament began to grow acute about 1640; Charles II returned in 1660; it is now 1680 and a full cycle has been completed.
9. To Dryden, "democracy" meant popular government. The "dregs of a democracy" would be mob rule.

1. A planet whose influence destines him to kingship.
2. After their exodus from Egypt under the leadership of Moses, whose "extended wand" separated the waters of the Red Sea so that they crossed over on dry land, the Israelites were led in their 40-year wandering in the wilderness by a pillar of cloud by day and a pillar of fire by night. See Exodus 13–14.
3. Cf. Joel 2.28.
4. Solemn promises of fidelity.

Or gathered ripe, or rot upon the tree.
Heaven has to all allotted, soon or late,
Some lucky revolution of their fate;
Whose motions if we watch and guide with skill
(For human good depends on human will),   255
Our Fortune rolls as from a smooth descent,
And from the first impression takes the bent;
But, if unseized, she glides away like wind,
And leaves repenting Folly far behind.
Now, now she meets you with a glorious prize,   260
And spreads her locks before her as she flies.[5]
Had thus old David, from whose loins you spring,
Not dared, when Fortune called him, to be king,
At Gath[6] an exile he might still remain,
And heaven's anointing[7] oil had been in vain.   265
Let his successful youth your hopes engage;
But shun the example of declining age;
Behold him setting in his western skies,
The shadows lengthening as the vapors rise.
He is not now, as when on Jordan's sand[8]   270
The joyful people thronged to see him land,
Covering the beach, and blackening all the strand;
But, like the Prince of Angels, from his height
Comes tumbling downward with diminished light;[9]
Betrayed by one poor plot to public scorn   275
(Our only blessing since his cursed return),
Those heaps of people which one sheaf did bind,
Blown off and scattered by a puff of wind.
What strength can he to your designs oppose,
Naked of friends, and round beset with foes?   280
If Pharaoh's[1] doubtful succor he should use,
A foreign aid would more incense the Jews:
Proud Egypt would dissembled friendship bring;
Foment the war, but not support the king:
Nor would the royal party e'er unite   285
With Pharaoh's arms to assist the Jebusite;
Or if they should, their interest soon would break,
And with such odious aid make David weak.
All sorts of men by my successful arts,
Abhorring kings, estrange their altered hearts   290
From David's rule: and 'tis the general cry,
'Religion, commonwealth, and liberty.'[2]

---

5. Achitophel gives to Fortune the traditional attributes of the allegorical personification of Opportunity: bald except for a forelock, she can be seized only as she approaches.
6. Brussels, where Charles spent his last years in exile. David took refuge from Saul in Gath (1 Samuel 27.4).
7. After God rejected Saul, He sent Samuel to anoint the boy David, as a token that he should

finally come to the throne (1 Samuel 16.1–13).
8. The seashore at Dover, where Charles landed (May 25, 1660).
9. Cf. the fall of Satan in *Paradise Lost*, which dims the brightness of the archangel. The choice of the undignified word "tumbling" is deliberate.
1. Louis XIV of France.
2. Cf. line 82 and note.

If you, as champion of the public good,
Add to their arms a chief of royal blood,
What may not Israel hope, and what applause   295
Might such a general gain by such a cause?
Not barren praise alone, that gaudy flower
Fair only to the sight, but solid power;
And nobler is a limited command,
Given by the love of all your native land,   300
Than a successive title,[3] long and dark,
Drawn from the moldy rolls of Noah's ark."
        What cannot praise effect in mighty minds,
When flattery soothes, and when ambition blinds!
Desire of power, on earth a vicious weed,   305
Yet, sprung from high, is of celestial seed:
In God 'tis glory; and when men aspire,
'Tis but a spark too much of heavenly fire.
The ambitious youth, too covetous of fame,
Too full of angels' metal[4] in his frame,   310
Unwarily was led from virtue's ways,
Made drunk with honor, and debauched with praise.
Half loath, and half consenting to the ill
(For loyal blood within him struggled still),
He thus replied: "And what pretense have I   315
To take up arms for public liberty?
My father governs with unquestioned right;
The faith's defender, and mankind's delight,
Good, gracious, just, observant of the laws:
And heaven by wonders has espoused his cause.   320
Whom has he wronged in all his peaceful reign?
Who sues for justice to his throne in vain?
What millions has he pardoned of his foes.
Whom just revenge did to his wrath expose?
Mild, easy, humble, studious of our good,   325
Inclined to mercy, and averse from blood;
If mildness ill with stubborn Israel suit,
His crime is God's beloved attribute.
What could he gain, his people to betray,
Or change his right for arbitrary sway?   330
Let haughty Pharaoh curse with such a reign
His fruitful Nile, and yoke a servile train.
If David's rule Jerusalem displease,
The Dog Star[5] heats their brains to this disease.
Why then should I, encouraging the bad,   335
Turn rebel and run popularly mad?

3. A title to the crown based on succession.
4. An alternative spelling of *mettle*, (i.e., spirit).
But a pun on "metal" is intended, as is obvious
from the pun "angel" (a purely intellectual being
and a coin). Ambition caused the revolt of the angels
in heaven.
5. Sirius, which in midsummer rises and sets with
the sun and is thus associated with the maddening
heat of the "dog days."

Were he a tyrant, who, by lawless might
Oppressed the Jews, and raised the Jebusite,
Well might I mourn; but nature's holy bands
Would curb my spirits and restrain my hands: 340
The people might assert[6] their liberty,
But what was right in them were crime in me.
His favor leaves me nothing to require,
Prevents my wishes, and outruns desire.
What more can I expect while David lives?   345
All but his kingly diadem he gives:
And that"—But there he paused; then sighing, said—
"Is justly destined for a worthier head.
For when my father from his toils shall rest
And late augment the number of the blest,   350
His lawful issue shall the throne ascend,
Or the collateral line,[7] where that shall end.
His brother, though oppressed with vulgar spite,
Yet dauntless, and secure of native right,
Of every royal virtue stands possessed;   355
Still dear to all the bravest and the best.
His courage foes, his friends his truth proclaim;
His loyalty the king, the world his fame.
His mercy even the offending crowd will find,
For sure he comes of a forgiving kind.[8]   360
Why should I then repine at heaven's decree,
Which gives me no pretense to royalty?
Yet O that fate, propitiously inclined,
Had raised my birth, or had debased my mind;
To my large soul not all her treasure lent,   365
And then betrayed it to a mean descent!
I find, I find my mounting spirits bold,
And David's part disdains my mother's mold.
Why am I scanted by a niggard birth?[9]
My soul disclaims the kindred of her earth;   370
And, made for empire, whispers me within,
'Desire of greatness is a godlike sin.' "
    Him staggering so when hell's dire agent found,[1]
While fainting Virtue scarce maintained her ground,
He pours fresh forces in, and thus replies: 375
    "The eternal god, supremely good and wise,
Imparts not these prodigious gifts in vain:
What wonders are reserved to bless your reign!
Against your will, your arguments have shown,
Such virtue's only given to guide a throne.   380

6. Claim.
7. In the event of Charles's dying without legitimate issue, the throne would constitutionally pass
to his brother James, or his descendants, the "collateral line."

8. Race, in the sense of family.
9. I.e., why am I limited by a sordid birth?
1. Observe the Miltonic inversion, which helps to
maintain the epic tone.

Not that your father's mildness I contemn,
But manly force becomes the diadem.
'Tis true he grants the people all they crave;
And more, perhaps, than subjects ought to have:
For lavish grants suppose a monarch tame,   385
And more his goodness than his wit[2] proclaim.
But when should people strive their bonds to break,
If not when kings are negligent or weak?
Let him give on till he can give no more,
The thrifty Sanhedrin[3] shall keep him poor;   390
And every shekel which he can receive,
Shall cost a limb of his prerogative.[4]
To ply him with new plots shall be my care;
Or plunge him deep in some expensive war;
Which when his treasure can no more supply,   395
He must, with the remains of kingship, buy.
His faithful friends our jealousies and fears
Call Jebusites, and Pharaoh's pensioners;
Whom when our fury from his aid has torn,
He shall be naked left to public scorn.   400
The next successor, whom I fear and hate,
My arts have made obnoxious to the state;
Turned all his virtues to his overthrow,
And gained our elders[5] to pronounce a foe.
His right, for sums of necessary gold,   405
Shall first be pawned, and afterward be sold;
Till time shall ever-wanting David draw,
To pass your doubtful title into law:
If not, the people have a right supreme
To make their kings; for kings are made for them.   410
All empire is no more than power in trust,
Which, when resumed, can be no longer just.
Succession, for the general good designed,
In its own wrong a nation cannot bind;
If altering that the people can relieve,   415
Better one suffer than a nation grieve.
The Jews well know their power: ere Saul they chose,[6]
God was their king, and God they durst depose.
Urge now your piety,[7] your filial name,
A father's right and fear of future fame;   420
The public good, that universal call,
To which even heaven submitted, answers all.

2. Intelligence.
3. The highest judicial counsel of the Jews; here,
Parliament.
4. The Whigs hoped to limit the special privileges
of the Crown (the royal "prerogative") by refusing
to vote money to Charles. He circumvented them
by living on French subsidies and refusing to summon Parliament.
5. The chief magistrates and rulers of the Jews.

Shaftesbury had won over ("gained") country
gentlemen and nobles to his hostile view of James.
6. Before Saul, the first king of Israel, came to the
throne, the Jews were governed by judges. Similarly Oliver Cromwell ("Saul") as Lord Protector
took over the reins of government, after he had
dissolved the Rump Parliament in 1653.
7. Dutifulness to a parent.

Nor let his love enchant your generous mind;
'Tis Nature's trick to propagate her kind.
Our fond begetters, who would never die,   425
Love but themselves in their posterity.
Or let his kindness by the effects be tried,
Or let him lay his vain pretense aside.
God said he loved your father; could he bring
A better proof than to anoint him king?   430
It surely showed he loved the shepherd well,
Who gave so fair a flock as Israel.
Would David have you thought his darling son?
What means he then, to alienate[8] the crown?
The name of godly he may blush to bear: 435
'Tis after God's own heart[9] to cheat his heir.
He to his brother gives supreme command;
To you a legacy of barren land,[1]
Perhaps the old harp, on which he thrums his lays,
Or some dull Hebrew ballad in your praise.   440
Then the next heir, a prince severe and wise,
Already looks on you with jealous eyes;
Sees through the thin disguises of your arts,
And marks your progress in the people's hearts.
Though now his mighty soul its grief contains,   445
He meditates revenge who least complains;
And, like a lion, slumbering in the way,
Or sleep dissembling, while he waits his prey,
His fearless foes within his distance draws,
Constrains his roaring, and contracts his paws;   450
Till at the last, his time for fury found,
He shoots with sudden vengeance from the ground;
The prostrate vulgar[2] passes o'er and spares,
But with a lordly rage his hunters tears.
Your case no tame expedients will afford: 455
Resolve on death, or conquest by the sword,
Which for no less a stake than life you draw;
And self-defense is nature's eldest law.
Leave the warm people no considering time;
For then rebellion may be thought a crime.   460
Prevail yourself of what occasion gives,
But try your title while your father lives;
And that your arms may have a fair pretense,[3]
Proclaim you take them in the king's defense;
Whose sacred life each minute would expose   465
To plots, from seeming friends, and secret foes.
And who can sound the depth of David's soul?

8. In law, to convey the title to property to another person.
9. An irony: cf. line 7, note.
1. James was given the title of generalissimo in 1678. In 1679 Monmouth was banished and withdrew to Holland.
2. Common people.
3. Pretext.

Perhaps his fear his kindness may control.
He fears his brother, though he loves his son,
For plighted vows too late to be undone.   470
If so, by force he wishes to be gained,
Like women's lechery, to seem constrained.[4]
Doubt not; but when he most affects the frown,
Commit a pleasing rape upon the crown.
Secure his person to secure your cause: 475
They who possess the prince, possess the laws."
    He said, and this advice above the rest
With Absalom's mild nature suited best:
Unblamed of life (ambition set aside),
Not stained with cruelty, nor puffed with pride,   480
How happy had he been, if destiny
Had higher placed his birth, or not so high!
His kingly virtues might have claimed a throne,
And blest all other countries but his own.
But charming greatness since so few refuse,   485
'Tis juster to lament him than accuse.
Strong were his hopes a rival to remove,
With blandishments to gain the public love;
To head the faction while their zeal was hot,
And popularly prosecute the Plot.   490
To further this, Achitophel unites
The malcontents of all the Israelites;
Whose differing parties he could wisely join,
For several ends, to serve the same design:
The best (and of the princes some were such),   495
Who thought the power of monarchy too much;
Mistaken men, and patriots in their hearts;
Not wicked, but seduced by impious arts.
By these the springs of property were bent,
And wound so high, they cracked the government.   500
The next for interest sought to embroil the state,
To sell their duty at a dearer rate;
And make their Jewish markets of the throne,
Pretending public good, to serve their own.
Others thought kings an useless heavy load,   505
Who cost too much, and did too little good.
These were for laying honest David by,
On principles of pure good husbandry.[5]
With them joined all the haranguers of the throng,
That thought to get preferment by the tongue.   510
Who follow next, a double danger bring,
Not only hating David, but the king:
The Solymaean rout,[6] well-versed of old
In godly faction, and in treason bold;

4. Forced.   6. I.e., London rabble. Solyma was a name for
5. Economy.   Jerusalem.

Cowering and quaking at a conqueror's sword, 515
But lofty to a lawful prince restored;
Saw with disdain an ethnic[7] plot begun,
And scorned by Jebusites to be outdone.
Hot Levites[8] headed these; who, pulled before
From the ark, which in the Judges' days they bore, 520
Resumed their cant, and with a zealous cry
Pursued their old beloved theocracy:
Where Sanhedrin and priest enslaved the nation,
And justified their spoils by inspiration:[9]
For who so fit for reign as Aaron's race,[1] 525
If once dominion they could found in grace?
These led the pack; though not of surest scent,
Yet deepest-mouthed[2] against the government.
A numerous host of dreaming saints[3] succeed,
Of the true old enthusiastic breed: 530
'Gainst form and order they their power employ,
Nothing to build, and all things to destroy.
But far more numerous was the herd of such,
Who think too little, and who talk too much.
These out of mere instinct, they knew not why, 535
Adored their fathers' God and property;
And, by the same blind benefit of fate,
The Devil and the Jebusite did hate:
Born to be saved, even in their own despite,
Because they could not help believing right. 540
Such were the tools; but a whole Hydra more
Remains, of sprouting heads too long to score.
Some of their chiefs were princes of the land:
In the first rank of these did Zimri[4] stand;
A man so various, that he seemed to be 545
Not one, but all mankind's epitome:
Stiff in opinions, always in the wrong;

---

7. Gentile; here, Roman Catholic.

8. I.e., Presbyterian clergymen. The tribe of Levi, assigned to duties in the tabernacle, carried the ark of the covenant during the 40-year sojourn in the wilderness (Numbers 4). Under the Commonwealth ("in the Judges' days") Presbyterianism became the state religion, and its clergy therefore "bore the ark." The Act of Uniformity (1662) forced the Presbyterian clergy out of their livings: in short, before the Popish Plot, they had been "pulled from the ark." They are represented here as joining the Whigs in the hope of restoring the Commonwealth, "their old beloved theocracy."

9. Observe in these lines the cluster of disparaging words: "cant," "zealous," "inspiration." Dryden shared Samuel Butler's contempt for the irrationality of Dissenters.

1. Priests had to be descendants of Aaron (Exodus 28.1; Numbers 18.7).

2. Loudest. The phrase is applied to hunting dogs. "Pack" and "scent" sustain the image.

3. A term used by certain Dissenters for those elected to salvation. The extreme fanaticism of the "saints" and their claims to inspiration are characterized as a form of religious madness ("enthusiastic").

4. George Villiers, 2nd duke of Buckingham (1628–1687), wealthy, brilliant, dissolute, unstable. He had been an influential member of the Cabal, but after 1673 had joined Shaftesbury in opposition to the Court party. This is the least political of the satirical portraits in the poem. Buckingham had been the chief author of *The Rehearsal* (1671), the play which satirized the heroic play and ridiculed Dryden in the character of Mr. Bayes. Politics gave Dryden an opportunity to retaliate. He comments on this portrait in his *Discourse Concerning the Original and Progress of Satire.* Dryden had two biblical Zimris in mind: the Zimri destroyed for his lustfulness and blasphemy (Numbers 25) and the conspirator and regicide of 1 Kings 16.8–20 and 2 Kings 9.31.

Was everything by starts, and nothing long;
But, in the course of one revolving moon,
Was chymist,[5] fiddler, statesman, and buffoon: 550
Then all for women, painting, rhyming, drinking,
Besides ten thousand freaks that died in thinking.
Blest madman, who could every hour employ,
With something new to wish, or to enjoy!
Railing[6] and praising were his usual themes; 555
And both (to show his judgment) in extremes:
So over-violent, or over-civil,
That every man, with him, was God or Devil.
In squandering wealth was his peculiar art:
Nothing went unrewarded but desert. 560
Beggared by fools, whom still he found[7] too late,
He had his jest, and they had his estate.
He laughed himself from court; then sought relief
By forming parties, but could ne'er be chief;
For, spite of him, the weight of business fell 565
On Absalom and wise Achitophel:
Thus, wicked but in will, of means bereft,
He left not faction, but of that was left.
     Titles and names 'twere tedious to rehearse
Of lords, below the dignity of verse. 570
Wits, warriors, Commonwealth's men, were the best;
Kind husbands, and mere nobles, all the rest.
And therefore, in the name of dullness, be
The well-hung Balaam and cold Caleb, free;
And canting Nadab[8] let oblivion damn, 575
Who made new porridge for the paschal lamb,
Let friendship's holy band some names assure;
Some their own worth, and some let scorn secure.
Nor shall the rascal rabble here have place,
Whom kings no titles gave, and God no grace: 580
Not bull-faced Jonas,[9] who could statutes draw
To mean rebellion, and make treason law.
But he, though bad, is followed by a worse,
The wretch who heaven's anointed dared to curse:
Shimei,[1] whose youth did early promise bring 585

5. Chemist.
6. Reviling, abusing.
7. Found out; "still": constantly.
8. The identities of Balaam, Caleb, and Nadab have not been certainly established, although various Whig nobles have been suggested. For Balaam see Numbers 22–24; for Caleb, Numbers 13–14; for Nadab, Leviticus 10.1–2. "Well-hung" may mean "fluent of speech" or "sexually potent" or both; "cold" would contrast with the second meaning of "well-hung." "Canting" points to a Nonconformist, as does the obscure line 576, for Dissenters referred to the Book of Common Prayer contemptuously as "porridge," a hodge-podge,

unsubstantial stuff. The "paschal lamb," the lamb slain at the Passover, is Christ.
9. Sir William Jones, Attorney General, had been largely responsible for the passage of the first Exclusion Bill by the House of Commons. He prosecuted the accused in the Popish Plot.
1. Shimei cursed and stoned David when he fled into the wilderness during Absalom's revolt (2 Samuel 16.5–14); his name is used here for one of the two sheriffs of London, Slingsby Bethel, a Whig, former republican, and virulent enemy of Charles. He packed juries with Whigs and so secured the acquittal of enemies of the court, among them Shaftesbury himself.

Of zeal to God and hatred to his king,
Did wisely from expensive sins refrain,
And never broke the Sabbath, but for gain;
Nor ever was he known an oath to vent,
Or curse, unless against the government.   590
Thus heaping wealth, by the most ready way
Among the Jews, which was to cheat and pray,
The city, to reward his pious hate
Against his master, chose him magistrate.
His hand a vare[2] of justice did uphold;   595
His neck was loaded with a chain of gold.
During his office, treason was no crime;
The sons of Belial[3] had a glorious time;
For Shimei, though not prodigal of pelf,
Yet loved his wicked neighbor as himself.   600
When two or three were gathered to declaim ⎤
Against the monarch of Jerusalem,   ⎬
Shimei was always in the midst of them;   ⎦
And if they cursed the king when he was by,
Would rather curse than break good company.   605
If any durst his factious friends accuse,
He packed a jury of dissenting Jews;
Whose fellow-feeling in the godly cause
Would free the suffering saint from human laws.
For laws are only made to punish those   610
Who serve the king, and to protect his foes.
If any leisure time he had from power
(Because 'tis sin to misemploy an hour),
His business was, by writing, to persuade
That kings were useless, and a clog to trade;   615
And, that his noble style he might refine,
No Rechabite[4] more shunned the fumes of wine.
Chaste were his cellars, and his shrieval board[5]
The grossness of a city feast abhorred:
His cooks, with long disuse, their trade forgot;   620
Cool was his kitchen, though his brains were hot,
Such frugal virtue malice may accuse,
But sure 'twas necessary to the Jews:
For towns once burnt[6] such magistrates require
As dare not tempt God's providence by fire.   625
With spiritual food he fed his servants well,
But free from flesh that made the Jews rebel;
And Moses' laws he held in more account,
For forty days of fasting in the mount.[7]

2. Staff.
3. Sons of wickedness. Cf. Milton, *Paradise Lost* 1.490–505. Dryden probably intended a pun on Balliol, the Oxford college in which leading Whigs stayed during the brief and fateful meeting of Parliament at Oxford in 1681.

4. An austere Jewish sect that drank no wine (Jeremiah 35.2–19).
5. Sheriff's dinner table.
6. London burned in 1666.
7. Mt. Sinai, where, during a fast of 40 days, Moses received the law (Exodus 34.28).

To speak the rest, who better are forgot,   630
Would tire a well-breathed witness of the Plot.
Yet, Corah,[8] thou shalt from oblivion pass:
Erect thyself, thou monumental brass,
High as the serpent of thy metal made,[9]
While nations stand secure beneath thy shade.   635
What though his birth were base, yet comets rise
From earthy vapors, ere they shine in skies.
Prodigious actions may as well be done
By weaver's issue,[1] as by prince's son.
This arch-attestor for the public good   640
By that one deed ennobles all his blood.
Who ever asked the witnesses' high race
Whose oath with martyrdom did Stephen grace?[2]
Ours was a Levite, and as times went then,
His tribe were God Almighty's gentlemen.   645
Sunk were his eyes, his voice was harsh and loud,
Sure signs he neither choleric[3] was nor proud:
His long chin proved his wit; his saintlike grace
A church vermilion, and a Moses' face.[4]
His memory, miraculously great,   650
Could plots, exceeding man's belief, repeat;
Which therefore cannot be accounted lies,
For human wit could never such devise.
Some future truths are mingled in his book;
But where the witness failed, the prophet spoke: 655
Some things like visionary flights appear;
The spirit caught him up, the Lord knows where,
And gave him his rabbinical degree,
Unknown to foreign university.[5]
His judgment yet his memory did excel;   660
Which pieced his wondrous evidence so well,
And suited to the temper of the times,
Then groaning under Jebusitic crimes.
Let Israel's foes suspect his heavenly call,
And rashly judge his writ apocryphal;[6]   665
Our laws for such affronts have forfeits made:
He takes his life, who takes away his trade.
Were I myself in witness Corah's place,
The wretch who did me such a dire disgrace

---

8. Or Korah, a rebellious Levite, swallowed up by the earth because of his crimes (Numbers 16). Corah is Titus Oates, the self-appointed, perjured, and "well-breathed" (long-winded) witness of the Plot.
9. Moses erected a brazen serpent to heal the Jews bitten by fiery serpents (Numbers 21.4–9). "Brass" also means "impudence" or "shamelessness."
1. Oates's father, a clergyman, belonged to an obscure family of ribbon weavers.
2. The first Christian martyr, accused by false wit-

nesses (Acts 6–7).
3. Prone to anger.
4. Moses' face shone when he came down from Mt. Sinai with the tables of the law (Exodus 34.29–30). Oates's face suggests high living, not spiritual illumination.
5. Oates falsely claimed to be a Doctor of Divinity in the University of Salamanca.
6. Not inspired, and hence excluded from Holy Writ.

Should whet my memory, though once forgot,   670
To make him an appendix of my plot.
His zeal to heaven made him his prince despise,
And load his person with indignities;
But zeal peculiar privilege affords,
Indulging latitude to deeds and words;   675
And Corah might for Agag's murder[7] call,
In terms as coarse as Samuel used to Saul.
What others in his evidence did join
(The best that could be had for love or coin),
In Corah's own predicament will fall;   680
For *witness* is a common name to all.
      Surrounded thus with friends of every sort,
Deluded Absalom forsakes the court:
Impatient of high hopes, urged with renown,
And fired with near possession of a crown.   685
The admiring crowd are dazzled with surprise,
And on his goodly person feed their eyes:
His joy concealed, he sets himself to show,
On each side bowing popularly[8] low;
His looks, his gestures, and his words he frames,   690
And with familiar ease repeats their names.
Thus formed by nature, furnished out with arts,
He glides unfelt into their secret hearts.
Then, with a kind compassionating look,
And sighs, bespeaking pity ere he spoke,   695
Few words he said; but easy those and fit,
More slow than Hybla-drops,[9] and far more sweet.
      "I mourn, my countrymen, your lost estate;
Though far unable to prevent your fate:
Behold a banished man, for your dear cause   700
Exposed a prey to arbitrary laws!
Yet oh! that I alone could be undone,
Cut off from empire, and no more a son!
Now all your liberties a spoil are made; ⎫
Egypt and Tyrus[1] intercept your trade,   ⎬   705
And Jebusites your sacred rites invade. ⎭
My father, whom with reverence yet I name,
Charmed into ease, is careless of his fame;
And, bribed with petty sums of foreign gold,
Is grown in Bathsheba's[2] embraces old;   710
Exalts his enemies, his friends destroys;
And all his power against himself employs.

---

7. Agag is probably one of the 5 Catholic peers
executed for the Popish Plot in 1680, most likely
Lord Stafford, against whom Oates fabricated testimony; almost certainly not, as is usually suggested, Sir Edmund Berry Godfrey (cf. title note).
For "Agag's murder" and Samuel's coarse terms to
Saul, see 1 Samuel 15.

8. "So as to please the crowd" (Johnson's *Dictionary*).
9. The famous honey of Hybla in Sicily.
1. France and Holland.
2. With whom David committed adultery (2
Samuel 11); here, Charles II's French mistress,
Louise de Keroualle, duchess of Portsmouth.

He gives, and let him give, my right away;
But why should he his own, and yours betray?
He only, he can make the nation bleed,   715
And he alone from my revenge is freed.
Take then my tears (with that he wiped his eyes),
'Tis all the aid my present power supplies:
No court-informer can these arms accuse;
These arms may sons against their fathers use: 720
And 'tis my wish, the next successor's reign
May make no other Israelite complain."
   Youth, beauty, graceful action seldom fail;
But common interest always will prevail;
And pity never ceases to be shown   725
To him who makes the people's wrongs his own.
The crowd (that still believe their kings oppress),
With lifted hands their young Messiah bless:
Who now begins his progress to ordain
With chariots, horsemen, and a numerous train;   730
From east to west his glories he displays,[3]
And, like the sun, the promised land surveys.
Fame runs before him as the morning star,
And shouts of joy salute him from afar:
Each house receives him as a guardian god,   735
And consecrates the place of his abode:
But hospitable treats did most commend
Wise Issachar,[4] his wealthy western friend.
This moving court, that caught the people's eyes,
And seemed but pomp, did other ends disguise: 740
Achitophel had formed it, with intent
To sound the depths, and fathom where it went,
The people's hearts; distinguish friends from foes,
And try their strength, before they came to blows.
Yet all was colored with a smooth pretense   745
Of specious love, and duty to their prince.
Religion, and redress of grievances,
Two names that always cheat and always please,
Are often urged; and good King David's life
Endangered by a brother and a wife.[5]   750
Thus, in a pageant show, a plot is made,
And peace itself is war in masquerade.
O foolish Israel! never warned by ill,
Still the same bait, and circumvented still!
Did ever men forsake their present ease,   755
In midst of health imagine a disease;

---

3. In 1680 Monmouth made a progress through the west of England, seeking popular support for his cause.
4. Thomas Thynne of Longleat. He entertained Monmouth on his journey in the west. "Wise" is

of course, ironic.
5. Titus Oates had sworn that both James, duke of York, and the queen were involved in a plot to poison Charles II.

Take pains contingent mischiefs to foresee,
Make heirs for monarchs, and for God decree?
What shall we think![6] Can people give away
Both for themselves and sons, their native sway?   760
Then they are left defenseless to the sword
Of each unbounded, arbitrary lord:
And laws are vain, by which we right enjoy,
If kings unquestioned can those laws destroy.
Yet if the crowd be judge of fit and just,   765
And kings are only officers in trust,
Then this resuming covenant was declared
When kings were made, or is forever barred.
If those who gave the scepter could not tie
By their own deed their own posterity,   770
How then could Adam bind his future race?
How could his forfeit on mankind take place?
Or how could heavenly justice damn us all,
Who ne'er consented to our father's fall?
Then kings are slaves to those whom they command,   775
And tenants to their people's pleasure stand.
Add, that the power for property allowed
Is mischievously seated in the crowd;
For who can be secure of private right,
If sovereign sway may be dissolved by might?   780
Nor is the people's judgment always true:
The most may err as grossly as the few;
And faultless kings run down, by common cry,
For vice, oppression, and for tyranny.
What standard is there in a fickle rout,   785
Which, flowing to the mark,[7] runs faster out?
Nor only crowds, but Sanhedrins may be
Infected with this public lunacy,
And share the madness of rebellious times,
To murder monarchs for imagined crimes.[8]   790
If they may give and take whene'er they please,
Not kings alone (the Godhead's images),
But government itself at length must fall
To nature's state, where all have right to all.
Yet, grant our lords the people kings can make,   795
What prudent men a settled throne would shake?
For whatsoe'er their sufferings were before,
That change they covet makes them suffer more.
All other errors but disturb a state,
But innovation is the blow of fate.   800

---

6. In the passage that follows, Dryden states his political philosophy. He bases the royal authority on a covenant entered into by the governor and the governed.

7. An obscure couplet, rare in Dryden. George R.

Noyes paraphrases it thus: "The fickle crowd is apparently compared to water, which, after rising to the *mark*, or boundary, it was intended to reach, overflows all the faster."

8. An allusion to the execution of Charles I.

If ancient fabrics nod, and threat to fall,
To patch the flaws, and buttress up the wall,
Thus far 'tis duty; but here fix the mark;
For all beyond it is to touch our ark.[9]
To change foundations, cast the frame anew,   805
Is work for rebels, who base ends pursue,
At once divine and human laws control,
And mend the parts by ruin of the whole.
The tampering world is subject to this curse,
To physic their disease into a worse.   810
    Now what relief can righteous David bring?
How fatal 'tis to be too good a king!
Friends he has few, so high the madness grows:
Who dare be such, must be the people's foes:
Yet some there were, even in the worst of days;   815
Some let me name, and naming is to praise.
    In this short file Barzillai[1] first appears;
Barzillai, crowned with honor and with years:
Long since, the rising rebels he withstood
In regions waste, beyond the Jordan's flood: 820
Unfortunately brave to buoy the State;
But sinking underneath his master's fate:
In exile with his godlike prince he mourned;
For him he suffered, and with him returned.
The court he practiced, not the courtier's art: 825
Large was his wealth, but larger was his heart:
Which well the noblest objects knew to choose,
The fighting warrior, and recording Muse.
His bed could once a fruitful issue boast;
Now more than half a father's name is lost.   830
His eldest hope,[2] with every grace adorned,
By me (so Heaven will have it) always mourned,
And always honored, snatched in manhood's prime
By unequal fates, and Providence's crime:
Yet not before the goal of honor won,   ⎫   835
All parts fulfilled of subject and of son;   ⎬
Swift was the race, but short the time to run. ⎭
O narrow circle, but of power divine,
Scanted in space, but perfect in thy line!
By sea, by land, thy matchless worth was known,   840
Arms thy delight, and war was all thy own:
Thy force, infused, the fainting Tyrians[3] propped;
And haughty Pharaoh found his fortune stopped.

9. Uzzah was struck dead because he sacrile-
giously touched the Ark of the Covenant. 2 Samuel 6. 6–7.
1. James Butler, duke of Ormond (1610–1688).
He was famous for his loyalty to the Stuart cause.
He fought for Charles I in Ireland, and when that
cause was hopeless, he joined Charles II in his exile

abroad. He spent a large fortune in behalf of the
king and continued to serve him loyally after the
Restoration.
2. Ormond's son, Thomas, earl of Ossory (1634–
1680), a famous soldier, and like his father devoted
to Charles II.
3. The Dutch.

Oh ancient honor! Oh unconquered hand,
Whom foes unpunished never could withstand!   845
But Israel was unworthy of thy name:
Short is the date of all immoderate fame.
It looks as Heaven our ruin had designed,
And durst not trust thy fortune and thy mind.
Now, free from earth, thy disencumbered soul   850
Mounts up, and leaves behind the clouds and starry pole:
From thence thy kindred legions mayst thou bring,
To aid the guardian angel of thy king.
Here stop my Muse, here cease thy painful flight;
No pinions can pursue immortal height: 855
Tell good Barzillai thou canst sing no more,
And tell thy soul she should have fled before:
Or fled she with his life, and left this verse
To hang on her departed patron's hearse?
Now take thy steepy flight from heaven, and see   860
If thou canst find on earth another *he*:
Another *he* would be too hard to find;
See then whom thou canst see not far behind.
Zadoc the priest,[4] whom, shunning power and place,
His lowly mind advanced to David's grace: 865
With him the Sagan of Jerusalem,
Of hospitable soul, and noble stem;
Him of the western dome, whose weighty sense
Flows in fit words and heavenly eloquence.
The prophets' sons, by such example led,   870
To learning and to loyalty were bred:
For colleges on bounteous kinds depend,
And never rebel was to arts a friend.
To these succeed the pillars of the laws,
Who best could plead, and best can judge a cause.   875
Next them a train of loyal peers ascend;
Sharp-judging Adriel, the Muses' friend,
Himself a Muse—in Sanhedrin's debate
True to his prince, but not a slave of state:
Whom David's love with honors did adorn,   880
That from his disobedient son were torn.
Jotham of piercing wit, and pregnant thought,
Indued by nature, and by learning taught
To move assemblies, who but only tried,
The worse a while, then chose the better side;   885
Nor chose alone, but turned the balance too;
So much the weight of one brave man can do.

4. William Sancroft, archbishop of Canterbury; the
Sagan is Henry Compton, bishop of London; "Him
of the western dome" is John Dolben, dean of
Westminster; "The prophets' sons" are the boys of
Westminster School, which Dryden had attended;
Adriel is John Sheffield, earl of Mulgrave; Jotham,
George Savile, marquis of Halifax; Hushai, Laur-
ence Hyde, earl of Rochester; and Amiel is Edward
Seymour, speaker of the House of Commons.

Hushai, the friend of David in distress,
In public storms, of manly steadfastness:
By foreign treaties he informed his youth,   890
And joined experience to his native truth.
His frugal care supplied the wanting throne,
Frugal for that, but bounteous of his own:
'Tis easy conduct when exchequers flow,
But hard the task to manage well the low;   895
For sovereign power is too depressed or high,
When kings are forced to sell, or crowds to buy.
Indulge one labor more, my weary Muse,
For Amiel: who can Amiel's praise refuse?
Of ancient race by birth, but nobler yet   900
In his own worth, and without title great:
The Sanhedrin long time as chief he ruled,
Their reason guided, and their passion cooled:
So dexterous was he in the crown's defence,
So formed to speak a loyal nation's sense,   905
That, as their band was Israel's tribes in small,
So fit was he to represent them all.
Now rasher charioteers the seat ascend,
Whose loose careers his steady skill commend:
They like the unequal ruler of the day,   910
Misguide the seasons, and mistake the way;
While he withdrawn at their mad labor smiles,
And safe enjoys the sabbath of his toils.
    These were the chief, a small but faithful band ⎤
Of worthies, in the breach who dared to stand, ⎬   915
And tempt the united fury of the land.   ⎦
With grief they viewed such powerful engines bent,
To batter down the lawful government:
A numerous faction, with pretended frights,
In Sanhedrins to plume the regal rights;   920
The true successor from the court removed:[5]
The Plot, by hireling witnesses, improved.
These ills they saw, and, as their duty bound,
They showed the king the danger of the wound:
That no concessions from the throne would please,   925
But lenitives[6] fomented the disease;
That Absalom, ambitious of the crown,
Was made the lure to draw the people down;
That false Achitophel's pernicious hate
Had turned the Plot to ruin Church and State: 930
The council violent, the rabble worse;
That Shimei taught Jerusalem to curse.
    With all these loads of injuries oppressed,
And long revolving in his careful breast,

---

5. The duke of York had been banished from Eng-   6. Any medicine that relieves pain.
land.

The event of things, at last, his patience tired,   935
Thus from his royal throne, by Heaven inspired,
The godlike David spoke: with awful fear
His train their Maker in their master hear.
    "Thus long have I, by native mercy swayed,
My wrongs dissembled, my revenge delayed: 940
So willing to forgive the offending age,
So much the father did the king assuage.
But now so far my clemency they slight,
The offenders question my forgiving right.
That one was made for many, they contend;   945
But 'tis to rule; for that's a monarch's end.
They call my tenderness of blood, my fear;
Though manly tempers can the longest bear.
Yet, since they will divert my native course,
'Tis time to show I am not good by force.   950
Those heaped affronts that haughty subjects bring,
Are burdens for a camel, not a king:
Kings are the public pillars of the State,
Born to sustain and prop the nation's weight:
If my young Samson will pretend a call   955
To shake the column, let him share the fall:[7]
But, oh, that yet he would repent and live!
How easy 'tis for parents to forgive!
With how few tears a pardon might be won
From nature, pleading for a darling son!   960
Poor pitied youth, by my paternal care
Raised up to all the height his frame could bear:
Had God ordained his fate for empire born,
He would have given his soul another turn:
Gulled[8] with a patriot's name, whose modern sense
Is one that would by law supplant his prince: 965
The people's brave, the politician's tool;
Never was patriot yet, but was a fool.
Whence comes it that religion and the laws
Should more be Absalom's than David's cause?   970
His old instructor, ere he lost his place,
Was never thought indued with so much grace.[9]
Good heavens, how faction can a patriot paint!
My rebel ever proves my people's saint:
Would *they* impose an heir upon the throne?   975
Let Sanhedrins be taught to give their own.
A king's at least a part of government,
And mine as requisite as their consent;
Without my leave a future king to choose,
Infers a right the present to depose: 980
True, they petition me to approve their choice;

7. Judges 16.   9. The earl of Shaftesbury.
8. Deceived.

But Esau's hands suit ill with Jacob's voice.[1]
My pious subjects for my safety pray,
Which to secure, they take my power away.
From plots and treasons Heaven preserve my years,   985
But save me most from my petitioners.
Unsatiate as the barren womb or grave;
God cannot grant so much as they can crave.
What then is left but with a jealous eye
To guard the small remains of royalty?   990
The law shall still direct my peaceful sway,
And the same law teach rebels to obey:
Votes shall no more established power control—
Such votes as make a part exceed the whole:
No groundless clamors shall my friends remove,   995
Nor crowds have power to punish ere they prove:
For gods and godlike kings, their care express,
Still to defend their servants in distress.
O that my power to saving were confined:
Why am I forced, like Heaven, against my mind,   1000
To make examples of another kind?
Must I at length the sword of justice draw?
O curst effects of necessary law!
How ill my fear they by my mercy scan!
Beware the fury of a patient man.   1005
Law they require, let Law then show her face;
They could not be content to look on Grace,
Her hinder parts, but with a daring eye
To tempt the terror of her front and die.[2]
By their own arts, 'tis righteously decreed,   1010
Those dire artificers of death shall bleed.
Against themselves their witnesses will swear,
Till viper-like their mother Plot they tear:
And suck for nutriment that bloody gore,
Which was their principle of life before.   1015
Their Belial with their Belzebub[3] will fight;
Thus on my foes, my foes shall do me right:
Nor doubt the event; for factious crowds engage,
In their first onset, all their brutal rage.
Then let 'em take an unresisted course,   1020
Retire and traverse, and delude their force:
But when they stand all breathless, urge the fight,
And rise upon 'em with redoubled might:
For lawful power is still superior found,
When long driven back, at length it stands the ground."   1025
    He said. The Almighty, nodding, gave consent;
And peals of thunder shook the firmament.

1. Genesis 27.22.
2. Moses was not allowed to see the countenance of Jehovah. Exodus 33. 20–23.
3. Belial, the incarnation of all evil; Beelzebub, a god of the Philistines.

Henceforth a series of new time began,
The mighty years in long procession ran:
Once more the godlike David was restored,   1030
And willing nations knew their lawful lord.

1681

Mac Flecknoe[1]

OR A SATIRE UPON THE TRUE-BLUE-PROTESTANT POET, T. S.

All human things are subject to decay,
And when fate summons, monarchs must obey.
This Flecknoe found, who, like Augustus,[2] young
Was called to empire, and had governed long;
In prose and verse, was owned, without dispute,   5
Through all the realms of Nonsense, absolute.
This aged prince, now flourishing in peace,
And blest with issue of a large increase,
Worn out with business, did at length debate
To settle the succession of the state;   10
And, pondering which of all his sons was fit
To reign, and wage immortal war with wit,
Cried: " 'Tis resolved; for nature pleads that he
Should only rule, who most resembles me.

1. The victim of this superb satire, which is cast in the form of a mock-heroic episode, is Thomas Shadwell (1640–1692), the playwright, with whom Dryden had been on good terms for a number of years, certainly as late as March 1678. Shadwell considered himself the successor of Ben Jonson and the champion of the type of comedy that Jonson had written, the "comedy of humors," in which each character is presented under the domination of a single psychological trait or eccentricity, his humor. His plays are not without merit, but they are often clumsy and prolix, and certainly much inferior to Jonson's. For many years he had conducted a public argument with Dryden on the merits of Jonson's comedies, which he thought Dryden undervalued. Exactly what moved Dryden to attack him is a matter of conjecture: he may simply have grown progressively bored and irritated by Shadwell and his tedious argument. The poem seems to have been written in late 1678 or 1679 and to have circulated only in manuscript, until it was printed in 1682 in a pirated edition by an obscure publisher. By that time, the two playwrights were alienated by politics as well as by literary quarrels. Shadwell was a violent Whig and the reputed author of a sharp attack on Dryden as the Tory author of *Absalom and Achitophel* and *The Medal*. It was probably for this reason that the printer added the subtitle referring to Shadwell's Whiggism in the phrase "true-blue-Protestant poet." Political passions were running high and sales would be helped if the poem seemed to refer to the events of the day.

Whereas Butler had debased and degraded his victims by using burlesque, caricature, and the grotesque, Dryden exposed Shadwell to ridicule by using the devices of mock-epic, which treats the low, mean, or absurd in the grand language, lofty style, and solemn tone of epic poetry. The obvious disparity between subject and style makes the satiric point. In 1678 an execrable Irish poet and playwright, Richard Flecknoe, died. Dryden conceived the idea of presenting Shadwell (the self-proclaimed heir of Ben Jonson, the laureate) as the son and successor of Flecknoe—hence *Mac* (i.e., son of) *Flecknoe*—from whom he inherits the throne of dullness. Flecknoe in the triple role of king, priest, and poet hails his successor, pronounces a panegyric on his perfect fitness for the throne, anoints and crowns him, foretells his glorious reign, and, as he sinks (leaden dullness cannot soar), leaves his mantle to fall symbolically upon Shadwell's shoulders. The poem abounds in literary allusions—to Roman legend and history and to the *Aeneid*; to Cowley's fragmentary epic, *The Davideis*, and to *Paradise Lost*; and to Shadwell's own plays. Biblical allusions add an unexpected dimension of incongruous dignity to the low scene. The coronation takes place in the City, to the plaudits of the citizens, who are fit to admire only what is dull. In 217 lines Dryden created an image of Shadwell which has fixed his reputation to this day.

2. In 31 B.C. Octavian became the first Roman emperor at the age of 32. He assumed the title Augustus in 27 B.C.

Sh——[3] alone my perfect image bears,   15
Mature in dullness from his tender years:
Sh—— alone, of all my sons, is he
Who stands confirmed in full stupidity.
The rest to some faint meaning make pretense,
But Sh—— never deviates into sense.   20
Some beams of wit on other souls may fall,
Strike through, and make a lucid interval;
But Sh——'s genuine night admits no ray,
His rising fogs prevail upon the day.
Besides, his goodly fabric[4] fills the eye,   25
And seems designed for thoughtless majesty:
Thoughtless as monarch oaks that shade the plain,
And, spread in solemn state, supinely reign.
Heywood and Shirley[5] were but types of thee,
Thou last great prophet of tautology.[6]   30
Even I, a dunce of more renown than they,
Was sent before but to prepare thy way;
And, coarsely clad in Norwich drugget,[7] came
To teach the nations in thy greater name.[8]
My warbling lute, the lute I whilom[9] strung,   35
When to King John of Portugal I sung,
Was but the prelude to that glorious day,
When thou on silver Thames didst cut thy way,
With well-timed oars before the royal barge,
Swelled with the pride of thy celestial charge;   40
And big with hymn, commander of a host,
The like was ne'er in Epsom blankets tossed.[1]
Methinks I see the new Arion[2] sail,
The lute still trembling underneath thy nail.
At thy well-sharpened thumb from shore to shore   45
The treble squeaks for fear, the basses roar;
Echoes from Pissing Alley Sh—— call,
And Sh—— they resound from Aston Hall.
About thy boat the little fishes throng,
As at the morning toast[3] that floats along.   50
Sometimes, as prince of thy harmonious band,

3. Thomas Shadwell. The initial and second letter of the name followed by a dash give the appearance, but only the appearance, of protecting Dryden's victim by concealing his name. A common device in the satire of the period.
4. His body. Shadwell was a corpulent man.
5. Thomas Heywood (ca. 1570–1641) and James Shirley (1596–1666), playwrights popular before the closing of the theaters in 1642 but now out of fashion. They are introduced here as "types" (i.e., prefigurings) of Shadwell, in the sense that Solomon was regarded as an Old Testament prefiguring of Christ, the "last [final] great prophet."
6. Unnecessary repetition of meaning in different words.
7. A coarse woolen cloth.

8. The parallel between Flecknoe, as forerunner of Shadwell, and John the Baptist, as forerunner of Jesus, is made plain in lines 32–34 by the use of details and even words taken from Matthew 3.3–4 and John 1.23.
9. Formerly. Flecknoe boasted of the patronage of the Portuguese king.
1. A reference to Shadwell's comedy *Epsom Wells* and to the farcical scene in his *Virtuoso*, in which Sir Samuel Hearty is tossed in a blanket.
2. A legendary Greek poet. Returning home by sea, he was robbed and thrown overboard by the sailors, but was saved by a dolphin which had been charmed by his music.
3. Sewage.

Thou wield'st thy papers in thy threshing hand,
St. André's[4] feet ne'er kept more equal time,
Not ev'n the feet of thy own *Psyche's* rhyme;
Though they in number as in sense excel: 55
So just, so like tautology, they fell,
That, pale with envy, Singleton[5] forswore   ⎫
The lute and sword, which he in triumph bore,   ⎬
And vowed he ne'er would act Villerius[6] more." ⎭
Here stopped the good old sire, and wept for joy   60
In silent raptures of the hopeful boy.
All arguments, but most his plays, persuade,
That for anointed[7] dullness he was made.

  Close to the walls which fair Augusta[8] bind
(The fair Augusta much to fears inclined),   65
An ancient fabric[9] raised to inform the sight,
There stood of yore, and Barbican it hight:
A watchtower once; but now, so fate ordains,
Of all the pile an empty name remains.
From its old ruins brothel houses rise,   70
Scenes of lewd loves, and of polluted joys,
Where their vast courts the mother-strumpets keep,
And, undisturbed by watch, in silence sleep.
Near these a Nursery[1] erects its head,
Where queens are formed, and future heroes bred;   75
Where unfledged actors learn to laugh and cry,   ⎫
Where infant punks[2] their tender voices try,   ⎬
And little Maximins[3] the gods defy.   ⎭
Great Fletcher[4] never treads in buskins here,
Nor greater Jonson dares in socks appear;   80
But gentle Simkin[5] just reception finds
Amidst this monument of vanished minds:
Pure clinches[6] the suburbian Muse affords,
And Panton[7] waging harmless war with words.
Here Flecknoe, as a place to fame well known,   85
Ambitiously design'd his Sh——'s throne;
For ancient Dekker[8] prophesied long since,   ⎫
That in this pile would reign a mighty prince,   ⎬
Born for a scourge of wit, and flail of sense;   ⎭

4. A French dancer who designed the choreography of Shadwell's opera *Psyche* (1675). Dryden's sneer in the next line at the mechanical metrics of the songs in *Psyche* is justified.
5. John Singleton (d. 1686), a musician at the Theatre Royal.
6. A character in Sir William Davenant's *Siege of Rhodes* (1656), the first English opera.
7. The anticipated phrase is "anointed *majesty.*" English kings are anointed with oil at their coronations.
8. London. The next line alludes to the fears excited by the Popish Plot (cf. *Absalom and Achitophel*).
9. Building.

1. The name of a training school for young actors.
2. Prostitutes.
3. Maximin is the cruel emperor in Dryden's *Tyrannic Love* (1669), notorious for his bombast.
4. John Fletcher (1579–1625), the playwright and collaborator with Francis Beaumont (ca. 1584–1616). "Buskins" and "socks" were the symbols of tragedy and comedy.
5. A popular character in low farces.
6. Puns.
7. Said to have been a celebrated punster.
8. Thomas Dekker (ca. 1572–1632), the playwright, whom Jonson had satirized in *The Poetaster.*

To whom true dullness should some *Psyches* owe,   90
But worlds of *Misers* from his pen should flow;
Humorists and *Hypocrites*[9] it should produce,
Whole Raymond families, and tribes of Bruce.
    Now Empress Fame had published the renown
Of Sh——'s coronation through the town.   95
Roused by report of Fame, the nations meet,
From near Bunhill, and distant Watling Street.[1]
No Persian carpets spread the imperial way,
But scattered limbs of mangled poets lay;
From dusty shops neglected authors come,   100
Martyrs of pies, and relics of the bum.[2]
Much Heywood, Shirley, Ogilby[3] there lay,
But loads of Sh—— almost choked the way.
Bilked stationers[4] for yeomen stood prepared,
And Herringman was captain of the guard.   105
The hoary prince in majesty appeared,
High on a throne of his own labors reared.
At his right hand our young Ascanius[5] sate,
Rome's other hope, and pillar of the state.
His brows thick fogs, instead of glories, grace,   110
And lambent dullness played around his face.
As Hannibal did to the altars come,
Sworn by his sire a mortal foe to Rome,[6]
So Sh——swore, nor should his vow be vain,
That he till death true dullness would maintain;   115
And, in his father's right, and realm's defense,
Ne'er to have peace with wit, nor truce with sense.
The king himself the sacred unction[7] made,
As king by office, and as priest by trade.
In his sinister[8] hand, instead of ball,   120
He placed a mighty mug of potent ale;
Love's Kingdom to his right he did convey,
At once his scepter, and his rule of sway;
Whose righteous lore the prince had practiced young,

9. Three of Shadwell's plays; *The Hypocrite*, a failure, was not published. "Raymond" and "Bruce" (line 94) are characters in *The Humorists* and *The Virtuoso* respectively.

1. Since Bunhill is about a quarter of a mile and Watling Street little more than half a mile from the site of the Nursery, where the coronation is held, Shadwell's fame is narrowly circumscribed. Moreover, his subjects live in the heart of the City, regarded by men of wit and fashion as the abode of bad taste and middle-class vulgarity.

2. Unsold books eventually went to bakers' shops and privies.

3. John Ogilby, a translator of Homer and Virgil, ridiculed by both Dryden and Pope as a bad poet.

4. Cheated publishers, who acted as "yeomen" of the guard, led by Henry Herringman, who until 1679 was the publisher of both Shadwell and Dryden.

5. Or Iulus, son of Aeneas; Virgil referred to him as "*spes altera Romae*" ("Rome's other hope"; *Aeneid* 12.168). As Troy fell, he was marked as favored by the gods when a flickering ("lambent") flame played round his head (*Aeneid* 2.680–84).

6. Hannibal, who almost conquered Rome in 216 B.C., during the 2nd Punic War, took this oath at the age of 9 (Livy 21.1).

7. The sacramental oil, used in the coronation.

8. Left. During his coronation a British monarch holds two symbols of kingship: a globe ("ball") representing the world in his left hand, a scepter in his right. In lines 121–27, Shadwell's symbols of monarchy—a mug of ale; Flecknoe's dreary play, *Love's Kingdom*; a crown of poppies—suggest heaviness, dullness, drowsiness. The poppies also refer obliquely to Shadwell's addiction to opium.

And from whose loins recorded *Psyche* sprung.   125
His temples, last, with poppies were o'erspread,
That nodding seemed to consecrate his head.
Just at that point of time, if fame not lie,
On his left hand twelve reverend owls did fly.[9]
So Romulus, 'tis sung, by Tiber's brook,   130
Presage of sway from twice six vultures took.
The admiring throng loud acclamations make,
And omens of his future empire take.
The sire then shook the honors[1] of his head,
And from his brows damps of oblivion shed   135
Full on the filial dullness: long he stood,   ⎫
Repelling from his breast the raging god;   ⎬
At length burst out in this prophetic mood: ⎭
    "Heavens bless my son, from Ireland let him reign
To far Barbadoes on the western main;[2]   140
Of his dominion may no end be known,
And greater than his father's be his throne;
Beyond *Love's Kingdom* let him stretch his pen!"
He paused, and all the people cried, "Amen."
Then thus continued he: "My son, advance   145
Still in new impudence, new ignorance.
Success let others teach, learn thou from me
Pangs without birth, and fruitless industry.
Let *Virtuosos* in five years be writ;
Yet not one thought accuse thy toil of wit.   150
Let gentle George[3] in triumph tread the stage,
Make Dorimant betray, and Loveit rage;
Let Cully, Cockwood, Fopling, charm the pit,
And in their folly show the writer's wit.
Yet still thy fools shall stand in thy defense,   155
And justify their author's want of sense.
Let 'em be all by thy own model made
Of dullness, and desire no foreign aid;
That they to future ages may be known,
Not copies drawn, but issue of thy own.   160
Nay, let thy men of wit too be the same,
All full of thee, and differing but in name.
But let no alien S—dl—y[4] interpose,
To lard with wit[5] thy hungry *Epsom* prose.
And when false flowers of rhetoric thou wouldst cull,   165
Trust nature, do not labor to be dull;

---

9. Birds of night, appropriate substitutes for the 12 vultures whose flight confirmed to Romulus the destined site of Rome, of which he was founder and king.
1. Ornaments, hence locks.
2. Shadwell's empire is vast but empty.
3. Sir George Etherege (ca. 1635–1691), a writer of brilliant comedies. In the next couplet Dryden names characters from his plays.
4. Sir Charles Sedley (1638–1701), wit, rake, poet, playwright. Dryden hints that he contributed more than the prologue to Shadwell's *Epsom Wells*.
5. The phrase "lard with wit" recalls a sentence in Burton's *Anatomy of Melancholy*: "They lard their lean books with the fat of others' works."

But write thy best, and top; and, in each line,
Sir Formal's[6] oratory will be thine:
Sir Formal, though unsought, attends thy quill,
And does thy northern dedications[7] fill.   170
Nor let false friends seduce thy mind to fame,
By arrogating Jonson's hostile name.
Let father Flecknoe fire thy mind with praise,
And uncle Ogilby thy envy raise.
Thou art my blood, where Jonson has no part: 175
What share have we in nature, or in art?
Where did his wit on learning fix a brand,
And rail at arts he did not understand?
Where made he love in Prince Nicander's vein,[8]
Or swept the dust in *Psyche's* humble strain?   180
Where sold he bargains,[9] 'whip-stitch, kiss my arse,'
Promised a play and dwindled to a farce?[1]
When did his Muse from Fletcher scenes purloin,
As thou whole Eth'rege dost transfuse to thine?
But so transfused, as oil on water's flow,   185
His always floats above, thine sinks below.
This is thy province, this thy wondrous way,
New humors to invent for each new play:
This is that boasted bias[2] of thy mind,
By which one way, to dullness, 'tis inclined;   190
Which makes thy writings lean on one side still,
And, in all changes, that way bends thy will.
Nor let thy mountain-belly make pretense
Of likeness; thine's a tympany[3] of sense.
A tun[4] of man in thy large bulk is writ,   195
But sure thou'rt but a kilderkin of wit.
Like mine, thy gentle numbers feebly creep;
Thy tragic Muse gives smiles, thy comic sleep.
With whate'er gall thou sett'st thyself to write,
Thy inoffensive satires never bite.   200
In thy felonious heart though venom lies,
It does but touch thy Irish pen,[5] and dies.
Thy genius calls thee not to purchase fame
In keen iambics,[6] but mild anagram.
Leave writing plays, and choose for thy command   205
Some peaceful province in acrostic land.

6. Sir Formal Trifle, the ridiculous and vapid orator in *The Virtuoso*.
7. Shadwell frequently dedicated his works to the duke of Newcastle and members of his family.
8. In *Psyche*.
9. To "sell bargains" is to answer an innocent question with a coarse or indecent phrase as in this line. "Whipstitch" is a nonsense word frequently used by Sir Samuel Hearty in *The Virtuoso*.
1. Low comedy which depends largely on situation rather than wit, consistently condemned by Dryden and other serious playwrights.
2. In bowling, the spin given to the bowl that causes it to swerve. Dryden closely parodies a passage in Shadwell's epilogue to *The Humorists*.
3. A swelling in some part of the body caused by wind.
4. A large wine cask. "Kilderkin": a very small cask.
5. Flecknoe was Irish, and so his son must be Irish. Ireland suggested only poverty, superstition, and barbarity to 17th-century Londoners.
6. Sharp satire.

There thou may'st wings display and altars raise,
And torture one poor word ten thousand ways.[7]
Or, if thou wouldst thy different talent suit,
Set thy own songs, and sing them to thy lute."   210
    He said: but his last words were scarcely heard ⎤
For Bruce and Longville had a trap prepared,   ⎬
And down they sent the yet declaiming bard.[8]   ⎦
Sinking he left his drugget robe behind,
Borne upwards by a subterranean wind.   215
The mantle fell to the young prophet's part,[9]
With double portion of his father's art.

ca. 1679   1682

To the Memory of Mr. Oldham[1]

Farewell, too little, and too lately known,
Whom I began to think and call my own:
For sure our souls were near allied, and thine
Cast in the same poetic mold with mine.
One common note on either lyre did strike,
And knaves and fools[2] we both abhorred alike.   5
To the same goal did both our studies drive;
The last set out the soonest did arrive.
Thus Nisus[3] fell upon the slippery place,
While his young friend performed and won the race.   10
O early ripe! to thy abundant store
What could advancing age have added more?
It might (what nature never gives the young)
Have taught the numbers[4] of thy native tongue.
But satire needs not those, and wit will shine   15
Through the harsh cadence of a rugged line.[5]
A noble error, and but seldom made,
When poets are by too much force betrayed.
Thy generous fruits, though gathered ere their prime, ⎤
Still showed a quickness;[6] and maturing time   ⎬ 20
But mellows what we write to the dull sweets of rhyme. ⎦

7. "Anagram": the transposition of letters in a word so as to make a new one; "acrostic": a poem in which the first letter of each line, read downward, makes up the name of the person or thing that is the subject of the poem; "wings" and "altars" refer to poems in the shape of these objects as in George Herbert's *Easter Wings* and *The Altar*. Dryden is citing instances of triviality and overingenuity in literature.
8. In *The Virtuoso*, Bruce and Longville play this trick on Sir Formal Trifle while he makes a speech.
9. When the prophet Elijah was carried to heaven in a chariot of fire borne on a whirlwind, his mantle fell on his successor, the younger prophet Elisha (2 Kings 2.8–14). Flecknoe, prophet of dullness,

naturally cannot ascend, but must sink.
1. John Oldham (1653–1683), the young poet whose *Satires upon the Jesuits* (1681) won Dryden's admiration. This elegy was published in Oldham's *Remains in Verse and Prose* (1684).
2. The objects of satire.
3. Nisus, on the point of winning a foot race, slipped in a pool of blood; his "young friend" was Euryalus (Virgil, *Aeneid* 5.315–39).
4. Metrics, verse.
5. Dryden repeats the Renaissance idea that the satirist should avoid smoothness and affect rough meters ("harsh cadence").
6. Sharpness of flavor.

Once more, hail and farewell;[7] farewell, thou young,
But ah too short, Marcellus[8] of our tongue;
Thy brows with ivy, and with laurels bound;[9]
But fate and gloomy night encompass thee around.   25

1684

A Song for St. Cecilia's Day[1]

1

From harmony, from heavenly harmony
    This universal frame began:
    When Nature[2] underneath a heap
        Of jarring atoms lay,
        And could not heave her head,   5
The tuneful voice was heard from high:
        "Arise, ye more than dead."
Then cold, and hot, and moist, and dry,
    In order to their stations leap,
        And Music's power obey.   10
From harmony, from heavenly harmony
    This universal frame began:
        From harmony to harmony
Through all the compass of the notes it ran,
The diapason[3] closing full in man.   15

2

What passion cannot Music raise and quell![4]
    When Jubal[5] struck the corded shell,

---

7. Dryden echoes the famous words that conclude Catullus's elegy to his brother: "*Atque in perpetuum, frater, ave atque vale*" ("And forever, brother, hail and farewell!").
8. The nephew of Augustus, adopted by him as his successor. After winning military fame as a youth, he died at the age of 20. Virgil celebrated him in the *Aeneid* 6.854–86; the last line of Dryden's poem is a reminiscence of *Aeneid* 6.866.
9. The poet's wreath. Cf. Milton's *Lycidas*, lines 1–2.
1. St. Cecilia, a Roman lady, was an early Christian martyr. She has long been regarded as the patroness of music and the supposed inventor of the organ. Celebrations of her festival day (November 22) in England were usually devoted to music and the praise of music, and from about 1683 to 1703 a "Musical Society" in London annually commemorated it with a religious service and a public concert. This concert always included an ode written and set to music for the occasion, of which the two by Dryden (*A Song for St. Cecilia's Day*, 1687, and *Alexander's Feast*, 1697) are the most distinguished. G. B. Draghi, an Italian brought to England by Charles II, set this ode to music, but Handel's fine score, composed in 1739, has completely obscured the original setting. Like

the ode to Mrs. Killigrew, this is an irregular ode in the manner of Cowley. In stanzas 3–6 Dryden boldly attempted to suggest in the sounds of his words the characteristic tones of the instruments mentioned.
2. Created nature, ordered by the Divine Wisdom out of chaos, which Dryden, adopting the physics of the Greek philosopher Epicurus, describes as composed of the warring and discordant ("jarring") atoms of the four elements: earth, fire, water, air ("cold," "hot," "moist," "dry").
3. The entire compass of tones in the scale. Dryden is thinking of the Chain of Being, the ordered creation from inanimate nature up to man, God's latest and final work. The just gradations of notes in a scale are analogous to the equally just gradations in the ascending scale of created beings. Both are the result of harmony.
4. The power of music to describe, evoke, or subdue emotion ("passion") is a frequent theme in 17th-century literature. In stanzas 2–6 the poet considers music as awakening religious awe, warlike courage, sorrow for unrequited love, jealousy and fury, and the impulse to worship God.
5. According to Genesis 4.21, the inventor of the lyre and the pipe. Dryden imagines Jubal's lyre to have been made of a tortoise shell ("corded shell").

His listening brethren stood around,
And, wondering, on their faces fell
To worship that celestial sound.   20
Less than a god they thought there could not dwell
    Within the hollow of that shell
    That spoke so sweetly and so well.
What passion cannot Music raise and quell!

                        3

The trumpet's loud clangor   25
    Excites us to arms,
With shrill notes of anger,
    And mortal alarms.
The double double double beat
    Of the thundering drum   30
Cries: "Hark! the foes come;
Charge, charge, 'tis too late to retreat."

                        4

The soft complaining flute
In dying notes discovers
The woes of hopeless lovers,   35
Whose dirge is whispered by the warbling lute.

                        5

Sharp violins[6] proclaim
Their jealous pangs, and desperation,
Fury, frantic indignation,
Depth of pains, and height of passion,   40
    For the fair, disdainful dame.

                        6

But O! what art can teach,
What human voice can reach,
The sacred organ's praise?
    Notes inspiring holy love,   45
Notes that wing their heavenly ways
    To mend the choirs above.

                        7

Orpheus[7] could lead the savage race;
And trees unrooted left their place,
    Sequacious of the lyre;   50
But bright Cecilia raised the wonder higher:
When to her organ vocal breath was given,
An angel heard, and straight appeared,[8]
    Mistaking earth for heaven.

---

6. A reference to the bright tone of the modern violin, introduced into England at the Restoration. The tone of the old-fashioned viol is much duller (Bronson).
7. A legendary poet, son of one of the Muses, who played so wonderfully on the lyre that wild beasts ("the savage race") grew tame and followed him, as did even rocks and trees. "Sequacious of": following.
8. According to the legend, it was Cecilia's piety, not her music, that brought an angel to visit her.

GRAND CHORUS

As from the power of sacred lays   55
   The spheres began to move,[9]
And sung the great Creator's praise
   To all the blest above;
So, when the last and dreadful hour
This crumbling pageant[1] shall devour,   60
The trumpet shall be heard on high,[2] ⎫
The dead shall live, the living die,   ⎬
And Music shall untune the sky.   ⎭

1687

Epigram on Milton[3]

Three poets, in three distant ages born,
Greece, Italy, and England did adorn.
The first in loftiness of thought surpassed,
The next in majesty, in both the last:
The force of Nature could no farther go;   5
To make a third, she joined the former two.

1688

Criticism   Because Dryden liked to talk about literature, he became a critic, indeed the first comprehensive critic in England. The Elizabethans, largely impelled by the example of Italian humanists, had produced an interesting and unsystematic body of critical writings. Dryden could look back to such pioneer works as George Puttenham's *Art of English Poesy* (1589), Sir Philip Sidney's *Defence of Poesy* (1595), Samuel Daniel's *Defense of Rhyme* (ca. 1603), and Ben Jonson's *Timber, or Discoveries* (1641). These and later writings Dryden knew, as he knew the ancients and the important contemporary French critics, notably Corneille, Rapin, and Boileau. Taken as a whole, his critical prefaces and dedications, which appeared between 1664 and 1700, are the work of a man of independent mind who has made his own synthesis of critical canons from wide reading, a great deal of thinking, and the constant practice of the art of writing. As a critic he is no one's disciple, and he has the saving grace of being always willing to change his mind.

9. As it was harmony which ordered the universe, so it was angelic song ("sacred lays") which put the celestial bodies ("spheres") in motion. The harmonious chord which results from the traditional "music of the spheres" is a hymn of "praise" sung by created nature to its "Creator."
1. The universe: the stage on which the drama of man's salvation has been acted out.
2. The "last trump" of 1 Corinthians 15.52, which

will announce the Resurrection and the Last Judgment. Dryden develops his theme of harmony as order in such a way as to give full emphasis of the splendid paradox ("Music shall *untune*") in the final line of the ode.
3. Engraved beneath the portrait of Milton in Jacob Tonson's edition of *Paradise Lost* (1688). The "three poets" are Homer, Virgil, Milton.

All but a very few of Dryden's critical works (most notably the *Essay of Dramatic Poesy*) grew out of the works to which they served as prefaces: comedies, heroic plays, tragedies, translations, poems of various sorts. Each work posed problems which Dryden was eager to discuss with his readers, and the topics that he treated proved to be important in the development of the new literature of which he was the principal apologist. He dealt with the processes of literary creation, the poet's relation to tradition, the forms of modern drama, the craft of poetry, and above all the genius of earlier poets: Shakespeare, Jonson, Chaucer, Juvenal, Horace, Homer, Virgil. For nearly forty years this voice was heard in the land, and when it was finally silenced, a set of critical standards had come into existence and a new age had been given its direction.

From An Essay of Dramatic Poesy[1]

[*Shakespeare and Ben Jonson Compared*]

"To begin, then, with Shakespeare. He was the man who of all modern, and perhaps ancient poets, had the largest and most comprehensive soul. All the images of Nature were still present to him, and he drew them, not laboriously, but luckily; when he describes anything, you more than see it, you feel it too. Those who accuse him to have wanted learning, give him the greater commendation: he was naturally learned; he needed not the spectacles of books to read Nature; he looked inwards, and found her there. I cannot say he is everywhere alike; were he so, I should do him injury to compare him with the greatest of mankind. He is many times flat, insipid; his comic wit degenerating into clenches, his serious swelling into bombast. But he is always great when some great occasion is presented to him; no man can say he ever had a fit subject for his wit and did not then raise himself as high above the rest of poets,

Quantum lenta solent inter viburna cupressi[2]

The consideration of this made Mr. Hales of Eton[3] say that there was no subject of which any poet ever writ, but he would produce it much

1. With the reopening of the theaters in 1660, older plays were revived, but, despite their power and charm, they seemed old-fashioned. Although new playwrights, ambitious to create a modern English drama, soon appeared, they were uncertain of their direction. What, if anything, useful could they learn from the dramatic practice of the ancients? Should they ignore the English dramatists of the late 16th and early 17th centuries? Should they make their example the vigorous contemporary drama of France? Dryden addresses himself to these and other problems in this essay, his first extended piece of criticism. Its purpose, he tells us, was "chiefly to vindicate the honor of our English writers from the censure of those who unjustly prefer the French before them." Its method is skeptical: Dryden presents several points of view, but imposes none. The form is a dialogue among friends, like the *Tusculan Disputations* or the *Brutus* of Cicero. Crites praises the drama of the ancients; Eugenius pro-

tests against their authority and argues for the idea of progress in the arts; Lisideius urges the excellence of French plays; Neander, speaking in the climactic position, defends the native tradition and the greatness of Shakespeare, Fletcher, and Jonson. The dialogue takes place on June 3, 1665, in a boat on the Thames. The four friends are rowed downstream to listen to the cannonading of the English and Dutch fleets, engaged in battle off the Suffolk coast. As the gunfire recedes they are assured of victory and order their boatman to return to London, and naturally enough they fall to discussing the number of bad poems that the victory will evoke, and then turn to other, related topics.

2. "As do cypresses among the bending shrubs" (Virgil, *Eclogues* 1.25).

3. The learned John Hales (1584–1656), provost of Eton. He is reputed to have said this to Jonson himself.

better treated of in Shakespeare; and however others are now generally preferred before him, yet the age wherein he lived, which had contemporaries with him Fletcher and Jonson, never equaled them to him in their esteem: and in the last king's[4] court, when Ben's reputation was at highest, Sir John Suckling,[5] and with him the greater part of the courtiers, set our Shakespeare far above him. . . .

"As for Jonson, to whose character I am now arrived, if we look upon him while he was himself (for his last plays were but his dotages), I think him the most learned and judicious writer which any theater ever had. He was a most severe judge of himself, as well as others. One cannot say he wanted wit, but rather that he was frugal of it. In his works you find little to retrench[6] or alter. Wit, and language, and humor also in some measure, we had before him; but something of art[7] was wanting to the drama till he came. He managed his strength to more advantage than any who preceded him. You seldom find him making love in any of his scenes or endeavoring to move the passions; his genius was too sullen and saturnine[8] to do it gracefully, especially when he knew he came after those who had performed both to such an height. Humor was his proper sphere:[9] and in that he delighted most to represent mechanic people.[1] He was deeply conversant in the ancients, both Greek and Latin, and he borrowed boldly from them: there is scarce a poet or historian among the Roman authors of those times whom he has not translated in Sejanus and Catiline.[2] But he has done his robberies so openly, that one may see he fears not to be taxed by any law. He invades authors like a monarch; and what would be theft in other poets is only victory in him. With the spoils of these writers he so represents old Rome to us, in its rites, ceremonies, and customs, that if one of their poets had written either of his tragedies, we had seen less of it than in him. If there was any fault in his language, 'twas that he weaved it too closely and laboriously, in his serious plays:[3] perhaps, too, he did a little too much Romanize our tongue, leaving the words which he translated almost as much Latin as he found them: wherein, though he learnedly followed the idiom of their language, he did not enough comply with the idiom of ours. If I would compare him with Shakespeare, I must acknowledge him the more correct poet, but Shakespeare the greater wit.[4] Shakespeare was the Homer, or father of our dramatic poets; Jonson was the Virgil, the pattern of elaborate writing; I admire him, but I love Shakespeare. To conclude of him; as he has given us the most correct plays, so in the precepts which he has laid down in his Discoveries, we have as many

---

4. Charles I.
5. Courtier, poet, playwright, much admired in Dryden's time for his wit and the easy naturalness of his style.
6. Delete.
7. Craftsmanship.
8. Heavy.
9. In Jonson's comedies the characters are seen under the domination of some psychological trait, ruling passion, or affectation—i.e., some

"humor"—which makes them unique and ridiculous.
1. I.e., artisans.
2. Jonson's two Roman plays, dated 1605 and 1611 respectively.
3. This is the reading of the first edition. Curiously enough, in the second edition Dryden altered the phrase to "in his comedies especially."
4. Genius.

and profitable rules for perfecting the stage, as any wherewith the French can furnish us."

1668

From A Discourse Concerning the Original and Progress of Satire[1]

[The Art of Satire]

* * * How easy is it to call rogue and villain, and that wittily! But how hard to make a man appear a fool, a blockhead, or a knave without using any of those opprobrious terms! To spare the grossness of the names, and to do the thing yet more severely, is to draw a full face, and to make the nose and cheeks stand out, and yet not to employ any depth of shadowing.[2] This is the mystery of that noble trade, which yet no master can teach to his apprentice; he may give the rules, but the scholar is never the nearer in his practice. Neither is it true that this fineness of raillery[3] is offensive. A witty man is tickled while he is hurt in this manner, and a fool feels it not. The occasion of an offense may possibly be given, but he cannot take it. If it be granted that in effect this way does more mischief; that a man is secretly wounded, and though he be not sensible himself, yet the malicious world will find it out for him; yet there is still a vast difference betwixt the slovenly butchering of a man, and the fineness of a stroke that separates the head from the body, and leaves it standing in its place. A man may be capable, as Jack Ketch's[4] wife said of his servant, of a plain piece of work, a bare hanging; but to make a malefactor die sweetly was only belonging to her husband. I wish I could apply it to myself, if the reader would be kind enough to think it belongs to me. The character of Zimri in my *Absalom*[5] is, in my opinion, worth the whole poem: it is not bloody, but it is ridiculous enough; and he, for whom it was intended, was too witty to resent it as an injury. If I had railed,[6] I might have suffered for it justly; but I managed my own work more happily, perhaps more dexterously. I avoided the mention of great crimes, and applied myself to the representing of blindsides, and little extravagancies; to which, the wittier a man is, he is generally

---

1. This passage is an excerpt from the long and rambling preface which served as the dedication of a translation of the satires of the Roman satirists Juvenal and Persius to Charles Sackville, 6th earl of Dorset. The translations were made by Dryden and other writers, among them William Congreve. Dryden traces the origin and development of verse satire in Rome, and in a very fine passage contrasts Horace and Juvenal as satiric poets. It is plain that he prefers the "tragic" satire of Juvenal to the urbane and laughing satire of Horace. But in the passage printed here he praises his own satiric character of Zimri (the duke of Buckingham) in

Absalom and Achitophel for the very reason that it is modeled on Horatian "raillery," not Juvenalian invective.
2. Early English miniaturists prided themselves on the art of giving roundness to the full face without painting in shadows.
3. Satirical mirth, good-natured satire.
4. A notorious public executioner of Dryden's time (d. 1686). His name later became a generic term for all members of his profession.
5. See *Absalom and Achitophel* 1.544–68.
6. Reviled, abused. Observe that the verb differed in meaning from its noun, defined above.

the more obnoxious.[7] It succeeded as I wished; the jest went round, and he was laughed at in his turn who began the frolic. * * *

1693

From The Preface to *Fables Ancient and Modern*[1]

[*In Praise of Chaucer*]

In the first place, as he is the father of English poetry, I hold him in the same degree of veneration as the Grecians held Homer, or the Romans Virgil. He is a perpetual fountain of good sense; learned in all sciences;[2] and, therefore, speaks properly on all subjects. As he knew what to say, so he knows also when to leave off; a continence which is practiced by few writers, and scarcely by any of the ancients, excepting Virgil and Horace. * * *

Chaucer followed Nature everywhere, but was never so bold to go beyond her; and there is a great difference of being *poeta* and *nimis poeta*,[3] if we may believe Catullus, as much as betwixt a modest behavior and affectation. The verse of Chaucer, I confess, is not harmonious to us; but 'tis like the eloquence of one whom Tacitus commends, it was *auribus istius temporis accommodata:*[4] they who lived with him, and some time after him, thought it musical; and it continues so, even in our judgment, if compared with the numbers[5] of Lydgate and Gower, his contemporaries; there is the rude sweetness of a Scotch tune in it, which is natural and pleasing, though not perfect. 'Tis true I cannot go so far as he who published the last edition of him;[6] for he would make us believe the fault is in our ears, and that there were really ten syllables in a verse where we find but nine; but this opinion is not worth confuting; 'tis so gross and obvious an error that common sense (which is a rule in everything but matters of faith and revelation) must convince the reader that equality of numbers in every verse which we call heroic[7] was either not known, or not always practiced in Chaucer's age. It were an

---

7. Liable.
1. Dryden's final work, published in the year of his death, was a collection of translations from Homer, Ovid, Boccaccio, and Chaucer, and one or two other pieces. The Preface, in many ways, is Dryden's ripest and finest critical essay. In it, he is not concerned with critical theory or with a formalistic approach to literature; he is simply a man, grown old in the reading and writing of poetry, who is eager to talk informally with his readers about some of his favorite authors. His praise of Chaucer (unusually sympathetic and perceptive for 1700) is animated by that love of great literature which is manifest in everything that Dryden wrote.
2. Branches of learning.
3. A poet ("*poeta*") and too much of a poet ("*nimis poeta*"). The phrase is not from Catullus but from

Martial (*Epigrams* 3.44).
4. "Suitable to the ears of that time." Tacitus was a Roman historian and writer on oratory (A.D. ca. 55–ca. 117).
5. Versification. John Lydgate (ca. 1370–ca. 1449) wrote poetry which shows the influence of Chaucer. John Gower (d. 1408), poet and friend of Chaucer.
6. Thomas Speght's Chaucer, which Dryden used, was first published in 1598; the second edition, published in 1602, was reprinted in 1687.
7. The pentameter line. In Dryden's time few readers knew how to pronounce Middle English, especially the syllabic *e*. Moreover, Chaucer's works were known only in corrupt printed texts. As a consequence Chaucer's verse seemed rough and irregular.

easy matter to produce some thousands of his verses which are lame for want of half a foot, and sometimes a whole one, and which no pronunciation can make otherwise. We can only say that he lived in the infancy of our poetry, and that nothing is brought to perfection at the first. * * *

He must have been a man of a most wonderful comprehensive nature, because, as it has been truly observed of him, he has taken into the compass of his *Canterbury Tales* the various manners and humors (as we now call them) of the whole English nation in his age. Not a single character has escaped him. All his pilgrims are severally distinguished from each other; and not only in their inclinations but in their very physiognomies and persons. Baptista Porta[8] could not have described their natures better than by the marks which the poet gives them. The matter and manner of their tales, and of their telling, are so suited to their different educations, humors, and callings that each of them would be improper in any other mouth. Even the grave and serious characters are distinguished by their several sorts of gravity: their discourses are such as belong to their age, their calling, and their breeding; such as are becoming of them, and of them only. Some of his persons are vicious, and some virtuous; some are unlearned, or (as Chaucer calls them) lewd, and some are learned. Even the ribaldry of the low characters is different: the Reeve, the Miller, and the Cook are several[9] men, and distinguished from each other as much as the mincing Lady Prioress and the broad-speaking, gap-toothed Wife of Bath. But enough of this; there is such a variety of game springing up before me that I am distracted in my choice, and know not which to follow. 'Tis sufficient to say, according to the proverb, that here is God's plenty. * * *

1700

8. Giambattista della Porta (ca. 1535–1615), author of a Latin treatise on physiognomy.
9. Different.

JONATHAN SWIFT
1667–1745

1704:	A *Tale of a Tub* and *The Battle of the Books*.
1710–14:	Alignment with Tories; political writings in defense of the Tory ministry.
1713:	Made Dean of St. Patrick's Cathedral, Dublin.
1726:	Publication of *Gulliver's Travels*.

Swift—a posthumous child—was born of English parents in Dublin. Through the generosity of an uncle he was educated at Kilkenny School and Trinity College, Dublin; but before he could fix on a career, the troubles that followed upon James II's abdication and his subsequent invasion of Ireland drove him along with other Anglo-Irish to England. Between 1689 and 1699 he was more or less continuously a member of the household of his kinsman Sir William Temple, an urban, civilized man, a retired diplomat, and a friend of King William. During these years Swift read widely; rather reluctantly decided on the church as a career and so took orders; and discovered his astonishing gifts as a satirist. About 1696–97 he wrote his powerful satires on corruptions in religion and learning, A *Tale of a Tub* and *The Battle of the Books*, which were published in 1704 and reached their final form only in the fifth edition of 1710. These were the years in which he slowly came to maturity. When at the age of thirty-two, he returned to Ireland as chaplain to the Lord Justice, the earl of Berkeley, he had a clear sense of his genius.

For the rest of his life Swift devoted his talents to politics and religion—not clearly separated at the time—and most of his works in prose were written to further a specific cause. As a clergyman, a spirited controversialist, and a devoted supporter of the Anglican Church as an institution no less important than the Crown itself, he was hostile to all who seemed to threaten his Church—Deists, freethinkers, Roman Catholics, Nonconformists, or merely Whig politicians. In 1710 he abandoned his old party, the Whig, because he disapproved of its indifference to the welfare of the Anglican Church in Ireland and of its desire to repeal the Test Act, which required all holders of offices of state to take the Sacrament according to the Anglican rites, thus excluding Roman Catholics and Dissenters. Welcomed by the Tories, he became the most brilliant political journalist of the day, serving the government of Oxford and Bolingbroke as editor of the party organ, the *Examiner*, and as author of its most powerful articles, as well as writing longer pamphlets in support of important policies, such as that favoring the Peace of Utrecht (1713). He was greatly valued by the two ministers, who admitted him to social intimacy, though never to their counsels. The reward of his services was not the English bishopric which he had a right to expect, but the deanship of St. Patrick's Cathedral in Dublin, which came to him in 1713, a year before the death of Queen Anne and the fall of the Tories put an end to all his hopes of preferment in England.

In Ireland, where he lived unwillingly, he became not only an efficient ecclesiastical administrator, but also, in 1724, the leader of Irish resistance to English oppression. Under the pseudonym of "M. B. Drapier," he published the famous series of public letters that aroused the country to refuse to accept £100,000 in new copper coins (minted in England by William Wood, who had obtained his patent through court corruption) which, it was feared, would further debase the coinage of the already poverty-stricken kingdom. Although his authorship of the letters was known to all Dublin, no one could be found to earn the £300 offered by the government for information as to the identity of the Drapier. Swift is still venerated in Ireland as a national hero. He earned the right to refer to himself in the epitaph that he wrote for his tomb as a vigorous defender of liberty.

His last years were less happy. Swift had suffered most of his adult life from what we now recognize as Ménière's syndrome, which affects the inner ear, causing dizziness, nausea, and deafness. After 1739, when he was seventy-two years old, his infirmities cut him off from his duties as dean, and from then on his social life dwindled. In 1742 guardians were appointed to administer his affairs, and his last three years were spent in gloom and lethargy. But this dark ending should not put his earlier life, so full of energy and humor, into a shadow. The writer of the satires was a man in full control of great intellectual powers.

He also had a gift for friendship. Swift was admired and loved by many of the distinguished men of his time. His friendships with Addison, Pope, Arbuthnot, Gay, Prior, Oxford, Bolingbroke, not to mention those with his less brilliant but amiable Irish circle, bear witness to his moral integrity and social charm. Nor was he, despite some of his writings, indifferent to women. Esther Johnson (Swift's "Stella") was the daughter of Temple's steward, and when Swift first knew her she was little more than a child. He educated her, formed her character, and came to love her as he was to love no other person. After Temple's death she moved to Dublin, where she and Swift met constantly, but never alone. To her he wrote the famous journal-letters, later published (1766) as *The Journal to Stella*, during his four-year residence in London when he was working with the Tories; and to her he wrote charming poems. Whether they were secretly married or whether they never married—and in either case why—has been often debated. A marriage of any sort seems most unlikely; and however perplexing their relationship was to others, it was obviously satisfying to each of them. Not even the violent passion that Swift awakened, no doubt unwittingly, in a much younger woman, Hester Vanhomrigh (pronounced V*an-úm-mer-y*), her pleadings and reproaches and early death, could unsettle his devotion to Stella. An enigmatic account of his relations with "Vanessa," as he called Vanhomrigh, is given in his poem *Cadenus and Vanessa*.

For all his involvement in public affairs, Swift seems to stand apart from his contemporaries—a striking figure even among the statesmen of the time, a man who towered above other writers by reason of his imagination, mordant wit, and emotional intensity. He has been called a misanthrope, a hater of mankind; and *Gulliver's Travels* has been considered an expression of savage misanthropy. It is true that Swift proclaimed himself a misanthrope in a letter to Pope, declaring that though he loved individuals, he hated "that animal called man" in general, and offering a new definition of the species as not *animal rationale* ("a rational animal"), but as merely *animal rationis capax* ("an animal *capable* of reason"). This, he declared, is the "great foundation" upon which his "misanthropy" was erected. Swift was stating not his hatred of his fellow creatures, but his antagonism to the current optimistic view that human nature is essentially good. To the "philanthropic" flattery that sentimentalism and Deistic rationalism were paying to human nature, Swift opposed a more ancient and plausible view: that human nature is deeply and permanently flawed, and that we can do nothing with or for the human race until we recognize its moral and intellectual limitations. In his epitaph he spoke of the "fierce indignation" which had torn his heart, an indignation that found superb expression in his greatest satires. It was provoked by the constant spectacle of creatures capable of reason, and therefore of reasonable conduct, steadfastly refusing to live up to their capabilities.

Swift is one of our greatest writers of prose. He defined a good style as "proper words in proper places," a more complex and difficult saying than at first appears. Clear, simple, concrete diction, uncomplicated syntax, economy and conciseness of language mark all of his writings. His is a style that shuns ornaments and singularity of all kinds, a style that grows more tense and controlled the more fierce the indignation that it is called upon to express. The virtues of his prose are those of his poetry, which shocks us with its hard look at the facts of life and the body. It is unpoetic poetry, devoid of, indeed as often as not mocking at, inspiration, romantic love, cosmetic beauty, easily assumed literary attitudes, and conventional poetic language. Like the prose it is predominantly satiric in purpose, but not without its moments of comedy and light-heartedness, though written most often not so much to divert as to reform the reader.

A Description of a City Shower

Careful observers may fortell the hour
(By sure prognostics) when to dread a shower:
While rain depends,[1] the pensive cat gives o'er
Her frolics, and pursues her tail no more.
Returning home at night, you'll find the sink[2]   5
Strike your offended sense with double stink.
If you be wise, then go not far to dine;
You'll spend in coach hire more than save in wine.
A coming shower your shooting corns presage,
Old achés throb, your hollow tooth will rage.   10
Sauntering in coffeehouse is Dulman[3] seen;
He damns the climate and complains of spleen.
   Meanwhile the South, rising with dabbled wings,
A sable cloud athwart the welkin flings,
That swilled more liquor than it could contain,   15
And, like a drunkard, gives it up again.
Brisk Susan whips her linen from the rope,
While the first drizzling shower is borne aslope:
Such is that sprinkling which some careless quean[4]
Flirts on you from her mop, but not so clean: 20
You fly, invoke the gods; then turning, stop
To rail; she singing, still whirls on her mop.
Not yet the dust had shunned the unequal strife,
But, aided by the wind, fought still for life,
And wafted with its foe by violent gust,   25
'Twas doubtful which was rain and which was dust.
Ah! where must needy poet seek for aid,
When dust and rain at once his coat invade?
Sole coat, where dust cemented by the rain
Erects the nap, and leaves a mingled stain.   30
   Now in contiguous drops the flood comes down,
Threatening with deluge this devoted town.
To shops in crowds the daggled[5] females fly,

---

1. Impends, is imminent. An example of elevated diction used frequently throughout the poem in order to gain a mock dignity, comically inappropriate to the homely and realistic subject.
2. Sewer.
3. A type name (from "dull man"), like Congreve's "Petulant" or "Witwoud." It was commonly believed at this time that the Englishman's tendency to melancholy ("the spleen") was attributable to the rainy climate.
4. Wench, slut.
5. Spattered with mud. "To cheapen": to bargain for.

Pretend to cheapen goods, but nothing buy.
The Templar[6] spruce, while every spout's abroach,   35
Stays till 'tis fair, yet seems to call a coach.
The tucked-up sempstress walks with hasty strides,
While streams run down her oiled umbrella's sides.
Here various kinds, by various fortunes led,
Commence acquaintance underneath a shed.   40
Triumphant Tories and desponding Whigs
Forget their feuds,[7] and join to save their wigs.
Boxed in a chair[8] the beau impatient sits,
While spouts run clattering o'er the roof by fits,
And ever and anon with frightful din   45
The leather sounds;[9] he trembles from within.
So when Troy chairmen bore the wooden steed,
Pregnant with Greeks impatient to be freed
(Those bully Greeks, who, as the moderns do,
Instead of paying chairmen, run them through),[1]   50
Laocoön struck the outside with his spear,
And each imprisoned hero quaked for fear.[2]
    Now from all parts the swelling kennels[3] flow,
And bear their trophies with them as they go:
Filth of all hues and odors seem to tell   55
What street they sailed from, by their sight and smell.
They, as each torrent drives with rapid force,
From Smithfield or St. Pulchre's shape their course,
And in huge confluence joined at Snow Hill ridge,
Fall from the conduit prone to Holborn Bridge.[4]   60
Sweepings from butchers' stalls, dung, guts, and blood,
Drowned puppies, stinking sprats,[5] all drenched in mud,
Dead cats, and turnip tops, come tumbling down the flood.[6]

1710

6. A young man engaged in studying law. In the literature of the period the Templar is usually depicted as neglecting his professional studies for the sake of dissipation and the pursuit of literature. Cf. the Member of the Inner Temple in *Spectator*
2. "Abroach": pouring out water.
7. The Whig ministry had just fallen and the Tories, led by Harley and St. John, were forming the government with which Swift was to be closely associated until the death of the queen in 1714.
8. Sedan chair.
9. The roof of the sedan chair was made of leather.
1. Run them through with their swords. The bully, always prone to violence, was a familiar figure in London streets and places of amusement.
2. *Aeneid* 2.40–53.
3. The open gutters in the middle of the street.

4. An accurate description of the drainage system of this part of London—the eastern edge of Holborn and West Smithfield, which lie outside the old walls west and east of Newgate. The great cattle and sheep markets were in Smithfield. The church of St. Sepulchre ("St. Pulchre's") stood opposite Newgate Prison. Holborn Conduit was at the foot of Snow Hill. It drained into Fleet Ditch, an evil-smelling open sewer, at Holborn Bridge.
5. Small herrings.
6. In Falkner's edition of Swift's *Works* (Dublin, 1735) a note almost certainly suggested by Swift points to the concluding triplet, with its resonant final alexandrine, as a burlesque of a mannerism of Dryden and other Restoration poets, and claims that Swift's ridicule banished the triplet from contemporary poetry.

Verses on the Death of Dr. Swift

Occasioned by Reading a Maxim in Rochefoucauld[1]

Dans l'adversité de nos meilleurs amis nous trouvons toujours quelque chose, qui ne nous déplaît pas.[2]

As Rochefoucauld his maxims drew
From nature, I believe 'em true:
They argue no corrupted mind
In him; the fault is in mankind.
This maxim more than all the rest   5
Is thought too base for human breast:
"In all distresses of our friends
We first consult our private ends,
While Nature, kindly bent to ease us,
Points out some circumstance to please us."   10
If this perhaps your patience move,[3]
Let reason and experience prove.
We all behold with envious eyes
Our equal raised above our size.
Who would not at a crowded show   15
Stand high himself, keep others low?
I love my friend as well as you,
But why should he obstruct my view?
Then let me have the higher post;
Suppose it but an inch at most.   20
If in a battle you should find
One, whom you love of all mankind,
Had some heroic action done,
A champion killed, or trophy won;
Rather than thus be overtopped,   25
Would you not wish his laurels cropped?
Dear honest Ned is in the gout,
Lies racked with pain, and you without:
How patiently you hear him groan!
How glad the case is not your own!   30
What poet would not grieve to see
His brethren write as well as he?
But rather than they should excel,
He'd wish his rivals all in hell.
Her end when Emulation misses,   35
She turns to envy, stings, and hisses:

---

1. François de la Rochefoucauld (1613–1680), writer of witty, cynical maxims. Writing to Pope (Nov. 26, 1725), Swift, opposing the optimistic philosophy that Pope and Bolingbroke were at that time developing, professed to have founded his whole character on these maxims.
2. "In the misfortune of our best friends we always find something that does not displease us."
3. Should agitate.

The strongest friendship yields to pride,
Unless the odds be on our side.
   Vain humankind! fantastic race!
Thy various follies who can trace?   40
Self-love, ambition, envy, pride,
Their empire in our hearts divide.
Give others riches, power, and station;
'Tis all on me an usurpation;
I have no title to aspire,   45
Yet, when you sink, I seem the higher.
In Pope I cannot read a line,
But with a sigh I wish it mine:
When he can in one couplet fix
More sense than I can do in six,   50
It gives me such a jealous fit,
I cry, "Pox take him and his wit!"
   I grieve to be outdone by Gay[4]
In my own humorous biting way.
Arbuthnot is no more my friend,   55
Who dares to irony pretend,
Which I was born to introduce,
Refined it first, and showed its use.
St. John,[5] as well as Pulteney, knows
That I had some repute for prose;   60
And, till they drove me out of date,
Could maul a minister of state.
If they have mortified my pride,
And made me throw my pen aside;
If with such talents Heaven hath blessed 'em,   65
Have I not reason to detest 'em?
   To all my foes, dear Fortune, send
Thy gifts, but never to my friend:
I tamely can endure the first,
But this with envy makes me burst.   70
   Thus much may serve by way of proem;
Proceed we therefore to our poem.
   The time is not remote, when I
Must by the course of nature die;
When, I foresee, my special friends   75
Will try to find their private ends:
Though it is hardly understood
Which way my death can do them good;

4. John Gay (1685–1732), author of the famous *Beggar's Opera* (1728), intimate friend of Swift and Pope. His *Trivia, or the Art of Walking the Streets of London* (1716) owes something to Swift's *City Shower*. Dr. John Arbuthnot, physician and wit, friend of Swift and Pope. See Pope's *Epistle to Dr. Arbuthnot*.
5. Henry St. John, Lord Bolingbroke (see note, Pope's *Essay on Man*. 1.1), though debarred from the House of Lords and from public office, had become the center of a group of Tories and discontented young Whigs (of whom William Pulteney was one) who united in opposing Sir Robert Walpole, the chief minister. They published a political periodical, the *Craftsman*, thus rivaling Swift in his role of political pamphleteer and enemy of Sir Robert.

Yet thus, methinks, I hear 'em speak:
"See how the Dean begins to break!   80
Poor gentleman! he droops apace!
You plainly find it in his face.
That old vertigo[6] in his head
Will never leave him till he's dead.
Besides, his memory decays;   85
He recollects not what he says;
He cannot call his friends to mind;
Forgets the place where last he dined;
Plies you with stories o'er and o'er,
He told them fifty times before.   90
How does he fancy we can sit
To hear his out-of-fashion wit?
But he takes up with younger folks,
Who for his wine will bear his jokes.
Faith, he must make his stories shorter,   95
Or change his comrades once a quarter;
In half the time he talks them round,
There must another set be found.
    "For poetry, he's past his prime;
He takes an hour to find a rhyme;   100
His fire is out, his wit decayed,
His fancy sunk, his Muse a jade.[7]
I'd have him throw away his pen—
But there's no talking to some men."
    And then their tenderness appears   105
By adding largely to my years:
"He's older than he would be reckoned,
And well remembers Charles the Second.
He hardly drinks a pint of wine;
And that, I doubt, is no good sign.   110
His stomach, too, begins to fail;
Last year we thought him strong and hale;
But now he's quite another thing;
I wish he may hold out till spring."
They hug themselves, and reason thus: 115
"It is not yet so bad with us."
    In such a case they talk in tropes,[8]
And by their fears express their hopes.
Some great misfortune to portend
No enemy can match a friend.   120
With all the kindness they profess,
The merit of a lucky guess
(When daily how-d'ye's come of course,
And servants answer, "Worse and worse!")

---

6. Johnson in his *Dictionary* authorizes Swift's
pronounciation: *ver-ti-go.*
7. A worn-out horse, in contrast to Pegasus, the
winged horse of Greek mythology, emblem of poetic
inspiration.
8. Figures of speech.

Would please 'em better, than to tell   125
That God be praised! the Dean is well.
Then he who prophesied the best,
Approves his foresight to the rest:
"You know I always feared the worst,
And often told you so at first."   130
He'd rather choose that I should die,
Than his prediction prove a lie.
Not one foretells I shall recover,
But all agree to give me over.

    Yet, should some neighbor feel a pain   135
Just in the parts where I complain,
How many a message would he send!
What hearty prayers that I should mend!
Inquire what regimen I kept;
What gave me ease, and how I slept,   140
And more lament, when I was dead,
Then all the snivelers round my bed.

    My good companions, never fear;
For though you may mistake a year,
Though your prognostics run too fast,   145
They must be verified at last.

    Behold the fatal day arrive!
"How is the Dean?"—"He's just alive."
Now the departing prayer is read.
"He hardly breathes"—"The Dean is dead."   150
Before the passing bell begun,
The news through half the town has run.
"Oh! may we all for death prepare!
What has he left? and who's his heir?"
"I know no more than what the news is;   155
'Tis all bequeathed to public uses."
"To public use! a perfect whim!
What had the public done for him?
Mere envy, avarice, and pride:
He gave it all—but first he died.   160
And had the Dean in all the nation
No worthy friend, no poor relation?
So ready to do strangers good,
Forgetting his own flesh and blood?"
Now Grub Street[9] wits are all employed;   165
With elegies the town is cloyed;
Some paragraph in every paper
To curse the Dean, or bless the Drapier.[1]

    The doctors, tender of their fame,

9. Originally a street in London largely inhabited by hack writers; later, a generic term applied to all such writers.

1. It was in the character of "M. B.," a Dublin drapier, that Swift aroused the Irish people to resistance against the importation of Wood's halfpence. See biographical introduction.

Wisely on me lay all the blame.   170
"We must confess his case was nice;[2]
But he would never take advice.
Had he been ruled, for aught appears,
He might have lived these twenty years:
For, when we opened him, we found,   175
That all his vital parts were sound."
    From Dublin soon to London spread,
'Tis told at court, "The Dean is dead."
Kind Lady Suffolk,[3] in the spleen,
Runs laughing up to tell the Queen.   180
The Queen, so gracious, mild and good,
Cries, "Is he gone? 'tis time he should.
He's dead, you say; why, let him rot:
I'm glad the medals were forgot.[4]
I promised him, I own; but when?   185
I only was the Princess then;
But now, as consort of the King,
You know, 'tis quite a different thing."
    Now Chartres,[5] at Sir Robert's levee,
Tells with a sneer the tidings heavy: 190
"Why, is he dead without his shoes?"
Cries Bob, "I'm sorry for the news:
Oh, were the wretch but living still,
And in his place my good friend Will![6]
Or had a miter on his head,   195
Provided Bolingbroke were dead!"
    Now Curll his shop from rubbish drains:[7]
Three genuine tomes of Swift's remains!
And then, to make them pass the glibber,
Revised by Tibbalds, Moore, and Cibber.[8]   200
He'll treat me as he does my betters,
Publish my will, my life, my letters;
Revive the libels born to die,
Which Pope must bear, as well as I.
    Here shift the scene, to represent   205
How those I love my death lament.
Poor Pope will grieve a month, and Gay
A week, and Arbuthnot a day.

---

2. Delicate; hence demanding careful diagnosis and treatment.
3. George II's mistress, with whom Swift became friendly during his visit to Pope in 1726. "In the spleen": in low spirits. The phrase is ironic, as "laughing" in the next line makes clear.
4. Queen Caroline had promised Swift some medals when she was princess of Wales during the same year.
5. Col. Francis Chartres, a debauchee often satirized by Pope; Sir Robert Walpole.
6. William Pulteney (see line 59 and its note.)
7. Edmund Curll, shrewd and disreputable book-

seller, published pirated works, scandalous biographies, and works falsely ascribed to notable writers of the time.
8. Lewis Theobald (1688–1744), Shakespeare scholar and editor, already enthroned as King of the Dunces in Pope's *Dunciad* (1728). Like Pope, Swift spells the name phonetically. James Moore-Smyth, poetaster and playwright, an enemy of Pope. Colley Cibber (1671–1757), comic actor, playwright, and supremely untalented poet laureate. He succeeded Theobald as King of the Dunces in the *Dunciad* of 1743.

St. John himself will scarce forbear
To bite his pen, and drop a tear.   210
The rest will give a shrug, and cry,
"I'm sorry—but we all must die!"
   Indifference clad in wisdom's guise
All fortitude of mind supplies:
For how can stony bowels melt   215
In those who never pity felt?
When *we* are lashed, *they* kiss the rod,
Resigning to the will of God.
   The fools, my juniors by a year,
Are tortured with suspense and fear;   220
Who wisely thought my age a screen,
When death approached, to stand between:
The screen removed, their hearts are trembling;
They mourn for me without dissembling.
   My female friends, whose tender hearts   225
Have better learned to act their parts,
Receive the news in doleful dumps:
"The Dean is dead (and what is trumps?)
Then, Lord have mercy on his soul!
(Ladies, I'll venture for the vole.)⁹   230
Six deans, they say, must bear the pall.
(I wish I knew what king to call.)
Madam, your husband will attend
The funeral of so good a friend?"
"No, madam, 'tis a shocking sight;   235
And he's engaged tomorrow night:
My Lady Club would take it ill,
If he should fail her at quadrille.
He loved the Dean—(I lead a heart)
But dearest friends, they say, must part.   240
His time was come; he ran his race;
We hope he's in a better place."
   Why do we grieve that friends should die?
No loss more easy to supply.
One year is past; a different scene!   245
No further mention of the Dean,
Who now, alas! no more is missed,
Than if he never did exist.
Where's now this favorite of Apollo?
Departed—and his works must follow,   250
Must undergo the common fate;
His kind of wit is out of date.
   Some country squire to Lintot¹ goes,
Inquires for Swift in verse and prose.
Says Lintot, "I have heard the name;   255

---

9. The equivalent in the card game quadrille of bidding a grand slam in bridge.

1. Bernard Lintot, the publisher of Pope's Homer and some of his early poems.

He died a year ago."—"The same."
He searches all the shop in vain.
"Sir, you may find them in Duck Lane:[2]
I sent them, with a load of books,
Last Monday to the pastry-cook's.[3]   260
To fancy they could live a year!
I find you're but a stranger here.
The Dean was famous in his time,
And had a kind of knack at rhyme.
His way of writing now is past: 265
The town has got a better taste.
I keep no antiquated stuff;
But spick and span I have enough.
Pray do but give me leave to show 'em:
Here's Colley Cibber's birthday poem.   270
This ode you never yet have seen
By Stephen Duck[4] upon the Queen.
Then here's a letter finely penned.
Against the *Craftsman*[5] and his friend;
It clearly shows that all reflection   275
On ministers is disaffection.
Next, here's Sir Robert's vindication,[6]
And Mr. Henley's last oration.[7]
The hawkers have not got them yet:
Your honor please to buy a set?   280
     "Here's Woolston's tracts,[8] the twelfth edition;
'Tis read by every politican:
The country members, when in town,
To all their boroughs send them down;
You never met a thing so smart;   285
The courtiers have them all by heart;
Those maids of honor (who can read)
Are taught to use them for their creed.
The reverend author's good intention
Has been rewarded with a pension.   290
He does an honor to his gown,
By bravely running priestcraft down;
He shows, as sure as God's in Gloucester,[9]
That Jesus was a grand impostor;
That all his miracles were cheats,   295
Performed as jugglers do their feats:
The Church had never such a writer;

2. London street where second-hand books and publishers' "remainders" were sold.
3. To be used as waste paper for lining baking dishes and wrapping parcels.
4. Stephen Duck, "the thresher poet," an agricultural laborer, whose mild poetic gifts brought him to the notice and patronage of Queen Caroline.
5. See line 59 and its note.
6. "Walpole hires a string of party scribblers who do nothing else but write in his defense" [Swift's note].
7. "Orator" John Henley, an Independent preacher, who dazzled unlearned audiences with his oratory and who wrote treatises on elocution.
8. Thomas Woolston (1670–1733), a freethinker, whose *Discourses on the Miracles of Our Saviour* had recently earned him notoriety.
9. Proverbially, Gloucestershire was full of monks.

A shame he has not got a miter!"
    Suppose me dead; and then suppose
A club assembled at the Rose;[1]   300
Where, from discourse of this and that,
I grow the subject of their chat.
And while they toss my name about,
With favor some, and some without,
One, quite indifferent in the cause,   305
My character impartial draws:
    "The Dean, if we believe report,
Was never ill received at court.
As for his works in verse and prose,
I own myself no judge of those;   310
Nor can I tell what critics thought 'em:
But this I know, all people bought 'em,
As with a moral view designed
To cure the vices of mankind.
    "His vein, ironically grave,   315
Exposed the fool and lashed the knave,
To steal a hint was never known,
But what he writ was all his own.
    "He never thought an honor done him,
Because a duke was proud to own him,   320
Would rather slip aside and choose
To talk with wits in dirty shoes;
Despised the fools with stars and garters,
So often seen caressing Chartres.
He never courted men in station,   325
Nor persons held in admiration;
Of no man's greatness was afraid,
Because he sought for no man's aid.
Though trusted long in great affairs,
He gave himself no haughty airs;   330
Without regarding private ends,
Spent all his credit for his friends;
And only chose the wise and good;
No flatterers, no allies in blood;
But succored virtue in distress,   335
And seldom failed of good success;
As numbers in their hearts must own,
Who, but for him, had been unknown.
    "With princes kept a due decorum,
But never stood in awe before 'em.   340
He followed David's lesson just;
In princes never put thy trust:[2]
And would you make him truly sour,
Provoke him with a slave in power.

---

1. A fashionable tavern in Covent Garden.   2. Psalm 146.3.

The Irish senate if you named,   345
With what impatience he declaimed!
Fair Liberty was all his cry,
For her he stood prepared to die;
For her he boldly stood alone;
For her he oft exposed his own.   350
Two kingdoms, just as faction led,
Had set a price upon his head,
But not a traitor could be found,
To sell him for six hundred pound.[3]
   "Had he but spared his tongue and pen,   355
He might have rose like other men;
But power was never in his thought,
And wealth he valued not a groat:
Ingratitude he often found,
And pitied those who meant the wound;   360
But kept the tenor of his mind,
To merit well of human kind:
Nor made a sacrifice of those
Who still were true, to please his foes.
He labored many a fruitless hour,   365
To reconcile his friends in power;
Saw mischief by a faction brewing,
While they pursued each other's ruin.
But finding vain was all his care,
He left the court in mere despair.[4]   370
   "And, oh! how short are human schemes!
Here ended all our golden dreams.
What St. John's skill in state affairs,
What Ormonde's[5] valor, Oxford's cares,
To save their sinking country lent,   375
Was all destroyed by one event.[6]
Too soon that precious life was ended,
On which alone our weal depended.
When up a dangerous faction starts,[7]
With wrath and vengeance in their hearts;   380
By solemn League and Covenant bound,

3. In 1714 the government offered £300 for the discovery of the author of Swift's *Public Spirit of the Whigs,* and in 1724 the Irish government offered a similar amount for the discovery of the author of the fourth of Swift's *Drapier's Letters.*
4. The antagonism between the two chief ministers (his dear friends), Robert Harley, earl of Oxford, and Bolingbroke paralyzed the Tory ministry in the crucial last months of Queen Anne's life and drove Swift to retirement in Ireland, whence he returned in 1714 to make a final effort to heal the breach and save the government. He failed and retired to the country in despair. There he received the news of Anne's death on August 1. The Hanoverian succession brought the Whigs back in triumph, ruined Swift's friends, and brought Swift's public life to a close.
5. James Butler, duke of Ormonde, who succeeded to the command of the English armies on the Continent, when, in 1711, the duke of Marlborough was stripped of his offices by Anne. He went into exile in 1714 and was active in Jacobite intrigue.
6. The death of Queen Anne.
7. Swift's view of the policies of the "dangerous faction" (the Whig party) is hardly impartial. He feared it especially because of its toleration of Dissenters, and so as an enemy of the Church of England.

To ruin, slaughter, and confound;
To turn religion to a fable,
And make the government a Babel;
Pervert the laws, disgrace the gown,   385
Corrupt the senate, rob the crown;
To sacrifice old England's glory,
And make her infamous in story:
When such a tempest shook the land,
How could unguarded Virtue stand?   390
With horror, grief, despair, the Dean
Beheld the dire destructive scene:
His friends in exile, or the Tower,[8]
Himself within the frown of power,
Pursued by base envenomed pens,   395
Far to the land of slaves and fens;[9]
A servile race in folly nursed,
Who truckle most, when treated worst.
    "By innocence and resolution,
He bore continual persecution;   400
While numbers to preferment rose,
Whose merits were to be his foes;
When even his own familiar friends,
Intent upon their private ends,
Like renegadoes now he feels,   405
Against him lifting up their heels.
    "The Dean did, by his pen, defeat
An infamous destructive cheat;[1]
Taught fools their interest how to know,
And gave them arms to ward the blow.   410
Envy has owned it was his doing,
To save that hapless land from ruin;
While they who at the steerage[2] stood,
And reaped the profit, sought his blood.
    "To save them from their evil fate,   415
In him was held a crime of state.
A wicked monster on the bench,[3]
Whose fury blood could never quench;
As vile and profligate a villain,
As modern Scroggs, or old Tresilian;[4]   420

---

8. Bolingbroke was in exile; Oxford was sent to the Tower by the Whigs.
9. Ireland.
1. The scheme to introduce Wood's copper halfpence into Ireland in 1723–24.
2. Literally the steering of a ship. Here the direction and management of public affairs in Ireland.
3. William Whitshed, Lord Chief Justice of the King's Bench of Ireland. In 1720, when the jury refused to find Swift's anonymous pamphlet *Proposal for the Universal Use of Irish Manufacture* wicked and seditious, Whitshed sent them back nine

times, hoping to force them to another verdict. In 1724 he presided over the trial of Harding, the printer of Swift's fourth *Drapier's Letter*, but again was unable, despite bullying, to force a verdict of guilty.
4. Sir William Scroggs, Lord Chief Justice of England at the time of the Popish Plot, 1678 (see Dryden's *Absalom and Achitophel*), was impeached for his misdemeanors in office in 1680. Sir Robert Tresilian punished with great severity in 1381 men who had participated in the Peasants' Revolt; he was impeached and in 1387 was hanged.

Who long all justice had discarded,
Nor feared he God, nor man regarded;
Vowed on the Dean his rage to vent,
And make him of his zeal repent:
But Heaven his innocence defends,   425
The grateful people stand his friends;
Not strains of law, nor judge's frown,
Nor topics brought to please the crown,
Nor witness hired, nor jury picked,
Prevail to bring him in convict.   430
          "In exile, with a steady heart,
He spent his life's declining part;
Where folly, pride, and faction sway,
Remote from St. John, Pope, and Gay.
          "His friendships there, to few confined,   435
Were always of the middling kind;
No fools of rank, a mongrel breed,
Who fain would pass for lords indeed:
Where titles give no right or power,
And peerage is a withered flower;   440
He would have held it a disgrace,
If such a wretch had known his face.
On rural squires, that kingdom's bane,
He vented oft his wrath in vain;
Biennial squires⁵ to market brought: 445
Who sell their souls, and votes for naught;
The nation stripped, go joyful back,
To rob the church, their tenants rack,
Go snacks with rogues and rapparees;⁶
And keep the peace to pick up fees;   450
In every job to have a share,
A jail or barrack to repair;
And turn the tax for public roads,
Commodious to their own abodes.
          "Perhaps I may allow the Dean   455
Had too much satire in his vein;
And seemed determined not to starve it,
Because no age could more deserve it.
Yet malice never was his aim;
He lashed the vice, but spared the name;   460
No individual could resent,
Where thousands equally were meant;
His satire points at no defect,
But what all mortals may correct;
For he abhorred that senseless tribe   465
Who call it humor when they gibe:
He spared a hump, or crooked nose,

5. Members of the Irish Parliament.   6. Highwaymen.

Whose owners set not up for beaux.
True genuine dullness moved his pity,
Unless it offered to be witty.   470
Those who their ignorance confessed,
He ne'er offended with a jest;
But laughed to hear an idiot quote
A verse from Horace learned by rote.
   "He knew an hundred pleasant stories,   475
With all the turns of Whigs and Tories:
Was cheerful to his dying day;
And friends would let him have his way.
   "He gave the little wealth he had
To build a house for fools and mad;[7]   480
And showed by one satiric touch,
No nation wanted it so much.
That kingdom he hath left his debtor,
I wish it soon may have a better."

1731   1739

From A Tale of a Tub

A Digression Concerning the Original, the Use, and Improvement of Madness in a Commonwealth[1]

Nor shall it any ways detract from the just reputation of his famous sect,[2] that its rise and institution are owing to such an author as I have described Jack to be, a person whose intellectuals were overturned, and his brain shaken out of its natural position; which we commonly suppose to be a distemper, and call by the name of madness or frenzy. For, if we take a survey of the greatest actions that have been performed in the world, under the influence of single men, which are the establishment of new empires by conquest, the advance and progress of new schemes in philosophy, and the contriving, as well as the propagating, of new religions, we shall find the authors of them all to have been persons whose natural reason had admitted great revolutions from their diet, their education, the prevalency of some certain temper, together with the particular influence of air and climate. Besides, there is something

---

7. Swift left funds to endow a hospital for the insane.

1. *A Tale of a Tub*, Swift's first major work, recounts the adventures of three brothers: Peter (Roman Catholicism), Martin (Luther, here regarded as inspiring the Church of England), and Jack (Calvin, the spirit of Protestant dissent). But the most memorable character of the book is its narrator, who interrupts the story with numerous digressions (including even "A Digression in Praise of Digressions"), and whose pride in learning and lack of common sense represent the zealous modern insanity that Swift takes as his target for satire.

"A Digression Concerning Madness," this narrator's masterpiece, is based on Swift's ironical doctrine of "the mechanical operation of the spirit": the notion that all spiritual and mental states derive from physical causes—in this case, the ascent of "vapors" to the brain. Beneath his whimsy, however, the author raises a fearful question: what right has any human being to trust that he is sane?

2. The Aeolists, who "maintain the original cause of all things to be wind," are equated by Swift with religious dissenters who believe themselves to be inspired.

individual in human minds, that easily kindles at the accidental approach and collision of certain circumstances, which, though of paltry and mean appearance, do often flame out into the greatest emergencies of life. For great turns are not always given by strong hands, but by lucky adaption, and at proper seasons; and it is of no import where the fire was kindled, if the vapor has once got up into the brain. For the upper region of man is furnished like the middle region of the air; the materials are formed from causes of the widest difference, yet produce at last the same substance and effect. Mists arise from the earth, steams from dunghills, exhalations from the sea, and smoke from fire; yet all clouds are the same in composition as well as consequences, and the fumes issuing from a jakes[3] will furnish as comely and useful a vapor as incense from an altar. Thus far, I suppose, will easily be granted me; and then it will follow, that as the face of nature never produces rain but when it is overcast and disturbed, so human understanding, seated in the brain, must be troubled and overspread by vapors, ascending from the lower faculties to water the invention and render it fruitful. Now, although these vapors, (as it hath been already said) are of as various original as those of the skies, yet the crop they produce differs both in kind and degree, merely according to the soil. I will produce two instances to prove and explain what I am now advancing.

A certain great prince[4] raised a mighty army, filled his coffers with infinite treasures, provided an invincible fleet, and all this without giving the least part of his design to his greatest ministers or his nearest favorites. Immediately the whole world was alarmed; the neighboring crowns in trembling expectation towards what point the storm would burst; the small politicians everywhere forming profound conjectures. Some believed he had laid a scheme for universal monarchy; others, after much insight, determined the matter to be a project for pulling down the Pope, and setting up the reformed religion, which had once been his own. Some again, of a deeper sagacity, sent him into Asia to subdue the Turk, and recover Palestine. In the midst of all these projects and preparations, a certain state-surgeon,[5] gathering the nature of the disease by these symptoms, attempted the cure, at one blow performed the operation, broke the bag, and out flew the vapor; nor did anything want to render it a complete remedy, only that the prince unfortunately happened to die in the performance. Now, is the reader exceeding curious to learn whence this vapor took its rise, which had so long set the nations at a gaze? What secret wheel, what hidden spring, could put into motion so wonderful an engine? It was afterwards discovered that the movement of this whole machine had been directed by an absent female, whose eyes had raised a protuberancy, and before emission, she was removed into an enemy's country. What should an unhappy prince

---

3. Latrine.
4. "This was Harry the Great of France" [Swift's note]. Henry IV (1553–1610), infatuated with the Princesse de Condé, whose husband had removed her to the Spanish Netherlands, prepared an expedition to bring her back.
5. "Ravillac, who stabbed Henry the Great in his coach" [Swift's note].

do in such ticklish circumstances as these? He tried in vain the poet's
never-failing receipt of *corpora quaeque*;[6] for,

> *Idque petit corpus mens unde est saucia amore:*
> *Unde feritur, eo tendit, gestitque coire.*—LUCRETIUS[7]

Having to no purpose used all peaceable endeavors, the collected part
of the semen, raised and inflamed, became adust, converted to choler,
turned head upon the spinal duct, and ascended to the brain. The very
same principle that influences a bully to break the windows of a whore
who has jilted him, naturally stirs up a great prince to raise mighty armies,
and dream of nothing but sieges, battles, and victories.

> ——*Teterrima belli*
> *Causa*——[8]

The other instance is what I have read somewhere in a very ancient
author, of a mighty king,[9] who, for the space of above thirty years, amused
himself to take and lose towns, beat armies, and be beaten, drive princes
out of their dominions; fright children from their bread and butter; burn,
lay waste, plunder, dragoon, massacre subject and stranger, friend and
foe, male and female. 'Tis recorded, that the philosophers of each country were in grave dispute upon causes natural, moral, and political, to
find out where they should assign an original solution of this phenomenon. At last the vapor or spirit, which animated the hero's brain, being
in perpetual circulation, seized upon that region of the human body, so
renowned for furnishing the *zibeta occidentalis*,[1] and gathering there
into a tumor, left the rest of the world for that time in peace. Of such
mighty consequence it is where those exhalations fix, and of so little
from whence they proceed. The same spirits which, in their superior
progress, would conquer a kingdom, descending upon the anus, conclude in a fistula.[2]

Let us next examine the great introducers of new schemes in philosophy, and search till we can find from what faculty of the soul the disposition arises in mortal man, of taking it into his head to advance new
systems with such an eager zeal, in things agreed on all hands impossible
to be known; from what seeds this disposition springs, and to what quality of human nature these grand innovators have been indebted for their
number of disciples. Because it is plain, that several of the chief among
them, both ancient and modern, were usually mistaken by their adversaries, and indeed by all except their own followers, to have been persons
crazed, or out of their wits; having generally proceeded, in the common

---

6. "Any available bodies."
7. "The body strives for that which sickens the mind
with love. . . . Stretches out toward that which
smites it, and yearns to couple" (*De Rerum Natura*
4.1048 ff.). "Adust": burned up.
8. "The most abominable cause of war" in olden
days, according to Horace, *Satires* 1.3.107–8, was
a whore.
9. "This is meant of the present French king"

[Louis XIV] [Swift's note].
1. "Paracelsus, who was so famous for chemistry,
tried an experiment upon human excrement, to
make a perfume of it, which when he had brought
to perfection, he called *zibeta occidentalis*, or
western-civet, the back parts of man . . . being the
west" [Swift's note].
2. Ulcer shaped like a pipe.

course of their words and actions, by a method very different from the
vulgar dictates of unrefined reason; agreeing for the most part in their
several models, with their present undoubted successors in the academy
of modern Bedlam[3] (whose merits and principles I shall farther examine
in due place). Of this kind were *Epicurus, Diogenes, Apollonius, Lucretius, Paracelsus, Descartes,*[4] and others, who, if they were now in the
world, tied fast, and separate from their followers, would, in this our
undistinguishing age, incur manifest danger of phlebotomy,[5] and whips,
and chains, and dark chambers, and straw. For what man, in the natural
state or course of thinking, did ever conceive it in his power to reduce
the notions of all mankind exactly to the same length, and breadth, and
height of his own? Yet this is the first humble and civil design of all
innovators in the empire of reason. Epicurus modestly hoped, that one
time or other a certain fortuitous concourse of all men's opinions, after
perpetual justlings, the sharp with the smooth, the light and the heavy,
the round and the square, would by certain *clinamina*[6] unite in the
notions of atoms and void, as these did in the originals of all things.
Cartesius reckoned to see, before he died, the sentiments of all philosophers, like so many lesser stars in his romantic system, wrapped and
drawn within his own vortex.[7] Now, I would gladly be informed, how it
is possible to account for such imaginations as these in particular men
without recourse to my phenomenon of vapors, ascending from the lower
faculties to overshadow the brain, and there distilling into conceptions
for which the narrowness of our mother-tongue has not yet assigned any
other name beside that of madness or frenzy. Let us therefore now conjecture how it comes to pass, that none of these great prescribers do ever
fail providing themselves and their notions with a number of implicit
disciples. And, I think, the reason is easy to be assigned: for there is a
peculiar string in the harmony of human understanding, which in several individuals is exactly of the same tuning. This, if you can dexterously screw up to its right key, and then strike gently upon it, whenever
you have the good fortune to light among those of the same pitch, they
will, by a secret necessary sympathy, strike exactly at the same time.
And in this one circumstance lies all the skill or luck of the matter; for
if you chance to jar the string among those who are either above or
below your own height, instead of subscribing to your doctrine, they will
tie you fast, call you mad, and feed you with bread and water. It is
therefore a point of the nicest conduct to distinguish and adapt this noble
talent, with respect to the differences of persons and of times. Cicero
understood this very well, when writing to a friend in England, with a
caution, among other matters, to beware of being cheated by our hack-

---

3. Bethlehem hospital, London's lunatic asylum.
4. Each of these famous speculative thinkers was
known as a materialist, hence suspected by Swift
of encouraging atheism.
5. Medical blood-letting.
6. Swerves. The Greek philosopher Epicurus held
that the universe was formed by atoms swerving

together; Swift implies that a similar miracle would
be required for men to join in agreement with Epicurus.
7. The physics of René Descartes (1596–1650) is
based on a theory of vortices; Swift considered the
theory pure romance.

ney-coachmen (who, it seems, in those days were as arrant rascals as
they are now), has these remarkable words: *Est quod gaudeas te in ista
loca venisse, ubi aliquid sapere viderere.*[8] For, to speak a bold truth, it is
a fatal miscarriage so ill to order affairs, as to pass for a fool in one
company, when in another you might be treated as a philosopher. Which
I desire some certain gentlemen of my acquaintance to lay up in their
hearts, as a very seasonable *innuendo.*

This, indeed, was the fatal mistake of that worthy gentleman, my
most ingenious friend, Mr. W—tt—n,[9] a person, in appearance, ordained
for great designs, as well as performances; whether you will consider his
notions or his looks. Surely no man ever advanced into the public with
fitter qualifications of body and mind, for the propagation of a new religion. Oh, had those happy talents, misapplied to vain philosophy, been
turned into their proper channels of dreams and visions, where distortion of mind and countenance are of such sovereign use, the base
detracting world would not then have dared to report that something is
amiss, that his brain has undergone an unlucky shake; which even his
brother modernists themselves, like ungrates, do whisper so loud, that it
reaches up to the very garret I am now writing in.

Lastly, whosoever pleases to look into the fountains of enthusiasm,[1]
from whence, in all ages, have eternally proceeded such fattening streams,
will find the springhead to have been as troubled and muddy as the
current. Of such great emolument is a tincture of this vapor, which the
world calls madness, that without its help, the world would not only be
deprived of those two great blessings, conquests and systems, but even
all mankind would unhappily be reduced to the same belief in things
invisible. Now, the former *postulatum* being held, that it is of no import
from what originals this vapor proceeds, but either in what angles it
strikes and spreads over the understanding, or upon what species of brain
it ascends; it will be a very delicate point to cut the feather, and divide
the several reasons to a nice and curious reader, how this numerical
difference in the brain can produce effects of so vast a difference from
the same vapor, as to be the sole point of individuation between Alexander the Great, Jack of Leyden[2] and Monsieur Descartes. The present
argument is the most abstracted that ever I engaged in; it strains my
faculties to their highest stretch; and I desire the reader to attend with
utmost perpensity; for I now proceed to unravel this knotty point.

There is in mankind a certain[3]   ·   ·   ·   ·   ·

---

8. "It is ground for rejoicing that you have come
to such places, where anyone can seem wise"
(Cicero, *Familiar Epistles* 7.10).
9. William Wotton (who had championed modern authors against Swift's patron, Sir William
Temple, a spokesman for the ancients) is ridiculed
in Swift's *Battle of the Books,* published in the same
volume as *A Tale of a Tub* (1704).
1. For much of the 18th century the word
"enthusiasm" (literally, "possessed by a god") signified a deluded belief in personal revelation.
2. John of Leyden, a tailor and prophet, briefly

established a revolutionary Anabaptist community, the "New Jerusalem," in the city of Münster
early in the 16th century.
3. "Here is another defect in the manuscript, but
I think the author did wisely, and that the matter
which thus strained his faculties, was not worth a
solution; and it were well if all metaphysical cobweb problems were no otherwise answered" [Swift's
note]. The Latin phrase ("Much is missing here")
indicates a gap in the text Swift pretends to be
"editing."

•   •   •   •   •   •   •   •   •

Hic multa   •   •   •   •   •   •
desiderantur.   •   •   •   •   •

•   •   •   •   •   And this I take to be a clear
solution of the matter.

Having therefore so narrowly passed through this intricate difficulty,
the reader will, I am sure, agree with me in the conclusion, that if the
moderns mean by madness, only a disturbance or transposition of the
brain, by force of certain vapors issuing up from the lower faculties, then
has this madness been the parent of all those mighty revolutions that
have happened in empire, in philosophy, and in religion. For the brain,
in its natural position and state of serenity, disposeth its owner to pass
his life in the common forms, without any thought of subduing multitudes to his own power, his reasons, or his visions; and the more he
shapes his understanding by the pattern of human learning, the less he
is inclined to form parties after his particular notions, because that instructs
him in his private infirmities, as well as in the stubborn ignorance of the
people. But when a man's fancy gets astride on his reason, when imagination is at cuffs with the senses, and common understanding, as well
as common sense, is kicked out of doors, the first proselyte he makes is
himself; and when that is once compassed, the difficulty is not so great
in bringing over others; a strong delusion always operating from without
as vigorously as from within. For cant[4] and vision are to the ear and the
eye, the same that tickling is to the touch. Those entertainments and
pleasures we most value in life, are such as dupe and play the wag with
the senses. For, if we take an examination of what is generally understood by happiness, as it has respect either to the understanding or the
senses, we shall find all its properties and adjuncts will herd under this
short definition, that it is a perpetual possession of being well deceived.
And first, with relation to the mind or understanding, 'tis manifest what
mighty advantages fiction has over truth; and the reason is just at our
elbow, because imagination can build nobler scenes, and produce more
wonderful revolutions, than fortune or nature will be at expense to furnish. Nor is mankind so much to blame in his choice thus determining
him, if we consider that the debate merely lies between things past and
things conceived; and so the question is only this: whether things that
have place in the imagination, may not as properly be said to exist, as
those that are seated in the memory; which may be justly held in the
affirmative, and very much to the advantage of the former, since this is
acknowledged to be the womb of things, and the other allowed to be no
more than the grave. Again, if we take this definition of happiness, and
examine it with reference to the senses, it will be acknowledged wonderfully adapt. How fading and insipid do all objects accost us, that are not
conveyed in the vehicle of delusion! How shrunk is everything, as it
appears in the glass of nature! So that if it were not for the assistance of

---

4. "Sudden exclamations, whining, unusual tones,   unlearned of the Presbyterians" (*Spectator* 147).
and in fine all praying and preaching like the

artificial mediums, false lights, refracted angles, varnish, and tinsel, there would be a mighty level in the felicity and enjoyments of mortal men. If this were seriously considered by the world, as I have a certain reason to suspect it hardly will, men would no longer reckon among their high points of wisdom, the art of exposing weak sides, and publishing infirmities; an employment, in my opinion, neither better nor worse than that of unmasking, which, I think, has never been allowed[5] fair usage, either in the world, or the playhouse.

In the proportion that credulity is a more peaceful possession of the mind than curosity, so far preferable is that wisdom, which converses about the surface, to that pretended philosophy which enters into the depth of things, and then comes gravely back with informations and discoveries, that in the inside they are good for nothing. The two senses, to which all objects first address themselves, are the sight and the touch; these never examine farther than the color, the shape, the size, and whatever other qualities dwell, or are drawn by art upon the outward of bodies; and then comes reason officiously with tools for cutting, and opening, and mangling, and piercing, offering to demonstrate, that they are not of the same consistence quite through. Now I take all this to be the last degree of perverting nature; one of whose eternal laws it is, to put her best furniture forward. And therefore, in order to save the charges of all such expensive anatomy for the time to come, I do here think fit to inform the reader, that in such conclusions as these, reason is certainly in the right, and that in most corporeal beings, which have fallen under my cognizance, the outside has been infinitely preferable to the in; whereof I have been farther convinced from some late experiments. Last week I saw a woman flayed, and you will hardly believe how much it altered her person for the worse. Yesterday I ordered the carcass of a beau to be stripped in my presence; when we were all amazed to find so many unsuspected faults under one suit of clothes. Then I laid open his brain, his heart, and his spleen; but I plainly perceived at every operation, that the farther we proceeded, we found the defects increase upon us in number and bulk; from all which, I justly formed this conclusion to myself: that whatever philosopher or projector[6] can find out an art to solder and patch up the flaws and imperfections of nature, will deserve much better of mankind, and teach us a more useful science, than that so much in present esteem, of widening and exposing them (like him who held anatomy to be the ultimate end of physic).[7] And he, whose fortunes and dispositions have placed him in a convenient station to enjoy the fruits of this noble art; he that can with Epicurus content his ideas with the films and images that fly off upon his senses from the superficies[8] of things; such a man, truly wise, creams off nature, leaving the sour and the dregs for philosophy and reason to lap up. This is the

5. Admitted to be.
6. Someone given to speculative experiments.
7. Medical practice.

8. Surfaces. Epicurus considered the senses, directly affected by objects, more trustworthy than reason.

sublime and refined point of felicity, called the possession of being well deceived; the serene peaceful state of being a fool among knaves.

But to return to madness. It is certain, that according to the system I have above deduced, every species thereof proceeds from a redundancy of vapors; therefore, as some kinds of frenzy give double strength to the sinews, so there are of other species, which add vigor, and life, and spirit to the brain. Now, it usually happens, that these active spirits, getting possession of the brain, resemble those that haunt other waste and empty dwellings, which for want of business, either vanish, and carry away a piece of the house, or else stay at home and fling it all out of the windows. By which are mystically displayed the two principal branches of madness, and which some philosophers, not considering so well as I, have mistaken to be different in their causes, over-hastily assigning the first to deficiency, and the other to redundance.

I think it therefore manifest, from what I have here advanced, that the main point of skill and address is to furnish employment for this redundancy of vapor, and prudently to adjust the season of it; by which means it may certainly become of cardinal and catholic emolument, in a commonwealth. Thus one man, choosing a proper juncture, leaps into a gulf, from thence proceeds a hero, and is called the saver of his country; another achieves the same enterprise, but unluckily timing it, has left the brand of madness fixed as a reproach upon his memory; upon so nice a distinction, are we taught to repeat the name of Curtius[9] with reverence and love, that of Empedocles with hatred and contempt. Thus also it is usually conceived, that the elder Brutus only personated the fool and madman for the good of the public; but this was nothing else than a redundancy of the same vapor long misapplied, called by the Latins, *ingenium par negotiis*;[1] or (to translate it as nearly as I can) a sort of frenzy, never in its right element, till you take it up in business of the state.

Upon all which, and many other reasons of equal weight, though not equally curious, I do here gladly embrace an opportunity I have long sought for, of recommending it as a very noble undertaking to Sir Edward Seymour, Sir Christopher Musgrave, Sir John Bowls, John How, Esq.,[2] and other patriots concerned, that they would move for leave to bring in a bill for appointing commissioners to inspect into Bedlam, and the parts adjacent; who shall be empowered to send for persons, papers, and records, to examine into the merits and qualifications of every student and professor, to observe with utmost exactness their several dispositions and behavior, by which means, duly distinguishing and adapting their talents, they might produce admirable instruments for the several offices

9. The Roman hero Marcus Curtius appeased the gods by hurling himself into an ominous crack in the earth of the Forum; Empedocles committed suicide by leaping into the crater of Mount Etna.

1. "A talent for business." Lucius Junius Brutus, like Hamlet, pretended madness to deceive his murderous uncle, Tarquin the Proud.
2. Members of Parliament.

in a state, . . . ,[3] civil, and military, proceeding in such methods as I shall here humbly propose. And I hope the gentle reader will give some allowance to my great solicitudes in this important affair, upon account of the high esteem I have borne that honorable society, whereof I had some time the happiness to be an unworthy member.

Is any student tearing his straw in piece-meal, swearing and blaspheming, biting his grate, foaming at the mouth, and emptying his piss-pot in the spectators' faces? Let the right worshipful the commissioners of inspection give him a regiment of dragoons, and send him into Flanders among the rest. Is another eternally talking, sputtering, gaping, bawling in a sound without period or article? What wonderful talents are here mislaid! Let him be furnished immediately with a green bag and papers, and threepence in his pocket,[4] and away with him to Westminster Hall. You will find a third gravely taking the dimensions of his kennel, a person of foresight and insight, though kept quite in the dark; for why, like Moses, *ecce cornuta erat ejus facies.*[5] He walks duly in one pace, entreats your penny with due gravity and ceremony, talks much of hard times, and taxes, and the whore of Babylon, bars up the wooden window of his cell constantly at eight o'clock, dreams of fire, and shop-lifters, and court-customers, and privileged places. Now, what a figure would all these acquirements amount to, if the owner were sent into the city[6] among his brethren! Behold a fourth, in much and deep conversation with himself, biting his thumbs at proper junctures, his countenance checkered with business and design, sometimes walking very fast, with his eyes nailed to a paper that he holds in his hands; a great saver of time, somewhat thick of hearing, very short of sight, but more of memory; a man ever in haste, a great hatcher and breeder of business, and excellent at the famous art of whispering nothing; a huge idolator of monosyllables and procrastination, so ready to give his word to everybody, that he never keeps it; one that has forgot the common meaning of words, but an admirable retainer of the sound; extremely subject to the looseness,[7] for his occasions are perpetually calling him away. If you approach his grate in his familiar intervals, "Sir," says he, "give me a penny, and I'll sing you a song; but give me the penny first." (Hence comes the common saying, and commoner practice, of parting with money for a song.) What a complete system of court skill is here described in every branch of it, and all utterly lost with wrong application! Accost the hole of another kennel, first stopping your nose, you will behold a surly, gloomy, nasty, slovenly mortal, raking in his own dung, and dabbling in his urine. The best part of his diet is the reversion of his own ordure, which expiring into steams, whirls perpetually about, and at last

---

3. Swift omits the third office, Ecclesiastical. "Instruments": useful persons.
4. "A lawyer's coach-hire" [Swift's note] from the Inns of Court to Westminster. Most lawyers carried green bags.
5. "Cornutus is either horned or shining, and by this term, Moses is described in the vulgar Latin

of the Bible" [Swift's note]. Swift puns on the Latin phrase ("Behold his face was shining") by suggesting someone kept in the dark through being "horned," i.e., a cuckold.
6. The commercial center of London.
7. Diarrhea.

re-infunds. His complexion is of a dirty yellow, with a thin scattered beard, exactly agreeable to that of his diet upon its first declination, like other insects, who having their birth and education in an excrement, from thence borrow their color and their smell. The student of this apartment is very sparing of his words, but somewhat over-liberal of his breath; he holds his hand out ready to receive your penny, and immediately upon receipt withdraws to his former occupations. Now, is it not amazing to think, the society of Warwick-lane[8] should have no more concern for the recovery of so useful a member, who, if one may judge from these appearances, would become the greatest ornament to that illustrious body? Another student struts up fiercely to your teeth, puffing with his lips, half squeezing out his eyes, and very graciously holds you out his hand to kiss. The keeper desires you not to be afraid of this professor, for he will do you no hurt; to him alone is allowed the liberty of the antechamber, and the orator of the place gives you to understand, that this solemn person is a tailor run mad with pride. This considerable student is adorned with many other qualities, upon which at present I shall not farther enlarge.------*Hark in your ear*[9]------I am strangely mistaken, if all his address, his motions, and his airs, would not then be very natural, and in their proper element.

I shall not descend so minutely, as to insist upon the vast number of beaux, fiddlers, poets, and politicians, that the world might recover by such a reformation; but what is more material, besides the clear gain redounding to the commonwealth, by so large an acquisition of persons to employ, whose talents and acquirements, if I may be so bold as to affirm it, are now buried, or at least misapplied; it would be a mighty advantage accruing to the public from this inquiry, that all these would very much excel, and arrive at great perfection in their several kinds; which, I think, is manifest from what I have already shown, and shall enforce by this one plain instance: that even I myself, the author of these momentous truths, am a person, whose imaginations are hard-mouthed,[1] and exceedingly disposed to run away with his reason, which I have observed from long experience to be a very light rider, and easily shook off; upon which account, my friends will never trust me alone, without a solemn promise to vent my speculations in this, or the like manner, for the universal benefit of human kind; which perhaps the gentle, courteous, and candid reader, brimful of that modern charity and tenderness usually annexed to his office, will be very hardly persuaded to believe.

1704

Gulliver's Travels

Gulliver's Travels is Swift's most universal satire. Although it is full of allusions to recent and contemporary historical events,

---

8. Royal College of Physicians.
9. "I cannot conjecture what the author means here, or how this chasm could be filled, though it is capable of more than one interpretation" [Swift's note].
1. (Of a horse) apt to reject control by the bit.

it is as valid today as it was in 1726, for its objects are man's moral nature and the defective political, economic, and social institutions which human imperfections call into being. Swift adopts an ancient satirical device: the imaginary voyage. Lemuel Gulliver, the narrator, is a ship's surgeon, a reasonably well-educated man, kindly, resourceful, cheerful, inquiring, patriotic, truthful, and rather unimaginative. He is, in short, a reasonably decent example of humanity, with whom we identify ourselves readily enough. He undertakes four voyages, all of which end disastrously among "several remote nations of the world." In the first, Gulliver is shipwrecked in the empire of Lilliput, where he finds himself a giant among a diminutive people, charmed by their miniature city and amused by their toylike prettiness. But in the end they prove to be treacherous, malicious, ambitious, vengeful, and cruel. As we read we grow disenchanted with the inhabitants of this fanciful kingdom, and then gradually we begin to recognize our likeness to them, especially in the disproportion between our natural pettiness and our boundless and destructive passions. In the second voyage, Gulliver is abandoned by his shipmates in Brobdingnag, a land of giants, creatures ten times as large as Europeans. Naturally enough, he assumes that such monsters must be brutes, but the reverse proves to be the case. Brobdingnag is something of a utopia, governed by a humane and enlightened prince who is the embodiment of moral and political wisdom. In the long interview in which Gulliver pridefully enlarges on the glories of England and her political institutions, the King reduces him to resentful silence by asking questions which reveal the difference between what is and what ought to be in human, especially British, institutions. In Brobdingnag, Gulliver finds himself a Lilliputian, his pride humbled by his helpless state and his human vanity diminished by the realization that his body must have seemed as disgusting to the Lilliputians as do the bodies of the Brobdingnagians to him.

In the third voyage, to Laputa, Swift is chiefly concerned with attacking extremes of theoretical and speculative reasoning, whether in science, politics, or economics. Much of this voyage is an allegory of political life under the administration of the Whig minister, Sir Robert Walpole. The final voyage sets Gulliver between a race of horses, Houyhnhnms (prounced *Hwínims*), who live entirely by reason except for a few well-controlled and muted social affections, and their slaves, the Yahoos, whose bodies are obscene caricatures of the human body, and who have no glimmer of reason, but are mere creatures of appetite and passion.

When *Gulliver's Travels* first appeared, everyone read it—children for the story, politicians for the satire of current affairs—and ever since it has retained a hold on readers of every kind. Almost unique in world literature, it is simple enough for a child, complex enough to carry an adult beyond his depth. Swift's art works on many levels. First of all, there is the sheer playfulness of the narrative. Through Gulliver's eyes, we gaze on marvel after marvel: a tiny girl who threads an invisible needle with invisible silk, or a white mare who threads a needle between pastern and hoof. The travels, like a fairy story, transport us to imaginary worlds that function with a perfect, fantastic logic different from our own; Swift exercises our sense of vision. But beyond that, he exercises our perceptions of meaning. In *Gulliver's Travels*, things are seldom what they seem; irony, probing or corrosive, underlies almost every word. During the last chapter, Gulliver insists that the example of the Houyhnhnms has made him incapable of telling a lie— but the oath he swears is quoted from Sinon, whose lies to the Trojans persuaded them to accept the Trojan *horse*. Swift trains us to read alertly, to look beneath the surface. Yet on its deepest level, the book does not offer final meanings, but a question: what sort of thing is man? Voyaging through imaginary worlds, we try to find ourselves. Are we prideful insects, or lords of creation? brutes, or reasonable beings? In the last voyage, Swift pushes such questions, and Gulliver himself, almost beyond endurance; hating his own humanity, Gulliver forgets who he is. For the reader, however, the outcome cannot be so clear. Swift does not set out to satisfy our minds, but to vex and unsettle them. And he leaves us at the moment when the mixed face of humanity—the pettiness of the Lilliputians, the savagery of the Yahoos, the innocence of Gulliver himself—begins to look strangely familiar, like our own faces in a mirror.

From Gulliver's Travels[1]

A Letter from Captain Gulliver to His Cousin Sympson

I hope you will be ready to own publicly, whenever you shall be called to it, that by your great and frequent urgency you prevailed on me to publish a very loose and uncorrect account of my travels; with direction to hire some young gentlemen of either University to put them in order, and correct the style, as my Cousin Dampier[2] did by my advice, in his book called A *Voyage round the World*. But I do not remember I gave you power to consent that anything should be omitted, and much less that anything should be inserted: therefore, as to the latter, I do here renounce everything of that kind; particularly a paragraph about her Majesty the late Queen Anne, of most pious and glorious memory; although I did reverence and esteem her more than any of human species. But you, or your interpolator, ought to have considered that as it was not my inclination, so was it not decent to praise any animal of our composition before my master Houyhnhnm; and besides, the fact was altogether false; for to my knowledge, being in England during some part of her Majesty's reign, she did govern by a chief Minister; nay, even by two successively; the first whereof was the Lord of Godolphin, and the second the Lord of Oxford; so that you have made me *say the thing that was not*. Likewise, in the account of the Academy of Projectors, and several passages of my discourse to my master Houyhnhnm, you have either omitted some material circumstances, or minced or changed them in such a manner, that I do hardly know mine own work. When

1. Swift's full title for this work was *Travels into Several Remote Nations of the World. In Four Parts. By Lemuel Gulliver, First a Surgeon, and then a Captain of several Ships*. In the first edition (1726), either the bookseller or Swift's friends Charles Ford, Pope, and others, who were concerned in getting the book anonymously into print, altered and omitted so much of the original manuscript (because of its dangerous political implications) that Swift was seriously annoyed. When, in 1735, the Dublin bookseller George Faulkner brought out an edition of Swift's works, the dean seems to have taken pains, surreptitiously, to see that a more authentic version of the work was published. This text is the basis of modern editions.

In this letter, first published in 1735, Swift complains, among other matters, of the alterations in his original text made by the publisher, Benjamin Motte, in the interest of what he considered political discretion.

2. William Dampier (1652–1715), the explorer, whose account of his circumnavigation of the globe Swift had read.

I formerly hinted to you something of this in a letter, you were pleased to answer that you were afraid of giving offense; that people in power were very watchful over the press; and apt not only to interpret, but to punish everything which looked like an *innuendo* (as I think you called it). But pray, how could that which I spoke so many years ago, and at above five thousand leagues distance, in another reign, be applied to any of the Yahoos, who now are said to govern the herd; especially, at a time when I little thought on or feared the unhappiness of living under them. Have not I the most reason to complain, when I see these very Yahoos carried by Houyhnhnms in a vehicle, as if these were brutes, and those the rational creatures? And, indeed, to avoid so monstrous and detestable a sight was one principal motive of my retirement hither.[3]

Thus much I thought proper to tell you in relation to yourself, and to the trust I reposed in you.

I do in the next place complain of my own great want of judgment, in being prevailed upon by the intreaties and false reasonings of you and some others, very much against mine own opinion, to suffer my travels to be published. Pray bring to your mind how often I desired you to consider, when you insisted on the motive of public good, that the Yahoos were a species of animals utterly incapable of amendment by precepts or examples; and so it hath proved; for instead of seeing a full stop put to all abuses and corruptions, at least in this little island, as I had reason to expect, behold, after above six months warning, I cannot learn that my book hath produced one single effect according to mine intentions; I desired you would let me know by a letter, when party and faction were extinguished; judges learned and upright; pleaders honest and modest, with some tincture of common sense; and Smithfield[4] blazing with pyramids of law books; the young nobility's education entirely changed; the physicians banished; the female Yahoos abounding in virtue, honor, truth, and good sense; courts and levees of great ministers thoroughly weeded and swept; wit, merit, and learning rewarded; all disgracers of the press in prose and verse, condemned to eat nothing but their own cotton,[5] and quench their thirst with their own ink. These, and a thousand other reformations, I firmly counted upon by your encouragement; as indeed they were plainly deducible from the precepts delivered in my book. And, it must be owned that seven months were a sufficient time to correct every vice and folly to which Yahoos are subject; if their natures had been capable of the least disposition to virtue or wisdom; yet so far have you been from answering mine expectation in any of your letters, that on the contrary, you are loading our carrier every week with libels, and keys, and reflections, and memoirs, and second parts; wherein I see myself accused of reflecting upon great statesfolk; of degrading human nature (for so they have still the confidence to style it) and of abusing the female sex. I find likewise, that the writers of those bundles are not

3. To Nottinghamshire.   5. Presumably their paper.
4. A part of London containing many bookshops.

agreed among themselves; for some of them will not allow me to be author of mine own travels; and others make me author of books to which I am wholly a stranger.

I find likewise that your printer hath been so careless as to confound the times, and mistake the dates of my several voyages and returns; neither assigning the true year, or the true month, or day of the month; and I hear the original manuscript is all destroyed, since the publication of my book. Neither have I any copy left; however, I have sent you some corrections, which you may insert, if ever there should be a second edition; and yet I cannot stand to them, but shall leave that matter to my judicious and candid readers, to adjust it as they please.

I hear some of our sea Yahoos find fault with my sea language, as not proper in many parts, nor now in use. I cannot help it. In my first voyages, while I was young, I was instructed by the oldest mariners, and learned to speak as they did. But I have since found that the sea Yahoos are apt, like the land ones, to become new fangled in their words; which the latter change every year; insomuch, as I remember upon each return to mine own country, their old dialect was so altered, that I could hardly understand the new. And I observe, when any Yahoo comes from London out of curiosity to visit me at mine own house, we neither of us are able to deliver our conceptions in a manner intelligible to the other.[6]

If the censure of Yahoos could any way affect me, I should have great reason to complain that some of them are so bold as to think my book of travels a mere fiction out of mine own brain; and have gone so far as to drop hints that the Houyhnhnms, and Yahoos have no more existence than the inhabitants of Utopia.

Indeed I must confess that as to the people of Lilliput, Brobdingrag (for so the word should have been spelled, and not erroneously Brobdingnag) and Laputa, I have never yet heard of any Yahoo so presumptuous as to dispute their being, or the facts I have related concerning them; because the truth immediately strikes every reader with conviction. And, is there less probability in my account of the Houyhnhnms or Yahoos, when it is manifest as to the latter, there are so many thousands even in this city, who only differ from their brother brutes in Houyhnhnmland, because they use a sort of a jabber, and do not go naked. I wrote for their amendment, and not their approbation. The united praise of the whole race would be of less consequence to me, than the neighing of those two degenerate Houyhnhnms I keep in my stable; because, from these, degenerate as they are, I still improve in some virtues, without any mixture of vice.

Do these miserable animals presume to think that I am so far degenerated as to defend my veracity; Yahoo as I am, it is well known through all Houyhnhnmland, that by the instructions and example of my illustrious master, I was able in the compass of two years (although I confess

---

6. Swift was the inveterate enemy of slang.

with the utmost difficulty) to remove that infernal habit of lying, shuffling, deceiving, and equivocating, so deeply rooted in the very souls of
all my species; especially the Europeans.

I have other complaints to make upon this vexatious occasion; but I
forbear troubling myself or you any further. I must freely confess that
since my last return, some corruptions of my Yahoo nature have revived
in me by conversing with a few of your species, and particularly those of
mine own family, by an unavoidable necessity; else I should never have
attempted so absurd a project as that of reforming the Yahoo race in this
kingdom; but I have now done with all such visionary schemes for ever.

1727?   1735

The Publisher to the Reader

The author of these travels, Mr. Lemuel Gulliver, is my ancient and
intimate friend; there is likewise some relation between us by the mother's side. About three years ago Mr. Gulliver, growing weary of the concourse of curious people coming to him at his house in Redriff,[1] made
a small purchase of land, with a convenient house, near Newark, in
Nottinghamshire, his native country; where he now lives retired, yet in
good esteem among his neighbors.

Although Mr. Gulliver were born in Nottinghamshire, where his father
dwelt, yet I have heard him say his family came from Oxfordshire; to
confirm which, I have observed in the churchyard at Banbury, in that
county, several tombs and monuments of the Gullivers.

Before he quitted Redriff, he left the custody of the following papers
in my hands, with the liberty to dispose of them as I should think fit. I
have carefully perused them three times; the style is very plain and simple; and the only fault I find is that the author, after the manner of
travelers, is a little too circumstantial. There is an air of truth apparent
through the whole; and indeed the author was so distinguished for his
veracity, that it became a sort of proverb among his neighbors at Redriff,
when anyone affirmed a thing, to say, it was as true as if Mr. Gulliver
had spoke it.

By the advice of several worthy persons, to whom, with the author's
permission, I communicated these papers, I now venture to send them
into the world; hoping they may be, at least for some time, a better
entertainment to our young noblemen, than the common scribbles of
politics and party.

This volume would have been at least twice as large, if I had not made
bold to strike out innumerable passages relating to the winds and tides,
as well as to the variations and bearings in the several voyages; together
with the minute descriptions of the management of the ship in storms,
in the style of sailors; likewise the account of the longitudes and lati-
tudes, wherein I have reason to apprehend that Mr. Gulliver may be a

1. Rotherhithe, a district in southern London, below Tower Bridge, then frequented by sailors.

little dissatisfied; but I was resolved to fit the work as much as possible to the general capacity of readers. However, if my own ignorance in sea affairs shall have led me to commit some mistakes, I alone am answerable for them; and if any traveler hath a curiosity to see the whole work at large, as it came from the hand of the author, I will be ready to gratify him.

As for any further particulars relating to the author, the reader will receive satisfaction from the first pages of the book.

RICHARD SYMPSON

Part 1. A Voyage to Lilliput

CHAPTER 1. *The author gives some account of himself and family; his first inducements to travel. He is shipwrecked, and swims for his life; gets safe on shore in the country of Lilliput; is made a prisoner, and carried up the country.*

My father had a small estate in Nottinghamshire; I was the third of five sons. He sent me to Emanuel College in Cambridge, at fourteen years old, where I resided three years, and applied myself close to my studies: but the charge of maintaining me (although I had a very scanty allowance) being too great for a narrow fortune, I was bound apprentice to Mr. James Bates, an eminent surgeon in London, with whom I continued four years; and my father now and then sending me small sums of money, I laid them out in learning navigation, and other parts of the mathematics, useful to those who intend to travel, as I always believed it would be some time or other my fortune to do. When I left Mr. Bates, I went down to my father; where, by the assistance of him and my uncle John, and some other relations, I got forty pounds, and a promise of thirty pounds a year to maintain me at Leyden:[1] there I studied physic two years and seven months, knowing it would be useful in long voyages.

Soon after my return from Leyden, I was recommended by my good master Mr. Bates, to be surgeon to the *Swallow*, Captain Abraham Pannell commander; with whom I continued three years and a half, making a voyage or two into the Levant[2] and some other parts. When I came back, I resolved to settle in London, to which Mr. Bates, my master, encouraged me; and by him I was recommended to several patients. I took part of a small house in the Old Jury; and being advised to alter my condition, I married Mrs.[3] Mary Burton, second daughter to Mr. Edmond Burton, hosier, in Newgate Street, with whom I received four hundred pounds for a portion.

But, my good master Bates dying in two years after, and I having few friends, my business began to fail; for my conscience would not suffer

---

1. The University of Leyden, in Holland, a center for the study of "physic" (medicine).
2. The eastern Mediterranean.

3. "Mrs." (pronounced "Mistress") designated any woman, married or unmarried. "Old Jury": a street (once "Old Jewry") in the City of London.

me to imitate the bad practice of too many among my brethren. Having therefore consulted with my wife, and some of my acquaintance, I determined to go again to sea. I was surgeon successively in two ships, and made several voyages, for six years, to the East and West Indies; by which I got some addition to my fortune. My hours of leisure I spent in reading the best authors, ancient and modern, being always provided with a good number of books; and when I was ashore, in observing the manners and dispositions of the people, as well as learning their language; wherein I had a great facility by the strength of my memory.

The last of these voyages not proving very fortunate, I grew weary of the sea, and intended to stay at home with my wife and family. I removed from the Old Jury to Fetter Lane, and from thence to Wapping, hoping to get business among the sailors; but it would not turn to account. After three years' expectation that things would mend, I accepted an advantageous offer from Captain William Prichard, master of the *Antelope*, who was making a voyage to the South Sea. We set sail from Bristol, May 4th, 1699, and our voyage at first was very prosperous.

It would not be proper, for some reasons, to trouble the reader with the particulars of our adventures in those seas: let it suffice to inform him, that in our passage from thence to the East Indies we were driven by a violent storm to the northwest of Van Diemen's Land.[4] By an observation, we found ourselves in the latitude of 30 degrees 2 minutes south. Twelve of our crew were dead by immoderate labor, and ill food, the rest were in a very weak condition. On the fifth of November, which was the beginning of summer in those parts, the weather being very hazy, the seamen spied a rock, within half a cable's length of the ship; but the wind was so strong, that we were driven directly upon it, and immediately split. Six of the crew, of whom I was one, having let down the boat into the sea, made a shift to get clear of the ship, and the rock. We rowed by my computation about three leagues, till we were able to work no longer, being already spent with labor while we were in the ship. We therefore trusted ourselves to the mercy of the waves; and in about half an hour the boat was overset by a sudden flurry from the north. What became of my companions in the boat, as well as of those who escaped on the rock, or were left in the vessel, I cannot tell; but conclude they were all lost. For my own part, I swam as fortune directed me, and was pushed forward by wind and tide. I often let my legs drop, and could feel no bottom; but when I was almost gone, and able to struggle no longer, I found myself within my depth; and by this time the storm was much abated. The declivity was so small, that I walked near a mile before I got to the shore, which I conjectured was about eight o'clock in the evening. I then advanced forward near half a mile, but could not discover any sign of houses or inhabitants; at least I was in so weak a condition, that I did not observe them. I was extremely tired, and with that, and the heat of the weather, and about half a pint of

4. Tasmania.

brandy that I drank as I left the ship, I found myself much inclined to sleep. I lay down on the grass, which was very short and soft, where I slept sounder than ever I remember to have done in my life, and as I reckoned, above nine hours; for when I awaked, it was just daylight. I attempted to rise, but was not able to stir: for as I happened to lie on my back, I found my arms and legs were strongly fastened on each side to the ground; and my hair, which was long and thick, tied down in the same manner. I likewise felt several slender ligatures across my body, from my armpits to my thighs. I could only look upwards; the sun began to grow hot, and the light offended my eyes. I heard a confused noise about me, but in the posture I lay, could see nothing except the sky. In a little time I felt something alive moving on my left leg, which advancing gently forward over my breast, came almost up to my chin; when bending my eyes downwards as much as I could, I perceived it to be a human creature not six inches high,[5] with a bow and arrow in his hands, and a quiver at his back. In the meantime, I felt at least forty more of the same kind (as I conjectured) following the first. I was in the utmost astonishment, and roared so loud, that they all ran back in a fright; and some of them, as I was afterwards told, were hurt with the falls they got by leaping from my sides upon the ground. However, they soon returned; and one of them, who ventured so far as to get a full sight of my face, lifting up his hands and eyes by way of admiration,[6] cried out in a shrill, but distinct voice, *Hekinah Degul:* the others repeated the same words several times, but I then knew not what they meant. I lay all this while, as the reader may believe, in great uneasiness; at length, struggling to get loose, I had the fortune to break the strings, and wrench out the pegs that fastened my left arm to the ground; for, by lifting it up to my face, I discovered the methods they had taken to bind me; and, at the same time, with a violent pull, which gave me excessive pain, I a little loosened the strings that tied down my hair on the left side; so that I was just able to turn my head about two inches. But the creatures ran off a second time, before I could seize them; whereupon there was a great shout in a very shrill accent; and after it ceased, I heard one of them cry aloud, *Tolgo phonac;* when in an instant I felt above an hundred arrows discharged on my left hand, which pricked me like so many needles; and besides they shot another flight into the air, as we do bombs in Europe, whereof many, I suppose, fell on my body (though I felt them not) and some on my face, which I immediately covered with my left hand. When this shower of arrows was over, I fell a groaning with grief and pain; and then striving again to get loose, they discharged another volley larger than the first, and some of them attempted with spears to stick me in the sides; but, by good luck, I had on me a buff jerkin,[7] which they could not pierce. I thought it the most prudent method to lie still; and my design was to continue so till night, when, my left hand being already loose, I could easily free myself: and as for the inhabitants, I had reason

5. Lilliput is scaled, fairly consistently, at one-twelfth of Gulliver's world.
6. Wonderment.
7. Leather jacket.

to believe I might be a match for the greatest armies they could bring
against me, if they were all of the same size with him that I saw. But
fortune disposed otherwise of me. When the people observed I was quiet,
they discharged no more arrows: but by the noise increasing, I knew
their numbers were greater; and about four yards from me, over-against
my right ear, I heard a knocking for above an hour, like people at work;
when turning my head that way, as well as the pegs and strings would
permit me, I saw a stage erected about a foot and a half from the ground,
capable of holding four of the inhabitatnts, with two or three ladders to
mount it: from whence one of them, who seemed to be a person of
quality, made me a long speech, whereof I understood not one syllable.
But I should have mentioned, that before the principal person began his
oration, he cried out three times, *Langro Dehul san:* (these words and
the former were afterwards repeated and explained to me). Whereupon
immediately about fifty of the inhabitants came, and cut the strings that
fastened the left side of my head, which gave me the liberty of turning
it to the right, and of observing the person and gesture of him who was
to speak. He appeared to be of a middle age, and taller than any of the
other three who attended him; whereof one was a page who held up his
train, and seemed to be somewhat longer than my middle finger; the
other two stood one on each side to support him. He acted every part of
an orator, and I could observe many periods[8] of threatenings, and others
of promises, pity and kindness. I answered in a few words, but in the
most submissive manner, lifting up my left hand and both my eyes to
the sun, as calling him for a witness; and being almost famished with
hunger, having not eaten a morsel for some hours before I left the ship,
I found the demands of nature so strong upon me, that I could not
forbear showing my impatience (perhaps against the strict rules of decency)
by putting my finger frequently on my mouth, to signify that I wanted
food. The Hurgo (for so they call a great lord, as I afterwards learned)
understood me very well. He descended from the stage, and commanded that several ladders should be applied to my sides, on which
above an hundred of the inhabitants mounted, and walked towards my
mouth, laden with baskets full of meat, which had been provided and
sent thither by the King's orders upon the first intelligence he received
of me. I observed there was the flesh of several animals, but could not
distinguish them by the taste. There were shoulders, legs, and loins shaped
like those of mutton, and very well dressed, but smaller than the wings
of a lark. I eat them by two or three at a mouthful, and took three loaves
at a time, about the bigness of musket bullets. They supplied me as fast
as they could, showing a thousand marks of wonder and astonishment
at my bulk and appetite. I then made another sign that I wanted drink.
They found by my eating that a small quantity would not suffice me;
and being a most ingenious people, they slung up with great dexterity
one of their largest hogsheads; then rolled it towards my hand, and beat

8. In rhetoric, complete, well-constructed sentences.

out the top; I drank it off at a draught, which I might well do, for it hardly held half a pint, and tasted like a small wine of Burgundy, but much more delicious. They brought me a second hogshead, which I drank in the same manner, and made signs for more, but they had none to give me. When I had performed these wonders, they shouted for joy, and danced upon my breast, repeating several times as they did at first, *Hekinah Degul*. They made me a sign that I should throw down the two hogsheads, but first warned the people below to stand out of the way, crying aloud, *Borach Mivola*, and when they saw the vessels in the air, there was an universal shout of *Hekinah Degul*. I confess I was often tempted, while they were passing backwards and forwards on my body, to seize forty or fifty of the first that came in my reach, and dash them against the ground. But the remembrance of what I had felt, which probably might not be the worst they could do; and the promise of honor I made them, for so I interpreted my submissive behavior, soon drove out those imaginations. Besides, I now considered myself as bound by the laws of hospitality to a people who had treated me with so much expense and magnificence. However, in my thoughts I could not sufficiently wonder at the intrepidity of these diminutive mortals, who durst venture to mount and walk on my body, while one of my hands was at liberty, without trembling at the very sight of so prodigious a creature as I must appear to them. After some time, when they observed that I made no more demands for meat, there appeared before me a person of high rank from his Imperial Majesty. His Excellency, having mounted on the small of my right leg, advanced forwards up to my face, with about a dozen of his retinue. And producing his credentials under the Signet Royal, which he applied[9] close to my eyes, spoke about ten minutes, without any signs of anger, but with a kind of determinate resolution; often pointing forwards, which, as I afterwards found, was towards the capital city, about half a mile distant, whither it was agreed by his Majesty in council that I must be conveyed. I answered in a few words, but to no purpose, and made a sign with my hand that was loose, putting it to the other (but over his Excellency's head, for fear of hurting him or his train) and then to my own head and body, to signify that I desired my liberty. It appeared that he understood me well enough; for he shook his head by way of disapprobation, and held his hand in a posture to show that I must be carried as a prisoner. However, he made other signs to let me understand that I should have meat and drink enough, and very good treatment. Whereupon I once more thought of attempting to break my bonds; but again, when I felt the smart of their arrows upon my face and hands, which were all in blisters, and many of the darts still sticking in them; and observing likewise that the number of my enemies increased; I gave tokens to let them know that they might do with me what they pleased. Upon this the *Hurgo* and his train withdrew, with much civility and cheerful countenances. Soon after I heard a general

9. Brought.

shout, with frequent repetitions of the words, *Peplom Selan*, and I felt great numbers of the people on my left side relaxing the cords to such a degree, that I was able to turn upon my right, and to ease myself with making water; which I very plentifully did, to the great astonishment of the people, who conjecturing by my motions what I was going to do, immediately opened to the right and left on that side, to avoid the torrent which fell with such noise and violence from me. But before this, they had daubed my face and both my hands with a sort of ointment very pleasant to the smell, which in a few minutes removed all the smart of their arrows. These circumstances, added to the refreshment I had received by their victuals and drink, which were very nourishing, disposed me to sleep. I slept about eight hours, as I was afterwards assured; and it was no wonder; for the physicians, by the Emperor's order, had mingled a sleeping potion in the hogsheads of wine.

It seems that upon the first moment I was discovered sleeping on the ground after my landing, the Emperor had early notice of it by an express; and determined in council that I should be tied in the manner I have related (which was done in the night while I slept), that plenty of meat and drink should be sent me, and a machine prepared to carry me to the capital city.

This resolution perhaps may appear very bold and dangerous, and I am confident would not be imitated by any prince in Europe on the like occasion; however, in my opinion it was extremely prudent as well as generous. For supposing these people had endeavored to kill me with their spears and arrows while I was asleep; I should certainly have awaked with the first sense of smart, which might so far have roused my rage and strength, as to enable me to break the strings wherewith I was tied; after which, as they were not able to make resistance, so they could expect no mercy.

These people are most excellent mathematicians, and arrived to a great perfection in mechanics by the countenance and encouragement of the Emperor, who is a renowned patron of learning. This prince hath several machines fixed on wheels, for the carriage of trees and other great weights. He often builds his largest men of war, whereof some are nine foot long, in the woods where the timber grows, and has them carried on these engines[1] three or four hundred yards to the sea. Five hundred carpenters and engineers were immediately set at work to prepare the greatest engine they had. It was a frame of wood raised three inches from the ground, about seven foot long and four wide, moving upon twenty-two wheels. The shout I heard was upon the arrival of this engine, which it seems set out in four hours after my landing. It was brought parallel to me as I lay. But the principal difficulty was to raise and place me in this vehicle. Eighty poles, each of one foot high, were erected for this purpose, and very strong cords of the bigness of packthread were fastened by hooks to many bandages, which the workmen had girt round my

---

1. Contrivances.

neck, my hands, my body, and my legs. Nine hundred of the strongest men were employed to draw up these cords by many pulleys fastened on the poles; and thus, in less than three hours, I was raised and slung into the engine, and there tied fast. All this I was told, for while the whole operation was performing, I lay in a profound sleep, by the force of that soporiferous[2] medicine infused into my liquor. Fifteen hundred of the Emperor's largest horses, each about four inches and a half high, were employed to draw me towards the metropolis, which, as I said, was half a mile distant.

About four hours after we began our journey, I awaked by a very ridiculous accident; for, the carriage being stopped a while to adjust something that was out of order, two or three of the young natives had the curiosity to see how I looked when I was asleep; they climbed up into the engine, and advancing very softly to my face, one of them, an officer in the guards, put the sharp end of his half-pike a good way up into my left nostril, which tickled my nose like a straw, and made me sneeze violently: whereupon they stole off unperceived, and it was three weeks before I knew the cause of my awaking so suddenly. We made a long march the remaining part of the day, and rested at night with five hundred guards on each side of me half with torches, and half with bows and arrows, ready to shoot me if I should offer to stir. The next morning at sunrise we continued our march, and arrived within two hundred yards of the city gates about noon. The Emperor and all his court came out to meet us, but his great officers would by no means suffer his Majesty to endanger his person by mounting on my body.

At the place where the carriage stopped, there stood an ancient temple, esteemed to be the largest in the whole kingdom, which having been polluted some years before by an unnatural murder,[3] was, according to the zeal of those people, looked on as profane, and therefore had been applied to common use, and all the ornaments and furniture carried away. In this edifice it was determined I should lodge. The great gate fronting to the north was about four foot high, and almost two foot wide, through which I could easily creep. On each side of the gate was a small window not above six inches from the ground: into that on the left side, the King's smiths conveyed fourscore and eleven chains, like those that hang to a lady's watch in Europe, and almost as large, which were locked to my left leg with six and thirty padlocks. Over against this temple, on the other side of the great highway, at twenty foot distance, there was a turret at least five foot high. Here the Emperor ascended with many principal lords of his court, to have an opportunity of viewing me, as I was told, for I could not see them. It was reckoned that above an hundred thousand inhabitants came out of the town upon the same errand; and in spite of my guards, I believe there could not be fewer than ten thousand, at several times, who mounted upon my body by the help of ladders. But a proclamation was soon issued to forbid it upon pain of

2. Inducing unnatural sleep.
3. Presumably a reference to the execution of

Charles I, who was sentenced in Westminster Hall.

death. When the workmen found it was impossible for me to break loose, they cut all the strings that bound me; whereupon I rose up with as melancholy a disposition as ever I had in my life. But the noise and astonishment of the people at seeing me rise and walk are not to be expressed. The chains that held my left leg were about two yards long, and gave me not only the liberty of walking backwards and forwards in a semicircle; but, being fixed within four inches of the gate, allowed me to creep in, and lie at my full length in the temple.

CHAPTER 2. *The Emperor of Lilliput, attended by several of the nobility, comes to see the author in his confinement. The Emperor's person and habit described. Learned men appointed to teach the author their language. He gains favor by his mild disposition. His pockets are searched, and his sword and pistols taken from him.*

When I found myself on my feet, I looked about me, and must confess I never beheld a more entertaining prospect. The country round appeared like a continued garden, and the inclosed fields, which were generally forty foot square, resembled so many beds of flowers. These fields were intermingled with woods of half a stang,[4] and the tallest trees, as I could judge, appeared to be seven foot high. I viewed the town on my left hand, which looked like the painted scene of a city in a theater.

I had been for some hours extremely pressed by the necessities of nature; which was no wonder, it being almost two days since I had last disburthened myself. I was under great difficulties between urgency and shame. The best expedient I could think on, was to creep into my house, which I accordingly did; and shutting the gate after me, I went as far as the length of my chain would suffer; and discharged my body of that uneasy load. But this was the only time I was ever guilty of so uncleanly an action; for which I cannot but hope the candid reader will give some allowance, after he hath maturely and impartially considered my case, and the distress I was in. From this time my constant practice was, as soon as I rose, to perform that business in open air, at the full extent of my chain, and due care was taken every morning before company came, that the offensive matter should be carried off in wheelbarrows by two servants appointed for that purpose. I would not have dwelt so long upon a circumstance, that perhaps at first sight may appear not very momentous, if I had not thought it necessary to justify my character in point of cleanliness to the world; which I am told some of my maligners have been pleased, upon this and other occasions, to call in question.

When this adventure was at an end, I came back out of my house, having occasion for fresh air. The Emperor was already descended from the tower, and advancing on horseback towards me, which had like to have cost him dear; for the beast, although very well trained, yet wholly unused to such a sight, which appeared as if a mountain moved before

4. A quarter of an acre.

him, reared up on his hinder feet: but that prince, who is an excellent horseman, kept his seat, until his attendants ran in, and held the bridle, while his Majesty had time to dismount. When he alighted, he surveyed me round with great admiration, but kept beyond the length of my chains. He ordered his cooks and butlers, who were already prepared, to give me victuals and drink, which they pushed forward in a sort of vehicles upon wheels until I could reach them. I took these vehicles, and soon emptied them all; twenty of them were filled with meat, and ten with liquor; each of the former afforded me two or three good mouthfuls, and I emptied the liquor of ten vessels, which was contained in earthen vials, into one vehicle, drinking it off at a draught; and so I did with the rest. The Empress, and young princes of the blood, of both sexes, attended by many ladies, sat at some distance in their chairs; but upon the accident that happened to the Emperor's horse, they alighted, and came near his person; which I am now going to describe. He is taller, by almost the breadth of my nail, than any of his court, which alone is enough to strike an awe into the beholders. His features are strong and masculine, with an Austrian lip, and arched nose, his complexion olive, his countenance[5] erect, his body and limbs well proportioned, all his motions graceful, and his deportment majestic. He was then past his prime, being twenty-eight years and three quarters old, of which he had reigned about seven, in great felicity, and generally victorious. For the better convenience of beholding him, I lay on my side, so that my face was parallel to his, and he stood but three yards off: however, I have had him since many times in my hand, and therefore cannot be deceived in the description. His dress was very plain and simple, the fashion of it between the Asiatic and the European; but he had on his head a light helmet of gold, adorned with jewels, and a plume on the crest. He held his sword drawn in his hand, to defend himself, if I should happen to break loose; it was almost three inches long, the hilt and scabbard were gold enriched with diamonds. His voice was shrill, but very clear and articulate, and I could distinctly hear it when I stood up. The ladies and courtiers were all most magnificently clad, so that the spot they stood upon seemed to resemble a petticoat spread on the ground, embroidered with figures of gold and silver. His Imperial Majesty spoke often to me, and I returned answers, but neither of us could understand a syllable. There were several of his priests and lawyers present (as I conjectured by their habits) who were commanded to address themselves to me, and I spoke to them in as many languages as I had the least smattering of, which were High and Low Dutch,[6] Latin, French, Spanish, Italian, and Lingua Franca; but all to no purpose. After about two hours the court retired, and I was left with a strong guard, to prevent the impertinence, and probably the malice of the rabble, who were very impatient to crowd about me as near as they durst; and some of them had the impudence to

---

5. Bearing, appearance. Swift is satirically idealizing George I, whom most of the British thought gross.

6. German and Dutch; "lingua franca": a jargon, based on Italian, used by traders in the Mediterranean.

shoot their arrows at me as I sat on the ground by the door of my house, whereof one very narrowly missed my left eye. But the colonel ordered six of the ringleaders to be seized, and thought no punishment so proper as to deliver them bound into my hands, which some of his soldiers accordingly did, pushing them forwards with the butt-ends of their pikes into my reach; I took them all in my right hand, put five of them into my coat-pocket; and as to the sixth, I made a countenance as if I would eat him alive. The poor man squalled terribly, and the colonel and his officer were in much pain, especially when they saw me take out my penknife: but I soon put them out of fear; for, looking mildly, and immediately cutting the strings he was bound with, I set him gently on the ground, and away he ran. I treated the rest in the same manner, taking them one by one out of my pocket, and I observed both the soldiers and people were highly obliged at this mark of my clemency, which was represented very much to my advantage at court.

Towards night I got with some difficulty into my house, where I lay on the ground, and continued to do so about a fortnight; during which time the Emperor gave orders to have a bed prepared for me. Six hundred beds of the common measure were brought in carriages, and worked up in my house; an hundred and fifty of their beds sewn together made up the breadth and length, and these were four double, which however kept me but very indifferently from the hardness of the floor, that was of smooth stone. By the same computation they provided me with sheets, blankets, and coverlets, tolerable enough for one who had been so long enured to hardships as I.

As the news of my arrival spread through the kingdom, it brought prodigious numbers of rich, idle, and curious people to see me; so that the villages were almost emptied, and great neglect of tillage and household affairs must have ensued, if his Imperial Majesty had not provided by several proclamations and orders of state against this inconveniency. He directed that those who had already beheld me should return home, and not presume to come within fifty yards of my house without license from court; whereby the secretaries of state got considerable fees.

In the mean time, the Emperor held frequent councils to debate what course should be taken with me; and I was afterwards assured by a particular friend, a person of great quality, who was as much in the secret as any, that the court was under many difficulties concerning me. They apprehended[7] my breaking loose, that my diet would be very expensive, and might cause a famine. Sometimes they determined to starve me, or at least to shoot me in the face and hands with poisoned arrows, which would soon dispatch me: but again they considered, that the stench of so large a carcass might produce a plague in the metropolis, and probably spread through the whole kingdom. In the midst of these consultations, several officers of the army went to the door of the great council chamber; and two of them being admitted, gave an account of my behavior

7. Anticipated with fear.

to the six criminals above-mentioned; which made so favorable an impression in the breast of his Majesty, and the whole board, in my behalf, that an imperial commission was issued out, obliging all the villages nine hundred yards round the city to deliver in every morning six beeves, forty sheep, and other victuals for my sustenance; together with a proportionable quantity of bread and wine, and other liquors: for the due payment of which his Majesty gave assignments[8] upon his treasury. For this prince lives chiefly upon his own demesnes; seldom except upon great occasions raising any subsidies upon his subjects, who are bound to attend him in his wars at their own expense. An establishment was also made of six hundred persons to be my domestics, who had board-wages allowed for their maintenance, and tents built for them very conveniently on each side of my door. It was likewise ordered, that three hundred tailors should make me a suit of clothes after the fashion of the country: that six of his Majesty's greatest scholars should be employed to instruct me in their language: and, lastly, that the Emperor's horses, and those of the nobility, and troops of guards, should be exercised in my sight, to accustom themselves to me. All these orders were duly put in execution; and in about three weeks I made a great progress in learning their language; during which time the Emperor frequently honored me with his visits, and was pleased to assist my masters in teaching me. We began already to converse together in some sort; and the first words I learned, were to express my desire that he would please to give me my liberty; which I every day repeated on my knees.[9] His answer, as I could apprehend, was, that this must be a work of time, not to be thought on without the advice of his council; and that first I must *Lumos kelmin pesso desmar lon emposo*; that is, swear a peace with him and his kingdom. However, that I should be used with all kindness; and he advised me to acquire by my patience and discreet behavior, the good opinion of himself and his subjects. He desired I would not take it ill, if he gave orders to certain proper officers to search me; for probably I might carry about me several weapons, which must needs be dangerous things, if they answered the bulk of so prodigious a person.[1] I said, his Majesty should be satisfied, for I was ready to strip myself, and turn up my pockets before him. This I delivered part in words, and part in signs. He replied, that by the laws of the kingdom, I must be searched by two of his officers; that he knew this could not be done without my consent and assistance; that he had so good an opinion of my generosity and justice, as to trust their persons in my hands; that whatever they took from me should be returned when I left the country, or paid for at the rate which I would set upon them. I took up the two officers in my hands, put them first into my coat-pockets, and then into every other pocket about me,

8. Formal mandates of revenue.

9. Gulliver's plea for liberty, and the threat of starvation or rebellion he represents to his captors, suggest the situation of Ireland with respect to England.

1. When the Whigs came into power in 1715, the leading Tories, who included Swift's friends Oxford and Bolingbroke (Robert Harley and Henry St. John) as well as Swift himself, were investigated by a Committee of Secrecy.

except my two fobs, and another secret pocket which I had no mind should be searched, wherein I had some little necessaries of no consequence to any but myself. In one of my fobs there was a silver watch, and in the other a small quantity of gold in a purse. These gentlemen, having pen, ink, and paper about them, made an exact inventory of everything they saw; and when they had done, desired I would set them down, that they might deliver it to the Emperor. This inventory I afterwards translated into English, and is word for word as follows.

Imprimis, In the right coat-pocket of the Great Man-Mountain (for so I interpret the words *Quinbus Flestrin*) after the strictest search, we found only one great piece of coarse cloth, large enough to be a foot-cloth for your Majesty's chief room of state. In the left pocket, we saw a huge silver chest, with a cover of the same metal, which we the searchers were not able to lift. We desired it should be opened; and one of us, stepping into it, found himself up to the mid leg in a sort of dust, some part whereof flying up to our faces, set us both a sneezing for several times together. In his right waistcoat-pocket, we found a prodigious bundle of white thin substances, folded one over another, about the bigness of three men, tied with a strong cable, and marked with black figures; which we humbly conceive to be writings; every letter almost half as large as the palm of our hands. In the left there was a sort of engine, from the back of which were extended twenty long poles, resembling the palisados[2] before your Majesty's court; wherewith we conjecture the Man-Mountain combs his head; for we did not always trouble him with questions, because we found it a great difficulty to make him understand us. In the large pocket on the right side of his middle cover (so I translate the word *ranfu-lo*, by which they meant my breeches) we saw a hollow pillar of iron, about the length of a man, fastened to a strong piece of timber, larger than the pillar; and upon one side of the pillar were huge pieces of iron sticking out, cut into strange figures; which we know not what to make of. In the left pocket, another engine of the same kind. In the smaller pocket on the right side, were several round flat pieces of white and red metal, of different bulk; some of the white, which seemed to be silver, were so large and heavy, that my comrade and I could hardly lift them. In the left pocket were two black pillars irregularly shaped: we could not, without difficulty, reach the top of them as we stood at the bottom of his pocket. One of them was covered, and seemed all of a piece; but at the upper end of the other, there appeared a white round substance, about twice the bigness of our heads. Within each of these was inclosed a prodigious plate of steel; which, by our orders, we obliged him to show us, because we apprehended they might be dangerous engines. He took them out of their cases, and told us,

2. Fences of stakes.

that in his own country his practice was to shave his beard with one
of these, and to cut his meat with the other. There were two pockets
which we could not enter: these he called his fobs; they were two
large slits cut into the top of his middle cover, but squeezed close
by the pressure of his belly. Out of the right fob hung a great silver
chain, with a wonderful kind of engine at the bottom. We directed
him to draw out whatever was at the end of the chain, which appeared
to be a globe, half silver, and half of some transparent metal: for on
the transparent side we saw certain strange figures circularly drawn,
and thought we could touch them, until we found our fingers stopped
with that lucid substance. He put this engine to our ears, which
made an incessant noise like that of a watermill. And we conjecture
it is either some unknown animal, or the god that he worships: but
we are more inclined to the latter opinion, because he assured us
(if we understood him right, for he expressed himself very imperfectly), that he seldom did any thing without consulting it. He called
it his oracle, and said it pointed out the time for every action of his
life. From the left fob he took out a net almost large enough for a
fisherman, but contrived to open and shut like a purse, and served
him for the same use: we found therein several massy pieces of
yellow metal, which if they be of real gold, must be of immense
value.

Having thus, in obedience to your Majesty's commands, diligently searched all his pockets, we observed a girdle[3] about his waist
made of the hide of some prodigious animal; from which, on the
left side, hung a sword of the length of five men; and on the right,
a bag or pouch divided into cells; each cell capable of holding three
of your Majesty's subjects. In one of these cells were several globes
or balls of a most ponderous metal, about the bigness of our heads,
and required a strong hand to lift them: the other cell contained a
heap of certain black grains, but of no great bulk or weight, for we
could hold above fifty of them in the palms of our hands.

This is an exact inventory of what we found about the body of
the Man-Mountain; who used us with great civility, and due respect
to your Majesty's commission. Signed and sealed on the fourth day
of the eighty-ninth moon of your Majesty's auspicious reign.

CLEFREN FRELOCK, MARSI FRELOCK.

When this inventory was read over to the Emperor, he directed me to
deliver up the several particulars. He first called for my scimitar, which
I took out, scabbard and all. In the meantime he ordered three thousand
of his choicest troops (who then attended him) to surround me at a
distance, with their bows and arrows just ready to discharge: but I did
not observe it; for my eyes were wholly fixed upon his Majesty. He then
desired me to draw my scimitar, which, although it had got some rust
by the sea water, was in most parts exceeding bright. I did so, and imme-

3. Belt.

diately all the troops gave a shout between terror and surprise; for the sun shone clear, and the reflection dazzled their eyes, as I waved the scimitar to and fro in my hand. His Majesty, who is a most magnanimous[4] prince, was less daunted than I could expect; he ordered me to return it into the scabbard, and cast it on the ground as gently as I could, about six foot from the end of my chain. The next thing he demanded was one of the hollow iron pillars, by which he meant my pocket-pistols. I drew it out, and at his desire, as well as I could, expressed to him the use of it, and charging it only with powder, which by the closeness of my pouch happened to escape wetting in the sea (an inconvenience that all prudent mariners take special care to provide against), I first cautioned the Emperor not to be afraid; and then I let it off in the air. The astonishment here was much greater than at the sight of my scimitar. Hundreds fell down as if they had been struck dead; and even the Emperor, although he stood his ground, could not recover himself in some time. I delivered up both my pistols in the same manner as I had done my scimitar, and then my pouch of powder and bullets; begging him that the former might be kept from fire; for it would kindle with the smallest spark, and blow up his imperial palace into the air. I likewise delivered up my watch, which the Emperor was very curious to see; and commanded two of his tallest yeomen of the guards to bear it on a pole upon their shoulders, as draymen in England do a barrel of ale. He was amazed at the continual noise it made, and the motion of the minute-hand, which he could easily discern; for their sight is much more acute than ours: he asked the opinions of his learned men about him, which were various and remote, as the reader may well imagine without my repeating; although indeed I could not very perfectly understand them. I then gave up my silver and copper money, my purse with nine large pieces of gold, and some smaller ones; my knife and razor, my comb and silver snuffbox, my handkerchief and journal book. My scimitar, pistols, and pouch, were conveyed in carriages to his Majesty's stores; but the rest of my goods were returned me.

I had, as I before observed, one private pocket which escaped their search, wherein there was a pair of spectacles (which I sometimes use for the weakness of my eyes), a pocket perspective,[5] and several other little conveniences; which, being of no consequence to the Emperor, I did not think myself bound in honor to discover, and I apprehended they might be lost or spoiled if I ventured them out of my possession.

CHAPTER 3. *The author diverts the Emperor and his nobility of both sexes in a very uncommon manner. The diversions of the court of Lilliput described. The author hath his liberty granted him upon certain conditions.*

---

4. Courageous, great-spirited. Magnanimity, the relation (direct or inverse) between the size of the body and the soul, is a central concern of the first two parts of the *Travels*.
5. Telescope.

My gentleness and good behavior had gained so far on the Emperor and his court, and indeed upon the army and people in general, that I began to conceive hopes of getting my liberty in a short time. I took all possible methods to cultivate this favorable disposition. The natives came by degrees to be less apprehensive of any danger from me. I would sometimes lie down, and let five or six of them dance on my hand. And at last the boys and girls would venture to come and play at hide-and-seek in my hair. I had now made a good progress in understanding and speaking their language. The Emperor had a mind one day to entertain me with several of the country shows; wherein they exceed all nations I have known, both for dexterity and magnificence. I was diverted with none so much as that of the rope-dancers, performed upon a slender white thread, extended about two foot, and twelve inches from the ground. Upon which I shall desire liberty, with the reader's patience, to enlarge a little.

This diversion is only practiced by those persons who are candidates for great employments, and high favor, at court. They are trained in this art from their youth, and are not always of noble birth, or liberal education. When a great office is vacant either by death or disgrace (which often happens) five or six of those candidates petition the Emperor to entertain his Majesty and the court with a dance on the rope; and whoever jumps the highest without falling, succeeds in the office. Very often the chief ministers themselves are commanded to show their skill, and to convince the Emperor that they have not lost their faculty. Flimnap,[6] the Treasurer, is allowed to cut a caper on the strait rope, at least an inch higher than any other lord in the whole empire. I have seen him do the summerset several times together upon a trencher[7] fixed on the rope, which is no thicker than a common packthread in England. My friend Reldresal, Principal Secretary for Private Affairs, is, in my opinion, if I am not partial, the second after the Treasurer; the rest of the great officers are much upon a par.

These diversions are often attended with fatal accidents, whereof great numbers are on record. I myself have seen two or three candidates break a limb. But the danger is much greater when the ministers themselves are commanded to show their dexterity; for, by contending to excel themselves and their fellows, they strain so far, that there is hardly one of them who hath not received a fall; and some of them two or three. I was assured, that a year or two before my arrival, Flimnap would have infallibly broke his neck, if one of the King's cushions,[8] that accidentally lay on the ground, had not weakened the force of his fall.

There is likewise another diversion, which is only shown before the Emperor and Empress, and first minister, upon particular occasions. The Emperor lays on a table three fine silken threads of six inches long.

6. Sir Robert Walpole, the Whig head of the government, notorious in Swift's circle for his political acrobatics.

7. Plate; "summerset": somersault.
8. A mistress of George I was supposed to have helped restore Walpole to office in 1721.

One is blue, the other red, and the third green.[9] These threads are proposed as prizes for those persons whom the Emperor hath a mind to distinguish by a peculiar mark of his favor. The ceremony is performed in his Majesty's great chamber of state; where the candidates are to undergo a trial of dexterity very different from the former, and such as I have not observed the least resemblance of in any other country of the old or the new world. The Emperor holds a stick in his hands, both ends parallel to the horizon, while the candidates, advancing one by one, sometimes leap over the stick, sometimes creep under it backwards and forwards several times, according as the stick is advanced or depressed. Sometimes the Emperor holds one end of the stick, and his first minister the other; sometimes the minister has it entirely to himself. Whoever performs his part with most agility, and holds out the longest in *leaping* and *creeping*, is rewarded with the blue-colored silk; the red is given to the next, and the green to the third, which they all wear girt twice round about the middle; and you see few great persons about this court who are not adorned with one of these girdles.

The horses of the army, and those of the royal stables, having been daily led before me, were no longer shy, but would come up to my very feet, without starting. The riders would leap them over my hand as I held it on the ground; and one of the Emperor's huntsmen, upon a large courser, took[1] my foot, shoe and all; which was indeed a prodigious leap. I had the good fortune to divert the Emperor one day after a very extraordinary manner. I desired he would order several sticks of two foot high, and the thickness of an ordinary cane, to be brought me; whereupon his Majesty commanded the master of his woods to give directions accordingly; and the next morning six woodmen arrived with as many carriages, drawn by eight horses to each. I took nine of these sticks, and fixing them firmly in the ground in a quadrangular figure, two foot and a half square, I took four other sticks, and tied them parallel at each corner, about two foot from the ground; then I fastened my handkerchief to the nine sticks that stood erect, and extended it on all sides till it was as tight as the top of a drum; and the four parallel sticks, rising about five inches higher than the handkerchief, served as ledges on each side. When I had finished my work, I desired the Emperor to let a troop of his best horse, twenty-four in number, come and exercise upon this plain. His Majesty approved of the proposal, and I took them up one by one in my hands, ready mounted and armed, with the proper officers to exercise them. As soon as they got into order, they divided into two parties, performed mock skirmishes, discharged blunt arrows, drew their swords, fled and pursued, attacked and retired; and in short discovered the best military discipline I ever beheld. The parallel sticks secured them and their horses from falling over the stage; and the Emperor was so much delighted, that he ordered this entertainment to be repeated several days; and once was pleased to be lifted up, and give the word of

9. The Orders of the Garter, the Bath, and the Thistle, conferred for services to the King.

1. Jumped over.

command; and, with great difficulty, persuaded even the Empress herself to let me hold her in her close chair[2] within two yards of the stage, from whence she was able to take a full view of the whole performance. It was my good fortune that no ill accident happened in these entertainments, only once a fiery horse that belonged to one of the captains pawing with his hoof struck a hole in my handkerchief, and his foot slipping, he overthrew his rider and himself; but I immediately relieved them both; for covering the hole with one hand, I set down the troop with the other, in the same manner as I took them up. The horse that fell was strained in the left shoulder, but the rider got no hurt, and I repaired my handkerchief as well as I could; however, I would not trust to the strength of it any more in such dangerous enterprises.

About two or three days before I was set at liberty, as I was entertaining the court with these kinds of feats, there arrived an express to inform his Majesty that some of his subjects, riding near the place where I was first taken up, had seen a great black substance lying on the ground, very oddly shaped, extending its edges round as wide as his Majesty's bed-chamber, and rising up in the middle as high as a man; that it was no living creature, as they at first apprehended, for it lay on the grass without motion, and some of them had walked round it several times; that by mounting upon each other's shoulders, they had got to the top, which was flat and even; and stamping upon it they found it was hollow within; that they humbly conceived it might be something belonging to the Man-Mountain, and if his Majesty pleased, they would undertake to bring it with only five horses. I presently[3] knew what they meant; and was glad at heart to receive this intelligence. It seems upon my first reaching the shore after our shipwreck, I was in such confusion, that before I came to the place where I went to sleep, my hat, which I had fastened with a string to my head while I was rowing, and had stuck on all the time I was swimming, fell off after I came to land; the string, as I conjecture, breaking by some accident which I never observed, but thought my hat had been lost at sea. I intreated his Imperial Majesty to give orders it might be brought to me as soon as possible, describing to him the use and the nature of it: and the next day the wagoners arrived with it, but not in a very good condition; they had bored two holes in the brim, within an inch and half of the edge, and fastened two hooks in the holes; these hooks were tied by a long cord to the harness, and thus my hat was dragged along for above half an English mile: but the ground in that country being extremely smooth and level, it received less damage than I expected.

Two days after this adventure, the Emperor, having ordered that part of his army which quarters in and about his metropolis to be in a readiness, took a fancy of diverting himself in a very singular manner. He desired I would stand like a colossus, with my legs as far asunder as I conveniently could. He then commanded his general (who was an old

2. An enclosed or sedan chair.   3. Immediately.

experienced leader, and a great patron of mine) to draw up the troops in close order, and march them under me; the foot[4] by twenty-four in a breast, and the horse by sixteen, with drums beating, colors flying, and pikes advanced. This body consisted of three thousand foot, and a thousand horse. His Majesty gave orders, upon pain of death, that every soldier in his march should observe the strictest decency with regard to my person; which, however, could not prevent some of the younger officers from turning up their eyes as they passed under me. And, to confess the truth, my breeches were at that time in so ill a condition, that they afforded some opportunities for laughter and admiration.

I had sent so many memorials and petitions for my liberty, that his Majesty at length mentioned the matter first in the cabinet, and then in a full council; where it was opposed by none, except Skyresh Bolgolam,[5] who was pleased, without any provocation, to be my mortal enemy. But it was carried against him by the whole board, and confirmed by the Emperor. That minister was *Galbet*, or Admiral of the Realm; very much in his master's confidence, and a person well versed in affairs, but of a morose and sour complexion.[6] However, he was at length persuaded to comply; but prevailed that the articles and conditions upon which I should be set free, and to which I must swear, should be drawn up by himself. These articles were brought to me by Skyresh Bolgolam in person, attended by two under-secretaries, and several persons of distinction. After they were read, I was demanded to swear to the performance of them; first in the manner of my own country, and afterwards in the method prescribed by their laws; which was to hold my right foot in my left hand, to place the middle finger of my right hand on the crown of my head, and my thumb on the tip of my right ear. But because the reader may perhaps be curious to have some idea of the style and manner of expression peculiar to that people, as well as to know the articles upon which I recovered my liberty, I have made a translation of the whole instrument,[7] word for word, as near as I was able; which I here offer to the public.

GOLBASTO MOMAREN EVLAME GURDILO SHEFIN MULLY ULLY GUE, most mighty Emperor of Lilliput, delight and terror of the universe, whose dominions extend five thousand blustrugs (about twelve miles in circumference) to the extremities of the globe; Monarch of all Monarchs; taller than the sons of men; whose feet press down to the center, and whose head strikes against the sun; at whose nod the princes of the earth shake their knees; pleasant as the spring, comfortable as the summer, fruitful as autumn, dreadful as winter. His most sublime Majesty proposeth to the Man-Mountain, lately arrived at our celestial dominions, the following articles, which by a solemn oath he shall be obliged to perform.

4. Foot-soldiers or infantry.
5. The earl of Nottingham, an enemy of Swift.
6. Disposition.
7. A formal legal document.

First, The Man-Mountain shall not depart from our dominions, without our license under our great seal.

Secondly, He shall not presume to come into our metropolis, without our express order; at which time the inhabitants shall have two hours warning, to keep within their doors.

Thirdly, The said Man-Mountain shall confine his walks to our principal high roads; and not offer to walk or lie down in a meadow, or field of corn.

Fourthly, As he walks the said roads, he shall take the utmost care not to trample upon the bodies of any of our loving subjects, their horses, or carriages, nor take any of our said subjects into his hands, without their own consent.

Fifthly, If an express require extraordinary dispatch, the Man-Mountain shall be obliged to carry in his pocket the messenger and horse, a six days' journey once in every moon, and return the said messenger back (if so required) safe to our Imperial Presence.

Sixthly, He shall be our ally against our enemies in the island of Blefuscu, and do his utmost to destroy their fleet, which is now preparing to invade us.

Seventhly, That the said Man-Mountain shall, at his times of leisure, be aiding and assisting to our workmen, in helping to raise certain great stones, towards covering the wall of the principal park, and other our royal buildings.

Eighthly, That the said Man-Mountain shall, in two moons' time, deliver in an exact survey of the circumference of our dominions by a computation of his own paces round the coast.

Lastly, That upon his solemn oath to observe all the above articles, the said Man-Mountain shall have a daily allowance of meat and drink sufficient for the support of 1,728 of our subjects; with free access to our Royal Person, and other marks of our favor. Given at our palace at Belfaborac the twelfth day of the ninety-first moon of our reign.

I swore and subscribed to these articles with great cheerfulness and content, although some of them were not so honorable as I could have wished; which proceeded wholly from the malice of Skyresh Bolgolam the High Admiral: whereupon my chains were immediately unlocked, and I was at full liberty: the Emperor himself in person did me the honor to be by at the whole ceremony. I made my acknowledgements by prostrating myself at his Majesty's feet: but he commanded me to rise; and after many gracious expressions, which, to avoid the censure of vanity, I shall not repeat, he added, that he hoped I should prove a useful servant, and well deserve all the favors he had already conferred upon me, or might do for the future.

The reader may please to observe, that in the last article for the recovery of my liberty, the Emperor stipulates to allow me a quantity of meat and drink, sufficient for the support of 1,728 Lilliputians. Some time after, asking a friend at court how they came to fix on that determinate number, he told me, that his Majesty's mathematicians, having taken the height of my body by the help of a quadrant, and finding it to exceed theirs in the proportion of twelve to one, they concluded from the similarity of their bodies, that mine must contain at least 1,728 of theirs, and consequently would require as much food as was necessary to support that number of Lilliputians. By which, the reader may conceive an idea of the ingenuity of that people, as well as the prudent and exact economy of so great a prince.

CHAPTER 4. *Mildendo, the metropolis of Lilliput, described, together with the Emperor's palace. A conversation between the author and a principal secretary, concerning the affairs of that empire; the author's offers to serve the Emperor in his wars.*

The first request I made after I had obtained my liberty, was, that I might have license to see Mildendo, the metropolis; which the Emperor easily granted me, but with a special charge to do no hurt, either to the inhabitants, or their houses. The people had notice by proclamation of my design to visit the town. The wall which encompassed it is two foot and an half high, and at least eleven inches broad, so that a coach and horses may be driven very safely round it; and it is flanked with strong towers at ten foot distance. I stepped over the great western gate, and passed very gently, and sideling[8] through the two principal streets, only in my short waistcoat, for fear of damaging the roofs and eaves of the houses with the skirts of my coat. I walked with the utmost circumspection, to avoid treading on any stragglers, who might remain in the streets, although the orders were very strict, that all people should keep in their houses, at their own peril. The garret windows and tops of houses were so crowded with spectators, that I thought in all my travels I had not seen a more populous place. The city is an exact square, each side of the wall being five hundred foot long. The two great streets, which run cross and divide it into four quarters, are five foot wide. The lanes and alleys, which I could not enter, but only viewed them as I passed, are from twelve to eighteen inches. The town is capable of holding five hundred thousand souls. The houses are from three to five stories. The shops and markets well provided.

The Emperor's palace is in the center of the city, where the two great streets meet. It is enclosed by a wall of two foot high, and twenty foot distant from the buildings. I had his Majesty's permission to step over this wall; and the space being so wide between that and the palace, I could easily view it on every side. The outward court is a square of forty foot, and includes two other courts: in the inmost are the royal apartments, which I was very desirous to see, but found it extremely difficult;

8. Sideways.

for the great gates, from one square into another, were but eighteen inches high, and seven inches wide. Now the buildings of the outer court were at least five foot high; and it was impossible for me to stride over them, without infinite damage to the pile, although the walls were strongly built of hewn stone, and four inches thick. At the same time the Emperor had a great desire that I should see the magnificence of his palace; but this I was not able to do till three days after, which I spent in cutting down with my knife some of the largest trees in the royal park, about an hundred yards distance from the city. Of these trees I made two stools, each about three foot high, and strong enough to bear my weight. The people having received notice a second time, I went again through the city to the palace, with my two stools in my hands. When I came to the side of the outer court, I stood upon one stool, and took the other in my hand: this I lifted over the roof, and gently set it down on the space between the first and second court, which was eight foot wide. I then stepped over the buildings very conveniently from one stool to the other, and drew up the first after me with a hooked stick. By this contrivance I got into the inmost court; and lying down upon my side, I applied my face to the windows of the middle stories, which were left open on purpose, and discovered the most splendid apartments that can be imagined. There I saw the Empress, and the young princes in their several lodgings, with their chief attendants about them. Her Imperial Majesty was pleased to smile very graciously upon me and gave me out of the window her hand to kiss.

But I shall not anticipate the reader with farther descriptions of this kind, because I reserve them for a greater work, which is now almost ready for the press; containing a general description of this empire, from its first erection, through a long series of princes, with a particular account of their wars and politics, laws, learning, and religion; their plants and animals, their peculiar manners and customs, with other matters very curious and useful; my chief design at present being only to relate such events and transactions as happened to the public, or to myself, during a residence of about nine months in that empire.

One morning, about a fortnight after I had obtained my liberty, Reldresal, Principal Secretary (as they style him) of Private Affairs, came to my house, attended only by one servant. He ordered his coach to wait at a distance, and desired I would give him an hour's audience; which I readily consented to, on account of his quality, and personal merits, as well as of the many good offices he had done me during my solicitations at court. I offered to lie down, that he might the more conveniently reach my ear; but he chose rather to let me hold him in my hand during our conversation. He began with compliments on my liberty, said he might pretend to some merit in it; but, however, added, that if it had not been for the present situation of things at court, perhaps I might not have obtained it so soon. For, said he, as flourishing a condition as we appear to be in to foreigners, we labor under two mighty evils; a violent faction at home, and the danger of an invasion by a most potent enemy from abroad. As to the first, you are to understand, that for above seventy moons past, there have been two struggling parties in the empire, under the names of *Tramecksan*, and *Slamecksan*,[9] from the high and low heels on their shoes, by which they distinguish themselves.

It is alleged indeed, that the high heels are most agreeable to our ancient constitution: but however this be, his Majesty hath determined to make use of only low heels in the administration of the government and all offices in the gift of the crown; as you cannot but observe; and particularly, that his Majesty's imperial heels are lower at least by a *drurr* than any of his court; (*drurr* is a measure about the fourteenth part of an inch). The animosities between these two parties run so high, that they will neither eat nor drink, nor talk with each other. We compute the *Tramecksan*, or High-Heels, to exceed us in number; but the power is wholly on our side. We apprehend his Imperial Highness, the heir to the crown, to have some tendency towards the High-Heels; at least we can plainly discover one of his heels higher than the other, which gives him a hobble in his gait.[1] Now, in the midst of these intestine disquiets, we are threatened with an invasion from the island of Blefuscu,[2] which is the other great empire of the universe, almost as large and powerful as this of his Majesty. For as to what we have heard you affirm, that there are other kingdoms and states in the world, inhabited by human creatures as large as yourself, our philosophers are in much doubt; and would rather conjecture that you dropped from the moon, or one of the stars; because it is certain, that an hundred mortals of your bulk would, in a short time, destroy all the fruits and cattle of his Majesty's dominions. Besides, our histories of six thousand moons make no mention of any other regions, than the two great empires of Lilliput and Blefuscu. Which two mighty powers have, as I was going to tell you, been engaged in a most obstinate war for six and thirty moons past. It began upon the following occasion. It is allowed on all hands, that the primitive way of breaking eggs before we eat them, was upon the larger end: but his present Majesty's grandfather, while he was a boy, going to eat an egg, and breaking it according to the ancient practice, happened to cut one of his fingers. Whereupon the Emperor his father published an edict, commanding all his subjects, upon great penalties, to break the smaller end of their eggs. The people so highly resented this law, that our histories tell us there have been six rebellions raised on that account; wherein one emperor lost his life, and another his crown.[3] These civil commotions were constantly fomented by the monarchs of Blefuscu; and when they were quelled, the exiles always fled for refuge to that empire. It is computed, that eleven thousand persons have, at several times, suffered death, rather than submit to break their eggs at the smaller end. Many hundred

9. Tory (High Church) and Whig (Low Church).
1. The Prince of Wales (later George II) had friends in both parties.
2. France.
3. Swift's satirical allegory of the strife between Catholics (Big-Endians) and Protestants (Little-Endians) touches on Henry VIII (who "broke" with the Pope), Charles I (who lost his life), and James II (who lost his crown).

large volumes have been published upon this controversy: but the books of the Big-Endians have been long forbidden, and the whole party rendered incapable by law of holding employments.[4] During the course of these troubles, the emperors of Blefuscu did frequently expostulate by their ambassadors, accusing us of making a schism in religion, by offending against a fundamental doctrine of our great prophet Lustrog, in the fifty-fourth chapter of the *Brundecral* (which is their Alcoran). This, however, is thought to be a mere strain upon the text: for the words are these; *That all true believers shall break their eggs at the convenient end*: and which is the convenient end, seems, in my humble opinion, to be left to every man's conscience, or at least in the power of the chief magistrate[5] to determine. Now the Big-Endian exiles have found so much credit in the Emperor of Blefuscu's court, and so much private assistance and encouragement from their party here at home, that a bloody war hath been carried on between the two empires for six and thirty moons with various success;[6] during which time we have lost forty capital ships, and a much greater number of smaller vessels, together with thirty thousand of our best seamen and soldiers; and the damage received by the enemy is reckoned to be somewhat greater than ours. However, they have now equipped a numerous fleet, and are just preparing to make a descent upon us; and his Imperial Majesty, placing great confidence in your valor and strength, hath commanded me to lay this account of his affairs before you.

I desired the Secretary to present my humble duty to the Emperor, and to let him know, that I thought it would not become me, who was a foreigner, to interfere with parties; but I was ready, with the hazard of my life, to defend his person and state against all invaders.

CHAPTER 5. *The author by an extraordinary stratagem prevents an invasion. A high title of honor is conferred upon him. Ambassadors arrive from the Emperor of Blefuscu, and sue for peace. The Empress's apartment on fire by an accident; the author instrumental in saving the rest of the palace.*

The empire of Blefuscu is an island situated to the north north-east side of Lilliput, from whence it is parted only by a channel of eight hundred yards wide. I had not yet seen it, and upon this notice of an intended invasion, I avoided appearing on that side of the coast, for fear of being discovered by some of the enemy's ships, who had received no intelligence of me; all intercourse between the two empires having been strictly forbidden during the war, upon pain of death; and an embargo laid by our Emperor upon all vessels whatsoever. I communicated to his Majesty a project I had formed of seizing the enemy's whole fleet; which,

4. The Test Act (1673) prevented Catholics and Nonconformists from holding office unless they accepted the Anglican sacrament.
5. Ruler, sovereign. Swift himself accepted the right
of the king to determine religious observances.
6. Reminiscent of the War of the Spanish Succession (1701–13).

as our scouts assured us, lay at anchor in the harbor ready to sail with the first fair wind. I consulted the most experienced seamen upon the depth of the channel, which they had often plumbed; who told me, that in the middle at high water it was seventy *glumgluffs* deep, which is about six foot of European measure; and the rest of it fifty *glumgluffs* at most. I walked to the northeast coast over against Blefuscu; where, lying down behind a hillock, I took out my small pocket perspective glass, and viewed the enemy's fleet at anchor, consisting of about fifty men of war, and a great number of transports: I then came back to my house, and gave order (for which I had a warrant) for a great quantity of the strongest cable and bars of iron. The cable was about as thick as packthread, and the bars of the length and size of a knitting-needle. I trebled the cable to make it stronger, and for the same reason I twisted three of the iron bars together, bending the extremities into a hook. Having thus fixed fifty hooks to as many cables, I went back to the northeast coast, and putting off my coat, shoes, and stockings, walked into the sea in my leathern jerkin, about half an hour before high water. I waded with what haste I could, and swam in the middle about thirty yards until I felt the ground; I arrived at the fleet in less than half an hour. The enemy was so frighted when they saw me, that they leaped out of their ships, and swam to shore, where there could not be fewer than thirty thousand souls. I then took my tackling, and fastening a hook to the hole at the prow of each, I tied all the cords together at the end. While I was thus employed, the enemy discharged several thousand arrows, many of which stuck in my hands and face; and besides the excessive smart, gave me much disturbance in my work. My greatest apprehension was for my eyes, which I should have infallibly lost, if I had not suddenly thought of an expedient. I kept, among other little necessaries, a pair of spectacles in a private pocket, which, as I observed before, had escaped the Emperor's searchers. These I took out, and fastened as strongly as I could upon my nose; and thus armed went on boldly with my work in spite of the enemy's arrows; many of which struck against the glasses of my spectacles, but without any other effect, further than a little to discompose them. I had now fastened all the hooks, and taking the knot in my hand, began to pull; but not a ship would stir, for they were all too fast by their anchors, so that the boldest part of my enterprise remained. I therefore let go the cord, and leaving the hooks fixed to the ships, I resolutely cut with my knife the cables that fastened the anchors, receiving about two hundred shots in my face and hands; then I took up the knotted end of the cables to which my hooks were tied; and with great ease drew fifty of the enemy's largest men-of-war after me.

The Blefuscudians, who had not the least imagination of what I intended, were at first confounded with astonishment. They had seen me cut the cables, and thought my design was only to let the ships run adrift, or fall foul on each other: but when they perceived the whole fleet moving in order, and saw me pulling at the end, they set up such a scream of grief and despair, that it is almost impossible to describe or conceive. When I had got out of danger, I stopped a while to pick out the arrows that stuck in my hands and face, and rubbed on some of the same ointment that was given me at my first arrival, as I have formerly mentioned. I then took off my spectacles, and waiting about an hour until the tide was a little fallen, I waded through the middle with my cargo, and arrived safe at the royal port of Lilliput.

The Emperor and his whole court stood on the shore, expecting the issue of this great adventure. They saw the ships move forward in a large half-moon, but could not discern me, who was up to my breast in water. When I advanced to the middle of the channel, they were yet more in pain, because I was under water to my neck. The Emperor concluded me to be drowned, and that the enemy's fleet was approaching in a hostile manner: but he was soon eased of his fears, for the channel growing shallower every step I made, I came in a short time within hearing; and holding up the end of the cable by which the fleet was fastened, I cried in a loud voice, Long live the most puissant Emperor of Lilliput! This great prince received me at my landing with all possible encomiums, and created me a *Nardac* upon the spot, which is the highest title of honor among them.

His Majesty desired I would take some other opportunity of bringing all the rest of his enemy's ships into his ports. And so unmeasurable is the ambition of princes, that he seemed to think of nothing less than reducing the whole empire of Blefuscu into a province, and governing it by a viceroy; of destroying the Big-Endian exiles, and compelling that people to break the smaller end of their eggs, by which he would remain sole monarch of the whole world. But I endeavored to divert him from this design, by many arguments drawn from the topics of policy as well as justice: and I plainly protested, that I would never be an instrument of bringing a free and brave people into slavery. And when the matter was debated in council, the wisest part of the ministry were of my opinion.

This open bold declaration of mine was so opposite to the schemes and politics of his Imperial Majesty, that he could never forgive me; he mentioned it in a very artful manner at council, where I was told that some of the wisest appeared, at least by their silence, to be of my opinion; but others, who were my secret enemies, could not forbear some expressions, which by a side-wind[7] reflected on me. And from this time began an intrigue between his Majesty and a junta of ministers maliciously bent against me, which broke out in less than two months, and had like to have ended in my utter destruction. Of so little weight are the greatest services to princes, when put into the balance with a refusal to gratify their passions.[8]

About three weeks after this exploit, there arrived a solemn embassy from Blefuscu, with humble offers of a peace; which was soon con-

7. Indirectly.
8. After a series of British naval victories, the Treaty of Utrecht (1713) had ended the war with France, but the Tory ministers who engineered the peace were subsequently accused of having sold out to the enemy.

cluded upon conditions very advantageous to our Emperor; wherewith I shall not trouble the reader. There were six ambassadors, with a train of about five hundred persons; and their entry was very magnificent, suitable to the grandeur of their master, and the importance of their business. When their treaty was finished, wherein I did them several good offices by the credit I now had, or at least appeared to have at court, their Excellencies, who were privately told how much I had been their friend, made me a visit in form. They began with many compliments upon my valor and generosity; invited me to that kingdom in the Emperor their master's name; and desired me to show them some proofs of my prodigious strength, of which they had heard so many wonders; wherein I readily obliged them, but shall not interrupt the reader with the particulars.

When I had for some time entertained their Excellencies to their infinite satisfaction and surprise, I desired they would do me the honor to present my most humble respects to the Emperor their master, the renown of whose virtues had so justly filled the whole world with admiration, and whose royal person I resolved to attend before I returned to my own country. Accordingly, the next time I had the honor to see our Emperor, I desired his general license to wait on the Blefuscudian monarch, which he was pleased to grant me, as I could plainly perceive, in a very cold manner; but could not guess the reason, till I had a whisper from a certain person, that Flimnap and Bolgolam had represented my intercourse with those ambassadors as a mark of disaffection, from which I am sure my heart was wholly free. And this was the first time I began to conceive some imperfect idea of courts and ministers.

It is to be observed, that these ambassadors spoke to me by an interpreter; the languages of both empires differing as much from each other as any two in Europe, and each nation priding itself upon the antiquity, beauty, and energy of their own tongues, with an avowed contempt for that of their neighbor; yet our Emperor, standing upon the advantage he had got by the seizure of their fleet, obliged them to deliver their credentials, and make their speech, in the Lilliputian tongue. And it must be confessed, that from the great intercourse of trade and commerce between both realms, from the continual reception of exiles, which is mutual among them, and from the custom in each empire to send their young nobility and richer gentry to the other, in order to polish themselves, by seeing the world, and understanding men and manners, there are few persons of distinction, or merchants, or seamen, who dwell in the maritime parts, but what can hold conversation in both tongues; as I found some weeks after, when I went to pay my respects to the Emperor of Blefuscu, which in the midst of great misfortunes, through the malice of my enemies, proved a very happy adventure to me, as I shall relate in its proper place.

The reader may remember, that when I signed those articles upon which I recovered my liberty, there were some which I disliked upon account of their being too servile, neither could any thing but an extreme necessity have forced me to submit. But being now a *Nardac*, of the highest rank in that empire, such offices[9] were looked upon as below my dignity, and the Emperor (to do him justice) never once mentioned them to me. However, it was not long before I had an opportunity of doing his Majesty, at least as I then thought, a most signal service. I was alarmed at midnight with the cries of many hundred people at my door; by which being suddenly awaked, I was in some kind of terror. I heard the word *burglum* repeated incessantly; several of the Emperor's court, making their way through the crowd, intreated me to come immediately to the palace, where her Imperial Majesty's apartment was on fire, by the carelessness of a maid of honor, who fell asleep while she was reading a romance. I got up in an instant; and orders being given to clear the way before me, and it being likewise a moonshine night, I made a shift to get to the palace without trampling on any of the people. I found they had already applied ladders to the walls of the apartment, and were well provided with buckets, but the water was at some distance. These buckets were about the size of a large thimble, and the poor people supplied me with them as fast as they could; but the flame was so violent, that they did little good. I might easily have stifled it with my coat, which I unfortunately left behind me for haste, and came away only in my leathern jerkin. The case seemed wholly desperate and deplorable; and this magnificent palace would have infallibly been burnt down to the ground, if, by a presence of mind, unusual to me, I had not suddenly thought of an expedient. I had the evening before drank plentifully of a most delicious wine, called *glimigrim* (the Blefuscudians call it *flunec*, but ours is esteemed the better sort), which is very diuretic. By the luckiest chance in the world, I had not discharged myself of any part of it. The heat I had contracted by coming very near the flames, and by my laboring to quench them, made the wine begin to operate by urine; which I voided in such a quantity, and applied so well to the proper places, that in three minutes the fire was wholly extinguished; and the rest of that noble pile, which had cost so many ages in erecting, preserved from destruction.

It was now daylight, and I returned to my house, without waiting to congratulate with the Emperor; because, although I had done a very eminent piece of service, yet I could not tell how his Majesty might resent the manner by which I had performed it: for, by the fundamental laws of the realm, it is capital[1] in any person, of what quality soever, to make water within the precincts of the palace. But I was a little comforted by a message from his Majesty, that he would give orders to the Grand Justiciary for passing my pardon in form; which, however, I could not obtain. And I was privately assured, that the Empress, conceiving the greatest abhorrence of what I had done,[2] removed to the most distant side of the court, firmly resolved that those buildings should never be

---

9. Duties.
1. Punishable by death.
2. Queen Anne, whom Swift called "a royal

prude," strongly objected to the coarseness of *A Tale of a Tub*.

repaired for her use; and, in the presence of her chief confidents, could not forbear vowing revenge.

CHAPTER 6. *Of the inhabitants of Lilliput; their learning, laws, and customs, the manner of educating their children. The author's way of living in that country. His vindication of a great lady.*

Although I intend to leave the description of this empire to a particular treatise, yet in the mean time I am content to gratify the curious reader with some general ideas. As the common size of the natives is somewhat under six inches, so there is an exact proportion in all other animals, as well as plants and trees: for instance, the tallest horses and oxen are between four and five inches in height, the sheep an inch and a half, more or less; their geese about the bigness of a sparrow; and so the several gradations downwards, till you come to the smallest, which, to my sight, were almost invisible; but nature hath adapted the eyes of the Lilliputians to all objects proper for their view: they see with great exactness, but at no great distance. And to show the sharpness of their sight towards objects that are near, I have been much pleased with observing a cook pulling[3] a lark, which was not so large as a common fly; and a young girl threading an invisible needle with invisible silk. Their tallest trees are about seven foot high; I mean some of those in the great royal park, the tops whereof I could but just reach with my fist clinched. The other vegetables[4] are in the same proportion; but this I leave to the reader's imagination.

I shall say but little at present of their learning, which for many ages hath flourished in all its branches among them: but their manner of writing is very peculiar; being neither from the left to the right, like the Europeans; nor from the right to the left, like the Arabians; nor from up to down, like the Chinese; nor from down to up, like the Cascagians;[5] but aslant from one corner of the paper to the other, like ladies in England.

They bury their dead with their heads directly downwards; because they hold an opinion that in eleven thousand moons they are all to rise again; in which period, the earth (which they conceive to be flat) will turn upside down, and by this means they shall, at their resurrection, be found ready standing on their feet. The learned among them confess the absurdity of this doctrine; but the practice still continues, in compliance to the vulgar.

There are some laws and customs in this empire very peculiar; and if they were not so directly contrary to those of my own dear country, I should be tempted to say a little in their justification. It is only to be wished, that they were as well executed. The first I shall mention relateth to informers. All crimes against the state are punished here with the utmost severity; but if the person accused make his innocence plainly to appear upon his trial, the accuser is immediately put to an ignominious

---

3. Plucking.
4. Plants.

5. Swift's invention.

death; and out of his goods or lands, the innocent person is quadruply recompensed for the loss of his time, for the danger he underwent, for the hardship of his imprisonment, and for all the charges he hath been at in making his defense. Or, if that fund be deficient, it is largely[6] supplied by the crown. The Emperor doth also confer on him some public mark of his favor; and proclamation is made of his innocence through the whole city.

They look upon fraud as a greater crime than theft, and therefore seldom fail to punish it with death; for they allege, that care and vigilance, with a very common understanding, may preserve a man's goods from thieves; but honesty hath no fence against superior cunning: and since it is necessary that there should be a perpetual intercourse of buying and selling, and dealing upon credit, where fraud is permitted or connived at, or hath no law to punish it, the honest dealer is always undone, and the knave gets the advantage. I remember when I was once interceding with the King for a criminal who had wronged his master of a great sum of money, which he had received by order, and ran away with; and happening to tell his Majesty, by way of extenuation, that it was only a breach of trust, the Emperor thought it monstrous in me to offer, as a defense, the greatest aggravation of the crime: and truly, I had little to say in return, farther than the common answer, that different nations had different customs; for, I confess, I was heartily ashamed.

Although we usually call reward and punishment the two hinges upon which all government turns, yet I could never observe this maxim to be put in practice by any nation, except that of Lilliput. Whoever can there bring sufficient proof that he hath strictly observed the laws of his country for seventy-three moons, hath a claim to certain privileges, according to his quality[7] and condition of life, with a proportionable sum of money out of a fund appropriated for that use: he likewise acquires the title of *Snilpall*, or *Legal*, which is added to his name, but doth not descend to his posterity. And these people thought it a prodigious defect of policy among us, when I told them that our laws were enforced only by penalties, without any mention of reward. It is upon this account that the image of Justice, in their courts of judicature, is formed with six eyes, two before, as many behind, and on each side one, to signify circumspection; with a bag of gold open in her right hand, and a sword sheathed in her left, to show she is more disposed to reward than to punish.

In choosing persons for all employments, they have more regard to good morals than to great abilities; for, since government is necessary to mankind, they believe that the common size of human understandings is fitted to some station or other; and that Providence never intended to make the management of public affairs a mystery, to be comprehended only by a few persons of sublime genius, of which there seldom are three born in an age: but they suppose truth, justice, temperance, and the like, to be in every man's power; the practice of which virtues, assisted

---

6. Fully.   7. Social position.

by experience and a good intention, would qualify any man for the service of his country, except where a course of study is required. But they thought the want of moral virtues was so far from being supplied by superior endowments of the mind, that employments could never be put into such dangerous hands as those of persons so qualified; and at least, that the mistakes committed by ignorance in a virtuous disposition would never be of such fatal consequence to the public weal, as the practices of a man whose inclinations led him to be corrupt, and had great abilities to manage, to multiply, and defend his corruptions.

In like manner, the disbelief of a divine Providence renders a man uncapable of holding any public station; for since kings avow themselves to be the deputies of Providence, the Lilliputians think nothing can be more absurd than for a prince to employ such men as disown the authority under which he acteth.

In relating these and the following laws, I would only be understood to mean the original institutions, and not the most scandalous corruptions into which these people are fallen by the degenerate nature of man. For as to that infamous practice of acquiring great employments by dancing on the ropes, or badges of favor and distinction by leaping over sticks, and creeping under them, the reader is to observe, that they were first introduced by the grandfather of the Emperor now reigning; and grew to the present height by the gradual increase of party and faction.

Ingratitude is among them a capital crime, as we read it to have been in some other countries; for they reason thus, that whoever makes ill returns to his benefactor, must needs be a common enemy to the rest of mankind, from whom he hath received no obligation; and therefore such a man is not fit to live.

Their notions relating to the duties of parents and children differ extremely from ours. For, since the conjunction of male and female is founded upon the great law of nature, in order to propagate and continue the species, the Lilliputians will needs have it, that men and women are joined together like other animals, by the motives of concupiscence; and that their tenderness towards their young proceedeth from the like natural principle: for which reason they will never allow, that a child is under any obligation to his father for begetting him, or to his mother for bringing him into the world; which, considering the miseries of human life, was neither a benefit in itself, nor intended so by his parents, whose thoughts in their love-encounters were otherwise employed. Upon these, and the like reasonings, their opinion is, that parents are the last of all others to be trusted with the education of their own children: and therefore they have in every town public nurseries, where all parents, except cottagers[8] and laborers, are obliged to send their infants of both sexes to be reared and educated when they come to the age of twenty moons; at which time they are supposed to have some rudiments of docility. These schools are of several kinds, suited to different qualities, and to both

---

8. Agricultural workers, peasants.

sexes. They have certain professors[9] well skilled in preparing children for such a condition of life as befits the rank of their parents, and their own capacities as well as inclinations. I shall first say something of the male nurseries, and then of the female.

The nurseries for males of noble or eminent birth are provided with grave and learned professors, and their several deputies. The clothes and food of the children are plain and simple. They are bred up in the principles of honor, justice, courage, modesty, clemency, religion, and love of their country; they are always employed in some business, except in the times of eating and sleeping, which are very short, and two hours for diversions, consisting of bodily exercises.[1] They are dressed by men until four years of age, and then are obliged to dress themselves, although their quality be ever so great; and the women attendants, who are aged proportionably to ours at fifty, perform only the most menial offices. They are never suffered to converse with servants, but go together in small or greater numbers to take their diversions, and always in the presence of a professor, or one of his deputies; whereby they avoid those early bad impressions of folly and vice to which our children are subject. Their parents are suffered to see them only twice a year; the visit is not to last above an hour; they are allowed to kiss the child at meeting and parting; but a professor, who always standeth by on those occasions, will not suffer them to whisper, or use any fondling expressions, or bring any presents of toys, sweetmeats, and the like.

The pension from each family for the education and entertainment[2] of a child, upon failure of due payment, is levied by the Emperor's officers.

The nurseries for children of ordinary gentlemen, merchants, traders, and handicrafts, are managed proportionably after the same manner; only those designed for trades are put out apprentices at seven years old; whereas those of persons of quality continue in their exercises until fifteen, which answers to one and twenty with us: but the confinement is gradually lessened for the last three years.

In the female nurseries, the young girls of quality are educated much like the males, only they are dressed by orderly servants of their own sex, but always in the presence of a professor or deputy, until they come to dress themselves, which is at five years old. And if it be found that these nurses ever presume to entertain the girls with frightful or foolish stories, or the common follies practiced by chambermaids among us, they are publicly whipped thrice about the city, imprisoned for a year, and banished for life to the most desolate parts of the country. Thus the young ladies there are as much ashamed of being cowards and fools as the men; and despise all personal ornaments beyond decency and cleanliness: neither did I perceive any difference in their education, made by their difference of sex, only that the exercises of the females were not altogether so robust; and that some rules were given them relating to domestic life,

9. Professional teachers.   2. Sustenance.
1. Activities.

and a smaller compass of learning was enjoined them: for their maxim is, that among people of quality, a wife should be always a reasonable and agreeable companion, because she cannot always be young. When the girls are twelve years old, which among them is the marriageable age, their parents or guardians take them home, with great expressions of gratitude to the professors, and seldom without tears of the young lady and her companions.

In the nurseries of females of the meaner sort, the children are instructed in all kinds of works proper for their sex, and their several degrees:[3] those intended for apprentices are dismissed at seven years old, the rest are kept to eleven.

The meaner families who have children at these nurseries are obliged, besides their annual pension, which is as low as possible, to return to the steward of the nursery a small monthly share of their gettings, to be a portion for the child; and therefore all parents are limited in their expenses by the law. For the Lilliputians think nothing can be more unjust, than that people, in subservience to their own appetites, should bring children into the world, and leave the burthen of supporting them on the public. As to persons of quality, they give security to appropriate a certain sum for each child, suitable to their condition; and these funds are always managed with good husbandry, and the most exact justice.

The cottagers and laborers keep their children at home, their business being only to till and cultivate the earth; and therefore their education is of little consequence to the public; but the old and diseased among them are supported by hospitals: for begging is a trade unknown in this empire.

And here it may perhaps divert the curious reader, to give some account of my domestic,[4] and my manner of living in this country, during a residence of nine months and thirteen days. Having a head mechanically turned, and being likewise forced by necessity, I had made for myself a table and chair convenient enough, out of the largest trees in the royal park. Two hundred sempstresses were employed to make me shirts, and linen for my bed and table, all of the strongest and coarsest kind they could get; which, however, they were forced to quilt together in several folds; for the thickest was some degrees finer than lawn. Their linen is usually three inches wide, and three foot make a piece. The sempstresses took my measure as I lay on the ground, one standing at my neck, and another at my mid-leg, with a strong cord extended, that each held by the end, while the third measured the length of the cord with a rule of an inch long. Then they measured my right thumb, and desired no more; for by a mathematical computation, that twice round the thumb is one round the wrist, and so on to the neck and the waist; and by the help of my old shirt, which I displayed on the ground before them for a pattern, they fitted me exactly. Three hundred tailors were employed in the same manner to make me clothes; but they had another

3. Various social ranks.   4. Household.

contrivance for taking my measure. I kneeled down, and they raised a ladder from the ground to my neck; upon this ladder one of them mounted, and let fall a plumb-line from my collar to the floor, which just answered the length of my coat; but my waist and arms I measured myself. When my clothes were finished, which was done in my house (for the largest of theirs would not have been able to hold them), they looked like the patchwork made by the ladies in England, only that mine were all of a color.

I had three hundred cooks to dress my victuals, in little convenient huts built about my house, where they and their families lived, and prepared me two dishes apiece. I took up twenty waiters in my hand, and placed them on the table; an hundred more attended below on the ground, some with dishes of meat, and some with barrels of wine, and other liquors, slung on their shoulders; all which the waiters above drew up as I wanted, in a very ingenious manner, by certain cords, as we draw the bucket up a well in Europe. A dish of their meat was a good mouthful, and a barrel of their liquor a reasonable draught. Their mutton yields to ours, but their beef is excellent. I have had a sirloin so large, that I have been forced to make three bites of it; but this is rare. My servants were astonished to see me eat it bones and all, as in our country we do the leg of a lark. Their geese and turkeys I usually eat at a mouthful, and I must confess they far exceed ours. Of their smaller fowl I could take up twenty or thirty at the end of my knife.

One day his Imperial Majesty, being informed of my way of living, desired that himself and his royal consort, with the young princes of the blood of both sexes, might have the happiness (as he was pleased to call it) of dining with me. They came accordingly, and I placed them upon chairs of state on my table, just over against me, with their guards about them. Flimnap the Lord High Treasurer attended there likewise, with his white staff; and I observed he often looked on me with a sour countenance, which I would not seem to regard, but eat more than usual, in honor to my dear country, as well as to fill the court with admiration. I have some private reasons to believe, that this visit from his Majesty gave Flimnap an opportunity of doing me ill offices to his master. That minister had always been my secret enemy, although he outwardly caressed me more than was usual to the moroseness of his nature. He represented to the Emperor the low condition of his treasury; that he was forced to take up money at great discount; that exchequer bills[5] would not circulate under nine per cent below par; that I had cost his Majesty above a million and a half of *sprugs* (their greatest gold coin, about the bigness of a spangle); and upon the whole, that it would be advisable in the Emperor to take the first fair occasion of dismissing me.

I am here obliged to vindicate the reputation of an excellent lady, who was an innocent sufferer upon my account. The Treasurer took a fancy to be jealous of his wife, from the malice of some evil tongues,

---

5. Government bills of credit. Walpole was noted as a canny financier.

who informed him that her Grace had taken a violent affection for my person; and the court-scandal ran for some time that she once came privately to my lodging. This I solemnly declare to be a most infamous falsehood, without any grounds, farther than that her Grace was pleased to treat me with all innocent marks of freedom and friendship. I own she came often to my house, but always publicly, nor ever without three more in the coach, who were usually her sister and young daughter, and some particular acquaintance; but this was common to many other ladies of the court. And I still appeal to my servants round, whether they at any time saw a coach at my door without knowing what persons were in it. On those occasions, when a servant had given me notice, my custom was to go immediately to the door; and, after paying my respects, to take up the coach and two horses very carefully in my hands (for if there were six horses, the postillion always unharnessed four) and placed them on a table, where I had fixed a moveable rim quite round, of five inches high, to prevent accidents. And I have often had four coaches and horses at once on my table full of company, while I sat in my chair leaning my face towards them; and when I was engaged with one set, the coachmen would gently drive the others round my table. I have passed many an afternoon very agreeably in these conversations. But I defy the Treasurer, or his two informers (I will name them, and let them make their best of it) Clustril and Drunlo, to prove that any person ever came to me *incognito*, except the Secretary Reldresal, who was sent by express command of his Imperial Majesty, as I have before related. I should not have dwelt so long upon this particular, if it had not been a point wherein the reputation of a great lady is so nearly concerned, to say nothing of my own; although I had the honor to be a *Nardac*, which the Treasurer himself is not; for all the world knows he is only a *Clumglum*, a title inferior by one degree, as that of a marquis is to a duke in England; yet I allow he preceded me in right of his post. These false informations, which I afterwards came to the knowledge of, by an accident not proper to mention, made the Treasurer show his lady for some time an ill countenance, and me a worse; for although he was at last undeceived and reconciled to her, yet I lost all credit with him; and found my interest decline very fast with the Emperor himself, who was indeed too much governed by that favorite.

CHAPTER 7. *The author, being informed of a design to accuse him of high treason, makes his escape to Blefuscu. His reception there.*

Before I proceed to give an account of my leaving this kingdom, it may be proper to inform the reader of a private intrigue which had been for two months forming against me.

I had been hitherto all my life a stranger to courts, for which I was unqualified by the meanness of my condition. I had indeed heard and read enough of the dispositions of great princes and ministers; but never expected to have found such terrible effects of them in so remote a country, governed, as I thought, by very different maxims from those in Europe.

When I was just preparing to pay my attendance on the Emperor of Blefuscu, a considerable person at court (to whom I had been very serviceable at a time when he lay under the highest displeasure of his Imperial Majesty) came to my house very privately at night in a close chair, and without sending his name, desired admittance. The chairmen were dismissed; I put the chair, with his Lordship in it, into my coat-pocket; and giving orders to a trusty servant to say I was indisposed and gone to sleep, I fastened the door of my house, placed the chair on the table, according to my usual custom, and sat down by it. After the common salutations were over, observing his Lordship's countenance full of concern, and enquiring into the reason, he desired I would hear him with patience, in a matter that highly concerned my honor and my life. His speech was to the following effect, for I took notes of it as soon as he left me.

You are to know, said he, that several committees of council have been lately called in the most private manner on your account: and it is but two days since his Majesty came to a full resolution.

You are very sensible that Skyresh Bolgolam (*Galbet*, or High Admiral) hath been your mortal enemy almost ever since your arrival. His original reasons I know not; but his hatred is much increased since your great success against Blefuscu, by which his glory, as Admiral, is obscured. This lord, in conjunction with Flimnap the High Treasurer, whose enmity against you is notorious on account of his lady, Limtoc the General, Lalcon the Chamberlain, and Balmuff the Grand Justiciary, have prepared articles of impeachment against you, for treason, and other capital crimes.[6]

This preface made me so impatient, being conscious of my own merits and innocence, that I was going to interrupt; when he entreated me to be silent, and thus proceeded.

Out of gratitude for the favors you have done me, I procured information of the whole proceedings, and a copy of the articles, wherein I venture my head for your service.

Articles of Impeachment against Quinbus Flestrin (*the* Man-Mountain).

ARTICLE 1

Whereas, by a statute made in the reign of his Imperial Majesty Calin Deffar Plune, it is enacted, that whoever shall make water within the precincts of the royal palace shall be liable to the pains and penalties of high treason: notwithstanding, the said Quinbus

---

6. After the Whigs had investigated Oxford and Bolingbroke, both were impeached for high trea- son, on charges of being sympathetic to the Jacob- ites and the French.

Flestrin, in open breach of the said law, under color of extinguish-
ing the fire kindled in the apartment of his Majesty's most dear
imperial consort, did maliciously, traitorously, and devilishly, by
discharge of his urine, put out the said fire kindled in the said apartment, lying and being within the precincts of the said royal palace;
against the statute in that case provided, etc., against the duty, etc.

ARTICLE 2

That the said Quinbus Flestrin, having brought the imperial fleet
of Blefuscu into the royal port, and being afterwards commanded
by his Imperial Majesty to seize all the other ships of the said empire
of Blefuscu, and reduce that empire to a province, to be governed
by a viceroy from hence; and to destroy and put to death not only
all the Big-Endian exiles, but likewise all the people of that empire
who would not immediately forsake the Big-Endian heresy: he, the
said Flestrin, like a false traitor against his most auspicious, serene,
Imperial Majesty, did petition to be excused from the said service,
upon pretense of unwillingness to force the consciences, or destroy
the liberties and lives of an innocent people.

ARTICLE 3

That, whereas certain ambassadors arrived from the court of Blefuscu to sue for peace in his Majesty's court: he the said Flestrin
did, like a false traitor, aid, abet, comfort, and divert the said
ambassadors; although he knew them to be servants to a prince who
was lately an open enemy to his Imperial Majesty, and in open war
against his said Majesty.

ARTICLE 4

That the said Quinbus Flestrin, contrary to the duty of a faithful
subject, is now preparing to make a voyage to the court and empire
of Blefuscu, for which he hath received only verbal license from
his Imperial Majesty; and under color of the said license, doth falsely
and traitorously intend to take the said voyage, and thereby to aid,
comfort, and abet the Emperor of Blefuscu, so late an enemy, and
in open war with his Imperial Majesty aforesaid.

There are some other articles, but these are the most important, of
which I have read you an abstract.

In the several debates upon this impeachment, it must be confessed
that his Majesty gave many marks of his great *lenity;* often urging the
services you had done him, and endeavoring to extenuate your crimes.
The Treasurer and Admiral insisted that you should be put to the most
painful and ignominious death, by setting fire on your house at night;

and the General was to attend with twenty thousand men armed with poisoned arrows, to shoot you on the face and hands. Some of your servants were to have private orders to strew a poisonous juice on your shirts and sheets, which would soon make you tear your own flesh, and die in the utmost torture. The General came into the same opinion; so that for a long time there was a majority against you. But his Majesty resolving, if possible, to spare your life, at last brought off[7] the Chamberlain.

Upon this incident, Reldresal, Principal Secretary for Private Affairs, who always approved[8] himself your true friend, was commanded by the Emperor to deliver his opinion, which he accordingly did; and therein justified the good thoughts you have of him. He allowed your crimes to be great; but that still there was room for mercy, the most commendable virtue in a prince, and for which his Majesty was so justly celebrated. He said, the friendship between you and him was so well known to the world, that perhaps the most honorable board might think him partial: however, in obedience to the command he had received, he would freely offer his sentiments. That if his Majesty, in consideration of your services, and pursuant to his own merciful disposition, would please to spare your life, and only give order to put out both your eyes, he humbly conceived, that by this expedient justice might in some measure be satisfied, and all the world would applaud the *lenity* of the Emperor, as well as the fair and generous proceedings of those who have the honor to be his counselors. That the loss of your eyes would be no impediment to your bodily strength, by which you might still be useful to his Majesty. That blindness is an addition to courage, by concealing dangers from us; that the fear you had for your eyes was the greatest difficulty in bringing over the enemy's fleet; and it would be sufficient for you to see by the eyes of the ministers, since the greatest princes do no more.

This proposal was received with the utmost disapprobation by the whole board. Bolgolam, the Admiral, could not preserve his temper; but rising up in fury, said, he wondered how the Secretary durst presume to give his opinion for preserving the life of a traitor: that the services you had performed were, by all true reasons of state, the great aggravation of your crimes; that you, who were able to extinguish the fire by discharge of urine in her Majesty's apartment (which he mentioned with horror), might, at another time, raise an inundation by the same means, to drown the whole palace; and the same strength which enabled you to bring over the enemy's fleet might serve, upon the first discontent, to carry it back: that he had good reasons to think you were a Big-Endian in your heart; and as treason begins in the heart before it appears in overt acts, so he accused you as a traitor on that account, and therefore insisted you should be put to death.

The Treasurer was of the same opinion; he showed to what straits his Majesty's revenue was reduced by the charge of maintaining you, which

7. Won over.   8. Proved.

would soon grow insupportable: that the Secretary's expedient of putting out your eyes was so far from being a remedy against this evil, that it would probably increase it; as it is manifest from the common practice of blinding some kind of fowl, after which they fed the faster, and grew sooner fat: that his sacred Majesty, and the council, who are your judges, were in their own consciences fully convinced of your guilt; which was a sufficient argument to condemn you to death, without the formal proofs required by the strict letter of the law.

But his Imperial Majesty, fully determined against capital punishment, was graciously pleased to say, that since the council thought the loss of your eyes too easy a censure, some other may be inflicted hereafter. And your friend the Secretary humbly desiring to be heard again, in answer to what the Treasurer had objected concerning the great charge his Majesty was at in maintaining you, said, that his Excellency, who had the sole disposal of the Emperor's revenue, might easily provide against this evil, by gradually lessening your establishment; by which, for want of sufficient food, you would grow weak and faint, and lose your appetite, and consequently decay and consume in a few months; neither would the stench of your carcass be then so dangerous, when it should become more than half diminished; and immediately upon your death, five or six thousand of his Majesty's subjects might, in two or three days, cut your flesh from your bones, take it away by cart-loads, and bury it in distant parts to prevent infection; leaving the skeleton as a monument of admiration to posterity.

Thus by the great friendship of the Secretary, the whole affair was compromised. It was strictly enjoined, that the project of starving you by degrees should be kept a secret; but the sentence of putting out your eyes was entered on the books; none dissenting except Bolgolam the Admiral, who being a creature of the Empress, was perpetually instigated by her Majesty to insist upon your death; she having borne perpetual malice against you, on account of that infamous and illegal method you took to extinguish the fire in her apartment.

In three days your friend the Secretary will be directed to come to your house, and read before you the articles of impeachment; and then to signify the great lenity and favor of his Majesty and council; whereby you are only condemned to the loss of your eyes, which his Majesty doth not question you will gratefully and humbly submit to; and twenty of his Majesty's surgeons will attend, in order to see the operation well performed, by discharging very sharp-pointed arrows into the balls of your eyes, as you lie on the ground.

I leave to your prudence what measures you will take; and to avoid suspicion, I must immediately return in as private a manner as I came.

His Lordship did so, and I remained alone, under many doubts and perplexities of mind.

It was a custom introduced by this prince and his ministry (very different, as I have been assured, from the practices of former times), that after the court had decreed any cruel execution, either to gratify the monarch's resentment, or the malice of a favorite, the Emperor always made a speech to his whole council, expressing his great lenity and tenderness, as qualities known and confessed by all the world. This speech was immediately published through the kingdom; nor did any thing terrify the people so much as those encomiums on his Majesty's mercy; because it was observed, that the more these praises were enlarged and insisted on, the more inhuman was the punishment, and the sufferer more innocent. Yet as to myself, I must confess, having never been designed for a courtier, either by my birth or education, I was so ill a judge of things, that I could not discover the lenity and favor of this sentence, but conceived it (perhaps erroneously) rather to be rigorous than gentle. I sometimes thought of standing my trial; for although I could not deny the facts alleged in the several articles, yet I hoped they would admit of some extenuations. But having in my life perused many state trials, which I ever observed to terminate as the judges thought fit to direct, I durst not rely on so dangerous a decision, in so critical a juncture, and against such powerful enemies. Once I was strongly bent upon resistance: for while I had liberty, the whole strength of that empire could hardly subdue me, and I might easily with stones pelt the metropolis to pieces; but I soon rejected that project with horror, by remembering the oath I had made to the Emperor, the favors I received from him, and the high title of *Nardac* he conferred upon me. Neither had I so soon learned the gratitude of courtiers, to persuade myself that his Majesty's present severities acquitted me of all past obligations.

At last I fixed upon a resolution, for which it is probable I may incur some censure, and not unjustly; for I confess I owe the preserving my eyes, and consequently my liberty, to my own great rashness and want of experience: because if I had then known the nature of princes and ministers, which I have since observed in many other courts, and their methods of treating criminals less obnoxious than myself, I should with great alacrity and readiness have submitted to so *easy* a punishment. But hurried on by the precipitancy of youth, and having his Imperial Majesty's license to pay my attendance upon the Emperor of Blefuscu, I took this opportunity, before the three days were elapsed, to send a letter to my friend the Secretary, signifying my resolution of setting out that morning for Blefuscu,[9] pursuant to the leave I had got; and without waiting for an answer, I went to that side of the island where our fleet lay. I seized a large man of war, tied a cable to the prow, and lifting up the anchors, I stripped myself, put my clothes (together with my coverlet, which I carried under my arm) into the vessel; and drawing it after me, between wading and swimming, arrived at the royal port of Blefuscu, where the people had long expected me. They lent me two guides to direct me to the capital city, which is of the same name; I held them in my hands until I came within two hundred yards of the gate; and desired them to signify my arrival to one of the secretaries, and let him

---

9. Before his trial for treason could be held, Bolingbroke had escaped to France.

know, I there waited his Majesty's commands. I had an answer in about an hour, that his Majesty, attended by the royal family, and great officers of the court, was coming out to receive me. I advanced a hundred yards; the Emperor, and his train, alighted from their horses, the Empress and ladies from their coaches; and I did not perceive they were in any fright or concern. I lay on the ground to kiss his Majesty's and the Empress's hand. I told his Majesty that I was come according to my promise, and with the license of the Emperor my master, to have the honor of seeing so mighty a monarch, and to offer him any service in my power, consistent with my duty to my own prince; not mentioning a word of my disgrace, because I had hitherto no regular information of it, and might suppose myself wholly ignorant of any such design; neither could I reasonably conceive that the Emperor would discover the secret while I was out of his power: wherein, however, it soon appeared I was deceived.

I shall not trouble the reader with the particular account of my reception at this court, which was suitable to the generosity of so great a prince; nor of the difficulties I was in for want of a house and bed, being forced to lie on the ground, wrapped up in my coverlet.

CHAPTER 8. *The author, by a lucky accident, finds means to leave Blefuscu; and, after some difficulties, returns safe to his native country.*

Three days after my arrival, walking out of curiosity to the northeast coast of the island, I observed, about half a league off, in the sea, somewhat that looked like a boat overturned. I pulled off my shoes and stockings, and wading two or three hundred yards, I found the object to approach nearer by force of the tide; and then plainly saw it to be a real boat, which I supposed might, by some tempest, have been driven from a ship. Whereupon I returned immediately towards the city, and desired his Imperial Majesty to lend me twenty of the tallest vessels he had left after the loss of his fleet, and three thousand seamen under the command of his Vice Admiral. This fleet sailed round, while I went back the shortest way to the coast where I first discovered the boat; I found the tide had driven it still nearer; the seamen were all provided with cordage, which I had beforehand twisted to a sufficient strength. When the ships came up, I stripped myself, and waded till I came within an hundred yards of the boat; after which I was forced to swim till I got up to it. The seamen threw me the end of the cord, which I fastened to a hole in the fore-part of the boat, and the other end to a man of war: but I found all my labor to little purpose; for being out of my depth, I was not able to work. In this necessity, I was forced to swim behind, and push the boat forwards as often as I could, with one of my hands; and the tide favoring me, I advanced so far, that I could just hold up my chin and feel the ground. I rested two or three minutes, and then gave the boat another shove, and so on till the sea was no higher than my armpits. And now the most laborious part being over, I took out my other cables which were stowed in one of the ships, and fastening them first to the boat, and then to nine of the vessels which attended me, the wind being favorable, the seamen towed, and I shoved till we arrived within forty yards of the shore; and waiting till the tide was out, I got dry to the boat, and by the assistance of two thousand men, with ropes and engines,[1] I made a shift to turn it on its bottom, and found it was but little damaged.

I shall not trouble the reader with the difficulties I was under by the help of certain paddles, which cost me ten days making, to get my boat to the royal port of Blefuscu; where a mighty concourse of people appeared upon my arrival, full of wonder at the sight of so prodigious a vessel. I told the Emperor that my good fortune had thrown this boat in my way, to carry me to some place from whence I might return into my native country; and begged his Majesty's orders for getting materials to fit it up, together with license to depart; which, after some kind expostulations, he was pleased to grant.

I did very much wonder, in all this time, not to have heard of any express relating to me from our Emperor to the court of Blefuscu. But I was afterwards given privately to understand, that his Imperial Majesty, never imagining I had the least notice of his designs, believed I was only gone to Blefuscu in performance of my promise, according to the license he had given me, which was well known at our court; and would return in a few days when that ceremony was ended. But he was at last in pain at my long absence; and, after consulting with the Treasurer, and the rest of that cabal, a person of quality was dispatched with the copy of the articles against me. This envoy had instructions to represent to the monarch of Blefuscu the great lenity of his master, who was content to punish me no further than with the loss of my eyes; that I had fled from justice, and if I did not return in two hours, I should be deprived of my title of *Nardac*, and declared a traitor. The envoy further added, that in order to maintain the peace and amity between both empires, his master expected, that his brother of Blefuscu would give orders to have me sent back to Lilliput, bound hand and foot, to be punished as a traitor.

The Emperor of Blefuscu, having taken three days to consult, returned an answer consisting of many civilities and excuses. He said, that as for sending me bound, his brother knew it was impossible; that although I had deprived him of his fleet, yet he owed great obligations to me for many good offices I had done him in making the peace. That however, both their Majesties would soon be made easy; for I had found a prodigious vessel on the shore, able to carry me on the sea, which he had given order to fit up with my own assistance and direction; and he hoped in a few weeks both empires would be freed from so insupportable an incumbrance.

With this answer the envoy returned to Lilliput, and the monarch of Blefuscu related to me all that had passed, offering me at the same time (but under the strictest confidence) his gracious protection, if I would

1. Mechanical contrivances.

continue in his service; wherein although I believed him sincere, yet I resolved never more to put any confidence in princes or ministers, where I could possibly avoid it; and therefore, with all due acknowledgements for his favorable intentions, I humbly begged to be excused. I told him, that since fortune, whether good or evil, had thrown a vessel in my way, I was resolved to venture myself in the ocean, rather than be an occasion of difference between two such mighty monarchs. Neither did I find the Emperor at all displeased; and I discovered by a certain accident, that he was very glad of my resolution, and so were most of his ministers.

These considerations moved me to hasten my departure somewhat sooner than I intended; to which the court, impatient to have me gone, very readily contributed. Five hundred workmen were employed to make two sails to my boat, according to my directions, by quilting thirteen fold of their strongest linen together. I was at the pains of making ropes and cables, by twisting ten, twenty or thirty of the thickest and strongest of theirs. A great stone that I happened to find, after a long search by the seashore, served me for an anchor. I had the tallow of three hundred cows for greasing my boat, and other uses. I was at incredible pains in cutting down some of the largest timber trees for oars and masts, wherein I was, however, much assisted by his Majesty's ship-carpenters, who helped me in smoothing them, after I had done the rough work.

In about a month, when all was prepared, I sent to receive his Majesty's commands, and to take my leave. The Emperor and royal family came out of the palace; I lay down on my face to kiss his hand, which he very graciously gave me: so did the Empress, and young princes of the blood. His Majesty presented me with fifty purses of two hundred *sprugs* apiece, together with his picture at full length, which I put immediately into one of my gloves, to keep it from being hurt. The ceremonies at my departure were too many to trouble the reader with at this time.

I stored the boat with the carcasses of an hundred oxen, and three hundred sheep, with bread and drink proportionable, and as much meat ready dressed as four hundred cooks could provide. I took with me six cows and two bulls alive, with as many ewes and rams, intending to carry them into my own country, and propagate the breed. And to feed them on board, I had a good bundle of hay, and a bag of corn.[2] I would gladly have taken a dozen of the natives; but this was a thing the Emperor would by no means permit; and besides a diligent search into my pockets, his Majesty engaged my honor not to carry away any of his subjects, although with their own consent and desire.

Having thus prepared all things as well as I was able, I set sail on the twenty-fourth day of September, 1701, at six in the morning; and when I had gone about four leagues to the northward, the wind being at southeast, at six in the evening, I descried a small island about half a league to the northwest. I advanced forward, and cast anchor on the lee-side of

---

2. Wheat.

the island, which seemed to be uninhabited. I then took some refreshment, and went to my rest. I slept well, and as I conjecture at least six hours; for I found the day broke in two hours after I awaked. It was a clear night; I eat my breakfast before the sun was up; and heaving anchor, the wind being favorable, I steered the same course that I had done the day before, wherein I was directed by my pocket compass. My intention was to reach, if possible, one of those islands which I had reason to believe lay to the northeast of Van Diemen's Land. I discovered nothing all that day; but upon the next, about three in the afternoon, when I had by my computation made twenty-four leagues from Blefuscu, I descried a sail steering to the southeast; my course was due east. I hailed her, but could get no answer; yet I found I gained upon her, for the wind slackened. I made all the sail I could, and in half an hour she spied me, then hung out her ancient,[3] and discharged a gun. It is not easy to express the joy I was in upon the unexpected hope of once more seeing my beloved country, and the dear pledges[4] I had left in it. The ship slackened her sails, and I came up with her between five and six in the evening, September 26; but my heart leapt within me to see her English colors. I put my cows and sheep into my coat-pockets and got on board with all my little cargo of provisions. The vessel was an English merchantman, returning from Japan by the North and South Seas;[5] the captain, Mr. John Biddel of Deptford, a very civil man, and an excellent sailor. We were now in the latitude of 30 degrees south; there were about fifty men in the ship; and here I met an old comrade of mine, one Peter Williams, who gave me a good character to the captain. This gentleman treated me with kindness, and desired I would let him know what place I came from last, and whither I was bound; which I did in few words; but he thought I was raving, and that the dangers I underwent had disturbed my head; whereupon I took my black cattle and sheep out of my pocket, which, after great astonishment, clearly convinced him of my veracity. I then showed him the gold given me by the Emperor of Blefuscu, together with his Majesty's picture at full length, and some other rarities of that country. I gave him two purses of two hundred *sprugs* each, and promised, when we arrived in England, to make him a present of a cow and a sheep big with young.

I shall not trouble the reader with a particular account of this voyage; which was very prosperous for the most part. We arrived in the Downs[6] on the 13th of April, 1702. I had only one misfortune, that the rats on board carried away one of my sheep; I found her bones in a hole, picked clean from the flesh. The rest of my cattle I got safe on shore, and set them a grazing in a bowling-green at Greenwich, where the fineness of the grass made them feed very heartily, though I had always feared the contrary; neither could I possibly have preserved them in so long a voyage, if the captain had not allowed me some of his best biscuit, which

---

3. Flag.
4. Hostages (i.e., his family).
5. North and South Pacific.

6. A rendezvous for ships off the southeast coast of England.

rubbed to powder, and mingled with water, was their constant food. The short time I continued in England, I made a considerable profit by showing my cattle to many persons of quality, and others: and before I began my second voyage, I sold them for six hundred pounds. Since my last return, I find the breed is considerably increased, especially the sheep; which I hope will prove much to the advantage of the woolen manufacture, by the fineness of the fleeces.

I stayed but two months with my wife and family; for my insatiable desire of seeing foreign countries would suffer me to continue no longer. I left fifteen hundred pounds with my wife, and fixed her in a good house at Redriff. My remaining stock I carried with me, part in money, and part in goods, in hopes to improve my fortunes. My eldest uncle, John, had left me an estate in land, near Epping, of about thirty pounds a year; and I had a long lease of the Black Bull in Fetter Lane, which yielded me as much more: so that I was not in any danger of leaving my family upon the parish.[7] My son Johnny, named so after his uncle, was at the grammar school, and a towardly[8] child. My daughter Betty (who is now well married, and has children) was then at her needlework. I took leave of my wife, and boy and girl, with tears on both sides; and went on board the *Adventure,* a merchant-ship of three hundred tons, bound for Surat, Captain John Nicholas of Liverpool, Commander. But my account of this voyage must be referred to the second part of my *Travels.*

Part 2. A Voyage to Brobdingnag

CHAPTER 1. *A great storm described. The longboat[1] sent to fetch water; the Author goes with it to discover the country. He is left on shore, is seized by one of the natives, and carried to a farmer's house. His reception there, with several accidents that happened there. A description of the inhabitants.*

Having been condemned by nature and fortune to an active and restless life, in ten months after my return I again left my native country, and took shipping in the Downs on the 20th day of June, 1702, in the *Adventure,* Captain John Nicholas, a Cornish man, Commander, bound for Surat.[2] We had a very prosperous gale till we arrived at the Cape of Good Hope, where we landed for fresh water, but discovering a leak we unshipped our goods and wintered there; for the Captain falling sick of an ague, we could not leave the Cape till the end of March. We then

---

7. On welfare (living on charity given by the parish).
8. Promising.
1. The largest boat carried by a merchant sailing vessel.
2. In India. The geography of the voyage is simple: The *Adventure,* after sailing up the east coast of Africa to about 5° south of the equator (the

"Line"), is blown past India into the Malay Archipelago, north of the islands of Buru and Ceram. The storm then drives the ship northward and eastward, away from the coast of Siberia ("Great Tartary") into the northeast Pacific, at that time unexplored. Brobdingnag lies somewhere in the vicinity of Alaska.

set sail, and had a good voyage till we passed the Straits of Madagascar;
but having got northward of that island, and to about five degrees south
latitude, the winds, which in those seas are observed to blow a constant
equal gale between the north and west from the beginning of December
to the beginning of May, on the 19th of April began to blow with much
greater violence and more westerly than usual, continuing so far twenty
days together, during which time we were driven a little to the east of
the Molucca Islands and about three degrees northward of the Line, as
our Captain found by an observation he took the 2nd of May, at which
time the wind ceased, and it was a perfect calm, whereat I was not a
little rejoiced. But he, being a man well experienced in the navigation
of those seas, bid us all prepare against a storm, which accordingly happened the day following: for a southern wind, called the southern mon-
soon, began to set in.

Finding it was likely to overblow,[3] we took in our spritsail, and stood
by to hand the foresail; but making foul weather, we looked the guns
were all fast, and handed the mizzen. The ship lay very broad off, so we
thought it better spooning before the sea, than trying or hulling. We
reefed the foresail and set him, we hauled aft the foresheet; the helm
was hard aweather. The ship wore bravely. We belayed the fore-down-
haul; but the sail was split, and we hauled down the yard and got the
sail into the ship, and unbound all the things clear of it. It was a very
fierce storm; the sea broke strange and dangerous. We hauled off upon
the lanyard of the whipstaff, and helped the man at helm. We would
not get down our topmast, but let all stand, because she scudded before
the sea very well, and we knew that the topmast being aloft, the ship was
the wholesomer, and made better way through the sea, seeing we had
searoom. When the storm was over, we set foresail and mainsail, and
brought the ship to. Then we set the mizzen, main topsail and the fore
topsail. Our course was east-northeast, the wind was at southwest. We
got the starboard tacks aboard, we cast off our weather braces and lifts;
we set in the lee braces, and hauled forward by the weather bowlings,
and hauled them tight, and belayed them, and hauled over the mizzen
tack to windward, and kept her full and by as near as she would lie.

During this storm, which was followed by a strong wind west-southwest, we were carried by my computation about five hundred leagues to
the east, so that the oldest sailor on board could not tell in what part of
the world we were. Our provisions held out well, our ship was stanch,
and our crew all in good health; but we lay in the utmost distress for
water. We thought it best to hold on the same course rather than turn
more northerly, which might have brought us to the northwest parts of
Great Tartary, and into the frozen sea.

On the 16th day of June, 1703, a boy on the topmast discovered land.
On the 17th we came in full view of a great island or continent (for we
knew not whether) on the south side whereof was a small neck of land

---

3. This paragraph is taken almost literally from   is ridiculing the use of technical terms by writers
Samuel Sturmy's *Mariner's Magazine* (1669). Swift   of popular voyages.

jutting out into the sea, and a creek[4] too shallow to hold a ship of above one hundred tons. We cast anchor within a league of this creek, and our Captain sent a dozen of his men well armed in the longboat, with vessels for water if any could be found. I desired his leave to go with them that I might see the country and make what discoveries I could. When we came to land we saw no river or spring, nor any sign of inhabitants. Our men therefore wandered on the shore to find out some fresh water near the sea, and I walked alone about a mile on the other side, where I observed the country all barren and rocky. I now began to be weary, and seeing nothing to entertain my curiosity, I returned gently down towards the creek; and the sea being full in my view, I saw our men already got into the boat, and rowing for life to the ship. I was going to hollow after them, although it had been to little purpose, when I observed a huge creature walking after them in the sea as fast as he could; he waded not much deeper than his knees and took prodigious strides, but our men had the start of him half a league, and the sea thereabouts being full of sharp-pointed rocks, the monster was not able to overtake the boat. This I was afterwards told, for I durst not stay to see the issue of that adventure, but ran as fast as I could the way I first went, and then climbed up a steep hill, which gave me some prospect of the country. I found it fully cultivated; but that which first surprised me was the length of the grass, which, in those grounds that seemed to be kept for hay, was about twenty foot high.[5]

I fell into a highroad, for so I took it to be, although it served to the inhabitants only as a footpath through a field of barley. Here I walked on for some time, but could see little on either side, it being now near harvest, and the corn[6] rising at least forty foot. I was an hour walking to the end of this field, which was fenced in with a hedge of at least one hundred and twenty foot high, and the trees so lofty that I could make no computation of their altitude. There was a stile to pass from this field into the next: it had four steps, and a stone to cross over when you came to the utmost. It was impossible for me to climb this stile, because every step was six foot high, and the upper stone above twenty. I was endeavoring to find some gap in the hedge when I discovered one of the inhabitants in the next field advancing towards the stile, of the same size with him whom I saw in the sea pursuing our boat. He appeared as tall as an ordinary spire-steeple, and took about ten yards at every stride, as near as I could guess. I was struck with the utmost fear and astonishment, and ran to hide myself in the corn, from whence I saw him at the top of the stile, looking back into the next field on the right hand; and heard him call in a voice many degrees louder than a speaking trumpet; but the noise was so high in the air that at first I certainly thought it was thunder. Whereupon seven monsters like himself came towards him with reaping hooks in their hands, each hook about the largeness of six

---

4. A small bay or cove, affording anchorage.
5. Swift's intention, not always carried out accurately, is that everything in Brobdingnag should

be, in relation to our familiar world, on a scale of ten to one.
6. Wheat, not maize.

scythes. These people were not so well clad as the first, whose servants
or laborers they seemed to be. For, upon some words he spoke, they
went to reap the corn in the field where I lay. I kept from them at as
great a distance as I could, but was forced to move with extreme difficulty, for the stalks of the corn were sometimes not above a foot distant,
so that I could hardly squeeze my body betwixt them. However, I made
a shift to go forward till I came to a part of the field where the corn had
been laid by the rain and wind; here it was impossible for me to advance
a step, for the stalks were so interwoven that I could not creep through,
and the beards of the fallen ears so strong and pointed that they pierced
through my clothes into my flesh. At the same time I heard the reapers
not above an hundred yards behind me. Being quite dispirited with toil,
and wholly overcome by grief and despair, I lay down between two ridges
and heartily wished I might there end my days. I bemoaned my desolate
widow and fatherless children; I lamented my own folly and willfulness
in attempting a second voyage against the advice of all my friends and
relations. In this terrible agitation of mind, I could not forbear thinking
of Lilliput, whose inhabitants looked upon me as the greatest prodigy
that ever appeared in the world; where I was able to draw an imperial
fleet in my hand, and perform those other actions which will be recorded
forever in the chronicles of that empire, while posterity shall hardly believe
them, although attested by millions. I reflected what a mortification it
must prove to me to appear as inconsiderable in this nation as one single
Lilliputian would be among us. But this I conceived was to be the least
of my misfortunes; for as human creatures are observed to be more savage and cruel in proportion to their bulk, what could I expect but to be
a morsel in the mouth of the first among these enormous barbarians
who should happen to seize me? Undoubtedly philosophers are in the
right when they tell us that nothing is great or little otherwise than by
comparison. It might have pleased fortune to let the Lilliputians find
some nation where the people were as diminutive with respect to them
as they were to me. And who knows but that even this prodigious race
of mortals might be equally overmatched in some distant part of the
world, whereof we have yet no discovery?

Scared and confounded as I was, I could not forbear going on with
these reflections; when one of the reapers approaching within ten yeards
of the ridge where I lay, made me apprehend that with the next step I
should be squashed to death under his foot, or cut in two with his reaping hook. And therefore when he was again about to move, I screamed
as loud as fear could make me. Whereupon the huge creature trod short,
and looking round about under him for some time, at last espied me as
I lay on the ground. He considered a while with the caution of one who
endeavors to lay hold on a small dangerous animal in such a manner
that it shall not be able either to scratch or to bite him, as I myself have
sometimes done with a weasel in England. At length he ventured to take
me up behind by the middle between his forefinger and thumb, and
brought me within three yards of his eyes, that he might behold my

shape more perfectly. I guessed his meaning, and my good fortune gave me so much presence of mind that I resolved not to struggle in the least as he held me in the air about sixty foot from the ground, although he grievously pinched my sides, for fear I should slip through his fingers. All I ventured was to raise mine eyes towards the sun, and place my hands together in a supplicating posture, and to speak some words in an humble melancholy tone, suitable to the condition I then was in. For I apprehended every moment that he would dash me against the ground, as we usually do any little hateful animal which we have a mind to destroy. But my good star would have it that he appeared pleased with my voice and gestures, and began to look upon me as a curiosity, much wondering to hear me pronounce articulate words, although he could not understand them. In the meantime I was not able to forbear groaning and shedding tears and turning my head towards my sides, letting him know, as well as I could, how cruelly I was hurt by the pressure of his thumb and finger. He seemed to apprehend my meaning; for, lifting up the lappet[7] of his coat, he put me gently into it, and immediately ran along with me to his master, who was a substantial farmer, and the same person I had first seen in the field.

The farmer having (as I supposed by their talk) received such an account of me as his servant could give him, took a piece of a small straw about the size of a walking staff, and therewith lifted up the lappets of my coat, which it seems he thought to be some kind of covering that nature had given me. He blew my hairs aside to take a better view of my face. He called his hinds[8] about him, and asked them (as I afterwards learned) whether they had ever seen in the fields any little creature that resembled me. He then placed me softly on the ground upon all four; but I got immediately up, and walked slowly backwards and forwards, to let those people see I had no intent to run away. They all sat down in a circle about me, the better to observe my motions. I pulled off my hat, and made a low bow towards the farmer; I fell on my knees, and lifted up my hands and eyes, and spoke several words as loud as I could; I took a purse of gold out of my pocket, and humbly presented it to him. He received it on the palm of his hand, then applied it close to his eye to see what it was, and afterwards turned it several times with the point of a pin (which he took out of his sleeve), but could make nothing of it. Whereupon I made a sign that he should place his hand on the ground; I then took the purse, and opening it, poured all the gold into his palm. There were six Spanish pieces of four pistoles each, beside twenty or thirty smaller coins. I saw him wet the tip of his little finger upon his tongue, and take up one of my largest pieces, and then another; but he seemed to be wholly ignorant what they were. He made me a sign to put them again into my purse, and the purse again into my pocket, which after offering to him several times, I thought it best to do.

The farmer by this time was convinced I must be a rational creature.

___

7. Flap or fold.   8. Farm servants.

He spoke often to me, but the sound of his voice pierced my ears like that of a water mill, yet his words were articulate enough. I answered as loud as I could in several languages, and he often laid his ear within two yards of me, but all in vain, for we were wholly unintelligible to each other. He then sent his servants to their work, and taking his handkerchief out of his pocket, he doubled and spread it on his hand, which he placed flat on the ground with the palm upwards, making me a sign to step into it, as I could easily do, for it was not above a foot in thickness. I thought it my part to obey, and for fear of falling, laid myself at full length upon the handkerchief, with the remainder of which he lapped me up to the head for further security, and in this manner carried me home to his house. There he called his wife, and showed me to her; but she screamed and ran back as women in England do at the sight of a toad or a spider. However, when she had a while seen my behavior, and how well I observed the signs her husband made, she was soon reconciled, and by degrees grew extremely tender of me.

It was about twelve at noon, and a servant brought in dinner. It was only one substantial dish of meat (fit for the plain condition of an husbandman) in a dish of about four-and-twenty foot diameter. The company were the farmer and his wife, three children, and an old grandmother. When they were sat down, the farmer placed me at some distance from him on the table, which was thirty foot high from the floor. I was in a terrible fright, and kept as far as I could from the edge, for fear of falling. The wife minced a bit of meat, then crumbled some bread on a trencher,[9] and placed it before me. I made her a low bow, took out my knife and fork, and fell to eat; which gave them exceeding delight. The mistress sent her maid for a small dram cup, which held about two gallons, and filled it with drink; I took up the vessel with much difficulty in both hands, and in a most respectful manner drank to her ladyship's health, expressing the words as loud as I could in English; which made the company laugh so heartily that I was almost deafened with the noise. This liquor tasted like a small cider,[1] and was not unpleasant. Then the master made me a sign to come to his trencher side; but as I walked on the table, being in great surprise all the time, as the indulgent reader will easily conceive and excuse, I happened to stumble against a crust, and fell flat on my face, but received no hurt. I got up immediately, and observing the good people to be in much concern, I took my hat (which I held under my arm out of good manners) and waving it over my head, made three huzzas to show I had got no mischief by my fall. But advancing forwards toward my master (as I shall henceforth call him), his youngest son who sat next him, an arch[2] boy of about ten years old, took me up by the legs, and held me so high in the air that I trembled every limb; but his father snatched me from him, and at the same time gave him such a box on the left ear as would have felled an European troop of horse to the earth, ordering him to be taken

9. A platter.   2. Mischievous.
1. I.e., weak cider.

from the table. But being afraid the boy might owe me a spite, and well remembering how mischievous all children among us naturally are to sparrows, rabbits, young kittens, and puppy dogs, I fell on my knees, and pointing to the boy, made my master to understand, as well as I could, that I desired his son might be pardoned. The father complied, and the lad took his seat again; whereupon I went to him and kissed his hand, which my master took, and made him stroke me gently with it.

In the midst of dinner, my mistress's favorite cat leaped into her lap. I heard a noise behind me like that of a dozen stocking weavers at work; and turning my head, I found it proceeded from the purring of this animal, who seemed to be three times larger than an ox, as I computed by the view of her head and one of her paws, while her mistress was feeding and stroking her. The fierceness of this creature's countenance altogether discomposed me, although I stood at the farther end of the table, about fifty foot off, and although my mistress held her fast for fear she might give a spring and seize me in her talons. But it happened there was no danger, for the cat took not the least notice of me when my master placed me within three yards of her. And as I have been always told, and found true by experience in my travels, that flying or discovering[3] fear before a fierce animal is a certain way to make it pursue or attack you, so I resolved in this dangerous juncture to show no manner of concern. I walked with intrepidity five or six times before the very head of the cat, and came within half a yard of her; whereupon she drew herself back, as if she were more afraid of me; I had less apprehension concerning the dogs, whereof three or four came into the room, as it is usual in farmers' houses; one of which was a mastiff, equal in bulk to four elephants, and a greyhound, somewhat taller than the mastiff, but not so large.

When dinner was almost done, the nurse came in with a child of a year old in her arms, who immediately spied me, and began a squall that you might have heard from London Bridge to Chelsea, after the usual oratory of infants, to get me for a plaything. The mother out of pure indulgence took me up, and put me towards the child, who presently seized me by the middle, and got my head in his mouth, where I roared so loud that the urchin was frighted and let me drop; and I should infallibly have broke my neck if the mother had not held her apron under me. The nurse to quiet her babe made use of a rattle, which was a kind of hollow vessel filled with great stones, and fastened by a cable to the child's waist: but all in vain, so that she was forced to apply the last remedy by giving it suck. I must confess no object ever disgusted me so much as the sight of her monstrous breast, which I cannot tell what to compare with so as to give the curious reader an idea of its bulk, shape, and color. It stood prominent six foot, and could not be less than sixteen in circumference. The nipple was about half the bigness of my head, and the hue both of that and the dug so varified with spots, pim-

3. Revealing.

ples, and freckles that nothing could appear more nauseous: for I had a near sight of her, she sitting down the more conveniently to give suck, and I standing on the table. This made me reflect upon the fair skins of our English ladies, who appear so beautiful to us, only because they are of our own size, and their defects not to be seen but through a magnifying glass, where we find by experiment that the smoothest and whitest skins look rough and coarse and ill colored.

I remember when I was at Lilliput, the complexion of those diminutive people appeared to me the fairest in the world; and talking upon this subject with a person of learning there, who was an intimate friend of mine, he said that my face appeared much fairer and smoother when he looked on me from the ground than it did upon a nearer view when I took him up in my hand and brought him close, which he confessed was at first a very shocking sight. He said he could discover great holes in my skin; that the stumps of my beard were ten times stronger than the bristles of a boar, and my complexion made up of several colors altogether disagreeable: although I must beg leave to say for myself that I am as fair as most of my sex and country and very little sunburnt by all my travels. On the other side, discoursing of the ladies in that Emperor's court, he used to tell me one had freckles, another too wide a mouth, a third too large a nose; nothing of which I was able to distinguish. I confess this reflection was obvious enough; which however I could not forbear, lest the reader might think those vast creatures were actually deformed: for I must do them justice to say they are a comely race of people; and particularly the features of my master's countenance, although he were but a farmer, when I beheld him from the height of sixty foot, appeared very well proportioned.

When dinner was done, my master went out to his laborers; and as I could discover by his voice and gesture, gave his wife a strict charge to take care of me. I was very much tired and disposed to sleep, which my mistress perceiving, she put me on her own bed, and covered me with a clean white handkerchief, but larger and coarser than the mainsail of a man-of-war.

I slept about two hours, and dreamed I was at home with my wife and children, which aggravated my sorrows when I awaked and found myself alone in a vast room, between two and three hundred foot wide, and above two hundred high, lying in a bed twenty yards wide. My mistress was gone about her household affairs, and had locked me in. The bed was eight yards from the floor. Some natural necessities required me to get down; I durst not presume to call, and if I had, it would have been in vain with such a voice as mine at so great a distance from the room where I lay to the kitchen where the family kept. While I was under these circumstances, two rats crept up the curtains, and ran smelling backwards and forwards on the bed. One of them came up almost to my face; whereupon I rose in a fright, and drew out my hanger[4] to defend

---

4. A short, broad sword.

myself. These horrible animals had the boldness to attack me on both sides, and one of them held his forefeet at my collar; but I had the good fortune to rip up his belly before he could do me any mischief. He fell down at my feet; and the other seeing the fate of his comrade, made his escape, but not without one good wound on the back, which I gave him as he fled, and made the blood run trickling from him. After this exploit I walked gently to and fro on the bed, to recover my breath and loss of spirits. These creatures were of the size of a large mastiff, but infinitely more nimble and fierce; so that if I had taken off my belt before I went to sleep, I must have infallibly been torn to pieces and devoured. I measured the tail of the dead rat, and found it to be two yards long, wanting an inch; but it went against my stomach to drag the carcass off the bed, where it lay still bleeding; I observed it had yet some life, but with a strong slash cross the neck, I thoroughly dispatched it.

Soon after, my mistress came into the room, who seeing me all bloody, ran and took me up in her hand. I pointed to the dead rat, smiling and making other signs to show I was not hurt, whereat she was extremely rejoiced, calling the maid to take up the dead rat with a pair of tongs, and throw it out of the window. Then she set me on a table, where I showed her my hanger all bloody, and wiping it on the lappet of my coat, returned it to the scabbard. I was pressed to do more than one thing, which another could not do for me, and therefore endeavored to make my mistress understand that I desired to be set down on the floor; which after she had done, my bashfulness would not suffer me to express myself farther than by pointing to the door, and bowing several times. The good woman with much difficulty at last perceived what I would be at, and taking me up again in her hand, walked into the garden, where she set me down. I went on one side about two hundred yards; and beckoning to her not to look or to follow me, I hid myself between two leaves of sorrel, and there discharged the necessities of nature.

I hope the gentle reader will excuse me for dwelling on these and the like particulars, which however insignificant they may appear to groveling vulgar[5] minds, yet will certainly help a philosopher to enlarge his thoughts and imagination, and apply them to the benefit of public as well as private life, which was my sole design in presenting this and other accounts of my travels to the world; wherein I have been chiefly studious of truth, without affecting any ornaments of learning or of style. But the whole scene of this voyage made so strong an impression on my mind, and is so deeply fixed in my memory, that in committing it to paper I did not omit one material circumstance; however, upon a strict review, I blotted out several passages of less moment which were in my first copy, for fear of being censured as tedious and trifling, whereof travelers are often, perhaps not without justice, accused.

---

5. Commonplace, uncultivated, in contrast to the scientist ("philosopher"); an irony.

CHAPTER 2. *A description of the farmer's daughter. The Author carried to a market town, and then to the metropolis. The particulars of his journey.*

My mistress had a daughter of nine years old, a child of towardly parts for her age, very dexterous at her needle, and skillful in dressing her baby.[6] Her mother and she contrived to fit up the baby's cradle for me against night: the cradle was put into a small drawer of a cabinet, and the drawer placed upon a hanging shelf for fear of the rats. This was my bed all the time I stayed with those people, although made more convenient by degrees as I began to learn their language, and make my wants known. This young girl was so handy, that after I had once or twice pulled off my clothes before her, she was able to dress and undress me, although I never gave her that trouble when she would let me do either myself. She made me seven shirts, and some other linen of as fine cloth as could be got, which indeed was coarser than sackcloth, and these she constantly washed for me with her own hands. She was likewise my schoolmistress to teach me the language: when I pointed to anything, she told me the name of it in her own tongue, so that in a few days I was able to call for whatever I had a mind to. She was very good-natured, and not above forty foot high, being little for her age. She gave me the name of *Grildrig*, which the family took up, and afterwards the whole kingdom. The word imports what the Latins call *nanunculus*, the Italian *homunceletino*,[7] and the English *mannikin*. To her I chiefly owe my preservation in that country: we never parted while I was there; I called her my *Glumdalclitch*, or little nurse: and I should be guilty of great ingratitude if I omitted this honorable mention of her care and affection towards me, which I heartily wish it lay in my power to requite as she deserves, instead of being the innocent but unhappy instrument of her disgrace, as I have too much reason to fear.

It now began to be known and talked of in the neighborhood that my master had found a strange animal in the field, about the bigness of a *splacknuck*, but exactly shaped in every part like a human creature, which it likewise imitated in all its actions: seemed to speak in a little language of its own, had already learned several words of theirs, went erect upon two legs, was tame and gentle, would come when it was called, do whatever it was bid, had the finest limbs in the world, and a complexion fairer than a nobleman's daughter of three years old. Another farmer who lived hard by, and was a particular friend of my master, came on a visit on purpose to inquire into the truth of this story. I was immediately produced, and placed upon a table, where I walked as I was commanded, drew my hanger, put it up again, made my reverence to my master's guest, asked him in his own language how he did, and told him

---

6. Doll.
7. The Latin and Italian words are Swift's own coinages, as, of course, are the various words from the Brobdingnagian language.

he was welcome, just as my little nurse had instructed me. This man, who was old and dimsighted, put on his spectacles to behold me better, at which I could not forbear laughing very heartily, for his eyes appeared like the full moon shining into a chamber at two windows. Our people, who discovered the cause of my mirth, bore me company in laughing, at which the old fellow was fool enough to be angry and out of countenance. He had the character of a great miser, and to my misfortune he well deserved it by the cursed advice he gave my master to show me as a sight upon a market day in the next town, which was half an hour's riding, about two and twenty miles from our house. I guessed there was some mischief contriving when I observed my master and his friend whispering long together, sometimes pointing at me; and my fears made me fancy that I overheard and understood some of their words. But the next morning Glumdalclitch, my little nurse, told me the whole matter, which she had cunningly picked out from her mother. The poor girl laid me on her bosom, and fell a weeping with shame and grief. She apprehended some mischief would happen to me from rude vulgar folks, who might squeeze me to death, or break one of my limbs by taking me in their hands. She had also observed how modest I was in my nature, how nicely I regarded my honor, and what an indignity I should conceive it to be exposed for money as a public spectacle to the meanest of the people. She said her papa and mamma had promised that Grildrig should be hers; but now she found they meant to serve her as they did last year, when they pretended to give her a lamb, and yet, as soon as it was fat, sold it to a butcher. For my own part, I may truly affirm that I was less concerned than my nurse. I had a strong hope, which never left me, that I should one day recover my liberty; and as to the ignominy of being carried about for a monster, I considered myself to be a perfect stranger in the country, and that such a misfortune could never be charged upon me as a reproach, if ever I should return to England; since the King of Great Britain himself, in my condition, must have undergone the same distress.

My master, pursuant to the advice of his friend, carried me in a box the next market day to the neighboring town, and took along with him his little daughter, my nurse, upon a pillion[8] behind him. The box was close on every side, with a little door for me to go in and out, and a few gimlet holes to let in air. The girl had been so careful to put the quilt of her baby's bed into it, for me to lie down on. However, I was terribly shaken and discomposed in this journey, although it were but of half an hour. For the horse went about forty foot at every step, and trotted so high that the agitation was equal to the rising and falling of a ship in a great storm, but much more frequent. Our journey was somewhat further than from London to St. Albans. My master alighted at an inn which he used to frequent; and after consulting a while with the innkeeper, and making some necessary preparations, he hired the *Grultrud*,

---

8. A pad attached to the hinder part of a saddle, on which a second person, usually a woman, could ride.

or crier, to give notice through the town of a strange creature to be seen
at the Sign of the Green Eagle, not so big as a *splacknuck* (an animal in
that country very finely shaped, about six foot long), and in every part
of the body resembling an human creature, could speak several words
and perform an hundred diverting tricks.

I was placed upon a table in the largest room of the inn, which might
be near three hundred foot square. My little nurse stood on a low stool
close to the table, to take care of me, and direct what I should do. My
master, to avoid a crowd, would suffer only thirty people at a time to see
me. I walked about on the table as the girl commanded; she asked me
questions as far as she knew my understanding of the language reached,
and I answered them as loud as I could. I turned about several times to
the company, paid my humble respects, said they were welcome, and
used some other speeches I had been taught. I took up a thimble filled
with liquor, which Glumdalclitch had given me for a cup, and drank
their health. I drew out my hanger, and flourished with it after the manner of fencers in England. My nurse gave me part of a straw, which I
exercised as pike, having learned the art in my youth. I was that day
shown to twelve sets of company, and as often forced to go over again
with the same fopperies, till I was half dead with weariness and vexation.
For those who had seen me made such wonderful reports that the people
were ready to break down the doors to come in. My master for his own
interest would not suffer anyone to touch me except my nurse; and, to
prevent danger, benches were set round the table at such a distance as
put me out of everybody's reach. However, an unlucky schoolboy aimed
a hazelnut directly at my head, which very narrowly missed me; otherwise, it came with so much violence that it would have infallibly knocked
out my brains, for it was almost as large as a small pumpion:[9] but I had
the satisfaction to see the young rogue well beaten, and turned out of
the room.

My master gave public notice that he would show me again the next
market day, and in the meantime he prepared a more convenient vehicle for me, which he had reason enough to do; for I was so tired with
my first journey, and with entertaining company for eight hours together,
that I could hardly stand upon my legs or speak a word. It was at least
three days before I recovered my strength; and that I might have no rest
at home, all the neighboring gentlemen from an hundred miles round,
hearing of my fame, came to see me at my master's own house. There
could not be fewer than thirty persons with their wives and children (for
the country is very populous); and my master demanded the rate of a full
room whenever he showed me at home, although it were only to a single
family. So that for some time I had but little ease every day of the week
(except Wednesday, which is their Sabbath) although I were not carried
to the town.

My master finding how profitable I was like to be, resolved to carry

9. Pumpkin.

me to the most considerable cities of the kingdom. Having therefore provided himself with all things necessary for a long journey, and settled his affairs at home, he took leave of his wife; and upon the 17th of August, 1703, about two months after my arrival, we set out for the metropolis, situated near the middle of that empire, and about three thousand miles distance from our house. My master made his daughter Glumdalclitch ride behind him. She carried me on her lap in a box tied about her waist. The girl had lined it on all sides with the softest cloth she could get, well quilted underneath, furnished it with her baby's bed, provided me with linen and other necessaries, and made everything as convenient as she could. We had no other company but a boy of the house, who rode after us with the luggage.

My master's design was to show me in all the towns by the way, and to step out of the road for fifty or an hundred miles to any village or person of quality's house where he might expect custom. We made easy journeys of not above seven or eight score miles a day: for Glumdalclitch, on purpose to spare me, complained she was tired with the trotting of the horse. She often took me out of my box at my own desire, to give me air and show me the country, but always held me fast by leading strings. We passed over five or six rivers many degrees broader and deeper than the Nile or the Ganges; and there was hardly a rivulet so small as the Thames at London Bridge. We were ten weeks in our journey, and I was shown in eighteen large towns, besides many large villages and private families.

On the 26th day of October, we arrived at the metropolis, called in their language *Lorbrulgrud*, or Pride of the Universe. My master took a lodging in the principal street of the city, not far from the royal palace, and put out bills in the usual form, containing an exact description of my person and parts. He hired a large room between three and four hundred foot wide. He provided a table sixty foot in diameter, upon which I was to act my part, and palisadoed it round three foot from the edge, and as many high, to prevent my falling over. I was shown ten times a day to the wonder and satisfaction of all people. I could now speak the language tolerably well, and perfectly understood every word that was spoken to me. Besides, I had learned their alphabet, and could make a shift to explain a sentence here and there; for Glumdalclitch had been my instructor while we were at home, and at leisure hours during our journey. She carried a little book in her pocket, not much larger than a Sanson's *Atlas*;[1] it was a common treatise for the use of young girls, giving a short account of their religion: out of this she taught me my letters, and interpreted the words.

CHAPTER 3. *The Author sent for to Court. The Queen buys him of his master, the farmer, and presents him to the King. He disputes with his Majesty's great scholars. An apartment at Court provided for the Author.*

1. I.e., over 2 feet long and about 2 feet wide.

He is in high favor with the Queen. He stands up for the honor of his own country. His quarrels with the Queen's dwarf.

The frequent labors I underwent every day made in a few weeks a very considerable change in my health: the more my master got by me, the more unsatiable he grew. I had quite lost my stomach, and was almost reduced to a skeleton. The farmer observed it, and concluding I soon must die, resolved to make as good a hand of me as he could. While he was thus reasoning and resolving with himself, a *Slardral*, or Gentleman Usher, came from Court, commanding my master to carry me immediately thither for the diversion of the Queen and her ladies. Some of the latter had already been to see me and reported strange things of my beauty, behavior, and good sense. Her Majesty and those who attended her were beyond measure delighted with my demeanor. I fell on my knees and begged the honor of kissing her Imperial foot; but this gracious princess held out her little finger towards me (after I was set on a table), which I embraced in both my arms, and put the tip of it, with the utmost respect, to my lip. She made me some general questions about my country and my travels, which I answered as distinctly and in as few words as I could. She asked whether I would be content to live at Court. I bowed down to the board of the table, and humbly answered that I was my master's slave, but if I were at my own disposal, I should be proud to devote my life to her Majesty's service. She then asked my master whether he were willing to sell me at a good price. He, who apprehended I could not live a month, was ready enough to part with me, and demanded a thousand pieces of gold, which were ordered him on the spot, each piece being about the bigness of eight hundred moidores;[2] but, allowing for the proportion of all things between that country and Europe, and the high price of gold among them, was hardly so great a sum as a thousand guineas would be in England. I then said to the Queen, since I was now her Majesty's most humble creature and vassal, I must beg the favor that Glumdalclitch, who had always tended me with so much care and kindness, and understood to do it so well, might be admitted into her service, and continue to be my nurse and instructor. Her Majesty agreed to my petition, and easily got the farmer's consent, who was glad enough to have his daughter preferred at Court; and the poor girl herself was not able to hide her joy. My late master withdrew, bidding me farewell, and saying he had left me in a good service; to which I replied not a word, only making him a slight bow.

The Queen observed my coldness, and when the farmer was gone out of the apartment, asked me the reason. I made bold to tell her Majesty that I owed no other obligation to my late master than his not dashing out the brains of a poor harmless creature found by chance in his field; which obligation was amply recompensed by the gain he had made in showing me through half the kingdom, and the price he had now sold

2. Portuguese coins.

me for. That the life I had since led was laborious enough to kill an animal of ten times my strength. That my health was much impaired by the continual drudgery of entertaining the rabble every hour of the day; and that if my master had not thought my life in danger, her Majestry would not have got so cheap a bargain. But as I was out of all fear of being ill treated under the protection of so great and good an Empress, the Ornament of Nature, the Darling of the World, the Delight of her Subjects, the Phoenix of the Creation; so I hoped my late master's apprehensions would appear to be groundless, for I already found my spirits to revive by the influence of her most august presence.

This was the sum of my speech, delivered with great improprieties and hesitation; the latter part was altogether framed in the style peculiar to that people, whereof I learned some phrases from Glumdalclitch, while she was carrying me to Court.

The Queen, giving great allowance for my defectiveness in speaking, was however surprised at so much wit and good sense in so diminutive an animal. She took me in her own hand, and carried me to the King, who was then retired to his cabinet.[3] His Majesty, a prince of much gravity, and austere countenance, not well observing my shape at first view, asked the Queen after a cold manner how long it was since she grew fond of a *splacknuck*; for such it seems he took me to be, as I lay upon my breast in her Majesty's right hand. But this princess, who hath an infinite deal of wit and humor, set me gently on my feet upon the scrutore,[4] and commanded me to give his Majesty an account of myself, which I did in a very few words; and Glumdalclitch, who attended at the cabinet door, and could not endure I should be out of her sight, being admitted, confirmed all that had passed from my arrival at her father's house.

The King, although he be as learned a person as any in his dominions, had been educated in the study of philosophy and particularly mathematics; yet when he observed my shape exactly, and saw me walk erect, before I began to speak, conceived I might be a piece of clockwork (which is in that country arrived to a very great perfection) contrived by some ingenious artist. But when he heard my voice, and found what I delivered to be regular and rational, he could not conceal his astonishment. He was by no means satisfied with the relation I gave him of the manner I came into his kingdom, but thought it a story concerted between Glumdalclitch and her father, who had taught me a set of words to make me sell at a higher price. Upon this imagination he put several other questions to me, and still received rational answers, no otherwise defective than by a foreign accent, and an imperfect knowledge in the language, with some rustic phrases which I had learned at the farmer's house, and did not suit the polite style of a court.

His Majesty sent for three great scholars who were then in their weekly waiting (according to the custom in that country). These gentlemen,

---

3. A private apartment.   4. Writing desk.

after they had a while examined my shape with much nicety, were of different opinions concerning me. They all agreed that I could not be produced according to the regular laws of nature, because I was not framed with a capacity of preserving my life, either by swiftness, or climbing of trees, or digging holes in the earth. They observed by my teeth, which they viewed with great exactness, that I was a carnivorous animal; yet most quadrupeds being an overmatch for me, and field mice, with some others, too nimble, they could not imagine how I should be able to support myself, unless I fed upon snails and other insects; which they offered, by many learned arguments, to evince that I could not possibly do. One of them seemed to think that I might be an embryo, or abortive birth. But this opinion was rejected by the other two, who observed my limbs to be perfect and finished, and that I had lived several years, as it was manifest from my beard, the stumps whereof they plainly discovered through a magnifying glass. They would not allow me to be a dwarf, because my littleness was beyond all degrees of comparison; for the Queen's favorite dwarf, the smallest ever known in that kingdom, was nearly thirty foot high. After much debate, they concluded unanimously that I was only *relplum scalcath*, which is interpreted literally, *lusus naturae*;[5] a determination exactly agreeable to the modern philosophy of Europe, whose professors, disdaining the old evasion of *occult causes*, whereby the followers of Aristotle endeavor in vain to disguise their ignorance, have invented this wonderful solution of all difficulties, to the unspeakable advancement of human knowledge.

After this decisive conclusion, I entreated to be heard a word or two. I applied myself to the King, and assured his Majesty that I came from a country which abounded with several millions of both sexes, and of my own stature, where the animals, trees, and houses were all in proportion, and where by consequence I might be as able to defend myself, and to find sustenance, as any of his Majesty's subjects could do here; which I took for a full answer to those gentlemen's arguments. To this they only replied with a smile of contempt, saying that the farmer had instructed me very well in my lesson. The King, who had a much better understanding, dismissing his learned men, sent for the farmer, who by good fortune was not yet gone out of town; having therefore first examined him privately, and then confronted him with me and the young girl, his Majesty began to think that what we told him might possibly be true. He desired the Queen to order that a particular care should be taken of me, and was of opinion that Glumdalclitch should still continue in her office of tending me, because he observed we had a great affection for each other. A convenient apartment was provided for her at Court; she had a sort of governess appointed to take care of her education, a maid to dress her, and two other servants for menial offices; but the care of me was wholly appropriated to herself. The Queen com-

5. One of nature's sports, or, roughly, freaks. Swift had contempt for both the medieval schoolmen, who discussed "occult causes," the unknown causes of observable effects, and modern scientists, who, he believed, often concealed their ignorance by using equally meaningless terms.

manded her own cabinetmaker to contrive a box that might serve me for a bedchamber, after the model that Glumdalclitch and I should agree upon. This man was a most ingenious artist, and according to my directions, in three weeks finished for me a wooden chamber of sixteen foot square and twelve high, with sash windows, a door, and two closets, like a London bedchamber. The board that made the ceiling was to be lifted up and down by two hinges, to put in a bed ready furnished by her Majesty's upholsterer, which Glumdalclitch took out every day to air, made it with her own hands, and letting it down at night, locked up the roof over me. A nice[6] workman, who was famous for little curiosities, undertook to make me two chairs, with backs and frames, of a substance not unlike ivory, and two tables, with a cabinet to put my things in. The room was quilted on all sides, as well as the floor and the ceiling, to prevent any accident from the carelessness of those who carried me, and to break the force of a jolt when I went in a coach. I desired a lock for my door to prevent rats and mice from coming in: the smith, after several attempts, made the smallest that ever was seen among them, for I have known a larger at the gate of a gentleman's house in England. I made a shift[7] to keep the key in a pocket of my own, fearing Glumdalclitch might lose it. The Queen likewise ordered the thinnest silks that could be gotten, to make me clothes, not much thicker than an English blanket, very cumbersome till I was accustomed to them. They were after the fashion of the kingdom, partly resembling the Persian, and partly the Chinese, and are a very grave, decent habit.

The Queen became so fond of my company that she could not dine without me. I had a table placed upon the same at which her Majesty ate, just at her left elbow, and a chair to sit on. Glumdalclitch stood upon a stool on the floor, near my table, to assist and take care of me. I had an entire set of silver dishes and plates, and other necessaries, which, in proportion to those of the Queen, were not much bigger than what I have seen of the same kind in a London toyshop,[8] for the furniture of a baby-house: these my little nurse kept in her pocket in a silver box and gave me at meals as I wanted them, always cleaning them herself. No person dined with the Queen but the two Princesses Royal, the elder sixteen years old, and the younger at that time thirteen and a month. Her Majesty used to put a bit of meat upon one of my dishes, out of which I carved for myself; and her diversion was to see me eat in miniature. For the Queen (who had indeed but a weak stomach) took up at one mouthful as much as a dozen English farmers could eat at a meal, which to me was for some time a very nauseous sight. She would craunch the wing of a lark, bones and all, between her teeth, although it were nine times as large as that of a full-grown turkey; and put a bit of bread into her mouth as big as two twelve-penny loaves. She drank out of a golden cup, above a hogshead at a draught. Her knives were twice as long as a scythe set straight upon the handle. The spoons, forks, and

---

6. Exact.   8. A shop for selling knickknacks.
7. Contrived.

other instruments were all in the same proportion. I remember when Glumdalclitch carried me out of curiosity to see some of the tables at Court, where ten or a dozen of these enormous knives and forks were lifted up together, I thought I had never till then beheld so terrible a sight.

It is the custom that every Wednesday (which, as I have before observed, was their Sabbath) the King and Queen, with the royal issue of both sexes, dine together in the apartment of his Majesty, to whom I was now become a favorite; and at these times my little chair and table were placed at his left hand, before one of the salt-cellars. This prince took a pleasure in conversing with me, inquiring into the manners, religion, laws, government, and learning of Europe; wherein I gave him the best account I was able. His apprehension was so clear, and his judgment so exact, that he made very wise reflections and observations upon all I said. But I confess that after I had been a little too copious in talking of my own beloved country, of our trade and wars by sea and land, of our schisms in religion and parties in the state, the prejudices of his education prevailed so far that he could not forbear taking me up in his right hand, and stroking me gently with the other, after an hearty fit of laughing, asked me whether I were a Whig or a Tory. Then turning to his first minister, who waited behind him with a white staff, near as tall as the mainmast of the *Royal Sovereign*,[9] he observed how contemptible a thing was human grandeur, which could be mimicked by such diminutive insects as I: "and yet," said he, "I dare engage, these creatures have their titles and distinctions of honor; they contrive little nests and burrows, that they call houses and cities; they make a figure in dress and equipage;[1] they love, they fight, they dispute, they cheat, they betray." And thus he continued on, while my color came and went several times with indignation to hear our noble country, the mistress of arts and arms, the scourge of France, the arbitress of Europe, the seat of virtue, piety, honor, and truth, the pride and envy of the world, so contemptuously treated.

But as I was not in a condition to resent injuries, so, upon mature thoughts, I began to doubt whether I were injured or no. For, after having been accustomed several months to the sight and converse of this people, and observed every object upon which I cast my eyes to be of proportionable magnitude, the horror I had first conceived from their bulk and aspect was so far worn off that if I had then beheld a company of English lords and ladies in their finery and birthday clothes,[2] acting their several parts in the most courtly manner of strutting and bowing and prating, to say the truth, I should have been strongly tempted to laugh as much at them as this King and his grandees did at me. Neither indeed could I forbear smiling at myself when the Queen used to place

---

9. At the English court the Lord Treasurer bore a white staff as the symbol of his office. The *Royal Sovereign* was one of the largest ships in the Royal Navy.

1. A carriage and horses, with attendant footmen.
2. Courtiers dressed with especial splendor on the monarch's birthday.

me upon her hand towards a looking glass, by which both our persons appeared before me in full view together; and there could be nothing more ridiculous than the comparison; so that I really began to imagine myself dwindled many degrees below my usual size.

Nothing angered and mortified me so much as the Queen's dwarf, who being of the lowest stature that was ever in that country (for I verily think he was not full thirty foot high) became so insolent at seeing a creature so much beneath him that he would always affect to swagger and look big as he passed by me in the Queen's antechamber, while I was standing on some table talking with the lords or ladies of the court; and he seldom failed of a smart word or two upon my littleness, against which I could only revenge myself by calling him brother, challenging him to wrestle, and such repartees as are usual in the mouths of Court pages. One day at dinner this malicious little cub was so nettled with something I had said to him that, raising himself upon the frame of Her Majesty's chair, he took me up by the middle, as I was sitting down, not thinking any harm, and let me drop into a large silver bowl of cream, and then ran away as fast as he could. I fell over head and ears, and if I had not been a good swimmer, it might have gone very hard with me; for Glumdalclitch in that instant happened to be at the other end of the room, and the Queen was in such a fright that she wanted presence of mind to assist me. But my little nurse ran to my relief, and took me out, after I had swallowed above a quart of cream. I was put to bed; however, I received no other damage than the loss of a suit of clothes, which was utterly spoiled. The dwarf was soundly whipped, and as further punishment, forced to drink up the bowl of cream into which he had thrown me; neither was he ever restored to favor: for soon after the Queen bestowed him to a lady of high quality, so that I saw him no more, to my very great satisfaction; for I could not tell to what extremity such a malicious urchin might have carried his resentment.

He had before served me a scurvy trick, which set the Queen a laughing, although at the same time she were heartily vexed, and would have immediately cashiered him,[3] if I had not been so generous as to intercede. Her Majesty had taken a marrow bone upon her plate, and after knocking out the marrow, placed the bone again in the dish, erect as it stood before; the dwarf watching his opportunity, while Glumdalclitch was gone to the sideboard, mounted upon the stool she stood on to take care of me at meals, took me up in both hands, and squeezing my legs together, wedged them into the marrow bone above my waist, where I stuck for some time, and made a very ridiculous figure. I believe it was near a minute before anyone knew what was become of me, for I thought it below me to cry out. But, as princes seldom get their meat hot, my legs were not scalded, only my stockings and breeches in a sad condition. The dwarf at my entreaty had no other punishment than a sound whipping.

---

3. Dismissed him.

I was frequently rallied by the Queen upon account of my fearfulness, and she used to ask me whether the people of my country were as great cowards as myself. The occasion was this. The kingdom is much pestered with flies in summer, and these odious insects, each of them as big as a Dunstable lark, hardly gave me any rest while I sat at dinner, with their continual humming and buzzing about my ears. They would sometimes alight upon my vituals, and leave their loathsome excrement or spawn behind, which to me was very visible, although not to the natives of that country, whose large optics were not so acute as mine in viewing smaller objects. Sometimes they would fix upon my nose or forehead, where they stung me to the quick, smelling very offensively; and I could easily trace that viscous matter, which our naturalists tell us enables those creatures to walk with their feet upwards upon a ceiling. I had much ado to defend myself against these detestable animals, and could not forbear starting when they came on my face. It was the common practice of the dwarf to catch a number of these insects in his hand, as schoolboys do among us, and let them out suddenly under my nose, on purpose to frighten me, and divert the Queen. My remedy was to cut them in pieces with my knife as they flew in the air, wherein my dexterity was much admired.

I remember one morning when Glumdalclitch had set me in my box upon a window, as she usually did in fair days to give me air (for I durst not venture to let the box be hung on a nail out of the window, as we do with cages in England), after I had lifted up one of my sashes, and sat down at my table to eat a piece of sweet cake for my breakfast, above twenty wasps, allured by the smell, came flying into the room, humming louder than the drones of as many bagpipes. Some of them seized my cake, and carried it piecemeal away; others flew about my head and face, confounding me with the noise, and putting me in the utmost terror of their stings. However, I had the courage to rise and draw my hanger, and attack them in the air. I dispatched four of them, but the rest got away, and I presently shut my window. These insects were as large as partridges; I took out their stings, found them an inch and a half long, and as sharp as needles. I carefully preserved them all, and having since shown them with some other curiosities in several parts of Europe, upon my return to England I gave three of them to Gresham College,[4] and kept the fourth for myself.

CHAPTER 4. *The country described. A proposal for correcting modern maps. The King's palace, and some account of the metropolis. The Author's way of traveling. The chief temple described.*

I now intend to give the reader a short description of this country, as far as I had traveled in it, which was not above two thousand miles round Lorbrulgrud the metropolis. For the Queen, whom I always attended,

4. The Royal Society, in its earliest years, met in Gresham College.

never went further when she accompanied the King in his progresses, and there stayed till his Majesty returned from viewing his frontiers. The whole extent of this prince's dominions reacheth about six thousand miles in length, and from three to five in breadth. From whence I cannot but conclude that our geographers of Europe are in a great error by supposing nothing but sea between Japan and California: for it was ever my opinion that there must be a balance of earth to counterpoise the great continent of Tartary; and therefore they ought to correct their maps and charts by joining this vast tract of land to the northwest parts of America, wherein I shall be ready to lend them my assistance.

The kingdom is a peninsula, terminated to the northeast by a ridge of mountains thirty miles high, which are altogether impassable by reason of the volcanoes upon the tops. Neither do the most learned know what sort of mortals inhabit beyond those mountains, or whether they be inhabited at all. On the three other sides it is bounded by the ocean. There is not one seaport in the whole kingdom; and those parts of the coasts into which the rivers issue are so full of pointed rocks, and the sea generally so rough, that there is no venturing with the smallest of their boats; so that these people are wholly excluded from any commerce with the rest of the world. But the large rivers are full of vessels, and abound with excellent fish, for they seldom get any from the sea, because the sea fish are of the same size with those in Europe, and consequently not worth catching; whereby it is manifest that nature, in the production of plants and animals of so extraordinary a bulk, is wholly confined to this continent, of which I leave the reasons to be determined by philosophers. However, now and then they take a whale that happens to be dashed against the rocks, which the common people feed on heartily. These whales I have known so large that a man could hardly carry one upon his shoulders; and sometimes for curiosity they are brought in hampers to Lorbrulgrud: I saw one of them in a dish at the King's table, which passed for a rarity, but I did not observe he was fond of it; for I think indeed the bigness disgusted him, although I have seen one somewhat larger in Greenland.

The country is well inhabited, for it contains fifty-one cities, near an hundred walled towns, and a great number of villages. To satisfy my curious reader, it may be sufficient to describe Lorbrulgrud. This city stands upon almost two equal parts on each side the river that passes through. It contains above eight thousand houses, and about six hundred thousand inhabitants. It is in length three *glongluns* (which make about fifty-four English miles) and two and a half in breadth, as I measured it myself in the royal map made by the King's order, which was laid on the ground on purpose for me, and extended an hundred feet; I paced the diameter and circumference several times barefoot, and computing by the scale, measured it pretty exactly.

The King's palace is no regular edifice, but an heap of buildings about seven miles round: the chief rooms are generally two hundred and forty foot high, and broad and long in proportion. A coach was allowed to

Glumdalclitch and me, wherein her governess frequently took her out
to see the town, or go among the shops; and I was always of the party,
carried in my box, although the girl at my own desire would often take
me out, and hold me in her hand, that I might more conveniently view
the houses and the people as we passed along the streets. I reckoned our
coach to be about a square of Westminster Hall, [5] but not altogether so
high; however, I cannot be very exact. One day the governess ordered
our coachman to stop at several shops, where the beggars, watching their
opportunity, crowded to the sides of the coach, and gave me the most
horrible spectacles that ever an English eye beheld. There was a woman
with a cancer in her breast, swelled to a monstrous size, full of holes, in
two or three of which I could have easily crept, and covered my whole
body. There was a fellow with a wen in his neck, larger than five wool-
packs, and another with a couple of wooden legs, each about twenty foot
high. But the most hateful sight of all was the lice crawling on their
clothes. I could see distinctly the limbs of these vermin with my naked
eye, much better than those of an European louse through a microscope, and their snouts with which they rooted like swine. They were
the first I had ever beheld; and I should have been curious enough to
dissect one of them if I had proper instruments (which I unluckily left
behind me in the ship), although indeed the sight was so nauseous that
it perfectly turned my stomach.

Besides the large box in which I was usually carried, the Queen ordered
a smaller one to be made for me, of about twelve foot square and ten
high, for the convenience of traveling, because the other was somewhat
too large for Glumdalclitch's lap, and cumbersome in the coach; it was
made by the same artist, whom I directed in the whole contrivance. This
traveling closet was an exact square with a window in the middle of three
of the squares, and each window was latticed with iron wire on the
outside, to prevent accidents in long journeys. On the fourth side, which
had no windows, two strong staples were fixed, through which the person that carried me, when I had a mind to be on horseback, put in a
leathern belt, and buckled it about his waist. This was always the office
of some grave trusty servant in whom I could confide, whether I attended
the King and Queen in their progresses, or were disposed to see the
gardens, or pay a visit to some great lady or minister of state in the court,
when Glumdalclitch happened to be out of order: for I soon began to be
known and esteemed among the greatest officers, I suppose more upon
account of their Majesties' favor than any merit of my own. In journeys,
when I was weary of the coach, a servant on horseback would buckle
my box, and place it on a cushion before him; and there I had a full
prospect of the country on three sides from my three windows. I had in
this closet a field bed and a hammock hung from the ceiling, two chairs
and a table, neatly screwed to the floor to prevent being tossed about by
the agitation of the horse or the coach. And having been long used to

5. The ancient hall, now incorporated into the Houses of Parliament, where the Law Courts then sat.
Swift presumably means the square of its breadth (just under 68 feet).

sea voyages, those motions, although sometimes very violent, did not much discompose me.

When I had a mind to see the town, it was always in my traveling closet, which Glumdalclitch held in her lap in a kind of open sedan, after the fashion of the country, borne by four men, and attended by two others in the Queen's livery. The people, who had often heard of me, were very curious to crowd about the sedan; and the girl was complaisant enough to make the bearers stop, and to take me in her hand that I might be more conveniently seen.

I was very desirous to see the chief temple, and particularly the tower belonging to it, which is reckoned the highest in the kingdom. Accordingly one day my nurse carried me thither, but I may truly say I came back disappointed; for the height is not above three thousand foot, reckoning from the ground to the highest pinnacle top; which, allowing for the difference between the size of those people and us in Europe, is no great matter for admiration, nor at all equal in proportion (if I rightly remember) to Salisbury steeple.[6] But, not to detract from a nation to which during my life I shall acknowledge myself extremely obliged, it must be allowed that whatever this famous tower wants in height is amply made up in beauty and strength. For the walls are near an hundred foot thick, built of hewn stone, whereof each is about forty foot square, and adorned on all sides with statues of gods and emperors cut in marble larger than the life, placed in their several niches. I measured a little finger which had fallen down from one of these statues, and lay unperceived among some rubbish, and found it exactly four foot and an inch in length. Glumdalclitch wrapped it up in a handkerchief, and carried it home in her pocket to keep among other trinkets, of which the girl was very fond, as children at her age usually are.

The King's kitchen is indeed a noble building, vaulted at top, and about six hundred foot high. The great oven is not so wide by ten paces as the cupola at St. Paul's:[7] for I measured the latter on purpose after my return. But if I should describe the kitchen grate, the prodigious pots and kettles, the joints of meat turning on the spits, with many other particulars, perhaps I should be hardly believed; at least a severe critic would be apt to think I enlarged a little, as travelers are often suspected to do. To avoid which censure, I fear I have run too much into the other extreme, and that if this treatise should happen to be translated into the language of Brobdingnag (which is the general name of that kingdom) and transmitted thither, the King and his people would have reason to complain that I had done them an injury by a false and diminutive representation.

His Majesty seldom keeps above six hundred horses in his stables: they are generally from fifty-four to sixty foot high. But when he goes abroad on solemn days, he is attended for state by a militia guard of five hundred

---

6. One of the most beautiful Gothic steeples in England is that of Salisbury Cathedral, 404 feet high.

7. The cupola of St. Paul's Cathedral in London is 108 feet in diameter.

horse, which indeed I thought was the most splendid sight that could be ever beheld, till I saw part of his army in battalia,[8] whereof I shall find another occasion to speak.

CHAPTER 5. *Several adventures that happened to the Author. The execution of a criminal. The Author shows his skill in navigation.*

I should have lived happy enough in that country if my littleness had not exposed me to several ridiculous and troublesome accidents, some of which I shall venture to relate. Glumdalclitch often carried me into the gardens of the court in my smaller box, and would sometimes take me out of it and hold me in her hand, or set me down to walk. I remember, before the dwarf left the Queen, he followed us one day into those gardens; and my nurse having set me down, he and I being close together near some dwarf apple trees, I must needs show my wit by a silly allusion between him and the trees, which happens to hold in their language as it doth in ours. Whereupon, the malicious rogue watching his opportunity, when I was walking under one of them, shook it directly over my head, by which a dozen apples, each of them near as large as a Bristol barrel, came tumbling about my ears; one of them hit me on the back as I chanced to stoop, and knocked me down flat on my face, but I received no other hurt; and the dwarf was pardoned at my desire, because I had given the provocation.

Another day Glumdalclitch left me on a smooth grassplot to divert myself while she walked at some distance with her governess. In the meantime there suddenly fell such a violent shower of hail that I was immediately by the force of it struck to the ground: and when I was down, the hailstones gave me such cruel bangs all over the body as if I had been pelted with tennis balls;[9] however I made a shift to creep on all four, and shelter myself by lying on my face on the lee side of a border of lemon thyme, but so bruised from head to foot that I could not go abroad in ten days. Neither is this at all to be wondered at, because nature in that country observing the same proportion through all her operations, a hailstone is near eighteen hundred times as large as one in Europe; which I can assert upon experience, having been so curious to weigh and measure them.

But a more dangerous accident happened to me in the same garden when my little nurse, believing she had put me in a secure place, which I often entreated her to do that I might enjoy my own thoughts, and having left my box at home to avoid the trouble of carrying it, went to another part of the garden with her governess and some ladies of her acquaintance. While she was absent and out of hearing, a small white spaniel belonging to one of the chief gardeners, having got by accident into the garden, happened to range near the place where I lay. The dog following the scent, came directly up, and taking me in his mouth, ran

8. Battle array.
9. 18th-century tennis balls, unlike the modern, were very hard.

straight to his master, wagging his tail, and set me gently on the ground. By good fortune he had been so well taught that I was carried between his teeth without the least hurt, or even tearing my clothes. But the poor gardener, who knew me well, and had a great kindness for me, was in a terrible fright. He gently took me up in both his hands, and asked me how I did; but I was so amazed and out of breath that I could not speak a word. In a few minutes I came to myself, and he carried me safe to my little nurse, who by this time had returned to the place where she left me, and was in cruel agonies when I did not appear nor answer when she called; she severely reprimanded the gardener on account of his dog. But the thing was hushed up and never known at court; for the girl was afraid of the Queen's anger; and truly, as to myself, I thought it would not be for my reputation that such a story should go about.

This accident absolutely determined Glumdalclitch never to trust me abroad for the future out of her sight. I had been long afraid of this resolution, and therefore concealed from her some little unlucky adventures that happened in those times when I was left by myself. Once a kite[1] hovering over the garden made a swoop at me, and if I had not resolutely drawn my hanger, and run under a thick espalier,[2] he would have certainly carried me away in his talons. Another time walking to the top of a fresh molehill, I fell to my neck in the hole through which that animal had cast up the earth, and coined some lie, not worth remembering, to excuse myself for spoiling my clothes. I likewise broke my right shin against the shell of a snail, which I happened to stumble over, as I was walking alone, and thinking on poor England.

I cannot tell whether I were more pleased or mortified to observe in those solitary walks that the smaller birds did not appear to be at all afraid of me; but would hop about within a yard distance, looking for worms and other food with as much indifference and security as if no creature at all were near them. I remember a thrush had the confidence to snatch out of my hand with his bill a piece of cake that Glumdalclitch had just given me for my breakfast. When I attempted to catch any of these birds, they would boldly turn against me, endeavoring to pick my fingers, which I durst not venture within their reach; and then they would hop back unconcerned to hunt for worms or snails, as they did before. But one day I took a thick cudgel, and threw it with all my strength so luckily at a linnet that I knocked him down, and seizing him by the neck with both my hands, ran with him in triumph to my nurse. However, the bird, who had only been stunned, recovering himself, gave me so many boxes with his wings on both sides of my head and body, though I held him at arm's length, and was out of the reach of his claws, that I was twenty times thinking to let him go. But I was soon relieved by one of our servants, who wrung off the bird's neck, and I had him next day for dinner, by the Queen's command. This linnet, as near as I can remember, seemed to be somewhat larger than an English swan.

---

1. A bird of prey.   2. A trellis on which fruit trees are trained.

The Maids of Honor often invited Glumdalclitch to their apartments, and desired she would bring me along with her, on purpose to have the pleasure of seeing and touching me. They would often strip me naked from top to toe and lay me at full length in their bosoms; wherewith I was much disgusted, because, to say the truth, a very offensive smell came from their skins, which I do not mention or intend to the disadvantage of those excellent ladies, for whom I have all manner of respect; but I conceive that my sense was more acute in proportion to my littleness, and that those illustrious persons were no more disagreeable to their lovers, or to each other, than people of the same quality are with us in England. And, after all, I found their natural smell was much more supportable than when they used perfumes, under which I immediately swooned away. I cannot forget that an intimate friend of mine in Lilliput took the freedom in a warm day, when I had used a good deal of exercise, to complain of a strong smell about me, although I am as little faulty that way as most of my sex: but I suppose his faculty of smelling was as nice with regard to me as mine was to that of this people. Upon this point, I cannot forbear doing justice to the Queen, my mistress, and Glumdalclitch, my nurse, whose persons were as sweet as those of any lady in England.

That which gave me most uneasiness among these Maids of Honor, when my nurse carried me to visit them, was to see them use me without any manner of ceremony, like a creature who had no sort of consequence. For they would strip themselves to the skin and put on their smocks in my presence, while I was placed on their toilet[3] directly before their naked bodies; which, I am sure, to me was very far from being a tempting sight, or from giving me any other emotions than those of horror and disgust. Their skins appeared so coarse and uneven, so variously colored, when I saw them near, with a mole here and there as broad as a trencher, and hairs hanging from it thicker than pack-threads, to say nothing further concerning the rest of their persons. Neither did they at all scruple, while I was by, to discharge what they had drunk, to the quantity of at least two hogsheads, in a vessel that held above three tuns. The handsomest among these Maids of Honor, a pleasant frolicsome girl of sixteen, would sometimes set me astride upon one of her nipples, with many other tricks, wherein the reader will excuse me for not being over particular. But I was so much displeased that I entreated Glumdalclitch to contrive some excuse for not seeing that young lady any more.

One day a young gentleman, who was nephew to my nurse's governess, came and pressed them both to see an execution. It was of a man who had murdered one of that gentleman's intimate acquaintance. Glumdalclitch was prevailed on to be of the company, very much against her inclination, for she was naturally tender-hearted: and as for myself, although I abhorred such kind of spectacles, yet my curiosity tempted

3. Toilet table.

me to see something that I thought must be extraordinary. The malefactor was fixed in a chair upon a scaffold erected for the purpose, and his
head cut off at a blow with a sword of about forty foot long. The veins
and arteries spouted up such a prodigious quantity of blood, and so high
in the air, that the great *jet d'eau*[4] at Versailles was not equal for the
time it lasted; and the head, when it fell on the scaffold floor, gave such
a bounce,[5] as made me start, although I were at least half an English
mile distant.

The Queen, who often used to hear me talk of my sea voyages, and
took all occasions to divert me when I was melancholy, asked me whether
I understood how to handle a sail or an oar, and whether a little exercise
of rowing might not be convenient for my health. I answered that I
understood both very well. For although my proper employment had
been to be surgeon or doctor to the ship, yet often, upon a pinch, I was
forced to work like a common mariner. But I could not see how this
could be done in their country, where the smallest wherry was equal to
a first-rate man-of-war among us, and such a boat as I could manage
would never live in any of their rivers. Her Majesty said, if I would
contrive a boat, her own joiner[6] should make it, and she would provide
a place for me to sail in. The fellow was an ingenious workman and, by
my instructions, in ten days finished a pleasure boat with all its tackling,
able conveniently to hold eight Europeans. When it was finished, the
Queen was so delighted that she ran with it in her lap to the King, who
ordered it to be put in a cistern full of water, with me in it, by way of
trial; where I could not manage my two sculls, or little oars, for want of
room. But the Queen had before contrived another project. She ordered
the joiner to make a wooden trough of three hundred foot long, fifty
broad, and eight deep; which being well pitched to prevent leaking, was
placed on the floor along the wall in an outer room of the palace. It had
a cock near the bottom to let out the water when it began to grow stale,
and two servants could easily fill it in half an hour. Here I often used to
row for my own diversion, as well as that of the Queen and her ladies,
who thought themselves well entertained with my skill and agility.
Sometimes I would put up my sail, and then my business was only to
steer, while the ladies gave me a gale with their fans; and when they
were weary, some of the pages would blow my sail forward with their
breath, while I showed my art by steering starboard or larboard as I
pleased. When I had done, Glumdalclitch always carried my boat into
her closet, and hung it on a nail to dry.

In this exercise I once met an accident which had like to have cost
me my life. For one of the pages having put my boat into the trough,
the governess who attended Glumdalclitch very officiously[7] lifted me up
to place me in the boat; but I happened to slip through her fingers, and
should have infallibly fallen down forty feet upon the floor, if by the

---

4. This fountain rose over 40 feet in the air.   6. A skilled woodworker.
5. A sudden noise.   7. Kindly, dutifully.

luckiest chance in the world I had not been stopped by a corking-pin[8] that stuck in the good gentlewoman's stomacher; the head of the pin passed between my shirt and the waistband of my breeches, and thus I was held by the middle in the air until Glumdalclitch ran to my relief.

Another time, one of the servants, whose office it was to fill my trough every third day with fresh water, was so careless to let a huge frog (not perceiving it) slip out of his pail. The frog lay concealed till I was put into my boat, but then seeing a resting place, climbed up, and made it lean so much on one side that I was forced to balance it with all my weight on the other, to prevent overturning. When the frog was got in, it hopped at once half the length of the boat, and then over my head, backwards and forwards, daubing my face and clothes with its odious slime. The largeness of its features made it appear the most deformed animal that can be conceived. However, I desired Glumdalclitch to let me deal with it alone. I banged it a good while with one of my sculls, and at last forced it to leap out of the boat.

But the greatest danger I ever underwent in that kingdom was from a monkey, who belonged to one of the clerks of the kitchen. Glumdalclitch had locked me up in her closet, while she went somewhere upon business or a visit. The weather being very warm, the closet window was left open, as well as the windows in the door of my bigger box, in which I usually lived, because of its largeness and conveniency. As I sat quietly meditating at my table, I heard something bounce in at the closet window, and skip about from one side to the other, whereat, although I was much alarmed, yet I ventured to look out, but stirred not from my seat; and then I saw this frolicsome animal, frisking and leaping up and down, till at last he came to my box, which he seemed to view with great pleasure and curiosity, peeping in at the door and every window. I retreated to the farther corner of my room, or box, but the monkey looking in at every side, put me into such a fright that I wanted presence of mind to conceal myself under the bed, as I might easily have done. After some time spent in peeping, grinning, and chattering, he at last espied me, and reaching one of his paws in at the door, as a cat does when she plays with a mouse, although I often shifted place to avoid him, he at length seized the lappet of my coat (which, being made of that country cloth, was very thick and strong) and dragged me out. He took me up in his right forefoot, and held me as a nurse does a child she is going to suckle, just as I have seen the same sort of creature do with a kitten in Europe: and when I offered to struggle, he squeezed me so hard that I thought it more prudent to submit. I have good reason to believe that he took me for a young one of his own species, by his often stroking my face very gently with his other paw. In these diversions he was interrupted by a noise at the closet door, as if somebody were opening it, whereupon he suddenly leaped up to the window at which he had come in, and thence

8. A pin of the largest size. "Stomacher": an ornamental covering for the front and upper part of the body.

upon the leads and gutters, walking upon three legs, and holding me in the fourth, till he clambered up to a roof that was next to ours. I heard Glumdalclitch give a shriek at the moment he was carrying me out. The poor girl was almost distracted: that quarter of the palace was all in an uproar; the servants ran for ladders; the monkey was seen by hundreds in the court, sitting upon the ridge of a building, holding me like a baby in one of his forepaws and feeding me with the other, by cramming into my mouth some victuals he had squeezed out of the bag on one side of his chaps, and patting me when I would not eat; whereat many of the rabble below could not forebear laughing; neither do I think they justly ought to be blamed, for without question the sight was ridiculous enough to everybody but myself. Some of the people threw up stones, hoping to drive the monkey down; but this was strictly forbidden, or else very probably my brains had been dashed out.

The ladders were now applied, and mounted by several men; which the monkey observing, and finding himself almost encompassed, not being able to make speed enough with his three legs, let me drop on a ridge tile, and made his escape. Here I sat for some time three hundred yards from the ground, expecting every moment to be blown down by the wind, or to fall by my own giddiness, and come tumbling over and over from the ridge to the eaves. But an honest lad, one of my nurse's footmen, climbed up, and putting me into his breeches pocket, brought me down safe.

I was almost choked with the filthy stuff the monkey had crammed down my throat; but my dear little nurse picked it out of my mouth with a small needle, and then I fell a vomiting, which gave me great relief. Yet I was so weak and bruised in the sides with the squeezes given me by this odious animal that I was forced to keep my bed a fortnight. The King, Queen, and all the Court sent every day to inquire after my health, and her Majesty made me several visits during my sickness. The monkey was killed, and an order made that no such animal should be kept about the palace.

When I attended the King after my recovery, to return him thanks for his favors, he was pleased to rally me a good deal upon this adventure. He asked me what my thoughts and speculations were while I lay in the monkey's paw, how I liked the victuals he gave me, his manner of feeding, and whether the fresh air on the roof had sharpened my stomach. He desired to know what I would have done upon such an occasion in my own country. I told his Majesty that in Europe we had no monkeys, except such as were brought for curiosities from other places, and so small that I could deal with a dozen of them together, if they presumed to attack me. And as for that monstrous animal with whom I was so lately engaged (it was indeed as large as an elephant), if my fears had suffered me to think so far as to make use of my hanger (looking fiercely and clapping my hand upon the hilt as I spoke) when he poked his paw into my chamber, perhaps I should have given him such a wound as

would have made him glad to withdraw it with more haste than he put
it in. This I delivered in a firm tone, like a person who was jealous lest
his courage should be called in question. However, my speech produced
nothing else besides a loud laughter, which all the respect due to his
Majesty from those about him could not make them contain. This made
me reflect how vain an attempt it is for a man to endeavor doing himself
honor among those who are out of all degree of equality or comparison
with him. And yet I have seen the moral of my own behavior very frequent in England since my return, where a little contemptible varlet,
without the least title to birth, person, wit, or common sense, shall presume to look with importance, and put himself upon a foot with the
greatest persons of the kingdom.

I was every day furnishing the court with some ridiculous story; and
Glumdalclitch, although she loved me to excess, yet was arch enough
to inform the Queen whenever I committed any folly that she thought
would be diverting to her Majesty. The girl, who had been out of order,
was carried by her governess to take the air about an hour's distance, or
thirty miles from town. They alighted out of the coach near a small
footpath in a field, and Glumdalclitch setting down my traveling box, I
went out of it to walk. There was a cow dung in the patch, and I must
needs try my activity by attempting to leap over it. I took a run, but
unfortunately jumped short, and found myself just in the middle up to
my knees. I waded through with some difficulty, and one of the footmen
wiped me as clean as he could with his handkerchief; for I was filthily
bemired, and my nurse confined me to my box till we returned home,
where the Queen was soon informed of what had passed and the footmen spread it about the Court, so that all the mirth, for some days, was
at my expense.

CHAPTER 6. *Several contrivances of the Author to please the King and
Queen. He shows his skill in music. The King inquires into the state of
Europe, which the Author relates to him. The King's observations thereon.*

I used to attend the King's levee[9] once or twice a week, and had often
seen him under the barber's hand, which indeed was at first very terrible
to behold. For the razor was almost twice as long as an ordinary scythe.
His Majesty, according to the custom of the country, was only shaved
twice a week. I once prevailed on the barber to give me some of the suds
or lather, out of which I picked forty or fifty of the strongest stumps of
hair. I then took a piece of fine wood, and cut it like the back of a comb,
making several holes in it at equal distance with as small a needle as I
could get from Glumdalclitch. I fixed in the stumps so artificially,[1]
scraping and sloping them with my knife towards the points, that I made
a very tolerable comb; which was a seasonable supply, my own being so

9. A morning reception held by a prince or noble-   1. Skillfully.
man, sometimes while dressing for the day.

much broken in the teeth that it was almost useless; neither did I know any artist in that country so nice and exact as would undertake to make me another.

And this puts me in mind of an amusement wherein I spent many of my leisure hours. I desired the Queen's woman to save for me the combings of her Majesty's hair, whereof in time I got a good quantity; and consulting with my friend the cabinetmaker, who had received general orders to do little jobs for me, I directed him to make two chair frames, no larger than those I had in my box, and then to bore little holes with a fine awl round those parts where I designed the backs and seats; through these holes I wove the strongest hairs I could pick out, just after the manner of cane chairs in England. When they were finished, I made a present of them to her Majesty, who kept them in her cabinet, and used to show them for curiosities, as indeed they were the wonder of every one that beheld them. The Queen would have made me sit upon one of these chairs, but I absolutely refused to obey her, protesting I would rather die a thousand deaths than place a dishonorable part of my body on those precious hairs that once adorned her Majesty's head. Of these hairs (as I had always a mechanical genius) I likewise made a neat little purse above five foot long, with her Majesty's name deciphered in gold letters, which I gave to Glumdalclitch by the Queen's consent. To say the truth, it was more for show than use, being not of strength to bear the weight of the larger coins; and therefore she kept nothing in it but some little toys[2] that girls are fond of.

The King, who delighted in music, had frequent consorts[3] at court, to which I was sometimes carried, and set in my box on a table to hear them; but the noise was so great that I could hardly distinguish the tunes. I am confident that all the drums and trumpets of a royal army, beating and sounding together just at your ears, could not equal it. My practice was to have my box removed from the places where the performers sat, as far as I could, then to shut the doors and windows of it, and draw the window curtains, after which I found their music not disagreeable.

I had learned in my youth to play a little upon the spinet. Glumdalclitch kept one in her chamber, and a master attended twice a week to teach her: I call it a spinet, because it somewhat resembled that instrument, and was played upon in the same manner. A fancy came into my head that I would entertain the King and Queen with an English tune upon this instrument. But this appeared extremely difficult: for the spinet was near sixty foot long, each key being almost a foot wide; so that, with my arms extended, I could not reach to above five keys, and to press them down required a good smart stroke with my fist, which would be too great a labor and to no purpose. The method I contrived was this: I prepared two round sticks about the bigness of common cudgels; they were thicker at one end than the other, and I covered the thicker ends with a piece of a mouse's skin, that by rapping on them I might neither

---

2. Trifles.   3. Concerts.

damage the tops of the keys, nor interrupt the sound. Before the spinet a bench was placed, about four foot below the keys, and I was put upon the bench. I ran sideling upon it that way and this, as fast as I could, banging the proper keys with my two sticks; and made a shift to play a jig, to the great satisfaction of both their Majesties: but it was the most violent exercise I ever underwent, and yet I could not strike above sixteen keys, nor, consequently, play the bass and treble together, as other artists do; which was a great disadvantage to my performance.

The King, who, as I before observed, was a prince of excellent understanding, would frequently order that I should be brought in my box and set upon the table in his closet. He would then command me to bring one of my chairs out of the box, and sit down within three yards distance upon the top of the cabinet, which brought me almost to a level with his face. In this manner I had several conversations with him. I one day took the freedom to tell his Majesty that the contempt he discovered towards Europe, and the rest of the world, did not seem answerable to those excellent qualities of mind that he was master of. That reason did not extend itself with the bulk of the body: on the contrary, we observed in our country that the tallest persons were usually least provided with it. That among other animals, bees and ants had the reputation of more industry, art, and sagacity than many of the larger kinds; and that, as inconsiderable as he took me to be, I hoped I might live to do his Majesty some signal service. The King heard me with attention, and began to conceive a much better opinion of me than he had before. He desired I would give him as exact an account of the government of England as I possibly could; because, as fond as princes commonly are of their own customs (for so he conjectured of other monarchs, by my former discourses), he should be glad to hear of anything that might deserve imitation.

Imagine with thyself, courteous reader, how often I then wished for the tongue of Demosthenes or Cicero, that might have enabled me to celebrate the praise of my own dear native country in a style equal to its merits and felicity.

I began my discourse by informing his Majesty that our dominions consisted of two islands, which composed three mighty kingdoms under one sovereign, beside our plantations in America. I dwelt long upon the fertility of our soil, and the temperature[4] of our climate. I then spoke at large upon the constitution of an English Parliament, partly made up of an illustrious body called the House of Peers, persons of the noblest blood, and of the most ancient and ample patrimonies. I described that extraordinary care always taken of their education in arts and arms, to qualify them for being counselors born to the king and kingdom; to have a share in the legislature, to be members of the highest Court of Judicature, from whence there could be no appeal; and to be champions always ready for the defense of their prince and country, by their valor,

4. Temperateness.

conduct, and fidelity. That these were the ornament and bulwark of the kingdom, worthy followers of their most renowned ancestors, whose honor had been the reward of their virtue, from which their posterity were never once known to degenerate. To these were joined several holy persons, as part of that assembly, under the title of Bishops, whose peculiar business it is to take care of religion, and of those who instruct the people therein. These were searched and sought out through the whole nation, by the prince and his wisest counselors, among such of the priesthood as were most deservedly distinguished by the sanctity of their lives and the depth of their erudition, who were indeed the spiritual fathers of the clergy and the people.

That the other part of the Parliament consisted of an assembly called the House of Commons, who were all principal gentlemen, freely picked and culled out by the people themselves, for their great abilities and love of their country, to represent the wisdom of the whole nation. And these two bodies make up the most august assembly in Europe, to whom, in conjunction with the prince, the whole legislature is committed.

I then descended to the Courts of Justice, over which the Judges, those venerable sages and interpreters of the law, presided, for determining the disputed rights and properties of men, as well as for the punishment of vice, and protection of innocence. I mentioned the prudent management of our treasury, the valor and achievements of our forces by sea and land. I computed the number of our people, by reckoning how many millions there might be of each religious sect, or political party among us. I did not omit even our sports and pastimes, or any other particular which I thought might redound to the honor of my country. And I finished all with a brief historical account of affairs and events in England for about an hundred years past.

This conversation was not ended under five audiences, each of several hours, and the King heard the whole with great attention, frequently taking notes of what I spoke, as well as memorandums of several questions he intended to ask me.

When I had put an end to these long discourses, his Majesty in a sixth audience consulting his notes, proposed many doubts, queries, and objections, upon every article. He asked what methods were used to cultivate the minds and bodies of our young nobility, and in what kind of business they commonly spent the first and teachable part of their lives. What course was taken to supply that assembly when any noble family became extinct. What qualifications were necessary in those who were to be created new lords. Whether the humor[5] of the prince, a sum of money to a Court lady or a prime minister, or a design of strengthening a party opposite to the public interest, ever happened to be motives in those advancements. What share of knowledge these lords had in the laws of their country, and how they came by it, so as to enable them to decide the properties of their fellow subjects in the last resort. Whether

5. Whim.

they were always so free from avarice, partialities, or want that a bribe or some other sinister view could have no place among them. Whether those holy lords I spoke of were constantly promoted to that rank upon account of their knowledge in religious matters, and the sanctity of their lives, had never been compliers with the times while they were common priests, or slavish prostitute chaplains to some nobleman, whose opinions they continued servilely to follow after they were admitted into that assembly.

He then desired to know what arts were practiced in electing those whom I called Commoners. Whether a stranger with a strong purse might not influence the vulgar voters to choose him before their own landlord or the most considerable gentleman in the neighborhood. How it came to pass that people were so violently bent upon getting into this assembly, which I allowed to be a great trouble and expense, often to the ruin of their families, without any salary or pension: because this appeared such an exalted strain of virtue and public spirit that his Majesty seemed to doubt it might possibly not be always sincere; and he desired to know whether such zealous gentlemen could have any views of refunding themselves for the charges and trouble they were at, by sacrificing the public good to the designs of a weak and vicious prince in conjunction with a corrupted ministry. He multiplied his questions, and sifted me thoroughly upon every part of this head, proposing numberless inquiries and objections, which I think it not prudent or convenient to repeat.

Upon what I said in relation to our Courts of Justice, his Majesty desired to be satisfied in several points: and this I was the better able to do, having been formerly almost ruined by a long suit in chancery, which was decreed for me with costs. He asked what time was usually spent in determining between right and wrong, and what degree of expense. Whether advocates and orators had liberty to plead in causes manifestly known to be unjust, vexatious, or oppressive. Whether party in religion or politics were observed to be of any weight in the scale of justice. Whether those pleading orators were persons educated in the general knowledge of equity, or only in provincial, national, and other local customs. Whether they or their judges had any part in penning those laws which they assumed the liberty of interpreting and glossing upon at their pleasure. Whether they had ever at different times pleaded for and against the same cause, and cited precedents to prove contrary opinions. Whether they were a rich or a poor corporation. Whether they received any pecuniary reward for pleading or delivering their opinions. And particularly whether they were ever admitted as members in the lower senate.

He fell next upon the management of our treasury, and said he thought my memory had failed me, because I computed our taxes at about five or six millions a year, and when I came to mention the issues,[6] he found

6. Expenditures.

they sometimes amounted to more than double, for the notes he had taken were very particular in this point; because he hoped, as he told me, that the knowledge of our conduct might be useful to him, and he could not be deceived in his calculations. But if what I told him were true, he was still at a loss how a kingdom could run out of its estate like a private person. He asked me, who were our creditors? and where we should find money to pay them? He wondered to hear me talk of such chargeable and extensive wars; that certainly we must be a quarrelsome people, or live among very bad neighbors, and that our generals must needs be richer than our kings.[7] He asked what business we had out of our own islands, unless upon the score of[8] trade or treaty or to defend the coasts with our fleet. Above all, he was amazed to hear me talk of a mercenary standing army[9] in the midst of peace, and among a free people. He said if we were governed by our own consent in the persons of our representatives, he could not imagine of whom we were afraid, or against whom we were to fight; and would hear my opinion whether a private man's house might not better be defended by himself, his children, and family, than by half a dozen rascals picked up at a venture[1] in the streets for small wages, who might get an hundred times more by cutting their throats.

He laughed at my odd kind of arithmetic (as he was pleased to call it) in reckoning the numbers of our people by a computation drawn from the several sects among us in religion and politics. He said he knew no reason why those who entertain opinions prejudicial to the public should be obliged to change, or should not be obliged to conceal them. And as it was tyranny in any government to require the first, so it was weakness not to enforce the second: for a man may be allowed to keep poisons in his closet, but not to vend them about for cordials.[2]

He observed that among the diversions of our nobility and gentry I had mentioned gaming.[3] He desired to know at what age this entertainment was usually taken up, and when it was laid down; how much of their time it employed; whether it ever went so high as to affect their fortunes; whether mean, vicious people, by their dexterity in that art, might not arrive at great riches, and sometimes keep our very nobles in dependence, as well as habituate them to vile companions, wholly take them from the improvement of their minds, and force them, by the losses they have received, to learn and practice that infamous dexterity upon others.

He was perfectly astonished with the historical account I gave him of our affairs during the last century, protesting it was only an heap of conspiracies, rebellions, murders, massacres, revolutions, banishments,

---

7. An allusion to the enormous fortune gained by the duke of Marlborough, formerly captain-general of the army, whom Swift detested.
8. For the sake of.
9. Since the declaration of the Bill of Rights (1689), a standing army without authorization by Parliament had been illegal. Swift and the Tories in general were vigilant in their opposition to such an army.
1. By chance.
2. Medicines to stimulate the heart, or, equally commonly, liqueurs.
3. Gambling.

the very worst effects that avarice, faction, hypocrisy, perfidiousness, cruelty, rage, madness, hatred, envy, lust, malice, or ambition could produce.

His Majesty in another audience was at the pains to recapitulate the sum of all I had spoken; compared the questions he made with the answers I had given; then taking me into his hands, and stroking me gently, delivered himself in these words, which I shall never forget nor the manner he spoke them in. "My little friend Grildrig, you have made a most admirable panegyric[4] upon your country. You have clearly proved that ignorance, idleness, and vice are the proper ingredients for qualifying a legislator. That laws are best explained, interpreted, and applied by those whose interests and abilities lie in perverting, confounding, and eluding them. I observe among you some lines of an institution which in its original might have been tolerable; but these half erased, and the rest wholly blurred and blotted by corruptions. It doth not appear from all you have said how any one virtue is required towards the procurement of any one station among you; much less that men are ennobled on account of their virtue, that priests are advanced for their piety or learning, soldiers for their conduct or valor, judges for their integrity, senators for the love of their country, or counselors for their wisdom. As for yourself," continued the King, "who have spent the greatest part of your life in traveling, I am well disposed to hope you may hitherto have escaped many vices of your country. But by what I have gathered from your own relation, and the answers I have with much pains wringed and extorted from you, I cannot but conclude the bulk of your natives to be the most pernicious race of little odious vermin that nature ever suffered to crawl upon the surface of the earth."

CHAPTER 7. *The Author's love of his country. He makes a proposal of much advantage to the King; which is rejected. The King's great ignorance in politics. The learning of that country very imperfect and confined. Their laws, and military affairs, and parties in the State.*

Nothing but an extreme love of truth could have hindered me from concealing this part of my story. It was in vain to discover my resentments, which were always turned into ridicule: and I was forced to rest with patience while my noble and most beloved country was so injuriously treated. I am heartily sorry as any of my readers can possibly be that such an occasion was given, but this prince happened to be so curious and inquisitive upon every particular that it could not consist either with gratitude or good manners to refuse giving him what satisfaction I was able. Yet thus much I may be allowed to say in my own vindication: that I artfully eluded many of his questions, and gave to every point a more favorable turn by many degrees than the strictness of truth would allow. For I have always borne that laudable partiality to my own coun-

---

4. A formal oration in praise of someone or something.

try, which Dionysius Halicarnassensis[5] with so much justice recommends to an historian. I would hide the frailties and deformities of my political mother, and place her virtues and beauties in the most advantageous light. This was my sincere endeavor in those many discourses I had with that mighty monarch, although it unfortunately failed of success.

But great allowances should be given to a King who lives wholly secluded from the rest of the world, and must therefore be altogether unacquainted with the manners and customs that most prevail in other nations: the want of which knowledge will ever produce many *prejudices*, and a certain *narrowness of thinking*, from which we and the politer countries of Europe are wholly exempted. And it would be hard indeed if so remote a prince's notions of virtue and vice were to be offered as a standard for all mankind.

To confirm what I have now said, and further, to show the miserable effects of a *confined education*, I shall here insert a passage which will hardly obtain belief. In hopes to ingratiate myself farther into his Majesty's favor, I told him of an invention discovered between three and four hundred years ago, to make a certain powder, into an heap of which the smallest spark of fire falling would kindle the whole in a moment, although it were as big as a mountain, and make it all fly up in the air together, with a noise and agitation greater than thunder. That a proper quantity of this powder rammed into an hollow tube of brass or iron, according to its bigness, would drive a ball of iron or lead with such violence and speed as nothing was able to sustain its force. That the largest balls thus discharged would not only destroy whole ranks of an army at once, but batter the strongest walls to the ground; sink down ships with a thousand men in each, to the bottom of the sea; and, when linked together by a chain, would cut through masts and rigging; divide hundreds of bodies in the middle, and lay all waste before them. That we often put this powder into large hollow balls of iron, and discharged them by an engine into some city we were besieging; which would rip up the pavements, tear the houses to pieces, burst and throw splinters on every side, dashing out the brains of all who came near. That I knew the ingredients very well, which were cheap and common; I understood the manner of compounding them, and could direct his workmen how to make those tubes of a size proportionable to all other things in his Majesty's kingdom, and the largest need not be above two hundred foot long; twenty or thirty of which tubes, charged with the proper quantity of powder and balls, would batter down the walls of the strongest town in his dominions in a few hours; or destroy the whole metropolis, if ever it should pretend to dispute his absolute commands. This I humbly offered to his Majesty as a small tribute of acknowledgement in return of so many marks that I had received of his royal favor and protection.

The King was struck with horror at the description I had given of those

5. A Greek rhetorician and historian, who flourished ca. 25 B.C. His history of Rome was written to reconcile the Greeks to their Roman masters.

terrible engines and the proposal I had made. He was amazed how so impotent and groveling an insect as I (these were his expressions) could entertain such inhuman ideas, and in so familiar a manner as to appear wholly unmoved at all the scenes of blood and desolation which I had painted as the common effects of those destructive machines; whereof he said some evil genius, enemy to mankind, must have been the first contriver. As for himself, he protested that although few things delighted him so much as new discoveries in art or in nature, yet he would rather lose half his kingdom than be privy[6] to such a secret, which he commanded me, as I valued my life, never to mention any more.

A strange effect of *narrow principles* and *short views!* that a prince possessed of every quality which procures veneration, love, and esteem; of strong parts, great wisdom, and profound learning; endued with admirable talents for government, and almost adored by his subjects; should from a *nice, unnecessary scruple,* whereof in Europe we can have no conception, let slip an opportunity put into his hands that would have made him absolute master of the lives, the liberties, and the fortunes of his people. Neither do I say this with the least intention to detract from the many virtues of that excellent King, whose character I am sensible will on this account be very much lessened in the opinion of an English reader: but I take this defect among them to have risen from their ignorance; they not having hitherto reduced politics into a science, as the more acute wits of Europe have done. For I remember very well, in a discourse one day with the King, when I happened to say there were several thousand books among us written upon the art of government, it gave him (directly contrary to my intention) a very mean opinion of our understandings. He professed both to abominate and despise all *mystery, refinement,* and *intrigue,* either in a prince or a minister. He could not tell what I meant by *secrets of state,* where an enemy or some rival nation were not in the case. He confined the knowledge of governing within very *narrow bounds:* to common sense and reason, to justice and lenity,[7] to the speedy determination of civil and criminal causes, with some other obvious topics which are not worth considering. And he gave it for his opinion that whoever could make two ears of corn or two blades of grass to grow upon a spot of ground where only one grew before would deserve better of mankind and do more essential service to his country than the whole race of politicians[8] put together.

The learning of this people is very defective, consisting only in morality, history, poetry, and mathematics; wherein they must be allowed to excel. But the last of these is wholly applied to what may be useful in life, to the improvement of agriculture and all mechanical arts; so that among us it would be little esteemed. And as to ideas, entities, abstractions, and transcendentals,[9] I could never drive the least conception into their heads.

6. To share secret knowledge.
7. Mildness.
8. By "politicians" Swift means something like our

modern "political scientists"—theorists.
9. In Swift's time, "transcendental" was practically synonymous with "metaphysical."

No law of that country must exceed in words the number of letters in their alphabet, which consists only in two and twenty. But indeed few of them extend even to that length. They are expressed in the most plain and simple terms, wherein those people are not mercurial[1] enough to discover above one interpretation. And to write a comment upon any law is a capital crime. As to the decision of civil causes, or proceedings against criminals, their precedents[2] are so few that they have little reason to boast of any extraordinary skill in either.

They have had the art of printing as well as the Chinese, time out of mind. But their libraries are not very large; for that of the King's, which is reckoned the biggest, doth not amount to above a thousand volumes, placed in a gallery of twelve hundred foot long, from whence I had liberty to borrow what books I pleased. The Queen's joiner had contrived in one of the Glumdalclitch's rooms a kind of wooden machine five and twenty foot high, formed like a standing ladder; the steps were each fifty foot long. It was indeed a movable pair of stairs, the lowest end placed at ten foot distance from the wall of the chamber. The book I had a mind to read was put up leaning against the wall. I first mounted to the upper step of the ladder, and turning my face towards the book began at the top of the page, and so walking to the right and left about eight or ten paces according to the length of the lines, till I had gotten a little below the level of mine eyes, and then descending gradually till I came to the bottom: after which I mounted again, and began the other page in the same manner, and so turned over the leaf, which I could easily do with both my hands, for it was as thick and stiff as a pasteboard, and in the largest folios[3] not above eighteen or twenty foot long.

Their style is clear, masculine, and smooth, but not florid; for they avoid nothing more than multiplying unnecessary words or using various expressions. I have perused many of their books, especially those in history and morality. Among the rest, I was much diverted with a little old treatise, which always lay in Glumdalclitch's bedchamber, and belonged to her governess, a grave elderly gentlewoman, who dealt in writings of morality and devotion. The book treats of the weakness of human kind, and is in little esteem, except among the women and the vulgar. However, I was curious to see what an author of that country could say upon such a subject. This writer went through all the usual topics of European moralists: showing how diminutive, contemptible, and helpless an animal was man in his own nature; how unable to defend himself from the inclemencies of the air, or the fury of wild beasts; how much he was excelled by one creature in strength, by another in speed, by a third in foresight, by a fourth in industry. He added that nature was degenerated in these latter declining ages of the world, and could now

---

1. Changeable.
2. A legal decision or a course of action which comes to serve as a rule in determining similar cases in the future. In the Fourth Voyage of *Gulliver's*

Travels, Gulliver is made to say: "It is a maxim among these lawyers that whatever hath been done before may legally be done again."
3. A book of the largest size.

produce only small abortive births in comparison of those in ancient times. He said it was very reasonable to think, not only that the species of men were originally much larger, but also that there must have been giants in former ages; which, as it is asserted by history and tradition, so it hath been confirmed by huge bones and skulls casually dug up in several parts of the kingdom, far exceeding the common dwindled race of man in our days. He argued that the very laws of nature absolutely required we should have been made in the beginning of a size more large and robust, not so liable to destruction from every little accident of a tile falling from a house, or a stone cast from the hand of a boy, or of being drowned in a little brook. From this way of reasoning, the author drew several moral applications useful in the conduct of life, but needless here to repeat. For my own part, I could not avoid reflecting how universally this talent was spread, of drawing lectures in morality, or indeed rather matter of discontent and repining, from the quarrels we raise with nature. And I believe, upon a strict inquiry, those quarrels might be shown as ill grounded among us as they are among that people.

As to their military affairs, they boast that the King's army consists of an hundred and seventy-six thousand foot and thirty-two thousand horse: if that may be called an army which is made up of tradesmen in the several cities, and farmers in the country, whose commanders are only the nobility and gentry, without pay or reward. They are indeed perfect enough in their exercises, and under very good discipline, wherein I saw no great merit; for how should it be otherwise, where every farmer is under the command of his own landlord, and every citizen under that of the principal men in his own city, chosen after the manner of Venice by ballot?

I have often seen the militia of Lorbrulgrud drawn out to exercise in a great field near the city, of twenty miles square. They were in all not above twenty-five thousand foot, and six thousand horse; but it was impossible for me to compute their number, considering the space of ground they took up. A cavalier mounted on a large steed might be about an hundred foot high. I have seen this whole body of horse, upon a word of command, draw their swords at once, and brandish them in the air. Imagination can figure nothing so grand, so surprising, and so astonishing. It looked as if ten thousand flashes of lightning were darting at the same time from every quarter of the sky.

I was curious to know how this prince, to whose dominions there is no access from any other country, came to think of armies, or to teach his people the practice of military discipline. But I was soon informed, both by conversation and reading their histories. For in the course of many ages they have been troubled with the same disease to which the whole race of mankind is subject: the nobility often contending for power, the people for liberty, and the King for absolute dominion. All which, however happily tempered by the laws of the kingdom, have been sometimes violated by each of the three parties, and have more than once occasioned civil wars, the last whereof was happily put an end to by this prince's grandfather in a general composition;[4] and the militia, then settled with common consent, hath been ever since kept in the strictest duty.

CHAPTER 8. *The King and Queen make a progress to the frontiers. The Author attends them. The manner in which he leaves the country very particularly related. He returns to England.*

I had always a strong impulse that I should some time recover my liberty, though it were impossible to conjecture by what means, or to form any project with the least hope of succeeding. The ship in which I sailed was the first ever known to be driven within sight of that coast; and the King had given strict orders that if at any time another appeared, it should be taken ashore, and with all its crew and passengers brought in a tumbrel[5] to Lorbrulgrud. He was strongly bent to get me a woman of my own size, by whom I might propagate the breed: but I think I should rather have died than undergone the disgrace of leaving a posterity to be kept in cages like tame canary birds, and perhaps in time sold about the kingdom to persons of quality for curiosities. I was indeed treated with much kindness: I was the favorite of a great King and Queen, and the delight of the whole Court, but it was upon such a foot as ill became the dignity of human kind. I could never forget those domestic pledges[6] I had left behind me. I wanted to be among people with whom I could converse upon even terms, and walk about the streets and fields without fear of being trod to death like a frog or a young puppy. But my deliverance came sooner than I expected, and in a manner not very common; the whole story and circumstances of which I shall faithfully relate.

I had now been two years in this country; and about the beginning of the third, Glumdalclitch and I attended the King and Queen in progress to the south coast of the kingdom. I was carried as usual in my traveling box, which, as I have already described, was a very convenient closet of twelve foot wide. I had ordered a hammock to be fixed by silken ropes from the four corners at the top, to break the jolts when a servant carried me before him on horseback, as I sometimes desired; and would often sleep in my hammock while we were upon the road. On the roof of my closet, set not directly over the middle of the hammock, I ordered the joiner to cut out a hole of a foot square to give me air in hot weather as I slept, which hole I shut at pleasure with a board that drew backwards and forwards through a groove.

When we came to our journey's end, the King thought proper to pass a few days at a palace he hath near Flanflasnic, a city within eighteen English miles of the seaside. Glumdalclitch and I were much fatigued; I had gotten a small cold, but the poor girl was so ill as to be confined

4. A political settlement based upon general   5. A farm wagon.
agreement of all parties.   6. His wife and children.

to her chamber. I longed to see the ocean, which must be the only scene of my escape, if ever it should happen. I pretended to be worse than I really was, and desired leave to take the fresh air of the sea with a page whom I was very fond of, and who had sometimes been trusted with me. I shall never forget with what unwillingness Glumdalclitch consented, nor the strict charge she gave the page to be careful of me, bursting at the same time into a flood of tears, as if she had some foreboding of what was to happen. The boy took me out in my box about half an hour's walk from the palace, towards the rocks on the seashore. I ordered him to set me down, and lifting up one of my sashes, cast many a wistful melancholy look towards the sea. I found myself not very well, and told the page that I had a mind to take a nap in my hammock, which I hoped would do me good. I got in, and the boy shut the window close down, to keep out the cold. I soon fell asleep: and all I can conjecture is that while I slept, the page, thinking no danger could happen, went among the rocks to look for birds' eggs; having before observed him from my window searching about, and picking up one or two in the clefts. Be that as it will, I found myself suddenly awaked with a violent pull upon the ring which was fastened at the top of my box for the conveniency of carriage. I felt my box raised very high in the air, and then borne forward with prodigious speed. The first jolt had like to have shaken me out of my hammock, but afterwards the motion was easy enough. I called out several times as loud as I could raise my voice, but all to no purpose. I looked towards my windows, and could see nothing but the clouds and sky. I heard a noise just over my head like the clapping of wings, and then began to perceive the woeful condition I was in; that some eagle had got the ring of my box in his beak, with an intent to let it fall on a rock, like a tortoise in a shell, and then pick out my body and devour it. For the sagacity and smell of this bird enable him to discover his quarry at a great distance, although better concealed than I could be within a two-inch board.

In a little time I observed the noise and flutter of wings to increase very fast, and my box was tossed up and down like a signpost in a windy day. I heard several bangs or buffets, as I thought, given to the eagle (for such I am certain it must have been that held the ring of my box in his beak), and then all on a sudden felt myself falling perpendicularly down for above a minute, but with such incredible swiftness that I almost lost my breath. My fall was topped by a terrible squash, that sounded louder to mine ears than the cataract of Niagara; after which I was quite in the dark for another minute, and then my box began to rise so high that I could see light from the tops of my windows. I now perceived that I was fallen into the sea. My box, by the weight of my body, the goods that were in, and the broad plates of iron fixed for strength at the four corners of the top and bottom, floated above five foot deep in water. I did then and do now suppose that the eagle which flew away with my box was pursued by two or three others, and forced to let me drop while he was defending himself against the rest, who hoped to share in the prey. The

plates of iron fastened at the bottom of the box (for those were the strongest) preserved the balance while it fell, and hindered it from being broken on the surface of the water. Every joint of it was well grooved, and
the door did not move on hinges, but up and down like a sash; which
kept my closet so tight that very little water came in. I got with much
difficulty out of my hammock, having first ventured to draw back the
slip-board on the roof already mentioned, contrived on purpose to let in
air, for want of which I found myself almost stifled.

How often did I then wish myself with my dear Glumdalclitch, from
whom one single hour had so far divided me! And I may say with truth
that in the midst of my own misfortune, I could not forbear lamenting
my poor nurse, the grief she would suffer for my loss, the displeasure of
the Queen, and the ruin of her fortune. Perhaps many travelers have
not been under greater difficulties and distress than I was at this juncture, expecting every moment to see my box dashed in pieces, or at least
overset by the first violent blast or a rising wave. A breach in one single
pane of glass would have been immediate death, nor could anything
have preserved the windows but the strong lattice wires placed on the
outside against accidents in traveling. I saw the water ooze in at several
crannies, although the leaks were not considerable, and I endeavored to
stop them as well as I could. I was not able to lift up the roof of my
closet, which otherwise I certainly should have done, and sat on the top
of it, where I might at least preserve myself from being shut up, as I may
call it, in the hold. Or, if I escaped these dangers for a day or two, what
could I expect but a miserable death of cold and hunger! I was four hours
under these circumstances, expecting and indeed wishing every moment
to be my last.

I have already told the reader that there were two strong staples fixed
upon that side of my box which had no window and into which the
servant, who used to carry me on horseback, would put a leathern belt,
and buckle it about his waist. Being in this disconsolate state, I heard,
or at least thought I heard, some kind of grating noise on that side of my
box where the staples were fixed; and soon after I began to fancy that the
box was pulled or towed along in the sea; for I now and then felt a sort
of tugging, which made the waves rise near the tops of my windows,
leaving me almost in the dark. This gave me some faint hopes of relief,
although I was not able to imagine how it could be brought about. I
ventured to unscrew one of my chairs, which were always fastened to
the floor; and having made a hard shift to screw it down again directly
under the slipping-board that I had lately opened, I mounted on the
chair, and putting my mouth as near as I could to the hole, I called for
help in a loud voice, and in all the languages I understood. I then fastened my handkerchief to a stick I usually carried, and thrusting it up
the hole, waved it several times in the air, that if any boat or ship were
near, the seamen might conjecture some unhappy mortal to be shut up
in the box.

I found no effect from all I could do, but plainly perceived my closet to be moved along; and in the space of an hour or better, that side of the box where the staples were, and had no window, struck against something that was hard. I apprehended it to be a rock, and found myself tossed more than ever. I plainly heard a noise upon the cover of my closet, like that of a cable, and the grating of it as it passed through the ring. I then found myself hoisted up by degrees at least three foot higher than I was before. Whereupon I again thrust up my stick and handkerchief, calling for help till I was almost hoarse. In return to which, I heard a great shout repeated three times, giving me such transports of joy as are not to be conceived but by those who feel them. I now heard a trampling over my head, and somebody calling through the hole with a loud voice in the English tongue: "If there be anybody below, let them speak." I answered, I was an Englishman, drawn by ill fortune into the greatest calamity that ever any creature underwent, and begged, by all that was moving, to be delivered out of the dungeon I was in. The voice replied, I was safe, for my box was fastened to their ship; and the carpenter should immediately come and saw an hole in the cover, large enough to pull me out. I answered, that was needless and would take up too much time, for there was no more to be done but let one of the crew put his finger into the ring, and take the box out of the sea into the ship, and so into the captain's cabin. Some of them, upon hearing me talk so wildly, thought I was mad; others laughed; for indeed it never came into my head that I was now got among people of my own stature and strength. The carpenter came, and in a few minutes sawed a passage about four foot square; then let down a small ladder, upon which I mounted, and from thence was taken into the ship in a very weak condition.

The sailors were all in amazement, and asked me a thousand questions, which I had no inclination to answer. I was equally confounded at the sight of so many pygmies, for such I took them to be, after having so long accustomed my eyes to the monstrous objects I had left. But the Captain, Mr. Thomas Wilcocks, an honest, worthy Shropshire man, observing I was ready to faint, took me into his cabin, gave me a cordial to comfort me, and made me turn in upon his own bed, advising me to take a little rest, of which I had great need. Before I went to sleep I gave him to understand that I had some valuable furniture in my box, too good to be lost, a fine hammock, an handsome field bed, two chairs, a table, and a cabinet; that my closet was hung on all sides, or rather quilted with silk and cotton; that if he would let one of the crew bring my closet into his cabin, I would open it before him and show him my goods. The Captain, hearing me utter these absurdities, concluded I was raving; however (I suppose to pacify me), he promised to give order as I desired, and going upon deck, sent some of his men down into my closet, from whence (as I afterwards found) they drew up all my goods and stripped off the quilting; but the chairs, cabinet, and bedstead, being screwed to the floor, were much damaged by the ignorance of the seamen, who tore them up by force. Then they knocked off some of the boards for the use of the ship; and when they had got all they had a mind for, let the hulk drop into the sea, which, by reason of many breaches made in the bottom and sides, sunk to rights.[7] And indeed I was glad not to have been a spectator of the havoc they made, because I am confident it would have sensibly touched me, by bringing former passages into my mind, which I had rather forget.

I slept some hours, but perpetually disturbed with dreams of the place I had left, and the dangers I had escaped. However, upon waking, I found myself much recovered. It was now about eight o'clock at night, and the Captain ordered supper immediately, thinking I had already fasted too long. He entertained me with great kindness, observing me not to look wildly, or talk inconsistently; and when we were left alone, desired I would give him a relation of my travels, and by what accident I came to be set adrift in that monstrous wooden chest. He said that about twelve o'clock at noon, as he was looking through his glass, he spied it at a distance, and thought it was a sail, which he had a mind to make,[8] being not much out of his course, in hopes of buying some biscuit, his own beginning to fall short. That, upon coming nearer, and finding his error, he sent out his longboat to discover what I was; that his men came back in a fright, swearing they had seen a swimming house. That he laughed at their folly, and went himself in the boat, ordering his men to take a strong cable along with them. That the weather being calm, he rowed round me several times, observed my windows, and the wire lattices that defended them. That he discovered two staples upon one side, which was all of boards, without any passage for light. He then commanded his men to row up to that side, and fastening a cable to one of the staples, ordered his men to tow my chest (as he called it) towards the ship. When it was there, he gave directions to fasten another cable to the ring fixed in the cover, and to raise up my chest with pulleys, which all the sailors were not able to do above two or three foot. He said they saw my stick and handkerchief thrust out of the hole, and concluded that some unhappy man must be shut up in the cavity. I asked whether he or the crew had seen any prodigious birds in the air about the time he first discovered me. To which he answered that, discoursing this matter with the sailors while I was asleep, one of them said he had observed three eagles flying towards the north, but remarked nothing of their being larger than the usual size (which I suppose must be imputed to the great height they were at), and he could not guess the reason of my question. I then asked the Captain how far he reckoned we might be from land; he said, by the best computation he could make, we were at least an hundred leagues. I assured him that he must be mistaken by almost half; for I had not left the country from whence I came above two hours before I dropped into the sea. Whereupon he began again to think that my brain was disturbed, of which he gave me a hint, and advised me to go to bed in a cabin he had provided. I assured him I was well refreshed with his good entertainment and company, and

---

7. At once; altogether.   8. Overtake.

as much in my senses as ever I was in my life. He then grew serious and desired to ask me freely whether I were not troubled in mind by the consciousness of some enormous crime, for which I was punished at the command of some prince, by exposing me in that chest, as great criminals in other countries have been forced to sea in a leaky vessel without provisions; for although he should be sorry to have taken so ill[9] a man into his ship, yet he would engage his word to set me safe on shore in the first port where we arrived. He added that his suspicions were much increased by some very absurd speeches I had delivered at first to the sailors, and afterwards to himself, in relation to my closet or chest, as well as by my odd looks and behavior while I was at supper.

I begged his patience to hear me tell my story, which I faithfully did from the last time I left England to the moment he first discovered me. And as truth always forceth its way into rational minds, so this honest, worthy gentleman, who had some tincture of learning, and very good sense, was immediately convinced of my candor and veracity. But further to confirm all I had said, I entreated him to give order that my cabinet should be brought, of which I kept the key in my pocket (for he had already informed me how the seamen disposed of my closet). I opened it in his presence and showed him the small collection of rarities I made in the country from whence I had been so strangely delivered. There was the comb I had contrived out of the stumps of the King's beard, and another of the same materials, but fixed into a paring of her Majesty's thumbnail, which served for the back. There was a collection of needles and pins from a foot to half a yard long; four wasp-stings, like joiners' tacks; some combings of the Queen's hair; a gold ring which one day she made me a present of in a most obliging manner, taking it from her little finger, and throwing it over my head like a collar. I desired the Captain would please to accept this ring in return for his civilities, which he absolutely refused. I showed him a corn that I had cut off with my own hand from a Maid of Honor's toe; it was about the bigness of a Kentish pippin,[1] and grown so hard that, when I returned to England, I got it hollowed into a cup and set in silver. Lastly, I desired him to see the breeches I had then on, which were made of a mouse's skin.

I could force nothing on him but a footman's tooth, which I observed him to examine with great curiosity, and found he had a fancy for it. He received it with abundance of thanks, more than such a trifle could deserve. It was drawn by an unskillful surgeon in a mistake from one of Glumdalclitch's men, who was afflicted with the toothache; but it was as sound as any in his head. I got it cleaned, and put it into my cabinet. It was about a foot long, and four inches in diameter.

The Captain was very well satisfied with this plain relation I had given him, and said he hoped when we returned to England I would oblige the world by putting it in paper and making it public. My answer was that I thought we were already overstocked with books of travels; that

9. Evil.   1. Apple.

nothing could now pass which was not extraordinary; wherein I doubted some authors less consulted truth than their own vanity or interest, or the diversion of ignorant readers. That my story could contain little besides common events, without those ornamental descriptions of strange plants, trees, birds, and other animals, or the barbarous customs and idolatry of savage people, with which most writers abound. However, I thanked him for his good opinion, and promised to take the matter into my thoughts.

He said he wondered at one thing very much, which was to hear me speak so loud, asking me whether the King or Queen of that country were thick of hearing. I told him it was what I had been used to for above two years past, and that I admired[2] as much at the voices of him and his men, who seemed to me only to whisper, and yet I could hear them well enough. But, when I spoke in that country, it was like a man talking in the street to another looking out from the top of a steeple, unless when I was placed on a table, or held in any person's hand. I told him I had likewise observed another thing: that when I first got into the ship, and the sailors stood all about me, I thought they were the most little contemptible creatures I had ever beheld. For indeed while I was in that prince's country, I could never endure to look in a glass after mine eyes had been accustomed to such prodigious objects, because the comparison gave me so despicable a conceit[3] of myself. The Captain said that while we were at supper he observed me to look at everything with a sort of wonder, and that I often seemed hardly able to contain my laughter; which he knew not well how to take, but imputed it to some disorder in my brain. I answered, it was very true; and I wondered how I could forbear, when I saw his dishes of the size of a silver threepence, a leg of pork hardly a mouthful, a cup not so big as a nutshell; and so I went on, describing the rest of his household stuff and provisions after the same manner. For, although the Queen had ordered a little equipage[4] of all things necessary for me while I was in her service, yet my ideas were wholly taken up with what I saw on every side of me, and I winked at my own littleness, as people do at their own faults. The Captain understood my raillery very well, and merrily replied with the old English proverb, that he doubted[5] mine eyes were bigger than my belly, for he did not observe my stomach so good, although I had fasted all day; and continuing in his mirth, protested he would have gladly given an hundred pounds to have seen my closet in the eagle's bill, and afterwards in its fall from so great an height into the sea; which would certainly have been a most astonishing object, worthy to have the description of it transmitted to future ages: and the comparison of Phaeton[6] was so obvious,

---

2. Wondered at.
3. Notion.
4. Furnishings.
5. Feared.

6. The son of Apollo, whose unsuccessful attempt to drive the chariot of the sun god resulted in his death, when he was hurled by Zeus from the sky and fell into the river Eridanus, where he drowned.

that he could not forbear applying it, although I did not much admire the conceit.

The Captain having been at Tonquin,[7] was in his return to England driven northeastward to the latitude of 44 degrees, and of longitude 143. But meeting a trade wind two days after I came on board him, we sailed southward a long time, and coasting New Holland[8] kept our course west-southwest, and then south-southwest till we doubled the Cape of Good Hope. Our voyage was very prosperous, but I shall not trouble the reader with a journal of it. The Captain called in at one or two ports, and sent in his longboat for provisions and fresh water; but I never went out of the ship till we came into the Downs,[9] which was on the third day of June, 1706, about nine months after my escape. I offered to leave my goods in security for payment of my freight; but the Captain protested he would not receive one farthing. We took kind leave of each other, and I made him promise he would come to see me at my house in Redriff.[1] I hired a horse and guide for five shillings, which I borrowed of the Captain.

As I was on the road, observing the littleness of the houses, the trees, the cattle, and the people, I began to think myself in Lilliput. I was afraid of trampling on every traveler I met, and often called aloud to have them stand out of the way, so that I had like to have gotten one or two broken heads for my impertinence.

When I came to my own house, for which I was forced to inquire, one of the servants opening the door, I bent down to go in (like a goose under a gate) for fear of striking my head. My wife ran out to embrace me, but I stooped lower than her knees, thinking she could otherwise never be able to reach my mouth. My daughter kneeled to ask my blessing, but I could not see her till she arose, having been so long used to stand with my head and eyes erect to above sixty foot; and then I went to take her up with one hand by the waist. I looked down upon the servants and one or two friends who were in the house, as if they had been pygmies and I a giant. I told my wife she had been too thrifty; for I found she had starved herself and her daughter to nothing. In short, I behaved myself so unaccountably that they were all of the Captain's opinion when he first saw me, and concluded I had lost my wits. This I mention as an instance of the great power of habit and prejudice.

In a little time I and my family and friends came to a right understanding; but my wife protested I should never go to sea any more, although my evil destiny so ordered that she had not power to hinder me; as the reader may know hereafter. In the meantime I here conclude the second part of my unfortunate voyages.

---

7. Tonkin, in Indochina.
8. Australia.
9. The sheltered anchorage between Goodwin Sands and the coast of Kent, near Deal.
1. Rotherhithe, on the south bank of the Thames, slightly below the City.

From *Part* 3. A Voyage to Laputa, Balnibarbi, Glubbdubdrib, Luggnagg, and Japan

[*The Flying Island of Laputa*][1]

CHAPTER 2. *The humors and dispositions of the Laputans described. An account of their learning. Of the King and his court. The author's reception there. The inhabitants subject to fears and disquietudes. An account of the women.*

At my alighting I was surrounded by a crowd of people, but those who stood nearest seemed to be of better quality. They beheld me with all the marks and circumstances of wonder; neither indeed was I much in their debt, having never till then seen a race of mortals so singular in their shapes, habits, and countenances. Their heads were all reclined to the right, or the left; one of their eyes turned inward, and the other directly up to the zenith. Their outward garments were adorned with the figures of suns, moons, and stars, interwoven with those of fiddles, flutes, harps, trumpets, guitars, harpsichords, and many more instruments of music, unknown to us in Europe.[2] I observed here and there many in the habits of servants, with a blown bladder fastened like a flail to the end of a short stick, which they carried in their hands. In each bladder was a small quantity of dried pease or little pebbles (as I was afterwards informed). With these bladders they now and then flapped the mouths and ears of those who stood near them, of which practice I could not then conceive the meaning. It seems, the minds of these people are so taken up with intense speculations, that they neither can speak, or attend to the discourses of others, without being roused by some external taction[3] upon the organs of speech and hearing; for which reason those persons who are able to afford it always keep a flapper (the original is *climenole*) in their family, as one of their domestics; nor ever walk abroad or make visits without him. And the business of this officer is, when two or more persons are in company, gently to strike with his bladder the mouth of him who is to speak, and the right ear of him or them to whom the speaker addresseth himself. This flapper is likewise employed diligently to attend his master in his walks, and upon occasion to give him a soft flap on his eyes, because he is always so wrapped up in cogitation, that he is in manifest danger of falling down every precipice, and bouncing his head against every post; and in the streets, of jostling others, or being jostled himself into the kennel.[4]

It was necessary to give the reader this information, without which he would be at the same loss with me, to understand the proceedings of these people, as they conducted me up the stairs to the top of the island,

---

1. In the first chapter of part 3 Gulliver starts on his third voyage, but is captured by pirates and set adrift. Just as he is about to despair, a vast flying island appears in the sky, and the inhabitants draw him up with pulleys.

2. The Laputans represent contemporary specu-

lation, deplored by Swift, about abstract theories of science, mathematics, and music. Both the Royal Society and Sir Isaac Newton took an interest in the mathematical basis of music.

3. Touch.
4. Gutter.

and from thence to the royal palace. While we were ascending, they forgot several times what they were about, and left me to myself, till their memories were again roused by their flappers; for they appeared altogether unmoved by the sight of my foreign habit and countenance, and by the shouts of the vulgar, whose thoughts and minds were more disengaged.

At last we entered the palace, and proceeded into the chamber of presence; where I saw the King seated on his throne, attended on each side by persons of prime quality. Before the throne was a large table filled with globes and spheres, and mathematical instruments of all kinds. His Majesty took not the least notice of us, although our entrance was not without sufficient noise, by the concourse of all persons belonging to the court. But he was then deep in a problem, and we attended at least an hour before he could solve it. There stood by him on each side a young page, with flaps in their hands, and when they saw he was at leisure, one of them gently struck his mouth, and the other his right ear; at which he started like one awaked on the sudden, and looking towards me, and the company I was in, recollected the occasion of our coming, whereof he had been informed before. He spoke some words, whereupon immediately a young man with a flap came up to my side, and flapped me gently on the right ear; but I made signs as well as I could, that I had no occasion for such an instrument; which as I afterwards found gave his Majesty and the whole court a very mean opinion of my understanding. The King, as far as I could conjecture, asked me several questions, and I addressed myself to him in all the languages I had. When it was found that I could neither understand nor be understood, I was conducted by his order to an apartment in his palace (this prince being distinguished above all his predecessors for his hospitality to strangers),[5] where two servants were appointed to attend me. My dinner was brought, and four persons of quality, whom I remembered to have seen very near the King's person, did me the honor to dine with me. We had two courses, of three dishes each. In the first course there was a shoulder of mutton, cut into an equilateral triangle; a piece of beef into a rhomboid; and a pudding into a cycloid. The second course was two ducks, trussed up into the form of fiddles; sausages and pudding resembling flutes and hautboys,[6] and a breast of veal in the shape of a harp. The servants cut our bread into cones, cylinders, parallelograms, and several other mathematical figures.

While we were at dinner, I made bold to ask the names of several things in their language, and those noble persons, by the assistance of their flappers, delighted to give me answers, hoping to raise my admiration of their great abilities, if I could be brought to converse with them. I was soon able to call for bread and drink, or whatever else I wanted.

5. George I, a patron of music and science, had filled his court with Hanoverians when he came to England in 1714.
6. Oboes.

After dinner my company withdrew, and a person was sent to me by the King's order, attended by a flapper. He brought with him pen, ink, and paper, and three or four books; giving me to understand by signs, that he was sent to teach me the language. We sat together four hours, in which time I wrote down a great number of words in columns, with the translations over against them. I likewise made a shift to learn several short sentences. For my tutor would order one of my servants to fetch something, to turn about, to make a bow, to sit, or stand, or walk, and the like. Then I took down the sentence in writing. He showed me also in one of his books the figures of the sun, moon, and stars, the zodiac, the tropics and polar circles, together with the denominations of many figures of planes and solids. He gave me the names and descriptions of all the musical instruments, and the general terms of art in playing on each of them. After he had left me, I placed all my words with their interpretations in alphabetical order. And thus in a few days, by the help of a very faithful memory, I got some insight into their language.

The word, which I interpret the *Flying* or *Floating Island*, is in the original *Laputa*; whereof I could never learn the true etymology. *Lap* in the old obsolete language signifieth *high*, and *untuh* a governor; from which they say by corruption was derived *Laputa*, from *Lapuntuh*. But I do not approve of this derivation, which seems to be a little strained. I ventured to offer to the learned among them a conjecture of my own, that *Laputa* was *quasi Lap outed*; *Lap* signifying properly the dancing of the sunbeams in the sea, and *outed* a wing, which however I shall not obtrude, but submit to the judicious reader.[7]

Those to whom the King had entrusted me, observing how ill I was clad, ordered a tailor to come next morning, and take my measure for a suit of clothes. This operator did his office after a different manner from those of his trade in Europe. He first took my altitude by a quadrant, and then, with rule and compasses, described the dimensions and out-lines of my whole body; all which he entered upon paper, and in six days brought my clothes very ill made, and quite out of shape, by hap-pening to mistake a figure in the calculation. But my comfort was, that I observed such accidents very frequent, and little regarded.

During my confinement for want of clothes, and by an indisposition that held me some days longer, I much enlarged my dictionary; and when I went next to court, was able to understand many things the King spoke, and to return him some kind of answers. His Majesty had given orders that the island should move northeast and by east, to the vertical point over Lagado, the metropolis of the whole kingdom, below upon the firm earth. It was about ninety leagues distant, and our voyage lasted four days and a half. I was not in the least sensible of the progressive motion made in the air by the island. On the second morning, about eleven o'clock, the King himself in person, attended by his nobility, courtiers, and officers, having prepared all their musical instruments,

7. Gulliver overlooks a likelier etymology: Spanish *la puta*, "the whore."

played on them for three hours without intermission, so that I was quite stunned with the noise; neither could I possibly guess the meaning, till my tutor informed me. He said, that the people of their island had their ears adapted to hear the music of the spheres, which always played at certain periods; and the court was now prepared to bear their part in whatever instrument they most excelled.

In our journey towards Lagado, the capital city, his Majesty ordered that the island should stop over certain towns and villages, from whence he might receive the petitions of his subjects. And to this purpose, several packthreads were let down with small weights at the bottom. On these packthreads the people strung their petitions, which mounted up directly like the scraps of paper fastened by schoolboys at the end of the string that holds their kite.[8] Sometimes we received wine and victuals from below, which were drawn up by pulleys.

The knowledge I had in mathematics gave me great assistance in acquiring their phraseology, which depended much upon that science and music; and in the latter I was not unskilled. Their ideas are perpetually conversant in lines and figures. If they would, for example, praise the beauty of a woman, or any other animal, they describe it by rhombs, circles, parallelograms, ellipses, and other geometrical terms; or else by words of art drawn from music, needless here to repeat. I observed in the King's kitchen all sorts of mathematical and musical instruments, after the figures of which they cut up the joints that were served to his Majesty's table.

Their houses are very ill built, the walls bevil, without one right angle in any apartment; and this defect ariseth from the contempt they bear for practical geometry; which they despise as vulgar and mechanic, those instructions they give being too refined for the intellectuals of their workmen; which occasions perpetual mistakes. And although they are dextrous enough upon a piece of paper, in the management of the rule, the pencil, and the divider, yet in the common actions and behavior of life I have not seen a more clumsy, awkward, and unhandy people, nor so slow and perplexed in their conceptions upon all other subjects, except those of mathematics and music. They are very bad reasoners, and vehemently given to opposition, unless when they happen to be of the right opinion, which is seldom their case. Imagination, fancy, and invention, they are wholly strangers to, nor have any words in their language by which those ideas can be expressed; the whole compass of their thoughts and mind being shut up within the two forementioned sciences.

Most of them, and especially those who deal in the astronomical part, have great faith in judicial astrology, although they are ashamed to own it publicly. But what I chiefly admired,[9] and thought altogether unaccountable, was the strong disposition I observed in them towards news and politics; perpetually enquiring into public affairs, giving their judg-

---

8. Petitioners, that is, might as well go fly a kite. Throughout this section Swift satirizes the "distance" of George I (who spent much of his time in Hanover) from his English subjects.
9. Wondered at.

ments in matters of state; and passionately disputing every inch of a party opinion. I have indeed observed the same disposition among most of the mathematicians I have known in Europe; although I could never discover the least analogy between the two sciences; unless those people suppose, that because the smallest circle hath as many degrees as the largest, therefore the regulation and management of the world require no more abilities than the handling and turning of a globe. But I rather take this quality to spring from a very common infirmity of human nature, inclining us to be more curious and conceited in matters where we have least concern, and for which we are least adapted either by study or nature.

These people are under continual disquietudes, never enjoying a minute's peace of mind; and their disturbances proceed from causes which very little affect the rest of mortals. Their apprehensions arise from several changes they dread in the celestial bodies. For instance; that the earth, by the continual approaches of the sun towards it, must in course of time be absorbed or swallowed up. That the face of the sun will by degrees be encrusted with its own effluvia,[1] and give no more light to the world. That the earth very narrowly escaped a brush from the tail of the last comet, which would have infallibly reduced it to ashes; and that the next, which they have calculated for one and thirty years hence, will probably destroy us.[2] For, if in its perihelion it should approach within a certain degree of the sun (as by their calculations they have reason to dread), it will conceive a degree of heat ten thousand times more intense than that of red-hot glowing iron; and in its absence from the sun, carry a blazing tail ten hundred thousand and fourteen miles long; through which if the earth should pass at the distance of one hundred thousand miles from the nucleus, or main body of the comet, it must in its passage be set on fire, and reduced to ashes. That the sun daily spending its rays without any nutriment to supply them, will at last be wholly consumed and annihilated; which must be attended with the destruction of this earth, and of all the planets that receive their light from it.

They are so perpetually alarmed with the apprehensions of these and the like impending dangers, that they can neither sleep quietly in their beds, nor have any relish for the common pleasures or amusements of life. When they meet an acquaintance in the morning, the first question is about the sun's health, how he looked at his setting and rising, and what hopes they have to avoid the stroke of the approaching comet. This conversation they are apt to run into with the same temper that boys discover in delighting to hear terrible stories of sprites and hobgoblins, which they greedily listen to, and dare not go to bed for fear.

The women of the island have abundance of vivacity; they contemn their husbands, and are exceedingly fond of strangers, whereof there is

---

1. Sunspots.

2. Halley's comet, some astronomers had feared, might strike the earth on its next appearance (1758).

All the disasters that disquiet the Laputans had occurred to English scientists as possible implications of Newtonian theory.

always a considerable number from the continent below, attending at court, either upon affairs of the several towns and corporations, or their own particular occasions; but are much despised, because they want the same endowments. Among these the ladies choose their gallants: but the vexation is, that they act with too much ease and security; for the husband is always so rapt in speculation, that the mistress and lover may proceed to the greatest familiarities before his face, if he be but provided with paper and implements, and without his flapper at his side.

The wives and daughters lament their confinement to the island, although I think it the most delicious spot of ground in the world; and although they live here in the greatest plenty and magnificence, and are allowed to do whatever they please, they long to see the world, and take the diversions of the metropolis, which they are not allowed to do without a particular license from the King; and this is not easy to be obtained, because the people of quality have found by frequent experience, how hard it is to persuade their women to return from below. I was told that a great court lady, who had several children, is married to the prime minister, the richest subject in the kingdom, a very graceful person, extremely fond of her, and lives in the finest palace of the island, went down to Lagado, on the pretense of health, there hid herself for several months, till the King sent a warrant to search for her, and she was found in an obscure eating-house all in rags, having pawned her clothes to maintain an old deformed footman, who beat her every day, and in whose company she was taken much against her will. And although her husband received her with all possible kindness, and without the least reproach, she soon after contrived to steal down again with all her jewels, to the same gallant, and hath not been heard of since.

This may perhaps pass with the reader rather for an European or English story, than for one of a country so remote. But he may please to consider, that the caprices of womankind are not limited by any climate or nation; and that they are much more uniform than can be easily imagined.

In about a month's time I had made a tolerable proficiency in their language, and was able to answer most of the King's questions, when I had the honor to attend him. His Majesty discovered not the least curiosity to enquire into the laws, government, history, religion, or manners of the countries where I had been; but confined his questions to the state of mathematics, and received the account I gave him with great contempt and indifference, though often roused by his flapper on each side. [3]

---

3. In the omitted chapters Gulliver visits countries that show the consequences of modern learning. After an account of the Flying Island, whose power of motion (derived from a giant magnet or loadstone) allows it to dominate the regions below, he descends to Balnibarbi, a once fertile land now ruined by the fanciful projects of impractical scientists. In the Grand Academy of Lagado he meets many professors who are contriving such perverse "improvements" as making clothes from cobwebs or breeding naked sheep. Then he visits the part of the academy devoted to speculative learning.

[The Academy of Lagado][4]

The first professor I saw was in a very large room, with forty pupils about him. After salutation, observing me to look earnestly upon a frame, which took up the greatest part of both the length and breadth of the room, he said, perhaps I might wonder to see him employed in a project for improving speculative knowledge by practical and mechanical operations. But the world would soon be sensible[5] of its usefulness, and he flattered himself that a more noble, exalted thought never sprang in any other man's head. Everyone knew how laborious the usual method is of attaining to arts and sciences; whereas by his contrivance the most ignorant person at a reasonable charge, and with a little bodily labor, may write books in philosophy, poetry, politics, law, mathematics, and theology, without the least assistance from genius or study. He then led me to the frame, about the sides whereof all his pupils stood in ranks. It was twenty foot square, placed in the middle of the room. The superficies[6] was composed of several bits of wood, about the bigness of a die, but some larger than others. They were all linked together by slender wires. These bits of wood were covered on every square with papers pasted on them; and on these papers were written all the words of their language in their several moods, tenses, and declensions, but without any order. The professor then desired me to observe, for he was going to set his engine[7] at work. The pupils at his command took each of them hold of an iron handle, whereof there were forty fixed round the edges of the frame; and giving them a sudden turn, the whole disposition[8] of the words was entirely changed. He then commanded six and thirty of the lads to read the several lines softly as they appeared upon the frame; and where they found three or four words together that might make part of a sentence, they dictated to the four remaining boys who were scribes. This work was repeated three or four times, and at every turn the engine was so contrived that the words shifted into new places, as the square bits of wood moved upside down.

Six hours a day the young students were employed in this labor; and the professor showed me several volumes in large folio already collected, of broken sentences, which he intended to piece together, and out of those rich materials to give the world a complete body of all arts and sciences; which however might be still improved, and much expedited, if the public would raise a fund for making and employing five hundred such frames in Lagado, and oblige the managers to contribute in common their several[9] collections.

He assured me, that this invention had employed all his thoughts from his youth, that he had emptied the whole vocabulary into his frame,

---

4. From Chapter 5. The Grand Academy of Lagado satirizes the Royal Society of London, an organization founded in 1662 to encourage the pursuit of scientific knowledge. Some of the projects described by Swift resemble the experiments or speculations of British scientists at the time, and at least one seems current today.
5. Aware.
6. Surface.
7. Contrivance.
8. Arrangement.
9. Separate.

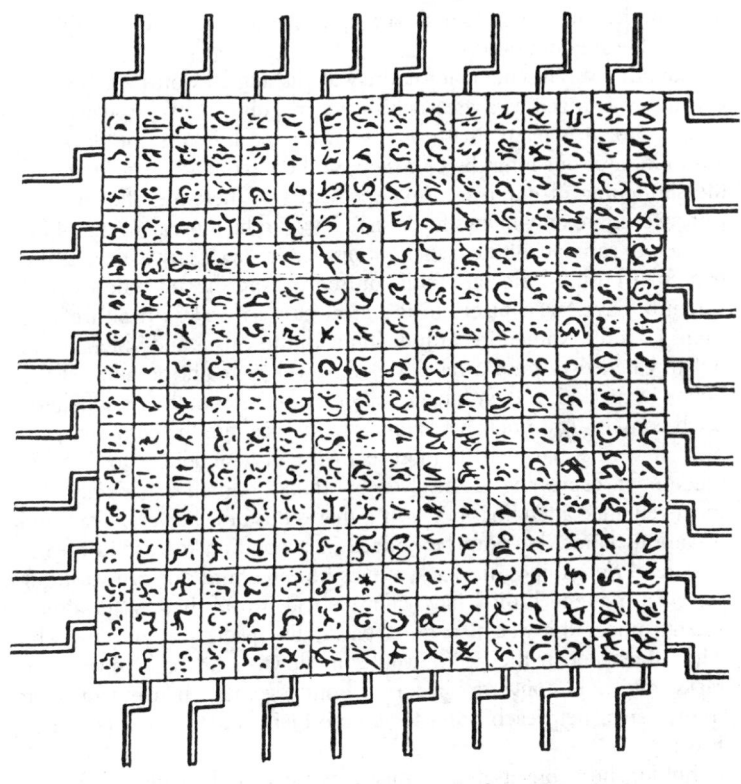

[A PRIMITIVE COMPUTER]

and made the strictest computation of the general proportion there is in books between the numbers of particles, nouns, and verbs, and other parts of speech.

I made my humblest acknowledgments to this illustrious person for his great communicativeness, and promised if ever I had the good fortune to return to my native country, that I would do him justice, as the sole inventor of this wonderful machine; the form and contrivance of which I desired leave to delineate upon paper as in the figure here annexed. I told him, although it were the custom of our learned in Europe to steal inventions from each other, who had thereby at least this advantage, that it became a controversy which was the right owner, yet I would take such caution, that he should have the honor entire without a rival.

We next went to the school of languages, where three professors sat in consultation upon improving that of their own country.[1]

The first project was to shorten discourse by cutting polysyllables into

1. Many contemporary scientists had proposed a philosophical language that would eliminate the treacherous disparity between words and things and thus allow accurate scientific discourse.

one, and leaving out verbs and participles, because in reality all things imaginable are but nouns.

The other was a scheme for entirely abolishing all words whatsoever; and this was urged as a great advantage in point of health as well as brevity. For it is plain, that every word we speak is in some degree a diminution of our lungs by corrosion, and consequently contributes to the shortening of our lives. An expedient was therefore offered, that since words are only names for *things*, it would be more convenient for all men to carry about them such *things* as were necessary to express the particular business they are to discourse on. And this invention would certainly have taken place, to the great ease as well as health of the subject,[2] if the women in conjunction with the vulgar and illiterate had not threatened to raise a rebellion, unless they might be allowed the liberty to speak with their tongues, after the manner of their forefathers. Such constant irreconcilable enemies to science[3] are the common people. However, many of the most learned and wise adhere to the new scheme of expressing themselves by *things*, which hath only this inconvenience attending it, that if a man's business be very great, and of various kinds, he must be obliged in proportion to carry a greater bundle of *things* upon his back, unless he can afford one or two strong servants to attend him. I have often beheld two of those sages almost sinking under the weight of their packs, like pedlars among us, who when they met in the streets would lay down their loads, open their sacks, and hold conversation for an hour together, then put up their implements, help each other to resume their burdens, and take their leave.

But for short conversations a man may carry implements in his pockets and under his arms, enough to supply him, and in his house he cannot be at a loss; therefore the room where company meet who practice this art is full of all *things* ready at hand, requisite to furnish matter for this kind of artificial converse.[4]

Another great advantage proposed by this invention was that it would serve as an universal language to be understood in all civilized nations, whose goods and utensils are generally of the same kind, or nearly resembling, so that their uses might easily be comprehended. And thus, ambassadors would be qualified to treat with foreign princes or ministers of state to whose tongues they were utter strangers.

I was at the mathematical school, where the master taught his pupils after a method scarce imaginable to us in Europe. The proposition and demonstration were fairly written on a thin wafer, with ink composed of a cephalic tincture.[5] This the student was to swallow upon a fasting stomach, and for three days following eat nothing but bread and water. As the wafer digested, the tincture mounted to his brain, bearing the

2. a. Person experimented on; b. topic of conversation. "Vulgar": common people.
3. Knowledge.
4. The Royal Society had sponsored a collection intended to contain one specimen of every thing in the world.
5. A solution or dye directed toward the head.

proposition along with it. But the success hath not hitherto been answerable, partly by some error in the *quantum*[6] or composition, and partly by the perverseness of lads, to whom this bolus is so nauseous that they generally steal aside, and discharge it upwards before it can operate; neither have they been yet persuaded to use so long an abstinence as the prescription requires.[7]

[The Struldbruggs]

CHAPTER 10. *The Luggnaggians commended. A particular description of the struldbruggs, with many conversations between the author and some eminent persons upon that subject.*

The Luggnaggians are a polite[8] and generous people, and although they are not without some share of that pride which is peculiar to all eastern countries, yet they show themselves courteous to strangers, especially such who are countenanced by the court. I had many acquaintance among persons of the best fashion, and being always attended by my interpreter, the conversation we had was not disagreeable.

One day in much good company, I was asked by a person of quality, whether I had seen any of their *struldbruggs* or *immortals*. I said I had not; and desired he would explain to me what he meant by such an appellation, applied to a mortal creature. He told me, that sometimes, although very rarely, a child happened to be born in a family with a red circular spot in the forehead, directly over the left eyebrow, which was an infallible mark that it should never die. The spot, as he described it, was about the compass of a silver threepence, but in the course of time grew larger, and changed its color; for at twelve years old it became green, so continued till five and twenty, then turned to a deep blue; at five and forty it grew coal black, and as large as an English shilling; but never admitted any farther alteration. He said these births were so rare, that he did not believe there could be above eleven hundred *struldbruggs* of both sexes in the whole kingdom, of which he computed about fifty in the metropolis, and among the rest a young girl born about three years ago. That these productions were not peculiar to any family, but a mere effect of chance; and the children of the *struldbruggs* themselves were equally mortal with the rest of the people.

I freely own myself to have been struck with inexpressible delight upon hearing this account: and the person who gave it me happening to understand the Balnibarbian language, which I spoke very well, I could not forbear breaking out into expressions perhaps a little too extravagant. I cried out as in a rapture: Happy nation, where every child hath at least

---

6. Amount. "Bolus": a large pill.
7. In the omitted chapters Gulliver hears projects for improving politics and offers some of his own. He sails to Glubbdubdrib, the Island of Sorcerers, where he talks with the spirits of the dead; he learns

that history is a pack of lies and that humanity has degenerated since ancient times. He is then received by the King of Luggnagg.
8. Refined, cultivated.

a chance for being immortal! Happy people who enjoy so many living examples of ancient virtue, and have masters ready to instruct them in the wisdom of all former ages! But happiest beyond all comparison are those excellent *struldbruggs*, who being born exempt from that universal calamity of human nature, have their minds free and disengaged, without the weight and depression of spirits caused by the continual apprehension of death. I discovered my admiration[9] that I had not observed any of these illustrious persons at court; the black spot on the forehead being so remarkable a distinction, that I could not have easily overlooked it; and it was impossible that his Majesty, a most judicious prince, should not provide himself with a good number of such wise and able counselors. Yet perhaps the virtue of those reverend sages was too strict for the corrupt and libertine manners of a court. And we often find by experience that young men are too opinionative[1] and volatile to be guided by the sober dictates of their seniors. However, since the King was pleased to allow me access to his royal person, I was resolved upon the very first occasion to deliver my opinion to him on this matter freely, and at large by the help of my interpreter; and whether he would please to take my advice or no, yet in one thing I was determined, that his Majesty having frequently offered me an establishment in this country, I would with great thankfulness accept the favor, and pass my life here in the conversation of those superior beings the *struldbruggs*, if they would please to admit me.

The gentleman to whom I addressed my discourse, because (as I have already observed) he spoke the language of Balnibarbi, said to me with a sort of a smile, which usually ariseth from pity to the ignorant, that he was glad of any occasion to keep me among them, and desired my permission to explain to the company what I had spoke. He did so; and they talked together for some time in their own language, whereof I understood not a syllable, neither could I observe by their countenances what impression my discourse had made on them. After a short silence the same person told me, that his friends and mine (so he thought fit to express himself) were very much pleased with the judicious remarks I had made on the great happiness and advantages of immortal life; and they were desirous to know in a particular manner, what scheme of living I should have formed to myself, if it had fallen to my lot to have been born a *struldbrugg*.

I answered, it was easy to be eloquent on so copious and delightful a subject, especially to me who have been often apt to amuse myself with visions of what I should do if I were a king, a general, or a great lord; and upon this very case I had frequently run over the whole system how I should employ myself, and pass the time if I were sure to live forever.

That, if it had been my good fortune to come into the world a *struldbrugg*, as soon as I could discover my own happiness by understanding the difference between life and death, I would first resolve by all arts and

9. Wonder.
1. Speculative, impractical. Note, in the next   sentence, Gulliver's own resolve to deliver his opinion.

methods whatsoever to procure myself riches: in the pursuit of which, by thrift and management, I might reasonably expect in about two hundred years to be the wealthiest man in the kingdom. In the second place, I would from my earliest youth apply myself to the study of arts and sciences, by which I should arrive in time to excel all others in learning. Lastly, I would carefully record every action and event of consequence that happened in the public, impartially draw the characters of the several successions of princes, and great ministers of state; with my own observations on every point. I would exactly set down the several changes in customs, languages, fashions of dress, diet and diversions. By all which acquirements, I should be a living treasury of knowledge and wisdom, and certainly become the oracle of the nation.

I would never marry after threescore, but live in an hospitable manner, yet still on the saving side. I would entertain myself in forming and directing the minds of hopeful young men, by convincing them from my own remembrance, experience and observation, fortified by numerous examples, of the usefulness of virtue in public and private life. But my choice and constant companions should be a set of my own immortal brotherhood, among whom I would elect a dozen from the most ancient down to my own contemporaries. Where any of these wanted fortunes, I would provide them with convenient lodges round my own estate, and have some of them always at my table, only mingling a few of the most valuable among you mortals, whom length of time would harden me to lose with little or no reluctance, and treat your posterity after the same manner; just as a man diverts himself with the annual succession of pinks and tulips in his garden, without regretting the loss of those which withered the preceding year.

These *struldbruggs* and I would mutually communicate our observations and memorials[2] through the course of time; remark the several gradations by which corruption steals into the world, and oppose it in every step, by giving perpetual warning and instruction to mankind; which, added to the strong influence of our own example, would probably prevent that continual degeneracy of human nature, so justly complained of in all ages.

Add to all this, the pleasure of seeing the various revolutions of states and empires; the changes in the lower and upper world;[3] ancient cities in ruins; and obscure villages become the seats of kings. Famous rivers lessening into shallow brooks; the ocean leaving one coast dry, and overwhelming another; the discovery of many countries yet unknown. Barbarity overrunning the politest nations, and the most barbarous becoming civilized. I should then see the discovery of the longitude, the perpetual motion, the universal medicine,[4] and many other great inventions brought to the utmost perfection.

2. Memories.
3. Earth and heaven; figuratively, common people and the ruling class. "Revolutions": cycles.
4. The *elixir vitae*, an alchemical formula to pre-serve life forever, was considered by Swift an impossible dream, like a method for calculating longitude at sea, or a perpetual motion machine.

What wonderful discoveries should we make in astronomy, by outliving and confirming our own predictions, by observing the progress and returns of comets, with the changes of motion in the sun, moon and stars.

I enlarged upon many other topics, which the natural desire of endless life and sublunary happiness could easily furnish me with. When I had ended, and the sum of my discourse had been interpreted as before to the rest of the company, there was a good deal of talk among them in the language of the country, not without some laughter at my expense. At last the same gentleman who had been my interpreter said, he was desired by the rest to set me right in a few mistakes, which I had fallen into through the common imbecility[5] of human nature, and upon that allowance was less answerable for them. That this breed of *struldbruggs* was peculiar to their country, for there were no such people either in Balnibarbi or Japan, where he had the honor to be ambassador from his Majesty, and found the natives in both those kingdoms very hard to believe that the fact was possible; and it appeared from my astonishment when he first mentioned the matter to me, that I received it as a thing wholly new, and scarcely to be credited. That in the two kingdoms above mentioned, where during his residence he had conversed very much, he observed long life to be the universal desire and wish of mankind. That whoever had one foot in the grave was sure to hold back the other as strongly as he could. That the oldest had still hopes of living one day longer, and looked on death as the greatest evil, from which nature always prompted him to retreat; only in this island of Luggnagg the appetite for living was not so eager, from the continual example of the *struldbruggs* before their eyes.

That the system of living contrived by me was unreasonable and unjust, because it supposed a perpetuity of youth, health, and vigor, which no man could be so foolish to hope, however extravagant he might be in his wishes. That the question therefore was not whether a man would choose to be always in the prime of youth, attended with prosperity and health; but how he would pass a perpetual life under all the usual disadvantages which old age brings along with it. For although few men will avow their desires of being immortal upon such hard conditions, yet in the two kingdoms before mentioned of Balnibarbi and Japan, he observed that every man desired to put off death for some time longer, let it approach ever so late; and he rarely heard of any man who died willingly, except he were incited by the extremity of grief or torture. And he appealed to me whether in those countries I had traveled, as well as my own, I had not observed the same general disposition.

After this preface he gave me a particular account of the *struldbruggs* among them. He said they commonly acted like mortals, till about thirty years old, after which by degrees they grew melancholy and dejected, increasing in both till they came to fourscore. This he learned from their

5. Weakness.

own confession; for otherwise there not being above two or three of that species born in an age, they were too few to form a general observation by. When they came to fourscore years, which is reckoned the extremity of living in this country, they had not only all the follies and infirmities of other old men, but many more which arose from the dreadful prospect of never dying. They were not only opinionative, peevish, covetous, morose, vain, talkative; but uncapable of friendship, and dead to all natural affection, which never descended below their grandchildren. Envy and impotent desires are their prevailing passions. But those objects against which their envy seems principally directed, are the vices of the younger sort, and the deaths of the old. By reflecting on the former, they find themselves cut off from all possibility of pleasure; and whenever they see a funeral, they lament and repine that others are gone to an harbor of rest, to which they themselves never can hope to arrive. They have no remembrance of anything but what they learned and observed in their youth and middle age, and even that is very imperfect. And for the truth or particulars of any fact, it is safer to depend on common traditions than upon their best recollections. The least miserable among them appear to be those who turn to dotage, and entirely lose their memories; these meet with more pity and assistance, because they want[6] many bad qualities which abound in others.

If a *struldbrugg* happen to marry one of his own kind, the marriage is dissolved of course by the courtesy of the kingdom, as soon as the younger of the two comes to be fourscore. For the law thinks it a reasonable indulgence, that those who are condemned without any fault of their own to a perpetual continuance in the world, should not have their misery doubled by the load of a wife.

As soon as they have completed the term of eighty years, they are looked on as dead in law; their heirs immediately succeed to their estates, only a small pittance is reserved for their support; and the poor ones are maintained at the public charge. After that period they are held incapable of any employment of trust or profit; they cannot purchase land, or take leases, neither are they allowed to be witnesses in any cause, either civil or criminal, not even for the decision of meers[7] and bounds.

At ninety they lose their teeth and hair; they have at that age no distinction of taste, but eat and drink whatever they can get, without relish or appetite. The diseases they were subject to still continue without increasing or diminishing. In talking they forget the common appellation of things, and the names of persons, even of those who are their nearest friends and relations. For the same reason they never can amuse themselves with reading, because their memory will not serve to carry them from the beginning of a sentence to the end, and by this defect they are deprived of the only entertainment whereof they might otherwise be capable.

The language of this country being always upon the flux, the *struld-*

6. Lack.   7. Boundaries.

bruggs of one age do not understand those of another; neither are they able after two hundred years to hold any conversation (farther than by a few general words) with their neighbors the mortals; and thus they lie under the disadvantage of living like foreigners in their own country.

This was the account given me of the *struldbruggs*, as near as I can remember. I afterwards saw five or six of different ages, the youngest not above two hundred years old, who were brought to me at several times by some of my friends; but although they were told that I was a great traveler, and had seen all the world, they had not the least curiosity to ask me a question; only desired I would give them *slumskudask*, or a token of remembrance; which is a modest way of begging, to avoid the law that strictly forbids it, because they are provided for by the public, although indeed with a very scanty allowance.

They are despised and hated by all sorts of people; when one of them is born, it is reckoned ominous, and their birth is recorded very particularly; so that you may know their age by consulting the registry, which however hath not been kept above a thousand years past, or at least hath been destroyed by time or public disturbances. But the usual way of computing how old they are, is by asking them what kings or great persons they can remember, and then consulting history; for infallibly the last prince in their mind did not begin his reign after they were fourscore years old.

They were the most mortifying sight I ever beheld; and the women more horrible than the men. Besides the usual deformities in extreme old age, they acquired an additional ghastliness in proportion to their number of years, which is not to be described; and among half a dozen I soon distinguished which was the oldest, although there were not above a century or two between them.

The reader will easily believe, that from what I had heard and seen, my keen appetite for perpetuity of life was much abated. I grew heartily ashamed of the pleasing visions I had formed; and thought no tyrant could invent a death into which I would not run with pleasure from such a life. The King heard of all that had passed between me and my friends upon this occasion, and rallied[8] me very pleasantly; wishing I would send a couple of *struldbruggs* to my own country, to arm our people against the fear of death; but this it seems is forbidden by the fundamental laws of the kingdom; or else I should have been well content with the trouble and expense of transporting them.

I could not but agree, that the laws of this kingdom relating to the *struldbruggs*, were founded upon the strongest reasons, and such as any other country would be under the necessity of enacting in the like circumstances. Otherwise, as avarice is the necessary consequent of old age, those immortals would in time become proprietors of the whole

8. Ridiculed.

nation, and engross[9] the civil power; which, for want of abilities to manage, must end in the ruin of the public.[1]

Part 4. A Voyage to the Country of the Houyhnhnms[1]

CHAPTER 1. *The Author sets out as Captain of a ship. His men conspire against him, confine him a long time to his cabin, set him on shore in an unknown land. He travels up into the country. The Yahoos, a strange sort of animal, described. The Author meets two Houyhnhnms.*

I continued at home with my wife and children about five months in a very happy condition, if I could have learned the lesson of knowing when I was well. I left my poor wife big with child, and accepted an advantageous offer made me to be Captain of the *Adventure*, a stout merchantman of 350 tons; for I understood navigation well, and being grown weary of a surgeon's employment at sea, which however I could exercise upon occasion, I took a skillful young man of that calling, one Robert Purefoy, into my ship. We set sail from Portsmouth upon the 7th day of September, 1710; on the 14th we met with Captain Pocock of Bristol, at Tenariff,[2] who was going to the Bay of Campeachy[3] to cut logwood. On the 16th he was parted from us by a storm; I heard since my return that his ship foundered and none escaped, but one cabin boy. He was an honest man and a good sailor, but a little too positive in his own opinions, which was the cause of his destruction, as it hath been of several others. For if he had followed my advice, he might at this time have been safe at home with his family as well as myself.

I had several men died in my ship of calentures,[4] so that I was forced to get recruits out of Barbadoes and the Leeward Islands, where I touched by the direction of the merchants who employed me; which I had soon too much cause to repent, for I found afterwards that most of them had been buccaneers. I had fifty hands on board; and my orders were that I should trade with the Indians in the South Sea, and make what discoveries I could. These rogues whom I had picked up debauched my other men, and they all formed a conspiracy to seize the ship and secure me; which they did one morning, rushing into my cabin, and binding me hand and foot, threatening to throw me overboard, if I offered to stir. I told them I was their prisoner, and would submit. This they made me swear to do, and then unbound me, only fastening one of my legs with a chain near my bed, and placed a sentry at my door with his piece charged, who was commanded to shoot me dead if I attempted my liberty. They sent me down victuals and drink, and took the government

9. Absorb, monopolize.
1. In the omitted chapter Gulliver sails to Japan, where a Dutch ship provides him passage back to Europe.
1. Pronounced Hwin-ims. The word suggests the neigh characteristic of a horse.

2. Teneriffe, one of the Canary Islands.
3. In the Gulf of Mexico.
4. "A distemper peculiar to sailors, in hot climates; wherein they imagine the sea to be green fields, and will throw themselves into it, if not restrained" (Johnson's *Dictionary*).

of the ship to themselves. Their design was to turn pirates and plunder the Spaniards, which they could not do, till they got more men. But first they resolved to sell the goods in the ship, and then go to Madagascar for recruits, several among them having died since my confinement. They sailed many weeks, and traded with the Indians; but I knew not what course they took, being kept close prisoner in my cabin, and expecting nothing less than to be murdered, as they often threatened me.

Upon the 9th day of May, 1711, one James Welch came down to my cabin; and said he had orders from the Captain to set me ashore. I expostulated with him, but in vain; neither would he so much as tell me who their new Captain was. They forced me into the longboat, letting me put on my best suit of clothes, which were as good as new, and a small bundle of linen, but no arms except my hanger; and they were so civil as not to search my pockets, into which I conveyed what money I had, with some other little necessaries. They rowed about a league, and then set me down on a strand. I desired them to tell me what country it was; they all swore, they knew no more than myself, but said that the Captain (as they called him) was resolved, after they had sold the lading, to get rid of me in the first place where they discovered land. They pushed off immediately, advising me to make haste, for fear of being overtaken by the tide, and bade me farewell.

In this desolate condition I advanced forward, and soon got upon firm ground, where I sat down on a bank to rest myself, and consider what I had best to do. When I was a little refreshed, I went up into the country, resolving to deliver myself to the first savages I should meet, and purchase my life from them by some bracelets, glass rings, and other toys, which sailors usually provide themselves with in those voyages, and whereof I had some about me. The land was divided by long rows of trees, not regularly planted, but naturally growing; there was great plenty of grass, and several fields of oats. I walked very circumspectly for fear of being surprised, or suddenly shot with an arrow from behind, or on either side. I fell into a beaten road, where I saw many tracks of human feet, and some of cows, but most of horses. At last I beheld several animals in a field, and one or two of the same kind sitting in trees. Their shape was very singular, and deformed, which a little discomposed me, so that I lay down behind a thicket to observe them better. Some of them coming forward near the place where I lay, gave me an opportunity of distinctly marking their form. Their heads and breasts were covered with a thick hair, some frizzled and others lank; they had beards like goats, and a long ridge of hair down their backs, and the fore parts of their legs and feet; but the rest of their bodies were bare, so that I might see their skins, which were of a brown buff color. They had no tails, nor any hair at all on their buttocks, except about the anus; which, I presume Nature had placed there to defend them as they sat on the ground; for this posture they used, as well as lying down, and often stood on their hind feet. They climbed high trees, as nimbly as a squirrel, for they had strong extended claws before and behind, terminating in sharp points,

and hooked. They would often spring, and bound, and leap with prodigious agility. The females were not so large as the males; they had long
lank hair on their heads, and only a sort of down on the rest of their
bodies, except about the anus, and pudenda. Their dugs hung between
their forefeet, and often reached almost to the ground as they walked.
The hair of both sexes was of several colors, brown, red, black, and
yellow. Upon the whole, I never beheld in all my travels so disagreeable
an animal, or one against which I naturally conceived so strong an
antipathy. So that thinking I had seen enough, full of contempt and
aversion, I got up and pursued the beaten road, hoping it might direct
me to the cabin of some Indian: I had not gone far when I met one of
these creatures full in my way, and coming up directly to me. The ugly
monster, when he saw me, distorted several ways every feature of his
visage, and stared as at an object he had never seen before; then
approaching nearer, lifted up his forepaw, whether out of curiosity or
mischief, I could not tell; but I drew my hanger, and gave him a good
blow with the flat side of it; for I durst not strike him with the edge,
fearing the inhabitants might be provoked against me, if they should
come to know that I had killed or maimed any of their cattle. When the
beast felt the smart, he drew back, and roared so loud, that a herd of at
least forty came flocking about me from the near field, howling and
making odious faces; but I ran to the body of a tree, and leaning my
back against it, kept them off, by waving my hanger. Several of this
cursed brood getting hold of the branches behind, leaped up into the
tree, from whence they began to discharge their excrements on my head;
however, I escaped pretty well, by sticking close to the stem of the tree,
but was almost stifled with the filth, which fell about me on every side.
    In the midst of this distress, I observed them all to run away on a
sudden as fast as they could; at which I ventured to leave the tree, and
pursue the road, wondering what it was that could put them into this
fright. But looking on my left hand, I saw a horse walking softly in the
field; which my persecutors having sooner discovered, was the cause of
their flight. The horse started a little when he came near me, but soon
recovering himself, looked full in my face with manifest tokens of wonder; he viewed my hands and feet, walking round me several times. I
would have pursued my journey, but he placed himself directly in the
way, yet looking with a very mild aspect, never offering the least violence. We stood gazing at each other for some time; at last I took the
boldness, to reach my hand towards his neck, with a design to stroke it;
using the common style and whistle of jockies when they are going to
handle a strange horse. But, this animal seeming to receive my civilities
with disdain, shook his head, and bent his brows, softly raising up his
left forefoot to remove my hand. Then he neighed three or four times,
but in so different a cadence, that I almost began to think he was speaking to himself in some language of his own.
    While he and I were thus employed, another horse came up; who
applying himself to the first in a very formal manner, they gently struck

each other's right hoof before, neighing several times by turns, and varying the sound, which seemed to be almost articulate. They went some paces off, as if it were to confer together, walking side by side, backward and forward, like persons deliberating upon some affair of weight; but often turning their eyes towards me, as it were to watch that I might not escape. I was amazed to see such actions and behavior in brute beasts; and concluded with myself that if the inhabitants of this country were endued with a proportionable degree of reason, they must needs be the wisest people upon earth. This thought gave me so much comfort, that I resolved to go forward until I could discover some house or village, or meet with any of the natives, leaving the two horses to discourse together as they pleased. But the first, who was a dapple grey, observing me to steal off, neighed after me in so expressive a tone that I fancied myself to understand what he meant; whereupon I turned back, and came near him, to expect his farther commands; but concealing my fear as much as I could; for I began to be in some pain, how this adventure might terminate; and the reader will easily believe I did not much like my present situation.

The two horses came up close to me, looking with great earnestness upon my face and hands. The grey steed rubbed my hat all round with his right fore hoof, and discomposed it so much that I was forced to adjust it better, by taking it off, and settling it again; whereat both he and his companion (who was a brown bay) appeared to be much surprised; the latter felt the lappet of my coat, and finding it to hang loose about me, they both looked with new signs of wonder. He stroked my right hand, seeming to admire the softness, and color; but he squeezed it so hard between his hoof and his pastern, that I was forced to roar; after which they both touched me with all possible tenderness. They were under great perplexity about my shoes and stockings, which they felt very often, neighing to each other, and using various gestures, not unlike those of a philosopher, when he would attempt to solve some new and difficult phenomenon.

Upon the whole, the behavior of these animals was so orderly and rational, so acute and judicious, that I at last concluded, they must needs be magicians, who had thus metamorphosed themselves upon some design; and seeing a stranger in the way, were resolved to divert themselves with him; or perhaps were really amazed at the sight of a man so very different in habit, feature, and complexion from those who might probably live in so remote a climate. Upon the strength of this reasoning, I ventured to address them in the following manner: "Gentlemen, if you be conjurers, as I have good cause to believe, you can understand any language; therefore I make bold to let your worships know that I am a poor distressed Englishman, driven by his misfortunes upon your coast; and I entreat one of you, to let me ride upon his back, as if he were a real horse, to some house or village, where I can be relieved. In return of which favor, I will make you a present of this knife and bracelet" (taking them out of my pocket). The two creatures stood silent while I spoke, seeming to listen with great attention; and when I had ended, they neighed frequently towards each other, as if they were engaged in serious conversation. I plainly observed, that their language expressed the passions very well, and the words might with little pains be resolved into an alphabet more easily than the Chinese.

I could frequently distinguish the word *Yahoo*,[5] which was repeated by each of them several times; and although it were impossible for me to conjecture what it meant, yet while the two horses were busy in conversation, I endeavored to practice this word upon my tongue; and as soon as they were silent, I boldly pronounced "Yahoo" in a loud voice, imitating, at the same time, as near as I could, the neighing of a horse; at which they were both visibly surprised, and the grey repeated the same word twice, as if he meant to teach me the right accent, wherein I spoke after him as well as I could, and found myself perceivably to improve every time, although very far from any degree of perfection. Then the bay tried me with a second word, much harder to be pronounced; but reducing it to the English orthography, may be spelt thus, *Houyhnhnm*. I did not succeed in this so well as the former, but after two or three farther trials, I had better fortune; and they both appeared amazed at my capacity.

After some farther discourse, which I then conjectured might relate to me, the two friends took their leaves, with the same compliment of striking each other's hoof; and the grey made me signs that I should walk before him; wherein I thought it prudent to comply, till I could find a better director. When I offered to slacken my pace, he would cry, "Hhuun, Hhuun"; I guessed his meaning, and gave him to understand, as well as I could that I was weary, and not able to walk faster; upon which, he would stand a while to let me rest.

CHAPTER 2. *The Author conducted by a Houyhnhnm to his house. The house described. The Author's reception. The food of the Houyhnhnms. The Author in distress for want of meat is at last relieved. His manner of feeding in that country.*

Having traveled about three miles, we came to a long kind of building, made of timber, stuck in the ground, and wattled across; the roof was low, and covered with straw. I now began to be a little comforted, and took out some toys, which travelers usually carry for presents to the savage Indians of America and other parts, in hopes the people of the house would be thereby encouraged to receive me kindly. The horse made me a sign to go in first; it was a large room with a smooth clay floor, and a rack and manger extending the whole length on one side. There were three nags, and two mares, not eating, but some of them sitting down upon their hams, which I very much wondered at; but wondered more to see the rest employed in domestic business; the last

---

5. Morley suggested that *Yahoo* was compounded from two expressions of disgust, *yah* and *ugh* (or *hoo*) common in the 18th century [Case's note].

seemed but ordinary cattle; however this confirmed my first opinion, that a people who could so far civilize brute animals must needs excel in wisdom all the nations of the world. The grey came in just after, and thereby prevented any ill treatment, which the others might have given me. He neighed to them several times in a style of authority, and received answers.

Beyond this room there were three others, reaching the length of the house, to which you passed through three doors, opposite to each other, in the manner of a vista; we went through the second room towards the third; here the grey walked in first, beckoning me to attend;[6] I waited in the second room, and got ready my presents, for the master and mistress of the house; they were two knives, three bracelets of false pearl, a small looking glass and a bead necklace. The horse neighed three or four times, and I waited to hear some answers in a human voice, but I heard no other returns than in the same dialect, only one or two a little shriller than his. I began to think that this house must belong to some person of great note among them, because there appeared so much ceremony before I could gain admittance. But, that a man of quality should be served all by horses, was beyond my comprehension. I feared my brain was disturbed by my sufferings and misfortunes; I roused myself, and looked about me in the room where I was left alone; this was furnished as the first, only after a more elegant manner. I rubbed my eyes often, but the same objects still occurred. I pinched my arms and sides, to awaken myself, hoping I might be in a dream. I then absolutely concluded that all these appearances could be nothing else but necromancy and magic. But I had no time to pursue these reflections; for the grey horse came to the door, and made me a sign to follow him into the third room; where I saw a very comely mare, together with a colt and foal, sitting on their haunches, upon mats of straw, not unartfully made, and perfectly neat and clean.

The mare soon after my entrance, rose from her mat, and coming up close, after having nicely observed my hands and face, gave me a most contemptuous look; then turning to the horse, I heard the word Yahoo often repeated betwixt them; the meaning of which word I could not then comprehend, although it were the first I had learned to pronounce; but I was soon better informed, to my everlasting mortification: for the horse beckoning to me with his head, and repeating the word, "Hhuun, Hhuun," as he did upon the road, which I understood was to attend him, led me out into a kind of court, where was another building at some distance from the house. Here we entered, and I saw three of those detestable creatures, which I first met after my landing, feeding upon roots, and the flesh of some animals, which I afterwards found to be that of asses and dogs, and now and then a cow dead by accident or disease. They were all tied by the neck with strong withes, fastened to a beam;

6. To wait.

they held their food between the claws of their forefeet, and tore it with their teeth.

The master horse ordered a sorrel nag, one of his servants, to untie the largest of these animals, and take him into a yard. The beast and I were brought close together; and our countenances diligently compared, both by master and servant, who thereupon repeated several times the word "Yahoo." My horror and astonishment are not to be described, when I observed, in this abominable animal, a perfect human figure; the face of it indeed was flat and broad, the nose depressed, the lips large, and the mouth wide; but these differences are common to all savage nations, where the lineaments of the countenance are distorted by the natives suffering their infants to lie groveling on the earth, or by carrying them on their backs, nuzzling with their face against the mother's shoulders. The forefeet of the Yahoo differed from my hands in nothing else but the length of the nails, the coarseness and brownness of the palms, and the hairiness on the backs. There was the same resemblance between our feet, with the same differences, which I knew very well, although the horses did not, because of my shoes and stockings; the same in every part of our bodies, except as to hairiness and color, which I have already described.

The great difficulty that seemed to stick with the two horses was to see the rest of my body so very different from that of a Yahoo, for which I was obliged to my clothes, whereof they had no conception; the sorrel nag offered me a root, which he held (after their manner, as we shall describe in its proper place) between his hoof and pastern; I took it in my hand, and having smelled it, returned it to him again as civilly as I could. He brought out of the Yahoo's kennel a piece of ass's flesh, but it smelled so offensively that I turned from it with loathing; he then threw it to the Yahoo, by whom it was greedily devoured. He afterwards showed me a wisp of hay, and a fetlock full of oats; but I shook my head, to signify that neither of these were food for me. And indeed, I now apprehended that I must absolutely starve, if I did not get to some of my own species; for as to those filthy Yahoos, although there were few greater lovers of mankind, at that time, than myself, yet I confess I never saw any sensitive being so detestable on all accounts; and the more I came near them, the more hateful they grew, while I stayed in that country. This the master horse observed by my behavior, and therefore sent the Yahoo back to his kennel. He then put his forehoof to his mouth, at which I was much surprised, although he did it with ease, and with a motion that appeared perfectly natural; and made other signs to know what I would eat; but I could not return him such an answer as he was able to apprehend; and if he had understood me, I did not see how it was possible to contrive any way for finding myself nourishment. While we were thus engaged, I observed a cow passing by; whereupon I pointed to her, and expressed a desire to let me go and milk her. This had its effect; for he led me back into the house, and ordered a mare-servant to open a room, where a good store of milk lay in earthen and wooden vessels, after a very orderly and cleanly manner. She gave me a large bowl full, of which I drank very heartily, and found myself well refreshed.

About noon I saw coming towards the house a kind of vehicle, drawn like a sledge by four Yahoos. There was in it an old steed, who seemed to be of quality; he alighted with his hind feet forward, having by accident got a hurt in his left forefoot. He came to dine with our horse, who received him with great civility. They dined in the best room, and had oats boiled in milk for the second course, which the old horse eat warm, but the rest cold. Their mangers were placed circular in the middle of the room, and divided into several partitions, round which they sat on their haunches upon bosses of straw. In the middle was a large rack with angles answering to every partition of the manger. So that each horse and mare eat their own hay, and their own mash of oats and milk, with much decency and regularity. The behavior of the young colt and foal appeared very modest; and that of the master and mistress extremely cheerful and complaisant to their guest. The grey ordered me to stand by him; and much discourse passed between him and his friend concerning me, as I found by the stranger's often looking on me, and the frequent repetition of the word Yahoo.

I happened to wear my gloves; which the master grey observing, seemed perplexed; discovering signs of wonder what I had done to my forefeet; he put his hoof three or four times to them, as if he would signify, that I should reduce them to their former shape, which I presently did, pulling off both my gloves, and putting them into my pocket. This occasioned farther talk, and I saw the company was pleased with my behavior, whereof I soon found the good effects. I was ordered to speak the few words I understood; and while they were at dinner, the master taught me the names for oats, milk, fire, water, and some others which I could readily pronounce after him, having from my youth a great facility in learning languages.

When dinner was done, the master horse took me aside, and by signs and words made me understand the concern he was in that I had nothing to eat. Oats in their tongue are called *hlunnh*. This word I pronounced two or three times; for although I had refused them at first, yet upon second thoughts, I considered that I could contrive to make a kind of bread, which might be sufficient with milk to keep me alive, till I could make my escape to some other country, and to creatures of my own species. The horse immediately ordered a white mare-servant of his family to bring me a good quantity of oats in a sort of wooden tray. These I heated before the fire as well as I could, and rubbed them till the husks came off, which I made a shift to winnow from the grain; I ground and beat them between two stones, then took water, and made them into a paste or cake, which I toasted at the fire, and eat warm with milk. It was at first a very insipid diet, although common enough in many parts of Europe, but grew tolerable by time; and having been often reduced to hard fare in my life, this was not the first experiment I had made how easily nature is satisfied. And I cannot but observe that I never had one hour's sickness, while I staid in this island. It is true, I sometimes made a shift to catch a rabbit, or bird, by springes[7] made of Yahoos' hairs; and I often gathered wholesome herbs, which I boiled, or eat as salads with my bread; and now and then, for a rarity, I made a little butter, and drank the whey. I was at first at a great loss for salt; but custom soon reconciled the want of it; and I am confident that the frequent use of salt among us is an effect of luxury, and was first introduced only as a provocative to drink; except where it is necessary for preserving of flesh in long voyages, or in places remote from great markets. For we observe no animal to be fond of it but man;[8] and as to myself, when I left this country, it was a great while before I could endure the taste of it in anything that I eat.

This is enough to say upon the subject of my diet, wherewith other travelers fill their books, as if the readers were personally concerned whether we fare well or ill. However, it was necessary to mention this matter, lest the world should think it impossible that I could find sustenance for three years in such a country, and among such inhabitants.

When it grew towards evening, the master horse ordered a place for me to lodge in; it was but six yards from the house, and separated from the stable of the Yahoos. Here I got some straw, and covering myself with my own clothes, slept very sound. But I was in a short time better accommodated, as the reader shall know hereafter, when I come to treat more particularly about my way of living.

CHAPTER 3. *The Author studious to learn the language, the Houyhnhnm his master assists in teaching him. The language described. Several Houyhnhnms of quality come out of curiosity to see the Author. He gives his master a short account of his voyage.*

My principal endeavor was to learn the language, which my master (for so I shall henceforth call him) and his children, and every servant of his house were desirous to teach me. For they looked upon it as a prodigy, that a brute animal should discover such marks of a rational creature. I pointed to everything, and enquired the name of it, which I wrote down in my journal book when I was alone, and corrected my bad accent, by desiring those of the family to pronounce it often. In this employment, a sorrel nag, one of the under servants, was very ready to assist me.

In speaking, they pronounce through the nose and throat, and their language approaches nearest to the High Dutch or German, of any I know in Europe; but is much more graceful and significant. The Emperor Charles V made almost the same observation, when he said, that if he were to speak to his horse, it should be in High Dutch.[9]

---

7. Snares.
8. Gulliver is, of course, in error. Many animals require salt.

9. The emperor is supposed to have said that he would speak to his God in Spanish, to his mistress in Italian, and to his horse in German.

The curiosity and impatience of my master were so great, that he spent many hours of his leisure to instruct me. He was convinced (as he afterwards told me) that I must be a Yahoo, but my teachableness, civility, and cleanliness astonished him; which were qualities altogether so opposite to those animals. He was most perplexed about my clothes, reasoning sometimes with himself whether they were a part of my body; for I never pulled them off till the family were asleep, and got them on before they waked in the morning. My master was eager to learn from whence I came; how I acquired those appearances of reason, which I discovered in all my actions; and to know my story from my own mouth, which he hoped he should soon do by the great proficiency I made in learning and pronouncing their words and sentences. To help my memory, I formed all I learned into the English alphabet, and writ the words down with the translations. This last, after some time, I ventured to do in my master's presence. It cost me much trouble to explain to him what I was doing; for the inhabitants have not the least idea of books or literature.

In about ten weeks time I was able to understand most of his questions; and in three months could give him some tolerable answers. He was extremely curious to know from what part of the country I came, and how I was taught to imitate a rational creature; because the Yahoos (whom he saw I exactly resembled in my head, hands, and face, that were only visible) with some appearance of cunning, and the strongest disposition to mischief, were observed to be the most unteachable of all brutes. I answered that I came over the sea, from a far place, with many others of my own kind, in a great hollow vessel made of the bodies of trees; that my companions forced me to land on this coast, and then left me to shift for myself. It was with some difficulty, and by the help of many signs, that I brought him to understand me. He replied that I must needs be mistaken, or that I *said the thing which was not*. (For they have no word in their language to express lying or falsehood.) He knew it was impossible that there could be a country beyond the sea, or that a parcel of brutes could move a wooden vessel whither they pleased upon water. He was sure no Houyhnhnm alive could make such a vessel, or would trust Yahoos to manage it.

The word Houyhnhnm, in their tongue, signifies a Horse; and in its etymology, the Perfection of Nature. I told my master that I was at a loss for expression, but would improve as fast as I could; and hoped in a short time I should be able to tell him wonders; he was pleased to direct his own mare, his colt, and foal, and the servants of the family to take all opportunities of instructing me; and every day for two or three hours, he was at the same pains himself; several horses and mares of quality in the neighborhood came often to our house, upon the report spread of a wonderful Yahoo, that could speak like a Houyhnhnm, and seemed in his words and actions to discover some glimmerings of reason. These delighted to converse with me; they put many questions, and received such answers as I was able to return. By all which advantages, I made so great a progress, that in five months from my arrival, I understood whatever was spoke, and could express myself tolerably well.

The Houyhnhnms who came to visit my master, out of a design of seeing and talking with me, could hardly believe me to be a right Yahoo, because my body had a different covering from others of my kind. They were astonished to observe me without the usual hair or skin, except on my head, face, and hands; but I discovered that secret to my master, upon an accident, which happened about a fortnight before.

I have already told the reader, that every night when the family were gone to bed, it was my custom to strip and cover myself with my clothes; it happened one morning early, that my master sent for me, by the sorrel nag, who was his valet; when he came, I was fast asleep, my clothes fallen off on one side, and my shirt above my waist. I awaked at the noise he made, and observed him to deliver his message in some disorder; after which he went to my master, and in a great fright gave him a very confused account of what he had seen; this I presently discovered; for going as soon as I was dressed, to pay my attendance upon his honor, he asked me the meaning of what his servant had reported; that I was not the same thing when I slept as I appeared to be at other times; that his valet assured him, some part of me was white, some yellow, at least not so white, and some brown.

I had hitherto concealed the secret of my dress, in order to distinguish myself as much as possible, from that cursed race of Yahoos; but now I found it in vain to do so any longer. Besides, I considered that my clothes and shoes would soon wear out, which already were in a declining condition, and must be supplied by some contrivance from the hides of Yahoos, or other brutes; whereby the whole secret would be known. I therefore told my master, that in the country from whence I came, those of my kind always covered their bodies with the hairs of certain animals prepared by art, as well for decency, as to avoid inclemencies of air both hot and cold; of which, as to my own person I would give him immediate conviction, if he pleased to command me; only desiring his excuse, if I did not expose those parts that Nature taught us to conceal. He said, my discourse was all very strange, but especially the last part; for he could not understand why Nature should teach us to conceal what Nature had given. That neither himself nor family were ashamed of any parts of their bodies; but however I might do as I pleased. Whereupon, I first unbuttoned my coat, and pulled it off. I did the same with my waistcoat; I drew off my shoes, stockings, and breeches. I let my shirt down to my waist, and drew up the bottom, fastening it like a girdle about my middle to hide my nakedness.

My master observed the whole performance with great signs of curiosity and admiration. He took up all my clothes in his pastern, one piece after another, and examined them diligently; he then stroked my body very gently, and looked round me several times; after which he said, it was plain I must be a perfect Yahoo; but that I differed very much from the rest of my species, in the whiteness and smoothness of my skin, my want of hair in several parts of my body, the shape and shortness of my claws behind and before, and my affectation of walking continually on my two hinder feet. He desired to see no more; and gave me leave to put on my clothes again, for I was shuddering with cold.

I expressed my uneasiness at his giving me so often the appellation of Yahoo, an odious animal, for which I had so utter an hatred and contempt. I begged he would forbear applying that word to me, and take the same order in his family, and among his friends whom he suffered to see me. I requested likewise, that the secret of my having a false covering to my body might be known to none but himself, at least as long as my present clothing should last; for as to what the sorrel nag his valet had observed, his honor might command him to conceal it.

All this my master very graciously consented to; and thus the secret was kept till my clothes began to wear out, which I was forced to supply by several contrivances, that shall hereafter be mentioned. In the meantime, he desired I would go on with my utmost diligence to learn their language, because he was more astonished at my capacity for speech and reason, than at the figure of my body, whether it were covered or no; adding that he waited with some impatience to hear the wonders which I promised to tell him.

From thenceforward he doubled the pains he had been at to instruct me; he brought me into all company, and made them treat me with civility, because, as he told them privately, this would put me into good humor, and make me more diverting.

Every day when I waited on him, beside the trouble he was at in teaching, he would ask me several questions concerning myself, which I answered as well as I could; and by those means he had already received some general ideas, although very imperfect. It would be tedious to relate the several steps, by which I advanced to a more regular conversation, but the first account I gave of myself in any order and length was to this purpose:

That, I came from a very far country, as I already had attempted to tell him, with about fifty more of my own species; that we traveled upon the seas, in a great hollow vessel made of wood, and larger than his honor's house. I described the ship to him in the best terms I could; and explained by the help of my handkerchief displayed, how it was driven forward by the wind. That, upon a quarrel among us, I was set on shore on this coast, where I walked forward without knowing whither, till he delivered me from the persecution of those execrable Yahoos. He asked me who made the ship, and how it was possible that the Houyhnhnms of my country would leave it to the management of brutes? My answer was that I durst proceed no farther in my relation, unless he would give me his word and honor that he would not be offended; and then I would tell him the wonders I had so often promised. He agreed; and I went on by assuring him, that the ship was made by creatures like myself, who in all the countries I had traveled, as well as in my own, were the only governing, rational animals; and that upon my arrival hither, I was as much astonished to see the Houyhnhnms act like rational beings, as he or his friends could be in finding some marks of reason in a creature he was pleased to call a Yahoo; to which I owned my resemblance in every part, but could not account for their degenerate and brutal nature. I said farther, that if good fortune ever restored me to my native country, to relate my travels hither, as I resolved to do, everybody would believe that I *said the thing which was not*; that I invented the story out of my own head; and with all possible respect to himself, his family, and friends, and under his promise of not being offended, our countrymen would hardly think it probable, that a Houyhnhnm should be the presiding creature of a nation, and a Yahoo the brute.

CHAPTER 4. *The Houyhnhnms' notion of truth and falsehood. The author's discourse disapproved by his master. The author gives a more particular account of himself, and the accidents of his voyage.*

My master heard me with great appearances of uneasiness in his countenance; because *doubting* or *not believing* are so little known in this country, that the inhabitants cannot tell how to behave themselves under such circumstances. And I remember in frequent discourses with my master concerning the nature of manhood, in other parts of the world, having occasion to talk of *lying* and *false representation*, it was with much difficulty that he comprehended what I meant; although he had otherwise a most acute judgment. For he argued thus: that the use of speech was to make us understand one another, and to receive information of facts; now if anyone *said the thing which was not*, these ends were defeated; because I cannot properly be said to understand him; and I am so far from receiving information, that he leaves me worse than in ignorance; for I am led to believe a thing *black* when it is *white*, and *short* when it is *long*. And these were all the notions he had concerning the faculty of *lying*, so perfectly well understood, and so universally practiced among human creatures.

To return from this digression; when I asserted that the Yahoos were the only governing animals in my country, which my master said was altogether past his conception, he desired to know, whether we had Houyhnhnms among us, and what was their employment; I told him we had great numbers; that in summer they grazed in the fields, and in winter were kept in houses, with hay and oats, where Yahoo servants were employed to rub their skins smooth, comb their manes, pick their feet, serve them with food, and make their beds. "I understand you well," said my master; "it is now very plain from all you have spoken, that whatever share of reason the Yahoos pretend to, the Houyhnhnms are your masters; I heartily wish our Yahoos would be so tractable." I begged his honor would please to excuse me from proceeding any farther, because I was very certain that the account he expected from me would be highly displeasing. But he insisted in commanding me to let him know the best and the worst; I told him he should be obeyed. I owned that the Houyhnhnms among us, whom we called Horses, were the most generous[1] and comely animal we had; that they excelled in strength and swiftness; and when they belonged to persons of quality, employed in traveling, racing, and drawing chariots, they were treated with much kindness and care, till they fell into diseases, or became foundered in the feet; but then they were sold, and used to all kind of drudgery till they died; after which their skins were stripped and sold for what they were worth, and their bodies left to be devoured by dogs and birds of prey. But the common race of horses had not so good fortune, being kept by farmers and carriers, and other mean people, who put them to greater labor, and feed them worse. I described as well as I could, our way of riding; the shape and use of a bridle, a saddle, a spur, and a whip; of harness and wheels. I added, that we fastened plates of a certain hard substance called iron at the bottom of their feet, to preserve their hoofs from being broken by the stony ways on which we often traveled.

My master, after some expressions of great indignation, wondered how we dared to venture upon a Houyhnhnm's back; for he was sure, that the weakest servant in his house would be able to shake off the strongest Yahoo; or by lying down, and rolling upon his back, squeeze the brute to death. I answered that our horses were trained up from three or four years old to the several uses we intended them for; that if any of them proved intolerably vicious, they were employed for carriages; that they were severely beaten while they were young for any mischievous tricks; that the males, designed for the common use of riding or draught, were generally castrated about two years after their birth, to take down their spirits, and make them more tame and gentle; that they were indeed sensible of rewards and punishments; but his honor would please to consider that they had not the least tincture of reason any more than the Yahoos in this country.

It put me to the pains of many circumlocutions to give my master a right idea of what I spoke; for their language doth not abound in variety of words, because their wants and passions are fewer than among us. But it is impossible to express his noble resentment at our savage treatment of the Houyhnhnm race; particularly after I had explained the manner and use of castrating horses among us, to hinder them from propagating their kind, and to render them more servile. He said, if it were possible there could be any country where Yahoos alone were endued with reason, they certainly must be the governing animal, because reason will in time always prevail against brutal strength. But, considering the frame of our bodies, and especially of mine, he thought no creature of equal bulk was so ill-contrived for employing that reason in the common offices of life; whereupon he desired to know whether those among whom I lived resembled me or the Yahoos of his country. I assured him that I was as well shaped as most of my age; but the younger and the females

1. Noble.

were much more soft and tender, and the skins of the latter generally as white as milk. He said I differed indeed from other Yahoos, being much more cleanly, and not altogether so deformed; but in point of real advantage, he thought I differed for the worse. That my nails were of no use either to my fore or hinder feet; as to my forefeet, he could not properly call them by that name, for he never observed me to walk upon them; that they were too soft to bear the ground; that I generally went with them uncovered, neither was the covering I sometimes wore on them of the same shape, or so strong as that on my feet behind. That I could not walk with any security; for if either of my hinder feet slipped, I must inevitably fall. He then began to find fault with other parts of my body; the flatness of my face, the prominence of my nose, my eyes placed directly in front, so that I could not look on either side without turning my head; that I was not able to feed myself without lifting one of my forefeet to my mouth; and therefore nature had placed those joints to answer that necessity. He knew not what could be the use of those several clefts and divisions in my feet behind; that these were too soft to bear the hardness and sharpness of stones without a covering made from the skin of some other brute; that my whole body wanted a fence against heat and cold, which I was forced to put on and off every day with tediousness and trouble. And lastly, that he observed every animal in his country naturally to abhor the Yahoos, whom the weaker avoided, and the stronger drove from them. So that supposing us to have the gift of reason, he could not see how it were possible to cure that natural antipathy which every creature discovered against us; nor consequently, how we could tame and render them serviceable. However, he would (as he said) debate the matter no farther, because he was more desirous to know my own story, the country where I was born, and the several actions and events of my life before I came hither.

I assured him how extremely desirous I was that he should be satisfied in every point; but I doubted much whether it would be possible for me to explain myself on several subjects whereof his honor could have no conception, because I saw nothing in his country to which I could resemble them. That however, I would do my best, and strive to express myself by similitudes, humbly desiring his assistance when I wanted proper words; which he was pleased to promise me.

I said, my birth was of honest parents, in an island called England, which was remote from this country, as many days journey as the strongest of his honor's servants could travel in the annual course of the sun. That I was bred a surgeon, whose trade it is to cure wounds and hurts in the body, got by accident or violence. That my country was governed by a female man, whom we called a queen. That I left it to get riches, whereby I might maintain myself and family when I should return. That in my last voyage, I was Commander of the ship and had about fifty Yahoos under me, many of which died at sea, and I was forced to supply them by others picked out from several nations. That our ship was twice in danger of being sunk; the first time by a great storm, and the second, by striking against a rock. Here my master interposed, by asking me, how I could persuade strangers out of different countries to venture with me, after the losses I had sustained, and the hazards I had run. I said, they were fellows of desperate fortunes, forced to fly from the places of their birth, on account of their poverty or their crimes. Some were undone by lawsuits; others spent all they had in drinking, whoring, and gaming; others fled for treason; many for murder, theft, poisoning, robbery, perjury, forgery, coining false money; for committing rapes or sodomy; for flying from their colors, or deserting to the enemy; and most of them had broken prison. None of these durst return to their native countries for fear of being hanged, or of starving in a jail; and therefore were under a necessity of seeking a livelihood in other places.

During this discourse, my master was pleased often to interrupt me. I had made use of many circumlocutions in describing to him the nature of the several crimes, for which most of our crew had been forced to fly their country. This labor took up several days conversation before he was able to comprehend me. He was wholly at a loss to know what could be the use or necessity of practicing those vices. To clear up which I endeavored to give him some ideas of the desire of power and riches; of the terrible effects of lust, intemperance, malice, and envy. All this I was forced to define and describe by putting of cases, and making suppositions. After which, like one whose imagination was struck with something never seen or heard of before, he would lift up his eyes with amazement and indignation. Power, government, war, law, punishment, and a thousand other things had no terms, wherein that language could express them; which made the difficulty almost insuperable to give my master any conception of what I meant; but being of an excellent understanding, much improved by contemplation and converse, he at last arrived at a competent knowledge of what human nature in our parts of the world is capable to perform; and desired I would give him some particular account of that land, which we call Europe, especially, of my own country.

CHAPTER 5. *The Author, at his master's commands, informs him of the state of England. The causes of war among the princes of Europe. The Author begins to explain the English Constitution.*

The reader may please to observe that the following extract of many conversations I had with my master contains a summary of the most material points, which were discoursed at several times for above two years; his honor often desiring fuller satisfaction as I farther improved in the Houyhnhnm tongue. I laid before him, as well as I could, the whole state of Europe; I discoursed of trade and manufactures, of arts and sciences; and the answers I gave to all the questions he made, as they arose upon several subjects, were a fund of conversation not to be exhausted. But I shall here only set down the substance of what passed between us concerning my own country, reducing it into order as well as I can, without any regard to time or other circumstances, while I strictly adhere to truth. My only concern is that I shall hardly be able to do justice to my master's arguments and expressions; which must needs suffer by my want of capacity, as well as by a translation into our barbarous English.

In obedience therefore to his honor's commands, I related to him the Revolution under the Prince of Orange; the long war with France entered into by the said Prince, and renewed by his successor the present queen; wherein the greatest powers of Christendom were engaged, and which still continued. I computed at his request, that about a million of Yahoos might have been killed in the whole progress of it; and perhaps a hundred or more cities taken, and five times as many ships burned or sunk.[2]

He asked me what were the usual causes or motives that made one country to go to war with another. I answered, they were innumerable; but I should only mention a few of the chief. Sometimes the ambition of princes, who never think they have land or people enough to govern; sometimes the corruption of ministers, who engage their master in a war in order to stifle or divert the clamor of the subjects against their evil administration. Difference in opinions hath cost many millions of lives; for instance, whether flesh be bread, or bread be flesh; whether the juice of a certain berry be blood or wine; whether whistling be a vice or a virtue; whether it be better to kiss a post, or throw it into the fire; what is the best color for a coat, whether black, white, red, or grey; and whether it should be long or short, narrow or wide, dirty or clean;[3] with many more. Neither are any wars so furious and bloody, or of so long continuance, as those occasioned by difference in opinion, especially if it be in things indifferent.[4]

Sometimes the quarrel between two princes is to decide which of them shall dispossess a third of his dominions, where neither of them pretend to any right. Sometimes one prince quarreleth with another, for fear the other should quarrel with him. Sometimes a war is entered upon, because the enemy is too strong, and sometimes because he is too weak. Sometimes our neighbors want the things which we have, or have the things which we want; and we both fight, till they take ours or give us theirs. It is a very justifiable cause of war to invade a country after the people have been wasted by famine, destroyed by pestilence, or embroiled by factions amongst themselves. It is justifiable to enter into a war against our nearest ally, when one of his towns lies convenient for us, or a territory of land, that would render our dominions round and compact. If a prince send forces into a nation, where the people are poor and ignorant, he may lawfully put half of them to death, and make slaves of the rest, in order to civilize and reduce them from their barbarous way of living. It is a very kingly, honorable, and frequent practice, when one prince desires

---

2. Gulliver relates recent English history: the Glorious Revolution of 1688 and the War of Spanish Succession (1703–13). He greatly exaggerates the casualties in the war.
3. Gulliver refers to the religious controversies of the Reformation and Counter Reformation: the doctrine of transubstantiation, the use of music in church services, the veneration of the crucifix, and the wearing of priestly vestments.
4. Of little consequence.

the assistance of another to secure him against an invasion, that the assistant, when he hath driven out the invader, should seize on the dominions himself, and kill, imprison, or banish the prince he came to relieve. Alliance by blood or marriage is a sufficient cause of war between princes; and the nearer the kindred is, the greater is their disposition to quarrel; poor nations are hungry, and rich nations are proud; and pride and hunger will ever be at variance. For these reasons, the trade of a soldier is held the most honorable of all others: because a soldier is a Yahoo hired to kill in cold blood as many of his own species, who have never offended him, as possibly he can.

There is likewise a kind of beggarly princes in Europe, not able to make war by themselves, who hire out their troops to richer nations for so much a day to each man; of which they keep three fourths to themselves, and it is the best part of their maintenance; such are those in many northern parts of Europe.[5]

"What you have told me," said my master, "upon the subject of war, doth indeed discover most admirably the effects of that reason you pretend to; however, it is happy that the shame is greater than the danger; and that Nature hath left you utterly uncapable of doing much mischief; for your mouths lying flat with your faces, you can hardly bite each other to any purpose, unless by consent. Then, as to the claws upon your feet before and behind, they are so short and tender, that one of our Yahoos would drive a dozen of yours before him. And therefore in recounting the numbers of those who have been killed in battle, I cannot but think that you have *said the thing which is not.*"

I could not forbear shaking my head and smiling a little at his ignorance. And, being no stranger to the art of war, I gave him a description of cannons, culverins, muskets, carabines, pistols, bullets, powder, swords, bayonets, battles, sieges, retreats, attacks, undermines, countermines, bombardments, sea fights; ships sunk with a thousand men; twenty thousand killed on each side; dying groans, limbs flying in the air; smoke, noise, confusion, trampling to death under horses' feet; flight, pursuit, victory; fields strewed with carcasses left for food to dogs, and wolves, and birds of prey; plundering, stripping, ravishing, burning, and destroying. And, to set forth the valor of my own dear countrymen, I assured him that I had seen them blow up a hundred enemies at once in a siege, and as many in a ship; and beheld the dead bodies drop down in pieces from the clouds, to the great diversion of all the spectators.

I was going on to more particulars, when my master commanded me silence. He said, whoever understood the nature of Yahoos might easily believe it possible for so vile an animal, to be capable of every action I had named, if their strength and cunning equaled their malice. But, as my discourse had increased his abhorrence of the whole species, so he found it gave him a disturbance in his mind, to which he was wholly a stranger before. He thought his ears being used to such abominable words,

---

5. A satiric glance at George I, who, as Elector of Hanover, had dealt in this trade.

might by degrees admit them with less detestation. That, although he hated the Yahoos of this country, yet he no more blamed them for their odious qualities, than he did a *gnnayh* (a bird of prey) for its cruelty, or a sharp stone for cutting his hoof. But, when a creature pretending to reason could be capable of such enormities, he dreaded lest the corruption of that faculty might be worse than brutality itself. He seemed therefore confident, that instead of reason, we were only possessed of some quality fitted to increase our natural vices; as the reflection from a troubled stream returns the image of an ill-shapen body, not only larger, but more distorted.

He added that he had heard too much upon the subject of war, both in this and some former discourses. There was another point which a little perplexed him at present. I had said that some of our crew left their country on account of being ruined by law: that I had already explained the meaning of the word; but he was at a loss how it should come to pass, that the law which was intended for every man's preservation, should be any man's ruin. Therefore he desired to be farther satisfied what I meant by law, and the dispensers thereof, according to the present practice in my own country; because he thought Nature and Reason were sufficient guides for a reasonable animal, as we pretended to be, in showing us what we ought to do, and what to avoid.

I assured his honor that law was a science wherein I had not much conversed, further than by employing advocates, in vain, upon some injustices that had been done me. However, I would give him all the satisfaction I was able.

I said there was a society of men among us, bred up from their youth in the art of proving by words multiplied for the purpose, that white is black, and black is white, according as they are paid. To this society all the rest of the people are slaves.

"For example. If my neighbor hath a mind to my cow, he hires a lawyer to prove that he ought to have my cow from me. I must then hire another to defend my right; it being against all rules of law that any man should be allowed to speak for himself. Now in this case, I who am the true owner lie under two great disadvantages. First, my lawyer being practiced almost from his cradle in defending falsehood is quite out of his element when he would be an advocate for justice, which as an office unnatural, he always attempts with great awkwardness, if not with ill-will. The second disadvantage is that my lawyer must proceed with great caution, or else he will be reprimanded by the judges, and abhorred by his brethren, as one who would lessen the practice of the law. And therefore I have but two methods to preserve my cow. The first is to gain over my adversary's lawyer with a double fee; who will then betray his client, by insinuating that he hath justice on his side. The second way is for my lawyer to make my cause appear as unjust as he can; by allowing the cow to belong to my adversary; and this if it be skillfully done, will certainly bespeak the favor of the bench.

"Now, your honor is to know that these judges are persons appointed to decide all controversies of property, as well as for the trial of criminals; and picked out from the most dextrous lawyers who are grown old or lazy; and having been biased all their lives against truth and equity, lie under such a fatal necessity of favoring fraud, perjury, and oppression, that I have known some of them to have refused a large bribe from the side where justice lay, rather than injure the faculty,[6] by doing anything unbecoming their nature or their office.

"It is a maxim among these lawyers, that whatever hath been done before may legally be done again; and therefore they take special care to record all the decisions formerly made against common justice and the general reason of mankind. These, under the name of *precedents*, they produce as authorities to justify the most iniquitous opinions; and the judges never fail of directing accordingly.

"In pleading, they studiously avoid entering into the merits of the cause; but are loud, violent, and tedious in dwelling upon all circumstances which are not to the purpose. For instance, in the case already mentioned, they never desire to know what claim or title my adversary hath to my cow; but whether the said cow were red or black; her horns long or short; whether the field I graze her in be round or square; whether she were milked at home or abroad; what diseases she is subject to, and the like. After which they consult precedents, adjourn the cause, from time to time, and in ten, twenty, or thirty years come to an issue.

"It is likewise to be observed, that this society hath a peculiar cant and jargon of their own, that no other mortal can understand, and wherein all their laws are written, which they take special care to multiply; whereby they have wholly confounded the very essence of truth and falsehood, of right and wrong; so that it will take thirty years to decide whether the field, left me by my ancestors for six generations, belong to me, or to a stranger three hundred miles off.

"In the trial of persons accused for crimes against the state, the method is much more short and commendable: the judge first sends to sound the disposition of those in power; after which he can easily hang or save the criminal, strictly preserving all the forms of law."

Here my master interposing said it was a pity that creatures endowed with such prodigious abilities of mind as these lawyers, by the description I gave of them must certainly be, were not rather encouraged to be instructors of others in wisdom and knowledge. In answer to which, I assured his honor that in all points out of their own trade, they were usually the most ignorant and stupid generation among us, the most despicable in common conversation, avowed enemies to all knowledge and learning; and equally disposed to pervert the general reason of mankind, in every other subject of discourse as in that of their own profession.

6. Profession.

CHAPTER 6. *A continuation of the state of England, under Queen Anne.*
The character of a first minister in the courts of Europe.

My master was yet wholly at a loss to understand what motives could
incite this race of lawyers to perplex, disquiet, and weary themselves by
engaging in a confederacy of injustice, merely for the sake of injuring
their fellow animals; neither could he comprehend what I meant in
saying they did it for hire. Whereupon I was at much pains to describe
to him the use of money, the materials it was made of, and the value of
the metals; that when a Yahoo had got a great store of his precious
substance, he was able to purchase whatever he had a mind to; the finest
clothing, the noblest houses, great tracts of land, the most costly meats
and drinks; and have his choice of the most beautiful females. Therefore
since money alone was able to perform all these feats, our Yahoos thought
they could never have enough of it to spend or to save, as they found
themselves inclined from their natural bent either to profusion or avarice. That the rich man enjoyed the fruit of the poor man's labor, and
the latter were a thousand to one in proportion to the former. That the
bulk of our people was forced to live miserably, by laboring every day
for small wages to make a few live plentifully. I enlarged myself much
on these and many other particulars to the same purpose, but his honor
was still to seek,[7] for he went upon a supposition that all animals had a
title to their share in the productions of the earth; and especially those
who presided over the rest. Therefore he desired I would let him know
what these costly meats were, and how any of us happened to want[8]
them. Whereupon I enumerated as many sorts as came into my head,
with the various methods of dressing them, which could not be done
without sending vessels by sea to every part of the world, as well for
liquors to drink, as for sauces, and innumerable other conveniencies. I
assured him, that this whole globe of earth must be at least three times
gone round, before one of our better female Yahoos could get her breakfast, or a cup to put it in. He said, "That must needs be a miserable
country which cannot furnish food for its own inhabitants." But what
he chiefly wondered at, was how such vast tracts of ground as I described,
should be wholly without fresh water, and the people put to the necessity
of sending over the sea for drink. I replied that England (the dear place
of my nativity) was computed to produce three times the quantity of
food, more than its inhabitants are able to consume, as well as liquors
extracted from grain, or pressed out of the fruit of certain trees, which
made excellent drink; and the same proportion in every other convenience of life. But, in order to feed the luxury and intemperance of the
males, and the vanity of the females, we sent away the greatest part of
our necessary things to other countries, from whence in return we brought
the materials of diseases, folly, and vice, to spend among ourselves. Hence

7. Still did not understand.   8. Lack.

it follows of necessity, that vast numbers of our people are compelled to seek their livelihood by begging, robbing, stealing, cheating, pimping, forswearing, flattering, suborning, forging, gaming, lying, fawning, hectoring, voting, scribbling, star gazing, poisoning, whoring, canting, libeling, freethinking, and the like occupations; every one of which terms, I was at much pains to make him understand.

That, wine was not imported among us from foreign countries, to supply the want of water or other drinks, but because it was a sort of liquid which made us merry, by putting us out of our senses; diverted all melancholy thoughts, begat wild extravagant imaginations in the brain, raised our hopes, and banished our fears; suspended every office of reason for a time, and deprived us of the use of our limbs, until we fell into a profound sleep; although it must be confessed, that we always awaked sick and dispirited; and that the use of this liquor filled us with diseases, which made our lives uncomfortable and short.

But beside all this, the bulk of our people supported themselves by furnishing the necessities or conveniencies of life to the rich, and to each other. For instance, when I am at home and dressed as I ought to be, I carry on my body the workmanship of an hundred tradesmen; the building and furniture of my house employ as many more; and five times the number to adorn my wife.

I was going on to tell him of another sort of people, who get their livelihood by attending the sick; having upon some occasions informed his honor that many of my crew had died of diseases. But here it was with the utmost difficulty that I brought him to apprehend what I meant. He could easily conceive that a Houyhnhnm grew weak and heavy a few days before his death; or by some accident might hurt a limb. But that nature, who worketh all things to perfection, should suffer any pains to breed in our bodies, he thought impossible; and desired to know the reason of so unaccountable an evil. I told him, we fed on a thousand things which operated contrary to each other; that we eat when we were not hungry, and drank without the provocation of thirst; that we sat whole nights drinking strong liquors without eating a bit, which disposed us to sloth, inflamed our bodies, and precipitated or prevented digestion. That, prostitute female Yahoos acquired a certain malady, which bred rottenness in the bones of those who fell into their embraces; that this and many other diseases were propagated from father to son; so that great numbers come into the world with complicated maladies upon them; that it would be endless to give him a catalogue of all diseases incident to human bodies; for they could not be fewer than five or six hundred, spread over every limb, and joint; in short, every part, external and intestine, having diseases appropriated to each. To remedy which, there was a sort of people bred up among us, in the profession or pretense of curing the sick. And because I had some skill in the faculty, I would in gratitude to his honor let him know the whole mystery and method by which they proceed.

Their fundamental is that all diseases arise from repletion; from whence they conclude, that a great evacuation of the body is necessary, either through the natural passage, or upwards at the mouth. Their next business is, from herbs, minerals, gums, oils, shells, salts, juices, seaweed, excrements, barks of trees, serpents, toads, frogs, spiders, dead men's flesh and bones, birds, beasts and fishes, to form a composition for smell and taste the most abominable, nauseous, and detestable, that they can possibly contrive, which the stomach immediately rejects with loathing, and this they call a vomit. Or else from the same storehouse, with some other poisonous additions, they command us to take in at the orifice above or below (just as the physician then happens to be disposed) a medicine equally annoying and disgustful to the bowels; which relaxing the belly, drives down all before it; and this they call a purge, or a clyster. For nature (as the physicians allege) having intended the superior anterior orifice only for the intromission of solids and liquids, and the inferior posterior for ejection, these artists ingeniously considering that in all diseases nature is forced out of her seat; therefore to replace her in it, the body must be treated in a manner directly contrary, by interchanging the use of each orifice; forcing solids and liquids in at the anus, and making evacuations at the mouth.

But, besides real diseases, we are subject to many that are only imaginary, for which the physicians have invented imaginary cures; these have their several names, and so have the drugs that are proper for them; and with these our female Yahoos are always infested.

One great excellency in this tribe is their skill at prognostics, wherein they seldom fail; their predictions in real diseases, when they rise to any degree of malignity, generally portending death, which is always in their power, when recovery is not, and therefore, upon any unexpected signs of amendment, after they have pronounced their sentence, rather than be accused as false prophets, they know how to approve[9] their sagacity to the world by a seasonable dose.

They are likewise of special use to husbands and wives, who are grown weary of their mates; to eldest sons, to great ministers of state, and often to princes.

I had formerly upon occasion discoursed with my master upon the nature of government in general, and particularly of our own excellent constitution, deservedly the wonder and envy of the whole world. But having here accidently mentioned a minister of state, he commanded me some time after to inform him what species of Yahoo I particularly meant by that appellation.

I told him that a first or chief minister of state, whom I intended to describe, was a creature wholly exempt from joy and grief, love and hatred, pity and anger; at least makes use of no other passions but a violent desire of wealth, power, and titles; that he applies his words to all uses, except to the indication of his mind; that he never tells a truth, but with an intent that you should take it for a lie; nor a lie, but with a

9. Prove.

design that you should take it for a truth; that those he speaks worst of behind their backs are in the surest way to preferment; and whenever he begins to praise you to others or to yourself, you are from that day forlorn. The worst mark you can receive is a promise, especially when it is confirmed with an oath; after which every wise man retires, and gives over all hopes.

There are three methods by which a man may rise to be chief minister: the first is by knowing how with prudence to dispose of a wife, a daughter, or a sister; the second, by betraying or undermining his predecessor; and the third is by a furious zeal in public assemblies against the corruptions of the court. But a wise prince would rather choose to employ those who practice the last of these methods; because such zealots prove always the most obsequious and subservient to the will and passions of their master. That, these ministers having all employments at their disposal, preserve themselves in power by bribing the majority of a senate or great council; and at last by an expedient called an Act of Indemnity[1] (whereof I described the nature to him) they secure themselves from after reckonings, and retire from the public, laden with the spoils of the nation.

The palace of a chief minister is a seminary to breed up others in his own trade; the pages, lackies, and porters, by imitating their master, become ministers of state in their several districts, and learn to excel in the three principal ingredients, of insolence, lying, and bribery. Accordingly, they have a subaltern court paid to them by persons of the best rank; and sometimes by the force of dexterity and impudence, arrive through several gradations to be successors to their lord.

He is usually governed by a decayed wench, or favorite footman, who are the tunnels through which all graces are conveyed, and may properly be called, in the last resort, the governors of the kingdom.

One day, my master, having heard me mention the nobility of my country, was pleased to make me a compliment which I could not pretend to deserve: that, he was sure, I must have been born of some noble family, because I far exceeded in shape, color, and cleanliness, all the Yahoos of his nation, although I seemed to fail in strength, and agility, which must be imputed to my different way of living from those other brutes; and besides, I was not only endowed with the faculty of speech, but likewise with some rudiments of reason, to a degree, that with all his acquaintance I passed for a prodigy.

He made me observe, that among the Houyhnhnms, the white, the sorrel, and the iron grey were not so exactly shaped as the bay, the dapple grey, and the black; nor born with equal talents of mind, or a capacity to improve them; and therefore continued always in the condition of servants, without ever aspiring to match out of their own race, which in that country would be reckoned monstrous and unnatural.

I made his honor my most humble acknowledgments for the good

1. An act passed at each session of Parliament to protect ministers of state who in good faith might have acted illegally.

opinion he was pleased to conceive of me; but assured him at the same time, that my birth was of the lower sort, having been born of plain, honest parents, who were just able to give me a tolerable education; that, nobility among us was altogether a different thing from the idea he had of it; that, our young noblemen are bred from their childhood in idleness and luxury; that, as soon as years will permit, they consume their vigor, and contract odious diseases among lewd females; and when their fortunes are almost ruined, they marry some woman of mean birth, disagreeable person, and unsound constitution, merely for the sake of money, whom they hate and despise. That, the productions of such marriages are generally scrofulous, rickety or deformed children; by which means the family seldom continues above three generations, unless the wife take care to provide a healthy father among her neighbors, or domestics, in order to improve and continue the breed. That a weak diseased body, a meager countenance, and sallow complexion are the true marks of noble blood; and a healthy robust appearance is so disgraceful in a man of quality, that the world concludes his real father to have been a groom or a coachman. The imperfections of his mind run parallel with those of his body; being a composition of spleen, dullness, ignorance, caprice, sensuality, and pride.

Without the consent of this illustrious body, no law can be enacted, repealed, or altered, and these nobles have likewise the decision of all our possessions without appeal.

CHAPTER 7. *The Author's great love of his native country. His master's observations upon the constitution and administration of England, as described by the Author, with parallel cases and comparisons. His master's observations upon human nature.*

The reader may be disposed to wonder how I could prevail on myself to give so free a representation of my own species, among a race of mortals who were already too apt to conceive the vilest opinion of humankind, from that entire congruity betwixt me and their Yahoos. But I must freely confess that the many virtues of those excellent quadrupeds placed in opposite view to human corruptions had so far opened my eyes, and enlarged my understanding, that I began to view the actions and passions of man in a very different light; and to think the honor of my own kind not worth managing;[2] which, besides, it was impossible for me to do before a person of so acute a judgment as my master, who daily convinced me of a thousand faults in myself, whereof I had not the least perception before, and which with us would never be numbered even among human infirmities. I had likewise learned from his example an utter detestation of all falsehood or disguise; and truth appeared so amiable to me, that I determined upon sacrificing everything to it.

Let me deal so candidly with the reader as to confess that there was

2. Taking care of.

yet a much stronger motive for the freedom I took in my representation of things. I had not been a year in this country, before I contracted such a love and veneration for the inhabitants, that I entered on a firm resolution never to return to humankind, but to pass the rest of my life among these admirable Houyhnhnms in the contemplation and practice of every virtue; where I could have no example or incitement to vice. But it was decreed by fortune, my perpetual enemy, that so great a felicity should not fall to my share. However, it is now some comfort to reflect that in what I said of my countrymen, I extenuated their faults as much as I durst before so strict an examiner; and upon every article, gave as favorable a turn as the matter would bear. For, indeed, who is there alive that will not be swayed by his bias and partiality to the place of his birth?

I have related the substance of several conversations I had with my master, during the greatest part of the time I had the honor to be in his service; but have indeed for brevity sake omitted much more than is here set down.

When I had answered all his questions, and his curiosity seemed to be fully satisfied; he sent for me one morning early, and commanding me to sit down at some distance (an honor which he had never before conferred upon me), he said he had been very seriously considering my whole story, as far as it related both to myself and my country; that, he looked upon us as a sort of animals to whose share, by what accident he could not conjecture, some small pittance of reason had fallen, whereof we made no other use than by its assistance to aggravate our natural corruptions, and to acquire new ones which nature had not given us. That we disarmed ourselves of the few abilities she had bestowed; had been very successful in multiplying our original wants, and seemed to spend our whole lives in vain endeavors to supply them by our own inventions. That, as to myself, it was manifest I had neither the strength or agility of a common Yahoo; that I walked infirmly on my hinder feet; had found out a contrivance to make my claws of no use or defense, and to remove the hair from my chin, which was intended as a shelter from the sun and the weather. Lastly, that I could neither run with speed, nor climb trees like my brethren (as he called them) the Yahoos in this country.

That our institutions of government and law were plainly owing to our gross defects in reason, and by consequence, in virtue; because reason alone is sufficient to govern a rational creature; which was therefore a character we had no pretense to challenge, even from the account I had given of my own people; although he manifestly perceived, that in order to favor them, I had concealed many particulars, and often *said the thing which was not.*

He was the more confirmed in this opinion, because he observed that I agreed in every feature of my body with other Yahoos, except where it was to my real disadvantage in point of strength, speed, and activity, the shortness of my claws, and some other particulars where Nature had no part; so, from the representation I had given him of our lives, our manners, and our actions, he found as near a resemblance in the disposition of our minds. He said the Yahoos were known to hate one another more than they did any different species of animals; and the reason usually assigned was the odiousness of their own shapes, which all could see in the rest, but not in themselves. He had therefore begun to think it not unwise in us to cover our bodies, and by that invention, conceal many of our deformities from each other, which would else be hardly supportable. But he now found he had been mistaken; and that the dissentions of those brutes in his country were owing to the same cause with ours, as I had described them. For, if (said he) you throw among five Yahoos as much food as would be sufficient for fifty, they will instead of eating peaceably, fall together by the ears, each single one impatient to have all to itself; and therefore a servant was usually employed to stand by while they were feeding abroad, and those kept at home were tied at a distance from each other. That, if a cow died of age or accident, before a Houyhnhnm could secure it for his own Yahoos, those in the neighborhood would come in herds to seize it, and then would ensue such a battle as I had described, with terrible wounds made by their claws on both sides, although they seldom were able to kill one another, for want of such convenient instruments of death as we had invented. At other times the like battles have been fought between the Yahoos of several neighborhoods without any visible cause; those of one district watching all opportunities to surprise the next before they are prepared. But if they find their project hath miscarried, they return home, and for want of enemies, engage in what I call a civil war among themselves.

That, in some fields of his country, there are certain shining stones of several colors, whereof the Yahoos are violently fond; and when part of these stones are fixed in the earth, as it sometimes happeneth, they will dig with their claws for whole days to get them out, and carry them away, and hide them by heaps in their kennels; but still looking round with great caution, for fear their comrades should find out their treasure. My master said he could never discover the reason of this unnatural appetite, or how these stones could be of any use to a Yahoo; but now he believed it might proceed from the same principle of avarice, which I had ascribed to mankind. That he had once, by way of experiment, privately removed a heap of these stones from the place where one of his Yahoos had buried it, whereupon, the sordid animal missing his treasure, by his loud lamenting brought the whole herd to the place, there miserably howled, then fell to biting and tearing the rest; began to pine away, would neither eat nor sleep, nor work, till he ordered a servant privately to convey the stones into the same hole, and hide them as before; which when his Yahoo had found, he presently recovered his spirits and good humor; but took care to remove them to a better hiding place; and hath ever since been a very serviceable brute.

My master farther assured me, which I also observed myself; that in the fields where these shining stones abound, the fiercest and most frequent battles are fought, occasioned by perpetual inroads of the neighboring Yahoos.

He said it was common when two Yahoos discovered such a stone in a field, and were contending which of them should be the proprietor, a third would take the advantage, and carry it away from them both; which my master would needs contend to have some resemblance with our suits at law; wherein I thought it for our credit not to undeceive him; since the decision he mentioned was much more equitable than many decrees among us; because the plaintiff and defendant there lost nothing beside the stone they contended for; whereas our courts of equity would never have dismissed the cause while either of them had anything left.

My master continuing his discourse said there was nothing that rendered the Yahoos more odious, than their undistinguished appetite to devour everything that came in their way, whether herbs, roots, berries, corrupted flesh of animals, or all mingled together; and it was peculiar in their temper, that they were fonder of what they could get by rapine or stealth at a greater distance, than much better food provided for them at home. If their prey held out, they would eat till they were ready to burst, after which nature had pointed out to them a certain root that gave them a general evacuation.

There was also another kind of root very juicy, but something rare and difficult to be found, which the Yahoos sought for with much eagerness, and would suck it with great delight; it produced the same effects that wine hath upon us. It would make them sometimes hug, and sometimes tear one another; they would howl and grin, and chatter, and reel, and tumble, and then fall asleep in the mud.

I did indeed observe that the Yahoos were the only animals in this country subject to any diseases; which however, were much fewer than horses have among us, and contracted not by any ill treatment they meet with, but by the nastiness and greediness of that sordid brute. Neither has their language any more than a general appellation for those maladies; which is borrowed from the name of the beast, and called *Hnea Yahoo*, or the Yahoo's Evil; and the cure prescribed is a mixture of their own dung and urine, forcibly put down the Yahoo's throat. This I have since often known to have been taken with success, and do here freely recommend it to my countrymen, for the public good, as an admirable specific against all diseases produced by repletion.

As to learning, government, arts, manufactures, and the like, my master confessed he could find little or no resemblance between the Yahoos of that country and those in ours. For he only meant to observe what parity there was in our natures. He had heard indeed some curious Houyhnhnms observe that in most herds there was a sort of ruling Yahoo (as among us there is generally some leading or principal stag in a park) who was always more deformed in body, and mischievous in disposition, than any of the rest. That this leader had usually a favorite as like himself as he could get, whose employment was to lick his master's feet and posteriors, and drive the female Yahoos to his kennel; for which he was now and then rewarded with a piece of ass's flesh. This favorite is hated by the whole herd; and therefore to protect himself, keeps always near the person of his leader. He usually continues in office till a worse can be found; but the very moment he is discarded, his successor, at the head of all the Yahoos in that district, young and old, male and female, come in a body, and discharge their excrements upon him from head to foot. But how far this might be applicable to our courts and favorites, and ministers of state, my master said I could best determine.

I durst make no return to this malicious insinuation, which debased human understanding below the sagacity of a common hound, who hath judgment enough to distinguish and follow the cry of the ablest dog in the pack, without being ever mistaken.

My master told me there were some qualities remarkable in the Yahoos, which he had not observed me to mention, or at least very slightly, in the accounts I had given him of humankind. He said, those animals, like other brutes, had their females in common; but in this they differed, that the she-Yahoo would admit the male while she was pregnant; and that the hes would quarrel and fight with the females as fiercely as with each other. Both which practices were such degrees of infamous brutality, that no other sensitive creature ever arrived at.

Another thing he wondered at in the Yahoos was their strange disposition to nastiness and dirt; whereas there appears to be a natural love of cleanliness in all other animals. As to the two former accusations, I was glad to let them pass without any reply, because I had not a word to offer upon them in defense of my species, which otherwise I certainly had done from my own inclinations. But I could have easily vindicated humankind from the imputation of singularity upon the last article, if there had been any swine in that country (as unluckily for me there were not) which although it may be a sweeter quadruped than a Yahoo, cannot I humbly conceive in justice pretend to more cleanliness; and so his honor himself must have owned, if he had seen their filthy way of feeding, and their custom of wallowing and sleeping in the mud.

My master likewise mentioned another quality, which his servants had discovered in several Yahoos, and to him was wholly unaccountable. He said, a fancy would sometimes take a Yahoo, to retire into a corner, to lie down and howl, and groan, and spurn away all that came near him, although he were young and fat, and wanted neither food nor water; nor did the servants imagine what could possibly ail him. And the only remedy they found was to set him to hard work, after which he would infallibly come to himself. To this I was silent out of partiality to my own kind; yet here I could plainly discover the true seeds of spleen,[3] which only seizeth on the lazy, the luxurious, and the rich; who, if they were forced to undergo the same regimen, I would undertake for the cure.

3. Hypochondria.

His Honor had farther observed, that a female Yahoo would often stand behind a bank or a bush, to gaze on the young males passing by, and then appear, and hide, using many antic gestures and grimaces; at which time it was observed, that she had a most offensive smell; and when any of the males advanced, would slowly retire, looking back, and with a counterfeit show of fear, run off into some convenient place where she knew the male would follow her.

At other times, if a female stranger came among them, three or four of her own sex would get about her, and stare and chatter, and grin, and smell her all over; and then turn off with gestures that seemed to express contempt and disdain.

Perhaps my master might refine a little in these speculations, which he had drawn from what he observed himself, or had been told by others; however, I could not reflect without some amazement, and much sorrow, that the rudiments of lewdness, coquetry, censure, and scandal, should have place by instinct in womankind.

I expected every moment that my master would accuse the Yahoos of those unnatural appetites in both sexes, so common among us. But Nature it seems hath not been so expert a schoolmistress; and these politer pleasures are entirely the productions of art and reason, on our side of the globe.

CHAPTER 8. *The Author relateth several particulars of the Yahoos. The great virtues of the Houyhnhnms. The education and exercises of their youth. Their general assembly.*

As I ought to have understood human nature much better than I supposed it possible for my master to do, so it was easy to apply the character he gave of the Yahoos to myself and my countrymen; and I believed I could yet make farther discoveries from my own observation. I therefore often begged his honor to let me go among the herds of Yahoos in the neighborhood; to which he always very graciously consented, being perfectly convinced that the hatred I bore those brutes would never suffer me to be corrupted by them; and his honor ordered one of his servants, a strong sorrel nag, very honest and good-natured, to be my guard; without whose protection I durst not undertake such adventures. For I have already told the reader how much I was pestered by those odious animals upon my first arrival. I afterwards failed very narrowly three or four times of falling into their clutches, when I happened to stray at any distance without my hanger. And I have reason to believe, they had some imagination that I was of their own species, which I often assisted myself, by stripping up my sleeves, and shewing my naked arms and breast in their sight, when my protector was with me; at which times they would approach as near as they durst, and imitate my actions after the manner of monkeys, but ever with great signs of hatred; as a tame jackdaw with cap and stockings is always persecuted by the wild ones, when he happens to be got among them.

They are prodigiously nimble from their infancy; however, I once caught a young male of three years old, and endeavored by all marks of tenderness to make it quiet; but the little imp fell a squalling, scratching, and biting with such violence, that I was forced to let it go; and it was high time, for a whole troop of old ones came about us at the noise; but finding the cub was safe (for away it ran) and my sorrel nag being by, they durst not venture near us. I observed the young animal's flesh to smell very rank, and the stink was somewhat between a weasel and a fox, but much more disagreeable. I forgot another circumstance (and perhaps I might have the reader's pardon, if it were wholly omitted) that while I held the odious vermin in my hands, it voided its filthy excrements of a yellow liquid substance, all over my clothes; but by good fortune there was a small brook hard by, where I washed myself as clean as I could; although I durst not come into my master's presence until I were sufficiently aired.

By what I could discover, the Yahoos appear to be the most unteachable of all animals, their capacities never reaching higher than to draw or carry burdens. Yet I am of opinion, this defect ariseth chiefly from a perverse, restive disposition. For they are cunning, malicious, treacherous and revengeful. They are strong and hardy, but of a cowardly spirit, and by consequence insolent, abject, and cruel. It is observed that the red-haired of both sexes are more libidinous and mischievous than the rest, whom yet they much exceed in strength and activity.

The Houyhnhnms keep the Yahoos for present use in huts not far from the house; but the rest are sent abroad to certain fields, where they dig up roots, eat several kinds of herbs, and search about for carrion, or sometimes catch weasels and *luhimuhs* (a sort of wild rat) which they greedily devour. Nature hath taught them to dig deep holes with their nails on the side of a rising ground, wherein they lie by themselves; only the kennels of the females are larger, sufficient to hold two or three cubs.

They swim from their infancy like frogs, and are able to continue long under water, where they often take fish, which the females carry home to their young. And upon this occasion, I hope the reader will pardon my relating an odd adventure.

Being one day abroad with my protector the sorrel nag, and the weather exceeding hot, I entreated him to let me bathe in a river that was near. He consented, and I immediately stripped myself stark naked, and went down softly into the stream. It happened that a young female Yahoo standing behind a bank, saw the whole proceeding; and inflamed by desire, as the nag and I conjectured, came running with all speed, and leaped into the water within five yards of the place where I bathed. I was never in my life so terribly frighted; the nag was grazing at some distance, not suspecting any harm; she embraced me after a most fulsome manner; I roared as loud as I could, and the nag came galloping towards me, whereupon she quitted her grasp, with the utmost reluctancy, and leaped upon the opposite bank, where she stood gazing and howling all the time I was putting on my clothes.

This was matter of diversion to my master and his family, as well as of mortification to myself. For now I could no longer deny that I was a real Yahoo, in every limb and feature, since the females had a natural propensity to me as one of their own species; neither was the hair of this brute of a red color (which might have been some excuse for an appetite a little irregular) but black as a sloe, and her countenance did not make an appearance altogether so hideous as the rest of the kind; for I think, she could not be above eleven years old.

Having already lived three years in this country, the reader I suppose will expect that I should, like other travelers, give him some account of the manners and customs of its inhabitants, which it was indeed my principal study to learn.

As these noble Houyhnhnms are endowed by Nature with a general disposition to all virtues, and have no conceptions or ideas of what is evil in a rational creature; so their grand maxim is to cultivate reason, and to be wholly governed by it. Neither is reason among them a point problematical as with us, where men can argue with plausibility on both sides of a question; but strikes you with immediate conviction; as it must needs do where it is not mingled, obscured, or discolored by passion and interest. I remember it was with extreme difficulty that I could bring my master to understand the meaning of the word "opinion," or how a point could be disputable; because reason taught us to affirm or deny only where we are certain; and beyond our knowledge we cannot do either. So that controversies, wranglings, disputes, and positiveness in false or dubious propositions are evils unknown among the Houyhnhnms. In the like manner when I used to explain to him our several systems of natural philosophy, he would laugh that a creature pretending to reason should value itself upon the knowledge of other people's conjectures, and in things, where that knowledge, if it were certain, could be of no use. Wherein he agreed entirely with the sentiments of Socrates, as Plato delivers them, which I mention as the highest honor I can do that prince of philosophers. I have often since reflected what destruction such a doctrine would make in the libraries of Europe; and how many paths to fame would be then shut up in the learned world.

Friendship and benevolence are the two principal virtues among the Houyhnhnms; and these not confined to particular objects, but universal to the whole race. For a stranger from the remotest part is equally treated with the nearest neighbor, and wherever he goes, looks upon himself as at home. They preserve decency and civility in the highest degrees, but are altogether ignorant of ceremony. They have no fondness for their colts or foals; but the care they take in educating them proceedeth entirely from the dictates of reason. And I observed my master to show the same affection to his neighbor's issue that he had for his own. They will have it that Nature teaches them to love the whole species, and it is reason only that maketh a distinction of persons, where there is a superior degree of virtue.

When the matron Houyhnhnms have produced one of each sex, they no longer accompany with their consorts, except they lose one of their issue by some casualty, which very seldom happens; but in such a case they meet again; or when the like accident befalls a person whose wife is past bearing, some other couple bestows on him one of their own colts, and then go together a second time, until the mother be pregnant. This caution is necessary to prevent the country from being overburdened with numbers. But the race of inferior Houyhnhnms bred up to be servants is not so strictly limited upon this article; these are allowed to produce three of each sex, to be domestics in the noble families.

In their marriages they are exactly careful to choose such colors as will not make any disagreeable mixture in the breed. Strength is chiefly valued in the male, and comeliness in the female; not upon the account of love, but to preserve the race from degenerating; for, where a female happens to excel in strength, a consort is chosen with regard to comeliness. Courtship, love, presents, jointures, settlements, have no place in their thoughts, or terms whereby to express them in their language. The young couple meet and are joined, merely because it is the determination of their parents and friends; it is what they see done every day; and they look upon it as one of the necessary actions in a reasonable being. But the violation of marriage, or any other unchastity, was never heard of; and the married pair pass their lives with the same friendship and mutual benevolence that they bear to all others of the same species who come in their way, without jealousy, fondness, quarreling, or discontent.

In educating the youth of both sexes, their method is admirable, and highly deserveth our imitation. These are not suffered to taste a grain of oats, except upon certain days, till eighteen years old; nor milk, but very rarely; and in summer they graze two hours in the morning, and as many in the evening, which their parents likewise observe; but the servants are not allowed above half that time; and a great part of the grass is brought home, which they eat at the most convenient hours when they can be best spared from work.

Temperance, industry, exercise, and cleanliness are the lessons equally enjoined to the young ones of both sexes; and my master thought it monstrous in us to give the females a different kind of education from the males, except in some articles of domestic management; whereby, as he truly observed, one half of our natives were good for nothing but bringing children into the world; and to trust the care of their children to such useless animals, he said was yet a greater instance of brutality.

But the Houyhnhnms train up their youth to strength, speed, and hardiness, by exercising them in running races up and down steep hills, or over hard stony grounds; and when they are all in a sweat, they are ordered to leap over head and ears into a pond or a river. Four times a year the youth of certain districts meet to show their proficiency in running, and leaping, and other feats of strength or agility; where the victor is rewarded with a song made in his or her praise. On this festival the servants drive a herd of Yahoos into the field, laden with hay, and oats, and milk for a repast to the Houyhnhnms; after which these brutes are immediately driven back again, for fear of being noisome to the assembly.

Every fourth year, at the vernal equinox, there is a representative council of the whole nation, which meets in a plain about twenty miles from our house, and continueth about five or six days. Here they inquire into the state and condition of the several districts; whether they abound or be deficient in hay or oats, or cows or Yahoos? And wherever there is any want (which is but seldom) it is immediately supplied by unanimous consent and contribution. Here likewise the regulation of children is settled: as for instance, if a Houyhnhnm hath two males, he changeth one of them with another who hath two females, and when a child hath been lost by any casualty, where the mother is past breeding, it is determined what family in the district shall breed another to supply the loss.

CHAPTER 9. *A grand debate at the general assembly of the Houyhnhnms, and how it was determined. The learning of the Houyhnhnms. Their buildings. Their manner of burials. The defectiveness of their language.*

One of these grand assemblies was held in my time, about three months before my departure, whither my master went as the representative of our district. In this council was resumed their old debate, and indeed, the only debate that ever happened in their country; whereof my master after his return gave me a very particular account.

The question to be debated was whether the Yahoos should be exterminated from the face of the earth. One of the members for the affirmative offered several arguments of great strength and weight, alleging that, as the Yahoos were the most filthy, noisome, and deformed animal which nature ever produced, so they were the most restive and indocible, mischievous, and malicious; they would privately suck the teats of the Houyhnhnms' cows; kill and devour their cats, trample down their oats and grass, if they were not continually watched; and commit a thousand other extravagancies. He took notice of a general tradition, that Yahoos had not been always in their country, but that many ages ago, two of these brutes appeared together upon a mountain; whether produced by the heat of the sun upon corrupted mud and slime, or from the ooze and froth of the sea, was never known. That these Yahoos engendered, and their brood in a short time grew so numerous as to overrun and infest the whole nation. That the Houyhnhnms to get rid of this evil, made a general hunting, and at last enclosed the whole herd; and destroying the older, every Houyhnhnm kept two young ones in a kennel, and brought them to such a degree of tameness as an animal so savage by nature can be capable of acquiring, using them for draft and carriage. That there seemed to be much truth in this tradition, and that those creatures could not be *ylnhniamshy* (or aborigines of the land) because of the violent hatred the Houyhnhnms as well as all other animals bore them; which although their evil disposition sufficiently deserved, could never have arrived at so high a degree, if they had been aborigines, or else they would have long since been rooted out. That the inhabitants taking a fancy to use the service of the Yahoos, had very imprudently neglected to cultivate the breed of asses, which were a comely animal, easily kept, more tame and orderly, without any offensive smell, strong enough for labor, although they yield to the other in agility of body; and if their braying be no agreeable sound, it is far preferable to the horrible howlings of the Yahoos.

Several others declared their sentiments to the same purpose, when my master proposed an expedient to the assembly, whereof he had indeed borrowed the hint from me. He approved of the tradition, mentioned by the honorable member, who spoke before; and affirmed, that the two Yahoos said to be first seen among them, had been driven thither over the sea; that coming to land, and being forsaken by their companions, they retired to the mountains, and degenerating by degrees, became in process of time much more savage than those of their own species in the country from whence these two originals came. The reason of his assertion was that he had now in his possession a certain wonderful Yahoo (meaning myself) which most of them had heard of, and many of them had seen. He then related to them how he first found me; that my body was all covered with an artificial composure of the skins and hairs of other animals; that I spoke in a language of my own, and had thoroughly learned theirs; that I had related to him the accidents which brought me thither; that when he saw me without my covering, I was an exact Yahoo in every part, only of a whiter color, less hairy and with shorter claws. He added how I had endeavored to persuade him that in my own and other countries the Yahoos acted as the governing, rational animal, and held the Houyhnhnms in servitude; that he observed in me all the qualities of a Yahoo, only a little more civilized by some tincture of reason, which however was in a degree as far inferior to the Houyhnhnm race as the Yahoos of their country were to me; that among other things, I mentioned a custom we had of castrating Houyhnhnms when they were young, in order to render them tame; that the operation was easy and safe; that it was no shame to learn wisdom from brutes, as industry is taught by the ant, and building by the swallow (for so I translate the world *lyhannh*, although it be a much larger fowl). That this invention might be practiced upon the younger Yahoos here, which, besides rendering them tractable and fitter for use, would in an age put an end to the whole species without destroying life. That in the meantime the Houyhnhnms should be exhorted to cultivate the breed of asses, which, as they are in all respects more valuable brutes, so they have this advantage, to be fit for service at five years old, which the other are not till twelve.

This was all my master thought fit to tell me at that time, of what passed in the grand council. But he was pleased to conceal one particular, which related personally to myself, whereof I soon felt the unhappy effect, as the reader will know in its proper place, and from whence I date all the succeeding misfortunes of my life.

The Houyhnhnms have no letters, and consequently, their knowledge is all traditional. But there happening few events of any moment among a people so well united, naturally disposed to every virtue, wholly governed by reason, and cut off from all commerce with other nations, the historical part is easily preserved without burdening their memories. I have already observed that they are subject to no diseases, and therefore can have no need of physicians. However, they have excellent medicines composed of herbs, to cure accidental bruises and cuts in the pastern or frog of the foot by sharp stones, as well as other maims and hurts in the several parts of the body.

They calculate the year by the revolution of the sun and the moon, but use no subdivisions into weeks. They are well enough acquainted with the motions of those two luminaries, and understand the nature of eclipses; and this is the utmost progress of their astronomy.

In poetry they must be allowed to excel all other mortals; wherein the justness of their similes, and the minuteness, as well as exactness of their descriptions, are indeed inimitable. Their verses abound very much in both of these, and usually contain either some exalted notions of friendship and benevolence, or the praises of those who were victors in races and other bodily exercises. Their buildings, although very rude and simple, are not inconvenient, but well contrived to defend them from all injuries of cold and heat. They have a kind of tree, which at forty years old loosens in the root, and falls with the first storm; it grows very straight, and being pointed like stakes with a sharp stone (for the Houyhnhnms know not the use of iron), they stick them erect in the ground about ten inches asunder, and then weave in oat straw, or sometimes wattles, betwixt them. The roof is made after the same manner, and so are the doors.

The Houyhnhnms use the hollow part between the pastern and the hoof of their forefeet as we do our hands, and this with greater dexterity than I could at first imagine. I have seen a white mare of our family thread a needle (which I lent her on purpose) with that joint. They milk their cows, reap their oats, and do all the work which requires hands in the same manner. They have a kind of hard flints, which by grinding against other stones they form into instruments that serve instead of wedges, axes, and hammers. With tools made of these flints, they likewise cut their hay, and reap their oats, which there groweth naturally in several fields; the Yahoos draw home the sheaves in carriages, and the servants tread them in certain covered huts, to get out the grain, which is kept in stores. They make a rude kind of earthen and wooden vessels, and bake the former in the sun.

If they can avoid casualties, they die only of old age, and are buried in the obscurest places that can be found, their friends and relations expressing neither joy nor grief at their departure; nor does the dying person discover the least regret that he is leaving the world, any more than if he were upon returning home from a visit to one of his neighbors; I remember my master having once made an appointment with a friend and his family to come to his house upon some affair of importance; on the day fixed, the mistress and her two children came very late; she made two excuses, first for her husband, who, as she said, happened that very morning to *lhnuwnh*. The word is strongly expressive in their language, but not easily rendered into English; it signifies, *to retire to his first Mother*. Her excuse for not coming sooner was that her husband dying late in the morning, she was a good while consulting her servants about a convenient place where his body should be laid; and I observed she behaved herself at our house, as cheerfully as the rest; she died about three months after.

They live generally to seventy or seventy-five years, very seldom to fourscore; some weeks before their death they feel a gradual decay, but without pain. During this time they are much visited by their friends, because they cannot go abroad with their usual ease and satisfaction. However, about ten days before their death, which they seldom fail in computing, they return the visits that have been made by those who are nearest in the neighborhood, being carried in a convenient sledge drawn by Yahoos; which vehicle they use, not only upon this occasion, but when they grow old, upon long journeys, or when they are lamed by any accident. And therefore when the dying Houyhnhnms return those visits, they take a solemn leave of their friends, as if they were going to some remote part of the country, where they designed to pass the rest of their lives.

I know not whether it may be worth observing, that the Houyhnhnms have no word in their language to express anything that is evil, except what they borrow from the deformities or ill qualities of the Yahoos. Thus they denote the folly of a servant, an omission of a child, a stone that cuts their feet, a continuance of foul or unseasonable weather, and the like, by adding to each the epithet of Yahoo. For instance, *hhnm Yahoo, whnaholm Yahoo, ynlhmndwihlma Yahoo*, and an ill-contrived house, *ynholmhnmrohlnw Yahoo*.

I could with great pleasure enlarge farther upon the manners and virtues of this excellent people; but intending in a short time to publish a volume by itself expressly upon that subject, I refer the reader thither. And in the meantime, proceed to relate my own sad catastrophe.

CHAPTER 10. *The Author's economy, and happy life among the Houyhnhnms. His great improvement in virtue, by conversing with them. Their conversations. The Author hath notice given him by his master that he must depart from the country. He falls into a swoon for grief, but submits. He contrives and finishes a canoe, by the help of a fellow servant, and puts to sea at a venture.*

I had settled my little economy to my own heart's content. My master had ordered a room to be made for me after their manner, about six yards from the house; the sides and floors of which I plastered with clay, and covered with rush mats of my own contriving; I had beaten hemp, which there grows wild, and made of it a sort of ticking; this I filled with the feathers of several birds I had taken with springes made of Yahoos' hairs, and were excellent food. I had worked two chairs with my knife, the sorrel nag helping me in the grosser and more laborious part. When my clothes were worn to rags, I made myself others with the skins of rabbits, and of a certain beautiful animal about the same size, called *nnuhnoh*, the skin of which is covered with a fine down. Of these I likewise made very tolerable stockings. I soled my shoes with wood which I cut from a tree, and fitted to the upper leather, and when this was worn out, I supplied it with the skins of Yahoos, dried in the sun. I often got honey out of hollow trees, which I mingled with water, or eat it with my bread. No man could more verify the truth of these two maxims, that *Nature is very easily satisfied*; and, that *Necessity is the mother of invention*. I enjoyed perfect health of body, and tranquility of mind; I did not feel the treachery or inconstancy of a friend, nor the inquiries of a secret or open enemy. I had no occasion of bribing, flattering, or pimping to procure the favor of any great man, or of his minion. I wanted no fence against fraud or oppression; here was neither physician to destroy my body, nor lawyer to ruin my fortune; no informer to watch my words and actions, or forge accusations against me for hire; here were no gibers, censurers, backbiters, pickpockets, highwaymen, housebreakers, attorneys, bawds, buffoons, gamesters, politicians, wits, splenetics, tedious talkers, controvertists, ravishers, murderers, robbers, virtuosos; no leaders or followers of party and faction; no encouragers to vice, by seducement or examples; no dungeons, axes, gibbets, whipping posts, or pillories; no cheating shopkeepers or mechanics; no pride, vanity or affectation; no fops, bullies, drunkards, strolling whores, or poxes; no ranting, lewd, expensive wives; no stupid, proud pedants; no importunate, overbearing, quarrelsome, noisy, roaring, empty, conceited, swearing companions; no scoundrels raised from the dust upon the merit of their vices; or nobility thrown into it on account of their virtues; no lords, fiddlers, judges, or dancing masters.

I had the favor of being admitted to several Houyhnhnms, who came to vist or dine with my master; where his honor graciously suffered me to wait in the room, and listen to their discourse. Both he and his company would often descend to ask me questions, and receive my answers. I had also sometimes the honor of attending my master in his visits to others. I never presumed to speak, except in answer to a question; and then I did it with inward regret, because it was a loss of so much time for improving myself; but I was infinitely delighted with the station of an humble auditor in such conversations, where nothing passed but what was useful, expressed in the fewest and most significant words; where (as I have already said) the greatest decency was observed, without the least degree of ceremony; where no person spoke without being pleased himself, and pleasing his companions; where there was no interruption, tediousness, heat, or difference of sentiments. They have a notion, that when people are met together, a short silence doth much improve conversation; this I found to be true; for during those little intermissions of talk, new ideas would arise in their minds, which very much enlivened the discourse. Their subjects are generally on friendship and benevolence; on order and economy; sometimes upon the visible operations of nature, or ancient traditions; upon the bounds and limits of virtue; upon the unerring rules of reason; or upon some determinations, to be taken at the next great assembly; and often upon the various excellencies of poetry. I may add, without vanity, that my presence often gave them sufficient matter for discourse, because it afforded my master an occasion of letting his friends into the history of me and my country, upon which they were all pleased to descant in a manner not very advantageous to human kind; and for that reason I shall not repeat what they said; only I may be allowed to observe that his honor, to my great admiration, appeared to understand the nature of Yahoos much better than myself. He went through all our vices and follies, and discovered many which I had never mentioned to him; by only supposing what qualities a Yahoo of their country, with a small proportion of reason, might be capable of exerting; and concluded, with too much probability, how vile as well as miserable such a creature must be.

I freely confess, that all the little knowledge I have of any value was acquired by the lectures I received from my master, and from hearing the discourses of him and his friends; to which I should be prouder to listen, than to dictate to the greatest and wisest assembly in Europe. I admired the strength, comeliness, and speed of the inhabitants; and such a constellation of virtues in such amiable persons produced in me the highest veneration. At first, indeed, I did not feel that natural awe which the Yahoos and all other animals bear towards them; but it grew upon me by degrees, much sooner than I imagined, and was mingled with a respectful love and gratitude, that they would condescend to distinguish me from the rest of my species.

When I thought of my family, my friends, my countrymen, or human race in general, I considered them as they really were, Yahoos in shape and disposition, perhaps a little more civilized, and qualified with the gift of speech; but making no other use of reason than to improve and multiply those vices, whereof their brethren in this country had only the share that nature allotted them. When I happened to behold the reflection of my own form in a lake or fountain, I turned away my face in horror and detestation of myself, and could better endure the sight of a common Yahoo than of my own person. By conversing with the Houyhnhnms, and looking upon them with delight, I fell to imitate their gait and gesture, which is now grown into a habit; and my friends often tell me in a blunt way, that I trot like a horse; which, however, I take for a great compliment; neither shall I disown, that in speaking I am apt to fall into the voice and manner of the Houyhnhnms, and hear myself ridiculed on that account without the least mortification.

In the midst of this happiness, when I looked upon myself to be fully settled for life, my master sent for me one morning a little earlier than his usual hour. I observed by his countenance that he was in some perplexity, and at a loss how to begin what he had to speak. After a short silence, he told me, he did not know how I would take what he was going to say; that, in the last general assembly, when the affair of the Yahoos was entered upon, the representatives had taken offense at his keeping a Yahoo (meaning myself) in his family more like a Houyhnhnm than a brute animal. That he was known frequently to converse with me, as if he could receive some advantage of pleasure in my company; that such a practice was not agreeable to reason or nature, or a thing ever heard of before among them. The assembly did therefore exhort him, either to employ me like the rest of my species, or command me to swim back to the place from whence I came. That the first of these expedients was utterly rejected by all the Houyhnhnms who had ever seen me at his house or their own; for, they alleged, that because I had some rudiments of reason, added to the natural pravity of those animals, it was to be feared, I might be able to seduce them into the woody and mountainous parts of the country, and bring them in troops by night to destroy the Houyhnhnms' cattle, as being naturally of the ravenous kind, and averse from labor.

My master added that he was daily pressed by the Houyhnhnms of the neighborhood to have the assembly's exhortation executed, which he could not put off much longer. He doubted it would be impossible for me to swim to another country; and therefore wished I would contrive some sort of vehicle resembling those I had described to him, that might carry me on the sea; in which work I should have the assistance of his own servants, as well as those of his neighbors. He concluded that for his own part he could have been content to keep me in his service as long as I lived; because he found I had cured myself of some bad habits and dispositions, by endeavoring, as far as my inferior nature was capable, to imitate the Houyhnhnms.

I should here observe to the reader, that a decree of the general assembly in this country is expressed by the word *hnhloayn*, which signifies an exhortation, as near as I can render it; for they have no conception how a rational creature can be compelled, but only advised, or exhorted; because no person can disobey reason without giving up his claim to be a rational creature.

I was struck with the utmost grief and despair at my master's discourse; and being unable to support the agonies I was under, I fell into a swoon at his feet; when I came to myself, he told me that he concluded I had been dead (for these people are subject to no such imbecilities of nature). I answered, in a faint voice, that death would have been too great an happiness; that although I could not blame the assembly's exhortation, or the urgency of his friends; yet in my weak and corrupt judgment, I thought it might consist with reason to have been less rigorous. That I could not swim a league, and probably the nearest land to theirs might be distant above an hundred; that many materials, necessary for making a small vessel to carry me off, were wholly wanting in this country, which, however, I would attempt in obedience and gratitude to his honor, although I concluded the thing to be impossible, and therefore looked on myself as already devoted[4] to destruction. That the certain prospect of an unnatural death was the least of my evils; for, supposing I should escape with life by some strange adventure, how could I think with temper[5] of passing my days among Yahoos, and relapsing into my old corruptions, for want of examples to lead and keep me within the paths of virtue. That I knew too well upon what solid reasons all the determinations of the wise Houyhnhnms were founded, not to be shaken by arguments of mine, a miserable Yahoo; and therefore after presenting him with my humble thanks for the offer of his servants' assistance in making a vessel, and desiring a reasonable time for so difficult a work, I told him I would endeavor to preserve a wretched being; and, if ever I returned to England, was not without hopes of being useful to my own species by celebrating the praises of the renowned Houyhnhnms, and proposing their virtues to the imitation of mankind.

My master in a few words made me a very gracious reply, allowed me the space of two months to finish my boat, and ordered the sorrel nag, my fellow servant (for so at this distance I may presume to call him), to follow my instructions, because I told my master that his help would be sufficient, and I knew he had a tenderness for me.

In his company my first business was to go to that part of the coast where my rebellious crew had ordered me to be set on shore. I got upon a height, and looking on every side into the sea, fancied I saw a small island towards the northeast; I took out my pocket glass, and could then clearly distinguish it about five leagues off, as I computed; but it appeared to the sorrel nag to be only a blue cloud; for, as he had no conception of any country besides his own, so he could not be as expert in distinguishing remote objects at sea, as we who so much converse in that element.

After I had discovered this island, I considered no farther; but resolved, it should, if possible, be the first place of my banishment, leaving the consequence to fortune.

I returned home, and consulting with the sorrel nag, we went into a copse at some distance, where I with my knive, and he with a sharp flint fastened very artificially,[6] after their manner, to a wooden handle, cut down several oak wattles about the thickness of a walking staff, and some larger pieces. But I shall not trouble the reader with a particular description of my own mechanics; let it suffice to say, that in six weeks time, with the help of the sorrel nag, who performed the parts that required most labor, I finished a sort of Indian canoe; but much larger, covering it with the skins of Yahoos, well stitched together, with hempen threads of my own making. My sail was likewise composed of the skins of the

4. Doomed.
5. Equanimity.

6. Artfully.

same animal; but I made use of the youngest I could get, the older being too tough and thick; and I likewise provided myself with four paddles. I laid in a stock of boiled flesh, of rabbits and fowls; and took with me two vessels, one filled with milk, and the other with water.

I tried my canoe in a large pond near my master's house, and then corrected in it what was amiss, stopping all the chinks with Yahoo's tallow, till I found it staunch, and able to bear me and my freight. And when it was as complete as I could possibly make it, I had it drawn on a carriage very gently by Yahoos, to the seaside, under the conduct of the sorrel nag and another servant.

When all was ready, and the day came for my departure, I took leave of my master and lady, and the whole family, my eyes flowing with tears and my heart quite sunk with grief. But his honor, out of curiosity, and perhaps (if I may speak it without vanity) partly out of kindness, was determined to see me in my canoe; and got several of his neighboring friends to accompany him. I was forced to wait above an hour for the tide, and then observing the wind very fortunately bearing towards the island to which I intended to steer my course, I took a second leave of my master; but as I was going to prostrate myself to kiss his hoof, he did me the honor to raise it gently to my mouth. I am not ignorant how much I have been censured for mentioning this last particular. Detractors are pleased to think it improbable that so illustrious a person should descend to give so great a mark of distinction to a creature so inferior as I. Neither have I forgot how apt some travelers are to boast of extraordinary favors they have received. But, if these censurers were better acquainted with the noble and courteous disposition of the Houyhnhnms, they would soon change their opinion. I paid my respects to the rest of the Houyhnhnms in his honor's company; then getting into my canoe, I pushed off from shore.

CHAPTER 11. *The Author's dangerous voyage. He arrives at New Holland, hoping to settle there. Is wounded with an arrow by one of the natives. Is seized and carried by force into a Portuguese ship. The great civilities of the Captain. The Author arrives at England.*

I began this desperate voyage on February 15, 1714 / 5,[7] at 9 o'clock in the morning. The wind was very favorable; however, I made use at first only of my paddles; but considering I should soon be weary, and that the wind might probably chop about, I ventured to set up my little sail, and thus, with the help of the tide, I went at the rate of a league and a half an hour, as near as I could guess. My master and his friends continued on the shore, till I was almost out of sight; and I often heard the sorrel nag (who always loved me) crying out, "*Hnuy illa nyha maiah Yahoo*" ("Take care of thyself, gentle Yahoo").

7. I.e., 1714. The year began on March 25.

My design was, if possible, to discover some small island uninhabited, yet sufficient by my labor to furnish me with necessaries of life, which I would have thought a greater happiness than to be first minister in the politest court of Europe, so horrible was the idea I conceived of returning to live in the society and under the government of Yahoos. For in such a solitude as I desired, I could at least enjoy my own thoughts, and reflect with delight on the virtues of those inimitable Houyhnhnms, without any opportunity of degenerating into the vices and corruptions of my own species.

The reader may remember what I related when my crew conspired against me, and confined me to my cabin, how I continued there several weeks, without knowing what course we took; and when I was put ashore in the longboat, how the sailors told me with oaths, whether true or false, that they knew not in what part of the world we were. However, I did then believe us to be about 10 degrees southward of the Cape of Good Hope, or about 45 degrees southern latitude, as I gathered from some general words I overheard among them, being I supposed to the southeast in their intended voyage to Madagascar. And although this were but little better than conjecture, yet I resolved to steer my course eastward, hoping to reach the southwest coast of New Holland, and perhaps some such island as I desired, lying westward of it. The wind was full west, and by six in the evening I computed I had gone eastward at least eighteen leagues; when I spied a very small island about half a league off, which I soon reached. It was nothing but a rock with one creek,[8] naturally arched by the force of tempests. Here I put in my canoe, and climbing a part of the rock, I could plainly discover land to the east, extending from south to north. I lay all night in my canoe; and repeating my voyage early in the morning, I arrived in seven hours to the southeast point of New Holland. This confirmed me in the opinion I have long entertained, that the maps and charts place this country at least three degrees more to the east than it really is; which thought I communicated many years ago to my worthy friend Mr. Herman Moll,[9] and gave him my reasons for it, although he hath rather chosen to follow other authors.

I saw no inhabitants in the place where I landed; and being unarmed, I was afraid of venturing far into the country. I found some shellfish on the shore, and eat them raw, not daring to kindle a fire, for fear of being discovered by the natives. I continued three days feeding on oysters and limpets, to save my own provisions; and I fortunately found a brook of excellent water, which gave me great relief.

On the fourth day, venturing out early a little too far, I saw twenty or thirty natives upon a height, not above five hundred yards from me. They were stark naked, men, women, and children round a fire, as I could discover by the smoke. One of them spied me, and gave notice to the rest; five of them advanced towards me, leaving the women and children at the fire. I made what haste I could to the shore, and getting

8. A bay.   9. A famous contemporary map maker.

into my canoe, shoved off; the savages observing me retreat, ran after me; and before I could get far enough into the sea, discharged an arrow, which wounded me deeply on the inside of my left knee. (I shall carry the mark to my grave.) I apprehended the arrow might be poisoned; and paddling out of the reach of their darts (being a calm day) I made a shift to suck the wound, and dress it as well as I could.

I was at a loss what to do, for I durst not return to the same landing place, but stood to the north, and was forced to paddle; for the wind, although very gentle, was against me, blowing northwest. As I was looking about for a secure landing place, I saw a sail to the north northeast, which appearing every minute more visible, I was in some doubt whether I should wait for them or no; but at last my detestation of the Yahoo race prevailed; and turning my canoe, I sailed and paddled together to the south, and got into the same creek from whence I set out in the morning, choosing rather to trust myself among these barbarians than live with European Yahoos. I drew up my canoe as close as I could to the shore, and hid myself behind a stone by the little brook, which, as I have already said, was excellent water.

The ship came within half a league of this creek, and sent out her longboat with vessels to take in fresh water (for the place it seems was very well known), but I did not observe it until the boat was almost on shore; and it was too late to seek another hiding place. The seamen at their landing observed my canoe, and rummaging it all over, easily conjectured that the owner could not be far off. Four of them well armed searched every cranny and lurking hole, till at last they found me flat on my face behind the stone. They gazed a while in admiration[1] at my strange uncouth dress; my coat made of skins, my wooden-soled shoes, and my furred stockings; from whence, however, they concluded I was not a native of the place, who all go naked. One of the seamen in Portuguese bid me rise, and asked who I was. I understood that language very well, and getting upon my feet, said I was a poor Yahoo, banished from the Houyhnhnms, and desired they would please to let me depart. They admired to hear me answer them in their own tongue, and saw by my complexion I must be an European; but were at a loss to know what I meant by Yahoos and Houyhnhnms, and at the same time fell a laughing at my strange tone in speaking, which resembled the neighing of a horse. I trembled all the while betwixt fear and hatred; I again desired leave to depart, and was gently moving to my canoe; but they laid hold on me, desiring to know what country I was of? whence I came? with many other questions. I told them I was born in England, from whence I came about five years ago, and then their country and ours was at peace. I therefore hoped they would not treat me as an enemy, since I meant them no harm, but was a poor Yahoo, seeking some desolate place where to pass the remainder of his unfortunate life.

When they began to talk, I thought I never heard or saw any thing so

1. Wonder.

unnatural; for it appeared to me as monstrous as if a dog or a cow should speak in England, or a Yahoo in Houyhnhnmland. The honest Portuguese were equally amazed at my strange dress, and the odd manner of delivering my words, which however they understood very well. They spoke to me with great humanity, and said they were sure their Captain would carry me *gratis* to Lisbon, from whence I might return to my own country; that two of the seamen would go back to the ship, to inform the Captain of what they had seen, and receive his orders; in the meantime, unless I would give my solemn oath not to fly, they would secure me by force. I thought it best to comply with their proposal. They were very curious to know my story, but I gave them very little satisfaction; and they all conjectured, that my misfortunes had impaired my reason. In two hours the boat, which went laden with vessels of water, returned with the Captain's commands to fetch me on board. I fell on my knees to preserve my liberty; but all was in vain, and the men having tied me with cords, heaved me into the boat, from whence I was taken into the ship, and from thence into the Captain's cabin.

His name was Pedro de Mendez; he was a very courteous and generous person; he entreated me to give some account of myself, and desired to know what I would eat or drink; said I should be used as well as himself, and spoke so many obliging things, that I wondered to find such civilities from a Yahoo. However, I remained silent and sullen; I was ready to faint at the very smell of him and his men. At last I desired something to eat out of my own canoe; but he ordered me a chicken and some excellent wine, and then directed that I should be put to bed in a very clean cabin. I would not undress myself, but lay on the bedclothes; and in half an hour stole out, when I thought the crew was at dinner; and getting to the side of the ship, was going to leap into the sea, and swim for my life, rather than continue among Yahoos. But one of the seamen prevented me, and having informed the Captain, I was chained to my cabin.

After dinner Don Pedro came to me, and desired to know my reason for so desperate an attempt; assured me he only meant to do me all the service he was able; and spoke so very movingly, that at last I descended to treat him like an animal which had some little portion of reason. I gave him a very short relation of my voyage; of the conspiracy against me by my own men; of the country where they set me on shore, and of my five years residence there. All which he looked upon as if it were a dream or a vision; whereat I took great offense; for I had quite forgot the faculty of lying, so peculiar to Yahoos in all countries where they preside, and consequently the disposition of suspecting truth in others of their own species. I asked him whether it were the custom of his country to *say the thing that was not?* I assured him I had almost forgot what he meant by falsehood; and if I had lived a thousand years in Houyhnhnmland, I should never have heard a lie from the meanest servant. That I was altogether indifferent whether he believed me or no; but however, in return for his favors, I would give so much allowance to the corruption of his nature, as to answer any objection he would please to make; and he might easily discover the truth.

The Captain, a wise man, after many endeavors to catch me tripping in some part of my story, at last began to have a better opinion of my veracity. But he added that since I professed so inviolable an attachment to truth, I must give him my word of honor to bear him company in this voyage without attempting anything against my life; or else he would continue me a prisoner till we arrived at Lisbon. I gave him the promise he required; but at the same time protested that I would suffer the greatest hardships rather than return to live among Yahoos.

Our voyage passed without any considerable accident. In gratitude to the Captain I sometimes sat with him at his earnest request, and strove to conceal my antipathy against humankind, although it often broke out; which he suffered to pass without observation. But the greatest part of the day, I confined myself to my cabin, to avoid seeing any of the crew. The Captain had often entreated me to strip myself of my savage dress, and offered to lend me the best suit of clothes he had. This I would not be prevailed on to accept, abhorring to cover myself with anything that had been on the back of a Yahoo. I only desired he would lend me two clean shirts, which having been washed since he wore them, I believed would not so much defile me. These I changed every second day, and washed them myself.

We arrived at Lisbon, Nov. 5, 1715. At our landing, the Captain forced me to cover myself with his cloak, to prevent the rabble from crowding about me. I was conveyed to his own house; and at my earnest request, he led me up to the highest room backwards.[2] I conjured him to conceal from all persons what I had told him of the Houyhnhnms; because the least hint of such a story would not only draw numbers of people to see me, but probably put me in danger of being imprisoned, or burned by the Inquisition. The Captain persuaded me to accept a suit of clothes newly made; but I would not suffer the tailor to take my measure; however, Don Pedro being almost of my size, they fitted me well enough. He accounted me with other necessaries, all new, which I aired for twenty-four hours before I would use them.

The Captain had no wife, nor above three servants, none of which were suffered to attend at meals; and his whole deportment was so obliging, added to very good human understanding, that I really began to tolerate his company. He gained so far upon me, that I ventured to look out of the back window. By degrees I was brought into another room, from whence I peeped into the street, but drew my head back in a fright. In a week's time he seduced me down to the door. I found my terror gradually lessened, but my hatred and contempt seemed to increase. I was at last bold enough to walk the street in his company, but kept my nose well stopped with rue, or sometimes with tobacco.

2. At the rear.

In ten days, Don Pedro, to whom I had given some account of my domestic affairs, put it upon me as a point of honor and conscience that I ought to return to my native country, and live at home with my wife and children. He told me there was an English ship in the port just ready to sail, and he would furnish me with all things necessary. It would be tedious to repeat his arguments, and my contradictions. He said it was altogether impossible to find such a solitary island as I had desired to live in; but I might command in my own house, and pass my time in a manner as recluse as I pleased.

I complied at last, finding I could not do better. I left Lisbon the 24th day of November, in an English merchantman, but who was the Master I never inquired. Don Pedro accompanied me to the ship, and lent me twenty pounds. He took kind leave of me, and embraced me at parting; which I bore as well as I could. During this last voyage I had no commerce with the Master, or any of his men; but pretending I was sick kept close in my cabin. On the fifth of December, 1715, we cast anchor in the Downs about nine in the morning, and at three in the afternoon I got safe to my house at Redriff.

My wife and family received me with great surprise and joy, because they concluded me certainly dead; but I must freely confess, the sight of them filled me only with hatred, disgust, and contempt; and the more, by reflecting on the near alliance I had to them. For although since my unfortunate exile from the Houyhnhnm country, I had compelled myself to tolerate the sight of Yahoos, and to converse with Don Pedro de Mendez; yet my memory and imaginations were perpetually filled with the virtues and ideas of those exalted Houyhnhnms. And when I began to consider that by copulating with one of the Yahoo species, I had become a parent of more, it struck me with the utmost shame, confusion, and horror.

As soon as I entered the house, my wife took me in her arms, and kissed me; at which, having not been used to the touch of that odious animal for so many years, I fell in a swoon for almost an hour. At the time I am writing, it is five years since my last return to England; during the first year I could not endure my wife or children in my presence, the very smell of them was intolerable; much less could I suffer them to eat in the same room. To this hour they dare not presume to touch my bread, or drink out of the same cup; neither was I ever able to let one of them take me by the hand. The first money I laid out was to buy two young stone-horses,[3] which I keep in a good stable, and next to them the groom is my greatest favorite; for I feel my spirits revived by the smell he contracts in the stable. My horses understand me tolerably well; I converse with them at least four hours every day. They are strangers to bridle or saddle; they live in great amity with me, and friendship to each other.

3. Stallions.

CHAPTER 12. *The Author's veracity. His design in publishing this work. His censure of those travelers who swerve from the truth. The Author clears himself from any sinister ends in writing. His native country commended. The right of the crown to those countries described by the Author is justified. The difficulty of conquering them. The Author takes his last leave of the reader; proposeth his manner of living for the future; gives good advice, and concludeth.*

Thus gentle reader, I have given thee a faithful history of my travels for sixteen years, and above seven months; wherein I have not been so studious of ornament as of truth. I could perhaps like others have astonished thee with strange improbable tales; but I rather chose to relate plain matter of fact in the simplest manner and style; because my principal design was to inform, and not to amuse thee.

It is easy for us who travel into remote countries, which are seldom visited by Englishmen or other Europeans, to form descriptions of wonderful animals both at sea and land. Whereas a traveler's chief aim should be to make men wiser and better, and to improve their minds by the bad as well as good example of what they deliver concerning foreign places.

I could heartily wish a law were enacted, that every traveler, before he were permitted to publish his voyages, should be obliged to make oath before the Lord High Chancellor that all he intended to print was absolutely true to the best of his knowledge; for then the world would no longer be deceived as it usually is, while some writers, to make their works pass the better upon the public, impose the grossest falsities on the unwary reader. I have perused several books of travels with great delight in my younger days; but, having since gone over most parts of the globe, and been able to contradict many fabulous accounts from my own observation, it hath given me a great disgust against this part of reading, and some indignation to see the credulity of mankind so impudently abused. Therefore, since my acquaintance were pleased to think my poor endeavors might not be unacceptable to my country; I imposed on myself as a maxim, never to be swerved from, that I would *strictly adhere to truth*; neither indeed can I be ever under the least temptation to vary from it, while I retain in my mind the lectures and example of my noble master, and the other illustrious Houyhnhnms, of whom I had so long the honor to be an humble hearer.

> ———*Nec si miserum Fortuna Sinonem*
> *Finxit, vanum etiam, mendacemque improba finget.*[4]

I know very well how little reputation is to be got by writings which require neither genius nor learning, nor indeed any other talent, except a good memory, or an exact *Journal*. I know likewise, that writers of travels, like dictionary-makers, are sunk into oblivion by the weight and bulk of those who come last, and therefore lie uppermost. And it is

---

4. Virgil, *Aeneid* 2. 79–80. ". . . nor if Fortune had moulded Sinon for misery, will she also in spite mould him as false and lying."

highly probable that such travelers who shall hereafter visit the countries described in this work of mine, may be detecting my errors (if there be any) and adding many new discoveries of their own, jostle me out of vogue, and stand in my place, making the world forget that ever I was an author. This indeed would be too great a mortification if I wrote for fame; but, as my sole intention was the PUBLIC GOOD, I cannot be altogether disappointed. For, who can read the virtues I have mentioned in the glorious Houyhnhnms, without being ashamed of his own vices, when he considers himself as the reasoning, governing animal of his country? I shall say nothing of those remote nations where Yahoos preside; amongst which the least corrupted are the Brobdingnagians, whose wise maxims in morality and government it would be our happiness to observe. But I forbear descanting further, and rather leave the judicious reader to his own remarks and applications.

I am not a little pleased that this work of mine can possibly meet with no censurers; for what objections can be made against a writer who relates only plain facts that happened in such distant countries, where we have not the least interest with respect either to trade or negotiations? I have carefully avoided every fault with which common writers of travels are often too justly charged. Besides, I meddle not the least with any party, but write without passion, prejudice, or ill-will against any man or number of men whatsoever. I write for the noblest end, to inform and instruct mankind, over whom I may, without breach of modesty, pretend to some superiority, from the advantages I received by conversing so long among the most accomplished Houyhnhnms. I write without any view towards profit or praise. I never suffer a word to pass that may look like a reflection, or possibly give the least offense even to those who are most ready to take it. So that, I hope, I may with justice pronounce myself an Author perfectly blameless; against whom the tribes of answerers, considerers, observers, reflectors, detecters, remarkers will never be able to find matter for exercising their talents.

I confess it was whispered to me that I was bound in duty as a subject of England, to have given in a memorial to a secretary of state, at my first coming over; because, whatever lands are discovered by a subject, belong to the Crown. But I doubt whether our conquests in the countries I treat of would be as easy as those of Ferdinando Cortez over the naked Americans. The Lilliputians, I think, are hardly worth the charge of a fleet and army to reduce them; and I question whether it might be prudent or safe to attempt the Brobdingnagians; or, whether an English army would be much at their ease with the Flying Island over their heads. The Houyhnhnms, indeed, appear not to be so well prepared for war, a science to which they are perfect strangers, and especially against missive weapons. However, supposing myself to be a minister of state, I could never give my advice for invading them. Their prudence, unanimity, unacquaintedness with fear, and their love of their country would amply supply all defects in the military art. Imagine twenty thousand of them breaking into the midst of an European army, confounding the ranks, overturning the carriages, battering the warriors' faces into mummy,[5] by terrible yerks[6] from their hinder hoofs: for they would well deserve the character given to Augustus, *Recalcitrat undique tutus.*[7] But instead of proposals for conquering that magnanimous nation, I rather wish they were in a capacity or disposition to send a sufficient number of their inhabitants for civilizing Europe; by teaching us the first principles of Honor, Justice, Truth, Temperance, public Spirit, Fortitude, Chastity, Friendship, Benevolence, and Fidelity. The names of all which Virtues are still retained among us in most languages, and are to be met with in modern as well as ancient authors, which I am able to assert from my own small reading.

But I had another reason which made me less forward to enlarge his majesty's dominions by my discoveries: to say the truth, I had conceived a few scruples with relation to the distributive justice of princes upon those occasions. For instance, a crew of pirates are driven by a storm they know not whither; at length a boy discovers land from the topmast; they go on shore to rob and plunder; they see an harmless people, are entertained with kindness, they give the country a new name, they take formal possession of it for the king, they set up a rotten plank or a stone for a memorial, they murder two or three dozen of the natives, bring away a couple more by force for a sample, return home, and get their pardon. Here commences a new dominion acquired with a title by Divine Right. Ships are sent with the first opportunity; the natives driven out or destroyed, their princes tortured to discover their gold; a free license given to all acts of inhumanity and lust; the earth reeking with the blood of its inhabitants: and this execrable crew of butchers employed in so pious an expedition is a *modern colony* sent to convert and civilize an idolatrous and barbarous people.

But this description, I confess, doth by no means affect the British nation, who may be an example to the whole world for their wisdom, care, and justice in planting colonies; their liberal endowments for the advancement of religion and learning; their choice of devout and able pastors to propagate Christianity; their caution in stocking their provinces with people of sober lives and conversations from this the Mother Kingdom; their strict regard to the distribution of justice, in supplying the civil administration through all their colonies with officers of the greatest abilities, utter strangers to corruption: and to crown all, by sending the most vigilant and virtuous governors, who have no other views than the happiness of the people over whom they preside, and the honor of the king their master.

But, as those countries which I have described do not appear to have any desire of being conquered, and enslaved, murdered, or driven out by colonies, nor abound either in gold, silver, sugar, or tobacco, I did humbly conceive they were by no means proper objects of our zeal, our valor, or our interest. However, if those whom it may concern, think fit

5. Pulp.
6. Kicks.

7. Horace, *Satires* 2.1.20. ". . . he kicks backward, at every point on his guard."

to be of another opinion, I am ready to depose, when I shall be lawfully called, that no European did ever visit these countries before me. I mean, if the inhabitants ought to be believed.

But, as to the formality of taking possession in my sovereign's name, it never came once into my thoughts; and if it had, yet as my affairs then stood, I should perhaps in point of prudence and self-preservation have put it off to a better opportunity.

Having thus answered the only objection that can be raised against me as a traveler, I here take a final leave of my courteous readers, and return to enjoy my own speculations in my little garden at Redriff; to apply those excellent lessons of virtue which I learned among the Houyhnhnms; to instruct the Yahoos of my own family as far as I shall find them docible animals; to behold my figure often in a glass, and thus if possible habituate myself by time to tolerate the sight of a human creature; to lament the brutality of Houyhnhnms in my own country, but always treat their persons with respect, for the sake of my noble master, his family, his friends, and the whole Houyhnhnm race, whom these of ours have the honor to resemble in all their lineaments, however their intellectuals came to degenerate.

I began last week to permit my wife to sit at dinner with me, at the farthest end of a long table; and to answer (but with the utmost brevity) the few questions I ask her. Yet the smell of a Yahoo continuing very offensive, I always keep my nose well stopped with rue, lavender, or tobacco leaves. And although it be hard for a man late in life to remove old habits, I am not altogether out of hopes in some time to suffer a neighbor Yahoo in my company, without the apprehensions I am yet under of his teeth or his claws.

My reconcilement to the Yahoo kind in general might not be so difficult, if they would be content with those vices and follies only which nature hath entitled them to. I am not in the least provoked at the sight of a lawyer, a pickpocket, a colonel, a fool, a lord, a gamester, a politician, a whoremonger, a physician, an evidence, a suborner, an attorney, a traitor, or the like: this is all according to the due course of things. But when I behold a lump of deformity, and diseases both in body and mind, smitten with pride, it immediately breaks all the measures of my patience; neither shall I be ever able to comprehend how such an animal and such a vice could tally together. The wise and virtuous Houyhnhnms, who abound in all excellencies that can adorn a rational creature, have no name for this vice in their language, which hath no terms to express anything that is evil, except those whereby they describe the detestable qualities of their Yahoos, among which they were not able to distinguish this of pride, for want of thoroughly understanding human nature, as it showeth itself in other countries, where that animal presides. But I, who had more experience, could plainly observe some rudiments of it among the wild Yahoos.

But the Houyhnhnms, who live under the government of reason, are no more proud of the good qualities they possess, than I should be for not wanting a leg or an arm, which no man in his wits would boast of, although he must be miserable without them. I dwell the longer upon this subject from the desire I have to make the society of an English Yahoo by any means not insupportable; and therefore I here entreat those who have any tincture of this absurd vice, that they will not presume to appear in my sight.

1726, 1735

A Modest Proposal[1]

FOR PREVENTING THE CHILDREN OF POOR PEOPLE IN IRELAND FROM BEING A BURDEN TO THEIR PARENTS OR COUNTRY, AND FOR MAKING THEM BENEFICIAL TO THE PUBLIC

It is a melancholy object to those who walk through this great town[2] or travel in the country, when they see the streets, the roads, and cabin doors, crowded with beggars of the female sex, followed by three, four, or six children, all in rags and importuning every passenger for an alms. These mothers, instead of being able to work for their honest livelihood, are forced to employ all their time in strolling to beg sustenance for their helpless infants, who, as they grow up, either turn thieves for want of work, or leave their dear native country to fight for the Pretender in Spain, or sell themselves to the Barbadoes.[3]

I think it is agreed by all parties that this prodigious number of children in the arms, or on the backs, or at the heels of their mothers, and frequently of their fathers, is in the present deplorable state of the kingdom a very great additional grievance; and therefore whoever could find out a fair, cheap, and easy method of making these children sound, useful members of the commonwealth would deserve so well of the public as to have his statue set up for a preserver of the nation.

But my intention is very far from being confined to provide only for the children of professed beggars; it is of a much greater extent, and shall take in the whole number of infants at a certain age who are born of

---

1. *A Modest Proposal* is an example of Swift's favorite satiric devices used with superb effect. Irony (from the deceptive adjective "modest" in the title to the very last sentence) pervades the piece. A rigorous logic deduces ghastly arguments from a shocking premise so quietly assumed that the reader assents before he is aware of what his assent implies. Parody, at which Swift is adept, allows him to glance sardonically at the by then familiar figure of the benevolent humanitarian (forerunner of the modern sociologist, social worker, economic planner) concerned to correct a social evil by means of a theoretically conceived plan. The proposer, as naïve as he is apparently logical and kindly, ignores and therefore emphasizes for the reader the enormity of his plan. The whole is an elaboration of a rather trite metaphor: "The English are devouring the Irish." But there is nothing trite about the pam-

phlet, which expresses in Swift's most controlled style his pity for the oppressed, ignorant, populous, and hungry Catholic peasants of Ireland, and his anger at the rapacious English absentee landlords, who were bleeding the country white with the silent approbation of Parliament, ministers, and the Crown.

2. Dublin.

3. James Francis Edward Stuart (1688–1766), the son of James II, was claimant ("Pretender") to the throne of England from which the Glorious Revolution had barred his succession. Catholic Ireland was loyal to him, and Irishmen joined him in his exile on the Continent. Because of the poverty in Ireland, many Irishmen emigrated to the West Indies and other British colonies in America; they paid their passage by binding themselves to work for a stated period for one of the planters.

parents in effect as little able to support them as those who demand our charity in the streets.

As to my own part, having turned my thoughts for many years upon this important subject, and maturely weighed the several schemes of other projectors,[4] I have always found them grossly mistaken in their computation. It is true, a child just dropped from its dam may be supported by her milk for a solar year, with little other nourishment; at most not above the value of two shillings, which the mother may certainly get, or the value in scraps, by her lawful occupation of begging; and it is exactly at one year old that I propose to provide for them in such a manner as instead of being a charge upon their parents or the parish, or wanting food and raiment for the rest of their lives, they shall on the contrary contribute to the feeding, and partly to the clothing, of many thousands.

There is likewise another great advantage in my scheme, that it will prevent those voluntary abortions, and that horrid practice of women murdering their bastard children, alas, too frequent among us, sacrificing the poor innocent babes, I doubt, more to avoid the expense than the shame, which would move tears and pity in the most savage and inhuman breast.

The number of souls in this kingdom[5] being usually reckoned one million and a half, of these I calculate there may be about two hundred thousand couple whose wives are breeders; from which number I subtract thirty thousand couples who are able to maintain their own children, although I apprehend there cannot be so many under the present distresses of the kingdom; but this being granted, there will remain an hundred and seventy thousand breeders. I again subtract fifty thousand for those women who miscarry, or whose children die by accident or disease within the year. There only remain an hundred and twenty thousand children of poor parents annually born. The question therefore is, how this number shall be reared and provided for, which, as I have already said, under the present situation of affairs, is utterly impossible by all the methods hitherto proposed. For we can neither employ them in handicraft or agriculture; we neither build houses (I mean in the country) nor cultivate land. They can very seldom pick up a livelihood by stealing till they arrive at six years old, except where they are of towardly[6] parts; although I confess they learn the rudiments much earlier, during which time they can however be looked upon only as probationers, as I have been informed by a principal gentleman in the county of Cavan, who protested to me that he never knew above one or two instances under the ages of six, even in a part of the kingdom so renowned for the quickest proficiency in that art.

I am assured by our merchants that a boy or a girl before twelve years old is no salable commodity; and even when they come to this age they will not yield above three pounds, or three pounds and half a crown at

4. Devisers of schemes.   6. Dutiful, tractable.
5. Ireland.

most on the Exchange; which cannot turn to account either to the parents or the kingdom, the charge of nutriment and rags having been at least four times that value.

I shall now therefore humbly propose my own thoughts, which I hope will not be liable to the least objection.

I have been assured by a very knowing American of my acquaintance in London, that a young healthy child well nursed is at a year old a most delicious, nourishing, and wholesome food, whether stewed, roasted, baked, or boiled; and I make no doubt that it will equally serve in a fricassee or a ragout.[7]

I do therefore humbly offer it to public consideration that of the hundred and twenty thousand children, already computed, twenty thousand may be reserved for breed, whereof only one fourth part to be males, which is more than we allow to sheep, black cattle, or swine; and my reason is that these children are seldom the fruits of marriage, a circumstance not much regarded by our savages, therefore one male will be sufficient to serve four females. That the remaining hundred thousand may at a year old be offered in sale to the persons of quality and fortune through the kingdom, always advising the mother to let them suck plentifully in the last month, so as to render them plump and fat for a good table. A child will make two dishes at an entertainment for friends; and when the family dines alone, the fore or hind quarter will make a reasonable dish, and seasoned with a little pepper or salt will be very good boiled on the fourth day, especially in winter.

I have reckoned upon a medium that a child just born will weigh twelve pounds, and in a solar year if tolerably nursed increaseth to twenty-eight pounds.

I grant this food will be somewhat dear, and therefore very proper for landlords, who, as they have already devoured most of the parents, seem to have the best title to the children.

Infant's flesh will be in season throughout the year, but more plentiful in March, and a little before and after. For we are told by a grave author, an eminent French physician,[8] that fish being a prolific diet, there are more children born in Roman Catholic countries about nine months after Lent than at any other season; therefore, reckoning a year after Lent, the markets will be more glutted than usual, because the number of popish infants is at least three to one in this kingdom; and therefore it will have one other collateral advantage, by lessening the number of Papists among us.

I have already computed the charge of nursing a beggar's child (in which list I reckon all cottagers, laborers, and four fifths of the farmers) to be about two shillings per annum, rags included; and I believe no gentleman would repine to give ten shillings for the carcass of a good fat child, which, as I have said, will make four dishes of excellent nutritive

---

7. A highly seasoned meat stew.   and a satirist, by no means grave.
8. François Rabelais (ca. 1494–1553), a humorist

meat, when he hath only some particular friend or his own family to dine with him. Thus the squire will learn to be a good landlord, and grow popular among the tenants; the mother will have eight shillings net profit, and be fit for the work till she produces another child.

Those who are more thrifty (as I must confess the times require) may flay the carcass; the skin of which artificially[9] dressed will make admirable gloves for ladies, and summer boots for fine gentlemen.

As to our city of Dublin, shambles[1] may be appointed for this purpose in the most convenient parts of it, and butchers we may be assured will not be wanting; although I rather recommend buying the children alive, and dressing them hot from the knife as we do roasting pigs.

A very worthy person, a true lover of his country, and whose virtues I highly esteem, was lately pleased in discoursing on this matter to offer a refinement upon my scheme. He said that many gentlemen of this kingdom, having of late destroyed their deer, he conceived that the want of venison might be well supplied by the bodies of young lads and maidens, not exceeding fourteen years of age nor under twelve, so great a number of both sexes in every county being now ready to starve for want of work and service; and these to be disposed of by their parents, if alive, or otherwise by their nearest relations. But with due deference to so excellent a friend and so deserving a patriot, I cannot be altogether in his sentiments; for as to the males, my American acquaintance assured me from frequent experience that their flesh was generally tough and lean, like that of our schoolboys, by continual exercise, and their taste disagreeable; and to fatten them would not answer the charge. Then as to the females, it would, I think with humble submission, be a loss to the public, because they soon would become breeders themselves; and besides, it is not improbable that some scrupulous people might be apt to censure such a practice (although indeed very unjustly) as a little bordering upon cruelty; which I confess, hath always been with me the strongest objection against any project, how well soever intended.

But in order to justify my friend, he confessed that this expedient was put into his head by the famous Psalmanazar,[2] a native of the island Formosa, who came from thence to London above twenty years ago, and in conversation told my friend that in his country when any young person happened to be put to death, the executioner sold the carcass to persons of quality as a prime dainty; and that in his time the body of a plump girl of fifteen, who was crucified for an attempt to poison the emperor, was sold to his Imperial Majesty's prime minister of state, and other great mandarins of the court, in joints from the gibbet, at four hundred crowns. Neither indeed can I deny that if the same use were made of several plump young girls in this town, who without one single

9. Skillfully.
1. Slaughterhouses.
2. George Psalmanazar (ca. 1679–1763), a famous imposter. A Frenchman, he imposed himself on English bishops, noblemen, and scientists as a Formosan. He wrote an entirely fictitious account of Formosa, in which he described human sacrifices and cannibalism.

groat to their fortunes cannot stir abroad without a chair, and appear at
the playhouse and assemblies in foreign fineries which they never will
pay for, the kingdom would not be the worse.

Some persons of a desponding spirit are in great concern about that
vast number of poor people who are aged, diseased, or maimed, and I
have been desired to employ my thoughts what course may be taken to
ease the nation of so grievous an encumbrance. But I am not in the least
pain upon that matter, because it is very well known that they are every
day dying and rotting by cold and famine, and filth and vermin, as fast
as can be reasonably expected. And as to the younger laborers, they are
now in almost as hopeful a condition. They cannot get work, and consequently pine away for want of nourishment to a degree that if at any
time they are accidentally hired to common labor, they have not strength
to perform it; and thus the country and themselves are happily delivered
from the evils to come.

I have too long digressed, and therefore shall return to my subject. I
think the advantages by the proposal which I have made are obvious and
many, as well as of the highest importance.

For first, as I have already observed, it would greatly lessen the number of Papists, with whom we are yearly overrun, being the principal
breeders of the nation as well as our most dangerous enemies; and who
stay at home on purpose to deliver the kingdom to the Pretender, hoping
to take their advantage by the absence of so many good Protestants, who
have chosen rather to leave their country than stay at home and pay
tithes against their conscience to an Episcopal curate.

Secondly, the poorer tenants will have something valuable of their
own, which by law may be made liable to distress,[3] and help to pay their
landlord's rent, their corn and cattle being already seized and money a
thing unknown.

Thirdly, whereas the maintenance of an hundred thousand children,
from two years old and upwards, cannot be computed at less than ten
shillings a piece per annum, the nation's stock will be thereby increased
fifty thousand pounds per annum, besides the profit of a new dish introduced to the tables of all gentlemen of fortune in the kingdom who have
any refinement in taste. And the money will circulate among ourselves,
the goods being entirely of our own growth and manufacture.

Fourthly, the constant breeders, besides the gain of eight shillings
sterling per annum by the sale of their children, will be rid of the charge
of maintaining them after the first year.

Fifthly, this food would likewise bring great custom to taverns, where
the vintners will certainly be so prudent as to procure the best receipts
for dressing it to perfection, and consequently have their houses frequented by all the fine gentlemen, who justly value themselves upon

3. Distraint, i.e., the seizing, through legal action, of property for the payment of debts and other obligations.

their knowledge in good eating; and a skillful cook, who understands how to oblige his guests, will contrive to make it as expensive as they please.

Sixthly, this would be a great inducement to marriage, which all wise nations have either encouraged by rewards or enforced by laws and penalties. It would increase the care and tenderness of mothers toward their children, when they were sure of a settlement for life to the poor babes, provided in some sort by the public, to their annual profit instead of expense. We should see an honest emulation among the married women, which of them could bring the fattest child to the market. Men would become as fond of their wives during the time of their pregnancy as they are now of their mares in foal, their cows in calf, or sows when they are ready to farrow; nor offer to beat or kick them (as is too frequent a practice) for fear of a miscarriage.

Many other advantages might be enumerated. For instance, the addition of some thousand carcasses in our exportation of barreled beef, the propagation of swine's flesh, and improvement in the art of making good bacon, so much wanted among us by the great destruction of pigs, too frequent at our tables, which are no way comparable in taste or magnificence to a well-grown, fat, yearling child, which roasted whole will make a considerable figure at a lord mayor's feast or any other public entertainment. But this and many others I omit, being studious of brevity.

Supposing that one thousand families in this city would be constant customers for infants' flesh, besides others who might have it at merry meetings, particularly weddings and christenings, I compute that Dublin would take off annually about twenty thousand carcasses, and the rest of the kingdom (where probably they will be sold somewhat cheaper) the remaining eighty thousand.

I can think of no one objection that will probably be raised against this proposal, unless it should be urged that the number of people will be thereby much lessened in the kingdom. This I freely own, and it was indeed one principal design in offering it to the world. I desire the reader will observe, that I calculate my remedy for this one individual kingdom of Ireland and for no other that ever was, is, or I think ever can be upon earth. Therefore let no man talk to me of other expedients: of taxing our absentees at five shillings a pound: of using neither clothes nor household furniture except what is of our own growth and manufacture: of utterly rejecting the materials and instruments that promote foreign luxury: of curing the expensiveness of pride, vanity, idleness, and gaming in our women: of introducing a vein of parsimony, prudence, and temperance: of learning to love our country, in the want of which we differ even from Laplanders and the inhabitants of Topinamboo:[4] of quitting

---

4. I.e., even Laplanders love their frozen, infertile country and the savage tribes of Brazil their jungle more than the Anglo-Irish love Ireland.

our animosities and factions, nor acting any longer like the Jews, who were murdering one another at the very moment their city was taken:[5] of being a little cautious not to sell our country and conscience for nothing: of teaching landlords to have at least one degree of mercy toward their tenants: lastly, of putting a spirit of honesty, industry, and skill into our shopkeepers; who, if a resolution could now be taken to buy only our native goods, would immediately unite to cheat and exact upon us in the price, the measure, and the goodness, nor could ever yet be brought to make one fair proposal of just dealing, though often and earnestly invited to it.[6]

Therefore I repeat, let no man talk to me of these and the like expedients, till he hath at least some glimpse of hope that there will ever be some hearty and sincere attempt to put them in practice.

But as to myself, having been wearied out for many years with offering vain, idle, visionary thoughts, and at length utterly despairing of success, I fortunately fell upon this proposal, which, as it is wholly new, so it hath something solid and real, of no expense and little trouble, full in our own power, and whereby we can incur no danger in disobliging England. For this kind of commodity will not bear exportation, the flesh being of too tender a consistence to admit a long continuance in salt, although perhaps I could name a country which would be glad to eat up our whole nation without it.[7]

After all, I am not so violently bent upon my own opinion as to reject any offer proposed by wise men, which shall be found equally innocent, cheap, easy, and effectual. But before something of that kind shall be advanced in contradiction to my scheme, and offering a better, I desire the author or authors will be pleased maturely to consider two points. First, as things now stand, how they will be able to find food and raiment for an hundred thousand useless mouths and backs. And secondly, there being a round million of creatures in human figure throughout this kingdom, whose sole subsistence put into a common stock would leave them in debt two millions of pounds sterling, adding those who are beggars by profession to the bulk of farmers, cottagers, and laborers, with their wives and children who are beggars in effect; I desire those politicians who dislike my overture, and may perhaps be so bold to attempt an answer, that they will first ask the parents of these mortals whether they would not at this day think it a great happiness to have been sold for food at a year old in the manner I prescribe, and thereby have avoided such a perpetual sense of misfortunes as they have since gone through by the oppression of landlords, the impossibility of paying rent without money or trade, the want of common sustenance, with neither house nor clothes to cover them from the inclemencies of the weather, and the

5. During the siege of Jerusalem by the Roman Emperor Titus, who captured and destroyed the city in A.D. 70, the city was torn by bloody fights between factions of fanatics.
6. Swift himself had made all these proposals in various pamphlets. In editions printed during his lifetime the various proposals were italicized to indicate that Swift is no longer being ironic.
7. I.e., England.

most inevitable prospect of entailing the like or greater miseries upon
their breed forever.

I profess, in the sincerity of my heart, that I have not the least personal
interest in endeavoring to promote this necessary work, having no other
motive than the public good of my country, by advancing our trade,
providing for infants, relieving the poor, and giving some pleasure to the
rich. I have no children by which I can propose to get a single penny;
the youngest being nine years old, and my wife past childbearing.

1729

ALEXANDER POPE
1688–1744

1711:   *Essay on Criticism.*
1712:   First version of *The Rape of the Lock.*
1713–26: Translating Homer, editing Shakespeare.
1728:   The *Dunciad* begins Pope's career as major verse sati-
        rist.
1733–34: The *Essay on Man* begins his career as ethical and
        philosophical poet.

Pope is the only important writer of his generation who was solely a man of
letters. Since he could not, as a Roman Catholic, attend a university, vote,
or hold public office, he was excluded from the sort of patronage that was
freely bestowed by statesmen on most writers during the reign of Anne. This
disadvantage he turned into a positive good, for the translation of Homer's
Iliad and *Odyssey*, which he undertook for profit as well as for fame, gave
him ample means to live the life of an independent suburban gentleman.
After 1718 he lived hospitably in his villa by the Thames at Twickenham
(then pronounced *Twit'nam*), entertaining his friends and converting his
five acres of land into a diminutive landscape garden. Almost exactly a century earlier, Shakespeare had earned enough to retire to a country estate at
Stratford—but he had been an actor-manager as well as a playwright; Pope
was the first English writer to demonstrate that literature alone could be a
gainful profession.

Ill health plagued Pope almost from birth. Delicate as a child, he was
early stunted and deformed by tuberculosis of the spine. His father, a well-
to-do London merchant, retired from business in the year of the poet's birth,
and about 1700 acquired a small property at Binfield in Windsor Forest. In
rural surroundings, as the boy's health improved, he early acquired his lifelong taste for natural beauty and for gardening. There he completed by wide
reading the desultory schooling that both his ill health and his religion had
made inevitable, and, encouraged by his father, he began also to develop
his precocious talent for poetry. But Pope was never to enjoy good health:

in later life he was troubled by violent headaches, and he suffered from easily exacerbated nerves, perhaps a price he had to pay for the sensitive and ardent temperament that helped make him one of our greatest poets.

Pope's first striking success as a poet was the *Essay on Criticism* (1711), which earned him the fame of Addison's approval and the notoriety of an intemperate personal attack from the critic John Dennis, who was angered by a casual reference to himself in the poem. *The Rape of the Lock*, both in its original shorter version of 1712 and in its more elaborate version of 1714, established the author as a master not only of metrics and of language, but also of witty, urbane satire. In the *Essay on Criticism*, Pope had excelled all his predecessors in writing a didactic poem after the example of Horace; in the *Rape*, he had written the most brilliant mock epic in the language. But there was another vein in Pope's youthful poetry, much of which, concerned as it is with natural beauty and love, reveals a temperament that in a later poet might have been called "Romantic." The *Pastorals* (1709), Pope's first publication, and *Windsor Forest* (1713; much of it was written earlier) abound in visual imagery and descriptive passages of ideally ordered nature; they remind us that Pope was an amateur painter. The *Elegy to the Memory of an Unfortunate Lady*, published in the collected poems of 1717, presents the high heroics of romantic love. And even the long task of translating Homer, the "dull duty" of editing Shakespeare, and, in middle age, his preoccupation with ethical and satirical poetry did not extinguish this side of Pope's nature and art. He learned to subordinate, but he did not cease to use, this sensitive awareness of visual beauty in his later poetry.

Pope's early poetry brought him to the attention of literary men, with whom he began to associate in the masculine world of coffeehouse and tavern. His fragile health never permitted him to live the rakish life that he would have liked, but it did not prevent his enjoying the company of some of the most distinguished authors of the time. Between 1706 and 1711 he came to know, among many others, William Congreve, William Walsh, the critic and poet, and Richard Steele and Joseph Addison. As it happened, all were Whigs. Pope could readily ignore politics in the excitement of taking his place among the leading wits of the town. But after the fall of the Whigs in 1710, and the formation of the Tory government under Robert Harley (later earl of Oxford) and Henry St. John (later Viscount Bolingbroke) party loyalties bred bitterness among the wits as among the politicians.

By 1712, Pope had made the acquaintance of another group of writers, all Tories, who soon became his intimate friends: Jonathan Swift, by then the close associate of Harley and St. John and the principal propagandist for their policies; Dr. John Arbuthnot, physician to the queen, a learned scientist, a wit, and a man of humanity and integrity; John Gay, the poet, who in 1728 was to produce the *Beggar's Opera*, the greatest theatrical success of the century; and the poet Thomas Parnell. It was among these men that Pope was to find his lifelong friends; and it was through them that he became the friend and admirer of Oxford, and later the intimate of Bolingbroke. In 1714 this group, at the instigation of Pope, formed a club which was to cooperate in a scheme for satirizing all sorts of false learning and pedantry. The friends proposed to write jointly the biography of a learned fool whom they named Martinus Scriblerus (Martin the Scribbler), whose life and opinions would be a running commentary on whatever they considered the abuses of learning and the follies of the learned. Some amusing episodes were later rewritten and published as the *Memoirs of Martinus Scriblerus* (1741). The real importance of the club, however, is that it fostered a satiric temper which was to find unexpected expression in such mature works of the friends as *Gulliver's Travels*, the *Dunciad*, and even, perhaps, the *Beggar's Opera*.

"The life of a wit is a warfare on earth," said Pope, generalizing from his own experience. His very success as a poet (and his astonishing precocity brought him success very early) made enemies among less talented writers, who were to plague him in pamphlets, verse satires, and squibs in the journals throughout his entire literary career. He was attacked for his writings, his religion, and his physical deformity. Though he smarted under the jibes of his detractors, he was a fighter who struck back, always giving better than he got. Pope's literary warfare began in 1713, when he announced his intention of translating the *Iliad* and sought subscribers to a deluxe edition of the work. Subscribers came in droves, but the Whig writers who surrounded Addison at Button's Coffee House did all they could through anonymous attacks to hinder the success of the venture. The eventual success of the first published installment of his *Iliad* in 1715 did not obliterate Pope's just resentment against Addison and his "little senate"; and this resentment found expression in the damaging portrait of Addison (under the name of Atticus), which, years after it was written, was included in Pope's *Epistle to Dr. Arbuthnot* (1735), lines 193–214. The not unjustified attacks on Pope's edition of Shakespeare (1725), especially those by the learned Shakespeare scholar Lewis Theobald (Pope always spelled and pronounced the name "Tibbald" in his satires), led to Theobald's appearance as king of the dunces in the *Dunciad* (1728). In this impressive poem Pope stigmatized his literary enemies as agents of all that he disliked and feared in the literary tendencies of his time—the vulgarization of taste and the arts consequent on the rapid growth of the reading public, the development of journalism, magazines, and other popular and cheap publications, which spread scandal, sensationalism, and political partisanship—in short the new commercial spirit of the nation, which was corrupting not only the arts, but, as Pope saw it, the national life itself.

In the 1730s Pope moved on to philosophical, ethical, and political subjects in the *Essay on Man*, the *Epistles to Several Persons*, and the *Imitations of Horace*. The reigns of George I and George II appeared to him, as to Swift and other Tories, a period of rapid moral, political, and cultural deterioration. The agents of decay seemed in one way or another related to the spread of moneyed (as opposed to landed) wealth, which accounted for the political corruption encouraged by Sir Robert Walpole and the court party, and the increasing influence in all aspects of the national life of a vulgar class of *nouveaux riches*. Pope assumed the role of the champion of traditional civilization: of right reason, humanistic learning, sound art, good taste, and public virtue. It was fortunate that most of his enemies seem to have been designed by nature to illustrate various degrees of unreason, pedantry, bad art, vulgar taste, and, at best, indifferent morals.

The satirist traditionally deals in generally prevalent evils and generally observable human types, not with particular individuals. So too with Pope; the bulk of his satire can be read and enjoyed without much biographical information. Usually in the late satires, as in the earlier *Rape*, he used fictional or type names, although he most often had an individual in mind—Sappho, Atossa, Atticus, Sporus; and when he named individuals (as he consistently did in the *Dunciad* and occasionally elsewhere), his purpose was to raise his victims to the bad eminence of typifying some sort of obliquity. To judge and censure the age, Pope also created the "I" of the satires (not identical with Alexander Pope of Twickenham). This fictional or semi-fictional figure is the detached observer, somewhat removed from City, town, and court, the centers of corruption; he is the friend of the virtuous, whose friendship for him testifies to his integrity; he is fond of peace, country life, the arts, morality, and truth, and he detests their opposites which flourish in the great world. In such an age, Pope implies, it is impossible for such a man—honest, truthful, blunt—not to write satire.

Pope was a master of style. From first to last, his verse is notable for its rhythmic variety, despite the apparently rigid metrical unit—the heroic couplet—in which he wrote; the precision of meaning and the harmony (or the expressive disharmony, when necessary) of his language; and the union of maximum conciseness with maximum complexity. Something of Pope's metrical variety and verbal harmony can be observed in even so short a passage as lines 71–76 of the pastoral *Summer* (1709), lines so lyrical that, in *Semele*, Handel set them to music. In the passage quoted below (as also in the following quotation), only those rhetorical stresses which distort the normal iambic flow of the verse have been marked; internal pauses within the line are indicated by single and double bars, alliteration and assonance by italics.

> Óh déign to visit our *forsaken seats*,
> The mossy *fountains* ‖ and the *green retreats!*
>
> Where'er yóu wálk ‖ cóol gáles shall *fan* the *glade*,
>
> Trées whére yóu sít ‖ shall crowd into a shade:
>
> Where'er yóu tŕead ‖ the bl*ush*ing *flowers* shall rise,
>
> And all thíngs *flóurish* where yóu túrn your eyes.

Pope has attained metrical variety by the free substitution of trochees and spondees for the normal iambs; he has achieved rhythmic variety by arranging phrases and clauses (units of syntax and logic) of different lengths within single lines and couplets, so that the passage moves with the sinuous fluency of thought and feeling; and he has not only chosen musical combinations of words, but has also subtly modulated the harmony of the passage by unobtrusive patterns of alliteration and assonance.

Contrast with this pastoral passage lines 16–25 of the *Epilogue to the Satires, Dialogue* 2 (1738), in which Pope is not making music, but is imitating actual conversation so realistically that the metrical pattern and the integrity of the couplet and individual line seem to be destroyed (though in fact they are very much present). In a dialogue with a friend who warns him that his satire is too personal, indeed mere libel, the poet-satirist replies:

> Yé státesmen, ‖ priests of one religion all!
>
> Yé trádesmen vile ‖ in army, court, or hall!
>
> Yé réverend atheists. ‖ F. Scandal! ‖ name them, ‖ Who?
>   P. Why that's the thing you bid me not to do.
>
> Whó stárved a sister, ‖ who foreswore a debt,

Í néver named; ‖ the town's inquiring yet.

The poisoning dame— | F. Yóu méan— | P. I don't— | F. Yóu dó.

P. Sée, nów Í kéep the secret, ‖ and nót yóu!

The bribing statesman— | F. Hóld, ‖ tóo hígh you go.

P. The bribed elector— ‖ F. Thére you stoop tóo lów.

In such a passage the language and rhythms of poetry merge with the language and rhythms of impassioned living speech.

A fine example of Pope's ability to derive the maximum of meaning from the most economic use of language and image is the description of the manor house in which lives old Cotta, the miser (*Epistle to Lord Bathurst*, lines 187–196):

> Like some lone Chartreuse stands the good old Hall,
> Silence without, and fasts within the wall;
> No raftered roofs with dance and tabor sound,
> No noontide bell invites the country round;
> Tenants with sighs the smokeless towers survey,
> And turn the unwilling steeds another way;
> Benighted wanderers, the forest o'er,
> Curse the saved candle and unopening door;
> While the gaunt mastiff growling at the gate,
> Affrights the beggar whom he longs to eat.

The first couplet of this passage, which associates the "Hall," symbol of English rural hospitality, with the Grande Chartreuse, the monastery in the French Alps, which, though a place of "silence" and "fasts" for the monks, afforded food and shelter to all travelers, clashes forcefully with the dismal details of Cotta's miserly dwelling; and the meaning of the scene is concentrated in the grotesque image of the last couplet: the half-starved watchdog and the frightened beggar confronting each other in mutual hunger.

But there is another sort of variety within Pope's work as a whole which derives from the poet's respect for the idea that the different kinds of literature have their different and appropriate styles. Thus the *Essay on Criticism*, an informal discussion of literary theory, is written, like Horace's *Art of Poetry*, a similarly didactic poem, in a plain style, the easy language of well-bred talk. *The Rape of the Lock*, being "a heroi-comical poem" (that is, a comic poem that treats trivial material in an epic style), employs the lofty heroic language that Dryden had perfected in his translation of Virgil, and introduces amusing parodies of passages in *Paradise Lost*; parodies later raised to truly Miltonic sublimity and complexity by the conclusion of the *Dunciad*. The grave epistles that make up the *Essay on Man*, a philosophical discussion of such majestic themes as the Creator and his creation, the universe, human nature, society, and happiness, are written in a stately forensic language and tone and constantly employ the traditional rhetorical figures. The *Imitations of Horace*, and, above all, the *Epistle to Dr. Arbuthnot*, his finest poem "in the Horatian way," reveal Pope's final mastery of the plain style of Horace's epistles and satires and justify his image of himself as the heir of the Roman poet. In short no other poet of the century can equal

Pope in the range of his materials, the diversity of his poetic styles, and his mastery of the poet's craft.

An Essay on Criticism

There is no pleasanter introduction to the canons of taste in the English Augustan age than Pope's *Essay on Criticism*. As Addison said in his review in *Spectator* 253, it assembles the "most known and most received observations on the subject of literature and criticism." Pope was attempting to do for his time what Horace, in his *Art of Poetry*, and what Nicolas Boileau (French poet of the age of Louis XIV), in his *L'Art Poétique*, had done for theirs. Horace is not only one of Pope's instructors in the principles of criticism; he is also Pope's model in this poem, especially in the simple, conversational language, the tone of well-bred ease, and the deliberately plain style.

In framing his critical creed, Pope did not try for novelty: he wished merely to give to generally accepted doctrines pleasing and memorable expression and make them useful to modern poets. Here one meets the key words of neoclassical criticism: *wit, Nature, ancients, rules, genius*. *Wit* in the poem is a word of many meanings—a clever remark, or the man who makes it; a conceit; liveliness of mind; inventiveness; fancy; genius; a genius; poetry itself, among others. *Nature* is an equally ambiguous word, meaning not "things out there," or "the outdoors," but most importantly that which is representative, universal, permanent in human experience as opposed to the idiosyncratic, the individual, the temporary. In line 21, "Nature" comes close to meaning "intuitive knowledge." In line 52, it means that half-personified power manifested in the cosmic order, which in its modes of working is a model for art. The reverence felt by most Augustans for the works of the great writers of ancient Greece and Rome raised the question how far the authority of these *ancients* extended. Were their works to be received as models to be conscientiously imitated? Were the *rules* received from them or deducible from their works to be accepted as prescriptive laws or merely convenient guides? Was individual *genius* to be bound by what has been conventionally held to be *Nature*, by the authority of the *ancients*, and by the legalistic pedantry of *rules*? Or could it go its own way?

In part 1 of the *Essay* Pope constructs a harmonious system in which he effects a compromise among all these conflicting forces—a compromise which is typically 18th century in spirit. Part 2 analyzes the causes of faulty criticism. Part 3 characterizes the good critic and praises the great critics of the past.

An Essay on Criticism

Part 1

'Tis hard to say, if greater want of skill
Appear in writing or in judging ill;
But of the two less dangerous is the offense
To tire our patience than mislead our sense.
Some few in that, but numbers err in this,   5

Ten censure[1] wrong for one who writes amiss;
A fool might once himself alone expose,
Now one in verse makes many more in prose.
    'Tis with our judgments as our watches, none
Go just alike, yet each believes his own.   10
In poets as true genius is but rare,
True taste as seldom is the critic's share;
Both must alike from Heaven derive their light,
These born to judge, as well as those to write.
Let such teach others who themselves excel,   15
And censure freely who have written well.
Authors are partial to their wit, 'tis true,
But are not critics to their judgment too?
    Yet if we look more closely, we shall find
Most have the seeds of judgment in their mind: 20
Nature affords at least a glimmering light;
The lines, though touched but faintly, are drawn right.
But as the slightest sketch, if justly traced,⎤
Is by ill coloring but the more disgraced, ⎬
So by false learning is good sense defaced:⎦   25
Some are bewildered in the maze of schools,
And some made coxcombs[2] Nature meant but fools.
In search of wit these lose their common sense,
And then turn critics in their own defense:
Each burns alike, who can, or cannot write,   30
Or with a rival's or an eunuch's spite.
All fools have still an itching to deride,
And fain would be upon the laughing side.
If Maevius[3] scribble in Apollo's spite,
There are who judge still worse than he can write.   35
    Some have at first for wits, then poets passed,
Turned critics next, and proved plain fools at last.
Some neither can for wits nor critics pass,
As heavy mules are neither horse nor ass.
Those half-learn'd witlings, numerous in our isle,   40
As half-formed insects on the banks of Nile;[4]
Unfinished things, one knows not what to call,
Their generation's so equivocal:
To tell[5] them would a hundred tongues require,
Or one vain wit's, that might a hundred tire.   45
    But you who seek to give and merit fame,
And justly bear a critic's noble name,
Be sure yourself and your own reach to know,
How far your genius, taste, and learning go;
Launch not beyond your depth, but be discreet,   50

---

1. Judge
2. Superficial pretenders to learning.
3. A silly poet alluded to contemptuously by Virgil in *Eclogue* 3 and by Horace in *Epode* 10.
4. The ancients believed that many forms of life were spontaneously generated in the fertile mud of the Nile.
5. Reckon, count.

And mark that point where sense and dullness meet.
    Nature to all things fixed the limits fit,
And wisely curbed proud man's pretending wit.
As on the land while here the ocean gains,
In other parts it leaves wide sandy plains;   55
Thus in the soul while memory prevails,
The solid power of understanding fails;
Where beams of warm imagination play,
The memory's soft figures melt away.
One science[6] only will one genius fit,   60
So vast is art, so narrow human wit.
Not only bounded to peculiar arts,
But oft in those confined to single parts.
Like kings we lose the conquests gained before,
By vain ambition still to make them more;   65
Each might his several province well command,
Would all but stoop to what they understand.
    First follow Nature, and your judgment frame
By her just standard, which is still the same;
Unerring Nature, still divinely bright,   70
One clear, unchanged, and universal light,
Life, force, and beauty must to all impart,
At once the source, and end, and test of art.
Art from that fund each just supply provides,
Works without show, and without pomp presides.   75
In some fair body thus the informing soul
With spirits feeds, with vigor fills the whole,
Each motion guides, and every nerve sustains;
Itself unseen, but in the effects remains.
Some, to whom Heaven in wit has been profuse,   80
Want as much more to turn it to its use;
For wit and judgment often are at strife,
Though meant each other's aid, like man and wife.
'Tis more to guide than spur the Muse's steed,
Restrain his fury than provoke his speed;   85
The wingèd courser,[7] like a generous horse,
Shows most true mettle when you check his course.
    Those rules of old discovered, not devised,
Are Nature still, but Nature methodized;
Nature, like liberty, is but restrained   90
By the same laws which first herself ordained.
    Hear how learn'd Greece her useful rules indites,
When to repress and when indulge our flights:
High on Parnassus' top her sons she showed,
And pointed out those arduous paths they trod;   95
Held from afar, aloft, the immortal prize,
And urged the rest by equal steps to rise.

6. Branch of learning.
7. Pegasus, associated with the Muses and poetic inspiration; "generous": spirited, highly bred.

Just precepts thus from great examples given,
She drew from them what they derived from Heaven.
The generous critic fanned the poet's fire,   100
And taught the world with reason to admire.
Then criticism the Muse's handmaid proved,
To dress her charms, and make her more beloved:
But following wits from that intention strayed,
Who could not win the mistress, wooed the maid;   105
Against the poets their own arms they turned,
Sure to hate most the men from whom they learned.
So modern 'pothecaries, taught the art
By doctors's bills[8] to play the doctor's part,
Bold in the practice of mistaken rules,   110
Prescribe, apply, and call their masters fools.
Some on the leaves of ancient authors prey,
Nor time nor moths e'er spoiled so much as they.
Some dryly plain, without invention's aid,
Write dull receipts[9] how poems may be made.   115
These leave the sense their learning to display,
And those explain the meaning quite away.
　　You then whose judgment the right course would steer,
Know well each ancient's proper character;
His fable,[1] subject, scope in every page;   120
Religion, country, genius of his age:
Without all these at once before your eyes,
Cavil you may, but never criticize.
Be Homer's works your study and delight,
Read them by day, and meditate by night;   125
Thence form your judgment, thence your maxims bring,
And trace the Muses upward to their spring.
Still with itself compared, his text peruse;
And let your comment be the Mantuan Muse.[2]
　　When first young Maro in his boundless mind   130
A work to outlast immortal Rome designed,
Perhaps he seemed above the critic's law,
And but from Nature's fountains scorned to draw;
But when to examine every part he came,
Nature and Homer were, he found, the same.   135
Convinced, amazed, he checks the bold design, ⎫
And rules as strict his labored work confine ⎬
As if the Stagirite[3] o'erlooked each line. ⎭
Learn hence for ancient rules a just esteem;

8. Prescriptions.
9. Formulas for preparing a dish; recipes. Pope himself wrote an amusing burlesque *Receipt to Make an Epic Poem*, first published in the *Guardian* 78 (1713).
1. Plot or story of a play or poem; "Scope": aim or purpose.
2. Virgil, the "young Maro" of the following line, was born in a village adjacent to Mantua in Italy;

hence "Mantuan Muse." His epic, the *Aeneid*, was modeled on Homer's *Iliad* and *Odyssey* and was considered to be a refinement on the Greek poems. Thus it could be thought of as a commentary ("comment") on Homer's poems.
3. Aristotle, native of Stagira, from whose *Poetics* later critics formulated strict rules for writing tragedy and the epic.

To copy Nature is to copy them.   140
    Some beauties yet no precepts can declare,
For there's a happiness as well as care.[4]
Music resembles poetry, in each   ⎫
Are nameless graces which no methods teach,   ⎬
And which a master hand alone can reach.   ⎭   145
If, where the rules not far enough extend
(Since rules were made but to promote their end)
Some lucky license answers to the full
The intent proposed, that license is a rule.
Thus Pegasus, a nearer way to take,   150
May boldly deviate from the common track.
Great wits sometimes may gloriously offend,
And rise to faults true critics dare not mend;
From vulgar bounds with brave disorder part,
And snatch a grace beyond the reach of art,   155
Which without passing through the judgment, gains
The heart, and all its end at once attains.
In prospects thus, some objects please our eyes, ⎫
Which out of Nature's common order rise,   ⎬
The shapeless rock, or hanging precipice.   ⎭   160
But though the ancients thus their rules invade
(As kings dispense with laws themselves have made)
Moderns, beware! or if you must offend
Against the precept, ne'er transgress its end;
Let it be seldom, and compelled by need;   165
And have at least their precedent to plead.
The critic else proceeds without remorse,
Seizes your fame, and puts his laws in force.
    I know there are, to whose presumptuous thoughts
Those freer beauties, even in them, seem faults.[5]   170
Some figures monstrous and misshaped appear,
Considered singly, or beheld too near,
Which, but proportioned to their light or place,
Due distance reconciles to form and grace.
A prudent chief not always must display   175
His powers in equal ranks and fair array,
But with the occasion and the place comply,
Conceal his force, nay seem sometimes to fly.
Those oft are stratagems which errors seem,
Nor is it Homer nods, but we that dream.   180
    Still green with bays each ancient altar stands
Above the reach of sacrilegious hands,
Secure from flames, from envy's fiercer rage,
Destructive war, and all-involving age.
See, from each clime the learn'd their incense bring!   185

---

4. I.e., no rules ("precepts") can explain ("declare', ("happiness"), not of painstaking labor ("care").
some beautiful effects in a work of art which can   5. Pronounced *fawts*.
be the result only of inspiration or good luck

Here in all tongues consenting[6] paeans ring!
In praise so just let every voice be joined,[7]
And fill the general chorus of mankind.
Hail, bards triumphant! born in happier days,
Immortal heirs of universal praise!   190
Whose honors with increase of ages grow,
As streams roll down, enlarging as they flow;
Nations unborn your mighty names shall sound,
And worlds applaud that must not yet be found!
Oh, may some spark of your celestial fire,   195
The last, the meanest of your sons inspire
(That on weak wings, from far, pursues your flights,
Glows while he reads, but trembles as he writes)
To teach vain wits a science little known,
To admire superior sense, and doubt their own!   200

Part 2

Of all the causes which conspire to blind
Man's erring judgment, and misguide the mind,
What the weak head with strongest bias rules,
Is pride, the never-failing vice of fools.
Whatever Nature has in worth denied,   205
She gives in large recruits[8] of needful pride;
For as in bodies, thus in souls, we find
What wants in blood and spirits swelled with wind:
Pride, where wit fails, steps in to our defense,
And fills up all the mighty void of sense.   210
If once right reason drives that cloud away,
Truth breaks upon us with resistless day.
Trust not yourself: but your defects to know,
Make use of every friend—and every foe.
A little learning is a dangerous thing;   215
Drink deep, or taste not the Pierian spring.[9]
There shallow draughts intoxicate the brain,
And drinking largely sobers us again.
Fired at first sight with what the Muse imparts,
In fearless youth we tempt[1] the heights of arts,   220
While from the bounded level of our mind
Short views we take, nor see the lengths behind;
But more advanced, behold with strange surprise
New distant scenes of endless science rise!
So pleased at first the towering Alps we try,   225
Mount o'er the vales, and seem to tread the sky,
The eternal snows appear already past,
And the first clouds and mountains seem the last;

6. Agreeing, concurring.
7. Pronounced *jined*.
8. Supplies.

9. The spring in Pieria on Mt. Olympus, sacred
to the Muses.
1. Attempt.

But, those attained, we tremble to survey
The growing labors of the lengthened way,   230
The increasing prospect tires our wandering eyes,
Hills peep o'er hills, and Alps on Alps arise!
    A perfect judge will read each work of wit
With the same spirit that its author writ:
Survey the whole, nor seek slight faults to find   235
Where Nature moves, and rapture warms the mind;
Nor lose, for that malignant dull delight,
The generous pleasure to be charmed with wit.
But in such lays as neither ebb nor flow,
Correctly cold, and regularly low,   240
That, shunning faults, one quiet tenor keep,
We cannot blame indeed—but we may sleep.
In wit, as nature, what affects our hearts
Is not the exactness of peculiar parts;
'Tis not a lip, or eye, we beauty call,   245
But the joint force and full result of all.
Thus when we view some well-proportioned dome
(The world's just wonder, and even thine, O Rome!),[2]
No single parts unequally surprise,
All comes united to the admiring eyes: 250
No monstrous height, or breadth, or length appear;
The whole at once is bold and regular.
    Whoever thinks a faultless piece to see,
Thinks what ne'er was, nor is, nor e'er shall be.
In every work regard the writer's end,   255
Since none can compass more than they intend;
And if the means be just, the conduct true,
Applause, in spite of trivial faults, is due.
As men of breeding, sometimes men of wit,
To avoid great errors must the less commit,   260
Neglect the rules each verbal critic lays,
For not to know some trifles is a praise.
Most critics, fond of some subservient art,
Still make the whole depend upon a part:
They talk of principles, but notions prize,   265
And all to one loved folly sacrifice.
    Once on a time La Mancha's knight,[3] they say,
A certain bard encountering on the way,
Discoursed in terms as just, with looks as sage,
As e'er could Dennis,[4] of the Grecian stage;   270
Concluding all were desperate sots and fools
Who durst depart from Aristotle's rules.

---

2. The dome of St. Peter's, designed by Michelangelo.
3. Don Quixote. The story comes not from Cer-
vantes' novel, but from a spurious sequel to it by
Don Alonzo Fernandez de Avellaneda.
4. John Dennis (1657–1734), though one of the
leading critics of the time, was frequently ridiculed
by the wits for his irascibility and his rather solemn
pomposity. Pope apparently did not know Dennis
personally, but his jibe at him in part 3 of this
poem incurred the critic's lasting animosity.

Our author, happy in a judge so nice,
Produced his play, and begged the knight's advice;
Made him observe the subject and the plot,   275
The manners, passions, unities; what not?
All which exact to rule were brought about,
Were but a combat in the lists left out.
"What! leave the combat out?" exclaims the knight.
"Yes, or we must renounce the Stagirite."   280
"Not so, by Heaven!" he answers in a rage,
"Knights, squires, and steeds must enter on the stage."
"So vast a throng the stage can ne'er contain."
"Then build a new, or act it in a plain."
    Thus critics of less judgment than caprice,   285
Curious,[5] not knowing, not exact, but nice,
Form short ideas, and offend in arts
(As most in manners), by a love to parts.
    Some to conceit[6] alone their taste confine,
And glittering thoughts struck out at every line;   290
Pleased with a work where nothing's just or fit,
One glaring chaos and wild heap of wit.
Poets, like painters, thus unskilled to trace
The naked nature and the living grace,
With gold and jewels cover every part,   295
And hide with ornaments their want of art.
    True wit is Nature to advantage dressed,
What oft was thought, but ne'er so well expressed;
Something whose truth convinced at sight we find,
That gives us back the image of our mind.   300
As shades more sweetly recommend the light,
So modest plainness sets off sprightly wit;
For works may have more wit than does them good,
As bodies perish through excess of blood.
    Others for language all their care express,   305
And value books, as women men, for dress.
Their praise is still—the style is excellent;
The sense they humbly take upon contènt.[7]
Words are like leaves; and where they most abound,
Much fruit of sense beneath is rarely found.   310
False eloquence, like the prismatic glass,
Its gaudy colors spreads on every place;[8]
The face of Nature we no more survey,
All glares alike, without distinction gay.
But true expression, like the unchanging sun, ⎤   315
Clears and improves whate'er it shines upon; ⎬
It gilds all objects, but it alters none.   ⎦

---

5. Laboriously careful. "Nice": minutely accurate, over refined.
6. Pointed wit, ingenuity and extravagance, or affectation in the use of figures, especially similes and metaphors.

7. Mere acquiescence.
8. A very up-to-date scientific reference. Newton's *Optics*, which treated of the prism and the spectrum, had been published in 1704, though his theories had been known earlier.

Expression is the dress of thought, and still
Appears more decent as more suitable.
A vile conceit in pompous words expressed   320
Is like a clown[9] in regal purple dressed:
For different styles with different subjects sort,
As several garbs with country, town, and court.
Some by old words to fame have made pretense,
Ancients in phrase, mere moderns in their sense.   325
Such labored nothings, in so strange a style,
Amaze the unlearn'd, and make the learned smile;
Unlucky as Fungoso[1] in the play,   ⎤
These sparks with awkward vanity display   ⎬
What the fine gentleman wore yesterday;   ⎦   330
And but so mimic ancient wits at best,
As apes our grandsires in their doublets dressed.
In words as fashions the same rule will hold,
Alike fantastic if too new or old:
Be not the first by whom the new are tried,   335
Nor yet the last to lay the old aside.
    But most by numbers[2] judge a poet's song,
And smooth or rough with them is right or wrong.
In the bright Muse though thousand charms conspire,
Her voice is all these tuneful fools admire,   340
Who haunt Parnassus but to please their ear,   ⎤
Not mend their minds; as some to church repair,   ⎬
Not for the doctrine, but the music there.   ⎦
These equal syllables alone require,
Though oft the ear the open vowels tire,[3]   345
While expletives[4] their feeble aid do join,
And ten low words oft creep in one dull line:
While they ring round the same unvaried chimes,
With sure returns of still expected rhymes;
Where'er you find "the cooling western breeze,"   350
In the next line, it "whispers through the trees";
If crystal streams "with pleasing murmurs creep,"
The reader's threatened (not in vain) with "sleep";
Then, at the last and only couplet fraught
With some unmeaning thing they call a thought,   355
A needless Alexandrine[5] ends the song
That, like a wounded snake, drags its slow length along.
Leave such to tune their own dull rhymes, and know
What's roundly smooth or languishingly slow;
And praise the easy vigor of a line   360

Where Denham's strength and Waller's sweetness join.[6]
True ease in writing comes from art, not chance,
As those move easiest who have learned to dance.
'Tis not enough no harshness gives offense,
The sound must seem an echo to the sense.   365
Soft is the strain when Zephyr gently blows,
And the smooth stream in smoother numbers flows;
But when loud surges lash the sounding shore,
The hoarse, rough verse should like the torrent roar.
When Ajax strives some rock's vast weight to throw,   370
The line too labors, and the words move slow;
Not so when swift Camilla scours the plain,
Flies o'er the unbending corn, and skims along the main.
Hear how Timotheus'[7] varied lays surprise,
And bid alternate passions fall and rise!   375
While at each change the son of Libyan Jove[8]
Now burns with glory, and then melts with love;
Now his fierce eyes with sparkling fury glow,
Now sighs steal out, and tears begin to flow:
Persians and Greeks like turns of nature[9] found   380
And the world's victor stood subdued by sound!
The power of music all our hearts allow,
And what Timotheus was is Dryden now.
    Avoid extremes; and shun the fault of such
Who still are pleased too little or too much.   385
At every trifle scorn to take offense:
That always shows great pride, or little sense.
Those heads, as stomachs, are not sure the best,
Which nauseate all, and nothing can digest.
Yet let not each gay turn thy rapture move;   390
For fools admire,[1] but men of sense approve:
As things seem large which we through mists descry,
Dullness is ever apt to magnify.
    Some foreign writers, some our own despise;
The ancients only, or the moderns prize.   395
Thus wit, like faith, by each man is applied
To one small sect, and all are damned beside.
Meanly they seek the blessing to confine,
And force that sun but on a part to shine,
Which not alone the southern wit sublimes,   400
But ripens spirits in cold northern climes;
Which from the first has shone on ages past,

---

6. Dryden, whom Pope echoes here, considered Sir John Denham (1615–1669) and Edmund Waller (1606–1687) to have been the principal shapers of the closed pentameter couplet. He had distinguished the "strength" of the one and the "sweetness" of the other.
7. The musician in Dryden's *Alexander's Feast.*

Pope retells the story of that poem in the following lines.
8. Alexander the Great.
9. Alternations of feelings.
1. Wonder. "Approve": judge favorably only after due deliberation.

Enlights the present, and shall warm the last;
Though each may feel increases and decays,
And see now clearer and now darker days.   405
Regard not then if wit be old or new,
But blame the false and value still the true.
    Some ne'er advance a judgment of their own,
But catch the spreading notion of the town;
They reason and conclude by precedent,   410
And own stale nonsense which they ne'er invent.
Some judge of authors' names, not works, and then
Nor praise nor blame the writings, but the men.
Of all this servile herd the worst is he
That in proud dullness joins with quality,   415
A constant critic at the great man's board,
To fetch and carry nonsense for my lord.
What woeful stuff this madrigal would be
In some starved hackney sonneteer or me!
But let a lord once own the happy lines,   420
How the wit brightens! how the style refines!
Before his sacred name flies every fault,
And each exalted stanza teems with thought!
    The vulgar thus through imitation err;
As oft the learn'd by being singular;   425
So much they scorn the crowd, that if the throng
By chance go right, they purposely go wrong.
So schismatics[2] the plain believers quit,
And are but damned for having too much wit.
Some praise at morning what they blame at night,   430
But always think the last opinion right.
A Muse by these is like a mistress used,
This hour she's idolized, the next abused;
While their weak heads like towns unfortified,
'Twixt sense and nonsense daily change their side.   435
Ask them the cause; they're wiser still, they say;
And still tomorrow's wiser than today.
We think our fathers fools, so wise we grow;
Our wiser sons, no doubt, will think us so.
Once school divines[3] this zealous isle o'erspread;   440
Who knew most sentences was deepest read.
Faith, Gospel, all seemed made to be disputed,
And none had sense enough to be confuted.
Scotists and Thomists now in peace remain
Amidst their kindred cobwebs in Duck Lane.[4]   445
If faith itself has different dresses worn,

---

2. Those who have divided the church on points
of theology. Pope stressed the first syllable, the
pronunciation approved by Johnson in his *Dictionary*.
3. The medieval theologians, such as the followers of Duns Scotus and St. Thomas Aquinas mentioned in line 444; "sentences" alludes to Peter Lombard's *Book of Sentences*, a book esteemed by Scholastic philosophers.
4. Street where publishers' remainders and second-hand books were sold.

What wonder modes in wit should take their turn?
Oft, leaving what is natural and fit,
The current folly proves the ready wit;
And authors think their reputation safe,   450
Which lives as long as fools are pleased to laugh.
   Some valuing those of their own side or mind,
Still make themselves the measure of mankind:
Fondly[5] we think we honor merit then,
When we but praise ourselves in other men.   455
Parties in wit attend on those of state,
And public faction doubles private hate.
Pride, Malice, Folly against Dryden rose,
In various shapes of parsons, critics, beaux;
But sense survived, when merry jests were past;   460
For rising merit will buoy up at last.
Might he return and bless once more our eyes,
New Blackmores and new Milbourns must arise.[6]
Nay, should great Homer lift his awful head,
Zoilus[7] again would start up from the dead.   465
Envy will merit, as its shade, pursue,
But like a shadow, proves the substance true;
For envied wit, like Sol eclipsed, makes known
The opposing body's grossness, not its own.
When first that sun too powerful beams displays,   470
It draws up vapors which obscure its rays;
But even those clouds at last adorn its way,
Reflect new glories, and augment the day.
   Be thou the first true merit to befriend;
His praise is lost who stays till all commend.   475
Short is the date, alas! of modern rhymes,
And 'tis but just to let them live betimes.
No longer now that golden age appears,
When patriarch wits survived a thousand years:
Now length of fame (our second life) is lost,   480
And bare threescore is all even that can boast;
Our sons their fathers' failing language see,
And such as Chaucer is shall Dryden be.[8]
So when the faithful pencil has designed
Some bright idea of the master's mind,   485
Where a new world leaps out at his command,
And ready Nature waits upon his hand;
When the ripe colors soften and unite,
And sweetly melt into just shade and light;

---

5. Foolishly.
6. Sir Richard Blackmore, physician and poet, had attacked Dryden for the immorality of his plays; the Rev. Luke Milbourn had attacked his translation of Virgil.
7. A Greek critic of the 4th century B.C., who wrote a book of carping criticism of Homer.

8. The radical changes that took place in the English language between the death of Chaucer in 1400 and the death of Dryden in 1700 suggested that in another 300 years Dryden would be unintelligible. Latin seemed the only means of attaining enduring fame.

When mellowing years their full perfection give,   490
And each bold figure just begins to live,
The treacherous colors the fair art betray,
And all the bright creation fades away!
    Unhappy wit, like most mistaken things,
Atones not for that envy which it brings.   495
In youth alone its empty praise we boast,
But soon the short-lived vanity is lost;
Like some fair flower the early spring supplies,
That gaily blooms, but even in blooming dies,
What is this wit, which must our cares employ?   500
The owner's wife, that other men enjoy;
Then most our trouble still when most admired,
And still the more we give, the more required;
Whose fame with pains we guard, but lose with ease,
Sure some to vex, but never all to please;   505
'Tis what the vicious fear, the virtuous shun,
By fools 'tis hated, and by knaves undone!
    If wit so much from ignorance undergo,
Ah, let not learning too commence its foe!
Of old those met rewards who could excel,   510
And such were praised who but endeavored well;
Though triumphs were to generals only due,
Crowns were reserved to grace the soldiers too.
Now they who reach Parnassus' lofty crown
Employ their pains to spurn some others down;   515
And while self-love each jealous writer rules,
Contending wits become the sport of fools;
But still the worst with most regret commend,
For each ill author is as bad a friend.
To what base ends, and by what abject ways,   520
Are mortals urged through sacred[9] lust of praise!
Ah, ne'er so dire a thirst of glory boast,
Nor in the critic let the man be lost!
Good nature and good sense must ever join;
To err is human, to forgive divine.   525
    But if in noble minds some dregs remain
Nor yet purged off, of spleen and sour disdain,
Discharge that rage on more provoking crimes,
Nor fear a dearth in these flagitious[1] times.
No pardon vile obscenity should find,   530
Though wit and art conspire to move your mind;
But dullness with obscenity must prove
As shameful sure as impotence in love.
In the fat age of pleasure, wealth, and ease
Sprung the rank weed, and thrived with large increase: 535

9. Accursed. The phrase imitates Virgil's "*auri*   3.57).
sacra famis," "accursed hunger for gold" (*Aeneid*   1. Scandalously wicked.

When love was all an easy monarch's[2] care,
Seldom at council, never in a war;
Jilts ruled the state, and statesmen farces writ;
Nay, wits had pensions, and young lords had wit;
The fair sat panting at a courtier's play,   540
And not a mask[3] went unimproved away;
The modest fan was lifted up no more,
And virgins smiled at what they blushed before.
The following license of a foreign reign
Did all the dregs of bold Socinus drain;[4]   545
Then unbelieving priests reformed the nation,
And taught more pleasant methods of salvation;
Where Heaven's free subjects might their rights dispute,
Lest God himself should seem too absolute;
Pulpits their sacred satire learned to spare,   550
And Vice admired to find a flatterer there!
Encouraged thus, wit's Titans braved the skies,
And the press groaned with licensed blasphemies.
These monsters, critics! with your darts engage,
Here point your thunder, and exhaust your rage!
Yet shun their fault, who, scandalously nice,
Will needs mistake an author into vice;
All seems infected that the infected spy,
As all looks yellow to the jaundiced eye.

Part 3

  Learn then what morals critics ought to show,   560
For 'tis but half a judge's task, to know.
'Tis not enough, taste, judgment, learning, join;
In all you speak, let truth and candor[5] shine:
That not alone what to your sense is due
All may allow; but seek your friendship too.   565
  Be silent always when you doubt your sense;
And speak, though sure, with seeming diffidence:
Some positive, persisting fops we know,
Who, if once wrong, will needs be always so;
But you, with pleasure own your errors past,   570
And make each day a critic[6] on the last.
  'Tis not enough, your counsel still be true;
Blunt truths more mischief than nice falsehoods do;
Men must be taught as if you taught them not,
And things unknown proposed as things forgot.   575

---

2. Charles II. The concluding lines of part 2 discuss the corruption of wit and poetry under this
monarch.
3. A woman wearing a mask.
4. The "foreign reign" refers to William III, a
Dutchman. Socinus was the name of two Italian
theologians of the 16th century who denied the
divinity of Jesus.
5. Kindness, impartiality.
6. Critique.

Without good breeding, truth is disapproved;
That only makes superior sense beloved.
    Be niggards of advice on no pretense;
For the worst avarice is that of sense.
With mean complacence[7] ne'er betray your trust,   580
Nor be so civil as to prove unjust.
Fear not the anger of the wise to raise;
Those best can bear reproof, who merit praise.
    'Twere well might critics still this freedom take;
But Appius reddens at each word you speak,   585
And stares, tremendous! with a threatening eye,
Like some fierce tyrant in old tapestry.[8]
Fear most to tax an honorable fool,
Whose right it is, uncensured to be dull;
Such, without wit, are poets when they please,   590
As without learning they can take degrees.[9]
Leave dangerous truths to unsuccessful satyrs,
And flattery to fulsome dedicators,
Whom, when they praise, the world believes no more,
Than when they promise to give scribbling o'er.   595
'Tis best sometimes your censure to restrain,
And charitably let the dull be vain:
Your silence there is better than your spite,
For who can rail so long as they can write?
Still humming on, their drowsy course they keep,   600
And lashed so long, like tops, are lashed asleep.[1]
False steps but help them to renew the race,
As, after stumbling, jades[2] will mend their pace.
What crowds of these, impenitently bold,
In sounds and jingling syllables grown old,   605
Still run on poets, in a raging vein,
Even to the dregs and squeezings of the brain,
Strain out the last dull droppings of their sense,
And rhyme with all the rage of impotence.
    Such shameless bards we have, and yet 'tis true,   610
There are as mad, abandoned critics too.
The bookful blockhead, ignorantly read,
With loads of learned lumber[3] in his head,
With his own tongue still edifies his ears,
And always listening to himself appears.   615
All books he reads, and all he reads assails,

---

7. Softness of manners; desire of pleasing.
8. "This picture was taken to himself by John Dennis, a furious old critic by profession, who, upon no other provocation, wrote against this Essay and its author, in a manner perfectly lunatic. . . ." [Pope's note, 1744]. Pope *did* intend to ridicule Dennis, whose *Appius and Virginia* had failed on the stage in 1709, and who was known for his stare

and his use of the word "tremendous." See line 270 above.
9. Honorary degrees were granted to unqualified men of rank. "Satyrs": satires.
1. Tops "sleep" when they spin so rapidly that they seem not to move.
2. Worthless, worn-out horses.
3. Rubbish.

From Dryden's *Fables* down to Durfey's *Tales.*[4]
With him, most authors steal their works, or buy;
Garth did not write his own *Dispensary.*[5]
Name a new play, and he's the poet's friend,   620
Nay showed his faults—but when would poets mend?
No place so sacred from such fops is barred,
Nor is Paul's church more safe than Paul's churchyard:[6]
Nay, fly to altars; *there* they'll talk you dead:
For fools rush in where angels fear to tread.   625
Distrustful sense with modest caution speaks,   ⎫
It still looks home, and short excursions makes;   ⎬
But rattling nonsense in full volleys breaks,   ⎭
And never shocked, and never turned aside,
Bursts out, resistless, with a thundering tide.   630
    But where's the man, who counsel can bestow,
Still pleased to teach, and yet not proud to know?
Unbiased, or[7] by favor, or by spite:
Not dully prepossessed, nor blindly right;
Though learned, well-bred; and though well-bred, sincere;   635
Modestly bold, and humanly severe:
Who to a friend his faults can freely show,
And gladly praise the merit of a foe?
Blessed with a taste exact, yet unconfined;
A knowledge both of books and humankind;   640
Gen'rous converse;[8] a soul exempt from pride;
And love to praise, with reason on his side?
    Such once were critics; such the happy few,
Athens and Rome in better ages knew.
The mighty Stagirite[9] first left the shore,   645
Spread all his sails, and durst the deeps explore;
He steered securely, and discovered far,
Led by the light of the Maeonian star.[1]
Poets, a race long unconfined, and free,
Still fond and proud of savage liberty,   650
Received his laws; and stood convinced 'twas fit,
Who conquered nature, should preside o'er wit.
    Horace still charms with graceful negligence,
And without method talks us into sense;
Will, like a friend, familiarly convey   655
The truest notions in the easiest[2] way.
He, who supreme in judgment, as in wit,

4. Dryden's *Fables* (1700), a set of translations, were among his most admired works; Thomas D'Urfey's *Tales* (1704) were notorious potboilers.
5. Samuel Garth (1661–1719), who had been accused of plagiarizing his mock-epic poem, *The Dispensary* (1699), was admired and defended by Pope.
6. Booksellers' district near St. Paul's Cathedral, whose aisles were used as a place to meet and do business.
7. Either.
8. Well-bred conversation.
9. Aristotle, whose *Poetics* founded the art of literary criticism, was born at Stagira.
1. Homer, who was supposed to have been born in Maeonia.
2. Least formal.

Might boldly censure, as he boldly writ,
Yet judged with coolness, though he sung with fire;
His precepts teach but what his works inspire.   660
Our critics take a contrary extreme,
They judge with fury, but they write with fle'me.[3]
Nor suffers Horace more in wrong translations
By wits, than critics[4] in as wrong quotations.
   See Dionysius[5] Homer's thoughts refine,   665
And call new beauties forth from every line!
   Fancy and art in gay Petronius[6] please,
The scholar's learning, with the courtier's ease.
   In grave Quintilian's[7] copious work, we find
The justest rules, and clearest method joined: 670
Thus useful arms in magazines[8] we place,
All ranged in order, and disposed with grace,
But less to please the eye, than arm the hand,
Still fit for use, and ready at command.
   Thee, bold Longinus![9] all the nine inspire,   675
And bless their critic with a poet's fire.
An ardent judge, who, zealous in his trust,
With warmth gives sentence, yet is always just;
Whose own example strengthens all his laws,
And is himself that great sublime he draws.   680
   Thus long succeeding critics justly reigned,
License repressed, and useful laws ordained.
Learning and Rome alike in empire grew;
And arts still followed where her eagles[1] flew;
From the same foes, at last, both felt their doom,   685
And the same age saw learning fall, and Rome.
With tyranny, then superstition joined,
As that the body, this enslaved the mind;
Much was believed, but little understood,
And to be dull was construed to be good;   690
A second deluge learning thus o'errun,
And the monks finished what the Goths begun.[2]
   At length Erasmus, that great, injured name
(The glory of the priesthood, and the shame!),[3]
Stemmed the wild torrent of a barb'rous age,   695
And drove those holy Vandals off the stage.

---

3. Phlegmatically.
4. I.e., than by critics. Phrases from Horace's *Art of Poetry* were quoted incessantly by critics.
5. Dionysius of Halicarnassus (1st century B.C.) wrote an important treatise on the artistic arrangement of words.
6. Author of the *Satyricon* (1st century A.D.).
7. Author of the *Institutio Oratoria* (ca. 95 A.D.), a famous treatise on rhetoric. Here as elsewhere, Pope's terms of praise are drawn from the author he is praising.
8. Storehouses or arsenals.

9. Supposed author of the influential treatise *On the Sublime* (1st century A.D.), greatly in vogue at the time of Pope. "Nine": the muses.
1. Emblems on the standards of the Roman army.
2. Pope thought that the scholastic theologians of the Middle Ages were "holy Vandals" who had "sacked" learning as the Goths and Vandals had sacked Rome.
3. Erasmus (1466–1536), the great humanist scholar, was the "glory" of the priesthood because of his goodness and learning, and its "shame" because he was persecuted.

But see! each Muse, in Leo's[4] golden days,
Starts from her trance, and trims her withered bays!
Rome's ancient Genius, o'er its ruins spread,
Shakes off the dust, and rears his reverend head.   700
Then sculpture and her sister-arts revive;
Stones leaped to form, and rocks began to live;
With sweeter notes each rising temple rung;
A Raphael painted, and a Vida[5] sung.
Immortal Vida: on whose honored brow   705
The poet's bays and critic's ivy grow:
Cremona now shall ever boast thy name,
As next in place to Mantua, next in fame![6]
   But soon by impious arms[7] from Latium chased,
Their ancient bounds the banished Muses passed;   710
Thence arts o'er all the northern world advance,
But critic-learning flourished most in France:
The rules a nation, born to serve, obeys;
And Boileau still in right of Horace sways.[8]
But we, brave Britons, foreign laws despised,   715
And kept unconquered—and uncivilized;
Fierce for the liberties of wit, and bold,
We still defied the Romans, as of old.
Yet some there were, among the sounder few
Of those who less presumed, and better knew,   720
Who durst assert the juster ancient cause,
And here restored wit's fundamental laws.
Such was the Muse, whose rules and practice tell,
"Nature's chief masterpiece is writing well."[9]
Such was Roscommon, not more learned than good,   725
With manners gen'rous as his noble blood;
To him the wit of Greece and Rome was known,
And every author's merit, but his own.
Such late was Walsh[1]—the Muse's judge and friend,
Who justly knew to blame or to commend;   730
To failings mild, but zealous for desert;
The clearest head, and the sincerest heart.
This humble praise, lamented shade! receive,
This praise at least a grateful Muse may give:
The Muse, whose early voice you taught to sing,   735

---

4. Leo X, pope from 1513 to 1521, was notable for his encouragement of artists. "Bays": the wreath of poetry.

5. "M. Hieronymus Vida, an excellent Latin poet, who writ an Art of Poetry in verse. He flourished in the time of Leo the Tenth" [Pope's note]. Raphael (1483–1520) painted many of his greatest works under the patronage of Leo X.

6. Vida came from Cremona, near Mantua, the birthplace of Virgil, his favorite poet.

7. German and Spanish troops sacked Rome in 1527. "Latium": Italy.

8. Boileau's *L'Art Poétique* (1674) regularized and modernized the lessons of Horace's *Art of Poetry*.

9. Quoted from an *Essay on Poetry* by John Sheffield, duke of Buckingham (1648–1721), who had befriended the young Pope. Wentworth Dillon, earl of Roscommon, wrote an important *Essay on Translated Verse* (1684).

1. William Walsh (1663–1708), whom Dryden once called "the best critic of our nation," and who had advised Pope to work at becoming the first great "correct" poet in English. The "Muse" here is Pope himself.

Prescribed her heights, and pruned her tender wing,
(Her guide now lost) no more attempts to rise,
But in low numbers[2] short excursions tries:
Content, if hence the unlearned their wants may view,
The learned reflect on what before they knew: 740
Careless of censure, nor too fond of fame;
Still pleased to praise, yet not afraid to blame;
Averse alike to flatter, or offend;
Not free from faults, nor yet too vain to mend.

1709   1711

The Rape of the Lock   *The Rape of the Lock* is based upon an actual episode that provoked a quarrel between two prominent Catholic families. Pope's friend John Caryll, to whom the poem is addressed (line 3), suggested that Pope write it, in the hope that a little laughter might serve to soothe ruffled tempers. Lord Petre had cut off a lock of hair from the head of the lovely Arabella Fermor (often spelled "Farmer" and doubtless so pronounced), much to the indignation of the lady and her relatives. In its original version of two cantos and 334 lines, published in 1712, *The Rape of the Lock* was a great success. In 1713 a new version was undertaken against the advice of Addison, who considered the poem perfect as it was first written. Pope greatly expanded the earlier version, adding the delightful "machinery" (i.e., the supernatural agents in epic action) of the Sylphs, Belinda's toilet, the card game, and the visit to the Cave of Spleen in canto 4. In 1717, with the addition of Clarissa's speech on good humor, the poem assumed its final form.

With supreme tact, delicate fancy, playful wit, and the gentlest satire, Pope elaborated the trivial episode which occasioned the poem into the semblance of an epic in miniature, the most nearly perfect "heroi-comical poem" in English. The poem abounds in parodies and echoes of the *Iliad*, the *Aeneid*, and *Paradise Lost*, thus constantly forcing the reader to compare small things with great. The familiar devices of epic are observed, but the incidents or characters are beautifully proportioned to the scale of mock epic. The *Rape* tells of war, but it is the drawing-room war between the sexes; it has its heroes and heroines, but they are beaux and belles; it has its supernatural characters ("machinery") but they are Sylphs (borrowed, as Pope tells us in his engaging dedicatory letter, from Rosicrucian lore)—creatures of the air, the souls of dead coquettes, with tasks appropriate to their nature— or the Gnome Umbriel, once a prude on earth; it has its epic game, played on the "velvet plain" of the card table, its feasting heroes, who sip coffee and gossip, its battle, fought with the clichés of compliment and conceits, with frowns and angry glances, with snuff and bodkin; it has the traditional epic journey to the underworld—here the Cave of Spleen, emblematic of the peevish ill nature of spoiled and hypochondriacal women. And Pope creates a world in which these actions take place, a world that is dense with beautiful objects: brocades, ivory and tortoise shell, cosmetics and diamonds, lacquered furniture, silver teapot, delicate chinaware. It is a world that is con-

2. Humble verses.

stantly in motion and that sparkles and glitters with light, whether the light of the sun, or of Belinda's eyes, or that light into which the "fluid" bodies of the Sylphs seem to dissolve as they flutter in shrouds and around the mast of Belinda's ship. Though Pope laughs at this world and its creatures—and remembers that a grimmer, darker world surrounds it (3.19–24 and 5.145–48)—he makes us very much aware of its beauty and its charm.

The epigraph may be translated, "I was unwilling, Belinda, to ravish your locks; but I rejoice to have conceded this to your prayers" (Martial, *Epigrams* 12.84.1–2). Pope substituted his heroine for Martial's Polytimus. The epigraph is intended to suggest that the poem was published at Miss Fermor's request.

The Rape of the Lock

An Heroi-Comical Poem

Nolueram, Belinda, tuos violare capillos;
sed juvat hoc precibus me tribuisse tuis.
—MARTIAL

TO MRS. ARABELLA FERMOR

MADAM,

It will be in vain to deny that I have some regard for this piece, since I dedicate it to you. Yet you may bear me witness, it was intended only to divert a few young ladies, who have good sense and good humor enough to laugh not only at their sex's little unguarded follies, but at their own. But as it was communicated with the air of a secret, it soon found its way into the world. An imperfect copy having been offered to a bookseller, you had the good nature for my sake to consent to the publication of one more correct; this I was forced to, before I had executed half my design, for the machinery was entirely wanting to complete it.

The machinery, Madam, is a term invented by the critics, to signify that part which the deities, angels, or demons are made to act in a poem; for the ancient poets are in one respect like many modern ladies: let an action be never so trivial in itself, they always make it appear of the utmost importance. These machines I determined to raise on a very new and odd foundation, the Rosicrucian[1] doctrine of spirits.

I know how disagreeable it is to make use of hard words before a lady; but 'tis so much the concern of a poet to have his works understood, and particularly by your sex, that you must give me leave to explain two or three difficult terms.

The Rosicrucians are a people I must bring you acquainted with. The best account I know of them is in a French book called *Le Comte de Gabalis*,[2] which both in its title and size is so like a novel, that many of the fair sex have read it for one by mistake. According to these gentlemen, the four elements are inhabited by spirits, which they call Sylphs,

1. A system of arcane philosophy introduced into England from Germany in the 17th century.

2. By the Abbé de Montfaucon de Villars, published in 1670.

Gnomes, Nymphs, and Salamanders. The Gnomes or Demons of earth delight in mischief; but the Sylphs, whose habitation is in the air, are the best-conditioned creatures imaginable. For they say, any mortals may enjoy the most intimate familiarities with these gentle spirits, upon a condition very easy to all true adepts, an inviolate preservation of chastity.

As to the following cantos, all the passages of them are as fabulous as the vision at the beginning, or the transformation at the end; (except the loss of your hair, which I always mention with reverence). The human persons are as fictitious as the airy ones; and the character of Belinda, as it is now managed, resembles you in nothing but in beauty.

If this poem had as many graces as there are in your person, or in your mind, yet I could never hope it should pass through the world half so uncensured as you have done. But let its fortune be what it will, mine is happy enough, to have given me this occasion of assuring you that I am, with the truest esteem,

MADAM,
Your most obedient, humble servant,
A. POPE

Canto 1

What dire offense from amorous causes springs,
What mighty contests rise from trivial things,
I sing—This verse to Caryll, Muse! is due:
This, even Belinda may vouchsafe to view:
Slight is the subject, but not so the praise,   5
If she inspire, and he approve my lays.
    Say what strange motive, Goddess! could compel
A well-bred lord to assault a gentle belle?
Oh, say what stranger cause, yet unexplored,
Could make a gentle belle reject a lord?   10
In tasks so bold can little men engage,
And in soft bosoms dwells such mighty rage?
    Sol through white curtains shot a timorous ray,
And oped those eyes that must eclipse the day.
Now lapdogs give themselves the rousing shake,   15
And sleepless lovers just at twelve awake:
Thrice rung the bell, the slipper knocked the ground,[3]
And the pressed watch returned a silver sound.
Belinda still her downy pillow pressed,
Her guardian Sylph prolonged the balmy rest: 20
'Twas he had summoned to her silent bed
The morning dream that hovered o'er her head.
A youth more glittering than a birthnight beau[4]
(That even in slumber caused her cheek to glow)

3. Summons to a maid. A "pressed watch" chimes the hour and the quarter-hour when the stem is pressed down.

4. Courtiers wore especially fine clothes on the sovereign's birthday.

Seemed to her ear his winning lips to lay,   25
And thus in whispers said, or seemed to say:
    "Fairest of mortals, thou distinguished care
Of thousand bright inhabitants of air!
If e'er one vision touched thy infant thought,
Of all the nurse and all the priest have taught,   30
Of airy elves by moonlight shadows seen,
The silver token, and the circled green,[5]
Or virgins visited by angel powers,
With golden crowns and wreaths of heavenly flowers,
Hear and believe! thy own importance know,   35
Nor bound thy narrow views to things below.
Some secret truths, from learned pride concealed,
To maids alone and children are revealed:
What though no credit doubting wits may give?
The fair and innocent shall still believe.   40
Know, then, unnumbered spirits round thee fly,
The light militia of the lower sky:
These, though unseen, are ever on the wing,
Hang o'er the box, and hover round the Ring.[6]
Think what an equipage thou hast in air,   45
And view with scorn two pages and a chair.[7]
As now your own, our beings were of old,
And once enclosed in woman's beauteous mold;
Thence, by a soft transition, we repair
From earthly vehicles to these of air.   50
Think not, when woman's transient breath is fled,
That all her vanities at once are dead:
Succeeding vanities she still regards,
And though she plays no more, o'erlooks the cards.
Her joy in gilded chariots, when alive,   55
And love of ombre,[8] after death survive.
For when the Fair in all their pride expire,
To their first elements[9] their souls retire:
The sprites of fiery termagants in flame
Mount up, and take a Salamander's name.[1]   60
Soft yielding minds to water glide away,
And sip, with Nymphs, their elemental tea.[2]
The graver prude sinks downward to a Gnome,
In search of mischief still on earth to roam.

---

5. According to popular belief fairies skim off the cream from jugs of milk left standing overnight and leave a coin ("silver token") in payment. Rings of bright green grass, which are common in England even in winter, were held to be due to the round dances of fairies.
6. The "box" in the theater and the fashionable circular drive ("Ring") in Hyde Park.
7. Sedan chair.
8. The popular card game. See 3.27 ff. and note.
9. The four elements out of which all things were believed to have been made were fire, water, earth, and air. One or another of these elements was supposed to be predominant in both the physical and psychological make-up of each human being. In this context they are spoken of as "humors."
1. Pope borrowed his supernatural beings from Rosicrucian mythology. Each element was inhabited by a spirit, as the following lines explain. The salamander is a lizardlike animal, in antiquity believed to live in fire.
2. Pronounce *tay*.

The light coquettes in Sylphs aloft repair,   65
And sport and flutter in the fields of air.
    "Know further yet; whoever fair and chaste
Rejects mankind, is by some Sylph embraced:
For spirits, freed from mortal laws, with ease
Assume what sexes and what shapes they please.[3]   70
What guards the purity of melting maids,
In courtly balls, and midnight masquerades,
Safe from the treacherous friend, the daring spark,
The glance by day, the whisper in the dark,
When kind occasion prompts their warm desires,   75
When music softens, and when dancing fires?
'Tis but their Sylph, the wise Celestials know,
Though Honor is the word with men below.
    "Some nymphs there are, too conscious of their face,
For life predestined to the Gnomes' embrace.   80
These swell their prospects and exalt their pride,
When offers are disdained, and love denied:
Then gay ideas[4] crowd the vacant brain,
While peers, and dukes, and all their sweeping train,
And garters, stars, and coronets[5] appear,   85
And in soft sounds, 'your Grace' salutes their ear.
'Tis these that early taint the female soul,
Instruct the eyes of young coquettes to roll,
Teach infant cheeks a bidden blush to know,
And little hearts to flutter at a beau.   90
    "Oft, when the world imagine women stray,
The Sylphs through mystic mazes guide their way,
Through all the giddy circle they pursue,
And old impertinence[6] expel by new.
What tender maid but must a victim fall   95
To one man's treat, but for another's ball?
When Florio speaks what virgin could withstand,
If gentle Damon did not squeeze her hand?
With varying vanities, from every part,
They shift the moving toyshop[7] of their heart;   100
Where wigs with wigs, with sword-knots sword-knots strive,
Beaux banish beaux, and coaches coaches drive.
This erring mortals levity may call;
Oh, blind to truth! the Sylphs contrive it all.
    "Of these am I, who thy protection claim,   105
A watchful sprite, and Ariel is my name.
Late, as I ranged the crystal wilds of air,
In the clear mirror of thy ruling star
I saw, alas! some dread event impend,

---

3. Cf. *Paradise Lost* 1.427–31; this is one of many
allusions to that poem in the *Rape*.
4. Showy images.
5. Emblems of nobility. "Your Grace" would be

a duchess.
6. Trifle.
7. A shop stocked with baubles and trifles.

Ere to the main this morning sun descend,   110
But Heaven reveals not what, or how, or where:
Warned by the Sylph, O pious maid, beware!
This to disclose is all thy guardian can:
Beware of all, but most beware of Man!"
He said; when Shock,[8] who thought she slept too long,   115
Leaped up, and waked his mistress with his tongue.
'Twas then, Belinda, if report say true,
Thy eyes first opened on a billet-doux;
Wounds, charms, and ardors were no sooner read,
But all the vision vanished from thy head.   120
And now, unveiled, the toilet stands displayed,
Each silver vase in mystic order laid.
First, robed in white, the nymph intent adores,
With head uncovered, the cosmetic powers.
A heavenly image in the glass appears;   125
To that she bends, to that her eyes she rears.
The inferior priestess, at her altar's side,
Trembling begins the sacred rites of Pride.
Unnumbered treasures ope at once, and here
The various offerings of the world appear;   130
From each she nicely culls with curious toil,
And decks the goddess with the glittering spoil.
This casket India's glowing gems unlocks,
And all Arabia breathes from yonder box.
The tortoise here and elephant unite,   135
Transformed to combs, the speckled and the white.
Here files of pins extend their shining rows,
Puffs, powders, patches, Bibles,[9] billet-doux.
Now awful Beauty puts on all its arms;
The fair each moment rises in her charms,   140
Repairs her smiles, awakens every grace,
And calls forth all the wonders of her face;
Sees by degrees a purer blush arise,
And keener lightnings quicken in her eyes.
The busy Sylphs surround their darling care,   145
These set the head, and those divide the hair,
Some fold the sleeve, whilst others plait the gown;
And Betty's[1] praised for labors not her own.

Canto 2

Not with more glories, in the ethereal plain,
The sun first rises o'er the purpled main,
Than, issuing forth, the rival of his beams

8. Belinda's lapdog; a "shock" was a long-haired
poodle.
9. It has been suggested that Pope intended here
not "Bibles," but "bibelots," (trinkets), but this
interpretation has not gained wide acceptance.
1. Belinda's maid, the "inferior priestess" mentioned in line 127.

Launched on the bosom of the silver Thames.
Fair nymphs and well-dressed youths around her shone,   5
But every eye was fixed on her alone.
On her white breast a sparkling cross she wore,
Which Jews might kiss, and infidels adore.
Her lively looks a sprightly mind disclose,
Quick as her eyes, and as unfixed as those: 10
Favors to none, to all she smiles extends;
Oft she rejects, but never once offends.
Bright as the sun, her eyes the gazers strike,
And, like the sun, they shine on all alike.
Yet graceful ease, and sweetness void of pride,   15
Might hide her faults, if belles had faults to hide:
If to her share some female errors fall,
Look on her face, and you'll forget 'em all.
    This nymph, to the destruction of mankind,
Nourished two locks which graceful hung behind   20
In equal curls, and well conspired to deck
With shining ringlets the smooth ivory neck.
Love in these labyrinths his slaves detains,
And mighty hearts are held in slender chains.
With hairy springes[2] we the birds betray,   25
Slight lines of hair surprise the finny prey,
Fair tresses man's imperial race ensnare,
And beauty draws us with a single hair.
    The adventurous Baron the bright locks admired,
He saw, he wished, and to the prize aspired.   30
Resolved to win, he meditates the way,
By force to ravish, or by fraud betray;
For when success a lover's toil attends,
Few ask if fraud or force attained his ends.
    For this, ere Phoebus rose, he had implored   35
Propitious Heaven, and every power adored,
But chiefly Love—to Love an altar built,
Of twelve vast French romances, neatly gilt.
There lay three garters, half a pair of gloves,
And all the trophies of his former loves.   40
With tender billet-doux he lights the pyre,
And breathes three amorous sighs to raise the fire.
Then prostrate falls, and begs with ardent eyes
Soon to obtain, and long possess the prize:
The powers gave ear, and granted half his prayer,   45
The rest the winds dispersed in empty air.
    But now secure the painted vessel glides,
The sunbeams trembling on the floating tides,
While melting music steals upon the sky,
And softened sounds along the waters die.   50

2. Snares; pronounced *sprin-jez*.

Smooth flow the waves, the zephyrs gently play,
Belinda smiled, and all the world was gay.
All but the Sylph—with careful thoughts oppressed,
The impending woe sat heavy on his breast.
He summons straight his denizens of air;   55
The lucid squadrons round the sails repair:
Soft o'er the shrouds aërial whispers breathe
That seemed but zephyrs to the train beneath.
Some to the sun their insect-wings unfold,
Waft on the breeze, or sink in clouds of gold.   60
Transparent forms too fine for mortal sight,
Their fluid bodies half dissolved in light,
Loose to the wind their airy garments flew,
Thin glittering textures of the filmy dew,
Dipped in the richest tincture of the skies,   65
Where light disports in ever-mingling dyes,
While every beam new transient colors flings,
Colors that change whene'er they wave their wings.
Amid the circle, on the gilded mast,
Superior by the head was Ariel placed;   70
His purple[3] pinions opening to the sun,
He raised his azure wand, and thus begun:
    "Ye Sylphs and Sylphids, to your chief give ear!
Fays, Fairies, Genïi, Elves, and Daemons, hear!
Ye know the spheres and various tasks assigned   75
By laws eternal to the aërial kind.
Some in the fields of purest ether play,
And bask and whiten in the blaze of day.
Some guide the course of wandering orbs on high,
Or roll the planets through the boundless sky.   80
Some less refined, beneath the moon's pale light
Pursue the stars that shoot athwart the night,
Or suck the mists in grosser air below,
Or dip their pinions in the painted bow,
Or brew fierce tempests on the wintry main,   85
Or o'er the glebe[4] distill the kindly rain.
Others on earth o'er human race preside,
Watch all their ways, and all their actions guide:
Of these the chief the care of nations own,
And guard with arms divine the British Throne.   90
    "Our humbler province is to tend the Fair,
Not a less pleasing, though less glorious care:
To save the powder from too rude a gale,
Nor let the imprisoned essences exhale;
To draw fresh colors from the vernal flowers;   95

3. In 18th-century poetic diction the word might
mean "blood-red," "purple," or simply (as is likely
here) "brightly colored." The word derives from
Virgil, *Eclogue* 9, 40, *purpureum*. An example of
the Latinate nature of some poetic diction of the
period.
4. Cultivated field.

To steal from rainbows e'er they drop in showers
A brighter wash;[5] to curl their waving hairs,
Assist their blushes, and inspire their airs,
Nay oft, in dreams invention we bestow,
To change a flounce, or add a furbelow.   100
    "This day black omens threat the brightest fair,
That e'er deserved a watchful spirit's care;
Some dire disaster, or by force or slight,
But what, or where, the Fates have wrapped in night:
Whether the nymph shall break Diana's law,[6]   105
Or some frail china jar receive a flaw,
Or stain her honor or her new brocade,
Forget her prayers, or miss a masquerade,
Or lose her heart, or necklace, at a ball;
Or whether Heaven has doomed that Shock must fall.   110
Haste, then, ye spirits! to your charge repair:
The fluttering fan be Zephyretta's care;
The drops[7] to thee, Brillante, we consign;
And, Momentilla, let the watch be thine;
Do thou, Crispissa,[8] tend her favorite Lock;   115
Ariel himself shall be the guard of Shock.
    "To fifty chosen Sylphs, of special note,
We trust the important charge, the petticoat;
Oft have we known that sevenfold fence to fail,
Though stiff with hoops, and armed with ribs of whale.   120
Form a strong line about the silver bound,
And guard the wide circumference around.
    "Whatever spirit, careless of his charge,
His post neglects, or leaves the fair at large,
Shall feel sharp vengeance soon o'ertake his sins,   125
Be stopped in vials, or transfixed with pins,
Or plunged in lakes of bitter washes lie,
Or wedged whole ages in a bodkin's eye;[9]
Gums and pomatums shall his flight restrain,
While clogged he beats his silken wings in vain,   130
Or alum styptics with contracting power
Shrink his thin essence like a riveled[1] flower:
Or, as Ixion[2] fixed, the wretch shall feel
The giddy motion of the whirling mill,
In fumes of burning chocolate shall glow,   135
And tremble at the sea that froths below!"
    He spoke; the spirits from the sails descend;
Some, orb in orb, around the nymph extend;

5. Cosmetic lotion.
6. Diana was the goddess of chastity.
7. Diamond earrings. Observe the appropriateness of the names of the Sylphs to their assigned functions.
8. From Latin *crispere*, to curl.
9. A "bodkin" is a blunt needle with a large eye, used for drawing ribbon through eyelets in the edging of women's garments.
1. To "rivel" is to "contract into wrinkles and corrugations" (Johnson's *Dictionary*).
2. In the Greek myth Ixion was punished in the underworld by being bound on an everturning wheel.

Some thread the mazy ringlets of her hair;
Some hang upon the pendants of her ear: 140
With beating hearts the dire event they wait,
Anxious, and trembling for the birth of Fate.

Canto 3

Close by those meads, forever crowned with flowers,
Where Thames with pride surveys his rising towers,
There stands a structure of majestic frame,
Which from the neighboring Hampton takes its name.[3]
Here Britain's statesmen oft the fall foredoom   5
Of foreign tyrants and of nymphs at home;
Here thou, great Anna! whom three realms obey,
Dost sometimes counsel take—and sometimes tea.
    Hither the heroes and the nymphs resort,
To taste awhile the pleasures of a court;   10
In various talk the instructive hours they passed,
Who gave the ball, or paid the visit last;
One speaks the glory of the British Queen,
And one describes a charming Indian screen;
A third interprets motions, looks, and eyes;   15
At every word a reputation dies.
Snuff, or the fan, supply each pause of chat,
With singing, laughing, ogling, and all that.
    Meanwhile, declining from the noon of day,
The sun obliquely shoots his burning ray;   20
The hungry judges soon the sentence sign,
And wretches hang that jurymen may dine;
The merchant from the Exchange returns in peace,
And the long labors of the toilet cease.
Belinda now, whom thirst of fame invites,   25
Burns to encounter two adventurous knights,
At ombre[4] singly to decide their doom,
And swells her breast with conquests yet to come.
Straight the three bands prepare in arms to join,
Each band the number of the sacred nine.   30
Soon as she spreads her hand, the aërial guard
Descend, and sit on each important card:
First Ariel perched upon a Matadore,
Then each according to the rank they bore;

3. Hampton Court, the royal palace, about 15
miles up the Thames from London.
4. The game of ombre which Belinda plays against
the baron and another young man is too complicated for complete explication here. Pope has
carefully arranged the cards so that Belinda wins.
The baron's hand is strong enough to be a threat,
but the third player's is of little account. The hand
is played exactly according to the rules of ombre,
and Pope's description of the cards is equally accurate. Each player holds nine cards (line 30). The
"Matadores" (line 33), when spades are trumps,
are "Spadillio" (line 49), the ace of spades; "Manillio" (line 51), the two of spades; "Basto" (line 53),
the ace of clubs; Belinda holds all three of these.
(For a more complete description of ombre, see
Appendix C, *The Rape of the Lock and Other
Poems*, ed. Geoffrey Tillotson, in the Twickenham Edition of Pope's poems, vol. 2.)

For Sylphs, yet mindful of their ancient race,   35
Are, as when women, wondrous fond of place.
   Behold, four Kings in majesty revered,
With hoary whiskers and a forky beard;
And four fair Queens whose hands sustain a flower,
The expressive emblem of their softer power;   40
Four Knaves in garbs succinct,[5] a trusty band,
Caps on their heads, and halberts in their hand;
And parti-colored troops, a shining train,
Draw forth to combat on the velvet plain.
   The skillful nymph reviews her force with care;   45
"Let Spades be trumps!" she said, and trumps they were.
   Now move to war her sable Matadores,
In show like leaders of the swarthy Moors.
Spadillio first, unconquerable lord!
Led off two captive trumps, and swept the board.   50
As many more Manillio forced to yield,
And marched a victor from the verdant field.
Him Basto followed, but his fate more hard
Gained but one trump and one plebeian card.
With his broad saber next, a chief in years,   55
The hoary Majesty of Spades appears,
Puts forth one manly leg, to sight revealed,
The rest his many-colored robe concealed.
The rebel Knave, who dares his prince engage,
Proves the just victim of his royal rage.   60
Even mighty Pam,[6] that kings and queens o'erthrew
And mowed down armies in the fights of loo,
Sad chance of war! now destitute of aid,
Falls undistinguished by the victor Spade.
   Thus far both armies to Belinda yield;   65
Now to the Baron fate inclines the field.
His warlike amazon her host invades,
The imperial consort of the crown of Spades.
The Club's black tyrant first her victim died,
Spite of his haughty mien and barbarous pride.   70
What boots the regal circle on his head,
His giant limbs, in state unwieldy spread?
That long behind he trails his pompous robe,
And of all monarchs only grasps the globe?
   The Baron now his Diamonds pours apace;   75
The embroidered King who shows but half his face,
And his refulgent Queen, with powers combined
Of broken troops an easy conquest find.
Clubs, Diamonds, Hearts, in wild disorder seen,
With throngs promiscuous strew the level green.   80
Thus when dispersed a routed army runs,

5. Girded up.
6. The knave of clubs, the highest trump in the game of loo.

Of Asia's troops, and Afric's sable sons,
With like confusion different nations fly,
Of various habit, and of various dye,
The pierced battalions disunited fall   85
In heaps on heaps; one fate o'erwhelms them all.
    The Knave of Diamonds tries his wily arts,
And wins (oh, shameful chance!) the Queen of Hearts.
At this, the blood the virgin's cheek forsook,
A livid paleness spreads o'er all her look;   90
She sees, and trembles at the approaching ill,
Just in the jaws of ruin, and Codille,[7]
And now (as oft in some distempered state)
On one nice trick depends the general fate.
An Ace of Hearts steps forth: the King unseen   95
Lurked in her hand, and mourned his captive Queen.
He springs to vengeance with an eager pace,
And falls like thunder on the prostrate Ace.
The nymph exulting fills with shouts the sky,
The walls, the woods, and long canals reply.   100
    O thoughtless mortals! ever blind to fate,
Too soon dejected, and too soon elate:
Sudden these honors shall be snatched away,
And cursed forever this victorious day.
    For lo! the board with cups and spoons is crowned,   105
The berries crackle, and the mill turns round;[8]
On shining altars of Japan[9] they raise
The silver lamp; the fiery spirits blaze:
From silver spouts the grateful liquors glide,
While China's earth receives the smoking tide.   110
At once they gratify their scent and taste,
And frequent cups prolong the rich repast.
Straight hover round the fair her airy band;
Some, as she sipped, the fuming liquor fanned,
Some o'er her lap their careful plumes displayed,   115
Trembling, and conscious of the rich brocade.
Coffee (which makes the politician wise,
And see through all things with his half-shut eyes)
Sent up in vapors to the Baron's brain
New stratagems, the radiant Lock to gain.   120
Ah, cease, rash youth! desist ere 'tis too late,
Fear the just Gods, and think of Scylla's fate![1]
Changed to a bird, and sent to flit in air,
She dearly pays for Nisus' injured hair!
    But when to mischief mortals bend their will,   125

7. The term applied to losing a hand at cards.
8. I.e., coffee is roasted and ground.
9. I.e., small, lacquered tables. The word "altars" suggests the ritualistic character of coffee drinking in Belinda's world.
1. Scylla, daughter of Nisus, was turned into a sea bird because, for the sake of her love for Minos of Crete, who was besieging her father's city of Megara, she cut from her father's head the purple lock on which his safety depended. She is not the Scylla of "Scylla and Charybdis."

How soon they find fit instruments of ill!
Just then, Clarissa drew with tempting grace
A two-edged weapon from her shining case:
So ladies in romance assist their knight,
Present the spear, and arm him for the fight.   130
He takes the gift with reverence, and extends
The little engine on his fingers' ends;
This just behind Belinda's neck he spread,
As o'er the fragrant steams she bends her head.
Swift to the Lock a thousand sprites repair,   135
A thousand wings, by turns, blow back the hair,
And thrice they twitched the diamond in her ear,
Thrice she looked back, and thrice the foe drew near.
Just in that instant, anxious Ariel sought
The close recesses of the virgin's thought;   140
As on the nosegay in her breast reclined,
He watched the ideas rising in her mind,
Sudden he viewed, in spite of all her art,
An earthly lover lurking at her heart.
Amazed, confused, he found his power expired,   145
Resigned to fate, and with a sigh retired.
        The Peer now spreads the glittering forfex[2] wide,
To enclose the Lock; now joins it, to divide.
Even then, before the fatal engine closed,
A wretched Sylph too fondly interposed;   150
Fate urged the shears, and cut the Sylph in twain
(But airy substance soon unites again):
The meeting points the sacred hair dissever
From the fair head, forever, and forever!
    Then flashed the living lightning from her eyes,   155
And screams of horror rend the affrighted skies.
Not louder shrieks to pitying heaven are cast,
When husbands, or when lapdogs breathe their last;
Or when rich china vessels fallen from high,
In glittering dust and painted fragments lie!   160
"Let wreaths of triumph now my temples twine,"
The victor cried, "the glorious prize is mine!
While fish in streams, or birds delight in air,
Or in a coach and six the British Fair,
As long as *Atalantis*[3] shall be read,   165
Or the small pillow grace a lady's bed,
While visits shall be paid on solemn days,
When numerous wax-lights in bright order blaze,
While nymphs take treats, or assignations give,
So long my honor, name, and praise shall live!   170
What Time would spare, from Steel receives its date,
And monuments, like men, submit to fate!

2. Scissors.
3. Mrs. Manley's *New Atalantis* (1709) was noto-   rious for its thinly concealed allusions to contemporary scandals.

Steel could the labor of the Gods destroy,
And strike to dust the imperial towers of Troy;
Steel could the works of mortal pride confound,   175
And hew triumphal arches to the ground.
What wonder then, fair nymph! thy hairs should feel,
The conquering force of unresisted Steel?"

Canto 4

But anxious cares the pensive nymph oppressed,
And secret passions labored in her breast.
Not youthful kings in battle seized alive,
Not scornful virgins who their charms survive,
Not ardent lovers robbed of all their bliss,   5
Not ancient ladies when refused a kiss,
Not tyrants fierce that unrepenting die,
Not Cynthia when her manteau's⁴ pinned awry,
E'er felt such rage, resentment, and despair,
As thou, sad virgin! for thy ravished hair.   10
For, that sad moment, when the Sylphs withdrew
And Ariel weeping from Belinda flew,
Umbriel,⁵ a dusky, melancholy sprite
As ever sullied the fair face of light,
Down to the central earth, his proper scene,   15
Repaired to search the gloomy Cave of Spleen.⁶
Swift on his sooty pinions flits the Gnome,
And in a vapor reached the dismal dome.
No cheerful breeze this sullen region knows,
The dreaded east is all the wind that blows.   20
Here in a grotto, sheltered close from air,
And screened in shades from day's detested glare,
She sighs forever on her pensive bed,
Pain at her side, and Megrim⁷ at her head.
Two handmaids wait the throne: alike in place   25
But differing far in figure and in face.
Here stood Ill-Nature like an ancient maid,
Her wrinkled form in black and white arrayed;
With store of prayers for mornings, nights, and noons,
Her hand is filled; her bosom with lampoons.   30
There Affectation, with a sickly mien,
Shows in her cheek the roses of eighteen,
Practiced to lisp, and hang the head aside,
Faints into airs, and languishes with pride,
On the rich quilt sinks with becoming woe,   35
Wrapped in a gown, for sickness and for show.
The fair ones feel such maladies as these,
When each new nightdress gives a new disease.

4. Negligee or loose robe.   6. Ill humor.
5. The name suggests shade and darkness.   7. Headache.

A constant vapor[8] o'er the palace flies,
Strange phantoms rising as the mists arise;   40
Dreadful as hermit's dreams in haunted shades,
Or bright as visions of expiring maids.
Now glaring fiends, and snakes on rolling spires,[9]
Pale specters, gaping tombs, and purple fires;
Now lakes of liquid gold, Elysian scenes,   45
And crystal domes, and angels in machines.[1]
    Unnumbered throngs on every side are seen
Of bodies changed to various forms by Spleen.
Here living teapots stand, one arm held out,
One bent; the handle this, and that the spout: 50
A pipkin[2] there, like Homer's tripod, walks;
Here sighs a jar, and there a goose pie talks;
Men prove with child, as powerful fancy works,
And maids, turned bottles, call aloud for corks.
    Safe passed the Gnome through this fantastic band,   55
A branch of healing spleenwort[3] in his hand.
Then thus addressed the Power: "Hail, wayward Queen!
Who rule the sex to fifty from fifteen:
Parent of vapors and of female wit,
Who give the hysteric or poetic fit,   60
On various tempers act by various ways,
Make some take physic, others scribble plays;
Who cause the proud their visits to delay,
And send the godly in a pet to pray.
A nymph there is that all your power disdains,   65
And thousands more in equal mirth maintains.
But oh! if e'er thy Gnome could spoil a grace,
Or raise a pimple on a beauteous face,
Like citron-waters[4] matrons' cheeks inflame,
Or change complexions at a losing game;   70
If e'er with airy horns[5] I planted heads,
Or rumpled petticoats, or tumbled beds,
Or caused suspicion when no soul was rude,
Or discomposed the headdress of a prude,
Or e'er to costive lapdog gave disease,   75
Which not the tears of brightest eyes could ease,
Hear me, and touch Belinda with chagrin:[6]
That single act gives half the world the spleen."

---

8. Emblematic of "the vapors," i.e., hypochondria, melancholy, peevishness, often affected by fashionable women.
9. Coils.
1. Mechanical devices used in the theaters for spectacular effects. The fantasies of neurotic women here merge with the sensational stage effects popular with contemporary audiences.
2. An earthen pot. In *Iliad* 18.373–77, Vulcan furnishes the gods with self-propelling "tripods" (three-legged stools).

3. An herb, efficacious against the spleen. Pope alludes to the golden bough that Aeneas and the Cumaean sybil carry with them for protection into the underworld in *Aeneid* 6.
4. Brandy flavored with orange or lemon peel.
5. Horns, the symbol of the cuckold, the man whose wife has been unfaithful to him; here "airy," because they exist only in the jealous suspicions of the husband, the victim of the mischievous Umbriel.
6. Ill humor.

The Goddess with a discontented air
Seems to reject him though she grants his prayer.   80
A wondrous bag with both her hands she binds,
Like that where once Ulysses held the winds;[7]
There she collects the force of female lungs,
Sighs, sobs, and passions, and the war of tongues.
A vial next she fills with fainting fears,   85
Soft sorrows, melting griefs, and flowing tears.
The Gnome rejoicing bears her gifts away,
Spreads his black wings, and slowly mounts to day.
    Sunk in Thalestris'[8] arms the nymph he found,
Her eyes dejected and her hair unbound.   90
Full o'er their heads the swelling bag he rent,
And all the Furies issued at the vent.
Belinda burns with more than mortal ire,
And fierce Thalestris fans the rising fire.
"O wretched maid!" she spread her hands, and cried   95
(While Hampton's echoes, "Wretched maid!" replied),
"Was it for this you took such constant care
The bodkin, comb, and essence to prepare?
For this your locks in paper durance bound,
For this with torturing irons wreathed around?   100
For this with fillets strained your tender head,
And bravely bore the double loads of lead?[9]
Gods! shall the ravisher display your hair,
While the fops envy, and the ladies stare!
Honor forbid! at whose unrivaled shrine   105
Ease, pleasure, virtue, all, our sex resign.
Methinks already I your tears survey,
Already hear the horrid things they say,
Already see you a degraded toast,
And all your honor in a whisper lost!   110
How shall I, then, your helpless fame defend?
'Twill then be infamy to seem your friend!
And shall this prize, the inestimable prize,
Exposed through crystal to the gazing eyes,
And heightened by the diamond's circling rays,   115
On that rapacious hand forever blaze?
Sooner shall grass in Hyde Park Circus grow,
And wits take lodgings in the sound of Bow;[1]
Sooner let earth, air, sea, to chaos fall,
Men, monkeys, lapdogs, parrots, perish all!"   120

---

7. Aeolus (later conceived of as god of the winds) gave Ulysses a bag containing all the winds adverse to his voyage home. When his ship was in sight of Ithaca, his companions opened the bag and the storms that ensued drove Ulysses far away (*Odyssey* 10.19 ff.).
8. The name is borrowed from a queen of the Amazons, hence a fierce and warlike woman.

Thalestris, according to legend, traveled 30 days in order to have a child by Alexander the Great. Plutarch denies the story.
9. The frame on which the elaborate coiffures of the day were arranged.
1. A person born within sound of the bells of St. Mary-le-Bow in Cheapside is said to be a cockney. No fashionable wit would have so vulgar an address.

She said; then raging to Sir Plume repairs,
And bids her beau demand the precious hairs
(Sir Plume of amber snuffbox justly vain,
And the nice conduct of a clouded cane).
With earnest eyes, and round unthinking face,   125
He first the snuffbox opened, then the case,
And thus broke out—"My Lord, why, what the devil!
Z——ds! damn the lock! 'fore Gad, you must be civil!
Plague on 't! 'tis past a jest—nay prithee, pox!
Give her the hair"—he spoke, and rapped his box.   130
    "It grieves me much," replied the Peer again,
"Who speaks so well should ever speak in vain.
But by this Lock, this sacred Lock I swear
(Which never more shall join its parted hair;
Which never more its honors shall renew,   135
Clipped from the lovely head where late it grew),
That while my nostrils draw the vital air,
This hand, which won it, shall forever wear."
He spoke, and speaking, in proud triumph spread
The long-contended honors[2] of her head.   140
    But Umbriel, hateful Gnome, forebears not so;
He breaks the vial whence the sorrows flow.
Then see! the nymph in beauteous grief appears,
Her eyes half languishing, half drowned in tears;
On her heaved bosom hung her drooping head,   145
Which with a sigh she raised, and thus she said:
    "Forever cursed be this detested day,
Which snatched my best, my favorite curl away!
Happy! ah, ten times happy had I been,
If Hampton Court these eyes had never seen!   150
Yet am not I the first mistaken maid,
By love of courts to numerous ills betrayed.
Oh, had I rather unadmired remained
In some lone isle, or distant northern land;
Where the gilt chariot never marks the way,   155
Where none learn ombre, none e'er taste bohea![3]
There kept my charms concealed from mortal eye,
Like roses that in deserts bloom and die.
What moved my mind with youthful lords to roam?
Oh, had I stayed, and said my prayers at home!   160
'Twas this the morning omens seemed to tell,
Thrice from my trembling hand the patch box[4] fell;
The tottering china shook without a wind,
Nay, Poll sat mute, and Shock was most unkind!
A Sylph too warned me of the threats of fate,   165
In mystic visions, now believed too late!

---

2. Ornaments, hence locks; a Latinism.   4. A box to hold the ornamental patches of court
3. A costly sort of tea.   plaster worn on the face by both sexes.

See the poor remnants of these slighted hairs!
My hands shall rend what e'en thy rapine spares.
These in two sable ringlets taught to break,
Once gave new beauties to the snowy neck;   170
The sister lock now sits uncouth, alone,
And in its fellow's fate foresees its own;
Uncurled it hangs, the fatal shears demands,
And tempts once more thy sacrilegious hands.
Oh, hadst thou, cruel! been content to seize   175
Hairs less in sight, or any hairs but these!"

Canto 5

She said: the pitying audience melt in tears.
But Fate and Jove had stopped the Baron's ears.
In vain Thalestris with reproach assails,
For who can move when fair Belinda fails?
Not half so fixed the Trojan[5] could remain,   5
While Anna begged and Dido raged in vain.
Then grave Clarissa graceful waved her fan;
Silence ensued, and thus the nymph began:
    "Say why are beauties praised and honored most,
The wise man's passion, and the vain man's toast?   10
Why decked with all that land and sea afford,
Why angels called, and angel-like adored?
Why round our coaches crowd the white-gloved beaux,
Why bows the side box from its inmost rows?
How vain are all these glories, all our pains,   15
Unless good sense preserve what beauty gains;
That men may say when we the front box grace,
'Behold the first in virtue as in face!'
Oh! if to dance all night, and dress all day,
Charmed the smallpox, or chased old age away,   20
Who would not scorn what housewife's cares produce,
Or who would learn one earthly thing of use?
To patch, nay ogle, might become a saint,
Nor could it sure be such a sin to paint.
But since, alas! frail beauty must decay,   25
Curled or uncurled, since locks will turn to gray;
Since painted, or not painted, all shall fade,
And she who scorns a man must die a maid;
What then remains but well our power to use,
And keep good humor still whate'er we lose?   30
And trust me, dear, good humor can prevail
When airs, and flights, and screams, and scolding fail.

5. Aeneas, who forsook Dido at the bidding of the gods, despite her reproaches and the supplications of her sister Anna. Virgil compares him to a steadfast oak that withstands a storm (*Aeneid* 4.437–43).

Beauties in vain their pretty eyes may roll;
Charms strike the sight, but merit wins the soul."[6]
   So spoke the dame, but no applause ensued;   35
Belinda frowned, Thalestris called her prude.
"To arms, to arms!" the fierce virago cries,
And swift as lightning to the combat flies.
All side in parties, and begin the attack;
Fans clap, silks rustle, and tough whalebones crack;   40
Heroes' and heroines' shouts confusedly rise,
And bass and treble voices strike the skies.
No common weapons in their hands are found,
Like Gods they fight, nor dread a mortal wound.
   So when bold Homer makes the Gods engage,   45
And heavenly breasts with human passions rage;
'Gainst Pallas, Mars; Latona, Hermes arms;
And all Olympus rings with loud alarms:
Jove's thunder roars, heaven trembles all around,
Blue Neptune storms, the bellowing deeps resound: 50
Earth shakes her nodding towers, the ground gives way,
And the pale ghosts start at the flash of day!
   Triumphant Umbriel on a sconce's[7] height
Clapped his glad wings, and sat to view the fight:
Propped on the bodkin spears, the sprites survey   55
The growing combat, or assist the fray.
   While through the press enraged Thalestris flies,
And scatters death around from both her eyes,
A beau and witling perished in the throng,
One died in metaphor, and one in song.   60
"O cruel nymph! a living death I bear,"
Cried Dapperwit, and sunk beside his chair.
A mournful glance Sir Fopling upwards cast,
"Those eyes are made so killing"—was his last.
Thus on Maeander's flowery margin lies   65
The expiring swan, and as he sings he dies.
   When bold Sir Plume had drawn Clarissa down,
Chloe stepped in, and killed him with a frown;
She smiled to see the doughty hero slain,
But, at her smile, the beau revived again.   70
   Now Jove suspends his golden scales in air,
Weighs the men's wits against the lady's hair;
The doubtful beam long nods from side to side;
At length the wits mount up, the hairs subside.
   See, fierce Belinda on the Baron flies,   75
With more than usual lightning in her eyes;
Nor feared the chief the unequal fight to try,

---

6. The speech is a close parody of Pope's own
translation of the speech of Sarpedon to Glaucus,
first published in 1709 and slightly revised in his
version of the *Iliad* (12.371–96).
7. Candlestick fastened on the wall.

Who sought no more than on his foe to die.
   But this bold lord with manly strength endued,
She with one finger and a thumb subdued: 80
Just where the breath of life his nostrils drew,
A charge of snuff the wily virgin threw;
The Gnomes direct, to every atom just,
The pungent grains of titillating dust.
Sudden, with starting tears each eye o'erflows,   85
And the high dome re-echoes to his nose.
   "Now meet thy fate," incensed Belinda cried,
And drew a deadly bodkin[8] from her side.
(The same, his ancient personage to deck,
Her great-great-grandsire wore about his neck,   90
In three seal rings; which after, melted down,
Formed a vast buckle for his widow's gown:
Her infant grandame's whistle next it grew,
The bells she jingled, and the whistle blew;
Then in a bodkin graced her mother' hairs,   95
Which long she wore, and now Belinda wears.)
   "Boast not my fall," he cried, "insulting foe!
Thou by some other shalt be laid as low.
Nor think to die dejects my lofty mind:
All that I dread is leaving you behind!   100
Rather than so, ah, let me still survive,
And burn in Cupid's flames—but burn alive."
   "Restore the Lock!" she cries; and all around
"Restore the Lock!" the vaulted roofs rebound.
Not fierce Othello in so loud a strain   105
Roared for the handkerchief that caused his pain.[9]
But see how oft ambitious aims are crossed,
And chiefs contend till all the prize is lost!
The lock, obtained with guilt, and kept with pain,
In every place is sought, but sought in vain: 110
With such a prize no mortal must be blessed,
So Heaven decrees! with Heaven who can contest?
   Some thought it mounted to the lunar sphere,
Since all things lost on earth are treasured there.
There heroes' wits are kept in ponderous vases,   115
And beaux' in snuffboxes and tweezer cases.
There broken vows and deathbed alms are found,
And lovers' hearts with ends of riband bound,
The courtier's promises, and sick man's prayers,
The smiles of harlots, and the tears of heirs,   120
Cages for gnats, and chains to yoke a flea,
Dried butterflies, and tomes of casuistry.
   But trust the Muse—she saw it upward rise,

8. An ornamental pin shaped like a dagger, to be   9. *Othello* 3.4.
worn in the hair.

Though marked by none but quick, poetic eyes
(So Rome's great founder to the heavens withdrew,[1]   125
To Proculus alone confessed in view);
A sudden star, it shot through liquid air,
And drew behind a radiant trail of hair.
Not Berenice's locks first rose so bright,[2]
The heavens bespangling with disheveled light.   130
The Sylphs behold it kindling as it flies,
And pleased pursue its progress through the skies.
   This the beau monde shall from the Mall[3] survey,
And hail with music its propitious ray.
This the blest lover shall for Venus take,   135
And send up vows from Rosamonda's Lake.[4]
This Partridge[5] soon shall view in cloudless skies,
When next he looks through Galileo's eyes;
And hence the egregious wizard shall foredoom
The fate of Louis, and the fall of Rome.   140
   Then cease, bright nymph! to mourn thy ravished hair,
Which adds new glory to the shining sphere!
Not all the tresses that fair head can boast,
Shall draw such envy as the Lock you lost.
For, after all the murders of your eye,   145
When, after millions slain, yourself shall die:
When those fair suns shall set, as set they must,
And all those tresses shall be laid in dust,
This Lock the Muse shall consecrate to fame,
And 'midst the stars inscribe Belinda's name.   150

1712   1714

Ode on Solitude[1]

Happy the man whose wish and care
   A few paternal acres bound,
Content to breathe his native air,
      In his own ground.

Whose herds with milk, whose fields with bread,   5
   Whose flocks supply him with attire,
Whose trees in summer yield him shade,
      In winter fire.

1. Romulus, the "founder" and first king of Rome, was snatched to heaven in a storm cloud while reviewing his army in the Campus Martius (Livy 1.16).

2. Berenice, the wife of Ptolemy III, dedicated a lock of her hair to the gods to ensure her husband's safe return from war. It was turned into a constellation.

3. A walk laid out by Charles II in St. James's Park, a resort for strollers of all sorts.

4. In St. James's Park; associated with unhappy lovers.

5. John Partridge, the astrologer whose annually published predictions had been amusingly satirized by Swift and other wits in 1708. "Galileo's eyes": i.e., a telescope.

1. The hint for this poem was taken from Horace's well-known *Epode* 2, which praises the simplicity and innocence of country life, a favorite literary theme in Pope's time.

Blest, who can unconcernedly find
　　Hours, days, and years slide soft away,   10
In health of body, peace of mind,
　　　　Quiet by day,

Sound sleep by night; study and ease,
　　Together mixed; sweet recreation;
And innocence, which most does please   15
　　　　With meditation.

Thus let me live, unseen, unknown;
　　Thus unlamented let me die;
Steal from the world, and not a stone
　　　　Tell where I lie.   20

ca. 1700–1709   1717, 1736

Epistle to Miss Blount[1]

On Her Leaving the Town, After the Coronation

As some fond virgin, whom her mother's care
Drags from the town to wholesome country air,
Just when she learns to roll a melting eye,
And hear a spark,[2] yet think no danger nigh;
From the dear man unwilling she must sever,   5
Yet takes one kiss before she parts forever:
Thus from the world fair Zephalinda[3] flew,
Saw others happy, and with sighs withdrew;
Not that their pleasures caused her discontent;
She sighed not that they stayed, but that she went.   10
　　She went to plain-work,[4] and to purling brooks,
Old-fashioned halls, dull aunts, and croaking rooks:
She went from opera, park, assembly, play,
To morning walks, and prayers three hours a day;
To part her time 'twixt reading and bohea,[5]   15
To muse, and spill her solitary tea,
Or o'er cold coffee trifle with the spoon,
Count the slow clock, and dine exact at noon;[6]
Divert her eyes with pictures in the fire,
Hum half a tune, tell stories to the squire;   20
Up to her godly garret after seven,
There starve and pray, for that's the way to heaven.

1. Teresa Blount, sister of Pope's lifelong friend
Martha Blount. The "coronation" was that of
George I (1714).
2. A fop, a beau.
3. A fanciful name adopted by Miss Blount.
4. "Needlework, as distinguished from embroidery" (Johnson's *Dictionary*).
5. A costly sort of tea.
6. The fashionable hour for dining in London was
three or four o'clock. A noon dinner is a sign of
old-fashioned rusticity.

Some squire, perhaps, you take delight to rack,
Whose game is whist, whose treat a toast in sack;
Who visits with a gun, presents you birds,   25
Then gives a smacking buss, and cries—"No words!"
Or with his hounds comes hollowing from the stable,
Makes love with nods and knees beneath a table;
Whose laughs are hearty, though his jests are coarse,
And loves you best of all things—but his horse.   30
    In some fair evening, on your elbow laid,
You dream of triumphs in the rural shade;
In pensive thought recall the fancied scene,
See coronations rise on every green:
Before you pass the imaginary sights   35
Of lords and earls and dukes and gartered knights,
While the spread fan o'ershades your closing eyes;
Then give one flirt,[7] and all the vision flies.
Thus vanish scepters, coronets, and balls,
And leave you in lone woods, or empty walls!   40
    So when your slave,[8] at some dear idle time
(Not plagued with headaches or the want of rhyme)
Stands in the streets, abstracted from the crew,
And while he seems to study, thinks of you;
Just when his fancy points[9] your sprightly eyes,   45
Or sees the blush of soft Parthenia[1] rise,
Gay[2] pats my shoulder, and you vanish quite;
Streets, chairs, and coxcombs rush upon my sight;
Vexed to be still in town, I knit my brow,
Look sour, and hum a tune—as you may now.   50

1717

An Essay on Man   Pope's philosophical poem, *An Essay on Man*,
is a fragment of an ambitious but never completed scheme for what the poet
referred to as his "ethic work," which was to have been a large survey of
human nature, society, and morals. The work is dedicated to Henry St. John
(pronounced *Sín-jun*), Viscount Bolingbroke (1678–1751), the brilliant,
though erratic, secretary of state in the Tory ministry of 1710–14, whom
Pope had come to know through Swift. After the accession of George I he
fled to France, attainted of treason, but was pardoned and allowed to return
in 1723. He settled near Pope at Dawley farm and a close friendship developed between the two men. In their conversations Bolingbroke, who fancied
himself a philosopher, helped Pope to formulate the optimistic system that
is expounded in this poem. Yet it is clear that the poem would have been
pretty much what it is had the two men never met, for it expresses doctrines
widely circulated and generally accepted at the time by enlightened minds
throughout Europe. The *Essay* gives memorable expression to ideas about

7. I.e., opens and closes her fan with a jerk.   1. Martha Blount.
8. I.e., Pope.   2. John Gay, the poet.
9. Notices.

the nature of the universe and man's place in it, ideas upon which eighteenth-century optimism rested.

Pope's purpose is to "vindicate the ways of God to man," a phrase that consciously echoes *Paradise Lost* 1.26. Like Milton, Pope faces the problem of the existence of evil in a world presumed to be the creation of a good God. *Paradise Lost* is Biblical in content, Christian in doctrine; the *Essay on Man* avoids all specifically Christian doctrines, not because Pope disbelieved them, but because "man," the subject of the poem, includes millions who never heard of Christianity, and Pope is concerned with the universal. Milton tells a mythological story. Pope writes in abstract terms.

The *Essay* is divided into four epistles. In the first Pope asserts the essential order and goodness of the universe and the rightness of our place in it. The other Epistles deal with how man may emulate in his nature and in society the cosmic harmony revealed in the first Epistle. The second seeks to show how he may attain a psychological harmony which can become the basis of a virtuous life through the co-operation of self-love and the passions (both necessary to our complete humanity) with reason, the controller and director. The third is concerned with man in society, which, it teaches, was created through the co-operation of self-love (the egoistic drives that motivate us) and social love (our dependence on others, our inborn benevolence). The fourth is concerned with happiness, which lies within the reach of all, for it is dependent upon virtue, which becomes possible when— though only when—self-love is transmuted into love of others and love of God. Such, in brief summary, are Pope's main ideas, expressed in many phrases so memorable that they have detached themselves from the poem and become a part of our daily speech.

From An Essay on Man

TO HENRY ST. JOHN, LORD BOLINGBROKE

Epistle 1. Of the Nature and State of Man, With Respect to the Universe

> Awake, my St. John! leave all meaner things
> To low ambition, and the pride of kings.
> Let us (since life can little more supply
> Than just to look about us and to die)
> Expatiate free[1] o'er all this scene of man;   5
> A mighty maze! but not without a plan;
> A wild, where weeds and flowers promiscuous shoot,
> Or garden, tempting with forbidden fruit.
> Together let us beat this ample field,
> Try what the open, what the covert yield;   10
> The latent tracts, the giddy heights, explore
> Of all who blindly creep, or sightless soar;
> Eye Nature's walks, shoot folly as it flies,
> And catch the manners living as they rise;

1. Range freely.

Laugh where we must, be candid[2] where we can;　　　　15
But vindicate the ways of God to man.[3]

    1. Say first, of God above, or man below,
What can we reason, but from what we know?
Of man, what see we but his station here,
From which to reason, or to which refer?　　　　20
Through worlds unnumbered though the God be known,
'Tis ours to trace him only in our own.
He, who through vast immensity can pierce,
See worlds on worlds compose one universe,
Observe how system into system runs,　　　　25
What other planets circle other suns,
What varied being peoples every star,
May tell why Heaven has made us as we are.
But of this frame the bearings, and the ties,
The strong connections, nice dependencies,　　　　30
Gradations just, has thy pervading soul
Looked through? or can a part contain the whole?
    Is the great chain, that draws all to agree,
And drawn supports, upheld by God, or thee?

    2. Presumptuous man! the reason wouldst thou find,　　　35
Why formed so weak, so little, and so blind?
First, if thou canst, the harder reason guess,
Why formed no weaker, blinder, and no less!
Ask of thy mother earth, why oaks are made
Taller or stronger than the weeds they shade?　　　　40
Or ask of yonder argent fields above,
Why Jove's satellites[4] are less than Jove?
    Of systems possible, if 'tis confessed
That Wisdom Infinite must form the best,
Where all must full or not coherent be,　　　　45
And all that rises, rise in due degree;
Then, in the scale of reasoning life, 'tis plain,
There must be, somewhere, such a rank as man:
And all the question (wrangle e'er so long)
Is only this, if God has placed him wrong?　　　　50
    Respecting man, whatever wrong we call,
May, must be right, as relative to all.
In human works, though labored on with pain,
A thousand movements scarce one purpose gain;
In God's, one single can its end produce;　　　　55
Yet serves to second too some other use.
So man, who here seems principal alone,
Perhaps acts second to some sphere unknown,
Touches some wheel, or verges to some goal;

---

2. Kindly.
3. Pope deliberately echoes *Paradise Lost* 1.26.

4. In his *Dictionary* Johnson notes and condemns Pope's giving his word four syllables, as in Latin.

'Tis but a part we see, and not a whole.   60
   When the proud steed shall know why man restrains
His fiery course, or drives him o'er the plains;
When the dull ox, why now he breaks the clod,
Is now a victim, and now Egypt's god:
Then shall man's pride and dullness comprehend   65
His actions', passions', being's use and end;
Why doing, suffering, checked, impelled; and why
This hour a slave, the next a deity.
   Then say not man's imperfect, Heaven in fault;
Say rather, man's as perfect as he ought;   70
His knowledge measured to his state and place,
His time a moment, and a point his space.
If to be perfect in a certain sphere,[5]
What matter, soon or late, or here or there?
The blest today is as completely so,   75
As who began a thousand years ago.

   3. Heaven from all creatures hides the book of Fate,
All but the page prescribed, their present state:
From brutes what men, from men what spirits know:
Or who could suffer being here below?   80
The lamb thy riot dooms to bleed today,
Had he thy reason, would he skip and play?
Pleased to the last, he crops the flowery food,
And licks the hand just raised to shed his blood.
O blindness to the future! kindly given,   85
That each may fill the circle marked by Heaven:
Who sees with equal eye, as God of all,
A hero perish, or a sparrow fall,
Atoms or systems[6] into ruin hurled,
And now a bubble burst, and now a world.   90
   Hope humbly then; with trembling pinions soar;
Wait the great teacher Death, and God adore!
What future bliss, he gives not thee to know,
But gives that hope to be thy blessing now.
Hope springs eternal in the human breast: 95
Man never is, but always to be blest:
The soul, uneasy and confined from home,
Rests and expatiates in a life to come.
   Lo! the poor Indian, whose untutored mind
Sees God in clouds, or hears him in the wind;   100
His soul proud Science never taught to stray
Far as the solar walk, or milky way;
Yet simple Nature to his hope has given,
Behind the cloud-topped hill, an humbler heaven;
Some safer world in depth of woods embraced,   105

5. I.e., in one's "state and place."   6. Solar systems.

Some happier island in the watery waste,
Where slaves once more their native land behold,
No fiends torment, no Christians thirst for gold!
To be, contents his natural desire,
He asks no angel's wing, no seraph's fire;   110
But thinks, admitted to that equal sky,
His faithful dog shall bear him company.

    4. Go, wiser thou! and, in thy scale of sense,
Weigh thy opinion against Providence;
Call imperfection what thou fancy'st such,   115
Say, here he gives too little, there too much;
Destroy all creatures for thy sport or gust,[7]
Yet cry, if man's unhappy, God's unjust;
If man alone engross not Heaven's high care,
Alone made perfect here, immortal there: 120
Snatch from his hand the balance and the rod,
Rejudge his justice, be the God of God!
In pride, in reasoning pride, our error lies;
All quit their sphere, and rush into the skies.
Pride still is aiming at the blest abodes,   125
Men would be angels, angels would be gods.
Aspiring to be gods, if angels fell,
Aspiring to be angels, men rebel:
And who but wishes to invert the laws
Of order, sins against the Eternal Cause.   130

    5. Ask for what end the heavenly bodies shine,
Earth for whose use? Pride answers, " 'Tis for mine:
For me kind Nature wakes her genial power,
Suckles each herb, and spreads out every flower;
Annual for me, the grape, the rose renew   135
The juice nectareous, and the balmy dew;
For me, the mine a thousand treasures brings;
For me, health gushes from a thousand springs;
Seas roll to waft me, suns to light me rise;
My footstool earth, my canopy the skies."   140
    But errs not Nature from this gracious end,
From burning suns when livid deaths descend,
When earthquakes swallow, or when tempests sweep
Towns to one grave, whole nations to the deep?
"No," 'tis replied, "the first Almighty Cause   145
Acts not by partial, but by general laws;
The exceptions few; some change since all began,
And what created perfect?"—Why then man?
If the great end be human happiness,
Then Nature deviates; and can man do less?   150

---

7. "Sense of tasting" (Johnson's *Dictionary*).

As much that end a constant course requires
Of showers and sunshine, as of man's desires;
As much eternal springs and cloudless skies,
As men forever temperate, calm, and wise.
If plagues or earthquakes break not Heaven's design,   155
Why then a Borgia, or a Catiline?[8]
Who knows but he whose hand the lightning forms,
Who heaves old ocean, and who wings the storms,
Pours fierce ambition in a Caesar's mind,
Or turns young Ammon[9] loose to scourge mankind?   160
From pride, from pride, our very reasoning springs;
Account for moral, as for natural things:
Why charge we Heaven in those, in these acquit?
In both, to reason right is to submit.
     Better for us, perhaps, it might appear,   165
Were there all harmony, all virtue here;
That never air or ocean felt the wind;
That never passion discomposed the mind:
But ALL subsists by elemental strife;
And passions are the elements of life.   170
The general ORDER, since the whole began,
Is kept in Nature, and is kept in man.

     6. What would this man? Now upward will he soar,
And little less than angel, would be more;
Now looking downwards, just as grieved appears   175
To want the strength of bulls, the fur of bears.
Made for his use all creatures if he call,
Say what their use, had he the powers of all?
Nature to these, without profusion, kind,
The proper organs, proper powers assigned;   180
Each seeming want compènsated of course,
Here with degrees of swiftness, there of force;
All in exact proportion to the state;
Nothing to add, and nothing to abate.
Each beast, each insect, happy in its own;   185
Is Heaven unkind to man, and man alone?
Shall he alone, whom rational we call,
Be pleased with nothing, if not blessed with all?
     The bliss of man (could pride that blessing find)
Is not to act or think beyond mankind;   190
No powers of body or of soul to share,
But what his nature and his state can bear.
Why has not man a microscopic eye?

8. The Renaissance Italian family of the Borgias were notorious for their crimes: ruthless lust for power, cruelty, rapaciousness, treachery, and murder (especially by poisoning); Cesare Borgia (1476–1507), son of Pope Alexander VI, is here referred to. Lucius Sergius Catiline (ca. 108–62 B.C.), an ambitious, greedy, and cruel conspirator against the Roman state, was denounced in Cicero's famous orations before the senate and in the Forum. 9. Alexander the Great.

For this plain reason, man is not a fly.
Say what the use, were finer optics given,   195
To inspect a mite, not comprehend the heaven?
Or touch, if tremblingly alive all o'er,
To smart and agonize at every pore?
Or quick effluvia[1] darting through the brain,
Die of a rose in aromatic pain?   200
If nature thundered in his opening ears,
And stunned him with the music of the spheres,
How would he wish that Heaven had left him still
The whispering zephyr, and the purling rill?
Who finds not Providence all good and wise,   205
Alike in what it gives, and what denies?

7. Far as creation's ample range extends,
The scale of sensual,[2] mental powers ascends:
Mark how it mounts, to man's imperial race,
From the green myriads in the peopled grass: 210
What modes of sight betwixt each wide extreme,
The mole's dim curtain, and the lynx's beam:[3]
Of smell, the headlong lioness between,
And hound sagacious[4] on the tainted green:
Of hearing, from the life that fills the flood,   215
To that which warbles through the vernal wood:
The spider's touch, how exquisitely fine!
Feels at each thread, and lives along the line:
In the nice[5] bee, what sense so subtly true
From poisonous herbs extracts the healing dew: 220
How instinct varies in the groveling swine,
Compared, half-reasoning elephant, with thine!
'Twixt that, and reason, what a nice barrier,[6]
Forever separate, yet forever near!
Remembrance and reflection how allied;   225
What thin partitions sense from thought divide:
And middle natures, how they long to join,
Yet never pass the insuperable line!
Without this just gradation, could they be
Subjected, these to those, or all to thee?   230
The powers of all subdued by thee alone,
Is not thy reason all these powers in one?

8. See, through this air, this ocean, and this earth,
All matter quick, and bursting into birth.

---

1. According to the philosophy of Epicurus (adopted by Robert Boyle, the chemist, and other 17th-century scientists), the senses are stirred to perception by being bombarded through the pores by steady streams of "effluvia," incredibly thin and tiny—but material—images of the objects which surround us.

2. Sensory.
3. One of several early theories of vision held that the eye casts a beam of light which makes objects visible.
4. Quick of scent.
5. Exact, accurate.
6. Pronounced *ba-réer*.

Above, how high progressive life may go!   235
Around, how wide! how deep extend below!
Vast Chain of Being! which from God began,
Natures ethereal, human, angel, man,
Beast, bird, fish, insect, what no eye can see,
No glass can reach! from Infinite to thee,   240
From thee to nothing.—On superior powers
Were we to press, inferior might on ours:
Or in the full creation leave a void,
Where, one step broken, the great scale's destroyed:
From Nature's chain whatever link you strike,   245
Tenth or ten thousandth, breaks the chain alike.
　　And, if each system in gradation roll
Alike essential to the amazing Whole,
The least confusion but in one, not all
That system only, but the Whole must fall.   250
Let earth unbalanced from her orbit fly,
Planets and suns run lawless through the sky,
Let ruling angels from their spheres be hurled,
Being on being wrecked, and world on world,
Heaven's whole foundations to their center nod,   255
And Nature tremble to the throne of God:
All this dread ORDER break—for whom? for thee?
Vile worm!—oh, madness, pride, impiety!

　　9. What if the foot, ordained the dust to tread,
Or hand, to toil, aspired to be the head?   260
What if the head, the eye, or ear repined
To serve mere engines to the ruling Mind?[7]
Just as absurd, to mourn the tasks or pains,   265
The great directing MIND of ALL ordains.
　　All are but parts of one stupendous whole,
Whose body Nature is, and God the soul;
That, changed through all, and yet in all the same,
Great in the earth, as in the ethereal frame,   270
Warms in the sun, refreshes in the breeze,
Glows in the stars, and blossoms in the trees,
Lives through all life, extends through all extent,
Spreads undivided, operates unspent,
Breathes in our soul, informs our mortal part,   275
As full, as perfect, in a hair as heart;
As full, as perfect, in vile man that mourns,
As the rapt seraph that adores and burns;
To him no high, no low, no great, no small;
He fills, he bounds, connects, and equals all.   280

　　10. Cease then, nor ORDER imperfection name:
Our proper bliss depends on what we blame.

---

7. Cf. 1 Corinthians 12.14–26.

Know thy own point: this kind, this due degree
Of blindness, weakness, Heaven bestows on thee.
Submit—In this, or any other sphere,   285
Secure to be as blest as thou canst bear:
Safe in the hand of one disposing Power,
Or in the natal, or the mortal hour.
All Nature is but art, unknown to thee;
All chance, direction, which thou canst not see;   290
All discord, harmony not understood;
All partial evil, universal good:
And, spite of pride, in erring reason's spite,
One truth is clear: Whatever IS, is RIGHT.

From Epistle 2. Of the Nature and State of Man With Respect to Himself, as an Individual[8]

1. Know then thyself, presume not God to scan;
The proper study of mankind is Man.
Placed on this isthmus of a middle state,
A being darkly wise, and rudely great:
With too much knowledge for the skeptic side,   5
With too much weakness for the Stoic's pride,
He hangs between; in doubt to act, or rest,
In doubt to deem himself a god, or beast;
In doubt his mind or body to prefer,
Born but to die, and reasoning but to err;   10
Alike in ignorance, his reason such,
Whether he thinks too little, or too much:
Chaos of thought and passion, all confused;
Still by himself abused, or disabused;
Created half to rise, and half to fall;   15
Great lord of all things, yet a prey to all;
Sole judge of truth, in endless error hurled:
The glory, jest, and riddle of the world!

                              *   *   *   1733

Epistle 2. To a Lady[1]

OF THE CHARACTERS OF WOMEN

Nothing so true as what you once let fall,
"Most women have no characters at all."

---

8. For the author's revisions while composing these lines, see "Poems in Process," below.
1. This is one of four poems that Pope grouped together under the title *Epistles to Several Persons*, but that have usually been known by the less appropriate title *Moral Essays*. They were con-

ceived as parts of Pope's ambitious "ethic work," of which only the first part, the *Essay on Man*, was completed. *Epistle* 1 treats the characters of men, *Epistle* 2 the characters of women. The other two epistles are concerned with the use of riches, a subject that engaged Pope's attention during the

Matter too soft a lasting mark to bear,
And best distinguished by black, brown, or fair.
    How many pictures[2] of one nymph we view,   5
All how unlike each other, all how true!
Arcadia's countess, here, in ermined pride,
Is, there, Pastora by a fountain side.
Here Fannia, leering on her own good man,
And there, a naked Leda with a swan.[3]   10
Let then the fair one beautifully cry,
In Magdalen's loose hair and lifted eye,
Or dressed in smiles of sweet Cecilia shine,[4]
With simpering angels, palms, and harps divine;
Whether the charmer sinner it, or saint it,   15
If folly grow romantic,[5] I must paint it.
    Come then, the colors and the ground[6] prepare!
Dip in the rainbow, trick her off in air;
Choose a firm cloud, before it fall, and in it
Catch, ere she change, the Cynthia[7] of this minute.   20
    Rufa, whose eye quick-glancing o'er the park,
Attracts each light gay meteor of a spark,
Agrees as ill with Rufa studying Locke,[8]
As Sappho's diamonds with her dirty smock,
Or Sappho at her toilet's greasy task,[9]   25
With Sappho fragrant at an evening masque:
So morning insects that in muck begun,

1730s, since he distrusted the influence on private morals and public life of the rapidly growing wealth of England under the first Hanoverians.

    Epistle 2 contains a series of brilliantly executed portraits (the metaphor of portrait painting dominates the poem) which among them illustrate the thesis that women are consistent only in being inconsistent. As we move from portrait to portrait, we not only observe ladies who are changeable and fickle in their own nature, but we also meet a variety of female characters—the affected, the slatternly, the soft-natured, the silly, the lewd, for instance—who remind us that ladies are as variegated as tulips (line 41).

    Are the portraits imaginary or do they represent women whom Pope knew and whom his readers could recognize? This question exercised the gossips of Pope's own time and after; and it has occupied the attention of Pope's editors and commentators ever since his death. Many of the portraits indubitably allude to actual women (Sappho); some doubtless are composite (Atossa); others are mere types. Questions of identity, however, pertain rather to Pope's biography and character than to his art. It should matter little if at all to the reader first approaching Pope's satire whether in fact Atossa is Sarah, duchess of Marlborough, or, as is much more likely, Katherine, duchess of Buckinghamshire, or, most likely of all, Katherine combined with a few traits of Sarah. Occasionally, perhaps, a lady's name might have hinted to some of Pope's contemporaries that a real person was

intended. Today the reader who is not a specialist will do well to neglect particular applications of Pope's satire and to concern himself with the generally, the permanently human, which is always the center of Pope's works.

    The "lady" of the title is Martha Blount (1690–1763), Pope's best-loved female friend, to whom he left the bulk of his property.

2. Ladies of the 17th and 18th centuries liked to have themselves painted in the costumes and attitudes of fanciful, mythological, or historical characters.

3. Leda was seduced by Zeus, who approached her in the form of a swan.

4. St. Mary Magdalen was often painted during the 17th century in the attitude described in line 12. St. Cecilia, the reputed inventor of the organ, was traditionally painted in the manner which Pope satirically glances at here.

5. Extravagant.

6. The first coatings of paint on the canvas before the figures in the picture are sketched in.

7. One of the names of Diana, goddess of the moon, a notoriously changeable heavenly body.

8. John Locke, author of *An Essay Concerning Human Understanding* (1690).

9. Lady Mary Wortley Montagu, though beautiful as a young woman, became notorious for her slatternly appearance and personal uncleanliness. Both Sappho and Lady Mary were female poets. "Flyblow": deposit their eggs.

Shine, buzz, and flyblow in the setting sun.
    How soft is Silia! fearful to offend,
The frail one's advocate, the weak one's friend: 30
To her, Calista proved her conduct nice,
And good Simplicius asks of her advice.
Sudden, she storms! she raves! You tip the wink,
But spare your censure; Silia does not drink.
All eyes may see from what the change arose,   35
All eyes may see—a pimple on her nose.
    Papillia,[1] wedded to her amorous spark,
Sighs for the shades—"How charming is a park!"
A park is purchased, but the fair he sees
All bathed in tears—"Oh, odious, odious trees!"   40
    Ladies, like variegated tulips, show;
'Tis to their changes half their charms we owe;
Fine by defect, and delicately weak,
Their happy spots the nice admirer take,
'Twas thus Calypso[2] once each heart alarmed,   45
Awed without virtue, without beauty charmed;
Her tongue bewitched as oddly as her eyes,
Less wit than mimic, more a wit than wise;
Strange graces still, and stranger flights she had,
Was just not ugly, and was just not mad;   50
Yet ne'er so sure your passion to create,
As when she touched the brink of all we hate.
    Narcissa's[3] nature, tolerably mild,
To make a wash,[4] would hardly stew a child;
Has even been proved to grant a lover's prayer,   55
And paid a tradesman once to make him stare,
Gave alms at Easter, in a Christian trim,
And made a widow happy, for a whim.
Why then declare good nature is her scorn,
When 'tis by that alone she can be borne?   60
Why pique all mortals, yet affect a name?
A fool to pleasure, yet a slave to fame:
Now deep in Taylor and the *Book of Martyrs*,[5]
Now drinking citron[6] with his Grace and Chartres.
Now conscience chills her, and now passion burns;   65
And atheism and religion take their turns;

---

1. The name comes from Latin for "butterfly."
2. The name is borrowed from the fascinating goddess who detained Odysseus on her island for seven years after the fall of Troy, thus preventing his return to his kingdom, Ithaca.
3. Type of extreme self-love. Narcissus, a beautiful youth, fell in love with his own image when he saw it reflected in a fountain.
4. Cosmetic lotion.
5. Jeremy Taylor, 17th-century Anglican divine, whose *Holy Living and Holy Dying* was often reprinted in the 18th century. John Foxe's *Acts and Monuments* (usually referred to as Foxe's *Book of Martyrs*), 1563, was a household book in most Protestant families in the 17th and 18th centuries; a record of the Protestants who perished for their faith under the persecution of Mary Tudor (1553–58), it was instrumental in keeping anti-Catholic sentiments alive.
6. I.e., citron-water, brandy flavored with lemon or orange peel. "His Grace" is usually said to be the duke of Wharton, an old enemy of Swift's and a notorious libertine; Francis Chartres: a debauchee often mentioned by Pope.

A very heathen in the carnal part,
Yet still a sad, good Christian at her heart.

    See Sin in state, majestically drunk;
Proud as a peeress, prouder as a punk;   70
Chaste to her husband, frank[7] to all beside,
A teeming mistress, but a barren bride.
What then? let blood and body bear the fault,
Her head's untouched, that noble seat of thought:
Such this day's doctrine—in another fit   75
She sins with poets through pure love of wit.
What has not fired her bosom or her brain?
Caesar and Tallboy,[8] Charles and Charlemagne.
As Helluo,[9] late dictator of the feast,
The nose of hautgout,[1] and the tip of taste,   80
Criticked your wine, and analyzed your meat,
Yet on plain pudding deigned at home to eat;
So Philomedé,[2] lecturing all mankind
On the soft passion, and the taste refined,
The address, the delicacy—stoops at once,   85
And makes her hearty meal upon a dunce.

    Flavia's a wit, has too much sense to pray;
To toast our wants and wishes, is her way;
Nor asks of God, but of her stars, to give
The mighty blessing, "while we live, to live."   90
Then all for death, that opiate of the soul!
Lucretia's dagger,[3] Rosamonda's bowl.
Say, what can cause such impotence of mind?
A spark too fickle, or a spouse too kind.
Wise wretch! with pleasures too refined to please,   95
With too much spirit to be e'er at ease,
With too much quickness ever to be taught,
With too much thinking to have common thought:
You purchase pain with all that joy can give,
And die of nothing but a rage to live.   100

    Turn then from wits; and look on Simo's mate,
No ass so meek, no ass so obstinate.
Or her, that owns her faults, but never mends,
Because she's honest, and the best of friends:
Or her, whose life the Church and scandal share,   105
Forever in a passion, or a prayer:
Or her, who laughs at hell, but (like her Grace)
Cries, "Ah! how charming, if there's no such place!"

---

7. "Liberal; generous" (Johnson's *Dictionary*).
8. A crude young man in Richard Brome's comedy *The Jovial Crew* (1641) or the opera adapted from the play (1731); "Charles," as F. W. Bateson points out, was a generic name for a footman in the period.
9. Latin for "glutton."
1. "Anything with a strong relish or strong scent,

as overkept venison" (Johnson's *Dictionary*).
2. The name is Pope's adaptation of a Greek epithet meaning "laughter-loving," frequently applied to Aphrodite, the goddess of love.
3. Lucretia, violated by Tarquin, committed suicide; according to tradition, the "fair Rosamonda," mistress of Henry II, was forced by Queen Eleanor to drink poison.

Or who in sweet vicissitude appears
Of mirth and opium, ratafie[4] and tears,   110
The daily anodyne, and nightly draught,
To kill those foes to fair ones, time and thought.
Woman and fool are two hard things to hit,
For true no-meaning puzzles more than wit.
   But what are these to great Atossa's mind?[5]   115
Scarce once herself, by turns all womankind!
Who, with herself, or others, from her birth
Finds all her life one warfare upon earth:
Shines in exposing knaves, and painting fools,
Yet is whate'er she hates and ridicules.   120
No thought advances, but her eddy brain
Whisks it about, and down it goes again.
Full sixty years the world has been her trade,
The wisest fool much time has ever made.
From loveless youth to unrespected age,   125
No passion gratified except her rage.
So much the fury still outran the wit,
The pleasure missed her, and the scandal hit.
Who breaks with her, provokes revenge from hell,
But he's a bolder man who dares be well:[6]   130
Her every turn with violence pursued,
Nor more a storm her hate than gratitude:
To that each passion turns, or soon or late;
Love, if it makes her yield, must make her hate:
Superiors? death! and equals? what a curse!   135
But an inferior not dependent? worse.
Offend her, and she knows not to forgive;
Oblige her, and she'll hate you while you live:
But die, and she'll adore you—Then the bust
And temple rise—then fall again to dust.   140
Last night, her lord was all that's good and great;
A knave this morning, and his will a cheat.
Strange! by the means defeated of the ends,
By spirit robbed of power, by warmth of friends,
By wealth of followers! without one distress   145
Sick of herself through very selfishness!
Atossa, cursed with every granted prayer,
Childless with all her children, wants an heir.
To heirs unknown descends the unguarded store,
Or wanders, Heaven-directed, to the poor.   150
   Pictures like these, dear Madam, to design,
Asks no firm hand, and no unerring line;
Some wandering touches, some reflected light,

---

4. "A fine liquor, prepared from the kernels of
apricots and spirits" (Johnson's *Dictionary*).
5. Atossa, daughter of Cyrus, Emperor of Persia
(d. 529 B.C.). If the duchess of Buckinghamshire
is alluded to, the name is appropriate, for she was
the natural daughter of James II.
6. Be in her favor.

Some flying stroke alone can hit 'em right:
For how should equal colors do the knack?[7]   155
Chameleons who can paint in white and black?
    "Yet Chloe sure was formed without a spot—"
Nature in her then erred not, but forgot.
"With every pleasing, every prudent part,
Say, what can Chloe want?"—She wants a heart.   160
She speaks, behaves, and acts just as she ought;
But never, never, reached one generous thought.
Virtue she finds too painful an endeavor,
Content to dwell in decencies forever.
So very reasonable, so unmoved,   165
As never yet to love, or to be loved.
She, while her lover pants upon her breast,
Can mark[8] the figures on an Indian chest;
And when she sees her friend in deep despair,
Observes how much a chintz exceeds mohair.   170
Forbid it Heaven, a favor or a debt
She e'er should cancel—but she may forget.
Safe is your secret still in Chloe's ear;
But none of Chloe's shall you ever hear.
Of all her dears she never slandered one,   175
But cares not if a thousand are undone.
Would Chloe know if you're alive or dead?
She bids her footman put it in her head.
Chloe is prudent—Would you too be wise?
Then never break your heart when Chloe dies.   180
    One certain portrait may (I grant) be seen,
Which Heaven has varnished out, and made a *Queen*:[9]
The same forever! and described by all
With Truth and Goodness, as with crown and ball.
Poets heap virtues, painters gems at will,   185
And show their zeal, and hide their want of skill.
'Tis well—but, artists! who can paint or write,
To draw the naked is your true delight.
That robe of quality so struts and swells,
None see what parts of Nature it conceals: 190
The exactest traits of body or of mind,
We owe to models of an humble kind.
If Queensberry[1] to strip there's no compelling,
'Tis from a handmaid we must take a Helen.
From peer or bishop 'tis no easy thing   195
To draw the man who loves his God, or king:
Alas! I copy (or my draft would fail)
From honest Mah'met[2] or plain Parson Hale.

7. Do the trick.
8. Pay attention to.
9. Pope refers as usual to Queen Caroline with
disapprobation.
1. The duchess of Queensberry, whom Pope val-

ued because of her kindness to his friend John Gay,
had been a famous beauty.
2. Mahomet, a Turkish servant of George I; Dr.
Stephen Hales was an Anglican clergyman and
friend of Pope.

But grant, in public men sometimes are shown,
A woman's seen in private life alone: 200
Our bolder talents in full light displayed;
Your virtues open fairest in the shade.
Bred to disguise, in public 'tis you hide;
There, none distinguish 'twixt your shame or pride,
Weakness or delicacy; all so nice,   205
That each may seem a virtue, or a vice.
    In men, we various ruling passions find;
In women, two almost divide the kind;
Those, only fixed, they first or last obey,
The love of pleasure, and the love of sway.   210
    That, Nature gives; and where the lesson taught
Is but to please, can pleasure seem a fault?
Experience, this; by man's oppression cursed,
They seek the second not to lose the first.
    Men, some to business, some to pleasure take;   215
But every woman is at heart a rake;
Men, some to quiet, some to public strife;
But every lady would be queen for life.
    Yet mark the fate of a whole sex of queens!
Power all their end, but beauty all the means: 220
In youth they conquer, with so wild a rage,
As leaves them scarce a subject in their age:
For foreign glory, foreign joy, they roam;
No thought of peace or happiness at home.
But wisdom's triumph is well-timed retreat,   225
As hard a science to the fair as great!
Beauties, like tyrants, old and friendless grown,
Yet hate repose, and dread to be alone,
Worn out in public, weary every eye,
Nor leave one sigh behind them when they die.   230
    Pleasures the sex, as children birds, pursue,
Still out of reach, yet never out of view,
Sure, if they catch, to spoil the toy at most,
To covet flying, and regret when lost:
At last, to follies youth could scarce defend,   235
It grows their age's prudence to pretend;
Ashamed to own they gave delight before,
Reduced to feign it, when they give no more:
As hags hold sabbaths,[3] less for joy than spite,
So these their merry, miserable night;   240
Still round and round the ghosts of beauty glide,
And haunt the places where their honor died.
    See how the world its veterans rewards!
A youth of frolics, an old age of cards;
Fair to no purpose, artful to no end,   245

---

3. Obscene rites popularly supposed to be held by   to evenings on which ladies entertained guests.
witches ("hags"); "night," in the next line, refers

Young without lovers, old without a friend;
A fop their passion, but their prize a sot;
Alive, ridiculous, and dead, forgot!
    Ah friend! to dazzle let the vain design;
To raise the thought, and touch the heart be thine!   250
That charm shall grow, while what fatigues the Ring[4]
Flaunts and goes down, an unregarded thing:
So when the sun's broad beam has tired the sight,
All mild ascends the moon's more sober light,
Serene in virgin modesty she shines,   255
And unobserved the glaring orb declines.
    Oh! blest with temper, whose unclouded ray
Can make tomorrow cheerful as today;
She, who can love a sister's charms, or hear
Sighs for a daughter with unwounded ear;   260
She, who ne'er answers till a husband cools,
Or, if she rules him, never shows she rules;
Charms by accepting, by submitting sways,
Yet has her humor most, when she obeys;
Lets fops or fortune fly which way they will;   265
Disdains all loss of tickets[5] or Codille;
Spleen, vapors, or smallpox, above them all,
And mistress of herself, though China[6] fall.
    And yet, believe me, good as well as ill,
Woman's at best a contradiction still.   270
Heaven, when it strives to polish all it can
Its last best work, but forms a softer man;
Picks from each sex, to make the favorite blest,
Your love of pleasure, our desire of rest:
Blends, in exception to all general rules,   275
Your taste of follies, with our scorn of fools:
Reserve with frankness, art with truth allied,
Courage with softness, modesty with pride;
Fixed principles, with fancy ever new;
Shakes all together, and produces—you.   280
    Be this a woman's fame: with this unblest,
Toasts live a scorn, and queens may die a jest.
This Phoebus promised (I forget the year)
When those blue eyes first opened on the sphere;
Ascendant Phoebus watched that hour with care,   285
Averted half your parents' simple prayer;
And gave you beauty, but denied the pelf
That buys your sex a tyrant o'er itself.
The generous god, who wit and gold refines,
And ripens spirits as he ripens mines,[7]   290

4. The fashionable drive in Hyde Park.
5. I.e., lottery tickets; "Codille": the loss of a hand
at the card games of ombre or quadrille.
6. Pope refers punningly to the chinaware which
fashionable women collected enthusiastically.

7. Phoebus Apollo, as god of poetry "ripens wit";
as god of the sun, he "ripens mines," for respectable scientific theory held that the sun's rays mature
precious metals in the earth.

Kept dross for duchesses, the world shall know it,
To you gave sense, good humor, and a poet.

1735, 1744

Epistle to Dr. Arbuthnot[1]

Advertisement
TO THE FIRST PUBLICATION OF THIS *Epistle*

This paper is a sort of bill of complaint, begun many years since, and
drawn up by snatches, as the several occasions offered. I had no thoughts
of publishing it, till it pleased some persons of rank and fortune (the
authors of *Verses to the Imitator of Horace*, and of an *Epistle to a Doctor
of Divinity from a Nobleman at Hampton Court*) to attack, in a very
extraordinary manner, not only my writings (of which, being public, the
public is judge) but my person, morals, and family, whereof, to those
who know me not, a truer information may be requisite. Being divided
between the necessity to say something of myself, and my own laziness
to undertake so awkward a task, I thought it the shortest way to put the
last hand to this epistle. If it have anything pleasing, it will be that by
which I am most desirous to please, the truth and the sentiment; and if
anything offensive, it will be only to those I am least sorry to offend, the
vicious or the ungenerous.

1. Dr. John Arbuthnot (1667–1735), to whom
Pope addressed his best-known verse epistle, was
distinguished both as a physician and as a man of
wit. He had been one of the liveliest members of
the Martinus Scriblerus Club, helping his friends
to create the character and shape the career of the
learned pedant whose *Memoirs* the Club had
undertaken to write.

Pope had long been meditating such a poem,
which was to be both an attack on his detractors
and a defense of his own character and career. In
his usual way he had jotted down hints, lines, couplets, fragments over a period of two decades, but
the poem might never have been completed had it
not been for two events: Arbuthnot, from his
deathbed, wrote to urge Pope to continue his
abhorrence of vice and to express it in his writings;
and during 1733, Pope was the victim of two bitter
attacks by "persons of rank and fortune," as the
"Advertisement" has it. The *Verses Addressed to
the Imitator of Horace* was the work of Lady Mary
Wortley Montagu, helped by her friend Lord
Hervey (pronounced "Harvey"), a close friend and
confidant of Queen Caroline; *An Epistle to a Doctor of Divinity from a Nobleman at Hampton Court*
was the work of Lord Hervey alone. Lady Mary, it
must be admitted, had provocation enough, especially in Pope's recent reference to her in *The First
Satire of the Second Book of Horace*, lines 83–84;
but Hervey had little to complain of beyond occasional covert references to him as "Lord Fanny."
At any rate, the two scurrilous attacks goaded Pope

into action, and the poem was completed by the
end of the summer of 1734.

The *Epistle* is a masterpiece of poetic rhetoric.
The very fact that it is addressed to Dr. Arbuthnot,
a man who had the general approbation of the world
because of his kindliness and probity, in some
degree seems to guarantee the integrity of the "I"
of the poem and to diminish the moral stature of
his enemies. This acquisition of virtue through
association, an effective stroke, is supported by every
device of persuasive rhetoric: reasonable argument
and emotional appeals, subtly suggestive imagery,
and superbly controlled shifts in tone and style
which help to sway the reader's judgment to the
side of the speaker. The poem opens in the flat
language of commonplace prose discourse, tinged
with a wry humor and a tone of exasperation: "Shut,
shut the door, good John! (fatigued, I said)" and as
it progresses it rises or falls in language and style
according to the emotions which the speaker
expresses—anger, contempt, amusement, sarcasm, mock self-pity, indignation, hatred, affection, gratitude, tenderness—to return at the end to
the homely tone of the opening.

It is not clear that Pope intended the poem to be
thought of as a dialogue, as it has usually been
printed since Warburton's edition of 1751. The
original edition, while suggesting interruptions in
the flow of the monologue, kept entirely to the
form of a letter. The introduction of the friend,
who speaks from time to time, of course converts
the original letter into a dramatic dialogue.

Many will know their own pictures in it, there being not a circumstance but what is true; but I have, for the most part, spared their names, and they may escape being laughed at, if they please.

I would have some of them know, it was owing to the request of the learned and candid friend to whom it is inscribed, that I make not as free use of theirs as they have done of mine. However, I shall have this advantage, and honor, on my side, that whereas, by their proceeding, any abuse may be directed at any man, no injury can possibly be done by mine, since a nameless character can never be found out, but by its truth and likeness. P.

P. Shut, shut the door, good John![2] (fatigued, I said),
Tie up the knocker, say I'm sick, I'm dead.
The Dog Star[3] rages! nay 'tis past a doubt
All Bedlam,[4] or Parnassus, is let out:
Fire in each eye, and papers in each hand,   5
They rave, recite, and madden round the land.
    What walls can guard me, or what shades can hide?
They pierce my thickets, through my grot[5] they glide,
By land, by water, they renew the charge,
They stop the chariot, and they board the barge.   10
No place is sacred, not the church is free;
Even Sunday shines no Sabbath day to me:
Then from the Mint[6] walks forth the man of rhyme,
Happy to catch me just at dinner time.
    Is there a parson, much bemused in beer,   15
A maudlin poetess, a rhyming peer,
A clerk foredoomed his father's soul to cross,
Who pens a stanza when he should engross?[7]
Is there who,[8] locked from ink and paper, scrawls
With desperate charcoal round his darkened walls?   20
All fly to Twit'nam,[9] and in humble strain
Apply to me to keep them mad or vain.
Arthur,[1] whose giddy son neglects the laws,
Imputes to me and my damned works the cause:
Poor Cornus[2] sees his frantic wife elope,   25
And curses wit, and poetry, and Pope.
    Friend to my life (which did not you prolong,

---

2. John Serle, Pope's gardener.
3. Sirius, associated with the period of greatest heat (and hence of madness) because it sets with the sun in late summer. August, in ancient Rome, was the season for reciting poetry.
4. Bethlehem Hospital for the insane in London.
5. The subterranean passage under the road that separated his house at Twickenham from his garden became, in Pope's hands, a romantic grotto ornamented with shells and mirrors.
6. A place in Southwark where debtors were free from arrest (they could not be arrested anywhere on Sundays).

7. Write out legal documents.
8. Is there some madman who, locked up without ink or paper. . . ?
9. I.e., Twickenham, Pope's villa on the bank of the Thames, a few miles above Hampton Court.
1. Arthur Moore, whose son, James Moore Smythe, dabbled in literature. Moore Smythe had earned Pope's enmity by using in one of his plays some unpublished lines from Pope's *Epistle to a Lady* in spite of Pope's objections.
2. Latin for "horn," the traditional emblem of the cuckold.

The world had wanted many an idle song)
What drop or nostrum[3] can this plague remove?
Or which must end me, a fool's wrath or love?   30
A dire dilemma! either way I'm sped,[4]
If foes, they write, if friends, they read me dead.
Seized and tied down to judge, how wretched I!
Who can't be silent, and who will not lie.
To laugh were want of goodness and of grace,   35
And to be grave exceeds all power of face.
I sit with sad civility, I read
With honest anguish and an aching head,
And drop at last, but in unwilling ears,
This saving counsel, "Keep your piece nine years."[5]   40
    "Nine years!" cries he, who high in Drury Lane,[6]
Lulled by soft zephyrs through the broken pane,
Rhymes ere he wakes, and prints before term[7] ends,
Obliged by hunger and request of friends:
"The piece, you think, is incorrect? why, take it,   45
I'm all submission, what you'd have it, make it."
    Three things another's modest wishes bound,
My friendship, and a prologue, and ten pound.
    Pitholeon[8] sends to me: "You know his Grace,
I want a patron; ask him for a place."   50
Pitholeon libeled me—"but here's a letter
Informs you, sir, 'twas when he knew no better.
Dare you refuse him? Curll[9] invites to dine,
He'll write a *Journal*, or he'll turn divine."[1]
Bless me! a packet.—" 'Tis a stranger sues,   55
A virgin tragedy, an orphan Muse."
If I dislike it, "Furies, death, and rage!"
If I approve, "Commend it to the stage."
There (thank my stars) my whole commission ends,
The players and I are, luckily, no friends.   60
Fired that the house reject him, " 'Sdeath, I'll print it,
And shame the fools—Your interest, sir, with Lintot!"[2]
Lintot, dull rogue, will think your price too much.
"Not, sir, if you revise it, and retouch."
All my demurs but double his attacks;   65
At last he whispers, "Do; and we go snacks."[3]
Glad of a quarrel, straight I clap the door,

3. Medicine.
4. Destroyed; killed (Johnson's *Dictionary*).
5. The advice of Horace in *Art of Poetry* (line 388).
6. I.e., living in a garret in Drury Lane, site of one of the theaters and the haunt of the profligate.
7. One of the four annual periods in which the law courts are in session and with which the publishing season coincided.
8. "A foolish poet of Rhodes, who pretended much to Greek" [Pope's note]; he is Leonard Welsted, who translated Longinus and had attacked and slandered Pope. See line 375.
9. Edmund Curll, shrewd and disreputable bookseller, published pirated works, works falsely ascribed to reputable writers, scandalous biographies, and other ephemera. Pope had often attacked him and had assigned to him a low role in the *Dunciad*.
1. I.e., he will attack Pope in the *London Journal* or write a treatise on theology, as Welsted in fact did.
2. Bernard Lintot, publisher of Pope's Homer and other early works.
3. Go shares.

"Sir, let me see your works and you no more."
 'Tis sung, when Midas' ears began to spring
(Midas, a sacred person and a king),
His very minister who spied them first,
(Some say his queen) was forced to speak, or burst.[4]
And is not mine, my friend, a sorer case,
When every coxcomb perks them in my face?
 A. Good friend, forbear! you deal in dangerous things.
I'd never name queens, ministers, or kings;
Keep close to ears, and those let asses prick;
'Tis nothing——P. Nothing? if they bite and kick?
Out with it, *Dunciad!* let the secret pass,
That secret to each fool, that he's an ass:
The truth once told (and wherefore should we lie?)
The queen of Midas slept, and so may I.
 You think this cruel? take it for a rule,
No creature smarts so little as a fool.
Let peals of laughter, Codrus! round thee break,
Thou unconcerned canst hear the mighty crack.
Pit, box, and gallery in convulsions hurled,
Thou stand'st unshook amidst a bursting world.
Who shames a scribbler? break one cobweb through,
He spins the slight, self-pleasing thread anew:
Destroy his fib or sophistry, in vain;
The creature's at his dirty work again,
Throned in the center of his thin designs,
Proud of a vast extent of flimsy lines.
Whom have I hurt? has poet yet or peer
Lost the arched eyebrow or Parnassian sneer?
And has not Colley[5] still his lord and whore?
His butchers Henley? his freemasons Moore?
Does not one table Bavius[6] still admit?
Still to one bishop Philips seem a wit?
Still Sappho[7]——A. Hold! for god's sake—you'll offend.
No names—be calm—learn prudence of a friend.
I too could write, and I am twice as tall;
But foes like these!——P. One flatterer's worse than all.
Of all mad creatures, if the learn'd are right,
It is the slaver kills, and not the bite.
A fool quite angry is quite innocent:
Alas! 'tis ten times worse when they repent.

70

75

80

85

90

95

100

105

4. Midas, king of ancient Lydia, had the bad taste to prefer the flute-playing of Pan to that of Apollo, whereupon the god endowed him with ass's ears. It was his barber (not his wife or his minister) who discovered the secret and whispered it into a hole in the earth. The reference to "queen" and "minister" makes it plain that Pope is alluding to George II, Queen Caroline, and Walpole.
5. Colley Cibber. The laureate John Henley, known as "Orator" Henley, an independent preacher of marked eccentricity, was popular among the lower orders, especially for his elocution.
6. The bad poet alluded to in Virgil's *Eclogue* 3. The "Bishop" is Hugh Boulter, bishop of Armagh; he had employed as his secretary Ambrose Philips (1674–1749), whose insipid and babbling simplicity of manner in poetry earned him the nickname of "Namby-Pamby."
7. Lady Mary Wortley Montagu.

One dedicates in high heroic prose,
And ridicules beyond a hundred foes;   110
One from all Grub Street[8] will my fame defend,
And, more abusive, calls himself my friend.
This prints my letters,[9] that expects a bribe,
And others roar aloud, "Subscribe, subscribe!"[1]
    There are, who to my person pay their court: 115
I cough like Horace, and, though lean, am short;
Ammon's great son[2] one shoulder had too high,
Such Ovid's nose, and "Sir! you have an eye—"
Go on, obliging creatures, make me see
All that disgraced my betters met in me.   120
Say for my comfort, languishing in bed,
"Just so immortal Maro[3] held his head":
And when I die, be sure you let me know
Great Homer died three thousand years ago.
    Why did I write? what sin to me unknown   125
Dipped me in ink, my parents', or my own?
As yet a child, nor yet a fool to fame,
I lisped in numbers, for the numbers came.
I left no calling for this idle trade,
No duty broke, no father disobeyed.   130
The Muse but served to ease some friend, not wife,
To help me through this long disease, my life,
To second, Arbuthnot! thy art and care,
And teach the being you preserved, to bear.[4]
    A. But why then publish? P. Granville the polite,   135
And knowing Walsh, would tell me I could write;
Well-natured Garth inflamed with early praise,
And Congreve loved, and Swift endured my lays;
The courtly Talbot, Somers, Sheffield, read;
Even mitered Rochester would nod the head,   140
And St. John's self (great Dryden's friends before)
With open arms received one poet more.[5]
Happy my studies, when by these approved!
Happier their author, when by these beloved!
From these the world will judge of men and books,   145

8. A term denoting the whole society of literary, political, and journalistic hack writers.
9. In 1726 Curll had surreptitiously acquired and published without permission some of Pope's letters to Henry Cromwell.
1. To ensure the financial success of a work, the public was often asked to "subscribe" to it by taking a certain number of copies before printing was undertaken. Pope's Homer was published thus.
2. Alexander the Great. "Ovid's nose": Ovid's family name Naso suggests the Latin word *nasus* ("nose"), hence the pun.
3. Virgil.

4. Endure.
5. The purpose of this list is to establish Pope as the successor of Dryden and thus to place him far above his Grub-Street persecutors. George Granville, Lord Lansdowne, poet and statesman; William Walsh, poet and critic; Sir Samuel Garth, physician and mock-epic poet; William Congreve, the playwright; the statesmen Charles Talbot, duke of Shrewsbury; Lord Sommers; John Sheffield, duke of Buckinghamshire; and Francis Atterbury, bishop of Rochester, had all been associated with Dryden in his later years and had all encouraged the young Pope.

Not from the Burnets, Oldmixons, and Cookes.[6]
    Soft were my numbers; who could take offense
While pure description held the place of sense?
Like gentle Fanny's[7] was my flowery theme,
A painted mistress, or a purling stream.   150
Yet then did Gildon[8] draw his venal quill;
I wished the man a dinner, and sat still.
Yet then did Dennis[9] rave in furious fret;
I never answered, I was not in debt.
If want provoked, or madness made them print,   155
I waged no war with Bedlam or the Mint.
    Did some more sober critic come abroad?
If wrong, I smiled; if right, I kissed the rod.
Pains, reading, study are their just pretense,
And all they want is spirit, taste, and sense.   160
Commas and points they set exactly right,
And 'twere a sin to rob them of their mite.
Yet ne'er one sprig of laurel graced these ribalds,
From slashing Bentley down to piddling Tibbalds.[1]
Each wight who reads not, and but scans and spells,   165
Each word-catcher that lives on syllables,
Even such small critics some regard may claim,
Preserved in Milton's or in Shakespeare's name.
Pretty! in amber to observe the forms
Of hairs, or straws, or dirt, or grubs, or worms!   170
The things, we know, are neither rich nor rare,
But wonder how the devil they got there.
    Were others angry? I excused them too;
Well might they rage; I gave them but their due.
A man's true merit 'tis not hard to find;   175
But each man's secret standard in his mind,
That casting weight[2] pride adds to emptiness,
This, who can gratify? for who can guess?
The bard[3] whom pilfered pastorals renown,
Who turns a Persian tale for half a crown,   180
Just writes to make his barrenness appear,
And strains from hard-bound brains eight lines a year:

---

6. Thomas Burnet, John Oldmixon, and Thomas
Cooke; Pope identifies them in a note as "authors
of secret and scandalous history."
7. John, Lord Hervey, whom Pope satirizes in the
character of Sporus, lines 305–33 below.
8. Charles Gildon, minor critic and scribbler, who,
Pope believed, early attacked him at the instigation
of Addison; hence "venal quill."
9. John Dennis (see Essay on Criticism, line 270
and its note).
1. Richard Bentley (1662–1742), the eminent
classical scholar, seemed to both Pope and Swift
the perfect type of the pedant: he is called "slashing" because, in his edition of Paradise Lost (1732),

he had set in square brackets all passages which he
disliked on the grounds they had been slipped into
the poem without the blind poet's knowledge. Lewis
Theobald (1688–1744), whose minute learning in
Elizabethan literature had enabled him to expose
Pope's defects as an editor of Shakespeare in 1726.
Pope made him King of the Dunces in the Dunciad (1728).
2. The weight that turns the scale; here, the
"deciding factor."
3. Ambrose Philips, Pope's rival in pastoral poetry
in 1709, when their pastorals were published in
Tonson's sixth Miscellany. Philips had also translated some Persian tales. Cf. line 100.

He, who still wanting, though he lives on theft,
Steals much, spends little, yet has nothing left;
And he who now to sense, now nonsense leaning,   185
Means not, but blunders round about a meaning:
And he whose fustian's so sublimely bad,
It is not poetry, but prose run mad:
All these, my modest satire bade translate,
And owned that nine such poets made a Tate.[4]   190
How did they fume, and stamp, and roar, and chafe!
And swear, not Addison himself was safe.

    Peace to all such! but were there one whose fires
True Genius kindles, and fair Fame inspires;
Blessed with each talent and each art to please,   195
And born to write, converse, and live with ease:
Should such a man, too fond to rule alone,
Bear, like the Turk, no brother near the throne;
View him with scornful, yet with jealous eyes,
And hate for arts that caused himself to rise;   200
Damn with faint praise, assent with civil leer,
And without sneering, teach the rest to sneer;
Willing to wound, and yet afraid to strike,
Just hint a fault, and hesitate dislike;
Alike reserved to blame or to commend,   205
A timorous foe, and a suspicious friend;
Dreading even fools; by flatterers besieged,
And so obliging that he ne'er obliged;
Like Cato, give his little senate[5] laws,
And sit attentive to his own applause;   210
While wits and Templars[6] every sentence raise,
And wonder with a foolish face of praise—
Who but must laugh, if such a man there be?
Who would not weep, if Atticus[7] were he?

    What though my name stood rubric[8] on the walls   215
Or plastered posts, with claps, in capitals?
Or smoking forth, a hundred hawkers' load,
On wings of winds came flying all abroad?
I sought no homage from the race that write;
I kept, like Asian monarchs, from their sight: 220
Poems I heeded (now berhymed so long)
No more than thou, great George! a birthday song.
I ne'er with wits or witlings passed my days

---

4. Nahum Tate (1652–1715), poet laureate (1692–1715). His popular rewriting of Shakespeare's's *King Lear* provided a happy ending; he wrote most of part 2 of *Absalom and Achitophel*. The line refers to the old adage that it takes nine tailors to make one man.

5. Addison's tragedy *Cato* had been a sensational success in 1713. Pope had written the prologue, in which occurs the line, "While Cato gives his little senate laws." The satirical reference here is to Addison in the role of arbiter of taste among his friends and admirers, mostly Whigs, at Button's Coffee House. It was these people who had worked against the success of Pope's Homer.

6. Law students.

7. Pope's satiric pseudonym for Addison; Atticus (109–32 B.C.) was a wealthy man of letters and a friend of Cicero, known as a wise and disinterested man.

8. In red letters. "Claps": posters.

To spread about the itch of verse and praise;
Nor like a puppy daggled through the town   225
To fetch and carry sing-song up and down;
Nor at rehearsals sweat, and mouthed, and cried,
With handkerchief and orange at my side;
But sick of fops, and poetry, and prate,
To Bufo[9] left the whole Castalian state.   230
   Proud as Apollo on his forkèd hill,[1]
Sat full-blown Bufo, puffed by every quill;
Fed with soft dedication all day long,
Horace and he went hand in hand in song.
His library (where busts of poets dead   235
And a true Pindar stood without a head)
Received of wits an undistinguished race,
Who first his judgment asked, and then a place:
Much they extolled his pictures, much his seat,[2]
And flattered every day, and some days eat: 240
Till grown more frugal in his riper days,
He paid some bards with port, and some with praise;
To some a dry rehearsal was assigned,
And others (harder still) he paid in kind.
Dryden alone (what wonder?) came not nigh;   245
Dryden alone escaped this judging eye:
But still the great have kindness in reserve;
He helped to bury whom he helped to starve.
   May some choice patron bless each gray goose quill!
May every Bavius have his Bufo still!   250
So when a statesman wants a day's defense,
Or Envy holds a whole week's war with Sense,
Or simple Pride for flattery makes demands,
May dunce by dunce be whistled off my hands!
Blessed be the great! for those they take away,   255
And those they left me—for they left me Gay;[3]
Left me to see neglected genius bloom,
Neglected die, and tell it on his tomb;
Of all thy blameless life the sole return
My verse, and Queensberry weeping o'er thy urn!   260
Oh, let me live my own, and die so too!
("To live and die is all I have to do")[4]
Maintain a poet's dignity and ease,
And see what friends, and read what books I please;
Above a patron, though I condescend   265

---

9. A type of tasteless patron of the arts. (*Bufo* means "toad" in Latin). The Castalian spring on Mt. Parnassus was sacred to Apollo and the Muses.
1. Mt. Parnassus had two peaks, one sacred to Apollo, one to Bacchus.
2. Pronounced *sate*, and rhymed in next line with "eat" (*ate*.) *Seat* means "estate."
3. John Gay (1685–1732), author of the *Beggar's Opera* (1728) and other delightful works, dear friend of Swift and Pope. His failure to obtain patronage from the court intensified Pope's hostility to the Whig administration and the queen. Gay spent the last years of his life under the protection of the duke and duchess of Queensberry.
4. A quotation from John Denham's poem, *Of Prudence.*

Sometimes to call a minister my friend.
I was not born for courts or great affairs;
I pay my debts, believe, and say my prayers,
Can sleep without a poem in my head,
Nor know if Dennis be alive or dead,   270
 Why am I asked what next shall see the light?
Heavens! was I born for nothing but to write?
Has life no joys for me? or (to be grave)
Have I no friend to serve, no soul to save?
"I found him close with Swift"—"Indeed? no doubt"   275
Cries prating Balbus, "something will come out."
'Tis all in vain, deny it as I will.
"No, such a genius never can lie still,"
And then for mine obligingly mistakes
The first lampoon Sir Will or Bubo makes.[5]   280
Poor guiltless I! and can I choose but smile,
When every coxcomb knows me by my style?
 Cursed be the verse, how well soe'er it flow,
That tends to make one worthy man my foe,
Give Virtue scandal, Innocence a fear,   285
Or from the soft-eyed virgin steal a tear!
But he who hurts a harmless neighbor's peace,
Insults fallen worth, or Beauty in distress,
Who loves a lie, lame Slander helps about,
Who writes a libel, or who copies out: 290
That fop whose pride affects a patron's name,
Yet absent, wounds an author's honest fame;
Who can your merit selfishly approve,
And show the sense of it without the love;
Who has the vanity to call you friend,   295
Yet wants the honor, injured, to defend;
Who tells whate'er you think, whate'er you say,
And, if he lie not, must at least betray:
Who to the dean and silver bell can swear,
And sees at Cannons what was never there:[6]   300
Who reads but with a lust to misapply,
Make satire a lampoon, and fiction, lie:
A lash like mine no honest man shall dread,
But all such babbling blockheads in his stead.
 Let Sporus[7] tremble—— A. What? that thing of silk,   305
Sporus, that mere white curd of ass's milk?[8]

---

5. Sir William Yonge, Whig politician and poe-
taster; George Bubb ("Bubo") Dodington was a
Whig patron of letters.
6. Pope's enemies had accused him of satirizing
Cannons, the ostentatious estate of the duke of
Chandos, in his description of Timon's villa in the
Epistle to Burlington. This Pope quite justly denied.
The bell of Timon's chapel was of silver, and there

preached a dean who "never mentions Hell to ears
polite."
7. John, Lord Hervey, effeminate courtier and
confidant of Queen Caroline; see title footnote. The
original Sporus was a boy, whom the Emperor Nero
publicly married (see Suetonius' life of Nero in The
Twelve Caesars).
8. Ass's milk was drunk by invalids.

Satire or sense, alas! can Sporus feel?
Who breaks a butterfly upon a wheel?
  P. Yet let me flap this bug with gilded wings,
This painted child of dirt, that stinks and stings;   310
Whose buzz the witty and the fair annoys,
Yet wit ne'er tastes, and beauty ne'er enjoys;
So well-bred spaniels civilly delight
In mumbling of the game they dare not bite.
Eternal smiles his emptiness betray,   315
As shallow streams run dimpling all the way.
Whether in florid impotence he speaks,
And, as the prompter breathes, the puppet squeaks;
Or at the ear of Eve,[9] familiar toad,
Half froth, half venom, spits himself abroad,   320
In puns, or politics, or tales, or lies,
Or spite, or smut, or rhymes, or blasphemies.
His wit all seesaw between *that* and *this*,
Now high, now low, now master up, now miss,
And he himself one vile antithesis.   325
Amphibious thing! that acting either part,
The trifling head or the corrupted heart,
Fop at the toilet, flatterer at the board,
Now trips a lady, and now struts a lord.
Eve's tempter thus the rabbins[1] have expressed,   330
A cherub's face, a reptile all the rest;
Beauty that shocks you, parts that none will trust,
Wit that can creep, and pride that licks the dust.
  Not Fortune's worshiper, nor Fashion's fool,
Not Lucre's madman, nor Ambition's tool,   335
Not proud, nor servile, be one poet's praise,
That if he pleased, he pleased by manly ways:
That flattery, even to kings, he held a shame,
And thought a lie in verse or prose the same:
That not in fancy's maze he wandered long,   340
But stooped[2] to truth, and moralized his song:
That not for fame, but Virtue's better end,
He stood the furious foe, the timid friend,
The damning critic, half approving wit,
The coxcomb hit, or fearing to be hit;   345
Laughed at the loss of friends he never had,
The dull, the proud, the wicked, and the mad;
The distant threats of vengeance on his head,
The blow unfelt, the tear he never shed;
The tale revived, the lie so oft o'erthrown,   350
The imputed trash, and dullness not his own;

---

9. "Eve" is the queen. The allusion is to *Paradise
Lost* 4.799–809.
1. Scholars of and authorities on Jewish law and
doctrine.
2. The falcon is said to "stoop" to its prey when it
swoops down and seizes it in flight.

The morals blackened when the writings 'scape,
The libeled person, and the pictured shape;[3]
Abuse on all he loved, or loved him, spread,
A friend in exile, or a father dead;   355
The whisper, that to greatness still too near,
Perhaps yet vibrates on his Sovereign's ear—
Welcome for thee, fair Virtue! all the past!
For thee, fair Virtue! welcome even the last!
   A. But why insult the poor, affront the great?   360
P. A knave's a knave to me in every state:
Alike my scorn, if he succeed or fail,
Sporus at court, or Japhet[4] in a jail,
A hireling scribbler, or a hireling peer,
Knight of the post[5] corrupt, or of the shire,   365
If on a pillory, or near a throne,
He gain his prince's ear, or lose his own.
   Yet soft by nature, more a dupe than wit,
Sappho[6] can tell you how this man was bit:
This dreaded satirist Dennis will confess   370
Foe to his pride, but friend to his distress:[7]
So humble, he has knocked at Tibbald's door,
Has drunk with Cibber, nay, has rhymed for Moore.
Full ten years slandered, did he once reply?
Three thousand suns went down on Welsted's lie.   375
To please a mistress one aspersed his life;
He lashed him not, but let her be his wife.
Let Budgell charge low Grub Street on his quill,
And write whate'er he pleased, except his will;[8]
Let the two Curlls of town and court,[9] abuse   380
His father, mother, body, soul, and muse.
Yet why? that father held it for a rule,
It was a sin to call our neighbor fool;
That harmless mother thought no wife a whore:
Hear this, and spare his family, James Moore!   385
Unspotted names, and memorable long,
If there be force in virtue, or in song.
   Of gentle blood (part shed in honor's cause,
While yet in Britain honor had applause)
Each parent sprung—— A. What fortune, pray?—— P. Their own,
And better got than Bestia's[1] from the throne.   391
Born to no pride, inheriting no strife,

---

3. Pope's deformity was frequently ridiculed and
occasionally caricatured.
4. Japhet Crook, a notorious forger.
5. One who lives by selling false evidence.
6. Lady Mary Wortley Montagu. "Bit": taken in;
deceived.
7. Pope wrote the prologue to Cibber's *Provoked
Husband* when that play was performed for Dennis's benefit, shortly before the old critic died.

8. Eustace Budgell attacked the *Grub Street Journal* for publishing what he took to be a squib by
Pope charging him with having forged the will of
Dr. Matthew Tindal.
9. I.e., the publisher and Lord Hervey.
1. Probably the duke of Marlborough, whose vast
fortune was made through the favor of Queen Anne.
The actual Bestia was a corrupt Roman consul.

Nor marrying discord in a noble wife,
Stranger to civil and religious rage,
The good man walked innoxious through his age.   395
No courts he saw, no suits would ever try,
Nor dared an oath,[2] nor hazarded a lie.
Unlearn'd, he knew no schoolman's subtle art,
No language but the language of the heart.
By nature honest, by experience wise,   400
Healthy by temperance, and by exercise;
His life, though long, to sickness passed unknown,
His death was instant, and without a groan.
Oh, grant me thus to live, and thus to die!
Who sprung from kings shall know less joy than I.   405
    O friend! may each domestic bliss be thine!
Be no unpleasing melancholy mine:
Me, let the tender office long engage,
To rock the cradle of reposing Age,
With lenient arts extend a mother's breath,   410
Make Languor smile, and smooth the bed of Death,
Explore the thought, explain the asking eye,
And keep a while one parent from the sky![3]
On cares like these if length of days attend,
May Heaven, to bless those days, preserve my friend,   415
Preserve him social, cheerful, and serene,
And just as rich as when he served a Queen![4]
A. Whether that blessing be denied or given,
Thus far was right—the rest belong to Heaven.

1735

The Dunciad: Book the Fourth

The fourth book of *The Dunciad*, Pope's last major work, was originally intended as a continuation of *An Essay on Man*. To Swift, the spiritual ancestor of the poem, Pope confided in 1736 that he was at work on a series of epistles on the uses of human reason and learning, to conclude with "a satire against the misapplication of all these, exemplified by pictures, characters, and examples." But the epistles never appeared; instead, the satire grew until it took their place. As Pope surveyed England in his last years, the complex literary and social order that had sustained him seemed to be crumbling. It was a time for desperate measures, for satire. And the means of retribution was at hand, in the structure of Pope's own *Dunciad*, the long work that had already impaled so many enemies.

2. As a Catholic, Pope's father refused to take the Oaths of Allegiance and Supremacy, and the oath against the Pope. He thus rendered himself vulnerable to the many repressive anti-Catholic laws then in force.

3. Pope was a tender and devoted son. His mother had died in 1733, and the earliest version of these lines dates from 1731, when the poet was nursing her through a serious illness.

4. Pope alludes to the fact that Arbuthnot, a man of strict probity, left the queen's service no wealthier than when he entered it.

The first *Dunciad*, published in three books in 1728, is a mock-epic reply to Pope's critics and other petty authors. Its hero and victim, Lewis Theobald, had attacked Pope's edition of Shakespeare (1725); other victims had offended Pope either by personal abuse or simply by ineptitude. Inspired by Dryden's *Mac Flecknoe*, the *Dunciad* celebrates the triumph of the hordes of Grub Street. Indeed, so many obscure hacks were mentioned that a *Dunciad Variorum* (1729) was soon required, in which mock-scholarly notes identify the victims, "since it is only in this monument that they must expect to survive." But a modern reader need not catch every reference to enjoy the dazzling wit of the poem, or the sheer sense of fun with which Pope remakes the London literary world into a tiny insane fairground of his own.

The New Dunciad (1742), however, plays a far more serious game: here Pope takes aim at the rot of the whole social fabric. The satire goes deep, and works at many levels. For convenience, these may be divided into four. 1) Politics: From 1721 to 1742 England had been ruled by the Whig supremacy of Robert Walpole, First Minister. To Pope and his circle, the immensely powerful Walpole (no friend of poets) seemed a crass and greedy vulgarian, like his monarch George II. It is no accident, in the kingdom of the *Dunciad*, that Dulness personified sits on a throne. 2) Society: Just as the action of the *Aeneid* had been the removal of the empire of Troy to Latium, the action of the *Dunciad*, according to Pope, is "the removal of the empire of Dulness from the City of London to the polite world, Westminster"; that is, the abdication of civility in favor of commerce and financial interests. In modern England authors write for money, and ministers govern for profit; conspicuous consumption (especially the consumption of paper by scribblers) has replaced the old values of the yeoman and the aristocrat. In 1743 Pope revised the original *Dunciad*, substituting the actor and poet laureate Colley Cibber for Theobald as the hero, and incorporating *The New Dunciad* as book four (the version printed here). Dulness, he implies, has achieved her final triumph; Cibber is laureate in England. 3) Education: The word "dunce" is derived from the scholastic philosopher John Duns Scotus (ca. 1265–1308), whose name had come to stand for silly and useless subtlety, logical hair-splitting. Pope, as an heir of the renaissance, believes that the central subject of education must always be its relevance for human behavior: "The proper study of mankind is Man," and moral philosophy, the relation of men to each other and to the world, should be the teacher's first and last concern. By contrast, Dunces waste their time on grammar (words alone) or the "science" of the collector (things alone); they never comprehend that word and thing, like spirit and matter, are essentially dead unless they join. 4) Religion: At its deepest level, the subject of the *Dunciad* is the undoing of God's creation. Many passages from Book Four echo *Paradise Lost*, and one of Pope's starting places seems to be Satan's threat (*Paradise Lost* 2.968–87) to return the world to its original darkness, chaos, and ancient night. The *Dunciad* ends in a great apocalypse, with a yawn that signals the death of *Logos*; as words have become meaningless, so has the whole creation, which the Lord called forth with words. Here Pope invokes, with terrifying intensity, the old idea that God was the first poet, whose poem was the world, and suggests that the sickness of the word has infected all nature. But there is one consolation: out of non-art itself, out of matter without spirit and substance without essence, the poet creates his own final artistic triumph, and makes a poem.

From The Dunciad

From *Book the Fourth*

Yet, yet a moment, one dim ray of light
Indulge, dread Chaos, and eternal Night!
Of darkness visible[1] so much be lent,
As half to show, half veil the deep intent.
Yet Powers![2] whose mysteries restored I sing,   5
To whom Time bears me on his rapid wing,
Suspend a while your force inertly strong,
Then take at once the poet and the song.
   Now flamed the Dog-star's[3] unpropitious ray,
Smote every brain, and withered every bay,[4]   10
Sick was the sun, the owl forsook his bower,
The moon-struck prophet felt the madding hour:
Then rose the seed[5] of Chaos, and of Night,
To blot out Order, and extinguish Light,
Of dull and venal a new world to mold,   15
And bring Saturnian[6] days of lead and gold.
   She mounts the throne: her head a cloud concealed,
In broad effulgence all below revealed,
('Tis thus aspiring Dulness ever shines)
Soft on her lap her Laureate son[7] reclines.   20
   Beneath her foot-stool, Science groans in chains,
And Wit dreads exile, penalties and pains.
There foamed rebellious Logic, gagged and bound,
There, stripped, fair Rhetoric languished on the ground;
His blunted arms by Sophistry are born,   25
And shameless Billingsgate[8] her robes adorn.
Morality, by her false guardians drawn,
Chicane in furs, and Casuistry in lawn,[9]
Gasps, as they straighten at each end the cord,
And dies, when Dulness gives her Page[1] the word.   30

[THE EDUCATOR]

   Now crowds on crowds around the Goddess press,   135
Each eager to present the first Address.[2]

1. Cf. *Paradise Lost* 1.63.
2. Chaos and Night, invoked in place of the Muse, since "the restoration of their empire is the action of the poem" [Pope].
3. Sirius, associated with the heat of summer and the madness of poets (see *Epistle to Dr. Arbuthnot*, line 3).
4. The laurel, whose garlands are bestowed on poets.
5. The Goddess Dulness.
6. Saturn ruled during the golden age; the new age of "gold" will be re-established by the dull and venal.

7. Colley Cibber, the poet laureate.
8. Fishmarket slang, which now covers the noble science of rhetoric.
9. Chicanery (legal trickery) wears the ermine robe of a judge; casuistry wears the linen sleeves of a bishop.
1. Sir Francis Page, a notorious "hanging judge"; court page, used to strangle criminals in Turkey; page of writing on which a dull author "kills" moral sentiments.
2. The Goddess, newly enthroned, is receiving petitions and congratulations.

Dunce scorning dunce beholds the next advance,
But fop shows fop superior complaisance.
When lo! a Specter[3] rose, whose index-hand
Held forth the virtue of the dreadful wand;   140
His beavered brow a birchen garland wears,[4]
Dropping with infant's blood, and mother's tears.
O'er every vein a shuddering horror runs;
Eton and Winton shake through all their sons.
All flesh is humbled, Westminster's bold race[5]   145
Shrink, and confess the Genius[6] of the place:
The pale boy-Senator yet tingling stands,
And holds his breeches close with both his hands.
    Then thus. "Since Man from beast by words is known,
Words are Man's province, words we teach alone.   150
When reason doubtful, like the Samian letter,[7]
Points him two ways, the narrower is the better.
Placed at the door of learning, youth to guide,
We never suffer it to stand too wide.
To ask, to guess, to know, as they commence,   155
As fancy opens the quick springs of sense,
We ply the memory, we load the brain,
Bind rebel wit, and double chain on chain,
Confine the thought, to exercise the breath;[8]
And keep them in the pale of words till death.   160
Whate'er the talents, or howe'er designed,
We hang one jingling padlock on the mind:
A poet the first day, he dips his quill;
And what the last? a very poet still.
Pity! the charm works only in our wall,   165
Lost, lost too soon in yonder House or Hall."[9]

[THE CARNATION AND THE BUTTERFLY]

    Then thick as locusts blackening all the ground,
A tribe,[1] with weeds and shells fantastic crowned,
Each with some wondrous gift approached the Power,
A nest, a toad, a fungus, or a flower.   400
But far the foremost, two, with earnest zeal,
And aspect ardent to the throne appeal.
    The first thus opened: "Hear thy suppliant's call,

---

3. The ghost of Dr. Busby, stern headmaster of Westminster School.
4. He wears a hat (beaver) and a garland of birch twigs, used for flogging. "Wand": cane used for beating.
5. Alumni of Westminster School, with a play on the justices and members of Parliament who meet at Westminster Hall.
6. I.e., admit that Dr. Busby is the presiding deity (Genius).
7. The letter Y, which Pythagoras (a native of

Samos) used as an emblem of the different roads of virtue and vice.
8. Students are taught only to recite the classic poets by heart.
9. The House of Commons and Westminster Hall, where law cases were heard. The eloquence learned by rote disappears on occasions for public speaking.
1. The Virtuosi, or amateur scientists and collectors.

Great Queen, and common Mother of us all!
Fair from its humble bed I reared this flower, 405
Suckled, and cheer'd, with air, and sun, and shower,
Soft on the paper ruff its leaves I spread,
Bright with the gilded button tipped its head,
Then throned in glass, and named it CAROLINE:[2]
Each maid cried, charming! and each youth, divine! 410
Did Nature's pencil ever blend such rays,
Such varied light in one promiscuous blaze?
Now prostrate! dead! behold that Caroline:
No maid cries, charming! and no youth, divine!
And lo the wretch! whose vile, whose insect lust 415
Laid this gay daughter of the Spring in dust.
Oh punish him, or to th' Elysian shades
Dismiss my soul, where no carnation fades."
  He ceased, and wept. With innocence of mien,
The accused stood forth, and thus addressed the Queen. 420
  "Of all th' enameled race,[3] whose silvery wing
Waves to the tepid zephyrs of the spring,
Or swims along the fluid atmosphere,
Once brightest shined this child of heat and air.
I saw, and started from its vernal bower 425
The rising game, and chased from flower to flower.
It fled, I followed; now in hope, now pain;
It stopped, I stopped; it moved, I moved again.
At last it fixed, 'twas on what plant it pleased,
And where it fixed, the beauteous bird[4] I seized: 430
Rose or carnation was below my care;
I meddle, Goddess! only in my sphere.
I tell the naked fact without disguise,
And, to excuse it, need but show the prize;
Whose spoils this paper offers to your eye, 435
Fair even in death! this peerless Butterfly."
  "My sons!" she answered, "both have done your parts;
Live happy both, and long promote our arts.
But hear a mother, when she recommends
To your fraternal care, our sleeping friends. 440
The common soul, of heaven's more frugal make,
Serves but to keep fools pert, and knaves awake:
A drowsy watchman, that just gives a knock,
And breaks our rest, to tell us what's a clock.[5]
Yet by some object every brain is stirred; 445
The dull may waken to a hummingbird;
The most recluse, discreetly opened, find
Congenial matter in the cockle-kind;[6]

2. Queen Caroline, an enthusiastic gardener, is an appropriate choice to lend her name to the perfect carnation.
3. Colored insects.
4. Insect.

5. Eighteenth-century watchmen kept guard in the streets and announced the hours.
6. Cockle-shells, popular with collectors, as were hummingbirds and varieties of moss.

The mind, in metaphysics at a loss,
May wander in a wilderness of moss;   450
The head that turns at super-lunar things,
Poised with a tail, may steer on Wilkins' wings.[7]
   "O! would the Sons of Men once think their eyes
And reason given them but to study *flies!*[8]
See Nature in some partial narrow shape,   455
And let the Author of the whole escape:
Learn but to trifle; or, who most observe,
To wonder at their Maker, not to serve."

[THE TRIUMPH OF DULNESS]

   Then blessing all,[9] "Go children of my care!
To practice now from theory repair.   580
All my commands are easy, short, and full:
My sons! be proud, be selfish, and be dull.
Guard my prerogative, assert my throne:
This nod confirms each privilege your own.
The cap and switch be sacred to his Grace;[1]   585
With staff and pumps[2] the Marquis lead the race;
From stage to stage the licensed[3] Earl may run,
Paired with his fellow-charioteer the Sun;
The learned baron butterflies design,
Or draw to silk Arachne's subtle line;[4]   590
The Judge to dance his brother Sergeant[5] call;
The Senator at cricket urge the ball;
The Bishop stow (pontific luxury!)
An hundred souls of turkeys in a pie;[6]
The sturdy squire to Gallic masters[7] stoop,   595
And drown his lands and manors in a Soup.
Others import yet nobler arts from France,
Teach kings to fiddle, and make senates dance.
Perhaps more high some daring son may soar,[8]
Proud to my list to add one monarch more;   600
And nobly conscious, Princes are but things
Born for First Ministers, as slaves for kings,
Tyrant supreme! shall three estates command,

7. John Wilkins (1614–1672), one of the founders of the Royal Society, had speculated "that a man may be able to fly, by the application of wings to his own body."
8. Cf. *An Essay on Man.* 1.189–96: "Say what the use, were finer optics given / T' inspect a mite, not comprehend the heaven?"
9. Having conferred her titles, Dulness bids each of the rulers of England to indulge in the triviality closest to his heart.
1. His Grace, a duke who loves horse-racing, is to use the cap and switch of a jockey.
2. Footmen, who wore pumps (low-cut shoes for

running), were matched in races.
3. The license required by the owner of a stage-coach; also, privileged or licentious.
4. A spiderweb.
5. A lawyer or legislative officer; formal ceremonies at the Inns of Court are said to have resembled a country dance, "a call of sergeants."
6. According to Pope, a hundred turkeys had been "not unfrequently deposited in one Pye in the Bishopric of Durham."
7. French chefs.
8. A bold, direct attack on Walpole.

And MAKE ONE MIGHTY DUNCIAD OF THE LAND!"
  More she had spoke, but yawned—All Nature nods: 605
What mortal can resist the Yawn of Gods?
Churches and chapels instantly it reached;
(St. James's first, for leaden Gilbert[9] preached)
Then catched the schools; the Hall scarce kept awake;
The Convocation gaped,[1] but could not speak: 610
Lost was the Nation's Sense,[2] nor could be found,
While the long solemn unison went round:
Wide, and more wide, it spread o'er all the realm;
Even Palinurus[3] nodded at the helm:
The vapor mild o'er each committee crept;   615
Unfinished treaties in each office slept;
And chiefless armies dozed out the campaign;
And navies yawned for orders on the main.
  O Muse! relate (for you can tell alone,
Wits have short memories, and dunces none)   620
Relate, who first, who last resigned to rest;
Whose heads she partly, whose completely blessed;
What charms could faction, what ambition lull,
The venal quiet, and entrance the dull;
'Till drowned was sense, and shame, and right, and wrong—   625
O sing, and hush the nations with thy song!

  In vain, in vain,—the all-composing Hour
Resistless falls: The Muse obeys the Power.
She comes! she comes![4] the sable throne behold
Of Night primeval, and of Chaos old!   630
Before her, Fancy's gilded clouds decay,
And all its varying rainbows die away.
Wit shoots in vain its momentary fires,
The meteor drops, and in a flash expires.
As one by one, at dread Medea's strain,   635
The sickening stars fade off the ethereal plain;[5]
As Argus' eyes by Hermes' wand oppressed,
Closed one by one to everlasting rest;[6]
Thus at her felt approach, and secret might,
Art after Art goes out, and all is Night.   640
See skulking Truth to her old cavern fled,[7]
Mountains of casuistry heaped o'er her head!
Philosophy, that leaned on Heaven before,

9. Dr. John Gilbert, dean of Exeter.
1. The Convocation, an assembly of clergy consulting on ecclesiastical affairs, had been adjourned since 1717.
2. A term for Parliament.
3. The pilot of Aeneas' ship; here Walpole.
4. Having triumphed in the contemporary world of affairs, Dulness (like her antitype Christ) has a Second Coming, a prophetic vision in which she extinguishes the light of the arts and sciences.
5. In Seneca's *Medea*, the stars obey the curse of Medea, a magician and avenger.
6. Argus, Hera's 100-eyed watchman, was charmed to sleep and slain by Hermes.
7. "Alluding to the saying of Democritus, that Truth lay at the bottom of a deep well" [Pope's note].

Shrinks to her second cause,[8] and is no more.
Physic[9] of Metaphysic begs defense,   645
And Metaphysic calls for aid on Sense!
See Mystery[1] to Mathematics fly!
In vain! they gaze, turn giddy, rave, and die.
Religion blushing veils her sacred fires,
And unawares Morality expires.   650
Nor public flame, nor private, dares to shine;
Nor human spark is left, nor glimpse divine!
Lo! thy dread Empire, CHAOS is restored;
Light dies before thy uncreating word:[2]
Thy hand, great Anarch! lets the curtain fall;   655
And Universal Darkness buries All.

1743

8. Science (philosophy) no longer accepts God as the first cause, or final explanation of how all things came to be; instead, it accepts only the second or material cause, and tries to account for all things by physical principles alone.

9. Natural science in general.
1. A religious truth known only through divine revelation.
2. Cf. God's first creating words in Genesis, "Let there be light."

SAMUEL JOHNSON
1709–1784

Johnson was famous as a talker in his own time, and his conversation (preserved by James Boswell and others) has been famous ever since. But his wisdom survives above all in his writings: a few superb poems; the grave *Rambler* essays, which established his reputation as a stylist and a moralist; the lessons about life in *Rasselas* and the *Lives of the Poets*; and literary criticism that ranks among the best in English. The virtues of the talk and the writings are the same. They come hot from a mind well stored with knowledge, searingly honest, humane, and quick to seize the unexpected but appropriate image of truth. Johnson's wit is timeless, for it deals with the great facts of human experience, with hope and happiness and loss and duty and the fear of death. Whatever topic he addresses, whatever the form in which he writes, he holds to one commanding purpose: to see life as it is.

Two examples must suffice here. When Mrs. Anna Williams wondered why a man should make a beast of himself through drunkenness, Johnson answered that "he who makes a beast of himself gets rid of the pain of being a man." In this reply Mrs. Williams' tired metaphor is so charged with an awareness of the dark aspects of human life that it comes almost unbearably alive. Such moments characterize Johnson's writings as well. For instance, in reviewing the book of a fatuous would-be philosopher who blandly explained away the pains of poverty by declaring that a kindly providence compensates the poor by making them more hopeful, more healthy, more capable of relishing small pleasures and less sensitive to small annoyances than the rich, Johnson retorted: "The poor indeed are insensible of many little vexations which sometimes embitter the possessions and pollute the enjoyment of the rich. They are not pained by casual incivility, or mortified by the mutilation of a compliment; but this happiness is like that of the malefactor who ceases to feel the cords that bind him when the pincers are tearing his flesh."

Johnson had himself known the pains of poverty. During his boyhood and youth, his father's financial circumstances steadily worsened, so that he was forced to leave Oxford before he had taken a degree. An early marriage to a well-to-do widow, Elizabeth ("Tetty") Porter, more than twenty years older than he, enabled him to open a school. But the school failed, and he moved to London to make his way as a writer. The years between 1737, when he first arrived there with his pupil David Garrick (later to become the leading actor of his generation), and 1755, when the publication of the *Dictionary* established his reputation, were very difficult. He supported himself at first as best he could by doing hack work for the *Gentleman's Magazine*, but gradually his own original writings began to attract attention.

In 1747 Johnson published the *Plan* of his *Dictionary*, and the next seven years were occupied in compiling it—although he had been sanguine enough to count on finishing it in three years. When in 1748 Dr. Adams, a friend from Oxford days, questioned his ability to carry out such a work alone in so short a time, and reminded him that the *Dictionary* of the French Academy had been compiled by forty academicians working for forty years, Johnson replied with humorous jingoism: "Sir, thus it is. This is the proportion. Let me see; forty times forty is sixteen hundred. As three to sixteen hundred, so is the proportion of an Englishman to a Frenchman."

Johnson's achievement in compiling the *Dictionary* becomes even greater when it is realized that he was writing some of his best essays and poems during the same period, for although the booksellers who published the *Dictionary* paid him what was then the large sum of £1575, it was not enough to enable him to support his household, buy materials, and pay the wages of the six assistants whom he employed year by year until the task was accomplished. He therefore had to exert himself to earn more money by writing. Thus, in 1749, his early tragedy *Irene* (pronounced *I-re-nĕ*) was produced at long last by his old friend Garrick, by then the manager of Drury Lane. The play was not a success, though Johnson made some profit from it. In the same year appeared his finest poem, *The Vanity of Human Wishes*. With the *Rambler* (1750–52) and the *Idler* (1758–60), two series of periodical essays, Johnson found a devoted audience; but his pleasure in success was tempered by the death of his wife in 1752. He never remarried.

Boswell said of the *Rambler* essays that "in no writings whatever can be found more bark and steel [i.e., quinine and iron] for the mind." Moral strength and health; the importance of applying reason to experience; the test of virtue by what we do, not what we say or "feel"; faith in God: these are the centers to which Johnson's moral writings always return. What Johnson uniquely offers us is the quality of his understanding of the human condition, based on wide reading but always ultimately referred to his own passionate and often anguished experience. Such understanding had to be fought for again and again.

Johnson is thought of as the great generalizer, but what gives his generalizations strength is that they are rooted in the particulars of his self-knowledge. He had constantly to fight against what he called "filling the mind" with illusions, in order to avoid the call of duty, his own black melancholy, and the realities of life. The portrait (largely a self-portrait) of Sober in *Idler* 31 is revealing: he occupies his idle hours with crafts and hobbies, and has now taken up chemistry—he "sits and counts the drops as they come from his retort, and forgets that, whilst a drop is falling, a moment flies away." So clear a vision is some distance away from the secure ease of the Addisonian essay.

His theme of themes is expressed in the title of his poem, *The Vanity of Human Wishes*, by which Johnson means the dangerous but all-pervasive illusion of what we now call wishful thinking, the feverish intrusion of desires and hopes that distort reality and lead to false expectations. Almost all of Johnson's major writings—verse satire, moral essay, or the prose fable *Rasselas* (1759)—express this theme. In *Rasselas* it is called "the hunger of imagination, which preys upon life," the seeing of things as one would like them to be, rather than as they are. The travelers who are the fable's protagonists pursue supposed guarantees of happiness; they reflect our naïve hopefulness, against the accumulation of contrary experience, that one choice of life will make us happy forever.

During this time of great activity, Johnson developed his characteristic style: the rotund periods, proceeding through balanced or parallel words; phrases or clauses moving to carefully controlled rhythms, in language that is characteristically general, often Latinate, and frequently polysyllabic. It is a style at the opposite extreme from Swift's simplicity or Addison's neatness. In Johnson's writings this style never becomes obscure or turgid, for even a very complex sentence reveals—as it should—the structure of the thought, and the learned words are always precisely used. While reading early scientists to collect words for the *Dictionary*, he developed a new vocabulary: for example, *obtund*, *exuberate*, *fugacity*, *frigorific*. But he used many of these strange words in conversation as well as in his writings, often with a peculiarly Johnsonian felicity, describing the operations of the mind with a scientific precision.

After Johnson received his pension in 1762, he no longer had to write for a living, and since he held that "no man but a blockhead" ever wrote for any other reason, he produced as little as he decently could during the last twenty years of his life. His edition of Shakespeare, long delayed, was published in 1765, with its fine preface and its fascinating notes. His last important work is the *Lives of the Poets*, which came out in two parts in 1779 and 1781. These biographical and critical prefaces were commissioned by a group of booksellers who had joined together to publish a large collection of the English poets and who wished to give their venture the prestige that it would acquire if Johnson took part in it. The poets to be included (except for four insisted on by Johnson) were selected by the booksellers according to current fashions. We have, therefore, a collection that begins with Cowley and Milton and ends with Gray and that omits poets whom we regard as "standard," such as Chaucer, Spenser, Sidney, Donne, and Marvell.

In the *Lives of the Poets* and in the earlier *Life of Richard Savage* (1744), Johnson did much to advance the art of biography in England. The public had long been familiar with biography as panegyric or as scandalous memoir, and therefore Johnson's insistence on truth, even about the subject's defects, and on concrete, often minute, details was a new departure, disliked by many readers. "The biographical part of literature is what I love most," Johnson said, for he found every biography useful in revealing human nature and the way we all live. His insistence on truth in biography (and knowing that Boswell intended to write his life, he insisted that he should write it truthfully) was due to his conviction that the more truthful such a work is the more useful it will be to all of us who are concerned with the business of living.

The ideal poet, according to Johnson, has a genius for making the familiar things we see every day seem new. The same might be said of Johnson himself as a critic. He is our great champion, in criticism, of common sense and the common reader. Without denying the right of the poet to flights of imagination, he also insists that poems must make sense, please readers, and help us not only to understand the world but to cope with it. Johnson holds poems to the truth, as he sees it: the principles of nature, logic, religion, and morality. Not even Shakespeare can be excused when "he sacrifices virtue to convenience" and "seems to write without any moral purpose." Yet Johnson is no worshiper of authority or mere "correctness." As a critic he is always the empiricist, testing theory, as he tested all notions, by experience. His determination to judge literature by its truth to life, not by abstract rules, is perfectly illustrated by his treatment of the doctrine of the three unities in the Preface to Shakespeare. Johnson is never afraid to state the obvious, whether the lack of human interest in *Paradise Lost* or Shakespeare's temptation by puns. But at its best, as in the praise of Milton or Shakespeare, his criticism engages some of the deepest questions about literature: why it endures, and how it helps us to endure.

The Vanity of Human Wishes[1]

In Imitation of the Tenth Satire of Juvenal

Let Observation, with extensive view,
Survey mankind, from China to Peru;
Remark each anxious toil, each eager strife,
And watch the busy scenes of crowded life;
Then say how hope and fear, desire and hate   5
O'erspread with snares the clouded maze of fate,

1. *The Vanity of Human Wishes* is an imitation of Juvenal's *Satire 10*. Although it closely follows the order and the ideas of the Latin poem, it remains a very personal work, for Johnson has used the Roman Stoic's satire as a means of expressing his own sense of the tragic and comic in human life. He has tried to reproduce in English verse the qualities he thought especially Juvenalian: stateliness, pointed sentences, declamatory grandeur. The poem is difficult because of the extreme compactness of the style: every line is forced to convey the greatest possible amount of meaning. Johnson's poetic theory demanded that the poet should deal in the general rather than the particular (cf. his phrase "the grandeur of generality"), but he certainly did not intend that the general should become the merely abstract: observe, for example, how he makes abstract nouns concrete, active, and dramatic by using them as subjects of active and dramatic verbs: "Hate *dogs* their flight, and Insult *mocks* their end" (line 78). But the difficulty of the poem is also related to its theme, the difficulty of seeing anything clearly on this earth. In a world of blindness and illusion, human beings must struggle to find a point of view that will not deceive them, and a happiness that can last.

For the author's revisions while composing this poem, see "Poems in Process," below.

Where wavering man, betrayed by venturous pride
To tread the dreary paths without a guide,
As treacherous phantoms in the mist delude,
Shuns fancied ills, or chases airy good;   10
How rarely Reason guides the stubborn choice,
Rules the bold hand, or prompts the suppliant voice;
How nations sink, by darling schemes oppressed,
When Vengeance listens to the fool's request.
Fate wings with every wish the afflictive dart,   15
Each gift of nature, and each grace of art;
With fatal heat impetuous courage glows,
With fatal sweetness elocution flows,
Impeachment stops the speaker's powerful breath,
And restless fire precipitates on death.   20
     But scarce observed, the knowing and the bold
Fall in the general massacre of gold;
Wide-wasting pest! that rages unconfined,
And crowds with crimes the records of mankind;
For gold his sword the hireling ruffian draws,   25
For gold the hireling judge distorts the laws;
Wealth heaped on wealth, nor truth nor safety buys,
The dangers gather as the treasures rise.
     Let History tell where rival kings command,
And dubious title shakes the madded land,   30
When statutes glean the refuse of the sword,
How much more safe the vassal than the lord;
Low skulks the hind beneath the rage of power,
And leaves the wealthy traitor[2] in the Tower,
Untouched his cottage, and his slumbers sound,   35
Though Confiscation's vultures hover round.
     The needy traveler, serene and gay,
Walks the wild heath, and sings his toil away.
Does envy seize thee? crush the upbraiding joy,
Increase his riches and his peace destroy;   40
New fears in dire vicissitude invade,
The rustling brake[3] alarms, and quivering shade,
Nor light nor darkness bring his pain relief,
One shows the plunder, and one hides the thief.
     Yet still one general cry the skies assails,   45
And gain and grandeur load the tainted gales;
Few know the toiling statesman's fear or care,
The insidious rival and the gaping heir.
     Once more, Democritus,[4] arise on earth,
With cheerful wisdom and instructive mirth,   50

2. Johnson first wrote "bonny traitor," recalling
the Jacobite uprising of 1745 and the execution of
four of its Scot leaders. "Hind": peasant.
3. Thicket.

4. A Greek philosopher of the late 5th century B.C.,
remembered as the "laughing philosopher" because
men's follies only moved him to mirth.

See motley life in modern trappings dressed,
And feed with varied fools the eternal jest:
Thou who couldst laugh where Want enchained Caprice,
Toil crushed Conceit, and man was of a piece;
Where Wealth unloved without a mourner died;   55
And scarce a sycophant was fed by Pride;
Where ne'er was known the form of mock debate,
Or seen a new-made mayor's unwieldy state;
Where change of favorites made no change of laws,
And senates heard before they judged a cause;   60
How wouldst thou shake at Britain's modish tribe,
Dart the quick taunt, and edge the piercing gibe?
Attentive truth and nature to descry,
And pierce each scene with philosophic eye,
To thee were solemn toys or empty show   65
The robes of pleasures and the veils of woe:
All aid the farce, and all thy mirth maintain,
Whose joys are causeless, or whose griefs are vain.
    Such was the scorn that filled the sage's mind,
Renewed at every glance on human kind;   70
How just that scorn ere yet thy voice declare,
Search every state, and canvass every prayer.
    Unnumbered suppliants crowd Preferment's gate,
Athirst for wealth, and burning to be great;
Delusive Fortune hears the incessant call,   75
They mount, they shine, evaporate, and fall.
On every stage the foes of peace attend,
Hate dogs their flight, and Insult mocks their end.
Love ends with hope, the sinking statesman's door
Pours in the morning worshiper no more;[5]   80
For growing names the weekly scribbler lies,
To growing wealth the dedicator flies;
From every room descends the painted face,
That hung the bright palladium[6] of the place;
And smoked in kitchens, or in auctions sold,   85
To better features yields the frame of gold;
For now no more we trace in every line
Heroic worth, benevolence divine:
The form distorted justifies the fall,
And Detestation rids the indignant wall.   90
    But will not Britain hear the last appeal,
Sign her foes' doom, or guard her favorites' zeal?
Through Freedom's sons no more remonstrance rings,
Degrading nobles and controlling kings;
Our supple tribes repress their patriot throats,   95

5. Statesmen gave interviews and received friends
and petitioners at levees, or morning receptions.
6. An image of Pallas Athena, which fell from
heaven and was preserved at Troy. Not until it was
stolen by Diomedes could the city fall to the Greeks.

And ask no questions but the price of votes,
With weekly libels and septennial ale.[7]
Their wish is full to riot and to rail.
    In full-blown dignity, see Wolsey[8] stand,
Law in his voice, and fortune in his hand: 100
To him the church, the realm, their powers consign,
Through him the rays of regal bounty shine;
Turned by his nod the stream of honor flows,
His smile alone security bestows:
Still to new heights his restless wishes tower, 105
Claim leads to claim, and power advances power;
Till conquest unresisted ceased to please,
And rights submitted, left him none to seize.
At length his sovereign frowns—the train of state
Mark the keen glance, and watch the sign to hate. 110
Where'er he turns, he meets a stranger's eye,
His suppliants scorn him, and his followers fly;
At once is lost the pride of awful state,
The golden canopy, the glittering plate,
The regal palace, the luxurious board, 115
The liveried army, and the menial lord.
With age, with cares, with maladies oppressed,
He seeks the refuge of monastic rest.
Grief aids disease, remembered folly stings,
And his last sighs reproach the faith of kings. 120
    Speak thou, whose thoughts at humble peace repine,
Shall Wolsey's wealth, with Wolsey's end be thine?
Or liv'st thou now, with safer pride content,
The wisest justice on the banks of Trent?
For why did Wolsey, near the steeps of fate, 125
On weak foundations raise the enormous weight?
Why but to sink beneath misfortune's blow,
With louder ruin to the gulfs below?
    What gave great Villiers[9] to the assassin's knife,
And fixed disease on Harley's closing life? 130
What murdered Wentworth, and what exiled Hyde,
By kings protected and to kings allied?
What but their wish indulged in courts to shine,
And power too great to keep or to resign?
    When first the college rolls receive his name, 135

7. Ministers and even the king freely bought support by bribing members of Parliament, who in
turn won elections by buying votes. "Weekly libels":
politically motivated lampoons published in the
weekly newspapers; "septennial ale": the ale given
away by candidates at parliamentary elections, held
at least every seven years.
8. Thomas Cardinal Wolsey (ca. 1475–1530), lord
chancellor and favorite of Henry VIII. Shakespeare dramatized his fall in *Henry VIII.*
9. George Villiers, 1st duke of Buckingham,
favorite of James I and Charles I, was assassinated

in 1628. Mentioned in the following lines are:
Robert Harley, earl of Oxford, chancellor of the
exchequer and later lord treasurer under Queen
Anne (1710–14), impeached and imprisoned by
the Whigs in 1715; Thomas Wentworth, earl of
Strafford, intimate and adviser of Charles I,
impeached by the Long Parliament and executed
1641; Edward Hyde, earl of Clarendon ("to kings
allied" because his daughter married James, duke
of York), lord chancellor under Charles II;
impeached in 1667, he fled to the Continent.

The young enthusiast quits his ease for fame;
Resistless burns the fever of renown
Caught from the strong contagion of the gown:
O'er Bodley's dome his future labors spread,
And Bacon's mansion trembles o'er his head.[1]   140
Are these thy views? proceed, illustrious youth,
And Virtue guard thee to the throne of Truth!
Yet should thy soul indulge the generous heat,
Till captive Science yields her last retreat;
Should Reason guide thee with her brightest ray,   145
And pour on misty Doubt resistless day;
Should no false kindness lure to loose delight,
Nor praise relax, nor difficulty fright;
Should tempting Novelty thy cell refrain,
And Sloth effuse her opiate fumes in vain;   150
Should Beauty blunt on fops her fatal dart,
Nor claim the triumph of a lettered heart;
Should no disease thy torpid veins invade,
Nor Melancholy's phantoms haunt thy shade;
Yet hope not life from grief or danger free,   155
Nor think the doom of man reversed for thee:
Deign on the passing world to turn thine eyes,
And pause a while from letters, to be wise;
There mark what ills the scholar's life assail,
Toil, envy, want, the patron, and the jail.   160
See nations slowly wise, and meanly just,
To buried merit raise the tardy bust.
If dreams yet flatter, once again attend,
Hear Lydiat's life, and Galileo's end.[2]
    Nor deem, when Learning her last prize bestows,   165
The glittering eminence exempt from foes;
See when the vulgar 'scapes, despised or awed,
Rebellion's vengeful talons seize on Laud.[3]
From meaner minds though smaller fines content,
The plundered palace, or sequestered rent;[4]   170
Marked out by dangerous parts he meets the shock,
And fatal Learning leads him to the block:
Around his tomb let Art and Genius weep,
But hear his death, ye blockheads, hear and sleep.
    The festal blazes, the triumphal show,   175
The ravished standard, and the captive foe,
The senate's thanks, the gazette's pompous tale,

1. "Bodley's dome" is the Bodleian Library, Oxford. Roger Bacon (ca. 1214–1294), scientist and philosopher, taught at Oxford, where his study, according to tradition, would collapse when a man greater than he should appear at Oxford.
2. Thomas Lydiat (1572–1646), Oxford scholar, died impoverished because of his Royalist sympathies. Galileo (1564–1642), the famous astronomer, was imprisoned as a heretic by the Inquisition in 1633; he died blind.
3. Appointed archbishop of Canterbury by Charles I, William Laud followed rigorously high-church policies and was executed by order of the Long Parliament in 1645.
4. During the Commonwealth, the estates of many Royalists were pillaged and their incomes confiscated ("sequestered") by the state.

With force resistless o'er the brave prevail.
Such bribes the rapid Greek[5] o'er Asia whirled,
For such the steady Romans shook the world;   180
For such in distant lands the Britons shine,
And stain with blood the Danube or the Rhine;
This power has praise that virtue scarce can warm,
Till fame supplies the universal charm.
Yet Reason frowns on War's unequal game,   185
Where wasted nations raise a single name,
And mortgaged states their grandsires' wreaths regret
From age to age in everlasting debt;
Wreaths which at last the dear-bought right convey
To rust on medals, or on stones decay.   190
    On what foundation stands the warrior's pride,
How just his hopes, let Swedish Charles[6] decide;
A frame of adamant, a soul of fire,
No dangers fright him, and no labors tire;
O'er love, o'er fear, extends his wide domain,   195
Unconquered lord of pleasure and of pain;
No joys to him pacific scepters yield,
War sounds the trump, he rushes to the field;
Behold surrounding kings their powers combine,
And one capitulate, and one resign;[7]   200
Peace courts his hand, but spreads her charms in vain;
"Think nothing gained," he cries, "till naught remain,
On Moscow's walls till Gothic standards fly,
And all be mine beneath the polar sky."
The march begins in military state,   205
And nations on his eye suspended wait;
Stern Famine guards the solitary coast,
And Winter barricades the realms of Frost;
He comes, nor want nor cold his course delay—
Hide, blushing Glory, hide Pultowa's day: 210
The vanquished hero leaves his broken bands,
And shows his miseries in distant lands;
Condemned a needy supplicant to wait,
While ladies interpose, and slaves debate.
But did not Chance at length her error mend?   215
Did no subverted empire mark his end?
Did rival monarchs give the fatal wound?
Or hostile millions press him to the ground?
His fall was destined to a barren strand,
A petty fortress, and a dubious hand;   220
He left the name at which the world grew pale,

---

5. Alexander the Great.
6. Charles XII of Sweden (1682–1718). Defeated
by the Russians at Poltava (1709), he escaped to
Turkey and tried to form an alliance against Russia
with the sultan. Returning to Sweden, he attacked

Norway and was killed in the attack on Fredriks-
hald.
7. Frederick IV of Denmark capitulated to Charles
in 1700; Augustus II of Poland resigned his throne
to Charles in 1704.

To point a moral, or adorn a tale.
    All times their scenes of pompous woes afford,
From Persia's tyrant to Bavaria's lord.[8]
In gay hostility, and barbarous pride,   225
With half mankind embattled at his side,
Great Xerxes comes to seize the certain prey,
And starves exhausted regions in his way;
Attendant Flattery counts his myriads o'er,
Till counted myriads soothe his pride no more;   230
Fresh praise is tried till madness fires his mind,
The waves he lashes, and enchains the wind;
New powers are claimed, new powers are still bestowed,
Till rude resistance lops the spreading god;
The daring Greeks deride the martial show,   235
And heap their valleys with the gaudy foe;
The insulted sea with humbler thought he gains,
A single skiff to speed his flight remains;
The encumbered oar scarce leaves the dreaded coast
Through purple billows and a floating host.   240
    The bold Bavarian, in a luckless hour,
Tries the dread summits of Caesarean power,
With unexpected legions bursts away,
And sees defenseless realms receive his sway;
Short sway! fair Austria spreads her mournful charms,   245
The queen, the beauty, sets the world in arms;
From hill to hill the beacon's rousing blaze
Spreads wide the hope of plunder and of praise;
The fierce Croatian, and the wild Hussar,[9]
With all the sons of ravage crowd the war;   250
The baffled prince, in honor's flattering bloom
Of hasty greatness finds the fatal doom;
His foes' derision, and his subjects' blame,
And steals to death from anguish and from shame.
    Enlarge my life with multitude of days!   255
In health, in sickness, thus the suppliant prays;
Hides from himself his state, and shuns to know,
That life protracted is protracted woe.
Time hovers o'er, impatient to destroy,
And shuts up all the passages of joy;   260
In vain their gifts the bounteous seasons pour,
The fruit autumnal, and the vernal flower;
With listless eyes the dotard views the store,
He views, and wonders that they please no more;
Now pall the tasteless meats, and joyless wines,   265
And Luxury with sighs her slave resigns.

---

8. Xerxes ("Persia's tyrant") invaded Greece and was totally defeated in the sea battle off Salamis, 480 B.C.; the Elector Charles Albert ("Bavaria's Lord") caused the War of the Austrian Succession (1740–48) when he contested the crown of the Empire with Maria Theresa ("Fair Austria" in line 245).

9. Hungarian light cavalry.

Approach, ye minstrels, try the soothing strain,
Diffuse the tuneful lenitives[1] of pain:
No sounds, alas! would touch the impervious ear,
Though dancing mountains witnessed Orpheus[2] near;   270
Nor lute nor lyre his feeble powers attend,
Nor sweeter music of a virtuous friend,
But everlasting dictates crowd his tongue,
Perversely grave, or positively wrong.
The still returning tale, and lingering jest,   275
Perplex the fawning niece and pampered guest,
While growing hopes scarce awe the gathering sneer,
And scarce a legacy can bribe to hear;
The watchful guests still hint the last offense;
The daughter's petulance, the son's expense,   280
Improve his heady rage with treacherous skill,
And mold his passions till they make his will.
    Unnumbered maladies his joints invade,
Lay siege to life and press the dire blockade;
But unextinguished avarice still remains,   285
And dreaded losses aggravate his pains;
He turns, with anxious heart and crippled hands,
His bonds of debt, and mortgages of lands;
Or views his coffers with suspicious eyes,
Unlocks his gold, and counts it till he dies.   290
But grant, the virtues of a temperate prime
Bless with an age exempt from scorn or crime;
An age that melts with unperceived decay,
And glides in modest innocence away;
Whose peaceful day Benevolence endears,   295
Whose night congratulating Conscience cheers;
The general favorite as the general friend:
Such age there is, and who shall wish its end?
    Yet even on this her load Misfortune flings,
To press the weary minutes' flagging wings;   300
New sorrow rises as the day returns,
A sister sickens, or a daughter mourns.
Now kindred Merit fills the sable bier,
Now lacerated Friendship claims a tear;
Year chases year, decay pursues decay,   305
Still drops some joy from withering life away;
New forms arise, and different views engage,
Superfluous lags the veteran[3] on the stage,
Till pitying Nature signs the last release,
And bids afflicted Worth retire to peace.   310
    But few there are whom hours like these await,
Who set unclouded in the gulfs of Fate.

1. Medicines that relieve pain.
2. A legendary poet who played on the lyre so   beautifully that wild beasts were spellbound.
3. A veteran of life, not of war.

From Lydia's monarch[4] should the search descend,
By Solon cautioned to regard his end,
In life's last scene what prodigies surprise,   315
Fears of the brave, and follies of the wise!
From Marlborough's eyes the streams of dotage flow,
And Swift expires a driveler and a show.[5]
  The teeming mother, anxious for her race,
Begs for each birth the fortune of a face: 320
Yet Vane could tell what ills from beauty spring;[6]
And Sedley cursed the form that pleased a king.
Ye nymphs of rosy lips and radiant eyes,
Whom Pleasure keeps too busy to be wise,
Whom Joys with soft varieties invite,   325
By day the frolic, and the dance by night;
Who frown with vanity, who smile with art,
And ask the latest fashion of the heart;
What care, what rules your heedless charms shall save,
Each nymph your rival, and each youth your slave?   330
Against your fame with Fondness Hate combines,
The rival batters, and the lover mines.
With distant voice neglected Virtue calls,
Less heard and less, the faint remonstrance falls;
Tired with contempt, she quits the slippery reign,   335
And Pride and Prudence take her seat in vain.
In crowd at once, where none the pass defend,
The harmless freedom, and the private friend.
The guardians yield, by force superior plied:
To Interest, Prudence; and to Flattery, Pride.   340
Now Beauty falls betrayed, despised, distressed,
And hissing Infamy proclaims the rest.
  Where then shall Hope and Fear their objects find?
Must dull Suspense corrupt the stagnant mind?
Must helpless man, in ignorance sedate,   345
Roll darkling down the torrent of his fate?
Must no dislike alarm, no wishes rise,
No cries invoke the mercies of the skies?
Inquirer, cease; petitions yet remain,
Which Heaven may hear, nor deem religion vain.   350
Still raise for good the supplicating voice,
But leave to Heaven the measure and the choice.
Safe in His power, whose eyes discern afar
The secret ambush of a specious prayer.
Implore His aid, in His decisions rest,   355

---

4. Croesus, a wealthy and fortunate king, was warned by Solon not to count himself happy till he ceased to live. He lost his crown to Cyrus the Great of Persia.
5. John Churchill, duke of Marlborough, England's brilliant general during most of the War of the Spanish Succession (1702–13); Jonathan Swift, who passed the last four years of his life in utter senility.
6. Anne Vane, mistress of Frederick, prince of Wales (son of George II). Catherine Sedley, mistress of James II.

Secure, whate'er He gives, He gives the best.
Yet when the sense of sacred presence fires,
And strong devotion to the skies aspires,
Pour forth thy fervors for a healthful mind,
Obedient passions, and a will resigned;   360
For love, which scarce collective man can fill;[7]
For patience sovereign o'er transmuted ill;
For faith, that panting for a happier seat,
Counts death kind Nature's signal of retreat:
These goods for man the laws of Heaven ordain,   365
These goods He grants, who grants the power to gain;
With these celestial Wisdom calms the mind,
And makes the happiness she does not find.

1749

On the Death of Dr. Robert Levet[1]

Condemned to Hope's delusive mine,
    As on we toil from day to day,
By sudden blasts, or slow decline,
    Our social comforts drop away.

Well tried through many a varying year,   5
    See Levet to the grave descend;
Officious,[2] innocent, sincere,
    Of every friendless name the friend.

Yet still he fills Affection's eye,
    Obscurely wise, and coarsely kind;   10
Nor, lettered Arrogance, deny
    Thy praise to merit unrefined.

When fainting Nature called for aid,
    And hovering Death prepared the blow,
His vigorous remedy displayed   15
    The power of art without the show.

In Misery's darkest cavern known,
    His useful care was ever nigh,
Where hopeless Anguish poured his groan,
    And lonely Want retired to die.   20

7. Which mankind as a whole can hardly over-
task.
1. An unlicensed physician, who lived in Johnson's house for many years and who died in 1782.
His practice was among the very poor. Boswell

wrote: "He was of a strange grotesque appearance,
stiff and formal in his manner, and seldom said a
word while any company was present."
2. "Kind, doing good offices" (Johnson's *Dictionary*).

No summons mocked by chill delay,
   No petty gain disdained by pride,
The modest wants of every day
   The toil of every day supplied.

His virtues walked their narrow round,   25
   Nor made a pause, nor left a void;
And sure the Eternal Master found
   The single talent well employed.[3]

The busy day, the peaceful night,
   Unfelt, uncounted, glided by;   30
His frame was firm, his powers were bright,
   Though now his eightieth year was nigh.

Then with no throbbing fiery pain,
   No cold gradations of decay,
Death broke at once the vital chain,   35
   And freed his soul the nearest way.

1783

Translation of Horace, *Odes*, Book 4.7[1]

The snow dissolved no more is seen,
The fields, and woods, behold, are green,
The changing year renews the plain,
The rivers know their banks again,
The spritely nymph and naked grace[2]   5
The mazy dance together trace.
The changing year's successive plan
Proclaims mortality to man.
Rough winter's blasts to spring give way,
Spring yields to summer's sovereign ray,   10
Then summer sinks in autumn's reign,
And winter chills the world again.
Her losses soon the moon supplies,
But wretched man, when once he lies
Where Priam[3] and his sons are laid,   15
Is naught but ashes and a shade.
Who knows if Jove who counts our score
Will toss us in a morning more?
What with your friend you nobly share

3. In the parable of the talents (Matthew 25.14–30), Jesus suggests that salvation will be granted to those who make good use of their abilities, however small.
1. Johnson composed this translation the month before his death.
2. One of the Three Graces, emblematic of beauty.
3. Last king of Troy, slain with his sons at the end of the Trojan War.

At least you rescue from your heir.   20
Not you, Torquatus, boast of Rome,
When Minos once has fixed your doom,[4]
Or eloquence, or splendid birth,
Or virtue shall replace on earth.
Hippolytus[5] unjustly slain   25
Diana calls to life in vain,
Nor can the might of Theseus rend
The chains of hell that hold his friend.[6]

1784

Rasselas   Johnson wrote *Rasselas* in January 1759, during the evenings
of one week, a remarkable instance of his ability to write rapidly and brilliantly under the pressure of necessity. His mother lay dying in Lichfield.
Her son, famous for his *Dictionary*, was nonetheless oppressed by poverty
and in great need of ready money with which to make her last days comfortable, pay her funeral expenses, and settle her small debts. He was paid
£100 for the first edition of *Rasselas*, but not in time to attend her deathbed
or her funeral.

Rasselas is a philosophical fable cast in the popular form of an Oriental
tale, a type of fiction that owed its popularity to the vogue of the *Arabian
Nights*, first translated into English in the early 18th century. Since the work
is a fable, we should not approach it as a novel: psychologically credible
characters and a series of intricately involved actions that lead to a necessary
resolution and conclusion are not to be found in *Rasselas*. Instead we are
meant to reflect on the ideas and to savor the melancholy resonance and
intelligence of the stately prose that expresses them. Johnson arranges the
incidents of the fable to test a variety of possible solutions to a problem: What
choice of life will bring us happiness? (*The Choice of Life* was his working
title for the book.) Many ways of life are examined in turn, and each is found
wanting. Johnson does not pretend to have solved the problem. Rather, he
locates the sources of discontent in a basic principle of human nature: the
"hunger of imagination which preys incessantly upon life" (chapter 32) and
which lures us to "listen with credulity to the whispers of fancy and pursue
with eagerness the phantoms of hope" (chapter 1). The tale is a gentle satire
on one of the perennial topics of satirists, the folly of all of us who stubbornly
cling to our illusions despite the evidence of experience. *Rasselas* is not all
darkness and gloom, for Johnson's theme invites comic as well as tragic
treatment, and some of the episodes evoke that laughter of the mind which
is the effect of high comedy. In its main theme, however—the folly of cherishing the dream of ever attaining unalloyed happiness in a world which can
never wholly satisfy our desires—and in many of the sayings of its characters,
especially of the sage Imlac, *Rasselas* expresses some of Johnson's own deepest convictions.

---

4. Sentence. L. Manlius Torquatus, a friend of
Horace and an advocate, is represented as pleading
his case before Minos, judge of the dead.
5. Phaedra, wife of Theseus, falsely accused his

chaste son Hippolytus of rape; Theseus brought
about the death of his son, and even Diana, goddess of chastity, could not restore him.
6. Pirithous, held prisoner with Theseus in Hell.

The History of Rasselas, Prince of Abyssinia

Chapter 1. Description of a Palace in a Valley

Ye who listen with credulity to the whispers of fancy, and pursue with eagerness the phantoms of hope; who expect that age will perform the promises of youth, and that the deficiencies of the present day will be supplied by the morrow—attend to the history of Rasselas, prince of Abyssinia.

Rasselas was the fourth son of the mighty emperor in whose dominions the Father of Waters[1] begins his course; whose bounty pours down the streams of plenty, and scatters over half the world the harvests of Egypt.

According to the custom which has descended from age to age among the monarchs of the torrid zone, Rasselas was confined in a private palace, with the other sons and daughters of Abyssinian royalty, till the order of succession should call him to the throne.

The place which the wisdom or policy of antiquity had destined for the residence of the Abyssinian princes was a spacious valley[2] in the kingdom of Amhara, surrounded on every side by mountains, of which the summits overhang the middle part. The only passage by which it could be entered was a cavern that passed under a rock, of which it has long been disputed whether it was the work of nature or of human industry. The outlet of the cavern was concealed by a thick wood, and the mouth which opened into the valley was closed with gates of iron, forged by the artificers of ancient days, so massy that no man could, without the help of engines, open or shut them.

From the mountains on every side rivulets descended that filled all the valley with verdure and fertility, and formed a lake in the middle, inhabited by fish of every species, and frequented by every fowl whom nature has taught to dip the wing in water. This lake discharged its superfluities by a stream, which entered a dark cleft of the mountain on the northern side, and fell with dreadful noise from precipice to precipice till it was heard no more.

The sides of the mountains were covered with trees, the banks of the brooks were diversified with flowers; every blast shook spices from the rocks, and every month dropped fruits upon the ground. All animals that bite the grass, or browse the shrub, whether wild or tame, wandered in this extensive circuit, secured from beasts of prey by the mountains which confined them. On one part were flocks and herds feeding in the pastures, on another all the beasts of chase frisking in the lawns; the sprightly kid was bounding on the rocks, the subtle monkey frolicking in

---

1. The Nile.
2. Johnson had read of the Happy Valley in the Portuguese Jesuit Father Lobo's book on Abyssinia, which he translated in 1735. The description in this and the immediately following paragraphs illustrates well enough Johnson's preference for the "general" over the "particular" (see chap. 10, below). It owes something to the description of the Garden in *Paradise Lost* 4, and Coleridge's *Kubla Khan* owes something to it.

the trees, and the solemn elephant reposing in the shade. All the diversities of the world were brought together, the blessings of nature were collected, and its evils extracted and excluded.

The valley, wide and fruitful, supplied its inhabitants with the necessaries of life, and all delights and superfluities were added at the annual visit which the emperor paid his children, when the iron gate was opened to the sound of music, and during eight days everyone that resided in the valley was required to propose whatever might contribute to make seclusion pleasant, to fill up the vacancies of attention, and lessen the tediousness of time. Every desire was immediately granted. All the artificers of pleasure were called to gladden the festivity; the musicians exerted the power of harmony, and the dancers showed their activity before the princes, in hope that they should pass their lives in this blissful captivity, to which those only were admitted whose performance was thought able to add novelty to luxury. Such was the appearance of security and delight which this retirement afforded, that they to whom it was new always desired that it might be perpetual; and as those on whom the iron gate had once closed were never suffered to return, the effect of longer experience could not be known. Thus every year produced new schemes of delight and new competitors for imprisonment.

The palace stood on an eminence, raised about thirty paces above the surface of the lake. It was divided into many squares or courts, built with greater or less magnificence according to the rank of those for whom they were designed. The roofs were turned into arches of massy stone, joined with a cement that grew harder by time, and the building stood from century to century, deriding the solstitial rains and equinoctial hurricanes, without need of reparation.

This house, which was so large as to be fully known to none but some ancient officers, who successively inherited the secrets of the place, was built as if suspicion herself had dictated the plan. To every room there was an open and secret passage; every square had a communication with the rest, either from the upper stories by private galleries, or by subterranean passages from the lower apartments. Many of the columns had unsuspected cavities, in which a long race of monarchs had reposited their treasures. They then closed up the opening with marble, which was never to be removed but in the utmost exigencies of the kingdom, and recorded their accumulations in a book, which was itself concealed in a tower, not entered but by the emperor, attended by the prince who stood next in succession.

Chapter 2. The Discontent of Rasselas in the Happy Valley

Here the sons and daughters of Abyssinia lived only to know the soft vicissitudes of pleasure and repose, attended by all that were skillful to delight, and gratified with whatever the senses can enjoy. They wandered in gardens of fragrance, and slept in the fortresses of security. Every art was practiced to make them pleased with their own condition.

The sages who instructed them told them of nothing but the miseries of public life, and described all beyond the mountains as regions of calamity, where discord was always raging, and where man preyed upon man.

To heighten their opinion of their own felicity, they were daily entertained with songs, the subject of which was the *happy valley*. Their appetites were excited by frequent enumerations of different enjoyments, and revelry and merriment was the business of every hour, from the dawn of morning to the close of even.

These methods were generally successful; few of the princes had ever wished to enlarge their bounds, but passed their lives in full conviction that they had all within their reach that art or nature could bestow, and pitied those whom fate had excluded from this seat of tranquility, as the sport of chance and the slaves of misery.

Thus they rose in the morning and lay down at night, pleased with each other and with themselves; all but Rasselas, who, in the twenty-sixth year of his age, began to withdraw himself from their pastimes and assemblies, and to delight in solitary walks and silent meditation. He often sat before tables covered with luxury, and forgot to taste the dainties that were placed before him; he rose abruptly in the midst of the song, and hastily retired beyond the sound of music. His attendants observed the change, and endeavored to renew his love of pleasure. He neglected their officiousness, repulsed their invitations, and spent day after day on the banks of rivulets sheltered with trees, where he sometimes listened to the birds in the branches, sometimes observed the fish playing in the stream, and anon cast his eyes upon the pastures and mountains filled with animals, of which some were biting the herbage, and some sleeping among the bushes.

This singularity of his humor made him much observed. One of the sages, in whose conversation he had formerly delighted, followed him secretly, in hope of discovering the cause of his disquiet. Rasselas, who knew not that anyone was near him, having for some time fixed his eyes upon the goats that were browsing among the rocks, began to compare their condition with his own.

"What," said he, "makes the difference between man and all the rest of the animal creation? Every beast that strays beside me has the same corporal necessities with myself; he is hungry, and crops the grass, he is thirsty, and drinks the stream, his thirst and hunger are appeased, he is satisfied, and sleeps; he rises again, and he is hungry, he is again fed, and is at rest. I am hungry and thirsty like him, but when thirst and hunger cease, I am not at rest; I am, like him, pained with want, but am not, like him, satisfied with fullness. The intermediate hours are tedious and gloomy; I long again to be hungry that I may again quicken my attention. The birds peck the berries or the corn, and fly away to the groves, where they sit in seeming happiness on the branches, and waste their lives in tuning one unvaried series of sounds. I likewise can call the lutanist and the singer, but the sounds that pleased me yesterday weary me today, and will grow yet more wearisome tomorrow. I can discover within me no power of perception which is not glutted with its proper pleasure, yet I do not feel myself delighted. Man has surely some latent sense for which this place affords no gratification, or he has some desires distinct from sense, which must be satisfied before he can be happy."

After this he lifted up his head, and seeing the moon rising, walked towards the palace. As he passed through the fields, and saw the animals around him, "Ye," said he, "are happy, and need not envy me that walk thus among you, burthened with myself; nor do I, ye gentle beings, envy your felicity, for it is not the felicity of man. I have many distresses from which ye are free; I fear pain when I do not feel it; I sometimes shrink at evils recollected, and sometimes start at evils anticipated. Surely the equity of Providence has balanced peculiar sufferings with peculiar enjoyments."

With observations like these the prince amused himself as he returned, uttering them with a plaintive voice, yet with a look that discovered him to feel some complacence in his own perspicacity, and to receive some solace of the miseries of life from consciousness of the delicacy with which he felt, and the eloquence with which he bewailed them. He mingled cheerfully in the diversions of the evening, and all rejoiced to find that his heart was lightened.

Chapter 3. The Wants of Him That Wants Nothing

On the next day his old instructor, imagining that he had now made himself acquainted with his disease of mind, was in the hope of curing it by counsel, and officiously sought an opportunity of conference, which the prince, having long considered him as one whose intellects were exhausted, was not very willing to afford. "Why," said he, "does this man thus intrude upon me; shall I be never suffered to forget those lectures which pleased only while they were new, and to become new again must be forgotten?" He then walked into the wood, and composed himself to his usual meditations; when, before his thoughts had taken any settled form, he perceived his pursuer at his side, and was at first prompted by his impatience to go hastily away; but, being unwilling to offend a man whom he had once reverenced and still loved, he invited him to sit down with him on the bank.

The old man, thus encouraged, began to lament the change which had been lately observed in the prince, and to inquire why he so often retired from the pleasures of the palace, to loneliness and silence. "I fly from pleasure," said the prince, "because pleasure has ceased to please; I am lonely because I am miserable, and am unwilling to cloud with my presence the happiness of others." "You, sir," said the sage, "are the first who has complained of misery in the *happy valley*. I hope to convince you that your complaints have no real cause. You are here in full possession of all that the emperor of Abyssinia can bestow; here is neither labor to be endured nor danger to be dreaded, yet here is all that labor or danger can procure or purchase. Look round and tell me which of your wants is without supply; if you want nothing, how are you unhappy?"

"That I want nothing," said the prince, "or that I know not what I want, is the cause of my complaint; if I had any known want, I should have a certain wish; that wish would excite endeavor, and I should not then repine to see the sun move so slowly towards the western mountain, or lament when the day breaks, and sleep will no longer hide me from myself. When I see the kids and the lambs chasing one another, I fancy that I should be happy if I had something to pursue. But, possessing all that I can want, I find one day and one hour exactly like another, except that the latter is still more tedious than the former. Let your experience inform me how the day may now seem as short as in my childhood, while nature was yet fresh and every moment showed me what I never had observed before. I have already enjoyed too much; give me something to desire."

The old man was surprised at this new species of affliction and knew not what to reply, yet was unwilling to be silent. "Sir," said he, "if you had seen the miseries of the world you would know how to value your present state." "Now," said the prince, "you have given me something to desire. I shall long to see the miseries of the world, since the sight of them is necessary to happiness."

Chapter 4. *The Prince Continues to Grieve and Muse*

At this time the sound of music proclaimed the hour of repast, and the conversation was concluded. The old man went away sufficiently discontented to find that his reasonings had produced the only conclusion which they were intended to prevent. But in the decline of life shame and grief are of short duration; whether it be that we bear easily what we have born long, or that, finding ourselves in age less regarded, we less regard others; or, that we look with slight regard upon afflictions, to which we know that the hand of death is about to put an end.

The prince, whose views were extended to a wider space, could not speedily quiet his emotions. He had been before terrified at the length of life which nature promised him, because he considered that in a long time much must be endured; he now rejoiced in his youth, because in many years much might be done.

This first beam of hope, that had been ever darted into his mind, rekindled youth in his cheeks, and doubled the luster of his eyes. He was fired with the desire of doing something, though he knew not yet with distinctness, either end or means.

He was now no longer gloomy and unsocial; but, considering himself as master of a secret stock of happiness, which he could enjoy only by concealing it, he affected to be busy in all schemes of diversion, and endeavored to make others pleased with the state of which he himself was weary. But pleasures never can be so multiplied or continued, as not to leave much of life unemployed; there were many hours, both of the night and day, which he could spend without suspicion in solitary thought. The load of life was much lightened: he went eagerly into the assemblies, because he supposed the frequency of his presence necessary to the success of his purposes; he retired gladly to privacy, because he had now a subject of thought.

His chief amusement was to picture to himself that world which he had never seen; to place himself in various conditions; to be entangled in imaginary difficulties, and to be engaged in wild adventures: but his benevolence always terminated his projects in the relief of distress, the detection of fraud, the defeat of oppression, and the diffusion of happiness.

Thus passed twenty months of the life of Rasselas. He busied himself so intensely in visionary bustle, that he forgot his real solitude; and, amidst hourly preparations for the various incidents of human affairs, neglected to consider by what means he should mingle with mankind.

One day, as he was sitting on a bank, he feigned to himself an orphan virgin robbed of her little portion[3] by a treacherous lover, and crying after him for restitution and redress. So strongly was the image impressed upon his mind, that he started up in the maid's defense, and ran forward to seize the plunderer with all the eagerness of real pursuit. Fear naturally quickens the flight of guilt. Rasselas could not catch the fugitive with his utmost efforts; but, resolving to weary, by perseverance, him whom he could not surpass in speed, he pressed on till the foot of the mountain stopped his course.

Here he recollected himself, and smiled at his own useless impetuosity. Then raising his eyes to the mountain, "This," said he, "is the fatal obstacle that hinders at once the enjoyment of pleasure, and the exercise of virtue. How long is it that my hopes and wishes have flown beyond this boundary of my life, which yet I never have attempted to surmount!"

Struck with this reflection, he sat down to muse, and remembered, that since he first resolved to escape from his confinement, the sun had passed twice over him in his annual course. He now felt a degree of regret with which he had never been before acquainted. He considered how much might have been done in the time which had passed, and left nothing real behind it. He compared twenty months with the life of man. "In life," said he, "is not to be counted the ignorance of infancy, or imbecility of age. We are long before we are able to think, and we soon cease from the power of acting. The true period of human existence may be reasonably estimated as forty years, of which I have mused away the four and twentieth part. What I have lost was certain, for I have certainly possessed it; but of twenty months to come who can assure me?"

The consciousness of his own folly pierced him deeply, and he was

3. Money or goods.

long before he could be reconciled to himself. "The rest of my time," said he, "has been lost by the crime or folly of my ancestors, and the absurd institutions of my country; I remember it with disgust, yet without remorse: but the months that have passed since new light darted into my soul, since I formed a scheme of reasonable felicity, have been squandered by my own fault. I have lost that which can never be restored: I have seen the sun rise and set for twenty months, an idle gazer on the light of heaven. In this time the birds have left the nest of their mother, and committed themselves to the woods and to the skies: the kid has forsaken the teat, and learned by degrees to climb the rocks in quest of independent sustenance. I only have made no advances, but am still helpless and ignorant. The moon, by more than twenty changes, admonished me of the flux of life; the stream that rolled before my feet upbraided my inactivity. I sat feasting on intellectual luxury, regardless alike of the examples of the earth, and the instructions of the planets. Twenty months are past, who shall restore them!"

These sorrowful meditations fastened upon his mind; he passed four months in resolving to lose no more time in idle resolves, and was awakened to more vigorous exertion by hearing a maid, who had broken a porcelain cup, remark that what cannot be repaired is not to be regretted.

This was obvious; and Rasselas reproached himself that he had not discovered it, having not known, or not considered, how many useful hints are obtained by chance, and how often the mind, hurried by her own ardor to distant views, neglects the truths that lie open before her. He, for a few hours, regretted his regret, and from that time bent his whole mind upon the means of escaping from the valley of happiness.

Chapter 5. The Prince Meditates His Escape

He now found that it would be very difficult to effect that which it was very easy to suppose effected. When he looked round about him, he saw himself confined by the bars of nature which had never yet been broken, and by the gate, through which none that once had passed it were ever able to return. He was now impatient as an eagle in a grate.[4] He passed week after week in clambering the mountains, to see if there was any aperture which the bushes might conceal, but found all the summits inaccessible by their prominence. The iron gate he despaired to open; for it was not only secured with all the power of art, but was always watched by successive sentinels, and was by its position exposed to the perpetual observation of all the inhabitants.

He then examined the cavern through which the waters of the lake were discharged; and, looking down at a time when the sun shone strongly upon its mouth, he discovered it to be full of broken rocks, which, though

---

4. Barred cage.

they permitted the stream to flow through many narrow passages, would stop any body of solid bulk. He returned discouraged and dejected; but, having now known the blessing of hope, resolved never to despair.

In these fruitless searches he spent ten months. The time, however, passed cheerfully away: in the morning he rose with new hope, in the evening applauded his own diligence, and in the night slept sound after his fatigue. He met a thousand amusements which beguiled his labor, and diversified his thoughts. He discerned the various instincts of animals, and properties of plants, and found the place replete with wonders, of which he purposed to solace himself with the contemplation, if he should never be able to accomplish his flight; rejoicing that his endeavors, though yet unsuccessful, had supplied him with a source of inexhaustible enquiry.

But his original curiosity was not yet abated; he resolved to obtain some knowledge of the ways of men. His wish still continued, but his hope grew less. He ceased to survey any longer the walls of his prison, and spared to search by new toils for interstices which he knew could not be found, yet determined to keep his design always in view, and lay hold on any expedient that time should offer.

Chapter 6. A Dissertation on the Art of Flying

Among the artists that had been allured into the happy valley, to labor for the accommodation and pleasure of its inhabitants, was a man eminent for his knowledge of the mechanic powers, who had contrived many engines[5] both of use and recreation. By a wheel, which the stream turned, he forced the water into a tower, whence it was distributed to all the apartments of the palace. He erected a pavillion in the garden, around which he kept the air always cool by artificial showers. One of the groves, appropriated to the ladies, was ventilated by fans, to which the rivulet that run through it gave a constant motion; and instruments of soft music were placed at proper distances, of which some played by the impulse of the wind, and some by the power of the stream.

This artist was sometimes visited by Rasselas, who was pleased with every kind of knowledge, imagining that the time would come when all his acquisitions should be of use to him in the open world. He came one day to amuse himself in his usual manner, and found the master busy in building a sailing chariot: he saw that the design was practicable upon a level surface, and with expressions of great esteem solicited its completion. The workman was pleased to find himself so much regarded by the prince, and resolved to gain yet higher honors. "Sir," said he, "you have seen but a small part of what the mechanic sciences can perform. I have been long of opinion, that, instead of the tardy conveyance of ships and chariots, man might use the swifter migration of wings;

---

5. Machines; "mechanic powers": the forces that cause things to move.

that the fields of air are open to knowledge, and that only ignorance and idleness need crawl upon the ground."

This hint rekindled the prince's desire of passing the mountains; having seen what the mechanist had already performed, he was willing to fancy that he could do more; yet resolved to inquire further before he suffered hope to afflict him by disappointment. "I am afraid," said he to the artist, "that your imagination prevails over your skill, and that you now tell me rather what you wish than what you know. Every animal has his element assigned him; the birds have the air, and man and beasts the earth." "So," replied the mechanist, "fishes have the water, in which yet beasts can swim by nature, and men by art. He that can swim needs not despair to fly: to swim is to fly in a grosser fluid, and to fly is to swim in a subtler. We are only to proportion our power of resistance to the different density of the matter through which we are to pass. You will be necessarily upborn by the air, if you can renew any impulse upon it, faster than the air can recede from the pressure."

"But the exercise of swimming," said the prince, "is very laborious; the strongest limbs are soon wearied; I am afraid the act of flying will be yet more violent, and wings will be of no great use, unless we can fly further than we can swim."

"The labor of rising from the ground," said the artist "will be great, as we see it in the heavier domestic fowls; but, as we mount higher, the earth's attraction, and the body's gravity, will be gradually diminished, till we shall arrive at a region where the man will float in the air without any tendency to fall: no care will then be necessary, but to move forwards, which the gentlest impulse will effect. You, Sir, whose curiosity is so extensive, will easily conceive with what pleasure a philosopher, furnished with wings, and hovering in the sky, would see the earth, and all its inhabitants, rolling beneath him, and presenting to him successively, by its diurnal motion, all the countries within the same parallel. How must it amuse the pendent spectator to see the moving scene of land and ocean, cities and deserts! To survey with equal security the marts of trade, and the fields of battle; mountains infested by barbarians, and fruitful regions gladdened by plenty, and lulled by peace! How easily shall we then trace the Nile through all his passage; pass over to distant regions, and examine the face of nature from one extremity of the earth to the other!"

"All this," said the prince, "is much to be desired, but I am afraid that no man will be able to breathe in these regions of speculation and tranquility. I have been told, that respiration is difficult upon lofty mountains, yet from these precipices, though so high as to produce great tenuity of the air, it is very easy to fall: therefore I suspect, that from any height, where life can be supported, there may be danger of too quick descent."

"Nothing," replied the artist, "will ever be attempted, if all possible objections must be first overcome. If you will favor my project I will try the first flight at my own hazard. I have considered the structure of all volant[6] animals, and find the folding continuity of the bat's wings most easily accommodated to the human form. Upon this model I shall begin my task tomorrow, and in a year expect to tower into the air beyond the malice or pursuit of man. But I will work only on this condition, that the art shall not be divulged, and that you shall not require me to make wings for any but ourselves."

"Why," said Rasselas, "should you envy others so great an advantage? All skill ought to be exerted for universal good; every man has owed much to others, and ought to repay the kindness that he has received."

"If men were all virtuous," returned the artist, "I should with great alacrity teach them all to fly. But what would be the security of the good, if the bad could at pleasure invade them from the sky? Against an army sailing through the clouds neither walls, nor mountains, nor seas, could afford any security. A flight of northern savages might hover in the wind, and light at once with irresistible violence upon the capital of a fruitful region that was rolling under them. Even this valley, the retreat of princes, the abode of happiness, might be violated by the sudden descent of some of the naked nations that swarm on the coast of the southern sea."

The prince promised secrecy, and waited for the performance, not wholly hopeless of success. He visited the work from time to time, observed its progress, and remarked many ingenious contrivances to facilitate motion, and unite levity with strength. The artist was every day more certain that he should leave vultures and eagles behind him, and the contagion of his confidence seized upon the prince.

In a year the wings were finished, and, on a morning appointed, the maker appeared furnished for flight on a little promontory: he waved his pinions a while to gather air, then leaped from his stand, and in an instant dropped into the lake. His wings, which were of no use in the air, sustained him in the water, and the prince drew him to land, half dead with terror and vexation.

Chapter 7. The Prince Finds a Man of Learning

The prince was not much afflicted by this disaster, having suffered himself to hope for a happier event, only because he had no other means of escape in view. He still persisted in his design to leave the happy valley by the first opportunity.

His imagination was now at a stand; he had no prospect of entering into the world; and, notwithstanding all his endeavors to support himself, discontent by degrees preyed upon him, and he began again to lose his thoughts in sadness, when the rainy season, which in these countries is periodical, made it inconvenient to wander in the woods.

The rain continued longer and with more violence than had been ever known; the clouds broke on the surrounding mountains, and the torrents streamed into the plain on every side, till the cavern was too

6. Able to fly.

narrow to discharge the water. The lake overflowed its banks, and all the level of the valley was covered with the inundation. The eminence, on which the palace was built, and some other spots of rising ground, were all that the eye could now discover. The herds and flocks left the pastures, and both the wild beasts and the tame retreated to the mountains.

This inundation confined all the princes to domestic amusements, and the attention of Rasselas was particularly seized by a poem, which Imlac rehearsed,[7] upon the various conditions of humanity. He commanded the poet to attend him in his apartment, and recite his verses a second time; then entering into familiar talk, he thought himself happy in having found a man who knew the world so well, and could so skilfully paint the scenes of life. He asked a thousand questions about things, to which, though common to all other mortals, his confinement from childhood had kept him a stranger. The poet pitied his ignorance, and loved his curiosity, and entertained him from day to day with novelty and instruction, so that the prince regretted the necessity of sleep, and longed till the morning should renew his pleasure.

As they were sitting together, the prince commanded Imlac to relate his history, and to tell by what accident he was forced, or by what motive induced, to close his life in the happy valley. As he was going to begin his narrative, Rasselas was called to a concert, and obliged to restrain his curiosity till the evening.

Chapter 8. The History of Imlac

The close of the day is, in the regions of the torrid zone, the only season of diversion and entertainment, and it was therefore midnight before the music ceased, and the princesses retired. Rasselas then called for his companion and required him to begin the story of his life.

"Sir," said Imlac, "my history will not be long: the life that is devoted to knowledge passes silently away, and is very little diversified by events. To talk in public, to think in solitude, to read and to hear, to inquire, and answer inquiries, is the business of a scholar. He wanders about the world without pomp or terror, and is neither known nor valued but by men like himself.

"I was born in the kingdom of Goiama, at no great distance from the fountain of the Nile. My father was a wealthy merchant, who traded between the inland countries of Africk and the ports of the red sea. He was honest, frugal and diligent, but of mean sentiments, and narrow comprehension: he desired only to be rich, and to conceal his riches, lest he should be spoiled[8] by the governors of the province."

"Surely," said the prince, "my father must be negligent of his charge, if any man in his dominions dares take that which belongs to another. Does he not know that kings are accountable for injustice permitted as well as done? If I were emperor, not the meanest of my subjects should

7. Recited.   8. Robbed.

be oppressed with impunity. My blood boils when I am told that a merchant durst not enjoy his honest gains for fear of losing them by the rapacity of power. Name the governor who robbed the people, that I may declare his crimes to the emperor."

"Sir," said Imlac, "your ardor is the natural effect of virtue animated by youth: the time will come when you will acquit your father, and perhaps hear with less impatience of the governor. Oppression is, in the Abyssinian dominions, neither frequent nor tolerated; but no form of government has been yet discovered, by which cruelty can be wholly prevented. Subordination supposes power on one part and subjection on the other; and if power be in the hands of men, it will sometimes be abused. The vigilance of the supreme magistrate may do much, but much will still remain undone. He can never know all the crimes that are committed, and can seldom punish all that he knows."

"This," said the prince, "I do not understand, but I had rather hear thee than dispute. Continue thy narration."

"My father," proceeded Imlac "originally intended that I should have no other education, than such as might qualify me for commerce; and discovering in me great strength of memory, and quickness of apprehension, often declared his hope that I should be some time the richest man in Abyssinia."

"Why," said the prince, "did thy father desire the increase of his wealth, when it was already greater than he durst discover or enjoy? I am unwilling to doubt thy veracity, yet inconsistencies cannot both be true."

"Inconsistencies," answered Imlac, "cannot both be right, but, imputed to man, they may both be true. Yet diversity is not inconsistency. My father might expect a time of greater security. However, some desire is necessary to keep life in motion, and he, whose real wants are supplied, must admit those of fancy."

"This," said the prince, "I can in some measure conceive. I repent that I interrupted thee."

"With this hope," proceeded Imlac, "he sent me to school; but when I had once found the delight of knowledge, and felt the pleasure of intelligence[9] and the pride of invention, I began silently to despise riches, and determined to disappoint the purpose of my father, whose grossness of conception raised my pity. I was twenty years old before his tenderness would expose me to the fatigue of travel, in which time I had been instructed, by successive masters, in all the literature of my native country. As every hour taught me something new, I lived in a continual course of gratifications; but, as I advanced towards manhood, I lost much of the reverence with which I had been used to look on my instructors; because, when the lesson was ended, I did not find them wiser or better than common men.

"At length my father resolved to initiate me in commerce, and, open-

9. Information or knowledge.

ing one of his subterranean treasuries, counted out ten thousand pieces of gold. 'This, young man,' said he, 'is the stock with which you must negotiate. I began with less than the fifth part, and you see how diligence and parsimony have increased it. This is your own to waste or to improve. If you squander it by negligence or caprice, you must wait for my death before you will be rich: if, in four years, you double your stock, we will thenceforward let subordination cease, and live together as friends and partners; for he shall always be equal with me, who is equally skilled in the art of growing rich.'

"We laid our money upon camels, concealed in bales of cheap goods, and travelled to the shore of the red sea. When I cast my eye on the expanse of waters my heart bounded like that of a prisoner escaped. I felt an unextinguishable curiosity kindle in my mind, and resolved to snatch this opportunity of seeing the manners of other nations, and of learning sciences unknown in Abyssinia.

"I remembered that my father had obliged me to the improvement of my stock, not by a promise which I ought not to violate, but by a penalty which I was at liberty to incur; and therefore determined to gratify my predominant desire, and by drinking at the fountains of knowledge, to quench the thirst of curiosity.

"As I was supposed to trade without connection with my father, it was easy for me to become acquainted with the master of a ship, and procure a passage to some other country. I had no motives of choice to regulate my voyage; it was sufficient for me that, wherever I wandered, I should see a country which I had not seen before. I therefore entered a ship bound for Surat,[1] having left a letter for my father declaring my intention.

Chapter 9. The History of Imlac Continued

"When I first entered upon the world of waters, and lost sight of land, I looked round about me with pleasing terror, and thinking my soul enlarged by the boundless prospect, imagined that I could gaze round for ever without satiety; but, in a short time, I grew weary of looking on barren uniformity, where I could only see again what I had already seen. I then descended into the ship, and doubted for a while whether all my future pleasures would not end like this in disgust and disappointment. Yet, surely, said I, the ocean and the land are very different; the only variety of water is rest and motion, but the earth has mountains and valleys, deserts and cities: it is inhabited by men of different customs and contrary opinions; and I may hope to find variety in life, though I should miss it in nature.

"With this thought I quieted my mind; and amused myself during the voyage, sometimes by learning from the sailors the art of navigation,

1. A port in India.

which I have never practiced, and sometimes by forming schemes for my conduct in different situations, in not one of which I have been ever placed.

"I was almost weary of my naval amusements when we landed safely at Surat. I secured my money, and purchasing some commodities for show, joined myself to a caravan that was passing into the inland country. My companions, for some reason or other, conjecturing that I was rich, and, by my inquiries and admiration, finding that I was ignorant, considered me as a novice whom they had a right to cheat, and who was to learn at the usual expense the art of fraud. They exposed me to the theft of servants, and the exaction of officers,[2] and saw me plundered upon false pretences, without any advantage to themselves, but that of rejoicing in the superiority of their own knowledge."

"Stop a moment," said the prince. "Is there such depravity in man, as that he should injure another without benefit to himself? I can easily conceive that all are pleased with superiority; but your ignorance was merely accidental, which, being neither your crime nor your folly, could afford them no reason to applaud themselves; and the knowledge which they had, and which you wanted, they might as effectually have shown by warning, as betraying you."

"Pride," said Imlac, "is seldom delicate, it will please itself with very mean advantages; and envy feels not its own happiness, but when it may be compared with the misery of others. They were my enemies because they grieved to think me rich, and my oppressors because they delighted to find me weak."

"Proceed," said the prince: "I doubt not of the facts which you relate, but imagine that you impute them to mistaken motives."

"In this company," said Imlac, "I arrived at Agra, the capital of Indostan, the city in which the great Mogul commonly resides. I applied myself to the language of the country, and in a few months was able to converse with the learned men; some of whom I found morose and reserved, and others easy and communicative; some were unwilling to teach another what they had with difficulty learned themselves; and some showed that the end of their studies was to gain the dignity of instructing.

"To the tutor of the young princes I recommended myself so much, that I was presented to the emperor as a man of uncommon knowledge. The emperor asked me many questions concerning my country and my travels; and though I cannot now recollect any thing that he uttered above the power of a common man, he dismissed me astonished at his wisdom, and enamored of his goodness.

"My credit was now so high, that the merchants, with whom I had traveled, applied to me for recommendations to the ladies of the court. I was surprised at their confidence of solicitation, and gently reproached them with their practices on the road. They heard me with cold indifference, and showed no tokens of shame or sorrow.

---

2. Officials or agents.

"They then urged their request with the offer of a bribe; but what I would not do for kindness I would not do for money; and refused them, not because they had injured me, but because I would not enable them to injure others; for I knew they would have made use of my credit to cheat those who should buy their wares.

"Having resided at Agra till there was no more to be learned, I traveled into Persia, where I saw many remains of ancient magnificence, and observed many new accommodations[3] of life. The Persians are a nation eminently social, and their assemblies afforded me daily opportunities of remarking characters and manners, and of tracing human nature through all its variations.

"From Persia I passed into Arabia, where I saw a nation at once pastoral and warlike; who live without any settled habitation; whose only wealth is their flocks and herds; and who have yet carried on, through all ages, an hereditary war with all mankind, though they neither covet nor envy their possessions.

Chapter 10. Imlac's History Continued.
A Dissertation upon Poetry

"Wherever I went, I found that poetry was considered as the highest learning, and regarded with a veneration somewhat approaching to that which man would pay to the angelic nature. And yet it fills me with wonder that, in almost all countries, the most ancient poets are considered as the best: whether it be that every other kind of knowledge is an acquisition gradually attained, and poetry is a gift conferred at once; or that the first poetry of every nation surprised them as a novelty, and retained the credit by consent which it received by accident at first; or whether, as the province of poetry is to describe nature and passion, which are always the same, the first writers took possession of the most striking objects for description and the most probable occurrences for fiction, and left nothing to those that followed them, but transcription of the same events, and new combinations of the same images—whatever be the reason, it is commonly observed that the early writers are in possession of nature, and their followers of art; that the first excel in strength and invention, and the latter in elegance and refinement.

"I was desirous to add my name to this illustrious fraternity. I read all the poets of Persia and Arabia, and was able to repeat by memory the volumes that are suspended in the mosque of Mecca. But I soon found that no man was ever great by imitation. My desire of excellence impelled me to transfer my attention to nature and to life. Nature was to be my subject, and men to be my auditors: I could never describe what I had not seen; I could not hope to move those with delight or terror, whose interests and opinions I did not understand.

"Being now resolved to be a poet, I saw everything with a new pur-

---

3. "Conveniences, things requisite to ease or refreshment" (Johnson's *Dictionary*).

pose; my sphere of attention was suddenly magnified; no kind of knowledge was to be overlooked. I ranged mountains and deserts for images and resemblances, and pictured upon my mind every tree of the forest and flower of the valley. I observed with equal care the crags of the rock and the pinnacles of the palace. Sometimes I wandered along the mazes of the rivulet, and sometimes watched the changes of the summer clouds. To a poet nothing can be useless. Whatever is beautiful, and whatever is dreadful, must be familiar to his imagination; he must be conversant with all that is awfully vast or elegantly little. The plants of the garden, the animals of the wood, the minerals of the earth, and meteors of the sky, must all concur to store his mind with inexhaustible variety: for every idea[4] is useful for the enforcement or decoration of moral or religious truth; and he who knows most will have most power of diversifying his scenes, and of gratifying his reader with remote allusions and unexpected instruction.

"All the appearances of nature I was therefore careful to study, and every country which I have surveyed has contributed something to my poetical powers."

"In so wide a survey," said the prince, "you must surely have left much unobserved. I have lived till now within the circuit of these mountains, and yet cannot walk abroad without the sight of something which I have never beheld before, or never heeded."

"The business of a poet," said Imlac, "is to examine, not the individual, but the species; to remark general properties and large appearances; he does not number the streaks of the tulip, or describe the different shades in the verdure of the forest. He is to exhibit in his portraits of nature such prominent and striking features as recall the original to every mind, and must neglect the minuter discriminations, which one may have remarked and another have neglected, for those characteristics which are alike obvious to vigilance and carelessness.

"But the knowledge of nature is only half the task of a poet; he must be acquainted likewise with all the modes of life. His character requires that he estimate the happiness and misery of every condition; observe the power of all the passions in all their combinations, and trace the changes of the human mind, as they are modified by various institutions and accidental influences of climate or custom, from the sprightliness of infancy to the despondence of decrepitude. He must divest himself of the prejudices of his age or country; he must consider right and wrong in their abstracted and invariable state; he must disregard present laws and opinions, and rise to general and transcendental[5] truths, which will always be the same. He must, therefore, content himself with the slow progress of his name, contemn the applause of his own time, and commit his claims to the justice of posterity. He must write as the interpreter of nature and the legislator of mankind, and consider himself as presid-

---

4. Mental image.
5. "General; pervading many particulars" (Johnson's *Dictionary*).

ing over the thoughts and manner of future generations, as a being superior to time and place.

"His labor is not yet at an end; he must know many languages and many sciences; and, that his style may be worthy of his thoughts, must by incessant practice familiarize to himself every delicacy of speech and grace of harmony."

Chapter 11. Imlac's Narrative Continued. A Hint on Pilgrimage

Imlac now felt the enthusiastic fit, and was proceeding to aggrandize his own profession, when the prince cried out: "Enough! thou hast convinced me that no human being can ever be a poet. Proceed with thy narration."

"To be a poet," said Imlac, "is indeed very difficult." "So difficult," returned the prince, "that I will at present hear no more of his labors. Tell me whither you went when you had seen Persia."

"From Persia," said the poet, "I traveled through Syria, and for three years resided in Palestine, where I conversed with great numbers of the northern and western nations of Europe, the nations which are now in possession of all power and all knowledge, whose armies are irresistible, and whose fleets command the remotest parts of the globe. When I compared these men with the natives of our own kingdom, and those that surround us, they appeared almost another order of beings. In their countries it is difficult to wish for anything that may not be obtained; a thousand arts, of which we never heard, are continually laboring for their convenience and pleasure; and whatever their own climate has denied them is supplied by their commerce."

"By what means," said the prince, "are the Europeans thus powerful, or why, since they can so easily visit Asia and Africa for trade or conquest, cannot the Asiatics and Africans invade their coasts, plant colonies in their ports, and give laws to their natural princes? The same wind that carries them back would bring us thither."

"They are more powerful, sir, than we," answered Imlac, "because they are wiser; knowledge will always predominate over ignorance, as man governs the other animals. But why their knowledge is more than ours, I know not what reason can be given, but the unsearchable will of the Supreme Being."

"When," said the prince with a sigh, "shall I be able to visit Palestine, and mingle with this mighty confluence of nations? Till that happy moment shall arrive, let me fill up the time with such representations as thou canst give me. I am not ignorant of the motive that assembles such numbers in that place, and cannot but consider it as the center of wisdom and piety, to which the best and wisest men of every land must be continually resorting."

"There are some nations," said Imlac, "that send few visitants to Palestine; for many numerous and learned sects in Europe concur to censure pilgrimage as superstitious, or deride it as ridiculous."

"You know," said the prince, "how little my life has made me acquainted with diversity of opinions. It will be too long to hear the arguments on both sides; you, that have considered them, tell me the result."

"Pilgrimage," said Imlac, "like many other acts of piety, may be reasonable or superstitious, according to the principles upon which it is performed. Long journeys in search of truth are not commanded. Truth, such as is necessary to the regulation of life, is always found where it is honestly sought. Change of place is no natural cause of the increase of piety, for it inevitably produces dissipation of mind. Yet, since men go every day to view the fields where great actions have been performed, and return with stronger impressions of the event, curiosity of the same kind may naturally dispose us to view that country whence our religion had its beginning; and I believe no man surveys those awful scenes without some confirmation of holy resolutions. That the Supreme Being may be more easily propitiated in one place than in another is the dream of idle superstition, but that some places may operate upon our own minds in an uncommon manner is an opinion which hourly experience will justify. He who supposes that his vices may be more successfully combated in Palestine, will, perhaps, find himself mistaken, yet he may go thither without folly; he who thinks they will be more freely pardoned, dishonors at once his reason and religion."

"These," said the prince, "are European distinctions. I will consider them another time. What have you found to be the effect of knowledge? Are those nations happier than we?"

"There is so much infelicity," said the poet, "in the world that scarce any man has leisure from his own distresses to estimate the comparative happiness of others. Knowledge is certainly one of the means of pleasure, as is confessed by the natural desire which every mind feels of increasing its ideas. Ignorance is mere privation, by which nothing can be produced; it is a vacuity in which the soul sits motionless and torpid for want of attraction; and, without knowing why, we always rejoice when we learn, and grieve when we forget. I am therefore inclined to conclude that if nothing counteracts the natural consequence of learning, we grow more happy as our minds take a wider range.

"In enumerating the particular comforts of life, we shall find many advantages on the side of the Europeans. They cure wounds and diseases with which we languish and perish. We suffer inclemencies of weather which they can obviate. They have engines for the despatch of many laborious works, which we must perform by manual industry. There is such communication between distant places that one friend can hardly be said to be absent from another. Their policy removes all public inconveniences; they have roads cut through their mountains, and bridges laid upon their rivers. And, if we descend to the privacies of life, their habitations are more commodious, and their possessions are more secure."

"They are surely happy," said the prince, "who have all these conve-

niencies, of which I envy none so much as the facility with which separated friends interchange their thoughts."

"The Europeans," answered Imlac, "are less unhappy than we, but
they are not happy. Human life is everywhere a state in which much is
to be endured, and little to be enjoyed."

Chapter 12. The Story of Imlac Continued

"I am not yet willing," said the prince, "to suppose that happiness is
so parsimoniously distributed to mortals; nor can believe but that, if I
had the choice of life, I should be able to fill every day with pleasure. I
would injure no man, and should provoke no resentment: I would relieve
every distress, and should enjoy the benedictions of gratitude. I would
choose my friends among the wise, and my wife among the virtuous;
and therefore should be in no danger from treachery, or unkindness. My
children should, by my care, be learned and pious, and would repay to
my age what their childhood had received. What would dare to molest
him who might call on every side to thousands enriched by his bounty,
or assisted by his power? And why should not life glide quietly away in
the soft reciprocation of protection and reverence? All this may be done
without the help of European refinements, which appear by their effects
to be rather specious than useful. Let us leave them and pursue our
journey."

"From Palestine," said Imlac, "I passed through many regions of Asia;
in the more civilized kingdoms as a trader, and among the barbarians of
the mountains as a pilgrim. At last I began to long for my native country,
that I might repose after my travels, and fatigues, in the places where I
had spent my earliest years, and gladden my old companions with the
recital of my adventures. Often did I figure to myself those, with whom
I had sported away the gay hours of dawning life sitting round me in its
evening, wondering at my tales, and listening to my counsels.

"When this thought had taken possession of my mind, I considered
every moment as wasted which did not bring me nearer to Abyssinia. I
hastened into Egypt, and, notwithstanding my impatience, was detained
ten months in the contemplation of its ancient magnificence, and in
enquiries after the remains of its ancient learning. I found in Cairo a
mixture of all nations; some brought thither by the love of knowledge,
some by the hope of gain, and many by the desire of living after their
own manner without observation, and of lying hid in the obscurity of
multitudes: for, in a city, populous as Cairo, it is possible to obtain at
the same time the gratifications of society, and the secrecy of solitude.

"From Cairo I traveled to Suez, and embarked on the red sea, passing
along the coast till I arrived at the port from which I had departed twenty
years before. Here I joined myself to a caravan and re-entered my native
country.

"I now expected the caresses of my kinsmen, and the congratulations of my friends, and was not without hope that my father, whatever value he had set upon riches, would own with gladness and pride a son who was able to add to the felicity and honor of the nation. But I was soon convinced that my thoughts were vain. My father had been dead fourteen years, having divided his wealth among my brothers, who were removed to some other provinces. Of my companions the greater part was in the grave, of the rest some could with difficulty remember me, and some considered me as one corrupted by foreign manners.

"A man used to vicissitudes is not easily dejected. I forgot, after a time, my disappointment, and endeavored to recommend myself to the nobles of the kingdom: they admitted me to their tables, heard my story, and dismissed me. I opened a school, and was prohibited to teach. I then resolved to sit down in the quiet of domestic life, and addressed a lady that was fond of my conversation, but rejected my suit, because my father was a merchant.

"Wearied at last with solicitation and repulses, I resolved to hide myself for ever from the world, and depend no longer on the opinion or caprice of others. I waited for the time when the gate of the *happy valley* should open, that I might bid farewell to hope and fear: the day came; my performance was distinguished with favor, and I resigned myself with joy to perpetual confinement."

"Hast thou here found happiness at last?" said Rasselas. "Tell me without reserve; art thou content with thy condition? or, dost thou wish to be again wandering and inquiring? All the inhabitants of this valley celebrate their lot, and, at the annual visit of the emperor, invite others to partake of their felicity."

"Great prince," said Imlac, "I shall speak the truth: I know not one of all your attendants who does not lament the hour when he entered this retreat. I am less unhappy than the rest, because I have a mind replete with images, which I can vary and combine at pleasure. I can amuse my solitude by the renovation of the knowledge which begins to fade from my memory, and by recollection of the accidents of my past life. Yet all this ends in the sorrowful consideration, that my acquirements are now useless, and that none of my pleasures can be again enjoyed. The rest, whose minds have no impression but of the present moment, are either corroded by malignant passions, or sit stupid in the gloom of perpetual vacancy."

"What passions can infest those," said the prince, "who have no trials? We are in a place where impotence precludes malice, and where all envy is repressed by community[6] of enjoyments."

"There may be community," said Imlac, "of material possessions, but there can never be community of love or of esteem. It must happen that one will please more than another; he that knows himself despised will always be envious; and still more envious and malevolent, if he is condemned to live in the presence of those who despise him. The invita-

6. Joint possession.

tions, by which they allure others to a state which they feel to be wretched, proceed from the natural malignity of hopeless misery. They are weary of themselves, and of each other, and expect to find relief in new companions. They envy the liberty which their folly has forfeited, and would gladly see all mankind imprisoned like themselves.

"From this crime, however, I am wholly free. No man can say that he is wretched by my persuasion. I look with pity on the crowds who are annually soliciting admission to captivity, and wish that it were lawful for me to warn them of their danger."

"My dear Imlac," said the prince, "I will open to thee my whole heart. I have long meditated an escape from the happy valley. I have examined the mountains on every side, but find myself insuperably barred: teach me the way to break my prison; thou shalt be the companion of my flight, the guide of my rambles, the partner of my fortune, and my sole director in the *choice of life*."

"Sir," answered the poet, "your escape will be difficult, and, perhaps, you may soon repent your curiosity. The world, which you figure to yourself smooth and quiet as the lake in the valley, you will find a sea foaming with tempests, and boiling with whirlpools: you will be sometimes overwhelmed by the waves of violence, and sometimes dashed against the rocks of treachery. Amidst wrongs and frauds, competitions and anxieties, you will wish a thousand times for these seats of quiet, and willingly quit hope to be free from fear."

"Do not seek to deter me from my purpose," said the prince: "I am impatient to see what thou hast seen; and, since thou art thyself weary of the valley, it is evident, that thy former state was better than this. Whatever be the consequence of my experiment, I am resolved to judge with my own eyes of the various conditions of men, and then to make deliberately my *choice of life*."

"I am afraid," said Imlac, "you are hindered by stronger restraints than my persuasions; yet, if your determination is fixed, I do not counsel you to despair. Few things are impossible to diligence and skill."

Chapter 13. Rasselas Discovers the Means of Escape

The prince now dismissed his favorite to rest, but the narrative of wonders and novelties filled his mind with perturbation. He revolved all that he had heard, and prepared innumerable questions for the morning.

Much of his uneasiness was now removed. He had a friend to whom he could impart his thoughts, and whose experience could assist him in his designs. His heart was no longer condemned to swell with silent vexation. He thought that even the *happy valley* might be endured with such a companion, and that, if they could range the world together, he should have nothing further to desire.

In a few days the water was discharged, and the ground dried. The prince and Imlac then walked out together to converse without the notice of the rest. The prince, whose thoughts were always on the wing, as he passed by the gate, said, with a countenance of sorrow, "Why art thou so strong, and why is man so weak?"

"Man is not weak" answered his companion; "knowledge is more than equivalent to force. The master of mechanics laughs at strength. I can burst the gate, but cannot do it secretly. Some other expedient must be tried."

As they were walking on the side of the mountain, they observed that the conies,[7] which the rain had driven from their burrows, had taken shelter among the bushes, and formed holes behind them, tending upwards in an oblique line. "It has been the opinion of antiquity," said Imlac, "that human reason borrowed many arts from the instinct of animals; let us, therefore, not think ourselves degraded by learning from the coney. We may escape by piercing the mountain in the same direction. We will begin where the summit hangs over the middle part, and labor upward till we shall issue out beyond the prominence."

The eyes of the prince, when he heard this proposal, sparkled with joy. The execution was easy, and the success certain.

No time was now lost. They hastened early in the morning to choose a place proper for their mine. They clambered with great fatigue among crags and brambles, and returned without having discovered any part that favored their design. The second and the third day were spent in the same manner, and with the same frustration. But, on the fourth, they found a small cavern, concealed by a thicket, where they resolved to make their experiment.

Imlac procured instruments proper to hew stone and remove earth, and they fell to their work on the next day with more eagerness than vigor. They were presently exhausted by their efforts, and sat down to pant upon the grass. The prince, for a moment, appeared to be discouraged. "Sir," said his companion, "practice will enable us to continue our labor for a longer time; mark, however, how far we have advanced, and you will find that our toil will some time have an end. Great works are performed, not by strength, but perseverance: yonder palace was raised by single stones, yet you see its height and spaciousness. He that shall walk with vigor three hours a day will pass in seven years a space equal to the circumference of the globe."

They returned to their work day after day, and, in a short time, found a fissure in the rock, which enabled them to pass far with very little obstruction. This Rasselas considered as a good omen. "Do not disturb your mind," said Imlac, "with other hopes or fears than reason may suggest: if you are pleased with prognostics of good, you will be terrified likewise with tokens of evil, and your whole life will be a prey to superstition. Whatever facilitates our work is more than an omen, it is a cause of success. This is one of those pleasing surprises which often happen to

7. Rabbits.

active resolution. Many things difficult to design prove easy to performance."

Chapter 14. *Rasselas and Imlac Receive an Unexpected Visit*

They had now wrought their way to the middle, and solaced their toil
with the approach of liberty, when the prince, coming down to refresh
himself with air, found his sister Nekayah standing before the mouth of
the cavity. He started and stood confused, afraid to tell his design, and
yet hopeless to conceal it. A few moments determined him to repose on
her fidelity, and secure her secrecy by a declaration without reserve.

"Do not imagine," said the princess, "that I came hither as a spy: I
had long observed from my window, that you and Imlac directed your
walk every day towards the same point, but I did not suppose you had
any better reason for the preference than a cooler shade, or more fragrant
bank; nor followed you with any other design than to partake of your
conversation. Since then not suspicion but fondness has detected you,
let me not lose the advantage of my discovery. I am equally weary of
confinement with yourself, and not less desirous of knowing what is
done or suffered in the world. Permit me to fly with you from this tasteless tranquility, which will yet grow more loathsome when you have left
me. You may deny me to accompany you, but cannot hinder me from
following."

The prince, who loved Nekayah above his other sisters, had no inclination to refuse her request, and grieved that he had lost an opportunity
of showing his confidence by a voluntary communication. It was therefore agreed that she should leave the valley with them; and that, in the
mean time, she should watch, lest any other straggler should, by chance
or curiosity, follow them to the mountain.

At length their labor was at an end; they saw light beyond the prominence, and, issuing to the top of the mountain, beheld the Nile, yet a
narrow current, wandering beneath them.

The prince looked round with rapture, anticipated all the pleasures of
travel, and in thought was already transported beyond his father's
dominions. Imlac, though very joyful at his escape, had less expectation
of pleasure in the world, which he had before tried, and of which he
had been weary.

Rasselas was so much delighted with a wider horizon, that he could
not soon be persuaded to return into the valley. He informed his sister
that the way was open, and that nothing now remained but to prepare
for their departure.

Chapter 15. *The Prince and Princess Leave the Valley,*
and See Many Wonders

The prince and princess had jewels sufficient to make them rich
whenever they came into a place of commerce, which, by Imlac's direc-

tion, they hid in their clothes, and, on the night of the next full moon, all left the valley. The princess was followed only by a single favorite, who did not know whither she was going.

They clambered through the cavity, and began to go down on the other side. The princess and her maid turned their eyes towards every part, and, seeing nothing to bound their prospect, considered themselves as in danger of being lost in a dreary vacuity. They stopped and trembled. "I am almost afraid," said the princess, "to begin a journey of which I cannot perceive an end, and to venture into this immense plain where I may be approached on every side by men whom I never saw." The prince felt nearly the same emotions, though he thought it more manly to conceal them.

Imlac smiled at their terrors, and encouraged them to proceed; but the princess continued irresolute till she had been imperceptibly drawn forward too far to return.

In the morning they found some shepherds in the field, who set milk and fruits before them. The princess wondered that she did not see a palace ready for her reception, and a table spread with delicacies; but, being faint and hungry, she drank the milk and ate the fruits, and thought them of a higher flavor than the products of the valley.

They traveled forward by easy journeys, being all unaccustomed to toil or difficulty, and knowing, that though they might be missed, they could not be pursued. In a few days they came into a more populous region, where Imlac was diverted with the admiration which his companions expressed at the diversity of manners, stations and employments.

Their dress was such as might not bring upon them the suspicion of having any thing to conceal, yet the prince, wherever he came, expected to be obeyed, and the princess was frighted, because those that came into her presence did not prostrate themselves before her. Imlac was forced to observe them with great vigilance, lest they should betray their rank by their unusual behavior, and detained them several weeks in the first village to accustom them to the sight of common mortals.

By degrees the royal wanderers were taught to understand that they had for a time laid aside their dignity, and were to expect only such regard as liberality and courtesy could procure. And Imlac, having, by many admonitions, prepared them to endure the tumults of a port, and the ruggedness of the commercial race, brought them down to the seacoast.

The prince and his sister, to whom every thing was new, were gratified equally at all places, and therefore remained for some months at the port without any inclination to pass further. Imlac was content with their stay, because he did not think it safe to expose them, unpracticed in the world, to the hazards of a foreign country.

At last he began to fear lest they should be discovered, and proposed to fix a day for their departure. They had no pretensions to judge for themselves, and referred the whole scheme to his direction. He therefore took passage in a ship to Suez; and, when the time came, with great difficulty prevailed on the princess to enter the vessel. They had a quick and prosperous voyage, and from Suez traveled by land to Cairo.

Chapter 16. *They Enter Cairo, and Find Every Man Happy*

As they approached the city, which filled the strangers with astonishment, "This," said Imlac to the prince, "is the place where travelers and merchants assemble from all the corners of the earth. You will here find men of every character and every occupation. Commerce is here honorable. I will act as a merchant, and you shall live as strangers, who have no other end of travel than curiosity. It will soon be observed that we are rich; our reputation will procure us access to all whom we shall desire to know; you will see all the conditions of humanity, and enable yourself at leisure to make your *choice of life.*"

They now entered the town, stunned by the noise, and offended by the crowds. Instruction had not yet so prevailed over habit, but that they wondered to see themselves pass undistinguished along the street, and met by the lowest of the people without reverence or notice. The princess could not at first bear the thought of being leveled with the vulgar,[8] and for some days continued in her chamber, where she was served by her favorite, Pekuah, as in the palace of the valley.

Imlac, who understood traffic,[9] sold part of the jewels the next day, and hired a house, which he adorned with such magnificence that he was immediately considered as a merchant of great wealth. His politeness attracted many acquaintance, and his generosity made him courted by many dependents. His table was crowded by men of every nation, who all admired his knowledge, and solicited his favor. His companions, not being able to mix in the conversation, could make no discovery of their ignorance or surprise, and were gradually initiated in the world as they gained knowledge of the language.

The prince had, by frequent lectures, been taught the use and nature of money; but the ladies could not for a long time comprehend what the merchants did with small pieces of gold and silver, or why things of so little use should be received as equivalent to the necessaries of life.

They studied the language two years, while Imlac was preparing to set before them the various ranks and conditions of mankind. He grew acquainted with all who had anything uncommon in their fortune or conduct. He frequented the voluptuous and the frugal, the idle and the busy, the merchants and the men of learning.

The prince being now able to converse with fluency, and having learned the caution necessary to be observed in his intercourse with strangers, began to accompany Imlac to places of resort, and to enter into all assemblies, that he might make his *choice of life.*

For some time he thought choice needless, because all appeared to

---

8. Ordinary people.   9. Commerce.

him equally happy. Wherever he went he met gaiety and kindness, and heard the song of joy or the laugh of carelessness. He began to believe that the world overflowed with universal plenty, and that nothing was withheld either from want or merit; that every hand showered liberality, and every heart melted with benevolence: "And who then," says he, "will be suffered to be wretched?"

Imlac permitted the pleasing delusion, and was unwilling to crush the hope of inexperience, till one day, having sat awhile silent, "I know not," said the prince, "what can be the reason that I am more unhappy than any of our friends. I see them perpetually and unalterably cheerful, but feel my own mind restless and uneasy. I am unsatisfied with those pleasures which I seem most to court; I live in the crowds of jollity, not so much to enjoy company as to shun myself, and am only loud and merry to conceal my sadness."

"Every man," said Imlac, "may, by examining his own mind, guess what passes in the minds of others; when you feel that your own gaiety is counterfeit, it may justly lead you to suspect that of your companions not to be sincere. Envy is commonly reciprocal. We are long before we are convinced that happiness is never to be found, and each believes it possessed by others, to keep alive the hope of obtaining it for himself. In the assembly where you passed the last night, there appeared such sprightliness of air, and volatility of fancy, as might have suited beings of an higher order, formed to inhabit serener regions, inaccessible to care or sorrow; yet, believe me, prince, there was not one who did not dread the moment when solitude should deliver him to the tyranny of reflection."

"This," said the prince, "may be true of others, since it is true of me; yet, whatever be the general infelicity of man, one condition is more happy than another, and wisdom surely directs us to take the least evil in the *choice of life*."

"The causes of good and evil," answered Imlac, "are so various and uncertain, so often entangled with each other, so diversified by various relations, and so much subject to accidents which cannot be foreseen, that he who would fix his condition upon incontestable reasons of preference must live and die inquiring and deliberating."

"But, surely," said Rasselas, "the wise men, to whom we listen with reverence and wonder, chose that mode of life for themselves which they thought most likely to make them happy."

"Very few," said the poet, "live by choice. Every man is placed in his present condition by causes which acted without his foresight, and with which he did not always willingly cooperate; and therefore you will rarely meet one who does not think the lot of his neighbor better than his own."

"I am pleased to think," said the prince, "that my birth has given me at least one advantage over others, by enabling me to determine for myself. I have here the world before me. I will review it at leisure; surely happiness is somewhere to be found."

Chapter 17. *The Prince Associates with Young Men
of Spirit and Gaiety*

Rasselas rose next day, and resolved to begin his experiments upon life. "Youth," cried he, "is the time of gladness: I will join myself to the young men, whose only business is to gratify their desires, and whose time is all spent in a succession of enjoyments."

To such societies he was readily admitted, but a few days brought him back weary and disgusted. Their mirth was without images,[1] their laughter without motive; their pleasures were gross and sensual, in which the mind had no part; their conduct was at once wild and mean; they laughed at order and at law, but the frown of power dejected, and the eye of wisdom abashed them.

The prince soon concluded, that he should never be happy in a course of life of which he was ashamed. He thought it unsuitable to a reasonable being to act without a plan, and to be sad or cheerful only by chance. "Happiness," said he, "must be something solid and permanent, without fear and without uncertainty."

But his young companions had gained so much of his regard by their frankness and courtesy, that he could not leave them without warning and remonstrance. "My friends," said he, "I have seriously considered our manners and our prospects, and find that we have mistaken our own interest. The first years of man must make provision for the last. He that never thinks never can be wise. Perpetual levity must end in ignorance; and intemperance, though it may fire the spirits for an hour, will make life short or miserable. Let us consider that youth is of no long duration, and that in maturer age, when the enchantments of fancy shall cease, and phantoms of delight dance no more about us, we shall have no comforts but the esteem of wise men, and the means of doing good. Let us, therefore, stop, while to stop is in our power: let us live as men who are sometime to grow old, and to whom it will be the most dreadful of all evils not to count their past years but by follies, and to be reminded of their former luxuriance of health only by the maladies which riot has produced."

They stared a while in silence one upon another, and, at last, drove him away by a general chorus of continued laughter.

The consciousness that his sentiments were just, and his intentions kind, was scarcely sufficient to support him against the horror of derision. But he recovered his tranquillity, and pursued his search.

Chapter 18. *The Prince Finds a Wise and Happy Man*

As he was one day walking in the street, he saw a spacious building which all were, by the open doors, invited to enter: he followed the stream of people, and found it a hall or school of declamation, in which

1. Ideas.

professors read lectures to their auditory. He fixed his eye upon a sage raised above the rest, who discoursed with great energy on the government of the passions. His look was venerable, his action graceful, his pronunciation clear, and his diction elegant. He showed with great strength of sentiment and variety of illustration that human nature is degraded and debased, when the lower faculties predominate over the higher; that when fancy, the parent of passion, usurps the dominion of the mind, nothing ensues but the natural effect of unlawful government, perturbation, and confusion; that she betrays the fortresses of the intellect to rebels, and excites her children to sedition against reason, their lawful sovereign. He compared reason to the sun, of which the light is constant, uniform and lasting; and fancy to a meteor, of bright but transitory luster, irregular in its motion, and delusive in its direction.

He then communicated the various precepts given from time to time for the conquest of passion, and displayed the happiness of those who had obtained the important victory, after which man is no longer the slave of fear, nor the fool of hope; is no more emaciated by envy, inflamed by anger, emasculated by tenderness, or depressed by grief; but walks on calmly through the tumults or the privacies of life, as the sun pursues alike his course through the calm or the stormy sky.

He enumerated many examples of heroes immovable by pain or pleasure, who looked with indifference on those modes or accidents to which the vulgar give the names of good and evil. He exhorted his hearers to lay aside their prejudices, and arm themselves against the shafts of malice or misfortune, by invulnerable patience; concluding that this state only was happiness, and that this happiness was in everyone's power.

Rasselas listened to him with the veneration due to the instructions of a superior being, and, waiting for him at the door, humbly implored the liberty of visiting so great a master of true wisdom. The lecturer hesitated a moment, when Rasselas put a purse of gold into his hand, which he received with a mixture of joy and wonder.

"I have found," said the prince at his return to Imlac, "a man who can teach all that is necessary to be known; who, from the unshaken throne of rational fortitude, looks down on the scenes of life changing beneath him. He speaks, and attention watches his lips. He reasons, and conviction closes his periods. This man shall be my future guide; I will learn his doctrines, and imitate his life."

"Be not too hasty," said Imlac, "to trust or to admire the teachers of morality: they discourse like angels, but they live like men."

Rasselas, who could not conceive how any man could reason so forcibly without feeling the cogency of his own arguments, paid his visit in a few days, and was denied admission. He had now learned the power of money, and made his way by a piece of gold to the inner apartment, where he found the philosopher in a room half darkened, with his eyes misty and his face pale. "Sir," said he, "you are come at a time when all human friendship is useless; what I suffer cannot be remedied, what I have lost cannot be supplied. My daughter, my only daughter, from whose tenderness I expected all the comforts of my age, died last night of a fever. My views, my purposes, my hopes are at an end; I am now a lonely being, disunited from society."

"Sir," said the prince, "mortality is an event by which a wise man can never be surprised; we know that death is always near, and it should therefore always be expected." "Young man," answered the philosopher, "you speak like one that has never felt the pangs of separation." "Have you then forgot the precepts," said Rasselas, "which you so powerfully enforced? Has wisdom no strength to arm the heart against calamity? Consider that external things are naturally variable, but truth and reason are always the same." "What comfort," said the mourner, "can truth and reason afford me? Of what effect are they now, but to tell me that my daughter will not be restored?"

The prince, whose humanity would not suffer him to insult misery with reproof, went away, convinced of the emptiness of rhetorical sound, and the inefficacy of polished periods and studied sentences.[2]

Chapter 19. A Glimpse of Pastoral Life

He was still eager upon the same inquiry; and having heard of a hermit that lived near the lowest cataract of the Nile, and filled the whole country with the fame of his sanctity, resolved to visit his retreat, and inquire whether that felicity which public life could not afford was to be found in solitude; and whether a man whose age and virtue made him venerable could teach any peculiar art of shunning evils, or enduring them.

Imlac and the princess agreed to accompany him, and, after the necessary preparations, they began their journey. Their way lay through fields, where shepherds tended their flocks and the lambs were playing upon the pasture. "This," said the poet, "is the life which has been often celebrated for its innocence and quiet; let us pass the heat of the day among the shepherds' tents, and know whether all our searches are not to terminate in pastoral simplicity."

The proposal pleased them, and they induced the shepherds, by small presents and familiar questions, to tell their opinion of their own state. They were so rude and ignorant, so little able to compare the good with the evil of the occupation, and so indistinct in their narratives and descriptions, that very little could be learned from them. But it was evident that their hearts were cankered with discontent; that they considered themselves as condemned to labor for the luxury of the rich, and looked up with stupid malevolence toward those that were placed above them.

The princess pronounced with vehemence that she would never suffer these envious savages to be her companions, and that she should not soon be desirous of seeing any more specimens of rustic happiness; but

---

2. Maxims or moral axioms; "periods": complete sentences.

could not believe that all the accounts of primeval pleasures were fabulous, and was yet in doubt whether life had anything that could be justly preferred to the placid gratifications of fields and woods. She hoped that the time would come, when, with a few virtuous and elegant companions, she could gather flowers planted by her own hand, fondle the lambs of her own ewe, and listen, without care, among brooks and breezes, to one of her maidens reading in the shade.

Chapter 20. The Danger of Prosperity

On the next day they continued their journey, till the heat compelled them to look round for shelter. At a small distance they saw a thick wood, which they no sooner entered than they perceived that they were approaching the habitations of men. The shrubs were diligently cut away to open walks where the shades were darkest; the boughs of opposite trees were artificially interwoven; seats of flowery turf were raised in vacant spaces, and a rivulet, that wantoned along the side of a winding path, had its banks sometimes opened into small basins, and its stream sometimes obstructed by little mounds of stone heaped together to increase its murmurs.

They passed slowly through the wood, delighted with such unexpected accommodations, and entertained each other with conjecturing what, or who, he could be, that, in those rude and unfrequented regions, had leisure and art for such harmless luxury.

As they advanced, they heard the sound of music, and saw youths and virgins dancing in the grove; and, going still further, beheld a stately palace built upon a hill surrounded with woods. The laws of eastern hospitality allowed them to enter, and the master welcomed them like a man liberal and wealthy.

He was skilful enough in appearances soon to discern that they were no common guests, and spread his table with magnificence. The eloquence of Imlac caught his attention, and the lofty courtesy of the princess excited his respect. When they offered to depart he entreated their stay, and was the next day still more unwilling to dismiss them than before. They were easily persuaded to stop, and civility grew up in time to freedom and confidence.

The prince now saw all the domestics cheerful, and all the face of nature smiling round the place, and could not forbear to hope that he should find here what he was seeking; but when he was congratulating the master upon his possessions, he answered with a sigh, "My condition has indeed the appearance of happiness, but appearances are delusive. My prosperity puts my life in danger; the Bassa of Egypt is my enemy, incensed only by my wealth and popularity. I have been hitherto protected against him by the princes of the country; but, as the favor of the great is uncertain, I know not how soon my defenders may be persuaded to share the plunder with the Bassa. I have sent my treasures into a distant country, and, upon the first alarm, am prepared to follow them.

Then will my enemies riot in my mansion, and enjoy the gardens which I have planted."

They all joined in lamenting his danger, and deprecating his exile; and the princess was so much disturbed with the tumult of grief and indignation, that she retired to her apartment. They continued with their kind inviter a few days longer, and then went forward to find the hermit.

Chapter 21. The Happiness of Solitude. The Hermit's History

They came on the third day, by the direction of the peasants, to the hermit's cell: it was a cavern in the side of a mountain, over-shadowed with palm-trees; at such a distance from the cataract, that nothing more was heard than a gentle uniform murmur, such as composed the mind to pensive meditation, especially when it was assisted by the wind whistling among the branches. The first rude essay of nature had been so much improved by human labor, that the cave contained several apartments, appropriated to different uses, and often afforded lodging to travelers, whom darkness or tempests happened to overtake.

The hermit sat on a bench at the door, to enjoy the coolness of the evening. On one side lay a book with pens and papers, on the other mechanical instruments of various kinds. As they approached him unregarded, the princess observed that he had not the countenance of a man that had found, or could teach, the way to happiness.

They saluted him with great respect, which he repaid like a man not unaccustomed to the forms of courts. "My children," said he, "if you have lost your way, you shall be willingly supplied with such conveniencies for the night as this cavern will afford. I have all that nature requires, and you will not expect delicacies in a hermit's cell."

They thanked him, and, entering, were pleased with the neatness and regularity of the place. The hermit set flesh and wine before them, though he fed only upon fruits and water. His discourse was cheerful without levity, and pious without enthusiasm.[3] He soon gained the esteem of his guests, and the princess repented of her hasty censure.

At last Imlac began thus: "I do not now wonder that your reputation is so far extended; we have heard at Cairo of your wisdom, and came hither to implore your direction for this young man and maiden in the *choice of life*."

"To him that lives well," answered the hermit, "every form of life is good; nor can I give any other rule for choice, than to remove from all apparent evil."

"He will remove most certainly from evil," said the prince, "who shall devote himself to that solitude which you have recommended by your example."

"I have indeed lived fifteen years in solitude," said the hermit, "but have no desire that my example should gain any imitators. In my youth

3. "A vain belief of private revelation; a vain confidence of divine favor or communication" (Johnson's *Dictionary*).

I professed arms, and was raised by degrees to the highest military rank. I have traversed wide countries at the head of my troops, and seen many battles and sieges. At last, being disgusted by the preferment of a younger officer, and feeling that my vigor was beginning to decay, I resolved to close my life in peace, having found the world full of snares, discord, and misery. I had once escaped from the pursuit of the enemy by the shelter of this cavern, and therefore chose it for my final residence. I employed artificers to form it into chambers, and stored it with all that I was likely to want.

"For some time after my retreat, I rejoiced like a tempest-beaten sailor at his entrance into the harbor, being delighted with the sudden change of the noise and hurry of war, to stillness and repose. When the pleasure of novelty went away, I employed my hours in examining the plants which grow in the valley, and the minerals which I collected from the rocks. But that inquiry is now grown tasteless and irksome. I have been for some time unsettled and distracted: my mind is disturbed with a thousand perplexities of doubt, and vanities of imagination, which hourly prevail upon me, because I have no opportunities of relaxation or diversion. I am sometimes ashamed to think that I could not secure myself from vice, but by retiring from the exercise of virtue, and begin to suspect that I was rather impelled by resentment, than led by devotion, into solitude. My fancy riots in scenes of folly, and I lament that I have lost so much, and have gained so little. In solitude, if I escape the example of bad men, I want likewise the counsel and conversation of the good. I have been long comparing the evils with the advantages of society, and resolve to return into the world tomorrow. The life of a solitary man will be certainly miserable, but not certainly devout."

They heard his resolution with surprise, but, after a short pause, offered to conduct him to Cairo. He dug up a considerable treasure which he had hid among the rocks, and accompanied them to the city, on which, as he approached it, he gazed with rapture.

Chapter 22. The Happiness of a Life Led According to Nature

Rasselas went often to an assembly of learned men, who met at stated times to unbend their minds and compare their opinions. Their manners were somewhat coarse, but their conversation was instructive, and their disputations acute, though sometimes too violent, and often continued till neither controvertist remembered upon what question they began. Some faults were almost general among them; everyone was desirous to dictate to the rest, and everyone was pleased to hear the genius or knowledge of another depreciated.

In this assembly Rasselas was relating his interview with the hermit, and the wonder with which he heard him censure a course of life which he had so deliberately chosen, and so laudably followed. The sentiments of the hearers were various. Some were of opinion that the folly of his choice had been justly punished by condemnation to perpetual perser-

verance. One of the youngest among them, with great vehemence, pronounced him an hypocrite. Some talked of the right of society to the
labor of individuals, and considered retirement as a desertion of duty.
Others readily allowed that there was a time when the claims of the
public were satisfied, and when a man might properly sequester himself,
to review his life and purify his heart.

One, who appeared more affected with the narrative than the rest,
thought it likely that the hermit would in a few years go back to his
retreat, and perhaps, if shame did not restrain, or death intercept him,
return once more from his retreat into the world. "For the hope of happiness," said he, "is so strongly impressed that the longest experience is
not able to efface it. Of the present state, whatever it be, we feel and are
forced to confess the misery; yet when the same state is again at a distance, imagination paints it as desirable. But the time will surely come
when desire will be no longer our torment, and no man shall be wretched
but by his own fault."

"This," said a philosopher who had heard him with tokens of great
impatience, "is the present condition of a wise man. The time is already
come when none are wretched but by their own fault. Nothing is more
idle than to inquire after happiness, which nature has kindly placed
within our reach. The way to be happy is to live according to nature, in
obedience to that universal and unalterable law with which every heart
is originally impressed; which is not written on it by precept, but engraven
by destiny, not instilled by education, but infused at our nativity. He
that lives according to nature will suffer nothing from the delusions of
hope, or importunities of desire; he will receive and reject with equabil-
ity of temper, and act or suffer as the reason of things shall alternately
prescribe. Other men may amuse themselves with subtle definitions, or
intricate ratiocination. Let them learn to be wise by easier means; let
them observe the hind of the forest, and the linnet of the grove; let them
consider the life of animals, whose motions are regulated by instinct;
they obey their guide, and are happy. Let us therefore, at length, cease
to dispute, and learn to live; throw away the encumbrance of precepts,
which they who utter them with so much pride and pomp do not understand, and carry with us this simple and intelligible maxim, that deviation from nature is deviation from happiness."

When he had spoken, he looked round him with a placid air, and
enjoyed the consciousness of his own beneficence. "Sir," said the prince
with great modesty, "as I, like all the rest of mankind, am desirous of
felicity, my closest attention has been fixed upon your discourse. I doubt
not the truth of a position which a man so learned has so confidently
advanced. Let me only know what it is to live according to nature."

"When I find young men so humble and so docile," said the philosopher, "I can deny them no information which my studies have enabled
me to afford. To live according to nature, is to act always with due regard
to the fitness arising from the relations and qualities of causes and effects;
to concur with the great and unchangeable scheme of universal felicity;

to co-operate with the general disposition and tendency of the present system of things."

The prince soon found that this was one of the sages whom he should understand less as he heard him longer. He therefore bowed and was silent; and the philosopher, supposing him satisfied, and the rest vanquished, rose up and departed with the air of a man that had co-operated with the present system.

Chapter 23. The Prince and his Sister Divide between Them the Work of Observation

Rasselas returned home full of reflections, doubtful how to direct his future steps. Of the way to happiness he found the learned and simple equally ignorant; but, as he was yet young, he flattered himself that he had time remaining for more experiments, and further inquiries. He communicated to Imlac his observations and his doubts, but was answered by him with new doubts, and remarks that gave him no comfort. He therefore discoursed more frequently and freely with his sister, who had yet the same hope with himself, and always assisted him to give some reason why, though he had been hitherto frustrated, he might succeed at last.

"We have hitherto," said she, "known but little of the world: we have never yet been either great or mean. In our own country, though we had royalty, we had no power, and in this we have not yet seen the private recesses of domestic peace. Imlac favors not our search, lest we should in time find him mistaken. We will divide the task between us: you shall try what is to be found in the splendor of courts, and I will range the shades of humbler life. Perhaps command and authority may be the supreme blessings, as they afford most opportunities of doing good: or, perhaps, what this world can give may be found in the modest habitations of middle fortune; too low for great designs, and too high for penury and distress."

Chapter 24. The Prince Examines the Happiness of High Stations

Rasselas applauded the design, and appeared next day with a splendid retinue at the court of the Bassa. He was soon distinguished for his magnificence, and admitted, as a prince whose curiosity had brought him from distant countries, to an intimacy with the great officers, and frequent conversation with the Bassa himself.

He was at first inclined to believe, that the man must be pleased with his own condition, whom all approached with reverence, and heard with obedience, and who had the power to extend his edicts to a whole kingdom. "There can be no pleasure," said he, "equal to that of feeling at once the joy of thousands all made happy by wise administration. Yet, since, by the law of subordination, this sublime delight can be in one nation but the lot of one, it is surely reasonable to think that there is some satisfaction more popular[4] and accessible, and that millions can hardly be subjected to the will of a single man, only to fill his particular breast with incommunicable content."

These thoughts were often in his mind, and he found no solution of the difficulty. But as presents and civilities gained him more familiarity, he found that almost every man who stood high in employment hated all the rest, and was hated by them, and that their lives were a continual succession of plots and detections, stratagems and escapes, faction and treachery. Many of those, who surrounded the Bassa, were sent only to watch and report his conduct; every tongue was muttering censure and every eye was searching for a fault.

At last the letters of revocation arrived, the Bassa was carried in chains to Constantinople, and his name was mentioned no more.

"What are we now to think of the prerogatives of power," said Rasselas to his sister; "is it without any efficacy to good? or, is the subordinate degree only dangerous, and the supreme safe and glorious? Is the Sultan the only happy man in his dominions? or, is the Sultan himself subject to the torments of suspicion, and the dread of enemies?"

In a short time the second Bassa was deposed. The Sultan, that had advanced him, was murdered by the Janisaries,[5] and his successor had other views and different favorites.

Chapter 25. The Princess Pursues Her Inquiry with More Diligence than Success

The princess, in the mean time, insinuated herself into many families; for there are few doors, through which liberality, joined with good humor, cannot find its way. The daughters of many houses were airy[6] and cheerful, but Nekayah had been too long accustomed to the conversation of Imlac and her brother to be much pleased with childish levity and prattle which had no meaning. She found their thoughts narrow, their wishes low, and their merriment often artificial. Their pleasures, poor as they were, could not be preserved pure, but were embittered by petty competitions and worthless emulation. They were always jealous of the beauty of each other; of a quality to which solicitude can add nothing, and from which detraction can take nothing away. Many were in love with triflers like themselves, and many fancied that they were in love when in truth they were only idle. Their affection was seldom fixed on sense or virtue, and therefore seldom ended but in vexation. Their grief, however, like their joy, was transient; everything floated in their mind unconnected with the past or future, so that one desire easily gave way to another, as a second stone cast into the water effaces and confounds the circles of the first.

4. Common.
5. Guards of the Turkish ruler.

6. "Gay; sprightly; full of mirth" (Johnson's *Dictionary*).

With these girls she played as with inoffensive animals, and found them proud of her countenance,[7] and weary of her company.

But her purpose was to examine more deeply, and her affability easily persuaded the hearts that were swelling with sorrow to discharge their secrets in her ear: and those whom hope flattered, or prosperity delighted, often courted her to partake their pleasures.

The princess and her brother commonly met in the evening in a private summer-house on the bank of the Nile, and related to each other the occurrences of the day. As they were sitting together, the princess cast her eyes upon the river that flowed before her. "Answer," said she, "great father of waters, thou that rollest thy floods through eighty nations, to the invocations of the daughter of thy native king. Tell me if thou waterest, through all thy course, a single habitation from which thou dost not hear the murmurs of complaint?"

"You are then," said Rasselas, "not more successful in private houses than I have been in courts." "I have, since the last partition of our provinces,"[8] said the princess, "enabled myself to enter familiarly into many families, where there was the fairest show of prosperity and peace, and know not one house that is not haunted by some fury that destroys its quiet.

"I did not seek ease among the poor, because I concluded that there it could not be found. But I saw many poor whom I had supposed to live in affluence. Poverty has, in large cities, very different appearances: it is often concealed in splendor, and often in extravagance. It is the care of a very great part of mankind to conceal their indigence from the rest: they support themselves by temporary expedients, and every day is lost in contriving for the morrow.

"This, however, was an evil, which, though frequent, I saw with less pain, because I could relieve it. Yet some have refused my bounties; more offended with my quickness to detect their wants, than pleased with my readiness to succor them: and others, whose exigencies compelled them to admit my kindness, have never been able to forgive their benefactress. Many, however, have been sincerely grateful without the ostentation of gratitude, or the hope of other favors."

Chapter 26. The Princess Continues Her Remarks upon Private Life

Nekayah, perceiving her brother's attention fixed, proceeded in her narrative.

"In families where there is or is not poverty, there is commonly discord. If a kingdom be, as Imlac tells us, a great family, a family likewise is a little kingdom, torn with factions and exposed to revolutions. An unpracticed observer expects the love of parents and children to be constant and equal; but this kindness seldom continues beyond the years of

---

7. Patronage, favor.   8. Division of our responsibilities.

infancy: in a short time the children become rivals to their parents. Benefits are allayed[9] by reproaches, and gratitude debased by envy.

"Parents and children seldom act in concert; each child endeavors to appropriate the esteem or fondness of the parents, and the parents, with yet less temptation, betray each other to their children. Thus, some place their confidence in the father, and some in the mother, and by degrees the house is filled with artifices and feuds.

"The opinions of children and parents, of the young and the old, are naturally opposite, by the contrary effects of hope and despondence, of expectation and experience, without crime or folly on either side. The colors of life in youth and age appear different, as the face of nature in spring and winter. And how can children credit the assertions of parents, which their own eyes show them to be false?

"Few parents act in such a manner as much to enforce their maxims by the credit of their lives. The old man trusts wholly to slow contrivance and gradual progression; the youth expects to force his way by genius, vigor, and precipitance. The old man pays regard to riches, and the youth reverences virtue. The old man deifies prudence; the youth commits himself to magnanimity and chance. The young man, who intends no ill, believes that none is intended, and therefore acts with openness and candor; but his father, having suffered the injuries of fraud, is impelled to suspect, and too often allured to practice it. Age looks with anger on the temerity of youth, and youth with contempt on the scrupulosity[1] of age. Thus parents and children, for the greatest part, live on to love less and less; and, if those whom nature has thus closely united are the torments of each other, where shall we look for tenderness and consolation?"

"Surely," said the prince, "you must have been unfortunate in your choice of acquaintance: I am unwilling to believe that the most tender of all relations is thus impeded in its effects by natural necessity."

"Domestic discord," answered she, "is not inevitably and fatally necessary, but yet is not easily avoided. We seldom see that a whole family is virtuous; the good and evil cannot well agree, and the evil can yet less agree with one another. Even the virtuous fall sometimes to variance, when their virtues are of different kinds, and tending to extremes. In general, those parents have most reverence who most deserve it; for he that lives well cannot be despised.

"Many other evils infest private life. Some are the slaves of servants whom they have trusted with their affairs. Some are kept in continual anxiety to the caprice of rich relations, whom they cannot please, and dare not offend. Some husbands are imperious, and some wives perverse; and, as it is always more easy to do evil than good, though the wisdom or virtue of one can very rarely make many happy, the folly or vice of one may often make many miserable."

9. To allay is "to joint anything to another, so as to abate its predominant qualities" (Johnson's *Dictionary*).

1. "Fear of acting in any manner" (Johnson's *Dictionary*).

"If such be the general effect of marriage," said the prince, "I shall for the future think it dangerous to connect my interest with that of another, lest I should be unhappy by my partner's fault."

"I have met," said the princess, "with many who live single for that reason; but I never found that their prudence ought to raise envy. They dream away their time without friendship, without fondness, and are driven to rid themselves of the day, for which they have no use, by childish amusements, or vicious delights. They act as beings under the constant sense of some known inferiority that fills their minds with rancor, and their tongues with censure. They are peevish at home, and malevolent abroad; and, as the outlaws of human nature, make it their business and their pleasure to disturb that society which debars them from its privileges. To live without feeling or exciting sympathy, to be fortunate without adding to the felicity of others, or afflicted without tasting the balm of pity, is a state more gloomy than solitude; it is not retreat but exclusion from mankind. Marriage has many pains, but celibacy has no pleasures."

"What then is to be done?" said Rasselas; "the more we inquire, the less we can resolve. Surely he is most likely to please himself that has no other inclination to regard."

Chapter 27. Disquisition upon Greatness

The conversation had a short pause. The prince, having considered his sister's observations, told her, that she had surveyed life with prejudice, and supposed misery where she did not find it. "Your narrative," says he, "throws yet a darker gloom upon the prospects of futurity: the predictions of Imlac were but faint sketches of the evils painted by Nekayah. I have been lately convinced that quiet is not the daughter of grandeur, or of power: that her presence is not to be bought by wealth, nor enforced by conquest. It is evident, that as any man acts in a wider compass, he must be more exposed to opposition from enmity or miscarriage from chance; whoever has many to please or to govern, must use the ministry of many agents, some of whom will be wicked, and some ignorant; by some he will be misled, and by others betrayed. If he gratifies one he will offend another: those that are not favored will think themselves injured; and, since favors can be conferred but upon few, the greater number will be always discontented.'

"The discontent," said the princess, "which is thus unreasonable, I hope that I shall always have spirit to despise, and you, power to repress."

"Discontent," answered Rasselas, "will not always be without reason under the most just or vigilant administration of public affairs. None, however attentive, can always discover that merit which indigence or faction may happen to obscure; and none, however powerful, can always reward it. Yet, he that sees inferior desert[2] advanced above him, will

---

2. Merit; one deserving reward.

naturally impute that preference to partiality or caprice; and, indeed, it can scarcely be hoped that any man, however magnanimous by nature, or exalted by condition, will be able to persist for ever in fixed and inexorable justice of distribution: he will sometimes indulge his own affections, and sometimes those of his favorites; he will permit some to please him who can never serve him; he will discover in those whom he loves qualities which in reality they do not possess; and to those, from whom he receives pleasure, he will in his turn endeavor to give it. Thus will recommendations sometimes prevail which were purchased by money, or by the more destructive bribery of flattery and servility.

"He that has much to do will do something wrong, and of that wrong must suffer the consequences; and, if it were possible that he should always act rightly, yet when such numbers are to judge of his conduct, the bad will censure and obstruct him by malevolence, and the good sometimes by mistake.

"The highest stations cannot therefore hope to be the abodes of happiness, which I would willingly believe to have fled from thrones and palaces to seats of humble privacy and placid obscurity. For what can hinder the satisfaction, or intercept the expectations, of him whose abilities are adequate to his employments, who sees with his own eyes the whole circuit of his influence, who chooses by his own knowledge all whom he trusts, and whom none are tempted to deceive by hope or fear? Surely he has nothing to do but to love and to be loved, to be virtuous and to be happy."

"Whether perfect happiness would be procured by perfect goodness," said Nekayah, "this world will never afford an opportunity of deciding. But this, at least, may be maintained, that we do not always find visible happiness in proportion to visible virtue. All natural and almost all political evils, are incident alike to the bad and good: they are confounded in the misery of a famine, and not much distinguished in the fury of a faction; they sink together in a tempest, and are driven together from their country by invaders. All that virtue can afford is quietness of conscience, a steady prospect of a happier state; this may enable us to endure calamity with patience; but remember that patience must suppose pain."

Chapter 28. Rasselas and Nekayah Continue Their Conversation

"Dear princess," said Rasselas, "you fall into the common errors of exaggeratory declamation, by producing, in a familiar disquisition,[3] examples of national calamities, and scenes of extensive misery, which are found in books rather than in the world, and which, as they are horrid, are ordained to be rare. Let us not imagine evils which we do not feel, nor injure life by misrepresentations. I cannot bear that querulous eloquence which threatens every city with a siege like that of Jeru-

---

3. Family discussion of a question.

salem,[4] that makes famine attend on every flight of locusts, and suspends pestilence on the wing of every blast that issues from the south.

"On necessary and inevitable evils, which overwhelm kingdoms at once, all disputation is vain: when they happen they must be endured. But it is evident, that these bursts of universal distress are more dreaded than felt: thousands and ten thousands flourish in youth, and wither in age, without the knowledge of any other than domestic evils, and share the same pleasures and vexations whether their kings are mild or cruel, whether the armies of their country pursue their enemies, or retreat before them. While courts are disturbed with intestine[5] competitions, and ambassadors are negotiating in foreign countries, the smith still plies his anvil, and the husbandman drives his plow forward; the necessaries of life are required and obtained, and the successive business of the seasons continues to make its wonted revolutions.

"Let us cease to consider what, perhaps, may never happen, and what, when it shall happen, will laugh at human speculation. We will not endeavor to modify the motions of the elements, or to fix the destiny of kingdoms. It is our business to consider what beings like us may perform; each laboring for his own happiness, by promoting within his circle, however narrow, the happiness of others.

"Marriage is evidently the dictate of nature; men and women were made to be companions of each other, and therefore I cannot be persuaded but that marriage is one of the means of happiness."

"I know not," said the princess, "whether marriage be more than one of the innumerable modes of human misery. When I see and reckon the various forms of connubial infelicity, the unexpected causes of lasting discord, the diversities of temper, the oppositions of opinion, the rude collisons of contrary desire where both are urged by violent impulses, the obstinate contests of disagreeing virtues, where both are supported by consciousness of good intention, I am sometimes disposed to think with the severer casuists of most nations, that marriage is rather permitted than approved, and that none, but by the instigation of a passion too much indulged, entangle themselves with indissoluble compacts."

"You seem to forget," replied Rasselas, "that you have, even now, represented celibacy as less happy than marriage. Both conditions may be bad, but they cannot both be worst. Thus it happens when wrong opinions are entertained, that they mutually destroy each other, and leave the mind open to truth."

"I did not expect," answered the princess, "to hear that imputed to falsehood which is the consequence only of frailty. To the mind, as to the eye, it is difficult to compare with exactness objects vast in their extent, and various in their parts. Where we see or conceive the whole at once we readily note the discriminations and decide the preference: but of two systems, of which neither can be surveyed by any human

4. In 70 A.D. the Romans, under Titus, besieged   5. Internal, domestic.
and destroyed Jerusalem.

being in its full compass of magnitude and multiplicity of complication, where is the wonder, that judging of the whole by parts, I am alternately affected by one and the other as either presses on my memory or fancy? We differ from ourselves just as we differ from each other, when we see only part of the question, as in the multifarious relations of politics and morality: but when we perceive the whole at once, as in numerical computations, all agree in one judgment, and none ever varies his opinion."

"Let us not add," said the prince, "to the other evils of life, the bitterness of controversy, nor endeavor to vie with each other in subtleties of argument. We are employed in a search, of which both are equally to enjoy the success, or suffer by the miscarriage. It is therefore fit that we assist each other. You surely conclude too hastily from the infelicity of marriage against its institution; will not the misery of life prove equally that life cannot be the gift of heaven? The world must be peopled by marriage, or peopled without it."

"How the world is to be peopled," returned Nekayah, "is not my care, and needs not be yours. I see no danger that the present generation should omit to leave successors behind them: we are not now inquiring for the world, but for ourselves."

Chapter 29. The Debate on Marriage Continued

"The good of the whole," says Rasselas, "is the same with the good of all its parts. If marriage be best for mankind it must be evidently best for individuals, or a permanent and necessary duty must be the cause of evil, and some must be inevitably sacrificed to the convenience of others. In the estimate which you have made of the two states, it appears that the incommodities of a single life are, in a great measure, necessary and certain, but those of the conjugal state accidental and avoidable.

"I cannot forbear to flatter myself that prudence and benevolence will make marriage happy. The general folly of mankind is the cause of general complaint. What can be expected but disappointment and repentance from a choice made in the immaturity of youth, in the ardor of desire, without judgment, without foresight, without inquiry after conformity of opinions, similarity of manners, rectitude of judgment, or purity of sentiment.

"Such is the common process of marriage. A youth and maiden meeting by chance, or brought together by artifice, exchange glances, reciprocate civilities, go home, and dream of one another. Having little to divert attention, or diversify thought, they find themselves uneasy when they are apart, and therefore conclude that they shall be happy together. They marry, and discover what nothing but voluntary blindness had before concealed; they wear out life in altercations, and charge nature with cruelty.

"From those early marriages proceeds likewise the rivalry of parents and children: the son is eager to enjoy the world before the father is

willing to forsake it, and there is hardly room at once for two generations. The daughter begins to bloom before the mother can be content
to fade, and neither can forbear to wish for the absence of the other.

"Surely all these evils may be avoided by that deliberation and delay
which prudence prescribes to irrevocable choice. In the variety and jollity of youthful pleasures life may be well enough supported without the
help of a partner. Longer time will increase experience, and wider views
will allow better opportunities of inquiry and selection: one advantage,
as least, will be certain; the parents will be visibly older than their children."

"What reason cannot collect," said Nekayah, "and what experiment
has not yet taught, can be known only from the report of others. I have
been told that late marriages are not eminently happy. This is a question
too important to be neglected, and I have often proposed it to those,
whose accuracy of remark, and comprehensiveness of knowledge, made
their suffrages[6] worthy of regard. They have generally determined that it
is dangerous for a man and woman to suspend their fate upon each
other, at a time when opinions are fixed, and habits are established;
when friendships have been contracted on both sides, when life has been
planned into method, and the mind has long enjoyed the contemplation
of its own prospects.

"It is scarcely possible that two traveling through the world under the
conduct of chance should have been both directed to the same path,
and it will not often happen that either will quit the track which custom
has made pleasing. When the desultory levity of youth has settled into
regularity, it is soon succeeded by pride ashamed to yield, or obstinacy
delighting to contend. And even though mutual esteem produces mutual
desire to please, time itself, as it modifies unchangeably the external
mien, determines likewise the direction of the passions, and gives an
inflexible rigidity to the manners. Long customs are not easily broken:
he that attempts to change the course of his own life very often labors in
vain; and how shall we do that for others which we are seldom able to
do for ourselves?"

"But surely," interposed the prince, "you suppose the chief motive of
choice forgotten or neglected. Whenever I shall seek a wife, it shall be
my first question, whether she be willing to be led by reason?"

"Thus it is," said Nekayah, "that philosophers are deceived. There
are a thousand familiar[6A] disputes which reason never can decide; questions that elude investigation, and make logic ridiculous; cases where
something must be done, and where little can be said. Consider the state
of mankind, and inquire how few can be supposed to act upon any
occasions, whether small or great, with all the reasons of action present
to their minds. Wretched would be the pair above all names of
wretchedness, who should be doomed to adjust by reason every morning
all the minute detail of a domestic day.

6. Opinions.
6A. Domestic.

"Those who marry at an advanced age will probably escape the encroachments of their children; but, in diminution of this advantage, they will be likely to leave them, ignorant and helpless, to a guardian's mercy: or, if that should not happen, they must at least go out of the world before they see those whom they love best either wise or great.

"From their children, if they have less to fear, they have less also to hope, and they lose, without equivalent, the joys of early love, and the convenience of uniting with manners pliant and minds susceptible of new impressions, which might wear away their dissimilitudes by long cohabitation, as soft bodies, by continual attrition, conform their surfaces to each other.

"I believe it will be found that those who marry late are best pleased with their children, and those who marry early with their partners."

"The union of these two affections," said Rasselas, "would produce all that could be wished. Perhaps there is a time when marriage might unite them, a time neither too early for the father, nor too late for the husband."

"Every hour," answered the princess, "confirms my prejudice in favor of the position so often uttered by the mouth of Imlac, 'That nature sets her gifts on the right hand and on the left.' Those conditions, which flatter hope and attract desire, are so constituted that, as we approach one, we recede from another. There are goods so opposed that we cannot seize both, but, by too much prudence, may pass between them at too great a distance to reach either. This is often the fate of long consideration; he does nothing who endeavors to do more than is allowed to humanity. Flatter not yourself with contrarieties of pleasure. Of the blessings set before you make your choice, and be content. No man can taste the fruits of autumn, while he is delighting his scent with the flowers of the spring: no man can, at the same time, fill his cup from the source and from the mouth of the Nile."

Chapter 30. Imlac Enters, and Changes the Conversation

Here Imlac entered, and interrupted them. "Imlac," said Rasselas, "I have been taking from the princess the dismal history of private life, and am almost discouraged from further search."

"It seems to me," said Imlac, "that while you are making the choice of life, you neglect to live. You wander about a single city, which, however large and diversified, can now afford few novelties, and forget that you are in a country, famous among the earliest monarchies for the power and wisdom of its inhabitants; a country where the sciences first dawned that illuminate the world, and beyond which the arts cannot be traced of civil society or domestic life.

"The old Egyptians have left behind them monuments of industry and power before which all European magnificence is confessed to fade away. The ruins of their architecture are the schools of modern builders, and from the wonders which time has spared we may conjecture, though uncertainly, what it has destroyed."

"My curiosity," said Rasselas, "does not very strongly lead me to survey piles of stone, or mounds of earth; my business is with man. I came hither not to measure fragments of temples, or trace choked aqueducts, but to look upon the various scenes of the present world."

"The things that are now before us," said the princess, "require attention, and deserve it. What have I to do with the heroes or the monuments of ancient times? with times which never can return, and heroes, whose form of life was different from all that the present condition of mankind requires or allows."

"To know anything," returned the poet, "we must know its effects; to see men we must see their works, that we may learn what reason has dictated, or passion has incited, and find what are the most powerful motives of action. To judge rightly of the present we must oppose it to the past; for all judgment is comparative, and of the future nothing can be known. The truth is, that no mind is much employed upon the present: recollection and anticipation fill up almost all our moments. Our passions are joy and grief, love and hatred, hope and fear. Of joy and grief the past is the object, and the future of hope and fear; even love and hatred respect the past, for the cause must have been before the effect.

"The present state of things is the consequence of the former, and it is natural to inquire what were the sources of the good that we enjoy, or of the evil that we suffer. If we act only for ourselves, to neglect the study of history is not prudent: if we are entrusted with the care of others, it is not just. Ignorance, when it is voluntary, is criminal; and he may properly be charged with evil who refused to learn how he might prevent it.

"There is no part of history so generally useful as that which relates the progress of the human mind, the gradual improvement of reason, the successive advances of science, the vicissitudes of learning and ignorance, which are the light and darkness of thinking beings, the extinction and resuscitation of arts, and all the revolutions of the intellectual world. If accounts of battles and invasions are peculiarly the business of princes, the useful or elegant arts are not to be neglected; those who have kingdoms to govern, have understandings to cultivate.

"Example is always more efficacious than precept. A soldier is formed in war, and a painter must copy pictures. In this, contemplative life has the advantage: great actions are seldom seen, but the labors of art are always at hand for those who desire to know what art has been able to perform.

"When the eye or the imagination is struck with any uncommon work the next transition of an active mind is to the means by which it was performed. Here begins the true use of such contemplation; we enlarge our comprehension by new ideas, and perhaps recover some art lost to mankind, or learn what is less perfectly known in our own country. At least we compare our own with former times, and either rejoice at our improvements, or, what is the first motion towards good, discover our defects."

"I am willing," said the prince, "to see all that can deserve my search."

"And I," said the princess, "shall rejoice to learn something of the manners of antiquity."

"The most pompous monument of Egyptian greatness, and one of the most bulky works of manual industry," said Imlac, "are the pyramids; fabrics[7] raised before the time of history, and of which the earliest narratives afford us only uncertain traditions. Of these the greatest is still standing, very little injured by time."

"Let us visit them tomorrow," said Nekayah. "I have often heard of the Pyramids, and shall not rest, till I have seen them within and without with my own eyes."

Chapter 31. They Visit the Pyramids

The resolution being thus taken, they set out the next day. They laid tents upon their camels, being resolved to stay among the pyramids till their curiosity was fully satisfied. They traveled gently, turned aside to everything remarkable, stopped from time to time and conversed with the inhabitants, and observed the various appearances of towns ruined and inhabited, of wild and cultivated nature.

When they came to the great pyramid, they were astonished at the extent of the base, and the height of the top. Imlac explained to them the principles upon which the pyramidal form was chosen for a fabric intended to coextend its duration with that of the world; he showed that its gradual diminution gave it such stability as defeated all the common attacks of the elements, and could scarcely be overthrown by earthquakes themselves, the least resistible of natural violence. A concussion that should shatter the pyramid would threaten the dissolution of the continent.

They measured all its dimensions, and pitched their tents at its foot. Next day they prepared to enter its interior apartments, and having hired the common guides, climbed up to the first passage, when the favorite of the princess, looking into the cavity, stepped back and trembled. "Pekuah," said the princess, "of what art thou afraid?" "Of the narrow entrance," answered the lady, "and of the dreadful gloom. I dare not enter a place which must surely be inhabited by unquiet souls. The original possessors of these dreadful vaults will start up before us, and perhaps shut us in forever." She spoke, and threw her arms round the neck of her mistress.

"If all your fear be of apparitions," said the prince, "I will promise you safety. There is no danger from the dead; he that is once buried will be seen no more."

"That the dead are seen no more," said Imlac, "I will not undertake

7. Buildings.

to maintain, against the concurrent and unvaried testimony of all ages, and of all nations. There is no people, rude or learned, among whom apparitions of the dead are not related and believed. This opinion, which perhaps prevails as far as human nature is diffused, could become universal only by its truth; those that never heard of one another would not have agreed in a tale which nothing but experience can make credible. That it is doubted by single cavilers can very little weaken the general evidence; and some who deny it with their tongues confess it by their fears.

"Yet I do not mean to add new terrors to those which have already seized upon Pekuah. There can be no reason why specters should haunt the pyramid more than other places, or why they should have power or will to hurt innocence and purity. Our entrance is no violation of their privileges; we can take nothing from them, how then can we offend them?"

"My dear Pekuah," said the princess, "I will always go before you, and Imlac shall follow you. Remember that you are the companion of the princess of Abyssinia."

"If the princess is pleased that her servant should die," returned the lady, "let her command some death less dreadful than enclosure in this horrid cavern. You know I dare not disobey you; I must go if you command me, but if I once enter, I never shall come back."

The princess saw that her fear was too strong for expostulation or reproof, and, embracing her, told her that she should stay in the tent till their return. Pekuah was yet not satisfied, but entreated the princess not to pursue so dreadful a purpose as that of entering the recesses of the pyramid. "Though I cannot teach courage," said Nekayah, "I must not learn cowardice, nor leave at last undone what I came hither only to do."

Chapter 32. They Enter the Pyramid

Pekuah descended to the tents, and the rest entered the pyramid. They passed through the galleries, surveyed the vaults of marble, and examined the chest in which the body of the founder is supposed to have been reposited. They then sat down in one of the most spacious chambers to rest a while before they attempted to return.

"We have now," said Imlac, "gratified our minds with an exact view of the greatest work of man, except the wall of China.

"Of the wall it is very easy to assign the motive. It secured a wealthy and timorous nation from the incursions of barbarians, whose unskillfulness in arts made it easier for them to supply their wants by rapine than by industry, and who from time to time poured in upon the habitations of peaceful commerce, as vultures descend upon domestic fowl. Their celerity and fierceness made the wall necessary, and their ignorance made it efficacious.

"But for the pyramids, no reason has ever been given adequate to the cost and labor of the work. The narrowness of the chambers proves that it could afford no retreat from enemies, and treasures might have been reposited at far less expense with equal security. It seems to have been erected only in compliance with that hunger of imagination which preys incessantly upon life, and must be always appeased by some employment. Those who have already all that they can enjoy must enlarge their desires. He that has built for use till use is supplied, must begin to build for vanity, and extend his plan to the utmost power of human performance, that he may not be soon reduced to form another wish.

"I consider this mighty structure as a monument of the insufficiency of human enjoyments. A king, whose power is unlimited, and whose treasures surmount all real and imaginary wants, is compelled to solace, by the erection of a pyramid, the satiety of dominion and tastelessness of pleasures, and to amuse the tediousness of declining life by seeing thousands laboring without end, and one stone, for no purpose, laid upon another. Whoever thou art, that, not content with a moderate condition, imaginest happiness in royal magnificence, and dreamest that command or riches can feed the appetite of novelty with perpetual gratifications, survey the pyramids, and confess thy folly!"

Chapter 33. *The Princess Meets with an Unexpected Misfortune*

They rose up, and returned through the cavity at which they had entered, and the princess prepared for her favorite a long narrative of dark labyrinths, and costly rooms, and of the different impressions which the varieties of the way had made upon her. But when they came to their train, they found every one silent and dejected: the men discovered[8] shame and fear in their countenances, and the women were weeping in the tents.

What had happened they did not try to conjecture, but immediately inquired. "You had scarcely entered into the pyramid," said one of the attendants, "when a troop of Arabs rushed upon us: we were too few to resist them, and too slow to escape. They were about to search the tents, set us on our camels, and drive us along before them, when the approach of some Turkish horsemen put them to flight; but they seized the lady Pekuah with her two maids, and carried them away: the Turks are now pursuing them by our instigation, but I fear they will not be able to overtake them."

The princess was overpowered with surprise and grief. Rasselas, in the first heat of his resentment, ordered his servants to follow him, and prepared to pursue the robbers with his saber in his hand. "Sir," said Imlac, "what can you hope from violence or valor? the Arabs are mounted on horses trained to battle and retreat; we have only beasts of burden. By leaving our present station we may lose the princess, but cannot hope to regain Pekuah."

8. Revealed, betrayed; "train": retinue.

In a short time the Turks returned, having not been able to reach the enemy. The princess burst out into new lamentations, and Rasselas could scarcely forbear to reproach them with cowardice; but Imlac was of opinion, that the escape of the Arabs was no addition to their misfortune, for, perhaps, they would have killed their captives rather than have resigned them.

Chapter 34. They Return to Cairo without Pekuah

There was nothing to be hoped from longer stay. They returned to Cairo repenting of their curiosity, censuring the negligence of the government, lamenting their own rashness which had neglected to procure a guard, imagining many expedients by which the loss of Pekuah might have been prevented, and resolving to do something for her recovery, though none could find any thing proper to be done.

Nekayah retired to her chamber, where her women attempted to comfort her, by telling her that all had their troubles, and that lady Pekuah had enjoyed much happiness in the world for a long time, and might reasonably expect a change of fortune. They hoped that some good would befall her wheresoever she was, and that their mistress would find another friend who might supply her place.

The princess made them no answer, and they continued the form of condolence, not much grieved in their hearts that the favorite was lost.

Next day the prince presented to the Bassa a memorial[9] of the wrong which he had suffered, and a petition for redress. The Bassa threatened to punish the robbers, but did not attempt to catch them, nor, indeed, could any account or description be given by which he might direct the pursuit.

It soon appeared that nothing would be done by authority. Governors, being accustomed to hear of more crimes than they can punish, and more wrongs than they can redress, set themselves at ease by indiscriminate negligence, and presently forget the request when they lose sight of the petitioner.

Imlac then endeavored to gain some intelligence by private agents. He found many who pretended to an exact knowledge of all the haunts of the Arabs, and to regular correspondence with their chiefs, and who readily undertook the recovery of Pekuah. Of these, some were furnished with money for their journey, and came back no more; some were liberally paid for accounts which a few days discovered to be false. But the princess would not suffer any means, however improbable, to be left untried. While she was doing something she kept her hope alive. As one expedient failed, another was suggested; when one messenger returned unsuccessful, another was dispatched to a different quarter.

Two months had now passed, and of Pekuah nothing had been heard; the hopes which they had endeavored to raise in each other grew more

9. Statement of facts.

languid, and the princess, when she saw nothing more to be tried, sunk down inconsolable in hopeless dejection. A thousand times she reproached herself with the easy compliance by which she permitted her favorite to stay behind her. "Had not my fondness," said she, "lessened my authority, Pekuah had not dared to talk of her terrors. She ought to have feared me more than specters. A severe look would have overpowered her; a peremptory command would have compelled obedience. Why did foolish indulgence prevail upon me? Why did I not speak and refuse to hear?"

"Great princess," said Imlac, "do not reproach yourself for your virtue, or consider that as blameable by which evil has accidentally been caused. Your tenderness for the timidity of Pekuah was generous and kind. When we act according to our duty, we commit the event to him by whose laws our actions are governed, and who will suffer none to be finally punished for obedience. When, in prospect of some good, whether natural or moral, we break the rules prescribed us, we withdraw from the direction of superior wisdom, and take all consequences upon ourselves. Man cannot so far know the connection of causes and events, as that he may venture to do wrong in order to do right. When we pursue our end by lawful means, we may always console our miscarriage by the hope of future recompense. When we consult only our own policy, and attempt to find a nearer way to good, by overleaping the settled boundaries of right and wrong, we cannot be happy even by success, because we cannot escape the consciousness of our fault; but, if we miscarry, the disappointment is irremediably embittered. How comfortless is the sorrow of him, who feels at once the pangs of guilt, and the vexation of calamity which guilt has brought upon him?

"Consider, princess, what would have been your condition, if the lady Pekuah had entreated to accompany you, and, being compelled to stay in the tents, had been carried away; or how would you have borne the thought, if you had forced her into the pyramid, and she had died before you in agonies of terror."

"Had either happened," said Nekayah, "I could not have endured life till now: I should have been tortured to madness by the remembrance of such cruelty, or must have pined away in abhorrence of myself."

"This at least," said Imlac, "is the present reward of virtuous conduct, that no unlucky consequence can oblige us to repent it."

Chapter 35. The Princess Languishes for Want of Pekuah

Nekayah, being thus reconciled to herself, found that no evil is insupportable but that which is accompanied with consciousness of wrong. She was, from that time, delivered from the violence of tempestuous sorrow, and sunk into silent pensiveness and gloomy tranquillity. She sat from morning to evening recollecting all that had been done or said by her Pekuah, treasured up with care every trifle on which Pekuah had set an accidental value, and which might recall to mind any little incident or careless conversation. The sentiments of her, whom she now expected to see no more, were treasured in her memory as rules of life, and she deliberated to no other end than to conjecture on any occasion what would have been the opinion and counsel of Pekuah.

The women, by whom she was attended, knew nothing of her real condition, and therefore she could not talk to them but with caution and reserve. She began to remit[1] her curiosity, having no great care to collect notions which she had no convenience of uttering. Rasselas endeavored first to comfort and afterwards to divert her; he hired musicians, to whom she seemed to listen, but did not hear them, and procured masters to instruct her in various arts, whose lectures, when they visited her again, were again to be repeated. She had lost her taste of pleasure and her ambition of excellence. And her mind, though forced into short excursions, always recurred to the image of her friend.

Imlac was every morning earnestly enjoined to renew his inquiries, and was asked every night whether he had yet heard of Pekuah, till not being able to return the princess the answer that she desired, he was less and less willing to come into her presence. She observed his backwardness, and commanded him to attend her. "You are not," said she, "to confound impatience with resentment, or to suppose that I charge you with negligence, because I repine at your unsuccessfulness. I do not much wonder at your absence; I know that the unhappy are never pleasing, and that all naturally avoid the contagion of misery. To hear complaints is wearisome alike to the wretched and the happy; for who would cloud by adventitious grief the short gleams of gaiety which life allows us? or who, that is struggling under his own evils, will add to them the miseries of another?

"The time is at hand, when none shall be disturbed any longer by the sighs of Nekayah: my search after happiness is now at an end. I am resolved to retire from the world with all its flatteries and deceits, and will hide myself in solitude, without any other care than to compose my thoughts, and regulate my hours by a constant succession of innocent occupations, till, with a mind purified from all earthly desires, I shall enter into that state, to which all are hastening, and in which I hope again to enjoy the friendship of Pekuah."

"Do not entangle your mind," said Imlac, "by irrevocable determinations, nor increase the burden of life by a voluntary accumulation of misery: the weariness of retirement will continue or increase when the loss of Pekuah is forgotten. That you have been deprived of one pleasure is no very good reason for rejection of the rest."

"Since Pekuah was taken from me," said the princess, "I have no pleasure to reject or to retain. She that has no one to love or trust has little to hope. She wants the radical principle of happiness. We may, perhaps, allow that what satisfaction this world can afford, must arise from the conjunction of wealth, knowledge and goodness: wealth is nothing but as it is bestowed, and knowledge nothing but as it is communicated: they must therefore be imparted to others, and to whom

---

1. To lay aside.

could I now delight to impart them? Goodness affords the only comfort which can be enjoyed without a partner, and goodness may be practised in retirement."

"How far solitude may admit goodness, or advance it, I shall not," replied Imlac, "dispute at present. Remember the confession of the pious hermit. You will wish to return into the world, when the image of your companion has left your thoughts." "That time," said Nekayah, "will never come. The generous frankness, the modest obsequiousness,[1] and the faithful secrecy of my dear Pekuah, will always be more missed, as I shall live longer to see vice and folly."

"The state of a mind oppressed with a sudden calamity," said Imlac, "is like that of the fabulous inhabitants of the new created earth, who, when the first night came upon them, supposed that day never would return. When the clouds of sorrow gather over us, we see nothing beyond them, nor can imagine how they will be dispelled: yet a new day succeeded to the night, and sorrow is never long without a dawn of ease. But they who restrain themselves from receiving comfort, do as the savages would have done, had they put out their eyes when it was dark. Our minds, like our bodies, are in continual flux; something is hourly lost, and something acquired. To lose much at once is inconvenient to either, but while the vital powers remain uninjured, nature will find the means of reparation. Distance has the same effect on the mind as on the eye, and while we glide along the stream of time, whatever we leave behind us is always lessening, and that which we approach increasing in magnitude. Do not suffer life to stagnate; it will grow muddy for want of motion: commit yourself again to the current of the world; Pekuah will vanish by degrees; you will meet in your way some other favorite, or learn to diffuse yourself in general conversation."

"At least," said the prince, "do not despair before all remedies have been tried: the inquiry after the unfortunate lady is still continued, and shall be carried on with yet greater diligence, on condition that you will promise to wait a year for the event, without any unalterable resolution."

Nekayah thought this a reasonable demand, and made the promise to her brother, who had been advised by Imlac to require it. Imlac had, indeed, no great hope of regaining Pekuah, but he supposed, that if he could secure the interval of a year, the princess would be then in no danger of a cloister.

Chapter 36. Pekuah Is Still Remembered. The Progress of Sorrow

Nekayah, seeing that nothing was omitted for the recovery of her favorite, and having, by her promise, set her intention of retirement at a distance, began imperceptibly to return to common cares and common pleasures. She rejoiced without her own consent at the suspension of her sorrows, and sometimes caught herself with indignation in the act

1. Obedience.

of turning away her mind from the remembrance of her, whom yet she resolved never to forget.

She then appointed a certain hour of the day for meditation on the merits and fondness of Pekuah, and for some weeks retired constantly at the time fixed, and returned with her eyes swollen and her countenance clouded. By degrees she grew less scrupulous, and suffered any important and pressing avocation to delay the tribute of daily tears. She then yielded to less occasions; sometimes forgot what she was indeed afraid to remember, and, at last, wholly released herself from the duty of periodical affliction.

Her real love of Pekuah was yet not diminished. A thousand occurrences brought her back to memory, and a thousand wants, which nothing but the confidence of friendship can supply, made her frequently regretted. She, therefore, solicited Imlac never to desist from inquiry, and to leave no art of intelligence untried, that, at least, she might have the comfort of knowing that she did not suffer by negligence or sluggishness. "Yet what," said she, "is to be expected from our pursuit of happiness, when we find the state of life to be such, that happiness itself is the cause of misery? Why should we endeavor to attain that, of which the possession cannot be secured? I shall henceforward fear to yield my heart to excellence, however bright, or to fondness, however tender, lest I should lose again what I have lost in Pekuah."

Chapter 37. The Princess Hears News of Pekuah

In seven months, one of the messengers, who had been sent away upon the day when the promise was drawn from the princess, returned, after many unsuccessful rambles, from the borders of Nubia, with an account that Pekuah was in the hands of an Arab chief, who possessed a castle or fortress on the extremity of Egypt. The Arab, whose revenue was plunder, was willing to restore her, with her two attendants, for two hundred ounces of gold.

The price was no subject of debate. The princess was in ecstasies when she heard that her favorite was alive, and might so cheaply be ransomed. She could not think of delaying for a moment Pekuah's happiness or her own, but entreated her brother to send back the messenger with the sum required. Imlac, being consulted, was not very confident of the veracity of the relator, and was still more doubtful of the Arab's faith, who might, if he were too liberally trusted, detain at once the money and the captives. He thought it dangerous to put themselves in the power of the Arab, by going into his district, and could not expect that the rover[2] would so much expose himself as to come into the lower country, where he might be seized by the forces of the Bassa.

It is difficult to negotiate where neither will trust. But Imlac, after some deliberation, directed the messenger to propose that Pekuah should

2. Robber.

be conducted by ten horsemen to the monastery of St. Anthony, which is situated in the deserts of Upper Egypt, where she should be met by the same number, and her ransom should be paid.

That no time might be lost, as they expected that the proposal would not be refused, they immediately began their journey to the monastery; and, when they arrived, Imlac went forward with the former messenger to the Arab's fortress. Rasselas was desirous to go with them, but neither his sister nor Imlac would consent. The Arab, according to the custom of his nation, observed the laws of hospitality with great exactness to those who put themselves into his power, and, in a few days, brought Pekuah with her maids, by easy journeys, to their place appointed, where receiving the stipulated price, he restored her with great respect to liberty and her friends, and undertook to conduct them back toward Cairo beyond all danger of robbery or violence.

The princess and her favorite embraced each other with transport too violent to be expressed, and went out together to pour the tears of tenderness in secret, and exchange professions of kindness and gratitude. After a few hours they returned into the refectory of the convent, where, in the presence of the prior and his brethren, the prince required of Pekuah the history of her adventures.

Chapter 38. The Adventures of the Lady Pekuah

"At what time, and in what manner, I was forced away," said Pekuah, "your servants have told you. The suddenness of the event struck me with surprise, and I was at first rather stupified than agitated with any passion of either fear or sorrow. My confusion was increased by the speed and tumult of our flight while we were followed by the Turks, who, as it seemed, soon despaired to overtake us, or were afraid of those whom they made a show of menacing.

"When the Arabs saw themselves out of danger they slackened their course, and, as I was less harassed by external violence, I began to feel more uneasiness in my mind. After some time we stopped near a spring shaded with trees in a pleasant meadow, where we were set upon the ground, and offered such refreshments as our masters were partaking. I was suffered to sit with my maids apart from the rest, and none attempted to comfort or insult us. Here I first began to feel the full weight of my misery. The girls sat weeping in silence, and from time to time looked on me for succor. I knew not to what condition we were doomed, nor could conjecture where would be the place of our captivity, or whence to draw any hope of deliverance. I was in the hands of robbers and savages, and had no reason to suppose that their pity was more than their justice, or that they would forbear the gratification of any ardor of desire, or caprice of cruelty. I, however, kissed my maids, and endeavored to pacify them by remarking, that we were yet treated with decency, and that, since we were now carried beyond pursuit, there was no danger of violence to our lives.

"When we were to be set again on horseback, my maids clung round me, and refused to be parted, but I commanded them not to irritate those who had us in their power. We traveled the remaining part of the day through an unfrequented and pathless country, and came by moonlight to the side of a hill, where the rest of the troop was stationed. Their tents were pitched, and their fires kindled, and our chief was welcomed as a man much beloved by his dependents.

"We were received into a large tent, where we found women who had attended their husbands in the expedition. They set before us the supper which they had provided, and I eat it rather to encourage my maids than to comply with any appetite of my own. When the meat was taken away they spread the carpets for repose. I was weary, and hoped to find in sleep that remission of distress which nature seldom denies. Ordering myself therefore to be undressed, I observed that the women looked very earnestly upon me, not expecting, I suppose, to see me so submissively attended. When my upper vest was taken off, they were apparently struck with the splendor of my clothes, and one of them timorously laid her hand upon the embroidery. She then went out, and, in a short time, came back with another woman, who seemed to be of higher rank, and greater authority. She did, at her entrance, the usual act of reverence, and, taking me by the hand, placed me in a smaller tent, spread with finer carpets, where I spent the night quietly with my maids.

"In the morning, as I was sitting on the grass, the chief of the troop came towards me: I rose up to receive him, and he bowed with great respect. 'Illustrious lady,' said he, 'my fortune is better than I had presumed to hope; I am told by my women that I have a princess in my camp.' 'Sir,' answered I, 'your women have deceived themselves and you; I am not a princess, but an unhappy stranger who intended soon to have left this country, in which I am now to be imprisoned for ever.' 'Whoever, or whencesoever, you are,' returned the Arab, 'your dress, and that of your servants, show your rank to be high, and your wealth to be great. Why should you, who can so easily procure your ransom, think yourself in danger of perpetual captivity? The purpose of my incursions is to increase my riches, or more properly to gather tribute. The sons of Ishmael[3] are the natural and hereditary lords of this part of the continent, which is usurped by late invaders, and low-born tryants, from whom we are compelled to take by the sword what is denied to justice. The violence of war admits no distinction; the lance that is lifted at guilt and power will sometimes fall on innocence and gentleness.'

" 'How little,' said I, 'did I expect that yesterday it should have fallen upon me.'

" 'Misfortunes,' answered the Arab, 'should always be expected. If the eye of hostility could learn reverence or pity, excellence like yours had been exempt from injury. But the angels of affliction spread their toils alike for the virtuous and the wicked, for the mighty and the mean. Do

---

3. Arabs, who claim descent from Ishmael, a son of Abraham.

not be disconsolate; I am not one of the lawless and cruel rovers of the desert; I know the rules of civil[4] life: I will fix your ransom, give a passport to your messenger, and perform my stipulation with nice punctuality.'

"You will easily believe that I was pleased with his courtesy; and finding that his predominant passion was desire of money, I began now to think my danger less, for I knew that no sum would be thought too great for the release of Pekuah. I told him that he should have no reason to charge me with ingratitude, if I was used with kindness, and that any ransom, which could be expected for a maid of common rank, would be paid, but that he must not persist to rate me as a princess. He said, he would consider what he should demand, and then, smiling, bowed and retired.

"Soon after the women came about me, each contending to be more officious[5] than the other, and my maids themselves were served with reverence. We traveled onward by short journeys. On the fourth day the chief told me, that my ransom must be two hundred ounces of gold, which I not only promised him, but told him, that I would add fifty more, if I and my maids were honorably treated.

"I never knew the power of gold before. From that time I was the leader of the troop. The march of every day was longer or shorter as I commanded, and the tents were pitched where I chose to rest. We now had camels and other conveniencies for travel, my own women were always at my side, and I amused myself with observing the manners of the vagrant nations,[6] and with viewing remains of ancient edifices with which these deserted countries appear to have been, in some distant age, lavishly embellished.

"The chief of the band was a man far from illiterate: he was able to travel by the stars or the compass, and had marked in his erratic expeditions such places as are most worthy the notice of a passenger.[7] He observed to me, that buildings are always best preserved in places little frequented, and difficult of access: for, when once a country declines from its primitive splendor, the more inhabitants are left, the quicker ruin will be made. Walls supply stones more easily than quarries, and palaces and temples will be demolished to make stables of granite, and cottages of porphyry.

Chapter 39. The Adventures of Pekuah Continued

"We wandered about in this manner for some weeks, whether, as our chief pretended, for my gratification, or, as I rather suspected, for some convenience of his own. I endeavored to appear contented where sullenness and resentment would have been of no use, and that endeavor conduced much to the calmness of my mind; but my heart was always

4. Civilized. "Nice punctuality": scrupulous exactness.
5. Ready to serve.
6. Nomads.
7. Traveler.

with Nekayah, and the troubles of the night much overbalanced the amusements of the day. My women, who threw all their cares upon their mistress, set their minds at ease from the time when they saw me treated with respect, and gave themselves up to the incidental alleviations of our fatigue without solicitude or sorrow. I was pleased with their pleasure, and animated with their confidence. My condition had lost much of its terror, since I found that the Arab ranged the country merely to get riches. Avarice is an uniform and tractable vice: other intellectual distempers are different in different constitutions of mind; that which sooths the pride of one will offend the pride of another; but to the favor of the covetous there is a ready way, bring money and nothing is denied.

"At last we came to the dwelling of our chief, a strong and spacious house built with stone in an island of the Nile, which lies, as I was told, under the tropic. 'Lady,' said the Arab, 'you shall rest after your journey a few weeks in this place, where you are to consider yourself as sovereign. My occupation is war: I have therefore chosen this obscure residence, from which I can issue unexpected, and to which I can retire unpursued. You may now repose in security: here are few pleasures, but here is no danger.' He then led me into the inner apartments, and seating me on the richest couch, bowed to the ground. His women, who considered me as a rival, looked on me with malignity; but being soon informed that I was a great lady detained only for my ransom, they began to vie with each other in obsequiousness and reverence.

"Being again comforted with new assurances of speedy liberty, I was for some days diverted from impatience by the novelty of the place. The turrets overlooked the country to a great distance, and afforded a view of many windings of the stream. In the day I wandered from one place to another as the course of the sun varied the splendor of the prospect, and saw many things which I had never seen before. The crocodiles and river-horses[8] are common in this unpeopled region, and I often looked upon them with terror, though I knew that they could not hurt me. For some time I expected to see mermaids and tritons, which, as Imlac has told me, the European travelers have stationed in the Nile, but no such beings ever appeared, and the Arab, when I inquired after them, laughed at my credulity.

"At night the Arab always attended me to a tower set apart for celestial observations, where he endeavored to teach me the names and courses of the stars. I had no great inclination to this study, but an appearance of attention was necessary to please my instructor, who valued himself for his skill, and, in a little while, I found some employment requisite to beguile the tediousness of time, which was to be passed always amidst the same objects. I was weary of looking in the morning on things from which I had turned away weary in the evening: I therefore was at last willing to observe the stars rather than do nothing, but could not always

---

8. Hippopotamuses.

compose my thoughts, and was very often thinking on Nekayah when others imagined me contemplating the sky. Soon after the Arab went upon another expedition, and then my only pleasure was to talk with my maids about the accident by which we were carried away, and the happiness that we should all enjoy at the end of our captivity."

"There were women in your Arab's fortress," said the princess, "why did you not make them your companions, enjoy their conversation, and partake their diversions? In a place where they found business or amusement, why should you alone sit corroded with idle melancholy? or why could not you bear for a few months that condition to which they were condemned for life?"

"The diversions of the women," answered Pekuah, "were only childish play, by which the mind accustomed to stronger operations could not be kept busy. I could do all which they delighted in doing by powers merely sensitive,[9] while my intellectual faculties were flown to Cairo. They ran from room to room as a bird hops from wire to wire in his cage. They danced for the sake of motion, as lambs frisk in a meadow. One sometimes pretended to be hurt that the rest might be alarmed, or hid herself that another might seek her. Part of their time passed in watching the progress of light bodies that floated on the river, and part in marking the various forms into which clouds broke in the sky.

"Their business was only needlework, in which I and my maids sometimes helped them; but you know that the mind will easily straggle from the fingers, nor will you suspect that captivity and absence from Nekayah could receive solace from silken flowers.

"Nor was much satisfaction to be hoped from their conversation: for of what could they be expected to talk? They had seen nothing; for they had lived from early youth in that narrow spot: of what they had not seen they could have no knowledge, for they could not read. They had no ideas but of the few things that were within their view, and had hardly names for anything but their clothes and their food. As I bore a superior character, I was often called to terminate their quarrels, which I decided as equitably as I could. If it could have amused me to hear the complaints of each against the rest, I might have been often detained by long stories, but the motives of their animosity were so small that I could not listen without intercepting the tale."

"How," said Rasselas, "can the Arab, whom you represented as a man of more than common accomplishments, take any pleasure in his seraglio, when it is filled only with women like these. Are they exquisitely beautiful?"

"They do not," said Pekuah, "want that unaffecting and ignoble beauty which may subsist without spriteliness or sublimity, without energy of thought or dignity of virtue. But to a man like the Arab such beauty was only a flower casually plucked and carelessly thrown away. Whatever

9. "Having sense or perception, but not reason" (Johnson's *Dictionary*).

pleasures he might find among them, they were not those of friendship or society. When they were playing about him he looked on them with inattentive superiority: when they vied for his regard he sometimes turned away disgusted. As they had no knowledge, their talk could take nothing from the tediousness of life: as they had no choice, their fondness, or appearance of fondness, excited in him neither pride nor gratitude; he was not exalted in his own esteem by the smiles of a woman who saw no other man, nor was much obliged by that regard, of which he could never know the sincerity, and which he might often perceive to be exerted not so much to delight him as to pain a rival. That which he gave, and they received, as love, was only a careless distribution of superfluous time, such love as man can bestow upon that which he despises, such as has neither hope nor fear, neither joy nor sorrow."

"You have reason, lady, to think yourself happy," said Imlac, "that you have been thus easily dismissed. How could a mind, hungry for knowledge, be willing, in an intellectual famine, to lose such a banquet as Pekuah's conversation?"

"I am inclined to believe," answered Pekuah, "that he was for some time in suspense; for, notwithstanding his promise, whenever I proposed to dispatch a messenger to Cairo, he found some excuse for delay. While I was detained in his house he made many incursions into the neighboring countries, and, perhaps, he would have refused to discharge me, had his plunder been equal to his wishes. He returned always courteous, related his adventures, delighted to hear my observations, and endeavored to advance my acquaintance with the stars. When I importuned him to send away my letters, he soothed me with professions of honor and sincerity; and, when I could be no longer decently denied, put his troop again in motion, and left me to govern in his absence. I was much afflicted by this studied procrastination, and was sometimes afraid that I should be forgotten; that you would leave Cairo, and I must end my days in an island of the Nile.

"I grew at last hopeless and dejected, and cared so little to entertain him, that he for a while more frequently talked with my maids. That he should fall in love with them, or with me, might have been equally fatal, and I was not much pleased with the growing friendship. My anxiety was not long; for, as I recovered some degree of cheerfulness, he returned to me, and I could not forbear to despise my former uneasiness.

"He still delayed to send for my ransom, and would, perhaps, never have determined, had not your agent found his way to him. The gold, which he would not fetch, he could not reject when it was offered. He hastened to prepare for our journey hither, like a man delivered from the pain of an intestine conflict. I took leave of my companions in the house, who dismissed me with cold indifference."

Nekayah, having heard her favorite's relation, rose and embraced her, and Rasselas gave her an hundred ounces of gold, which she presented to the Arab for the fifty that were promised.

Chapter 40. The History of a Man of Learning

They returned to Cairo, and were so well pleased at finding them-selves together, that none of them went much abroad. The prince began to love learning, and one day declared to Imlac, that he intended to devote himself to science,[1] and pass the rest of his days in literary soli-tude.

"Before you make your final choice," answered Imlac, "you ought to examine its hazards, and converse with some of those who are grown old in the company of themselves. I have just left the observatory of one of the most learned astronomers in the world, who has spent forty years in unwearied attention to the motions and appearances of the celestial bodies, and has drawn out his soul in endless calculations. He admits a few friends once a month to hear his deductions and enjoy his discov-eries. I was introduced as a man of knowledge worthy of his notice. Men of various ideas and fluent conversation are commonly welcome to those whose thoughts have been long fixed upon a single point, and who find the images of other things stealing away. I delighted him with my remarks, he smiled at the narrative of my travels, and was glad to forget the con-stellations, and descend for a moment into the lower world.

"On the next day of vacation I renewed my visit, and was so fortunate as to please him again. He relaxed from that time the severity of his rule, and permitted me to enter at my own choice. I found him always busy, and always glad to be relieved. As each knew much which the other was desirous of learning, we exchanged our notions with great delight. I perceived that I had every day more of his confidence, and always found new cause of admiration in the profundity of his mind. His comprehen-sion is vast, his memory capacious and retentive, his discourse is methodical, and his expression clear.

"His integrity and benevolence are equal to his learning. His deepest researches and most favorite studies are willingly interrupted for any opportunity of doing good by his counsel or his riches. To his closest retreat, at his most busy moments, all are admitted that want his assis-tance: 'For though I exclude idleness and pleasure, I will never,' says he, 'bar my doors against charity. To man is permitted the contempla-tion of the skies, but the practice of virtue is commanded.' "

"Surely," said the princess, "this man is happy."

"I visited him," said Imlac, "with more and more frequency, and was every time more enamored of his conversation: he was sublime without haughtiness, courteous without formality, and communicative without ostentation. I was at first, great princess, of your opinion, thought him the happiest of mankind, and often congratulated him on the blessing that he enjoyed. He seemed to hear nothing with indifference but the praises of his condition, to which he always returned a general answer, and diverted the conversation to some other topic.

1. Knowledge.

"Amidst this willingness to be pleased, and labor to please, I had quickly reason to imagine that some painful sentiment pressed upon his mind. He often looked up earnestly towards the sun, and let his voice fall in the midst of his discourse. He would sometimes, when we were alone, gaze upon me in silence with the air of a man who longed to speak what he was yet resolved to suppress. He would often send for me with vehement injunctions of haste, though, when I came to him, he had nothing extraordinary to say. And sometimes, when I was leaving him, he would call me back, pause a few moments and then dismiss me.

Chapter 41. The Astronomer Discovers the Cause of His Uneasiness

"At last the time came when the secret burst his reserve. We were sitting together last night in the turret of his house, watching the emersion of a satellite of Jupiter. A sudden tempest clouded the sky, and disappointed our observation. We sat a while silent in the dark, and then he addressed himself to me in these words: 'Imlac, I have long considered thy friendship as the greatest blessing of my life. Integrity without knowledge is weak and useless, and knowledge without integrity is dangerous and dreadful. I have found in thee all the qualities requisite for trust, benevolence, experience, and fortitude. I have long discharged an office which I must soon quit at the call of nature, and shall rejoice in the hour of imbecility[2] and pain to devolve it upon thee.'

"I thought myself honored by this testimony, and protested that whatever could conduce to his happiness would add likewise to mine.

" 'Hear, Imlac, what thou wilt not without difficulty credit. I have possessed for five years the regulation of weather, and the distribution of the seasons: the sun has listened to my dictates, and passed from tropic to tropic by my direction; the clouds, at my call, have poured their waters, and the Nile has overflowed at my command; I have restrained the rage of the dog-star, and mitigated the fervors of the crab.[3] The winds alone, of all the elemental powers, have hitherto refused my authority, and multitudes have perished by equinoctial tempests which I found myself unable to prohibit or restrain. I have administered this great office with exact justice, and made to the different nations of the earth an impartial dividend of rain and sunshine. What must have been the misery of half the globe, if I had limited the clouds to particular regions, or confined the sun to either side of the equator?' "

Chapter 42. The Opinion of the Astronomer Is Explained and Justified

"I suppose he discovered in me, through the obscurity of the room, some tokens of amazement and doubt, for, after a short pause, he proceeded thus:

2. Feebleness.
3. Fourth sign of the Zodiac (Cancer). Sirius, "the dog-star," was supposed to cause the heat ("dog-days") of summer.

" 'Not to be easily credited will neither surprise nor offend me; for I am, probably, the first of human beings to whom this trust has been imparted. Nor do I know whether to deem this distinction a reward or punishment; since I have possessed it I have been far less happy than before, and nothing but the consciousness of good intention could have enabled me to support the weariness of unremitted vigilance.'

" 'How long, Sir, said I, has this great office been in your hands?'

" 'About ten years ago,' said he, 'my daily observations of the changes of the sky led me to consider, whether, if I had the power of the seasons, I could confer greater plenty upon the inhabitants of the earth. This contemplation fastened on my mind, and I sat days and nights in imaginary dominion, pouring upon this country and that the showers of fertility, and seconding every fall of rain with a due proportion of sunshine. I had yet only the will to do good, and did not imagine that I should ever have the power.

" 'One day as I was looking on the fields withering with heat, I felt in my mind a sudden wish that I could send rain on the southern mountains, and raise the Nile to an inundation. In the hurry of my imagination I commanded rain to fall, and, by comparing the time of my command, with that of the inundation, I found that the clouds had listened to my lips.'

" 'Might not some other cause,' said I, 'produce this concurrence? the Nile does not always rise on the same day.'

" 'Do not believe,' said he with impatience, 'that such objections could escape me: I reasoned long against my own conviction, and labored against truth with the utmost obstinacy. I sometimes suspected myself of madness, and should not have dared to impart this secret but to a man like you, capable of distinguishing the wonderful from the impossible, and the incredible from the false.'

" 'Why, Sir,' said I, 'do you call that incredible, which you know, or think you know, to be true?'

" 'Because,' said he, 'I cannot prove it by any external evidence; and I know too well the laws of demonstration to think that my conviction ought to influence another, who cannot, like me, be conscious of its force. I therefore shall not attempt to gain credit by disputation. It is sufficient that I feel this power, that I have long possessed, and every day exerted it. But the life of man is short, the infirmities of age increase upon me, and the time will soon come when the regulator of the year must mingle with the dust. The care of appointing a successor has long disturbed me; the night and the day have been spent in comparisons of all the characters which have come to my knowledge, and I have yet found none so worthy as thyself.

Chapter 43. The Astronomer Leaves Imlac His Directions

" 'Hear therefore, what I shall impart, with attention, such as the welfare of a world requires. If the task of a king be considered as difficult, who has the care only of a few millions, to whom he cannot do much good or harm, what must be the anxiety of him, on whom depends the action of the elements, and the great gifts of light and heat!—Hear me therefore with attention.

" 'I have diligently considered the position of the earth and sun, and formed innumerable schemes in which I changed their situation. I have sometimes turned aside the axis of the earth, and sometimes varied the ecliptic of the sun: but I have found it impossible to make a disposition by which the world may be advantaged; what one region gains, another loses by any imaginable alteration, even without considering the distant parts of the solar system with which we are unacquainted. Do not, therefore, in thy administration of the year, indulge thy pride by innovation; do not please thyself with thinking that thou canst make thyself renowned to all future ages, by disordering the seasons. The memory of mischief is no desirable fame. Much less will it become thee to let kindness or interest prevail. Never rob other countries of rain to pour it on thine own. For us the Nile is sufficient.'

"I promised that when I possessed the power, I would use it with inflexible integrity, and he dismissed me, pressing my hand. 'My heart,' said he, 'will be now at rest, and my benevolence will no more destroy my quiet: I have found a man of wisdom and virtue, to whom I can cheerfully bequeath the inheritance of the sun.' "

The prince heard this narration with very serious regard, but the princess smiled, and Pekuah convulsed herself with laughter. "Ladies," said Imlac, "to mock the heaviest of human afflictions is neither charitable nor wise. Few can attain this man's knowledge, and few practice his virtues; but all may suffer his calamity. Of the uncertainties of our present state, the most dreadful and alarming is the uncertain continuance of reason."

The princess was recollected, and the favorite was abashed. Rasselas, more deeply affected, inquired of Imlac, whether he thought such maladies of the mind frequent, and how they were contracted.

Chapter 44. The Dangerous Prevalence[4] of Imagination

"Disorders of intellect," answered Imlac, "happen much more often than superficial observers will easily believe. Perhaps, if we speak with rigorous exactness, no human mind is in its right state. There is no man whose imagination does not sometimes predominate over his reason, who can regulate his attention wholly by his will, and whose ideas will come and go at his command. No man will be found in whose mind airy notions do not sometimes tyrannize, and force him to hope or fear beyond the limits of sober probability. All power of fancy over reason is a degree of insanity; but while this power is such as we can control and repress, it is not visible to others, nor considered as any depravation of

4. Predominance.

the mental faculties; it is not pronounced madness but when it comes ungovernable, and apparently influences speech or action.

"To indulge the power of fiction, and send imagination out upon the wing, is often the sport of those who delight too much in silent speculation. When we are alone we are not always busy; the labor of excogitation is too violent to last long; the ardor of inquiry will sometimes give way to idleness or satiety. He who has nothing external that can divert him must find pleasure in his own thoughts, and must conceive himself what he is not; for who is pleased with what he is? He then expatiates in boundless futurity, and culls from all imaginable conditions that which for the present moment he should most desire, amuses his desires with impossible enjoyments, and confers upon his pride unattainable dominion. The mind dances from scene to scene, unites all pleasures in all combinations, and riots in delights which nature and fortune, with all their bounty, cannot bestow.

"In time, some particular train of ideas fixes the attention; all other intellectual gratifications are rejected; the mind, in weariness or leisure, recurs constantly to the favorite conception, and feasts on the luscious falsehood, whenever she is offended with the bitterness of truth. By degrees the reign of fancy is confirmed; she grows first imperious, and in time despotic. Then fictions begin to operate as realities, false opinions fasten upon the mind, and life passes in dreams of rapture or of anguish.

"This, sir, is one of the dangers of solitude, which the hermit has confessed not always to promote goodness, and the astronomer's misery has proved to be not always propitious to wisdom."

"I will no more," said the favorite, "imagine myself the queen of Abyssinia. I have often spent the hours which the princess gave to my own disposal, in adjusting ceremonies and regulating the court; I have repressed the pride of the powerful, and granted the petitions of the poor; I have built new palaces in more happy situations, planted groves upon the tops of mountains, and have exulted in the beneficence of royalty, till, when the princess entered, I had almost forgotten to bow down before her."

"And I," said the princess, "will not allow myself any more to play the shepherdess in my waking dreams. I have often soothed my thoughts with the quiet and innocence of pastoral employments, till I have in my chamber heard the winds whistle, and the sheep bleat; sometimes freed the lamb entangled in the thicket, and sometimes with my crook encountered the wolf. I have a dress like that of the village maids, which I put on to help my imagination, and a pipe on which I play softly, and suppose myself followed by my flocks."

"I will confess," said the prince, "an indulgence of fantastic delight more dangerous than yours. I have frequently endeavored to image the possibility of a perfect government, by which all wrong should be restrained, all vice reformed, and all the subjects preserved in tranquility and innocence. This thought produced innumerable schemes of reformation, and dictated many useful regulations and salutary edicts. This has been the sport, and sometimes the labor, of my solitude; and I start, when I think with how little anguish I once supposed the death of my father and my brothers."

"Such," says Imlac, "are the effects of visionary schemes; when we first form them, we know them to be absurd, but familiarize them by degrees, and in time lose sight of their folly."

Chapter 45. They Discourse with an Old Man

The evening was now far past, and they rose to return home. As they walked along the bank of the Nile, delighted with the beams of the moon quivering on the water, they saw at a small distance an old man, whom the prince had often heard in the assembly of the sages. "Yonder," said he, "is one whose years have calmed his passions, but not clouded his reason. Let us close the disquisitions of the night by inquiring what are his sentiments of his own state, that we may know whether youth alone is to struggle with vexation, and whether any better hope remains for the latter part of life."

Here the sage approached and saluted them. They invited him to join their walk, and prattled a while, as acquaintance that had unexpectedly met one another. The old man was cheerful and talkative, and the way seemed short in his company. He was pleased to find himself not disregarded, accompanied them to their house, and, at the prince's request, entered with them. They placed him in the seat of honor, and set wine and conserves before him.

"Sir," said the princess, "an evening walk must give to a man of learning like you pleasures which ignorance and youth can hardly conceive. You know the qualities and the causes of all that you behold, the laws by which the river flows, the periods in which the planets perform their revolutions. Everything must supply you with contemplation, and renew the consciousness of your own dignity."

"Lady," answered he, "let the gay and the vigorous expect pleasure in their excursions; it is enough that age can obtain ease. To me the world has lost its novelty; I look round, and see what I remember to have seen in happier days. I rest against a tree, and consider that in the same shade I once disputed upon the annual overflow of the Nile with a friend who is now silent in the grave. I cast my eyes upward, fix them on the changing moon, and think with pain on the vicissitudes of life. I have ceased to take much delight in physical truth; for what have I to do with those things which I am soon to leave?"

"You may at least recreate[5] yourself," said Imlac, "with the recollection of an honorable and useful life, and enjoy the praise which all agree to give you."

"Praise," said the sage with a sigh, "is to an old man an empty sound. I have neither mother to be delighted with the reputation of her son, nor

5. Refresh.

wife to partake the honors of her husband. I have outlived my friends and my rivals. Nothing is now of much importance; for I cannot extend my interest beyond myself. Youth is delighted with applause, because it is considered as the earnest of some future good, and because the prospect of life is far extended; but to me, who am now declining to decrepitude, there is little to be feared from the malevolence of men, and yet less to be hoped from their affection or esteem. Something they may yet take away, but they can give me nothing. Riches would now be useless, and high employment would be pain. My retrospect of life recalls to my view many opportunities of good neglected, much time squandered upon trifles, and more lost in idleness and vacancy. I leave many great designs unattempted, and many great attempts unfinished. My mind is burthened with no heavy crime, and therefore I compose myself to tranquility; endeavor to abstract my thoughts from hopes and cares which, though reason knows them to be vain, still try to keep their old possession of the heart; expect,[6] with serene humility, that hour which nature cannot long delay; and hope to possess, in a better state, that happiness which here I could not find, and that virtue which here I have not attained."

He arose and went away, leaving his audience not much elated with the hope of long life. The prince consoled himself with remarking that it was not reasonable to be disappointed by this account; for age had never been considered as the season of felicity, and if it was possible to be easy in decline and weakness, it was likely that the days of vigor and alacrity might be happy; that the noon of life might be bright, if the evening could be calm.

The princess suspected that age was querulous and malignant, and delighted to repress the expectations of those who had newly entered the world. She had seen the possessors of estates look with envy on their heirs, and known many who enjoy pleasure no longer than they can confine it to themselves.

Pekuah conjectured that the man was older than he appeared, and was willing to impute his complaints to delirious dejection; or else supposed that he had been unfortunate, and was therefore discontented. "For nothing," said she, "is more common than to call our own condition the condition of life."

Imlac, who had no desire to see them depressed, smiled at the comforts which they could so readily procure to themselves, and remembered that, at the same age, he was equally confident of unmingled prosperity, and equally fertile of consolatory expedients. He forebore to force upon them unwelcome knowledge, which time itself would too soon impress. The princess and her lady retired; the madness of the astronomer hung upon their minds, and they desired Imlac to enter upon his office, and delay next morning the rising of the sun.

6. Await.

Chapter 46. The Princess and Pekuah Visit the Astronomer

The princess and Pekuah, having talked in private of Imlac's astronomer, thought his character at once so amiable and so strange, that they
could not be satisfied without a nearer knowledge, and Imlac was requested
to find the means of bringing them together.

This was somewhat difficult; the philosopher had never received any
visits from women, though he lived in a city that had in it many Europeans who followed the manners of their own countries, and many from
other parts of the world that lived there with European liberty. The
ladies would not be refused, and several schemes were proposed for the
accomplishment of their design. It was proposed to introduce them as
strangers in distress, to whom the sage was always accessible; but, after
some deliberation, it appeared, that by this artifice, no acquaintance
could be formed, for their conversation would be short, and they could
not decently importune him often. "This," said Rasselas, "is true; but I
have yet a stronger objection against the misrepresentation of your state.
I have always considered it as treason against the great republic of human
nature, to make any man's virtues the means of deceiving him, whether
on great or little occasions. All imposture weakens confidence and chills
benevolence. When the sage finds that you are not what you seemed,
he will feel the resentment natural to a man who, conscious of great
abilities, discovers that he has been tricked by understandings meaner
than his own, and, perhaps, the distrust, which he can never afterwards
wholly lay aside, may stop the voice of counsel, and close the hand of
charity; and where will you find the power of restoring his benefactions
to mankind, or his peace to himself?"

To this no reply was attempted, and Imlac began to hope that their
curiosity would subside; but next day Pekuah told him, she had now
found an honest pretense for a visit to the astronomer, for she would
solicit permission to continue under him the studies in which she had
been initiated by the Arab, and the princess might go with her either as
a fellow-student, or because a woman could not decently come alone.
"I am afraid," said Imlac, "that he will be soon weary of your company:
men advanced far in knowledge do not love to repeat the elements of
their art, and I am not certain, that even of the elements, as he will
deliver them connected with inferences, and mingled with reflections,
you are a very capable auditress." "That," said Pekuah, "must be my
care: I ask of you only to take me thither. My knowledge is, perhaps,
more than you imagine it, and by concurring always with his opinions I
shall make him think it greater than it is."

The astronomer, in pursuance of this resolution, was told, that a foreign lady, traveling in search of knowledge, had heard of his reputation,
and was desirous to become his scholar. The uncommonness of the
proposal raised at once his surprise and curiosity, and when, after a short
deliberation, he consented to admit her, he could not stay without impatience till the next day.

The ladies dressed themselves magnificently, and were attended by Imlac to the astronomer, who was pleased to see himself approached with respect by persons of so splendid an appearance. In the exchange of the first civilities he was timorous and bashful; but when the talk became regular, he recollected his powers, and justified the character which Imlac had given. Inquiring of Pekuah what could have turned her inclination towards astronomy, he received from her a history of her adventure at the pyramid, and of the time passed in the Arab's island. She told her tale with ease and elegance, and her conversation took possession of his heart. The discourse was then turned to astronomy: Pekuah displayed what she knew: he looked upon her as a prodigy of genius, and entreated her not to desist from a study which she had so happily begun.

They came again and again, and were every time more welcome than before. The sage endeavored to amuse them, that they might prolong their visits, for he found his thoughts grow brighter in their company; the clouds of solicitude vanished by degrees, as he forced himself to entertain them, and he grieved when he was left at their departure to his old employment of regulating the seasons.

The princess and her favorite had now watched his lips for several months, and could not catch a single word from which they could judge whether he continued, or not, in the opinion of his preternatural commission. They often contrived to bring him to an open declaration, but he easily eluded all their attacks, and on which side soever they pressed him escaped from them to some other topic.

As their familiarity increased they invited him often to the house of Imlac, where they distinguished him by extraordinary respect. He began gradually to delight in sublunary pleasures. He came early and departed late; labored to recommend himself by assiduity and compliance; excited their curiosity after new arts, that they might still want his assistance; and when they made any excursion of pleasure or inquiry, entreated to attend them.

By long experience of his integrity and wisdom, the prince and his sister were convinced that he might be trusted without danger; and lest he should draw any false hopes from the civilities which he received, discovered to him their condition, with the motives of their journey, and required his opinion on the choice of life.

"Of the various conditions which the world spreads before you, which you shall prefer," said the sage, "I am not able to instruct you. I can only tell that I have chosen wrong. I have passed my time in study without experience; in the attainment of sciences which can, for the most part, be but remotely useful to mankind. I have purchased knowledge at the expense of all the common comforts of life: I have missed the endearing elegance of female friendship, and the happy commerce of domestic tenderness. If I have obtained any prerogatives above other students, they have been accompanied with fear, disquiet, and scrupulosity; but even of these prerogatives, whatever they were, I have, since my thoughts have been diversified by more intercourse with the world, begun to question the reality. When I have been for a few days lost in pleasing dissipation, I am always tempted to think that my inquiries have ended in error, and that I have suffered much, and suffered it in vain."

Imlac was delighted to find that the sage's understanding was breaking through its mists, and resolved to detain him from the planets till he should forget his task of ruling them, and reason should recover its original influence.

From this time the astronomer was received into familiar friendship, and partook of all their projects and pleasures: his respect kept him attentive, and the activity of Rasselas did not leave much time unengaged. Something was always to be done; the day was spent in making observations which furnished talk for the evening, and the evening was closed with a scheme for the morrow.

The sage confessed to Imlac, that since he had mingled in the gay tumults of life, and divided his hours by a succession of amusements, he found the conviction of his authority over the skies fade gradually from his mind, and began to trust less to an opinion which he never could prove to others, and which he now found subject to variation from causes in which reason had no part. "If I am accidentally left alone for a few hours," said he, "my inveterate persuasion rushes upon my soul, and my thoughts are chained down by some irresistible violence, but they are soon disentangled by the prince's conversation, and instantaneously released at the entrance of Pekuah. I am like a man habitually afraid of specters, who is set at ease by a lamp, and wonders at the dread which harassed him in the dark, yet, if his lamp be extinguished, feels again the terrors which he knows that when it is light he shall feel no more. But I am sometimes afraid lest I indulge my quiet by criminal negligence, and voluntarily forget the great charge with which I am intrusted. If I favor myself in a known error, or am determined by my own ease in a doubtful question of this importance, how dreadful is my crime!"

"No disease of the imagination," answered Imlac, "is so difficult of cure, as that which is complicated with the dread of guilt: fancy and conscience then act interchangeably upon us, and so often shift their places, that the illusions of one are not distinguished from the dictates of the other. If fancy presents images not moral or religious, the mind drives them away when they give it pain, but when melancholic notions take the form of duty, they lay hold on the faculties without opposition, because we are afraid to exclude or banish them. For this reason the superstitious are often melancholy, and the melancholy almost always superstitious.

"But do not let the suggestions of timidity overpower your better reason: the danger of neglect can be but as the probability of the obligation, which, when you consider it with freedom, you find very little, and that little growing every day less. Open your heart to the influence of the light, which, from time to time, breaks in upon you: when scruples importune you, which you in your lucid moments know to be vain, do not stand to parley, but fly to business or to Pekuah, and keep this thought always prevalent, that you are only one atom of the mass of humanity, and have neither such virtue nor vice, as that you should be singled out for supernatural favors or afflictions."

Chapter 47. The Prince Enters, and Brings a New Topic

"All this," said the astronomer, "I have often thought, but my reason has been so long subjugated by an uncontrollable and overwhelming idea, that it durst not confide in its own decisions. I now see how fatally I betrayed my quiet, by suffering chimeras to prey upon me in secret; but melancholy shrinks from communication, and I never found a man before, to whom I could impart my troubles, though I had been certain of relief. I rejoice to find my own sentiments confirmed by yours, who are not easily deceived, and can have no motive or purpose to deceive. I hope that time and variety will dissipate the gloom that has so long surrounded me, and the latter part of my days will be spent in peace."

"Your learning and virtue," said Imlac, "may justly give you hopes."

Rasselas then entered with the princess and Pekuah, and inquired whether they had contrived any new diversion for the next day. "Such," said Nekayah, "is the state of life, that none are happy but by the anticipation of change: the change itself is nothing; when we have made it, the next wish is to change again. The world is not yet exhausted; let me see something tomorrow which I never saw before."

"Variety," said Rasselas, "is so necessary to content, that even the happy valley disgusted me by the recurrence of its luxuries; yet I could not forbear to reproach myself with impatience, when I saw the monks of St. Anthony support without complaint, a life, not of uniform delight, but uniform hardship."

"Those men," answered Imlac, "are less wretched in their silent convent than the Abyssinian princes in their prison of pleasure. Whatever is done by the monks is incited by an adequate and reasonable motive. Their labor supplies them with necessaries; it therefore cannot be omitted, and is certainly rewarded. Their devotion prepares them for another state, and reminds them of its approach, while it fits them for it. Their time is regularly distributed; one duty succeeds another, so that they are not left open to the distraction of unguided choice, nor lost in the shades of listless inactivity. There is a certain task to be performed at an appropriated hour; and their toils are cheerful, because they consider them as acts of piety, by which they are always advancing towards endless felicity."

"Do you think," said Nekayah, "that the monastic rule is a more holy and less imperfect state than any other? May not he equally hope for future happiness who converses openly with mankind, who succors the distressed by his charity, instructs the ignorant by his learning, and contributes by his industry to the general system of life; even though he should omit some of the mortifications which are practiced in the cloister, and allow himself such harmless delights as his condition may place within his reach?"

"This," said Imlac, "is a question which has long divided the wise, and perplexed the good. I am afraid to decide on either part. He that lives well in the world is better than he that lives well in a monastery. But perhaps everyone is not able to stem the temptations of public life; and if he cannot conquer, he may properly retreat. Some have little power to do good, and have likewise little strength to resist evil. Many are weary of their conflicts with adversity, and are willing to eject those passions which have long busied them in vain. And many are dismissed by age and diseases from the more laborious duties of society. In monasteries the weak and timorous may be happily sheltered, the weary may repose, and the penitent may meditate. Those retreats of prayer and contemplation have something so congenial to the mind of man, that, perhaps, there is scarcely one that does not purpose to close his life in pious abstraction with a few associates serious as himself."

"Such," said Pekuah, "has often been my wish, and I have heard the princess declare, that she should not willingly die in a crowd."

"The liberty of using harmless pleasures," proceeded Imlac, "will not be disputed; but it is still to be examined what pleasures are harmless. The evil of any pleasure that Nekayah can image is not in the act itself, but in its consequences. Pleasure, in itself harmless, may become mischievous, by endearing to us a state which we know to be transient and probatory,[7] and withdrawing our thoughts from that, of which every hour brings us nearer to the beginning, and of which no length of time will bring us to the end. Mortification is not virtuous in itself, nor has any other use, but that it disengages us from the allurements of sense. In the state of future perfection, to which we all aspire, there will be pleasure without danger, and security without restraint."

The princess was silent, and Rasselas, turning to the astronomer, asked him, whether he could not delay her retreat, by showing her something which she had not seen before.

"Your curiosity," said the sage, "has been so general, and your pursuit of knowledge so vigorous, that novelties are not now very easily to be found: but what you can no longer procure from the living may be given by the dead. Among the wonders of this country are the catacombs, or the ancient repositories, in which the bodies of the earliest generations were lodged, and where, by the virtue of the gums which embalmed them, they yet remain without corruption."

"I know not," said Rasselas, "what pleasure the sight of the catacombs can afford; but, since nothing else is offered, I am resolved to view them, and shall place this with many other things which I have done, because I would do something."

They hired a guard of horsemen, and the next day visited the cata-

---

7. Serving as a trial or test.

combs. When they were about to descend into the sepulchral caves, "Pekuah," said the princess, "we are now again invading the habitations of the dead; I know that you will stay behind; let me find you safe when I return." "No, I will not be left," answered Pekuah; "I will go down between you and the prince."

They then all descended, and roved with wonder through the labyrinth of subterraneous passages, where the bodies were laid in rows on either side.

Chapter 48. Imlac Discourses on the Nature of the Soul

"What reason," said the prince, "can be given, why the Egyptians should thus expensively preserve those carcasses which some nations consume with fire, others lay to mingle with the earth, and all agree to remove from their sight, as soon as decent rites can be performed?"

"The original of ancient customs," said Imlac, "is commonly unknown; for the practice often continues when the cause has ceased; and concerning superstitious ceremonies it is vain to conjecture; for what reason did not dictate reason cannot explain. I have long believed that the practice of embalming arose only from tenderness to the remains of relations or friends, and to this opinion I am more inclined, because it seems impossible that this care should have been general: had all the dead been embalmed, their repositories must in time have been more spacious than the dwellings of the living. I suppose only the rich or honorable were secured from corruption, and the rest left to the course of nature.

"But it is commonly supposed that the Egyptians believed the soul to live as long as the body continued undissolved, and therefore tried this method of eluding death."

"Could the wise Egyptians," said Nekayah, "think so grossly of the soul? If the soul could once survive its separation, what could it afterwards receive or suffer from the body?"

"The Egyptians would doubtless think erroneously," said the astronomer, "in the darkness of heathenism, and the first dawn of philosophy. The nature of the soul is still disputed amidst all our opportunities of clearer knowledge: some yet say, that it may be material, who, nevertheless, believe it to be immortal."

"Some," answered Imlac, "have indeed said that the soul is material, but I can scarcely believe that any man has thought it, who knew how to think; for all the conclusions of reason enforce the immateriality of mind, and all the notices of sense and investigations of science concur to prove the unconsciousness of matter.

"It was never supposed that cogitation is inherent in matter, or that every particle is a thinking being. Yet if any part of matter be devoid of thought, what part can we suppose to think? Matter can differ from matter only in form, density, bulk, motion, and direction of motion: to which of these, however varied or combined, can consciousness be annexed? To be round or square, to be solid or fluid, to be great or little, to be moved slowly or swiftly one way or another, are modes of material existence, all equally alien from the nature of cogitation. If matter be once without thought, it can only be made to think by some new modification, but all the modifications which it can admit are equally unconnected with cogitative powers."

"But the materialists," said the astronomer, "urge that matter may have qualities with which we are unacquainted."

"He who will determine," returned Imlac, "against that which he knows, because there may be something which he knows not; he that can set hypothetical possibility against acknowledged certainty, is not to be admitted among reasonable beings. All that we know of matter is, that matter is inert, senseless and lifeless; and if this conviction cannot be opposed but by referring us to something that we know not, we have all the evidence that human intellect can admit. If that which is known may be overruled by that which is unknown, no being, not omniscient, can arrive at certainty."

"Yet let us not," said the astronomer, "too arrogantly limit the Creator's power."

"It is no limitation of omnipotence," replied the poet, "to suppose that one thing is not consistent with another, that the same proposition cannot be at once true and false, that the same number cannot be even and odd, that cogitation cannot be conferred on that which is created incapable of cogitation."

"I know not," said Nekayah, "any great use of this question. Does that immateriality, which, in my opinion, you have sufficiently proved, necessarily include eternal duration?"

"Of immateriality," said Imlac, "our ideas are negative, and therefore obscure. Immateriality seems to imply a natural power of perpetual duration as a consequence of exemption from all causes of decay: whatever perishes, is destroyed by the solution of its contexture,[8] and separation of its parts; nor can we conceive how that which has no parts, and therefore admits no solution, can be naturally corrupted or impaired."

"I know not," said Rasselas, "how to conceive anything without extension: what is extended must have parts, and you allow, that whatever has parts may be destroyed."

"Consider your own conceptions," replied Imlac, "and the difficulty will be less. You will find substance without extension. An ideal form is no less real than material bulk: yet an ideal form has no extension. It is no less certain, when you think on a pyramid, that your mind possesses the idea of a pyramid, than that the pyramid itself is standing. What space does the idea of a pyramid occupy more than the idea of a grain of corn? or how can either idea suffer laceration? As is the effect such is the cause; as thought is, such is the power that thinks; a power impassive and indiscerptible."[9]

---

8. Dissolution of its structure.   9. Not to be separated.

"But the Being," said Nekayah, "whom I fear to name, the Being which made the soul, can destroy it."

"He, surely, can destroy it," answered Imlac, "since, however unperishable, it receives from a superior nature its power of duration. That it will not perish by any inherent cause of decay, or principle of corruption, may be shown by philosophy; but philosophy can tell no more. That it will not be annihilated by him that made it, we must humbly learn from higher authority."

The whole assembly stood a while silent and collected. "Let us return," said Rasselas, "from this scene of mortality. How gloomy would be these mansions of the dead to him who did not know that he shall never die; that what now acts shall continue its agency, and what now thinks shall think on for ever. Those that lie here stretched before us, the wise and the powerful of ancient times, warn us to remember the shortness of our present state: they were, perhaps, snatched away while they were busy, like us, in the choice of life."

"To me," said the princess, "the choice of life is become less important; I hope hereafter to think only on the choice of eternity."

They then hastened out of the caverns, and, under the protection of their guard, returned to Cairo.

Chapter 49. The Conclusion, in Which Nothing Is Concluded

It was now the time of the inundation of the Nile: a few days after their visit to the catacombs, the river began to rise.

They were confined to their house. The whole region being under water gave them no invitation to any excursions, and being well supplied with materials for talk, they diverted themselves with comparisons of the different forms of life which they had observed, and with various schemes of happiness which each of them had formed.

Pekuah was never so much charmed with any place as the convent of St. Anthony, where the Arab restored her to the princess, and wished only to fill it with pious maidens, and to be made prioress of the order; she was weary of expectation and disgust,[1] and would gladly be fixed in some unvariable state.

The princess thought that, of all sublunary things, knowledge was the best: she desired first to learn all sciences, and then purposed to found a college of learned women, in which she would preside, that, by conversing with the old and educating the young, she might divide her time between the acquisition and communication of wisdom, and raise up for the next age models of prudence, and patterns of piety.

The prince desired a little kingdom, in which he might administer justice in his own person, and see all the parts of government with his own eyes; but he could never fix the limits of his dominion, and was always adding to the number of his subjects.

1. Aversion.

Imlac and the astronomer were contented to be driven along the stream of life, without directing their course to any particular port.

Of these wishes that they had formed, they well knew that none could be obtained. They deliberated a while what was to be done, and resolved, when the inundation should cease, to return to Abyssinia.[2]

1759

Rambler No. 4[1]

[*On Fiction*]

Saturday, March 31, 1750

Simul et jucunda et idonea dicere vitae.
—HORACE, *Art of Poetry*, 334
And join both profit and delight in one.
—CREECH

The works of fiction with which the present generation seems more particularly delighted are such as exhibit life in its true state, diversified only by accidents that daily happen in the world, and influenced by passions and qualities which are really to be found in conversing with mankind.

This kind of writing may be termed, not improperly, the comedy of romance, and is to be conducted nearly by the rules of comic poetry. Its province is to bring about natural events by easy means, and to keep up curiosity without the help of wonder: it is therefore precluded from the machines[2] and expedients of the heroic romance, and can neither employ giants to snatch away a lady from the nuptial rites, nor knights to bring her back from captivity; it can neither bewilder its personages in deserts, nor lodge them in imaginary castles.

I remember a remark made by Scaliger upon Pontanus,[3] that all his writings are filled with the same images; and that if you take from him his lilies and his roses, his satyrs and his dryads, he will have nothing left that can be called poetry. In like manner, almost all the fictions of the last age will vanish if you deprive them of a hermit and a wood, a battle and a shipwreck.

Why this wild strain of imagination found reception so long in polite and learned ages, it is not easy to conceive; but we cannot wonder that

2. Probably not, as is often suggested, to the Happy Valley, which the travelers earlier fled as a prison. Presumably the travelers return, with whatever wisdom they have gained, but also with their cherished illusions, to share the common destiny of mankind.

1. The *Rambler*, almost wholly written by Johnson himself, appeared every Tuesday and Saturday from Mar. 20, 1750, to Mar. 14, 1752—years in which Johnson was writing the *Dictionary*. It is a successor of the *Tatler* and the *Spectator*, but it is much more serious in tone than the earlier periodicals. Johnson's reputation as a moralist and a stylist was established by these essays; because of them Boswell first conceived the ambition to seek Johnson's acquaintance.

2. The technical term in neoclassical critical theory for the supernatural agents who intervene in human affairs in epic and tragedy.

3. Julius Caesar Scaliger (1484–1558) critized the Latin poems of the Italian poet Jovianus Pontanus (1426–1503).

while readers could be procured, the authors were willing to continue it; for when a man had by practice gained some fluency of language, he had no further care than to retire to his closet, let loose his invention, and heat his mind with incredibilities; a book was thus produced without fear of criticism, without the toil of study, without knowledge of nature, or acquaintance with life.

The task of our present writers is very different; it requires, together with that learning which is to be gained from books, that experience which can never be attained by solitary diligence, but must arise from general converse and accurate observation of the living world. Their performances have, as Horace expresses it, *plus oneris quanto veniae minus*,[4] little indulgence, and therefore more difficulty. They are engaged in portraits of which everyone knows the original, and can detect any deviation from exactness of resemblance. Other writings are safe, except from the malice of learning, but these are in danger from every common reader; as the slipper ill executed was censured by a shoemaker who happened to stop in his way at the Venus of Apelles.[5]

But the fear of not being approved as just copiers of human manners is not the most important concern that an author of this sort ought to have before him. These books are written chiefly to the young, the ignorant, and the idle, to whom they serve as lectures of conduct, and introductions into life. They are the entertainment of minds unfurnished with ideas, and therefore easily susceptible of impressions; not fixed by principles, and therefore easily following the current of fancy; not informed by experience, and consequently open to every false suggestion and partial account.

That the highest degree of reverence should be paid to youth, and that nothing indecent should be suffered to approach their eyes or ears, are precepts extorted by sense and virtue from an ancient writer by no means eminent for chastity of thought.[6] The same kind, though not the same degree, of caution, is required in everything which is laid before them, to secure them from unjust prejudices, perverse opinions, and incongruous combinations of images.

In the romances formerly written, every transaction and sentiment was so remote from all that passes among men that the reader was in very little danger of making any applications to himself; the virtues and crimes were equally beyond his sphere of activity; and he amused himself with heroes and with traitors, deliverers and persecutors, as with beings of another species, whose actions were regulated upon motives of their own, and who had neither faults nor excellencies in common with himself.

But when an adventurer is leveled with the rest of the world, and acts in such scenes of the universal drama as may be the lot of any other

4. *Epistles* 2.1.170.
5. According to Pliny the Younger (*Naturalis Historia* 35.85), the Greek painter Apelles of Kos (4th century B.C.) corrected the drawing of a sandal after hearing a shoemaker criticize it as faulty, but when the flattered artisan dared to find fault with the drawing of a leg, the artist bade him "stick to his last."
6. Juvenal, *Satires* 14.1–58.

man, young spectators fix their eyes upon him with closer attention, and hope, by observing his behavior and success, to regulate their own practices when they shall be engaged in the like part.

For this reason these familiar histories may perhaps be made of greater use than the solemnities of professed morality, and convey the knowledge of vice and virtue with more efficacy than axioms and definitions. But if the power of example is so great as to take possession of the memory by a kind of violence, and produce effects almost without the intervention of the will, care ought to be taken that when the choice is unrestrained, the best examples only should be exhibited; and that which is likely to operate so strongly should not be mischievous or uncertain in its effects.

The chief advantage which these fictions have over real life is that their authors are at liberty, though not to invent, yet to select objects, and to cull from the mass of mankind those individuals upon which the attention ought most to be employed; as a diamond, though it cannot be made, may be polished by art, and placed in such situation as to display that luster which before was buried among common stones.

It is justly considered as the greatest excellency of art to imitate nature; but it is necessary to distinguish those parts of nature which are most proper for imitation: greater care is still required in representing life, which is so often discolored by passion or deformed by wickedness. If the world be promiscuously described, I cannot see of what use it can be to read the account; or why it may not be as safe to turn the eye immediately upon mankind as upon a mirror which shows all that presents itself without discrimination.

It is therefore not a sufficient vindication of a character that it is drawn as it appears; for many characters ought never to be drawn: nor of a narrative that the train of events is agreeable to observation and experience; for that observation which is called knowledge of the world will be found much more frequently to make men cunning than good. The purpose of these writings is surely not only to show mankind, but to provide that they may be seen hereafter with less hazard; to teach the means of avoiding the snares which are laid by Treachery for Innocence, without infusing any wish for that superiority with which the betrayer flatters his vanity; to give the power of counteracting fraud without the temptation to practice it; to initiate youth by mock encounters in the art of necessary defense, and to increase prudence without impairing virtue.

Many writers, for the sake of following nature, so mingle good and bad qualities in their principal personages that they are both equally conspicuous; and as we accompany them through their adventures with delight, and are led by degrees to interest ourselves in their favor, we lose the abhorrence of their faults because they do not hinder our pleasure, or perhaps regard them with some kindness for being united with so much merit.

There have been men indeed splendidly wicked, whose endowments threw a brightness on their crimes, and whom scarce any villainy made perfectly detestable because they never could be wholly divested of their excellencies; but such have been in all ages the great corrupters of the world, and their resemblance ought no more to be preserved than the art of murdering without pain.

Some have advanced, without due attention to the consequence of this notion, that certain virtues have their correspondent faults, and therefore that to exhibit either apart is to deviate from probability. Thus men are observed by Swift to be "grateful in the same degree as they are resentful." This principle, with others of the same kind, supposes man to act from a brute impulse, and pursue a certain degree of inclination without any choice of the object; for, otherwise, though it should be allowed that gratitude and resentment arise from the same constitution of the passions, it follows not that they will be equally indulged when reason is consulted; yet, unless that consequence be admitted, this sagacious maxim becomes an empty sound, without any relation to practice or to life.

Nor is it evident that even the first motions to these effects are always in the same proportion. For pride, which produces quickness of resentment, will obstruct gratitude by unwillingness to admit that inferiority which obligation implies; and it is very unlikely that he who cannot think he receives a favor will acknowledge or repay it.

It is of the utmost importance to mankind that positions of this tendency should be laid open and confuted; for while men consider good and evil as springing from the same root, they will spare the one for the sake of the other, and in judging, if not of others at least of themselves, will be apt to estimate their virtues by their vices. To this fatal error all those will contribute who confound the colors of right and wrong, and, instead of helping to settle their boundaries, mix them with so much art that no common mind is able to disunite them.

In narratives where historical veracity has no place, I cannot discover why there should not be exhibited the most perfect idea of virtue; of virtue not angelical, nor above probability (for what we cannot credit, we shall never imitate), but the highest and purest that humanity can reach, which, exercised in such trials as the various revolutions of things shall bring upon it, may, by conquering some calamities and enduring others, teach us what we may hope, and what we can perform. Vice (for vice is necessary to be shown) should always disgust; nor should the graces of gaiety, nor the dignity of courage, be so united with it as to reconcile it to the mind. Wherever it appears, it should raise hatred by the malignity of its practices, and contempt by the meanness of its stratagems: for while it is supported by either parts or spirit, it will be seldom heartily abhorred. The Roman tyrant was content to be hated if he was but feared;[7] and there are thousands of the readers of romances willing to be thought wicked if they may be allowed to be wits. It is therefore to be steadily inculcated that virtue is the highest proof of understanding,

---

7. The emperor Tiberius. See Suetonius's *Lives of the Caesars.*

and the only solid basis of greatness; and that vice is the natural consequence of narrow thoughts; that it begins in mistake, and ends in ignominy.

Rambler No. 60

[*Biography*]

Saturday, October 13, 1750

—Quid sit pulchrum, quid turpe, quid utile, quid non,
Plenius ac melius Chrysippo et Crantore dicit.
—HORACE, *Epistles*, 1.2. 3–4

> Whose works the beautiful and base contain,
> Of vice and virtue more instructive rules,
> Than all the sober sages of the schools.
> —FRANCIS

All joy or sorrow for the happiness or calamities of others is produced
by an act of the imagination, that realizes the event, however fictitious,
or approximates it, however remote, by placing us, for a time, in the
condition of him whose fortune we contemplate; so that we feel, while
the deception lasts, whatever motions would be excited by the same good
or evil happening to ourselves.

Our passions are therefore more strongly moved, in proportion as we
can more readily adopt the pains or pleasure proposed to our minds, by
recognizing them as once our own, or considering them as naturally
incident to our state of life. It is not easy for the most artful writer to give
us an interest in happiness or misery, which we think ourselves never
likely to feel, and with which we have never yet been made acquainted.
Histories of the downfall of kingdoms, and revolutions of empires, are
read with great tranquility; the imperial tragedy pleases common auditors only by its pomp of ornament, and grandeur of ideas; and the man
whose faculties have been engrossed by business, and whose heart never
fluttered but at the rise or fall of stocks, wonders how the attention can
be seized, or the affections agitated, by a tale of love.

Those parallel circumstances, and kindred images to which we readily
conform our minds, are, above all other writings, to be found in narratives of the lives of particular persons; and therefore no species of writing
seems more worthy of cultivation than biography, since none can be
more delightful or more useful, none can more certainly enchain the
heart by irresistible interest, or more widely diffuse instruction to every
diversity of condition.

The general and rapid narratives of history, which involve a thousand
fortunes in the business of a day, and complicate innumerable incidents
in one great transaction, afford few lessons applicable to private life,
which derives its comforts and its wretchedness from the right or wrong
management of things, which nothing but their frequency makes con-

siderable, *Parva si non fiunt quotidie*, says Pliny,[1] and which can have no place in those relations which never descend below the consultation of senates, the motions of armies, and the schemes of conspirators.

I have often thought that there has rarely passed a life of which a judicious and faithful narrative would not be useful. For, not only every man has in the mighty mass of the world great numbers in the same condition with himself, to whom his mistakes and miscarriages, escapes and expedients, would be of immediate and apparent use; but there is such an uniformity in the state of man, considered apart from adventitious and separable decorations and disguises, that there is scarce any possibility of good or ill, but is common to humankind. A great part of the time of those who are placed at the greatest distance by fortune, or by temper, must unavoidably pass in the same manner; and though, when the claims of nature are satisfied, caprice, and vanity, and accident, begin to produce discriminations and peculiarities, yet the eye is not very heedful or quick, which cannot discover the same causes still[2] terminating their influence in the same effects, though sometimes accelerated, sometimes retarded, or perplexed by multiplied combinations. We are all prompted by the same motives, all deceived by the same fallacies, all animated by hope, obstructed by danger, entangled by desire, and seduced by pleasure.

It is frequently objected to relations of particular lives, that they are not distinguished by any striking or wonderful vicissitudes. The scholar who passed his life among his books, the merchant who conducted only his own affairs, the priest whose sphere of action was not extended beyond that of his duty, are considered as no proper objects of public regard, however they might have excelled in their several stations, whatever might have been their learning, integrity, and piety. But this notion arises from false measures of excellence and dignity, and must be eradicated by considering, that in the esteem of uncorrupted reason, what is of most use is of most value.

It is, indeed, not improper to take honest advantages of prejudice, and to gain attention by a celebrated name; but the business of the biographer is often to pass slightly over those performances and incidents, which produce vulgar greatness, to lead the thoughts into domestic privacies, and display the minute details of daily life, where exterior appendages are cast aside, and men excel each other only by prudence and by virtue. The account of Thuanus[3] is, with great propriety, said by its author to have been written, that it might lay open to posterity the private and familiar character of that man, *cujus ingenium et candorem ex ipsius scriptis sunt olim semper miraturi*, whose candor and genius will to the end of time be by his writings preserved in admiration.

There are many invisible circumstances which, whether we read as

---

1. Pliny the Younger, *Epistles* 3.1. Johnson translates the phrase in the preceding clause.
2. Always
3. Jacques-Auguste de Thou (1553–1617), an important French historian, of whom Nicholas Rigault wrote a brief biography, a sentence of which Johnson quotes and translates below.

inquirers after natural or moral knowledge, whether we intend to enlarge our science, or increase our virtue, are more important than public occurrences. Thus Sallust, the great master of nature, has not forgot, in his account of Catiline,[4] to remark that *his walk was now quick, and again slow*, as an indication of a mind revolving something with violent commotion. Thus the story of Melancthon[5] affords a striking lecture on the value of time, by informing us that when he made an appointment, he expected not only the hour, but the minute to be fixed, that the day might not run out in the idleness of suspense; and all the plans and enterprises of De Witt are now of less importance to the world, than that part of his personal character, which represents him as careful of his health, and negligent of his life.[6]

But biography has often been allotted to writers who seem very little acquainted with the nature of their task, or very negligent about the performance. They rarely afford any other account than might be collected from public papers, but imagine themselves writing a life when they exhibit a chronological series of actions or preferments; and so little regard the manners or behavior of their heroes, that more knowledge may be gained of a man's real character, by a short conversation with one of his servants, than from a formal and studied narrative, begun with his pedigree, and ended with his funeral.

If now and then they condescend to inform the world of particular facts, they are not always so happy as to select the most important. I know not well what advantage posterity can receive from the only circumstance by which Tickell has distinguished Addison from the rest of mankind, the irregularity of his pulse:[7] nor can I think myself overpaid for the time spent in reading the life of Malherbe, by being enabled to relate, after the learned biographer,[8] that Malherbe had two predominant opinions; one, that the looseness of a single woman might destroy all her boast of ancient descent; the other, that the French beggars made use very improperly and barbarously of the phrase *noble gentleman*, because either word included the sense of both.

There are, indeed, some natural reasons why these narratives are often written by such as were not likely to give much instruction or delight, and why most accounts of particular persons are barren and useless. If a life be delayed till interest and envy are at an end, we may hope for impartiality, but must expect little intelligence; for the incidents which give excellence to biography are of a volatile and evanescent kind, such as soon escape the memory, and are rarely transmitted by tradition. We know how few can portray a living acquaintance, except by his most prominent and observable particularities, and the grosser features of his mind; and it may be easily imagined how much of this little knowledge

---

4. Sallust, a Roman historian of the first century B.C., wrote an account of Catiline's conspiracy against the Roman state.

5. Camerarius wrote a life of Melancthon, a German theologian of the 16th century.

6. Sir William Temple, characterizing the Dutch statesman John De Witt.

7. From Thomas Tickell's preface to Addision's *Works* (1721).

8. The life of the French poet François de Malherbe (1555–1628) was written by Honorat de Racan.

may be lost in imparting it, and how soon a succession of copies will lose all resemblance of the original.

If the biographer writes from personal knowledge, and makes haste to gratify the public curiosity, there is danger lest his interest, his fear, his gratitude, or his tenderness, overpower his fidelity, and tempt him to conceal, if not to invent. There are many who think it an act of piety to hide the faults or failings of their friends, even when they can no longer suffer by their detection; we therefore see whole ranks of characters adorned with uniform panegyric, and not to be known from one another, but by extrinsic and casual circumstances. "Let me remember," says Hale, "when I find myself inclined to pity a criminal, that there is likewise a pity due to the country."[9] If we owe regard to the memory of the dead, there is yet more respect to be paid to knowledge, to virtue, and to truth.

A Dictionary of the English Language

Before Johnson no standard dictionary of the English language existed. The want had troubled speakers of English for some time, both because Italian and French academies had produced major dictionaries of their own tongues, and because, in the absence of any authority, English seemed likely to change utterly from one generation to another. Many eighteenth-century authors feared that their own language would soon become obsolete: as Pope wrote in *An Essay on Criticism*,

> Our sons their fathers' failing language see,
> And such as Chaucer is shall Dryden be.

A dictionary could help retard such change; and commercially it would be a book that everyone would need to buy. In 1746 a group of London publishers commissioned Johnson, still an unknown author, to undertake the project. He hoped to finish it in three years; it took him nine. But the quantity and quality of work he accomplished, aided only by six part-time assistants, made him famous as "Dictionary Johnson." The *Dictionary* remained a standard reference book for one hundred years.

Johnson's achievement is notable in three respects: its size (40,000 words); the wealth of illustrative quotations; and the excellence of the definitions. No earlier English dictionary rivaled the scope of Johnson's two large folio volumes. About 114,000 quotations, gathered from the best English writers from Sidney to the eighteenth century, exemplify the usage of words as well as their meanings. Above all it was the definitions, however, which established the authority of Johnson's *Dictionary*. A small selection is only too likely to concentrate on a few amusing or notorious definitions; but the great majority are full, clear, and totally free from eccentricity. Indeed, many of them are still repeated in modern dictionaries. Language, Johnson knew, cannot be fixed once and for all; many of the words he defines have radically changed meaning since the eighteenth century. Yet Johnson did more than any man of his time to preserve the ideal of a standard English.

---

9. From Gilbert Burnet's *Life and Death of Sir Matthew Hale* (1682).

From A Dictionary of the English Language

From *Preface*

* * *

A large work is difficult because it is large, even though all its parts might singly be performed with facility; where there are many things to be done, each must be allowed its share of time and labor, in the proportion only which it bears to the whole; nor can it be expected that the stones which form the dome of a temple should be squared and polished like the diamond of a ring.

Of the event of this work, for which, having labored it with so much application, I cannot but have some degree of parental fondness, it is natural to form conjectures. Those who have been persuaded to think well of my design will require that it should fix our language, and put a stop to those alterations which time and chance have hitherto been suffered to make in it without opposition. With this consequence I will confess that I flattered myself for a while;[1] but now begin to fear that I have indulged expectation which neither reason nor experience can justify. When we see men grow old and die at a certain time one after another, from century to century, we laugh at the elixir that promises to prolong life to a thousand years; and with equal justice may the lexicographer be derided, who being able to produce no example of a nation that has preserved their words and phrases from mutability, shall imagine that his dictionary can embalm his language and secure it from corruption and decay, that it is in his power to change sublunary nature, or clear the world at once from folly, vanity, and affectation.

With this hope, however, academies have been instituted, to guard the avenues of their languages, to retain fugitives, and repulse intruders; but their vigilance and activity have hitherto been vain; sounds are too volatile and subtle for legal restraints; to enchain syllables, and to lash the wind, are equally the undertakings of pride, unwilling to measure its desires by its strength. The French language has visibly changed under the inspection of the academy;[2] the style of Amelot's translation of father Paul is observed by Le Courayer to be *un peu passé*;[3] and no Italian will maintain that the diction of any modern writer is not perceptibly different from that of Boccace, Machiavel, or Caro.[4]

Total and sudden transformations of a language seldom happen; conquests and migrations are now very rare: but there are other causes of

1. Johnson's *Plan* (1747) had called for "a dictionary by which the pronunciation of our language may be fixed, and its attainment facilitated; by which its purity may be preserved, its use ascertained, and its duration lengthened."
2. The French academy, founded to purify the French language, had produced a dictionary in 1694; but revisions were necessary within a few years.

3. "A bit old-fashioned." Le Courayer's translation (1736) of Father Paolo Sarpi's *History of the Council of Trent* superseded Amelot's (1683).
4. Like Boccaccio (1313–1375) and Machiavelli (1469–1527), Annibale Caro (1507–1566) was a classic Italian stylist whose work had preceded the dictionary published in 1612 by the Italian academy.

change, which, though slow in their operation, and invisible in their progress, are perhaps as much superior to human resistance as the revolutions of the sky, or intumescence[5] of the tide. Commerce, however necessary, however lucrative, as it depraves the manners, corrupts the language; they that have frequent intercourse with strangers, to whom they endeavor to accommodate themselves, must in time learn a mingled dialect, like the jargon which serves the traffickers[6] on the Mediterranean and Indian coasts. This will not always be confined to the exchange, the warehouse, or the port, but will be communicated by degrees to other ranks of the people, and be at last incorporated with the current speech.

There are likewise internal causes equally forcible. The language most likely to continue long without alteration would be that of a nation raised a little, and but a little, above barbarity, secluded from strangers, and totally employed in procuring the conveniencies of life; either without books, or, like some of the Mahometan countries, with very few: men thus busied and unlearned, having only such words as common use requires, would perhaps long continue to express the same notions by the same signs. But no such constancy can be expected in a people polished by arts, and classed by subordination, where one part of the community is sustained and accommodated by the labor of the other. Those who have much leisure to think, will always be enlarging the stock of ideas, and every increase of knowledge, whether real or fancied, will produce new words, or combinations of words. When the mind is unchained from necessity, it will range after convenience; when it is left at large in the fields of speculation, it will shift opinions; as any custom is disused, the words that expressed it must perish with it; as any opinion grows popular, it will innovate speech in the same proportion as it alters practice.

As by the cultivation of various sciences, a language is amplified, it will be more furnished with words deflected from their original sense; the geometrician will talk of a courtier's zenith, or the eccentric virtue of a wild hero, and the physician of sanguine expectations and phlegmatic delays.[7] Copiousness of speech will give opportunities to capricious choice, by which some words will be preferred, and others degraded; vicissitudes of fashion will enforce the use of new, or extend the signification of known terms. The tropes[8] of poetry will make hourly encroachments, and the metaphorical will become the current sense: pronunciation will be varied by levity or ignorance, and the pen must at length comply with the tongue; illiterate writers will at one time or other, by public infatuation, rise into renown, who, not knowing the original import of words, will use them with colloquial licentiousness, confound distinc-

---

5. Swelling.
6. Traders.
7. "Zenith" (the point of the sky directly overhead) and "eccentric" (deviating from the center) were originally astronomical and geometrical terms;

"sanguine" and "phlegmatic" once referred only to the physiological predominance of blood or phlegm.
8. "A change of a word from its original signification" (Johnson's *Dictionary*).

tion, and forget propriety. As politeness increases, some expressions will be considered as too gross and vulgar for the delicate, others as too formal and ceremonious for the gay and airy; new phrases are therefore adopted, which must, for the same reasons, be in time dismissed. Swift, in his petty treatise on the English language,[9] allows that new words must sometimes be introduced, but proposes that none should be suffered to become obsolete. But what makes a word obsolete, more than general agreement to forbear it? and how shall it be continued, when it conveys an offensive idea, or recalled again in the mouths of mankind, when it has once by disuse become unfamiliar, and by unfamiliarity unpleasing.

There is another cause of alteration more prevalent than any other, which yet in the present state of the world cannot be obviated. A mixture of two languages will produce a third distinct from both, and they will always be mixed, where the chief part of education, and the most conspicuous accomplishment, is skill in ancient or in foreign tongues. He that has long cultivated another language, will find its words and combinations crowd upon his memory; and haste and negligence, refinement and affectation, will obtrude borrowed terms and exotic expressions.

The great pest of speech is frequency of translation. No book was every turned from one language into another, without imparting something of its native idiom; this is the most mischievous and comprehensive innovation; single words may enter by thousands, and the fabric of the tongue continue the same, but new phraseology changes much at once; it alters not the single stones of the building, but the order[1] of the columns. If an academy should be established for the cultivation of our style, which I, who can never wish to see dependence multiplied, hope the spirit of English liberty will hinder or destroy, let them, instead of compiling grammars and dictionaries, endeavor with all their influence to stop the license of translators, whose idleness and ignorance, if it be suffered to proceed, will reduce us to babble a dialect of France.

If the changes that we fear be thus irresistible, what remains but to acquiesce with silence, as in the other insurmountable distresses of humanity? It remains that we retard what we cannot repel, that we palliate what we cannot cure. Life may be lengthened by care, though death cannot be ultimately defeated: tongues, like governments, have a natural tendency to degeneration; we have long preserved our constitution, let us make some struggles for our language.

In hope of giving longevity to that which its own nature forbids to be immortal, I have devoted this book, the labor of years, to the honor of my country, that we may no longer yield the palm of philology without a contest to the nations of the continent. The chief glory of every people arises from its authors: whether I shall add anything by my own writings to the reputation of English literature, must be left to time. Much of my

---

9. *A Proposal for Correcting, Improving, and Ascertaining the English Tongue* (1712). "Petty": little.

1. Architectural mode (Doric, etc.), which determines the style and proportions of columns.

life has been lost under the pressures of disease; much has been trifled away; and much has always been spent in provision for the day that was passing over me; but I shall not think my employment useless or ignoble, if by my assistance foreign nations, and distant ages, gain access to the propagators of knowledge, and understand the teachers of truth; if my labors afford light to the repositories of science, and add celebrity to Bacon, to Hooker, to Milton, and to Boyle.[2]

When I am animated by this wish, I look with pleasure on my book, however defective; and deliver it to the world with the spirit of a man that has endeavored well. That it will immediately become popular I have not promised to myself: a few wild blunders and risible absurdities, from which no work of such multiplicity was ever free, may for a time furnish folly with laughter, and harden ignorance in contempt; but useful diligence will at last prevail, and there never can be wanting some who distinguish desert;[3] who will consider that no dictionary of a living tongue ever can be perfect, since while it is hastening to publication, some words are budding, and some falling away; that a whole life cannot be spent upon syntax and etymology, and that even a whole life would not be sufficient; that he, whose design includes whatever language can express, must often speak of what he does not understand; that a writer will sometimes be hurried by eagerness to the end, and sometimes faint with weariness under a task, which Scaliger compares to the labors of the anvil and the mine;[4] that what is obvious is not always known, and what is known is not always present; that sudden fits of inadvertency will surprise vigilance, slight avocations[5] will reduce attention, and casual eclipses of the mind will darken learning; and that the writer shall often in vain trace his memory at the moment of need, for that which yesterday he knew with intuitive readiness, and which will come uncalled into his thoughts tomorrow.

In this work, when it shall be found that much is omitted, let it not be forgotten that much likewise is performed; and though no book was ever spared out of tenderness to the author, and the world is little solicitous to know whence proceeded the faults of that which it condemns; yet it may gratify curiosity to inform it, that the *English Dictionary* was written with little assistance of the learned, and without any patronage of the great;[6] not in the soft obscurities of retirement, or under the shelter of academic bowers, but amidst inconvenience and distraction, in sickness and in sorrow: and it may repress the triumph of malignant criticism to observe, that if our language is not here fully displayed, I have only failed in an attempt which no human powers have hitherto completed. If the lexicons of ancient tongues, now immutably fixed, and comprised

---

2. Richard Hooker wrote *The Laws of Ecclesiastical Polity* (1594–97), a famous defense of the Church of England. Robert Boyle (1627–1691) was a leading physicist and chemist. "Science": knowledge.
3. Merit.
4. Joseph Justus Scaliger (1540–1609), a great scholar and lexicographer, wrote Latin verses suggesting that criminals should be condemned to lexicography.
5. Whatever calls one aside.
6. In a famous letter to Lord Chesterfield, Johnson expressed his resentment of patrons who failed to make good their promises.

in a few volumes, be yet, after the toil of successive ages, inadequate and delusive; if the aggregated knowledge and cooperating diligence of the Italian academicians did not secure them from the censure of Beni;[7] if the embodied critics of France, when fifty years had been spent upon their work, were obliged to change its economy,[8] and give their second edition another form, I may surely be contented without the praise of perfection, which, if I could obtain, in this gloom of solitude, what would it avail me? I have protracted my work till most of those whom I wished to please have sunk into the grave,[9] and success and miscarriage are empty sounds: I therefore dismiss it with frigid tranquility, having little to fear or hope from censure or from praise.

[*Some Definitions: A Small Anthology*][1]

ANTHO′LOGY. *n.*

1. A collection of flowers.

To CANT. *v.*

To talk in the jargon of particular professions, or in any kind of formal affected language, or with a peculiar and studied tone of voice.

> Men *cant* endlessly about *materia forma*; and hunt chimeras by rules of art, or dress up ignorance in words of bulk or sound, which may stop up the mouth of inquiry.—*Glanville's Scepsis Scientifica.*

ENTHU′SIASM. *n.*

1. A vain belief of private revelation; a vain confidence of divine favor or communication.

> *Enthusiasm* is founded neither on reason nor divine revelation, but rises from the conceits of a warmed or overweening brain.—*Locke.*

GE′NIUS. *n.*

1. The protecting or ruling power of men, places, or things.

> And as I awake, sweet music breathe,
> Sent by some spirit to mortals good,
> Or th' unseen *genius* of the wood.—*Milton.*

2. A man endowed with superior faculties.

3. Mental power or faculties.

4. Disposition of nature by which anyone is qualified for some peculiar employment.

5. Nature; disposition.

IMA′GINATION. *n.*

1. Fancy; the power of forming ideal pictures; the power of representing things absent to one's self or others.

2. Conception; image in the mind; idea.

3. Contrivance; scheme.

LEXICO′GRAPHER. *n.*

A writer of dictionaries; a harmless drudge, that busies himself in tracing the original, and detailing the signification of words.

---

7. Paolo Beni's *L'Anticrusca* (1612) violently attacked the first edition of the *Vocabolario* (the Italian dictionary).
8. Organization.

9. Johnson's wife had died three years earlier.
1. Johnson's definitions include etymologies and illustrative quotations, some of which are omitted in this selection.

MELANCHO'LY. *n.*

1. A disease, supposed to proceed from a redundance of black bile.
2. A kind of madness, in which the mind is always fixed on one object.
3. A gloomy, pensive, discontented temper.

NA'TURE. *n.*

1. An imaginary being supposed to preside over the material and animal world.

> Thou, *nature*, art my goddess; to thy law
> My services are bound.—*Shakespeare.*

2. The native state or properties of anything, by which it is discriminated from others.
3. The constitution of an animated body.
4. Disposition of mind; temper.
5. The regular course of things.
6. The compass of natural existence.
7. Natural affection, or reverence; native sensations.
8. The state or operation of the material world.
9. Sort; species.
10. Sentiments or images adapted to nature, or comformable to truth and reality.
11. Physics; the science which teaches the qualities of things.

> *Nature* and *nature's* laws lay hid in night,
> God said, Let Newton be, and all was light.—*Pope.*

NE'TWORK. *n.*

Anything reticulated or decussated, at equal distances, with interstices between the intersections.

OATS. *n.*

A grain, which in England is generally given to horses, but in Scotland supports the people.

PA'STERN. *n.*

1. The knee of an horse.[2]

PA'TRON. *n.*

1. One who countenances, supports, or protects. Commonly a wretch who supports with insolence, and is paid with flattery.

PE'NSION. *n.*

An allowance made to anyone without an equivalent. In England it is generally understood to mean pay given to a state hireling for treason to his country.[3]

SA'TIRE. *n.*

A poem in which wickedness or folly is censured. Proper *satire* is distinguished, by the generality of the reflections, from a *lampoon*, which

---

2. "A lady once asked him how he came to define *Pastern* the *knee* of a horse: instead of making an elaborate defense, as she expected, he at once answered, 'Ignorance, Madam, pure ignorance' " (Boswell).

3. In 1762 Johnson was awarded a pension, but he did not revise the definition in later editions.

is aimed against a particular person; but they are too frequently confounded.

TO'RY. *n.*

One who adheres to the ancient constitution of the state, and the apostolical hierarchy of the church of England, opposed to a whig.

> The knight is more a *tory* in the country than the town, because it more advances his interest.—*Addison.*

WHIG. *n.*

2. The name of a faction.

> Whoever has a true value for church and state, should avoid the extremes of *whig* for the sake of the former, and the extremes of tory on the account of the latter.—*Swift.*

WIT. *n.*

1. The powers of the mind; the mental faculties; the intellects. This is the original signification.

2. Imagination; quickness of fancy.

3. Sentiments produced by quickness of fancy.

4. A man of fancy.

5. A man of genius.

6. Sense; judgment.

7. In the plural. Sound mind; intellect not crazed.

8. Contrivance; strategem; power of expedients.

1755

From The Preface to Shakespeare[1]

[*Shakespeare's Excellence. General Nature*]

That praises are without reason lavished on the dead, and that the honors due only to excellence are paid to antiquity, is a complaint likely to be always continued by those who, being able to add nothing to truth, hope for eminence from the heresies of paradox; or those who, being forced by disappointment upon consolatory expedients, are willing to hope from posterity what the present age refuses, and flatter themselves that the regard which is yet denied by envy will be at last bestowed by time.

---

1. This, the finest piece of Shakespeare criticism in the 18th century, is the culmination of a critical tradition that began with Nicholas Rowe's edition of the plays in 1709 (indeed with Dryden's critical remarks on Shakespeare) and that was continued by subsequent editors, notably Pope, Lewis Theobald, and William Warburton. Johnson's topics are in the main the conventional ones of 18th-century Shakespeare criticism: Shakespeare as the poet of nature, not of learning; as the creator of memorable characters; as a poet who supremely expresses and evokes the passions. Johnson follows his tradition in weighing Shakespeare's poetic virtues against his faults and finding that the virtues outweigh the faults. No one has praised Shakespeare more nobly and generously. The *Preface* is most original when Johnson attacks and dismisses the long-standing reverence in critical theory for the unities of time and place. By appealing to the experience of the playgoer, he demonstrates that, thanks to the imagination of the spectator, the playwright need not contain his action within a period of twenty-four hours or restrict it to one place throughout the drama.

Johnson's edition of Shakespeare also contained footnotes and brief introductions to each of the plays. We reprint here the introductory headnote to the two *Henry IV* plays.

Antiquity, like every other quality that attracts the notice of mankind, has undoubtedly votaries that reverence it not from reason but from prejudice. Some seem to admire indiscriminately whatever has been long preserved, without considering that time has sometimes cooperated with chance; all perhaps are more willing to honor past than present excellence; and the mind contemplates genius through the shades of age, as the eye surveys the sun through artificial opacity. The great contention of criticism is to find the faults of the moderns and the beauties of the ancients. While an author is yet living we estimate his powers by his worst performance; and when he is dead we rate them by his best.

To works, however, of which the excellence is not absolute and definite, but gradual and comparative; to works not raised upon principles demonstrative and scientific, but appealing wholly to observation and experience, no other test can be applied than length of duration and continuance of esteem. What mankind have long possessed they have often examined and compared; and if they persist to value the possession, it is because frequent comparisons have confirmed opinion in its favor. As among the works of nature no man can properly call a river deep or a mountain high, without the knowledge of many mountains and many rivers; so in the productions of genius, nothing can be styled excellent till it has been compared with other works of the same kind. Demonstration[2] immediately displays its power and has nothing to hope or fear from the flux of years; but works tentative and experimental must be estimated by their proportion to the general and collective ability of man, as it is discovered in a long succession of endeavors. Of the first building that was raised, it might be with certainty determined that it was round or square, but whether it was spacious or lofty must have been referred to time. The Pythagorean scale of numbers[3] was at once discovered to be perfect; but the poems of Homer we yet know not to transcend the common limits of human intelligence, but by remarking that nation after nation, and century after century, has been able to do little more than transpose his incidents, new name his characters, and paraphrase his sentiments.

The reverence due to writings that have long subsisted arises, therefore, not from any credulous confidence in the superior wisdom of past ages, or gloomy persuasion of the degeneracy of mankind, but is the consequence of acknowledged and indubitable positions, that what has been longest known has been most considered, and what is most considered is best understood.

The poet of whose works I have undertaken the revision may now begin to assume the dignity of an ancient and claim the privilege of established fame and prescriptive veneration. He has long outlived his century, the term commonly fixed as the test of literary merit.[4] Whatever advantages he might once derive from personal allusions, local cus-

---

2. "The highest degree of deducible or argumental evidence" (Johnson's *Dictionary*).
3. Pythagoras discovered the ratios that determine

the principal intervals of the musical scale.
4. Horace, *Epistles* 2.1.39.

toms, or temporary opinions, have for many years been lost; and every topic of merriment or motive of sorrow which the modes of artificial life afforded him now only obscure the scenes which they once illuminated. The effects of favor and competition are at an end; the tradition of his friendships and his enmities has perished; his works support no opinion with arguments nor supply any faction with invectives; they can neither indulge vanity nor gratify malignity; but are read without any other reason than the desire of pleasure, and are therefore praised only as pleasure is obtained; yet, thus unassisted by interest or passion, they have passed through variations of taste and changes of manners, and, as they devolved from one generation to another, have received new honors at every transmission.

But because human judgment, though it be gradually gaining upon certainty, never becomes infallible, and approbation, though long continued, may yet be only the approbation of prejudice or fashion, it is proper to inquire by what peculiarities of excellence Shakespeare has gained and kept the favor of his countrymen.

Nothing can please many, and please long, but just representations of general nature. Particular manners can be known to few, and therefore few only can judge how nearly they are copied. The irregular combinations of fanciful invention may delight awhile by that novelty of which the common satiety of life sends us all in quest; but the pleasures of sudden wonder are soon exhausted, and the mind can only repose on the stability of truth.

Shakespeare is, above all writers, at least above all modern writers, the poet of nature, the poet that holds up to his readers a faithful mirror of manners and of life. His characters are not modified by the customs of particular places, unpracticed by the rest of the world; by the peculiarities of studies or professions, which can operate but upon small numbers; or by the accidents of transient fashions or temporary opinions: they are the genuine progeny of common humanity, such as the world will always supply and observation will always find. His persons act and speak by the influence of those general passions and principles by which all minds are agitated and the whole system of life is continued in motion. In the writings of other poets a character is too often an individual: in those of Shakespeare it is commonly a species.

It is from this wide extension of design that so much instruction is derived. It is this which fills the plays of Shakespeare with practical axioms and domestic wisdom. It was said of Euripides[5] that every verse was a precept; and it may be said of Shakespeare that from his works may be collected a system of civil and economical prudence. Yet his real power is not shown in the splendor of particular passages, but by the progress of his fable and the tenor of his dialogue; and he that tries to recommend him by select quotations will succeed like the pedant in Hierocles[6] who,

5. The Greek tragic poet (ca. 480–406 B.C.). The observation is Cicero's.

6. Hierocles of Alexandria, a Greek philosopher of the 5th century A.D.

when he offered his house to sale, carried a brick in his pocket as a specimen.

It will not easily be imagined how much Shakespeare excels in accommodating his sentiments to real life but by comparing him with other authors. It was observed of the ancient schools of declamation that the more diligently they were frequented, the more was the student disqualified for the world, because he found nothing there which he should ever meet in any other place. The same remark may be applied to every stage but that of Shakespeare. The theater, when it is under any other direction, is peopled by such characters as were never seen, conversing in a language which was never heard, upon topics which will never arise in the commerce of mankind. But the dialogue of this author is often so evidently determined by the incident which produces it, and is pursued with so much ease and simplicity, that it seems scarcely to claim the merit of fiction, but to have been gleaned by diligent selection out of common conversation and common occurrences.

Upon every other stage the universal agent is love, by whose power all good and evil is distributed and every action quickened or retarded. To bring a lover, a lady, and a rival into the fable; to entangle them in contradictory obligations, perplex them with oppositions of interest, and harass them with violence of desires inconsistent with each other; to make them meet in rapture, and part in agony; to fill their mouths with hyperbolical joy and outrageous sorrow; to distress them as nothing human ever was distressed; to deliver them as nothing human ever was delivered, is the business of a modern dramatist. For this, probability is violated, life is misrepresented, and language is depraved. But love is only one of many passions; and as it has no great influence upon the sum of life, it has little operation in the dramas of a poet who caught his ideas from the living world and exhibited only what he saw before him. He knew that any other passion, as it was regular or exorbitant, was a cause of happiness or calamity.

Characters thus ample and general were not easily discriminated and preserved; yet perhaps no poet ever kept his personages more distinct from each other. I will not say with Pope that every speech may be assigned to the proper speaker,[7] because many speeches there are which have nothing characteristical; but perhaps though some may be equally adapted to every person, it will be difficult to find that any can be properly transferred from the present possessor to another claimant. The choice is right when there is reason for choice.

Other dramatists can only gain attention by hyperbolical or aggravated characters, by fabulous and unexampled excellence or depravity, as the writers of barbarous romances invigorated the reader by a giant and a dwarf; and he that should form his expectations of human affairs from the play or from the tale would be equally deceived. Shakespeare has no

_____

7. In the preface to his edition of Shakespeare's plays (1725).

heroes; his scenes are occupied only by men, who act and speak as the reader thinks that he should himself have spoken or acted on the same occasion; even where the agency is supernatural, the dialogue is level with life. Other writers disguise the most natural passions and most frequent incidents so that he who contemplates them in the book will not know them in the world: Shakespeare approximates[8] the remote, and familiarizes the wonderful; the event which he represents will not happen, but, if it were possible, its effects would probably be such as he has assigned; and it may be said that he has not only shown human nature as it acts in real exigencies, but as it would be found in trials to which it cannot be exposed.

This therefore is the praise of Shakespeare, that his drama is the mirror of life; that he who has mazed his imagination in following the phantoms which other writers raise up before him, may here be cured of his delirious ecstasies by reading human sentiments in human language, by scenes from which a hermit may estimate the transactions of the world, and a confessor predict the progress of the passions.

[Shakespeare's Faults. The Three Dramatic Unities]

Shakespeare with his excellencies has likewise faults, and faults sufficient to obscure and overwhelm any other merit. I shall show them in the proportion in which they appear to me, without envious malignity or superstitious veneration. No question can be more innocently discussed than a dead poet's pretensions to renown; and little regard is due to that bigotry which sets candor[1] higher than truth.

His first defect is that to which may be imputed most of the evil in books or in men. He sacrifices virtue to convenience, and is so much more careful to please than to instruct that he seems to write without any moral purpose. From his writings indeed a system of social duty may be selected, for he that thinks reasonably must think morally, but his precepts and axioms drop casually from him; he makes no just distribution of good or evil, nor is always careful to show in the virtuous a disapprobation of the wicked; he carries his persons indifferently through right and wrong, and at the close dismisses them without further care, and leaves their examples to operate by chance. This fault the barbarity of his age cannot extenuate; for it is always a writer's duty to make the world better, and justice is a virtue independent on time or place.

The plots are often so loosely formed that a very slight consideration may improve them, and so carelessly pursued that he seems not always fully to comprehend his own design. He omits opportunities of instructing or delighting which the train of his story seems to force upon him, and apparently rejects those exhibitions which would be more affecting for the sake of those which are more easy.

It may be observed that in many of his plays the latter part is evidently

---

8. Brings near.   1. Kindness.

neglected. When he found himself near the end of his work, and in view of his reward, he shortened the labor to snatch the profit. He therefore remits his efforts where he should most vigorously exert them, and his catastrophe is improbably produced or imperfectly represented.

He had no regard to distinction of time or place, but gives to one age or nation, without scruple, the customs, institutions, and opinions of another, at the expense not only of likelihood but of possibility. These faults Pope has endeavored, with more zeal than judgment, to transfer to his imagined interpolators. We need not wonder to find Hector quoting Aristotle, when we see the loves of Theseus and Hippolyta combined with the Gothic mythology of fairies.[2] Shakespeare, indeed, was not the only violator of chronology, for in the same age Sidney, who wanted not the advantages of learning, has, in his *Arcadia*, confounded the pastoral with the feudal times, the days of innocence, quiet, and security with those of turbulence, violence, and adventure.

In his comic scenes he is seldom very successful when he engages his characters in reciprocations of smartness and contests of sarcasm; their jests are commonly gross, and their pleasantry licentious; neither his gentlemen nor his ladies have much delicacy, nor are sufficiently distinguished from his clowns by any appearance of refined manners. Whether he represented the real conversation of his time is not easy to determine: the reign of Elizabeth is commonly supposed to have been a time of stateliness, formality, and reserve; yet perhaps the relaxations of that severity were not very elegant. There must, however, have been always some modes of gaiety preferable to others, and a writer ought to choose the best.

In tragedy his performance seems constantly to be worse as his labor is more. The effusions of passion, which exigence forces out, are for the most part striking and energetic; but whenever he solicits his invention, or strains his faculties, the offspring of his throes is tumor,[3] meanness, tediousness, and obscurity.

In narration he affects a disproportionate pomp of diction and a wearisome train of circumlocution, and tells the incident imperfectly in many words which might have been more plainly delivered in few. Narration in dramatic poetry is naturally tedious, as it is unanimated and inactive, and obstructs the progress of the action; it should therefore always be rapid and enlivened by frequent interruption. Shakespeare found it an encumbrance, and instead of lightening it by brevity, endeavored to recommend it by dignity and splendor.

His declamations or set speeches are commonly cold and weak, for his power was the power of nature; when he endeavored, like other tragic writers, to catch opportunities of amplification and, instead of inquiring what the occasion demanded, to show how much his stores of knowledge could supply, he seldom escapes without the pity or resentment of his reader.

---

2. In *Troilus and Cressida*, 2.2.166, and in *Mid-summer Night's Dream*, respectively.   3. Inflated grandeur, false magnificence.

It is incident to him to be now and then entangled with an unwieldy sentiment which he cannot well express, and will not reject; he struggles with it awhile, and, if it continues stubborn, comprises it in words such as occur, and leaves it to be disentangled and evolved by those who have more leisure to bestow upon it.

Not that always where the language is intricate the thought is subtle, or the image always great where the line is bulky; the equality of words to things is very often neglected, and trivial sentiments and vulgar[4] ideas disappoint the attention, to which they are recommended by sonorous epithets and swelling figures.

But the admirers of this great poet have most reason to complain when he approaches nearest to his highest excellence, and seems fully resolved to sink them in dejection and mollify them with tender emotions by the fall of greatness, the danger of innocence, or the crosses of love. What he does best, he soon ceases to do. He is not long soft and pathetic without some idle conceit or contemptible equivocation. He no sooner begins to move than he counteracts himself; and terror and pity, as they are rising in the mind, are checked and blasted by sudden frigidity.

A quibble[5] is to Shakespeare what luminous vapors are to the traveler: he follows it at all adventures; it is sure to lead him out of his way, and sure to engulf him in the mire. It has some malignant power over his mind, and its fascinations are irresistible. Whatever be the dignity or profundity of his disquisitions, whether he be enlarging knowledge or exalting affection, whether he be amusing[6] attention with incidents, or enchaining it in suspense, let but a quibble spring up before him, and he leaves his work unfinished. A quibble is the golden apple for which he will always turn aside from his career[7] or stoop from his elevation. A quibble, poor and barren as it is, gave him such delight that he was content to purchase it by the sacrifice of reason, propriety, and truth. A quibble was to him the fatal Cleopatra for which he lost the world, and was content to lose it.

It will be thought strange that in enumerating the defects of this writer, I have not yet mentioned his neglect of the unities; his violation of those laws which have been instituted and established by the joint authority of poets and critics.

For his other deviations from the art of writing, I resign him to critical justice without making any other demand in his favor than that which must be indulged to all human excellence: that his virtues be rated with his failings. But from the censure which this irregularity may bring upon him I shall, with due reverence to that learning which I must oppose, adventure to try how I can defend him.

His histories, being neither tragedies nor comedies, are not subject to

---

4. "Mean; low; being of the common rate" (Johnson's *Dictionary*).

5. Pun.

6. "To entertain with tranquility; to fill with thoughts that engage the mind, without distracting it" (Johnson's *Dictionary*).

7. In Greek legend Atalanta refused to marry any man who could not defeat her in a foot race. Hippomenes won her by dropping, as he ran, three of the golden apples of the Hesperides, which she paused to pick up.

any of their laws; nothing more is necessary to all the praise which they expect than that the changes of action be so prepared as to be understood; that the incidents be various and affecting, and the characters consistent, natural, and distinct. No other unity is intended, and therefore none is to be sought.

In his other works he has well enough preserved the unity of action. He has not, indeed, an intrigue regularly perplexed and regularly unraveled: he does not endeavor to hide his design only to discover it, for this is seldom the order of real events, and Shakespare is the poet of nature: but his plan has commonly what Aristotle requires,[8] a beginning, a middle, and an end; one event is concatenated with another, and the conclusion follows by easy consequence. There are, perhaps, some incidents that might be spared, as in other poets there is much talk that only fills up time upon the stage; but the general system makes gradual advances, and the end of the play is the end of expectation.

To the unities of time and place he has shown no regard; and perhaps a nearer view of the principles on which they stand will diminish their value and withdraw from them the veneration which, from the time of Corneille,[9] they have very generally received, by discovering that they have given more trouble to the poet than pleasure to the auditor.

The necessity of observing the unities of time and place arises from the supposed necessity of making the drama credible. The critics hold it impossible that an action of months or years can be possibly believed to pass in three hours; or that the spectator can suppose himself to sit in the theater while ambassadors go and return between distant kings, while armies are levied and towns besieged, while an exile wanders and returns, or till he whom they saw courting his mistress shall lament the untimely fall of his son. The mind revolts from evident falsehood, and fiction loses its force when it departs from the resemblance of reality.

From the narrow limitation of time necessarily arises the contraction of place. The spectator who knows that he saw the first act at Alexandria cannot suppose that he sees the next at Rome, at a distance to which not the dragons of Medea could, in so short a time, have transported him; he knows with certainty that he has not changed his place; and he knows that place cannot change itself, that what was a house cannot become a plain, that what was Thebes can never be Persepolis.

Such is the triumphant language with which a critic exults over the misery of an irregular poet, and exults commonly without resistance or reply. It is time, therefore, to tell him by the authority of Shakespeare that he assumes, as an unquestionable principle, a position which, while his breath is forming it into words, his understanding pronounces to be false. It is false that any representation is mistaken for reality; that any dramatic fable in its materiality was ever credible or, for a single moment, was ever credited.

The objection arising from the impossibility of passing the first hour

8. *Poetics* 7.
9. Pierre Corneille (1606–1684), the French

playwright, discussed the unities in his *Discours des trois unités* (1660).

at Alexandria and the next at Rome supposes that when the play opens
the spectator really imagines himself at Alexandria, and believes that his
walk to the theater has been a voyage to Egypt, and that he lives in the
days of Antony and Cleopatra. Surely he that imagines this may imagine
more. He that can take the stage at one time for the palace of the Ptol-
emies may take it in half an hour for the promontory of Actium. Delusion, if delusion be admitted, has no certain limitation; if the spectator
can be once persuaded that his old acquaintances are Alexander and
Caesar, that a room illuminated with candles is the plain of Pharsalia or
the bank of Granicus, he is in a state of elevation above the reach of
reason or of truth, and from the heights of empyrean poetry may despise
the circumscriptions of terrestrial nature. There is no reason why a mind
thus wandering in ecstasy should count the clock, or why an hour should
not be a century in that calenture[1] of the brain that can make the stage
a field.

The truth is that the spectators are always in their senses, and know,
from the first act to the last, that the stage is only a stage, and that the
players are only players. They came to hear a certain number of lines
recited with just gesture and elegant modulation. The lines relate to
some action, and an action must be in some place; but the different
actions that complete a story may be in places very remote from each
other; and where is the absurdity of allowing that space to represent first
Athens, and then Sicily, which was always known to be neither Sicily
nor Athens but a modern theater?

By supposition, as place is introduced, time may be extended; the
time required by the fable elapses, for the most part, between the acts;
for, of so much of the action as is represented, the real and poetical
duration is the same. If, in the first act, preparations for war against
Mithridates are represented to be made in Rome, the event of the war
may, without absurdity, be represented, in the catastrophe, as happening in Pontus; we know that there is neither war nor preparation for war;
we know that we are neither in Rome nor Pontus, that neither Mithridates nor Lucullus are before us. The drama exhibits successive imitations of successive actions; and why may not the second imitation represent
an action that happened years after the first, if it be so connected with it
that nothing but time can be supposed to intervene? Time is, of all
modes of existence, most obsequious[2] to the imagination; a lapse of years
is as easily conceived as a passage of hours. In contemplation we easily
contract the time of real actions, and therefore willingly permit it to be
contracted when we only see their imitation.

It will be asked how the drama moves if it is not credited. It is credited
with all the credit due to a drama. It is credited, whenever it moves, as
a just picture of a real original; as representing to the auditor what he

---

1. A delirium produced by tropical heat, which
causes sailors to leap into the sea under the delusion that it is a green field.
2. "Obedient; compliant" (Johnson's *Dictionary*).

would himself feel if he were to do or suffer what is there feigned to be suffered or to be done. The reflection that strikes the heart is not that the evils before us are real evils, but that they are evils to which we ourselves may be exposed. If there be any fallacy, it is not that we fancy the players, but that we fancy ourselves, unhappy for a moment; but we rather lament the possibility than suppose the presence of misery, as a mother weeps over her babe when she remembers that death may take it from her. The delight of tragedy proceeds from our consciousness of fiction; if we thought murders and treasons real, they would please no more.

Imitations produce pain or pleasure, not because they are mistaken for realities, but because they bring realities to mind. When the imagination is recreated by a painted landscape, the trees are not supposed capable to give us shade or the fountains coolness; but we consider how we should be pleased with such fountains playing beside us and such woods waving over us. We are agitated in reading the history of *Henry the Fifth*; yet no man takes his book for the field of Agincourt. A dramatic exhibition is a book recited with concomitants that increase or diminish its effect. Familiar comedy is often more powerful on the theater than in the page; imperial tragedy is always less. The humor of Petruchio may be heightened by grimace; but what voice or what gesture can hope to add dignity or force to the soliloquy of Cato?[3]

A play read affects the mind like a play acted. It is therefore evident that the action is not supposed to be real; and it follows that between the acts a longer or shorter time may be allowed to pass, and that no more account of space or duration is to be taken by the auditor of a drama than by the reader of a narrative, before whom may pass in an hour the life of a hero or the revolutions of an empire.

Whether Shakespeare knew the unities and rejected them by design or deviated from them by happy ignorance, it is, I think, impossible to decide and useless to inquire. We may reasonably suppose that, when he rose to notice, he did not want[4] the counsels and admonitions of scholars and critics, and that he at last deliberately persisted in a practice which he might have begun by chance. As nothing is essential to the fable but unity of action, and as the unities of time and place arise evidently from false assumptions, and, by circumscribing the extent of the drama, lessen its variety, I cannot think it much to be lamented that they were not known by him, or not observed: nor, if such another poet could arise, should I very vehemently reproach him that his first act passed at Venice and his next in Cyprus.[5] Such violations of rules merely positive become the comprehensive genius of Shakespeare, and such censures are suitable to the minute and slender criticism of Voltaire.

---

3. Petruchio is the hero of Shakespeare's comedy *The Taming of the Shrew*. In Addison's tragedy *Cato* (5.1), the hero soliloquizes on immortality shortly before committing suicide.
4. Lack.
5. As is the case in *Othello*.

Non usque adeo permiscuit imis
Longus summa dies, ut non, si voce Metelli
Serventur leges, malint a Caesare tolli.[6]

Yet when I speak thus slightly of dramatic rules, I cannot but recollect how much wit and learning may be produced against me; before such authorities I am afraid to stand: not that I think the present question one of those that are to be decided by mere authority, but because it is to be suspected that these precepts have not been so easily received but for better reasons than I have yet been able to find. The result of my inquiries, in which it would be ludicrous to boast of impartiality, is that the unities of time and place are not essential to a just drama, that though they may sometimes conduce to pleasure, they are always to be sacrificed to the nobler beauties of variety and instruction; and that a play written with nice observation of critical rules is to be contemplated as an elaborate curiosity, as the product of superfluous and ostentatious art, by which is shown rather what is possible than what is necessary.

He that without diminution of any other excellence shall preserve all the unities unbroken deserves the like applause with the architect who shall display all the orders of architecture in a citadel without any deduction for its strength; but the principal beauty of a citadel is to exclude the enemy, and the greatest graces of a play are to copy nature and instruct life. * * *

[Henry IV]

None of Shakespeare's plays are more read than the first and second parts of *Henry the fourth*. Perhaps no author has ever in two plays afforded so much delight. The great events are interesting, for the fate of kingdoms depends upon them; the slighter occurrences are diverting, and, except one or two, sufficiently probable; the incidents are multiplied with wonderful fertility of invention, and the characters diversified with the utmost nicety of discernment, and the profoundest skill in the nature of man.

The prince, who is the hero both of the comic and tragic part, is a young man of great abilities and violent passions, whose sentiments are right, though his actions are wrong; whose virtues are obscured by negligence, and whose understanding is dissipated by levity. In his idle hours he is rather loose than wicked, and when the occasion forces out his latent qualities, he is great without effort, and brave without tumult. The trifler is roused into a hero, and the hero again reposes in the trifler. This character is great, original, and just.[7]

Percy is a rugged soldier, choleric, and quarrelsome, and has only the soldier's virtues, generosity and courage.

6. Lucan, *Pharsalia* 3.138–40: "The course of time has not wrought such confusion that the laws would not rather be trampled on by Caesar than saved by Metellus."
7. Exact.

But Falstaff, unimitated, unimitable Falstaff, how shall I describe thee? Thou compound of sense and vice; of sense which may be admired but not esteemed, of vice which may be despised, but hardly detested. Falstaff is a character loaded with faults, and with those faults which naturally produce contempt. He is a thief, and a glutton, a coward, and a boaster, always ready to cheat the weak, and prey upon the poor; to terrify the timorous and insult the defenseless. At once obsequious and malignant, he satirizes in their absence those whom he lives by flattering. He is familiar with the prince only as an agent of vice, but of this familiarity he is so proud as not only to be supercilious and haughty with common men, but to think his interest of importance to the duke of Lancaster. Yet the man thus corrupt, thus despicable, makes himself necessary to the prince that despises him, by the most pleasing of all qualities, perpetual gaiety, by an unfailing power of exciting laughter, which is the more freely indulged, as his wit is not of the splendid or ambitious kind, but consists in easy escapes and sallies of levity, which make sport but raise no envy. It must be observed that he is stained with no enormous or sanguinary crimes, so that his licentiousness is not so offensive but that it may be borne for his mirth.

The moral to be drawn from this representation is that no man is more dangerous than he that with a will to corrupt, hath the power to please; and that neither wit nor honesty ought to think themselves safe with such a companion when they see Henry seduced by Falstaff.

From LIVES OF THE POETS

From Cowley[1]

[Metaphysical Wit]

Wit, like all other things subject by their nature to the choice of man, has its changes and fashions, and at different times takes different forms. About the beginning of the seventeenth century appeared a race of writers that may be termed the metaphysical poets,[2] of whom in a criticism on the works of Cowley it is not improper to give some account.

The metaphysical poets were men of learning, and to show their learning was their whole endeavor; but, unluckily resolving to show it in rhyme, instead of writing poetry they only wrote verses, and very often such verses as stood the trial of the finger better than of the ear; for the

1. Abraham Cowley (1618–1667) was much admired during the middle of the 17th century. His reputation began to decline before 1700, but he was remembered as a writer of false wit, especially in his love poems *The Mistress*.
2. Presumably Johnson took this now common designation from a hint in Dryden's *Discourse*

Concerning the Original and Progress of Satire, 1693. Dryden condemned Donne because "he affects the metaphysics . . . and perplexes the minds of the fair sex with nice speculations of philosophy, when he should engage their hearts, and entertain them with the softnesses of love" (*Essays*, ed. W. P. Ker, 2.19).

modulation was so imperfect that they were only found to be verses by counting the syllables.

If the father of criticism[3] has rightly denominated poetry *tekhnē mimē-tikè, an imitative art*, these writers will without great wrong lose their right to the name of poets, for they cannot be said to have imitated anything: they neither copied nature nor life; neither painted the forms of matter nor represented the operations of intellect.

Those however who deny them to be poets allow them to be wits. Dryden confesses of himself and his contemporaries that they fall below Donne in it, but maintains that they surpass him in poetry.[4]

If wit be well described by Pope as being "that which has been often thought, but was never before so well expressed,"[5] they certainly never attained nor ever sought it, for they endeavored to be singular in their thoughts, and were careless of their diction. But Pope's account of wit is undoubtedly erroneous; he depresses it below its natural dignity, and reduces it from strength of thought to happiness of language.

If by a more noble and more adequate conception that be considered as wit which is at once natural and new, that which though not obvious is, upon its first production, acknowledged to be just; if it be that which he that never found it, wonders how he missed; to wit of this kind the metaphysical poets have seldom risen. Their thoughts are often new, but seldom natural; they are not obvious, but neither are they just;[6] and the reader, far from wondering that he missed them, wonders more frequently by what perverseness of industry they were ever found.

But wit, abstracted from its effects upon the hearer, may be more rigorously and philosophically considered as a kind of *discordia concors;*[7] a combination of dissimilar images, or discovery of occult resemblances in things apparently unlike. Of wit, thus defined, they have more than enough. The most heterogeneous ideas are yoked by violence together; nature and art are ransacked for illustrations, comparisons, and allusions; their learning instructs, and their subtlety surprises; but the reader commonly thinks his improvement dearly bought, and, though he sometimes admires, is seldom pleased.

From this account of their compositions it will be readily inferred that they were not successful in representing or moving the affections. As they were wholly employed on something unexpected and surprising, they had no regard to that uniformity of sentiment which enables us to conceive and to excite the pains and the pleasure of other minds: they never inquired what on any occasion they should have said or done, but wrote rather as beholders than partakers of human nature; as beings looking upon good and evil, impassive and at leisure; as Epicurean deities making remarks on the actions of men and the vicissitudes of life, without interest and without emotion. Their courtship was void of fondness

3. Aristotle in his *Poetics.*
4. *Discourse . . . of Satire* (Ker 2.102).
5. *Essay on Criticism,* lines 297–98.
6. Exact, proper.
7. Literally, "a harmonious discord." Johnson is

himself being witty in using this phrase, a familiar philosophical concept denoting the general harmony of God's creation despite its manifold and often contradictory particulars.

and their lamentation of sorrow. Their wish was only to say what they hoped had been never said before.

Nor was the sublime more within their reach than the pathetic; for they never attempted that comprehension and expanse of thought which at once fills the whole mind, and of which the first effect is sudden astonishment, and the second rational admiration. Sublimity is produced by aggregation, and littleness by dispersion. Great thoughts are always general, and consist in positions not limited by exceptions, and in descriptions not descending to minuteness. It is with great propriety that subtlety, which in its original import means exility[8] of particles, is taken in its metaphorical meaning for nicety of distinction. Those writers who lay on the watch for novelty could have little hope of greatness; for great things cannot have escaped former observation. Their attempts were always analytic: they broke every image into fragments, and could no more represent by their slender conceits and labored particularities the prospects of nature or the scenes of life, than he who dissects a sunbeam with a prism can exhibit the wide effulgence of a summer noon.

What they wanted however of the sublime they endeavored to supply by hyperbole;[9] their amplification had no limits: they left not only reason but fancy behind them, and produced combinations of confused magnificence that not only could not be credited, but could not be imagined.

Yet great labor directed by great abilities is never wholly lost: if they frequently threw away their wit upon false conceits, they likewise sometimes struck out unexpected truth: if their conceits were farfetched, they were often worth the carriage.[1] To write on their plan it was at least necessary to read and think. No man could be born a metaphysical poet, nor assume the dignity of a writer by descriptions copied from descriptions, by imitations borrowed from imitations, by traditional imagery and hereditary similes, by readiness of rhyme and volubility of syllables.

1779

From Milton[1]

[Lycidas]

One of the poems on which much praise has been bestowed is *Lycidas*; of which the diction is harsh,[2] the rhymes uncertain, and the num-

---

8. Thinness.
9. An image heightened beyond reality (see Johnson's *Dictionary*).
1. In the *Life of Addison*, Johnson wrote: "A simile may be compared to lines converging at a point, and is more excellent as the lines approach from greater distance . . ."
1. Johnson's treatment of Milton as man and poet gave great offense to many ardent Miltonians in his own day and damaged his reputation as a critic

in the following century. He did not admire Milton's character, and he detested his politics and religion. But no one has praised *Paradise Lost* more handsomely. Especially offensive in the 19th century was his attack on *Lycidas*. Johnson disliked modern pastorals, recognizing that the tradition had been worn threadbare. His views on the genre may be read in *Ramblers* 36 and 37.
2. This notorious word does not mean "unmelodious," but "strained, forced, affected, or labored."

bers unpleasing. What beauty there is, we must therefore seek in the sentiments and images. It is not to be considered as the effusion of real passion; for passion runs not after remote allusions and obscure opinions. Passion plucks no berries from the myrtle and ivy, nor calls upon Arethuse and Mincius, nor tells of "rough satyrs and fauns with cloven heel." Where there is leisure for fiction there is little grief.

In this poem there is no nature, for there is no truth; there is no art, for there is nothing new. Its form is that of a pastoral, easy, vulgár, and therefore disgusting:[3] whatever images it can supply are long ago exhausted; and its inherent improbability always forces dissatisfaction on the mind. When Cowley tells of Hervey that they studied together, it is easy to suppose how much he must miss the companion of his labors and the partner of his discoveries;[4] but what image of tenderness can be excited by these lines!

> We drove afield, and both together heard
> What time the grayfly winds her sultry horn,
> Battening our flocks with the fresh dews of night.

We know that they never drove afield, and that they had no flocks to batten; and though it be allowed that the representation may be allegorical, the true meaning is so uncertain and remote that it is never sought because it cannot be known when it is found.

Among the flocks and copses and flowers appear the heathen deities, Jove and Phoebus, Neptune and Aeolus, with a long train of mythological imagery, such as a college easily supplies. Nothing can less display knowledge or less exercise invention than to tell how a shepherd has lost his companion and must now feed his flocks alone, without any judge of his skill in piping; and how one god asks another god what is become of Lycidas, and how neither god can tell. He who thus grieves will excite no sympathy; he who thus praises will confer no honor.

This poem has yet a grosser fault. With these trifling fictions are mingled the most awful and sacred truths, such as ought never to be polluted with such irreverent combinations. The shepherd likewise is now a feeder of sheep, and afterwards an ecclesiastical pastor, a superintendent of a Christian flock. Such equivocations are always unskillful; but here they are indecent,[5] and at least approach to impiety, of which, however, I believe the writer not to have been conscious.

Such is the power of reputation justly acquired that its blaze drives away the eye from nice examination. Surely no man could have fancied that he read *Lycidas* with pleasure had he not known its author.

[L'Allegro, Il Penseroso]

Of the two pieces, *L'Allegro* and *Il Penseroso*, I believe opinion is uniform; every man that reads them, reads them with pleasure. The

---

3. I.e., displeasing ("disgusting") because its stale conventionality made it "vulgar" by putting it within the reach of the many.

4. Cowley's *On the Death of Mr. William Hervey* (1656).

5. Unbecoming, lacking in decorum.

author's design is not, what Theobald[1] has remarked, merely to show how objects derived their colors from the mind, by representing the operation of the same things upon the gay and the melancholy temper, or upon the same man as he is differently disposed; but rather how, among the successive variety of appearances, every disposition of mind takes hold on those by which it may be gratified.

The *cheerful* man hears the lark in the morning; the *pensive* man hears the nightingale in the evening. The *cheerful* man sees the cock strut, and hears the horn and hounds echo in the wood; then walks "not unseen" to observe the glory of the rising sun or listen to the singing milkmaid, and view the labors of the plowman and the mower; then casts his eyes about him over scenes of smiling plenty, and looks up to the distant tower, the residence of some fair inhabitant: thus he pursues rural gaiety through a day of labor or of play, and delights himself at night with the fanciful narratives of superstitious ignorance.

The *pensive* man at one time walks "unseen" to muse at midnight, and at another hears the sullen curfew. If the weather drives him home he sits in a room lighted only by "glowing embers"; or by a lonely lamp outwatches the North Star to discover the habitation of separate souls, and varies the shades of meditation by contemplating the magnificent or pathetic scenes of tragic and epic poetry. When the morning comes, a morning gloomy with rain and wind, he walks into the dark trackless woods, falls asleep by some murmuring water, and with melancholy enthusiasm expects some dream of prognostication or some music played by aerial performers.

Both Mirth and Melancholy are solitary, silent inhabitants of the breast that neither receive nor transmit communication: no mention is therefore made of a philosophical friend or a pleasant companion. The seriousness does not arise from any participation of calamity, nor the gaiety from the pleasures of the bottle.

The man of *cheerfulness* having exhausted the country tries what "towered cities" will afford, and mingles with scenes of splendor, gay assemblies, and nuptial festivities; but he mingles a mere spectator as, when the learned comedies of Jonson or the wild dramas of Shakespeare are exhibited, he attends the theater.

The *pensive* man never loses himself in crowds, but walks the cloister or frequents the cathedral. Milton probably had not yet forsaken the Church.

Both his characters delight in music; but he seems to think that cheerful notes would have obtained from Pluto a complete dismission of Eurydice, of whom solemn sounds only procured a conditional release.

For the old age of Cheerfulness he makes no provision; but Melancholy he conducts with great dignity to the close of life. His Cheerfulness is without levity, and his Pensiveness without asperity.

Through these two poems the images are properly selected and nicely

---

1. Lewis Theobald (1688–1744), the editor of Shakespeare and the enemy of Pope.

distinguished, but the colors of the diction seem not sufficiently discriminated. I know not whether the characters are kept sufficiently apart. No mirth can, indeed, be found in his melancholy; but I am afraid that I always meet some melancholy in his mirth. They are two noble efforts of imagination.

[Paradise Lost]

Those little pieces may be dispatched without much anxiety; a greater work calls for greater care. I am now to examine *Paradise Lost*, a poem which, considered with respect to design, may claim the first place, and with respect to performance the second, among the productions of the human mind.

By the general consent of critics the first praise of genius is due to the writer of an epic poem, as it requires an assemblage of all the powers which are singly sufficient for other compositions. Poetry is the art of uniting pleasure with truth, by calling imagination to the help of reason. Epic poetry undertakes to teach the most important truths by the most pleasing precepts, and therefore relates some great event in the most affecting manner. History must supply the writer with the rudiments of narration, which he must improve and exalt by a nobler art, must animate by dramatic energy, and diversify by retrospection and anticipation; morality must teach him the exact bounds and different shades of vice and virtue; from policy and the practice of life he has to learn the discriminations of character and the tendency of the passions, either single or combined; and physiology must supply him with illustrations and images. To put these materials to poetical use is required an imagination capable of painting nature and realizing fiction. Nor is he yet a poet till he has attained the whole extension of his language, distinguished all the delicacies of phrase, and all the colors of words, and learned to adjust their different sounds to all the varieties of metrical modulation.

Bossu is of opinion that the poet's first work is to find a *moral*, which his fable is afterwards to illustrate and establish.[1] This seems to have been the process only of Milton: the moral of other poems is incidental and consequent; in Milton's only it is essential and intrinsic. His purpose was the most useful and the most arduous: "to vindicate the ways of God to man"; to show the reasonableness of religion, and the necessity of obedience to the Divine Law.

To convey this moral there must be a *fable*, a narration artfully constructed, so as to excite curiosity and surprise expectation. In this part of his work Milton must be confessed to have equaled every other poet. He has involved in his account of the Fall of Man the events which preceded, and those that were to follow it: he has interwoven the whole system of theology with such propriety that every part appears to be nec-

---

1. Père le Bossu wrote a treatise on the epic poem, *Traité du Poëme Épique*, 1675, much admired during the late 17th and early 18th centuries.

essary, and scarcely any recital is wished shorter for the sake of quickening the progress of the main action.

The subject of an epic poem is naturally an event of great importance. That of Milton is not the destruction of a city, the conduct of a colony, or the foundation of an empire. His subject is the fate of worlds, the revolutions of heaven and of earth; rebellion against the Supreme King raised by the highest order of created beings; the overthrow of their host and the punishment of their crime; the creation of a new race of reasonable creatures; their original happiness and innocence, their forfeiture of immortality, and their restoration to hope and peace.

Great events can be hastened or retarded only by persons of elevated dignity. Before the greatness displayed in Milton's poem all other greatness shrinks away. The weakest of his agents are the highest and noblest of human beings, the original parents of mankind; with whose actions the elements consented; on whose rectitude or deviation of will depended the state of terrestrial nature and the condition of all the future inhabitants of the globe.

Of the other agents in the poem, the chief are such as it is irreverence to name on slight occasions. The rest were lower powers;

> of which the least could wield
> Those elements, and arm him with the force
> Of all their regions;[2]

powers which only the control of Omnipotence restrains from laying creation waste, and filling the vast expanse of space with ruin and confusion. To display the motives and actions of beings thus superior, so far as human reason can examine them or human imagination represent them, is the task which this mighty poet has undertaken and performed.

In the examination of epic poems much speculation is commonly employed upon the *characters*. The characters in the *Paradise Lost* which admit of examination are those of angels and of man; of angels good and evil, of man in his innocent and sinful state.

Among the angels the virtue of Raphael is mild and placid, of easy condescension and free communication; that of Michael is regal and lofty, and, as may seem, attentive to the dignity of his own nature. Abdiel and Gabriel appear occasionally, and act as every incident requires; the solitary fidelity of Abdiel is very amiably painted.[3]

Of the evil angels the characters are more diversified. To Satan, as Addison observes, such sentiments are given as suit "the most exalted and most depraved being."[4] Milton has been censured by Clarke for the impiety which sometimes breaks from Satan's mouth. For there are thoughts, as he justly remarks, which no observation of character can justify, because no good man would willingly permit them to pass, however transiently, through his own mind.[5] To make Satan speak as a rebel,

---

2. *Paradise Lost* 6.221.   4. *Spectator* 303.
3. *Paradise Lost* 5.803 ff.   5. John Clarke, *Essay upon Study*, 1731.

without any such expressions as might taint the reader's imagination, was indeed one of the great difficulties in Milton's undertaking, and I cannot but think that he has extricated himself with great happiness. There is in Satan's speeches little that can give pain to a pious ear. The language of rebellion cannot be the same with that of obedience. The malignity of Satan foams in haughtiness and obstinacy; but his expressions are commonly general, and no otherwise offensive than as they are wicked.

The other chiefs of the celestial rebellion are very judiciously discriminated in the first and second books; and the ferocious character of Moloch appears, both in the battle and the council, with exact consistency.

To Adam and Eve are given during their innocence such sentiments as innocence can generate and utter. Their love is pure benevolence and mutual veneration; their repasts are without luxury and their diligence without toil. Their addresses to their Maker have little more than the voice of admiration and gratitude. Fruition left them nothing to ask, and Innocence left them nothing to fear.

But with guilt enter distrust and discord, mutual accusation, and stubborn self-defense; they regard each other with alienated minds, and dread their Creator as the avenger of their transgression. At last they seek shelter in his mercy, soften to repentance, and melt in supplication. Both before and after the Fall the superiority of Adam is diligently sustained.

Of the *probable* and the *marvelous*,[6] two parts of a vulgar epic poem which immerge the critic in deep consideration, the *Paradise Lost* requires little to be said. It contains the history of a miracle, of Creation and Redemption; it displays the power and the mercy of the Supreme Being: the probable therefore is marvelous, and the marvelous is probable. The substance of the narrative is truth; and as truth allows no choice, it is, like necessity, superior to rule. To the accidental or adventitious parts, as to every thing human, some slight exceptions may be made. But the main fabric is immovably supported.

It is justly remarked by Addison[7] that this poem has, by the nature of its subject, the advantage above all others, that it is universally and perpetually interesting. All mankind will, through all ages, bear the same relation to Adam and to Eve, and must partake of that good and evil which extend to themselves.

Of the *machinery*, so called from *theòs apò mēkhanēs*[8] by which is meant the occasional interposition of supernatural power, another fertile topic of critical remarks, here is no room to speak, because every thing is done under the immediate and visible direction of Heaven; but the rule is so far observed that no part of the action could have been accomplished by any other means.

Of *episodes*[9] I think there are only two, contained in Raphael's rela-

6. Actions in an epic poem which are wonderful because they exceed the probable.
7. *Spectator* 273.
8. Aristotle, *Poetics* 15.10. "Deus ex machina," the intervention of supernatural powers into the affairs of men.
9. Incidental but related narratives within an epic poem. Johnson is citing *Paradise Lost* 5.577 ff. and 11.334 ff.

tion of the war in heaven and Michael's prophetic account of the changes to happen in this world. Both are closely connected with the great action; one was necessary to Adam as a warning, the other as a consolation.

To the completeness or *integrity* of the design nothing can be objected; it has distinctly and clearly what Aristotle requires, a beginning, a middle, and an end. There is perhaps no poem of the same length from which so little can be taken without apparent mutilation. Here are no funeral games, nor is there any long description of a shield. The short digressions at the beginning of the third, seventh, and ninth books might doubtless be spared; but superfluities so beautiful who would take away? or who does not wish that the author of the *Iliad* had gratified succeeding ages with a little knowledge of himself? Perhaps no passages are more frequently or more attentively read than those extrinsic paragraphs; and since the end of poetry is pleasure, that cannot be unpoetical with which all are pleased.

The questions, whether the action of the poem be strictly *one*,[1] whether the poem can be properly termed *heroic*, and who is the hero, are raised by such readers as draw their principles of judgment rather from books than from reason. Milton, though he entitled *Paradise Lost* only a "poem," yet calls it himself "heroic song."[2] Dryden, petulantly and indecently, denies the heroism of Adam because he was overcome; but there is no reason why the hero should not be unfortunate except established practice, since success and virtue do not go necessarily together. Cato is the hero of Lucan, but Lucan's authority will not be suffered by Quintilian to decide. However, if success be necessary, Adam's deceiver was at last crushed; Adam was restored to his Maker's favor, and therefore may securely resume his human rank.

After the scheme and fabric of the poem must be considered its component parts, the sentiments, and the diction.

The *sentiments*, as expressive of manners or appropriated to characters, are for the greater part unexceptionably just. Splendid passages containing lessons of morality or precepts of prudence occur seldom. Such is the original formation of this poem that as it admits no human manners till the Fall, it can give little assistance to human conduct. Its end is to raise the thoughts above sublunary cares or pleasures. Yet the praise of that fortitude, with which Abdiel maintained his singularity of virtue against the scorn of multitudes, may be accommodated to all times; and Raphael's reproof of Adam's curiosity after the planetary motions, with the answer returned by Adam, may be confidently opposed to any rule of life which any poet has delivered.[3]

The thoughts which are occasionally called forth in the progress are such as could only be produced by an imagination in the highest degree fervid and active, to which materials were supplied by incessant study and unlimited curiosity. The heat of Milton's mind might be said to

---

1. I.e., a single action dealing with a single character.   2. *Paradise Lost* 9.25.
3. *Paradise Lost* 8.65 ff.

sublimate his learning, to throw off into his work the spirit of science, unmingled with its grosser parts.

He had considered creation in its whole extent, and his descriptions are therefore learned. He had accustomed his imagination to unrestrained indulgence, and his conceptions therefore were extensive. The characteristic quality of his poem is sublimity. He sometimes descends to the elegant, but his element is the great. He can occasionally invest himself with grace; but his natural port is gigantic loftiness. He can please when pleasure is required; but it is his peculiar power to astonish.

He seems to have been well acquainted with his own genius, and to know what it was that Nature had bestowed upon him more bountifully than upon others; the power of displaying the vast, illuminating the splendid, enforcing the awful, darkening the gloomy, and aggravating the dreadful: he therefore chose a subject on which too much could not be said, on which he might tire his fancy without the censure of extravagance.

*   *   *

The defects and faults of *Paradise Lost*, for faults and defects every work of man must have, it is the business of impartial criticism to discover. As in displaying the excellence of Milton I have not made long quotations, because of selecting beauties there had been no end, I shall in the same general manner mention that which seems to deserve censure; for what Englishman can take delight in transcribing passages, which, if they lessen the reputation of Milton, diminish in some degree the honor of our country?

*   *   *

The plan of *Paradise Lost* has this inconvenience, that it comprises neither human actions nor human manners. The man and woman who act and suffer are in a state which no other man or woman can ever know. The reader finds no transaction in which he can be engaged, beholds no condition in which he can by any effort of imagination place himself; he has, therefore, little natural curiosity or sympathy.

We all, indeed, feel the effects of Adam's disobedience; we all sin like Adam, and like him must all bewail our offenses; we have restless and insidious enemies in the fallen angels, and in the blessed spirits we have guardians and friends; in the Redemption of mankind we hope to be included: in the description of heaven and hell we are surely interested, as we are all to reside hereafter either in the regions of horror or of bliss.

But these truths are too important to be new: they have been taught to our infancy; they have mingled with our solitary thoughts and familiar conversation, and are habitually interwoven with the whole texture of life. Being therefore not new they raise no unaccustomed emotion in the mind: what we knew before, we cannot learn; what is not unexpected, cannot surprise.

Of the ideas suggested by these awful scenes, from some we recede with reverence, except when stated hours require their association; and from others we shrink with horror, or admit them only as salutary inflictions, as counterpoises to our interests and passions. Such images rather obstruct the career of fancy than incite it.

Pleasure and terror are indeed the genuine sources of poetry; but poetical pleasure must be such as human imagination can at least conceive, and poetical terror such as human strength and fortitude may combat. The good and evil of Eternity are too ponderous for the wings of wit; the mind sinks under them in passive helplessness, content with calm belief and humble adoration.

Known truths however may take a different appearance, and be conveyed to the mind by a new train of intermediate images. This Milton has undertaken, and performed with pregnancy and vigor of mind peculiar to himself. Whoever considers the few radical positions which the Scriptures afforded him will wonder by what energetic operation he expanded them to such extent and ramified them to so much variety, restrained as he was by religious reverence from licentiousness of fiction.

Here is a full display of the united force of study and genius; of a great accumulation of materials, with judgment to digest and fancy to combine them: Milton was able to select from nature or from story, from ancient fable or from modern science, whatever could illustrate or adorn his thoughts. An accumulation of knowledge impregnated his mind, fermented by study and exalted by imagination.

* * *

But original deficience cannot be supplied. The want of human interest is always felt. *Paradise Lost* is one of the books which the reader admires and lays down, and forgets to take up again. None ever wished it longer than it is. Its perusal is a duty rather than a pleasure. We read Milton for instruction, retire harassed and overburdened, and look elsewhere for recreation; we desert our master, and seek for companions.

* * *

Dryden remarks that Milton has some flats among his elevations.[4] This is only to say that all the parts are not equal. In every work one part must be for the sake of others; a palace must have passages, a poem must have transitions. It is no more to be required that wit should always be blazing than that the sun should always stand at noon. In a great work there is a vicissitude[5] of luminous and opaque parts, as there is in the world a succession of day and night. Milton, when he has expatiated in the sky, may be allowed sometimes to revisit earth; for what other author ever soared so high or sustained his flight so long?

* * *

4. Preface to *Sylvae*; see Essays (ed. W. P. Ker),   5. Change.
I.268.

The highest praise of genius is original invention. Milton cannot be said to have contrived the structure of an epic poem, and therefore owes reverence to that vigor and amplitude of mind to which all generations must be indebted for the art of poetical narration, for the texture of the fable, the variation of incidents, the interposition of dialogue, and all the stratagems that surprise and enchain attention. But of all the borrowers from Homer Milton is perhaps the least indebted. He was naturally a thinker for himself, confident of his own abilities and disdainful of help or hindrance; he did not refuse admission to the thoughts or images of his predecessors, but he did not seek them. From his contemporaries he neither courted nor received support; there is in his writings nothing by which the pride of other authors might be gratified or favor gained, no exchange of praise or solicitation of support. His great works were performed under discountenance and in blindness, but difficulties vanished at his touch; he was born for whatever is arduous; and his work is not the greatest of heroic poems, only because it is not the first.

1779

From Pope

[Pope's Intellectual Character. Pope and Dryden Compared]

Of his intellectual character, the constituent and fundamental principle was good sense, a prompt and intuitive perception of consonance and propriety. He saw immediately, of his own conceptions, what was to be chosen, and what to be rejected; and, in the works of others, what was to be shunned, and what to be copied.

But good sense alone is a sedate and quiescent quality, which manages its possessions well, but does not increase them; it collects few materials for its own operations, and preserves safety, but never gains supremacy. Pope had likewise genius; a mind active, ambitious, and adventurous, always investigating, always aspiring; in its widest searches still longing to go forward, in its highest flights still wishing to be higher; always imagining something greater than it knows, always endeavoring more than it can do.

To assist these powers, he is said to have had great strength and exactness of memory. That which he had heard or read was not easily lost; and he had before him not only what his own meditation suggested, but what he had found in other writers that might be accommodated to his present purpose.

These benefits of nature he improved by incessant and unwearied diligence; he had recourse to every source of intelligence, and lost no opportunity of information; he consulted the living as well as the dead; he read his compositions to his friends, and was never content with mediocrity when excellence could be attained. He considered poetry as the business of his life, and however he might seem to lament his occupation, he followed it with constancy: to make verses was his first labor, and to mend them was his last.

From his attention to poetry he was never diverted. If conversation offered anything that could be improved, he committed it to paper; if a thought, or perhaps an expression more happy than was common, rose to his mind, he was careful to write it; an independent distich was preserved for an opportunity of insertion, and some little fragments have been found containing lines, or parts of lines, to be wrought upon at some other time.

He was one of those few whose labor is their pleasure; he was never elevated to negligence, nor wearied to impatience; he never passed a fault unamended by indifference, nor quitted it by despair. He labored his works first to gain reputation, and afterwards to keep it.

Of composition there are different methods. Some employ at once memory and invention, and, with little intermediate use of the pen, form and polish large masses by continued meditation, and write their productions only when, in their own opinion, they have completed them. It is related of Virgil[1] that his custom was to pour out a great number of verses in the morning, and pass the day in retrenching exuberances and correcting inaccuracies. The method of Pope, as may be collected from his translation, was to write his first thoughts in his first words, and gradually to amplify, decorate, rectify, and refine them.

With such faculties and such dispositions, he excelled every other writer in *poetical prudence*; he wrote in such a manner as might expose him to few hazards. He used almost always the same fabric of verse; and, indeed, by those few essays which he made of any other, he did not enlarge his reputation. Of this uniformity the certain consequence was readiness and dexterity. By perpetual practice, language had in his mind a systematical arrangement; having always the same use for words, he had words so selected and combined as to be ready at his call. This increase of facility he confessed himself to have perceived in the progress of his translation.

But what was yet of more importance, his effusions were always voluntary, and his subjects chosen by himself. His independence secured him from drudging at a task, and laboring upon a barren topic: he never exchanged praise for money, nor opened a shop of condolence or congratulation. His poems, therefore, were scarce ever temporary. He suffered coronations and royal marriages to pass without a song, and derived no opportunities from recent events, nor any popularity from the accidental disposition of his readers. He was never reduced to the necessity of soliciting the sun to shine upon a birthday, of calling the Graces and Virtues to a wedding, or of saying what multitudes have said before him. When he could produce nothing new, he was at liberty to be silent.

His publications were for the same reason never hasty. He is said to have sent nothing to the press till it had lain two years under his inspec-

---

1. By Suetonius in his brief life of the poet.

tion: it is at least certain that he ventured nothing without nice examination. He suffered the tumult of imagination to subside, and the novelties of invention to grow familiar. He knew that the mind is always enamored of its own productions, and did not trust his first fondness. He consulted his friends, and listened with great willingness to criticism; and, what was of more importance, he consulted himself, and let nothing pass against his own judgment.

He professed to have learned his poetry from Dryden, whom, whenever an opportunity was presented, he praised through his whole life with unvaried liberality; and perhaps his character may receive some illustration, if he be compared with his master.

Integrity of understanding and nicety of discernment were not allotted in a less proportion to Dryden than to Pope. The rectitude of Dryden's mind was sufficiently shown by the dismission of his poetical prejudices, and the rejection of unnatural thoughts and rugged numbers. But Dryden never desired to apply all the judgment that he had. He wrote, and professed to write, merely for the people; and when he pleased others, he contented himself. He spent no time in struggles to rouse latent powers; he never attempted to make that better which was already good, nor often to mend what he must have known to be faulty. He wrote, as he tells us, with very little consideration; when occasion or necessity called upon him, he poured out what the present moment happened to supply, and, when once it had passed the press, ejected it from his mind; for when he had no pecuniary interest, he had no further solicitude.

Pope was not content to satisfy; he desired to excel, and therefore always endeavored to do his best: he did not court the candor, but dared the judgment of his reader, and, expecting no indulgence from others, he showed none to himself. He examined lines and words with minute and punctilious observation, and retouched every part with indefatigable diligence, till he had left nothing to be forgiven.

For this reason he kept his pieces very long in his hands, while he considered and reconsidered them. The only poems which can be supposed to have been written with such regard to the times as might hasten their publication were the two satires of *Thirty-Eight*; of which Dodsley[2] told me that they were brought to him by the author, that they might be fairly copied. "Almost every line," he said, "was then written twice over; I gave him a clean transcript, which he sent some time afterwards to me for the press, with almost every line written twice over a second time."

His declaration, that his care for his works ceased at their publication, was not strictly true. His parental attention never abandoned them; what he found amiss in the first edition, he silently corrected in those that followed. He appears to have revised the *Iliad*, and freed it from some of its imperfections; and the *Essay on Criticism* received many improvements after its first appearance. It will seldom be found that he altered

---

2. Robert Dodsley, the publisher.

without adding clearness, elegance, or vigor. Pope had perhaps the judgment of Dryden; but Dryden certainly wanted the diligence of Pope.

In acquired knowledge, the superiority must be allowed to Dryden, whose education was more scholastic, and who before he became an author had been allowed more time for study, with better means of information. His mind has a larger range, and he collects his images and illustrations from a more extensive circumference of science. Dryden knew more of man in his general nature, and Pope in his local manners. The notions of Dryden were formed by comprehensive speculation, and those of Pope by minute attention. There is more dignity in the knowledge of Dryden, and more certainty in that of Pope.

Poetry was not the sole praise of either; for both excelled likewise in prose; but Pope did not borrow his prose from his predecessor. The style of Dryden is capricious and varied, that of Pope is cautious and uniform; Dryden obeys the motions of his own mind, Pope constrains his mind to his own rules of composition; Dryden is sometimes vehement and rapid; Pope is always smooth, uniform, and gentle. Dryden's page is a natural field, rising into inequalities, and diversified by the varied exuberance of abundant vegetation; Pope's is a velvet lawn, shaven by the scythe, and leveled by the roller.

Of genius, that power which constitutes a poet; that quality without which judgment is cold and knowledge is inert; that energy which collects, combines, amplifies, and animates; the superiority must, with some hesitation, be allowed to Dryden. It is not to be inferred that of this poetical vigor Pope had only a little, because Dryden had more; for every other writer since Milton must give place to Pope; and even of Dryden it must be said that if he has brighter paragraphs, he has not better poems. Dryden's performances were always hasty, either excited by some external occasion, or extorted by domestic necessity; he composed without consideration, and published without correction. What his mind could supply at call, or gather in one excursion, was all that he sought, and all that he gave. The dilatory caution of Pope enabled him to condense his sentiments, to multiply his images, and to accumulate all that study might produce, or chance might supply. If the flights of Dryden therefore are higher, Pope continues longer on the wing. If of Dryden's fire the blaze is brighter, of Pope's the heat is more regular and constant. Dryden often surpasses expectation, and Pope never falls below it. Dryden is read with frequent astonishment, and Pope with perpetual delight.

This parallel will, I hope, when it is well considered, be found just; and if the reader should suspect me, as I suspect myself, of some partial fondness for the memory of Dryden, let him not too hastily condemn me; for meditation and inquiry may, perhaps, show him the reasonableness of my determination.

1781

The Romantic Period
1798-1832

1789–1815: Revolutionary and Napoleonic period in France. 1789: The Revolution begins with the assembly of the States-General in May and the storming of the Bastille on July 14.—1793: King Louis XVI executed; England joins the alliance against France.—1793–94: The Reign of Terror under Robespierre.—1804: Napoleon crowned emperor.—1815: Napoleon defeated at Waterloo.

1798: *Lyrical Ballads* published anonymously by William Wordsworth and Samuel Taylor Coleridge.

1811–20: The Regency—George, Prince of Wales, acts as regent for George III, who was declared incurably insane.

1820: Accession of George IV.

1832: The Reform Bill carried in Parliament.

THE POLITICAL BACKGROUND: REVOLUTION AND REACTION

Following the common usage of historians of English literature, we shall denote by the "Romantic period" the span between the year 1798, in which Wordsworth and Coleridge published their *Lyrical Ballads*, and 1832, when Sir Walter Scott died, when other major writers of the earlier century were either dead or no longer productive, and when passage of the first Reform Bill inaugurated the Victorian era of cautious readjustment of political power to the economic and social realities of a new industrial age. This was a turbulent period, during which England experienced the ordeal of change from a primarily agricultural society, where wealth and power had been concentrated in the landholding aristocracy, to a modern industrial nation, in which the balance of economic power shifted to large-scale employers, who found themselves ranged against an immensely enlarging and increasingly restive working class. And this change occurred in a context of the American Revolution and then of the much more radical French Revolution, of wars, of economic cycles of inflation and depression, and of the constant threat to the social structure from imported revolutionary ideologies to which the ruling classes responded by heresy hunts and the repression of traditional liberties.

The early period of the French Revolution, marked by the Declaration of the Rights of Man and the storming of the Bastille to release imprisoned political offenders, evoked enthusiastic support from English liberals and radicals alike. Two influential books indicate the radical social thinking stimulated by the Revolution. Tom Paine's *Rights of Man* (1791–92) justified the French Revolution against Edmund Burke's attack in his *Reflections on the Revolution in France* (1790), and advocated for England a democratic republic which was to be achieved, if lesser pressures failed, by popular revolution. More important as an influence on Wordsworth, Shelley, and other poets was William Godwin's *Inquiry Concerning Political Justice* (1793), which foretold an inevitable but peaceful evolution of society to a final stage in which all property would be equally distributed and all government would wither away. Later, however, English sympathizers dropped off as the Revolution followed its increasingly grim and violent course: the accession to power by Jacobin extremists; the "September Massacres" of the imprisoned and helpless nobility in 1792, followed by the execution of the royal family; the invasion by the French Republic of the Rhineland and Netherlands, and its offer of armed assistance to all countries desiring to overthrow their governments, which brought England into the war against France; the guillotining of thousands in the Reign of Terror under Robespierre; and, after the execution in their turn of the men who had directed the Terror, the emergence of Napoleon first as dictator and then as emperor of France. As Wordsworth wrote in *The Prelude* (11.206–9),

> become Oppressors in their turn,
> Frenchmen had changed a war of self-defence
> For one of Conquest, losing sight of all
> Which they had struggled for. . . .

For Wordsworth and other English observers of liberal inclinations, these events posed a dilemma which has become familiar since the 1920s, in our parallel era of wars, revolutions, and the struggle by competing social ideologies—liberals had no side they could wholeheartedly espouse. Napoleon, the child and champion of the French Revolution, had become an archaggressor, a despot, and the founder of a new dynasty; yet almost all those who opposed him did so for the wrong reasons, with the result that his final defeat at Waterloo in 1815 proved to be the triumph, not of progress and reform, but of reactionary despotisms throughout continental Europe.

In England this period was one of harsh repressive measures. Public meetings were prohibited, habeas corpus was suspended for the first time in over a hundred years, and advocates of even moderate political change were charged with high treason in time of war. The Napoleonic wars put an end to reform, and to almost all genuine political life in England, for more than three decades.

Yet this was the very time when profound economic and social changes were creating a desperate need for corresponding changes in political arrangements, and new classes—manufacturing, rather than agricultural—were beginning to demand a power in government proportionate to their wealth. The "Industrial Revolution"—the shift in manufacturing that resulted from the invention of power-driven machinery to replace hand labor—had begun in the mid-eighteenth century with improvements in machines for processing textiles, and was given immense impetus when James Watt perfected the steam engine in 1765. In the succeeding decades steam replaced wind and water as the primary source of power in one after another type of manufacturing; and at once, after centuries of almost imperceptibly slow change, there began that ever-accelerating alteration in economic and social conditions which shows no signs of slowing down in the foreseeable future. A new laboring population massed in the sprawling mill towns which burgeoned in central and northern England. In rural communities the destruction of home industry was accompanied by a rapid growth of the process—lamented by Oliver Goldsmith in *The Deserted Village* as early as 1770—of enclosing the old open-field and communally worked farms into privately owned agricultural holdings. This process was necessary for the more efficient methods of agriculture and animal breeding required to supply a growing population (although some of the land thus acquired was turned into vast private parks); in any case, it created a new landless class which either migrated to the industrial towns or remained as farm laborers, subsisting on starvation wages eked out by an inadequate dole. The landscape of England began to take on its modern appearance—the hitherto open rural areas subdivided into a checkerboard of fields enclosed by hedges and stone walls, with the factories of the industrial and trading cities casting a pall of smoke over vast areas of jerry-built houses and slum tenements. Meanwhile, the population was becoming increasingly polarized into what Disraeli later called the "Two Nations"—the two classes of capital and labor, the large owner or trader and the possessionless wageworker, the rich and the poor.

No attempt was made to regulate this shift from the old economic world to the new, not only because of inertia and the power of vested interests, but because even liberal reformers were dominated by the social philosophy of laissez-faire. This theory of "let alone" holds that the general welfare can be ensured only by the free operation of economic laws; the government must maintain a policy of strict noninterference and leave people to pursue their private interests. For the great majority of the laboring class the results of this policy were inadequate wages, long hours of work under harsh discipline in sordid conditions, and the large-scale employment of women and children for tasks that destroyed both the body and the spirit. Reports by investigating committees on the coal mines, where male and female children of ten or even five years of age were harnessed to heavy coal-sledges which they dragged by crawling on their hands and knees, read like scenes from Dante's *Inferno*. In 1815 the conclusion of the French war, when the enlargement of the working force by demobilized troops coincided with the fall in the wartime demand for goods, brought on the first modern industrial depression. Since the workers had no vote and were prevented by law from unionizing, their sole recourse was to petitions, protest meetings, agitation, and hunger riots, which only frightened the ruling class into more repressive measures. In addition the introduction of new machines caused technological unemployment, and this provoked sporadic attempts by dispossessed workers to destroy the machines. After one such outbreak the House of Lords—despite Lord Byron's eloquent protest—passed a bill (1812) making death the penalty for destroying the frames used for weaving in the stocking industry. In 1819 meetings of workers were organized to demand parliamentary reform. In August of that year, a huge but orderly assembly at St. Peter's Fields, Manchester, was wantonly charged by troops, who killed nine and severely injured hundreds more; this was the notorious "Peterloo Massacre," so named as a parody on the Battle of Waterloo. The event incited Shelley to write his great poems for the working class, *England in 1819, Song: "Men of England,"* and *To Sidmouth and Castlereagh.*

Suffering was largely confined to the poor, however, for all this while the landed classes, the industrialists, and many of the merchants prospered. In

London the Regency period (1811–20) was for the leisure class a time of lavish display and moral laxity. In the provinces, the gentry in their country houses carried on their familial and social concerns—reflected in the novels of Jane Austen—almost untouched by great national and international events.

As in earlier English history, women constituted a deprived class which cut across social classes, for they were widely regarded as inferior to men in intellect and in all but domestic talents, were provided limited schooling and no facilities for higher education, had only lowly vocations open to them, were subjected to a special, rigid code of sexual behavior, and possessed (especially after marriage) almost no legal rights. In the revolutionary period, women finally acquired a strong and eloquent champion. Mary Wollstonecraft, who in 1790 wrote an early defense of the French Revolution, A Vindication of the Rights of Men, followed this two years later with A Vindication of the Rights of Woman, a founding classic of the feminist movement. Wollstonecraft asserted that women possess equal intellectual capacity and talents with men, and demanded for them greater equality of social, educational, and vocational privileges. The cause of women's rights, however, was not taken up by effective proponents until the Victorian era, and even partial achievement of its aims was delayed until well along in the twentieth century.

But the pressures for reform in the privileges of men, as distinct from women, could not be eliminated in the early nineteenth century, especially since political disabilities were not limited to laborers. Gradually the working-class reformers acquired the support of the middle classes and the liberal Whigs. Finally, at a time of acute economic distress, and after unprecedented agitation and disorders that threatened to break out into revolution, the first Reform Bill was carried in 1832, amid widespread rejoicing. It eliminated the rotten boroughs (depopulated areas whose seat in Commons was at the disposal of a nobleman), redistributed parliamentary representation to include the new industrial cities, and extended the vote. Although about half the middle class, almost all the working class, and all women remained still without a franchise, the principle of peaceful adjustment of conflicting interests by parliamentary majority had been firmly established; and reform was to go on until, by stages, England acquired universal adult suffrage.

"THE SPIRIT OF THE AGE"

Attempts at a single definition of Romanticism fall far short of matching the variegated facts of a time which exceeds almost all other ages of English literature in the range and diversity of its achievements. No writer in Wordsworth's lifetime thought of himself as a "Romantic"; the word was not applied until half a century later, by English historians. Contemporary critics and reviewers treated them as independent individuals, or else grouped them (often invidiously, but with some basis in fact) into a number of separate schools: "the Lake School" of Wordsworth, Coleridge, and Robert Southey; "the Cockney School," a derogatory term for the Londoners Leigh Hunt, Hazlitt, and associated writers, including John Keats; and "the Satanic School" of Byron, Shelley, and their followers.

Many of the major writers, however, did feel that there was something distinctive about their time—not a shared doctrine or literary quality, but a pervasive intellectual and imaginative climate, which some of them called "the spirit of the age." They had the sense that (as Keats said in one of his sonnets) "Great spirits now on earth are sojourning," and that there was evidence all about of that release of energy, experimental boldness, and creative power which marks a literary renaissance. In his *Defence of Poetry* Shelley claimed that the literature of the age "has arisen as it were from a new birth," and that "an electric life burns" within the words of its best writers, which is "less their spirit than the spirit of the age." Shelley explained this literary spirit as an accompaniment of political and social revolution, and other writers agreed. Francis Jeffrey, foremost conservative reviewer of the day, connected "the revolution in our literature" with "the agitations of the French Revolution, and the discussions as well as the hopes and terrors to which it gave occasion." William Hazlitt, who published a book of essays called *The Spirit of the Age*, described how, in his early youth, the French Revolution seemed "the dawn of a new era, a new impulse had been given to men's minds." The new poetry of the school of Wordsworth, he maintained, "had its origin in the French Revolution. . . . It was a time of promise, a renewal of the world—and of letters."

The imagination of Romantic writers was, indeed, preoccupied with the fact and idea of revolution. In the early period of the French Revolution all the leading English writers except Edmund Burke were in sympathy with it, and Robert Burns, William Blake, Wordsworth, Coleridge, Southey, and Mary Wollstonecraft were among its fervent adherents. Later, even after the first boundless expectations had been disappointed by the events in France, the younger writers, including Hazlitt, Hunt, Shelley, and Byron, felt that its example, when purged of its errors, still comprised humanity's best hope. The Revolution generated a pervasive feeling that this was a great age of new beginnings when, by discarding inherited procedures and outworn customs, everything was possible, and not only in the political and social realm but in intellectual and literary enterprises as well. In his *Prelude* Wordsworth wrote the classic description of the intoxicating spirit of the early 1790s, with "France standing on the top of golden hours, / And human nature seeming born again," so that "the whole Earth, / The beauty wore of promise." Something of this sense of suddenly limitless possibilities survived the shock of first disappointment at events in France and carried over to the year 1797, when Wordsworth and Coleridge, in excited daily communion, set out to revolutionize, on grounds analogous to the politics of democracy, the theory and practice of poetry. The product of these discussions was the *Lyrical Ballads* of 1798.

POETIC THEORY AND POETIC PRACTICE

Wordsworth undertook to justify the new poetry by a critical manifesto or statement of poetic principles, in the form of an extended Preface to the second edition of *Lyrical Ballads* in 1800, which he enlarged still further in the third edition of 1802. In it he set himself in opposition to the literary *ancien régime*, those writers of the preceding century who, in his view, had imposed on poetry artificial conventions that distorted its free and natural development. Many of Wordsworth's later critical writings were attempts to clarify, buttress, or qualify points made in his first declaration. Coleridge declared that the Preface was "half a child of my own brain"; and although he soon developed doubts about some of Wordsworth's unguarded statements, and undertook to correct them in *Biographia Literaria* (1817), he did not question the necessity of Wordsworth's attempt to overturn the reigning tradition. In the course of the eighteenth century there had been increasing opposition to the tradition of Dryden, Pope, and Johnson, and especially in the 1740s and later, there had emerged many of the critical concepts, as well as a number of the poetic subjects and forms, that were later exploited by Wordsworth and his contemporaries. Wordsworth's Preface nevertheless deserves its reputation as a turning point in English literature, for Wordsworth gathered up isolated ideas, organized them into a coherent theory based on explicit critical principles, and made them the rationale for his own massive achievements as a poet. We can conveniently use the concepts in this extremely influential essay as points of departure for a survey of distinctive elements in the theory and poetry of the Romantic period.

1. The Concept of Poetry and the Poet

Eighteenth-century theorists had regarded poetry as primarily an imitation of human life—in a frequent figure, "a mirror held up to nature"—which the poet artfully renders and puts into an order designed to instruct and give artistic pleasure to the reader. Wordsworth, on the other hand, repeatedly described all good poetry as, at the moment of composition, "the spontaneous overflow of powerful feelings." Reversing earlier theory, he thus located the source of a poem not in the outer world, but in the individual poet, and specified that the essential materials of a poem were not external people and events, but the inner feelings of the author, or at any rate, external objects only after these have been transformed or irradiated by the author's feelings. Other Romantic theories, however diverse in other aspects, concurred on this crucial point by referring primarily to the mind, emotions, and imagination of the poet, instead of to the outer world, for the origin, content, and defining attributes of a poem. Many writers identified poetry (in metaphors parallel to Wordsworth's "overflow") as the "expression" or "utterance" or "exhibition" of emotion. Blake and Shelley described a poem as an embodiment of the poet's imaginative vision, which they opposed to the ordinary world of common experience. Coleridge introduced into English criticism an organic theory of the imaginative process and the poetic product, based on the model of the growth of a plant. That is, he conceived a great work of literature to be a self-originating and self-organizing process that begins with a seedlike idea in the poet's imagination, grows by assimilating both the poet's feelings and the diverse materials of sense-experience, and evolves into an organic whole in which the parts are integrally related to each other and to the whole.

In accordance with the view that poetry expresses the poet's own feelings and temperament, the lyric poem written in the first person, earlier regarded as a minor kind, became a major Romantic form, and was often described as the most essentially poetic of all the genres. And in the Romantic lyric the "I" often is not a conventionally typical lyric speaker, such as the Petrarchan lover or Cavalier gallant of Elizabethan and seventeenth-century love poems, but has recognizable characteristics of the poet in his own person and circumstances. In the poems of Wordsworth, Coleridge, Shelley, and Keats the experiences and states of mind expressed by the lyric speaker often accord closely with the known facts of the poet's life and with the personal confessions in his letters and journals. Even in his ostensibly fictional writings, narrative and dramatic, Byron usually invites his readers to identify the hero with the author, whether the hero is presented romantically (as in *Childe Harold, Manfred*, or the Oriental tales) or in an ironic perspective (as in *Don Juan*). An extreme instance of this tendency is Wordsworth's *Prelude*, which is a poem of epic length and epic seriousness about the growth of the poet's own mind.

The Prelude exemplifies two other important tendencies in the period. Like Blake, Coleridge in his early poems, and later on Shelley, Wordsworth presents himself as what he calls "a chosen son," or "Bard." That is, he assumes the persona and voice of a poet-prophet, modeled on Milton and the prophets in the Bible, and puts himself forward as a spokesman for traditional Western civilization at a time of profound crisis—a time, as Wordsworth said in book 2 of *The Prelude*, "of dereliction and dismay" and the "melancholy waste of hopes o'erthrown." As bards, Wordsworth and his visionary fellow poets set out to revise the Biblical promise of divine redemption by reconstituting the grounds of hope and pronouncing the coming of a time in which a renewed humanity will inhabit a renovated earth on which men and women will feel thoroughly at home. *The Prelude* also represents a central literary form of English, as of European Romanticism—a long work about the formation of the self, often centering on a crisis, and presented in the radical metaphor of an interior journey in quest of one's true identity and destined spiritual home. Major examples of this form are Blake's *Milton*, the crucial episode of Asia's underground journey in Shelley's *Prometheus Unbound*, and Keats's *Endymion* and the *Fall of Hyperion*. In contemporary prose, we find equivalent developments: the subjectivity of the personal essays of Lamb, Hazlitt, and Leigh Hunt, and the currency of spiritual autobiography, whether fictionalized (Thomas Carlyle's *Sartor Resartus*) or presented as fact (Coleridge's *Biographia Literaria*, Thomas De Quincey's *Confessions of an English Opium Eater* and *Autobiographic Sketches*).

2. Poetic Spontaneity and Freedom

Wordsworth defined good poetry not merely as the overflow but as "the *spontaneous* overflow" of feelings. In traditional aesthetic theory, poetry had been regarded as supremely an art—an art which in modern times could be practiced successfully only by poets who had assimilated classical precedents, were aware of the "rules" governing the kind of poem they were writing, and (except for the felicities which, as Pope said, are "beyond the reach of art") deliberately employed tested means to achieve foreknown effects upon an audience. But to Wordsworth, although the composition of a poem originates from "emotion recollected in tranquillity," and may be preceded and followed by reflection, the immediate act of composition must be spontaneous—that is, arising from impulse, and free from all rules and the artful manipulation of means to foreseen ends—if the product is to be a genuine poem. Other important Romantic critics also voiced declarations of artistic independence. Keats listed as an "axiom" that "if poetry comes not as naturally as the leaves to a tree it had better not come at all." Blake insisted that he wrote from "Inspiration and Vision" and that his long "prophetic" poem *Milton* was given to him by an agency not himself and "produced without Labor or Study." Shelley also maintained that it is "an error to assert that the finest passages of poetry are produced by labor and study," and suggested instead that they are the products of an unconscious creativity: "A great statue or picture grows under the power of the artist as a child in the mother's womb." "The definition of genius," Hazlitt remarked, "is that it acts unconsciously." The surviving manuscripts of the Romantic poets, however, as well as the testimony of observers, show that they worked and reworked their texts no less arduously—if perhaps more immediately under the impetus of first conception—than the poets of earlier ages. Coleridge, who believed that truth lies in a union of opposites, came closer to the facts of Romantic practice when he claimed that the act of composing poetry involves the psychological contraries "of passion and of will, of *spontaneous* impulse and of *voluntary* purpose."

The emphasis in this period on the free activity of the imagination is related to an insistence on the essential role of instinct, intuition, and the feelings of "the heart" to supplement the judgments of the purely logical faculty, "the head," whether in the province of artistic beauty, philosophical and religious truth, or moral goodness. "Deep thinking," Coleridge wrote, "is attainable only by a man of deep feeling, and all truth is a species of revelation"; hence, "a metaphysical solution that does not tell you something in the heart is grievously to be suspected as apocryphal."

3. Romantic "Nature Poetry"

In his Preface Wordsworth wrote that "I have at all times endeavored to look steadily at my subject"; and in a supplementary Essay he complained that from Dryden through Pope there is scarcely an image from external nature "from which it can be inferred that the eye of the poet had been steadily fixed on his object." A glance at the table of contents of any collection of Romantic poems will show the degree to which the natural scene has become a primary poetic subject, while Wordsworth, Shelley, and even more Coleridge and Keats, described natural phenomena with an accuracy of observation which had no earlier match in its ability to capture the sensuous nuance.

Because of the prominence of landscape in this period, "Romantic poetry" has to the popular mind become almost synonymous with "nature poetry." Neither Romantic theory nor practice, however, justifies the opinion that the aim of this poetry was description for its own sake. Wordsworth in fact insisted that the ability to observe and describe objects accurately, although a necessary, is not at all a sufficient condition for poetry, "as its exercise supposes all the higher qualities of the mind to be passive, and in a state of subjection to external objects." And while most of the great Romantic lyrics—Wordsworth's *Tintern Abbey* and *Ode: Intimations of Immortality*, Coleridge's *Frost at Midnight* and *Dejection*, Shelley's *Ode to the West Wind*, Keats's *Nightingale*—begin with an aspect or change of aspect in the natural scene, this serves only as stimulus to the most characteristic human activity, that of thinking. Romantic "nature poems" are in fact meditative poems, in which the presented scene usually serves to raise an emotional problem or personal crisis whose development and resolution constitute the organizing principle of the poem. As Wordsworth said in his Prospectus to *The Recluse*, not nature, but "the Mind of Man" is "my haunt, and the main region of my song."

In addition, Romantic poems habitually imbue the landscape with human life, passion, and expressiveness. In part such descriptions represent the poetic equivalent of the metaphysical concept of nature, which had developed in deliberate revolt against the world views of the scientific philosophers of the seventeenth and eighteenth centuries, who had posited as the ultimate reality a mechanical world consisting of physical particles in motion. What is needed in philosophy, Coleridge wrote, is "the substitution of life and intelligence . . . for the philosophy of mechanism, which, in everything that is most worthy of the human intellect, strikes *Death.*" But for many Romantic poets it was clearly also a matter of immediate experience to respond to the outer universe as a living entity which participates in the feelings of the observer. James Thomson and other descriptive poets of the preceding century had depicted the created universe as giving direct access to God, and even as itself possessing the attributes of divinity; in *Tintern Abbey* and other poems Wordsworth exhibits toward the landscape attitudes and sentiments which human beings had earlier felt not only for God, but also for a father, a mother, or a beloved. Elsewhere, as in the great passage on crossing Simplon Pass (*The Prelude* 6.625 ff.), Wordsworth also revives the ancient theological concept that God's creation constitutes a symbol system, a physical revelation parallel to Revelation in the Scriptures—

> Characters of the great Apocalypse,
> The types and symbols of Eternity,
> Of first, and last, and midst, and without end.

This view of natural objects as corresponding to an inner or a spiritual world served also as the understructure for a tendency, especially by Blake and Shelley, to write a symbolist poetry in which a rose, a sunflower, a mountain, a cave, or a cloud is presented as an object instinct with a significance beyond itself. "I always seek in what I see," Shelley said, "the likeness of something beyond the present and tangible object." And by Blake mere nature, as perceived by the physical eye and unhumanized by the imagination, was spurned "as the dirt upon my feet, no part of me."

4. The Glorification of the Commonplace

In two lectures on Wordsworth, Hazlitt declared that the school of poetry founded by Wordsworth was the literary equivalent of the French Revolution, translating political changes into poetical experiments. "Kings and queens were dethroned from their rank and station in legitimate tragedy or epic poetry, as they were decapitated elsewhere. . . . The paradox [these poets] set out with was that all things are by nature equally fit subjects for poetry; or that if there is any preference to be given, those that are the meanest and most unpromising are the best."

Hazlitt had in mind Wordsworth's statement that the aim of *Lyrical Ballads* was "to choose incidents and situations from common life" and to use a "selection of language really spoken by men," for which the source and model is "humble and rustic life." As Hazlitt shrewdly saw, this was more a social than a distinctively literary definition of the proper materials and language for poetry. Versifiers of the later decades of the eighteenth century had experimented in the simple treatment of simple subjects, and Robert Burns—like Wordsworth, a sympathizer with the French Revolution—had achieved great poetic success in the serious representation of humble life in a language really spoken by rustics. But Wordsworth buttressed his poetic practice by a theory which inverted the traditional hierarchy of poetic genres, subjects, and style by elevating humble and rustic life and the plain style, earlier appropriate only to the lowly pastoral, into the principal subject and medium for poetry in general. And in his own practice, as Hazlitt also noted, Wordsworth went even further, and turned for the subjects of his serious poems not only to humble people but to the ignominious, the outcast, the delinquent—to "convicts, female vagrants, gypsies . . . idiot boys and mad mothers," as well as to "peasants, peddlers, and village barbers." Hence the outrage of Lord Byron, who alone among his great contemporaries insisted that Dryden and Pope had laid out the proper road for poetry, and who—in spite of his liberalism in politics—maintained allegiance both to aristocratic proprieties and traditional poetic decorum:

> "Peddlers," and "Boats," and "Wagons"! Oh! ye shades
> Of Pope and Dryden, are we come to this?

But in his democratization of poetry, Hazlitt insisted, Wordsworth was "the most original poet now living." And certainly Wordsworth in *Lyrical Ballads* was, in this respect, more radical than any of his contemporaries. He effected an immense enlargement of our imaginative sympathies and brought into the province of serious literature a range of materials and interests which are still being explored by writers of the present day.

It should be noted, however, that Wordsworth's aim in *Lyrical Ballads* was not to represent the actual world, but, as he announced in his Preface, to throw over "situations from common life . . . a certain coloring of imagination, whereby ordinary things should be presented to the mind in an unusual aspect." As this passage indicates, Wordsworth's concern in his poetry was not only with "common life" but with "ordinary *things*"; no one can read his poems without noticing the extraordinary reverence which he attaches to words which in earlier writers had been derogatory—words like "common," "ordinary," "everyday," "humble," whether applied to people or to objects in the visible scene. His aim throughout is to shake us out of the lethargy of custom so as to refresh our sense of wonder—indeed, of divinity—in the everyday, the commonplace, the trivial, and the lowly.

Samuel Johnson had said that "wonder is a pause of reason" and that "all wonder is the effect of novelty upon ignorance." But for many Romantic critics, to arouse in the sophisticated mind that sense of wonder felt by the ignorant and the innocent was a primary power of imagination and a major function of poetry. Commenting on the special imaginative quality of Wordsworth's early poetry (*Biographia*, chapter 6), Coleridge remarked: "To combine the child's sense of wonder and novelty with the appearances, which every day for perhaps forty years had rendered familiar . . . this is the character and privilege of genius," and its prime service is to awaken in the reader "freshness of sensation" in the representation of "familiar objects." Poetry, said Shelley in his *Defence of Poetry*, "reproduces the common universe" but "purges from our inward sight the film of familiarity which obscures from us the wonder of our being," and "creates anew the universe, after it has been blunted by reiteration." And in Carlyle's *Sartor Resartus* (1833–34), the chief—indeed the only—effect of the conversion of the protagonist from despairing unbelief is that he is able to sustain a sense of the "Natural Supernaturalism" in ordinary experience and so overcome the "custom" which "blinds us to the miraculousness of daily-recurring miracles." The great power of the imagination is that it makes the old world new again.

5. The Supernatural and "Strangeness in Beauty"

In most of his poems Coleridge, like Wordsworth, dealt with the everyday things of this world, and in *Frost at Midnight* he showed how well he too could achieve the effect of wonder in the familiar. But according to the agreed division of labor in *Lyrical Ballads*, Coleridge's function, he tells us, was to achieve wonder by a frank violation of natural laws and the ordinary course of events, in poems of which "the incidents and agents were to be, in part at least, supernatural." And in *The Ancient Mariner, Christabel*, and *Kubla Khan*, he opened up to poetry the realm of mystery and magic, in which materials from ancient folklore, superstition, and demonology are used to impress upon the reader the sense of the working of occult powers and unknown modes of being. Such poems are usually set in the distant past or in faraway places, or both; the milieu of *Kubla Khan*, for example, exploits the exoticism both of the Middle Ages and of the Orient. Next to Coleridge, the greatest master of this Romantic mode—in which supernatural events have a profound psychological import—was John Keats. In *La Belle Dame sans Merci* and *The Eve of St. Agnes* he adapted the old forms of ballad and romance to modern sophisticated use and, like Coleridge, established a medieval setting for events that violate our sense of realism and the natural order. Hence the term "medieval revival," frequently attached to the Romantic period, which comprehends also the ballad imitations and some of the verse tales and historical novels of Sir Walter Scott.

Another side of the tendency that Walter Pater later called "the addition of strangeness to beauty" was the Romantic interest in unusual modes of experience, of a kind that earlier writers had largely ignored as either too trivial or too aberrant for serious literary concern. Blake, Wordsworth, and Coleridge in their poetry explored visionary states of consciousness that are common among children but violate the standard categories of adult judgment. Coleridge was interested in mesmerism (what we now call hypnotism), and, like Blake and Shelley, studied the literature of the occult and the esoteric. Coleridge also shared with De Quincey a concern with dreams and nightmares; both authors exploited in their writings the heightened consciousness and distorted perceptions they experienced under their addiction to opium. Byron made repeated use of the fascination of the forbidden and the appeal of the terrifying Satanic hero. And Keats was extraordinarily sensitive to the ambivalences of human experience—to the mingling, at their highest intensity, of pleasure and pain, to the destructiveness of love, and to the erotic quality of the longing for death. These phenomena had already been explored by eighteenth-century writers of terror tales and Gothic fiction, and later in the nineteenth century all of them, sometimes exaggerated to blatant perversity, became the special literary province of Charles Baudelaire, Algernon Charles Swinburne, and writers of the European "Decadence."

INDIVIDUALISM, INFINITE STRIVING, AND NONCONFORMITY

Through the greater part of the eighteenth century, men and women had for the most part been viewed as limited beings in a strictly ordered and essentially unchanging world. A variety of philosophical and religious systems in this century coincided in a distrust of radical innovation, a respect for the precedents established through the ages by the common sense of humanity, and the recommendation to set accessible goals and avoid extremes, whether in politics, intellect, morality, or art. Many of the great literary works of the period joined in attacking "pride," or aspirations beyond the limits natural to our species. "The bliss of man," Pope wrote in *An Essay on Man*, "(could pride that blessing find) / Is not to act or think beyond mankind."

> This kind, this due degree
> Of blindness, weakness, Heaven bestows on thee.
> Submit.

The Romantic period, the age of burgeoning free enterprise and revolutionary hope, was also an age of radical individualism, in which both the philosophers and poets put an immensely higher estimate on human potentialities and powers. In German post-Kantian philosophy, which generated many of the characteristic ideas of European Romanticism, the human mind—what was called the "Subject" or "Ego"—took over various functions which had hitherto been the sole prerogative of Divinity. Most prominent was the rejection of a central eighteenth-century concept of the mind as a mirrorlike recipient of a universe already created, and its replacement by the new concept of the mind as itself the creator of the universe it perceives. The English founders of the new poetry also described the mind as creating its own experience. In Blake, the mind creates its proper milieu only if it rejects the material world; in Coleridge and Wordsworth, the mind creates in collaboration with something given to it from without. Mind, wrote Coleridge in 1801, is "not passive" but "made in God's Image, and that too in the sublimest sense—the Image of the *Creator*." And Wordsworth declared in *The Prelude* (2.258–61) that the individual mind

> Doth, like an Agent of the one great Mind,
> Create, creator and receiver both,
> Working but in alliance with the works
> Which it beholds.

Many Romantic writers also agreed that the mind has access beyond sense to the infinite, through a special faculty they called either Reason or Imagination. In *The Prelude* (6.600 ff.) Wordsworth describes a flash of imagination "that has revealed / The invisible world," and affirms:

> Our destiny, our being's heart and home,
> Is with infinitude, and only there;
> With hope it is, hope that can never die,
> Effort, and expectation, and desire,
> And something evermore about to be.

The aspect of humanity that, to the moralists of the preceding age, had been an essential sin, or tragic error, now becomes a glory and a triumph: the human being refuses to submit to limitations and, though finite, persists in setting infinite, hence inaccessible goals. Wordsworth characteristically goes on to declare that "under such banners militant, the soul / Seeks for no trophies, struggles for no spoils"; for him, the militant striving ends in physical quietism and moral fortitude. But for other writers, especially in Germany, the proper human aim is ceaseless activity—a *"Streben nach dem Unendlichen,"* a striving for the infinite. This view is epitomized by Goethe's Faust, who in his quest for the unattainable violates ordinary moral limits, yet wins salvation by his very insatiability, which never stoops to contentment with any possibilities offered by this finite world. Infinite longing—in Shelley's phrase, "the desire of the moth for a star"—was a recurrent theme also in the English literature of the day. "Less than everything," Blake announced, "cannot satisfy man." Shelley's *Alastor* and Keats's *Endymion* both represent the quest for an indefinable and inaccessible goal, and Byron's *Manfred* has for its hero a man whose "powers and will" reach beyond the limits of that human clay "which clogs the ethereal essence," so that "his aspirations / Have been beyond the dwellers of the earth."

In a parallel fashion, Romantic theorists of art rejected the neoclassic ideal of a limited intention, perfectly accomplished, in favor of "the glory of the imperfect," in which the very failures of artists attest the unlimited reach of their aims. And in their own work, Romantic writers deliberately put themselves in competition with the greatest of their predecessors and experimented boldly in poetic language, versification, and design. Especially in their longer poems they struck out in new directions, and in the space of a few decades produced an astonishing variety of forms constructed on novel principles of organization and style. Blake's symbolic lyrics and visionary "prophetic" poems; Coleridge's haunting ballad-narrative of sin and retribution, *The Ancient Mariner*; Wordsworth's epiclike spiritual autobiography, *The Prelude*; Shelley's cosmic symbolic drama, *Prometheus Unbound*; Keats's great sequence of *Odes* on the irreconcilable conflict in basic human desires; Byron's ironic survey of all European civilization, *Don Juan*—one can say of each of them, as Shelley said of Byron's poem, that it was "something wholly new and relative to the age."

The great eighteenth-century writers had typically dealt with men and women as members of an organized, and usually an urban, society; of this society authors regarded themselves to be integral parts, its highest standards were those that they spoke for, and to it as their audience they addressed themselves. Some Romantic writers, on the other hand, deliberately isolated themselves from society in order to give scope to their individual vision. Wordsworth's projected masterwork he entitled *The Recluse*, and he described himself as "musing in solitude" on its subject, "the individual Mind that keeps her own / Inviolate retirement." And in almost all Wordsworth's poems, long or short, the words "single," "solitary," "by oneself," "alone" constitute a leitmotif; his imagination is released by the sudden apparition of a single figure or object, stark against an undifferentiated background. Coleridge also, and still more strikingly Byron and Shelley, represented a solitary protagonist who is separated from society because he has rejected it, or because it has rejected him. These last three poets introduced what became a persistent theme in many Victorian and modern writers—the theme of exile, of the disinherited mind that cannot find a spiritual home in its native land and society or anywhere in the modern world. The solitary Romantic nonconformist was sometimes also a great sinner. Writers of that time were fascinated by the outlaws of myth, legend, or history—Cain, Satan, Faust, the Wandering Jew, or the great, flawed figure of Napoleon—about whom they wrote and on whom they modeled a number of their villains or their heroes. In Coleridge's *Ancient Mariner* (as in Wordsworth's *Guilt and Sorrow* and *Peter Bell*) the guilty outcast—"alone, alone, all, all alone"—is made to realize and expiate his sin against the community of living things, so that he may reassume his place in the social order. But in Byron the violator of conventional laws and limits remains proudly unrepentant. His hero Manfred, a compound of guilt and superhuman greatness, cannot be defeated by death, successfully defying the demons who, in the tradition of Marlowe's *Dr. Faustus*, have come to drag his soul to hell: I "was my own destroyer, and will be / My own hereafter . . . / Back, ye baffled fiends!" A more reputable

Romantic hero, who turns up frequently in Byron and other writers and is made the protagonist of Shelley's greatest poem, is the Prometheus of Greek mythology. He shares with Satan the status of superlative nonconformity, since he sets himself in opposition to deity itself; unlike Satan, however, he is the champion rather than the enemy of the human race.

APOCALYPTIC EXPECTATIONS

Nowhere is the Romantic combination of boundless aspiration and the reliance on the power of the individual mind and imagination better exhibited than in the literary treatment of the ultimate hope of humanity. The French Revolution had aroused in many sympathizers the millennial expectations that are profoundly rooted in Hebrew and Christian tradition. "Few persons but those who have lived in it," Robert Southey reminisced in 1824, "can conceive or comprehend what the memory of the French Revolution was, nor what a visionary world seemed to open upon those who were just entering it. Old things seemed passing away, and nothing was dreamt of but the regeneration of the human race." Southey's language—like that of Wordsworth, Coleridge, Hazlitt, and other writers when they described their early Revolutionary fervor—is Biblical; and it reflects the extent to which, in England, the Revolution was championed by members of radical Protestant sects, who envisioned it on the model of Biblical prophecy.

The Bible ends with the book of Apocalypse (literally, "Revelation"), prophesying a return of human beings to their lost Edenic felicity, first in the millennium ("a thousand years") of an earthly kingdom, then in the eternity of "a new heaven and a new earth"; this consummation of history is symbolized as a marriage between the New Jerusalem and Christ the Lamb. At the outbreak of the French Revolution, Joseph Priestley and other Unitarian leaders hailed that event as the stage preceding the millennium prophesied in Revelation. Coleridge and Wordsworth, in their early poems, also interpreted the Revolution as the violent preliminary to the new earth and heaven of apocalyptic prophecy. And Blake's *The French Revolution* (1791) and *America, a Prophecy* (1793) represented both these revolutions as apocalyptic portents of the last days of the fallen world.

When the later events in France dashed their faith in political revolution as a means to the millennium, a number of Romantic writers salvaged their apocalyptic hope by giving it a new interpretation. They transferred the agency of apocalypse from mass action to the individual mind—from a political to a spiritual revolution—and proposed that "the new earth and new heaven" of Revelation is available here, now, to all of us, if only we can make our visionary imagination triumph over our senses and sensebound understanding. Hence the extraordinary Romantic emphasis on a new way of *seeing* (which is regarded as the restoration of a lost earlier way of seeing) as the chief aim in life. Blake's "Prophetic Books," for example, all deal with some aspects of the Fall and Redemption, and represent apocalypse as the recovery of the imaginative vision of things as they really are, seen "through and not with the eye." "The Nature of my Work is Visionary or Imaginative; it is an Endeavor to Restore what the Ancients called the Golden Age." This concept of the imaginative re-creation of the old earth is still expressed by Romantic poets in the original Biblical metaphor of a marriage—although now it is not a marriage of the New Jerusalem with the Lamb, but a conjunction of the inner faculties into spiritual unity, or else a marriage between the mind and the external world. Coleridge put this latter version succinctly in *Dejec-*

tion: An Ode; it is the inner condition of "Joy," at life's highest moments, "Which, wedding nature to us, gives in dower / A new earth and new heaven." Wordsworth announced as his "high argument" in the Prospectus to *The Recluse* (the same theme serves as underpattern for *The Prelude*) that "Paradise, and groves Elysian" are not "a history only of departed things"—

> For the discerning intellect of Man
> When wedded to this goodly universe
> In love and holy passion, shall find these
> A simple produce of the common day.

In Shelley's *Prometheus Unbound*, Prometheus represents archetypal humanity whose total change in moral being frees the imaginative capacity to envision, and to achieve, a regenerate world; the fourth act symbolizes this event in the mode of a marriage festival in which the whole cosmos participates.

Carlyle's *Sartor Resartus*, to mention one other example, is the history of an individual's savage spiritual crisis and conversion, which turns out to be the achievement of an individual apocalypse: "And I awoke to a new Heaven and a new Earth." But, as Carlyle goes on to indicate, this new earth is the old earth, seen by his protagonist as though miraculously re-created, because he has learned to substitute the "Imaginative" faculty for what Carlyle represents as the chief faculty of the eighteenth-century Enlightenment, the "Logical, Mensurative faculty," or "Understanding." Writing in 1830–31, at the close of the period historians have labeled "Romantic," Carlyle thus summed up the tendency of a generation of writers to retain the ancient faith in apocalypse, but to interpret it not as a change of the world, but as a change in our imaginative vision, or world view.

THE FAMILIAR ESSAY

At the close of the eighteenth century, reviews and magazines were written largely by hacks who acceded to the political bias and financial interests of the publisher and advertisers. The essays they included were weak imitations of the type established nearly a century earlier by single-essay periodicals such as the *Tatler* and the *Spectator*. In 1802, however, the *Edinburgh Review* inaugurated the modern type of periodical publication. It allowed considerable latitude to its writers, set its literary standards high, and was able to meet these standards by paying its contributors rates good enough to command the best talents of the day.

The immediate success of this new enterprise stimulated the founding of rival reviews and magazines. (A "review," usually issued four times yearly, consisted primarily of essays on important books and discussions of contemporary issues; a "magazine" was a monthly publication that printed more miscellaneous materials, including a high proportion of original essays, poems, and stories.) In 1820 appeared the *London Magazine*, liberal in politics and contemporary in literary interests; in its short but notable career until 1829 it printed the work of a group of brilliant writers, including the three men who soon established themselves as the greatest essayists of the age—Lamb, Hazlitt, and De Quincey. These new periodicals not only elevated the essay in literary dignity and quality but revolutionized its form and substance. They competed strenuously for talent, paying well enough so that an author (at least one as prolific as Hazlitt) could earn a living as a free-lance essayist. Since allotment of space was flexible, each topic could find its appropriate length, instead of being held to the Procrustean brevity of the earlier essays modeled on Addison and Steele; in consequence, the new essays tended to be from two to four times as long as the eighteenth-century form. And writers were treated as serious practitioners who were competent, within broad limits, to write as they pleased.

Under these new conditions the "familiar essay"—a commentary on a non-technical subject written in a relaxed and intimate manner—flourished, and in a fashion that to some degree paralleled the course of Romantic poetry. Each of the three major essayists was in fact closely associated with important poets and supported at least some of the new poetic developments in critical commentaries whose perceptiveness and discrimination render them permanently valuable. Like the poets, these essayists were personal and subjective; their essays are often candidly autobiographical, reminiscent, self-analytic; and when the writers treated other matters than themselves, they tended to do so impressionistically, so that the material is seen reflected in the temperament of the essayist. The subject matter of the essays, like that of the poetry, exhibits an extension of range and sympathy far beyond the earlier limits of the leisure class and its fashionable concerns, to comprehend clerks, chimney sweeps, poor relations, handball players, prizefighters, and murderers. Most strikingly, the essayists resemble the poets in rebelling against eighteenth-century conventions to revive prose forms long disused and to develop new prose styles and structural principles. The result was a notable variety of achievements, ranging from Hazlitt's hard-hitting plain style and seemingly casual order of topics, through Lamb's delicately contrived rhetoric and meticulously controlled organization, to De Quincey's elaborate experiments in applying to prose the rhythms, harmonies, and thematic structure of music.

THE DRAMA

Although favorable to the essay, literary conditions in the early nineteenth century were unfavorable in the extreme to writing for the stage. By a licensing act which was not repealed until 1843, only the Drury Lane and Covent Garden theaters had the right to produce "legitimate"—that is to say, spoken—drama; the other theaters were restricted by law to entertainments in which there could be no dialogue except to music, and so put on mainly dancing, pantomime, and various types of musical plays. The two monopoly theaters were vast and ill-lighted, and their audiences were noisy and unruly; as a result, actors played in a grandiose and orotund style. To succeed under such conditions, plays had also to be blatant and magniloquent, so that the drama of that period (fettered also by rigid moral and political censorship) tended to the extremes of either farce or melodrama. None of the plays written by the professional playwrights of the time are read nowadays, and they survive mainly in the limbo of scholarly monographs on the history of the theater.

Nonetheless, attracted irresistibly by the example of their idolized Shakespeare, all the greatest Romantic poets, and many minor ones, tried their hand at poetic plays. Some of these were deliberate closet drama—Byron's *Manfred* and Shelley's *Prometheus Unbound*, for example, can hardly be visualized, much less produced—but others were expressly written for the stage. The poets, however, lacked experience with the hard necessities of the practical theater, and they were for the most part unable to throw off the artifice of an archaic style dominated by Elizabethan and Jacobean models.

Above all, the genius of an age which excelled in subjective or visionary literary forms was ill adapted to the theater, which is a peculiarly social genre and must represent a variety of credible characters. Even Byron, the only important poet of his generation to produce major work in a literary kind— satire—which requires a highly developed social sensibility, did not succeed as a practical dramatist. His stage plays, while readable, mainly exhibit various aspects of the Byronic hero; they lack theatrical vigor and variety, and their thin-skinned author wisely refused to let them be put on before the merciless and demonstrative audiences of his day. Coleridge achieved a minor hit with his tragedy *Remorse*, which ran for twenty nights at the Drury Lane in 1813. The most successful Romantic dramatist was, surprisingly, Shelley. In *The Cenci* (1820) Shelley, with extraordinary tact and genuine theatrical acumen, converts a true story of the Italian Renaissance—of a monstrous father who violates his daughter and is in turn murdered by her—into a powerful version of his own central fable of the instinctive desire of evil to destroy, by degrading, the defiant individual, and of the moral triumph of the unconquerable single spirit, even in death. The play was not staged, however, until long after Shelley's death.

THE NOVEL

Two new types of fiction were prominent in the late eighteenth century. One was the "Gothic novel," which had been inaugurated in 1764 by Horace Walpole's *Castle of Otranto: A Gothic Story*, and continued by Clara Reeve in *The Champion of Virtue: A Gothic Story* (1777). The term derives from the frequent setting of these tales in a gloomy castle of the Middle Ages, but it has been extended to a larger group of novels, set somewhere in the past, which exploit the possibilities of mystery and terror in sullen, craggy landscapes; decaying mansions with dank dungeons, secret passages, and stealthy ghosts; chilling supernatural phenomena; and, often, persecution of a beautiful maiden by an obsessed and haggard villain. These novels opened up to later fiction the dark, irrational side of human nature—the savage egoism, the perverse impulses, and the nightmarish terrors that lie beneath the controlled and ordered surface of the conscious mind. Some of the most powerful and influential writings in the mode were by women—they doubtless afforded a fictional release for the submerged desires and compensatory fantasies of that rigidly restricted and disadvantaged class. In her *Mysteries of Udolpho* (1794), and better still in *The Italian* (1797), Ann Radcliffe developed the figure of the mysterious and solitary *homme fatal*, torturing others because himself tortured by unspeakable guilt, who, though a villain, usurps the place of the hero in the reader's interest. Matthew Gregory Lewis in *The Monk* (1797), which he wrote at the age of twenty, has a similar protagonist, and brings to the fore the elements of diabolism, sensuality, and sadistic perversion which were pungent but submerged components in Radcliffe's Gothic formula. Gothicism is apparent also in Romantic poetry: in Coleridge's medieval terror poem *Christabel*, in Byron's recurrent hero-villain, and in Shelley's inclinations (fostered by his early love for Gothic tales and his own youthful trials in that form) toward the fantastic, the macabre, and the exploration of the realm of the unconscious mind and of such aberrations as incest.

The second fictional mode popular at the turn of the century was the novel of purpose, often written to propagate the new social and political theories current in the period of the French Revolution. The best examples combine didactic intention with elements of Gothic terror. William God-win, the political philosopher, wrote *Caleb Williams* (1794) to illustrate the thesis that the lower classes are helplessly subject to the power and privilege of the ruling class, but he did so in the form of a chilling story about the relentless pursuit and persecution by a wealthy squire of his young secretary, who has come upon evidence that the squire has committed murder. Mary Shelley—Shelley's wife and the daughter of Mary Wollstonecraft, author of *A Vindication of the Rights of Woman*—wrote a thematic novel of terror which not only is a literary classic but has become a popular myth. Her *Frankenstein* (1817) transforms a story about a fabricated monster into a powerful representation of the moral distortion imposed on an individual who, because he diverges from the norm, is rejected by society.

The Romantic period produced two major novelists, Jane Austen and Sir Walter Scott. Jane Austen (1775–1817) is one of the greatest of English novelists, yet she is the only important author who seems to be untouched by the political, intellectual, and artistic revolutions of her age. Charlotte Brontë, speaking for the Romantic sensibility, complained that Jane Aus-ten's novels lack warmth, enthusiasm, energy; "she ruffles her reader by nothing vehement, disturbs him by nothing profound. The passions are per-fectly unknown to her." But Austen deliberately elected to work within the circumference of her own experience—the life of provincial English gentle-folk—and to maintain the decorum of the novel of manners, based on such eighteenth-century antecedents as the comedy of manners of William Con-greve and Richard Brinsley Sheridan and the novels of earlier women authors, Fanny Burney and Maria Edgeworth. Within these elected limits both of subject and form, Austen achieved a fully particularized setting within which to examine and criticize the values men and women live by in their everyday social lives.

Sense and Sensibility and *Northanger Abbey* poke fun at two later eight-eenth-century deviations from the humanistic norm, the cult of sensibility and the taste for Gothic terrors. Austen's other novels, published between 1813 and 1818—*Mansfield Park, Persuasion,* and best of all, *Pride and Prej-udice* and *Emma*—all deal with the subject of getting married. This was in fact a central preoccupation and problem for the young leisure-class lady of that age, who had no career open to her outside of domesticity; Austen, however, chose the subject because it provided her with the best realistic opportunities for testing her heroines' practical sense and moral integrity, their degree of knowledge of the world and of themselves, and their capacity to demonstrate grace under social and financial pressure.

Sir Walter Scott (1771–1832) was contemporary with Jane Austen, and admired her greatly, but his work in fiction was at an extreme from hers. In 1814, with the anonymous *Waverley,* he turned from narrative verse (in which Byron had displaced him in popularity) to narrative prose and man-aged to write almost thirty long works of fiction in the eighteen years before he died. They are in the mode which he himself defined as romance, "the interest of which turns upon marvelous and uncommon incidents," in con-trast to the novel such as Jane Austen wrote, in which "the events are accommodated to the ordinary train of human events, and the modern state of society." Scott's originality lay in opening up to fiction the rich and lively realm of history; he sometimes alters the order of events for novelistic pur-poses, yet he maintains fidelity to the spirit of the past and a meticulous accuracy in antiquarian detail. His great series of Scottish novels, including

Guy Mannering, The Antiquary, Old Mortality, Rob Roy, and (most enduringly) *The Heart of Midlothian,* are rooted in historical events from the
seventeenth century up to his own time; *Ivanhoe* is set in thirteenth-century
England and *Kenilworth* in the age of Elizabeth; and *Quentin Durward,* the
best of his Continental romances, has for background the French Court of
the fifteenth century.

Like Byron, Scott wrote with dash and grandiosity in a kind of sustained
improvisation; his plotting is often loose, his romantic lovers pallid, and his
kings and chieftains large-scale puppets. But in his great scenes of action
there are a scope and sweep not to be exceeded in fiction until the appearance of Leo Tolstoy's *War and Peace* in the 1860s. And although, unlike
his liberal Romantic contemporaries, Scott's political sympathies were aristocratic and feudal, his most vivid and convincing characters are members
of the middle and lower classes. His tradesmen, servants, peasantry, social
outcasts, and demented old women, speaking a rich Scottish vernacular (Scott's
language, like Robert Burns's in verse, tended to become stilted and conventional when he wrote in standard English), compose a populous world in
which each person is an individual, rooted in the circumstances of his time
and place and class and occupation.

Scott had an immense international vogue, equaling that of Byron and
Goethe, and became the acknowledged master of some of the greatest nineteenth-century novelists, including Balzac and Tolstoy. Jane Austen, on the
other hand, during her lifetime was admired only by a limited group of
English readers. Her novels have, however, demonstrated greater staying
power. Scott's combination of casualness in design and prodigality in detail
puts off many readers who have formed their sensibilities on the well-made
novel of the present century. But even after the achievements of such craftsmen in the form as Henry James, Jane Austen remains the sovereign of the
intricate, spare, and ironic art of the novel of manners.

WILLIAM BLAKE
1757–1827

1783:   *Poetical Sketches,* his first book of poems.
1794:   *Songs of Innocence and of Experience.*
1804–20:   The two last and greatest "prophetic" poems,
           Milton and *Jerusalem.*

What Blake called his "Spiritual Life" was as varied, free, and dramatic as his "Corporeal Life" was simple, limited, and unadventurous. His father was a London haberdasher. His only formal education was in art: at the age of ten he entered a drawing school and later studied for a time at the school of the Royal Academy of Arts. At fourteen he served as apprentice for seven years to a well-known engraver, James Basire, read widely in his free time, and began to try his hand at poetry. At twenty-four he married Catherine Boucher, daughter of a market gardener. She was then illiterate, but Blake taught her to read and to help him in his engraving and printing. In the early and somewhat sentimentalized biographies, Catherine is represented as an ideal wife for an unorthodox and impecunious genius. Blake, however, must have been a trying domestic partner, and his vehement attacks on the torment caused by a possessive, jealous female will, which reached their height in 1793 and remained prominent in his writings for another decade, probably reflect a troubled period at home. The couple were childless.

The Blakes for a time enjoyed a moderate prosperity while Blake gave drawing lessons, illustrated books, and engraved designs made by other artists. When the demand for his work slackened, Blake in 1800 moved to a cottage at Felpham, on the Sussex seacoast, under the patronage of the wealthy poetaster, biographer, and amateur of the arts, William Hayley, who with the best of narrow intentions tried to transform Blake into a conventional artist and breadwinner. But the caged eagle soon rebelled. Hayley, Blake wrote, "is the Enemy of my Spiritual Life while he pretends to be the Friend of my Corporeal."

At Felpham in 1803 occurred an event that left a permanent mark on Blake's mind and art. He had an altercation with one John Schofield, a private in the Royal Dragoons. Blake ordered the soldier out of his garden and, when the soldier replied with threats and curses against Blake and his wife, pushed him the fifty yards to the inn where he was quartered. Schofield brought charges that Blake had uttered seditious statements about King and country. Since England was at war with France, sedition was a hanging offense. Blake was acquitted—an event, according to a newspaper account, "which so gratified the auditory that the court was . . . thrown into an uproar by their noisy exultations." Nevertheless Schofield, his fellow soldier Cock, and other participants in the trial haunted Blake's imagination and were enlarged to demonic characters who play a sinister role in *Jerusalem.* The event exacerbated Blake's sense that ominous forces were at work in the contemporary world and led him to complicate the symbolic obliquities by which he veiled the unorthodoxy of his religious and moral opinions, as well as the radicalism of the many allusions to contemporary affairs that he worked into his poems.

After three years at Felpham Blake moved back to London, determined to follow his "Divine Vision" though it meant a life of isolation, misunderstanding, and poverty. When his one great bid for public recognition, a one-man show put on in 1809, proved a total failure, Blake passed into almost complete obscurity. Only when he was in his sixties did he finally attract a small but devoted group of young painters who served as an audience for his work and his talk. Blake's old age was serene, self-confident, and joyous, largely free from the bursts of irascibility with which he had earlier responded to the shallowness and blindness of the English public. He died in his seventieth year.

Blake's first book of poems, *Poetical Sketches*, which he had printed when he was twenty-six years old, showed his dissatisfaction with the reigning poetic tradition and his restless quest for new forms and techniques. For lyric models he turned back to the Elizabethan and early seventeenth-century poets, to the Ossianic poems, and to Collins, Thomas Chatterton, and other eighteenth-century writers outside the tradition of Pope; he also experimented with partial rhymes and novel rhythms and employed bold figures of speech that at times approximate symbols. In 1788 he began to experiment with relief etching, the method, used to produce most of his books of poems, that he called "illuminated printing." Working directly on a copper plate with pens, brushes, and an acid-resistant medium, he wrote the text in reverse (so that it would print in the normal order) and also drew the illustration; he then etched the plate in acid to eat away the untreated copper and leave the design standing in relief. The pages printed from such plates were colored by hand ("illuminated") in water colors and stitched together to make up a volume. This process was laborious and time consuming, and Blake printed very few copies of his books; for example, of *Songs of Innocence and of Experience* twenty-eight copies (both complete and incomplete) are known to exist; of *The Book of Thel*, sixteen; of *The Marriage of Heaven and Hell*, nine; and of *Jerusalem*, five.

It must be remembered that to read Blake's poem in a printed text is to see only an abstraction from an integral and mutually illuminating combination of words and design. In this mode of relief etching, he published *Songs of Innocence* (1789), then added supplementary poems and printed *Songs of Innocence and of Experience* in 1794. The two groups of poems represent the world as it is envisioned by what he calls "two contrary states of the human soul." In the best of the songs of experience, such as *The Tyger* and *London*, Blake achieved his mature lyric technique of compressed metaphor and symbol which explode into a multiplicity of references.

Gradually Blake's thinking about human history and his experience of life and suffering articulated themselves in the "Giant Forms" and their actions, which constitute a complete mythology. As Los said, speaking for all imaginative artists, "I must Create a System or be enslaved by another Man's." This coherent but constantly altering and enlarging system composed the subject matter, first of Blake's "minor prophecies," completed by 1795, and then of the major prophetic books on which he continued working until about 1820: *The Four Zoas, Milton,* and *Jerusalem.*

In his sixties Blake gave up poetry to devote himself to pictorial art. In the course of his life he produced hundreds of paintings and engravings, many of them illustrations for the work of other poets, including a representation of Chaucer's Canterbury pilgrims, a superb set of designs for the Book of Job, and a series of illustrations of Dante, on which he was still hard at work when he died. At the time of his death Blake was little known as an artist and almost entirely unknown as a poet. In the mid-nineteenth century he acquired a group of admirers among the Pre-Raphaelites, who regarded him as a precursor. Since the mid 1920s, Blake has finally come into his own, both in poetry and painting, as one of the most dedicated, intellectually challenging, and astonishingly original of artists.

The explication of Blake's cryptic prophetic books has been the preoccupation of many scholars. Blake wrote them in the persona, or "voice," of "the Bard! / Who Present, Past, & Future sees"—that is, as a British poet who follows Spenser, and especially Milton, in a lineage going back to the prophets of the Bible. "The Nature of my Work," he said, "is Visionary or Imaginative." What Blake meant by the key terms "vision" and "imagination," however, is often misinterpreted by taking literally what he, speaking the traditional language of his great predecessors, intended in a figurative sense. "That which can be made Explicit to the Idiot," Blake declared, "is not worth my care." Blake was a born ironist who enjoyed mystifying his well-meaning but literal-minded friends and who took a defiant pleasure in shocking the dull and complacent "angels" of his day by being deliberately outrageous in representing his work and opinions.

Blake declared that "all he knew was in the Bible" and that "The Old & New Testaments are the Great Code of Art." This is an exaggeration of the truth that all his prophetic writings deal, in various formulations, with some aspects of the overall Biblical plot of the creation and fall of man, the history of the generations of man in the fallen world, redemption, and the promise of a recovery of Eden and of a New Jerusalem. These events, however, Blake interprets in what he calls "the spiritual sense." For such a procedure he had considerable precedent, not in the Neoplatonic and occult thinkers with whom some modern commentators align him, but in the "spiritual" interpreters of the Bible among the radical Protestant sects in seventeenth- and eighteenth-century England. In *The French Revolution, America: A Prophecy, Europe: A Prophecy,* and the trenchant prophetic satire, *The Marriage of Heaven and Hell*—all of which Blake wrote in the early 1790s while he was an ardent supporter of the French Revolution—he, like Wordsworth, Coleridge, Southey, and a number of radical English theologians, represented the contemporary Revolution as the purifying violence that, according to Biblical prophecy, was the portent of the imminent redemption of humanity and the world. In Blake's later poems, Orc, the fiery spirit of revolution, gives way as a central personage to Los, the type of the visionary imagination in the fallen world. Even in his early writings, however, Blake had represented historical revolution as correlative with a radical change effected within the mind and imagination of man, so that the replacement of Orc by Los does not indicate Blake's recantation of former beliefs, but a shift of emphasis from an apocalypse by revolution to an apocalypse by imagination.

BLAKE'S MATURE MYTH

Blake's first attempt to articulate his full myth of humanity's present, past, and future was *The Four Zoas,* begun in 1796 or 1797. A passage from the opening statement of its theme exemplifies the long verse line (what Blake called "the march of long resounding strong heroic verse") in which he wrote his Prophetic Books and will serve also to outline the myth, or visualizable imaginative form, in which Blake's thought embodied itself:

Four Mighty Ones are in every Man; a Perfect Unity
Cannot Exist, but from the Universal Brotherhood of Eden,
The Universal Man. To Whom be Glory Evermore, Amen. . . .
Los was the fourth immortal starry one, & in the Earth
Of a bright Universe Empery attended day & night
Days & nights of revolving joy, Urthona was his name
In Eden; in the Auricular Nerves of Human life
Which is the Earth of Eden, he his Emanations propagated. . . .
                    Daughter of Beulah, Sing
His fall into Division & his Resurrection to Unity.

    Blake's mythical premise, or starting point, is not a transcendent God but the "Universal Man" who is himself God and who incorporates the cosmos as well. (Blake elsewhere describes this founding image as "the Human Form Divine" and names him "Albion.") The fall, in this myth, is not the fall of man away from God but a falling apart of primal man, a "fall into Division." In this event the original sin is what Blake calls "Selfhood," the attempt of an isolated part to be self-sufficient. The breakup of the all-inclusive Universal Man in Eden into exiled parts, it is evident, identifies the fall of man with the creation—both of man and of nature, as we ordinarily know them, as well as of a sky god who is alien from humanity. Universal Man divides first into the "Four Mighty Ones" who are the Zoas, or chief powers and component aspects of man, and these in turn divide sexually into male Spectres and female Emanations. (Thus in the quoted passage the Zoa known in the unfallen state of Eden as Urthona, the imaginative power, separates into the form of Los in the fallen world.) In addition to Eden there are three successively lower "states" of being in the fallen world, which Blake calls Beulah (a pastoral condition of easy and relaxed innocence, without clash of "contraries"), Generation (the realm of common human experience, suffering, and conflicting contraries), and Ulro (Blake's hell, the lowest state, or limit, of bleak rationality, tyranny, static negation, and isolated Selfhood). The fallen world moves through the cycles of its history, successively approaching and falling away from redemption, until, by the agency of the Redeemer (who is equated with the human imagination and is most potently operative in the prophetic poet), it will culminate in an apocalypse. In terms of his controlling image of the Universal Man, Blake describes this apocalypse as a return to the original, undivided condition, "his Resurrection to Unity."

    Although Blake did not know it, he shared with a number of contemporary German philosophers the point of view—it has in our own time become the prevailing point of view—that our fall (or the malaise of modern culture) is essentially a mode of psychic disintegration and of resultant alienation from oneself, one's world, and one's fellow human beings, and that our hope of recovery lies in a process of reintegration. As an imaginative poet, however, Blake does not present this view in abstract conceptual terms, but embodies it in picturable agents acting out an epic plot. What is confusing to many readers is that Blake uses different ways of representing the same vision of men and women in the world. For example, Blake alternates with his image of the division of Primal Man, the representation of the fall as a catastrophic alteration, in individual human beings, from imaginative vision to physical eyesight. The result of this alteration was that the cosmos, which in the original mode of unified imaginative perception had been beheld as human and one, came to be seen as a multitude of isolated individuals in a dehumanized and alien nature. Conversely, the apocalypse toward which Blake—the imaginative artist who as an individual represents the mythical type-figure Los—is always working, is to enable all men and women to break through to a restored unity of vision. By such a vision all beings, together with the world they inhabit, will again be perceived as sharing the one life and the one humanity of that "Universal Brotherhood," the Human Form Divine, who is imaged as creating such a universe by the very act of so envisioning it.

Blake decries, as the mythical being "Vala," what we ordinarily mean by "nature," the material universe perceived by the senses. It would, however, be a mistake to equate his views with ascetic otherworldliness. Blake does not look forward to a consummation that will wipe out the natural world and replace it by a transcendental substitute. Blake maintained, on the contrary, that we achieve redemption by liberating and intensifying the bodily senses—as he said, by "an improvement of sensual enjoyment"—and by attaining and sustaining that mode of vision that does not cancel the fallen world, but transfigures it, by revealing the lineaments of its eternal imaginative form. That is what Blake means when, in A Vision of the Last Judgment (included below), he says that "The Nature of my Work is Visionary or Imaginative," and that in the moment of apocalyptic redemption "Error or Creation will be Burned Up & then & not till then Truth or Eternity will appear. It is Burnt up the Moment Men cease to behold it." Accordingly, in the apocalypse that concludes Jerusalem, the reunion of Albion the Universal Man with Jerusalem, his emanation, is accompanied by a freeing of man's senses and results in the recovery of a lost mode of vision that sees a nature which, because it is humanized, is a place where all individuals, united as One Man, can feel at home.

The text for all of Blake's writings is that of The Complete Poetry and Prose of William Blake, edited by David V. Erdman and Harold Bloom (revised edition, Berkeley, 1982). Blake's erratic spelling and punctuation have been altered when the original form might mislead the reader. The editors are grateful for the expert advice of Joseph Viscomi and Robert Essick in editing the selections from Blake.

From POETICAL SKETCHES[1]

To Spring[2]

O thou, with dewy locks, who lookest down
Thro' the clear windows of the morning; turn

---

1. *Poetical Sketches*, Blake's only volume of poems to be set in type, went to press in 1783, but was never put on sale. A preface written by an anonymous friend apologized for the poems on the ground that they had been composed between the ages of 12 and 20. Although, like the work of other youthful poets, they echo earlier writers (especially Spenser, Shakespeare, and Milton), many of them show remarkable originality. Some are radical experiments in meter and rhyme; *To the Evening Star*, like *To Spring*, is a sonnet without rhyme,

and shows great boldness in its use of metaphor (lines 8–10); while in the *Song* ("How sweet I roam'd"), the images begin to assume the added reach of meaning that characterizes Blake's mature symbolism.

2. *Poetical Sketches* includes four poems, each in the form of an invocation to one of the four seasons. *To Spring* is thronged with echoes from the poetry of the Old Testament, as well as from Milton.

Thine angel eyes upon our western isle,
Which in full choir hails thy approach, O Spring!

The hills tell each other, and the list'ning   5
Vallies hear; all our longing eyes are turned
Up to thy bright pavillions: issue forth,
And let thy holy feet visit our clime.

Come o'er the eastern hills, and let our winds
Kiss thy perfumed garments; let us taste   10
Thy morn and evening breath; scatter thy pearls
Upon our love-sick land that mourns for thee.

O deck her forth with thy fair fingers; pour
Thy soft kisses on her bosom; and put
Thy golden crown upon her languish'd head,   15
Whose modest tresses were bound up for thee!

                                                        1783

To the Evening Star

Thou fair-hair'd angel of the evening,
Now, while the sun rests on the mountains, light
Thy bright torch of love;[3] thy radiant crown
Put on, and smile upon our evening bed!
Smile on our loves; and, while thou drawest the   5
Blue curtains of the sky, scatter thy silver dew
On every flower that shuts its sweet eyes
In timely sleep. Let thy west wind sleep on
The lake; speak silence with thy glimmering eyes,
And wash the dusk with silver. Soon, full soon,   10
Dost thou withdraw; then the wolf rages wide,
And the lion glares thro' the dun forest:
The fleeces of our flocks are cover'd with
Thy sacred dew: protect them with thine influence.[4]

                                                        1783

Song

How sweet I roam'd from field to field,
And tasted all the summer's pride,
'Till I the prince of love[5] beheld,
Who in the sunny beams did glide!

3. The evening star is Venus, goddess of love.   power of stars over humans.
4. In astrology, the technical term for the occult 5. In Greek myth, Eros or Cupid.

He shew'd me lilies for my hair,   5
    And blushing roses for my brow;
He led me through his gardens fair,
    Where all his golden pleasures grow.

With sweet May dews my wings were wet,
    And Phoebus fir'd my vocal rage;[6]   10
He caught me in his silken net,
    And shut me in his golden cage.

He loves to sit and hear me sing,
    Then, laughing, sports and plays with me;
Then stretches out my golden wing,   15
    And mocks my loss of liberty.

1783

To the Muses

Whether on Ida's[7] shady brow,
    Or in the chambers of the East,
The chambers of the sun, that now
    From antient melody have ceas'd;

Whether in Heav'n ye wander fair,   5
    Or the green corners of the earth,
Or the blue regions of the air,
    Where the melodious winds have birth;

Whether on chrystal rocks ye rove,
    Beneath the bosom of the sea   10
Wand'ring in many a coral grove,
    Fair Nine,[8] forsaking Poetry!

How have you left the antient love
    That bards of old enjoy'd in you![9]
The languid strings do scarcely move!   15
    The sound is forc'd, the notes are few!

1783

. . .

---

6. Fervor.
7. Ida is a mountain in southern Phrygia, celebrated in classical mythology.
8. The nine Muses.

9. The poem is Blake's lament, in the diction of
later 18-century poetry, over the failure of the
inspiration manifested by the "bards," the older
British poet-prophets.

All Religions Are One[1]

The Voice of one crying in the Wilderness[2]

The Argument. As the true method of knowledge is experiment the true faculty of knowing must be the faculty which experiences. This faculty I treat of.

PRINCIPLE 1st. That the Poetic Genius is the true Man, and that the body or outward form of Man is derived from the Poetic Genius. Likewise that the forms of all things are derived from their Genius, which by the Ancients was call'd an Angel & Spirit & Demon.

PRINCIPLE 2d. As all men are alike in outward form, So (and with the same infinite variety) all are alike in the Poetic Genius.

PRINCIPLE 3d. No man can think write or speak from his heart, but he must intend truth. Thus all sects of Philosophy are from the Poetic Genius, adapted to the weaknesses of every individual.

PRINCIPLE 4. As none by travelling over known lands can find out the unknown, So from already acquired knowledge Man could not acquire more. Therefore an universal Poetic Genius exists.

PRINCIPLE 5. The Religions of all Nations are derived from each Nation's different reception of the Poetic Genius, which is every where call'd the Spirit of Prophecy.

PRINCIPLE 6. The Jewish & Christian Testaments are An original derivation from the Poetic Genius. This is necessary from the confined nature of bodily sensation.

Principle 7th. As all men are alike (tho' infinitely various), So all Religions & as all similars have one source.

The true Man is the source, he being the Poetic Genius.

There Is No Natural Religion[3]

[a]

The Argument. Man has no notion of moral fitness but from Education. Naturally he is only a natural organ subject to Sense.

I. Man cannot naturally Percieve but through his natural or bodily organs.

---

1. This and the following two little tracts are early illuminated works, probably etched in 1788. They are directed both against 18th-century Deism or "natural religion" (which bases its religious tenets not on scriptural revelation, but on evidences of God in the natural or "organic" world) and against Christian orthodoxy, whose creed is based on a particular Scripture. In this first tract, Blake ironically accepts the Deistic view that all particular religions are variants of the one true religion, but rejects the Deists' "Argument" that this religion is grounded on reasoning from sense-experience. He attributes the one religion instead to the innate possession by all men of "Poetic Genius"—that is, of a capacity for imaginative vision.

2. Applied in the Gospels (e.g., Matthew 3.3) to John the Baptist, regarded as fulfilling the prophecy in Isaiah 39.3. Blake applies the phrase to himself, as a later prophetic voice in an alien time.

3. In this tract, Blake presents his version of English empiricism, which derives all mental content (including the evidences from which, in "natural religion," reason is held to prove the existence of God) from perceptions by the physical senses.

II. Man by his reasoning power can only compare & judge of what he has already perciev'd.

III. From a perception of only 3 senses or 3 elements none could deduce a fourth or fifth.

IV. None could have other than natural or organic thoughts if he had none but organic perceptions.

V. Man's desires are limited by his perceptions; none can desire what he has not perciev'd.

VI. The desires & perceptions of man, untaught by any thing but organs of sense, must be limited to objects of sense.

There Is No Natural Religion[4]

[b]

I. Man's perceptions are not bounded by organs of perception; he percieves more than sense (tho' ever so acute) can discover.

II. Reason, or the ratio[5] of all we have already known, is not the same that it shall be when we know more.

[III lacking]

IV. The bounded is loathed by its possessor. The same dull round even of a universe would soon become a mill with complicated wheels.

V. If the many become the same as the few when possess'd, More! More! is the cry of a mistaken soul. Less than All cannot satisfy Man.

VI. If any could desire what he is incapable of possessing, despair must be his eternal lot.

VII. The desire of Man being Infinite, the possession is Infinite & himself Infinite.

Application. He who sees the Infinite in all things sees God. He who sees the Ratio only sees himself only.

Conclusion. If it were not for the Poetic or Prophetic character the Philosophic & Experimental would soon be at the ratio of all things, & stand still unable to do other than repeat the same dull round over again.

Therefore God becomes as we are, that we may be as he is.

1788

---

4. In this third document, Blake presents his assertions (in opposition to those in the preceding tract) that knowledge is not limited to the physical senses, but is as unbounded as the infinite desires of humankind and its godlike capacity for infinite vision.

5. In Latin, *ratio* signifies both "reason" and "calculation." Blake applies the term derogatorily to the 18th-century concept of reason as a calculating faculty whose operations are limited to sense-perceptions.

From SONGS OF INNOCENCE AND OF EXPERIENCE[1]

SHEWING THE TWO CONTRARY STATES OF THE HUMAN SOUL

From SONGS OF INNOCENCE

Introduction

Piping down the valleys wild
Piping songs of pleasant glee
On a cloud I saw a child,
And he laughing said to me,

"Pipe a song about a Lamb";   5
So I piped with merry chear;
"Piper pipe that song again"—
So I piped, he wept to hear.

"Drop thy pipe thy happy pipe
Sing thy songs of happy chear";   10
So I sung the same again
While he wept with joy to hear.

"Piper sit thee down and write
In a book that all may read"—
So he vanish'd from my sight.   15
And I pluck'd a hollow reed,

And I made a rural pen,
And I stain'd the water clear,
And I wrote my happy songs
Every child may joy to hear.   20

1789

---

1. *Songs of Innocence* was etched in 1789, and in 1794 was combined with additional poems under the title *Songs of Innocence and of Experience*; this collection was reprinted at various later times with varying arrangements of the poems. In his songs of innocence Blake assumes the stance that he is writing "happy songs / Every child may joy to hear," but they do not all depict an innocent and happy world; many of them incorporate injustice, evil, and suffering. These aspects of the fallen world, however, are represented as they appear to a "state" of the human soul that Blake calls "innocence," and which he expresses in a simple pastoral language, in the tradition of Isaac Watts's widely read *Divine Songs for Children* (1715). The vision of the same world, as it appears to the "contrary" state of the soul that Blake calls "experience," is an ugly and terrifying one of poverty, disease, prostitution, war, and social, institutional, and sexual repression, epitomized in the ghastly representation of modern London. Though each stands as an independent poem, a number of the songs of innocence have a matched counterpart, or "contrary," in the songs of experience. Thus *Infant Joy* is paired with *Infant Sorrow*, and the meek *Lamb* reveals its other aspect of divinity in the flaming, wrathful *Tyger*.

In Blake's later writings the "contrary states" become a dialectic of contraries, according to which naïve innocence must necessarily pass through and assimilate the opposing state of experience if it is to move on, by an act of imagination, to the third state—in Northrop Frye's phrase, one of "organized innocence"—that includes but transcends both the others.

The Ecchoing Green

The Sun does arise,
And make happy the skies.
The merry bells ring
To welcome the Spring.
The sky-lark and thrush,   5
The birds of the bush,
Sing louder around,
To the bells' chearful sound.
While our sports shall be seen
On the Ecchoing Green.   10

Old John with white hair
Does laugh away care,
Sitting under the oak,
Among the old folk.
They laugh at our play,   15
And soon they all say:
"Such, such were the joys.
When we all, girls & boys,
In our youth-time were seen,
On the Ecchoing Green."   20

Till the little ones weary
No more can be merry
The sun does descend,
And our sports have an end:
Round the laps of their mothers,   25
Many sisters and brothers,
Like birds in their nest,
Are ready for rest;
And sport no more seen,
On the darkening Green.   30

                                          1789

The Lamb

Little Lamb, who made thee?
  Dost thou know who made thee?
Gave thee life & bid thee feed,
By the stream & o'er the mead;
Gave thee clothing of delight,   5
Softest clothing wooly bright;
Gave thee such a tender voice,
Making all the vales rejoice!

Little Lamb who made thee?
Dost thou know who made thee?   10

Little Lamb I'll tell thee,
Little Lamb I'll tell thee!
He is callèd by thy name,
For he calls himself a Lamb;
He is meek & he is mild,   15
He became a little child;
I a child & thou a lamb,
We are callèd by his name.
Little Lamb God bless thee.
Little Lamb God bless thee.   20

1789

The Little Black Boy

My mother bore me in the southern wild,
And I am black, but O! my soul is white;
White as an angel is the English child,
But I am black as if bereav'd of light.

My mother taught me underneath a tree,   5
And sitting down before the heat of day,
She took me on her lap and kissèd me,
And pointing to the east, began to say:

"Look on the rising sun: there God does live
And gives his light, and gives his heat away;   10
And flowers and trees and beasts and men receive
Comfort in morning, joy in the noon day.

"And we are put on earth a little space,
That we may learn to bear the beams of love,
And these black bodies and this sun-burnt face   15
Is but a cloud, and like a shady grove.

"For when our souls have learn'd the heat to bear,
The cloud will vanish; we shall hear his voice,
Saying: 'Come out from the grove, my love & care,
And round my golden tent like lambs rejoice.' "   20

Thus did my mother say, and kissèd me;
And thus I say to little English boy:
When I from black and he from white cloud free,
And round the tent of God like lambs we joy,

I'll shade him from the heat till he can bear   25
To lean in joy upon our father's knee.
And then I'll stand and stroke his silver hair,
And be like him, and he will then love me.

1789

The Chimney Sweeper

When my mother died I was very young,
And my father sold me while yet my tongue
Could scarcely cry " 'weep! 'weep! 'weep! 'weep!" [2]
So your chimneys I sweep & in soot I sleep.

There's little Tom Dacre, who cried when his head   5
That curl'd like a lamb's back, was shav'd, so I said,
"Hush, Tom! never mind it, for when your head's bare,
You know that the soot cannot spoil your white hair."

And so he was quiet, & that very night,
As Tom was a-sleeping he had such a sight!   10
That thousands of sweepers, Dick, Joe, Ned, & Jack,
Were all of them lock'd up in coffins of black;

And by came an Angel who had a bright key,
And he open'd the coffins & set them all free;
Then down a green plain, leaping, laughing they run,   15
And wash in a river and shine in the Sun.

Then naked & white, all their bags left behind,
They rise upon clouds, and sport in the wind.
And the Angel told Tom, if he'd be a good boy,
He'd have God for his father & never want joy.   20

And so Tom awoke; and we rose in the dark
And got with our bags & our brushes to work.
Tho' the morning was cold, Tom was happy & warm;
So if all do their duty, they need not fear harm.

1789

The Divine Image

To Mercy, Pity, Peace, and Love,
All pray in their distress,

---

2. The child's lisping attempt at the chimney sweeper's street cry, "Sweep! Sweep!"

And to these virtues of delight
Return their thankfulness.

For Mercy, Pity, Peace, and Love,   5
Is God, our father dear:
And Mercy, Pity, Peace, and Love,
Is Man, his child and care.

For Mercy has a human heart,
Pity, a human face,   10
And Love, the human form divine,
And Peace, the human dress.

Then every man of every clime,
That prays in his distress,
Prays to the human form divine,   15
Love, Mercy, Pity, Peace.

And all must love the human form,
In heathen, Turk, or Jew.
Where Mercy, Love, & Pity dwell,
There God is dwelling too.   20

                                                          1789

Holy Thursday[3]

'Twas on a Holy Thursday, their innocent faces clean,
The children walking two & two, in red & blue & green;
Grey headed beadles[4] walkd before with wands as white as snow,
Till into the high dome of Paul's they like Thames' waters flow.

O what a multitude they seemd, these flowers of London town!   5
Seated in companies they sit with radiance all their own.
The hum of multitudes was there, but multitudes of lambs,
Thousands of little boys & girls raising their innocent hands.

Now like a mighty wind they raise to heaven the voice of song,
Or like harmonious thunderings the seats of heaven among.   10
Beneath them sit the agèd men, wise guardians of the poor;
Then cherish pity, lest you drive an angel from your door.[5]

ca. 1784   1789

---

3. In the English church, the Thursday celebrating the ascension of Jesus (39 days after Easter). It was the custom on this day to march the children from the charity schools of London to a service at St. Paul's Cathedral.

4. Lower church officers, one of whose duties is to keep order.

5. "Be not forgetful to entertain strangers: for thereby some have entertained angels unawares" (Hebrews 13.2).

Nurse's Song

When the voices of children are heard on the green
And laughing is heard on the hill,
My heart is at rest within my breast
And everything else is still.

"Then come home my children, the sun is gone down   5
And the dews of night arise;
Come, come, leave off play, and let us away
Till the morning appears in the skies."

"No, no, let us play, for it is yet day
And we cannot go to sleep;   10
Besides, in the sky, the little birds fly
And the hills are all coverd with sheep."

"Well, well, go & play till the light fades away
And then go home to bed."
The little ones leaped & shouted & laugh'd   15
And all the hills ecchoèd.

ca. 1784   1789

Infant Joy

"I have no name,
I am but two days old."
What shall I call thee?
"I happy am,
Joy is my name."   5
Sweet joy befall thee!

Pretty joy!
Sweet joy but two days old,
Sweet joy I call thee;
Thou dost smile,   10
I sing the while—
Sweet joy befall thee.

1789

From SONGS OF EXPERIENCE

Introduction

Hear the voice of the Bard!
Who Present, Past, & Future sees;
Whose ears have heard
The Holy Word
That walk'd among the ancient trees;[1]   5

Calling the lapsèd Soul
And weeping in the evening dew,
That might controll
The starry pole,
And fallen, fallen light renew![2]   10

"O Earth, O Earth, return!
Arise from out the dewy grass;
Night is worn,
And the morn
Rises from the slumberous mass.   15

"Turn away no more;
Why wilt thou turn away?
The starry floor
The watry shore[3]
Is giv'n thee till the break of day."   20

1794

Earth's Answer[4]

Earth rais'd up her head,
From the darkness dread & drear.
Her light fled:
Stony dread!
And her locks cover'd with grey despair.   5

---

1. Genesis 3.8: "And [Adam and Eve] heard the voice of the Lord God walking in the garden in the cool of the day." The Bard, or poet-prophet, whose imagination is not bound by time, has heard the voice of the Lord in Eden. The call (the syntax leaves it ambiguous whether it is "the Bard" or the Holy Word" whose voice does the calling) is to the fallen ("lapsèd") soul and to the fallen earth; the behest is to turn full to the light and stop the endless natural cycle of alternating light and darkness.

2. The likely syntax is that "Soul" is the subject of "might controll"; the sense would be that the fallen Soul could, if it would, renew the fallen light.
3. In Blake's recurrent symbolism, the starry sky ("floor") signifies rigid rational order, and the sea signifies chaos.
4. The Earth's answer explains why she, the natural world, cannot by her unaided endeavors renew the fallen light.

"Prison'd on watry shore
Starry Jealousy does keep my den,
Cold and hoar
Weeping o'er
I hear the Father of the ancient men.[5]   10

"Selfish father of men,
Cruel, jealous, selfish fear!
Can delight
Chain'd in night
The virgins of youth and morning bear?   15

"Does spring hide its joy
When buds and blossoms grow?
Does the sower
Sow by night,
Or the plowman in darkness plow?   20

"Break this heavy chain
That does freeze my bones around;
Selfish! vain!
Eternal bane!
That free Love with bondage bound."   25

1794

The Clod & the Pebble

"Love seeketh not Itself to please,
Nor for itself hath any care;
But for another gives its ease,
And builds a Heaven in Hell's despair."

    So sang a little Clod of Clay,   5
    Trodden with the cattle's feet;
    But a Pebble of the brook,
    Warbled out these metres meet:

"Love seeketh only Self to please,
To bind another to its delight;   10
Joys in another's loss of ease,
And builds a Hell in Heaven's despite."

1794

---

5. This is the character that Blake later named "Urizen" in his prophetic works. He imposes the perceptual and moral tyranny that binds the mind to time and space and imposes on sexual desire (as on all modes of human energy) the bondage of selfishness, fear, secrecy, shame, and jealousy.

Holy Thursday

Is this a holy thing to see,
In a rich and fruitful land,
Babes reduced to misery,
Fed with cold and usurous hand?

Is that trembling cry a song?   5
Can it be a song of joy?
And so many children poor?
It is a land of poverty!

And their sun does never shine,
And their fields are bleak & bare,   10
And their ways are fill'd with thorns;
It is eternal winter there.

For where-e'er the sun does shine,
And where-e'er the rain does fall,
Babe can never hunger there,   15
Nor poverty the mind appall.

1794

The Chimney Sweeper

A little black thing among the snow
Crying " 'weep, 'weep," in notes of woe!
"Where are thy father & mother? say?"
"They are both gone up to the church to pray.

"Because I was happy upon the heath,   5
And smil'd among the winter's snow;
They clothed me in the clothes of death,
And taught me to sing the notes of woe.

"And because I am happy, & dance & sing,
They think they have done me no injury,   10
And are gone to praise God & his Priest & King,
Who make up a heaven of our misery."

1790–92   1794

Nurse's Song

When the voices of children are heard on the green
And whisperings are in the dale,

The days of my youth rise fresh in my mind,
My face turns green and pale.

Then come home my children, the sun is gone down   5
And the dews of night arise;
Your spring & your day are wasted in play,
And your winter and night in disguise.

1794

The Sick Rose

O Rose, thou art sick.
The invisible worm
That flies in the night
In the howling storm

Has found out thy bed   5
Of crimson joy,
And his dark secret love
Does thy life destroy.

1794

The Tyger[6]

Tyger! Tyger! burning bright
In the forests of the night,
What immortal hand or eye
Could frame thy fearful symmetry?

In what distant deeps or skies   5
Burnt the fire of thine eyes?
On what wings dare he aspire?
What the hand dare seize the fire?

And what shoulder, & what art,
Could twist the sinews of thy heart?   10
And when thy heart began to beat,
What dread hand? & what dread feet?

What the hammer? what the chain?
In what furnace was thy brain?
What the anvil? what dread grasp   15
Dare its deadly terrors clasp?

6. For the author's revisions while composing *The Tyger*, see "Poems in Process," below.

When the stars[7] threw down their spears
And water'd heaven with their tears,
Did he smile his work to see?
Did he who made the Lamb make thee?   20

Tyger! Tyger! burning bright
In the forests of the night,
What immortal hand or eye
Dare frame thy fearful symmetry?

1790–92   1794

My Pretty Rose Tree

A flower was offerd to me;
Such a flower as May never bore,
But I said, "I've a Pretty Rose-tree,"
And I passed the sweet flower o'er.

Then I went to my Pretty Rose-tree,   5
To tend her by day and by night.
But my Rose turnd away with jealousy,
And her thorns were my only delight.

1794

Ah Sun-Flower

Ah Sun-flower! weary of time,
Who countest the steps of the Sun,
Seeking after that sweet golden clime
Where the traveller's journey is done;

Where the Youth pined away with desire,   5
And the pale Virgin shrouded in snow,
Arise from their graves and aspire,
Where my Sun-flower wishes to go.

1794

The Garden of Love

I went to the Garden of Love,
And saw what I never had seen:

---

7. The stars in their courses often serve Blake as a symbol of cold rationality and imposed regularity.

A Chapel was built in the midst,
Where I used to play on the green.

And the gates of this Chapel were shut,   5
And "Thou shalt not" writ over the door;
So I turn'd to the Garden of Love,
That so many sweet flowers bore,

And I saw it was filled with graves,
And tomb-stones where flowers should be;   10
And Priests in black gowns were walking their rounds,
And binding with briars my joys & desires.

1794

London

I wander thro' each charter'd[8] street,
Near where the charter'd Thames does flow,
And mark in every face I meet
Marks of weakness, marks of woe.

In every cry of every Man,   5
In every Infant's cry of fear,
In every voice, in every ban,[9]
The mind-forg'd manacles I hear:

How the Chimney-sweeper's cry
Every blackning Church appalls,   10
And the hapless Soldier's sigh
Runs in blood down Palace walls.

But most thro' midnight streets I hear
How the youthful Harlot's curse
Blasts the new-born Infant's tear,[1]   15
And blights with plagues the Marriage hearse.[2]

1794

---

8. "Given liberty," but also, ironically, "pre-empted as private property, and rented out."
9. The various meanings of "ban" are relevant (political and legal prohibition, curse, public condemnation) as well as "banns" (marriage proclamation).
1. Most critics read this line as implying prenatal blindness, resulting from a parent's venereal disease (the "plagues" of line 16) by earlier infection from the harlot.
2. In the older sense of "hearse": converts the marriage bed into a bier. Or possibly, since the current sense of the word had also come into use in Blake's day, "converts the marriage coach into a funeral hearse."

The Human Abstract[3]

Pity would be no more,
If we did not make somebody Poor;
And Mercy no more could be,
If all were as happy as we;

And mutual fear brings peace,   5
Till the selfish loves increase;
Then Cruelty knits a snare,
And spreads his baits with care.

He sits down with holy fears,
And waters the ground with tears;   10
Then Humility takes its root
Underneath his foot.

Soon spreads the dismal shade
Of Mystery over his head;
And the Catterpiller and Fly   15
Feed on the Mystery.

And it bears the fruit of Deceit,
Ruddy and sweet to eat;
And the Raven his nest has made
In its thickest shade.   20

The Gods of the earth and sea,
Sought thro' Nature to find this Tree,
But their search was all in vain:
There grows one in the Human Brain.

1790–92   1794

Infant Sorrow

My mother groand! my father wept.
Into the dangerous world I leapt,
Helpless, naked, piping loud;
Like a fiend hid in a cloud.

Struggling in my father's hands,
Striving against my swadling bands;   5

---

3. The matched contrary to *The Divine Image* in *Songs of Innocence*. The virtues of the earlier poem, "Mercy, Pity, Peace, and Love," are now seen as exploitation, cruelty, conflict, and hypocritical humility—the seed in the human brain of the Tree of Mystery, which darkens both the moral and natural world.

Bound and weary I thought best
To sulk upon my mother's breast.

1794

A Poison Tree

I was angry with my friend:
I told my wrath, my wrath did end.
I was angry with my foe:
I told it not, my wrath did grow.

And I waterd it in fears,   5
Night & morning with my tears;
And I sunnèd it with smiles,
And with soft deceitful wiles.

And it grew both day and night,
Till it bore an apple bright.   10
And my foe beheld it shine,
And he knew that it was mine,

And into my garden stole,
When the night had veild the pole;
In the morning glad I see   15
My foe outstretchd beneath the tree.

1794

To Tirzah[4]

Whate'er is Born of Mortal Birth
Must be consumèd with the Earth
To rise from Generation free;
Then what have I to do with thee?[5]

The Sexes sprung from Shame & Pride,   5
Blow'd[6] in the morn, in evening died;
But Mercy changd Death into Sleep;
The Sexes rose to work & weep.

4. Tirzah was the capital of the northern kingdom of Israel and is conceived by Blake in opposition to Jerusalem, capital of the southern kingdom of Judah, whose tribes had been redeemed from captivity. In his poem, which was added to late versions of *Songs of Experience*, Tirzah represents the natural mother of the mortal body, with its restricted senses and enslaved desires. Blake anticipates his emancipation from this bondage to the cycle of generation by the redemptive triumph of the imaginative over the natural body.
5. Echoing the words of Christ to his mother at the marriage in Cana, John 2.4: "Woman, what have I to do with thee? mine hour is not yet come."
6. Blossomed.

Thou, Mother of my Mortal part,
With cruelty didst mould my Heart,   10
And with false self-deceiving tears
Didst bind my Nostrils, Eyes, & Ears.

Didst close my Tongue in senseless clay
And me to Mortal Life betray.
The Death of Jesus set me free;   15
Then what have I to do with thee?

ca. 1805

A Divine Image[7]

Cruelty has a Human Heart
And Jealousy a Human Face,
Terror, the Human Form Divine,
And Secrecy, the Human Dress.

The Human Dress is forgèd Iron,   5
The Human Form, a fiery Forge,
The Human Face, a Furnace seal'd,
The Human Heart, its hungry Gorge.[8]

1790–91

• • •

The Book of Thel

Although Blake dated the etched poem 1789, its composition probably extended to 1791, so that he was working on it at the time he was writing the *Songs of Innocence* and some of the *Songs of Experience*. *The Book of Thel* treats the same two "states" and implies the need to pass from primitive innocence through experience in order to achieve a higher, organized innocence; now, however, Blake employs the narrative instead of the lyrical mode and embodies aspects of the developing myth which was fully enacted in his later prophetic books. And like the major prophecies, this poem is written in the fourteener, a long line of seven stresses.

Thel—her name probably derives from a Greek word for "wish" or "will" and suggests the timid failure of a desire to fulfill itself—is a virgin dwelling in the Vales of Har, which is equivalent to the sheltered condition of pastoral peace and innocence in Blake's *Songs of Innocence* and will develop into the "Beulah" of his prophetic books. In the fragile beauty of this realm of unrealized potentiality, Thel lives a two-dimensional mirror image of existence (line 9). The Lily of the Valley and the Cloud try to comfort her by describing their content with their roles in the cycle of innocent existence. Thel, however, since she is a human potentiality, finds such comfort inap-

7. Blake omitted this poem from all but one copy of *Songs of Experience*, probably because *The Human Abstract* served as a more comprehensive and subtle contrary to *The Divine Image*, in *Songs of Innocence*.

8. Maw, stomach.

plicable to her condition of unfulfillment and uselessness, as a virgin without a male contrary and as a shepherdess whose sheep run no risks and need no care. The Clod of Clay then speaks for her child, the voiceless Worm, an emblem of phallic generation and a devourer of the mortal body in the fallen world; but the maternal Clay sees the role of the Worm, as well as her own, only from the perspective of essential ignorance: "But how this is, sweet maid, I know not, and I cannot know." In her capacity, however, as the substance from which is formed the mortal body of man, the Clay invites Thel to try the experiment of dying into embodied life. With an abrupt and brutal shift in language and tone, part 4 expresses the shock of the revelation to Thel of the world of Generation and Experience—a revelation from which she flees in terror back to her sheltered, if unfulfilling, paradise.

The reader does not need to be an adept in Blakean mythology to recognize the symbolic reach of this poem in ordinary human experience—the elemental failure of nerve to meet the challenge of life as it is, the timid incapacity to risk the conflict, physicality, pain, and loss without which there is no possibility either of growth or of creativity.

The Book of Thel

PLATE 1[1]

THEL'S MOTTO

Does the Eagle know what is in the pit?
Or wilt thou go ask the Mole?
Can Wisdom be put in a silver rod?
Or Love in a golden bowl?[2]

1

The daughters of Mne[3] Seraphim led round their sunny flocks,
All but the youngest; she in paleness sought the secret air,
To fade away like morning beauty from her mortal day;
Down by the river of Adona[4] her soft voice is heard,
And thus her gentle lamentation falls like morning dew: 5

"O life of this our spring! why fades the lotus of the water?
Why fade these children of the spring? born but to smile & fall.
Ah! Thel is like a watry bow, and like a parting cloud,
Like a reflection in a glass, like shadows in the water,
Like dreams of infants, like a smile upon an infant's face,   10

---

1. The plate numbers identify the page, each with its own pictorial design, as originally printed by Blake. They are reproduced here because they are frequently used in references to Blake's writings.
2. Ecclesiastes 12.5–6 describes a time when "fears shall be in the way . . . and desire shall fail: because man goeth to his long home, and the mourners go about the streets: Or ever the silver cord be loosed, or the golden bowl be broken." Blake presumably changed the silver cord to a rod in order to make

it, with the golden bowl, a sexual symbol.
3. In his earlier poem *Tiriel*, Blake adopted the name "Mnetha" for the goddess of the vales of Har. Thel, the abbreviated form of this name indicates, is one of the daughters of the angelic Mnetha. In the Bible, Seraphim are the highest order of angels.
4. Possibly suggesting an equation of the Vales of Har to Spenser's Garden of Adonis in *The Faerie Queene* 3.6, as well as to the paradisal garden in Genesis (in line 14).

Like the dove's voice, like transient day, like music in the air.
Ah! gentle may I lay me down, and gentle rest my head,
And gentle sleep the sleep of death, and gentle hear the voice
Of him that walketh in the garden in the evening time."[5]

The Lilly of the valley breathing in the humble grass   15
Answer'd the lovely maid and said: "I am a watry weed,
And I am very small, and love to dwell in lowly vales;
So weak, the gilded butterfly scarce perches on my head;
Yet I am visited from heaven, and he that smiles on all
Walks in the valley and each morn over me spreads his hand,   20
Saying: 'Rejoice, thou humble grass, thou new-born lilly flower,
Thou gentle maid of silent valleys and of modest brooks;
For thou shalt be clothed in light, and fed with morning manna,
Till summer's heat melts thee beside the fountains and the springs
To flourish in eternal vales.' Then why should Thel complain?   25

PLATE 2
Why should the mistress of the vales of Har utter a sigh?"

She ceasd & smild in tears, then sat down in her silver shrine.

Thel answerd: "O thou little virgin of the peaceful valley,
Giving to those that cannot crave, the voiceless, the o'ertired;
Thy breath doth nourish the innocent lamb, he smells thy milky
     garments,   5
He crops thy flowers, while thou sittest smiling in his face,
Wiping his mild and meekin[6] mouth from all contagious taints.
Thy wine doth purify the golden honey; thy perfume,
Which thou dost scatter on every little blade of grass that springs,
Revives the milkèd cow, & tames the fire-breathing steed.   10
But Thel is like a faint cloud kindled at the rising sun:
I vanish from my pearly throne, and who shall find my place?"

"Queen of the vales," the Lilly answered, "ask the tender cloud,
And it shall tell thee why it glitters in the morning sky,
And why it scatters its bright beauty thro' the humid air.   15
Descend, O little cloud, & hover before the eyes of Thel."

The Cloud descended, and the Lilly bowd her modest head,
And went to mind her numerous charge among the verdant grass.

PLATE 3
                                    2
"O little Cloud," the virgin said, "I charge thee tell to me,
Why thou complainest not when in one hour thou fade away:

---

5. Genesis 3.8: "And they heard the voice of the   day."
Lord God walking in the garden in the cool of the   6. Humble.

Then we shall seek thee but not find; ah, Thel is like to Thee.
I pass away, yet I complain, and no one hears my voice."

The Cloud then shew'd his golden head & his bright form emerg'd,   5
Hovering and glittering on the air before the face of Thel.

"O virgin, know'st thou not our steeds drink of the golden springs
Where Luvah[7] doth renew his horses? Look'st thou on my youth,
And fearest thou because I vanish and am seen no more,
Nothing remains? O maid, I tell thee, when I pass away,   10
It is to tenfold life, to love, to peace, and raptures holy:
Unseen descending, weigh my light wings upon balmy flowers,
And court the fair eyed dew, to take me to her shining tent;
The weeping virgin trembling kneels before the risen sun,
Till we arise link'd in a golden band, and never part,   15
But walk united, bearing food to all our tender flowers."

"Dost thou O little Cloud? I fear that I am not like thee;
For I walk through the vales of Har and smell the sweetest flowers,
But I feed not the little flowers; I hear the warbling birds,
But I feed not the warbling birds; they fly and seek their food;   20
But Thel delights in these no more, because I fade away,
And all shall say, 'Without a use this shining woman liv'd,
Or did she only live to be at death the food of worms?' "

The Cloud reclind upon his airy throne and answer'd thus:

"Then if thou art the food of worms, O virgin of the skies,   25
How great thy use, how great thy blessing! Every thing that lives
Lives not alone, nor for itself; fear not, and I will call
The weak worm from its lowly bed, and thou shalt hear its voice.
Come forth, worm of the silent valley, to thy pensive queen."

The helpless worm arose, and sat upon the Lilly's leaf,   30
And the bright Cloud saild on, to find his partner in the vale.

PLATE 4

3
Then Thel astonish'd view'd the Worm upon its dewy bed.

"Art thou a Worm? Image of weakness, art thou but a Worm?
I see thee like an infant wrapped in the Lilly's leaf;
Ah, weep not, little voice, thou can'st not speak, but thou can'st weep.
Is this a Worm? I see thee lay helpless & naked, weeping,   5
And none to answer, none to cherish thee with mother's smiles."

7. The earliest mention in Blake's work of one of his "Giant Forms," the Zoas. Luvah is the mythical embodiment of the passional and sexual aspect of humankind. He is represented here, like the Greek Phoebus Apollo, as the driver of the chariot of the sun; he repairs to the Vales of Har simply in order to rest and water his horses. The cloud in this passage describes the cycle of water, from cloud to rain and (by the vaporizing action of the sun on water) back to the cloud.

The Clod of Clay heard the Worm's voice, & raisd her pitying head;
She bow'd over the weeping infant, and her life exhal'd
In milky fondness; then on Thel she fix'd her humble eyes.

"O beauty of the vales of Har! we live not for ourselves;   10
Thou seest me the meanest thing, and so I am indeed;
My bosom of itself is cold, and of itself is dark,

PLATE 5
But he that loves the lowly, pours his oil upon my head,
And kisses me, and binds his nuptial bands around my breast,
And says: 'Thou mother of my children, I have lovèd thee,
And I have given thee a crown that none can take away.'
But how this is, sweet maid, I know not, and I cannot know;   5
I ponder, and I cannot ponder; yet I live and love."

The daughter of beauty wip'd her pitying tears with her white veil,
And said: "Alas! I know not this, and therefore did I weep.
That God would love a Worm, I knew, and punish the evil foot
That, wilful, bruis'd its helpless form; but that he cherish'd it   10
With milk and oil I never knew; and therefore did I weep,
And I complaind in the mild air, because I fade away,
And lay me down in thy cold bed, and leave my shining lot."

"Queen of the vales," the matron Clay answered, "I heard thy sighs,
And all thy moans flew o'er my roof, but I have call'd them down.   15
Wilt thou, O Queen, enter my house? 'tis given thee to enter
And to return; fear nothing, enter with thy virgin feet."

PLATE 6
                              4
The eternal gates' terrific porter lifted the northern bar:[8]
Thel enter'd in & saw the secrets of the land unknown.
She saw the couches of the dead, & where the fibrous roots
Of every heart on earth infixes deep its restless twists:
A land of sorrows & of tears where never smile was seen.   5

She wanderd in the land of clouds thro' valleys dark, listning
Dolours & lamentations; waiting oft beside a dewy grave,
She stood in silence, listning to the voices of the ground,
Till to her own grave plot she came, & there she sat down,
And heard this voice of sorrow breathed from the hollow pit: 10

"Why cannot the Ear be closed to its own destruction?
Or the glistning Eye to the poison of a smile?

---

8. Homer, in *Odyssey* 13, described the Cave of
the Naiades, of which the northern gate is for mortals and the southern gate for gods. The Neopla-
tonist Porphyro had allegorized it as an account of
the descent of the soul into matter and then its
return. Blake has Thel use the northern gate to
pass from the state before birth into incarnate life.

Why are Eyelids stord with arrows ready drawn,
Where a thousand fighting men in ambush lie?
Or an Eye of gifts & graces, show'ring fruits & coinèd gold?   15
Why a Tongue impress'd with honey from every wind?
Why an Ear, a whirlpool fierce to draw creations in?
Why a Nostril wide inhaling terror, trembling, & affright?
Why a tender curb upon the youthful burning boy?
Why a little curtain of flesh on the bed of our desire?"[9]   20

The Virgin started from her seat, & with a shriek
Fled back unhinderd till she came into the vales of Har.

1789–91

Visions of the Daughters of Albion   This work, dated 1793 on

the title page, is one of Blake's early illuminated books, and like his later
and longer prophetic works it is written in what Blake called "the long
resounding strong heroic verse" of seven-foot lines. It has only three characters and a very simple plot. Unlike the timorous heroine of *The Book of
Thel*, the virgin Oothoon (probably pronounced as two syllables, Oothoon)
dares to assume the stage of adult sexuality (symbolized by her plucking a
marigold and placing it between her breasts) and sets out exultantly to join
her lover Theotormon, whose realm is the Atlantic Ocean. In her flight she
is waylaid and raped by Bromion in the figure of a thunderstorm, 1.16–17.
The jealous Theotormon, condemning the victim as well as the rapist, binds
the two "back to back" in a cave and sits weeping on the threshold. The rest
of the work consists of monologues by each of the three characters, who
remain frozen in these postures; the concluding speech (5.3 and following)
is a sustained oration by Oothoon. Throughout this stage tableau the Daughters
of Albion serve as a chorus of witnesses and auditors who, in a recurrent
single-line refrain, echo the "woes" and "sighs" of Oothoon but not her call
to rebellion.

    This simple drama is densely significant, for the three characters are human
archetypes, and the events and speeches, as Blake's compressed allusions
reveal, are the vehicle of multiple meanings with diverse areas of application. Blake's abrupt opening word, which he stresses by etching it in very
large letters, is "Enslav'd," and the work as a whole expresses his view that
contemporary men, and even more women, in a spiritual parallel to shackled and branded black slaves, are in bondage to prevailing concepts, codes,
and customs in all aspects of human perception, thought, and behavior.
Thus Oothoon (her name is adapted from a character in James Macpherson's pretended translations from the ancient British bard, Ossian) is in one
aspect a woman who has been raped, bound, and limited to an unsatisfactory option between two lovers, the one brutal and the other ineffectual. In
this aspect, as indicated by the refrain of the Daughters of Albion (that is,
contemporary Englishwomen), she represents in dramatized form the disabilities and slavelike status of all women in a male-dominated society. But

9. The voice from Thel's grave describes how
experience would seem to her timid and shrinking
temperament, should she elect to live out her life
in the human world. The catalogue of experience
runs through the various senses to end with touch,
the primary sexual sense.

Oothoon is also "the soft soul of America" (1.3); that is, she is the feminine aspect of the revolutionary nation which only a decade earlier had won political emancipation, yet tolerated an agricultural system that involved black slavery. In this dimension Bromion's rape of her, and his allusions to branding and scourging and to impregnating her, signify that Oothoon represents the situation of black female slaves, and at the same time the 'crass economic exploitation by slave-owning planters of her "soft American plains" (1.20–2.2). Oothoon's plucking the marigold, furthermore, turns out to signalize not only her sexual liberation, but also her liberation from constrictive sensible and moral perception to achieve the imaginative vision of "the breaking day" (2.24 and following)—that is, of the revolutionary promise of the highest human potentialities.

Correlatively the boastful Bromion (whose name is derived from the Greek word for "roarer") shows himself in his speeches to be not only a sexual exploiter of women, but a cruel slave owner whose aims are limited to the acquisition of "riches and ease." He reveals also that he is an exponent of mastery by force—a force that is manifested in war, an oppressive legal system, and a religious morality dependent on the threat of punishment in hell (4.19–24). Theotormon (whose name suggests, etymologically, "God-twisted" or "God-tormented") is represented even less sympathetically. Broken-spirited, paralyzed by a puritanical religion and its prohibitions, he despairs of the power of human "thought" (the vision of higher possibilities) to make any change in the human condition, denies the possibility of any "joys" in this life, and, rationalizing his own incapacities, can only decry and bewail Oothoon's daring to think and act other than he does (3.22–4.11).

Prominent in Oothoon's passionate closing oration is her celebration of the joys of a free and abundant sexual life for both women and men. The theme of sexual liberation serves Blake, however, as what Shelley, justifying the overt sexuality of his own poetry, was later to describe "as a kind of type or expression" of other, related human themes. In Blake's poem, these themes had already been introduced in the speeches of Bromion and Theotormon, but Oothoon corrects their warped perspectives. From her standpoint of imaginative vision she recognizes that Urizen (a name Blake uses here for the first time) is a "mistaken Demon"—a tyrannical, calculating, avaricious, and jealous god mistakenly worshipped by a self-enslaved mankind. She discerns also that narrow egoism, the "self-love that envies all," is the common root of a hypocritical "selfish holiness" and of the replacement of an outgoing sexuality by the solitary "self-enjoyings of self-denial." To this self-centeredness she attributes also the reduction of reality from the unboundedness of human "thoughts" to the contracted world perceived by the physical senses, as well as the tyranny of uniform laws imposed by science on the varied life of the natural world and of uniform moral laws imposed on the variousness of individual human identities. Above all she recognizes that the love of self is the root cause of human acquisitiveness, whether manifested in the commercial system, an institutionalized religion, a jealous possessiveness in love, or the insistence on the property rights established by a contractual but loveless marriage.

The period 1791–93, during which Blake composed *Visions of the Daughters of Albion*, was not only the heady time when the revolutionary spirit had spread from America to France, and effected reverberations in England; it was also the time of sporadic rebellions by slaves in the western hemisphere, and of widespread debate in the English Parliament, pulpits, and journals of several motions and bills to abolish the slave trade. Blake himself, while composing the *Visions*, had illustrated the sadistic punishments inflicted on slaves in engravings he made for J. G. Stedman's *A Narrative, of a Five Years' Expedition, against the Revolted Negroes of Surinam.* (See David Erdman, *Blake: Prophet against Empire*, chapter 10.) And Blake's championing of women's liberation very likely owed much to his acquaintance with Mary Wollstonecraft, one of whose books he had illustrated in 1791, and who, like him, was among the authors who gathered at the home of Joseph Johnson, the radical publisher. Blake's views parallel a number of those expressed in Wollstonecraft's *Vindications of the Rights of Woman*, published in 1792, a year before the *Visions*. Blake, however, in his characteristic way, radicalized some of the proposals of the most radical feminist af the time and wove them into an inclusive design in which, as David Erdman has put it, freedom in all its modes "is indivisible."

Visions of the Daughters of Albion
The Eye sees more than the Heart knows.

PLATE iii

The Argument

I loved Theotormon
And I was not ashamed
I trembled in my virgin fears
And I hid in Leutha's vale!

I plucked Leutha's flower,   5
And I rose up from the vale;
But the terrible thunders tore
My virgin mantle in twain.

PLATE 1
Visions

ENSLAV'D, the Daughters of Albion weep: a trembling lamentation
Upon their mountains; in their valleys, sighs toward America.

For the soft soul of America, Oothoon wandered in woe,
Along the vales of Leutha seeking flowers to comfort her;
And thus she spoke to the bright Marygold of Leutha's vale: 5

"Art thou a flower! art thou a nymph! I see thee now a flower,
Now a nymph! I dare not pluck thee from thy dewy bed!"

The Golden nymph replied: "Pluck thou my flower Oothoon the mild.
Another flower shall spring, because the soul of sweet delight
Can never pass away." She ceas'd & closd her golden shrine.   10

Then Oothoon pluck'd the flower saying, "I pluck thee from thy bed,
Sweet flower, and put thee here to glow between my breasts,
And thus I turn my face to where my whole soul seeks."

Over the waves she went in wing'd exulting swift delight;
And over Theotormon's reign took her impetuous course.   15

Bromion rent her with his thunders. On his stormy bed
Lay the faint maid, and soon her woes appalld his thunders hoarse.

Bromion spoke: "Behold this harlot here on Bromion's bed,
And let the jealous dolphins sport around the lovely maid;
Thy soft American plains are mine, and mine thy north & south: 20
Stampt with my signet[1] are the swarthy children of the sun:
They are obedient, they resist not, they obey the scourge:
Their daughters worship terrors and obey the violent.

PLATE 2
Now thou maist marry Bromion's harlot, and protect the child
Of Bromion's rage, that Oothoon shall put forth in nine moons'
    time."[2]

Then storms rent Theotormon's limbs; he rolld his waves around,
And folded his black jealous waters round the adulterate pair;
Bound back to back in Bromion's caves terror & meekness dwell.   5

At entrance Theotormon sits wearing the threshold hard
With secret tears; beneath him sound like waves on a desart shore
The voice of slaves beneath the sun, and children bought with money,
That shiver in religious caves beneath the burning fires
Of lust, that belch incessant from the summits of the earth.   10

Oothoon weeps not: she cannot weep! her tears are locked up;
But she can howl incessant, writhing her soft snowy limbs,
And calling Theotormon's Eagles to prey upon her flesh.[3]

"I call with holy voice! kings of the sounding air,
Rend away this defiled bosom that I may reflect   15
The image of Theotormon on my pure transparent breast."

The Eagles at her call descend & rend their bleeding prey;
Theotormon severely smiles; her soul reflects the smile,
As the clear spring mudded with feet of beasts grows pure & smiles.

1. A small seal or stamp. The allusion is to the branding of black slaves by their owners.
2. The context of the violence that Bromion inflicted on black female slaves (line 23) suggests that the raped and pregnant Oothoon represents this class of oppressed women, among others. (Pregnancy enhanced the market value of a young slave.)
3. Oothoon's sufferings under Theotormon's unjust condemnation are implicitly paralleled to Zeus' punishment of Prometheus (for befriending mankind) by setting an eagle to devour his ever-regenerating liver.

The Daughters of Albion hear her woes, & eccho back her sighs.   20

"Why does my Theotormon sit weeping upon the threshold,
And Oothoon hovers by his side, perswading him in vain?
I cry, 'Arise O Theotormon, for the village dog
Barks at the breaking day, the nightingale has done lamenting,
The lark does rustle in the ripe corn, and the Eagle returns   25
From nightly prey, and lifts his golden beak to the pure east,
Shaking the dust from his immortal pinions to awake
The sun that sleeps too long. Arise my Theotormon, I am pure;
Because the night is gone that clos'd me in its deadly black.'
They told me that the night & day were all that I could see;   30
They told me that I had five senses to inclose me up,
And they inclos'd my infinite brain into a narrow circle,
And sunk my heart into the Abyss, a red round globe hot burning,
Till all from life I was obliterated and erased.
Instead of morn arises a bright shadow, like an eye   35
In the eastern cloud,[4] instead of night a sickly charnel house,
That Theotormon hears me not! to him the night and morn
Are both alike: a night of sighs, a morning of fresh tears;

PLATE 3
And none but Bromion can hear my lamentations.

"With what sense is it that the chicken shuns the ravenous hawk?
With what sense does the tame pigeon measure out the expanse?
With what sense does the bee form cells? have not the mouse & frog
Eyes and ears and sense of touch? yet are their habitations   5
And their pursuits as different as their forms and as their joys.
Ask the wild ass why he refuses burdens, and the meek camel
Why he loves man; is it because of eye, ear, mouth, or skin,
Or breathing nostrils? No, for these the wolf and tyger have.
Ask the blind worm the secrets of the grave, and why her spires   10
Love to curl round the bones of death; and ask the rav'nous snake
Where she gets poison, & the wing'd eagle why he loves the sun,
And then tell me the thoughts of man, that have been hid of old.[5]

"Silent I hover all the night, and all day could be silent,
If Theotormon once would turn his loved eyes upon me.   15
How can I be defild when I reflect thy image pure?
Sweetest the fruit that the worm feeds on, & the soul prey'd on by woe,
The new wash'd lamb ting'd with the village smoke, & the bright swan

---

4. The contrast is between the physical sun perceived by the constricted ("inclos'd") sensible eye
and "the breaking day" (line 24) of a new era, perceived by Oothoon's liberated vision.
5. Oothoon implies that "thoughts" (i.e., imagi-

native powers) are as native to humanity as the
animal instincts are to other living species. In his
response, 3.23 and following, Theotormon
despairingly denies the validity of "thoughts," in
this sense.

By the red earth[6] of our immortal river: I bathe my wings,
And I am white and pure to hover round Theotormon's breast." 20

Then Theotormon broke his silence, and he answered:

"Tell me what is the night or day to one o'erflowd with woe?
Tell me what is a thought? & of what substance is it made?
Tell me what is a joy? & in what gardens do joys grow?
And in what rivers swim the sorrows? and upon what mountains 25

PLATE 4
Wave shadows of discontent? and in what houses dwell the wretched
Drunken with woe, forgotten, and shut up from cold despair?

"Tell me where dwell the thoughts, forgotten till thou call them forth?
Tell me where dwell the joys of old! & where the ancient loves?
And when will they renew again & the night of oblivion past? 5
That I might traverse times & spaces far remote and bring
Comforts into a present sorrow and a night of pain.
Where goest thou, O thought? to what remote land is thy flight?
If thou returnest to the present moment of affliction
Wilt thou bring comforts on thy wings and dews and honey and balm,
Or poison from the desart wilds, from the eyes of the envier?" 11

Then Bromion said, and shook the cavern with his lamentation:

"Thou knowest that the ancient trees seen by thine eyes have fruit;
But knowest thou that trees and fruits flourish upon the earth
To gratify senses unknown? trees beasts and birds unknown: 15
Unknown, not unpercievd, spread in the infinite microscope,
In places yet unvisited by the voyager, and in worlds
Over another kind of seas, and in atmospheres unknown?
Ah! are there other wars, beside the wars of sword and fire?
And are there other sorrows, beside the sorrows of poverty? 20
And are there other joys, beside the joys of riches and ease?
And is there not one law for both the lion and the ox?[7]
And is there not eternal fire, and eternal chains?
To bind the phantoms of existence from eternal life?"

Then Oothoon waited silent all the day and all the night, 25

PLATE 5
But when the morn arose, her lamentation renewd.
The Daughters of Albion hear her woes, & eccho back her sighs.

---

6. "Red earth" is the etymological meaning of the Hebrew name "Adam" (compare *The Marriage of Heaven and Hell*, 2.13). The "immortal river," accordingly, can be taken to refer to the "river" that "went out of Eden" (Genesis 2.10).
7. The last line of *The Marriage of Heaven and Hell* proclaims: "One Law for the Lion & Ox is Oppression."

"O Urizen! Creator of men! mistaken Demon of heaven:
Thy joys are tears! thy labour vain, to form men to thine image.
How can one joy absorb another? are not different joys   5
Holy, eternal, infinite! and each joy is a Love.

"Does not the great mouth laugh at a gift? & the narrow eyelids mock
At the labour that is above payment? and wilt thou take the ape
For thy councellor? or the dog for a schoolmaster to thy children?
Does he who contemns poverty, and he who turns with
          abhorrence   10
From usury, feel the same passion, or are they moved alike?
How can the giver of gifts experience the delights of the merchant?
How the industrious citizen the pains of the husbandman?
How different far the fat fed hireling with hollow drum,
Who buys whole corn fields into wastes,[8] and sings upon the
          heath: 15
How different their eye and ear! how different the world to them!
With what sense does the parson claim the labour of the farmer?
What are his nets & gins[9] & traps? & how does he surround him
With cold floods of abstraction, and with forests of solitude,
To build him castles and high spires, where kings & priests may dwell?
Till she who burns with youth, and knows no fixed lot, is bound   21
In spells of law to one she loaths; and must she drag the chain
Of life, in weary lust? must chilling murderous thoughts obscure
The clear heaven of her eternal spring? to bear the wintry rage
Of a harsh terror, driv'n to madness, bound to hold a rod   25
Over her shrinking shoulders all the day, & all the night
To turn the wheel of false desire, and longings that wake her womb
To the abhorred birth of cherubs in the human form
That live a pestilence & die a meteor & are no more;
Till the child dwell with one he hates, and do the deed he loaths,   30
And the impure scourge force his seed into its unripe birth
E'er yet his eyelids can behold the arrows of the day?[1]

"Does the whale worship at thy footsteps as the hungry dog?
Or does he scent the mountain prey, because his nostrils wide
Draw in the ocean? does his eye discern the flying cloud   35
As the raven's eye? or does he measure the expanse like the vulture?
Does the still spider view the cliffs where eagles hide their young?
Or does the fly rejoice because the harvest is brought in?
Does not the eagle scorn the earth & despise the treasures beneath?
But the mole knoweth what is there, & the worm shall tell it thee.   40
Does not the worm erect a pillar in the mouldering church yard,

---

8. Probably a compressed allusion both to the
wealthy landowner who converts fertile fields into
a game preserve, and to the recruiting officer ("with
hollow-drum") who strips the land of its agricultural laborers.

9. Snares.
1. The description is apparently of begetting children in loveless marriages, from one generation to
the next.

PLATE 6
And a palace of eternity in the jaws of the hungry grave?
Over his porch these words are written: 'Take thy bliss O Man!
And sweet shall be thy taste & sweet thy infant joys renew!'

"Infancy, fearless, lustful, happy! nestling for delight
In laps of pleasure; Innocence! honest, open, seeking   5
The vigorous joys of morning light, open to virgin bliss,
Who taught thee modesty, subtil modesty? Child of night & sleep,
When thou awakest wilt thou dissemble all thy secret joys,
Or wert thou not awake when all this mystery was disclos'd?
Then com'st thou forth a modest virgin, knowing to dissemble,   10
With nets found under thy night pillow to catch virgin joy,
And brand it with the name of whore, & sell it in the night,
In silence, ev'n without a whisper, and in seeming sleep.[2]
Religious dreams and holy vespers light thy smoky fires;
Once were thy fires lighted by the eyes of honest morn.   15
And does my Theotormon seek this hypocrite modesty,
This knowing, artful, secret, fearful, cautious, trembling hypocrite?
Then is Oothoon a whore indeed! and all the virgin joys
Of life are harlots, and Theotormon is a sick man's dream,
And Oothoon is the crafty slave of selfish holiness.   20

"But Oothoon is not so; a virgin fill'd with virgin fancies
Open to joy and to delight where ever beauty appears.
If in the morning sun I find it, there my eyes are fix'd

PLATE 7
In happy copulation; if in evening mild, wearied with work,
Sit on a bank and draw the pleasures of this free born joy.

"The moment of desire! the moment of desire! The virgin
That pines for man shall awaken her womb to enormous joys
In the secret shadows of her chamber; the youth shut up from   5
The lustful joy shall forget to generate & create an amorous image
In the shadows of his curtains and in the folds of his silent pillow.
Are not these the places of religion? the rewards of continence?
The self enjoyings of self denial? Why dost seek religion?
Is it because acts are not lovely, that thou seekest solitude,   10
Where the horrible darkness is impressed with reflections of desire?

"Father of Jealousy,[3] be thou accursed from the earth!
Why hast thou taught my Theotormon this accursed thing?
Till beauty fades from off my shoulders, darken'd and cast out,
A solitary shadow wailing on the margin of non-entity.   15

2. Oothoon contrasts the natural, innocent sensuality of an infant to the socially acquired, hypocritical modesty of the adult virgin; the latter is

Theotormon's concept of female virtue.
3. I.e., Urizen (5.3), the false creator-god.

"I cry, Love! Love! Love! happy happy Love! free as the mountain wind!
Can that be Love, that drinks another as a sponge drinks water?
That clouds with jealousy his nights, with weepings all the day,
To spin a web of age around him, grey and hoary! dark!
Till his eyes sicken at the fruit that hangs before his sight.   20
Such is self-love that envies all! a creeping skeleton
With lamplike eyes watching around the frozen marriage bed.

"But silken nets and traps of adamant[4] will Oothoon spread,
And catch for thee girls of mild silver, or of furious gold;
I'll lie beside thee on a bank & view their wanton play   25
In lovely copulation bliss on bliss with Theotormon:
Red as the rosy morning, lustful as the first born beam,
Oothoon shall view his dear delight, nor e'er with jealous cloud
Come in the heaven of generous love; nor selfish blightings bring.

"Does the sun walk in glorious raiment on the secret floor   30

PLATE 8
Where the cold miser spreads his gold? or does the bright cloud drop
On his stone threshold? does his eye behold the beam that brings
Expansion to the eye of pity? or will he bind himself
Beside the ox to thy hard furrow? does not that mild beam blot
The bat, the owl, the glowing tyger, and the king of night?   5
The sea fowl takes the wintry blast for a cov'ring to her limbs,
And the wild snake the pestilence to adorn him with gems & gold.
And trees & birds & beasts & men behold their eternal joy.
Arise you little glancing wings, and sing your infant joy!
Arise and drink your bliss, for every thing that lives is holy!"[5]   10

Thus every morning wails Oothoon, but Theotormon sits
Upon the margind ocean conversing with shadows dire.

The Daughters of Albion hear her woes, & eccho back her sighs.

1791–93

                                                                     1793

The Marriage of Heaven and Hell   This, the most immediately
accessible of Blake's longer works, is a vigorous, deliberately outrageous, and
at times comic, onslaught against the timidly conventional and self-right-
eous members of society, as well as against many of the stock opinions of
orthodox Christian piety and morality. The seeming simplicity of Blake's
satiric attitude, however, is deceptive.

4. A legendary stone believed to be unbreakable.   5. This last phrase is also the concluding line of
(The name is derived from the Greek word for dia-   "A Song of Liberty," appended to The Marriage of
mond.)   Heaven and Hell, below.

Initially, Blake accepts the terminology of standard Christian morality ("what the religious call Good & Evil") but reverses its values. In this conventional use Evil, which is manifested by the class of beings called Devils and which consigns wrongdoers to the orthodox Hell, is everything associated with the body and its desires and consists essentially of energy, abundance, act, freedom. And conventional Good, which is manifested by Angels and guarantees its adherents a place in the orthodox Heaven, is associated with the Soul (regarded as entirely separate from the body) and consists of the contrary qualities of reason, restraint, passivity, and prohibition. Blandly adopting this current nomenclature, Blake elects to assume the diabolic persona—what he calls "the voice of the Devil"—and to utter "Proverbs of Hell." This ironic stance produces a vein of satire which is in the great eighteenth-century tradition of sustained ironic reversal, represented by works such as Jonathan Swift's Modest Proposal.

But the transvaluation of standard criteria is only a first stage in Blake's complex irony, designed to startle the reader into recognizing the inadequacy of conventional moral categories and stock responses. As he also says in the opening summary, "Without Contraries is no progression," and "Reason and Energy" are both "necessary to Human existence." It turns out that Blake subordinates his satiric reversal of conventional values under a more inclusive point of view, according to which the real Good, as distinguished from the merely ironic Good, is not instinctual abandon but a "marriage," or union of the contraries, of desire and restraint, energy and reason, the promptings of Hell and the denials of Heaven—or as Blake calls these contraries, in the comprehensive terms he introduces in plate 16, "the Prolific" and "the Devouring." These two classes, he adds, "should be enemies," and "whoever tries to reconcile them seeks to destroy existence." When Blake speaks not as moral satirist but as serious moralist, the good life is that abundant and strenuous life he describes as the sustained tension, without victory or suppression, of co-present oppositions.

Blake was stimulated to write this unique work in response to the books of the visionary Swedish theologian Emanuel Swedenborg, whom he had at first admired but then had come to recognize as a conventional Angel in the disguise of a radical Devil. In plate 3 the writings of Swedenborg are described as the winding clothes Blake discards as he is resurrected from the tomb of his past self, as a poet-prophet who heralds the apocalyptic promise of his age. For Blake wrote The Marriage of Heaven and Hell in the early 1790s, during the bright early years of the French Revolution, when he shared the expectations of a number of radical Englishmen, including the young poets Wordsworth, Coleridge, and Southey, that the Revolution was the universal violence which had been predicted by the Biblical prophets as a stage immediately preceding the millennium. The double role of The Marriage as both satire and revolutionary prophecy is made explicit in A Song of Liberty, which Blake etched in 1792 and added as a coda.

The Marriage of Heaven and Hell

PLATE 2

The Argument

Rintrah[1] roars & shakes his fires in the burdend air;
Hungry clouds swag[2] on the deep.

Once meek, and in a perilous path,
The just man kept his course along
The vale of death.   5
Roses are planted where thorns grow,
And on the barren heath
Sing the honey bees.

Then the perilous path was planted,
And a river, and a spring,   10
On every cliff and tomb;
And on the bleached bones
Red clay[3] brought forth;

Till the villain left the paths of ease,
To walk in perilous paths, and drive   15
The just man into barren climes.

Now the sneaking serpent walks
In mild humility,
And the just man rages in the wilds
Where lions roam.   20

Rintrah roars & shakes his fires in the burdend air;
Hungry clouds swag on the deep.

PLATE 3

As a new heaven is begun, and it is now thirty-three years since its
advent, the Eternal Hell revives.[4] And lo! Swedenborg is the Angel sit-

1. Rintrah plays the role of the angry Old Testament prophet Elijah as well as of John the Baptist, the voice "crying in the wilderness" (Matthew 3), preparing the way for Christ the Messiah. It has been plausibly suggested that stanzas 2–5 summarize the course of Biblical history to the present time. "Once" (line 3) refers to Old Testament history after the fall of man; "Then" (line 9) is the time of the birth of Christ; "Till" (line 14) identifies the era when Christianity was perverted into an institutional religion; and "Now" (line 17) is the time of the wrathful portent of the French Revolution. In this final era, the hypocritical serpent represents the priest of the "angels" in the poem, while "the just man" is embodied in Blake himself, a raging poet and prophet in the guise of a Devil.

2. Sag, hang down.

3. In Hebrew, the literal meaning of "Adam," or created man. There is a probable reference to the birth of the Redeemer, the new Adam.

4. The Swedish scientist and religious philosopher Emanuel Swedenborg (1688–1772) had predicted, on the basis of his visions, that the Last Judgment and the coming of the Kingdom of Heaven would occur in 1757. This was precisely the year of Blake's birth. Now, in 1790, Blake is thirty-three, the age at which Christ had been resurrected from the tomb; appropriately, Blake rises from the tomb of his past life in his new role as imaginative artist who will redeem his age. But, Blake ironically comments, the works he will

ting at the tomb; his writings are the linen clothes folded up. Now is the dominion of Edom, & the return of Adam into Paradise; see Isaiah xxxiv & XXXV Chap.[5]

Without Contraries is no progression. Attraction and Repulsion, Reason and Energy, Love and Hate, are necessary to Human existence.

From these contraries spring what the religious call Good & Evil. Good is the passive that obeys Reason. Evil is the active springing from Energy.

Good is Heaven. Evil is Hell.

PLATE 4

The Voice of the Devil

All Bibles or sacred codes have been the causes of the following Errors:

1. That Man has two real existing principles; Viz: a Body & a Soul.

2. That Energy, calld Evil, is alone from the Body, & that Reason, calld Good, is alone from the Soul.

3. That God will torment Man in Eternity for following his Energies.

But the following Contraries to these are True:

1. Man has no Body distinct from his Soul; for that calld Body is a portion of Soul discernd by the five Senses, the chief inlets of Soul in this age.

2. Energy is the only life, and is from the Body; and Reason is the bound or outward circumference of Energy.

3. Energy is Eternal Delight.

PLATE 5

Those who restrain desire, do so because theirs is weak enough to be restrained; and the restrainer or reason usurps its place & governs the unwilling.

And being restraind, it by degrees becomes passive, till it is only the shadow of desire.

The history of this is written in *Paradise Lost*,[6] & the Governor or Reason is call'd Messiah.

---

engrave in his resurrection will constitute the Eternal Hell, the contrary inevitably brought into simultaneous being by Swedenborg's limited New Heaven.

5. Isaiah 34 prophesies "the day of the Lord's vengeance," a time of violent destruction and bloodshed; Isaiah 35 prophesies the redemption to follow, in which "the desert shall . . . blossom as the rose," "in the wilderness shall waters break out, and streams in the desert," and "no lion shall be there," but "an highway shall be there . . . and it shall be called the way of holiness." (Cf. "The Argument," lines 3–11, 20.) Blake combines with these chapters Isaiah 63, in which "Edom" is the place from

which comes the man whose garments are red with the blood he has spilled; for as he says, "the day of vengeance is in mine heart, and the year of my redeemed is come." Blake interprets this last phrase as predicting the time when Adam would regain his lost Paradise.

With reference to affairs in 1790, Edom represents France, and the red man coming from Edom (to England) is the spirit of the French Revolution, which Blake interprets as a portent of apocalyptic redemption and the recovery of Paradise.

6. What follows, to the end of this section, is Blake's "diabolical" reading of Milton's *Paradise Lost*.

And the original Archangel, or possessor of the command of the heavenly host, is calld the Devil or Satan, and his children are call'd Sin & Death.[7]

But in the Book of Job, Milton's Messiah is call'd Satan.[8]

For this history has been adopted by both parties.

It indeed appear'd to Reason as if Desire was cast out; but the Devil's account is, that the Messi[PL 6]ah fell, & formed a heaven of what he stole from the Abyss.

This is shewn in the Gospel, where he prays to the Father to send the comforter or Desire that Reason may have Ideas to build on;[9] the Jehovah of the Bible being no other than he who dwells in flaming fire. Know that after Christ's death, he became Jehovah.

But in Milton, the Father is Destiny, the Son, a Ratio of the five senses,[1] & the Holy-ghost, Vacuum!

Note. The reason Milton wrote in fetters when he wrote of Angels & God, and at liberty when of Devils & Hell, is because he was a true Poet and of the Devil's party without knowing it.

A Memorable Fancy[2]

As I was walking among the fires of hell, delighted with the enjoyments of Genius, which to Angels look like torment and insanity, I collected some of their Proverbs; thinking that as the sayings used in a nation mark its character, so the Proverbs of Hell shew the nature of Infernal wisdom better than any description of buildings or garments.

When I came home, on the abyss of the five senses, where a flat sided steep frowns over the present world, I saw a mighty Devil folded in black clouds, hovering on the sides of the rock; with cor[PL 7]roding fires he wrote the following sentence[3] now perceived by the minds of men, & read by them on earth:

How do you know but ev'ry Bird that cuts the airy way,
Is an immense world of delight, clos'd by your senses five?

Proverbs of Hell[4]

In seed time learn, in harvest teach, in winter enjoy.
Drive your cart and your plow over the bones of the dead.
The road of excess leads to the palace of wisdom.

7. Satan's giving birth to Sin and then incestuously begetting Death upon her is described in *Paradise Lost* 2.745 ff.; the war in heaven, referred to three lines below, in which the Messiah defeated Satan and drove him out of heaven, is described in 6.824 ff.

8. In the Book of Job, Satan plays the role of Job's moral accuser and physical tormentor.

9. Possibly John 14.16–17, where Christ says he "will pray the Father, and he shall give you another Comforter . . . even the Spirit of truth."

1. The Latin *ratio* means both "reason" and "sum." Blake applies the term to the 18th-century view, following the empirical philosophy of John Locke, that the content of the mind, upon which the faculty of reason operates, is limited to the sum of the experience acquired by the five senses.

2. A parody of what Swedenborg called "memorable relations" of his literal-minded visions of the eternal world.

3. The "mighty Devil" is Blake, as he sees himself reflected in the shiny plate on which he is etching this very passage with "corroding fires"—i.e., acid. See also the third from last sentence in plate 14.

4. A "diabolic" version of the Book of Proverbs in the Old Testament.

Prudence is a rich ugly old maid courted by Incapacity.
He who desires but acts not, breeds pestilence.   5
The cut worm forgives the plow.
Dip him in the river who loves water.
A fool sees not the same tree that a wise man sees.
He whose face gives no light, shall never become a star.
Eternity is in love with the productions of time.   10
The busy bee has no time for sorrow.
The hours of folly are measur'd by the clock; but of wisdom, no clock
    can measure.
All wholsom food is caught without a net or a trap.
Bring out number, weight, & measure in a year of dearth.
No bird soars too high, if he soars with his own wings.   15
A dead body revenges not injuries.
The most sublime act is to set another before you.
If the fool would persist in his folly he would become wise.
Folly is the cloke of knavery.
Shame is Pride's cloke.   20

PLATE 8
Prisons are built with stones of Law, Brothels with bricks of Religion.
The pride of the peacock is the glory of God.
The lust of the goat is the bounty of God.
The wrath of the lion is the wisdom of God.
The nakedness of woman is the work of God.   25
Excess of sorrow laughs. Excess of joy weeps.
The roaring of lions, the howling of wolves, the raging of the stormy
    sea, and the destructive sword, are portions of eternity too great for
    the eye of man.
The fox condemns the trap, not himself.
Joys impregnate. Sorrows bring forth.
Let man wear the fell of the lion, woman the fleece of the sheep.   30
The bird a nest, the spider a web, man friendship.
The selfish smiling fool & the sullen frowning fool shall be both thought
    wise, that they may be a rod.
What is now proved was once only imagin'd.
The rat, the mouse, the fox, the rabbit watch the roots; the lion, the
    tyger, the horse, the elephant, watch the fruits.
The cistern contains; the fountain overflows.   35
One thought fills immensity.
Always be ready to speak your mind, and a base man will avoid you.
Every thing possible to be believ'd is an image of truth.
The eagle never lost so much time as when he submitted to learn of the
    crow.

PLATE 9
The fox provides for himself, but God provides for the lion.   40
Think in the morning, Act in the noon, Eat in the evening, Sleep in
    the night.

He who has sufferd you to impose on him knows you.
As the plow follows words, so God rewards prayers.
The tygers of wrath are wiser than the horses of instruction.
Expect poison from the standing water.   45
You never know what is enough unless you know what is more than
    enough.
Listen to the fool's reproach! it is a kingly title!
The eyes of fire, the nostrils of air, the mouth of water, the beard of
    earth.
The weak in courage is strong in cunning.
The apple tree never asks the beech how he shall grow, nor the lion
    the horse, how he shall take his prey.   50
The thankful reciever bears a plentiful harvest.
If others had not been foolish, we should be so.
The soul of sweet delight can never be defil'd.
When thou seest an Eagle, thou seest a portion of Genius; lift up thy
    head!
As the catterpiller chooses the fairest leaves to lay her eggs on, so the
    priest lays his curse on the fairest joys.   55
To create a little flower is the labour of ages.
Damn braces; Bless relaxes.
The best wine is the oldest, the best water the newest.
Prayers plow not! Praises reap not!
Joys laugh not! Sorrows weep not!   60

PLATE 10
The head Sublime, the heart Pathos, the genitals Beauty, the hands &
    feet Proportion.
As the air to a bird or the sea to a fish, so is contempt to the contempti-
    ble.
The crow wish'd every thing was black, the owl that every thing was
    white.
Exuberance is Beauty.
If the lion was advised by the fox, he would be cunning.   65
Improvement makes strait roads, but the crooked roads without
    Improvement are roads of Genius.
Sooner murder an infant in its cradle than nurse unacted desires.
Where man is not, nature is barren.
Truth can never be told so as to be understood, and not be believ'd.
                    Enough! or Too much.   70

_____

PLATE 11
    The ancient Poets animated all sensible objects with Gods or Geniuses,
calling them by the names and adorning them with the properties of
woods, rivers, mountains, lakes, cities, nations, and whatever their
enlarged & numerous senses could perceive.

And particularly they studied the genius of each city & country, placing it under its mental deity.

Till a system was formed, which some took advantage of & enslav'd
the vulgar by attempting to realize or abstract the mental deities from
their objects; thus began Priesthood,

Choosing forms of worship from poetic tales.

And at length they pronounced that the Gods had ordered such things.

Thus men forgot that All deities reside in the human breast.

PLATE 12

A Memorable Fancy[5]

The Prophets Isaiah and Ezekiel dined with me, and I asked them
how they dared so roundly to assert that God spake to them; and whether
they did not think at the time that they would be misunderstood, & so
be the cause of imposition.

Isaiah answer'd: "I saw no God, nor heard any, in a finite organical
perception; but my senses discover'd the infinite in every thing, and as I
was then perswaded, & remain confirm'd, that the voice of honest indignation is the voice of God, I cared not for consequences, but wrote."

Then I asked: "Does a firm perswasion that a thing is so, make it so?"

He replied: "All poets believe that it does, & in ages of imagination
this firm perswasion removed mountains; but many are not capable of a
firm perswasion of any thing."

Then Ezekiel said: "The philosophy of the East taught the first principles of human perception. Some nations held one principle for the
origin & some another; we of Israel taught that the Poetic Genius (as
you now call it) was the first principle and all the others merely derivative, which was the cause of our despising the Priests & Philosophers of
other countries, and prophecying that all Gods [PL 13] would at last be
proved to originate in ours & to be the tributaries of the Poetic Genius;
it was this that our great poet, King David, desired so fervently & invokes
so pathetically, saying by this he conquers enemies & governs kingdoms;
and we so loved our God, that we cursed in his name all the deities of
surrounding nations, and asserted that they had rebelled; from these
opinions the vulgar came to think that all nations would at last be subject
to the Jews."

"This," said he, "like all firm perswasions, is come to pass, for all
nations believe the Jews' code and worship the Jews' god, and what greater
subjection can be?"

I heard this with some wonder, & must confess my own conviction.
After dinner I ask'd Isaiah to favour the world with his lost works; he said
none of equal value was lost. Ezekiel said the same of his.

5. Blake parodies Swedenborg's accounts, in his *Memorable Relations*, of his conversations with the
inhabitants during his spiritual trips to heaven.

I also asked Isaiah what made him go naked and barefoot three years? He answered, "the same that made our friend Diogenes, the Grecian."[6]

I then asked Ezekiel why he eat dung, & lay so long on his right & left side?[7] He answered, "the desire of raising other men into a perception of the infinite; this the North American tribes practise, & is he honest who resists his genius or conscience only for the sake of present ease or gratification?"

PLATE 14

The ancient tradition that the world will be consumed in fire at the end of six thousand years is true, as I have heard from Hell.

For the cherub with his flaming sword is hereby commanded to leave his guard at the tree of life;[8] and when he does, the whole creation will be consumed, and appear infinite and holy, whereas it now appears finite & corrupt.

This will come to pass by an improvement of sensual enjoyment.

But first the notion that man has a body distinct from his soul is to be expunged; this I shall do, by printing in the infernal method, by corrosives, which in Hell are salutary and medicinal, melting apparent surfaces away, and displaying the infinite which was hid.[9]

If the doors of perception were cleansed every thing would appear to man as it is, infinite.

For man has closed himself up, till he sees all things thro' narrow chinks of his cavern.

PLATE 15

A Memorable Fancy

I was in a Printing house in Hell & saw the method in which knowledge is transmitted from generation to generation.

In the first chamber was a Dragon-Man, clearing away the rubbish from a cave's mouth; within, a number of Dragons were hollowing the cave.

In the second chamber was a Viper folding round the rock & the cave, and others adorning it with gold, silver, and precious stones.

In the third chamber was an Eagle with wings and feathers of air; he caused the inside of the cave to be infinite; around were numbers of Eagle-like men, who built palaces in the immense cliffs.

In the fourth chamber were Lions of flaming fire, raging around & melting the metals into living fluids.

---

6. In Isaiah 20.2–3, the prophet, at the command of the Lord, walked "naked and bare-foot" for three years. Diogenes was the 4th-century Greek Cynic whose extreme repudiation of civilized customs gave rise to anecdotes that he had renounced clothing.
7. The Lord gave these instructions to the prophet Ezekiel, 4.4–6.

8. In Genesis 3.24, when the Lord drove Adam and Eve from the Garden of Eden, he had placed Cherubim and a flaming sword at the eastern end "to keep the way of the tree of life."
9. See "A Memorable Fancy," plates 6–7 above, footnote 3.

In the fifth chamber were Unnam'd forms, which cast the metals into the expanse.

There they were receiv'd by Men who occupied the sixth chamber, and took the forms of books & were arranged in libraries.[1]

PLATE 16

The Giants who formed this world into its sensual existence, and now seem to live in it in chains, are in truth the causes of its life & the sources of all activity; but the chains are the cunning of weak and tame minds which have power to resist energy; according to the proverb, the weak in courage is strong in cunning.

Thus one portion of being is the Prolific, the other, the Devouring; to the Devourer it seems as if the producer was in his chains, but it is not so; he only takes portions of existence and fancies that the whole.

But the Prolific would cease to be Prolific unless the Devourer as a sea received the excess of his delights.[2]

Some will say, "Is not God alone the Prolific?" I answer, "God only Acts & Is, in existing beings or Men."

These two classes of men are always upon earth, & they should be enemies; whoever tries [PL 17] to reconcile them seeks to destroy existence.

Religion is an endeavour to reconcile the two.

Note. Jesus Christ did not wish to unite but to separate them, as in the Parable of sheep and goats! & he says, "I came not to send Peace but a Sword."[3]

Messiah or Satan or Tempter was formerly thought to be one of the Antediluvians[4] who are our Energies.

A Memorable Fancy

An Angel came to me and said: "O pitiable foolish young man! O horrible! O dreadful state! consider the hot burning dungeon thou art preparing for thyself to all eternity, to which thou art going in such career."

I said: "Perhaps you will be willing to shew me my eternal lot, & we will contemplate together upon it and see whether your lot or mine is most desirable."

So he took me thro' a stable & thro' a church & down into the church vault at the end of which was a mill; thro' the mill we went, and came to a cave; down the winding cavern we groped our tedious way till a void boundless as a nether sky appeared beneath us, & we held by the roots

---

1. In this Memorable Fancy Blake allegorizes his procedure in designing, etching, printing, and binding his works of imaginative genius.
2. The "Giants" in this section are human creative energies, called "the Prolific," in their rela-
tion to their indispensable contrary, "the Devourer."
3. The parable of the sheep and the goats is in Matthew 25.32–33; the saying of Christ, in Matthew 10.34.
4. Those who lived before Noah's flood.

of trees and hung over this immensity, but I said: "If you please, we will commit ourselves to this void, and see whether Providence is here also, if you will not I will." But he answered: "Do not presume, O young man, but as we here remain, behold thy lot which will soon appear when the darkness passes away."[5]

So I remain with him sitting in the twisted [PL 18] root of an oak; he was suspended in a fungus which hung with the head downward into the deep.

By degrees we beheld the infinite Abyss, fiery as the smoke of a burning city; beneath us at an immense distance was the sun, black but shining; round it were fiery tracks on which revolv'd vast spiders, crawling after their prey, which flew, or rather swum in the infinite deep, in the most terrific shapes of animals sprung from corruption; & the air was full of them, & seemed composed of them; these are Devils, and are called Powers of the air. I now asked my companion which was my eternal lot? He said, "Between the black & white spiders."

But now, from between the black & white spiders a cloud and fire burst and rolled thro the deep, blackning all beneath, so that the nether deep grew black as a sea & rolled with a terrible noise. Beneath us was nothing now to be seen but a black tempest, till looking east between the clouds & the waves, we saw a cataract of blood mixed with fire, and not many stones' throw from us appeared and sunk again the scaly fold of a monstrous serpent. At last to the east, distant about three degrees, appeared a fiery crest above the waves. Slowly it reared like a ridge of golden rocks till we discovered two globes of crimson fire, from which the sea fled away in clouds of smoke. And now we saw it was the head of Leviathan; his forehead was divided into streaks of green & purple like those on a tyger's forehead; soon we saw his mouth & red gills hang just above the raging foam, tinging the black deep with beams of blood, advancing toward [PL 19] us with all the fury of a spiritual existence.

My friend the Angel climb'd up from his station into the mill. I remain'd alone, & then this appearance was no more, but I found myself sitting on a pleasant bank beside a river by moon light, hearing a harper who sung to the harp, & his theme was: "The man who never alters his opinion is like standing water, & breeds reptiles of the mind."

But I arose, and sought for the mill, & there I found my Angel, who surprised asked me how I escaped?

I answerd: "All that we saw was owing to your metaphysics: for when you ran away, I found myself on a bank by moonlight hearing a harper. But now we have seen my eternal lot, shall I shew you yours? He laughd at my proposal; but I by force suddenly caught him in my arms, & flew

5. The "stable" is that where Jesus was born, which, allegorically, leads to the "church" founded in his name and to the "vault" where this institution effectually buried him. The "mill" in Blake is a symbol of mechanical and analytic philosophy; through this the pilgrims pass into the twisting cave of rationalistic theology and descend to an underworld which is an empty abyss. The point of this

Blakean equivalent of a carnival fun house is that only after you have thoroughly confused yourself by this tortuous approach, and only if you then (as in the next two paragraphs) stare at this topsy-turvy emptiness long enough, will the void gradually assume the semblance of the comic horrors of the fantasied hell of angelic orthodoxy.

westerly thro' the night, til we were elevated above the earth's shadow; then I flung myself with him directly into the body of the sun. Here I clothed myself in white, & taking in my hand Swedenborg's volumes, sunk from the glorious clime, and passed all the planets till we came to Saturn. Here I staid to rest & then leap'd into the void between Saturn & the fixed stars.[6]

"Here," said I, "is your lot, in this space, if space it may be calld." Soon we saw the stable and the church, & I took him to the altar and open'd the Bible, and lo! it was a deep pit, into which I descended, driving the Angel before me. Soon we saw seven houses of brick;[7] one we enterd; in it were a [PL 20] number of monkeys, baboons, & all of that species, chaind by the middle, grinning and snatching at one another, but withheld by the shortness of their chains. However, I saw that they sometimes grew numerous, and then the weak were caught by the strong, and with a grinning aspect, first coupled with & then devourd, by pluck-ing off first one limb and then another till the body was left a helpless trunk. This, after grinning & kissing it with seeming fondness, they devourd too; and here & there I saw one savourily picking the flesh off of his own tail. As the stench terribly annoyd us both, we went into the mill, & I in my hand brought the skeleton of a body, which in the mill was Aristotle's Analytics.[8]

So the Angel said: "Thy phantasy has imposed upon me, & thou oughtest to be ashamed."

I answerd: "We impose on one another, & it is but lost time to con-verse with you whose works are only Analytics."

Opposition is true Friendship.

PLATE 21

I have always found that Angels have the vanity to speak of themselves as the only wise; this they do with a confident insolence sprouting from systematic reasoning.

Thus Swedenborg boasts that what he writes is new; tho' it is only the Contents or Index of already publish'd books.

A man carried a monkey about for a shew, & because he was a little wiser than the monkey, grew vain, and conceiv'd himself as much wiser than seven men. It is so with Swedenborg; he shews the folly of churches & exposes hypocrites, till he imagines that all are religious, & himself the single [PL 22] one on earth that ever broke a net.

Now hear a plain fact: Swedenborg has not written one new truth. Now hear another: he has written all the old falshoods.

And now hear the reason: He conversed with Angels who are all reli-

---

6. In the Ptolemaic world picture, Saturn was in the outermost planetary sphere; beyond it was the sphere of the fixed stars.
7. The "seven churches which are in Asia," to which John addresses the Book of Revelation 1.4.

Blake now forces upon the angel his own diabolic view of angelic Biblical exegesis, theological spec-ulation and disputation, and Hell.
8. Aristotle's treatises on logic.

gious, & conversed not with Devils, who all hate religion, for he was incapable thro' his conceited notions.

Thus Swedenborg's writings are a recapitulation of all superficial opinions, and an analysis of the more sublime, but no further.

Have now another plain fact: Any man of mechanical talents may from the writings of Paracelsus or Jacob Behmen[9] produce ten thousand volumes of equal value with Swedenborg's, and from those of Dante or Shakespear, an infinite number.

But when he has done this, let him not say that he knows better than his master, for he only holds a candle in sunshine.

A Memorable Fancy

Once I saw a Devil in a flame of fire, who arose before an Angel that sat on a cloud, and the Devil utterd these words:

"The worship of God is, Honouring his gifts in other men, each according to his genius, and loving the [PL 23] greatest men best. Those who envy or calumniate great men hate God, for there is no other God."

The Angel hearing this became almost blue; but mastering himself, he grew yellow, & at last white, pink, & smiling, and then replied:

"Thou Idolater, is not God One? & is not he visible in Jesus Christ? and has not Jesus Christ given his sanction to the law of ten commandments, and are not all other men fools, sinners, & nothings?"

The Devil answer'd; "Bray a fool in a mortar with wheat, yet shall not his folly be beaten out of him.[1] If Jesus Christ is the greatest man, you ought to love him in the greatest degree. Now hear how he has given his sanction to the law of ten commandments: did he not mock at the sabbath, and so mock the sabbath's God? murder those who were murderd because of him? turn away the law from the woman taken in adultery? steal the labor of others to support him? bear false witness when he omitted making a defence before Pilate? covet when he pray'd for his disciples, and when he bid them shake off the dust of their feet against such as refused to lodge them?[2] I tell you, no virtue can exist without breaking these ten commandments. Jesus was all virtue, and acted from im[PL 24]pulse, not from rules."

When he had so spoken, I beheld the Angel, who stretched out his arms embracing the flame of fire, & he was consumed and arose as Elijah.[3]

Note. This Angel, who is now become a Devil, is my particular friend;

---

9. Paracelsus (1493–1541), a Swiss physician and a pioneer in empirical medicine, was also a prominent theorist of the occult. Behmen is Jakob Boehme (1575–1624), a German shoemaker who developed a theosophical system which has had persisting influence both on theological and metaphysical speculation.

1. "Though thou shouldst bray a fool in a mortar among wheat with a pestle, yet will not his foolishness depart from him" (Proverbs 27.22). "Bray":

pound into small pieces.

2. See Mark 2.27 ("the sabbath was made for man"); John 7.2 ff. (on the woman taken in adultery); Matthew 35.13–14 (Christ's silence before Pilate); Matthew 10.4 ("whosoever shall not receive you . . . when ye depart . . . shake off the dust of your feet").

3. In II Kings 2.11, the prophet Elijah "went up by a whirlwind into heaven," borne by "a chariot of fire."

we often read the Bible together in its infernal or diabolical sense, which the world shall have if they behave well.

I have also The Bible of Hell,[4] which the world shall have whether they will or no.

One Law for the lion & Ox is Oppression.

1790–93   1790–93

PLATE 25

A Song of Liberty[1]

1. The Eternal Female groand! it was heard over all the Earth.

2. Albion's[2] coast is sick, silent; the American meadows faint!

3. Shadows of Prophecy shiver along by the lakes and the rivers and mutter across the ocean. France, rend down thy dungeon![3]

4. Golden Spain, burst the barriers of old Rome!

5. Cast thy keys, O Rome,[4] into the deep down falling, even to eternity down falling,

6. And weep.[5]

7. In her trembling hands she took the new born terror, howling.

8. On those infinite mountains of light now barr'd out by the Atlantic sea,[6] the new born fire stood before the starry king!

9. Flag'd with grey brow'd snows and thunderous visages, the jealous wings wav'd over the deep.

10. The speary hand burned aloft, unbuckled was the shield, forth went the hand of jealousy among the flaming hair, and [PL 26] hurl'd the new born wonder thro' the starry night.

11. The fire, the fire, is falling!

12. Look up! look up! O citizen of London, enlarge thy countenance! O Jew, leave counting gold! return to thy oil and wine. O African! black African! (Go, wingèd thought, widen his forehead.)

13. The fiery limbs, the flaming hair, shot like the sinking sun into the western sea.

14. Wak'd from his eternal sleep, the hoary element[7] roaring fled away:

15. Down rushd, beating his wings in vain, the jealous king; his grey brow'd councellors, thunderous warriors, curl'd veterans, among helms,

---

4. I.e., the poems and designs that Blake is working on.
1. Blake etched this poem in 1792 and sometimes bound it as an appendix to *The Marriage of Heaven and Hell*. It recounts the birth, manifested in the contemporary events in France, of the flaming Spirit of Revolution (whom Blake later called Orc), and describes his conflict with the tyrannical sky god (whom Blake later called Urizen). The poem ends with the portent of the Spirit of Revolution shattering the ten commandments, or prohibitions against political, religious, and moral liberty, and bringing in a free and joyous new world.

2. England's.
3. The political prison, the Bastille, was destroyed by the French revolutionaries in 1789.
4. The keys of Rome, a symbol of Papal power.
5. "Jesus wept" (John 11.35).
6. The legendary continent of Atlantis, sunk beneath the sea; Blake uses it to represent the condition before the fall. "Starry king": Blake often uses the stars, in their fixed courses, as symbol of the law-governed Newtonian universe.
7. The sea, which to Blake represents a devouring chaos, such as had swallowed Atlantis.

and shields, and chariots, horses, elephants; banners, castles, slings and rocks,

16. Falling, rushing, ruining! buried in the ruins, on Urthona's[8] dens;

17. All night beneath the ruins; then, their sullen flames faded, emerge round the gloomy king,

18. With thunder and fire, leading his starry hosts thro' the waste wilderness [PL 27] he promulgates his ten commands, glancing his beamy eyelids over the deep in dark dismay,

19. Where the son of fire in his eastern cloud, while the morning plumes her golden breast,

20. Spurning the clouds written with curses, stamps the stony law[9] to dust, loosing the eternal horses from the dens of night, crying:

"Empire is no more! and now the lion & wolf shall cease."[1]

Chorus

Let the Priests of the Raven of dawn, no longer in deadly black, with hoarse note curse the sons of joy. Nor his accepted brethren, whom, tyrant, he calls free, lay the bound or build the roof. Nor pale religious letchery call that virginity, that wishes but acts not!

For every thing that lives is Holy.

1792   1792

POEMS FROM BLAKE'S NOTEBOOK[1]

Mock on, Mock on, Voltaire, Rousseau

Mock on, Mock on, Voltaire, Rousseau;[2]
Mock on, Mock on, 'tis all in vain.
You throw the sand against the wind,
And the wind blows it back again;

And every sand becomes a Gem   5
Reflected in the beams divine;
Blown back, they blind the mocking Eye,
But still in Israel's paths they shine.

---

8. In the later Prophetic Books, Urthona is the unfallen form of Los, who in the fallen world represents the poetic imagination, the agent working for the regeneration of humanity.
9. I.e., the ten commandments (verse 18), which the "finger of God" had written on "tables [tablets] of stone" (Exodus 31.18).
1. Cf. Isaiah's prophecy, 65.17–25, of "new heavens and a new earth," when "the wolf and the lamb shall feed together, and the lion shall eat straw like the bullock."

1. A commonplace book in which Blake drew sketches and jotted down verses and memoranda between the late 1780s and 1810. It is known as the "Rossetti Manuscript" because it later came into the possession of the poet and painter Dante Gabriel Rossetti. These poems were first published in imperfect form in 1863, then transcribed from the manuscript by Geoffrey Keynes in 1935.
2. Blake regards both Voltaire and Rousseau as representing rationalism and Deism.

The Atoms of Democritus
And Newton's Particles of light[3]   10
Are sands upon the Red sea shore,
Where Israel's tents do shine so bright.

Never Pain to Tell Thy Love

Never pain to tell thy love
Love that never told can be,
For the gentle wind does move
Silently, invisibly.

I told my love, I told my love,   5
I told her all my heart,
Trembling, cold, in ghastly fears—
Ah, she doth depart.

Soon as she was gone from me
A traveller came by   10
Silently, invisibly—
O, was no deny.

I Askèd a Thief

I askèd a thief to steal me a peach,
He turned up his eyes;
I ask'd a lithe lady to lie her down,
Holy & meek she cries.

As soon as I went   5
An angel came.
He wink'd at the thief
And smild at the dame—

And without one word said
Had a peach from the tree   10
And still as a maid
Enjoy'd the lady.

1796   • • •

---

3. Democritus (460–362 B.C.) proposed that atoms were the ultimate components of the universe; Newton in his *Opticks* hypothesized that light consisted of minute material particles.

And Did Those Feet[1]

And did those feet in ancient time
Walk upon England's mountains green?
And was the holy Lamb of God
On England's pleasant pastures seen?

And did the Countenance Divine   5
Shine forth upon our clouded hills?
And was Jerusalem builded here,
Among those dark Satanic Mills?[2]

Bring me my Bow of burning gold,
Bring me my Arrows of desire,   10
Bring me my Spear; O clouds unfold!
Bring me my Chariot of fire!

I will not cease from Mental Fight,
Nor shall my Sword sleep in my hand,
Till we have built Jerusalem   15
In England's green & pleasant Land.

ca. 1804–10   ca. 1804–10

From A Vision of the Last Judgment[1]

For the Year 1810
Additions to Blake's Catalogue of Pictures &c

The Last Judgment [will be] when all those are Cast away who trouble
Religion with Questions concerning Good & Evil or Eating of the Tree
of those Knowledges or Reasonings which hinder the Vision of God
turning all into a Consuming fire. When Imaginative Art & Science &

1. These quatrains occur in the Preface to Blake's
prophetic poem *Milton*. There is an ancient belief,
still current in parts of England, that Jesus came
to England with Joseph of Arimathea. Blake adapts
the legend to his own conception of a spiritual Israel,
in which the significance of Biblical events is as
relevant to England as to Palestine. By a particularly Blakean irony, this poem of mental war in
the service of apocalyptic desire is widely used as a
hymn by those of us whom Blake called "angels."
2. There may be an allusion here to industrial
England; but the mill is primarily Blake's symbol
for a mechanistic and utilitarian world view,
according to which, as he said elsewhere, "the same
dull round, even of a universe" becomes "a mill
with complicated wheels."
1. In this essay Blake describes and comments on
his painting of the Last Judgment, now lost, which

is said to have measured seven by five feet and to
have included a thousand figures. The text has been
transcribed and rearranged, as the sequence of the
pages indicates, from the scattered fragments in
Blake's Notebook. The opening and closing parts
are reprinted here as Blake's fullest, although cryptic, statements of what he means by "vision." These
sections deal with the relations of imaginative vision
to allegory, Greek fable, and the Biblical story; to
uncurbed human passion and intellectual power;
to conventional and coercive virtue; to what is seen
by the "corporeal" eye; to the arts; and to the Last
Judgment and the apocalyptic redemption of man
and of the created world—an apocalypse which is
to be achieved by the triumph over the bodily eye
of human imagination, as manifested in the creative artist.

all Intellectual Gifts, all the Gifts of the Holy Ghost, are lookd upon as of no use & only Contention remains to Man, then the Last Judgment begins, & its Vision is seen by the Imaginative Eye of Every one according to the situation he holds.

[PAGE 68] The Last Judgment is not Fable or Allegory but Vision. Fable or Allegory are a totally distinct & inferior kind of Poetry. Vision, or Imagination, is a Representation of what Eternally Exists, Really & Unchangeably. Fable or Allegory is Formd by the daughters of Memory. Imagination is Surrounded by the daughters of Inspiration, who in the aggregate are calld Jerusalem. [P 69] Fable is Allegory, but what Critics call The Fable is Vision itself. [P 68] The Hebrew Bible & the Gospel of Jesus are not Allegory, but Eternal Vision, or Imagination of All that Exists. Note here that Fable or Allegory is Seldom without some Vision. *Pilgrim's Progress* is full of it, the Greek Poets the same; but Allegory & Vision ought to be known as Two Distinct Things, & so calld for the Sake of Eternal Life. Plato has made Socrates say that Poets & Prophets do not know or Understand what they write or Utter; this is a most Pernicious Falshood. If they do not, pray is an inferior Kind to be calld Knowing? Plato confutes himself.[2]

The Last Judgment is one of these Stupendous Visions. I have represented it as I saw it. To different People it appears differently, as [P 69] every thing else does; for tho on Earth things seem Permanent, they are less permanent than a Shadow, as we all know too well.

The Nature of Visionary Fancy, or Imagination, is very little Known, & the Eternal nature & permanence of its ever Existent Images is considered as less permanent than the things of Vegetative & Generative Nature; yet the Oak dies as well as the Lettuce, but Its Eternal Image & Individuality never dies, but renews by its seed. Just so the Imaginative Image returns by the seed of Contemplative Thought. The Writings of the Prophets illustrate these conceptions of the Visionary Fancy by their various sublime & Divine Images as seen in the Worlds of Vision. * * *

Let it here be Noted that the Greek Fables originated in Spiritual Mystery [P 72] & Real Visions, Which are lost & clouded in Fable & Allegory, while the Hebrew Bible & the Greek Gospel are Genuine, Preservd by the Saviour's Mercy. The Nature of my Work is Visionary or Imaginative; it is an Endeavour to Restore what the Ancients calld the Golden Age.

[PAGE 69] This world of Imagination is the World of Eternity; it is the Divine bosom into which we shall all go after the death of the Vegetated body. This World of Imagination is Infinite & Eternal, whereas the world of Generation, or Vegetation, is Finite & Temporal. There Exist in that Eternal World the Permanent Realities of Every Thing which we see reflected in this Vegetable Glass of Nature.

All Things are comprehended in their Eternal Forms in the Divine [P 70] body of the Saviour, the True Vine of Eternity, The Human Imag-

---

2. In Plato's dialogue *Ion*, in which Socrates traps Ion into admitting that, since poets compose by inspiration, they do so without knowing what they are doing.

ination, who appeard to Me as Coming to Judgment among his Saints & throwing off the Temporal that the Eternal might be Establishd. Around him were seen the Images of Existences according to a certain order suited to my Imaginative Eye. * * *

[PAGE 87] Men are admitted into Heaven not because they have curbed & governd their Passions, or have No Passions, but because they have Cultivated their Understandings. The Treasures of Heaven are not Negations of Passion, but Realities of Intellect from which All the Passions Emanate Uncurbed in their Eternal Glory. The Fool shall not enter into Heaven, let him be ever so Holy. Holiness is not The price of Enterance into Heaven. Those who are cast out Are All Those who, having no Passions of their own because No Intellect, Have spent their lives in Curbing & Governing other People's by the Various arts of Poverty & Cruelty of all kinds. Wo Wo Wo to you Hypocrites! Even Murder the Courts of Justice, more merciful than the Church, are compelld to allow, is not done in Passion but in Cool Blooded Design & Intention.

The Modern Church Crucifies Christ with the Head Downwards.

[PAGE 92] Many persons such as Paine & Voltaire, with some of the Ancient Greeks, say: "We will not converse concerning Good & Evil; we will live in Paradise & Liberty."[3] You may do so in Spirit, but not in the Mortal Body as you pretend, till after the last Judgment; for in Paradise they have no Corporeal & Mortal Body—that originated with the Fall & was calld Death & cannot be removed but by a Last Judgment; while we are in the world of Mortality we Must Suffer. The Whole Creation Groans to be deliverd; there will always be as many Hypocrites born as Honest Men & they will always have superior Power in Mortal Things. You cannot have Liberty in this World without what you call Moral Virtue, & you cannot have Moral Virtue without the Slavery of that half of the Human Race who hate what you call Moral Virtue.

* * *

Thinking as I do that the Creator of this World is a very Cruel Being, & being a Worshipper of Christ, I cannot help saying: "The Son, O how unlike the Father!" First God Almighty comes with a Thump on the Head. Then Jesus Christ comes with a balm to heal it.

The Last Judgment is an Overwhelming of Bad Art & Science. Mental Things are alone Real; what is Calld Corporeal Nobody Knows of its dwelling Place; it is in Fallacy & its Existence an Imposture. Where is the Existence Out of Mind or Thought? Where is it but in the Mind of a Fool? Some People flatter themselves that there will be No Last Judgment, & [P 95] that Bad Art will be adopted & mixed with Good Art, That Error or Experiment will make a Part of Truth, & they Boast that it is its Foundation. These People flatter themselves; I will not Flatter

3. Blake represents Thomas Paine, author of *The Rights of Man* (1791), and Voltaire, the great author of the French Enlightenment, as proponents of the possibility of restoring an earthly paradise by polit- ical revolution. Such had been Blake's own view in the early 1790s; see, e.g., *The Marriage of Heaven and Hell*, above.

them. Error is Created; Truth is Eternal. Error or Creation will be Burned Up, & then & not till then Truth or Eternity will appear. It is Burnt up the Moment Men cease to behold it. I assert for My self that I do not behold the Outward Creation & that to me it is hindrance & not Action; it is as the Dirt upon my feet, No part of Me. "What," it will be Questioned, "When the Sun rises, do you not see a round Disk of fire somewhat like a Guinea?" O no no, I see an Innumerable company of the Heavenly host crying "Holy Holy Holy is the Lord God Almighty." I question not my Corporeal or Vegetative Eye any more than I would Question a Window concerning a Sight: I look thro it & not with it.

1810   1810

WILLIAM WORDSWORTH
1770–1850

1791–92:	In France during the early period of the Revolution.
1797:	With his sister, Dorothy, at Alfoxden House, Somersetshire, near Coleridge at Nether Stowey.
1798:	First edition of *Lyrical Ballads*.
1799:	William and Dorothy settle at Grasmere, in the Lake District.
1800:	Second edition of *Lyrical Ballads* in two volumes, with the famous Preface.
1807:	*Poems in Two Volumes*; end of the great decade.

Wordsworth was born in Cockermouth in West Cumberland, just on the northern fringe of the English Lake District. When his mother died, the eight-year-old boy was sent to school at Hawkshead, near Esthwaite Lake, in the heart of that thinly settled region which he and Coleridge were to transform into the poetic center of England. William and his three brothers boarded in the cottage of Ann Tyson, who gave the boys simple comfort, ample affection, and freedom to roam the countryside at will. A vigorous, willful, and sometimes moody boy, William spent his free days and sometimes "half the night" in the sports and rambles described in the first two books of *The Prelude*, "drinking in" (to use one of his favorite metaphors) the natural sights and sounds, and getting to know the cottagers, shepherds, and solitary wanderers who moved through his imagination into his later poetry. He also found time to read voraciously in the books owned by his young headmaster, William Taylor, who encouraged him in his inclination to poetry.

John Wordsworth, the poet's father, died suddenly when William was thirteen, leaving to his five children mainly the substantial sum owed him by Lord Lonsdale, whom he had served as attorney and as steward of the huge Lonsdale estate. That harsh and litigious nobleman managed to keep from paying the debt until he died in 1802. Wordsworth was nevertheless able to go up to St. John's College, Cambridge, in 1787, where he found very little in the limited curriculum of that time to appeal to him. He took his degree in 1791 without distinction.

During the summer vacation of his third year at Cambridge (1790), Wordsworth and his closest college friend, the Welshman Robert Jones, journeyed on foot through France and the Alps (described in *The Prelude* 6) at the time when the French were joyously celebrating the first anniversary of the fall of the Bastille. Upon completing his course at Cambridge, Wordsworth spent four months in London, set off on another walking tour with Robert Jones through Wales (the time of the memorable ascent of Mount Snowdon in *The Prelude* 14), and then went back alone to France in order to master the language and qualify as a traveling tutor.

During his year in France (between November 1791 and December 1792) Wordsworth became a fervent "democrat" and proselyte of the French Revolution—which seemed to him, as to many other generous spirits, to promise a "glorious renovation"—and he had a love affair with Annette Vallon, the impetuous and warm-hearted daughter of a French surgeon at Blois. It seems clear that Wordsworth and Annette planned to marry, despite their difference in religion and political inclinations (Annette belonged to an old Catholic family whose sympathies were Royalist). But almost immediately after a daughter, Caroline, was born, lack of funds forced Wordsworth back to England. The outbreak of war between England and France made it impossible for him to rejoin Annette until they had drifted so far apart in sympathies that a permanent union no longer seemed desirable. Wordsworth's agonies of guilt, his divided loyalties between England and France, his gradual disillusion with the course of the Revolution in France—as he describes them in *The Prelude* 10 and 11—brought him to the verge of an emotional breakdown, when "sick, wearied out with contrarieties," he "yielded up moral questions in despair." His suffering, his near-collapse, and the successful effort, after his sharp break with his past, to re-establish "a saving intercourse with my true self," are the experiences that underlie many of his greatest poems.

At this critical point a young friend, Raisley Calvert, died and left Wordsworth a sum of money just sufficient to enable him to live by his poetry. He settled in a rent-free cottage at Racedown, Dorsetshire, with his beloved sister, Dorothy, who now began her long career as confidante, inspirer, and secretary. At that same time Wordsworth met Samuel Taylor Coleridge; two years later he moved to Alfoxden House, Somersetshire, to be near Coleridge, who lived four miles away at Nether Stowey. Here, his recovery complete, he entered at the age of twenty-seven upon the delayed springtime of his poetic career.

Even while he had been an undergraduate at Cambridge, Coleridge had detected signs of genius in Wordsworth's rather conventional poem about his tour in the Alps, *Descriptive Sketches*, published in 1793. Now he hailed Wordsworth unreservedly as "the best poet of the age." The two men met almost daily, talked for hours about poetry, and composed prolifically. So close was their association that they almost lost the sense of individual proprietorship in a composition. We find the same phrases occurring in poems by Wordsworth and Coleridge, as well as in the remarkable journals that Dorothy kept at the time; the two poets collaborated in some writings and freely traded thoughts and passages for others; and Coleridge even undertook to complete a few poems that Wordsworth had left unfinished.

The result of their joint efforts was a small volume, published anonymously in 1798, *Lyrical Ballads, with a Few Other Poems*. It opened with Coleridge's *Ancient Mariner*, included three other poems by Coleridge, a number of Wordsworth's verse anecdotes and psychological studies of humble people, some lyrics in which Wordsworth celebrated impulses from a vernal wood, and closed with Wordsworth's great descriptive and meditative poem in blank verse (not a "lyrical ballad," but one of the "other poems" of the title), *Tintern Abbey*. No other book of poems in English so plainly announces a new literary departure. William Hazlitt said that when he heard Coleridge read some of these newly written poems aloud, "the sense of a new style and a new spirit in poetry came over me," with something of the effect "that arises from the turning up of the fresh soil, or of the first welcome breath of spring." The professional reviewers were less enthusiastic. Nevertheless *Lyrical Ballads* sold out in two years, and Wordsworth published over his own name a new edition, dated 1800, to which he added a second volume of poems, many of them written in homesickness during a long, cold, and friendless winter that he and Dorothy had spent in Goslar, Germany, 1798–99. In his famous Preface to this edition, planned, like so many of the poems, in close consultation with Coleridge, Wordsworth enunciated the principles of the new criticism which served as rationale for the new poetry. Notable among the other works written in this prolific period is his austere and powerful tragic poem *The Ruined Cottage*.

Late in 1799 Wordsworth and Dorothy moved back permanently to their native lakes, settling at Grasmere in the little house later named Dove Cottage. Coleridge, following them, rented Greta Hall at Keswick, thirteen miles away. In 1802 Wordsworth finally came into his father's inheritance and, after an amicable settlement with Annette Vallon, married Mary Hutchinson, a Lake Country woman whom he had known since childhood. The course of his existence after that time was broken by various disasters: the drowning in 1805 of his favorite brother John, a sea captain whose ship was wrecked in a storm; the death of two of his five children in 1812; a gradual estrangement from Coleridge, culminating in an open quarrel (1810) from which they were not completely reconciled for almost two decades; and, from the 1830s on, the physical and mental decline of his sister, Dorothy. The life of his middle age, however, was one of steadily increasing prosperity and reputation, as well as of political and religious conservatism. In 1813 an appointment as Stamp Distributor (that is, revenue collector) for Westmorland was concrete evidence of his recognition as a national poet. Gradually his residences, as he moved into more and more commodious quarters, became standard stops for tourists; he was awarded honorary degrees and, in 1843, appointed poet laureate. He died in 1850 at the age of eighty; only then did his executors publish his masterpiece, *The Prelude*, the autobiographical poem which he had written in two parts in 1799, expanded to its full length in 1805, and then continued to revise almost to the last decade of his long life.

Most of Wordsworth's greatest poetry had been written by 1807, when he published *Poems in Two Volumes*; and after *The Excursion* (1814) and the first collected edition of his poems (1815), although he continued to write voluminously, there is a conspicuous decline in his powers as a poet. The causes of what is often called "Wordsworth's anticlimax" have been much debated; the principal cause seems to be inherent in the very nature of his most characteristic writing. Wordsworth is above all the poet of the remem-

brance of things past, or as he himself put it, of "emotion recollected in
tranquillity." Some object or event in the present triggers a sudden renewal
of feelings he had experienced in youth; the result is a poem exhibiting the
sharp discrepancy between what Wordsworth called "two consciousnesses":
himself as he is now and himself as he once was. But one's early emotional
experience is not an inexhaustible resource for poetry. As Basil Willey has
said, Wordsworth as a poet "was living upon capital"; and he knew it. As he
says in *The Prelude* 12, while describing the recurrence of "spots of time"
from his memories of childhood:

> The days gone by
> Return upon me almost from the dawn
> Of life: the hiding places of Man's power
> Open; I would approach them, but they close.
> I see by glimpses now; when age comes on,
> May scarcely see at all.

The past that Wordsworth recollected was one of emotional turmoil which
is ordered, in the calmer present, into a hard-won equilibrium. The result
was a poetry of excitation in calm; genius, as Wordsworth said, is "born to
thrive by interchange / Of peace and excitation" (*Prelude* 13.1–10). As time
went on, however, the precarious equilibrium of his great creative period
became a habit, and Wordsworth finally gained what, in the *Ode to Duty*
(composed in 1804), he longed for, "a repose which ever is the same"—but
at the expense of the agony and excitation which, under the calm surface,
empowers his best and most characteristic poems.

Occasionally in his middle and later life a jolting experience would revive
the intensity of Wordsworth's remembered emotion, and also his earlier
poetic strength. The moving sonnet *Surprised by Joy*, for example, was written in his forties at the abrupt realization that time was beginning to diminish his grief at the death some years earlier of his little daughter Catherine.
And when Wordsworth was sixty-five years old, the sudden report of the
death of James Hogg called up the memory of other and greater poets whom
Wordsworth had loved and outlived; the result was an "Extempore Effusion," written in a return to the simple quatrains of the early *Lyrical Ballads*
and with a recovery of the great elegiac voice which had uttered the dirges
to Lucy, thirty-five years before.

From LYRICAL BALLADS OF 1798

We Are Seven[1]

————A simple Child,
That lightly draws its breath,
And feels its life in every limb,
What should it know of death?

---

1. "Written at Alfoxden in the spring of 1798. . . .
The little girl who is the heroine I met within the
area of Goodrich Castle in the year 1793" (Wordsworth). Wordsworth also tells us that he composed
the last line of the last stanza first, and that Coleridge contributed the initial stanza.

I met a little cottage Girl: 5
She was eight years old, she said;
Her hair was thick with many a curl
That clustered round her head.

She had a rustic, woodland air,
And she was wildly clad: 10
Her eyes were fair, and very fair;
—Her beauty made me glad.

"Sisters and brothers, little Maid,
How many may you be?"
"How many? Seven in all," she said,   15
And wondering looked at me.

"And where are they? I pray you tell."
She answered, "Seven are we;
And two of us at Conway dwell,
And two are gone to sea.   20

"Two of us in the church-yard lie,
My sister and my brother;
And, in the church-yard cottage, I
Dwell near them with my mother."

"You say that two at Conway dwell,   25
And two are gone to sea,
Yet ye are seven! I pray you tell,
Sweet Maid, how this may be."

Then did the little Maid reply,
"Seven boys and girls are we;   30
Two of us in the church-yard lie,
Beneath the church-yard tree."

"You run about, my little Maid,
Your limbs they are alive;
If two are in the church-yard laid,   35
Then ye are only five."

"Their graves are green, they may be seen,"
The little Maid replied,
"Twelve steps or more from my mother's door,
And they are side by side.   40

"My stockings there I often knit,
My kerchief there I hem;
And there upon the ground I sit,
And sing a song to them.

"And often after sun-set, Sir,   45
When it is light and fair,
I take my little porringer,[2]
And eat my supper there.

"The first that died was sister Jane;
In bed she moaning lay,   50
Till God released her of her pain;
And then she went away.

"So in the church-yard she was laid;
And, when the grass was dry,
Together round her grave we played,   55
My brother John and I.

"And when the ground was white with snow,
And I could run and slide,
My brother John was forced to go,
And he lies by her side."   60

"How many are you, then," said I,
"If they two are in heaven?"
Quick was the little Maid's reply,
"O Master! we are seven."

"But they are dead; those two are dead!   65
Their spirits are in heaven!"
'Twas throwing words away; for still
The little Maid would have her will,
And said, "Nay, we are seven!"

1798   1798

Lines Written in Early Spring

I heard a thousand blended notes,
While in a grove I sate reclined,
In that sweet mood when pleasant thoughts
Bring sad thoughts to the mind.

To her fair works did Nature link   5
The human soul that through me ran;
And much it grieved my heart to think
What man has made of man.

2. Bowl for porridge.

Through primrose tufts, in that green bower,
The periwinkle[1] trailed its wreaths,   10
And 'tis my faith that every flower
Enjoys the air it breathes.

The birds around me hopped and played,
Their thoughts I cannot measure:—
But the least motion which they made,   15
It seemed a thrill of pleasure.

The budding twigs spread out their fan,
To catch the breezy air;
And I must think, do all I can,
That there was pleasure there.   20

If this belief from heaven be sent,
If such be Nature's holy plan,[2]
Have I not reason to lament
What man has made of man?

1798   1798

Expostulation and Reply[1]

"Why, William, on that old grey stone,
Thus for the length of half a day,
Why, William, sit you thus alone,
And dream your time away?

"Where are your books?—that light bequeathed   5
To Beings else forlorn and blind!
Up! up! and drink the spirit breathed
From dead men to their kind.

"You look round on your Mother Earth,
As if she for no purpose bore you;   10
As if you were her first-born birth,
And none had lived before you!"

One morning thus, by Esthwaite lake,
When life was sweet, I knew not why,

---

1. A trailing evergreen plant with small blue flowers (U.S. myrtle).
2. The version of these two lines in the *Lyrical Ballads* of 1798 reads: "If I these thoughts may not prevent, / If such be of my creed the plan."
1. This and the following companion-poem have often been attacked—and defended—as Wordsworth's solemn deliverance on the comparative merits of nature and of books. But they are a dialogue between two friends who rally one another by the usual device of overstating parts of a whole truth. Wordsworth said that the pieces originated in a conversation "with a friend who was somewhat unreasonably attached to modern books of moral philosophy," and also that the lore of "a wise passiveness" made the poem a favorite among Quakers.

To me my good friend Matthew spake,   15
And thus I made reply.

"The eye—it cannot choose but see;
We cannot bid the ear be still;
Our bodies feel, where'er they be,
Against or with our will.   20

"Nor less I deem that there are Powers
Which of themselves our minds impress;
That we can feed this mind of ours
In a wise passiveness.

"Think you, 'mid all this mighty sum   25
Of things for ever speaking,
That nothing of itself will come,
But we must still be seeking?

"—Then ask not wherefore, here, alone,
Conversing[2] as I may,   30
I sit upon this old grey stone,
And dream my time away."

Spring 1798   1798

The Tables Turned

An Evening Scene on the Same Subject

Up! up! my Friend, and quit your books;
Or surely you'll grow double:
Up! up! my Friend, and clear your looks;
Why all this toil and trouble?

The sun, above the mountain's head,   5
A freshening lustre mellow
Through all the long green fields has spread,
His first sweet evening yellow.

Books! 'tis a dull and endless strife:
Come, hear the woodland linnet,[1]   10
How sweet his music! on my life,
There's more of wisdom in it.

And hark! how blithe the throstle[2] sings!
He, too, is no mean preacher:

---

2. In the old sense of "communing" (with the   1. A small finch, common in Europe.
"things forever speaking").   2. The song thrush.

Come forth into the light of things,   15
Let Nature be your Teacher.

She has a world of ready wealth,
Our minds and hearts to bless—
Spontaneous wisdom breathed by health,
Truth breathed by cheerfulness.   20

One impulse from a vernal wood
May teach you more of man,
Of moral evil and of good,
Than all the sages can.

Sweet is the lore which Nature brings;   25
Our meddling intellect
Mis-shapes the beauteous forms of things:—
We murder to dissect.

Enough of Science and of Art;
Close up those barren leaves;   30
Come forth, and bring with you a heart
That watches and receives.

1798   1798

Lines[1]

Composed a Few Miles above Tintern Abbey, on Revisiting the Banks of the Wye during a Tour, July 13, 1798

Five years have past; five summers, with the length
Of five long winters! and again I hear
These waters, rolling from their mountain-springs
With a soft inland murmur.—Once again
Do I behold these steep and lofty cliffs,   5
That on a wild secluded scene impress
Thoughts of more deep seclusion; and connect
The landscape with the quiet of the sky.
The day is come when I again repose
Here, under this dark sycamore, and view   10
These plots of cottage-ground, these orchard-tufts,

1. "No poem of mine was composed under circumstances more pleasant for me to remember than this. I began it upon leaving Tintern, after crossing the Wye, and concluded it just as I was entering Bristol in the evening, after a ramble of 4 or 5 days, with my sister. Not a line of it was altered, and not any part of it written down till I reached Bristol" (Wordsworth). The poem was printed as the last item in *Lyrical Ballads*.

Wordsworth had first visited the Wye valley and the ruins of Tintern Abbey, in Monmouthshire, while on a solitary walking tour in August 1793, when he was 23 years old. The puzzling difference between the present landscape and the remembered "picture of the mind" (line 61) gives rise to an intricately organized meditation, in which the poet reviews his past, evaluates the present, and (through his sister as intermediary) anticipates the future; he ends by rounding back quietly upon the scene which had been his point of departure.

Which at this season, with their unripe fruits,
Are clad in one green hue, and lose themselves
'Mid groves and copses. Once again I see
These hedge-rows, hardly hedge-rows, little lines   15
Of sportive wood run wild: these pastoral farms,
Green to the very door; and wreaths of smoke
Sent up, in silence, from among the trees!
With some uncertain notice, as might seem
Of vagrant dwellers in the houseless woods,   20
Or of some Hermit's cave, where by his fire
The Hermit sits alone.

                    These beauteous forms,
Through a long absence, have not been to me
As is a landscape to a blind man's eye:
But oft, in lonely rooms, and 'mid the din   25
Of towns and cities, I have owed to them
In hours of weariness, sensations sweet,
Felt in the blood, and felt along the heart;
And passing even into my purer mind,
With tranquil restoration:—feelings too   30
Of unremembered pleasure: such, perhaps,
As have no slight or trivial influence
On that best portion of a good man's life,
His little, nameless, unremembered, acts
Of kindness and of love. Nor less, I trust,   35
To them I may have owed another gift,
Of aspect more sublime; that blessed mood,
In which the burthen of the mystery,
In which the heavy and the weary weight
Of all this unintelligible world,   40
Is lightened:—that serene and blessed mood,
In which the affections gently lead us on,—
Until, the breath of this corporeal frame
And even the motion of our human blood
Almost suspended, we are laid asleep   45
In body, and become a living soul:
While with an eye made quiet by the power
Of harmony, and the deep power of joy,
We see into the life of things.

                    If this
Be but a vain belief, yet, oh! how oft—   50
In darkness and amid the many shapes
Of joyless daylight; when the fretful stir
Unprofitable, and the fever of the world,
Have hung upon the beatings of my heart—
How oft, in spirit, have I turned to thee,   55

O sylvan Wye! thou wanderer thro' the woods,
How often has my spirit turned to thee!

   And now, with gleams of half-extinguished thought,
With many recognitions dim and faint,
And somewhat of a sad perplexity,   60
The picture of the mind revives again:
While here I stand, not only with the sense
Of present pleasure, but with pleasing thoughts
That in this moment there is life and food
For future years. And so I dare to hope,   65
Though changed, no doubt, from what I was when first
I came among these hills; when like a roe
I bounded o'er the mountains, by the sides
Of the deep rivers, and the lonely streams,
Wherever nature led: more like a man   70
Flying from something that he dreads, than one
Who sought the thing he loved. For nature then
(The coarser pleasures of my boyish days,
And their glad animal movements all gone by)
To me was all in all.—I cannot paint   75
What then I was. The sounding cataract
Haunted me like a passion: the tall rock,
The mountain, and the deep and gloomy wood,
Their colours and their forms, were then to me
An appetite; a feeling and a love,   80
That had no need of a remoter charm,
By thought supplied, nor any interest
Unborrowed from the eye.—That time is past,
And all its aching joys are now no more,
And all its dizzy raptures.[2] Not for this   85
Faint[3] I, nor mourn nor murmur; other gifts
Have followed; for such loss, I would believe,
Abundant recompense. For I have learned
To look on nature, not as in the hour
Of thoughtless youth; but hearing oftentimes   90
The still, sad music of humanity,
Nor harsh nor grating, though of ample power
To chasten and subdue. And I have felt
A presence that disturbs me with the joy

---

2. Lines 66 ff. contain Wordsworth's famed description of the three stages of his growing up, defined in terms of his evolving relations to the natural scene: the young boy's purely physical responsiveness (lines 73–74); the post-adolescent's aching, dizzy, and equivocal passions—a love which is more like dread (lines 67–72, 75–85: this was his state of mind on the occasion of his first visit); his present state (lines 85 ff.), in which for the first time he adds thought to sense. All his knowledge of human suffering, so painfully acquired in the interim, chastens him while it enriches the visible scene like a chord of music; he has gained also awareness of an immanent "presence" which links his mind and all the elements of the external world.

3. Lose heart.

Of elevated thoughts; a sense sublime   95
Of something far more deeply interfused,
Whose dwelling is the light of setting suns,
And the round ocean and the living air,
And the blue sky, and in the mind of man:
A motion and a spirit, that impels   100
All thinking things, all objects of all thought,
And rolls through all things. Therefore am I still
A lover of the meadows and the woods,
And mountains; and of all that we behold
From this green earth; of all the mighty world   105
Of eye, and ear,—both what they half create,[4]
And what perceive; well pleased to recognise
In nature and the language of the sense,
The anchor of my purest thoughts, the nurse,
The guide, the guardian of my heart, and soul   110
Of all my moral being.

            Nor perchance,
If I were not thus taught, should I the more
Suffer my genial spirits[5] to decay:
For thou art with me here upon the banks
Of this fair river; thou my dearest Friend,[6]   115
My dear, dear Friend; and in thy voice I catch
The language of my former heart, and read
My former pleasures in the shooting lights
Of thy wild eyes. Oh! yet a little while
May I behold in thee what I was once,   120
My dear, dear Sister! and this prayer I make,
Knowing that Nature never did betray
The heart that loved her; 'tis her privilege,
Through all the years of this our life, to lead
From joy to joy: for she can so inform   125
The mind that is within us, so impress
With quietness and beauty, and so feed
With lofty thoughts, that neither evil tongues,
Rash judgments, nor the sneers of selfish men,
Nor greetings where no kindness is, nor all   130
The dreary intercourse of daily life,
Shall e'er prevail against us, or disturb
Our cheerful faith, that all which we behold

---

4. The fact that apparent changes in the sensible world have turned out to be projected by the changing mind of the observer gives evidence that the faculties "half create" the world; the part that is "perceived" (line 107) is what has remained unchanged between the two visits. This view that the "creative sensibility" contributes to its own perceptions is often reiterated in the early books of *The Prelude.*

5. Creative powers. ("Genial" is here the adjectival form of the noun "genius.") The sense of lines 111–13 is: "Perhaps, even if I had not learned to look at nature in the way I have just described, I would not have suffered a decay in my creative powers."

6. His sister Dorothy.

Is full of blessings. Therefore let the moon
Shine on thee in thy solitary walk; 135
And let the misty mountain-winds be free
To blow against thee: and, in after years,
When these wild ecstasies shall be matured
Into a sober pleasure; when thy mind
Shall be a mansion for all lovely forms, 140
Thy memory be as a dwelling-place
For all sweet sounds and harmonies; oh! then,
If solitude, or fear, or pain, or grief,
Should be thy portion, with what healing thoughts
Of tender joy wilt thou remember me, 145
And these my exhortations! Nor, perchance—
If I should be where I no more can hear
Thy voice, nor catch from thy wild eyes these gleams
Of past existence[7]—wilt thou then forget
That on the banks of this delightful stream 150
We stood together; and that I, so long
A worshipper of Nature, hither came
Unwearied in that service; rather say
With warmer love—oh! with far deeper zeal
Of holier love. Nor wilt thou then forget, 155
That after many wanderings, many years
Of absence, these steep woods and lofty cliffs,
And this green pastoral landscape, were to me
More dear, both for themselves and for thy sake!

July 1798 1798

Preface to *Lyrical Ballads* (1802)

To the first edition of *Lyrical Ballads*, published jointly with Coleridge in 1798, Wordsworth prefixed an "Advertisement" which asserted that the major number of the poems were "to be considered as experiments" to determine "how far the language of conversation in the middle and lower classes of society is adapted to the purposes of poetic pleasure." In the second, two-volume edition of 1800 Wordsworth, relying on frequent conversations with Coleridge, expanded the Advertisement into a Preface which justified the new poetry not as experiments, but as exemplifying the principles of all good poetry. The Preface was enlarged for the third edition of *Lyrical Ballads*, published two years later; this last version of 1802 is the one that is reprinted here.

The Preface deserves its reputation as a revolutionary manifesto about the nature of poetry. Like most radical statements, however, it claims to go back to the implicit principles that governed the great poetry of the past but have been perverted in recent practice. Most discussions of the Preface, following the lead of Coleridge in his *Biographia Literaria*, have focused on Words-worth's assertions about the valid language of poetry, on which he bases his

---

7. I.e., equivalent to his own "past existence" five years earlier (cf. lines 116–19).

attack on the "poetic diction" of eighteenth-century poets. As Coleridge pointed out, Wordsworth's argument about this issue is far from clear. It is apparent, however, that Wordsworth undertook to overthrow the basic theory, as well as the reigning practice, of neoclassic poetry. That is, his Preface implicitly denies the traditional assumption that the poetic genres constitute a hierarchy, from epic and tragedy at the top down through comedy, satire, pastoral, to the short lyric at the lower reaches of the poetic scale; he also rejects the traditional principle of "decorum," according to which the subject matter (especially the social class of the protagonists) and the level of diction of a poem must conform to the status of the literary kind on the poetic scale.

When Wordsworth asserted in the Preface that he deliberately chose to represent "incidents and situations from common life," he translated his democratic sympathies into critical terms, justifying his use of peasants, children, outcasts, criminals, and idiot boys as serious subjects of poetic and even tragic concern. He also undertook to write in "a selection of language really used by men," on the grounds that there can be no "essential difference between the language of prose and metrical composition." In making this claim, Wordsworth subverted the neoclassic principle that the language of a poem must be elevated over standard speech by a special diction and by artful figures of speech, in order to match the language to the height and dignity of a particular genre. Wordsworth's own views about the valid language of poetry are based on the new and radical premise that "all good poetry is the spontaneous overflow of powerful feelings"—spontaneous, that is, at the moment of composition, even though the process is influenced by prior thought and acquired poetic skill. The equivalence which Wordsworth claims, therefore, between the valid language of poems and the prose language "really spoken by men" is not one of vocabulary nor of syntax, but an equivalence in emotional genesis—instead of consisting in contrived and artful constructions, both forms of language originate spontaneously, as the words and figures which, as Keats later put it, are "the true voice of feeling."

Wordsworth's assertions about the materials and diction of poetry have been immensely influential in expanding the range of serious literature to include the common people and ordinary things and events, as well as in justifying a poetry of sincerity rather than of artifice, expressed in the ordinary language of its time. But in the long view, other aspects of his Preface have been no less significant in establishing its importance, not only as a turning point in English criticism but also as a central document in modern culture. Wordsworth attributed to imaginative literature the primary role in keeping human beings emotionally alive and morally sensitive—that is, keeping them essentially human—in the modern era of a technological and increasingly urban society, with its mass media and mass culture that threaten, as he foresaw, to blunt the mind's "discriminatory powers" and to "reduce it to a state of almost savage torpor." However radical their particular application by Wordsworth, the values that permeate his Preface are the central humanistic values of the eighteenth-century Enlightenment—that is, the use, as a standard, of elements that are essential, simple, universal, and permanent in human nature. The great subjects of poetry, Wordsworth claims, are "the essential passions of the heart" and "the great and simple affections," as these qualities interact with "the beautiful and permanent forms of nature" and are expressed in a "naked and simple" language that is "adapted to interest mankind permanently." The great poet is not the practitioner of an artistic craft designed to satisfy the refined "taste" of a literary connoisseur. He is instead, Wordsworth says in a memorable phrase, "a man speaking to men," who is motivated by and affirms the primal human values—the joy of life, reverence for all manifestations of life, and the grandeur of the pleasure principle which is the expression of the life force and the natural sign of any activity that enhances life. In opposition to all the modern forces that tend to divide—or, as we now say, to "alienate"—human beings from their own essential nature, from outer nature, and from their fellows, Wordsworth places the burden of sustaining human connections primarily on the poet: "He is the rock of defense of human nature; an upholder and preserver, carrying everywhere with him relationship and love."

From Preface to *Lyrical Ballads, with Pastoral and Other Poems* (1802)

[*The Subject and Language of Poetry*]

The first volume of these poems has already been submitted to general perusal. It was published, as an experiment, which, I hoped, might be of some use to ascertain, how far, by fitting to metrical arrangement a selection of the real language of men in a state of vivid sensation, that sort of pleasure and that quantity of pleasure may be imparted, which a poet may rationally endeavour to impart.

I had formed no very inaccurate estimate of the probable effect of those poems: I flattered myself that they who should be pleased with them would read them with more than common pleasure: and, on the other hand, I was well aware, that by those who should dislike them they would be read with more than common dislike. The result has differed from my expectation in this only, that I have pleased a greater number than I ventured to hope I should please.

For the sake of variety, and from a consciousness of my own weakness, I was induced to request the assistance of a friend, who furnished me with the poems of the *Ancient Mariner*, the *Foster-Mother's Tale*, the *Nightingale*, and the poem entitled *Love*. I should not, however, have requested this assistance, had I not believed that the poems of my friend would in a great measure have the same tendency as my own, and that, though there would be found a difference, there would be found no discordance in the colours of our style; as our opinions on the subject of poetry do almost entirely coincide.[1]

Several of my friends are anxious for the success of these poems from a belief, that, if the views with which they were composed were indeed realized, a class of poetry would be produced, well adapted to interest mankind permanently, and not unimportant in the multiplicity, and in

1. "The friend" of course is Coleridge. When he read this preface and the new poems included in the 1802 edition of *Lyrical Ballads*, Coleridge wrote to Robert Southey that although Wordsworth's Preface of 1800 had been "half a child of my own brain," he now suspects that "there is a radical difference in our theoretical opinions respecting poetry—this I shall endeavour to go to the bottom of." The results of this endeavor are Coleridge's discussions of Wordsworth's Preface in *Biographia Literaria*, chapters 14 and 17.

the quality of its moral relations: and on this account they have advised me to prefix a systematic defence of the theory upon which the poems were written. But I was unwilling to undertake the task, because I knew that on this occasion the reader would look coldly upon my arguments, since I might be suspected of having been principally influenced by the selfish and foolish hope of *reasoning* him into an approbation of these particular poems: and I was still more unwilling to undertake the task, because, adequately to display my opinions, and fully to enforce my arguments, would require a space wholly disproportionate to the nature of a preface. For to treat the subject with the clearness and coherence of which I believe it susceptible, it would be necessary to give a full account of the present state of the public taste in this country, and to determine how far this taste is healthy or depraved; which, again, could not be determined, without pointing out, in what manner language and the human mind act and re-act on each other, and without retracing the revolutions, not of literature alone, but likewise of society itself. I have therefore altogether declined to enter regularly upon this defence; yet I am sensible, that there would be some impropriety in abruptly obtruding upon the public, without a few words of introduction, poems so materially different from those upon which general approbation is at present bestowed.

It is supposed, that by the act of writing in verse an author makes a formal engagement that he will gratify certain known habits of association; that he not only thus apprizes the reader that certain classes of ideas and expressions will be found in his book, but that others will be carefully excluded. This exponent or symbol held forth by metrical language must in different eras of literature have excited very different expectations: for example, in the age of Catullus, Terence, and Lucretius and that of Statius or Claudian,[2] and in our own country, in the age of Shakespeare and Beaumont and Fletcher, and that of Donne and Cowley, or Dryden, or Pope. I will not take upon me to determine the exact import of the promise which by the act of writing in verse an author, in the present day, makes to his reader; but I am certain, it will appear to many persons that I have not fulfilled the terms of an engagement thus voluntarily contracted. They who have been accustomed to the gaudiness and inane phraseology of many modern writers, if they persist in reading this book to its conclusion, will, no doubt, frequently have to struggle with feelings of strangeness and awkwardness: they will look round for poetry, and will be induced to inquire by what species of courtesy these attempts can be permitted to assume that title. I hope therefore the reader will not censure me, if I attempt to state what I have proposed to myself to perform; and also (as far as the limits of a preface will permit) to explain some of the chief reasons which have determined me in the choice of my purpose: that at least he may be spared any unpleasant

---

2. Wordsworth's implied contrast is between the naturalness and simplicity of the first three Roman poets (who wrote in the last two centuries B.C.) and the elaborate artifice of the last two Roman poets (Statius wrote in the 1st and Claudian in the 4th century A.D.).

feeling of disappointment, and that I myself may be protected from the most dishonorable accusation which can be brought against an author, namely, that of an indolence which prevents him from endeavouring to ascertain what is his duty, or, when this duty is ascertained, prevents him from performing it.

The principal object, then, which I proposed to myself in these poems was to choose incidents and situations from common life, and to relate or describe them, throughout, as far as was possible, in a selection of language really used by men; and, at the same time, to throw over them a certain colouring of imagination, whereby ordinary things should be presented to the mind in an unusual way; and, further, and above all, to make these incidents and situations interesting by tracing in them, truly though not ostentatiously, the primary laws of our nature: chiefly, as far as regards the manner in which we associate ideas in a state of excitement.[3] Low and rustic life was generally chosen, because in that condition, the essential passions of the heart find a better soil in which they can attain their maturity, are less under restraint, and speak a plainer and more emphatic language; because in that condition of life our elementary feelings co-exist in a state of greater simplicity, and, consequently, may be more accurately contemplated, and more forcibly communicated; because the manners of rural life germinate from those elementary feelings; and, from the necessary character of rural occupations, are more easily comprehended; and are more durable; and lastly, because in that condition the passions of men are incorporated with the beautiful and permanent forms of nature. The language, too, of these men is adopted (purified indeed from what appear to be its real defects, from all lasting and rational causes of dislike or disgust) because such men hourly communicate with the best objects from which the best part of language is originally derived; and because, from their rank in society and the sameness and narrow circle of their intercourse, being less under the influence of social vanity they convey their feelings and notions in simple and unelaborated expressions. Accordingly, such a language, arising out of repeated experience and regular feelings, is a more permanent, and a far more philosophical language, than that which is frequently substituted for it by poets, who think that they are conferring honour upon themselves and their art, in proportion as they separate themselves from the sympathies of men, and indulge in arbitrary and capricious habits of expression, in order to furnish food for fickle tastes, and fickle appetites, of their own creation.[4]

I cannot, however, be insensible of the present outcry against the triviality and meanness both of thought and language, which some of my contemporaries have occasionally introduced into their metrical compositions; and I acknowledge, that this defect, where it exists, is more dishonorable to the writer's own character than false refinement or

3. Cf. Coleridge's account of their plan in *Biographia Literaria*, the beginning of chapter 14.
4. "It is worth while here to observe that the affecting parts of Chaucer are almost always expressed in language pure and universally intelligible even to this day" [Wordsworth's note].

arbitrary innovation, though I should contend at the same time that it is far less pernicious in the sum of its consequences. From such verses the poems in these volumes will be found distinguished at least by one mark of difference, that each of them has a worthy *purpose*. Not that I mean to say, that I always began to write with a distinct purpose formally conceived; but I believe that my habits of meditation have so formed my feelings, as that my descriptions of such objects as strongly excite those feelings, will be found to carry along with them a *purpose*. If in this opinion I am mistaken, I can have little right to the name of a poet. For all good poetry is the spontaneous overflow of powerful feelings: but though this be true, poems to which any value can be attached, were never produced on any variety of subjects but by a man who, being possessed of more than usual organic sensibility, had also thought long and deeply. For our continued influxes of feeling are modified and directed by our thoughts, which are indeed the representatives of all our past feelings; and, as by contemplating the relation of these general representatives to each other we discover what is really important to men, so, by the repetition and continuance of this act, our feelings will be connected with important subjects, till at length, if we be originally possessed of much sensibility, such habits of mind will be produced, that, by obeying blindly and mechanically the impulses of those habits, we shall describe objects, and utter sentiments, of such a nature and in such connection with each other, that the understanding of the being to whom we address ourselves, if he be in a healthful state of association, must necessarily be in some degree enlightened, and his affections ameliorated.

I have said that each of these poems has a purpose. I have also informed my reader what this purpose will be found principally to be: namely, to illustrate the manner in which our feelings and ideas are associated in a state of excitement. But, speaking in language somewhat more appropriate, it is to follow the fluxes and refluxes of the mind when agitated by the great and simple affections of our nature. This object I have endeavored in these short essays to attain by various means; by tracing the maternal passion through many of its more subtile windings, as in the poems of the *Idiot Boy* and the *Mad Mother*; by accompanying the last struggles of a human being, at the approach of death, cleaving in solitude to life and society, as in the poem of the *Forsaken Indian*; by shewing, as in the stanzas entitled *We Are Seven*, the perplexity and obscurity which in childhood attend our notion of death, or rather our utter inability to admit that notion; or by displaying the strength of fraternal, or to speak more philosophically, of moral attachment when early associated with the great and beautiful objects of nature, as in *The Brothers*; or, as in the Incident of *Simon Lee*, by placing my reader in the way of receiving from ordinary moral sensations another and more salutary impression than we are accustomed to receive from them. It has also been part of my general purpose to attempt to sketch characters under the influence of less impassioned feelings, as in the *Two April Mornings*, *The Fountain, The Old Man Travelling, The Two Thieves*, &c., characters of which the elements are simple, belonging rather to nature than to manners, such as exist now, and will probably always exist, and which from their constitution may be distinctly and profitably contemplated. I will not abuse the indulgence of my reader by dwelling longer upon this subject; but it is proper that I should mention one other circumstance which distinguishes these poems from the popular poetry of the day; it is this, that the feeling therein developed gives importance to the action and situation, and not the action and situation to the feeling. My meaning will be rendered perfectly intelligible by referring my reader to the poems entitled *Poor Susan* and the *Childless Father*, particularly to the last stanza of the latter poem.

I will not suffer a sense of false modesty to prevent me from asserting, that I point my reader's attention to this mark of distinction, far less for the sake of these particular poems than from the general importance of the subject. The subject is indeed important! For the human mind is capable of being excited without the application of gross and violent stimulants; and he must have a very faint perception of its beauty and dignity who does not know this, and who does not further know, that one being is elevated above another, in proportion as he possesses this capability. It has therefore appeared to me, that to endeavour to produce or enlarge this capability is one of the best services in which, at any period, a writer can be engaged; but this service, excellent at all times, is especially so at the present day. For a multitude of causes, unknown to former times, are now acting with a combined force to blunt the discriminating powers of the mind, and, unfitting it for all voluntary exertion, to reduce it to a state of almost savage torpor. The most effective of these causes are the great national events which are daily taking place, and the increasing accumulation of men in cities, where the uniformity of their occupations produces a craving for extraordinary incident, which the rapid communication of intelligence hourly gratifies.[5] To this tendency of life and manners the literature and theatrical exhibitions of the country have conformed themselves. The invaluable works of our elder writers, I had almost said the works of Shakespeare and Milton, are driven into neglect by frantic novels, sickly and stupid German tragedies,[6] and deluges of idle and extravagant stories in verse.— When I think upon this degrading thirst after outrageous stimulation, I am almost ashamed to have spoken of the feeble effort with which I have endeavoured to counteract it; and, reflecting upon the magnitude of the general evil, I should be oppressed with no dishonorable melancholy, had I not a deep impression of certain inherent and indestructible qualities of the human mind, and likewise of certain powers in the great and permanent objects that act upon it which are equally inherent and inde-

5. This was the period of the wars against France, of industrial urbanization, and of the rapid proliferation in England of daily newspapers.
6. Wordsworth had in mind the "Gothic" terror novels by writers such as Ann Radcliffe and Mat-

thew Gregory Lewis, and the sentimental melodrama, then immensely popular in England, of August von Kotzebue and his German contemporaries.

structible; and did I not further add to this impression a belief, that the time is approaching when the evil will be systematically opposed, by men of greater powers, and with far more distinguished success.

Having dwelt thus long on the subjects and aim of these poems, I shall request the reader's permission to apprize him of a few circumstances relating to their *style*, in order, among other reasons, that I may not be censured for not having performed what I never attempted. The reader will find that personifications of abstract ideas rarely occur in these volumes; and, I hope, are utterly rejected as an ordinary device to elevate the style, and raise it above prose. I have proposed to myself to imitate, and, as far as is possible, to adopt the very language of men; and assuredly such personifications do not make any natural or regular part of that language. They are, indeed, a figure of speech occasionally prompted by passion, and I have made use of them as such; but I have endeavoured utterly to reject them as a mechanical device of style, or as a family language which writers in metre seem to lay claim to by prescription. I have wished to keep my reader in the company of flesh and blood, persuaded that by so doing I shall interest him. I am, however, well aware that others who pursue a different track may interest him likewise; I do not interfere with their claim, I only wish to prefer a different claim of my own. There will also be found in these volumes little of what is usually called poetic diction;[7] I have taken as much pains to avoid it as others ordinarily take to produce it; this I have done for the reason already alleged, to bring my language near to the language of men, and further, because the pleasure which I have proposed to myself to impart is of a kind very different from that which is supposed by many persons to be the proper object of poetry. I do not know how, without being culpably particular, I can give my reader a more exact notion of the style in which I wished these poems to be written than by informing him that I have at all times endeavoured to look steadily at my subject, consequently, I hope that there is in these poems little falsehood of description, and that my ideas are expressed in language fitted to their respective importance. Something I must have gained by this practice, as it is friendly to one property of all good poetry, namely, good sense; but it has necessarily cut me off from a large portion of phrases and figures of speech which from father to son have long been regarded as the common inheritance of poets. I have also thought it expedient to restrict myself still further, having abstained from the use of many expressions, in themselves proper and beautiful, but which have been foolishly repeated by bad poets, till such feelings of disgust are connected with them as it is scarcely possible by any art of association to overpower.

If in a poem there should be found a series of lines, or even a single line, in which the language, though naturally arranged and according to the strict laws of metre, does not differ from that of prose, there is a numerous class of critics, who, when they stumble upon these prosaisms

7. In the sense of words, phrases, and figures of speech not commonly used in conversation or prose which are regarded as especially appropriate to poetry.

as they call them, imagine that they have made a notable discovery, and exult over the poet as over a man ignorant of his own profession. Now these men would establish a canon of criticism which the reader will conclude he must utterly reject, if he wishes to be pleased with these volumes. And it would be a most easy task to prove to him, that not only the language of a large portion of every good poem, even of the most elevated character, must necessarily, except with reference to the metre, in no respect differ from that of good prose, but likewise that some of the most interesting parts of the best poems will be found to be strictly the language of prose, when prose is well written. The truth of this assertion might be demonstrated by innumerable passages from almost all the poetical writings, even of Milton himself. I have not space for much quotation; but, to illustrate the subject in a general manner, I will here adduce a short composition of Gray, who was at the head of those who by their reasonings have attempted to widen the space of separation betwixt prose and metrical composition, and was more than any other man curiously elaborate in the structure of his own poetic diction.[8]

> In vain to me the smiling mornings shine,
> And reddening Phoebus lifts his golden fire:
> The birds in vain their amorous descant join,
> Or cheerful fields resume their green attire:
> These ears, alas! for other notes repine;
> *A different object do these eyes require;*
> *My lonely anguish melts no heart but mine;*
> *And in my breast the imperfect joys expire;*
> Yet Morning smiles the busy race to cheer,
> And new-born pleasure brings to happier men;
> The fields to all their wonted tribute bear;
> To warm their little loves the birds complain.
> *I fruitless mourn to him that cannot hear*
> *And weep the more because I weep in vain.*

It will easily be perceived that the only part of this sonnet which is of any value is the lines printed in italics: it is equally obvious, that, except in the rhyme, and in the use of the single word "fruitless" for fruitlessly, which is so far a defect, the language of these lines does in no respect differ from that of prose.

By the foregoing quotation I have shewn that the language of prose may yet be well adapted to poetry; and I have previously asserted that a large portion of the language of every good poem can in no respect differ from that of good prose. I will go further. I do not doubt that it may be safely affirmed, that there neither is, nor can be, any essential difference between the language of prose and metrical composition. We are fond of tracing the resemblance between poetry and painting, and, accordingly, we call them sisters: but where shall we find bonds of connection

---

8. Thomas Gray had written, in a letter to Richard West, that "the language of the age is never the language of poetry." The poem that follows is Gray's *Sonnet on the Death of Richard West.*

sufficiently strict to typify the affinity betwixt metrical and prose composition? They both speak by and to the same organs; the bodies in which both of them are clothed may be said to be of the same substance, their affections are kindred and almost identical, not necessarily differing even in degree; poetry[9] sheds no tears "such as Angels weep,"[1] but natural and human tears; she can boast of no celestial ichor[2] that distinguishes her vital juices from those of prose; the same human blood circulates through the veins of them both.

* * *

["What Is a Poet?"]

Taking up the subject, then, upon general grounds, I ask what is meant by the word "poet"? What is a poet? To whom does he address himself? And what language is to be expected from him? He is a man speaking to men: a man, it is true, endued with more lively sensibility, more enthusiasm and tenderness, who has a greater knowledge of human nature, and a more comprehensive soul, than are supposed to be common among mankind; a man pleased with his own passions and volitions, and who rejoices more than other men in the spirit of life that is in him; delighting to contemplate similar volitions and passions as manifested in the goings-on of the universe, and habitually impelled to create them where he does not find them. To these qualities he has added a disposition to be affected more than other men by absent things as if they were present; an ability of conjuring up in himself passions, which are indeed far from being the same as those produced by real events, yet (especially in those parts of the general sympathy which are pleasing and delightful) do more nearly resemble the passions produced by real events, than any thing which, from the motions of their own minds merely, other men are accustomed to feel in themselves; whence, and from practice, he has acquired a greater readiness and power in expressing what he thinks and feels, and especially those thoughts and feelings which, by his own choice, or from the structure of his own mind, arise in him without immediate external excitement.

But, whatever portion of this faculty we may suppose even the greatest poet to possess, there cannot be a doubt but that the language which it will suggest to him, must, in liveliness and truth, fall far short of that which is uttered by men in real life, under the actual pressure of those passions, certain shadows of which the poet thus produces, or feels to be produced, in himself. However exalted a notion we would wish to cher-

---

9. "I here use the word 'poetry' (though against my own judgment) as opposed to the word prose, and synonymous with metrical composition. But much confusion has been introduced into criticism by this contradistinction of poetry and prose, instead of the more philosophical one of poetry and matter of fact, or science. The only strict antithesis to prose is metre; nor is this, in truth, a *strict* antithesis; because lines and passages of metre so naturally occur in writing prose, that it would be scarcely possible to avoid them, even were it desirable" [Wordsworth's note].

1. *Paradise Lost* 1.620.

2. In Greek mythology, the fluid in the veins of the gods.

ish of the character of a poet, it is obvious, that, while he describes and imitates passions, his situation is altogether slavish and mechanical, compared with the freedom and power of real and substantial action and suffering. So that it will be the wish of the poet to bring his feelings near to those of the persons whose feelings he describes, nay, for short spaces of time perhaps, to let himself slip into an entire delusion, and even confound and identify his own feelings with theirs; modifying only the language which is thus suggested to him, by a consideration that he describes for a particular purpose, that of giving pleasure. Here, then, he will apply the principle on which I have so much insisted, namely, that of selection; on this he will depend for removing what would otherwise be painful or disgusting in the passion; he will feel that there is no necessity to trick out or to elevate nature: and, the more industriously he applies this principle, the deeper will be his faith that no words, which his fancy or imagination can suggest, will be to be compared with those which are the emanations of reality and truth.

But it may be said by those who do not object to the general spirit of these remarks, that, as it is impossible for the poet to produce upon all occasions language as exquisitely fitted for the passion as that which the real passion itself suggests, it is proper that he should consider himself as in the situation of a translator, who deems himself justified when he substitutes excellences of another kind for those which are unattainable by him; and endeavours occasionally to surpass his original, in order to make some amends for the general inferiority to which he feels that he must submit. But this would be to encourage idleness and unmanly despair. Further, it is the language of men who speak of what they do not understand; who talk of poetry as a matter of amusement and idle pleasure; who will converse with us as gravely about a *taste* for poetry, as they express it, as if it were a thing as indifferent as a taste for rope-dancing, or Frontiniac[3] or sherry. Aristotle, I have been told, hath said, that poetry is the most philosophic of all writing;[4] it is so: its object is truth, not individual and local, but general, and operative; not standing upon external testimony, but carried alive into the heart by passion; truth which is its own testimony, which gives strength and divinity to the tribunal to which it appeals, and receives them from the same tribunal. Poetry is the image of man and nature. The obstacles which stand in the way of the fidelity of the biographer and historian, and of their consequent utility, are incalculably greater than those which are to be encountered by the poet who has an adequate notion of the dignity of his art. The poet writes under one restriction only, namely, that of the necessity of giving immediate pleasure to a human being possessed of that information which may be expected from him, not as a lawyer, a physician, a mariner, an astronomer or a natural philosopher, but as a man. Except this one restriction, there is no object standing between

3. A sweet wine made from muscat grapes.
4. Aristotle in fact said that "poetry is more philosophic than history, since its statements are of the nature of universals, whereas those of history are singulars" (*Poetics* 1451b).

the poet and the image of things; between this, and the biographer and historian there are a thousand.

Nor let this necessity of producing immediate pleasure be considered as a degradation of the poet's art. It is far otherwise. It is an acknowledgment of the beauty of the universe, an acknowledgment the more sincere because it is not formal, but indirect; it is a task light and easy to him who looks at the world in the spirit of love: further, it is a homage paid to the native and naked dignity of man, to the grand elementary principle of pleasure, by which he knows, and feels, and lives, and moves.[5] We have no sympathy but what is propagated by pleasure: I would not be misunderstood; but wherever we sympathize with pain it will be found that the sympathy is produced and carried on by subtle combinations with pleasure. We have no knowledge, that is, no general principles drawn from the contemplation of particular facts, but what has been built up by pleasure, and exists in us by pleasure alone. The man of science, the chemist and mathematician, whatever difficulties and disgusts they may have had to struggle with, know and feel this. However painful may be the objects with which the anatomist's knowledge is connected, he feels that his knowledge is pleasure; and where he has no pleasure he has no knowledge. What then does the poet? He considers man and the objects that surround him as acting and re-acting upon each other, so as to produce an infinite complexity of pain and pleasure; he considers man in his own nature and in his ordinary life as contemplating this with a certain quantity of immediate knowledge, with certain convictions, intuitions, and deductions which by habit become of the nature of intuitions; he considers him as looking upon this complex scene of ideas and sensations, and finding every where objects that immediately excite in him sympathies which, from the necessities of his nature, are accompanied by an overbalance of enjoyment.

To this knowledge which all men carry about with them, and to these sympathies in which without any other discipline than that of our daily life we are fitted to take delight, the poet principally directs his attention. He considers man and nature as essentially adapted to each other,[6] and the mind of man as naturally the mirror of the fairest and most interesting qualities of nature. And thus the poet, prompted by this feeling of pleasure which accompanies him through the whole course of his studies, converses with general nature with affections akin to those, which, through labour and length of time, the man of science has raised up in himself, by conversing with those particular parts of nature which are the objects of his studies. The knowledge both of the poet and the man of science is pleasure; but the knowledge of the one cleaves to us as a necessary part of our existence, our natural and unalienable inheritance; the other is a personal and individual acquisition, slow to come to us, and by no habitual and direct sympathy connecting us with our fellow-

---

5. A bold echo of the words of St. Paul, that in God "we live, and move, and have our being" (Acts 17.28).

6. On the mutual adaptation of man's mind and nature, see below, Wordsworth's Prospectus to *The Recluse*, lines 63–71.

beings. The man of science seeks truth as a remote and unknown benefactor; he cherishes and loves it in his solitude: the poet, singing a song in which all human beings join with him, rejoices in the presence of truth as our visible friend and hourly companion. Poetry is the breath and finer spirit of all knowledge; it is the impassioned expression which is in the countenance of all science. Emphatically may it be said of the poet, as Shakespeare hath said of man, "that he looks before and after."[7] He is the rock of defence of human nature; an upholder and preserver, carrying everywhere with him relationship and love. In spite of difference of soil and climate, of language and manners, of laws and customs, in spite of things silently gone out of mind and things violently destroyed, the poet binds together by passion and knowledge the vast empire of human society, as it is spread over the whole earth, and over all time. The objects of the poet's thoughts are every where; though the eyes and senses of man are, it is true, his favorite guides, yet he will follow wheresoever he can find an atmosphere of sensation in which to move his wings. Poetry is the first and last of all knowledge—it is as immortal as the heart of man. If the labours of men of science should ever create any material revolution, direct or indirect, in our condition, and in the impressions which we habitually receive, the poet will sleep then no more than at present, but he will be ready to follow the steps of the man of science, not only in those general indirect effects, but he will be at his side, carrying sensation into the midst of the objects of the science itself. The remotest discoveries of the chemist, the botanist, or mineralogist, will be as proper objects of the poet's art as any upon which it can be employed, if the time should ever come when these things shall be familiar to us, and the relations under which they are contemplated by the followers of these respective sciences shall be manifestly and palpably material to us as enjoying and suffering beings.[8] If the time should ever come when what is now called science, thus familiarized to men, shall be ready to put on, as it were, a form of flesh and blood, the poet will lend his divine spirit to aid the transfiguration, and will welcome the being thus produced, as a dear and genuine inmate of the household of man.—It is not, then, to be supposed that any one, who holds that sublime notion of poetry which I have attempted to convey, will break in upon the sanctity and truth of his pictures by transitory and accidental ornaments, and endeavour to excite admiration of himself by arts, the necessity of which must manifestly depend upon the assumed meanness of his subject.

What I have thus far said applies to poetry in general; but especially to those parts of composition where the poet speaks through the mouth of his characters; and upon this point it appears to have such weight that I will conclude, there are few persons, of good sense, who would not allow that the dramatic parts of composition are defective, in proportion

---

7. *Hamlet* 4.4.37.
8. Wordsworth is at least right in anticipating the poetry of the machine; he himself wrote an early instance, the sonnet *Steamboats, Viaducts, and Railways*.

as they deviate from the real language of nature, and are coloured by a diction of the poet's own, either peculiar to him as an individual poet, or belonging simply to poets in general, to a body of men who, from the circumstance of their compositions being in metre, it is expected will employ a particular language.

It is not, then, in the dramatic parts of composition that we look for this distinction of language; but still it may be proper and necessary where the poet speaks to us in his own person and character. To this I answer by referring my reader to the description which I have before given of a poet. Among the qualities which I have enumerated as principally conducing to form a poet, is implied nothing differing in kind from other men, but only in degree. The sum of what I have there said is, that the poet is chiefly distinguished from other men by a greater promptness to think and feel without immediate external excitement, and a greater power in expressing such thoughts and feelings as are produced in him in that manner. But these passions and thoughts and feelings are the general passions and thoughts and feelings of men. And with what are they connected? Undoubtedly with our moral sentiments and animal sensations, and with the causes which excite these; with the operations of the elements and the appearances of the visible universe; with storm and sun-shine, with the revolutions of the seasons, with cold and heat, with loss of friends and kindred, with injuries and resentments, gratitude and hope, with fear and sorrow. These, and the like, are the sensations and objects which the poet describes, as they are the sensations of other men, and the objects which interest them. The poet thinks and feels in the spirit of the passions of men. How, then, can his language differ in any material degree from that of all other men who feel vividly and see clearly? It might be *proved* that it is impossible. But supposing that this were not the case, the poet might then be allowed to use a peculiar language, when expressing his feelings for his own gratification, or that of men like himself. But poets do not write for poets alone, but for men. Unless therefore we are advocates for that admiration which depends upon ignorance, and that pleasure which arises from hearing what we do not understand, the poet must descend from this supposed height, and, in order to excite rational sympathy, he must express himself as other men express themselves. * * *

[*"Emotion Recollected in Tranquillity"*]

I have said that poetry is the spontaneous overflow of powerful feelings: it takes its origin from emotion recollected in tranquillity: the emotion is contemplated till by a species of reaction the tranquillity gradually disappears, and an emotion, kindred to that which was before the subject of contemplation, is gradually produced, and does itself actually exist in the mind. In this mood successful composition generally begins, and in a mood similar to this it is carried on; but the emotion, of whatever kind and in whatever degree, from various causes is qualified by various pleasures, so that in describing any passions whatsoever, which are voluntarily described, the mind will upon the whole be in a state of enjoyment. Now, if nature be thus cautious in preserving in a state of enjoyment a being thus employed, the poet ought to profit by the lesson thus held forth to him, and ought especially to take care, that whatever passions he communicates to his reader, those passions, if his reader's mind be sound and vigorous, should always be accompanied with an overbalance of pleasure. Now the music of harmonious metrical language, the sense of difficulty overcome, and the blind association of pleasure which has been previously received from works of rhyme or metre of the same or similar construction, an indistinct perception perpetually renewed of language closely resembling that of real life, and yet, in the circumstance of metre, differing from it so widely, all these imperceptibly make up a complex feeling of delight, which is of the most important use in tempering the painful feeling which will always be found intermingled with powerful descriptions of the deeper passions. This effect is always produced in pathetic and impassioned poetry; while, in lighter compositions, the ease and gracefulness with which the poet manages his numbers are themselves confessedly a principal source of the gratification of the reader. I might perhaps include all which it is *necessary* to say upon this subject by affirming, what few persons will deny, that, of two descriptions, either of passions, manners, or characters, each of them equally well executed, the one in prose and the other in verse, the verse will be read a hundred times where the prose is read once. * * *

I know that nothing would have so effectually contributed to further the end which I have in view, as to have shewn of what kind the pleasure is, and how the pleasure is produced, which is confessedly produced by metrical composition essentially different from that which I have here endeavoured to recommend: for the reader will say that he has been pleased by such composition; and what can I do more for him? The power of any art is limited; and he will suspect, that, if I propose to furnish him with new friends, it is only upon condition of his abandoning his old friends. Besides, as I have said, the reader is himself conscious of the pleasure which he has received from such composition, composition to which he has peculiarly attached the endearing name of poetry; and all men feel an habitual gratitude, and something of an honorable bigotry for the objects which have long continued to please them: we not only wish to be pleased, but to be pleased in that particular way in which we have been accustomed to be pleased. There is a host of arguments in these feelings; and I should be the less able to combat them successfully, as I am willing to allow, that, in order entirely to enjoy the poetry which I am recommending, it would be necessary to give up much of what is ordinarily enjoyed. But, would my limits have permitted me to point out how this pleasure is produced, I might have removed many obstacles, and assisted my reader in perceiving that the powers of language are not so limited as he may suppose; and that it is possible that poetry may give other enjoyments, of a purer, more lasting, and more exquisite nature. This part of my subject I have not altogether neglected; but it has been less my present aim to prove, that the interest excited by some other kinds of poetry is less vivid, and less worthy of the nobler powers of the mind, than to offer reasons for presuming, that, if the object which I have proposed to myself were adequately attained, a species of poetry would be produced, which is genuine poetry; in its nature well adapted to interest mankind permanently, and likewise important in the multiplicity and quality of its moral relations.

From what has been said, and from a perusal of the poems, the reader will be able clearly to perceive the object which I have proposed to myself: he will determine how far I have attained this object; and, what is a much more important question, whether it be worth attaining; and upon the decision of these two questions will rest my claim to the approbation of the public.

1800, 1802

Strange Fits of Passion Have I Known[1]

Strange fits of passion have I known:
And I will dare to tell,
But in the Lover's ear alone,
What once to me befel.

When she I loved looked every day   5
Fresh as a rose in June,
I to her cottage bent my way,
Beneath an evening moon.

Upon the moon I fixed my eye,
All over the wide lea;   10
With quickening pace my horse drew nigh
Those paths so dear to me.

And now we reached the orchard-plot;
And, as we climbed the hill,
The sinking moon to Lucy's cot   15
Came near, and nearer still.

In one of those sweet dreams I slept,
Kind Nature's gentlest boon!

1. This and the four following pieces are often grouped by editors as the "Lucy poems," even though *A Slumber Did My Spirit Seal* does not identify the "she" who is the subject of that poem. All but the last were written in 1799, while Wordsworth and his sister were in Germany, and home- sick. There has been diligent speculation about the identity of Lucy, but it remains speculation; the one certainty is that she is not the girl of Wordsworth's *Lucy Gray*, below. "Fits of passion" (line 1): in an archaic sense, "sudden moods of intense grief."

And all the while my eyes I kept
On the descending moon.   20

My horse moved on; hoof after hoof
He raised, and never stopped:
When down behind the cottage roof,
At once, the bright moon dropped.

What fond and wayward thoughts will slide   25
Into a Lover's head!
"O mercy!" to myself I cried,
"If Lucy should be dead!"[2]

1799   1800

She Dwelt among the Untrodden Ways[1]

She dwelt among the untrodden ways
    Beside the springs of Dove,[2]
A Maid whom there were none to praise
    And very few to love:

A violet by a mossy stone   5
    Half hidden from the eye!
—Fair as a star, when only one
    Is shining in the sky.

She lived unknown, and few could know
    When Lucy ceased to be;   10
But she is in her grave, and, oh,
    The difference to me!

1799   1800

Three Years She Grew

Three years she grew in sun and shower,
Then Nature said, "A lovelier flower
On earth was never sown;
This Child I to myself will take;
She shall be mine, and I will make   5
A Lady of my own.[1]

---

2. An additional stanza in an earlier MS version demonstrates how a poem may profit by omitting a passage which is, in itself, excellent poetry: "I told her this: her laughter light / Is ringing in my ears; / And when I think upon that night / My eyes are dim with tears."
1. For the author's revisions while composing this poem, see "Poems in Process," below.
2. There are several rivers by this name in England, including one in the Lake Country.
1. I.e., Lucy was three years old when Nature made this promise; line 37 makes clear that Lucy had reached the maturity foretold in the sixth stanza when she died.

"Myself will to my darling be
Both law and impulse: and with me
The Girl, in rock and plain,
In earth and heaven, in glade and bower,   10
Shall feel an overseeing power
To kindle or restrain.

"She shall be sportive as the fawn
That wild with glee across the lawn
Or up the mountain springs;   15
And hers shall be the breathing balm,
And hers the silence and the calm
Of mute insensate things.

"The floating clouds their state shall lend
To her; for her the willow bend;   20
Nor shall she fail to see
Even in the motions of the Storm
Grace that shall mould the Maiden's form
By silent sympathy.

"The stars of midnight shall be dear   25
To her; and she shall lean her ear
In many a secret place
Where rivulets dance their wayward round,
And beauty born of murmuring sound
Shall pass into her face.   30

"And vital feelings of delight
Shall rear her form to stately height,
Her virgin bosom swell;
Such thoughts to Lucy I will give
While she and I together live   35
Here in this happy dell."

Thus Nature spake—the work was done—
How soon my Lucy's race was run!
She died, and left to me
This heath, this calm, and quiet scene;   40
The memory of what has been,
And never more will be.

1799   1800

A Slumber Did My Spirit Seal

A slumber did my spirit seal;
   I had no human fears:

She seemed a thing that could not feel
   The touch of earthly years.

No motion has she now, no force;   5
   She neither hears nor sees;
Rolled round in earth's diurnal[1] course,
   With rocks, and stones, and trees.

1799   1800

I Travelled among Unknown Men

I travelled among unknown men,
   In lands beyond the sea;
Nor, England! did I know till then
   What love I bore to thee.

'Tis past, that melancholy dream!   5
   Nor will I quit thy shore
A second time; for still I seem
   To love thee more and more.

Among thy mountains did I feel
   The joy of my desire;   10
And she I cherished turned her wheel
   Beside an English fire.

Thy mornings showed, thy nights concealed
   The bowers where Lucy played;
And thine too is the last green field   15
   That Lucy's eyes surveyed.

ca. 1801   1807

Nutting[1]

—————————It seems a day
(I speak of one from many singled out)
One of those heavenly days that cannot die;
When, in the eagerness of boyish hope,
I left our cottage-threshold, sallying forth   5
With a huge wallet o'er my shoulder slung,
A nutting-crook in hand; and turned my steps
Tow'rd some far-distant wood, a Figure quaint,

1. Daily.
1. Wordsworth said that this passage, written in Germany in 1798, was "intended as part of a poem on my own mind [*The Prelude*], but struck out as not being wanted there." He published it in the second edition of *Lyrical Ballads*, 1800.

Tricked out in proud disguise of cast-off weeds[2]
Which for that service had been husbanded,   10
By exhortation of my frugal Dame[3]—
Motley accoutrement, of power to smile
At thorns, and brakes, and brambles,—and, in truth,
More raggèd than need was! O'er pathless rocks,
Through beds of matted fern, and tangled thickets,   15
Forcing my way, I came to one dear nook
Unvisited, where not a broken bough
Drooped with its withered leaves, ungracious sign
Of devastation; but the hazels rose
Tall and erect, with tempting clusters hung,   20
A virgin scene!—A little while I stood,
Breathing with such suppression of the heart
As joy delights in; and, with wise restraint
Voluptuous, fearless of a rival, eyed
The banquet;—or beneath the trees I sate   25
Among the flowers, and with the flowers I played;
A temper known to those, who, after long
And weary expectation, have been blest
With sudden happiness beyond all hope.
Perhaps it was a bower beneath whose leaves   30
The violets of five seasons re-appear
And fade, unseen by any human eye;
Where fairy water-breaks[4] do murmur on
For ever; and I saw the sparkling foam,
And—with my cheek on one of those green stones   35
That, fleeced with moss, under the shady trees,
Lay round me, scattered like a flock of sheep—
I heard the murmur and the murmuring sound,
In that sweet mood when pleasure loves to pay
Tribute to ease; and, of its joy secure,   40
The heart luxuriates with indifferent things,
Wasting its kindliness on stocks[5] and stones,
And on the vacant air. Then up I rose,
And dragged to earth both branch and bough, with crash
And merciless ravage: and the shady nook   45
Of hazels, and the green and mossy bower,
Deformed and sullied, patiently gave up
Their quiet being: and, unless I now
Confound my present feelings with the past,
Ere from the mutilated bower I turned   50
Exulting, rich beyond the wealth of kings,
I felt a sense of pain when I beheld

---

2. Clothes.
3. Ann Tyson, with whom Wordsworth lodged
while at Hawkshead grammar school.
4. Places where the flow of a stream is broken by
rocks.
5. Tree stumps. ("Stocks and stones" is a conventional expression for "inanimate things.")

The silent trees, and saw the intruding sky.—
Then, dearest Maiden,[6] move along these shades
In gentleness of heart; with gentle hand   55
Touch—for there is a spirit in the woods.

1798   1800

The Ruined Cottage
Wordsworth wrote *The Ruined Cottage* in
1797–98, but revised it several times before he finally published an expanded
rendering of the story as book 1 of *The Excursion*, in 1814. Not until 1949
was *The Ruined Cottage*, as an independent poem, made available in the
fifth volume of *The Poetical Works of William Wordsworth*, edited by Ernest
de Selincourt and Helen Darbishire, who printed a version known as "MS.
B." The version reprinted here is, however, from "MS. D," dating 1799, as
transcribed by James Butler in the Cornell Wordsworth volume, *"The Ruined
Cottage" and "The Pedlar"* (1979).

This is a shorter and better poem than the one reprinted in *The Poetical
Works*. The latter lacks the great concluding passage, lines 493–538, and
includes in part 1 more than 250 lines describing the youthful development
of the peddler that are extraneous to the narrative proper and soften the hard
naturalism of the story by introducing into it, at considerable length, the
peddler's faith that nature teaches "deeply the lesson deep of love." The
version in the first book of *The Excursion* is longer still, and attempts to
mitigate the impact of Margaret's sufferings even more, by attributing to her
a Christian piety which is conventional rather than deeply realized. In the
version reprinted here, we confront the bleak facts of "a tale of silent suffering"—suffering which is undeserved, unrationalized, and irremissive. The
event is "a common tale," and it poses the implicit question, What are we
to make of human life, in which such things happen?

The peddler's recovery of heart turns, unexpectedly, on his recognition
that this human tragedy takes place within the unceasing and neutral operation—as the narrator says, "the calm oblivious tendencies"—of nature, which
silently goes about the process of assimilating the human artifacts that have
been wrought from it back into its own independent and continuing life. In
a reversal as extreme as Wordsworth could make it, the peddler declares: "I
turned away / And walked along my road in happiness." By his artistry
Wordsworth carries us along in imagination so that we too, whatever our
own beliefs, feel what it is to be able to look upon and master the fact of
human suffering, unsupported by any creed of a beneficent power, whether
in or out of nature.

Beyond any of Wordsworth's writings, even *Michael*, *The Ruined Cottage*
demonstrates that distinctive quality which the critic Walter Raleigh identified more than a half century ago as Wordsworth's "calm and almost terrible
strength."

---

6. In a MS passage, originally intended to lead up to *Nutting*, the maiden is called Lucy.

The Ruined Cottage

First Part

'Twas summer and the sun was mounted high.
Along the south the uplands feebly glared
Through a pale steam, and all the northern downs
In clearer air ascending shewed far off
Their surfaces with shadows dappled o'er   5
Of deep embattled clouds: far as the sight
Could reach those many shadows lay in spots
Determined and unmoved, with steady beams
Of clear and pleasant sunshine interposed;
Pleasant to him who on the soft cool moss   10
Extends his careless limbs beside the root
Of some huge oak whose aged branches make
A twilight of their own, a dewy shade
Where the wren warbles while the dreaming man,
Half-conscious of that soothing melody,   15
With side-long eye looks out upon the scene,
By those impending branches made more soft,
More soft and distant. Other lot was mine.
Across a bare wide Common I had toiled
With languid feet which by the slipp'ry ground   20
Were baffled still, and when I stretched myself
On the brown earth my limbs from very heat
Could find no rest nor my weak arm disperse
The insect host which gathered round my face
And joined their murmurs to the tedious noise   25
Of seeds of bursting gorse that crackled round.
I rose and turned towards a group of trees
Which midway in that level stood alone,
And thither come at length, beneath a shade
Of clustering elms that sprang from the same root   30
I found a ruined house, four naked walls
That stared upon each other. I looked round
And near the door I saw an aged Man,
Alone, and stretched upon the cottage bench;
An iron-pointed staff lay at his side.   35
With instantaneous joy I recognized
That pride of nature and of lowly life,
The venerable Armytage, a friend
As dear to me as is the setting sun.
                  Two days before   40
We had been fellow-travellers. I knew
That he was in this neighbourhood and now
Delighted found him here in the cool shade.
He lay, his pack of rustic merchandize

Pillowing his head—I guess he had no thought   45
Of his way-wandering life. His eyes were shut;
The shadows of the breezy elms above
Dappled his face. With thirsty heat oppress'd
At length I hailed him, glad to see his hat
Bedewed with water-drops, as if the brim   50
Had newly scoop'd a running stream. He rose
And pointing to a sun-flower bade me climb
The [   ]¹ wall where that same gaudy flower
Looked out upon the road. It was a plot
Of garden-ground, now wild, its matted weeds   55
Marked with the steps of those whom as they pass'd,
The goose-berry trees that shot in long lank slips,
Or currants hanging from their leafless stems
In scanty strings, had tempted to o'erleap
The broken wall. Within that cheerless spot,   60
Where two tall hedgerows of thick willow boughs
Joined in a damp cold nook, I found a well
Half-choked [with willow flowers and weeds.]²
I slaked my thirst and to the shady bench
Returned, and while I stood unbonneted   65
To catch the motion of the cooler air
The old Man said, "I see around me here
Things which you cannot see: we die, my Friend,
Nor we alone, but that which each man loved
And prized in his peculiar nook of earth   70
Dies with him or is changed, and very soon
Even of the good is no memorial left.
The Poets in their elegies and songs
Lamenting the departed call the groves,
They call upon the hills and streams to mourn,   75
And senseless rocks, nor idly; for they speak
In these their invocations with a voice
Obedient to the strong creative power
Of human passion. Sympathies there are
More tranquil, yet perhaps of kindred birth,   80
That steal upon the meditative mind
And grow with thought. Beside yon spring I stood
And eyed its waters till we seemed to feel
One sadness, they and I. For them a bond
Of brotherhood is broken: time has been   85
When every day the touch of human hand
Disturbed their stillness, and they ministered
To human comfort. When I stooped to drink,
A spider's web hung to the water's edge,
And on the wet and slimy foot-stone lay   90

1. The brackets here and in later lines mark blank spaces left unfilled in the MS.

2. Wordsworth penciled the bracketed phrase into a gap left in the MS.

The useless fragment of a wooden bowl;
It moved my very heart. The day has been
When I could never pass this road but she
Who lived within these walls, when I appeared,
A daughter's welcome gave me, and I loved her   95
As my own child. O Sir! the good die first,
And they whose hearts are dry as summer dust
Burn to the socket. Many a passenger
Has blessed poor Margaret for her gentle looks
When she upheld the cool refreshment drawn   100
From that forsaken spring, and no one came
But he was welcome, no one went away
But that it seemed she loved him. She is dead,
The worm is on her cheek, and this poor hut,
Stripp'd of its outward garb of household flowers,   105
Of rose and sweet-briar, offers to the wind
A cold bare wall whose earthy top is tricked
With weeds and the rank spear-grass. She is dead,
And nettles rot and adders sun themselves
Where we have sate together while she nurs'd   110
Her infant at her breast. The unshod Colt,
The wandring heifer and the Potter's ass,
Find shelter now within the chimney-wall
Where I have seen her evening hearth-stone blaze
And through the window spread upon the road   115
Its chearful light.—You will forgive me, Sir,
But often on this cottage do I muse
As on a picture, till my wiser mind
Sinks, yielding to the foolishness of grief.

    She had a husband, an industrious man,   120
Sober and steady; I have heard her say
That he was up and busy at his loom
In summer ere the mower's scythe had swept
The dewy grass, and in the early spring
Ere the last star had vanished. They who pass'd   125
At evening, from behind the garden-fence
Might hear his busy spade, which he would ply
After his daily work till the day-light
Was gone and every leaf and flower were lost
In the dark hedges. So they pass'd their days   130
In peace and comfort, and two pretty babes
Were their best hope next to the God in Heaven.
—You may remember, now some ten years gone,
Two blighting seasons when the fields were left
With half a harvest.[3] It pleased heaven to add   135

3. As James Butler points out in his introduction, Wordsworth is purposely distancing his story in time. The "two blighting seasons" in fact occurred in 1794–95, only a few years before Wordsworth wrote *The Ruined Cottage*, when a bad harvest was followed by one of the worst winters on record; much of the seed grain was destroyed in the ground, and the price of wheat nearly doubled.

A worse affliction in the plague of war:
A happy land was stricken to the heart;
'Twas a sad time of sorrow and distress:
A wanderer among the cottages,
I with my pack of winter raiment saw   140
The hardships of that season: many rich
Sunk down as in a dream among the poor,
And of the poor did many cease to be,
And their place knew them not. Meanwhile, abridg'd
Of daily comforts, gladly reconciled   145
To numerous self-denials, Margaret
Went struggling on through those calamitous years
With chearful hope: but ere the second autumn
A fever seized her husband. In disease
He lingered long, and when his strength returned   150
He found the little he had stored to meet
The hour of accident or crippling age
Was all consumed. As I have said, 'twas now
A time of trouble; shoals of artisans
Were from their daily labour turned away   155
To hang for bread on parish charity,
They and their wives and children—happier far
Could they have lived as do the little birds
That peck along the hedges or the kite
That makes her dwelling in the mountain rocks.   160
Ill fared it now with Robert, he who dwelt
In this poor cottage; at his door he stood
And whistled many a snatch of merry tunes
That had no mirth in them, or with his knife
Carved uncouth figures on the heads of sticks,   165
Then idly sought about through every nook
Of house or garden any casual task
Of use or ornament, and with a strange,
Amusing but uneasy novelty
He blended where he might the various tasks   170
Of summer, autumn, winter, and of spring.
But this endured not; his good-humour soon
Became a weight in which no pleasure was,
And poverty brought on a petted[4] mood
And a sore temper: day by day he drooped,   175
And he would leave his home, and to the town
Without an errand would he turn his steps
Or wander here and there among the fields.
One while he would speak lightly of his babes
And with a cruel tongue: at other times   180
He played with them wild freaks of merriment:
And 'twas a piteous thing to see the looks

---

4. Ill-tempered.

Of the poor innocent children. 'Every smile,'
Said Margaret to me here beneath these trees,
'Made my heart bleed.' " At this the old Man paus'd   185
And looking up to those enormous elms
He said, "'Tis now the hour of deepest noon,
At this still season of repose and peace,
This hour when all things which are not at rest
Are chearful, while this multitude of flies   190
Fills all the air with happy melody,
Why should a tear be in an old man's eye?
Why should we thus with an untoward mind
And in the weakness of humanity
From natural wisdom turn our hearts away,   195
To natural comfort shut our eyes and ears,
And feeding on disquiet thus disturb
The calm of Nature with our restless thoughts?"

END OF THE FIRST PART

Second Part

He spake with somewhat of a solemn tone:
But when he ended there was in his face   200
Such easy chearfulness, a look so mild
That for a little time it stole away
All recollection, and that simple tale
Passed from my mind like a forgotten sound.
A while on trivial things we held discourse,   205
To me soon tasteless. In my own despite
I thought of that poor woman as of one
Whom I had known and loved. He had rehearsed
Her homely tale with such familiar power,
With such a[n active]⁵ countenance, an eye   210
So busy, that the things of which he spake
Seemed present, and, attention now relaxed,
There was a heartfelt chillness in my veins.
I rose, and turning from that breezy shade
Went out into the open air and stood   215
To drink the comfort of the warmer sun.
Long time I had not stayed ere, looking round
Upon that tranquil ruin, I returned
And begged of the old man that for my sake
He would resume his story. He replied,   220
"It were a wantonness and would demand
Severe reproof, if we were men whose hearts
Could hold vain dalliance with the misery
Even of the dead, contented thence to draw
A momentary pleasure never marked   225

5. Penciled by Wordsworth into a gap left in the MS.

By reason, barren of all future good.
But we have known that there is often found
In mournful thoughts, and always might be found,
A power to virtue friendly; were't not so,
I am a dreamer among men, indeed   230
An idle dreamer. 'Tis a common tale,
By moving accidents[6] uncharactered,
A tale of silent suffering, hardly clothed
In bodily form, and to the grosser sense
But ill adapted, scarcely palpable   235
To him who does not think. But at your bidding
I will proceed.
                    While thus it fared with them
To whom this cottage till that hapless year
Had been a blessed home, it was my chance
To travel in a country far remote,   240
And glad I was when, halting by yon gate
That leads from the green lane, again I saw
These lofty elm-trees. Long I did not rest:
With many pleasant thoughts I cheer'd my way
O'er the flat common. At the door arrived,   245
I knocked, and when I entered with the hope
Of usual greeting, Margaret looked at me
A little while, then turned her head away
Speechless, and sitting down upon a chair
Wept bitterly. I wist not what to do   250
Or how to speak to her. Poor wretch! at last
She rose from off her seat—and then, oh Sir!
I cannot tell how she pronounced my name:
With fervent love, and with a face of grief
Unutterably helpless, and a look   255
That seem'd to cling upon me, she enquir'd
If I had seen her husband. As she spake
A strange surprize and fear came to my heart,
Nor had I power to answer ere she told
That he had disappeared—just two months gone.   260
He left his house; two wretched days had passed,
And on the third by the first break of light,
Within her casement full in view she saw
A purse of gold.[7] 'I trembled at the sight,'
Said Margaret, 'for I knew it was his hand   265
That placed it there, and on that very day
By one, a stranger, from my husband sent,
The tidings came that he had joined a troop

---

6. Othello speaks "of most disastrous chances: / Of moving accidents by flood and field, / Of hairbreadth 'scapes . . ." (*Othello* 1.3.135).
7. The "bounty" that her husband had been paid for enlisting in the militia. The shortage of volunteers and England's sharply rising military needs had in some counties forced the bounty up from about £1 in 1757 to more than £16 in 1796 (J. R. Western, *English Militia in the Eighteenth Century*, 1965, p. 276).

Of soldiers going to a distant land.
He left me thus—Poor Man! he had not heart   270
To take a farewell of me, and he feared
That I should follow with my babes, and sink
Beneath the misery of a soldier's life.'
This tale did Margaret tell with many tears:
And when she ended I had little power   275
To give her comfort, and was glad to take
Such words of hope from her own mouth as serv'd
To cheer us both: but long we had not talked
Ere we built up a pile of better thoughts,
And with a brighter eye she looked around   280
As if she had been shedding tears of joy.
We parted. It was then the early spring;
I left her busy with her garden tools;
And well remember, o'er that fence she looked,
And while I paced along the foot-way path   285
Called out, and sent a blessing after me
With tender chearfulness and with a voice
That seemed the very sound of happy thoughts.
    I roved o'er many a hill and many a dale
With this my weary load, in heat and cold,   290
Through many a wood, and many an open ground,
In sunshine or in shade, in wet or fair,
Now blithe, now drooping, as it might befal,
My best companions now the driving winds
And now the 'trotting brooks'[8] and whispering trees   295
And now the music of my own sad steps,
With many a short-lived thought that pass'd between
And disappeared. I came this way again
Towards the wane of summer, when the wheat
Was yellow, and the soft and bladed grass   300
Sprang up afresh and o'er the hay-field spread
Its tender green. When I had reached the door
I found that she was absent. In the shade
Where now we sit I waited her return.
Her cottage in its outward look appeared   305
As chearful as before; in any shew
Of neatness little changed, but that I thought
The honeysuckle crowded round the door
And from the wall hung down in heavier wreathes,
And knots of worthless stone-crop[9] started out   310
Along the window's edge, and grew like weeds
Against the lower panes. I turned aside
And stroll'd into her garden.—It was chang'd:
The unprofitable bindweed spread his bells
From side to side and with unwieldy wreaths   315

8. The quotation is from Robert Burns (To Wil-   9. A plant with yellow flowers that grows on walls
liam Simpson, line 87).   and rocks.

Had dragg'd the rose from its sustaining wall
And bent it down to earth; the border-tufts—
Daisy and thrift and lowly camomile
And thyme—had straggled out into the paths
Which they were used to deck. Ere this an hour   320
Was wasted. Back I turned my restless steps,
And as I walked before the door it chanced
A stranger passed, and guessing whom I sought
He said that she was used to ramble far.
The sun was sinking in the west, and now   325
I sate with sad impatience. From within
Her solitary infant cried aloud.
The spot though fair seemed very desolate,
The longer I remained more desolate.
And, looking round, I saw the corner-stones,   330
Till then unmark'd, on either side the door
With dull red stains discoloured and stuck o'er
With tufts and hairs of wool, as if the sheep
That feed upon the commons thither came
Familiarly and found a couching-place   335
Even at her threshold.—The house-clock struck eight;
I turned and saw her distant a few steps.
Her face was pale and thin, her figure too
Was chang'd. As she unlocked the door she said,
'It grieves me you have waited here so long,   340
But in good truth I've wandered much of late
And sometimes, to my shame I speak, have need
Of my best prayers to bring me back again.'
While on the board she spread our evening meal
She told me she had lost her elder child,   345
That he for months had been a serving-boy
Apprenticed by the parish. 'I perceive
You look at me, and you have cause. Today
I have been travelling far, and many days
About the fields I wander, knowing this   350
Only, that what I seek I cannot find.
And so I waste my time: for I am changed;
And to myself,' said she, 'have done much wrong,
And to this helpless infant. I have slept
Weeping, and weeping I have waked; my tears   355
Have flow'd as if my body were not such
As others are, and I could never die.
But I am now in mind and in my heart
More easy, and I hope,' said she, 'that heaven
Will give me patience to endure the things   360
Which I behold at home.' It would have grieved
Your very heart to see her. Sir, I feel
The story linger in my heart. I fear
'Tis long and tedious, but my spirit clings

To that poor woman: so familiarly   365
Do I perceive her manner, and her look
And presence, and so deeply do I feel
Her goodness, that not seldom in my walks
A momentary trance comes over me;
And to myself I seem to muse on one   370
By sorrow laid asleep or borne away,
A human being destined to awake
To human life, or something very near
To human life, when he shall come again
For whom she suffered. Sir, it would have griev'd   375
Your very soul to see her: evermore
Her eye-lids droop'd, her eyes were downward cast;
And when she at her table gave me food
She did not look at me. Her voice was low,
Her body was subdued. In every act   380
Pertaining to her house-affairs appeared
The careless stillness which a thinking mind
Gives to an idle matter—still she sighed,
But yet no motion of the breast was seen,
No heaving of the heart. While by the fire   385
We sate together, sighs came on my ear;
I knew not how, and hardly whence they came.
I took my staff, and when I kissed her babe
The tears stood in her eyes. I left her then
With the best hope and comfort I could give;   390
She thanked me for my will, but for my hope
It seemed she did not thank me.
                              I returned
And took my rounds along this road again
Ere on its sunny bank the primrose flower
Had chronicled the earliest day of spring.   395
I found her sad and drooping; she had learn'd
No tidings of her husband: if he lived
She knew not that he lived; if he were dead
She knew not he was dead. She seemed the same
In person [or]¹ appearance, but her house   400
Bespoke a sleepy hand of negligence;
The floor was neither dry nor neat, the hearth
Was comfortless [   ],
The windows too were dim, and her few books,
Which, one upon the other, heretofore   405
Had been piled up against the corner-panes
In seemly order, now with straggling leaves
Lay scattered here and there, open or shut
As they had chanced to fall. Her infant babe
Had from its mother caught the trick of grief   410

---

1. The word "or" here was erased; later MSS read "and."

And sighed among its playthings. Once again
I turned towards the garden-gate and saw
More plainly still that poverty and grief
Were now come nearer to her: the earth was hard,
With weeds defaced and knots of withered grass;   415
No ridges there appeared of clear black mould,
No winter greenness; of her herbs and flowers
It seemed the better part were gnawed away
Or trampled on the earth; a chain of straw
Which had been twisted round the tender stem   420
Of a young apple-tree lay at its root;
The bark was nibbled round by truant sheep.
Margaret stood near, her infant in her arms,
And seeing that my eye was on the tree
She said, 'I fear it will be dead and gone   425
Ere Robert come again.' Towards the house
Together we returned, and she inquired
If I had any hope. But for her Babe
And for her little friendless Boy, she said,
She had no wish to live, that she must die   430
Of sorrow. Yet I saw the idle loom
Still in its place. His Sunday garments hung
Upon the self-same nail, his very staff
Stood undisturbed behind the door. And when
I passed this way beaten by Autumn winds   435
She told me that her little babe was dead
And she was left alone. That very time,
I yet remember, through the miry lane
She walked with me a mile, when the bare trees
Trickled with foggy damps, and in such sort   440
That any heart had ached to hear her begg'd
That wheresoe'er I went I still would ask
For him whom she had lost. We parted then,
Our final parting, for from that time forth
Did many seasons pass ere I returned   445
Into this tract again.
                          Five tedious years
She lingered in unquiet widowhood,
A wife and widow. Needs must it have been
A sore heart-wasting. I have heard, my friend,
That in that broken arbour she would sit   450
The idle length of half a sabbath day—
There, where you see the toadstool's lazy head—
And when a dog passed by she still would quit
The shade and look abroad. On this old Bench
For hours she sate, and evermore her eye   455
Was busy in the distance, shaping things
Which made her heart beat quick. Seest thou that path?
(The green-sward now has broken its grey line)

There to and fro she paced through many a day
Of the warm summer, from a belt of flax   460
That girt her waist spinning the long-drawn thread
With backward steps.—Yet ever as there passed
A man whose garments shewed the Soldier's red,
Or crippled Mendicant in Sailor's garb,
The little child who sate to turn the wheel   465
Ceased from his toil, and she with faltering voice,
Expecting still to learn her husband's fate,
Made many a fond inquiry; and when they
Whose presence gave no comfort were gone by,
Her heart was still more sad. And by yon gate   470
Which bars the traveller's road she often stood
And when a stranger horseman came, the latch
Would lift, and in his face look wistfully,
Most happy if from aught discovered there
Of tender feeling she might dare repeat   475
The same sad question. Meanwhile her poor hut
Sunk to decay, for he was gone whose hand
At the first nippings of October frost
Closed up each chink and with fresh bands of straw
Chequered the green-grown thatch. And so she lived   480
Through the long winter, reckless and alone,
Till this reft house by frost, and thaw, and rain
Was sapped; and when she slept the nightly damps
Did chill her breast, and in the stormy day
Her tattered clothes were ruffled by the wind   485
Even at the side of her own fire. Yet still
She loved this wretched spot, nor would for worlds
Have parted hence; and still that length of road
And this rude bench one torturing hope endeared,
Fast rooted at her heart, and here, my friend,   490
In sickness she remained, and here she died,
Last human tenant of these ruined walls."
     The old Man ceased: he saw that I was mov'd;
From that low Bench, rising instinctively,
I turned aside in weakness, nor had power   495
To thank him for the tale which he had told.
I stood, and leaning o'er the garden-gate
Reviewed that Woman's suff'rings, and it seemed
To comfort me while with a brother's love
I blessed her in the impotence of grief.   500
At length [towards] the [Cottage I returned]²
Fondly, and traced with milder interest
That secret spirit of humanity
Which, 'mid the calm oblivious tendencies
Of nature, 'mid her plants, her weeds, and flowers,   505

2. The words inside the brackets were added in MS. E.

And silent overgrowings, still survived.
The old man, seeing this, resumed and said,
"My Friend, enough to sorrow have you given,
The purposes of wisdom ask no more;
Be wise and chearful, and no longer read   510
The forms of things with an unworthy eye.
She sleeps in the calm earth, and peace is here.
I well remember that those very plumes,
Those weeds, and the high spear-grass on that wall,
By mist and silent rain-drops silver'd o'er,   515
As once I passed did to my heart convey
So still an image of tranquillity,
So calm and still, and looked so beautiful
Amid the uneasy thoughts which filled my mind,
That what we feel of sorrow and despair   520
From ruin and from change, and all the grief
The passing shews of being leave behind,
Appeared an idle dream that could not live
Where meditation was. I turned away
And walked along my road in happiness."   525
   He ceased. By this the sun declining shot
A slant and mellow radiance which began
To fall upon us where beneath the trees
We sate on that low bench, and now we felt,
Admonished thus, the sweet hour coming on.   530
A linnet warbled from those lofty elms,
A thrush sang loud, and other melodies,
At distance heard, peopled the milder air.
The old man rose and hoisted up his load.
Together casting then a farewell look   535
Upon those silent walls, we left the shade
And ere the stars were visible attained
A rustic inn, our evening resting-place.

THE END

1797–ca. 1799   1949

Michael[1]

A *Pastoral Poem*

If from the public way you turn your steps
Up the tumultuous brook of Green-head Ghyll,[2]

1. This poem is founded on the actual misfortunes of a family at Grasmere. Wordsworth wrote to Thomas Poole, on April 9, 1801, that he had attempted to picture a man "agitated by two of the most powerful affections of the human heart; the parental affection, and the love of property, *landed* property, including the feelings of inheritance, home, and personal and family independence." The subtitle shows Wordsworth's shift of the term "pastoral" from aristocratic make-believe to the tragic suffering of people in what he called "humble and rustic life."

2. Greenhead Ghyll (a ghyll is a ravine forming the bed of a stream) is not far from Wordsworth's cottage at Grasmere. The other places named in the poem are also in that vicinity.

You will suppose that with an upright path
Your feet must struggle; in such bold ascent
The pastoral mountains front you, face to face.
But, courage! for around that boisterous brook   5
The mountains have all opened out themselves,
And made a hidden valley of their own.
No habitation can be seen; but they
Who journey thither find themselves alone
With a few sheep, with rocks and stones, and kites[3]   10
That overhead are sailing in the sky.
It is in truth an utter solitude;
Nor should I have made mention of this Dell
But for one object which you might pass by,
Might see and notice not. Beside the brook   15
Appears a straggling heap of unhewn stones!
And to that simple object appertains
A story—unenriched with strange events,
Yet not unfit, I deem, for the fireside,
Or for the summer shade. It was the first   20
Of those domestic tales that spake to me
Of Shepherds, dwellers in the valleys, men
Whom I already loved;—not verily
For their own sakes, but for the fields and hills   25
Where was their occupation and abode.
And hence this Tale, while I was yet a Boy
Careless of books, yet having felt the power
Of Nature, by the gentle agency
Of natural objects, led me on to feel   30
For passions that were not my own, and think
(At random and imperfectly indeed)
On man, the heart of man, and human life.
Therefore, although it be a history
Homely and rude, I will relate the same   35
For the delight of a few natural hearts;
And, with yet fonder feeling, for the sake
Of youthful Poets, who among these hills
Will be my second self when I am gone.

    Upon the forest-side in Grasmere Vale   40
There dwelt a Shepherd, Michael was his name;
An old man, stout of heart, and strong of limb.
His bodily frame had been from youth to age
Of an unusual strength: his mind was keen,
Intense, and frugal, apt for all affairs,   45
And in his shepherd's calling he was prompt
And watchful more than ordinary men.
Hence had he learned the meaning of all winds,

---

3. Hawks.

Of blasts of every tone; and, oftentimes,
When others heeded not, he heard the South   50
Make subterraneous music, like the noise
Of bagpipers on distant Highland hills.
The Shepherd, at such warning, of his flock
Bethought him, and he to himself would say,
"The winds are now devising work for me!"   55
And, truly, at all times, the storm, that drives
The traveller to a shelter, summoned him
Up to the mountains: he had been alone
Amid the heart of many thousand mists,
That came to him, and left him, on the heights.   60
So lived he till his eightieth year was past.
And grossly that man errs, who should suppose
That the green valleys, and the streams and rocks,
Were things indifferent to the Shepherd's thoughts.
Fields, where with cheerful spirits he had breathed 65
The common air; hills, which with vigorous step
He had so often climbed; which had impressed
So many incidents upon his mind
Of hardship, skill or courage, joy or fear;
Which, like a book, preserved the memory   70
Of the dumb animals, whom he had saved,
Had fed or sheltered, linking to such acts
The certainty of honourable gain;
Those fields, those hills—what could they less? had laid
Strong hold on his affections, were to him   75
A pleasurable feeling of blind love,
The pleasure which there is in life itself.

His days had not been passed in singleness.
His Helpmate was a comely matron, old—
Though younger than himself full twenty years.   80
She was a woman of a stirring life,
Whose heart was in her house: two wheels she had
Of antique form; this large, for spinning wool;
That small, for flax; and if one wheel had rest,
It was because the other was at work.   85
The Pair had but one inmate in their house,
An only Child, who had been born to them
When Michael, telling o'er his years, began
To deem that he was old,—in shepherd's phrase,
With one foot in the grave. This only Son,   90
With two brave sheep-dogs tried in many a storm,
The one of an inestimable worth,
Made all their household. I may truly say,
That they were as a proverb in the vale
For endless industry. When day was gone,   95
And from their occupations out of doors

The Son and Father were come home, even then,
Their labour did not cease; unless when all
Turned to the cleanly supper-board, and there,
Each with a mess of pottage and skimmed milk,   100
Sat round the basket piled with oaten cakes,
And their plain home-made cheese. Yet when the meal
Was ended, Luke (for so the Son was named)
And his old Father both betook themselves
To such convenient work as might employ   105
Their hands by the fire-side; perhaps to card
Wool for the Housewife's spindle, or repair
Some injury done to sickle, flail, or scythe,
Or other implement of house or field.

    Down from the ceiling, by the chimney's edge,   110
That in our ancient uncouth country style
With huge and black projection overbrowed
Large space beneath, as duly as the light
Of day grew dim the Housewife hung a lamp;
An aged utensil, which had performed   115
Service beyond all others of its kind.
Early at evening did it burn—and late,
Surviving comrade of uncounted hours,
Which, going by from year to year, had found,
And left the couple neither gay perhaps   120
Nor cheerful, yet with objects and with hopes,
Living a life of eager industry.
And now, when Luke had reached his eighteenth year,
There by the light of his old lamp they sate,
Father and Son, while far into the night   125
The Housewife plied her own peculiar work,
Making the cottage through the silent hours
Murmur as with the sound of summer flies.
This light was famous in its neighbourhood,
And was a public symbol of the life   130
That thrifty Pair had lived. For, as it chanced,
Their cottage on a plot of rising ground
Stood single, with large prospect, north and south,
High into Easedale, up to Dunmail-Raise,
And westward to the village near the lake;   135
And from this constant light, so regular
And so far seen, the House itself, by all
Who dwelt within the limits of the vale,
Both old and young, was named THE EVENING STAR.

    Thus living on through such a length of years,   140
The Shepherd, if he loved himself, must needs
Have loved his Helpmate; but to Michael's heart
This son of his old age was yet more dear—

Less from instinctive tenderness, the same
Fond spirit that blindly works in the blood of all—   145
Than that a child, more than all other gifts
That earth can offer to declining man,
Brings hope with it, and forward-looking thoughts,
And stirrings of inquietude, when they
By tendency of nature needs must fail.   150
Exceeding was the love he bare to him,
His heart and his heart's joy! For oftentimes
Old Michael, while he was a babe in arms,
Had done him female service, not alone
For pastime and delight, as is the use   155
Of fathers, but with patient mind enforced
To acts of tenderness; and he had rocked
His cradle, as with a woman's gentle hand.

    And, in a later time, ere yet the Boy
Had put on boy's attire, did Michael love,   160
Albeit of a stern unbending mind,
To have the Young-one in his sight, when he
Wrought in the field, or on his shepherd's stool
Sate with a fettered sheep before him stretched
Under the large old oak, that near his door   165
Stood single, and, from matchless depth of shade,
Chosen for the Shearer's covert from the sun,
Thence in our rustic dialect was called
The CLIPPING TREE, a name which yet it bears.
There, while they two were sitting in the shade,   170
With others round them, earnest all and blithe,
Would Michael exercise his heart with looks
Of fond correction and reproof bestowed
Upon the Child, if he disturbed the sheep
By catching at their legs, or with his shouts   175
Scared them, while they lay still beneath the shears.

    And when by Heaven's good grace the boy grew up
A healthy Lad, and carried in his cheek
Two steady roses that were five years old;
Then Michael from a winter coppice[4] cut   180
With his own hand a sapling, which he hooped
With iron, making it throughout in all
Due requisites a perfect shepherd's staff,
And gave it to the Boy; wherewith equipt
He as a watchman oftentimes was placed   185
At gate or gap, to stem or turn the flock;
And, to his office prematurely called,
There stood the urchin, as you will divine,

---

4. Grove of small trees.

Something between a hindrance and a help;
And for this cause not always, I believe,   190
Receiving from his Father hire of praise;
Though nought was left undone which staff, or voice,
Or looks, or threatening gestures, could perform.

But soon as Luke, full ten years old, could stand
Against the mountain blasts; and to the heights,   195
Not fearing toil, nor length of weary ways,
He with his Father daily went, and they
Were as companions, why should I relate
That objects which the Shepherd loved before
Were dearer now? that from the Boy there came   200
Feelings and emanations—things which were
Light to the sun and music to the wind;
And that the old Man's heart seemed born again?

Thus in his Father's sight the Boy grew up:
And now, when he had reached his eighteenth year,   205
He was his comfort and his daily hope.

While in this sort the simple household lived
From day to day, to Michael's ear there came
Distressful tidings. Long before the time
Of which I speak, the Shepherd had been bound   210
In surety for his brother's son, a man
Of an industrious life, and ample means;
But unforeseen misfortunes suddenly
Had prest upon him; and old Michael now
Was summoned to discharge the forfeiture,   215
A grievous penalty, but little less
Than half his substance. This unlooked-for claim,
At the first hearing, for a moment took
More hope out of his life than he supposed
That any old man ever could have lost.   220
As soon as he had armed himself with strength
To look his trouble in the face, it seemed
The Shepherd's sole resource to sell at once
A portion of his patrimonial fields.
Such was his first resolve; he thought again,   225
And his heart failed him. "Isabel," said he,
Two evenings after he had heard the news,
"I have been toiling more than seventy years,
And in the open sunshine of God's love
Have we all lived; yet if these fields of ours   230
Should pass into a stranger's hand, I think
That I could not lie quiet in my grave.
Our lot is a hard lot; the sun himself
Has scarcely been more diligent than I;

And I have lived to be a fool at last   235
To my own family. An evil man
That was, and made an evil choice, if he
Were false to us; and if he were not false,
There are ten thousand to whom loss like this
Had been no sorrow. I forgive him;—but   240
'Twere better to be dumb than to talk thus.

 "When I began, my purpose was to speak
Of remedies and of a cheerful hope.
Our Luke shall leave us, Isabel; the land
Shall not go from us, and it shall be free;   245
He shall possess it, free as is the wind
That passes over it. We have, thou know'st,
Another kinsman—he will be our friend
In this distress. He is a prosperous man,
Thriving in trade—and Luke to him shall go,   250
And with his kinsman's help and his own thrift
He quickly will repair this loss, and then
He may return to us. If here he stay,
What can be done? Where every one is poor,
What can be gained?"
       At this the old Man paused,   255
And Isabel sat silent, for her mind
Was busy, looking back into past times.
There's Richard Bateman,[5] thought she to herself,
He was a parish-boy—at the church-door
They made a gathering for him, shillings, pence   260
And halfpennies, wherewith the neighbours bought
A basket, which they filled with pedlar's wares;
And, with this basket on his arm, the lad
Went up to London, found a master there,
Who, out of many, chose the trusty boy   265
To go and overlook his merchandise
Beyond the seas; where he grew wondrous rich,
And left estates and monies to the poor,
And, at his birth-place, built a chapel floored
With marble, which he sent from foreign lands.   270
These thoughts, and many others of like sort,
Passed quickly through the mind of Isabel,
And her face brightened. The old Man was glad,
And thus resumed:—"Well, Isabel! this scheme
These two days, has been meat and drink to me.   275
Far more than we have lost is left us yet.
—We have enough—I wish indeed that I
Were younger;—but this hope is a good hope.
Make ready Luke's best garments, of the best

5. "The story alluded to here is well known in the   on the road leading from Kendal to Ambleside"
country. The chapel is called Ings Chapel and is   [Wordsworth's note].

Buy for him more, and let us send him forth   280
To-morrow, or the next day, or to-night:
—If he *could* go, the Boy should go to-night."

Here Michael ceased, and to the fields went forth
With a light heart. The Housewife for five days
Was restless morn and night, and all day long   285
Wrought on with her best fingers to prepare
Things needful for the journey of her son.
But Isabel was glad when Sunday came
To stop her in her work: for, when she lay
By Michael's side, she through the last two nights   290
Heard him, how he was troubled in his sleep:
And when they rose at morning she could see
That all his hopes were gone. That day at noon
She said to Luke, while they two by themselves
Were sitting at the door, "Thou must not go: 295
We have no other Child but thee to lose,
None to remember—do not go away,
For if thou leave thy Father he will die."
The Youth made answer with a jocund voice;
And Isabel, when she had told her fears,   300
Recovered heart. That evening her best fare
Did she bring forth, and all together sat
Like happy people round a Christmas fire.

With daylight Isabel resumed her work;
And all the ensuing week the house appeared   305
As cheerful as a grove in Spring: at length
The expected letter from their kinsman came,
With kind assurances that he would do
His utmost for the welfare of the Boy;
To which, requests were added, that forthwith   310
He might be sent to him. Ten times or more
The letter was read over; Isabel
Went forth to show it to the neighbours round;
Nor was there at that time on English land
A prouder heart than Luke's. When Isabel   315
Had to her house returned, the old Man said,
"He shall depart to-morrow." To this word
The Housewife answered, talking much of things
Which, if at such short notice he should go,
Would surely be forgotten. But at length   320
She gave consent, and Michael was at ease.

Near the tumultuous brook of Green-head Ghyll,
In that deep valley, Michael had designed
To build a Sheep-fold;[6] and, before he heard

---

6. Pen for sheep. "A sheepfold in these mountains is an unroofed building of stone walls, with different
divisions" [Wordsworth's note].

The tidings of his melancholy loss,   325
For this same purpose he had gathered up
A heap of stones, which by the streamlet's edge
Lay thrown together, ready for the work.
With Luke that evening thitherward he walked:
And soon as they had reached the place he stopped,   330
And thus the old Man spake to him:—"My Son,
To-morrow thou wilt leave me: with full heart
I look upon thee, for thou art the same
That wert a promise to me ere thy birth,
And all thy life hast been my daily joy.   335
I will relate to thee some little part
Of our two histories; 'twill do thee good
When thou art from me, even if I should touch
On things thou canst not know of.——After thou
First cam'st into the world—as oft befals   340
To new-born infants—thou didst sleep away
Two days, and blessings from thy Father's tongue
Then fell upon thee. Day by day passed on,
And still I loved thee with increasing love.
Never to living ear came sweeter sounds   345
Than when I heard thee by our own fire-side
First uttering, without words, a natural tune;
While thou, a feeding babe, didst in thy joy
Sing at thy Mother's breast. Month followed month,
And in the open fields my life was passed   350
And on the mountains; else I think that thou
Hadst been brought up upon thy Father's knees.
But we were playmates, Luke: among these hills,
As well thou knowest, in us the old and young
Have played together, nor with me didst thou   355
Lack any pleasure which a boy can know."
Luke had a manly heart; but at these words
He sobbed aloud. The old Man grasped his hand,
And said, "Nay, do not take it so—I see
That these are things of which I need not speak.   360
—Even to the utmost I have been to thee
A kind and a good Father: and herein
I but repay a gift which I myself
Received at others' hands; for, though now old
Beyond the common life of man, I still   365
Remember them who loved me in my youth.
Both of them sleep together: here they lived,
As all their Forefathers had done; and when
At length their time was come, they were not loth
To give their bodies to the family mould.   370
I wished that thou should'st live the life they lived:
But, 'tis a long time to look back, my Son,
And see so little gain from threescore years.

These fields were burthened[7] when they came to me;
Till I was forty years of age, not more   375
Than half of my inheritance was mine.
I toiled and toiled; God blessed me in my work,
And till these three weeks past the land was free.
—It looks as if it never could endure
Another Master. Heaven forgive me, Luke,   380
If I judge ill for thee, but it seems good
That thou should'st go."
                              At this the old Man paused;
Then, pointing to the stones near which they stood,
Thus, after a short silence, he resumed:
"This was a work for us; and now, my Son,   385
It is a work for me. But, lay one stone—
Here, lay it for me, Luke, with thine own hands.
Nay, Boy, be of good hope;—we both may live
To see a better day. At eighty-four
I still am strong and hale;—do thou thy part;   390
I will do mine.—I will begin again
With many tasks that were resigned to thee:
Up to the heights, and in among the storms,
Will I without thee go again, and do
All works which I was wont to do alone,   395
Before I knew thy face.—Heaven bless thee, Boy!
Thy heart these two weeks has been beating fast
With many hopes; it should be so—yes—yes—
I knew that thou could'st never have a wish
To leave me, Luke: thou hast been bound to me   400
Only by links of love: when thou art gone,
What will be left to us!—But, I forget
My purposes. Lay now the corner-stone,
As I requested; and hereafter, Luke,
When thou art gone away, should evil men   405
Be thy companions, think of me, my Son,
And of this moment; hither turn thy thoughts,
And God will strengthen thee: amid all fear
And all temptation, Luke, I pray that thou
May'st bear in mind the life thy Fathers lived,   410
Who, being innocent, did for that cause
Bestir them in good deeds. Now, fare thee well—
When thou return'st, thou in this place wilt see
A work which is not here: a covenant
'Twill be between us; but, whatever fate   415
Befal thee, I shall love thee to the last,
And bear thy memory with me to the grave."

    The Shepherd ended here; and Luke stooped down,
And, as his Father had requested, laid

7. Mortgaged.

The first stone of the Sheep-fold. At the sight   420
The old Man's grief broke from him; to his heart
He pressed his Son, he kissèd him and wept;
And to the house together they returned.
—Hushed was that House in peace, or seeming peace,
Ere the night fell:—with morrow's dawn the Boy   425
Began his journey, and when he had reached
The public way, he put on a bold face;
And all the neighbours, as he passed their doors,
Came forth with wishes and with farewell prayers,
That followed him till he was out of sight.   430

    A good report did from their Kinsman come,
Of Luke and his well-doing: and the Boy
Wrote loving letters, full of wondrous news,
Which, as the Housewife phrased it, were throughout
"The prettiest letters that were ever seen."   435
Both parents read them with rejoicing hearts.
So, many months passed on: and once again
The Shepherd went about his daily work
With confident and cheerful thoughts; and now
Sometimes when he could find a leisure hour   440
He to that valley took his way, and there
Wrought at the Sheep-fold. Meantime Luke began
To slacken in his duty; and, at length,
He in the dissolute city gave himself
To evil courses: ignominy and shame   445
Fell on him, so that he was driven at last
To seek a hiding-place beyond the seas.

    There is a comfort in the strength of love;
'Twill make a thing endurable, which else
Would overset the brain, or break the heart: 450
I have conversed with more than one who well
Remember the old Man, and what he was
Years after he had heard this heavy news.
His bodily frame had been from youth to age
Of an unusual strength. Among the rocks   455
He went, and still looked up to sun and cloud,
And listened to the wind; and, as before
Performed all kinds of labour for his sheep,
And for the land, his small inheritance.
And to that hollow dell from time to time   460
Did he repair, to build the Fold of which
His flock had need. 'Tis not forgotten yet
The pity which was then in every heart
For the old Man—and 'tis believed by all
That many and many a day he thither went,   465
And never lifted up a single stone.

There, by the Sheep-fold, sometimes was he seen
Sitting alone, or with his faithful Dog,
Then old, beside him, lying at his feet.
The length of full seven years, from time to time,   470
He at the building of this Sheep-fold wrought,
And left the work unfinished when he died.
Three years, or little more, did Isabel
Survive her Husband: at her death the estate
Was sold, and went into a stranger's hand.   475
The Cottage which was named the EVENING STAR
Is gone—the ploughshare has been through the ground
On which it stood; great changes have been wrought
In all the neighbourhood:—yet the oak is left
That grew beside their door; and the remains   480
Of the unfinished Sheep-fold may be seen
Beside the boisterous brook of Green-head Ghyll.

Oct. 11–Dec. 9, 1800   1800

Resolution and Independence[1]

1

There was a roaring in the wind all night;
The rain came heavily and fell in floods;
But now the sun is rising calm and bright;
The birds are singing in the distant woods;
Over his own sweet voice the Stock-dove broods;   5
The Jay makes answer as the Magpie chatters;
And all the air is filled with pleasant noise of waters.

2

All things that love the sun are out of doors;
The sky rejoices in the morning's birth;
The grass is bright with rain-drops;—on the moors   10
The hare is running races in her mirth;
And with her feet she from the plashy earth
Raises a mist; that, glittering in the sun,
Runs with her all the way, wherever she doth run.

3

I was a Traveller then upon the moor;   15
I saw the hare that raced about with joy;
I heard the woods and distant waters roar;

1. Wordsworth tells us that "I was in the state of feeling described in the beginning of the poem, while crossing over Barton Fell from Mr. Clarkson's, at the foot of Ullswater, towards Askam. The image of the hare I then observed on the ridge of the Fell." Eighteen months later, these events, recollected in tranquility, were transformed into this poem of personal crisis, mastered by an imaginative process of spontaneous mythmaking. The metamorphoses of the still old man (stanzas 8 ff.) end when he modulates into the archetypal figure of the eternal and haunted wanderer, of whom Coleridge's Ancient Mariner had been the most recent embodiment. Unlike Coleridge's, however, Wordsworth's is a natural supernaturalism, for the old leech gatherer remains stubbornly matter-of-fact.

Or heard them not, as happy as a boy:
The pleasant season did my heart employ:
My old remembrances went from me wholly;   20
And all the ways of men, so vain and melancholy.

4

But, as it sometimes chanceth, from the might
Of joy in minds that can no further go,
As high as we have mounted in delight
In our dejection do we sink as low;   25
To me that morning did it happen so;
And fears and fancies thick upon me came;
Dim sadness—and blind thoughts, I knew not, nor could name.

5

I heard the sky-lark warbling in the sky;
And I bethought me of the playful hare: 30
Even such a happy Child of earth am I;
Even as these blissful creatures do I fare;
Far from the world I walk, and from all care;
But there may come another day to me—
Solitude, pain of heart, distress, and poverty.   35

6

My whole life I have lived in pleasant thought,
As if life's business were a summer mood;
As if all needful things would come unsought
To genial faith, still rich in genial good;
But how can He expect that others should   40
Build for him, sow for him, and at his call
Love him, who for himself will take no heed at all?

7

I thought of Chatterton,[2] the marvellous Boy,
The sleepless Soul that perished in his pride;
Of Him who walked in glory and in joy   45
Following his plough, along the mountain-side:[3]
By our own spirits are we deified:
We Poets in our youth begin in gladness;
But thereof come in the end despondency and madness.

8

Now, whether it were by peculiar grace,   50
A leading from above, a something given,
Yet it befel, that, in this lonely place,
When I with these untoward thoughts had striven,
Beside a pool bare to the eye of heaven
I saw a Man before me unawares: 55
The oldest man he seemed that ever wore grey hairs.

2. Thomas Chatterton (1752–1770), a poet of great talent who, in his loneliness and dire poverty, poisoned himself at the age of 17 and so became the prime Romantic symbol of neglected young genius.

3. Robert Burns, also considered at that time as a natural poet who died young and poor, without adequate recognition.

9

As a huge stone is sometimes seen to lie
Couched on the bald top of an eminence;
Wonder to all who do the same espy,
By what means it could thither come, and whence;   60
So that it seems a thing endued with sense:
Like a sea-beast crawled forth, that on a shelf
Of rock or sand reposeth, there to sun itself;

10

Such seemed this Man,[4] not all alive nor dead,
Nor all asleep—in his extreme old age: 65
His body was bent double, feet and head
Coming together in life's pilgrimage;
As if some dire constraint of pain, or rage
Of sickness felt by him in times long past,
A more than human weight upon his frame had cast.   70

11

Himself he propped, limbs, body, and pale face,
Upon a long grey staff of shaven wood:
And, still as I drew near with gentle pace,
Upon the margin of that moorish flood
Motionless as a cloud the old Man stood,   75
That heareth not the loud winds when they call;
And moveth all together, if it move at all.

12

At length, himself unsettling, he the pond
Stirred with his staff, and fixedly did look
Upon the muddy water, which he conned,   80
As if he had been reading in a book:
And now a stranger's privilege I took;
And, drawing to his side, to him did say,
"This morning gives us promise of a glorious day."

13

A gentle answer did the old Man make,   85
In courteous speech which forth he slowly drew:
And him with further words I thus bespake,
"What occupation do you there pursue?
This is a lonesome place for one like you."
Ere he replied, a flash of mild surprise   90
Broke from the sable orbs of his yet-vivid eyes.

14

His words came feebly, from a feeble chest,
But each in solemn order followed each,

4. In Wordsworth's own analysis of this passage, he says that the stone is endowed with something of life, the sea beast is stripped of some of its life to assimilate it to the stone, and the old man divested of enough life and motion to make "the two objects unite and coalesce in just comparison." He used the passage to demonstrate his theory of how the "conferring, the abstracting, and the modifying powers of the Imagination . . . are all brought into conjunction" (Preface to the *Poems* of 1815). Compare Coleridge's brief definitions of the imagination in *Biographia Literaria*, Chapter 13.

With something of a lofty utterance drest—
Choice word and measured phrase, above the reach   95
Of ordinary men; a stately speech;
Such as grave Livers[5] do in Scotland use,
Religious men, who give to God and man their dues.

                    15
He told, that to these waters he had come
To gather leeches,[6] being old and poor: 100
Employment hazardous and wearisome!
And he had many hardships to endure:
From pond to pond he roamed, from moor to moor;
Housing, with God's good help, by choice or chance;
And in this way he gained an honest maintenance.   105

                    16
The old Man still stood talking by my side;
But now his voice to me was like a stream
Scarce heard; nor word from word could I divide;
And the whole body of the Man did seem
Like one whom I had met with in a dream;   110
Or like a man from some far region sent,
To give me human strength, by apt admonishment.

                    17
My former thoughts returned: the fear that kills;
And hope that is unwilling to be fed;
Cold, pain, and labour, and all fleshly ills;   115
And mighty Poets in their misery dead.
—Perplexed, and longing to be comforted,
My question eagerly did I renew,
"How is it that you live, and what is it you do?"

                    18
He with a smile did then his words repeat;   120
And said, that, gathering leeches, far and wide
He travelled; stirring thus about his feet
The waters of the pools where they abide.
"Once I could meet with them on every side;
But they have dwindled long by slow decay;   125
Yet still I persevere, and find them where I may."

                    19
While he was talking thus, the lonely place,
The old Man's shape, and speech—all troubled me:
In my mind's eye I seemed to see him pace
About the weary moors continually,   130
Wandering about alone and silently.
While I these thoughts within myself pursued,
He, having made a pause, the same discourse renewed.

5. Those who live gravely.   water, stirred the water to attract them and, when
6. Leeches were used to draw blood for curative   they fastened themselves to his legs, picked them
purposes. A leech gatherer, bare legged in shallow   off.

20

And soon with this he other matter blended,
Cheerfully uttered, with demeanour kind,   135
But stately in the main; and when he ended,
I could have laughed myself to scorn to find
In that decrepit Man so firm a mind.
"God," said I, "be my help and stay[7] secure;
I'll think of the Leech-gatherer on the lonely moor!"   140

May 3–July 4, 1802   1807

I Wandered Lonely as a Cloud

I wandered lonely as a cloud
That floats on high o'er vales and hills,
When all at once I saw a crowd,
A host, of golden daffodils;
Beside the lake, beneath the trees,   5
Fluttering and dancing in the breeze.

Continuous as the stars that shine
And twinkle on the milky way,
They stretched in never-ending line
Along the margin of a bay: 10
Ten thousand saw I at a glance,
Tossing their heads in sprightly dance.

The waves beside them danced; but they
Out-did the sparkling waves in glee:
A poet could not but be gay,   15
In such a jocund company:
I gazed—and gazed—but little thought
What wealth the show to me had brought:

For oft, when on my couch I lie
In vacant or in pensive mood,   20
They flash upon that inward eye
Which is the bliss of solitude;
And then my heart with pleasure fills,
And dances with the daffodils.

1804   1807

My Heart Leaps Up

My heart leaps up when I behold
A rainbow in the sky:

7. Support (a noun).

> So was it when my life began;
> So is it now I am a man;
> So be it when I shall grow old,   5
>   Or let me die!
> The Child is father of the Man;
> And I could wish my days to be
> Bound each to each by natural piety.[1]

Mar. 26, 1802   1807

Ode: Intimations of Immortality   Wordsworth said about this
Ode to Isabella Fenwick:

This was composed during my residence at Town End, Grasmere; two years at least passed between the writing of the four first stanzas and the remaining part. To the attentive and competent reader the whole sufficiently explains itself; but there may be no harm in adverting here to particular feelings or *experiences* of my own mind on which the structure of the poem partly rests. Nothing was more difficult for me in childhood than to admit the notion of death as a state applicable to my own being. I have said elsewhere [in the opening stanza of We Are Seven]:

> —A simple child,
> That lightly draws its breath,
> And feels its life in every limb,
> What should it know of death!—

But it was not so much from [feelings] of animal vivacity that *my* difficulty came as from a sense of the indomitableness of the spirit within me. I used to brood over the stories of Enoch and Elijah, and almost to persuade myself that, whatever might become of others, I should be translated, in something of the same way, to heaven. With a feeling congenial to this, I was often unable to think of external things as having external existence, and I communed with all that I saw as something not apart from, but inherent in, my own immaterial nature. Many times while going to school have I grasped at a wall or tree to recall myself from this abyss of idealism to the reality. At that time I was afraid of such processes. In later periods of life I have deplored, as we have all reason to do, a subjugation of an opposite character, and have rejoiced over the remembrances, as is expressed in the lines—

> Obstinate questionings
> Of sense and outward things,
> Fallings from us, vanishings; etc.

---

1. As distinguished from piety based on the Scriptures, in which God makes the rainbow the token of his covenant with Noah and all his descendants (Genesis 9.12–17). The religious sentiment that binds Wordsworth's mature self to that of his childhood is a continuing responsiveness to the miracle of ordinary things.

To that dreamlike vividness and splendor which invest objects of sight in childhood, everyone, I believe, if he would look back, could bear testimony, and I need not dwell upon it here: but having in the Poem regarded it as presumptive evidence of a prior state of existence, I think it right to protest against a conclusion, which has given pain to some good and pious persons, that I meant to inculcate such a belief. It is far too shadowy a notion to be recommended to faith, as more than an element in our instincts of immortality. But let us bear in mind that, though the idea is not advanced in revelation, there is nothing there to contradict it, and the fall of Man presents an analogy in its favor. Accordingly, a pre-existent state has entered into the popular creeds of many nations; and, among all persons acquainted with classic literature, is known as an ingredient in Platonic philosophy. Archimedes said that he could move the world if he had a point whereon to rest his machine. Who has not felt the same aspirations as regards the world of his own mind? Having to wield some of its elements when I was impelled to write this Poem on the 'Immortality of the Soul,' I took hold of the notion of pre-existence as having sufficient foundation in humanity for authorizing me to make for my purpose the best use of it I could as a Poet. (Wordsworth)

As Wordsworth says, Plato held the doctrine that the soul is immortal and exists separately from the body both before birth and after death. But while the *Ode* proposes that the soul only gradually loses "the vision splendid" after birth, Plato maintained the contrary: that the knowledge of the eternal Ideas, which the soul had acquired by direct acquaintance, is totally lost at the instant of birth, and must be gradually "recollected" by philosophical discipline in the course of this life (*Phaedo* 73–77). Wordsworth's metaphorical use of the concept of preexistence in his poem resembles more closely the view of some Neoplatonists that the glory of the unborn soul is gradually quenched by its descent into the darkness of matter.

Wordsworth was troubled by objections to the Christian heterodoxy of this apparent claim for the preexistence, as against the orthodox belief in the survival, of the soul. He insisted that he did not intend to assert this as doctrine, but only to use it as a poetic postulate, enabling him to deal "as a poet" with an experience to which everyone, as he says, "if he would look back, could bear testimony." This experience is a universal human one: that the loss of youth involves the loss of a freshness and radiance investing all experience. Coleridge's *Dejection: An Ode*, which he wrote after he had heard the first four stanzas of Wordsworth's poem, employs a similar figurative technique for a comparable, though more devastating, experience of loss. As with all poems so large and rich as this one of Wordsworth's, there are divergent interpretations of its purport, emphases, and organization. But most commentators agree that the poem offers two different perspectives on the fact that growing up is also a stage on the way to death, and almost all agree that it is one of the greatest instances of the very difficult form of the irregular English ode. The Catholic poet G. M. Hopkins remarked: "For my part I should think St. George and St. Thomas of Canterbury wore roses in heaven for England's sake on the day that *Ode*, not without their intercession, was penned."

The original published version of this poem had as its title only "Ode," and then as epigraph *"Paulo maiora canamus"* ("Let us sing of somewhat higher things") from Virgil's *Eclogue 4.*

Ode

Intimations of Immortality from Recollections of Early Childhood

The Child is Father of the Man;
And I could wish my days to be
Bound each to each by natural piety.[1]

1

There was a time when meadow, grove, and stream,
The earth, and every common sight,
     To me did seem
     Apparelled in celestial light,
The glory and the freshness of a dream.   5
It is not now as it hath been of yore;—
     Turn wheresoe'er I may,
     By night or day,
The things which I have seen I now can see no more.

2

     The Rainbow comes and goes,   10
     And lovely is the Rose,
     The Moon doth with delight
Look round her when the heavens are bare,
     Waters on a starry night
     Are beautiful and fair;   15
     The sunshine is a glorious birth;
     But yet I know, where'er I go,
That there hath past away a glory from the earth.

3

Now, while the birds thus sing a joyous song,
     And while the young lambs bound   20
     As to the tabor's sound,[2]
To me alone there came a thought of grief:
A timely utterance[3] gave that thought relief,
     And I again am strong:
The cataracts blow their trumpets from the steep;   25
No more shall grief of mine the season wrong;
I hear the Echoes through the mountains throng,
The Winds come to me from the fields of sleep,[4]

1. The concluding lines of Wordsworth's *My Heart Leaps Up,* above.
2. A tabor is a small drum often used to beat time for dancing.
3. Perhaps *My Heart Leaps Up,* perhaps *Resolution and Independence,* perhaps not a poem at all.

4. Of the many suggested interpretations, the simplest is "from the fields where they were sleeping." Wordsworth often associated a rising wind with the revival of spirit and of poetic inspiration; see, e.g., the opening passage of *The Prelude.*

And all the earth is gay;
          Land and sea   30
     Give themselves up to jollity,
          And with the heart of May
     Doth every Beast keep holiday;—
          Thou Child of Joy,
Shout round me, let me hear thy shouts, thou happy
     Shepherd-boy!   35

                              4

Ye blessed Creatures, I have heard the call
     Ye to each other make; I see
The heavens laugh with you in your jubilee;
     My heart is at your festival,
          My head hath its coronal,[5]   40
The fulness of your bliss, I feel—I feel it all.
          Oh evil day! if I were sullen
          While Earth herself is adorning,
               This sweet May-morning,
          And the Children are culling   45
               On every side,
          In a thousand valleys far and wide,
          Fresh flowers; while the sun shines warm,
And the Babe leaps up on his Mother's arm:—
          I hear, I hear, with joy I hear!   50
     —But there's a Tree, of many, one,
A single Field which I have looked upon,
Both of them speak of something that is gone:
          The Pansy at my feet
          Doth the same tale repeat: 55
Whither is fled the visionary gleam?
Where is it now, the glory and the dream?

                              5

Our birth is but a sleep and a forgetting:
The Soul that rises with us, our life's Star,[6]
          Hath had elsewhere its setting,   60
          And cometh from afar:
          Not in entire forgetfulness,
          And not in utter nakedness,
But trailing clouds of glory do we come
          From God, who is our home: 65
Heaven lies about us in our infancy!
Shades of the prison-house begin to close
          Upon the growing Boy,
But He beholds the light, and whence it flows,
          He sees it in his joy;   70
The Youth, who daily farther from the east
          Must travel, still is Nature's Priest,

5. Circlet of wild flowers, with which the shep-   6. The sun, as metaphor for the soul.
herd boys trimmed their hats in May.

And by the vision splendid
Is on his way attended;
At length the Man perceives it die away,   75
And fade into the light of common day.

6

Earth fills her lap with pleasures of her own;
Yearnings she hath in her own natural kind,
And, even with something of a Mother's mind,
          And no unworthy aim,   80
          The homely[7] Nurse doth all she can
To make her Foster-child, her Inmate Man,
          Forget the glories he hath known,
And that imperial palace whence he came.

7

Behold the Child among his new-born blisses,   85
A six years' Darling of a pigmy size!
See, where 'mid work of his own hand he lies,
Fretted[8] by sallies of his mother's kisses,
With light upon him from his father's eyes!
See, at his feet, some little plan or chart,   90
Some fragment from his dream of human life,
Shaped by himself with newly-learnèd art;
          A wedding or a festival,
          A mourning or a funeral;
          And this hath now his heart,   95
          And unto this he frames his song:
          Then will he fit his tongue
To dialogues of business, love, or strife;
          But it will not be long
          Ere this be thrown aside,   100
          And with new joy and pride
The little Actor cons another part;
Filling from time to time his "humorous stage"[9]
With all the Persons, down to palsied Age,
That Life brings with her in her equipage;   105
          As if his whole vocation
          Were endless imitation.

8

Thou, whose exterior semblance doth belie
          Thy Soul's immensity;
Thou best Philosopher, who yet dost keep   110
Thy heritage, thou Eye among the blind,
That, deaf and silent, read'st the eternal deep,
Haunted for ever by the eternal mind,—
          Mighty Prophet! Seer blest!

7. In the old sense, "simple and friendly."
8. "Irritated," or possibly in the old sense, "checkered over."
9. From a sonnet by the Elizabethan poet Samuel Daniel. In Daniel's age, "humorous" meant "capricious," and also referred to the various characters and temperaments ("humors") represented in drama.

On whom those truths do rest,   115
Which we are toiling all our lives to find,
In darkness lost, the darkness of the grave;
Thou, over whom thy Immortality
Broods like the Day, a Master o'er a Slave,
A Presence which is not to be put by;   120
Thou little Child, yet glorious in the might
Of heaven-born freedom on thy being's height,
Why with such earnest pains dost thou provoke
The years to bring the inevitable yoke,
Thus blindly with thy blessedness at strife?   125
Full soon thy Soul shall have her earthly freight,
And custom lie upon thee with a weight,
Heavy as frost, and deep almost as life!

9

O joy! that in our embers
Is something that doth live,   130
That nature yet remembers
What was so fugitive!
The thought of our past years in me doth breed
Perpetual benediction: not indeed
For that which is most worthy to be blest;   135
Delight and liberty, the simple creed
Of Childhood, whether busy or at rest,
With new-fledged hope still fluttering in his breast:—
Not for these I raise
The song of thanks and praise;   140
But for those obstinate questionings
Of sense and outward things,
Fallings from us, vanishings;
Blank misgivings of a Creature
Moving about in worlds not realised,[1]   145
High instincts before which our mortal Nature
Did tremble like a guilty Thing surprised:
But for those first affections,
Those shadowy recollections,
Which, be they what they may,   150
Are yet the fountain light of all our day,
Are yet a master light of all our seeing;
Uphold us, cherish, and have power to make
Our noisy years seem moments in the being
Of the eternal Silence: truths that wake,   155
To perish never;
Which neither listlessness, nor mad endeavour,
Nor Man nor Boy,
Nor all that is at enmity with joy,
Can utterly abolish or destroy!   160

---

1. Not seeming real; see Wordsworth's comment in the headnote to the *Ode*.

Hence in a season of calm weather
  Though inland far we be,
Our Souls have sight of that immortal sea
  Which brought us hither,
  Can in a moment travel thither,   165
And see the Children sport upon the shore,
And hear the mighty waters rolling evermore.

                    10

Then sing, ye Birds, sing, sing a joyous song!
    And let the young Lambs bound
    As to the tabor's sound!   170
We in thought will join your throng,
    Ye that pipe and ye that play,
    Ye that through your hearts to-day
    Feel the gladness of the May!
What though the radiance which was once so bright   175
Be now for ever taken from my sight,
    Though nothing can bring back the hour
Of splendour in the grass, of glory in the flower;
      We will grieve not, rather find
      Strength in what remains behind;   180
      In the primal sympathy
      Which having been must ever be;
      In the soothing thoughts that spring
      Out of human suffering;
      In the faith that looks through death,   185
In years that bring the philosophic mind.

                    11

And O, ye Fountains, Meadows, Hills, and Groves,
Forebode not any severing of our loves!
Yet in my heart of hearts I feel your might;
I only have relinquished one delight   190
To live beneath your more habitual sway.
I love the Brooks which down their channels fret,
Even more than when I tripped lightly as they;
The innocent brightness of a new-born Day
      Is lovely yet;   195
The Clouds that gather round the setting sun
Do take a sober colouring from an eye
That hath kept watch o'er man's mortality;
Another race hath been, and other palms are won.[2]
Thanks to the human heart by which we live,   200
Thanks to its tenderness, its joys, and fears,
To me the meanest flower that blows can give
Thoughts that do often lie too deep for tears.

1802–04   1807

2. In Greece, foot races were often run for the prize of a branch or wreath of palm. Wordsworth's line echoes Paul, I Corinthians 9.24, who uses such races as a metaphor for life: "Know ye not that they which run in a race run all, but one receiveth the prize?"

Ode to Duty[1]

Jam non consilio bonus, sed more eò perductus, ut non tantum rectè facere possim, sed nisi rectè facere non possim.

Stern Daughter of the Voice of God![2]
O Duty! if that name thou love
Who art a light to guide, a rod
To check the erring, and reprove;
Thou, who art victory and law   5
When empty terrors overawe;
From vain temptations dost set free;
And calm'st the weary strife of frail humanity!

There are who ask not if thine eye
Be on them; who, in love and truth,   10
Where no misgiving is, rely
Upon the genial sense[3] of youth:
Glad Hearts! without reproach or blot;
Who do thy work, and know it not:
Oh! if through confidence misplaced   15
They fail, thy saving arms, dread Power! around them cast.

Serene will be our days and bright,
And happy will our nature be,
When love is an unerring light,
And joy its own security.   20
And they a blissful course may hold
Even now, who, not unwisely bold,
Live in the spirit of this creed;
Yet seek thy firm support, according to their need.

---

1. "This Ode . . . is on the model of Gray's *Ode to Adversity* which is copied from Horace's *Ode to Fortune*. Many and many a time have I been twitted by my wife and sister for having forgotten this dedication of myself to the stern lawgiver" (Wordsworth).

This poem merits its reputation as a departure from Wordsworth's earlier forms and ideas. In it he abandons the descriptive-meditative pattern of his *Tintern Abbey* and *Ode: Intimations of Immortality* and reverts to the standard 18th-century form of an ode addressed to a personified abstraction. The poem also represents Wordsworth's reversion from his youthful reliance on natural impulse to a more orthodox ethical tradition. It makes no reference to that "Nature" which earlier had constituted for Wordsworth "both law and impulse," and, in *Tintern Abbey*, had been called "The guide, the guardian of my heart, and soul / Of all my moral being." The Duty, "Stern Daughter of the Voice of God," to which Wordsworth now commends himself, is the same concept as Milton's "right reason," God's representative in man, which Christian humanists had developed by combining the stern morality of the pagan Stoics with the concept of the inner voice of the Christian "conscience." (In one MS variant Wordsworth described Duty as "sent from God" to keep us to the road "which conscience hath pronounced the best.")

The epigraph is translated, "Now I am not good by conscious intent, but have been so trained by habit that I not only can act rightly but am unable to act other than rightly." Added in 1837, it is an adaptation from *Moral Epistles* 120.10 by Seneca (4 B.C.–A.D. 65), Stoic philosopher and writer of tragedies.

2. Cf. *Paradise Lost* 9.652–54: "God so commanded, and left that Command / Sole Daughter of his voice; the rest, we live / Law to ourselves, our Reason is our Law."

3. Innate vitality.

I, loving freedom, and untried;   25
No sport of every random gust,
Yet being to myself a guide,
Too blindly have reposed my trust:
And oft, when in my heart was heard
Thy timely mandate, I deferred   30
The task, in smoother walks to stray;
But thee I now would serve more strictly, if I may.

Through no disturbance of my soul,
Or strong compunction[4] in me wrought,
I supplicate for thy control;   35
But in the quietness of thought:
Me this unchartered freedom tires;
I feel the weight of chance-desires:
My hopes no more must change their name,
I long for a repose that ever is the same.   40

Stern Lawgiver! yet thou dost wear
The Godhead's most benignant grace;
Nor know we any thing so fair
As is the smile upon thy face:
Flowers laugh before thee on their beds   45
And fragrance in thy footing treads;
Thou dost preserve the stars from wrong;[5]
And the most ancient heavens, through Thee, are fresh and strong.

To humbler functions, awful Power!
I call thee: I myself commend   50
Unto thy guidance from this hour;
Oh, let my weakness have an end!
Give unto me, made lowly wise,[6]
The spirit of self-sacrifice;
The confidence of reason give;
And in the light of truth thy Bondman let me live!

1804   1807

4. In the older sense, "sting of conscience," "remorse."
5. Wordsworth's parallel between the moral law and the laws governing the motion of the stars is illuminated by Kant's famous statement: "Two things fill the mind with ever new and increasing admiration and awe . . . the starry heavens above and the moral law within."
6. Another echo from Milton, whose Christian-humanist ethic pervades this ode. The angel Raphael had advised Adam (*Paradise Lost* 8.173–74), "Be lowly wise: / Think only what concerns thee and thy being."

The Solitary Reaper[1]

Behold her, single in the field,
Yon solitary Highland Lass!
Reaping and singing by herself;
Stop here, or gently pass!
Alone she cuts and binds the grain,   5
And sings a melancholy strain;
O listen! for the Vale profound
Is overflowing with the sound.

No Nightingale did ever chaunt
More welcome notes to weary bands   10
Of travellers in some shady haunt,
Among Arabian sands:
A voice so thrilling ne'er was heard
In spring-time from the Cuckoo-bird,
Breaking the silence of the seas   15
Among the farthest Hebrides.

Will no one tell me what she sings?[2]—
Perhaps the plaintive numbers flow
For old, unhappy, far-off things,
And battles long ago: 20
Or is it some more humble lay,
Familiar matter of to-day?
Some natural sorrow, loss, or pain,
That has been, and may be again?

Whate'er the theme, the Maiden sang   25
As if her song could have no ending;
I saw her singing at her work,
And o'er the sickle bending;—
I listened, motionless and still;
And, as I mounted up the hill,   30
The music in my heart I bore,
Long after it was heard no more.

Nov. 5, 1805   1807

---

1. One of the rare poems not based on Words-worth's own experience. The poet tells us that it was suggested by a passage in Thomas Wilkinson's *Tour of Scotland* (1824), which he had seen in MS: "Passed by a female who was reaping alone, she sung in Erse [the Gaelic language of Scotland] as she bended over her sickle, the sweetest human voice I ever heard. Her strains were tenderly melancholy, and felt delicious long after they were heard no more."
2. The poet does not understand Erse, the lan-guage in which she sings.

Elegiac Stanzas

Suggested by a Picture of Peele Castle, in a Storm, Painted by Sir George Beaumont[1]

I was thy neighbour once, thou rugged Pile!
Four summer weeks I dwelt in sight of thee:
I saw thee every day; and all the while
Thy Form was sleeping on a glassy sea.

So pure the sky, so quiet was the air!   5
So like, so very like, was day to day!
Whene'er I looked, thy Image still was there;
It trembled, but it never passed away.

How perfect was the calm! it seemed no sleep;
No mood, which season takes away, or brings: 10
I could have fancied that the mighty Deep
Was even the gentlest of all gentle Things.

Ah! THEN, if mine had been the Painter's hand,
To express what then I saw; and add the gleam,
The light that never was, on sea or land,   15
The consecration, and the Poet's dream;

I would have planted thee, thou hoary Pile
Amid a world how different from this!
Beside a sea that could not cease to smile;
On tranquil land, beneath a sky of bliss.   20

Thou shouldst have seemed a treasure-house divine
Of peaceful years; a chronicle of heaven;—
Of all the sunbeams that did ever shine
The very sweetest had to thee been given.

A Picture had it been of lasting ease,   25
Elysian[2] quiet, without toil or strife;
No motion but the moving tide, a breeze,
Or merely silent Nature's breathing life.

Such, in the fond illusion of my heart,
Such Picture would I at that time have made: 30

1. Sir George Beaumont, a wealthy landscape painter, was Wordsworth's patron and close friend. Peele Castle is on a promontory opposite Rampside, Lancashire, where Wordsworth had spent a month in 1794, twelve years before he saw Beaumont's painting. A current tendency is to interpret this poem as an expression of Wordsworth's loss of faith in nature. It should be noted, however, that the focus of the poem is not on an altered view of nature, but on an altered knowledge of human life and on the moral values necessary to manage the inevitability of loss and suffering.
2. Referring to Elysium, in classical mythology the peaceful place where those favored by the gods dwelled after death.

And seen the soul of truth in every part,
A stedfast peace that might not be betrayed.

So once it would have been,—'tis so no more;
I have submitted to a new control:
A power is gone, which nothing can restore;   35
A deep distress hath humanised my Soul.[3]

Not for a moment could I now behold
A smiling sea, and be what I have been:
The feeling of my loss will ne'er be old;
This, which I know, I speak with mind serene.   40

Then, Beaumont, Friend! who would have been the Friend,
If he had lived, of Him whom I deplore,[4]
This work of thine I blame not, but commend;
This sea in anger, and that dismal shore.

O 'tis a passionate Work!—yet wise and well,   45
Well chosen is the spirit that is here;
That Hulk which labours in the deadly swell,
This rueful sky, this pageantry of fear!

And this huge Castle, standing here sublime,
I love to see the look with which it braves,   50
Cased in the unfeeling armour of old time,
The lightning, the fierce wind, and trampling waves.

Farewell, farewell the heart that lives alone,
Housed in a dream, at distance from the Kind![5]
Such happiness, wherever it be known,   55
Is to be pitied; for 'tis surely blind.

But welcome fortitude, and patient cheer,
And frequent sights of what is to be borne!
Such sights, or worse, as are before me here.—
Not without hope we suffer and we mourn.   60

Summer 1806   1807

---

3. Captain John Wordsworth, William's brother,   4. Mourn.
had been drowned in a shipwreck on Feb. 5, 1805.   5. Humankind.
He is referred to in lines 41–42.

SONNETS

Composed upon Westminster Bridge, September 3, 1802[1]

Earth has not any thing to show more fair:
Dull would he be of soul who could pass by
A sight so touching in its majesty:
This City now doth, like a garment, wear
The beauty of the morning; silent, bare,   5
Ships, towers, domes, theatres, and temples lie
Open unto the fields, and to the sky;
All bright and glittering in the smokeless air.
Never did sun more beautifully steep
In his first splendour, valley, rock, or hill;   10
Ne'er saw I, never felt, a calm so deep!
The river glideth at his own sweet will:
Dear God! the very houses seem asleep;
And all that mighty heart is lying still!

1802   1807

It Is a Beauteous Evening

It is a beauteous evening, calm and free,
The holy time is quiet as a Nun
Breathless with adoration; the broad sun
Is sinking down in its tranquillity;
The gentleness of heaven broods o'er the Sea: 5
Listen! the mighty Being is awake,
And doth with his eternal motion make
A sound like thunder—everlastingly.
Dear Child! dear Girl! that walkest with me here,[2]
If thou appear untouched by solemn thought,   10
Thy nature is not therefore less divine:
Thou liest in Abraham's bosom[3] all the year;
And worshipp'st at the Temple's inner shrine,
God being with thee when we know it not.

August 1802   1807

---

1. The date of this experience was not Sept. 3, but July 31, 1802; its occasion was a trip to France. (See Dorothy Wordsworth's *Grasmere Journals* for July 1802.) The conflict of feelings attending Wordsworth's brief return to France, where he had once been a revolutionist and the lover of Annette Vallon, evoked a number of personal and political sonnets, among them the two which follow.

2. Dorothy Wordsworth's *Grasmere Journals* for July 1802 identify the child walking with Wordsworth as Caroline, his natural daughter by Annette Vallon.
3. Where the souls destined for heaven rest after death. Luke 16.22: "And it came to pass, that the beggar died, and was carried by the angels into Abraham's bosom."

London, 1802[4]

Milton! thou should'st be living at this hour:
England hath need of thee: she is a fen
Of stagnant waters: altar, sword, and pen,
Fireside, the heroic wealth of hall and bower,
Have forfeited their ancient English dower   5
Of inward happiness. We are selfish men;
Oh! raise us up, return to us again;
And give us manners, virtue, freedom, power.
Thy soul was like a Star, and dwelt apart:
Thou hadst a voice whose sound was like the sea: 10
Pure as the naked heavens, majestic, free,
So didst thou travel on life's common way,
In cheerful godliness; and yet thy heart
The lowliest duties on herself did lay.

September 1802   1807

The World Is Too Much with Us

The world is too much with us; late and soon,
Getting and spending, we lay waste our powers:
Little we see in Nature that is ours;
We have given our hearts away, a sordid boon![5]
This Sea that bares her bosom to the moon;   5
The winds that will be howling at all hours,
And are up-gathered now like sleeping flowers;
For this, for every thing, we are out of tune;
It moves us not.—Great God! I'd rather be
A Pagan suckled in a creed outworn;   10
So might I, standing on this pleasant lea,
Have glimpses that would make me less forlorn;
Have sight of Proteus rising from the sea;
Or hear old Triton blow his wreathèd horn.[6]

1802–04   1807

---

4. One of a series "written immediately after my
return from France to London, when I could not
but be struck, as here described, with the vanity
and parade of our own country . . . as contrasted
with the quiet, and I may say the desolation, that
the revolution had produced in France" (Wordsworth).
5. Gift; it is the act of giving the heart away that is
sordid.

6. Proteus: an old man of the sea who (in the
Odyssey) could assume a variety of shapes. *Triton:*
a sea deity, usually represented as blowing on a
conch shell. The description of Proteus echoes
Paradise Lost 3.603–4, and that of Triton echoes
Spenser's *Colin Clout's Come Home Again,* lines
244–45. Spenser and Milton are the two English
poets with whom Wordsworth most closely allied
himself.

Surprised by Joy[7]

Surprised by joy—impatient as the Wind
I turned to share the transport—Oh! with whom
But Thee, deep buried in the silent tomb,
That spot which no vicissitude can find?
Love, faithful love, recalled thee to my mind—   5
But how could I forget thee? Through what power,
Even for the least division of an hour,
Have I been so beguiled as to be blind
To my most grievous loss!—That thought's return
Was the worst pang that sorrow ever bore,   10
Save one, one only, when I stood forlorn,
Knowing my heart's best treasure was no more;
That neither present time, nor years unborn
Could to my sight that heavenly face restore.

1812–15   1815

Mutability[8]

From low to high doth dissolution climb,
And sink from high to low, along a scale
Of awful notes, whose concord shall not fail;
A musical but melancholy chime,
Which they can hear who meddle not with crime,   5
Nor avarice, nor over-anxious care.
Truth fails not; but her outward forms that bear
The longest date do melt like frosty rime,
That in the morning whitened hill and plain
And is no more; drop like the tower sublime   10
Of yesterday, which royally did wear
His crown of weeds, but could not even sustain
Some casual shout that broke the silent air,
Or the unimaginable touch of Time.

1821   1822

---

7. "This was in fact suggested by my daughter Catherine, long after her death" (Wordsworth). Catherine Wordsworth died June 4, 1812, at the age of 4.

8. This great sonnet was included in an otherwise rather pedestrian sequence, *Ecclesiastical Sonnets*, dealing with the history and ceremonies of the Church of England.

Steamboats, Viaducts, and Railways[9]

Motions and Means, on land and sea at war
With old poetic feeling, not for this,
Shall ye, by Poets even, be judged amiss!
Nor shall your presence, howsoe'er it mar
The loveliness of Nature, prove a bar   5
To the Mind's gaining that prophetic sense
Of future change, that point of vision, whence
May be discovered what in soul ye are.
In spite of all that beauty may disown
In your harsh features, Nature doth embrace   10
Her lawful offspring in Man's art; and Time,
Pleased with your triumphs o'er his brother Space,
Accepts from your bold hands the proffered crown
Of hope, and smiles on you with cheer sublime.

1833   • • •   1835

Extempore Effusion upon the Death of James Hogg[1]

When first, descending from the moorlands,
I saw the Stream of Yarrow[2] glide
Along a bare and open valley,
The Ettrick Shepherd[3] was my guide.

When last along its banks I wandered,   5
Through groves that had begun to shed
Their golden leaves upon the pathways,
My steps the Border-minstrel[4] led.

The mighty Minstrel breathes no longer,
'Mid mouldering ruins low he lies;   10

---

9. In late middle age Wordsworth demonstrates, as he had predicted in the Preface to *Lyrical Ballads*, that the poet will assimilate to his subject matter the "material revolution" produced by science. Unlike most poets, furthermore, he boldly accepts as evidences of man's progress even the unlovely encroachments of technology upon his beloved natural scene.

1. Wordsworth's niece relates how he was deeply moved by finding unexpectedly in a newspaper an account of the death of the poet James Hogg. "Half an hour afterwards he came into the room where the ladies were sitting and asked Miss Hutchinson [his sister-in-law] to write down some lines which he had just composed." All the poets named here, several of Wordsworth's closest friends among them, had died between 1832 and 1835.

2. A river in the southeast of Scotland.

3. James Hogg, the "Ettrick Shepherd" (he was born in Ettrick Forest, and was for a time a shepherd), was discovered as a writer by Sir Walter Scott, and became well known as a poet, essayist, and editor.

4. Sir Walter Scott.

And death upon the braes[5] of Yarrow,
Has closed the Shepherd-poet's eyes:

Nor has the rolling year twice measured,
From sign to sign, its stedfast course,
Since every mortal power of Coleridge   15
Was frozen at its marvellous source;

The rapt One, of the godlike forehead,
The heaven-eyed creature sleeps in earth:
And Lamb, the frolic and the gentle,
Has vanished from his lonely hearth.   20

Like clouds that rake the mountain-summits,
Or waves that own no curbing hand,
How fast has brother followed brother,
From sunshine to the sunless land!

Yet I, whose lids from infant slumber   25
Were earlier raised, remain to hear
A timid voice, that asks in whispers,
"Who next will drop and disappear?"

Our haughty life is crowned with darkness,
Like London with its own black wreath,   30
On which with thee, O Crabbe![6] forth-looking,
I gazed from Hampstead's breezy heath.

As if but yesterday departed,
Thou too art gone before; but why,
O'er ripe fruit, seasonably gathered,   35
Should frail survivors heave a sigh?

Mourn rather for that holy Spirit,
Sweet as the spring, as ocean deep;
For Her[7] who, ere her summer faded,
Has sunk into a breathless sleep.   40

No more of old romantic sorrows,
For slaughtered Youth or love-lorn Maid!
With sharper grief is Yarrow smitten,
And Ettrick mourns with her their Poet dead.

Nov. 21, 1835   1835

---

5. The sloping banks of a stream.
6. George Crabbe, the poet of rural and village life.
7. Felicia Hemans, a minor but prolific poet, who died when only 42. She is best known in America for *The Landing of the Pilgrim Fathers* and "The Boy Stood on the Burning Deck."

Prospectus
to *The Recluse*[1]

On Man, on Nature, and on Human Life,
Musing in solitude, I oft perceive
Fair trains of imagery before me rise,
Accompanied by feelings of delight
Pure, or with no unpleasing sadness mixed;   5
And I am conscious of affecting thoughts
And dear remembrances, whose presence soothes
Or elevates the Mind, intent to weigh
The good and evil of our mortal state.
—To these emotions, whencesoe'er they come,   10
Whether from breath of outward circumstance,
Or from the Soul—an impulse to herself—
I would give utterance in numerous verse.[2]
Of Truth, of Grandeur, Beauty, Love, and Hope,
And melancholy Fear subdued by Faith;   15
Of blessed consolations in distress;
Of moral strength, and intellectual Power;
Of joy in widest commonalty spread;
Of the individual Mind that keeps her own
Inviolate retirement, subject there   20
To Conscience only, and the law supreme
Of that Intelligence which governs all—
I sing:—"fit audience let me find though few!"[3]

    So prayed, more gaining than he asked, the Bard—
In holiest mood. Urania,[4] I shall need   25
Thy guidance, or a greater Muse, if such

1. Through most of his poetic life Wordsworth labored intermittently at a long philosophic poem called *The Recluse*, which he intended to be his masterwork. As Wordsworth described this project in the Preface to *The Excursion* (1814), it was to consist of an autobiographical introduction (the poem now called *The Prelude*) and three long parts; of these three he completed only book 1 of part 1 ("Home at Grasmere") and part 2, called *The Excursion*. In the Preface to *The Excursion*, Wordsworth printed this long extract (the concluding section of "Home at Grasmere") to serve "as a kind of *Prospectus* of the design and scope of the whole Poem"—i.e., of the entire *Recluse*.

The first version of this "Prospectus" may have been drafted as early as 1798 or 1800. In language resonant with echoes from *Paradise Lost*, Wordsworth announces an undertaking which he conceives to be no less inspired and sublime than Milton's. In it he will move higher than Milton's heaven and deeper than Milton's hell, past scenes evoking greater fear than hell and greater awe than Jehovah; but without ever leaving "the Mind of

Man—/ My haunt, and the main region of my song" (lines 40–41). And his "high argument" is that Paradise can be regained; not, however, as in Revelation 21 and in Milton, by the marriage between the New Jerusalem and Christ the Lamb, but by a marriage between the "intellect of Man" and "this goodly universe," and the resulting new "creation . . . which they with blended might / Accomplish" (lines 47–71). In no other. passage does Wordsworth reveal so clearly the extent to which he assimilates in his poetry the Biblical scheme of Milton's epic—assigning, however, the active role, from creation to redemption, to the human faculties, in their vital interaction with the external universe.

2. Harmonious verse; an echo of *Paradise Lost* 5.150. The inspiring "breath of outward circumstance" parallels the "correspondent breeze" in the opening passage of *The Prelude*, just below.
3. *Paradise Lost* 7.31.
4. The Muse whom Milton had invoked in *Paradise Lost* 7.1–39.

Descend to earth or dwell in highest heaven!
For I must tread on shadowy ground, must sink
Deep—and, aloft ascending, breathe in worlds
To which the heaven of heavens[5] is but a veil.   30
All strength—all terror, single or in bands,
That ever was put forth in personal form—
Jehovah—with his thunder, and the choir
Of shouting Angels, and the empyreal thrones—
I pass them unalarmed. Not Chaos, not   35
The darkest pit of lowest Erebus,[6]
Nor aught of blinder vacancy, scooped out
By help of dreams—can breed such fear and awe
As fall upon us often when we look
Into our Minds, into the Mind of Man—   40
My haunt, and the main region of my song.
—Beauty—a living Presence of the earth,
Surpassing the most fair ideal Forms
Which craft of delicate Spirits hath composed
From earth's materials—waits upon my steps;   45
Pitches her tents before me as I move,
An hourly neighbour. Paradise, and groves
Elysian,[7] Fortunate Fields—like those of old
Sought in the Atlantic Main—why should they be
A history only of departed things,   50
Or a mere fiction of what never was?
For the discerning intellect of Man,
When wedded to this goodly universe
In love and holy passion, shall find these
A simple produce of the common day.   55
—I, long before the blissful hour arrives,
Would chant, in lonely peace, the spousal[8] verse
Of this great consummation:—and, by words
Which speak of nothing more than what we are,
Would I arouse the sensual from their sleep   60
Of Death, and win the vacant and the vain
To noble raptures; while my voice proclaims
How exquisitely the individual Mind
(And the progressive powers perhaps no less
Of the whole species) to the external World   65
Is fitted:—and how exquisitely, too—
Theme this but little heard of among men—
The external World is fitted to the Mind;

---

5. In *Paradise Lost* the dwelling place, beyond the visible heaven, of God and his angels. For line 34, see *Paradise Lost* 2.430: "O progeny of Heaven, empyreal thrones!"
6. In classical myth, a dark region of the underworld; often used as a name for hell by Christian writers.
7. Elysium, in Greek myth, was the place where mortals favored by the gods live a happy life after death. It was sometimes identified with the "Islands of the Blessed," reputed to be located far out in the western sea—hence "sought in the Atlantic Main." See Horace, *Epodes* 16.
8. Marital; hence a "spousal verse" is an epithalamion.

And the creation (by no lower name
Can it be called) which they with blended might   70
Accomplish:—this is our high argument.[9]
—Such grateful haunts foregoing, if I oft
Must turn elsewhere—to travel near the tribes
And fellowships of men, and see ill sights
Of madding passions mutually inflamed;   75
Must hear Humanity in fields and groves
Pipe solitary anguish; or must hang
Brooding above the fierce confederate storm
Of sorrow, barricadoed[1] evermore
Within the walls of cities—may these sounds   80
Have their authentic comment; that even these
Hearing, I be not downcast or forlorn!—
Descend, prophetic Spirit! that inspir'st
The human Soul of universal earth,
Dreaming on things to come;[2] and dost possess   85
A metropolitan temple[3] in the hearts
Of mighty Poets; upon me bestow
A gift of genuine insight; that my Song
With star-like virtue in its place may shine,
Shedding benignant influence, and secure,   90
Itself, from all malevolent effect
Of those mutations that extend their sway
Throughout the nether sphere![4]—And if with this
I mix more lowly matter; with the thing
Contemplated, describe the Mind and Man   95
Contemplating; and who, and what he was—
The transitory Being that beheld
This Vision; when and where, and how he lived;[5]—
Be not this labour useless. If such theme
May sort with highest objects, then—dread Power!   100
Whose gracious favour is the primal source
Of all illumination—may my Life
Express the image of a better time,
More wise desires, and simpler manners;—nurse
My Heart in genuine freedom:—all pure thoughts   105
Be with me;—so shall thy unfailing love
Guide, and support, and cheer me to the end!

ca. 1798–1814   1814

---

9. Theme, as in *Paradise Lost* 1.24: "the height
of this great argument."
1. Barricaded, as in *Paradise Lost* 8.241: "Fast we
found, fast shut / Of The dismal gates, and barricadoed strong. . . ."
2. Cf. "the prophetic soul / Of the wide world
dreaming on things to come" (Shakespeare, Sonnet 107).

3. The primary church of a religion.
4. In the Ptolemaic world picture, the spheres of
the heavenly bodies were immutable, and only the
earth (the "nether sphere," or region below the
sphere of the moon) was subject to change. Compare *Paradise Lost* 7.375 and 10.656–64.
5. Wordsworth thus justifies *The Prelude* and the
autobiographical sections of *The Recluse*.

The Prelude   *The Prelude* is Wordsworth's crowning achievement, the greatest and most original long poem since Milton's *Paradise Lost*. Its existence, however, was unknown to the public until after Wordsworth's death in 1850. When, three months later, *The Prelude* was published from manuscript, its title was given to it by the poet's wife; Wordsworth himself had referred to it variously as "the poem to Coleridge," "the poem on the growth of my own mind," and "the poem on my own poetical education."

For some seventy-five years this posthumous publication of 1850 was the only known text of *The Prelude*. Then in 1926 Ernest de Selincourt, working from manuscripts, printed an earlier version of the poem that Wordsworth had completed in 1805. Since that time other scholars have established the existence of a still earlier and much shorter version of *The Prelude*, in two parts, which Wordsworth had composed in 1798–99. The following seems to have been the process of composition that produced the three extant versions of the poem:

1. The *Two-Part Prelude* of 1799. Wordsworth originally planned, early in 1798, to include an account of his own development as a poet in his projected but never-completed philosophical poem *The Recluse* (see the title footnote to the Prospectus for *The Recluse*, above). While living in Germany during the autumn and winter of 1798–99, he composed a number of passages about his early experiences with nature. What had been intended to be part of *The Recluse*, however, quickly evolved into an independent autobiographical poem, and by late 1799, when Wordsworth settled with his sister Dorothy at Grasmere, he had written a poem in two parts, 978 lines in length, which takes his life from infancy, through his years at Hawkshead School, to the age of seventeen. This poem corresponds, by and large, to the contents of books 1 and 2 of the later versions of *The Prelude*.

2. The 1805 *Prelude*. Late in 1801 Wordsworth began to expand the poem on his poetic life, and in 1804 he set to work intensively on the project. His initial plan was to write it in five books. Before he completed the five-book poem, however, he decided to enlarge it still further, to incorporate an account of his experiences in France and of his mental crisis after the failure of his hopes in the French Revolution, and to end the poem with his settlement at Grasmere and his taking up the great task of *The Recluse*. He completed this poem, in thirteen books, in May 1805. This is the version that Wordsworth read to Coleridge after the latter's return from Malta (see Coleridge's *To William Wordsworth*, below).

3. The 1850 *Prelude*. For the next thirty-five years Wordsworth tinkered with the text, polishing the style and qualifying some of its radical statements about the divine sufficiency of the human mind in its communion with nature; he did not, however, in any essential way alter its subject matter or overall design. *The Prelude* that was published in July 1850 is in fourteen books and was printed from a fair copy; it incorporated Wordsworth's latest revisions, which had been made in 1839, as well as some alterations introduced by his literary executors. The selections printed below are from Wordsworth's final version of his autobiographical poem.

When Wordsworth enlarged the two-part *Prelude* of 1799, he not only made it a poem of epic length but also heightened the style and introduced various thematic parallels with earlier epics, especially *Paradise Lost*. (For a central example, see Wordsworth's version of Milton's enterprise to "justify the ways of God to men," in 14.162–70, 384–89, below.) The expanded poem, however, is a personal history which turns on a mental crisis and recovery, and for such a narrative design the chief prototype is not the classical or Christian epic, but the spiritual autobiography of crisis. St. Augustine's *Confessions* established this great Christian form late in the fourth century, and it has had an uninterrupted history in European literature ever since. Among the scores of prose versions of the spiritual autobiography are the Catholic Dante's *Vita Nuova (The New Life)* and the Puritan Bunyan's *Grace Abounding to the Chief of Sinners*. Its greatest poetic instance is Dante's *Divine Comedy*, an allegorical account of the narrator's spiritual journey from earth through hell, purgatory, and paradise, back to earth.

As in *The Divine Comedy*, and in Augustine's *Confessions* itself, Wordsworth's recurrent metaphor is that of a journey, whose end—as T. S. Eliot put it in *Four Quartets*, his adaptation of the same form—is in its beginning, and in which it turns out that the end of the journey is "to arrive where we started / And know the place for the first time" (see the Quartet *Little Gidding*, below, lines 241–42). Wordsworth's *Prelude* opens with a literal journey whose chosen goal (1.72, 106–7) is "a known Vale whither my feet should turn"—that is, the Vale of Grasmere. There are a number of later journeys, of which the most important are the crossing of the Alps in book 6 and, at the beginning of the final book, the ascent of Mount Snowdon which culminates in a definitive vision. In the course of the poem, however, such literal journeys become the metaphoric vehicle for an interior journey in a quest, both within the poet's memory and in his poetic enterprise itself, for his lost early self and his proper spiritual home. The poem ends by adverting to its own beginning, and leaves the poet settled in the Vale of Grasmere, ready finally to begin his great enterprise, *The Recluse* (14.302–11, 374–85).

In reading *The Prelude* as autobiography, we readily forget how traditional it is in both voice and form; and in our understandable preoccupation with its great poetic moments we are apt to neglect the artistry of its overall structure. Although the narrator is the actual Wordsworth, addressing himself to the English people of his own troubled age, he adopts a personal and a prophetic stance that goes back through Milton and Spenser to the poets and prophets of the Bible. And although the separate episodes are events from Wordsworth's own life, he does not describe these events as they had seemed to him at the time, but as they are interpreted in distant retrospect, reordered in sequence, and shaped into the inherited design of crisis and recovery, from which the author emerges as a different self in a transformed world.

Wordsworth, however, changes the traditional spiritual history in a radical way: he converts what had earlier been the supernatural Christian agencies of its providential plot into secular and humanistic terms. The true protagonist in Wordsworth's poem turns out, in fact, to be a power of his own mind which is capable of transforming the natural world with which it interacts; he calls this power "Imagination." "This faculty," he reveals in the last book (14.193 ff.), "hath been the feeding source of our long labor," and he goes on to say that the account of its appearance, development, loss, and restoration has constituted the submerged plot of the poem in its entirety. *The Prelude* has been called the greatest religious poem of the nineteenth century. Its religion, however, despite some pious phrases and passages that Wordsworth cautiously inserted into the 1850 text, is not an inherited creed, nor even a religion of Nature, but rather a faith in the redeeming power of "the mind of man" which, the closing lines declare, compared with the unchanging earth, is "In beauty exalted, as it is itself / Of quality and fabric more divine."

The text reprinted here is that established from the surviving printer's copy by W. J. B. Owen in the Cornell Wordsworth volume, *The Fourteen-Book Prelude* (1985).

From THE PRELUDE

OR

GROWTH OF A POET'S MIND

AN AUTOBIOGRAPHICAL POEM

Book First
Introduction, Childhood, and School-time

O there is blessing in this gentle breeze,
A visitant that, while he fans my cheek,
Doth seem half-conscious of the joy he brings
From the green fields, and from yon azure sky.
Whate'er his mission, the soft breeze can come   5
To none more grateful than to me; escaped
From the vast City,[1] where I long have pined
A discontented Sojourner—Now free,
Free as a bird to settle where I will.
What dwelling shall receive me? in what vale   10
Shall be my harbour? underneath what grove
Shall I take up my home? and what clear stream
Shall with its murmur lull me into rest?
The earth is all before me:[2] with a heart
Joyous, nor scared at its own liberty,   15
I look about; and should the chosen guide
Be nothing better than a wandering cloud,
I cannot miss my way. I breathe again;
Trances of thought and mountings of the heart
Come fast upon me: it is shaken off,   20
That burthen of my own unnatural self,
The heavy weight of many a weary day
Not mine, and such as were not made for me.
Long months of peace (if such bold word accord
With any promises of human life),   25
Long months of ease and undisturbed delight
Are mine in prospect; whither shall I turn,
By road or pathway, or through trackless field,

---

1. London. Wordsworth uses this city as a type, symbolizing a place of spiritual bondage from which he has finally escaped.
2. One of many echoes from *Paradise Lost*, where the line is applied to Adam and Eve as, at the conclusion of the poem, they begin their new life after being expelled from Eden: "The world was all before them" (12.646).

Up hill or down, or shall some floating thing
Upon the River point me out my course?   30
Dear Liberty! Yet what would it avail,
But for a gift that consecrates the joy?
For I, methought, while the sweet breath of heaven
Was blowing on my body, felt, within,
A correspondent breeze, that gently moved   35
With quickening virtue,[3] but is now become
A tempest, a redundant[4] energy,
Vexing its own creation. Thanks to both,
And their congenial[5] powers that, while they join
In breaking up a long continued frost,   40
Bring with them vernal promises, the hope
Of active days urged on by flying hours;
Days of sweet leisure taxed with patient thought
Abstruse, nor wanting punctual service high,
Matins and vespers, of harmonious verse![6]   45
        Thus far, O Friend![7] did I, not used to make
A present joy the matter of a Song,[8]
Pour forth, that day, my soul in measured strains,
That would not be forgotten, and are here
Recorded:—to the open fields I told   50
A prophecy:—poetic numbers came
Spontaneously, to clothe in priestly robe
A renovated Spirit singled out,
Such hope was mine, for holy services:
My own voice cheered me, and, far more, the mind's   55
Internal echo of the imperfect sound;
To both I listened, drawing from them both
A chearful confidence in things to come.
        Content, and not unwilling now to give
A respite to this passion, I paced on   60
With brisk and eager steps; and came at length
To a green shady place where down I sate
Beneath a tree, slackening my thoughts by choice,

---

3. Revivifying power. ("To quicken" is to give or
restore life.)
4. Abundant, exuberant.
5. Kindred.
6. I.e., verses equivalent to morning prayers
(matins) and evening prayers (vespers). The opening passage (lines 1–45), which Wordsworth calls
in book 7, line 4, a "glad preamble," replaces the
traditional epic device, such as Milton had adopted
in Paradise Lost, of an opening prayer to the Muse
for inspiration. To be "inspired," in the literal sense,
is to be breathed or blown into by a divinity (in
Latin spirare means both "to breathe" and "to
blow"). Wordsworth begins his poem with a
"blessing" from an outer "breeze," which (lines 34–
45) is called the "breath of heaven" and evokes in
him a correspondent inner breeze that signalizes a
springlike revival of his spirit after a wintry season,
and also a burst of poetic power that he goes on to
equate (lines 50–54) with the utterances of Biblical
prophets when inspired by the Holy Spirit. The
revivifying breeze and breath, at once material and
spiritual, recurs in The Prelude as a kind of leitmotif; it also serves as the radical metaphor of other
Romantic poems such as Coleridge's Eolian Harp
and Dejection: An Ode, and Shelley's Ode to the
West Wind (below).
7. Samuel Taylor Coleridge, to whom Wordsworth addresses the whole of the Prelude. For Coleridge's response, after the poem was read to him,
see To William Wordsworth, below.
8. In the Preface to Lyrical Ballads Wordsworth
says that his poetry usually originates in "emotion
recollected in tranquillity"; hence not, as in the
preceding preamble, during the experience that it
records.

And settling into gentler happiness.
'Twas Autumn, and a clear and placid day,   65
With warmth, as much as needed, from a sun
Two hours declined towards the west, a day
With silver clouds, and sunshine on the grass,
And, in the sheltered and the sheltering grove,
A perfect stillness. Many were the thoughts   70
Encouraged and dismissed, till choice was made
Of a known Vale whither my feet should turn,[9]
Nor rest till they had reached the very door
Of the one Cottage which methought I saw.
No picture of mere memory ever looked   75
So fair; and while upon the fancied scene
I gazed with growing love, a higher power
Than Fancy gave assurance of some work
Of glory, there forthwith to be begun,
Perhaps too there performed.[1] Thus long I mused,   80
Nor e'er lost sight of what I mused upon,
Save where, amid the stately grove of Oaks,
Now here—now there—an acorn, from its cup
Dislodged, through sere leaves rustled, or at once
To the bare earth dropped with a startling sound.   85
      From that soft couch I rose not, till the sun
Had almost touched the horizon; casting then
A backward glance upon the curling cloud
Of city smoke, by distance ruralized,
Keen as a Truant or a Fugitive,   90
But as a Pilgrim resolute, I took,
Even with the chance equipment of that hour,
The road that pointed tow'rd the chosen Vale.
      It was a splendid evening: and my Soul
Once more made trial of her strength, nor lacked   95
Eolian visitations;[2] but the harp
Was soon defrauded, and the banded host
Of harmony dispersed in straggling sounds;
And lastly utter silence! "Be it so;
Why think of any thing but present good?"   100
So, like a Home-bound Labourer, I pursued
My way, beneath the mellowing sun, that shed
Mild influence;[3] nor left in me one wish
Again to bend the sabbath of that time[4]
To a servile yoke. What need of many words?   105

9. Grasmere, where Wordsworth settled with his
sister Dorothy in December 1799. Wordsworth uses
his walk to that "Vale" to symbolize a new stage in
the journey of his life—a stage in which he returns
to what he calls (in the title of the opening book of
The Recluse, designed to follow The Prelude) "Home
at Grasmere."
1. I.e., The Recluse, which Wordsworth planned
to be his major poetic work.

2. Influences to which his soul responded as an
Eolian harp responds to gusts of a breeze. For a
description of this instrument, see the footnote to
Coleridge's The Eolian Harp, below.
3. Paradise Lost 7.374–75: "The Pleiades [i.e., a
cluster of stars] before him danced / Shedding sweet
influence." "Influence" is an astrological term for
the effect of stars on human life.
4. That time of rest.

A pleasant loitering journey, through three days
Continued, brought me to my hermitage.
I spare to tell of what ensued, the life
In common things,—the endless store of things
Rare, or at least so seeming, every day   110
Found all about me in one neighbourhood;
The self-congratulation,[5] and from morn
To night unbroken cheerfulness serene.
But speedily an earnest longing rose
To brace myself to some determined aim,   115
Reading or thinking; either to lay up
New stores, or rescue from decay the old
By timely interference: and therewith
Came hopes still higher, that with outward life
I might endue some airy phantasies   120
That had been floating loose about for years;
And to such Beings temperately deal forth
The many feelings that oppressed my heart.
That hope hath been discouraged; welcome light
Dawns from the East, but dawns—to disappear   125
And mock me with a sky that ripens not
Into a steady morning: if my mind,
Remembering the bold promise of the past,
Would gladly grapple with some noble theme,
Vain is her wish: where'er she turns, she finds   130
Impediments from day to day renewed.
    And now it would content me to yield up
Those lofty hopes awhile for present gifts
Of humbler industry. But, O dear Friend!
The Poet, gentle Creature as he is,   135
Hath, like the Lover, his unruly times,
His fits when he is neither sick nor well,
Though no distress be near him but his own
Unmanageable thoughts: his mind, best pleas'd
While she, as duteous as the Mother Dove,   140
Sits brooding,[6] lives not always to that end,
But, like the innocent Bird, hath goadings on
That drive her, as in trouble, through the groves:
With me is now such passion, to be blamed
No otherwise than as it lasts too long.   145
    When as becomes a Man who would prepare
For such an arduous Work, I through myself
Make rigorous inquisition, the report
Is often chearing; for I neither seem
To lack that first great gift, the vital Soul,   150
Nor general Truths, which are themselves a sort

---

5. Self-rejoicing.
6. Echoing Milton's reference to the original act
of creation in his invocation to the Holy Spirit:

Thou "Dove-like satst brooding on the vast Abyss /
And mad'st it pregnant" (*Paradise Lost* 1.21–22).

Of Elements and Agents, Under-powers,
Subordinate helpers of the living Mind:
Nor am I naked of external things,
Forms, images, nor numerous other aids   155
Of less regard, though won perhaps with toil,
And needful to build up a Poet's praise.
Time, place, and manners do I seek, and these
Are found in plenteous store, but no where such
As may be singled out with steady choice: 160
No little band of yet remembered names
Whom I in perfect confidence might hope
To summon back from lonesome banishment,
And make them dwellers in the hearts of men
Now living, or to live in future years.   165
Sometimes the ambitious Power of choice, mistaking
Proud spring-tide swellings for a regular sea,
Will settle on some British theme, some old
Romantic Tale by Milton left unsung:[7]
More often turning to some gentle place   170
Within the groves of Chivalry, I pipe
To Shepherd Swains, or seated, harp in hand,
Amid reposing knights by a River side
Or fountain, listen to the grave reports
Of dire enchantments faced, and overcome   175
By the strong mind, and Tales of warlike feats
Where spear encountered spear, and sword with sword
Fought, as if conscious of the blazonry
That the shield bore, so glorious was the strife;
Whence inspiration for a song that winds   180
Through ever changing scenes of votive quest,[8]
Wrongs to redress, harmonious tribute paid
To patient courage and unblemished truth,
To firm devotion, zeal unquenchable,
And Christian meekness hallowing faithful loves.[9]   185
Sometimes, more sternly moved, I would relate
How vanquished Mithridates northward passed,
And, hidden in the cloud of years, became
Odin, the Father of a Race by whom
Perished the Roman Empire;[1] how the friends   190
And followers of Sertorius, out of Spain
Flying, found shelter in the Fortunate Isles;
And left their usages, their arts, and laws

---

7. In *Paradise Lost* 9.24–41 Milton relates that, in seeking a subject for his epic poem, he rejected "fabled Knights" and medieval romance.
8. A quest undertaken to fulfill a vow.
9. An echo of the prefatory statement to Spenser's *Faerie Queene*, line 9: "Fierce warres and faithfull loves shall moralize my song."
1. Mithridates VI, king of Pontus, was defeated by the Roman Pompey in 66 B.C. In chapter 10 of his *Decline and Fall of the Roman Empire*, Edward Gibbon associates him with Odin, a chieftain of the Goths, who hoped to produce descendants who would wreak revenge upon the conquering Romans. All the protagonists that Wordsworth considered for his poem were heroes in fights against tyranny.

To disappear by a slow gradual death;
To dwindle and to perish, one by one,   195
Starved in those narrow bounds: but not the soul
Of Liberty, which fifteen hundred years
Survived, and, when the European came
With skill and power that might not be withstood,
Did, like a pestilence, maintain its hold,   200
And wasted down by glorious death that Race
Of natural Heroes;[2]—or I would record
How, in tyrannic times, some high-souled Man,
Unnamed among the chronicles of Kings,
Suffered in silence for truth's sake: or tell   205
How that one Frenchman, through continued force
Of meditation on the inhuman deeds
Of those who conquered first the Indian isles,
Went, single in his ministry, across
The Ocean;—not to comfort the Oppressed,   210
But, like a thirsty wind, to roam about,
Withering the Oppressor:[3]—how Gustavus sought
Help at his need in Dalecarlia's mines:[4]
How Wallace fought for Scotland,[5] left the name
Of Wallace to be found, like a wild flower,   215
All over his dear Country, left the deeds
Of Wallace, like a family of Ghosts,
To people the steep rocks and river banks,
Her natural sanctuaries, with a local soul
Of independence and stern liberty.   220
Sometimes it suits me better to invent
A Tale from my own heart, more near akin
To my own passions, and habitual thoughts,
Some variegated Story, in the main
Lofty, but the unsubstantial Structure melts   225
Before the very sun that brightens it,
Mist into air dissolving! Then, a wish,
My last and favourite aspiration, mounts,
With yearning, tow'rds some philosophic Song
Of Truth that cherishes our daily life;[6]   230
With meditations passionate, from deep
Recesses in man's heart, immortal verse
Thoughtfully fitted to the Orphean lyre;[7]

2. Sertorius, a Roman general allied with Mithridates, fought off the armies of Pompey and others until he was assassinated in 72 B.C. There is a legend that after his death his followers, to escape Roman tyranny, fled from Spain to the Canary Islands (known in ancient times as "the Fortunate Isles," line 192), where their descendants flourished until subjugated and decimated by invading Spaniards late in the 15th century.
3. "Dominique de Gourges, a French gentleman who went in 1568 to Florida to avenge the massacre of the French by the Spaniards there" [footnote in *The Prelude* of 1850].
4. Gustavus I of Sweden; in the 16th century he mustered supporters in Dalecarlia, a mining district, who helped free Sweden from the tyranny of Denmark.
5. William Wallace, the Scottish national hero, fought against the English until captured and executed in 1305.
6. I.e., *The Recluse*.
7. The lyre of Orpheus, who in Greek myth was able to enchant not only human listeners but the natural world by his singing and playing.

But from this awful burthen I full soon
Take refuge, and beguile myself with trust   235
That mellower years will bring a riper mind
And clearer insight. Thus my days are passed
In contradiction; with no skill to part
Vague longing, haply bred by want of power,
From paramount impulse—not to be withstood;   240
A timorous capacity from prudence;
From circumspection, infinite delay.[8]
Humility and modest awe themselves
Betray me, serving often for a cloke
To a more subtile selfishness; that now   245
Locks every function up in blank reserve,[9]
Now dupes me, trusting to an anxious eye
That with intrusive restlessness beats off
Simplicity, and self-presented truth.
    Ah! better far than this, to stray about   250
Voluptuously,[1] through fields and rural walks,
And ask no record of the hours, resigned
To vacant musing, unreproved neglect
Of all things, and deliberate holiday:
Far better never to have heard the name   255
Of zeal and just ambition, than to live
Baffled and plagued by a mind that every hour
Turns recreant to her task, takes heart again,
Then feels immediately some hollow thought
Hang like an interdict[2] upon her hopes.   260
This is my lot; for either still I find
Some imperfection in the chosen theme;
Or see of absolute accomplishment
Much wanting, so much wanting, in myself
That I recoil and droop, and seek repose   265
In listlessness from vain perplexity;
Unprofitably travelling toward the grave,
Like a false Steward who hath much received,
And renders nothing back.[3]
               Was it for this[4]
That one, the fairest of all rivers, loved   270
To blend his murmurs with my Nurse's song;
And, from his alder shades and rocky falls,
And from his fords and shallows, sent a voice
That flowed along my dreams? For this didst Thou,
O Derwent! winding among grassy holms[5]   275

---

8. The syntax is complex and inverted; in outline, the sense of lines 238–42 is: "With no ability ('skill') to distinguish longing from impulse, timid capacity from prudence, delay from carefulness ('circumspection')."
9. Absolute inaction.
1. Luxuriously, sensuously.

2. Pronounced "interdite": prohibition.
3. The reference is to the parable of the false steward in Matthew 25.14–30.
4. The *Two-Part Prelude* that Wordsworth wrote in 1798–99 begins at this point.
5. Flat ground next to a river.

Where I was looking on, a Babe in arms,
Make ceaseless music, that composed my thoughts
To more than infant softness, giving me,
Amid the fretful dwellings of mankind,
A foretaste, a dim earnest, of the calm   280
That Nature breathes among the hills and groves?
    When he had left the mountains, and received
On his smooth breast the shadow of those Towers
That yet survive, a shattered Monument
Of feudal sway, the bright blue River passed   285
Along the margin of our Terrace Walk;[6]
A tempting Playmate whom we dearly loved.
O many a time have I, a five years' Child,
In a small mill-race severed from his stream,
Made one long bathing of a summer's day;   290
Basked in the sun, and plunged, and basked again,
Alternate all a summer's day, or scoured[7]
The sandy fields, leaping through flow'ry groves
Of yellow ragwort; or when rock and hill,
The woods and distant Skiddaw's[8] lofty height,   295
Were bronzed with deepest radiance, stood alone
Beneath the sky, as if I had been born
On Indian plains, and from my Mother's hut
Had run abroad in wantonness, to sport,
A naked Savage, in the thunder shower.   300
    Fair seed-time had my soul, and I grew up
Fostered alike by beauty and by fear;[9]
Much favoured in my birth-place, and no less
In that beloved Vale[1] to which erelong
We were transplanted—there were we let loose   305
For sports of wider range. Ere I had told
Ten birth-days, when among the mountain slopes
Frost, and the breath of frosty wind, had snapped
The last autumnal Crocus, 'twas my joy,
With store of Springes[2] o'er my Shoulder slung,   310
To range the open heights where woodcocks ran
Along the smooth green turf. Through half the night,
Scudding away from snare to snare, I plied
That anxious visitation;—moon and stars
Were shining o'er my head; I was alone,   315

6. The Derwent River flows by Cockermouth
Castle and then past the garden terrace behind
Wordsworth's father's house in Cockermouth,
Cumberland.
7. Run swiftly over.
8. A mountain 9 miles east of Cockermouth.
9. Wordsworth introduces here a dialectic that plays
a central role in the evolution of *The Prelude*. He
represents his mind, confronting nature, as fostered in its growth by two antithetic principles, one
associated with love and the other with fear. These
principles correspond to the two main categories,
"the beautiful" and "the sublime," into which theorists of the landscape during the preceding century had classified the antithetic aspects of the
natural scene. See, e.g., 1.351–56, 466–75, 546.
In the concluding book, this antithesis is finally
resolved; see below, 14.162–70 and note.
1. The valley of Esthwaite, the location of Hawkshead, where Wordsworth attended school.
2. Bird snares.

And seemed to be a trouble to the peace
That dwelt among them. Sometimes it befel,
In these night-wanderings, that a strong desire
O'erpowered my better reason, and the Bird
Which was the Captive of another's toil[3]   320
Became my prey; and when the deed was done
I heard, among the solitary hills,
Low breathings coming after me, and sounds
Of undistinguishable motion, steps
Almost as silent as the turf they trod.   325
　　　Nor less, when Spring had warmed the cultured[4] Vale,
Roved we as plunderers where the Mother-bird
Had in high places built her lodge; though mean
Our object, and inglorious, yet the end[5]
Was not ignoble. Oh! when I have hung   330
Above the Raven's nest, by knots of grass
And half-inch fissures in the slippery rock
But ill-sustained; and almost (so it seemed)
Suspended by the blast that blew amain,
Shouldering the naked crag; Oh, at that time,   335
While on the perilous ridge I hung alone,
With what strange utterance did the loud dry wind
Blow through my ears! the sky seemed not a sky
Of earth, and with what motion moved the clouds!
　　　Dust as we are, the immortal Spirit grows   340
Like harmony in music; there is a dark
Inscrutable workmanship that reconciles
Discordant elements, makes them cling together
In one society. How strange that all
The terrors, pains, and early miseries,   345
Regrets, vexations, lassitudes, interfused
Within my mind, should e'er have borne a part,
And that a needful part, in making up
The calm existence that is mine when I
Am worthy of myself! Praise to the end!   350
Thanks to the means which Nature deigned to employ!
Whether her fearless visitings or those
That came with soft alarm like hurtless lightning
Opening the peaceful clouds, or she would use
Severer interventions, ministry   355
More palpable, as best might suit her aim.[6]
　　　One summer evening (led by her) I found
A little Boat tied to a Willow-tree
Within a rocky cave, its usual home.
Strait I unloosed her chain, and, stepping in,   360
Pushed from the shore. It was an act of stealth

3. "Snare," or else "labor."
4. Cultivated.
5. Outcome.

6. A restatement of the double ministry of nature described in line 302; what follows is a second example of discipline by fear.

And troubled pleasure, nor without the voice
Of mountain-echoes did my Boat move on,
Leaving behind her still, on either side,
Small circles glittering idly in the moon,   365
Until they melted all into one track
Of sparkling light. But now, like one who rows
(Proud of his skill) to reach a chosen point
With an unswerving line, I fixed my view
Upon the summit of a craggy ridge,   370
The horizon's utmost boundary; for above
Was nothing but the stars and the grey sky.
She was an elfin Pinnace;[7] lustily
I dipped my oars into the silent lake;
And, as I rose upon the stroke, my boat   375
Went heaving through the Water like a swan:
When, from behind that craggy Steep, till then
The horizon's bound, a huge peak, black and huge,
As if with voluntary power instinct,
Upreared its head.[8]—I struck, and struck again,   380
And, growing still in stature, the grim Shape
Towered up between me and the stars, and still,
For so it seemed, with purpose of its own
And measured motion, like a living Thing
Strode after me. With trembling oars I turned,   385
And through the silent water stole my way
Back to the Covert of the Willow-tree;
There, in her mooring-place, I left my Bark,—
And through the meadows homeward went, in grave
And serious mood; but after I had seen   390
That spectacle, for many days, my brain
Worked with a dim and undetermined sense
Of unknown modes of being; o'er my thoughts
There hung a darkness, call it solitude
Or blank desertion. No familiar Shapes   395
Remained, no pleasant images of trees,
Of sea or Sky, no colours of green fields,
But huge and mighty Forms, that do not live
Like living men, moved slowly through the mind
By day, and were a trouble to my dreams.   400
    Wisdom and Spirit of the Universe!
Thou Soul that art the eternity of thought,
That giv'st to forms and images a breath
And everlasting Motion! not in vain,
By day or star-light, thus from my first dawn   405
Of Childhood didst thou intertwine for me

7. Small boat.
8. In order to direct his boat in a straight line, the rower (sitting facing the stern of the boat) has fixed his eye on a point on the ridge of the nearby shore, which blocks out the landscape behind. As he moves farther out, the black peak rears into his altering angle of vision and seems to stride closer with each stroke of the oars. "Instinct" (line 379): endowed.

The passions that build up our human Soul,
Not with the mean and vulgar[9] works of man,
But with high objects, with enduring things,
With life and nature, purifying thus   410
The elements of feeling and of thought,
And sanctifying, by such discipline,
Both pain and fear; until we recognize
A grandeur in the beatings of the heart.
    Nor was this fellowship vouchsafed to me   415
With stinted kindness. In November days
When vapours, rolling down the valley, made
A lonely scene more lonesome; among woods
At noon, and 'mid the calm of summer nights,
When, by the margin of the trembling Lake,   420
Beneath the gloomy hills homeward I went
In solitude, such intercourse was mine:
Mine was it, in the fields both day and night,
And by the waters, all the summer long.
    —And in the frosty season, when the sun   425
Was set, and visible for many a mile,
The cottage windows blazed through twilight gloom,
I heeded not their summons;—happy time
It was indeed for all of us; for me
It was a time of rapture!—Clear and loud   430
The village Clock toll'd six—I wheeled about,
Proud and exulting like an untired horse
That cares not for his home.—All shod with steel,
We hissed along the polished ice, in games
Confederate, imitative of the chase   435
And woodland pleasures,—the resounding horn,
The Pack loud-chiming and the hunted hare.
So through the darkness and the cold we flew,
And not a voice was idle: with the din
Smitten, the precipices rang aloud;   440
The leafless trees and every icy crag
Tinkled like iron; while far distant hills
Into the tumult sent an alien sound
Of melancholy, not unnoticed while the stars,
Eastward, were sparkling clear, and in the west   445
The orange sky of evening died away.
Not seldom from the uproar I retired
Into a silent bay,—or sportively
Glanced sideway,[1] leaving the tumultous throng
To cut across the reflex[2] of a star   450
That fled, and, flying still before me, gleamed
Upon the glassy plain: and oftentimes,
When we had given our bodies to the wind,

9. Commonplace.   2. Reflection.
1. Moved off obliquely.

And all the shadowy banks on either side
Came sweeping through the darkness, spinning still   455
The rapid line of motion, then at once
Have I, reclining back upon my heels,
Stopped short; yet still the solitary cliffs
Wheeled by me—even as if the earth had rolled
With visible motion her diurnal[3] round!   460
Behind me did they stretch in solemn train,[4]
Feebler and feebler, and I stood and watched
Till all was tranquil as a dreamless sleep.
    Ye presences of Nature, in the sky,
And on the earth! Ye visions of the hills!   465
And Souls of lonely places![5] can I think
A vulgar hope was yours when ye employed
Such ministry, when ye, through many a year,
Haunting me thus among my boyish sports,
On caves and trees, upon the woods and hills,   470
Impressed upon all forms the characters[6]
Of danger or desire; and thus did make
The surface of the universal earth
With triumph and delight, with hope and fear,
Work[7] like a sea?
                        Not uselessly employed,   475
Might I pursue this theme through every change
Of exercise and play, to which the year
Did summon us in his delightful round.
    —We were a noisy crew; the sun in heaven
Beheld not vales more beautiful than ours,   480
Nor saw a Band in happiness and joy
Richer, or worthier of the ground they trod.
I could record with no reluctant voice
The woods of Autumn, and their hazel bowers
With milk-white clusters hung; the rod and line,   485
True symbol of hope's foolishness, whose strong
And unreproved enchantment led us on,
By rocks and pools shut out from every star
All the green summer, to forlorn cascades
Among the windings hid of mountain brooks.   490
—Unfading recollections! at this hour
The heart is almost mine with which I felt,
From some hill-top on sunny afternoons,
The paper-Kite, high among fleecy clouds,
Pull at her rein, like an impatient Courser;   495
Or, from the meadows sent on gusty days,
Beheld her breast the wind, then suddenly

---

3. Daily.
4. Succession.
5. Wordsworth refers both to a single "Spirit" or
"Soul" of the universe as a whole (e.g., lines 401–

2 above) and to plural "Presences" and "Souls"
inanimating the various parts of the universe.
6. Signs.
7. Seethe.

Dashed headlong, and rejected by the storm.
　　Ye lowly Cottages in which we dwelt,
A ministration of your own was yours!   500
Can I forget you, being as ye were
So beautiful among the pleasant fields
In which ye stood? or can I here forget
The plain and seemly countenance with which
Ye dealt out your plain Comforts? Yet had ye   505
Delights and exultations of your own.
Eager and never weary, we pursued
Our home-amusements by the warm peat-fire
At evening, when with pencil, and smooth slate
In square divisions parcelled out, and all   510
With crosses and with cyphers scribbled o'er,
We schemed and puzzled, head opposed to head,
In strife too humble to be named in verse;[8]
Or round the naked table, snow-white deal,[9]
Cherry, or maple, sate in close array,   515
And to the Combat, Lu or Whist, led on
A thick-ribbed Army, not as in the world
Neglected and ungratefully thrown by
Even for the very service they had wrought,
But husbanded through many a long campaign.   520
Uncouth assemblage was it, where no few
Had changed their functions; some, plebeian cards
Which Fate, beyond the promise of their birth,
Had dignified, and called to represent
The Persons of departed Potentates.   525
Oh, with what echoes on the board they fell!
Ironic diamonds; Clubs, Hearts, Diamonds, Spades,
A congregation piteously akin!
Cheap matter offered they to boyish wit,
Those sooty Knaves, precipitated down   530
With scoffs and taunts like Vulcan out of heaven;[1]
The paramount Ace, a moon in her eclipse,
Queens gleaming through their Splendor's last decay,
And Monarchs surly at the wrongs sustained
By royal visages.[2] Meanwhile abroad   535
Incessant rain was falling, or the frost
Raged bitterly, with keen and silent tooth;
And, interrupting oft that eager game,
From under Esthwaite's splitting fields of ice
The pent-up air, struggling to free itself,   540
Gave out to meadow-grounds and hills, a loud

8. I.e., ticktacktoe. Wordsworth pokes fun at 18th-
century poetic diction, which avoided homely terms
by using circumlocutions.
9. Pine, or fir.
1. Vulcan was the Roman god of fire and forge.
His mother, Hera, when he was born lame, threw

him down from Olympus, the abode of the gods.
2. Wordsworth implicitly parallels the boys' card
games to the mock-epic description of the aristocratic game of ombre in Pope's *The Rape of the
Lock* 3.37–98.

Protracted yelling, like the noise of wolves
Howling in Troops along the Bothnic Main.[3]
   Nor, sedulous[4] as I have been to trace
How Nature by extrinsic passion first   545
Peopled the mind with forms sublime or fair[5]
And made me love them, may I here omit
How other pleasures have been mine, and joys
Of subtler origin; how I have felt,
Not seldom even in that tempestuous time,   550
Those hallowed and pure motions of the sense
Which seem, in their simplicity, to own
An intellectual[6] charm;—that calm delight
Which, if I err not, surely must belong
To those first-born[7] affinities that fit   555
Our new existence to existing things,
And, in our dawn of being, constitute
The bond of union between life and joy.
   Yes, I remember when the changeful earth
And twice five summers on my mind had stamped   560
The faces of the moving year, even then
I held unconscious intercourse with beauty
Old as creation, drinking in a pure
Organic pleasure from the silver wreaths
Of curling mist, or from the level plain   565
Of waters, colored by impending[8] clouds.
   The sands of Westmorland, the creeks and bays
Of Cumbria's[9] rocky limits, they can tell
How, when the Sea threw off his evening shade,
And to the Shepherd's hut on distant hills   570
Sent welcome notice of the rising moon,
How I have stood, to fancies such as these
A Stranger, linking with the Spectacle
No conscious memory of a kindred sight,
And bringing with me no peculiar sense   575
Of quietness or peace, yet have I stood,
Even while mine eye hath moved o'er many a league[1]
Of shining water, gathering, as it seemed,
Through every hair-breadth in that field of light,
New pleasure, like a bee among the flowers.   580
   Thus oft amid those fits of vulgar[2] joy
Which, through all seasons, on a Child's pursuits
Are prompt Attendants; 'mid that giddy bliss
Which like a tempest works along the blood

---

3. A northern gulf of the Baltic Sea.
4. Diligent.
5. The passion at first was "extrinsic" because it was felt not for nature itself but for nature as associated with the outdoor activities he loved. Wordsworth now goes on to distinguish other "subtler" pleasures, felt in the very process of sensing the natural objects.
6. Spiritual, as opposed to sense perceptions.
7. Innate.
8. Overhanging.
9. Cumberland's.
1. A league is approximately three miles.
2. Ordinary, commonplace.

And is forgotten: even then I felt 585
Gleams like the flashing of a shield,—the earth
And common face of Nature spake to me
Rememberable things; sometimes, 'tis true,
By chance collisions and quaint accidents
(Like those ill-sorted unions, work supposed 590
Of evil-minded fairies), yet not vain
Nor profitless, if haply they impressed
Collateral[3] objects and appearances,
Albeit lifeless then, and doomed to sleep
Until maturer seasons called them forth 595
To impregnate and to elevate the mind.
—And, if the vulgar joy by its own weight
Wearied itself out of the memory,
The scenes which were a witness of that joy
Remained, in their substantial lineaments 600
Depicted on the brain, and to the eye
Were visible, a daily sight: and thus
By the impressive discipline of fear,
By pleasure and repeated happiness,
So frequently repeated, and by force 605
Of obscure feelings representative
Of things forgotten; these same scenes so bright,
So beautiful, so majestic in themselves,
Though yet the day was distant, did become
Habitually dear; and all their forms 610
And changeful colours by invisible links
Were fastened to the affections.[4]
                          I began
My Story early, not misled, I trust,
By an infirmity of love for days
Disowned by memory,[5] fancying flowers where none, 615
Not even the sweetest, do or can survive
For him at least whose dawning day they cheered;
Nor will it seem to Thee, O Friend! so prompt
In sympathy, that I have lengthened out,
With fond and feeble tongue, a tedious tale. 620
Meanwhile, my hope has been, that I might fetch
Invigorating thoughts from former years;
Might fix the wavering balance of my mind,
And haply meet reproaches too, whose power
May spur me on, in manhood now mature, 625
To honorable toil. Yet should these hopes
Prove vain, and thus should neither I be taught
To understand myself, nor thou to know
With better knowledge how the heart was framed

---

3. Accompanying but subordinate.
4. Feelings.
5. I.e., he fears that he may have been attributing later thoughts and feelings to a time of life he can no longer remember.

Of him thou lovest, need I dread from thee   630
Harsh judgments, if the Song be loth to quit
Those recollected hours that have the charm
Of visionary things, those lovely forms
And sweet sensations that throw back our life,
And almost make remotest infancy   635
A visible scene, on which the sun is shining?
    One end at least hath been attained—my mind
Hath been revived; and, if this genial[6] mood
Desert me not, forthwith shall be brought down
Through later years the story of my life: 640
The road lies plain before me,—'tis a theme
Single, and of determined bounds; and hence
I chuse it rather, at this time, than work
Of ampler or more varied argument,
Where I might be discomfited and lost;   645
And certain hopes are with me that to thee
This labour will be welcome, honoured Friend!

Book Second
School-time continued

Thus far, O Friend! have we, though leaving much
Unvisited, endeavoured to retrace
The simple ways in which my childhood walked,
Those chiefly, that first led me to the love
Of rivers, woods, and fields. The passion yet   5
Was in its birth, sustained, as might befal,
By nourishment that came unsought; for still,
From week to week, from month to month, we lived
A round of tumult. Duly[1] were our games
Prolonged in summer till the day-light failed;   10
No chair remained before the doors, the bench
And threshold steps were empty; fast asleep
The Labourer, and the old Man who had sate,
A later Lingerer, yet the revelry
Continued, and the loud uproar; at last,   15
When all the ground was dark, and twinkling stars
Edged the black clouds, home and to bed we went,
Feverish, with weary joints and beating minds.
Ah! is there One who ever has been young
Nor needs a warning voice to tame the pride   20
Of intellect, and virtue's self-esteem?[2]
One is there,[3] though the wisest and the best
Of all mankind, who covets not at times

6. Productive, creative.   need to be warned not to overrate the achieve-
1. Appropriately.   ments of age?
2. I.e., does anyone who has once been young   3. I.e., "Is there anyone . . . ?"

Union that cannot be; who would not give,
If so he might, to duty and to truth   25
The eagerness of infantine desire?
A tranquillizing spirit presses now
On my corporeal frame, so wide appears
The vacancy between me and those days,
Which yet have such self-presence[4] in my mind,   30
That, musing on them, often do I seem
Two consciousnesses, conscious of myself
And of some other Being. A rude mass
Of native rock, left midway in the Square
Of our small market Village, was the goal   35
Or centre of these sports; and, when, returned
After long absence, thither I repaired,
Gone was the old grey stone, and in its place
A smart Assembly-room usurped the ground
That had been ours.[5] There let the fiddle scream,   40
And be ye happy! Yet, my Friends,[6] I know
That more than one of you will think with me
Of those soft starry nights, and that old Dame
From whom the Stone was named, who there had sate
And watched her table with its huckster's wares   45
Assiduous, through the length of sixty years.
—We ran a boisterous course, the year span round
With giddy motion. But the time approached
That brought with it a regular desire
For calmer pleasures, when the winning forms   50
Of Nature were collaterally attached[7]
To every scheme of holiday delight,
And every boyish sport, less grateful[8] else
And languidly pursued.
             When summer came,
Our pastime was, on bright half-holidays,   55
To sweep along the plain of Windermere
With rival oars; and the selected bourne[9]
Was now an Island musical with birds
That sang and ceased not; now a sister isle,
Beneath the oaks' umbrageous[1] covert, sown   60
With lilies of the valley like a field;
And now a third small island, where survived,
In solitude, the ruins of a shrine
Once to our Lady dedicate, and served
Daily with chaunted rites.[2] In such a race,   65
So ended, disappointment could be none,

4. Actuality, existence.
5. The Hawkshead Town Hall, built in 1790.
6. Coleridge and John Wordsworth (William's brother), who had visited Hawkshead together with William in November 1799.
7. Associated as an accompaniment.
8. Pleasing.
9. Destination.
1. Shaded.
2. The island of Lady Holm, former site of a chapel dedicated to the Virgin Mary.

Uneasiness, or pain, or jealousy;
We rested in the Shade, all pleased alike,
Conquered and Conqueror. Thus the pride of strength,
And the vain-glory of superior skill,   70
Were tempered, thus was gradually produced
A quiet independence of the heart:
And, to my Friend who knows me, I may add,
Fearless of blame, that hence, for future days,
Ensued a diffidence and modesty;   75
And I was taught to feel, perhaps too much,
The self-sufficing power of solitude.
     Our daily meals were frugal, Sabine fare![3]
More than we wished we knew the blessing then
Of vigorous hunger—hence corporeal strength   80
Unsapped by delicate viands; for, exclude
A little weekly stipend,[4] and we lived
Through three divisions of the quartered year
In pennyless poverty. But now, to school
From the half-yearly holidays returned,   85
We came with weightier purses, that sufficed
To furnish treats more costly than the Dame
Of the old grey stone, from her scanty board, supplied.
Hence rustic dinners on the cool green ground,
Or in the woods, or by a river side,   90
Or shady fountains,[5] while among the leaves
Soft airs were stirring, and the mid-day sun
Unfelt shone brightly round us in our joy.
     Nor is my aim neglected if I tell
How sometimes, in the length of those half years,   95
We from our funds drew largely—proud to curb,
And eager to spur on, the gallopping Steed:
And with the cautious Inn-keeper, whose Stud
Supplied our want, we haply might employ
Sly subterfuges, if the Adventure's bound   100
Were distant, some famed Temple where of yore
The Druids worshipped,[6] or the antique Walls
Of that large Abbey which within the Vale
Of Nightshade, to St Mary's honour built,
Stands yet, a mouldering Pile, with fractured arch,   105
Belfry, and Images, and living Trees;
A holy Scene![7]—Along the smooth green Turf
Our Horses grazed:—to more than inland peace
Left by the west wind sweeping overhead

---

3. Like the meals of the Roman poet Horace on his Sabine farm.
4. In his last year at school Wordsworth had an allowance of sixpence a week, and his younger brother Christopher threepence. After the Mid-summer and Christmas holidays (line 85), the boys received a larger sum, ranging up to a guinea.
5. Springs, streams.
6. The stone circle at Swinside, on the lower Duddon River, mistakenly believed at the time to have been a Druid temple.
7. Furness Abbey, some 20 miles south of Hawks-head.

From a tumultuous ocean, trees and towers   110
In that sequestered Valley may be seen
Both silent and both motionless alike;
Such the deep shelter that is there, and such
The safeguard for repose and quietness.
    Our Steeds remounted, and the summons given,   115
With whip and spur we through the Chauntry[8] flew
In uncouth race, and left the cross-legged Knight
And the Stone-abbot, and that single Wren
Which one day sang so sweetly in the Nave
Of the old Church, that, though from recent Showers   120
The earth was comfortless, and, touched by faint
Internal breezes, sobbings of the place
And respirations, from the roofless walls
The shuddering ivy dripped large drops, yet still
So sweetly 'mid the gloom the invisible Bird   125
Sang to herself, that there I could have made
My dwelling-place, and lived for ever there
To hear such music. Through the Walls we flew,
And down the Valley, and, a circuit made
In wantonness of heart, through rough and smooth   130
We scampered homewards. Oh, ye rocks and streams,
And that still Spirit shed from evening air!
Even in this joyous time I sometimes felt
Your presence, when with slackened step we breathed[9]
Along the sides of the steep hills, or when,   135
Lighted by gleams of moonlight from the sea,
We beat with thundering hoofs the level sand.
    Midway on long Winander's Eastern shore,
Within the crescent of a pleasant Bay,
A Tavern stood, no homely-featured House,   140
Primeval like its neighbouring Cottages;
But 'twas a splendid place, the door beset
With Chaises, Grooms, and Liveries,—and within
Decanters, Glasses, and the blood-red Wine.
In ancient times, or ere the Hall was built   145
On the large Island, had this Dwelling been
More worthy of a Poet's love, a Hut
Proud of its one bright fire and sycamore shade.[1]
But, though the rhymes were gone that once inscribed
The threshold, and large golden characters   150
Spread o'er the spangled sign-board had dislodged
The old Lion, and usurped his place in slight
And mockery of the rustic Painter's hand,
Yet to this hour the spot to me is dear
With all its foolish pomp. The garden lay   155

8. A chapel endowed for masses to be sung to the donor.
9. Stopped to let the horses catch their breath.

1. The tavern was the White Lion at Bowness; the Hall (line 145) on Belle Isle in Lake Windermere had been built in the early 1780s.

Upon a slope surmounted by the plain
Of a small Bowling-green: beneath us stood
A grove, with gleams of water through the trees
And over the tree-tops; nor did we want
Refreshment, strawberries, and mellow cream.   160
There, while through half an afternoon we played
On the smooth platform, whether skill prevailed
Or happy blunder triumphed, bursts of glee
Made all the mountains ring. But ere night-fall,
When in our pinnace we returned, at leisure   165
Over the shadowy Lake, and to the beach
Of some small Island steered our course with one,
The Minstrel of our Troop,[2] and left him there,
And rowed off gently, while he blew his flute
Alone upon the rock,—Oh then the calm   170
And dead still water lay upon my mind
Even with a weight of pleasure, and the sky,
Never before so beautiful, sank down
Into my heart, and held me like a dream!
    Thus were my sympathies enlarged, and thus   175
Daily the common range of visible things
Grew dear to me: already I began
To love the sun; a boy I loved the sun,
Not as I since have loved him, as a pledge
And surety of our earthly life, a light   180
Which we behold, and feel we are alive;
Nor for his bounty to so many worlds,
But for this cause, that I had seen him lay
His beauty on the morning hills, had seen
The western mountain touch his setting orb,   185
In many a thoughtless hour, when, from excess
Of happiness, my blood appear'd to flow
For its own pleasure, and I breathed with joy;
And from like feelings, humble though intense,
To patriotic and domestic love   190
Analogous, the moon to me was dear;
For I would dream away my purposes,
Standing to gaze upon her while she hung
Midway between the hills, as if she knew
No other region; but belonged to thee,   195
Yea, appertained by a peculiar right
To thee, and thy grey huts,[3] thou one dear Vale!
    Those incidental charms which first attached
My heart to rural objects, day by day
Grew weaker, and I hasten on to tell   200
How Nature, intervenient[4] till this time

2. Identified by Christopher Wordsworth, *Mem-*   3. Cottages built of gray stones.
oirs (1857), as Robert Greenwood, who became   4. I.e., entering incidentally into his other con-
Senior Fellow of Trinity College, Cambridge.   cerns.

And secondary, now at length was sought
For her own sake. But who shall[5] parcel out
His intellect, by geometric rules,
Split like a province into round and square?   205
Who knows the individual hour in which
His habits were first sown, even as a seed?
Who that shall point, as with a wand, and say,
"This portion of the river of my mind
Came from yon fountain"? Thou, my friend! art one   210
More deeply read in thy own thoughts; to thee
Science[6] appears but what in truth she is,
Not as our glory and our absolute boast,
But as a succedaneum,[7] and a prop
To our infirmity. No officious slave   215
Art thou of that false secondary power[8]
By which we multiply distinctions, then
Deem that our puny boundaries are things
That we perceive, and not that we have made.
To thee, unblinded by these formal arts,   220
The unity of all hath been revealed;
And thou wilt doubt with me, less aptly skilled
Than many are to range the faculties
In scale and order, class the cabinet
Of their sensations,[9] and in voluble phrase[1]   225
Run through the history and birth of each
As of a single independent thing.
Hard task, vain hope, to analyse the mind,
If each most obvious and particular thought,
Not in a mystical and idle sense,   230
But in the words of reason deeply weighed,
Hath no beginning.
    Blest the infant Babe,
(For with my best conjecture I would trace
Our Being's earthly progress) blest the Babe,
Nursed in his Mother's arms, who sinks to sleep   235
Rocked on his Mother's breast; who, when his soul
Claims manifest kindred with a human soul,
Drinks in the feelings of his Mother's eye![2]
For him, in one dear Presence, there exists
A virtue which irradiates and exalts   240
Objects through widest intercourse of sense.
No outcast he, bewildered and depressed;
Along his infant veins are interfused

---

5. Is able to.
6. In the old sense of "learning."
7. In medicine, a drug substituted for a different drug. Wordsworth, however, uses the term to signify a remedy, or palliative.
8. The analytic faculty, as opposed to the power to apprehend "the unity of all" (line 221).

9. To classify, as if arranged in a display case.
1. In fluent phraseology.
2. Like the modern psychologist, Wordsworth recognizes the importance of earliest infancy in the development of the individual mind, although he had then to invent the terms with which to analyze the process.

The gravitation and the filial bond
Of nature that connect him with the world.   245
Is there a flower to which he points with hand
Too weak to gather it, already love
Drawn from love's purest earthly fount for him
Hath beautified that flower; already shades
Of pity cast from inward tenderness   250
Do fall around him upon aught that bears
Unsightly marks of violence or harm.
Emphatically such a Being lives,
Frail Creature as he is, helpless as frail,
An inmate of this active universe.   255
For feeling has to him imparted power
That through the growing faculties of sense
Doth, like an Agent of the one great Mind,
Create, creator and receiver both,
Working but in alliance with the works   260
Which it beholds.[3]—Such, verily, is the first
Poetic spirit of our human life,
By uniform control of after years
In most abated or suppressed, in some,
Through every change of growth and of decay,   265
Preeminent till death.
                              From early days,
Beginning not long after that first time
In which, a Babe, by intercourse of touch,
I held mute dialogues with my Mother's heart,[4]
I have endeavoured to display the means   270
Whereby this infant sensibility,
Great birth-right of our being, was in me
Augmented and sustained. Yet is a path
More difficult before me, and I fear
That, in its broken windings, we shall need   275
The chamois'[5] sinews, and the eagle's wing:
For now a trouble came into my mind
From unknown causes. I was left alone,
Seeking the visible world, nor knowing why.
The props of my affections were removed,[6]   280
And yet the building stood, as if sustained
By its own spirit! All that I beheld
Was dear, and hence to finer influxes[7]

---

3. The infant, in the sense of security and love shed by his mother's presence on outer things, perceives what would otherwise be an alien world as a place to which he has a relationship like that of a son to a mother (lines 239–45). On such grounds Wordsworth asserts that the mind partially creates, by altering, the world it seems simply to perceive.
4. I.e., both infant and mother feel the pulse of the other's heart.
5. A very agile species of antelope inhabiting mountainous regions of Europe.
6. Wordsworth's mother had died the month before his eighth birthday. It is unclear from the context whether the "trouble" that came into his mind (line 276) refers to the loss of his mother, in whose arms he had established his initial relationship to the natural world, or to the mysterious processes of the continued development and diversification of this relationship.
7. Influences.

The mind lay open, to a more exact
And close communion. Many are our joys   285
In youth, but Oh! what happiness to live
When every hour brings palpable access
Of knowledge, when all knowledge is delight,
And sorrow is not there! The seasons came,
And every season, wheresoe'er I moved,   290
Unfolded transitory qualities
Which, but for this most watchful power of love,
Had been neglected, left a register
Of permanent relations, else unknown.[8]
Hence life, and change, and beauty; solitude   295
More active even than "best society,"[9]
Society made sweet as solitude
By inward concords, silent, inobstrusive;
And gentle agitations of the mind
From manifold distinctions, difference   300
Perceived in things where, to the unwatchful eye,
No difference is, and hence, from the same source,
Sublimer joy: for I would walk alone
Under the quiet stars, and at that time
Have felt whate'er there is of power in sound   305
To breathe an elevated mood, by form
Or Image unprofaned: and I would stand,
If the night blackened with a coming storm,
Beneath some rock, listening to notes that are
The ghostly[1] language of the ancient earth,   310
Or make their dim abode in distant winds.
Thence did I drink the visionary power;
And deem not profitless those fleeting moods
Of shadowy exultation: not for this,
That they are kindred to our purer mind   315
And intellectual life;[2] but that the soul,
Remembering how she felt, but what she felt
Remembering not, retains an obscure sense[3]
Of possible sublimity, whereto
With growing faculties she doth aspire,   320
With faculties still growing, feeling still
That, whatsoever point they gain, they yet
Have something to pursue.[4]
                              And not alone
'Mid gloom and tumult, but no less 'mid fair
And tranquil scenes, that universal power   325

---

8. I.e., had it not been for the watchful power of
love (line 291), the "transitory qualities" would have
been neglected, and the "permanent relations" now
recorded in his memory would have been unknown.
9. A partial quotation of a line spoken by Adam
to Eve in *Paradise Lost* 9.249: "For solitude sometimes is best society."

1. Disembodied.
2. I.e., not because they are related to the non-
sensuous ("intellectual") aspect of our life.
3. Pronounced *ăn ŏbscūre sénse*.
4. Compare the revelation, while crossing Simplon Pass, that our destiny is with "something
evermore about to be," below, 6.604–608.

And fitness in the latent qualities
And essences of things, by which the mind
Is moved with feelings of delight, to me
Came strengthened with a superadded soul,
A virtue not its own.—My morning walks   330
Were early;—oft before the hours of School
I travelled round our little Lake, five miles
Of pleasant wandering; happy time! more dear
For this, that One was by my side, a Friend
Then passionately loved;[5] with heart how full   335
Would he peruse these lines! for many years
Have since flowed in between us, and, our minds
Both silent to each other, at this time
We live as if those hours had never been.
Nor seldom did I lift our Cottage latch   340
Far earlier, and ere one smoke-wreath had risen
From human dwelling, or the thrush, high perched,
Piped to the woods his shrill *reveillé*,[6] sate
Alone upon some jutting eminence
At the first gleam of dawn-light, when the Vale,   345
Yet slumbering, lay in utter solitude.
How shall I seek the origin, where find
Faith in the marvellous things which then I felt?
Oft in those moments such a holy calm
Would overspread my soul, that bodily eyes   350
Were utterly forgotten, and what I saw
Appeared like something in myself, a dream,
A prospect[7] in the mind.
                          'Twere long to tell
What spring and autumn, what the winter snows,
And what the summer shade, what day and night,   355
Evening and morning, sleep and waking thought,
From sources inexhaustible, poured forth
To feed the spirit of religious love,
In which I walked with Nature. But let this
Be not forgotten, that I still retained   360
My first creative sensibility,[8]
That by the regular action of the world
My soul was unsubdued. A plastic[9] power
Abode with me, a forming hand, at times
Rebellious, acting in a devious mood,   365
A local Spirit of his own, at war
With general tendency, but, for the most,
Subservient strictly to external things
With which it communed. An auxiliar light

---

5. Identified as John Fleming in a note to the edition of 1850.
6. Military parlance for a signal call.
7. Scene.

8. I.e., the creative perception manifested by the babe in his mother's arms, above.
9. Shaping, formative.

Came from my mind which on the setting sun   370
Bestowed new splendor; the melodious birds,
The fluttering breezes, fountains that ran on
Murmuring so sweetly in themselves, obeyed
A like dominion; and the midnight storm
Grew darker in the presence of my eye;   375
Hence my obeisance, my devotion hence,
And hence my transport.[1]
                              Nor should this, perchance,
Pass unrecorded, that I still[2] had loved
The exercise and produce of a toil
Than analytic industry to me   380
More pleasing, and whose character I deem
Is more poetic, as resembling more
Creative agency. The Song would speak
Of that interminable building reared
By observation of affinities   385
In objects where no brotherhood exists
To passive minds. My seventeenth year was come;
And, whether from this habit rooted now
So deeply in my mind, or from excess
Of the great social principle of life   390
Coercing all things into sympathy,
To unorganic Natures were transferred
My own enjoyments; or the Power of truth,
Coming in revelation, did converse
With things that really are;[3] I, at this time,   395
Saw blessings spread around me like a sea.
Thus while the days flew by and years passed on,
From Nature overflowing on my soul
I had received so much, that every thought
Was steeped in feeling; I was only then   400
Contented when with bliss ineffable
I felt the sentiment of Being spread
O'er all that moves, and all that seemeth still;
O'er all that, lost beyond the reach of thought
And human knowledge, to the human eye   405
Invisible, yet liveth to the heart;
O'er all that leaps, and runs, and shouts, and sings,
Or beats the gladsome air; o'er all that glides
Beneath the wave, yea, in the wave itself,
And mighty depth of waters. Wonder not   410
If high the transport, great the joy I felt,
Communing in this sort through earth and Heaven
With every form of Creature, as it looked

1. Exaltation.
2. Always.
3. Wordsworth is careful to indicate that there are alternative explanations for his sense that life pervades the inorganic as well as the organic world: it may be the result either of a way of perceiving habitual since infancy, or of a projection of his own inner life, or else it may be the perception of an objective truth.

Towards the Uncreated with a countenance
Of adoration, with an eye of love.[4]   415
One song they sang, and it was audible,
Most audible, then, when the fleshly ear,
O'ercome by humblest prelude of that strain,
Forgot her functions and slept undisturbed.
  If this be error, and another faith   420
Find easier access to the pious mind,[5]
Yet were I grossly destitute of all
Those human sentiments that make this earth
So dear, if I should fail with grateful voice
To speak of you, Ye Mountains, and Ye Lakes,   425
And sounding Cataracts, Ye Mists and Winds
That dwell among the Hills where I was born.
If in my Youth I have been pure in heart,
If, mingling with the world, I am content
With my own modest pleasures, and have lived,   430
With God and Nature communing, removed
From little enmities and low desires,
The gift is yours: if in these times of fear,
This melancholy waste[6] of hopes o'erthrown,
If, 'mid indifference and apathy   435
And wicked exultation, when good men,
On every side, fall off, we know not how,
To selfishness, disguised in gentle names
Of peace and quiet and domestic love,
Yet mingled, not unwillingly, with sneers   440
On visionary minds; if, in this time
Of dereliction and dismay,[7] I yet
Despair not of our Nature, but retain
A more than Roman confidence, a faith
That fails not, in all sorrow my support,   445
The blessing of my life, the gift is yours,
Ye Winds and sounding Cataracts, 'tis yours,
Ye Mountains! thine, O Nature! Thou hast fed
My lofty speculations; and in thee,
For this uneasy heart of ours, I find   450
A never-failing principle of joy
And purest passion.
                    Thou, my Friend! wert reared
In the great City, 'mid far other scenes;[8]
But we, by different roads, at length have gained
The self-same bourne.[9] And for this cause to Thee   455

---

4. Wordsworth did not add lines 412–14, giving a Christian frame to his experience of the "one life," until the last revision of *The Prelude*, 1839.
5. With lines 416–21, compare *Tintern Abbey*, lines 43–50.
6. Wasteland.
7. The era, some ten years after the outbreak of the French Revolution, was one of violent reaction, in which many earlier sympathizers were recanting their radical beliefs.
8. A reminiscence of Coleridge's *Frost at Midnight* (see below), lines 51–52: "For I was reared / In the great city, pent 'mid cloisters dim."
9. Destination.

I speak, unapprehensive of contempt,
The insinuated scoff of coward tongues,
And all that silent language which so oft,
In conversation between Man and Man,
Blots from the human countenance all trace   460
Of beauty and of love. For Thou hast sought
The truth in solitude, and, since the days
That gave thee liberty, full long desired,
To serve in Nature's Temple, thou hast been
The most assiduous of her Ministers,[1]   465
In many things my Brother, chiefly here
In this our deep devotion.
                          Fare Thee well!
Health, and the quiet of a healthful mind,
Attend Thee! seeking oft the haunts of Men,
And yet more often living with thyself   470
And for thyself, so haply shall thy days
Be many, and a blessing to mankind.

From Book Third
Residence at Cambridge

[*Experiences at St. John's College. The "Heroic Argument"*]

It was a dreary Morning when the Wheels
Rolled over a wide plain o'erhung with clouds,
And nothing cheered our way till first we saw
The long-roof'd Chapel of King's College lift
Turrets, and pinnacles in answering files   5
Extended high above a dusky grove.
    Advancing, we espied upon the road
A Student, clothed in Gown and tasselled Cap,
Striding along, as if o'ertasked by Time
Or covetous of exercise and air.   10
He passed—nor was I Master of my eyes
Till he was left an arrow's flight behind.
As near and nearer to the Spot we drew,
It seemed to suck us in with an eddy's force;
Onward we drove beneath the Castle, caught,   15
While crossing Magdalene Bridge, a glimpse of Cam,
And at the *Hoop* alighted, famous Inn![1]
    My Spirit was up, my thoughts were full of hope;
Some friends I had, acquaintances who there

1. Wordsworth may be recalling the conclusion of
Coleridge's *France: An Ode* (1798) where, disillu-
sioned about the promise of liberty by the French
Revolution, he writes that, while standing on a "sea-
cliff's verge," "O Liberty! my spirit felt thee there."
Wordsworth added lines 461–64 some years after

Coleridge's death in 1834.
1. Wordsworth renders some of his early college
experiences, when he was a callow country boy
(lines 34–35), in a deliberately inflated, or mock-
epic, manner. "Cam" (line 16) is the river that
flows through Cambridge.

Seemed friends, poor simple School-boys! now hung round   20
With honor and importance: in a world
Of welcome faces up and down I roved;
Questions, directions, warnings, and advice
Flowed in upon me, from all sides; fresh day
Of pride and pleasure! to myself I seemed   25
A man of business and expence, and went
From shop to shop, about my own affairs,
To Tutor or to Tailor, as befel,
From street to street, with loose and careless mind.
   I was the Dreamer, they the dream: I roamed   30
Delighted through the motley spectacle;
Gowns grave or gaudy, Doctors, Students, Streets,
Courts, Cloisters, flocks of Churches, gateways, towers.
Migration strange for a Stripling of the Hills,
A Northern Villager! As if the change   35
Had waited on some Fairy's wand, at once
Behold me rich in monies; and attired
In splendid garb, with hose of silk, and hair
Powdered like rimy trees,[2] when frost is keen.
My lordly dressing-gown, I pass it by,   40
With other signs of manhood that supplied
The lack of beard.—The weeks went roundly on
With invitations, suppers, wine and fruit,
Smooth housekeeping within, and all without
Liberal, and suiting Gentleman's array!   45
   The Evangelist St. John my Patron was;[3]
Three gothic Courts are his, and in the first
Was my abiding-place, a nook obscure!
Right underneath, the College Kitchens made
A humming sound, less tuneable than bees,   50
But hardly less industrious; with shrill notes
Of sharp command and scolding intermixed.
Near me hung Trinity's loquacious Clock,
Who never let the quarters, night or day,
Slip by him unproclaimed, and told the hours   55
Twice over, with a male and female voice.
Her pealing Organ was my neighbour too;
And from my pillow, looking forth by light
Of moon or favoring stars, I could behold
The Antechapel, where the Statue stood   60
Of Newton, with his prism,[4] and silent face:
The marble index of a Mind for ever
Voyaging through strange seas of Thought, alone.
   Of College labors, of the Lecturer's room

2. The fashion was for men to wear their hair
powdered. "Rimy": covered with rime, frosted over.
3. Wordsworth was a student at St. John's College, Cambridge University, from 1787 to 1791.
Book 3 deals with his first year there.

4. In the west end of Trinity Chapel, adjoining
St. John's College, stands Roubiliac's statue of
Newton holding the prism with which he had con-
ducted the experiments described in his Optics.

All studded round, as thick as chairs could stand,   65
With loyal Students faithful to their books,
Half-and-half Idlers, hardy Recusants,[5]
And honest Dunces—of important days,
Examinations when the man was weighed
As in a balance! of excessive hopes,   70
Tremblings withal, and commendable fears;
Small jealousies, and triumphs good or bad,
Let others, that know more, speak as they know.
Such glory was but little sought by me
And little won. Yet, from the first crude days   75
Of settling time in this untried abode,
I was disturbed at times by prudent thoughts,
Wishing to hope, without a hope; some fears
About my future worldly maintenance;[6]
And, more than all, a strangeness in the mind,   80
A feeling that I was not for that hour,
Nor for that place. But wherefore be cast down?
For (not to speak of Reason and her pure
Reflective acts to fix the moral law
Deep in the conscience; nor of Christian Hope   85
Bowing her head before her Sister Faith
As one far mightier),[7] hither I had come,
Bear witness, Truth, endowed with holy powers
And faculties, whether to work or feel.
Oft when the dazzling shew no longer new   90
Had ceased to dazzle, ofttimes did I quit
My Comrades, leave the Crowd, buildings and groves,
And as I paced alone the level fields
Far from those lovely sights and sounds sublime
With which I had been conversant, the mind   95
Drooped not, but there into herself returning
With prompt rebound, seemed fresh as heretofore.
At least I more distinctly recognized
Her native instincts; let me dare to speak
A higher language, say that now I felt   100
What independent solaces were mine
To mitigate the injurious sway of place
Or circumstance, how far soever changed
In youth, or to be changed in manhood's prime;
Or, for the few who shall be called to look   105
On the long shadows, in our evening years,
Ordained Precursors to the night of death.
As if awakened, summoned, roused, constrained,
I looked for universal things, perused

5. Those who refused to work at their studies.
6. Wordsworth was troubled by the expectation of
his family that he would be appointed a Fellow of
St. John's College.
7. This pious qualification, lines 83–87, was added
by Wordsworth in late revisions of *The Prelude*. In
the version of 1805, he wrote: "I was a chosen son. / For
hither I had come with holy powers / And faculties, whether to work or feel."

The common countenance of earth and sky;   110
Earth no where unembellished by some trace
Of that first paradise whence man was driven;
And sky whose beauty and bounty are expressed
By the proud name she bears, the name of heaven.
I called on both to teach me what they might;   115
Or, turning the mind in upon herself,
Pored, watched, expected, listened, spread my thoughts
And spread them with a wider creeping; felt
Incumbencies more awful,[8] visitings
Of the Upholder, of the tranquil Soul   120
That tolerates the indignities of Time;
And, from his centre of eternity
All finite motions overruling, lives
In glory immutable. But peace!—enough
Here to record I had ascended now   125
To such community with highest truth.
—A track pursuing, not untrod before,
From strict analogies by thought supplied,
Or consciousnesses not to be subdued,
To every natural form, rock, fruit or flower,   130
Even the loose stones that cover the high-way,
I gave a moral life; I saw them feel,
Or linked them to some feeling: the great mass
Lay bedded in a quickening[9] soul, and all
That I beheld respired with inward meaning.   135
Add, that whate'er of Terror or of Love
Or Beauty, Nature's daily face put on
From transitory passion, unto this
I was as sensitive as waters are
To the sky's influence: in a kindred mood   140
Of passion, was obedient as a lute
That waits upon the touches of the wind.[1]
Unknown, unthought of, yet I was most rich;
I had a world about me; 'twas my own,
I made it; for it only lived to me,   145
And to the God who sees into the heart.
Such sympathies, though rarely, were betrayed
By outward gestures and by visible looks:
Some called it madness—so, indeed, it was,
If child-like fruitfulness in passing joy,   150
If steady moods of thoughtfulness, matured
To inspiration, sort with such a name;
If prophecy be madness; if things viewed
By Poets in old time, and higher up
By the first men, earth's first inhabitants,   155
May in these tutored days no more be seen

8. I.e., the weight of more awe-inspiring moods.   1. I.e., as a wind harp.
9. Life-giving.

With undisordered sight. But, leaving this,
It was no madness: for the bodily eye
Amid my strongest workings evermore
Was searching out the lines of difference   160
As they lie hid in all external forms,
Near or remote, minute or vast, an eye
Which from a tree, a stone, a withered leaf,
To the broad ocean, and the azure heavens
Spangled with kindred multitudes of Stars,   165
Could find no surface where its power might sleep;
Which spake perpetual logic to my Soul,
And by an unrelenting agency
Did bind my feelings, even as in a chain.
    And here, O friend! have I retraced my life   170
Up to an eminence, and told a tale
Of matters which not falsely may be called
The glory of my Youth. Of genius, power,
Creation, and Divinity itself,
I have been speaking, for my theme has been   175
What passed within me. Not of outward things
Done visibly for other minds; words, signs,
Symbols, or actions, but of my own heart
Have I been speaking, and my youthful mind.
O Heavens! how awful is the might of Souls   180
And what they do within themselves, while yet
The yoke of earth is new to them, the world
Nothing but a wild field where they were sown.
This is, in truth, heroic argument,
This genuine prowess, which I wished to touch   185
With hand however weak,[2] but in the main
It lies far hidden from the reach of words.
Points have we, all of us, within our Souls,
Where all stand single: this I feel, and make
Breathings for incommunicable powers.[3]   190
But is not each a memory to himself?
And, therefore, now that we must quit this theme,
I am not heartless;[4] for there's not a man
That lives who hath not known his god-like hours,
And feels not what an empire we inherit,   195
As natural Beings, in the strength of Nature.
    No more:—for now into a populous plain
We must descend.—A Traveller I am
Whose tale is only of himself; even so,
So be it, if the pure of heart be prompt   200
To follow, and if Thou, O honored Friend!

2. Wordsworth describes the innovative epic theme
("heroic argument") for his projected long poem.
Cf. his Prospectus to *The Recluse*, above, lines 25–
41.

3. This obscure assertion may mean that he tries,
inadequately, to express the inexpressible.
4. Disheartened.

Who in these thoughts art ever at my side,
Support, as heretofore, my fainting steps.[5]

* * *

Thus in submissive idleness, my Friend,
The laboring time of Autumn, Winter, Spring,
Eight months! rolled pleasingly away—the ninth
Came and returned me to my native hills.   635

From Book Fourth
Summer Vacation[1]

[*The Walks with His Terrier. The Circuit of the Lake*]

Among the favorites whom it pleased me well
To see again, was one, by ancient right
Our Inmate, a rough terrier of the hills,   95
By birth and call of nature pre-ordained
To hunt the badger, and unearth the fox,
Among the impervious crags; but having been
From youth our own adopted, he had passed
Into a gentler service. And when first   100
The boyish spirit flagged, and day by day
Along my veins I kindled with the stir,
The fermentation and the vernal heat
Of poesy, affecting private shades
Like a sick lover, then this Dog was used   105
To watch me, an attendant and a friend
Obsequious to my steps, early and late,
Though often of such dilatory walk
Tired, and uneasy at the halts I made.
A hundred times when, roving high and low,   110
I have been harrassed with the toil of verse,
Much pains and little progress, and at once
Some lovely Image in the Song rose up
Full-formed, like Venus rising from the Sea;[2]
Then have I darted forwards and let loose   115
My hand upon his back, with stormy joy;
Caressing him again, and yet again.
And when at evening on the public Way
I sauntered, like a river murmuring
And talking to itself, when all things else   120
Are still, the Creature trotted on before—
Such was his custom; but whene'er he met
A passenger[3] approaching, he would turn

---

5. The terms of this behest to Coleridge suggests the relation to Dante of Virgil, his guide in the *Inferno*.
1. Wordsworth returned to Hawkshead for his first summer vacation, 1788.
2. Aphrodite (the Roman Venus), goddess of love, was born from the foam of the sea.
3. A foot traveler.

To give me timely notice; and, straitway,
Grateful for that admonishment, I hushed   125
My voice, composed my gait, and with the air
And mien of one whose thoughts are free, advanced
To give and take a greeting, that might save
My name from piteous rumours, such as wait
On men suspected to be crazed in brain.   130
    Those walks, well worthy to be prized and loved,
Regretted! that word too was on my tongue,
But they were richly laden with all good,
And cannot be remembered but with thanks
And gratitude, and perfect joy of heart;   135
Those walks, in all their freshness, now came back,
Like a returning Spring. When first I made
Once more the circuit of our little Lake,
If ever happiness hath lodged with man,
That day consummate[4] happiness was mine,   140
Wide-spreading, steady, calm, contemplative.
The sun was set, or setting, when I left
Our cottage door, and evening soon brought on
A sober hour,—not winning or serene,
For cold and raw the air was, and untuned: 145
But as a face we love is sweetest then
When sorrow damps it; or, whatever look
It chance to wear, is sweetest if the heart
Have fulness in herself, even so with me
It fared that evening. Gently did my Soul   150
Put off her veil, and, self-transmuted, stood
Naked, as in the presence of her God.[5]
While on I walked, a comfort seemed to touch
A heart that had not been disconsolate;
Strength came where weakness was not known to be,   155
At least not felt; and restoration came,
Like an intruder, knocking at the door
Of unacknowledged weariness. I took
The balance, and with firm hand weighed myself.
—Of that external scene which round me lay   160
Little, in this abstraction, did I see,
Remembered less; but I had inward hopes
And swellings of the Spirit: was rapt and soothed,
Conversed with promises; had glimmering views
How life pervades the undecaying mind,   165
How the immortal Soul with God-like power
Informs, creates, and thaws the deepest sleep
That time can lay upon her;[6] how on earth,

4. Perfect (pronounced *consúmmate*).
5. In Exodus 34.30–34, when Moses descended
from Mount Sinai, he wore a veil to hide from the
Israelites the shining of his face, but removed the
veil when, in privacy, he talked to God.

6. "Informs" and "creates" are probably to be read
as intransitive verbs, while "thaws" has "sleep" for
its direct object. "Sleep" Wordsworth uses, here
and elsewhere in *The Prelude*, for the deadening
effect of routine experience.

Man, if he do but live within the light
Of high endeavours, daily spreads abroad   170
His being armed with strength that cannot fail.
Nor was there want of milder thoughts, of love,
Of innocence, and holiday repose;
And more than pastoral quiet 'mid the stir
Of boldest projects; and a peaceful end   175
At last, or glorious, by endurance won.
Thus musing, in a wood I sate me down,
Alone, continuing there to muse; the slopes
And heights, meanwhile, were slowly overspread
With darkness; and before a rippling breeze   180
The long lake lengthened out its hoary line:
And in the sheltered coppice[7] where I sate,
Around me from among the hazel leaves,
Now here, now there, moved by the straggling wind,
Came ever and anon a breath-like sound,   185
Quick as the pantings of the faithful Dog,
The off and on Companion of my walk;
And such, at times, believing them to be,
I turned my head, to look if he were there;
Then into solemn thought I passed once more.   190

["The Surface of Past Time." The Walk Home from the Dance. The Discharged Soldier]

As one who hangs down-bending from the side
Of a slow-moving boat, upon the breast
Of a still water, solacing himself
With such discoveries as his eye can make,
Beneath him, in the bottom of the deep,   260
Sees many beauteous sights, weeds, fishes, flowers,
Grots, pebbles, roots of trees, and fancies more;
Yet often is perplexed, and cannot part
The shadow from the substance, rocks and sky,
Mountains and clouds reflected in the depth   265
Of the clear flood, from things which there abide
In their true Dwelling: now is crossed by gleam
Of his own image, by a sun-beam now,
And wavering motions, sent he knows not whence,
Impediments that make his task more sweet—   270
Such pleasant office have we long pursued,
Incumbent o'er the surface of past time,
With like success, nor often have appeared
Shapes fairer, or less doubtfully discerned
Than these to which the Tale, indulgent Friend!   275

7. A clump of small trees and underbrush.

Would now direct thy notice.[8] Yet in spite
Of pleasure won and knowledge not withheld,
There was an inner falling-off. I loved,
Loved deeply, all that had been loved before,
More deeply even than ever: but a swarm   280
Of heady schemes, jostling each other, gawds,[9]
And feast, and dance, and public revelry;
And sports, and games (too grateful in themselves,
Yet in themselves less grateful, I believe,
Than as they were a badge, glossy and fresh,   285
Of manliness and freedom) all conspired
To lure my mind from firm habitual quest
Of feeding pleasures;[1] to depress the zeal
And damp those daily yearnings which had once been mine—
A wild unworldly-minded youth, given up   290
To his own eager thoughts. It would demand
Some skill, and longer time than may be spared,
To paint these vanities, and how they wrought
In haunts where they, till now, had been unknown.
It seemed the very garments that I wore   295
Preyed on my strength, and stopped the quiet stream
Of self-forgetfulness.
                          Yes, that heartless[2] chase
Of trivial pleasures was a poor exchange
For books and nature at that early age.
'Tis true some casual knowledge might be gained   300
Of character or life; but at that time,
Of manners put to School[3] I took small note;
And all my deeper passions lay elsewhere.
Far better had it been to exalt the mind
By solitary Study; to uphold   305
Intense desire through meditative peace.
And yet, for chastisement of these regrets,
The memory of one particular hour
Doth here rise up against me.—'Mid a throng
Of Maids and Youths, old Men and Matrons staid,   310
A medley of all tempers,[4] I had passed
The night in dancing, gaiety, and mirth;
With din of instruments, and shuffling feet,
And glancing forms, and tapers glittering,
And unaimed prattle flying up and down—   315
Spirits upon the stretch, and here and there
Slight shocks of young love-liking interspersed,
Whose transient pleasure mounted to the head,

---

8. In this sustained simile Wordsworth describes
his endeavors to distinguish facts from fancies, and
his present self from his former self, in his remembrance of things past.
9. Amusements, pastimes.

1. Pleasures that would nourish the mind.
2. Dispirited, without deep feeling.
3. Made a subject of systematic study.
4. Temperaments, types of character.

And tingled through the veins. Ere we retired
The cock had crowed; and now the eastern sky   320
Was kindling, not unseen from humble copse
And open field through which the pathway wound
That homeward led my steps. Magnificent
The Morning rose, in memorable pomp,
Glorious as e'er I had beheld; in front   325
The Sea lay laughing at a distance;—near,
The solid mountains shone bright as the clouds,
Grain-tinctured, drenched in empyrean light;[5]
And, in the meadows and the lower grounds,
Was all the sweetness of a common dawn;   330
Dews, vapours, and the melody of birds;
And Labourers going forth to till the fields.

　　Ah! need I say, dear Friend, that to the brim
My heart was full: I made no vows, but vows
Were then made for me; bond unknown to me   335
Was given, that I should be, else sinning greatly,
A dedicated Spirit.[6] On I walked
In thankful blessedness which yet survives.

　　Strange rendezvous my mind was at that time,
A party-colored shew of grave and gay,   340
Solid and light, short-sighted and profound;
Of inconsiderate habits and sedate,
Consorting in one mansion, unreproved.
The worth I knew of powers that I possessed,
Though slighted and too oft misused. Besides,   345
That summer, swarming as it did with thoughts
Transient and idle, lacked not intervals
When Folly from the frown of fleeting Time
Shrunk, and the Mind experienced in herself
Conformity as just as that of old[7]   350
To the end and written spirit of God's works,
Whether held forth in Nature or in Man,
Through pregnant vision, separate or conjoined.

　　When from our better selves we have too long
Been parted by the hurrying world, and droop,   355
Sick of its business, of its pleasures tired,
How gracious, how benign is Solitude!
How potent a mere image of her sway!
Most potent when impressed upon the mind
With an appropriate human centre—Hermit   360
Deep in the bosom of the Wilderness;
Votary[8] (in vast Cathedral, where no foot

5. The "empyrean" in ancient belief was the outer sphere of the universe, composed of pure fire. "Grain-tinctured": crimson colored.
6. Wordsworth describes later in *The Prelude* his discovery that the specific vocation to which he felt dedicated was to be the agent of a new kind of poetry. See 13.232 ff.
7. I.e., an immediacy of response similar to his mental experience before he indulged in these present distractions.
8. A person devoted to God's service.

Is treading and no other face is seen)
Kneeling at prayer; or Watchman on the top
Of Lighthouse beaten by Atlantic Waves;   365
Or as the soul of that great Power is met
Sometimes embodied on a public road,
When, for the night deserted, it assumes
A character of quiet more profound
Than pathless Wastes.
                    Once, when those summer Months   370
Were flown, and Autumn brought its annual shew
Of oars with oars contending, sails with sails,
Upon Winander's[9] spacious breast, it chanced
That—after I had left a flower-decked room
(Whose in-door pastime, lighted-up, survived   375
To a late hour) and spirits overwrought[1]
Were making night do penance for a day
Spent in a round of strenuous idleness—
My homeward course led up a long ascent
Where the road's watery surface, to the top   380
Of that sharp rising, glittered to the moon
And bore the semblance of another stream
Stealing with silent lapse[2] to join the brook
That murmured in the Vale. All else was still;
No living thing appeared in earth or air,   385
And, save the flowing Water's peaceful voice,
Sound was there none: but lo! an uncouth shape
Shewn by a sudden turning of the road,
So near, that, slipping back into the shade
Of a thick hawthorn, I could mark him well,   390
Myself unseen. He was of stature tall,
A span[3] above man's *common* measure tall.
Stiff, lank, and upright;—a more meagre[4] man
Was never seen before by night or day.
Long were his arms, pallid his hands;—his mouth   395
Looked ghastly[5] in the moonlight. From behind,
A mile-stone propped him; I could also ken
That he was clothed in military garb,
Though faded, yet entire. Companionless,
No dog attending, by no staff sustained   400
He stood; and in his very dress appeared
A desolation, a simplicity
To which the trappings of a gaudy world
Make a strange background. From his lips erelong

9. Lake Winandermere's (Windermere's).
1. Worked up to a high pitch. Wordsworth is describing a party at which the "pastime" had been dancing. The description of the meeting with the discharged soldier that follows was written in 1798 as an independent poem, which Wordsworth later incorporated in *The Prelude*.
2. Flowing. Wordsworth is remembering a description which his sister, Dorothy, had entered into her journal in January 1798, a few days before he composed this passage: "The road to the village of Holford glittered like another stream."
3. About 9 inches (the distance between extended thumb and little finger).
4. Lean, emaciated.
5. Ghostly.

Issued low muttered sounds, as if of pain   405
Or some uneasy thought; yet still his form
Kept the same awful steadiness;—at his feet
His shadow lay and moved not. From self-blame
Not wholly free, I watched him thus; at length
Subduing my heart's specious cowardice,[6]   410
I left the shady nook where I had stood,
And hailed him. Slowly, from his resting-place
He rose; and, with a lean and wasted arm
In measured gesture lifted to his head,
Returned my salutation: then resumed   415
His station as before; and when I asked
His history, the Veteran, in reply,
Was neither slow nor eager; but, unmoved,
And with a quiet uncomplaining voice,
A stately air of mild indifference,   420
He told, in few plain words, a Soldier's tale—
That in the Tropic Islands he had served,
Whence he had landed, scarcely three weeks past,
That on his landing he had been dismissed,
And now was travelling towards his native home.[7]   425
This heard, I said in pity, "Come with me."
He stooped, and straightway from the ground took up
An oaken staff, by me yet unobserved—
A staff which must have dropped from his slack hand
And lay till now neglected in the grass.   430
   Though weak his step and cautious, he appeared
To travel without pain, and I beheld,
With an astonishment but ill suppressed,
His ghastly figure moving at my side;
Nor could I, while we journeyed thus, forbear   435
To turn from present hardships to the past,
And speak of war, battle, and pestilence,
Sprinkling this talk with questions, better spared,
On what he might himself have seen or felt.
He all the while was in demeanour calm,   440
Concise in answer; solemn and sublime
He might have seemed, but that in all he said
There was a strange half-absence, as of one
Knowing too well the importance of his theme,
But feeling it no longer. Our discourse   445
Soon ended, and together on we passed,
In silence, through a wood, gloomy and still.
Up-turning then along an open field,
We reached a Cottage. At the door I knocked,
And earnestly to charitable care   450

---

6. I.e., he had been deceiving himself in thinking
that the motive for his delay was not cowardice.
7. The Tropic Islands are the West Indies. Tens
of thousands of British soldiers serving there contracted tropical fevers and died, or else were rendered unfit for further service and discharged.

Commended him, as a poor friendless Man
Belated, and by sickness overcome.
Assured that now the Traveller would repose
In comfort, I entreated, that henceforth
He would not linger in the public ways,   455
But ask for timely furtherance and help,
Such as his state required.—At this reproof,
With the same ghastly mildness in his look,
He said, "My trust is in the God of Heaven,
And in the eye of him who passes me."   460
  The Cottage door was speedily unbarred,
And now the Soldier touched his hat once more
With his lean hand; and, in a faltering voice
Whose tone bespake reviving interests
Till then unfelt, he thanked me; I returned   465
The farewell blessing of the patient Man,
And so we parted. Back I cast a look,
And lingered near the door a little space;
Then sought with quiet heart my distant home.
  This passed, and He who deigns to mark with care   470
By what rules governed, with what end in view
This Work proceeds, *he* will not wish for more.

From Book Fifth
Books

[*The Boy of Winander*]

  There was a Boy;[1]—ye knew him well, Ye Cliffs
And Islands of Winander!—many a time
At evening, when the earliest stars began
To move along the edges of the hills,
Rising or setting, would he stand alone,   370
Beneath the trees, or by the glimmering lake;
And there, with fingers interwoven, both hands
Pressed closely palm to palm and to his mouth
Uplifted, he, as through an instrument,
Blew mimic hootings to the silent owls   375
That they might answer him.—And they would shout
Across the watery Vale, and shout again,
Responsive to his call,—with quivering peals,
And long halloos, and screams, and echoes loud
Redoubled and redoubled; concourse wild   380
Of jocund din! and when a lengthened pause
Of silence came, and baffled his best skill,
Then, sometimes, in that silence, while he hung

---

1. In an early MS version of this passage Wordsworth uses the first-person pronoun; the experience he describes was thus apparently his own.

Listening, a gentle shock of mild surprize
Has carried far into his heart the voice   385
Of mountain torrents; or the visible scene
Would enter unawares into his mind
With all its solemn imagery, its rocks,
Its woods, and that uncertain heaven, received
Into the bosom of the steady lake.[2]   390
    This Boy was taken from his Mates, and died
In childhood, ere he was full twelve years old.
Fair is the Spot, most beautiful the Vale
Where he was born: the grassy Church-yard hangs
Upon a slope above the Village School;   395
And through that Church-yard when my way has led
On summer evenings, I believe that there
A long half-hour together I have stood
Mute—looking at the grave in which he lies!
    Even now appears before the mind's clear eye   400
That self-same Village Church; I see her sit
(The thronèd Lady whom erewhile we hailed)
On her green hill, forgetful of this Boy
Who slumbers at her feet, forgetful, too,
Of all her silent neighbourhood of graves,   405
And listening only to the gladsome sounds
That, from the rural School ascending, play
Beneath her, and about her. May she long
Behold a race of Young Ones like to those
With whom I herded! (easily, indeed,   410
We might have fed upon a fatter soil
Of Arts and Letters, but be that forgiven)
A race of *real* children; not too wise,
Too learnèd, or too good: but wanton, fresh,
And bandied up and down by love and hate;   415
Not unresentful where self-justified;
Fierce, moody, patient, venturous, modest, shy;
Mad at their sports like withered leaves in winds:
Though doing wrong and suffering, and full oft
Bending beneath our life's mysterious weight   420
Of pain, and doubt, and fear; yet yielding not
In happiness to the happiest upon earth.
Simplicity in habit, truth in speech,
Be these the daily strengtheners of their minds!
May books and nature be their early joy!   425
And knowledge, rightly honored with that name,
Knowledge not purchased by the loss of power!

---

2. Coleridge wrote of the last line and a half ("that uncertain heaven . . . lake"): "Had I met these lines running wild in the deserts of Arabia, I should instantly have screamed out, 'Wordsworth.' "

["The Mystery of Words"]

Here must we pause; this only let me add,
From heart-experience, and in humblest sense
Of modesty, that he, who, in his youth,
A daily Wanderer among woods and fields,
With living Nature hath been intimate,   590
Not only in that raw unpractised time
Is stirred to extasy, as others are,
By glittering verse; but, further, doth receive,
In measure only dealt out to himself,
Knowledge and increase of enduring joy   595
From the great Nature that exists in works
Of mighty Poets.[3] Visionary Power
Attends the motions of the viewless[4] winds
Embodied in the mystery of words:
There darkness makes abode, and all the host   600
Of shadowy things work endless changes there,
As in a mansion like their proper home.
Even forms and substances are circumfused
By that transparent veil with light divine;
And, through the turnings intricate of verse,   605
Present themselves as objects recognized,
In flashes, and with glory not their own.
     Thus far a scanty record is deduced
Of what I owed to Books in early life;
Their later influence yet remains untold;   610
But as this work was taking in my mind
Proportions that seemed larger than had first
Been meditated, I was indisposed
To any further progress, at a time
When these acknowledgments were left unpaid.   615

From Book Sixth
Cambridge, and the Alps

["Human Nature Seeming Born Again"]

When the third summer freed us from restraint,[1]
A youthful Friend, he too a Mountaineer,
Not slow to share my wishes, took his staff,   325
And, sallying forth, we journeyed, side by side,

3. Having found a set of symbols in nature,
Wordsworth now finds nature in the symbol systems of "mighty poets."
4. Invisible.
1. After reviewing briefly his second and third years
at Cambridge, Wordsworth here describes his trip

through France and Switzerland with a college
friend, Robert Jones, in the succeeding summer
vacation, 1790. France was then in the "golden
hours" of the early period of the Revolution; the
fall of the Bastille had occurred on July 14 of the
preceding year.

Bound to the distant Alps. A hardy slight
Did this unprecedented course imply
Of College studies and their set rewards;[2]
Nor had, in truth, the scheme been formed by me   330
Without uneasy forethought of the pain,
The censures, and ill-omening of those
To whom my worldly interests were dear.
But Nature then was Sovereign in my mind,
And mighty Forms, seizing a youthful fancy,   335
Had given a charter[3] to irregular hopes.
In any age of uneventful calm
Among the Nations, surely would my heart
Have been possessed by similar desire;
But Europe at that time was thrilled with joy,   340
France standing on the top of golden hours,
And human nature seeming born again.

[Crossing Simplon Pass]

* * * That very day,
From a bare ridge we also first beheld   525
Unveiled the summit of Mont Blanc, and grieved
To have a soulless image on the eye
Which had usurped upon a living thought
That never more could be.[4] The wondrous Vale
Of Chamouny stretched far below, and soon   530
With its dumb cataracts, and streams of ice,
A motionless array of mighty waves,
Five rivers broad and vast, made rich amends,
And reconciled us to realities.
There small birds warble from the leafy trees,   535
The eagle soars high in the element;
There doth the Reaper bind the yellow sheaf,
The Maiden spread the hay-cock in the sun,
While Winter like a well-tamed lion walks,
Descending from the Mountain to make sport   540
Among the Cottages by beds of flowers.
   Whate'er in this wide circuit we beheld,
Or heard, was fitted to our unripe state
Of intellect and heart. With such a book
Before our eyes we could not chuse but read   545
Lessons of genuine brotherhood, the plain
And universal reason of mankind,
The truths of Young and Old. Nor, side by side
Pacing, two social Pilgrims, or alone

2. English universities allow much longer vaca-
tions than those in America, on the optimistic
assumption that they will be used primarily for
intensive study. Wordsworth is facing his final
examinations in the next college year.

3. Privileged freedom.
4. The "image" is the actual sight of Mont Blanc,
as against what the poet has imagined the famous
Swiss mountain to be. Chamonix (see line 530) is
a valley in eastern France, north of Mont Blanc.

Each with his humour,[5] could we fail to abound   550
In dreams and fictions pensively composed,
Dejection taken up for pleasure's sake,
And gilded sympathies; the willow wreath,[6]
And sober posies of funeral flowers
Gathered, among those solitudes sublime,   555
From formal gardens of the Lady Sorrow,
Did sweeten many a meditative hour.
      Yet still in me with those soft luxuries
Mixed something of stern mood, an under thirst
Of vigor seldom utterly allayed.   560
And from that source how different a sadness
Would issue, let one incident make known.
When from the Vallais we had turned, and clomb
Along the Simplon's steep and rugged road,[7]
Following a band of Muleteers, we reached   565
A halting-place where all together took
Their noon-tide meal. Hastily rose our Guide,
Leaving *us* at the Board; awhile we lingered,
Then paced the beaten downward way that led
Right to a rough stream's edge and there broke off.   570
The only track now visible was one
That from the torrent's further brink held forth
Conspicuous invitation to ascend
A lofty mountain. After brief delay
Crossing the unbridged stream, that road we took   575
And clomb with eagerness, till anxious fears
Intruded, for we failed to overtake
Our Comrades gone before. By fortunate chance,
While every moment added doubt to doubt,
A Peasant met us, from whose mouth we learned   580
That to the Spot which had perplexed us first
We must descend, and there should find the road,
Which in the stony channel of the Stream
Lay a few steps, and then along its banks,
And that our future course, all plain to sight,   585
Was downwards, with the current of that Stream.
Loth to believe what we so grieved to hear,
For still we had hopes that pointed to the clouds,
We questioned him again, and yet again;
But every word that from the Peasant's lips   590
Came in reply, translated by our feelings,
Ended in this, *that we had crossed the Alps*.[8]

---

5. Temperament, or state of mind.
6. Symbolizing sorrow. "Gilded": laid on like gilt; i.e., superficial. "Posies": small bunches of flowers.
7. The Simplon Pass through the Alps. "Clomb": climbed.
8. As Dorothy Wordsworth baldly put it later on, "The ambition of youth was disappointed at these tidings." The visionary experience that follows (lines 593–617) occurred not in the Alps but at the time of writing the passage, as the 1805 text explicitly says: "Imagination! lifting up itself / Before the eye and progress of my Song."

Imagination—here the Power so called
Through sad incompetence of human speech—
That awful Power rose from the Mind's abyss   595
Like an unfathered vapour[9] that enwraps
At once some lonely Traveller. I was lost,
Halted without an effort to break through;
But to my conscious soul I now can say,
"I recognize thy glory"; in such strength   600
Of usurpation, when the light of sense
Goes out, but with a flash that has revealed
The invisible world, doth Greatness make abode,
There harbours, whether we be young or old;
Our destiny, our being's heart and home,   605
Is with infinitude, and only there;
With hope it is, hope that can never die,
Effort, and expectation, and desire,
And something evermore about to be.[1]
Under such banners militant the Soul   610
Seeks for no trophies, struggles for no spoils,
That may attest her prowess, blest in thoughts
That are their own perfection and reward,
Strong in herself, and in beatitude[2]
That hides her like the mighty flood of Nile   615
Poured from his fount of Abyssinian clouds
To fertilize the whole Egyptian plain.
      The melancholy slackening that ensued
Upon those tidings by the Peasant given
Was soon dislodged; downwards we hurried fast   620
And, with the half-shaped road, which we had missed,
Entered a narrow chasm. The brook and road
Were fellow-Travellers in this gloomy Strait,
And with them did we journey several hours
At a slow pace. The immeasurable height   625
Of woods decaying, never to be decayed,
The stationary blasts of waterfalls,
And in the narrow rent at every turn
Winds thwarting winds, bewildered and forlorn,
The torrents shooting from the clear blue sky,   630
The rocks that muttered close upon our ears,
Black drizzling crags that spake by the way-side
As if a voice were in them, the sick sight
And giddy prospect of the raving stream,
The unfettered clouds, and region of the Heavens,   635
Tumult and peace, the darkness and the light—
Were all like workings of one mind, the features

9. Sudden vapor from no apparent source.
1. At the time, Wordsworth had not been able to
understand why he had felt such grievous disappointment at finding that he had already crossed
the Alps, while still expecting to climb upward (lines
587–92). Now, a flash of vision reveals the symbolic significance of that experience: that the glory
of humankind is to aim infinitely high, even though
our capabilities are finite.
2. The ultimate blessedness or happiness.

Of the same face, blossoms upon one tree,
Characters of the great Apocalypse,[3]
The types and symbols of Eternity,   640
Of first and last, and midst, and without end.[4]

From Book Seventh
Residence in London[1]

[*The Blind Beggar*]

As the black storm upon the mountain top
Sets off the sunbeam in the Valley, so   620
That huge fermenting Mass of human-kind
Serves as a solemn background or relief
To single forms and objects, whence they draw,
For feeling and contemplative regard,
More than inherent liveliness and power.   625
How oft amid those overflowing streets
Have I gone forward with the Crowd, and said
Unto myself, "The face of every one
That passes by me is a mystery!"
Thus have I looked, nor ceased to look, oppressed   630
By thoughts of what and whither, when and how,
Until the Shapes before my eyes became
A second-sight procession, such as glides
Over still mountains, or appears in dreams.
And once, far-travelled in such mood, beyond   635
The reach of common indication, lost
Amid the moving pageant, I was smitten
Abruptly with the view (a sight not rare)
Of a blind Beggar who, with upright face,
Stood propped against a Wall; upon his chest   640
Wearing a written paper to explain
His Story, whence he came, and who he was.
Caught by the spectacle, my mind turned round
As with the might of waters; an apt type
This Label seemed, of the utmost we can know   645
Both of ourselves and of the universe;
And on the Shape of that unmoving Man,
His steadfast face, and sightless eyes, I gazed
As if admonished from another world.
Though reared upon the base of outward things,   650

3. The objects in this natural scene, exhibiting a
coincidence of all opposites, are like the written
words of the Apocalypse—i.e., of the Book of Revelation, the last book of the New Testament.
4. Cf. Revelation 1.8: "I am Alpha and Omega,
the beginning and the ending, saith the Lord"; the
phrase is repeated in 21.6, after the fulfillment of

the last things. In *Paradise Lost* 5.153–65 Milton
says that the things created declare their Creator,
and calls on all to extol "him first, him last, him
midst, and without end."
1. Wordsworth spent three and a half months in
London in 1791.

Structures like these the excited Spirit mainly
Builds for herself. Scenes different there are,
Full-formed, that take, with small internal help,
Possession of the faculties—the peace
That comes with night; the deep solemnity   655
Of Nature's intermediate hours of rest,
When the great tide of human life stands still,
The business of the day to come—unborn,
Of that gone by—locked up as in the grave;[2]
The blended calmness of the heavens and earth,   660
Moonlight, and stars, and empty streets, and sounds
Unfrequent as in deserts: at late hours
Of winter evenings when unwholesome rains
Are falling hard, with people yet astir,
The feeble salutation from the voice   665
Of some unhappy woman, now and then
Heard as we pass; when no one looks about,
Nothing is listened to. But these, I fear,
Are falsely catalogued;[3] things that are, are not,
As the mind answers to them, or the heart   670
Is prompt or slow to feel. * * *

From Book Eighth
Retrospect, Love of Nature leading
to Love of Man[1]

[*The Shepherd in the Mist. Man Still Subordinate to Nature*]

        * * * A rambling School-boy, thus
I felt his presence in his own domain
As of a Lord and Master; or a Power
Or Genius,[2] under Nature, under God
Presiding; and severest solitude   260
Had more commanding looks when he was there.
When up the lonely brooks on rainy days
Angling I went, or trod the trackless hills
By mists bewildered, suddenly mine eyes
Have glanced upon him distant a few steps,   265
In size a Giant, stalking through thick fog,
His sheep like Greenland bears;[3] or, as he stepped

---

2. The sonnet *Composed upon Westminster Bridge* (above) describes a similar response to London when its "mighty heart is lying still."
3. I.e., mistakenly classified as scenes (lines 652–54) whose effects on the perceiver depend but little on contributions by the perceiving mind.
1. In this book Wordsworth reviews the first 21 years of his life in order to trace the transfer of his earlier feelings for nature to shepherds and other humble people who carry on their lonely duties almost as though they were animate parts of the

landscape (cf. *Michael*, lines 1–39). Wordsworth's central concern is to describe the early development in his relatively inexperienced mind of an image, or conceptual model, of the largeness, worth, and almost sacred dignity of generic Man (lines 256–81), an image which proved invulnerable to the acid bath of his later experience of the vulgarity, meanness, and evil of which individuals are capable (lines 317–22).
2. Presiding spirit.
3. Polar bears.

Beyond the boundary line of some hill-shadow,
His form hath flashed upon me, glorified
By the deep radiance of the setting sun:[4]   270
Or him have I descried in distant sky,
A solitary object and sublime,
Above all height! like an aerial cross
Stationed alone upon a spiry rock
Of the Chartreuse, for worship.[5] Thus was Man   275
Ennobled outwardly before my sight,
And thus my heart was early introduced
To an unconscious love and reverence
Of human nature; hence the human Form
To me became an index of delight,   280
Of grace, and honor, power, and worthiness.
Meanwhile this Creature, spiritual almost
As those of Books, but more exalted far;
Far more of an imaginative Form
Than the gay Corin of the groves, who lives   285
For his own fancies, or to dance by the hour
In coronal, with Phillis in the midst[6]—
Was, for the purposes of Kind,[7] a Man
With the most common; husband, father; learned,
Could teach, admonish, suffered with the rest   290
From vice and folly, wretchedness and fear;
Of this I little saw, cared less for it;
But something must have felt.
                                        Call ye these appearances
Which I beheld of Shepherds in my youth,
This sanctity of Nature given to man—   295
A shadow, a delusion, ye who pore
On the dead letter, miss the spirit of things;
Whose truth is not a motion or a shape
Instinct with vital functions, but a Block
Or waxen image which yourselves have made,   300
And ye adore. But blessed be the God
Of Nature and of Man, that this was so,
That men before my inexperienced eyes
Did first present themselves thus purified,
Removed, and to a distance that was fit.   305
And so we all of us in some degree
Are led to knowledge, whencesoever led
And howsoever; were it otherwise,
And we found evil fast as we find good

---

4. A "glory" is a mountain phenomenon in which
the enlarged figure of a person is seen projected by
the sun upon the mist, with a radiance about its
head. Cf. Coleridge's *Dejection*, line 54.
5. In his tour of the Alps Wordsworth had been
deeply impressed by the Chartreuse, a Carthusian
monastery in the French Alps, with its soaring cross

visible against the sky. There is an overtone here
of the Christlike divinity investing the "common"
man (line 289).
6. Corin and Phillis, dancing in their coronals, or
wreaths of flowers, were stock characters in earlier
pastoral literature.
7. I.e., in carrying out the tasks of humankind.

In our first years, or think that it is found,   310
How could the innocent heart bear up and live?
But doubly fortunate my lot; not here
Alone, that something of a better life
Perhaps was round me than it is the privilege
Of most to move in, but that first I looked   315
At Man through objects that were great or fair,
First communed with him by their help. And thus
Was founded a sure safeguard and defence
Against the weight of meanness, selfish cares,
Coarse manners, vulgar passions, that beat in   320
On all sides from the ordinary world
In which we traffic. Starting from this point,
I had my face turned tow'rd the truth, began
With an advantage furnished by that kind
Of prepossession without which the soul   325
Receives no knowledge that can bring forth good,
No genuine insight ever comes to her.
From the restraint of over-watchful eyes
Preserved, I moved about, year after year
Happy, and now most thankful, that my walk   330
Was guarded from too early intercourse
With the deformities of crowded life,
And those ensuing laughters and contempts
Self-pleasing, which, if we would wish to think
With a due reverence on earth's rightful Lord,   335
Here placed to be the Inheritor of heaven,[8]
Will not permit us; but pursue the mind
That to devotion willingly would rise,
Into the Temple, and the Temple's heart.[9]
    Yet deem not, Friend, that human-kind with me   340
Thus early took a place preeminent;
Nature herself was at this unripe time
But secondary to my own pursuits
And animal activities, and all
Their trivial pleasures:[1] and when these had drooped   345
And gradually expired, and Nature, prized
For her own sake, became my joy, even then—
And upwards through late youth, until not less
Than two and twenty summers had been told—
Was Man in my affections and regards   350
Subordinate to her; her visible Forms
And viewless[2] agencies: a passion she,
A rapture often, and immediate love
Ever at hand; *he* only a delight

---

8. This pious line was a later addition to the version of 1805.
9. I.e., into the devotional recesses of the innermost mind.

1. Cf. his account of the stages of his development in *Tintern Abbey*, lines 65–92 and note.
2. Invisible.

Occasional, an accidental grace,   355
His hour being not yet come. * * *

From Book Ninth
Residence in France[1]

[*Paris and Orléans. Becomes a "Patriot"*]

Even as a River—partly (it might seem)
Yielding to old remembrances, and swayed
In part by fear to shape a way direct
That would engulph him soon in the ravenous Sea—
Turns, and will measure back his course, far back,   5
Seeking the very regions which he crossed
In his first outset; so have we, my Friend!
Turned and returned with intricate delay.
Or as a Traveller, who has gained the brow
Of some aerial Down,[2] while there he halts   10
For breathing-time, is tempted to review
The region left behind him; and if aught
Deserving notice have escaped regard,
Or been regarded with too careless eye,
Strives, from that height, with one, and yet one more   15
Last look, to make the best amends he may,
So have we lingered. Now we start afresh
With courage, and new hope risen on our toil.
Fair greetings to this shapeless eagerness,
Whene'er it comes! needful in work so long,   20
Thrice needful to the argument which now
Awaits us! Oh, how much unlike the past![3]
   Free as a Colt, at pasture on the hill,
I ranged at large through London's wide Domain
Month after Month. Obscurely did I live,   25
Not seeking frequent intercourse with men
By literature, or elegance, or rank
Distinguished. Scarcely was a year thus spent[4]
Ere I forsook the crowded Solitude;
With less regret for its luxurious pomp   30
And all the nicely-guarded shews of Art,
Than for the humble Bookstalls in the Streets,
Exposed to eye and hand where'er I turned.

1. Wordsworth's second visit to France, while he was 21 and 22 years of age (1791–92), came during a crucial period of the French Revolution. This book deals with his stay at Paris, Orléans, and Blois, when he developed his passionate partisanship for the French people and the revolutionary cause.
2. Treeless high land.
3. This preface parallels in function Milton's preface to the equivalent ninth book of *Paradise Lost*, in which he announces that, having narrated the blameless life of Adam and Eve in Eden, he "now must change / Those notes to tragic," and tell of their fall. "Argument": theme.
4. His stay in London in fact lasted only four or five months, January–May 1791.

—France lured me forth, the realm that I had crossed
So lately, journeying toward the snow-clad Alps.   35
But now relinquishing the scrip and staff[5]
And all enjoyment which the summer sun
Sheds round the steps of those who meet the day
With motion constant as his own, I went
Prepared to sojourn in a pleasant Town   40
Washed by the current of the stately Loire.[6]
     Through Paris lay my readiest course, and there
Sojourning a few days, I visited
In haste each spot, of old or recent fame,
The latter chiefly; from the field of Mars   45
Down to the suburbs of St. Anthony;
And from Mont Martyr southward to the Dome
Of Genevieve.[7] In both her clamorous Halls,
The National Synod[8] and the Jacobins,
I saw the Revolutionary Power   50
Toss like a Ship at anchor, rocked by storms;
The Arcades I traversed, in the Palace huge
Of Orleans,[9] coasted round and round the line
Of Tavern, Brothel, Gaming-house, and Shop,
Great rendezvous of worst and best, the walk   55
Of all who had a purpose, or had not;
I stared, and listened with a Stranger's ears
To Hawkers and Haranguers, hubbub wild!
And hissing Factionists, with ardent eyes,
In knots, or pairs, or single. Not a look   60
Hope takes, or Doubt or Fear are forced to wear,
But seemed there present, and I scanned them all,
Watched every gesture uncontrollable
Of anger, and vexation, and despite,
All side by side, and struggling face to face   65
With Gaiety and dissolute Idleness.
—Where silent zephyrs sported with the dust
Of the Bastille,[1] I sate in the open sun,
And from the rubbish gathered up a stone
And pocketed the Relic in the guise   70
Of an Enthusiast; yet, in honest truth,
I looked for Something that I could not find,
Affecting more emotion than I felt;

5. The "scrip" (the bag or knapsack) and the "staff"
are the traditional emblems of the foot pilgrim.
6. Orléans, on the Loire River, where Wordsworth stayed from December 1791 until he moved
to Blois early the next year.
7. The "field of Mars" (the Champ de Mars), where
Louis XVI swore fidelity to the new constitution.
"The suburbs of St. Anthony": Faubourg St.
Antoine, near the Bastille, a working-class quarter
and center of revolutionary violence. "Mont Martyr": Montmartre, a hill on which revolutionary
meetings were held. The "Dome of Geneviève"

became the Panthéon, a burial place for notable
Frenchmen.
8. The newly formed National Assembly. "Jacobins": the club of radical democratic revolutionists,
named for the ancient convent of St. Jacques, their
meeting place.
9. The arcades in the courtyard of the Palais
d'Orléans, a fashionable shopping center and Parisian rendezvous.
1. The political prison of the Bastille had been
demolished, after it had been stormed and sacked
on July 14, 1789.

For 'tis most certain that these various sights,
However potent their first shock, with me   75
Appeared to recompence the Traveller's pains
Less than the painted Magdalene of Le Brun,[2]
A Beauty exquisitely wrought, with hair
Dishevelled, gleaming eyes, and rueful cheek
Pale, and bedropp'd with everflowing tears.   80
    But hence to my more permanent Abode
I hasten;[3] there by novelties in speech,
Domestic manners, customs, gestures, looks,
And all the attire of ordinary life,
Attention was engrossed; and, thus amused,   85
I stood 'mid those concussions unconcerned,
Tranquil almost, and careless as a flower
Glassed in a green-house, or a Parlour shrub
That spreads its leaves in unmolested peace
While every bush and tree, the country through,   90
Is shaking to the roots; indifference this
Which may seem strange; but I was unprepared
With needful knowledge, had abruptly passed
Into a theatre whose stage was filled,
And busy with an action far advanced.   95
Like Others I had skimmed, and sometimes read
With care, the master pamphlets of the day;[4]
Nor wanted such half-insight as grew wild
Upon that meagre soil, helped out by talk
And public news; but having never seen   100
A Chronicle that might suffice to shew
Whence the main Organs[5] of the public Power
Had sprung, their transmigrations when and how
Accomplished, giving thus unto events
A form and body; all things were to me   105
Loose and disjointed, and the affections left
Without a vital interest. At that time,
Moreover, the first storm was overblown,
And the strong hand of outward violence
Locked up in quiet.[6] For myself, I fear   110
Now, in connection with so great a Theme,
To speak (as I must be compelled to do)
Of one so unimportant; night by night
Did I frequent the formal haunts of men
Whom, in the City, privilege of birth   115
Sequestered from the rest: societies

---

2. A theatrical painting of the weeping Mary
Magdalene by Charles Le Brun (1619–1690), then
regarded as a religious masterpiece.
3. In Orléans.
4. Wordsworth probably refers to the numerous
English pamphlets (including Thomas Paine's
Rights of Man, part 1, and Mary Wollstonecraft's
A *Vindication of the Rights of Men*) published in

response to Edmund Burke's attack on the Revolution, *Reflections on the Revolution in France*
(1790).
5. Institutions, instruments.
6. After the storming of the Bastille in 1789 there
was a period of calm until the massacre of 3,000
Royalists in September 1792, after the deposition
and imprisonment of Louis XVI.

Polished in Arts, and in punctilio[7] versed;
Whence, and from deeper causes, all discourse
Of good and evil of the time was shunned
With scrupulous care: but these restrictions soon   120
Proved tedious, and I gradually withdrew
Into a noisier world, and thus erelong
Became a Patriot;[8] and my heart was all
Given to the People, and my love was theirs.

From Book Tenth
France continued[1]

[The Revolution: Paris and England]

Cheared with this hope,[2] to Paris I returned;
And ranged, with ardor heretofore unfelt,
The spacious City, and in progress passed   50
The Prison where the unhappy Monarch lay,[3]
Associate with his Children and his Wife,
In Bondage; and the Palace lately stormed,
With roar of Cannon, by a furious Host.
I crossed the Square (an empty Area then!)   55
Of the Carousel, where so late had lain
The Dead, upon the Dying heaped; and gazed
On this and other Spots, as doth a Man
Upon a Volume whose contents he knows
Are memorable, but from him locked up,   60
Being written in a tongue he cannot read;
So that he questions the mute leaves with pain,
And half-upbraids their silence. But, that night,
I felt most deeply in what world I was,
What ground I trod on, and what air I breathed.   65
High was my Room and lonely, near the roof
Of a large Mansion or Hotel,[4] a Lodge
That would have pleased me in more quiet times,
Nor was it wholly without pleasure, then.
With unextinguished taper I kept watch,   70
Reading at intervals; the fear gone by
Pressed on me almost like a fear to come.
I thought of those September massacres,
Divided from me by one little month,

---

7. The niceties of social manners.
8. I.e., became committed to the people's side in the Revolution.
1. At this period, October 1792–August 1794, Wordsworth's revolutionary enthusiasm was at its height.
2. Wordsworth's "hope" was that the moderates were now taking over and would eliminate further violence.
3. I.e., the "Temple" (it had once housed the religious Order of Templars), where Louis XVI was held prisoner. "The Palace" (line 53) is the Tuileries; in front of this is the great square of "the Carousel" (line 56), where a number of the mob storming the palace had been killed.
4. A town house.

Saw them and touched;[5] the rest was conjured up   75
From tragic fictions, or true history,
Remembrances and dim admonishments.
The Horse is taught his manage,[6] and no Star
Of wildest course but treads back his own steps;
For the spent hurricane the air provides   80
As fierce a Successor; the tide retreats
But to return out of its hiding place
In the great Deep; all things have second birth;
The earthquake is not satisfied at once;
And in this way I wrought upon myself   85
Until I seemed to hear a voice that cried
To the whole City, "Sleep no more."[7] The Trance
Fled with the Voice to which it had given birth,
But vainly comments of a calmer mind
Promised soft peace and sweet forgetfulness.   90
The place, all hushed and silent as it was,
Appeared unfit for the repose of Night,
Defenceless as a wood where Tygers roam.

        * * * In this frame of mind,
Dragged by a chain of harsh necessity,
So seemed it,—now I thankfully acknowledge,
Forced by the gracious providence of Heaven—
To England I returned,[8] else (though assured   225
That I both was, and must be, of small weight,
No better than a Landsman on the deck
Of a ship struggling with a hideous storm)
Doubtless I should have then made common cause
With some who perished, haply perished too,[9]   230
A poor mistaken and bewildered offering,
Should to the breast of Nature have gone back
With all my resolutions, all my hopes,
A Poet only to myself, to Men
Useless, and even, belovèd Friend, a Soul   235
To thee unknown![1]

              * * *

What then were my emotions, when in Arms
Britain put forth her free-born strength in league,
O pity and shame! with those confederate Powers?[2]   265

5. I.e., his imagination of the September Massacres was so vivid as to be palpable.
6. The French *manège*, the prescribed action and paces of a trained horse.
7. "Methought I heard a voice cry, 'Sleep no more!/Macbeth does murder sleep' " (*Macbeth* 2.2.34–36).
8. Forced by the "harsh necessity" of a lack of money, Wordsworth returned to England late in 1792.
9. Wordsworth had allied his sympathies with the party of the Girondins, almost all of whom were guillotined or committed suicide.
1. Wordsworth did not meet Coleridge, the "beloved Friend," until 1795.
2. England joined the war against France in February 1793. The great moral crisis which almost

Not in my single self alone I found,
But in the minds of all ingenuous Youth,
Change and subversion from that hour. No shock
Given to my moral nature had I known
Down to that very moment; neither lapse   270
Nor turn of sentiment that might be named
A revolution, save at this one time;
All else was progress on the self-same path
On which, with a diversity of pace,
I had been travelling: this a stride at once   275
Into another region.—As a light
And pliant hare-bell swinging in the breeze
On some gray rock, its birth-place, so had I
Wantoned, fast rooted on the ancient tower
Of my beloved Country, wishing not   280
A happier fortune than to wither there.
Now was I from that pleasant station torn
And tossed about in whirlwind. I rejoiced,
Yea, afterwards, truth most painful to record!
Exulted, in the triumph of my Soul,   285
When Englishmen by thousands were o'erthrown,
Left without glory on the field, or driven,
Brave hearts, to shameful flight.[3] It was a grief,—
Grief call it not, 'twas any thing but that,—
A conflict of sensations without name,   290
Of which *he* only who may love the sight
Of a Village Steeple as I do can judge,
When, in the Congregation bending all
To their great Father, prayers were offered up,
Or praises, for our Country's victories,   295
And, 'mid the simple Worshippers, perchance
I only, like an uninvited Guest,
Whom no one owned, sate silent, shall I add,
Fed on the day of vengeance yet to come?

[*The Reign of Terror. Nightmares*]

—Domestic carnage now filled the whole year
With Feast-days; old Men from the Chimney-nook,
The Maiden from the bosom of her Love,
The Mother from the Cradle of her Babe,
The Warrior from the Field, all perished, all,   360
Friends, enemies, of all parties, ages, ranks,
Head after head, and never heads enough

wrecked Wordsworth's life began with this sudden split between his profound attachments to the English land (the development of which he had described in the early books of *The Prelude*) and his later but heartfelt identification with the cause of the French Revolution. What had seemed a single and coherent development suddenly became split into conflicting parts.

3. The French defeated the English in the battle of Hondschoote, Sept. 6, 1793.

For those that bade them fall.[4] They found their joy,
They made it, proudly eager as a Child
(If like desires of innocent little ones   365
May with such heinous appetites be compared),
Pleased in some open field to exercise
A toy that mimics with revolving wings
The motion of a windmill, though the air
Do of itself blow fresh and make the Vanes   370
Spin in his eyesight, *that* contents him not,
But, with the play-thing at arm's length, he sets
His front against the blast, and runs amain
That it may whirl the faster.

                      *   *   *

Most melancholy at that time, O Friend!
Were my day-thoughts, my nights were miserable;
Through months, through years, long after the last beat
Of those atrocities, the hour of sleep   400
To me came rarely charged with natural gifts,
Such ghastly Visions had I of despair
And tyranny, and implements of death,
And innocent victims sinking under fear,
And momentary hope, and worn-out prayer,   405
Each in his separate cell, or penned in crowds
For sacrifice, and struggling with forced mirth
And levity in dungeons where the dust
Was laid with tears. Then suddenly the scene
Changed, and the unbroken dream entangled me   410
In long orations which I strove to plead
Before unjust tribunals—with a voice
Labouring, a brain confounded, and a sense
Death-like of treacherous desertion, felt
In the last place of refuge, my own soul.   415

From Book Eleven
France, concluded[1]

[Retrospect: "Bliss Was It in That Dawn." Recourse to "Reason's Naked Self"]

O pleasant exercise of hope and joy![2]   105
For mighty were the Auxiliars which then stood

---

4. A description of the height of the Reign of Terror under Robespierre; in 1794, 1,376 people were guillotined in Paris in 49 days. "Feast-days" (line 357): i.e., festivals celebrated by human slaughter ("carnage").
1. Book 11 deals with the year from August 1794 through September 1795: Wordsworth's growing disillusionment with the French Revolution, his

recourse to abstract theories of man and politics, his despair and nervous breakdown, and the beginning of his recovery when he moved from London to Racedown.
2. Wordsworth in this passage turns back to the summer of 1792, when his enthusiasm for the Revolution was at its height.

Upon our side, we who were strong in Love!
Bliss was it in that dawn to be alive,
But to be young was very Heaven! O times,
In which the meagre, stale, forbidding ways   110
Of custom, law, and statute, took at once
The attraction of a Country in Romance!
When Reason seemed the most to assert her rights,
When most intent on making of herself
A prime Enchantress—to assist the work   115
Which then was going forward in her name!
Not favored spots alone, but the whole earth
The beauty wore of promise—that which sets
(As at some moments might not be unfelt
Among the bowers of Paradise itself)   120
The budding rose above the rose full blown.[3]
What Temper at the prospect did not wake
To happiness unthought of? The inert
Were roused, and lively natures rapt away![4]
They who had fed their Childhood upon dreams,   125
The play-fellows of Fancy, who had made
All powers of swiftness, subtilty, and strength
Their ministers,—who in lordly wise had stirred
Among the grandest objects of the Sense,
And dealt with whatsoever they found there   130
As if they had within some lurking right
To wield it;—they, too, who of gentle mood
Had watched all gentle motions, and to these
Had fitted their own thoughts, schemers more mild,
And in the region of their peaceful selves;—   135
Now was it that *both* found, the Meek and Lofty
Did both find helpers to their hearts' desire,
And stuff at hand, plastic[5] as they could wish,—
Were called upon to exercise their skill,
Not in Utopia,—subterranean Fields,—   140
Or some secreted Island, Heaven knows where!
But in the very world, which is the world
Of all of us,—the place where in the end
We find our happiness, or not at all!
    Why should I not confess that Earth was then   145
To me what an Inheritance new-fallen
Seems, when the first time visited, to one
Who thither comes to find in it his home?
He walks about and looks upon the spot
With cordial transport, moulds it and remoulds,   150
And is half-pleased with things that are amiss,
'Twill be such joy to see them disappear.

3. A statement of the Romantic theme of the glory
of the imperfect, which sets a higher value on
promise than on achievement. "Temper" (line 122):
temperament.
4. Enraptured; carried away by enthusiasm.
5. Malleable.

An active partisan, I thus convoked[6]
From every object pleasant circumstance
To suit my ends; I moved among mankind   155
With genial feelings still[7] predominant;
When erring, erring on the better part,
And in the kinder spirit; placable,
Indulgent, as not uninformed that men
See as they have been taught, and that Antiquity[8]   160
Gives rights to error; and aware no less
That throwing off oppression must be work
As well of licence as of liberty;
And above all, for this was more than all,
Not caring if the wind did now and then   165
Blow keen upon an eminence that gave
Prospect so large into futurity;
In brief, a Child of Nature, as at first,
Diffusing only those affections wider
That from the cradle had grown up with me,   170
And losing, in no other way than light
Is lost in light, the weak in the more strong.
   In the main outline, such, it might be said,
Was my condition, till with open war
Britain opposed the Liberties of France;[9]   175
This threw me first out of the pale[1] of love,
Soured, and corrupted, upwards to the source,
My sentiments; was not,[2] as hitherto,
A swallowing up of lesser things in great;
But change of them into their contraries;   180
And thus a way was opened for mistakes
And false conclusions, in degree as gross,
In kind more dangerous. What had been a pride
Was now a shame; my likings and my loves
Ran in new channels, leaving old ones dry,   185
And hence a blow that in maturer age
Would but have touched the judgement, struck more deep
Into sensations near the heart; meantime,
As from the first, wild theories were afloat
To whose pretensions sedulously urged[3]   190
I had but lent a careless ear, assured
That time was ready to set all things right,
And that the multitude so long oppressed
Would be oppressed no more.
                 But when events
Brought less encouragement, and unto these   195
The immediate proof of principles no more

---

6. Called up.
7. Always.
8. Classical antiquity.
9. On Feb. 11, 1793, England declared war against

France.
1. Enclosure.
2. I.e., there was not (in my sentiments). . . .
3. Diligently argued for.

Could be entrusted, while the events themselves,
Worn out in greatness, stripped of novelty,
Less occupied the mind; and sentiments
Could through my understanding's natural growth   200
No longer keep their ground, by faith maintained
Of inward consciousness, and hope that laid
Her hand upon her object; evidence
Safer, of universal application, such
As could not be impeached, was sought elsewhere.   205
    But now, become Oppressors in their turn,
Frenchmen had changed a war of self-defence
For one of Conquest, losing sight of all
Which they had struggled for:[4] and mounted up,
Openly in the eye of Earth and Heaven,   210
The scale of Liberty.[5] I read her doom
With anger vexed, with disappointment sore,
But not dismayed, nor taking to the shame
Of a false Prophet. While resentment rose,
Striving to hide, what nought could heal, the wounds   215
Of mortified presumption, I adhered
More firmly to old tenets, and, to prove[6]
Their temper, strained them more; and thus, in heat
Of contest, did opinions every day
Grow into consequence, till round my mind   220
They clung, as if they were its life, nay more,
The very being of the immortal Soul.
    This was the time when, all things tending fast
To depravation, speculative schemes
That promised to abstract the hopes of Man   225
Out of his feelings, to be fixed thenceforth
For ever in a purer element,
Found ready welcome.[7] Tempting region *that*
For Zeal to enter and refresh herself,
Where passions had the privilege to work,   230
And never hear the sound of their own names:
But, speaking more in charity, the dream
Flattered the young, pleased with extremes, nor least
With that which makes our Reason's naked self
The object of its fervour. * * *   235

---

4. In late 1794 and early 1795 French troops had successes in Spain, Italy, Holland, and Germany—even though, in the constitution written in 1790, they had renounced all foreign conquest.
5. I.e., the desire for power now outweighed the love of liberty.
6. Test; the figure is that of testing a tempered steel sword.
7. I.e., schemes which undertook to separate ("abstract") people's hopes for future happiness from reliance on the emotional part of human nature, and instead to ground those hopes on their rational natures ("a purer element"). The allusion is primarily to William Godwin's *Inquiry Concerning Political Justice* (1793), which attempted to ground ethical and political principles, and the expectation of human progress, on rational principles.

[Crisis, Breakdown, and Recovery]

I summoned my best skill, and toiled, intent
To anatomize[8] the frame of social life,   280
Yea, the whole body of society
Searched to its heart. Share with me, Friend! the wish
That some dramatic tale indued with shapes
Livelier, and flinging out less guarded words
Than suit the Work we fashion, might set forth   285
What then I learned, or think I learned, of truth,
And the errors into which I fell, betrayed
By present objects, and by reasonings false
From their beginnings, inasmuch as drawn
Out of a heart that had been turned aside   290
From Nature's way by outward accidents,
And which was thus confounded more and more,
Misguided and misguiding. So I fared,
Dragging all precepts, judgments, maxims, creeds,
Like culprits to the bar; calling the mind,   295
Suspiciously, to establish in plain day
Her titles[9] and her honors, now believing,
Now disbelieving, endlessly perplexed
With impulse, motive, right and wrong, the ground
Of obligation, what the rule and whence   300
The sanction, till, demanding formal *proof*
And seeking it in every thing, I lost
All feeling of conviction, and, in fine,[1]
Sick, wearied out with contrarieties,
Yielded up moral questions in despair.   305
    This was the crisis of that strong disease,
This the soul's last and lowest ebb; I drooped,
Deeming our blessed Reason of least use
Where wanted most. * * *

                    * * * Then it was,
Thanks to the bounteous Giver of all good!
That the beloved Woman[2] in whose sight   335
Those days were passed, now speaking in a voice
Of sudden admonition—like a brook
That does but *cross* a lonely road, and now
Seen, heard, and felt, and caught at every turn,
Companion never lost through many a league—   340
Maintained for me a saving intercourse
With my true self:[3] for, though bedimmed and changed

8. Analyze.
9. Legal entitlements.
1. In the end.
2. After a long separation, Dorothy Wordsworth came to live with her brother at Racedown in 1795, and remained a permanent member of his household.
3. Dorothy and the renewed influence of nature (line 349) healed the inner fracture between his earlier and later self, which Wordsworth had described in book 10.268 ff.

Both as a clouded and a waning moon,
She whispered still that brightness would return,
She in the midst of all preserved me still   345
A Poet, made me seek beneath that name,
And that alone, my office upon earth.
And lastly, as hereafter will be shewn,
If willing audience fail not, Nature's self,
By all varieties of human love   350
Assisted, led me back through opening day
To those sweet counsels between head and heart
Whence grew that genuine knowledge fraught with peace
Which, through the later sinkings of this cause,
Hath still upheld me, and upholds me now   355
In the catastrophe (for so they dream,
And nothing less), when, finally to close
And rivet down the gains of France, a Pope
Is summoned in, to crown an Emperor:[4]
This last opprobrium, when we see a people   360
That once looked up in faith, as if to Heaven
For manna, take a lesson from the Dog
Returning to his vomit. * * *

Book Twelfth
Imagination and Taste, how impaired and restored[1]

Long time have human ignorance and guilt
Detained us, on what spectacles of woe
Compelled to look, and inwardly oppressed
With sorrow, disappointment, vexing thoughts,
Confusion of the judgment, zeal decayed,   5
And, lastly, utter loss of hope itself
And things to hope for! Not with these began
Our Song, and not with these our Song must end.[2]
Ye motions of delight, that haunt the sides
Of the green hills; ye breezes and soft airs,   10
Whose subtile intercourse with breathing flowers,
Feelingly watched, might teach Man's haughty race
How without injury to take, to give
Without offence; ye who, as if to shew
The wondrous influence of power gently used,   15
Bend the complying heads of lordly pines,
And with a touch shift the stupendous clouds
Through the whole compass of the sky; ye brooks

4. The ultimate blow to liberal hopes for France
occurred when on Dec. 2, 1804, Napoleon summoned Pope Pius VII to officiate at the ceremony
elevating him to Emperor. At the last moment,
Napoleon took the crown and donned it himself.
1. Book 12 reviews the "impairment" and gradual
recovery of Wordsworth's creative sensibility in
response to the natural world.
2. The reference is back to the joyous preamble
with which *The Prelude* began. Wordsworth goes
on (line 10) to invoke the breeze described in the
opening line of the poem.

Muttering along the stones, a busy noise
By day, a quiet sound in silent night;   20
Ye waves that out of the great deep steal forth
In a calm hour to kiss the pebbly shore,
Not mute, and then retire, fearing no storm;
And you, ye Groves, whose ministry it is
To interpose the covert of your shades,   25
Even as a sleep, between the heart of man
And outward troubles, between man himself,
Not seldom, and his own uneasy heart!
Oh that I had a music and a voice
Harmonious as your own, that I might tell   30
What Ye have done for me! The morning shines,
Nor heedeth Man's perverseness; Spring returns,
I saw the Spring return and could rejoice,
In common with the Children of her love
Piping on boughs, or sporting on fresh fields,   35
Or boldly seeking pleasure nearer heaven
On wings that navigate cerulean skies.
So neither were complacency[3] nor peace
Nor tender yearnings wanting for my good
Through those distracted times;[4] in Nature still   40
Glorying, I found a counterpoise in her,
Which, when the Spirit of evil reached its height,
Maintained for me a secret happiness.
　　This Narrative, my Friend, hath chiefly told
Of intellectual power,[5] fostering love,   45
Dispensing truth, and over men and things,
Where reason yet might hesitate, diffusing
Prophetic sympathies of genial faith.
So was I favored, such my happy lot,
Until that natural graciousness of mind   50
Gave way to overpressure from the times
And their disastrous issues. What availed,
When spells forbade the Voyager to land,
That fragrant notice of a pleasant shore
Wafted at intervals from many a bower   55
Of blissful gratitude and fearless peace?
Dare I avow that wish was mine to see,
And hope that future times *would* surely see,
The man to come parted as by a gulph
From him who had been, that I could no more   60
Trust the elevation which had made me one
With the great Family that still survives
To illuminate the abyss of ages past,
Sage, Warrior, Patriot, Hero?—for it seemed

---

3. Satisfaction.
4. I.e., the period of spiritual crisis that he had
described in 11.293–309, above.

5. The power of the integral mind (as distinguished from the limited capacity of "reason" alone,
line 47).

That their best virtues were not free from taint   65
Of something false and weak, that could not stand
The open eye of Reason.[6] Then I said,
"Go to the Poets; they will speak to thee
More perfectly of purer Creatures; yet
If Reason be nobility in Man,   70
Can aught be more ignoble than the Man
Whom they delight in, blinded as he is
By prejudice, the miserable slave
Of low ambition, or distempered love?"
    In such strange passion (if I may once more   75
Review the past) I warred against myself,
A Bigot to a New Idolatry;
Like a cowled Monk who hath forsworn the world,
Zealously labour'd to cut off my heart
From all the sources of her former strength;   80
And as by simple waving of a Wand
The wizard instantaneously dissolves
Palace or grove, even so could I unsoul
As readily by syllogistic words[7]
Those mysteries of being which have made,   85
And shall continue evermore to make,
Of the whole human race one brotherhood.
    What wonder, then, if to a mind so far
Perverted, even the visible Universe
Fell under the dominion of a taste   90
Less Spiritual, with microscopic view
Was scanned, as I had scanned the moral world?[8]
    Oh Soul of Nature, excellent and fair!
That didst rejoice with me, with whom I too
Rejoiced, through early Youth, before the winds   95
And roaring waters, and in lights and shades
That marched and countermarched about the hills
In glorious apparition, powers on whom
I daily waited, now all eye and now
All ear; but never long without the heart   100
Employed, and Man's unfolding intellect!

6. This passage is both elliptical and contorted in its syntax. The fragrance wafted to the sailor from the shore—i.e., his remembered experiences of human feelings of gratitude and love (lines 54–56)—serve also as evidence of the shared emotions that had earlier united him to the family of past humanity (lines 61–63). The "spells" that prevented the sailor from landing on that shore (line 53) consist of his fascination with a limited mode of analytic reasoning, which engendered the hope that in the future people would be purely rational beings, hence utterly different from the feelingful, passionate creatures of the past (lines 58–60). This mode of reasoning, in addition, not only made Wordsworth distrust the earlier emotional evidences of his unity with humanity, but also led him to believe that the actions of even the greatest men recorded in human history were tainted, because motivated by feelings rather than by reason alone (lines 64–67).

    In his allusions to the rational "spells" and his hope for a new type of mankind Wordsworth is describing the period in his life when he had succumbed to the views of William Godwin's *Enquiry Concerning Political Justice* (1793), which derogated the role of the feelings and passions as motives and confidently anticipated a future in which the actions of humanity will be determined solely by dispassionate reason.

7. Logical reasoning.

8. I.e., the habit of logical analysis perverted his perception of the natural world.

Oh Soul of Nature! that, by laws divine
Sustained and governed, still dost overflow
With an impassioned life, what feeble ones
Walk on this earth! how feeble have I been   105
When thou wert in thy strength! Nor this through stroke
Of human suffering, such as justifies
Remissness and inaptitude of mind,
But through presumption;[9] even in pleasure pleased
Unworthily, disliking here, and there   110
Liking; by rules of mimic Art transferred
To things above all Art; but more,—for this,
Although a strong infection of the age,
Was never much my habit—giving way
To a comparison of scene with scene,   115
Bent overmuch on superficial things,
Pampering myself with meagre novelties
Of colour and proportion, to the moods
Of time and season, to the moral power,
The affections and the spirit of the Place,   120
Insensible.[1] Nor only did the love
Of sitting thus in judgment interrupt
My deeper feelings, but another cause,
More subtile and less easily explained,
That almost seems inherent in the Creature,   125
A twofold frame of body and of mind.
I speak in recollection of a time
When the bodily eye, in every stage of life
The most despotic of our senses, gained
Such strength in *me* as often held my mind   130
In absolute dominion. Gladly here,
Entering upon abstruser Argument,
Could I endeavour to unfold the means
Which Nature studiously employs to thwart
This tyranny, summons all the senses each   135
To counteract the other, and themselves,
And makes them all, and the Objects with which all
Are conversant, subservient in their turn
To the great ends of Liberty and Power.[2]
But leave we this: enough that my delights   140
(Such as they were) were sought insatiably.
Vivid the transport, vivid, though not profound;
I roamed from hill to hill, from rock to rock,

9. Presumptuousness, arrogance.
1. Unresponsive. Wordsworth has described his
temporary participation in the cult of the picturesque—i.e., judging a natural scene by criteria
derived from the "Art" of landscape painting (lines
11–12)—and then, his acquired and longer-lasting
tendency to judge the comparative value of natural
scenes by superficial, purely aesthetic criteria (lines
115–18).

2. I.e., the ways in which Nature uses an individual's other senses to counteract the tyranny of the
eye—as well as the tyranny of any other single
sense—so as to make all the senses (and the external objects they enable us to perceive) subordinate
to the free, creative power of the human mind.
Later in this book Wordsworth attributes this power
of free creativity to the imagination.

Still craving combinations of new forms,
New pleasure, wider empire for the sight, 145
Proud of her own endowments, and rejoiced
To lay the inner faculties asleep.
Amid the turns and counterturns, the strife
And various trials of our complex being,
As we grow up, such thraldom of that sense[3] 150
Seems hard to shun. And yet I knew a Maid,
A young Enthusiast, who escaped these bonds;[4]
Her eye was not the Mistress of her heart;
Far less did rules prescribed by passive taste
Or barren intermeddling subtleties 155
Perplex her mind; but, wise as women are
When genial circumstance[5] hath favoured them,
She welcomed what was given and craved no more;
Whate'er the scene presented to her view,
That was the best, to that she was attuned 160
By her benign simplicity of life
And through a perfect happiness of Soul
Whose variegated feelings were in this
Sisters, that they were each some new delight.
Birds in the bower, and lambs in the green field, 165
Could they have known her, would have loved; methought
Her very presence such a sweetness breathed
That flowers, and trees, and even the silent hills,
And every thing she looked on should have had
An intimation how she bore herself 170
Towards them and to all creatures. God delights
In such a being; for her common thoughts
Are piety, her life is gratitude.
    Even like this Maid, before I was called forth
From the retirement of my native hills, 175
I loved whate'er I saw: nor lightly loved,
But most intensely; never dreamt of aught
More grand, more fair, more exquisitely framed
Than those few nooks to which my happy feet
Were limited. I had not at that time 180
Lived long enough, nor in the least survived
The first diviner influence of this world
As it appears to unaccustomed eyes.
Worshipping then among the depth of things
As piety ordained,[6] could I submit 185
To measured admiration, or to aught
That should preclude humility and love?
I felt, observed, and pondered; did not judge,

---

3. I.e., subservience to the sense of sight.
4. Mary Hutchinson, whom Wordsworth had known since childhood, and whom he married in 1802.
5. Beneficent conditions (of a woman's life).
6. In the text of 1805 the phrase had been: "As my soul bade me."

Yea, never thought of judging; with the gift
Of all this glory filled and satisfied.   190
And afterwards, when through the gorgeous Alps
Roaming, I carried with me the same heart:[7]
In truth, the degradation,[8] howsoe'er
Induced, effect in whatsoe'er degree
Of custom that prepares a partial scale   195
In which the little oft outweighs the great,
Or any other cause that hath been named;
Or lastly, aggravated by the times,
And their empassioned sounds,[9] which well might make
The milder minstrelsies of rural scenes   200
Inaudible, was transient; I had known
Too forcibly, too early in my life,
Visitings of imaginative power
For this to last: I shook the habit off
Entirely and for ever, and again   205
In Nature's presence stood, as now I stand,
A sensitive Being, a *creative* Soul.
     There are in our existence spots of time,[1]
That with distinct pre-eminence retain
A renovating virtue, whence, depressed   210
By false opinion and contentious thought,
Or aught of heavier or more deadly weight,
In trivial occupations, and the round
Of ordinary intercourse, our minds
Are nourished and invisibly repaired;   215
A virtue by which pleasure is inhanced,
That penetrates, enables us to mount,
When high, more high, and lifts us up when fallen.
This efficacious Spirit chiefly lurks
Among those passages of life that give   220
Profoundest knowledge how and to what point
The mind is lord and master—outward sense
The obedient Servant of her will. Such moments
Are scattered every where, taking their date
From our first Childhood. I remember well   225
That once, while yet my inexperienced hand
Could scarcely hold a bridle, with proud hopes
I mounted, and we journied towards the hills:

---

7. In his walk across the Alps in 1790, described
in book 6 above.
8. I.e., the deterioration (of a full, unreflective
response to nature) that he has described in 12.109–
151.
9. I.e., by the high passions aroused by the French
Revolution. Wordsworth speculates that these may
have been a contributing factor in diminishing his
attention and responsiveness to the natural world.
1. Moments of experience in which something
ordinary (line 254) suddenly becomes profoundly

significant; since this significance is bestowed by
the perceiver, it demonstrates the freedom and
creative power of the imaginative mind (lines 220–
23, 275–77). The remembrance of such moments
nourishes and repairs the mind in periods of
depression or distraction when the imagination flags
(lines 210–15). Wordsworth also recognizes (lines
277–86) that the recollection of such spots of time
from his early life is the source of his greatest poetry,
and that this source is not inexhaustible.

An ancient Servant of my Father's house
Was with me, my encourager and Guide.   230
We had not travelled long ere some mischance
Disjoined me from my Comrade, and, through fear
Dismounting, down the rough and stony Moor
I led my horse, and, stumbling on, at length
Came to a bottom,[2] where in former times   235
A Murderer had been hung in iron chains.
The Gibbet mast[3] had mouldered down, the bones
And iron case were gone, but on the turf
Hard by, soon after that fell deed was wrought,
Some unknown hand had carved the Murderer's name.   240
The monumental Letters were inscribed
In times long past, but still from year to year,
By superstition of the neighbourhood,
The grass is cleared away, and to that hour
The characters were fresh and visible.   245
A casual glance had shewn them, and I fled,
Faultering and faint and ignorant of the road:
Then, reascending the bare common, saw
A naked Pool that lay beneath the hills,
The Beacon on its summit, and, more near,   250
A Girl who bore a Pitcher on her head,
And seemed with difficult steps to force her way
Against the blowing wind. It was in truth
An ordinary sight; but I should need
Colors and words that are unknown to man   255
To paint the visionary dreariness
Which, while I looked all round for my lost Guide,
Invested Moorland waste and naked Pool,
The Beacon crowning the lone eminence,
The Female and her garments vexed and tossed   260
By the strong wind.—When, in the blessed hours
Of early love, the loved One[4] at my side,
I roamed, in daily presence of this scene,
Upon the naked Pool and dreary Crags,
And on the melancholy Beacon, fell   265
A spirit of pleasure, and Youth's golden gleam;
And think ye not with radiance more sublime
For these remembrances, and for the power
They had left behind? So feeling comes in aid
Of feeling, and diversity of strength   270
Attends us, if but once we have been strong.
Oh! mystery of Man, from what a depth
Proceed thy honors! I am lost, but see
In simple child-hood something of the base
On which thy greatness stands; but this I feel,   275

2. Valley.   hangings.
3. The post of the T-shaped structure used for   4. Mary Hutchinson.

That from thyself it comes, that thou must give,
Else never canst receive. The days gone by
Return upon me almost from the dawn
Of life: the hiding-places of Man's power
Open; I would approach them, but they close.   280
I see by glimpses now; when age comes on
May scarcely see at all, and I would give,
While yet we may, as far as words can give,
Substance and life to what I feel, enshrining,
Such is my hope, the spirit of the past   285
For future restoration.—Yet another
Of these memorials.
                    One Christmas-time, [5]
On the glad Eve of its dear holidays,
Feverish, and tired, and restless, I went forth
Into the fields, impatient for the sight   290
Of those led Palfreys[6] that should bear us home,
My Brothers and myself. There rose a Crag
That, from the meeting point of two highways
Ascending, overlooked them both, far stretched;
Thither, uncertain on which road to fix   295
My expectation, thither I repaired,
Scout-like, and gained the summit; 'twas a day
Tempestuous, dark, and wild, and on the grass
I sate, half-sheltered by a naked wall;
Upon my right hand couched a single sheep,   300
Upon my left a blasted hawthorn stood:
With those Companions at my side, I sate,
Straining my eyes intensely, as the mist
Gave intermitting prospect of the copse
And plain beneath. Ere we to School returned   305
That dreary time, ere we had been ten days
Sojourners in my Father's House, he died,[7]
And I and my three Brothers, Orphans then,
Followed his Body to the Grave. The Event,
With all the sorrow that it brought, appeared   310
A chastisement; and when I called to mind
That day so lately passed, when from the Crag
I looked in such anxiety of hope,
With trite reflections of morality,
Yet in the deepest passion, I bowed low   315
To God, who thus corrected my desires;
And afterwards, the wind and sleety rain
And all the business[8] of the Elements,
The single Sheep, and the one blasted tree,
And the bleak music of that old stone wall,   320

5. In 1783; Wordsworth, aged 13, was at Hawkshead School with two of his brothers.
6. Small saddle horses.

7. John Wordsworth died on Dec. 30, 1783; William's mother had died 5 years earlier.
8. Busy-ness; motions.

The noise of wood and water, and the mist
That on the line of each of those two Roads
Advanced in such indisputable shapes;[9]
All these were kindred spectacles and sounds
To which I oft repaired, and thence would drink   325
As at a fountain; and on winter nights,
Down to this *very* time, when storm and rain
Beat on my roof, or haply at noon-day,
While in a grove I walk whose lofty trees,
Laden with summer's thickest foliage, rock   330
In a strong wind, some working of the spirit,
Some inward agitations, thence are brought,[1]
Whate'er their office, whether to beguile
Thoughts over-busy in the course they took,
Or animate an hour of vacant ease.   335

From Book Thirteenth
Subject concluded

[*Return to "Life's Familiar Face"*]

From Nature doth emotion come, and moods
Of calmness equally are Nature's gift:
This is her glory; these two attributes
Are sister horns that constitute her strength.[1]
Hence Genius,[2] born to thrive by interchange   5
Of peace and excitation, finds in her
His best and purest friend, from her receives
That energy by which he seeks the truth,
From her that happy stillness of the mind
Which fits him to receive it, when unsought.   10
   Such benefit the humblest intellects
Partake of, each in their degree: 'tis mine
To speak of what myself have known and felt.
Smooth task! for words find easy way, inspired
By gratitude and confidence in truth.   15
Long time in search of knowledge did I range
The field of human life, in heart and mind
Benighted, but the dawn beginning now
To reappear,[3] 'twas proved that not in vain
I had been taught to reverence a Power   20
That is the visible quality and shape
And image of right reason,[4] that matures

---

9. Pronounced *indispútáble shápes*; i.e., shapes one
did not dare question.
1. Another instance of Wordsworth's inner response
to an outer breeze (cf. 1.33–38).
1. In the Old Testament, the horn of an animal
signifies power.

2. A person capable of creativity.
3. I.e., he is beginning to recover from the spiritual crisis recorded in 11.293–309, above.
4. Wordsworth follows Milton's use of the term
"right reason" to denote a human faculty that is
inherently attuned to truth.

Her processes by steadfast laws, gives birth
To no impatient or fallacious hopes,
No heat of passion or excessive zeal,   25
No vain conceits,—provokes to no quick turns
Of self-applauding intellect,—but trains
To meekness, and exalts by humble faith;[5]
Holds up before the mind, intoxicate
With present objects, and the busy dance   30
Of things that pass away, a temperate shew
Of objects that endure; and by this course
Disposes her, when over-fondly set
On throwing off incumbrances, to seek
In Man, and in the frame of social life,   35
Whate'er there is desireable and good
Of kindred permanence, unchanged in form
And function, or through strict vicissitude
Of life and death revolving. Above all
Were re-established now those watchful thoughts   40
Which (seeing little worthy or sublime
In what the Historian's pen so much delights
To blazon, Power and Energy detached
From moral purpose) early tutored me
To look with feelings of fraternal love   45
Upon the unassuming things that hold
A silent station in this beauteous world.[6]
    Thus moderated, thus composed, I found
Once more in Man an object of delight,
Of pure imagination, and of love;   50
And, as the horizon of my mind enlarged,
Again I took the intellectual eye[7]
For my Instructor, studious more to see
Great Truths, than touch and handle little ones.
Knowledge was given accordingly; my trust   55
Became more firm in feelings that had stood
The test of such a trial; clearer far
My sense of excellence—of right and wrong:
The promise of the present time retired
Into its true proportions; sanguine[8] schemes,   60
Ambitious projects, pleased me less; I sought
For present good in life's familiar face,
And built thereon my hopes of good to come.

5. In the text of 1805: "but lifts / The being into magnanimity."

6. Here Wordsworth begins his account of how he came to feel bonds to, and to love, the silent, lowly, common things whose celebration he considers to be his special vocation as an innovative poet-prophet; see lines 301–8.

7. Perception by the integral mind.

8. Optimistic. Wordsworth apparently refers back to his earlier "ambitious projects" for a long poem, described in 1.166–220 above, as well as to the optimistic schemes for mankind that had been engendered by his commitment to the French Revolution.

[*Discovery of His Poetic Subject. Salisbury Plain.*
Sight of "a New World"]

Here, calling up to mind what then I saw,[9]   220
A youthful Traveller, and see daily now
In the familiar circuit of my home,
Here might I pause and bend in reverence
To Nature, and the power of human minds,
To Men as they are Men within themselves.   225
How oft high service is performed within,
When all the external Man is rude in shew!
Not like a Temple rich with pomp and gold,
But a mere mountain Chapel that protects
Its simple Worshippers from sun and shower.   230
Of these, said I, shall be my song, of these,
If future years mature me for the task,
Will I record the praises, making Verse
Deal boldly with substantial things; in truth
And sanctity of passion speak of these,   235
That justice may be done, obeisance paid
Where it is due: thus haply shall I teach,
Inspire, through unadulterated[1] ears
Pour rapture, tenderness, and hope, my theme
No other than the very heart of Man   240
As found among the best of those who live
Not unexalted by religious faith,
Nor uninformed by Books, good books, though few,
In Nature's presence: thence may I select
Sorrow, that is not sorrow, but delight,   245
And miserable love that is not pain
To hear of, for the glory that redounds
Therefrom to human kind and what we are.
Be mine to follow with no timid step
Where knowledge leads me; it shall be my pride   250
That I have dared to tread this holy ground,
Speaking no dream, but things oracular,
Matter not lightly to be heard by those
Who to the letter of the outward promise
Do read the invisible Soul,[2] by Men adroit   255
In speech, and for communion with the world
Accomplished, minds whose faculties are then
Most active when they are most eloquent,

---

9. Wordsworth has described, as part of his imaginative recovery, his learning to look again with sympathy upon "the unassuming things that hold / A silent station in this beauteous world," and his finding again "in Man an object of delight." Now he shows how, in reaction against his concern with great actions detached from moral purpose which constituted the French Revolution, he came to embrace the poetic doctrines of the Preface to *Lyr*-*ical Ballads*. He will write of simple, lowly people, whose patient endurance of suffering redounds to the glory of humankind, and who speak a language which is the spontaneous overflow of powerful feelings (lines 263–64).

1. Uncorrupted.

2. I.e., this doctrine will not be lightly accepted by those who judge inner worth by exterior seeming.

And elevated most, when most admired.
Men may be found of other mold than these, 260
Who are their own Upholders, to themselves
Encouragement, and energy, and will,
Expressing liveliest thoughts in lively words
As native passion dictates.[3] Others, too,
There are, among the walks of homely life, 265
Still higher, men for contemplation framed,
Shy, and unpractised in the strife of phrase,[4]
Meek men, whose very souls perhaps would sink
Beneath them, summoned to such intercourse:
Theirs is the language of the heavens, the power, 270
The thought, the image, and the silent joy;
Words are but under-agents in their Souls;
When they are grasping with their greatest strength
They do not breathe among them;[5] this I speak
In gratitude to God, who feeds our hearts 275
For his own service; knoweth, loveth us
When we are unregarded by the world.
    Also, about this time did I receive
Convictions still more strong than heretofore
Not only that the inner frame is good, 280
And graciously composed, but that, no less,
Nature for all conditions wants not power
To consecrate, if we have eyes to see,
The outside of her Creatures, and to breathe
Grandeur upon the very humblest face 285
Of human life. I felt that the array
Of act and circumstance, and visible form,
Is mainly, to the pleasure of the mind,
What passion makes them, that meanwhile the forms
Of Nature have a passion in themselves 290
That intermingles with those works of man
To which she summons him; although the works
Be mean, have nothing lofty of their own;
And that the Genius of the Poet hence
May boldly take his way among mankind 295
Wherever Nature leads, that he hath stood
By Nature's side among the Men of old,
And so shall stand for ever. Dearest Friend,
If thou partake the animating faith
That Poets, even as Prophets, each with each 300
Connected in a mighty scheme of truth,
Have each his own peculiar faculty,
Heaven's gift, a sense that fits him to perceive

3. In his Preface to *Lyrical Ballads* of 1800,
Wordsworth said that he chose characters from low
and rustic life because in them "the essential passions of the heart . . . are less under restraint, and
speak a plainer and more emphatic language."

4. The rhetoric of controversy.
5. I.e., even in the greatest strength of their intuitive grasp, they do not utter words, which (line
272) are for them merely subsidiary to the fullness
of their response to an experience.

Objects unseen before, thou wilt not blame
The humblest of this band[6] who dares to hope   305
That unto him hath also been vouchsafed
An insight, that in some sort he possesses
A Privilege, whereby a Work of his,
Proceeding from a source of untaught things,
Creative and enduring, may become   310
A Power like one of Nature's. To a hope
Not less ambitious once among the Wilds
Of Sarum's Plain[7] my youthful Spirit was raised;
There, as I ranged at will the pastoral downs[8]
Trackless and smooth, or paced the bare white roads   315
Lengthening in solitude their dreary line,
Time with his retinue of ages fled
Backwards, nor checked his flight until I saw
Our dim Ancestral Past in Vision clear;[9]
Saw multitudes of men, and here and there   320
A single Briton clothed in Wolf-skin vest,
With shield and stone-axe, stride across the wold;[1]
The voice of Spears was heard, the rattling spear
Shaken by arms of mighty bone, in strength,
Long mouldered, of barbaric majesty.   325
I called on Darkness—but before the word
Was uttered, midnight darkness seemed to take
All objects from my sight; and lo! again
The Desart visible by dismal flames;
It is the Sacrificial Altar, fed   330
With living Men—how deep the groans! the voice
Of those that crowd the giant wicker thrills
The monumental hillocks,[2] and the pomp
Is for both worlds, the living and the dead.
At other moments (for through that wide waste   335
Three summer days I roamed) where'er the Plain
Was figured o'er with circles, lines, or mounds,
That yet survive, a work, as some divine,[3]
Shaped by the Druids, so to represent
Their knowledge of the heavens, and image forth   340
The constellations; gently was I charmed
Into a waking dream, a reverie

---

6. Wordsworth himself.
7. Salisbury Plain, which Wordsworth crossed on
foot and alone in the summer of 1793.
8. Open hills used to pasture sheep.
9. Wordsworth shared the common, but mistaken, belief of his time that Stonehenge, the giant
megalithic structure on the Plain, had been a temple of the Celtic priests, the Druids, and that the
Druids had there performed the rite of human sacrifice; hence the imaginings and vision that he goes
on to relate.
1. High open country.
2. The many bronze age burial mounds on Salisbury Plain. "Giant wicker": Aylett Sammes, in
Britannia Antiqua Illustrata (1676), had described,
as a rite of the ancient Britons, that they wove a
huge wicker structure in the shape of a man, filled
it with living humans, and set it afire.
3. Conjecture (a verb).

That with believing eyes, where'er I turned,
Beheld long-bearded Teachers with white wands
Uplifted, pointing to the starry sky   345
Alternately, and Plain below, while breath
Of music swayed their motions, and the Waste
Rejoiced with them and me in those sweet Sounds.
     This for the past, and things that may be viewed
Or fancied, in the obscurity of years   350
From monumental hints:[4] and thou, O Friend!
Pleased with some unpremeditated strains
That served those wanderings to beguile, hast said
That then and there my mind had exercised
Upon the vulgar forms of present things,   355
The actual world of our familiar days,
Yet higher power, had caught from them a tone,
An image, and a character, by books
Not hitherto reflected.[5] Call we this
A partial[6] judgement—and yet why? for *then*   360
We were as Strangers; and I may not speak
Thus wrongfully of verse, however rude,
Which on thy young imagination, trained
In the great City, broke like light from far.
Moreover, each man's mind is to herself   365
Witness and judge; and I remember well
That in Life's every-day appearances
I seemed about this time to gain clear sight
Of a new world, a world, too, that was fit
To be transmitted and to other eyes   370
Made visible, as ruled by those fixed laws
Whence spiritual dignity originates,
Which do both give it being and maintain
A balance, an ennobling interchange
Of action from without, and from within;   375
The excellence, pure function, and best power
Both of the object seen, and eye that sees.

---

4. I.e., from what the monumental remains on Salisbury Plain suggested to him.
5. Wordsworth refers to an event that Coleridge narrates in *Biographia Literaria*, chapter 4 (see below). In November 1795, Wordsworth had read to Coleridge a MS version of his poem *Adventures on Salisbury Plain*. What impressed Coleridge, as he tells us, was Wordsworth's "fine balance of truth in observing with the imaginative faculty in modifying the objects observed, and above all, the orig-

inal gift of spreading . . . the depth and height of the ideal world, around forms, incidents, and situations of which, for the common view, custom had bedimmed all the luster." "This," Coleridge concludes, "is the character and privilege of genius."
6. Biased (in Wordsworth's favor). "We were as Strangers" (line 361) because, though Coleridge and Wordsworth had met in September 1795, they did not become close friends until 1797.

From Book Fourteenth
Conclusion

[The Vision on Mount Snowdon. Fear vs. Love Resolved.
Imagination]

In one of those Excursions (may they ne'er
Fade from remembrance!), through the Northern tracts
Of Cambria ranging with a youthful Friend,
I left Bethgellert's huts at couching-time,
And westward took my way, to see the sun   5
Rise from the top of Snowdon.[1] To the door
Of a rude Cottage at the Mountain's base
We came, and rouzed the Shepherd who attends
The adventurous Stranger's steps, a trusty Guide;
Then, cheered by short refreshment, sallied forth.   10
—It was a close, warm, breezeless summer night,
Wan, dull, and glaring,[2] with a dripping fog
Low-hung and thick, that covered all the sky.
But, undiscouraged, we began to climb
The mountain-side. The mist soon girt us round,   15
And, after ordinary Travellers' talk
With our Conductor, pensively we sank
Each into commerce with his private thoughts:
Thus did we breast the ascent, and by myself
Was nothing either seen or heard that checked   20
Those musings or diverted, save that once
The Shepherd's Lurcher,[3] who, among the crags,
Had to his joy unearthed a Hedgehog, teased
His coiled-up Prey with barkings turbulent.
This small adventure, for even such it seemed   25
In that wild place, and at the dead of night,
Being over and forgotten, on we wound
In silence as before. With forehead bent
Earthward, as if in opposition set
Against an enemy, I panted up   30
With eager pace, and no less eager thoughts.
Thus might we wear a midnight hour away,
Ascending at loose distance each from each,
And I, as chanced, the foremost of the Band:
When at my feet the ground appeared to brighten,   35

1. Wordsworth climbed Mt. Snowdon—the
highest peak in Wales ("Cambria"), and some 10
miles from the sea—with Robert Jones, the friend
with whom he had also tramped through the Alps
(book 6). The climb started from the village of
Bethgelert at "couching-time" (line 4), the time of
night when the sheep lie down to sleep. This event
had taken place in 1791 (or possibly 1793); Wordsworth presents it out of its chronological order to
introduce at this point a great natural "type" or
"emblem" (lines 66, 70) for the mind, and especially for the activity of the imagination, whose
"restoration" he has described in the two preceding books.
2. In north of England dialect, "glairie," applied
to the weather, means dull, rainy.
3. A crossbred dog, used to hunt hares.

And with a step or two seemed brighter still;
Nor was time given to ask, or learn, the cause;
For instantly a light upon the turf
Fell like a flash; and lo! as I looked up,
The Moon hung naked in a firmament   40
Of azure without cloud, and at my feet
Rested a silent sea of hoary mist.
A hundred hills their dusky backs upheaved
All over this still Ocean;[4] and beyond,
Far, far beyond, the solid vapours stretched,   45
In Headlands, tongues, and promontory shapes,
Into the main Atlantic, that appeared
To dwindle, and give up his majesty,
Usurped upon far as the sight could reach.
Not so the ethereal Vault; encroachment none   50
Was there, nor loss;[5] only the inferior stars
Had disappeared, or shed a fainter light
In the clear presence of the full-orbed Moon;
Who, from her sovereign elevation, gazed
Upon the billowy ocean, as it lay   55
All meek and silent, save that through a rift
Not distant from the shore whereon we stood,
A fixed, abysmal, gloomy breathing-place,
Mounted the roar of waters—torrents—streams
Innumerable, roaring with one voice!   60
Heard over earth and sea, and in that hour,
For so it seemed, felt by the starry heavens.
      When into air had partially dissolved
That Vision, given to Spirits of the night,
And three chance human Wanderers, in calm thought   65
Reflected, it appeared to me the type
Of a majestic Intellect, its acts
And its possessions, what it has and craves,
What in itself it is, and would become.
There I beheld the emblem of a Mind   70
That feeds upon infinity, that broods
Over the dark abyss, intent to hear
Its voices issuing forth to silent light
In one continuous stream; a mind sustained
By recognitions of transcendent power   75
In sense, conducting to ideal form;
In soul, of more than mortal privilege.[6]
One function, above all, of such a mind
Had Nature shadowed there, by putting forth,

4. In Milton's description of the creation of the world, "the mountains huge appear / Emergent, and their broad bare backs upheave / Into the clouds" (*Paradise Lost*, 7.285–87).
5. The mist projected in various shapes over the Atlantic Ocean, but did not "encroach" upon the heavens overhead.
6. The sense of lines 74–77 seems to be that the mind of someone who is gifted beyond the ordinary lot of mortals recognizes its power to transcend the senses by converting sensory objects into ideal forms.

'Mid circumstances awful and sublime,   80
That mutual domination which she loves
To exert upon the face of outward things,
So moulded, joined, abstracted; so endowed
With interchangeable supremacy,
That Men least sensitive see, hear, perceive,   85
And cannot chuse but feel. The power which all
Acknowledge when thus moved, which Nature thus
To bodily sense exhibits, is the express
Resemblance of that glorious faculty
That higher minds bear with them as their own.[7]   90
This is the very spirit in which they deal
With the whole compass of the universe:
They, from their native selves, can send abroad
Kindred mutations; for themselves create
A like existence; and whene'er it dawns   95
Created for them, catch it;—or are caught
By its inevitable mastery,
Like angels stopped upon the wing by sound
Of harmony from heaven's remotest spheres.
Them the enduring and the transient both   100
Serve to exalt; they build up greatest things
From least suggestions; ever on the watch,
Willing to work and to be wrought upon,
They need not extraordinary calls
To rouse them, in a world of life they live;   105
By sensible impressions not enthralled,
But, by their quickening impulse, made more prompt
To hold fit converse with the spiritual world,
And with the generations of mankind
Spread over time, past, present, and to come,   110
Age after age, till Time shall be no more.
Such minds are truly from the Deity,
For they are powers; and hence the highest bliss
That flesh can know is theirs,—the consciousness
Of whom they are, habitually infused   115
Through every image, and through every thought,
And all affections[8] by communion raised
From earth to heaven, from human to divine.
Hence endless occupation for the Soul,
Whether discursive or intuitive;[9]   120
Hence chearfulness for acts of daily life,
Emotions which best foresight need not fear,

---

7. The "glorious faculty" is the imagination, which
in its exhibition of mastery over sense—through its
power to alter and re-create what is given to it in
perception (lines 93–105)—is analogous to that
aspect of the outer scene in which the ordinary
landscape is transfigured by the moonlit mist.
Compare the mind as "lord and master" of out-

ward sense in 12.221–23.
8. Feelings, emotions.
9. An echo of *Paradise Lost* 5.488. The "discursive" reason undertakes to reach truths through a
logical sequence of premises, observations, and
conclusions; the "intuitive" reason comprehends
truths immediately.

Most worthy then of trust when most intense:
Hence, amid ills that vex, and wrongs that crush
Our hearts, if here the words of holy Writ   125
May with fit reverence be applied, that peace
Which passeth understanding,[1]—that repose
In moral judgements which from this pure source
Must come, or will by Man be sought in vain.
    Oh! who is he that hath his whole life long   130
Preserved, enlarged, this freedom in himself?
For this alone is genuine Liberty.
Where is the favoured Being who hath held
That course, unchecked, unerring, and untired,
In one perpetual progress smooth and bright?   135
—A humbler destiny have we retraced,
And told of lapse and hesitating choice,
And backward wanderings along thorny ways:
Yet, compassed round by Mountain Solitudes
Within whose solemn temple I received   140
My earliest visitations, careless then
Of what was given me; and which now I range
A meditative, oft a suffering Man,
Do I declare, in accents which, from truth
Deriving chearful confidence, shall blend   145
Their modulation with these vocal streams,
That, whatsoever falls my better mind
Revolving[2] with the accidents of life
May have sustained, that, howsoe'er misled,
Never did I, in quest of right and wrong,   150
Tamper with conscience from a private aim;
Nor was in any public hope the dupe
Of selfish passions; nor did ever yield,
Wilfully, to mean cares or low pursuits;
But shrunk with apprehensive jealousy   155
From every combination which might aid
The tendency, too potent in itself,
Of use and custom to bow down the Soul
Under a growing weight of vulgar sense,
And substitute a universe of death[3]   160
For that which moves with light and life informed,
Actual, divine, and true. To fear and love,
To love as prime and chief, for there fear ends,
Be this ascribed; to early intercourse
In presence of sublime or beautiful forms   165
With the adverse principles of pain and joy—
Evil, as one is rashly named by men

---

1. Philippians 4.7: "the peace of God, which passeth all understanding." This passage of Christian
piety was added by Wordsworth in a late revision.
2. An allusion to the ancient concept of fortune's
revolving wheel.
3. Milton's description of hell in *Paradise Lost*,
2.622–23: "A universe of death, which God by
curse / Created evil. . . ."

Who know not what they speak. By love subsists
All lasting grandeur, by pervading love;
That gone, we are as dust.[4]—Behold the fields   170
In balmy spring-time full of rising flowers
And joyous Creatures; see that Pair, the lamb
And the lamb's Mother, and their tender ways
Shall touch thee to the heart; thou callest this love,
And not inaptly so, for love it is,   175
Far as it carries thee. In some green Bower
Rest, and be not alone, but have thou there
The One who is thy choice of all the world:
There linger, listening, gazing with delight
Impassioned, but delight how pitiable!   180
Unless this love by a still higher love
Be hallowed, love that breathes not without awe;
Love that adores, but on the knees of prayer,
By heaven inspired; that frees from chains the soul,
Bearing in union with the purest, best   185
Of earth-born passions, on the wings of praise,
A mutual tribute to the Almighty's Throne.[5]

    This spiritual love acts not, nor can exist
Without Imagination,[6] which in truth
Is but another name for absolute power   190
And clearest insight, amplitude of mind,
And reason, in her most exalted mood.
This faculty hath been the feeding source
Of our long labor: we have traced the stream
From the blind cavern whence is faintly heard   195
Its natal murmur; followed it to light
And open day; accompanied its course
Among the ways of Nature; for a time
Lost sight of it, bewildered and engulphed;
Then given it greeting as it rose once more   200
In strength, reflecting from its placid breast
The works of man, and face of human life;
And lastly, from its progress have we drawn
Faith in life endless, the sustaining thought
Of human being, Eternity, and God.[7]   205

---

4. Wordsworth's mind, he had said early in *The Prelude*, had been "fostered alike by beauty and by fear" (1.302 and footnote); that is, by the opposing but equally necessary principles of the beautiful and the terrifying, or "sublime," aspects of nature. Now, in his conclusion, the principles of fear and pain are said to be mistakenly equated with "evil," and to be ultimately transcended by their "adverse principles" of love and joy. This passage is equivalent to the theodicy of *Paradise Lost*, in which Milton justifies evil and pain ("the ways of God to men," 1.26) by reference to the fall and redemption; Wordsworth, however, translates this into a natural theodicy of the interaction of man's mind with the external world. Cf. the Prospectus to *The Recluse*, above, lines 8–9, and the title footnote.

5. In place of lines 182–87, the text of 1805 has: ". . . a love that comes into the heart / With awe and a diffusive sentiment. / Thy love is human merely: this proceeds / More from the brooding soul, and is divine."

6. Cf. Shelley's *Defence of Poetry*: "The great secret of morals is love; or a going out of our own nature. . . . The great instrument of moral good is the imagination."

7. The 1805 version reads: "The feeling of life endless, the great thought / By which we live, Infinity and God."

—Imagination having been our theme,
So also hath that intellectual love,
For they are each in each, and cannot stand
Dividually.[8]—Here must thou be, O Man!
Power to thyself; no Helper hast thou here;   210
Here keepest thou in singleness thy state;
No other can divide with thee this work;
No secondary hand can intervene
To fashion this ability; 'tis thine,
The prime and vital principle is thine   215
In the recesses of thy nature, far
From any reach of outward fellowship,
Else is not thine at all. * * *

[Conclusion: "The Mind of Man"]

And now, O Friend![9] this History is brought
To its appointed close: the discipline
And consummation of a Poet's mind
In every thing that stood most prominent   305
Have faithfully been pictured; we have reached
The time (our guiding object from the first)
When we may, not presumptuously, I hope,
Suppose my powers so far confirmed, and such
My knowledge, as to make me capable   310
Of building up a Work that shall endure.
                    * * *
                              Having now
Told what best merits mention, further pains
Our present purpose seems not to require,
And I have other tasks. Recall to mind
The mood in which this labour was begun.   375
O Friend! the termination of my course
Is nearer now, much nearer; yet even then,
In that distraction, and intense desire,
I said unto the life which I had lived,
Where art thou? Hear I not a voice from thee   380
Which 'tis reproach to hear?[1] Anon I rose
As if on wings, and saw beneath me stretched
Vast prospect of the world which I had been
And was; and hence this Song, which like a Lark
I have protracted, in the unwearied heavens   385
Singing, and often with more plaintive voice
To earth attempered and her deep-drawn sighs,

8. Separately.
9. Coleridge.
1. As he approaches the end, Wordsworth recalls
the beginning of *The Prelude*. The reproachful voice
is that which asked the question, "Was it for this?"
in 1.269 ff. This query called forth a vision of his
remembered life, which he proceeded to explore
in search of both the sources of his poetic powers
and the impediments to their fulfillment. The
"Song" (line 384) describing this quest, which he
then began, is the poem he is now completing.

Yet centering all in love, and in the end
All gratulant, if rightly understood.[2]
                      * * *
Oh! yet a few short years of useful life,
And all will be complete, thy[3] race be run,
Thy monument of glory will be raised;
Then, though, too weak to tread the ways of truth,   435
This Age fall back to old idolatry,
Though Men return to servitude as fast
As the tide ebbs, to ignominy and shame
By Nations sink together,[4] we shall still
Find solace—knowing what we have learnt to know,   440
Rich in true happiness if allowed to be
Faithful alike in forwarding a day
Of firmer trust, joint laborers in the Work
(Should Providence such grace to us vouchsafe)
Of their deliverance,[5] surely yet to come.   445
Prophets of Nature, we to them will speak
A lasting inspiration, sanctified
By reason, blest by faith: what we have loved
Others will love, and we will teach them how,
Instruct them how the mind of Man becomes   450
A thousand times more beautiful than the earth
On which he dwells, above this Frame of things
(Which 'mid all revolutions in the hopes
And fears of Men doth still remain unchanged)
In beauty exalted, as it is itself   455
Of quality and fabric more divine.[6]

1798–1839   1850

2. The poet finds that suffering and frustration are justified, when seen as part of the overall design of the life he has just reviewed. The passage echoes the conclusion of Pope's theodicy (the justification of evil) in *An Essay on Man*, 1.291–92: "All discord, harmony not understood;/ All partial evil, universal good." "Gratulant": expressing joy.
3. Coleridge's.
4. I.e., though men—whole nations of them together—sink to ignominy and shame.

5. In the 1805 text, the term was "redemption." Wordsworth reaffirms his belief in a millennial outcome of human history, though he now bases that belief not on political "revolutions" (cf. line 453) but on a revolution in the mind of man.
6. Cf. Wordsworth's assertion that "the Mind of Man" is "My haunt, and the main region of my song" in the Prospectus to *The Recluse*, lines 40–41.

SAMUEL TAYLOR COLERIDGE
1772–1834

1797: At Nether Stowey, Somersetshire; the Wordsworths settle nearby, at Alfoxden.
1798: *Lyrical Ballads*, which included *The Ancient Mariner* and several other poems by Coleridge.

1800: Moves to Greta Hall, Keswick, thirteen miles from the Wordsworths at Grasmere.

1816: Final residence at Highgate, near London, under the care of Dr. James Gillman.

1817: *Biographia Literaria.*

In *The Prelude* Wordsworth, recording his gratitude to the mountains, lakes, and winds "that dwell among the hills where I was born," commiserates with Coleridge because "thou, my Friend! wert reared / In the great City, 'mid far other scenes." Coleridge had in fact been born in the small town of Ottery St. Mary, in rural Devonshire; but upon the death of his father he had been sent to school at Christ's Hospital, in London. He was a dreamy, enthusiastic, and extraordinarily precocious schoolboy; Charles Lamb, his schoolmate and lifelong friend, in his essay on Christ's Hospital has given us a vivid sketch of Coleridge's loneliness, his learning, and his eloquence. When in 1791 Coleridge went up to Jesus College, Cambridge, he was an accomplished scholar; but he found little intellectual stimulation at the university, fell into idleness, dissoluteness, and debt, and in despair fled to London and enlisted in the Light Dragoons under the alias of Silas Tomkyn Comberbache—probably the most inept cavalryman in the long history of the British army. Although rescued by his brothers and sent back to Cambridge, he left in 1794 without a degree.

In June 1794 Coleridge met Robert Southey, then a student at Oxford who, like himself, had poetic aspirations, was a radical in religion and politics, and sympathized with the republican experiment in France. Together the two young men planned to establish an ideal democratic community in America for which Coleridge coined the name "Pantisocracy," signifying an equal rule by all. A plausible American real-estate agent persuaded them that the ideal location would be on the banks of the Susquehanna, in Pennsylvania. Twelve men undertook to go; and since perpetuation of the scheme required offspring, hence wives, Coleridge dutifully became engaged to Sara Fricker, conveniently at hand as the sister of Southey's fiancée. The Pantisocracy scheme collapsed, but at Southey's insistence Coleridge went through with the marriage, "resolved," as he said, "but wretched." Later Coleridge's radicalism waned, and he became a conservative—a highly philosophical one—in politics, and a staunch Anglican in religion.

Despite its inauspicious beginning, Coleridge was at first happy in his marriage. In 1795 he met Wordsworth, and at once judged him to be "the best poet of the age." When in 1797 Wordsworth brought his sister, Dorothy, to settle at Alfoxden, only three miles from the Coleridges at Nether Stowey, the period of intimate communication and poetic collaboration began which was the golden time of Coleridge's life. An annuity of £150, granted to Coleridge by Thomas and Josiah Wedgwood, sons of the founder of the famous pottery firm, came just in time to deflect him from assuming a post as a Unitarian minister. After their momentous joint publication of *Lyrical Ballads* in 1798, Coleridge and the Wordsworths spent a winter in Germany, where Coleridge attended the University of Göttingen and began the lifelong study of Kant and the post-Kantian German philosophers and critics which helped to alter profoundly his thinking about philosophy, religion, and aesthetics.

Back in England, Coleridge in 1800 followed the Wordsworths to the Lake District, settling at Greta Hall, Keswick. He had become gradually disaffected from his wife, and in 1799 he fell helplessly and hopelessly in love with Sara Hutchinson, whose sister, Mary, Wordsworth married three years later. All his life Coleridge had suffered from numerous painful physical ailments; Wordsworth has described how sometimes, in a sudden spasm of agony, Coleridge would "throw himself down and writhe like a worm upon the ground." According to the standard medical prescription of the time, Coleridge had long been taking laudanum (opium dissolved in alcohol). In 1800–01 heavy dosages taken for attacks of rheumatism made opium a necessity to him, and Coleridge soon recognized that the drug was a worse evil than the diseases it did not cure. *Dejection: An Ode*, published in 1802, was Coleridge's despairing farewell to health, happiness, and poetic creativity. A two-year sojourn on the Mediterranean island of Malta, intended to restore his health, instead completed his decline. When he returned to England in the late summer of 1806 he was a broken man, an inveterate drug addict, estranged from his wife, suffering from agonies of remorse, and subject to terrifying nightmares of guilt and despair from which his own shrieks awakened him. A bitter quarrel with Wordsworth in 1810 marked the nadir of his life and expectations.

Under these conditions Coleridge's literary efforts, however sporadic and fragmentary, were little short of heroic. In 1808 he gave his first course of public lectures in London, and in the next eleven years followed these with other series on both literary and philosophical topics. He wrote for newspapers and single-handedly undertook to write, publish, and distribute a periodical, *The Friend*, which lasted for some fourteen months after January 1809. A tragedy, *Remorse*, had in 1813 a very successful run of twenty performances at the Drury Lane Theatre. In 1816 he took up residence at Highgate, a northern suburb of London, under the supervision of the excellent and endlessly forbearing physician James Gillman, who managed to control, although not to eliminate, Coleridge's consumption of opium. The next three years were Coleridge's most sustained period of literary activity: while continuing to lecture and to write for the newspapers on a variety of subjects, he published the *Biographia Literaria*, *Zapolya* (a drama), a book consisting of the essays in *The Friend* (revised and greatly enlarged), two collections of poems, and several important treatises on philosohical and religious subjects; in these last he undertook to establish a philosophical basis for the Trinitarian theology to which he had turned after his youthful period of Unitarianism.

The remaining years of his life, which he spent with Dr. and Mrs. Gillman, were quieter and happier than any he had known since the turn of the century. He came to a peaceful understanding with his wife and was reconciled with Wordsworth, with whom he toured the Rhineland in 1828. His rooms at Highgate became a center for friends, for the London literati, and for a steady stream of pilgrims from England and America. They came to hear one of the wonders of the age, the Sage of Highgate's conversation— or monologue—for even in his decline, Coleridge's talk never lost the almost incantatory power which Hazlitt has immortalized in *My First Acquaintance with Poets*. When he died, Coleridge left his friends with the sense that an incomparable intellect had vanished from the world. "The most *wonderful* man that I have ever known," Wordsworth declared, his voice breaking; and Charles Lamb: "His great and dear spirit haunts me. . . . Never saw I his likeness, nor probably the world can see again."

Coleridge's friends, however, abetted by his own merciless self-judgments, set current the opinion, still common, that he was great in promise but not in performance. Even in his buoyant youth, before opium had drained his strength and weakened his will, he described his own character as "indolence capable of energies"; and it is true that while his mind was incessantly active and fertile, he lacked application and staying power. He also manifested early in life a profound sense of guilt and a need for public expiation. After drug addiction sapped his strength and will, even while it reinforced his emotional problems, he often adapted (or simply adopted) passages from other writers, with little or no acknowledgment, and sometimes in a context that seems designed at once to obfuscate his literary obligations and to reveal the subterfuge. Whatever the tangled motives for his procedure, Coleridge has repeatedly been charged with plagiarism, from his day to our own. After *The Ancient Mariner*, most of the poems he completed were written, like the first version of *Dejection: An Ode*, in a spasm of intense effort. Writings which required sustained planning and application were either left unfinished or, like the *Biographia Literaria*, made up of brilliant sections eked out with filler, sometimes lifted from other writers, in a desperate effort to meet a deadline. Many of his best speculations Coleridge merely confided to his notebooks and the ears of his friends, incorporated in letters, and poured out upon the margins of his own and other people's books.

Even so, it is only when measured against his own immense potentialities that Coleridge's achievements appear limited. In opposition to the prevailing British philosophy of empiricism and associationism, Coleridge for most of his mature life expounded his views of the mind as creative in perception, intuitive in its discovery of the first premises of metaphysics and religion, and capable of a poetic re-creation of the world of sense by the fusing and formative power of the "secondary imagination." Within the decade after Coleridge died, John Stuart Mill, an acute student of contemporary thought, announced that Coleridge was one of "the two great seminal minds of England," the most important instigator and representative of the conservative intellectual movement of the day. Time has proved Mill's estimate of Coleridge to be just, for his influence is strongly evident in nineteenth-century English and American traditions of philosophical idealism, enlightened political conservatism, and liberal interpretations of Trinitarian theology. By present consensus, Coleridge is also one of the greatest and most influential of literary theorists; his ideas became central points of reference even in many of the New Critics of the middle of the present century who depreciated the Romantic poetry for which Coleridge, in his criticism, attempted to provide a rationale. And Coleridge's writings in verse, though small in bulk, are the work of a major and notably original poet.

In the course of a few years, he wrote his poems of mystery and demonism, *The Ancient Mariner*, *Christabel*, and *Kubla Khan*. No less impressive in their own way are the blank-verse poems of the lonely and meditative mind which, by an extension of his term for one of them, are called "Conversation Poems"; in the best of these, *Frost at Midnight*, Coleridge perfected the characteristic pattern of integrally related description and meditation which Wordsworth immediately adopted in *Tintern Abbey*. Coleridge himself adapted this pattern to the larger requirements of *Dejection*, a high achievement in a genre in which few poets have been successful, the irregular English ode. The verse epistle *To William Wordsworth* is at once a most insightful comment about *The Prelude*, a superb tribute to a friend whom Coleridge thought the greatest poet since Milton, and a moving elegy on the death of his own poetic power. But even when he had mainly given up poetry, after 1805, Coleridge continued to write occasional short lyrics (represented below) which are remarkable equally for their quality, their diversity, and the extent to which they have been neglected by anthologists.

The Eolian Harp[1]

Composed at Clevedon, Somersetshire

My pensive Sara! thy soft cheek reclined
Thus on mine arm, most soothing sweet it is
To sit beside our Cot, our Cot o'ergrown
With white-flowered Jasmin, and the broad-leaved Myrtle,
(Meet emblems they of Innocence and Love!)   5
And watch the clouds, that late were rich with light,
Slow saddening round, and mark the star of eve
Serenely brilliant (such should Wisdom be)
Shine opposite! How exquisite the scents
Snatched from yon bean-field! and the world *so* hushed!   10
The stilly murmur of the distant Sea
Tells us of silence.

        And that simplest Lute,
Placed length-ways in the clasping casement, hark!
How by the desultory breeze caressed,
Like some coy maid half yielding to her lover,   15
It pours such sweet upbraiding, as must needs
Tempt to repeat the wrong! And now, its strings
Boldlier swept, the long sequacious[2] notes
Over delicious surges sink and rise,

---

1. Named for Aeolus, god of the winds, the harp has strings stretched over a rectangular sounding box. The strings are tuned in unison. When placed in an opened window, the harp (also called "Eolian lute," "Eolian lyre," "wind harp") responds to the altering wind by sequences of musical chords. This instrument, which seems to voice nature's own music, was a favorite household furnishing in the period, and was repeatedly alluded to in Romantic poetry; see Geoffrey Grigson, *The Harp of Aeolus and Other Essays* (1947). It served also as one of the recurrent Romantic images for the mind—either the mind in poetic inspiration, as in the last stanza of Shelley's *Ode to the West Wind*, or else the mind in perception, responding to an intellectual breeze by trembling into consciousness, as in this poem, lines 44–48. Coleridge, however, no sooner puts forward this concept than he retracts it, for it comes too close to the heresy of pantheism, which identifies God with the nature that, in the orthodox view, is His creation.

Coleridge wrote this poem to Sara Fricker, whom he married on Oct. 4, 1795, and took to a cottage at Clevedon, overlooking the Bristol Channel. He later several times expanded and altered the short original version; the famous lines 26–29, for example, were not incorporated until 1817. The poem was Coleridge's first achievement in the important Romantic form of the sustained blank-verse lyric of description and meditation, in the mode of conversation addressed to a silent auditor—a form that he perfected in *Frost at Midnight*, and that Wordsworth adopted for *Tintern Abbey*.

2. Successive.

Such a soft floating witchery of sound   20
As twilight Elfins make, when they at eve
Voyage on gentle gales from Fairy-Land,
Where Melodies round honey-dropping flowers,
Footless and wild, like birds of Paradise,[3]
Nor pause, nor perch, hovering on untamed wing!   25
O! the one Life within us and abroad,
Which meets all motion and becomes its soul,
A light in sound, a sound-like power in light,
Rhythm in all thought, and joyance everywhere—
Methinks, it should have been impossible   30
Not to love all things in a world so filled;
Where the breeze warbles, and the mute still air
Is Music slumbering on her instrument.

    And thus, my Love! as on the midway slope
Of yonder hill I stretch my limbs at noon,   35
Whilst through my half-closed eyelids I behold
The sunbeams dance, like diamonds, on the main,
And tranquil muse upon tranquillity:
Full many a thought uncalled and undetained,
And many idle flitting phantasies,   40
Traverse my indolent and passive brain,
As wild and various as the random gales
That swell and flutter on this subject Lute!

    And what if all of animated nature
Be but organic Harps diversely framed,   45
That tremble into thought, as o'er them sweeps
Plastic and vast, one intellectual breeze,
At once the Soul of each, and God of all?

    But thy more serious eye a mild reproof
Darts, O belovèd Woman! nor such thoughts   50
Dim and unhallowed dost thou not reject,
And biddest me walk humbly with my God.
Meek Daughter in the family of Christ!
Well hast thou said and holily dispraised
These shapings of the unregenerate mind;   55
Bubbles that glitter as they rise and break
On vain Philosophy's aye-babbling spring.
For never guiltless may I speak of him,
The Incomprehensible! save when with awe
I praise him, and with Faith that inly *feels*;   60
Who with his saving mercies healèd me,
A sinful and most miserable man,

3. Brilliantly colored birds, found in New Guinea and adjacent islands. The native practice of removing the legs when preparing the skin led Europeans to believe that the birds were footless and spent their lives hovering in the air and feeding on nectar.

Wildered and dark, and gave me to possess
Peace, and this Cot, and thee, heart-honored Maid!

1795–1817   1796, 1817

This Lime-Tree Bower My Prison

Addressed to Charles Lamb, of the India House, London

In the June of 1797 some long-expected friends paid a visit to the author's
cottage; and on the morning of their arrival, he met with an accident,
which disabled him from walking during the whole time of their stay.
One evening, when they had left him for a few hours, he composed
the following lines in the garden-bower.[1]

Well, they are gone, and here must I remain,
This lime-tree bower my prison! I have lost
Beauties and feelings, such as would have been
Most sweet to my remembrance even when age
Had dimmed mine eyes to blindness! They, meanwhile,   5
Friends, whom I never more may meet again,
On springy[2] heath, along the hill-top edge,
Wander in gladness, and wind down, perchance,
To that still roaring dell, of which I told;
The roaring dell, o'erwooded, narrow, deep,   10
And only speckled by the mid-day sun;
Where its slim trunk the ash from rock to rock
Flings arching like a bridge;—that branchless ash,
Unsunned and damp, whose few poor yellow leaves
Ne'er tremble in the gale, yet tremble still,   15
Fanned by the waterfall! and there my friends
Behold the dark green file of long lank weeds,
That all at once (a most fantastic sight!)
Still nod and drip beneath the dripping edge
Of the blue clay-stone.

                  Now, my friends emerge   20
Beneath the wide wide Heaven—and view again
The many-steepled tract magnificent
Of hilly fields and meadows, and the sea,
With some fair bark, perhaps, whose sails light up
The slip of smooth clear blue betwixt two Isles   25
Of purple shadow! Yes! they wander on
In gladness all; but thou, methinks, most glad,

---

1. The time was in fact July 1797; the visiting
friends were William and Dorothy Wordsworth and
Charles Lamb; the accident was the fault of Mrs.
Coleridge—"dear Sara," Coleridge wrote, "accidentally emptied a skillet of boiling milk on my
foot"; and the bower consisted of lime (i.e., linden) trees in the garden of Thomas Poole, next
door to Coleridge's cottage at Nether Stowey. Coleridge related these facts in a letter to Robert
Southey, July 17, 1797, in which he transcribed
the first version of this fine "conversation poem."
2. *"Elastic,* I mean" [Coleridge's note].

My gentle-hearted Charles! for thou hast pined
And hungered after Nature, many a year,
In the great City pent,[3] winning thy way   30
With sad yet patient soul, through evil and pain
And strange calamity![4] Ah! slowly sink
Behind the western ridge, thou glorious Sun!
Shine in the slant beams of the sinking orb,
Ye purple heath-flowers! richlier burn, ye clouds!   35
Live in the yellow light, ye distant groves!
And kindle, thou blue Ocean! So my friend
Struck with deep joy may stand, as I have stood,
Silent with swimming sense; yea, gazing round
On the wide landscape, gaze till all doth seem   40
Less gross than bodily; and of such hues
As veil the Almighty Spirit, when yet he makes
Spirits perceive his presence.

             A delight
Comes sudden on my heart, and I am glad
As I myself were there! Nor in this bower,   45
This little lime-tree bower, have I not marked
Much that has soothed me. Pale beneath the blaze
Hung the transparent foliage; and I watched
Some broad and sunny leaf, and loved to see
The shadow of the leaf and stem above   50
Dappling its sunshine! And that walnut-tree
Was richly tinged, and a deep radiance lay
Full on the ancient ivy, which usurps
Those fronting elms, and now, with blackest mass
Makes their dark branches gleam a lighter hue   55
Through the late twilight: and though now the bat
Wheels silent by, and not a swallow twitters,
Yet still the solitary humblebee
Sings in the bean-flower! Henceforth I shall know
That Nature ne'er deserts the wise and pure;   60
No plot so narrow, be but Nature there,
No waste so vacant, but may well employ
Each faculty of sense, and keep the heart
Awake to Love and Beauty! and sometimes
'Tis well to be bereft of promised good,   65
That we may lift the soul, and contemplate
With lively joy the joys we cannot share.
My gentle-hearted Charles! when the last rook
Beat its straight path along the dusky air
Homewards, I blessed it! deeming its black wing   70
(Now a dim speck, now vanishing in light)

3. Despite Coleridge's claim, Lamb eminently preferred London over what he called "dead Nature".

4. Some 10 months earlier Charles Lamb's sister, Mary, had stabbed her mother to death in a fit of insanity.

Had crossed the mighty Orb's dilated glory,
While thou stood'st gazing; or, when all was still,
Flew creeking o'er thy head, and had a charm
For thee, my gentle-hearted Charles, to whom   75
No sound is dissonant which tells of Life.

1797   1800

The Rime of the Ancient Mariner[1]

IN SEVEN PARTS

*Facile credo, plures esse Naturas invisibiles quam visibiles in rerum
universitate. Sed horum [sic] omnium familiam quis nobis enarrabit?
et gradus et cognationes et discrimina et singulorum munera? Quid
agunt? quae loca habitant? Harum rerum notitiam semper ambivit
ingenium humanum, nunquam attigit. Juvat, interea, non diffiteor,
quandoque in animo, tanquam in tabulâ, majoris et melioris mundi
imaginem contemplari: ne mens assuefacta hodiernae vitae minutiis se
contrahat nimis, et tota subsidat in pusillas cogitationes. Sed veritati
interea invigilandum est, modusque servandus, ut certa ab incertis,
diem a nocte, distinguamus.*

T. BURNET, *Archaeol. Phil.* p. 68.[2]

Argument

How a Ship, having first sailed to the Equator, was driven by storms
to the cold Country towards the South Pole; how the Ancient Mariner
cruelly and in contempt of the laws of hospitality killed a Seabird and
how he was followed by many and strange Judgments: and in what manner he came back to his own Country.

1. Coleridge describes the origin of this poem in
the opening section of chapter 14 of *Biographia
Literaria*. In a comment made to the Rev. Alexander Dyce in 1835, and in a note on *We Are
Seven* dictated in 1843, Wordsworth added some
details. The poem, based on a dream of Coleridge's friend Cruikshank, was originally planned as
a collaboration between the two friends, to pay the
expense of a walking tour they took with Dorothy
Wordsworth in November 1797. Before he dropped
out of the enterprise, Wordsworth suggested the
shooting of the albatross and the navigation of the
ship by the dead men; he also contributed lines
13–16 and 226–27.

The version of *The Ancient Mariner* printed in
Lyrical Ballads (1798) contained many archaic
words and spellings. In later editions Coleridge
greatly improved the poem by pruning the archaisms and by other revisions; he also added the Latin

epigraph and the marginal glosses.
2. "I readily believe that there are more invisible
than visible Natures in the universe. But who will
explain for us the family of all these beings, and
the ranks and relations and distinguishing features
and functions of each? What do they do? What
places do they inhabit? The human mind has always
sought the knowledge of these things, but never
attained it. Meanwhile I do not deny that it is
helpful sometimes to contemplate in the mind, as
on a tablet, the image of a greater and better world,
lest the intellect, habituated to the petty things of
daily life, narrow itself and sink wholly into trivial
thoughts. But at the same time we must be watchful for the truth and keep a sense of proportion, so
that we may distinguish the certain from the
uncertain, day from night." Adapted by Coleridge
from Thomas Burnet, *Archaeologiae philosophicae*
(1692).

Part 1

It is an ancient Mariner
And he stoppeth one of three.
—"By thy long gray beard and glittering eye,
Now wherefore stopp'st thou me?

The Bridegroom's doors are opened wide, 5
And I am next of kin;
The guests are met, the feast is set:
May'st hear the merry din."

He holds him with his skinny hand,
"There was a ship," quoth he. 10
"Hold off! unhand me, graybeard loon!"
Eftsoons[3] his hand dropped he.

He holds him with his glittering eye—
The Wedding-Guest stood still,
And listens like a three years' child: 15
The Mariner hath his will.[4]

The Wedding-Guest sat on a stone:
He cannot choose but hear;
And thus spake on that ancient man,
The bright-eyed Mariner. 20

"The ship was cheered, the harbor cleared,
Merrily did we drop

Below the kirk,[5] below the hill,
Below the lighthouse top.

The Sun came up upon the left, 25
Out of the sea came he!
And he shone bright, and on the right
Went down into the sea.

Higher and higher every day,
Till over the mast at noon[6]—" 30
The Wedding-Guest here beat his breast,
For he heard the loud bassoon.

The bride hath paced into the hall,
Red as a rose is she;
Nodding their heads before her goes 35
The merry minstrelsy.

---

3. At once.
4. I.e., the Mariner has gained control of the will
of the Wedding Guest by hypnosis—or, as it was
called in Coleridge's time, by "mesmerism."
5. Church.
6. The ship had reached the equator (the "Line").

The Wedding-Guest he beat his breast,
Yet he cannot choose but hear;
And thus spake on that ancient man,
The bright-eyed Mariner.   40

The ship driven by a
storm toward the
South Pole.

"And now the STORM-BLAST came, and he
Was tyrannous and strong;
He struck with his o'ertaking wings,
And chased us south along.

With sloping masts and dipping prow,   45
As who pursued with yell and blow
Still treads the shadow of his foe,
And forward bends his head,
The ship drove fast, loud roared the blast,
And southward aye we fled.   50

And now there came both mist and snow,
And it grew wondrous cold:
And ice, mast-high, came floating by,
As green as emerald.

The land of ice, and
of fearful sounds
where no living thing
was to be seen.

And through the drifts the snowy clifts   55
Did send a dismal sheen:
Nor shapes of men nor beasts we ken—
The ice was all between.

The ice was here, the ice was there,
The ice was all around: 60
It cracked and growled, and roared and howled,
Like noises in a swound![7]

Till a great sea bird,
called the Albatross,
came through the
snow-fog, and was
received with great joy
and hospitality.

At length did cross an Albatross,
Thorough the fog it came;
As if it had been a Christian soul,   65
We hailed it in God's name.

It ate the food it ne'er had eat,
And round and round it flew.
The ice did split with a thunder-fit;
The helmsman steered us through!   70

And lo! the Albatross
proveth a bird of good
omen, and followeth
the ship as it returned
northward through fog
and floating ice.

And a good south wind sprung up behind;
The Albatross did follow,
And every day, for food or play,
Came to the mariner's hollo!

7. Swoon.

In mist or cloud, on mast or shroud,[8]   75
It perched for vespers nine;
Whiles all the night, through fog-smoke white,
Glimmered the white Moon-shine."

"God save thee, ancient Mariner!
From the fiends, that plague thee thus!—   80
Why look'st thou so?"—With my crossbow
I shot the ALBATROSS.

Part 2

The Sun now rose upon the right:[9]
Out of the sea came he,
Still hid in mist, and on the left   85
Went down into the sea.

And the good south wind still blew behind,
But no sweet bird did follow,
Nor any day for food or play
Came to the mariners' hollo!   90

And I had done a hellish thing,
And it would work 'em woe:
For all averred, I had killed the bird
That made the breeze to blow.
Ah wretch! said they, the bird to slay,   95
That made the breeze to blow!

Nor dim nor red, like God's own head,
The glorious Sun uprist:
Then all averred, I had killed the bird
That brought the fog and mist.
'Twas right, said they, such birds to slay,
That bring the fog and mist.   100

The fair breeze blew, the white foam flew,
The furrow followed free;
We were the first that ever burst   105
Into that silent sea.

Down dropped the breeze, the sails dropped down,
'Twas sad as sad could be;

8. Rope supporting the mast.
9. Having rounded Cape Horn, the ship heads north into the Pacific.

And we did speak only to break
The silence of the sea! 110

All in a hot and copper sky,
The bloody Sun, at noon,
Right up above the mast did stand,
No bigger than the Moon.

Day after day, day after day, 115
We stuck, nor breath nor motion;
As idle as a painted ship
Upon a painted ocean.

And the Albatross begins to be avenged.

Water, water, everywhere,
And all the boards did shrink; 120
Water, water, everywhere,
Nor any drop to drink.

The very deep did rot: O Christ!
That ever this should be!
Yea, slimy things did crawl with legs 125
Upon the slimy sea.

About, about, in reel and rout
The death-fires[1] danced at night;
The water, like a witch's oils,
Burnt green, and blue and white. 130

A Spirit had followed them; one of the invisible inhabitants of this planet, neither departed souls nor angels; concerning whom the learned Jew, Josephus, and the Platonic Constaninopolitan, Michael Psellus, may be consulted. They are very numerous, and there is no climate or element without one or more.

And some in dreams assurèd were
Of the Spirit that plagued us so;
Nine fathom deep he had followed us
From the land of mist and snow.

And every tongue, through utter drought, 135
Was withered at the root;
We could not speak, no more than if
We had been choked with soot.

The shipmates, in their sore distress, would fain throw the whole guilt on the ancient Mariner: in sign whereof they hang the dead sea bird round his neck.

Ah! well-a-day! what evil looks 140
Had I from old and young!
Instead of the cross, the Albatross
About my neck was hung. 140

---

1. The corposant, or St. Elmo's fire, an atmospheric electricity on a ship's mast or rigging, believed by superstitious sailors to portend disaster.

Part 3

There passed a weary time. Each throat
Was parched, and glazed each eye.
A weary time! a weary time!   145
How glazed each weary eye,
When looking westward, I beheld
A something in the sky.

The ancient Mariner beholdeth a sign in the element afar off.

At first it seemed a little speck,
And then it seemed a mist;   150
It moved and moved, and took at last
A certain shape, I wist.[2]

A speck, a mist, a shape, I wist!
And still it neared and neared:
As if it dodged a water-sprite,   155
It plunged and tacked and veered.

At its nearer approach, it seemeth him to be a ship; and at a dear ransom he freeth his speech from the bonds of thirst.

With throats unslaked, with black lips baked,
We could nor laugh nor wail;
Through utter drought all dumb we stood!
I bit my arm, I sucked the blood,   160
And cried, A sail! a sail!

A flash of joy;

With throats unslaked, with black lips baked,
Agape they heard me call:
Gramercy![3] they for joy did grin,
And all at once their breath drew in,   165
As they were drinking all.

And horror follows. For can it be a ship that comes onward without wind or tide?

See! see! (I cried) she tacks no more!
Hither to work us weal;[4]
Without a breeze, without a tide,
She steadies with upright keel!   170

The western wave was all aflame.
The day was well nigh done!
Almost upon the western wave
Rested the broad bright Sun;
When that strange shape drove suddenly   175
Betwixt us and the Sun.

It seemeth him but the skeleton of a ship.

And straight the Sun was flecked with bars,
(Heaven's Mother send us grace!)
As if through a dungeon grate he peered
With broad and burning face.   180

2. Knew.   4. Benefit.
3. From the French *grand-merci*, "great thanks."

And its ribs are seen
as bars on the face
of the setting Sun.

Alas! (thought I, and my heart beat loud)
How fast she nears and nears!
Are those *her* sails that glance in the Sun,
Like restless gossameres?[5]

The Specter-Woman
and her Deathmate,
and no other on
board the skeleton
ship.

Are those *her* ribs through which the Sun   185
Did peer, as through a grate?
And is that Woman all her crew?
Is that a DEATH? and are there two?
Is DEATH that woman's mate?

Like vessel, like
crew!

Her lips were red, *her* looks were free,
Her locks were yellow as gold: 190
Her skin was as white as leprosy,
The Night-mare LIFE-IN-DEATH was she,
Who thicks man's blood with cold.

Death and Life-in-
Death have diced for
the ship's crew, and
she (the latter)
winneth the ancient
Mariner.

The naked hulk alongside came,   195
And the twain were casting dice;
"The game is done! I've won! I've won!"
Quoth she, and whistles thrice.

No twilight within
the courts of the
Sun.

The Sun's rim dips; the stars rush out:
At one stride comes the dark;   200
With far-heard whisper, o'er the sea,
Off shot the spectre-bark.

At the rising of the
Moon,

We listened and looked sideways up!
Fear at my heart, as at a cup,
My lifeblood seemed to sip!   205
The stars were dim, and thick the night,
The steersman's face by his lamp gleamed white;
From the sails the dew did drip—
Till clomb above the eastern bar
The hornèd Moon, with one bright star   210
Within the nether tip.[6]

One after another,

One after one, by the star-dogged Moon,
Too quick for groan or sigh,
Each turned his face with a ghastly pang,
And cursed me with his eye.   215

His shipmates drop
down dead.

Four times fifty living men,
(And I heard nor sigh nor groan)
With heavy thump, a lifeless lump,
They dropped down one by one.

5. Filmy cobwebs floating in the air.   6. An omen of impending evil.

*But Life-in-Death
begins her work on
the ancient Mariner.*

The souls did from their bodies fly—   220
They fled to bliss or woe!
And every soul, it passed me by,
Like the whizz of my crossbow!

Part 4

*The Wedding-Guest
feareth that a Spirit
is talking to him;*

"I fear thee, ancient Mariner!
I fear thy skinny hand!   225
And thou art long, and lank, and brown,
As is the ribbed sea-sand.

I fear thee and thy glittering eye,
And thy skinny hand, so brown."—

*But the ancient
Mariner assureth
him of his bodily
life, and proceedeth
to relate his horrible
penance.*

Fear not, fear not, thou Wedding-Guest!   230
This body dropped not down.

Alone, alone, all, all alone,
Alone on a wide wide sea!
And never a saint took pity on
My soul in agony.   235

*He despiseth the
creatures of the
calm,*

The many men, so beautiful!
And they all dead did lie:
And a thousand thousand slimy things
Lived on; and so did I.

*And envieth that
they should live,
and so many lie
dead.*

I looked upon the rotting sea,   240
And drew my eyes away;
I looked upon the rotting deck,
And there the dead men lay.

I looked to heaven, and tried to pray;
But or ever a prayer had gushed,   245
A wicked whisper came, and made
My heart as dry as dust.

I closed my lids, and kept them close,
And the balls like pulses beat;
For the sky and the sea, and the sea and the sky250
Lay like a load on my weary eye,
And the dead were at my feet.

*But the curse liveth
for him in the eye
of the dead men.*

The cold sweat melted from their limbs,
Nor rot nor reek did they:
The look with which they looked on me   255
Had never passed away.

An orphan's curse would drag to hell
A spirit from on high;
But oh! more horrible than that
Is the curse in a dead man's eye!   260
Seven days, seven nights, I saw that curse,
And yet I could not die.

In his loneliness and fixedness he yearneth towards the journeying Moon, and the stars that still sojourn, yet still move onward; and everywhere the blue sky belongs to them, and is their appointed rest, and their native country and their own natural homes, which they enter

The moving Moon went up the sky,
And nowhere did abide:
Softly she was going up,   265
And a star or two beside—

Her beams bemocked the sultry main,
Like April hoar-frost spread;
But where the ship's huge shadow lay,
The charmèd water burnt alway   270
A still and awful red.

unannounced, as lords that are certainly expected and yet there is a silent joy at their arrival.

By the light of the Moon he beholdeth God's creatures of the great calm.

Beyond the shadow of the ship,
I watched the water snakes:
They moved in tracks of shining white,
And when they reared, the elfish light   275
Fell off in hoary flakes.

Within the shadow of the ship
I watched their rich attire:
Blue, glossy green, and velvet black,
They coiled and swam; and every track   280
Was a flash of golden fire.

Their beauty and their happiness.

O happy living things! no tongue
Their beauty might declare:
A spring of love gushed from my heart,

He blesseth them in his heart.

And I blessed them unaware: 285
Sure my kind saint took pity on me,
And I blessed them unaware.

The spell begins to break.

The self-same moment I could pray;
And from my neck so free
The Albatross fell off, and sank   290
Like lead into the sea.

Part 5

Oh sleep! it is a gentle thing,
Beloved from pole to pole!
To Mary Queen the praise be given!

She sent the gentle sleep from Heaven,   295
That slid into my soul.

By grace of the holy Mother, the ancient Mariner is refreshed with rain.

The silly[7] buckets on the deck,
That had so long remained,
I dreamt that they were filled with dew;
And when I awoke, it rained.   300

My lips were wet, my throat was cold,
My garments all were dank;
Sure I had drunken in my dreams,
And still my body drank.

I moved, and could not feel my limbs: 305
I was so light—almost
I thought that I had died in sleep,
And was a blessed ghost.

He heareth sounds and seeth strange sights and commotions in the sky and the element.

And soon I heard a roaring wind:
It did not come anear;   310
But with its sound it shook the sails,
That were so thin and sere.

The upper air burst into life!
And a hundred fire-flags sheen,[8]
To and fro they were hurried about!   315
And to and fro, and in and out,
The wan stars danced between.

And the coming wind did roar more loud,
And the sails did sigh like sedge;[9]
And the rain poured down from one black
     cloud;   320
The Moon was at its edge.

The thick black cloud was cleft, and still
The Moon was at its side:
Like waters shot from some high crag,
The lightning fell with never a jag,   325
A river steep and wide.

The bodies of the ship's crew are inspirited, and the ship moves on;

The loud wind never reached the ship,
Yet now the ship moved on!
Beneath the lightning and the Moon
The dead men gave a groan.   330

7. Simple, homely.
8. Shone. These are the Aurora Australis, or Southern Lights.
9. A rushlike plant growing in wet soil.

They groaned, they stirred, they all uprose,
Nor spake, nor moved their eyes;
It had been strange, even in a dream,
To have seen those dead men rise.

The helmsman steered, the ship moved on;   335
Yet never a breeze up-blew;
The mariners all 'gan work the ropes,
Where they were wont to do;
They raised their limbs like lifeless tools—
We were a ghastly crew.   340

The body of my brother's son
Stood by me, knee to knee:
The body and I pulled at one rope,
But he said nought to me.

But not by the souls
of the men, nor by
demons of earth or
middle air, but by a
blessed troop of
angelic spirits, sent
down by the
invocation of the
guardian saint.

"I fear thee, ancient Mariner!"   345
Be calm, thou Wedding Guest!
'Twas not those souls that fled in pain,
Which to their corses[1] came again,
But a troop of spirits blest:

For when it dawned—they dropped their arms,   350
And clustered round the mast;
Sweet sounds rose slowly through their mouths,
And from their bodies passed.

Around, around, flew each sweet sound,
Then darted to the Sun;   355
Slowly the sounds came back again,
Now mixed, now one by one.

Sometimes a-dropping from the sky
I heard the sky-lark sing;
Sometimes all little birds that are,   360
How they seemed to fill the sea and air
With their sweet jargoning![2]

And now 'twas like all instruments,
Now like a lonely flute;
And now it is an angel's song,   365
That makes the heavens be mute.

It ceased; yet still the sails made on
A pleasant noise till noon,

---

1. Corpses.   2. In Middle English, "warbling."

A noise like of a hidden brook
In the leafy month of June,   370
That to the sleeping woods all night
Singeth a quiet tune.

Till noon we quietly sailed on,
Yet never a breeze did breathe:
Slowly and smoothly went the ship,   375
Moved onward from beneath.

The lonesome Spirit
from the South Pole   Under the keel nine fathom deep,
carries on the ship   From the land of mist and snow,
as far as the Line,   The spirit slid: and it was he
in obedience to the   That made the ship to go.   380
angelic troop, but   The sails at noon left off their tune,
still requireth   And the ship stood still also.
vengeance.

The Sun, right up above the mast,
Had fixed her to the ocean:
But in a minute she 'gan stir,   385
With a short uneasy motion—
Backwards and forwards half her length
With a short uneasy motion.

Then like a pawing horse let go,
She made a sudden bound: 390
It flung the blood into my head,
And I fell down in a swound.

The Polar Spirit's
fellow demons, the   How long in that same fit I lay,
invisible inhabitants I have not[3] to declare;
of the element, take   But ere my living life returned,   395
part in his wrong;   I heard and in my soul discerned
and two of them   Two voices in the air.
relate, one to the
other, that penance
long and heavy for   "Is it he?" quoth one, "Is this the man?
the ancient Mariner   By him who died on cross,
hath been accorded   With his cruel bow he laid full low   400
to the Polar Spirit,   The harmless Albatross.
who returneth
southward.
                        The spirit who bideth by himself
                        In the land of mist and snow,
                        He loved the bird that loved the man
                        Who shot him with his bow."   405

The other was a softer voice,
As soft as honeydew:

3. I.e., have not the knowledge.

Quoth he, "The man hath penance done,
And penance more will do."

Part 6

FIRST VOICE

"But tell me, tell me! speak again,   410
Thy soft response renewing—
What makes that ship drive on so fast?
What is the ocean doing?"

SECOND VOICE

"Still as a slave before his lord,
The ocean hath no blast;   415
His great bright eye most silently
Up to the Moon is cast—

If he may know which way to go;
For she guides him smooth or grim.
See, brother, see! how graciously   420
She looketh down on him."

FIRST VOICE

*The Mariner hath
been cast into a
trance; for the
angelic power caus-
eth the vessel to
drive northward
faster than human
life could endure.*

"But why drives on that ship so fast,
Without or wave or wind?"

SECOND VOICE

"The air is cut away before,
And closes from behind.   425

Fly, brother, fly! more high, more high!
Or we shall be belated:
For slow and slow that ship will go,
When the Mariner's trance is abated."

*The supernatural
motion is retarded;
the Mariner awakes,
and his penance
begins anew.*

I woke, and we were sailing on   430
As in a gentle weather:
'Twas night, calm night, the moon was high;
The dead men stood together.

All stood together on the deck,
For a charnel-dungeon fitter: 435
All fixed on me their stony eyes,
That in the Moon did glitter.

The pang, the curse, with which they died,
Had never passed away:

I could not draw my eyes from theirs,   440
Nor turn them up to pray.

The curse is finally expiated.
And now this spell was snapped: once more
I viewed the ocean green,
And looked far forth, yet little saw
Of what had else been seen—   445

Like one, that on a lonesome road
Doth walk in fear and dread,
And having once turned round walks on,
And turns no more his head;
Because he knows, a frightful fiend   450
Doth close behind him tread.

But soon there breathed a wind on me,
Nor sound nor motion made:
Its path was not upon the sea,
In ripple or in shade.   455

It raised my hair, it fanned my cheek
Like a meadow-gale of spring—
It mingled strangely with my fears,
Yet it felt like a welcoming.

Swiftly, swiftly flew the ship,   460
Yet she sailed softly too:
Sweetly, sweetly blew the breeze—
On me alone it blew.

And the ancient Mariner beholdeth his native country.
Oh! dream of joy! is this indeed
The lighthouse top I see?   465
Is this the hill? is this the kirk?
Is this mine own countree?

We drifted o'er the harbor bar,
And I with sobs did pray—
O let me be awake, my God!   470
Or let me sleep alway.

The harbor bay was clear as glass,
So smoothly it was strewn!
And on the bay the moonlight lay,
And the shadow of the Moon.   475

The rock shone bright, the kirk no less,
That stands above the rock:
The moonlight steeped in silentness
The steady weathercock.

And the bay was white with silent light,   480
Till rising from the same,

Full many shapes, that shadows were,
In crimson colors came.

A little distance from the prow
Those crimson shadows were: 485
I turned my eyes upon the deck—
Oh, Christ! what saw I there!

Each corse lay flat, lifeless and flat,
And, by the holy rood!
A man all light, a seraph[4] man,   490
On every corse there stood.

This seraph band, each waved his hand:
It was a heavenly sight!
They stood as signals to the land,
Each one a lovely light;   495

This seraph band, each waved his hand,
No voice did they impart—
No voice; but oh! the silence sank
Like music on my heart.

But soon I heard the dash of oars,   500
I heard the Pilot's cheer;
My head was turned perforce away
And I saw a boat appear.

The Pilot and the Pilot's boy,
I heard them coming fast: 505
Dear Lord in Heaven! it was a joy
The dead men could not blast.

I saw a third—I heard his voice:
It is the Hermit good!
He singeth loud his godly hymns   510
That he makes in the wood.
He'll shrieve my soul, he'll wash away
The Albatross's blood.

Part 7

This Hermit good lives in that wood
Which slopes down to the sea.   515

4. A shining celestial being, highest in the ranks of the angels. "Rood": cross.

How loudly his sweet voice he rears!
He loves to talk with marineres
That come from a far countree.

He kneels at morn, and noon, and eve—
He hath a cushion plump: 520
It is the moss that wholly hides
The rotted old oak-stump.

The skiff-boat neared: I heard them talk,
"Why, this is strange, I trow!
Where are those lights so many and fair,   525
That signal made but now?"

"Strange, by my faith!" the Hermit said—
"And they answered not our cheer!
The planks looked warped! and see those sails,
How thin they are and sere!   530
I never saw aught like to them,
Unless perchance it were

Brown skeletons of leaves that lag
My forest-brook along;
When the ivy tod[5] is heavy with snow,   535
And the owlet whoops to the wolf below,
That eats the she-wolf's young."

"Dear Lord! it hath a fiendish look,"
(The Pilot made reply)
"I am a-feared"—"Push on, push on!"   540
Said the Hermit cheerily.

The boat came closer to the ship,
But I nor spake nor stirred;
The boat came close beneath the ship,
And straight a sound was heard.   545

*The ship suddenly
sinketh.*   Under the water it rumbled on,
Still louder and more dread:
It reached the ship, it split the bay;
The ship went down like lead.

*The ancient
Mariner is saved
in the Pilot's
boat.*   Stunned by that loud and dreadful sound,   550
Which sky and ocean smote,
Like one that hath been seven days drowned
My body lay afloat;
But swift as dreams, myself I found
Within the Pilot's boat.   555

5. Clump of ivy.

Upon the whirl, where sank the ship,
The boat spun round and round;
And all was still, save that the hill
Was telling of the sound.

I moved my lips—the Pilot shrieked   560
And fell down in a fit;
The holy Hermit raised his eyes,
And prayed where he did sit.

I took the oars: the Pilot's boy,
Who now doth crazy go,   565
Laughed loud and long, and all the while
His eyes went to and fro.
"Ha! ha!" quoth he, "full plain I see,
The Devil knows how to row."

And now, all in my own countree,   570
I stood on the firm land!
The Hermit stepped forth from the boat,
And scarcely he could stand.

The ancient Mariner earnestly entreateth the Hermit to shrieve him; and the penance of life falls on him.

"O shrieve me, shrieve me, holy man!"
The Hermit crossed his brow.[6]   575
"Say quick," quoth he, "I bid thee say—
What manner of man art thou?"

Forthwith this frame of mine was wrenched
With a woeful agony,
Which forced me to begin my tale;   580
And then it left me free.

And ever and anon throughout his future life an agony constraineth him to travel from land to land;

Since then, at an uncertain hour,
That agony returns:
And till my ghastly tale is told,
This heart within me burns.   585

I pass, like night, from land to land;
I have strange power of speech;
That moment that his face I see,
I know the man that must hear me:
To him my tale I teach.   590

What loud uproar bursts from that door!
The wedding-guests are there:
But in the garden-bower the bride

---

6. Made the sign of the cross on his forehead. "Shrieve me" (line 574): hear my confession and grant me absolution.

And bride-maids singing are:
And hark the little vesper bell,   595
Which biddeth me to prayer!

O Wedding-Guest! this soul hath been
Alone on a wide wide sea:
So lonely 'twas, that God himself
Scarce seemèd there to be.   600

O sweeter than the marriage feast,
'Tis sweeter far to me,
To walk together to the kirk
With a goodly company!—

To walk together to the kirk,   605
And all together pray,
While each to his great Father bends,
Old men, and babes, and loving friends
And youths and maidens gay!

*And to teach, by
his own example,
love and reverence to
all things that God
made and loveth.*

Farewell, farewell! but this I tell   610
To thee, thou Wedding-Guest!
He prayeth well, who loveth well
Both man and bird and beast.

He prayeth best, who loveth best
All things both great and small;   615
For the dear God who loveth us,
He made and loveth all.[7]

The Mariner, whose eye is bright,
Whose beard with age is hoar,
Is gone: and now the Wedding-Guest   620
Turned from the bridegroom's door.

He went like one that hath been stunned,
And is of sense forlorn:[8]
A sadder and a wiser man,
He rose the morrow morn.   625

1797–1816   1798, 1817

---

7. Coleridge said in 1830, answering the objection of the poet Mrs. Barbauld that the poem "lacked a moral": "I told her that in my own judgment the poem had too much; and that the only, or chief fault, if I might say so, was the obtrusion of the moral sentiment so openly on the reader as a principle or cause of action in a work of pure imagination. It ought to have had no more moral than the *Arabian Nights'* tale of the merchant's sitting down to eat dates by the side of a well and throwing the shells aside, and lo! a genie starts up and says he *must* kill the aforesaid merchant *because* one of the date shells had, it seems, put out the eye of the genie's son."
8. Forsaken.

Kubla Khan

Or, A Vision in a Dream. A Fragment

The following fragment is here published at the request of a poet of great and deserved celebrity,[1] and, as far as the author's own opinions are concerned, rather as a psychological curiosity, than on the ground of any supposed *poetic* merits.

In the summer of the year 1797, the author, then in ill health, had retired to a lonely farmhouse between Porlock and Linton, on the Exmoor confines of Somerset and Devonshire. In consequence of a slight indisposition, an anodyne had been prescribed, from the effects of which he fell asleep in his chair at the moment that he was reading the following sentence, or words of the same substance, in *Purchas's Pilgrimage*: "Here the Khan Kubla commanded a palace to be built, and a stately garden thereunto. And thus ten miles of fertile ground were inclosed with a wall."[2] The author continued for about three hours in a profound sleep, at least of the external senses,[3] during which time he has the most vivid confidence that he could not have composed less than from two to three hundred lines; if that indeed can be called composition in which all the images rose up before him as *things*, with a parallel production of the correspondent expressions, without any sensation or consciousness of effort. On awaking he appeared to himself to have a distinct recollection of the whole, and taking his pen, ink, and paper, instantly and eagerly wrote down the lines that are here preserved. At this moment he was unfortunately called out by a person on business from Porlock, and detained by him above an hour, and on his return to his room, found, to his no small surprise and mortification, that though he still retained some vague and dim recollection of the general purport of the vision, yet, with the exception of some eight or ten scattered lines and images, all the rest had passed away like the images on the surface of a stream into which a stone has been cast, but, alas! without the after restoration of the latter!

> Then all the charm
> Is broken—all that phantom world so fair
> Vanishes, and a thousand circlets spread,
> And each misshape[s] the other. Stay awhile,
> Poor youth! who scarcely dar'st lift up thine eyes—
> The stream will soon renew its smoothness, soon

---

1. Lord Byron.

2. "In Xamdu did Cublai Can build a stately Palace, encompassing sixteene miles of plaine ground with a wall, wherein are fertile Meddowes, pleasant Springs, delightfull Streames, and all sorts of beasts of chase and game, and in the middest thereof a sumptuous house of pleasure, which may be removed from place to place." From Samuel Purchas, *Purchas his Pilgrimage* (1613). The historical Kublai Khan founded the Mongol dynasty in China in the 13th century.

3. In a note on a manuscript copy of *Kubla Khan*, Coleridge gave a more precise account of the nature of this "sleep": "This fragment with a good deal more, not recoverable, composed, in a sort of reverie brought on by two grains of opium, taken to check a dysentery, at a farmhouse between Porlock and Linton, a quarter of a mile from Culbone Church, in the fall of the year, 1797."

The visions will return! And lo, he stays,
And soon the fragments dim of lovely forms
Come trembling back, unite, and now once more
The pool becomes a mirror.
    [From Coleridge's *The Picture; or, the Lover's Resolution*,
lines 91–100]

    Yet from the still surviving recollections in his mind, the author
has frequently purposed to finish for himself what had been originally,
as it were, given to him. Σαμερον αδιον ασω: but the tomorrow is yet
to come.[4]

    As a contrast to this vision, I have annexed a fragment of a very dif-
ferent character, describing with equal fidelity the dream of pain and
disease.[5]

In Xanadu did Kubla Khan
A stately pleasure dome decree:
Where Alph,[6] the sacred river, ran
Through caverns measureless to man
    Down to a sunless sea.   5
So twice five miles of fertile ground
With walls and towers were girdled round:
And there were gardens bright with sinuous rills,
Where blossomed many an incense-bearing tree;
And here were forests ancient as the hills,   10
Enfolding sunny spots of greenery.

But oh! that deep romantic chasm which slanted
Down the green hill athwart a cedarn cover!
A savage place! as holy and enchanted
As e'er beneath a waning moon was haunted   15
By woman wailing for her demon lover!
And from this chasm, with ceaseless turmoil seething,
As if this earth in fast thick pants were breathing,
A mighty fountain momently was forced:
Amid whose swift half-intermitted burst   20
Huge fragments vaulted like rebounding hail,
Or chaffy grain beneath the thresher's flail:
And 'mid these dancing rocks at once and ever
It flung up momently the sacred river.
Five miles meandering with a mazy motion   25

4. The Greek may be translated, "I shall sing a sweeter song today." In the edition of 1834, Σαμερον ("today") was changed to Αυριον ("tomorrow"). Coleridge had in mind Theocritus, *Idyls* 1.145: ἐσ ὑστερον αδιον ἀσω ("I shall sing a sweeter song on a later day").

    A number of Coleridge's assertions in this pref-ace have been debated by critics: whether the poem was written in 1797 or later; whether it was actually composed in a "dream" or opium reverie; even whether it is a fragment or in fact complete. All critics agree, however, that this visionary poem of daemonic inspiration is much more than a mere "psychological curiosity."

5. Coleridge is referring to his poem *The Pains of Sleep*.

6. Derived probably from the Greek river Alpheus, which flows into the Ionian Sea. Its waters were fabled to rise again in Sicily as the fountain of Are-thusa; see Milton's *Lycidas*, lines 85 and 132.

Through wood and dale the sacred river ran,
Then reached the caverns measureless to man,
And sank in tumult to a lifeless ocean:
And 'mid this tumult Kubla heard from far
Ancestral voices prophesying war!　　　　　　　　　30
　　The shadow of the dome of pleasure
　　Floated midway on the waves;
　　Where was heard the mingled measure
　　From the fountain and the caves.
It was a miracle of rare device,　　　　　　　　　35
A sunny pleasure dome with caves of ice!

　　A damsel with a dulcimer
　　In a vision once I saw:
　　It was an Abyssinian maid,
　　And on her dulcimer she played,　　　　　　　40
　　Singing of Mount Abora.[7]
　　Could I revive within me
　　Her symphony and song,
　　To such a deep delight 'twould win me,
That with music loud and long,　　　　　　　　　45
I would build that dome in air,
That sunny dome! those caves of ice!
And all who heard should see them there,
And all should cry, Beware! Beware!
His flashing eyes, his floating hair!　　　　　　　50
Weave a circle round him thrice,[8]
And close your eyes with holy dread,
For he on honeydew hath fed,
And drunk the milk of Paradise.[9]

ca. 1797–98　　　　　　　　　　　　　　　　　　1816

Christabel[1]

Preface

　　The first part of the following poem was written in the year 1797, at
Stowey, in the county of Somerset. The second part, after my return

---

7. Apparently a reminiscence of *Paradise Lost*
4.280–82: "where Abassin Kings their issue
guard, / Mount Amara, though this by some supposed / True Paradise under the Ethiop Line."
8. A magic ritual, to protect the inspired poet from
intrusion.
9. Lines 50 ff. echo in part the description, in Plato's *Ion* 533–34, of inspired poets, who are "like
Bacchic maidens who draw milk and honey from
the rivers when they are under the influence of
Dionysus but not when they are in their right
mind."

1. Coleridge had planned to publish *Christabel* in
the second edition of *Lyrical Ballads* (1800), but
had not been able to complete the poem. When
Christabel was finally published in 1816 in its present fragmentary state, he still had hopes of finishing it, for the Preface contained this sentence
(deleted in the edition of 1834): "But as, in my
very first conception of the tale, I had the whole
present to my mind, with the wholeness, no less
than the liveliness of a vision, I trust that I shall be
able to embody in verse the three parts yet to come,
in the course of the present year."

from Germany, in the year 1800, at Keswick, Cumberland. It is probable that if the poem had been finished at either of the former periods, or if even the first and second part had been published in the year 1800, the impression of its originality would have been much greater than I dare at present expect. But for this I have only my own indolence to blame. The dates are mentioned for the exclusive purpose of precluding charges of plagiarism or servile imitation from myself. For there is amongst us a set of critics, who seem to hold that every possible thought and image is traditional; who have no notion that there are such things as fountains in the world, small as well as great; and who would therefore charitably derive every rill they behold flowing, from a perforation made in some other man's tank. I am confident, however, that as far as the present poem is concerned, the celebrated poets[2] whose writings I might be suspected of having imitated, either in particular passages, or in the tone and the spirit of the whole, would be among the first to vindicate me from the charge, and who, on any striking coincidence, would permit me to address them in this doggerel version of two monkish Latin hexameters.

'Tis mine and it is likewise yours;
But an if this will not do;
Let it be mine, good friend! for I
Am the poorer of the two.

I have only to add that the meter of Christabel is not, properly speaking, irregular, though it may seem so from its being founded on a new principle: namely, that of counting in each line the accents, not the syllables.[3] Though the latter may vary from seven to twelve, yet in each line the accents will be found to be only four. Nevertheless, this occasional variation in number of syllables is not introduced wantonly, or for the mere ends of convenience, but in correspondence with some transition in the nature of the imagery or passion.

Part 1

'Tis the middle of night by the castle clock,
And the owls have awakened the crowing cock;
Tu—whit!——Tu—whoo!
And hark, again! the crowing cock,
How drowsily it crew.   5

---

2. Sir Walter Scott and Lord Byron, who had read and admired *Christabel* while it circulated in manuscript. Coleridge has in mind Scott's *Lay of the Last Minstrel* (1805) and Byron's *Siege of Corinth* (1816), which showed the influence of *Christabel*, especially in their meter.
3. Much of the older English versification, following the example of Anglo-Saxon poetry, had been based on stress, or "accent," and some of it shows as much freedom in varying the number of syllables as does *Christabel*. The poem, however, is a radical departure from the theory and practice of versification in the 18th century, which had been based on a recurrent number of syllables in each line.

Sir Leoline, the Baron rich,
Hath a toothless mastiff bitch;
From her kennel beneath the rock
She maketh answer to the clock,
Four for the quarters, and twelve for the hour;   10
Ever and aye, by shine and shower,
Sixteen short howls, not over loud;
Some say she sees my lady's shroud.

Is the night chilly and dark?
The night is chilly, but not dark.   15
The thin gray cloud is spread on high,
It covers but not hides the sky.
The moon is behind, and at the full;
And yet she looks both small and dull.
The night is chill, the cloud is gray: 20
'Tis a month before the month of May,
And the spring comes slowly up this way.

The lovely lady, Christabel,
Whom her father loves so well,
What makes her in the wood so late,   25
A furlong from the castle gate?
She had dreams all yesternight
Of her own betrothèd knight;
And she in the midnight wood will pray
For the weal[4] of her lover that's far away.   30

She stole along, she nothing spoke.
The sighs she heaved were soft and low,
And naught was green upon the oak
But moss and rarest mistletoe:[5]
She kneels beneath the huge oak tree,   35
And in silence prayeth she.

The lady sprang up suddenly,
The lovely lady, Christabel!
It moaned as near, as near can be,
But what it is she cannot tell.—   40
On the other side it seems to be,
Of the huge, broad-breasted, old oak tree.

The night is chill; the forest bare;
Is it the wind that moaneth bleak?
There is not wind enough in the air   45
To move away the ringlet curl

4. Well-being.
5. In Celtic Britain the mistletoe (a parasitic plant) had been held in veneration when it was found growing—as it rarely does—on an oak tree. (Its usual host is the apple tree.)

From the lovely lady's cheek—
There is not wind enough to twirl
The one red leaf, the last of its clan,
That dances as often as dance it can,   50
Hanging so light, and hanging so high,
On the topmost twig that looks up at the sky.

Hush, beating heart of Christabel!
Jesu, Maria, shield her well!
She folded her arms beneath her cloak,   55
And stole to the other side of the oak.
    What sees she there?

There she sees a damsel bright,
Dressed in a silken robe of white,
That shadowy in the moonlight shone: 60
The neck that made that white robe wan,
Her stately neck, and arms were bare;
Her blue-veined feet unsandaled were,
And wildly glittered here and there
The gems entangled in her hair.   65
I guess, 'twas frightful there to see
A lady so richly clad as she—
Beautiful exceedingly!

"Mary mother, save me now!"
Said Christabel, "And who art thou?"   70

The lady strange made answer meet,
And her voice was faint and sweet—
"Have pity on my sore distress,
I scarce can speak for weariness:
Stretch forth thy hand, and have no fear!"   75
Said Christabel, "How camest thou here?"
And the lady, whose voice was faint and sweet,
Did thus pursue her answer meet:—

"My sire is of a noble line,
And my name is Geraldine: 80
Five warriors seized me yestermorn,
Me, even me, a maid forlorn:
They choked my cries with force and fright,
And tied me on a palfrey white.
The palfrey was as fleet as wind,   85
And they rode furiously behind.
They spurred amain,[6] their steeds were white:
And once we crossed the shade of night.

6. At top speed.

As sure as Heaven shall rescue me,
I have no thought what men they be;   90
Nor do I know how long it is
(For I have lain entranced, I wis[7])
Since one, the tallest of the five,
Took me from the palfrey's back,
A weary woman, scarce alive.   95
Some muttered words his comrades spoke:
He placed me underneath this oak;
He swore they would return with haste;
Whither they went I cannot tell—
I thought I heard, some minutes past,   100
Sounds as of a castle bell.
Stretch forth thy hand," thus ended she,
"And help a wretched maid to flee."

Then Christabel stretched forth her hand,
And comforted fair Geraldine: 105
"O well, bright dame! may you command
The service of Sir Leoline;
And gladly our stout chivalry
Will he send forth and friends withal
To guide and guard you safe and free   110
Home to your noble father's hall."

She rose: and forth with steps they passed
That strove to be, and were not, fast.
Her gracious stars the lady blessed,
And thus spake on sweet Christabel: 115
"All our household are at rest,
The hall as silent as the cell;
Sir Leoline is weak in health,
And may not well awakened be,
But we will move as if in stealth,   120
And I beseech your courtesy,
This night, to share your couch with me."

They crossed the moat, and Christabel
Took the key that fitted well;
A little door she opened straight,   125
All in the middle of the gate;
The gate that was ironed within and without,
Where an army in battle array had marched out.
The lady sank, belike through pain,
And Christabel with might and main   130
Lifted her up, a weary weight,

---

7. I believe; Coleridge's misinterpretation of the Middle English adverb "ywis," meaning "certainly."

Over the threshold of the gate:[8]
Then the lady rose again,
And moved, as she were not in pain.

So free from danger, free from fear,   135
They crossed the court: right glad they were.
And Christabel devoutly cried
To the lady by her side,
"Praise we the Virgin all divine
Who hath rescued thee from thy distress!"   140
"Alas, alas!" said Geraldine,
"I cannot speak for weariness."
So free from danger, free from fear,
They crossed the court: right glad they were.

Outside her kennel, the mastiff old   145
Lay fast asleep, in moonshine cold.
The mastiff old did not awake,
Yet she an angry moan did make!
And what can ail the mastiff bitch?
Never till now she uttered yell   150
Beneath the eye of Christabel.
Perhaps it is the owlet's scritch:
For what can ail the mastiff bitch?

They passed the hall, that echoes still,
Pass as lightly as you will!   155
The brands were flat, the brands were dying,
Amid their own white ashes lying;
But when the lady passed, there came
A tongue of light, a fit of flame;
And Christabel saw the lady's eye,   160
And nothing else saw she thereby,
Save the boss of the shield of Sir Leoline tall,
Which hung in a murky old niche in the wall.
"O softly tread," said Christabel,
"My father seldom sleepeth well."   165

Sweet Christabel her feet doth bare,
And jealous of the listening air
They steal their way from stair to stair,
Now in glimmer, and now in gloom,
And now they pass the Baron's room,   170
As still as death, with stifled breath!
And now have reached her chamber door;

---

8. According to legend, a witch cannot cross the threshold by her own power because it has been blessed against evil spirits.

And now doth Geraldine press down
The rushes[9] of the chamber floor.

The moon shines dim in the open air,   175
And not a moonbeam enters here.
But they without its light can see
The chamber carved so curiously,
Carved with figures strange and sweet,
All made out of the carver's brain,   180
For a lady's chamber meet:
The lamp with twofold silver chain
Is fastened to an angel's feet.

The silver lamp burns dead and dim;
But Christabel the lamp will trim.   185
She trimmed the lamp, and made it bright,
And left it swinging to and fro,
While Geraldine, in wretched plight,
Sank down upon the floor below.

"O weary lady, Geraldine,   190
I pray you, drink this cordial wine!
It is a wine of virtuous powers;
My mother made it of wild flowers."

"And will your mother pity me,
Who am a maiden most forlorn?"   195
Christabel answered—"Woe is me!
She died the hour that I was born.
I have heard the gray-haired friar tell
How on her deathbed she did say,
That she should hear the castle bell   200
Strike twelve upon my wedding day.
O mother dear! that thou wert here!"
"I would," said Geraldine, "she were!"

But soon with altered voice, said she—
"Off, wandering mother! Peak and pine!   205
I have power to bid thee flee."
Alas! what ails poor Geraldine?
Why stares she with unsettled eye?
Can she the bodiless dead espy?
And why with hollow voice cries she,   210
"Off, woman, off! this hour is mine—
Though thou her guardian spirit be,
Off, woman, off! 'tis given to me."

9. Often used as a floor covering in the Middle Ages.

Then Christabel knelt by the lady's side,
And raised to heaven her eyes so blue—   215
"Alas!" said she, "this ghastly ride—
Dear lady! it hath 'wildered you!"
The lady wiped her moist cold brow,
And faintly said, " 'tis over now!"

Again the wild-flower wine she drank: 220
Her fair large eyes 'gan glitter bright,
And from the floor whereon she sank,
The lofty lady stood upright:
She was most beautiful to see,
Like a lady of a far countrée.   225

And thus the lofty lady spake—
"All they who live in the upper sky,
Do love you, holy Christabel!
And you love them, and for their sake
And for the good which me befell,   230
Even I in my degree will try,
Fair maiden, to requite you well.
But now unrobe yourself; for I
Must pray, ere yet in bed I lie."

Quoth Christabel, "So let it be!"   235
And as the lady bade, did she.
Her gentle limbs did she undress,
And lay down in her loveliness.

But through her brain of weal and woe
So many thoughts moved to and fro,   240
That vain it were her lids to close;
So halfway from the bed she rose,
And on her elbow did recline
To look at the lady Geraldine.

Beneath the lamp the lady bowed,   245
And slowly rolled her eyes around;
Then drawing in her breath aloud,
Like one that shuddered, she unbound
The cincture[1] from beneath her breast:
Her silken robe, and inner vest,   250
Dropped to her feet, and full in view,
Behold! her bosom and half her side——
A sight to dream of, not to tell!
O shield her! shield sweet Christabel!

1. Belt.

Yet Geraldine nor speaks nor stirs;   255
Ah! what a stricken look was hers!
Deep from within she seems halfway
To lift some weight with sick assay,[2]
And eyes the maid and seeks delay;
Then suddenly, as one defied,   260
Collects herself in scorn and pride,
And lay down by the maiden's side!—
And in her arms the maid she took,
   Ah well-a-day!
And with low voice and doleful look   265
These words did say:
"In the touch of this bosom there worketh a spell,
Which is lord of thy utterance, Christabel!
Thou knowest tonight, and wilt know tomorrow,
This mark of my shame, this seal of my sorrow;   270
  But vainly thou warrest,
   For this is alone in
  Thy power to declare,
   That in the dim forest
  Thou heard'st a low moaning,   275
And found'st a bright lady, surpassingly fair;
And didst bring her home with thee in love and in charity,
To shield her and shelter her from the damp air."

The Conclusion to Part 1

It was a lovely sight to see
The lady Christabel, when she   280
Was praying at the old oak tree.
  Amid the jaggèd shadows
  Of mossy leafless boughs,
  Kneeling in the moonlight,
  To make her gentle vows: 285
Her slender palms together pressed,
Heaving sometimes on her breast;
Her face resigned to bliss or bale[3]—
Her face, oh call it fair not pale,
And both blue eyes more bright than clear,   290
Each about to have a tear.

With open eyes (ah woe is me!)
Asleep, and dreaming fearfully,
Fearfully dreaming, yet, I wis,
Dreaming that alone, which is—   295
O sorrow and shame! Can this be she,

---

2. Attempt.   3. Evil, sorrow.

The lady, who knelt at the old oak tree?
And lo! the worker of these harms,
That holds the maiden in her arms,
Seems to slumber still and mild,
As a mother with her child.   300

A star hath set, a star hath risen,
O Geraldine! since arms of thine
Have been the lovely lady's prison.
O Geraldine! one hour was thine—   305
Thou'st had thy will! By tairn[4] and rill,
The night birds all that hour were still.
But now they are jubilant anew,
From cliff and tower, tu—whoo! tu—whoo!
Tu—whoo! tu—whoo! from wood and fell![5]   310

And see! the lady Christabel
Gathers herself from out her trance;
Her limbs relax, her countenance
Grows sad and soft; the smooth thin lids
Close o'er her eyes; and tears she sheds—   315
Large tears that leave the lashes bright!
And oft the while she seems to smile
As infants at a sudden light!

Yea, she doth smile, and she doth weep,
Like a youthful hermitess,   320
Beauteous in a wilderness,
Who, praying always, prays in sleep.
And, if she move unquietly,
Perchance, 'tis but the blood so free
Comes back and tingles in her feet.   325
No doubt, she hath a vision sweet.
What if her guardian spirit 'twere,
What if she knew her mother near?
But this she knows, in joys and woes,
That saints will aid if men will call: 330
For the blue sky bends over all!

Part 2

"Each matin bell," the Baron saith,
"Knells us back to a world of death."
These words Sir Leoline first said,
When he rose and found his lady dead: 335
These words Sir Leoline will say
Many a morn to his dying day!

---

4. Tarn, a mountain pool.   5. Elevated moor, or hill.

And hence the custom and law began
That still at dawn the sacristan,
Who duly pulls the heavy bell,   340
Five and forty beads must tell[6]
Between each stroke—a warning knell,
Which not a soul can choose but hear
From Bratha Head to Wyndermere.[7]

Saith Bracy the bard, "So let it knell!   345
And let the drowsy sacristan
Still count as slowly as he can!
There is no lack of such, I ween,
As well fill up the space between.
In Langdale Pike[8] and Witch's Lair,   350
And Dungeon Ghyll[9] so foully rent,
With ropes of rock and bells of air
Three sinful sextons' ghosts are pent,
Who all give back, one after t'other,
The death note to their living brother;   355
And oft too, by the knell offended,
Just as their one! two! three! is ended,
The devil mocks the doleful tale
With a merry peal from Borodale."

The air is still! through mist and cloud   360
That merry peal comes ringing loud;
And Geraldine shakes off her dread,
And rises lightly from the bed;
Puts on her silken vestments white,
And tricks her hair in lovely plight,[1]   365
And nothing doubting of her spell
Awakens the lady Christabel.
"Sleep you, sweet lady Christabel?
I trust that you have rested well."

And Christabel awoke and spied   370
The same who lay down by her side—
O rather say, the same whom she
Raised up beneath the old oak tree!
Nay, fairer yet! and yet more fair!
For she belike hath drunken deep   375
Of all the blessedness of sleep!
And while she spake, her looks, her air
Such gentle thankfulness declare,
That (so it seemed) her girded vests

6. Pray while "telling" (keeping count on) the beads
of a rosary. "Sacristan" (line 339): sexton.
7. These and the following names are of localities
in the English Lake Country.

8. Peak
9. Ravine forming the bed of a stream.
1. Plait.

Grew tight beneath her heaving breasts. 380
"Sure I have sinned!" said Christabel,
"Now heaven be praised if all be well!"
And in low faltering tones, yet sweet,
Did she the lofty lady greet
With such perplexity of mind 385
As dreams too lively leave behind.

So quickly she rose, and quickly arrayed
Her maiden limbs, and having prayed
That He, who on the cross did groan,
Might wash away her sins unknown, 390
She forthwith led fair Geraldine
To meet her sire, Sir Leoline.

The lovely maid and the lady tall
Are pacing both into the hall,
And pacing on through page and groom, 395
Enter the Baron's presence-room.

The Baron rose, and while he pressed
His gentle daughter to his breast,
With cheerful wonder in his eyes
The lady Geraldine espies, 400
And gave such welcome to the same,
As might beseem so bright a dame!

But when he heard the lady's tale,
And when she told her father's name,
Why waxed Sir Leoline so pale, 405
Murmuring o'er the name again,
Lord Roland de Vaux of Tryermaine?

Alas! they had been friends in youth;
But whispering tongues can poison truth;
And constancy lives in realms above; 410
And life is thorny; and youth is vain;
And to be wroth with one we love
Doth work like madness in the brain.
And thus it chanced, as I divine,
With Roland and Sir Leoline. 415
Each spake words of high disdain
And insult to his heart's best brother:
They parted—ne'er to meet again!
But never either found another
To free the hollow heart from paining— 420
They stood aloof, the scars remaining,
Like cliffs which had been rent asunder;
A dreary sea now flows between—

But neither heat, nor frost, nor thunder,
Shall wholly do away, I ween,   425
The marks of that which once hath been.

Sir Leoline, a moment's space,
Stood gazing on the damsel's face:
And the youthful Lord of Tryermaine
Came back upon his heart again.   430

O then the Baron forgot his age,
His noble heart swelled high with rage;
He swore by the wounds in Jesu's side
He would proclaim it far and wide,
With trump and solemn heraldry,   435
That they, who thus had wronged the dame,
Were base as spotted infamy!
"And if they dare deny the same,
My herald shall appoint a week,
And let the recreant traitors seek   440
My tourney court—that there and then
I may dislodge their reptile souls
From the bodies and forms of men!"
He spake: his eye in lightning rolls!
For the lady was ruthlessly seized; and he kenned   445
In the beautiful lady the child of his friend!

And now the tears were on his face,
And fondly in his arms he took
Fair Geraldine, who met the embrace,
Prolonging it with joyous look.   450
Which when she viewed, a vision fell
Upon the soul of Christabel,
The vision of fear, the touch and pain!
She shrunk and shuddered, and saw again—
(Ah, woe is me! Was it for thee,   455
Thou gentle maid! such sights to see?)

Again she saw that bosom old,
Again she felt that bosom cold,
And drew in her breath with a hissing sound:
Whereat the Knight turned wildly round,   460
And nothing saw, but his own sweet maid
With eyes upraised, as one that prayed.

The touch, the sight, had passed away,
And in its stead that vision blest,
Which comforted her after-rest   465
While in the lady's arms she lay,
Had put a rapture in her breast,

And on her lips and o'er her eyes
Spread smiles like light!
                  With new surprise,
"What ails then my belovèd child?"   470
The Baron said—His daughter mild
Made answer, "All will yet be well!"
I ween, she had no power to tell
Aught else: so mighty was the spell.

Yet he, who saw this Geraldine,   475
Had deemed her sure a thing divine:
Such sorrow with such grace she blended,
As if she feared she had offended
Sweet Christabel, that gentle maid!
And with such lowly tones she prayed   480
She might be sent without delay
Home to her father's mansion.
                    "Nay!
Nay, by my soul!" said Leoline.
"Ho! Bracy the bard, the charge be thine!
Go thou, with music sweet and loud,   485
And take two steeds with trappings proud,
And take the youth whom thou lov'st best
To bear thy harp, and learn thy song,
And clothe you both in solemn vest,
And over the mountains haste along,   490
Lest wandering folk, that are abroad,
Detain you on the valley road.

"And when he has crossed the Irthing flood,
My merry bard! he hastes, he hastes
Up Knorren Moor, through Halegarth Wood,   495
And reaches soon that castle good
Which stands and threatens Scotland's wastes.

"Bard Bracy! bard Bracy! your horses are fleet,
Ye must ride up the hall, your music so sweet,
More loud than your horses' echoing feet!   500
And loud and loud to Lord Roland call,
Thy daughter is safe in Langdale hall!
Thy beautiful daughter is safe and free—
Sir Leoline greets thee thus through me!
He bids thee come without delay   505
With all thy numerous array
And take thy lovely daughter home:
And he will meet thee on the way
With all his numerous array
White with their panting palfreys' foam: 510
And, by mine honor! I will say,

That I repent me of the day
When I spake words of fierce disdain
To Roland de Vaux of Tryermaine!—
For since that evil hour hath flown,   515
Many a summer's sun hath shone;
Yet ne'er found I a friend again
Like Roland de Vaux of Tryermaine."

The lady fell, and clasped his knees,
Her face upraised, her eyes o'erflowing;   520
And Bracy replied, with faltering voice,
His gracious Hail on all bestowing!—
"Thy words, thou sire of Christabel,
Are sweeter than my harp can tell;
Yet might I gain a boon of thee,   525
This day my journey should not be,
So strange a dream hath come to me,
That I had vowed with music loud
To clear yon wood from thing unblest,
Warned by a vision in my rest!   530
For in my sleep I saw that dove,
That gentle bird, whom thou dost love,
And call'st by thy own daughter's name—
Sir Leoline! I saw the same
Fluttering, and uttering fearful moan,   535
Among the green herbs in the forest alone.
Which when I saw and when I heard,
I wondered what might ail the bird;
For nothing near it could I see,
Save the grass and green herbs underneath the old tree. 540

"And in my dream methought I went
To search out what might there be found;
And what the sweet bird's trouble meant,
That thus lay fluttering on the ground.
I went and peered, and could descry   545
No cause for her distressful cry;
But yet for her dear lady's sake
I stooped, methought, the dove to take,
When lo! I saw a bright green snake
Coiled around its wings and neck.   550
Green as the herbs on which it couched,
Close by the dove's its head it crouched;
And with the dove it heaves and stirs,
Swelling its neck as she swelled hers!
I woke; it was the midnight hour,   555
The clock was echoing in the tower;
But though my slumber was gone by,
This dream it would not pass away—

It seems to live upon my eye!
And thence I vowed this selfsame day   560
With music strong and saintly song
To wander through the forest bare,
Lest aught unholy loiter there."

Thus Bracy said: the Baron, the while,
Half-listening heard him with a smile;   565
Then turned to Lady Geraldine,
His eyes made up of wonder and love;
And said in courtly accents fine,
"Sweet maid, Lord Roland's beauteous dove,
With arms more strong than harp or song,   570
Thy sire and I will crush the snake!"
He kissed her forehead as he spake,
And Geraldine in maiden wise
Casting down her large bright eyes,
With blushing cheek and courtesy fine   575
She turned her from Sir Leoline;
Softly gathering up her train,
That o'er her right arm fell again;
And folded her arms across her chest,
And couched her head upon her breast,   580
And looked askance at Christabel——
Jesu, Maria, shield her well!

A snake's small eye blinks dull and shy;
And the lady's eyes they shrunk in her head,
Each shrunk up to a serpent's eye,   585
And with somewhat of malice, and more of dread,
At Christabel she looked askance!—
One moment—and the sight was fled!
But Christabel in dizzy trance
Stumbling on the unsteady ground   590
Shuddered aloud, with a hissing sound;
And Geraldine again turned round,
And like a thing, that sought relief,
Full of wonder and full of grief,
She rolled her large bright eyes divine   595
Wildly on Sir Leoline.

The maid, alas! her thoughts are gone,
She nothing sees—no sight but one!
The maid, devoid of guile and sin,
I know not how, in fearful wise,   600
So deeply had she drunken in
That look, those shrunken serpent eyes,
That all her features were resigned
To this sole image in her mind:

And passively did imitate   605
That look of dull and treacherous hate!
And thus she stood, in dizzy trance,
Still picturing that look askance
With forced unconscious sympathy
Full before her father's view—   610
As far as such a look could be
In eyes so innocent and blue!

And when the trance was o'er, the maid
Paused awhile, and inly prayed:
Then falling at the Baron's feet,   615
"By my mother's soul do I entreat
That thou this woman send away!"
She said: and more she could not say:
For what she knew she could not tell,
O'ermastered by the mighty spell.   620

Why is thy cheek so wan and wild,
Sir Leoline? Thy only child
Lies at thy feet, thy joy, thy pride,
So fair, so innocent, so mild;
The same, for whom thy lady died!   625
O by the pangs of her dear mother
Think thou no evil of thy child!
For her, and thee, and for no other,
She prayed the moment ere she died:
Prayed that the babe for whom she died,   630
Might prove her dear lord's joy and pride!
    That prayer her deadly pangs beguiled,
            Sir Leoline!
    And wouldst thou wrong thy only child,
            Her child and thine?   635

Within the Baron's heart and brain
If thoughts, like these, had any share,
They only swelled his rage and pain,
And did but work confusion there.
His heart was cleft with pain and rage,   640
His cheeks they quivered, his eyes were wild,
Dishonoured thus in his old age;
Dishonoured by his only child,
And all his hospitality
To the wronged daughter of his friend   645
By more than woman's jealousy
Brought thus to a disgraceful end—
He rolled his eye with stern regard
Upon the gentle minstrel bard,
And said in tones abrupt, austere—   650

"Why, Bracy! dost thou loiter here?
I bade thee hence!" The bard obeyed;
And turning from his own sweet maid,
The agèd knight, Sir Leoline,
Led forth the lady Geraldine!   655

The Conclusion to Part 2

A little child, a limber elf,
Singing, dancing to itself,
A fairy thing with red round cheeks,
That always finds, and never seeks,
Makes such a vision to the sight   660
As fills a father's eyes with light;
And pleasures flow in so thick and fast
Upon his heart, that he at last
Must needs express his love's excess
With words of unmeant bitterness.   665
Perhaps 'tis pretty to force together
Thoughts so all unlike each other;
To mutter and mock a broken charm,
To dally with wrong that does no harm.
Perhaps 'tis tender too and pretty   670
At each wild word to feel within
A sweet recoil of love and pity.
And what, if in a world of sin
(O sorrow and shame should this be true!)
Such giddiness of heart and brain   675
Comes seldom save from rage and pain,
So talks as it's most used to do.

1797–1801   1816

Frost at Midnight[1]

The Frost performs its secret ministry,
Unhelped by any wind. The owlet's cry
Came loud—and hark, again! loud as before.
The inmates of my cottage, all at rest,
Have left me to that solitude, which suits   5
Abstruser musings: save that at my side
My cradled infant slumbers peacefully.
'Tis calm indeed! so calm, that it disturbs
And vexes meditation with its strange
And extreme silentness. Sea, hill, and wood,   10

---

1. The scene is Coleridge's cottage at Nether Stowey; the infant in line 7 is his son Hartley.

This populous village! Sea, and hill, and wood,
With all the numberless goings-on of life,
Inaudible as dreams! the thin blue flame
Lies on my low-burnt fire, and quivers not;
Only that film,[2] which fluttered on the grate,   15
Still flutters there, the sole unquiet thing.
Methinks its motion in this hush of nature
Gives it dim sympathies with me who live,
Making it a companionable form,
Whose puny flaps and freaks the idling Spirit   20
By its own moods interprets, everywhere
Echo or mirror seeking of itself,
And makes a toy of Thought.

                     But O! how oft,
How oft, at school, with most believing mind,
Presageful, have I gazed upon the bars,   25
To watch that fluttering *stranger!* and as oft
With unclosed lids, already had I dreamt
Of my sweet birthplace,[3] and the old church tower,
Whose bells, the poor man's only music, rang
From morn to evening, all the hot fair-day,   30
So sweetly, that they stirred and haunted me
With a wild pleasure, falling on mine ear
Most like articulate sounds of things to come!
So gazed I, till the soothing things, I dreamt,
Lulled me to sleep, and sleep prolonged my dreams!   35
And so I brooded all the following morn,
Awed by the stern preceptor's face,[4] mine eye
Fixed with mock study on my swimming book:
Save if the door half opened, and I snatched
A hasty glance, and still my heart leaped up,   40
For still I hoped to see the *stranger's* face,
Townsman, or aunt, or sister more beloved,
My playmate when we both were clothed alike![5]

    Dear Babe, that sleepest cradled by my side,
Whose gentle breathings, heard in this deep calm,   45
Fill up the interspersèd vacancies
And momentary pauses of the thought!
My babe so beautiful! it thrills my heart
With tender gladness, thus to look at thee,
And think that thou shalt learn far other lore,   50

---

2. "In all parts of the kingdom these films are called *strangers* and supposed to portend the arrival of some absent friend" [Coleridge's note]. The "film" is a piece of soot fluttering on the bar of the grate.
3. Coleridge was born at Ottery St. Mary, Devonshire, but went to school in London, beginning at the age of 9.

4. The "stern preceptor" at Coleridge's school, Christ's Hospital, was the Rev. James Boyer, whom Coleridge describes in *Biographia Literaria*, chap. 1.
5. I.e., when both Coleridge and his sister Ann still wore infant clothes.

And in far other scenes! For I was reared
In the great city, pent 'mid cloisters dim,
And saw nought lovely but the sky and stars.
But *thou*, my babe! shalt wander like a breeze
By lakes and sandy shores, beneath the crags   55
Of ancient mountain, and beneath the clouds,
Which image in their bulk both lakes and shores
And mountain crags: so shalt thou see and hear
The lovely shapes and sounds intelligible
Of that eternal language, which thy God   60
Utters, who from eternity doth teach
Himself in all, and all things in himself.
Great universal Teacher! he shall mold
Thy spirit, and by giving make it ask.

    Therefore all seasons shall be sweet to thee,   65
Whether the summer clothe the general earth
With greenness, or the redbreast sit and sing
Betwixt the tufts of snow on the bare branch
Of mossy apple tree, while the nigh thatch
Smokes in the sun-thaw; whether the eave-drops fall   70
Heard only in the trances of the blast,
Or if the secret ministry of frost
Shall hang them up in silent icicles,
Quietly shining to the quiet Moon.

February 1798   1798

Dejection: An Ode[1]

> Late, late yestreen I saw the new Moon,
> With the old Moon in her arms;
> And I fear, I fear, my master dear!
> We shall have a deadly storm.
> *Ballad of Sir Patrick Spence*

1

Well! If the bard was weather-wise, who made
The grand old ballad of Sir Patrick Spence,

1. This poem originated in a verse letter of 340 lines, called *A Letter to ———*, that Coleridge wrote on the night of Apr. 4, 1802, after hearing the opening stanzas of *Ode: Intimations of Immortality*, which Wordsworth had just composed. The *Letter* was addressed to Sara Hutchinson (whom Coleridge sometimes called "Asra"), the sister of Wordsworth's fiancée, Mary. It picked up the theme of a loss in the quality of perceptual experience which Wordsworth had presented at the beginning of his *Ode*. In his original poem, Coleridge lamented at length his unhappy marriage and the hopelessness of his love for Sara Hutchinson. In the next six months Coleridge deleted more than half the original lines, revised and reordered the remaining passages, and so transformed a long verse confession into the compact and dignified *Dejection: An Ode*. He published the *Ode*, in substantially its present form, on Oct. 4, 1802, Wordsworth's wedding day—and also the seventh anniversary of Coleridge's own disastrous marriage to Sara Fricker. Note Coleridge's use of marriage as a metaphor in lines 49 and 67–70.

This night, so tranquil now, will not go hence
Unroused by winds, that ply a busier trade
Than those which mold yon cloud in lazy flakes,   5
Or the dull sobbing draft, that moans and rakes
Upon the strings of this Aeolian lute,[2]
    Which better far were mute.
    For lo! the New-moon winter-bright!
    And overspread with phantom light,   10
    (With swimming phantom light o'erspread
    But rimmed and circled by a silver thread)
I see the old Moon in her lap, foretelling
    The coming-on of rain and squally blast.
And oh! that even now the gust were swelling,   15
    And the slant night shower driving loud and fast!
Those sounds which oft have raised me, whilst they awed,
    And sent my soul abroad,
Might now perhaps their wonted[3] impulse give,
Might startle this dull pain, and make it move and live!   20

2

A grief without a pang, void, dark, and drear,
    A stifled, drowsy, unimpassioned grief,
    Which finds no natural outlet, no relief,
        In word, or sigh, or tear—
O Lady!,[4] in this wan and heartless mood,   25
To other thoughts by yonder throstle wooed,
    All this long eve, so balmy and serene,
Have I been gazing on the western sky,
    And its peculiar tint of yellow green:
And still I gaze—and with how blank an eye!   30
And those thin clouds above, in flakes and bars,
That give away their motion to the stars;
Those stars, that glide behind them or between,
Now sparkling, now bedimmed, but always seen:
Yon crescent Moon, as fixed as if it grew   35
In its own cloudless, starless lake of blue;
I see them all so excellently fair,
I see, not feel, how beautiful they are!

3

    My genial[5] spirits fail;
    And what can these avail   40
To lift the smothering weight from off my breast?
    It were a vain endeavour,
    Though I should gaze forever
On that green light that lingers in the west:

---

2. A stringed instrument played upon by the wind;
see Coleridge's *The Eolian Harp*, note 1.
3. Customary.
4. In the original version "Sara"—i.e., Sara
Hutchinson. After intervening versions, in which
the poem was addressed first to "William" (Wordsworth) and then to "Edmund," Coleridge introduced the noncommittal "Lady" in 1817.
5. In its old use as the adjectival form of "genius":
"My innate powers fail."

I may not hope from outward forms to win   45
The passion and the life, whose fountains are within.

4

O Lady! we receive but what we give,
And in our life alone does Nature live:
Ours is her wedding garment, ours her shroud![6]
   And would we aught behold, of higher worth,   50
Than that inanimate cold world allowed
To the poor loveless ever-anxious crowd,
   Ah! from the soul itself must issue forth
A light, a glory,[7] a fair luminous cloud
      Enveloping the Earth—   55
And from the soul itself must there be sent
   A sweet and potent voice, of its own birth,
Of all sweet sounds the life and element!

5

O pure of heart! thou need'st not ask of me
What this strong music in the soul may be!   60
What, and wherein it doth exist,
This light, this glory, this fair luminous mist,
This beautiful and beauty-making power.
   Joy,[8] virtuous Lady! Joy that ne'er was given,
Save to the pure, and in their purest hour,   65
Life, and Life's effluence, cloud at once and shower,
Joy, Lady! is the spirit and the power,
Which wedding Nature to us gives in dower
   A new Earth and new Heaven,[9]
Undreamt of by the sensual and the proud—   70
Joy is the sweet voice, Joy the luminous cloud—
      We in ourselves rejoice!
And thence flows all that charms or ear or sight,
   All melodies the echoes of that voice,
All colors a suffusion from that light.   75

6

There was a time when, though my path was rough,
   This joy within me dallied with distress,
And all misfortunes were but as the stuff
   Whence Fancy made me dreams of happiness:
For hope grew round me, like the twining vine,   80
And fruits, and foliage, not my own, seemed mine.

6. I.e., whether nature is experienced as "inanimate" (line 51) or in living interchange with the observer depends on the apathy or joyous vitality of the observer's own spirit.
7. Coleridge commonly used "glory" not in the sense of a halo, merely, but as a term for a mountain phenomenon in which a walker sees his own figure projected by the sun in the mist, enlarged, and with a circle of light around its head.
8. Coleridge often uses "Joy" for a sense of abounding vitality and of harmony between one's inner life and the life of nature. He sometimes calls the contrary "exsiccation," or spiritual dryness.
9. The sense becomes clearer if line 68 is punctuated in the way that Coleridge himself punctuated it when quoting the passage in one of his essays: "Which, wedding Nature to us, gives in dower." The idea is that "Joy" is the condition which (overcoming the alienation between mind and its milieu) marries us to "Nature," and gives by way of wedding portion ("dower") the experience of a renovated world.

But now afflictions bow me down to earth:
Nor care I that they rob me of my mirth;
        But oh! each visitation
Suspends what nature gave me at my birth,   85
    My shaping spirit of Imagination.
For not to think of what I needs must feel,
    But to be still and patient, all I can;
And haply by abstruse research to steal
        From my own nature all the natural man—   90
    This was my sole resource, my only plan:
Till that which suits a part infects the whole,
And now is almost grown the habit of my soul.

                              7

Hence, viper thoughts, that coil around my mind,
        Reality's dark dream!   95
I turn from you, and listen to the wind,
    Which long has raved unnoticed. What a scream
Of agony by torture lengthened out
That lute sent forth! Thou Wind, that rav'st without,
    Bare crag, or mountain tairn,[1] or blasted tree,   100
Or pine grove whither woodman never clomb,
Or lonely house, long held the witches' home,
    Methinks were fitter instruments for thee,
Mad lutanist! who in this month of showers,
Of dark-brown gardens, and of peeping flowers,   105
Mak'st devils' yule,[2] with worse than wintry song,
The blossoms, buds, and timorous leaves among.
    Thou actor, perfect in all tragic sounds!
Thou mighty poet, e'en to frenzy bold!
        What tell'st thou now about?   110
        'Tis of the rushing of an host in rout,
    With groans, of trampled men, with smarting wounds—
At once they groan with pain, and shudder with the cold!
But hush! there is a pause of deepest silence!
    And all that noise, as of a rushing crowd,   115
With groans, and tremulous shudderings—all is over—
    It tells another tale, with sounds less deep and loud!
        A tale of less affright,
        And tempered with delight,
As Otway's[3] self had framed the tender lay—   120
        'Tis of a little child
        Upon a lonesome wild,
Not far from home, but she hath lost her way:
And now moans low in bitter grief and fear,
And now screams loud, and hopes to make her mother hear.   125

1. Tarn, or mountain pool.
2. Christmas as, in a perverted form, it is celebrated by devils.
3. Thomas Otway (1652–1685), a dramatist noted

for the pathos of his tragic passages. The poet originally named was "William," and the allusion was
probably to Wordsworth's *Lucy Gray*.

8

'Tis midnight, but small thoughts have I of sleep:
Full seldom may my friend such vigils keep!
Visit her, gentle Sleep! with wings of healing,
    And may this storm be but a mountain birth,[4]
May all the stars hang bright above her dwelling,   130
    Silent as though they watched the sleeping Earth!
        With light heart may she rise,
        Gay fancy, cheerful eyes,
    Joy lift her spirit, joy attune her voice;
To her may all things live, from pole to pole,   135
Their life the eddying of her living soul!
    O simple spirit, guided from above,
Dear Lady! friend devoutest of my choice,
Thus mayest thou ever, evermore rejoice.

Apr. 4, 1802   1802, 1817

To William Wordsworth

Composed on the Night after His Recitation of a Poem on the Growth of an Individual Mind[1]

Friend of the wise! and teacher of the good!
Into my heart have I received that lay
More than historic, that prophetic lay
Wherein (high theme by thee first sung aright)
Of the foundations and the building up   5
Of a Human Spirit thou hast dared to tell
What may be told, to the understanding mind
Revealable; and what within the mind
By vital breathings secret as the soul
Of vernal growth, oft quickens in the heart   10
Thoughts all too deep for words![2]—

                                        Theme hard as high!
Of smiles spontaneous, and mysterious fears
(The first-born they of Reason and twin birth),
Of tides obedient to external force,
And currents self-determined, as might seem,   15

4. Probably, "May this be a typical mountain storm, short though violent," although it is possible that Coleridge intended an allusion to Horace's phrase, "The mountain labored and brought forth a mouse."
1. This was the poem (later called *The Prelude*) addressed to Coleridge, which Wordsworth had completed in 1805. After Coleridge returned from Malta, very low in health and spirits, Wordsworth read the poem aloud to him during the even-

ings of almost two weeks. Coleridge wrote most of the present response immediately after the reading was completed, on Jan. 7, 1807.
2. Wordsworth had described the effect on his mind of the animating breeze ("vital breathings") in *The Prelude*, 1.1–44. "Thoughts . . . words" echoes the last line of Wordsworth's *Intimations* ode. Coleridge goes on to summarize the major themes and events of *The Prelude*.

Or by some inner Power; of moments awful,
Now in thy inner life, and now abroad,
When power streamed from thee, and thy soul received
The light reflected, as a light bestowed—
Of fancies fair, and milder hours of youth,   20
Hyblean[3] murmurs of poetic thought
Industrious in its joy, in vales and glens
Native or outland, lakes and famous hills!
Or on the lonely high-road, when the stars
Were rising; or by secret mountain streams,   25
The guides and the companions of thy way!

Of more than Fancy, of the Social Sense
Distending wide, and man beloved as man,
Where France in all her towns lay vibrating
Like some becalmèd bark beneath the burst   30
Of Heaven's immediate thunder, when no cloud
Is visible, or shadow on the main.
For thou wert there, thine own brows garlanded,
Amid the tremor of a realm aglow,
Amid a mighty nation jubilant,   35
When from the general heart of human kind
Hope sprang forth like a full-born deity!
——Of that dear Hope afflicted and struck down,
So summoned homeward, thenceforth calm and sure
From the dread watchtower of man's absolute self,   40
With light unwaning on her eyes, to look
Far on—herself a glory to behold,
The Angel of the vision! Then (last strain)
Of Duty, chosen Laws controlling choice,
Action and joy!—An Orphic song[4] indeed,   45
A song divine of high and passionate thoughts
To their own music chaunted!

                         O great bard!
Ere yet that last strain dying awed the air,
With stedfast eye I viewed thee in the choir
Of ever-enduring men. The truly great   50
Have all one age, and from one visible space
Shed influence! They, both in power and act,
Are permanent, and Time is not with them,
Save as it worketh for them, they in it.
Nor less a sacred roll, than those of old,   55
And to be placed, as they, with gradual fame

---

3. Sweet; Hybla, in ancient Sicily, was famous for
its honey.
4. As enchanting and oracular as the song of the
legendary Orpheus. There may also be an allusion
to the Orphic mysteries, involving spiritual death
and rebirth; see lines 61–66. "The Angel of the
vision" (line 43) probably alludes to "the great vision
of the guarded mount" in Milton's *Lycidas*, line
161.

Among the archives of mankind, thy work
Makes audible a linkèd lay of Truth,
Of Truth profound a sweet continuous lay,
Not learnt, but native, her own natural notes!   60
Ah! as I listened with a heart forlorn,
The pulses of my being beat anew:
And even as Life returns upon the drowned,[5]
Life's joy rekindling roused a throng of pains—
Keen pangs of Love, awakening as a babe   65
Turbulent, with an outcry in the heart;
And fears self-willed, that shunned the eye of Hope;
And Hope that scarce would know itself from Fear;
Sense of past Youth, and Manhood come in vain,
And Genius given, and Knowledge won in vain;   70
And all which I had culled in wood-walks wild,
And all which patient toil had reared, and all,
Commune with thee had opened out—but flowers
Strewed on my corse, and borne upon my bier,
In the same coffin, for the self-same grave!   75

That way no more! and ill beseems it me,
Who came a welcomer in herald's guise,
Singing of Glory, and Futurity,
To wander back on such unhealthful road,
Plucking the poisons of self-harm! And ill   80
Such intertwine beseems triumphal wreaths
Strewed before thy advancing!

                          Nor do thou,
Sage bard! impair the memory of that hour
Of thy communion with my nobler mind[6]
By pity or grief, already felt too long!   85
Nor let my words import more blame than needs.
The tumult rose and ceased: for Peace is nigh
Where Wisdom's voice has found a listening heart.
Amid the howl of more than wintry storms,
The Halcyon[7] hears the voice of vernal hours   90
Already on the wing.

                 Eve following eve,[8]
Dear tranquil time, when the sweet sense of Home
Is sweetest! moments for their own sake hailed
And more desired, more precious, for thy song,
In silence listening, like a devout child,   95
My soul lay passive, by thy various strain

---

5. A death-in-life is also described in, e.g., *Dejection* and *Epitaph*.
6. I.e., during the early association between the two poets (1797–98).
7. A fabled bird, able to calm the sea, where it nested in winter.
8. The evenings during which Wordsworth read his poem aloud.

Driven as in surges now beneath the stars,
With momentary stars of my own birth,
Fair constellated foam, still darting off
Into the darkness; now a tranquil sea,   100
Outspread and bright, yet swelling to the moon.

And when—O friend! my comforter and guide!
Strong in thyself, and powerful to give strength!—
Thy long sustainèd song finally closed,
And thy deep voice had ceased—yet thou thyself   105
Wert still before my eyes, and round us both
That happy vision of belovèd faces—
Scarce conscious, and yet conscious of its close
I sate, my being blended in one thought
(Thought was it? or aspiration? or resolve?)   110
Absorbed, yet hanging still upon the sound—
And when I rose, I found myself in prayer.

1807   1817

Recollections of Love

1

How warm this woodland wild recess!
    Love surely hath been breathing here;
    And this sweet bed of heath, my dear!
Swells up, then sinks with faint caress,
    As if to have you yet more near.   5

2

Eight springs have flown since last I lay
    On seaward Quantock's heathy hills,[1]
    Where quiet sounds from hidden rills
Float here and there, like things astray,
    And high o'erhead the sky-lark shrills.   10

3

No voice as yet had made the air
    Be music with your name; yet why
    That asking look? that yearning sigh?
That sense of promise every where?
    Belovèd! flew your spirit by?   15

4

As when a mother doth explore
    The rose mark on her long-lost child,
    I met, I loved you, maiden mild!
As whom I long had loved before—
    So deeply had I been beguiled.   20

1. Near Nether Stowey, Somerset, where Coleridge had lived 1796–98.

5

You stood before me like a thought,
   A dream remembered in a dream.
   But when those meek eyes first did seem
To tell me, Love within you wrought—
   O Greta,[2] dear domestic stream!   25

6

Has not, since then, Love's prompture deep,
   Has not Love's whisper evermore
   Been ceaseless, as thy gentle roar?
Sole voice, when other voices sleep,
   Dear under-song in clamor's hour.   30

ca. 1807   1817

On Donne's Poetry[1]

With Donne, whose muse on dromedary[2] trots,
Wreathe iron pokers into true-love knots;
Rhyme's sturdy cripple, fancy's maze and clue,
Wit's forge and fire-blast, meaning's press and screw.

ca. 1818   1836

Work without Hope

Lines Composed 21st February 1825

All Nature seems at work. Slugs leave their lair—
The bees are stirring—birds are on the wing—
And Winter slumbering in the open air,
Wears on his smiling face a dream of Spring!
And I the while, the sole unbusy thing,   5
Nor honey make, nor pair, nor build, nor sing.

Yet well I ken the banks where amaranths[1] blow,
Have traced the fount whence streams of nectar flow.
Bloom, O ye amaranths! bloom for whom ye may,
For me ye bloom not! Glide, rich streams, away!   10
With lips unbrightened, wreathless brow, I stroll:
And would you learn the spells that drowse my soul?
Work without Hope draws nectar in a sieve,
And Hope without an object cannot live.

1825   1828

2. The river Greta, which flowed past Coleridge's home in Keswick, in the Lake Country.

1. Donne as a poet had been in eclipse for most of the 18th century. This terse and penetrating comment shows the Romantic poet's great, though ironically qualified, respect for the master of the metaphysical style.

2. The one-humped Arabian camel, trained for riding.

1. Mythical flowers that bloom perpetually.

Epitaph[1]

Stop, Christian passer-by!—Stop, child of God,
And read with gentle breast. Beneath this sod
A poet lies, or that which once seemed he.
O, lift one thought in prayer for S. T. C.;
That he who many a year with toil of breath   5
Found death in life, may here find life in death!
Mercy for praise—to be forgiven for[2] fame
He asked, and hoped, through Christ. Do thou the same!

1833   1834

Biographia Literaria

Biographia Literaria   In March 1815 Coleridge was preparing a collected edition of his poems, and planned to include "a general preface . . . on the principles of philosophic and genial criticism." Characteristically, the materials developed as Coleridge worked on them until, on July 29, he declared that the preface had been extended into a complete work, "an Autobiographia Literaria"; it was to consist of two main parts, "my literary life and opinions, as far as poetry and *poetical* criticism [are] concerned," and a critique of Wordsworth's theory of poetic diction. This work was ready by September 17, 1815, but the *Biographia Literaria*, in two volumes, was not published until July 1817. The delay was caused by a series of miscalculations by his printer, which forced Coleridge to add miscellaneous materials needed to eke out the length of his original manuscript.

The critique of Wordsworth's theory of diction, which Coleridge had been planning ever since 1802, when he had detected "a radical difference in our theoretical opinions respecting poetry," is long, detailed, and subtly reasoned. In the selection from chapter 17, below, Coleridge agrees with Wordsworth's general aim of reforming the artifices of modern poetic diction, but he sharply denies Wordsworth's claim that there is no essential difference between the language of poetry and the language really spoken by men. The other selections printed here are devoted mainly to the central principle of Coleridge's own critical theory, the distinction between the mechanical "fancy" and the organic "imagination." Thus the biographical section of the *Biographia* (chapters 1 and 4), dealing with the development of his poetic taste and theory, describes his gradual realization, climaxed by his first exposure to Wordsworth's poetry, "that fancy and imagination were two distinct and widely different faculties." The conclusion to chapter 13 tersely summarizes this distinction, and the definition of poetry, at the end of chapter 14, develops at somewhat greater length the nature of the process and products of the "synthetic and magical power . . . of imagination." These cryptic paragraphs have proved to be the most widely discussed, disputed, and influential passages ever written by an English critic.

---

1. Written by Coleridge the year before he died. One version that he sent in a letter had as title: "Epitaph on a Poet little known, yet better known by the Initials of his name than by the Name Itself."

2. " 'For' in the sense of 'instead of' " [Coleridge's note].

From Biographia Literaria

From Chapter 1
[The discipline of his taste at school][1]

At school I enjoyed the inestimable advantage of a very sensible, though at the same time a very severe master. He[2] early molded my taste to the preference of Demosthenes to Cicero, of Homer and Theocritus to Virgil, and again of Virgil to Ovid. He habituated me to compare Lucretius (in such extracts as I then read), Terence, and, above all, the chaster poems of Catullus not only with the Roman poets of the so-called silver and brazen ages but with even those of the Augustan era; and, on grounds of plain sense and universal logic, to see and assert the superiority of the former in the truth and nativeness both of their thoughts and diction. At the same time that we were studying the Greek tragic poets, he made us read Shakespeare and Milton as lessons; and they were the lessons, too, which required most time and trouble to *bring up*, so as to escape his censure. I learnt from him that poetry, even that of the loftiest and, seemingly, that of the wildest odes, had a logic of its own as severe as that of science; and more difficult, because more subtle, more complex, and dependent on more, and more fugitive, causes. In the truly great poets, he would say, there is a reason assignable, not only for every word, but for the position of every word; and I well remember that, availing himself of the synonyms to the Homer of Didymus,[3] he made us attempt to show, with regard to each, *why* it would not have answered the same purpose, and *wherein* consisted the peculiar fitness of the word in the original text.

In our own English compositions (at least for the last three years of our school education) he showed no mercy to phrase, metaphor, or image unsupported by a sound sense, or where the same sense might have been conveyed with equal force and dignity in plainer words. Lute, harp, and lyre, muse, muses, and inspirations, Pegasus, Parnassus, and Hippocrene were all an abomination to him. In fancy I can almost hear him now, exclaiming, "Harp? Harp? Lyre? Pen and ink, boy, you mean! Muse, boy, muse? Your nurse's daughter, you mean! Pierian spring? Oh, aye! the cloister pump, I suppose!" Nay, certain introductions, similes, and examples were placed by name on a list of interdiction. Among the similes there was, I remember, that of the manchineel fruit,[4] as suiting equally well with too many subjects, in which, however, it yielded the palm at once to the example of Alexander and Clytus,[5] which was equally good and apt whatever might be the theme. Was it ambition?

---

1. Coleridge heads each chapter of the *Biographia* with a list of topics. In instances where we excerpt from chapters, we introduce these headings in brackets before the relevant selection.
2. "The Rev. James Bowyer, many years Head Master of the Grammar School, Christ's Hospital" [Coleridge's note].
3. Didymus of Alexandria (ca. 65 B.C.–A.D. 10) was the author of a commentary on the text of Homer.
4. Poisonous, though attractive in appearance.
5. Plutarch's *Life* of Alexander the Great relates that the king killed his friend Clytus in a drunken quarrel.

Alexander and Clytus! Flattery? Alexander and Clytus! Anger? Drunkenness? Pride? Friendship? Ingratitude? Late repentance? Still, still Alexander and Clytus! At length, the praises of agriculture having been exemplified in the sagacious observation that, had Alexander been holding the plow, he would not have run his friend Clytus through with a spear, this tried and serviceable old friend was banished by public edict in *secula seculorum*.[6] I have sometimes ventured to think that a list of this kind or an *index expurgatorius*[7] of certain well-known and ever returning phrases, both introductory and transitional, including the large assortment of modest egoisms and flattering illeisms,[8] etc., etc., might be hung up in our law courts and both Houses of Parliament with great advantage to the public as an important saving of national time, an incalculable relief to his Majesty's ministers; but, above all, as insuring the thanks of country attorneys and their clients, who have private bills to carry through the House.

Be this as it may, there was one custom of our master's which I cannot pass over in silence, because I think it imitable and worthy of imitation. He would often permit our theme exercises, under some pretext of want of time, to accumulate till each lad had four or five to be looked over. Then placing the whole number *abreast* on his desk, he would ask the writer why this or that sentence might not have found as appropriate a place under this or that other thesis; and if no satisfying answer could be returned and two faults of the same kind were found in one exercise, the irrevocable verdict followed, the exercise was torn up, and another on the same subject to be produced, in addition to the tasks of the day. The reader will, I trust, excuse this tribute of recollection to a man whose severities, even now, not seldom furnish the dreams by which the blind fancy would fain interpret to the mind the painful sensations of distempered sleep; but neither lessen nor dim the deep sense of my moral and intellectual obligations. He sent us to the university excellent Latin and Greek scholars and tolerable Hebraists. Yet our classical knowledge was the least of the good gifts which we derived from his zealous and conscientious tutorage. He is now gone to his final reward, full of years and full of honors, even of those honors which were dearest to his heart as gratefully bestowed by that school, and still binding him to the interests of that school, in which he had been himself educated and to which during his whole life he was a dedicated thing. * * *

[Bowles's sonnets]

I had just entered on my seventeenth year, when the sonnets of Mr. Bowles,[9] twenty in number, and just then published in a quarto pamphlet, were first made known and presented to me by a schoolfellow

6. Forever ("for centuries of centuries").
7. Index of things to be deleted.
8. Excessive use of the pronoun "he" (in Latin, *ille*).

9. William Lisle Bowles (1762–1850) published in 1789 two editions of a collection of sonnets setting forth the meditations evoked from a traveler by the changing scene.

who had quitted us for the university and who, during the whole time that he was in our first form (or in our school language, a Grecian),[1] had been my patron and protector. I refer to Dr. Middleton, the truly learned and every way excellent Bishop of Calcutta. * * *

It was a double pleasure to me, and still remains a tender recollection, that I should have received from a friend so revered the first knowledge of a poet by whose works, year after year, I was so enthusiastically delighted and inspired. My earliest acquaintances will not have forgotten the undisciplined eagerness and impetuous zeal with which I laboured to make proselytes, not only of my companions, but of all with whom I conversed, of whatever rank and in whatever place. As my school finances did not permit me to purchase copies, I made, within less than a year and a half, more than forty transcriptions, as the best presents I could offer to those who had in any way won my regard. And with almost equal delight did I receive the three or four following publications of the same author.

Though I have seen and known enough of mankind to be well aware that I shall perhaps stand alone in my creed, and that it will be well if I subject myself to no worse charge than that of singularity, I am not therefore deterred from avowing that I regard and ever have regarded the obligations of intellect among the most sacred of the claims of gratitude. A valuable thought, or a particular train of thoughts, gives me additional pleasure when I can safely refer and attribute it to the conversation or correspondence of another. My obligations to Mr. Bowles were indeed important and for radical good. At a very premature age, even before my fifteenth year, I had bewildered myself in metaphysics and in theological controversy. Nothing else pleased me. History and particular facts lost all interest in my mind. Poetry (though for a schoolboy of that age I was above par in English versification and had already produced two or three compositions which, I may venture to say without reference to my age, were somewhat above mediocrity, and which had gained me more credit than the sound good sense of my old master was at all pleased with), poetry itself, yea novels and romances, became insipid to me. In my friendless wanderings on our leave-days (for I was an orphan, and had scarce any connections in London), highly was I delighted if any passenger, especially if he were dressed in black,[2] would enter into conversation with me. For I soon found the means of directing it to my favorite subjects

> Of providence, fore-knowledge, will, and fate,
> Fixed fate, free will, fore-knowledge absolute,
> And found no end, in wandering mazes lost.[3]

This preposterous pursuit was, beyond doubt, injurious both to my natural powers and to the progress of my education. It would perhaps have been destructive had it been continued; but from this I was auspiciously

---

1. Gifted students in the final class at Christ's Hospital who were being prepared for a university.
2. I.e., if he were a clergyman.
3. *Paradise Lost* 2.559–61.

withdrawn, partly indeed by an accidental introduction to an amiable family,[4] chiefly however by the genial influence of a style of poetry so tender and yet so manly, so natural and real, and yet so dignified and harmonious, as the sonnets, etc., of Mr. Bowles! Well were it for me, perhaps, had I never relapsed into the same mental disease; if I had continued to pluck the flower and reap the harvest from the cultivated surface, instead of delving in the unwholesome quicksilver mines of metaphysic depths. But if in after time I have sought a refuge from bodily pain and mismanaged sensibility in abstruse researches, which exercised the strength and subtlety of the understanding without awakening the feelings of the heart; still there was a long and blessed interval, during which my natural faculties were allowed to expand and my original tendencies to develop themselves: my fancy, and the love of nature, and the sense of beauty in forms and sounds.

[Comparison between the poets before and since Mr. Pope]

The second advantage which I owe to my early perusal and admiration of these poems (to which let me add, though known to me at a somewhat later period, the *Lewesdon Hill* of Mr. Crow)[5] bears more immediately on my present subject. Among those with whom I conversed there were, of course, very many who had formed their taste and their notions of poetry from the writings of Mr. Pope and his followers: or to speak more generally, in that school of French poetry condensed and invigorated by English understanding which had predominated from the last century. I was not blind to the merits of this school, yet as from inexperience of the world and consequent want of sympathy with the general subjects of these poems they gave me little pleasure, I doubtless undervalued the *kind*, and with the presumption of youth withheld from its masters the legitimate name of poets. I saw that the excellence of this kind consisted in just and acute observations on men and manners in an artificial state of society as its matter and substance, and in the logic of wit conveyed in smooth and strong epigrammatic couplets as its *form*. Even when the subject was addressed to the fancy or the intellect, as in the *Rape of the Lock* or the *Essay on Man*; nay, when it was a consecutive narration, as in that astonishing product of matchless talent and ingenuity, Pope's translation of the *Iliad*; still a *point* was looked for at the end of each second line, and the whole was as it were a sorites or, if I may exchange a logical for a grammatical metaphor, a *conjunction disjunctive*,[6] of epigrams. Meantime the matter and diction seemed to me characterized not so much by poetic thoughts as by thoughts *translated* into the language of poetry. On this last point I had occasion to

4. The family of Mary Evans, with whom Coleridge fell in love in 1788.
5. William Crow(e) (1745–1829) published in 1788 *Lewesdon Hill*, a long poem in blank verse which, like Bowles's sonnets, combined descriptions of the natural scene with associated moral and personal reflections.
6. A word which connects the parts of a sentence but expresses an alternative or opposition: "or," "but," "lest," etc. "Sorites": a sequence of interconnected syllogisms.

render my own thoughts gradually more and more plain to myself by frequent amicable disputes concerning Darwin's *Botanic Garden*,[7] which for some years was greatly extolled, not only by the *reading* public in general, but even by those whose genius and natural robustness of understanding enabled them afterwards to act foremost in dissipating these "painted mists" that occasionally rise from the marshes at the foot of Parnassus. During my first Cambridge vacation I assisted a friend in a contribution for a literary society in Devonshire, and in this I remember to have compared Darwin's work to the Russian palace of ice, glittering, cold, and transitory. In the same essay too I assigned sundry reasons, chiefly drawn from a comparison of passages in the Latin poets with the original Greek from which they were borrowed, for the preference of Collins's odes to those of Gray, and of the simile in Shakespeare:

> How like a younker or a prodigal
> The scarfed bark puts from her native bay,
> Hugged and embraced by the strumpet wind!
> How like the prodigal doth she return,
> With over-weathered ribs and ragged sails,
> Lean, rent and beggared by the strumpet wind![8]

to the imitation in the *Bard:*

> Fair laughs the morn, and soft the zephyr blows
> While proudly riding o'er the azure realm
> In gallant trim the gilded vessel goes;
> YOUTH on the prow, and PLEASURE at the helm;
> Regardless of the sweeping whirlwind's sway,
> That, hushed in grim repose, expects its evening prey.[9]

(In which, by the bye, the words "realm" and "sway" are rhymes dearly purchased.) I preferred the original, on the ground that in the imitation it depended wholly in the compositor's putting, or not putting, a small capital both in this and in many other passages of the same poet whether the words should be personifications or mere abstracts. I mention this because, in referring various lines in Gray to their original in Shakespeare and Milton, and in the clear perception how completely all the propriety was lost in the transfer, I was at that early period led to a conjecture which, many years afterwards, was recalled to me from the same thought having been started in conversation, but far more ably, and developed more fully, by Mr. Wordsworth; namely, that this style of poetry which I have characterized above as translations of prose thoughts into poetic language had been kept up by, if it did not wholly arise from, the custom of writing Latin verses and the great importance attached to these exercises in our public schools. Whatever might have been the case in the fifteenth century, when the use of the Latin tongue was so

7. Published in 1789–91 by Erasmus Darwin (1731–1802); a long poem in closed couplets, presenting the science of botany in elaborate allegories.
8. *Merchant of Venice* 2.6.14–19.
9. Thomas Gray, *The Bard* (1757).

general among learned men that Erasmus is said to have forgotten his native language; yet in the present day it is not to be supposed that a youth can think in Latin, or that he can have any other reliance on the force or fitness of his phrases but the authority of the author from whence he had adopted them. Consequently he must first prepare his thoughts and then pick out from Virgil, Horace, Ovid, or perhaps more compendiously, from his *Gradus*,[1] halves and quarters of lines in which to embody them.

I never object to a certain degree of disputatiousness in a young man from the age of seventeen to that of four or five and twenty, provided I find him always arguing on one side of the question. The controversies occasioned by my unfeigned zeal for the honor of a favorite contemporary, then known to me only by his works, were of great advantage in the formation and establishment of my taste and critical opinions. In my defense of the lines running into each other instead of closing at each couplet, and of natural language, neither bookish nor vulgar, neither redolent of the lamp nor of the kennel, such as *I will remember thee*; instead of the same thought tricked up in the rag-fair finery of

> ———Thy image on her wing
> Before my FANCY'S eye shall MEMORY bring,

I had continually to adduce the meter and diction of the Greek poets from Homer to Theocritus inclusive; and still more of our elder English poets from Chaucer to Milton. Nor was this all. But as it was my constant reply to authorities brought against me from later poets of great name that no authority could avail in opposition to Truth, Nature, Logic, and the Laws of Universal Grammar; actuated too by my former passion for metaphysical investigations, I labored at a solid foundation on which permanently to ground my opinions in the component faculties of the human mind itself and their comparative dignity and importance. According to the faculty or source from which the pleasure given by any poem or passage was derived I estimated the merit of such poem or passage. As the result of all my reading and meditation, I abstracted two critical aphorisms, deeming them to comprise the conditions and criteria of poetic style: first, that not the poem which we have *read*, but that to which we *return* with the greatest pleasure, possesses the genuine power and claims the name of *essential* poetry. Second, that whatever lines can be translated into other words of the same language without diminution of their significance, either in sense of association or in any worthy feeling, are so far vicious in their diction. Be it however observed that I excluded from the list of worthy feelings the pleasure derived from mere novelty in the reader, and the desire of exciting wonderment at his powers in the author. Oftentimes since then, in perusing French tragedies, I have fancied two marks of admiration at the end of each line, as

---

1. *Gradus ad Parnassum* ("Stairway to Parnassus"), a dictionary of Latin words, synonyms, and descriptive epithets, illustrated from the Latin poets. It was long used as a school text in Latin composition.

hieroglyphics of the author's own admiration at his own cleverness. Our genuine admiration of a great poet is a continuous undercurrent of feeling; it is everywhere present, but seldom anywhere as a separate excitement. I was wont boldly to affirm that it would be scarcely more difficult to push a stone out from the pyramids with the bare hand than to alter a word, or the position of a word, in Milton or Shakespeare (in their most important works at least), without making the author say something else, or something worse, than he does say. One great distinction I appeared to myself to see plainly, between even the characteristic faults of our elder poets and the false beauties of the moderns. In the former, from Donne to Cowley, we find the most fantastic out-of-the-way thoughts, but in the most pure and genuine mother English; in the latter, the most obvious thoughts, in language the most fantastic and arbitrary. Our faulty elder poets sacrificed the passion and passionate flow of poetry to the subtleties of intellect and to the starts of wit; the moderns to the glare and glitter of a perpetual yet broken and heterogeneous imagery, or rather to an amphibious something, made up half of image and half of abstract[2] meaning. The one sacrificed the heart to the head, the other both heart and head to point and drapery. * * *

From *Chapter 4*
[*Mr. Wordsworth's earlier poems*]

* * * During the last year of my residence at Cambridge, I became acquainted with Mr. Wordsworth's first publication, entitled *Descriptive Sketches*;[3] and seldom, if ever, was the emergence of an original poetic genius above the literary horizon more evidently announced. In the form, style, and manner of the whole poem, and in the structure of the particular lines and periods, there is a harshness and acerbity connected and combined with words and images all a-glow which might recall those products of the vegetable world, where gorgeous blossoms rise out of the hard and thorny rind and shell within which the rich fruit was elaborating. The language was not only peculiar and strong, but at times knotty and contorted, as by its own impatient strength; while the novelty and struggling crowd of images, acting in conjunction with the difficulties of the style, demanded always a greater closeness of attention than poetry (at all events than descriptive poetry) has a right to claim. It not seldom therefore justified the complaint of obscurity. In the following extract I have sometimes fancied that I saw an emblem of the poem itself and of the author's genius as it was then displayed:

> 'Tis storm; and hid in mist from hour to hour,
> All day the floods a deepening murmur pour;

---

2. "I remember a ludicrous instance in the poem of a young tradesman: 'No more will I endure Love's pleasing pain, / Or round my *heart's leg* tie his galling chain' " [Coleridge's note].
3. Published 1793, the year before Coleridge left Cambridge; a long descriptive-meditative poem in closed couplets, recounting Wordsworth's walking tour in the Alps in 1790. Wordsworth describes the same tour in *The Prelude*, book 6.

The sky is veiled, and every cheerful sight:
Dark is the region as with coming night;
And yet what frequent bursts of overpowering light!
Triumphant on the bosom of the storm,
Glances the fire-clad eagle's wheeling form;
Eastward, in long perspective glittering, shine
The wood-crowned cliffs that o'er the lake recline;
Wide o'er the Alps a hundred streams unfold,
At once to pillars turned that flame with gold;
Behind his sail the peasant strives to shun
The West, that burns like one dilated sun,
Where in a mighty crucible expire
The mountains, glowing hot, like coals of fire.[4]

The poetic Psyche, in its process to full development, undergoes as many changes as its Greek namesake, the butterfly.[5] And it is remarkable how soon genius clears and purifies itself from the faults and errors of its earliest products; faults which, in its earliest compositions, are the more obtrusive and confluent because, as heterogeneous elements which had only a temporary use, they constitute the very *ferment* by which themselves are carried off. Or we may compare them to some diseases, which must work on the humors and be thrown out on the surface in order to secure the patient from their future recurrence. I was in my twenty-fourth year when I had the happiness of knowing Mr. Wordsworth personally;[6] and, while memory lasts, I shall hardly forget the sudden effect produced on my mind by his recitation of a manuscript poem which still remains unpublished, but of which the stanza and tone of style were the same as those of *The Female Vagrant* as originally printed in the first volume of the *Lyrical Ballads*.[7] There was here no mark of strained thought or forced diction, no crowd or turbulence of imagery, and, as the poet hath himself well described in his lines on revisiting the Wye, manly reflection and human associations had given both variety and an additional interest to natural objects which in the passion and appetite of the first love they had seemed to him neither to need or permit.[8] The occasional obscurities, which had risen from an imperfect control over the resources of his native language, had almost wholly disappeared, together with that worse defect of arbitrary and illogical phrases, at once hackneyed and fantastic, which hold so distinguished a place in the *technique* of ordinary poetry and will, more or less, alloy the earlier poems of the truest genius, unless the attention has been specifically directed to their worthlessness and incongruity. I did not perceive anything particular in the mere style of the poem alluded to during its recitation, except indeed such difference as was not separable from the thought and

4. *Descriptive Sketches* (1815 version), lines 332 ff.
5. "In Greek, Psyche is the common name for the soul and the butterfly" [Coleridge's note].
6. The meeting occurred in September 1795.
7. *Salisbury Plain* (1793–94), which was left in manuscript until Wordsworth published a revised version in 1842 under the title *Guilt and Sorrow*. An excerpt from *Salisbury Plain* was printed as *The Female Vagrant*, in *Lyrical Ballads* (1798).
8. Wordsworth's *Tintern Abbey*, lines 76 ff.

manner; and the Spenserian stanza which always, more or less, recalls to the reader's mind Spenser's own style, would doubtless have authorized in my then opinion a more frequent descent to the phrases of ordinary life than could, without an ill effect, have been hazarded in the heroic couplet. It was not however the freedom from false taste, whether as to common defects or to those more properly his own, which made so unusual an impression on my feelings immediately, and subsequently on my judgment. It was the union of deep feeling with profound thought; the fine balance of truth in observing with the imaginative faculty in modifying the objects observed; and above all the original gift of spreading the tone, the *atmosphere*, and with it the depth and height of the ideal world, around forms, incidents, and situations of which, for the common view, custom had bedimmed all the luster, had dried up the sparkle and the dewdrops. "To find no contradiction in the union of old and new, to contemplate the Ancient of Days and all his works with feelings as fresh as if all had then sprang forth at the first creative fiat, characterizes the mind that feels the riddle of the world and may help to unravel it. To carry on the feelings of childhood into the powers of manhood; to combine the child's sense of wonder and novelty with the appearances which every day for perhaps forty years had rendered familiar;

> With sun and moon and stars throughout the year,
> And man and woman;[9]

this is the character and privilege of genius, and one of the marks which distinguish genius from talents. And therefore it is the prime merit of genius, and its most unequivocal mode of manifestation, so to represent familiar objects as to awaken in the minds of others a kindred feeling concerning them, and that freshness of sensation which is the constant accompaniment of mental no less than of bodily convalescence. Who has not a thousand times seen snow fall on water? Who has not watched it with a new feeling from the time that he has read Burns' comparison of sensual pleasure

> To snow that falls upon a river
> A moment white—then gone forever![1]

In poems, equally as in philosophic disquisitions, genius produces the strongest impressions of novelty while it rescues the most admitted truths from the impotence caused by the very circumstance of their universal admission. Truths of all others the most awful and mysterious, yet being at the same time of universal interest, are too often considered as *so* true, that they lose all the life and efficiency of truth and lie bedridden in the dormitory of the soul side by side with the most despised and exploded errors." *The Friend*, p. 76, no. 5.[2]

9. Altered from Milton's sonnet *To Mr. Cyriack Skinner upon His Blindness.*
1. Altered from Burns, *Tam o' Shanter*, lines 61–62.
2. *The Friend* was a periodical published by Coleridge (1809–10).

[*On fancy and imagination—The investigation of the distinction
important to the fine arts*]

This excellence, which in all Mr. Wordsworth's writings is more or
less predominant and which constitutes the character of his mind, I no
sooner felt than I sought to understand. Repeated meditations led me
first to suspect (and a more intimate analysis of the human faculties,
their appropriate marks, functions, and effects, matured my conjecture
into full conviction) that fancy and imagination were two distinct and
widely different faculties, instead of being, according to the general belief,
either two names with one meaning, or at furthest the lower and higher
degree of one and the same power. It is not, I own, easy to conceive a
more apposite translation of the Greek *phantasia* than the Latin *imagi-
natio*; but it is equally true that in all societies there exists an instinct of
growth, a certain collective unconscious good sense working progressively to desynonymize those words originally of the same meaning which
the conflux of dialects had supplied to the more homogeneous languages, as the Greek and German: and which the same cause, joined
with accidents of translation from original works of different countries,
occasion in mixed languages like our own. The first and most important
point to be proved is, that two conceptions perfectly distinct are confused
under one and the same word, and (this done) to appropriate that word
exclusively to one meaning, and the synonym (should there be one) to
the other. But if (as will be often the case in the arts and sciences) no
synonym exists, we must either invent or borrow a word. In the present
instance the appropriation had already begun and been legitimated in
the derivative adjective: Milton had a highly *imaginative*, Cowley a very
fanciful, mind. If therefore I should succeed in establishing the actual
existence of two faculties generally different, the nomenclature would
be at once determined. To the faculty by which I had characterized
Milton we should confine the term *imagination*; while the other would
be contra-distinguished as *fancy*. Now were it once fully ascertained that
this division is no less grounded in nature than that of delirium from
mania, or Otway's

Lutes, lobsters, seas of milk, and ships of amber,[3]

from Shakespeare's

What! have his daughters brought him to this pass?[4]

or from the preceding apostrophe to the elements, the theory of the fine
arts and of poetry in particular could not, I thought, but derive some
additional and important light. It would in its immediate effects furnish
a torch of guidance to the philosophical critic, and ultimately to the poet
himself. In energetic minds truth soon changes by domestication into
power; and from directing in the discrimination and appraisal of the

3. Thomas Otway, in *Venice Preserved* (1682),   4. *King Lear* 3.4.63.
wrote "laurels" in place of "lobsters" (5.2.151).

product becomes influencive in the production. To admire on principle is the only way to imitate without loss of originality. * * *

From *Chapter 13*
[*On the imagination, or esemplastic[5] power*]

* * * The IMAGINATION, then, I consider either as primary, or secondary. The primary IMAGINATION I hold to be the living power and prime agent of all human perception, and as a repetition in the finite mind of the eternal act of creation in the infinite I AM. The secondary I consider as an echo of the former, coexisting with the conscious will, yet still as identical with the primary in the *kind* of its agency, and differing only in *degree*, and in the *mode* of its operation. It dissolves, diffuses, dissipates, in order to recreate; or where this process is rendered impossible, yet still, at all events, it struggles to idealize and to unify. It is essentially *vital*, even as all objects (*as* objects) are essentially fixed and dead.

FANCY, on the contrary, has no other counters to play with but fixities and definites. The fancy is indeed no other than a mode of memory emancipated from the order of time and space; and blended with, and modified by that empirical phenomenon of the will which we express by the word CHOICE. But equally with the ordinary memory it must receive all its materials ready made from the law of association.[6] * * *

Chapter 14
Occasion of the Lyrical Ballads, and the objects originally proposed—Preface to the second edition—The ensuing controversy, its causes and acrimony—Philosophic definitions of a poem and poetry with scholia.[7]

During the first year that Mr. Wordsworth and I were neighbours,[8] our conversations turned frequently on the two cardinal points of poetry, the power of exciting the sympathy of the reader by a faithful adherence to the truth of nature, and the power of giving the interest of novelty by the modifying colors of imagination.[9] The sudden charm which accidents of light and shade, which moonlight or sunset diffused over a known and familiar landscape, appeared to represent the practicability of combining both. These are the poetry of nature. The thought suggested itself

5. Coleridge coined this word and used it to mean "molding into unity."

6. Coleridge conceives God's creation to be a continuing process, which has an analogy in the creative perception ("primary imagination") of all human minds. The creative process is repeated, or "echoed," on still a third level, by the "secondary imagination" of the poet, which dissolves the products of primary perception in order to shape them into a new and unified creation—the imaginative passage or poem. The "fancy," on the other hand, can only manipulate "fixities and definites" which, linked by association, come to it ready-made from perception. Its products, therefore, are not re-creations (echoes of God's original creative process), but mosaic-like reassemblies of existing bits and pieces.

7. Additional remarks, after a philosophic demonstration.

8. At Nether Stowey and Alfoxden, Somerset, in 1797.

9. Cf. Wordsworth's account in his Preface to *Lyrical Ballads*, above.

(to which of us I do not recollect) that a series of poems might be composed of two sorts. In the one, the incidents and agents were to be, in part at least, supernatural; and the excellence aimed at was to consist in the interesting of the affections by the dramatic truth of such emotions as would naturally accompany such situations, supposing them real. And real in *this* sense they have been to every human being who, from whatever source of delusion, has at any time believed himself under supernatural agency. For the second class, subjects were to be chosen from ordinary life; the characters and incidents were to be such as will be found in every village and its vicinity where there is a meditative and feeling mind to seek after them, or to notice them when they present themselves.

In this idea originated the plan of the *Lyrical Ballads*; in which it was agreed that my endeavours should be directed to persons and characters supernatural, or at least romantic; yet so as to transfer from our inward nature a human interest and a semblance of truth sufficient to procure for these shadows of imagination that willing suspension of disbelief for the moment, which constitutes poetic faith. Mr. Wordsworth, on the other hand, was to propose to himself as his object to give the charm of novelty to things of every day, and to excite a feeling analogous to the supernatural, by awakening the mind's attention from the lethargy of custom and directing it to the loveliness and the wonders of the world before us; an inexhaustible treasure, but for which, in consequence of the film of familiarity and selfish solicitude, we have eyes yet see not, ears that hear not, and hearts that neither feel nor understand.[1]

With this view I wrote *The Ancient Mariner*, and was preparing, among other poems, *The Dark Ladie*, and the *Christabel*, in which I should have more nearly realized my ideal than I had done in my first attempt. But Mr. Wordsworth's industry had proved so much more successful and the number of his poems so much greater, that my compositions, instead of forming a balance, appeared rather an interpolation of heterogeneous matter.[2] Mr. Wordsworth added two or three poems written in his own character, in the impassioned, lofty, and sustained diction which is characteristic of his genius. In this form the *Lyrical Ballads* were published; and were presented by him, as an *experiment*,[3] whether subjects which from their nature rejected the usual ornaments and extra-colloquial style of poems in general might not be so managed in the language of ordinary life as to produce the pleasurable interest which it is the peculiar business of poetry to impart. To the second edition[4] he added a preface of considerable length; in which, notwithstanding some passages of apparently a contrary import, he was understood to contend for the extension of this style to poetry of all kinds, and to reject as vicious and indefensible all phrases and forms of style that were not

---

1. Cf. Isaiah 6.9–10.
2. The first edition of *Lyrical Ballads*, published anonymously in 1798, contained 19 poems by Wordsworth, 4 by Coleridge.
3. "Experiments" was the word used by Wordsworth in his "Advertisement" to the first edition.
4. Of 1800.

included in what he (unfortunately, I think, adopting an equivocal expression) called the language of *real* life. From this preface, prefixed to poems in which it was impossible to deny the presence of original genius, however mistaken its direction might be deemed, arose the whole long-continued controversy.[5] For from the conjunction of perceived power with supposed heresy I explain the inveteracy and in some instances, I grieve to say, the acrimonious passions with which the controversy has been conducted by the assailants.

Had Mr. Wordsworth's poems been the silly, the childish things which they were for a long time described as being; had they been really distinguished from the compositions of other poets merely by meanness of language and inanity of thought; had they indeed contained nothing more than what is found in the parodies and pretended imitations of them; they must have sunk at once, a dead weight, into the slough of oblivion, and have dragged the preface along with them. But year after year increased the number of Mr. Wordsworth's admirers. They were found too not in the lower classes of the reading public, but chiefly among young men of strong sensibility and meditative minds; and their admiration (inflamed perhaps in some degree by opposition) was distinguished by its intensity, I might almost say, by its *religious* fervor. These facts, and the intellectual energy of the author, which was more or less consciously felt where it was outwardly and even boisterously denied, meeting with sentiments of aversion to his opinions and of alarm at their consequences, produced an eddy of criticism which would of itself have borne up the poems by the violence with which it whirled them round and round. With many parts of this preface, in the sense attributed to them and which the words undoubtedly seem to authorize, I never concurred; but, on the contrary objected to them as erroneous in principle, and as contradictory (in appearance at least) both to other parts of the same preface and to the author's own practice in the greater number of the poems themselves. Mr. Wordsworth in his recent collection[6] has, I find, degraded this prefatory disquisition to the end of his second volume, to be read or not at the reader's choice. But he has not, as far as I can discover, announced any change in his poetic creed. At all events, considering it as the source of a controversy in which I have been honored more than I deserve by the frequent conjunction of my name with his, I think it expedient to declare once for all in what points I coincide with his opinions, and in what points I altogether differ. But in order to render myself intelligible I must previously, in as few words as possible, explain my ideas, first, of a POEM; and secondly, of POETRY itself, in *kind* and in *essence*.

The office of philosophical *disquisition* consists in just *distinction*; while it is the privilege of the philosopher to preserve himself constantly aware that distinction is not division. In order to obtain adequate notions of any truth, we must intellectually separate its distinguishable parts; and

5. The controversy over Wordsworth's theory and poetical practice in the literary journals of the day. 6. Wordsworth's *Poems*, 2 vols., 1815.

this is the technical *process* of philosophy. But having so done, we must then restore them in our conceptions to the unity in which they actually coexist; and this is the *result* of philosophy. A poem contains the same elements as a prose composition; the difference therefore must consist in a different combination of them, in consequence of a different object proposed. According to the difference of the object will be the difference of the combination. It is possible that the object may be merely to facilitate the recollection of any given facts or observations by artificial arrangement; and the composition will be a poem, merely because it is distinguished from prose by meter, or by rhyme, or by both conjointly. In this, the lowest sense, a man might attribute the name of a poem to the well-known enumeration of the days in the several months:

> Thirty days hath September,
> April, June, and November, etc.

and others of the same class and purpose. And as a particular pleasure is found in anticipating the recurrence of sounds and quantities, all compositions that have this charm superadded, whatever be their contents, *may* be entitled poems.

So much for the superficial *form*. A difference of object and contents supplies an additional ground of distinction. The immediate purpose may be the communication of truths; either of truth absolute and demonstrable, as in works of science; or of facts experienced and recorded, as in history. Pleasure, and that of the highest and most permanent kind, may *result* from the *attainment* of the end; but it is not itself the immediate end. In other works the communication of pleasure may be the immediate purpose; and though truth, either moral or intellectual, ought to be the *ultimate* end, yet this will distinguish the character of the author, not the class to which the work belongs. Blessed indeed is that state of society in which the immediate purpose would be baffled by the perversion of the proper ultimate end; in which no charm of diction or imagery could exempt the Bathyllus even of an Anacreon, or the Alexis of Virgil,[7] from disgust and aversion!

But the communication of pleasure may be the immediate object of a work not metrically composed; and that object may have been in a high degree attained, as in novels and romances. Would then the mere superaddition of meter, with or without rhyme, entitle *these* to the name of poems? The answer is that nothing can permanently please which does not contain in itself the reason why it is so, and not otherwise. If meter be superadded, all other parts must be made consonant with it. They must be such as to justify the perpetual and distinct attention to each part which an exact correspondent recurrence of accent and sound are calculated to excite. The final definition then, so deduced, may be thus worded. A poem is that species of composition which is opposed to

---

7. The reference is to poems of homosexual love. "Bathyllus" was a beautiful boy praised by Anacreon, a Greek lyric poet (ca. 560–475 B.C.);   "Alexis" was a young man loved by the shepherd Corydon in Virgil's *Eclogues* 2.

works of science by proposing for its *immediate* object pleasure, not truth; and from all other species (having *this* object in common with it) it is discriminated by proposing to itself such delight from the *whole* as is compatible with a distinct gratification from each component *part*.

Controversy is not seldom excited in consequence of the disputants attaching each a different meaning to the same word; and in few instances has this been more striking than in disputes concerning the present subject. If a man chooses to call every composition a poem which is rhyme, or measure, or both, I must leave his opinion uncontroverted. The distinction is at least competent to characterize the writer's intention. If it were subjoined that the whole is likewise entertaining or affecting as a tale or as a series of interesting reflections, I of course admit this as another fit ingredient of a poem and an additional merit. But if the definition sought for be that of a *legitimate* poem, I answer it must be one the parts of which mutually support and explain each other; all in their proportion harmonizing with, and supporting the purpose and known influences of metrical arrangement. The philosophic critics of all ages coincide with the ultimate judgment of all countries in equally denying the praises of a just poem on the one hand to a series of striking lines or distichs,[8] each of which absorbing the whole attention of the reader to itself disjoins it from its context and makes it a separate whole, instead of a harmonizing part; and on the other hand, to an unsustained composition, from which the reader collects rapidly the general result unattracted by the component parts. The reader should be carried forward, not merely or chiefly by the mechanical impulse of curiosity, or by a restless desire to arrive at the final solution; but by the pleasurable activity of mind excited by the attractions of the journey itself. Like the motion of a serpent, which the Egyptians made the emblem of intellectual power; or like the path of sound through the air; at every step he pauses and half recedes, and from the retrogressive movement collects the force which again carries him onward. *"Praecipitandus est* liber *spiritus,"* says Petronius Arbiter most happily.[9] The epithet *liber* here balances the preceding verb; and it is not easy to conceive more meaning condensed in fewer words.

But if this should be admitted as a satisfactory character of a poem, we have still to seek for a definition of poetry. The writings of Plato, and Bishop Taylor, and the *Theoria Sacra* of Burnet,[1] furnish undeniable proofs that poetry of the highest kind may exist without meter, and even without the contradistinguishing objects of a poem. The first chapter of Isaiah (indeed a very large proportion of the whole book) is poetry in the most emphatic sense; yet it would be not less irrational than strange to assert that pleasure, and not truth, was the immediate object of the

8. Pairs of lines.
9. "The *free* spirit [of the poet] must be hurled onward." From the *Satyricon*, by the lively Roman satirist Petronius Arbiter (1st century A.D.).
1. Bishop Jeremy Taylor (1613–1667), author of *Holy Living* and *Holy Dying*; Thomas Burnet

(1635?–1715), author of *The Sacred Theory of the Earth*. Coleridge greatly admired the elaborate and sonorous prose of both these writers; he took from a work by Burnet the Latin motto for *The Ancient Mariner*.

prophet. In short, whatever *specific* import we attach to the word poetry, there will be found involved in it, as a necessary consequence, that a poem of any length neither can be, nor ought to be, all poetry.[2] Yet if a harmonious whole is to be produced, the remaining parts must be preserved in *keeping* with the poetry; and this can be no otherwise effected than by such a studied selection and artificial arrangement as will partake of *one*, though not a *peculiar*, property of poetry. And this again can be no other than the property of exciting a more continuous and equal attention than the language of prose aims at, whether colloquial or written.

My own conclusions on the nature of poetry, in the strictest use of the word, have been in part anticipated in the preceding disquisition on the fancy and imagination. What is poetry? is so nearly the same question with, what is a poet? that the answer to the one is involved in the solution of the other. For it is a distinction resulting from the poetic genius itself, which sustains and modifies the images, thoughts, and emotions of the poet's own mind.

The poet, described in *ideal* perfection, brings the whole soul of man into activity, with the subordination of its faculties to each other, according to their relative worth and dignity. He diffuses a tone and spirit of unity that blends and (as it were) *fuses*, each into each, by that synthetic and magical power to which we have exclusively appropriated the name of imagination. This power, first put in action by the will and understanding and retained under their irremissive, though gentle and unnoticed, control *(laxis effertur habenis[3])* reveals itself in the balance or reconciliation of opposite or discordant qualities:[4] of sameness, with difference; of the general, with the concrete; the idea, with the image; the individual, with the representative; the sense of novelty and freshness, with old and familiar objects; a more than usual state of emotion, with more than usual order; judgment ever awake and steady self-possession, with enthusiasm and feeling profound or vehement; and while it blends and harmonizes the natural and the artificial, still subordinates art to nature; the manner to the matter; and our admiration of the poet to our sympathy with the poetry. "Doubtless," as Sir John Davies observes of the soul (and his words may with slight alteration be applied, and even more appropriately, to the poetic IMAGINATION):

> Doubtless this could not be, but that she turns
> Bodies to spirit by sublimation strange,
> As fire converts to fire the things it burns,
> As we our food into our nature change.

2. Coleridge does not use the word "poetry" in the usual way, as a term for the class of all metrical compositions, or of all "poems," but to designate those passages, whether in verse or prose, produced by the mind of genius in its supreme moments of imaginative activity.

3. I.e., driven with loosened reins.
4. Here Coleridge introduces the concept that the highest poetry incorporates and reconciles opposite or discordant elements; under the names of "irony" and "paradox," this concept became a primary criterion of the American New Critics.

From their gross matter she abstracts their forms,
    And draws a kind of quintessence from things;
Which to her proper nature she transforms,
    To bear them light on her celestial wings.

Thus does she, when from individual states
    She doth abstract the universal kinds;
Which then reclothed in divers names and fates
    Steal access through our senses to our minds.[5]

Finally, GOOD SENSE is the BODY of poetic genius, FANCY its DRAPERY, MOTION its LIFE, and IMAGINATION the SOUL that is everywhere, and in each; and forms all into one graceful and intelligent whole.

From *Chapter 17*
[*Examination of the tenets peculiar to Mr. Wordsworth*]

As far then as Mr. Wordsworth in his preface contended, and most ably contended, for a reformation in our poetic diction, as far as he has evinced the truth of passion, and the *dramatic* propriety of those figures and metaphors in the original poets which, stripped of their justifying reasons and converted into mere artifices of connection or ornament, constitute the characteristic falsity in the poetic style of the moderns; and as far as he has, with equal acuteness and clearness, pointed out the process by which this change was effected and the resemblances between that state into which the reader's mind is thrown by the pleasurable confusion of thought from an unaccustomed train of words and images and that state which is induced by the natural language of impassioned feeling, he undertook a useful task and deserves all praise, both for the attempt and for the execution. The provocations to this remonstrance in behalf of truth and nature were still of perpetual recurrence before and after the publication of this preface. * * *

My own differences from certain supposed parts of Mr. Wordsworth's theory ground themselves on the assumption that his words had been rightly interpreted, as purporting that the proper diction for poetry in general consists altogether in a language taken, with due exceptions, from the mouths of men in real life, a language which actually constitutes the natural conversation of men under the influence of natural feelings.[6] My objection is, first, that in *any* sense this rule is applicable only to *certain* classes of poetry; secondly, that even to these classes it is not applicable, except in such a sense as hath never by anyone (as far as I know or have read) been denied or doubted; and, lastly, that as far as, and in that degree in which it is *practicable*, yet as a *rule* it is useless, if not injurious, and therefore either need not or ought not to be practiced. * * *

5. Adapted from John Davies' *Nosce Teipsum* ("Know Thyself"), a philosophical poem (1599).
6. Wordsworth, Preface to *Lyrical Ballads* (1800): "A selection of the real language of men in a state of vivid sensation. . . . Low and rustic life was generally chosen. . . . The language, too, of these men is adopted. . . ."

[*Rustic life (above all,* low *and rustic life) especially unfavorable to the formation of a human diction—The best parts of language the products of philosophers, not clowns[7] or shepherds*]

As little can I agree with the assertion that from the objects with which the rustic hourly communicates the best part of language is formed. For first, if to communicate with an object implies such an acquaintance with it, as renders it capable of being discriminately reflected on; the distinct knowledge of an uneducated rustic would furnish a very scanty vocabulary. The few things, and modes of action, requisite for his bodily conveniences, would alone be individualized; while all the rest of nature would be expressed by a small number of confused general terms. Secondly, I deny that the words and combinations of words derived from the objects, with which the rustic is familiar, whether with distinct or confused knowledge, can be justly said to form the *best* part of language. It is more than probable that many classes of the brute creation possess discriminating sounds, by which they can convey to each other notices of such objects as concern their food, shelter, or safety. Yet we hesitate to call the aggregate of such sounds a language, otherwise than metaphorically. The best part of human language, properly so called, is derived from reflection on the acts of the mind itself. It is formed by a voluntary appropriation of fixed symbols to internal acts, to processes and results of imagination, the greater part of which have no place in the consciousness of uneducated man; though in civilized society, by imitation and passive remembrance of what they hear from their religious instructors and other superiors, the most uneducated share in the harvest which they neither sowed or reaped. * * *

[*The language of Milton as much the language of* real *life, yea, incomparably more so than that of the cottager*]

Here let me be permitted to remind the reader that the positions which I controvert are contained in the sentences—"a selection of the REAL language of men"; "the language of these men (i.e., men in low and rustic life) I propose to myself to imitate, and as far as possible to adopt the very language of men." "Between the language of prose and that of metrical composition there neither is, nor can be any essential difference." It is against these exclusively that my opposition is directed.

I object, in the very first instance, to an equivocation in the use of the word "real." Every man's language varies according to the extent of his knowledge, the activity of his faculties, and the depth or quickness of his feelings. Every man's language has, first, its *individualities;* secondly, the common properties of the *class* to which he belongs; and thirdly, words and phrases of *universal* use. The language of Hooker, Bacon, Bishop Taylor, and Burke differs from the common language of the learned class only by the superior number and novelty of the thoughts

7. Rustic people.

and relations which they had to convey. The language of Algernon Sidney[8] differs not at all from that which every well-educated gentleman would wish to write, and (with due allowances for the undeliberateness and less connected train of thinking natural and proper to conversation) such as he would wish to talk. Neither one nor the other differ half as much from the general language of cultivated society as the language of Mr. Wordsworth's homeliest composition differs from that of a common peasant. For "real" therefore we must substitute *ordinary,* or *lingua communis.*[9] And this, we have proved, is no more to be found in the phraseology of low and rustic life than in that of any other class. Omit the peculiarities of each, and the result of course must be common to all. And assuredly the omissions and changes to be made in the language of rustics before it could be transferred to any species of poem, except the drama or other professed imitation, are at least as numerous and weighty as would be required in adapting to the same purpose the ordinary language of tradesmen and manufacturers. Not to mention that the language so highly extolled by Mr. Wordsworth varies in every county, nay, in every village, according to the accidental character of the clergyman, the existence or nonexistence of schools; or even, perhaps, as the exciseman, publican, or barber happen to be, or not to be, zealous politicians and readers of the weekly newspaper *pro bono publico.*[1] Anterior to cultivation the *lingua communis* of every country, as Dante has well observed, exists every where in parts and no where as a whole.[2]

Neither is the case rendered at all more tenable by the addition of the words "in a state of excitement."[3] For the nature of a man's words, when he is strongly affected by joy, grief, or anger, must necessarily depend on the number and quality of the general truths, conceptions, and images, and of the words expressing them, with which his mind had been previously stored. For the property of passion is not to *create,* but to set in increased activity. At least, whatever new connections of thoughts or images, or (which is equally, if not more than equally, the appropriate effect of strong excitement) whatever generalizations of truth or experience the heat of passion may produce, yet the terms of their conveyance must have pre-existed in his former conversations, and are only collected and crowded together by the unusual stimulation. It is indeed very possible to adopt in a poem the unmeaning repetitions, habitual phrases, and other blank counters which an unfurnished or confused understanding interposes at short intervals in order to keep hold of his subject which is still slipping from him, and to give him time for recollection; or in mere aid of vacancy, as in the scanty companies of a country stage the same player pops backwards and forwards, in order to prevent the appearance of empty spaces, in the procession of *Macbeth* or *Henry*

8. Algernon Sidney (1622–1683), republican soldier and statesmen, author of *Discourses Concerning Government.*
9. "The common language."
1. "For the public welfare."
2. In *De vulgari eloquentia* ("On the Speech of the People") Dante discusses—and affirms—the fitness for poetry of the unlocalized Italian vernacular.
3. Wordsworth: "the manner in which we associate ideas in a state of excitement."

VIIIth. But what assistance to the poet or ornament to the poem these can supply, I am at a loss to conjecture. Nothing assuredly can differ either in origin or in mode more widely from the apparent tautologies of intense and turbulent feeling in which the passion is greater and of longer endurance than to be exhausted or satisfied by a single representation of the image or incident exciting it. Such repetitions I admit to be a beauty of the highest kind; as illustrated by Mr. Wordsworth himself from the song of Deborah. "At her feet he bowed, he fell, he lay down; at her feet he bowed, he fell; where he bowed, there he fell down dead."[4]

1815   1817

4. Judges 5.27. Cited by Wordsworth in a note to *The Thorn* as an example of the natural tautology of "impassioned feelings."

GEORGE GORDON, LORD BYRON
1788–1824

1812:   *Childe Harold*, cantos 1 and 2.
1813–14:   The Oriental tales, including *The Giaour, The Corsair, Lara.*
1816:   Separation from Lady Byron; leaves England, never to return.
1818:   Begins *Don Juan.*
1823:   Joins the Greek war for liberation from the Turks.

In his *History of English Literature,* written in the late 1850s, the French critic Hippolyte Taine gave only a few condescending pages to Wordsworth, Coleridge, Shelley, and Keats, and then devoted a long enthusiastic chapter to Lord Byron, "the greatest and most English of these artists; he is so great and so English that from him alone we shall learn more truths of his country and of his age than from all the rest together." This comment reflects the fact that Byron had achieved an immense European reputation during his own lifetime, while his English contemporaries were admired only by small coteries in England and America; through much of the nineteenth century he continued to be rated as one of the greatest of English poets and the very prototype of literary Romanticism. His influence was felt everywhere, not only among minor writers—in the two or three decades after his death, most European poets struck Byronic attitudes—but among the major poets and novelists (including Goethe in Germany, Balzac and Stendhal in France, Pushkin and Dostoevsky in Russia, and Melville in America), painters (especially Delacroix), and composers (especially Beethoven and Berlioz).

These facts may surprise the student who is aware of the modern estimate of Byron as the least consequential of the great Romantic poets, whose achievements have little in common with the distinctive innovations of Wordsworth, Coleridge, Keats, or Shelley. Only Shelley, among these writers, thought highly of either Byron or his work; while Byron spoke slightingly of all of them except Shelley, and in fact insisted that, measured against the poetic practice of Alexander Pope, he and his contemporaries were "all in the wrong, one as much as another . . . we are upon a wrong revolutionary poetical system, or systems, not worth a damn in itself." Byron's masterpiece, *Don Juan*, is an instance of that favorite neoclassic type, a satire against modern civilization, and shares many of the aims and methods of Pope, Swift, Voltaire, and Sterne. Even Byron's lyrics are old-fashioned: many are in the eighteenth-century gentlemanly mode of witty extemporization and epigram *(Written after Swimming from Sestos to Abydos)* or continue the Cavalier tradition of the elaborate development of a compliment to a lady *(She Walks in Beauty* and *There Be None of Beauty's Daughters)*.

Byron's chief claim to be considered an arch-Romantic is that he provided his age with what Taine called its "ruling personage; that is, the model that contemporaries invest with their admiration and sympathy." This personage is the "Byronic hero." He occurs in various guises in Byron's writings, but from the first sketch in the opening canto of *Childe Harold*, and in the verse romances and dramas that follow, his persistent character is that of a moody, passionate, and remorse-torn but unrepentant wanderer. In his developed form, as we find it in his drama *Manfred*, he is an alien, mysterious, and gloomy spirit, immensely superior in his passions and powers to the common run of humanity, whom he regards with disdain. He harbors the torturing memory of an enormous, nameless guilt that drives him toward an inevitable doom. He is in his isolation absolutely self-reliant, inflexibly pursuing his own ends according to his self-generated moral code against any opposition, human or supernatural. And he exerts an attraction on other characters which is the more compelling because it involves their terror at his obliviousness to ordinary human concerns and values. This figure, infusing the archrebel in a nonpolitical form with a strong erotic interest, embodied the implicit yearnings of Byron's time, was imitated in life as well as in art, and helped shape the intellectual as well as the cultural history of the later nineteenth century. The literary descendants of the Byronic hero include Heathcliff in *Wuthering Heights*, Captain Ahab in *Moby-Dick*, and the hero of Pushkin's great poem *Eugene Onegin*. Bertrand Russell, in his *History of Western Philosophy*, gives a chapter to Byron—not because he was a systematic thinker, but because "Byronism," the attitude of "Titanic cosmic self-assertion," established an outlook and a stance toward humanity and the world that entered nineteenth-century philosophy and eventually helped to form Nietzsche's concept of the Superman, the hero who stands outside the jurisdiction of the ordinary criteria of good and evil.

Byron's contemporaries insisted on identifying the author with his fictional characters. But Byron's letters and the testimony of his friends show that, except for recurrent moods of black depression, his own temperament was in many respects antithetic to that of his heroes. He was passionate and willful, but when in good humor he could be very much a man of the world in the eighteenth-century style—gregarious, lively, tolerant, and a witty conversationalist capable of taking an ironic attitude toward his own activities as well as those of other men. The aloof hauteur he exhibited in public was largely a mask to hide his diffidence when in a strange company; he possessed devoted friends, both men and women, and among them he was usually unassuming, companionable, sometimes even exuberant, and tactful; to his household dependents he was unfailingly generous and tenaciously loyal. But though Byronism was largely a fiction, produced by a collaboration between Byron's imagination and that of his public, the fiction was historically more important than the poet in his actual person.

Byron was descended from two aristocratic families, both of them colorful, violent, and dissolute. His grandfather was an admiral nicknamed "Foulweather Jack"; his great-uncle was the fifth Baron Byron, known to his rural neighbors as the "Wicked Lord," who was tried by his peers for killing his kinsman William Chaworth in a drunken duel; his father, Captain John Byron, was a rake and fortune-hunter who rapidly dissipated the patrimony of two wealthy wives. Byron's mother was a Scotswoman, Catherine Gordon of Gight, the last descendant of a line of lawless Scottish lairds. After her husband died (Byron was then three), she brought up her son in near-poverty in Aberdeen, where he was indoctrinated with the Calvinistic morality of Scottish Presbyterianism. Mrs. Byron was an ill-educated and almost pathologically irascible woman who nevertheless had an abiding love for her son; they fought violently when together, but corresponded affectionately enough when apart, until her death in 1811.

When Byron was ten, the death of his great-uncle, preceded by that of more immediate heirs to the title, made him the sixth Lord Byron. In a fashion suitable to his new eminence he was sent to Harrow School, then to Trinity College, Cambridge. He had been born with a clubfoot, which was made worse by inept medical treatment, and this defect all his life caused him physical suffering and agonized embarrassment. His lameness made him avid for athletic prowess; he played cricket and made himself an expert boxer, fencer, and horseman, and a powerful swimmer. He was also sexually precocious; when only seven, he fell in love with a little cousin, Mary Duff, and so violently that ten years later news of her marriage threw him into convulsions. Both at Cambridge and at his ancestral estate of Newstead, he engaged with more than ordinary zeal in the expensive pursuits and fashionable dissipations of a young Regency lord. As a result, despite a sizable and increasing income, he got into financial difficulties from which he did not entirely extricate himself until late in his life. In the course of his schooling he formed many close friendships, the most important with John Cam Hobhouse, a sturdy political liberal and commonsense moralist who exerted a steadying influence throughout Byron's turbulent life.

Despite his distractions at the university, Byron found time to try his hand at lyric verse, some of which was published in 1807 in a slim and conventional volume entitled *Hours of Idleness*. This was treated with unmerited harshness by the pontifical *Edinburgh Review*, and Byron was provoked to write in reply his first important poem, *English Bards and Scotch Reviewers*, a vigorous satire in the couplet style of the late eighteenth-century followers of Pope, in which he incorporated skillful but tactless ridicule of all his major poetic contemporaries, including Scott, Wordsworth, and Coleridge.

After attaining his A.M. degree and his majority, Byron set out with Hobhouse in 1809 on a tour through Portugal and Spain to Malta, and then to little-known Albania, Greece, and Asia Minor. In this adventurous two-year excursion, he accumulated materials which he wove into most of his important poems, including his last work, *Don Juan*. The first literary product was *Childe Harold*; he wrote the opening two cantos while on the tour which the poem describes, published them in 1812 soon after his return to England, and, in his own oft-quoted phrase, "awoke one morning and found myself famous." He became the celebrity of fashionable London, enjoying an unprecedented literary success, which he soon increased by his series of highly readable Near Eastern verse tales; in these the Byronic hero, in various embodiments, flaunts his misanthropy and undergoes a variety of violent and romantic adventures that current gossip attributed to the author himself. In his chronic shortage of money, Byron could well have used the huge income from these publications, but instead maintained his status as an aristocratic amateur by giving the royalties away. Occupying his inherited seat in the House of Lords, he also became briefly active on the extreme liberal side of the Whig party and spoke courageously in defense of the Nottingham weavers who, made desperate by technological unemployment, had resorted to destroying the new textile machines; he also supported other liberal measures, including that of Catholic Emancipation.

In the meantime he found himself besieged by women. He was extraordinarily handsome—"so beautiful a countenance," Coleridge wrote, "I scarcely ever saw . . . his eyes the open portals of the sun—things of light, and for light." Because of a constitutional tendency to obesity, however, Byron was able to maintain his beauty only by recurring again and again to a starvation diet of biscuits, soda water, and strong cathartics. Often as a result of female initiative rather than his own, Byron entered into a sequence of liaisons with ladies of fashion. One of these, the flamboyant, eccentric, and hysterical young Lady Caroline Lamb, caused him so much distress by her frenzied pursuit and public tantrums that Byron turned for relief to marriage with Annabella Milbanke, who was in every way Lady Caroline's opposite, for she was naïve, unworldly, intellectual (with a special passion for mathematics), and not a little priggish; she persuaded herself that she could make Byron over in her own image. This ill-starred marriage produced a daughter (Augusta Ada) and many scenes in which Byron, goaded by financial difficulties, behaved so frantically that his wife suspected his sanity; after only one year, the union ended in a legal separation. The final blow came when Lady Byron discovered her husband's incestuous relations with his half sister, Augusta Leigh. The two had been raised apart, so that they were almost strangers when they met as adults; also, Byron seems to have had one attribute in common with the Byronic hero—a compulsion to try forbidden experience (including, as we now know, homosexual love affairs), joined with a tendency to court his own destruction. Byron's affection for his sister, however guilty, was genuine, and endured all through his life. This affair proved a delicious morsel even to the jaded palate of the dissolute Regency society; Byron was ostracized by all but a few friends, and finally forced to leave England forever on April 25, 1816.

Byron now resumed the travels incorporated in the third and fourth cantos of *Childe Harold*. At Geneva he lived for several months in close and intellectually fruitful relation to Shelley, who was accompanied by his wife, Mary Wollstonecraft Shelley, and by his wife's stepsister Claire Clairmont—a misguided girl of seventeen who had forced herself upon Byron while he was still in England and who in January 1817 bore him a daughter, Allegra. In the fall of 1817 Byron established himself in Venice, where he inaugurated various affairs that culminated in a period of frenzied debauchery that, he estimated, involved more than two hundred women, mainly of the lower class. This period was also one of great literary creativity: often working through the later hours of the night, he finished his tragedy *Manfred*, wrote the fourth canto of *Childe Harold*, and after turning out *Beppo*, a short preview of the narrative style and stanza of *Don Juan*, began the composition of *Don Juan* itself. In the colloquial ottava rima, he finally learned to write poetry as well as he had written the prose of his superbly vivid, informative, and witty letters.

Exhausted and bored by promiscuity, Byron in 1819 settled into a placid and relatively faithful relationship with Teresa Guiccioli, the young wife of the elderly Count Alessandro Guiccioli; according to the Italian upper-class mores of the times, having contracted a marriage of convenience, she could now with propriety attach Byron to herself as a *cavaliere servente*. Through Teresa's nationalistic family, the Gambas, Byron became involved in the Carbonari plot against Austrian control over northern Italy. When the Gambas were forced by the authorities to move to Pisa, Byron followed them there, and for the second time joined Shelley. There grew up about the two friends the "Pisan Circle," which in addition to the Gambas included Shelley's wife Mary and his friends Thomas Medwin and Edward and Jane Williams, as well as the Greek nationalist leader Prince Mavrocordatos, the picturesque Irish Count Taaffe, and the flamboyant and mendacious adventurer Edward Trelawny, who seems to have stepped out of one of Byron's romances. The circle was gradually broken up, first by Shelley's anger over Byron's treatment of his daughter, Allegra (Byron had sent the child to be brought up as a Catholic in an Italian convent, where she died of a fever in 1822); then by the expulsion of the Gambas, whom Byron followed to Genoa; and finally by the drowning of Shelley and Williams in July 1822.

Byron meanwhile had been steadily at work on a series of closet tragedies (including *Cain, Sardanapalus,* and *Marino Faliero*) and on his superb satire, *The Vision of Judgment.* But increasingly he devoted himself to the continuation of *Don Juan.* He had always been diffident in his self-judgments and easily swayed by literary advice. But now, confident that he had at last found his métier and was accomplishing a masterpiece, he kept on, in spite of persistent objections against the supposed immorality of the poem by the English public, by his publisher John Murray, by his friends and well-wishers, and by his extremely decorous mistress, the Countess Guiccioli—by almost everyone, in fact, except the idealist Shelley, who thought *Juan* incomparably better than anything he himself could write and insisted "that every word of it is pregnant with immortality."

Byron finally broke off literature for action when he organized an expedition to assist in the Greek war for independence from the Turks. He knew too well the conditions in Greece, and had too skeptical an estimate of human nature, to entertain hope of success; but he was bored with love, with the domesticity of his relations to Teresa, and in some moods, with life itself. Also, since his own writings had helped to kindle European enthusiasm for the Greek cause, he now felt honor-bound to try what could be done. In the dismal, marshy town of Missolonghi he lived a Spartan existence, training troops whom he had himself subsidized and exhibiting great practical grasp and power of leadership amid a chaos of factionalism, intrigue, and military ineptitude. Worn out, he succumbed to a series of feverish attacks and died just after he had reached his thirty-sixth birthday. To this day Byron is revered by the Greek people as a national hero.

Students of Byron still feel, as his friends had felt, the magnetism of his volatile temperament. As Mary Shelley wrote six years after his death, when she read Thomas Moore's edition of his *Letters and Journals:* "The Lord Byron I find there is our Lord Byron—the fascinating—faulty—childish—philosophical being—daring the world—docile to a private circle—impetuous and indolent—gloomy and yet more gay than any other. . . . [I become] reconciled (as I used to in his lifetime) to those waywardnesses which annoyed me when he was away, through the delightful and buoyant tone of his conversation and manners." Of his inner discordances, Byron himself was well aware; he told his friend Lady Blessington: "I am so changeable, being everything by turns and nothing long—I am such a strange *mélange* of good and evil, that it would be difficult to describe me." Yet he remained faithful to his code: a determination always to tell the truth as he saw it about the world and about himself (his refusal to suppress or conceal any of his moods is in part what made him seem so contradictory) and a dedication to the freedom of nations and individuals. As he went on to say to Lady Blessington: "There are but two sentiments to which I am constant—a strong love of liberty, and a detestation of cant."

Written after Swimming from Sestos to Abydos[1]

1

If, in the month of dark December,
    Leander, who was nightly wont
(What maid will not the tale remember?)
    To cross thy stream, broad Hellespont!

2

If, when the wintry tempest roared,   5
    He sped to Hero, nothing loath,
And thus of old thy current poured,
    Fair Venus! how I pity both!

3

For *me*, degenerate modern wretch,
    Though in the genial month of May,   10
My dripping limbs I faintly stretch,
    And think I've done a feat today.

4

But since he crossed the rapid tide,
    According to the doubtful story,
To woo—and—Lord knows what beside,   15
    And swam for Love, as I for Glory;

5

'Twere hard to say who fared the best:
    Sad mortals! thus the gods still plague you!
He lost his labor, I my jest;
    For he was drowned, and I've the ague.   20

1810   1812

1. The Hellespont (now called the Dardanelles) is the narrow strait between Europe and Asia. In the ancient story, retold in Christopher Marlowe's *Hero and Leander*, young Leander of Abydos, on the Asian side, swam nightly to visit Hero, a priestess of the goddess Venus at Sestos, until he was drowned when he made the attempt in a storm. Byron and a young Lt. Ekenhead swam the Hellespont in the reverse direction on May 3, 1810. Byron alternated between complacency and humor in his many references to the event. In a note to the poem, he mentions that the distance was "upwards of four English miles, though the actual breadth is barely one. The rapidity of the current is such that no boat can row directly across. . . . The water was extremely cold, from the melting of the mountain snows."

When We Two Parted

When we two parted
   In silence and tears,
Half broken-hearted
   To sever for years,
Pale grew thy cheek and cold,   5
   Colder thy kiss;
Truly that hour foretold
   Sorrow to this.

The dew of the morning
   Sunk chill on my brow—   10
It felt like the warning
   Of what I feel now.
Thy vows are all broken,
   And light is thy fame;
I hear thy name spoken,   15
   And share in its shame.

They name thee before me,
   A knell to mine ear;
A shudder comes o'er me—
   Why wert thou so dear?   20
They know not I knew thee,
   Who knew thee too well—
Long, long shall I rue thee,
   Too deeply to tell.

In secret we met—   25
   In silence I grieve,
That thy heart could forget,
   Thy spirit deceive.
If I should meet thee
   After long years,   30
How should I greet thee?—
   With silence and tears.

1813   1816

She Walks in Beauty[1]

1
She walks in beauty, like the night
Of cloudless climes and starry skies;

1. One of the lyrics in *Hebrew Melodies* (1815), written to be set to adaptations of traditional Jewish tunes by the young musician Isaac Nathan. Byron wrote the lines the morning after he had met his beautiful young cousin by marriage, Mrs. Robert John Wilmot, who wore a black mourning gown brightened with spangles.

And all that's best of dark and bright
   Meet in her aspect and her eyes:
Thus mellowed to that tender light
   Which heaven to gaudy day denies.

2

One shade the more, one ray the less,
   Had half impaired the nameless grace
Which waves in every raven tress,
   Or softly lightens o'er her face;   10
Where thoughts serenely sweet express
   How pure, how dear their dwelling place.

3

And on that cheek, and o'er that brow,
   So soft, so calm, yet eloquent,
The smiles that win, the tints that glow,   15
   But tell of days in goodness spent,
A mind at peace with all below,
   A heart whose love is innocent!

June 12, 1814   1815

Stanzas for Music

There Be None of Beauty's Daughters

1

There be none of Beauty's daughters
   With a magic like thee;
And like music on the waters
   Is thy sweet voice to me:
When, as if its sound were causing   5
The charmèd ocean's pausing,
The waves lie still and gleaming,
And the lulled winds seem dreaming;

2

And the midnight moon is weaving
   Her bright chain o'er the deep;
Whose breast is gently heaving,   10
   As an infant's asleep:
So the spirit bows before thee,
To listen and adore thee;
With a full but soft emotion,   15
Like the swell of summer's ocean.

1816   1816

Darkness[1]

I had a dream, which was not all a dream.
The bright sun was extinguished, and the stars
Did wander darkling[2] in the eternal space,
Rayless, and pathless, and the icy earth
Swung blind and blackening in the moonless air;   5
Morn came and went—and came, and brought no day,
And men forgot their passions in the dread
Of this their desolation; and all hearts
Were chilled into a selfish prayer for light:
And they did live by watchfires—and the thrones,   10
The palaces of crownèd kings—the huts,
The habitations of all things which dwell,
Were burnt for beacons; cities were consumed,
And men were gathered round their blazing homes
To look once more into each other's face;   15
Happy were those who dwelt within the eye
Of the volcanoes, and their mountain torch:
A fearful hope was all the world contained;
Forests were set on fire—but hour by hour
They fell and faded—and the crackling trunks   20
Extinguished with a crash—and all was black.
The brows of men by the despairing light
Wore an unearthly aspect, as by fits
The flashes fell upon them; some lay down
And hid their eyes and wept; and some did rest   25
Their chins upon their clenchèd hands, and smiled;
And others hurried to and fro, and fed
Their funeral piles with fuel, and looked up
With mad disquietude on the dull sky,
The pall of a past world; and then again   30
With curses cast them down upon the dust,
And gnashed their teeth and howled: the wild birds shrieked
And, terrified, did flutter on the ground,
And flap their useless wings; the wildest brutes
Came tame and tremulous; and vipers crawled   35
And twined themselves among the multitude,
Hissing, but stingless—they were slain for food;
And War, which for a moment was no more,
Did glut himself again—a meal was bought
With blood, and each sate sullenly apart   40
Gorging himself in gloom: no love was left;
All earth was but one thought—and that was death
Immediate and inglorious; and the pang
Of famine fed upon all entrails—men

---

1. A powerfully imagined blank-verse description
of the end of life on earth—a speculation hardly

less common in Byron's time than in ours.
2. In the dark.

Died, and their bones were tombless as their flesh;   45
The meager by the meager were devoured,
Even dogs assailed their masters, all save one,
And he was faithful to a corse, and kept
The birds and beasts and famished men at bay,
Till hunger clung[3] them, or the dropping dead   50
Lured their lank jaws; himself sought out no food,
But with a piteous and perpetual moan,
And a quick desolate cry, licking the hand
Which answered not with a caress—he died.
The crowd was famished by degrees; but two   55
Of an enormous city did survive,
And they were enemies; they met beside
The dying embers of an altar place,
Where had been heaped a mass of holy things
For an unholy usage; they raked up,   60
And shivering scraped with their cold skeleton hands
The feeble ashes, and their feeble breath
Blew for a little life, and made a flame
Which was a mockery; then they lifted up
Their eyes as it grew lighter, and beheld   65
Each other's aspects—saw, and shrieked, and died—
Even of their mutual hideousness they died,
Unknowing who he was upon whose brow
Famine had written Fiend. The world was void,
The populous and the powerful was a lump   70
Seasonless, herbless, treeless, manless, lifeless—
A lump of death—a chaos of hard clay.
The rivers, lakes, and ocean all stood still,
And nothing stirred within their silent depths;
Ships sailorless lay rotting on the sea,   75
And their masts fell down piecemeal: as they dropped
They slept on the abyss without a surge—
The waves were dead; the tides were in their grave,
The Moon, their mistress, had expired before;
The winds were withered in the stagnant air,   80
And the clouds perished; Darkness had no need
Of aid from them—She was the Universe.

1816   1816

So We'll Go No More A-Roving[1]

1

So we'll go no more a-roving
So late into the night,

---

3. Withered.
1. Composed in the Lenten aftermath of a spell of   feverish dissipation in the Carnival season in Venice, and included in a letter to Thomas Moore,

> Though the heart be still as loving,
>   And the moon be still as bright.
>
>   2
> For the sword outwears its sheath,   5
>   And the soul wears out the breast,
> And the heart must pause to breathe,
>   And Love itself have rest.
>
>   3
> Though the night was made for loving,
>   And the day returns too soon,   10
> Yet we'll go no more a-roving
>   By the light of the moon.

1817   1836

When a Man Hath No Freedom to Fight for at Home[1]

> When a man hath no freedom to fight for at home,
>   Let him combat for that of his neighbors;
> Let him think of the glories of Greece and of Rome,
>   And get knocked on his head for his labors.
>
> To do good to mankind is the chivalrous plan,   5
>   And is always as nobly requited;
> Then battle for freedom wherever you can,
>   And, if not shot or hanged, you'll get knighted.

Nov. 5, 1820   1824

Childe Harold's Pilgrimage

Childe Harold is a travelogue, narrated by a melancholy, passionate, well-read, and very eloquent tourist. Byron wrote most of the first two cantos while on the tour through Spain, Portugal, Albania, and Greece which these cantos describe; when he published them, in 1812, they made him at one stroke the best known and most talked about English poet. Byron took up *Childe Harold* again in 1816, during the European tour he made after the breakup of his marriage. Canto 3, published in 1816, moves through Belgium, up the Rhine, then to Switzerland and the Alps. Canto 4, published in 1818, describes the great cities and monuments of Italy.

Byron chose for his poem the Spenserian stanza, and like James Thomson (in the *Castle of Indolence*) and other eighteenth-century predecessors, he

---

Feb. 28, 1817. Byron wrote, "I find 'the sword wearing out the scabbard,' though I have but just turned the corner of twenty-nine." The poem is based on the refrain of a Scottish song, *The Jolly Beggar*: "And we'll gang nae mair a roving / Sae late into the nicht. . . ."

1. The ironist's attitude toward gratuitous enlistment in a foreign war for national freedom—a cause to which Byron gave his own life less than four years later.

attempted in the first canto to imitate, in a seriocomic fashion, the archaic language of his Elizabethan model. (The word "Childe" itself is the ancient term for a young noble awaiting knighthood.) But he soon dropped the archaisms; and in the last two cantos he adapts Spenser's mellifluous stanza to his own assured and brassy magniloquence.

In the Preface to his first two cantos, Byron had insisted that the narrator, Childe Harold, was "a fictitious character," merely "the child of imagination." But in the manuscript version of these cantos, he had himself called his hero "Childe Burun," the early form of his own family name; the world insisted on identifying the character as well as the travels of the protagonist with those of the author; and in the fourth canto Byron, abandoning the third-person *dramatis persona*, spoke out frankly in the first person.

In its shock tactics of apostrophes, imperatives, exclamations, hyperbole, and abrupt changes in subject, pace, and mood, the style of *Childe Harold* is without close parallel in English; to it Goethe applied the terms *Keckheit, Kühnheit, und Grandiosität:* "daring, dash, and grandiosity." It is no small feat in the author to have converted a meticulously accurate tourist's record of scenes, memorials, and museums into a dramatic and passionate experience. The result is like seeing Europe by flashes of lightning, for everything is presented, not as it is in itself, but as it affects the violent sensibility of that new cultural phenomenon, the Romantic Man of Feeling.

From Childe Harold's Pilgrimage

A ROMAUNT[1]

From *Canto* 1

["SIN'S LONG LABYRINTH"]

Oh, thou! in Hellas deemed of heavenly birth,
Muse! formed or fabled at the minstrel's will!
Since shamed full oft by later lyres on earth,
Mine dares not call thee from thy sacred hill:
Yet there I've wandered by the vaunted rill;   5
Yes! sighed o'er Delphi's long-deserted shrine,
Where, save that feeble fountain, all is still;
Nor mote my shell awake the weary Nine[2]
To grace so plain a tale—this lowly lay of mine.

2

Whilome[3] in Albion's isle there dwelt a youth,   10
Who ne in virtue's ways did take delight;

---

1. A romance, or narrative of adventure.
2. The "shell" is a lyre (Hermes is fabled to have invented the lyre by stretching strings over the hollow of a tortoise shell); the "Nine" are the Muses, whose "vaunted rill" (line 5) was the Castalian spring. "Mote": may.
3. Once upon a time.

But spent his days in riot most uncouth,
And vexed with mirth the drowsy ear of Night.
Ah, me! in sooth he was a shameless wight,
Sore given to revel and ungodly glee;   15
Few earthly things found favor in his sight
Save concubines and carnal companie,
And flaunting wassailers[4] of high and low degree.

3

Childe Harold was he hight—but whence his name
And lineage long, it suits me not to say;   20
Suffice it that perchance they were of fame,
And had been glorious in another day:
But one sad losel[5] soils a name for aye,
However mighty in the olden time;
Nor all that heralds rake from coffined clay,   25
Nor florid prose, nor honeyed lies of rhyme,
Can blazon evil deeds, or consecrate a crime.

4

Childe Harold basked him in the noontide sun,
Disporting there like any other fly;
Nor deemed before his little day was done   30
One blast might chill him into misery.
But long ere scarce a third of his passed by,
Worse than adversity the Childe befell;
He felt the fullness of satiety:
Then loathed he in his native land to dwell,   35
Which seemed to him more lone than eremite's[6] sad cell.

5

For he through Sin's long labyrinth had run,
Nor made atonement when he did amiss;
Had sighed to many though he loved but one,
And that loved one, alas! could ne'er be his.   40
Ah, happy she! to 'scape from him whose kiss
Had been pollution unto aught so chaste;
Who soon had left her charms for vulgar bliss,
And spoiled her goodly lands to gild his waste,
Nor calm domestic peace had ever deigned to taste.   45

6

And now Childe Harold was sore sick at heart,
And from his fellow bacchanals would flee;
'Tis said, at times the sullen tear would start,
But Pride congealed the drop within his ee:[7]
Apart he stalked in joyless reverie,   50

---

4. Noisy, insolent drinkers (Byron is thought to
refer to his own youthful carousing with friends at
Newstead Abbey).
5. Rascal. Byron's great-uncle, the 5th Lord Byron,
had killed a kinsman in a drunken duel.
6. A religious hermit.
7. Eye.

And from his native land resolved to go,
And visit scorching climes beyond the sea;
With pleasure drugged, he almost longed for woe,
And e'en for change of scene would seek the shades below.

From *Canto* 3

["ONCE MORE UPON THE WATERS"]

1

Is thy face like thy mother's, my fair child!
Ada![1] sole daughter of my house and heart?
When last I saw thy young blue eyes they smiled,
And then we parted—not as now we part,
But with a hope.—
          Awaking with a start,   5
The waters heave around me; and on high
The winds lift up their voices; I depart,
Whither I know not; but the hour's gone by,
When Albion's[2] lessening shores could grieve or glad mine eye.

2

Once more upon the waters! yet once more!   10
And the waves bound beneath me as a steed
That knows his rider. Welcome to their roar!
Swift be their guidance, wheresoe'er it lead!
Though the strained mast should quiver as a reed,
And the rent canvas fluttering strew the gale,   15
Still must I on; for I am as a weed,
Flung from the rock on Ocean's foam, to sail
Where'er the surge may sweep, the tempest's breath prevail.

3

In my youth's summer[3] I did sing of One,
The wandering outlaw of his own dark mind;   20
Again I seize the theme, then but begun,
And bear it with me, as the rushing wind
Bears the cloud onwards: in that tale I find
The furrows of long thought, and dried-up tears,
Which, ebbing, leave a sterile track behind,   25
O'er which all heavily the journeying years
Plod the last sands of life—where not a flower appears.

4

Since my young days of passion—joy, or pain—
Perchance my heart and harp have lost a string,

1. Byron's daughter, Augusta Ada, born in December 1816, a month before her parents separated. Byron's "hope" (line 5) had been for a reconciliation, but he was never to see Ada again.
2. England's.
3. Byron wrote canto 1 at age 21; he is now 28.

And both may jar:[4] it may be that in vain   30
    I would essay as I have sung to sing.
Yet, though a dreary strain, to this I cling,
    So that it wean me from the weary dream
Of selfish grief or gladness—so it fling
    Forgetfulness around me—it shall seem   35
To me, though to none else, a not ungrateful theme.

                        5

He, who grown agèd in this world of woe,
    In deeds, not years, piercing the depths of life,
So that no wonder waits him—nor below
    Can love, or sorrow, fame, ambition, strife,   40
Cut to his heart again with the keen knife
    Of silent, sharp endurance—he can tell
Why thought seeks refuge in lone caves, yet rife
    With airy images, and shapes which dwell
Still unimpaired, though old, in the soul's haunted cell.   45

                        6

'Tis to create, and in creating live
    A being more intense, that we endow
With form our fancy, gaining as we give
    The life we image, even as I do now.
What am I? Nothing: but not so art thou,   50
    Soul of my thought![5] with whom I traverse earth,
Invisible but gazing, as I glow
    Mixed with thy spirit, blended with thy birth,
And feeling still with thee in my crushed feelings' dearth.

                        7

Yet must I think less wildly—I *have* thought   55
    Too long and darkly, till my brain became,
In its own eddy boiling and o'erwrought,
    A whirling gulf of phantasy and flame:
And thus, untaught in youth my heart to tame,
    My springs of life were poisoned. 'Tis too late!   60
Yet am I changed; though still enough the same
    In strength to bear what time can not abate,
And feed on bitter fruits without accusing Fate.

                        8

Something too much of this—but now 'tis past,
    And the spell closes with its silent seal.[6]   65
Long absent HAROLD reappears at last;
    He of the breast which fain no more would feel,
Wrung with the wounds which kill not but ne'er heal;
    Yet Time, who changes all, had altered him
In soul and aspect as in age: years steal   70
    Fire from the mind as vigor from the limb,
And life's enchanted cup but sparkles near the brim.

---

4. Sound discordant.
5. I.e., Childe Harold, his literary creation.

6. I.e., he sets the seal of silence on his personal
tale ("spell").

9

His had been quaffed too quickly, and he found
The dregs were wormwood; but he filled again,
And from a purer fount, on holier ground,   75
And deemed its spring perpetual; but in vain!
Still round him clung invisibly a chain
Which galled forever, fettering though unseen,
And heavy though it clanked not; worn with pain,
Which pined although it spoke not, and grew keen,   80
Entering with every step he took through many a scene.

10

Secure in guarded coldness, he had mixed
Again in fancied safety with his kind,
And deemed his spirit now so firmly fixed
And sheathed with an invulnerable mind,   85
That, if no joy, no sorrow lurked behind;
And he, as one, might 'midst the many stand
Unheeded, searching through the crowd to find
Fit speculation—such as in strange land
He found in wonderworks of God and Nature's hand.   90

11

But who can view the ripened rose, nor seek
To wear it? who can curiously behold
The smoothness and the sheen of beauty's cheek,
Nor feel the heart can never all grow old?
Who can contemplate Fame through clouds unfold   95
The star which rises o'er her steep, nor climb?
Harold, once more within the vortex, rolled
On with the giddy circle, chasing Time,
Yet with a nobler aim than in his youth's fond[7] prime.

12

But soon he knew himself the most unfit   100
Of men to herd with Man, with whom he held
Little in common; untaught to submit
His thoughts to others, though his soul was quelled
In youth by his own thoughts; still uncompelled,
He would not yield dominion of his mind   105
To spirits against whom his own rebelled,
Proud though in desolation; which could find
A life within itself, to breathe without mankind.

13

Where rose the mountains, there to him were friends;
Where rolled the ocean, thereon was his home;   110
Where a blue sky, and glowing clime, extends,
He had the passion and the power to roam;
The desert, forest, cavern, breaker's foam,
Were unto him companionship; they spake

---

7. Foolish.

A mutual language, clearer than the tome   115
    Of his land's tongue, which he would oft forsake
For Nature's pages glassed[8] by sunbeams on the lake.

                                    14
Like the Chaldean,[9] he could watch the stars,
    Till he had peopled them with beings bright
As their own beams; and earth, and earth-born jars,   120
    And human frailties, were forgotten quite:
    Could he have kept his spirit to that flight
He had been happy; but this clay will sink
    Its spark immortal, envying it the light
To which it mounts, as if to break the link   125
That keeps us from yon heaven which woos us to its brink.

                                    15
But in Man's dwellings he became a thing
    Restless and worn, and stern and wearisome,
Drooped as a wild-born falcon with clipped wing,
    To whom the boundless air alone were home: 130
    Then came his fit again, which to o'ercome,
As eagerly the barred-up bird will beat
    His breast and beak against his wiry dome
    Till the blood tinge his plumage, so the heat
Of his impeded soul would through his bosom eat.   135

                                    16
Self-exiled Harold wanders forth again,
    With nought of hope left—but with less of gloom;
The very knowledge that he lived in vain,
    That all was over on this side the tomb,
    Had made Despair a smilingness assume,   140
Which, though 'twere wild—as on the plundered wreck
    Where mariners would madly meet their doom
    With draughts intemperate on the sinking deck—
Did yet inspire a cheer which he forebore to check.

                            [WATERLOO]

                                    17
Stop!—for thy tread is on an Empire's dust!   145
    An Earthquake's spoil is sepulchered below!
Is the spot marked with no colossal bust,
    Nor column trophied for triumphal show?
    None; but the moral's truth tells simpler so,
As the ground was before, thus let it be—   150
    How that red rain hath made the harvest grow!
    And is this all the world has gained by thee,
Thou first and last of fields, king-making Victory?

8. Made glassy.
9. A people of ancient Babylonia, expert in astronomy.

18

And Harold stands upon this place of skulls,
The grave of France, the deadly Waterloo![1]
How in an hour the power which gave annuls   155
Its gifts, transferring fame as fleeting too!
In "pride of place" here last the eagle flew,[2]
Then tore with bloody talon the rent plain,
Pierced by the shaft of banded nations, through;   160
Ambition's life and labors all were vain;
He wears the shattered links of the world's broken chain.[3]

19

Fit retribution! Gaul[4] may champ the bit
And foam in fetters—but is Earth more free?
Did nations combat to make *One* submit;   165
Or league to teach all kings true sovereignty?
What! shall reviving Thralldom again be
The patched-up idol of enlightened days?
Shall we, who struck the Lion down, shall we
Pay the Wolf homage? proffering lowly gaze   170
And servile knees to thrones? No; *prove*[5] before ye praise!

20

If not, o'er one fallen despot boast no more!
In vain fair cheeks were furrowed with hot tears
For Europe's flowers long rooted up before
The trampler of her vineyards; in vain years   175
Of death, depopulation, bondage, fears,
Have all been borne, and broken by the accord
Of roused-up millions: all that most endears
Glory is when the myrtle wreathes a sword
Such as Harmodius drew on Athens' tyrant lord.[6]   180

21

There was a sound of revelry by night,
And Belgium's capital had gathered then
Her Beauty and her Chivalry, and bright
The lamps shone o'er fair women and brave men;[7]
A thousand hearts beat happily; and when   185
Music arose with its voluptuous swell,
Soft eyes looked love to eyes which spake again,
And all went merry as a marriage bell—
But hush! hark! a deep sound strikes like a rising knell!

1. Napoleon's defeat at Waterloo, near Brussels, had occurred only the year before, on June 18, 1815.
2. The eagle was the standard of Napoleon. "Pride of place" is a term from falconry meaning the highest point of flight (cf. *Macbeth* 2.4.12).
3. Napoleon was then a prisoner at St. Helena.
4. France. Byron, like Shelley and other liberals, saw the defeat of the Napoleonic tyranny as also a victory for tyrannous kings and the forces of extreme reaction throughout Europe.
5. Await the test (proof) of experience.
6. In 514 B.C. Harmodius and Aristogeiton, hiding their daggers in myrtle (symbol of love), killed Hipparchus, tyrant of Athens.
7. A famous ball, given by the duchess of Richmond on the eve of the battle of Quatre Bras, which opened the conflict at Waterloo.

22

Did ye not hear it?—No; 'twas but the wind,   190
Or the car rattling o'er the stony street;
On with the dance! let joy be unconfined;
No sleep till morn, when Youth and Pleasure meet
To chase the glowing Hours with flying feet—
But hark!—that heavy sound breaks in once more,   195
As if the clouds its echo would repeat;
And nearer, clearer, deadlier than before!
Arm! Arm! it is—it is—the cannon's opening roar!

23

Within a windowed niche of that high hall
Sate Brunswick's fated chieftain;[8] he did hear   200
That sound the first amidst the festival,
And caught its tone with Death's prophetic ear;
And when they smiled because he deemed it near,
His heart more truly knew that peal too well
Which stretched his father on a bloody bier,   205
And roused the vengeance blood alone could quell:
He rushed into the field, and, foremost fighting, fell.

24

Ah! then and there was hurrying to and fro,
And gathering tears, and tremblings of distress,
And cheeks all pale, which but an hour ago   210
Blushed at the praise of their own loveliness;
And there were sudden partings, such as press
The life from out young hearts, and choking sighs
Which ne'er might be repeated; who could guess
If ever more should meet those mutual eyes,   215
Since upon night so sweet such awful morn could rise!

25

And there was mounting in hot haste: the steed,
The mustering squadron, and the clattering car,
Went pouring forward with impetuous speed,
And swiftly forming in the ranks of war;   220
And the deep thunder peal on peal afar;
And near, the beat of the alarming drum
Roused up the soldier ere the morning star;
While thronged the citizens with terror dumb,
Or whispering, with white lips—"The foe! They come! they come!"

26

And wild and high the "Cameron's gathering"[9] rose!   226
The war-note of Lochiel, which Albyn's hills
Have heard, and heard, too, have her Saxon foes—
How in the noon of night that pibroch[1] thrills,

8. The duke of Brunswick, nephew of George III of England, was killed in the battle of Quatre Bras, just as his father, commanding the Prussian army against Napoleon, had been killed at Auerstedt in 1806 (line 205).

9. The clan song of the Camerons, whose chief was called "Lochiel," after his estate. "Albyn's" (line 227): Scotland's.

1. Bagpipe music, usually warlike in character.

Savage and shrill! But with the breath which fills 230
Their mountain pipe, so fill the mountaineers
With the fierce native daring which instills
The stirring memory of a thousand years,
And Evan's, Donald's fame[2] rings in each clansman's ears!

27

And Ardennes[3] waves above them her green leaves, 235
Dewy with nature's teardrops, as they pass,
Grieving, if aught inanimate e'er grieves,
Over the unreturning brave—alas!
Ere evening to be trodden like the grass
Which now beneath them, but above shall grow 240
In its next verdure, when this fiery mass
Of living valor, rolling on the foe
And burning with high hope, shall molder cold and low.

28

Last noon beheld them full of lusty life,
Last eve in Beauty's circle proudly gay, 245
The midnight brought the signal-sound of strife,
The morn the marshaling in arms—the day
Battle's magnificently-stern array!
The thunderclouds close o'er it, which when rent
The earth is covered thick with other clay, 250
Which her own clay shall cover, heaped and pent,
Rider and horse—friend, foe—in one red burial blent!

[NAPOLEON]

36

There sunk the greatest, nor the worst of men,[4]
Whose spirit antithetically mixed
One moment of the mightiest, and again
On little objects with like firmness fixed,
Extreme in all things! hadst thou been betwixt, 320
Thy throne had still been thine, or never been;
For daring made thy rise as fall: thou seek'st
Even now to reassume the imperial mien,
And shake again the world, the Thunderer of the scene!

37

Conqueror and captive of the earth art thou! 325
She trembles at thee still, and thy wild name
Was ne'er more bruited in men's minds than now
That thou art nothing, save the jest of Fame,
Who wooed thee once, thy vassal, and became
The flatterer of thy fierceness, till thou wert 330

---

2. Sir Evan and Donald Cameron, famous warriors in the Stuart cause in the 17th and 18th centuries.
3. A forested region covering parts of Belgium, France, and Luxembourg.
4. Napoleon, here portrayed with many of the characteristics of the Byronic hero.

A god unto thyself; nor less the same
To the astounded kingdoms all inert,
Who deemed thee for a time whate'er thou didst assert.

38

Oh, more or less than man—in high or low,
Battling with nations, flying from the field;   335
Now making monarchs' necks thy footstool, now
More than thy meanest soldier taught to yield;
An empire thou couldst crush, command, rebuild,
But govern not thy pettiest passion, nor,
However deeply in men's spirits skilled,   340
Look through thine own, nor curb the lust of war,
Nor learn that tempted Fate will leave the loftiest star.

39

Yet well thy soul hath brooked the turning tide
With that untaught innate philosophy,
Which, be it wisdom, coldness, or deep pride,   345
Is gall and wormwood to an enemy.
When the whole host of hatred stood hard by,
To watch and mock thee shrinking, thou hast smiled
With a sedate and all-enduring eye—
When Fortune fled her spoiled and favorite child,   350
He stood unbowed beneath the ills upon him piled.

40

Sager than in thy fortunes; for in them
Ambition steeled thee on too far to show
That just habitual scorn, which could contemn
Men and their thoughts; 'twas wise to feel, not so   355
To wear it ever on thy lip and brow,
And spurn the instruments thou wert to use
Till they were turned unto thine overthrow:
'Tis but a worthless world to win or lose;
So hath it proved to thee and all such lot[5] who choose.   360

41

If, like a tower upon a headlong rock,
Thou hadst been made to stand or fall alone,
Such scorn of man had helped to brave the shock;
But men's thoughts were the steps which paved thy throne,
Their admiration thy best weapon shone;   365
The part of Philip's son[6] was thine, not then
(Unless aside thy purple had been thrown)
Like stern Diogenes[7] to mock at men;
For sceptered cynics earth were far too wide a den.

---

5. An inversion: "all who choose such lot" (i.e., who choose to play such a game of chance).
6. Alexander the Great, son of Philip of Macedon.
7. The Greek philosopher of Cynicism, contemporary of Alexander. It is related that Alexander was so struck by his independence of mind that he said, "If I were not Alexander, I should wish to be Diogenes"; hence the allusion in lines 367 and 369.

42

But quiet to quick bosoms is a hell,   370
And *there* hath been thy bane; there is a fire
And motion of the soul which will not dwell
In its own narrow being, but aspire
Beyond the fitting medium of desire;
And, but once kindled, quenchless evermore,   375
Preys upon high adventure, nor can tire
Of aught but rest; a fever at the core,
Fatal to him who bears, to all who ever bore.

43

This makes the madmen who have made men mad
By their contagion; Conquerors and Kings,   380
Founders of sects and systems, to whom add
Sophists, Bards, Statesmen, all unquiet things
Which stir too strongly the soul's secret springs,
And are themselves the fools to those they fool;
Envied, yet how unenviable! what stings   385
Are theirs! One breast laid open were a school
Which would unteach mankind the lust to shine or rule.

44

Their breath is agitation, and their life
A storm whereon they ride, to sink at last;
And yet so nursed and bigoted to strife,   390
That should their days, surviving perils past,
Melt to calm twilight, they feel overcast
With sorrow and supineness, and so die;
Even as a flame unfed which runs to waste
With its own flickering, or a sword laid by,   395
Which eats into itself and rusts ingloriously.

45

He who ascends to mountain tops, shall find
The loftiest peaks most wrapped in clouds and snow;
He who surpasses or subdues mankind,
Must look down on the hate of those below.   400
Though high *above* the sun of glory glow,
And far *beneath* the earth and ocean spread,
Round him are icy rocks, and loudly blow
Contending tempests on his naked head,
And thus reward the toils which to those summits led.[8]   405

*   *   *

52

Thus Harold inly said, and passed along,   460
Yet not insensibly to all which here
Awoke the jocund birds to early song
In glens which might have made even exile dear:

8. In the stanzas here omitted, Harold is abruptly sent sailing up the Rhine, meditating on the "thousand battles" that "have assailed thy banks."

Though on his brow were graven lines austere,
And tranquil sternness which had ta'en the place   465
Of feelings fierier far but less severe,
Joy was not always absent from his face,
But o'er it in such scenes would steal with transient trace.

53

Nor was all love shut from him, though his days
Of passion had consumed themselves to dust.   470
It is in vain that we would coldly gaze
On such as smile upon us; the heart must
Leap kindly back to kindness, though disgust
Hath weaned it from all worldlings: thus he felt,
For there was soft remembrance, and sweet trust   475
In one fond breast,[9] to which his own would melt,
And in its tenderer hour on that his bosom dwelt.

54

And he had learned to love—I know not why,
For this in such as him seems strange of mood—
The helpless looks of blooming infancy,   480
Even in its earliest nurture; what subdued,
To change like this, a mind so far imbued
With scorn of man, it little boots to know;
But thus it was; and though in solitude
Small power the nipped affections have to grow,   485
In him this glowed when all beside had ceased to glow.

55

And there was one soft breast, as hath been said,
Which unto his was bound by stronger ties
Than the church links withal; and, though unwed,
That love was pure, and, far above disguise,   490
Had stood the test of mortal enmities
Still undivided, and cemented more
By peril, dreaded most in female eyes;
But this was firm, and from a foreign shore
Well to that heart might his these absent greetings pour! 495

[SWITZERLAND]

68

Lake Leman[1] woos me with its crystal face,
The mirror where the stars and mountains view   645
The stillness of their aspect in each trace
Its clear depth yields of their far height and hue:
There is too much of man here, to look through
With a fit mind the might which I behold;
But soon in me shall Loneliness renew   650

---

9. Commentators agree that the reference is to   1. Lake Geneva, in Switzerland.
Byron's half sister, Augusta Leigh.

Thoughts hid, but not less cherished than of old,
Ere mingling with the herd had penned me in their fold.

69

To fly from, need not be to hate, mankind:
All are not fit with them to stir and toil,
Nor is it discontent to keep the mind   655
Deep in its fountain, lest it overboil
In the hot throng, where we become the spoil
Of our infection, till too late and long
We may deplore and struggle with the coil,[2]
In wretched interchange of wrong for wrong   660
Midst a contentious world, striving where none are strong.

70

There, in a moment, we may plunge our years
In fatal penitence, and in the blight
Of our own soul turn all our blood to tears,
And color things to come with hues of night;   665
The race of life becomes a hopeless flight
To those that walk in darkness: on the sea,
The boldest steer but where their ports invite,
But there are wanderers o'er Eternity
Whose bark drives on and on, and anchored ne'er shall be.   670

71

Is it not better, then, to be alone,
And love earth only for its earthly sake?
By the blue rushing of the arrowy Rhone,
Or the pure bosom of its nursing lake,
Which feeds it as a mother who doth make   675
A fair but froward infant her own care,
Kissing its cries away as these awake—
Is it not better thus our lives to wear,
Than join the crushing crowd, doomed to inflict or bear?

72

I live not in myself, but I become   680
Portion of that around me; and to me
High mountains are a feeling, but the hum
Of human cities torture: I can see
Nothing to loathe in nature, save to be
A link reluctant in a fleshly chain,   685
Classed among creatures, when the soul can flee,
And with the sky, the peak, the heaving plain
Of ocean, or the stars, mingle, and not in vain.[3]

2. Tumult.
3. Byron had lived in close contact with Shelley at Geneva and had toured the lake with him. At that time, he was introduced to concepts of nature in the poetry of Wordsworth, whom Shelley had pressed on Byron's attention; these ideas are reflected in canto 3, but the voice is Byron's own. He said of this canto: "I was half mad during the time of its composition, between metaphysics, mountains, lakes, love unextinguishable, thoughts unutterable, and the nightmare of my own delinquencies." He then adds, with a typical shift to self-irony, "I should, many a good day, have blown my brains out, but for the recollection that it would have given pleasure to my mother-in-law."

73

And thus I am absorbed, and this is life:
I look upon the peopled desert past,   690
As on a place of agony and strife,
Where, for some sin, to sorrow I was cast,
To act and suffer, but remount at last
With a fresh pinion; which I feel to spring,
Though young, yet waxing vigorous, as the blast   695
Which it would cope with, on delighted wing,
Spurning the clay-cold bonds which round our being cling.

74

And when, at length, the mind shall be all free
From what it hates in this degraded form,
Reft of its carnal life, save what shall be   700
Existent happier in the fly and worm—
When elements to elements conform,
And dust is as it should be, shall I not
Feel all I see, less dazzling, but more warm?
The bodiless thought? the Spirit of each spot?   705
Of which, even now, I share at times the immortal lot?

75

Are not the mountains, waves, and skies a part
Of me and of my soul, as I of them?
Is not the love of these deep in my heart
With a pure passion? should I not contemn   710
All objects, if compared with these? and stem
A tide of suffering, rather than forego
Such feelings for the hard and worldly phlegm
Of those whose eyes are only turned below,
Gazing upon the ground, with thoughts which dare not glow?   715

76

But this is not my theme; and I return
To that which is immediate, and require
Those who find contemplation in the urn,[4]
To look on One, whose dust was once all fire,
A native of the land where I respire   720
The clear air for a while—a passing guest,
Where he became a being—whose desire
Was to be glorious; 'twas a foolish quest,
The which to gain and keep he sacrificed all rest.[5]

77

Here the self-torturing sophist, wild Rousseau,   725
The apostle of affliction, he who threw
Enchantment over passion, and from woe
Wrung overwhelming eloquence, first drew

---

4. I.e., those who find matter for meditation in
an urn containing the ashes of the dead.
5. Jean-Jacques Rousseau, who had been born in
Geneva in 1712. Byron's characterization is based

on Rousseau's novel *La Nouvelle Héloise*, as well
as on his *Confessions*. It clearly influenced Shelley's representation of Rousseau 6 years later in his
Triumph of Life (1822), lines 180 ff.; see below.

The breath which made him wretched; yet he knew
How to make madness beautiful, and cast   730
O'er erring deeds and thoughts a heavenly hue
Of words, like sunbeams, dazzling as they past
The eyes, which o'er them shed tears feelingly and fast.

78

His love was passion's essence—as a tree
On fire by lightning; with ethereal flame   735
Kindled he was, and blasted; for to be
Thus, and enamored, were in him the same.
But his was not the love of living dame,
Nor of the dead who rise upon our dreams,
But of ideal beauty, which became   740
In him existence, and o'erflowing teems
Along his burning page, distempered though it seems.

*   *   *

85

Clear, placid Leman! thy contrasted lake,
With the wild world I dwelt in, is a thing
Which warns me with its stillness to forsake
Earth's troubled waters for a purer spring.
This quiet sail is as a noiseless wing   800
To waft me from distraction; once I loved
Torn ocean's roar, but thy soft murmuring
Sounds sweet as if a sister's voice reproved,
That I with stern delights should e'er have been so moved. 805

86

It is the hush of night, and all between
Thy margin and the mountains, dusk, yet clear,
Mellowed and mingling, yet distinctly seen,
Save darkened Jura,[6] whose capped heights appear
Precipitously steep; and drawing near,   810
There breathes a living fragrance from the shore,
Of flowers yet fresh with childhood; on the ear
Drops the light drip of the suspended oar,
Or chirps the grasshopper one good-night carol more.

87

He is an evening reveler, who makes   815
His life an infancy, and sings his fill;
At intervals, some bird from out the brakes[7]
Starts into voice a moment, then is still.
There seems a floating whisper on the hill,
But that is fancy, for the starlight dews   820
All silently their tears of love instill,
Weeping themselves away, till they infuse
Deep into Nature's breast the spirit of her hues.

6. The mountain range between Switzerland and   7. Thickets.
France, visible from Lake Geneva.

88

Ye stars! which are the poetry of heaven!
If in your bright leaves we would read the fate　　825
Of men and empires—'tis to be forgiven,
That in our aspirations to be great,
Our destinies o'erleap their mortal state,
And claim a kindred with you; for ye are
A beauty and a mystery, and create　　830
In us such love and reverence from afar
That fortune—fame—power—life have named themselves a Star.

89

All heaven and earth are still—though not in sleep,
But breathless, as we grow when feeling most;
And silent, as we stand in thoughts too deep—　　835
All heaven and earth are still. From the high host
Of stars to the lulled lake and mountain coast,
All is concentered in a life intense,
Where not a beam, nor air, nor leaf is lost,
But hath a part of being, and a sense　　840
Of that which is of all Creator and defense.

90

Then stirs the feeling infinite, so felt
In solitude, where we are *least* alone;
A truth, which through our being then doth melt
And purifies from self: it is a tone,　　845
The soul and source of music, which makes known
Eternal harmony, and sheds a charm,
Like to the fabled Cytherea's zone,[8]
Binding all things with beauty—'twould disarm
The specter Death, had he substantial power to harm.　　850

91

Not vainly did the early Persian make
His altar the high places and the peak
Of earth-o'ergazing mountains, and thus take
A fit and unwalled temple, there to seek
The Spirit, in whose honor shrines are weak,　　855
Upreared of human hands. Come, and compare
Columns and idol-dwellings, Goth or Greek,
With Nature's realms of worship, earth and air,
Nor fix on fond abodes to circumscribe thy prayer!

92

The sky is changed!—and such a change! Oh night,　　860
And storm, and darkness, ye are wondrous strong,
Yet lovely in your strength, as is the light
Of a dark eye in woman! Far along,
From peak to peak, the rattling crags among,
Leaps the live thunder! Not from one lone cloud,　　865

---

8. The sash of Venus, which conferred the power to attract love.

But every mountain now hath found a tongue,
And Jura answers, through her misty shroud,
Back to the joyous Alps, who call to her aloud!

93

And this is in the night—Most glorious night!
Thou wert not sent for slumber! let me be   870
A sharer in thy fierce and far delight—
A portion of the tempest and of thee!
How the lit lake shines, a phosphoric sea,
And the big rain comes dancing to the earth!
And now again 'tis black—and now, the glee   875
Of the loud hills shakes with its mountain mirth,
As if they did rejoice o'er a young earthquake's birth.

94

Now, where the swift Rhone cleaves his way between
Heights which appear as lovers who have parted
In hate, whose mining depths so intervene   880
That they can meet no more, though brokenhearted!
Though in their souls, which thus each other thwarted,
Love was the very root of the fond rage
Which blighted their life's bloom, and then departed—
Itself expired, but leaving them an age   885
Of years all winters—war within themselves to wage:

95

Now, where the quick Rhone thus hath cleft his way,
The mightiest of the storms hath ta'en his stand:
For here, not one, but many, make their play,
And fling their thunderbolts from hand to hand,   890
Flashing and cast around: of all the band,
The brightest through these parted hills hath forked
His lightnings—as if he did understand,
That in such gaps as desolation worked,
There the hot shaft should blast whatever therein lurked.   895

96

Sky—mountains—river—winds—lake—lightnings! ye,
With night, and clouds, and thunder, and a soul
To make these felt and feeling, well may be
Things that have made me watchful; the far roll
Of your departing voices, is the knoll[9]   900
Of what in me is sleepless—if I rest.
But where of ye, oh tempests! is the goal?
Are ye like those within the human breast?
Or do ye find at length, like eagles, some high nest?

97

Could I embody and unbosom now   905
That which is most within me—could I wreak
My thoughts upon expression, and thus throw

9. Knell (old form).

Soul, heart, mind, passions, feelings, strong or weak,
All that I would have sought, and all I seek,
Bear, know, feel—and yet breathe—into *one* word,   910
And that one word were lightning, I would speak;
But as it is, I live and die unheard,
With a most voiceless thought, sheathing it as a sword.

98

The morn is up again, the dewy morn,
With breath all incense and with cheek all bloom,   915
Laughing the clouds away with playful scorn,
And living as if earth contained no tomb—
And glowing into day; we may resume
The march of our existence; and thus I,
Still on thy shores, fair Leman! may find room   920
And food for meditation, nor pass by
Much, that may give us pause, if pondered fittingly.

*　*　*

113

I have not loved the world, nor the world me;[1]
I have not flattered its rank breath, nor bowed   1050
To its idolatries a patient knee—
Nor coined my cheek to smiles—nor cried aloud
In worship of an echo; in the crowd
They could not deem me one of such; I stood
Among them, but not of them; in a shroud   1055
Of thoughts which were not their thoughts, and still could,
Had I not filed[2] my mind, which thus itself subdued.

114

I have not loved the world, nor the world me—
But let us part fair foes; I do believe,
Though I have found them not, that there may be   1060
Words which are things, hopes which will not deceive,
And virtues which are merciful nor weave
Snares for the failing: I would also deem
O'er others' griefs that some sincerely grieve;
That two, or one, are almost what they seem—   1065
That goodness is no name, and happiness no dream.

115

My daughter! with thy name this song begun—
My daughter! with thy name thus much shall end!—
I see thee not—I hear thee not—but none
Can be so wrapped in thee; thou art the friend   1070
To whom the shadows of far years extend:
Albeit my brow thou never shouldst behold,
My voice shall with thy future visions blend,

---

1. Harold utters this soliloquy as he stands at the summit of an Alpine pass, looking southward upon Italy.

2. Defiled. In a note Byron refers to *Macbeth* 3.1.64 ("For Banquo's issue have I filed my mind").

And reach into thy heart—when mine is cold—
A token and a tone even from thy father's mold.   1075

116

To aid thy mind's development—to watch
Thy dawn of little joys—to sit and see
Almost thy very growth—to view thee catch
Knowledge of objects—wonders yet to thee!
To hold thee lightly on a gentle knee,   1080
And print on thy soft cheek a parent's kiss—
This, it should seem, was not reserved for me;
Yet this was in my nature—as it is,
I know not what is there, yet something like to this.

117

Yet, though dull Hate as duty should be taught,   1085
I know that thou wilt love me; though my name
Should be shut from thee, as a spell still fraught
With desolation, and a broken claim;
Though the grave closed between us—'twere the same;
I know that thou wilt love me; though to drain   1090
My blood from out thy being were an aim
And an attainment—all would be in vain—
Still thou wouldst love me, still that more than life retain.

118

The child of love—though born in bitterness
And nurtured in convulsion! Of thy sire   1095
These were the elements, and thine no less.
As yet such are around thee, but thy fire
Shall be more tempered and thy hope far higher.
Sweet be thy cradled slumbers! O'er the sea,
And from the mountains where I now respire,   1100
Fain would I waft such blessing upon thee,
As, with a sigh, I deem thou mightst have been to me!

1812, 1816, 1818

The Vision of Judgment[1]

By *Quevedo Redivivus*[2]

SUGGESTED BY THE COMPOSITION SO ENTITLED BY THE AUTHOR
OF *Wat Tyler*

"A Daniel come to judgment! yea, a Daniel!
I thank thee, Jew, for teaching me that word."[3]

1

Saint Peter sat by the celestial gate:
    His keys were rusty, and the lock was dull,
So little trouble had been given of late;
    Not that the place by any means was full,
But since the Gallic era "eighty-eight"[4]   5
    The devils had ta'en a longer, stronger pull,
And "a pull altogether," as they say
At sea—which drew most souls another way.

2

The angels all were singing out of tune,
    And hoarse with having little else to do,   10
Excepting to wind up the sun and moon,
    Or curb a runaway young star or two,
Or wild colt of a comet, which too soon
    Broke out of bounds o'er th' ethereal blue,
Splitting some planet with its playful tail,   15
As boats are sometimes by a wanton whale.

3

The guardian seraphs had retired on high,
    Finding their charges past all care below;

1. Although originally an ardent supporter of the French Revolution, Robert Southey early became a Tory and in 1813 was appointed poet laureate. Four years after the appointment he was dismayed by the unauthorized publication of his radical poetical drama *Wat Tyler*, which he had written in 1794 but had prudently left in MS. Byron reminds him of it in the subtitle. When King George III died in 1820—Shelley in his sonnet *England in 1819* had called him, accurately enough, "an old, mad, blind, despised, and dying king"—Southey did his official duty by writing *A Vision of Judgment* (1821). In this fulsome eulogy George III goes to heaven, confounds such detractors as John Wilkes and Junius, and obtains a testimonial of noble character from his old enemy, George Washington. The vision ends with the king, beatified, ceremoniously admitted to heaven.
    Byron, responding to reports that Southey was vilifying him, had ridiculed the poet in his "Dedication" to canto 1 of *Don Juan*. In the Preface to his *Vision of Judgment*, Southey then exhibited his bad judgment by denouncing Byron as head of the "Satanic School" of poetry, combining "lascivious" passages with "a satanic spirit of pride and audacious impiety." Byron immediately responded with *The Vision of Judgment*, in which he purports to tell the true story of how, with the unwitting help of Southey, King George had really managed to get into heaven. The poem is in the genre of the satiric attack on literary "dunces" by Dryden and Pope, but is written in the ottava rima stanza and the easy colloquial manner of Byron's *Don Juan*. In its quick, sure characterization, the pace and economy of its narrative, its inventiveness in detail, and above all the high spirits and unfailing good humor with which the author demolishes his opponent, this poem represents Byron the satirist at his masterful best.
2. "Quevedo Revived." Quevedo was a 17th-century Spanish author of *Sueños*, "Visions," written in prose and predominantly satirical in tone.
3. Quoted, not quite accurately, from *The Merchant of Venice*, 4.1.340–41.
4. The last year of the old régime in France, before the outbreak of the Revolution in 1789.

Terrestrial business filled nought in the sky
  Save the recording angel's black bureau;   20
Who found, indeed, the facts to multiply
  With such rapidity of vice and woe,
That he had stripped off both his wings in quills,
And yet was in arrear of human ills.

4

His business so augmented of late years,   25
  That he was forced, against his will no doubt
(Just like those cherubs, earthly ministers),
  For some resource to turn himself about,
And claim the help of his celestial peers,
  To aid him ere he should be quite worn out   30
By the increased demand for his remarks;
Six angels and twelve saints were named his clerks.

5

This was a handsome board—at least for heaven;
  And yet they had even then enough to do,
So many conquerors' cars were daily driven,   35
  So many kingdoms fitted up anew;
Each day too slew its thousands six or seven,
  Till at the crowning carnage, Waterloo,
They threw their pens down in divine disgust—
The page was so besmeared with blood and dust.   40

6

This by the way; 'tis not mine to record
  What angels shrink from: even the very devil
On this occasion his own work abhorred,
  So surfeited with the infernal revel:
Though he himself had sharpened every sword,   45
  It almost quenched his innate thirst of evil.
(Here Satan's sole good work deserves insertion—
'Tis, that he has both generals in reversion.)[5]

7

Let's skip a few short years of hollow peace,
  Which peopled earth no better, hell as wont,   50
And heaven none—they form the tyrant's lease,
  With nothing but new names subscribed upon 't;
'Twill one day finish: meantime they increase,
  "With seven heads and ten horns," and all in front,
Like Saint John's foretold beast;[6] but ours are born   55
Less formidable in the head than horn.

8

In the first year of freedom's second dawn[7]
  Died George the Third; although no tyrant, one

5. I.e., Satan has the legal right to the possession,
after their deaths, of both Napoleon and Wellington, the commanding officers at the Battle of
Waterloo.
6. The Book of Revelation describes such a beast,
13.1.
7. 1820 was a year of new revolutionary movements in Italy and other countries of southern
Europe.

Who shielded tyrants, till each sense withdrawn
    Left him nor mental nor external sun: 60
A better farmer ne'er brushed dew from lawn,
    A worse king never left a realm undone!
He died—but left his subjects still behind,
One half as mad—and t'other no less blind.

9

He died! his death made no great stir on earth;   65
    His burial made some pomp; there was profusion
Of velvet, gilding, brass, and no great dearth
    Of aught but tears—save those shed by collusion.
For these things may be bought at their true worth;
    Of elegy there was the due infusion—   70
Bought also; and the torches, cloaks, and banners,
Heralds, and relics of old Gothic manners,

10

Formed a sepulchral melodrame. Of all
    The fools who flocked to swell or see the show,
Who cared about the corpse? The funeral   75
    Made the attraction, and the black the woe.
There throbbed not there a thought which pierced the pall;
    And when the gorgeous coffin was laid low,
It seemed the mockery of hell to fold
The rottenness of eighty years in gold.   80

11

So mix his body with the dust! It might
    Return to what it *must* far sooner, were
The natural compound left alone to fight
    Its way back into earth, and fire, and air;
But the unnatural balsams[8] merely blight   85
    What nature made him at his birth, as bare
As the mere million's base unmummied clay—
Yet all his spices but prolong decay.

12

He's dead—and upper earth with him has done;
    He's buried; save the undertaker's bill,   90
Or lapidary scrawl,[9] the world is gone
    For him, unless he left a German will;
But where's the proctor who will ask his son?[1]
    In whom his qualities are reigning still,
Except that household virtue, most uncommon,   95
Of constancy to a bad, ugly woman.

13

"God save the king!" It is a large economy
    In God to save the like; but if he will

---

8. Embalming fluids.
9. Inscription cut into a stone monument.
1. A King's Proctor is an official who intervenes
in the probate of a will when chicanery is suspected. Byron alludes to the scandal that the will
of George I, of the German House of Hanover,
had been hidden by his son, George II, who was
the grandfather of the late George III.

Be saving, all the better; for not one am I
   Of those who think damnation better still:
I hardly know too if not quite alone am I
   In this small hope of bettering future ill
By circumscribing, with some slight restriction,
The eternity of hell's hot jurisdiction.   100

14

I know this is unpopular; I know   105
   'Tis blasphemous; I know one may be damned
For hoping no one else may e'er be so;
   I know my catechism; I know we're crammed
With the best doctrines till we quite o'erflow;
   I know that all save England's church have shammed,   110
And that the other twice two hundred churches
And synagogues have made a *damned* bad purchase.

15

God help us all! God help me too! I am,
   God knows, as helpless as the devil can wish,
And not a whit more difficult to damn,   115
   Than is to bring to land a late-hooked fish,
Or to the butcher to purvey the lamb;
   Not that I'm fit for such a noble dish,
As one day will be that immortal fry
Of almost everybody born to die.   120

16

Saint Peter sat by the celestial gate,
   And nodded o'er his keys; when, lo! there came
A wondrous noise he had not heard of late—
   A rushing sound of wind, and stream, and flame;
In short, a roar of things extremely great,   125
   Which would have made aught save a saint exclaim;
But he, with first a start and then a wink,
Said, "There's another star gone out, I think!"

17

But ere he could return to his repose,
   A cherub flapped his right wing o'er his eyes—   130
At which St. Peter yawned, and rubbed his nose:
   "Saint porter," said the angel, "prithee rise!"
Waving a goodly wing, which glowed, as glows
   An earthly peacock's tail, with heavenly dyes:
To which the saint replied, "Well, what's the matter?   135
"Is Lucifer come back with all this clatter?"

18

"No," quoth the cherub; "George the Third is dead."
   "And who *is* George the Third?" replied the apostle:
"*What George? what Third?*" "The king of England," said
   The angel. "Well! he won't find kings to jostle   140
Him on his way; but does he wear his head;
   Because the last we saw here had a tustle,

And ne'er would have got into heaven's good graces,
Had he not flung his head in all our faces.[2]

19

"He was, if I remember, king of France;   145
    That head of his, which could not keep a crown
On earth, yet ventured in my face to advance
    A claim to those of martyrs—like my own:
If I had had my sword, as I had once
    When I cut ears off, I had cut him down;[3]   150
But having but my *keys*, and not my brand,
I only knocked his head from out his hand.

20

"And then he set up such a headless howl,
    That all the saints came out and took him in;
And there he sits by St. Paul, cheek by jowl;   155
    That fellow Paul—the parvenu! The skin
Of St. Bartholomew,[4] which makes his cowl
    In heaven, and upon earth redeemed his sin
So as to make a martyr, never sped
Better than did this weak and wooden head.   160

21

"But had it come up here upon its shoulders,
    There would have been a different tale to tell:
The fellow-feeling in the saint's beholders
    Seems to have acted on them like a spell;
And so this very foolish head heaven solders   165
    Back on its trunk: it may be very well,
And seems the custom here to overthrow
Whatever has been wisely done below."

22

The angel answered, "Peter! do not pout:
    The king who comes has head and all entire,   170
And never knew much what it was about—
    He did as doth the puppet—by its wire,
And will be judged like all the rest, no doubt:
    My business and your own is not to inquire
Into such matters, but to mind our cue—   175
Which is to act as we are bid to do."

23

While thus they spake, the angelic caravan,
    Arriving like a rush of mighty wind,
Cleaving the fields of space, as doth the swan
    Some silver stream (say Ganges, Nile, or Inde,   180
Or Thames, or Tweed), and 'midst them an old man

2. Louis XVI, who had been guillotined in January 1793.
3. When the officers came to take Jesus, "Simon
Peter having a sword drew it, and smote the high

priest's servant, and cut off his right ear" (John
18.10). "Brand" (line 151) is archaic for "sword."
4. According to tradition, the martyred St. Bartholomew was flayed alive.

With an old soul, and both extremely blind,
Halted before the gate, and in his shroud
Seated their fellow traveler on a cloud.

24

But bringing up the rear of this bright host   185
   A Spirit of a different aspect waved
His wings, like thunder clouds above some coast
   Whose barren beach with frequent wrecks is paved;
His brow was like the deep when tempest-tossed;
   Fierce and unfathomable thoughts engraved   190
Eternal wrath on his immortal face,
And *where* he gazed a gloom pervaded space.

25

As he drew near, he gazed upon the gate
   Ne'er to be entered more by him or Sin,
With such a glance of supernatural hate,   195
   As made Saint Peter wish himself within;
He pattered with his keys at a great rate,
   And sweated through his apostolic skin:
Of course his perspiration was but ichor,[5]
Or some such other spiritual liquor.   200

26

The very cherubs huddled all together,
   Like birds when soars the falcon; and they felt
A tingling to the tip of every feather,
   And formed a circle like Orion's belt
Around their poor old charge; who scarce knew whither   205
   His guards had led him, though they gently dealt
With royal manes[6] (for by many stories,
And true, we learn the angels all are Tories).

27

As things were in this posture, the gate flew
   Asunder, and the flashing of its hinges   210
Flung over space an universal hue
   Of many-colored flame, until its tinges
Reached even our speck of earth, and made a new
   Aurora borealis spread its fringes
O'er the North Pole; the same seen, when ice-bound,   215
By Captain Parry's[7] crew, in "Melville's Sound."

28

And from the gate thrown open issued beaming
   A beautiful and mighty Thing of Light,
Radiant with glory, like a banner streaming
   Victorious from some world-o'erthrowing fight: 220
My poor comparisons must needs be teeming

5. The fluid in the veins of the classical gods.
6. In Roman religion, spirits of the dead (pronounced mā'nēz).

7. Capt. William Edward Parry, in his account of his *Voyage in 1819–20*, in search of a northwest passage.

With earthly likenesses, for here the night
Of clay obscures our best conceptions, saving
Johanna Southcote,[8] or Bob Southey raving.

                    29

'Twas the archangel Michael: all men know   225
    The make of angels and archangels, since
There's scarce a scribbler has not one to show,
    From the fiends' leader to the angels' prince.
There also are some altarpieces, though
    I really can't say that they much evince   230
One's inner notions of immortal spirits;
But let the connoisseurs explain *their* merits.

                    30

Michael flew forth in glory and in good;
    A goodly work of him from whom all glory
And good arise; the portal past—he stood;   235
    Before him the young cherubs and saints hoary—
(I say *young*, begging to be understood
    By looks, not years; and should be very sorry
To state, they were not older than St. Peter,
But merely that they seemed a little sweeter).   240

                    31

The cherubs and the saints bowed down before
    That arch-angelic hierarch, the first
Of essences angelical, who wore
    The aspect of a god; but this ne'er nursed
Pride in his heavenly bosom, in whose core   245
    No thought, save for his Master's service, durst
Intrude, however glorified and high;
He knew him but the viceroy of the sky.

                    32

He and the somber silent Spirit met—
    They knew each other both for good and ill;   250
Such was their power, that neither could forget
    His former friend and future foe; but still
There was a high, immortal, proud regret
    In either's eye, as if 'twere less their will
Than destiny to make the eternal years   255
Their date of war, and their "champ clos"[9] the spheres.

                    33

But here they were in neutral space: we know
    From Job, that Satan hath the power to pay
A heavenly visit thrice a year or so;
    And that the "sons of God," like those of clay,   260

8. Joanna Southcott (1750–1814) was a servant girl who, claiming direct communications from the Almighty, became head of a religious sect. In 1813 she proclaimed that she was about to give birth to a son, Shiloh, who would redeem the world. The pregnancy turned out to be a tumor, of which she died the following year.
9. "Enclosed field," the arena for knightly tournaments.

Must keep him company;[1] and we might show
   From the same book, in how polite a way
The dialogue is held between the Powers
Of Good and Evil—but 'twould take up hours.

34

And this is not a theologic tract,   265
   To prove with Hebrew and with Arabic
If Job be allegory or a fact,
   But a true narrative; and thus I pick
From out the whole but such and such an act
   As sets aside the slightest thought of trick.   270
'Tis every tittle true, beyond suspicion,
And accurate as any other vision.

35

The spirits were in neutral space, before
   The gate of heaven; like eastern thresholds is
The place where Death's grand cause is argued o'er,[2]   275
   And souls despatched to that world or to this;
And therefore Michael and the other wore
   A civil aspect: though they did not kiss,
Yet still between his Darkness and his Brightness
There passed a mutual glance of great politeness.   280

36

The Archangel bowed, not like a modern beau,
   But with a graceful oriental bend,
Pressing one radiant arm just where below
   The heart in good men is supposed to tend.
He turned as to an equal, not too low,   285
   But kindly; Satan met his ancient friend
With more hauteur, as might an old Castilian
Poor noble meet a mushroom rich civilian.[3]

37

He merely bent his diabolic brow
   An instant; and then raising it, he stood   290
In act to assert his right or wrong, and show
   Cause why King George by no means could or should
Make out a case to be exempt from woe
   Eternal, more than other kings, endued
With better sense and hearts, whom history mentions,   295
Who long have "paved hell with their good intentions."[4]

38

Michael began: "What wouldst thou with this man,
   Now dead, and brought before the Lord? What ill
Hath he wrought since his mortal race began,

---

1. "There was a day when the sons of God came to present themselves before the Lord, and Satan came also among them" (Job 1.6).
2. The gateways of walled cities in the Middle East were sometimes used for public debates and to administer justice.
3. Byron contrasts ancient Spanish noblemen with *nouveaux riches* who spring up as rapidly as mushrooms.
4. An old English proverb.

That thou canst claim him? Speak! and do thy will,   300
If it be just: if in this earthly span
   He hath been greatly failing to fulfil
His duties as a king and mortal, say,
And he is thine; if not, let him have way."

39

"Michael!" replied the Prince of Air, "even here,   305
   Before the Gate of him thou servest, must
I claim my subject: and will make appear
   That as he was my worshipper in dust,
So shall he be in spirit, although dear
   To thee and thine, because nor wine nor lust   310
Were of his weaknesses; yet on the throne
He reigned o'er millions to serve me alone.

40

"Look to *our* earth, or rather *mine*; it was,
   Once, *more* thy master's: but I triumph not
In this poor planet's conquest; nor, alas!   315
   Need he thou servest envy me my lot:
With all the myriads of bright worlds which pass
   In worship round him, he may have forgot
Yon weak creation of such paltry things:
I think few worth damnation save their kings—   320

41

"And these but as a kind of quitrent,[5] to
   Assert my right as lord: and even had
I such an inclination, 'twere (as you
   Well know) superfluous; they are grown so bad,
That hell has nothing better left to do   325
   Than leave them to themselves: so much more mad
And evil by their now internal curse,
Heaven cannot make them better, nor I worse.

42

"Look to the earth, I said, and say again:
   When this old, blind, mad, helpless, weak, poor worm   330
Began in youth's first bloom and flush to reign,
   The world and he both wore a different form,
And much of earth and all the watery plain
   Of ocean called him king: through many a storm
His isles had floated on the abyss of time;   335
For the rough virtues chose them for their clime.

43

"He came to his scepter young; he leaves it old:
   Look to the state in which he found his realm,
And left it; and his annals too behold,
   How to a minion first he gave the helm,[6]   340
How grew upon his heart a thirst for gold,

---

5. A fixed rent, paid in place of services to a feudal   6. The unpopular earl of Bute, whom George III
lord.   made Prime Minister in 1802.

The beggar's vice, which can but overwhelm
The meanest hearts; and for the rest, but glance
Thine eye along America and France.

44

" 'Tis true, he was a tool from first to last   345
   (I have the workmen safe); but as a tool
So let him be consumed. From out the past
   Of ages, since mankind have known the rule
Of monarchs—from the bloody rolls amassed
   Of sin and slaughter—from the Caesars' school,   350
Take the worst pupil; and produce a reign
More drenched with gore, more cumbered with the slain.

45

"He ever warred with freedom and the free:
   Nations as men, home subjects, foreign foes,
So that[7] they uttered the word 'Liberty!'   355
   Found George the Third their first opponent. Whose
History was ever stained as his will be
   With national and individual woes?
I grant his household abstinence; I grant
His neutral virtues, which most monarchs want;   360

46

"I know he was a constant consort; own
   He was a decent sire, and middling lord.
All this is much, and most upon a throne;
   As temperance, if at Apicius' board,[8]
Is more than at an anchorite's[9] supper shown.   365
   I grant him all the kindest can accord;
And this was well for him, but not for those
Millions who found him what oppression chose.

47

"The New World shook him off; the Old yet groans
   Beneath what he and his prepared, if not   370
Completed: he leaves heirs on many thrones
   To all his vices, without what begot
Compassion for him—his tame virtues; drones
   Who sleep, or despots who have now forgot
A lesson which shall be re-taught them, wake   375
Upon the thrones of earth; but let them quake!

48

"Five millions of the primitive,[1] who hold
   The faith which makes ye great on earth, implored
A *part* of that vast *all* they held of old—
   Freedom to worship—not alone your Lord,   380
Michael, but you, and you, Saint Peter! Cold

---

7. Provided that.
8. I.e., at the table of Apicius (a famed Roman gourmet in the time of Augustus).
9. A religious hermit's.

1. The Irish Catholics. In 1795 George had opposed the Catholic Emancipation Bill, which would have given Roman Catholics the right to hold public offices (line 383).

Must be your souls, if you have not abhorred
The foe to Catholic participation
In all the license of a Christian nation.

49

"True! he allowed them to pray God; but as   385
    A consequence of prayer, refused the law
Which would have placed them upon the same base
    With those who did not hold the saints in awe."
But here Saint Peter started from his place,
    And cried, "You may the prisoner withdraw: 390
Ere heaven shall ope her portals to this Guelph,[2]
While I am guard, may I be damned myself!

50

"Sooner will I with Cerberus[3] exchange
    My office (and *his* is no sinecure)
Than see this royal Bedlam bigot range   395
    The azure fields of heaven, of that be sure!"
"Saint!" replied Satan, "you do well to avenge
    The wrongs he made your satellites endure;
And if to this exchange you should be given,
I'll try to coax *our* Cerberus up to heaven."   400

51

Here Michael interposed: "Good saint! and devil!
    Pray, not so fast; you both outrun discretion.
Saint Peter! you were wont to be more civil!
    Satan! excuse this warmth of his expression,
And condescension to the vulgar's level: 405
    Even saints sometimes forget themselves in session.
Have you got more to say?"—"No."—"If you please,
I'll trouble you to call your witnesses."

52

Then Satan turned and waved his swarthy hand,
    Which stirred with its electric qualities   410
Clouds farther off than we can understand,
    Although we find him sometimes in our skies;
Infernal thunder shook both sea and land
    In all the planets, and hell's batteries
Let off the artillery, which Milton mentions   415
As one of Satan's most sublime inventions.[4]

53

This was a signal unto such damned souls
    As have the privilege of their damnation
Extended far beyond the mere controls
    Of worlds past, present, or to come; no station   420

2. The House of Hanover was descended from the German Guelphs.
3. The three-headed dog guarding the entrance to Hades.
4. In *Paradise Lost* 6.469 ff., Satan announces his invention of the cannon for use in the war in heaven.

Is theirs particularly in the rolls
  Of hell assigned; but where their inclination
Or business carries them in search of game,
They may range freely—being damned the same.

        54

They're proud of this—as very well they may,   425
  It being a sort of knighthood, or gilt key
Stuck in their loins;[5] or like to an "entré"
  Up the back stairs, or such freemasonry.
I borrow my comparisons from clay,
  Being clay myself. Let not those spirits be   430
Offended with such base low likenesses;
We know their posts are nobler far than these.

        55

When the great signal ran from heaven to hell—
  About ten million times the distance reckoned
From our sun to its earth, as we can tell   435
  How much time it takes up, even to a second,
For every ray that travels to dispel
  The fogs of London, through which, dimly beaconed,
The weathercocks are gilt some thrice a year,
If that the *summer* is not too severe—   440

        56

I say that I can tell—'twas half a minute:
  I know the solar beams take up more time
Ere, packed up for their journey, they begin it;
  But then their telegraph[6] is less sublime,
And if they ran a race, they would not win it   445
  'Gainst Satan's couriers bound for their own clime.
The sun takes up some years for every ray
To reach its goal—the devil not half a day.

        57

Upon the verge of space, about the size
  Of half-a-crown, a little speck appeared   450
(I've seen a something like it in the skies
  In the Aegean, ere a squall); it neared,
And, growing bigger, took another guise;
  Like an aërial ship it tacked, and steered,
Or *was* steered (I am doubtful of the grammar   455
Of the last phrase, which makes the stanza stammer—

        58

But take your choice); and then it grew a cloud;
  And so it was—a cloud of witnesses.
But such a cloud! No land e'er saw a crowd
  Of locusts numerous as the heavens saw these;   460
They shadowed with their myriads space; their loud

5. A gold key hung from the belt betokens certain official positions at the English court.

6. In its original sense, any apparatus for transmitting signals at a distance.

And varied cries were like those of wild geese
(If nations may be likened to a goose),
And realized the phrase of "hell broke loose."[7]

59

Here crashed a sturdy oath of stout John Bull,   465
   Who damned away his eyes as heretofore:
There Paddy brogued "By Jasus!"—"What's your wull?"
   The temperate Scot exclaimed: the French ghost swore
In certain terms I shan't translate in full,
   As the first coachman will; and 'midst the war,   470
The voice of Jonathan was heard to express,
"*Our* president is going to war, I guess."[8]

60

Besides there were the Spaniard, Dutch, and Dane;
   In short, an universal shoal of shades,
From Otaheite's isle[9] to Salisbury Plain,   475
   Of all climes and professions, years and trades,
Ready to swear against the good king's reign,
   Bitter as clubs in cards are against spades;
All summoned by this grand "subpoena," to
Try if kings mayn't be damned like me or you.   480

61

When Michael saw this host, he first grew pale,
   As angels can; next, like Italian twilight,
He turned all colors—as a peacock's tail,
   Or sunset streaming through a Gothic skylight
In some old abbey, or a trout not stale,   485
   Or distant lightning on the horizon *by* night,
Or a fresh rainbow, or a grand review
Of thirty regiments in red, green, and blue.

62

Then he addressed himself to Satan: "Why—
   My good old friend, for such I deem you, though   490
Our different parties make us fight so shy,
   I ne'er mistake you for a *personal* foe;
Our difference is *political*, and I
   Trust that, whatever may occur below,
You know my great respect for you: and this   495
Makes me regret whate'er you do amiss—

63

"Why, my dear Lucifer, would you abuse
   My call for witnesses? I did not mean
That you should half of earth and hell produce;
   'Tis even superfluous, since two honest, clean,   500
True testimonies are enough: we lose

---

7. *Paradise Lost* 4.918.
8. "Brother Jonathan" was the name applied to America and Americans, now replaced by "Uncle Sam"; the "I guess" was intended by Byron as an obvious Americanism. This was written during the troubled Anglo-American relations after the War of 1812.
9. The old name for Tahiti.

Our time, nay, our eternity, between
The accusation and defense: if we
Hear both, 'twill stretch our immortality."

64

Satan replied, "To me the matter is   505
   Indifferent, in a personal point of view:
I can have fifty better souls than this
   With far less trouble than we have gone through
Already; and I merely argued his
   Late majesty of Britain's case with you   510
Upon a point of form: you may dispose
Of him; I've kings enough below, God knows!"

65

Thus spoke the Demon (late called "multifaced"
   By multo-scribbling Southey).[1] "Then we'll call
One or two persons of the myriads placed   515
   Around our congress, and dispense with all
The rest," quoth Michael: "Who may be so graced
   As to speak first? there's choice enough—who shall
It be?" Then Satan answered, "There are many;
But you may choose Jack Wilkes[2] as well as any."   520

66

A merry, cock-eyed, curious-looking sprite
   Upon the instant started from the throng,
Dressed in a fashion now forgotten quite;
   For all the fashions of the flesh stick long
By people in the next world; where unite   525
   All the costumes since Adam's, right or wrong,
From Eve's fig leaf down to the petticoat,
Almost as scanty, of days less remote.

67

The spirit looked around upon the crowds
   Assembled, and exclaimed, "My friends of all   530
The spheres, we shall catch cold amongst these clouds;
   So let's to business: why this general call?
If those are freeholders I see in shrouds,
   And 'tis for an election that they bawl,
Behold a candidate with unturned coat!   535
Saint Peter, may I count upon your vote?"

68

"Sir," replied Michael, "you mistake; these things
   Are of a former life, and what we do
Above is more august; to judge of kings
   Is the tribunal met: so now you know."   540

1. In A Vision of Judgment 5.70.
2. John Wilkes (1727–1797), noted libertine, wit, and courageous political radical who in 1764 was expelled from the House of Commons and driven into exile for his libelous attack on George III in his weekly periodical, The North Briton. He later came back to England, became Lord Mayor of London, and was triumphantly returned to Parliament. For an example of the wit and aplomb for which Byron admired Wilkes, see Boswell's account of Samuel Johnson's dinner with him in volume 1 of this anthology.

"Then I presume those gentlemen with wings,"
   Said Wilkes, "are cherubs; and that soul below
Looks much like George the Third, but to my mind
A good deal older—Bless me! is he blind?"

69

"He is what you behold him, and his doom   545
   Depends upon his deeds," the Angel said.
"If you have aught to arraign in him, the tomb
   Gives license to the humblest beggar's head
To lift itself against the loftiest."—"Some,"
   Said Wilkes, "don't wait to see them laid in lead,   550
For such a liberty—and I, for one,
Have told them what I thought beneath the sun."

70

"Above the sun repeat, then, what thou hast
   To urge against him," said the Archangel. "Why,"
Replied the spirit, "since old scores are past,   555
   Must I turn evidence? In faith, not I.
Besides, I beat him hollow at the last,
   With all his Lords and Commons:[3] in the sky
I don't like ripping up old stories, since
His conduct was but natural in a prince.   560

71

"Foolish, no doubt, and wicked, to oppress
   A poor unlucky devil without a shilling;
But then I blame the man himself much less
   Than Bute and Grafton,[4] and shall be unwilling
To see him punished here for their excess,   565
   Since they were both damned long ago, and still in
Their place below: for me, I have forgiven,
And vote his 'habeas corpus' into heaven."

72

"Wilkes," said the Devil, "I understand all this;
   You turned to half a courtier ere you died,[5]   570
And seem to think it would not be amiss
   To grow a whole one on the other side
Of Charon's ferry;[6] you forget that his
   Reign is concluded; whatsoe'er betide,
He won't be sovereign more: you've lost your labor   575
For at the best he will but be your neighbor.

73

"However, I knew what to think of it,
   When I beheld you in your jesting way
Flitting and whispering round about the spit
   Where Belial, upon duty for the day,   580

---

3. In 1782 Wilkes succeeded in getting the House of Commons to erase the record of his expulsion.
4. The duke of Grafton, like the earl of Bute, was a minister subservient to George III.

5. Wilkes in his latter years softened his opposition and moved in higher social circles.
6. In Greek mythology, Charon ferried the dead to the underworld across the river Styx.

With Fox's lard was basting William Pitt,[7]
   His pupil; I knew what to think, I say:
That fellow even in hell breeds farther ills;
   I'll have him *gagged*—'twas one of his own bills.[8]

74

"Call Junius!"[9] From the crowd a shadow stalked,   585
   And at the name there was a general squeeze,
So that the very ghosts no longer walked
   In comfort, at their own aërial ease,
But were all rammed, and jammed (but to be balked,
   As we shall see), and jostled hands and knees,   590
Like wind compressed and pent within a bladder,
Or like a human colic, which is sadder.

75

The shadow came—a tall, thin, gray-haired figure,
   That looked as it had been a shade on earth;
Quick in its motions, with an air of vigor,   595
   But nought to mark its breeding or its birth:
Now it waxed little, then again grew bigger,
   With now an air of gloom, or savage mirth;
But as you gazed upon its features, they
Changed every instant—to *what*, none could say.   600

76

The more intently the ghosts gazed, the less
   Could they distinguish whose the features were;
The Devil himself seemed puzzled even to guess;
   They varied like a dream—now here, now there;
And several people swore from out the press,   605
   They knew him perfectly; and one could swear
He was his father: upon which another
Was sure he was his mother's cousin's brother:

77

Another, that he was a duke, or knight,
   An orator, a lawyer, or a priest,   610
A nabob,[1] a man-midwife; but the wight
   Mysterious changed his countenance at least
As oft as they their minds: though in full sight
   He stood, the puzzle only was increased;
The man was a phantasmagoria in   615
Himself—he was so volatile and thin.

---

7. Charles James Fox, statesman and political opponent of William Pitt, prime minister under George III, was notably corpulent.
8. The Alien and Sedition Bills of 1795 severely restricted freedom of speech and of the press.
9. Pseudonym of the writer of a brilliant series of letters (1769–71) attacking supporters of George III and the king himself. His identity is an unsolved political mystery; among more than fifty possibilities proposed are Edmund Burke, John Horne Tooke, and Sir Philip Francis, mentioned in lines 631–32. When the letters were published as a book, the title page read: *Letters of Junius, Stat Nominis Umbra* ("he stands, the shadow of a name"); hence the allusions, lines 593 ff., 667. The Latin phrase is from Lucan's *Pharsalia* 1.135.
1. A man of great wealth, especially one who has returned to England with a fortune acquired in India.

78

The moment that you had pronounced him *one*,
    Presto! his face changed, and he was another;
And when that change was hardly well put on,
    It varied, till I don't think his own mother   620
(If that he had a mother) would her son
    Have known, he shifted so from one to t'other;
Till guessing from a pleasure grew a task,
At this epistolary "Iron Mask."[2]

79

For sometimes he like Cerberus would seem—   625
    "Three gentlemen at once" (as sagely says
Good Mrs. Malaprop);[3] then you might deem
    That he was not even *one*; now many rays
Were flashing round him; and now a thick steam
    Hid him from sight—like fogs on London days: 630
Now Burke, now Tooke, he grew to people's fancies,
And certes often like Sir Philip Francis.

80

I've an hypothesis—'tis quite my own;
    I never let it out till now, for fear
Of doing people harm about the throne,   635
    And injuring some minister or peer,
On whom the stigma might perhaps be blown;
    It is—my gentle public, lend thine ear!
'Tis, that what Junius we are wont to call
Was *really, truly*, nobody at all.   640

81

I don't see wherefore letters should not be
    Written without hands, since we daily view
Them written without heads; and books, we see,
    Are filled as well without the latter too:
And really till we fix on somebody   645
    For certain sure to claim them as his due,
Their author, like the Niger's mouth,[4] will bother
The world to say if *there* be mouth or author.

82

"And who and what art thou?" the Archangel said.
    "For *that* you may consult my title page,"   650
Replied this mighty shadow of a shade;
    "If I have kept my secret half an age,
I scarce shall tell it now."—"Canst thou upbraid,"
    Continued Michael, "George Rex, or allege
Aught further?" Junius answered, "You had better   655
First ask him for *his* answer to my letter:

2. "The Man in the Iron Mask" was a state prisoner in the reign of Louis XIV, whose identity was
thus concealed.
3. A character in R. B. Sheridan's *The Rivals*, who
comically misused words; the term "malapropism"
derives from her name.
4. Several recent British expeditions to explore the
course of the river Niger, in western Africa, had
ended in failure.

83

"My charges upon record will outlast
    The brass of both his epitaph and tomb."
"Repent'st thou not," said Michael, "of some past
    Exaggeration? something which may doom   660
Thyself if false, as him if true? Thou wast
    Too bitter—is it not so?—in thy gloom
Of passion?"—"Passion!" cried the phantom dim,
"I loved my country, and I hated him.

84

"What I have written, I have written:[5] let   665
    The rest be on his head or mine!" So spoke
Old "Nominis Umbra"; and while speaking yet,
    Away he melted in celestial smoke.
Then Satan said to Michael, "Don't forget
    To call George Washington, and John Horne Tooke,[6]   670
And Franklin"—but at this time there was heard
A cry for room, though not a phantom stirred.

85

At length with jostling, elbowing, and the aid
    Of cherubim appointed to that post,
The devil Asmodeus[7] to the circle made   675
    His way, and looked as if his journey cost
Some trouble. When his burden down he laid,
    "What's this?" cried Michael; "why, 'tis not a ghost?"
"I know it," quoth the incubus; "but he
Shall be one, if you leave the affair to me.   680

86

"Confound the renegado! I have sprained
    My left wing, he's so heavy; one would think
Some of his works about his neck were chained.
    But to the point; while hovering o'er the brink
Of Skiddaw (where as usual it still rained),[8]   685
    I saw a taper, far below me, wink,
And stooping, caught this fellow at a libel—
No less on history than the Holy Bible.

87

"The former is the devil's scripture, and
    The latter yours, good Michael: so the affair   690
Belongs to all of us, you understand.
    I snatched him up just as you see him there,
And brought him off for sentence out of hand:
    I've scarcely been ten minutes in the air—
At least a quarter it can hardly be: 695
I dare say that his wife is still at tea."

---

5. Said by Pilate, John 19.22.
6. A prominent English opponent of the war against the American colonies; see note to line 585.
7. The devil in Le Sage's *Le Diable Boiteux* ("The Lame Devil"), published 1707, who carries Don Cleofas to the summit of San Salvador.
8. Mount Skiddaw, near Southey's home in the Lake Country.

88

Here Satan said, "I know this man of old,
  And have expected him for some time here;
A sillier fellow you will scarce behold,
  Or more conceited in his petty sphere: 700
But surely it was not worth while to fold
  Such trash below your wing, Asmodeus dear:
We had the poor wretch safe (without being bored
With carriage) coming of his own accord.

89

"But since he's here, let's see what he has done."   705
  "Done!" cried Asmodeus, "he anticipates
The very business you are now upon,
  And scribbles as if head clerk to the Fates.
Who knows to what his ribaldry may run,
  When such an ass as this, like Balaam's,[9] prates?"   710
"Let's hear," quoth Michael, "What he has to say:
You know we're bound to that in every way."

90

Now the bard, glad to get an audience, which
  By no means often was his case below,
Began to cough, and hawk, and hem, and pitch   715
  His voice into that awful note of woe
To all unhappy hearers within reach
  Of poets when the tide of rhyme's in flow;
But stuck fast with his first hexameter,
Not one of all whose gouty feet would stir.   720

91

But ere the spavined dactyls[1] could be spurred
  Into recitative, in great dismay
Both cherubim and seraphim were heard
  To murmur loudly through their long array;
And Michael rose ere he could get a word   725
  Of all his foundered verses under way,
And cried, "For God's sake stop, my friend! 'twere best—
Non Di, non homines[2]—you know the rest."

92

A general bustle spread throughout the throng,
  Which seemed to hold all verse in detestation;   730
The angels had of course enough of song
  When upon service; and the generation
Of ghosts had heard too much in life, not long
  Before, to profit by a new occasion:

---

9. Balaam's ass was granted speech in Numbers
22.28 ff.
1. Southey's A Vision of Judgment was written in
dactylic hexameters, a very awkward measure in
English. A "spavined" horse is a lame one.

2. Horace, Art of Poetry 372–73: "mediocribus esse
poetis / Non homines, non di, non concessere col-
umnae" ("mediocrity in poets has never been tolerated by either men, or gods, or booksellers").

The monarch, mute till then, exclaimed, "What! what!   735
Pye[3] come again? No more—no more of that!"

93

The tumult grew; an universal cough
   Convulsed the skies, as during a debate,
When Castlereagh[4] has been up long enough
   (Before he was first minister of state,   740
I mean—the *slaves hear now*); some cried "Off, off!"
   As at a farce; till, grown quite desperate,
The bard Saint Peter prayed to interpose
(Himself an author)[5] only for his prose.

94

The varlet was not an ill-favored knave;   745
   A good deal like a vulture in the face,
With a hook nose and a hawk's eye, which gave
   A smart and sharper-looking sort of grace
To his whole aspect, which, though rather grave,
   Was by no means so ugly as his case;   750
But that, indeed, was hopeless as can be,
Quite a poetic felony "*de se*."[6]

95

Then Michael blew his trump, and stilled the noise
   With one still greater, as is yet the mode
On earth besides; except some grumbling voice,   755
   Which now and then will make a slight inroad
Upon decorous silence, few will twice
   Lift up their lungs when fairly overcrowed;
And now the bard could plead his own bad cause,
With all the attitudes of self-applause.   760

96

He said—(I only give the heads)—he said,
   He meant no harm in scribbling; 'twas his way
Upon all topics; 'twas, besides, his bread,
   Of which he buttered both sides; 'twould delay
Too long the assembly (he was pleased to dread),   765
   And take up rather more time than a day,
To name his works—he would but cite a few—
"Wat Tyler"—"Rhymes on Blenheim"—"Waterloo."

97

He had written praises of a regicide;[7]
   He had written praises of all kings whatever;   770
He had written for republics far and wide,

---

3. Henry James Pye, an inept and much ridiculed poet, Southey's predecessor as poet laureate.
4. Viscount Castlereagh was foreign secretary when Byron wrote his poem. "The slaves hear now" (line 741): i.e., now that he is prime minister, members of the House of Commons listen obsequiously.
5. The reference is to the first and second epistles of Peter, very short books in the New Testament.
6. A felony "upon himself"; i.e., suicide.
7. In an early poem on Henry Martin, one of the judges who had condemned Charles I to be beheaded.

And then against them bitterer than ever:
For pantisocracy[8] he once had cried
    Aloud, a scheme less moral than 'twas clever;
Then grew a hearty anti-jacobin—   775
Had turned his coat—and would have turned his skin.

                98

He had sung against all battles, and again
    In their high praise and glory; he had called
Reviewing "the ungentle craft,"[9] and then
    Become as base a critic as e'er crawled—   780
Fed, paid, and pampered by the very men
    By whom his muse and morals had been mauled:
He had written much blank verse, and blanker prose,
And more of both than anybody knows.

                99

He had written Wesley's life—here turning round   785
    To Satan, "Sir, I'm ready to write yours,
In two octavo volumes, nicely bound,
    With notes and preface, all that most allures
The pious purchaser; and there's no ground
    For fear, for I can choose my own reviewers: 790
So let me have the proper documents,
That I may add you to my other saints."

               100

Satan bowed, and was silent. "Well, if you,
    With amiable modesty, decline
My offer, what says Michael? There are few   795
    Whose memoirs could be rendered more divine.
Mine is a pen of all work; not so new
    As it was once, but I would make you shine
Like your own trumpet. By the way, my own
Has more of brass in it, and is as well blown.   800

               101

"But talking about trumpets, here's my Vision!
    Now you shall judge, all people; yes, you shall
Judge with my judgment, and by my decision
    Be guided who shall enter heaven or fall.
I settle all these things by intuition,   805
    Times present, past, to come, heaven, hell, and all,
Like King Alfonso.[1] When I thus see double,
I save the Deity some worlds of trouble."

              102

He ceased, and drew forth an MS; and no
    Persuasion on the part of devils, saints,   810

---

8. An ideal community that Southey and Coleridge, in 1794–95, had planned to set up in America on the banks of the Susquehanna. The scheme was utopian, but in no way immoral.
9. In Southey's *The Remains of Henry Kirke White*, vol. 1 (1808).

1. "King Alphonso [of Castile, in the 13th century], speaking of the Ptolemean system, said that had he been consulted at the creation of the world, he would have spared the Maker some absurdities" [Byron's note].

Or angels, now could stop the torrent; so
  He read the first three lines of the contents;
But at the fourth, the whole spiritual show
  Had vanished, with variety of scents,
Ambrosial and sulphureous, as they sprang,   815
Like lightning, off from his "melodious twang."[2]

103

Those grand heroics acted as a spell:
  The angels stopped their ears and plied their pinions;
The devils ran howling, deafened, down to hell;
  The ghosts fled, gibbering, for their own dominions—   820
(For 'tis not yet decided where they dwell,
  And I leave every man to his opinions);
Michael took refuge in his trump—but, lo!
His teeth were set on edge, he could not blow!

104

Saint Peter, who has hitherto been known   825
  For an impetuous saint, upraised his keys,
And at the fifth line knocked the poet down;
  Who fell like Phaëton,[3] but more at ease,
Into his lake, for there he did not drown;
  A different web being by the Destinies   830
Woven for the Laureate's final wreath, whene'er
Reform shall happen either here or there.

105

He first sank to the bottom—like his works,
  But soon rose to the surface—like himself;
For all corrupted things are buoyed like corks,   835
  By their own rottenness, light as an elf,
Or wisp that flits o'er a morass: he lurks,
  It may be, still, like dull books on a shelf,
In his own den, to scrawl some "Life" or "Vision,"
As Welborn says—"the devil turned precisian."[4]   840

106

As for the rest, to come to the conclusion
  Of this true dream, the telescope is gone
Which kept my optics free from all delusion,
  And showed me what I in my turn have shown;
All I saw farther, in the last confusion,   845
  Was, that King George slipped into heaven for one;
And when the tumult dwindled to a calm,
I left him practicing the hundredth psalm.[5]

1821   1822

---

2. John Aubrey in his *Miscellanies upon Various Subjects* (1696) had described a ghost that vanished "with a curious perfume, and most melodious twang."
3. Phaethon, son of Apollo, tried to drive his father's chariot, the sun. He could not control the horses and was struck down into the sea by a thunderbolt of Zeus. The satiric point is that Apollo is the god of poetry as well as of the sun.
4. A "precisian" is a Puritan. Spoken by Welborn in Massinger's play, *A New Way to Pay Old Debts* (1626) 1.1.6.
5. Which contains the relevant line, "Enter into his gates with thanksgiving."

Don Juan   Byron began his masterpiece (pronounced in the English fashion, *Don Joó-un*) in July of 1818, published it in installments beginning with cantos 1 and 2 in 1819, and continued working on it almost until his death. He extemporized the poem from episode to episode; "I *have* no plan," he said, "I *had* no plan; but I had or have materials." The work was composed with remarkable speed (the 888 lines of canto 13, for example, were accomplished within a week), and it aims at the effect of improvisation and scope rather than of compression; it asks to be read rapidly, at a conversational pace.

The poem breaks off with the sixteenth canto, but even in its unfinished state *Don Juan* is the longest satirical poem, and indeed one of the longest poems of any kind, in English. Its hero, the Spanish libertine, had in the original legend been superhuman in his sexual energy and wickedness. Throughout Byron's version the unspoken but persistent joke is that this violent and archetypal *homme fatal* of European legend is in fact more acted upon than active. Unfailingly amiable and well-intentioned, he is guilty largely of youth, charm, and a courteous and compliant spirit. The ladies do all the rest.

The chief models for the poem were the Italian seriocomic versions of medieval chivalric romances; the genre had been introduced by Pulci in the fifteenth century and achieved its greatest success in Ariosto's *Orlando Furioso* (1532). From these writers Byron caught the mixed moods and violent oscillations between the sublime and the ridiculous, as well as the easy, colloquial management of the complex ottava rima—an eight-line stanza in which the initial interlaced rhymes *(ababab)* build up to the comic turn in the pat couplet *(cc)*. Byron was influenced in the English use of this Italian form by a mildly amusing poem published in 1817, under the pseudonym of "Whistlecraft," by his friend John Hookham Frere. Other recognizable antecedents of *Don Juan* are Swift's *Gulliver's Travels* and Johnson's *Rasselas*, which had employed the naïve traveler as a satiric device, and Laurence Sterne's novel, *Tristram Shandy*, with its comic exploitation of a narrative medium blatantly subject to the whimsy of the author. But even the most original literary works play variations upon inherited conventions. Shelley at once recognized his friend's poem for what it was, "something wholly new and relative to the age."

Byron's most trusted literary advisers thought the poem unacceptably immoral, and John Murray took the precaution of printing the first two installments without identifying either Byron as the author or himself as the publisher. More recently, however, a common complaint has been not that *Don Juan* is immoral, but that it is morally nihilistic—that the poem is destructive without limit, since it proposes no positive values as a base for the satire, but sees life, in the words of one critic, as "a strange meaningless pageant." Yet Byron himself insisted that *Don Juan* is "a *satire* on *abuses* of the present state of society" and "the most moral of poems." Though the final phrase exaggerates, it has a foundation of truth. What the poem most frequently attacks, in love, religion, and social relations, are very considerable vices—sham, hypocrisy, complacency, oppression, greed, and lust. Furthermore the satire constantly, though silently, assumes as moral positives the qualities of courage, loyalty, generosity, and, above all, candor; it merely implies that these virtues are excessively rare, and that the modern world is not constituted to reward, to encourage, or even to recognize them when they make their appearance. And the poem is zestfully on the side of life, in its abundant variety. "As to *Don Juan*," Byron wrote elatedly to a friend, "confess—confess, you dog and be candid. . . . It may be profligate, but is it not *life*, is it not *the thing*?"

It is a mistake to look to *Don Juan* primarily for the story. The controlling element is not the narrative but the narrator, and his temperament gives the work its unity. The poem is really an incessant monologue, in the course of which a story manages to be told. It opens with the first-person pronoun and immediately lets us into the storyteller's predicament: "I want a hero. . . ." The voice then goes on, for almost two thousand stanzas, with effortless volubility and bewildering shifts of mood and perspective, using the occasion of Juan's misadventures to confide to us the speaker's thoughts and devastating judgments upon the major institutions, activities, and values of Western society.

What Byron discovered in *Don Juan* was how to give literary expression to those aspects of his temperament which, in real life, his self-consciousness and reserve permitted him to display only in the security of a circle of intimate friends or in his wonderfully vivacious letters to people he trusted. The poet who in his brilliantly successful youth created the gloomy and misanthropic Byronic hero, in his later and sadder life created a character (not the hero, but the narrator of *Don Juan*) who is one of the great, and one of the most complex, comic inventions in literature.

From Don Juan

Fragment[1]

I would to heaven that I were so much clay,
　　As I am blood, bone, marrow, passion, feeling—
Because at least the past were passed away—
　　And for the future—(but I write this reeling,
Having got drunk exceedingly today,   5
　　So that I seem to stand upon the ceiling)
I say—the future is a serious matter—
And so—for God's sake—hock[2] and soda water!

From *Canto* 1

[JUAN AND DONNA JULIA]

1

I want a hero: an uncommon want,
　　When every year and month sends forth a new one,
Till, after cloying the gazettes with cant,
　　The age discovers he is not the true one;
Of such as these I should not care to vaunt,   5
　　I'll therefore take our ancient friend Don Juan—

---

1. This stanza was written on the back of part of the MS of canto 1. For the author's revisions while composing 2 stanzas of *Don Juan*, see "Poems in Process," below.
2. A white Rhine wine, from the German *Hochheimer*.

We all have seen him, in the pantomime,[1]
Sent to the devil somewhat ere his time.

                    *   *   *

                    5
Brave men were living before Agamemnon[2]
    And since, exceeding valorous and sage,
A good deal like him too, though quite the same none;   35
    But then they shone not on the poet's page,
And so have been forgotten—I condemn none,
    But can't find any in the present age
Fit for my poem (that is, for my new one);
So, as I said, I'll take my friend Don Juan.   40

                    6
Most epic poets plunge *"in medias res"*[3]
    (Horace makes this the heroic turnpike road),
And then your hero tells, whene'er you please,
    What went before—by way of episode,
While seated after dinner at his ease,   45
    Beside his mistress in some soft abode,
Palace, or garden, paradise, or cavern,
Which serves the happy couple for a tavern.

                    7
That is the usual method, but not mine—
    My way is to begin with the beginning;   50
The regularity of my design
    Forbids all wandering as the worst of sinning,
And therefore I shall open with a line
    (Although it cost me half an hour in spinning)
Narrating somewhat of Don Juan's father,   55
And also of his mother, if you'd rather.

                    8
In Seville was he born, a pleasant city,
    Famous for oranges and women—he
Who has not seen it will be much to pity,
    So says the proverb—and I quite agree;   60
Of all the Spanish towns is none more pretty,
    Cadiz perhaps—but that you soon may see—
Don Juan's parents lived beside the river,
A noble stream, and called the Guadalquivir.

                    9
His father's name was Jóse[4]—*Don*, of course,   65
    A true Hidalgo, free from every stain
Of Moor or Hebrew blood, he traced his source

---

1. The Juan legend was a popular subject in
English pantomime.
2. In Homer's *Iliad*, the king commanding the
Greeks in the siege of Troy. This line is translated
from an ode by Horace.
3. "Into the middle of things" (Horace, *Art of Poetry*
148).
4. Normally "José"; Byron transferred the accent
for his meter.

Through the most Gothic gentlemen of Spain;
A better cavalier ne'er mounted horse,
   Or, being mounted, e'er got down again,   70
Than Jóse, who begot our hero, who
Begot—but that's to come—Well, to renew:

          10
His mother was a learned lady, famed
   For every branch of every science known—
In every Christian language ever named,   75
   With virtues equaled by her wit alone:
She made the cleverest people quite ashamed,
   And even the good with inward envy groan,
Finding themselves so very much exceeded
In their own way by all the things that she did.   80

          11
Her memory was a mine: she knew by heart
   All Calderon and greater part of Lopé,[5]
So that if any actor missed his part
   She could have served him for the prompter's copy;
For her Feinagle's[6] were an useless art,   85
   And he himself obliged to shut up shop—he
Could never make a memory so fine as
That which adorned the brain of Donna Inez.

          12
Her favorite science was the mathematical,
   Her noblest virtue was her magnanimity,   90
Her wit (she sometimes tried at wit) was Attic[7] all,
   Her serious sayings darkened to sublimity;
In short, in all things she was fairly what I call
   A prodigy—her morning dress was dimity,
Her evening silk, or, in the summer, muslin,   95
And other stuffs, with which I won't stay puzzling.

          13
She knew the Latin—that is, "the Lord's prayer,"
   And Greek—the alphabet—I'm nearly sure;
She read some French romances here and there,
   Although her mode of speaking was not pure;   100
For native Spanish she had no great care,
   At least her conversation was obscure;
Her thoughts were theorems, her words a problem,
As if she deemed that mystery would ennoble 'em.

      *   *   *

          22
'Tis pity learned virgins ever wed
   With persons of no sort of education,   170

5. Lope de Vega and Calderón de la Barca, the great Spanish dramatists of the early 17th century.
6. Gregor von Feinagle, a German expert on the art of memory, who had lectured in England in 1811.
7. Athenian. The common phrase "Attic salt" signifies the famed wit of the Athenians.

Or gentlemen, who, though well born and bred,
   Grow tired of scientific conversation:
I don't choose to say much upon this head,
   I'm a plain man, and in a single station,
But—Oh! ye lords of ladies intellectual,   175
Inform us truly, have they not henpecked you all?

23

Don Jóse and his lady quarreled—*why*,
   Not any of the many could divine,
Though several thousand people chose to try,
    'Twas surely no concern of theirs nor mine;   180
I loathe that low vice, curiosity;
   But if there's anything in which I shine,
'Tis in arranging all my friends' affairs,
Not having, of my own, domestic cares.

24

And so I interfered, and with the best   185
   Intentions, but their treatment was not kind;
I think the foolish people were possessed,
   For neither of them could I ever find,
Although their porter afterwards confessed—
   But that's no matter, and the worst's behind,   190
For little Juan o'er me threw, downstairs,
A pail of housemaid's water unawares.

25

A little curly-headed, good-for-nothing,
   And mischief-making monkey from his birth;
His parents ne'er agreed except in doting   195
   Upon the most unquiet imp on earth;
Instead of quarreling, had they been but both in
   Their senses, they'd have sent young master forth
To school, or had him soundly whipped at home,
To teach him manners for the time to come.   200

26

Don Jóse and the Donna Inez led
   For some time an unhappy sort of life,
Wishing each other, not divorced, but dead;
   They lived respectably as man and wife,
Their conduct was exceedingly well-bred,   205
   And gave no outward signs of inward strife,
Until at length the smothered fire broke out,
And put the business past all kind of doubt.

27

For Inez called some druggists and physicians,
   And tried to prove her loving lord was *mad*,[8]   210
But as he had some lucid intermissions,

---

8. Lady Byron had thought her husband might be insane, and sought medical advice on the matter. This and other passages obviously allude to his wife, although Byron insisted that Donna Inez was not intended to be a caricature of Lady Byron.

She next decided he was only *bad*;
Yet when they asked her for her depositions,
   No sort of explanation could be had,
Save that her duty both to man and God   215
Required this conduct—which seemed very odd.

28

She kept a journal, where his faults were noted,
   And opened certain trunks of books and letters,
All which might, if occasion served, be quoted;
   And then she had all Seville for abettors,   220
Besides her good old grandmother (who doted);
   The hearers of her case became repeaters,
Then advocates, inquisitors, and judges,
Some for amusement, others for old grudges.

29

And then this best and meekest woman bore   225
   With such serenity her husband's woes,
Just as the Spartan ladies did of yore,
   Who saw their spouses killed, and nobly chose
Never to say a word about them more—
   Calmly she heard each calumny that rose,   230
And saw *his* agonies with such sublimity,
That all the world exclaimed, "What magnanimity!"

*   *   *

32

Their friends had tried at reconciliation,
   Then their relations, who made matters worse   250
('Twere hard to tell upon a like occasion
   To whom it may be best to have recourse—
I can't say much for friend or yet relation);
   The lawyers did their utmost for divorce,
But scarce a fee was paid on either side   255
Before, unluckily, Don Jóse died.

33

He died: and most unluckily, because
   According to all hints I could collect
From counsel learned in those kinds of laws
   (Although their talk's obscure and circumspect),   260
His death contrived to spoil a charming cause;
   A thousand pities also with respect
To public feeling, which on this occasion
Was manifested in a great sensation.

*   *   *

37

Dying intestate, Juan was sole heir
   To a chancery suit,[9] and messuages, and lands,   290

9. A suit in what was then the highest English court, notorious for its delays. "Messuages": houses and
the adjoining lands.

Which, with a long minority and care,
    Promised to turn out well in proper hands:
Inez became sole guardian, which was fair,
    And answered but to nature's just demands;
An only son left with an only mother   295
Is brought up much more wisely than another.

                        38
Sagest of women, even of widows, she
    Resolved that Juan should be quite a paragon,
And worthy of the noblest pedigree
    (His sire was of Castile, his dam from Aragon).   300
Then for accomplishments of chivalry,
    In case our lord the king should go to war again,
He learned the arts of riding, fencing, gunnery,
And how to scale a fortress—or a nunnery.

                        39
But that which Donna Inez most desired,   305
    And saw into herself each day before all
The learned tutors whom for him she hired,
    Was that his breeding should be strictly moral:
Much into all his studies she inquired,
    And so they were submitted first to her, all,   310
Arts, sciences, no branch was made a mystery
To Juan's eyes, excepting natural history. [1]

                        40
The languages, especially the dead,
    The sciences, and most of all the abstruse,
The arts, at least all such as could be said   315
    To be the most remote from common use,
In all these he was much and deeply read;
    But not a page of anything that's loose,
Or hints continuation of the species,
Was ever suffered, lest he should grow vicious.   320

                        41
His classic studies made a little puzzle,
    Because of filthy loves of gods and goddesses,
Who in the earlier ages raised a bustle,
    But never put on pantaloons or bodices;
His reverend tutors had at times a tussle,   325
    And for their *Aeneids*, *Iliads*, and *Odysseys*,
Were forced to make an odd sort of apology,
For Donna Inez dreaded the mythology.

                        42
Ovid's a rake, as half his verses show him,
    Anacreon's morals are a still worse sample,   330
Catullus scarcely has a decent poem,
    I don't think Sappho's *Ode* a good example,

---

1. Which includes biology and physiology.

Although Longinus tells us there is no hymn
   Where the sublime soars forth on wings more ample,[2]
But Virgil's songs are pure, except that horrid one   335
Beginning with *"Formosum Pastor Corydon."*[3]

43

Lucretius' irreligion[4] is too strong
   For early stomachs, to prove wholesome food;
I can't help thinking Juvenal[5] was wrong,
   Although no doubt his real intent was good,   340
For speaking out so plainly in his song,
   So much indeed as to be downright rude;
And then what proper person can be partial
To all those nauseous epigrams of Martial?

44

Juan was taught from out the best edition,   345
   Expurgated by learned men, who place,
Judiciously, from out the schoolboy's vision,
   The grosser parts; but fearful to deface
Too much their modest bard by this omission,
   And pitying sore his mutilated case,   350
They only add them all in an appendix,[6]
Which saves, in fact, the trouble of an index.

*   *   *

52

For my part I say nothing—nothing—but
   This I will say—my reasons are my own—   410
That if I had an only son to put
   To school (as God be praised that I have none)
'Tis not with Donna Inez I would shut
   Him up to learn his catechism alone,
No—no—I'd send him out betimes to college,   415
For there it was I picked up my own knowledge.

53

For there one learns—'tis not for me to boast,
   Though I acquired—but I pass over *that,*
As well as all the Greek I since have lost:
   I say that there's the place—but *"Verbum sat,"*[7]   420
I think I picked up too, as well as most,
   Knowledge of matters—but no matter *what*—
I never married—but, I think, I know
That sons should not be educated so.

---

2. The Greek rhetorician Longinus praises a passage from Sappho in *On the Sublime* 10.
3. Virgil's *Eclogue* 2 begins: "The shepherd, Corydon, burned with love for the handsome Alexis."
4. In *De rerum natura* ("On the Nature of Things") Lucretius sets out to show that the universe can be explained without reference to any god.

5. The Latin satires of Juvenal attacked the corruption of Roman society in the 1st century A.D.
6. "Fact! There is, or was, such an edition, with all the obnoxious epigrams of Martial placed by themselves at the end" [Byron's note].
7. "A word [to the wise] is sufficient" (Latin).

54

Young Juan now was sixteen years of age,   425
    Tall, handsome, slender, but well knit: he seemed
Active, though not so sprightly, as a page;
    And everybody but his mother deemed
Him almost man; but she flew in a rage
    And bit her lips (for else she might have screamed)   430
If any said so, for to be precocious
Was in her eyes a thing the most atrocious.

55

Amongst her numerous acquaintance, all
    Selected for discretion and devotion,
There was the Donna Julia, whom to call   435
    Pretty were but to give a feeble notion
Of many charms in her as natural
    As sweetness to the flower, or salt to ocean,
Her zone[8] to Venus, or his bow to Cupid
(But this last simile is trite and stupid).   440

56

The darkness of her Oriental eye
    Accorded with her Moorish origin
(Her blood was not all Spanish, by the by;
    In Spain, you know, this is a sort of sin).
When proud Granada fell, and, forced to fly,   445
    Boabdil wept,[9] of Donna Julia's kin
Some went to Africa, some stayed in Spain,
Her great-great-grandmamma chose to remain.

57

She married (I forget the pedigree)
    With an hidalgo,[1] who transmitted down   450
His blood less noble than such blood should be;
    At such alliances his sires would frown,
In that point so precise in each degree
    That they bred *in and in*, as might be shown,
Marrying their cousins—nay, their aunts, and nieces,   455
Which always spoils the breed, if it increases.

58

This heathenish cross restored the breed again,
    Ruined its blood, but much improved its flesh;
For from a root the ugliest in old Spain
    Sprung up a branch as beautiful as fresh;   460
The sons no more were short, the daughters plain:
    But there's a rumor which I fain would hush,
'Tis said that Donna Julia's grandmamma
Produced her Don more heirs at love than law.

---

8. Girdle.
9. The last Moorish king of Granada (then a province in Spain) wept when his capital fell to the
Spaniards (1492).
1. A Spanish nobleman of the lower class.

59

However this might be, the race went on   465
    Improving still through every generation,
Until it centered in an only son,
    Who left an only daughter; my narration
May have suggested that this single one
    Could be but Julia (whom on this occasion   470
I shall have much to speak about), and she
Was married, charming, chaste, and twenty-three.

60

Her eye (I'm very fond of handsome eyes)
    Was large and dark, suppressing half its fire
Until she spoke, then through its soft disguise   475
    Flashed an expression more of pride than ire,
And love than either; and there would arise
    A something in them which was not desire,
But would have been, perhaps, but for the soul
Which struggled through and chastened down the whole.   480

61

Her glossy hair was clustered o'er a brow
    Bright with intelligence, and fair, and smooth;
Her eyebrow's shape was like the aërial bow,
    Her cheek all purple with the beam of youth,
Mounting, at times, to a transparent glow,   485
    As if her veins ran lightning; she, in sooth,
Possessed an air and grace by no means common:
Her stature tall—I hate a dumpy woman.

62

Wedded she was some years, and to a man
    Of fifty, and such husbands are in plenty;   490
And yet, I think, instead of such a ONE
    'Twere better to have TWO of five-and-twenty,
Especially in countries near the sun:
    And now I think on 't, "mi vien in mente,"[2]
Ladies even of the most uneasy virtue   495
Prefer a spouse whose age is short of thirty.

63

'Tis a sad thing, I cannot choose but say,
    And all the fault of that indecent sun,
Who cannot leave alone our helpless clay,
    But will keep baking, broiling, burning on,   500
That howsoever people fast and pray,
    The flesh is frail, and so the soul undone:
What men call gallantry, and gods adultery,
Is much more common where the climate's sultry.

2. "It comes to my mind" (Italian).

64

Happy the nations of the moral North!   505
   Where all is virtue, and the winter season
Sends sin, without a rag on, shivering forth
   ('Twas snow that brought St. Anthony to reason);[3]
Where juries cast up what a wife is worth
   By laying whate'er sum, in mulct,[4] they please on   510
The lover, who must pay a handsome price,
Because it is a marketable vice.

65

Alfonso was the name of Julia's lord,
   A man well looking for his years, and who
Was neither much beloved nor yet abhorred: 515
   They lived together as most people do,
Suffering each other's foibles by accord,
   And not exactly either *one* or *two*;
Yet he was jealous, though he did not show it,
For jealousy dislikes the world to know it.

*   *   *

69

Juan she saw, and, as a pretty child,   545
   Caressed him often—such a thing might be
Quite innocently done, and harmless styled,
   When she had twenty years, and thirteen he;
But I am not so sure I should have smiled
   When he was sixteen, Julia twenty-three;   550
These few short years make wondrous alterations,
Particularly amongst sunburnt nations.

70

Whate'er the cause might be, they had become
   Changed; for the dame grew distant, the youth shy,
Their looks cast down, their greetings almost dumb,   555
   And much embarrassment in either eye;
There surely will be little doubt with some
   That Donna Julia knew the reason why,
But as for Juan, he had no more notion
Than he who never saw the sea, of ocean.   560

71

Yet Julia's very coldness still was kind,
   And tremulously gentle her small hand
Withdrew itself from his, but left behind
   A little pressure, thrilling, and so bland
And slight, so very slight, that to the mind   565
   'Twas but a doubt; but ne'er magician's wand

---

3. "For the particulars of St. Anthony's recipe for   *Lives of the Saints*" [Byron's note].
hot blood in cold weather, see Mr. Alban Butler's   4. By way of a fine or legal penalty.

Wrought change with all Armida's[5] fairy art
Like what this light touch left on Juan's heart.

72

And if she met him, though she smiled no more,
    She looked a sadness sweeter than her smile,   570
As if her heart had deeper thoughts in store
    She must not own, but cherished more the while,
For that compression in its burning core;
    Even innocence itself has many a wile,
And will not dare to trust itself with truth,   575
And love is taught hypocrisy from youth.

✻ ✻ ✻

75

Poor Julia's heart was in an awkward state;
    She felt it going, and resolved to make
The noblest efforts for herself and mate,   595
    For honor's, pride's, religion's, virtue's sake;
Her resolutions were most truly great,
    And almost might have made a Tarquin[6] quake;
She pray'ed the Virgin Mary for her grace,
As being the best judge of a lady's case.   600

76

She vowed she never would see Juan more,
    And next day paid a visit to his mother,
And looked extremely at the opening door,
    Which, by the Virgin's grace, let in another;
Grateful she was, and yet a little sore—   605
    Again it opens, it can be no other,
'Tis surely Juan now—No! I'm afraid
That night the Virgin was no further prayed.

77

She now determined that a virtuous woman
    Should rather face and overcome temptation,   610
That flight was base and dastardly, and no man
    Should ever give her heart the least sensation;
That is to say, a thought beyond the common
    Preference, that we must feel upon occasion,
For people who are pleasanter than others,   615
But then they only seem so many brothers.

78

And even if by chance—and who can tell?
    The devil's so very sly—she should discover
That all within was not so very well,
    And, if still free, that such or such a lover   620

---

5. The sorceress who seduces Rinaldo in Tasso's *Jerusalem Delivered.*
6. A member of a legendary family of Roman kings

noted for tyranny and cruelty; perhaps a reference specifically to Lucius Tarquinus, the villain of Shakespeare's *The Rape of Lucrece.*

Might please perhaps, a virtuous wife can quell
   Such thoughts, and be the better when they're over;
And if the man should ask, 'tis but denial:
I recommend young ladies to make trial.

79

And then there are such things as love divine,   625
   Bright and immaculate, unmixed and pure,
Such as the angels think so very fine,
   And matrons, who would be no less secure,
Platonic, perfect, "just such love as mine":
   Thus Julia said—and thought so, to be sure,   630
And so I'd have her think, were I the man
On whom her reveries celestial ran.

* * *

86

So much for Julia. Now we'll turn to Juan.
   Poor little fellow! he had no idea
Of his own case, and never hit the true one;
   In feelings quick as Ovid's Miss Medea,[7]
He puzzled over what he found a new one,   685
   But not as yet imagined it could be a
Thing quite in course, and not at all alarming,
Which, with a little patience, might grow charming.

* * *

90

Young Juan wandered by the glassy brooks,
   Thinking unutterable things; he threw
Himself at length within the leafy nooks   715
   Where the wild branch of the cork forest grew;
There poets find materials for their books,
   And every now and then we read them through,
So that their plan and prosody are eligible,
Unless, like Wordsworth, they prove unintelligible.   720

91

He, Juan (and not Wordsworth), so pursued
   His self-communion with his own high soul,
Until his mighty heart, in its great mood,
   Had mitigated part, though not the whole
Of its disease; he did the best he could   725
   With things not very subject to control,
And turned, without perceiving his condition,
Like Coleridge, into a metaphysician.

92

He thought about himself, and the whole earth,
   Of man the wonderful, and of the stars,   730

---

7. In *Metamorphoses* 7, Ovid tells the story of Medea's mad infatuation for Jason.

And how the deuce they ever could have birth;
    And then he thought of earthquakes, and of wars,
How many miles the moon might have in girth,
    Of air-balloons, and of the many bars
To perfect knowledge of the boundless skies—   735
And then he thought of Donna Julia's eyes.

93

In thoughts like these true wisdom may discern
    Longings sublime, and aspirations high,
Which some are born with, but the most part learn
    To plague themselves withal, they know not why: 740
'Twas strange that one so young should thus concern
    His brain about the action of the sky;
If *you* think 'twas philosophy that this did,
I can't help thinking puberty assisted.

94

He pored upon the leaves, and on the flowers,   745
    And heard a voice in all the winds; and then
He thought of wood nymphs and immortal bowers,
    And how the goddesses came down to men:
He missed the pathway, he forgot the hours,
    And when he looked upon his watch again,   750
He found how much old Time had been a winner—
He also found that he had lost his dinner.

*   *   *

103

'Twas on a summer's day—the sixth of June—
    I like to be particular in dates,
Not only of the age, and year, but moon;
    They are a sort of post house, where the Fates   820
Change horses, making history change its tune,
    Then spur away o'er empires and o'er states,
Leaving at last not much besides chronology,
Excepting the post-obits[8] of theology.

104

'Twas on the sixth of June, about the hour   825
    Of half-past six—perhaps still nearer seven—
When Julia sate within as pretty a bower
    As e'er held houri in that heathenish heaven
Described by Mahomet, and Anacreon Moore,[9]
    To whom the lyre and laurels have been given,   830
With all the trophies of triumphant song—
He won them well, and may he wear them long!

---

8. I.e., post-obit bonds (*post obitum*, "after death"): loans to an heir which fall due after the death of the person whose estate he is to inherit. Byron's meaning is probably that only theology purports to tell us what rewards are due in heaven.

9. Byron's friend the poet Thomas Moore, who had translated the *Odes* of Anacreon; Byron is alluding to the tale of *Paradise and the Peri* in Moore's Oriental poem *Lalla Rookh*.

105

She sate, but not alone; I know not well
   How this same interview had taken place,
And even if I knew, I should not tell—   835
   People should hold their tongues in any case;
No matter how or why the thing befell,
   But there were she and Juan, face to face—
When two such faces are so, 'twould be wise,
But very difficult, to shut their eyes.   840

106

How beautiful she looked! her conscious[1] heart
   Glowed in her cheek, and yet she felt no wrong.
Oh Love! how perfect is thy mystic art,
   Strengthening the weak, and trampling on the strong,
How self-deceitful is the sagest part   845
   Of mortals whom thy lure hath led along—
The precipice she stood on was immense,
So was her creed[2] in her own innocence.

107

She thought of her own strength, and Juan's youth,
   And of the folly of all prudish fears,   850
Victorious virtue, and domestic truth,
   And then of Don Alfonso's fifty years:
I wish these last had not occurred, in sooth,
   Because that number rarely much endears,
And through all climes, the snowy and the sunny,   855
Sounds ill in love, whate'er it may in money.

*　*　*

113

The sun set, and up rose the yellow moon:
   The devil's in the moon for mischief; they
Who called her CHASTE, methinks, began too soon
   Their nomenclature; there is not a day,   900
The longest, not the twenty-first of June,
   Sees half the business in a wicked way
On which three single hours of moonshine smile—
And then she looks so modest all the while.

114

There is a dangerous silence in that hour,   905
   A stillness, which leaves room for the full soul
To open all itself, without the power
   Of calling wholly back its self-control;
The silver light which, hallowing tree and tower,
   Sheds beauty and deep softness o'er the whole,   910
Breathes also to the heart, and o'er it throws
A loving languor, which is not repose.

---

1. Feelingful.   2. Belief.

115

And Julia sate with Juan, half embraced
    And half retiring from the glowing arm,
Which trembled like the bosom where 'twas placed;   915
    Yet still she must have thought there was no harm,
Or else 'twere easy to withdraw her waist;
    But then the situation had its charm,
And then—God knows what next—I can't go on;
I'm almost sorry that I e'er begun.   920

116

Oh Plato! Plato! you have paved the way,
    With your confounded fantasies, to more
Immoral conduct by the fancied sway
    Your system feigns o'er the controlless core
Of human hearts, than all the long array   925
    Of poets and romancers: You're a bore,
A charlatan, a coxcomb—and have been,
At best, no better than a go-between.

117

And Julia's voice was lost, except in sighs,
    Until too late for useful conversation;   930
The tears were gushing from her gentle eyes,
    I wish, indeed, they had not had occasion,
But who, alas! can love, and then be wise?
    Not that remorse did not oppose temptation;
A little still she strove, and much repented,   935
And whispering "I will ne'er consent"—consented.

               *   *   *

126

'Tis sweet to win, no matter how, one's laurels
    By blood or ink; 'tis sweet to put an end
To strife; 'tis sometimes sweet to have our quarrels,
    Particularly with a tiresome friend:
Sweet is old wine in bottles, ale in barrels;   1005
    Dear is the helpless creature we defend
Against the world; and dear the schoolboy spot
We ne'er forget, though there we are forgot.

127

But sweeter still than this, than these, than all,
    Is first and passionate love—it stands alone,   1010
Like Adam's recollection of his fall;
    The tree of knowledge has been plucked—all's known—
And life yields nothing further to recall
    Worthy of this ambrosial sin, so shown,
No doubt in fable, as the unforgiven   1015
Fire which Prometheus[3] filched for us from heaven.

               *   *   *

3. The Titan Prometheus incurred the wrath of Zeus by stealing fire from heaven for humans.

133

Man's a phenomenon, one knows not what,
   And wonderful beyond all wondrous measure;
'Tis pity though, in this sublime world, that
   Pleasure's a sin, and sometimes sin's a pleasure;   1060
Few mortals know what end they would be at,
   But whether glory, power, or love, or treasure,
The path is through perplexing ways, and when
The goal is gained, we die, you know—and then—

134

What then?—I do not know, no more do you—   1065
   And so good night.—Return we to our story:
'Twas in November, when fine days are few,
   And the far mountains wax a little hoary,
And clap a white cape on their mantles blue;
   And the sea dashes round the promontory,   1070
And the loud breaker boils against the rock,
And sober suns must set at five o'clock.

135

'Twas, as the watchmen say, a cloudy night;
   No moon, no stars, the wind was low or loud
By gusts, and many a sparkling hearth was bright   1075
   With the piled wood, round which the family crowd;
There's something cheerful in that sort of light,
   Even as a summer sky's without a cloud:
I'm fond of fire, and crickets, and all that,
A lobster salad, and champagne, and chat.   1080

136

'Twas midnight—Donna Julia was in bed,
   Sleeping, most probably—when at her door
Arose a clatter might awake the dead,
   If they had never been awoke before,
And that they have been so we all have read,   1085
   And are to be so, at the least, once more;
The door was fastened, but with voice and fist
First knocks were heard, then "Madam—Madam—hist!

137

"For God's sake, Madam—Madam—here's my master,
   With more than half the city at his back—   1090
Was ever heard of such a cursed disaster!
   'Tis not my fault—I kept good watch—Alack!
Do, pray, undo the bolt a little faster—
   They're on the stair just now, and in a crack
Will all be here; perhaps he yet may fly—   1095
Surely the window's not so *very* high!"

138

By this time Don Alfonso was arrived,
   With torches, friends, and servants in great number;
The major part of them had long been wived,

And therefore paused not to disturb the slumber   1100
Of any wicked woman, who contrived
    By stealth her husband's temples to encumber:[4]
Examples of this kind are so contagious,
Were *one* not punished, *all* would be outrageous.

139

I can't tell how, or why, or what suspicion   1105
    Could enter into Don Alfonso's head;
But for a cavalier of his condition[5]
    It surely was exceedingly ill-bred,
Without a word of previous admonition,
    To hold a levee[6] round his lady's bed   1110
And summon lackeys, armed with fire and sword,
To prove himself the thing he most abhorred.

140

Poor Donna Julia! starting as from sleep
    (Mind that I do not say she had not slept),
Began at once to scream, and yawn, and weep;   1115
    Her maid, Antonia, who was an adept,
Contrived to fling the bedclothes in a heap,
    As if she had just now from out them crept:
I can't tell why she should take all this trouble
To prove her mistress had been sleeping double.   1120

141

But Julia mistress, and Antonia maid,
    Appeared like two poor harmless women, who
Of goblins, but still more of men, afraid,
    Had thought one man might be deterred by two,
And therefore side by side were gently laid,   1125
    Until the hours of absence should run through,
And truant husband should return, and say,
"My dear, I was the first who came away."

142

Now Julia found at length a voice, and cried,
    "In heaven's name, Don Alfonso, what d'ye mean?   1130
Has madness seized you? would that I had died
    Ere such a monster's victim I had been!
What may this midnight violence betide,
    A sudden fit of drunkenness or spleen?
Dare you suspect me, whom the thought would kill?   1135
Search, then, the room!"—Alfonso said, "I will."

143

He searched, *they* searched, and rummaged everywhere,
    Closet and clothes-press, chest and window seat,
And found much linen, lace, and seven pair
    Of stockings, slippers, brushes, combs, complete,   1140
With other articles of ladies fair,

4. Horns growing on the forehead was the tradi-   5. Rank.
tional emblem of the cuckolded husband.   6. Morning reception.

To keep them beautiful, or leave them neat:
Arras[7] they pricked and curtains with their swords,
And wounded several shutters, and some boards.

144

Under the bed they searched, and there they found—   1145
    No matter what—it was not that they sought;
They opened windows, gazing if the ground
    Had signs or footmarks, but the earth said nought;
And then they stared each other's faces round:
    'Tis odd, not one of all these seekers thought,   1150
And seems to me almost a sort of blunder,
Of looking *in* the bed as well as under.

145

During this inquisition Julia's tongue
    Was not asleep—"Yes, search and search," she cried,
"Insult on insult heap, and wrong on wrong!   1155
    It was for this that I became a bride!
For this in silence I have suffered long
    A husband like Alfonso at my side;
But now I'll bear no more, nor here remain,
If there be law or lawyers in all Spain.   1160

146

"Yes, Don Alfonso! husband now no more,
    If ever you indeed deserved the name,
Is 't worthy of your years?—you have threescore—
    Fifty, or sixty, it is all the same—
Is't wise or fitting, causeless to explore   1165
    For facts against a virtuous woman's fame?
Ungrateful, perjured, barbarous Don Alfonso,
How dare you think your lady would go on so?"

*   *   *

159

The Senhor Don Alfonso stood confused;   1265
    Antonia bustled round the ransacked room,
And, turning up her nose, with looks abused
    Her master, and his myrmidons, of whom
Not one, except the attorney, was amused;
    He, like Achates,[8] faithful to the tomb,   1270
So there were quarrels, cared not for the cause,
Knowing they must be settled by the laws.

160

With prying snub nose, and small eyes, he stood,
    Following Antonia's motions here and there,
With much suspicion in his attitude;   1275
    For reputations he had little care;
So that a suit or action were made good,

---

7. A tapestry hanging on a wall.
8. The *fidus Achates* ("faithful Achates") of

Virgil's *Aeneid*, whose loyalty to Aeneas has
become proverbial.

Small pity had he for the young and fair,
And ne'er believed in negatives, till these
Were proved by competent false witnesses.   1280

161

But Don Alfonso stood with downcast looks,
    And, truth to say, he made a foolish figure;
When, after searching in five hundred nooks,
    And treating a young wife with so much rigor,
He gained no point, except some self-rebukes,   1285
    Added to those his lady with such vigor
Had poured upon him for the last half hour,
Quick, thick, and heavy—as a thundershower.

162

At first he tried to hammer an excuse,
    To which the sole reply was tears, and sobs,   1290
And indications of hysterics, whose
    Prologue is always certain throes, and throbs,
Gasps, and whatever else the owners choose—
    Alfonso saw his wife, and thought of Job's;[9]
He saw too, in perspective, her relations,   1295
And then he tried to muster all his patience.

163

He stood in act to speak, or rather stammer,
    But sage Antonia cut him short before
The anvil of his speech received the hammer,
    With "Pray, sir, leave the room, and say no more,   1300
Or madam dies."—Alfonso muttered, "D—n her,"
    But nothing else, the time of words was o'er;
He cast a rueful look or two, and did,
He knew not wherefore, that which he was bid.

164

With him retired his *"posse comitatus,"*[1]
    The attorney last, who lingered near the door   1305
Reluctantly, still tarrying there as late as
    Antonia let him—not a little sore
At this most strange and unexplained *"hiatus"*
    In Don Alfonso's facts, which just now wore   1310
An awkward look; as he revolved the case,
The door was fastened in his legal face.

165

No sooner was it bolted, than—Oh shame!
    Oh sin! Oh sorrow! and Oh womankind!
How can you do such things and keep your fame,   1315
    Unless this world, and t' other too, be blind?
Nothing so dear as an unfilched good name!
    But to proceed—for there is more behind:

---

9. Job's wife had advised her afflicted husband to "curse God, and die" (Job 2.9).
1. The complete form of the modern word "posse" (*posse comitatus* means literally "power of the county," i.e., the body of citizens summoned by a sheriff to preserve order in the county).

With much heartfelt reluctance be it said,
Young Juan slipped, half-smothered, from the bed.   1320

166

He had been hid—I don't pretend to say
    How, nor can I indeed describe the where—
Young, slender, and packed easily, he lay,
    No doubt, in little compass, round or square;
But pity him I neither must nor may   1325
    His suffocation by that pretty pair;
'Twere better, sure, to die so, than be shut
With maudlin Clarence in his malmsey butt.[2]

*   *   *

169

What's to be done? Alfonso will be back   1345
    The moment he has sent his fools away.
Antonia's skill was put upon the rack,
    But no device could be brought into play—
And how to parry the renewed attack?
    Besides, it wanted but few hours of day: 1350
Antonia puzzled; Julia did not speak,
But pressed her bloodless lip to Juan's cheek.

170

He turned his lip to hers, and with his hand
    Called back the tangles of her wandering hair;
Even then their love they could not all command,   1355
    And half forgot their danger and despair:
Antonia's patience now was at a stand—
    "Come, come, 'tis no time now for fooling there,"
She whispered, in great wrath—"I must deposit
This pretty gentleman within the closet."   1360

*   *   *

173

Now, Don Alfonso entering, but alone,
    Closed the oration of the trusty maid:
She loitered, and he told her to be gone,
    An order somewhat sullenly obeyed;   1380
However, present remedy was none,
    And no great good seemed answered if she stayed:
Regarding both with slow and sidelong view,
She snuffed the candle, curtsied, and withdrew.

174

Alfonso paused a minute—then begun   1385
    Some strange excuses for his late proceeding;
He would not justify what he had done,
    To say the best, it was extreme ill-breeding;

---

2. The duke of Clarence, brother of Richard III, was reputed to have been assassinated by being drowned in a cask ("butt") of malmsey, a sweet and aromatic wine.

But there were ample reasons for it, none
   Of which he specified in this his pleading: 1390
His speech was a fine sample, on the whole,
   Of rhetoric, which the learned call *"rigmarole."*[3]

*   *   *

180

Alfonso closed his speech, and begged her pardon,
   Which Julia half withheld, and then half granted,
And laid conditions, he thought very hard on,   1435
   Denying several little things he wanted:
He stood like Adam lingering near his garden,
   With useless penitence perplexed and haunted,
Beseeching she no further would refuse,
When, lo! he stumbled o'er a pair of shoes.   1440

181

A pair of shoes!—what then? not much, if they
   Are such as fit with ladies' feet, but these
(No one can tell how much I grieve to say)
   Were masculine; to see them, and to seize,
Was but a moment's act.—Ah! well-a-day!   1445
   My teeth begin to chatter, my veins freeze—
Alfonso first examined well their fashion,
And then flew out into another passion.

182

He left the room for his relinquished sword,
   And Julia instant to the closet flew.   1450
"Fly, Juan, fly! for heaven's sake—not a word—
   The door is open—you may yet slip through
The passage you so often have explored—
   Here is the garden key—Fly—fly—Adieu!
Haste—haste! I hear Alfonso's hurrying feet—   1455
Day has not broke—there's no one in the street."

183

None can say that this was not good advice,
   The only mischief was, it came too late;
Of all experience 'tis the usual price,
   A sort of income tax laid on by fate: 1460
Juan had reached the room door in a trice,
   And might have done so by the garden gate,
But met Alfonso in his dressing gown,
Who threatened death—so Juan knocked him down.

184

Dire was the scuffle, and out went the light;
   Antonia cried out "Rape!" and Julia "Fire!"   1465
But not a servant stirred to aid the fight.
   Alfonso, pommeled to his heart's desire,

3. Illogical sequence of vague statements.

Swore lustily he'd be revenged this night;
   And Juan, too, blasphemed an octave higher;
His blood was up: though young, he was a Tartar,[4]   1470
And not at all disposed to prove a martyr.

185

Alfonso's sword had dropped ere he could draw it,
   And they continued battling hand to hand,
For Juan very luckily ne'er saw it;   1475
   His temper not being under great command,
If at that moment he had chanced to claw it,
   Alfonso's days had not been in the land
Much longer.—Think of husbands', lovers' lives!
And how ye may be doubly widows—wives!   1480

186

Alfonso grappled to detain the foe,
   And Juan throttled him to get away,
And blood ('twas from the nose) began to flow;
   At last, as they more faintly wrestling lay,
Juan contrived to give an awkward blow,   1485
   And then his only garment quite gave way;
He fled, like Joseph,[5] leaving it; but there,
I doubt, all likeness ends between the pair.

187

Lights came at length, and men, and maids, who found
   An awkward spectacle their eyes before;   1490
Antonia in hysterics, Julia swooned,
   Alfonso leaning, breathless, by the door;
Some half-torn drapery scattered on the ground,
   Some blood, and several footsteps, but no more:
Juan the gate gained, turned the key about,   1495
And liking not the inside, locked the out.

188

Here ends this canto.—Need I sing, or say,
   How Juan, naked, favored by the night,
Who favors what she should not, found his way,
   And reached his home in an unseemly plight?   1500
The pleasant scandal which arose next day,
   The nine days' wonder which was brought to light,
And how Alfonso sued for a divorce,
Were in the English newspapers, of course.

189

If you would like to see the whole proceedings,   1505
   The depositions, and the cause at full,
The names of all the witnesses, the pleadings
   Of counsel to nonsuit,[6] or to annul,

---

4. "To catch a Tartar" is to tackle someone too strong for his assailant.
5. In Genesis 39.7 ff. the chaste Joseph flees from the advances of Potiphar's wife, leaving "his garment in her hand."
6. Judgment against the plaintiff for failure to establish his case.

There's more than one edition, and the readings
   Are various, but they none of them are dull;   1510
The best is that in shorthand ta'en by Gurney,[7]
Who to Madrid on purpose made a journey.

190

But Donna Inez, to divert the train
   Of one of the most circulating scandals
That had for centuries been known in Spain,   1515
   At least since the retirement of the Vandals,[8]
First vowed (and never had she vowed in vain)
   To Virgin Mary several pounds of candles;
And then, by the advice of some old ladies,
She sent her son to be shipped off from Cadiz.   1520

191

She had resolved that he should travel through
   All European climes, by land or sea,
To mend his former morals, and get new,
   Especially in France and Italy
(At least this is the thing most people do).   1525
   Julia was sent into a convent; she
Grieved, but, perhaps, her feelings may be better
Shown in the following copy of her letter:

192

"They tell me 'tis decided; you depart:
   'Tis wise—'tis well, but not the less a pain;   1530
I have no further claim on your young heart,
   Mine is the victim, and would be again;
To love too much has been the only art
   I used—I write in haste, and if a stain
Be on this sheet, 'tis not what it appears;   1535
My eyeballs burn and throb, but have no tears.

193

"I loved, I love you, for this love have lost
   State, station, heaven, mankind's, my own esteem,
And yet cannot regret what it hath cost,
   So dear is still the memory of that dream;   1540
Yet, if I name my guilt, 'tis not to boast,
   None can deem harshlier of me than I deem:
I trace this scrawl because I cannot rest—
I've nothing to reproach, or to request.

194

"Man's love is of man's life a thing apart,   1545
   'Tis woman's whole existence; man may range
The court, camp, church, the vessel, and the mart;
   Sword, gown, gain, glory, offer in exchange
Pride, fame, ambition, to fill up his heart,

---

7. William B. Gurney, official shorthand writer for the houses of Parliament and a famous court reporter.

8. The Germanic tribe which overran Spain and other parts of southern Europe in the 4th and 5th centuries, notorious for rape and violence.

And few there are whom these cannot estrange;   1550
Men have all these resources, we but one,
To love again, and be again undone.

195

"You will proceed in pleasure, and in pride,
    Beloved and loving many; all is o'er
For me on earth, except some years to hide   1555
    My shame and sorrow deep in my heart's core;
These I could bear, but cannot cast aside
    The passion which still rages as before,
And so farewell—forgive me, love me—No,
That word is idle now—but let it go.   1560

196

"My breast has been all weakness, is so yet;
    But still I think I can collect my mind;
My blood still rushes where my spirit's set,
    As roll the waves before the settled wind;
My heart is feminine, nor can forget—   1565
    To all, except one image, madly blind;
So shakes the needle,[9] and so stands the pole,
As vibrates my fond heart to my fixed soul.

197

"I have no more to say, but linger still,
    And dare not set my seal upon this sheet,   1570
And yet I may as well the task fulfil,
    My misery can scarce be more complete:
I had not lived till now, could sorrow kill;
    Death shuns the wretch who fain the blow would meet,
And I must even survive this last adieu,   1575
And bear with life, to love and pray for you!"

198

This note was written upon gilt-edged paper
    With a neat little crow-quill, slight and new;
Her small white hand could hardly reach the taper,[1]
    It trembled as magnetic needles do,   1580
And yet she did not let one tear escape her;
    The seal a sunflower; "*Elle vous suit partout*,"[2]
The motto, cut upon a white cornelian;
The wax was superfine, its hue vermilion.

199

This was Don Juan's earliest scrape; but whether   1585
    I shall proceed with his adventures is
Dependent on the public altogether;
    We'll see, however, what they say to this,
Their favor in an author's cap's a feather,
    And no great mischief's done by their caprice;   1590

---

9. Of a compass.
1. The candle (in order to melt wax to seal the

letter).
2. "She follows you everywhere" (French).

And if their approbation we experience,
Perhaps they'll have some more about a year hence.

                    200

My poem's epic, and is meant to be
    Divided in twelve books; each book containing,
With love, and war, a heavy gale at sea,   1595
    A list of ships, and captains, and kings reigning,
New characters; the episodes are three;
    A panoramic view of hell's in training,
After the style of Virgil and of Homer,
So that my name of Epic's no misnomer.   1600

                    201

All these things will be specified in time,
    With strict regard to Aristotle's rules,
The *Vade Mecum*[3] of the true sublime,
    Which makes so many poets, and some fools:
Prose poets like blank verse, I'm fond of rhyme,   1605
    Good workmen never quarrel with their tools;
I've got new mythological machinery,
And very handsome supernatural scenery.

                    202

There's only one slight difference between
    Me and my epic brethren gone before,   1610
And here the advantage is my own, I ween
    (Not that I have not several merits more,
But this will more peculiarly be seen):
    They so embellish that 'tis quite a bore
Their labyrinth of fables to thread through,   1615
Whereas this story's actually true.

                    203

If any person doubt it, I appeal
    To history, tradition, and to facts,
To newspapers, whose truth all know and feel,
    To plays in five, and operas in three acts;   1620
All these confirm my statement a good deal,
    But that which more completely faith exacts
Is that myself, and several now in Seville,
Saw Juan's last elopment with the devil.[4]

                    204

If ever I should condescend to prose,   1625
    I'll write poetical commandments, which
Shall supersede beyond all doubt all those
    That went before; in these I shall enrich
My text with many things that no one knows,
    And carry precept to the highest pitch: 1630

3. Handbook; literally "go with me" (Latin). Byron
is deriding the neoclassic view that Aristotle's *Poetics* proposes "rules" for writing epic and tragedy.

4. The usual plays on the Juan legend ended with
Juan in hell; an early 20th-century version is George
Bernard Shaw's *Man and Superman.*

I'll call the work "Longinus o'er a Bottle,
Or Every Poet his *own* Aristotle."

205

Thou shalt believe in Milton, Dryden, Pope;[5]
   Thou shalt not set up Wordsworth, Coleridge, Southey;
Because the first is crazed beyond all hope,   1635
   The second drunk, the third so quaint and mouthy:
With Crabbe it may be difficult to cope,
   And Campbell's Hippocrene[6] is somewhat drouthy:
Thou shalt not steal from Samuel Rogers, nor
Commit—flirtation with the muse of Moore.[7]   1640

206

Thou shalt not covet Mr. Sotheby's Muse,[8]
   His Pegasus, nor anything that's his;
Thou shalt not bear false witness like "the Blues"[9]
   (There's one, at least, is very fond of this);
Thou shalt not write, in short, but what I choose: 1645
   This is true criticism, and you may kiss—
Exactly as you please, or not—the rod;
But if you don't, I'll lay it on, by G—d!

207

If any person should presume to assert
   This story is not moral, first I pray   1650
That they will not cry out before they're hurt,
   Then that they'll read it o'er again, and say
(But, doubtless, nobody will be so pert)
   That this is not a moral tale, though gay;
Besides, in Canto Twelfth, I mean to show   1655
The very place where wicked people go.

*   *   *

213

But now at thirty years my hair is gray
   (I wonder what it will be like at forty?
I thought of a peruke[1] the other day)—
   My heart is not much greener; and, in short, I   1700
Have squandered my whole summer while 'twas May,
   And feel no more the spirit to retort; I
Have spent my life, both interest and principal,
And deem not, what I deemed, my soul invincible.

---

5. This is one of many passages, in prose and verse, in which Byron vigorously defended Dryden and Pope against his Romantic contemporaries.
6. Fountain on Mt. Helicon whose waters supposedly gave inspiration (pronounced *Hip'-ocreen*).
7. George Crabbe, whom Byron admired, was the author of *The Village* (1783) and other realistic poems of rural life. Thomas Campbell, Samuel Rogers, and Thomas Moore were lesser poets of the Romantic period; the last two were close friends

of Byron's.
8. William Sotheby, contemporary poet and translator, was a wealthy man (see line 1642). Pegasus was the winged horse symbolizing poetic inspiration.
9. I.e., "Bluestockings," a contemporary term for pedantic lady intellectuals, among whom Byron numbered his wife (line 1644).
1. Wig.

214

No more—no more—Oh! never more on me   1705
   The freshness of the heart can fall like dew,
Which out of all the lovely things we see
   Extracts emotions beautiful and new,
Hived in our bosoms like the bag o' the bee:
   Think'st thou the honey with those objects grew?   1710
Alas! 'twas not in them, but in thy power
To double even the sweetness of a flower.

215

No more—no more—Oh! never more, my heart,
   Canst thou be my sole world, my universe!
Once all in all, but now a thing apart,   1715
   Thou canst not be my blessing or my curse:
The illusion's gone forever, and thou art
   Insensible, I trust, but none the worse,
And in thy stead I've got a deal of judgment,
Though heaven knows how it ever found a lodgment.   1720

216

My days of love are over; me no more
   The charms of maid, wife, and still less of widow
Can make the fool of which they made before—
   In short, I must not lead the life I did do;
The credulous hope of mutual minds is o'er,   1725
   The copious use of claret is forbid too,
So for a good old-gentlemanly vice,
I think I must take up with avarice.

217

Ambition was my idol, which was broken
   Before the shrines of Sorrow and of Pleasure;   1730
And the two last have left me many a token
   O'er which reflection may be made at leisure:
Now, like Friar Bacon's brazen head, I've spoken,
   "Time is, Time was, Time's past,"[2] a chymic treasure
Is glittering youth, which I have spent betimes—   1735
My heart in passion, and my head on rhymes.

218

What is the end of fame? 'tis but to fill
   A certain portion of uncertain paper:
Some liken it to climbing up a hill,
   Whose summit, like all hills, is lost in vapor;   1740
For this men write, speak, preach, and heroes kill,
   And bards burn what they call their "midnight taper,"
To have, when the original is dust,
A name, a wretched picture, and worse bust.[3]

2. Spoken by a bronze bust in Robert Greene's comedy *Friar Bacon and Friar Bungay* (1594). "Chymic": alchemic; i.e., the "treasure" is counterfeit gold.

3. Byron was unhappy with the portrait bust of him recently made by the Danish sculptor Thorwaldsen.

219

What are the hopes of man? Old Egypt's King   1745
    Cheops erected the first pyramid
And largest, thinking it was just the thing
    To keep his memory whole, and mummy hid:
But somebody or other rummaging
    Burglariously broke his coffin's lid: 1750
Let not a monument give you or me hopes,
Since not a pinch of dust remains of Cheops.

220

But I, being fond of true philosophy,
    Say very often to myself, "Alas!
All things that have been born were born to die,   1755
    And flesh (which Death mows down to hay) is grass;
You've passed your youth not so unpleasantly,
    And if you had it o'er again—'twould pass—
So thank your stars that matters are no worse,
And read your Bible, sir, and mind your purse."   1760

221

But for the present, gentle reader! and
    Still gentler purchaser! the bard—that's I—
Must, with permission, shake you by the hand,
    And so your humble servant, and good-by!
We meet again, if we should understand   1765
    Each other; and if not, I shall not try
Your patience further than by this short sample—
'Twere well if others followed my example.

222

"Go, little book, from this my solitude!
    I cast thee on the waters—go thy ways!   1770
And if, as I believe, thy vein be good,
    The world will find thee after many days."
When Southey's read, and Wordsworth understood,
    I can't help putting in my claim to praise—
The four first rhymes are Southey's, every line:[4]   1775
For God's sake, reader! take them not for mine!

From *Canto* 2

[THE SHIPWRECK]

8

But to our tale: the Donna Inez sent
    Her son to Cadiz only to embark;
To stay there had not answered her intent,
    But why?—we leave the reader in the dark—   60
'Twas for a voyage that the young man was meant,
    As if a Spanish ship were Noah's ark,

---

4. The lines occur in the last stanza of Southey's *Epilogue to the Lay of the Laureate*.

To wean him from the wickedness of earth,
And send him like a dove of promise forth.

9

Don Juan bade his valet pack his things   65
   According to direction, then received
A lecture and some money: for four springs
   He was to travel; and though Inez grieved
(As every kind of parting has its stings),
   She hoped he would improve—perhaps believed: 70
A letter, too, she gave (he never read it)
Of good advice—and two or three of credit.

10

In the meantime, to pass her hours away,
   Brave Inez now set up a Sunday school
For naughty children, who would rather play   75
   (Like truant rogues) the devil, or the fool;
Infants of three years old were taught that day,
   Dunces were whipped or set upon a stool:
The great success of Juan's education,
Spurred her to teach another generation.   80

11

Juan embarked—the ship got under way,
   The wind was fair, the water passing rough;
A devil of a sea rolls in that bay,
   As I, who've crossed it oft, know well enough;
And, standing upon deck, the dashing spray   85
   Flies in one's face, and makes it weather-tough:
And there he stood to take, and take again,
His first—perhaps his last—farewell of Spain.

12

I can't but say it is an awkward sight
   To see one's native land receding through   90
The growing waters; it unmans one quite,
   Especially when life is rather new:
I recollect Great Britain's coast looks white,
   But almost every other country's blue,
When gazing on them, mystified by distance,   95
We enter on our nautical existence.

*   *   *

17

And Juan wept, and much he sighed and thought,
   While his salt tears dropped into the salt sea,   130
"Sweets to the sweet" (I like so much to quote;
   You must excuse this extract—'tis where she,
The Queen of Denmark, for Ophelia brought
   Flowers to the grave);[1] and, sobbing often, he

---

1. *Hamlet* 5.1.243.

Reflected on his present situation,   135
And seriously resolved on reformation.

18

"Farewell, my Spain! a long farewell!" he cried,
    "Perhaps I may revisit thee no more,
But die, as many an exiled heart hath died,
    Of its own thirst to see again thy shore: 140
Farewell, where Guadalquivir's waters glide!
    Farewell, my mother! and, since all is o'er,
Farewell, too, dearest Julia!"—(here he drew
Her letter out again, and read it through).

19

"And oh! if e'er I should forget, I swear—   145
    But that's impossible, and cannot be—
Sooner shall this blue ocean melt to air,
    Sooner shall earth resolve itself to sea,
Than I resign thine image, oh, my fair!
    Or think of anything, excepting thee;   150
A mind diseased no remedy can physic"—
(Here the ship gave a lurch, and he grew seasick.)

20

"Sooner shall heaven kiss earth"—(here he fell sicker)
    "Oh, Julia! what is every other woe?—
(For God's sake let me have a glass of liquor;   155
    Pedro, Battista, help me down below.)
Julia, my love—(you rascal, Pedro, quicker)—
    Oh, Julia!—(this cursed vessel pitches so)—
Beloved Julia, hear me still beseeching!"
(Here he grew inarticulate with retching.)   160

21

He felt that chilling heaviness of heart,
    Or rather stomach, which, alas! attends,
Beyond the best apothecary's art,
    The loss of love, the treachery of friends,
Or death of those we dote on, when a part   165
    Of us dies with them as each fond hope ends:
No doubt he would have been much more pathetic,
But the sea acted as a strong emetic.[2]

*   *   *

49

'Twas twilight, and the sunless day went down   385
    Over the waste of waters; like a veil,
Which, if withdrawn, would but disclose the frown
    Of one whose hate is masked but to assail.
Thus to their hopeless eyes the night was shown,
    And grimly darkled o'er their faces pale,   390

2. In stanzas 22–48 (here omitted) the ship, bound for Leghorn, runs into a violent storm and is battered
into a helpless, sinking wreck.

And the dim desolate deep: twelve days had Fear
Been their familiar, and now Death was here.

50

Some trial had been making at a raft,
    With little hope in such a rolling sea,
A sort of thing at which one would have laughed,   395
    If any laughter at such times could be,
Unless with people who too much have quaffed,
    And have a kind of wild and horrid glee,
Half epileptical, and half hysterical—
Their preservation would have been a miracle.   400

51

At half-past eight o'clock, booms, hencoops, spars,
    And all things, for a chance, had been cast loose
That still could keep afloat the struggling tars,
    For yet they strove, although of no great use:
There was no light in heaven but a few stars,   405
    The boats put off o'ercrowded with their crews;
She gave a heel, and then a lurch to port,
And, going down head foremost—sunk, in short.

52

Then rose from sea to sky the wild farewell—
    Then shrieked the timid, and stood still the brave—   410
Then some leaped overboard with dreadful yell,
    As eager to anticipate their grave;
And the sea yawned around her like a hell,
    And down she sucked with her the whirling wave,
Like one who grapples with his enemy,   415
And strives to strangle him before he die.

53

And first one universal shriek there rushed,
    Louder than the loud ocean, like a crash
Of echoing thunder; and then all was hushed,
    Save the wild wind and the remorseless dash   420
Of billows; but at intervals there gushed,
    Accompanied with a convulsive splash,
A solitary shriek, the bubbling cry
Of some strong swimmer in his agony.

* * *

56

Juan got into the longboat, and there
    Contrived to help Pedrillo[3] to a place;
It seemed as if they had exchanged their care,
    For Juan wore the magisterial face
Which courage gives, while poor Pedrillo's pair   445
    Of eyes were crying for their owner's case:

---

3. Juan's tutor.

Battista, though (a name called shortly Tita),
Was lost by getting at some aqua-vita.[4]

57

Pedro, his valet, too, he tried to save,
    But the same cause, conducive to his loss,   450
Left him so drunk, he jumped into the wave,
    As o'er the cutter's edge he tried to cross,
And so he found a wine-and-watery grave;
    They could not rescue him although so close,
Because the sea ran higher every minute,   455
And for the boat—the crew kept crowding in it.

*　*　*

66

'Tis thus with people in an open boat,
    They live upon the love of life, and bear
More than can be believed, or even thought,
    And stand like rocks the tempest's wear and tear;
And hardship still has been the sailor's lot,   525
    Since Noah's ark went cruising here and there;
She had a curious crew as well as cargo,
Like the first old Greek privateer, the *Argo*.[5]

67

But man is a carnivorous production,
    And must have meals, at least one meal a day;   530
He cannot live, like woodcocks, upon suction,[6]
    But, like the shark and tiger, must have prey;
Although his anatomical construction
    Bears vegetables, in a grumbling way,
Your laboring people think beyond all question   535
Beef, veal, and mutton, better for digestion.

68

And thus it was with this our hapless crew;
    For on the third day there came on a calm,
And though at first their strength it might renew,
    And lying on their weariness like balm,   540
Lulled them like turtles sleeping on the blue
    Of ocean, when they woke they felt a qualm,
And fell all ravenously on their provision,
Instead of hoarding it with due precision.

*　*　*

72

The seventh day,[7] and no wind—the burning sun
    Blistered and scorched, and, stagnant on the sea,   570

---

4. Brandy.
5. In the Greek myth, the *Argo* is the ship on which Jason set out in quest of the Golden Fleece. Byron ironically calls it a "privateer" (a private ship licensed by a government in wartime to attack and pillage enemy vessels).

6. Woodcocks probe the turf with long flexible bills, seeming to suck air as they feed.
7. On the fourth day the crew had killed and eaten Juan's pet spaniel. Byron based the episode of cannibalism that follows on various historical accounts of disasters at sea.

They lay like carcasses; and hope was none,
   Save in the breeze that came not; savagely
They glared upon each other—all was done,
   Water, and wine, and food—and you might see
The longings of the cannibal arise   575
   (Although they spoke not) in their wolfish eyes.

73

At length one whispered his companion, who
   Whispered another, and thus it went round,
And then into a hoarser murmur grew,
   An ominous, and wild, and desperate sound;   580
And when his comrade's thought each sufferer knew,
   'Twas but his own, suppressed till now, he found:
And out they spoke of lots for flesh and blood,
And who should die to be his fellow's food.

74

But ere they came to this, they that day shared   585
   Some leathern caps, and what remained of shoes;
And then they looked around them, and despaired,
   And none to be the sacrifice would choose;
At length the lots were torn up, and prepared,
   But of materials that must shock the Muse—   590
Having no paper, for the want of better,
They took by force from Juan Julia's letter.

75

The lots were made, and marked, and mixed, and handed
   In silent horror, and their distribution
Lulled even the savage hunger which demanded,   595
   Like the Promethean vulture,[8] this pollution;
None in particular had sought or planned it,
   'Twas nature gnawed them to this resolution,
By which none were permitted to be neuter—
And the lot fell on Juan's luckless tutor.   600

76

He but requested to be bled to death:
   The surgeon had his instruments, and bled
Pedrillo, and so gently ebbed his breath,
   You hardly could perceive when he was dead.
He died as born, a Catholic in faith,   605
   Like most in the belief in which they're bred,
And first a little crucifix he kissed,
And then held out his jugular and wrist.

77

The surgeon, as there was no other fee,
   Had his first choice of morsels for his pains;   610
But being thirstiest at the moment, he
   Preferred a draft from the fast-flowing veins:

---

8. Because Prometheus had stolen fire from heaven to give to humans, Zeus punished him by nailing him to a mountain peak, where an eagle fed on his ever-renewing liver.

Part was divided, part thrown in the sea,
   And such things as the entrails and the brains
Regaled two sharks, who followed o'er the billow—   615
The sailors ate the rest of poor Pedrillo.

78

The sailors ate him, all save three or four,
   Who were not quite so fond of animal food;
To these was added Juan, who, before
   Refusing his own spaniel, hardly could   620
Feel now his appetite increased much more;
   'Twas not to be expected that he should,
Even in extremity of their disaster,
Dine with them on his pastor and his master.

79

'Twas better that he did not; for, in fact,   625
   The consequence was awful in the extreme;
For they, who were most ravenous in the act,
   Went raging mad—Lord! how they did blaspheme!
And foam and roll, with strange convulsions racked,
   Drinking salt water like a mountain stream,   630
Tearing, and grinning, howling, screeching, swearing,
And, with hyena laughter, died despairing.

*   *   *

103

As they drew nigh the land, which now was seen
   Unequal in its aspect here and there,
They felt the freshness of its growing green,
   That waved in forest tops, and smoothed the air,   820
And fell upon their glazed eyes like a screen
   From glistening waves, and skies so hot and bare—
Lovely seemed any object that should sweep
Away the vast, salt, dread, eternal deep.

104

The shore looked wild, without a trace of man,   825
   And girt by formidable waves; but they
Were mad for land, and thus their course they ran,
   Though right ahead the roaring breakers lay:
A reef between them also now began
   To show its boiling surf and bounding spray,   830
But finding no place for their landing better,
They ran the boat for shore—and overset her.

105

But in his native stream, the Guadalquivir,
   Juan to lave his youthful limbs was wont;
And having learnt to swim in that sweet river,   835
   Had often turned the art to some account:
A better swimmer you could scarce see ever,

He could, perhaps, have passed the Hellespont,
As once (a feat on which ourselves we prided)
Leander, Mr. Ekenhead, and I did.[9]   840

106

So, here, though faint, emaciated, and stark,
  He buoyed his boyish limbs, and strove to ply
With the quick wave, and gain, ere it was dark,
  The beach which lay before him, high and dry:
The greatest danger here was from a shark,   845
  That carried off his neighbor by the thigh;
As for the other two, they could not swim,
So nobody arrived on shore but him.

107

Nor yet had he arrived but for the oar,
  Which, providentially for him, was washed   850
Just as his feeble arms could strike no more,
  And the hard wave o'erwhelmed him as 'twas dashed
Within his grasp; he clung to it, and sore
  The waters beat while he thereto was lashed;
At last, with swimming, wading, scrambling, he   855
Rolled on the beach, half senseless, from the sea:

108

There, breathless, with his digging nails he clung
  Fast to the sand, lest the returning wave,
From whose reluctant roar his life he wrung,
  Should suck him back to her insatiate grave: 860
And there he lay, full length, where he was flung,
  Before the entrance of a cliff-worn cave,
With just enough of life to feel its pain,
And deem that it was saved, perhaps, in vain.

109

With slow and staggering effort he arose,   865
  But sunk again upon his bleeding knee
And quivering hand; and then he looked for those
  Who long had been his mates upon the sea;
But none of them appeared to share his woes,
  Save one, a corpse, from out the famished three,   870
Who died two days before, and now had found
An unknown barren beach for burial ground.

110

And as he gazed, his dizzy brain spun fast,
  And down he sunk; and as he sunk, the sand
Swam round and round, and all his senses passed: 875
  He fell upon his side, and his stretched hand
Drooped dripping on the oar (their jurymast),
  And, like a withered lily, on the land

9. Like Leander in the myth, Byron and Lt. Ekenhead had swum the Hellespont on May 3, 1810. See *Written After Swimming from Sestos to Abydos*, above.

His slender frame and pallid aspect lay,
As fair a thing as e'er was formed of clay.   880

[JUAN AND HAIDÉE]

111

How long in his damp trance young Juan lay
    He knew not, for the earth was gone for him,
And time had nothing more of night nor day
    For his congealing blood, and senses dim;
And how this heavy faintness passed away   885
    He knew not, till each painful pulse and limb,
And tingling vein seemed throbbing back to life,
For Death, though vanquished, still retired with strife.

112

His eyes he opened, shut, again unclosed,
    For all was doubt and dizziness; he thought   890
He still was in the boat, and had but dozed,
    And felt again with his despair o'erwrought,
And wished it death in which he had reposed,
    And then once more his feelings back were brought,
And slowly by his swimming eyes was seen   895
A lovely female face of seventeen.

113

'Twas bending close o'er his, and the small mouth
    Seemed almost prying into his for breath;
And chafing him, the soft warm hand of youth
    Recalled his answering spirits back from death;   900
And, bathing his chill temples, tried to soothe
    Each pulse to animation, till beneath
Its gentle touch and trembling care, a sigh
To these kind efforts made a low reply.

114

Then was the cordial poured, and mantle flung   905
    Around his scarce-clad limbs; and the fair arm
Raised higher the faint head which o'er it hung;
    And her transparent cheek, all pure and warm,
Pillowed his deathlike forehead; then she wrung
    His dewy curls, long drenched by every storm;   910
And watched with eagerness each throb that drew
A sigh from his heaved bosom—and hers, too.

115

And lifting him with care into the cave,
    The gentle girl, and her attendant—one
Young, yet her elder, and of brow less grave,   915
    And more robust of figure—then begun
To kindle fire, and as the new flames gave
    Light to the rocks that roofed them, which the sun

Had never seen, the maid, or whatsoe'er
She was, appeared distinct, and tall, and fair.   920

116

Her brow was overhung with coins of gold,
   That sparkled o'er the auburn of her hair,
Her clustering hair, whose longer locks were rolled
   In braids behind; and though her stature were
Even of the highest for a female mold,   925
   They nearly reached her heel; and in her air
There was a something which bespoke command,
As one who was a lady in the land.

117

Her hair, I said, was auburn; but her eyes
   Were black as death, their lashes the same hue,   930
Of downcast length, in whose silk shadow lies
   Deepest attraction; for when to the view
Forth from its raven fringe the full glance flies,
   Ne'er with such force the swiftest arrow flew;
'Tis as the snake late coiled, who pours his length,   935
And hurls at once his venom and his strength.

*   *   *

123

And these two tended him, and cheered him both
   With food and raiment, and those soft attentions,
Which are (as I must own) of female growth,
   And have ten thousand delicate inventions: 980
They made a most superior mess of broth,
   A thing which poesy but seldom mentions,
But the best dish that e'er was cooked since Homer's
Achilles ordered dinner for newcomers.[1]

124

I'll tell you who they were, this female pair,
   Lest they should seem princesses in disguise;   985
Besides, I hate all mystery, and that air
   Of claptrap, which your recent poets prize;
And so, in short, the girls they really were
   They shall appear before your curious eyes,   990
Mistress and maid; the first was only daughter
Of an old man, who lived upon the water.

125

A fisherman he had been in his youth,
   And still a sort of fisherman was he;
But other speculations were, in sooth,
   Added to his connection with the sea,   995
Perhaps not so respectable, in truth:

1. A reference to the lavish feast with which Achilles entertained Ajax, Phoenix, and Ulysses (*Iliad* 9.193 ff.).

A little smuggling, and some piracy,
Left him, at last, the sole of many masters
Of an ill-gotten million of piasters.[2]   1000
                        126
A fisher, therefore, was he—though of men,
    Like Peter the Apostle[3]—and he fished
For wandering merchant vessels, now and then,
    And sometimes caught as many as he wished;
The cargoes he confiscated, and gain   1005
    He sought in the slave market too, and dished
Full many a morsel for that Turkish trade,
By which, no doubt, a good deal may be made.
                        127
He was a Greek, and on his isle had built
    (One of the wild and smaller Cyclades)[4]   1010
A very handsome house from out his guilt,
    And there he lived exceedingly at ease;
Heaven knows what cash he got or blood he spilt,
    A sad[5] old fellow was he, if you please;
But this I know, it was a spacious building,   1015
Full of barbaric carving, paint, and gilding.
                        128
He had an only daughter, called Haidée,
    The greatest heiress of the Eastern Isles;
Besides, so very beautiful was she,
    Her dowry was as nothing to her smiles: 1020
Still in her teens, and like a lovely tree
    She grew to womanhood, and between whiles
Rejected several suitors, just to learn
How to accept a better in his turn.
                        129
And walking out upon the beach, below   1025
    The cliff, towards sunset, on that day she found,
Insensible—not dead, but nearly so—
    Don Juan, almost famished, and half drowned;
But being naked, she was shocked, you know,
    Yet deemed herself in common pity bound,   1030
As far as in her lay, "to take him in,
A stranger"[6] dying, with so white a skin.
                        130
But taking him into her father's house
    Was not exactly the best way to save,
But like conveying to the cat the mouse,   1035
    Or people in a trance into their grave;
Because the good old man had so much "*νοῦς*,"[7]

2. Near Eastern coins.
3. Christ's words to Peter and Andrew, both fishermen: "Follow me, and I will make you fishers of
men" (Matthew 4.19).
4. A group of islands in the Aegean Sea.

5. In the playful sense: "wicked."
6. Cf. Matthew 25.35: "I was a stranger, and ye
took me in."
7. Nous, "intelligence"; in England, pronounced
so as to rhyme with "mouse."

Unlike the honest Arab thieves so brave,
He would have hospitably cured the stranger
And sold him instantly when out of danger.   1040

131

And therefore, with her maid, she thought it best
  (A virgin always on her maid relies)
To place him in the cave for present rest:
  And when, at last, he opened his black eyes,
Their charity increased about their guest;   1045
  And their compassion grew to such a size,
It opened half the turnpike gates to heaven—
(St. Paul says 'tis the toll which must be given).[8]

*   *   *

141

And Haidée met the morning face to face;
  Her own was freshest, though a feverish flush
Had dyed it with the headlong blood, whose race
  From heart to cheek is curbed into a blush,
Like to a torrent which a mountain's base,   1125
  That overpowers some Alpine river's rush,
Checks to a lake, whose waves in circles spread;
Or the Red Sea—but the sea is not red.

142

And down the cliff the island virgin came,
  And near the cave her quick light footsteps drew,   1130
While the sun smiled on her with his first flame,
  And young Aurora[9] kissed her lips with dew,
Taking her for a sister; just the same
  Mistake you would have made on seeing the two,
Although the mortal, quite as fresh and fair,   1135
Had all the advantage, too, of not being air.

143

And when into the cavern Haidée stepped
  All timidly, yet rapidly, she saw
That like an infant Juan sweetly slept;
  And then she stopped, and stood as if in awe   1140
(For sleep is awful), and on tiptoe crept
  And wrapped him closer, lest the air, too raw,
Should reach his blood, then o'er him still as death
Bent, with hushed lips, that drank his scarce-drawn breath.

*   *   *

148

And she bent o'er him, and he lay beneath,
  Hushed as the babe upon its mother's breast,
Drooped as the willow when no winds can breathe,

---

8. 1 Corinthians 13.13.   9. The dawn.

Lulled like the depth of ocean when at rest,   1180
Fair as the crowning rose of the whole wreath,
  Soft as the callow cygnet[1] in its nest;
In short, he was a very pretty fellow,
Although his woes had turned him rather yellow.

149

He woke and gazed, and would have slept again,   1185
  But the fair face which met his eyes forbade
Those eyes to close, though weariness and pain
  Had further sleep a further pleasure made;
For woman's face was never formed in vain
  For Juan, so that even when he prayed   1190
He turned from grisly saints, and martyrs hairy,
To the sweet portraits of the Virgin Mary.

150

And thus upon his elbow he arose,
  And looked upon the lady, in whose cheek
The pale contended with the purple rose,   1195
  As with an effort she began to speak;
Her eyes were eloquent, her words would pose,
  Although she told him, in good modern Greek,
With an Ionian accent, low and sweet,
That he was faint, and must not talk, but eat.   1200

*   *   *

168

And every day by daybreak—rather early
  For Juan, who was somewhat fond of rest—
She came into the cave, but it was merely
  To see her bird reposing in his nest;   1340
And she would softly stir his locks so curly,
  Without disturbing her yet slumbering guest,
Breathing all gently o'er his cheek and mouth,
As o'er a bed of roses the sweet South.[2]

169

And every morn his color freshlier came,   1345
  And every day helped on his convalescence;
'Twas well, because health in the human frame
  Is pleasant, besides being true love's essence,
For health and idleness to passion's flame
  Are oil and gunpowder; and some good lessons   1350
Are also learnt from Ceres[3] and from Bacchus,
Without whom Venus will not long attack us.

170

While Venus fills the heart (without heart really
  Love, though good always, is not quite so good),
Ceres presents a plate of vermicelli—   1355

---

1. Young swan.   3. Goddess of the grain.
2. The south wind.

For love must be sustained like flesh and blood—
While Bacchus pours out wine, or hands a jelly:
   Eggs, oysters, too, are amatory food;
But who is their purveyor from above
Heaven knows—it may be Neptune, Pan, or Jove.   1360

     171

When Juan woke he found some good things ready,
   A bath, a breakfast, and the finest eyes
That ever made a youthful heart less steady,
   Besides her maid's, as pretty for their size;
But I have spoken of all this already—   1365
   And repetition's tiresome and unwise—
Well—Juan, after bathing in the sea,
Came always back to coffee and Haidée.

     172

Both were so young, and one so innocent,
   That bathing passed for nothing; Juan seemed   1370
To her, as 'twere, the kind of being sent,
   Of whom these two years she had nightly dreamed,
A something to be loved, a creature meant
   To be her happiness, and whom she deemed
To render happy; all who joy would win   1375
Must share it—Happiness was born a twin.

     173

It was such pleasure to behold him, such
   Enlargement of existence to partake
Nature with him, to thrill beneath his touch,
   To watch him slumbering, and to see him wake: 1380
To live with him forever were too much;
   But then the thought of parting made her quake:
He was her own, her ocean-treasure, cast
Like a rich wreck—her first love, and her last.

     174

And thus a moon rolled on, and fair Haidée   1385
   Paid daily visits to her boy, and took
Such plentiful precautions, that still he
   Remained unknown within his craggy nook;
At last her father's prows put out to sea,
   For certain merchantmen upon the look,
Not as of yore to carry off an Io,[4]   1390
But three Ragusan vessels, bound for Scio.[5]

     175

Then came her freedom, for she had no mother,
   So that, her father being at sea, she was
Free as a married woman, or such other   1395
   Female, as where she likes may freely pass,

---

4. Io, a mistress of Zeus persecuted by his jealous wife, Hera, was kidnapped by Phoenician merchants.

5. Ragusa (or Dubrovnik) is an Adriatic port; Scio is the Italian name for Chios, an island near Turkey.

Without even the encumbrance of a brother,
    The freest she that ever gazed on glass:
I speak of Christian lands in this comparison,
Where wives, at least, are seldom kept in garrison.   1400
176
Now she prolonged her visits and her talk
    (For they must talk), and he had learnt to say
So much as to propose to take a walk—
    For little had he wandered since the day
On which, like a young flower snapped from the stalk,   1405
    Drooping and dewy on the beach he lay—
And thus they walked out in the afternoon,
And saw the sun set opposite the moon.
177
It was a wild and breaker-beaten coast,
    With cliffs above, and a broad sandy shore,   1410
Guarded by shoals and rocks as by an host,
    With here and there a creek, whose aspect wore
A better welcome to the tempest-tossed;
    And rarely ceased the haughty billow's roar,
Save on the dead long summer days, which make   1415
The outstretched ocean glitter like a lake.
178
And the small ripple spilt upon the beach
    Scarcely o'erpass'd the cream of your champagne,
When o'er the brim the sparkling bumpers reach,
    That spring dew of the spirit! the heart's rain!   1420
Few things surpass old wine; and they may preach
    Who please—the more because they preach in vain—
Let us have wine and woman, mirth and laughter,
Sermons and soda water the day after.
179
Man, being reasonable, must get drunk;   1425
    The best of life is but intoxication:
Glory, the grape, love, gold, in these are sunk
    The hopes of all men, and of every nation;
Without their sap, how branchless were the trunk
    Of life's strange tree, so fruitful on occasion: 1430
But to return—Get very drunk; and when
You wake with headache, you shall see what then.
180
Ring for your valet—bid him quickly bring
    Some hock and soda water, then you'll know
A pleasure worthy Xerxes the great king;[6]   1435
    For not the blest sherbet, sublimed with snow,
Nor the first sparkle of the desert spring,

---

6. Xerxes, 5th-century Persian king, was said to have offered a reward to anyone who could discover a
new kind of pleasure.

Nor Burgundy in all its sunset glow,
After long travel, ennui, love, or slaughter,
Vie with that draught of hock and soda water.   1440

181

The coast—I think it was the coast that I
    Was just describing—Yes, it *was* the coast—
Lay at this period quiet as the sky,
    The sands untumbled, the blue waves untossed,
And all was stillness, save the sea bird's cry,   1445
    And dolphin's leap, and little billow crossed
By some low rock or shelve, that made it fret
Against the boundary it scarcely wet.

182

And forth they wandered, her sire being gone,
    As I have said, upon an expedition;   1450
And mother, brother, guardian, she had none,
    Save Zoë, who, although with due precision
She waited on her lady with the sun,
    Thought daily service was her only mission,
Bringing warm water, wreathing her long tresses,   1455
And asking now and then for cast-off dresses.

183

It was the cooling hour, just when the rounded
    Red sun sinks down behind the azure hill,
Which then seems as if the whole earth it bounded,
    Circling all nature, hushed, and dim, and still,   1460
With the far mountain crescent half surrounded
    On one side, and the deep sea calm and chill
Upon the other, and the rosy sky,
With one star sparkling through it like an eye.

184

And thus they wandered forth, and hand in hand,   1465
    Over the shining pebbles and the shells,
Glided along the smooth and hardened sand,
    And in the worn and wild receptacles
Worked by the storms, yet worked as it were planned,
    In hollow halls, with sparry roofs and cells,   1470
They turned to rest; and, each clasped by an arm,
Yielded to the deep twilight's purple charm.

185

They looked up to the sky, whose floating glow
    Spread like a rosy ocean, vast and bright;
They gazed upon the glittering sea below,   1475
    Whence the broad moon rose circling into sight;
They heard the wave's splash, and the wind so low,
    And saw each other's dark eyes darting light
Into each other—and, beholding this,
Their lips drew near, and clung into a kiss;   1480

186

A long, long kiss, a kiss of youth, and love,
   And beauty, all concentrating like rays
Into one focus, kindled from above;
   Such kisses as belong to early days,
Where heart, and soul, and sense, in concert move,   1485
   And the blood's lava, and the pulse a blaze,
Each kiss a heart-quake—for a kiss's strength,
I think, it must be reckoned by its length.

187

By length I mean duration; theirs endured
   Heaven knows how long—no doubt they never reckoned;   1490
And if they had, they could not have secured
   The sum of their sensations to a second:
They had not spoken; but they felt allured,
   As if their souls and lips each other beckoned,
Which, being joined, like swarming bees they clung—   1495
Their hearts the flowers from whence the honey sprung.

188

They were alone, but not alone as they
   Who shut in chambers think it loneliness;
The silent ocean, and the starlight bay,
   The twilight glow, which momently grew less,   1500
The voiceless sands, and dropping caves, that lay
   Around them, made them to each other press,
As if there were no life beneath the sky
Save theirs, and that their life could never die.

189

They feared no eyes nor ears on that lone beach,   1505
   They felt no terrors from the night, they were
All in all to each other: though their speech
   Was broken words, they *thought* a language there—
And all the burning tongues the passions teach
   Found in one sigh the best interpreter   1510
Of nature's oracle—first love—that all
Which Eve has left her daughters since her fall.

190

Haidée spoke not of scruples, asked no vows,
   Nor offered any; she had never heard
Of plight and promises to be a spouse,   1515
   Or perils by a loving maid incurred;
She was all which pure ignorance allows,
   And flew to her young mate like a young bird;
And never having dreamt of falsehood, she
Had not one word to say of constancy.[7]   1520

---

7. Byron said, with reference to Haidée: "I was, and am, penetrated with the conviction that women only know evil from men, whereas men have no criterion to judge of purity or goodness but woman."

191
She loved, and was beloved—she adored,
     And she was worshiped; after nature's fashion,
Their intense souls, into each other poured,
     If souls could die, had perished in that passion—
But by degrees their senses were restored,   1525
     Again to be o'ercome, again to dash on;
And, beating 'gainst *his* bosom, Haidée's heart
Felt as if never more to beat apart.

192
Alas! they were so young, so beautiful,
     So lonely, loving, helpless, and the hour   1530
Was that in which the heart is always full,
     And, having o'er itself no further power,
Prompts deeds eternity cannot annul,
     But pays off moments in an endless shower
Of hell-fire—all prepared for people giving   1535
Pleasure or pain to one another living.

193
Alas! for Juan and Haidée! they were
     So loving and so lovely—till then never,
Excepting our first parents, such a pair
     Had run the risk of being damned forever;   1540
And Haidée, being devout as well as fair,
     Had, doubtless, heard about the Stygian river, [8]
And hell and purgatory—but forgot
Just in the very crisis she should not.

194
They look upon each other, and their eyes   1545
     Gleam in the moonlight; and her white arm clasps
Round Juan's head, and his around hers lies
     Half buried in the tresses which it grasps;
She sits upon his knee, and drinks his sighs,
     He hers, until they end in broken gasps;   1550
And thus they form a group that's quite antique,
Half naked, loving, natural, and Greek.

195
And when those deep and burning moments passed,
     And Juan sunk to sleep within her arms,
She slept not, but all tenderly, though fast,   1555
     Sustained his head upon her bosom's charms;
And now and then her eye to heaven is cast,
     And then on the pale cheek her breast now warms,
Pillowed on her o'erflowing heart, which pants
With all it granted, and with all it grants.   1560

8. The Styx, which flows through Hades.

196

An infant when it gazes on a light,
    A child the moment when it drains the breast,
A devotee when soars the Host[9] in sight,
    An Arab with a stranger for a guest,
A sailor when the prize has struck[1] in fight,   1565
    A miser filling his most hoarded chest,
Feel rapture; but not such true joy are reaping
As they who watch o'er what they love while sleeping.

197

For there it lies so tranquil, so beloved,
    All that it hath of life with us is living;   1570
So gentle, stirless, helpless, and unmoved,
    And all unconscious of the joy 'tis giving;
All it hath felt, inflicted, passed, and proved,
    Hushed into depths beyond the watcher's diving;
There lies the thing we love with all its errors   1575
And all its charms, like death without its terrors.

198

The lady watched her lover—and that hour
    Of Love's, and Night's, and Ocean's solitude,
O'erflowed her soul with their united power;
    Amidst the barren sand and rocks so rude   1580
She and her wave-worn love had made their bower,
    Where nought upon their passion could intrude,
And all the stars that crowded the blue space
Saw nothing happier than her glowing face.

199

Alas! the love of women! it is known   1585
    To be a lovely and a fearful thing;
For all of theirs upon that die is thrown,
    And if 'tis lost, life hath no more to bring
To them but mockeries of the past alone,
    And their revenge is as the tiger's spring,   1590
Deadly, and quick, and crushing; yet, as real
Torture is theirs, what they inflict they feel.

200

They are right; for man, to man so oft unjust,
    Is always so to women; one sole bond
Awaits them, treachery is all their trust;   1595
    Taught to conceal, their bursting hearts despond
Over their idol, till some wealthier lust
    Buys them in marriage—and what rests beyond?
A thankless husband, next a faithless lover,
Then dressing, nursing, praying, and all's over.   1600

---

9. The Eucharistic wafer.   1. Has lowered its flag in token of surrender.

201

Some take a lover, some take drams or prayers,
   Some mind their household, others dissipation,
Some run away, and but exchange their cares,
   Losing the advantage of a virtuous station;
Few changes e'er can better their affairs,   1605
   Theirs being an unnatural situation,
From the dull palace to the dirty hovel:
Some play the devil, and then write a novel.[2]

202

Haidée was Nature's bride, and knew not this;
   Haidée was Passion's child, born where the sun   1610
Showers triple light, and scorches even the kiss
   Of his gazelle-eyed daughters; she was one
Made but to love, to feel that she was his
   Who was her chosen: what was said or done
Elsewhere was nothing. She had nought to fear,   1615
Hope, care, nor love beyond, her heart beat *here*.

203

And oh! that quickening of the heart, that beat!
   How much it costs us! yet each rising throb
Is in its cause as its effect so sweet,
   That Wisdom, ever on the watch to rob   1620
Joy of its alchemy, and to repeat
   Fine truths; even Conscience, too, has a tough job
To make us understand each good old maxim,
So good—I wonder Castlereagh[3] don't tax 'em.

204

And now 'twas done—on the lone shore were plighted   1625
   Their hearts; the stars, their nuptial torches, shed
Beauty upon the beautiful they lighted:
   Ocean their witness, and the cave their bed,
By their own feelings hallowed and united,
   Their priest was Solitude, and they were wed: 1630
And they were happy, for to their young eyes
Each was an angel, and earth paradise.

*   *   *

208

But Juan! had he quite forgotten Julia?
   And should he have forgotten her so soon?
I can't but say it seems to me most truly a
   Perplexing question; but, no doubt, the moon   1660
Does these things for us, and whenever newly a
   Strong palpitation rises, 'tis her boon,

2. The impetuous and hysterical Lady Caroline Lamb, having thrown herself at Byron and been after a time rejected, incorporated incidents from the affair in her novel *Glenarvon* (1816).
3. Robert Stewart, Viscount Castlereagh, British foreign secretary from 1812 to 1822.

Else how the devil is it that fresh features
Have such a charm for us poor human creatures?

209

I hate inconstancy—I loathe, detest,   1665
   Abhor, condemn, abjure the mortal made
Of such quicksilver clay that in his breast
   No permanent foundation can be laid;
Love, constant love, has been my constant guest—
   And yet last night, being at a masquerade,   1670
I saw the prettiest creature, fresh from Milan,
Which gave me some sensations like a villain.

210

But soon Philosophy came to my aid,
   And whispered, "Think of every sacred tie!"
"I will, my dear Philosophy!" I said,   1675
   "But then her teeth, and then, oh, Heaven! her eye!
I'll just inquire if she be wife or maid,
   Or neither—out of curiosity."
"Stop!" cried Philosophy, with air so Grecian
(Though she was masked then as a fair Venetian);   1680

211

"Stop!" so I stopped.—But to return: that which
   Men call inconstancy is nothing more
Than admiration due where nature's rich
   Profusion with young beauty covers o'er
Some favored object; and as in the niche   1685
   A lovely statue we almost adore,
This sort of adoration of the real
Is but a heightening of the "beau ideal."[4]

212

'Tis the perception of the beautiful,
   A fine extension of the faculties,   1690
Platonic, universal, wonderful,
   Drawn from the stars, and filtered through the skies,
Without which life would be extremely dull;
   In short, it is the use of our own eyes,
With one or two small senses added, just   1695
To hint that flesh is formed of fiery dust.

213

Yet 'tis a painful feeling, and unwilling,
   For surely if we always could perceive
In the same object graces quite as killing
   As when she rose upon us like an Eve,   1700
'Twould save us many a heartache, many a shilling
   (For we must get them anyhow, or grieve),
Whereas, if one sole lady pleased forever,
How pleasant for the heart, as well as liver!

4. Ideal beauty.

* * *

216

In the meantime, without proceeding more
    In this anatomy, I've finished now
Two hundred and odd stanzas as before,
    That being about the number I'll allow
Each canto of the twelve, or twenty-four;
    And, laying down my pen, I make my bow,
Leaving Don Juan and Haidée to plead
For them and theirs with all who deign to read.

1725

From *Canto 3*

[JUAN AND HAIDÉE]

1

Hail, Muse! et cetera.—We left Juan sleeping,
    Pillowed upon a fair and happy breast,
And watched by eyes that never yet knew weeping,
    And loved by a young heart, too deeply blest
To feel the poison through her spirit creeping,
    Or know who rested there, a foe to rest,
Had soiled the current of her sinless years,
And turned her pure heart's purest blood to tears!

5

2

Oh, Love! what is it in this world of ours
    Which makes it fatal to be loved? Ah why
With cypress branches[1] hast thou wreathed thy bowers,
    And made thy best interpreter a sigh?
As those who dote on odors pluck the flowers,
    And place them on their breast—but place to die—
Thus the frail beings we would fondly cherish
Are laid within our bosoms but to perish.

10

15

3

In her first passion woman loves her lover,
    In all the others all she loves is love,
Which grows a habit she can ne'er get over,
    And fits her loosely—like an easy glove,
As you may find, whene'er you like to prove her:
    One man alone at first her heart can move;
She then prefers him in the plural number,
Not finding that the additions much encumber.

20

4

I know not if the fault be men's or theirs;
    But one thing's pretty sure; a woman planted[2]
(Unless at once she plunge for life in prayers)
    After a decent time must be gallanted:

25

1. Signifying sorrow.
2. Abandoned (from the French *planter là*, to leave in the lurch).

Although, no doubt, her first of love affairs
  Is that to which her heart is wholly granted;   30
Yet there are some, they say, who have had *none*,
But those who have ne'er end with only *one*.

5

'Tis melancholy, and a fearful sign
  Of human frailty, folly, also crime,
That love and marriage rarely can combine,   35
  Although they both are born in the same clime;
Marriage from love, like vinegar from wine—
  A sad, sour, sober beverage—by time
Is sharpened from its high celestial flavor,
Down to a very homely household savor.   40

6

There's something of antipathy, as 'twere,
  Between their present and their future state;
A kind of flattery that's hardly fair
  Is used until the truth arrives too late—
Yet what can people do, except despair?
  The same things change their names at such a rate;   45
For instance—passion in a lover's glorious,
But in a husband is pronounced uxorious.

7

Men grow ashamed of being so very fond;
  They sometimes also get a little tired
(But that, of course, is rare), and then despond: 50
  The same things cannot always be admired,
Yet 'tis "so nominated in the bond,"[3]
  That both are tied till one shall have expired.
Sad thought! to lose the spouse that was adorning   55
Our days, and put one's servants into mourning.

8

There's doubtless something in domestic doings
  Which forms, in fact, true love's antithesis;
Romances paint at full length people's wooings,
  But only give a bust of marriages;   60
For no one cares for matrimonial cooings,
  There's nothing wrong in a connubial kiss:
Think you, if Laura had been Petrarch's wife,
He would have written sonnets all his life?

9

All tragedies are finished by a death,   65
  All comedies are ended by a marriage;
The future states of both are left to faith,
  For authors fear description might disparage
The worlds to come of both, or fall beneath,
  And then both worlds would punish their miscarriage;   70

---

3. *Shylock*: "Is it so nominated in the bond?" (*The Merchant of Venice* 4.1.259).

So leaving each their priest and prayer book ready,
They say no more of Death or of the Lady.[4]

                    10
The only two that in my recollection
    Have sung of heaven and hell, or marriage, are
Dante and Milton, and of both the affection   75
    Was hapless in their nuptials, for some bar
Of fault or temper ruined the connection
    (Such things, in fact, it don't ask much to mar);
But Dante's Beatrice and Milton's Eve
Were not drawn from their spouses, you conceive.   80

                    11
Some persons say that Dante meant theology
    By Beatrice, and not a mistress—I,
Although my opinion may require apology,
    Deem this a commentator's phantasy,
Unless indeed it was from his own knowledge he   85
    Decided thus, and showed good reason why;
I think that Dante's more abstruse ecstatics
Meant to personify the mathematics.

                    12
Haidée and Juan were not married, but
    The fault was theirs, not mine: it is not fair,   90
Chaste reader, then, in any way to put
    The blame on me, unless you wish they were;
Then if you'd have them wedded, please to shut
    The book which treats of this erroneous pair,
Before the consequences grow too awful;   95
'Tis dangerous to read of loves unlawful.

                    13
Yet they were happy—happy in the illicit
    Indulgence of their innocent desires;
But more imprudent grown with every visit,
    Haidée forgot the island was her sire's;   100
When we have what we like, 'tis hard to miss it,
    At least in the beginning, ere one tires;
Thus she came often, not a moment losing,
Whilst her piratical papa was cruising.

                    14
Let not his mode of raising cash seem strange,   105
    Although he fleeced the flags of every nation,
For into a prime minister but change
    His title, and 'tis nothing but taxation;
But he, more modest, took an humbler range
    Of life, and in an honester vocation   110
Pursued o'er the high seas his watery journey,
And merely practiced as a sea attorney.

4. Alluding to a popular ballad, *Death and the Lady*.

15

The good old gentleman had been detained
   By winds and waves, and some important captures;
And, in the hope of more, at sea remained,   115
   Although a squall or two had damped his raptures,
By swamping one of the prizes; he had chained
   His prisoners, dividing them like chapters
In numbered lots; they all had cuffs and collars,
And averaged each from ten to a hundred dollars.   120

*   *   *

19

Then having settled his marine affairs,   145
   Despatching single cruisers here and there,
His vessel having need of some repairs,
   He shaped his course to where his daughter fair
Continued still her hospitable cares;
   But that part of the coast being shoal and bare,   150
And rough with reefs which ran out many a mile,
His port lay on the other side o' the isle.

20

And there he went ashore without delay,
   Having no customhouse nor quarantine
To ask him awkward questions on the way   155
   About the time and place where he had been:
He left his ship to be hove down next day,
   With orders to the people to careen;[5]
So that all hands were busy beyond measure,
In getting out goods, ballast, guns, and treasure.   160

*   *   *

From *Canto* 4

[JUAN AND HAIDÉE]

3

As boy, I thought myself a clever fellow,
   And wished that others held the same opinion;
They took it up when my days grew more mellow,
   And other minds acknowledged my dominion: 20
Now my sere fancy "falls into the yellow
   Leaf,"[1] and Imagination droops her pinion,
And the sad truth which hovers o'er my desk
Turns what was once romantic to burlesque.

4

And if I laugh at any mortal thing,   25
   'Tis that I may not weep; and if I weep,

5. To tip a vessel on its side in order to clean and
repair its hull.

1. Cf. *Macbeth* 5.3.22–23: "My way of life / Is
fall'n into the sear, the yellow leaf."

'Tis that our nature cannot always bring
   Itself to apathy, for we must steep
Our hearts first in the depths of Lethe's spring,
   Ere what we least wish to behold will sleep: 30
Thetis baptized her mortal son in Styx;[2]
A mortal mother would on Lethe fix.

           5

Some have accused me of a strange design
   Against the creed and morals of the land,
And trace it in this poem every line: 35
   I don't pretend that I quite understand
My own meaning when I would be *very* fine;
   But the fact is that I have nothing planned,
Unless it were to be a moment merry,
A novel word in my vocabulary.   40

           6

To the kind reader of our sober clime
   This way of writing will appear exotic;
Pulci[3] was sire of the half-serious rhyme,
   Who sang when chivalry was more Quixotic,
And reveled in the fancies of the time,   45
   True knights, chaste dames, huge giants, kings despotic;
But all these, save the last, being obsolete,
I chose a modern subject as more meet.

           7

How I have treated it, I do not know;
   Perhaps no better than they have treated me   50
Who have imputed such designs as show
   Not what they saw, but what they wished to see:
But if it gives them pleasure, be it so;
   This is a liberal age, and thoughts are free:
Meantime Apollo plucks me by the ear,   55
And tells me to resume my story here.

        * * *

           29

Now pillowed cheek to cheek, in loving sleep,   225
   Haidée and Juan their siesta took,
A gentle slumber, but it was not deep,
   Forever and anon a something shook
Juan, and shuddering o'er his frame would creep;
   And Haidée's sweet lips murmured like a brook   230
A wordless music, and her face so fair
Stirred with her dream, as rose-leaves with the air;

---

2. The river in Hades into which the nymph Thetis dipped Achilles, to make him invulnerable.
Lethe, another river in Hades, brings oblivion of
life.

3. Author of the *Morgante Maggiore*, prototype of
the Italian seriocomic romance from which Byron
derived the stanza and manner of *Don Juan*. See
the introduction to *Don Juan*.

30

Or as the stirring of a deep clear stream
   Within an Alpine hollow, when the wind
Walks o'er it, was she shaken by the dream,   235
   The mystical usurper of the mind—
O'erpowering us to be whate'er may seem
   Good to the soul which we no more can bind;
Strange state of being! (for 'tis still to be)
Senseless to feel, and with sealed eyes to see.   240

31

She dreamed of being alone on the seashore,
   Chained to a rock; she knew not how, but stir
She could not from the spot, and the loud roar
   Grew, and each wave rose roughly, threatening her;
And o'er her upper lip they seemed to pour,   245
   Until she sobbed for breath, and soon they were
Foaming o'er her lone head, so fierce and high—
Each broke to drown her, yet she could not die.

32

Anon—she was released, and then she strayed
   O'er the sharp shingles[4] with her bleeding feet,   250
And stumbled almost every step she made;
   And something rolled before her in a sheet,
Which she must still pursue howe'er afraid;
   'Twas white and indistinct, nor stopped to meet
Her glance nor grasp, for still she gazed and grasped,   255
And ran, but it escaped her as she clasped.

33

The dream changed—in a cave she stood, its walls
   Were hung with marble icicles; the work
Of ages on its water-fretted halls,
   Where waves might wash, and seals might breed and lurk;   260
Her hair was dripping, and the very balls
   Of her black eyes seemed turned to tears, and murk
The sharp rocks looked below each drop they caught,
Which froze to marble as it fell, she thought.

34

And wet, and cold, and lifeless at her feet,   265
   Pale as the foam that frothed on his dead brow,
Which she essayed in vain to clear (how sweet
   Were once her cares, how idle seemed they now!),
Lay Juan, nor could aught renew the beat
   Of his quenched heart; and the sea dirges low   270
Rang in her sad ears like a mermaid's song,
And that brief dream appeared a life too long.

35

And gazing on the dead, she thought his face
   Faded, or altered into something new—

4. Loose pebbles.

Like to her father's features, till each trace   275
    More like and like to Lambro's aspect grew—
With all his keen worn look and Grecian grace;
    And starting, she awoke, and what to view?
Oh! Powers of Heaven! what dark eye meets she there?
'Tis—'tis her father's—fixed upon the pair!   280

                    36
Then shrieking, she arose, and shrieking fell,
    With joy and sorrow, hope and fear, to see
Him whom she deemed a habitant where dwell
    The ocean-buried, risen from death, to be
Perchance the death of one she loved too well: 285
    Dear as her father had been to Haidée,
It was a moment of that awful kind—
I have seen such—but must not call to mind.

                    37
Up Juan sprung to Haidée's bitter shriek,
    And caught her falling, and from off the wall   290
Snatched down his saber, in hot haste to wreak
    Vengeance on him who was the cause of all:
Then Lambro, who till now forbore to speak,
    Smiled scornfully, and said, "Within my call,
A thousand scimitars await the word;   295
Put up, young man, put up your silly sword."

                    38
And Haidée clung around him; "Juan, 'tis—
    'Tis Lambro—'tis my father! Kneel with me—
He will forgive us—yes—it must be—yes.
    Oh! dearest father, in this agony   300
Of pleasure and of pain—even while I kiss
    Thy garment's hem with transport, can it be
That doubt should mingle with my filial joy?
Deal with me as thou wilt, but spare this boy."

                    39
High and inscrutable the old man stood,   305
    Calm in his voice, and calm within his eye—
Not always signs with him of calmest mood:
    He looked upon her, but gave no reply;
Then turned to Juan, in whose cheek the blood
    Oft came and went, as there resolved to die;   310
In arms, at least, he stood, in act to spring
On the first foe whom Lambro's call might bring.

                    40
"Young man, your sword"; so Lambro once more said:
    Juan replied, "Not while this arm is free."
The old man's cheek grew pale, but not with dread,   315
    And drawing from his belt a pistol, he
Replied, "Your blood be then on your own head."
    Then looked close at the flint, as if to see

'Twas fresh—for he had lately used the lock[5]—
And next proceeded quietly to cock.   320

41

It has a strange quick jar upon the ear,
   That cocking of a pistol, when you know
A moment more will bring the sight to bear
   Upon your person, twelve yards off, or so;
A gentlemanly distance,[6] not too near,   325
   If you have got a former friend for foe;
But after being fired at once or twice,
The ear becomes more Irish, and less nice.[7]

42

Lambro presented, and one instant more
   Had stopped this Canto, and Don Juan's breath,   330
When Haidée threw herself her boy before;
   Stern as her sire: "On me," she cried, "let death
Descend—the fault is mine; this fatal shore
   He found—but sought not. I have pledged my faith;
I love him—I will die with him: I knew   335
Your nature's firmness—know your daughter's too."

43

A minute past, and she had been all tears,
   And tenderness, and infancy; but now
She stood as one who championed human fears—
   Pale, statue-like, and stern, she wooed the blow;   340
And tall beyond her sex, and their compeers,[8]
   She drew up to her height, as if to show
A fairer mark; and with a fixed eye scanned
Her father's face—but never stopped his hand.

44

He gazed on her, and she on him: 'twas strange   345
   How like they looked! the expression was the same;
Serenely savage, with a little change
   In the large dark eye's mutual-darted flame;
For she, too, was as one who could avenge,
   If cause should be—a lioness, though tame;   350
Her father's blood before her father's face
Boiled up, and proved her truly of his race.

45

I said they were alike, their features and
   Their stature differing but in sex and years;
Even to the delicacy of their hand   355
   There was resemblance, such as true blood wears;
And now to see them, thus divided, stand
   In fixed ferocity, when joyous tears,

---

5. The part of the gun that explodes the charge.
6. I.e., dueling distance.
7. Finicky. Byron alludes to the propensity of hot-

headed young Irishmen to fight duels.
8. I.e., she was the match in height of Lambro
and Juan.

And sweet sensations, should have welcomed both,
Show what the passions are in their full growth.   360

46

The father paused a moment, then withdrew
  His weapon, and replaced it; but stood still,
And looking on her, as to look her through,
   "Not *I*," he said, "have sought this stranger's ill;
Not *I* have made this desolation: few   365
  Would bear such outrage, and forbear to kili;
But I must do my duty—how thou hast
Done thine, the present vouches for the past.

47

"Let him disarm; or, by my father's head,
  His own shall roll before you like a ball!"   370
He raised his whistle as the word he said,
  And blew; another answered to the call,
And rushing in disorderly, though led,
   And armed from boot to turban, one and all,
Some twenty of his train came, rank on rank;   375
He gave the word, "Arrest or slay the Frank."[9]

48

Then, with a sudden movement, he withdrew
  His daughter; while compressed within his clasp,
'Twixt her and Juan interposed the crew;
   In vain she struggled in her father's grasp—   380
His arms were like a serpent's coil: then flew
  Upon their prey, as darts an angry asp,
The file of pirates; save the foremost, who
Had fallen, with his right shoulder half cut through.

49

The second had his cheek laid open; but   385
  The third, a wary, cool old sworder, took
The blows upon his cutlass, and then put
  His own well in; so well, ere you could look,
His man was floored, and helpless at his foot,
  With the blood running like a little brook   390
From two smart saber gashes, deep and red—
One on the arm, the other on the head.

50

And then they bound him where he fell, and bore
  Juan from the apartment: with a sign
Old Lambro bade them take him to the shore,   395
  Where lay some ships which were to sail at nine.
They laid him in a boat, and plied the oar
   Until they reached some galliots,[1] placed in line;
On board of one of these, and under hatches,
They stowed him, with strict orders to the watches.   400

9. Term used in the Near East to designate a western European.

1. A small, fast galley, propelled by both oars and sails.

*   *   *

58

The last sight which she saw was Juan's gore,
    And he himself o'ermastered and cut down;
His blood was running on the very floor
    Where late he trod, her beautiful, her own;   460
Thus much she viewed an instant and no more—
    Her struggles ceased with one convulsive groan;
On her sire's arm, which until now scarce held
Her writhing, fell she like a cedar felled.

59

A vein had burst, and her sweet lips' pure dyes   465
    Were dabbled with the deep blood which ran o'er;
And her head drooped, as when the lily lies
    O'ercharged with rain: her summoned handmaids bore
Their lady to her couch with gushing eyes;
    Of herbs and cordials they produced their store,   470
But she defied all means they could employ,
Like one life could not hold, nor death destroy.

60

Days lay she in that state unchanged, though chill—
    With nothing livid,[4] still her lips were red;
She had no pulse, but death seemed absent still;   475
    No hideous sign proclaimed her surely dead;
Corruption came not in each mind to kill
    All hope; to look upon her sweet face bred
New thoughts of life, for it seemed full of soul—
She had so much, earth could not claim the whole.   480

*   *   *

69

Twelve days and nights she withered thus; at last,   545
    Without a groan, or sigh, or glance, to show
A parting pang, the spirit from her passed:
    And they who watched her nearest could not know
The very instant, till the change that cast
    Her sweet face into shadow, dull and slow,   550
Glazed o'er her eyes—the beautiful, the black—
Oh! to possess such luster—and then lack!

70

She died, but not alone; she held within
    A second principle of life, which might
Have dawned a fair and sinless child of sin;   555
    But closed its little being without light,
And went down to the grave unborn, wherein
    Blossom and bough lie withered with one blight;

2. North African.   4. I.e., though she was ashen pale.
3. A violent, hot, dust-laden desert wind.

In vain the dews of Heaven descend above
The bleeding flower and blasted fruit of love.   560

71

Thus lived—thus died she; never more on her
    Shall sorrow light, or shame. She was not made
Through years or moons the inner weight to bear,
    Which colder hearts endure till they are laid
By age in earth; her days and pleasures were   565
    Brief, but delightful—such as had not stayed
Long with her destiny; but she sleeps well
By the seashore, whereon she loved to dwell.

72

That isle is now all desolate and bare,
    Its dwellings down, its tenants passed away;   570
None but her own and father's grave is there,
    And nothing outward tells of human clay;
Ye could not know where lies a thing so fair,
    No stone is there to show, no tongue to say
What was; no dirge, except the hollow sea's,   575
Mourns o'er the beauty of the Cyclades.

73

But many a Greek maid in a loving song
    Sighs o'er her name; and many an islander
With her sire's story makes the night less long;
    Valor was his, and beauty dwelt with her: 580
If she loved rashly, her life paid for wrong—
    A heavy price must all pay who thus err,
In some shape; let none think to fly the danger,
For soon or late Love is his own avenger.

74

But let me change this theme, which grows too sad,   585
    And lay this sheet of sorrows on the shelf;
I don't much like describing people mad,
    For fear of seeming rather touched myself—
Besides I've no more on this head to add;
    And as my Muse is a capricious elf,   590
We'll put about, and try another tack
With Juan, left half-killed some stanzas back. [5]

1818–23

1819–24

---

5. Juan's adventures continue. He is sold as a slave
in Constantinople to an enamored Sultana; she
disguises him as a girl and adds him to her husband's harem for convenience of access. Juan
escapes, joins the Russian army that is besieging
Ismail, and so distinguishes himself in the capture
of the town that he is sent with despatches to St.
Petersburg. There he becomes "man-mistress" to
the insatiable Catherine the Great; as the result of
her assiduous attentions, he falls into a physical
decline and, for a salutary change of scene and
climate, is sent on a diplomatic mission to England.
In canto 16, the last that Byron finished, he is in
the middle of an amorous adventure while a guest
at the medieval country mansion of an English
nobleman, Lord Henry Amundeville, and his very
beautiful wife.

PERCY BYSSHE SHELLEY
1792–1822

1811: Is expelled from Oxford and elopes with Harriet Westbrook.
1818: Leaves England for Italy, never to return.
1819: The great year: *Prometheus Unbound, The Cenci,* and some
of his best lyrics, including *Ode to the West Wind.*
1820: Settles in Pisa and its vicinity; the "Pisan Circle."

Shelley, although a radical nonconformist in every aspect of his life and thought, emerged from a solidly conservative background. His ancestors had been Sussex aristocrats since early in the seventeenth century; his grandfather, Sir Bysshe Shelley, made himself the richest man in Horsham, Sussex; his father, Timothy Shelley, was a hardheaded and conventional member of Parliament. Percy Shelley himself was in line for a baronetcy and, as befitted his station, was sent to be educated at Eton and Oxford. He was slight of build, eccentric in manner, and unskilled in sports or fighting, and as a consequence was mercilessly baited by older and stronger boys. Even then he saw the petty tyranny of schoolmasters and schoolmates as representative of man's general inhumanity to man, and dedicated his life to a war against injustice and oppression. He describes the experience in the Dedication to *Laon and Cythna* (later called *The Revolt of Islam*):

> So without shame, I spake:—"I will be wise,
> And just, and free, and mild, if in me lies
> Such power, for I grow weary to behold
> The selfish and the strong still tyrannise
> Without reproach or check." I then controuled
> My tears, my heart grew calm, and I was meek and bold.

At Oxford in the autumn of 1810 Shelley's closest friend was Thomas Jefferson Hogg, a self-centered and self-confident young man who shared Shelley's love of philosophy and scorn of orthodoxy. The two collaborated on a pamphlet, *The Necessity of Atheism,* which claimed that God's existence cannot be proved on empirical grounds. Shelley refused to repudiate the document, as demanded by the authorities; to his great shock and grief, he was peremptorily expelled, terminating a university career that had lasted only six months. This event opened a breach between Shelley and his father that widened over the years.

Shelley went to London, where, eager for a test of his zeal for social justice, he took up the cause of Harriet Westbrook, the pretty and warm-hearted daughter of a well-to-do tavern keeper, whose father, Shelley wrote to Hogg, "has persecuted her in a most horrible way by endeavoring to compel her to go to school." Harriet threw herself on Shelley's protection, and "gratitude and admiration," he wrote, "all demand that I shall love her *forever.*" He eloped with Harriet to Edinburgh and married her, against his conviction that marriage was a tyrannical and degrading social institution.

He was then eighteen years of age, and his bride sixteen. The young couple moved restlessly from place to place, living on a small allowance granted reluctantly by their families. In February 1812, accompanied by Harriet's sister Eliza, they traveled to Dublin to distribute Shelley's *Address to the Irish People* and otherwise take part in the movement for Catholic emancipation and for the amelioration of the oppressed and poverty-stricken people.

Back in London, Shelley became a disciple of the radical social philosopher William Godwin, author of the *Inquiry concerning Political Justice*. In 1813 he printed privately his first important work, *Queen Mab*, a long prophetic poem set in the fantastic frame of the journey of a disembodied soul through space, to whom the fairy Mab reveals in visions the woeful past, the dreadful present, and the utopian future. Announcing that "there is no God!" Mab decries institutional religion and codified morality as the roots of social evil. She prophesies that, under the rule of the goddess Necessity, all institutions will wither away, and humanity will return to its natural condition of goodness and felicity.

In the following spring Shelley, who had drifted apart from Harriet, fell in love with the beautiful Mary Wollstonecraft Godwin, daughter of Mary Wollstonecraft and William Godwin. Acting according to his conviction that cohabitation without love is immoral, he abandoned Harriet, fled to France with Mary (taking along her half sister, Claire Clairmont), and—still acting in accordance with his belief in nonexclusive love—invited Harriet to come live with them in the relationship of a sister. Shelley's elopement with Mary outraged her father, despite the facts that his theoretical views of marriage had been no less radical than Shelley's and that Shelley, himself in financial difficulties, had earlier taken over Godwin's very substantial debts. When he returned to London, Shelley found that the general public, his family, and most of his friends regarded him not only as an atheist and revolutionary, but also as a gross immoralist. When two years later Harriet, pregnant by an unknown lover, drowned herself in a fit of despair, the courts denied Shelley the custody of their two children. Shelley married Mary Godwin and in 1818 moved to Italy; thereafter he saw himself in the role of an alien and outcast, scorned and rejected by the human race to whose welfare he had dedicated his powers and his life.

In Italy he resumed his restless existence, moving from town to town and house to house. His health was usually bad. Although the death of his grandfather in 1815 had provided a substantial income, he dissipated so much of it by his warmhearted but improvident support of William Godwin, Leigh Hunt, and other indigent pensioners that he was constantly short of money and harried by creditors. Within nine months, in 1818–19, Clara and William, the beloved children of Percy and Mary Shelley, both died. This tragedy threw Mary into a state of apathy and self-absorption that destroyed the earlier harmony of her relationship with her husband, and from which even the birth of another son, Percy Florence, could not entirely rescue her.

In these desperate circumstances, in a state sometimes verging on despair, and knowing that he almost entirely lacked an audience, Shelley wrote his greatest works. In 1819 he completed his masterpiece, *Prometheus Unbound*, and a fine tragedy, *The Cenci*. He wrote also numerous lyric poems; a visionary call for a proletarian revolution, *The Mask of Anarchy*; a discerning and witty satire on Wordsworth, *Peter Bell the Third*; and a penetrating political essay, *A Philosophical View of Reform*. His works of the next two years include *A Defence of Poetry*; *Epipsychidion*, a rhapsodic vision of love as a union, beyond earthly limits, with what the title identifies as "the soul out of my soul"; *Adonais*, his noble elegy on the death of Keats; and *Hellas*, a lyrical drama evoked by the Greek war for liberation from the Turks, in which he again projected his vision of a coming golden age. These writings, unlike the early *Queen Mab*, are the products of a mind enlarged and chastened by tragic experience, deepened by incessant philosophical speculation, and richly stored with the harvest of his reading—which Shelley carried on, as his friend Hogg said, "in season and out of season, at table, in bed, and especially during a walk," until he became one of the most erudite of poets. His delight in scientific discoveries and speculations continued, but his earlier zest for Gothic terrors and the social theories of the radical eighteenth-century optimists gave way to an absorption in Greek tragedy, Milton's *Paradise Lost*, and the Bible. While he did not give up his hopes for a millennial future (he wore a ring with the motto *Il buon tempo verrà*—"the good time will come"), he now attributed the evils of present society to humanity's own moral failures and grounded the possibility of radical social reform upon a prior reform of the moral and imaginative faculties through the redeeming power of love. Though often thought of as a simple-minded doctrinaire, Shelley in fact possessed a complex and energetically inquisitive intelligence which never halted at a fixed mental position; his writings represent stages in a ceaseless exploration.

The poems of Shelley's maturity also show the influence of his study of Plato and the Neoplatonists. Shelley found congenial the Platonic division of the cosmos into two worlds—the ordinary world of change, mortality, evil, and suffering, and the criterion world of perfect and eternal Forms, of which the world of sense-experience is only a distant and illusory reflection. The earlier interpretations of Shelley as a downright Platonic idealist, however, have been drastically modified by modern investigations of his reading and writings. He was a close student of English empirical philosophy, which limits knowledge to valid reasoning upon what is given in sense-experience, and within this tradition he felt a special affinity to the radical skepticism of David Hume. Shelley was indeed an idealist, but, as C. E. Pulos has shown in *The Deep Truth: A Study of Shelley's Scepticism*, his was "a qualified idealism," holding provisionally to the ideas envisioned by an imagination that transcends experience, but refusing to assert that these ideas are anything more than high possibilities. As Shelley wrote, we quickly reach "the verge where words abandon us, and what wonder if we grow dizzy to look down the dark abyss of how little we know." Many of his major poems express his sense of the limits of certain knowledge and his refusal to let his intuitions and hopes harden into a philosophical or religious creed. To the skeptical idealism of the mature Shelley (see, for example, the notes to his great lyrics from *Hellas*), the hope in the ultimate redemption of life by love and imagination is not a certainty but a moral obligation. We must, he asserts, cling to hope because its contrary, despair about human possibility, is self-fulfilling, by ensuring the permanence of the conditions before which the mind has surrendered its aspirations. Hope does not guarantee achievement, but it keeps open the possibility of achievement, and so releases the imaginative and creative powers that are its only available means.

When in 1820 the Shelleys settled finally at Pisa, he came closer to finding contentment than at any other time in his adult life. A group of friends, Shelley's "Pisan Circle," gathered around them, including for a while Lord

Byron and the swashbuckling young Cornishman Edward Trelawny. Chief in Shelley's affections, however, were Edward Williams, a retired lieutenant of a cavalry regiment serving in India, and his charming common-law wife, Jane, with whom Shelley carried on a flirtation and to whom he addressed some of his best lyrics and verse letters. The end came suddenly, and in a way previsioned in the ecstatic last stanza of *Adonais*, where he had described his spirit as a ship driven by a violent storm out into the dark unknown. On July 8, 1822, Shelley and Edward Williams were sailing their open boat, the *Don Juan*, from Leghorn to their summer house near Lerici, on the Gulf of Spezia. A violent squall blew up and swamped the boat. When several days later the bodies were washed ashore they were cremated, and Shelley's ashes were buried in the Protestant Cemetery at Rome, near the graves of John Keats and William Shelley, the poet's young son. He left unfinished *The Triumph of Life*, which was a new departure that, in the estimation of many readers, promised to be his greatest poem. Byron, who did not pay moral compliments lightly, wrote to John Murray at the time of Shelley's death: "You were all brutally mistaken about Shelley, who was, without exception, the *best* and least selfish man I ever knew. I never knew one who was not a beast in comparison."

To many critics of the mid-twentieth century (and despite the reverence toward him of W. B. Yeats, an admitted master of the poetry these critics most admired), Shelley was a favorite resort for supposed examples of intellectual and emotional immaturity, shoddy workmanship, and incoherent imagery. In recent years, however, he has been the subject of many sympathetic critics, whose studies have clarified the complex and coherent structure of his symbolism and have increasingly confirmed Wordsworth's recognition that "Shelley is one of the best *artists* of us all: I mean in workmanship of style." Shelley's expansion of the metrical and stanzaic resources of verse is without recent parallel in the history of English literature. Furthermore, his successful poems show an astonishing range of voice, from the controlled passion of *Ode to the West Wind*, through the calm and heroic dignity of the utterances of Prometheus, to the approximation to the inexpressible in the description of Asia's transfiguration and in the visionary conclusion of *Adonais*. Most surprising, for a poet who almost entirely lacked an audience, is the assured urbanity, the effortless command of the tone and language of a cultivated man of the world, exemplified in passages that Shelley wrote all through his mature career and especially in the lyrics and verse letters that he composed during the last year of his life.

TEXTUAL NOTE

The publication of Shelley's writings has had a tangled history. Shelley had no chance to correct proofs for many of the poems published during his lifetime, especially those that appeared in periodicals, while a number of his poems were not printed until after his death. As a result, standard editions of Shelley's collected poems—and the selections and anthologies that have been based on these editions—have included important errors and deviations from the poet's probable intentions.

The texts below are those prepared by Donald H. Reiman and Sharon B. Powers for *Shelley's Poetry and Prose*, A Norton Critical Edition (1977); Reiman has also edited for this anthology a few poems not included in that edition. The texts are based on Shelley's extant holograph manuscripts and transcripts, on first editions of the various works, and on any later editions that may have incorporated the author's own changes; they also take advantage of specialized editions and textual studies by various Shelley scholars.

The detailed rationale is provided in Reiman and Powers' Textual Introduction. Shelley's spellings have been kept (though in part regularized according to the poet's own preferred forms), as well as Shelley's punctuation of those texts that he himself prepared for printing. The modern reader should remember that Shelley's punctuation, in the common fashion of his time, was primarily rhetorical rather than syntactical. That is, a punctuation mark indicates a phrasal pause in the reading; there is an increasingly longer pause in the sequence: comma, semicolon, colon, period, and dash. Also, Shelley often relied on the natural pause at the end of a line of verse, where modern usage would call for a comma or other mark of punctuation.

Mutability

We are as clouds that veil the midnight moon;
    How restlessly they speed, and gleam, and quiver,
Streaking the darkness radiantly!—yet soon
    Night closes round, and they are lost for ever:

Or like forgotten lyres,[1] whose dissonant strings   5
    Give various response to each varying blast,
To whose frail frame no second motion brings
    One mood or modulation like the last.

We rest.—A dream has power to poison sleep;
    We rise.—One wandering thought pollutes the day;   10
We feel, conceive or reason, laugh or weep;
    Embrace fond woe, or cast our cares away:

It is the same!—For, be it joy or sorrow,
    The path of its departure still is free:
Man's yesterday may ne'er be like his morrow;   15
    Nought may endure but Mutability.

ca. 1814–15   1816

To Wordsworth[2]

Poet of Nature, thou hast wept to know
That things depart which never may return:
Childhood and youth, friendship and love's first glow,
Have fled like sweet dreams, leaving thee to mourn.
These common woes I feel. One loss is mine   5

---

1. Wind harps.
2. Shelley's grieved comment on the poet of nature   and of social radicalism after his views had become conservative.

Which thou too feel'st, yet I alone deplore.
Thou wert as a lone star, whose light did shine
On some frail bark in winter's midnight roar:
Thou hast like to a rock-built refuge stood
Above the blind and battling multitude: 10
In honoured poverty thy voice did weave
Songs consecrate to truth and liberty,—
Deserting these, thou leavest me to grieve,
Thus having been, that thou shouldst cease to be.

ca. 1814–15   1816

Alastor; or, The Spirit of Solitude

According to Shelley's friend Thomas Love Peacock, the poet was "at a loss for a title, and I proposed that which he adopted: Alastor, or the Spirit of Solitude. The Greek word *Alastor* is an evil genius. . . . I mention the true meaning of the word because many have supposed *Alastor* to be the name of the hero" *(Memoirs of Shelley)*. Peacock's definition of an *alastor* as "an *evil* genius" has compounded the problems that many readers have found in interpreting this work: the term "evil" does not seem to fit the attitude to the poet's solitary quest expressed within the poem; the poem seems to clash with some statements in Shelley's Preface; and the first and second paragraphs within the Preface seem inconsistent with each other. These problems, however, are largely resolved if we recognize that, in his first major achievement (he was only twenty-three when he wrote *Alastor*), Shelley established his characteristic procedure of working with multiple perspectives. Both Preface and poem explore alternative and conflicting possibilities in what Shelley calls "doubtful knowledge"—matters which are humanly essential but in which no certainty is humanly possible.

The first paragraph of the Preface explains the "allegorical" plot. By "allegorical" Shelley means that the poem, like medieval and Renaissance allegories such as Dante's *Divine Comedy* and Spenser's *Faerie Queene*, represents a spiritual need and aspiration in the vehicle of a journey and quest in the physical world. Shelley's protagonist reaches a stage at which the natural object within the world "cease to suffice," for he envisions a "Being," a female Other who will answer to all that is best in his own self and will fulfill the requirements of his "intellectual faculties," "imagination," and "the functions of sense." He commits himself to the search for "a prototype" of this vision in the real world, but since his desires are infinite and the world's possibilities are limited, his quest is doomed to end in his early death.

The second paragraph proceeds to pass judgment upon such a Poet in terms of the values of "actual men"—the requirements of human and social life in this world. Since the visionary Poet turned away from both human and natural community in search of the projected demands of his own psyche, his lot can be said to have been "avenged" by the *alastor*, the spirit of solitude, in the sense of "solitude" as alienation from both nature and humanity. The Preface goes on, however, passionately to elevate the moral status of such a visionary over the status of a second class of "meaner spirits" who also "keep aloof from sympathies with their kind," but only because they ignobly lack any capacity to project their imagination beyond their own narrow selves, and so are "morally dead." The Preface leaves open a possibility which Shelley proceeded to explore in *Prometheus Unbound* and other poems—the possibility that there exists a third class of men who sustain an imaginative vision but undertake to realize it, not in self-centered solitude, but by effecting a transformation in human nature, society, and milieu.

The diverse attitudes expressed within the poem itself are clarified, once we realize that the story is narrated—as the many echoes from Wordsworth in the opening invocation suggest—in the persona of a Wordsworthian poet for whom nature suffices both to the demands of his imagination and to his need for community. This narrator-poet proceeds to tell, with insight and compassion, but from his own perspective, the history of a nameless visionary Poet who, having himself passed through a Wordsworthian phase, then gives up everything in the quest for a goal beyond possibility.

In this early poem Shelley established a form, conceptual frame, and imagery for the Romantic quest which not only shaped his own later poems but also served as a paradigm for the writings of many other poets, from Byron's *Manfred* and Keats's *Endymion* and invocation to *The Fall of Hyperion* to the quest-poems of Shelley's later admirer William Butler Yeats.

Alastor; or, The Spirit of Solitude

Preface

The poem entitled "ALASTOR," may be considered as allegorical of one of the most interesting situations of the human mind. It represents a youth of uncorrupted feelings and adventurous genius led forth by an imagination inflamed and purified through familiarity with all that is excellent and majestic, to the contemplation of the universe. He drinks deep of the fountains of knowledge, and is still insatiate. The magnificence and beauty of the external world sinks profoundly into the frame of his conceptions, and affords to their modifications a variety not to be exhausted. So long as it is possible for his desires to point towards objects thus infinite and unmeasured, he is joyous, and tranquil, and self-possessed. But the period arrives when these objects cease to suffice. His mind is at length suddenly awakened and thirsts for intercourse with an intelligence similar to itself. He images to himself the Being whom he loves. Conversant with speculations of the sublimest and most perfect natures, the vision in which he embodies his own imaginations unites all of wonderful, or wise, or beautiful, which the poet, the philosopher, or the lover could depicture. The intellectual faculties, the imagination, the functions of sense, have their respective requisitions on the sympathy of corresponding powers in other human beings. The Poet is represented as uniting these requisitions, and attaching them to a single image.[1] He

1. Shelley's view that the object of love is an idealized antitype to all that is best within the self is clarified by a passage in his *Essay on Love*, which may have been written at about the time of *Alastor*: "We dimly see within our intellectual nature . . . the ideal prototype of every thing excellent or lovely that we are capable of conceiving as belonging to the nature of men. . . . [This is] a soul within our soul. . . . The discovery of its anti-type . . . in such proportion as the type within demands; this is the invisible and unattainable point to which Love tends; and . . . without the possession of which there is no rest nor respite to the heart over which it rules."

seeks in vain for a prototype of his conception. Blasted by his disappointment, he descends to an untimely grave.

The picture is not barren of instruction to actual men. The Poet's self-centred seclusion was avenged by the furies of an irresistible passion pursuing him to speedy ruin. But that Power which strikes the luminaries of the world with sudden darkness and extinction, by awakening them to too exquisite a perception of its influences, dooms to a slow and poisonous decay those meaner spirits that dare to abjure its dominion. Their destiny is more abject and inglorious as their delinquency is more contemptible and pernicious. They who, deluded by no generous error, instigated by no sacred thirst of doubtful knowledge, duped by no illustrious superstition, loving nothing on this earth, and cherishing no hopes beyond, yet keep aloof from sympathies with their kind, rejoicing neither in human joy nor mourning with human grief; these, and such as they, have their apportioned curse. They languish, because none feel with them their common nature. They are morally dead. They are neither friends, nor lovers, nor fathers, nor citizens of the world, nor benefactors of their country. Among those who attempt to exist without human sympathy, the pure and tender-hearted perish through the intensity and passion of their search after its communities, when the vacancy of their spirit suddenly makes itself felt. All else, selfish, blind, and torpid, are those unforeseeing multitudes who constitute, together with their own, the lasting misery and loneliness of the world. Those who love not their fellow-beings live unfruitful lives, and prepare for their old age a miserable grave.

> "The good die first,
> And those whose hearts are dry as summer dust,
> Burn to the socket!"[2]

December 14, 1815.

Alastor; or, The Spirit of Solitude

Nondum amabam, et amare amabam, quærebam quid amarem, amans amare.—*Confess. St. August.*[3]

Earth, ocean, air, beloved brotherhood!
If our great Mother[4] has imbued my soul

2. Quoted from Wordsworth's *The Excursion* 1.519–21; the passage occurs in *The Ruined Cottage* (above, lines 96–98), which Wordsworth reworked into the first book of *The Excursion* (1814).
3. Condensed from a passage in St. Augustine, *Confessions* 3.1: "Not yet did I love, though I loved to love, seeking what I might love, loving to love." Augustine thus describes his state of mind when he was addicted to illicit sexual love; the true object of his desire, which compels the tortuous spiritual

journey of his life, he later discovered to be the infinite and transcendent God.
4. Nature, invoked as the common mother of the elements and of the poet.
5. Wordsworth, *My Heart Leaps Up* (above, lines 9–10): "And I could wish my days to be / Bound each to each by natural piety." Wordsworth also used these lines as the epigraph to his *Ode: Intimations of Immortality.*

With aught of natural piety[5] to feel
Your love, and recompense the boon with mine;[6]
If dewy morn, and odorous noon, and even,   5
With sunset and its gorgeous ministers,[7]
And solemn midnight's tingling silentness;
If autumn's hollow sighs in the sere wood,
And winter robing with pure snow and crowns
Of starry ice the grey grass and bare boughs;   10
If spring's voluptuous pantings when she breathes
Her first sweet kisses, have been dear to me;
If no bright bird, insect, or gentle beast
I consciously have injured, but still loved
And cherished these my kindred; then forgive   15
This boast, beloved brethren, and withdraw
No portion of your wonted favour now!

   Mother of this unfathomable world!
Favour my solemn song, for I have loved
Thee ever, and thee only; I have watched   20
Thy shadow, and the darkness of thy steps,
And my heart ever gazes on the depth
Of thy deep mysteries. I have made my bed
In charnels and on coffins, where black death
Keeps record of the trophies won from thee,   25
Hoping to still these obstinate questionings[8]
Of thee and thine, by forcing some lone ghost,
Thy messenger, to render up the tale
Of what we are. In lone and silent hours,
When night makes a weird sound of its own stillness,   30
Like an inspired and desperate alchymist
Staking his very life on some dark hope,
Have I mixed awful talk and asking looks
With my most innocent love, until strange tears
Uniting with those breathless kisses, made   35
Such magic as compels the charmed night
To render up thy charge: . . . and, though ne'er yet
Thou hast unveil'd thy inmost sanctuary,
Enough from incommunicable dream,
And twilight phantasms, and deep noonday thought,   40
Has shone within me, that serenely now
And moveless, as a long-forgotten lyre
Suspended in the solitary dome
Of some mysterious and deserted fane,[9]
I wait thy breath, Great Parent, that my strain   45
May modulate with murmurs of the air,

6. I.e., with my love.
7. The sunset colors.
8. *Ode: Intimations of Immortality*, line 143: ". . .
those obstinate questionings / Of sense and outward things. . . ."

9. Temple. The narrator calls on the Mother, his
natural muse, to make him her wind harp. Cf. the
opening passage of Wordsworth's *Prelude*, Coleridge's *Dejection: An Ode*, and the conclusions of
Shelley's *Ode to the West Wind* and of *Adonais*.

And motions of the forests and the sea,
And voice of living beings, and woven hymns
Of night and day, and the deep heart of man.[1]

There was a Poet whose untimely tomb   50
No human hands with pious reverence reared,
But the charmed eddies of autumnal winds
Built o'er his mouldering bones a pyramid
Of mouldering leaves in the waste wilderness:—
A lovely youth,—no mourning maiden decked   55
With weeping flowers, or votive cypress wreath,[2]
The lone couch of his everlasting sleep:—
Gentle, and brave, and generous,—no lorn[3] bard
Breathed o'er his dark fate one melodious sigh:
He lived, he died, he sung, in solitude.   60
Strangers have wept to hear his passionate notes,
And virgins, as unknown he past, have pined
And wasted for fond love of his wild eyes.
The fire of those soft orbs has ceased to burn,
And Silence, too enamoured of that voice,   65
Locks its mute music in her rugged cell.

By solemn vision, and bright silver dream,
His infancy was nurtured. Every sight
And sound from the vast earth and ambient air,
Sent to his heart its choicest impulses.   70
The fountains of divine philosophy
Fled not his thirsting lips, and all of great
Or good, or lovely, which the sacred past
In truth or fable consecrates, he felt
And knew. When early youth had past, he left   75
His cold fireside and alienated home
To seek strange truths in undiscovered lands.
Many a wide waste and tangled wilderness
Has lured his fearless steps; and he has bought
With his sweet voice and eyes, from savage men,   80
His rest and food. Nature's most secret steps
He like her shadow has pursued, where'er
The red volcano overcanopies
Its fields of snow and pinnacles of ice
With burning smoke, or where bitumen lakes[4]   85
On black bare pointed islets ever beat
With sluggish surge, or where the secret caves
Rugged and dark, winding among the springs
Of fire and poison, inaccessible

---

1. Cf. Wordsworth, *Tintern Abbey*, lines 94 ff.: "A presence . . . / Whose dwelling is . . . the round ocean and the living air, / And the blue sky, and in the mind of man; / A motion and a spirit. . . ."

2. "Votive": offered to fulfill a vow to the gods. The cypress represented mourning.
3. Abandoned.
4. Lakes of pitch, flowing from a volcano.

To avarice or pride, their starry domes   90
Of diamond and of gold expand above
Numberless and immeasurable halls,
Frequent[5] with crystal column, and clear shrines
Of pearl, and thrones radiant with chrysolite.[6]
Nor had that scene of ampler majesty   95
Than gems or gold, the varying roof of heaven
And the green earth lost in his heart its claims
To love and wonder; he would linger long
In lonesome vales, making the wild his home,
Until the doves and squirrels would partake   100
From his innocuous hand his bloodless food,[7]
Lured by the gentle meaning of his looks,
And the wild antelope, that starts whene'er
The dry leaf rustles in the brake,[8] suspend
Her timid steps to gaze upon a form   105
More graceful than her own.

            His wandering step
Obedient to high thoughts, has visited
The awful ruins of the days of old:
Athens, and Tyre, and Balbec,[9] and the waste
Where stood Jerusalem, the fallen towers   110
Of Babylon, the eternal pyramids,
Memphis and Thebes,[1] and whatsoe'er of strange
Sculptured on alabaster obelisk,
Or jasper tomb, or multilated sphinx,
Dark Æthiopia in her desert hills   115
Conceals. Among the ruined temples there,
Stupendous columns, and wild images
Of more than man, where marble dæmons watch
The Zodiac's brazen mystery,[2] and dead men
Hang their mute thoughts on the mute walls around,[3]   120
He lingered, poring on memorials
Of the world's youth, through the long burning day
Gazed on those speechless shapes, nor, when the moon
Filled the mysterious halls with floating shades
Suspended he that task, but ever gazed   125
And gazed, till meaning on his vacant mind
Flashed like strong inspiration, and he saw
The thrilling secrets of the birth of time.

---

5. Crowded.
6. An olive-green stone.
7. Shelley was himself a vegetarian.
8. Thicket.
9. Tyre: once an important commercial city on the Phoenician coast. Balbec: an ancient city in Syria.

1. Memphis: the ruined capital of Lower Egypt. Thebes: the ancient capital of Upper Egypt.
2. In the temple of Isis at Denderah, Egypt, the Zodiac is represented on the ceiling. "Daemons": in Greek mythology demons were not evil spirits but minor deities, or attendant spirits.
3. I.e., by quotations inscribed in the stone.

Meanwhile an Arab maiden brought his food,
Her daily portion, from her father's tent,   130
And spread her matting for his couch, and stole
From duties and repose to tend his steps:—
Enamoured, yet not daring for deep awe
To speak her love:—and watched his nightly sleep,
Sleepless herself, to gaze upon his lips   135
Parted in slumber, whence the regular breath
Of innocent dreams arose: then, when red morn
Made paler the pale moon, to her cold home
Wildered,[4] and wan, and panting, she returned.

The Poet wandering on, through Arabie   140
And Persia, and the wild Carmanian waste,[5]
And o'er the aërial mountains which pour down
Indus and Oxus[6] from their icy caves,
In joy and exultation held his way;
Till in the vale of Cashmire, far within   145
Its loneliest dell, where odorous plants entwine
Beneath the hollow rocks a natural bower,
Beside a sparkling rivulet he stretched
His languid limbs. A vision on his sleep
There came, a dream of hopes that never yet   150
Had flushed his cheek. He dreamed a veiled maid
Sate near him, talking in low solemn tones.
Her voice was like the voice of his own soul
Heard in the calm of thought; its music long,
Like woven sounds of streams and breezes, held   155
His inmost sense suspended in its web
Of many-coloured woof and shifting hues.
Knowledge and truth and virtue were her theme,
And lofty hopes of divine liberty,
Thoughts the most dear to him, and poesy,   160
Herself a poet.[7] Soon the solemn mood
Of her pure mind kindled through all her frame
A permeating fire: wild numbers then
She raised, with voice stifled in tremulous sobs
Subdued by its own pathos: her fair hands   165
Were bare alone, sweeping from some strange harp
Strange symphony, and in their branching veins
The eloquent blood told an ineffable tale.
The beating of her heart was heard to fill
The pauses of her music, and her breath   170
Tumultuously accorded with those fits

---

4. Astray, bewildered.
5. A desert in southern Persia.
6. Rivers in Asia.
7. The envisioned maiden embodies all three

qualities specified in the Preface: intellect (line 158), imagination (lines 160–61), and the sexual and other "functions of sense" (lines 176 ff.).

Of intermitted song. Sudden she rose,
As if her heart impatiently endured
Its bursting burthen: at the sound he turned,
And saw by the warm light of their own life   175
Her glowing limbs beneath the sinuous veil
Of woven wind, her outspread arms now bare,
Her dark locks floating in the breath of night,
Her beamy bending eyes, her parted lips
Outstretched, and pale, and quivering eagerly.   180
His strong heart sunk and sickened with excess
Of love. He reared his shuddering limbs and quelled
His gasping breath, and spread his arms to meet
Her panting bosom: . . . she drew back a while,
Then, yielding to the irresistible joy,   185
With frantic gesture and short breathless cry
Folded his frame in her dissolving arms.
Now blackness veiled his dizzy eyes, and night
Involved and swallowed up the vision; sleep,
Like a dark flood suspended in its course,   190
Rolled back its impulse on his vacant brain.

　　Roused by the shock he started from his trance—
The cold white light of morning, the blue moon
Low in the west, the clear and garish hills,
The distinct valley and the vacant woods,   195
Spread round him where he stood. Whither have fled
The hues of heaven that canopied his bower
Of yesternight? The sounds that soothed his sleep,
The mystery and the majesty of Earth,
The joy, the exultation? His wan eyes   200
Gaze on the empty scene as vacantly
As ocean's moon looks on the moon in heaven.
The spirit of sweet human love has sent
A vision to the sleep of him who spurned
Her choicest gifts. He eagerly pursues   205
Beyond the realms of dream that fleeting shade;
He overleaps the bounds. Alas! alas!
Were limbs, and breath, and being intertwined
Thus treacherously? Lost, lost, for ever lost,
In the wide pathless desart of dim sleep,   210
That beautiful shape! Does the dark gate of death
Conduct to thy mysterious paradise,
O Sleep?[8] Does the bright arch of rainbow clouds,
And pendent mountains seen in the calm lake,
Lead only to a black and watery depth,   215
While death's blue vault, with loathliest vapours hung,
Where every shade which the foul grave exhales

---

8. I.e., is death the only access to this maiden of his dream?

Hides its dead eye from the detested day,
Conduct,[9] O Sleep, to thy delightful realms?
This doubt with sudden tide flowed on his heart,   220
The insatiate hope which it awakened, stung
His brain even like despair.
                                    While day-light held
The sky, the Poet kept mute conference
With his still soul. At night the passion came,
Like the fierce fiend of a distempered dream,   225
And shook him from his rest, and led him forth
Into the darkness.—As an eagle grasped
In folds of the green serpent, feels her breast
Burn with the poison, and precipitates[1]
Through night and day, tempest, and calm, and cloud,   230
Frantic with dizzying anguish, her blind flight
O'er the wide aëry wilderness:[2] thus driven
By the bright shadow of that lovely dream,
Beneath the cold glare of the desolate night,
Through tangled swamps and deep precipitous dells,   235
Startling with careless step the moon-light snake,
He fled. Red morning dawned upon his flight,
Shedding the mockery of its vital hues
Upon his cheek of death. He wandered on
Till vast Aornos seen from Petra's steep[3]   240
Hung o'er the low horizon like a cloud;
Through Balk,[4] and where the desolated tombs
Of Parthian kings scatter to every wind
Their wasting dust, wildly he wandered on,
Day after day, a weary waste of hours,   245
Bearing within his life the brooding care
That ever fed on its decaying flame.
And now his limbs were lean; his scattered hair
Sered by the autumn of strange suffering
Sung dirges in the wind; his listless hand   250
Hung like dead bone within its withered skin;
Life, and the lustre that consumed it, shone
As in a furnace burning secretly
From his dark eyes alone. The cottagers,
Who ministered with human charity   255
His human wants, beheld with wondering awe
Their fleeting visitant. The mountaineer,
Encountering on some dizzy precipice
That spectral form, deemed that the Spirit of wind
With lightning eyes, and eager breath, and feet   260

9. "Conduct" is a singular subjunctive verb; its subject is "vault" (line 216).
1. Hastens.
2. The eagle and serpent locked in mortal combat is a recurrent image in Shelley's poems; see *Prometheus Unbound* 3.1.72–73, below.

3. Aornos is a high mountain and Petra ("the rock") a mountain stronghold in the northern part of Ancient Arabia.
4. Balk is the ancient Bactria; it is now part of Afghanistan, but in ancient times was Persian. The Parthians (line 243) inhabited northern Persia.

Disturbing not the drifted snow, had paused
In its career: the infant would conceal
His troubled visage in his mother's robe
In terror at the glare of those wild eyes,
To remember their strange light in many a dream   265
Of after-times; but youthful maidens, taught
By nature, would interpret half the woe
That wasted him, would call him with false names
Brother, and friend,[5] would press his pallid hand
At parting, and watch, dim through tears, the path   270
Of his departure from their father's door.

    At length upon the lone Chorasmian shore[6]
He paused, a wide and melancholy waste
Of putrid marshes. A strong impulse urged
His steps to the sea-shore. A swan was there,   275
Beside a sluggish stream among the reeds.
It rose as he approached, and with strong wings
Scaling the upward sky, bent its bright course
High over the immeasurable main.
His eyes pursued its flight.—"Thou hast a home,   280
Beautiful bird; thou voyagest to thine home,
Where thy sweet mate will twine her downy neck
With thine, and welcome thy return with eyes
Bright in the lustre of their own fond joy.
And what am I that I should linger here,   285
With voice far sweeter than thy dying notes,
Spirit more vast than thine, frame more attuned
To beauty, wasting these surpassing powers
In the deaf air, to the blind earth, and heaven
That echoes not my thoughts?" A gloomy smile   290
Of desperate hope wrinkled his quivering lips.
For sleep, he knew, kept most relentlessly
Its precious charge,[7] and silent death exposed,
Faithless perhaps as sleep, a shadowy lure,
With doubtful smile mocking its own strange charms.   295

    Startled by his own thoughts he looked around.
There was no fair fiend[8] near him, not a sight
Or sound of awe but in his own deep mind.
A little shallop[9] floating near the shore
Caught the impatient wandering of his gaze.   300
It had been long abandoned, for its sides
Gaped wide with many a rift, and its frail joints

5. The maidens call him "false" (i.e., mistaken) names signifying an affectionate earthly relationship instead of his unearthly love.
6. The shore of Lake Aral in modern Russia, about 175 miles east of the Caspian Sea.
7. I.e., the maiden in the sleeper's dream. The passage goes on to express the skeptical fear that neither sleep nor death may yield the Poet his desire.
8. Apparently, he suspects there may have been an external agent luring him to the death described in the preceding lines.
9. A light, open boat.

waste; 305

aves. 310

315

vision floats
sweep of odorous winds
splendent clouds, so rapidly
along the dark and ruffled waters fled
The straining boat.—A whirlwind swept it on, 320
With fierce gusts and precipitating force,
Through the white ridges of the chafed sea.
The waves arose. Higher and higher still
Their fierce necks writhed beneath the tempest's scourge
Like serpents struggling in a vulture's grasp. 325
Calm and rejoicing in the fearful war
Of wave running on wave, and blast on blast
Descending, and black flood on whirlpool driven
With dark obliterating course, he sate:
As if their genii were the ministers 330
Appointed to conduct him to the light
Of those beloved eyes, the Poet sate
Holding the steady helm. Evening came on,
The beams of sunset hung their rainbow hues
High 'mid the shifting domes of sheeted spray 335
That canopied his path o'er the waste deep;
Twilight, ascending slowly from the east,
Entwin'd in duskier wreaths her braided locks
O'er the fair front and radiant eyes of day;
Night followed, clad with stars. On every side 340
More horribly the multitudinous streams
Of ocean's mountainous waste to mutual war
Rushed in dark tumult thundering, as to mock
The calm and spangled sky. The little boat
Still fled before the storm; still fled, like foam 345
Down the steep cataract of a wintry river;
Now pausing on the edge of the riven wave;
Now leaving far behind the bursting mass
That fell, convulsing ocean. Safely fled—

As if that frail and wasted human form,
Had been an elemental god.[1]
                    At midnight
The moon arose: and lo! the etherial cliffs[2]
Of Caucasus, whose icy summits shone
Among the stars like sunlight, and around
Whose cavern'd base the whirlpools and the waves
Bursting and eddying irresistibly
Rage and resound for ever.—Who shall save?—
The boat fled on,—the boiling torrent drove,—
The crags closed round with black and jagged arms,
The shattered mountain overhung the sea,
And faster still, beyond all human speed,
Suspended on the sweep of the smooth wave,
The little boat was driven. A cavern there
Yawned, and amid its slant and winding depths
Ingulphed the rushing sea. The boat fled on   365
With unrelaxing speed.—"Vision and Love!"
The Poet cried aloud, "I have beheld
The path of thy departure. Sleep and death
Shall not divide us long!"

                    The boat pursued
The winding of the cavern.[3] Day-light shone   370
At length upon that gloomy river's flow;
Now, where the fiercest war among the waves
Is calm, on the unfathomable stream
The boat moved slowly. Where the mountain, riven,
Exposed those black depths to the azure sky,   375
Ere yet the flood's enormous volume fell
Even to the base of Caucasus, with sound
That shook the everlasting rocks, the mass
Filled with one whirlpool all that ample chasm;
Stair above stair the eddying waters rose,   380
Circling immeasurably fast, and laved
With alternating dash the knarled roots
Of mighty trees, that stretched their giant arms
In darkness over it. I' the midst was left,
Reflecting, yet distorting every cloud,   385
A pool of treacherous and tremendous calm.
Seized by the sway of the ascending stream,
With dizzy swiftness, round, and round, and round,
Ridge after ridge the straining boat arose,
Till on the verge of the extremest curve,   390
Where, through an opening of the rocky bank,
The waters overflow, and a smooth spot

1. A god of one of the natural elements; see line 1.
2. I.e., cliffs high in the air.

3. A boat beating upstream within a cave, like the eagle and serpent, is a recurrent Shelleyan image. See, e.g., *Prometheus Unbound* 2.98–110, below.

Of glassy quiet mid those battling tides
Is left, the boat paused shuddering.—Shall it sink
Down the abyss? Shall the reverting stress   395
Of that resistless gulph embosom it?
Now shall it fall?—A wandering stream of wind,
Breathed from the west, has caught the expanded sail,
And, lo! with gentle motion, between banks
Of mossy slope, and on a placid stream,   400
Beneath a woven grove it sails, and, hark!
The ghastly torrent mingles its far roar,
With the breeze murmuring in the musical woods.
Where the embowering trees recede, and leave
A little space of green expanse, the cove   405
Is closed by meeting banks, whose yellow flowers
For ever gaze on their own drooping eyes,
Reflected in the crystal calm. The wave
Of the boat's motion marred their pensive task,
Which nought but vagrant bird, or wanton wind,   410
Or falling spear-grass, or their own decay
Had e'er disturbed before. The Poet longed
To deck with their bright hues his withered hair,
But on his heart its solitude returned,
And he forbore.[4] Not the strong impulse hid   415
In those flushed cheeks, bent eyes, and shadowy frame,
Had yet performed its ministry: it hung
Upon his life, as lightning in a cloud
Gleams, hovering ere it vanish, ere the floods
Of night close over it.   420
                    The noonday sun
Now shone upon the forest, one vast mass
Of mingling shade, whose brown magnificence
A narrow vale embosoms. There, huge caves,
Scooped in the dark base of their aëry rocks
Mocking[5] its moans, respond and roar for ever.   425
The meeting boughs and implicated[6] leaves
Wove twilight o'er the Poet's path, as led
By love, or dream, or god, or mightier Death,
He sought in Nature's dearest haunt, some bank,
Her cradle, and his sepulchre. More dark   430
And dark the shades accumulate. The oak,
Expanding its immense and knotty arms,
Embraces the light beech. The pyramids
Of the tall cedar overarching, frame
Most solemn domes within, and far below.   435

4. Another recurrent image: flowers overhanging their own reflection. The "yellow flowers" (line 406), probably narcisssus, may signify, in this passage, the temptation of the Poet to be satisfied with the projection of his own earthly nature. But his need for a supermundane Other revives, and "the strong impulse," his *alastor*, drives him on.
5. As often in Shelley, "mocking" has a double sense: mimicking, as well as ridiculing, the sounds of the forest (line 421).
6. Intertwined.

Like clouds suspended in an emerald sky,
The ash and the acacia floating hang
Tremulous and pale. Like restless serpents, clothed
In rainbow and in fire, the parasites,
Starred with ten thousand blossoms, flow around   440
The grey trunks, and, as gamesome infants' eyes,
With gentle meanings, and most innocent wiles,
Fold their beams round the hearts of those that love,
These twine their tendrils with the wedded boughs
Uniting their close union;[7] the woven leaves   445
Make net-work of the dark blue light of day,
And the night's noontide clearness, mutable
As shapes in the weird clouds. Soft mossy lawns
Beneath these canopies extend their swells,
Fragrant with perfumed herbs, and eyed with blooms   450
Minute yet beautiful. One darkest glen
Sends from its woods of musk-rose, twined with jasmine,
A soul-dissolving odour, to invite
To some more lovely mystery. Through the dell,
Silence and Twilight here, twin-sisters, keep   455
Their noonday watch, and sail among the shades,
Like vaporous shapes half seen; beyond, a well,
Dark, gleaming, and of most translucent wave,
Images all the woven boughs above,
And each depending leaf, and every speck   460
Of azure sky, darting between their chasms;
Nor aught else in the liquid mirror laves
Its portraiture, but some inconstant star
Between one foliaged lattice twinkling fair,
Or, painted bird, sleeping beneath the moon,   465
Or gorgeous insect floating motionless,
Unconscious of the day, ere yet his wings
Have spread their glories to the gaze of noon.

    Hither the Poet came. His eyes beheld
Their own wan light through the reflected lines   470
Of his thin hair, distinct in the dark depth
Of that still fountain; as the human heart,
Gazing in dreams over the gloomy grave,
Sees its own treacherous likeness there. He heard
The motion of the leaves, the grass that sprung   475
Startled and glanced and trembled even to feel
An unaccustomed presence, and the sound
Of the sweet brook that from the secret springs
Of that dark fountain rose. A Spirit seemed
To stand beside him—clothed in no bright robes   480
Of shadowy silver or enshrining light,

7. These embracements and diverse modes of "union" apparently exemplify the communion of things within the natural world that to the Poet does not suffice.

Borrowed from aught the visible world affords
Of grace, or majesty, or mystery;—
But, undulating woods, and silent well,
And leaping rivulet, and evening gloom   485
Now deepening the dark shades, for speech assuming
Held commune with him, as if he and it
Were all that was,—only . . . when his regard
Was raised by intense pensiveness, . . . two eyes,
Two starry eyes, hung in the gloom of thought,   490
And seemed with their serene and azure smiles
To beckon him.[8]

         Obedient to the light
That shone within his soul, he went, pursuing
The windings of the dell.—The rivulet
Wanton and wild, through many a green ravine   495
Beneath the forest flowed. Sometimes it fell
Among the moss with hollow harmony
Dark and profound. Now on the polished stones
It danced; like childhood laughing as it went:
Then, through the plain in tranquil wanderings crept,   500
Reflecting every herb and drooping bud
That overhung its quietness.—"O stream!
Whose source is inaccessibly profound,
Whither do thy mysterious waters tend?
Thou imagest my life. Thy darksome stillness,   505
Thy dazzling waves, thy loud and hollow gulphs,
Thy searchless[9] fountain, and invisible course
Have each their type in me: and the wide sky,
And measureless ocean may declare as soon
What oozy cavern or what wandering cloud   510
Contains thy waters, as the universe
Tell where these living thoughts reside, when stretched
Upon thy flowers my bloodless limbs shall waste
I' the passing wind!"

        Beside the grassy shore
Of the small stream he went; he did impress   515
On the green moss his tremulous step, that caught
Strong shuddering from his burning limbs. As one
Roused by some joyous madness from the couch
Of fever, he did move; yet, not like him,
Forgetful of the grave, where, when the flame   520
Of his frail exultation shall be spent,
He must descend. With rapid steps he went

---

8. In this temptation to rest content, the "Spirit"—
clothed in material things but lacking "light" (line
481)—gives the momentary impression that there
is no ideal beyond itself (lines 486–88). But then,

in intense meditation, the Poet sees the eyes of the
maiden of his vision and, obedient to his inner
light, reassumes his quest (lines 491–93).
9. Undiscoverable.

Beneath the shade of trees, beside the flow
Of the wild babbling rivulet; and now
The forest's solemn canopies were changed   525
For the uniform and lightsome[1] evening sky.
Grey rocks did peep from the spare moss, and stemmed
The struggling brook: tall spires of windlestrae[2]
Threw their thin shadows down the rugged slope,
And nought but knarled roots[3] of antient pines   530
Branchless and blasted, clenched with grasping roots
The unwilling soil. A gradual change was here,
Yet ghastly. For, as fast years flow away,
The smooth brow gathers, and the hair grows thin
And white, and where irradiate[4] dewy eyes   535
Had shone, gleam stony orbs:—so from his steps
Bright flowers departed, and the beautiful shade
Of the green groves, with all their odorous winds
And musical motions. Calm, he still pursued
The stream, that with a larger volume now   540
Rolled through the labyrinthine dell; and there
Fretted a path through its descending curves
With its wintry speed. On every side now rose
Rocks, which, in unimaginable forms,
Lifted their black and barren pinnacles   545
In the light of evening, and its precipice[5]
Obscuring the ravine, disclosed above,
Mid toppling stones, black gulphs and yawning caves,
Whose windings gave ten thousand various tongues
To the loud stream. Lo! where the pass expands   550
Its stony jaws, the abrupt mountain breaks,
And seems, with its accumulated crags,
To overhang the world: for wide expand
Beneath the wan stars and descending moon
Islanded seas, blue mountains, mighty streams,   555
Dim tracts and vast, robed in the lustrous gloom
Of leaden-coloured even, and fiery hills
Mingling their flames with twilight, on the verge
Of the remote horizon. The near scene,
In naked and severe simplicity,   560
Made contrast with the universe. A pine,[6]
Rock-rooted, stretched athwart the vacancy
Its swinging boughs, to each inconstant blast
Yielding one only response, at each pause
In most familiar cadence, with the howl   565
The thunder and the hiss of homeless streams
Mingling its solemn song, whilst the broad river,

1. Illuminated.
2. Scottish dialect for "windlestraw"—tall, dried stalks of grass.
3. Apparently an error for "trunks."
4. Used adjectivally: illumined, brilliant.
5. Headlong fall (of the stream, line 540).
6. Pine trees in Shelley often signify persistence and steadfastness amid change and vicissitudes.

Foaming and hurrying o'er its rugged path,
Fell into that immeasurable void
Scattering its waters to the passing winds.   570

   Yet the grey precipice and solemn pine
And torrent, were not all;—one silent nook
Was there. Even on the edge of that vast mountain,
Upheld by knotty roots and fallen rocks,
It overlooked in its serenity   575
The dark earth, and the bending vault of stars.
It was a tranquil spot, that seemed to smile
Even in the lap of horror. Ivy clasped
The fissured stones with its entwining arms,
And did embower with leaves for ever green,   580
And berries dark, the smooth and even space
Of its inviolated floor, and here
The children of the autumnal whirlwind bore,
In wanton sport, those bright leaves, whose decay,
Red, yellow, or etherially pale,   585
Rivals the pride of summer. 'Tis the haunt
Of every gentle wind, whose breath can teach
The wilds to love tranquillity. One step,
One human step alone, has ever broken
The stillness of its solitude:—one voice   590
Alone inspired its echoes,—even that voice
Which hither came, floating among the winds,
And led the loveliest among human forms
To make their wild haunts the depository
Of all the grace and beauty that endued   595
Its motions, render up its majesty,
Scatter its music on the unfeeling storm,
And to the damp leaves and blue cavern mould,
Nurses of rainbow flowers and branching moss,
Commit the colours of that varying cheek,   600
That snowy breast, those dark and drooping eyes.

   The dim and horned moon[7] hung low, and poured
A sea of lustre on the horizon's verge
That overflowed its mountains. Yellow mist
Filled the unbounded atmosphere, and drank   605
Wan moonlight even to fulness: not a star
Shone, not a sound was heard; the very winds,
Danger's grim playmates, on that precipice
Slept, clasped in his embrace.—O, storm of death!
Whose sightless[8] speed divides this sullen night: 610
And thou, colossal Skeleton, that, still
Guiding its irresistible career

---

7. Crescent-shaped, with the points curved in.   8. Invisible; or perhaps "unseeing."

In thy devastating omnipotence,
Art king of this frail world, from the red field
Of slaughter, from the reeking hospital,   615
The patriot's sacred couch, the snowy bed
Of innocence, the scaffold and the throne,
A mighty voice invokes thee. Ruin calls
His brother Death. A rare and regal prey
He hath prepared, prowling around the world;   620
Glutted with which thou mayst repose, and men
Go to their graves like flowers or creeping worms,
Nor ever more offer at thy dark shrine
The unheeded tribute of a broken heart.

When on the threshold of the green recess   625
The wanderer's footsteps fell, he knew that death
Was on him. Yet a little, ere it fled,
Did he resign his high and holy soul
To images of the majestic past,
That paused within his passive being now,   630
Like winds that bear sweet music, when they breathe
Through some dim latticed chamber. He did place
His pale lean hand upon the rugged trunk
Of the old pine. Upon an ivied stone
Reclined his languid head, his limbs did rest,   635
Diffused and motionless, on the smooth brink
Of that obscurest chasm;—and thus he lay,
Surrendering to their final impulses
The hovering powers of life. Hope and despair,
The torturers, slept; no mortal pain or fear   640
Marred his repose, the influxes of sense,
And his own being unalloyed by pain,
Yet feebler and more feeble, calmly fed
The stream of thought, till he lay breathing there
At peace, and faintly smiling:—his last sight   645
Was the great moon, which o'er the western line
Of the wide world her mighty horn suspended,
With whose dun[9] beams inwoven darkness seemed
To mingle. Now upon the jagged hills
It rests, and still as the divided frame   650
Of the vast meteor[1] sunk, the Poet's blood,
That ever beat in mystic sympathy
With nature's ebb and flow, grew feebler still:
And when two lessening points of light alone
Gleamed through the darkness, the alternate gasp   655
Of his faint respiration scarce did stir
The stagnate night:[2]—till the minutest ray

---

9. Darkened, dimmed.
1. I.e., the moon; "meteor" was once used for any phenomenon within the earth's atmosphere.
2. The Poet's life ebbs in consonance with the descent of the "horned moon," to the moment when only the two "points of light"—its horns—show above the hills.

Was quenched, the pulse yet lingered in his heart.
It paused—it fluttered. But when heaven remained
Utterly black, the murky shades involved   660
An image, silent, cold, and motionless,
As their own voiceless earth and vacant air.
Even as a vapour[3] fed with golden beams
That ministered on sunlight, ere the west
Eclipses it, was now that wonderous frame—   665
No sense, no motion, no divinity—
A fragile lute, on whose harmonious strings
The breath of heaven did wander—a bright stream
Once fed with many-voiced waves—a dream
Of youth, which night and time have quenched for ever,   670
Still, dark, and dry, and unremembered now.

  O, for Medea's wondrous alchemy,
Which wheresoe'er it fell made the earth gleam
With bright flowers, and the wintry boughs exhale
From vernal blooms fresh fragrance![4] O, that God,   675
Profuse of poisons, would concede the chalice
Which but one living man has drained,[5] who now,
Vessel of deathless wrath, a slave that feels
No proud exemption in the blighting curse
He bears, over the world wanders for ever,   680
Lone as incarnate death! O, that the dream
Of dark magician in his visioned cave,[6]
Raking the cinders of a crucible
For life and power, even when his feeble hand
Shakes in its last decay, were the true law   685
Of this so lovely world! But thou art fled
Like some frail exhalation; which the dawn
Robes in its golden beams,—ah! thou hast fled!
The brave, the gentle, and the beautiful,
The child of grace and genius. Heartless things   690
Are done and said i' the world, and many worms
And beasts and men live on, and mighty Earth
From sea and mountain, city and wilderness,
In vesper low or joyous orison,[7]
Lifts still its solemn voice:—but thou art fled—   695
Thou canst no longer know or love the shapes
Of this phantasmal scene, who have to thee
Been purest ministers, who are, alas!
Now thou art not. Upon those pallid lips

3. I.e., a cloud. "Ministered on" (line 664): attended, acted as a servant to.
4. Medea brewed a magic potion to rejuvenate the dying Aeson; where some of the potion spilled on the ground, flowers sprang up (Ovid, *Metamorphoses* 7.275 ff.).
5. The Wandering Jew; according to a medieval legend, he had taunted Christ on the way to His crucifixion and was condemned to wander the world, deathless, until Christ's second coming.
6. Cave in which he has visions. The "dark magician" is an alchemist attempting to produce the elixir of enduring life.
7. Prayer; "vesper": evening prayer.

So sweet even in their silence, on those eyes   700
That image sleep in death, upon that form
Yet safe from the worm's outrage, let no tear
Be shed—not even in thought. Nor, when those hues
Are gone, and those divinest lineaments,
Worn by the senseless[8] wind, shall live alone   705
In the frail pauses of this simple strain,
Let not high verse, mourning the memory
Of that which is no more, or painting's woe
Or sculpture, speak in feeble imagery
Their own cold powers. Art and eloquence,   710
And all the shews o' the world are frail and vain
To weep a loss that turns their lights to shade.
It is a woe too "deep for tears,"[9] when all
Is reft at once, when some surpassing Spirit,
Whose light adorned the world around it, leaves   715
Those who remain behind, not sobs or groans,
The passionate tumult of a clinging hope;
But pale despair and cold tranquillity,
Nature's vast frame, the web of human things,
Birth and the grave, that are not as they were.   720

1815   1816

Mont Blanc[1]

Lines Written in the Vale of Chamouni

1

The everlasting universe of things
Flows through the mind, and rolls its rapid waves,

---

8. Unfeeling.
9. From the last line of Wordsworth's *Ode: Intimations of Immortality:* "Thoughts that do often lie too deep for tears."
1. Mont Blanc, near the French border with Italy, is the highest mountain in the Alps. When he conceived the poem, Shelley was standing on a bridge over the Arve River in the Valley of Chamonix, in what is now southeastern France.
  Shelley wrote of this poem: "It was composed under the immediate impression of the deep and powerful feelings excited by the objects which it attempts to describe; and, as an indisciplined overflowing of the soul, rests its claim to approbation on an attempt to imitate the untamable wildness and inaccessible solemnity from which those feelings sprang."
  Shelley's comment points to two important attributes of *Mont Blanc*. First, he attempts, as in other poems (supremely in *Ode to the West Wind*), to make the poem iconic, or directly imitative of the alternating "wildness" and "solemnity" of the scene and the consonant thought and feelings it evokes. Second, this work belongs to the genre of

the "local" poem, a descriptive-meditative presentation of a precisely identified landscape. In this respect it resembles Wordsworth's *Tintern Abbey*, the major influence on *Mont Blanc*. Shelley's poem, like Wordsworth's, poses the question of the significance of the interchange between nature and the human mind; he proposes, however, a very different answer to that question.
  The poem raises the central problem about the nature of "Power," the ultimate principle behind all natural and mental process. The symbol of this Power is the river Arve (lines 16–17), which has its "secret throne" at the summit of Mont Blanc. Shelley's answer is austerely skeptical. He postulates only that "the power is there," at the inaccessible peak, but refuses to invest it with anthropomorphic intentions or values.
  What we do know is that this Power, as it descends from its secret throne into the human ken, remorselessly destroys all things (lines 100–20); yet in its simultaneous form as a river (lines 120–26), it with equal moral indifference is the "breath and blood of distant lands," and the source of life-giving rain. It is the enlightened human will alone

Now dark—now glittering—now reflecting gloom—
Now lending splendour, where from secret springs
The source of human thought its tribute brings   5
Of waters,—with a sound but half its own.
Such as a feeble brook will oft assume
In the wild woods, among the mountains lone,
Where waterfalls around it leap forever,
Where woods and winds contend, and a vast river   10
Over its rocks ceaselessly bursts and raves.

                        2

Thus thou, Ravine of Arve—dark, deep Ravine—
Thou many-coloured, many-voiced vale,
Over whose pines, and crags, and caverns sail
Fast cloud shadows and sunbeams: awful[2] scene,   15
Where Power in likeness of the Arve comes down
From the ice gulphs that gird his secret throne,
Bursting through these dark mountains like the flame
Of lightning through the tempest;—thou dost lie,
Thy giant brood of pines around thee clinging,   20
Children of elder time, in whose devotion
The chainless winds still come and ever came
To drink their odours, and their mighty swinging
To hear—an old and solemn harmony;
Thine earthly rainbows stretched across the sweep   25
Of the etherial waterfall, whose veil
Robes some unsculptured[3] image; the strange sleep
Which when the voices of the desart fail
Wraps all in its own deep eternity;—
Thy caverns echoing to the Arve's commotion,   30
A loud, lone sound no other sound can tame;
Thou art pervaded with that ceaseless motion,
Thou art the path of that unresting sound—
Dizzy Ravine! and when I gaze on thee
I seem as in a trance sublime and strange   35
To muse on my own separate phantasy,
My own, my human mind, which passively
Now renders and receives fast influencings,
Holding an unremitting interchange
With the clear universe of things around;[4]   40
One legion of wild thoughts, whose wandering wings
Now float above thy darkness, and now rest
Where that or thou art no unbidden guest,
In the still cave of the witch Poesy,[5]

which can convert this purposeless destroyer and
preserver to its own human ends, even to the revolutionary end of total reform (lines 80–83).
2. Awe-inspiring.
3. I.e., not formed by humans.
4. This passage is remarkably parallel to a passage
Shelley could not have read in *The Prelude*, published in 1850, in which Wordsworth discovers, in
the landscape viewed from Mount Snowdon, the
"type" or "emblem" of the human mind in its
interchange with nature. See *The Prelude* 14.63
ff., above.
5. I.e., in that part of the mind which creates
poetry.

Seeking among the shadows that pass by   45
Ghosts of all things that are, some shade of thee,
Some phantom, some faint image; till the breast
From which they fled recalls them, thou art there![6]

                              3

Some say that gleams of a remoter world
Visit the soul in sleep,—that death is slumber,   50
And that its shapes the busy thoughts outnumber
Of those who wake and live.—I look on high;
Has some unknown omnipotence unfurled
The veil of life and death? or do I lie
In dream, and does the mightier world of sleep   55
Spread far around and inaccessibly
Its circles? For the very spirit fails,
Driven like a homeless cloud from steep to steep
That vanishes among the viewless[7] gales!
Far, far above, piercing the infinite sky,   60
Mont Blanc appears,—still, snowy, and serene—
Its subject mountains their unearthly forms
Pile around it, ice and rock; broad vales between
Of frozen floods, unfathomable deeps,
Blue as the overhanging heaven, that spread   65
And wind among the accumulated steeps;
A desart peopled by the storms alone,
Save when the eagle brings some hunter's bone,
And the wolf tracts[8] her there—how hideously
Its shapes are heaped around! rude, bare, and high,   70
Ghastly, and scarred, and riven.—Is this the scene
Where the old Earthquake-dæmon[9] taught her young
Ruin? Were these their toys? or did a sea
Of fire, envelope once this silent snow?
None can reply—all seems eternal now.   75
The wilderness has a mysterious tongue
Which teaches awful doubt, or faith so mild,
So solemn, so serene, that man may be
But for such faith[1] with nature reconciled;
Thou hast a voice, great Mountain, to repeal   80
Large codes of fraud and woe; not understood
By all, but which[2] the wise, and great, and good
Interpret, or make felt, or deeply feel.

---

6. I.e., the thoughts (line 41) seek, in the poet's
creative faculty, some shade, phantom, or image
of the Arve; and when the breast, which has forgotten these images, recalls them again—there,
suddenly, does the Arve exist.
7. Invisible.
8. Tracks, traces.
9. A "daemon" is a supernatural being, halfway
between mortals and the gods; here, it represents

the force that makes earthquakes.
1. I.e., "simply by holding such faith." In Shelley's balance of possibilities, the landscape is equally
capable of instilling such a Wordsworthian faith
(in the possibility of reconciling man and nature,
lines 78–79), or the "awful" (i.e., "awesome") doubt
(that nature is totally alien to human ends and values).
2. The reference is to "voice," line 80.

4

The fields, the lakes, the forests, and the streams,
Ocean, and all the living things that dwell   85
Within the dædal[3] earth; lightning, and rain,
Earthquake, and fiery flood, and hurricane,
The torpor of the year when feeble dreams
Visit the hidden buds, or dreamless sleep
Holds every future leaf and flower;—the bound   90
With which from that detested trance they leap;
The works and ways of man, their death and birth,
And that of him and all that his may be;
All things that move and breathe with toil and sound
Are born and die; revolve, subside and swell.   95
Power dwells apart in its tranquillity
Remote, serene, and inaccessible:
And *this*, the naked countenance of earth,
On which I gaze, even these primæval mountains
Teach the adverting mind. The glaciers creep   100
Like snakes that watch their prey, from their far fountains,
Slow rolling on; there, many a precipice,
Frost and the Sun in scorn of mortal power
Have piled: dome, pyramid, and pinnacle,
A city of death, distinct with many a tower   105
And wall impregnable of beaming ice.
Yet not a city, but a flood of ruin
Is there, that from the boundaries of the sky
Rolls its perpetual stream; vast pines are strewing
Its destined path, or in the mangled soil   110
Branchless and shattered stand: the rocks, drawn down
From yon remotest waste, have overthrown
The limits of the dead and living world,
Never to be reclaimed. The dwelling-place
Of insects, beasts, and birds, becomes its spoil;   115
Their food and their retreat for ever gone,
So much of life and joy is lost. The race
Of man, flies far in dread; his work and dwelling
Vanish, like smoke before the tempest's stream,
And their place is not known. Below, vast caves   120
Shine in the rushing torrents' restless gleam,
Which from those secret chasms in tumult welling[4]
Meet in the vale, and one majestic River,
The breath and blood of distant lands, for ever
Rolls its loud waters to the ocean waves,   125
Breathes its swift vapours to the circling air.

3. Intricately formed; derived from Daedalus, builder of the labyrinth in Crete.
4. This description (as well as that in lines 9–11) seems to be an echo of Coleridge's description of the chasm and sacred river in the recently published *Kubla Khan*, lines 12–24. The "majestic River" (line 123) is the Arve, which flows into Lake Geneva.

5

Mont Blanc yet gleams on high:—the power is there,
The still and solemn power of many sights,
And many sounds, and much of life and death.
In the calm darkness of the moonless nights,   130
In the lone glare of day, the snows descend
Upon that Mountain; none beholds them there,
Nor when the flakes burn in the sinking sun,
Or the star-beams dart through them:—Winds contend
Silently there, and heap the snow with breath   135
Rapid and strong, but silently! Its home
The voiceless lightning in these solitudes
Keeps innocently, and like vapour broods
Over the snow. The secret strength of things
Which governs thought, and to the infinite dome   140
Of heaven is as a law, inhabits thee!
And what were thou,[5] and earth, and stars, and sea,
If to the human mind's imaginings
Silence and solitude were vacancy?

1816   1817

Hymn to Intellectual Beauty[1]

1

The awful shadow of some unseen Power
　　Floats though unseen amongst us,—visiting
　　This various world with as inconstant wing
As summer winds that creep from flower to flower.—
Like moonbeams that behind some piny mountain shower,[2]   5
　　　　It visits with inconstant glance
　　　　Each human heart and countenance;
Like hues and harmonies of evening,—
　　　　Like clouds in starlight widely spread,—
　　　　Like memory of music fled,—   10
　　　　Like aught that for its grace may be
Dear, and yet dearer for its mystery.

2

Spirit of BEAUTY, that dost consecrate
　　With thine own hues all thou dost shine upon
　　Of human thought or form,—where art thou gone?   15
Why dost thou pass away and leave our state,
This dim vast vale of tears, vacant and desolate?

5. Mont Blanc.
1. "Intellectual" means "non-sensible." "Intellectual Beauty" is thus beyond access by sense experience; it is simply postulated to account for occasional states of awareness which lend splendor, grace, and truth both to experience of the natural world and to man's moral consciousness. To this mystery (stanzas 5–7) Shelley had, at its early visitation, dedicated his powers, and to it he now prays as he passes the noon of life (stanza 7).
2. "Shower" is a verb.

Ask why the sunlight not forever
Weaves rainbows o'er yon mountain river,
Why aught should fail and fade that once is shewn,   20
   Why fear and dream and death and birth
   Cast on the daylight of this earth
   Such gloom,—why man has such a scope
For love and hate, despondency and hope?

3

No voice from some sublimer world hath ever   25
   To sage or poet these responses given—
   Therefore the name of God and ghosts and Heaven,
Remain the records of their vain endeavour,[3]
Frail spells—whose uttered charm might not avail to sever,
   From all we hear and all we see,   30
   Doubt, chance, and mutability.
Thy light alone—like mist o'er mountains driven,
   Or music by the night wind sent
   Through strings of some still instrument,[4]
   Or moonlight on a midnight stream,   35
Gives grace and truth to life's unquiet dream.

4

Love, Hope, and Self-esteem, like clouds depart
   And come, for some uncertain moments lent.
   Man were immortal, and omnipotent,
Didst thou, unknown and awful as thou art,   40
Keep with thy glorious train firm state within his heart.[5]
    Thou messenger of sympathies,
    That wax and wane in lovers' eyes—
Thou—that to human thought art nourishment,
   Like darkness to a dying flame!   45
   Depart not as thy shadow came,
   Depart not—lest the grave should be,
Like life and fear, a dark reality.

5

While yet a boy I sought for ghosts, and sped
   Through many a listening chamber, cave and ruin,   50
   And starlight wood, with fearful steps pursuing
Hopes of high talk with the departed dead.
I called on poisonous names with which our youth is fed;[6]
   I was not heard—I saw them not—
   When musing deeply on the lot   55
Of life, at that sweet time when winds are wooing
   All vital things that wake to bring
   News of buds and blossoming,—

---

3. The names (line 27) are nothing better than
guesses at identifying the mystery by religious philosophers and poets (line 26).
4. A wind harp.
5. I.e., "man would be immortal . . . if thou didst

keep. . . ."
6. Lines 49–52 refer to Shelley's youthful experiments with magic. The "poisonous names" in line
53 are apparently those in the prayers he had been
taught as a child.

Sudden, thy shadow fell on me;
I shrieked, and clasped my hands in extacy!   60

6

I vowed that I would dedicate my powers
   To thee and thine—have I not kept the vow?
    With beating heart and streaming eyes, even now
I call the phantoms of a thousand hours
Each from his voiceless grave: they have in visioned bowers   65
    Of studious zeal or love's delight
    Outwatched with me the envious night[7]—
They know that never joy illumed my brow
    Unlinked with hope that thou wouldst free
    This world from its dark slavery,   70
    That thou—O awful LOVELINESS,
Wouldst give whate'er these words cannot express.

7

The day becomes more solemn and serene
   When noon is past—there is a harmony
   In autumn, and a lustre in its sky,   75
Which through the summer is not heard or seen,
As if it could not be, as if it had not been!
    Thus let thy power, which like the truth
    Of nature on my passive youth
Descended, to my onward life supply   80
    Its calm—to one who worships thee,
    And every form containing thee,
    Whom, SPIRIT fair, thy spells did bind
To fear[8] himself, and love all human kind.

1816   1817

Ozymandias[1]

I met a traveller from an antique land,
Who said—"Two vast and trunkless legs of stone
Stand in the desert. . . . Near them, on the sand,
Half sunk a shattered visage lies, whose frown,
And wrinkled lip, and sneer of cold command,   5
Tell that its sculptor well those passions read
Which yet survive, stamped on these lifeless things,
The hand that mocked them, and the heart that fed;[2]
And on the pedestal, these words appear:

---

7. I.e., stayed up until the night, envious of their
delight, had reluctantly departed.
8. Probably in the old sense: to stand in awe of.
1. According to Diodorus Siculus, Greek historian of the 1st century B.C., the largest statue in
Egypt had the inscription: "I am Ozymandias, king
of kings; if anyone wishes to know what I am and
where I lie, let him surpass me in some of my
exploits." Ozymandias was the Greek name for
Ramses II of Egypt, 13th century B.C.
2. "The hand" is the sculptor's, who had "mocked"
(both imitated and derided) the sculptured passions; "the heart" is the king's, which has "fed" his
passions.

My name is Ozymandias, King of Kings,   10
Look on my Works, ye Mighty, and despair!
Nothing beside remains. Round the decay
Of that colossal Wreck, boundless and bare
The lone and level sands stretch far away."

1817   1818

Stanzas Written in Dejection— December 1818, near Naples[1]

The Sun is warm, the sky is clear,
The waves are dancing fast and bright,
Blue isles and snowy mountains wear
The purple noon's transparent might,
The breath of the moist earth is light   5
Around its unexpanded buds;
Like many a voice of one delight
The winds, the birds, the Ocean-floods;
The City's voice itself is soft, like Solitude's.

I see the Deep's untrampled floor   10
With green and purple seaweeds strown;
I see the waves upon the shore
Like light dissolved in star-showers, thrown;
I sit upon the sands alone;
The lightning of the noontide Ocean   15
Is flashing round me, and a tone
Arises from its measured motion,
How sweet! did any heart now share in my emotion.

Alas, I have nor hope nor health
Nor peace within nor calm around,   20
Nor that content surpassing wealth
The sage[2] in meditation found,
And walked with inward glory crowned;
Nor fame nor power nor love nor leisure—
Others I see whom these surround,   25
Smiling they live and call life pleasure:
To me that cup has been dealt in another measure.

Yet now despair itself is mild,
Even as the winds and waters are;
I could lie down like a tired child   30

---

1. Shelley's first wife, Harriet, had drowned herself; Clara, his baby daughter by Mary Shelley,
had just died; and Shelley himself was plagued by
ill health, pain, financial worries, and the sense

that he had failed as a poet.
2. Probably the Roman emperor Marcus Aurelius
(2nd century A.D.), Stoic philosopher who wrote
12 books of Meditations.

And weep away the life of care
Which I have borne and yet must bear
Till Death like Sleep might steal on me,
And I might feel in the warm air
My cheek grow cold, and hear the Sea   35
Breathe o'er my dying brain its last monotony.

Some might lament that I were cold,
As I, when this sweet day is gone,[3]
Which my lost heart, too soon grown old,
Insults with this untimely moan—   40
They might lament,—for I am one
Whom men love not, and yet regret;
Unlike this day, which, when the Sun
Shall on its stainless glory set,
Will linger though enjoyed, like joy in Memory yet.   45

1818   1824

A Song: "Men of England"[1]

Men of England, wherefore plough
For the lords who lay ye low?
Wherefore weave with toil and care
The rich robes your tyrants wear?

Wherefore feed and clothe and save   5
From the cradle to the grave
Those ungrateful drones who would
Drain your sweat—nay, drink your blood?

Wherefore, Bees of England, forge
Many a weapon, chain, and scourge,   10
That these stingless drones may spoil
The forced produce of your toil?

Have ye leisure, comfort, calm,
Shelter, food, love's gentle balm?
Or what is it ye buy so dear   15
With your pain and with your fear?

The seed ye sow, another reaps;
The wealth ye find, another keeps;
The robes ye weave, another wears;
The arms ye forge, another bears.   20

3. I.e., as I will lament this sweet day when it has
gone.
1. This and the following poem were written at a
time of turbulent unrest, after the return of troops
from the Napoleonic Wars had precipitated a great
economic depression. The *Song*, expressing Shelley's hope for a proletarian revolution, was originally planned as one of a series for workingmen; it
has become, as the poet wished, a hymn of the
British labor movement.

Sow seed—but let no tyrant reap:
Find wealth—let no impostor heap:
Weave robes—let not the idle wear:
Forge arms—in your defence to bear.

Shrink to your cellars, holes, and cells—   25
In halls ye deck another dwells.
Why shake the chains ye wrought? Ye see
The steel ye tempered glance on ye.

With plough and spade and hoe and loom
Trace your grave and build your tomb   30
And weave your winding-sheet—till fair
England be your Sepulchre.

1819   1839

England in 1819

An old, mad, blind, despised, and dying King;[1]
Princes, the dregs of their dull race, who flow
Through public scorn,—mud from a muddy spring;
Rulers who neither see nor feel nor know,
But leechlike to their fainting country cling   5
Till they drop, blind in blood, without a blow.
A people starved and stabbed in th' untilled field;[2]
An army, whom liberticide and prey
Makes as a two-edged sword to all who wield;
Golden and sanguine laws[3] which tempt and slay;   10
Religion Christless, Godless—a book sealed;
A senate, Time's worst statute, unrepealed[4]—
Are graves from which a glorious Phantom[5] may
Burst, to illumine our tempestuous day.

1819   1839

The Indian Girl's Song[1] [The Indian Serenade]

I arise from dreams of thee
In the first sleep of night—
The winds are breathing low
And the stars are burning bright.

1. George III, who had been declared insane in 1811; he died in 1820.
2. Alluding to the "Peterloo Massacre" on Aug. 16, 1819; in St. Peter's field, near Manchester, a troop of cavalry had charged into a crowd attending a peaceful rally in support of parliamentary reform. "Peterloo" is an ironic combination of "Waterloo" and "St. Peter's."
3. Laws bought with gold, and leading to blood-shed.
4. The law imposing disabilities upon Dissenters and Roman Catholics.
5. I.e., a revolution.
1. Usually entitled *The Indian Serenade*. Shelley's title makes it clear that the poem is not a personal utterance but a dramatic lyric, sung by an imagined East Indian girl; it manifests the conventional extravagance of an Oriental love poem.

I arise from dreams of thee—   5
And a spirit in my feet
Has borne me—Who knows how?
To thy chamber window, sweet!—

The wandering airs they faint
On the dark silent stream—   10
The champak[2] odours fail
Like sweet thoughts in a dream;
The nightingale's complaint—
It dies upon her heart—
As I must die on thine   15
O beloved as thou art!

O lift me from the grass!
I die, I faint, I fail!
Let thy love in kisses rain
On my lips and eyelids pale.   20
My cheek is cold and white, alas!
My heart beats loud and fast.
Oh press it close to thine again
Where it will break at last.

1819   1822

Ode to the West Wind[1]

1

O wild West Wind, thou breath of Autumn's being,
Thou, from whose unseen presence the leaves dead
Are driven, like ghosts from an enchanter fleeing,

Yellow, and black, and pale, and hectic[2] red,
Pestilence-stricken multitudes: O Thou,   5
Who chariotest to their dark wintry bed

1. "This poem was conceived and chiefly written in a wood that skirts the Arno, near Florence, and on a day when that tempestuous wind, whose temperature is at once mild and animating, was collecting the vapours which pour down the autumnal rains" [Shelley's note]. As in other major Romantic poems—for example, the opening of Wordsworth's *Prelude*, Coleridge's *Dejection*, and the conclusion to Shelley's *Adonais*—the rising wind, linked with the cycle of the seasons, is presented as the outer correspondent to an inner change from apathy to spiritual vitality, and from imaginative sterility to a burst of creative power that is paralleled to the inspiration of the Biblical prophets. In Hebrew, Latin, Greek, and many other languages, the words for wind, breath, soul, and inspiration

2. An Indian species of magnolia, bearing fragrant orange flowers.
are all identical or related. Thus Shelley's west wind is a "spirit" (the Latin *spiritus*: wind, breath, soul, and the root word in "inspiration"), the "breath of Autumn's being," which on earth, sky, and sea destroys in the autumn in order to revivify in the spring. Around this central image the poem weaves various cycles of death and regeneration—vegetational, human, and divine.

Shelley's 14-line stanza, developed from the interlaced 3-line units of the Italian *terza rima* (*aba bcb cdc*, etc.), consists of a set of four such tercets, closed by a couplet rhyming with the middle line of the preceding tercet: *aba bcb cdc ded ee*.

2. The kind of fever which occurs in tuberculosis.

The winged seeds, where they lie cold and low,
Each like a corpse within its grave, until
Thine azure sister of the Spring[3] shall blow

Her clarion[4] o'er the dreaming earth, and fill   10
(Driving sweet buds like flocks to feed in air)
With living hues and odours plain and hill:

Wild Spirit, which art moving everywhere;
Destroyer and Preserver; hear, O hear!

2

Thou on whose stream, 'mid the steep sky's commotion,   15
Loose clouds like Earth's decaying leaves are shed,
Shook from the tangled boughs of Heaven and Ocean,[5]

Angels of rain and lightning: there are spread
On the blue surface of thine aery surge,
Like the bright hair uplifted from the head   20

Of some fierce Mænad,[6] even from the dim verge
Of the horizon to the zenith's height,
The locks of the approaching storm. Thou Dirge

Of the dying year, to which this closing night
Will be the dome of a vast sepulchre,   25
Vaulted with all thy congregated might

Of vapours,[7] from whose solid atmosphere
Black rain and fire and hail will burst: O hear!

3

Thou who didst waken from his summer dreams
The blue Mediterranean, where he lay,   30
Lulled by the coil of his chrystalline streams,[8]

Beside a pumice isle in Baiæ's bay,[9]
And saw in sleep old palaces and towers
Quivering within the wave's intenser day,[1]

All overgrown with azure moss and flowers   35
So sweet, the sense faints picturing them! Thou
For whose path the Atlantic's level powers

3. The west wind that will blow in the spring.
4. A high, shrill trumpet.
5. The fragmentary clouds ("leaves") are torn by the wind from the larger and higher clouds ("boughs"), which are formed by a union of air with vapor drawn up by the sun from the ocean. "Angels" (line 18) suggests the old sense: messengers, harbingers.
6. A female votary who danced frenziedly in the worship of Dionysus (Bacchus), the Greek god of wine and vegetation. As vegetation god, he was

fabled to die in the fall and to be resurrected in the spring.
7. Clouds.
8. The currents that flow in the Mediterranean Sea, sometimes with a visible difference in color.
9. "Pumice": a porous volcanic stone. "Baiae's bay," west of Naples, was the locale of imposing villas erected by Roman emperors.
1. Shelley once observed that, when reflected in water, colors are "more vivid yet blended with more harmony."

Cleave themselves into chasms, while far below
The sea-blooms and the oozy woods which wear
The sapless foliage of the ocean, know   40

Thy voice, and suddenly grow grey with fear,
And tremble and despoil themselves:[2] O hear!

4

If I were a dead leaf thou mightest bear;
If I were a swift cloud to fly with thee;
A wave to pant beneath thy power, and share   45

The impulse of thy strength, only less free
Than thou, O Uncontrollable! If even
I were as in my boyhood, and could be

The comrade of thy wanderings over Heaven,
As then, when to outstrip thy skiey speed   50
Scarce seemed a vision; I would ne'er have striven

As thus with thee in prayer in my sore need.
Oh! lift me as a wave, a leaf, a cloud!
I fall upon the thorns of life! I bleed!

A heavy weight of hours has chained and bowed   55
One too like thee: tameless, and swift, and proud.

5

Make me thy lyre,[3] even as the forest is:
What if my leaves are falling like its own!
The tumult of thy mighty harmonies

Will take from both a deep, autumnal tone,   60
Sweet though in sadness. Be thou, Spirit fierce,
My spirit! Be thou me, impetuous one!

Drive my dead thoughts over the universe
Like withered leaves to quicken a new birth!
And, by the incantation of this verse,   65

Scatter, as from an unextinguished hearth
Ashes and sparks, my words among mankind!
Be through my lips to unawakened Earth

The trumpet of a prophecy![4] O Wind,
If Winter comes, can Spring be far behind?   70

1819   1820

2. "The vegetation at the bottom of the sea . . . sympathizes with that of the land in the change of seasons" [Shelley's note].
3. The Eolian lyre, which responds to the wind with rising and falling musical chords.
4. A reference back to the "clarion" of line 10, as well as an allusion to the last trumpet of the apocalypse in Revelation 11.15.

Prometheus Unbound Shelley composed this work in Italy between the autumn of 1818 and the close of 1819 and published it the following summer. Upon its completion he wrote in a letter, "It is a drama, with characters and mechanism of a kind yet unattempted; and I think the execution is better than any of my former attempts." It is based upon the *Prometheus Bound* of Aeschylus, which dramatizes the sufferings of Prometheus, unrepentant champion of humanity, who, because he had stolen fire from heaven, was condemned by Zeus to be chained to Mount Caucasus and to be tortured by a vulture feeding upon his liver; in a lost sequel, Aeschylus reconciled Prometheus with his oppressor. Shelley continued Aeschylus' story, but transformed it into a symbolic drama about the origin of evil and its elimination. In such earlier writings as *Queen Mab* Shelley had expressed his belief that injustice and suffering can be eliminated by an external revolution which will wipe out or radically reform the causes of evil, which are existing social, political, and religious institutions. Implicit in *Prometheus Unbound*, on the other hand, is the view that both the origin of evil and the possibility of reform are the moral responsibility of men and women themselves. Social chaos and wars are a gigantic projection of human moral disorder and inner division and conflict; tyrants are the outer representatives of the tyranny of our baser over our better elements; hatred for others is an expression of self-contempt; and successful political reform is impossible unless we have first reformed our own nature at its roots, by substituting selfless love for divisive hate. Shelley thus incorporates into his secular myth (of universal regeneration by an apocalypse of the moral imagination of the human race) the ethical teaching of Christ on the Mount, as well as the highest classical morality represented in the *Prometheus* of Aeschylus. And Shelley warns (4.562 ff.) that even should such a victory take place—the reintegration of splintered humanity, with a consequent restoration of moral and political order and a release of all our creative powers in art and science—the price of its continuation is an unremitting vigilance lest the serpent deep in human nature should break loose and start the cycle all over again.

Shelley wrote in his Preface that Prometheus is, "as it were, the type of the highest perfection of moral and intellectual nature." But he also warned that it is a mistake to suppose that the poem contains "a reasoned system on the theory of human life. Didactic poetry is my abhorrence." *Prometheus Unbound* is not a dramatized philosophical essay, nor a moral allegory, but a large and intricate imaginative construction that involves premises about human nature and the springs of morality and creativity. The non-Christian poet Yeats called it one of "the sacred books of the world," and the Christian critic C. S. Lewis found in it poetic powers matched only by Dante.

From Prometheus Unbound

A *Lyrical Drama in Four Acts*

Audisne hæc Amphiarae, sub terram abdite?[1]

From Act 1

SCENE: A *Ravine of Icy Rocks in the Indian Caucasus.* PRO-
METHEUS *is discovered bound to the Precipice.* PANTHEA and
IONE *are seated at his feet. Time, Night. During the Scene,
Morning slowly breaks.*

PROMETHEUS. Monarch of Gods and Dæmons,[1] and all Spirits
  But One, who throng those bright and rolling Worlds
  Which Thou and I alone of living things
  Behold with sleepless eyes! regard this Earth
  Made multitudinous with thy slaves, whom thou   5
  Requitest for knee-worship, prayer and praise,
  And toil, and hecatombs[2] of broken hearts,
  With fear and self contempt and barren hope;
  Whilst me, who am thy foe, eyeless in hate,[3]
  Hast thou made reign and triumph, to thy scorn,   10
  O'er mine own misery and thy vain revenge.—
  Three thousand years of sleep-unsheltered hours
  And moments—aye[4] divided by keen pangs
  Till they seemed years, torture and solitude,
  Scorn and despair,—these are mine empire:—   15
  More glorious far than that which thou surveyest
  From thine unenvied throne, O Mighty God!
  Almighty, had I deigned[5] to share the shame
  Of thine ill tyranny, and hung not here
  Nailed to this wall of eagle-baffling mountain,   20
  Black, wintry, dead, unmeasured; without herb,
  Insect, or beast, or shape or sound of life.
  Ah me, alas, pain, pain ever, forever!

No change, no pause, no hope!—Yet I endure.
I ask the Earth, have not the mountains felt?   25

1. Cicero, *Tusculan Disputations* 2.60: "Do you hear this, O Amphiaraus, concealed under the earth?" In Greek myth, Amphiaraus was a seer; fleeing from an unsuccessful assault on Thebes, he was saved from his pursuers by Zeus, who by a thunderbolt opened a cleft in the earth that swallowed him up.

In his *Disputations*, Cicero is arguing for the Stoic doctrine of man's need to master pain and suffering. He quotes this line (a Latin translation from Aeschylus' lost drama *Epigoni*) in the course of an anecdote about Dionysius of Heraclea, who, tormented by kidney stones, abjures the doctrine of his Stoic teacher Zeno that pain is not an evil.

By way of reproof his fellow-Stoic Cleanthes strikes his foot on the ground and utters this line; Cicero interprets it as an appeal to Zeno the Stoic master (under the name of Amphiaraus).

1. Prometheus is addressing Jupiter. "Daemons" are supernatural beings, intermediary between gods and mortals. The "One" in the next line is Demogorgon; see 2.4, below.
2. Large sacrificial offerings.
3. Blinded by hate.
4. Always.
5. I.e., you would have been all-powerful, if I had deigned.

I ask yon Heaven—the all-beholding Sun,
Has it not seen? The Sea, in storm or calm,
Heaven's ever-changing Shadow, spread below—
Have its deaf waves not heard my agony?
Ah me, alas, pain, pain ever, forever!   30

The crawling glaciers pierce me with the spears
Of their moon-freezing chrystals; the bright chains
Eat with their burning cold into my bones.
Heaven's winged hound, polluting from thy lips
His beak in poison not his own, tears up   35
My heart;[6] and shapeless sights come wandering by,
The ghastly people of the realm of dream,
Mocking me: and the Earthquake-fiends are charged
To wrench the rivets from my quivering wounds
When the rocks split and close again behind;   40
While from their loud abysses howling throng
The genii of the storm, urging the rage
Of whirlwind, and afflict me with keen hail.
And yet to me welcome is Day and Night,
Whether one breaks the hoar frost of the morn,   45
Or starry, dim, and slow, the other climbs
The leaden-coloured East; for then they lead
Their wingless, crawling Hours,[7] one among whom
—As some dark Priest hales the reluctant victim—
Shall drag thee, cruel King, to kiss the blood   50
From these pale feet,[8] which then might trample thee
If they disdained not such a prostrate slave.
Disdain? Ah no! I pity thee.[9]—What Ruin
Will hunt thee undefended through wide Heaven!
How will thy soul, cloven to its depth with terror,   55
Gape like a Hell within! I speak in grief,
Not exultation, for I hate no more,
As then, ere misery made me wise.—The Curse
Once breathed on thee I would recall. Ye Mountains,
Whose many-voiced Echoes, through the mist   60
Of cataracts, flung the thunder of that spell!
Ye icy Springs, stagnant with wrinkling frost,
Which vibrated to hear me, and then crept
Shuddering through India! Thou serenest Air,
Through which the Sun walks burning without beams!   65
And ye swift Whirlwinds, who on poised wings
Hung mute and moveless o'er yon hushed abyss,
As thunder louder than your own made rock

6. The vulture, tearing daily at Prometheus' heart, was kissed by Jupiter by way of reward.
7. The Hours were represented in Greek myth and art by human figures with wings. "Hales" (line 49): drags.
8. One of a number of implied parallels between the agony of Prometheus and the passion of Christ.

9. At this early point occurs the crisis of the action: the beginning of Prometheus' change of heart from hate to compassion, consummated in lines 303–5. The rest of the symbolic drama gradually unfolds the consequences of this moral triumph—of which Prometheus himself is unaware.

The orbed world! If then my words had power
—Though I am changed so that aught evil wish   70
Is dead within, although no memory be
Of what is hate—let them not lose it now![1]
What was that curse? for ye all heard me speak.[2]

*   *   *

PHANTASM

Fiend, I defy thee! with a calm, fixed mind,
  All that thou canst inflict I bid thee do;
Foul Tyrant both of Gods and Humankind,
    One only being shalt thou not subdue.   265
      Rain then thy plagues upon me here,
      Ghastly disease and frenzying fear;
      And let alternate frost and fire
      Eat into me, and be thine ire
Lightning and cutting hail and legioned forms   270
Of furies, driving by upon the wounding storms.

Aye, do thy worst. Thou art Omnipotent.
  O'er all things but thyself I gave thee power,
And my own will. Be thy swift mischiefs sent
    To blast mankind, from yon etherial tower.   275
      Let thy malignant spirit move
      Its darkness over those I love:
      On me and mine I imprecate[3]
      The utmost torture of thy hate
And thus devote to sleepless agony   280
This undeclining head while thou must reign on high.

But thou who art the God and Lord—O thou
  Who fillest with thy soul this world of woe,
To whom all things of Earth and Heaven do bow
    In fear and worship—all-prevailing foe!   285
      I curse thee! let a sufferer's curse
      Clasp thee, his torturer, like remorse,
      Till thine Infinity shall be
      A robe of envenomed agony;[4]
And thine Omnipotence a crown of pain   290
To cling like burning gold round thy dissolving brain.

Heap on thy soul by virtue of this Curse
  Ill deeds, then be thou damned, beholding good,

---

1. Let my words not lose their power now.
2. In the passage here omitted, none dares to repeat
the curse Prometheus had proclaimed against
Jupiter for fear of that god's vengeance. Prometheus is finally forced to call up the Phantasm of
Jupiter himself, who, in the next excerpt, repeats

the words of Prometheus' curse.
3. Invoke, pray for.
4. Like the poisoned shirt of the centaur Nessus,
which consumed Hercules' flesh when he put it
on. The next 2 lines allude to the mock crowning
of Christ with a crown of thorns.

Both infinite as is the Universe,
   And thou, and thy self-torturing solitude.   295
      An awful Image of calm power
      Though now thou sittest, let the hour
      Come, when thou must appear to be
      That which thou art internally.
And after many a false and fruitless crime   300
Scorn track thy lagging fall through boundless space and time.

                                     [The Phantasm vanishes.]

PROMETHEUS. Were these my words, O Parent?
THE EARTH.   They were thine.
PROMETHEUS. It doth repent me: words are quick and vain;
   Grief for awhile is blind, and so was mine.
   I wish no living thing to suffer pain.   305

THE EARTH

     Misery, O misery to me,
     That Jove at length should vanquish thee.[5]
     Wail, howl aloud, Land and Sea,
     The Earth's rent heart shall answer ye.
Howl, Spirits of the living and the dead,   310
Your refuge, your defence lies fallen and vanquished.

FIRST ECHO

Lies fallen and vanquished?

SECOND ECHO

   Fallen and vanquished!

IONE[6]

Fear not—'tis but some passing spasm,
   The Titan is unvanquished still.[7]   315

               *   *   *

FURY. Behold, an emblem—those who do endure
   Deep wrongs for man, and scorn and chains, but heap   595
   Thousand-fold torment on themselves and him.
PROMETHEUS. Remit the anguish of that lighted stare—
   Close those wan lips—let that thorn-wounded brow

5. Earth mistakes mercy for submission, and therefore interprets Prometheus' moral victory as his defeat.
6. Ione, Panthea, and Asia (in the following scene) are sisters and Oceanids—i.e., daughters of Oceanus.
7. In the omitted passage the herald Mercury, at Jupiter's command, brings a group of Furies (in Greek myth, avengers of crimes against the gods) who tempt Prometheus to despair by revealing the loathsome potentialities for evil in mankind's conscious and unconscious mind. In the climactic temptation, a Fury tears aside a veil to reveal a representation ("emblem," line 594) of the suffering Christ on the cross.

Stream not with blood—it mingles with thy tears
Fix, fix those tortured orbs in peace and death   600
So thy sick throes shake not that crucifix,
So those pale fingers play not with thy gore.—
O horrible! Thy name I will not speak,
It hath become a curse.[8] I see, I see
The wise, the mild, the lofty and the just,   605
Whom thy slaves hate for being like to thee,
Some hunted by foul lies from their heart's home,
An early-chosen, late-lamented home,
As hooded ounces cling to the driven hind,[9]
Some linked to corpses in unwholesome cells: 610
Some—hear I not the multitude laugh loud?—
Impaled in lingering fire: and mighty realms
Float by my feet like sea-uprooted isles
Whose sons are kneaded down in common blood
By the red light of their own burning homes.   615
FURY. Blood thou canst see, and fire; and canst hear groans;
    Worse things, unheard, unseen, remain behind.
PROMETHEUS. Worse?
FURY: In each human heart terror survives
    The ravin it has gorged:[1] he loftiest fear
    All that they would disdain to think were true: 620
    Hypocrisy and custom make their minds
    The fanes[2] of many a worship, now outworn.
    They dare not devise good for man's estate
    And yet they know not that they do not dare.
    The good want power, but to weep barren tears.   625
    The powerful goodness want: worse need for them.
    The wise want love, and those who love want wisdom;
    And all best things are thus confused to ill.
    Many are strong and rich,—and would be just,—
    But live among their suffering fellow men   630
    As if none felt: they know not what they do.[3]
PROMETHEUS. Thy words are like a cloud of winged snakes
    And yet, I pity those they torture not.
FURY. Thou pitiest them? I speak no more!   [Vanishes.]
PROMETHEUS.   Ah woe!
    Ah woe! Alas! pain, pain ever, forever!   635
    I close my tearless eyes, but see more clear
    Thy works within my woe-illumed mind,
    Thou subtle Tyrant![4] . . . Peace is in the grave—
    The grave hides all things beautiful and good—
    I am a God and cannot find it there,   640
    Nor would I seek it: for, though dread revenge,

---

9. Female deer. "Ounces" are cheetahs, or leopards, used in hunting (hoods were sometimes placed
over their eyes to make them easier to control).
1. The prey that it has greedily devoured.
2. Temples.
3. The Fury ironically echoes Christ's plea for
forgiveness of his crucifiers: "Father, forgive them:

for they know not what they do" (Luke 23.24). Lines
625–28 are Shelley's comment on his own age of
political reaction and oppression. This passage
underlies Yeats's description of the troubled era after
World War I in *The Second Coming* (below), lines
3–8.
4. Jupiter (also addressed as "fierce King," line 642).

This is defeat, fierce King, not victory.
The sights with which thou torturest gird my soul
With new endurance, till the hour arrives
When they shall be no types of things which are.   645
PANTHEA. Alas! what sawest thou?
PROMETHEUS.   There are two woes:
To speak and to behold; thou spare me one.[5]
Names are there, Nature's sacred watchwords—they
Were borne aloft in bright emblazonry.[6]
The nations thronged around, and cried aloud   650
As with one voice, "Truth, liberty and love!"
Suddenly fierce confusion fell from Heaven
Among them—there was strife, deceit and fear;
Tyrants rushed in, and did divide the spoil.
This was the shadow of the truth I saw.   655
THE EARTH. I felt thy torture, Son, with such mixed joy
As pain and Virtue give.—To cheer thy state
I bid ascend those subtle and fair spirits
Whose homes are the dim caves of human thought
And who inhabit, as birds wing the wind,   660
Its world-surrounding ether;[7] they behold
Beyond that twilight realm, as in a glass,
The future—may they speak comfort to thee![8]

✶   ✶   ✶

From Act 2

SCENE 4—*The Cave of* DEMOGORGON. ASIA *and* PANTHEA.[1]

PANTHEA. What veiled form sits on that ebon throne?
ASIA. The veil has fallen! . . .
PANTHEA.   I see a mighty Darkness
Filling the seat of power; and rays of gloom
Dart round, as light from the meridian Sun,
Ungazed upon and shapeless—neither limb   5

---

5. I.e., spare me the woe of speaking (about what I have beheld).
6. As in a brilliant display of banners.
7. A medium, weightless and infinitely elastic, once supposed to permeate the universe.
8. The speech of the Earth ushers in a troop of spirits representing the noble and virtuous potentialities of the mind, on which rests the hope of a future felicity for humanity. "Glass": mirror.
1. Act II has opened with Asia—the feminine principle and embodiment of love, who was separated from Prometheus at the moment of his fall into divisive hate—in a lovely Indian valley at the first hour of the dawn of the spring season of redemption. Asia and her sister Panthea have been led, by a sweet and irresistible compulsion, first to the portal and then down into the depths of the cave of Demogorgon—the central enigma of Shelley's poem.
    Commentators have usually equated Demogorgon with necessity, but the interpretation, though

pertinent, is too confining. More flexibly, he can be thought of as process, the inexorable way in which things evolve. But the ultimate mover of that process—the ultimate reason for the way things are—must remain, Shelley skeptically insists, a mystery beyond the limits of accessible knowledge. Demogorgon, like the inaccessible Power represented by the Arve in *Mont Blanc* (above), is implacable, neutral, and the more terrifying because he himself is ignorant of the principle that controls him. He serves merely to stimulate Asia to ask once more the ultimate and persistent questions about the "why" of creation, good, and evil. But "the deep truth is imageless" (line 116). Demogorgon can give merely riddling answers, which in fact stimulate Asia herself to bring to full awareness what she had obscurely known already (lines 121–23). The one question he can answer unequivocally is not "why" but "when": the hour in the process when Prometheus shall arise. That hour (line 128) is now.

Nor form—nor outline;[2] yet we feel it is
A living Spirit.
DEMOGORGON.   Ask what thou wouldst know.
ASIA. What canst thou tell?
DEMOGORGON.   All things thou dar'st demand.
ASIA. Who made the living world?
DEMOGORGON.   God.
ASIA.   Who made all
  That it contains—thought, passion, reason, will,   10
  Imagination?
DEMOGORGON. God, Almighty God.
ASIA. Who made that sense[3] which, when the winds of Spring
  In rarest visitation, or the voice
  Of one beloved heard in youth alone,
  Fills the faint eyes with falling tears, which dim   15
  The radiant looks of unbewailing flowers,
  And leaves this peopled earth a solitude
  When it returns no more?
DEMOGORGON.   Merciful God.
ASIA. And who made terror, madness, crime, remorse,
  Which from the links of the great chain of things   20
  To every thought within the mind of man
  Sway and drag heavily—and each one reels
  Under the load towards the pit of death;
  Abandoned hope, and love that turns to hate;
  And self-contempt, bitterer to drink than blood;   25
  Pain whose unheeded and familiar speech
  Is howling and keen shrieks, day after day;
  And Hell, or the sharp fear of Hell?[4]
DEMOGORGON.   He reigns.
ASIA. Utter his name—a world pining in pain
  Asks but his name; curses shall drag him down.   30
DEMOGORGON. He reigns.
ASIA.   I feel, I know it—who?
DEMOGORGON.   He reigns.
ASIA. Who reigns? There was the Heaven and Earth at first
  And Light and Love;—then Saturn,[5] from whose throne
  Time fell, an envious shadow; such the state
  Of the earth's primal spirits beneath his sway   35
  As the calm joy of flowers and living leaves
  Before the wind or sun has withered them
  And semivital worms; but he refused
  The birthright of their being, knowledge, power,
  The skill which wields the elements, the thought   40
  Which pierces this dim Universe like light,

2. Echoing Milton's description of Death, *Paradise Lost* 2.666–73.
3. Presumably the sense by which one is aware of the "unseen Power" that Shelley calls "Intellectual Beauty"; see *Hymn to Intellectual Beauty*, stanza 2.
4. The nouns "hope," "love," etc. (lines 24–28), are all objects of the verb "made" (line 19).
5. In Greek myth, Saturn's reign was the golden age. In Shelley's version, Saturn refused to grant mortals knowledge and science, so that it was an age of ignorant innocence in which the deepest human needs remained unfulfilled.

Self-empire and the majesty of love,
For thirst of which they fainted. Then Prometheus
Gave wisdom, which is strength, to Jupiter
And with this law alone: "Let man be free,"   45
Clothed him with the dominion of wide Heaven.
To know nor faith nor love nor law, to be
Omnipotent but friendless, is to reign;
And Jove now reigned; for on the race of man
First famine, and then toil, and then disease,   50
Strife, wounds, and ghastly death unseen before,
Fell; and the unseasonable seasons drove,
With alternating shafts of frost and fire,
Their shelterless, pale tribes to mountain caves;
And in their desart[6] hearts fierce wants he sent   55
And mad disquietudes, and shadows idle
Of unreal good, which levied mutual war,
So ruining the lair wherein they raged.
Prometheus saw, and waked the legioned hopes
Which sleep within folded Elysian flowers,   60
Nepenthe, Moly, Amaranth,[7] fadeless blooms;
That they might hide with thin and rainbow wings
The shape of Death; and Love he sent to bind
The disunited tendrils of that vine
Which bears the wine of life, the human heart;   65
And he tamed fire which, like some beast of prey,
Most terrible, but lovely, played beneath
The frown of man, and tortured to his will
Iron and gold, the slaves and signs of power,
And gems and poisons, and all subtlest forms,   70
Hidden beneath the mountains and the waves.
He gave man speech, and speech created thought,
Which is the measure of the Universe;
And Science struck the thrones of Earth and Heaven
Which shook, but fell not; and the harmonious mind   75
Poured itself forth in all-prophetic song,
And music lifted up the listening spirit
Until it walked, exempt from mortal care,
Godlike, o'er the clear billows of sweet sound;
And human hands first mimicked and then mocked[8]   80
With moulded limbs more lovely than its own
The human form, till marble grew divine,
And mothers, gazing, drank the love men see
Reflected in their race, behold, and perish.[9]—
He told the hidden power of herbs and springs,   85

---

6. Empty, forsaken.
7. These are medicinal drugs and flowers in Greek myth. Asia is describing (lines 59–97) the various sciences and arts given to humans by Prometheus, the culture-bringer.
8. I.e., sculptors first merely reproduced, but later improved upon ("mocked" in the sense of heightened) the beauty of the human form.
9. Expectant mothers looked at the beautiful statues so that their children might, by prenatal influence, be born with that beauty which makes beholders die of love.

And Disease drank and slept—Death grew like sleep.—
He taught the implicated[1] orbits woven
Of the wide-wandering stars, and how the Sun
Changes his lair, and by what secret spell
The pale moon is transformed, when her broad eye   90
Gazes not on the interlunar[2] sea;
He taught to rule, as life directs the limbs,
The tempest-winged chariots of the Ocean,
And the Celt knew the Indian.[3] Cities then
Were built, and through their snow-like columns flowed   95
The warm winds, and the azure æther shone,
And the blue sea and shadowy hills were seen . . .
Such the alleviations of his state
Prometheus gave to man—for which he hangs
Withering in destined pain—but who rains down   100
Evil, the immedicable plague, which while
Man looks on his creation like a God
And sees that it is glorious, drives him on,
The wreck of his own will, the scorn of Earth,
The outcast, the abandoned, the alone?—   105
Not Jove: while yet his frown shook Heaven, aye when
His adversary from adamantine chains
Cursed him, he trembled like a slave. Declare
Who is his master? Is he too a slave?
DEMOGORGON. All spirits are enslaved which serve things evil: 110
    Thou knowest if Jupiter be such or no.
ASIA. Whom calledst thou God?
DEMOGORGON.   I spoke but as ye speak—
    For Jove is the supreme of living things.
ASIA. Who is the master of the slave?
DEMOGORGON.   —If the Abysm
    Could vomit forth its secrets:—but a voice   115
    Is wanting, the deep truth is imageless;[4]
    For what would it avail to bid thee gaze
    On the revolving world? what to bid speak
    Fate, Time, Occasion, Chance and Change? To these
    All things are subject but eternal Love.   120
ASIA. So much I asked before, and my heart gave
    The response thou hast given; and of such truths
    Each to itself must be the oracle.—
    One more demand . . . and do thou answer me
    As my own soul would answer, did it know   125
    That which I ask.—Prometheus shall arise
    Henceforth the Sun of this rejoicing world:
    When shall the destined hour arrive?

---

1. Intertwined.
2. The phase between old and new moons, when
the moon is invisible.
3. The reference is to the ships in which the Celtic

(here, non-Greco-Roman) races of Europe were
able to sail to India.
4. I.e., ultimate truths can be neither known nor
expressed.

DEMOGORGON.   Behold![5]
ASIA. The rocks are cloven, and through the purple night
   I see Cars drawn by rainbow-winged steeds   130
   Which trample the dim winds—in each there stands
   A wild-eyed charioteer, urging their flight.
   Some look behind, as fiends pursued them there
   And yet I see no shapes but the keen stars:
   Others with burning eyes lean forth, and drink   135
   With eager lips the wind of their own speed,
   As if the thing they loved fled on before,
   And now—even now they clasped it; their bright locks
   Stream like a comet's flashing hair: they all
   Sweep onward.—
DEMOGORGON.   These are the immortal Hours   140
   Of whom thou didst demand.—One waits for thee.
ASIA. A Spirit with a dreadful countenance
   Checks its dark chariot by the craggy gulph.
   Unlike thy brethren, ghastly charioteer,
   What art thou? whither wouldst thou bear me? Speak!   145
SPIRIT. I am the shadow of a destiny
   More dread than is my aspect—ere yon planet
   Has set, the Darkness[6] which ascends with me
   Shall wrap in lasting night Heaven's kingless throne.
ASIA. What meanest thou?
PANTHEA.   That terrible shadow floats   150
   Up from its throne, as may the lurid[7] smoke
   Of earthquake-ruined cities o'er the sea.—
   Lo! it ascends the Car . . . the coursers fly
   Terrified; watch its path among the stars
   Blackening the night!
ASIA.   Thus I am answered—strange!   155
PANTHEA. See, near the verge[8] another chariot stays;
   An ivory shell inlaid with crimson fire
   Which comes and goes within its sculptured rim
   Of delicate strange tracery—the young Spirit
   That guides it, has the dovelike eyes of hope.   160
   How its soft smiles attract the soul!—as light
   Lures winged insects[9] through the lampless air.

SPIRIT

My coursers are fed with the lightning,
   They drink of the whirlwind's stream
And when the red morning is brightning   165
   They bathe in the fresh sunbeam;

---

5. Demogorgon's answer is a gesture: he points to
the approaching chariots ("Cars").
6. Demogorgon, who is ascending (lines 150–55)
to effect the dethronement of Jupiter.
7. Red-glaring.

8. Horizon.
9. The ancient image of the soul, or *psyche*, was
a moth. The chariot described here will carry Asia
to a reunion with Prometheus.

They have strength for their swiftness, I deem:
    Then ascend with me, daughter of Ocean.

I desire—and their speed makes night kindle;
    I fear—they outstrip the Typhoon;   170
Ere the cloud piled on Atlas[1] can dwindle
    We encircle the earth and the moon:
    We shall rest from 'long labours at noon:
    Then ascend with me, daughter of Ocean.

SCENE 5—*The Car pauses within a Cloud on the Top of a
snowy Mountain.* ASIA, PANTHEA, *and the* SPIRIT OF THE
HOUR.

SPIRIT

On the brink of the night and the morning
    My coursers are wont to respire,[2]
But the Earth has just whispered a warning
    That their flight must be swifter than fire:
    They shall drink the hot speed of desire!   5

ASIA. Thou breathest on their nostrils—but my breath
    Would give them swifter speed.
SPIRIT.   Alas, it could not.
PANTHEA. O Spirit! pause and tell whence is the light
    Which fills the cloud? the sun is yet unrisen.
SPIRIT. The sun will rise not until noon.[3]—Apollo   10
    Is held in Heaven by wonder—and the light
    Which fills this vapour, as the aerial hue
    Of fountain-gazing roses fills the water,
    Flows from thy mighty sister.
PANTHEA.   Yes, I feel . . .
ASIA. What is it with thee, sister? Thou art pale.   15
PANTHEA. How thou art changed! I dare not look on thee;
    I feel, but see thee not. I scarce endure
    The radiance of thy beauty.[4] Some good change
    Is working in the elements which suffer
    Thy presence thus unveiled.—The Nereids tell   20
    That on the day when the clear hyaline
    Was cloven at thy uprise, and thou didst stand
    Within a veined shell,[5] which floated on
    Over the calm floor of the chrystal sea,
    Among the Ægean isles, and by the shores   25
    Which bear thy name, love, like the atmosphere

---

1. A mountain in North Africa, which the Greeks
regarded as so high that it supported the heavens.
2. Catch their breath.
3. Noon will be the time of the reunion between
Prometheus and Asia.
4. In an earlier scene, Panthea had envisioned in
a dream the radiant and eternal inner form of Prometheus emerging through his "wound-worn

limbs." The corresponding transfiguration of Asia,
prepared for by her descent to the underworld, now
takes place.
5. The story told by the Nereids (sea nymphs) serves
to associate Asia with Aphrodite, goddess of love,
emerging (as in Botticelli's painting) from the
Mediterranean on a seashell. "Hyaline": the glassy
sea.

Of the sun's fire filling the living world,
Burst from thee, and illumined Earth and Heaven
And the deep ocean and the sunless caves,
And all that dwells within them; till grief cast   30
Eclipse upon the soul from which it came:
Such art thou now, nor is it I alone,
Thy sister, thy companion, thine own chosen one,
But the whole world which seeks thy sympathy.
Hearest thou not sounds i' the air which speak the love   35
Of all articulate beings? Feelest thou not
The inanimate winds enamoured of thee?—List!   [*Music.*]
ASIA. Thy words are sweeter than aught else but his
Whose echoes they are—yet all love is sweet,
Given or returned; common as light is love   40
And its familiar voice wearies not ever.
Like the wide Heaven, the all-sustaining air,
It makes the reptile equal to the God . . .
They who inspire it most are fortunate
As I am now; but those who feel it most   45
Are happier still, after long sufferings
As I shall soon become.
PANTHEA.   List! Spirits speak.

VOICE (*in the air, singing*)[6]

Life of Life! thy lips enkindle
    With their love the breath between them
And thy smiles before they dwindle   50
    Make the cold air fire; then screen them
In those looks where whoso gazes
Faints, entangled in their mazes.

Child of Light! thy limbs are burning
    Through the vest which seems to hide them   55
As the radiant lines of morning
    Through the clouds ere they divide them,
And this atmosphere divinest
Shrouds thee wheresoe'er thou shinest.

Fair are others;—none beholds thee   60
    But thy voice sounds low and tender
Like the fairest, for it folds thee
    From the sight, that liquid splendour,
And all feel, yet see thee never
As I feel now, lost forever!   65

Lamp of Earth! where'er thou movest
    Its dim shapes are clad with brightness
And the souls of whom thou lovest

---

6. The voice attempts to describe, in a dizzying whirl of optical paradoxes, what it feels like to look upon the naked essence of love and beauty.

Walk upon the winds with lightness
Till they fail, as I am failing,   70
Dizzy, lost . . . yet unbewailing!

ASIA

My soul is an enchanted Boat
Which, like a sleeping swan, doth float
Upon the silver waves of thy sweet singing,
     And thine doth like an Angel sit   75
     Beside the helm conducting it
Whilst all the winds with melody are ringing.
     It seems to float ever—forever—
     Upon that many winding River
     Between mountains, woods, abysses,   80
     A Paradise of wildernesses,
Till like one in slumber bound
Borne to the Ocean, I float down, around,
Into a Sea profound, of ever-spreading sound.

     Meanwhile thy spirit lifts its pinions[7]   85
     In Music's most serene dominions,
Catching the winds that fan that happy Heaven.
     And we sail on, away, afar,
     Without a course—without a star—
But by the instinct of sweet Music driven   90
     Till, through Elysian garden islets
     By thee, most beautiful of pilots,
     Where never mortal pinnace[8] glided,
     The boat of my desire is guided—
Realms where the air we breathe is Love   95
Which in the winds and on the waves doth move,
Harmonizing this Earth with what we feel above.

     We have past Age's icy caves,
     And Manhood's dark and tossing waves
And Youth's smooth ocean, smiling to betray;   100
     Beyond the glassy gulphs we flee
     Of shadow-peopled Infancy,
Through Death and Birth to a diviner day,[9]
     A Paradise of vaulted bowers
     Lit by downward-gazing flowers   105
     And watery paths that wind between
     Wildernesses calm and green,
Peopled by shapes too bright to see,
And rest, having beheld—somewhat like thee,
Which walk upon the sea, and chaunt melodiously!   110

7. Wings.
8. Small boat.
9. Asia is describing what it feels like to be transfigured—in the image of moving backward in the stream of time, through youth and infancy and birth itself, in order to die to this life and be born again to a "diviner" existence.

From Act 3

SCENE 1—*Heaven.* JUPITER *on his Throne;* THETIS *and the other Deities assembled.*

JUPITER. Ye congregated Powers of Heaven who share
   The glory and the strength of him ye serve,
   Rejoice! henceforth I am omnipotent.
   All else had been subdued to me—alone
   The soul of man, like unextinguished fire,   5
   Yet burns towards Heaven with fierce reproach and doubt
   And lamentation and reluctant prayer,
   Hurling up insurrection, which might make
   Our antique empire insecure, though built
   On eldest faith, and Hell's coeval,[1] fear.   10
   And though my curses through the pendulous[2] air
   Like snow on herbless peaks, fall flake by flake
   And cling to it[3]—though under my wrath's night
   It climb the crags of life, step after step,
   Which wound it, as ice wounds unsandalled feet,   15
   It yet remains supreme o'er misery,
   Aspiring . . . unrepressed; yet soon to fall:
   Even now have I begotten a strange wonder,
   That fatal Child,[4] the terror of the Earth,
   Who waits but till the destined Hour arrive,   20
   Bearing from Demogorgon's vacant throne
   The dreadful might of ever living limbs
   Which clothed that awful spirit unbeheld—
   To redescend, and trample out the spark . . .[5]

   Pour forth Heaven's wine, Idæan Ganymede,[6]   25
   And let it fill the dædal cups like fire
   And from the flower-inwoven soil divine
   Ye all triumphant harmonies arise
   As dew from Earth under the twilight stars;
   Drink! be the nectar circling through your veins   30
   The soul of joy, ye everliving Gods,
   Till exultation burst in one wide voice
   Like music from Elysian winds.—
                       And thou
   Ascend beside me, veiled in the light
   Of the desire which makes thee one with me,   35
   Thetis, bright Image of Eternity!—

1. Of the same age.
2. Suspending.
3. "It" (as also in lines 14 and 16) is "the soul of man," line 5.
4. The son of Jupiter and Thetis; Jupiter believes that he has begotten a child who will assume the bodily form of the conquered Demogorgon and then

return to announce his victory and the defeat of the resistance of Prometheus.
5. The "spark" of Prometheus' defiance.
6. Ganymede had been seized on Mt. Ida by an eagle and carried to heaven to be Jupiter's cup-bearer. "Daedal" (line 26): skillfully wrought (from the name of the Greek craftsman Daedalus).

When thou didst cry, "Insufferable might![7]
God! spare me! I sustain not the quick flames,
The penetrating presence; all my being,
Like him whom the Numidian seps[8] did thaw   40
Into a dew with poison, is dissolved,
Sinking through its foundations"—even then
Two mighty spirits, mingling, made a third
Mightier than either—which unbodied now
Between us, floats, felt although unbeheld,   45
Waiting the incarnation, which ascends—
Hear ye the thunder of the fiery wheels
Griding[9] the winds?—from Demogorgon's throne.—
Victory! victory! Feel'st thou not, O World,
The Earthquake of his chariot thundering up   50
Olympus?

> [*The Car of the* HOUR *arrives.* DEMOGORGON *descends and moves
> towards the Throne of* JUPITER.]

        Awful Shape, what art thou? Speak!
DEMOGORGON. Eternity—demand no direr name.
Descend, and follow me down the abyss;
I am thy child,[1] as thou wert Saturn's child,
Mightier than thee; and we must dwell together   55
Henceforth in darkness.—Lift thy lightnings not.
The tyranny of Heaven none may retain,
Or reassume, or hold succeeding thee . . .
Yet if thou wilt—as 'tis the destiny
Of trodden worms to writhe till they are dead—   60
Put forth thy might.
JUPITER.   Detested prodigy!
Even thus beneath the deep Titanian prisons[2]
I trample thee! . . . thou lingerest?
                         Mercy! mercy!
No pity—no release, no respite! . . . Oh,
That thou wouldst make mine enemy my judge.   65
Even where he hangs, seared by my long revenge
On Caucasus—he would not doom me thus.—
Gentle and just and dreadless, is he not
The monarch of the world?[3] what then art thou? . . .
No refuge! no appeal—. . .
              Sink with me then—   70
We two will sink in the wide waves of ruin

---

7. This description of the sexual union of Jupiter and Thetis is a grotesque parody of the reunion of Prometheus and Asia.
8. A serpent of Numidia (North Africa) whose bite was thought to cause putrefaction.
9. Cutting with a rasping sound.
1. Ironically, and in a figurative sense: Demogorgon's function follows from Jupiter's actions.
2. After they overthrew the Titans, Jupiter and the Olympian gods had imprisoned them in Tartarus, deep beneath the earth.
3. The ultimate irony: Jupiter appeals to those very qualities of Prometheus for which he has hitherto persecuted him, begging for a mercy which Prometheus has already granted him; but Prometheus' change from vengefulness to mercy is in fact the cause of Jupiter's present downfall.

Even as a vulture and a snake outspent
Drop, twisted in inextricable fight,[4]
Into a shoreless sea.—Let Hell unlock
Its mounded Oceans of tempestuous fire,   75
And whelm on them into the bottomless void
The desolated world and thee and me,
The conqueror and the conquered, and the wreck
Of that for which they combated.
                          Ai! Ai!
The elements obey me not . . . I sink . . .   80
Dizzily down—ever, forever, down—
And, like a cloud, mine enemy above
Darkens my fall with victory!—Ai! Ai![5]

From SCENE 4—*A Forest. In the Background a Cave.* PRO-
METHEUS, ASIA, PANTHEA, IONE, *and the* SPIRIT OF THE
EARTH.[6]

*   *   *

[*The* SPIRIT OF THE HOUR *enters.*]

PROMETHEUS. We feel what thou hast heard and seen—yet speak.
SPIRIT OF THE HOUR. Soon as the sound had ceased whose thunder
       filled
The abysses of the sky, and the wide earth,
There was a change . . . the impalpable thin air   100
And the all-circling sunlight were transformed
As if the sense of love dissolved in them
Had folded itself round the sphered world.
My vision then grew clear and I could see
Into the mysteries of the Universe.[7]   105
Dizzy as with delight I floated down,
Winnowing the lightsome air with languid plumes,
My coursers sought their birthplace in the sun
Where they henceforth will live exempt from toil,
Pasturing flowers of vegetable fire—   110
And where my moonlike car will stand within
A temple, gazed upon by Phidian forms,[8]
Of thee, and Asia and the Earth, and me
And you fair nymphs, looking the love we feel,
In memory of the tidings it has borne,   115

4. The eagle (or vulture) and the snake locked in
equal combat—a favorite Shelleyan image; cf.
Alastor, lines 227–32, above.
5. Jupiter's scream is to be imagined diminishing
to silence.
6. After Jupiter's annihilation (described in scene
2), Hercules unbinds Prometheus, who is reunited
with Asia and retires to a cave "where we will sit
and talk of time and change / . . . ourselves
unchanged." In the speech which concludes the
act (reprinted here) the Spirit of the Hour describes

what happened in the human world when he
sounded the apocalyptic trumpet.
7. I.e., the earth's atmosphere clarifies, no longer
refracting the sunlight, and so allows the Spirit of
the Hour to see what is happening on earth.
8. The crescent-shaped ("moonlike") chariot, its
apocalyptic mission accomplished, will be frozen
to stone, and will be surrounded by the sculptured
forms of other agents in the drama. Phidias (5th
century B.C.) was the noblest of Greek sculptors.

Beneath a dome fretted with graven flowers,
Poised on twelve columns of resplendent stone
And open to the bright and liquid sky.
Yoked to it by an amphisbænic snake[9]
The likeness of those winged steeds will mock[1]   120
The flight from which they find repose.—Alas,
Whither has wandered now my partial[2] tongue
When all remains untold which ye would hear!—
As I have said, I floated to the Earth:
It was, as it is still, the pain of bliss   125
To move, to breathe, to be; I wandering went
Among the haunts and dwellings of mankind
And first was disappointed not to see
Such mighty change as I had felt within
Expressed in outward things; but soon I looked,   130
And behold! thrones were kingless, and men walked
One with the other even as spirits do,
None fawned, none trampled; hate, disdain or fear,
Self-love or self-contempt on human brows
No more inscribed, as o'er the gate of hell,   135
"All hope abandon, ye who enter here";[3]
None frowned, none trembled, none with eager fear
Gazed on another's eye of cold command
Until the subject of a tyrant's will
Became, worse fate, the abject of his own[4]   140
Which spurred him, like an outspent horse, to death.
None wrought his lips in truth-entangling lines
Which smiled the lie his tongue disdained to speak;
None with firm sneer trod out in his own heart
The sparks of love and hope, till there remained   145
Those bitter ashes, a soul self-consumed,
And the wretch crept, a vampire among men,
Infecting all with his own hideous ill.
None talked that common, false, cold, hollow talk
Which makes the heart deny the *yes* it breathes   150
Yet question that unmeant hypocrisy
With such a self-mistrust as has no name.
And women too, frank, beautiful and kind
As the free Heaven which rains fresh light and dew
On the wide earth, past; gentle, radiant forms,   155
From custom's evil taint exempt and pure;
Speaking the wisdom once they could not think,
Looking emotions once they feared to feel
And changed to all which once they dared not be,
Yet being now, made Earth like Heaven—nor pride   160
Nor jealousy nor envy nor ill shame,

9. A mythical snake with a head at either end; it serves here as a symbolic warning that a reversal of the process is always possible.
1. "Imitate" and also, in their immobility, "mock at" the flight they represent.
2. "Biased," or, possibly, "telling only part of the story."
3. The inscription over the gate of hell in Dante's *Inferno* 3.9.
4. I.e.,, he was so abjectly enslaved that his own will accorded with the tyrants's will.

The bitterest of those drops of treasured gall,
Spoilt the sweet taste of the nepenthe,[5] love.

Thrones, altars, judgement-seats and prisons; wherein
And beside which, by wretched men were borne   165
Sceptres, tiaras, swords and chains, and tomes
Of reasoned wrong glozed on[6] by ignorance,
Were like those monstrous and barbaric shapes,
The ghosts of a no more remembered fame,
Which from their unworn obelisks[7] look forth   170
In triumph o'er the palaces and tombs
Of those who were their conquerors, mouldering round.
Those imaged to the pride of Kings and Priests
A dark yet mighty faith, a power as wide
As is the world it wasted, and are now   175
But an astonishment; even so the tools
And emblems of its last captivity
Amid the dwellings of the peopled Earth,
Stand, not o'erthrown, but unregarded now.
And those foul shapes, abhorred by God and man—   180
Which under many a name and many a form
Strange, savage, ghastly, dark and execrable
Were Jupiter,[8] the tyrant of the world;
And which the nations panic-stricken served
With blood, and hearts broken by long hope, and love   185
Dragged to his altars soiled and garlandless
And slain amid men's unreclaiming tears,
Flattering the thing they feared, which fear was hate—
Frown, mouldering fast, o'er their abandoned shrines.
The painted veil, by those who were, called life,[9]   190
Which mimicked, as with colours idly spread,
All men believed and hoped, is torn aside—
The loathsome mask has fallen, the man remains
Sceptreless, free, uncircumscribed—but man:
Equal, unclassed, tribeless, and nationless,   195
Exempt from awe, worship, degree,—the King
Over himself; just, gentle, wise—but man:
Passionless? no—yet free from guilt or pain
Which were, for his will made, or suffered them,
Nor yet exempt, though ruling them like slaves,   200
From chance and death and mutability,
The clogs of that which else might oversoar
The loftiest star of unascended Heaven
Pinnacled dim in the intense inane.[1]

5. A drug (probably opium) that brings forgetfulness of pain and sorrow.
6. Annotated, explained.
7. The Egyptian obelisks (tapering shafts of stone), brought to Rome by its conquering armies, included hieroglyphs which—since they were still undeciphered in Shelley's time—seemed "monstrous and barbaric shapes" (line 168).
8. The "foul shapes" (line 180) were statues of the gods who, whatever their names, were all really manifestations of Jupiter.
9. I.e., which was thought to be life by men as they were before their regeneration.
1. I.e., a dim point in the extreme of empty space. The sense of lines 198–204 is: if regenerate man were to be released from all earthly and biological impediments ("clogs"), he would become what even the stars are not—a pure ideal.

From Act 4[1]

SCENE—A *Part of the Forest near the Cave of* PROMETHEUS.

*   *   *

IONE.   Even whilst we speak
   New notes arise . . . What is that awful sound?   185
PANTHEA. 'Tis the deep music of the rolling world,
   Kindling within the strings of the waved air
   Æolian modulations.[2]
IONE.   Listen too,
   How every pause is filled with under-notes,
   Clear, silver, icy, keen, awakening tones   190
   Which pierce the sense and live within the soul
   As the sharp stars pierce Winter's chrystal air
   And gaze upon themselves within the sea.
PANTHEA. But see, where through two openings in the forest
   Which hanging branches overcanopy,   195
   And where two runnels of a rivulet
   Between the close moss violet-inwoven
   Have made their path of melody, like sisters
   Who part with sighs that they may meet in smiles,
   Turning their dear disunion to an isle   200
   Of lovely grief, a wood of sweet sad thoughts;
   Two visions of strange radiance float upon
   The Ocean-like inchantment of strong sound
   Which flows intenser, keener, deeper yet
   Under the ground and through the windless air.   205
IONE. I see a chariot like that thinnest boat
   In which the Mother of the Months is borne
   By ebbing light into her western cave
   When she upsprings from interlunar dreams,[3]
   O'er which is curved an orblike canopy   210
   Of gentle darkness, and the hills and woods
   Distinctly seen through that dusk aery veil

---

1. The original drama, completed in the spring of 1819, consisted of three acts. Later that year Shelley added a jubilant fourth act. In Revelation 21, the apocalyptic replacement of the old world by "a new heaven and new earth" had been symbolized by the marriage of the Lamb with the New Jerusalem. Shelley's fourth act, somewhat like the conclusion of Blake's *Jerusalem*, expands this figure into a cosmic epithalamion, representing a union of divided elements which enacts everywhere the reunion of Prometheus and Asia that is taking place off-stage.
   Shelley's model is the Renaissance masque, which combines song and dance with spectacular displays. Panthea and Ione serve as commentators on the action, which is divided into three episodes. In the first episode, omitted here, the purified "Spirits of the human mind" unite in a ritual dance with the Hours of the glad new day. In the second episode (below, lines 194–318), there appear emblematic representations of the moon and the earth, each bearing an infant whose hour has come round at last; Shelley based this description in part on chap. 1 of Ezekiel, the vision of the chariot of divine glory, which had traditionally been interpreted as a portent of apocalypse. The third episode (lines 319–502) is the bacchanalian dance of the love-intoxicated moon around her brother and paramour, the rejuvenescent earth. By way of coda (lines 549 to the end), Demogorgon calls upon all beings to hear his proclamation of the moral significance of this great drama of humanity's self-betrayal and self-redemption.
2. Evoking music like that of the Eolian harp.
3. I.e., the chariot is a thin crescent-shape, like the new moon, when it carries within it the outline of the old moon ("Mother of the Months") to the cave where she is reborn during the "interlunar" period—i.e., when the moon is entirely invisible.

Regard[4] like shapes in an enchanter's glass;
Its wheels are solid clouds, azure and gold,
Such as the genii of the thunderstorm   215
Pile on the floor of the illumined sea
When the Sun rushes under it; they roll
And move and grow as with an inward wind.
Within it sits a winged Infant, white
Its countenance, like the whiteness of bright snow,   220
Its plumes are as feathers of sunny frost,
Its limbs gleam white, through the wind-flowing folds
Of its white robe, woof of ætherial pearl.
Its hair is white,—the brightness of white light
Scattered in strings,[5] yet its two eyes are Heavens   225
Of liquid darkness, which the Deity
Within, seems pouring, as a storm is poured
From jagged clouds, out of their arrowy lashes,
Tempering the cold and radiant air around
With fire that is not brightness;[6] in its hand   230
It sways a quivering moonbeam, from whose point
A guiding power directs the chariot's prow
Over its wheeled clouds, which as they roll
Over the grass and flowers and waves, wake sounds
Sweet as a singing rain of silver dew.   235
PANTHEA. And from the other opening in the wood
          Rushes with loud and whirlwind harmony
          A sphere, which is as many thousand spheres,
          Solid as chrystal, yet through all its mass
          Flow, as through empty space, music and light: 240
          Ten thousand orbs involving and involved,[7]
          Purple and azure, white and green and golden,
          Sphere within sphere, and every space between
          Peopled with unimaginable shapes
          Such as ghosts dream dwell in the lampless deep 245
          Yet each intertranspicuous,[8] and they whirl
          Over each other with a thousand motions
          Upon a thousand sightless[9] axles spinning
          And with the force of self-destroying swiftness,
          Intensely, slowly, solemnly roll on—   250
          Kindling with mingled sounds, and many tones,

4. Look, appear.
5. The infant resembles "one like unto the Son of man" in Revelation 1.13–14: "His head and his hairs were white like wool, as white as snow." The description that follows, of the light radiated from the infant's eyes, echoes the description in Ezekiel's vision, 1.27–28, of the "brightness round about" that "was the appearance of the likeness of the glory of the Lord."
6. Shelley knew, from the account by Sir Humphry Davy, Herschel's discovery (1800) that there are what Herschel called "dark rays"—i.e., infrared radiation; Davy suggested that the moon gave off such rays.

7. The transparent sphere is an emblem of earth. The description of its spinning and that of its interior orbs echoes both Ezekiel 1.15–17—"the appearance of the wheels and their work . . . was as it were a wheel in the middle of a wheel"—and *Paradise Lost* 5.620–24, which describes the "mystical dance" of the angels in heaven, whose movements resemble the revolving spheres of the planets: "mazes intricate, / Eccentric, intervolved, yet regular / Then most, when most irregular they seem."
8. Transparent, so that each can be seen through the others.
9. Invisible.

Intelligible words and music wild.—
With mighty whirl the multitudinous Orb
Grinds the bright brook into an azure mist
Of elemental subtlety, like light,   255
And the wild odour of the forest flowers,
The music of the living grass and air,
The emerald light of leaf-entangled beams
Round its intense, yet self-conflicting[1] speed,
Seem kneaded into one aerial mass   260
Which drowns the sense. Within the Orb itself,
Pillowed upon its alabaster arms
Like to a child o'erwearied with sweet toil,
On its own folded wings and wavy hair
The Spirit of the Earth is laid asleep,   265
And you can see its little lips are moving
Amid the changing light of their own smiles
Like one who talks of what he loves in dream—
IONE. 'Tis only mocking[2] the Orb's harmony . . .
PANTHEA. And from a star upon its forehead, shoot,   270
Like swords of azure fire, or golden spears
With tyrant-quelling myrtle[3] overtwined,
Embleming Heaven and Earth united now,
Vast beams like spokes of some invisible wheel
Which whirl as the Orb whirls, swifter than thought,   275
Filling the abyss with sunlike lightenings,
And perpendicular now, and now transverse,
Pierce the dark soil, and as they pierce and pass
Make bare the secrets of the Earth's deep heart,[4]
Infinite mine of adamant[5] and gold,   280
Valueless[6] stones and unimagined gems,
And caverns on chrystalline columns poised
With vegetable silver overspread,
Wells of unfathomed fire, and watersprings
Whence the great Sea, even as a child, is fed   285
Whose vapours clothe Earth's monarch mountain-tops
With kingly, ermine snow; the beams flash on
And make appear the melancholy ruins
Of cancelled cycles;[7] anchors, beaks of ships,
Planks turned to marble, quivers, helms and spears   290
And gorgon-headed targes,[8] and the wheels
Of scythed chariots,[9] and the emblazonry
Of trophies, standards and armorial beasts[1]

---

1. Because its component spheres are spinning in opposed directions.
2. Imitating.
3. The myrtle, sacred to Venus, symbolizes love.
4. I.e., the star on the infant's forehead radiates penetrating beams which (like modern X rays) reveal what lies beneath the surface of the earth.
5. Very hard rock.
6. Priceless.
7. I.e., of civilizations that flourished, then disappeared.
8. Shields embossed with a gorgon's head. "Helms": helmets.
9. Ancient war chariots sometimes had steel blades fastened to the revolving wheels.
1. Animals in heraldic insignia.

Round which Death laughed, sepulchred emblems
Of dead Destruction, ruin within ruin!   295
The wrecks beside of many a city vast,
Whose population which the Earth grew over
Was mortal but not human;[2] see, they lie,
Their monstrous works and uncouth skeletons,
Their statues, homes, and fanes;[3] prodigious shapes   300
Huddled in grey annihilation, split,
Jammed in the hard black deep; and over these
The anatomies[4] of unknown winged things,
And fishes which were isles of living scale,
And serpents, bony chains, twisted around   305
The iron crags, or within heaps of dust
To which the tortuous strength of their last pangs
Had crushed the iron crags;—and over these
The jagged alligator and the might
Of earth-convulsing behemoth,[5] which once   310
Were monarch beasts, and on the slimy shores
And weed-overgrown continents of Earth
Increased and multiplied like summer worms
On an abandoned corpse, till the blue globe
Wrapt Deluge round it like a cloak, and they   315
Yelled, gaspt and were abolished; or some God
Whose throne was in a Comet, past, and cried—
"Be not!"—and like my words they were no more.[6]

THE EARTH

The joy, the triumph, the delight, the madness,
The boundless, overflowing, bursting gladness,   320
The vaporous exultation, not to be confined![7]
    Ha! ha! the animation of delight
    Which wraps me, like an atmosphere of light,
And bears me as a cloud is borne by its own wind!

THE MOON

    Brother mine, calm wanderer,   325
    Happy globe of land and air,
Some Spirit[8] is darted like a beam from thee,

2. That is, a prehuman race of beings which once overspread the earth.
3. Temples.
4. Skeletons.
5. The huge land animal described in Job 40.15–24.
6. According to the theory of "Catastrophism" proposed by G. F. Cuvier, *Researches on Fossil Bones* (1812), successive geologic layers of fossils are evidence of a sequence of catastrophes—volcanic upheavals and gigantic floods—each of which wiped out the forms of life that then existed. Shel-

ley proposes two hypotheses (lines 314–18): either such floods originated from some cataclysm on earth, or else they were prodigious tides caused by the gravitational pull of a passing comet.
    In writing this passage, Shelley recalled Keats's *Endymion* 3.123–36, which described the remains on the ocean floor of extinct cultures and animal species.
7. Literally, the earth's gases are bursting out through its volcanoes.
8. Physically, the gravitational force exerted by the earth on the satellite moon.

Which penetrates my frozen frame
And passes with the warmth of flame—
With love and odour and deep melody   330
Through me, through me!—

THE EARTH

Ha! ha! the caverns of my hollow mountains,
My cloven fire-crags, sound-exulting fountains
Laugh with a vast and inextinguishable laughter.
    The Oceans and the Desarts and the Abysses   335
    And the deep air's unmeasured wildernesses
Answer from all their clouds and billows, echoing after.

    They cry aloud as I do—"Sceptred Curse,[9]
    Who all our green and azure Universe
Threatenedst to muffle round with black destruction, sending   340
    A solid cloud to rain hot thunderstones,
    And splinter and knead down my children's bones,
All I bring forth, to one void mass battering and blending,

    "Until each craglike tower and storied column,
    Palace and Obelisk and Temple solemn,   345
My imperial mountains crowned with cloud and snow and fire,
    My sea-like forests, every blade and blossom
    Which finds a grave or cradle in my bosom,
Were stamped by thy strong hate into a lifeless mire,

    "How art thou sunk, withdrawn, cover'd—drunk up   350
    By thirsty nothing, as the brackish[1] cup
Drained by a Desert-troop—a little drop for all;
    And from beneath, around, within, above,
    Filling thy void annihilation, Love
Bursts in like light on caves cloven by the thunderball."   355

THE MOON

    The snow upon my lifeless mountains
    Is loosened into living fountains,
My solid Oceans flow and sing and shine
    A spirit from my heart bursts forth,
    It clothes with unexpected birth   360
My cold bare bosom: Oh! it must be thine
      On mine, on mine!

    Gazing on thee I feel, I know,
    Green stalks burst forth, and bright flowers grow
And living shapes upon my bosom move: 365

---

9. Jupiter.   1. Slightly salty.

Music is in the sea and air,
Winged clouds soar here and there,
Dark with the rain new buds are dreaming of:
'Tis Love, all Love!

THE EARTH

It interpenetrates my granite mass,   370
Through tangled roots and trodden clay doth pass
Into the utmost leaves and delicatest flowers;
Upon the winds, among the clouds 'tis spread,
It wakes a life in the forgotten dead,
They breathe a spirit up from their obscurest bowers   375

And like a storm, bursting its cloudy prison
With thunder and with whirlwind, has arisen
Out of the lampless caves of unimagined being,
With earthquake shock and swiftness making shiver
Thought's stagnant chaos, unremoved forever,   380
Till Hate and Fear and Pain, light-vanquished shadows, fleeing,

Leave Man, who was a many-sided mirror
Which could distort to many a shape of error
This true fair world of things—a Sea reflecting Love;
Which over all his kind, as the Sun's Heaven   385
Gliding o'er Ocean, smooth, serene and even,
Darting from starry depths radiance and light, doth move,

Leave Man, even as a leprous child is left
Who follows a sick beast to some warm cleft
Of rocks, through which the might of healing springs is poured: 390
Then when it wanders home with rosy smile
Unconscious, and its mother fears awhile
It is a Spirit—then weeps on her child restored.[2]

Man, oh, not men![3] a chain of linked thought,
Of love and might to be divided not,   395
Compelling the elements with adamantine stress—
As the Sun rules,[4] even with a tyrant's gaze,
The unquiet Republic of the maze
Of Planets, struggling fierce towards Heaven's free wilderness.

Man, one harmonious Soul of many a soul   400
Whose nature is its own divine controul
Where all things flow to all, as rivers to the sea;

2. A reminiscence of the legend of King Bladud of Britain, who, a banished leper, was following a lost swine and stumbled upon a hot spring (now in the town of Bath), which cured him.

3. Human society, once splintered by hate, is now united by love into a single macrocosmic "Man."
4. By gravitational force.

Familiar acts are beautiful through love;
  Labour and Pain and Grief in life's green grove
Sport like tame beasts—none knew how gentle they could be!   405

His Will, with all mean passions, bad delights,
  And selfish cares, its trembling satellites,
A spirit ill to guide, but mighty to obey,
  Is as a tempest-winged ship, whose helm
Love rules, through waves which dare not overwhelm,   410
Forcing Life's wildest shores to own its sovereign sway.

All things confess his strength.—Through the cold mass
  Of marble and of colour his dreams pass;
Bright threads, whence mothers weave the robes their children wear;
  Language is a perpetual Orphic song,[5]   415
  Which rules with Dædal harmony a throng
Of thoughts and forms, which else senseless and shapeless were.

The Lightning is his slave;[6] Heaven's utmost deep
  Gives up her stars, and like a flock of sheep
They pass before his eye, are numbered, and roll on!   420
  The Tempest is his steed,—he strides the air;
  And the abyss shouts from her depth laid bare,
"Heaven, hast thou secrets? Man unveils me; I have none."

THE MOON

The shadow of white Death has past
From my path in Heaven at last,
A clinging shroud of solid frost and sleep—   425
And through my newly-woven bowers
Wander happy paramours
Less mighty, but as mild as those who keep
Thy vales more deep.   430

THE EARTH

As the dissolving warmth of Dawn may fold
A half-unfrozen dewglobe, green and gold
And chrystalline, till it becomes a winged mist
And wanders up the vault of the blue Day,
Outlives the noon, and on the Sun's last ray   435
Hangs o'er the Sea—a fleece of fire and amethyst—

THE MOON

Thou art folded, thou art lying
In the light which is undying

---

5. Like the music of Orpheus, which attracted and controlled beasts, rocks, and trees. "Daedal" (line 416): skillful, intricate.

6. The Earth describes regenerate man's scientific and technological triumphs.

Of thine own joy and Heaven's smile divine;
All suns and constellations shower 440
On thee a light, a life, a power
Which doth array thy sphere—thou pourest thine
On mine, on mine!

THE EARTH

I spin beneath my pyramid of night[7]
Which points into the Heavens, dreaming delight, 445
Murmuring victorious joy in my enchanted sleep;
As a youth lulled in love-dreams, faintly sighing,
Under the shadow of his beauty lying
Which round his rest a watch of light and warmth doth
keep.

THE MOON

As in the soft and sweet eclipse 450
When soul meets soul on lovers' lips,
High hearts are calm and brightest eyes are dull;
So when thy shadow falls on me[8]
Then am I mute and still,—by thee
Covered; of thy love, Orb most beautiful, 455
Full, oh, too full!—

Thou art speeding round the Sun,
Brightest World of many a one,
Green and azure sphere, which shinest
With a light which is divinest 460
Among all the lamps of Heaven
To whom life and light is given;
I, thy chrystal paramour,
Borne beside thee by a power
Like the polar Paradise, 465
Magnet-like, of lovers' eyes;[9]
I, a most enamoured maiden
Whose weak brain is overladen
With the pleasure of her love—
Maniac-like around thee move, 470
Gazing, an insatiate bride,
On thy form from every side
Like a Mænad round the cup
Which Agave lifted up
In the weird Cadmæan forest.[1]— 475

7. The conical shadow cast by the earth as it intercepts the sun's light.
8. In the eclipse of the moon, when it enters the earth's shadow.
9. As it circles the earth, the moon spins at a rate that keeps the same side constantly toward it.

1. The Maenads were female participants in the ecstatic worship of Dionysus (Bacchus). Agave, daughter of King Cadmus, in a blind frenzy tore her own son Pentheus to bits when he was caught spying on the Dionysiac rites.

Brother, wheresoe'er thou soarest
I must hurry, whirl and follow
Through the Heavens wide and hollow,
Sheltered by the warm embrace
Of thy soul, from hungry space,   480
Drinking, from thy sense and sight
Beauty, majesty, and might,
As a lover or chameleon
Grows like what it looks upon,
As a violet's gentle eye   485
Gazes on the azure sky
Until its hue grows like what it beholds,
As a grey and watery mist
Glows like solid amethyst
Athwart the western mountains it enfolds,   490
When the sunset sleeps
    Upon its snow—

THE EARTH

And the weak day weeps[2]
    That it should be so.
O gentle Moon, the voice of thy delight   495
Falls on me like thy clear and tender light
Soothing the seaman, borne the summer night
    Through isles forever calm;
O gentle Moon, thy chrystal accents pierce
The caverns of my Pride's deep Universe,   500
Charming the tyger Joy, whose tramplings fierce
    Made wounds, which need thy balm.

*   *   *

DEMOGORGON

Man, who wert once a despot and a slave,—
    A dupe and a deceiver,—a Decay,   550
A Traveller from the cradle to the grave
    Through the dim night of this immortal Day:

ALL

Speak—thy strong words may never pass away.

DEMOGORGON

This is the Day which down the void Abysm
At the Earth-born's spell[3] yawns for Heaven's Despotism,   555
    And Conquest is dragged Captive through the Deep;[4]

---

2. I.e., with the dew at nightfall.
3. Prometheus' spell—i.e., his magically effective
words of pity, in place of vengefulness.

4. Ephesians 4.8: "When [Christ] ascended up on
high, he led captivity captive."

Love from its awful throne of patient power
In the wise heart, from the last giddy hour
   Of dread endurance, from the slippery, steep,
And narrow verge of crag-like Agony, springs   560
And folds over the world its healing wings.

Gentleness, Virtue, Wisdom and Endurance,—
These are the seals of that most firm assurance
   Which bars the pit over Destruction's strength;
And if, with infirm hand, Eternity,   565
Mother of many acts and hours, should free
   The serpent that would clasp her with his length[5]—
These are the spells by which to reassume
An empire o'er the disentangled Doom.[6]

To suffer woes which Hope thinks infinite;   570
To forgive wrongs darker than Death or Night;
   To defy Power which seems Omnipotent;
To love, and bear; to hope, till Hope creates
From its own wreck the thing it contemplates;
   Neither to change nor falter nor repent: 575
This, like thy glory, Titan! is to be
Good, great and joyous, beautiful and free;
This is alone Life, Joy, Empire and Victory.

1818–19   1820

The Cloud

I bring fresh showers for the thirsting flowers,
   From the seas and streams;
I bear light shade for the leaves when laid
   In their noon-day dreams.
From my wings are shaken the dews that waken   5
   The sweet buds every one,
When rocked to rest on their mother's[1] breast,
   As she dances about the Sun.
I wield the flail of the lashing hail,
   And whiten the green plains under,   10
And then again I dissolve it in rain,
   And laugh as I pass in thunder.

I sift the snow on the mountains below,
   And their great pines groan aghast;

---

5. A final reminder that the serpent incessantly struggles to break loose and start the cycle of humanity's fall all over again. Felicity must continue to be earned.

6. Shelley's four cardinal virtues (line 562), which seal the serpent in the pit, also constitute the magic formulas ("spells") by which to remaster him, should he again break loose. These virtues are expanded upon in the concluding lines (570–75).

1. The earth's.

And all the night 'tis my pillow white,   15
    While I sleep in the arms of the blast.
Sublime on the towers of my skiey bowers,
    Lightning my pilot sits;
In a cavern under is fettered the thunder,
    It struggles and howls at fits;[2]   20
Over Earth and Ocean, with gentle motion,
    This pilot is guiding me,
Lured by the love of the genii that move
    In the depths of the purple sea;[3]
Over the rills, and the crags, and the hills,   25
    Over the lakes and the plains,
Wherever he dream, under mountain or stream,
    The Spirit he loves remains;
And I all the while bask in Heaven's blue smile,[4]
    Whilst he is dissolving in rains.   30

The sanguine Sunrise, with his meteor eyes,[5]
    And his burning plumes outspread,
Leaps on the back of my sailing rack,[6]
    When the morning star shines dead;
As on the jag of a mountain crag,   35
    Which an earthquake rocks and swings,
An eagle alit one moment may sit
    In the light of its golden wings.
And when Sunset may breathe, from the lit Sea beneath,
    Its ardours of rest and of love,
And the crimson pall[7] of eve may fall   40
    From the depth of Heaven above,
With wings folded I rest, on mine aëry nest,
    As still as a brooding dove.

That orbed maiden with white fire laden   45
    Whom mortals call the Moon,
Glides glimmering o'er my fleece-like floor,
    By the midnight breezes strewn;
And wherever the beat of her unseen feet,
    Which only the angels hear,   50
May have broken the woof,[8] of my tent's thin roof,
    The stars peep behind her, and peer;
And I laugh to see them whirl and flee,
    Like a swarm of golden bees,
When I widen the rent in my wind-built tent,   55
    Till the calm rivers, lakes, and seas,

---

2. Fitfully.
3. I.e., atmospheric electricity, guiding the cloud (line 18), discharges as lightning when "lured" by the attraction of an opposite charge.
4. The upper part of the cloud remains exposed to the sun.

5. Bright as a burning meteor. The following line refers to the sun's corona.
6. High, broken clouds, driven by the wind.
7. Coverlet of rich material.
8. Texture.

Like strips of the sky fallen through me on high,
    Are each paved with the moon and these.[9]

I bind the Sun's throne with a burning zone[1]
    And the Moon's with a girdle of pearl;   60
The volcanos are dim and the stars reel and swim
    When the whirlwinds my banner unfurl.
From cape to cape, with a bridge-like shape,
    Over a torrent sea,
Sunbeam-proof, I hang like a roof—   65
    The mountains its columns be!
The triumphal arch, through which I march
    With hurricane, fire, and snow,
When the Powers of the Air, are chained to my chair,
    Is the million-coloured Bow;   70
The sphere-fire[2] above its soft colours wove
    While the moist Earth was laughing below.

I am the daughter of Earth and Water,
    And the nursling of the Sky;
I pass through the pores, of the ocean and shores;   75
    I change, but I cannot die—
For after the rain, when with never a stain
    The pavilion of Heaven is bare,
And the winds and sunbeams, with their convex gleams,
    Build up the blue dome of Air[3]—   80
I silently laugh at my own cenotaph,[4]
    And out of the caverns of rain,
Like a child from the womb, like a ghost from the tomb,
    I arise, and unbuild it again.—

1820   1820

To a Sky-Lark[1]

Hail to thee, blithe Spirit!
    Bird thou never wert—
That from Heaven, or near it,
    Pourest thy full heart
In profuse strains of unpremeditated art.   5

9. The stars reflected in the water.
1. Girdle, belt.
2. The sunlight.
3. The blue color of the sky; the phenomenon, as Shelley indicates, results from the way "sunbeams" are filtered by the earth's atmosphere.
4. The memorial monument of the dead cloud is the cloudless blue dome of the sky. (The point is that a cenotaph is a monument that does not con-

tain a corpse.)
1. The European skylark is a small bird that sings only in flight, often when it is too high to be visible. This bird, freed from the bonds of earth and soaring beyond the reach of all the physical senses except hearing, is made the emblem of a nonmaterial spirit of pure joy, beyond the possibility of human experience; see lines 15, 31.

    Higher still and higher
      From the earth thou springest
    Like a cloud of fire;
      The blue deep thou wingest,
And singing still dost soar, and soaring ever singest.   10

    In the golden lightning
      Of the sunken Sun—
O'er which clouds are brightning,
      Thou dost float and run;
Like an unbodied joy whose race is just begun.   15

    The pale purple even
      Melts around thy flight,
    Like a star of Heaven
      In the broad day-light
Thou art unseen,—but yet I hear thy shrill delight,   20

    Keen as are the arrows
      Of that silver sphere,[2]
    Whose intense lamp narrows
      In the white dawn clear
Until we hardly see—we feel that it is there.   25

    All the earth and air
      With thy voice is loud,
    As when Night is bare
      From one lonely cloud
The moon rains out her beams—and Heaven is overflowed.   30

    What thou art we know not;
      What is most like thee?
From rainbow clouds there flow not
      Drops so bright to see
As from thy presence showers a rain of melody.   35

    Like a Poet hidden
      In the light of thought,
    Singing hymns unbidden,
      Till the world is wrought
To sympathy with hopes and fears it heeded not: 40

    Like a high-born maiden
      In a palace-tower,
    Soothing her love-laden
      Soul in secret hour,
With music sweet as love—which overflows her bower: 45

2. The morning star.

Like a glow-worm golden
    In a dell of dew,
Scattering unbeholden
    Its aerial hue
Among the flowers and grass which screen it from the view: 50

Like a rose embowered
    In its own green leaves—
By warm winds deflowered—
    Till the scent it gives
Makes faint with too much sweet those heavy-winged
    thieves:³   55

Sound of vernal showers
    On the twinkling grass,
Rain-awakened flowers,
    All that ever was
Joyous, and clear and fresh, thy music doth surpass.   60

Teach us, Sprite⁴ or Bird,
    What sweet thoughts are thine;
I have never heard
    Praise of love or wine
That panted forth a flood of rapture so divine: 65

Chorus Hymeneal⁵
    Or triumphal chaunt
Matched with thine would be all
    But an empty vaunt,
A thing wherein we feel there is some hidden want.   70

What objects are the fountains
    Of thy happy strain?
What fields or waves or mountains?
    What shapes of sky or plain?
What love of thine own kind? what ignorance of pain?   75

With thy clear keen joyance
    Languor cannot be—
Shadow of annoyance
    Never came near thee;
Thou lovest—but ne'er knew love's sad satiety.   80

Waking or asleep,
    Thou of death must deem
Things more true and deep

---

3. The "warm winds," line 53.   5. Marital (from Hymen, Greek god of marriage).
4. Spirit.

Than we mortals dream,
Or how could thy notes flow in such a chrystal stream?   85

We look before and after,
    And pine for what is not—
Our sincerest laughter
    With some pain is fraught—
Our sweetest songs are those that tell of saddest thought.   90

Yet if we could scorn
    Hate and pride and fear;
If we were things born
    Not to shed a tear,
I know not how thy joy we ever should come near.   95

Better than all measures
    Of delightful sound—
Better than all treasures
    That in books are found—
Thy skill to poet were, thou Scorner of the ground!   100

Teach me half the gladness
    That thy brain must know,
Such harmonious madness
    From my lips would flow
The world should listen then—as I am listening now.   105

1820   1820

To ———— [Music, When Soft Voices Die]

Music, when soft voices die,
Vibrates in the memory.—
Odours, when sweet violets sicken,
Live within the sense they quicken.—

Rose leaves, when the rose is dead,   5
Are heaped for the beloved's bed[1]—
And so thy thoughts,[2] when thou art gone,
Love itself shall slumber on.

1821   1824

---

1. The bed of the dead rose.   2. I.e., my thoughts of thee.

O World, O Life, O Time[1]

O World, O Life, O Time,
  On whose last steps I climb,
Trembling at that where I had stood before,
  When will return the glory of your prime?
    No more, O never more!   5

  Out of the day and night
  A joy has taken flight—
Fresh spring and summer [   ] and winter hoar
  Move my faint heart with grief, but with delight
    No more, O never more!   10

1824

Choruses from *Hellas*[1]

Worlds on Worlds[2]

Worlds on worlds are rolling ever
  From creation to decay,
Like the bubbles on a river
  Sparkling, bursting, borne away.
  But *they*[3] are still immortal   5
  Who through Birth's orient[4] portal
And Death's dark chasm hurrying to and fro,
  Clothe their unceasing flight
  In the brief dust and light
Gathered around their chariots as they go;   10
  New shapes they still may weave,
  New Gods, new Laws receive,
Bright or dim are they as the robes they last
  On Death's bare ribs had cast.

---

1. For the author's revisions while composing this poem, see "Poems in Process," below.

1. *Hellas*, a closet drama written in the autumn of 1821, was inspired by the Greek war for independence against the Turks. In his Preface Shelley declared that he viewed this revolution as auguring the final overthrow of all tyranny. The choruses below are sung by Greek captive women. The first chorus describes the entrance of Christ into the revolving cycle of history; the second chorus concludes the drama.

2. "The popular notions of Christianity are represented in this chorus as true in their relation to the worship they superseded . . . without considering their merits in a relation more universal. . . . The concluding verses indicate a progressive state of more or less exalted existence. . . . Let it not be supposed that I mean to dogmatise upon a subject [i.e., the problem of evil, and the possibility of its future elimination] upon which all men are equally ignorant. . . . That there is a true solution to the riddle, and that in our present state that solution is unattainable by us, are propositions that may be regarded as equally certain: meanwhile, as it is the province of the poet to attach himself to those ideas which exalt and ennoble humanity, let him be permitted to have conjectured the condition of that futurity towards which we are all impelled by an inextinguishable thirst for immortality . . ." [Shelley's note].

3. The immortal "beings which inhabit the planets and . . . clothe themselves in matter" [Shelley's note].

4. Eastern.

A Power from the unknown God,   15
    A Promethean Conqueror,[5] came;
Like a triumphal path he trod
    The thorns of death and shame.
A mortal shape to him
    Was like the vapour dim   20
Which the orient planet animates with light;
    Hell, Sin, and Slavery came
    Like bloodhounds mild and tame,
Nor preyed, until their Lord had taken flight;
    The moon of Mahomet[6]   25
    Arose, and it shall set,
While blazoned as on Heaven's immortal noon
    The cross leads generations on.[7]

Swift as the radiant shapes of sleep
    From one whose dreams are Paradise   30
Fly, when the fond wretch wakes to weep,
    And Day peers forth with her blank eyes;
So fleet, so faint, so fair,
    The Powers of earth and air
Fled from the folding star[8] of Bethlehem: 35
    Apollo, Pan, and Love,
    And even Olympian Jove
Grew weak, for killing Truth had glared on them;
    Our hills and seas and streams,
    Dispeopled of their dreams,   40
Their waters turned to blood, their dew to tears,
    Wailed for the golden years.

The World's Great Age[9]

The world's great age begins anew,
    The golden years return,[1]
The earth doth like a snake renew
    Her winter weeds[2] outworn;

5. Christ, whom Shelley compares to Prometheus, who brought fire and the arts of civilization to humankind.
6. The crescent, emblem of Mohammedanism, which was founded six centuries after the birth of Christ.
7. The Roman emperor Constantine was converted to Christianity when he saw a bright cross imposed on the sun at noon.
8. The star of evening, the time when sheep are driven into the sheepfold. Shelley goes on to describe the pagan gods of earth and Olympus fleeing before the star of Bethlehem.
9. "Prophecies of wars, and rumours of wars, etc., may safely be made by poet or prophet in any age, but to anticipate however darkly a period of regeneration and happiness is a more hazardous exercise of the faculty which bards possess or fain. It will remind the reader . . . of Isaiah and Virgil, whose ardent spirits . . . saw the possible and perhaps approaching state of society in which the 'lion shall lie down with the lamb,' and 'omnis feret omnia tellus.' Let these great names be my authority and excuse" [Shelley's note]. The quotations are from Isaiah's millennial prophecy (e.g., chapters 25, 45), and Virgil's prediction, in Eclogue 4, of a return of the golden age, when "all the earth will produce all things."
1. In Greek myth, the first period of history, when Saturn reigned, was the golden age.
2. Clothes (especially mourning garments) as well as dead vegetation.

Heaven smiles, and faiths and empires gleam 5
Like wrecks of a dissolving dream.

A brighter Hellas rears its mountains
 From waves serener far,
A new Peneus[3] rolls his fountains
 Against the morning-star, 10
Where fairer Tempes bloom, there sleep
Young Cyclads[4] on a sunnier deep.

A loftier Argo[5] cleaves the main,
 Fraught with a later prize;
Another Orpheus[6] sings again, 15
 And loves, and weeps, and dies;
A new Ulysses leaves once more
Calypso[7] for his native shore.

O, write no more the tale of Troy,
 If earth Death's scroll must be! 20
Nor mix with Laian[8] rage the joy
 Which dawns upon the free;
Although a subtler Sphinx renew
Riddles of death Thebes never knew.

Another Athens shall arise, 25
 And to remoter time
Bequeath, like sunset to the skies,
 The splendour of its prime,
And leave, if nought so bright may live,
All earth can take or Heaven can give. 30

Saturn and Love their long repose
 Shall burst, more bright and good
Than all who fell, than One who rose,
 Than many unsubdued;[9]
Not gold, not blood their altar dowers 35
But votive tears and symbol flowers.

O cease! must hate and death return?
 Cease! must men kill and die?

3. The river that flows through the beautiful vale of Tempe (line 11).
4. The Cyclades, islands in the Aegean Sea.
5. On which Jason sailed in his quest for the Golden Fleece.
6. The legendary player on the lyre who was torn to pieces by the frenzied Thracian women while he was mourning the death of his wife, Eurydice.
7. The nymph deserted by Ulysses on his voyage back from the Trojan War to his native Ithaca.
8. King Laius of Thebes was killed in a quarrel by his son Oedipus, who did not recognize his father.

Shortly thereafter, Oedipus delivered Thebes from the ravages of the Sphinx by answering its riddle (lines 23–24).
9. "Saturn and Love were among the deities of a real or imaginary state of innocence and happiness. 'All' those 'who fell' [are] the Gods of Greece, Asia, and Egypt; the 'One who rose' [is] Jesus Christ . . . and the 'many unsubdued' [are] the monstrous objects of the idolatry of China, India, the Antarctic islands, and the native tribes of America" [Shelley's note].

> Cease! drain not to its dregs the urn
>   Of bitter prophecy.
> The world is weary of the past,
> O might it die or rest at last!

40

1821   1822

Adonais

An Elegy on the Death of John Keats, Author of Endymion, Hyperion, etc.[1]

> [Thou wert the morning star among the living,
>   Ere thy fair light had fled—
> Now, having died, thou art as Hesperus, giving
>   New splendour to the dead.][2]

1

> I weep for Adonais—he is dead!
> O, weep for Adonais! though our tears
> Thaw not the frost which binds so dear a head!
> And thou, sad Hour,[3] selected from all years
> To mourn our loss, rouse thy obscure compeers,
> And teach them thine own sorrow, say: with me
> Died Adonais; till the Future dares
> Forget the Past, his fate and fame shall be
> An echo and a light unto eternity!

5

1. John Keats died in Rome on Feb. 23, 1821, and was buried there in the Protestant Cemetery. Shelley had met Keats, had invited him to be his guest at Pisa, and had gradually come to recognize him as "among the writers of the highest genius who have adorned our age" (Preface to Adonais). The name "Adonais" is derived from Adonis, the handsome youth who had been loved by the goddess Venus and slain by a wild boar; the function of the beast in this poem is attributed to the anonymous author of a vituperative review of Keats's Endymion in the Quarterly Review, April 1818 (now known to be John Wilson Croker), whom Shelley mistakenly believed to be responsible for Keats's illness and death.

Shelley described Adonais in a letter as a "highly wrought piece of art." Its artistry consists in part in the care with which it follows the conventions of the pastoral elegy, established more than 2,000 years earlier by the Greek Sicilian poets Theocritus, Bion, and Moschus—Shelley had himself translated into English Bion's Lament for Adonis and Moschus' Lament for Bion. We recognize the centuries-old poetic ritual in many verbal echoes, and in such devices as the mournful and accusing invocation to a muse (stanzas 2–4), the sympathetic partici-

pation of nature in the death of the poet (stanzas 14–17), the procession of appropriate mourners (stanzas 30–35), the denunciation of unworthy practitioners of the pastoral or literary art (stanzas 17, 27–29, 36–37); and above all in the turn from despair at the finality of human death (lines 1, 64, 190: "He will awake no more, oh, never more!") to consolation in the sudden and contradictory discovery that the grave is a gate to a higher existence (line 343: "Peace, peace! he is not dead, he doth not sleep"). These familiar elements Shelley transforms into a densely symbolic poetic construction; Adonais ranks with Milton's Lycidas among the supreme examples of the exacting form of the pastoral elegy.

2. Shelley prefixed to Adonais a Greek epigram, attributed to Plato; this is Shelley's own translation of the Greek. (See also The Triumph of Life, below, footnote to line 259.) The planet Venus appears both as the morning star, Lucifer, and the evening star, Hesperus or Vesper. Shelley makes of this phenomenon a key symbol for Adonais' triumph over death, in stanzas 44–46.

3. Shelley follows the classical mode of personifying the hours, which mark the passage of time and turn of the seasons.

2

Where wert thou mighty Mother,[4] when he lay,   10
When thy Son lay, pierced by the shaft which flies
In darkness?[5] where was lorn Urania
When Adonais died? With veiled eyes,
'Mid listening Echoes, in her Paradise
She sate, while one,[6] with soft enamoured breath,   15
Rekindled all the fading melodies,
With which, like flowers that mock the corse[7] beneath,
He had adorned and hid the coming bulk of death.

3

O, weep for Adonais—he is dead!
Wake, melancholy Mother, wake and weep!   20
Yet wherefore? Quench within their burning bed
Thy fiery tears, and let thy loud heart keep
Like his, a mute and uncomplaining sleep;
For he is gone, where all things wise and fair
Descend;—oh, dream not that the amorous Deep[8]   25
Will yet restore him to the vital air;
Death feeds on his mute voice, and laughs at our despair.

4

Most musical of mourners, weep again!
Lament anew, Urania!—He[9] died,
Who was the Sire of an immortal strain,   30
Blind, old, and lonely, when his country's pride,
The priest, the slave, and the liberticide,
Trampled and mocked with many a loathed rite
Of lust and blood; he went, unterrified,
Into the gulph of death; but his clear Sprite[1]   35
Yet reigns o'er earth; the third among the sons of light.[2]

5

Most musical of mourners, weep anew!
Not all to that bright station dared to climb;
And happier they their happiness who knew,
Whose tapers yet burn through that night of time   40
In which suns perished; others more sublime,
Struck by the envious wrath of man or God,
Have sunk, extinct in their refulgent prime;
And some yet live, treading the thorny road,
Which leads, through toil and hate, to Fame's serene abode.   45

4. Urania. She had originally been the Muse of
astronomy, but the name was also an epithet for
Venus. Shelley converts Venus Urania, who in
Greek myth had been the lover of Adonis, into the
mother of Adonais.
5. The allusion is to the anonymity of the review
of *Endymion*. "Lorn": abandoned.
6. I.e., the echo of Keats's voice in his poems.
7. Corpse.
8. Abyss.

9. Milton, regarded as precursor of the great poetic
tradition in which Keats wrote: he had adopted
Urania as the muse of *Paradise Lost*. Lines 31–35
describe Milton's life during the restoration of the
Stuart monarchy.
1. Spirit.
2. The three are Milton and his great predecessors
in epic poetry, Homer and Dante. The stanza following describes the lot of other poets, up to Shelley's own time.

6

But now, thy youngest, dearest one, has perished
The nursling of thy widowhood, who grew,
Like a pale flower by some sad maiden cherished,
And fed with true love tears, instead of dew;[3]
Most musical of mourners, weep anew!   50
Thy extreme[4] hope, the loveliest and the last,
The bloom, whose petals nipt before they blew[5]
Died on the promise of the fruit, is waste;
The broken lily lies—the storm is overpast.

7

To that high Capital,[6] where kingly Death   55
Keeps his pale court in beauty and decay,
He came; and bought, with price of purest breath,
A grave among the eternal.—Come away!
Haste, while the vault of blue Italian day
Is yet his fitting charnel-roof! while still   60
He lies, as if in dewy sleep he lay;
Awake him not! surely he takes his fill
Of deep and liquid rest, forgetful of all ill.

8

He will awake no more, oh, never more!—
Within the twilight chamber spreads apace,   65
The shadow of white Death, and at the door
Invisible Corruption waits to trace
His extreme way to her dim dwelling-place;
The eternal Hunger sits, but pity and awe
Soothe her pale rage, nor dares she to deface   70
So fair a prey, till darkness, and the law
Of change, shall 'oer his sleep the mortal curtain draw.

9

O, weep for Adonais!—The quick[7] Dreams,
The passion-winged Ministers of thought,
Who were his flocks,[8] whom near the living streams   75
Of his young spirit he fed, and whom he taught
The love which was its music, wander not,—
Wander no more, from kindling brain to brain,
But droop there, whence they sprung; and mourn their lot
Round the cold heart, where, after their sweet pain,   80
They ne'er will gather strength, or find a home again.

10

And one[9] with trembling hands clasps his cold head,
And fans him with her moonlight wings, and cries;

---

3. An allusion to an incident in Keats's *Isabella*.
4. Last, as well as highest.
5. Bloomed.
6. Rome.
7. Living.

8. The products of Keats's imagination, figuratively represented (according to pastoral convention) as his sheep.
9. One of the Dreams (line 73).

"Our love, our hope, our sorrow, is not dead;
See, on the silken fringe of his faint eyes,   85
Like dew upon a sleeping flower, there lies
A tear some Dream has loosened from his brain."
Lost Angel of a ruined Paradise!
She knew not 'twas her own; as with no stain
She faded, like a cloud which had outwept its rain.   90

                          11
One from a lucid[1] urn of starry dew
Washed his light limbs as if embalming them;
Another clipt her profuse locks, and threw
The wreath upon him, like an anadem,[2]
Which frozen tears instead of pearls begem;   95
Another in her wilful grief would break
Her bow and winged reeds, as if to stem
A greater loss with one which was more weak;
And dull the barbed fire against his frozen cheek.

                          12
Another Splendour on his mouth alit,   100
That mouth, whence it was wont to draw the breath
Which gave it strength to pierce the guarded wit,[3]
And pass into the panting heart beneath
With lightning and with music: the damp death
Quenched its caress upon his icy lips;   105
And, as a dying meteor stains a wreath
Of moonlight vapour, which the cold night clips,[4]
It flushed through his pale limbs, and past to its eclipse.

                          13
And others came . . . Desires and Adorations,
Winged Persuasions and veiled Destinies,   110
Splendours, and Glooms, and glimmering Incarnations
Of hopes and fears, and twilight Phantasies;
And Sorrow, with her family of Sighs,
And Pleasure, blind with tears, led by the gleam
Of her own dying smile instead of eyes,   115
Came in slow pomp;—the moving pomp might seem
Like pageantry of mist on an autumnal stream.

                          14
All he had loved, and moulded into thought,
From shape, and hue, and odour, and sweet sound,
Lamented Adonais. Morning sought   120
Her eastern watchtower, and her hair unbound,
Wet with the tears which should adorn the ground,
Dimmed the aerial eyes that kindle day;
Afar the melancholy thunder moaned,

---

1. Luminous.   3. The cautious intellect (of the listener).
2. A rich garland.   4. Embraces.

Pale Ocean in unquiet slumber lay,   125
And the wild winds flew round, sobbing in their dismay.

15

Lost Echo sits amid the voiceless mountains,
And feeds her grief with his remembered lay,
And will no more reply to winds or fountains,
Or amorous birds perched on the young green spray,   130
Or herdsman's horn, or bell at closing day;
Since she can mimic not his lips, more dear
Than those for whose disdain she pined away
Into a shadow of all sounds:[5]—a drear
Murmur, between their songs, is all the woodmen hear.   135

16

Grief made the young Spring wild, and she threw down
Her kindling buds, as if she Autumn were,
Or they dead leaves; since her delight is flown
For whom should she have waked the sullen year?
To Phoebus was not Hyacinth so dear[6]   140
Nor to himself Narcissus, as to both
Thou Adonais: wan they stand and sere[7]
Amid the faint companions of their youth,
With dew all turned to tears; odour, to sighing ruth. [8]

17

Thy spirit's sister, the lorn nightingale[9]   145
Mourns not her mate with such melodious pain;
Not so the eagle, who like thee could scale
Heaven, and could nourish in the sun's domain
Her mighty youth with morning,[1] doth complain,
Soaring and screaming round her empty nest,   150
As Albion[2] wails for thee: the curse of Cain
Light on his[3] head who pierced thy innocent breast,
And scared the angel soul that was its earthly guest!

18

Ah woe is me! Winter is come and gone,
But grief returns with the revolving year;   155
The airs and streams renew their joyous tone;
The ants, the bees, the swallows reappear;
Fresh leaves and flowers deck the dead Seasons' bier;
The amorous birds now pair in every brake,
And build their mossy homes in field and brere;[4]   160

5. Because of her unrequited love for Narcissus, who was enamored of his own reflection (line 141), the nymph Echo pined away until she was only a reflected sound.
6. Young Hyacinthus was loved by Phoebus Apollo, who accidentally killed him in a game of quoits. Apollo made the hyacinth flower spring from his blood.
7. Dried, withered.

8. Pity.
9. To whom Keats had written *Ode to a Nightingale.*
1. In the legend, the aged eagle, to renew his youth, flies toward the sun until his old plumage is burned off and the film cleared from his eyes.
2. England.
3. The reviewer of *Endymion.*
4. Briar. "Brake": thicket.

And the green lizard, and the golden snake,
Like unimprisoned flames, out of their trance awake.

19

Through wood and stream and field and hill and Ocean
A quickening life from the Earth's heart has burst
As it has ever done, with change and motion,   165
From the great morning of the world when first
God dawned on Chaos; in its stream immersed
The lamps of Heaven flash with a softer light;
All baser things pant with life's sacred thirst;
Diffuse themselves; and spend in love's delight,   170
The beauty and the joy of their renewed might.

20

The leprous corpse touched by this spirit tender
Exhales itself in flowers of gentle breath;
Like incarnations of the stars, when splendour
Is changed to fragrance, they illumine death   175
And mock the merry worm that wakes beneath;
Nought we know, dies. Shall that alone which knows
Be as a sword consumed before the sheath
By sightless lightning?[5]—th' intense atom glows
A moment, then is quenched in a most cold repose.   180

21

Alas! that all we loved of him should be,
But for our grief, as if it had not been,
And grief itself be mortal! Woe is me!
Whence are we, and why are we? of what scene
The actors or spectators? Great and mean   185
Meet massed in death, who lends what life must borrow.
As long as skies are blue, and fields are green,
Evening must usher night, night urge the morrow,
Month follow month with woe, and year wake year to sorrow.

22

He will awake no more, oh, never more!   190
"Wake thou," cried Misery, "childless Mother, rise
Out of thy sleep, and slake,[6] in thy heart's core,
A wound more fierce than his with tears and sighs."
And all the Dreams that watched Urania's eyes,
And all the Echoes whom their sister's song[7]   195
Had held in holy silence, cried: "Arise!"
Swift as a Thought by the snake Memory stung,
From her ambrosial rest the fading Splendour[8] sprung.

23

She rose like an autumnal Night, that springs
Out of the East, and follows wild and drear   200

5. The sword is the mind which knows; the sheath
is its vehicle, the material body. "Sightless": invisible.

6. Assuage.
7. I.e., the Echo in line 127.
8. Urania.

The golden Day, which, on eternal wings,
Even as a ghost abandoning a bier,
Had left the Earth a corpse. Sorrow and fear
So struck, so roused, so rapt Urania;
So saddened round her like an atmosphere   205
Of stormy mist; so swept her on her way
Even to the mournful place where Adonais lay.

24

Out of her secret Paradise she sped,
Through camps and cities rough with stone, and steel,
And human hearts, which to her aery tread   210
Yielding not, wounded the invisible
Palms of her tender feet where'er they fell:
And barbed tongues, and thoughts more sharp than they
Rent the soft Form they never could repel,
Whose sacred blood, like the young tears of May,   215
Paved with eternal flowers that undeserving way.

25

In the death chamber for a moment Death
Shamed by the presence of that living Might
Blushed to annihilation, and the breath
Revisited those lips, and life's pale light   220
Flashed through those limbs, so late her dear delight.
"Leave me not wild and drear and comfortless,
As silent lightning leaves the starless night!
Leave me not!" cried Urania: her distress
Roused Death: Death rose and smiled, and met her vain caress.   225

26

"Stay yet awhile! speak to me once again;
Kiss me, so long but as a kiss may live;
And in my heartless[9] breast and burning brain
That word, that kiss shall all thoughts else survive
With food of saddest memory kept alive,   230
Now thou art dead, as if it were a part
Of thee, my Adonais! I would give
All that I am to be as thou now art!
But I am chained to Time, and cannot thence depart!

27

"Oh gentle child, beautiful as thou wert,   235
Why didst thou leave the trodden paths of men
Too soon, and with weak hands though mighty heart
Dare the unpastured dragon in his den?[1]
Defenceless as thou wert, oh where was then
Wisdom the mirrored shield, or scorn the spear?[2]   240
Or hadst thou waited the full cycle, when

---

9. Because her heart had been given to Adonais.
1. I.e., the hostile reviewers.
2. The allusion is to Perseus, who had cut off

Medusa's head while avoiding the direct sight of
her (which would have turned him to stone) by
looking only at her reflection in his shield.

Thy spirit should have filled its crescent sphere,[3]
The monsters of life's waste had fled from thee like deer.

28

"The herded wolves, bold only to pursue;
The obscene ravens, clamorous o'er the dead; 245
The vultures to the conqueror's banner true
Who feed where Desolation first has fed,
And whose wings rain contagion;—how they fled,
When like Apollo, from his golden bow,
The Pythian of the age[4] one arrow sped 250
And smiled!—The spoilers tempt no second blow,
They fawn on the proud feet that spurn them lying low.

29

"The sun comes forth, and many reptiles spawn;
He sets, and each ephemeral insect then
Is gathered into death without a dawn, 255
And the immortal stars awake again;
So is it in the world of living men:
A godlike mind soars forth, in its delight
Making earth bare and veiling heaven,[5] and when
It sinks, the swarms that dimmed or shared its light 260
Leave to its kindred lamps[6] the spirit's awful night."

30

Thus ceased she: and the mountain shepherds came,
Their garlands sere, their magic mantles rent;
The Pilgrim of Eternity,[7] whose fame
Over his living head like Heaven is bent, 265
An early but enduring monument,
Came, veiling all the lightnings of his song
In sorrow; from her wilds Ierne sent
The sweetest lyrist of her saddest wrong,[8]
And love taught grief to fall like music from his tongue. 270

31

Midst others of less note, came one frail Form,[9]
A phantom among men; companionless
As the last cloud of an expiring storm
Whose thunder is its knell; he, as I guess,
Had gazed on Nature's naked loveliness, 275
Actæon-like, and now he fled astray
With feeble steps o'er the world's wilderness,

---

3. When thy spirit, like the full moon, should have reached its maturity.
4. Byron, who had directed against critics of the age his satiric poem *English Bards and Scotch Reviewers* (1809). The allusion is to Apollo, called "the Pythian" because he had slain the dragon Python.
5. As the sun reveals the earth but veils the other stars.
6. The other stars (i.e., creative minds), of lesser brilliance than the sun.
7. Byron, who had referred to his Childe Harold as one of the "wanderers o'er eternity" (3.669).
8. Thomas Moore (1779–1852), from Ireland ("Ierne"), who had written poems about the oppression of his native land.
9. Shelley himself, represented in one of his aspects—that of "weakness"—rather than of the "Power" of the poet who wrote *Prometheus Unbound* (see lines 281–82).

And his own thoughts, along that rugged way,
Pursued, like raging hounds, their father and their prey.[1]

32

A pardlike[2] Spirit beautiful and swift—   280
A Love in desolation masked;—a Power
Girt round with weakness;—it can scarce uplift
The weight of the superincumbent hour;[3]
It is a dying lamp, a falling shower,
A breaking billow;—even whilst we speak   285
Is it not broken? On the withering flower
The killing sun smiles brightly: on a cheek
The life can burn in blood, even while the heart may break.

33

His head was bound with pansies overblown,
And faded violets, white, and pied, and blue;   290
And a light spear topped with a cypress cone,
Round whose rude shaft dark ivy tresses grew[4]
Yet dripping with the forest's noonday dew,
Vibrated, as the ever-beating heart
Shook the weak hand that grasped it; of that crew   295
He came the last, neglected and apart;
A herd-abandoned deer struck by the hunter's dart.

34

All stood aloof, and at his partial[5] moan
Smiled through their tears; well knew that gentle band
Who in another's fate now wept his own;   300
As in the accents of an unknown land,
He sung new sorrow; sad Urania scanned
The Stranger's mien, and murmured: "who art thou?"
He answered not, but with a sudden hand
Made bare his branded and ensanguined brow,   305
Which was like Cain's or Christ's[6]—Oh! that it should be so!

35

What softer voice is hushed over the dead?
Athwart what brow is that dark mantle thrown?
What form leans sadly o'er the white death-bed,
In mockery of monumental stone,[7]   310
The heavy heart heaving without a moan?
If it be He,[8] who, gentlest of the wise,
Taught, soothed, loved, honoured the departed one;
Let me not vex, with inharmonious sighs
The silence of that heart's accepted sacrifice.   315

1. Actaeon, while hunting, came upon the naked
Diana bathing, and as a punishment was turned
into a stag and torn to pieces by his own hounds.
2. Leopard-like.
3. The heavy, overhanging hour of Keats's death.
4. Like the thyrsus, the leaf-entwined and cone-
topped staff carried by Dionysus. The pansies are
emblems of sorrowful thought; the cypress is an
emblem of mourning.

5. Sympathetic.
6. His bloody ("ensanguined") brow bore a mark
like that with which God had branded Cain for
murdering Abel—or like that left by Christ's crown
of thorns.
7. In imitation of a memorial statue.
8. Leigh Hunt, close friend of both Keats and
Shelley.

36

Our Adonais has drunk poison—oh!
What deaf and viperous murderer could crown
Life's early cup with such a draught of woe?
The nameless worm[9] would now itself disown:
It felt, yet could escape the magic tone   320
Whose prelude held all envy, hate, and wrong,
But what was howling in one breast alone,
Silent with expectation of the song,[1]
Whose master's hand is cold, whose silver lyre unstrung.

37

Live thou, whose infamy is not thy fame!   325
Live! fear no heavier chastisement from me,
Thou noteless blot on a remembered name!
But be thyself, and know thyself to be!
And ever at thy season be thou free
To spill the venom when thy fangs o'erflow: 330
Remorse and Self-contempt shall cling to thee;
Hot Shame shall burn upon thy secret brow,
And like a beaten hound tremble thou shalt—as now.

38

Nor let us weep that our delight is fled
Far from these carrion kites[2] that scream below;   335
He wakes or sleeps with the enduring dead;
Thou canst not soar where he is sitting now.—
Dust to the dust! but the pure spirit shall flow
Back to the burning fountain whence it came,
A portion of the Eternal,[3] which must glow   340
Through time and change, unquenchably the same,
Whilst thy cold embers choke the sordid hearth of shame.

39

Peace, peace! he is not dead, he doth not sleep—
He hath awakened from the dream of life—
'Tis we, who lost in stormy visions, keep   345
With phantoms an unprofitable strife,
And in mad trance, strike with our spirit's knife
Invulnerable nothings.—We decay
Like corpses in a charnel; fear and grief
Convulse us and consume us day by day,   350
And cold hopes swarm like worms within our living clay.

40

He has outsoared the shadow of our night;[4]
Envy and calumny and hate and pain,

9. Snake; the anonymous reviewer.
1. The promise of later greatness in Keats's early
poems "held . . . silent" the expression of all
malignant feelings except the reviewer's.
2. Large birds of prey; a species of hawk.
3. Shelley adopts for this poem the Neoplatonic
view that all life and all forms emanate from the

Absolute, the eternal One. The Absolute is imaged
as both a radiant light source and an overflowing
fountain, which circulates continuously through
the dross of matter (stanza 43) and back to its source.
4. He has soared beyond the shadow cast by the
earth as it intercepts the sun's light.

And that unrest which men miscall delight,
Can touch him not and torture not again;   355
From the contagion of the world's slow stain
He is secure, and now can never mourn
A heart grown cold, a head grown grey in vain;
Nor, when the spirit's self has ceased to burn,
With sparkless ashes load an unlamented urn.   360

41

He lives, he wakes—'tis Death is dead, not he;
Mourn not for Adonais.—Thou young Dawn
Turn all thy dew to splendour, for from thee
The spirit thou lamentest is not gone;
Ye caverns and ye forests, cease to moan!   365
Cease ye faint flowers and fountains, and thou Air
Which like a mourning veil thy scarf hadst thrown
O'er the abandoned Earth, now leave it bare
Even to the joyous stars which smile on its despair![5]

42

He is made one with Nature: there is heard   370
His voice in all her music, from the moan
Of thunder, to the song of night's sweet bird;[6]
He is a presence to be felt and known
In darkness and in light, from herb and stone,
Spreading itself where'er that Power may move   375
Which has withdrawn his being to its own;
Which wields the world with never wearied love,
Sustains it from beneath, and kindles it above.

43

He is a portion of the loveliness
Which once he made more lovely: he doth bear   380
His part, while the one Spirit's plastic[7] stress
Sweeps through the dull dense world, compelling there,
All new successions to the forms they wear;
Torturing th' unwilling dross that checks its flight
To its own likeness, as each mass may bear;[8]   385
And bursting in its beauty and its might
From trees and beasts and men into the Heaven's light.

44

The splendours of the firmament of time
May be eclipsed, but are extinguished not;
Like stars to their appointed height they climb   390
And death is a low mist which cannot blot
The brightness it may veil.[9] When lofty thought
Lifts a young heart above its mortal lair,

---

5. Shelley's science is, as usual, accurate: it is the envelope of air around the earth which, by diffusing and reflecting sunlight, veils the stars.
6. The nightingale, in allusion to Keats's *Ode to a Nightingale*.
7. Formative, shaping.

8. I.e., to the degree that a particular substance will permit.
9. The radiance of stars (i.e., of poets) persists, even when they are temporarily "eclipsed" by another heavenly body, or obscured by the veil of the earth's atmosphere.

And love and life contend in it, for what
Shall be its earthly doom, the dead live there[1]   395
And move like winds of light on dark and stormy air.

45

The inheritors of unfulfilled renown[2]
Rose from their thrones, built beyond mortal thought,
Far in the Unapparent. Chatterton
Rose pale, his solemn agony had not   400
Yet faded from him; Sidney, as he fought
And as he fell and as he lived and loved
Sublimely mild, a Spirit without spot,
Arose; and Lucan, by his death approved:[3]
Oblivion as they rose shrank like a thing reproved.   405

46

And many more, whose names on Earth are dark
But whose transmitted effluence cannot die
So long as fire outlives the parent spark,
Rose, robed in dazzling immortality.
"Thou art become as one of us," they cry,   410
"It was for thee yon kingless sphere has long
Swung blind in unascended majesty,
Silent alone amid an Heaven of song.
Assume thy winged throne, thou Vesper of our throng!"[4]

47

Who mourns for Adonais? oh come forth   415
Fond wretch! and know thyself and him aright.
Clasp with thy panting soul the pendulous[5] Earth;
As from a centre, dart thy spirit's light
Beyond all worlds, until its spacious might
Satiate the void circumference: then shrink   420
Even to a point within our day and night;[6]
And keep thy heart light lest it make thee sink
When hope has kindled hope, and lured thee to the brink.

48

Or go to Rome, which is the sepulchre
O, not of him, but of our joy: 'tis nought   425
That ages, empires, and religions there
Lie buried in the ravage they have wrought;
For such as he can lend,—they[7] borrow not

---

1. I.e., in the thought of the "young heart" (line
393). "Doom": destiny.
2. Poets who (like Keats) died young, before
achieving their full measure of fame: Thomas
Chatterton (1752–1770) committed suicide at 17;
Sir Philip Sidney (1554–1586) died in battle at 32;
and the Roman poet Lucan (A.D. 39–65) killed
himself at 26 to escape a sentence of death for having plotted against the tyrant Nero.
3. Justified, proved worthy.
4. Adonais assumes his place in the sphere of Vesper, the evening star, hitherto unoccupied ("kingless"), hence also "silent" amid the music of the

other spheres.
5. Suspended, floating in space.
6. The poet bids the wretch who is foolish ("fond")
enough to mourn Adonais to stretch his imagination so as to reach the poet's own cosmic viewpoint, and then allow it to contract ("shrink") back
to its ordinary vantage point on earth—where,
unlike Adonais in his heavenly place, we have an
alternation of day and night (line 421).
7. Poets like Keats, who can bestow ("lend") glory,
as opposed to the Roman conquerors, who borrowed glory from those they conquered.

Glory from those who made the world their prey;
And he is gathered to the kings of thought   430
Who waged contention with their time's decay,
And of the past are all that cannot pass away.

                            49
Go thou to Rome,—at once the Paradise,
The grave, the city, and the wilderness;
And where its wrecks like shattered mountains rise,   435
And flowering weeds, and fragrant copses[8] dress
The bones of Desolation's nakedness
Pass, till the Spirit of the spot shall lead
Thy footsteps to a slope of green access[9]
Where, like an infant's smile, over the dead,   440
A light of laughing flowers along the grass is spread.

                            50
And grey walls moulder round,[1] on which dull Time
Feeds, like slow fire upon a hoary brand;[2]
And one keen pyramid with wedge sublime,[3]
Pavilioning the dust of him who planned   445
This refuge for his memory, doth stand
Like flame transformed to marble; and beneath,
A field is spread, on which a newer band
Have pitched in Heaven's smile their camp of death
Welcoming him we lose with scarce extinguished breath.   450

                            51
Here pause: these graves are all too young as yet
To have outgrown the sorrow which consigned
Its charge to each; and if the seal is set,
Here, on one fountain of a mourning mind,[4]
Break it not thou! too surely shalt thou find   455
Thine own well full, if thou returnest home,
Of tears and gall. From the world's bitter wind
Seek shelter in the shadow of the tomb.
What Adonais is, why fear we to become?

                            52
The One remains, the many change and pass;   460
Heaven's light forever shines, Earth's shadows fly;
Life, like a dome of many-coloured glass,
Stains the white radiance of Eternity,
Until Death tramples it to fragments.[5]—Die,
If thou wouldst be with that which thou dost seek!   465

---

8. Undergrowth. In Shelley's time the ruins of
ancient Rome were overgrown with weeds and
shrubbery.
9. The Protestant Cemetery, Keats's burial place.
The next line is a glancing allusion to Shelley's 3-
year-old son William, also buried there.
1. The wall of ancient Rome formed one boundary of the cemetery.
2. A burning log.
3. The tomb of Caius Cestius, a Roman tribune,

just outside the cemetery.
4. Shelley's mourning for his son.
5. Earthly life colors ("stains") the pure white light
of the One, which is the source of all light (see
lines 339–40 and note). The azure sky, flowers,
etc., of lines 466–68 exemplify earthly colors that,
however beautiful, fall far short of the "glory" of
the pure Light which they transmit, but also refract
("transfuse").

Follow where all is fled!—Rome's azure sky,
Flowers, ruins, statues, music, words, are weak
The glory they transfuse with fitting truth to speak.

53

Why linger, why turn back, why shrink, my Heart?
Thy hopes are gone before; from all things here   470
They have departed; thou shouldst now depart!
A light is past from the revolving year,
And man, and woman; and what still is dear
Attracts to crush, repels to make thee wither.
The soft sky smiles,—the low wind whispers near: 475
'Tis Adonais calls! oh, hasten thither,
No more let Life divide what Death can join together.

54

That Light whose smile kindles the Universe,
That Beauty in which all things work and move,
That Benediction which the eclipsing Curse   480
Of birth can quench not, that sustaining Love
Which through the web of being blindly wove
By man and beast and earth and air and sea,
Burns bright or dim, as each are mirrors of[6]
The fire for which all thirst;[7] now beams on me,   485
Consuming the last clouds of cold mortality.

55

The breath whose might I have invoked in song[8]
Descends on me; my spirit's bark is driven,
Far from the shore, far from the trembling throng
Whose sails were never to the tempest given;   490
The massy earth and sphered skies are riven!
I am borne darkly, fearfully, afar;
Whilst burning through the inmost veil of Heaven,
The soul of Adonais, like a star,
Beacons from the abode where the Eternal are.   495

1821   1821

A Dirge

Rough wind, that moanest loud
Grief too sad for song;
Wild wind, when sullen cloud
Knells all the night long;
Sad storm, whose tears are vain,   5

6. I.e., according to the degree that each reflects.
7. The "thirst" of the human spirit is to return to
the fountain and fire (the "burning fountain," line
339) which is its source.

8. Two years earlier, Shelley had "invoked" (prayed
to, and also asked for) "the breath of Autumn's
being" in his Ode to the West Wind.

Bare woods, whose branches strain,
Deep caves and dreary main,—
   Wail, for the world's wrong!

When the Lamp Is Shattered

When the lamp is shattered
The light in the dust lies dead—
   When the cloud is scattered
The rainbow's glory is shed—
   When the lute is broken   5
Sweet tones are remembered not—
   When the lips have spoken
Loved accents are soon forgot.

   As music and splendour
Survive not the lamp and the lute,   10
   The heart's echoes render
No song when the spirit is mute—
   No song—but sad dirges
Like the wind through a ruined cell
   Or the mournful surges   15
That ring the dead seaman's knell.

   When hearts have once mingled
Love first leaves the well-built nest[1]—
   The weak one is singled
To endure what it once possest.   20
   O Love! who bewailest
The frailty of all things here,
   Why choose you the frailest[2]
For your cradle, your home and your bier?

   Its passions will rock thee   25
As the storms rock the ravens on high—
   Bright Reason will mock thee
Like the Sun from a wintry sky—
   From thy nest every rafter
Will rot, and thine eagle home[3]   30
   Leave thee naked to laughter
When leaves fall and cold winds come.

1. Love abandons first the sturdier heart.   3. Like the lofty, and therefore exposed, nest of
2. I.e., the human heart.   the eagle.

To Jane. The Invitation[1]

Best and brightest, come away—
Fairer far than this fair day
Which like thee to those in sorrow
Comes to bid a sweet good-morrow
To the rough year just awake   5
In its cradle on the brake.[2]—
The brightest hour of unborn spring
Through the winter wandering
Found, it seems, this halcyon[3] morn
To hoar February born;   10
Bending from Heaven in azure mirth
It kissed the forehead of the earth
And smiled upon the silent sea,
And bade the frozen streams be free
And waked to music all their fountains,   15
And breathed upon the frozen mountains,
And like a prophetess of May
Strewed flowers upon the barren way,
Making the wintry world appear
Like one on whom thou smilest, dear.   20

Away, away from men and towns
To the wild wood and the downs,
To the silent wilderness
Where the soul need not repress
Its music lest it should not find   25
An echo in another's mind,
While the touch of Nature's art
Harmonizes heart to heart.—
I leave this notice on my door
For each accustomed visitor—   30
"I am gone into the fields
To take what this sweet hour yields.
Reflexion, you may come tomorrow,
Sit by the fireside with Sorrow—
You, with the unpaid bill, Despair,   35
You, tiresome verse-reciter Care,
I will pay you in the grave,
Death will listen to your stave[4]—
Expectation too, be off!
To-day is for itself enough—   40
Hope, in pity mock not woe

1. "Jane" is Jane Williams, the common-law wife
of Edward Williams, Shelley's close friend. This
invitation to an outdoor excursion exemplifies
Shelley's grace and urbanity, writing in the ancient
tradition of the verse letter.
2. Thicket.
3. Calm and peaceful.
4. Stanza, set of verses.

With smiles, nor follow where I go;
Long having lived on thy sweet food,
At length I find one moment's good
After long pain—with all your love   45
This you never told me of."

Radiant Sister of the day,
Awake, arise and come away
To the wild woods and the plains
And the pools where winter-rains   50
Image all their roof of leaves,
Where the pine its garland weaves
Of sapless green and ivy dun
Round stems that never kiss the Sun—
Where the lawns and pastures be   55
And the sandhills of the sea—
Where the melting hoar-frost wets
The daisy-star that never sets,
And wind-flowers, and violets
Which yet join not scent to hue   60
Crown the pale year weak and new,
When the night is left behind
In the deep east dun and blind
And the blue noon is over us,
And the multitudinous   65
Billows murmur at our feet
Where the earth and ocean meet,
And all things seem only one
In the universal Sun.—

1822   1824

A Defence of Poetry

In 1820 Shelley's good friend Thomas Love Peacock published an ironic essay, *The Four Ages of Poetry*, implicitly directed against the towering claims for poetry and the poetic imagination by his Romantic contemporaries. Peacock adopted the premise of Wordsworth and other Romantic critics—that poetry in its origin was a primitive use of language and mind—but from this premise he proceeded to draw the conclusion that poetry has become a useless anachronism in this age of science and technology. Peacock was himself a poet, as well as the best contemporary prose satirist, and Shelley saw the joke; but he also recognized that the view which Peacock, as a satirist, had only half-humorously assumed was very close to that actually held in his day by Utilitarian philosophers and material-minded laymen who either attacked or contemptuously ignored the imaginative faculty and its achievements. He therefore undertook, as he good-humoredly wrote to Peacock, "to break a lance with you . . . in honor of my mistress Urania," even though he was only "the knight of the shield of shadow and the lance of gossamere." The result was *The Defence of Poetry*, planned to consist of three parts. The last two parts were never written, and even the existing section, written in 1821, remained unpublished until 1840, eighteen years after Shelley's death. For many decades Shelley's *Defence* was regarded as one of the classic essays in literary criticism. Its reputation, however, diminished in the era of the New Criticism, during the middle decades of the present century, when the chief interest was in applied commentary and the kind of critical theory that provides useful distinctions for the close analysis of particular literary texts. But Shelley's main enterprise, although different, is no less valid, and a rarer achievement in the history of critical writings. His emphasis is on the universal and permanent forms, qualities, and values that all great poems, as products of imagination, possess in common—on those aspects, as he puts it, in which time, person, and place "are convertible with respect to the highest poetry without injuring it as poetry." Shelley's position thus parallels that of William Blake, and has analogues to that of "archetypal" criticism in our own time. More than this: Shelley extends the term "poet" to comprehend all the creative minds that break out of the limitations of their age and place to approximate what he regards as enduring and general forms of value—including not only writers in verse and prose, but artists, legislators, and prophets, as well as the founders of a new organization of society, morality, or religion.

The range of the *Defence* gives it unequaled importance as a ringing claim for the validity and indispensability of the visionary and creative imagination in all the great human concerns. And no later writer has exceeded the cogency of Shelley's attack on our acquisitive society and its narrowly material concept of utility and progress. This bias has permitted the human race to make enormous progress in science and in material well-being without a proportionate development of our "poetical faculty," the moral imagination—with the result, as Shelley says, that "man, having enslaved the elements, remains himself a slave."

From A Defence of Poetry

or Remarks Suggested by an Essay Entitled "The Four Ages of Poetry"

According to one mode of regarding those two classes of mental action, which are called reason and imagination, the former may be considered as mind contemplating the relations borne by one thought to another, however produced; and the latter, as mind acting upon those thoughts so as to colour them with its own light, and composing from them, as from elements, other thoughts, each containing within itself the principle of its own integrity. The one[1] is the *to poiein*,[2] or the principle of synthesis, and has for its objects those forms which are common to universal nature and existence itself; the other is the *to logizein*,[3] or principle of analysis, and its action regards the relations of things, simply as

---

1. "The one" is the imagination; "the other" (later in the sentence) is the reason.
2. Making. The Greek word from which the English term "poet" derives means "maker," and "maker" was often used as equivalent to "poet" by

Renaissance critics such as Sir Philip Sidney in his *Defence of Poesy*, which Shelley had carefully studied.
3. Calculating, reasoning.

relations; considering thoughts, not in their integral unity, but as the algebraical representations which conduct to certain general results. Reason is the enumeration of quantities already known; imagination is the perception of the value of those quantities, both separately and as a whole. Reason respects the differences, and imagination the similitudes of things. Reason is to Imagination as the instrument to the agent, as the body to the spirit, as the shadow to the substance.

* * *

In the youth of the world, men dance and sing and imitate natural objects, observing[4] in these actions, as in all others, a certain rhythm or order. And, although all men observe a similar, they observe not the same order, in the motions of the dance, in the melody of the song, in the combinations of language, in the series of their imitations of natural objects. For there is a certain order or rhythm belonging to each of these classes of mimetic representation, from which the hearer and the spectator receive an intenser and purer pleasure than from any other: the sense of an approximation to this order has been called taste, by modern writers. Every man in the infancy of art, observes an order which approximates more or less closely to that from which this highest delight results: but the diversity is not sufficiently marked, as that its gradations should be sensible, except in those instances where the predominance of this faculty of approximation to the beautiful (for so we may be permitted to name the relation between this highest pleasure and its cause) is very great. Those in whom it exists in excess are poets, in the most universal sense of the word; and the pleasure resulting from the manner in which they express the influence of society or nature upon their own minds, communicates itself to others, and gathers a sort of reduplication from that community. Their language is vitally metaphorical; that is, it marks the before unapprehended relations of things, and perpetuates their apprehension, until the words which represent them, become through time signs for portions or classes of thoughts[5] instead of pictures of integral thoughts; and then if no new poets should arise to create afresh the associations which have been thus disorganized, language will be dead to all the nobler purposes of human intercourse. These similitudes or relations are finely said by Lord Bacon to be "the same footsteps of nature impressed upon the various subjects of the world"[6]—and he considers the faculty which perceives them as the storehouse of axioms common to all knowledge. In the infancy of society every author is necessarily a poet, because language itself is poetry; and to be a poet is to apprehend the true and the beautiful, in a word the good which exists in the relation, subsisting, first between existence and perception, and secondly between perception and expression. Every original language near to its source is in itself the chaos of a cyclic poem:[7] the copiousness

4. Following, obeying.
5. I.e., abstract concepts.
6. Bacon, *De Augmentis Scientiarum* ("On the

Enlargement of the Sciences"), 1.3.
7. A group of poems (e.g., "the Arthurian cycle") that deal with the same subject.

of lexicography[8] and the distinctions of grammar are the works of a later age, and are merely the catalogue and the form of the creations of Poetry. But Poets, or those who imagine and express this indestructible order, are not only the authors of language and of music, of the dance and architecture and statuary and painting: they are the institutors of laws, and the founders of civil society and the inventors of the arts of life and the teachers, who draw into a certain propinquity with the beautiful and the true that partial apprehension of the agencies of the invisible world which is called religion.[9] Hence all original religions are allegorical, or susceptible of allegory, and like Janus[1] have a double face of false and true. Poets, according to the circumstances of the age and nation in which they appeared, were called in the earlier epochs of the world legislators or prophets:[2] a poet essentially comprises and unites both these characters. For he not only beholds intensely the present as it is, and discovers those laws according to which present things ought to be ordered, but he beholds the future in the present, and his thoughts are the germs of the flower and the fruit of latest time. Not that I assert poets to be prophets in the gross sense of the word, or that they can foretell the form as surely as they foreknow the spirit of events: such is the pretence of superstition which would make poetry an attribute of prophecy, rather than prophecy an attribute of poetry. A Poet participates in the eternal, the infinite, and the one; as far as relates to his conceptions, time and place and number are not. The grammatical forms which express the moods of time, and the difference of persons and the distinction of place are convertible with respect to the highest poetry without injuring it as poetry, and the choruses of Æschylus, and the book of Job, and Dante's Paradise would afford, more than any other writings, examples of this fact, if the limits of this essay did not forbid citation. The creations of sculpture, painting, and music, are illustrations still more decisive.

* * *

A poem is the very image of life expressed in its eternal truth. There is this difference between a story and a poem, that a story is a catalogue of detached facts, which have no other bond of connexion than time, place, circumstance, cause and effect; the other is the creation of actions according to the unchangeable forms of human nature, as existing in the mind of the creator, which is itself the image of all other minds. The one is partial, and applies only to a definite period of time, and a certain combination of events which can never again recur; the other is universal, and contains within itself the germ of a relation to whatever motives or actions have place in the possible varieties of human nature. Time, which destroys the beauty and the use of the story of particular

8. The making of a dictionary.
9. Here Shelley enlarges the scope of the term "poetry" to denote all the creative achievements, or imaginative breakthroughs, of mankind, including noninstitutional religious insights.
1. Roman god of beginnings and endings, often

represented by two heads facing in opposite directions.
2. Sir Philip Sidney had pointed out, in his *Defence of Poesy*, that *vates*, the Roman term for poet, signifies "a diviner, fore-seer, or Prophet."

facts, stript of the poetry which should invest them, augments that of Poetry, and for ever develops new and wonderful applications of the eternal truth which it contains. Hence epitomes have been called the moths of just history;[3] they eat out the poetry of it. The story of particular facts is as a mirror which obscures and distorts that which should be beautiful: Poetry is a mirror which makes beautiful that which is distorted.

The parts of a composition may be poetical, without the composition as a whole being a poem. A single sentence may be considered as a whole though it be found in a series of unassimilated portions; a single word even may be a spark of inextinguishable thought. And thus all the great historians, Herodotus, Plutarch, Livy,[4] were poets; and although the plan of these writers, especially that of Livy, restrained them from developing this faculty in its highest degree, they make copious and ample amends for their subjection, by filling all the interstices of their subjects with living images.

Having determined what is poetry, and who are poets, let us proceed to estimate its effects upon society.

Poetry is ever accompanied with pleasure: all spirits on which it falls, open themselves to receive the wisdom which is mingled with its delight. In the infancy of the world, neither poets themselves nor their auditors are fully aware of the excellence of poetry: for it acts in a divine and unapprehended manner, beyond and above consciousness; and it is reserved for future generations to contemplate and measure the mighty cause and effect in all the strength and splendour of their union. Even in modern times, no living poet ever arrived at the fulness of his fame; the jury which sits in judgement upon a poet, belonging as he does to all time, must be composed of his peers: it must be impanelled by Time from the selectest of the wise of many generations. A Poet is a nightingale, who sits in darkness and sings to cheer its own solitude with sweet sounds; his auditors are as men entranced by the melody of an unseen musician, who feel that they are moved and softened, yet know not whence or why. The poems of Homer and his contemporaries were the delight of infant Greece; they were the elements of that social system which is the column upon which all succeeding civilization has reposed. Homer embodied the ideal perfection of his age in human character; nor can we doubt that those who read his verses were awakened to an ambition of becoming like to Achilles, Hector and Ulysses: the truth and beauty of friendship, patriotism and persevering devotion to an object, were unveiled to the depths in these immortal creations: the sentiments of the auditors must have been refined and enlarged by a sympathy with such great and lovely impersonations, until from admiring they imitated, and from imitation they identified themselves with the objects of

3. By Bacon in *The Advancement of Learning* 2.2.4. "Epitomes": abstracts, summaries.
4. Herodotus (ca. 480–ca. 425 B.C.) wrote the first systematic history of Greece; Plutarch (ca. 46–ca. 120 A.D.) wrote *Parallel Lives* of eminent Greeks and Romans; Titus Livius (59 B.C.–A.D. 17) wrote an immense history of Rome.

their admiration. Nor let it be objected, that these characters are remote from moral perfection, and that they can by no means be considered as edifying patterns for general imitation. Every epoch under names more or less specious has deified its peculiar errors; Revenge is the naked Idol of the worship of a semi-barbarous age; and Self-deceit is the veiled Image of unknown evil before which luxury and satiety lie prostrate. But a poet considers the vices of his contemporaries as the temporary dress in which his creations must be arrayed, and which cover without concealing the eternal proportions of their beauty. An epic or dramatic personage is understood to wear them around his soul, as he may the antient armour or the modern uniform around his body; whilst it is easy to conceive a dress more graceful than either. The beauty of the internal nature cannot be so far concealed by its accidental vesture, but that the spirit of its form shall communicate itself to the very disguise, and indicate the shape it hides from the manner in which it is worn. A majestic form and graceful motions will express themselves through the most barbarous and tasteless costume. Few poets of the highest class have chosen to exhibit the beauty of their conceptions in its naked truth and splendour; and it is doubtful whether the alloy of costume, habit, etc., be not necessary to temper this planetary music[5] for mortal ears.

The whole objection, however, of the immorality of poetry[6] rests upon a misconception of the manner in which poetry acts to produce the moral improvement of man. Ethical science[7] arranges the elements which poetry has created, and propounds schemes and proposes examples of civil and domestic life: nor is it for want of admirable doctrines that men hate, and despise, and censure, and deceive, and subjugate one another. But Poetry acts in another and diviner manner. It awakens and enlarges the mind itself by rendering it the receptacle of a thousand unapprehended combinations of thought. Poetry lifts the veil from the hidden beauty of the world, and makes familiar objects be as if they were not familiar; it reproduces[8] all that it represents, and the impersonations clothed in its Elysian light stand thenceforward in the minds of those who have once contemplated them, as memorials of that gentle and exalted content[9] which extends itself over all thoughts and actions with which it coexists. The great secret of morals is Love; or a going out of our own nature, and an identification of ourselves with the beautiful which exists in thought, action, or person, not our own. A man, to be greatly good, must imagine intensely and comprehensively; he must put himself in the place of another and of many others; the pains and pleasures of his species must become his own. The great instrument of moral good is the imagination;[1] and poetry administers to the effect by acting upon the cause.

5. The music made by the revolving crystalline spheres of the planets, inaudible to human ears.
6. In the preceding paragraph Shelley has been implicitly dealing with the charge, voiced by Plato in his *Republic*, that poetry is immoral because it represents evil characters acting evilly.
7. Moral philosophy.
8. Produces anew, recreates.

9. Contentment (pronounced con-tént).
1. Central to Shelley's theory is the concept (developed by 18th-century philosophers) of the sympathetic imagination—the faculty by which an individual is enabled to identify with the thoughts and feelings of others. Shelley claims that the faculty which in poetry enables us to share the joys and sufferings of invented characters is also the basis

Poetry enlarges the circumference of the imagination by replenishing it with thoughts of ever new delight, which have the power of attracting and assimilating to their own nature all other thoughts, and which form new intervals and interstices whose void for ever craves fresh food. Poetry strengthens that faculty which is the organ of the moral nature of man, in the same manner as exercise strengthens a limb. A Poet therefore would do ill to embody his own conceptions of right and wrong, which are usually those of his place and time, in his poetical creations, which participate in neither. By this assumption of the inferior office of interpreting the effect, in which perhaps after all he might acquit himself but imperfectly, he would resign the glory in a participation in the cause.[2] There was little danger that Homer, or any of the eternal Poets, should have so far misunderstood themselves as to have abdicated this throne of their widest dominion. Those in whom the poetical faculty, though great, is less intense, as Euripides, Lucan, Tasso, Spenser, have frequently affected[3] a moral aim, and the effect of their poetry is diminished in exact proportion to the degree in which they compel us to advert to this purpose.[4]

*   *   *

It is difficult to define pleasure in its highest sense; the definition involving a number of apparent paradoxes. For, from an inexplicable defect of harmony in the constitution of human nature, the pain of the inferior is frequently connected with the pleasures of the superior portions of our being. Sorrow, terror, anguish, despair itself are often the chosen expressions of an approximation to the highest good. Our sympathy in tragic fiction depends on this principle; tragedy delights by affording a shadow of the pleasure which exists in pain. This is the source also of the melancholy which is inseparable from the sweetest melody. The pleasure that is in sorrow is sweeter than the pleasure of pleasure itself. And hence the saying, "It is better to go to the house of mourning, than to the house of mirth."[5] Not that this highest species of pleasure is necessarily linked with pain. The delight of love and friendship, the ecstasy of the admiration of nature, the joy of the perception and still more of the creation of poetry is often wholly unalloyed.

The production and assurance of pleasure in this highest sense is true utility. Those who produce and preserve this pleasure are Poets or poetical philosophers.

of all morality, for it compels us to feel for others as we feel for ourselves.

2. The "effect," or the explicit moral standards into which imaginative insights are translated at a particular time or place, is contrasted to the "cause" of all morality, the imagination itself.

3. Euripides, Greek writer of tragedies, 5th century B.C.; Lucan, Roman poet, 1st century, author of the *Pharsalia*; Tasso, Italian poet of the 16th century, author of *Jerusalem Delivered*, an epic poem about a crusade. "Affected.": assumed,

adopted.

4. In the omitted passage Shelley reviews the history of drama and poetry in relation to civilization and morality, and proceeds to refute the charge that poets are less useful than "reasoners and merchants." He begins by defining utility in terms of pleasure, and then distinguishes between the lower (physical and material) and the higher (imaginative) pleasures.

5. Ecclesiastes 7.2.

The exertions of Locke, Hume, Gibbon, Voltaire, Rousseau,[6] and their disciples, in favour of oppressed and deluded humanity, are entitled to the gratitude of mankind. Yet it is easy to calculate the degree of moral and intellectual improvement which the world would have exhibited, had they never lived. A little more nonsense would have been talked for a century or two; and perhaps a few more men, women, and children, burnt as heretics. We might not at this moment have been congratulating each other on the abolition of the Inquisition in Spain.[7] But it exceeds all imagination to conceive what would have been the moral condition of the world if neither Dante, Petrarch, Boccaccio, Chaucer, Shakespeare, Calderon, Lord Bacon, nor Milton, had ever existed; if Raphael and Michael Angelo had never been born; if the Hebrew poetry had never been translated; if a revival of the study of Greek literature had never taken place; if no monuments of antient sculpture had been handed down to us; and if the poetry of the religion of the antient world had been extinguished together with its belief. The human mind could never, except by the intervention of these excitements, have been awakened to the invention of the grosser sciences, and that application of analytical reasoning to the aberrations of society, which it is now attempted to exalt over the direct expression of the inventive and creative faculty itself.

We have more moral, political and historical wisdom, than we know how to reduce into practice; we have more scientific and economical knowledge than can be accommodated to the just distribution of the produce which it multiplies. The poetry in these systems of thought, is concealed by the accumulation of facts and calculating processes. There is no want of knowledge respecting what is wisest and best in morals, government, and political economy, or at least, what is wiser and better than what men now practise and endure. But we let "*I dare not* wait upon *I would*, like the poor cat i' the adage."[8] We want the creative faculty to imagine that which we know; we want the generous impulse to act that which we imagine; we want the poetry of life: our calculations have outrun conception; we have eaten more than we can digest. The cultivation of those sciences which have enlarged the limits of the empire of man over the external world, has, for want of the poetical faculty, proportionally circumscribed those of the internal world; and man, having enslaved the elements, remains himself a slave. To what but a cultivation of the mechanical arts in a degree disproportioned to the presence of the creative faculty, which is the basis of all knowledge, is to be attributed the abuse of all invention for abridging and combining labour, to the exasperation of the inequality of mankind? From what other cause has it arisen that these inventions which should have lightened, have added a weight to the curse imposed on Adam? Poetry, and the principle of

6. In a note Shelley says that although Peacock had classified Rousseau with these other thinkers of the 17th and 18th centuries, "he was essentially a poet. The others, even Voltaire, were mere reasoners."

7. The Inquisition had been suspended in 1820, the year before Shelley wrote this essay; it was not abolished permanently until 1834.

8. *Macbeth* 1.7.44–45.

Self, of which money is the visible incarnation, are the God and Mammon of the world.[9]

The functions of the poetical faculty are two-fold; by one it creates new materials of knowledge, and power and pleasure; by the other it engenders in the mind a desire to reproduce and arrange them according to a certain rhythm and order which may be called the beautiful and the good. The cultivation of poetry is never more to be desired than at periods when, from an excess of the selfish and calculating principle, the accumulation of the materials of external life exceed the quantity of the power of assimilating them to the internal laws of human nature. The body has then become too unwieldy for that which animates it.

Poetry is indeed something divine. It is at once the centre and circumference of knowledge; it is that which comprehends all science, and that to which all science must be referred. It is at the same time the root and blossom of all other systems of thought; it is that from which all spring, and that which adorns all; and that which, if blighted, denies the fruit and the seed, and withholds from the barren world the nourishment and the succession of the scions of the tree of life. It is the perfect and consummate surface and bloom of things; it is as the odour and the colour of the rose to the texture of the elements which compose it, as the form and the splendour of unfaded beauty to the secrets of anatomy and corruption. What were Virtue, Love, Patriotism, Friendship etc.—what were the scenery of this beautiful Universe which we inhabit—what were our consolations on this side of the grave—and what were our aspirations beyond it—if Poetry did not ascend to bring light and fire from those eternal regions where the owl-winged faculty of calculation dare not ever soar? Poetry is not like reasoning, a power to be exerted according to the determination of the will. A man cannot say, "I will compose poetry." The greatest poet even cannot say it: for the mind in creation is as a fading coal which some invisible influence, like an inconstant wind, awakens to transitory brightness: this power arises from within, like the colour of a flower which fades and changes as it is developed, and the conscious portions of our natures are unprophetic either of its approach or its departure.[1] Could this influence be durable in its original purity and force, it is impossible to predict the greatness of the results; but when composition begins, inspiration is already on the decline, and the most glorious poetry that has ever been communicated to the world is probably a feeble shadow of the original conception of the poet. I appeal to the greatest Poets of the present day, whether it be not an error to assert that the finest passages of poetry are produced by labour and study. The toil and the delay recommended by critics can be justly interpreted to mean no more than a careful observation of the inspired moments, and an artificial connexion of the spaces between their suggestions by the

9. "Ye cannot serve God and Mammon" (Matthew 6.24).
1. This passage reiterates the ancient belief that the highest poetry is "inspired," and therefore occurs independently of the intention, effort, or consciousness of the poet. Unlike earlier critics, however, Shelley attributes such poetry not to a god or muse but to the unconscious depths of the poet's own mind.

intertexture of conventional expressions; a necessity only imposed by the limitedness of the poetical faculty itself. For Milton conceived the Paradise Lost as a whole before he executed it in portions. We have his own authority also for the Muse having "dictated" to him the "unpremeditated song,"[2] and let this be an answer to those who would allege the fifty-six various readings of the first line of the Orlando Furioso.[3] Compositions so produced are to poetry what mosaic is to painting. This instinct and intuition of the poetical faculty is still more observable in the plastic and pictorial arts: a great statue or picture grows under the power of the artist as a child in the mother's womb; and the very mind which directs the hands in formation is incapable of accounting to itself for the origin, the gradations, or the media of the process.

Poetry is the record of the best and happiest[4] moments of the happiest and best minds. We are aware of evanescent visitations of thought and feeling sometimes associated with place or person, sometimes regarding our own mind alone, and always arising unforeseen and departing unbidden, but elevating and delightful beyond all expression: so that even in the desire and the regret they leave, there cannot but be pleasure, participating as it does in the nature of its object. It is as it were the interpenetration of a diviner nature through our own; but its footsteps are like those of a wind over a sea, where the coming calm erases, and whose traces remain only as on the wrinkled sand which paves it. These and corresponding conditions of being are experienced principally by those of the most delicate sensibility and the most enlarged imagination; and the state of mind produced by them is at war with every base desire. The enthusiasm of virtue, love, patriotism, and friendship is essentially linked with these emotions; and whilst they last, self appears as what it is, an atom to a Universe. Poets are not only subject to these experiences as spirits of the most refined organization, but they can colour all that they combine with the evanescent hues of this etherial world; a word, or a trait in the representation of a scene or a passion, will touch the enchanted chord, and reanimate, in those who have ever experienced these emotions, the sleeping, the cold, the buried image of the past. Poetry thus makes immortal all that is best and most beautiful in the world; it arrests the vanishing apparitions which haunt the interlunations[5] of life, and veiling them or in language or in form sends them forth among mankind, bearing sweet news of kindred joy to those with whom their sisters abide—abide, because there is no portal of expression from the caverns of the spirit which they inhabit into the universe of things. Poetry redeems from decay the visitations of the divinity in man.

Poetry turns all things to loveliness; it exalts the beauty of that which is most beautiful, and it adds beauty to that which is most deformed; it marries exultation and horror, grief and pleasure, eternity and change;

2. *Paradise Lost* 9:21–24.
3. The epic poem by the 16th-century Italian poet Ariosto, noted for his care in composition.
4. In the double sense of "most joyous" and "most

apt or felicitous in invention."
5. The dark intervals between the old and new moons.

it subdues to union under its light yoke all irreconcilable things. It transmutes all that it touches, and every form moving within the radiance of its presence is changed by wondrous sympathy to an incarnation of the spirit which it breathes; its secret alchemy turns to potable gold[6] the poisonous waters which flow from death through life; it strips the veil of familiarity from the world, and lays bare the naked and sleeping beauty which is the spirit of its forms.

All things exist as they are perceived: at least in relation to the percipient. "The mind is its own place, and of itself can make a heaven of hell, a hell of heaven."[7] But poetry defeats the curse which binds us to be subjected to the accident of surrounding impressions. And whether it spreads its own figured curtain or withdraws life's dark veil from before the scene of things, it equally creates for us a being within our being. It makes us the inhabitants of a world to which the familiar world is a chaos. It reproduces the common universe of which we are portions and percipients, and it purges from our inward sight the film of familiarity which obscures from us the wonder of our being. It compels us to feel that which we perceive, and to imagine that which we know. It creates anew the universe after it has been annihilated in our minds by the recurrence of impressions blunted by reiteration.[8] It justifies that bold and true word of Tasso: *Non merita nome di creatore, se non Iddio ed il Poeta.*[9]

A Poet, as he is the author to others of the highest wisdom, pleasure, virtue and glory, so he ought personally to be the happiest, the best, the wisest, and the most illustrious of men. As to his glory, let Time be challenged to declare whether the fame of any other institutor of human life be comparable to that of a poet. That he is the wisest, the happiest, and the best, inasmuch as he is a poet, is equally incontrovertible: the greatest poets have been men of the most spotless virtue, of the most consummate prudence, and, if we could look into the interior of their lives, the most fortunate of men: and the exceptions, as they regard those who possessed the poetic faculty in a high yet inferior degree, will be found on consideration to confirm rather than destroy the rule. Let us for a moment stoop to the arbitration of popular breath, and usurping and uniting in our own persons the incompatible characters of accuser, witness, judge and executioner, let us decide without trial, testimony, or form that certain motives of those who are "there sitting where we dare not soar"[1] are reprehensible. Let us assume that Homer was a drunkard, that Virgil was a flatterer, that Horace was a coward, that Tasso was a madman, that Lord Bacon was a peculator, that Raphael was a libertine, that Spenser was a poet laureate.[2] It is inconsistent with this

6. Alchemists aimed to produce a drinkable form of gold that would be an elixir of life, curing all diseases.
7. Satan's speech, *Paradise Lost* 1.254–55.
8. Shelley's version of a widespread Romantic doctrine that the poetic imagination transforms the familiar into the miraculous and recreates the old world into a new world. See, e.g., Coleridge's *Bio*

graphia Literaria, above, chap. 4, on "freshness of sensation."
9. "No one merits the name of Creator except God and the Poet." Quoted by Pierantonio Serassi in his *Life of Torquato Tasso* (1785).
1. *Paradise Lost* 4.829.
2. Charges, some of them valid, which had in fact been made against these men. "Peculator": a mis

division of our subject to cite living poets, but Posterity has done ample justice to the great names now referred to. Their errors have been weighed and found to have been dust in the balance; if their sins "were as scarlet, they are now white as snow";[3] they have been washed in the blood of the mediator and the redeemer Time. Observe in what a ludicrous chaos the imputations of real or fictitious crime have been confused in the contemporary calumnies against poetry and poets;[4] consider how little is, as it appears—or appears, as it is; look to your own motives, and judge not, lest ye be judged.

Poetry, as has been said, in this respect differs from logic, that it is not subject to the controul of the active powers of the mind, and that its birth and recurrence has no necessary connexion with consciousness or will. It is presumptuous to determine that these[5] are the necessary conditions of all mental causation, when mental effects are experienced insusceptible of being referred to them. The frequent recurrence of the poetical power, it is obvious to suppose, may produce in the mind an habit of order and harmony correlative with its own nature and with its effects upon other minds. But in the intervals of inspiration, and they may be frequent without being durable, a poet becomes a man, and is abandoned to the sudden reflux of the influences under which others habitually live. But as he is more delicately organized than other men, and sensible to pain and pleasure, both his own and that of others, in a degree unknown to them, he will avoid the one and pursue the other with an ardour proportioned to this difference. And he renders himself obnoxious to calumny,[6] when he neglects to observe the circumstances under which these objects of universal pursuit and flight have disguised themselves in one another's garments.

But there is nothing necessarily evil in this error, and thus cruelty, envy, revenge, avarice, and the passions purely evil, have never formed any portion of the popular imputations on the lives of poets.

I have thought it most favourable to the cause of truth to set down these remarks according to the order in which they were suggested to my mind, by a consideration of the subject itself, instead of following that of the treatise that excited me to make them public.[7] Thus although devoid of the formality of a polemical reply; if the view they contain be just, they will be found to involve a refutation of the doctrines of the Four Ages of Poetry, so far at least as regards the first division of the subject. I can readily conjecture what should have moved the gall of the learned and intelligent author of that paper; I confess myself, like him, unwilling to be stunned by the Theseids of the hoarse Codri of the day. Bavius and Mævius[8] undoubtedly are, as they ever were, insufferable

---

appropriator of public money. Raphael is the 16th-century Italian painter. The use of "poet laureate" as a derogatory term was a dig at Robert Southey, who held that honor at the time of Shelley's writing.

3. Isaiah 1.18.

4. Shelley alludes especially to the charges of immorality by contemporary reviewers against Lord Byron and himself.

5. I.e., consciousness or will. Shelley again proposes that some mental processes are unconscious—outside our control or awareness.

6. Exposed to slander.

7. Peacock's Four Ages of Poetry.

8. Would-be poets satirized by Virgil and Horace. "Theseids": epic poems about Theseus. Codrus

persons. But it belongs to a philosophical critic to distinguish rather than confound.

The first part of these remarks has related to Poetry in its elements and principles; and it has been shewn, as well as the narrow limits assigned them would permit, that what is called poetry, in a restricted sense, has a common source with all other forms of order and of beauty according to which the materials of human life are susceptible of being arranged, and which is poetry in an universal sense.

The second part[9] will have for its object an application of these principles to the present state of the cultivation of Poetry, and a defence of the attempt to idealize the modern forms of manners and opinions, and compel them into a subordination to the imaginative and creative faculty. For the literature of England, an energetic developement of which has ever preceded or accompanied a great and free developement of the national will, has arisen as it were from a new birth. In spite of the low-thoughted envy which would undervalue contemporary merit, our own will be a memorable age in intellectual achievements, and we live among such philosophers and poets as surpass beyond comparison any who have appeared since the last national struggle for civil and religious liberty.[1] The most unfailing herald, companion, and follower of the awakening of a great people to work a beneficial change in opinion or institution, is Poetry. At such periods there is an accumulation of the power of communicating and receiving intense and impassioned conceptions respecting man and nature. The persons in whom this power resides, may often, as far as regards many portions of their nature, have little apparent correspondence with that spirit of good of which they are the ministers. But even whilst they deny and abjure, they are yet compelled to serve, the Power which is seated upon the throne of their own soul. It is impossible to read the compositions of the most celebrated writers of the present day without being startled with the electric life which burns within their words. They measure the circumference and sound the depths of human nature with a comprehensive and all-penetrating spirit, and they are themselves perhaps the most sincerely astonished at its manifestations, for it is less their spirit than the spirit of the age.[2] Poets are the hierophants[3] of an unapprehended inspiration, the mirrors of the gigantic shadows which futurity casts upon the present, the words which express what they understand not; the trumpets which sing to battle, and feel not what they inspire: the influence which is moved not, but moves.[4] Poets are the unacknowledged legislators of the World.

1821   1840

(plural "Codri") was the Roman author of a long, dull *Theseid* attacked by Juvenal and others.

9. Shelley, however, completed only the first part of his *Defence*.

1. In the age of Milton and the English Civil War.

2. By "the spirit of the age" Shelley identifies what was later to be called "the Romantic movement" in contemporary literature and philosophy; he recognized its greatness, as well as its relation to the ferment of ideas and aspirations effected by the French Revolution.

3. Priests who are expositors of sacred mysteries.

4. Aristotle had said that God is the "Unmoved Mover" of the universe.

JOHN KEATS
1795–1821

1817: *Poems*, Keats's first book.

1818: *Endymion*.

1819: Keats's *annus mirabilis*, in which he writes almost all his greatest poems.

1820: Publishes the volume *Lamia, Isabella, The Eve of St. Agnes, and Other Poems*.

No major poet has had a less propitious origin. Keats's father was head stableman at a London livery stable; he married his employer's daughter and inherited the business. Mrs. Keats, by all reports, was a strongly sensuous woman, and a rather casual but affectionate mother to her five children— John (the first-born), his three brothers (one of whom died in infancy), and a sister. Keats was sent to the Reverend John Clarke's private school at Enfield, where he was a noisy, high-spirited boy; despite his small stature (when full-grown, he was barely over five feet in height), he distinguished himself in skylarking and fistfights. Here he had the good fortune to have as a teacher Charles Cowden Clarke, son of the headmaster, who later became himself a man of letters; he encouraged Keats's passion for reading and, both at school and in the course of their later friendship, introduced him to Spenser and other poets, to music, and to the theater.

When Keats was eight his father was killed by a fall from a horse, and when he was fourteen, his mother died of tuberculosis. Although the livery stable had prospered, and £8,000 had been left in trust to the children by Keats's grandmother, the estate remained tied up in the law courts for all of Keats's lifetime. The children's guardian, Richard Abbey, was an unimaginative and practical-minded businessman; he took Keats out of school at the age of fifteen and bound him apprentice to Thomas Hammond, a surgeon and apothecary at Edmonton. In 1815 Keats carried on his medical studies at Guy's Hospital, London, and the next year qualified to practice as an apothecary-surgeon—but almost immediately, over his guardian's protests, he abandoned medicine for poetry.

This decision was influenced by Keats's friendship with Leigh Hunt, then editor of the *Examiner* and a leading political radical, poet, and prolific writer of criticism and periodical essays. Hunt, the first successful author of Keats's acquaintance, added his enthusiastic encouragement of Keats's poetic efforts to that of Clarke. More important, he introduced him to writers greater than Hunt himself, Hazlitt, Lamb, and Shelley, as well as to Benjamin Robert Haydon, painter of grandiose historical and religious canvases. Through Hunt Keats also met John Hamilton Reynolds, and then Charles Wentworth Dilke and Charles Brown, men who became his intimate friends and provided him with an essential circumstance for a fledgling poet, a sympathetic and appreciative audience.

The rapidity and sureness of Keats's development has no match. He did not even undertake poetry until his eighteenth year, and for the next few years produced album verse which was at best merely competent and at times manifested an arch sentimentality. Suddenly, in 1816, he spoke out loud and bold in *On First Looking into Chapman's Homer*, a major sonnet in the grand style. Later that same year he wrote *Sleep and Poetry*, in which he laid out for himself a poetic program deliberately modeled on the careers of the greatest poets, asking only

> for ten years, that I may overwhelm
> Myself in poesy; so I may do the deed
> That my own soul has to itself decreed.

For even while his health was good, Keats felt a foreboding of early death and applied himself to his art with a desperate urgency. In 1817 he went on to compose *Endymion*, an ambitious undertaking of more than 4,000 lines. It is a profuse and often obscure allegory of the poet's quest for an ideal feminine counterpart and a flawless happiness beyond earthly possibility; in a number of passages, however, it already exhibits the sure movement and phrasing of his mature poetic style. But Keats's critical judgment and aspiration exceeded his achievement: long before he completed it, he declared impatiently that he carried on with the "slipshod" *Endymion* only as a poetic exercise and "trial of invention" and began to block out the more ambitious *Hyperion*, conceived on the model of Milton's *Paradise Lost* in that most demanding of forms, the epic poem. The extent of his success in achieving the Miltonic manner is one of the reasons why Keats left off before *Hyperion* was finished, for he recognized that he was uncommonly susceptible to poetic influences, and regarded this as a threat to his individuality. "I will write independently," he insisted. "The Genius of Poetry must work out its own salvation in a man." He had refused the chance of intimacy with Shelley "that I might have my own unfettered scope"; he had broken away from Leigh Hunt's influence lest he get "the reputation of Hunt's *élève* [pupil]"; now he shied away from domination by Milton's distinctive and powerfully infectious style.

With the year 1818 began a series of disappointments and disasters which culminated in Keats's mortal illness. Sentimental legend used to fix the blame upon two anonymous articles: a scurrilous attack on Keats as a member of the "Cockney School" (that is, Leigh Hunt's radical literary circle in London) which appeared in the heavily Tory *Blackwood's Magazine*, and a savage mauling of *Endymion* in the *Quarterly Review*. Shelley gave impetus to this myth by his description of Keats in *Adonais* as "a pale flower," and Byron, who knew even less about him, asserted that he was "snuffed out by an article." But in fact, Keats had the good sense to recognize that the attacks were motivated by Tory bias and class snobbery, and he had already passed his own severe judgment on *Endymion*: "My own domestic criticism," he said, "has given me pain without comparison beyond what *Blackwood* or the *Quarterly* could possibly inflict." More important was the financial distress of his brother George and his young bride, who had just emigrated to Kentucky and lost their money in an ill-advised investment; Keats, himself always short of funds, had now to turn to literary journeywork to eke out the family income. His younger brother Tom contracted tuberculosis, and the poet, in devoted attendance upon him through the later months of 1818, helplessly watched him waste away until his death that December. In the summer of that year Keats had taken a strenuous walking tour in the English Lake Country, Scotland, and Ireland; it was a glorious adventure, but a totally exhausting one in wet, cold weather, and he returned in August with a chronically ulcerated throat made increasingly ominous by the shadow of the tuberculosis which had killed his mother and brother. And in the late fall of 1818 Keats fell unwillingly, helplessly in love with Fanny Brawne. This pretty, vivacious, and mildly flirtatious girl of eighteen had little interest in poetry, but she possessed an alert and sensible mind, loved Keats sincerely, and might well have made him an excellent wife. They became engaged, but Keats's dedication to poetry, his poverty, and his growing illness made marriage impossible and love a torment.

In this period of acute distress and emotional turmoil, within five years of his first trying his hand at poetry, Keats achieved the culmination of his brief poetic career. Between January and September of 1819, masterpiece followed masterpiece in astonishing succession: *The Eve of St. Agnes, La Belle Dame sans Merci,* all of the "great odes," *Lamia,* and a sufficient number of fine sonnets to make him, with Wordsworth, the major Romantic craftsman in that form. All of these poems possess the distinctive qualities of the work of his maturity: a slow-paced, gracious movement; a concreteness of description in which all the senses—tactile, gustatory, kinetic, organic, as well as visual and auditory—combine to give the total apprehension of an experience; an intense delight at the sheer existence of things outside himself, the poet seeming to lose his own identity in the fullness of identification with the object he contemplates; and a concentrated felicity of phrasing which reminded his friends, as it has many critics since, of the language of Shakespeare. And under the richly sensuous surface we find Keats's characteristic presentation of all experience as a tangle of inseparable but irreconcilable opposites. He finds melancholy in delight, and pleasure in pain; he feels the highest intensity of love as an approximation to death; he inclines equally toward a life of indolence and "sensation" and toward a life of thought; he is aware both of the attraction of an imaginative dream world without "disagreeables" and the remorseless pressure of the actual; he aspires at the same time for aesthetic detachment and for social responsibility.

His letters, no less remarkable than his poetry, show that Keats felt on his pulses the conflicts he dramatized in his major poems. Above all, they reveal him wrestling with the problem of evil and suffering—what to make of our lives in the discovery that "the world is full of misery and heartbreak, pain, sickness and oppression." To the end of his life, with stubborn courage, he refused to seek comfort by substituting for the complexity and contradictions of experience either the simplicity of inherited philosophical doctrines or the absolutes of a religious creed. At the close of his poetic career, in the latter part of 1819, Keats began to rework the epic *Hyperion* into the form of a dream vision which he called *The Fall of Hyperion.* In the introductory section of this fragment the poet is told by the prophetess Moneta that he has hitherto been merely a dreamer; he must know that

> The poet and the dreamer are distinct,
> Diverse, sheer opposite, antipodes,

and that the height of poetry can be reached only by

> those to whom the miseries of the world
> Are misery, and will not let them rest.

He was seemingly planning to undertake a new direction and subject matter, when death intervened.

On the night of February 3, 1820, he coughed up some blood. He refused to evade the truth: "I cannot be deceived in that colour; that drop of blood is my death warrant. I must die." That spring and summer a series of hemorrhages rapidly weakened him. In the autumn he allowed himself to be persuaded to seek the milder climate of Italy in the company of Joseph Severn, a young painter; but these last months were only what he called "a posthumous existence." He died in Rome on February 23, 1821, and was buried in the Protestant Cemetery. At times the agony of his disease, the apparent frustration of his hopes for great poetic achievement, and the despair of his passion for Fanny Brawne combined to compel even Keats's brave spirit to bitterness, resentment, and jealousy, but he always recovered his gallantry. His last letter, written to Charles Brown, concludes: "I can scarcely bid you good bye even in a letter. I always made an awkward bow. God bless you! John Keats."

No one can read Keats's poems and letters without an undersense of the tragic waste of so extraordinary an intellect and genius cut off so early. What he might have accomplished is beyond conjecture; what we do know is that his achievement, when he stopped writing at the age of twenty-four, greatly exceeds that at the same age of Chaucer, Shakespeare, or Milton.

The texts of the poems were prepared by Jack Stillinger for his edition of *The Poems of John Keats* (Cambridge, Mass., 1978).

On First Looking into Chapman's Homer[1]

> Much have I travell'd in the realms of gold,
>   And many goodly states and kingdoms seen;
>   Round many western islands have I been
> Which bards in fealty to Apollo hold.
> Oft of one wide expanse had I been told   5
>   That deep-brow'd Homer ruled as his demesne;[2]
>   Yet did I never breathe its pure serene[3]
> Till I heard Chapman speak out loud and bold:
> Then felt I like some watcher of the skies
>   When a new planet swims into his ken;   10
> Or like stout Cortez when with eagle eyes
>   He star'd at the Pacific—and all his men
> Look'd at each other with a wild surmise—
>   Silent, upon a peak in Darien.

October 1816   1816

---

1. Keats's former schoolteacher, Charles Cowden Clarke, introduced him to Homer in the robust translation of the Elizabethan poet George Chapman. They read through the night, and Keats walked home at dawn; this sonnet, his first great poem, reached Clarke by the ten o'clock mail that same morning. That it was Balboa, not Cortez, who caught his first sight of the Pacific from the heights of Darien, in Panama, matters to history but not to poetry.

2. Realm, feudal possession.

3. Clear expanse of air.

From Sleep and Poetry[1]

["*O for Ten Years*"]

O for ten years, that I may overwhelm
Myself in poesy; so I may do the deed
That my own soul has to itself decreed.
Then will I pass the countries that I see
In long perspective, and continually   100
Taste their pure fountains. First the realm I'll pass
Of Flora, and old Pan:[2] sleep in the grass,
Feed upon apples red, and strawberries,
And choose each pleasure that my fancy sees;
Catch the white-handed nymphs in shady places,   105
To woo sweet kisses from averted faces,—
Play with their fingers, touch their shoulders white
Into a pretty shrinking with a bite
As hard as lips can make it: till agreed,
A lovely tale of human life we'll read.   110
And one will teach a tame dove how it best
May fan the cool air gently o'er my rest;
Another, bending o'er her nimble tread,
Will set a green robe floating round her head,
And still will dance with ever varied ease,   115
Smiling upon the flowers and the trees:
Another will entice me on, and on
Through almond blossoms and rich cinnamon;
Till in the bosom of a leafy world
We rest in silence, like two gems upcurl'd   120
In the recesses of a pearly shell.

    And can I ever bid these joys farewell?
Yes, I must pass them for a nobler life,
Where I may find the agonies, the strife
Of human hearts: for lo! I see afar,   125
O'er sailing the blue cragginess, a car[3]
And steeds with streamy manes—the charioteer

---

1. At the early age of 21, Keats set himself a rigorous regimen of poetic training modeled on the course followed by the greatest poets. Virgil had established the pattern of beginning with pastoral writing and proceeding gradually to the point at which he was ready to undertake the epic, and this pattern had been deliberately followed by Spenser and Milton. Keats's version of this program, as he describes it here, is to begin with the realm of "Flora, and old Pan" (line 102) and, within ten years, to climb up to the level of poetry dealing with "the agonies, the strife / Of human hearts" (lines 124–25). The latter achievement Keats found best represented among his contemporaries by

Wordsworth and, less successfully, by Shelley; Keats's vision of the chariot of poesy (lines 125–154) echoes Shelley's allegorical visions. The program Keats set himself is illuminated by his analysis of Wordsworth's progress in his letter to J. H. Reynolds of May 3, 1818, below.
2. I.e., the carefree pastoral world. Flora was the Roman goddess of flowers, and Pan the Greek god of pastures, woods, and animal life.
3. This chariot, with its "charioteer" (line 127), represents the higher poetic imagination, which bodies forth the matters "of delight, of mystery, and fear" (line 138) that characterize the grander poetic forms.

Looks out upon the winds with glorious fear:
And now the numerous tramplings quiver lightly
Along a huge cloud's ridge; and now with sprightly   130
Wheel downward come they into fresher skies,
Tipt round with silver from the sun's bright eyes.
Still downward with capacious whirl they glide;
And now I see them on a green-hill's side
In breezy rest among the nodding stalks.   135
The charioteer with wond'rous gesture talks
To the trees and mountains; and there soon appear
Shapes of delight, of mystery, and fear,
Passing along before a dusky space
Made by some mighty oaks: as they would chase   140
Some ever-fleeting music on they sweep.
Lo! how they murmur, laugh, and smile, and weep:
Some with upholden hand and mouth severe;
Some with their faces muffled to the ear
Between their arms; some, clear in youthful bloom,   145
Go glad and smilingly athwart the gloom;
Some looking back, and some with upward gaze;
Yes, thousands in a thousand different ways
Flit onward—now a lovely wreath of girls
Dancing their sleek hair into tangled curls;   150
And now broad wings. Most awfully intent,
The driver of those steeds is forward bent,
And seems to listen: O that I might know
All that he writes with such a hurrying glow.

    The visions all are fled—the car is fled   155
Into the light of heaven, and in their stead
A sense of real things comes doubly strong,
And, like a muddy stream, would bear along
My soul to nothingness: but I will strive
Against all doubtings, and will keep alive   160
The thought of that same chariot, and the strange
Journey it went.

                    *   *   *

October–December 1816   1817

On Seeing the Elgin Marbles[1]

My spirit is too weak—mortality
    Weighs heavily on me like unwilling sleep,

1. Lord Elgin had brought to England in 1806 the marble statues and friezes which adorned the Parthenon at Athens; in 1816 they were purchased by the government for the British Museum. Keats's response to his first sight of these time-worn memorials of Grecian artistry is characteristically intense, mixed, and subtly analyzed.

And each imagined pinnacle and steep
Of godlike hardship tells me I must die
Like a sick eagle looking at the sky.   5
Yet 'tis a gentle luxury to weep
That I have not the cloudy winds to keep
Fresh for the opening of the morning's eye.
Such dim-conceived glories of the brain
    Bring round the heart an undescribable feud;   10
So do these wonders a most dizzy pain,
    That mingles Grecian grandeur with the rude
Wasting of old time—with a billowy main—
A sun—a shadow of a magnitude.

Mar. 1 or 2, 1817   1817

From Endymion: A Poetic Romance[1]

"The stretched metre of an antique song"

INSCRIBED TO THE MEMORY OF THOMAS CHATTERTON

Preface

Knowing within myself the manner in which this Poem has been produced, it is not without a feeling of regret that I make it public.

What manner I mean, will be quite clear to the reader, who must soon perceive great inexperience, immaturity, and every error denoting a feverish attempt, rather than a deed accomplished. The two first books, and indeed the two last, I feel sensible are not of such completion as to warrant their passing the press; nor should they if I thought a year's castigation would do them any good;—it will not: the foundations are too sandy. It is just that this youngster should die away: a sad thought

---

1. This poem of more than 4,000 lines (based on the classical myth of a mortal beloved by the goddess of the moon) tells of Endymion's long and agonized search for an immortal goddess whom he had seen in several visions. In the course of his wanderings he comes upon an Indian maid who had been abandoned by the followers of Bacchus, and to his utter despair succumbs to a sensual passion for her, in apparent betrayal of his love for his heavenly ideal. In the resolution, the Indian maid reveals that she is herself Cynthia (Diana), goddess of the moon, the celestial subject of his earlier visions.

Keats set himself to writing a long poem before he was entirely ready in range of knowledge, clarity of thought, or stylistic assurance; the poem reaches a high level only in isolated passages. The interpretation that seems best to fit the text is that ideal love and imaginative beauty are to be found only by way of instinctual impulses and earthly sexuality, which the ideal repeats, in one of Keats's phrases, "in a finer tone." The poem is so cloudy, however, that its purport is disputed. But Keats has disarmed all external criticism by his self-criticism in the candid and insightful Preface, which has become a classic statement of the characteristics of unripe genius.

The verse epigraph is adapted from Shakespeare's Sonnet 17, line 12: "And stretchèd meter of an antique song." Thomas Chatterton (1752–70), to whom *Endymion* is inscribed, wrote a number of brilliant pseudo-archaic poems which he attributed to an imaginary 15th-century poet, Thomas Rowley. Reduced to despair by neglect and poverty, Chatterton poisoned himself with arsenic when he was only 17. He came to be greatly admired in the Romantic period. Wordsworth, in *Resolution and Independence*, lines 43–44, called him "the marvelous Boy, / the sleepless Soul that perished in his pride," and Keats described him as "the most English of poets except Shakespeare."

for me, if I had not some hope that while it is dwindling I may be plotting, and fitting myself for verses fit to live.

This may be speaking too presumptuously, and may deserve a punishment: but no feeling man will be forward to inflict it: he will leave me alone, with the conviction that there is not a fiercer hell than the failure in a great object. This is not written with the least atom of purpose to forestall criticisms of course, but from the desire I have to conciliate men who are competent to look, and who do look with a zealous eye, to the honour of English literature.

The imagination of a boy is healthy, and the mature imagination of a man is healthy; but there is a space of life between, in which the soul is in a ferment, the character undecided, the way of life uncertain, the ambition thick-sighted: thence proceeds mawkishness, and all the thousand bitters which those men I speak of must necessarily taste in going over the following pages.

I hope I have not in too late a day touched the beautiful mythology of Greece, and dulled its brightness: for I wish to try once more,[2] before I bid it farewel.

Teignmouth, April 10, 1818

From *Book* 1

[A THING OF BEAUTY]

A thing of beauty is a joy for ever:
Its loveliness increases; it will never
Pass into nothingness; but still will keep
A bower quiet for us, and a sleep
Full of sweet dreams, and health, and quiet breathing.   5
Therefore, on every morrow, are we wreathing
A flowery band to bind us to the earth,
Spite of despondence, of the inhuman dearth
Of noble natures, of the gloomy days,
Of all the unhealthy and o'er-darkened ways   10
Made for our searching: yes, in spite of all,
Some shape of beauty moves away the pall
From our dark spirits. Such the sun, the moon,
Trees old, and young sprouting a shady boon
For simple sheep; and such are daffodils   15
With the green world they live in; and clear rills
That for themselves a cooling covert make
'Gainst the hot season; the mid forest brake,[3]
Rich with a sprinkling of fair musk-rose blooms:
And such too is the grandeur of the dooms[4]   20
We have imagined for the mighty dead;
All lovely tales that we have heard or read:

2. In *Hyperion*, which Keats was already planning.

3. Thicket.
4. Judgments.

An endless fountain of immortal drink,
Pouring unto us from the heaven's brink. [5]

Nor do we merely feel these essences   25
For one short hour; no, even as the trees
That whisper round a temple become soon
Dear as the temple's self, so does the moon,
The passion poesy, glories infinite,
Haunt us till they become a cheering light   30
Unto our souls, and bound to us so fast,
That, whether there be shine, or gloom o'ercast,
They alway must be with us, or we die.

Therefore, 'tis with full happiness that I
Will trace the story of Endymion.   35
The very music of the name has gone
Into my being, and each pleasant scene
Is growing fresh before me as the green
Of our own vallies. * * *

[THE "PLEASURE THERMOMETER"]

"Peona![6] ever have I long'd to slake
    My thirst for the world's praises: nothing base,   770
No merely slumberous phantasm, could unlace
The stubborn canvas for my voyage prepar'd—
Though now 'tis tatter'd; leaving my bark bar'd
And sullenly drifting: yet my higher hope
Is of too wide, too rainbow-large a scope,   775
To fret at myriads of earthly wrecks.
Wherein lies happiness? In that which becks
Our ready minds to fellowship divine,
A fellowship with essence; till we shine,
Full alchemiz'd,[7] and free of space. Behold   780

---

5. The poet sets up, and searches to resolve, the basic opposition between the inevitably "mortal" pleasures in this life and the conceived possibility of "immortal" delight. Thus "essences" (line 25) seem to be the things of beauty in this world, purged of the mutability that is inescapable in ordinary experience. The central passage dealing with this theme is below, book 1, lines 777 ff.
6. The sister to whom Endymion confides his troubles. Of lines 769–857, Keats wrote to his publisher, John Taylor: "When I wrote it, it was the regular stepping of the Imagination towards a Truth. My having written that Argument will perhaps be of the greatest Service to me of anything I ever did—It set before me at once the gradations of Happiness even like a kind of Pleasure Thermometer, and is my first step towards the chief attempt in the Drama—the playing of different Natures with Joy and Sorrow." The gradations on

this "Pleasure Thermometer" mark the stages on the way to what Keats calls "happiness" (line 777)—his secular version of the religious concept of "felicity" which, in the orthodox view, is to be achieved by a surrender of oneself to God. For Keats the way to happiness lies through a fusion of ourselves, first sensuously, with the lovely objects of nature and art (lines 781–97), then on a higher level, with other human beings through "love and friendship" (line 801) and, ultimately, sexual love. By this "self-destroying," or loss of personal identity through our imaginative identification with a beloved person outside ourselves, we escape from the material limits and the self-centered condition of ordinary experience, to achieve a "fellowship with essence," which is a kind of immortality within our mortal existence (line 844).
7. Transformed by alchemy from a base to a precious metal.

The clear religion of heaven! Fold
A rose leaf round thy finger's taperness,
And soothe thy lips: hist, when the airy stress
Of music's kiss impregnates the free winds,
And with a sympathetic touch unbinds   785
Eolian[8] magic from their lucid wombs:
Then old songs waken from enclouded tombs;
Old ditties sigh above their father's grave;
Ghosts of melodious prophecyings rave
Round every spot where trod Apollo's foot;   790
Bronze clarions awake, and faintly bruit,[9]
Where long ago a giant battle was;
And, from the turf, a lullaby doth pass
In every place where infant Orpheus slept.
Feel we these things?—that moment have we stept   795
Into a sort of oneness, and our state
Is like a floating spirit's. But there are
Richer entanglements, enthralments far
More self-destroying, leading, by degrees,
To the chief intensity: the crown of these   800
Is made of love and friendship, and sits high
Upon the forehead of humanity.
All its more ponderous and bulky worth
Is friendship, whence there ever issues forth
A steady splendour; but at the tip-top   805
There hangs by unseen film, an orbed drop
Of light, and that is love: its influence,
Thrown in our eyes, genders a novel sense,
At which we start and fret; till in the end,
Melting into its radiance, we blend,   810
Mingle, and so become a part of it,—
Nor with aught else can our souls interknit
So wingedly: when we combine therewith,
Life's self is nourish'd by its proper pith,[1]
And we are nurtured like a pelican brood.[2]   815
Aye, so delicious is the unsating food,
That men, who might have tower'd in the van
Of all the congregated world, to fan
And winnow from the coming step of time
All chaff of custom, wipe away all slime   820
Left by men-slugs and human serpentry,
Have been content to let occasion die,
Whilst they did sleep in love's elysium.
And, truly, I would rather be struck dumb,
Than speak against this ardent listlessness: 825
For I have ever thought that it might bless

---

8. From Aeolus, god of winds.
9. Make a sound.
1. Its own elemental substance.

2. Young pelicans were once thought to feed on their mother's flesh; so our life is nourished by another's life, with which it fuses in love.

The world with benefits unknowingly;
As does the nightingale, upperched high,
And cloister'd among cool and bunched leaves—
She sings but to her love, nor e'er conceives   830
How tiptoe Night holds back her dark-grey hood.[3]
Just so may love, although 'tis understood
The mere commingling of passionate breath,
Produce more than our searching witnesseth:
What I know not: but who, of men, can tell   835
That flowers would bloom, or that green fruit would swell
To melting pulp, that fish would have bright mail,
The earth its dower of river, wood, and vale,
The meadows runnels, runnels pebble-stones,
The seed its harvest, or the lute its tones,   840
Tones ravishment, or ravishment its sweet,
If human souls did never kiss and greet?

     "Now, if this earthly love has power to make
Men's being mortal, immortal; to shake
Ambition from their memories, and brim   845
Their measure of content; what merest whim,
Seems all this poor endeavour after fame,
To one, who keeps within his stedfast aim
A love immortal, an immortal too.
Look not so wilder'd; for these things are true,   850
And never can be born of atomies[4]
That buzz about our slumbers, like brain-flies,
Leaving us fancy-sick. No, no, I'm sure,
My restless spirit never could endure
To brood so long upon one luxury,   855
Unless it did, though fearfully, espy
A hope beyond the shadow of a dream."

April–November 1817   1818

On Sitting Down to Read *King Lear* Once Again[1]

O golden-tongued Romance, with serene lute!
  Fair plumed syren, queen of far-away!
  Leave melodizing on this wintry day,
Shut up thine olden pages, and be mute.
Adieu! for, once again, the fierce dispute   5
  Betwixt damnation and impassion'd clay
  Must I burn through; once more humbly assay

3. I.e., in order better to hear.
4. Mites, tiny flying insects.
1. Keats pauses, while revising *Endymion: A Poetic Romance*, to read again Shakespeare's great tragedy. The word "syren" (line 2) indicates Keats's

feeling that "Romance" was enticing him from the poet's prime duty, to deal with "the agonies, the strife / Of human hearts" (*Sleep and Poetry*, lines 124–125).

The bitter-sweet of this Shakespearean fruit.
Chief Poet! and ye clouds of Albion,[2]
   Begetters of our deep eternal theme!   10
When through the old oak forest I am gone,
   Let me not wander in a barren dream:
But, when I am consumed in the fire,
Give me new phoenix[3] wings to fly at my desire.

Jan. 22, 1818   1838

When I Have Fears That I May Cease To Be[1]

When I have fears that I may cease to be
   Before my pen has glean'd my teeming brain,
Before high piled books, in charactry,[2]
   Hold like rich garners the full ripen'd grain;
When I behold, upon the night's starr'd face,   5
   Huge cloudy symbols of a high romance,
And think that I may never live to trace
   Their shadows, with the magic hand of chance;
And when I feel, fair creature of an hour,
   That I shall never look upon thee more,   10
Never have relish in the fairy power
   Of unreflecting love;—then on the shore
Of the wide world I stand alone, and think
Till love and fame to nothingness do sink.

January 1818   1848

To Homer

Standing aloof in giant ignorance,
   Of thee I hear and of the Cyclades,[1]
As one who sits ashore and longs perchance
   To visit dolphin-coral in deep seas.
So wast thou blind;—but then the veil was rent,   5
   For Jove uncurtain'd heaven to let thee live,
And Neptune made for thee a spumy tent,
   And Pan made sing for thee his forest-hive;
Aye on the shores of darkness there is light,
   And precipices show untrodden green,   10

2. Albion is the old Celtic name for England; *King Lear* is set in Celtic Britain. The "oak forest" of line 11 refers either to *King Lear* or to the romance, *Endymion*.
3. The fabulous bird which periodically burns itself to death in order to rise anew from the ashes.
1. The first, and one of the most successful, of Keats's attempts at the sonnet in the Shakespearean rhyme scheme.
2. Characters; printed letters of the alphabet.
1. A group of islands in the Aegean Sea, off Greece; Keats's allusion is to his ignorance of the Greek language.

There is a budding morrow in midnight,
    There is a triple sight in blindness keen;
Such seeing hadst thou, as it once befel
To Dian, Queen of Earth, and Heaven, and Hell.[2]

1818   1848

The Eve of St. Agnes[1]

1

St. Agnes' Eve—Ah, bitter chill it was!
The owl, for all his feathers, was a-cold;
The hare limp'd trembling through the frozen grass,
And silent was the flock in woolly fold:
Numb were the Beadsman's[2] fingers, while he told   5
His rosary, and while his frosted breath,
Like pious incense from a censer old,
Seem'd taking flight for heaven, without a death,
Past the sweet Virgin's picture, while his prayer he saith.

2

His prayer he saith, this patient, holy man;   10
Then takes his lamp, and riseth from his knees,
And back returneth, meagre, barefoot, wan,
Along the chapel aisle by slow degrees:
The sculptur'd dead, on each side, seem to freeze,
Emprison'd in black, purgatorial rails: 15
Knights, ladies, praying in dumb orat'ries,[3]
He passeth by; and his weak spirit fails
To think[4] how they may ache in icy hoods and mails.

3

Northward he turneth through a little door,
And scarce three steps, ere Music's golden tongue   20
Flatter'd[5] to tears this aged man and poor;

2. In later cults Diana was worshiped as a three-figured goddess, the deity of nature and of the moon, as well as queen of hell. The "triple sight" which blind Homer paradoxically commands is of these three regions, and also of heaven, sea, and earth (the realms of Jove, Neptune, and Pan, lines 6–8).

1. St. Agnes, martyred ca. 303 at the age of 13, is the patron saint of virgins. Legend has it that if a virtuous young girl performs the proper ritual, she will dream of her future husband on the evening before St. Agnes's Day, which falls on Jan. 21. Keats combines this superstition with the Romeo and Juliet theme of young love thwarted by feuding families and tells the story in a sequence of evolving Spenserian stanzas. The luxurious product has been called "a colored dream," but it is a complexly meaningful dream, in which the strong contrasts of heat and cold, crimson and silver, youth and age, revelry and austere penance, sensuality and chastity, life and death, hell and heaven, assume symbolic values. They figure forth the extremes of spirituality and of grossness that are involved in sexuality, the difference between the dream and the reality of passion, and the ambivalences at the center of both human love and the imagination. The poem is Keats's first complete success in sustained narrative.

For the author's revisions while composing stanzas 26 and 30 of The Eve of St. Agnes, see "Poems in Process," below.

2. A "beadsman" is paid to pray for his benefactor. He "tells" (counts) the beads of his rosary, to keep track of his prayers.

3. Silent chapels.

4. I.e., when he thinks.

5. Beguiled, charmed.

But no—already had his deathbell rung;
The joys of all his life were said and sung:
His was harsh penance on St. Agnes' Eve:
Another way he went, and soon among   25
Rough ashes sat he for his soul's reprieve,
And all night kept awake, for sinners' sake to grieve.

4

That ancient Beadsman heard the prelude soft;
And so it chanc'd, for many a door was wide,
From hurry to and fro. Soon, up aloft,   30
The silver, snarling trumpets 'gan to chide:
The level chambers, ready with their pride,[6]
Were glowing to receive a thousand guests:
The carved angels, ever eager-eyed,
Star'd, where upon their heads the cornice rests,   35
With hair blown back, and wings put cross-wise on their breasts.

5

At length burst in the argent revelry,[7]
With plume, tiara, and all rich array,
Numerous as shadows haunting fairily
The brain, new stuff'd, in youth, with triumphs gay   40
Of old romance. These let us wish away,
And turn, sole-thoughted, to one Lady there,
Whose heart had brooded, all that wintry day,
On love, and wing'd St. Agnes' saintly care,
As she had heard old dames full many times declare.   45

6

They told her how, upon St. Agnes' Eve,
Young virgins might have visions of delight,
And soft adorings from their loves receive
Upon the honey'd middle of the night,
If ceremonies due they did aright;   50
As, supperless to bed they must retire,
And couch supine their beauties, lily white;
Nor look behind, nor sideways, but require
Of heaven with upward eyes for all that they desire.

7

Full of this whim was thoughtful Madeline: 55
The music, yearning like a god in pain,
She scarcely heard: her maiden eyes divine,
Fix'd on the floor, saw many a sweeping train
Pass by—she heeded not at all: in vain
Came many a tiptoe, amorous cavalier,   60
And back retir'd, not cool'd by high disdain;
But she saw not: her heart was otherwhere:
She sigh'd for Agnes' dreams, the sweetest of the year.

6. Ostentation.   7. Silver-clad revelers.

8

She danc'd along with vague, regardless eyes,
Anxious her lips, her breathing quick and short: 65
The hallow'd hour was near at hand: she sighs
Amid the timbrels,[8] and the throng'd resort
Of whisperers in anger, or in sport;
'Mid looks of love, defiance, hate, and scorn,
Hoodwink'd with faery fancy;[9] all amort,   70
Save to St. Agnes and her lambs unshorn,[1]
And all the bliss to be before to-morrow morn.

9

So, purposing each moment to retire,
She linger'd still. Meantime, across the moors,
Had come young Porphyro, with heart on fire   75
For Madeline. Beside the portal doors,
Buttress'd from moonlight,[2] stands he, and implores
All saints to give him sight of Madeline,
But for one moment in the tedious hours,
That he might gaze and worship all unseen;   80
Perchance speak, kneel, touch, kiss—in sooth such things have been.

10

He ventures in: let no buzz'd whisper tell:
All eyes be muffled, or a hundred swords
Will storm his heart, Love's fev'rous citadel:
For him, those chambers held barbarian hordes,   85
Hyena foemen, and hot-blooded lords,
Whose very dogs would execrations howl
Against his lineage: not one breast affords
Him any mercy, in that mansion foul,
Save one old beldame,[3] weak in body and in soul.   90

11

Ah, happy chance! the aged creature came,
Shuffling along with ivory-headed wand,[4]
To where he stood, hid from the torch's flame,
Behind a broad hall-pillar, far beyond
The sound of merriment and chorus bland:[5]   95
He startled her; but soon she knew his face,
And grasp'd his fingers in her palsied hand,
Saying, "Mercy, Porphyro! hie thee from this place;
They are all here to-night, the whole blood-thirsty race!

12

"Get hence! get hence! there's dwarfish Hildebrand;   100
He had a fever late, and in the fit

8. Small drums.
9. She was blinded ("hoodwink'd"—as though the
eyes were covered by a hood) by her charmed
imagination. "All amort": as though dead.
1. On St. Agnes's Day it was the custom to offer
lambs' wool at the altar, to be made into cloth by
nuns.

2. Sheltered from the moonlight by the buttresses
(the supports projecting from the wall).
3. Old (and usually, homely) woman; an ironic
development in English from the French meaning, "lovely lady."
4. Staff.
5. Soft.

He cursed thee and thine, both house and land:
Then there's that old Lord Maurice, not a whit
More tame for his gray hairs—Alas me! flit!
Flit like a ghost away."—"Ah, Gossip[6] dear,   105
We're safe enough; here in this arm-chair sit,
And tell me how"—"Good Saints! not here, not here;
Follow me, child, or else these stones will be thy bier."

13

He follow'd through a lowly arched way,
Brushing the cobwebs with his lofty plume,   110
And as she mutter'd "Well-a—well-a-day!"
He found him in a little moonlight room,
Pale, lattic'd, chill, and silent as a tomb.
"Now tell me where is Madeline," said he,
"O tell me, Angela, by the holy loom   115
Which none but secret sisterhood may see,
When they St. Agnes' wool are weaving piously."

14

"St. Agnes! Ah! it is St. Agnes' Eve—
Yet men will murder upon holy days:
Thou must hold water in a witch's sieve,[7]   120
And be liege-lord of all the Elves and Fays,
To venture so: it fills me with amaze
To see thee, Porphyro!—St. Agnes' Eve!
God's help! my lady fair the conjuror plays[8]
This very night: good angels her deceive!   125
But let me laugh awhile, I've mickle[9] time to grieve."

15

Feebly she laugheth in the languid moon,
While Porphyro upon her face doth look,
Like puzzled urchin on an aged crone
Who keepeth clos'd a wond'rous riddle-book,   130
As spectacled she sits in chimney nook.
But soon his eyes grew brilliant, when she told
His lady's purpose; and he scarce could brook[1]
Tears, at the thought of those enchantments cold,
And Madeline asleep in lap of legends old.   135

16

Sudden a thought came like a full-blown rose,
Flushing his brow, and in his pained heart
Made purple riot: then doth he propose
A stratagem, that makes the beldame start:
"A cruel man and impious thou art: 140
Sweet lady, let her pray, and sleep, and dream
Alone with her good angels, far apart

---

6. In the old sense: godmother, or old friend.
7. A sieve made to hold water by witchcraft.
8. I.e., in her attempt to evoke the vision of her lover.

9. Much.
1. "Brook" ordinarily means "endure"; here Keats apparently uses it for "restrain."

From wicked men like thee. Go, go!—I deem
Thou canst not surely be the same that thou didst seem."

17

"I will not harm her, by all saints I swear,"   145
Quoth Porphyro: "O may I ne'er find grace
When my weak voice shall whisper its last prayer,
If one of her soft ringlets I displace,
Or look with ruffian passion in her face:
Good Angela, believe me by these tears;   150
Or I will, even in a moment's space,
Awake, with horrid shout, my foemen's ears,
And beard them, though they be more fang'd than wolves and bears."

18

"Ah! why wilt thou affright a feeble soul?
A poor, weak, palsy-stricken, churchyard thing,   155
Whose passing-bell[2] may ere the midnight toll;
Whose prayers for thee, each morn and evening,
Were never miss'd."—Thus plaining,[3] doth she bring
A gentler speech from burning Porphyro;
So woful, and of such deep sorrowing,   160
That Angela gives promise she will do
Whatever he shall wish, betide her weal or woe.

19

Which was, to lead him, in close secrecy,
Even to Madeline's chamber, and there hide
Him in a closet, of such privacy   165
That he might see her beauty unespied,
And win perhaps that night a peerless bride,
While legion'd fairies pac'd the coverlet,
And pale enchantment held her sleepy-eyed.
Never on such a night have lovers met,   170
Since Merlin paid his Demon all the monstrous debt.[4]

20

"It shall be as thou wishest," said the Dame:
"All cates[5] and dainties shall be stored there
Quickly on this feast-night: by the tambour frame[6]
Her own lute thou wilt see: no time to spare,   175
For I am slow and feeble, and scarce dare
On such a catering trust my dizzy head.
Wait here, my child, with patience; kneel in prayer
The while: Ah! thou must needs the lady wed,
Or may I never leave my grave among the dead."   180

21

So saying, she hobbled off with busy fear.
The lover's endless minutes slowly pass'd;

---

2. Death knell.
3. Complaining.
4. Probably the episode in the Arthurian legends
in which Merlin, the magician, lost his life when

the wily Vivien turned one of his own spells against
him.
5. Delicacies.
6. A drum-shaped embroidery frame.

The dame return'd, and whisper'd in his ear
To follow her; with aged eyes aghast
From fright of dim espial. Safe at last,   185
Through many a dusky gallery, they gain
The maiden's chamber, silken, hush'd, and chaste;
Where Porphyro took covert, pleas'd amain.[7]
His poor guide hurried back with agues in her brain.

22

Her falt'ring hand upon the balustrade,   190
Old Angela was feeling for the stair,
When Madeline, St. Agnes' charmed maid,
Rose, like a mission'd spirit,[8] unaware:
With silver taper's light, and pious care,
She turn'd, and down the aged gossip led   195
To a safe level matting. Now prepare,
Young Porphyro, for gazing on that bed;
She comes, she comes again, like ring-dove fray'd[9] and fled.

23

Out went the taper as she hurried in;
Its little smoke, in pallid moonshine, died: 200
She clos'd the door, she panted, all akin
To spirits of the air, and visions wide:
No uttered syllable, or, woe betide!
But to her heart, her heart was voluble,
Paining with eloquence her balmy side;   205
As though a tongueless nightingale should swell
Her throat in vain, and die, heart-stifled, in her dell.

24

A casement high and triple-arch'd there was,
All garlanded with carven imag'ries
Of fruits, and flowers, and bunches of knot-grass,   210
And diamonded with panes of quaint device,
Innumerable of stains and splendid dyes,
As are the tiger-moth's deep-damask'd wings;
And in the midst, 'mong thousand heraldries,
And twilight saints, and dim emblazonings,   215
A shielded scutcheon blush'd with blood of queens and kings.[1]

25

Full on this casement shone the wintry moon,
And threw warm gules[2] on Madeline's fair breast,
As down she knelt for heaven's grace and boon;[3]
Rose-bloom fell on her hands, together prest,   220
And on her silver cross soft amethyst,
And on her hair a glory, like a saint:

---

7. Mightily.
8. Like an angel sent on a mission.
9. Frightened.
1. I.e., among the genealogical emblems ("heraldries") and other devices ("emblazonings"), a
heraldic shield signified by its colors that the family was of royal blood.
2. In heraldry, the color red.
3. Gift, blessing.

She seem'd a splendid angel, newly drest,
  Save wings, for heaven:—Porphyro grew faint:
She knelt, so pure a thing, so free from mortal taint.   225

26

  Anon his heart revives: her vespers done,
Of all its wreathed pearls her hair she frees;
Unclasps her warmed jewels one by one;
Loosens her fragrant boddice; by degrees
Her rich attire creeps rustling to her knees: 230
Half-hidden, like a mermaid in sea-weed,
Pensive awhile she dreams awake, and sees,
  In fancy, fair St. Agnes in her bed,
But dares not look behind, or all the charm is fled.

27

  Soon, trembling in her soft and chilly nest,   235
In sort of wakeful swoon, perplex'd[4] she lay,
Until the poppied warmth of sleep oppress'd
Her soothed limbs, and soul fatigued away;
Flown, like a thought, until the morrow-day;
Blissfully haven'd both from joy and pain;   240
Clasp'd like a missal where swart Paynims pray;[5]
  Blinded alike from sunshine and from rain,
As though a rose should shut, and be a bud again.

28

  Stol'n to this paradise, and so entranced,
Porphyro gazed upon her empty dress,   245
And listen'd to her breathing, if it chanced
To wake into a slumberous tenderness;
Which when he heard, that minute did he bless,
And breath'd himself: then from the closet crept,
Noiseless as fear in a wide wilderness,   250
  And over the hush'd carpet, silent, stept,
And 'tween the curtains peep'd, where, lo!—how fast she slept.

29

  Then by the bed-side, where the faded moon
Made a dim, silver twilight, soft he set
A table, and, half anguish'd, threw thereon   255
A cloth of woven crimson, gold, and jet:—
O for some drowsy Morphean amulet![6]
The boisterous, midnight, festive clarion,[7]
The kettle-drum, and far-heard clarionet,
  Affray his ears, though but in dying tone:—   260
The hall door shuts again, and all the noise is gone.

---

4. In a confused state between waking and sleeping.
5. Variously interpreted; perhaps: held tightly, cherished (or else kept shut, fastened with a clasp), like a Christian prayer book ("missal") in a land where the religion is that of dark-skinned pagans ("swart Paynims").
6. Sleep-producing charm.
7. High-pitched trumpet.

30

And still she slept an azure-lidded sleep,
In blanched linen, smooth, and lavender'd,
While he from forth the closet brought a heap
Of candied apple, quince, and plum, and gourd;[8]   265
With jellies soother than the creamy curd,
And lucent syrops, tinct with cinnamon;
Manna and dates, in argosy transferr'd
From Fez,[9] and spiced dainties, every one,
From silken Samarcand to cedar'd Lebanon.   270

31

These delicates he heap'd with glowing hand
On golden dishes and in baskets bright
Of wreathed silver: sumptuous they stand
In the retired quiet of the night,
Filling the chilly room with perfume light.—   275
"And now, my love, my seraph[1] fair, awake!
Thou art my heaven, and I thine eremite:[2]
Open thine eyes, for meek St. Agnes' sake,
Or I shall drowse beside thee, so my soul doth ache."

32

Thus whispering, his warm, unnerved arm   280
Sank in her pillow. Shaded was her dream
By the dusk curtains:—'twas a midnight charm
Impossible to melt as iced stream:
The lustrous salvers in the moonlight gleam;
Broad golden fringe upon the carpet lies: 285
It seem'd he never, never could redeem
From such a stedfast spell his lady's eyes;
So mus'd awhile, entoil'd in woofed phantasies.[3]

33

Awakening up, he took her hollow lute,—
Tumultuous,—and, in chords that tenderest be,   290
He play'd an ancient ditty, long since mute,
In Provence call'd, "La belle dame sans mercy":[4]
Close to her ear touching the melody;—
Wherewith disturb'd, she utter'd a soft moan:
He ceased—she panted quick—and suddenly   295
Her blue affrayed eyes wide open shone:
Upon his knees he sank, pale as smooth-sculptured stone.

34

Her eyes were open, but she still beheld,
Now wide awake, the vision of her sleep:

---

8. Melon. According to the legend, the dream lover would bring the virgin a feast of delicacies.
9. I.e., jellies softer ("soother") than the curds of cream, clear ("lucent") syrups tinged with cinnamon, and sweet gums ("manna") and dates transported in a great merchant ship ("argosy") from Fez.

1. One of the highest order of angels.
2. A religious hermit.
3. Entangled in a weave of fantasies.
4. "The Lovely Lady without Pity," title of a work by the medieval poet Alain Chartier. Keats later adopted the title for his own ballad.

There was a painful change, that nigh expell'd   300
The blisses of her dream so pure and deep:
At which fair Madeline began to weep,
And moan forth witless words with many a sigh;
While still her gaze on Porphyro would keep;
Who knelt, with joined hands and piteous eye,   305
Fearing to move or speak, she look'd so dreamingly.

                                35
"Ah, Porphyro!" said she, "but even now
Thy voice was at sweet tremble in mine ear,
Made tuneable with every sweetest vow;
And those sad eyes were spiritual and clear: 310
How chang'd thou art! how pallid, chill, and drear!
Give me that voice again, my Porphyro,
Those looks immortal, those complainings dear!
Oh leave me not in this eternal woe,
For if thou diest, my love, I know not where to go."   315

                                36
Beyond a mortal man impassion'd far
At these voluptuous accents, he arose,
Ethereal, flush'd, and like a throbbing star
Seen mid the sapphire heaven's deep repose;
Into her dream he melted, as the rose   320
Blendeth its odour with the violet,—
Solution sweet: meantime the frost-wind blows
Like Love's alarum pattering the sharp sleet
Against the window-panes; St. Agnes' moon hath set.

                                37
'Tis dark: quick pattereth the flaw-blown[5] sleet: 325
"This is no dream, my bride, my Madeline!"
'Tis dark: the iced gusts still rave and beat:
"No dream, alas! alas! and woe is mine!
Porphyro will leave me here to fade and pine.—
Cruel! what traitor could thee hither bring?   330
I curse not, for my heart is lost in thine,
Though thou forsakest a deceived thing;—
A dove forlorn and lost with sick unpruned wing."

                                38
"My Madeline! sweet dreamer! lovely bride!
Say, may I be for aye thy vassal blest?   335
Thy beauty's shield, heart-shap'd and vermeil[6] dyed?
Ah, silver shrine, here will I take my rest
After so many hours of toil and quest,
A famish'd pilgrim,—saved by miracle.
Though I have found, I will not rob thy nest   340
Saving of thy sweet self; if thou think'st well
To trust, fair Madeline, to no rude infidel.

5. Gust-blown.   6. Vermilion.

39

"Hark! 'tis an elfin-storm from faery land,
Of haggard[7] seeming, but a boon indeed:
Arise—arise! the morning is at hand;—   345
The bloated wassaillers[8] will never heed:—
Let us away, my love, with happy speed;
There are no ears to hear, or eyes to see,—
Drown'd all in Rhenish and the sleepy mead:[9]
Awake! arise! my love, and fearless be,   350
For o'er the southern moors I have a home for thee."

40

She hurried at his words, beset with fears,
For there were sleeping dragons all around,
At glaring watch, perhaps, with ready spears—
Down the wide stairs a darkling[1] way they found.—   355
In all the house was heard no human sound.
A chain-droop'd lamp was flickering by each door;
The arras, rich with horseman, hawk, and hound,
Flutter'd in the besieging wind's uproar;
And the long carpets rose along the gusty floor.   360

41

They glide, like phantoms, into the wide hall;
Like phantoms, to the iron porch, they glide;
Where lay the Porter, in uneasy sprawl,
With a huge empty flaggon by his side:
The wakeful bloodhound rose, and shook his hide,   365
But his sagacious eye an inmate owns:[2]
By one, and one, the bolts full easy slide:—
The chains lie silent on the footworn stones;—
The key turns, and the door upon its hinges groans.

42

And they are gone: ay, ages long ago   370
These lovers fled away into the storm.
That night the Baron dreamt of many a woe,
And all his warrior-guests, with shade and form
Of witch, and demon, and large coffin-worm,
Were long be-nightmar'd. Angela the old   375
Died palsy-twitch'd, with meagre face deform;
The Beadsman, after thousand aves[3] told,
For aye unsought for slept among his ashes cold.

January–February 1819   1820

---

7. Wild, untamed (originally, a wild hawk).
8. Drunken carousers.
9. Rhine wine and the sleep-producing mead (a heavy fermented drink made with honey).

1. In the dark.
2. Acknowledges a member of the household.
3. The prayers beginning Ave Maria ("Hail Mary").

Bright Star, Would I Were Stedfast as Thou Art[1]

Bright star, would I were stedfast as thou art—
　　Not in lone splendor hung aloft the night,
And watching, with eternal lids apart,
　　Like nature's patient, sleepless eremite,[2]
The moving waters at their priestlike task   5
　　Of pure ablution[3] round earth's human shores,
Or gazing on the new soft-fallen mask
　　Of snow upon the mountains and the moors;
No—yet still stedfast, still unchangeable,
　　Pillow'd upon my fair love's ripening breast,   10
To feel for ever its soft swell and fall,
　　Awake for ever in a sweet unrest,
Still, still to hear her tender-taken breath,
And so live ever—or else swoon to death.[4]

1819   1838

La Belle Dame sans Merci: A Ballad[1]

1

O what can ail thee, knight at arms,
　　Alone and palely loitering?
The sedge has wither'd from the lake,
　　And no birds sing.

2

O what can ail thee, knight at arms,   5
　　So haggard and so woe-begone?
The squirrel's granary is full,
　　And the harvest's done.

3

I see a lily on thy brow
　　With anguish moist and fever dew,   10
And on thy cheeks a fading rose
　　Fast withereth too.

1. While on a tour of the Lake Country in 1818, Keats had said that the austere scenes "refine one's sensual vision into a sort of north star which can never cease to be open lidded and steadfast over the wonders of the great Power"; the thought developed into this sonnet. Keats drafted this poem in 1819, then copied it into his volume of Shakespeare's poems, at the end of September or beginning of October 1820, while on the way to his death in Italy.
2. Hermit, religious solitary.
3. Washing, as part of a religious rite.
4. In the earlier version: "Half passionless, and so swoon on to death."
1. The title, though not the subject matter, was taken from a medieval poem by Alain Chartier and means "The Lovely Lady without Pity." The story of a mortal destroyed by his love for a supernatural *femme fatale* has been told repeatedly in myth, fairy tale, and ballad, but never so hauntingly. Conducive to this effect is the suspension achieved by shortening to two stresses the final line of each stanza. We print here Keats's earlier version of the poem, as transcribed by Charles Brown. The version published in 1820, "Ah, what can ail thee, wretched wight," is a rare instance in which Keats weakened a poem by revision.
　　Keats imitates a frequent procedure of folk ballads by casting the poem into the dialogue form. The first three stanzas are addressed to the knight, and the rest of the poem is his reply.

                                    4
I met a lady in the meads,
    Full beautiful, a fairy's child;
Her hair was long, her foot was light,   15
        And her eyes were wild.
                                    5
I made a garland for her head,
    And bracelets too, and fragrant zone;[2]
She look'd at me as she did love,
        And made sweet moan.   20
                                    6
I set her on my pacing steed,
    And nothing else saw all day long,
For sidelong would she bend, and sing
        A fairy's song.
                                    7
She found me roots of relish sweet,   25
    And honey wild, and manna dew,
And sure in language strange she said—
        I love thee true.
                                    8
She took me to her elfin grot,
    And there she wept, and sigh'd full sore,   30
And there I shut her wild wild eyes
        With kisses four.
                                    9
And there she lulled me asleep,
    And there I dream'd—Ah! woe betide!
The latest[3] dream I ever dream'd   35
        On the cold hill's side.
                                    10
I saw pale kings, and princes too,
    Pale warriors, death pale were they all;
They cried—"La belle dame sans merci
        Hath thee in thrall!"   40
                                    11
I saw their starv'd lips in the gloam
    With horrid warning gaped wide,
And I awoke and found me here
        On the cold hill's side.
                                    12
And this is why I sojourn here,   45
    Alone and palely loitering,
Though the sedge is wither'd from the lake,
        And no birds sing.

April 1819   1820

---

2. Belt, girdle (of flowers).   3. Last.

Ode to Psyche[1]

O Goddess! hear these tuneless numbers, wrung
    By sweet enforcement and remembrance dear,
And pardon that thy secrets should be sung
    Even into thine own soft-conchèd[2] ear:
Surely I dreamt to-day, or did I see   5
    The winged Psyche with awaken'd eyes?[3]
I wander'd in a forest thoughtlessly,
    And, on the sudden, fainting with surprise,
Saw two fair creatures, couched side by side
    In deepest grass, beneath the whisp'ring roof   10
    Of leaves and trembled blossoms, where there ran
        A brooklet, scarce espied:
'Mid hush'd, cool-rooted flowers, fragrant-eyed,
    Blue, silver-white, and budded Tyrian,[4]
They lay calm-breathing on the bedded grass;   15
    Their arms embraced, and their pinions[5] too;
    Their lips touch'd not, but had not bade adieu,
As if disjoined by soft-handed slumber,
And ready still past kisses to outnumber
    At tender eye-dawn of aurorean love:[6]   20
        The winged boy I knew;
But who wast thou, O happy, happy dove?
        His Psyche true!

O latest born and loveliest vision far
    Of all Olympus' faded hierarchy![7]   25

1. This poem initiated the sequence of great odes that Keats wrote in the spring of 1819. It is copied into the same journal-letter which included the *Sonnet to Sleep* and several other sonnets, as well as a comment about "endeavoring to discover a better sonnet stanza than we have." It is therefore likely that Keats's experiments with sonnet schemes led to the development of the intricate and varied stanzas of his odes, and also that he abandoned the sonnet upon discovering the richer possibilities of the more spacious form. In his journal-letter, on April 30, he said that of all his poems up to that time, *Psyche* "is the first and the only one with which I have taken even moderate pains. I have for the most part dashed off my lines in a hurry. This I have done leisurely—I think it reads the more richly for it and will I hope encourage me to write other things in even a more peaceable and healthy spirit." In the story told by the Roman author Apuleius in the 2nd century, Psyche was a lovely mortal beloved by Cupid, "the winged boy," son of Venus. After various tribulations, imposed by Venus because she was jealous of Psyche's beauty, Psyche was wedded to Cupid and translated to heaven as an immortal.

The tendency in recent criticism is to read the *Ode* as a quasi allegory, in which Psyche (in Greek: soul, or mind) represents "the human-soul-in-love" (Harold Bloom) or else the modern inward-oriented poetry of the mind (W. J. Bate). To this latter-day goddess, Keats in the last two stanzas promises to establish a place of worship within "some untrodden region" of his own mind, with himself as poet-priest and prophet.
2. Soft and shaped like a seashell.
3. Another of Keats's inquiries into the relation of dreams to poetic vision; see, e.g., *Sleep and Poetry* and the concluding lines of *Ode to a Nightingale*.
4. The purple dye anciently made in Tyre.
5. Wings.
6. Aurora was the goddess of the dawn.
7. The ranks of the classic gods of Mt. Olympus. "You must recollect that Psyche was not embodied as a goddess before the time of Apuleius the Platonist who lived after the Augustan age, and consequently the goddess was never worshiped or sacrificed to with any of the ancient fervor—and perhaps never thought of in the old religion" (Keats, journal-letter under date of Apr. 30, 1819).

Fairer than Phoebe's sapphire-region'd star,[8]
   Or Vesper, amorous glow-worm of the sky;
Fairer than these, though temple thou hast none,
    Nor altar heap'd with flowers;
Nor virgin-choir to make delicious moan   30
    Upon the midnight hours;
No voice, no lute, no pipe, no incense sweet
   From chain-swung censer teeming;
No shrine, no grove, no oracle, no heat
    Of pale-mouth'd prophet dreaming.   35

O brightest! though too late for antique vows,
   Too, too late for the fond believing lyre,
When holy were the haunted forest boughs,
    Holy the air, the water, and the fire;
Yet even in these days so far retir'd   40
    From happy pieties, thy lucent fans,[9]
    Fluttering among the faint Olympians,
I see, and sing, by my own eyes inspired.
So let me be thy choir, and make a moan
    Upon the midnight hours;   45
Thy voice, thy lute, thy pipe, thy incense sweet
   From swinged censer teeming;
Thy shrine, thy grove, thy oracle, thy heat
    Of pale-mouth'd prophet dreaming.

Yes, I will be thy priest, and build a fane[1]   50
    In some untrodden region of my mind,
Where branched thoughts, new grown with pleasant pain,
    Instead of pines shall murmur in the wind:
Far, far around shall those dark-cluster'd trees
   Fledge[2] the wild-ridged mountains steep by steep;   55
And there by zephyrs, streams, and birds, and bees,
    The moss-lain Dryads[3] shall be lull'd to sleep;
And in the midst of this wide quietness
A rosy sanctuary will I dress
With the wreath'd trellis of a working brain,   60
    With buds, and bells, and stars without a name,
With all the gardener Fancy e'er could feign,
    Who breeding flowers, will never breed the same:
And there shall be for thee all soft delight
    That shadowy thought can win,   65
A bright torch, and a casement ope at night,
    To let the warm Love[4] in!

April 1819   1820

8. The moon, supervised by the goddess Phoebe
(Diana). "Vesper" (line 27): the evening star.
9. Shining wings.
1. Temple.

2. I.e., the trees shall stand, rank against rank,
like layers of feathers.
3. Wood nymphs.
4. I.e., Cupid, god of love.

Ode to a Nightingale[1]

1

My heart aches, and a drowsy numbness pains
  My sense, as though of hemlock[2] I had drunk,
Or emptied some dull opiate to the drains
  One minute past, and Lethe-wards[3] had sunk:
'Tis not through envy of thy happy lot,   5
  But being too happy in thine happiness,—
    That thou, light-winged Dryad of the trees,
      In some melodious plot
  Of beechen green, and shadows numberless,
    Singest of summer in full-throated ease.   10

2

O, for a draught of vintage! that hath been
  Cool'd a long age in the deep-delved earth,
Tasting of Flora[4] and the country green,
  Dance, and Provençal song,[5] and sunburnt mirth!
O for a beaker full of the warm South,   15
  Full of the true, the blushful Hippocrene,[6]
    With beaded bubbles winking at the brim,
      And purple-stained mouth;
  That I might drink, and leave the world unseen,
    And with thee fade away into the forest dim: 20

3

Fade far away, dissolve, and quite forget
  What thou among the leaves hast never known,
The weariness, the fever, and the fret
  Here, where men sit and hear each other groan;
Where palsy shakes a few, sad, last gray hairs,   25
  Where youth grows pale, and spectre-thin, and dies;[7]
    Where but to think is to be full of sorrow
      And leaden-eyed despairs,
  Where Beauty cannot keep her lustrous eyes,
    Or new Love pine at them beyond to-morrow.   30

4

Away! away! for I will fly to thee,
  Not charioted by Bacchus and his pards,

---

1. Charles Brown, with whom Keats was then living in Hampstead, wrote: "In the spring of 1819 a nightingale had built her nest near my house. Keats felt a tranquil and continual joy in her song; and one morning he took his chair from the breakfast table to the grass plot under a plum tree, where he sat for two or three hours. When he came into the house, I perceived he had some scraps of paper in his hand, and these he was quietly thrusting behind the books. On inquiry, I found those scraps, four or five in number, contained his poetic feeling on the song of our nightingale."
2. A poisonous herb, not the North American evergreen tree.
3. Toward Lethe, the river in Hades whose waters cause forgetfulness.
4. Roman goddess of flowers, or the flowers themselves.
5. Provence, in southern France, was in the late Middle Ages renowned for its troubadours, the writers and singers of love songs.
6. Pronounced *Hip'-ocreen:* fountain of the Muses on Mt. Helicon; hence, the waters of inspiration, here applied metaphorically to a beaker of wine.
7. Keats's brother, Tom, wasted by tuberculosis, had died the preceding winter.

But on the viewless wings of Poesy,[8]
  Though the dull brain perplexes and retards:
Already with thee! tender is the night,   35
    And haply the Queen-Moon is on her throne,
      Cluster'd around by all her starry Fays;[9]
        But here there is no light,
Save what from heaven is with the breezes blown
    Through verdurous[1] glooms and winding mossy ways.   40

                              5

I cannot see what flowers are at my feet,
  Nor what soft incense hangs upon the boughs,
But, in embalmed[2] darkness, guess each sweet
    Wherewith the seasonable month endows
The grass, the thicket, and the fruit-tree wild;   45
    White hawthorn, and the pastoral eglantine;[3]
      Fast fading violets cover'd up in leaves;
        And mid-May's eldest child,
The coming musk-rose, full of dewy wine,
    The murmurous haunt of flies on summer eves.   50

                              6

Darkling[4] I listen; and, for many a time
  I have been half in love with easeful Death,
Call'd him soft names in many a mused[5] rhyme,
    To take into the air my quiet breath;
Now more than ever seems it rich to die,   55
    To cease upon the midnight with no pain,
      While thou art pouring forth thy soul abroad
        In such an ecstasy!
Still wouldst thou sing, and I have ears in vain—
    To thy high requiem become a sod.   60

                              7

Thou wast not born for death, immortal Bird!
  No hungry generations tread thee down;
The voice I hear this passing night was heard
    In ancient days by emperor and clown:
Perhaps the self-same song that found a path   65
    Through the sad heart of Ruth,[6] when, sick for home,
      She stood in tears amid the alien corn;
        The same that oft-times hath
Charm'd magic casements, opening on the foam
    Of perilous seas, in faery lands forlorn.   70

---

8. I.e., not by getting drunk on wine (the "vintage" of stanza 2), but on the invisible ("viewless")
wings of the poetic imagination. (Bacchus, god of
wine, was sometimes represented in a chariot drawn
by "pards"—leopards.)
9. Fairies.
1. Green-foliaged.
2. Perfumed.

3. Sweetbrier, or honeysuckle.
4. In darkness.
5. Meditated. An earlier poem ("rhyme") by Keats
which called on "easeful Death" is the sonnet
Bright Star, Would I Were Stedfast as Thou
Art.
6. The young widow in the Biblical Book of Ruth.
"Corn" (line 67): i.e., wheat.

8

Forlorn![7] the very word is like a bell
   To toll me back from thee to my sole self!
Adieu! the fancy[8] cannot cheat so well
   As she is fam'd to do, deceiving elf
Adieu! adieu! thy plaintive anthem[9] fades   75
     Past the near meadows, over the still stream,
        Up the hill-side; and now 'tis buried deep
        In the next valley-glades:
   Was it a vision, or a waking dream?
   Fled is that music:—Do I wake or sleep?[1]   80

May 1819   1819

Ode on a Grecian Urn[1]

1

Thou still unravish'd bride of quietness,
   Thou foster-child of silence and slow time,
Sylvan[2] historian, who canst thus express
   A flowery tale more sweetly than our rhyme:
What leaf-fring'd legend haunts about thy shape   5
   Of deities or mortals, or of both,
     In Tempe or the dales of Arcady?[3]
   What men or gods are these? What maidens loth?
   What mad pursuit? What struggle to escape?
     What pipes and timbrels? What wild ecstasy?   10

2

Heard melodies are sweet, but those unheard
   Are sweeter; therefore, ye soft pipes, play on;
Not to the sensual ear,[4] but, more endear'd,
   Pipe to the spirit ditties of no tone:

---

7. One critic has said that "forlorn"—which means "long past" as well as "sorrowful"—"has its feet in two worlds," the faeryland of imagination and the woe of reality to which the word reawakens the lyric speaker.
8. I.e., imagination, "the viewless wings of Poesy" of line 33.
9. Hymn.
1. See *Ode to Psyche*, note to line 6.
1. This urn, with its sculptured reliefs of Dionysian ecstasies, panting young lovers in flight and pursuit, a pastoral piper under spring foliage, and the quiet celebration of communal pieties, resembles parts of various vases, sculptures, and paintings; but it existed in all its particulars only in Keats's imagination. In the urn—which captures moments of intense experience in attitudes of grace and immobilizes them in marble—Keats found the perfect correlative for his concern with the longing for permanence in a world of change. The inter-

pretation of the details with which he develops this concept, however, is hotly disputed, all the way from the opening phrase—is "still" an adverb ("as yet") or an adjective ("motionless")?—to the two concluding lines, which have already accumulated as much critical discussion as the "two-handed engine" in Milton's *Lycidas* or the cruxes in Shakespeare's plays. These disputes testify to the enigmatic richness of meaning in the five stanzas, and show that the ode has become a central point of reference in the criticism of the English lyric.
2. Rustic, representing a woodland scene.
3. Tempe is a beautiful valley in Greece which has come to represent supreme rural beauty. The "dales of Arcady" are the valleys of Arcadia, a state in ancient Greece often used as a symbol of the pastoral ideal.
4. The ear of sense (as opposed to that of the "spirit," or imagination).

Fair youth, beneath the trees, thou canst not leave   15
  Thy song, nor ever can those trees be bare;
    Bold lover, never, never canst thou kiss,
Though winning near the goal—yet, do not grieve;
    She cannot fade, though thou hast not thy bliss,
  For ever wilt thou love, and she be fair!   20

                          3

Ah, happy, happy boughs! that cannot shed
  Your leaves, nor ever bid the spring adieu;
And, happy melodist, unwearied,
  For ever piping songs for ever new;
More happy love! more happy, happy love!   25
    For ever warm and still to be enjoy'd,
      For ever panting, and for ever young;
All breathing human passion far above,
    That leaves a heart high-sorrowful and cloy'd,
      A burning forehead, and a parching tongue.   30

                          4

Who are these coming to the sacrifice?
  To what green altar, O mysterious priest,
Lead'st thou that heifer lowing at the skies,
  And all her silken flanks with garlands drest?
What little town by river or sea shore,   35
    Or mountain-built with peaceful citadel,
      Is emptied of this folk, this pious morn?
And, little town, thy streets for evermore
    Will silent be; and not a soul to tell
      Why thou art desolate, can e'er return.   40

                          5

O Attic[5] shape! Fair attitude! with brede
  Of marble men and maidens overwrought,[6]
With forest branches and the trodden weed;
    Thou, silent form, dost tease us out of thought
As doth eternity: Cold Pastoral!   45
    When old age shall this generation waste,
      Thou shalt remain, in midst of other woe
Than ours, a friend to man, to whom thou say'st,
  "Beauty is truth, truth beauty,"[7]—that is all
      Ye know on earth, and all ye need to know.   50

1819   1820

---

5. Greek. Attica was the region of Greece in which Athens was located.
6. Ornamented all over ("overwrought") with an interwoven pattern ("brede").
7. The quotation marks around this phrase are found in the volume of poems Keats published in 1820; but there are no quotation marks in the version printed in *Annals of the Fine Arts* that same year, or in the four transcripts of the poem made by Keats's friends. This discrepancy has multiplied the diversity of critical interpretations of the last

two lines. Leading critics disagree whether the whole of these lines is said by the urn, or "Beauty is truth, truth beauty" by the urn and the rest by the lyric speaker; whether the "ye" in the last line is addressed to the lyric speaker, to the readers, to the urn, or to the figures on the urn; whether "all ye know" is that beauty is truth, or this plus the statement in lines 46–48; and whether "beauty is truth" is a profound metaphysical proposition, or an overstatement uttered in the course of a dramatic dialogue, or simply nonsensical.

Ode on Melancholy This is Keats's best-known statement of his recurrent theme of the mingled contrarieties of life. The remarkable last stanza, in which Melancholy becomes a veiled goddess in a mystery religion, implies that it is the tragic human destiny that beauty, joy, and life itself owe not only their quality but their value to the fact that they are transitory and turn into their opposites.

The poem once had the following initial stanza, which Keats canceled in MS:

> Though you should build a bark of dead men's bones,
>   And rear a phantom gibbet for a mast,
> Stitch creeds together for a sail, with groans
>   To fill it out, bloodstained and aghast;
> Although your rudder be a Dragon's tail,
>   Long sever'd, yet still hard with agony,
>   Your cordage large uprootings from the skull
> Of bald Medusa: certes you would fail
>   To find the Melancholy, whether she
>   Dreameth in any isle of Lethe dull.

Ode on Melancholy

1

No, no, go not to Lethe,[1] neither twist
     Wolf's-bane, tight-rooted, for its poisonous wine;
Nor suffer thy pale forehead to be kiss'd
     By nightshade,[2] ruby grape of Proserpine;
Make not your rosary of yew-berries,[3]   5
     Nor let the beetle, nor the death-moth be
          Your mournful Psyche,[4] nor the downy owl
A partner in your sorrow's mysteries;[5]
     For shade to shade will come too drowsily,
          And drown the wakeful anguish of the soul.[6]   10

2

But when the melancholy fit shall fall
     Sudden from heaven like a weeping cloud,
That fosters the droop-headed flowers all,
     And hides the green hill in an April shroud;
Then glut thy sorrow on a morning rose,   15
     Or on the rainbow of the salt sand-wave,
          Or on the wealth of globed peonies;
Or if thy mistress some rich anger shows,

---

1. The waters of forgetfulness in Hades.
2. "Nightshade" and "wolfsbane" (line 2) are poisonous plants. Proserpine is the wife of Pluto and queen of the infernal regions.
3. A symbol of death.
4. In ancient times Psyche (the soul) was sometimes represented as a butterfly or moth, fluttering out of the mouth of a dying man. The allusion

may also be to the death's-head moth, which has skull-like markings on its back. The "beetle" of line 6 refers to replicas of the large black beetle, the scarab, which were often placed by Egyptians in their tombs as a symbol of resurrection.
5. Secret religious rites.
6. I.e., sorrow needs contrast to sustain its intensity.

Emprison her soft hand, and let her rave,
　　And feed deep, deep upon her peerless eyes.　　　　20

3

She[7] dwells with Beauty—Beauty that must die;
　　And Joy, whose hand is ever at his lips
Bidding adieu; and aching Pleasure nigh,
　　Turning to poison while the bee-mouth sips:
Ay, in the very temple of Delight　　　　　　　25
　　Veil'd Melancholy has her sovran shrine,
　　　　Though seen of none save him whose strenuous tongue
Can burst Joy's grape against his palate fine;[8]
His soul shall taste the sadness of her might,
　　And be among her cloudy trophies hung.[9]　　　　30

1819　　　　　　　　　　　　　　　　　　　　　　1820

Ode on Indolence[1]

"They toil not, neither do they spin."[2]

1

One morn before me were three figures seen,
　　With bowed necks, and joined hands, side-faced;
And one behind the other stepp'd serene,
　　In placid sandals, and in white robes graced:
They pass'd, like figures on a marble urn,　　　　5
　　When shifted round to see the other side;
　　　　They came again: as when the urn once more
Is shifted round, the first seen shades return;
　　And they were strange to me, as may betide
　　　　With vases, to one deep in Phidian[3] lore.　　　　10

2

How is it, shadows, that I knew ye not?
　　How came ye muffled in so hush a masque?
Was it a silent deep-disguised plot
　　To steal away, and leave without a task
My idle days? Ripe was the drowsy hour;　　　　15
　　The blissful cloud of summer-indolence
　　　　Benumb'd my eyes; my pulse grew less and less;

---

7. Melancholy, personified as a goddess whose chief place of worship ("shrine," line 26) is located "in the very temple of Delight" (line 25).
8. Sensitive, subtly discriminative.
9. A reference to the Greek and Roman practice of hanging trophies in the temples of the gods.
1. On Mar. 19, 1819, Keats wrote to George and Georgiana Keats: "This morning I am in a sort of temper indolent and supremely careless. . . . Neither Poetry, nor Ambition, nor Love have any alertness of countenance as they pass by me:

they seem rather like three figures on a greek vase—a Man and two women—whom no one but myself could distinguish in their disguisement. This is the only happiness; and is a rare instance of advantage in the body overpowering the Mind." The ode was probably written soon after this time, but was not published until 1848, long after the poet's death.
2. Matthew 6.28.
3. Phidias was the great Athenian sculptor of the 5th century B.C. who designed the marble sculptures for the Parthenon.

Pain had no sting, and pleasure's wreath no flower.
O, why did ye not melt, and leave my sense
Unhaunted quite of all but—nothingness? 20

3

A third time pass'd they by, and, passing, turn'd
Each one the face a moment whiles to me;
Then faded, and to follow them I burn'd
And ached for wings, because I knew the three:
The first was a fair maid, and Love her name; 25
The second was Ambition, pale of cheek,
And ever watchful with fatigued eye;
The last, whom I love more, the more of blame
Is heap'd upon her, maiden most unmeek,—
I knew to be my demon Poesy. 30

4

They faded, and, forsooth! I wanted wings:
O folly! What is Love? and where is it?
And for that poor Ambition—it springs
From a man's little heart's short fever-fit;
For Poesy!—no,—she has not a joy,— 35
At least for me,—so sweet as drowsy noons,
And evenings steep'd in honied indolence;
O, for an age so shelter'd from annoy,
That I may never know how change the moons,
Or hear the voice of busy common-sense! 40

5

A third time came they by;—alas! wherefore?
My sleep had been embroider'd with dim dreams;
My soul had been a lawn besprinkled o'er
With flowers, and stirring shades, and baffled beams:
The morn was clouded, but no shower fell, 45
Though in her lids hung the sweet tears of May;
The open casement press'd a new-leaved vine,
Let in the budding warmth and throstle's lay;
O shadows! 'twas a time to bid farewell!
Upon your skirts had fallen no tears of mine. 50

6

So, ye three ghosts, adieu! Ye cannot raise
My head cool-bedded in the flowery grass;
For I would not be dieted with praise,
A pet-lamb in a sentimental farce![4]
Fade softly from my eyes, and be once more 55
In masque-like figures on the dreamy urn;
Farewell! I yet have visions for the night,

4. In a letter of June 9, 1819, Keats wrote: "I have been very idle lately, very averse to writing; both from the overpowering idea of our dead poets and from abatement of my love of fame. I hope I am a little more of a Philosopher than I was, conse- quently a little less of a versifying Pet-lamb. . . . You will judge of my 1819 temper when I tell you that the thing I have most enjoyed this year has been writing an ode to Indolence."

And for the day faint visions there is store;
    Vanish, ye phantoms, from my idle spright,[5]
Into the clouds, and never more return!   60

Spring 1819   1848

Lamia   Keats himself cited, as the source of his plot, a story in Robert
Burton's *Anatomy of Melancholy* (1621): "One Menippus Lycius, a young
man twenty-five years of age, that going betwixt Cenchreas and Corinth,
met such a phantasm in the habit of a fair gentlewoman, which, taking him
by the hand, carried him home to her house, in the suburbs of Corinth.
. . . The young man, a philosopher, otherwise staid and discreet, able to
moderate his passions, though not this of love, tarried with her a while to
his great content, and at last married her, to whose wedding, amongst other
guests, came Apollonius; who, by some probable conjectures, found her out
to be a serpent, a lamia; and that all her furniture was, like Tantalus' gold,
described by Homer, no substance but mere illusions. When she saw herself
descried, she wept, and desired Apollonius to be silent, but he would not
be moved, and thereupon she, plate, house, and all that was in it, vanished
in an instant: many thousands took notice of this fact, for it was done in the
midst of Greece."

In ancient demonology, a "lamia"—pronounced *lā'·mĭ·a*—was a monster in woman's form who preyed on human beings. There are various clues
(see especially part 2, lines 229–38) that Keats invested the ancient legend
with allegorical significance. Its interpretation, however, and even the inclination of Keats's own sympathies in the contest between Lamia and Apollonius, have been disputed. It is possible that Keats simply failed to make up
his mind, or wavered in the course of composition. What seems more likely,
however, is that he intended to present an inevitably fatal situation, in which
no one is entirely blameless or blameworthy, and no character is meant to
monopolize either our sympathy or antipathy. Lamia is an enchantress, a
liar, and a calculating expert in *amour*; but she apparently intends no harm,
is genuinely in love, and is very beautiful. And both male protagonists exhibit
culpable extremes. Lycius, though an attractive young lover, is gullible, a
slave to his passions, and capable of gratuitous cruelty; while Apollonius,
though realistically clear-sighted, is rigid, puritanical, and inhumane.

The poem, written between late June and early September 1819, is a
return, after the Spenserian stanzas of *The Eve of St. Agnes*, to the pentameter couplets Keats had used in *Endymion* and other early narrative poems.
But Keats had in the meantime been studying John Dryden's closed and
strong-paced couplets. The initial lines of Dryden's version of Boccaccio's
story *Cymon and Iphigenia* show the kind of narrative model that helped
Keats make the technical transition from the fluent but sprawling gracefulness of the opening of *Endymion* to the vigor and economy of the opening
of *Lamia*:

      In that sweet isle where Venus keeps her court,
      And every grace, and all the loves, resort;

5. Spirit.

Where either sex is formed of softer earth,
And takes the bent of pleasure from their birth;
There lived a Cyprian lord, above the rest
Wise, wealthy, with a numerous issue blessed. . . .

Lamia

Part 1

Upon a time, before the faery broods
Drove Nymph and Satyr from the prosperous woods,[1]
Before King Oberon's bright diadem,
Sceptre, and mantle, clasp'd with dewy gem,
Frighted away the Dryads and the Fauns   5
From rushes green, and brakes,[2] and cowslip'd lawns,
The ever-smitten Hermes empty left
His golden throne, bent warm on amorous theft:[3]
From high Olympus had he stolen light,
On this side of Jove's clouds, to escape the sight   10
Of his great summoner, and made retreat
Into a forest on the shores of Crete.
For somewhere in that sacred island dwelt
A nymph, to whom all hoofed Satyrs knelt;
At whose white feet the languid Tritons[4] poured   15
Pearls, while on land they wither'd and adored.
Fast by the springs where she to bathe was wont,
And in those meads where sometime she might haunt,
Were strewn rich gifts, unknown to any Muse,
Though Fancy's casket were unlock'd to choose.   20
Ah, what a world of love was at her feet!
So Hermes thought, and a celestial heat
Burnt from his winged heels to either ear,
That from a whiteness, as the lily clear,
Blush'd into roses 'mid his golden hair,   25
Fallen in jealous curls about his shoulders bare.[5]

    From vale to vale, from wood to wood, he flew,
Breathing upon the flowers his passion new,
And wound with many a river to its head,
To find where this sweet nymph prepar'd her secret bed: 30
In vain; the sweet nymph might nowhere be found,

---

1. Nymphs and satyrs—like the dryads and fauns in line 5—were all minor classical deities of the woods and fields, said here to have been driven off by Oberon, king of the fairies, who were supernatural beings of the postclassical era.
2. Thickets.
3. Hermes (or Mercury), wing-footed messenger at the summons of Jove (line 11), was notoriously amorous.
4. Minor sea gods.
5. The curls clung jealously to his bare shoulders. This line is the first of a number of Alexandrines, a 6-foot line, used to vary the metrical movement—a device that Keats learned from Dryden. Another such device is the triplet, occurring first in lines 61–63.

And so he rested, on the lonely ground,
Pensive, and full of painful jealousies
Of the Wood-Gods, and even the very trees.
There as he stood, he heard a mournful voice,   35
Such as once heard, in gentle heart, destroys
All pain but pity: thus the lone voice spake:
"When from this wreathed tomb shall I awake!
When move in a sweet body fit for life,
And love, and pleasure, and the ruddy strife   40
Of hearts and lips! Ah, miserable me!"
The God, dove-footed,[6] glided silently
Round bush and tree, soft-brushing, in his speed,
The taller grasses and full-flowering weed,
Until he found a palpitating snake,   45
Bright, and cirque-couchant[7] in a dusky brake.

She was a gordian[8] shape of dazzling hue,
Vermilion-spotted, golden, green, and blue;
Striped like a zebra, freckled like a pard,
Eyed like a peacock,[9] and all crimson barr'd;   50
And full of silver moons, that, as she breathed,
Dissolv'd, or brighter shone, or interwreathed
Their lustres with the gloomier tapestries—
So rainbow-sided, touch'd with miseries,
She seem'd, at once, some penanced lady elf,   55
Some demon's mistress, or the demon's self.
Upon her crest she wore a wannish[1] fire
Sprinkled with stars, like Ariadne's tiar:[2]
Her head was serpent, but ah, bitter-sweet!
She had a woman's mouth with all its pearls[3] complete: 60
And for her eyes: what could such eyes do there
But weep, and weep, that they were born so fair?
As Proserpine still weeps for her Sicilian air.[4]
Her throat was serpent, but the words she spake
Came, as through bubbling honey, for Love's sake,   65
And thus; while Hermes on his pinions lay,
Like a stoop'd falcon[5] ere he takes his prey.

"Fair Hermes, crown'd with feathers, fluttering light,
I had a splendid dream of thee last night:
I saw thee sitting, on a throne of gold,   70
Among the Gods, upon Olympus old,

---

6. Quietly as a dove.
7. Lying in a circular coil.
8. Intricately twisted, like the knot tied by King Gordius, which no one could undo.
9. Having multicolored spots, like the "eyes" in a peacock's tail. "Pard": leopard.
1. Rather dark.
2. Ariadne, who was transformed into a constel-

lation, had been represented in a painting by Titian wearing a symbolic crown, or tiara ("tiar"), of stars.
3. "Pearls" had become almost a synonym for teeth in Elizabethan poetry.
4. Proserpine had been carried off to Hades by Pluto from the field of Enna, in Sicily.
5. "Stoop" is the term for the plunge of a falcon upon his prey.

The only sad one; for thou didst not hear
The soft, lute-finger'd Muses chaunting clear,
Nor even Apollo when he sang alone,
Deaf to his throbbing throat's long, long melodious moan.   75
I dreamt I saw thee, robed in purple flakes,
Break amorous through the clouds, as morning breaks,
And, swiftly as a bright Phœbean dart,[6]
Strike for the Cretan isle; and here thou art!
Too gentle Hermes, hast thou found the maid?"   80
Whereat the star of Lethe[7] not delay'd
His rosy eloquence, and thus inquired:
"Thou smooth-lipp'd serpent, surely high inspired!
Thou beauteous wreath, with melancholy eyes,
Possess whatever bliss thou canst devise,   85
Telling me only where my nymph is fled,—
Where she doth breathe!" "Bright planet, thou hast said,"
Return'd the snake, "but seal with oaths, fair God!"
"I swear," said Hermes, "by my serpent rod,
And by thine eyes, and by thy starry crown!"   90
Light flew his earnest words, among the blossoms blown.
Then thus again the brilliance feminine:
"Too frail of heart! for this lost nymph of thine,
Free as the air, invisibly, she strays
About these thornless wilds; her pleasant days   95
She tastes unseen; unseen her nimble feet
Leave traces in the grass and flowers sweet;
From weary tendrils, and bow'd branches green,
She plucks the fruit unseen, she bathes unseen:
And by my power is her beauty veil'd   100
To keep it unaffronted, unassail'd
By the love-glances of unlovely eyes,
Of Satyrs, Fauns, and blear'd Silenus'[8] sighs.
Pale grew her immortality, for woe
Of all these lovers, and she grieved so   105
I took compassion on her, bade her steep
Her hair in weïrd[9] syrops, that would keep
Her loveliness invisible, yet free
To wander as she loves, in liberty.
Thou shalt behold her, Hermes, thou alone,   110
If thou wilt, as thou swearest, grant my boon!"
Then, once again, the charmed God began
An oath, and through the serpent's ears it ran
Warm, tremulous, devout, psalterian.[1]

---

6. A ray of Phoebus Apollo, god of the sun.
7. Hermes, when he appeared like a star on the banks of Lethe, in the darkness of Hades. (One of Hermes' offices was to guide the souls of the dead to the lower regions.)

8. Silenus was a satyr, tutor of Bacchus, and usually represented as drunk.
9. Magical: Keats makes the word a dissyllable.
1. Either "like a psalm" or "like the sound of the psaltery" (an ancient stringed instrument).

Ravish'd, she lifted her Circean[2] head,   115
Blush'd a live damask, and swift-lisping said,
"I was a woman, let me have once more
A woman's shape, and charming as before.
I love a youth of Corinth—O the bliss!
Give me my woman's form, and place me where he is.   120
Stoop, Hermes, let me breathe upon thy brow,
And thou shalt see thy sweet nymph even now."
The God on half-shut feathers sank serene,
She breath'd upon his eyes, and swift was seen
Of both the guarded nymph near-smiling on the green.   125
It was no dream; or say a dream it was,
Real are the dreams of Gods, and smoothly pass
Their pleasures in a long immortal dream.
One warm, flush'd moment, hovering, it might seem
Dash'd by the wood-nymph's beauty, so he burn'd;   130
Then, lighting on the printless verdure, turn'd
To the swoon'd serpent, and with languid arm,
Delicate, put to proof the lythe Caducean charm.[3]
So done, upon the nymph his eyes he bent
Full of adoring tears and blandishment,   135
And towards her stept: she, like a moon in wane,
Faded before him, cower'd, nor could restrain
Her fearful sobs, self-folding like a flower
That faints into itself at evening hour:
But the God fostering her chilled hand,   140
She felt the warmth, her eyelids open'd bland,[4]
And, like new flowers at morning song of bees,
Bloom'd, and gave up her honey to the lees.[5]
Into the green-recessed woods they flew;
Nor grew they pale, as mortal lovers do.   145

    Left to herself, the serpent now began
To change; her elfin blood in madness ran,
Her mouth foam'd, and the grass, therewith besprent,[6]
Wither'd at dew so sweet and virulent;
Her eyes in torture fix'd, and anguish drear,   150
Hot, glaz'd, and wide, with lid-lashes all sear,
Flash'd phosphor and sharp sparks, without one cooling tear.
The colours all inflam'd throughout her train,
She writh'd about, convuls'd with scarlet pain:
A deep volcanian[7] yellow took the place   155
Of all her milder-mooned body's grace;

---

2. Like that of Circe, the enchantress in the *Odys-*
sey. "Live damask" (line 116): a living damask rose
(large and fragrant pink rose).
3. I.e., put to the test the magic of the flexible
Caduceus (Hermes' official staff).

4. Softly.
5. Dregs.
6. Sprinkled.
7. The yellow of sulphur (thrown up by a volcano)
replaced her former silvery moon color.

And, as the lava ravishes the mead,
Spoilt all her silver mail, and golden brede;[8]
Made gloom of all her frecklings, streaks and bars,
Eclips'd her crescents, and lick'd up her stars: 160
So that, in moments few, she was undrest
Of all her sapphires, greens, and amethyst,
And rubious-argent:[9] of all these bereft,
Nothing but pain and ugliness were left.
Still shone her crown; that vanish'd, also she   165
Melted and disappear'd as suddenly;
And in the air, her new voice luting soft,
Cried, "Lycius! gentle Lycius!"—Borne aloft
With the bright mists about the mountains hoar
These words dissolv'd: Crete's forests heard no more.   170

     Whither fled Lamia, now a lady bright,
A full-born beauty new and exquisite?
She fled into that valley they pass o'er
Who go to Corinth from Cenchreas' shore;[1]
And rested at the foot of those wild hills,   175
The rugged founts of the Peræan rills,
And of that other ridge whose barren back
Stretches, with all its mist and cloudy rack,
South-westward to Cleone. There she stood
About a young bird's flutter from a wood,   180
Fair, on a sloping green of mossy tread,
By a clear pool, wherein she passioned[2]
To see herself escap'd from so sore ills,
While her robes flaunted with the daffodils.

     Ah, happy Lycius!—for she was a maid   185
More beautiful than ever twisted braid,
Or sigh'd, or blush'd, or on spring-flowered lea[3]
Spread a green kirtle to the minstrelsy:
A virgin purest lipp'd, yet in the lore
Of love deep learned to the red heart's core: 190
Not one hour old, yet of sciential brain
To unperplex bliss from its neighbour pain;
Define their pettish limits, and estrange
Their points of contact, and swift counterchange;[4]
Intrigue with the specious chaos,[5] and dispart   195
Its most ambiguous atoms with sure art;

8. "Mail": interlinked rings, as in a coat of armor. "Brede": embroidery, interwoven pattern.
9. Silvery red.
1. Cenchrea (Keats's "Cenchreas") was a harbor of Corinth, in southern Greece.
2. Felt intense excitement.
3. Meadow. "Kirtle" (line 188): gown.
4. I.e., of knowledgeable ("sciential") brain to disentangle ("unperplex") bliss from its closely related pain, to define their quarreled-over ("pettish") limits, and to separate out ("estrange") their points of contact and the swift changes of each condition into its opposite. Cf. Keats's Ode on Melancholy, lines 21–26.
5. I.e., turn to her own artful purpose the seeming ("specious") chaos.

As though in Cupid's college she had spent
Sweet days a lovely graduate, still unshent,[6]
And kept his rosy terms in idle languishment.

Why this fair creature chose so fairly   200
By the wayside to linger, we shall see;
But first 'tis fit to tell how she could muse
And dream, when in the serpent prison-house,
Of all she list,[7] strange or magnificent:
How, ever, where she will'd, her spirit went;   205
Whether to faint Elysium, or where
Down through tress-lifting waves the Nereids[8] fair
Wind into Thetis' bower by many a pearly stair;
Or where God Bacchus drains his cups divine,
Stretch'd out, at ease, beneath a glutinous pine;   210
Or where in Pluto's gardens palatine
Mulciber's columns gleam in far piazzian line.[9]
And sometimes into cities she would send
Her dream, with feast and rioting to blend;
And once, while among mortals dreaming thus,   215
She saw the young Corinthian Lycius
Charioting foremost in the envious race,
Like a young Jove with calm uneager face,
And fell into a swooning love of him.
Now on the moth-time of that evening dim   220
He would return that way, as well she knew,
To Corinth from the shore; for freshly blew
The eastern soft wind, and his galley now
Grated the quaystones with her brazen prow
In port Cenchreas, from Egina isle   225
Fresh anchor'd; whither he had been awhile
To sacrifice to Jove, whose temple there
Waits with high marble doors for blood and incense rare.
Jove heard his vows, and better'd his desire;
For by some freakful chance he made retire   230
From his companions, and set forth to walk,
Perhaps grown wearied of their Corinth talk:
Over the solitary hills he fared,
Thoughtless at first, but ere eve's star appeared
His phantasy was lost, where reason fades,   235
In the calm'd twilight of Platonic shades.[1]
Lamia beheld him coming, near, more near—
Close to her passing, in indifference drear,
His silent sandals swept the mossy green;

---

6. Unspoiled. "Rosy terms" (line 199): the terms
spent studying in "Cupid's college."
7. Wished.
8. Sea nymphs, of whom Thetis (line 208, the
mother of Achilles) was one.

9. I.e., columns made by Mulciber (Vulcan, god
of fire and metalworking) gleam in long lines around
open courts (piazzas). "Palatine": palatial.
1. I.e., he was absorbed in musing about the
obscurities of Plato's philosophy.

So neighbour'd to him, and yet so unseen   240
She stood: he pass'd, shut up in mysteries,
His mind wrapp'd like his mantle, while her eyes
Follow'd his steps, and her neck regal white
Turn'd—syllabling thus, "Ah, Lycius bright,
And will you leave me on the hills alone?   245
Lycius, look back! and be some pity shown."
He did; not with cold wonder fearingly,
But Orpheus-like at an Eurydice;[2]
For so delicious were the words she sung,
It seem'd he had lov'd them a whole summer long: 250
And soon his eyes had drunk her beauty up,
Leaving no drop in the bewildering cup,
And still the cup was full,—while he, afraid
Lest she should vanish ere his lip had paid
Due adoration, thus began to adore;   255
Her soft look growing coy, she saw his chain so sure:
"Leave thee alone! Look back! Ah, Goddess, see
Whether my eyes can ever turn from thee!
For pity do not this sad heart belie[3]—
Even as thou vanishest so I shall die.   260
Stay! though a Naiad of the rivers, stay!
To thy far wishes will thy streams obey:
Stay! though the greenest woods be thy domain,
Alone they can drink up the morning rain:
Though a descended Pleiad,[4] will not one   265
Of thine harmonious sisters keep in tune
Thy spheres, and as thy silver proxy shine?
So sweetly to these ravish'd ears of mine
Came thy sweet greeting, that if thou shouldst fade
Thy memory will waste me to a shade:—   270
For pity do not melt!"—"If I should stay,"
Said Lamia, "here, upon this floor of clay,
And pain my steps upon these flowers too rough,
What canst thou say or do of charm enough
To dull the nice[5] remembrance of my home?   275
Thou canst not ask me with thee here to roam
Over these hills and vales, where no joy is,—
Empty of immortality and bliss!
Thou art a scholar, Lycius, and must know
That finer spirits cannot breathe below   280
In human climes, and live: Alas! poor youth,
What taste of purer air hast thou to soothe
My essence? What serener palaces,

2. As Orpheus looked at Eurydice in Hades. Orpheus was allowed by Pluto to lead Eurydice back to earth on condition that he not look back at her, but he could not resist doing so, hence lost her once more.

3. Be false to.
4. One of the seven sisters composing the constellation Pleiades.
5. Detailed, minutely accurate.

Where I may all my many senses please,
And by mysterious sleights a hundred thirsts appease?   285
It cannot be—Adieu!" So said, she rose
Tiptoe with white arms spread. He, sick to lose
The amorous promise of her lone complain,
Swoon'd, murmuring of love, and pale with pain.
The cruel lady, without any show   290
Of sorrow for her tender favourite's woe,
But rather, if her eyes could brighter be,
With brighter eyes and slow amenity,
Put her new lips to his, and gave afresh
The life she had so tangled in her mesh: 295
And as he from one trance was wakening
Into another, she began to sing,
Happy in beauty, life, and love, and every thing,
A song of love, too sweet for earthly lyres,
While, like held breath, the stars drew in their panting fires.   300
And then she whisper'd in such trembling tone,
As those who, safe together met alone
For the first time through many anguish'd days,
Use other speech than looks; bidding him raise
His drooping head, and clear his soul of doubt,   305
For that she was a woman, and without
Any more subtle fluid in her veins
Than throbbing blood, and that the self-same pains
Inhabited her frail-strung heart as his.
And next she wonder'd how his eyes could miss   310
Her face so long in Corinth, where, she said,
She dwelt but half retir'd, and there had led
Days happy as the gold coin could invent
Without the aid of love; yet in content
Till she saw him, as once she pass'd him by,   315
Where 'gainst a column he leant thoughtfully
At Venus' temple porch, 'mid baskets heap'd
Of amorous herbs and flowers, newly reap'd
Late on that eve, as 'twas the night before
The Adonian feast;[6] whereof she saw no more,   320
But wept alone those days, for why should she adore?
Lycius from death awoke into amaze,
To see her still, and singing so sweet lays;
Then from amaze into delight he fell
To hear her whisper woman's lore so well;   325
And every word she spake entic'd him on
To unperplex'd delight[7] and pleasure known.
Let the mad poets say whate'er they please
Of the sweets of Fairies, Peris,[8] Goddesses,
There is not such a treat among them all,   330

6. The feast of Adonis, beloved by Venus.   see line 192.
7. I.e., delight not mixed with its neighbor, pain;   8. Fairylike creatures in Persian mythology.

Haunters of cavern, lake, and waterfall,
As a real woman, lineal indeed
From Pyrrha's pebbles[9] or old Adam's seed.
Thus gentle Lamia judg'd, and judg'd aright,
That Lycius could not love in half a fright,   335
So threw the goddess off, and won his heart
More pleasantly by playing woman's part,
With no more awe than what her beauty gave,
That, while it smote, still guaranteed to save.
Lycius to all made eloquent reply,   340
Marrying to every word a twinborn sigh;
And last, pointing to Corinth, ask'd her sweet,
If 'twas too far that night for her soft feet.
The way was short, for Lamia's eagerness
Made, by a spell, the triple league decrease   345
To a few paces; not at all surmised
By blinded Lycius, so in her comprized.[1]
They pass'd the city gates, he knew not how,
So noiseless, and he never thought to know.

    As men talk in a dream, so Corinth all,   350
Throughout her palaces imperial,
And all her populous streets and temples lewd,[2]
Mutter'd, like tempest in the distance brew'd,
To the wide-spreaded night above her towers.
Men, women, rich and poor, in the cool hours,   355
Shuffled their sandals o'er the pavement white,
Companion'd or alone; while many a light
Flared, here and there, from wealthy festivals,
And threw their moving shadows on the walls,
Or found them cluster'd in the corniced shade   360
Of some arch'd temple door, or dusky colonnade.

    Muffling his face, of greeting friends in fear,
Her fingers he press'd hard, as one came near
With curl'd gray beard, sharp eyes, and smooth bald crown,
Slow-stepp'd, and robed in philosophic gown: 365
Lycius shrank closer, as they met and past,
Into his mantle, adding wings to haste,
While hurried Lamia trembled: "Ah," said he,
"Why do you shudder, love, so ruefully?
Why does your tender palm dissolve in dew?"—   370
"I'm wearied," said fair Lamia: "tell me who
Is that old man? I cannot bring to mind
His features:—Lycius! wherefore did you blind
Yourself from his quick eyes?" Lycius replied,

9. Descended from the pebbles with which, in   1. Bound up, absorbed.
Greek myth, Pyrrha and Deucalion repeopled the   2. Temples of Venus, whose worship sometimes
earth after the flood.   involved ritual prostitution.

" 'Tis Apollonius sage, my trusty guide   375
And good instructor; but to-night he seems
The ghost of folly haunting my sweet dreams."

    While yet he spake they had arrived before
A pillar'd porch, with lofty portal door,
Where hung a silver lamp, whose phosphor glow   380
Reflected in the slabbed steps below,
Mild as a star in water; for so new,
And so unsullied was the marble hue,
So through the crystal polish, liquid fine,
Ran the dark veins, that none but feet divine   385
Could e'er have touch'd there. Sounds Æolian[3]
Breath'd from the hinges, as the ample span
Of the wide doors disclos'd a place unknown
Some time to any, but those two alone,
And a few Persian mutes, who that same year   390
Were seen about the markets: none knew where
They could inhabit; the most curious
Were foil'd, who watch'd to trace them to their house:
And but the flitter-winged verse must tell,
For truth's sake, what woe afterwards befel,   395
'Twould humour many a heart to leave them thus,
Shut from the busy world of more incredulous.

Part 2

Love in a hut, with water and a crust,
Is—Love, forgive us!—cinders, ashes, dust;
Love in a palace is perhaps at last
More grievous torment than a hermit's fast:—
That is a doubtful tale from faery land,   5
Hard for the non-elect to understand.
Had Lycius liv'd to hand his story down,
He might have given the moral a fresh frown,
Or clench'd it quite: but too short was their bliss
To breed distrust and hate, that make the soft voice hiss.   10
Besides, there, nightly, with terrific glare,
Love, jealous grown of so complete a pair,
Hover'd and buzz'd his wings, with fearful roar,
Above the lintel of their chamber door,
And down the passage cast a glow upon the floor.   15

    For all this came a ruin: side by side
They were enthroned, in the even tide,
Upon a couch, near to a curtaining
Whose airy texture, from a golden string,

3. Like sounds from the wind harp (Aeolus is god of winds), which responds musically to a current of air.

Floated into the room, and let appear   20
Unveil'd the summer heaven, blue and clear,
Betwixt two marble shafts:—there they reposed,
Where use had made it sweet, with eyelids closed,
Saving a tythe which love still open kept,
That they might see each other while they almost slept;   25
When from the slope side of a suburb hill,
Deafening the swallow's twitter, came a thrill
Of trumpets—Lycius started—the sounds fled,
But left a thought, a buzzing in his head.
For the first time, since first he harbour'd in   30
That purple-lined palace of sweet sin,
His spirit pass'd beyond its golden bourn
Into the noisy world almost forsworn.
The lady, ever watchful, penetrant,
Saw this with pain, so arguing a want   35
Of something more, more than her empery[4]
Of joys; and she began to moan and sigh
Because he mused beyond her, knowing well
That but a moment's thought is passion's passing bell.[5]
"Why do you sigh, fair creature?" whisper'd he: 40
"Why do you think?" return'd she tenderly:
"You have deserted me;—where am I now?
Not in your heart while care weighs on your brow:
No, no, you have dismiss'd me; and I go
From your breast houseless: ay, it must be so."   45
He answer'd, bending to her open eyes,
Where he was mirror'd small in paradise,
"My silver planet, both of eve and morn![6]
Why will you plead yourself so sad forlorn,
While I am striving how to fill my heart   50
With deeper crimson, and a double smart?
How to entangle, trammel up and snare
Your soul in mine, and labyrinth you there
Like the hid scent in an unbudded rose?
Ay, a sweet kiss—you see your mighty woes.[7]   55
My thoughts! shall I unveil them? Listen then!
What mortal hath a prize, that other men
May be confounded and abash'd withal,
But lets it sometimes pace abroad majestical,
And triumph, as in thee I should rejoice   60
Amid the hoarse alarm of Corinth's voice.
Let my foes choke, and my friends shout afar,
While through the thronged streets your bridal car
Wheels round its dazzling spokes."—The lady's cheek
Trembled; she nothing said, but, pale and meek,   65

4. Empire.
5. Death knell.
6. The planet Venus, which is both the morning
and the evening star.
7. Playfully: "You see how great your troubles
were!"

Arose and knelt before him, wept a rain
Of sorrows at his words; at last with pain
Beseeching him, the while his hand she wrung,
To change his purpose. He thereat was stung,
Perverse, with stronger fancy to reclaim   70
Her wild and timid nature to his aim:
Besides, for all his love, in self despite,
Against his better self, he took delight
Luxurious in her sorrows, soft and new.
His passion, cruel grown, took on a hue   75
Fierce and sanguineous as 'twas possible
In one whose brow had no dark veins to swell.
Fine was the mitigated fury, like
Apollo's presence when in act to strike
The serpent—Ha, the serpent! certes, she   80
Was none. She burnt, she lov'd the tyranny,
And, all subdued, consented to the hour
When to the bridal he should lead his paramour.
Whispering in midnight silence, said the youth,
"Sure some sweet name thou hast, though, by my truth,   85
I have not ask'd it, ever thinking thee
Not mortal, but of heavenly progeny,
As still I do. Hast any mortal name,
Fit appellation for this dazzling frame?
Or friends or kinsfolk on the citied earth,   90
To share our marriage feast and nuptial mirth?"
"I have no friends," said Lamia, "no, not one;
My presence in wide Corinth hardly known:
My parents' bones are in their dusty urns
Sepulchred, where no kindled incense burns,   95
Seeing all their luckless race are dead, save me,
And I neglect the holy rite for thee.
Even as you list invite your many guests;
But if, as now it seems, your vision rests
With any pleasure on me, do not bid   100
Old Apollonius—from him keep me hid."
Lycius, perplex'd at words so blind and blank,
Made close inquiry; from whose touch she shrank,
Feigning a sleep; and he to the dull shade
Of deep sleep in a moment was betray'd.   105

    It was the custom then to bring away,
The bride from home at blushing shut of day,
Veil'd, in a chariot, heralded along
By strewn flowers, torches, and a marriage song,
With other pageants: but this fair unknown   110
Had not a friend. So being left alone,
(Lycius was gone to summon all his kin)
And knowing surely she could never win

His foolish heart from its mad pompousness,
She set herself, high-thoughted, how to dress   115
The misery in fit magnificence.
She did so, but 'tis doubtful how and whence
Came, and who were her subtle servitors.
About the halls, and to and from the doors,
There was a noise of wings, till in short space   120
The glowing banquet-room shone with wide-arched grace.
A haunting music, sole perhaps and lone
Supportress of the faery-roof, made moan
Throughout, as fearful the whole charm might fade.
Fresh carved cedar, mimicking a glade   125
Of palm and plantain, met from either side,
High in the midst, in honour of the bride:
Two palms and then two plantains, and so on,
From either side their stems branch'd one to one
All down the aisled place; and beneath all   130
There ran a stream of lamps straight on from wall to wall.
So canopied, lay an untasted feast
Teeming with odours. Lamia, regal drest,
Silently paced about, and as she went,
In pale contented sort of discontent,   135
Mission'd her viewless servants to enrich
The fretted[8] splendour of each nook and niche.
Between the tree-stems, marbled plain at first,
Came jasper pannels; then, anon, there burst
Forth creeping imagery of slighter trees,   140
And with the larger wove in small intricacies.
Approving all, she faded at self-will,
And shut the chamber up, close, hush'd and still,
Complete and ready for the revels rude,
When dreadful[9] guests would come to spoil her solitude.   145

    The day appear'd, and all the gossip rout.
O senseless Lycius! Madman! wherefore flout
The silent-blessing fate, warm cloister'd hours,
And show to common eyes these secret bowers?
The herd approach'd; each guest, with busy brain,   150
Arriving at the portal, gaz'd amain,[1]
And enter'd marveling: for they knew the street,
Remember'd it from childhood all complete
Without a gap, yet ne'er before had seen
That royal porch, that high-built fair demesne;[2]   155
So in they hurried all, maz'd, curious and keen:
Save one, who look'd thereon with eye severe,
And with calm-planted steps walk'd in austere;
'Twas Apollonius: something too he laugh'd,

8. Adorned with fretwork (interlaced patterns).   1. Intently.
9. Terrifying.   2. Estate.

As though some knotty problem, that had daft[3]   160
His patient thought, had now begun to thaw,
And solve and melt:—'twas just as he foresaw.

He met within the murmurous vestibule
His young disciple. " 'Tis no common rule,
Lycius," said he, "for uninvited guest   165
To force himself upon you, and infest
With an unbidden presence the bright throng
Of younger friends; yet must I do this wrong,
And you forgive me." Lycius blush'd, and led
The old man through the inner doors broad-spread;   170
With reconciling words and courteous mien
Turning into sweet milk the sophist's spleen.

Of wealthy lustre was the banquet-room,
Fill'd with pervading brilliance and perfume:
Before each lucid pannel fuming stood   175
A censer fed with myrrh and spiced wood,
Each by a sacred tripod held aloft,
Whose slender feet wide-swerv'd upon the soft
Wool-woofed[4] carpets: fifty wreaths of smoke
From fifty censers their light voyage took   180
To the high roof, still mimick'd as they rose
Along the mirror'd walls by twin-clouds odorous.
Twelve sphered tables, by silk seats insphered,
High as the level of a man's breast rear'd
On libbard's[5] paws, upheld the heavy gold   185
Of cups and goblets, and the store thrice told
Of Ceres' horn,[6] and, in huge vessels, wine
Come from the gloomy tun with merry shine.
Thus loaded with a feast the tables stood,
Each shrining in the midst the image of a God.   190

When in an antichamber every guest
Had felt the cold full sponge to pleasure press'd,
By minist'ring slaves, upon his hands and feet,
And fragrant oils with ceremony meet
Pour'd on his hair, they all mov'd to the feast   195
In white robes, and themselves in order placed
Around the silken couches, wondering
Whence all this mighty cost and blaze of wealth could spring.

Soft went the music the soft air along,
While fluent Greek a vowel'd undersong   200
Kept up among the guests, discoursing low

3. Baffled, bewildered.
4. Woven.
5. Leopard's.

6. The horn of plenty, overflowing with the products of Ceres, goddess of vegetation.

At first, for scarcely was the wine at flow;
But when the happy vintage touch'd their brains,
Louder they talk, and louder come the strains
Of powerful instruments:—the gorgeous dyes,   205
The space, the splendour of the draperies,
The roof of awful richness, nectarous cheer,
Beautiful slaves, and Lamia's self, appear,
Now, when the wine has done its rosy deed,
And every soul from human trammels freed,   210
No more so strange; for merry wine, sweet wine,
Will make Elysian shades not too fair, too divine.

     Soon was God Bacchus at meridian height;
Flush'd were their cheeks, and bright eyes double bright:
Garlands of every green, and every scent   215
From vales deflower'd, or forest-trees branch-rent,
In baskets of bright osier'd[7] gold were brought
High as the handles heap'd, to suit the thought
Of every guest; that each, as he did please,
Might fancy-fit his brows, silk-pillow'd at his ease.   220

     What wreath for Lamia? What for Lycius?
What for the sage, old Apollonius?
Upon her aching forehead be there hung
The leaves of willow and of adder's tongue;[8]
And for the youth, quick, let us strip for him   225
The thyrsus,[9] that his watching eyes may swim
Into forgetfulness; and, for the sage,
Let spear-grass and the spiteful thistle wage
War on his temples. Do not all charms fly
At the mere touch of cold philosophy?[1]   230
There was an awful[2] rainbow once in heaven:
We know her woof, her texture; she is given
In the dull catalogue of common things.
Philosophy will clip an Angel's wings,
Conquer all mysteries by rule and line,   235
Empty the haunted air, and gnomed mine[3]—
Unweave a rainbow, as it erewhile made
The tender-person'd Lamia melt into a shade.

     By her glad Lycius sitting, in chief place,
Scarce saw in all the room another face,   240
Till, checking his love trance, a cup he took

7. Plaited. An "osier" is a willow rod used in weaving baskets.
8. A fern whose spikes resemble a serpent's tongue.
9. The vine-covered staff of Bacchus, used to signify drunkenness.
1. "Philosophy" in the sense of "natural philosophy," or science. Benjamin Haydon tells in his *Autobiography* how, at a hard-drinking and high-spirited dinner party, Keats had agreed with Charles Lamb (to what extent jokingly, is not clear) that Newton's *Optics* "had destroyed all the poetry of the rainbow by reducing it to the prismatic colors."
2. Awe-inspiring.
3. Gnomes were guardians of mines.

Full brimm'd, and opposite sent forth a look
'Cross the broad table, to beseech a glance
From his old teacher's wrinkled countenance,
And pledge him.[4] The bald-head philosopher   245
Had fix'd his eye, without a twinkle or stir
Full on the alarmed beauty of the bride,
Brow-beating her fair form, and troubling her sweet pride.
Lycius then press'd her hand, with devout touch,
As pale it lay upon the rosy couch: 250
'Twas icy, and the cold ran through his veins;
Then sudden it grew hot, and all the pains
Of an unnatural heat shot to his heart.
"Lamia, what means this? Wherefore dost thou start?
Know'st thou that man?" Poor Lamia answer'd not.   255
He gaz'd into her eyes, and not a jot
Own'd[5] they the lovelorn piteous appeal:
More, more he gaz'd: his human senses reel:
Some hungry spell that loveliness absorbs;
There was no recognition in those orbs.   260
"Lamia!" he cried—and no soft-toned reply.
The many heard, and the loud revelry
Grew hush; the stately music no more breathes;
The myrtle[6] sicken'd in a thousand wreaths.
By faint degrees, voice, lute, and pleasure ceased;   265
A deadly silence step by step increased,
Until it seem'd a horrid presence there,
And not a man but felt the terror in his hair.
"Lamia!" he shriek'd; and nothing but the shriek
With its sad echo did the silence break.   270
"Begone, foul dream!" he cried, gazing again
In the bride's face, where now no azure vein
Wander'd on fair-spaced temples; no soft bloom
Misted the cheek; no passion to illume
The deep-recessed vision:—all was blight;   275
Lamia, no longer fair, there sat a deadly white.
"Shut, shut those juggling[7] eyes, thou ruthless man!
Turn them aside, wretch! or the righteous ban
Of all the Gods, whose dreadful images
Here represent their shadowy presences,   280
May pierce them on the sudden with the thorn
Of painful blindness; leaving thee forlorn,
In trembling dotage to the feeblest fright
Of conscience, for their long offended might,
For all thine impious proud-heart sophistries,   285
Unlawful magic, and enticing lies.
Corinthians! look upon that gray-beard wretch!
Mark how, possess'd, his lashless eyelids stretch

4. Drink a toast to him.   6. Sacred to Venus, hence an emblem of love.
5. Acknowledged.   7. Deceiving, full of trickery.

Around his demon eyes! Corinthians, see!
My sweet bride withers at their potency." 290
"Fool!" said the sophist, in an under-tone
Gruff with contempt; which a death-nighing moan
From Lycius answer'd, as heart-struck and lost,
He sank supine beside the aching ghost.
"Fool! Fool!" repeated he, while his eyes still 295
Relented not, nor mov'd; "from every ill
Of life have I preserv'd thee to this day,
And shall I see thee made a serpent's prey?"
Then Lamia breath'd death breath; the sophist's eye,
Like a sharp spear, went through her utterly, 300
Keen, cruel, perceant,[8] stinging: she, as well
As her weak hand could any meaning tell,
Motion'd him to be silent; vainly so,
He look'd and look'd again a level—No!
"A Serpent!" echoed he; no sooner said, 305
Than with a frightful scream she vanished:
And Lycius' arms were empty of delight,
As were his limbs of life, from that same night.
On the high couch he lay!—his friends came round—
Supported him—no pulse, or breath they found, 310
And, in its marriage robe, the heavy body wound.

July–August 1819   1820

To Autumn[1]

1

Season of mists and mellow fruitfulness,
    Close bosom-friend of the maturing sun;
Conspiring with him how to load and bless
    With fruit the vines that round the thatch-eves run;
To bend with apples the moss'd cottage-trees, 5
    And fill all fruit with ripeness to the core;
        To swell the gourd, and plump the hazel shells
    With a sweet kernel; to set budding more,
And still more, later flowers for the bees,
Until they think warm days will never cease, 10
        For summer has o'er-brimm'd their clammy cells.

2

Who hath not seen thee oft amid thy store?
    Sometimes whoever seeks abroad may find
    Thee sitting careless on a granary floor,

8. Piercing.
1. Two days after this serene and gracious ode was
composed, Keats wrote to J. H. Reynolds: "I never
liked stubble fields so much as now—Aye, better
than the chilly green of the spring. Somehow a
stubble plain looks warm—in the same way that
some pictures look warm—this struck me so much
in my Sunday's walk that I composed upon it."
    For the author's revisions while composing *To
Autumn*, see "Poems in Process," below.

Thy hair soft-lifted by the winnowing[2] wind;   15
Or on a half-reap'd furrow sound asleep,
   Drows'd with the fume of poppies, while thy hook[3]
   Spares the next swath and all its twined flowers:
And sometimes like a gleaner thou dost keep
   Steady thy laden head across a brook;   20
   Or by a cyder-press, with patient look,
     Thou watchest the last oozings hours by hours.

3

Where are the songs of spring? Ay, where are they?
   Think not of them, thou hast thy music too,—
While barred clouds bloom the soft-dying day,   25
   And touch the stubble-plains with rosy hue;
Then in a wailful choir the small gnats mourn
   Among the river sallows,[4] borne aloft
   Or sinking as the light wind lives or dies;
And full-grown lambs loud bleat from hilly bourn;[5]   30
   Hedge-crickets sing; and now with treble soft
   The red-breast whistles from a garden-croft;[6]
     And gathering swallows twitter in the skies.

Sept. 19, 1819   1820

Letters   Keats's letters serve as a running commentary on his life, reading, thinking, and writing. They demonstrate an extraordinary intelligence, whose very lack of academic or philosophical training gives its expression a freedom from jargon and standard categories that is equally challenging and rewarding to the reader. Keats's early reputation as a poet of pure luxury, sensation, and art for art's sake has undergone a radical change since, in the present century, critics began to pay close attention to his letters. For Keats thought hard and persistently about life and art, and any seed of an ethical or critical idea that he picked up from his intellectual contemporaries (Hazlitt, Coleridge, Wordsworth) instantly germinated and flourished in the rich soil of his imagination. What T. S. Eliot said about the metaphysical poets applies equally to Keats in his letters: his "mode of feeling was directly and freshly altered by [his] reading and thought." And like Donne, he looked not only into the heart but, literally, "into the cerebral cortex, the nervous system, and the digestive tract." A number of Keats's casual comments on the poet and on poetry included below—especially those dealing with what we now call empathy, and with "negative capability"—have become standard points of reference in aesthetic theory. But Keats himself regarded nothing that he said as ultimate; each statement constituted only a stage in his continuing exploration into what he called "the mystery."

   The text below is that of the edition of the *Letters* by Hyder E. Rollins (1958), which reproduces the original MSS precisely, so that the reader may follow Keats's pen as, throwing spelling and grammar to the winds, it strains to keep up with the rush of his thoughts.

---

2. To "winnow" is to fan the chaff from the grain.   5. Region.
3. Scythe.   6. A "croft" is an enclosed plot of farm land.
4. Willows.

LETTERS

To Benjamin Bailey[1]

[The Authenticity of the Imagination]

[November 22, 1817]

My dear Bailey,

    * * * O I wish I was as certain of the end of all your troubles as that of your momentary start about the authenticity of the Imagination. I am certain of nothing but of the holiness of the Heart's affections and the truth of Imagination—What the imagination seizes as Beauty must be truth[2]—whether it existed before or not—for I have the same Idea of all our Passions as of Love they are all in their sublime, creative of essential Beauty—In a Word, you may know my favorite Speculation by my first Book and the little song I sent in my last[3]—which is a representation from the fancy of the probable mode of operating in these Matters—The Imagination may be compared to Adam's dream[4]—he awoke and found it truth. I am the more zealous in this affair, because I have never yet been able to perceive how any thing can be known for truth by consequitive reasoning[5]—and yet it must be—Can it be that even the greatest Philosopher ever ~~when~~ arrived at his goal without putting aside numerous objections—However it may be, O for a Life of Sensations[6] rather than of Thoughts! It is "a Vision in the form of Youth" a Shadow of reality to come—and this consideration has further conv[i]nced me for it has come as auxiliary to another favorite Speculation of mine, that we shall enjoy ourselves here after by having what we called happiness on Earth repeated in a finer tone and so repeated[7]—And yet such a fate can only befall those who delight in sensation rather than hunger as you do after Truth—Adam's dream will do here and seems to be a conviction that Imagination and its empyreal reflection is the same as human Life and its spiritual repetition. But as I was saying—the simple imaginative Mind may have its rewards in the repeti[ti]on of its own silent Working coming continually on the spirit with a fine suddenness—to compare great things with small—have you never by being surprised with an old Melody—in a delicious place—by a delicious voice, fe[l]t over again your very speculations and surmises at the time it first operated on your soul—do you not remember forming to yourself the singer's face more beautiful that[8] it was possible and yet with the elevation of the Moment

---

1. Bailey was one of Keats's closest friends. Keats had stayed with him the month before at Oxford, where Bailey was an undergraduate.
2. The phrase occurs in a poetic context at the close of *Ode on a Grecian Urn.* Try substituting "real," or "reality," where Keats uses the word "truth."
3. The song was "O Sorrow," from book 4 of *Endymion.*
4. In *Paradise Lost* 8.452–90, Adam dreams that Eve has been created, and awakes to find her real.

Adam also describes an earlier prefigurative dream in the same work, 8.283–311.
5. Consecutive reasoning—reasoning that moves by logical steps.
6. Probably not only sense experiences, but also the intuitive perceptions of truths, as opposed to truth achieved by consecutive reasoning.
7. Cf. the "Pleasure Thermometer" in *Endymion,* book 1, lines 777 ff., above.
8. For "than."

you did not think so—even then you were mounted on the Wings of Imagination so high—that the Prototype must be here after—that delicious face you will see—What a time! I am continually running away from the subject—sure this cannot be exactly the case with a complex Mind—one that is imaginative and at the same time careful of its fruits—who would exist partly on sensation partly on thought—to whom it is necessary that years should bring the philosophic Mind[9]—such an one I consider your's and therefore it is necessary to your eternal Happiness that you not only ~~have~~ drink this old Wine of Heaven which I shall call the redigestion of our most ethereal Musings on Earth; but also increase in knowledge and know all things. I am glad to hear you are in a fair Way for Easter—you will soon get through your unpleasant reading and then!—but the world is full of troubles and I have not much reason to think myself pesterd with many—I think Jane or Marianne has a better opinion of me than I deserve—for really and truly I do not think my Brothers illness connected with mine—you know more of the real Cause than they do—nor have I any chance of being rack'd as you have been[1]— you perhaps at one time thought there was such a thing as Worldly Happiness to be arrived at, at certain periods of time marked out—you have of necessity from your disposition been thus led away—I scarcely remember counting upon any Happiness—I look not for it if it be not in the present hour—nothing startles me beyond the Moment. The setting sun will always set me to rights—or if a Sparrow come before my Window I take part in its existince and pick about the Gravel. The first thing that strikes me on hea[r]ing a Misfortune having befalled another is this. "Well it cannot be helped.—he will have the pleasure of trying the resourses of his spirit, and I beg now my dear Bailey that hereafter should you observe any thing cold in me not to but[2] it to the account of heartlessness but abstraction—for I assure you I sometimes feel not the influence of a Passion or Affection during a whole week—and so long this sometimes continues I begin to suspect myself and the genuiness of my feelings at other times—thinking them a few barren Tragedy-tears. * * *

Your affectionate friend

John Keats—

To George and Thomas Keats

[Negative Capability]

[December 21, 27 (?), 1817]

My dear Brothers

I must crave your pardon for not having written ere this. * * * I spent Friday evening with Wells[1] & went the next morning to see *Death on*

---

9. An echo of Wordsworth, *Ode: Intimations of Immortality*, line 187.
1. Keats's friends Jane and Mariane Reynolds feared that his ill health at this time threatened tuberculosis, from which his brother Tom was suffering.

Bailey had recently experienced pain (been "racked") because of an unsuccessful love affair.
2. For "put."
1. Charles Wells, a former schoolmate of Tom Keats.

the Pale horse. It is a wonderful picture, when West's age is considered;[2] But there is nothing to be intense upon; no women one feels mad to kiss; no face swelling into reality. the excellence of every Art is its intensity, capable of making all disagreeables evaporate, from their being in close relationship with Beauty & Truth[3]—Examine King Lear & you will find this examplified throughout; but in this picture we have unpleasantness without any momentous depth of speculation excited, in which to bury its repulsiveness—The picture is larger than Christ rejected—I dined with Haydon[4] the sunday after you left, & had a very pleasant day, I dined too (for I have been out too much lately) with Horace Smith & met his two Brothers with Hill & Kingston & one Du Bois,[5] they only served to convince me, how superior humour is to wit in respect to enjoyment—These men say things which make one start, without making one feel, they are all alike; their manners are alike; they all know fashionables; they have a mannerism in their very eating & drinking, in their mere handling a Decanter—They talked of Kean[6] & his low company—Would I were with that company instead of yours said I to myself! I know such like acquaintance will never do for me & yet I am going to Reynolds, on wednesday—Brown & Dilke[7] walked with me & back from the Christmas pantomime.[8] I had not a dispute but a disquisition with Dilke, on various subjects; several things dovetailed in my mind, & at once it struck me, what quality went to form a Man of Achievement especially in Literature & which Shakespeare possessed so enormously—I mean *Negative Capability*,[9] that is when man is capable of being in uncertainties, Mysteries, doubts, without any irritable reaching after fact & reason—Coleridge, for instance, would let go by a fine isolated verisimilitude caught from the Penetralium[1] of mystery, from being incapable of remaining content with half knowledge. This pursued through Volumes would perhaps take us no further than this, that with a great poet the sense of Beauty overcomes every other consideration, or rather obliterates all consideration.

---

2. Benjamin West (1738–1820), painter of historical pictures, was an American who moved to England and became president of the Royal Academy. The "Christ Rejected" mentioned a few sentences farther on is also by West.

3. Keats's solution to a problem at least as old as Aristotle's *Poetics:* why do we take pleasure in the aesthetic representation of a subject which in life would be ugly or painful?

4. Keats's close friend Benjamin Haydon, painter of large-scale historical and religious pictures.

5. Horace Smith was one of the best-known literary wits of the day; the others mentioned were men of letters or of literary interests.

6. Edmund Kean, noted Shakespearean actor of the early 19th century.

7. John Hamilton Reynolds, Charles Armitage Brown, and Charles Wentworth Dilke were all writers and friends of Keats. Keats interrupted the writing of this letter after the dash; beginning with "Brown & Dilke" he is writing several days after the preceding sentences.

8. Christmas pantomimes were performed each year at Drury Lane and Covent Garden.

9. This famous and elusive phrase has accumulated a heavy body of commentary. Two points may be offered here: (1) Keats is concerned with a central aesthetic question of his day: to distinguish between what was called the "objective" poet, who simply and impersonally presents his material, and the "subjective" or "sentimental" poet, who presents his material as it appears when viewed through his personal interests, beliefs, and feelings. The poet of "negative capability" is the objective poet. (See the letter to Reynolds, Feb. 3, 1818, below.) (2) Keats goes on to propose that, within a poem, the presentation of subject matter in an artistic form that appeals to our "sense of Beauty" is enough, independently of its truth or falsity when considered outside the poem.

1. The Latin *penetralia* signified the innermost and most secret parts of a temple.

Shelley's poem[2] is out & there are words about its being objected too, as much as Queen Mab was. Poor Shelley I think he has his Quota of good qualities, in sooth la!! Write soon to your most sincere friend & affectionate Brother

John

To John Hamilton Reynolds[1]

[*Wordsworth's Poetry*]

[February 3, 1818]

My dear Reynolds,

* * * It may be said that we ought to read our Contemporaries. that Wordsworth &c should have their due from us. but for the sake of a few fine imaginative or domestic passages, are we to be bullied into a certain Philosophy engendered in the whims of an Egotist[2]—Every man has his speculations, but every man does not brood and peacock over them till he makes a false coinage and deceives himself—Many a man can travel to the very bourne[3] of Heaven, and yet want confidence to put down his halfseeing. Sancho[4] will invent a Journey heavenward as well as any body. We hate poetry that has a palpable design upon us—and if we do not agree, seems to put its hand in its breeches pocket. Poetry should be great & unobtrusive, a thing which enters into one's soul, and does not startle it or amaze it with itself but with its subject.—How beautiful are the retired flowers! how would they lose their beauty were they to throng into the highway crying out, "admire me I am a violet! dote upon me I am a primrose! Modern poets differ from the Elizabethans in this. Each of the moderns like an Elector of Hanover governs his petty state, & knows how many straws are swept daily from the Causeways in all his dominions & has a continual itching that all the Housewives should have their coppers well scoured: the antients were ~~Emperors of large~~ Emperors of vast Provinces, they had only heard of the remote ones and scarcely cared to visit them.—I will cut all this—I will have no more of Wordsworth or Hunt[5] in particular—Why should we be of the tribe of Manasseh, when we can wander with Esau?[6] why should we kick against

2. *Laon and Cythna* (1817), which dealt with incest and had to be recalled by the author; it was revised and republished as *The Revolt of Islam* (1818). *Queen Mab* (1813) was a youthful poem in which Shelley presented his radical program for the achievement of a millennial earthly state by the elimination of "kings, priests, and statesmen," and the reform of human institutions.

1. Reynolds, a close friend, was at this time an insurance clerk and also an able poet and man of letters.

2. Keats immensely admired Wordsworth, as succeeding letters will show, and learned more from him than from any poetic contemporary. He had reservations, however, about the subjective and

didactic qualities of Wordsworth's poetry (see the letter to George and Thomas Keats, above)—reservations which, in some moods, he stated in unflattering terms.

3. Boundary.

4. Sancho Panza, the earthy squire in *Don Quixote*.

5. Leigh Hunt, a poet who earlier had strongly influenced Keats's style.

6. I.e., why should we carry on a conventional way of life (as did the tribe of Manasseh in Old Testament history) when we can become adventurers (like Esau, who sold his birthright in Genesis 25.29–34 and became an outlaw).

the Pricks, when we can walk on Roses? Why should we be owls, when we can be Eagles? Why be teased with "nice Eyed wagtails," when we have in sight "the Cherub Contemplation"?[7]—Why with Wordsworths "Matthew with a bough of wilding in his hand" when we can have Jacques "under an oak &c"[8]—The secret of the Bough of Wilding will run through your head faster than I can write it—Old Matthew spoke to him some years ago on some nothing, & because he happens in an Evening Walk to imagine the figure of the old man—he must stamp it down in black & white, and it is henceforth sacred—I don't mean to deny Wordsworth's grandeur & Hunt's merit, but I mean to say we need not be teazed with grandeur & merit—when we can have them uncontaminated & unobtrusive. Let us have the old Poets, & robin Hood[9] Your letter and its sonnets gave me more pleasure than will the 4th Book of Childe Harold[1] & the whole of any body's life & opinions. * * *

Yr sincere friend and Coscribbler

John Keats.

To John Taylor[1]

[Keats's Axioms in Poetry]

[February 27, 1818]

My dear Taylor,

Your alteration strikes me as being a great improvement—the page looks much better. * * * It is a sorry thing for me that any one should have to overcome Prejudices in reading my Verses—that affects me more than any hypercriticism on any particular Passage. In *Endymion* I have most likely but moved into the Go-cart from the leading strings. In Poetry I have a few Axioms, and you will see how far I am from their Centre. 1st I think Poetry should surprise by a fine excess and not by Singularity—it should strike the Reader as a wording of his own highest thoughts, and appear almost a Remembrance—2nd Its touches of Beauty should never be half way therby making the reader breathless instead of content: the rise, the progress, the setting of imagery should like the Sun come natural natural too him—shine over him and set soberly although in magnificence leaving him in the Luxury of twilight—but it is easier to think what Poetry should be than to write it—and this leads me on to another axiom. That if Poetry comes not as naturally as the Leaves to a tree it had better not come at all. However it may be with me I cannot help looking into new countries with "O for a Muse of fire to ascend!"[2]—

7. The first phrase is from Hunt's *Nymphs*, the second from Milton's *Il Penseroso* (line 54).

8. The Wordsworth phrase is from his poem *The Two April Mornings* (a "wilding" is a wild apple tree). For Jacques "under an oak," see *As You Like It*, 2.1.31.

9. A reference to two sonnets on Robin Hood, written by Reynolds, which he had sent to Keats.

1. Canto 4 of Byron's *Childe Harold* was being eagerly awaited by English readers.

1. Partner in the publishing firm of Taylor and Hessey, to whom Keats wrote this letter while *Endymion* was being put through the press.

2. Altered from Shakespeare's *Henry V*, Prologue, line 1.

If Endymion serves me as a Pioneer perhaps I ought to be content. I have great reason to be content, for thank God I can read and perhaps understand Shakspeare to his depths, and I have I am sure many friends, who, if I fail, will attribute any change in my Life and Temper to Humbleness rather than to Pride—to a cowering under the Wings of great Poets rather than to a Bitterness that I am not appreciated. I am anxious to get Endymion printed that I may forget it and proceed. * * *

Your sincere and oblig^d friend

Your sincere and obligᵈ friend
John Keats—

P.S. You shall have a sho[r]t *Preface* in good time—

To John Hamilton Reynolds

[*Milton, Wordsworth, and the Chambers of Human Life*]

[May 3, 1818]

My dear Reynolds.

* * * Were I to study physic or rather Medicine again,—I feel it would not make the least difference in my Poetry; when the Mind is in its infancy a Bias ~~in~~ is in reality a Bias, but when we have acquired more strength, a Bias becomes no Bias. Every department of knowledge we see excellent and calculated towards a great whole. I am so convinced of this, that I am glad at not having given away my medical Books, which I shall again look over to keep alive the little I know thitherwards; and moreover intend through you and Rice to become a sort of Pipcivilian.[1] An extensive knowledge is needful to thinking people—it takes away the heat and fever; and helps, by widening speculation, to ease the Burden of the Mystery:[2] a thing I begin to understand a little, and which weighed upon you in the most gloomy and true sentence in your Letter. The difference of high Sensations with and without knowledge appears to me this—in the latter case we are falling continually ten thousand fathoms deep and being blown up again without wings and with all [the] horror of a ~~Case~~ bare shoulderd Creature—in the former case, our shoulders are fledged,[3] and we go thro' the same ~~Fir~~ air and space without fear. * * *

You say "I fear there is little chance of any thing else in this life." You seem by that to have been going through with a more painful and acute ~~test~~ zest the same labyrinth that I have—I have come to the same conclusion thus far. My Branchings out therefrom have been numerous: one of them is the consideration of Wordsworth's genius and as a help, in the manner of gold being the meridian Line of worldly wealth,—how he differs from Milton.[4]—And here I have nothing but surmises, from

---

1. Apparently, "a small-scale layman." James Rice, a lawyer, was one of Keats's favorite friends.
2. *Tintern Abbey*, line 38. Here begins Keats's remarkably insightful expansion of the significance of this and other phrases and passages in Wordsworth.
3. Grow wings.

4. I.e., as gold is the standard of material wealth (in the way that the meridian line of Greenwich Observatory, England, is the reference for measuring degrees of longitude), so Milton is the standard of poetic value, by which we may measure Wordsworth.

an uncertainty whether Miltons apparently less anxiety for Humanity
proceeds from his seeing further or no than Wordsworth: And whether
Wordsworth has in truth epic passions, and martyrs himself to the human
heart, the main region of his song[5]—In regard to his genius alone—we
find what he says true as far as we have experienced and we can judge
no further but by larger experience—for axioms in philosophy are not
axioms until they are proved upon our pulses: We read fine——things
but never feel them to thee[6] full until we have gone the same steps as
the Author.—I know this is not plain; you will know exactly my meaning when I say, that now I shall relish Hamlet more than I ever have
done—Or, better—You are sensible no man can set down Venery[7] as a
bestial or joyless thing until he is sick of it and therefore all philosophiz-
ing on it would be mere wording. Until we are sick, we understand
not;—in fine, as Byron says, "Knowledge is Sorrow";[8] and I go on to say
that "Sorrow is Wisdom"—and further for aught we can know for certainty! "Wisdom is folly." * * *

I will return to Wordsworth—whether or no he has an extended vision
or a circumscribed grandeur—whether he is an eagle in his nest, or on
the wing—And to be more explicit and to show you how tall I stand by
the giant, I will put down a simile of human life as far as I now perceive
it; that is, to the point to which I say we both have arrived at—Well—I
compare human life to a large Mansion of Many Apartments, two of
which I can only describe, the doors of the rest being as yet shut upon
me—The first we step into we call the infant or thoughtless Chamber,
in which we remain as long as we do not think—We remain there a
long while, and notwithstanding the doors of the second Chamber remain
wide open, showing a bright appearance, we care not to hasten to it; but
are at length imperceptibly impelled by the awakening of the thinking
principle—within us—we no sooner get into the second Chamber, which
I shall call the Chamber of Maiden-Thought,[9] than we become intoxicated with the light and the atmosphere, we see nothing but pleasant
wonders, and think of delaying there for ever in delight: However among
the effects this breathing is father of is that tremendous one of sharpening one's vision into the ~~head~~ heart and nature of Man—of convincing
ones nerves that the World is full of Misery and Heartbreak, Pain, Sickness and oppression—whereby This Chamber of Maiden Thought
becomes gradually darken'd and at the same time on all sides of it many
doors are set open—but all dark—all leading to dark passages—We see
not the ballance of good and evil. We are in a Mist—We are now in
that state—We feel the "burden of the Mystery," To this point was
Wordsworth come, as far as I can conceive when he wrote "Tintern
Abbey" and it seems to me that his Genius is explorative of those dark
Passages. Now if we live, and go on thinking, we too shall explore them.
he is a Genius and superior [to] us, in so far as he can, more than we,

---

5. Cf. "Prospectus" to *The Recluse*, above, line 41.

6. For "the."

7. Sexual indulgence.

8. *Manfred* 1.1.10: "Sorrow is knowledge."

9. I.e., innocent thought, with the implication (as
in "maiden voyage") of a first undertaking.

make discoveries, and shed a light in them—Here I must think Wordsworth is deeper than Milton—though I think it has depended more upon
the general and gregarious advance of intellect, than individual greatness
of Mind—From the Paradise Lost and the other Works of Milton, I
hope it is not too presuming, even between ourselves to say, his Philosophy, human and divine, may be tolerably understood by one not much
advanced in years, In his time englishmen were just emancipated from
a great superstition—and Men had got hold of certain points and resting
places in reasoning which were too newly born to be doubted, and too
much ~~oppressed~~ opposed by the Mass of Europe not to be thought etherial and authentically divine—who could gainsay his ideas on virtue,
vice, and Chastity in Comus, just at the time of the dismissal of Cod-
pieces[1] and a hundred other disgraces? who would not rest satisfied with
his hintings at good and evil in the Paradise Lost, when just free from
the inquisition and burrning in Smithfield?[2] The Reformation produced
such immediate and greats benefits, that Protestantism was considered
under the immediate eye of heaven, and its own remaining Dogmas and
superstitions, then, as it were, regenerated, constituted those resting places
and seeming sure points of Reasoning—from that I have mentioned,
Milton, whatever he may have thought in the sequel,[3] appears to have
been content with these by his writings—He did not think into the human
heart, as Wordsworth has done—Yet Milton as a Philosop[h]er, had sure
as great powers as Wordsworth—What is then to be inferr'd? O many
things—It proves there is really a grand march of intellect—, It proves
that a mighty providence subdues the mightiest Minds to the service of
the time being, whether it be in human Knowledge or Religion— * * *
Tom[4] has spit a leetle blood this afternoon, and that is rather a damper—
but I know—the truth is there is something real in the World Your third
Chamber of Life shall be a lucky and a gentle one—stored with the wine
of love—and the Bread of Friendship— * * *

                                        Your affectionate friend
                                                John Keats.

To Richard Woodhouse[1]

[A Poet Has No Identity]

                                                [October 27, 1818]

My dear Woodhouse,
     Your Letter gave me a great satisfaction; more on account of its friend-
liness, than any relish of that matter in it which is accounted so accept-

---

1. In the 15th and 16th centuries the codpiece was
a flap, often ornamental, that covered an opening
in the front of men's breeches.
2. An open place northwest of the walls of the City
of London where, in the 16th century, heretics
were burned.
3. Later on.

4. Keats's younger brother, then 18, who was dying
of tuberculosis.
1. Woodhouse was a young lawyer with literary
interests who early recognized Keats's talents and
prepared, or preserved, MS copies of many of his
poems and letters.

able in the "genus irritabile"[2] The best answer I can give you is in a clerklike manner to make some observations on two principle points, which seem to point like indices into the midst of the whole pro and con, about genius, and views and atchievements and ambition and cœtera. 1st As to the poetical Character itself, (I mean that sort of which, if I am any thing, I am a Member; that sort distinguished from the wordsworthian or egotistical sublime; which is a thing per se and stands alone) it is not itself—it has no self—it is every thing and nothing—It has no character—it enjoys light and shade; it lives in gusto, be it foul or fair, high or low, rich or poor, mean or elevated—It has as much delight in conceiving an Iago as an Imogen.[3] What shocks the virtuous philosop[h]er, delights the camelion[4] Poet. It does no harm from its relish of the dark side of things any more than from its taste for the bright one; because they both end in speculation.[5] A Poet is the most unpoetical of any thing in existence; because he has no Identity—he is continually in for[6]—and filling some other Body—The Sun, the Moon, the Sea and Men and Women who are creatures of impulse are poetical and have about them an unchangeable attribute—the poet has none; no identity—he is certainly the most unpoetical of all God's Creatures. If then he has no self, and if I am a Poet, where is the Wonder that I should say I would ~~right~~ write no more? Might I not at that very instant [have] been cogitating on the Characters of saturn and Ops?[7] It is a wretched thing to confess; but is a very fact that not one word I ever utter can be taken for granted as an opinion growing out of my identical nature—how can it, when I have no nature? When I am in a room with People if I ever am free from speculating on creations of my own brain, then not myself goes home to myself: but the identity of every one in the room begins to to press upon me[8] that, I am in a very little time an[ni]hilated—not only among Men; it would be the same in a Nursery of children: I know not whether I make myself wholly understood: I hope enough so to let you see that no dependence is to be placed on what I said that day.

In the second place I will speak of my views, and of the life I purpose to myself—I am ambitious of doing the world some good: if I should be spared that may be the work of maturer years—in the interval I will assay to reach to as high a summit in Poetry as the nerve[9] bestowed upon me will suffer. The faint conceptions I have of Poems to come brings the blood frequently into my forehead—All I hope is that I may not lose all interest in human affairs—that the solitary indifference I feel for applause even from the finest Spirits, will not blunt any acuteness of vision I may

2. "The irritable race," a phrase Horace had applied to poets (*Epistles* 2.2.102).
3. Iago is the villain in Shakespeare's *Othello* and Imogen the virtuous heroine in his *Cymbeline*.
4. The chameleon is a lizard that camouflages itself by changing its color to match its surroundings.
5. "In speculation" here may mean "in contemplation"—i.e., without affecting our practical judgment or actions.

6. Instead of "in for," Keats may have intended to write "informing."
7. Characters in Keats's *Hyperion*. Woodhouse had recently written Keats to express concern at a remark by the poet that, since former writers had preempted the best poetic materials and styles, there was nothing new left for the modern poet.
8. Perhaps "*so* to press upon me."
9. Sinew.

have. I do not think it will—I feel assured I should write from the mere yearning and fondness I have for the Beautiful even if my night's labours should be burnt every morning and no eye ever shine upon them. But even now I am perhaps not speaking from myself; but from some character in whose soul I now live. I am sure however that this next sentence is from myself. I feel your anxiety, good opinion and friendliness in the highest degree, and am

Your's most sincerely
John Keats

To George and Georgiana Keats[1]

["The Vale of Soul-Making"]

[February 14–May 3, 1819]

My dear Brother & Sister—

* * * I have this moment received a note from Haslam[2] in which he expects the death of his Father who has been for some time in a state of insensibility—his mother bears up he says very well—I shall go to twon[3] tommorrow to see him. This is the world—thus we cannot expect to give way many hours to pleasure—Circumstances are like Clouds continually gathering and bursting—While we are laughing the seed of some trouble is put into he the wide arable land of events—while we are laughing it sprouts is[4] grows and suddenly bears a poison fruit which we must pluck—Even so we have leisure to reason on the misfortunes of our friends; our own touch us too nearly for words. Very few men have ever arrived at a complete disinterestedness of Mind: very few have been influenced by a pure desire of the benefit of others—in the greater part of the Benefactors of & to Humanity some meretricious motive has sullied their greatness—some melodramatic scenery has facinated them—From the manner in which I feel Haslam's misfortune I perceive how far I am from any humble standard of disinterestedness—Yet this feeling ought to be carried to its highest pitch, as there is no fear of its ever injuring society—which it would do I fear pushed to an extremity—For in wild nature the Hawk would loose his Breakfast of Robins and the Robin his of Worms The Lion must starve as well as the swallow—The greater part of Men make their way with the same instinctiveness, the same unwandering eye from their purposes, the same animal eagerness as the Hawk—The Hawk wants a Mate, so does the Man—look at them both they set about it and procure on[e] in the same manner—They want both a nest and they both set about one in the same manner—they get their food in the same manner—The noble animal Man for his

---

1. Keats's brother and his wife, who had emigrated to Louisville, Kentucky, in 1818. This is part of a long letter that Keats wrote over a period of several months. The date of the first extract is March 19.

2. William Haslam, a young businessman and close friend.
3. For "town."
4. For "it."

amusement smokes his pipe—the Hawk balances about the Clouds—that is the only difference of their leisures. This it is that makes the Amusement of Life—to a speculative Mind. I go among the Feilds and catch a glimpse of a stoat[5] or a fieldmouse peeping out of the withered grass—the creature hath a purpose and its eyes are bright with it—I go amongst the buildings of a city and I see a Man hurrying along—to what? The Creature has a purpose and his eyes are bright with it. But then as Wordsworth says, "we have all one human heart"[6]—there is an ellectric fire in human nature tending to purify—so that among these human creature[s] there is continually some birth of new heroism—The pity is that we must wonder at it: as we should at finding a pearl in rubbish—I have no doubt that thousands of people never heard of have had hearts comp[l]etely disinterested: I can remember but two—Socrates and Jesus—their Histories evince it—What I heard a little time ago, Taylor observe with respect to Socrates, may be said of Jesus—That he was so great as man that though he transmitted no writing of his own to posterity, we have his Mind and his sayings and his greatness handed to us by others. It is to be lamented that the history of the latter was written and revised by Men interested in the pious frauds of Religion. Yet through all this I see his splendour. Even here though I myself am pursueing the same instinctive course as the veriest human animal you can think of—I am however young writing at random—straining at particles of light in the midst of a great darkness—without knowing the bearing of any one assertion of any one opinion. Yet may I not in this be free from sin?[7] May there not be superior beings amused with any graceful, though instinctive attitude my mind my[8] fall into, as I am entertained with the alertness of a Stoat or the anxiety of a Deer? Though a quarrel in the streets is a thing to be hated, the energies displayed in it are fine; the commonest Man shows a grace in his quarrel—By a superior being our reasoning[s] may take the same tone—though erroneous they may be fine—This is the very thing in which consists poetry; and if so it is not so fine a thing as philosophy—For the same reason that an eagle is not so fine a thing as a truth—Give me this credit—Do you not think I strive—to know myself? Give me this credit—and you will not think that on my own accou[n]t I repeat Milton's lines

> "How charming is divine Philosophy
> Not harsh and crabbed as dull fools suppose
> But musical as is Apollo's lute"—[9]

No—no for myself—feeling grateful as I do to have got into a state of mind to relish them properly—Nothing ever becomes real till it is expe-

5. A weasel.
6. *The Old Cumberland Beggar*, line 153.
7. Keats speculates that though his instinctive course is not, any more than an animal's, "disinterested" (free from selfish interests), it may still, like an animal's, be natural, hence innocent and possessed of an innate grace and beauty. He fur-

ther supposes that this may be the nature of poetry, also, as distinguished from the deliberate and self-conscious process of philosophical reasoning. Compare the letter on "Negative Capability," begun on Dec. 21, 1817, above.
8. For "may."
9. *Comus*, lines 475–77.

rienced—Even a Proverb is no proverb to you till your Life has illustrated it— * * *

* * * I have been reading lately two very different books Robertson's America and Voltaire's Siecle De Louis xiv[1] It is like walking arm and arm between Pizarro and the great-little Monarch.[2] In How lementabl[e] a case do we see the great body of the people in both instances: in the first, where Men might seem to inherit quiet of Mind from unsophisticated senses; from uncontamination of civilisation; and especially from their being as it were estranged from the mutual helps of Society and its mutual injuries—and thereby more immediately under the Protection of Providence—even there they had mortal pains to bear as bad; or even worse than Baliffs,[3] Debts and Poverties of civilised Life—The whole appears to resolve into this—that Man is originally "a poor forked creature"[4] subject to the same mischances as the beasts of the forest, destined to hardships and disquietude of some kind or other. If he improves by degrees his bodily accommodations and comforts—at each stage, at each accent there are waiting for him a fresh set of annoyances—he is mortal and there is still a heaven with its Stars abov[e] his head. The most interesting question that can come before us is, How far by the persevering endeavours of a seldom appearing Socrates Mankind may be made happy—I can imagine such happiness carried to an extreme—but what must it end in?—Death—and who could in such a case bear with death—the whole troubles of life which are now frittered away in a series of years, would the[n] be accumulated for the last days of a being who instead of hailing its approach, would leave this world as Eve left Paradise—But in truth I do not at all believe in this sort of perfectibility—the nature of the world will not admit of it—the inhabitants of the world will correspond to itself—Let the fish philosophise the ice away from the Rivers in winter time and they shall be at continual play in the tepid delight of summer. Look at the Poles and at the sands of Africa, Whirlpools and volcanoes—Let men exterminate them and I will say that they may arrive at earthly Happiness—The point at which Man may arrive is as far as the paralel state in inanimate nature and no further—For instance suppose a rose to have sensation, it blooms on a beautiful morning it enjoys itself—but there comes a cold wind, a hot sun—it can not escape it, it cannot destroy its annoyances—they are as native to the world as itself: no more can man be happy in spite, the world[l]y elements will prey upon his nature—The common cognomen of this world among the misguided and superstitious is "a vale of tears" from which we are to be redeemed by a certain arbitrary interposition of God and taken to Heaven—What a little circumscribe[d] straightened notion! Call the world

---

1. William Robertson, *The History of America* (1777—Keats was reading the 10th ed., 4 vols., 1803); Voltaire, *Le Siècle de Louis XIV*, 5 vols. (1751). In this second extract from the journal-letter Keats is writing toward the end of April (on the 21st or 28th).

2. Francisco Pizarro, the Spanish explorer whose

exploits are described in Robertson's *America*. The "Monarch" is Louis XIV.

3. Bailiffs: officers of the law whose duties included making arrests for bad debts.

4. *King Lear* 3.4.106–108. Lear says: "Unaccommodated man is no more but such a poor, bare, forked animal as thou art."

if you Please "The vale of Soul-making" Then you will find out the use of the world (I am speaking now in the highest terms for human nature admitting it to be immortal which I will here take for granted for the purpose of showing a thought which has struck me concerning it) I say "*Soul making*" Soul as distinguished from an Intelligence—There may be intelligences or sparks of the divinity in millions—but they are not Souls ~~the~~ till they acquire identities, till each one is personally itself. I[n]telligences are atoms of perception—they know and they see and they are pure, in short they are God—how then are Souls to be made? How then are these sparks which are God to have identity given them— so as ever to possess a bliss peculiar to each ones individual existence? How, but by the medium of a world like this? This point I sincerely wish to consider because I think it a grander system of salvation than the chrysteain religion—or rather it is a system of Spirit-creation[5]—This is effected by three grand materials acting the one upon the other for a series of years—These three Materials are the *Intelligence*—the *human heart* (as distinguished from intelligence or Mind) and the *World* or *Elemental space* suited for the proper action of *Mind and Heart* on each other for the purpose of forming the *Soul* or *Intelligence destined to possess the sense of Identity*. I can scarcely express what I but dimly perceive—and yet I think I perceive it—that you may judge the more clearly I will put it in the most homely form possible—I will call the *world* a School instituted for the purpose of teaching little children to read—I will call the *human heart* the *horn Book*[6] used in that School— and I will call the *Child able to read, the Soul* made from that *school* and its *hornbook*. Do you not see how necessary a World of Pains and troubles is to school an Intelligence and make it a soul? A Place where the heart must feel and suffer in a thousand diverse ways! Not merely is the Heart a Hornbook, It is the Minds Bible, it is the Minds experience, it is the teat from which the Mind or intelligence sucks its identity—As various as the Lives of Men are—so various become their souls, and thus does God make individual beings, Souls, Identical Souls of the sparks of his own essence—This appears to me a faint sketch of a system of Salvation which does not affront our reason and humanity—I am convinced that many difficulties which christians labour under would vanish before it—There is one wh[i]ch even now Strikes me—the Salvation of Children—In them the Spark or intelligence returns to God without any identity—it having had no time to learn of, and be altered by, the heart—or seat of the human Passions—It is pretty generally sus-

---

5. Keats is struggling for an analogy that will embody his solution to the ancient riddle of evil, as an alternative to what he understands to be the Christian view: that evil exists as a test of the individual's merit of salvation in heaven, and this world is only a proving ground for a later and better life. Keats proposes that the function of the human experience of sorrow and pain is to feed and discipline the formless and unstocked "intelligence" that we possess at birth, and thus to shape it into a rich and coherent "identity," or "soul." This result provides a justification ("salvation") for our suffering in terms of our earthly life itself: that is, experience is its own reward. The passage is Keats's version of what Wordsworth says in the last two stanzas of his *Ode: Intimations of Immortality*.

6. A child's primer, which used to consist of a sheet of paper mounted on thin wood, protected by a sheet of transparent horn.

pected that the chr[i]stian scheme has been coppied from the ancient
persian and greek Philosophers. Why may they not have made this simple thing even more simple for common apprehension by introducing
Mediators and Personages in the same manner as in the hethen mythology abstractions are personified—Seriously I think it probable that this
System of Soul-making—may have been the Parent of all the more palpable and personal Schemes of Redemption, among the Zoroastrians
the Christians and the Hindoos. For as one part of the human species
must have their carved Jupiter; so another part must have the palpable
and named Mediatior and saviour, their Christ their Oromanes and their
Vishnu[7]—If what I have said should not be plain enough, as I fear it
may not be, I will but[8] you in the place where I began in this series of
thoughts—I mean, I began by seeing how man was formed by circumstances—and what are circumstances?—but touchstones of his heart—?
and what are touch stones?—but proovings of his hearrt?—and what are
proovings of his heart but fortifiers or alterers of his nature? and what is
his altered nature but his soul?—and what was his soul before it came
into the world and had These provings and alterations and perfection-
ings?—An intelligences—without Identity—and how is this Identity to
be made? Through the medium of the Heart? And how is the heart to
become this Medium but in a world of Circumstances?—There now I
think what with Poetry and Theology you may thank your Stars that my
pen is not very long winded— * * *

   This is the 3^d of May & every thing is in delightful forwardness; the
violets are not withered, before the peeping of the first rose; You must
let me know every thing, how parcels go & come, what papers you have,
& what Newspapers you want, & other things—God bless you my dear
Brother & Sister

Your ever Affectionate Brother
John Keats—

To Fanny Brawne

[Fanny Brawne as Keats's "Fair Star"]

[July 25, 1819]

My sweet Girl,
   I hope you did not blame me much for not obeying your request of a
Letter on Saturday: we have had four in our small room playing at cards
night and morning leaving me no undisturb'd opportunity to write. Now
Rice and Martin are gone I am at liberty. Brown to my sorrow confirms
the account you give of your ill health. You cannot conceive how I ache
to be with you: how I would die for one hour——for what is in the

---

7. Oromanes (Ahriman) was the principle of evil,
locked in a persisting struggle with Ormazd, the
principle of good, in the Zoroastrian religion.

Vishnu was the deity who creates and preserves the
world, in Hindu belief.
8. For "put."

world? I say you cannot conceive; it is impossible you should look with such eyes upon me as I have upon you: it cannot be. Forgive me if I wander a little this evening, for I have been all day employ'd in a very abstr[a]ct Poem[1] and I am in deep love with you—two things which must excuse me. I have, believe me, not been an age in letting you take possession of me; the very first week I knew you I wrote myself your vassal; but burnt the Letter as the very next time I saw you I thought you manifested some dislike to me. If you should ever feel for Man at the first sight what I did for you, I am lost. Yet I should not quarrel with you, but hate myself if such a thing were to happen—only I should burst if the thing were not as fine as a Man as you are as a Woman. Perhaps I am too vehement, then fancy me on my knees, especially when I mention a part of you Letter which hurt me; you say speaking of Mr. Severn[2] "but you must be satisfied in knowing that I admired you much more than your friend." My dear love, I cannot believe there ever was or ever could be any thing to admire in me especially as far as sight goes—I cannot be admired, I am not a thing to be admired. You are, I love you; all I can bring you is a swooning admiration of your Beauty. I hold that place among Men which snub-nos'd brunettes with meeting eyebrows do among women—they are trash to me—unless I should find one among them with a fire in her heart like the one that burns in mine. You absorb me in spite of myself—you alone: for I look not forward with any pleasure to what is call'd being settled in the world; I tremble at domestic cares—yet for you I would meet them, though if it would leave you the happier I would rather die than do so. I have two luxuries to brood over in my walks, your Loveliness and the hour of my death. O that I could have possession of them both in the same minute. I hate the world: it batters too much the wings of my self-will, and would I could take a sweet poison from your lips to send me out of it. From no others would I take it. I am indeed astonish'd to find myself so careless of all cha[r]ms but yours—remembring as I do the time when even a bit of ribband was a matter of interest with me. What softer words can I find for you after this—what it is I will not read. Nor will I say more here, but in a Postscript answer any thing else you may have mentioned in your Letter in so many words—for I am distracted with a thousand thoughts. I will imagine you Venus tonight and pray, pray, pray to your star like a Hethen.[3]

Your's ever, fair Star,
John Keats.

---

1. Probably *Hyperion*.
2. Joseph Severn, who later looked after Keats during his mortal illness in Rome.
3. See Keats's sonnet, *Bright Star*, for parallels to this and other remarks in the present letter.

To Percy Bysshe Shelley[1]

["*Load Every Rift with Ore*"]

[August 16, 1820]

My dear Shelley,

I am very much gratified that you, in a foreign country, and with a mind almost over occupied, should write to me in the strain of the Letter beside me. If I do not take advantage of your invitation it will be prevented by a circumstance I have very much at heart to prophesy[2]—There is no doubt that an english winter would put an end to me, and do so in a lingering hateful manner, therefore I must either voyage or journey to Italy as a soldier marches up to a battery. My nerves at present are the worst part of me, yet they feel soothed when I think that come what extreme may, I shall not be destined to remain in one spot long enough to take a hatred of any four particular bed-posts. I am glad you take any pleasure in my poor Poem;[3]—which I would willingly take the trouble to unwrite, if possible, did I care so much as I have done about Reputation. I received a copy of the Cenci,[4] as from yourself from Hunt. There is only one part of it I am judge of; the Poetry, and dramatic effect, which by many spirits now a days is considered the mammon. A modern work it is said must have a purpose,[5] which may be the God— *an artist* must serve Mammon—he must have "self concentration" selfishness perhaps. You I am sure will forgive me for sincerely remarking that you might curb your magnanimity and be more of an artist, and "load every rift"[6] of your subject with ore. The thought of such discipline must fall like cold chains upon you, who perhaps never sat with your wings furl'd for six Months together. And is not this extraordina[r]y talk for the writer of Endymion? whose mind was like a pack of scattered cards—I am pick'd up and sorted to a pip.[7] My Imagination is a Monastry and I am its Monk—you must explain my metap[cs8] to yourself. I am in expectation of Prometheus[9] every day. Could I have my own wish for its interest effected you would have it still in manuscript—or be but now putting an end to the second act. I remember you advising me not to publish my first-blights, on Hampstead heath—I am returning advice

---

1. Written in reply to a letter urging Keats (who was ill) to spend the winter with the Shelleys in Pisa.

2. His own death.

3. Keats's *Endymion*, Shelley had written, contains treasures, "though treasures poured forth with indistinct profusion." Keats here responds with advice in kind.

4. Shelley's blank-verse tragedy, *The Cenci*, had been published in the spring of 1820.

5. Wordsworth had said this in his Preface to *Lyrical Ballads*. For "Mammon" see Matthew 6.24, and Luke 16.13: "Ye cannot serve God and mammon."

6. Spenser, *The Faerie Queene* 2.7.28: "With rich metall loaded every rifte."

7. Perfectly ordered; all the suits in the deck matched up ("pips" are the conventional spots on playing cards).

8. I.e., "metaphysics."

9. *Prometheus Unbound*, of which Shelley had promised Keats a copy.

1. Keats's volume of 1820, including *Lamia*, *The Eve of St. Agnes*, and the odes. When Shelley drowned, he had this small book open in his pocket.

upon your hands. Most of the Poems in the volume I send you[1] have been written above two years, and would never have been publish'd but from a hope of gain; so you see I am inclined enough to take your advice now. I must exp[r]ess once more my deep sense of your kindness, adding my sincere thanks and respects for M[rs] Shelley. In the hope of soon seeing you I remain

most sincerely yours,
John Keats—

To Charles Brown[1]

[Keats's Last Letter]

Rome. 30 November 1820.

My dear Brown,

'Tis the most difficult thing in the world to me to write a letter. My stomach continues so bad, that I feel it worse on opening any book,— yet I am much better than I was in Quarantine.[2] Then I am afraid to encounter the proing and conning of any thing interesting to me in England. I have an habitual feeling of my real life having past, and that I am leading a posthumous existence. God knows how it would have been—but it appears to me—however, I will not speak of that subject. I must have been at Bedhampton nearly at the time you were writing to me from Chichester—how unfortunate—and to pass on the river too! There was my star predominant![3] I cannot answer any thing in your letter, which followed me from Naples to Rome, because I am afraid to look it over again. I am so weak (in mind) that I cannot bear the sight of any hand writing of a friend I love so much as I do you. Yet I ride the little horse,—and, at my worst, even in Quarantine, summoned up more puns, in a sort of desperation, in one week than in any year of my life. There is one thought enough to kill me—I have been well, healthy, alert &c, walking with her[4]—and now—the knowledge of contrast, feeling for light and shade, all that information (primitive sense) necessary for a poem are great enemies to the recovery of the stomach. There, you rogue, I put you to the torture,—but you must bring your philosophy to bear—as I do mine, really—or how should I be able to live? D[r] Clarke is very attentive to me; he says, there is very little the matter with my lungs, but my stomach, he says, is very bad. I am well disappointed in hearing good news from George,—for it runs in my head we shall all die young. I have not written to x x x x x yet,[5] which he must think very

---

1. Written to Keats's friend Charles Armitage Brown from the house on the Spanish Stairs, leading up from the Piazza di Spagna, where Keats was being tended in his mortal illness by the devoted Joseph Severn.
2. When it landed at Naples, Keats's ship had been quarantined for 10 miserably hot days.

3. *The Winter's Tale* 1.2.201–202: "It is a bawdy planet, that will strike / Where 'tis predominant."
4. Fanny Brawne.
5. Charles Brown, whose MS transcription is the only text for this letter, substituted crosses for the names of Keats's friends in order to conceal their identities.

neglectful; being anxious to send him a good account of my health, I have delayed it from week to week. If I recover, I will do all in my power to correct the mistakes made during sickness; and if I should not, all my faults will be forgiven. I shall write to x x x to-morrow, or next day. I will write to x x x x x in the middle of next week. Severn is very well, though he leads so dull a life with me. Remember me to all friends, and tell x x x x I should not have left London without taking leave of him, but from being so low in body and mind. Write to George as soon as you receive this, and tell him how I am, as far as you can guess;—and also a note to my sister—who walks about my imagination like a ghost—she is so like Tom.[6] I can scarcely bid you good bye even in a letter. I always made an awkward bow.

God bless you!
John Keats.

6. George was John Keats's younger brother; his only sister was Fanny Keats; Tom, the youngest   brother, whom Fanny closely resembled, had died of tuberculosis on Dec. 1, 1818.

The Victorian Age

1832-1901

1832:	The First Reform Bill.
1837:	Victoria becomes queen.
1846:	The Corn Laws repealed.
1850:	Tennyson succeeds Wordsworth as Poet Laureate.
1851:	The Great Exhibition in London.
1859:	Charles Darwin's *Origin of Species* published.
1870–71:	Franco-Prussian War.
1901:	Death of Victoria.

AN AGE OF EXPANSION

In 1897 Mark Twain was visiting London during the Diamond Jubilee celebrations honoring the sixtieth anniversary of Queen Victoria's coming to the throne. "British history is two thousand years old," Twain observed, "and yet in a good many ways the world has moved farther ahead since the Queen was born than it moved in all the rest of the two thousand put together." And if the whole world had "moved" during that long lifetime and reign of Victoria's, it was in her own country itself that the expansionist movement was most marked and dramatic, a movement that brought England to its highest point of development as a world power.

In the eighteenth century the pivotal city of Western civilization had been Paris; by the second half of the nineteenth century this center of influence had shifted to London, a city which expanded from about two million inhabitants when Victoria came to the throne to six and one half million at the time of her death. The rapid growth of London is one of the many indications of the most important development of the age: the shift from a way of life based on the ownership of land to a modern urban economy based on trade and manufacturing. "We have been living, as it were, the life of three hundred years in thirty" was the impression formed by Dr. Thomas Arnold during the early stages of England's industrialization. By the end of the century—after the resources of steam power had been more fully exploited for fast railways and iron ships, for looms, printing presses, and farmers' combines, and after the introduction of the telegraph, intercontinental cable, photography, anesthetics, and universal compulsory education—a late Victorian could look back with astonishment on these developments during his lifetime. Walter Besant, one of these late Victorians, observed that so completely transformed were "the mind and habits of the ordinary Englishman" by 1897, "that he would not, could he see him, recognize his own grandfather."

Because England was the first country to become industrialized, her transformation was an especially painful one, but being first had a compensation: it was profitable. An early start enabled England to capture markets all over the globe. Her cotton and other manufactured products were exported in English ships, a merchant fleet whose size was without parallel in other countries. The profits gained from her trade led also to extensive capital investments in all continents (especially in the underdeveloped sections of her own Empire) so that after England had become the world's workshop, London became, from 1870 on, the world's banker.

The effect of these developments on Victorian character has been described by the historian David Thomson. The period, he says in *England and the Nineteenth Century* (1950), "is one of strenuous activity and dynamic change, of ferment of ideas and recurrent social unrest, of great inventiveness and expansion." And he adds:

> The whole meaning of Victorian England is lost if it is thought of as a country of stuffy complacency and black top-hatted moral priggery. Its frowsty crinolines and dingy hansom cabs, its gas-lit houses and over-ornate draperies, concealed a people engaged in a tremendously exciting adventure—the daring experiment of fitting industrial man into a democratic society. Their failures, faults, and ludicrous shortcomings are all too apparent: but the days when Mr. Lytton Strachey could afford to laugh at the foibles of the "Eminent Victorians" have passed, and we must ask ourselves the question of whether we *can* laugh at our great-grandfathers' attempts to solve problems to which we have so far failed to find an answer. At least the Victorians found greatness, stability, and peace: and the whole world, marveling, envied them for it.

The reactions of Victorian writers to the fast-paced expansion of England were various. Thomas Babington Macaulay (1800–1859) relished the spectacle as wholly delightful. During the prosperous 1850s Macaulay's essays and histories, with their recitations of the statistics of industrial growth, constituted a Hymn to Progress as well as a celebration of the superior qualities of the English people—"the greatest and most highly civilized people that ever the world saw." And later in the century there were lesser jingoists whose writings confidently pointed out the reasons for further national self-congratulation. More representative, perhaps, was Tennyson, whose capacity to relish industrial change was only sporadic. Much of the time he felt instead that leadership in commerce and industry was being paid for at a terrible price in human happiness. In their experience a so-called progress had been gained only by abandoning the traditional rhythms of life and traditional patterns of human relationships which had sustained mankind for centuries. In the melancholy poetry of Matthew Arnold this note is often struck:

> For what wears out the life of mortal men?
> 'Tis that from change to change their being rolls;
> 'Tis that repeated shocks, again, again,
> Exhaust the energy of strongest souls.

An occasional ride on a roller coaster may be exhilarating, but to be chained aboard for a lifetime is a nightmare.

Accounts of the Victorian state of mind can be wildly contradictory when interpretations focus on one side of this set of attitudes and exclude the other. Thus *The Lyttletons: A Family Chronicle* (1975) asserts that during the period from 1830 to 1880 "the educated classes of England believed that they had the answer to everything. . . . It was an age of certainty and of faith only paralleled by the great cathedral-building epoch of the Middle Ages." But according to *The Finer Optic* (also 1975), this same period was one of "agony and confusion. The Victorians felt . . . a desperate pessimism based on the fear of . . . experience with no meaning beyond itself." To restore focus, it can be said that although most perceptive Victorians did share a sense of satisfaction in the industrial and political preeminence of England during the period, they also suffered from an anxious sense of something lost, a sense too of being displaced persons in a world made alien by technological changes which had been exploited too quickly for the adaptive powers of the human psyche. In this respect, as in many others, the Victorians may remind us of their English-speaking counterparts in America during the second half of the twentieth century who have taken over a leading position in the Western world with similar mixed feelings of satisfaction and anxiety.

DIFFERENT CRITICAL REACTIONS TO THE VICTORIAN AGE

To suggest a similarity between the Victorians and ourselves (a similarity, not an identity) seems a necessary preliminary for a reading of their writings. In the earlier decades of the twentieth century such an understanding perspective was conspicuously absent. It was then the fashion for most literary critics to treat their Victorian predecessors as somewhat absurd creatures with whose way of life they had little in common. Lytton Strachey's skillful puncturing of over-inflated Victorian balloons is characteristic of the attitudes of the Georgian period (1911–36). A subtler example occurs in Virginia Woolf's *Orlando*, a delightful fictionalized survey of English literature from Elizabethan times to 1928, in which the Victorians are presented in terms of dampness, rain, and proliferating vegetation:

> Ivy grew in unparalleled profusion. Houses that had been of bare stone were smothered in greenery. . . . And just as the ivy and the evergreen rioted in the damp earth outside, so did the same fertility show itself within. The life of the average woman was a succession of childbirths. . . . Giant cauliflowers towered deck above deck till they rivaled . . . the elm trees themselves. Hens laid incessantly eggs of no special tint. . . . The whole sky itself as it spread wide above the British Isles was nothing but a vast feather bed.

This witty description not only identifies a distinguishing quality of Victorian life and literature—creative energy—but it reveals that the author of the passage did not admire such creative energy. In fact, she felt terrified by it as if it might smother her. Woolf was the daughter of Sir Leslie Stephen (1832–1904), himself an eminent Victorian. Growing up under such towering shadows, she and her generation felt an understandable need to mock their predecessors.

The Georgian reaction against the Victorians is now only a matter of the history of taste, but its aftereffects still sometimes crop up when the term "Victorian" is employed in an exclusively pejorative sense. Most of us would rather be called a thief than a prude, and if the connotation of "Victorian" is narrowed down to suggest "prude" and nothing else, we remain seriously hampered in enjoying to the full what the Victorian writers accomplished.

Sympathy may not be essential, but condescension is fatal to understanding. Happily, the note of condescension has all but disappeared from critical studies of more recent date. Indeed the pendulum has swung far to the other side. In *In Bluebeard's Castle* (1971) the critic George Steiner notes how most of us are affected by images of the past which are "often as highly structured and selective as myths," in particular an image of a lost garden of Eden. For Steiner, the lost Eden is located in the golden age of Victoria, "that great summer" of human civilization. "Our sensibility locates that garden in England and western Europe between ca. the 1820s and 1915." Steiner's evaluation would have astounded earlier twentieth-century critics to whom Victorian England seemed not Eden but Hell.

But to revert from image and myth to history leads to a second difficulty about the term "Victorian." For a period almost seventy years in length we can hardly expect our generalizations to be uniformly applicable. As a preliminary corrective it is helpful to subdivide the age into three phases: Early Victorian (1832–48); Mid-Victorian (1848–70); Late Victorian (1870–1901). It may also be convenient to subdivide the Late phase by considering the final decade, the nineties, as a bridge between two centuries.

THE EARLY PERIOD (1832–48): A TIME OF TROUBLES

The early phase has been sometimes characterized as the Time of Troubles. In 1832 the passing of a Reform Bill had seemed to satisfy many of the demands of the middle classes, who were gradually taking over control of England's economy. The bill extended the right to vote to all males owning property worth ten pounds or more in annual rent. In effect the voting public hereafter included the lower middle classes but not the working classes (the latter had to wait their turn until 1867 when a second Reform Bill was passed). Even more important than the extension of the franchise was the virtual abolition in 1832 of an archaic electoral system whereby some of the new industrial cities were unrepresented in Parliament while "rotten boroughs" (communities that had become depopulated) elected the nominees of the local squire. Because it broke up the monopoly of power that the conservative landowners had so long enjoyed (the Tory party had been in office almost continuously from 1783 until 1830), the Reform Bill represents the beginning of a new age. Yet this celebrated piece of legislation could hardly be expected to solve all the economic, social, and political problems that had been building up while England was developing into a modern democratic and industrialized state. In the early 1840s a severe depression, with widespread unemployment, led to rioting. Even without the provocation of unemployment, conditions in the new industrial and coal-mining areas were sufficiently inflammatory to create fears of revolution. Workers and their families in the slums of such cities as Manchester lived like packs of rats in a sewer, and the conditions under which women and children toiled in mines and factories were unimaginably brutal. Elizabeth Barrett's poem *The Cry of the Children* (1843) may strike us as exaggerated, but it was based upon reliable evidence concerning children of five years of age who dragged heavy tubs of coal through low-ceilinged mine passages for sixteen hours a day. Life in early Victorian mines and factories was much like Thomas Hobbes's "state of nature"—"poor, nasty, brutish, and short."

The owners of mines and factories regarded themselves as innocent of blame for such conditions, for they were wedded to an economic theory of laissez-faire, which assumed that unregulated working conditions would ultimately benefit everyone. A sense of the seemingly hopeless complexity of the situation during the Hungry 1840s is provided by an entry for 1842 in the diary of the statesman Charles Greville, an entry written at the same time that Carlyle was making his contribution to the "Condition of England Question," *Past and Present*. Conditions in the north of England, Greville reports, were "appalling."

> There is an immense and continually increasing population, no adequate demand for labor, . . . no confidence, but a universal alarm, disquietude, and discontent. Nobody can sell anything. . . . Certainly I have never seen . . . so serious a state of things as that which now stares us in the face; and this after thirty years of uninterrupted peace, and the most ample scope afforded for the development of all our resources. . . . One remarkable feature in the present condition of affairs is that nobody can account for it, and nobody pretends to be able to point out any remedy.

In reality many remedies were being pointed out. One of the most striking was put forward by the Chartists, a large organization of workingmen. In 1838 the organization drew up a "People's Charter" advocating the extension of the right to vote, the use of secret balloting, and other legislative reforms. For ten years the Chartist leaders engaged in agitation to have their program adopted by Parliament. Their fiery speeches, addressed to large mobs of discontented people, alarmed those who were not themselves suffering from hunger. In *Locksley Hall*, Tennyson seems to have had the Chartist mobs in mind when he pictured the threat posed by this time of troubles: "Slowly comes a hungry people, as a lion, creeping nigher, / Glares at one that nods and winks behind a slowly-dying fire." Although in the eyes of posterity the Chartist program seems an eminently reasonable one, it was premature in the 1840s. More immediately feasible was the agitation to abolish the high tariffs on imported grains, tariffs known as the Corn Laws (the word "corn" in England refers to wheat and other grains). These high tariffs had been established to protect English farm products from having to compete with low-priced products imported from abroad. Landowners and farmers fought to keep these tariffs in force so that high prices for their wheat would be assured, but the rest of the population suffered severely from the exorbitant price of bread or, in years of bad crops, from scarcity of food. In 1845 serious crop failures in England and the outbreak of potato blight in Ireland, convinced Sir Robert Peel, the Tory Prime Minister, that traditional protectionism must be abandoned. In 1846 the Corn Laws were repealed by Parliament, and the way was paved for the introduction of a system of Free Trade whereby goods could be imported with the payment of only minimal tariff duties. Although Free Trade did not eradicate the slums of Manchester, it worked well for many years and helped to relieve the major crisis of the Victorian economy. In 1848, when armed revolutions were exploding violently in every country in Europe, England was relatively unaffected. A monster Chartist demonstration fizzled out harmlessly in London, and Englishmen settled down to enjoy two decades of prosperity.

This Time of Troubles left its mark on some early Victorian literature. "Insurrection is a most sad necessity," Carlyle writes in his *Past and Present*, "and governors who must wait for that to instruct them are surely getting into the fatalest courses." A similar refrain runs through Carlyle's history *The French Revolution* (1837). Memories of the French Reign of Terror lasted longer than memories of Trafalgar and Waterloo, memories freshened by later out-breaks of civil strife, "the red fool-fury of the Seine" as Tennyson described one of the violent overturnings of government in France. It is the novelists of the 1840s and early 1850s, however, who show the most marked response to the industrial and political scene. Vivid records of these conditions are to be found in the fiction of Charles Kingsley (1819–1875), Elizabeth Gaskell (1810–1865), and Benjamin Disraeli (1804–1881), a novelist who became prime minister. For his novel *Sybil* (1845) Disraeli chose an appropriate subtitle, *The Two Nations*—a phrase that pointed up the line dividing the England of the rich from the other nation, the England of the poor.

THE MID-VICTORIAN PERIOD (1848–70): ECONOMIC PROSPERITY AND RELIGIOUS CONTROVERSY

In the decades following the Time of Troubles some Victorian writers, such as Dickens, continued to make critical attacks on the shortcomings of the Victorian social scene. Even more critical and indignant than Dickens was John Ruskin, who abandoned the criticism of art during this period in order to expose the faults of Victorian industry and commerce, as in his *The Stones of Venice* (1853), which combines a history of architecture with stern prophecies about the doom of technological culture, or in his attacks upon laissez-faire economics in *Unto This Last* (1862). Generally speaking, how-ever, the "solid substance" of the novels of Anthony Trollope (1815–1882)—as Robert Adam has described it—is a more characteristic reflection of the mid-Victorian attitude toward the social and political scene than are Rus-kin's lamentations. As Adam said of Trollope in 1983: "His books are solidly put together, as befits the world of fixed values and stable institutions that he describes; aided, perhaps, by a bit of nostalgia, they have regained in our time some of the popularity they had in their own." Overall, this second phase of the Victorian period had many harassing problems, but it was a time of prosperity. On the whole its institutions worked well. Even the badly bungled war against Russia in the Crimea (1854–56) did not seriously affect the growing sense of satisfaction that the challenging difficulties of the 1840s had been solved or would be solved by English wisdom and energy. The monarchy was proving its worth in a modern setting. The queen and her husband, Prince Albert, were themselves models of middle class domesticity and devotion to duty. The aristocracy was discovering that Free Trade was enriching rather than impoverishing their estates; agriculture flourished together with trade and industry. And through a succession of Factory Acts in Parliament, which restricted child labor and limited hours of employ-ment, the condition of the working classes was also being gradually improved. When we speak of Victorian complacency or stability or optimism, we are usually referring to this mid-Victorian phase—"The Age of Improvement," as the historian Asa Briggs has called it. "Of all the decades in our history," writes G. M. Young, "a wise man would choose the eighteen-fifties to be young in."

In 1851 Prince Albert opened the Great Exhibition in Hyde Park where a gigantic glass greenhouse, the Crystal Palace, had been erected to display the exhibits of modern industry and science. The Crystal Palace was one of the first buildings constructed according to modern architectural principles in which materials such as glass and iron are employed for purely functional ends (much late Victorian furniture, on the other hand, with its fantastic and irrelevant ornamentation, was constructed according to the opposite principle). The building itself, as well as the exhibits, symbolized the triumphant feats of Victorian technology. As Benjamin Disraeli wrote to a friend in 1862: "It is a privilege to live in this age of rapid and brilliant events. What an error to consider it a utilitarian age. It is one of infinite romance."

In the strenuous assertiveness of some of Robert Browning's poetry one might detect parallels to the confident mood inspired by the Great Exhibition. Generally, however, most mid-Victorian poetry and critical prose was less preoccupied with technology, economics, and politics than with the conflict between religion and science. This conflict was not, of course, altogether a new one. Tennyson's *In Memoriam* (1850), like much mid-Victorian literature, carries on the religious debates of earlier decades. These debates, in their earlier form, had been generally between the Utilitarians, the followers of Jeremy Bentham (1772–1832) and the philosophical conservatives, the followers of Samuel Taylor Coleridge. As John Stuart Mill demonstrates in his excellent essays on Bentham and Coleridge, these two writers divided between them the allegiance of all thoughtful people in England. Bentham and his disciples were reformers of a distinctive cast of mind. Their aim was to test all institutions in the light of human reason in order to determine whether such institutions were useful—that is, whether they contributed to the greatest happiness of the greatest numbers. This "Utilitarian" test was an extremely effective method of correcting inefficiencies in government administration: the drastic remodeling of the Civil Service in Victorian England was a tribute to Benthamite thinking. But such a test, if applied to a long-established institution like the Church of England, or to religious belief in general, could have, and did have, disruptive effects. Was religious belief useful for the needs of a reasonable person? To the Benthamites the answer was evident: religious belief was merely an outmoded superstition. This answer was emphatically stated in a letter by Harriet Martineau (1802–1876), a Utilitarian writer and freethinker: "There is no *theory* of a God, of an author of Nature, of an origin of the universe, which is not utterly repugnant to my faculties; which is not (to my feelings) so irreverent as to make me blush; so misleading as to make me mourn."

Opponents of Utilitarianism, including Coleridge, argued that Bentham's view of human nature was unrealistically narrow, that people had always needed a faith as profoundly as they had needed food, and that if reason seemed to demonstrate the irrelevance of religion then reason must be an inadequate mode of arriving at truth. These anti-Utilitarians were of two types. The first were those such as Carlyle, who abandoned institutional Christianity yet sought to retain some sort of substitute religious belief—a quest that is vividly described in his spiritual autobiography, *Sartor Resartus*. Others, led by John Henry Newman, argued that only a powerful, dogmatic, and traditional religious institution could withstand the attacks of irreverent thinkers of the Benthamite stamp. In the 1830s and 1840s (before he was converted to Roman Catholicism), Newman became the leader of an impressive crusade to strengthen the Church of England. The movement he headed is known under various names including "The Oxford Movement," because it originated at Oxford University, or as "Tractarianism," because Newman and his conservative followers developed their arguments in defense of a High Church in a series of pamphlets or tracts. Whatever name it went by, Newman's campaign produced a lively controversy. When Arthur Hugh Clough and Matthew Arnold were at Oxford in the early 1840s, the university was seething with religious debates, debates that were to have a marked effect on the poetry written by both men in the 1850s.

In mid-Victorian England these controversies continued, but with an added intensification. Leadership in the anticlerical position passed gradually from the Utilitarians to some of the leaders of science, in particular to Thomas Henry Huxley, who popularized the theories of Charles Darwin. Although many English scientists were themselves men of strong religious convictions, the impact of their scientific discoveries seemed consistently damaging to established faiths. Complaining about the "flimsiness" of his own religious faith in 1851, Ruskin exclaimed: "If only the Geologists would let me alone, I could do very well, but those dreadful hammers! I hear the clink of them at the end of every cadence of the Bible verses."

The damage lamented by Ruskin was effected in two ways. First the scientific attitude of mind was applied towards a study of the Bible itself. This kind of investigation, developed especially in Germany, was known as the "Higher Criticism." Instead of treating the Bible as a sacredly infallible document, scientifically minded scholars examined it as a mere text of history and presented evidence about its composition that believers, especially in Protestant countries, found disconcerting, to say the least. A noteworthy example of such Higher Criticism studies was David Friedrich Strauss's *Das Leben Jesu*, which was translated by George Eliot in 1846 as *The Life of Jesus*. The second kind of damage was effected by the view of humanity implicit in the discoveries of geology and astronomy, the new and "Terrible Muses" of literature, as Tennyson called them in a late poem. Geology, by extending the history of the earth backwards millions of years, reduced the stature of the human race in time. John Tyndall, an eminent physicist, said in an address at Belfast in 1874 that in the eighteenth century, men had an "unwavering trust" in the "chronology of the Old Testament," but in Victorian times men have had to become accustomed to

> the idea that not for six thousand, nor for sixty thousand, nor for six thousand thousand, but for aeons embracing untold millions of years, this earth has been the theater of life and death. The riddle of the rocks has been read by the geologist and paleontologist, from sub-Cambrian depths to the deposits thickening over the sea bottoms of today. And upon the leaves of that stone book are . . . stamped the characters, plainer and surer than those formed by the ink of history, which carry the mind back into abysses of past time.

The discoveries of astronomers, by extending a knowledge of stellar distances to dizzying expanses, were likewise disconcerting. Carlyle's friend, John Sterling, remarked in a letter of 1837 how geology "gives one the same sort of bewildering view of the abysmal extent of Time that Astronomy does of Space." To Tennyson's speaker in *Maud* (1855) the stars are "innumerable" tyrants of "iron skies." They are "Cold fires, yet with power to burn and brand / His nothingness into man."

In the mid-Victorian period biology reduced mankind even further into "nothingness." Darwin's great treatise, *The Origin of Species* (1859), was interpreted by the nonscientific public in a variety of ways. Some chose to assume that evolution was synonymous with progress, but most readers recognized that Darwin's theory of natural selection conflicted not only with the concept of creation derived from the Bible but also with long-established assumptions of the values attached to humanity's special role in the world. Darwin's later treatise, *The Descent of Man* (1871), raised more explicitly the haunting question of our identification with the animal kingdom. If the principle of survival of the fittest was accepted as the key to conduct, there remained the inquiry: fittest for what? As John Fowles noted in 1968, Darwin's theories made the Victorians feel "infinitely isolated." "By the 1860s the great iron structures of their philosophies, religions, and social stratifications were already beginning to look dangerously corroded to the more perspicacious."

Disputes about evolutionary science, like the disputes about the Oxford Movement, are a reminder that beneath the placidly prosperous surface of the mid-Victorian age there were serious conflicts and anxieties. In the same year as the Great Exhibition, with its celebration of the triumphs of trade and industry, Charles Kingsley wrote, "The young men and women of our day are fast parting from their parents and each other; the more thoughtful are wandering either towards Rome, towards sheer materialism, or towards an unchristian and unphilosophic spiritualism."

THE LATE PERIOD (1870–1901): DECAY OF VICTORIAN VALUES

The third phase of the Victorian age is more difficult to categorize. At first glance its point of view seems merely an extension of mid-Victorianism whose golden glow lingered on through the Jubilee years of 1887 and 1897 (years celebrating the fiftieth and sixtieth anniversaries of the queen's accession) down to 1914. For many Victorians, this final phase of the century was a time of serenity and security, the age of house parties and long weekends in the country. In the amber of Henry James's prose is immortalized a sense of the comfortable pace of these pleasant, well-fed gatherings. Life in London, too, was for many an exhilarating heyday. In *My Life and Loves*, the Irish-American Frank Harris, often a severe critic of the English scene, records his recollections of the gaiety of London in the 1880s: "London: who would give even an idea of its varied delights: London, the center of civilization, the queen city of the world without a peer in the multitude of its attractions, as superior to Paris as Paris is to New York." Yet as the leading social critic of the 1860s, Matthew Arnold, had tried to show, there were anomalies in the seemingly smooth-working institutions of mid-Victorian England, and after 1870 flaws became evident. Some of the flaws developed out of issues of long standing such as relations with the Irish, and, a related issue, the status of Roman Catholics in England. The "Irish Question," as it was called, became especially divisive in the 1880s when Home Rule for Ireland became a topic of heated debate—a proposed reform that was unsuccessfully advocated by Prime Minister Gladstone and other leaders. And outside of England were other developments that challenged Victorian stability and security. The sudden emergence of Bismarck's Germany after the defeat of France in 1871 was progressively to confront England with powerful threats to her naval and military position and also to her exclusive preeminence in trade and industry. The recovery of the United States after the Civil War likewise provided new and serious competition. In 1873 and 1874 such severe economic depressions occurred that the rate of emigration rose to an alarming degree. Another threat to the domestic balance of power was the growth of labor as a political and economic force. In 1867, under Disraeli's guidance, a second Reform Bill had been passed which extended the right to vote to sections of the working classes, and this, together with the subsequent development of trade unions, made labor a political force to be reckoned with. The Labor Party represented a wide variety of shades of socialism. Some labor leaders were disciples of the Tory-Socialism of John Ruskin and shared his idealistic conviction that the middle-class economic and political system, with its distrust of state interference, was irresponsible and immoral. Other labor leaders had been infected instead by the revolutionary theories of Karl Marx and Friedrich Engels as expounded in their *Communist Manifesto* of 1847 and in Marx's *Capital* (1867, 1885, 1895). Perhaps the first English author of note to be connected with Marxism was the poet and painter William Morris. Morris, himself a man of some independent means, was too much of an individualist to follow consistently an orthodox Marxist line, but he did share with Marx a conviction that utopia could be achieved only after the working classes had, by revolution, taken control of government and industry.

In much of the literature of this final phase of Victorianism we can sense an overall change of attitudes. Some of the late Victorian writers expressed the change openly by simply attacking the major mid-Victorian idols. Samuel Butler (1835–1902), for example, set about demolishing Darwin, Tennyson, and Prime Minister Gladstone, figures whose aura of authority reminded him of his own father. For the more worldly and casual-mannered Prime Minister Disraeli, on the other hand, Butler could express considerable admiration: "Earnestness was his greatest danger, but if he did not quite overcome it (as who indeed can? it is the last enemy that shall be subdued), he managed to veil it with a fair amount of success." In his novel, *The Way of All Flesh*, much of which was written in the 1870s, Butler satirized family life, in particular the tyrannical self-righteousness of a Victorian father, his own father (a clergyman) serving as his model. Butler's open revolt was perhaps premature. More typical were Walter Pater and his followers, writers who concluded that the striving of their predecessors was ultimately pointless, that the answers to our problems are not to be found, and that our role is to enjoy the fleeting moments of beauty in "this short day of frost and sun." It is symptomatic of this shift in point of view that Edward FitzGerald's beautiful translation of the *Rubáiyát of Omar Khayyám* (1859), with its melancholy theme that life's problems are insoluble, went virtually unnoticed in the 1860s but became a popular favorite in subsequent decades.

THE NINETIES

The changes in attitude that had begun cropping up in the 1870s became much more conspicuous in the final decade of the century and give the nineties a special aura of notoriety. Of course the changes were not in evidence everywhere. Throughout the Empire at its outposts in India and Africa—an Empire which by 1890 comprised more than a quarter of all the territory on the surface of the world—Englishmen were building railways and administering governments with the same strenuous dedication to duty as in the mid-Victorian period. The stories of Kipling and Conrad variously record the struggles of such men. Also embodying the strenuous task of sustaining an Empire were the soldiers and sailors who fought in various colonial wars, most notably in the war against the Boers in South Africa (1899–1902). But back in England, Victorian standards were breaking down on several fronts. One colorful embodiment of changing values was Victoria's son and heir, Edward Prince of Wales, who was entering his fiftieth year as the nineties began. A pleasure-seeking, easygoing person, Edward was the antithesis of his father, Prince Albert, an earnest-minded intellectual who had devoted his life to hard work and to administrative responsibilities. Edward's carry-ings-on were a favorite topic for newspaper articles, one of which noted how this father of five children "openly maintained scandalous relations with ballet dancers and chorus singers." The familiar epithet "Gay Nineties," however inadequate to characterize the decade, evokes the rakish life style of Victoria's son.

Much of the writing of the decade illustrates a breakdown of a different sort. Melancholy, not gaiety, is characteristic of its spirit. Artists of the nineties, representing the aesthetic movement, were very much aware of living at the end of a great century, and often cultivated a deliberately *fin-de-siècle* ("end-of-century") pose. A studied languor, a weary sophistication, a search for new ways of titillating jaded palates can be found in both the poetry and the prose of the period. *The Yellow Book,* a periodical which ran from 1894 to 1897, is generally taken to represent the aestheticism of the nineties. The startling black-and-white drawings and designs of its art editor, Aubrey Beardsley (1872–1898), the prose of George Moore and Max Beerbohm, and the poetry of Ernest Dowson illustrate different aspects of the movement. In 1893, an Austrian critic, Max Nordau, summed up what seemed to him to be happening, in a book that was as sensational as its title: *Degeneration.*

From a different perspective, an evaluation of the nineties directly contrary to Nordau's could be argued for, perhaps entitled "Regeneration." The final decade can be viewed, that is, as either the beginning of a great future movement in literature or as the ending and death of another great movement in literature. Possibly it may be more fruitful to see this transitional decade as both a beginning and an ending. In his essay, "The Nineties," Helmut Gerber offers a useful generalization (applicable to the 1790s as well as to the 1890s) on this point. According to Gerber, it seems to be "that at the ends of centuries . . . human beings, but artists in particular, are infected by a sense of death, decay, agony, old gods falling, cultural decline, on the one hand, or by a sense of regeneration . . . on the other."

In Dickens's *David Copperfield* (1850), the hero affirms: "I have always been thoroughly in earnest." Forty-five years later, Wilde's comedy, *The Importance of Being Earnest,* turns this typical mid-Victorian word, "earnest," into a pun, a key joke in this comic spectacle of earlier Victorian values being turned upside down. As Richard Le Gallienne (a novelist of the nineties) remarked in *The Romantic Nineties* (1926): "Wilde made dying Victorianism laugh at itself, and it may be said to have died of the laughter."

EARNESTNESS, RESPECTABILITY, AND THE EVANGELICALS

Wilde's decades, the 1880s and 1890s, when being earnest was apparently not important, can be legitimately overlooked if we are trying to categorize the Victorian age as a whole instead of distinguishing the stages of its development. Why has the term "earnest" been so often applied to the typical Victorian writers? It should be noted that the quality of earnestness (or as some historians call it, more appropriately, "eagerness") was not strained. It did not exclude high spirits and humor. An age which relished the comic genius of Dickens and Thackeray, the grotesque humor of Browning and Carlyle, the nonsensical whimsy of Edward Lear and Lewis Carroll, was not exclusively dedicated to mere solemnity. Nevertheless the general Victorian preference for earnestness of spirit was firmly rooted and can best be accounted for by distinguishing it not from what came after but from what went before it.

The connections between literature in the Romantic and Victorian ages are close. Victorian poets as different as Browning and Swinburne both derive from Shelley. Tennyson is a follower of Keats, Arnold is a follower of Wordsworth, and many other instances of such continuity and influence may be cited. Most Victorian writers, both in poems and in essays, grappled with the same religious issues that had been a central concern for Wordsworth, Blake, and Shelley. As M. H. Abrams demonstrates in *Natural Supernaturalism* (1971), the post-Romantics from Tennyson through Yeats continued the Romantic endeavor to salvage "the cardinal values of their religious heritage by reconstituting them in a way that would make them intellectually acceptable, as well as emotionally pertinent, for the time being."

A dividing point, however, may be observed in Carlyle's well-known advice to his contemporaries in 1834: "Close thy *Byron*; open thy *Goethe*." Carlyle's advice could be interpreted in two ways. The first is with reference to literary forms. A Victorian writer might avoid the wild excesses, the lack of controlled form of much Romantic writing; Byron himself foresaw that such a reformation was necessary. "We are all on a wrong tack ('Lakers' and all)," he wrote. "Our successors will have to go back to the riding school . . . and learn to ride the great horse." Some of Byron's Victorian successors ignored his prediction; they too rode Pegasus bareback as casually as he had done. Yet several Victorian poets, Tennyson in particular, do fulfill Byron's prediction. The energy of Romantic literature persists, but it is channeled into a stricter concern for disciplined forms. It is significant that the Romantic poet most influential in the Victorian age was Keats, the most form-conscious of the Romantics, rather than Byron.

Carlyle himself was not primarily concerned with a chastening of literary forms. He was saying, in effect: "Stop moping. There is work to be done, work that requires the earnest efforts of all of us." A similar message was made, also in 1834, by the popular novelist, Edward Bulwer-Lytton, in his *England and the English*. "When Byron passed away," Lytton reported, ". . . we turned to the actual and practical career of life: we awoke from the morbid, the dreaming, 'the moonlight and dimness of the mind,' and by a natural reaction addressed ourselves to the active and daily objects which lay before us."

And to address themselves to the "actual and practical" meant for the Victorians that their "natural reaction" was directed not only against the excesses of Romanticism but also against the life-style of many of Byron's aristocratic contemporaries who had flourished in the previous decades and who had embodied the worldly-minded code of the Regency, with its preference for a happy-go-lucky enjoyment of the physical pleasures of life, for fox hunting and hard drinking and lounging. Lord Melbourne, Victoria's first prime minister, embodied such a view of life and found himself out of place under the new dispensation—an "autumn rose" as Strachey called him. Carlyle's gospel, on the other hand, was soon to be extremely timely for the new generation. From 1830 on there developed what the historian Arnold Toynbee called a "challenge." The earnest strivings of the Victorians provided the needed "response." A speech made by the heroine of *Jane Eyre* sums up these developments. After she refuses to accept a proposal to become the mistress of the loose-living Mr. Rochester, and he is bewailing his lonely lot, Jane Eyre advises him sternly: "Mr. Rochester . . . we are born to strive and endure—you as well as I: do so."

A further indication of the timeliness of Carlyle's call to action in *Sartor Resartus* is its Evangelical tone. In its strictest sense "Evangelical" refers to part of a branch of the Church of England called the Low Church. Zealously dedicated to good causes (they were responsible for the emancipation of all the slaves in the British Empire as early as 1833), advocates of a strict puritan code of morality, and righteously censorious of worldliness in others, the Evangelicals became a powerful and active minority in the early part of the nineteenth century. Much of their power depended on the fact that their view of life and religion was virtually identical with that of a much larger group, the Nonconformists—that is, the Baptists, Methodists, Congregationalists, and other Protestant sects which did not conform to the tenets of the Established Church (the Church of England has been, in effect, a state church). When united for action with this large group of sects—Dissenters as they were called—a group whose membership included a generous proportion of successful businessmen, the Evangelicals were a formidable force.

Finally, the term "Evangelical" has been loosely applied to cover any kind of enthusiastic concern for reform. It is thus used to describe anyone infected with the *spirit* of the Evangelical movement even though he or she does not subscribe to its ethical code or its beliefs. Victorian earnestness may therefore be explained partly as a response to a challenging situation and partly as rooted in an active religious movement that left its stamp on agnostics as well as on believers. George Eliot is an example of this Evangelical legacy. After having abandoned Christianity and having flouted convention by living for years with a married man, she devoted her novels to painstaking analyses of problems of conscience and moral choice. It would be difficult to name a Victorian writer of any consequence who remained an Evangelical in the true sense of the term; it would be equally difficult to name one who was not affected by what Evangelicalism had stood for.

The code of puritanism and respectability advocated by the Nonconformists and Evangelicals is symbolized by the joyless Victorian Sunday. In 1837, a new Sunday Observance Bill (strenuously opposed by Charles Dickens) was introduced into Parliament. Although the Bill did not quite pass, the Sober Sunday ritual became established by custom if not by law. To later generations, even more repressive was the puritans' standard of sexual behavior, with its intense concern for female innocence—or, as its opponents contended, for female ignorance. The history of Victorian asceticism is nevertheless much more complex than common supposition allows, as may be suggested by the fact that in 1850, 8,000 prostitutes were known by the police to be operating in London. In the city of Leeds, a few years earlier, statistics indicate that there were two churches and 39 chapels or meeting houses to compete with 451 taverns and 98 brothels. For useful correctives to the commonly accepted suppositions about Victorian puritanism, a reader may consult Steven Marcus's sensational disclosures of sexual habits in mid-nineteenth-century England in his *The Other Victorians* (1966), and also the more scholarly history by Peter Gay: *The Bourgeois Experience: Victoria to Freud,* of which the first volume *(Education of the Senses)* was published in 1984.

The middle-class puritan code was largely derived from the Old Testament, but it also reflected commercial experience in which sobriety, hard work, and a joyless abstention from worldly pleasures paid off, paradoxically enough, in worldly success. Intermixed with this ascetic code was an insistence upon respectability—an insistence reflecting the insecurity of a newly powerful class in a fluid society, a class anxious to have a fixed set of manners by which to live and to measure themselves and the families of others. Hence developed the phenomenon of "Mrs. Grundyism": conformity in its worst sense—that is, external conformity.

It is against this background that John Stuart Mill's essay *On Liberty* (1859) should be read. The status of liberty in Victorian England was actually one of the most outstanding achievements of the age. For continental agitators of left, right, or center in politics, Victorian England was the land of freedom, an asylum where the policeman (who was unarmed) was a friendly protector instead of an instrument of tyranny. To this asylum flocked General Torrijos (whose plot against the Spanish monarchy involved Tennyson); Mazzini, the Italian nationalist; Louis Napoleon of France; Kossuth, the Hungarian patriot; Prince Metternich of Austria; and Karl Marx himself, whose major work, *Capital*, was conceived in the Reading Room of the British Museum. The Victorian achievement in religious as well as political freedom is also impressive. Atheist orators such as Charles Bradlaugh enjoyed the privilege of addressing large audiences. In 1844, Friedrich Engels (not usually friendly toward the English scene) observed: "England is unquestionably the freest—that is, the least unfree—country in the world, North America not excepted."

Under such circumstances, why did Mill consider liberty a problem? Mill was inspired by his experience that individuality is threatened not merely by political tyrannies or entrenched religions. It is threatened also by the less tangible pressures exerted by society itself, in particular by the middle-class conventions which weighed upon the nonconformist in society rather than upon the Nonconformist in religion. In Hardy's late-Victorian novel, *Jude the Obscure*, a novel which contributed to the breakdown of the puritan code in literature, it is revealing that when the heroine resolves to leave her husband she justifies her action by citing a passage from Mill's *On Liberty*.

THE ROLE OF WOMEN IN VICTORIAN LIFE AND LITERATURE

Hardy's heroine might also have cited a later treatise by Mill on a different aspect of liberty: *The Subjection of Women* (1869), in which he boldly challenged long-established assumptions about women's roles in society. Like Mary Wollstonecraft's *A Vindication of the Rights of Women* (1792), Mill's treatise brings libertarian arguments for reform in the privileges of men to apply to the status of women. It was not only the political revolutions of the times, however, that provided a basis for change in woman's position, but the Industrial Revolution as well. The explosive growth of the textile industries brought hundreds of thousands of lower-class women into factory jobs with grueling working conditions. In its disruption of family life and in its similarity to male labor, women's factory work presented an increasing challenge to traditional ideas of woman's sphere. In quite a different way, however, the strains of modernization motivated a renewed emphasis on home and family that enforced the separation between men's work and women's work. All of these changes brought to the fore what Victorians called The Woman Question, which concerned issues of sexual inequality in politics, economic life, education, and social intercourse. In the political area, it was abundantly evident that women continued to rank as second-class citizens. Like millions of working-class men, they could not vote or hold office except the highest office of queen (and Victoria was in general an antifeminist).

Petitions to Parliament advocating women's suffrage were introduced as early as the 1840s, but they did not become law until 1918. Less prolonged was the agitation to allow married women to own and handle their own property, which culminated successfully in the passing of the Married Women's Property Acts (1870–1908). The Factory Acts, which had been passed earlier, corrected some of the worst aspects of women's employment in the mines and factories, including the reduction of the sixteen-hour day; in this instance, however, the argument for reform was based not on women's equality but on the earlier chivalric view of their comparative frailty of physique.

In addition to pressuring Parliament for legal reform, feminists worked to enlarge educational opportunities for women. In 1837 none of England's three universities was open to women. Tennyson's long poem *The Princess* (1847), with its fantasy of a women's college from whose precincts all males are excluded, was inspired by contemporary discussions of the need for women to obtain an education more advanced than that provided by the popular finishing schools such as Miss Pinkerton's Academy in Thackeray's *Vanity Fair*. Although by the end of the poem, Princess Ida has repented of her Amazonian scheme, she and the prince look forward to a future in which man will be "more of woman, she of man." The poem reflects a climate of opinion that led in 1848 to the establishment of the first women's college in London, an example later recommended by Thomas Henry Huxley, a strong advocate of advanced education for women. By the end of Victoria's reign, women could take degrees at twelve universities or university colleges and could study, although not earn a degree, at Oxford and Cambridge.

There was also agitation for improved employment opportunities for women. Writers as diverse as Charlotte Brontë, Elizabeth Barrett Browning, and Florence Nightingale complained that middle-class women were taught trivial accomplishments in order to fill up days in which there was nothing important to do. The problem of nothing to do was acute in quite a different way for what contemporary journalists called surplus or redundant women, that is, the women in the population who remained unmarried because of the imbalance in numbers between the sexes. Such women (of whom there were approximately half a million in mid-Victorian England) had few employment opportunities, none of them attractive or profitable. Emigration was frequently proposed as a solution to the problem, but the number of single female emigrants was never high enough to affect significantly the population imbalance. Bad working conditions and underemployment drove thousands of women into prostitution, which became increasingly professionalized in the nineteenth century. The only occupation at which an unmarried middle-class woman could earn a living and maintain some claim to gentility was that of a governess, but a governess could expect no security of employment, minimal wages, and an ambiguous status, somewhere between servant and family member, that isolated her within the household. Perhaps because the governess so clearly indicated the precariousness of the unmarried middle-class woman's status in Victorian England, the governess novel, of which the most famous examples are *Jane Eyre* and *Vanity Fair*, became a popular genre through which to explore woman's role in society.

As such novels indicate, Victorian society was preoccupied not only with legal and economic limitations on women's lives but with the nature of woman itself. In *The Subjection of Women*, John Stuart Mill argues that "what is now called the nature of women is eminently an artificial thing—the result of forced repression in some directions, unnatural stimulation in others." In Tennyson's *The Princess*, the king voices a more traditional view of woman's role:

> Man for the field and woman for the hearth:
> Man for the sword and for the needle she:
> Man with the head and woman with the heart:
> Man to command and woman to obey.

The king's relegation of women to the hearth and heart reflects an ideology that claimed that woman had a special nature peculiarly fit for her domestic role. Most aptly epitomized by the title of Coventry Patmore's immensely popular poem *The Angel in the House* (1854–62), this concept of womanhood stressed woman's purity and selflessness. Protected and enshrined within the home, her role was to create a place of peace where man could take refuge from the difficulties of modern life. In *Of Queen's Gardens*, John Ruskin writes:

> This is the true nature of home—it is the place of Peace; the shelter, not only from all injury, but from all terror, doubt, and division. In so far as it is not this, it is not home; so far as the anxieties of the outer life penetrate into it, and the inconsistently-minded, unknown, unloved, or hostile society of the outer world is allowed either by husband or wife to cross the threshold, it ceases to be home; it is then only a part of that outer world which you have roofed over, and lighted fire in. But so far as it is a sacred place, a vestal temple, a temple of the hearth watched over by Household Gods, . . . so far it vindicates the name, and fulfills the praise, of home.

Such an exalted conception of home placed great pressure on the woman who ran it to be, in Ruskin's words, "enduringly, incorruptibly good; instinctively, infallibly wise—wise, not for self-development, but for self-renunciation." It is easy to recognize the oppressive aspects of this ideology. Paradoxically, however, it was used not only by antifeminists, eager to keep woman in her place, but by some feminists as well, in justifying the special contribution that woman could make to public life.

In his preface to *The Portrait of a Lady* (1881), Henry James writes: "Millions of presumptuous girls, intelligent or not intelligent, daily affront their destiny, and what is it open to their destiny to *be*, at the most, that we should make an ado about it?" Every major Victorian novelist makes the "ado" that James describes in addressing the question of woman's vocation. Ultimately, as Victorian novels illustrate, the basic problem was not only political, economic, and educational. It was how women were regarded, and regarded themselves, as members of a society. In the final pages of our section on Victorian Issues, the vigorous debate about the problem is represented under the title The Woman Question.

THE DIVERSITY OF VICTORIAN LITERATURE

The weight of the puritan code on the literature of early and mid-Victorian England was, as we might expect, considerable. It was most evident in the novels, for novels were commonly read aloud in family gatherings, and the need to avoid topics which might cause embarrassment to young girls established taboos that novelists could not dare ignore, although they might sometimes skillfully circumvent them. Thackeray and others offered protests, but it was not until near the end of the century or later that the novelists broke clear of those restrictions. The poets and essayists fared better. When Browning was writing *The Ring and the Book* he was obviously unconcerned about whether his poem might raise blushes on prudish cheeks, and Swinburne's *Poems and Ballads* flouts the taboos in the manner of the French poets whom he admired (of his Victorian contemporaries Swinburne remarked that "their ears are the chastest part about them"). Both volumes appeared in the 1860s at the same time as the essays of Matthew Arnold with their attacks on the narrowness of the puritan middle-class mind.

Too much can be made of the importance of these taboos as literary conventions in the Victorian age. A much more significant kind of pressure from the Victorian audience on its writers, one that they were themselves inclined to comply with, was the desire on the part of readers to be guided and edified. The newly expanding reading public, despite its air of solid confidence, wanted help from its authors, and its authors were understandably flattered by the request. Only a few, such as Dante Gabriel Rossetti, ignored it; the others all exhibit, in varying degrees, an air of prophecy and mission. Carlyle in his lectures *On Heroes* identifies the writer or "Poet" such as Shakespeare with the great prophets such as Mahomet, and in his own writings it is evident that he sought to make his mark as a seer rather than as a mere man of letters. The very high status that even Matthew Arnold claimed for literature is evident in his statement that "most of what now passes with us for religion and philosophy will be replaced by poetry." Perhaps the most extreme example of a Victorian writer with a sense of mission is, however, John Ruskin, a writer who had opinions on every topic. Tennyson, here as in most instances, is more representative. To provide firm guidance in problems of science and religion, the destiny of nations and daily life, was a task that sometimes appealed to Tennyson and sometimes appalled him. As we might expect, several of his poems are concerned with the dilemma of writers' divided duty toward their public and their art—a dilemma that has become even more acute in the twentieth century as the reading public has further expanded.

The existence of this dilemma may help to explain another characteristic of Victorian literature: its variety both in style and in subject matter. Variety is in part a symptom of the Victorian writers' bold independence and their zest for literary experiment for its own sake, but it is also a symptom of an absence of any final general agreement concerning the function of literature and art in a democratic society. Writers and their audiences might usually agree that instruction was a desirable attribute of a work of literature, but what was to constitute the instruction and what was the appropriate mode in which to convey it?

It is among the poets that the search for appropriate modes is most evident. All of them seem driven to experiment in a variety of ways. In versification, although making considerable use of traditional forms such as the sonnet, most of them preferred experimenting with new or unusual metrical patterns, as did Swinburne, Gerard Manley Hopkins, and, later, Thomas Hardy. In line with their metrical experiments are their experiments in the art of narrative poetry. The chief challenge facing the writer of a "modern poem," according to Dwight Culler, has been "not steam but the novel," and the development of poetic narrative in the Victorian age bears out his point. As the novel emerged as one of the dominant forms of literature, the poets sought new ways of telling stories in verse; examples of such attempts include Tennyson's *Maud*, Elizabeth Barrett Browning's *Aurora Leigh*, and

Robert Browning's *The Ring and the Book*. Some of the poets, such as George Meredith, William Morris, and Emily Brontë, novelists as well as poets, were especially aware that poetry can offer unusual resources for the writer of narratives, as demonstrated by the compression and intensification of Morris's early poems or Meredith's *Modern Love*. Others, in particular Arthur Hugh Clough, sought to write narrative poems as if they were novels, poems that are long, casual in tone, and usually prosaic in style.

To illustrate the diversity of styles in Victorian writing, two poems, published within the space of three years, may be compared. Tennyson's *The Lotos-Eaters* (1842) is in the grand manner of English poetry, the culmination of a poetic tradition emphasizing beautiful cadences and vowel sounds: "To watch the crisping ripples on the beach, / And tender curving lines of creamy spray." In Browning's *The Bishop Orders his Tomb* (1845), the colloquial tone of the speaker, as he hisses his hatred of a rival, seems to belong to a different century: "Shrewd was that snatch from out the corner south / He graced his carrion with, God curse the same!" And if we ignore the stylistic differences here and concentrate upon a possible similarity—that both poems, like many Victorian writings, evoke the past of myth and history—what is to be done to align these works with other works of the same period? What resemblance is there to Dickens's *Oliver Twist* (1838), for example, with its realistic scenes of a sordid workhouse, or to Carlyle's *Past and Present* (1843) with its idiosyncratic manner of exposing the sufferings of the Victorian poor, or to John Ruskin's *Modern Painters* (1843) with its rhapsodic celebrations of alpine scenery and romantic sunsets? As a result, most candid literary historians admit that while we may confidently identify the distinguishing characteristics of individual Victorian writers, of a Browning, a Dickens, or a Newman, it is extremely difficult to devise satisfactory statements about Victorian literature that are generally applicable to most or all of these writers. This admission is distressing to tidy minds, but in itself it tells us something distinctive about Victorian literature as a whole.

What we can perhaps isolate is what Jerome Buckley calls the "temper" of Victorian literature, a state of mind and emotion already described in this introduction as an eager or earnest response to the expanding horizons of nineteenth-century life. We also encounter some frequently recurring subjects in Victorian literature, including a preoccupation with humanity's relationship to God, and also an acute awareness of time, past, present, and future. Among the poets (and the novelists as well) one topic that links their writings together is love, for love, despite the reputed strain of puritanism in the age, is as prominent in Victorian poetry as it had been in the time of John Donne and his followers. Although the Victorian poets, unlike their seventeenth-century predecessors, rarely made witty proposals for gathering rosebuds, they explored other aspects of love relationships, such as the timeless equilibrium of lovers pictured by D. G. Rossetti, or the poignant experience of isolation by Arnold and Christina Rossetti, or the hostility of partners of a shattered marriage in Meredith's *Modern Love*. All these aspects, and more, are present in the poetry of Robert Browning, and his comprehensive exploration of such relationships links him to his contemporaries. In reviewing Browning's volume, *Men and Women*, William Morris (himself a fine love poet) praised some of the monologues dealing with religious issues, but added that these, "as it is in all art, in all life," however fine, were "but a supplement to the love-poems."

VICTORIAN PROSE

If Victorian poets and novelists write extensively of love and personal relationships, there is also a large body of writings in which these subjects are relatively subordinate, writings categorized as nonfictional prose. Although the term is clumsy and also not quite exact (for practitioners of nonfictional prose such as Carlyle and Pater resorted, on occasion, to fictional narratives), it has its uses to distinguish these prose writers from the novelists.

On behalf of their kinds of writing, Pater argued, in his essay on *Style* (1889), that prose was "the special and opportune art of the modern world." His contention was not that prose is superior to verse but that it more readily conveys the "chaotic variety and complexity" of modern life, the "incalculable" intellectual diversity of the "master currents of the present time." Whether prose is a more appropriate medium than verse to communicate the "chaotic variety" of an age remains a matter of dispute, but what Pater says of the age itself would be much more generally agreed upon. Toward this condition of their age the Victorian writers of nonfictional prose responded in a variety of ways and in a variety of styles. All sought in their distinctive manners to create some sort of order out of the chaos. Pater himself, coming to maturity late in the century, differs from the others in his distaste for controversy. By writing critical essays celebrating a beautifully ordered world of art and literature, Pater sought to rise above the flux and chaos which he saw as characteristic of his century. His predecessors were more engaged in shaping and reconstructing the social order. All of them use prose primarily as an instrument of persuasion and argument. On a wide range of controversial topics—religious, political, or aesthetic—they seek to convince a reader to share their convictions and values. Their modes of persuasion differ. Mill and Huxley rely on clear reasoning, logical argument, and the kind of lucid style favored by essayists of the eighteenth century, uncolored by the emotional heightening of romanticism. Carlyle and Ruskin, in much of their writing, seem closer to the seventeenth century than to the eighteenth. Their "polyphonic" style, as it has been called, has affinities with the prose rhythms of Sir Thomas Browne and Robert Burton. It is a style that also appeals to the eye as well as the ear, and, by a combination of vivid effects, plays upon the feelings of the reader. Poetic passages in Newman and Arnold also play upon our feelings, but much of their writing is less mannered and more in the relatively straightforward vein of Mill and Huxley.

However various their styles, all of these Victorian prose writers were linked by a common concern for the fate of humanity in an industrial, democratic, and increasingly secularized society. Of their interlocking debates on education, leadership, and the role of science and religion, C. F. Harrold aptly says: "What they wrote constitutes a fascinating chapter in the history of the English mind, and also provides a perspective for viewing much that continues to perplex the world. Above all, a survey of their beliefs and assumptions will illuminate the richness of their prose, a prose which is often highly allusive, sometimes deceptively simple, and always susceptible to fresh and profitable interpretation as the symbol of their thought and the eloquent expression of their convictions."

VICTORIAN DRAMA AND THEATER

If the Victorian age can lay claim to greatness for its poetry, its prose, and its novels, it would be difficult to make such a high claim for its plays, at least until the final decade of the century. Here we must distinguish between playwriting on the one hand and theatrical activity on the other. For the theater itself, throughout the period, was a flourishing and popular institution, in which were performed not merely conventional dramas but a rich variety of theatrical entertainments, many with lavish spectacular effects— burlesques, extravaganzas, highly scenic and altered versions of Shakespeare's plays, melodramas, pantomimes, musicals. Robert Corrigan gives figures that suggest the extent of the popularity of such entertainment: "In the decade between 1850 and 1860 the number of theaters built throughout the country was doubled, and in the middle of the sixties, in London alone, 150,000 would be attending the theater on any given day. Only when we realize that the theatre was to Victorian England what television is to us today will we be able to comprehend both its wide appeal and its limited artistic achievement." As might be expected, the soaring popularity of Victorian stage performances lured some of the major writers of the age, such as Tennyson and Browning and Henry James, to try their hands at writing plays, but the results were disappointing. Successful plays on stage were written by lesser lights of literature (except for the remarkable comic operas of W. S. Gilbert and Arthur Sullivan). New Victorian plays, as Robertson Davies comments, "are extremely numerous, and they are, in the main, undistinguished by literary merit, though many of them are not nearly so bad as people who have not studied them suppose." Davies's book, *The Mirror of Nature* (1983), is an important corrective to the formerly established practice of dismissing all Victorian plays as deplorable melodramas. What Davies is recommending is that we approach such plays and the whole Victorian theater scene with "imaginative sympathy." In any event, in the 1890s appeared the lively dramatic masterpieces of Oscar Wilde and George Bernard Shaw; no apologies are thereafter required.

THE VICTORIAN NOVEL

It will be obvious that any estimate of Victorian literature has to take into account the outstanding achievements of the Victorian novelists. From the time of Charles Dickens (1812–1870), early in the period (his first novel, *Pickwick Papers*, was published in the same year as Victoria became queen), to the final decade when the late novels of Thomas Hardy (1840–1928) such as his *Tess of the D'Urbervilles* (1891) appeared, a long line of novelists continued to turn out monumental masterpieces that delighted their contemporaries and that continue to delight readers today, as is evident by their being among the most readily available books in English.

After Dickens's epoch-making early novels had appeared on the scene in the 1830s, each subsequent decade featured the emergence of new novelists of stature such as Charlotte Brontë (1816–1855) and Emily Brontë (1818–1848) in the 1840s, and William Makepeace Thackeray (1811–1863) whose prominence in the 1850s was a challenge to Dickens's continued preeminence and popularity. In the 1860s, Anthony Trollope (1815–1882) established himself as a portraitist of mid-Victorian society, and in the 1870s, George Eliot (1819–1880) published what is generally regarded as her finest novel, *Middlemarch* (1872), although she had already established her reputation earlier with *Adam Bede* (1859) and *The Mill on the Floss* (1860). In the 1880s, George Meredith (1828–1909)—a less well-known novelist today— finally began to receive adequate attention from the critics and public for novels he had published earlier such as *The Ordeal of Richard Feverel* (1859). In addition to these major novelists from Dickens to Hardy, several note-worthy names could be cited of writers who contributed to the rich variety of the Victorian novel, such as Elizabeth Gaskell (1810–1865), Wilkie Collins (1824–1889), and George Gissing (1857–1903).

Often these novelists confront the same issues and employ similar styles as their contemporaries among the poets and essayists (the stylistic affinities between Browning and Dickens, for example, are striking). One significant difference, however, is that the novelists for the most part do not share the preoccupation of the Victorian poets and essayists with humanity's relationship to God. Like their greatest predecessors—Fielding, Richardson, and Jane Austen—most of the Victorian novelists were primarily concerned with people in society and with those aspects of experience categorized by the title of Lionel Trilling's essay: "Manners, Morals and the Novel," to which we can add an additional topic—Money. Typically these stories center on the struggles of a protagonist, male or female, to find himself or herself in relation to other men and women, in love or marriage, with family or neighbors, or with associates in his or her working career. Occasionally such a search may take on quasi-religious dimensions, as in the later novels of Thomas Hardy or in Emily Brontë's *Wuthering Heights* (1847), and more indirectly, in George Eliot's novels, with their persistent concern with the role of free will and fate in the lives of their characters. On the whole, however, the major Victorian novelists were less occupied with people's relation to God than with their relation to other people.

And for the most part, the other people were the reader's contemporaries. The historical novel, as established by Sir Walter Scott, remained popular throughout the post-Romantic period, but it was a form especially congenial to the lesser novelists, such as Bulwer-Lytton (*The Last Days of Pompeii*, 1834) or Charles Reade (*The Cloister and the Hearth*, 1861). While the major novelists occasionally tried their hand at historical fiction, their preference was for the contemporary or the recent past. Whether the story was set in the rural landscapes of Eliot's Warwickshire and Hardy's Wessex, Trollope's cathedral towns, or Dickens's fogbound London, readers expected a representation of daily nineteenth-century life that would be recognizably familiar to them.

To satisfy such expectations they were provided with a rich fare. Dickens was praised by Walter Bagehot for having described London "like a special correspondent for posterity." His contemporaries and successors among the novelists were also skillful reporters, and most of them were more scrupulously concerned with detailed realism than he had been. Disputes about the degree of Dickens's realism have persisted among critical readers from his day to ours, but what is now generally recognized is that he was much more than a brilliant reporter, and that the heightening and stylization of his novels produce effects like poetic drama that are very different from straightforward realism. "Every writer of fiction," he said, "although he may not adopt the dramatic form, writes, in effect, for the stage." The attitude to this aspect of his writing by other novelists is of crucial importance in understanding how the Victorian novel developed. Among Dickens's rivals and successors there was a common agreement that the stagey aspect of his novels was his most glaring fault, and each of the novelists in turn set out to correct that fault by an example of what he or she believed was a more realistic representation of life. Thackeray's masterpiece, *Vanity Fair* (1848), has to a modern reader many mannerisms of its own, but is much less blatantly mannered than a characteristic Dickens novel. "The Art of Novels," Thackeray affirmed in a letter, "*is* to represent nature: to convey as strongly as possible the sentiment of reality." In Thackeray's disciple, Anthony Trollope, and later in the drab narratives of George Gissing, a lesser figure, there is a similar reduction of stagelike scenes and effects. In George Eliot this reaction against novelistic theatricalism took a more influential turn: she set out to explore what the theatrical writer rarely explores—the inner lives of her characters. Early in the twentieth century, the young D. H. Lawrence, beginning his career as a novelist, remarked to a friend: "You see, it was really George Eliot who started it all, and how wild they all were with her for doing it. It was she who started putting all the action inside. Before, you know, with Fielding and the others, it had been outside. Now I wonder which is right?" Lawrence himself decided, as a practicing novelist, that Fielding and his Victorian followers could be as right as George Eliot, but most early twentieth-century novelists preferred to follow Eliot's example and concentrate on the inner lives of their characters; and critical readers, adapting their tastes to the new mode, were disposed at that time to undervalue Victorian novels which had portrayed people acting rather than people recollecting, or reflecting, or trying to come to a decision.

Contributing to this underevaluation of the Victorian achievement was the assumption that novels published in serial form (as Victorian novels had usually been published) must be slapdash productions altogether deficient in art, or as Henry James characterized them, "large loose baggy monsters." James's affectionate derogation is applicable to such a novel as Dickens's early *Pickwick Papers*, but it does not apply at all to some of Dickens's later novels such as *Bleak House* (a masterpiece of narrative construction), Eliot's *Middlemarch* (1872), Hardy's *Jude the Obscure* (1895), or the tight and intricate plotting of Wilkie Collins's detective novel, *The Moonstone* (1868). Serial publication, as later critics have come to recognize, did not necessarily preclude artful storytelling, and it had advantages to offset the possible disadvantages of fragmentation. Publication by installments challenged the novelists to sustain the interest of their readers; in every single number they had to entertain them or, to use the traditional critical term, to provide delight. Like an actor or public speaker, the Victorian novelists had a sense, during the very process of writing their books, of how their audience was responding to their performance. And it was an audience that offered a special challenge because of its exceptional diversity; Victorian readers ranged from the sophisticated and well-read lawyer to the semiliterate household servant. The present-day division of the novel-reading public into highbrow, middlebrow, and lowbrow existed only in embryonic form in the Victorian age, and did not become a significant controlling influence on the novelist until late in the century.

This popular genre is thus especially representative of all but the religious attitudes that have been emphasized in this account of the Victorian period: the earnest sense of responsibility, the occasional lapses of taste, and the overflowing creative energy of its writers. Near the end of his life Thackeray drew a comparison between himself and Dickens: "I am played out. All I can do now is to bring out my old puppets. . . . But, if he live to be ninety, Dickens will still be creating new characters. In his art that man is marvelous." Wrung from a novelist whose own writings occupy more than twenty thick volumes, this compliment is quintessentially Victorian.

ELIZABETH BARRETT BROWNING
1806–1861

During her lifetime, Elizabeth Barrett Browning was England's most famous woman poet. Passionately admired by contemporaries as diverse as Ruskin, Swinburne, and Emily Dickinson for her moral and emotional ardor and her energetic engagement with the issues of her day, she was more famous than her husband at the time of her death. Her work fell into disrepute with the Modernist reaction against what was seen as the inappropriate didacticism and rhetorical excess of Victorian poetry, but recently scholars, interested in her exploration of what it means to be a woman poet, have initiated a revaluation of her work.

Barrett Browning received an unusual education for a woman of her time. Availing herself of her brother's tutor, she studied Latin and Greek. She read voraciously in history, philosophy, and literature and began to write poetry from an early age—her first volume of poetry was published when she was thirteen. But as her intellectual and literary powers matured, her personal life became increasingly circumscribed both by ill health and by a tyrannically protective father, who had forbidden any of his eleven children to marry. By the age of thirty-nine, Elizabeth Barrett was a prominent woman of letters who lived in semiseclusion as an invalid in her father's house, where she occasionally received visitors in her room. One of these visitors was Robert Browning, who, moved by his admiration of her poetry, wrote to tell her "I do as I say, love these books with all my heart—and I love you too." He thereby initiated a courtship that culminated in 1846 in their secret marriage and elopement to Italy, for which her father never forgave her. Once in Italy, she regained much health and strength, bearing and raising a son, Pen, to whom she was ardently devoted, and becoming deeply involved in Italian nationalist politics.

Her poetry is characterized by a fervent moral sensibility. In her early work, she tended to use the visionary modes of Romantic narrative poetry, but turned increasingly to contemporary topics, particularly liberal causes of her day. For example, in 1843, when government investigations had exposed the exploitation of children employed in coal mines and factories, she wrote *The Cry of the Children*, of which the following stanza is typical:

> "For oh," say the children, "we are weary,
>   And we cannot run or leap;
> If we cared for any meadows, it were merely
>   To drop down in them and sleep.
> Our knees tremble sorely in the stooping,
>   We fall upon our faces, trying to go;
> And, underneath our heavy eyelids drooping,
>   The reddest flower would look as pale as snow.
> For, all day, we drag our burden tiring
>   Through the coal dark, underground;
> Or, all day, we drive the wheels of iron
>   In the factories round and round."

In later poems, she took up the cause of Italian nationalism, which, the critic Sandra M. Gilbert has recently argued, provided her a subject through which to enact her own struggle for poetic identity.

For many years Elizabeth Barrett Browning was best known for her *Sonnets from the Portuguese*, a sequence of forty-four sonnets in which she recorded the stages of her love for Robert Browning, a sequence she presented under the guise of a translation from the Portuguese language. But increasingly her verse novel *Aurora Leigh* (1857) has attracted critical attention. The poem depicts the growth of a woman poet and is thus, as Cora Kaplan observes, the first work in English by a woman writer in which the heroine herself is an author. When Barrett Browning first envisioned the poem, she wrote, "My chief *intention* just now is the writing of a sort of novel-poem . . . running into the midst of our conventions, and rushing into drawing-rooms and the like 'where angels fear to tread'; and so, meeting face to face and without mask the Humanity of the age, and speaking the truth as I conceive of it out plainly." The poem is a female *Prelude*, a portrait of the artist as a young woman committed to a socially inclusive realist art. It is a daring work both in its presentation of social issues concerning women and in its claims for Aurora's poetic vocation; on her twentieth birthday, in order to pursue her career as a poet, Aurora refuses a proposal of marriage from her cousin Romney, who wants her to be his helpmate in the liberal causes he has embraced. Later in the poem she rescues a fallen woman and takes her to Italy, where they settle together and confront a chastened Romney.

Immensely popular in its own day, *Aurora Leigh* had extravagant admirers (like Ruskin, who asserted that it was the greatest poem written in English) and critics who found fault with both its poetry and its morality. With its crowded canvas and melodramatic plot, it seems closer to the novel than to poetry, but it is important to view the poem in the context of the debate about appropriate poetic subject that engaged other Victorian poets. Unlike Arnold, who felt that the present age had not produced actions heroic enough to be the subjects of a great poetry, and unlike Tennyson, who used Arthurian legend to represent contemporary concerns, Barrett Browning felt that the present age contained the materials for an epic poetry. Virginia Woolf writes that "Elizabeth Barrett was inspired by a flash of true genius when she rushed into the drawing-room and said that here, where we live and work, is the true place for the poet." And whatever its faults, *Aurora Leigh* succeeds in giving us what Woolf describes as "a sense of life in general, of people who are unmistakably Victorian, wrestling with the problems of their own time, all brightened, intensified, and compacted by the fire of poetry. . . . Aurora Leigh, with her passionate interest in social questions, her conflict as artist and woman, her longing for knowledge and freedom, is the true daughter of her age."

To George Sand[1]

A *Desire*

Thou large-brained woman and large-hearted man,
Self-called George Sand! whose soul, amid the lions
Of thy tumultuous senses, moans defiance
And answers roar for roar, as spirits can:
I would some mild miraculous thunder ran   5
Above the applauded circus,[2] in appliance
Of thine own nobler nature's strength and science,
Drawing two pinions, white as wings of swan,
From thy strong shoulders, to amaze the place
With holier light! that thou to woman's claim   10
And man's, mightst join beside the angel's grace
Of a pure genius sanctified from blame,
Till child and maiden pressed to thine embrace
To kiss upon thy lips a stainless fame.

1844

To George Sand

A *Recognition*

True genius, but true woman! dost deny
The woman's nature with a manly scorn,
And break away the gauds[1] and armlets worn
By weaker women in captivity?
Ah, vain denial! that revolted cry   5
Is sobbed in by a woman's voice forlorn,—
Thy woman's hair, my sister, all unshorn
Floats back dishevelled strength in agony,
Disproving thy man's name: and while before
The world thou burnest in a poet-fire,   10
We see thy woman-heart beat evermore
Through the large flame. Beat purer, heart, and higher,
Till God unsex thee on the heavenly shore
Where unincarnate spirits purely aspire!

1844

---

1. French Romantic novelist (1804–1876), famous for her unconventional ideas and behavior. Elizabeth Barrett Browning discovered her writing when she was an invalid, "a prisoner," and asserts that George Sand, together with Balzac, "kept the color in my life." Barrett Browning defended Sand's genius to her less sympathetic friends, who were critical of Sand's morality; she writes to her friend Mary Russell Mitford, a contemporary novelist and dramatist, "She is eloquent as a fallen angel. . . . A true woman of genius!—but of a womanhood tired of itself, and scorned by *her*, while she bears it burning above her head."

2. A Roman spectacle in which Christians were martyred by fighting lions.

1. Ornaments.

From Sonnets from the Portuguese

21

Say over again, and yet once over again,
That thou dost love me. Though the word repeated
Should seem "a cuckoo song,"[1] as thou dost treat it,
Remember, never to the hill or plain,
Valley and wood, without her cuckoo strain   5
Comes the fresh Spring in all her green completed.
Belovèd, I, amid the darkness greeted
By a doubtful spirit voice, in that doubt's pain
Cry, "Speak once more—thou lovest!" Who can fear
Too many stars, though each in heaven shall roll,   10
Too many flowers, though each shall crown the year?
Say thou dost love me, love me, love me—toll
The silver iterance![2]—only minding, Dear,
To love me also in silence with thy soul.

22

When our two souls stand up erect and strong,
Face to face, silent, drawing nigh and nigher,
Until the lengthening wings break into fire
At either curved point—what bitter wrong
Can the earth do to us, that we should not long   5
Be here contented? Think. In mounting higher,
The angels would press on us and aspire
To drop some golden orb of perfect song
Into our deep, dear silence. Let us stay
Rather on earth, Belovèd,—where the unfit   10
Contrarious moods of men recoil away
And isolate pure spirits, and permit
A place to stand and love in for a day,
With darkness and the death-hour rounding it.

32

The first time that the sun rose on thine oath
To love me, I looked forward to the moon
To slacken all those bonds which seemed too soon
And quickly tied to make a lasting troth.
Quick-loving hearts, I thought, may quickly loathe;   5
And, looking on myself, I seemed not one
For such man's love!—more like an out-of-tune
Worn viol, a good singer would be wroth
To spoil his song with, and which, snatched in haste,

---

1. The cuckoo has a repeating call.   2. Repetition.

Is laid down at the first ill-sounding note.   10
I did not wrong myself so, but I placed
A wrong on *thee*. For perfect strains may float
'Neath master-hands, from instruments defaced—
And great souls, at one stroke, may do and dote.

43

How do I love thee? Let me count the ways.
I love thee to the depth and breadth and height
My soul can reach, when feeling out of sight
For the ends of Being and ideal Grace.
I love thee to the level of everyday's   5
Most quiet need, by sun and candlelight.
I love thee freely, as men strive for Right;
I love thee purely, as they turn from Praise.
I love thee with the passion put to use
In my old griefs, and with my childhood's faith.   10
I love thee with a love I seemed to lose
With my lost saints—I love thee with the breath,
Smiles, tears, of all my life!—and, if God choose,
I shall but love thee better after death.

1845–47   1850

A Year's Spinning

1

He listened at the porch that day,
   To hear the wheel go on, and on;
And then it stopped, ran back away,
   While through the door he brought the sun:
   But now my spinning is all done.   5

2

He sat beside me, with an oath
   That love ne'er ended, once begun;
I smiled—believing for us both,
   What was the truth for only one:
   And now my spinning is all done.   10

3

My mother cursed me that I heard
   A young man's wooing as I spun:
Thanks, cruel mother, for that word—
   For I have, since, a harder known!
   And now my spinning is all done.   15

4

I thought—O God!—my first-born's cry
   Both voices to mine ear would drown:

I listened in mine agony—
   It was the *silence* made me groan!
And now my spinning is all done.   20

5

Bury me 'twixt my mother's grave,
   (Who cursed me on her death-bed lone)
And my dead baby's (God it save!)
   Who, not to bless me, would not moan.
   And now my spinning is all done.   25

6

A stone upon my heart and head,
   But no name written on the stone!
Sweet neighbours, whisper low instead,
   "This sinner was a loving one—
   And now her spinning is all done."   30

7

And let the door ajar remain,
   In case he should pass by anon;
And leave the wheel out very plain,—
   That HE, when passing in the sun,
   May see the spinning is all done.   35

1850

From Aurora Leigh

From *Book* 1

[THE FEMININE EDUCATION OF AURORA LEIGH][1]

Then, land!—then, England! oh, the frosty cliffs[2]
Looked cold upon me. Could I find a home
Among those mean red houses through the fog?
And when I heard my father's language first
From alien lips which had no kiss for mine   255
I wept aloud, then laughed, then wept, then wept,
And some one near me said the child was mad
Through much sea-sickness. The train swept us on:
Was this my father's England? the great isle?
The ground seemed cut up from the fellowship   260
Of verdure, field from field,[3] as man from man;
The skies themselves looked low and positive,
As almost you could touch them with a hand,
And dared to do it they were so far off

---

1. Aurora Leigh, the only child of an Italian mother and an English father, has been raised in Italy by her father since her mother's death when Aurora was 4 years old. When she was 13, her father also died, and the orphaned girl has been sent to England to live with her father's maiden sister, who is to be responsible for the girl's education.
2. The white chalk cliffs at Dover.
3. English fields were separated from each other by hedgerows.

From God's celestial crystals;[4] all things blurred   265
And dull and vague. Did Shakespeare and his mates
Absorb the light here?—not a hill or stone
With heart to strike a radiant colour up
Or active outline on the indifferent air.

I think I see my father's sister stand   270
Upon the hall-step of her country-house
To give me welcome. She stood straight and calm,
Her somewhat narrow forehead braided tight
As if for taming accidental thoughts
From possible pulses;[5] brown hair pricked with gray   275
By frigid use of life (she was not old,
Although my father's elder by a year),
A nose drawn sharply, yet in delicate lines;
A close mild mouth, a little soured about
The ends, through speaking unrequited loves   280
Or peradventure niggardly half-truths;
Eyes of no colour,—once they might have smiled,
But never, never have forgot themselves
In smiling; cheeks, in which was yet a rose
Of perished summers, like a rose in a book,   285
Kept more for ruth[6] than pleasure,—if past bloom,
Past fading also.
                    She had lived, we'll say,
A harmless life, she called a virtuous life,
A quiet life, which was not life at all
(But that, she had not lived enough to know),   290
Between the vicar and the county squires,
The lord-lieutenant[7] looking down sometimes
From the empyrean to assure their souls
Against chance vulgarisms, and, in the abyss,
The apothecary,[8] looked on once a year   295
To prove their soundness of humility.
The poor-club[9] exercised her Christian gifts
Of knitting stockings, stitching petticoats,
Because we are of one flesh, after all,
And need one flannel[1] (with a proper sense   300
Of difference in the quality)—and still
The book-club, guarded from your modern trick
Of shaking dangerous questions from the crease,[2]
Preserved her intellectual. She had lived
A sort of cage-bird life, born in a cage,   305

---

4. Perhaps a reference to the ancient notion that the sky was composed of several crystalline spheres orbiting around the earth.
5. I.e., pulsation in her temples from excitement.
6. Remorse.
7. Governor of the county.
8. Pharmacist, who in England at the time could prescribe as well as sell medicine.
9. Club devoted to making things for the poor.
1. Flannel petticoat.
2. The fold between two pages of a book, which had to be cut to open the pages. Presumably more modern books revealed more dangerous material when the crease was cut.

Accounting that to leap from perch to perch
Was act and joy enough for any bird.
Dear heaven, how silly are the things that live
In thickets, and eat berries!
                                    I, alas,
A wild bird scarcely fledged, was brought to her cage,   310
And she was there to meet me. Very kind.
Bring the clean water, give out the fresh seed.

She stood upon the steps to welcome me,
Calm, in black garb. I clung about her neck,—
Young babes, who catch at every shred of wool   315
To draw the new light closer, catch and cling
Less blindly. In my ears my father's word
Hummed ignorantly, as the sea in shells,
"Love, love, my child." She, black there with my grief,
Might feel my love— she was his sister once—   320
I clung to her. A moment she seemed moved,
Kissed me with cold lips, suffered me to cling,
And drew me feebly through the hall into
The room she sat in.
                              There, with some strange spasm
Of pain and passion, she wrung loose my hands   325
Imperiously, and held me at arm's length,
And with two grey-steel naked-bladed eyes
Searched through my face,—ay, stabbed it through and through,
Through brows and cheeks and chin, as if to find
A wicked murderer in my innocent face,   330
If not here, there perhaps. Then, drawing breath,
She struggled for her ordinary calm—
And missed it rather,—told me not to shrink,
As if she had told me not to lie or swear,—
"She loved my father and would love me too   335
As long as I deserved it." Very kind.

I understood her meaning afterward;
She thought to find my mother in my face,
And questioned it for that. For she, my aunt,
Had loved my father truly, as she could,   340
And hated, with the gall of gentle souls,
My Tuscan[3] mother who had fooled away
A wise man from wise courses, a good man
From obvious duties, and, depriving her,
His sister, of the household precedence,   345
Had wronged his tenants, robbed his native land,
And made him mad, alike by life and death,
In love and sorrow. She had pored for years

---

3. From Tuscany, a region in central Italy.

What sort of woman could be suitable
To her sort of hate, to entertain it with,   350
And so, her very curiosity
Became hate too, and all the idealism
She ever used in life was used for hate,
Till hate, so nourished, did exceed at last
The love from which it grew, in strength and heat,   355
And wrinkled her smooth conscience with a sense
Of disputable virtue (say not, sin)
When Christian doctrine was enforced at church.

And thus my father's sister was to me
My mother's hater. From that day she did   360
Her duty to me (I appreciate it
In her own word as spoken to herself),
Her duty, in large measure, well pressed out
But measured always. She was generous, bland,
More courteous than was tender, gave me still   365
The first place,—as if fearful that God's saints
Would look down suddenly and say "Herein
You missed a point, I think, through lack of love."
Alas, a mother never is afraid
Of speaking angerly to any child,   370
Since love, she knows, is justified of love.

And I, I was a good child on the whole,
A meek and manageable child. Why not?
I did not live, to have the faults of life:
There seemed more true life in my father's grave   375
Than in all England. Since *that* threw me off
Who fain would cleave (his latest will, they say,
Consigned me to his land), I only thought
Of lying quiet there where I was thrown
Like sea-weed on the rocks, and suffering her   380
To prick me to a pattern with her pin,[4]
Fibre from fibre, delicate leaf from leaf,
And dry out from my drowned anatomy
The last sea-salt left in me.
                              So it was.
I broke the copious curls upon my head   385
In braids, because she liked smooth-ordered hair.
I left off saying my sweet Tuscan words
Which still at any stirring of the heart
Came up to float across the English phrase
As lilies *(Bene* or *Che che),*[5] because   390
She liked my father's child to speak his tongue.
I learnt the collects[6] and the catechism,

4. As in embroidery.
5. No, no, indeed; "*Bene*": it is well.
6. Seasonal opening prayers in the Anglican church service.

The creeds,[7] from Athanasius back to Nice,
The Articles, the Tracts *against* the times[8]
(By no means Buonaventure's "Prick of Love"),[9]   395
And various popular synopses of
Inhuman doctrines never taught by John,[1]
Because she liked instructed piety.
I learnt my complement of classic French
(Kept pure of Balzac and neologism)[2]   400
And German also, since she liked a range
Of liberal education,—tongues,[3] not books.
I learnt a little algebra, a little
Of the mathematics,—brushed with extreme flounce
The circle of the sciences, because   405
She misliked women who are frivolous.
I learnt the royal genealogies
Of Oviedo, the internal laws
Of the Burmese empire,—by how many feet
Mount Chimborazo outsoars Teneriffe,   410
What navigable river joins itself
To Lara, and what census of the year five
Was taken at Klagenfurt,[4]—because she liked
A general insight into useful facts.
I learnt much music,—such as would have been   415
As quite impossible in Johnson's day[5]
As still it might be wished—fine sleights of hand
And unimagined fingering, shuffling off
The hearer's soul through hurricanes of notes
To a noisy Tophet;[6] and I drew . . . costumes   420
From French engravings, nereids[7] neatly draped
(With smirks of simmering godship): I washed in[8]
Landscapes from nature (rather say, washed out).
I danced the polka and Cellarius,[9]
Spun glass, stuffed birds, and modeled flowers in wax,   425
Because she liked accomplishments in girls.
I read a score of books on womanhood
To prove, if women do not think at all,
They may teach thinking (to a maiden aunt

---

7. Articles of Christian faith such as those proclaimed at the early church council held at Nicaea.
8. In the 1830s, leaders of the conservative High
Church party, such as Newman, had published
Tracts for the Times, which expounded arguments
against efforts by liberals to modernize the Anglican Church. Aurora's version of the title is hence
ironic. "Articles": the 39 articles are the principles
of faith of the Church of England.
9. Saint Buonaventure's doctrine that the power
of the heart to love leads to higher illumination
than the power of the mind to reason.
1. I.e., the author of the gospel.
2. A new word or expression. "Balzac": A French
novelist (1799–1850) whose realism would have
made him improper reading for a young lady.

3. I.e., languages.
4. A town in Austria; "Lara": a town in Spain on
the river Arlanza; "Teneriffe": a mountain in the
Canary Islands; "Mount Chimborazo": one of the
highest peaks of the Andes; "Oviedo": a 16th-cen-
tury Spanish historian who wrote a book on the
genealogies of the grandees of Spain.
5. An allusion to the story about Samuel Johnson,
who, when told how difficult a piece of music was
that a young lady was playing, replied, "I would it
had been impossible."
6. Hell.
7. Sea nymphs.
8. As in painting with watercolors.
9. A kind of waltz.

Or else the author),—books that boldly assert   430
Their right of comprehending husband's talk
When not too deep, and even of answering
With pretty "may it please you," or "so it is,"—
Their rapid insight and fine aptitude,
Particular worth and general missionariness,   435
As long as they keep quiet by the fire
And never say "no" when the world says "ay,"
For that is fatal,—their angelic reach
Of virtue, chiefly used to sit and darn,
And fatten household sinners,—their, in brief,   440
Potential faculty in everything
Of abdicating power in it: she owned
She liked a woman to be womanly,
And English women, she thanked God and sighed
(Some people always sigh in thanking God),   445
Were models to the universe. And last
I learnt cross-stitch,[1] because she did not like
To see me wear the night with empty hands
A-doing nothing. So, my shepherdess
Was something after all (the pastoral saints   450
Be praised for't), leaning lovelorn with pink eyes
To match her shoes, when I mistook the silks;
Her head uncrushed by that round weight of hat
So strangely similar to the tortoise shell
Which slew the tragic poet.[2]

              By the way,   455
The works of women are symbolical.
We sew, sew, prick our fingers, dull our sight,
Producing what? A pair of slippers, sir,
To put on when you're weary—or a stool
To stumble over and vex you . . . "curse that stool!"   460
Or else at best, a cushion, where you lean
And sleep, and dream of something we are not
But would be for your sake. Alas, alas!
This hurts most, this—that, after all, we are paid
The worth of our work, perhaps.

              In looking down   465
Those years of education (to return)
I wonder if Brinvilliers suffered more
In the water-torture[3] . . . flood succeeding flood
To drench the incapable throat and split the veins . . .
Than I did. Certain of your feebler souls   470
Go out in such a process; many pine
To a sick, inodorous light; my own endured:

---

1. As in needlepoint.
2. According to tradition, the Greek playwright
Aeschylus was killed by an eagle, who, mistaking
his bald head for a stone, dropped a tortoise on it
to break the shell.
3. Marie Marguerite, Marquise de Brinvilliers, a
celebrated criminal who was beheaded in 1676,
was tortured by having water forced down her throat.

I had relations in the Unseen, and drew
The elemental nutriment and heat
From nature, as earth feels the sun at nights,   475
Or as a babe sucks surely in the dark.
I kept the life thrust on me, on the outside
Of the inner life with all its ample room
For heart and lungs, for will and intellect,
Inviolable by conventions. God,   480
I thank thee for that grace of thine!
                              At first
I felt no life which was not patience,—did
The thing she bade me, without heed to a thing
Beyond it, sat in just the chair she placed,
With back against the window, to exclude   485
The sight of the great lime-tree on the lawn,[4]
Which seemed to have come on purpose from the woods
To bring the house a message,—ay, and walked
Demurely in her carpeted low rooms,
As if I should not, harkening my own steps,   490
Misdoubt I was alive. I read her books,
Was civil to her cousin, Romney Leigh,
Gave ear to her vicar, tea to her visitors,
And heard them whisper, when I changed a cup
(I blushed for joy at that),—"The Italian child,   495
For all her blue eyes and her quiet ways,
Thrives ill in England: she is paler yet
Than when we came the last time; she will die."

From *Book 2*

[ROMNEY'S PROPOSAL AND AURORA'S REFUSAL][1]

                              "Is it so,"
I said, "my cousin? is the world so bad,
While I hear nothing of it through the trees?   305
The world was always evil,—but so bad?"

"So bad, Aurora. Dear, my soul is grey
With poring over the long sum of ill;
So much for vice, so much for discontent,   310
So much for the necessities of power,
So much for the connivances of fear,
Coherent in statistical despairs
With such a total of distracted life, . . .

4. Perhaps a reference to Coleridge's *This Lime-Tree Bower My Prison*, in which the lime-tree becomes the vehicle of a realization that Nature never deserts the wise and pure even when they seem to be cut off from her most beautiful vistas.
1. At the beginning of this book, Romney, having just discovered Aurora's book of poems, comes upon her crowning herself with an ivy wreath upon her twentieth birthday. He proceeds to tell her that a woman cannot be a great poet and to lecture her upon the evils of the day.

To see it down in figures on a page.
Plain, silent, clear, as God sees through the earth
The sense of all the graves,—that's terrible
For one who is not God, and cannot right
The wrong he looks on. May I choose indeed,
But vow away my years, my means, my aims,   320
Among the helpers, if there's any help
In such a social strait? The common blood
That swings along my veins is strong enough
To draw me to this duty."
                          Then I spoke.
"I have not stood long on the strand of life,   325
And these salt waters have had scarcely time
To creep so high up as to wet my feet:
I cannot judge these tides—I shall, perhaps.
A woman's always younger than a man
At equal years, because she is disallowed   330
Maturing by the outdoor sun and air,
And kept in long-clothes past[2] the age to walk.
Ah well, I know you men judge otherwise!
You think a woman ripens, as a peach,
In the cheeks chiefly. Pass it to me now;   335
I'm young in age, and younger still, I think,
As a woman. But a child may say amen
To a bishop's prayer and feel the way it goes,
And I, incapable to loose the knot
Of social questions, can approve, applaud   340
August compassion, Christian thoughts that shoot
Beyond the vulgar white of personal aims.
Accept my reverence."
                      There he glowed on me
With all his face and eyes. "No other help?"
Said he—"no more than so?"
                          "What help?" I asked.   345
"You'd scorn my help,—as Nature's self, you say,
Has scorned to put her music in my mouth
Because a woman's. Do you now turn round
And ask for what a woman cannot give?"

"For what she only can, I turn and ask,"   350
He answered, catching up my hands in his,
And dropping on me from his high-eaved brow
The full weight of his soul,—"I ask for love,
And that, she can; for life in fellowship
Through bitter duties—that, I know she can;   355
For wifehood—will she?"
                        "Now," I said, "may God

---

2. I.e., in baby clothes.

witness 'twixt us two!" and with the word,
ɔseemed[3] I floated into a sudden light
ɔove his stature,—"am I proved too weak
To stand alone, yet strong enough to bear   360
Such leaners on my shoulder? poor to think,
Yet rich enough to sympathise with thought?
Incompetent to sing, as blackbirds can,
Yet competent to love, like HIM?"
                               I paused;
Perhaps I darkened, as the lighthouse will   365
That turns upon the sea. "It's always so.
Anything does for a wife."
                        "Aurora, dear,
And dearly honoured,"—he pressed in at once
With eager utterance,—"you translate me ill.
I do not contradict my thought of you   370
Which is most reverent, with another thought
Found less so. If your sex is weak for art
(And I, who said so, did but honour you
By using truth in courtship), it is strong
For life and duty. Place your fecund heart   375
In mine, and let us blossom for the world
That wants[4] love's colour in the grey of time.
My talk, meanwhile, is arid to you, ay,
Since all my talk can only set you where
You look down coldly on the arena-heaps[5]   380
Of headless bodies, shapeless, indistinct!
The Judgment-Angel scarce would find his way
Through such a heap of generalised distress
To the individual man with lips and eyes,
Much less Aurora. Ah, my sweet, come down,   385
And hand in hand we'll go where yours shall touch
These victims, one by one! till, one by one,
The formless, nameless trunk of every man
Shall seem to wear a head with hair you know,
And every woman catch your mother's face   390
To melt you into passion."
                     "I am a girl,"
I answered slowly; "you do well to name
My mother's face. Though far too early, alas,
God's hand did interpose 'twixt it and me,
I know so much of love as used to shine   395
In that face and another. Just so much;
No more indeed at all. I have not seen
So much love since, I pray you pardon me,
As answers even to make a marriage with
In this cold land of England. What you love   400

3. It seemed to me.
4. Lacks.

5. I.e., heaps of bodies slain in, for example, the games in the Roman arena.

Is not a woman, Romney, but a cause:
You want a helpmate, not a mistress, sir,
A wife to help your ends,—in her no end.
Your cause is noble, your ends excellent,
But I, being most unworthy of these and that,   405
Do otherwise conceive of love. Farewell."

"Farewell, Aurora? you reject me thus?"
He said.
        "Sir, you were married long ago.
You have a wife already whom you love,
Your social theory. Bless you both, I say.   410
For my part, I am scarcely meek enough
To be the handmaid of a lawful spouse.
Do I look a Hagar,[6] think you?"
                     "So you jest."

"Nay, so, I speak in earnest," I replied.
"You treat of marriage too much like, at least,   415
A chief apostle: you would bear with you
A wife . . . a sister . . . shall we speak it out?
A sister of charity."
           "Then, must it be
Indeed farewell? And was I so far wrong
In hope and in illusion, when I took   420
The woman to be nobler than the man,
Yourself the noblest woman in the use
And comprehension of what love is,—love,
That generates the likeness of itself
Through all heroic duties? so far wrong,   425
In saying bluntly, venturing truth on love,
'Come, human creature, love and work with me,'—
Instead of 'Lady, thou art wondrous fair,
'And, where the Graces[7] walk before, the Muse
'Will follow at the lightning of their eyes,   430
'And where the Muse walks, lovers need to creep:
'Turn round and love me, or I die of love.' "

With quiet indignation I broke in.
"You misconceive the question like a man,
Who sees a woman as the complement   435
Of his sex merely. You forget too much
That every creature, female as the male,
Stands single in responsible act and thought
As also in birth and death. Whoever says
To a loyal woman, 'Love and work with me,'   440
Will get fair answers if the work and love,

6. Servant of Sarah, Abraham's wife. Because
Sarah was barren, Hagar bore a child of Abraham
for Sarah (Genesis 16).
7. Greek goddesses of charm and beauty.

Being good themselves, are good for her—the best
She was born for. Women of a softer mood,
Surprised by men when scarcely awake to life,
Will sometimes only hear the first word, love,   445
And catch up with it any kind of work,
Indifferent, so that dear love go with it.
I do not blame such women, though, for love,
They pick much oakum;[8] earth's fanatics make
Too frequently heaven's saints. But *me* your work   450
Is not the best for,—nor your love the best,
Nor able to commend the kind of work
For love's sake merely. Ah, you force me, sir,
To be overbold in speaking of myself:
I too have my vocation,—work to do,   455
The heavens and earth have set me since I changed
My father's face for theirs, and, though your world
Were twice as wretched as you represent,
Most serious work, most necessary work
As any of the economists'. Reform,   460
Make trade a Christian possibility,
And individual right no general wrong;
Wipe out earth's furrows of the Thine and Mine,
And leave one green for men to play at bowls,[9]
With innings for them all! . . . What then, indeed,   465
If mortals are not greater by the head
Than any of their prosperities? what then,
Unless the artist keep up open roads
Betwixt the seen and unseen,—bursting through
The best of your conventions with his best,   470
The speakable, imaginable best
God bids him speak, to prove what lies beyond
Both speech and imagination? A starved man
Exceeds a fat beast: we'll not barter, sir,
The beautiful for barley.—And, even so,   475
I hold you will not compass your poor ends
Of barley-feeding and material ease,
Without a poet's individualism
To work your universal. It takes a soul,
To move a body: it takes a high-souled man,   480
To move the masses, even to a cleaner style:[1]
It takes the ideal, to blow a hair's-breadth off
The dust of the actual.—Ah, your Fouriers[2] failed,
Because not poets enough to understand
That life develops from within.——For me,   485

8. The tangled mass of fibers made by untwisting
strands of rope, used for caulking the seams of boats.
Picking oakum was a well-known occupation of
prisoners.
9. A form of outdoor bowling.

1. Enclosure for pigs.
2. Charles Fourier (1772–1837) was a celebrated
socialist writer who proposed a system of social
reform that Barrett Browning would have found
rather mechanical.

Perhaps I am not worthy, as you say,
Of work like this: perhaps a woman's soul
Aspires, and not creates: yet we aspire,
And yet I'll try out your perhapses, sir,
And if I fail . . . why, burn me up my straw   490
Like other false works—I'll not ask for grace;
Your scorn is better, cousin Romney. I
Who love my art, would never wish it lower
To suit my stature. I may love my art.
You'll grant that even a woman may love art,   495
Seeing that to waste true love on anything
Is womanly, past question."
                              I retain
The very last word which I said that day,
As you the creaking of the door, years past,
Which let upon you such disabling news   500
You ever after have been graver. He,
His eyes, the motions in his silent mouth,
Were fiery points on which my words were caught,
Transfixed for ever in my memory
For his sake, not their own. And yet I know   505
I did not love him . . . nor he me . . . that's
          sure . . .
And what I said is unrepented of,
As truth is always. Yet . . . a princely man!—
If hard to me, heroic for himself!
He bears down on me through the slanting years,   510
The stronger for the distance. If he had loved,
Ay, loved me, with that retributive face, . . .
I might have been a common woman now
And happier, less known and less left alone,
Perhaps a better woman after all,   515
With chubby children hanging on my neck
To keep me low and wise. Ah me, the vines
That bear such fruit are proud to stoop with it.
The palm stands upright in a realm of sand.
And I, who spoke the truth then, stand upright,   520
Still worthy of having spoken out the truth,
By being content I spoke it though it set
Him there, me here.—O woman's vile remorse,
To hanker after a mere name, a show,
A supposition, a potential love!   525
Does every man who names love in our lives
Become a power for that? is love's true thing
So much best to us, that what personates love
Is next best? A potential love, forsooth!
I'm not so vile. No, no—he cleaves, I think,   530
This man, his image,—chiefly for the wrong
And shock he gave my life, in finding me

Precisely where the devil of my youth
Had set me, on those mountain-peaks of hope
All glittering with the dawn-dew, all erect   535
And famished for the noon,—exclaiming, while
I looked for empire and much tribute, "Come,
I have some worthy work for thee below.
Come, sweep my barns and keep my hospitals,
And I will pay thee with a current coin   540
Which men give women."

From *Book 5*

[POETS AND THE PRESENT AGE]

The critics say that epics have died out
With Agamemnon and the goat-nursed gods;[5]   140
I'll not believe it. I could never deem,
As Payne Knight[6] did (the mythic mountaineer
Who travelled higher than he was born to live,
And showed sometimes the goitre[7] in his throat
Discoursing of an image seen through fog),   145
That Homer's heroes measured twelve feet high.
They were but men:—his Helen's hair turned grey
Like any plain Miss Smith's who wears a front;[8]
And Hector's infant whimpered at a plume[9]
As yours last Friday at a turkey-cock.   150
All actual heroes are essential men,
And all men possible heroes: every age,
Heroic in proportions, double-faced,
Looks backward and before, expects a morn
And claims an epos.[1]
                        Ay, but every age   155
Appears to souls who live in 't (ask Carlyle)[2]
Most unheroic. Ours, for instance, ours:
The thinkers scout it, and the poets abound
Who scorn to touch it with a finger-tip:
A pewter age,[3]—mixed metal, silver-washed;   160
An age of scum, spooned off the richer past,
An age of patches for old gaberdines,[4]
An age of mere transition,[5] meaning nought

5. Zeus was nursed by a goat.
6. Richard Payne Knight (1750–1824), a classical philologist, who, upon England's acquisition of the Parthenon marbles, claimed that Lord Elgin had wasted his labor, because they were not all Greek.
7. A disease often contracted in high mountain areas because of the low iodine content of the water.
8. A piece of false hair worn by women over the forehead.
9. In an episode in the *Iliad*, Hector tries to take his infant son in his arms, but the child clings to his nurse, frightened of his father's helmet and crest.

1. An epic poem.
2. In *Heroes and Hero-Worship* (1841), Carlyle argues that the present age needs a renewed perception of the heroic.
3. Barrett Browning is alluding to the convention, which originates in Hesiod, of describing civilization's decline through a succession of ages named for increasingly less precious materials, i.e., the golden age, the silver age, the bronze age.
4. Coats made of gabardine.
5. In *The Spirit of the Age* (1831), John Stuart Mill calls the present age "an age of transition."

Except that what succeeds must shame it quite
If God please. That's wrong thinking, to my mind,   165
And wrong thoughts make poor poems.
                              Every age,
Through being beheld too close, is ill-discerned
By those who have not lived past it. We'll suppose
Mount Athos carved, as Alexander schemed,
To some colossal statue of a man.[6]   170
The peasants, gathering brushwood in his ear,
Had guessed as little as the browsing goats
Of form or feature of humanity
Up there,—in fact, had travelled five miles off
Or ere the giant image broke on them,   175
Full human profile, nose and chin distinct,
Mouth, muttering rhythms of silence up the sky
And fed at evening with the blood of suns;
Grand torso,—hand, that flung perpetually
The largesse of a silver river down   180
To all the country pastures. 'Tis even thus
With times we live in,—evermore too great
To be apprehended near.
                              But poets should
Exert a double vision; should have eyes
To see near things as comprehensively   185
As if afar they took their point of sight,
And distant things as intimately deep
As if they touched them. Let us strive for this.
I do distrust the poet who discerns
No character or glory in his times,   190
And trundles back his soul five hundred years,
Past moat and drawbridge, into a castle-court,
To sing—oh, not of lizard or of toad
Alive i' the ditch there,—'twere excusable,
But of some black chief, half knight, half sheep-lifter,   195
Some beauteous dame, half chattel and half queen,
As dead as must be, for the greater part,
The poems made on their chivalric bones;
And that's no wonder: death inherits death.

Nay, if there's room for poets in this world   200
A little overgrown (I think there is),
Their sole work is to represent the age,
Their age, not Charlemagne's,[7]—this live, throbbing age,
That brawls, cheats, maddens, calculates, aspires,
And spends more passion, more heroic heat,   205

6. Dionocrates, a sculptor, is said to have suggested to Alexander that Mount Athos be carved
into the statue of a conqueror with a city in his left
hand and a basin in his right, where all the waters
of the region could be collected and used to water
the pasture lands below.
7. Frankish conqueror (768–814), who created a
European empire.

Betwixt the mirrors of its drawing-rooms,
Than Roland[8] with his knights at Roncesvalles.
To flinch from modern varnish, coat or flounce,
Cry out for togas and the picturesque,
Is fatal,—foolish too. King Arthur's self   210
Was commonplace to Lady Guenever;
And Camelot to minstrels seemed as flat
As Fleet Street[9] to our poets.
                              Never flinch,
But still, unscrupulously epic, catch
Upon the burning lava of a song
The full-veined, heaving, double-breasted Age: 215
That, when the next shall come, the men of that
May touch the impress with reverent hand, and say
"Behold,—behold the paps[1] we all have sucked!
This bosom seems to beat still, or at least   220
It sets ours beating: this is living art,
Which thus presents and thus records true life."

1853–56   1857

A Musical Instrument

1

What was he doing, the great god Pan,[1]
    Down in the reeds by the river?
Spreading ruin and scattering ban,[2]
Splashing and paddling with hoofs of a goat,
And breaking the golden lilies afloat   5
    With the dragon-fly on the river.

2

He tore out a reed, the great god Pan,
    From the deep cool bed of the river:
The limpid water turbidly ran,
And the broken lilies a-dying lay,   10
And the dragon-fly had fled away,
    Ere he brought it out of the river.

3

High on the shore sat the great god Pan
    While turbidly flowed the river;
And hacked and hewed as a great god can,   15

---

8. Legendary medieval hero, whose adventures are told in the epic poem *Chanson de Roland*.
9. Street in London, a center for book shops and newspaper and publishing offices.
1. Breasts.
1. God of woods, fields, and flocks, having a human body with goat's legs, horns, and ears. According to legend, a nymph, Syrinx, when escaping from Pan's pursuit of her, was metamorphosed into a reed in a stream. One version of the legend (the one used here) has Pan making this single reed into a shepherd's pipe, in shape like a flute. In another version, he makes a pipe out of seven reeds in a row, an invention named in honor of the nymph.
2. Curses, malediction.

With his hard bleak steel at the patient reed,
Till there was not a sign of the leaf indeed
   To prove it fresh from the river.

4

He cut it short, did the great god Pan,
   (How tall it stood in the river!)   20
Then drew the pith,[3] like the heart of a man,
Steadily from the outside ring,
And notched the poor dry empty thing
   In holes, as he sat by the river.

5

"This is the way," laughed the great god Pan   25
   (Laughed while he sat by the river),
"The only way, since gods began
To make sweet music, they could succeed."
Then, dropping his mouth to a hole in the reed,
   He blew in power by the river.   30

6

Sweet, sweet, sweet, O Pan!
   Piercing sweet by the river!
Blinding sweet, O great god Pan!
The sun on the hill forgot to die,
And the lilies revived, and the dragon-fly   35
   Came back to dream on the river.

7

Yet half a beast is the great god Pan,
   To laugh as he sits by the river,
Making a poet out of a man:
The true gods sigh for the cost and pain,—   40
For the reed which grows nevermore again
   As a reed with the reeds in the river.

1860   1860

Mother and Poet[1]

(Turin, After News from Gaeta, 1861)

1

DEAD! One of them shot by the sea in the east,
   And one of them shot in the west by the sea.
Dead! both my boys! When you sit at the feast
   And are wanting a great song for Italy free,
     Let none look at *me*!   5

---

3. Central tissue.
1. The speaker is the Italian poet and patriot Laura
Savio of Turin, both of whose sons were killed in
the struggle for the unification of Italy, one in the
attack on the fortress at Ancona, the other at the
siege of Gaeta, the last stronghold of the Neapolitan government.

2

Yet I was a poetess only last year,
    And good at my art, for a woman, men said;
But *this* woman, *this*, who is agonised here,
        —The east sea and west sea rhyme on in her
            head
            For ever instead.   10

3

What art can a woman be good at? Oh, vain!
    What art *is* she good at, but hurting her breast
With the milk-teeth of babes, and a smile at the
            pain?
    Ah boys, how you hurt! you were strong as you
            pressed,
            And I proud, by that test.   15

4

What art's for a woman? To hold on her knees
    Both darlings! to feel all their arms round her
            throat,
Cling, strangle a little! to sew by degrees
    And 'broider the long-clothes and neat little coat;
            To dream and to doat.   20

5

To teach them . . . It stings there! *I* made them
            indeed
    Speak plain the word *country*. *I* taught them, no
            doubt,
That a country's a thing men should die for at need.
    I prated of liberty, rights, and about
            The tyrant cast out.   25

6

And when their eyes flashed . . . O my beautiful
            eyes! . . .
    I exulted; nay, let them go forth at the wheels
Of the guns, and denied not. But then the surprise
    When one sits quite alone! Then one weeps, then
            one kneels!
            God, how the house feels!   30

7

At first, happy news came, in gay letters moiled[2]
    With my kisses,—of camp-life and glory, and
            how
They both loved me; and, soon coming home to be
            spoiled
    In return would fan off every fly from my brow
            With their green laurel-bough.[3]   35

2. Moistened.
3. A laurel crown is the conventional mark of a poet's fame.

8

Then was triumph at Turin: "Ancona was free!"
   And some one came out of the cheers in the street,
With a face pale as stone, to say something to me.
   My Guido was dead! I fell down at his feet,
         While they cheered in the street.   40

9

I bore it; friends soothed me; my grief looked sub-
         lime
   As the ransom of Italy. One boy remained
To be leant on and walked with, recalling the time
   When the first grew immortal, while both of us
         strained
         To the height he had gained.   45

10

And letters still came, shorter, sadder, more strong,
   Writ now but in one hand, "I was not to faint,—
One loved me for two—would be with me ere
         long:
And Viva l'Italia!—he died for, our saint,
         Who forbids our complaint."   50

11

My Nanni would add, "he was safe, and aware
   Of a presence that turned off the balls,[4]—was im-
         prest
It was Guido himself, who knew what I could bear,
   And how 'twas impossible, quite dispossessed
         To live on for the rest."   55

12

On which, without pause, up the telegraph line
   Swept smoothly the next news from Gaeta:—Shot.
Tell his mother. Ah, ah, "his," "their" mother,—
         not "mine,"
   No voice says "My mother" again to me. What!
         You think Guido forgot?   60

13

Are souls straight so happy that, dizzy with Heaven,
   They drop earth's affections, conceive not of woe?
I think not. Themselves were too lately forgiven
   Through THAT Love and Sorrow which recon-
         ciled so
         The Above and Below.   65

14

O Christ of the five wounds, who look'dst through
         the dark
   To the face of thy mother! consider, I pray,

4. Cannon balls.

How we common mothers stand desolate, mark,
 Whose sons, not being Christs, die with eyes
   turned away
  And no last word to say!   70

        15

Both boys dead? but that's out of nature. We all
 Have been patriots, yet each house must always
   keep one.
'Twere imbecile, hewing out roads to a wall;
 And, when Italy's made, for what end is it done
  If we have not a son?   75

        16

Ah, ah, ah! when Gaeta's taken, what then?
 When the fair wicked queen sits no more at her
   sport
Of the fire-balls of death crashing souls out of men?
 When the guns of Cavalli with final retort
  Have cut the game short?[5]   80

        17

When Venice and Rome keep their new jubilee,[6]
 When your flag takes all heaven for its white,
   green, and red,
When *you* have your country from mountain to sea,
 When King Victor has Italy's crown on his head,
  (And *I* have my Dead)—   85

        18

What then? Do not mock me. Ah, ring your bells
   low,
 And burn your lights faintly! *My* country is
   there,
Above the star pricked by the last peak of snow:
 My Italy's THERE, with my brave civic Pair,
  To disfranchise despair!   90

        19

Forgive me. Some women bear children in strength,
 And bite back the cry of their pain in self-scorn;
But the birth-pangs of nations will wring us at length
 Into wail such as this—and we sit on forlorn
  When the man-child is born.   95

        20

Dead! One of them shot by the sea in the east,
 And one of them shot in the west by the sea.
Both! both my boys! If in keeping the feast

---

5. Cavalli was the general commanding the siege of Gaeta; "the fair wicked queen" was Maria, wife of Frances II, the last ruler of the Neapolitan government, who retreated to Gaeta.
6. The celebration when they too will have been united with the rest of Italy under King Victor Emmanuel. In 1861, when the poem was written, they were the two cities that were still independent of the new state.

You want a great song for your Italy free,
　　Let none look at *me*!   100

ALFRED, LORD TENNYSON
1809–1892

1830:　*Poems, Chiefly Lyrical.*
1833:　Death of Arthur Hallam.
1842:　*Poems.*
1850:　*In Memoriam.* Tennyson appointed poet laureate.
1859:　*Idylls of the King* (first four books).

Whether or not Alfred Tennyson was the greatest of the Victorian poets, as affirmed by many critics today, there is no doubt that in his own lifetime he was the most popular of poets. On the bookshelves of almost every family of readers in England and the United States, from 1850 onwards, were the works of a man who had incontestably gained the title that Walt Whitman longed for: "The Poet of the People" (Whitman, in fact, called Tennyson, colorfully, "The Boss"). Popularity inevitably provided provocation for a reaction in the decades following his death. In the course of repudiating their Victorian predecessors, the Edwardians and Georgians established the fashion of making fun of Tennyson's great achievements. Samuel Butler (1835–1902), who anticipated early twentieth-century tastes, has a characteristic entry in his *Notebooks*: "Talking it over, we agreed that Blake was no good because he learnt Italian at sixty in order to study Dante, and we knew Dante was no good because he was so fond of Virgil, and Virgil was no good because Tennyson ran him, and as for Tennyson—well, Tennyson goes without saying." In the second half of the twentieth century, Butler's confident assumption that Tennyson's poetry was simply contemptible no longer "goes without saying." The delights to be found in this superb "lord of language"—as Tennyson himself addresses his favorite predecessor, Virgil— have been rediscovered, and Tennyson's stature as one of the major poets of any age has been re-established. In 1892, the year of his death, he himself had made an accurate prophecy of his changing status in his lines on *Poets and Critics*:

　　　　　What is true at last will tell:
　　　　　Few at first will place thee well;
　　　　Some too low would have thee shine,
　　　　Some too high—no fault of thine—
　　　　　Hold thine own, and work thy will!

　Like his poetry, Tennyson's life and character have been reassessed in the twentieth century. To many of his contemporaries he seemed a remote wizard, secure in his laureate's robes, a man whose life had been sheltered, marred only by the loss of his best friend in youth. During much of his career Tennyson may have been isolated, but his was not a sheltered life in the real sense of the word. Although he grew up in a parsonage, it was not the kind of parsonage one encounters in the novels of Jane Austen. It was a household dominated by frictions and loyalties and broodings over ancestral inheritances, in which the children showed marked strains of instability and eccentricity.

Alfred was the fourth son in a family of twelve children. One of his brothers had to be confined to an insane asylum for life; another was long a victim of the opium habit; another had violent quarrels with his father, the Reverend Dr. George Tennyson, who had become a drunkard. This father, a man of considerable learning, had himself been born the eldest son of a wealthy landowner and had therefore expected to be heir to his family's estates. Instead he was disinherited in favor of his younger brother and had to make his own livelihood by joining the clergy, a profession which he disliked. After George Tennyson had settled in a small rectory in Somersby, his brooding sense of dissatisfaction led to increasingly violent bouts of drunkenness, despite which he was nevertheless still able to serve as tutor for his sons in classical and modern languages to prepare them for entering the university.

Before leaving this strange household for Cambridge, Alfred had already demonstrated a flair for writing verse—precocious exercises in the manner of Milton or Byron or the Elizabethan dramatists. He had even published a volume in 1827, in collaboration with his brother Charles, *Poems by Two Brothers*. This feat drew him to the attention of a group of gifted undergraduates at Cambridge, the "Apostles," who encouraged him to devote his life to poetry. Up until this time, the young man had known scarcely anyone outside the circle of his own family. Despite his massive frame and powerful physique, he was painfully shy, and the friendships he found at Cambridge, as well as the intellectual and political discussions in which he participated, served to give him confidence and to widen his horizons as a poet. The most important of these friendships was with Arthur Hallam, a leader of the Apostles, who later became engaged to Tennyson's sister. Hallam's sudden death, in 1833, seemed an overwhelming calamity to his friend. Not only the long elegy *In Memoriam* but many of Tennyson's other poems are tributes to this early friendship.

Alfred's career at Cambridge was interrupted and finally broken off in 1831 by family dissensions and financial need, and he returned home to study and practice the craft of poetry. His early volumes (1830 and 1832) were attacked as "obscure" or "affected" by some of the reviewers. Tennyson suffered acutely under hostile criticism, but he also profited from it. His volume of 1842 demonstrated a remarkable advance in taste and technical excellence, and in 1850 he at last attained fame and full critical recognition with *In Memoriam*. In the same year he became poet laureate in succession to Wordsworth. The struggle during the previous twenty years had been made especially painful by the long postponement of his marriage to Emily Sellwood, with whom he had fallen in love in 1836 but could not marry, because of poverty, until 1850.

His life thereafter was a comfortable one. He was as popular as Byron had been, and his fame lasted for much longer. The earnings from his poetry (sometimes exceeding £10,000 a year) enabled him to purchase a house in the country and to enjoy the kind of seclusion he liked. His notoriety was enhanced, like that of G. B. Shaw and Walt Whitman, by his colorful appearance. Huge and shaggy, in cloak and broadbrimmed hat, gruff in manner as a farmer, he impressed everyone as what is called a "character." The pioneer photographer Julia Cameron, who took magnificent portraits of him, called him "the most beautiful old man on earth." He also had a booming voice, when reading his poetry, that electrified listeners much as Dylan Thomas electrified audiences in the twentieth century: "mouthing out his hollow o's and a's, / Deep-chested music." Moreover, for many Victorian readers, he seemed not only a great poetical phrasemaker and a striking individual but also a wise man whose occasional pronouncements on politics or world affairs represented the national voice itself. In 1884 he accepted a peerage. In 1892 he died and was buried in Westminster Abbey.

It is often said that success was bad for Tennyson, and that after *In Memoriam* his poetic power seriously declined. That in his last forty-two years certain of his mannerisms became accentuated is true. One of the difficulties of his dignified blank verse was, as he said himself, that it is hard to describe commonplace objects and "at the same time to retain poetical elevation." This difficulty is evident, for example, in *Enoch Arden* (1864), a long blank verse narrative of everyday life in a fishing village, in which a basketful of fish is ornately described as "Enoch's ocean spoil / In ocean-smelling osier." In others of his later poems, those dealing with national affairs, there is also an increased shrillness of tone—a mannerism accentuated by Tennyson's realizing that like Dickens he had a vast public behind him to back up his pronouncements.

It is foolish, however, to try to shelve all of Tennyson's later productions. In 1855 he published his experimental monologue *Maud*, perhaps his finest long poem. In 1859 he published four books of his *Idylls of the King*, a large-scale epic which occupied most of his energies in the second half of his career. About this late poem, completed in twelve books, in 1888, there is less agreement. Some readers consider it to be complacent—mere "lollipops," as Carlyle called it. Yet *Idylls of the King* is not simply a hymn to progress. It records, instead, a cycle of change from a society that has emerged from a wasteland into civilization but which may revert to a wasteland once more. In any event, even if this ambitious epic does not always show Tennyson in his best vein, there is no sign of decline in his late lyrics. The eighty-year-old poet who wrote *Crossing the Bar* had certainly not lost his touch.

The problem of Tennyson's development is really of more significance for the period before 1850 rather than afterwards. W. H. Auden has stated that Tennyson had "the finest ear, perhaps, of any English poet." The interesting point is that Tennyson did not "have" such an ear: he developed it. Studies of the original versions of his poems in the 1830 and 1832 volumes demonstrate that not only was his taste uncertain at the outset of his career but that his sense of meter was originally unreliable. The harmonics he was to achieve from 1842 onwards had to be learned just as a pianist with a weak left hand has to overcome his weakness by constant exercise. Like Chaucer or Keats or Pope, Tennyson studied his predecessors assiduously to perfect his technique. Anyone wanting to learn the traditional craft of English verse can study with profit the various stages of revision that such poems as *The Lotos-Eaters* were subjected to by this painstaking and artful poet.

If the early Tennyson was uncertain of meter, he had other skills that were immediately in evidence. One of these was a capacity for linking scenery to states of mind. As early as 1835, J. S. Mill identified the special kind of scene-painting to be found in early poems such as *Mariana*: ". . . not the power of producing that rather vapid species of composition usually termed descriptive poetry . . . but the power of *creating* scenery, in keeping with some state of human feeling so fitted to it as to be the embodied symbol of it, and to summon up the state of feeling itself, with a force not to be surpassed by anything but reality."

A second aspect of Tennyson's early development was his increased preoccupation with problems of his day. If Mill praised his capacity to render landscape, he also urged, in his review, Tennyson's further responsibilities—to "cultivate, and with no half devotion, philosophy as well as poetry." Advice of this kind Tennyson was already predisposed to heed. The death of Hallam, the religious uncertainties which he had himself experienced, together with his own extensive study of writings by geologists, astronomers, and biologists, led him to confront many of the religious issues that bewildered his generation and later generations. The result was *In Memoriam* (1850), a long elegy written over a period of seventeen years embodying the poet's reflections on man's relation to God and to nature.

Was Tennyson intellectually equipped to deal with the great questions raised in *In Memoriam*? The answer may depend on a reader's religious and philosophical presuppositions. Some, such as T. H. Huxley, considered Tennyson an intellectual giant, a thinker who had mastered the scientific thought of his century and fully confronted the issues it raised. Others dismissed Tennyson, in this phase, as a lightweight. Auden went so far as to call him the "stupidest" of English poets. We might say more accurately that his mind was slow, ponderous, brooding, and we should add that for the composition of *In Memoriam* such qualities of mind were assets, not liabilities. In these terms we can understand when Tennyson's poetry really fails to measure up: it is when he writes of events of the moment over which his thoughts and feelings have had no time to brood. Several of his poems are essentially newspaper pieces. They are Letters to the Editor, in effect, with the ephemeral heat and simplicity we expect of such productions. *The Charge of the Light Brigade*, inspired by a report in *The Times* of a cavalry charge at Balaclava during the Crimean War, is one of the best of his productions in this category.

Tennyson's poems of contemporary events were inevitably popular in his own day. So too were those poems where, as in *Locksley Hall*, he dipped into the future. The technological changes wrought by Victorian inventors and engineers fascinated him. Sometimes they gave him an assurance of human progress as swaggeringly exultant as that of Macaulay. At other times the horrors of industrialism's by-products in the slums, the bloodshed of war, the greed of the newly rich, destroyed his hopes that man was evolving upwards. Such a late poem as *The Dawn* embodies an attitude which he found in Virgil: "Thou majestic in thy sadness at the doubtful doom of human kind."

For despite Tennyson's fascination with technological developments, he was essentially a poet of the countryside, a man whose whole being was conditioned by the recurring rhythms of rural rather than urban life. He had the countryman's awareness of traditional roots and his sense of the past. It is appropriate that most of his best poems are about the past, not about the present or future. The past is his great theme: his own past (as in *In the*

Valley of Cauteretz), his country's past (as in *The Idylls of the King*), the past of mankind, the past of the world itself:

> There rolls the deep where grew the tree.
>   O earth, what changes hast thou seen!
> There where the long street roars hath been
>   The stillness of the central sea.

Tennyson is the first major writer to express this awareness of the vast extent of geological time that has haunted human consciousness since Victorian scientists exposed the history of the earth's crust. In his more usual vein, however, it is the recorded past of mankind that inspires him, the classical past in particular. Classical themes, as Douglas Bush has noted, "generally banished from his mind what was timid, parochial, sentimental . . . and evoked his special gifts and most authentic emotions, his rich and wistful sense of the past, his love of nature, and his power of style."

One returns, finally then, to the question of language. At the time of his death, a critic complained that Tennyson was merely "a discoverer of words rather than of ideas." The same complaint has been made by George Bernard Shaw and others—not about Tennyson but about Shakespeare.

Mariana[1]

"Mariana in the moated grange."
Measure for Measure

With blackest moss the flower-plots
    Were thickly crusted, one and all;
The rusted nails fell from the knots
    That held the pear to the gable wall.
The broken sheds looked sad and strange: 5
    Unlifted was the clinking latch;
    Weeded and worn the ancient thatch
Upon the lonely moated grange.
        She only said, "My life is dreary,
            He cometh not," she said;   10
        She said, "I am aweary, aweary,
            I would that I were dead!"

Her tears fell with the dews at even;
    Her tears fell ere the dews were dried;
She could not look on the sweet heaven,   15
    Either at morn or eventide.
After the flitting of the bats,
    When thickest dark did trance[2] the sky,

1. Mariana, in Shakespeare's *Measure for Measure* 3.1.277), waits in a grange (an outlying farmhouse) for her lover who has deserted her.
2. Traverse (noted by R. W. Hill).

She drew her casement curtain by,
And glanced athwart the glooming flats.   20
   She only said, "The night is dreary,
     He cometh not," she said;
   She said, "I am aweary, aweary,
     I would that I were dead!"

Upon the middle of the night,   25
   Waking she heard the nightfowl crow;
The cock sung out an hour ere light;
   From the dark fen the oxen's low
Came to her; without hope of change,
   In sleep she seemed to walk forlorn,   30
   Till cold winds woke the gray-eyed morn
About the lonely moated grange.
   She only said, "The day is dreary,
     He cometh not," she said;
   She said, "I am aweary, aweary,   35
     I would that I were dead!"

About a stonecast from the wall
   A sluice with blackened waters slept,
And o'er it many, round and small,
   The clustered marish-mosses[3] crept.   40
Hard by a poplar shook alway,
   All silver-green with gnarlèd bark:
For leagues no other tree did mark
The level waste, the rounding gray.
   She only said, "My life is dreary,   45
     He cometh not," she said;
   She said, "I am aweary, aweary,
     I would that I were dead!"

And ever when the moon was low,
   And the shrill winds were up and away,   50
In the white curtain, to and fro,
   She saw the gusty shadow sway.
But when the moon was very low,
   And wild winds bound within their cell,[4]
   The shadow of the poplar fell   55
Upon her bed, across her brow.
   She only said, "The night is dreary,
     He cometh not," she said;
   She said, "I am aweary, aweary,
     I would that I were dead!"   60

3. "The little marsh-moss lumps that float on the surface of water" [Tennyson's comment].
4. According to Virgil, Aeolus, god of winds, kept the winds imprisoned in a cave. See *Aeneid* 1.50–59.

All day within the dreamy house,
    The doors upon their hinges creaked;
The blue fly sung in the pane; the mouse
    Behind the moldering wainscot shrieked,[5]
Or from the crevice peered about.   65
    Old faces glimmered through the doors,
    Old footsteps trod the upper floors,
Old voices called her from without.
        She only said, "My life is dreary,
            He cometh not," she said;   70
        She said, "I am aweary, aweary,
            I would that I were dead!"

The sparrow's chirrup on the roof,
    The slow clock ticking, and the sound
Which to the wooing wind aloof   75
    The poplar made, did all confound
Her sense; but most she loathed the hour
    When the thick-moted sunbeam lay
    Athwart the chambers, and the day
Was sloping toward his western bower.   80
        Then, said she, "I am very dreary,
            He will not come," she said;
        She wept, "I am aweary, aweary,
            Oh God, that I were dead!"

                                   1830

Sonnet

She took the dappled partridge flecked with blood,
    And in her hand the drooping pheasant bare,
    And by his feet she held the woolly hare,
And like a master painting where she stood,
Looked some new goddess of an English wood.   5
    Nor could I find an imperfection there,
    Nor blame the wanton act that showed so fair—
To me whatever freak[1] she plays is good.
Hers is the fairest Life that breathes with breath,
    And *their* still plumes and azure eyelids closed   10
        Made quiet Death so beautiful to see
That Death lent grace to Life and Life to Death
    And in one image Life and Death reposed,
        To make my love an Immortality.

ca. 1830   1931

5. Cf. "And a time for the wind . . . to shake the wainscot where the fieldmouse trots / And to shake the tattered arras. . . ." (T. S. Eliot, *Four Quar-* *tets: East Coker*, lines 11–13).
1. Prank.

The Lady of Shalott

Part 1

On either side the river lie
Long fields of barley and of rye,
That clothe the wold[1] and meet the sky;
And through the field the road runs by
    To many-towered Camelot;[2]   5
And up and down the people go,
Gazing where the lilies blow[3]
Round an island there below,
    The island of Shalott.

Willows whiten, aspens quiver,   10
Little breezes dusk and shiver
Through the wave that runs forever
By the island in the river
    Flowing down to Camelot.
Four gray walls, and four gray towers,   15
Overlook a space of flowers,
And the silent isle imbowers
    The Lady of Shalott.

By the margin, willow-veiled,
Slide the heavy barges trailed   20
By slow horses; and unhailed
The shallop[4] flitteth silken-sailed
    Skimming down to Camelot:
But who hath seen her wave her hand?
Or at the casement seen her stand?   25
Or is she known in all the land,
    The Lady of Shalott?

Only reapers, reaping early
In among the bearded barley,
Hear a song that echoes cheerly   30
From the river winding clearly,
    Down to towered Camelot;
And by the moon the reaper weary,
Piling sheaves in uplands airy,
Listening, whispers " 'Tis the fairy   35
    Lady of Shalott."

---

1. Rolling plains.
2. Legendary city in which King Arthur's palace was located.

3. Bloom.
4. A light open boat.

Part 2

There she weaves by night and day
A magic web with colors gay.
She has heard a whisper say,
A curse is on her if she stay   40
     To look down to Camelot.
She knows not what the curse may be,
And so she weaveth steadily,
And little other care hath she,
     The Lady of Shalott.   45

And moving through a mirror clear[5]
That hangs before her all the year,
Shadows of the world appear.
There she sees the highway near
     Winding down to Camelot;   50
There the river eddy whirls,
And there the surly village churls,
And the red cloaks of market girls,
     Pass onward from Shalott.

Sometimes a troop of damsels glad,   55
An abbot on an ambling pad,[6]
Sometimes a curly shepherd lad,
Or long-haired page in crimson clad,
     Goes by to towered Camelot;
And sometimes through the mirror blue   60
The knights come riding two and two:
She hath no loyal knight and true,
     The Lady of Shalott.

But in her web she still delights
To weave the mirror's magic' sights,
For often through the silent nights   65
A funeral, with plumes and lights
     And music, went to Camelot;
Or when the moon was overhead,
Came two young lovers lately wed: 70
"I am half sick of shadows," said
     The Lady of Shalott.

Part 3

A bowshot from her bower eaves,
He rode between the barley sheaves,

---

5. Weavers used mirrors, placed facing their looms, in order to see the progress of their work.
6. Easy-paced horse.

The sun came dazzling through the leaves,   75
And flamed upon the brazen greaves[7]
    Of bold Sir Lancelot.
A red-cross knight[8] forever kneeled
To a lady in his shield,
That sparkled on the yellow field,   80
    Beside remote Shalott.

The gemmy bridle glittered free,
Like to some branch of stars we see
Hung in the golden Galaxy.
The bridle bells rang merrily   85
    As he rode down to Camelot;
And from his blazoned baldric[9] slung
A mighty silver bugle hung,
And as he rode his armor rung,
    Beside remote Shalott.   90

All in the blue unclouded weather
Thick-jeweled shone the saddle leather,
The helmet and the helmet-feather
Burned like one burning flame together,
    As he rode down to Camelot;   95
As often through the purple night,
Below the starry clusters bright,
Some bearded meteor, trailing light,
    Moves over still Shalott.

His broad clear brow in sunlight glowed;   100
On burnished hooves his war horse trode;
From underneath his helmet flowed
His coal-black curls as on he rode,
    As he rode down to Camelot.
From the bank and from the river   105
He flashed into the crystal mirror,
"Tirra lirra," by the river
    Sang Sir Lancelot.

She left the web, she left the loom,
She made three paces through the room,   110
She saw the water lily bloom,
She saw the helmet and the plume,
    She looked down to Camelot.
Out flew the web and floated wide;
The mirror cracked from side to side;   115
"The curse is come upon me," cried
    The Lady of Shalott.

---

7. Armor protecting the leg below the knee.
8. Cf. Spenser's *Faerie Queene* 1 and 3.2.17–25.

9. A richly decorated sash worn diagonally across
the breast.

Part 4

In the stormy east wind straining,
The pale yellow woods were waning,
The broad stream in his banks complaining,   120
Heavily the low sky raining
    Over towered Camelot;
Down she came and found a boat
Beneath a willow left afloat,
And round about the prow she wrote   125
    The Lady of Shalott.

And down the river's dim expanse
Like some bold seër in a trance,
Seeing all his own mischance—
With a glassy countenance   130
    Did she look to Camelot.
And at the closing of the day
She loosed the chain, and down she lay;
The broad steam bore her far away,
    The Lady of Shalott.   135

Lying, robed in snowy white
That loosely flew to left and right—
The leaves upon her falling light—
Through the noises of the night
    She floated down to Camelot;   140
And as the boat-head wound along
The willowy hills and fields among,
They heard her singing her last song,
    The Lady of Shalott.

Heard a carol, mournful, holy,   145
Chanted loudly, chanted lowly,
Till her blood was frozen slowly,
And her eyes were darkened wholly,
    Turned to towered Camelot.
For ere she reached upon the tide   150
The first house by the waterside,
Singing in her song she died,
    The Lady of Shalott.

Under tower and balcony,
By garden wall and gallery,
A gleaming shape she floated by,   155
Dead-pale between the houses high,
    Silent into Camelot.
Out upon the wharfs they came,
Knight and burgher, lord and dame,   160

And round the prow they read her name,
  The Lady of Shalott.

Who is this? and what is here?
And in the lighted palace near
Died the sound of royal cheer;   165
And they crossed themselves for fear,
  All the knights at Camelot:
But Lancelot mused a little space;
He said, "She has a lovely face;
God in his mercy lend her grace,   170
  The Lady of Shalott."

1832   1832, 1842

The Lotos-Eaters[1]

"Courage!" he[2] said, and pointed toward the land,
"This mounting wave will roll us shoreward soon."
In the afternoon they came unto a land[3]
In which it seemèd always afternoon.
All round the coast the languid air did swoon,   5
Breathing like one that hath a weary dream.
Full-faced above the valley stood the moon;
And, like a downward smoke, the slender stream
Along the cliff to fall and pause and fall did seem.

A land of streams! some, like a downward smoke, 10
Slow-dropping veils of thinnest lawn,[4] did go;
And some through wavering lights and shadows broke,
Rolling a slumbrous sheet of foam below.
They saw the gleaming river seaward flow
From the inner land; far off, three mountaintops 15
Three silent pinnacles of aged snow,
Stood sunset-flushed; and, dewed with showery drops,
Up-clomb the shadowy pine above the woven copse.

---

1. Based on a short episode from the *Odyssey* (9.82–97) in which the weary Greek veterans of the Trojan War are tempted by a desire to abandon their long voyage homeward. As Odysseus later reported: "On the tenth day we set foot on the land of the lotos-eaters who eat a flowering food. . . . I sent forth certain of my company [who] . . . mixed with the men of the lotos-eaters who gave . . . them of the lotos to taste. Now whosoever of them did eat the honey-sweet fruit of the lotos had no more wish to bring tidings nor to come back, but there he chose to abide . . . forgetful of his homeward way."
  Tennyson expands Homer's brief account into an elaborate picture of weariness and the desire for rest and death. The descriptions in the first stanzas are similar to Spenser's *Faerie Queene* (2.6), and employ the same stanza form. The final section derives, in part, from Lucretius' conception of the gods in *De rerum natura*.
2. Odysseus (or Ulysses).
3. The repetition of "land" from line 1 was deliberate; Tennyson said that this "no rhyme" was "lazier" in its effect. Compare "afternoon" (lines 3–4) and the rhyming of "adown" and "down" (lines 19, 21).
4. A fine, thin linen.

The charmèd sunset lingered low adown
In the red West; through mountain clefts the dale   20
Was seen far inland, and the yellow down[5]
Bordered with palm, and many a winding vale
And meadow, set with slender galingale;[6]
A land where all things always seemed the same!
And round about the keel with faces pale,   25
Dark faces pale against that rosy flame,
The mild-eyed melancholy Lotos-eaters came.

Branches they bore of that enchanted stem,
Laden with flower and fruit, whereof they gave
To each, but whoso did receive of them   30
And taste, to him the gushing of the wave
Far far away did seem to mourn and rave
On alien shores; and if his fellow spake,
His voice was thin, as voices from the grave;
And deep-asleep he seemed, yet all awake,   35
And music in his ears his beating heart did make.

They sat them down upon the yellow sand,
Between the sun and moon upon the shore;
And sweet it was to dream of Fatherland,
Of child, and wife, and slave; but evermore   40
Most weary seemed the sea, weary the oar,
Weary the wandering fields of barren foam,
Then some one said, "We will return no more";
And all at once they sang, "Our island home[7]
Is far beyond the wave; we will no longer roam."   45

Choric Song[8]

1

There is sweet music here that softer falls
Than petals from blown roses on the grass,
Or night-dews on still waters between walls
Of shadowy granite, in a gleaming pass;
Music that gentlier on the spirit lies,   50
Than tired eyelids upon tired eyes;[9]
Music that brings sweet sleep down from the blissful skies.
Here are cool mosses deep,
And through the moss the ivies creep,
And in the stream the long-leaved flowers weep,
And from the craggy ledge the poppy hangs in sleep.

5. An open plain on high ground.
6. A plant resembling tall coarse grass.
7. Ithaca.
8. Sung by the mariners.

9. Tennyson wanted the word to be pronounced as *tie-yerd* rather than *tier'd* or *tire-èd*, thus "making the word neither monosyllable or disyllabic, but a dreamy child of the two."

2

Why are we weighed upon with heaviness,
And utterly consumed with sharp distress,
While all things else have rest from weariness?
All things have rest: why should we toil alone,   60
We only toil, who are the first of things,
And make perpetual moan,
Still from one sorrow to another thrown;
Nor ever fold our wings,
And cease from wanderings,   65
Nor steep our brows in slumber's holy balm;
Nor harken what the inner spirit sings,
"There is no joy but calm!"—
Why should we only toil, the roof and crown of things?[1]

3

Lo! in the middle of the wood,   70
The folded leaf is wooed from out the bud
With winds upon the branch, and there
Grows green and broad, and takes no care,
Sun-steeped at noon, and in the moon
Nightly dew-fed; and turning yellow   75
Falls, and floats adown the air.
Lo! sweetened with summer light,
The full-juiced apple, waxing over-mellow,
Drops in a silent autumn night.
All its allotted length of days   80
The flower ripens in its place,
Ripens and fades, and falls, and hath no toil,
Fast-rooted in the fruitful soil.

4

Hateful is the dark blue sky,
Vaulted o'er the dark blue sea.   85
Death is the end of life; ah, why
Should life all labor be?
Let us alone. Time driveth onward fast,
And in a little while our lips are dumb.
Let us alone. What is it that will last?   90
All things are taken from us, and become
Portions and parcels of the dreadful past.
Let us alone. What pleasure can we have
To war with evil? Is there any peace
In ever climbing up the climbing wave?   95
All things have rest, and ripen toward the grave
In silence—ripen, fall, and cease:
Give us long rest or death, dark death, or dreamful ease.[2]

1. Cf.: "Why then dost thou, O man, that of them
all / Art Lord, and eke of nature Sovereaine, / Wilfully . . . wast thy joyous houres in needlesse paine
. . . ?" (Spenser's *Faerie Queene*, 2.6.17).

2. Cf.: "Sleepe after toyle, port after stormie seas, /
Ease after warre, death after life does greatly please."
(*Faerie Queen*, 1.9.40).

5

How sweet it were, hearing the downward stream,
With half-shut eyes ever to seem
Falling asleep in a half-dream!   100
To dream and dream, like yonder amber light,
Which will not leave the myrrh-bush on the height;
To hear each other's whispered speech;
Eating the Lotos day by day,
To watch the crisping[3] ripples on the beach,   105
And tender curving lines of creamy spray;
To lend our hearts and spirits wholly
To the influence of mild-minded melancholy;
To muse and brood and live again in memory,
With those old faces of our infancy   110
Heaped over with a mound of grass,
Two handfuls of white dust, shut in an urn of brass!

6

Dear is the memory of our wedded lives,
And dear the last embraces of our wives
And their warm tears; but all hath suffered change;   115
For surely now our household hearths are cold,
Our sons inherit us, our looks are strange,
And we should come like ghosts to trouble joy.
Or else the island princes[4] overbold
Have eat our substance, and the minstrel sings   120
Before them of the ten years' war in Troy,
And our great deeds, as half-forgotten things.
Is there confusion in the little isle?
Let what is broken so remain.
The Gods are hard to reconcile;   125
'Tis hard to settle order once again.
There *is* confusion worse than death,
Trouble on trouble, pain on pain,
Long labor unto aged breath,
Sore tasks to hearts worn out by many wars   130
And eyes grown dim with gazing on the pilot-stars.

7

But, propped on beds of amaranth[5] and moly,
How sweet—while warm airs lull us, blowing lowly—
With half-dropped eyelid still,
Beneath a heaven dark and holy,   135
To watch the long bright river drawing slowly
His waters from the purple hill—
To hear the dewy echoes calling
From cave to cave through the thick-twined vine—
To watch the emerald-colored water falling   140

---

3 Curling.
4. Penelope's suitors.

5. A legendary unfading flower. "Moly": a flower
with magical properties mentioned by Homer.

Through many a woven acanthus[6] wreath divine!
Only to hear and see the far-off sparkling brine,
Only to hear were sweet, stretched out beneath the pine.

8

The Lotos blooms below the barren peak,   145
The Lotos blows by every winding creek;
All day the wind breathes low with mellower tone;
Through every hollow cave and alley lone
Round and round the spicy downs the yellow Lotos dust is blown.
We have had enough of action, and of motion we,   150
Rolled to starboard, rolled to larboard, when the surge was seething free,
Where the wallowing monster spouted his foam-fountains in the sea.
Let us swear an oath, and keep it with an equal mind,
In the hollow Lotos land to live and lie reclined
On the hills like Gods together, careless of mankind.   155
For they lie beside their nectar, and the bolts[7] are hurled
Far below them in the valleys, and the clouds are lightly curled
Round their golden houses, girdled with the gleaming world;
Where they smile in secret, looking over wasted lands,
Blight and famine, plague and earthquake, roaring deeps and fiery
    sands,   160
Clanging fights, and flaming towns, and sinking ships, and praying hands.
But they smile, they find a music centered in a doleful song
Steaming up, a lamentation and an ancient tale of wrong,
Like a tale of little meaning though the words are strong;
Chanted from an ill-used race of men that cleave the soil,   165
Sow the seed, and reap the harvest with enduring toil,
Storing yearly little dues of wheat, and wine and oil;
Till they perish and they suffer—some, 'tis whispered—down in hell
Suffer endless anguish, others in Elysian valleys dwell,
Resting weary limbs at last on beds of asphodel.[8]   170
Surely, surely, slumber is more sweet than toil, the shore
Than labor in the deep mid-ocean, wind and wave and oar;
O, rest ye, brother mariners, we will not wander more.

                                                    1832, 1842

Ulysses[1]

It little profits that an idle king,
By this still hearth, among these barren crags,

---

6. A plant resembling a thistle. Its leaves were the model for ornaments on Corinthian columns.
7. Thunderbolts.
8. A yellow lilylike flower supposed to grow in the Elysian valleys.
1. According to Dante, after the fall of Troy, Ulysses never returned to his island-home of Ithaca. Instead he persuaded some of his followers to seek new experiences by a voyage of exploration westward out beyond the straits of Gibraltar. In his inspiring speech to his aging crew he said: "Consider your origin: you were not made to live as brutes, but to pursue virtue and knowledge" (*Inferno* 26). Tennyson modified Dante's version by combining it with Homer's account in his *Odyssey* (19–24). Thus Tennyson has Ulysses make his speech in Ithaca some time after his return home to his reunion with his wife, Penelope, and his son,

Matched with an aged wife, I mete and dole
Unequal laws[2] unto a savage race,
That hoard, and sleep, and feed, and know not me.   5

    I cannot rest from travel; I will drink
Life to the lees. All times I have enjoyed
Greatly, have suffered greatly, both with those
That loved me, and alone; on shore, and when
Through scudding drifts[3] the rainy Hyades   10
Vexed the dim sea. I am become a name;
For always roaming with a hungry heart
Much have I seen and known—cities of men
And manners, climates, councils, governments,
Myself not least, but honored of them all—   15
And drunk delight of battle with my peers,
Far on the ringing plains of windy Troy,
I am a part of all that I have met;
Yet all experience is an arch wherethrough
Gleams that untraveled world whose margin fades   20
Forever and forever when I move.
How dull it is to pause, to make an end,
To rust unburnished, not to shine in use!
As though to breathe were life! Life piled on life
Were all too little, and of one to me   25
Little remains; but every hour is saved
From that eternal silence, something more,
A bringer of new things; and vile it were
For some three suns to store and hoard myself,
And this gray spirit yearning in desire   30
To follow knowledge like a sinking star,
Beyond the utmost bound of human thought.

    This is my son, mine own Telemachus,
To whom I leave the scepter and the isle—
Well-loved of me, discerning to fulfill   35
This labor, by slow prudence to make mild
A rugged people, and through soft degrees
Subdue them to the useful and the good.
Most blameless is he, centered in the sphere
Of common duties, decent not to fail   40
In offices of tenderness, and pay
Meet adoration to my household gods,
When I am gone. He works his work, I mine.

Telemachus, and, presumably, his resumption of administrative responsibilities involved in governing his kingdom.

    Tennyson himself stated that this poem expressed his own "need of going forward and braving the struggle of life" after the death of Hallam.

2. Measure out rewards and punishments.

3. Driving showers of spray and rain; the "Hyades" are a group of stars whose rising was assumed to be followed by rain.

There lies the port; the vessel puffs her sail;
There gloom the dark, broad seas. My mariners,   45
Souls that have toiled, and wrought, and thought with me—
That ever with a frolic welcome took
The thunder and the sunshine, and opposed
Free hearts, free foreheads—you and I are old;
Old age hath yet his honor and his toil.   50
Death closes all; but something ere the end,
Some work of noble note, may yet be done,
Not unbecoming men that strove with Gods.
The lights begin to twinkle from the rocks;
The long day wanes; the slow moon climbs; the deep   55
Moans round with many voices. Come, my friends,
'Tis not too late to seek a newer world.
Push off, and sitting well in order smite
The sounding furrows; for my purpose holds
To sail beyond the sunset, and the baths   60
Of all the western stars,[4] until I die.
It may be that the gulfs will wash us down;
It may be we shall touch the Happy Isles,[5]
And see the great Achilles, whom we knew.
Though much is taken, much abides; and though   65
We are not now that strength which in old days
Moved earth and heaven, that which we are, we are—
One equal temper of heroic hearts,
Made weak by time and fate, but strong in will
To strive, to seek, to find, and not to yield.   70

1833   1842

Tithonus[1]

The woods decay, the woods decay and fall,
The vapors weep their burthen to the ground,
Man comes and tills the field and lies beneath,
And after many a summer dies the swan.[2]
Me only cruel immortality   5
Consumes; I wither slowly in thine arms,[3]
Here at the quiet limit of the world,
A white-haired shadow roaming like a dream
The ever-silent spaces of the East,

---

4. The outer ocean or river which, in Greek cosmology, surrounded the flat circle of the earth, and into which the stars descended.
5. In Greek myth, the Islands of the Blessed, a paradise of perpetual summer, were thought to be located in the far-western ocean. They were peopled by great heroes who, without having died, had been translated there by the gods and made immortal. In later versions of the myth, the heroes

became immortal after their deaths. Achilles, who had been killed at Troy, would have been one of these heroes.
1. Tithonus, a Trojan prince, was loved by the goddess of the dawn, Eos or Aurora, who obtained for him the gift of living forever but neglected to obtain for him the gift of everlasting youth.
2. Some species of swans live for at least 50 years.
3. I.e., the arms of Eos.

Far-folded mists, and gleaming halls of morn.   10
   Alas! for this gray shadow, once a man—
So glorious in his beauty and thy choice,
Who madest him thy chosen, that he seemed
To his great heart none other than a God!
I asked thee, "Give me immortality."   15
Then didst thou grant mine asking with a smile,
Like wealthy men who care not how they give.
But thy strong Hours indignant worked their wills,
And beat me down and marred and wasted me,
And though they could not end me, left me maimed   20
To dwell in presence of immortal youth,
Immortal age beside immortal youth,
And all I was in ashes. Can thy love,
Thy beauty, make amends, though even now,
Close over us, the silver star,[4] thy guide,   25
Shines in those tremulous eyes that fill with tears
To hear me? Let me go; take back thy gift.
Why should a man desire in any way
To vary from the kindly race of men,
Or pass beyond the goal of ordinance[5]   30
Where all should pause, as is most meet for all?
   A soft air fans the cloud apart; there comes
A glimpse of that dark world where I was born.
Once more the old mysterious glimmer steals
From thy pure brows, and from thy shoulders pure,   35
And bosom beating with a heart renewed.
Thy cheek begins to redden through the gloom,
Thy sweet eyes brighten slowly close to mine,
Ere yet they blind the stars, and the wild team[6]
Which love thee, yearning for thy yoke, arise,   40
And shake the darkness from their loosened manes,
And beat the twilight into flakes of fire.
   Lo! ever thus thou growest beautiful
In silence, then before thine answer given
Departest, and thy tears are on my cheek.   45
   Why wilt thou ever scare me with thy tears,
And make me tremble lest a saying learnt,
In days far-off, on that dark earth, be true?
"The Gods themselves cannot recall their gifts."
   Ay me! ay me! with what another heart   50
In days far-off, and with what other eyes
I used to watch—if I be he that watched—
The lucid outline forming round thee; saw
The dim curls kindle into sunny rings;
Changed with thy mystic change, and felt my blood   55
Glow with the glow that slowly crimsoned all

---

4. The morning star that precedes the dawn.   6. The horses that draw Eos' chariot into the sky
5. What is decreed or ordained as human destiny.   at daybreak.

Thy presence and thy portals, while I lay,
Mouth, forehead, eyelids, growing dewy-warm
With kisses balmier than half-opening buds
Of April, and could hear the lips that kissed   60
Whispering I knew not what of wild and sweet,
Like that strange song I heard Apollo sing,
While Ilion like a mist rose into towers.[7]
    Yet hold me not forever in thine East;
How can my nature longer mix with thine?   65
Coldly thy rosy shadows bathe me, cold
Are all thy lights, and cold my wrinkled feet
Upon thy glimmering thresholds, when the steam
Floats up from those dim fields about the homes
Of happy men that have the power to die,   70
And grassy barrows of the happier dead.
Release me, and restore me to the ground.
Thou seest all things, thou wilt see my grave;
Thou wilt renew thy beauty morn by morn,
I earth in earth forget these empty courts,   75
And thee returning on thy silver wheels.

1833, 1859   1860

Break, Break, Break

Break, break, break,
    On thy cold gray stones, O Sea!
And I would that my tongue could utter
    The thoughts that arise in me.

O, well for the fisherman's boy,   5
    That he shouts with his sister at play!
O, well for the sailor lad,
    That he sings in his boat on the bay!

And the stately ships go on
    To their haven under the hill;   10
But O for the touch of a vanished hand,
    And the sound of a voice that is still!

Break, break, break,
    At the foot of thy crags, O Sea!
But the tender grace of a day that is dead   15
    Will never come back to me.

1834   1842

7. The walls of Troy (Ilion) were supposed to have been built to the strains of Apollo's music.

The Eagle: A Fragment

He clasps the crag with crooked hands;
Close to the sun in lonely lands,
Ringed with the azure world, he stands.

The wrinkled sea beneath him crawls:
He watches from his mountain walls,   5
And like a thunderbolt he falls.

1851

Locksley Hall[1]

Comrades, leave me here a little, while as yet 'tis early morn;
Leave me here, and when you want me, sound upon the bugle horn.

'Tis the place, and all around it, as of old, the curlews call,
Dreary gleams[2] about the moorland flying over Locksley Hall;

Locksley Hall, that in the distance overlooks the sandy tracts,   5
And the hollow ocean-ridges roaring into cataracts.

Many a night from yonder ivied casement, ere I went to rest,
Did I look on great Orion sloping slowly to the west.

Many a night I saw the Pleiads,[3] rising through the mellow shade,
Glitter like a swarm of fireflies tangled in a silver braid.   10

Here about the beach I wandered, nourishing a youth sublime
With the fairy tales of science, and the long result of time;

When the centuries behind me like a fruitful land reposed;
When I clung to all the present for the promise that it closed;[4]

When I dipped into the future far as human eye could see,   15
Saw the vision of the world and all the wonder that would be.—

In the spring a fuller crimson comes upon the robin's breast;
In the spring the wanton lapwing gets himself another crest;

1. The situation in this poem—of a young man's being jilted by a girl who chose to marry a wealthy landowner—may have been suggested to Tennyson by the experience of his brother. Frederick Tennyson, a hot-tempered man, had fallen in love with his cousin, Julia Tennyson, and was similarly unsuccessful. It may also have been inspired by Tennyson's own frustrated courtship of Rosa Baring, who rejected the young poet in favor of a wealthy suitor. Concerning the ranting tone of the speaker (a tone accentuated by the heavily marked trochaic meter), Tennyson himself said: "The whole poem represents young life, its good side, its deficiencies, and its yearnings."
2. Tennyson stated that "gleams" does not refer to "curlews" flying but to streaks of light.
3. The Pleiades, a seven-starred constellation.
4. Enclosed.

In the spring a livelier iris changes on the burnished dove;[5]
In the spring a young man's fancy lightly turns to thoughts of love.   20

Then her check was pale and thinner than should be for one so young,
And her eyes on all my motions with a mute observance hung.

And I said, "My cousin Amy, speak, and speak the truth to me,
Trust me, cousin, all the current of my being sets to thee."

On her pallid cheek and forehead came a color and a light,   25
As I have seen the rosy red flushing in the northern night.

And she turned—her bosom shaken with a sudden storm of sighs—
All the spirit deeply dawning in the dark of hazel eyes—

Saying, "I have hid my feelings, fearing they should do me wrong";
Saying, "Dost thou love me, cousin?" weeping, "I have loved thee
          long."   30

Love took up the glass of Time, and turned it in his glowing hands;
Every moment, lightly shaken, ran itself in golden sands.

Love took up the harp of Life, and smote on all the chords with
          might;
Smote the chord of Self, that, trembling, passed in music out of
          sight.

Many a morning on the moorland did we hear the copses ring,   35
And her whisper thronged my pulses with the fullness of the spring.

Many an evening by the waters did we watch the stately ships,
And our spirits rushed together at the touching of the lips.

O my cousin, shallow-hearted! O my Amy, mine no more!
O the dreary, dreary moorland! O the barren, barren shore!   40

Falser than all fancy fathoms, falser than all songs have sung,
Puppet to a father's threat, and servile to a shrewish tongue!

Is it well to wish thee happy?—having known me—to decline
On a range of lower feelings and a narrower heart than mine!

Yet it shall be; thou shalt lower to his level day by day,   45
What is fine within thee growing coarse to sympathize with clay.

As the husband is, the wife is; thou art mated with a clown,[6]
And the grossness of his nature will have weight to drag thee down.

5. Rainbow-like colors of a dove's throat plumage are intensified in the mating season.
6. Boor.

He will hold thee, when his passion shall have spent its novel force,
Something better than his dog, a little dearer than his horse.   50

What is this? his eyes are heavy; think not they are glazed with wine.
Go to him, it is thy duty; kiss him, take his hand in thine.

It may be my lord is weary, that his brain is overwrought;
Soothe him with thy finer fancies, touch him with thy lighter
    thought.

He will answer to the purpose, easy things to understand—   55
Better thou wert dead before me, though I slew thee with my hand!

Better thou and I were lying, hidden from the heart's disgrace,
Rolled in one another's arms, and silent in a last embrace.

Cursed be the social wants that sin against the strength of youth!
Cursed be the social lies that warp us from the living truth!   60

Cursed be the sickly forms that err from honest Nature's rule!
Cursed be the gold that gilds the straitened[7] forehead of the fool!

Well—'tis well that I should bluster!—Hadst thou less unworthy proved—
Would to God—for I had loved thee more than ever wife was loved.

Am I mad, that I should cherish that which bears but bitter fruit?   65
I will pluck it from my bosom, though my heart be at the root.

Never, though my mortal summers to such length of years should
    come
As the many-wintered crow[8] that leads the clanging rookery home.

Where is comfort? in division of the records of the mind?
Can I part her from herself, and love her, as I knew her, kind?   70

I remember one that perished; sweetly did she speak and move;
Such a one do I remember, whom to look at was to love.

Can I think of her as dead, and love her for the love she bore?
No—she never loved me truly; love is love for evermore.

Comfort? comfort scorned of devils! this is truth the poet[9] sings,   75
That a sorrow's crown of sorrow is remembering happier things.

Drug thy memories, lest thou learn it, lest thy heart be put to proof,
In the dead unhappy night, and when the rain is on the roof.

---

7. Narrowed.
8. A rook, a long-lived bird.

9. Dante (*Inferno* 5.121–23).

Like a dog, he hunts in dreams, and thou art staring at the wall,
Where the dying night-lamp flickers, and the shadows rise and fall.   80

Then a hand shall pass before thee, pointing to his drunken sleep,
To thy widowed[1] marriage-pillows, to the tears that thou wilt weep.

Thou shalt hear the "Never, never," whispered by the phantom years.
And a song from out the distance in the ringing of thine ears;

And an eye shall vex thee, looking ancient kindness on thy pain.   85
Turn thee, turn thee on thy pillow; get thee to thy rest again.

Nay, but Nature brings thee solace; for a tender voice will cry.
'Tis a purer life than thine, a lip to drain thy trouble dry.

Baby lips will laugh me down; my latest rival brings thee rest.
Baby fingers, waxen touches, press me from the mother's breast.   90

O, the child too clothes the father with a dearness not his due.
Half is thine and half is his; it will be worthy of the two.

O, I see thee old and formal, fitted to thy petty part,
With a little hoard of maxims preaching down a daughter's heart.

"They were dangerous guides the feelings—she herself was not
          exempt—
Truly, she herself had suffered"—Perish in thy self-contempt!

Overlive it—lower yet—be happy! wherefore should I care?
I myself must mix with action, lest I wither by despair.

What is that which I should turn to, lighting upon days like these?
Every door is barred with gold, and opens but to golden keys.   100

Every gate is thronged with suitors, all the markets overflow.
I have but an angry fancy; what is that which I should do?

I had been content to perish, falling on the foeman's ground,
When the ranks are rolled in vapor, and the winds are laid with
          sound.[2]

But the jingling of the guinea helps the hurt that Honor feels,   105
And the nations do but murmur, snarling at each other's heels.

Can I but relive in sadness? I will turn that earlier page.
Hide me from my deep emotion, O thou wondrous Mother-Age![3]

1. Presumably figurative. Her marriage having
become a mockery, she is widowed.
2. It was once believed that the firing of artillery
stilled the winds.

3. A happier past at life's beginning, which generated a more confident anticipation of the future.
See also line 185.

Make me feel the wild pulsation that I felt before the strife,
When I heard my days before me, and the tumult of my life;   110

Yearning for the large excitement that the coming years would yield,
Eager-hearted as a boy when first he leaves his father's field,

And at night along the dusky highway near and nearer drawn,
Sees in heaven the light of London flaring like a dreary dawn;

And his spirit leaps within him to be gone before him then,   115
Underneath the light he looks at, in among the throngs of men;

Men, my brothers, men the workers, ever reaping something new;
That which they have done but earnest[4] of the things that they
        shall do.

For I dipped into the future, far as human eye could see,
Saw the Vision of the world, and all the wonder that would be;   120

Saw the heavens fill with commerce, argosies of magic sails,[5]
Pilots of the purple twilight, dropping down with costly bales;

Heard the heavens fill with shouting, and there rained a ghastly dew
From the nations' airy navies grappling in the central blue;

Far along the world-wide whisper of the south wind rushing
        warm,   125
With the standards of the peoples plunging through the thunder-
        storm;

Till the war drum throbbed no longer, and the battle flags were
        furled
In the Parliament of man, the Federation of the world.

There the common sense of most shall hold a fretful realm in awe,
And the kindly earth shall slumber, lapped in universal law.   130

So I triumphed ere my passion sweeping through me left me dry,
Left me with the palsied heart, and left me with the jaundiced eye;

Eye, to which all order festers, all things here are out of joint.
Science moves, but slowly, slowly, creeping on from point to point;

Slowly comes a hungry people, as a lion, creeping nigher,   135
Glares at one that nods and winks behind a slowly-dying fire.

Yet I doubt not through the ages one increasing purpose runs,
And the thoughts of men are widened with the process of the suns.

4. A pledge.   5. Probably airships, such as balloons.

What is that to him that reaps not harvest of his youthful joys,
Though the deep heart of existence beat forever like a boy's? 140

Knowledge comes, but wisdom lingers, and I linger on the shore,
And the individual withers, and the world is more and more.

Knowledge comes, but wisdom lingers, and he bears a laden breast,
Full of sad experience, moving toward the stillness of his rest.

Hark, my merry comrades call me, sounding on the bugle horn, 145
They to whom my foolish passion were a target for their scorn.

Shall it not be scorn to me to harp on such a moldered string?
I am shamed through all my nature to have loved so slight a thing.

Weakness to be wroth with weakness! woman's pleasure, woman's
    pain—
Nature made them blinder motions bounded in a shallower brain. 150

Woman is the lesser man, and all thy passions, matched with mine,
Are as moonlight unto sunlight, and as water unto wine—

Here at least, where nature sickens, nothing. Ah, for some retreat
Deep in yonder shining Orient, where my life began to beat.

Where in wild Mahratta-battle[6] fell my father evil-starred— 155
I was left a trampled orphan, and a selfish uncle's ward.

Or to burst all links of habit—there to wander far away,
On from island unto island at the gateways of the day.

Larger constellations burning, mellow moons and happy skies,
Breadths of tropic shade and palms in cluster, knots of Paradise. 160

Never comes the trader, never floats an European flag,
Slides the bird o'er lustrous woodland, swings the trailer[7] from the
    crag;

Droops the heavy-blossomed bower, hangs the heavy-fruited tree—
Summer isles of Eden lying in dark purple spheres of sea.

There methinks would be enjoyment more than in this march of
    mind,
In the steamship, in the railway, in the thoughts that shake man-
    kind.

6. A reference to wars waged by a Hindu people against the British forces in India (1803 and 1817).
7. A vine.

There the passions cramped no longer shall have scope and breath-
    ing space;
I will take some savage woman, she shall rear my dusky race.

Iron-jointed, supple-sinewed, they shall dive, and they shall run,
Catch the wild goat by the hair, and hurl their lances in the sun;   170

Whistle back the parrot's call, and leap the rainbows of the brooks,
Not with blinded eyesight poring over miserable books—

Fool, again the dream, the fancy! but I *know* my words are wild,
But I count the gray barbarian lower than the Christian child.

I, to herd with narrow foreheads, vacant of our glorious gains,   175
Like a beast with lower pleasures, like a beast with lower pains!

Mated with a squalid savage—what to me were sun or clime?
I the heir of all the ages, in the foremost files of time—

I that rather held it better men should perish one by one,
Than that earth should stand at gaze like Joshua's moon in
    Ajalon![8]   180

Not in vain the distance beacons. Forward, forward let us range,
Let the great world spin forever down the ringing grooves[9] of change.

Through the shadow of the globe we sweep into the younger day;
Better fifty years of Europe than a cycle of Cathay.[1]

Mother-Age—for mine I knew not—help me as when life begun;   185
Rift the hills, and roll the waters, flash the lightnings, weigh the sun.

O, I see the crescent promise of my spirit hath not set.
Ancient founts of inspiration well through all my fancy yet.

Howsoever these things be, a long farewell to Locksley Hall!
Now for me the woods may wither, now for me the roof-tree fall.   190

Comes a vapor from the margin, blackening over heath and holt,
Cramming all the blast before it, in its breast a thunderbolt.

Let it fall on Locksley Hall, with rain or hail, or fire or snow;
For the mighty wind arises, roaring seaward, and I go.

1837–38   1842

8. At the command of Joshua, the sun and moon stood still while the Israelites completed the slaughter of their enemies in the valley of Ajalon (Joshua 10.12–13).

9. Railroad tracks. Tennyson at one time had the impression that train wheels ran in grooved rails.
1. China, regarded in the 19th century as a static, unprogressive country.

From THE PRINCESS[1]

Sweet and Low

Sweet and low, sweet and low,
    Wind of the western sea,
Low, low, breathe and blow,
    Wind of the western sea!
Over the rolling waters go,   5
Come from the dying moon, and blow,
    Blow him again to me;
While my little one, while my pretty one, sleeps.

Sleep and rest, sleep and rest,
    Father will come to thee soon;   10
Rest, rest, on mother's breast,
    Father will come to thee soon;
Father will come to his babe in the nest,
Silver sails all out of the west
    Under the silver moon;   15
Sleep, my little one, sleep, my pretty one, sleep.

1850

The Splendor Falls

The splendor falls on castle walls
    And snowy summits old in story;
The long light shakes across the lakes,
    And the wild cataract leaps in glory.
Blow, bugle, blow, set the wild echoes flying,   5
Blow, bugle; answer, echoes, dying, dying, dying.

O, hark, O, hear! how thin and clear,
    And thinner, clearer, farther going!
O, sweet and far from cliff and scar[2]
    The horns of Elfland faintly blowing!   10
Blow, let us hear the purple glens replying,
Blow, bugle; answer, echoes, dying, dying, dying.

O love, they die in yon rich sky,
    They faint on hill or field or river;
Our echoes roll from soul to soul,   15
    And grow forever and forever.

1. *The Princess* (1847), a long narrative poem, contains interludes in which occasional songs are sung. The 6 of these in our selection, some of which first appeared in later editions of the poem, rank among the finest of Tennyson's lyrics, and various 19th- and 20th-century composers have set them to music.
2. Mountainside.

Blow, bugle, blow, set the wild echoes flying,
And answer, echoes, answer, dying, dying, dying.

1850

Tears, Idle Tears[3]

Tears, idle tears, I know not what they mean,
Tears from the depth of some divine despair
Rise in the heart, and gather to the eyes,
In looking on the happy autumn-fields,
And thinking of the days that are no more.   5

Fresh as the first beam glittering on a sail,
That brings our friends up from the underworld,
Sad as the last which reddens over one
That sinks with all we love below the verge;
So sad, so fresh, the days that are no more.   10

Ah, sad and strange as in dark summer dawns
The earliest pipe of half-awakened birds
To dying ears, when unto dying eyes
The casement slowly grows a glimmering square;
So sad, so strange, the days that are no more.   15

Dear as remembered kisses after death,
And sweet as those by hopeless fancy feigned
On lips that are for others; deep as love,
Deep as first love, and wild with all regret;
O Death in Life, the days that are no more!   20

1847

Ask Me No More

Ask me no more: the moon may draw the sea;
    The cloud may stoop from heaven and take the shape,
    With fold to fold, of mountain or of cape;
But O too fond, when have I answered thee?
                Ask me no more.   5

Ask me no more: what answer should I give?
    I love not hollow cheek or faded eye:

---

3. Tennyson commented: "This song came to me on the yellowing autumn-tide at Tintern Abbey, full for me of its bygone memories." This locale would be for him associated both with Wordsworth's *Tintern Abbey* and with memories of Hallam, who was buried across the Bristol Channel in this area. "It is what I have always felt even from a boy, and what as a boy I called the 'passion of the past.' And it is so always with me now; it is the distance that charms me in the landscape, the picture and the past, and not the immediate today in which I move."

Yet, O my friend, I will not have thee die!
Ask me no more, lest I should bid thee live;
             Ask me no more.   10

Ask me no more: thy fate and mine are sealed;
    I strove against the stream and all in vain;
    Let the great river take me to the main.
No more, dear love, for at a touch I yield;
             Ask me no more.   15

1850

Now Sleeps the Crimson Petal

Now sleeps the crimson petal, now the white;
Nor waves the cypress in the palace walk;
Nor winks the gold fin in the porphyry font.
The firefly wakens; waken thou with me.

Now droops the milk-white peacock like a ghost,   5
And like a ghost she glimmers on to me.

Now lies the Earth all Danaë[4] to the stars,
And all thy heart lies open unto me.

Now slides the silent meteor on, and leaves
A shining furrow, as thy thoughts in me.   10

Now folds the lily all her sweetness up,
And slips into the bosom of the lake.
So fold thyself, my dearest, thou, and slip
Into my bosom and be lost in me.

1847

Come Down, O Maid[5]

Come down, O maid, from yonder mountain height.
What pleasure lives in height (the shepherd sang),
In height and cold, the splendor of the hills?
But cease to move so near the heavens, and cease
To glide a sunbeam by the blasted pine,   5
To sit a star upon the sparkling spire;

4. Danaë, a Greek princess, was confined in a metal tower by her father to prevent suitors from coming near her. Zeus, however, succeeded in visiting her in the form of a shower of gold. Their offspring was the hero Perseus.
5. Written during Tennyson's visit to the Swiss Alps in 1846, after he had seen Mount Jungfrau ("The Maiden").

And come, for Love is of the valley, come,
For Love is of the valley, come thou down
And find him; by the happy threshold, he,
Or hand in hand with Plenty in the maize,   10
Or red with spirted purple of the vats,
Or foxlike in the vine;[6] nor cares to walk
With Death and Morning on the Silver Horns,[7]
Nor wilt thou snare him in the white ravine,
Nor find him dropped upon the firths of ice,[8]   15
That huddling slant in furrow-cloven falls
To roll the torrent out of dusky doors.[9]
But follow; let the torrent dance thee down
To find him in the valley; let the wild
Lean-headed eagles yelp alone, and leave   20
The monstrous ledges there to slope, and spill
Their thousand wreaths of dangling water-smoke,
That like a broken purpose waste in air.
So waste not thou, but come; for all the vales
Await thee; azure pillars of the hearth[1]   25
Arise to thee; the children call, and I
Thy shepherd pipe, and sweet is every sound,
Sweeter thy voice, but every sound is sweet;
Myriads of rivulets hurrying through the lawn,
The moan of doves in immemorial elms,   30
And murmuring of innumerable bees.

                                               1847

["The Woman's Cause Is Man's"][2]

    "Blame not thyself too much," I said, "nor blame
Too much the sons of men and barbarous laws;   240
These were the rough ways of the world till now.
Henceforth thou hast a helper, me, that know
The woman's cause is man's: they rise or sink
Together, dwarfed or godlike, bond or free:
For she that out of Lethe scales with man   245
The shining steps of Nature, shares with man
His nights, his days, moves with him to one goal,
Stays all the fair young planet in her hands—

---

6. This image comes from the Song of Solomon
2.15.
7. Mountain peaks.
8. Glaciers.
9. Heaps of rock and refuse at the base of a glacier
through which the mountain torrent forces its way
down to the valley below.
1. Columns of smoke from the houses in the valley.
2. *The Princess* tells the story of a prince who courts

the young and beautiful Princess Ida, who has
established a university from which men are
excluded; she has also vowed she will never marry.
At the end she is persuaded that her feminist
experiment was a failure, but the prince assures
her that ideal relations between men and women
may be achieved in the future. Our selection, covering the prince's key speech, is from book 7, lines
239–91.

If she be small, slight-natured, miserable,
How shall men grow? but work no more alone!   250
Our place is much: as far as in us lies
We two will serve them both in aiding her—
Will clear away the parasitic forms
That seem to keep her up but drag her down—
Will leave her space to burgeon out of all   255
Within her—let her make herself her own
To give or keep, to live and learn and be
All that not harms distinctive womanhood.
For woman is not undevelopt man,
But diverse: could we make her as the man,   260
Sweet Love were slain: his dearest bond is this,
Not like to like, but like in difference.
Yet in the long years liker must they grow;
The man be more of woman, she of man;
He gain in sweetness and in moral height,   265
Nor lose the wrestling thews that throw the world;
She mental breadth, nor fail in childward care,
Nor lose the childlike in the larger mind;
Till at the last she set herself to man,
Like perfect music unto noble words;   270
And so these twain, upon the skirts of Time,
Sit side by side, full-summed in all their powers,
Dispensing harvest, sowing the To-be,
Self-reverent each and reverencing each,
Distinct in individualities,   275
But like each other even as those who love.
Then comes the statelier Eden back to men:
Then reign the world's great bridals, chaste and calm:
Then springs the crowning race of humankind.
May these things be!"
                    Sighing she spoke "I fear
They will not."   280
          "Dear, but let us type them now
In our own lives, and this proud watchword rest
Of equal; seeing either sex alone
Is half itself, and in true marriage lies
Nor equal, nor unequal: each fulfils   285
Defect in each, and always thought in thought,
Purpose in purpose, will in will, they grow,
The single pure and perfect animal,
The two-celled heart beating, with one full stroke,
Life."
          And again sighing she spoke: "A dream   290
That once was mine! what woman taught you this?"

1839–47   1847

In Memoriam A. H. H.   Like most of Tennyson's writings, *In Memoriam* shows his debt to earlier poetry. In its celebration of male friendship, as Christopher Ricks has shown, the poem has many affinities with Shakespeare's *Sonnets*, and as an elegy it is of course in the tradition of Milton's *Lycidas* and Shelley's *Adonais*. Its structure, however, is strikingly different. Resembling a song cycle more than a symphony, it is made up of individual lyric units, seemingly self-sustaining, that may be enjoyed by themselves even though the full pleasure to be derived from each component depends upon its relationship to the poem as a whole. The circumstances of the poem's composition help to explain how this new kind of elegy was evolved. The sudden death of Arthur Hallam at the age of twenty-two had a profound effect on Tennyson. The young poet had cherished Hallam not only as his closest friend and the fiancé of his sister but as an all-wise counselor upon whose judgment he depended for guidance. This fatherly prop having been pulled away, Tennyson was overwhelmed with doubts about the meaning of life and man's role in the universe, doubts reinforced by his own study of geology and other sciences. As a kind of poetic diary recording the variety of his feelings and reflections he began to compose a series of lyrics. These "short swallow-flights of song," as he calls them, written at intervals over a period of seventeen years, were later arranged into one long elegy in which a progressive development from despair to some sort of hope, as in section 95, is recorded.

Some of the early sections of the poem resemble traditional pastoral elegies, including those portraying the voyage during which Hallam's body was brought to England for burial (sections 9–15 and 19). Other early sections portraying the speaker's loneliness, in which even Christmas festivities seem joyless (section 28–30), are more distinctive. With the passage of time, indicated by anniversaries and by recurring changes of the seasons, the speaker comes to accept the loss and to assert his belief in life and in an afterlife. In particular the recurring Christmases (section 28, 78, 104) indicate the stages of his development, yet the pattern of progress in the poem is not a simple unimpeded movement upwards. Dramatic conflicts recur throughout. Thus the most intense expression of doubt occurs not at the beginning of *In Memoriam* but as late as sections 54, 55, and 56.

The quatrain form in which the whole poem is written is usually called the *"In Memoriam* stanza," although it had been occasionally used by earlier poets. So rigid a form taxed Tennyson's ingenuity in achieving variety, but it is one of several means by which the diverse parts of the poem are knitted together.

The introductory section, consisting of eleven stanzas, is commonly referred to as the "Prologue," although Tennyson did not assign a title to it. It was written in 1849 after the rest of the poem was complete.

From IN MEMORIAM A. H. H.

OBIIT MDCCCXXXIII[1]

Strong Son of God, immortal Love,
     Whom we, that have not seen thy face,

---

1. Died 1833.

By faith, and faith alone, embrace,
Believing where we cannot prove;[2]

Thine are these orbs[3] of light and shade;   5
   Thou madest Life in man and brute;
   Thou madest Death; and lo, thy foot
Is on the skull which thou hast made.

Thou wilt not leave us in the dust:
   Thou madest man, he knows not why,   10
   He thinks he was not made to die;
And thou hast made him: thou art just.

Thou seemest human and divine,
   The highest, holiest manhood, thou.
   Our wills are ours, we know not how;   15
Our wills are ours, to make them thine.

Our little systems[4] have their day;
   They have their day and cease to be;
   They are but broken lights of thee,
And thou, O Lord, art more than they.   20

We have but faith: we cannot know,
   For knowledge is of things we see;
   And yet we trust it comes from thee,
A beam in darkness: let it grow.

Let knowledge grow from more to more,   25
   But more of reverence in us dwell;
   That mind and soul, according well,
May make one music as before,[5]

But vaster. We are fools and slight;
   We mock thee when we do not fear: 30
   But help thy foolish ones to bear;
Help thy vain worlds to bear thy light.

Forgive what seemed my sin in me,
   What seemed my worth since I began;
   For merit lives from man to man,   35
And not from man, O Lord, to thee.

---

2. See John 20.24–29, in which Jesus rebukes
Thomas for his doubts concerning the Resurrection: "Blessed are they that have not seen, and yet
have believed." For first line of poem, cf. Love, by
George Herbert: "Immortal Love, Author of this
great frame, / Sprung from that beauty which can
never fade, How hath Man parceled out Thy glorious name, / And thrown it on the dust which
Thou hast made?" [noted by R. W. Hill].
3. Planets.
4. Systems of religion and philosophy.
5. As in the days of fixed religious faith.

Forgive my grief for one removed,
    Thy creature, whom I found so fair.
      I trust he lives in thee, and there
I find him worthier to be loved.   40

Forgive these wild and wandering cries,
    Confusions of a wasted[6] youth;
      Forgive them where they fail in truth,
And in thy wisdom make me wise.

1849

1

I held it truth, with him who sings
    To one clear harp in divers tones,[7]
      That men may rise on stepping stones
Of their dead selves to higher things.

But who shall so forecast the years   5
    And find in loss a gain to match?
      Or reach a hand through time to catch
The far-off interest of tears?

Let Love clasp Grief lest both be drowned,
    Let darkness keep her raven gloss.   10
      Ah, sweeter to be drunk with loss,
To dance with Death, to beat the ground,

Than that the victor Hours should scorn
    The long result of love, and boast,
      "Behold the man that loved and lost,   15
But all he was is overworn."

2

Old yew, which graspest at the stones
    That name the underlying dead,
      Thy fibers net the dreamless head,
Thy roots are wrapped about the bones.

The seasons bring the flower again,   5
    And bring the firstling to the flock;
      And in the dusk of thee the clock
Beats out the little lives of men.

O, not for thee the glow, the bloom,
    Who changest not in any gale,   10
      Nor branding summer suns avail
To touch thy thousand years of gloom;[8]

---

6. Desolated.
7. Identified by Tennyson as Goethe.
8. The ancient yew tree, growing in the grounds near the clock tower and church where Hallam was to be buried, seems neither to blossom in spring nor change from its dark mournful color in summer.

And gazing on thee, sullen tree,
   Sick for[9] thy stubborn hardihood,
   I seem to fail from out my blood   15
And grow incorporate into thee.

3

O Sorrow, cruel fellowship,
   O Priestess in the vaults of Death,
   O sweet and bitter in a breath,
What whispers from thy lying lip?

"The stars," she whispers, "blindly run;   5
   A web is woven across the sky;
   From out waste places comes a cry,
And murmurs from the dying sun;

"And all the phantom, Nature, stands—
   With all the music in her tone,   10
   A hollow echo of my own—
A hollow form with empty hands."

And shall I take a thing so blind,
   Embrace her[1] as my natural good;
   Or crush her, like a vice of blood,   15
Upon the threshold of the mind?

4

To Sleep I give my powers away;
   My will is bondsman to the dark;
   I sit within a helmless bark,
And with my heart I muse and say:

O heart, how fares it with thee now,   5
   That thou should fail from thy desire,
   Who scarcely darest to inquire,
"What is it makes me beat so low?"

Something it is which thou hast lost,
   Some pleasure from thine early years.   10
   Break thou deep vase of chilling tears,
That grief hath shaken into frost![2]

Such clouds of nameless trouble cross
   All night below the darkened eyes;
   With morning wakes the will, and cries,   15
"Thou shalt not be the fool of loss."

---

9. Envying or longing to share.
1. I.e., sorrow.
2. Tennyson comments: "Water can be brought below freezing-point and not turn into ice—if it be kept still; but if it be moved suddenly it turns into ice and may break a vase."

5

I sometimes hold it half a sin
   To put in words the grief I feel;
   For words, like Nature, half reveal
And half conceal the Soul within.

But, for the unquiet heart and brain,
   A use in measured language lies;   5
   The sad mechanic exercise,
Like dull narcotics, numbing pain.

In words, like weeds,[3] I'll wrap me o'er,
   Like coarsest clothes against the cold;   10
   But that large grief which these enfold
Is given in outline and no more.

6

One writes, that "Other friends remain,"
   That "Loss is common to the race"—
   And common is the commonplace,
And vacant chaff well meant for grain.

That loss is common would not make   5
   My own less bitter, rather more:
   Too common! Never morning wore
To evening, but some heart did break.

O father, wheresoe'er thou be,
   Who pledgest[4] now thy gallant son;   10
   A shot, ere half thy draft be done,
Hath stilled the life that beat from thee.

O mother, praying God will save
   Thy sailor—while thy head is bowed,
   His heavy-shotted hammock-shroud   15
Drops in his vast and wandering grave.

Ye know no more than I who wrought
   At that last hour to please him well;[5]
   Who mused on all I had to tell,
And something written, something thought;   20

Expecting still his advent home;
   And ever met him on his way
   With wishes, thinking, "here today,"
Or "here tomorrow will he come."

3. Garments.
4. Toasts.
5. According to Tennyson's son, his father had discovered that he had been writing a letter to Hallam during the very hour when his friend died.

O somewhere, meek, the unconscious dove,   25
    That sittest ranging[6] golden hair;
    And glad to find thyself so fair,
Poor child, that waitest for thy love!

For now her father's chimney glows
    In expectation of a guest;   30
    And thinking "this will please him best,"
She takes a riband or a rose;

For he will see them on tonight;
    And with the thought her color burns;
    And, having left the glass, she turns   35
Once more to set a ringlet right;

And, even when she turned, the curse
    Had fallen, and her future Lord
    Was drowned in passing through the ford,
Or killed in falling from his horse.   40

O what to her shall be the end?
    And what to me remains of good?
    To her, perpetual maidenhood,
And unto me no second friend.

7

Dark house,[7] by which once more I stand
    Here in the long unlovely street,
    Doors, where my heart was used to beat
So quickly, waiting for a hand,

A hand that can be clasped no more—   5
    Behold me, for I cannot sleep,
    And like a guilty thing I creep
At earliest morning to the door.

He is not here; but far away
    The noise of life begins again,   10
    And ghastly through the drizzling rain
On the bald street breaks the blank day.

*   *   *

9

Fair ship, that from the Italian shore
    Sailest the placid ocean-plains
With my lost Arthur's loved remains,
    Spread thy full wings, and waft him o'er.

6. Arranging.
7. House on Wimpole Street, in London, where Hallam had lived.

So draw him home to those that mourn   5
   In vain; a favorable speed
   Ruffle thy mirrored mast, and lead
Through prosperous floods his holy urn.

All night no ruder air perplex
   Thy sliding keel, till Phosphor,[8] bright   10
   As our pure love, through early light
Shall glimmer on the dewey decks.

Sphere all your lights around, above;
   Sleep, gentle heavens, before the prow;
   Sleep, gentle winds, as he sleeps now,   15
My friend, the brother of my love;

My Arthur, whom I shall not see
   Till all my widowed race be run;
   Dear as the mother to the son,
More than my brothers are to me.   20

10

I hear the noise about thy keel;
   I hear the bell struck in the night;
   I see the cabin window bright;
I see the sailor at the wheel.

Thou bring'st the sailor to his wife,   5
   And traveled men from foreign lands;
   And letters unto trembling hands;
And, thy dark freight, a vanished life.

So bring him; we have idle dreams;
   This look of quiet flatters thus   10
   Our home-bred fancies. O, to us,
The fools of habit, sweeter seems

To rest beneath the clover sod,
   That takes the sunshine and the rains,
   Or where the kneeling hamlet drains   15
The chalice of the grapes of God;[9]

Than if with thee the roaring wells
   Should gulf him fathom-deep in brine,
   And hands so often clasped in mine,
Should toss with tangle[1] and with shells.   20

11

Calm is the morn without a sound,
   Calm as to suit a calmer grief,

---

8. The morning star.
9. Referring to a burial inside a church building
rather than in the churchyard.
1. Seaweed.

And only through the faded leaf
The chestnut pattering to the ground;

Calm and deep peace on this high wold,[2]   5
    And on these dews that drench the furze,
    And all the silvery gossamers
That twinkle into green and gold;

Calm and still light on yon great plain
    That sweeps with all its autumn bowers,   10
    And crowded farms and lessening towers,
To mingle with the bounding main;

Calm and deep peace in this wide air,
    These leaves that redden to the fall,
    And in my heart, if calm at all,   15
If any calm, a calm despair;

Calm on the seas, and silver sleep,
    And waves that sway themselves in rest,
    And dead calm in that noble breast
Which heaves but with the heaving deep.[3]   20

                    12
Lo, as a dove when up she springs
    To bear through Heaven a tale of woe,
    Some dolorous message knit below
The wild pulsation of her wings;

Like her I go; I cannot stay;   5
    I leave this mortal ark behind,[4]
    A weight of nerves without a mind,
And leave the cliffs, and haste away

O'er ocean-mirrors rounded large,
    And reach the glow of southern skies,   10
    And see the sails at distance rise,
And linger weeping on the marge,

And saying; "Comes he thus, my friend?
    Is this the end of all my care?"
    And circle moaning in the air: 15
"Is this the end? Is this the end?"

---

2. High and open countryside.
3. It is now the autumn of 1833, and the poet imagines that Hallam's body was already being brought back by ship to England. The date of the actual voyage seems to have been later in the year.
4. According to Christopher Ricks, the account of the imagined flight of the soul refers to Genesis 8.8, when Noah first sends a dove from the ark to discover whether the flood has subsided, "but the dove found no rest for the sole of her foot, and she returned unto him into the ark, for the waters were on the face of the earth."

And forward dart again, and play
   About the prow, and back return
   To where the body sits, and learn
That I have been an hour away.   20

13

Tears of the widower, when he sees
   A late-lost form that sleep reveals,
   And moves his doubtful arms, and feels
Her place is empty, fall like these;

Which weep a loss forever new,   5
   A void where heart on heart reposed;
   And, where warm hands have pressed and closed,
Silence, till I be silent too;

Which weep the comrade of my choice,
   An awful thought, a life removed,   10
   The human-hearted man I loved,
A Spirit, not a breathing voice.

Come, Time, and teach me, many years,
   I do not suffer in a dream;
   For now so strange do these things seem,   15
Mine eyes have leisure for their tears,

My fancies time to rise on wing,
   And glance about the approaching sails,
   As though they brought but merchants' bales,
And not the burthen that they bring.[5]   20

14

If one should bring me this report,
   That thou[6] hadst touched the land today,
   And I went down unto the quay;
And found thee lying in the port;

And standing, muffled round with woe,   5
   Should see thy passengers in rank
   Come stepping lightly down the plank
And beckoning unto those they know;

And if along with these should come
   The man I held as half divine,   10
   Should strike a sudden hand in mine,
And ask a thousand things of home;

---

5. The speaker asks Time to teach him to confront the awesome fact of what has happened (line
10) so that he will not delude himself by fancying
the ship is bearing only merchandise and not the
body of his friend.
6. I.e., the ship.

And I should tell him all my pain,
   And how my life had drooped of late,
   And he should sorrow o'er my state   15
And marvel what possessed my brain;

And I perceived no touch of change,
   No hint of death in all his frame,
   But found him all in all the same,
I should not feel it to be strange.   20

15

Tonight the winds begin to rise
   And roar from yonder dropping day;
   The last red leaf is whirled away,
The rooks are blown about the skies;

The forest cracked, the waters curled,   5
   The cattle huddled on the lea;
   And wildly dashed on tower and tree
The sunbeam strikes along the world:

And but for fancies, which aver
   That all thy motions gently pass   10
   Athwart a plane of molten glass,
I scarce could brook the strain and stir

That makes the barren branches loud;
   And but for fear it is not so,
   The wild unrest that lives in woe   15
Would dote and pore on yonder cloud

That rises upward always higher,
   And onward drags a laboring breast,
   And topples round the dreary west,
A looming bastion fringed with fire.   20

*   *   *

19

The Danube to the Severn[7] gave
   The darkened heart that beat no more;
   They laid him by the pleasant shore,
And in the hearing of the wave.

There twice a day the Severn fills;   5
   The salt sea water passes by,
   And hushes half the babbling Wye,[8]
And makes a silence in the hills.

---

7. Hallam died at Vienna on the Danube. His burial place is on the banks of the Severn, a tidal river in the southwest of England.
8. The water of the Wye River, a tributary of the Severn, is dammed up as the tide flows in, and its sound is silenced until, with the turn of the tide, its "wave" once more becomes "vocal" (lines 13–14); these stanzas were written at Tintern Abbey in the Wye River country.

The Wye is hushed nor moved along,
    And hushed my deepest grief of all,   10
    When filled with tears that cannot fall,
I brim with sorrow drowning song.

The tide flows down, the wave again
    Is vocal in its wooded walls;
    My deeper anguish also falls,   15
And I can speak a little then.

*   *   *

21

I sing to him that rests below,
    And, since the grasses round me wave,
    I take the grasses of the grave,[9]
And make them pipes whereon to blow.

The traveler hears me now and then,   5
    And sometimes harshly will he speak:
    "This fellow would make weakness weak,
And melt the waxen hearts of men."

Another answers: "Let him be,
    He loves to make parade of pain,   10
    That with his piping he may gain
The praise that comes to constancy."

A third is wroth: "Is this an hour
    For private sorrow's barren song,
    When more and more the people throng   15
The chairs and thrones of civil power?

"A time to sicken and to swoon,
    When Science reaches forth her arms[1]
    To feel from world to world, and charms
Her secret from the latest moon?"[2]   20

Behold, ye speak an idle thing;
    Ye never knew the sacred dust.
    I do but sing because I must,
And pipe but as the linnets sing:

And one is glad; her note is gay,   25
    For now her little ones have ranged;
    And one is sad; her note is changed,
Because her brood is stolen away.

9. The speaker assumes that the burial was in the churchyard; in fact, Hallam's body was interred in a vault inside St. Andrews church at Clevedon, Somersetshire, on Jan. 3, 1834. See section 10, lines 11–16.
1. Astronomical instruments such as telescopes.
2. Probably alluding to the discovery in 1846, of the planet Neptune and its moon.

22

The path by which we twain did go,
    Which led by tracts that pleased us well,
    Through four sweet years arose and fell,
From flower to flower, from snow to snow;

And we with singing cheered the way,   5
    And, crowned with all the season lent,
    From April on to April went,
And glad at heart from May to May.

But where the path we walked began
    To slant the fifth autumnal slope,[3]   10
    As we descended following Hope,
There sat the Shadow feared of man;

Who broke our fair companionship,
    And spread his mantle dark and cold,
    And wrapped thee formless in the fold,   15
And dulled the murmur on thy lip,

And bore thee where I could not see
    Nor follow, though I walk in haste,
    And think that somewhere in the waste
The Shadow sits and waits for me.   20

23

Now, sometimes in my sorrow shut,
    Or breaking into song by fits,
    Alone, alone, to where he sits,
The Shadow cloaked from head to foot,

Who keeps the keys of all the creeds,   5
    I wander, often falling lame,
    And looking back to whence I came,
Or on to where the pathway leads;

And crying, How changed from where it ran
    Through lands where not a leaf was dumb,   10
    But all the lavish hills would hum
The murmur of a happy Pan;

When each by turns was guide to each,
    And Fancy light from Fancy caught,
    And Thought leapt out to wed with Thought   15
Ere Thought could wed itself with Speech;

And all we met was fair and good,
    And all was good that Time could bring,

---

3. Hallam died in early autumn (Sept. 15, 1833) in the fifth year of the friendship.

And all the secret of the Spring
   Moved in the chambers of the blood;   20

And many an old philosophy
   On Argive heights divinely sang,
   And round us all the thicket rang
To many a flute of Arcady.[4]

24

And was the day of my delight
   As pure and perfect as I say?
   The very source and fount of day
Is dashed with wandering isles of night.[5]

If all was good and fair we met,   5
   This earth had been the Paradise
   It never looked to human eyes
Since our first sun arose and set.

And is it that the haze of grief
   Makes former gladness loom so great?   10
   The lowness of the present state,
That sets the past in this relief?

Or that the past will always win
   A glory from its being far,
   And orb into the perfect star   15
We saw not when we moved therein?[6]

25

I know that this was Life—the track
   Whereon with equal feet we fared;
   And then, as now, the day prepared
The daily burden for the back.

But this it was that made me move   5
   As light as carrier birds in air;
   I loved the weight I had to bear,
Because it needed help of Love;

Nor could I weary, heart or limb,
   When mighty Love would cleave in twain   10
   The lading[7] of a single pain,
And part it, giving half to him.

---

4. Sheep-raising region in Greece associated with pastoral poetry; Argos ("Argive heights") was a Greek city renowned for its music.
5. Moving spots on the sun.
6. The speaker speculates whether past experiences seem so much more "pure and perfect" (line 2) than present ones because they are far distant from us in time just as our planet Earth would have the deceptive appearance of being a perfect orb if we viewed it from a great distance in space, as from another planet. See *Locksley Hall Sixty Years After*, lines 187–92.
7. Burden.

26

Still onward winds the dreary way;
    I with it, for I long to prove
    No lapse of moons can canker Love,
Whatever fickle tongues may say.

And if that eye which watches guilt   5
    And goodness, and hath power to see
    Within the green the mouldered tree,
And towers fallen as soon as built—

O, if indeed that eye foresee
    Or see—in Him is no before—   10
    In more of life true life no more
And Love the indifference to be,

Then might I find, ere yet the morn
    Breaks hither over Indian seas,
    That Shadow waiting with the keys,   15
To shroud me from my proper scorn.[8]

27

I envy not in any moods
    The captive void of noble rage,
    The linnet born within the cage,
That never knew the summer woods;

I envy not the beast that takes   5
    His license in the field of time,
    Unfettered by the sense of crime,
To whom a conscience never wakes;

Nor, what may count itself as blest,
    The heart that never plighted troth   10
    But stagnates in the weeds of sloth;
Nor any want-begotten rest.[9]

I hold it true, whate'er befall;
    I feel it, when I sorrow most;
    'Tis better to have loved and lost   15
Than never to have loved at all.

28

The time draws near the birth of Christ.[1]
    The moon is hid, the night is still;
    The Christmas bells from hill to hill
Answer each other in the mist.

---

8. The Deity, being outside time, sees (rather than foresees) whether or not the rest of life ("more of life," line 11) will be pointless. If pointless then the way for the speaker to deal with his self-scorn ("proper scorn") might be to seek death.

9. Complacency resulting from some deficiency or "want."

1. The first Christmas after Hallam's death (1833); the setting is Tennyson's family home in Lincolnshire.

Four voices of four hamlets round,   5
    From far and near, on mead and moor,
    Swell out and fail, as if a door
Were shut between me and the sound;

Each voice four changes[2] on the wind,
    That now dilate, and now decrease,   10
    Peace and goodwill, goodwill and peace,
Peace and goodwill, to all mankind.

This year I slept and woke with pain,
    I almost wished no more to wake,
    And that my hold on life would break   15
Before I heard those bells again;

But they my troubled spirit rule,
    For they controlled me when a boy;
    They bring me sorrow touched with joy,
The merry, merry bells of Yule.   20

29

With such compelling cause to grieve
    As daily vexes household peace,
    And chains regret to his decease,
How dare we keep our Christmas eve;

Which brings no more a welcome guest   5
    To enrich the threshold of the night
    With showered largess of delight
In dance and song and game and jest?

Yet go, and while the holly boughs
    Entwine the cold baptismal font,   10
    Make one wreath more for Use and Wont,[3]
That guard the portals of the house;

Old sisters of a day gone by,
    Gray nurses, loving nothing new;
    Why should they miss their yearly due   15
Before their time? They too will die.

30

With trembling fingers did we weave
    The holly round the Christmas hearth;
    A rainy cloud possessed the earth,
And sadly fell our Christmas eve.

At our old pastimes in the hall   5
    We gamboled, making vain pretense

---

2. Different sequences in which church bells are pealed.
3. Personifying the spirits who expect customary observances of the Christmas season to be followed.

Of gladness, with an awful sense
Of one mute Shadow watching all.

We paused: the winds were in the beech;
　　We heard them sweep the winter land;　　　10
　　And in a circle hand-in-hand
Sat silent, looking each at each.

Then echo-like our voices rang;
　　We sung, though every eye was dim,
　　A merry song we sang with him　　　15
Last year; impetuously we sang.

We ceased; a gentler feeling crept
　　Upon us: surely rest is meet.[4]
　　"They rest," we said, "their sleep is sweet,"
And silence followed, and we wept.　　　20

Our voices took a higher range;
　　Once more we sang: "They do not die
　　Nor lose their mortal sympathy,
Nor change to us, although they change;

"Rapt[5] from the fickle and the frail　　　25
　　With gathered power, yet the same,
　　Pierces the keen seraphic flame
From orb to orb,[6] from veil to veil."

Rise, happy morn, rise, holy morn,
　　Draw forth the cheerful day from night:　　　30
　　O Father, touch the east, and light
The light that shone when Hope was born.

＊　＊　＊

34

My own dim life should teach me this,
　　That life shall live forevermore,
　　Else earth is darkness at the core,
And dust and ashes all that is;

This round of green, this orb of flame,　　　5
　　Fantastic beauty; such as lurks
　　In some wild poet, when he works
Without a conscience or an aim.[7]

4. Proper or appropriate.
5. Carried away from.
6. The angelic spirit ("flame") of the dead moves from star to star.

7. Perhaps Thomas Lovell Beddoes, a brilliantly promising but erratic poet, admired by Tennyson, who committed suicide in 1849.

What then were God to such as I?
  'Twere hardly worth my while to choose   10
  Of things all mortal, or to use
A little patience ere I die;

'Twere best at once to sink to peace,
  Like birds the charming serpent draws,[8]
  To drop head-foremost in the jaws   15
Of vacant darkness and to cease.

35

Yet if some voice that man could trust
  Should murmur from the narrow house,
  "The cheeks drop in, the body bows;
Man dies, nor is there hope in dust";

Might I not say? "Yet even here,   5
  But for one hour, O Love, I strive
  To keep so sweet a thing alive."
But I should turn mine ears and hear

The moanings of the homeless sea,
  The sound of streams that swift or slow   10
  Draw down Aeonian hills,[9] and sow
The dust of continents to be;

And Love would answer with a sigh,
  "The sound of that forgetful shore
  Will change my sweetness more and more,   15
Half-dead to know that I shall die."

O me, what profits it to put
  An idle case? If Death were seen
  At first as Death, Love had not been,
Or been in narrowest working shut,   20

Mere fellowship of sluggish moods,
  Or in his coarsest Satyr-shape
  Had bruised the herb and crushed the grape,
And basked and battened in the woods.[1]

* * *

39

Old warder of these buried bones,
  And answering now my random stroke

---

8. Some snakes are reputed to capture their prey by casting a charm.
9. Hills that are aeons old, seemingly everlasting.
1. Lines 18 ff. may be paraphrased: if we knew death to be final and that no afterlife were possible, love could not exist except on a primitive or bestial level.

With fruitful cloud and living smoke,
Dark yew, that graspest at the stones

And dippest toward the dreamless head,   5
    To thee too comes the golden hour
    When flower is feeling after flower;[2]
But Sorrow—fixed upon the dead,

And darkening the dark graves of men—
    What whispered from her lying lips?   10
    Thy gloom is kindled at the tips,[3]
And passes into gloom again.

                    *   *   *

                    47
That each, who seems a separate whole,
    Should move his rounds,[4] and fusing all
    The skirts[5] of self again, should fall
Remerging in the general Soul,

Is faith as vague as all unsweet.   5
    Eternal form shall still divide
    The eternal soul from all beside;
And I shall know him when we meet;

And we shall sit at endless feast,
    Enjoying each the other's good.   10
    What vaster dream can hit the mood
Of Love on earth? He seeks at least

Upon the last and sharpest height,
    Before the spirits fade away,
    Some landing place, to clasp and say,   15
"Farewell! We lose ourselves in light."

                    48
If these brief lays, of Sorrow born,
    Were taken to be such as closed
    Grave doubts and answers here proposed,
Then these were such as men might scorn.

Her[6] care is not to part and prove;   5
    She takes, when harsher moods remit,
    What slender shade of doubt may flit,
And makes it vassal unto love;

And hence, indeed, she sports with words,
  But better serves a wholesome law,   10
  And holds it sin and shame to draw
The deepest measure from the chords;

Nor dare she trust a larger lay,
  But rather loosens from the lip
  Short swallow-flights of song, that dip   15
Their wings in tears, and skim away.

*   *   *

50

Be near me when my light is low,
  When the blood creeps, and the nerves prick
  And tingle; and the heart is sick,
And all the wheels of being slow.

Be near me when the sensuous frame
  Is racked with pangs that conquer trust;
  And Time, a maniac scattering dust,
And Life, a Fury slinging flame.

Be near me when my faith is dry,
  And men the flies of latter spring,   10
  That lay their eggs, and sting and sing
And weave their petty cells and die.

Be near me when I fade away,
  To point the term of human strife,
  And on the low dark verge of life   15
The twilight of eternal day.

*   *   *

54

O, yet we trust that somehow good
  Will be the final goal of ill,
  To pangs of nature, sins of will,
Defects of doubt, and taints of blood;

That nothing walks with aimless feet;
  That not one life shall be destroyed,
  Or cast as rubbish to the void,
When God hath made the pile complete;

That not a worm is cloven in vain;
  That not a moth with vain desire   10
  Is shriveled in a fruitless fire,
Or but subserves another's gain.

Behold, we know not anything;
   I can but trust that good shall fall
   At last—far off—at last, to all,   15
And every winter change to spring.

So runs my dream; but what am I?
   An infant crying in the night;
   An infant crying for the light,
And with no language but a cry.   20

55

The wish, that of the living whole
   No life may fail beyond the grave,
   Derives it not from what we have
The likest God within the soul?

Are God and Nature then at strife,   5
   That Nature lends such evil dreams?
   So careful of the type[7] she seems,
So careless of the single life,

That I, considering everywhere
   Her secret meaning in her deeds,   10
   And finding that of fifty seeds
She often brings but one to bear,

I falter where I firmly trod,
   And falling with my weight of cares
   Upon the great world's altar-stairs   15
That slope through darkness up to God,

I stretch lame hands of faith, and grope,
   And gather dust and chaff, and call
   To what I feel is Lord of all,
And faintly trust the larger hope.[8]   20

56

"So careful of the type?" but no.
   From scarpèd[9] cliff and quarried stone
   She[1] cries, "A thousand types are gone;
I care for nothing, all shall go.

"Thou makest thine appeal to me: 5
   I bring to life, I bring to death;
   The spirit does but mean the breath:
I know no more." And he, shall he,

Man, her last work, who seemed so fair,
   Such splendid purpose in his eyes,   10

7. Species.
8. As expressed in lines 1–2 of this section.
9. Cut away so that the strata are exposed.
1. Nature.

Who rolled the psalm to wintry skies,
Who built him fanes[2] of fruitless prayer,

Who trusted God was love indeed
   And love Creation's final law—
   Though Nature, red in tooth and claw   15
With ravine, shrieked against his creed—

Who loved, who suffered countless ills,
   Who battled for the True, the Just,
   Be blown about the desert dust,
Or sealed within the iron hills?[3]   20

No more? A monster then, a dream,
   A discord. Dragons of the prime,
   That tare[4] each other in their slime,
Were mellow music matched with[5] him.

O life as futile, then, as frail!   25
   O for thy voice to soothe and bless!
   What hope of answer, or redress?
Behind the veil, behind the veil.

57

Peace; come away:[6] the song of woe
   Is after all an earthly song.
   Peace; come away: we do him wrong
To sing so wildly: let us go.

Come; let us go: your cheeks are pale;   5
   But half my life I leave behind.
   Methinks my friend is richly shrined;
But I shall pass, my work will fail.

Yet in these ears, till hearing dies,
   One set slow bell will seem to toll   10
   The passing of the sweetest soul
That ever looked with human eyes.

I hear it now, and o'er and o'er,
   Eternal greetings to the dead;
   And "Ave,[7] Ave, Ave," said,   15
"Adieu, adieu," forevermore.

*   *   *

2. Temples.
3. Preserved like fossils in rock.
4. Tore (archaic).
5. In comparison with.

6. Perhaps addressed to Emily Tennyson, the poet's sister and Hallam's fiancée.
7. Hail.

67

When on my bed the moonlight falls,
  I know that in thy place of rest
  By that broad water of the west[8]
There comes a glory on the walls:

Thy marble bright in dark appears,   5
  As slowly steals a silver flame
  Along the letters of thy name,
And o'er the number of thy years.

The mystic glory swims away,
  From off my bed the moonlight dies;   10
  And closing eaves of wearied eyes
I sleep till dusk is dipped in gray;

And then I know the mist is drawn
  A lucid veil from coast to coast,
  And in the dark church like a ghost   15
Thy tablet glimmers to the dawn.

*   *   *

72

Risest thou thus, dim dawn, again,[9]
  And howlest, issuing out of night,
  With blasts that blow the poplar white,
And lash with storm the streaming pane?

Day, when my crowned estate[1] begun   5
  To pine in that reverse of doom,[2]
  Which sickened every living bloom,
And blurred the splendor of the sun;

Who usherest in the dolorous hour
  With thy quick tears that make the rose   10
  Pull sideways, and the daisy close
Her crimson fringes to the shower;

Who mightst have heaved a windless flame
  Up the deep East, or, whispering, played
  A checker-work of beam and shade   15
Along the hills, yet looked the same,

As wan, as chill, as wild as now;
  Day, marked as with some hideous crime,

---

8. The Severn River.
9. Sept. 15, 1834, the first anniversary of Hallam's death.

1. State of happiness.
2. The reversal or disaster which doom brought upon him when Hallam died.

When the dark hand struck down through time,
And canceled nature's best: but thou,   20

Lift as thou mayst thy burthened brows
    Through clouds that drench the morning star,
    And whirl the ungarnered sheaf afar,
And sow the sky with flying boughs,

And up thy vault with roaring sound   25
    Climb thy thick noon, disastrous day;
    Touch thy dull goal of joyless gray,
And hide thy shame beneath the ground.

*   *   *

78

Again at Christmas[3] did we weave
    The holly round the Christmas hearth;
    The silent snow possessed the earth,
And calmly fell our Christmas eve.

The yule clog[4] sparkled keen with frost,   5
    No wing of wind the region swept,
    But over all things brooding slept
The quiet sense of something lost.

As in the winters left behind,
    Again our ancient games had place,   10
    The mimic picture's[5] breathing grace,
And dance and song and hoodman-blind.

Who showed a token of distress?
    No single tear, no mark of pain—
    O sorrow, then can sorrow wane?   15
O grief, can grief be changed to less?

O last regret, regret can die!
    No—mixed with all this mystic frame,
    Her[6] deep relations are the same,
But with long use her tears are dry.   20

*   *   *

82

I wage not any feud with Death
    For changes wrought on form and face;

---

3. The second Christmas (1834) after Hallam's
death.
4. Log.
5. A game in which the participants pose in the

manner of some famous statue or painting and the
spectators try to guess what work of art is being
mimicked.
6. I.e., sorrow's.

No lower life that earth's embrace
May breed with him can fright my faith.

Eternal process moving on,   5
    From state to state the spirit walks;
    And these are but the shattered stalks,
Or ruined chrysalis of one.

Nor blame I Death, because he bare
    The use of virtue out of earth;   10
    I know transplanted human worth
Will bloom to profit, otherwhere.

For this alone on Death I wreak
    The wrath that garners in my heart:
    He put our lives so far apart   15
We cannot hear each other speak.

83

Dip down upon the northern shore,
    O sweet new-year[7] delaying long;
    Thou doest expectant Nature wrong;
Delaying long, delay no more.

What stays thee from the clouded noons,   5
    Thy sweetness from its proper place?
    Can trouble live with April days,
Or sadness in the summer moons?

Bring orchis, bring the foxglove spire,
    The little speedwell's[8] darling blue,   10
    Deep tulips dashed with fiery dew,
Laburnums, dropping-wells of fire.

O thou, new-year, delaying long,
    Delayest the sorrow in my blood,
    That longs to burst a frozen bud   15
And flood a fresher throat with song.

           *   *   *

86

Sweet after showers, ambrosial air,
    That rollest from the gorgeous gloom
    Of evening over brake and bloom
And meadow, slowly breathing bare

The round of space,[9] and rapt below   5
    Through all the dewy-tasseled wood,

7. Spring of 1835.
8. A blue spring flower.

9. Air that is slowly clearing the clouds from the sky.

And shadowing down the hornèd flood[1]
In ripples, fan my brows and blow

The fever from my cheek, and sigh
 The full new life that feeds thy breath   10
 Throughout my frame, till Doubt and Death,
Ill brethren, let the fancy fly

From belt to belt of crimson seas
 On leagues of odor streaming far,
 To where in yonder orient star   15
A hundred spirits whisper "Peace."

87

I passed beside the reverend walls[2]
 In which of old I wore the gown;
 I roved at random through the town,
And saw the tumult of the halls;

And heard once more in college fanes   5
 The storm their high-built organs make,
 And thunder-music, rolling, shake
The prophet blazoned on the panes;

And caught once more the distant shout,
 The measured pulse of racing oars   10
 Among the willows; paced the shores
And many a bridge, and all about

The same gray flats again, and felt
 The same, but not the same; and last
 Up that long walk of limes I passed   15
To see the rooms in which he dwelt.

Another name was on the door.
 I lingered; all within was noise
 Of songs, and clapping hands, and boys
That crashed the glass and beat the floor;   20

Where once we held debate, a band
 Of youthful friends,[3] on mind and art,
 And labor, and the changing mart,
And all the framework of the land;

When one would aim an arrow fair,   25
 But send it slackly from the string;

---

1. "Between two promontories." [Tennyson's comment].
2. Of Trinity College, Cambridge University.

3. The "Apostles," an undergraduate club to which Tennyson and Hallam had belonged.

And one would pierce an outer ring,
And one an inner, here and there;

And last the master bowman, he,
   Would cleave the mark. A willing ear   30
   We lent him. Who but hung to hear
The rapt oration flowing free

From point to point, with power and grace
   And music in the bounds of law,[4]
   To those conclusions when we saw   35
The God within him light his face,

And seem to lift the form, and glow
   In azure orbits heavenly-wise;
   And over those ethereal eyes
The bar of Michael Angelo?[5]   40

88

Wild bird, whose warble, liquid sweet,
   Rings Eden through the budded quicks,[6]
   O tell me where the senses mix,
O tell me where the passions meet,

Whence radiate: fierce extremes employ   45
   Thy spirits in the darkening leaf,[7]
   And in the midmost heart of grief
Thy passion clasps a secret joy;

And I—my harp would prelude woe—
   I cannot all command the strings;   50
   The glory of the sum of things
Will flash along the chords and go.

89

Witch elms that counterchange the floor
   Of this flat lawn with dusk and bright;[8]
   And thou, with all thy breadth and height
Of foliage, towering sycamore;

How often, hither wandering down,   5
   My Arthur found your shadows fair,
   And shook to all the liberal air
The dust and din and steam of town!

4. An essay presented by Arthur Hallam at Cambridge in 1831 provides an example of his skill in theological argument while still an undergraduate (see *The Writings of Arthur Hallam*, edited by T. H. V. Motter, 1943, pp. 198–213).
5. Hallam, like Michelangelo, had a prominent ridge of bone above his eyes.
6. Hawthorn hedges. The "wild bird" is presumably a nightingale.
7. Cf. Keats's *Ode to a Nightingale* (lines 10 and 60).
8. Shadows of the elm tree checker the lawn at Somersby, the Tennysons' country home.

He brought an eye for all he saw;
   He mixed in all our simple sports;   10
     They pleased him, fresh from brawling courts
And dusty purlieus of the law.[9]

O joy to him in this retreat,
   Immantled in ambrosial dark,
     To drink the cooler air, and mark   15
The landscape winking through the heat!

O sound to rout the brood of cares,
   The sweep of scythe in morning dew,
     The gust that round the garden flew,
And tumbled half the mellowing pears!   20

O bliss, when all in circle drawn
   About him, heart and ear were fed
     To hear him, as he lay and read
The Tuscan poets[1] on the lawn!

Or in the all-golden afternoon   25
   A guest, or happy sister, sung,
     Or here she brought the harp and flung
A ballad to the brightening moon.

Nor less it pleased in livelier moods,
   Beyond the bounding hill to stray,   30
     And break the livelong summer day
With banquet in the distant woods;

Whereat we glanced from theme to theme,
   Discussed the books to love or hate,
     Or touched the changes of the state,   35
Or threaded some Socratic dream;[2]

But if I praised the busy town,
   He loved to rail against it still,
     For "ground in yonder social mill
We rub each other's angles down,   40

"And merge," he said, "in form and gloss
   The picturesque of man and man."
     We talked: the stream beneath us ran,
The wine-flask lying couched in moss,

---

9. Hallam became a law student in London after
leaving Cambridge.
1. Petrarch and Dante.

2. I.e., worked our way through some discourse
of Socrates (as recorded by Plato).

Or cooled within the glooming wave; 45
  And last, returning from afar,
  Before the crimson-circled star[3]
Had fallen into her father's grave,

And brushing ankle-deep in flowers,
  We heard behind the woodbine veil 50
  The milk that bubbled in[4] the pail,
And buzzings of the honeyed hours.

*   *   *

91

When rosy plumelets tuft the larch,
  And rarely[5] pipes the mounted thrush,
  Or underneath the barren bush
Flits by the sea-blue bird[6] of March;

Come, wear the form by which I know 5
  Thy spirit in time among thy peers;
  The hope of unaccomplished years
Be large and lucid round thy brow.

When summer's hourly-mellowing change
  May breathe, with many roses sweet, 10
  Upon the thousand waves of wheat
That ripple round the lowly grange,

Come; not in watches of the night,
  But where the sunbeam broodeth warm,
  Come, beauteous in thine after form, 15
And like a finer light in light.

*   *   *

93

I shall not see thee. Dare I say
  No spirit ever brake the band
  That stays him from the native land
Where first he walked when clasped in clay?[7]

No visual shade of someone lost, 5
  But he, the Spirit himself, may come
  Where all the nerve of sense is numb,
Spirit to Spirit, Ghost to Ghost.

3. Venus, which will sink into the west as the sun has done. According to the nebular hypothesis, planets were flung from the sun into the outer spaces of our solar system; in this sense the sun is the "father" of planets.

4. Into.
5. Exquisitely.
6. Kingfisher.
7. I.e., when he was alive and clothed in flesh.

Oh, therefore from thy sightless[8] range
   With gods in unconjectured bliss,   10
   Oh, from the distance of the abyss
Of tenfold-complicated change,

Descend, and touch, and enter; hear
   The wish too strong for words to name,
   That in this blindness of the frame[9]   15
My Ghost may feel that thine is near.

94

How pure at heart and sound in head,
   With what divine affections bold
   Should be the man whose thought would hold
An hour's communion with the dead.

In vain shalt thou, or any, call   5
   The spirits from their golden day,
   Except, like them, thou too canst say,
My spirit is at peace with all.

They haunt the silence of the breast,
   Imaginations calm and fair,   10
   The memory like a cloudless air,
The conscience as a sea at rest;

But when the heart is full of din,
   And doubt beside the portal waits,
   They can but listen at the gates,   15
And hear the household jar within.

95

By night we lingered on the lawn,
   For underfoot the herb was dry;
   And genial warmth; and o'er the sky
The silvery haze of summer drawn;

And calm that let the tapers burn   5
   Unwavering: not a cricket chirred;
   The brook alone far off was heard,
And on the board the fluttering urn.[1]

And bats went round in fragrant skies,
   And wheeled or lit the filmy shapes[2]   10
   That haunt the dusk, with ermine capes
And woolly breasts and beaded eyes;

---

8. Invisible.
9. The living body.
1. Urn to boil water for tea or coffee, heated by a
fluttering flame.
2. The white-winged night moths called ermine moths.

While now we sang old songs that pealed
　　From knoll to knoll, where, couched at ease,
　　The white kine[3] glimmered, and the trees　　　　15
Laid their dark arms[4] about the field.

But when those others, one by one,
　　Withdrew themselves from me and night,
　　And in the house light after light
Went out, and I was all alone,　　　　20

A hunger seized my heart; I read
　　Of that glad year which once had been,
　　In those fallen leaves which kept their green,
The noble letters of the dead.

And strangely on the silence broke　　　　25
　　The silent-speaking words, and strange
　　Was love's dumb cry defying change
To test his worth; and strangely spoke

The faith, the vigor, bold to dwell
　　On doubts that drive the coward back,　　　　30
　　And keen through wordy snares to track
Suggestion to her inmost cell.

So word by word, and line by line,
　　The dead man touched me from the past,
　　And all at once it seemed at last　　　　35
The[5] living soul was flashed on mine.

And mine in this was wound, and whirled
　　About empyreal heights of thought,
　　And came on that which is, and caught
The deep pulsations of the world,　　　　40

Aeonian music[6] measuring out
　　The steps of Time—the shocks of Chance—
　　The blows of Death. At length my trance
Was canceled, stricken through with doubt.[7]

---

3. Cows.
4. Cast the shadows of their branches.
5. Printed "His" in the first edition; and line 37 read, in the first edition, "And mine in his was wound."
6. The music of the universe which has pulsated for aeons of time.
7. In a letter of 1874 replying to an inquiry about his experience of mystical trances, Tennyson wrote: "A kind of waking trance I have frequently had, quite up from boyhood, when I have been all alone. This has generally come upon me through repeating my own name two or three times to myself

silently, till all at once, as if were out of the intensity of the consciousness of individuality, the individuality itself seemed to dissolve and fade away into boundless being, and this not a confused state, but the clearest of the clearest, the surest of the surest, the weirdest of the weirdest, utterly beyond words, where death was an almost laughable impossibility, the loss of personality (if so it were) seeming no extinction but the only true life. . . . This might . . . be the state which St. Paul describes, 'Whether in the body I cannot tell, or whether out of the body I cannot tell.' . . . I am ashamed of my feeble description. Have I not said

Vague words! but ah, how hard to frame   45
    In matter-molded forms of speech,
    Or even for intellect to reach
Through memory that which I became.

Till now the doubtful dusk revealed
    The knolls once more where, couched at ease,   50
    The white kine glimmered, and the trees
Laid their dark arms about the field;

And sucked from out the distant gloom
    A breeze began to tremble o'er
    The large leaves of the sycamore,   55
And fluctuate all the still perfume,

And gathering freshlier overhead,
    Rocked the full-foliaged elms, and swung
    The heavy-folded rose, and flung
The lilies to and fro, and said,   60

"The dawn, the dawn," and died away;
    And East and West, without a breath,
    Mixed their dim lights, like life and death,
To broaden into boundless day.

96

You say, but with no touch of scorn,
    Sweet-hearted, you,[8] whose light blue eyes
    Are tender over drowning flies,
You tell me, doubt is Devil-born.

I know not: one[9] indeed I knew   5
    In many a subtle question versed,
    Who touched a jarring lyre at first,
But ever strove to make it true;

Perplexed in faith, but pure in deeds,
    At last he beat his music out.   10
    There lives more faith in honest doubt,
Believe me, than in half the creeds.

He fought his doubts and gathered strength,
    He would not make his judgment blind,
    He faced the specters of the mind   15
And laid them; thus he came at length

---

the state is utterly beyond words? But in a moment, when I come back to my normal state of 'sanity,' I am ready to fight for *mein liebes Ich* [my dear self], and hold that it will last for aeons of aeons."—

Alfred Lord Tennyson: A Memoir, 1897, 1, 320.
8. A woman of simple faith.
9. Hallam.

To find a stronger faith his own,
    And Power was with him in the night,
    Which makes the darkness and the light,
And dwells not in the light alone,   20

But in the darkness and the cloud,[1]
    As over Sinaï's peaks of old,
    While Israel made their gods of gold,
Although the trumpet blew so loud.

       *   *   *

99

Risest thou thus, dim dawn, again,[2]
    So loud with voices of the birds,
    So thick with lowings of the herds,
Day, when I lost the flower of men;

Who tremblest through thy darkling red   5
    On yon swollen brook that bubbles fast[3]
    By meadows breathing of the past,
And woodlands holy to the dead;

Who murmurest in the foliage eaves
    A song that slights the coming care,[4]   10
    And Autumn laying here and there
A fiery finger on the leaves;

Who wakenest with thy balmy breath
    To myriads on the genial earth,
    Memories of bridal, or of birth,[5]   15
And unto myriads more, of death.

Oh, wheresoever those[6] may be,
    Betwixt the slumber of the poles,
    Today they count as kindred souls;
They know me not, but mourn with me.   20

       *   *   *

103

On that last night before we went
From out the doors where I was bred,[7]

---

1. See Exodus 19.16–25. After veiling Mount Sinai in a "cloud" of smoke, God addressed Moses from the darkness.
2. Sept. 15, 1835, the second anniversary of Hallam's death.
3. Reflections of the clouded red light of dawn quiver on the surface of the fast-moving water.
4. I.e., disregards future events such as death or the coming of autumn. Cf. Shelley's *Ode to the West Wind*.
5. Cf. *Epilogue*, below, lines 117–28.
6. I.e., the "myriads" who remember death.
7. In 1837 Tennyson and his family moved away from their home in Lincolnshire, which had been closely associated with his friendship with Hallam. In section 104 the move seems to occur in 1835, the year of the third Christmas after Hallam's death.

I dreamed a vision of the dead,
Which left my after-morn content.

Methought I dwelt within a hall,   5
  And maidens with me; distant hills
  From hidden summits fed with rills
A river sliding by the wall.

The hall with harp and carol rang.
  They sang of what is wise and good   10
  And graceful. In the center stood
A statue veiled, to which they sang;

And which, though veiled, was known to me,
  The shape of him I loved, and love
  Forever. Then flew in a dove   15
And brought a summons from the sea;

And when they learnt that I must go,
  They wept and wailed, but led the way
  To where the little shallop[8] lay
At anchor in the flood below;   20

And on by many a level mead,
  And shadowing bluff that made the banks,
  We glided winding under ranks
Of iris and the golden reed;

And still as vaster grew the shore   25
  And rolled the floods in grander space,
  The maidens gathered strength and grace
And presence, lordlier than before;

And I myself, who sat apart
  And watched them, waxed in every limb;   30
  I felt the thews of Anakim,[9]
The pulses of a Titan's heart;

As one would sing the death of war,
  And one would chant the history
  Of that great race which is to be,[1]   35
And one the shaping of a star;

Until the forward-creeping tides
  Began to foam, and we to draw

8. A light open boat.
9. Plural of *Anak*; i.e., a reference to the giant sons of Anak. See Numbers 13.33. The Titans (line

32) were giants of Greek mythology.
1. See the account of the "crowning race" in *Epilogue*, below, lines 128–44.

From deep to deep, to where we saw
A great ship lift her shining sides.[2]   40

The man we loved was there on deck,
    But thrice as large as man he bent
    To greet us. Up the side I went,
And fell in silence on his neck;

Whereat those maidens with one mind   45
    Bewailed their lot; I did them wrong:
    "We served thee here," they said, "so long,
And wilt thou leave us now behind?"

So rapt[3] I was, they could not win
    An answer from my lips, but he   50
    Replying, "Enter likewise ye
And go with us:" they entered in.

And while the wind began to sweep
    A music out of sheet and shroud,
    We steered her toward a crimson cloud   55
That landlike slept along the deep.

104

The time draws near the birth of Christ;[4]
    The moon is hid, the night is still;
    A single church below the hill
Is pealing, folded in the mist.

A single peal of bells below,   5
    That wakens at this hour of rest
    A single murmur in the breast,
That these are not the bells I know.

Like strangers' voices here they sound,
    In lands where not a memory strays,   10
    Nor landmark breathes of other days,
But all is new unhallowed ground.

105

Tonight ungathered let us leave
    This laurel, let this holly stand:[5]
    We live within the stranger's land,
And strangely falls our Christmas eve.

2. Cf. *Morte d'Arthur*, lines 255–322, in which Bedivere is left behind as Arthur's barge, the ship of death, sails away. In the present dream vision, not only is the speaker taken aboard but also his companions, who represent the creative arts of this world—"all the human powers and talents that do not pass with life but go along with it," as Tenny- son said of this passage.
3. Entranced.
4. See note 7 to section 103.
5. Cf. section 29 in which the family in their for- mer home still continued to gather holly. In the new home, in "stranger's land," the customary observances lapse.

Our father's dust is left alone   5
   And silent under other snows:
   There in due time the woodbine blows,
The violet comes, but we are gone.

No more shall wayward grief abuse
   The genial hour with mask and mime;   10
   For change of place, like growth of time,
Has broke the bond of dying use.

Let cares that petty shadows cast,
   By which our lives are chiefly proved,
   A little spare the night I loved,   15
And hold it solemn to the past.

But let no footstep beat the floor,
   Nor bowl of wassail mantle warm;[6]
   For who would keep an ancient form
Through which the spirit breathes no more?   20

Be neither song, nor game, nor feast;
   Nor harp be touched, nor flute be blown;
   No dance, no motion, save alone
What lightens in the lucid east

Of rising worlds[7] by yonder wood.   25
   Long sleeps the summer in the seed;
   Run out your measured arcs, and lead
The closing cycle rich in good.

106

Ring out, wild bells, to the wild sky,
   The flying cloud, the frosty light:
   The year is dying in the night;
Ring out, wild bells, and let him die.

Ring out the old, ring in the new,   5
   Ring, happy bells, across the snow:
   The year is going, let him go;
Ring out the false, ring in the true.

Ring out the grief that saps the mind,
   For those that here we see no more;   10
   Ring out the feud of rich and poor,
Ring in redress to all mankind.

Ring out a slowly dying cause,
   And ancient forms of party strife;

6. I.e., no bowl of hot punch warms the mantelpiece.

7. "The scintillating motion of the stars that rise"
[Tennyson's note].

Ring in the nobler modes of life,   15
With sweeter manners, purer laws.

Ring out the want, the care, the sin,
    The faithless coldness of the times:
    Ring out, ring out my mournful rhymes,
But ring the fuller minstrel in.   20

Ring out false pride in place and blood,
    The civic slander and the spite;
    Ring in the love of truth and right,
Ring in the common love of good.

Ring out old shapes of foul disease;   25
    Ring out the narrowing lust of gold;
    Ring out the thousand wars of old,
Ring in the thousand years of peace.

Ring in the valiant man and free,
    The larger heart, the kindlier hand;   30
    Ring out the darkness of the land,
Ring in the Christ that is to be.[8]

107

It is the day when he was born.[9]
    A bitter day that early sank
    Behind a purple-frosty bank
Of vapor, leaving night forlorn.

The time admits not flowers or leaves   5
    To deck the banquet. Fiercely flies
    The blast of North and East, and ice
Makes daggers at the sharpened eaves,

And bristles all the brakes and thorns
    To yon hard crescent, as she hangs   10
    Above the wood which grides[1] and clangs
Its leafless ribs and iron horns

Together, in the drifts[2] that pass
    To darken on the rolling brine
    That breaks the coast. But fetch the wine,   15
Arrange the board and brim the glass;

Bring in great logs and let them lie,
    To make a solid core of heat;

---

8. These allusions to the second coming of Christ and to the millennium are derived from Revelation 20, but Tennyson has interpreted the Biblical account in his own way. He once told his son of his conviction that "the forms of Christian religion would alter; but that the spirit of Christ would still grow from more to more."
9. February 1.
1. Clashes with a strident noise.
2. Either cloud-drifts or clouds of snow.

Be cheerful-minded, talk and treat
Of all things even as he were by;   20

We keep the day. With festal cheer,
    With books and music, surely we
    Will drink to him, whate'er he be,
And sing the songs he loved to hear.

                    108

I will not shut me from my kind,
    And, lest I stiffen into stone,
    I will not eat my heart alone,
Nor feed with sighs a passing wind:

What profit lies in barren faith,   5
    And vacant yearning, though with might
    To scale the heaven's highest height,
Or dive below the wells of Death?

What find I in the highest place,
    But mine own phantom chanting hymns?   10
    And on the depths of death there swims
The reflex of a human face.[3]

I'll rather take what fruit may be
    Of sorrow under human skies:
    'Tis held that sorrow makes us wise,   15
Whatever wisdom sleep with thee.[4]

                    109

Heart-affluence in discursive talk
    From household fountains never dry;
    The critic clearness of an eye
That saw through all the Muses' walk;[5]

Seraphic intellect and force   5
    To seize and throw the doubts of man;
    Impassioned logic, which outran
The hearer in its fiery course;

High nature amorous of the good,
    But touched with no ascetic gloom;   10
    And passion pure in snowy bloom
Through all the years of April blood;

A love of freedom rarely felt,
    Of freedom in her regal seat

Of England; not the schoolboy heat,   15
The blind hysterics of the Celt;[6]

And manhood fused with female grace
    In such a sort, the child would twine
    A trustful hand, unasked, in thine,
And find his comfort in thy face;   20

All these have been, and thee mine eyes
    Have looked on: if they looked in vain,
    My shame is greater who remain,
Nor let thy wisdom make me wise.

* * *

115

Now fades the last long streak of snow,
    Now burgeons every maze of quick[7]
    About the flowering squares, and thick
By ashen roots the violets blow.

Now rings the woodland loud and long,   5
    The distance takes a lovelier hue,
    And drowned in yonder living blue
The lark becomes a sightless song.

Now dance the lights on lawn and lea,
    The flocks are whiter down the vale,   10
    And milkier every milky sail
On winding stream or distant sea;

Where now the seamew pipes, or dives
    In yonder greening gleam, and fly
    The happy birds, that change their sky   15
To build and brood, that live their lives

From land to land; and in my breast
    Spring wakens too, and my regret
    Becomes an April violet,
And buds and blossoms like the rest.   20

* * *

118

Contèmplate all this work of Time,
    The giant laboring in his youth;
    Nor dream of human love and truth,
As dying Nature's earth and lime;

---

6. In particular the French at the time of the Rev-   7. Hawthorn hedges. "Squares": fields.
olution of 1789. See also section 127, lines 7–8.

But trust that those we call the dead   5
   Are breathers of an ampler day
   For ever nobler ends. They[8] say,
The solid earth whereon we tread

In tracts of fluent heat began,
   And grew to seeming-random forms,   10
   The seeming prey of cyclic storms,
Till at the last arose the man;

Who throve and branched from clime to clime,
   The herald of a higher race,
   And of himself in higher place   15
If so he type[9] this work of time

Within himself, from more to more;
   Or, crowned with attributes of woe
   Like glories, move his course, and show
That life is not as idle ore,   20

But iron dug from central gloom,
   And heated hot with burning fears,
   And dipped in baths of hissing tears,
And battered with the shocks of doom

To shape and use. Arise and fly   25
   The reeling Faun, the sensual feast;
   Move upward, working out the beast,
And let the ape and tiger die.

119

Doors, where my heart was used to beat
   So quickly, not as one that weeps
   I come once more; the city sleeps;
I smell the meadow in the street;

I hear a chirp of birds; I see   5
   Betwixt the black fronts long-withdrawn
   A light blue lane of early dawn,
And think of early days and thee,

And bless thee, for thy lips are bland,
   And bright the friendship of thine eye;   10
   And in my thoughts with scarce a sigh
I take the pressure of thine hand.

120

I trust I have not wasted breath:
   I think we are not wholly brain,

---

8. Geologists and astronomers.   9. Emulate, prefigure as a type.

Magnetic mockeries;[1] not in vain,
Like Paul[2] with beasts, I fought with Death;

Not only cunning casts in clay: 5
    Let Science prove we are, and then
    What matters Science unto men,
At least to me? I would not stay.

Let him, the wiser man who springs
    Hereafter, up from childhood shape   10
    His action like the greater ape,
But I was *born* to other things.

121

Sad Hesper[3] o'er the buried sun
    And ready, thou, to die with him,
    Thou watchest all things ever dim
And dimmer, and a glory done.

The team is loosened from the wain,[4]   5
    The boat is drawn upon the shore;
    Thou listenest to the closing door,
And life is darkened in the brain.

Bright Phosphor,[5] fresher for the night,
    By thee the world's great work is heard   10
    Beginning, and the wakeful bird;
Behind thee comes the greater light.[6]

The market boat is on the stream,
    And voices hail it from the brink;
    Thou hear'st the village hammer clink,   15
And see'st the moving of the team.

Sweet Hesper-Phosphor, double name[7]
    For what is one, the first, the last,
    Thou, like my present and my past,
Thy place is changed; thou art the same.   20

*   *   *

123

There rolls the deep where grew the tree.
O earth, what changes hast thou seen!

---

1. Mechanisms operated by responses to electrical forces.
2. 1 Corinthians 15.32.
3. Evening star.
4. Hay wagon.
5. Morning star.
6. Cf. Genesis 1.16: "The greater light to rule the day."
7. The same planet, Venus, is both evening star and morning star.

There where the long street roars hath been
The stillness of the central sea.[8]

The hills are shadows, and they flow
 From form to form, and nothing stands;
 They melt like mist, the solid lands,
Like clouds they shape themselves and go.

But in my spirit will I dwell,
 And dream my dream, and hold it true;   10
 For though my lips may breathe adieu,
I cannot think the thing farewell.

124

That which we dare invoke to bless;
 Our dearest faith; our ghastliest doubt;
 He, They, One, All; within, without;
The Power in darkness whom we guess—

I found Him not in world or sun,
 Or eagle's wing, or insect's eye,[9]   5
 Nor through the questions men may try,
The petty cobwebs we have spun.

If e'er when faith had fallen asleep,
 I heard a voice, "believe no more,"   10
 And heard an ever-breaking shore
That tumbled in the Godless deep,

A warmth within the breast would melt
 The freezing reason's colder part,
 And like a man in wrath the heart   15
Stood up and answered, "I have felt."

No, like a child in doubt and fear:
 But that blind clamor made me wise;
 Then was I as a child that cries,
But, crying, knows his father near;   20

And what I am beheld again
 What is, and no man understands;
 And out of darkness came the hands
That reach through nature, molding men.

---

8. Cf. a passage from Sir Charles Lyell's *The Principles of Geology* (1832), a book well-known to Tennyson. In discussing the "interchange of sea and land" that has occurred "on the surface of our globe" Lyell remarks: "In the Mediterranean alone, many flourishing inland towns and a still greater number of ports now stand where the sea rolled its waves since the era when civilized nations first grew in Europe."

9. He does not discover satisfactory proof of God's existence in the 18th-century argument that because objects in nature are designed there must exist a designer.

* * *

126

Love is and was my lord and king,
    And in his presence I attend
    To hear the tidings of my friend,
Which every hour his couriers bring.

Love is and was my king and lord,   5
    And will be, though as yet I keep
    Within the court on earth, and sleep
Encompassed by his faithful guard,

And hear at times a sentinel
    Who moves about from place to place,   10
    And whispers to the worlds of space,
In the deep night, that all is well.

127

And all is well, though faith and form[1]
    Be sundered in the night of fear;
    Well roars the storm to those that hear
A deeper voice across the storm,

Proclaiming social truth shall spread,   5
    And justice, even though thrice again
    The red fool-fury of the Seine
Should pile her barricades with dead.[2]

But ill for him that wears a crown,
    And him, the lazar,[3] in his rags!   10
    They tremble, the sustaining crags;
The spires of ice are toppled down,

And molten up, and roar in flood;
    The fortress crashes from on high,
    The brute earth lightens[4] to the sky,   15
And the great Aeon[5] sinks in blood,

And compassed by the fires of hell,
    While thou, dear spirit, happy star,
    O'erlook'st the tumult from afar,
And smilest, knowing all is well.   20

---

1. Traditional institutions through which faith was formerly expressed, such as the Church. See Carlyle's essay, *Characteristics*, above.
2. Revolutionary uprisings in France, in each of which a king lost his throne (line 9): in 1789 against Louis XVI, in 1830 against Charles X, and in 1848 against Louis Philippe. The third (line 6) would

have been a prophecy if, as Tennyson recollected, section 126 was finished at a date earlier than 1848.
3. Pauper suffering from disease.
4. Is lit up by fire.
5. A vast tract of time, here perhaps modern western civilization.

*   *   *

129

Dear friend, far off, my lost desire,
  So far, so near in woe and weal,
  O loved the most, when most I feel
There is a lower and a higher;

Known and unknown, human, divine;   5
  Sweet human hand and lips and eye;
  Dear heavenly friend that canst not die,
Mine, mine, forever, ever mine;

Strange friend, past, present, and to be;
  Loved deeplier, darklier understood;   10
  Behold, I dream a dream of good,
And mingle all the world with thee.

130

Thy voice is on the rolling air
  I hear thee where the waters run;
  Thou standest in the rising sun,
And in the setting thou art fair.

What art thou then? I cannot guess;   5
  But though I seem in star and flower
  To feel thee some diffusive power,
I do not therefore love thee less.

My love involves the love before;
  My love is vaster passion now;   10
  Tho' mix'd with God and Nature thou,
I seem to love thee more and more.

Far off thou art, but ever nigh;
  I have thee still, and I rejoice;
  I prosper, circled with thy voice;   15
I shall not lose thee tho' I die.

131

O living will[6] that shalt endure
  When all that seems shall suffer shock,
  Rise in the spiritual rock,[7]
Flow through our deeds and make them pure,

That we may lift from out of dust   5
  A voice as unto him that hears,
  A cry above the conquered years
To one that with us works, and trust,

6. Tennyson later commented that he meant here the moral will of mankind.
7. Christ (see 1 Corinthians 10.4).

With faith that comes of self-control,
   The truths that never can be proved   10
   Until we close with all we loved,
And all we flow from, soul in soul.

From *Epilogue*[8]

*   *   *

And rise, O moon, from yonder down,
   Till over down and over dale   110
   All night the shining vapor sail
And pass the silent-lighted town,

The white-faced halls, the glancing rills,
   And catch at every mountain head,
   And o'er the friths[9] that branch and spread   115
Their sleeping silver through the hills;

And touch with shade the bridal doors,
   With tender gloom the roof, the wall;
   And breaking let the splendor fall
To spangle all the happy shores   120

By which they rest, and ocean sounds,
   And, star and system rolling past,
   A soul shall draw from out the vast
And strike his being into bounds,

And, moved through life of lower phase,   125
   Result in man,[1] be born and think,
   And act and love, a closer link
Betwixt us and the crowning race

Of those that, eye to eye, shall look
   On knowledge; under whose command   130
   Is Earth and Earth's, and in their hand
Is Nature like an open book;

No longer half-akin to brute,
   For all we thought and loved and did,
   And hoped, and suffered, is but seed   135
Of what in them is flower and fruit;

---

8. The *Epilogue* describes the wedding day of Tennyson's sister Cecilia to Edmund Lushington. At the conclusion (reprinted here) the speaker reflects upon their moonlit wedding night and the kind of offspring that will result from their union.
9. Inlets of the sea.

1. A child will be conceived and will develop in embryo through various stages. This development is similar to the evolution of man from the animal to the human level and perhaps to a future higher stage of development.

Whereof the man that with me trod
   This planet was a noble type
   Appearing ere the times were ripe,
That friend of mine who lives in God,   140

That God, which ever lives and loves,
   One God, one law, one element,
   And one far-off divine event,
To which the whole creation moves.

1833–50   1850

The Charge of the Light Brigade[1]

1

Half a league, half a league,
Half a league onward,
All in the valley of Death
   Rode the six hundred.
"Forward the Light Brigade!   5
Charge for the guns!" he said.
Into the valley of Death
   Rode the six hundred.

2

"Forward, the Light Brigade!"
Was there a man dismayed?   10
Not though the soldier knew
   Someone had blundered.
Theirs not to make reply,
Theirs not to reason why,
Theirs but to do and die.   15
Into the valley of Death
   Rode the six hundred.

3

Cannon to right of them,
Cannon to left of them,
Cannon in front of them   20
   Volleyed and thundered;
Stormed at with shot and shell,
Boldly they rode and well,
Into the jaws of Death,
Into the mouth of hell   25
   Rode the six hundred.

1. During the Crimean War, owing to confusion of orders, a brigade of British cavalry charged some entrenched batteries of Russian artillery. This blunder cost the lives of three fourths of the 600 horsemen engaged (see Cecil Woodham-Smith, *The Reason Why*, 1954). Tennyson rapidly composed his "ballad" (as he called the poem) after reading an account of the battle in a newspaper.

4

Flashed all their sabers bare,
Flashed as they turned in air
Sab'ring the gunners there,
Charging an army, while   30
    All the world wondered.
Plunged in the battery smoke
Right through the line they broke;
Cosssack and Russian
Reeled from the saber stroke   35
    Shattered and sundered.
Then they rode back, but not,
    Not the six hundred.

5

Cannon to right of them,
Cannon to left of them,   40
Cannon behind them
    Volleyed and thundered;
Stormed at with shot and shell,
While horse and hero fell.
They that had fought so well   45
Came through the jaws of Death,
Back from the mouth of hell,
All that was left of them,
    Left of six hundred.

6

When can their glory fade?   50
O the wild charge they made!
    All the world wondered.
Honor the charge they made!
Honor the Light Brigade,
Noble six hundred!   55

1854   1854

From Maud[1]

Part 1

6

* * *

5

Ah, what shall I be at fifty
Should Nature keep me alive,   220

1. Tennyson described this experimental long poem as a "monodrama," in which a speaker tells his story in a sequence of short lyrics, in varying meters—a method which requires the reader to fill in the events of the action on the evidence of the speaker's shifting emotional states. The speaker is a young man, living alone in the country, whose disillusionment after his father's suicide has left him

If I find the world so bitter
When I am but twenty-five?
Yet, if she were not a cheat,
If Maud were all that she seemed,
And her smile were all that I dreamed,[2]   225
Then the world were not so bitter
But a smile could make it sweet.

*   *   *

8

Perhaps the smile and tender tone
Came out of her pitying womanhood,
For am I not, am I not, here alone
So many a summer since she died,   255
My mother, who was so gentle and good?
Living alone in an empty house,
Here half-hid in the gleaming wood,
Where I hear the dead at midday moan,
And the shrieking rush of the wainscot mouse,   260
And my own sad name in corners cried,
When the shiver of dancing leaves is thrown
About its echoing chambers wide,
Till a morbid hate and horror have grown
Of a world in which I have hardly mixed,   265
And a morbid eating lichen fixed
On a heart half turned to stone.

*   *   *

10

I have played with her when a child;
She remembers it now we meet.
Ah, well, well, well, I *may* be beguiled
By some coquettish deceit.
Yet, if she were not a cheat,   280
And Maud were all that she seemed,
And her smile had all that I dreamed,
Then the world were not so bitter
But a smile could make it sweet.

full of a bitterness that borders on madness. He is restored to sanity and intense happiness when he discovers that Maud, the beautiful daughter of a local landowner, accepts his love for her. Our selections focus on the stages of this love affair. In the early sections he is fearful of love itself ("And most of all would I flee from the cruel madness of love"), and he is suspicious that Maud is stony-hearted and will make a fool of him. When she accepts his proposal, he is, at first, deliriously exultant, but, later, serene and secure. Subse-

quent sections of the poem (not represented here) show how the resolution of his problems is shattered when he loses Maud after killing her brother in a duel. Eventually he finds a fresh resolution by enlisting to fight against Russia in the Crimean War.

Tennyson called the poem "a little *Hamlet*, the history of a morbid, poetic soul, under the blighting influence of a recklessly speculative age."
2. On a previous day he had encountered Maud and was surprised by her smiling at him.

8

She came to the village church,
And sat by a pillar alone;
An angel watching an urn
Wept over her, carved in stone;
And once, but once, she lifted her eyes,   305
And suddenly, sweetly, strangely blushed
To find they were met by my own;
And suddenly, sweetly, my heart beat stronger
And thicker, until I heard no longer
The snowy-banded, dilettante,   310
Delicate-handed priest intone;
And thought, is it pride? and mused and sighed,
"No surely, now it cannot be pride."

11

1

O let the solid ground
    Not fail beneath my feet
Before my life has found   400
    What some have found so sweet;
Then let come what come may,
What matter if I go mad,
I shall have had my day.

2

Let the sweet heavens endure,   405
    Not close and darken above me
Before I am quite quite sure
    That there is one to love me;
Then let come what come may
To a life that has been so sad,   410
I shall have had my day.

12

1

Birds in the high Hall-garden
    When twilight was falling,
Maud, Maud, Maud, Maud,
    They were crying and calling.   415

2

Where was Maud? in our wood;
    And I, who else, was with her,
Gathering woodland lilies,
    Myriads blow together.

3

Birds in our wood[3] sang   420
   Ringing through the valleys,
Maud is here, here, here
   In among the lilies.

4

I kissed her slender hand,
   She took the kiss sedately;   425
Maud is not seventeen,
   But she is tall and stately.

5

I to cry out on pride
   Who have won her favor!
O Maud were sure of Heaven   430
   If lowliness[4] could save her.

6

I know the way she went
   Home with her maiden posy,
For her feet have touched the meadows
   And left the daisies rosy.[5]   435

7

Birds in the high Hall-garden
   Were crying and calling to her,
Where is Maud, Maud, Maud?
   One is come to woo her.

8

Look, a horse at the door,   440
   And little King Charley snarling,[6]
Go back, my lord, across the moor,
   You are not her darling.

16

*   *   *

3

Catch not my breath, O clamorous heart,
Let not my tongue be a thrall to my eye,
For I must tell her before we part,
I must tell her, or die.[7]   570

---

3. The wood in the valley of the speaker's small country estate. Here the "little birds" (as Tennyson called them in a note) are responding, in a sort of duet, to the caws of the rooks in the garden of Maud's family estate.
4. Meekness.
5. As Tennyson explained: "If you tread on the daisy [English variety], it turns up a rosy underside."
6. Maud's dog snarls at the aristocratic visitor who is the speaker's rival for Maud's hand.
7. He is about to propose to Maud, who will accept him.

18

1

I have led her home, my love, my only friend.
There is none like her, none.   600
And never yet so warmly ran my blood
And sweetly, on and on
Calming itself to the long-wished-for end,
Full to the banks, close on the promised good.

2

None like her, none.   605
Just now the dry-tongued laurels' pattering talk
Seemed her light foot along the garden walk,
And shook my heart to think she comes once more,
But even then I heard her close the door;
The gates of heaven are closed, and she is gone.   610

3

There is none like her, none,
Nor will be when our summers have deceased.
O, art thou[8] sighing for Lebanon
In the long breeze that streams to thy delicious East,
Sighing for Lebanon,   615
Dark cedar, though thy limbs have here increased,
Upon a pastoral slope as fair,
And looking to the South and fed
With honeyed rain and delicate air,
And haunted by the starry head   620
Of her whose gentle will has changed my fate,
And made my life a perfumed altar-flame;
And over whom thy darkness must have spread
With such delight as theirs of old, thy great
Forefathers of the thornless garden, there   625
Shadowing the snow-limbed Eve from whom she came?

4

Here will I lie, while these long branches sway,
And you fair stars that crown a happy day
Go in and out as if at merry play,
Who am no more so all forlorn   630
As when it seemed far better to be born
To labor and the mattock-hardened hand
Than nursed at ease and brought to understand
A sad astrology,[9] the boundless plan
That makes you tyrants in your iron skies,   635
Innumerable, pitiless, passionless eyes,
Cold fires, yet with power to burn and brand
His nothingness into man.

---

8. The vast old cedar tree in Maud's garden, addressed in a 14-line question about its ancestry on Mount Lebanon in Syria and its ultimate   ancestry in Eden. See Song of Solomon 5.15.
9. Astronomy.

5

But now shine on, and what care I,
Who in this stormy gulf have found a pearl   640
The countercharm of space and hollow sky,[1]
And do accept my madness, and would die
To save from some slight shame one simple girl?—

6

Would die, for sullen-seeming Death may give
More life to Love than is or ever was   645
In our low world, where yet 'tis sweet to live.
Let no one ask me how it came to pass;
It seems that I am happy, that to me
A livelier emerald twinkles in the grass,
A purer sapphire melts into the sea.   650

7

Not die, but live a life of truest breath,
And teach true life to fight with mortal wrongs.
O, why should Love, like men in drinking songs,
Spice his fair banquet with the dust of death?[2]
Make answer, Maud my bliss,   655
Maud made my Maud by that long loving kiss,
Life of my life, wilt thou not answer this?
"The dusky strand of Death inwoven here
With dear Love's tie, makes Love himself more dear."

8

Is that enchanted moan only the swell   660
Of the long waves that roll in yonder bay?
And hark the clock within, the silver knell
Of twelve sweet hours that passed in bridal white,
And died to live, long as my pulses play;
But now by this my love has closed her sight   665
And given false death[3] her hand, and stolen away
To dreamful wastes where footless fancies dwell
Among the fragments of the golden day.
May nothing there her maiden grace affright!
Dear heart, I feel with thee the drowsy spell.   670
My bride to be, my evermore delight,
My own heart's heart, my ownest own, farewell;
It is but for a little space I go.
And ye[4] meanwhile far over moor and fell
Beat to the noiseless music of the night!   675
Has our whole earth gone nearer to the glow
Of your soft splendors that you look so bright?
I have climbed nearer out of lonely hell.
Beat, happy stars, timing with things below,
Beat with my heart more blest than heart can tell,   680

---

1. Something that calms his former fears of the   of love by linking it with death?
vastness of space revealed by modern astronomy.   3. I.e., sleep.
2. I.e., why do we try to intensify the experience   4. The stars.

Blest, but for some dark undercurrent woe
That seems to draw——but it shall not be so;
Let all be well, be well.

*   *   *

Part 2

4[5]

1

O that 'twere possible
After long grief and pain
To find the arms of my true love
Round me once again!

2

When I was wont to meet her   145
In the silent woody places
By the home that gave me birth,
We stood tranced in long embraces
Mixt with kisses sweeter sweeter
Than anything on earth.   150

3

A shadow flits before me,
Not thou, but like to thee:
Ah Christ, that it were possible
For one short hour to see
The souls we loved, that they might tell us   155
What and where they be.

4

It leads me forth at evening,
It lightly winds and steals
In a cold white robe before me,
When all my spirit reels   160
At the shouts, the leagues of lights
And the roaring of the wheels.

*   *   *

1855

In the Valley of Cauteretz[1]

All along the valley, stream that flashest white,
Deepening thy voice with the deepening of the night,
All along the valley, where thy waters flow,

5. This excerpt from part 2 of *Maud* was originally a separate lyric, written in 1833–34 and published in 1837. Tennyson wrote that a friend
"begged me to weave a story round this poem, and
so *Maud* came into being." The lyric expresses the
speaker's longing for reunion with Maud, who has
died by this point in the poem.
1. A valley in the French Pyrenees visited by Tennyson and Hallam in 1830 and revisited by Tennyson in 1861.

I walked with one I loved two and thirty years ago.
All along the valley, while I walked today,   5
The two and thirty years were a mist that rolls away;
For all along the valley, down thy rocky bed,
Thy living voice to me was as the voice of the dead,
And all along the valley, by rock and cave and tree,
The voice of the dead was a living voice to me.   10

1861   1864

Idylls of the King

Idylls of the King   When John Milton was considering subjects suitable for an epic poem, one of those he entertained was the story of the Christian British king, Arthur, a semilegendary leader of about 500 A.D. who fought off the heathen Saxon invaders who had swarmed into Britain after the withdrawal of the Roman legions. Tennyson likewise saw that the Arthurian story had epic potential and selected it for his lifework as "the greatest of all poetical subjects." At intervals, over a period of fifty years, he labored over the twelve books that make up his *Idylls of the King*, completing the work in 1888.

The principal source of Tennyson's stories of Arthur and his knights was Sir Thomas Malory's *Morte Darthur*, a version which Malory translated into English prose from French sources in 1470. As Talbot Donaldson has suggested, one basis of the appeal of the Arthurian stories, like the legends of Robin Hood and stories of the American West, is that all three represent the struggle of individuals to restore order in situations of chaos and anarchy, a task performed in the face of "seemingly overwhelming odds." The individual stories in Tennyson's *Idylls* have the same basic appeal, but the overall design of the whole poem is more ambitious and impressive. The *Idylls of the King* represent the rise and fall of a civilization. They imply that after 2000 years of Christianity, Western civilization may be going through a cycle in which it must confront the possibilities of a renewal in the future or an apocalyptic extinction. The first book, *The Coming of Arthur*, introduces the basic myth of a springtime hero transforming a wasteland and inspiring faith and hope in the highest values of civilized life among his devoted followers. Succeeding books move through summer and autumn and culminate in the bleak wintry scene of Arthur's last battle in which his order perishes in a civil war; the leader of the enemy forces is his own nephew, Sir Modred.

Throughout the later books of the *Idylls* the forces of opposition grow in strength, and disaffections infect leading figures of the Round Table itself. The most glaring example is the adulterous relationship between Guinevere, Arthur's "sumptuous" queen (as Tennyson once described her), and the king's chief lieutenant and friend, Sir Lancelot. Many other fallings away subsequently come to light, such as the perfidious betrayal by Sir Gawain in *Pelleas and Ettarre*, and the cynical conduct of Sir Tristram, whose story is told in the bitter tenth book, *The Last Tournament*. Even Merlin, Arthur's trusted magician and counselor, becomes corrupted and can perform no further offices for the king (*Merlin and Vivien*). These accumulating signs of decline and fall figure prominently in the two late idylls that make up the following selections.

From Idylls of the King

The Passing of Arthur[1]

That story which the bold Sir Bedivere,[2]
First made and latest left of all the knights,
Told, when the man was no more than a voice
In the white winter of his age, to those
With whom he dwelt, new faces, other minds.   5

    For on their march to westward, Bedivere,
Who slowly paced among the slumbering host,
Heard in his tent the moanings of the King:

    "I found Him in the shining of the stars,
I marked Him in the flowering of His fields,   10
But in His ways with men I find Him not.
I waged His wars, and now I pass and die.
O me! for why is all around us here
As if some lesser god had made the world,
But had not force to shape it as he would,   15
Till the High God behold it from beyond,
And enter it, and make it beautiful?
Or else as if the world were wholly fair,
But that these eyes of men are dense and dim,
And have not power to see it as it is: 20
Perchance, because we see not to the close;—
For I, being simple, thought to work His will,
And have but stricken with the sword in vain;
And all whereon I learned in wife and friend
Is traitor to my peace, and all my realm   25
Reels back into the beast, and is no more.
My God, thou has forgotten me in my death:[3]
Nay—God my Christ—I pass but shall not die."

    Then, ere that last weird battle in the west,
There came on Arthur sleeping, Gawain killed   30
In Lancelot's war, the ghost of Gawain blown
Along a wandering wind, and past his ear
Went shrilling. "Hollow, hollow all delight!
Hail, King! tomorrow thou shalt pass away.
Farewell! there is an isle of rest for thee.   35

1. The principal source for this idyll was Sir Thomas Malory's *Morte Darthur* 21.4–5. Preceding the action of this idyll, Arthur had been in France with his nephew Gawain fighting against the forces of Lancelot. Learning at that time of the gathering of an army against him in England, under the leadership of his nephew Modred, Arthur returned there to engage in his last battle. Upon landing at Dover, Gawain was slain.

2. A knight who had long been close to the king described in *The Coming of Arthur*: "Bedivere, the first of all his knights / knighted by Arthur at his crowning."

3. Cf. "My God, my God, why hast thou forsaken me?" Matthew 27.46.

And I am blown along a wandering wind,
And hollow, hollow, hollow all delight."
And fainter onward, like wild birds that change
Their season in the night and wail their way
From cloud to cloud, down the long wind the dream   40
Shrilled; but in going mingled with dim cries
Far in the moonlit haze among the hills,
As of some lonely city sacked by night,
When all is lost, and wife and child with wail
Pass to new lords; and Arthur woke and called,   45
"Who spake? A dream. O light upon the wind,
Thine, Gawain, was the voice—are these dim cries
Thine? or doth all that haunts the waste and wild
Mourn, knowing it will go along with me?"

    This heard the bold Sir Bedivere and spake: 50
"O me, my King, let pass whatever will,
Elves, and the harmless glamor of the field;[4]
But in their stead thy name and glory cling
To all high places like a golden cloud
Forever: but as yet thou shalt not pass.   55
Light was Gawain in life, and light in death
Is Gawain, for the ghost is as the man;
And care not thou for dreams from him, but rise—
I hear the steps of Modred in the west,
And with him many of thy people, and knights   60
Once thine, whom thou hast loved, but grosser grown
Than heathen, spitting at their vows and thee.
Right well in heart they know thee for the King.
Arise, go forth and conquer as of old."

    Then spake King Arthur to Sir Bedivere: 65
"Far other is this battle in the west
Whereto we move, than when we strove in youth,
And brake the petty kings, and fought with Rome,
Or thrust the heathen from the Roman wall,
And shook him through the north. Ill doom is mine   70
To war against my people and my knights.
The king who fights his people fights himself.
And they thy knights, who loved me once, the stroke
That strikes them dead is as my death to me.
Yet let us hence, and find or feel a way   75
Through this blind haze, which ever since I saw
One lying in the dust at Almesbury,[5]
Hath folded in the passes of the world."

4. Tennyson said the reference is to "the legends which cluster round the King's name." One legend told of the elves' bestowing gifts on Arthur as a child.

5. The convent to which Guinevere had withdrawn; during the king's farewell visit to her there, she had lain in the dust at his feet.

Then rose the King and moved his host by night,
And ever pushed Sir Modred, league by league,   80
Back to the sunset bound of Lyonnesse[6]—
A land of old upheaven from the abyss
By fire, to sink into the abyss again;
Where fragments of forgotten peoples dwelled,
And the long mountains ended in a coast   85
Of ever-shifting sand, and far away
The phantom circle of a moaning sea.
There the pursuer could pursue no more,
And he that fled no further fly the King;
And there, that day when the great light of heaven   90
Burned at his lowest in the rolling year,
On the waste sand by the waste sea they closed.
Nor ever yet had Arthur fought a fight
Like this last, dim, weird battle of the west.
A deathwhite mist slept over sand and sea: 95
Whereof the chill, to him who breathed it, drew
Down with his blood, till all his heart was cold
With formless fear; and even on Arthur fell
Confusion, since he saw not whom he fought.
For friend and foe were shadows in the mist,   100
And friend slew friend not knowing whom he slew;
And some had visions out of golden youth,
And some beheld the faces of old ghosts
Look in upon the battle; and in the mist
Was many a noble deed, many a base,   105
And chance and craft and strength in single fights,
And ever and anon with host to host
Shocks, and the splintering spear, the hard mail hewn,
Shield-breakings, and the clash of brands, the crash
Of battleaxes on shattered helms, and shrieks   110
After the Christ, of those who falling down
Looked up for heaven, and only saw the mist;
And shouts of heathen and the traitor knights,
Oaths, insult, filth, and monstrous blasphemies,
Sweat, writhings, anguish, laboring of the lungs   115
In that close mist, and cryings for the light,
Moans of the dying, and voices of the dead.

    Last, as by some one deathbed after wail
Of suffering, silence follows, or through death
Or deathlike swoon, thus over all that shore,   120
Save for some whisper of the seething seas,
A dead hush fell; but when the dolorous day
Grew drearier toward twilight falling, came
A bitter wind, clear from the North, and blew

---

6. Legendary land extending west from Cornwall, which sank into the sea.

The mist aside, and with that wind the tide   125
Rose, and the pale King glanced across the field
Of battle: but no man was moving there;
Nor any cry of Christian heard thereon,
Nor yet of heathen; only the wan wave
Brake in among dead faces, to and fro   130
Swaying the helpless hands, and up and down
Tumbling the hollow helmets of the fallen,
And shivered brands that once had fought with Rome,
And rolling far along the gloomy shores
The voice of days of old and days to be.   135

    Then spake King Arthur to Sir Bedivere,
And whiter than the mist that all day long
Had held the field of battle was the King:

    "Hearest thou this great voice that shakes the world,
And wastes the narrow realm whereon we move,   140
And beats upon the faces of the dead,
My dead, as though they had not died for me?—
O Bedivere, for on my heart hath fallen
Confusion, till I know not what I am,
Nor whence I am, nor whether I be King.   145
Behold, I seem but King among the dead."

    Then spake the bold Sir Bedivere: "My King,
King everywhere! and so the dead have kings,
There also will I worship thee as King.
Yet still thy life is whole, and still I live   150
Who love thee; but who hates thee, he that brought
The heathen back among us, yonder stands,
Modred, unharmed, the traitor of thine house."

    Then spake the King: "My house hath been my doom.
But call not thou this traitor of my house   155
Who hath but dwelled beneath one roof with me.
My house are rather they who sware my vows,
Yea, even while they brake them, owned me King.
And well for thee, saying in my dark hour,
When all the purport of my throne hath failed,   160
That quick or dead thou holdest me for King.
King am I, whatsoever be their cry;
And one last act of kinghood shalt thou see
Yet, ere I pass." And uttering this the King
Made at the man: then Modred smote his liege   165
Hard on that helm which many a heathen sword
Had beaten thin; while Arthur at one blow,
Striking the last stroke with Excalibur,
Slew him, and all but slain himself, he fell.

So all day long the noise of battle rolled   170
Among the mountains by the winter sea;
Until King Arthur's Table, man by man,
Had fallen in Lyonnesse about their lord,
King Arthur. Then, because his wound was deep,
The old Sir Bedivere uplifted him,   175
And bore him to a chapel nigh the field,
A broken chancel with a broken cross,
That stood on a dark strait of barren land:
On one side lay the Ocean, and on one
Lay a great water, and the moon was full.   180

Then spake King Arthur to Sir Bedivere:
"The sequel of today unsolders all
The goodliest fellowship of famous knights
Whereof this world holds record. Such a sleep
They sleep—the men I loved. I think that we   185
Shall never more, at any future time,
Delight our souls with talk of knightly deeds,
Walking about the gardens and the halls
Of Camelot, as in the days that were.
I perish by this people which I made,—   190
Though Merlin sware that I should come again
To rule once more;[7] but, let what will be, be,
I am so deeply smitten through the helm
That without help I cannot last til morn.
Thou therefore take my brand[8] Excalibur,   195
Which was my pride: for thou rememberest how
In those old days, one summer noon, an arm
Rose up from out the bosom of the lake,
Clothed in white samite,[9] mystic, wonderful,
Holding the sword—and how I rowed across   200
And took it, and have worn it, like a king;
And, wheresoever I am sung or told
In aftertime, this also shall be known:
But now delay not: take Excalibur,
And fling him far into the middle mere:[1]   205
Watch what thou seëst, and lightly[2] bring me word."

To him replied the bold Sir Bedivere:
"It is not meet, Sir King, to leave thee thus,
Aidless, alone, and smitten through the helm—
A little thing may harm a wounded man;   210
Yet I thy hest[3] will all perform at full,
Watch what I see, and lightly bring thee word."

7. Cf. Malory 21.7: "Some men yet say in many parts of England that King Arthur is not dead, but by the will of our Lord in another place. And men say that he will come again."
8. Sword.
9. A rich, heavy silk.
1. Middle of the lake.
2. Quickly.
3. Command.

So saying, from the ruined shrine he stepped,
And in the moon athwart the place of tombs,
Where lay the mighty bones of ancient men,   215
Old knights, and over them the sea-wind sang
Shrill, chill, with flakes of foam. He, stepping down
By zigzag paths, and juts of pointed rock,
Came on the shining levels of the lake.

There drew he forth the brand Excalibur,   220
And o'er him, drawing it, the winter moon,
Brightening the skirts of a long cloud, ran forth
And sparkled keen with frost against the hilt:
For all the haft twinkled with diamond sparks,
Myriads of topaz-lights, and jacinth-work[4]   225
Of subtlest jewelry. He gazed so long
That both his eyes were dazzled as he stood,
This way and that dividing the swift mind,
In act to throw: but at the last it seemed
Better to leave Excalibur concealed   230
There in the many-knotted waterflags,
That whistled stiff and dry about the marge.
So strode he back slow to the wounded King.

Then spake King Arthur to Sir Bedivere:
"Hast thou performed my mission which I gave?   235
What is it thou hast seen? or what hast heard?"

And answer made the bold Sir Bedivere:
"I heard the ripple washing in the reeds,
And the wild water lapping on the crag."

To whom replied King Arthur, faint and pale: 240
"Thou hast betrayed thy nature and thy name.
Not rendering true answer, as beseemed
Thy fëalty, nor like a noble knight:
For surer sign had followed, either hand,
Or voice, or else a motion of the mere.   245
This is a shameful thing for men to lie.
Yet now, I charge thee, quickly go again,
As thou art lief[5] and dear, and do the thing
I bade thee, watch, and lightly bring me word."

Then went Sir Bedivere the second time   250
Across the ridge, and paced beside the mere,
Counting the dewy pebbles, fixed in thought;
But when he saw the wonder of the hilt,

---

4. A "jacinth" is a red gem.   5. Beloved.

How curiously[6] and strangely chased, he smote
His palms together, and he cried aloud: 255

"And if indeed I cast the brand away,
Surely a precious thing, one worthy note,
Should thus be lost forever from the earth,
Which might have pleased the eyes of many men.
What good should follow this, if this were done?   260
What harm, undone? Deep harm to disobey,
Seeing obedience is the bond of rule.
Were it well to obey then, if a king demand
An act unprofitable, against himself?
The King is sick, and knows not what he does.   265
What record, or what relic of my lord
Should be to aftertime, but empty breath
And rumors of a doubt? But were this kept,
Stored in some treasure-house of mighty kings,
Some one might show it at a joust of arms,   270
Saying, 'King Arthur's sword, Excalibur,
Wrought by the lonely maiden of the Lake.
Nine years she wrought it, sitting in the deeps
Upon the hidden bases of the hills.'
So might some old man speak in the aftertime   275
To all the people, winning reverence.
But now much honor and much fame were lost."

So spake he, clouded with his own conceit,[7]
And hid Excalibur the second time,
And so strode back slow to the wounded king.   280

Then spoke King Arthur, breathing heavily:
"What is it thou hast seen? or what hast heard?"

And answer made the bold Sir Bedivere:
"I heard the water lapping on the crag,
And the long ripple washing in the reeds."   285

To whom replied King Arthur, much in wrath:
"Ah, miserable and unkind, untrue,
Unknightly, traitor-hearted! Woe is me!
Authority forgets a dying king,
Laid widowed of the power in his eye   290
That bowed the will. I see thee what thou art,
For thou, the latest-left of all my knights,
In whom should meet the offices of all,
Thou wouldst betray me for the precious hilt;
Either from lust of gold, or like a girl   295

6. Skillfully. "Chased": adorned.   7. Vain and foolish fancies.

Valuing the giddy pleasure of the eyes.
Yet, for a man may fail in duty twice,
And the third time may prosper, get thee hence:
But, if thou spare to fling Excalibur,
I will arise and slay thee with my hands."   300

    Then quickly rose Sir Bedivere, and ran,
And, leaping down the ridges lightly, plunged
Among the bullrush beds, and clutched the sword,
And strongly wheeled and threw it. The great brand
Made lightnings in the splendor of the moon,   305
And flashing round and round and whirled in an arch,
Shot like a streamer of the northern morn,
Seen where the moving isles of winter shock[8]
By night, with noises of the Northern Sea.
So flashed and fell the brand Excalibur: 310
But ere he dipped the surface, rose an arm
Clothed in white samite, mystic, wonderful,
And caught him by the hilt, and brandished him
Three times, and drew him under in the mere.
And lightly went the other to the King.   315

    Then spoke King Arthur, drawing thicker breath:
"Now see I by thine eyes that this is done.
Speak out: what is it thou hast heard, or seen?"

    And answer made the bold Sir Bedivere:
"Sir King, I closed mine eyelids, lest the gems   320
Should blind my purpose, for I never saw,
Nor shall see, here or elsewhere, till I die,
Not though I live three lives of mortal men,
So great a miracle as yonder hilt.
Then with both hands I flung him, wheeling him;   325
But when I looked again, behold an arm,
Clothed in white samite, mystic, wonderful,
That caught him by the hilt, and brandished him
Three times, and drew him under in the mere."

    And answer made King Arthur, breathing hard: 330
"My end draws nigh; 'tis time that I were gone.
Make broad thy shoulders to receive my weight,
And bear me to the margin; yet I fear
My wound hath taken cold, and I shall die."

    So saying, from the pavement he half rose,   335
Slowly, with pain, reclining on his arm,
And looking wistfully with wide blue eyes

8. I.e., where the icebergs collide. "Northern morn": the northern lights.

As in a picture. Him Sir Bedivere
Remorsefully regarded through his tears,
And would have spoken, but he found not words;   340
Then took with care, and kneeling on one knee,
O'er both his shoulders drew the languid hands,
And rising bore him through the place of tombs.

But, as he walked, King Arthur panted hard,
Like one that feels a nightmare on his bed   345
When all the house is mute. So sighed the King,
Muttering and murmuring at his ear, "Quick, quick!
I fear it is too late, and I shall die."
But the other swiftly strode from ridge to ridge,
Clothed with his breath, and looking, as he walked,   350
Larger than human on the frozen hills.
He heard the deep behind him, and a cry
Before. His own thought drove him like a goad.
Dry clashed his harness in the icy caves
And barren chasms, and all to left and right   355
The bare black cliff clanged round him, as he based
His feet on juts of slippery crag that rang
Sharp-smitten with the dint of armèd heels—
And on a sudden, lo! the level lake,
And the long glories of the winter moon.   360

Then saw they how there hove a dusky barge,
Dark as a funeral scarf from stem to stern,
Beneath them; and descending they were ware
That all the decks were dense with stately forms,
Black-stoled, black-hooded, like a dream—by these   365
Three Queens with crowns of gold: and from them rose
A cry that shivered to the tingling stars,
And, as it were one voice, an agony
Of lamentation, like a wind that shrills
All night in a waste land, where no one comes,   370
Or hath come, since the making of the world.

Then murmured Arthur, "Place me in the barge."
So to the barge they came. There those three Queens
Put forth their hands, and took the King, and wept.
But she, that rose the tallest of them all   375
And fairest, laid his head upon her lap,
And loosed the shattered casque,[9] and chafed his hands,
And called him by his name, complaining loud,
And dropping bitter tears against a brow
Striped with dark blood: for all his face was white   380
And colorless, and like the withered moon

9. Helmet.

Smote by the fresh beam of the springing east;
And all his greaves and cuisses dashed with drops
Of onset;[1] and the light and lustrous curls—
That made his forehead like a rising sun   385
High from the daïs-throne—were parched with dust;
Or, clotted into points and hanging loose,
Mixed with the knightly growth that fringed his lips.
So like a shattered column lay the King;
Not like that Arthur who, with lance in rest,   390
From spur to plume a star of tournament,
Shot through the lists at Camelot, and charged
Before the eyes of ladies and of kings.

　　Then loudly cried the bold Sir Bedivere:
"Ah! my Lord Arthur, whither shall I go?   395
Where shall I hide my forehead and my eyes?
For now I see the true old times are dead,
When every morning brought a noble chance,
And every chance brought out a noble knight.
Such times have been not since the light that led   400
The holy Elders with the gift of myrrh.[2]
But now the whole Round Table is dissolved
Which was an image of the mighty world,
And I, the last, go forth companionless,
And the days darken round me, and the years,   405
Among new men, strange faces, other minds."

　　And slowly answered Arthur from the barge:
"The old order changeth, yielding place to new,
And God fulfills himself in many ways,
Lest one good custom should corrupt the world.   410
Comfort thyself: what comfort is in me?
I have lived my life, and that which I have done
May He within himself make pure! but thou,
If thou shouldst never see my face again,
Pray for my soul. More things are wrought by prayer   415
Than this world dreams of. Wherefore, let thy voice
Rise like a fountain for me night and day.
For what are men better than sheep or goats
That nourish a blind life within the brain,
If, knowing God, they lift not hands of prayer   420
Both for themselves and those who call them friend?
For so the whole round earth is every way
Bound by gold chains about the feet of God.
But now farewell. I am going a long way
With these thou seëst—if indeed I go   425

---

1. "Greaves": armor to protect the leg below the knee; "cuisses": armor to protect the front of the thighs; "onset": blood from battle.

2. I.e., the star that guided the three kings ("Elders") to the Christ Child at Bethlehem.

(For all my mind is clouded with a doubt)—
To the island-valley of Avilion;[3]
Where falls not hail, or rain, or any snow,
Nor ever wind blows loudly: but it lies
Deep-meadowed, happy, fair with orchard lawns   430
And bowery hollows crowned with summer sea,
Where I will heal me of my grievous wound."

So said he, and the barge with oar and sail
Moved from the brink, like some full-breasted swan
That, fluting a wild carol ere her death,   435
Ruffles her pure cold plume, and takes the flood
With swarthy webs. Long stood Sir Bedivere
Revolving many memories, till the hull
Looked one black dot against the verge of dawn,
And on the mere the wailing died away.   440

But when that moan had passed for evermore,
The stillness of the dead world's winter dawn
Amazed him, and he groaned, "The King is gone."
And therewithal came on him the weird rhyme,[4]
"From the great deep to the great deep he goes."   445

Whereat he slowly turned and slowly clomb
The last hard footstep of that iron crag;
Thence marked the black hull moving yet, and cried,
"He passes to be King among the dead,
And after healing of his grievous wound   450
He comes again; but—if he come no more—
O me, be yon dark Queens in yon black boat,
Who shrieked and wailed, the three whereat we gazed
On that high day, when, clothed with living light,
They stood before his throne in silence, friends   455
Of Arthur, who should help him at his need?"

Then from the dawn it seemed there came, but faint
As from beyond the limit of the world,
Like the last echo born of a great cry,
Sounds, as if some fair city were one voice   460
Around a king returning from his wars.

Thereat once more he moved about, and clomb
Even to the highest he could climb, and saw,
Straining his eyes beneath an arch of hand,
Or thought he saw, the speck that bare the King,   465

---

3. Avalon, in Celtic mythology and medieval romance, the Vale of the Blessed where heroes enjoyed life after death.
4. A mysterious prophecy in verse had been spoken by Merlin concerning Arthur's birth: "Sun, rain, and sun! and where is he who knows? From the great deep to the great deep he goes" (*The Coming of Arthur*, lines 409–10).

Down that long water opening on the deep
Somewhere far off, pass on and on, and go
From less to less and vanish into light.
And the new sun rose bringing the new year.

1833–69   1869

Northern Farmer[1]

New Style

1
Dosn't thou 'ear my 'erse's[2] legs, as they canters awaäy?
Proputty,[3] proputty, proputty—that's what I 'ears 'em saäy.
Proputty, proputty, proputty—Sam, thou's an ass for thy paaïns:
Theer's moor sense i' one o' 'is legs, nor in all thy braaïns.

2
Woä—theer's a craw[4] to pluck wi' tha, Sam: yon's parson's
        'ouse—   5
Dosn't thou knaw that a man mun be eäther a man or a mouse?
Time to think on it then; for thou'll be twenty to weeäk.[5]
Proputty, proputty—woä then woä—let ma 'ear mysèn[6] speäk.

3
Me an' thy muther, Sammy, 'as beän a-talkin' o' thee;
Thou's beän talkin' to muther, an' she beän a tellin' it me.   10
Thou'll not marry for munny—thou's sweet upo' parson's lass—
Noä—thou'll marry for luvv—an' we boäth on us thinks tha an ass.

4
Seeäd her todaäy goä by—Saäint's-daäy—they was ringing the bells.
She's a beauty thou thinks—an' soä is scoors o' gells,[7]
Them as 'as munny an' all—wot's a beauty?—the flower as blaws.   15
But proputty, proputty sticks, an' proputty, proputty graws.

5
Do'ant be stunt:[8] taäke time; I knaws what maäkes tha sa mad.
Warn't I craäzed fur the lasses mysèn when I wur a lad?
But I knawed a Quaäker feller as often 'as towd[9] ma this:
"Doänt thou marry for munny, but goä wheer munny is!"   20

6
An' I went wheer munny war; an' thy muther coom to 'and,
Wi' lots o' munny laaïd by, an' a nicetish bit o' land.

1. This monologue exemplifies the diversity of
Tennyson's talents. A passionate attachment to land
and property, which was portrayed sympathetically
by Wordsworth in *Michael*, is here represented
humorously. The harsh common sense of the
farmer's attitude toward love and marriage is reinforced by his jaw-breaking north English dialect.
    This is the second of a pair of monologues in
dialect. In the first, *Northern Farmer: Old Style*,
the speaker is a bailiff who has spent his life supervising the farmlands of a wealthy squire. In the
second, the "new style" farmer is himself an independent landowner.
2. Horse's.
3. Property.
4. Crow.
5. This week.
6. Myself.
7. Scores of girls.
8. Stubborn.
9. Told.

Maäybe she warn't a beauty:—I niver giv it a thowt—
But warn't she as good to cuddle an' kiss as a lass as 'ant nowt?[1]

7

Parson's lass 'ant nowt, an' she weänt 'a nowt[2] when 'e's deäd,   25
Mun be a guvness,[3] lad, or summut, and addle[4] her breäd:
Why? fur 'e's nobbut[5] a curate, an' weänt niver get hissèn clear,
An' 'e maäde the bed as 'e ligs[6] on afoor 'e coomed to the shere.

8

An' thin 'e coomed to the parish wi' lots o' Varsity debt,
Stook to his taaïl they did, an' 'e 'ant got shut on 'em[7] yet.   30
An' 'e ligs on 'is back i' the grip,[8] wi' noan to lend 'im a shuvv,
Woorse nor a far-weltered yowe:[9] fur, Sammy, 'e married fur luvv.

9

Luvv? what's luvv? thou can luvv thy lass an' 'er munny too,
Maäkin' 'em goä togither, as they've good right to do.
Couldn' I luvv thy muther by cause o' 'er munny laaïd by?   35
Naäy—fur I luvved 'er a vast sight moor fur it: reäson why.

10

Ay an' thy muther says thou wants to marry the lass,
Cooms of a gentleman burn:[1] an' we boäth on us think tha an ass.
Woä then, proputty, wiltha?—an ass as near as mays nowt[2]—
Woä then, wiltha? dangtha!—the bees is as fell as owt.[3]   40

11

Breäk me a bit o' the esh[4] for his 'eäd, lad, out o' the fence!
Gentleman burn! what's gentleman burn? is it shillins an' pence?
Proputty, proputty's ivrything 'ere, an', Sammy, I'm blest
If it isn't the saäme oop yonder, fur them as 'as it's the best.

12

Tis'n them as 'as munny as breäks into 'ouses an' steäls,   45
Them as 'as coäts to their backs an' taäkes their regular meäls.
Noä, but it's them as niver knaws wheer a meäl's to be 'ad.
Taäke my word for it, Sammy, the poor in a loomp is bad.

13

Them or thir feythers, tha sees, mun 'a beän a laäzy lot,
Fur work mun 'a gone to the gittin' whiniver munny was got.   50
Feyther 'ad ammost nowt; leästways 'is munny was 'id.
But 'e tued an' moiled[5] 'issèn deäd, an' 'e died a good un, 'e did.

14

Loök thou theer wheer Wrigglesby beck[6] cooms out by the 'ill!
Feyther run oop[7] to the farm, an' I runs oop to the mill;
An' I'll run oop to the brig,[8] an' that thou'll live to see;   55
And if thou marries a good un I'll leäve the land to thee.

---

1. Has nothing.
2. Won't have anything.
3. Must be a governess.
4. Earn.
5. Nothing but.
6. Lies; "shere": shire.
7. Rid of them.
8. Ditch.
9. Ewe lying on her back.

1. Born.
2. Makes nothing.
3. The flies are as mean as anything.
4. A branch of ash leaves (to keep the flies off the horse's head).
5. Toiled and drudged.
6. Brook.
7. I.e., father's property ran up.
8. Bridge.

15

Thim's my noätions, Sammy, wheerby I meäns to stick;
But if thou marries a bad un, I'll leäve the land to Dick.—
Coom oop, propputty, proputty—that's what I 'ears 'im saäy—
Proputty, proputty, proputty—canter an' canter awaäy.   60

1869

Flower in the Crannied Wall

Flower in the crannied wall,
I pluck you out of the crannies,
I hold you here, root and all, in my hand,
Little flower—but if I could understand
What you are, root and all, and all in all,   5
I should know what God and man is.

1869

"Frater Ave atque Vale"[1]

Row us out from Desenzano,[2] to your Sirmione row!
So they rowed, and there we landed—"O venusta Sirmio!"
There to me through all the groves of olive in the summer glow,
There beneath the Roman ruin where the purple flowers grow,
Came that "Ave atque Vale" of the Poet's hopeless woe,   5
Tenderest of Roman poets nineteen hundred years ago,
"Frater Ave atque Vale"—as we wandered to and fro
Gazing at the Lydian[3] laughter of the Garda Lake below
Sweet Catullus's all-but-island olive-silvery Sirmio!

1880   1883

The Dawn

"You are but children."
—EGYPTIAN PRIEST TO SOLON

Red of the Dawn!
Screams of a babe in the red-hot palms of a Moloch[1] of Tyre,
Man with his brotherless dinner on man in the tropical wood,

1. "Brother, hail and farewell," a line from an elegy by the Roman poet Catullus on the death of his brother (101.10). Tennyson himself had recently lost his brother Charles.
2. A town on Lake Garda in Italy, which Tennyson visited in 1880. Sirmione is a beautiful peninsula jutting into the lake, on which Catullus had his summer home. Catullus's poem in honor of the locality includes the phrase "O venusta Sirmio!" ("O lovely Sirmio!").
3. The Etruscans, who settled near Lake Garda, were thought to be descended from the Lydians of Asia Minor.
1. A god to whom children were sacrificed as burnt offerings.

Priests in the name of the Lord passing souls through fire to the fire,
Head-hunters and boats of Dahomey[2] that float upon human blood!   5

Red of the Dawn!
Godless fury of peoples, and Christless frolic of kings,
    And the bolt of war dashing down upon cities and blazing farms,
    For Babylon was a child newborn, and Rome was a babe in arms,
And London and Paris and all the rest are as yet but in leading
        strings.   10

Dawn not Day,
While scandal is mouthing a bloodless name at *her* cannibal feast,
    And rake-ruined bodies and souls go down in a common wreck,
    And the Press of a thousand cities is prized for it smells of the beast,
Or easily violates virgin Truth for a coin or a check.   15

Dawn not Day!
Is it Shame, so few should have climbed from the dens in the level
        below,
    Men, with a heart and a soul, no slaves of a four-footed will?
    But if twenty million of summers are stored in the sunlight still,
We are far from the noon of man, there is time for the race to grow.   20

Red of the Dawn!
Is it turning a fainter red? So be it, but when shall we lay
    The Ghost of the Brute that is walking and haunting us yet, and be
        free?
    In a hundred, a thousand winters? Ah, what will *our* children be?
The men of a hundred thousand, a million summers away?   25

1892

Crossing the Bar[1]

Sunset and evening star,
    And one clear call for me!
And may there be no moaning of the bar,[2]
    When I put out to sea,

But such a tide as moving seems asleep,   5
    Too full for sound and foam,
When that which drew from out the boundless deep
    Turns again home.

2. West African country in which the custom of
human sacrifice persisted in the 19th century. In
1892, after a war, Dahomey became a French colony.
1. Although not the last poem written by Tenny-

son, *Crossing the Bar* appears, at his request, as
the final poem in all collections of his work.
2. Mournful sound of the ocean beating on a sand
bar at the mouth of a harbor.

Twilight and evening bell,
   And after that the dark!   10
And may there be no sadness of farewell,
   When I embark;

For though from out our bourne[3] of Time and Place
   The flood may bear me far,
I hope to see my Pilot face to face   15
   When I have crossed the bar.

1889   1889

3. Boundary.

ROBERT BROWNING
1812–1889

1846:   Marriage to Elizabeth Barrett and residence in Italy.
1855:   *Men and Women* published.
1861:   Death of Elizabeth Barrett Browning.
1868–69:   *The Ring and the Book* published.

During the years of his marriage Robert Browning was sometimes referred to as "Mrs. Browning's husband." Elizabeth Barrett, who seems to us now a lesser figure, was at that time a famous poet while her husband was a relatively unknown experimenter whose poems were greeted with misunderstanding or indifference. Not until the 1860s did he at last gain a public and become recognized as the rival or equal of Tennyson. In the twentieth century his reputation has persisted, but in an unusual way: his poetry is admired by two groups of readers widely different in tastes. To one group his work is a moral tonic. Such readers appreciate him as a man who lived bravely and as a writer who showed life to be a joyful battle, the imperfections of this world being remedied, under the dispensations of an all-loving God, by the perfections of the next. Typical of this group are the Browning Societies that have flourished in England and America. Members of these societies usually regard their poet as a wise philosopher and religious teacher who resolved the doubts which had troubled Arnold and Tennyson and which have continued to trouble later generations of less confident writers.

    A second group of readers enjoy Browning less for his attempt to solve problems of religious doubt than for his attempt to solve the problems of how poetry should be written. Such poets as Ezra Pound and Robert Lowell have valued him as a major artist; they have recognized that more than any other nineteenth-century poet (even including Hopkins), it was Browning who energetically hacked through a trail that has subsequently become the main road of twentieth-century poetry. In *Poetry and the Age* (1953) Randall Jarrell remarked how "the dramatic monologue, which once had depended for its effect upon being a departure from the norm of poetry, now became in one form or another the norm." Later poets such as Edward Lucie-Smith in England and Richard Howard in America are especially close to Browning's mode. In 1969, Howard dedicated a volume of monologues to Browning: "to the great poet of otherness . . . who said, as I should like to say, 'I'll tell my state as though 'twere none of mine.' "

The dramatic monologue, as Browning uses it, enables the reader, speaker, and poet to be located at an appropriate distance from each other, aligned in such a way that readers must work *through* the words of the speaker toward the meaning of the poet themselves. For example, in the well-known early monologue *My Last Duchess*, we listen to the Duke as he speaks of his dead wife, and it is almost as if we were overhearing a man talking into the telephone of a booth adjacent to ours. From his one-sided conversation we piece together the situation, both past and present, and we infer what sort of woman the Duchess really was, and what sort of man is the Duke. Ultimately we may also infer what the poet himself thinks of the speaker he has created. In this instance, from evidence outside the poem we know that Browning had a special aversion for domestic tyrants. His own father-in-law was to provide him with a striking example of the breed, and it is revealing that in his longest poem, *The Ring and the Book*, he once more explored the story of another domestic tyrant who, like the Duke, was irritated by his wife's virtues. Yet from *My Last Duchess* itself, if we exclude external evidence, it is interesting to note how persuasive is the Duke's own side of the story:

> She had
> A heart—how shall I say?—too soon made glad,
> Too easily impressed; she liked whate'er
> She looked on, and her looks went everywhere.

Although Browning contrives that our verdict as jurors will be a just one, he does allow us a considerable amount of latitude. And in some of his later monologues we are really obliged to grope toward a choice. In reading *A Grammarian's Funeral*, for example, can we be sure that the central character is a hero? Or is he merely a fool? Browning has not made the answer easy for us.

In addition to his experiments with the dramatic monologue Browning also made experiments with language and syntax. The grotesque rhymes and jaw-breaking diction which he often employs have been repugnant to some critics; George Santayana, for instance, dismissed him as a clumsy barbarian. But to those who understand Browning's aims, the incongruities of language are not literally incongruous but functional, a humorous and appropriate counterpart to an imperfect world. Ezra Pound's tribute to "Old Hippety-Hop o' the accents," as he addresses Browning, is both affectionate and memorable:

> Heart that was big as the bowels of Vesuvius
> Words that were winged as her sparks in eruption,
> Eagled and thundered as Jupiter Pluvius
> Sound in your wind past all signs o' corruption.

This capacity to attract the admiration of such a diversity of readers, sophisticated and unsophisticated, is one of several ways in which Browning's writings can be likened to those of Dickens and Shakespeare.

The personal life of Robert Browning falls into three phases: his years as a child and young bachelor, as a husband, and as a widower. Each of these phases is most appropriately considered in relation to his development as a poet.

He was born in Camberwell, a London suburb, within a few months of the births of Dickens and Thackeray. His father, a bank clerk, was a learned man with an extensive library. His mother was a kindly, religious-minded woman, interested in music, whose love for her brilliant son was warmly reciprocated. Until the time of his marriage at the age of thirty-four Browning was rarely absent from his parents' home. He attended a boarding school near Camberwell, traveled a little (to Russia and Italy), and was a student at the University of London for a short period, but he preferred to pursue his education at home where he was tutored in foreign languages, music, boxing, and horsemanship, and where he read omnivorously. From this unusual education he acquired a store of knowledge upon which to draw for the background of his poems.

The "obscurity" of which his contemporaries complained in his earlier poetry may be partly accounted for by the circumstances of Browning's education. He was inclined to assume that his out-of-the-ordinary learning was generally shared by educated readers. Often it was not. But the obscurity of such poems as *Sordello* (1840) is attributable not only to the nature of Browning's learning but to the poet's anxious desire to avoid exposing himself too explicitly before his readers. His first poem, *Pauline*, published when he was twenty-one, had been modeled on the example of Shelley, the most personal of poets. When a review by John Stuart Mill pointed out that the young author was parading a "morbid state" of self-worship, Browning was overwhelmed with embarrassment. He resolved to avoid confessional writings thereafter.

One way of reducing the personal element in his poetry was to write plays instead of soul-searching narratives or lyrics. In 1836, encouraged by the actor W. C. Macready, Browning began work on his first play, *Strafford*, a historical tragedy that lasted only four nights when it was produced at a London theater in 1837. For ten years the young writer struggled to produce other plays that would better hold the attention of an audience, but as stage productions they all remained failures. Browning nevertheless profited from this otherwise disheartening experience. Writing dialogue for actors led him to explore another form more congenial to his genius, the dramatic monologue, a form that enabled him through imaginary speakers to avoid explicit autobiography and yet did not demand that these speakers act out their story with the speed or the simplifications that stage production demands. As William Irvine notes: "In Browning's monologues, murderers recollect, but do not commit, their murders." His first collection of such monologues, *Dramatic Lyrics*, appeared in 1842. Unlike Tennyson's volume, appearing the same year, *Dramatic Lyrics* was as poorly received by reviewers and public as Browning's plays had been.

Browning's resolution to avoid the subjective manner of Shelley did not preclude his being influenced by the earlier poet in other ways. At fourteen, when he first discovered Shelley's works, he became an atheist and liberal. Although he grew away from the atheism, after a struggle, and also the extreme phases of his liberalism, he retained from Shelley's influence something permanent and more difficult to define: an ardent dedication to ideals (often undefined ideals) and an energetic striving toward goals (often undefined goals). This quality of aspiration is much more mixed with earthiness—even worldliness—in Browning's character than in Shelley's. To soar upwards on a skylark's wing was not to Browning's taste. He is more like Robert Frost's swinger of birches who climbs a tree toward heaven but is anxious to swing down to earth again before getting too far away.

Yet the element of worldliness should not obscure from us Browning's ardent romanticism. His love affair with Elizabeth Barrett was romantic in several of the senses of that hard-worked adjective. It is easy to see why the well-known story of their courtship has been retold by novelists, dramatists, and movie-producers, for the situation had the dramatic ingredients of Browning's own favorite story of St. George rescuing the maiden from the dragon. Almost everything seemed unpropitious when Browning met Elizabeth Barrett in 1845. She was six years older than he was, a semi-invalid, jealously guarded by her possessively tyrannical father. But love, as the poet was to say later, is best, and love swept aside all obstacles. After their elopement to Italy, the former semi-invalid was soon enjoying good health and a full life. The husband likewise seemed to thrive during the years of this remarkable marriage. Like many English poets he was especially at ease in the warm lands of the Mediterranean. His most memorable volume of poems, *Men and Women* (1855), reflects his enjoyment of Italy: its picturesque landscapes and lively street scenes as well as its monuments from the past— its Renaissance past in particular, a period of expanding energies which was congenial to his own expansive temperament.

The happy fifteen-year sojourn in Italy ended in 1861 with Elizabeth's death. The widower returned to London with his son. During the twenty-eight years remaining to him, the quantity of verse he produced did not diminish. Nor, during the first decade, did it decrease in quality. *Dramatis Personae* (1864) is a volume containing some of his finest monologues, such as *Caliban upon Setebos*. And in 1868 he published his greatest single poem, *The Ring and the Book*, which was inspired by his discovery of an old book of legal records concerning a murder trial in seventeenth-century Rome. His poem tells the story of a brutally sadistic husband, Count Guido Franceschini (who has much in common with the duke in *My Last Duchess*). The middle-aged Guido grows dissatisfied with his young wife, Pompilia, and accuses her of having adulterous relations with a handsome priest who, like St. George, had tried to rescue her from the dragon's den in which her husband confined her. Eventually Guido stabs his wife to death and is himself executed. In a series of twelve books Browning retells this tale of violence, presenting it from the contrasting points of view of participants and spectators. Because of its vast scale, *The Ring and the Book* is like a Victorian novel, but in its experiments with multiple points of view it anticipates later novels such as Conrad's *Lord Jim*. (Unlike Tennyson's major long poem, *The Idylls of the King*, Browning's twelve monologues do not lend themselves to excerpting.)

After *The Ring and the Book* several more volumes appeared. In general Browning's writings during the last two decades of his life suffer from a certain mechanical repetition of mannerism and an excess of argumentation—faults into which he may have been led by the unqualified enthusiasm of his admirers, for it was during this period that he gained his great following. When he died, in 1889, he was buried in Westminster Abbey.

During these London years Browning became abundantly fond of social life. He dined at the homes of friends and at clubs, where he enjoyed port wine and conversation. He would talk loudly and emphatically about many topics—except his own poetry, about which he was usually reticent. His reticence bothered many of his admirers. American women visiting in London, after having looked forward to meeting the author whose poems had inspired them to higher things, were disappointed—almost appalled—when they met the man at a dinner party. He did not "look like a poet." His late poem *House* may show why he gave such an impression. Behind the façade of the hearty diner-out, Browning could live and think as he pleased, just as he had discovered in writing his monologues the advantage, for him, of indirect speaking. Each speaker of monologue provides a mask for the poet.

Despite his bursts of outspokenness, Browning's character is thus not so clearly known to us as that of Tennyson or Arnold or Carlyle. Hardy once said that Browning's character seemed to him "*the* literary puzzle of the nineteenth century." To solve the puzzle one biographer, Betty Miller, has tried to show that Browning was not such a happy and confident person as he is usually represented to have been, an impression that can be reinforced by the note of desperation in such poems as *Childe Roland*. And although later biographies correct the eccentricities of this interpretation, they also demonstrate that Browning was a complex figure. Like Yeats, he was a poet preoccupied with masks. On the occasion of his burial in Westminster Abbey, his friend Henry James reflected that many oddities and many great writers have been buried there, "but none of the odd ones have been so great and none of the great ones been so odd."

Just as Browning's character is harder to identify than that of Tennyson, so also are his poems more difficult to relate to the age in which they were written than are the sometimes topical poems of Tennyson. Our first impression may be that there is no connection whatever. Bishops and painters of the Renaissance, physicians of the Roman Empire, musicians of eighteenth-century Germany—as we explore this gallery of talking portraits we seem to be in a world of time long past, remote from the world of steam engines and disputes about human beings' descent from the ape.

Yet our first impression is misleading. Many of these portraits explore problems that confronted Browning's contemporaries, especially problems of faith and doubt, good and evil, and problems of the function of the artist in modern life. *Caliban upon Setebos*, for example, is a highly topical critique of Darwinism and of natural (as opposed to supernatural) religions. Browning's own attitude towards these topics is partially concealed because of his use of speakers and of settings from earlier ages, yet we do encounter certain recurrent religious assumptions that we can safely assign to the poet himself. The most recurrent is that God has created an imperfect world as a kind of testing ground, a "vale of soul-making," as Keats had said. It followed, for Browning's purposes, that the human soul must be immortal and that heaven itself be perfect. As Abt Vogler affirms: "On the earth the broken arcs; in the heaven, a perfect round." Armed with such a faith, Browning gives the impression that he was himself untroubled by the doubts that gnawed at the hearts of Arnold and Clough and Tennyson. The "evidence" presented by historical criticism of the Bible he could dismiss as simply irrelevant, just as D. H. Lawrence, a later romantic, disposed of evolution by contending that he did not feel the evidence for it in his solar plexus.

This kind of religious conviction attracts many readers who expect poetry to provide uplift and reassurances. Other readers find it an insurmountable obstacle, as fatuous as Macaulay's faith in progress. To what extent our capacity to enjoy the writings of authors is hindered if their religious positions seem repellent to us is one of the most important problems in modern criticism. The problem is much too vast to explore here, but there is at least room to insert a qualifying clause to modify the indictment that Browning's critics too hastily draw up against his cheerful religious position. A blind optimist might be simply unreadable, but Browning's optimism was not blind. Few writers, in fact, seem to have been more aware of the existence of evil. His gallery of villains—murderers, sadistic husbands, mean and petty manipulators—is an extraordinary one. Nothing is more essential to a fair-minded study of his poetry than our recognition that his apparent optimism is consistently being tested by his bringing to light the evils of human nature. Readers who prefer to dispose of his writings by pinning them down in a formulated phrase, instead of reading them with attention, invariably cite the following lines as summing up all of Browning:

> God's in his heaven—
> All's right with the world!

But if we turn to the poem in which these lines appear, we have to modify our formulation. *Pippa Passes* is a collection of sordid tales such as one encounters on the front page of the most lurid style of newspaper. The heroine, who works in a sweatshop 364 days a year, is about to be sent to Rome as a prostitute; a man and woman living in adultery have just murdered the woman's husband; a waspish set of bohemians have tricked a youth into marriage. Because Pippa's innocence seems to counteract the sordidness of the other scenes, we may say afterwards that God is in his heaven. But that all's right with the world is merely affirmed by the girl; the poem does not show it.

A second aspect of Browning's poetry that separates it from the Victorian age is its style. The most representative Victorian poets such as Tennyson or Dante Gabriel Rossetti write in the manner of Keats, Milton, Spenser, and of classical poets such as Virgil. Theirs is the central stylistic tradition in English poetry, one which favors smoothly polished texture and pleasing liquidity of sound. Browning draws from a different tradition, more colloquial and discordant, a tradition which includes the poetry of John Donne, the soliloquies of Shakespeare, the comic verse of the early nineteenth-century poet Thomas Hood, and certain features of the narrative style of Chaucer. Of most significance are Browning's affinities with Donne. Both poets sacrifice, on occasion, the pleasures of harmony and of a consistent elevation of tone by using a harshly discordant style and unexpected juxtapositions that startle us into an awareness of a world of everyday realities and trivialities. Readers who dislike this kind of poetry in Browning or in Donne argue that it suffers from prosiness. Oscar Wilde once described the novelist George Meredith as "a prose Browning." And so, he added, was Browning. Wilde's joke may help us to relate Browning to his contemporaries. For if Browning seems out of step with his fellow Victorian poets, he is by no means out of step with his contemporaries in prose. The grotesque, which plays such a prominent role in the style and subject matter of Carlyle and Dickens, and in the aesthetic theories of John Ruskin, is equally prominent in Browning's verse:

Fee, faw, fum! bubble and squeak!
Blessedest Thursday's the fat of the week.
Rumble and tumble, sleek and rough,
Stinking and savory, smug and gruff.

These opening lines of *Holy-Cross Day* display a kind of noisy jocularity in presenting a situation of grave seriousness similar to that used by Carlyle in his *Sartor Resartus*. It was fitting that Browning and Carlyle remained good friends, even though the elder writer kept urging Browning to give up verse in favor of prose.

The link between Browning and the Victorian prose writers is not limited to style. With the later generation of Victorian novelists, George Eliot, George Meredith, and Henry James, Browning shares a central preoccupation. Like Eliot in particular, he was interested in exposing the devious ways in which our minds work and the complexity of our motives. "My stress lay on incidents in the development of a human soul," he wrote; "little else is worth study." His psychological insights can be illustrated in such a poem as *The Bishop Orders His Tomb*. Although this is a spoken monologue, not an inner monologue in the manner of James Joyce, the insight into the workings of the mind is similarly acute. As in reading Joyce, we must be on our guard to follow the rapid shifts of the speaker's mental processes as jumps are made from one cluster of associations to another. A further challenge for the reader of Browning is to identify what has been left out. As was remarked in a letter by the 1890s poet, Ernest Dowson, Browning's "masterpieces in verse" demonstrate both "subtlety" and "the tact of omission." *My Last Duchess*, he added, "is pure Henry James."

But Browning's role as a forerunner of twentieth-century literature should not blind us to his essential Victorianism. Energy is the most characteristic aspect of his writing, and energy is perhaps the most characteristic aspect of Victorian literature in general. Often, of course, such energy was misdirected. Gerard Manley Hopkins identified this failing precisely when he complained of Browning's "Broad Church" way of talking, like "a man bouncing up from table with his mouth full of bread and cheese and saying that he meant to stand no blasted nonsense." At its best, however, such buoyancy is a virtue imparting a creative vitality to all of Browning's writings.

Porphyria's Lover[1]

The rain set early in tonight,
    The sullen wind was soon awake,
It tore the elm-tops down for spite,
    And did its worst to vex the lake:
    I listened with heart fit to break.   5
When glided in Porphyria; straight
    She shut the cold out and the storm,

---

1. One of a pair of monologues originally published under the title *Madhouse Cells*, a title that emphasized the abnormal state of mind of the speaker.

And kneeled and made the cheerless grate
    Blaze up, and all the cottage warm;
      Which done, she rose, and from her form   10
Withdrew the dripping cloak and shawl,
    And laid her soiled gloves by, untied
Her hat and let the damp hair fall,
    And, last, she sat down by my side
      And called me. When no voice replied,   15
She put my arm about her waist,
    And made her smooth white shoulder bare,
And all her yellow hair displaced,
    And, stooping, made my cheek lie there,
      And spread, o'er all, her yellow hair,   20
Murmuring how she loved me—she
    Too weak, for all her heart's endeavor,
To set its struggling passion free
    From pride, and vainer ties dissever,
      And give herself to me forever.   25
But passion sometimes would prevail,
    Nor could tonight's gay feast restrain
A sudden thought of one so pale
    For love of her, and all in vain:
      So, she was come through wind and rain.   30
Be sure I looked up at her eyes
    Happy and proud; at last I knew
Porphyria worshiped me: surprise
    Made my heart swell, and still it grew
      While I debated what to do.   35
That moment she was mine, mine, fair,
    Perfectly pure and good: I found
A thing to do, and all her hair
    In one long yellow string I wound
      Three times her little throat around,   40
And strangled her. No pain felt she;
    I am quite sure she felt no pain.
As a shut bud that holds a bee,
    I warily oped her lids: again
      Laughed the blue eyes without a stain.   45
And I untightened next the tress
    About her neck; her cheek once more
Blushed bright beneath my burning kiss:
    I propped her head up as before,
      Only, this time my shoulder bore   50
Her head, which droops upon it still:
    The smiling rosy little head,
So glad it has its utmost will,
    That all it scorned at once is fled,
      And I, its love, am gained instead!   55
Porphyria's love: she guessed not how

Her darling one wish would be heard.
And thus we sit together now,
  And all night long we have not stirred,
  And yet God has not said a word!   60

1834   1836, 1842

Soliloquy of the Spanish Cloister[1]

1

Gr-r-r—there go, my heart's abhorrence!
  Water your damned flowerpots, do!
If hate killed men, Brother Lawrence,
  God's blood, would not mine kill you!
What? your myrtle bush wants trimming?   5
  Oh, that rose has prior claims—
Needs its leaden vase filled brimming?
  Hell dry you up with its flames!

2

At the meal we sit together:
  Salve tibi![2] I must hear   10
Wise talk of the kind of weather,
  Sort of season, time of year:
Not a plenteous cork crop: scarcely
  Dare we hope oak-galls,[3] *I doubt:*
What's the Latin name for "parsley"?   15
  What's the Greek name for Swine's Snout?[4]

3

Whew! We'll have our platter burnished,
  Laid with care on our own shelf!
With a fire-new spoon we're furnished,
  And a goblet for ourself,   20
Rinsed like something sacrificial
  Ere 'tis fit to touch our chaps[5]—
Marked with L. for our initial!
  (He-he! There his lily snaps!)

4

Saint, forsooth! While brown Dolores   25
  Squats outside the Convent bank
With Sanchicha, telling stories,
  Steeping tresses in the tank,
Blue-black, lustrous, thick like horsehairs,
  —Can't I see his dead eye glow,   30

1. No period of history is specified in this poem.
2. "Hail to thee!" This and other speeches in italics in this stanza are supposed to be the words of Brother Lawrence.
3. Abnormal outgrowths on oak trees, used for tanning.
4. In the 19th century, "Swine's Snout" meant dandelion.
5. Jaws.

Bright as 'twere a Barbary corsair's?[6]
    (That is, if he'd let it show!)

5

When he finishes refection,[7]
    Knife and fork he never lays
Cross-wise, to my recollection,   35
    As do I, in Jesu's praise.
I the Trinity illustrate,
    Drinking watered orange pulp—
In three sips the Arian[8] frustrate;
    While he drains his at one gulp.   40

6

Oh, those melons? If he's able
    We're to have a feast! so nice!
One goes to the Abbot's table,
    All of us get each a slice.
How go on your flowers? None double?   45
    Not one fruit-sort can you spy?
Strange!—And I, too, at such trouble,
    Keep them close-nipped on the sly!

7

There's a great text in Galatians,[9]
    Once you trip on it, entails   50
Twenty-nine distinct damnations,
    One sure, if another fails:
If I trip him just a-dying,
    Sure of heaven as sure can be,
Spin him round and send him flying
    Off to hell, a Manichee?[1]   55

8

Or, my scrofulous French novel
    On gray paper with blunt type!
Simply glance at it, you grovel
    Hand and foot in Belial's gripe: 60
If I double down its pages
    At the woeful sixteenth print,
When he gathers his greengages,
    Ope a sieve and slip it in't?

9

Or, there's Satan!—one might venture   65
    Pledge one's soul to him,[2] yet leave

---

6. Pirate of the Barbary Coast of northern Africa, renowned for fierceness and lechery.

7. Dinner.

8. Heretical followers of Arius (256–336), who denied the divinity of the Trinity.

9. The speaker hopes to obtain Lawrence's damnation by luring him into a heresy, this to be accomplished by exposing him to the difficult task of interpreting "Galatians" in an unswervingly orthodox way. In Galatians 5.15–23, St. Paul specifies an assortment of "works of the flesh" that lead to damnation, which could make up a total of "twenty-nine."

1. A heretic, a follower of the Persian prophet of the 3rd century, Mani.

2. The speaker would pledge his own soul to Satan in return for blasting Lawrence and his "rose-acacia," but the pledge would be so cleverly worded that the speaker would not have to pay, himself, his debt to Satan. There would be an escape-clause, a "flaw in the indenture," for himself.

Such a flaw in the indenture
   As he'd miss till, past retrieve,
Blasted lay that rose-acacia
   We're so proud of! *Hy, Zy, Hine* . . .[3]   70
'St, there's Vespers! *Plena gratiâ*
   Ave, Virgo![4] Gr-r-r—you swine!

ca. 1839   1842

My Last Duchess[1]

FERRARA

That's my last Duchess painted on the wall,
Looking as if she were alive. I call
That piece a wonder, now: Frà Pandolf's[2] hands
Worked busily a day, and there she stands.
Will 't please you sit and look at her? I said   5
"Frà Pandolf" by design, for never read
Strangers like you that pictured countenance,
The depth and passion of its earnest glance,
But to myself they turned (since none puts by
The curtain I have drawn for you, but I)   10
And seemed as they would ask me, if they durst,
How such a glance came there; so, not the first
Are you to turn and ask thus. Sir, 'twas not
Her husband's presence only, called that spot
Of joy into the Duchess' cheek: perhaps   15
Frà Pandolf chanced to say "Her mantle laps
Over my lady's wrist too much," or "Paint
Must never hope to reproduce the faint
Half-flush that dies along her throat": such stuff
Was courtesy, she thought, and cause enough   20
For calling up that spot of joy. She had
A heart—how shall I say?—too soon made glad,
Too easily impressed; she liked whate'er
She looked on, and her looks went everywhere.
Sir, 'twas all one! My favor at her breast,   25
The dropping of the daylight in the West,
The bough of cherries some officious fool
Broke in the orchard for her, the white mule
She rode with round the terrace—all and each

---

3. Perhaps the opening of a mysterious curse against Lawrence.
4. "Full of grace, Hail, Virgin!" The speaker's twisted state of mind may be reflected in his mixed-up version of the prayer to Mary: "Ave, Maria, gratia plena."
1. The poem is based on incidents in the life of Alfonso II, duke of Ferrara in Italy, whose first wife, Lucrezia, a young girl, died in 1561 after 3 years of marriage. Following her death, the duke negotiated through an agent to marry a niece of the count of Tyrol. Browning represents the duke as addressing this agent.
2. Brother Pandolf, an imaginary painter.

Would draw from her alike the approving speech,   30
Or blush, at least. She thanked men—good! but thanked
Somehow—I know not how—as if she ranked
My gift of a nine-hundred-years-old name
With anybody's gift. Who'd stoop to blame
This sort of trifling? Even had you skill   35
In speech—(which I have not)—to make your will
Quite clear to such an one, and say, "Just this
Or that in you disgusts me; here you miss,
Or there exceed the mark"—and if she let
Herself be lessoned so, nor plainly set   40
Her wits to yours, forsooth, and made excuse
—E'en then would be some stooping; and I choose
Never to stoop. Oh sir, she smiled, no doubt,
Whene'er I passed her; but who passed without
Much the same smile? This grew; I gave commands;   45
Then all smiles stopped together. There she stands
As if alive. Will 't please you rise? We'll meet
The company below, then. I repeat,
The Count your master's known munificence
Is ample warrant that no just pretense   50
Of mine for dowry will be disallowed;
Though his fair daughter's self, as I avowed
At starting, is my object. Nay, we'll go
Together down, sir. Notice Neptune, though,
Taming a sea horse, thought a rarity,   55
Which Claus of Innsbruck[3] cast in bronze for me!

1842   1842

Home-Thoughts, from Abroad

1

Oh, to be in England
Now that April's there,
And whoever wakes in England
Sees, some morning, unaware,
That the lowest boughs and the brushwood sheaf   5
Round the elm-tree bole are in tiny leaf,
While the chaffinch sings on the orchard bough
In England—now!

2

And after April, when May follows,
And the whitethroat builds, and all the swallows!   10
Hark, where my blossomed peartree in the hedge
Leans to the field and scatters on the clover
Blossoms and dewdrops—at the bent spray's edge—

3. An unidentified or imaginary sculptor. The count of Tyrol had his capital at Innsbruck.

That's the wise thrush; he sings each song twice over,
Lest you should think he never could recapture
The first fine careless rapture!
And though the fields look rough with hoary dew,
All will be gay when noontide wakes anew
The buttercups, the little children's dower
—Far brighter than this gaudy melon-flower!

ca. 1845   1845

Home-Thoughts, from the Sea

Nobly, nobly Cape Saint Vincent[1] to the northwest died away;
Sunset ran, one glorious blood-red, reeking into Cadiz Bay;
Bluish 'mid the burning water, full in face Trafalgar[2] lay;
In the dimmest northeast distance dawned Gibraltar grand and gray;
"Here and here did England help me: how can I help England?"
        —say,
Whoso turns as I, this evening, turn to God to praise and pray,
While Jove's planet[3] rises yonder, silent over Africa.

1844   1845

The Bishop Orders His Tomb at Saint Praxed's Church[1]

Rome, 15—

Vanity, saith the preacher, vanity![2]
Draw round my bed: is Anselm keeping back?
Nephews—sons mine . . . ah God, I know not! Well—
She, men would have to be your mother once,
Old Gandolf envied me, so fair she was!
What's done is done, and she is dead beside,
Dead long ago, and I am Bishop since,

1. Off the coast of Portugal, scene of British naval victory under Admiral Nelson (1797).
2. A cape in Spain, where Nelson won his great victory over Napoleon's fleets (1805).
3. Jupiter.
1. In *Fra Lippo Lippi* Browning represents the dawn of the Renaissance in Italy, with its fresh zest for man's experiences in this world. In the present monologue he portrays a later stage of the Renaissance when such worldliness, full-blown, had infected even some of the leading churchmen of Italy. Browning's portrait of the dying bishop is, however, not primarily a satire against corruption in the church. It is a brilliant exposition of the workings of a mind, a mind that has been conditioned by special historical circumstances. The Victorian historian of art, John Ruskin, said of this poem: "I know of no other piece of modern English, prose or poetry, in which there is so much told, as in these lines, of the Renaissance spirit—its worldliness, inconsistency, pride, hypocrisy, ignorance of itself, love of art, of luxury, and of good Latin. It is nearly all that I have said of the central Renaissance in thirty pages of the *Stones of Venice*, put into as many lines, Browning's also being the antecedent work."
    St. Praxed's Church was named in honor of St. Praxedes, a Roman virgin of the 2nd century who gave her riches to poor Christians. Both the bishop and his predecessor, Gandolf, are imaginary persons.
2. Cf. Ecclesiastes 1.2.

And as she died so must we die ourselves,
And thence ye may perceive the world's a dream.
Life, how and what is it? As here I lie   10
In this state chamber, dying by degrees,
Hours and long hours in the dead night, I ask
"Do I live, am I dead?" Peace, peace seems all.
Saint Praxed's ever was the church for peace;
And so, about this tomb of mine. I fought   15
With tooth and nail to save my niche, ye know:
—Old Gandolf cozened[3] me, despite my care;
Shrewd was that snatch from out the corner south
He graced his carrion with, God curse the same!
Yet still my niche is not so cramped but thence   20
One sees the pulpit o' the epistle side,[4]
And somewhat of the choir, those silent seats,
And up into the aery dome where live
The angels, and a sunbeam's sure to lurk:
And I shall fill my slab of basalt[5] there,   25
And 'neath my tabernacle[6] take my rest,
With those nine columns round me, two and two,
The odd one at my feet where Anselm stands:
Peach-blossom marble all, the rare, the ripe
As fresh-poured red wine of a mighty pulse.[7]   30
—Old Gandolf with his paltry onion-stone,[8]
Put me where I may look at him! True peach,
Rosy and flawless: how I earned the prize!
Draw close: that conflagration of my church
—What then? So much was saved if aught were missed!   35
My sons, ye would not be my death? Go dig
The white-grape vineyard where the oil-press stood,
Drop water gently till the surface sink,
And if ye find . . . Ah God, I know not, I! . . .
Bedded in store of rotten fig leaves soft,   40
And corded up in a tight olive-frail,[9]
Some lump, ah God, of *lapis lazuli*,[1]
Big as a jew's head cut off at the nape,[2]
Blue as a vein o'er the Madonna's breast . . .
Sons, all have I bequeathed you, villas, all,   45
That brave Frascati[3] villa with its bath,
So, let the blue lump poise between my knees,

---

3. Cheated.
4. The Epistles of the New Testament are read from the right-hand side of the altar (as one faces it).
5. Dark-colored igneous rock.
6. Stone canopy or tentlike roof, presumably supported by the "nine columns" under which the sculptured effigy of the bishop would lie on the slab of basalt.
7. Browning uses "pulse" in the special sense of a pulpy mash of fermented grapes from which a strong

wine might be poured off. In a later poem, the *Epilogue* to *Pacchiarotto*, he likens such wine to "viscous blood" that has been "squeezed gold" from the "pulp" of the grapes.
8. An inferior marble that peels in layers.
9. Basket for holding olives.
1. Valuable bright blue stone.
2. Perhaps a reference to the head of John the Baptist, cut off at the request of Salomé.
3. Suburb of Rome, used as a resort by wealthy Italians.

Like God the Father's globe on both his hands
Ye worship in the Jesu Church[4] so gay,
For Gandolf shall not choose but see and burst!   50
Swift as a weaver's shuttle fleet our years:[5]
Man goeth to the grave, and where is he?
Did I say basalt for my slab, sons? Black[6]—
'Twas ever antique-black I meant! How else
Shall ye contrast my frieze[7] to come beneath?   55
The bas-relief in bronze ye promised me,
Those Pans and Nymphs ye wot of, and perchance
Some tripod, thyrsus, with a vase or so,
The Saviour at his sermon on the mount,
Saint Praxed in a glory, and one Pan   60
Ready to twitch the Nymph's last garment off,
And Moses with the tables[8] . . . but I know
Ye mark me not! What do they whisper thee,
Child of my bowels, Anselm? Ah, ye hope
To revel down my villas while I gasp   65
Bricked o'er with beggar's moldy travertine[9]
Which Gandolf from his tomb-top chuckles at!
Nay, boys, ye love me—all of jasper, then!
'Tis jasper ye stand pledged to, lest I grieve
My bath must needs be left behind, alas!   70
One block, pure green as a pistachio nut,
There's plenty jasper somewhere in the world—
And have I not Saint Praxed's ear to pray
Horses for ye, and brown Greek manuscripts,
And mistresses with great smooth marbly limbs?   75
—That's if ye carve my epitaph aright,
Choice Latin, picked phrase, Tully's[1] every word,
No gaudy ware like Gandolf's second line—
Tully, my masters? Ulpian[2] serves his need!
And then how I shall lie through centuries,   80
And hear the blessed mutter of the mass,
And see God made and eaten all day long,[3]
And feel the steady candle flame, and taste
Good strong thick stupefying incense-smoke!
For as I lie here, hours of the dead night,   85

---

4. Il Gesù, a Jesuit church in Rome. On the altar of this church, the figure of an angel (rather than God) holds a huge lump of lapis lazuli in his hands.
5. Cf. Job 7.6.
6. Black marble.
7. Continuous band of sculpture.
8. The "bas-relief" (or sculpture in which the figures do not project far from the background surface) would consist of a mixture of pagan and religious scenes (lines 57–62). Among the former would be a "tripod," on which priestesses at the oracle of Delphi sat to make their prophecies, and a "thyrsus," a long staff carried in processions in honor of Bacchus, the god of wine. The religious scenes would include St. Praxed with her halo ("a glory") and Moses with the stone tablets ("tables") on which the Ten Commandments were written. Such intermingling of pagan and Christian traditions, characteristic of the Renaissance, had been attacked in 1841 in Contrasts, a book on architecture by A. W. Pugin, a Roman Catholic.
9. Italian limestone.
1. A familiar name for Marcus Tullius Cicero, whose writing was the model, during the Renaissance, of classical Latin prose.
2. Late Latin prose-writer, not considered a model of good style.
3. Reference to the doctrine of transubstantiation.

Dying in state and by such slow degrees,
I fold my arms as if they clasped a crook,[4]
And stretch my feet forth straight as stone can point,
And let the bedclothes, for a mortcloth,[5] drop
Into great laps and folds of sculptor's-work: 90
And as yon tapers dwindle, and strange thoughts
Grow, with a certain humming in my ears,
About the life before I lived this life,
And this life too, popes, cardinals, and priests,
Saint Praxed at his sermon on the mount,[6]   95
Your tall pale mother with her talking eyes,
And new-found agate urns as fresh as day,
And marble's language, Latin pure, discreet
—Aha, ELUCESCEBAT[7] quoth our friend?
No Tully, said I, Ulpian at the best!   100
Evil and brief hath been my pilgrimage.[8]
All *lapis*, all, sons! Else I give the Pope
My villas! Will ye ever eat my heart?
Ever your eyes were as a lizard's quick,
They glitter like your mother's for my soul,   105
Or ye would heighten my impoverished frieze,
Pierce out its starved design, and fill my vase
With grapes, and add a vizor and a Term,[9]
And to the tripod ye would tie a lynx
That in his struggle throws the thyrsus down,   110
To comfort me on my entablature[1]
Whereon I am to lie till I must ask
"Do I live, am I dead?" There, leave me, there!
For ye have stabbed me with ingratitude
To death—ye wish it—God, ye wish it! Stone—   115
Gritstone,[2] a-crumble! Clammy squares which sweat
As if the corpse they keep were oozing through—
And no more *lapis* to delight the world!
Well go! I bless ye. Fewer tapers there,
But in a row: and, going, turn your backs   120
—Aye, like departing altar-ministrants,
And leave me in my church, the church for peace,
That I may watch at leisure if he leers—
Old Gandolf, at me, from his onion-stone,
As still he envied me, so fair she was!   125

1844   1845

---

4. Bishop's staff or crozier.
5. Rich cloth spread over a dead body or coffin.
6. The bishop is confusing St. Praxed (a woman) with Christ—an indication that his mind is wandering.
7. Word from Gandolf's epitaph meaning "he was illustrious." The bishop considers the form of the verb to be in "gaudy" bad taste. If the epitaph had been copied from Cicero instead of from Ulpian,

the word would have been *elucebat*.
8. Cf. Genesis 47.9.
9. Statue of Terminus, the Roman god of boundaries, usually represented without arms. "Vizor": part of a helmet, often represented in sculpture.
1. Horizontal platform supporting a statue or effigy.
2. Coarse sandstone such as that used for grindstones.

Meeting at Night[1]

1

The gray sea and the long black land;
And the yellow half-moon large and low;
And the startled little waves that leap
In fiery ringlets from their sleep,
As I gain the cove with pushing prow,   5
And quench its speed i' the slushy sand.

2

Then a mile of warm sea-scented beach;
Three fields to cross till a farm appears;
A tap at the pane, the quick sharp scratch
And blue spurt of a lighted match,   10
And a voice less loud, through its joys and fears,
Than the two hearts beating each to each!

1845

Parting at Morning

Round the cape of a sudden came the sea,
And the sun looked over the mountain's rim:
And straight was a path of gold for him,[1]
And the need of a world of men for me.

1845

A Toccata of Galuppi's[1]

1

Oh, Galuppi, Baldassaro, this is very sad to find!
I can hardly misconceive you; it would prove me deaf and blind;
But although I take your meaning, 'tis with such a heavy mind!

2

Here you come with your old music, and here's all the good it brings.
What, they lived once thus at Venice where the merchants were the

---

1. This poem and the one which follows it appeared originally under the single title *Night and Morning*. The speaker in both is a man.
1. The sun.
1. There are three speakers in this short poem. The first is a 19th-century scientist in England who is listening to a musical composition by Baldassaro Galuppi (1706–1785), a Venetian. The music evokes for this scientist the voice of the dead composer (the third speaker) who comments upon the pointless and butterfly-like frivolity of his 18th-

century contemporaries. The second group of voices is made up of comments by members of Galuppi's audience as they respond to the different moods of his clavichord-playing during a party which the scientist imagines to have taken place in Venice.

   A "toccata" is defined in Grove's *Dictionary of Music* as a "touch-piece, or a composition intended to exhibit the touch and execution of the performer." The same authority states that "no particular composition was taken as the basis of the poem."

kings,   5
Where Saint Mark's is, where the Doges used to wed the sea with rings?[2]

                                      3

Aye, because the sea's the street there; and 'tis arched by . . . what you
    call
. . . Shylock's bridge[3] with houses on it, where they kept the carnival:
I was never out of England—it's as if I saw it all.

                                      4

Did young people take their pleasure when the sea was warm in May? 10
Balls and masks[4] begun at midnight, burning ever to midday,
When they made up fresh adventures for the morrow, do you say?

                                      5

Was a lady such a lady, cheeks so round and lips so red—
On her neck the small face buoyant, like a bellflower on its bed,
O'er the breast's superb abundance where a man might base his
    head?   15

                                      6

Well, and it was graceful of them—they'd break talk off and afford
—She, to bite her mask's black velvet—he, to finger on his sword,
While you sat and played toccatas, stately at the clavichord?[5]

                                      7

What? Those lesser thirds so plaintive, sixths diminished, sigh on sigh,
Told them something? Those suspensions, those solutions—"Must we
    die?"   20
Those commiserating sevenths[6]—"Life might last! we can but try!"

                                      8

"Were you happy?"—"Yes."—"And are you still as happy?"—"Yes.
    And you?"
—"Then, more kisses!"—"Did I stop them, when a million seemed so
    few?"
Hark, the dominant's persistence till it must be answered to!

                                      9

So, an octave struck the answer. Oh, they praised you, I dare say!   25
"Brave Galuppi! that was music; good alike at grave and gay!
I can always leave off talking when I hear a master play!"

                                      10

Then they left you for their pleasure: till in due time, one by one,
Some with lives that came to nothing, some with deeds as well
    undone,   29
Death stepped tacitly and took them where they never see the sun.

---

2. An annual ceremony in which the doge, the
Venetian chief magistrate, threw a ring into the
water to symbolize the bond between his city, with
its maritime empire, and the sea.
3. The Rialto, a bridge over the Grand Canal.
4. Masquerades.
5. A keyboard instrument in which the strings are
struck by metal hammers. As a mechanism it
resembles a piano, but the sound is more like that
of a harpsichord.
6. This term and others in these lines all refer to
the technical devices used by Galuppi to produce
alternating moods in his music, conflict in each
instance being resolved into harmony. Thus the
"dominant" (the fifth note of the scale), after being
persistently sounded, is answered by a resolving
chord (lines 24–25).

11

But when I sit down to reason, think to take my stand nor swerve,
While I triumph o'er a secret wrung from nature's close reserve,
In you come with your cold music till I creep through every nerve.

12

Yes, you, like a ghostly cricket, creaking where a house was burned:
"Dust and ashes, dead and done with, Venice spent what Venice
    earned.   35
The soul, doubtless, is immortal—where a soul can be discerned.

13

"Yours for instance: you know physics, something of geology,
Mathematics are your pastime; souls shall rise in their degree;
Butterflies may dread extinction—you'll not die, it cannot be!

14

"As for Venice and her people, merely born to bloom and drop,   40
Here on earth they bore their fruitage, mirth and folly were the crop:
What of soul was left, I wonder, when the kissing had to stop?

15

"Dust and ashes!" So you creak it, and I want[7] the heart to scold.
Dear dead women, with such hair, too—what's become of all the gold
Used to hang and brush their bosoms? I feel chilly and grown old.   45

ca. 1847   1855

Love Among the Ruins[1]

1

Where the quiet-colored end of evening smiles,
    Miles and miles
On the solitary pastures where our sheep
    Half-asleep
Tinkle homeward through the twilight, stray or stop   5
    As they crop—
Was the site once of a city great and gay
    (So they say),
Of our country's very capital, its prince
    Ages since   10
Held his court in, gathered councils, wielding far
    Peace or war.

2

Now—the country does not even boast a tree,
    As you see,

---

7. Lack.
1. The ruins may be those of such cities as Babylon or Nineveh or one of the Etruscan cities of Italy.
   The unusual stanza used in this poem was invented by Browning. The contrast between past and present, which is the core of the poem, is reinforced by devoting one half of each stanza to the past and the other half to the present.

To distinguish slopes of verdure, certain rills   15
    From the hills
Intersect and give a name to (else they run
    Into one),
Where the domed and daring palace shot its spires
    Up like fires   20
O'er the hundred-gated circuit of a wall
    Bounding all,
Made of marble, men might march on nor be pressed,
    Twelve abreast.

3

And such plenty and perfection, see, of grass   25
    Never was!
Such a carpet as, this summertime, o'erspreads
    And embeds
Every vestige of the city, guessed alone,
    Stock or stone—   30
Where a multitude of men breathed joy and woe
    Long ago;
Lust of glory pricked their hearts up, dread of shame
    Struck them tame;
And that glory and that shame alike, the gold   35
    Bought and sold.

4

Now—the single little turret that remains
    On the plains,
By the caper overrooted, by the gourd
    Overscored,   40
While the patching houseleek's[2] head of blossom winks
    Through the chinks—
Marks the basement whence a tower in ancient time
    Sprang sublime,
And a burning ring, all round, the chariots traced   45
    As they raced,
And the monarch and his minions and his dames
    Viewed the games.

5

And I know, while thus the quiet-colored eve
    Smiles to leave   50
To their folding, all our many-tinkling fleece
    In such peace,
And the slopes and rills in undistinguished gray
    Melt away—
That a girl with eager eyes and yellow hair   55
    Waits me there
In the turret whence the charioteers caught soul
    For the goal,

2. Common European plant, with petals clustered in the shape of rosettes.

When the king looked, where she looks now, breathless, dumb
    Till I come.   60

6

But he looked upon the city, every side,
    Far and wide,
All the mountains topped with temples, all the glades'
    Colonnades,
All the causeys,[3] bridges, aqueducts—and then,   65
    All the men!
When I do come, she will speak not, she will stand,
    Either hand
On my shoulder, give her eyes the first embrace
    Of my face,   70
Ere we rush, ere we extinguish sight and speech
    Each on each.

7

In one year they sent a million fighters forth
    South and north,
And they built their gods a brazen pillar high   75
    As the sky,
Yet reserved a thousand chariots in full force—
    Gold, of course.
Oh heart! oh blood that freezes, blood that burns!
    Earth's returns   80
For whole centuries of folly, noise, and sin!
    Shut them in,
With their triumphs and their glories and the rest!
    Love is best.

1853   1855

"Childe Roland to the Dark Tower Came"[1]

(*See Edgar's Song in "Lear"*)

1

My first thought was, he lied in every word,
    That hoary cripple, with malicious eye

---

3. Causeways or roads raised above low ground.
1. Browning stated that this poem "came upon me as a kind of dream,"and that it was written in one day. Although the poem was among those of his own writings that pleased him most, he was reluctant to explain what the dream (or nightmare) signified. He once agreed with a friend's suggestion that the meaning might be expressed in the statement: "He that endureth to the end shall be saved." Most readers have responded to the poem in this way, finding in the story of Roland's quest an inspiring expression of defiance and courage. Other readers find the poem to be more expressive of despair than of enduring hope, and it is at least

true that the landscape is as grim and nightmare-like as in such 20th-century writings as T. S. Eliot's *Hollow Men* or Franz Kafka's *Penal Colony*. It has been said of *Childe Roland* that every reader can be his own allegorist.

The lines from Shakespeare's *King Lear* (187–90), from which the title is taken, are spoken when Lear is about to enter a hovel on the heath, and Edgar, feigning madness, chants the fragment of a song reminiscent of quests and challenges in fairy tales: "Child Rowland to the dark tower came; / His word was still / 'Fie, foh, and fum! / I smell the blood of a British man." A "childe" is a youth of gentle birth, usually a candidate for knighthood.

    Askance[2] to watch the working of his lie
On mine, and mouth scarce able to afford
Suppression of the glee, that pursed and scored   5
        Its edge, at one more victim gained thereby.

2

What else should he be set for, with his staff?
        What, save to waylay with his lies, ensnare
        All travelers who might find him posted there,
And ask the road? I guessed what skull-like laugh   10
Would break, what crutch 'gin write my epitaph
        For pastime in the dusty thoroughfare,

3

If at his counsel I should turn aside
        Into that ominous tract which, all agree,
        Hides the Dark Tower, Yet acquiescingly   15
I did turn as he pointed: neither pride
Nor hope rekindling at the end descried,
        So much as gladness that some end might be.

4

For, what with my whole world-wide wandering,
        What with my search drawn out through years, my hope   20
        Dwindled into a ghost not fit to cope
With that obstreperous joy success would bring,
I hardly tried now to rebuke the spring
        My heart made, finding failure in its scope.

5

As when a sick man very near to death   25
        Seems dead indeed, and feels begin and end
        The tears and takes the farewell of each friend,
And hears one bid the other go, draw breath
Freelier outside ("since all is o'er," he saith,
        "And the blow fallen no grieving can amend"),   30

6

While some discuss if near the other graves
        Be room enough for this, and when a day
        Suits best for carrying the corpse away,
With care about the banners, scarves and staves:
And still the man hears all, and only craves   35
        He may not shame such tender love and stay.

7

Thus, I had so long suffered in this quest,
        Heard failure prophesied so oft, been writ
        So many times among "The Band"—to wit,
The knights who to the Dark Tower's search addressed   40
Their steps—that just to fail as they, seemed best,
        And all the doubt was now—should I be fit?

2. Squinting sidewise.

8

So, quiet as despair, I turned from him,
  That hateful cripple, out of his highway
  Into the path he pointed. All the day   45
Had been a dreary one at best, and dim
Was settling to its close, yet shot one grim
  Red leer to see the plain catch its estray.[3]

9

For mark! no sooner was I fairly found
  Pledged to the plain, after a pace or two, 50
  Than, pausing to throw backward a last view
O'er the safe road, 'twas gone; gray plain all round:
Nothing but plain to the horizon's bound.
  I might go on; naught else remained to do.

10

So, on I went. I think I never saw   55
  Such starved ignoble nature; nothing throve:
  For flowers—as well expect a cedar grove!
But, cockle,[4] spurge, according to their law
Might propagate their kind, with none to awe,
  You'd think; a burr had been a treasure trove. 60

11

No! penury, inertness and grimace,
  In some strange sort, were the land's portion. "See
  Or shut your eyes," said Nature peevishly,
"It nothing skills: I cannot help my case;
'Tis the Last Judgment's fire must cure this place, 65
  Calcine[5] its clods and set my prisoners free."

12

If there pushed any ragged thistle stalk
  Above its mates, the head was chopped; the bents[6]
  Were jealous else. What made those holes and rents
In the dock's[7] harsh swarth leaves, bruised as to balk 70
All hope of greenness? 'tis a brute must walk
  Pashing their life out, with a brute's intents.

13

As for the grass, it grew as scant as hair
  In leprosy; thin dry blades pricked the mud
  Which underneath looked kneaded up with blood. 75
One stiff blind horse, his every bone a-stare,
Stood stupefied, however he came there:
  Thrust out past service from the devil's stud!

14

Alive? he might be dead for aught I know,
  With that red gaunt and colloped[8] neck a-strain, 80

---

3. Literally, a domestic animal that has strayed
away from its home.
4. A weed that bears burrs. "Spurge" is a bitter-
juiced weed.

5. Turn to powder by heat.
6. Coarse, stiff grasses.
7. Coarse plant.
8. Ridged.

And shut eyes underneath the rusty mane;
Seldom went such grotesqueness with such woe;
I never saw a brute I hated so;
    He must be wicked to deserve such pain.
15

I shut my eyes and turned them on my heart.   85
    As a man calls for wine before he fights,
    I asked one draught of earlier, happier sights,
Ere fitly I could hope to play my part.
Think first, fight afterwards—the soldier's art:
    One taste of the old time sets all to rights.   90
16

Not it! I fancied Cuthbert's reddening face
    Beneath its garniture of curly gold,
    Dear fellow, till I almost felt him fold
An arm in mine to fix me to the place,
That way he used. Alas, one night's disgrace!   95
    Out went my heart's new fire and left it cold.
17

Giles then, the soul of honor—there he stands
    Frank as ten years ago when knighted first.
    What honest man should dare (he said) he durst.
Good—but the scene shifts—faugh! what hangman hands   100
Pin to his breast a parchment? His own bands
    Read it. Poor traitor, spit upon and cursed!
18

Better this present than a past like that;
    Back therefore to my darkening path again!
    No sound, no sight as far as eye could strain.   105
Will the night send a howlet[9] or a bat?
I asked: when something on the dismal flat
    Came to arrest my thoughts and change their train.
19

A sudden little river crossed my path
    As unexpected as a serpent comes.   110
    No sluggish tide congenial to the glooms;
This, as it frothed by, might have been a bath
For the fiend's glowing hoof—to see the wrath
    Of its black eddy bespate[1] with flakes and spumes.
20

So petty yet so spiteful! All along,   115
  Low scrubby alders kneeled down over it;
    Drenched willows flung them headlong in a fit
Of mute despair, a suicidal throng:
The river which had done them all the wrong,
    Whate'er that was, rolled by, deterred no whit.   120

9. Owl.   1. Bespattered.

21

Which, while I forded—good saints, how I feared
    To set my foot upon a dead man's cheek,
    Each step, or feel the spear I thrust to seek
For hollows, tangled in his hair or beard!
—It may have been a water rat I speared,   125
    But, ugh! it sounded like a baby's shriek.

22

Glad was I when I reached the other bank.
    Now for a better country. Vain presage!
    Who were the strugglers, what war did they wage,
Whose savage trample thus could pad the dank   130
Soil to a plash? Toads in a poisoned tank,
    Or wild cats in a red-hot iron cage—

23

The fight must so have seemed in that fell cirque.[2]
    What penned them there, with all the plain to choose?
    No footprint leading to that horrid mews,[3]   135
None out of it. Mad brewage set to work
Their brains, no doubt, like galley slaves the Turk
    Pits for his pastime, Christians against Jews.

24

And more than that—a furlong on—why, there!
    What bad use was that engine for, that wheel,   140
    Or brake,[4] not wheel—that harrow fit to reel
Men's bodies out like silk? with all the air
Of Tophet's[5] tool, on earth left unaware,
    Or brought to sharpen its rusty teeth of steel.

25

Then came a bit of stubbed ground, once a wood,   145
    Next a marsh, it would seem, and now mere earth
    Desperate and done with; (so a fool finds mirth,
Makes a thing and then mars it, till his mood
Changes and off he goes!) within a rood[6]
    Bog, clay and rubble, sand and stark black dearth.   150

26

Now blotches rankling, colored gay and grim,
    Now patches where some leanness of the soil's
    Broke into moss or substances like boils;
Then came some palsied oak, a cleft in him
Like a distorted mouth that splits its rim   155
    Gaping at death, and dies while it recoils.

27

And just as far as ever from the end!
    Naught in the distance but the evening, naught

---

2. Dreadful arena.
3. Enclosed stable yard.
4. A toothed machine used for separating the fibers

of flax or hemp. Here an instrument of torture.
5. Hell's. See also Jeremiah 19.4–5.
6. Quarter acre of land.

To point my footstep further! At the thought,
A great black bird, Apollyon's[7] bosom friend,   160
Sailed past, nor beat his wide wing dragon-penned[8]
    That brushed my cap—perchance the guide I sought.

28

For, looking up, aware I somehow grew,
    'Spite of the dusk, the plain had given place
    All round to mountains—with such name to grace   165
Mere ugly heights and heaps now stolen in view.
How thus they had surprised me—solve it, you!
    How to get from them was no clearer case.

29

Yet half I seemed to recognize some trick
    Of mischief happened to me, God knows when—   170
    In a bad dream perhaps. Here ended, then,
Progress this way. When, in the very nick
Of giving up, one time more, came a click
    As when a trap shuts—you're inside the den!

30

Burningly it came on me all at once,   175
    This was the place! those two hills on the right,
    Crouched like two bulls locked horn in horn in fight;
While to the left, a tall scalped mountain . . . Dunce,
Dotard, a-dozing at the very nonce,[9]
    After a life spent training for the sight!   180

31

What in the midst lay but the Tower itself?
    The round squat turret, blind as the fool's heart,[1]
    Built of brown stone, without a counterpart
In the whole world. The tempest's mocking elf
Points to the shipman thus the unseen shelf   185
    He strikes on, only when the timbers start.

32

Not see? because of night perhaps?—why, day
    Came back again for that! before it left,
    The dying sunset kindled through a cleft:
The hills, like giants at a hunting, lay,   190
Chin upon hand, to see the game at bay—
    "Now stab and end the creature—to the heft!"[2]

33

Not hear? when noise was everywhere! it tolled
    Increasing like a bell. Names in my ears
    Of all the lost adventurers my peers—   195
How such a one was strong, and such was bold,

---

7. In Revelation 9.11, Apollyon is "an angel of the bottomless pit." In Bunyan's *Pilgrim's Progress*, he is a hideous "monster"; "he had wings like a dragon."
8. With wings or pinions like those of a dragon.

9. Moment.
1. Cf. "the fool hath said in his heart, There is no God" (Psalms 14.1).
2. Handle of dagger or sword.

And such was fortunate, yet each of old
    Lost, lost! one moment knelled the woe of years.

34

There they stood, ranged along the hillsides, met
    To view the last of me, a living frame   200
    For one more picture! in a sheet of flame
I saw them and I knew them all. And yet
Dauntless the slug-horn[3] to my lips I set,
    And blew. *"Childe Roland to the Dark Tower came."*

1852					1855

Fra Lippo Lippi[1]

I am poor brother Lippo, by your leave!
You need not clap your torches to my face.
Zooks,[2] what's to blame? you think you see a monk!
What, 'tis past midnight, and you go the rounds,
And here you catch me at an alley's end   5
Where sportive ladies leave their doors ajar?
The Carmine's[3] my cloister: hunt it up,
Do—harry out, if you must show your zeal,
Whatever rat, there, haps on his wrong hole,
And nip each softling of a wee white mouse,   10
Weke, weke, that's crept to keep him company!
Aha, you know your betters! Then, you'll take
Your hand away that's fiddling on my throat,
And please to know me likewise. Who am I?
Why, one, sir, who is lodging with a friend   15
Three streets off—he's a certain . . . how d'ye call?
Master—a . . . Cosimo of the Medici,[4]
I' the house that caps the corner. Boh! you were best!
Remember and tell me, the day you're hanged,
How you affected such a gullet's gripe![5]   20
But you,[6] sir, it concerns you that your knaves
Pick up a manner nor discredit you:
Zooks, are we pilchards,[7] that they sweep the streets

3. This Scottish word meant the war cry or slogan (*slug-horn*) of a clan about to engage in battle, but in 1770 the poet Chatterton was misled into using it to mean a kind of trumpet or horn. Browning followed Chatterton's example, although the original meaning would also be relevant here.
1. This monologue portrays the dawn of the Renaissance in Italy at a point when the medieval attitude toward life and art was about to be displaced by a fresh appreciation of earthly pleasures. It was from Giorgio Vasari's *Lives of the Painters* that Browning derived most of his information about the life of the Florentine painter and friar, Lippo Lippi (1406–1469), but the theory of art propounded by Lippi in the poem was developed by the poet himself.

2. A shortened version of "Gadzooks," a mild oath now obscure in meaning but perhaps resembling a phrase still in use: "God's truth."
3. Santa Maria del Carmine, a church and cloister of the Carmelite order of friars to which Lippi belonged.
4. Lippi's patron, banker and virtual ruler of Florence.
5. I.e., how you had the arrogance to choke the gullet of someone with my connections.
6. The officer in charge of the patrol of policemen or watchmen.
7. Small fish.

And count fair prize what comes into this net?
He's Judas to a tittle, that man is![8]   25
Just such a face! Why, sir, you make amends.
Lord, I'm not angry! Bid your hangdogs go
Drink out this quarter-florin to the health
Of the munificent House that harbors me
(And many more beside, lads! more beside!)   30
And all's come square again. I'd like his face—
His, elbowing on his comrade in the door
With the pike and lantern—for the slave that holds
John Baptist's head a-dangle by the hair
With one hand ("Look you, now," as who should say)   35
And his weapon in the other, yet unwiped!
It's not your chance to have a bit of chalk,
A wood-coal or the like? or you should see!
Yes, I'm the painter, since you style me so.
What, brother Lippo's doings, up and down,   40
You know them and they take you? like enough!
I saw the proper twinkle in your eye—
'Tell you, I liked your looks at very first.
Let's sit and set things straight now, hip to haunch.
Here's spring come, and the nights one makes up bands   45
To roam the town and sing out carnival,[9]
And I've been three weeks shut within my mew,[1]
A-painting for the great man, saints and saints
And saints again. I could not paint all night—
Ouf! I leaned out of window for fresh air.   50
There came a hurry of feet and little feet,
A sweep of lute-strings, laughs, and whiffs of song—
Flower o' the broom,
Take away love, and our earth is a tomb!
Flower o' the quince,   55
I let Lisa go, and what good in life since?[2]
Flower o' the thyme—and so on. Round they went.
Scarce had they turned the corner when a titter
Like the skipping of rabbits by moonlight—three slim shapes,
And a face that looked up . . . zooks, sir, flesh and blood, 60
That's all I'm made of! Into shreds it went,
Curtain and counterpane and coverlet,
All the bed-furniture—a dozen knots,
There was a ladder! Down I let myself,
Hands and feet, scrambling somehow, and so dropped,   65
And after them. I came up with the fun
Hard by Saint Laurence,[3] hail fellow, well met—
Flower o' the rose,

8. I.e., one of the watchmen has a face that would serve as a model for a painting of Judas.
9. Season of revelry before the commencement of Lent.

1. Private den.
2. This and other interspersed flower-songs are called *stornelli* in Italy.
3. San Lorenzo, a church in Florence.

If I've been merry, what matter who knows!
And so as I was stealing back again
To get to bed and have a bit of sleep
Ere I rise up tomorrow and go work
On Jerome knocking at his poor old breast
With his great round stone to subdue the flesh,[4]
You snap me of the sudden. Ah, I see!
Though your eye twinkles still, you shake your head—
Mine's shaved—a monk, you say—the sting's in that!
If Master Cosimo announced himself,
Mum's the word naturally; but a monk!
Come, what am I a beast for? tell us, now!
I was a baby when my mother died
And father died and left me in the street.
I starved there, God knows how, a year or two
On fig skins, melon parings, rinds and shucks,
Refuse and rubbish. One fine frosty day,
My stomach being empty as your hat,
The wind doubled me up and down I went.
Old Aunt Lapaccia trussed me with one hand
(Its fellow was a stinger as I knew),
And so along the wall, over the bridge,
By the straight cut to the convent. Six words there,
While I stood munching my first bread that month:
"So, boy, you're minded," quoth the good fat father
Wiping his own mouth, 'twas refection time[5]—
"To quit this very miserable world?
Will you renounce" . . . "the mouthful of bread?" thought I;
By no means! Brief, they made a monk of me;
I did renounce the world, its pride and greed,
Palace, farm, villa, shop, and banking house,
Trash, such as these poor devils of Medici
Have given their hearts to—all at eight years old.
Well, sir, I found in time, you may be sure,
'Twas not for nothing—the good bellyful,
The warm serge and the rope that goes all round,
And day-long blessed idleness beside!
"Let's see what the urchin's fit for"—that came next.
Not overmuch their way, I must confess.
Such a to-do! They tried me with their books:
Lord, they'd have taught me Latin in pure waste!
Flower o' the clove,
All the Latin I construe is "amo," I love!
But, mind you, when a boy starves in the streets
Eight years together, as my fortune was,
Watching folk's faces to know who will fling
The bit of half-stripped grape bunch he desires,

70

75

80

85

90

95

100

105

110

115

---

4. A picture of St. Jerome (ca. 340–420), whose ascetic observances were hardly a congenial sub- ject for such a painter as Lippi.
5. Mealtime.

And who will curse or kick him for his pains—
Which gentleman processional and fine,
Holding a candle to the Sacrament,
Will wink and let him lift a plate and catch
The droppings of the wax to sell again,   120
Or holla for the Eight[6] and have him whipped—
How say I?—nay, which dog bites, which lets drop
His bone from the heap of offal in the street—
Why, soul and sense of him grow sharp alike,
He learns the look of things, and none the less   125
For admonition from the hunger-pinch.
I had a store of such remarks, be sure,
Which, after I found leisure, turned to use.
I drew men's faces on my copybooks,
Scrawled them within the antiphonary's marge,[7]   130
Joined legs and arms to the long music-notes,
Found eyes and nose and chin for A's and B's,
And made a string of pictures of the world
Betwixt the ins and outs of verb and noun,
On the wall, the bench, the door. The monks looked black.   135
"Nay," quoth the Prior,[8] "turn him out, d' ye say?
In no wise. Lose a crow and catch a lark.
What if at last we get our man of parts,
We Carmelites, like those Camaldolese
And Preaching Friars,[9] to do our church up fine   140
And put the front on it that ought to be!"
And hereupon he bade me daub away.
Thank you! my head being crammed, the walls a blank,
Never was such prompt disemburdening.
First, every sort of monk, the black and white,   145
I drew them, fat and lean: then, folk at church,
From good old gossips waiting to confess
Their cribs of barrel droppings, candle ends—
To the breathless fellow at the altar-foot,
Fresh from his murder, safe and sitting there   150
With the little children round him in a row
Of admiration, half for his beard and half
For that white anger of his victim's son
Shaking a fist at him with one fierce arm,
Signing himself with the other because of Christ   155
(Whose sad face on the cross sees only this
After the passion[1] of a thousand years)
Till some poor girl, her apron o'er her head
(Which the intense eyes looked through), came at eve
On tiptoe, said a word, dropped in a loaf,   160
Her pair of earrings and a bunch of flowers

---

6. Florentine magistrates.
7. Margin of music book used for choral singing.
8. Head of a Carmelite convent.

9. Benedictine and Dominican religious orders, respectively.
1. Sufferings.

(The brute took growling), prayed, and so was gone.
I painted all, then cried "'Tis ask and have;
Choose, for more's ready!"—laid the ladder flat,
And showed my covered bit of cloister wall.   165
The monks closed in a circle and praised loud
Till checked, taught what to see and not to see,
Being simple bodies—"That's the very man!
Look at the boy who stoops to pat the dog!
That woman's like the Prior's niece who comes   170
To care about his asthma: it's the life!"
But there my triumph's straw-fire flared and funked;[2]
Their betters took their turn to see and say:
The Prior and the learned pulled a face
And stopped all that in no time. "How? what's here?   175
Quite from the mark of painting, bless us all!
Faces, arms, legs and bodies like the true
As much as pea and pea! it's devil's game!
Your business is not to catch men with show,
With homage to the perishable clay,   180
But lift them over it, ignore it all,
Make them forget there's such a thing as flesh.
Your business is to paint the souls of men—
Man's soul, and it's a fire, smoke . . . no, it's not . . .
It's vapor done up like a newborn babe—   185
(In that shape when you die it leaves your mouth)
It's . . . well, what matters talking, it's the soul!
Give us no more of body than shows soul!
Here's Giotto,[3] with his Saint a-praising God,
That sets us praising—why not stop with him?   190
Why put all thoughts of praise out of our head
With wonder at lines, colors, and what not?
Paint the soul, never mind the legs and arms!
Rub all out, try at it a second time.
Oh, that white smallish female with the breasts,   195
She's just my niece . . . Herodias,[4] I would say—
Who went and danced and got men's heads cut off!
Have it all out!" Now, is this sense, I ask?
A fine way to paint soul, by painting body
So ill, the eye can't stop there, must go further   200
And can't fare worse! Thus, yellow does for white
When what you put for yellow's simply black,
And any sort of meaning looks intense
When all beside itself means and looks naught.
Why can't a painter lift each foot in turn,   205

2. Went up in smoke.
3. Great Florentine painter (1276–1337), whose
stylized pictures of religious subjects were admired
as models of pre-Renaissance art.
4. Herodias, also called Salomé, had the same

name as her mother, Herodias, sister-in-law of King
Herod. The daughter's dance coincided with the
beheading of John the Baptist, who had aroused
her mother's displeasure. See Matthew 14.1–2.

Left foot and right foot, go a double step,
Make his flesh liker and his soul more like,
Both in their order? Take the prettiest face,
The Prior's niece . . . patron-saint—is it so pretty
You can't discover if it means hope, fear,   210
Sorrow or joy? won't beauty go with these?
Suppose I've made her eyes all right and blue,
Can't I take breath and try to add life's flash,
And then add soul and heighten them threefold?
Or say there's beauty with no soul at all—   215
(I never saw it—put the case the same—)
If you get simple beauty and naught else,
You get about the best thing God invents:
That's somewhat: and you'll find the soul you have missed,
Within yourself, when you return him thanks.   220
"Rub all out!" Well, well, there's my life, in short,
And so the thing has gone on ever since.
I'm grown a man no doubt, I've broken bounds:
You should not take a fellow eight years old
And make him swear to never kiss the girls.   225
I'm my own master, paint now as I please—
Having a friend, you see, in the Corner-house![5]
Lord, it's fast holding by the rings in front—
Those great rings serve more purposes than just
To plant a flag in, or tie up a horse!   230
And yet the old schooling sticks, the old grave eyes
Are peeping o'er my shoulder as I work,
The heads shake still—"It's art's decline, my son!
You're not of the true painters, great and old;
Brother Angelico's the man, you'll find;   235
Brother Lorenzo stands his single peer:[6]
Fag on at flesh, you'll never make the third!"
Flower o' the pine,
You keep your mistr . . . manners, and I'll stick to mine!
I'm not the third, then: bless us, they must know!   240
Don't you think they're the likeliest to know,
They with their Latin? So, I swallow my rage,
Clench my teeth, suck my lips in tight, and paint
To please them—sometimes do and sometimes don't;
For, doing most, there's pretty sure to come   245
A turn, some warm eve finds me at my saints—
A laugh, a cry, the business of the world—
(Flower o' the peach,
Death for us all, and his own life for each!)
And my whole soul revolves, the cup runs over,   250
The world and life's too big to pass for a dream,
And I do these wild things in sheer despite,

5. The Medici palace.   naco (1370–1425), whose paintings were in the
6. Fra Angelico (1387–1455) and Lorenzo Mo-   approved traditional manner.

And play the fooleries you catch me at,
In pure rage! The old mill-horse, out at grass
After hard years, throws up his stiff heels so,   255
Although the miller does not preach to him
The only good of grass is to make chaff.[7]
What would men have? Do they like grass or no—
May they or mayn't they? all I want's the thing
Settled forever one way. As it is,   260
You tell too many lies and hurt yourself:
You don't like what you only like too much,
You do like what, if given you at your word,
You find abundantly detestable.
For me, I think I speak as I was taught;   265
I always see the garden and God there
A-making man's wife: and, my lesson learned,
The value and significance of flesh,
I can't unlearn ten minutes afterwards.

You understand me: I'm a beast, I know.   270
But see, now—why, I see as certainly
As that the morning star's about to shine,
What will hap some day. We've a youngster here
Comes to our convent, studies what I do,
Slouches and stares and lets no atom drop: 275
His name is Guidi[8]—he'll not mind the monks—
They call him Hulking Tom, he lets them talk—
He picks my practice up—he'll paint apace,
I hope so—though I never live so long,
I know what's sure to follow. You be judge!   280
You speak no Latin more than I, belike;
However, you're my man, you've seen the world
—The beauty and the wonder and the power,
The shapes of things, their colors, lights and shades,
Changes, surprises—and God made it all!   285
—For what? Do you feel thankful, aye or no,
For this fair town's face, yonder river's line,
The mountain round it and the sky above,
Much more the figures of man, woman, child,
These are the frame to? What's it all about?   290
To be passed over, despised? or dwelt upon,
Wondered at? oh, this last of course!—you say.
But why not do as well as say—paint these
Just as they are, careless what comes of it?
God's works—paint any one, and count it crime   295

7. Straw.
8. Guidi or Masaccio (1401–1428), a painter who
may have been Lippi's master rather than his pupil,
although Browning, in a letter to the press in 1870,
argued that Lippi had been born earlier. Like Lippi,
Masaccio was in revolt against the medieval theory
of art. His frescoes in the chapel of Santa Maria
del Carmine (Fra Lippo's church) are considered
his masterpiece.

To let a truth slip. Don't object, "His works
Are here already; nature is complete:
Suppose you reproduce her—(which you can't)
There's no advantage! You must beat her, then."
For, don't you mark? we're made so that we love　　　　300
First when we see them painted, things we have passed
Perhaps a hundred times nor cared to see;
And so they are better, painted—better to us,
Which is the same thing. Art was given for that;
God uses us to help each other so,　　　　305
Lending our minds out. Have you noticed, now,
Your cullion's[9] hanging face? A bit of chalk,
And trust me but you should, though! How much more,
If I drew higher things with the same truth!
That were to take the Prior's pulpit-place,　　　　310
Interpret God to all of you! Oh, oh,
It makes me mad to see what men shall do
And we in our graves! This world's no blot for us,
Nor blank; it means intensely, and means good:
To find its meaning is my meat and drink.　　　　315
"Aye, but you don't so instigate to prayer!"
Strikes in the Prior: "when your meaning's plain
It does not say to folk—remember matins,
Or, mind you fast next Friday!" Why, for this
What need of art at all? A skull and bones,　　　　320
Two bits of stick nailed crosswise, or, what's best,
bell to chime the hour with, does as well.
I painted a Saint Laurence[1] six months since
At Prato, splashed the fresco in fine style:
"How looks my painting, now the scaffold's down?"　　　　325
I ask a brother: "Hugely," he returns—
"Already not one phiz of your three slaves
Who turn the Deacon off his toasted side,
But it's scratched and prodded to our heart's content,
The pious people have so eased their own　　　　330
With coming to say prayers there in a rage:
We get on fast to see the bricks beneath.
Expect another job this time next year,
For pity and religion grow i' the crowd—
Your painting serves its purpose!" Hang the fools!　　　　335

—That is—you'll not mistake an idle word
Spoke in a huff by a poor monk, God wot,
Tasting the air this spicy night which turns
The unaccustomed head like Chianti wine!
Oh, the church knows! don't misreport me, now!　　　　340

---

9. Rascal's.
1. A scene representing the fiery martyrdom of
Saint Laurence; a "fresco" is painted quickly on
fresh plaster over a surface of bricks. Prato is a town
near Florence.

It's natural a poor monk out of bounds
Should have his apt word to excuse himself:
And hearken how I plot to make amends.
I have bethought me: I shall paint a piece
. . . There's for you! Give me six months, then go, see   345
Something in Sant' Ambrogio's!² Bless the nuns!
They want a cast o' my office.³ I shall paint
God in the midst, Madonna and her babe,
Ringed by a bowery flowery angel brood,
Lilies and vestments and white faces, sweet   350
As puff on puff of grated orris-root⁴
When ladies crowd to Church at midsummer.
And then i' the front, of course a saint or two—
Saint John, because he saves the Florentines,
Saint Ambrose, who puts down in black and white   355
The convent's friends and gives them a long day,
And Job, I must have him there past mistake,
The man of Uz (and Us without the z,
Painters who need his patience). Well, all these
Secured at their devotion, up shall come   360
Out of a corner when you least expect,
As one by a dark stair into a great light,
Music and talking, who but Lippo! I!—
Mazed, motionless and moonstruck—I'm the man!
Back I shrink—what is this I see and hear?   365
I, caught up with my monk's things by mistake,
My old serge gown and rope that goes all round,
I, in this presence, this pure company!
Where's a hole, where's a corner for escape?
Then steps a sweet angelic slip of a thing   370
Forward, puts out a soft palm—"Not so fast!"
—Addresses the celestial presence, "nay—
He made you and devised you, after all,
Though he's none of you! Could Saint John there draw—
His camel-hair⁵ make up a painting-brush?   375
We come to brother Lippo for all that,
Iste perfecit opus!"⁶ So, all smile—
I shuffle sideways with my blushing face
Under the cover of a hundred wings
Thrown like a spread of kirtles when you're gay   380
And play hot cockles,⁷ all the doors being shut,
Till, wholly unexpected, in there pops
The hothead husband! Thus I scuttle off

2. A convent church in Florence.
3. Sample of my work. The completed painting, which Browning saw in Florence, is Lippi's *Coronation of the Virgin*.
4. Powder (like talcum) made from sweet-smelling roots of a flower.
5. "And John was clothed with camel's hair" (Mark 1.6).
6. "This man made the work." In this painting, as later completed, these words appear beside a figure which Browning took to be Lippi's self-portrait.
7. A game in which a player wears a blindfold. "Kirtles": skirts.

To some safe bench behind, not letting go
The palm of her, the little lily thing   385
That spoke the good word for me in the nick,
Like the Prior's niece . . . Saint Lucy, I would say.
And so all's saved for me, and for the church
A pretty picture gained. Go, six months hence!
Your hand, sir, and good-by: no lights, no lights!   390
The street's hushed, and I know my own way back,
Don't fear me! There's the gray beginning. Zooks!

ca. 1853   1855

The Last Ride Together

1

I said—Then, dearest, since 'tis so,
Since now at length my fate I know,
Since nothing all my love avails,
Since all, my life seemed meant for, fails,
    Since this was written and needs must be—   5
My whole heart rises up to bless
Your name in pride and thankfulness!
Take back the hope you gave—I claim
Only a memory of the same,
—And this beside, if you will not blame,   10
Your leave for one more last ride with me.

2

My mistress bent that brow of hers;
Those deep dark eyes where pride demurs
When pity would be softening through,
Fixed me a breathing-while or two   15
    With life or death in the balance: right!
The blood replenished me again;
My last thought was at least not vain:
I and my mistress, side by side
Shall be together, breathe and ride,   20
So, one day more am I deified.
    Who knows but the world may end tonight?

3

Hush! if you saw some western cloud
All billowy-bosomed, over-bowed
By many benedictions—sun's   25
And moon's and evening star's at once—
    And so, you, looking and loving best,
Conscious grew, your passion drew
Cloud, sunset, moonrise, star-shine too,
Down on you, near and yet more near,   30
Till flesh must fade for heaven was here!—

Thus leant she and lingered [1]—joy and fear!
    Thus lay she a moment on my breast.
           4

Then we begin to ride. My soul
Smoothed itself out, a long-cramped scroll   35
Freshening and fluttering in the wind.
Past hopes already lay behind.
    What need to strive with a life awry?
Had I said that, had I done this,
So might I gain, so might I miss.   40
Might she have loved me? just as well
She might have hated, who can tell!
Where had I been now if the worst befell?
    And here we are riding, she and I.
           5

Fail I alone, in words and deeds?   45
Why, all men strive and who succeeds?
We rode; it seemed my spirit flew,
Saw other regions, cities new,
    As the world rushed by on either side.
I thought—All labor, yet no less   50
Bear up beneath their unsuccess.
Look at the end of work, contrast
The petty done, the undone vast,
This present of theirs with the hopeful past!
    I hoped she would love me; here we ride.   55
           6

What hand and brain went ever paired?
What heart alike conceived and dared?
What act proved all its thought had been?
What will but felt the fleshly screen?
    We ride and I see her bosom heave.   60
There's many a crown for who can reach.
Ten lines, a statesman's life in each! [2]
The flag stuck on a heap of bones,
A soldier's doing! what atones?
They scratch his name on the Abbey stones. [3]   65
    My riding is better, by their leave.
           7

What does it all mean, poet? Well,
Your brains beat into rhythm, you tell
What we felt only; you expressed
You hold things beautiful the best,   70
    And pace them in rhyme so, side by side.
'Tis something, nay 'tis much: but then,

---

1. Before she mounts her horse.
2. If a man tries hard enough, he may be crowned
with what seems to be success. He might become,
for example, an eminent "statesman." Yet his only
memorial would be a short sketch of his career ("ten
lines") in some history or biographical dictionary.
3. He is honored by burial in Westminster Abbey.

Have you yourself what's best for men?
Are you—poor, sick, old ere your time—
Nearer one whit your own sublime   75
Than we who never have turned a rhyme?
    Sing, riding's a joy! For me, I ride.

8

And you, great sculptor—so, you gave
A score of years to Art, her slave,
And that's your Venus, whence we turn   80
To yonder girl that fords the burn![4]
    You acquiesce, and shall I repine?
What, man of music, you grown gray
With notes and nothing else to say,
Is this your sole praise from a friend,   85
"Greatly his opera's strains intend,
But in music we know how fashions end!"
    I gave my youth; but we ride, in fine.[5]

9

Who knows what's fit for us? Had fate
Proposed bliss here should sublimate   90
My being—had I signed the bond—
Still one must lead some life beyond,
    Have a bliss to die with, dim-descried.
This foot once planted on the goal,
This glory-garland round my soul,   95
Could I descry such? Try and test!
I sink back shuddering from the quest.
Earth being so good, would Heaven seem best?[6]
    Now, Heaven and she are beyond this ride.

10

And yet—she has not spoke so long!   100
What if heaven be that, fair and strong
At life's best, with our eyes upturned
Whither life's flower is first discerned,
    We, fixed so, ever should so abide?
What if we still ride on, we two   105
With life forever old yet new,
Changed not in kind but in degree,
The instant made eternity—
And heaven just prove that I and she
    Ride, ride together, forever ride?   110

                 1855

---

4. Crosses the brook.
5. In short.
6. If fate had decreed that he could possess his mistress fully, life on earth would have been so blissful that heaven could offer nothing for him to look forward to after death. Hence (he argues) to preserve "a bliss to die with" (line 93), it is better that she never really became his on earth.

Andrea del Sarto [1]

(*called "The Faultless Painter"*)

But do not let us quarrel any more,
No, my Lucrezia; bear with me for once:
Sit down and all shall happen as you wish.
You turn your face, but does it bring your heart?
I'll work then for your friend's friend, never fear,　　　　5
Treat his own subject after his own way,
Fix his own time, accept too his own price,
And shut the money into this small hand
When next it takes mine. Will it? tenderly?
Oh, I'll content him—but tomorrow, Love!　　　　10
I often am much wearier than you think,
This evening more than usual, and it seems
As if—forgive now—should you let me sit
Here by the window with your hand in mine
And look a half-hour forth on Fiesole,[2]　　　　15
Both of one mind, as married people use,
Quietly, quietly the evening through,
I might get up tomorrow to my work
Cheerful and fresh as ever. Let us try.
Tomorrow, how you shall be glad for this!　　　　20
Your soft hand is a woman of itself,
And mine the man's bared breast she curls inside.
Don't count the time lost, neither; you must serve
For each of the five pictures we require:
It saves a model. So! keep looking so—　　　　25
My serpentining beauty, rounds on rounds![3]
—How could you ever prick those perfect ears,
Even to put the pearl there! oh, so sweet—
My face, my moon, my everybody's moon,
Which everybody looks on and calls his,　　　　30
And, I suppose, is looked on by in turn,

---

1. This portrait of Andrea del Sarto (1486–1531) was derived from a biography written by his pupil, Giorgio Vasari, author of *The Lives of the Painters*. Vasari's account seeks to explain why his Florentine master, one of the most skillful painters of the Renaissance, never altogether fulfilled the promise he had shown early in his career and why he had never arrived (in Vasari's opinion) at the level of such artists as Raphael. Vasari noted that Andrea suffered from "a certain timidity of mind . . . which rendered it impossible that those evidences of ardor and animation, which are proper to the more exalted character, should ever appear in him."
　　Browning also follows Vasari's account of Andrea's marriage to a beautiful widow, Lucrezia, "an artful woman who made him do as she pleased

in all things." Vasari reports that Andrea's "immoderate love for her soon caused him to neglect the studies demanded by his art," and that this infatuation had "more influence over him than the glory and honor towards which he had begun to make such hopeful advances."
　　Browning's poem has often been praised for its exposition of a paradoxical theory of success and failure, but it has other qualities as well. Its slow-paced, enervated blank verse, its setting of a quiet evening in autumn, its comparative lack of the movement and noise that we expect in Browning's energetic verse create a unity of impression that is unobtrusive yet effective.
2. A suburb on the hills overlooking Florence.
3. Coils of hair like the coils of a serpent.

While she looks—no one's: very dear, no less.[4]
You smile? why, there's my picture ready made,
There's what we painters call our harmony!
A common grayness silvers everything[5]—   35
All in a twilight, you and I alike
—You, at the point of your first pride in me
(That's gone you know)—but I, at every point;
My youth, my hope, my art, being all toned down
To yonder sober pleasant Fiesole.   40
There's the bell clinking from the chapel top;
That length of convent wall across the way
Holds the trees safer, huddled more inside;
The last monk leaves the garden; days decrease,
And autumn grows, autumn in everything.   45
Eh? the whole seems to fall into a shape
As if I saw alike my work and self
And all that I was born to be and do,
A twilight-piece. Love, we are in God's hand.
How strange now, looks the life he makes us lead;   50
So free we seem, so fettered fast we are!
I feel he laid the fetter: let it lie!
This chamber for example—turn your head—
All that's behind us! You don't understand
Nor care to understand about my art,   55
But you can hear at least when people speak:
And that cartoon,[6] the second from the door
—It is the thing, Love! so such things should be—
Behold Madonna!—I am bold to say.
I can do with my pencil what I know,   60
What I see, what at bottom of my heart
I wish for, if I ever wish so deep—
Do easily, too—when I say, perfectly,
I do not boast, perhaps: yourself are judge,
Who listened to the Legate's[7] talk last week,   65
And just as much they used to say in France.
At any rate 'tis easy, all of it!
No sketches first, no studies, that's long past:
I do what many dream of, all their lives,
—Dream? strive to do, and agonize to do,   70
And fail in doing. I could count twenty such
On twice your fingers, and not leave this town,
Who strive—you don't know how the others strive
To paint a little thing like that you smeared
Carelessly passing with your robes afloat—   75
Yet do much less, so much less, Someone[8] says

4. Her affections are centered upon no one person, not even upon her husband, yet she is nevertheless dear to him.
5. The predominant color in many of Andrea's
paintings is silver gray.
6. Drawing.
7. A deputy of the Pope.
8. Probably Michelangelo (1475–1564).

(I know his name, no matter)—so much less!
Well, less is more, Lucrezia: I am judged.
There burns a truer light of God in them,
In their vexed beating stuffed and stopped-up brain,   80
Heart, or whate'er else, than goes on to prompt
This low-pulsed forthright craftsman's hand of mine.
Their works drop groundward, but themselves, I know,
Reach many a time a heaven that's shut to me,
Enter and take their place there sure enough,   85
Though they come back and cannot tell the world.
My works are nearer heaven, but I sit here.
The sudden blood of these men! at a word—
Praise them, it boils, or blame them, it boils too.
I, painting from myself and to myself,   90
Know what I do, am unmoved by men's blame
Or their praise either. Somebody remarks
Morello's[9] outline there is wrongly traced,
His hue mistaken; what of that? or else,
Rightly traced and well ordered; what of that?   95
Speak as they please, what does the mountain care?
Ah, but a man's reach should exceed his grasp,
Or what's a heaven for? All is silver-gray
Placid and perfect with my art: the worse!
I know both what I want and what might gain,   100
And yet how profitless to know, to sigh
"Had I been two, another and myself,
Our head would have o'erlooked the world!"[1] No doubt.
Yonder's a work now, of that famous youth
The Urbinate[2] who died five years ago.   105
('Tis copied, George Vasari sent it me.)[3]
Well, I can fancy how he did it all,
Pouring his soul, with kings and popes to see,
Reaching, that heaven might so replenish him,
Above and through his art—for it gives way;   110
That arm is wrongly put—and there again—
A fault to pardon in the drawing's lines,
Its body, so to speak: its soul is right,
He means right—that, a child may understand.
Still, what an arm! and I could alter it: 115
But all the play, the insight and the stretch—
Out of me, out of me! And wherefore out?
Had you enjoined them on me, given me soul,
We might have risen to Rafael, I and you!
Nay, Love, you did give all I asked, I think—   120

9. A mountain peak outside Florence.
1. I.e., if I had been both an aspiring, dedicated, and soul-conscious artist as well as a faultless craftsman, the combination would have been unsurpassable. See also line 140 ("we half-men").
2. Raphael (1483–1520), born at Urbino.
3. In saying that the painting is a copy, Andrea may perhaps be concerned to prevent Lucrezia from selling it.

More than I merit, yes, by many times.
But had you—oh, with the same perfect brow,
And perfect eyes, and more than perfect mouth,
And the low voice my soul hears, as a bird
The fowler's pipe,[4] and follows to the snare—⁣⁣⁣⁣⁣⁣⁣⁣⁣⁣ 125
Had you, with these the same, but brought a mind!
Some women do so. Had the mouth there urged
"God and the glory! never care for gain.
The present by the future, what is that?
Live for fame, side by side with Agnolo![5]⁣⁣⁣⁣⁣⁣⁣⁣⁣⁣ 130
Rafael is waiting: up to God, all three!"
I might have done it for you. So it seems:
Perhaps not. All is as God overrules.
Beside, incentives come from the soul's self;
The rest avail not. Why do I need you?⁣⁣⁣⁣⁣⁣⁣⁣⁣⁣ 135
What wife had Rafael, or has Agnolo?
In this world, who can do a thing, will not;
And who would do it, cannot, I perceive:
Yet the will's somewhat—somewhat, too, the power—
And thus we half-men struggle. At the end,⁣⁣⁣⁣⁣⁣⁣⁣⁣⁣ 140
God, I conclude, compensates, punishes.
'Tis safer for me, if the award be strict,
That I am something underrated here.
Poor this long while, despised, to speak the truth.
I dared not, do you know, leave home all day,⁣⁣⁣⁣⁣⁣⁣⁣⁣⁣ 145
For fear of chancing on the Paris lords.
The best is when they pass and look aside;
But they speak sometimes; I must bear it all.
Well may they speak! That Francis,[6] that first time,
And that long festal year at Fontainebleau!⁣⁣⁣⁣⁣⁣⁣⁣⁣⁣ 150
I surely then could sometimes leave the ground,
Put on the glory, Rafael's daily wear,
In that humane great monarch's golden look—
One finger in his beard or twisted curl
Over his mouth's good mark that made the smile,⁣⁣⁣⁣⁣⁣⁣⁣⁣⁣ 155
One arm about my shoulder, round my neck,
The jingle of his gold chain in my ear,
I painting proudly with his breath on me,
All his court round him, seeing with his eyes,
Such frank French eyes, and such a fire of souls⁣⁣⁣⁣⁣⁣⁣⁣⁣⁣ 160
Profuse, my hand kept plying by those hearts—
And, best of all, this, this, this face beyond,
This in the background, waiting on my work,
To crown the issue with a last reward!

4. Whistle or call used by hunters to lure wildfowl into range.
5. Michelangelo.
6. King Francis I of France had invited Andrea to his court at Fontainebleau and warmly encouraged him in his painting. On returning to Flor- ence, however, Andrea is reputed to have stolen some funds entrusted to him by Francis, and to please Lucrezia he built a house with the money. Now he is afraid of being insulted by "Paris lords" on the streets.

A good time, was it not, my kingly days? 165
And had you not grown restless . . . but I know—
'Tis done and past; 'twas right, my instinct said;
Too live the life grew, golden and not gray,
And I'm the weak-eyed bat no sun should tempt
Out of the grange whose four walls make his world.[7] 170
How could it end in any other way?
You called me, and I came home to your heart.
The triumph was—to reach and stay there; since
I reached it ere the triumph, what is lost?
Let my hands frame your face in your hair's gold, 175
You beautiful Lucrezia that are mine!
"Rafael did this, Andrea painted that;
The Roman's is the better when you pray,
But still the other's Virgin was his wife—"
Men will excuse me. I am glad to judge 180
Both pictures in your presence; clearer grows
My better fortune, I resolve to think.
For, do you know, Lucrezia, as God lives,
Said one day Agnolo, his very self,
To Rafael . . . I have known it all these years . . . 185
(When the young man was flaming out his thoughts
Upon a palace wall for Rome to see,
Too lifted up in heart because of it)
"Friend, there's a certain sorry little scrub
Goes up and down our Florence, none cares how, 190
Who, were he set to plan and execute
As you are, pricked on by your popes and kings,
Would bring the sweat into that brow of yours!"
To Rafael's—And indeed the arm is wrong.
I hardly dare . . . yet, only you to see, 195
Give the chalk here—quick, thus the line should go!
Aye, but the soul! he's Rafael! rub it out!
Still, all I care for, if he spoke the truth,
(What he? why, who but Michel Agnolo?
Do you forget already words like those?) 200
If really there was such a chance, so lost—
Is, whether you're—not grateful—but more pleased.
Well, let me think so. And you smile indeed!
This hour has been an hour! Another smile?
If you would sit thus by me every night 205
I should work better, do you comprehend?
I mean that I should earn more, give you more.
See, it is settled dusk now; there's a star;
Morello's gone, the watch-lights show the wall,
The cue-owls[8] speak the name we call them by. 210

7. The bat, a creature of evening, thrives best in the confines of the "four walls" of a farm building ("grange"). See also line 261 in which Andrea thinks of heaven as a place of four walls.
8. An owl whose cry sounds like the Italian word *ciù*.

Come from the window, love—come in, at last,
Inside the melancholy little house
We built to be so gay with. God is just.
King Francis may forgive me: oft at nights
When I look up from painting, eyes tired out,   215
The walls become illumined, brick from brick
Distinct, instead of mortar, fierce bright gold,
That gold of his I did cement them with!
Let us but love each other. Must you go?
That Cousin here again? he waits outside?   220
Must see you—you, and not with me? Those loans?
More gaming debts to pay?[9] you smiled for that?
Well, let smiles buy me! have you more to spend?
While hand and eye and something of a heart
Are left me, work's my ware, and what's it worth?   225
I'll pay my fancy. Only let me sit
The gray remainder of the evening out,
Idle, you call it, and muse perfectly
How I could paint, were I but back in France,
One picture, just one more—the Virgin's face,   230
Not yours this time! I want you at my side
To hear them—that is, Michel Agnolo—
Judge all I do and tell you of its worth.
Will you? Tomorrow, satisfy your friend.
I take the subjects for his corridor,   235
Finish the portrait out of hand—there, there,
And throw him in another thing or two
If he demurs; the whole should prove enough
To pay for this same Cousin's freak. Beside,
What's better and what's all I care about,   240
Get you the thirteen scudi[1] for the ruff!
Love, does that please you? Ah, but what does he,
The Cousin! What does he to please you more?

    I am grown peaceful as old age tonight.
I regret little, I would change still less.   245
Since there my past life lies, why alter it?
The very wrong to Francis!—it is true
I took his coin, was tempted and complied,
And built this house and sinned, and all is said.
My father and my mother died of want.[2]   250
Well, had I riches of my own? you see
How one gets rich! Let each one bear his lot.
They were born poor, lived poor, and poor they died:

9. Lucrezia's "Cousin" (or lover or "friend") owes
gambling debts to a creditor. Andrea has already
contracted (lines 5–10) to pay off these debts by
painting some pictures according to the creditor's
specifications. Now he agrees to pay off further

debts.
1. Italian coins.
2. According to Vasari, Andrea's infatuation for
Lucrezia prompted him to stop supporting his
poverty-stricken parents.

And I have labored somewhat in my time
And not been paid profusely. Some good son   255
Paint my two hundred pictures—let him try!
No doubt, there's something strikes a balance. Yes,
You loved me quite enough, it seems tonight.
This must suffice me here. What would one have?
In heaven, perhaps, new chances, one more chance—   260
Four great walls in the New Jerusalem,
Meted on each side by the angel's reed,[3]
For Leonard,[4] Rafael, Agnolo and me
To cover—the three first without a wife,
While I have mine! So—still they overcome   265
Because there's still Lucrezia—as I choose.

Again the Cousin's whistle! Go, my Love.

ca. 1853   1855

Two in the Campagna[1]

1

I wonder do you feel today
    As I have felt since, hand in hand,
We sat down on the grass, to stray
    In spirit better through the land,
This morn of Rome and May?   5

2

For me, I touched a thought, I know,
    Has tantalized me many times,
(Like turns of thread the spiders throw
    Mocking across our path) for rhymes
To catch at and let go.   10

3

Help me to hold it! First it left
    The yellowing fennel,[2] run to seed
There, branching from the brickwork's cleft,
    Some old tomb's ruin: yonder weed
Took up the floating weft,[3]   15

4

Where one small orange cup amassed
    Five beetles—blind and green they grope
Among the honey-meal: and last,
    Everywhere on the grassy slope
I traced it. Hold it fast!   20

3. Measuring rod. For "New Jerusalem," see Revelation 21.10–21.
4. Leonardo da Vinci (1452–1519).
1. The Campagna is the name for the level plains and pasture lands near Rome where the ruins of ancient cities are overrun with wild flowers.
2. A yellow-flowered plant from which a pungent spice is derived.
3. Threads crossing from side to side of a web.

5

The champaign[4] with its endless fleece
　　Of feathery grasses everywhere!
Silence and passion, joy and peace,
　　An everlasting wash of air—
Rome's ghost since her decease.　　　　　　　25

6

Such life here, through such lengths of hours,
　　Such miracles performed in play,
Such primal naked forms of flowers,
　　Such letting nature have her way
While heaven looks from its towers!　　　　30

7

How say you? Let us, O my dove,
　　Let us be unashamed of soul,
As earth lies bare to heaven above!
　　How is it under our control
To love or not to love?　　　　　　　　　35

8

I would that you were all to me,
　　You that are just so much, no more.
Nor yours nor mine, nor slave nor free!
　　Where does the fault lie? What the core
O' the wound, since wound must be?　　　40

9

I would I could adopt your will,
　　See with your eyes, and set my heart
Beating by yours, and drink my fill
　　At your soul's springs—your part my part
In life, for good and ill.　　　　　　　　45

10

No. I yearn upward, touch you close,
　　Then stand away. I kiss your cheek,
Catch your soul's warmth—I pluck the rose
　　And love it more than tongue can speak—
Then the good minute goes.　　　　　　　50

11

Already how am I so far
　　Out of that minute? Must I go
Still like the thistle-ball, no bar,
　　Onward, whenever light winds blow,
Fixed by no friendly star?[5]　　　　　　　55

12

Just when I seemed about to learn!
　　Where is the thread now? Off again!
The old trick! Only I discern—

---

4. Here, the Campagna.　　　　　　　5. See Shakespeare's Sonnet 116.

Infinite passion, and the pain
Of finite hearts that yearn.   60

1854   1855

A Grammarian's Funeral[1]

Shortly After the Revival of Learning in Europe

Let us begin and carry up this corpse,
    Singing together.
Leave we the common crofts, the vulgar thorpes[2]
    Each in its tether[3]
Sleeping safe on the bosom of the plain,   5
    Cared for till cock-crow:
Look out if yonder be not day again
    Rimming the rock-row!
That's the appropriate country; there, man's thought,
    Rarer, intenser,   10
Self-gathered for an outbreak, as it ought,
    Chafes in the censer.
Leave we the unlettered plain its herd and crop;[4]
    Seek we sepulture
On a tall mountain, citied to the top,   15
    Crowded with culture!
All the peaks soar, but one the rest excels;
    Clouds overcome it;
No! yonder sparkle is the citadel's
    Circling its summit.   20
Thither our path lies; wind we up the heights:
    Wait ye the warning?
Our low life was the level's and the night's;
    He's for the morning.
Step to a tune, square chests, erect each head,   25
    'Ware[5] the beholders!
This is our master, famous, calm, and dead,
    Borne on our shoulders.

1. The speaker is one of the students who are bearing the body of their scholarly master to the mountaintop for burial. The student's defense of the dead grammarian's idealistic dedication to knowledge and faith in a future life is expressed in some of the harshest-sounding and most laborious verse ever written by Browning. It is this grotesque combination of opposites (soaring idealism in conjunction with harsh or petty realities) that gives *A Grammarian's Funeral* its distinctive tone.

No model for the grammarian has been specifically identified. Browning seems to have had in mind the kind of early Renaissance scholar whose devotion to the Greek language made it possible for others to enjoy the more recognizably significant aspects of the revival of learning.
2. "Crofts" are small tracts of land farmed by peasants; "thorpes" are villages.
3. Restricted to a narrow sphere like an animal tied to a stake.
4. Flatlands at the base of the mountain which are populated by illiterate shepherds and peasants. "Sepulture": burial place.
5. Look out for!

Sleep, crop and herd! sleep, darkling thorpe and croft,
    Safe from the weather!   30
He, whom we convoy to his grave aloft,
    Singing together,
He was a man born with thy face and throat,
    Lyric Apollo![6]
Long he lived nameless: how should spring take note   35
    Winter would follow?
Till lo, the little touch, and youth was gone!
    Cramped and diminished,
Moaned he, "New measures, other feet anon!
    My dance is finished?"   40
No, that's the world's way: (keep the mountain-side,
    Make for the city!)
He knew the signal, and stepped on with pride
    Over men's pity;
Left play for work, and grappled with the world   45
    Bent on escaping:
"What's in the scroll," quoth he, "thou keepest furled?
    Show me their shaping,
Theirs who most studied man, the bard and sage—
    Give!"—So, he gowned him,[7]   50
Straight got by heart that book to its last page:
    Learned, we found him.
Yea, but we found him bald too, eyes like lead,
    Accents uncertain:
"Time to taste life," another would have said,   55
    "Up with the curtain!"
This man said rather, "Actual life comes next?
    Patience a moment!
Grant I have mastered learning's crabbed text,
    Still there's the comment.[8]   60
Let me know all! Prate not of most or least,
    Painful or easy!
Even to the crumbs I'd fain eat up the feast,
    Aye, nor feel queasy."
Oh, such a life as he resolved to live,   65
    When he had learned it,
When he had gathered all books had to give!
    Sooner, he spurned it.
Image the whole, then execute the parts—
    Fancy the fabric   70
Quite, ere you build, ere steel strike fire from quartz,
    Ere mortar dab brick!

(Here's the town gate reached: there's the market place
    Gaping before us.)

---

6. God of music and embodiment of male beauty.   8. Commentaries or annotations upon a text.
7. Dressed in academic gown; became a scholar.

Yea, this in him was the peculiar grace   75
    (Hearten our chorus!)
That before living he'd learn how to live—
    No end to learning:
Earn the means first—God surely will contrive
    Use for our earning.   80
Others mistrust and say, "But time escapes:
    Live now or never!"
He said, "What's time? Leave Now for dogs and apes!
    Man has Forever."
Back to his book then: deeper drooped his head: 85
    Calculus[9] racked him:
Leaden before, his eyes grew dross of lead:
    Tussis[1] attacked him.
"Now, master, take a little rest!"—not he!
    (Caution redoubled,   90
Step two abreast, the way winds narrowly!)
    Not a whit troubled
Back to his studies, fresher than at first,
    Fierce as a dragon
He (soul-hydroptic[2] with a sacred thirst)   95
    Sucked at the flagon.
Oh, if we draw a circle premature,
    Heedless of far gain,
Greedy for quick returns of profit, sure
    Bad is our bargain!   100
Was it not great? did not he throw on God
    (He loves the burthen)—
God's task to make the heavenly period
    Perfect the earthen?
Did not he magnify the mind, show clear   105
    Just what it all meant?
He would not discount life, as fools do here,
    Paid by installment.
He ventured neck or nothing—heaven's success
    Found, or earth's failure: 110
"Wilt thou trust death or not?" He answered "Yes:
    Hence with life's pale lure!"
That low man seeks a little thing to do,
    Sees it and does it:
This high man, with a great thing to pursue,   115
    Dies ere he knows it.
That low man goes on adding one to one,
    His hundred's soon hit:
This high man, aiming at a million,
    Misses an unit.[3]   120

---

9. A stone such as a gallstone.
1. A cough.
2. Insatiably soul-thirsty.

3. A small item such as some trifling worldly pleasure.

That, has the world here—should he need the next,
    Let the world mind him!
This, throws himself on God, and unperplexed
    Seeking shall find him.
So, with the throttling hands of death at strife,   125
    Ground he at grammar;
Still, through the rattle, parts of speech were rife:
    While he could stammer
He settled *Hoti's* business—let it be!—
    Properly based *Oun*—   130
Gave us the doctrine of the enclitic *De*,[4]
    Dead from the waist down.
Well, here's the platform, here's the proper place:
    Hail to your purlieus,
All ye highfliers of the feathered race,   135
    Swallows and curlews!
Here's the top peak; the multitude below
    Live, for they can, there:
This man decided not to Live but Know—
    Bury this man there?   140
Here—here's his place, where meteors shoot, clouds form,
    Lightnings are loosened,
Stars come and go! Let joy break with the storm,
    Peace let the dew send!
Lofty designs must close in like effects: 145
    Loftily lying,
Leave him—still loftier than the world suspects,
    Living and dying.

ca. 1854   1855

A Woman's Last Word

1

Let's contend no more, Love,
    Strive nor weep:
All be as before, Love,
    —Only sleep!

2

What so wild as words are?   5
    I and thou
In debate, as birds are,
    Hawk on bough!

3

See the creature stalking
    While we speak!   10

4. "*Hoti*," "*Oun*," and "*De*" are Greek particles meaning "that," "then," and "toward." An unaccented word such as *de* is "enclitic" when it affects the accentuation of a word adjacent to it. In a letter of 1863 Browning commented to Tennyson that he wanted his grammarian to have been working on "the biggest of the littlenesses."

Hush and hide the talking,
    Cheek on cheek!

          4

What so false as truth is,
    False to thee?
Where the serpent's tooth is   15
    Shun the tree—

          5

Where the apple reddens
    Never pry—
Lest we lose our Edens,
    Eve and I.   20

          6

Be a god and hold me
    With a charm!
Be a man and fold me
    With thine arm!

          7

Teach me, only teach, Love!   25
    As I ought
I will speak thy speech, Love,
    Think thy thought—

          8

Meet, if thou require it,
    Both demands,
Laying flesh and spirit   30
    In thy hands.

          9

That shall be tomorrow
    Not tonight:
I must bury sorrow   35
    Out of sight:

          10

—Must a little weep, Love
    (Foolish me!),
And so fall asleep, Love,
    Loved by thee.   40

          1855

An Epistle Containing the Strange Medical Experience of Karshish, the Arab Physician[1]

Karshish, the picker-up of learning's crumbs,
The not-incurious in God's handiwork

---

1. The letter is written in the year 66 A.D., when the Romans, under Vespasian, were to invade Palestine. During a journey across the country, Karshish, whose name in Arabic means "one who gathers" (or, roughly, "the picker-up of learning's crumbs"), has been collecting information on medical and scientific developments he has encountered. The "case" which has intrigued him

(This man's-flesh he hath admirably made,
Blown like a bubble, kneaded like a paste,
To coop up and keep down on earth a space
That puff of vapor from his mouth, man's soul)[2]   5
—To Abib, all-sagacious in our art,
Breeder in me of what poor skill I boast,
Like me inquisitive how pricks and cracks
Befall the flesh through too much stress and strain,   10
Whereby the wily vapor fain would slip
Back and rejoin its source before the term,—
And aptest in contrivance (under God)
To baffle it by deftly stopping such:—
The vagrant[3] Scholar to his Sage at home   15
Sends greeting (health and knowledge, fame with peace)
Three samples of true snakestone[4]—rarer still,
One of the other sort, the melon-shaped,
(But fitter, pounded fine, for charms than drugs)
And writeth now the twenty-second time.   20

        My journeyings were brought to Jericho:
Thus I resume. Who studious in our art
Shall count a little labor unrepaid?
I have shed sweat enough, left flesh and bone
On many a flinty furlong of this land.   25
Also, the country-side is all on fire
With rumors of a marching hitherward:
Some say Vespasian cometh, some, his son.[5]
A black lynx snarled and pricked a tufted ear;
Lust of my blood inflamed his yellow balls:[6]   30
I cried and threw my staff and he was gone.
Twice have the robbers stripped and beaten me,
And once a town declared me for a spy;
But at the end, I reach Jerusalem,
Since this poor covert where I pass the night,   35
This Bethany,[7] lies scarce the distance thence
A man with plague-sores at the third degree
Runs till he drops down dead. Thou laughest here!
'Sooth,[8] it elates me, thus reposed and safe,
To void the stuffing of my travel-scrip[9]   40
And share with thee whatever Jewry yields.
A viscid choler is observable

In tertians,[1] I was nearly bold to say;
And falling-sickness[2] hath a happier cure
Than our school wots[3] of: there's a spider here   45
Weaves no web, watches on the ledge of tombs,
Sprinkled with mottles on an ash-gray back;
Take five and drop them . . . but who knows his mind,
The Syrian runagate[4] I trust this to?
His service payeth me a sublimate[5]   50
Blown up his nose to help the ailing eye.
Best wait: I reach Jerusalem at morn,
There set in order my experiences,
Gather what most deserves, and give thee all—
Or I might add, Judea's gum-tragacanth[6]   55
Scales off in purer flakes, shines clearer-grained,
Cracks 'twixt the pestle and the porphyry,[7]
In fine exceeds our produce. Scalp-disease
Confounds me, crossing so with leprosy—
Thou hadst admired one sort I gained at Zoar[8]—   60
But zeal outruns discretion. Here I end.

Yet stay: my Syrian blinketh gratefully,
Protesteth his devotion is my price—
Suppose I write what harms not, though he steal?
I half resolve to tell thee, yet I blush,   65
What set me off a-writing first of all.
An itch I had, a sting to write, a tang!
For, be it this town's barrenness—or else
The Man[9] had something in the look of him—
His case has struck me far more than 'tis worth.   70
So, pardon if—(lest presently I lose
In the great press of novelty at hand
The care and pains this somehow stole from me)
I bid thee take the thing while fresh in mind,
Almost in sight—for, wilt thou have the truth?   75
The very man is gone from me but now,
Whose ailment is the subject of discourse.
Thus then, and let thy better wit help all!

'Tis but a case of mania—subinduced[1]
By epilepsy, at the turning-point   80
Of trance prolonged unduly some three days:
When, by the exhibition[2] of some drug
Or spell, exorcization, stroke of art

1. A sticky bile is observable in fevers occurring
every other day.
2. Epilepsy.
3. Knows.
4. Renegade.
5. Pays me for a medicine.
6. A salve derived from a plant.

7. A hard rock against which the substance is
pounded with a pestle.
8. Town north of the Dead Sea.
9. Lazarus.
1. Brought about as a result of something else.
2. Administration.

Unknown to me and which 'twere well to know,
The evil thing out-breaking all at once   85
Left the man whole and sound of body indeed,—
But, flinging (so to speak) life's gates too wide,
Making a clear house of it too suddenly,
The first conceit[3] that entered might inscribe
Whatever it was minded on the wall   90
So plainly at that vantage, as it were,
(First come, first served) that nothing subsequent
Attaineth to erase those fancy-scrawls
The just-returned and new-established soul
Hath gotten now so thoroughly by heart   95
That henceforth she will read or these or none.
And first—the man's own firm conviction rests
That he was dead (in fact they buried him)
—That he was dead and then restored to life
By a Nazarene physician of his tribe: 100
—'Sayeth, the same bade "Rise," and he did rise.
"Such cases are diurnal,"[4] thou wilt cry.
Not so this figment!—not, that such a fume,[5]
Instead of giving way to time and health,
Should eat itself into the life of life,   105
As saffron[6] tingeth flesh, blood, bones and all!
For see, how he takes up the after-life.
The man—it is one Lazarus a Jew,
Sanguine,[7] proportioned, fifty years of age,
The body's habit wholly laudable,[8]   110
As much, indeed, beyond the common health
As he were made and put aside to show.
Think, could we penetrate by any drug
And bathe the wearied soul and worried flesh,
And bring it clear and fair, by three days' sleep!   115
Whence has the man the balm that brightens all?
This grown man eyes the world now like a child.
Some elders of his tribe, I should premise,[9]
Led in their friend, obedient as a sheep,
To bear my inquisition. While they spoke,   120
Now sharply, now with sorrow,—told the case,—
He listened not except I spoke to him,
But folded his two hands and let them talk,
Watching the flies that buzzed: and yet no fool.
And that's a sample how his years must go.   125
Look, if a beggar, in fixed middle-life,
Should find a treasure,—can he use the same
With straitened habits and with tastes starved small,

3. Idea.   same name, also used as a spice.
4. Occur every day.   7. Robust.
5. A vapor standing for a hallucinated belief.   8. Healthy.
6. Yellow-colored dye made from the plant of the   9. Set forth beforehand.

And take at once to his impoverished brain
The sudden element that changes things,   130
That sets the undreamed-of rapture at his hand
And puts the cheap old joy in the scorned dust?
Is he not such an one as moves to mirth—
Warily parsimonious, when no need,
Wasteful as drunkenness at undue times?   135
All prudent counsel as to what befits
The golden mean, is lost on such an one:
The man's fantastic will is the man's law.
So here—we call the treasure knowledge, say,
Increased beyond the fleshly faculty—   140
Heaven opened to a soul while yet on earth,
Earth forced on a soul's use while seeing heaven:
The man is witless of the size, the sum,
The value in proportion of all things,
Or whether it be little or be much.   145
Discourse to him of prodigious armaments
Assembled to besiege his city now,
And of the passing of a mule with gourds—
'Tis one! Then take it on the other side,
Speak of some trifling fact,—he will gaze rapt   150
With stupor at its very littleness
(Far as I see), as if in that indeed
He caught prodigious import, whole results;
And so will turn to us the bystanders
In ever the same stupor (note this point)   155
That we too see not with his opened eyes.
Wonder and doubt come wrongly into play,
Preposterously, at cross-purposes.
Should his child sicken unto death,—why, look
For scarce abatement of his cheerfulness,   160
Or pretermission[1] of the daily craft!
While a word, gesture, glance from that same child
At play or in the school or laid asleep,
Will startle him to an agony of fear,
Exasperation, just as like. Demand   165
The reason why—" 'tis but a word," object—
"A gesture"—he regards thee as our lord[2]
Who lived there in the pyramid alone,
Looked at us (dost thou mind?) when, being young,
We both would unadvisedly recite   170
Some charm's beginning, from that book of his,
Able to bid the sun throb wide and burst
All into stars, as suns grown old are wont.
Thou and the child have each a veil alike
Thrown o'er your heads, from under which ye both   175

1. Interruption.
2. A magician or wise man under whom Karshish   and Abib had studied.

Stretch your blind hands and trifle with a match
Over a mine of Greek fire,[3] did ye know!
He holds on firmly to some thread of life—
(It is the life to lead perforcedly)
Which runs across some vast distracting orb   180
Of glory on either side that meager thread,
Which, conscious of, he must not enter yet—
The spiritual life around the earthly life:
The law of that is known to him as this,[4]
His heart and brain move there, his feet stay here.   185
So is the man perplexed with impulses
Sudden to start off crosswise, not straight on,
Proclaiming what is right and wrong across,
And not along, this black thread through the blaze—
"It should be" balked by "here it cannot be."   190
And oft the man's soul springs into his face
As if he saw again and heard again
His sage that bade him "Rise" and he did rise.
Something, a word, a tick o' the blood[5] within
Admonishes: then back he sinks at once   195
To ashes, who was very fire before,
In sedulous recurrence to his trade
Whereby he earneth him the daily bread;
And studiously the humbler for that pride,
Professedly the faultier that he knows   200
God's secret, while he holds the thread of life.
Indeed the especial marking of the man
Is prone submission to the heavenly will—
Seeing it, what it is, and why it is.
'Sayeth,[6] he will wait patient to the last   205
For that same death which must restore his being
To equilibrium, body loosening soul
Divorced even now by premature full growth:
He will live, nay, it pleaseth him to live
So long as God please, and just how God please.   210
He even seeketh not to please God more
(Which meaneth, otherwise) than as God please.
Hence, I perceive not he affects[7] to preach
The doctrine of his sect whate'er it be,
Make proselytes as madmen thirst to do: 215
How can he give his neighbor the real ground,
His own conviction? Ardent as he is—
Call his great truth a lie, why, still the old
"Be it as God please" reassureth him.
I probed the sore[8] as thy disciple should: 220

---

3. Weapon made of sulphur, naphtha, and salt-   5. Pulse beat.
peter.   6. He says.
4. I.e., he knows the law of the spiritual life as 7. Aspires.
well as that of the earthly life.   8. Investigated the case.

"How, beast," said I, "this stolid carelessness
Sufficeth thee, when Rome is on her march
To stamp out like a little spark thy town,
Thy tribe, thy crazy tale and thee at once?"
He merely looked with his large eyes on me.   225
The man is apathetic, you deduce?
Contrariwise, he loves both old and young,
Able and weak, affects[9] the very brutes
And birds—how say I? flowers of the field—
As a wise workman recognizes tools   230
In a master's workshop, loving what they make.
Thus is the man, as harmless as a lamb:
Only impatient, let him do his best,
At ignorance and carelessness and sin—
An indignation which is promptly curbed: 235
As when in certain travels I have feigned
To be an ignoramus in our art
According to some preconceived design,
And happed to hear the land's practitioners
Steeped in conceit sublimed[1] by ignorance,   240
Prattle fantastically on disease,
Its cause and cure—and I must hold my peace!

    Thou wilt object—Why have I not ere this
Sought out the sage himself, the Nazarene
Who wrought this cure, inquiring at the source,   245
Conferring with the frankness that befits?
Alas! it grieveth me, the learnèd leech[2]
Perished in a tumult many years ago,
Accused,—our learning's fate,—of wizardry,
Rebellion, to the setting up a rule   250
And creed prodigious as described to me.
His death, which happened when the earthquake fell[3]
(Prefiguring, as soon appeared, the loss
To occult learning in our lord the sage
Who lived there in the pyramid alone)   255
Was wrought by the mad people—that's their wont!
On vain recourse, as I conjecture it,
To his tried virtue, for miraculous help—
How could he stop the earthquake? That's their way!
The other imputations must be lies: 260
But take one, though I loathe to give it thee,
In mere respect for any good man's fame.
(And after all, our patient Lazarus
Is stark mad; should we count on what he says?
Perhaps not: though in writing to a leech   265

---

9. Has affection for.
1. Exalted. "Conceit": foolish fancy.
2. Doctor.

3. The earthquake at the time of Christ's crucifixion reported in Matthew 27.51.

'Tis well to keep back nothing of a case.)
This man so cured regards the curer, then,
As—God forgive me! who but God himself,
Creator and sustainer of the world,
That came and dwelt in flesh on it awhile!   270
—'Sayeth that such an one was born and lived,
Taught, healed the sick, broke bread at his own house,
Then died, with Lazarus by, for aught I know,
And yet was . . . what I said nor choose repeat,
And must have so avouched himself, in fact,   275
In hearing of this very Lazarus
Who saith—but why all this of what he saith?
Why write of trivial matters, things of price
Calling at every moment for remark?
I noticed on the margin of a pool   280
Blue-flowering borage, the Aleppo[4] sort,
Aboundeth, very nitrous. It is strange!

Thy pardon for this long and tedious case,
Which, now that I review it, needs must seem
Unduly dwelt on, prolixly set forth!   285
Nor I myself discern in what is writ
Good cause for the peculiar interest
And awe indeed this man has touched me with.
Perhaps the journey's end, the weariness
Had wrought upon me first. I met him thus: 290
I crossed a ridge of short sharp broken hills
Like an old lion's cheek teeth. Out there came
A moon made like a face with certain spots
Multiform, manifold and menacing:
Then a wind rose behind me. So we met   295
In this old sleepy town at unaware,
The man and I. I send thee what is writ.
Regard it as a chance, a matter risked
To this ambiguous Syrian—he may lose,
Or steal, or give it thee with equal good,   300
Jerusalem's repose shall make amends
For time this letter wastes, thy time and mine;
Till when, once more thy pardon and farewell!

The very God! think, Abib; dost thou think?
So, the All-Great, were the All-Loving too—   305
So, through the thunder comes a human voice
Saying, "O heart I made, a heart beats here!
Face, my hands fashioned, see it in myself!
Thou hast no power nor mayst conceive of mine,
But love I gave thee, with myself to love,   310

---

4. Town in northern Syria. "Borage": herb used medicinally that contains nitre.

And thou must love me who have died for thee!"
The madman saith He said so: it is strange.

1855

Caliban upon Setebos   Two closely related controversies of the
Victorian period led Browning to write this poem (whose title means "Caliban's thoughts about Setebos"). The first, stimulated by Darwin, was concerned with man's origins and his relation to other animals (the poem teems
with animal life; in 295 lines, as Park Honan has shown, there are sixty-
three references to animals). Caliban, the half-man and half-monster of
Shakespeare's *Tempest*, provided the poet with a model of how the mind of
a primitive creature may operate. The second controversy concerned the
nature of God and God's responsibility for the existence of suffering in the
world. Like many men, Caliban thinks of God's nature as similar to his own.
His anthropomorphic conception of the deity, whom he calls Setebos, is
confined to what he has observed of life on his island and to what he has
observed of himself. From the former derives his "natural theology," that is,
his identifying the character of God from evidences provided by nature rather
than from the evidence of supernatural revelation. From the latter, his
observation of his own character, derives Caliban's conception of God's willful power. Caliban himself admires power and thinks of God in Calvinistic
terms as a being who selects at random some creatures who are to be saved
and others who are to be condemned to suffer.

An obstacle for the reader is Caliban's use of the third person pronoun.
He says that he "never speaks his mind save housed as now"—that is, he
thinks if he is adequately hidden under the slush in his cave, the deity will
not catch him thinking; he may remind us of the hero of George Orwell's
1984 trying to evade the Thought Police. But to make especially sure of not
being caught, Caliban refers to himself in the third person. Thus " 'Will
sprawl" means "Caliban will sprawl" (an apostrophe before the verb usually
indicates that Caliban himself is the implied subject). When he feels that
Setebos will not hear him, he then slips into the first person (e.g., line 56
or 68). The deity is also referred to in the third person but with an initial
capital letter ("He").

Caliban upon Setebos

Or Natural Theology in the Island

"Thou thoughtest that I was altogether such a one as thyself."[1]

['Will sprawl, now that the heat of day is best,
Flat on his belly in the pit's much mire,
With elbows wide, fists clenched to prop his chin.
And, while he kicks both feet in the cool slush,
And feels about his spine small eft-things[2] course,   5

1. Psalms 50:21. The speaker is God.   2. Water lizards.

Run in and out each arm, and make him laugh:
And while above his head a pompion plant,[3]
Coating the cave-top as a brow its eye,
Creeps down to touch and tickle hair and beard,
And now a flower drops with a bee inside,　　　　　　　　10
And now a fruit to snap at, catch and crunch—
He looks out o'er yon sea which sunbeams cross
And recross till they weave a spider web
(Meshes of fire, some great fish breaks at times)
And talks to his own self, howe'er he please,　　　　　　15
Touching that other, whom his dam[4] called God.
Because to talk about Him, vexes—ha,
Could He but know! and time to vex is now,
When talk is safer than in wintertime.
Moreover Prosper[5] and Miranda sleep　　　　　　　　20
In confidence he drudges at their task,
And it is good to cheat the pair, and gibe,
Letting the rank tongue blossom into speech.]

Setebos, Setebos, and Setebos!
'Thinketh, He dwelleth i' the cold o' the moon.　　　　　25

'Thinketh He made it, with the sun to match,
But not the stars; the stars came otherwise;
Only made clouds, winds, meteors, such as that:
Also this isle, what lives and grows thereon,
And snaky sea which rounds and ends the same.　　　　30

'Thinketh, it came of being ill at ease:
He hated that He cannot change His cold,
Nor cure its ache. 'Hath spied an icy fish
That longed to 'scape the rock-stream where she lived,
And thaw herself within the lukewarm brine　　　　　35
O' the lazy sea her stream thrusts far amid,
A crystal spike 'twixt two warm walls of wave;[6]
Only, she ever sickened, found repulse
At the other kind of water, not her life,
(Green-dense and dim-delicious, bred o' the sun)　　　　40
Flounced back from bliss she was not born to breathe,
And in her old bounds buried her despair,
Hating and loving warmth alike: so He.

'Thinketh, He made thereat the sun, this isle,
Trees and the fowls here, beast and creeping thing.　　45
Yon otter, sleek-wet, black, lithe as a leech;

---

3. Pumpkin plant.
4. Caliban's mother, Sycorax.
5. Prospero the magician, who is Caliban's master

in *The Tempest*. Miranda is Prospero's daughter.
6. I.e., the thin stream of cold water which is driven
into the warm ocean like a spike between walls.

Yon auk,[7] one fire-eye in a ball of foam,
That floats and feeds; a certain badger brown
He hath watched hunt with that slant white-wedge eye
By moonlight; and the pie[8] with the long tongue   50
That pricks deep into oakwarts for a worm,
And says a plain word when she finds her prize,
But will not eat the ants; the ants themselves
That build a wall of seeds and settled stalks
About their hole—He made all these and more,   55
Made all we see, and us, in spite: how else?
He could not, Himself, make a second self
To be His mate; as well have made Himself:
He would not make what he mislikes or slights,
An eyesore to Him, or not worth His pains: 60
But did, in envy, listlessness, or sport,
Make what Himself would fain, in a manner, be—
Weaker in most points, stronger in a few,
Worthy, and yet mere playthings all the while,
Things He admires and mocks too—that is it.   65
Because, so brave, so better though they be,
It nothing skills if He begin to plague.[9]
Look now, I melt a gourd-fruit into mash,
Add honeycomb and pods, I have perceived,
Which bite like finches when they bill and kiss—   70
Then, when froth rises bladdery,[1] drink up all,
Quick, quick, till maggots scamper through my brain;
Last, throw me on my back i' the seeded thyme,
And wanton, wishing I were born a bird.
Put case, unable to be what I wish,   75
I yet could make a live bird out of clay:
Would not I take clay, pinch my Caliban
Able to fly?—for, there, see, he hath wings,
And great comb like the hoopoe's[2] to admire,
And there, a sting to do his foes offense,   80
There, and I will that he begin to live,
Fly to yon rock-top, nip me off the horns
Of griggs[3] high up that make the merry din,
Saucy through their veined wings, and mind me not.
In which feat, if his leg snapped, brittle clay,   85
And he lay stupid-like—why, I should laugh;
And if he, spying me, should fall to weep,
Beseech me to be good, repair his wrong,
Bid his poor leg smart less or grow again—
Well, as the chance were, this might take or else   90

---

7. Sea bird.
8. Magpie.
9. I.e., our superior virtues are of no help to us if
God elects to inflict plagues upon us.

1. Bubbly.
2. Bird with bright plumage.
3. Grasshoppers.

Not take my fancy: I might hear his cry,
And give the mankin three sound legs for one,
Or pluck the other off, leave him like an egg,
And lessoned he was mine and merely clay.
Were this no pleasure, lying in the thyme,　　　　　　　95
Drinking the mash, with brain become alive,
Making and marring clay at will? So He.

'Thinketh, such shows nor right nor wrong in Him,
Nor kind, nor cruel: He is strong and Lord.
'Am strong myself compared to yonder crabs　　　　100
That march now from the mountain to the sea;
'Let twenty pass, and stone the twenty-first,
Loving not, hating not, just choosing so.
'Say, the first straggler that boasts purple spots
Shall join the file, one pincer twisted off;　　　　　105
'Say, this bruised fellow shall receive a worm,
And two worms he whose nippers end in red;
As it likes me each time, I do: so He.

Well then, 'supposeth He is good i' the main,
Placable if His mind and ways were guessed,　　　　110
But rougher than His handiwork, be sure!
Oh, He hath made things worthier than Himself,
And envieth that, so helped, such things do more
Than He who made them! What consoles but this?
That they, unless through Him, do naught at all,　　115
And must submit: what other use in things?
'Hath cut a pipe of pithless elder-joint
That, blown through, gives exact the scream o' the jay
When from her wing you twitch the feathers blue:
Sound this, and little birds that hate the jay　　　　120
Flock within stone's throw, glad their foe is hurt:
Put case such pipe could prattle and boast forsooth,
"I catch the birds, I am the crafty thing,
I make the cry my maker cannot make
With his great round mouth; he must blow through mine!"　　125
Would not I smash it with my foot? So He.

But wherefore rough, why cold and ill at ease?
Aha, that is a question! Ask, for that,
What knows—the something over Setebos
That made Him, or He, may be, found and fought,　　130
Worsted, drove off and did to nothing,[4] perchance.
There may be something quiet o'er His head,
Out of His reach, that feels nor joy nor grief,
Since both derive from weakness in some way.

4. Completely overcame.

I joy because the quails come; would not joy   135
Could I bring quails here when I have a mind:
This Quiet, all it hath a mind to, doth.
'Esteemeth stars the outposts of its couch,
But never spends much thought nor care that way.
It may look up, work up—the worse for those   140
It works on! 'Careth but for Setebos[5]
The many-handed as a cuttlefish,
Who, making Himself feared through what He does,
Looks up, first, and perceives he cannot soar
To what is quiet and hath happy life;   145
Next looks down here, and out of very spite
Makes this a bauble-world to ape yon real,
These good things to match those as hips[6] do grapes.
'Tis solace making baubles, aye, and sport.
Himself peeped late, eyed Prosper at his books   150
Careless and lofty, lord now of the isle:
Vexed, 'stitched a book of broad leaves, arrow-shaped,
Wrote thereon, he knows what, prodigious words;
Has peeled a wand and called it by a name;
Weareth at whiles for an enchanter's robe   155
The eyed skin of a supple oncelot;[7]
And hath an ounce[8] sleeker than youngling mole,
A four-legged serpent he makes cower and couch,
Now snarl, now hold its breath and mind his eye,
And saith she is Miranda and my wife: 160
'Keeps for his Ariel[9] a tall pouch-bill crane
He bids go wade for fish and straight disgorge;
Also a sea beast, lumpish, which he snared,
Blinded the eyes of, and brought somewhat tame,
And split its toe-webs, and now pens the drudge   165
In a hole o'the rock and calls him Caliban;
A bitter heart that bides its time and bites.
'Plays thus at being Prosper in a way,
Taketh his mirth with make-believes: so He.

His dam held that the Quiet made all things   170
Which Setebos vexed only: 'holds not so.
Who made them weak, meant weakness He might vex.
Had He meant other, while His hand was in,
Why not make horny eyes no thorn could prick,
Or plate my scalp with bone against the snow,   175
Or overscale my flesh 'neath joint and joint,
Like an orc's[1] armor? Aye—so spoil His sport!
He is the One now: only He doth all.

5. Caliban is concerned to appease only Setebos, not the other deity—the Quiet.
6. Hard fruits produced by wild roses.
7. Browning may have invented this term from the Spanish *oncela* or from the French *ocelot*. Both words signify a leopard or spotted wildcat.
8. A large, ferocious leopard, 6 or 7 feet in length.
9. In *The Tempest*, a spirit who serves Prospero.
1. Killer whale's.

'Saith, He may like, perchance, what profits Him.
Aye, himself loves what does him good; but why?   180
'Gets good no otherwise. This blinded beast
Loves whoso places flesh-meat on his nose,
But, had he eyes, would want no help, but hate
Or love, just as it liked him: He hath eyes.
Also it pleaseth Setebos to work,   185
Use all His hands, and exercise much craft,
By no means for the love of what is worked.
'Tasteth, himself, no finer good i' the world
When all goes right, in this safe summertime,
And he wants little, hungers, aches not much,   190
Than trying what to do with wit and strength.
'Falls to make something: 'piled yon pile of turfs,
And squared and stuck there squares of soft white chalk,
And, with a fish-tooth, scratched a moon on each,
And set up endwise certain spikes of tree,   195
And crowned the whole with a sloth's skull a-top,
Found dead i' the woods, too hard for one to kill.
No use at all i' the work, for work's sole sake;
'Shall some day knock it down again: so He.

'Saith He is terrible: watch His feats in proof!   200
One hurricane will spoil six good months' hope.
He hath a spite against me, that I know,
Just as He favors Prosper, who knows why?
So it is, all the same, as well I find.
'Wove wattles half the winter, fenced them firm   205
With stone and stake to stop she-tortoises
Crawling to lay their eggs here: well, one wave,
Feeling the foot of Him upon its neck,
Gaped as a snake does, lolled out its large tongue,
And licked the whole labor flat; so much for spite.   210
'Saw a ball[2] flame down late (yonder it lies)
Where, half an hour before, I slept i' the shade:
Often they scatter sparkles: there is force!
'Dug up a newt He may have envied once
And turned to stone, shut up inside a stone.   215
Please Him and hinder this?—What Prosper does?[3]
Aha, if He would tell me how! Not He!
There is the sport: discover how or die!
All need not die, for of the things o' the isle
Some flee afar, some dive, some run up trees;   220
Those at His mercy—why, they please Him most
When . . . when . . . well, never try the same way twice!
Repeat what act has pleased, He may grow wroth.

2. Meteorite.
3. I.e., shall I please Setebos, as Prospero does, and thus prevent my being punished as the newt was punished?

You must not know His ways, and play Him off,
Sure of the issue. 'Doth the like himself: 225
'Spareth a squirrel that it nothing fears
But steals the nut from underneath my thumb,
And when I threat, bites stoutly in defense:
'Spareth an urchin[4] that contrariwise
Curls up into a ball, pretending death   230
For fright at my approach: the two ways please.
But what would move my choler more than this,
That either creature counted on its life
Tomorrow and next day and all days to come,
Saying, forsooth, in the inmost of its heart,   235
"Because he did so yesterday with me,
And otherwise with such another brute,
So must he do henceforth and always."—Aye?
Would teach the reasoning couple what "must" means!
'Doth as he likes, or wherefore Lord? So He.   240

'Conceiveth all things will continue thus,
And we shall have to live in fear of Him
So long as He lives, keeps His strength: no change,
If He have done His best, make no new world
To please Him more, so leave off watching this—   235
If He surprise not even the Quiet's self
Some strange day—or, suppose, grow into it
As grubs grow butterflies: else, here are we,
And there is He, and nowhere help at all.
'Believeth with the life, the pain shall stop.   250
His dam held different, that after death
He both plagued enemies and feasted friends:
Idly![5] He doth His worst in this our life,
Giving just respite lest we die through pain,
Saving last pain for worst—with which, an end.   255
Meanwhile, the best way to escape His ire
Is, not to seem too happy. 'Sees, himself,
Yonder two flies, with purple films and pink,
Bask on the pompion-bell above: kills both.
'Sees two black painful beetles roll their ball   260
On head and tail as if to save their lives:
Moves them the stick away they strive to clear.

Even so, 'would have Him misconceive, suppose
This Caliban strives hard and ails no less,
And always, above all else, envies Him;   265
Wherefore he mainly dances on dark nights,
Moans in the sun, gets under holes to laugh,

4. Hedgehog.
5. I.e., Caliban thinks his mother's opinion was wrong or idle. God's sport with man is confined to this
world: there is no afterlife.

And never speaks his mind save housed as now:
Outside, 'groans, curses. If He caught me here,
O'erheard this speech, and asked "What chucklest at?"   270
'Would, to appease Him, cut a finger off,
Or of my three kid yearlings burn the best,
Or let the toothsome apples rot on tree,
Or push my tame beast for the orc to taste:
While myself lit a fire, and made a song   275
And sung it, *"What I hate, be consecrate*
To celebrate Thee and Thy state, no mate
For Thee; what see for envy in poor me?"
Hoping the while, since evils sometimes mend,
Warts rub away and sores are cured with slime,   280
That some strange day, will either the Quiet catch
And conquer Setebos, or likelier He
Decrepit may doze, doze, as good as die.

———————————

[What, what? A curtain o'er the world at once!
Crickets stop hissing; not a bird—or, yes,   285
There scuds His raven that has told Him all!
It was fool's play this prattling! Ha! The wind
Shoulders the pillared dust, death's house o'the move,[6]
And fast invading fires begin! White blaze—
A tree's head snaps—and there, there, there, there, there,   290
His thunder follows! Fool to gibe at Him!
Lo! 'Lieth flat and loveth Setebos!
'Maketh his teeth meet through his upper lip,
Will let those quails fly, will not eat this month
One little mess of whelks,[7] so he may 'scape!]   295

ca. 1860   1864

Prospice[1]

Fear death?—to feel the fog in my throat,
     The mist in my face,
When the snows begin, and the blasts denote
     I am nearing the place,
The power of the night, the press of the storm,   5
     The post of the foe;
Where he stands, the Arch Fear in a visible form,
     Yet the strong man must go:
For the journey is done and the summit attained,
     And the barriers fall,   10
Though a battle's to fight ere the guerdon be gained,
     The reward of it all.

———————————

6. The whirlwind stirs up a column of dust that   7. Shellfish.
Caliban associates with a house of death.   1. The title means "Look forward."

I was ever a fighter, so—one fight more,
    The best and the last!
I would hate that death bandaged my eyes, and forbore,   15
    And bade me creep past.
No! let me taste the whole of it, fare like my peers
    The heroes of old,
Bear the brunt, in a minute pay glad life's arrears
    Of pain, darkness, and cold.   20
For sudden the worst turns the best to the brave,
    The black minute's at end,
And the elements' rage, the fiend-voices that rave,
    Shall dwindle, shall blend,
Shall change, shall become first a peace out of pain,   25
    Then a light, then thy breast,
O thou soul of my soul![2] I shall clasp thee again,
    And with God be the rest!

ca. 1861   1864

Abt Vogler[1]

(After he has Been Extemporizing Upon the Musical Instrument of His Invention)

1

Would that the structure brave, the manifold music I build,
    Bidding my organ obey, calling its keys to their work,
Claiming each slave of the sound, at a touch, as when Solomon willed
    Armies of angels that soar, legions of demons that lurk,
Man, brute, reptile, fly—alien of end and of aim,   5
    Adverse, each from the other heaven-high, hell-deep removed—
Should rush into sight at once as he named the ineffable Name,[2]
    And pile him a palace straight, to pleasure the princess[3] he loved!

2

Would it might tarry like his, the beautiful building of mine,
    This which my keys in a crowd pressed and importuned to raise!   10
Ah, one and all, how they helped, would dispart now and now combine,
    Zealous to hasten the work, heighten their master his praise!

2. Browning's wife.
1. Georg Joseph Vogler (1749–1814), a German priest and musician, held the honorary title of *Abbé* or *Abt*. As a composer, teacher, and designer of musical instruments he was well known in his own day, but he was most famous as an extemporizer at the organ. Browning's soliloquy represents Vogler at the organ joyfully improvising a piece of music and then reflecting upon the ephemeral existence of such a unique work of art and of its possible relation to God's purposes in heaven and on earth.

A characteristic feature of *Abt Vogler* is the use of exceptionally long sentences, densely packed with details, which may evoke for us the effects of rolling organ music. The resulting movement is markedly different from the brisk staccato rhythms of *A Toccata of Galuppi's*.

The "musical instrument of his invention" is a compact organ called the Orchestrion.
2. According to Jewish legend, King Solomon (because he possessed a seal inscribed with the "ineffable Name" of God) had the power of compelling the demons of earth and air to perform his bidding.
3. Pharoah's daughter (1 Kings 7.8).

And one would bury his brow with a blind plunge down to hell,
    Burrow awhile and build, broad on the roots of things,
Then up again swim into sight, having based me my palace well,   15
    Founded it, fearless of flame, flat on the nether springs.

3

And another would mount and march, like the excellent minion he was,
    Aye, another and yet another, one crowd but with many a crest,
Raising my rampired walls of gold as transparent as glass,
    Eager to do and die, yield each his place to the rest: 20
For higher still and higher (as a runner tips with fire,
    When a great illumination surprises a festal night—
Outlining round and round Rome's dome from space to spire)[4]
    Up, the pinnacled glory reached, and the pride of my soul was in
        sight.

4

In sight? Not half! for it seemed, it was certain, to match man's birth, 25
    Nature in turn conceived, obeying an impulse as I;
And the emulous heaven yearned down, made effort to reach the earth,
    As the earth had done her best, in my passion, to scale the sky:
Novel splendors burst forth, grew familiar and dwelt with mine,
    Not a point nor peak but found and fixed its wandering star;   30
Meteor-moons, balls of blaze: and they did not pale nor pine,
    For earth had attained to heaven, there was no more near nor far.

5

Nay more; for there wanted not who walked in the glare and glow,
    Presences plain in the place; or, fresh from the Protoplast,[5]
Furnished for ages to come, when a kindlier wind should blow,   35
    Lured now to begin and live, in a house to their liking at last;
Or else the wonderful Dead who have passed through the body and
    gone,
    But were back once more to breathe in an old world worth their
        new:
What never had been, was now; what was, as it shall be anon;   39
    And what is—shall I say, matched both? for I was made perfect too.

6

All through my keys that gave their sounds to a wish of my soul,
    All through my soul that praised as its wish flowed visibly forth,
All through music and me! For think, had I painted the whole,
    Why, there it had stood, to see, nor the process so wonderworth:
Had I written the same, made verse—still, effect proceeds from cause,45
    Ye know why the forms are fair, ye hear how the tale is told;
It is all triumphant art, but art in obedience to laws,
    Painter and poet are proud in the artist-list enrolled—

---

4. On festival nights the dome of St. Peter's in Rome is illuminated by a series of lights ignited by a torchbearer.

5. The original or archetypal form of a species.

The "presences" from this source are beings of the future, not yet existing, who are "lured" into life by the music.

7

But here is the finger of God, a flash of the will that can,
　　Existent behind all laws, that made them and, lo, they are!　　50
And I know not if, save in this, such gift be allowed to man,
　　That out of three sounds he frame, not a fourth sound, but a star.[6]
Consider it well: each tone of our scale in itself is naught;
　　It is everywhere in the world—loud, soft, and all is said:
Give it to me to use! I mix it with two in my thought:　　55
　　And, there! Ye have heard and seen: consider and bow the head!

8

Well, it is gone at last, the palace of music I reared;
　　Gone! and the good tears start, the praises that come too slow;
For one is assured at first, one scarce can say that he feared,
　　That he even gave it a thought, the gone thing was to go.　　60
Never to be again! But many more of the kind
　　As good, nay, better perchance: is this your comfort to me?
To me, who must be saved because I cling with my mind
　　To the same, same self, same love, same God: aye, what was, shall
　　　be.

9

Therefore to whom turn I but to thee, the ineffable Name?　　65
　　Builder and maker, thou, of houses not made with hands![7]
What, have fear of change from thee who art ever the same?
　　Doubt that thy power can fill the heart that thy power expands?
There shall never be one lost good! What was, shall live as before;
　　The evil is null, is naught, is silence implying sound;　　70
What was good shall be good, with, for evil, so much good more;
　　On the earth the broken arcs; in the heaven, a perfect round.

10

All we have willed or hoped or dreamed of good shall exist;
　　Not its semblance, but itself; no beauty, nor good, nor power
Whose voice has gone forth, but each survives for the melodist　　75
　　When eternity affirms the conception of an hour.
The high that proved too high, the heroic for earth too hard,
　　The passion that left the ground to lose itself in the sky,
Are music sent up to God by the lover and the bard;
　　Enough that he heard it once: we shall hear it by-and-by.　　80

11

And what is our failure here but a triumph's evidence
　　For the fullness of the days? Have we withered or agonized?
Why else was the pause prolonged but that singing might issue thence?
　　Why rushed the discords in but that harmony should be prized?
Sorrow is hard to bear, and doubt is slow to clear,　　85
　　Each sufferer says his say, his scheme of the weal and woe:

6. I.e., the musician's combining of 3 notes into a new harmonic unit is a creative act as miraculous as the creation of a star.

7. See 2 Corinthians 5.1, in which St. Paul speaks of "a building of God, an house not made with hands, eternal in the heavens."

But God has a few of us whom he whispers in the ear;
    The rest may reason and welcome: 'tis we musicians know.

12

Well, it is earth with me; silence resumes her reign:
    I will be patient and proud, and soberly acquiesce.   90
Give me the keys. I feel for the common chord again,
    Sliding by semitones, till I sink to the minor—yes,
And I blunt it into a ninth, and I stand on alien ground,
    Surveying awhile the heights I rolled from into the deep;
Which, hark, I have dared and done, for my resting place is found,   95
    The C Major of this life:[8] so, now I will try to sleep.

1864

Rabbi Ben Ezra[1]

1

    Grow old along with me!
    The best is yet to be,
The last of life, for which the first was made:
    Our times are in His hand
    Who saith, "A whole I planned,   5
Youth shows but half; trust God: see all nor be afraid!"

2

    Not that, amassing flowers,
    Youth sighed, "Which rose make ours,
Which lily leave and then as best recall?"
    Not that, admiring stars,   10
    It yearned, "Nor Jove, nor Mars;
Mine be some figured flame which blends, transcends them all!"

3

    Not for such hopes and fears
    Annulling youth's brief years,
Do I remonstrate: folly wide the mark!   15
    Rather I prize the doubt
    Low kinds exist without,
Finished and finite clods, untroubled by a spark.

4

    Poor vaunt of life indeed,
    Were man but formed to feed   20
On joy, to solely seek and find and feast:
    Such feasting ended, then
    As sure an end to men;
Irks care the crop-full bird? Frets doubt the maw-crammed beast?[2]

8. C major: a key without sharps or flats, representing the plane of ordinary life. "Ninth": a discord which requires resolution.
1. The speaker, Abraham Ibn Ezra (ca. 1092–1167), was an eminent biblical scholar of Spain, but Browning makes little attempt to present him as a distinct individual or to relate him to the age in which he lived. Unlike the more characteristic monologues, *Rabbi Ben Ezra* is not dramatic but declamatory.
2. I.e., does care disturb a bird whose gullet ("crop") is full of food? does doubt trouble an animal whose stomach ("maw") is full?

5

Rejoice we are allied   25
    To That which doth provide
And not partake, effect and not receive!
    A spark disturbs our clod;
    Nearer we hold of God
Who gives, than of His tribes that take, I must believe.   30

6

Then, welcome each rebuff
    That turns earth's smoothness rough,
Each sting that bids nor sit nor stand but go!
    Be our joys three parts pain!
    Strive, and hold cheap the strain;   35
Learn, nor account the pang; dare, never grudge the throe![3]

7

For thence—a paradox
    Which comforts while it mocks—
Shall life succeed in that it seems to fail:
    What I aspired to be,   40
    And was not, comforts me:
A brute I might have been, but would not sink i' the scale.

8

What is he but a brute
    Whose flesh has soul to suit,
Whose spirit works lest arms and legs want play?   45
    To man, propose this test—
    Thy body at its best,
How far can that project thy soul on its lone way?

9

Yet gifts should prove their use:
    I own the Past profuse   50
Of power each side, perfection every turn:
    Eyes, ears took in their dole,
    Brain treasured up the whole;
Should not the heart beat once, "How good to live and learn"?

10

Not once beat, "Praise be Thine!   55
    I see the whole design,
I, who saw power, see now love perfect too:
    Perfect I call Thy plan:
    Thanks that I was a man!
Maker, remake, complete—I trust what Thou shalt do!"   60

11

For pleasant is this flesh;
    Our soul, in its rose-mesh[4]
Pulled ever to the earth, still yearns for rest;
    Would we some prize might hold

3. Anguish.   4. The body, which holds the soul in its net.

To match those manifold   65
Possessions of the brute—gain most, as we did best!

12

Let us not always say,
"Spite of this flesh today
I strove, made head, gained ground upon the whole!"
As the bird wings and sings,   70
Let us cry, "All good things
Are ours, nor soul helps flesh more, now, than flesh helps soul!"

13

Therefore I summon age
To grant youth's heritage,
Life's struggle having so far reached its term: 75
Thence shall I pass, approved
A man, for aye removed
From the developed brute; a god though in the germ.

14

And I shall thereupon
Take rest, ere I be gone
Once more on my adventure brave and new;[5]   80
Fearless and unperplexed,
When I wage battle next,
What weapons to select, what armor to indue.[6]

15

Youth ended, I shall try
My gain or loss thereby;
Leave the fire ashes,[7] what survives is gold:
And I shall weigh the same,
Give life its praise or blame:
Young, all lay in dispute; I shall know, being old.   90

16

For note, when evening shuts,
A certain moment cuts
The deed off, calls the glory from the gray:
A whisper from the west
Shoots—"Add this to the rest,   95
Take it and try its worth: here dies another day."

17

So, still within this life,
Though lifted o'er its strife,
Let me discern, compare, pronounce at last,
"This rage was right i' the main,
That acquiescence vain: 100
The Future I may face now I have proved the Past."

18

For more is not reserved
To man, with soul just nerved

---

5. In the next life.   7. If the fire leaves ashes.
6. Put on.

To act tomorrow what he learns today: 105
       Here, work enough to watch
       The Master work, and catch
Hints of the proper craft, tricks of the tool's true play.

19

       As it was better, youth
       Should strive, through acts uncouth,   110
Toward making, than repose on aught found made:
       So, better, age, exempt
       From strife, should know, than tempt[8]
Further. Thou waitedst age: wait death nor be afraid!

20

       Enough now, if the Right   115
       And Good and Infinite
Be named here, as thou callest thy hand thine own,
       With knowledge absolute,
       Subject to no dispute
From fools that crowded youth, nor let thee feel alone.[9]   120

21

       Be there, for once and all,
       Severed great minds from small,
Announced to each his station in the Past!
       Was I, the world arraigned,[1]
       Were they, my soul disdained,   125
Right? Let age speak the truth and give us peace at last!

22

       Now, who shall arbitrate?
       Ten men love what I hate,
Shun what I follow, slight what I receive;
       Ten, who in ears and eyes   130
       Match me: we all surmise,
They this thing, and I that: whom shall my soul believe?

23

       Not on the vulgar mass
       Called "work," must sentence pass,
Things done, that took the eye and had the price;   135
       O'er which, from level stand,
       The low world laid its hand,
Found straightway to its mind, could value in a trice:

24

       But all, the world's coarse thumb
       And finger failed to plumb,   140
So passed in making up the main account;
       All instincts immature,

---

8. Attempt.

9. Stanzas 20 and 21 affirm that in age we can more readily think independently than in youth. Maturity enables us to ignore the pressure of hav-ing to conform to the thinking of the crowd of small-minded people.

1. Was I, whom the world arraigned.

All purposes unsure,
That weighed not as his work, yet swelled the man's amount:

25

    Thoughts hardly to be packed   145
    Into a narrow act,
Fancies that broke through language and escaped;
    All I could never be,
    All, men ignored in me,
This, I was worth to God, whose wheel[2] the pitcher shaped.   150

26

    Aye, note that Potter's wheel,
    That metaphor! and feel
Why time spins fast, why passive lies our clay—
    Thou, to whom fools propound,[3]
    When the wine makes its round,   155
"Since life fleets, all is change; the Past gone, seize today!"

27

    Fool! All that is, at all,
    Lasts ever, past recall;
Earth changes, but thy soul and God stand sure:
    What entered into thee,   160
    That was, is, and shall be:
Time's wheel runs back or stops: Potter and clay endure.

28

    He fixed thee 'mid this dance
    Of plastic circumstance,
This Present, thou, forsooth, wouldst fain arrest:[4]   165
    Machinery just meant
    To give thy soul its bent,
Try thee and turn thee forth, sufficiently impressed.

29

    What though the earlier grooves
    Which ran the laughing loves   170
Around thy base,[5] no longer pause and press?
    What though, about thy rim,
    Skull-things in order grim
Grow out, in graver mood, obey the sterner stress?

30

    Look not thou down but up!
    To uses of a cup,   175
The festal board, lamp's flash, and trumpet's peal,
    The new wine's foaming flow,
    The Master's lips a-glow!
Thou, heaven's consummate cup, what need'st thou with earth's
      wheel?   180

---

2. The potting-wheel on which the speaker's highest qualities of soul were shaped into an enduring "pitcher" by God. See Isaiah 64.8.
3. Perhaps addressed to Omar Khayyám, whose poem, *The Rubáiyát*, urged men to eat, drink, and be merry. Edward FitzGerald's translation of Omar's poem had appeared in 1859.
4. I.e., you would be glad to stop ("arrest") time at this present point of your life.
5. Base of the clay pitcher.

31

But I need, now as then,
    Thee, God, who moldest men;
And since, not even while the whirl was worst,
        Did I—to the wheel of life
        With shapes and colors rife,   185
Bound dizzily—mistake my end, to slake Thy thirst:

32

        So, take and use Thy work:
        Amend what flaws may lurk,
What strain o' the stuff, what warpings past the aim!
        My times be in Thy hand!   190
        Perfect the cup as planned!
Let age approve of youth, and death complete the same!

ca. 1862   1864

Epilogue to *Asolando*[1]

At the midnight in the silence of the sleep-time,
    When you[2] set your fancies free,
Will they pass to where—by death, fools think, imprisoned—
Low he lies who once so loved you, whom you loved so,
        —Pity me?   5
Oh to love so, be so loved, yet so mistaken!
    What had I on earth to do
With the slothful, with the mawkish, the unmanly?
Like the aimless, helpless, hopeless, did I drivel
        —Being—who?   10

One who never turned his back but marched breast forward,
    Never doubted clouds would break,
Never dreamed, though right were worsted, wrong would triumph,
Held we fall to rise, are baffled to fight better,
        Sleep to wake.   15

No, at noonday in the bustle of man's work-time
    Greet the unseen[3] with a cheer!
Bid him forward, breast and back as either should be,
"Strive and thrive!" cry, "Speed—fight on, fare ever
        There as here!"   20

1889   1890

1. The final poem in *Asolando*, a volume published on the day of Browning's death. Browning
is said to have recognized that because the third
stanza sounded "like bragging" he ought to consider canceling it. "But it's the simple truth," he
added, "and as it's true, it shall stand."
2. Any loved person who survives the speaker.
3. The speaker, after he is dead.

MATTHEW ARNOLD
1822–1888

1853: *Poems* (with Preface) published.
1857: Elected Professor of Poetry at Oxford.
1869: *Culture and Anarchy* published.
1888: *Essays in Criticism: Second Series.*

How is a full and enjoyable life to be lived in a modern industrial society? This was the recurrent topic in the poetry and prose of Matthew Arnold. In his poetry the question itself is raised; in his prose some answers are attempted. Arnold's mode of posing such questions may not always satisfy us, and his answers may sometimes be simply wrong. What is less excusable, as he himself said of Ruskin, is that he could be not only wrong but dogmatic when he was wrong. On the whole, however, his writings have fared well with posterity. "The misapprehensiveness of his age is exactly what a poet is sent to remedy," wrote Browning. Oddly enough it is to Arnold's work rather than to Browning's that the statement seems more appropriate. And its applicability to Arnold has persisted from Victorian times to ours, in part because the "misapprehensiveness" has also persisted.

Matthew Arnold was born in Laleham, a village in the valley of the Thames. That his childhood was spent in the vicinity of a river seems appropriate, for clear-flowing streams were later to appear in his poems as symbols of serenity. At six, Arnold was moved to Rugby School, where his father, Dr. Thomas Arnold, had become headmaster. As a clergyman Dr. Arnold was a leader of the liberal or Broad Church and hence one of the principal opponents of John Henry Newman. As a headmaster he became famous as an educational reformer, a teacher who instilled into his pupils an earnest preoccupation with moral and social issues and also an awareness of the connection between liberal studies and modern life. At Rugby his eldest son, Matthew, was directly exposed to the powerful force of the father's mind and character. The son's attitude toward this force was a mixture of attraction and repulsion. That he was permanently influenced by his father is evident in his poems and in his writings on religion and politics, but like many sons of clergymen, he made a determined effort in his youth to be different. At Oxford he behaved like a character from one of Evelyn Waugh's early novels. Elegantly and colorfully dressed, alternately languid or merry in manner, he attracted attention as a dandy whose irreverent jokes irritated his more solemn undergraduate friends and acquaintances. "His manner displeases, from its seeming foppery," wrote Charlotte Brontë after talking with the young man. "The shade of Dr. Arnold," she added, "seemed to me to frown on his young representative." With Rugby School's standards of earnestness, thus, the son of Dr. Arnold appeared to have no connection. Even his studies did not seem to occupy him seriously. By a session of cramming, he managed to earn second-class honors in his final examinations, a near disaster that was redeemed by his election to a fellowship at Oriel College.

Arnold's biographers usually dismiss his youthful frivolity of spirit as a temporary pose or mask, but it was more. It remained to color his prose style, brightening his most serious criticism with geniality and wit. For most readers the jauntiness of his prose is a virtue, although for others it is offensive. Anyone suspicious of urbanity and irony would applaud Whitman's sour comment that Arnold is "one of the dudes of literature." A more appropriate estimate of his manner is provided by Arnold's own description of Sainte-Beuve as a critic: "a critic of measure, not exuberant; of the center, not provincial . . . with gay and amiable temper, his manner as good as his matter—the '*critique souriant*' [smiling critic]."

Unlike Tennyson or Carlyle, Arnold had to confine his writing and reading to his spare time. In 1847 he took the post of private secretary to Lord Lansdowne, and in 1851, the year of his marriage, he became an inspector of schools, a position which he held for thirty-five years. Although his work as an inspector may have reduced his output as a writer, it had several advantages. His extensive traveling in England took him to the homes of the more ardently Protestant middle classes, and when he criticized the dullness of middle-class life (as he often did), Arnold knew his subject intimately. His position also led to travel on the Continent to study the schools of Europe. As a critic of English education he was thus able to make helpful comparisons and to draw on a stock of fresh ideas in the same way as in his literary criticism he used his knowledge of French, German, Italian, and classical literatures to measure the achievements of English writers. Despite the monotony of much of his work as an inspector, Arnold became convinced of its importance. It was work that contributed to what he regarded as the most important need of his century: the development of a satisfactory system of education for the middle classes.

In 1849 Arnold published *The Strayed Reveler*, the first of his volumes of poetry. Eight years later, as a tribute to his poetic achievement, he was elected to the professorship of poetry at Oxford, a part-time position which he held for ten years. Later, like Dickens and Thackeray before him, Arnold toured America in order to make money by lecturing. For his two visits (1883 and 1886) there was the further inducement of seeing his daughter Lucy, who had married an American. Two years after his second visit to the United States, Arnold died of a sudden heart attack.

Arnold's career as a writer can be divided roughly into four periods. In the 1850s appeared most of his poems; in the 1860s, his literary criticism and social criticism; in the 1870s, his religious and educational writings; and in the 1880s, his second set of essays in literary criticism.

About his career as a poet, two questions are repeatedly asked. The first is whether his poetry is as effective or better than his prose; the second is why he virtually stopped writing poetry after 1860. The first has, of course, been variously answered. Many would endorse Tennyson's request in a letter: "Tell Mat not to write any more of those prose things like *Literature and Dogma*, but to give us something like his *Thyrsis, Scholar Gypsy,* or *Forsaken Merman.*" At the opposite extreme is a recent critic, J. D. Jump, who has a high regard for Arnold's prose but considers only one of the poems to have merit: *Dover Beach.* Such readers complain, and with good cause, of Arnold's bad habits as a poet: for example, his excessive reliance upon italics instead of upon meter as a method of emphasizing the meaning of a line. Or they cite the prosy flatness with which he opens his fine sonnet *To a Friend:* "Who prop, thou ask'st, in these bad days, my mind?" Contrariwise, when Arnold leaves the flat plane of versified reflections and attempts to scale the heights of what he called "the grand style," there is a different kind of uncertainty which becomes evident, as in *Sohrab and Rustum*, in the over-elaborated similes. Yet the success of such lovely poems as *Thyrsis* is more than enough to overcome the indictments of the critics. Often, as in *Thyrsis*, he is at his best as a poet of nature. Settings of seashore or river or mountaintop provide something more than picturesque backdrops for these poems; they function to draw the meaning together. A concern for rendering outdoor nature may seem a curious accomplishment for so sophisticated a writer, but as his contemporaries noted, Arnold is in this respect, as in several others, similar to Thomas Gray.

Arnold's own verdict on the qualities of his poetry is a reasonable one. In a letter to his mother, in 1869, he writes: "My poems represent, on the whole, the main movement of mind of the last quarter of a century, and thus they will probably have their day as people become conscious to themselves of what that movement of mind is, and interested in the literary productions which reflect it. It might be fairly urged that I have less poetical sentiment than Tennyson, and less intellectual vigor and abundance than Browning; yet, because I have perhaps more of a fusion of the two than either of them, and have more regularly applied that fusion to the main line of modern development, I am likely enough to have my turn, as they have had theirs."

The emphasis in the letter upon "movement of mind" suggests that Arnold's poetry and prose should be studied together. Such an approach can be fruitful provided that it does not obscure the important difference between Arnold the poet and Arnold the critic. T. S. Eliot once said of his own writings that "in one's prose reflections one may be legitimately occupied with ideals, whereas in the writing of verse, one can deal only with actuality." Arnold's writings provide a nice verification of Eliot's seeming paradox. As a poet he usually records his own experiences, his own feelings of loneliness and isolation as a lover, his longing for a serenity that he cannot find, his melancholy sense of the passing of youth (more than for many men, Arnold's thirtieth birthday was an awesome landmark after which he felt, he said, "three parts iced over"). Above all he records his despair in a universe in which man's role seemed as incongruous as it was later to seem to Thomas Hardy. In a memorable passage of his *Stanzas from the Grande Chartreuse* he describes himself as "wandering between two worlds, one dead, / The other powerless to be born." And addressing the representatives of a faith which seems to him dead, he cries: "Take me, cowled forms, and fence me round, / Till I possess my soul again."

As a poet, then, like T. S. Eliot and W. H. Auden, Arnold provides a record of a sick individual in a sick society. This was "actuality" as he experienced it. As a prose-writer, a formulator of "ideals," he seeks a different role. It is the role of what Auden calls the "healer" of a sick society, or as he himself called Goethe, the "Physician of the iron age." And in this difference we have a clue to the question previously raised: why did Arnold virtually abandon the writing of poetry and shift into criticism? Among other reasons, he abandoned it because he was dissatisfied with the kind of poetry he himself was writing.

In one of his excellent letters to his friend Arthur Hugh Clough in the 1850s (letters which provide the best insight we have into Arnold's mind and tastes) this note of dissatisfaction is struck: "I am glad you like the *Gypsy Scholar*—but what does it *do* for you? Homer *animates*—Shakespeare *ani-*

mates—in its poor way I think *Sohrab and Rustum animates*—the *Gypsy Scholar* at best awakens a pleasing melancholy. But this is not what we want." It is evident that early in his career Arnold had evolved a theory of what poetry should do for its readers, a theory based, in part, on his impression of what classical poetry had achieved. To help make life bearable, poetry, in Arnold's view, must bring joy. As he says in the preface to his *Poems* in 1853, it must "inspirit and rejoice the reader"; it must "convey a charm, and infuse delight." Such a demand does not exclude tragic poetry but does exclude works "in which suffering finds no vent in action; in which a continual state of mental distress is prolonged." Of Charlotte Brontë's novel *Villette* he says witheringly: "The writer's mind contains nothing but hunger, rebellion, and rage. . . . No fine writing can hide this thoroughly, and it will be fatal to her in the long run." Judged by such a standard, most nineteenth-century poems, including *Empedocles on Etna* and others by Arnold, were unsatisfactory. And when Arnold tried himself to write poems which would meet his own requirements—*Sohrab and Rustum* or *Balder Dead*—he was not at his best. By the late 1850s he thus found himself at a dead end. By turning aside to literary criticism he was able partially to escape the dilemma. In his prose his melancholy and "morbid" personality was subordinated to the resolutely cheerful and purposeful character he had created for himself by an effort of will.

Arnold's two volumes of *Essays in Criticism* (1865 and 1888) repeatedly show how authors as different as Marcus Aurelius, Tolstoy, Homer, and Wordsworth provide the virtues he sought in his reading. Among these virtues was plainness of style. Although he could on occasion recommend the richness of language of such poets as Keats or Tennyson—their "natural magic" as he himself called it—Arnold's usual preference was for literature that was unadorned. And beyond stylistic excellences the principal virtue he admired as a critic was what he called the quality of "high seriousness." Given a world in which formal religion appeared to be of subordinate importance, it became increasingly important to Arnold that the poet must be a serious thinker who could offer guidance for his readers. Arnold's attitude towards religion helps to account for his finally asking perhaps too much from literature. Excessive expectations underlie his most glaring blunder as a critic: his solemnly inadequate discussion of Chaucer's lack of high seriousness in *The Study of Poetry*.

In *The Function of Criticism* it is apparent that Arnold regarded good literary criticism, as he regarded literature itself, as a potent force in producing a civilized society. From a close study of this basic essay one could forecast the third stage of his career: his excursion into the criticism of society which was to culminate in *Culture and Anarchy* (1869) and *Friendship's Garland* (1871).

Arnold's starting point as a critic of society is different from that of Carlyle and John Ruskin. The older prophets attacked the Victorian middle classes on the grounds of their materialism, their selfish indifference to the sufferings of the poor—their immorality, in effect. Arnold argued instead that the "Philistines," as he called them, were not so much wicked as ignorant, narrow-minded, and suffering from the dullness of their private lives. This novel analysis was reinforced by Arnold's conviction that the world of the future, both in England and America, would be a middle-class world, a world dominated therefore by a class inadequately equipped for leadership and inadequately equipped to enjoy civilized living.

To establish this point, Arnold employed cajolery, satire, and even quotations from the newspapers with considerable effect. He also employed catchwords (such as "sweetness and light") which have remained useful slogans even though they are an obstacle to understanding the complexities of his position. His view of civilization, for example, was pared down to a four-point formula of the four "powers": conduct, intellect and knowledge, beauty, social life and manners. The formula was simple and workable. Applying it to French or American civilizations, he had a scale by which to show up the virtues of different countries as well as their inadequacies. Applying the formula to his own country, Arnold usually awarded the Victorian middle classes an "A" in the first category (of conduct) but a failing grade in the other three categories.

Arnold's relentless exposure of middle-class narrow-mindedness eventually led him into the arena of religious controversy. As a critic of religious institutions he was arguing, in effect, that just as the middle classes did not know how to lead full lives, so also did they not know how to read the Bible intelligently or attend church intelligently. Of the Christian religion he remarked that there are two things "that surely must be clear to anybody with eyes in his head. One is, that men cannot do without it; the other that they cannot do with it as it is." His three full-length studies of the Bible, including *Literature and Dogma* (1873), are best considered in this way as a postscript to his social criticism. The Bible, to Arnold, was a great work of literature like the *Odyssey*, and the Church of England was a great national institution like Parliament. Both Bible and church must be preserved not because historical Christianity was credible but because both, when properly understood, were agents of what he called "culture"—they contributed to making mankind more civilized.

The term *culture* is perhaps Arnold's most familiar catchword, although what he meant by it has sometimes been misunderstood. For him the term connotes the qualities of an open-minded intelligence (as described in *The Function of Criticism*)—a refusal to take things on authority. But the word also connotes a full awareness of man's past and a capacity to enjoy the best works of art, literature, history, and philosophy that have come down to us from that past. As a way of viewing life in all its aspects, including the social, political, and religious, culture represents for Arnold the most effective way of curing the ills of a sick society. It is his principal prescription.

To attempt to define culture brings one to a final aspect of Arnold's career as a critic: his writings on education, in which he sought to make cultural values, as he said, "prevail." Most obviously these writings comprise his reply to Huxley in his admirably reasoned essay, *Literature and Science*, as well as his volumes of official reports written as an inspector of schools. Less obviously they comprise all of his prose. At the core of these writings is his belief that good education is the crucial need for modern man. Arnold was essentially a great teacher raised to the nth degree. He has the faults of a teacher: a tendency to repeat himself, to lean too hard on formulated phrases, and he displays something of the lectern manner at times. He also has the great teacher's virtues, in particular the virtue of skillfully conveying to us the conviction on which all his arguments are based. This conviction is that the humanist tradition of which he is the expositor can enable the individual man or woman to live life more fully as well as to change the course of society. For these values Arnold fought. He boxed with the gloves on—kid gloves, his opponents used to say—and he provided a lively exhibition of footwork that is a pleasure in itself for us to witness. Yet the gracefulness of the display should not obscure the fact that he is landing hard blows squarely on what Carlyle called the vast blockheadism.

Although his lifelong attacks against the inadequacies of puritanism make Arnold one of the most anti-Victorian figures of the Victorian age, there is an assumption behind his attacks that is itself characteristically Victorian. This assumption is that the puritan middle classes *can* be changed, that they are, as we would more clumsily say, educable. In 1852, writing to Clough on the subject of equality (a political objective in which he believed by conviction if not by instinct), he observed: "I am more and more convinced that the world tends to become more comfortable for the mass, and more uncomfortable for those of any natural gift or distinction—and it is as well perhaps that it should be so—for hitherto the gifted have astonished and delighted the world, but not trained or inspired or in any real way changed it." Arnold's gifts as a poet and critic enabled him to do both: to delight the world and also to change it.

To a Friend

Who prop, thou ask'st in these bad days, my mind?—
He much, the old man,[1] who, clearest-souled of men,
Saw The Wide Prospect, and the Asian Fen,
And Tmolus hill, and Smyrna bay, though blind.

Much he, whose friendship I not long since won,   5
That halting slave, who in Nicopolis[2]
Taught Arrian, when Vespasian's brutal son[3]
Cleared Rome of what most shamed him. But be his

My special thanks, whose even-balanced soul,
From first youth tested up to extreme old age,   10
Business could not make dull, nor passion wild;

Who saw life steadily, and saw it whole;
The mellow glory of the Attic stage,
Singer of sweet Colonus,[4] and its child.

1848   1849

---

1. Homer, who was reputed to have been born in Smyrna, a seaport of what is now Turkey. From Smyrna he saw across the sea to Europe ("The Wide Prospect") as well as to the nearby marshes ("Fen") and mountain ranges ("Tmolus hill") of Asia Minor.
2. Epictetus, a lame philosopher who was exiled to Nicopolis where he taught Stoicism to Arrian,
a Greek historian.
3. I.e., the Emperor Domitian (81–96). Because the philosophers had "shamed" him, he had ordered their expulsion from Rome.
4. Sophocles (496–406 B.C.), a native of Colonus, sang of his town in his *Oedipus at Colonus*.

The Forsaken Merman[1]

Come, dear children, let us away;
Down and away below!
Now my brothers call from the bay,
Now the great winds shoreward blow,
Now the salt tides seaward flow;　　　　　　　　　　5
Now the wild white horses play,
Champ and chafe and toss in the spray.
Children dear, let us away!
This way, this way!

Call her once before you go—　　　　　　　　　　10
Call once yet!
In a voice that she will know:
"Margaret! Margaret!"
Children's voices should be dear
(Call once more) to a mother's ear;　　　　　　　　　　15
Children's voices, wild with pain—
Surely she will come again!
Call her once and come away;
This way, this way!
"Mother dear, we cannot stay!　　　　　　　　　　20
The wild white horses foam and fret."
Margaret! Margaret!

Come, dear children, come away down;
Call no more!
One last look at the white-walled town,　　　　　　　　　　25
And the little gray church on the windy shore,
Then come down!
She will not come though you call all day;
Come away, come away!

Children dear, was it yesterday　　　　　　　　　　30
We heard the sweet bells over the bay?
In the caverns where we lay,
Through the surf and through the swell,
The far-off sound of a silver bell?
Sand-strewn caverns, cool and deep,　　　　　　　　　　35
Where the winds are all asleep;
Where the spent lights quiver and gleam,
Where the salt weed sways in the stream,
Where the sea beasts, ranged all round,
Feed in the ooze of their pasture ground;　　　　　　　　　　40

1. For a comparison of Arnold's skillful telling of this story with the Danish version from which he derived it, see C. B. Tinker and H. F. Lowry: *The Poetry of Arnold: A Commentary* (1940), pp. 129–132.

Where the sea snakes coil and twine,
Dry their mail and bask in the brine;
Where great whales come sailing by,
Sail and sail, with unshut eye,
Round the world for ever and aye?   45
When did music come this way?
Children dear, was it yesterday?

Children dear, was it yesterday
(Call yet once) that she went away?
Once she sate with you and me,   50
On a red gold throne in the heart of the sea,
And the youngest sate on her knee.
She combed its bright hair, and she tended it well,
When down swung the sound of a far-off bell.
She sighed, she looked up through the clear green sea;   55
She said: "I must go, for my kinsfolk pray
In the little gray church on the shore today.
'Twill be Easter time in the world—ah me!
And I lose my poor soul, Merman! here with thee."
I said: "Go up, dear heart, through the waves;   60
Say thy prayer, and come back to the kind sea-caves!"
She smiled, she went up through the surf in the bay.
Children dear, was it yesterday?

     Children dear, were we long alone?
"The sea grows stormy, the little ones moan;   65
Long prayers," I said, "in the world they say;
Come!" I said; and we rose through the surf in the bay.
We went up the beach, by the sandy down
Where the sea-stocks bloom, to the white-walled town;
Through the narrow paved streets, where all was still,   70
To the little gray church on the windy hill.
From the church came a murmur of folk at their prayers,
But we stood without in the cold blowing airs.
We climbed on the graves, on the stones worn with rains,
And we gazed up the aisle through the small leaded panes. 75
She sate by the pillar; we saw her clear:
"Margaret, hist! come quick, we are here!
Dear heart," I said, "we are long alone;
The sea grows stormy, the little ones moan."
But, ah, she gave me never a look,   80
For her eyes were sealed to the holy book!
Loud prays the priest; shut stands the door.
Come away, children, call no more!
Come away, come down, call no more!

     Down, down, down!   85
Down to the depths of the sea!

She sits at her wheel in the humming town,
Singing most joyfully.
Hark what she sings: "O joy, O joy,
For the humming street, and the child with its toy!   90
For the priest, and the bell, and the holy well;
For the wheel where I spun,
And the blessed light of the sun!"
And so she sings her fill,
Singing most joyfully,   95
Till the spindle drops from her hand,
And the whizzing wheel stands still.
She steals to the window, and looks at the sand,
And over the sand at the sea;
And her eyes are set in a stare;   100
And anon there breaks a sigh,
And anon there drops a tear,
From a sorrow-clouded eye,
And a heart sorrow-laden,
A long, long sigh;   105
For the cold strange eyes of a little Mermaiden
And the gleam of her golden hair.

Come away, away children;
Come children, come down!
The hoarse wind blows coldly;   110
Lights shine in the town.
She will start from her slumber
When gusts shake the door;
She will hear the winds howling,
Will hear the waves roar.   115
We shall see, while above us
The waves roar and whirl,
A ceiling of amber,
A pavement of pearl.
Singing: "Here came a mortal,   120
But faithless was she!
And alone dwell forever
The kings of the sea."

But, children, at midnight,
When soft the winds blow,   125
When clear falls the moonlight,
When spring tides are low;
When sweet airs come seaward
From heaths starred with broom,
And high rocks throw mildly   130
On the blanched sands a gloom;
Up the still, glistening beaches,
Up the creek we will hie,

Over banks of bright seaweed
The ebb-tide leaves dry.   135
We will gaze, from the sand-hills,
At the white, sleeping town;
At the church on the hillside—
And then come back down.
Singing: "There dwells a loved one,   140
But cruel is she!
She left lonely forever
The kings of the sea."

1849

Isolation. To Marguerite[1]

We were apart; yet, day by day,
I bade my heart more constant be.
I bade it keep the world away,
And grow a home for only thee;
Nor feared but thy love likewise grew,   5
Like mine, each day, more tried, more true.

The fault was grave! I might have known,
What far too soon, alas! I learned—
The heart can bind itself alone,
And faith may oft be unreturned.   10
Self-swayed our feelings ebb and swell—
Thou lov'st no more—Farewell! Farewell!

Farewell!—and thou, thou lonely heart,[2]
Which never yet without remorse
Even for a moment didst depart   15
From thy remote and spherèd course
To haunt the place where passions reign—
Back to thy solitude again!

Back with the conscious thrill of shame
Which Luna[3] felt, that summer night,   20
Flash through her pure immortal frame,
When she forsook the starry height
To hang over Endymion's sleep
Upon the pine-grown Latmian steep.

1. Addressed to a girl Arnold is reputed to have
met in Switzerland in the 1840s. It has been commonly assumed that she was French or Swiss, but
some recent biographies speculate she might have
been Mary Claude, a girl Arnold knew in England
at this same period, who, although English, had
connections with Germany and had translated

German prose and verse.
2. Presumably the speaker's heart, not Marguerite's.
3. Luna (or Diana), the goddess of chastity and of
the moon, fell in love with Endymion, a handsome shepherd, whom she discovered asleep on
Mt. Latmos.

Yet she, chaste queen, had never proved   25
How vain a thing is mortal love,
Wandering in Heaven, far removed.
But thou hast long had place to prove
This truth—to prove, and make thine own:
"Thou hast been, shalt be, art, alone."   30

Or, if not quite alone, yet they
Which touch thee are unmating things—
Ocean and clouds and night and day;
Lorn autumns and triumphant springs;
And life, and others' joy and pain,   35
And love, if love, of happier men.

Of happier men—for they, at least,
Have *dreamed* two human hearts might blend
In one, and were through faith released
From isolation without end   40
Prolonged; nor knew, although not less
Alone than thou, their loneliness.

1849   1857

To Marguerite—Continued

Yes! in the sea of life enisled,
With echoing straits between us thrown,
Dotting the shoreless watery wild,
We mortal millions live *alone*.
The islands feel the enclasping flow,   5
And then their endless bounds they know.

But when the moon their hollows lights,
And they are swept by balms of spring,
And in their glens, on starry nights,
The nightingales divinely sing;   10
And lovely notes, from shore to shore,
Across the sounds and channels pour—

Oh! then a longing like despair
Is to their farthest caverns sent;
For surely once, they feel, we were   15
Parts of a single continent!
Now round us spreads the watery plain—
Oh might our marges meet again!

Who ordered that their longing's fire
Should be, as soon as kindled, cooled?   20
Who renders vain their deep desire?—

A God, a God their severance ruled!
And bade betwixt their shores to be
The unplumbed, salt, estranging sea.

1849   1852

The Buried Life

Light flows our war of mocking words, and yet,
Behold, with tears mine eyes are wet!
I feel a nameless sadness o'er me roll.
Yes, yes, we know that we can jest,
We know, we know that we can smile!   5
But there's a something in this breast,
To which thy light words bring no rest,
And thy gay smiles no anodyne.
Give me thy hand, and hush awhile,
And turn those limpid eyes on mine,   10
And let me read there, love! thy inmost soul.

Alas! is even love too weak
To unlock the heart, and let it speak?
Are even lovers powerless to reveal
To one another what indeed they feel?   15
I knew the mass of men concealed
Their thoughts, for fear that if revealed
They would by other men be met
With blank indifference, or with blame reproved;
I knew they lived and moved   20
Tricked in disguises, alien to the rest
Of men, and alien to themselves—and yet
The same heart beats in every human breast!

But we, my love!—doth a like spell benumb
Our hearts, our voices?—must we too be dumb?   25

Ah! well for us, if even we,
Even for a moment, can get free
Our heart, and have our lips unchained;
For that which seals them hath been deep-ordained!

Fate, which foresaw   30
How frivolous a baby man would be—
By what distractions he would be possessed,
How he would pour himself in every strife,
And well-nigh change his own identity—
That it might keep from his capricious play   35
His genuine self, and force him to obey

Even in his own despite his being's law,
Bade through the deep recesses of our breast
The unregarded river of our life
Pursue with indiscernible flow its way;   40
And that we should not see
The buried stream, and seem to be
Eddying at large in blind uncertainty,
Though driving on with it eternally.

But often, in the world's most crowded streets,[1]   45
But often, in the din of strife,
There rises an unspeakable desire
After the knowledge of our buried life;
A thirst to spend our fire and restless force
In tracking out our true, original course;   50
A longing to inquire
Into the mystery of this heart which beats
So wild, so deep in us—to know
Whence our lives come and where they go.
And many a man in his own breast then delves,   55
But deep enough, alas! none ever mines.
And we have been on many thousand lines,
And we have shown, on each, spirit and power;
But hardly have we, for one little hour,
Been on our own line, have we been ourselves—   60
Hardly had skill to utter one of all
The nameless feelings that course through our breast,
But they course on forever unexpressed.
And long we try in vain to speak and act
Our hidden self, and what we say and do   65
Is eloquent, is well—but 'tis not true!
And then we will no more be racked
With inward striving, and demand
Of all the thousand nothings of the hour
Their stupefying power;   70
Ah yes, and they benumb us at our call!
Yet still, from time to time, vague and forlorn,
From the soul's subterranean depth upborne
As from an infinitely distant land,
Come airs, and floating echoes, and convey   75
A melancholy into all our day.[2]

Only—but this is rare—
When a beloved hand is laid in ours,

---

1. This passage, like many others in Arnold's
poetry, illustrates the impact on his writings of
Wordsworth. In this instance cf. Wordsworth's
Tintern Abbey, lines 25–27: "But oft, in lonely
rooms, and 'mid the din / Of towns and cities, I
have owed to them, / In hours of weariness, sen-

sations sweet."
2. Cf. Wordsworth's *Ode: Intimations of Immortality*, lines 151–53: "Those shadowy recollections, / Which, be they what they may, / Are yet
the fountain light of all our day."

When, jaded with the rush and glare
Of the interminable hours,   80
Our eyes can in another's eyes read clear,
When our world-deafened ear
Is by the tones of a loved voice caressed—
A bolt is shot back somewhere in our breast,
And a lost pulse of feeling stirs again.   85
The eye sinks inward, and the heart lies plain,
And what we mean, we say, and what we would, we know.
A man becomes aware of his life's flow,
And hears its winding murmur; and he sees
The meadows where it glides, the sun, the breeze.   90

And there arrives a lull in the hot race
Wherein he doth forever chase
That flying and elusive shadow, rest.
An air of coolness plays upon his face,
And an unwonted calm pervades his breast.   95
And then he thinks he knows
The hills where his life rose,
And the sea where it goes.

1852

Memorial Verses[1]

April 1850

Goethe in Weimar sleeps, and Greece,
Long since, saw Byron's struggle cease.
But one such death remained to come;
The last poetic voice is dumb—
We stand today by Wordsworth's tomb.   5

When Byron's eyes were shut in death,
We bowed our head and held our breath.
He taught us little; but our soul
Had *felt* him like the thunder's roll.
With shivering heart the strife we saw   10
Of passion with eternal law;
And yet with reverential awe
We watched the fount of fiery life
Which served for that Titanic strife.

1. This elegy was written shortly after Wordsworth had died in April 1850, at the age of 80.
Arnold had known the poet as a man and deeply
admired his writings—as is evident not only in this
poem but in his late essay, *Wordsworth*. Byron,
who died in Greece in 1824, had affected Arnold
profoundly in his youth, but later that strenuous
"Titanic" poetry seemed to him less satisfactory,
its value limited by its lack of serenity. His final
verdict on Byron can be encountered in his essay
in *Essays in Criticism: Second Series*. Goethe, who
died in 1832, was regarded by Arnold as a great
philosophical poet and the most significant man of
letters of the early 19th century.

When Goethe's death was told, we said: 15
Sunk, then, is Europe's sagest head.
Physician of the iron age,
Goethe has done his pilgrimage.
He took the suffering human race,
He read each wound, each weakness clear;   20
And struck his finger on the place,
And said: *Thou ailest here, and here!*
He looked on Europe's dying hour
Of fitful dream and feverish power;
His eye plunged down the weltering strife,   25
The turmoil of expiring life—
He said: *The end is everywhere,*
Art still has truth, take refuge there!
And he was happy, if to know
Causes of things, and far below   30
His feet to see the lurid flow
Of terror, and insane distress,
And headlong fate, be happiness.

And Wordsworth!—Ah, pale ghosts, rejoice!
For never has such soothing voice   35
Been to your shadowy world conveyed,
Since erst, at morn, some wandering shade
Heard the clear song of Orpheus[2] come
Through Hades, and the mournful gloom.
Wordsworth has gone from us—and ye,   40
Ah, may ye feel his voice as we!
He too upon a wintry clime
Had fallen—on this iron time
Of doubts, disputes, distractions, fears.
He found us when the age had bound   45
Our souls in its benumbing round;
He spoke, and loosed our heart in tears.
He laid us as we lay at birth
On the cool flowery lap of earth,
Smiles broke from us and we had ease;   50
The hills were round us, and the breeze
Went o'er the sunlit fields again;
Our foreheads felt the wind and rain.
Our youth returned; for there was shed
On spirits that had long been dead,   55
Spirits dried up and closely furled,
The freshness of the early world.

Ah! since dark days still bring to light
Man's prudence and man's fiery might,

2. By means of his beautiful music, Orpheus won   of his dead wife, Eurydice.
his way through Hades in his search for the shade

Time may restore us in his course   60
Goethe's sage mind and Byron's force;
But where will Europe's latter hour
Again find Wordsworth's healing power?
Others will teach us how to dare,
And against fear our breast to steel;   65
Others will strengthen us to bear—
But who, ah! who, will make us feel?
The cloud of mortal destiny,
Others will front it fearlessly—
But who, like him, will put it by?   70

Keep fresh the grass upon his grave
O Rotha,[3] with thy living wave!
Sing him thy best! for few or none
Hears thy voice right, now he is gone.

1850   1850

The Scholar Gypsy

The story of a seventeenth-century student who left Oxford and joined a band of gypsies had made a strong impression on Arnold. In the poem he wistfully imagines that the spirit of this scholar is still to be encountered in the Cumner countryside near Oxford, having achieved immortality by a serene pursuit of the secret of human existence. Like Keats's nightingale, the scholar has escaped "the weariness, the fever, and the fret" of modern life.

At the outset, the poet addresses a shepherd who has been helping him in his search for traces of the scholar. The shepherd is addressed as "you." After line 61, with the shift to "thou" and "thy," the person addressed is the scholar himself, and the poet thereafter sometimes uses the pronoun "we" to indicate he is speaking for all mankind of later generations.

About the setting Arnold wrote to his brother Tom on May 15, 1857: "You alone of my brothers are associated with that life at Oxford, the *freest* and most delightful part, perhaps, of my life, when with you and Clough and Walrond I shook off all the bonds and formalities of the place, and enjoyed the spring of life and that unforgotten Oxfordshire and Berkshire country. Do you remember a poem of mine called 'The Scholar Gipsy'? It was meant to fix the remembrance of those delightful wanderings of ours in the Cumner Hills."

The passage from Joseph Glanvill's *Vanity of Dogmatizing* (1661) that inspired the poem was included by Arnold as a note:

There was very lately a lad in the University of Oxford, who was by his poverty forced to leave his studies there; and at last to join himself to a company of vagabond gypsies. Among these extravagant people, by the insinuating subtilty of his carriage, he quickly got so much of their love and esteem as that they discovered to him their mystery. After he had been a pretty while exercised in the trade, there chanced to ride by a

3. A river near Wordsworth's burial place.

couple of scholars, who had formerly been of his acquaintance. They
quickly spied out their old friend among the gypsies; and he gave them
an account of the necessity which drove him to that kind of life, and
told them that the people he went with were not such imposters as they
were taken for, but that they had a traditional kind of learning among
them, and could do wonders by the power of imagination, their fancy
binding that of others: that himself had learned much of their art, and
when he had compassed the whole secret, he intended, he said, to leave
their company, and give the world an account of what he had learned.

The Scholar Gypsy

Go, for they call you, shepherd, from the hill;
  Go, shepherd, and untie the wattled cotes![1]
    No longer leave thy wistful flock unfed,
    Nor let thy bawling fellows rack their throats,
      Nor the cropped herbage shoot another head.   5
        But when the fields are still,
    And the tired men and dogs all gone to rest,
      And only the white sheep are sometimes seen
      Cross and recross the strips of moon-blanched green,
  Come, shepherd, and again begin the quest!   10

Here, where the reaper was at work of late—
  In this high field's dark corner, where he leaves
    His coat, his basket, and his earthen cruse,[2]
    And in the sun all morning binds the sheaves,
      Then here, at noon, comes back his stores to use—   15
        Here will I sit and wait,
    While to my ear from uplands far away
      The bleating of the folded[3] flocks is borne,
      With distant cries of reapers in the corn[4]—
  All the live murmur of a summer's day.   20

Screened is this nook o'er the high, half-reaped field,
  And here till sundown, shepherd! will I be.
    Through the thick corn the scarlet poppies peep,
    And round green roots and yellowing stalks I see
      Pale pink convolvulus in tendrils creep;   25
        And air-swept lindens yield
    Their scent, and rustle down their perfumed showers
      Of bloom on the bent grass[5] where I am laid,
      And bower me from the August sun with shade;
  And the eye travels down to Oxford's towers.   30

1. Sheepfolds woven from sticks.   4. Grain or wheat.
2. Pot or jug for carrying his drink.   5. A stiff kind of grass.
3. Penned up.

And near me on the grass lies Glanvill's book—
 Come, let me read the oft-read tale again!
  The story of the Oxford scholar poor,
 Of pregnant parts[6] and quick inventive brain,
  Who, tired of knocking at preferment's door,   35
   One summer morn forsook
 His friends, and went to learn the gypsy lore,
  And roamed the world with that wild brotherhood,
  And came, as most men deemed, to little good,
 But came to Oxford and his friends no more.   40

But once, years after, in the country lanes,
 Two scholars, whom at college erst he knew,
  Met him, and of his way of life inquired;
 Whereat he answered, that the gypsy crew,
  His mates, had arts to rule as they desired   45
   The workings of men's brains,
 And they can bind them to what thoughts they will.
  "And I," he said, "the secret of their art,
  When fully learned, will to the world impart;
 But it needs heaven-sent moments for this skill."   50

This said, he left them, and returned no more.—
 But rumors hung about the countryside,
  That the lost Scholar long was seen to stray,
 Seen by rare glimpses, pensive and tongue-tied,
  In hat of antique shape, and cloak of grey,   55
   The same the gypsies wore.
 Shepherds had met him on the Hurst[7] in spring;
  At some lone alehouse in the Berkshire moors,
  On the warm ingle-bench,[8] the smock-frocked boors
 Had found him seated at their entering,   60

But, 'mid their drink and clatter, he would fly.
 And I myself seem half to know thy looks,
  And put the shepherds, wanderer! on thy trace;
 And boys who in lone wheatfields scare the rooks[9]
  I ask if thou hast passed their quiet place;   65
   Or in my boat I lie
 Moored to the cool bank in the summer heats,
  'Mid wide grass meadows which the sunshine fills,
  And watch the warm, green-muffled Cumner hills,
 And wonder if thou haunt'st their shy retreats.   70

---

6. Teeming with ideas.
7. A hill near Oxford. All the place names in the poem (except those in the final 2 stanzas) refer to the country-side near Oxford.
8. Fireside bench. "Boors," here, are rustics.
9. Boys hired to frighten crows away from eating wheat grains.

For most, I know, thou lov'st retired ground!
  Thee at the ferry Oxford riders blithe,
    Returning home on summer nights, have met
  Crossing the stripling Thames[1] at Bab-lock-hithe,
    Trailing in the cool stream thy fingers wet,   75
      As the punt's rope chops round;[2]
  And leaning backward in a pensive dream,
    And fostering in thy lap a heap of flowers
    Plucked in shy fields and distant Wychwood bowers,
  And thine eyes resting on the moonlit stream.   80

And then they land, and thou art seen no more!—
  Maidens, who from the distant hamlets come
    To dance around the Fyfield elm in May,
  Oft through the darkening fields have seen thee roam,
    Or cross a stile into the public way.   85
      Oft thou hast given them store
  Of flowers—the frail-leafed, white anemone,
    Dark bluebells drenched with dews of summer eves,
    And purple orchises with spotted leaves—
  But none hath words she can report of thee.   90

And, above Godstow Bridge, when hay time's here
  In June, and many a scythe in sunshine flames,
    Men who through those wide fields of breezy grass
  Where black-winged swallows haunt the glittering Thames,
    To bathe in the abandoned lasher pass,[3]   95
      Have often passed thee near
  Sitting upon the river bank o'ergrown;
    Marked thine outlandish garb, thy figure spare,
    Thy dark vague eyes, and soft abstracted air—
  But, when they came from bathing, thou wast gone!   100

At some lone homestead in the Cumner hills,
  Where at her open door the housewife darns,
    Thou hast been seen, or hanging on a gate
  To watch the threshers in the mossy barns.
    Children, who early range these slopes and late   105
      For cresses from the rills,
  Have known thee eying, all an April day,
    The springing pastures and the feeding kine;
    And marked thee, when the stars come out and shine,
  Through the long dewy grass move slow away.   110

---

1. I.e., the narrow upper reaches of the river before it broadens out to its full width.
2. The scholar's flat-bottomed boat ("punt") is tied up by a rope at the river bank near the ferry crossing like the speaker's boat (in the previous stanza), which was "moored to the cool bank." The motion of the boat as it is stirred by the current of the river causes the chopping sound of the rope in the water.
3. Water that spills over a dam or weir.

In autumn, on the skirts of Bagley Wood—
    Where most the gypsies by the turf-edged way
      Pitch their smoked tents, and every bush you see
    With scarlet patches tagged and shreds of grey,
      Above the forest ground called Thessaly—   115
        The blackbird, picking food,
    Sees thee, nor stops his meal, nor fears at all;
      So often has he known thee past him stray,
      Rapt, twirling in thy hand a withered spray,
    And waiting for the spark from heaven to fall.   120

And once, in winter, on the causeway chill
    Where home through flooded fields foot-travelers go,
      Have I not passed thee on the wooden bridge,
    Wrapped in thy cloak and battling with the snow,
      Thy face tow'rd Hinksey and its wintry ridge?   125
        And thou hast climbed the hill,
    And gained the white brow of the Cumner range;
      Turned once to watch, while thick the snowflakes fall,
      The line of festal light in Christ Church hall[4]—
    Then sought thy straw in some sequestered grange.   130

But what—I dream! Two hundred years are flown
    Since first thy story ran through Oxford halls,
      And the grave Glanvill did the tale inscribe
    That thou wert wandered from the studious walls
      To learn strange arts, and join a gypsy tribe;   135
        And thou from earth art gone
    Long since, and in some quiet churchyard laid—
      Some country nook, where o'er thy unknown grave
      Tall grasses and white flowering nettles wave,
    Under a dark, red-fruited yew tree's shade.   140

—No, no, thou hast not felt the lapse of hours!
    For what wears out the life of mortal men?
      'Tis that from change to change their being rolls;
    'Tis that repeated shocks, again, again,
      Exhaust the energy of strongest souls   145
        And numb the elastic powers.
    Till having used our nerves with bliss and teen,[5]
      And tired upon a thousand schemes our wit,
      To the just-pausing Genius[6] we remit
    Our worn-out life, and are—what we have been.   150

Thou hast not lived, why should'st thou perish, so?
    Thou hadst *one* aim, *one* business, *one* desire;

---

4. The dining hall of an Oxford college.
5. Vexation.

6. Perhaps the spirit of the universe, which pauses
briefly to receive back the life given to us.

Else wert thou long since numbered with the dead!
Else hadst thou spent, like other men, thy fire!
    The generations of thy peers are fled,   155
        And we ourselves shall go;
But thou possessest an immortal lot,
    And we imagine thee exempt from age
    And living as thou liv'st on Glanvill's page,
Because thou hadst—what we, alas! have not.   160

For early didst thou leave the world, with powers
    Fresh, undiverted to the world without,
        Firm to their mark, not spent on other things;
    Free from the sick fatigue, the languid doubt,
        Which much to have tried, in much been baffled, brings.   165
            O life unlike to ours!
    Who fluctuate idly without term or scope,
        Of whom each strives, nor knows for what he strives,
        And each half[7] lives a hundred different lives;
    Who wait like thee, but not, like thee, in hope.   170

Thou waitest for the spark from heaven! and we,
    Light half-believers of our casual creeds,
        Who never deeply felt, nor clearly willed,
    Whose insight never has borne fruit in deeds,
        Whose vague resolves never have been fulfilled;   175
            For whom each year we see
    Breeds new beginnings, disappointments new;
        Who hesitate and falter life away,
        And lose tomorrow the ground won today—
    Ah! do not we, wanderer! await it too?   180

Yes, we await it!—but it still delays,
    And then we suffer! and amongst us one,[8]
        Who most has suffered, takes dejectedly
    His seat upon the intellectual throne;
        And all his store of sad experience he   185
            Lays bare of wretched days;
    Tells us his misery's birth and growth and signs,
        And how the dying spark of hope was fed,
        And how the breast was soothed, and how the head,
    And all his hourly varied anodynes.   190

This for our wisest! and we others pine,
    And wish the long unhappy dream would end,
        And waive all claim to bliss, and try to bear;
    With close-lipped patience for our only friend,
        Sad patience, too near neighbor to despair—   195

7. An adverb modifying "lives."
8. Probably Goethe, although possibly referring to

Tennyson, whose *In Memoriam* had appeared in
1850.

But none has hope like thine!
Thou through the fields and through the woods dost stray,
  Roaming the countryside, a truant boy,
  Nursing thy project in unclouded joy,
And every doubt long blown by time away.   200

O born in days when wits were fresh and clear,
  And life ran gaily as the sparkling Thames;
    Before this strange disease of modern life,
  With its sick hurry, its divided aims,
    Its heads o'ertaxed, its palsied hearts, was rife—   205
      Fly hence, our contact fear!
  Still fly, plunge deeper in the bowering wood!
    Averse, as Dido[9] did with gesture stern
    From her false friend's approach in Hades turn,
  Wave us away, and keep thy solitude!   210

Still nursing the unconquerable hope,
  Still clutching the inviolable shade,
    With a free, onward impulse brushing through,
  By night, the silvered branches of the glade—
    Far on the forest skirts, where none pursue.   215
      On some mild pastoral slope
  Emerge, and resting on the moonlit pales
    Freshen thy flowers as in former years
    With dew, or listen with enchanted ears,
  From the dark dingles,[1] to the nightingales!   220

But fly our paths, our feverish contact fly!
  For strong the infection of our mental strife,
    Which, though it gives no bliss, yet spoils for rest;
  And we should win thee from thy own fair life,
    Like us distracted, and like us unblest.   225
      Soon, soon thy cheer would die,
  Thy hopes grow timorous, and unfixed thy powers,
    And thy clear aims be cross and shifting made;
    And then thy glad perennial youth would fade,
  Fade, and grow old at last, and die like ours.   230

Then fly our greetings, fly our speech and smiles!
  —As some grave Tyrian trader, from the sea,
    Descried at sunrise an emerging prow
  Lifting the cool-haired creepers stealthily,
    The fringes of a southward-facing brow   235
      Among the Aegean isles;
  And saw the merry Grecian coaster come,
    Freighted with amber grapes, and Chian wine,

9. Dido committed suicide after her lover, Aeneas,   Hades, she turned sternly away from him.
deserted her. When he later encountered her in   1. Small deep valleys.

Green, bursting figs, and tunnies[2] steeped in brine—
And knew the intruders on his ancient home,　　　　　240

The young lighthearted masters of the waves—
　And snatched his rudder, and shook out more sail;
　　And day and night held on indignantly
　O'er the blue Midland waters with the gale,
　　Betwixt the Syrtes[3] and soft Sicily,　　　　　245
　　　To where the Atlantic raves
　Outside the western straits; and unbent sails
　　There, where down cloudy cliffs, through sheets of foam,
　　Shy traffickers, the dark Iberians[4] come;
And on the beach undid his corded bales.[5]　　　　　250

1853

Dover Beach

　The sea is calm tonight.
　The tide is full, the moon lies fair
　Upon the straits—on the French coast the light
　Gleams and is gone; the cliffs of England stand,
　Glimmering and vast, out in the tranquil bay.　　　5
　Come to the window, sweet is the night air!
　Only, from the long line of spray
　Where the sea meets the moon-blanched land,
　Listen! you hear the grating roar[1]
　Of pebbles which the waves draw back, and fling,　　10
　At their return, up the high strand,
　Begin, and cease, and then again begin,
　With tremulous cadence slow, and bring
　The eternal note of sadness in.

2. Tuna fish.
3. Shoals off the coast of North Africa.
4. Dark inhabitants of Spain and Portugal—perhaps associated with gypsies.
5. The elaborate simile of the final two stanzas has been variously interpreted. The trader from Tyre is disconcerted when, peering out through the foliage ("fringes") that screens his hiding place, he sees noisy intruders entering his harbor. Like the Scholar Gypsy, when similarly intruded upon by hearty extroverts, he resolves to flee and seek a new home.

The reference (line 249) to the Iberians as "shy traffickers" (traders) is explained by Kenneth Allott as having been derived from Herodotus' History (4.196). Herodotus describes a distinctive method of selling goods established by Carthaginian merchants who used to sail through the straits of Gibraltar to trade with the inhabitants of the coast of West Africa. The Carthaginians would leave bales of their merchandise on display along the beaches and, without having seen their prospective customers, would return to their ships. The shy natives would then come down from their inland hiding places and set gold beside the bales they wished to buy. When the natives withdrew in their turn, the Carthaginians would return to the beach and decide whether payments were adequate, a process repeated until agreement was reached. On the Atlantic coasts this method of bargaining persisted into the 19th century. As William Beloe, a translator of Herodotus, noted in 1844: "In this manner they transact their exchange without seeing one another, or without the least instance of dishonesty . . . on either side." For the solitary Tyrian trader such a procedure, with its avoidance of contact (line 221), would have been especially appropriate.

1. Cf. Wordsworth's It Is a Beauteous Evening: "Listen! the mighty Being is awake, / And doth with his eternal motion make / A sound like thunder—everlastingly."

Sophocles long ago   15
Heard it on the Aegean, and it brought
Into his mind the turbid ebb and flow
Of human misery;[2] we
Find also in the sound a thought,
Hearing it by this distant northern sea.   20

The Sea of Faith
Was once, too, at the full, and round earth's shore
Lay like the folds of a bright girdle furled.[3]
But now I only hear
Its melancholy, long, withdrawing roar,   25
Retreating, to the breath
Of the night wind, down the vast edges drear
And naked shingles[4] of the world.

Ah, love, let us be true
To one another! for the world, which seems   30
To lie before us like a land of dreams,
So various, so beautiful, so new,
Hath really neither joy, nor love, nor light,
Nor certitude, nor peace, nor help for pain;
And we are here as on a darkling plain   35
Swept with confused alarms of struggle and flight,
Where ignorant armies[5] clash by night.

ca. 1851   1867

Stanzas from the Grande Chartreuse[1]

Through Alpine meadows soft-suffused
With rain, where thick the crocus blows,
Past the dark forges long disused,
The mule track from Saint Laurent goes.
The bridge is crossed, and slow we ride,   5
Through forest, up the mountainside.

2. See Sophocles' *Antigone*, lines 583 ff.
3. This difficult line means, in general, that at high tide the sea envelops the land closely. Its forces are "gathered" up (to use Wordsworth's term for it) like the "folds" of bright clothing ("girdle") which have been compressed ("furled"). At ebb tide, as the sea retreats, it is unfurled and spread out. It still surrounds the shoreline but not as an "enclasping flow" (as Arnold speaks of the sea in *To Marguerite, Continued*).
4. Beaches covered with pebbles.
5. Perhaps the revolutions of 1848 or a reference to the siege of Rome by the French in 1849. The date of composition of the poem is unknown, although generally assumed to be 1851.
1. A monastery situated high in the French Alps. It was established in 1084 by St. Bruno, founder of the Carthusians (line 30), whose austere regimen of solitary contemplation, fasting, and religious exercises (lines 37–44) had remained virtually unchanged for centuries. Arnold visited the site Sept. 7, 1851, accompanied by his bride. His account may be compared with that by Wordsworth (*Prelude* 6. 416–88) who had made a similar visit in 1790.

The autumnal evening darkens round,
The wind is up, and drives the rain;
While, hark! far down, with strangled sound
Doth the Dead Guier's[2] stream complain,   10
Where that wet smoke, among the woods,
Over his boiling cauldron broods.

Swift rush the spectral vapors white
Past limestone scars[3] with ragged pines,
Showing—then blotting from our sight!—   15
Halt—through the cloud-drift something shines!
High in the valley, wet and drear,
The huts of Courrerie appear.

Strike leftward! cries our guide; and higher
Mounts up the stony forest way.   20
At last the encircling trees retire;
Look! through the showery twilight grey
What pointed roofs are these advance?—
A palace of the Kings of France?

Approach, for what we seek is here!   25
Alight, and sparely sup, and wait
For rest in this outbuilding near;
Then cross the sward and reach that gate.
Knock; pass the wicket! Thou art come
To the Carthusians' world-famed home.   30

The silent courts, where night and day
Into their stone-carved basins cold
The splashing icy fountains play—
The humid corridors behold!
Where, ghostlike in the deepening night,   35
Cowled forms brush by in gleaming white.

The chapel, where no organ's peal
Invests the stern and naked prayer—
With penitential cries they kneel
And wrestle; rising then, with bare   40
And white uplifted faces stand,
Passing the Host from hand to hand;[4]

2. The Guiers Mort river flows down from the monastery and joins the Guiers Vif in the valley below. Wordsworth speaks of the two rivers as "the sister streams of Life and Death."
3. Precipices.
4. Arnold, during his short visit, may not actually have witnessed the service of the Mass in the monastery. The consecrated wafer (the Host) is not passed from the hand of the officiating priest to the hands of the communicant (as is the practice in Arnold's own Anglican church) but placed, instead, on the tongue of the communicant (who kneels rather than stands). See Tinker and Lowry, *The Poetry of Matthew Arnold: A Commentary,* pp. 249–51.

Each takes, and then his visage wan
Is buried in his cowl once more.
The cells!—the suffering Son of Man   45
Upon the wall—the knee-worn floor—
And where they sleep, that wooden bed,
Which shall their coffin be, when dead![5]

The library, where tract and tome
Not to feed priestly pride are there,   50
To hymn the conquering march of Rome,
Nor yet to amuse, as ours are!
They paint of souls the inner strife,
Their drops of blood, their death in life.

The garden, overgrown—yet mild,   55
See, fragrant herbs[6] are flowering there!
Strong children of the Alpine wild
Whose culture is the brethren's care;
Of human tasks their only one,
And cheerful works beneath the sun.   60

Those halls, too, destined to contain
Each its own pilgrim-host of old,
From England, Germany, or Spain—
All are before me! I behold
The House, the Brotherhood austere!   65
—And what am I, that I am here?

For rigorous teachers seized my youth,
And purged its faith, and trimmed its fire,
Showed me the high, white star of Truth,
There bade me gaze, and there aspire.   70
Even now their whispers pierce the gloom:
What dost thou in this living tomb?

Forgive me, masters of the mind![7]
At whose behest I long ago
So much unlearnt, so much resigned—   75
I come not here to be your foe!
I seek these anchorites, not in ruth,[8]
To curse and to deny your truth;

5. A Carthusian is buried on a wooden plank but does not sleep in a coffin.
6. From which the liqueur, Chartreuse, is manufactured. Sales of this liqueur provide the principal revenues for upkeep of the monastery.
7. Writers whose insistence upon testing religious beliefs in the light of fact and reason persuaded Arnold that faith in Christianity (especially in the Roman Catholic or Anglo Catholic forms) was no longer tenable in the modern world.
8. Remorse for having adopted the rationalist view of Christianity.

Not as their friend, or child, I speak!
But as, on some far northern strand,   80
Thinking of his own Gods, a Greek
In pity and mournful awe might stand
Before some fallen Runic stone—[9]
For both were faiths, and both are gone.

Wandering between two worlds, one dead,   85
The other powerless to be born,
With nowhere yet to rest my head,
Like these, on earth I wait forlorn.
Their faith, my tears, the world deride—
I come to shed them at their side.   90

Oh, hide me in your gloom profound,
Ye solemn seats of holy pain!
Take me, cowled forms, and fence me round,
Till I possess my soul again;
Till free my thoughts before me roll,   95
Not chafed by hourly false control!

For the world cries your faith is now
But a dead time's exploded dream;
My melancholy, sciolists[1] say,
Is a passed mode, an outworn theme—   100
As if the world had ever had
A faith, or sciolists been sad!

Ah, if it _be_ passed, take away,
At least, the restlessness, the pain;
Be man henceforth no more a prey   105
To these out-dated stings again!
The nobleness of grief is gone—
Ah, leave us not the fret alone!

But—if you[2] cannot give us ease—
Last of the race of them who grieve   110
Here leave us to die out with these
Last of the people who believe!
Silent, while years engrave the brow;
Silent—the best are silent now.

---

9. A monument inscribed in Teutonic letters (runes), emblematic of a Nordic religion that has become extinct. The relic reminds the Greek that his own religion is likewise dying and will soon be extinct.

1. Superficial-minded persons who pretend to know the answers to all questions.

2. It is not clear whether the speaker has resumed addressing his "rigorous teachers" (line 67) or (as would seem more likely) a combination of the sciolists, who scorn the speaker's melancholy and the worldly, who scorn the faith of the monks. See his address to the "sons of the world" (lines 160–68).

Achilles[3] ponders in his tent, 115
The kings of modern thought[4] are dumb;
Silent they are, though not content,
And wait to see the future come.
They have the grief men had of yore,
But they contend and cry no more. 120

Our fathers[5] watered with their tears
This sea of time whereon we sail,
Their voices were in all men's ears
Who passed within their puissant hail.
Still the same ocean round us raves, 125
But we stand mute, and watch the waves.

For what availed it, all the noise
And outcry of the former men?—
Say, have their sons achieved more joys,
Say, is life lighter now than then? 130
The sufferers died, they left their pain—
The pangs which tortured them remain.

What helps it now, that Byron bore,
With haughty scorn which mocked the smart,
Through Europe to the Aetolian shore[6] 135
The pageant of his bleeding heart?
That thousands counted every groan,
And Europe made his woe her own?

What boots it, Shelley! that the breeze
Carried thy lovely wail away, 140
Musical through Italian trees
Which fringe thy soft blue Spezzian bay?[7]
Inheritors of thy distress
Have restless hearts one throb the less?

Or are we easier, to have read, 145
O Obermann![8] the sad, stern page,
Which tells us how thou hidd'st thy head
From the fierce tempest of thine age
In the lone brakes of Fontainebleau,
Or chalets near the Alpine snow? 150

---

3. Achilles, after the death of Patroclus, refused to participate in the Trojan war; hence similar to modern intellectual leaders who refuse to speak out about their frustrated sense of alienation.
4. Variously but never satisfactorily identified as Newman or Carlyle (the latter was said to have preached the gospel of silence in 40 volumes). Another advocate of stoical silence was the French poet Alfred de Vigny (1797–1863).
5. Predecessors among the Romantic writers such as Byron.
6. Region in Greece where Byron died.
7. The Gulf of Spezzia in Italy, where Shelley was drowned.
8. Melancholy hero of *Obermann* (1804), a novel by Senancour.

Ye slumber in your silent grave!
The world, which for an idle day
Grace to your mood of sadness gave,
Long since hath flung her weeds[9] away.
The eternal trifler[1] breaks your spell;   155
But we—we learnt your lore too well!

Years hence, perhaps, may dawn an age,
More fortunate, alas! than we,
Which without hardness will be sage,
And gay without frivolity.   160
Sons of the world, oh, speed those years;
But, while we wait, allow our tears!

Allow them! We admire with awe
The exulting thunder of your race;
You give the universe your law,   165
You triumph over time and space!
Your pride of life, your tireless powers,
We laud them, but they are not ours.

We are like children reared in shade
Beneath some old-world abbey wall,   170
Forgotten in a forest glade,
And secret from the eyes of all.
Deep, deep the greenwood round them waves,
Their abbey, and its close[2] of graves!

But, where the road runs near the stream,   175
Oft through the trees they catch a glance
Of passing troops in the sun's beam—
Pennon, and plume, and flashing lance!
Forth to the world those soldiers fare,
To life, to cities, and to war!   180

And through the wood, another way,
Faint bugle notes from far are borne,
Where hunters gather, staghounds bay,[3]
Round some fair forest-lodge at morn.
Gay dames are there, in sylvan green;   185
Laughter and cries—those notes between!

The banners flashing through the trees
Make their blood dance and chain their eyes;
That bugle music on the breeze
Arrests them with a charmed surprise.   190

---

9. Mourning clothes.
1. The sciolist, as in line 99.
2. Enclosure.

3. Cf. the contrast between recluses and hunters in *The Scholar Gypsy*, lines 71–81.

Banner by turns and bugle woo:
Ye shy recluses, follow too!

O children, what do ye reply?—
"Action and pleasure, will ye roam
Through these secluded dells to cry   195
And call us?—but too late ye come!
Too late for us your call ye blow,
Whose bent was taken long ago.

"Long since we pace this shadowed nave;
We watch those yellow tapers shine,   200
Emblems of hope over the grave,
In the high altar's depth divine;
The organ carries to our ear
Its accents of another sphere.[4]

"Fenced early in this cloistral round   205
Of reverie, of shade, of prayer,
How should we grow in other ground?
How can we flower in foreign air?
—Pass, banners, pass, and bugles, cease;
And leave our desert to its peace!"   210

1852(?)   1855

Thyrsis[1]

A Monody, to Commemorate the Author's Friend, Arthur Hugh Clough, Who Died at Florence, 1861

How changed is here each spot man makes or fills!
    In the two Hinkseys[2] nothing keeps the same;
        The village street its haunted mansion lacks,
    And from the sign is gone Sibylla's name,[3]
    And from the roofs the twisted chimney stacks—   5

---

4. The organ music is from the abbey in the greenwood (line 174), as contrasted with the monastery on the mountain-top in which there is no organ (line 37).
1. In the 1840s, at Oxford, Clough had been one of Arnold's closest friends. After the death of this fellow poet, 20 years later, Arnold revisited the Thames valley countryside which they had explored together. The familiar scenes prompted him to review the changes wrought by time on the ideals shared in his Oxford days with Clough, ideals symbolized, in part, by a distant elm and by the story of the Scholar Gypsy. The survival of these ideals in the face of the difficulties of modern life is the subject of this elegy. Unlike Tennyson in such elegies as *In Memoriam*, Arnold rarely touches here upon other kinds of immortality.

As a framework for his elegy, Arnold draws on the same Greek and Latin pastoral tradition from which Milton's *Lycidas* and Shelley's *Adonais* were derived. Hence Clough is referred to by one of the traditional names for a shepherd-poet, Thyrsis, and Arnold himself as Corydon. The sense of distancing which results from this traditional elegiac mode is reduced considerably by the realism of the setting with its bleak wintry landscape at twilight, a landscape which is brightened, in turn, by evocations of the return of hopeful springtime.
2. The villages of North Hinksey and South Hinksey.
3. Sibylla Kerr had been the proprietress of a tavern in South Hinksey.

Are ye too changed, ye hills?
See, 'tis no foot of unfamiliar men
    Tonight from Oxford up your pathway strays!
    Here came I often, often, in old days—
Thyrsis and I; we still had Thyrsis then.   10

Runs it not here, the track by Childsworth Farm,
    Past the high wood, to where the elm tree crowns
        The hill behind whose ridge the sunset flames?
    The signal-elm, that looks on Ilsley Downs,
        The Vale, the three lone weirs, the youthful Thames?—   15
            This winter eve is warm,
    Humid the air! leafless, yet soft as spring,
        The tender purple spray on copse and briers!
        And that sweet city with her dreaming spires,
    She needs not June for beauty's heightening,   20

Lovely all times she lies, lovely tonight!—
    Only, methinks, some loss of habit's power
        Befalls me wandering through this upland dim.
    Once passed I blindfold here, at any hour;
        Now seldom come I, since I came with him.   25
            That single elm tree bright
    Against the west—I miss it! is it gone?
        We prized it dearly; while it stood, we said,
        Our friend, the Gypsy Scholar, was not dead;
    While the tree lived, he in these fields lived on.   30

Too rare, too rare, grow now my visits here,
    But once I knew each field, each flower, each stick;
        And with the countryfolk acquaintance made
    By barn in threshing time, by new-built rick.
        Here, too, our shepherd pipes we first assayed.   35
            Ah me! this many a year
    My pipe is lost, my shepherd's holiday!
        Needs must I lose them, needs with heavy heart
        Into the world and wave of men depart;
    But Thyrsis of his own will went away.[4]   40

It irked him to be here, he could not rest.
    He loved each simple joy the country yields,
        He loved his mates; but yet he could not keep,[5]
    For that a shadow loured on the fields,
        Here with the shepherds and the silly[6] sheep.   45
            Some life of men unblest
    He knew, which made him droop, and filled his head.

4. Arnold left Oxford out of the necessity for earning a living; Clough left as a matter of principle
when in 1848 he resigned a fellowship rather than
subscribe to the creed of the Anglican Church.
5. Stay.
6. Innocent.

He went; his piping took a troubled sound
   Of storms[7] that rage outside our happy ground;
He could not wait their passing, he is dead.   50

So, some tempestuous morn in early June,
   When the year's primal burst of bloom is o'er,
     Before the roses and the longest day—
   When garden walks and all the grassy floor
     With blossoms red and white of fallen May   55
       And chestnut flowers are strewn—
So have I heard the cuckoo's parting cry,
   From the wet field, through the vexed garden trees,
   Come with the volleying rain and tossing breeze:
The bloom is gone, and with the bloom go I!   60

Too quick despairer, wherefore wilt thou go?
   Soon will the high Midsummer pomps come on,
     Soon will the musk carnations break and swell,
   Soon shall we have gold-dusted snapdragon,
     Sweet-William with his homely cottage-smell,   65
       And stocks in fragrant blow;
Roses that down the alleys shine afar,
   And open, jasmine-muffled lattices,
   And groups under the dreaming garden trees,
And the full moon, and the white evening star.   70

He hearkens not! light comer, he is flown!
   What matters it? next year he will return,
     And we shall have him in the sweet spring days,
   With whitening hedges, and uncrumpling fern,
     And bluebells trembling by the forest ways,   75
       And scent of hay new-mown.
But Thyrsis never more we swains shall see,
   See him come back, and cut a smoother reed,
   And blow a strain the world at last shall heed—
For Time, not Corydon, hath conquered thee!   80

Alack, for Corydon no rival now!—
   But when Sicilian shepherds lost a mate,
     Some good survivor with his flute would go,
   Piping a ditty sad for Bion's fate;[8]
     And cross the unpermitted ferry's flow,[9]   85
       And relax Pluto's brow,
And make leap up with joy the beauteous head
   Of Proserpine, among whose crownèd hair

---

7. Religious and political controversies.
8. Moschus, a Greek poet, composed a pastoral elegy upon the death of the poet Bion in Sicily.
9. The river Styx across which the dead were fer-ried to the underworld where Pluto ruled with his queen, Proserpine. In spring, Proserpine's return-ing above ground in Sicily would cause the flowers to blossom.

Are flowers first opened on Sicilian air,
And flute his friend, like Orpheus, from the dead.[1]　　90

O easy access to the hearer's grace
　　When Dorian shepherds[2] sang to Proserpine!
　　　　For she herself had trod Sicilian fields,
　　She knew the Dorian water's gush divine,
　　　　She knew each lily white which Enna yields,[3]　　95
　　　　　　Each rose with blushing face;
　　She loved the Dorian pipe, the Dorian strain.
　　　　But ah, of our poor Thames she never heard!
　　　　Her foot the Cumner cowslips never stirred;
　　And we should tease her with our plaint in vain!　　100

Well! wind-dispersed and vain the words will be,
　　Yet, Thyrsis, let me give my grief its hour
　　　　In the old haunt, and find our tree-topped hill!
　　Who, if not I, for questing here hath power?
　　　　I know the wood which hides the daffodil,　　105
　　　　　　I know the Fyfield tree,
　　I know what white, what purple fritillaries[4]
　　　　The grassy harvest of the river fields,
　　　　Above by Ensham, down by Sandford, yields,
　　And what sedged brooks are Thames's tributaries;　　110

I know these slopes; who knows them if not I?—
　　But many a dingle[5] on the loved hillside,
　　　　With thorns once studded, old, white-blossomed trees,
　　Where thick the cowslips grew, and far descried
　　　　High towered the spikes of purple orchises,　　115
　　　　　　Hath since our day put by
　　The coronals of that forgotten time;
　　　　Down each green bank hath gone the plowboy's team,
　　　　And only in the hidden brookside gleam
　　Primroses, orphans of the flowery prime.　　120

Where is the girl, who by the boatman's door,
　　Above the locks, above the boating throng,
　　　　Unmoored our skiff when through the Wytham flats,
　　Red loosestrife[6] and blond meadowsweet among
　　　　And darting swallows and light water-gnats,　　125
　　　　　　We tracked the shy Thames shore?
　　Where are the mowers, who, as the tiny swell
　　　　Of our boat passing heaved the river grass,

1. Orpheus' music enabled him to enter the "unpermitted" realms of the dead and to bring his wife, Eurydice, back with him to the land of the living.
2. The Dorian Greeks had colonized Sicily, the home of pastoral poetry.
3. From a meadow near Enna, a Sicilian town, Proserpine had been carried off to the underworld by Pluto (or Dis).
4. Flowers commonly found in moist meadows.
5. Small deep valley.
6. Flowers which grow on banks of streams.

Stood with suspended scythe to see us pass?—
They all are gone, and thou art gone as well!   130

Yes, thou art gone! and round me too the night
  In ever-nearing circle weaves her shade.
    I see her veil draw soft across the day,
  I feel her slowly chilling breath invade
    The cheek grown thin, the brown hair sprent[7] with grey;   135
      I feel her finger light
  Laid pausefully upon life's headlong train;
    The foot less prompt to meet the morning dew,
    The heart less bounding at emotion new,
  And hope, once crushed, less quick to spring again.   140

And long the way appears, which seemed so short
  To the less practiced eye of sanguine youth;
    And high the mountaintops, in cloudy air,
  The mountaintops where is the throne of Truth,
    Tops in life's morning sun so bright and bare!   145
      Unbreachable the fort
  Of the long-battered world uplifts its wall;
    And strange and vain the earthly turmoil grows,
    And near and real the charm of thy repose,
  And night as welcome as a friend would fall.   150

But hush! the upland hath a sudden loss
  Of quiet!—Look, adown the dusk hillside,
    A troop of Oxford hunters going home,
  As in old days, jovial and talking, ride!
    From hunting with the Berkshire hounds they come.   155
      Quick! let me fly, and cross
  Into yon farther field!—'Tis done; and see,
    Backed by the sunset, which doth glorify
    The orange and pale violet evening sky,
  Bare on its lonely ridge, the Tree! the Tree!   160

I take the omen! Eve lets down her veil,
  The white fog creeps from bush to bush about,
    The west unflushes, the high stars grow bright,
  And in the scattered farms the lights come out.
    I cannot reach the signal-tree tonight,   165
      Yet, happy omen, hail!
  Hear it from thy broad lucent Arno vale[8]
    (For there thine earth-forgetting eyelids keep
    The morningless and unawakening sleep
  Under the flowery oleanders pale),   170

----

7. Sprinkled.
8. Clough was buried in Florence, which is situated in the valley of the Arno River.

Hear it, O Thyrsis, still our tree is there!—
    Ah, vain! These English fields, this upland dim,
      These brambles pale with mist engarlanded,
      That lone, sky-pointing tree, are not for him;
        To a boon southern country he is fled,   175
          And now in happier air,
    Wandering with the great Mother's[9] train divine
      (And purer or more subtle soul than thee,
      I trow, the mighty Mother doth not see)
    Within a folding of the Apennine,[1]   180

Thou hearest the immortal chants of old!—
    Putting his sickle to the perilous grain
      In the hot cornfield of the Phrygian king,[2]
    For thee the Lityerses song again
      Young Daphnis with his silver voice doth sing;   185
        Sings his Sicilian fold,
    His sheep, his hapless love, his blinded eyes—
      And how a call celestial round him rang,
      And heavenward from the fountain brink he sprang,
    And all the marvel of the golden skies.   190

There thou art gone, and me thou leavest here
    Sole in these fields! yet will I not despair.
      Despair I will not, while I yet descry
      'Neath the mild canopy of English air
        That lonely tree against the western sky.   195
        Still, still these slopes, 'tis clear,
    Our Gypsy Scholar haunts, outliving thee!
      Fields where soft sheep from cages pull the hay,
      Woods with anemones in flower till May,
    Know him a wanderer still; then why not me?   200

A fugitive and gracious light he seeks,
    Shy to illumine; and I seek it too.
      This does not come with houses or with gold,
      With place, with honor, and a flattering crew;
        'Tis not in the world's market bought and sold—   205

9. Demeter (whose name may mean Earth Mother) was worshiped as the goddess of agriculture. The "immortal chants" (line 181) would be sung in her honor by her followers, members of the "train divine" (line 176).
1. Mountains near Florence.
2. Arnold includes a note from Servius's commentary on Virgil's *Eclogues:* "Daphnis, the ideal Sicilian shepherd of Greek pastoral poetry, was said to have followed into Phrygia his mistress Piplea, who had been carried off by robbers, and to have found her in the power of the king of Phrygia, Lityerses. Lityerses used to make strangers try a contest with him in reaping corn, and to put them to death if he overcame them. Hercules arrived in time to save Daphnis, took upon himself the reaping contest with Lityerses, overcame him, and slew him. The Lityerses song connected with this tradition was, like the Linus song, one of the early plaintive strains of Greek popular poetry, and used to be sung by corn reapers. Other traditions represented Daphnis as beloved by a nymph who exacted from him an oath to love no one else. He fell in love with a princess, and was struck blind by the jealous nymph. Mercury, who was his father, raised him to heaven, and made a fountain spring up in the place from which he ascended. At this fountain the Sicilians offered yearly sacrifices."

But the smooth-slipping weeks
Drop by, and leave its seeker still untired;
    Out of the heed of mortals he is gone,
    He wends unfollowed, he must house alone;
Yet on he fares, by his own heart inspired.   210

Thou too, O Thyrsis, on like quest wast bound;
    Thou wanderedst with me for a little hour!
        Men gave thee nothing; but this happy quest,
    If men esteemed thee feeble, gave thee power,
        If men procured thee trouble, gave thee rest.   215
            And this rude Cumner ground,
    Its fir-topped Hurst, its farms, its quiet fields,
        Here cam'st thou in thy jocund youthful time,
        Here was thine height of strength, thy golden prime!
And still the haunt beloved a virtue yields.   220

What though the music of thy rustic flute
    Kept not for long its happy, country tone;
        Lost it too soon, and learnt a stormy note[3]
    Of men contention-tossed, of men who groan,
        Which tasked thy pipe too sore, and tired thy throat—   225
            It failed, and thou wast mute!
    Yet hadst thou always visions of our light,
        And long with men of care thou couldst not stay,
        And soon thy foot resumed its wandering way,
Left human haunt, and on alone till night.   230

Too rare, too rare, grow now my visits here!
    'Mid city noise, not, as with thee of yore,
        Thyrsis! in reach of sheep-bells is my home.
    —Then through the great town's harsh, heart-wearying roar,
        Let in thy voice a whisper often come,   235
            To chase fatigue and fear:
    Why faintest thou? I wandered till I died.
        Roam on! The light we sought is shining still.
        Dost thou ask proof? Our tree yet crowns the hill,
Our Scholar travels yet the loved hillside.   240

                                                    1866

Growing Old[1]

What is it to grow old?
    Is it to lose the glory of the form,

3. Clough's poetry often dealt with contemporary religious problems.
1. Arnold's poem may have been prompted as a rejoinder to Browning's enthusiastic picture of old age in *Rabbi Ben Ezra* (1864).

The luster of the eye?
Is it for beauty to forego her wreath?
—Yes, but not this alone.   5

Is it to feel our strength—
Not our bloom only, but our strength—decay?
Is it to feel each limb
Grow stiffer, every function less exact,
Each nerve more loosely strung?   10

Yes, this, and more; but not
Ah, 'tis not what in youth we dreamed 'twould be!
'Tis not to have our life
Mellowed and softened as with sunset glow,
A golden day's decline.   15

'Tis not to see the world
As from a height, with rapt prophetic eyes,
And heart profoundly stirred;
And weep, and feel the fullness of the past,
The years that are no more.   20

It is to spend long days
And not once feel that we were ever young;
It is to add, immured
In the hot prison of the present, month
To month with weary pain.   25

It is to suffer this,
And feel but half, and feebly, what we feel.
Deep in our hidden heart
Festers the dull remembrance of a change,
But no emotion—none.   30

It is—last stage of all—
When we are frozen up within, and quite
The phantom of ourselves,
To hear the world applaud the hollow ghost
Which blamed the living man.   35

1867

From The Function of Criticism at the Present Time[1]

Many objections have been made to a proposition which, in some remarks of mine on translating Homer,[2] I ventured to put forth; a proposition about criticism, and its importance at the present day. I said: "Of the literature of France and Germany, as of the intellect of Europe in general, the main effort, for now many years, has been a critical effort; the endeavor, in all branches of knowledge, theology, philosophy, history, art, science, to see the object as in itself it really is." I added, that owing to the operation in English literature of certain causes, "almost the last thing for which one would come to English literature is just that very thing which now Europe most desires—criticism"; and that the power and value of English literature was thereby impaired. More than one rejoinder declared that the importance I here assigned to criticism was excessive, and asserted the inherent superiority of the creative effort of the human spirit over its critical effort. And the other day, having been led by a Mr. Shairp's excellent notice of Wordsworth[3] to turn again to his biography, I found, in the words of this great man, whom I, for one, must always listen to with the profoundest respect, a sentence passed on the critic's business, which seems to justify every possible disparagement of it. Wordsworth says in one of his letters:

> The writers in these publications (the Reviews), while they prosecute their inglorious employment, cannot be supposed to be in a state of mind very favorable for being affected by the finer influences of a thing so pure as genuine poetry.

And a trustworthy reporter of his conversation quotes a more elaborate judgment to the same effect:

> Wordsworth holds the critical power very low, infinitely lower than the inventive; and he said today that if the quantity of time consumed in writing critiques on the works of others were given to original composition, of whatever kind it might be, it would be much better employed; it would make a man find out sooner his

---

1. This essay served as an introduction to Arnold's volume of *Essays in Criticism* (1865). As a declaration of intentions, it can serve as a standard for measuring his total accomplishment in criticism. The essay makes us aware that criticism, for Arnold, meant a great deal more than casual book reviewing or mere censoriousness. He was not a Utilitarian, yet his object in this essay is to show that good criticism is useful. Creative writers, he argues, can profit in a special way from good criticism, but all of us can also derive from it benefits of the greatest value. In particular, we may develop a civilized attitude of mind in which to examine the social, political, aesthetic, and religious problems which confront us.

2. *On Translating Homer* (1861).

3. J. C. Shairp's essay *Wordsworth: The Man and the Poet* was published in 1864. Arnold comments in a footnote: "I cannot help thinking that a practice, common in England during the last century, and still followed in France, of printing a notice of this kind—a notice by a competent critic—to serve as an introduction to an eminent author's works, might be revived among us with advantage. To introduce all succeeding editions of Wordsworth, Mr. Shairp's notice might, it seems to me, excellently serve; it is written from the point of view of an admirer, nay, of a discipline, and that is right; but then the disciple must be also, as in this case he is, a critic, a man of letters, not, as too often happens, some relation or friend with no qualification for his task except affection for his author."

own level, and it would do infinitely less mischief. A false or malicious criticism may do much injury to the minds of others; a stupid invention, either in prose or verse, is quite harmless.

It is almost too much to expect of poor human nature, that a man capable of producing some effect in one line of literature, should, for the greater good of society, voluntarily doom himself to impotence and obscurity in another. Still less is this to be expected from men addicted to the composition of the "false or malicious criticism" of which Wordsworth speaks. However, everybody would admit that a false or malicious criticism had better never have been written. Everybody, too, would be willing to admit, as a general proposition, that the critical faculty is lower than the inventive. But is it true that criticism is really, in itself, a baneful and injurious employment; is it true that all time given to writing critiques on the works of others would be much better employed if it were given to original composition, of whatever kind this may be? Is it true that Johnson had better have gone on producing more Irenes[4] instead of writing his Lives of the Poets; nay, is it certain that Wordsworth himself was better employed in making his Ecclesiastical Sonnets[5] than when he made his celebrated Preface so full of criticism, and criticism of the works of others? Wordsworth was himself a great critic, and it is to be sincerely regretted that he has not left us more criticism; Goethe was one of the greatest of critics, and we may sincerely congratulate ourselves that he has left us so much criticism. Without wasting time over the exaggeration which Wordsworth's judgment on criticism clearly contains, or over an attempt to trace the causes—not difficult, I think, to be traced—which may have led Wordsworth to this exaggeration, a critic may with advantage seize an occasion for trying his own conscience, and for asking himself of what real service, at any given moment, the practice of criticism either is or may be made to his own mind and spirit, and to the minds and spirits of others.

The critical power is of lower rank than the creative. True; but in assenting to this proposition, one or two things are to be kept in mind. It is undeniable that the exercise of a creative power, that a free creative activity, is the highest function of man; it is proved to be so by man's finding in it his true happiness. But it is undeniable, also, that men may have the sense of exercising this free creative activity in other ways than in producing great works of literature or art; if it were not so, all but a very few men would be shut out from the true happiness of all men. They may have it in well-doing, they may have it in learning, they may have it even in criticizing. This is one thing to be kept in mind. Another is, that the exercise of the creative power in the production of great works of literature or art, however high this exercise of it may rank, is not at

4. *Irene* is the name of a clumsy play by Samuel Johnson.
5. A sonnet sequence by Wordsworth, usually regarded as minor verse. The Preface is to his *Lyrical Ballads* of 1800.

all epochs and under all conditions possible; and that therefore labor may be vainly spent in attempting it, which might with more fruit be used in preparing for it, in rendering it possible. This creative power works with elements, with materials; what if it has not those materials, those elements, ready for its use? In that case it must surely wait till they are ready. Now, in literature—I will limit myself to literature, for it is about literature that the question arises—the elements with which the creative power works are ideas; the best ideas on every matter which literature touches, current at the time. At any rate we may lay it down as certain that in modern literature no manifestation of the creative power not working with these can be very important or fruitful. And I say *current* at the time, not merely accessible at the time; for creative literary genius does not principally show itself in discovering new ideas, that is rather the business of the philosopher. The grand work of literary genius is a work of synthesis and exposition, not of analysis and discovery; its gift lies in the faculty of being happily inspired by a certain intellectual and spiritual atmosphere, by a certain order of ideas, when it finds itself in them; of dealing divinely with these ideas, presenting them in the most effective and attractive combinations—making beautiful works with them, in short. But it must have the atmosphere, it must find itself amidst the order of ideas, in order to work freely; and these it is not so easy to command. This is why great creative epochs in literature are so rare, this is why there is so much that is unsatisfactory in the productions of many men of real genius; because, for the creation of a masterwork of literature two powers must concur, the power of the man and the power of the moment, and the man is not enough without the moment; the creative power has, for its happy exercise, appointed elements, and those elements are not in its own control.

Nay, they are more within the control of the critical power. It is the business of the critical power, as I said in the words already quoted, "in all branches of knowledge, theology, philosophy, history, art, science, to see the object as in itself it really is." Thus it tends, at last, to make an intellectual situation of which the creative power can profitably avail itself. It tends to establish an order of ideas, if not absolutely true, yet true by comparison with that which it displaces; to make the best ideas prevail. Presently these new ideas reach society, the touch of truth is the touch of life, and there is a stir and growth everywhere; out of this stir and growth come the creative epochs of literature.

Or, to narrow our range, and quit these considerations of the general march of genius and of society—considerations which are apt to become too abstract and impalpable—everyone can see that a poet, for instance, ought to know life and the world before dealing with them in poetry; and life and the world being in modern times very complex things, the creation of a modern poet, to be worth much, implies a great critical effort behind it; else it must be a comparatively poor, barren, and short-lived affair. This is why Byron's poetry had so little endurance in it, and

Goethe's so much; both Byron and Goethe had a great productive power, but Goethe's was nourished by a great critical effort providing the true materials for it, and Byron's was not; Goethe knew life and the world, the poet's necessary subjects, much more comprehensively and thoroughly than Byron. He knew a great deal more of them, and he knew them much more as they really are.

It has long seemed to me that the burst of creative activity in our literature, through the first quarter of this century, had about it in fact something premature; and that from this cause its productions are doomed, most of them, in spite of the sanguine hopes which accompanied and do still accompany them, to prove hardly more lasting than the productions of far less splendid epochs. And this prematureness comes from its having proceeded without having its proper data, without sufficient materials to work with. In other words, the English poetry of the first quarter of this century, with plenty of energy, plenty of creative force, did not know enough. This makes Byron so empty of matter, Shelley so incoherent, Wordsworth even, profound as he is, yet so wanting in completeness and variety. Wordsworth cared little for books, and disparaged Goethe. I admire Wordsworth, as he is, so much that I cannot wish him different; and it is vain, no doubt, to imagine such a man different from what he is, to suppose that he *could* have been different. But surely the one thing wanting to make Wordsworth an even greater poet than he is—his thought richer, and his influence of wider application—was that he should have read more books, among them, no doubt, those of that Goethe whom he disparaged without reading him.

But to speak of books and reading may easily lead to a misunderstanding here. It was not really books and reading that lacked to our poetry at this epoch: Shelley had plenty of reading, Coleridge had immense reading. Pindar and Sophocles—as we all say so glibly, and often with so little discernment of the real import of what we are saying—had not many books; Shakespeare was no deep reader. True; but in the Greece of Pindar and Sophocles, in the England of Shakespeare, the poet lived in a current of ideas in the highest degree animating and nourishing to the creative power; society was, in the fullest measure, permeated by fresh thought, intelligent and alive. And this state of things is the true basis for the creative power's exercise, in this it finds its data, its materials, truly ready for its hand; all the books and reading in the world are only valuable as they are helps to this. Even when this does not actually exist, books and reading may enable a man to construct a kind of semblance of it in his own mind, a world of knowledge and intelligence in which he may live and work. This is by no means an equivalent to the artist for the nationally diffused life and thought of the epochs of Sophocles or Shakespeare; but, besides that it may be a means of preparation for such epochs, it does really constitute, if many share in it, a quickening and sustaining atmosphere of great value. Such an atmosphere the many-sided learning and the long and widely combined critical effort of Germany formed for Goethe, when he lived and worked. There was no national glow of life and thought there as in the Athens of Pericles[6] or the England of Elizabeth. That was the poet's weakness. But there was a sort of equivalent for it in the complete culture and unfettered thinking of a large body of Germans. That was his strength. In the England of the first quarter of this century there was neither a national glow of life and thought, such as we had in the age of Elizabeth, nor yet a culture and a force of learning and criticism such as were to be found in Germany. Therefore the creative power of poetry wanted, for success in the highest sense, materials and a basis; a thorough interpretation of the world was necessarily denied to it.

At first sight it seems strange that out of the immense stir of the French Revolution and its age should not have come a crop of works of genius equal to that which came out of the stir of the great productive time of Greece, or out of that of the Renascence, with its powerful episode the Reformation. But the truth is that the stir of the French Revolution took a character which essentially distinguished it from such movements as these. These were, in the main, disinterestedly intellectual and spiritual movements; movements in which the human spirit looked for its satisfaction in itself and in the increase play of its own activity. The French Revolution took a political, practical character. The movement, which went on in France under the old *régime*, from 1700 to 1789, was far more really akin than that of the Revolution itself to the movement of the Renascence; the France of Voltaire and Rousseau told far more powerfully upon the mind of Europe than the France of the Revolution. Goethe reproached this last expressly with having "thrown quiet culture back." Nay, and the true key to how much in our Byron, even in our Wordsworth, is this!—that they had their source in a great movement of feeling, not in a great movement of mind. The French Revolution, however—that object of so much blind love and so much blind hatred—found undoubtedly its motive power in the intelligence of men, and not in their practical sense; this is what distinguishes it from the English Revolution of Charles the First's time. This is what makes it a more spiritual event than our Revolution, an event of much more powerful and worldwide interest, though practically less successful; it appeals to an order of ideas which are universal, certain, permanent. 1789 asked of a thing, Is it rational? 1642 asked of a thing, Is it legal? or, when it went furthest, Is it according to conscience? This is the English fashion, a fashion to be treated, within its own sphere, with the highest respect; for its success, within its own sphere, has been prodigious. But what is law in one place is not law in another; what is law here today is not law even here tomorrow; and as for conscience, what is binding on one man's conscience is not binding on another's. The old woman who threw her stool at the head of the surpliced minister in St. Giles's Church at Edinburgh[7] obeyed an impulse to which millions of the human race

---

6. Pericles (d. 429 B.C.), the leading statesman of Athens during a period of the city's most outstanding achievements in art, literature, and politics.

7. In 1637 rioting broke out in Scotland against a new kind of church service prescribed by Charles

may be permitted to remain strangers. But the prescriptions of reason are absolute, unchanging, of universal validity; *to count by tens is the easiest way of counting*—that is a proposition of which everyone, from here to the Antipodes, feels the force; at least I should say so if we did not live in a country where it is not impossible that any morning we may find a letter in the *Times* declaring that a decimal coinage is an absurdity.[8] That a whole nation should have been penetrated with an enthusiasm for pure reason, and with an ardent zeal for making its prescriptions triumph, is a very remarkable thing, when we consider how little of mind, or anything so worthy and quickening as mind, comes into the motives which alone, in general, impel great masses of men. In spite of the extravagant direction given to this enthusiasm, in spite of the crimes and follies in which it lost itself, the French Revolution derives from the force, truth, and universality of the ideas which it took for its law, and from the passion with which it could inspire a multitude for these ideas, a unique and still living power; it is—it will probably long remain—the greatest, the most animating event in history. And as no sincere passion for the things of the mind, even though it turn out in many respects an unfortunate passion, is ever quite thrown away and quite barren of good, France has reaped from hers one fruit—the natural and legitimate fruit though not precisely the grand fruit she expected: she is the country in Europe where *the people* is most alive.

But the mania for giving an immediate political and practical application to all these fine ideas of the reason was fatal. Here an Englishman is in his element: on this theme we can all go on for hours. And all we are in the habit of saying on it has undoubtedly a great deal of truth. Ideas cannot be too much prized in and for themselves, cannot be too much lived with; but to transport them abruptly into the world of politics and practice, violently to revolutionize this world to their bidding—that is quite another thing. There is the world of ideas and there is the world of practice; the French are often for suppressing the one and the English the other; but neither is to be suppressed. A member of the House of Commons said to me the other day: "That a thing is an anomaly, I consider to be no objection to it whatever." I venture to think he was wrong; that a thing is an anomaly *is* an objection to it, but absolutely and in the sphere of ideas: it is not necessarily, under such and such circumstances, or at such and such a moment, an objection to it in the sphere of politics and practice. Joubert[9] has said beautifully: "*C'est la force et le droit qui règlent toutes choses dans le monde; la force en attendant le droit.*"—"Force and right are the governors of this world; force till right is ready." *Force till right is ready*; and till right is ready, force, the existing order of things, is justified, is the legitimate ruler. But right

---

1. The riot was started by an old woman hurling a stool at a clergyman.
8. In 1863 a proposal in Parliament to introduce the French decimal system for weights and measures had provoked articles in the *Times* defending the English system (of ounces and pounds or inches and feet) as more practical.
9. Joseph Joubert (1754–1824), French moralist about whom Arnold wrote one of his *Essays in Criticism*.

is something moral, and implies inward recognition, free assent of the will; we are not ready for right—*right*, so far as we are concerned, is *not ready*—until we have attained this sense of seeing it and willing it. The way in which for us it may change and transform force, the existing order of things, and become, in its turn, the legitimate ruler of the world, should depend on the way in which, when our time comes, we see it and will it. Therefore for other people enamored of their own newly discerned right, to attempt to impose it upon us as ours, and violently to substitute their right for our force, is an act of tyranny, and to be resisted. It sets at nought the second great half of our maxim, *force till right is ready*. This was the grand error of the French Revolution; and its movement of ideas, by quitting the intellectual sphere and rushing furiously into the political sphere, ran, indeed a prodigious and memorable course, but produced no such intellectual fruit as the movement of ideas of the Renascence, and created, in opposition to itself, what I may call an *epoch of concentration*. The great force of that epoch of concentration was England; and the great voice of that epoch of concentration was Burke.[1] It is the fashion to treat Burke's writings on the French Revolution as superannuated and conquered by the event; as the eloquent but unphilosophical tirades of bigotry and prejudice. I will not deny that they are often disfigured by the violence and passion of the moment, and that in some directions Burke's view was bounded, and his observation therefore at fault. But on the whole, and for those who can make the needful corrections, what distinguishes these writings is their profound, permanent, fruitful, philosophical truth, They contain the true philosophy of an epoch of concentration, dissipate the heavy atmosphere which its own nature is apt to engender round it, and make its resistance rational instead of mechanical.

But Burke is so great because, almost alone in England, he brings thought to bear upon politics, he saturates politics with thought. It is his accident that his ideas were at the service of an epoch of concentration, not of an epoch of expansion; it is his characteristic that he so lived by ideas, and had such a source of them welling up within him, that he could float even an epoch of concentration and English Tory politics with them. It does not hurt him that Dr. Price[2] and the Liberals were enraged with him; it does not even hurt him that George the Third and the Tories were enchanted with him. His greatness is that he lived in a world which neither English Liberalism nor English Toryism is apt to enter—the world of ideas, not the world of catchwords and party habits. So far is it from being really true of him that he "to party gave up what was meant for mankind,"[3] that at the very end of his fierce struggle with the French Revolution, after all his invectives against its false pretensions, hollowness, and madness, with his sincere convictions of its mis-

---

1. Edmund Burke (1729–1797), prominent statesman and author of *Reflections on the French Revolution* (1790), which expressed the conservative opposition to revolutionary theories.

2. Richard Price (1723–1791), a pro-revolutionary clergyman who was an opponent of Burke's.

3. See Oliver Goldsmith's poem, *Retaliation* (1774).

chievousness, he can close a memorandum on the best means of combating it, some of the last pages[4] he ever wrote—the *Thoughts on French Affairs*, in December 1791—with these striking words:

> The evil is stated, in my opinion, as it exists. The remedy must be where power, wisdom, and information, I hope, are more united with good intentions than they can be with me. I have done with this subject, I believe, forever. It has given me many anxious moments for the last two years. *If a great change is to be made in human affairs, the minds of men will be fitted to it; the general opinions and feelings will draw that way. Every fear, every hope will forward it; and then they who persist in opposing this mighty current in human affairs, will appear rather to resist the decrees of Providence itself, than the mere designs of men. They will not be resolute and firm, but perverse and obstinate.*

That return of Burke upon himself has always seemed to me one of the finest things in English literature, or indeed in any literature. That is what I call living by ideas: when one side of a question has long had your earnest support, when all your feelings are engaged, when you hear all round you no language but one, when your party talks this language like a steam engine and can imagine no other—still to be able to think, still to be irresistibly carried, if so it be, by the current of thought to the opposite side of the question, and, like Balaam,[5] to be unable to speak anything *but what the Lord has put in your mouth.* I know nothing more striking, and I must add that I know nothing more un-English.

For the Englishman in general is like my friend the Member of Parliament, and believes, point-blank, that for a thing to be an anomaly is absolutely no objection to it whatever. He is like the Lord Auckland of Burke's day, who, in a memorandum on the French Revolution, talks of certain "miscreants, assuming the name of philosophers, who have presumed themselves capable of establishing a new system of society." The Englishman has been called a political animal, and he values what is political and practical so much that ideas easily become objects of dislike in his eyes, and thinkers, "miscreants," because ideas and thinkers have rashly meddled with politics and practice. This would be all very well if the dislike and neglect confined themselves to ideas transported out of their own sphere, and meddling rashly with practice; but they are inevitably extended to ideas as such, and to the whole life of intelligence; practice is everything, a free play of the mind is nothing. The notion of the free play of the mind upon all subjects being a pleasure in itself, being an object of desire, being an essential provider of elements without which a nation's spirit, whatever compensations it may have for them, must, in the long run, die of inanition, hardly enters

4. Arnold was mistaken, Burke continued to write for another 6 years after 1791. According to Arnold's editor, R. H. Super, the mistake was caused by misunderstanding a passage in one of Burke's letters.

5. Cf. Numbers 22.38.

into an Englishman's thoughts. It is noticeable that the word *curiosity*, which in other languages is used in a good sense, to mean, as a high and fine quality of man's nature, just this disinterested love of a free play the mind on all subjects, for its own sake—it is noticeable, I say, that bad and has in our language no sense of the kind, no sense but a rather exercise disparaging one. But criticism, real criticism, is essentially the know the best very quality. It obeys an instinct prompting it to try to practice, politic at is known and thought in the world, irrespectively of and thought as the nd everything of the kind; and to value knowledge other considerations w approach this best, without the intrusion of any think, little original symp tever. This is an instinct for which there is, I there was of it has undergo y in the practical English nature, and what suppression in the epoch of co a long benumbing period of blight and Revolution. entration which followed the French

But epochs of concentration cannot well endure forever; epochs of expansion, in the due course of things, follow them. Such an epoch of expansion seems to be opening in this country. In the first place all danger of a hostile forcible pressure of foreign ideas upon our practice has long disappeared; like the traveler in the fable, therefore, we begin to wear our cloak a little more loosely.[6] Then, with a long peace, the ideas of Europe steal gradually and amicably in, and mingle, though in infinitesimally small quantities at a time, with our own notions. Then, too, in spite of all that is said about the absorbing and brutalizing influence of our passionate material progress, it seems to me indisputable that this progress is likely, though not certain, to lead in the end to an apparition of intellectual life; and that man, after he has made himself perfectly comfortable and has now to determine what to do with himself next, may begin to remember that he has a mind, and that the mind may be made the source of great pleasure. I grant it is mainly the privilege of faith, at present, to discern this end to our railways, our business, and our fortune-making; but we shall see if, here as elsewhere, faith is not in the end the true prophet. Our ease, our traveling, and our unbounded liberty to hold just as hard and securely as we please to the practice to which our notions have given birth, all tend to beget an inclination to deal a little more freely with these notions themselves, to canvass them a little, to penetrate a little into their real nature. Flutterings of curiosity, in the foreign sense of the word, appear amongst us, and it is in these that criticism must look to find its account. Criticism first; a time of true creative activity, perhaps—which, as I have said, must inevitably be preceded amongst us by a time of criticism—hereafter, when criticism has done its work.

It is of the last importance that English criticism should clearly discern what rule for its course, in order to avail itself of the field now opening to it, and to produce fruit for the future, it ought to take. The

---

6. See Aesop's fable of the wind and the sun.

rule may be summed up in one word—*disinterestedness*.[7] And how is criticism to show disinterestedness? By keeping aloof from what is called "the practical view of things"; by resolutely following the law of its own nature, which is to be a free play of the mind on all subjects which it touches. By steadily refusing to lend itself to any of those ulterior, political, practical considerations about ideas, which plenty of people will be sure to attach to them, which perhaps ought often to be attached to them, which in this country at any rate are certainly attached to them quite sufficiently, but which criticism has really nothing to do with. Its business is, as I have said, simply to know the best that is known and thought in the world, and by in its turn making this known, to create a current of true and fresh ideas. Its business is to do this with inflexible honesty, with due ability; but its business is to do no more, and to leave alone all questions of practical consequences and applications, questions which will never fail to have due prominence given to them. Else criticism, besides being really false to its own nature, merely continues in the old rut which it has hitherto followed in this country, and will certainly miss the chance now given to it. For what is at present the bane of criticism in this country? It is that practical considerations cling to it and stifle it. It subserves interests not its own. Our organs of criticism are organs of men and parties having practical ends to serve, and with them those practical ends are the first thing and the play of mind the second; so much play of mind as is compatible with the prosecution of those practical ends is all that is wanted. An organ like the *Revue des Deux Mondes*,[8] having for its main function to understand and utter the best that is known and thought in the world, existing, it may be said, as just an organ for a free play of the mind, we have not. But we have the *Edinburgh Review*, existing as an organ of the old Whigs, and for as much play of mind as may suit its being that; we have the *Quarterly Review*, existing as an organ of the Tories, and for as much play of mind as may suit its being that; we have the *British Quarterly Review*, existing as an organ of the political Dissenters, and for as much play of mind as may suit its being that; we have the *Times*, existing as an organ of the common, satisfied, well-to-do Englishman, and for as much play of mind as may suit its being that. And so on through all the various fractions, political and religious, of our society; every fraction has, as such, its organ of criticism, but the notion of combining all fractions in the common pleasure of a free disinterested play of mind meets with no favor. Directly this play of mind wants to have more scope, and to forget the pressure of practical considerations a little, it is checked, it is made to feel the chain. We saw this the other day in the extinction, so much to be regretted, of the *Home and Foreign Review*.[9] Perhaps in no organ of criticism in this country was there so much knowledge, so much play

7. This key word in Arnold's argument connotes independence and objectivity of mind. It should not be confused, as it often is, with mere lack of interest.

8. An international magazine of exceptionally high quality, founded in Paris in 1829.
9. A liberal Catholic periodical, founded in 1862, which ceased publication in 1864.

of mind; but these could not save it. The *Dublin Review* subordinates play of mind to the practical business of English and Irish Catholicism, and lives. It must needs be that men should act in sects and parties, that each of these sects and parties should have its organ, and should make this organ subserve the interests of its action; but it would be well, too, that there should be a criticism, not the minister of these interests, not their enemy, but absolutely and entirely independent of them. No other criticism will ever attain any real authority or make any real way towards its end—the creating a current of true and fresh ideas.

It is because criticism has so little kept in the pure intellectual sphere, has so little detached itself from practice, has been so directly polemical and controversial, that it has so ill accomplished, in this country, its best spiritual work, which is to keep man from a self-satisfaction which is retarding and vulgarizing, to lead him towards perfection, by making his mind dwell upon what is excellent in itself, and the absolute beauty and fitness of things. A polemical practical criticism makes men blind even to the ideal imperfection of their practice, makes them willingly assert its ideal perfection, in order the better to secure it against attack; and clearly this is narrowing and baneful for them. If they were reassured on the practical side, speculative considerations of ideal perfection they might be brought to entertain, and their spiritual horizon would thus gradually widen. Sir Charles Adderley[1] says to the Warwickshire farmers:

> Talk of the improvement of breed! Why, the race we ourselves represent, the men and women, the old Anglo-Saxon race, are the best breed in the whole world. . . . The absence of a too enervating climate, too unclouded skies, and a too luxurious nature, has produced so vigorous a race of people, and has rendered us so superior to all the world.

Mr. Roebuck[2] says to the Sheffield cutlers:

> I look around me and ask what is the state of England? Is not property safe? Is not every man able to say what he likes? Can you not walk from one end of England to the other in perfect security? I ask you whether, the world over or in past history, there is anything like it? Nothing. I pray that our unrivaled happiness may last.

Now obviously there is a peril for poor human nature in words and thoughts of such exuberant self-satisfaction, until we find ourselves safe in the streets of the Celestial City.

> *Das wenige verschwindet leicht dem Blicke*
> *Der vorwärts sieht, wie viel noch übrig bleibt—*[3]

---

1. 1814–1905; conservative politician and wealthy landowner.
2. John Arthur Roebuck (1801–1879), radical politician and representative in Parliament for the industrial city of Sheffield.
3. Goethe's *Iphigenie auf Tauris* 1.2.91–92.

says Goethe; "the little that is done seems nothing when we look forward and see how much we have yet to do." Clearly this is a better line of reflection for weak humanity, so long as it remains on this earthly field of labor and trial.

But neither Sir Charles Adderley nor Mr. Roebuck is by nature inaccessible to considerations of this sort. They only lose sight of them owing to the controversial life we all lead, and the practical form which all speculation takes with us. They have in view opponents whose aim is not ideal, but practical; and in their zeal to uphold their own practice against these innovators, they go so far as even to attribute to this practice an ideal perfection. Somebody has been wanting to introduce a six-pound franchise,[4] or to abolish church-rates, or to collect agricultural statistics by force, or to diminish local self-government. How natural, in reply to such proposals, very likely improper or ill-timed, to go a little beyond the mark and to say stoutly, "Such a race of people as we stand, so superior to all the world! The old Anglo-Saxon race, the best breed in the whole world! I pray that our unrivaled happiness may last! I ask you whether, the world over or in past history, there is anything like it?" And so long as criticism answers this dithyramb by insisting that the old Anglo-Saxon race would be still more superior to all others if it had no church-rates, or that our unrivaled happiness would last yet longer with a six-pound franchise, so long will the strain, "The best breed in the whole world!" swell louder and louder, everything ideal and refining will be lost out of sight, and both the assailed and their critics will remain in a sphere, to say the truth, perfectly unvital, a sphere in which spiritual progression is impossible. But let criticism leave church-rates and the franchise alone, and in the most candid spirit, without a single lurking thought of practical innovation, confront with our dithyramb this paragraph on which I stumbled in a newspaper immediately after reading Mr. Roebuck:

> A shocking child murder has just been committed at Nottingham. A girl named Wragg left the workhouse there on Saturday morning with her young illegitimate child. The child was soon afterwards found dead on Mapperly Hills, having been strangled. Wragg is in custody.

Nothing but that; but, in juxtaposition with the absolute eulogies of Sir Charles Adderley and Mr. Roebuck, how eloquent, how suggestive are those few lines! "Our old Anglo-Saxon breed, the best in the whole world!"—how much that is harsh and ill-favored there is in this best! Wragg! If we are to talk of ideal perfection, of "the best in the whole world," has anyone reflected what a touch of grossness in our race, what an original shortcoming in the more delicate spiritual perceptions, is shown by the natural growth amongst us of such hideous names—Hig-

---

4. A radical proposal to extend the right to vote to anyone owning land worth £6 annual rent.   "Church-rates": taxes supporting the Church of England.

ginbottom, Stiggins, Bugg! In Ionia and Attica they were luckier in this respect than "the best race in the world"; by the Ilissus[5] there was no Wragg, poor thing! And "our unrivaled happiness"—what an element of grimness, bareness, and hideousness mixes with it and blurs it; the workhouse, the dismal Mapperly Hills[6]—how dismal those who have seen them will remember—the gloom, the smoke, the cold, the strangled illegitimate child! "I ask you whether, the world over or in past history, there is anything like it?" Perhaps not, one is inclined to answer; but at any rate, in that case, the world is very much to be pitied. And the final touch—short, bleak and inhuman: *Wragg is in custody.* The sex lost in the confusion of our unrivaled happiness; or (shall I say?) the superfluous Christian name lopped off by the straightforward vigor of our old Anglo-Saxon breed! There is profit for the spirit in such contrasts as this; criticism serves the cause of perfection by establishing them. By eluding sterile conflict, by refusing to remain in the sphere where alone narrow and relative conceptions have any worth and validity, criticism may diminish its momentary importance, but only in this way has it a chance of gaining admittance for those wider and more perfect conceptions to which all its duty is really owed. Mr. Roebuck will have a poor opinion of an adversary who replies to his defiant songs of triumph only by murmuring under his breath, *Wragg is in custody;* but in no other way will these songs of triumph be induced gradually to moderate themselves, to get rid of what in them is excessive and offensive, and to fall into a softer and truer key.

It will be said that it is a very subtle and indirect action which I am thus prescribing for criticism, and that, by embracing in this manner the Indian virtue of detachment and abandoning the sphere of practical life, it condemns itself to a slow and obscure work. Slow and obscure it may be, but it is the only proper work of criticism. The mass of mankind will never have any ardent zeal for seeing things as they are; very inadequate ideas will always satisfy them. On these inadequate ideas reposes, and must repose, the general practice of the world. That is as much as saying that whoever sets himself to see things as they are will find himself one of a very small circle; but it is only by this small circle resolutely doing its own work that adequate ideas will ever get current at all. The rush and roar of practical life will always have a dizzying and attracting effect upon the most collected spectator, and tend to draw him into its vortex; most of all will this be the case where that life is so powerful as it is in England. But it is only by remaining collected, and refusing to lend himself to the point of view of the practical man, that the critic can do the practical man any service, and it is only by the greatest sincerity in pursuing his own course, and by at last convincing even the practical man of his sincerity, that he can escape misunderstandings which perpetually threaten him.

For the practical man is not apt for fine distinctions, and yet in these

---

5. A stream in Attica, Greece.
6. Adjacent to the coal-mining and industrial area

of Nottingham (later associated with the writings of D. H. Lawrence).

distinctions truth and the highest culture greatly find their account. But
it is not easy to lead a practical man—unless you reassure him as to your
practical intentions, you have no chance of leading him—to see that a
thing which he has always been used to look at from one side only,
which he greatly values, and which, looked at from that side, quite
deserves, perhaps, all the prizing and admiring which he bestows upon
it—that this thing, looked at from another side, may appear much less
beneficent and beautiful, and yet retain all its claims to our practical
allegiance. Where shall we find language innocent enough, how shall
we make the spotless purity of our intentions evident enough, to enable
us to say to the political Englishman that the British Constitution itself,
which, seen from the practical side, looks such a magnificent organ of
progress and virtue, seen from the speculative side—with its compro-
mises, its love of facts, its horror of theory, its studied avoidance of clear
thoughts—that, seen from this side, our august Constitution sometimes
looks—forgive me, shade of Lord Somers![7]—a colossal machine for the
manufacture of Philistines?[8] How is Cobbett[9] to say this and not be misunderstood, blackened as he is with the smoke of a lifelong conflict in
the field of political practice? how is Mr. Carlyle to say it and not be
misunderstood, after his furious raid into this field with his *Latter-day
Pamphlets?* how is Mr. Ruskin, after his pugnacious political economy?[1]
I say, the critic must keep out of the region of immediate practice in the
political, social, humanitarian sphere if he wants to make a beginning
for that more free speculative treatment of things, which may perhaps
one day make its benefits felt even in this sphere, but in a natural and
thence irresistible manner.

* * *

If I have insisted so much on the course which criticism must take
where politics and religion are concerned, it is because, where these
burning matters are in question, it is most likely to go astray. I have
wished, above all, to insist on the attitude which criticism should adopt
towards things in general; on its right tone and temper of mind. But then
comes another question as to the subject matter which literary criticism
should most seek. Here, in general, its course is determined for it by the
idea which is the law of its being; the idea of a disinterested endeavor to
learn and propagate the best that is known and thought in the world,
and thus to establish a current of fresh and true ideas. By the very nature
of things, as England is not all the world, much of the best that is known
and thought in the world cannot be of English growth, must be foreign;
by the nature of things, again, it is just this that we are least likely to

---

7. John Somers (1651–1716), statesman responsible for formulating the Declaration of Rights.
8. The unenlightened middle classes whose opposition to the men of culture is parallel to the biblical tribe which fought against the people of Israel,
"the children of light." Arnold's repeated use of
this parallel has established the term in our lan-

guage.
9. William Cobbett (1762–1835), vehement
reformer whose political position anticipated that
of Dickens.
1. Reference to *Unto this Last* (1862) in which
Ruskin shifted from art criticism to an attack on
traditional theories of economics.

know, while English thought is streaming in upon us from all sides, and takes excellent care that we shall not be ignorant of its existence. The English critic of literature, therefore, must dwell much on foreign thought, and with particular heed on any part of it, which, while significant and fruitful in itself, is for any reason specially likely to escape him. Again, judging is often spoken of as the critic's one business, and so in some sense it is; but the judgment which almost insensibly forms itself in a fair and clear mind, along with fresh knowledge, is the valuable one; and thus knowledge, and ever fresh knowledge, must be the critic's great concern for himself. And it is by communicating fresh knowledge, and letting his own judgment pass along with it—but insensibly, and in the second place, not the first, as a sort of companion and clue, not as an abstract lawgiver—that the critic will generally do most good to his readers. Sometimes, no doubt, for the sake of establishing an author's place in literature, and his relation to a central standard (and if this is not done, how are we to get at our *best in the world?*) criticism may have to deal with a subject matter so familiar that fresh knowledge is out of the question, and then it must be all judgment; an enunciation and detailed application of principles. Here the great safeguard is never to let oneself become abstract, always to retain an intimate and lively consciousness of the truth of what one is saying, and, the moment this fails us, to be sure that something is wrong. Still under all circumstances, this mere judgment and application of principles is, in itself, not the most satisfactory work to the critic; like mathematics, it is tautological, and cannot well give us, like fresh learning, the sense of creative activity.

But stop, some one will say; all this talk is of no practical use to us whatever; this criticism of yours is not what we have in our minds when we speak of criticism; when we speak of critics and criticism, we mean critics and criticism of the current English literature of the day; when you offer to tell criticism its function, it is to this criticism that we expect you to address yourself. I am sorry for it, for I am afraid I must disappoint these expectations. I am bound by my own definition of criticism: *a disinterested endeavor to learn and propagate the best that is known and thought in the world.* How much of current English literature comes into this "best that is known and thought in the world"? Not very much I fear; certainly less, at this moment, than of the current literature of France or Germany. Well, then, am I to alter my definition of criticism, in order to meet the requirements of a number of practicing English critics, who, after all, are free in their choice of a business? That would be making criticism lend itself just to one of those alien practical considerations, which, I have said, are so fatal to it. One may say, indeed, to those who have to deal with the mass—so much better disregarded—of current English literature, that they may at all events endeavor, in dealing with this, to try it, so far as they can, by the standard of the best that is known and thought in the world; one may say, that to get anywhere near this standard, every critic should try and possess one great literature, at least, besides his own; and the more unlike his own, the better. But, after all, the criticism I am really concerned with—the criticism which alone can much help us for the future, the criticism which, throughout Europe, is at the present day meant, when so much stress is laid on the importance of criticism and the critical spirit—is a criticism which regards Europe as being, for intellectual and spiritual purposes, one great confederation, bound to a joint action and working to a common result, and whose members have, for their proper outfit, a knowledge of Greek, Roman, and Eastern antiquity, and of one another. Special, local, and temporary advantages being put out of account, that modern nation will in the intellectual and spiritual sphere make most progress, which most thoroughly carries out this program. And what is that but saying that we too, all of us, as individuals, the more thoroughly we carry it out, shall make the more progress?

There is so much inviting us!—what are we to take? what will nourish us in growth towards perfection? That is the question which, with the immense field of life and of literature lying before him, the critic has to answer; for himself first, and afterwards for others. In this idea of the critic's business the essays brought together in the following pages have had their origin; in this idea, widely different as are their subjects, they have, perhaps, their unity.

I conclude with what I said at the beginning: to have the sense of creative activity is the great happiness and the great proof of being alive, and it is not denied to criticism to have it; but then criticism must be sincere, simple, flexible, ardent, ever widening its knowledge. Then it may have, in no contemptible measure, a joyful sense of creative activity; a sense which a man of insight and conscience will prefer to what he might derive from a poor, starved, fragmentary, inadequate creation. And at some epochs no other creation is possible.

Still, in full measure, the sense of creative activity belongs only to genuine creation; in literature we must never forget that. But what true man of letters ever can forget it? It is no such common matter for a gifted nature to come into possession of a current of true and living ideas, and to produce amidst the inspiration of them, that we are likely to underrate it. The epochs of Aeschylus and Shakespeare make us feel their preeminence. In an epoch like those is, no doubt, the true life of literature; there is the promised land, towards which criticism can only beckon. That promised land it will not be ours to enter, and we shall die in the wilderness: but to have desired to enter it, to have saluted it from afar, is already, perhaps, the best distinction among contemporaries; it will certainly be the best title to esteem with posterity.

1864, 1865

From Maurice de Guérin[1]

[A *Definition of Poetry*]

The grand power of poetry is its interpretative power; by which I mean, not a power of drawing out in black and white an explanation of the mystery of the universe, but the power of so dealing with things as to awaken in us a wonderfully full, new, and intimate sense of them, and of our relations with them. When this sense is awakened in us, as to objects without us, we feel ourselves to be in contact with the essential nature of those objects, to be no longer bewildered and oppressed by them, but to have their secret, and to be in harmony with them; and this feeling calms and satisfies us as no other can. Poetry, indeed, interprets in another way besides this; but one of its two ways of interpreting, of exercising its highest power, is by awakening this sense in us. I will not now inquire whether this sense is illusive, whether it can be proved not to be illusive, whether it does absolutely make us possess the real nature of things; all I say is, that poetry can awaken it in us, and that to awaken it is one of the highest powers of poetry. The interpretations of science do not give us this intimate sense of objects as the interpretations of poetry give it; they appeal to a limited faculty, and not to the whole man. * * *

I have said that poetry interprets in two ways; it interprets by expressing, with magical felicity, the physiognomy and movement of the outward world, and it interprets by expressing, with inspired conviction, the ideas and laws of the inward world of man's moral and spiritual nature. In other words, poetry is interpretative both by having *natural magic* in it, and by having *moral profundity*. In both ways it illuminates man; it gives him a satisfying sense of reality; it reconciles him with himself and the universe. Thus Aeschylus's "drásanti pathein"[2] and his "anērithmon gélasma"[3] are alike interpretative. Shakespeare interprets both when he says,

> Full many a glorious morning have I seen,
> Flatter the mountaintops with sovereign eye;[4]

and when he says,

> There's a divinity that shapes our ends,
> Rough-hew them as we will.[5]

These great poets unite in themselves the faculty of both kinds of interpretation, the naturalistic and the moral. But it is observable that in the

---

1. 1810–1839; a minor French poet. The essay was included in *Essays in Criticism: First Series*.
2. "The doer must suffer." From Aeschylus' *Choephori* (line 313).

3. "Countless laughter." From Aeschylus' *Prometheus Bound* (line 90).
4. Shakespeare, *Sonnets* 33.1–2.
5. *Hamlet* 5.2.10–11.

poets who unite both kinds, the latter (the moral) usually ends by making itself the master. In Shakespeare the two kinds seem wonderfully to balance one another; but even in him the balance leans; his expression tends to become too little sensuous and simple, too much intellectualized. The same thing may be yet more strongly affirmed of Lucretius and of Wordsworth. In Shelley there is not a balance of the two gifts, nor even a coexistence of them, but there is a passionate straining after them both, and this is what makes Shelley, as a man, so interesting; I will not now inquire how much Shelley achieves as a poet, but whatever he achieves, he in general fails to achieve natural magic in his expression; in Mr. Palgrave's charming *Treasury*[6] may be seen a gallery of his failures.[7] But in Keats and Guérin, in whom the faculty of naturalistic interpretations is overpoweringly predominant, the natural magic is perfect; when they speak of the world they speak like Adam naming by divine inspiration the creatures; their expression corresponds with the thing's essential reality.

1863, 1865

From Culture and Anarchy[1]

From *Chapter* 1. *Sweetness and Light*

The impulse of the English race towards moral development and self-conquest has nowhere so powerfully manifested itself as in Puritanism. Nowhere has Puritanism found so adequate an expression as in the religious organization of the Independents.[2] The modern Independents have a newspaper, the *Nonconformist*, written with great sincerity and ability. The motto, the standard, the profession of faith which this organ of theirs carries aloft, is: "The Dissidence of Dissent and the Protestantism

6. Francis Palgrave's anthology of poems, *The Golden Treasury*, was first published in 1861.

7. "Compare, for example, his *Lines Written in the Euganean Hills*, with Keats's *Ode to Autumn* . . . The latter piece *renders* Nature; the former *tries to render* her. I will not deny, however, that Shelley has natural magic in his rhythm; what I deny is, that he has it in his language. It always seems to me that the right sphere for Shelley's genius was the sphere of music, not of poetry; the medium of sounds he can master, but to master the more difficult medium of words he has neither intellectual force enough nor sanity enough" [Arnold's note].

1. As a critic of social life, Arnold sought to test Victorian institutions according to whether they seemed to him civilized. A characteristic quality of the civilized state of mind is summed up, for his purposes, in his formula "sweetness and light," a phrase suggesting reasonableness of temper and intellectual insight. Arnold derived the phrase from a fable contrasting the spider with the bee in Swift's *Battle of the Books*. The spider (representing a narrow, self-centered, and uncultured mind) spins out

of itself "nothing at all but flybane and cobweb." The bee (representing a cultured mind that has drawn nourishment from the humanist tradition) ranges far and wide and brings to its hive honey and also wax out of which candles may be made. Therefore the bee, Swift says, furnishes mankind "with the two noblest of things, which are sweetness and light."

The following excerpts illustrate aspects of Arnold's indictment of the middle classes for their lack of sweetness and light. The first and third expose the narrowness and dullness of middle-class Puritan religious institutions in both the 17th and 19th centuries. The second, "Doing As One Likes," shows the limitations of the middle-class political bias and the irresponsibility of *laissez faire*. Here Arnold is most close to Carlyle and Ruskin. These 3 extracts indicate why it has been said that Matthew Arnold discovered the foibles of Main Street 50 years before Sinclair Lewis exposed them in his novels of American life.

2. A 17th-century Puritan group (of which Cromwell was an adherent), allied with the Congregationalists.

of the Protestant religion." There is sweetness and light, and an ideal of
complete harmonious human perfection! One need not go to culture
and poetry to find language to judge it. Religion, with its instinct for
perfection, supplies language to judge it, language, too, which is in our
mouths every day. "Finally, be of one mind, united in feeling," says St.
Peter.[3] There is an ideal which judges the Puritan ideal: "The Dissidence of Dissent and the Protestantism of the Protestant religion!" And
religious organizations like this are what people believe in, rest in, would
give their lives for! Such, I say, is the wonderful virtue of even the beginnings of perfection, of having conquered even the plain faults of our
animality, that the religious organization which has helped us to do it
can seem to us something precious, salutary, and to be propagated, even
when it wears such a brand of imperfection on its forehead as this. And
men have got such a habit of giving to the language of religion a special
application, of making it a mere jargon, that for the condemnation which
religion itself passes on the shortcomings of their religious organizations
they have no ear; they are sure to cheat themselves and to explain this
condemnation away. They can only be reached by the criticism which
culture, like poetry, speaking of language not to be sophisticated, and
resolutely testing these organizations by the ideal of a human perfection
complete on all sides, applies to them.

But men of culture and poetry, it will be said, are again and again
failing, and failing conspicuously, in the necessary first stage to a harmonious perfection, in the subduing of the great obvious faults of our
animality, which it is the glory of these religious organizations to have
helped us to subdue. True, they do often so fail. They have often been
without the virtues as well as the faults of the Puritan; it has been one of
their dangers that they so felt the Puritan's faults that they too much
neglected the practice of his virtues. I will not, however, exculpate them
at the Puritan's expense. They have often failed in morality, and morality is indispensable. And they have been punished for their failure, as
the Puritan has been rewarded for his performance. They have been
punished wherein they erred; but their ideal of beauty, of sweetness and
light, and a human nature complete on all its sides, remains the true
ideal of perfection still; just as the Puritan's ideal of perfection remains
narrow and inadequate, although for what he did well he has been richly
rewarded. Notwithstanding the mighty results of the Pilgrim Fathers'
voyage, they and their standard of perfection are rightly judged when we
figure to ourselves Shakespeare or Virgil—souls in whom sweetness and
light, and all that in human nature is most humane, were eminent—
accompanying them on their voyage, and think what intolerable company Shakespeare and Virgil would have found them! In the same way
let us judge the religious organizations which we see all around us. Do
not let us deny the good and the happiness which they have accomplished; but do not let us fail to see clearly that their idea of human

3. Cf. 1 Peter 3.8.

perfection is narrow and inadequate, and that the Dissidence of Dissent and the Protestantism of the Protestant religion will never bring humanity to its true goal. As I said with regard to wealth: Let us look at the life of those who live in and for it—so I say with regard to the religious organizations. Look at the life imaged in such a newspaper the Non-conformist—a life of jealousy of the Establishment,[4] disputes, tea-meetings, openings of chapels, sermons; and then think of as an ideal of a human life completing itself on all sides, and aspiring with all its organs after sweetness, light, and perfection!

From *Chapter 2. Doing As One Likes*

* * *

When I began to speak of culture, I insisted on our bondage to machinery, on our proneness to value machinery as an end in itself, without looking beyond it to the end for which alone, in truth, it is valuable. Freedom, I said, was one of those things which we thus worshiped in itself, without enough regarding the ends for which freedom is to be desired. In our common notions and talk about freedom, we eminently show our idolatry of machinery. Our prevalent notion is—and I quoted a number of instances to prove it—that it is a most happy and important thing for a man merely to be able to do as he likes. On what he is to do when he is thus free to do as he likes, we do not lay so much stress. Our familiar praise of the British Constitution under which we live, is that it is a system of checks—a system which stops and paralyzes any power in interfering with the free action of individuals. To this effect Mr. Bright,[5] who loves to walk in the old ways of the Constitution, said forcibly in one of his great speeches, what many other people are every day saying less forcibly, that the central idea of English life and politics is *the assertion of personal liberty*. Evidently this is so; but evidently, also, as feudalism, which with its ideas, and habits of subordination was for many centuries silently behind the British Constitution, dies out, and we are left with nothing but our system of checks, and our notion of its being the great right and happiness of an Englishman to do as far as possible what he likes, we are in danger of drifting towards anarchy. We have not the notion, so familiar on the Continent and to antiquity, of *the State*—the nation in its collective and corporate character, entrusted with stringent powers for the general advantage, and controlling individual wills in the name of an interest wider than that of individuals. We say, what is very true, that this notion is often made instrumental to tyranny; we say that a State is in reality made up of the individuals who compose it, and that every individual is the best judge of his own interests. Our leading class is an aristocracy, and no aristocracy likes the notion of a State-authority greater than itself, with a stringent administrative machinery superseding the decorative inutilities of

4. The Church of England or the Established Church.   5. John Bright, 19th-century orator and reformer.

lord-lieutenancy, deputy-lieutenancy, and the *posse comitatus*,[6] which are all in its own hands. Our middle class, the great representative of trade and Dissent, with its maxims of every man for himself in business, every man for himself in religion, dreads a powerful administration which might somehow interfere with it; and besides, it has its own decorative inutilities of vestrymanship and guardianship, which are to this class what lord-lieutenancy and the county magistracy are to the aristocratic class, and a stringent administration might either take these functions out of its hands, or prevent its exercising them in its own comfortable, independent manner, as at present.

Then as to our working class. This class, pressed constantly by the hard daily compulsion of material wants, is naturally the very center and stronghold of our national idea, that it is man's ideal right and felicity to do as he likes. I think I have somewhere related how M. Michelet[7] said to me of the people of France, that it was "a nation of barbarians civilized by the conscription." He meant that through their military service the idea of public duty and of discipline was brought to the mind of these masses, in other respects so raw and uncultivated. Our masses are quite as raw and uncultivated as the French; and so far from their having the idea of public duty and of discipline, superior to the individual's self-will, brought to their mind by a universal obligation of military service, such as that of the conscription—so far from their having this, the very idea of a conscription is so at variance with our English notion of the prime right and blessedness of doing as one likes, that I remember the manager of the Clay Cross works in Derbyshire told me during the Crimean war, when our want of soldiers was much felt and some people were talking of a conscription, that sooner than submit to a conscription the population of that district would flee to the mines, and lead a sort of Robin Hood life underground.

For a long time, as I have said, the strong feudal habits of subordination and deference continued to tell upon the working class. The modern spirit has now almost entirely dissolved those habits, and the anarchical tendency of our worship of freedom in and for itself, of our superstitious faith, as I say, in machinery, is becoming very manifest. More and more, because of this our blind faith in machinery, because of our want of light to enable us to look beyond machinery to the end for which machinery is valuable, this and that man, and this and that body of men, all over the country, are beginning to assert and put in practice an Englishman's right to do what he likes; his right to march where he likes, meet where he likes, enter where he likes, hoot as he likes, threaten as he likes, smash as he likes.[8] All this, I say, tends to anarchy; and though a number of excellent people, and particularly my friends of the Liberal or progressive party, as they call themselves, are kind enough to reassure

6. I.e., "power of the county"—a feudal method of enforcing law by local authorities instead of by agencies of the central government.
7. Jules Michelet (1798–1874), French historian.

8. Reference to the riots of 1866 in which a London mob demolished the iron railings enclosing Hyde Park.

us by saying that these are trifles, that a few transient outbreaks of rowdyism signify nothing, that our system of liberty is one which itself cures all the evils which it works, that the educated and intelligent classes stand in overwhelming strength and majestic repose, ready, like our military force in riots, to act at a moment's notice—yet one finds that one's Liberal friends generally say this because they have such faith in themselves and their nostrums, when they shall return, as the public welfare requires, to place and power. But this faith of theirs one cannot exactly share, when one has so long had them and their nostrums at work, and see that they have not prevented our coming to our present embarrassed condition. And one finds, also, that the outbreaks of rowdyism tend to become less and less of trifles, to become more frequent rather than less frequent; and that meanwhile our educated and intelligent classes remain in their majestic repose, and somehow or other, whatever happens, their overwhelming strength, like our military force in riots, never does act.

How indeed, *should* their overwhelming strength act, when the man who gives an inflammatory lecture, or breaks down the park railings, or invades a Secretary of State's office, is only following an Englishman's impulse to do as he likes; and our own conscience tells us that we ourselves have always regarded this impulse as something primary and sacred? Mr. Murphy[9] lectures at Birmingham, and showers on the Catholic population of that town "words," says the Home Secretary, "only fit to be addressed to thieves or murderers." What then? Mr. Murphy has his own reasons of several kinds. He suspects the Roman Catholic Church of designs upon Mrs. Murphy; and he says if mayors and magistrates do not care for their wives and daughters, he does. But, above all, he is doing as he likes; or, in worthier language, asserting his personal liberty. "I will carry out my lectures if they walk over my body as a dead corpse, and I say to the Mayor of Birmingham that he is my servant while I am in Birmingham, and as my servant he must do his duty and protect me." Touching and beautiful words, which find a sympathetic chord in every British bosom! The moment it is plainly put before us that a man is asserting his personal liberty, we are half disarmed; because we are believers in freedom, and not in some dream of a right reason to which the assertion of our freedom is to be subordinated. Accordingly, the Secretary of State had to say that although the lecturer's language was "only fit to be addressed to thieves or murderers," yet, "I do not think he is to be deprived, I do not think that anything I have said could justify the inference that he is to be deprived, of the right of protection in a place built by him for the purpose of these lectures; because the language was not language which afforded grounds for a criminal prosecution." No, nor to be silenced by Mayor, or Home Secretary, or any administrative authority on earth, simply on their notion of what is discreet and reasonable! This is in perfect consonance with our public opinion, and with our national love for the assertion of personal liberty.

9. An orator whose inflammatory anti-Catholic public speech *The Errors of the Roman Church* led to rioting in Birmingham and other cities in 1867.

* * *

From *Chapter 5. Porro Unum Est Necessarium*[1]

* * *

* * * Sweetness and light evidently have to do with the bent or side in humanity which we call Hellenic. Greek intelligence has obviously for its essence the instinct for what Plato calls the true, firm, intelligible law of things; the law of light, of seeing things as they are. Even in the ~tural sciences, where the Greeks had not time and means adequately they'v this instinct, and where we have gone a great deal further than ground o.is this instinct which is the root of the whole matter and the of the Greeks, 'r success; and this instinct the world has mainly learnt tion of it. Greek ar, uch as they are humanity's most signal manifesta-impulse to see things as they ~ Greek beauty, have their root in the same rest on fidelity to nature—the bes. ~ture—inasmuch as Greek art and beauty nation of what this best nature is. To ~y we work for sweetness and light, then, is only another way of saying that we work for Hellenism. But, oh! cry many people, sweetness and light are not enough; you must put strength or energy along with them, and make a kind of trinity of strength, sweetness and light, and then, perhaps, you may do some good. That is to say, we are to join Hebraism, strictness of the moral conscience, and manful walking by the best light we have, together with Hellenism, inculcate both, and rehearse the praises of both.

Or, rather, we may praise both in conjunction, but we must be careful to praise Hebraism most. "Culture," says an acute, though somewhat rigid critic, Mr. Sidgwick,[2] "diffuses sweetness and light. I do not undervalue these blessings, but religion gives fire and strength, and the world wants fire and strength even more than sweetness and light." By religion, let me explain, Mr. Sidgwick here means particularly that Puritanism on the insufficiency of which I have been commenting and to which he says I am unfair. Now, no doubt, it is possible to be a fanatical partisan of light and the instincts which push us to it, a fanatical enemy of strictness of moral conscience and the instincts which push us to it. A fanaticism of this sort deforms and vulgarizes the well-known work, in some respects so remarkable, of the late Mr. Buckle.[3] Such a fanaticism carries its own mark with it, in lacking sweetness; and its own penalty, in that, lacking sweetness, it comes in the end to lack light too. And the Greeks—the great exponents of humanity's bent for sweetness and light united, of its perception that the truth of things must be at the same time beauty—singularly escaped the fanaticism which we moderns, whether

---

1. Luke 10.42: "But one thing is needful." This chapter develops a contrast established in chap. 4 between *Hebraism* (Puritan morality and energetic devotion to work) and *Hellenism* (cultivation of the aesthetic and intellectual understanding of life). The Puritan middle classes, according to Arnold, think that the "one thing needful" is the Hebraic form of virtue.

2. Henry Sidgwick, philosopher (1838–1900), whose article on Arnold appeared in *Macmillan's Magazine*, August 1867.

3. Henry Thomas Buckle (1821–1862), author of *A History of Civilization*.

we Hellenize or whether we Hebraize, are so apt to show. They arrived—though failing, as has been said, to give adequate practical satisfaction to the claims of man's moral side—at the idea of a comprehensive adjustment of the claims of both the sides in man, the moral as well as the intellectual, of a full estimate of both, and of a reconciliation of both; an idea which is philosophically of the greatest value, and the best of lessons for us moderns. So we ought to have no difficulty in conceding to Mr. Sidgwick that manful walking by the best light one has—fire and strength as he calls it—has its high value as well as culture, the endeavor to see things in their truth and beauty, the pursuit of sweetness and light. But whether at this or that time, and to this or that, or persons, one ought to insist most on the praises of fire and, think, on on the praises of sweetness and light, must depend, on those particular the circumstances and needs of that particular indeed any glance at the persons. And all that we have been saying with the most respectable and world around us, shows that with the ruling force is now, and long has been, a Puritan strongest part of us, the ruling force is now, and long has been, a Puritan force—the care for fire and strength, strictness of conscience, Hebraism, rather than the care for sweetness and light, spontaneity of consciousness, Hellenism.

Well, then, what is the good of our now rehearsing the praises of fire and strength to ourselves, who dwell too exclusively on them already? When Mr. Sidgwick says so broadly, that the world wants fire and strength even more than sweetness and light, is he not carried away by a turn for broad generalization? does he not forget that the world is not all of one piece, and every piece with the same needs at the same time? It may be true that the Roman world at the beginning of our era, or Leo the Tenth's Court at the time of the Reformation, or French society in the eighteenth century,[4] needed fire and strength even more than sweetness and light. But can it be said that the Barbarians who overran the empire needed fire and strength even more than sweetness and light; or that the Puritans needed them more; or that Mr. Murphy, the Birmingham lecturer, and the Rev. W. Cattle[5] and his friends, need them more?

The Puritan's great danger is that he imagines himself in possession of a rule telling him the *unum necessarium*, or one thing needful, and that he then remains satisfied with a very crude conception of what this rule really is and what it tells him, thinks he has now knowledge and henceforth needs only to act, and, in this dangerous state of assurance and self-satisfaction, proceeds to give full swing to a number of the instincts of his ordinary self. Some of the instincts of his ordinary self he has, by the help of his rule of life, conquered; but others which he has not conquered by this help he is so far from perceiving to need subjugation, and to be instincts of an inferior self, that he even fancies it to be his

---

4. Societies representing an excess of sophisticated worldliness as at the courts of such a Roman emperor as Nero (A.D. 54–68), or Pope Leo X (1513–1521), or Louis XV (1715–1774).

5. A Nonconformist clergyman who was chairman of the anti-Catholic meeting addressed by Murphy in 1867. See "Doing As One Likes," above.

right a., duty, in virtue of having conquered a limited part of himself, to give u. hecked swing to the remainder. He is, I say, a victim of Hebraism, b .he tendency to cultivate strictness of conscience rather than spontanei. of consciousness. And what he wants is a larger conception of human .ature, showing him the number of other points at which his nature m. come to its best, besides the points which he himself knows and thi. of. There is no *unum necessarium*, or one thing needful, which can 1. human nature from the obligation of trying to come to its best at all the points. The real *unum necessarium* for us is to come to our best at all p.nts. Instead of our "one thing needful," justifying in us vulgarity, h.deo..ess, ignorance, violence—our vulgarwh.hideousness, ignorance, vi..ce, are really so many touchstones any rate, in which we one thing needful, d which prove that in the state, at force which encourages us to stand it is not all we want. And as the ground we have is Hebraism, so the f..ch and fast by the rule and back upon this rule, and to try the very gr. which encourages us to go stand, is Hellenism—a turn for giving our co. on which we appear to enlarging its range. And what I say is, not that F.lenism is always for everybody more wanted than Hebraism, but that fo. he Rev. W. Cattle at this particular moment, and for the great major. of us his fellow countrymen, it is more wanted.

* * *

1868, 1869

From The Study of Poetry[1]

"The future of poetry is immense, because in poetry, where it is worthy of its high destinies, our race, as time goes on, will find an ever surer and surer stay. There is not a creed which is not shaken, not an accredited dogma which is not shown to be questionable, not a received tradition which does not threaten to dissolve. Our religion has materialized itself in the fact, in the supposed fact; it has attached its emotion to the fact, and now the fact is failing it. But for poetry the idea is everything; the rest is a world of illusion, of divine illusion. Poetry attaches its emotion to the idea; the idea *is* the fact. The strongest part of our religion today is its unconscious poetry."

1. Aside from its vindication of the importance of literature, this essay is an interesting example of the variety of Arnold's own reading. To know literature in only one language seemed to him not to know literature. His personal *Notebooks* show that throughout his active life he continued to read books in French, German, Italian, Latin, and Greek. His favorite authors in these languages are used by him as a means of testing English poetry. The testing is sometimes a severe one. Readers may also protest that despite Arnold's own wit, his essay is limited by an incomplete recognition of the values of comic literature, a shortcoming abundantly evident in the discussion of Chaucer. Nevertheless, whether we agree or disagree with some of Arnold's verdicts, we can be attracted by the combination of traditionalism and impressionism on which these verdicts are based, and we can enjoy the memorable phrasemaking in which the verdicts are expressed. *The Study of Poetry* has been extraordinarily potent in shaping literary tastes in England and in America.

Let me be permitted to quote these words of my own, as uttering the thought which should, in my opinion, go with us and govern us in all our study of poetry. In the present work[2] it is the course of one great contributory stream to the world-river of poetry that we are invited to follow. We are here invited to trace the stream of English poetry. But whether we set ourselves, as here, to follow only one of the several streams that make the mighty river of poetry, or whether we seek to know them all, our governing thought should be the same. We should conceive of poetry worthily, and more highly than it has been the custom to conceive of it. We should conceive of it as capable of higher uses, and called to higher destinies, than those which in general men have assigned to it hitherto. More and more mankind will discover that we have to turn to poetry to interpret life for us, to console us, to sustain us. Without poetry, our science will appear incomplete; and most of what now passes with us for religion and philosophy will be replaced by poetry. Science, I say, will appear incomplete without it. For finely and truly does Wordsworth call poetry "the impassioned expression which is in the countenance of all science";[3] and what is a countenance without its expression? Again, Wordsworth finely and truly calls poetry "the breath and finer spirit of all knowledge": our religion, parading evidences such as those on which the popular mind relies now; our philosophy, pluming itself on its reasonings about causation and finite and infinite being; what are they but the shadows and dreams and false shows of knowledge? The day will come when we shall wonder at ourselves for having trusted to them, for having taken them seriously; and the more we perceive their hollowness, the more we shall prize "the breath and finer spirit of knowledge" offered to us by poetry.

But if we conceive thus highly of the destinies of poetry, we must also set our standard for poetry high, since poetry, to be capable of fulfilling such high destinies, must be poetry of a high order of excellence. We must accustom ourselves to a high standard and to a strict judgment. * * *

The best poetry is what we want; the best poetry will be found to have a power of forming, sustaining, and delighting us, as nothing else can. A clearer, deeper sense of the best in poetry, and of the strength and joy to be drawn from it, is the most precious benefit which we can gather from a poetical collection such as the present. And yet in the very nature and conduct of such a collection there is inevitably something which tends to obscure in us the consciousness of what our benefit should be, and to distract us from the pursuit of it. We should therefore steadily set it before our minds at the outset, and should compel ourselves to revert constantly to the thought of it as we proceed.

Yes; constantly in reading poetry, a sense for the best, the really excellent, and of the strength and joy to be drawn from it, should be present in our minds and should govern our estimate of what we read. But this

2. An anthology of English poetry for which Arnold's essay served as the introduction.
3. See Wordsworth's Preface to *Lyrical Ballads*.

real estimate, the only true one, is liable to be superseded, if we are not watchful, by two other kinds of estimate, the historic estimate and the personal estimate, both of which are fallacious. A poet or a poem may count to us historically, they may count to us on grounds personal to ourselves, and they may count to us really. They may count to us historically. The course of development of a nation's language, thought, and poetry, is profoundly interesting; and by regarding a poet's work as a stage in this course of development we may easily bring ourselves to make it of more importance as poetry than in itself it really is, we may come to use a language of quite exaggerated praise in criticizing it; in short, to overrate it. So arises in our poetic judgments the fallacy caused by the estimate which we may call historic. Then, again, a poet or a poem may count to us on grounds personal to ourselves. Our personal affinities, likings, and circumstances, have great power to sway our estimate of this or that poet's work, and to make us attach more importance to it as poetry than in itself it really possesses, because to us it is, or has been, of high importance. Here also we overrate the object of our interest, and apply to it a language of praise which is quite exaggerated. And thus we get the source of a second fallacy in our poetic judgments—the fallacy caused by an estimate which we may call personal.

*   *   *

* * * The historic estimate is likely in especial to affect our judgment and our language when we are dealing with ancient poets; the personal estimate when we are dealing with poets our contemporaries, or at any rate modern. The exaggerations due to the historic estimate are not in themselves, perhaps, of very much gravity. Their report hardly enters the general ear; probably they do not always impose even on the literary men who adopt them. But they lead to a dangerous abuse of language. So we hear Caedmon,[4] amongst our own poets, compared to Milton. I have already noticed the enthusiasm of one accomplished French critic for "historic origins."[5] Another eminent French critic, M. Vitet, comments upon that famous document of the early poetry of his nation, the *Chanson de Roland*.[6] It is indeed a most interesting document. The *joculator* or *jongleur*[7] Taillefer, who was with William the Conqueror's army at Hastings, marched before the Norman troops, so said the tradition, singing "of Charlemagne and of Roland and of Oliver, and of the vassals who died at Roncevaux"; and it is suggested that in the *Chanson de Roland* by one Turoldus or *Théroulde*, a poem preserved in a manuscript of the twelfth century in the Bodleian Library at Oxford, we have certainly the matter, perhaps even some of the words, of the chant which Taillefer sang. The poem has vigor and freshness; it is not without pathos.

---

4. 7th-century Old English poet.

5. Charles d'Héricault, a critic cited earlier, in a passage omitted here. Arnold had mildly reprimanded him for his "historical" bias in praising a 15th-century poet, Clément Marot, at the expense of such classical 17th-century poets as Racine.

6. 11th-century epic poem in Old French which tells of the wars of Charlemagne against the Moors in Spain, and of the bravery of the French leaders, Roland and Oliver.

7. I.e., minstrel.

But M. Vitet is not satisfied with seeing in it a document of some poetic value, and of very high historic and linguistic value; he sees in it a grand and beautiful work, a monument of epic genius. In its general design he finds the grandiose conception, in its details he finds the constant union of simplicity with greatness, which are the marks, he truly says, of the genuine epic, and distinguish it from the artificial epic of literary ages. One thinks of Homer; this is the sort of praise which is given to Homer, and justly given. Higher praise there cannot well be, and it is the praise due to epic poetry of the highest order only, and to no other. Let us try, then, the *Chanson de Roland* at its best. Roland, mortally wounded, lays himself down under a pine tree, with his face turned towards Spain and the enemy—

> *De plusurs choses à remembrer li prist,*
> *De tantes teres cume li bers cunquist,*
> *De dulce France, des humes de sun lign,*
> *De Carlemagne sun seignor ki l'nurrit.*[8]

That is primitive work, I repeat, with an undeniable poetic quality of its own. It deserves such praise, and such praise is sufficient for it. But now turn to Homer—

> Hōs pháto toùs d'ēdē kátechen phusízoos aîa
> ēn Lakedaímoni aûthi phílē en patrídi gaíē.[9]

We are here in another world, another order of poetry altogether; here is rightly due such supreme praise as that which M. Vitet gives to the *Chanson de Roland.* If our words are to have any meaning, if our judgments are to have any solidity, we must not heap that supreme praise upon poetry of an order immeasurably inferior.

Indeed there can be no more useful help for discovering what poetry belongs to the class of the truly excellent, and can therefore do us most good, than to have always in one's mind lines and expressions of the great masters, and to apply them as a touchstone to other poetry. Of course we are not to require this other poetry to resemble them; it may be very dissimilar. But if we have any tact we shall find them, when we have lodged them well in our minds, an infallible touchstone for detecting the presence or absence of high poetic quality, and also the degree of this quality, in all other poetry which we may place beside them. Short passages, even single lines, will serve our turn quite sufficiently. Take the two lines which I have just quoted from Homer, the poet's comment on Helen's mention of her brothers—or take his

8. "'Then began he to call many things to remembrance—all the lands which his valor conquered and pleasant France, and the men of his lineage, and Charlemagne his liege lord who nourished him.' *Chanson de Roland* 3.939–42" [Arnold's note].

9. "'So said she; they long since in Earth's soft arms were reposing,/There, in their own dear land, their fatherland, Lacedaemon.' *Iliad* 3.243–44 (translated by Dr. Hawtrey)" [Arnold's note].

A deilō, tí sphōi dómen Pēléi ánakti
thnētō? humeis d'estòn agērō t' athanátō te.
ē hina dustēnoisi met' andrásin alge' echēton[1]

the address of Zeus to the horses of Peleus—or take finally his

Kaì sé géron, tò prìn mèn akoúomen olbion eînai:[2]

the words of Achilles to Priam, a suppliant before him. Take that incomparable line and a half of Dante, Ugolino's tremendous words—

Io no piangeva; sì dentro impietrai.
Piangevan elli . . .[3]

take the lovely words of Beatrice to Virgil—

Io son fatta da Dio, sua mercè, tale,
Che la vostra miseria non mi tange,
Nè fiamma d'esto incendio non m'assale . . .[4]

take the simple, but perfect, single line—

In la sua volontade è nostra pace.[5]

Take of Shakespeare a line or two of Henry the Fourth's expostulation with sleep—

Wilt thou upon the high and giddy mast
Seal up the shipboy's eyes, and rock his brains
In cradle of the rude imperious surge . . .[6]

and take, as well, Hamlet's dying request to Horatio—

If thou didst ever hold me in thy heart,
Absent thee from felicity awhile,
And in this harsh world draw thy breath in pain,
To tell my story . . .[7]

Take of Milton that Miltonic passage—

Darkened so, yet shone
Above them all the archangel; but his face
Deep scars of thunder had intrenched, and care
Sat on his faded cheek . . .[8]

add two such lines as—

1. " 'Ah, unhappy pair, why gave we you to King Peleus, to a mortal? but ye are without old age, and immortal. Was it that with men born to misery ye might have sorrow?' *Iliad* 17.443–45" [Arnold's note].
2. " 'Nay, and thou too, old man, in former days wast, as we hear, happy.' *Iliad* 14.543" [Arnold's note].
3. " 'I wailed not, so of stone I grew within; *they* wailed.' *Inferno* 33.49–50" [Arnold's note].
4. " 'Of such sort hath God, thanked be His mercy, made me, that your misery toucheth me not, neither doth the flame of this fire strike me.' *Inferno* 2.91–93" [Arnold's note].
5. " 'In His will is our peace.' *Paradiso* 3.85" [Arnold's note].
6. *2 Henry IV* 3.1.18–20.
7. *Hamlet* 5.2.357–60.
8. *Paradise Lost* 1.599–602.

> And courage never to submit or yield
> And what is else not to be overcome . . .[9]

and finish with the exquisite close to the loss of Proserpine, the loss

> . . . which cost Ceres all that pain
> To seek her through the world.[1]

These few lines, if we have tact and can use them, are enough even of themselves to keep clear and sound our judgments about poetry, to save us from fallacious estimates of it, to conduct us to a real estimate.

The specimens I have quoted differ widely from one another, but they have in common this: the possession of the very highest poetical quality. If we are thoroughly penetrated by their power, we shall find that we have acquired a sense enabling us, whatever poetry may be laid before us, to feel the degree in which a high poetical quality is present or wanting there. Critics give themselves great labor to draw out what in the abstract constitutes the characters of a high quality of poetry. It is much better simply to have recourse to concrete examples—to take specimens of poetry of the high, the very highest quality, and to say: The characters of a high quality of poetry are what is expressed *there*. They are far better recognized by being felt in the verse of the master, than by being perused in the prose of the critic. Nevertheless if we are urgently pressed to give some critical account of them, we may safely, perhaps, venture on laying down, not indeed how and why the characters arise, but where and in what they arise. They are in the matter and substance of the poetry, and they are in its manner and style. Both of these, the substance and matter on the one hand, the style and manner on the other, have a mark, an accent, of high beauty, worth, and power. But if we are asked to define this mark and accent in the abstract, our answer must be: No, for we should thereby be darkening the question, not clearing it. The mark and accent are as given by the substance and matter of that poetry, by the style and manner of that poetry, and of all other poetry which is akin to it in quality.

Only one thing we may add as to the substance and matter of poetry, guiding ourselves by Aristotle's profound observation that the superiority of poetry over history consists in its possessing a higher truth and a higher seriousness (philosophōteron kai spoudaióteron).[2] Let us add, therefore, to what we have said, this: that the substance and matter of the best poetry acquire their special character from possessing, in an eminent degree, truth and seriousness. We may add yet further, what is in itself evident, that to the style and manner of the best poetry their special character, their accent, is given by their diction, and, even yet more, by their movement. And though we distinguish between the two characters the two accents, of superiority, yet they are nevertheless vitally con-

9. *Ibid.* 1.108–9.　　　　　2. Aristotle, *Poetics* 9.
1. *Ibid.* 4.271–72.

nected one with the other. The superior character of truth and seriousness, in the matter and substance of the best poetry, is inseparable from
the superiority of diction and movement marking its style and manner.
The two superiorities are closely related, and are in steadfast proportion
one to the other. So far as high poetic truth and seriousness are wanting
to a poet's matter and substance, so far also, we may be sure, will a high
poetic stamp of diction and movement be wanting to his style and manner. In proportion as this high stamp of diction and movement, again,
is absent from a poet's style and manner, we shall find, also, that high
poetic truth and seriousness are absent from his substance and matter.

So stated, these are but dry generalities; their whole force lies in their
application. And I could wish every student of poetry to make the application of them for himself. Made by himself, the application would
impress itself upon his mind far more deeply than made by me. Neither
will my limits allow me to make any full application of the generalities
above propounded; but in the hope of bringing out, at any rate, some
significance in them, and of establishing an important principle more
firmly by their means, I will, in the space which remains to me, follow
rapidly from the commencement the course of our English poetry with
them in my view.

*   *   *

Chaucer's * * * poetical importance does not need the assistance of
the historic estimate; it is real. He is a genuine source of joy and strength,
which is flowing still for us and will flow always. He will be read, as
time goes on, far more generally than he is read now. His language is a
cause of difficulty for us; but so also, and I think in quite as great a
degree, is the language of Burns. In Chaucer's case, as in that of Burns,
it is a difficulty to be unhesitatingly accepted and overcome.

If we ask ourselves wherein consists the immense superiority of Chaucer's poetry over the romance poetry—why it is that in passing from this
to Chaucer we suddenly feel ourselves to be in another world, we shall
find that his superiority is both in the substance of his poetry and in the
style of his poetry. His superiority in substance is given by his large, free,
simple, clear yet kindly view of human life—so unlike the total want, in
the romance poets, of all intelligent command of it. Chaucer has not
their helplessness; he has gained the power to survey the world from a
central, a truly human point of view. We have only to call to mind the
Prologue to *The Canterbury Tales*. The right comment upon it is Dryden's: "It is sufficient to say, according to the proverb, that *here is God's
plenty*." And again: "He is a perpetual fountain of good sense."[3] It is by
a large, free, sound representation of things, that poetry, this high criticism of life, has truth of substance; and Chaucer's poetry has truth of
substance.

3. Both quotations are from Dryden's preface to his *Fables* (1700).

Of his style and manner, if we think first of the romance poetry and then of Chaucer's divine liquidness of diction, his divine fluidity of movement, it is difficult to speak temperately. They are irresistible, and justify all the rapture with which his successors speak of his "gold dew-drops of speech."[4] Johnson misses the point entirely when he finds fault with Dryden for ascribing to Chaucer the first refinement of our numbers, and says that Gower[5] also can show smooth numbers and easy rhymes. The refinement of our numbers means something far more than this. A nation may have versifiers with smooth numbers and easy rhymes, and yet may have no real poetry at all. Chaucer is the father of our splendid English poetry; he is our "well of English undefiled,"[6] because by the lovely charm of his diction, the lovely charm of his movement, he makes an epoch and founds a tradition. In Spenser, Shakespeare, Milton, Keats, we can follow the tradition of the liquid diction, the fluid movement, of Chaucer; at one time it is his liquid diction of which in these poets we feel the virtue, and at another time it is his fluid movement. And the virtue is irresistible.

Bounded as is my space, I must yet find room for an example of Chaucer's virtue, as I have given examples to show the virtue of the great classics. I feel disposed to say that a single line is enough to show the charm of Chaucer's verse; that merely one line like this—

O martyr souded[7] in virginitee!

has a virtue of manner and movement such as we shall not find in all the verse of romance poetry—but this is saying nothing. The virtue is such as we shall not find, perhaps, in all English poetry, outside the poets whom I have named as the special inheritors of Chaucer's tradition. A single line, however, is too little if we have not the strain of Chaucer's verse well in our memory; let us take a stanza. It is from *The Prioress's Tale*, the story of the Christian child murdered in a Jewry—

> My throte is cut unto my nekke-bone
> Saidè this child, and as by way of kinde
> I should have deyd, yea, longè time agone;
> But Jesu Christ, as ye in bookès finde,
> Will that his glory last and be in minde,
> And for the worship of his mother dere
> Yet may I sing O *Alma* loud and clere.

Wordsworth has modernized this Tale, and to feel how delicate and evanescent is the charm of verse, we have only to read Wordsworth's first three lines of this stanza after Chaucer's—

---

4. *The Life of Our Lady*, a poem by John Lydgate (ca. 1370-ca. 1451).

5. John Gower (ca. 1325–1408), friend of Chaucer and author of the *Confessio Amantis*, a long poem in octosyllabic couplets.

6. Said of Chaucer by Spenser (*Faerie Queene* 4.2.32).

7. "The French *soudé*: soldered, fixed fast" [Arnold's note]. The line is from the Prioress's Tale (line 127): Chaucer wrote "souded to" rather than "souded in."

> My throat is cut unto the bone, I trow,
> Said this young child, and by the law of kind
> I should have died, yea, many hours ago.

The charm is departed. It is often said that the power of liquidness and fluidity in Chaucer's verse was dependent upon a free, a licentious dealing with language, such as is now impossible; upon a liberty, such as Burns too enjoyed, of making words like *neck*, *bird*, into a dissyllable by adding to them, and words like *cause*, *rhyme*, into a dissyllable by sounding the *e* mute. It is true that Chaucer's fluidity is conjoined with this liberty, and is admirably served by it; but we ought not to say that it was dependent upon it. It was dependent upon his talent. Other poets with a like liberty do not attain to the fluidity of Chaucer; Burns himself does not attain to it. Poets, again, who have a talent akin to Chaucer's, such as Shakespeare or Keats, have known how to attain to his fluidity without the like liberty.

And yet Chaucer is not one of the great classics. His poetry transcends and effaces, easily and without effort, all the romance poetry of Catholic Christendom; it transcends and effaces all the English poetry contemporary with it, it transcends and effaces all the English poetry subsequent to it down to the age of Elizabeth. Of such avail is poetic truth of substance, in its natural and necessary union with poetic truth of style. And yet, I say, Chaucer is not one of the great classics. He has not their accent. What is wanting to him is suggested by the mere mention of the name of the first great classic of Christendom, the immortal poet who died eighty years before Chaucer—Dante. The accent of such verse as

In la sua volontade è nostra pace . . .

is altogether beyond Chaucer's reach; we praise him, but we feel that this accent is out of the question for him. It may be said that it was necessarily out of the reach of any poet in the England of that stage of growth. Possibly; but we are to adopt a real, not a historic, estimate of poetry. However we may account for its absence, something is wanting, then, to the poetry of Chaucer, which poetry must have before it can be placed in the glorious class of the best. And there is no doubt what that something is. It is the spoudaiótes, the high and excellent seriousness, which Aristotle assigns as one of the grand virtues of poetry. The substance of Chaucer's poetry, his view of things and his criticism of life, has largeness, freedom, shrewdness, benignity; but it has not this high seriousness. Homer's criticism of life has it, Dante's has it, Shakespeare's has it. It is this chiefly which gives to our spirits what they can rest upon; and with the increasing demands of our modern ages upon poetry, this virtue of giving us what we can rest upon will be more and more highly esteemed. A voice from the slums of Paris, fifty or sixty years after Chaucer, the voice of poor Villon[8] out of his life of riot and crime, has at its

---

8. François Villon (1431–1484), French poet and vagabond.

happy moments (as, for instance, in the last stanza of *La Belle Heaul-mière*)[9] more of this important poetic virtue of seriousness than all the productions of Chaucer. But its apparition in Villon, and in men like Villon, is fitful; the greatness of the great poets, the power of their criticism of life, is that their virtue is sustained.

To our praise, therefore, of Chaucer as a poet there must be this limitation: he lacks the high seriousness of the great classics, and therewith an important part of their virtue. Still, the main fact for us to bear in mind about Chaucer is his sterling value according to that real estimate which we firmly adopt for all poets. He has poetic truth of substance, though he has not high poetic seriousness, and corresponding to his truth of substance he has an exquisite virtue of style and manner. With him is born our real poetry.

For my present purpose I need not dwell on our Elizabethan poetry, or on the continuation and close of this poetry in Milton. We all of us profess to be agreed in the estimate of this poetry; we all of us recognize it as great poetry, our greatest, and Shakespeare and Milton as our poetical classics. The real estimate, here, has universal currency. With the next age of our poetry divergency and difficulty begin. An historic estimate of that poetry has established itself; and the question is, whether it will be found to coincide with the real estimate.

The age of Dryden, together with our whole eighteenth century which followed it, sincerely believed itself to have produced poetical classics of its own, and even to have made advance, in poetry, beyond all its predecessors. Dryden regards as not seriously disputable the opinion "that the sweetness of English verse was never understood or practiced by our fathers."[1] Cowley could see nothing at all in Chaucer's poetry. Dryden heartily admired it, and, as we have seen, praised its matter admirably; but of its exquisite manner and movement all he can find to say is that "there is the rude sweetness of a Scotch tune in it, which is natural and pleasing, though not perfect."[2] Addison, wishing to praise Chaucer's numbers, compares them with Dryden's own. And all through the eighteenth century, and down even into our own times, the stereotyped phrase of approbation for good verse found in our early poetry has been, that it even approached the verse of Dryden, Addison, Pope, and Johnson.

Are Dryden and Pope poetical classics? Is the historic estimate, which represents them as such, and which has been so long established that it cannot easily give way, the real estimate? Wordsworth and Coleridge, as is well known, denied it; but the authority of Wordsworth and Coleridge

---

9. "The name *Heaulmière* is said to be derived from a headdress (helm) worn as a mask by courtesans. In Villon's ballad, a poor old creature of this class laments her days of youth and beauty. The last stanza of the ballad runs thus—'*Ainsi le bon temps regretons / Entre nous, pauvres vieilles sottes, / Assises bas, à croppetons, / Tout en ung tas comme pelottes; / A petit feu de chenevottes / Tost allumées, tost estaincles, / Et jadis fusmes si mignottes! / Ainsi en prend à maintz et maintes.'*

[It may be translated:] 'Thus amongst ourselves we regret the good time, poor silly old things, low-seated on our heels, all in a heap like so many balls; by a little fire of hemp stalks, soon lighted, soon spent. And once we were such darlings! So fares it with many and many a one' " [Arnold's note].

1. Dryden's *Essay on Dramatic Poesy*. Cowley is the poet Abraham Cowley (1618–1667).

2. Dryden's preface to his *Fables*.

does not weigh much with the young generation, and there are many signs to show that the eighteenth century and its judgments are coming into favor again. Are the favorite poets of the eighteenth century classics?

It is impossible within my present limits to discuss the question fully. And what man of letters would not shrink from seeming to dispose dictatorially of the claims of two men who are, at any rate, such masters in letters as Dryden and Pope; two men of such admirable talent, both of them, and one of them, Dryden, a man, on all sides, of such energetic and genial power? And yet, if we are to gain the full benefit from poetry, we must have the real estimate of it. I cast about for some mode of arriving, in the present case, at such an estimate without offense. And perhaps the best way is to begin, as it is easy to begin, with cordial praise.

When we find Chapman, the Elizabethan translator of Homer, expressing himself in his preface thus: "Though truth in her very nakedness sits in so deep a pit, that from Gades to Aurora and Ganges few eyes can sound her, I hope yet those few here will so discover and confirm that, the date being out of her darkness in this morning of our poet, he shall now gird his temples with the sun," we pronounce that such a prose is intolerable. When we find Milton writing: "And long it was not after, when I was confirmed in this opinion, that he, who would not be frustrate of his hope to write well hereafter in laudable things, ought himself to be a true poem"[3]—we pronounce that such a prose has its own grandeur, but that it is obsolete and inconvenient. But when we find Dryden telling us: "What Virgil wrote in the vigor of his age, in plenty and at ease, I have undertaken to translate in my declining years; struggling with wants, oppressed with sickness, curbed in my genius, liable to be misconstrued in all I write"[4]—then we exclaim that here at last we have the true English prose, a prose such as we would all gladly use if we only knew how. Yet Dryden was Milton's contemporary.

But after the Restoration the time had come when our nation felt the imperious need of a fit prose. So, too, the time had likewise come when our nation felt the imperious need of freeing itself from the absorbing preoccupation which religion in the Puritan age had exercised. It was impossible that this freedom should be brought about without some negative excess, without some neglect and impairment of the religious life of the soul; and the spiritual history of the eighteenth century shows us that the freedom was not achieved without them. Still, the freedom was achieved; the preoccupation, an undoubtedly baneful and retarding one if it had continued, was got rid of. And as with religion amongst us at that period, so it was also with letters. A fit prose was a necessity; but it was impossible that a fit prose should establish itself amongst us without some touch of frost to the imaginative life of the soul. The needful qualities for a fit prose are regularity, uniformity, precision, balance. The men of letters, whose destiny it may be to bring their nation to the attainment of a fit prose, must of necessity, whether they work in prose

3. Milton's *Apology for Smectymnuus.*
4. Dryden's *Postscript to the Reader* in his translation of Virgil.

or in verse, give a predominating, an almost exclusive attention to the qualities of regularity, uniformity, precision, balance. But an almost exclusive attention to these qualities involves some repression and silencing of poetry.

We are to regard Dryden as the puissant and glorious founder, Pope as the splendid high priest, of our age of prose and reason, of our excellent and indispensable eighteenth century. For the purposes of their mission and destiny their poetry, like their prose, is admirable. Do you ask me whether Dryden's verse, take it almost where you will, is not good?

> A milk-white Hind, immortal and unchanged,
> Fed on the lawns and in the forest ranged.[5]

I answer: Admirable for the purposes of the inaugurator of an age of prose and reason. Do you ask me whether Pope's verse, take it almost where you will, is not good?

> To Hounslow Heath I point, and Banstead Down;
> Thence comes your mutton, and these chicks my own.[6]

I answer: Admirable for the purposes of the high priest of an age of prose and reason. But do you ask me whether such verse proceeds from men with an adequate poetic criticism of life, from men whose criticism of life has a high seriousness, or even, without that high seriousness, has poetic largeness, freedom, insight, benignity? Do you ask me whether the application of ideas to life in the verse of these men, often a powerful application, no doubt, is a powerful *poetic* application? Do you ask me whether the poetry of these men has either the matter or the inseparable manner of such an adequate poetic criticism; whether it has the accent of

> Absent thee from felicity awhile . . .

or of

> And what is else not to be overcome . . .

or of

> O martyr souded in virginitee!

I answer: It has not and cannot have them; it is the poetry of the builders of an age of prose and reason. Though they may write in verse, though they may in a certain sense be masters of the art of versification, Dryden and Pope are not classics of our poetry, they are classics of our prose.

Gray is our poetical classic of that literature and age; the position of Gray is singular, and demands a word of notice here. He has not the volume or the power of poets who, coming in times more favorable, have attained to an independent criticism of life. But he lived with the great poets, he lived, above all, with the Greeks, through perpetually

---

5. *The Hind and the Panther* 1.1–2.   6. *Imitations of Horace*, Satire 2.2.143–44.

studying and enjoying them; and he caught their poetic point of view for regarding life, caught their poetic manner. The point of view and the manner are not self-sprung in him, he caught them of others; and he had not the free and abundant use of them. But whereas Addison and Pope never had the use of them, Gray had the use of them at times. He is the scantiest and frailest of classics in our poetry, but he is a classic.[7]

* * *

At any rate the end to which the method and the estimate are designed to lead, and from leading to which, if they do lead to it, they get their whole value—the benefit of being able clearly to feel and deeply to enjoy the best, the truly classic, in poetry—is an end, let me say it once more at parting, of supreme importance. We are often told that an era is opening in which we are to see multitudes of a common sort of readers, and masses of a common sort of literature; that such readers do not want and could not relish anything better than such literature, and that to provide it is becoming a vast and profitable industry. Even if good literature entirely lost currency with the world, it would still be abundantly worth while to continue to enjoy it by oneself. But it never will lose currency with the world, in spite of momentary appearances; it never will lose supremacy. Currency and supremacy are insured to it, not indeed by the world's deliberate and conscious choice, but by something far deeper—by the instinct of self-preservation in humanity.

1880

7. After Gray the only other poet discussed by Arnold is Burns. We have omitted this evaluation. In it, Arnold concludes that "Burns, like Chaucer, comes short of the high seriousness of the great classics."

GERARD MANLEY HOPKINS
1844–1889

1866: Converts to Roman Catholic Church.
1877: Ordained a Jesuit priest.
1918: Posthumous publication of his poems.

Of Gerard Manley Hopkins, it has been said that the most important date in his career was 1918, twenty-nine years after his death, for it was then that the first publication of his poems made them accessible to the world of readers. During his lifetime, these remarkable poems, most of them celebrating the wonders of God's creation, had been known only to a small circle of friends, including his literary executor, the poet Robert Bridges, who waited until 1918 before releasing them to a publisher. Partly because his work was first made public in a twentieth-century volume, but especially because of his striking experiments in meter and diction, Hopkins was widely

hailed as a pioneering figure of "modern" literature, miraculously unconnected with his fellow Victorian poets (who during the 1920s and 1930s were
largely out of fashion among critical readers). And this way of classifying and
evaluating his writings has long persisted. In 1936 a substantial selection of
his poems led off *The Faber Book of Modern Verse*, one of the most influential anthologies of the century, featuring poets such as W. H. Auden,
Dylan Thomas, and T. S. Eliot (the only one whose selections occupy more
pages than those allotted to Hopkins). And the first four editions of *The
Norton Anthology of English Literature* (1962–1979) grouped Hopkins with
these same twentieth-century poets. To reclassify him, as we are now doing,
is not to repudiate his earlier reputation as a "modern," but rather to suggest
that his work can be better understood and appreciated if it is restored to the
Victorian world out of which it developed.

Hopkins was born near London into a large and cultivated family in comfortable circumstances. After a brilliant career at Highgate School, he entered
Oxford in 1863, where he was exposed to a variety of Victorian ways of
thinking, both secular and religious. Among influential leaders at Oxford
was Matthew Arnold, professor of poetry, but more important for Hopkins
was his tutor, Walter Pater, an aesthetician whose emphasis on the intense
apprehension of sensuous beauty struck a responsive chord in Hopkins. At
Oxford he was also exposed to the liberal theology of the master of his college
(Balliol), Benjamin Jowett, whose Broad Church position corresponded to
the moderate Anglicanism of Hopkins's own family. But Hopkins became
increasingly attracted first to the High Church movement, represented at
Oxford by Edward Pusey, and then to Roman Catholicism. Profoundly
influenced by John Henry Newman's account in *Apologia Pro Vita Sua* of
his conversion to Rome and by subsequent conversations with Newman
himself, Hopkins entered the Roman Catholic Church in 1866. The
estrangement from his family that resulted from his conversion was very
painful for him; his parents' letters to him were so "terrible" (he reported to
Newman) that he could not bear to "read them twice." And this alienation
was heightened by his decision not only to become a Roman Catholic but
to become a priest, and, in particular, a Jesuit priest, for in the eyes of many
Victorian Protestants, the Jesuit order was regarded with a special distrust.
For the rest of his life, Hopkins served as a parish priest and teacher in
various places, among them Wales, Liverpool, and Glasgow. In 1885 he
was appointed professor of classics at University College in Dublin, where
Newman had served as rector in the 1850s, and where James Joyce would
be enrolled as a student at the turn of the century.

At school and at Oxford in the early 1860s, Hopkins had written a few
traditional poems in the vein of Keats. He burned most of these early writings after his conversion (although drafts survive), for he believed that his
vocation must require renouncing such personal satisfactions as the writing
of poems. Only after his superiors in the Church encouraged him to do so
did he resume writing poetry, but during the seven years of silence, as his
letters show, he had been thinking about experimenting with what he called
a "new rhythm." The result, in 1875, was his rhapsodic lyric-narrative, *The
Wreck of the Deutschland*, a long ode about the wreck of a ship in which
five Franciscan nuns were drowned. The style of the poem was so distinctive
that the editor of the Jesuit magazine to which he had submitted it "dared
not print it," as Hopkins himself reported. During the remaining fourteen
years of his life, Hopkins continued to write poems but never again submit-

ted them for publication, partly because he was convinced that poetic fame was incompatible with his religious vocation but also because of a fear that readers would be discouraged by the eccentricity of his work.

Hopkins's sense of his own singularity gives us an indication of the organizing structure of his poetry. Drawing upon the theology of Duns Scotus, a medieval philosopher, he felt that everything in the universe was characterized by what he called *inscape*, the distinctive design that constitutes individual identity. This identity is not static but dynamic. Each being in the universe "selves," that is, enacts its identity. And man or woman, the most highly selved, the most individually distinctive being in the universe, recognizes the inscape of other beings in an act that Hopkins calls *instress*, the apprehension of an object in an intense thrust of energy toward it that enables one to realize its specific distinctiveness. Ultimately the instress of inscape leads one to Christ, for the individual identity of any object is the stamp of divine creation upon it. In the act of instress, therefore, man or woman becomes a celebrant of the divine, at once recognizing God's creation and enacting his or her own God-given identity within it.

Poetry for Hopkins enacts this celebration. It is instress, and it realizes the inscape of its subject in its own distinctive design. Hopkins wrote, "But as air, melody, is what strikes me most of all in music and design in painting, so design, pattern or what I am in the habit of calling 'inscape' is what I above all aim at in poetry." In order to create inscape, Hopkins seeks to give each poem a unique design that captures the initial inspiration when he is "caught" by his subject. Many of the characteristics of Hopkins's style—his disruption of conventional syntax, his coining and compounding of words, his use of ellipsis and repetition—can be understood as ways of representing the stress and action of the brain in moments of inspiration. He creates compounds to represent the unique interlocking of the characteristics of an object—"piece-bright," "dapple-dawn-drawn," "blue-bleak." He omits syntactical connections to fuse qualities more intensely—"the dearest freshness deep down things." He creates puns in order to suggest how God's creation rhymes and chimes in a divine patterning. He violates conventional syntactic order to represent the shape of mental experience. In the act of imaginative apprehension, a language particular to the moment generates itself.

Hopkins also uses a new rhythm to give each poem its distinctive design. In the new metric system he created, which he called *sprung rhythm*, lines have a given number of stresses, but the number and placement of unstressed syllables is highly variable. Here, for example, is the way in which Hopkins scanned the first three lines of *The Windhover*. (An accent marks a stressed syllable; a curved line marks what Hopkins calls "outriders"—syllables added to a foot in order to create what Hopkins terms an "extra-metrical effect," involving a stronger stress on the preceding strong syllable and a short pause after the outrider.)

> I caúght this mórning mórning's mínion, kíng-
>   dom of dáylight's dáuphin, dapple-dáwn-drawn Fálcon, in his ríding
> Of the rólling level underneáth him steady aír, and stríding . . .

Hopkins argued that sprung rhythm was the natural rhythm of common speech and written prose, as well as of music. He found a model for it in Old English poetry and in nursery rhymes, but he claimed that it had not been used in English poetry since the Elizabethan age.

The density and difficulty that result from Hopkins's unconventional rhythm and syntax make his poetry seem modern, but his concern with the imagination's shaping of the natural world puts him very much in the Romantic tradition, and his creation of a rough and difficult style, designed to capture the mind's own motion, resembles the style of Browning. "A horrible thing has happened to me," Hopkins wrote in 1864, "I have begun to *doubt* Tennyson." He goes on to criticize Tennyson for using the grand style as a smooth and habitual poetic speech. Like Swinburne, Pater, and Henry James as well as Browning, Hopkins displays a new mannerism, characteristic of the latter part of the nineteenth century, which paradoxically combines an elaborate aestheticism with a more complex representation of consciousness.

In Hopkins's early poetry, his singular apprehension of the beauty of individual objects always brings him to an ecstatic illumination of the presence of God. But in his late poems, the so called "terrible sonnets," his distinctive individuality comes to isolate him from the God who made him thus. In an early journal entry, Hopkins writes, "To me there is no resemblance: searching nature, I taste *self* but at one tankard, that of my own being." In the terrible sonnets, Hopkins confronts the solipsism to which his own stress on individuality seems to lead him. Like the mad speakers of so many Victorian dramatic monologues, he cannot escape a world solely of his own imagining. Yet even these poems of despair, which seem so distinctively modern, reflect a traditional religious vision, the dark night of the soul as described by earlier religious writers such as Saint Ignatius Loyola, the founder of the Jesuit order.

In his introduction to *The Oxford Book of Modern Verse*, Yeats calls Hopkins's poetry "a last development of poetical diction." Yeats's remark indicates the anomaly that Hopkins's work poses. Perhaps it is only appropriate for a writer who stressed the uniqueness of inscape to strike us with the individuality of his achievement.

God's Grandeur

The world is charged with the grandeur of God.
   It will flame out, like shining from shook foil;[1]
   It gathers to a greatness, like the ooze of oil
Crushed.[2] Why do men then now not reck his rod?
Generations have trod, have trod, have trod;   5
   And all is seared with trade; bleared, smeared with toil;
   And wears man's smudge and shares man's smell: the soil
Is bare now, nor can foot feel, being shod.

And for[3] all this, nature is never spent;
   There lives the dearest freshness deep down things;   10
And though the last lights off the black West went
   Oh, morning, at the brown brink eastward, springs—

1. Hopkins explained this image in a letter: "I mean foil in its sense of leaf or tinsel. . . . Shaken gold-foil gives off broad glares like sheet lightning and also, and this is true of nothing else, owing to its zigzag dints and creasings and network of small many cornered facets, a sort of fork lightning too."
2. E.g., from the crushing of olives.
3. Despite.

Because the Holy Ghost over the bent
  World broods with warm breast and with ah! bright wings.

1877   1918

The Starlight Night

Look at the stars! look, look up at the skies!
  O look at all the fire-folk sitting in the air!
  The bright boroughs, the circle-citadels there!
Down in dim woods the diamond delves![1] the elves'-eyes!
The grey lawns cold where gold, where quickgold[2] lies!   5
  Wind-beat whitebeam! airy abeles[3] set on a flare!
  Flake-doves sent floating forth at a farmyard scare!—
Ah well! it is all a purchase, all is a prize.

Buy then! bid then!—What?—Prayer, patience, alms, vows.
Look, look: a May-mess,[4] like on orchard boughs!   10
  Look! March-bloom, like on mealed-with-yellow sallows![5]
These are indeed the barn; withindoors house
The shocks. This piece-bright paling[6] shuts the spouse
  Christ home, Christ and his mother and all his hallows.[7]

1877   1918

Spring

Nothing is so beautiful as Spring—
  When weeds, in wheels, shoot long and lovely and lush;
  Thrush's eggs look little low heavens, and thrush
Through the echoing timber does so rinse and wring
The ear, it strikes like lightnings to hear him sing;   5
  The glassy peartree leaves and blooms, they brush
  The descending blue; that blue is all in a rush
With richness; the racing lambs too have fair their fling.

What is all this juice and all this joy?
  A strain of the earth's sweet being in the beginning   10
In Eden garden.—Have, get, before it cloy,

1. Mines or pits.
2. Coined by analogy with quicksilver. The star-light night resembles the lawns below it where the dew, reflecting the starlight, looks like gold.
3. White poplars. The leaves of these trees, being white on the underside, give off a "whitebeam" when blown by the wind.
4. A profusion of growing things such as May blossoms.
5. Willows, here with yellow spots like meal.
6. Fence in which each individual slat is bright.
"Shocks": sheaves of grain; perhaps also jarring events as in "the thousand natural shocks that flesh is heir to" (Hamlet).
7. Saints.

Before it cloud, Christ, lord, and sour with sinning,
    Innocent mind and Mayday in girl and boy,
      Most, O maid's child,[1] thy choice and worthy the winning.

1877   1918

The Windhover:[1]

To Christ our Lord

I caught this morning morning's minion,[2] king-
    dom of daylight's dauphin,[3] dapple-dawn-drawn Falcon, in
        his riding
Of the rolling level underneath him steady air, and striding
High there, how he rung upon the rein of a wimpling[4] wing
In his ecstasy! then off, off forth on swing,   5
    As a skate's heel sweeps smooth on a bow-bend: the hurl
        and gliding
Rebuffed the big wind. My heart in hiding
Stirred for a bird,—the achieve of, the mastery of the thing!

Brute beauty and valour and act, oh, air, pride, plume, here
    Buckle![5] AND the fire that breaks from thee then, a billion   10
Times told lovelier, more dangerous, O my chevalier![6]

No wonder of it: shéer plód makes plough down sillion[7]
Shine, and blue-bleak embers, ah my dear,
    Fall, gall[8] themselves, and gash gold-vermilion.

1877   1918

Pied[1] Beauty

Glory be to God for dappled things—
    For skies of couple-colour as a brinded[2] cow;
      For rose-moles all in stipple upon trout that swim;
Fresh-firecoal chestnut-falls,[3] finches' wings;
    Landscape plotted and pieced—fold, fallow, and plough;[4]   5
    And áll trádes, their gear and tackle and trim.[5]

---

1. Jesus, son of the Virgin Mary.
1. A small falcon.
2. Darling.
3. A prince who is heir to the French throne.
4. Rippling. "Rung upon the rein": circled at the end of a rein.
5. The verb can be read as imperative or indicative. All three meanings of "buckle" are relevant: to prepare for action, to fasten together, to collapse.
6. Knight.

7. The ridge between two furrows of a ploughed field.
8. Break the surface of.
1. "Pied": of two or more colors in blotches, variegated.
2. Brownish orange in color with streaks of gray.
3. Freshly fallen chestnuts, bright as coals.
4. Divided into fields used as pastures ("fold"), lying fallow, or ploughed for cultivation. The landscape thus appears like rectangles of different colors.
5. Equipment.

All things counter, original, spare,[6] strange;
  Whatever is fickle, freckled (who knows how?)
    With swift, slow; sweet, sour; adazzle, dim;
He fathers-forth whose beauty is past change: 10
                Praise him.

1877   1918

Hurrahing in Harvest

Summer ends now; now, barbarous in beauty, the stooks[1] rise
Around; up above, what wind-walks! what lovely
    behavior
Of silk-sack clouds! has wilder, wilful-wavier
Meal-drift moulded ever and melted across skies?

I walk, I lift up, I lift up heart, eyes,   5
Down all that glory in the heavens to glean our Saviour;
And, éyes, heárt, what looks, what lips yet gave you a
Rapturous love's greeting of realer, of rounder replies?

And the azurous hung hills are his world-wielding shoulder
Majestic—as a stallion stalwart, very-violet-sweet!—   10
These things, these things were here and but the beholder
Wanting; which two when they once meet,
The heart rears wings bold and bolder
And hurls for him, O half hurls earth for him off under his
    feet.

1877   1918

Binsey Poplars

felled 1879

My aspens dear, whose airy cages quelled,
Quelled or quenched in leaves the leaping sun,
All felled, felled, are all felled;
  Of a fresh and following folded rank
        Not spared, not one   5
        That dandled a sandalled
      Shadow that swam or sank
On meadow and river and wind-wandering
  weed-winding bank.

---

6. Rare. "Counter": contrary.   1. Sheaves of grain.

O if we but knew what we do   10
          When we delve[1] or hew—
      Hack and rack[2] the growing green!
          Since country is so tender
      To touch, her being só slender,
      That, like this sleek and seeing ball[3]   15
      But a prick will make no eye at all,

      Where we, even where we mean
          To mend her we end her,
          When we hew or delve:
After-comers cannot guess the beauty been.   20
      Ten or twelve, only ten or twelve
          Strokes of havoc únselve[4]
          The sweet especial scene,
      Rural scene, a rural scene,
      Sweet especial rural scene.   25

1879   1918

Duns Scotus's Oxford[1]

Towery city and branchy between towers;
Cuckoo-echoing, bell-swarmèd, lark-charmèd, rook-racked,
      river-rounded;
The dapple-eared lily below thee; that country and town did
Once encounter in, here coped[2] and poisèd powers;

Thou hast a base and brickish skirt[3] there, sours   5
That neighbour-nature thy grey beauty is grounded
Best in; graceless growth, thou hast confounded
Rural rural keeping[4]—folk, flocks, and flowers.

Yet ah! this air I gather and I release
He lived on; these weeds and waters, these walls are what   10
He haunted who of all men most sways my spirits to peace;

1. Dig.
2. Torture.
3. The eye.
4. Rob it of self.
1. Duns Scotus, the 13th-century theologian, lectured at Oxford about 1301. His idea that individuality is the final perfection of any creature influenced Hopkins's conception of inscape. When Hopkins came upon two of Scotus's commentaries in 1872, he wrote that he was immediately "flush with a new stroke of enthusiasm . . . when I took in any inscape of the sky or sea I thought of Scotus."
2. Set off against one another.
3. Red brick housing developments and industrial complex, built in the 19th century on the north edge of Oxford, are in marked contrast with the "gray" stone buildings of the medieval city.
4. The brickish skirt has destroyed the way in which the rural landscape and the old city have tended and preserved each other.

Of realty[5] the rarest-veinèd unraveller; a not
Rivalled insight, be rival Italy or Greece;
Who fired France for Mary without spot.[6]

1879   1918

Felix Randal

Felix Randal the farrier,[1] O is he dead then? my duty all
    ended,
Who have watched his mould of man, big-boned and hardy-
    handsome
Pining, pining, till time when reason rambled in it and some
Fatal four disorders, fleshed there, all contended?

Sickness broke him. Impatient, he cursed at first, but mended   5
Being anointed[2] and all; though a heavenlier heart began some
Months earlier, since I had our sweet reprieve and ransom[3]
Tendered to him. Ah well, God rest him all road ever[4] he
    offended!

This seeing the sick endears them to us, us too it endears.
My tongue had taught thee comfort, touch had quenched thy   10
    tears,
Thy tears that touched my heart, child, Felix, poor Felix
    Randal;

How far from then forethought of, all thy more boisterous
    years,
When thou at the random[5] grim forge, powerful amidst peers,
Didst fettle[6] for the great grey drayhorse his bright and battering
    sandal!

1880   1918

Spring and Fall:

to a young child

Márgarét, áre you gríeving
Over Goldengrove unleaving?

---

5. Reality.
6. In Paris, Scotus was the first to defend the doctrine of the Immaculate Conception, that Mary
was born without original sin.
1. Blacksmith.
2. In Extreme Unction, the sacrament for the

dying.
3. Holy Communion preceded by confession and
absolution.
4. In whatever way.
5. Built with stones of irregular size and shape.
6. Prepare.

Leáves, líke the things of man, you
With your fresh thoughts care for, can you?
Áh! ás the heart grows older   5
It will come to such sights colder
By and by, nor spare a sigh
Though worlds of wanwood leafmeal[1] lie;
And yet you *will* weep and know why.
Now no matter, child, the name: 10
Sórrow's spríngs áre the same.
Nor mouth had, no nor mind, expressed
What heart heard of, ghost[2] guessed:
It ís the blight man was born for,
It is Margaret you mourn for.

1880   1918

[As Kingfishers Catch Fire]

As kingfishers catch fire, dragonflies draw flame;
    As tumbled over rim in roundy wells
    Stones ring; like each tucked[1] string tells, each hung bell's
Bow swung finds tongue to fling out broad its name;
Each mortal thing does one thing and the same: 5
    Deals out that being indoors each one dwells;
    Selves[2]—goes itself; *myself* it speaks and spells,
Crying *What I do is me: for that I came.*

Í say more: the just man justices;[3]
    Keeps gráce: thát keeps all his goings graces;   10
Acts in God's eye what in God's eye he is—
    Chríst. For Christ plays in ten thousand places,
Lovely in limbs, and lovely in eyes not his
    To the Father through the features of men's faces.

1881   1918

[Carrion Comfort][1]

Not, I'll not, carrion comfort, Despair, not feast on thee,[2]
Not untwist—slack they may be—these last strands of man
In me ór, most weary, cry *I can no more.* I can;
Can something, hope, wish day come, not choose not to be.

---

1. Wan forest with scattered leaves. "Leafmeal" is
coined by analogy with piecemeal.
2. Spirit.
1. Plucked.
2. Fulfills its individuality. "Indoors": within.
3. Acts in a just manner.

1. The title of this poem was supplied by Bridges.
It is one of the "terrible sonnets," as are the three
following poems.
2. The satisfaction of giving in to despair as a kind
of "comfort" is implicitly likened to a vulture's satisfaction in feasting upon dead flesh.

But ah, but O thou terrible, why wouldst thou rude on me   5
Thy wring-world right foot rock?[3] lay a lionlimb against me?
    scan
With darksome devouring eyes my bruisèd bones? and fan,
O in turns of tempest, me heaped there; me frantic to avoid
    thee and flee?

Why? That my chaff might fly; my grain lie, sheer and clear.
Nay in all that toil, that coil,[4] since (seems) I kissed the rod,   10
Hand rather,[5] my heart lo! lapped strength, stole joy, would
    laugh, chéer.
Cheer whom though? The Hero whose heaven-handling flung
    me, fóot tród
Me? or me that fought him? O which one? is it each one?
    That night, that year
Of now done darkness I wretch lay wrestling with (my God!)
    my God.

1885   1918

[No Worst, There Is None]

No worst, there is none. Pitched past pitch of grief,
More pangs will, schooled at forepangs, wilder wring.
Comforter, where, where is your comforting?
Mary, mother of us, where is your relief?
My cries heave, herds-long;[1] huddle in a main, a chief-   5
woe, world-sorrow; on an age-old anvil wince and sing—
Then lull, then leave off. Fury had shrieked "No ling-
ering! Let me be fell: force[2] I must be brief."
O the mind, mind has mountains; cliffs of fall
Frightful, sheer, no-man-fathomed. Hold them cheap   10
May who ne'er hung there. Nor does long our small
Durance[3] deal with that steep or deep. Here! creep,
Wretch, under a comfort serves in a whirlwind: all
Life death does end and each day dies with sleep.

1885   1918

[I Wake and Feel the Fell of Dark, Not Day]

I wake and feel the fell[1] of dark, not day.
What hours, O what black hoürs we have spent

3. I.e., why wouldst thou roughly against me rock
thy right foot that wrings the world.
4. Tumult.
5. I.e., the hand that wields the rod.
1. Like the succession of cries made by cattle that

have been following one another in a long line.
2. Perforce. "Fell": fierce.
3. Endurance.
1. Skin of an animal.

This night! what sights you, heart, saw; ways you went!
And more must, in yet longer light's delay.

With witness I speak this. But where I say   5
Hours I mean years, mean life. And my lament
Is cries countless, cries like dead letters[2] sent
To dearest him that lives alas! away.

I am gall, I am heartburn. God's most deep decree
Bitter would have me taste: my taste was me;   10
Bones built in me, flesh filled, blood brimmed the curse.

Selfyeast of spirit a dull dough sours. I see
The lost are like this, and their scourge to be
As I am mine, their sweating selves; but worse.

1885   1918

[Thou Art Indeed Just, Lord]

*Justus quidem tu es, Domine, si disputem tecum; verumtamen
justa loquar ad te: Quare via impiorum prosperatur? &c.*[1]

Thou art indeed just, Lord, if I contend
With thee; but, sir, so what I plead is just.
Why do sinners' ways prosper? and why must
Disappointment all I endeavour end?

Wert thou my enemy, O thou my friend,   5
How wouldst thou worse, I wonder, than thou dost
Defeat, thwart me? Oh, the sots and thralls of lust
Do in spare hours more thrive than I that spend,

Sir, life upon thy cause. See, banks and brakes[2]
Now, leavèd how thick! lacèd they are again   10
With fretty chervil,[3] look, and fresh wind shakes

Them; birds build—but not I build; no, but strain,
Time's eunuch, and not breed one work that wakes.
Mine, O thou lord of life, send my roots rain.

1889   1918

---

2. Letters undelivered or returned to the sender by
the post office.
1. "Righteous art thou, O Lord, when I plead with
thee: yet let me talk with thee of thy judgments:
Wherefore doth the way of the wicked prosper?"
(Jeremiah 12.1). The Latin was Hopkins's title.
2. Thickets.
3. A kind of parsley.

The Twentieth Century

1914–18:	World War I.
1918:	Gerard Manley Hopkins's poetry published.
1922:	T. S. Eliot's *The Waste Land*.
1922:	James Joyce's *Ulysses*.
1930:	Period of depression and unemployment begins.
1939–45:	World War II.

HISTORICAL BACKGROUND

The period, which for convenience we call "the twentieth century," begins really with the late nineteenth, when the sense of the passing of a major phase of English history was already in the air. Queen Victoria's Jubilee in 1887 and, even more, her Diamond Jubilee in 1897 were felt even by contemporaries to mark the end of an era. As the nineteenth century drew to a close there were many manifestations of a weakening of traditional stabilities. The aesthetic movement, with its insistence on "art for art's sake," assaulted the assumptions about the nature and function of art held by ordinary middle-class readers, deliberately, provocatively. It helped to widen the breach between artists and writers on the one hand and the "Philistine" public on the other—a breach whose earlier symptom was Matthew Arnold's war on the Philistines in *Culture and Anarchy* and which was later to result in the "alienation of the artist" that has since become a commonplace of criticism. This breach was more than a purely English matter. From France came the tradition of the bohemian life that scorned the limits imposed by conventional ideas of respectability, together with other notions of the artist as rejecting and rejected by ordinary society, which in different ways fostered the view of the alienated artist. The life and work of the French Symbolist poets in France, the early novels of Thomas Mann in Germany (especially *Buddenbrooks*, 1901), and Joyce's *Portrait of the Artist as a Young Man* (1916) show some of the very different ways in which this attitude revealed itself in literature all over Europe. In England, the growth of popular education as a result of the Education Act of 1870, which finally made elementary education compulsory and universal, led to the rapid emergence of a large, unsophisticated literary public at whom new kinds of journalism, in particular the cheap "yellow press," were directed. A public that was literate but not in any real sense educated increased steadily throughout the nineteenth century, and one result of this was the splitting up of the audience for literature into "highbrows," "lowbrows," and "middlebrows." Although in earlier periods there had been different kinds of audience for different kinds of writing, the split now developed with unprecedented speed and to an unprecedented degree because of the mass production of "popular" literature for the semiliterate. The fragmentation of the reading public now merged with the artist's war on the Philistine (and indeed was one of the causes of that war in the first place) to widen the gap between popular art and art esteemed only by the sophisticated and the expert.

Another manifestation—or at least accompaniment—of the end of the Victorian age was the rise of various kinds of pessimism and stoicism. The novels and poetry of Thomas Hardy show one kind of pessimism (and it *was* pessimism, even if Hardy himself repudiated the term), and the poems of A. E. Housman show another variety, while a real or affected stoicism is to be found not only in these writers but also in many minor writers of the last decade of the nineteenth century and the first decade of the twentieth. Examples of this stoicism—the determination to stand for human dignity by enduring bravely, with a "stiff upper lip," whatever fate may bring—range from Robert Louis Stevenson's essays and the rhetorically assertive poems of the editor and journalist W. E. Henley, to Rudyard Kipling's *Jungle Books* and many of his short stories, the last stanza of Housman's *The Chestnut Casts His Flambeaux* ("Bear them we can, and if we can we must") and Yeats's "They know that Hamlet and Lear are gay."

Although the high tide of anti-Victorianism was marked by the publication in 1918 of that classic of ironic debunking, *Eminent Victorians* by Lytton Strachey (1880–1932), the criticism of the normal attitudes and preconceptions of the Victorian middle classes first became really violent in the last two decades of the nineteenth century. No one could have been more savage in his attacks on the Victorian conceptions of the family, education, and religion than Samuel Butler, whose novel *The Way of All Flesh* (completed in 1884, posthumously published in 1903) is still the bitterest indictment in English literature of the Victorian way of life. The chorus of questioning of Victorian assumptions grew ever louder as the century drew to an end; sounding prominently in it was the voice of the young Bernard Shaw, one of Butler's greatest admirers. The position of women, too, was rapidly changing during this period. The Married Woman's Property Act of 1882, which allowed married women to own property in their own right; the admission of women to the universities at different times during the latter part of the century; the fight for women's suffrage, which was not won until 1918 (and not fully won until 1928)—these events marked a change in the attitude to women and in the part they played in the national life as well as in the relation between the sexes, which is reflected in a variety of ways in the literature of the period.

The Boer War (1899–1902), fought by the British to establish political and economic control over the Boer republics of South Africa, marked both the high point of and the reaction against British imperialism. It was a war against which many British intellectuals protested and one which the British in the end were slightly ashamed of having won. The development of the British Empire into the British Commonwealth (an association of self-governing countries) continued in fits and starts throughout the first half of the twentieth century, with imperialist and anti-imperialist sentiment often meeting head on; writers as far apart as Kipling and E. M. Forster occupied themselves with the problem. The Irish question also caused a great deal of excitement from the beginning of the period until well into the 1920s. A steadily rising Irish nationalism protested with increasing violence against the political subordination of Ireland to the British Crown and government. In World War I some Irish nationalists sought German help in rebelling against Britain, and this exacerbated feeling on both sides. No one can fully understand William Butler Yeats or James Joyce without some awareness of the Irish struggle for independence, the feelings of Anglo-Irish literary people on this burning topic, and the way in which the Irish Literary Revival of the late nineteenth and early twentieth centuries (with which Yeats was much concerned) reflected a determination to achieve a vigorous national life culturally even if the road seemed blocked politically.

Edwardian England (1901–10) was very conscious of being no longer Victorian. Edward VII stamped his extrovert and self-indulgent character on the decade in which he reigned. It was a vulgar age of conspicuous enjoyment by those who could afford it, and writers and artists kept well away from implication in high society (though there were some conspicuous exceptions): in general, there was no equivalent in this period of Queen Victoria's interest in Tennyson. The alienation of artists and intellectuals was proceeding apace. From 1910 (when George V came to the throne) until war broke out in August 1914, Britain achieved a temporary equilibrium between Victorian earnestness and Edwardian flashiness; in retrospect that "Georgian" period seems peculiarly golden, the last phase of assurance and stability before the old order throughout Europe broke up in violence with results that are still with us. Yet even then, under the surface, there was restlessness and experimentation. If this was the age of Rupert Brooke, it was also the age of T. S. Eliot's first experiments in a radically new kind of poetry.

"Edwardian" as a term applied to English cultural history suggests a period in which the social and economic stabilities of the Victorian age—country houses with numerous servants, a flourishing and confident middle class, a strict hierarchy of social classes—remained unimpaired, though on the level of ideas there was a sense of change and liberation. "Georgian" refers largely to the lull before the storm of World War I. That war, as our selection of the war poets makes clear, produced some major shifts in attitude.

The postwar disillusion of the 1920s was, it might be said, a spiritual matter, just as Eliot's Waste Land was a spiritual and not a literal wasteland. Depression and unemployment in the early 1930s, followed by the rise of Hitler and the cruel shadow of Fascism and Nazism over Europe, with its threat of another war, represented another sort of wasteland which produced another sort of effect on poets and novelists. The impotence of capitalist governments in the face of Hitlerism combined with economic dislocation to turn the majority of young intellectuals (and not only intellectuals) in the 1930s to the political left. The 1930s were the red decade, because only the left seemed to offer any solution. The early poetry of W. H. Auden and his contemporaries cried out for "the death of the old gang" (in Auden's phrase) and a clean sweep politically and economically, while the right-wing army's rebellion against the left-wing republican government in Spain, which started in the summer of 1936 and soon led to full-scale civil war, was regarded as a rehearsal for an inevitable second world war and thus further emphasized the inadequacy of politicians. Yet though all this is reflected passionately in the literature of the period, particularly in the poetry, it was not accompanied by any interesting developments in technique; many younger writers were more anxious to express their attitudes than to construct new kinds of works of art. The outbreak of World War II in September 1939, following very shortly on Hitler's pact with Russia, which shocked and disillusioned so many of the young Left-wing writers, marked the sudden end of the red decade; the concern of writers in Britain now was to maintain their integrity and indeed their existence in what was from the beginning expected to be a long and destructive war. This they did surprisingly well, but nevertheless the struggle brought inevitable exhaustion and, winning a war, Great Britain lost an empire. India, long the jewel in the imperial crown, came to independence in 1947 and, although she and the newly formed Muslim State of Pakistan elected to remain within the British Commonwealth, other former dominions did not. The Irish Republic withdrew from the Commonwealth in 1949, and the republic of South Africa in 1961. While Britain was engaged in a painful reappraisal of her place in the world, countries that had lost the war—West Germany and Japan—were, in economic terms, winning the peace that followed.

Less obvious, but no less significant for English literature, were changes on the national scene. London, as the capital of the Empire, had long dominated the culture as well as the politics and the economy of the British Isles. London spoke for Britain in the impeccable southern English intonations of the radio announcers of the state-owned British Broadcasting Corporation (known as the BBC); but from the 1960s this changed. Regional dialects were admitted to the air waves. Regional radio and television stations sprang up. The Arts Council, which had subsidized the nation's drama, literature, music, painting, and plastic arts from London, delegated much of its grant-giving responsibility to regional arts councils. This gave a new confidence to writers and artists outside London, and has since contributed to a notable renaissance of regional literature. At its best, this builds on the native tradition of Yeats and Hardy, transcending the narrowly provincial to achieve a true universality.

POETRY

The years leading up to World War I saw the start of a poetic revolution. The Imagist movement, influenced by the philosopher-poet T. E. Hulme's insistence on hard, clear, precise images and encouraged by the modernist American poet, Ezra Pound, who was then living in London, fought against romantic fuzziness and facile emotionalism in poetry. The movement developed simultaneously on both sides of the Atlantic, and its early members included Amy Lowell, Richard Aldington, Hilda Doolittle, John Gould Fletcher, and F. S. Flint. As Flint explained in an article in March 1913, Imagists insisted on "direct treatment of the 'thing,' whether subjective or objective," on the avoidance of all words "that did not contribute to the presentation," and on a freer metrical movement than a strict adherence to "the sequence of a metronome" could allow. All this encouraged precision in imagery and freedom of rhythmic movement, but more was required for the production of poetry of any real scope and interest. Imagism went in for the short, sharply etched, descriptive lyric, but it had no technique for the production of longer and more complex poems. Other new ideas about poetry helped to provide this technique. Sir Herbert Grierson's great edition of the poems of John Donne in 1912 both reflected and helped to encourage a new enthusiasm for seventeenth-century metaphysical poetry. The revival of interest in metaphysical wit brought with it a desire on the part of some pioneering poets to introduce into their poetry a much higher degree of intellectual complexity than had been found among the Victorians or the Georgians. The full subtlety of French Symbolist poetry also now came to be appreciated; it had been admired in the nineties, but for its dreamy suggestiveness rather than for its imagistic precision and complexity. At the same time a need was felt to bring poetic language and rhythms closer to those of conversation, or at least to spice the formalities of poetic utterance with echoes of the colloquial and even the slangy. Irony, which made possible several levels of discourse simultaneously, and wit, with the use of puns (banished from serious poetry for over two hundred years), helped to achieve that union of thought and passion which T. S. Eliot, in his review of Grierson's anthology of metaphysical poetry (1921), saw as characteristic of the metaphysicals and wished to bring back into modern poetry. A new critical and a new creative movement in poetry went hand in hand, with Eliot the high priest of both. It was Eliot who extended the scope of Imagism by bringing the English metaphysicals and the French Symbolists (as well as the English Jacobean dramatists) to the rescue, thus adding new criteria of complexity and allusiveness to the criteria of concreteness and precision stressed by the Imagists. It was Eliot, too, who introduced into modern English and American poetry the kind of irony achieved by shifting suddenly from the formal to the colloquial or by oblique allusions to objects or ideas that contrasted sharply with those carried by the surface meaning of the poem. Thus between, say, 1911 (the first year of the Georgian poets) and 1922 (the year of the publication of *The Waste Land*) a major revolution occurred in English— and for that matter American—poetic theory and practice—one which determined the way in which most serious poets and critics now think about their art. This revolution was by no means an isolated literary phenomenon. Writers on both sides of the English Channel were influenced by the French Impressionist, Postimpressionist, and Cubist painters' radical re-examination of the nature of reality. Ezra Pound wrote books about the French sculptor Henri Gaudier-Brzeska and the American composer George Antheil. Wilfred Owen wrote in 1918: "I suppose I am doing in poetry what the advanced composers are doing in music"; and T. S. Eliot, while writing *The Waste Land* three years later, was so impressed by a performance of the composer Stravinsky's *Le Sacre du Printemps* that he stood up at the end and cheered.

The posthumous publication by Robert Bridges in 1918 of the poetry of Gerard Manley Hopkins encouraged experimentation in language and rhythms. Hopkins combined absolute precision of the individual image with a complex ordering of images and a new kind of metrical patterning. The young poets of the early 1930s—W. H. Auden, Stephen Spender, C. Day Lewis—were much influenced by Hopkins as well as by Eliot (then the presiding genius of modern English and American poetry) and by a variety of other poets from the sixteenth-century John Skelton to Wilfred Owen.

Meanwhile the remarkable career of W. B. Yeats, stretching across the whole modern period, showed how a truly great poet can reflect the varying developments of his age yet maintain an unmistakably individual accent. Beginning among the aesthetes of the nineties, turning later to a more tough and spare ironic language without losing his characteristic verbal magic, working out his own notions of symbolism and bringing them in different ways into his poetry, developing in his full maturity a rich symbolic and metaphysical poetry with its own curiously haunting cadences and its imagery both shockingly realistic and movingly suggestive, Yeats's work is itself a history of English Poetry between 1890 and 1939. Yet he is always Yeats, unique and inimitable—without doubt the greatest English-speaking poet of his age.

In his poem *Remembering the Thirties*, Donald Davie declared: "A neutral tone is nowadays preferred." That tone—the coolly clinical tone of W. H. Auden—dominated the poetry of the decade, but as it ended and World War II began, a neutral tone gave way to the vehemence of what came to be known as the New Apocalypse. The poets of this movement, the most notable of whom was Dylan Thomas, owed something of their audacity and violence to the example of the French Surrealist poets and painters, who sought to express, often by free association, the operation of the subconscious mind. Many of these, such as Salvador Dali and Pablo Picasso, were both poets and painters, whose poetry was introduced to English readers in translations and in A *Short History of Surrealism* (1936) by David Gascoyne, one of the poets of the New Apocalypse. With the coming of the 1950s, however, the pendulum swung back again. A new generation of poets, that included Donald Davie, Thom Gunn, and Philip Larkin, reacted against what seemed to them the verbal excesses of Dylan Thomas, Edith Sitwell, and others. "The Movement," as this new group came to be called, aimed once again for a neutral tone, a purity of diction, in which to render an unpretentious fidelity to experience. Philip Larkin, its most notable exponent, explicitly rejected the imported modernism of Pound and Eliot in favor of a native tradition represented in this century by Thomas Hardy. That tradition now flourishes in the work of Tony Harrison and Seamus Heaney. Other of the younger poets, following the example of Craig Raine and taking their name—the Martian School—from his poem, A *Martian Sends a Postcard Home*, once again look to the painters for their inspiration. "Look" is the operative word, for the eye is paramount in their poetry, an eye that sees the world with the freshness of a child or a painter or a visitor from Mars, and records what it sees with an often exuberant wit.

In 1912, Edward Marsh introduced the first of his anthologies of *Georgian Poetry* with the claim that "English poetry is now once again putting on a new strength and beauty." That claim can be made with more justice today; and perhaps with more justice than it could have been made at any point in the years between.

FICTION

The years 1912 to 1930 were the Heroic Age of the modern novel, the age of Joseph Conrad, James Joyce, D. H. Lawrence, Virginia Woolf, and E. M. Forster. One can trace three major influences on the changes in attitude and technique in the fiction of this period. The first is the novelists' realization that the general background of belief which united them with their public in a common sense of what was significant in experience had disappeared. The public values of the Victorian novel, in which major crises of plot could be shown through changes in the social or financial or marital status of the chief characters, gave way to more personally conceived notions of value, dependent on the novelists' own intuitions and sensibilities rather than on public agreement. "To believe that your impressions hold good for others," Woolf once wrote (discussing Jane Austen), "is to be released from the cramp and confinement of personality." Modern novelists could no longer believe this: they had to fall back on personality, drawing their criteria of significance in human affairs (and thus their principles of selection) from their own intuitions, so that they needed to find ways of convincing readers that their own sense of what was significant in experience was truly valid. A new technical burden was thus imposed on the novelist's prose, for it had now to build up a world of values instead of drawing on an existing world of values. Woolf tried to solve the problem by using some of the devices of poetry in order to suggest the novelist's own sense of value and vision of the world. Joyce, on the other hand, made no attempt to convey a single personal attitude, but reacted to the breakdown of public values by employing a kind of writing so multiple in its implications that it conveyed numerous points of view simultaneously, the author remaining totally objective and committed to none of them—a mode which required remarkable technical virtuosity.

The second influence on the changes in attitude and technique in the modern novel was a new view of time; time was not a series of chronological moments to be presented by the novelist in sequence with an occasional deliberate retrospect ("this reminded him of," "she recalled that"), but as a continuous flow in the consciousness of the individual, with the "already" continuously merging into the "not yet" and retrospect merging into anticipation. This influence is closely bound up with a third: the new notions of the nature of consciousness, which derived in a general way from the pioneer explorations of the subconscious by Sigmund Freud and Carl Jung, but were also part of the spirit of the age and discernible even in those novelists who had not read either of these psychologists. Consciousness is multiple; the past is always present in it at some level and is continually coloring one's present reaction. Marcel Proust in France, in his great novel sequence *Remembrance of Things Past* (1913–28), had explored the ways in which the past impinges on the present and consciousness is determined by memory. The view that we *are* our memories, that our present is the sum of our past, that if we dig into the human consciousness we can tell the whole truth about people without waiting for a chronological sequence of time to take them through a series of testing circumstances, inevitably led to a technical revolution in the novel. For now, by exploring in depth into consciousness and memory rather than proceeding lengthwise along the dimension of time, a novelist could write a novel concerned ostensibly with only one day of the hero's life (Joyce's *Ulysses* and Woolf's *Mrs. Dalloway*). This view of multiple levels of consciousness existing simultaneously, coupled with the view of time as a constant flow rather than a series of separate moments, meant that novelists preferred to plunge into the consciousness of their characters in order to tell their stories rather than to provide external frameworks of chronological narrative. The "stream-of-consciousness" technique, where the author tries to render directly the very fabric of a character's consciousness without reporting it in formal, quoted remarks, was developed in the 1920s as an important new technique of the English novel. It made for more difficult reading, at least for those accustomed only to the methods of the older English novel. No "porch" was constructed at the front of the novel to put the reader in possession of necessary preliminary information: such information emerged, as the novel progressed, from the consciousness of each character as it responded to the present with echoes of its past. No conventional signposts were put up to tell readers where they were, for that was felt to interfere with the immediacy of the impression. But once readers learn how to find their way in this unsignposted territory, they are rewarded by new delicacies of perception and new subtleties of presentation.

Concentration on the "stream of consciousness" and on the association of ideas within the individual consciousness led inevitably to stress on the essential loneliness of the individual. For all consciousnesses are unique and isolated, and if this unique, private world is the real world in which we live, if the public values to which we must pay lip service in the social world in which we move are not the real values which give meaning to our personalities, then we are all condemned to live in the prison of our own incommunicable consciousness. How is true communication possible in such a world? The public gestures imposed upon us by society never correspond to our real inward needs. They are conventional in the bad sense, mechanical, imposing a crude standardization on the infinite subtlety of experience. If we do try to give out a sign from our real selves, that sign is bound to be misunderstood when read by some other self in the light of that self's quite other personality. The theme of such modern fiction is thus the possibility of love, the establishment of emotional communication, in a community of private consciousnesses. This is, in different ways, the theme of Joyce, of Lawrence, of Woolf, and of Forster, and (on a rather different scale and not always so directly) of Conrad. The search for communion and the inescapable isolation of Leopold Bloom in *Ulysses* is symbolic of the human condition as seen by the modern novelist. Similar investigations of this basic condition are Forster's explorations of the conventions which seem to be helps to living but which in fact prevent true human contacts, and Woolf's projection of the relation between the self's need for privacy and the self's need for genuine communication. The theme of all Lawrence's novels is human relationships, the ideal of which he restlessly explored with shifting emphasis throughout his career; such relationships can be all too easily distorted by the mechanical conventions of society, by notions of respectability or propriety, by all the shams and frauds of middle-class life, by the demands of power or money or success. One might almost say that the greatest modern novels are about the difficulty, and at the same time the inevitability, of being human. The dilemma of the human condition is never really solved in these novels; but knowledge that the dilemma is shared—a knowledge so brilliantly conveyed in *Ulysses* and so wryly proffered by Forster—can both illuminate and comfort.

Not all the novelists of the period, of course, were concerned with these themes or employed the new techniques appropriate to them. The "documentary" novelists, such as Arnold Bennett and John Galsworthy (and, in some at least of his novels, H. G. Wells), presented, often with great skill, the changing social scene, showing considerable insight and sympathy in recording aspects of it through the behavior of their imagined characters. Woolf called these writers "materialists," maintaining that they were content to deal with externals and did not go on to explore those aspects of consciousness, of our true inward life, in which human reality resides. She was perhaps judging unfairly, by standards that were not applicable to their sort of fiction; but modern criticism has on the whole agreed with her.

The short story in this century has benefited from the new techniques of exploration in depth. A great consciousness of the symbolic uses to which objects and incidents can be put and a greater subtlety in the ways in which patterns of suggestiveness are built up below the quietly realistic surface can be found in the short stories of writers so different from each other as Joyce, Katherine Mansfield, Lawrence, Forster, Doris Lessing, Edna O'Brien, and Susan Hill. Mansfield learned from the Russian short-story writer Anton Chekhov how to use the casual-seeming incidents of ordinary life in such a way as to set up haunting overtones of meaning. The apparently inconsequential surface masking the carefully organized substructure is found in much modern fiction (perhaps most of all in *Ulysses*): it is one of the results of the coming together, in the novel and the short story, of realism and symbolism, of contemporary probability and timeless significance. These things of course come together in great fiction of all ages; but modern writers contrive their coexistence with greater self-consciousness than their predecessors.

DRAMA

Modern drama begins in a sense with the witty drawing-room comedies of Oscar Wilde; yet Wilde founded no dramatic school. His wit was personal and generative of paradoxes for their own sake. Bernard Shaw brought still another kind of wit into drama—not Wilde's light-hearted sparkle nor yet the assured sophistication of the Restoration dramatists, but the provocative paradox that was meant to tease and disturb, to challenge the complacency of the audience. Shaw's discussion plays were given dramatic life through the mastery of theatrical techniques which he learned during his years as a dramatic critic. In his general attitudes he represents the anti-Victorianism of the late Victorians; his long life should not obscure the fact that his first— and some of his best—plays belong to the nineties. Other attempts by twentieth-century dramatists to debate social questions on the stage—by Galsworthy, for example—deserve respect for their humanity and intelligence and sometimes for their theatrical craftsmanship, but they lack Shaw's verbal and intellectual brilliance and his superb capacity to entertain.

We must turn to Ireland to find another really impressive variety of dramatic activity. The Irish Literary Theatre was founded in 1899, with Yeats's early play *The Countess Cathleen* as its first production. The founders— Yeats, Lady Gregory, George Moore, and Edward Martyn—wanted to make a contribution to an Irish literary revival, but they were influenced also by the Independent Theatre in London, founded in 1891 by J. T. Grein in order to encourage new developments in the drama. In 1902 the Irish Literary Theatre was able to maintain a permanent all-Irish company and changed its name to the Irish National Theatre, which moved in 1904 to the Abbey Theatre, by which name it has since been known. Many of the plays produced at the Abbey Theatre were only of local and ephemeral interest. But J. M. Synge's use of the speech and imagination of Irish country people, Yeats's powerful symbolic use of themes from old Irish legend, and Sean O'Casey's use of the Irish civil war as a background for plays combining tragic melodrama, humor of character, and irony of circumstance, brought new kinds of vitality to the theater. T. S. Eliot attempted with considerable success to revive a ritual poetic drama in England with his *Murder in the Cathedral* (1935). His later attempts to combine religious symbolism with the box-office appeal of an entertaining society comedy (as in *The Cocktail Party*, 1950), though impressive technical achievements, were not wholly successful: the combination of contemporary social chatter with profound religious symbolism produces both an unevenness of tone and disturbing shifts in levels of realism. Elsewhere in modern drama the conflict between realism and symbolism (first clearly seen in Ibsen) is acted out in a variety of ways.

In spite of the achievements of Shaw, Yeats, and Eliot, it cannot be said of the drama, as it can of poetry and fiction in the first half of the century, that a technical revolution occurred that changed the whole course of literary history with respect to that particular literary form. The reformers of the 1890s invoked the name of the great Norwegian playwright Henrik Ibsen:

like Shaw they saw him as essentially a critic of middle-class society rather than (as critics tend to see him today) as an essentially poetic dramatist experimenting with symbolic modes of expression. This may be the reason why the influence of Ibsen soon petered out in run-of-the-mill plays of humanitarian social concern. The staple of the London West End theater remained social comedy stiffened by occasional irony and sweetened by sentimentality (Noel Coward was one of the best, as well as most successful, purveyors of this sort of fare).

The course of British and Irish drama during the first half of the century may have been less revolutionary than developments in poetry and fiction over the same period, but its revolution was to come, and since the end of World War II it has been the major area of literary innovation. There is no accounting for the emergence of genius. In the history of cultural movements, it appears sporadically and less often singly than in constellations, as if it were the property of great "stars" to attract lesser. A factor in the emergence of such a constellation in twentieth-century British and Irish drama has been the role played by the BBC in commissioning and promoting new work. Wartime verse plays, written for radio by Louis MacNeice and other poets, helped prepare the audience that in the late 1940s and early 1950s rapturously received the verse plays of Christopher Fry. It seemed that these were about to bring a new kind of poetic life into English drama. But Fry's exuberantly witty use of metaphor soon lost its appeal, and by the late 1950s a very different kind of drama brought vitality to the British theater. John Osborne's *Look Back In Anger* was produced at the Royal Court Theatre in 1956. Angrily, violently, and in an unadorned and sometimes brutally colloquial dialogue, it thrust upon the audience the revelation of psychological and social problems left unresolved, or even exacerbated, by the welfare state. *The Entertainer* (1957) was similar in its brash virtuosity; Osborne's third play, *Luther* (1960), shows him moving out of a preoccupation with a restricted part of the contemporary social scene to wider concerns and a freer use of imagination. Arnold Wesker was another Royal Court discovery and became the most prominent of the so-called "kitchen sink" playwrights. In a trilogy that began with *Chicken Soup with Barley* (1958), he explored, though less stridently than Osborne, related social and psychological problems. Joan Littlewood's Theatre Workshop introduced another kind of vigorous new theatricalism, with an impromptu-seeming kind of play made up of numerous small scenes: distinctive examples are Brendan Behan's *The Quare Fellow* (1956) and Shelagh Delaney's *A Taste of Honey* (1958). Another significant factor in the recent resurgence of British drama has been the interaction of such innovative directors as Peter Brook and Peter Hall with the outstanding playwrights of the period and with several generations of superlative actors.

It is clear, however, that the major star in the constellation of playwrights that has emerged in the last three decades is Samuel Beckett. Friend and amanuensis of the major star of an earlier literary constellation, James Joyce, Beckett changed the course of English drama with his first play, written in French in 1948 and translated by the author himself as *Waiting for Godot* (1953), which strongly influenced a younger group of playwrights that includes Harold Pinter, the South African Athol Fugard, and Tom Stoppard. These, now at the height of their powers, have benefited from the variety of outlets for their work—large stage, small stage, film, radio, and television—and have helped to make London once again the capital city of the theater world.

THOMAS HARDY
1840–1928

1872–96:   Career as novelist, ending with *Jude the Obscure*.
1898:   *Wessex Poems*, first collection of poetry.

Thomas Hardy was born near Dorchester, in that area of southwest England that he was to make the "Wessex" of his novels. He attended local schools until the age of fifteen, when he was apprenticed to a Dorchester architect with whom he worked for six years. In 1861 he went to London to continue his studies and to practice as an architect. Meanwhile he was completing his general education informally through his own erratic reading, and becoming more and more interested in both fiction and poetry. After some early attempts at writing both short stories and poems, he decided to concentrate on fiction. His first novel was rejected by the publishers in 1868 on the advice of George Meredith, who nevertheless advised Hardy to write another. The result was *Desperate Remedies*, published anonymously in 1871, followed the next year by his first real success (also published anonymously), *Under the Greenwood Tree*. Hardy's career as a novelist was now well launched; he gave up his architectural work and produced a series of novels that ended with *Jude the Obscure* in 1896. The hostile reception of this novel sent him back to poetry. His remarkable epic-drama of the Napoleonic Wars, *The Dynasts*, came out in three parts between 1903 and 1908; after this he wrote mostly lyric poetry.

Hardy's novels, set in a predominantly rural "Wessex," show the forces of nature outside and inside man combining to shape human destiny. Against a background of immemorial agricultural labor, with ancient monuments such as Stonehenge or an old Roman amphitheater reminding us of the human past, he presents characters at the mercy of their own passions or finding temporary salvation in the age-old rhythms of rural work or rural recreation. Men and women in Hardy's fiction are not masters of their fates; they are at the mercy of the indifferent forces which manipulate their behavior and their relations with others; but they can achieve dignity through endurance, and heroism through simple strength of character. The characteristic Victorian novelist—e.g., Dickens and Thackeray—was concerned with the behavior and problems of people in a given social milieu, which he described in detail; Hardy preferred to go directly for the elemental in human behavior with a minimum of contemporary social detail. Most of Hardy's novels are tragic, though *Under the Greenwood Tree* has an idyllic character possessed by no other of his novels. But even here the happy ending is achieved only by ending the story with the marriage of the hero and heroine and refusing to go further; the texture of the narrative, for all its moments of gaiety and charm, has already suggested the bitter ironies of which life is capable. His later work explores those ironies with sometimes an almost malevolent staging of coincidence in order to emphasize the disparity between human desire and ambition on the one hand and what fate has in store for the characters on the other. But fate is not a wholly external force. Men and women are driven by the demands of their own nature as much as by anything from outside them. *Tess of the D'Urbervilles* (1891) is the story of an intelligent and sensitive girl, daughter of a poor family, driven to murder and so to death by hanging, by a concatenation of events and circumstances so bitterly ironic that many readers find it the darkest of Hardy's novels, while others would award that distinction to *Jude the Obscure*, the disturbingly powerful account of an ambitious rustic trapped between his intellect and his sensuality and as a result delivered to destruction.

Hardy himself denied that he was a pessimist, calling himself a "meliorist," i.e., one who believes that the world may be made better by human effort. But there is little sign of "meliorism" in either his most important novels or his lyric poetry. In his poems—which alone are represented here because no extract could do justice to Hardy's power as a novelist—many of his characteristic attitudes and ideas and many of his favorite situations can be found. A number of his poems are verse anecdotes illustrating the perversity of fate, the disastrous or ironic coincidence. But his best poems go beyond this mood to present with quiet gravity and a carefully controlled elegiac feeling some aspect of human sorrow or loss or frustration or regret, always projected through a particular, fully realized situation. *Hap* shows Hardy in the characteristic mood of complaining about the irony of human destiny in a universe ruled by chance; but a poem such as *The Walk* (one of a group of poems written after the death of his first wife in 1912) gives, with remarkable power, concrete embodiment to a sense of loss. That power— we see it also in *A Broken Appointment*—is achieved through a kind of verbal as well as an emotional integrity. Hardy's poetry, like his prose, often has a self-taught air about it; both can be odd or pretentious or awkward or clumsy. But at their best both his poetry and his prose have an air of persuasive authenticity. The association of a given emotion with particular visual memories in *Neutral Tones*, for example, is impressive because it carries such extraordinary conviction; and it carries that conviction because the rhythms and rhymes are handled so as to suggest the kind of utterance actually wrung from the poet (consider, e.g., the curious dead fall of "They had fallen from an ash, and were gray"). At the same time, Hardy will use an antique or a poetic word or phrase ("thereby," "a-wing") if it fits in with the movement of the poem and keeps him from having to stop and search for something more deft: the result is an effect not of artificiality but of spontaneity. Hardy's use of ballad rhythms often helps to give an elemental quality to his poetry, suggesting that this incident or situation, carefully particularized though it is, nevertheless stands for some profound and recurring themes in human experience.

The sadness in Hardy—his inability to believe in the government of the world by a benevolent God, his sense of the waste and frustration involved in human life, his insistent irony when faced with moral or metaphysical questions—is part of the late Victorian mood. We can see something like it in A. E. Housman, and there is an earlier version of Victorian pessimism in Edward FitzGerald's *Rubáiyát of Omar Khayyám*, published when Hardy was nineteen. What has been termed "the disappearance of God" affected him more deeply than many of his contemporaries, because until he was twenty-five he seriously considered entering the Church. Yet his characteristic themes and attitudes cannot be related simply to the reaction to new scientific and philosophical ideas (Darwin's theory of evolution, for example) that we see in so many forms in late nineteenth-century literature. The favorite poetic mood of both Tennyson and Arnold was also an elegiac one (e.g., in Tennyson's *Break, Break, Break* and Arnold's *Dover Beach*), but this is not Hardy's mood. The sad-sweet cadences of Victorian self-pity are not to be found in Hardy's poetry, which is sterner, as though braced by a long look at the worst. It is this sternness—sometimes amounting to ruggedness—together with his verbal and emotional integrity, his refusal ever to surrender to mere poetic fashion, his quietly searching individual accent, that has helped to bring about the steady rise in Hardy's poetic reputation, so that today he is regarded not only as a distinguished novelist but also as a great English poet.

Hap[1]

If but some vengeful god would call to me
From up the sky, and laugh: "Thou suffering thing,
Know that thy sorrow is my ecstasy,
That thy love's loss is my hate's profiting!"

Then would I bear it, clench myself, and die,   5
Steeled by the sense of ire unmerited;
Half-eased in that a Powerfuller than I
Had willed and meted[2] me the tears I shed.

But not so. How arrives it joy lies slain,
And why unblooms the best hope ever sown?   10
—Crass Casualty obstructs the sun and rain,
And dicing Time for gladness casts a moan. . . .
These purblind Doomsters[3] had as readily strown
Blisses about my pilgrimage as pain.

1866   1898

The Impercipient

(At a Cathedral Service)

That with this bright believing band
        I have no claim to be,
That faiths by which my comrades stand
        Seem fantasies to me,
And mirage-mists their Shining Land,   5
        Is a strange destiny.

Why thus my soul should be consigned
        To infelicity,
Why always I must feel as blind
        To sights my brethren see,   10

---

1. I.e., chance (as also "Casualty," line 11).   3. Half-blind judges.
2. Alotted, given.

Why joys they have found I cannot find,
    Abides a mystery.

Since heart of mine knows not that ease
    Which they know; since it be
That He who breathes All's Well to these   15
    Breathes no All's-Well to me,
My lack might move their sympathies
    And Christian charity!

I am like a gazer who should mark
    An inland company   20
Standing upfingered, with, "Hark! hark!
    The glorious distant sea!"
And feel, "Alas, 'tis but yon dark
    And wind-swept pine to me!"

Yet I would bear my shortcomings   25
    With meet tranquillity,
But for the charge that blessed things
    I'd liefer not have be.
O, doth a bird beshorn of wings
    Go earth-bound wilfully!   30

    • • •

Enough. As yet disquiet clings
    About us. Rest shall we.

        1898

Neutral Tones

We stood by a pond that winter day,
And the sun was white, as though chidden of God,
And a few leaves lay on the starving sod;
    —They had fallen from an ash, and were gray.

Your eyes on me were as eyes that rove   5
Over tedious riddles of years ago;
And some words played between us to and fro
    On which lost the more by our love.

The smile on your mouth was the deadest thing
Alive enough to have strength to die;   10
And a grin of bitterness swept thereby
    Like an ominous bird a-wing. . .

Since then, keen lessons that love deceives,
And wrings with wrong, have shaped to me

Your face, and the God-curst sun, and a tree,   15
   And a pond edged with grayish leaves.

1867   1898

I Look into My Glass[1]

I look into my glass,
And view my wasting skin,
And say, "Would God it came to pass
My heart had shrunk as thin!"

For then, I, undistrest   5
By hearts grown cold to me,
Could lonely wait my endless rest
With equanimity.

But Time, to make me grieve,
Part steals, lets part abide;   10
And shakes this fragile frame at eve
With throbbings of noontide.

1898

A Broken Appointment

   You did not come,
And marching Time drew on, and wore me numb.—
Yet less for loss of your dear presence there
Than that I thus found lacking in your make
That high compassion which can overbear   5
Reluctance for pure lovingkindness' sake
Grieved I, when, as the hope-hour stroked its sum,
   You did not come.

   You love not me,
And love alone can lend you loyalty;   10
—I know and knew it. But, unto the store
Of human deeds divine in all but name,
Was it not worth a little hour or more
To add yet this: Once you, a woman, came
To soothe a time-torn man; even though it be   15
   You love not me?

1902

1. Mirror.

Drummer Hodge

1

They throw in Drummer Hodge, to rest
    Uncoffined—just as found:
His landmark is a kopje-crest[1]
    That breaks the veldt around;
And foreign constellations west[2]   5
    Each night above his mound.

2

Young Hodge the Drummer never knew—
    Fresh from his Wessex home—
The meaning of the broad Karoo,[3]
    The Bush, the dusty loam,   10
And why uprose to nightly view
    Strange stars amid the gloam.

3

Yet portion of that unknown plain
    Will Hodge for ever be;
His homely Northern breast and brain   15
    Grow to some Southern tree,
And strange-eyed constellations reign
    His stars eternally.

1899   1902

The Darkling[1] Thrush

I leant upon a coppice gate[2]
    When Frost was spectre-gray,
And Winter's dregs made desolate
    The weakening eye of day.
The tangled bine-stems[3] scored the sky   5
    Like strings of broken lyres,
And all mankind that haunted nigh
    Had sought their household fires.

The land's sharp features seemed to be
    The Century's corpse outleant,[4]   10
His crypt the cloudy canopy,
    The wind his death-lament.

---

1. South African Dutch (Afrikaans) word for a small hill. "Veldt": Afrikaans for a plain or prairie. The poem is a lament for an English soldier killed in the Boer War (1899–1902).
2. Set. The "foreign constellations" are those visible only in the southern hemisphere.
3. A dry table-land region in South Africa (usually spelled "Karroo"). "The Bush": British Colonial word for an uncleared area of land.

1. In the dark.
2. Gate leading to a small wood or thicket.
3. Twining stems of shrubs.
4. Leaning out (of its coffin). This poem was written on Dec. 31, 1900, the last day of the 19th century.

The ancient pulse of germ and birth
    Was shrunken hard and dry,
And every spirit upon earth   15
    Seemed fervourless as I.

At once a voice arose among
    The bleak twigs overhead
In a full-hearted evensong
    Of joy illimited;   20
An aged thrush, frail, gaunt, and small,
    In blast-beruffled plume,
Had chosen thus to fling his soul
    Upon the growing gloom.

So little cause for carolings   25
    Of such ecstatic sound
Was written on terrestrial things
    Afar or nigh around,
That I could think there trembled through
    His happy good-night air   30
Some blessed Hope, whereof he knew
    And I was unaware.

1900   1901

The Ruined Maid

"O 'Melia, my dear, this does everything crown!
Who could have supposed I should meet you in Town?
And whence such fair garments, such prosperi-ty?"—
"O didn't you know I'd been ruined?" said she.

—"You left us in tatters, without shoes or socks,   5
Tired of digging potatoes, and spudding up docks;[1]
And now you've gay bracelets and bright feathers three!"—
"Yes: that's how we dress when we're ruined," said she.

—"At home in the barton[2] you said 'thee' and 'thou,'
And 'thik oon,' and 'theäs oon,' and 't'other'; but now   10
Your talking quite fits 'ee for high compa-ny!"—
"Some polish is gained with one's ruin," said she.

—"Your hands were like paws then, your face blue and bleak
But now I'm bewitched by your delicate cheek,
And your little gloves fit as on any la-dy!"—   15
"We never do work when we're ruined," said she.

---

1. Digging up a species of thick-rooted weed.   2. Farmyard.

—"You used to call home-life a hag-ridden dream,
And you'd sigh, and you'd sock;[3] but at present you seem
To know not of megrims[4] or melancho-ly!"—
"True. One's pretty lively when ruined," said she.   20

—"I wish I had feathers, a fine sweeping gown,
And a delicate face, and could strut about Town!"—
"My dear—a raw country girl, such as you be,
Cannot quite expect that. You ain't ruined," said she.

1866   1901

Channel Firing[1]

That night your great guns, unawares,
Shook all our coffins as we lay,
And broke the chancel[2] window-squares,
We thought it was the Judgment-day

And sat upright. While drearisome   5
Arose the howl of wakened hounds:
The mouse let fall the altar-crumb,
The worms drew back into the mounds,

The glebe cow[3] drooled. Till God called, "No;
It's gunnery practice out at sea   10
Just as before you went below;
The world is as it used to be:

"All nations striving strong to make
Red war yet redder. Mad as hatters
They do no more for Christès[4] sake   15
Than you who are helpless in such matters.

"That this is not the judgment-hour
For some of them's a blessed thing,
For if it were they'd have to scour
Hell's floor for so much threatening. . . .   20

"Ha, ha. It will be warmer when
I blow the trumpet (if indeed
I ever do; for you are men,
And rest eternal sorely need)."

3. Sigh.
4. Low spirits.
1. Written in April 1914, when Anglo-German naval rivalry was growing steadily more acute; the title refers to gunnery practice in the English Channel. Four months later (August 4) World War

I broke out.
2. Part of church nearest to the altar.
3. I.e., cow on a small plot of land belonging to a cottage (a "glebe" is a small field).
4. The archaic spelling and pronunciation suggest a ballad note of doom.

So down we lay again. "I wonder,   25
Will the world ever saner be,"
Said one, "than when He sent us under
In our indifferent century!"

And many a skeleton shook his head.
"Instead of preaching forty year,"
My neighbour Parson Thirdly said,   30
"I wish I had stuck to pipes and beer."

Again the guns disturbed the hour,
Roaring their readiness to avenge,
As far inland as Stourton Tower,   35
And Camelot, and starlit Stonehenge.[5]

1914   1914

The Convergence of the Twain

(Lines on the Loss of the *Titanic*)[1]

1

In a solitude of the sea
Deep from human vanity,
And the Pride of Life that planned her, stilly couches
she.

2

Steel chambers, late the pyres
Of her salamandrine fires,[2]   5
Cold currents thrid, and turn to rhythmic tidal lyres.

3

Over the mirrors meant
To glass the opulent
The sea-worm crawls—grotesque, slimed, dumb, in-
different.

4

Jewels in joy designed   10
To ravish the sensuous mind
Lie lightless, all their sparkles bleared and black and
blind.

5. Stonehenge is the famous prehistoric stone circle on Salisbury Plain; Camelot was the legendary
location of King Arthur's court and the Round
Table. There is a real river Stour in Dorset, and a
town called Stour Head, which Hardy calls
"Stourton."
1. The *Titanic* was the largest and most luxurious
ocean liner of her day. Considered unsinkable, she
sank with great loss of life on April 15, 1912, on
her maiden voyage from Southampton to America, after colliding with an iceberg.
2. Probably "fires in which nothing could survive"
(although, since the salamander is a lizardlike animal supposed to be able to live in fire, "salamandrine" usually means "able to resist or to live in
fire"). In the next line, "thrid" is the archaic past
tense of the verb "thread."

5

Dim moon-eyed fishes near
Gaze at the gilded gear
And query: "What does this vaingloriousness down
        here?" . . .   15

6

Well: while was fashioning
This creature of cleaving wing,
The Immanent Will[3] that stirs and urges everything

7

Prepared a sinister mate
For her—so gaily great—   20
A Shape of Ice, for the time far and dissociate.

8

And as the smart ship grew
In stature, grace, and hue,
In shadowy silent distance grew the Iceberg too.

9

Alien they seemed to be: 25
No mortal eye could see
The intimate welding of their later history,

10

Or sign that they were bent
By paths coincident
On being anon twin halves of one august event,   30

11

Till the Spinner of the Years
Said "Now!" And each one hears,
And consummation comes, and jars two hemispheres.

1912   1912, 1914

Ah, Are You Digging on My Grave?

"Ah, are you digging on my grave
        My loved one?—planting rue?"[1]
—"No: yesterday he went to wed
One of the brightest wealth has bred.
'It cannot hurt her now,' he said,   5
        'That I should not be true.' "

"Then who is digging on my grave?
        My nearest dearest kin?"
—"Ah, no; they sit and think, 'What use!

---

3. The force (blind, but slowly gaining consciousness throughout history) which drives the world,
according to Hardy's philosophy.

1. A yellow-flowered herb, traditionally an emblem
of sorrow ("rue" is also an archaic word for "sorrow").

What good will planting flowers produce?   10
No tendance of her mound can loose
    Her spirit from Death's gin.' "[2]

"But some one digs upon my grave?
    My enemy?—prodding sly?"
—"Nay: when she heard you had passed the Gate   15
That shuts on all flesh soon or late,
She thought you no more worth her hate,
    And cares not where you lie."

"Then, who is digging on my grave?
    Say—since I have not guessed!"   20
—"O it is I, my mistress dear,
Your little dog, who still lives near,
And much I hope my movements here
    Have not disturbed your rest?"

"Ah, yes! *You* dig upon my grave . . .   25
    Why flashed it not on me
That one true heart was left behind!
What feeling do we ever find
To equal among human kind
    A dog's fidelity!"   30

"Mistress, I dug upon your grave
    To bury a bone, in case
I should be hungry near this spot
When passing on my daily trot.
I am sorry, but I quite forgot   35
    It was your resting-place."

                    1914

Under the Waterfall

"Whenever I plunge my arm, like this,
In a basin of water, I never miss
The sweet sharp sense of a fugitive day
Fetched back from its thickening shroud of gray.
        Hence the only prime   5
        And real love-rhyme
        That I know by heart,
        And that leaves no smart,
Is the purl of a little valley fall
About three spans wide and two spans tall   10

2. Trap.

Over a table of solid rock,
And into a scoop of the self-same block;
The purl of a runlet that never ceases
In stir of kingdoms, in wars, in peaces;
With a hollow boiling voice it speaks   15
And has spoken since hills were turfless peaks."

"And why gives this the only prime
Idea to you of a real love-rhyme?
And why does plunging your arm in a bowl
Full of spring water, bring throbs to your soul?"   20

"Well, under the fall, in a crease of the stone,
Though where precisely none ever has known,
Jammed darkly, nothing to show how prized,
And by now with its smoothness opalized,
                Is a drinking-glass: 25
                For, down that pass
                My lover and I
                Walked under a sky
Of blue with a leaf-wove awning of green,
In the burn of August, to paint the scene,   30
And we placed our basket of fruit and wine
By the runlet's rim, where we sat to dine;
And when we had drunk from the glass together,
Arched by the oak-copse from the weather,
I held the vessel to rinse in the fall,   35
Where it slipped, and sank, and was past recall,
Though we stooped and plumbed the little abyss
With long bared arms. There the glass still is.
And, as said, if I thrust my arm below
Cold water in basin or bowl, a throe[1]   40
From the past awakens a sense of that time,
And the glass we used, and the cascade's rhyme.
The basin seems the pool, and its edge
The hard smooth face of the brook-side ledge,
And the leafy pattern of china-ware   45
The hanging plants that were bathing there.

"By night, by day, when it shines or lours,
There lies intact that chalice of ours,
And its presence adds to the rhyme of love
Persistently sung by the fall above.   50
No lip has touched it since his and mine
In turns therefrom sipped lovers' wine."

                                                    1914

1. Violent pang.

The Walk

You did not walk with me
Of late to the hill-top tree
    By the gated ways,
    As in earlier days;
    You were weak and lame,   5
    So you never came,
And I went alone, and I did not mind,
Not thinking of you as left behind.

    I walked up there to-day
    Just in the former way: 10
        Surveyed around
        The familiar ground
        By myself again:
        What difference, then?
Only that underlying sense   15
Of the look of a room on returning thence.

1912–13   1914

The Voice

Woman much missed, how you call to me, call to me,
Saying that now you are not as you were
When you had changed from the one who was all to me,
But as at first, when our day was fair.

Can it be you that I hear? Let me view you, then,   5
Standing as when I drew near to the town
Where you would wait for me: yes, as I knew you then,
Even to the original air-blue gown!

Or is it only the breeze, in its listlessness
Travelling across the wet mead to me here,   10
You being ever dissolved to wan wistlessness,[1]
Heard no more again far or near?

    Thus I; faltering forward,
    Leaves around me falling,
Wind oozing thin through the thorn from norward,[2]
    And the woman calling.

December 1912   1914

1. Inattention.   2. Northward.

The Workbox

"See, here's the workbox, little wife,
   That I made of polished oak."
He was a joiner,[1] of village life;
   She came of borough folk.[2]

He holds the present up to her   5
   As with a smile she nears
And answers to the profferer,
   "'Twill last all my sewing years!"

"I warrant it will. And longer too.
   'Tis a scantling[3] that I got   10
Off poor John Wayward's coffin, who
   Died of they knew not what.

"The shingled pattern that seems to cease
   Against your box's rim
Continues right on in the piece   15
   That's underground with him.

"And while I worked it made me think
   Of timber's varied doom;
One inch where people eat and drink,
   The next inch in a tomb.   20

"But why do you look so white, my dear,
   And turn aside your face?
You knew not that good lad, I fear,
   Though he came from your native place?"

"How could I know that good young man,   25
   Though he came from my native town,
When he must have left far earlier than
   I was a woman grown?"

"Ah, no. I should have understood!
   It shocked you that I gave   30
To you one end of a piece of wood
   Whose other is in a grave?"

"Don't, dear, despise my intellect,
   Mere accidental things
Of that sort never have effect   35
   On my imaginings."

---

1. Carpenter.
2. Townspeople.
3. Small piece of wood.

Yet still her lips were limp and wan,
   Her face still held aside,
As if she had known not only John,
   But known of what he died.   40

1914

During Wind and Rain

They sing their dearest songs—
   He, she, all of them—yea,
Treble and tenor and bass,
    And one to play;
With the candles mooning each face. . . .   5
    Ah, no; the years O!
How the sick leaves reel down in throngs!

They clear the creeping moss—
   Elders and juniors—aye,
Making the pathways neat   10
    And the garden gay;
And they build a shady seat. . . .
    Ah, no; the years, the years;
See, the white storm-birds wing across.

They are blithely breakfasting all—   15
   Men and maidens—yea,
Under the summer tree,
    With a glimpse of the bay,
While pet fowl come to the knee. . . .
    Ah, no; the years O!   20
And the rotten rose is ript from the wall.

They change to a high new house,
   He, she, all of them—aye,
Clocks and carpets and chairs
    On the lawn all day,   25
And brightest things that are theirs. . . .
    Ah, no; the years, the years;
Down their carved names the rain-drop ploughs.

1917

In Time of "The Breaking of Nations"[1]

1

Only a man harrowing clods
  In a slow silent walk

---

1. Cf. "Thou art my battle axe and weapon of war: for with thee will I break in pieces the nations" (Jeremiah 51.20). The poem was written during World War I.

With an old horse that stumbles and nods
   Half asleep as they stalk.

2

Only thin smoke without flame   5
   From the heaps of couch-grass;
Yet this will go onward the same
   Though Dynasties pass.

3

Yonder a maid and her wight[2]
   Come whispering by: 10
War's annals will cloud into night
   Ere their story die.

1915   1916

He Never Expected Much

[or]
A Consideration
[A *reflection*] *on My Eighty-Sixth Birthday*

Well, World, you have kept faith with me,
         Kept faith with me;
Upon the whole you have proved to be
         Much as you said you were.
Since as a child I used to lie
Upon the leaze[1] and watch the sky,   5
Never, I own, expected I
         That life would all be fair.

'Twas then you said, and since have said,
         Times since have said,   10
In that mysterious voice you shed
         From clouds and hills around:
"Many have loved me desperately,
Many with smooth serenity,
While some have shown contempt of me   15
         Till they dropped underground.

"I do not promise overmuch,
         Child; overmuch;
Just neutral-tinted haps[2] and such,"
         You said to minds like mine.   20
Wise warning for your credit's sake!
Which I for one failed not to take,

And hence could stem such strain and ache
As each year might assign.

1926   1928

JOSEPH CONRAD
1857–1924

1875–94:   Career as a seaman.
1895:   *Almayer's Folly.*
1904:   *Nostromo.*

Joseph Conrad was born Jozef Teodor Konrad Nalecz Korzeniowski in Poland (then under Russian rule), son of a Polish patriot who suffered exile in Russia for his Polish nationalist activities and died in 1869, leaving Conrad to be brought up by a maternal uncle. At the age of fifteen he amazed his family and friends by announcing his passionate desire to go to sea; he was eventually allowed to go to Marseilles in 1874, and from there he made a number of voyages on French merchant ships to Martinique and the West Indies. In 1878 he signed on an English ship which brought him to the east coast English port of Lowestoft, where (still as an ordinary seaman) he joined the crew of a small coasting vessel plying between Lowestoft and Newcastle. In six voyages between these two ports he learned English. Thus launched on a career in the British merchant service, Conrad sailed on a variety of British ships to the Orient and elsewhere and eventually gained his master's certificate in 1886, the year when he became a naturalized British subject. He received his first command in 1888, and in 1890 took a steamboat up the Congo River in nightmarish circumstances (described in *Heart of Darkness*) which produced severe illness and permanently haunted his imagination. In the early 1890s he was already thinking of turning some of his Malayan experiences into English fiction, and in 1892–93, when serving as first mate on the *Torrens* sailing from London to Adelaide, he revealed to a sympathetic passenger that he had begun a novel (*Almayer's Folly*), while on the return journey he impressed John Galsworthy, who was on board, with his conversation. Though possessed of a master's certificate, Conrad found it difficult to get the kind of job as master that he wished, and occasionally he had to serve in lesser capacities. His difficulty in obtaining a command, together with the interest aroused by *Almayer's Folly* when it was published in 1895, helped to turn him away from the sea to a career as a writer. He settled in London and in 1896 married an English girl; this son of a Polish patriot turned merchant seaman turned writer was henceforth an English novelist.

Conrad was for a long time regarded as a sea writer whose exotic descriptions of eastern landscapes and exploitation of the romantic atmosphere of Malaya and other unfamiliar regions gave his work a special kind of richness and splendor. But this is only one, and not in the last analysis the most important, aspect of his work. More and more Conrad used the sea and the circumstances of life on shipboard or in remote eastern settlements as means of exploring certain profound moral ambiguities in human experience. In *The Nigger of the "Narcissus"* (1897) he shows how a dying Negro seaman corrupts the morale of a ship's crew by the very fact that his plight produces sympathy, thus symbolically presenting one of his commonest themes—the necessity and at the same time the dangers of human contact. In *Lord Jim* (1900), using the device of an intermediate narrator, he probes the meaning of a gross failure of duty on the part of a romantic and idealistic young sailor, and by presenting the hero's history from a series of different points of view keeps the moral questioning continuing to the end. The use of intermediate narrators and multiple points of view is common in Conrad; it is his favorite way of suggesting the complexity of experience and the difficulty of judging human actions.

This notion of the difficulty of true communion, coupled with the idea that communion can be unexpectedly forced on us—sometimes with someone who may be on the surface our moral opposite, so that we can at times be compelled into a mysterious recognition of our opposite as our true self—is found in many of Conrad's works; it provides one of the underlying themes of *The Secret Sharer* (1912). This story can be enjoyed for the clarity and power with which Conrad renders the atmosphere of the Gulf of Siam as felt by a young sea captain on taking on his first command, but it also uses situation and incident symbolically in order to suggest some of the paradoxes of identity and sympathy.

Other stories and novels explore the ways in which the codes we live by are tested in moments of crisis, revealing either their inadequacy or our own. Imagination can corrupt (as with Lord Jim), or save (as in *The Shadow Line*, 1917); and there are times when total lack of it can see a man through (Captain M'Whirr in *Typhoon*, 1902), though a similar lack in other circumstances can render a man comically ridiculous (Captain Mitchell in *Nostromo*, 1904).

Nostromo, a profound and subtle study of the corrupting effects of politics and "material interests" on personal relationships (set in an imaginary South American republic), is often regarded as Conrad's greatest work. His two other political novels—*The Secret Agent* (1906) and *Under Western Eyes* (1910)—have also recently come into their own. The latter is the story of a Russian student who becomes involuntarily associated with antigovernment violence in Czarist Russia and is irresistibly maneuvered by circumstances into a position where, although a government spy, he has to pretend to be a revolutionary among revolutionaries. This is the ultimate in human loneliness and incommunicability—when you must consistently pretend to be the opposite of what you are. It is a story of Dostoyevskian power, and shows a very different Conrad from the picturesque sea-dreamer pictured by the earlier critics. Conrad was as much a pessimist as Hardy, but he projected his pessimism in subtler ways. He was also a great master of English prose, an astonishing fact when we realize that he was twenty-one before he learned any English, and that to the end of his life he spoke English with a thick foreign accent.

Heart of Darkness is derived from Conrad's personal experience in the Congo in 1890. Like Marlow, the narrator of the story, Conrad had as a child determined one day to visit the heart of Africa. "It was in 1868, when nine years old or thereabouts, that while looking at a map of Africa at the time and putting my finger on the blank space then representing the unsolved mystery of that continent, I said to myself with absolute assurance and an amazing audacity which are no longer in my character now: 'When I grow up I shall go *there*' " (*A Personal Record*, 1912).

Conrad was promised a job as a Congo River pilot through the influence of his distant cousin Marguerite Poradowska, who lived in Brussels and knew important officials of the Belgian company which exploited the Congo. At this time the Congo, though nominally an independent state, the Congo Free State (État Indépendent du Congo), was virtually the personal property of Leopold II, king of the Belgians, who made a fortune out of it. Later, the appalling abuses involved in the naked colonial exploitation that went on in the Congo were exposed to public view, and international criticism compelled the setting up of a committee of inquiry in 1904. What Conrad saw in 1890 shocked him profoundly and shook his view of the moral basis of all exploring and trading in newly discovered countries and indeed of civilization in general. *"Heart of Darkness* is experience, too,"* Conrad wrote in his 1917 "Author's Note," "but it is experience pushed a little (and only very little) beyond the actual facts of the case for the perfectly legitimate, I believe, purpose of bringing it home to the minds and bosoms of the readers." And later he told Edward Garnett: "Before the Congo I was just a mere animal."

Conrad arrived in Africa in May 1890 and made his way up the Congo River very much as described in *Heart of Darkness*. At Kinshasa (which Conrad spells Kinchassa) on Stanley Pool, which he reached after an exhausting 200-mile trek from Matadi, near the mouth of the river, Conrad was much taken aback to learn that the steamer of which he was to be captain had been damaged and was undergoing repairs. He was sent as supernumerary on another steamer to learn the river. This other steamer was sent to Stanley Falls to collect and bring back to Kinshasa one Georges Antoine Klein, an agent of the company who had fallen gravely ill and who in fact died on board. Klein was the original of Kurtz. Conrad himself then fell seriously ill, and eventually returned to London in January 1891 without ever having actually served as a Congo River pilot, the job for which he went out to Africa. The Congo experience permanently impaired his health: it also permanently haunted his imagination. The nightmare atmosphere of *Heart of Darkness* is an accurate reflection of Conrad's own response to his traumatic experience.

The theme of the story is partly the "choice of nightmares" facing the white man in the Congo—either to become like the wholly commercially minded manager, who sees Africa, its people, and its resources solely as instruments of financial gain, or to become like Kurtz, the self-tortured and corrupted idealist. The manager is a "hollow man" (T. S. Eliot quoted from this story in his poem of that title); his only objections to Kurtz are commercial, not moral; Kurtz's methods are "unsound" and would therefore lose the company money. Kurtz finally recognizes the moral horror of his having succumbed to the dark temptations which African life posed for the white man. "He had summed up—he had judged." But the story also has other levels of meaning, and the counterpointing of Western civilization in Europe with what that civilization has done in Africa (see the concluding interview between Marlow and Kurtz's "intended"—based on a real interview between Conrad and the dead Klein's fiancée) throws up several of these.

Heart of Darkness

1

The *Nellie*, a cruising yawl, swung to her anchor without a flutter of the sails, and was at rest. The flood had made, the wind was nearly calm, and being bound down the river, the only thing for it was to come to and wait for the turn of the tide.

The sea-reach of the Thames stretched before us like the beginning of an interminable waterway. In the offing the sea and the sky were welded together without a joint, and in the luminous space the tanned sails of the barges drifting up with the tide seemed to stand still in red clusters of canvas sharply peaked, with gleams of varnished spirits. A haze rested on the low shores that ran out to sea in vanishing flatness. The air was dark above Gravesend,[1] and farther back still seemed condensed into a mournful gloom, brooding motionless over the biggest, and the greatest, town on earth.

The Director of Companies was our captain and our host. We four affectionately watched his back as he stood in the bows looking to seaward. On the whole river there was nothing that looked half so nautical. He resembled a pilot, which to a seaman is trustworthiness personified. It was difficult to realise his work was not out there in the luminous estuary, but behind him, within the brooding gloom.

Between us there was, as I have already said somewhere, the bond of the sea. Besides holding our hearts together through long periods of separation, it had the effect of making us tolerant of each other's yarns—and even convictions. The Lawyer—the best of old fellows—had, because of his many years and many virtues, the only cushion on deck, and was lying on the only rug. The Accountant had brought out already a box of dominoes, and was toying architecturally with the bones. Marlow sat cross-legged right aft, leaning against the mizzenmast. He had sunken cheeks, a yellow complexion, a straight back, an ascetic aspect, and, with his arms dropped, the palms of hands outwards, resembled an idol. The Director, satisfied the anchor had good hold, made his way aft and sat down amongst us. We exchanged a few words lazily. Afterwards there was silence on board the yacht. For some reason or other we did not begin that game of dominoes. We felt meditative, and fit for nothing but placid staring. The day was ending in a serenity of still and exquisite brilliance. The water shone pacifically; the sky, without a speck, was a benign immensity of unstained light; the very mist on the Essex marshes was like a gauzy and radiant fabric, hung from the wooded rises inland, and draping the low shores in diaphanous folds. Only the gloom to the west, brooding over the upper reaches, became more sombre every minute, as if angered by the approach of the sun.

And at last, in its curved and imperceptible fall, the sun sank low,

---

1. River port on the south bank of the Thames some 24 miles east (downriver) of London.

and from glowing white changed to a dull red without rays and without heat, as if about to go out suddenly, stricken to death by the touch of that gloom brooding over a crowd of men.

Forthwith a change came over the waters, and the serenity became less brilliant but more profound. The old river in its broad reach rested unruffled at the decline of day, after ages of good service done to the race that peopled its banks, spread out in the tranquil dignity of a waterway leading to the uttermost ends of the earth. We looked at the venerable stream not in the vivid flush of a short day that comes and departs for ever, but in the august light of abiding memories. And indeed nothing is easier for a man who has, as the phrase goes, "followed the sea" with reverence and affection, than to evoke the great spirit of the past upon the lower reaches of the Thames. The tidal current runs to and fro in its unceasing service, crowded with memories of men and ships it has borne to the rest of home or to the battles of the sea. It had known and served all the men of whom the nation is proud, from Sir Francis Drake to Sir John Franklin,[2] knights all, titled and untitled—the great knights-errant of the sea. It had borne all the ships whose names are like jewels flashing in the night of time, from the *Golden Hind* returning with her round flanks full of treasure, to be visited by the Queen's Highness and thus pass out of the gigantic tale, to the *Erebus* and *Terror*, bound on other conquests—and that never returned. It had known the ships and the men. They had sailed from Deptford, from Greenwich, from Erith—the adventurers and the settlers; kings' ships and the ships of men on 'Change; captains, admirals, the dark "interlopers" of the Eastern trade, and the commissioned "generals" of East India fleets.[3] Hunters for gold or pursuers of fame, they all had gone out on that stream, bearing the sword, and often the torch, messengers of the might within the land, bearers of a spark from the sacred fire. What greatness had not floated on the ebb of that river into the mystery of an unknown earth! . . . The dreams of men, the seed of commonwealths, the germs of empires.

The sun set; the dusk fell on the stream, and lights began to appear along the shore. The Chapman lighthouse, a three-legged thing erect on a mud-flat, shone strongly. Lights of ships moved in the fairway[4]—a great stir of lights going up and going down. And farther west on the upper reaches the place of the monstrous town was still marked ominously on the sky, a brooding gloom in sunshine, a lurid glare under the stars.

---

2. Sir Francis Drake (ca. 1540–1596), Elizabethan naval hero and explorer, sailed round the world in his ship *The Golden Hind*. Queen Elizabeth knighted Drake on board his ship, loaded with captured Spanish treasure, on his return. Sir John Franklin (1786–1847), Arctic explorer, in 1845 commanded an expedition consisting of the ships *Erebus* and *Terror* in search of the Northwest passage. The ships never returned.
3. Deptford, on the south bank of the Thames, on the eastern edge of London, once (but no longer)

an important dockyard. Greenwich is on the south bank of the Thames immediately east of Deptford. Erith is some 8 miles further east. "Change" is the Stock Exchange. "Interlopers" were private ships muscling in on the monopoly of the East India Company, which was founded in 1600, lost its trading monopoly in 1813, and transferred its governmental functions to the Crown in 1858.
4. Navigable part of a river, through which ships enter and depart.

"And this also," said Marlow suddenly, "has been one of the dark places of the earth."

He was the only man of us who still "followed the sea." The worst that could be said of him was that he did not represent his class. He was a seaman, but he was a wanderer too, while most seamen lead, if one may so express it, a sedentary life. Their minds are of the stay-at-home order, and their home is always with them—the ship; and so is their country—the sea. One ship is very much like another, and the sea is always the same. In the immutability of their surroundings the foreign shores, the foreign faces, the changing immensity of life, glide past, veiled not by a sense of mystery but by a slightly disdainful ignorance; for there is nothing mysterious to a seaman unless it be the sea itself, which is the mistress of his existence and as incrutable as Destiny. For the rest, after his hours of work, a casual stroll or a casual spree on shore suffices to unfold for him the secret of a whole continent, and generally he finds the secret not worth knowing. The yarns of seamen have a direct simplicity, the whole meaning of which lies within the shell of a cracked nut. But Marlow was not typical (if his propensity to spin yarns be excepted), and to him the meaning of an episode was not inside like a kernel but outside, enveloping the tale which brought it out only as a glow brings out a haze, in the likeness of one of these misty halos that sometimes are made visible by the spectral illumination of moonshine.

His remark did not seem at all surprising. It was just like Marlow. It was accepted in silence. No one took the trouble to grunt even; and presently he said, very slow:

"I was thinking of very old times, when the Romans first came here, nineteen hundred years ago—the other day. . . . Light came out of this river since—you say Knights? Yes; but it is like a running blaze on a plain, like a flash of lightning in the clouds. We live in the flicker—may it last as long as the old earth keeps rolling! But darkness was here yesterday. Imagine the feelings of a commander of a fine—what d'ye call 'em?—trireme[5] in the Mediterranean, ordered suddenly to the north; run overland across the Gauls in a hurry; put in charge of one of these craft the legionaries—a wonderful lot of handy men they must have been too—used to build, apparently by the hundred, in a month or two, if we may believe what we read. Imagine him here—the very end of the world, a sea the colour of lead, a sky the colour of smoke, a kind of ship about as rigid as a concertina—and going up this river with stores, or orders, or what you like. Sandbanks, marshes, forests, savages—precious little to eat fit for a civilised man, nothing but Thames water to drink. No Falernian wine here, no going ashore. Here and there a military camp lost in a wilderness, like a needle in a bundle of hay—cold, fog, tempests, disease, exile, and death—death skulking in the air, in the water, in the bush. They must have been dying like flies here. Oh yes—he did it. Did it very well, too, no doubt, and without thinking much

5. Ancient Greek and Roman galley with three ranks of oars.

about it either, except afterwards to brag of what he had gone through in his time, perhaps. They were men enough to face the darkness. And perhaps he was cheered by keeping his eye on a chance of promotion to the fleet at Ravenna[6] by and by, if he had good friends in Rome and survived the awful climate. Or think of a decent young citizen in a toga—perhaps too much dice, you know—coming out here in the train of some prefect, or tax-gatherer, or trader, even, to mend his fortunes. Land in a swamp, march through the woods, and in some inland post feel the savagery, the utter savagery, had closed round him—all that mysterious life of the wilderness that stirs in the forest, in the jungles, in the hearts of wild men. There's no initiation either into such mysteries. He has to live in the midst of the incomprehensible, which is also detestable. And it has a fascination, too, that goes to work upon him. The fascination of the abomination—you know. Imagine the growing regrets, the longing to escape, the powerless disgust, the surrender, the hate."

He paused.

"Mind," he began again, lifting one arm from the elbow, the palm of the hand outwards, so that, with his legs folded before him, he had the pose of a Buddha preaching in European clothes and without a lotus-flower—"Mind, none of us would feel exactly like this. What saves us is efficiency—the devotion to efficiency. But these chaps were not much account, really. They were no colonists; their administration was merely a squeeze, and nothing more, I suspect. They are conquerors, and for that you want only brute force—nothing to boast of, when you have it, since your strength is just an accident arising from the weakness of others. They grabbed what they could get for the sake of what was to be got. It was just robbery with violence, aggravated murder on a great scale, and men going at it blind—as is very proper for those who tackle a darkness. The conquest of the earth, which mostly means the taking it away from those who have a different complexion or slightly flatter noses than ourselves, is not a pretty thing when you look into it too much. What redeems it is the idea only. An idea at the back of it; not a sentimental pretence but an idea; and an unselfish belief in the idea—something you can set up, and bow down before, and offer a sacrifice to. . . ."

He broke off. Flames glided in the river, small green flames, red flames, white flames, pursuing, overtaking, joining, crossing each other—then separating slowly or hastily. The traffic of the great city went on in the deepening night upon the sleepless river. We looked on, waiting patiently—there was nothing else to do till the end of the flood; but it was only after a long silence, when he said, in a hesitating voice, "I suppose you fellows remember I did once turn fresh-water sailor for a bit," that we knew we were fated, before the ebb began to run, to hear about one of Marlow's inconclusive experiences.

"I don't want to bother you much with what happened to me personally," he began, showing in this remark the weakness of many tellers of

6. City in northern Italy once directly on the Adriatic Sea and an important naval station in Roman times. Now about 6 miles from the sea, connected with it by a canal.

tales who seem so often unaware of what their audience would best like to hear; "yet to understand the effect of it on me you ought to know how I got out there, what I saw, how I went up that river to the place where I first met the poor chap. It was the farthest point of navigation and the culminating point of my experience. It seemed somehow to throw a kind of light on everything about me—and into my thoughts. It was sombre enough too—and pitiful—not extraordinary in any way—not very clear either. No, not very clear. And yet it seemed to throw a kind of light.

"I had then, as you remember, just returned to London after a lot of Indian Ocean, Pacific, China Seas—a regular dose of the East—six years or so, and I was loafing about, hindering you fellows in your work and invading your homes, just as though I had got a heavenly mission to civilise you. It was very fine for a time, but after a bit I did get tired of resting. Then I began to look for a ship—I should think the hardest work on earth. But the ships wouldn't even look at me. And I got tired of that game too.

"Now when I was a little chap I had a passion for maps. I would look for hours at South America, or Africa, or Australia, and lose myself in all the glories of exploration. At that time there were many blank spaces on the earth, and when I saw one that looked particularly inviting on a map (but they all look that) I would put my finger on it and say, When I grow up I will go there. The North Pole was one of these places, I remember. Well, I haven't been there yet, and shall not try now. The glamour's off. Other places were scattered about the Equator, and in every sort of latitude all over the two hemispheres. I have been in some of them, and . . . well, we won't talk about that. But there was one yet—the biggest, the most blank, so to speak—that I had a hankering after.

"True, by this time it was not a blank space any more. It had got filled since my boyhood with rivers and lakes and names. It had ceased to be a blank space of delightful mystery—a white patch for a boy to dream gloriously over. It had become a place of darkness. But there was in it one river especially, a mighty big river, that you could see on the map, resembling an immense snake uncoiled, with its head in the sea, its body at rest curving afar over a vast country, and its tail lost in the depths of the land. And as I looked at the map of it in a shop-window, it fascinated me as a snake would a bird—a silly little bird. Then I remembered there was a big concern, a Company for trade on that river. Dash it all! I thought to myself, they can't trade without using some kind of craft on that lot of fresh water—steamboats! Why shouldn't I try to get charge of one? I went on along Fleet Street, but could not shake off the idea. The snake had charmed me.

"You understand it was a Continental concern, that Trading Society; but I have a lot of relations living on the Continent, because it's cheap and not so nasty as it looks, they say.

"I am sorry to own I began to worry them. This was already a fresh departure for me. I was not used to get things that way, you know. I always went my own road and on my own legs where I had a mind to go. I wouldn't have believed it of myself; but, then—you see—I felt somehow I must get there by hook or by crook. So I worried them. The men said, 'My dear fellow,' and did nothing. Then—would you believe it?—I tried the women. I, Charlie Marlow, set the women to work—to get a job. Heavens! Well, you see, the notion drove me. I had an aunt, a dear enthusiastic soul. She wrote: 'It will be delightful. I am ready to do anything, anything for you. It is a glorious idea. I know the wife of a very high personage in the Administration, and also a man who has lots of influence with,' etc. etc. She was determined to make no end of fuss to get me appointed skipper of a river steamboat, if such was my fancy.

"I got my appointment—of course; and I got it very quick. It appears the Company had received news that one of their captains had been killed in a scuffle with the natives. This was my chance, and it made me the more anxious to go. It was only months and months afterwards, when I made the attempt to recover what was left of the body, that I heard the original quarrel arose from a misunderstanding about some hens. Yes, two black hens. Fresleven—that was the fellow's name, a Dane—thought himself wronged somehow in the bargain, so he went ashore and started to hammer the chief of the village with a stick. Oh, it didn't surprise me in the least to hear this, and at the same time to be told that Fresleven was the gentlest, quietest creature that ever walked on two legs. No doubt he was; but he had been a couple of years already out there engaged in the noble cause, you know, and he probably felt the need at last of asserting his self-respect in some way. Therefore he whacked the old nigger mercilessly, while a big crowd of his people watched him, thunderstruck, till some man—I was told the chief's son—in desperation at hearing the old chap yell, made a tentative jab with a spear at the white man—and of course it went quite easy between the shoulder-blades. Then the whole population cleared into the forest, expecting all kinds of calamities to happen, while, on the other hand, the steamer Fresleven commanded left also in a bad panic, in charge of the engineer, I believe. Afterwards nobody seemed to trouble much about Fresleven's remains, till I got out and stepped into his shoes. I couldn't let it rest, though; but when an opportunity offered at last to meet my predecessor, the grass growing through his ribs was tall enough to hide his bones. They were all there. The supernatural being had not been touched after he fell. And the village was deserted, the huts gaped black, rotting, all askew within the fallen enclosures. A calamity had come to it, sure enough. The people had vanished. Mad terror had scattered them, men, women, and children, through the bush, and they had never returned. What became of the hens I don't know either. I should think the cause of progress got them, anyhow. However, through this glorious affair I got my appointment, before I had fairly begun to hope for it.

"I flew around like mad to get ready, and before forty-eight hours I was crossing the Channel to show myself to my employers, and sign the contract. In a very few hours I arrived in a city that always makes me think of a whited sepulchre. Prejudice no doubt. I had no difficulty in finding the Company's offices. It was the biggest thing in the town, and everybody I met was full of it. They were going to run an oversea empire, and make no end of coin by trade.

"A narrow and deserted street in deep shadow, high houses, innumerable windows with venetian blinds, a dead silence, grass sprouting between the stones, imposing carriage archways right and left, immense double doors standing ponderously ajar. I slipped through one of these cracks, went up a swept and ungarnished staircase, as arid as a desert, and opened the first door I came to. Two women, one fat and the other slim, sat on straw-bottomed chairs, knitting black wool. The slim one got up and walked straight at me—still knitting with downcast eyes—and only just as I began to think of getting out of her way, as you would for a somnambulist, stood still, and looked up. Her dress was as plain as an umbrella-cover, and she turned round without a word and preceded me into a waiting-room. I gave my name, and looked about. Deal table in the middle, plain chairs all round the walls, on one end a large shining map, marked with all the colours of a rainbow. There was a vast amount of red—good to see at any time, because one knows that some real work is done in there, a deuce of a lot of blue, a little green, smears of orange, and, on the East Coast, a purple patch, to show where the jolly pioneers of progress drink the jolly lager-beer. However, I wasn't going into any of these. I was going into the yellow. Dead in the centre. And the river was there—fascinating—deadly—like a snake. Ough! A door opened, a white-haired secretarial head, but wearing a compassionate expression, appeared, and a skinny forefinger beckoned me into the sanctuary. Its light was dim, and a heavy writing desk squatted in the middle. From behind that structure came out an impression of pale plumpness in a frockcoat. The great man himself. He was five feet six, I should judge, and had his grip on the handle-end of ever so many millions. He shook hands, I fancy, murmured vaguely, was satisfied with my French. *Bon voyage.*

"In about forty-five seconds I found myself again in the waiting-room with the compassionate secretary, who, full of desolation and sympathy, made me sign some document. I believe I undertook amongst other things not to disclose any trade secrets. Well, I am not going to.

"I began to feel slightly uneasy. You know I am not used to such ceremonies, and there was something ominous in the atmosphere. It was just as though I had been let into some conspiracy—I don't know—something not quite right; and I was glad to get out. In the outer room the two women knitted black wool feverishly. People were arriving, and the younger one was walking back and forth introducing them. The old one sat on her chair. Her flat cloth slippers were propped up on a foot-warmer, and a cat reposed on her lap. She wore a starched white affair on her head, had a wart on one cheek, and silver-rimmed spectacles hung on the tip of her nose. She glanced at me above the glasses. The swift and indifferent placidity of that look troubled me. Two youths with foolish and cheery countenances were being piloted over, and she threw at them the same quick glance of unconcerned wisdom. She seemed to know all about them and about me too. An eerie feeling came over me. She seemed uncanny and fateful. Often far away there I thought of these two, guarding the door of Darkness, knitting black wool as for a warm pall, one introducing, introducing continuously to the unknown, the other scrutinising the cheery and foolish faces with unconcerned old eyes. *Ave!* Old knitter of black wool. *Morituri te salutant.*[7] Not many of those she looked at ever saw her again—not half, by a long way.

"There was yet a visit to the doctor. 'A simple formality,' assured me the secretary, with an air of taking an immense part in all my sorrows. Accordingly a young chap wearing his hat over the left eyebrow, some clerk I suppose—there must have been clerks in the business, though the house was as still as a house in a city of the dead—came from some-where upstairs, and led me forth. He was shabby and careless, with ink-stains on the sleeves of his jacket, and his cravat was large and billowy, under a chin shaped like the toe of an old boot. It was a little too early for the doctor, so I proposed a drink, and thereupon he developed a vein of joviality. As we sat over our vermuths he glorified the Company's business, and by and by I expressed casually my surprise at him not going out there. He became very cool and collected all at once. 'I am not such a fool as I look, quoth Plato to his disciples,' he said senten-tiously, emptied his glass with great resolution, and we rose.

"The old doctor felt my pulse, evidently thinking of something else the while. 'Good, good for there,' he mumbled, and then with a certain eagerness asked me whether I would let him measure my head. Rather surprised, I said Yes, when he produced a thing like callipers and got the dimensions back and front and every way, taking notes carefully. He was an unshaven little man in a threadbare coat like a gaberdine, with his feet in slippers, and I thought him a harmless fool. 'I always ask leave, in the interests of science, to measure the crania of those going out there,' he said. 'And when they come back too?' I asked. 'Oh, I never see them,' he remarked; 'and, moreover, the changes take place inside, you know.' He smiled, as if at some quiet joke. 'So you are going out there. Famous. Interesting too.' He gave me a searching glance, and made another note. 'Ever any madness in your family?' he asked, in a matter-of-fact tone. I felt very annoyed. 'Is that question in the interests of science too?' 'It would be,' he said, without taking notice of my irri-tation, 'interesting for science to watch the mental changes of individu-als, on the spot, but . . .' 'Are you an alienist?'[8] I interrupted. 'Every doctor should be—a little,' answered that original imperturbably. 'I have a little theory which you Messieurs who go out there must help me to prove. This is my share in the advantages my country shall reap from

7. "Hail! . . . Those who are about to die salute you." The Roman gladiators' salute to the Emperor on entering the arena.

8. Doctor who treats mental diseases. (The term has now been replaced by "psychiatrist.")

the possession of such a magnificent dependency. The mere wealth I leave to others. Pardon my questions, but you are the first Englishman coming under my observation . . .' I hastened to assure him I was not in the least typical. 'If I were,' said I, 'I wouldn't be talking like this with you.' 'What you say is rather profound, and probably erroneous,' he said, with a laugh. 'Avoid irritation more than exposure to the sun. Adieu. How do you English say, eh? Good-bye. Ah! Good-bye. Adieu. In the tropics one must before everything keep calm.' . . . He lifted a warning forefinger. . . . '*Du calme, du calme. Adieu.*'

"One thing more remained to do—say good-bye to my excellent aunt. I found her triumphant. I had a cup of tea—the last decent cup of tea for many days—and in a room that most soothingly looked just as you would expect a lady's drawing-room to look, we had a long quiet chat by the fireside. In the course of these confidences it became quite plain to me I had been represented to the wife of the high dignitary, and goodness knows to how many more people besides, as an exceptional and gifted creature—a piece of good fortune for the Company—a man you don't get hold of every day. Good heavens! and I was going to take charge of a two-penny-halfpenny river-steamboat with a penny whistle attached! It appeared, however, I was also one of the Workers, with a capital—you know. Something like an emissary of light, something like a lower sort of apostle. There had been a lot of such rot let loose in print and talk just about that time, and the excellent woman, living right in the rush of all that humbug, got carried off her feet. She talked about 'weaning those ignorant millions from their horrid ways,' till, upon my word, she made me quite uncomfortable. I ventured to hint that the Company was run for profit.

" 'You forget, dear Charlie, that the labourer is worthy of his hire,' she said brightly. It's queer how out of touch with truth women are. They live in a world of their own, and there had never been anything like it, and never can be. It is too beautiful altogether, and if they were to set it up it would go to pieces before the first sunset. Some confounded fact we men have been living contentedly with ever since the day of creation would start up and knock the whole thing over.

"After this I got embraced, told to wear flannel, be sure to write often, and so on—and I left. In the street—I don't know why—a queer feeling came to me that I was an impostor. Odd thing that I, who used to clear out for any part of the world at twenty-four hours' notice, with less thought than most men give to the crossing of a street, had a moment—I won't say of hesitation, but of startled pause, before this commonplace affair. The best way I can explain it to you is by saying that, for a second or two, I felt as though, instead of going to the centre of a continent, I were about to set off for the centre of the earth.

"I left in a French steamer, and she called in every blamed port they have out there, for, as far as I could see, the sole purpose of landing soldiers and custom-house officers. I watched the coast. Watching a coast as it slips by the ship is like thinking about an enigma. There it is

before you—smiling, frowning, inviting, grand, mean, insipid, or savage, and always mute with an air of whispering, Come and find out.
This one was almost featureless, as if still in the making, with an aspect
of monotonous grimness. The edge of a colossal jungle, so dark green
as to be almost black, fringed with white surf, ran straight, like a ruled
line, far, far away along a blue sea whose glitter was blurred by a creeping mist. The sun was fierce, the land seemed to glisten and drip with
steam. Here and there greyish-whitish specks showed up clustered inside
the white surf, with a flag flying above them perhaps—settlements some
centuries old, and still no bigger than pin-heads on the untouched expanse
of their background. We pounded along, stopped, landed soldiers; went
on, landed custom-house clerks to levy toll in what looked like a God-
forsaken wilderness, with a tin shed and a flag-pole lost in it; landed
more soldiers—to take care of the custom-house clerks presumably. Some,
I heard, got drowned in the surf; but whether they did or not, nobody
seemed particularly to care. They were just flung out there, and on we
went. Every day the coast looked the same, as though we had not moved;
but we passed various places—trading places—with names like Gran'
Bassam, Little Popo; names that seemed to belong to some sordid farce
acted in front of a sinister back-cloth. The idleness of a passenger, my
isolation amongst all these men with whom I had no point of contact,
the oily and languid sea, the uniform sombreness of the coast, seemed
to keep me away from the truth of things, within the toil of a mournful
and senseless delusion. The voice of the surf heard now and then was a
positive pleasure, like the speech of a brother. It was something natural,
that had its reason, that had a meaning. Now and then a boat from the
shore gave one a momentary contact with reality. It was paddled by black
fellows. You could see from afar the white of their eyeballs glistening.
They shouted, sang; their bodies streamed with perspiration; they had
faces like grotesque masks—these chaps; but they had bone, muscle, a
wild vitality, an intense energy of movement, that was as natural and
true as the surf along their coast. They wanted no excuse for being there.
They were a great comfort to look at. For a time I would feel I belonged
still to a world of straightforward facts; but the feeling would not last
long. Something would turn up to scare it away. Once, I remember, we
came upon a man-of-war anchored off the coast. There wasn't even a
shed there, and she was shelling the bush. It appears the French had
one of their wars going on thereabouts. Her ensign dropped limp like a
rag; the muzzles of the long six-inch guns stuck out all over the low hull;
the greasy, slimy swell swung her up lazily and let her down, swaying
her thin masts. In the empty immensity of earth, sky, and water, there
she was, incomprehensible, firing into a continent. Pop, would go one
of the six-inch guns; a small flame would dart and vanish, a little white
smoke would disappear, a tiny projectile would give a feeble screech—
and nothing happened. Nothing could happen. There was a touch of
insanity in the proceeding, a sense of lugubrious drollery in the sight;
and it was not dissipated by somebody on board assuring me earnestly

there was a camp of natives—he called them enemies!—hidden out of
sight somewhere.

"We gave her her letters (I heard the men in that lonely ship were
dying of fever at the rate of three a day) and went on. We called at some
more places with farcical names, where the merry dance of death and
trade goes on in a still and earthy atmosphere as of an overheated cata-
comb; all along the formless coast bordered by dangerous surf, as if Nature
herself had tried to ward off intruders; in and out of rivers, streams of
death in life, whose banks were rotting into mud, whose waters, thick-
ened into slime, invaded the contorted mangroves, that seemed to writhe
at us in the extremity of an impotent despair. Nowhere did we stop long
enough to get a particularised impression, but the general sense of vague
and oppressive wonder grew upon me. It was like a weary pilgrimage
amongst hints for nightmares.

"It was upward of thirty days before I saw the mouth of the big river.
We anchored off the seat of the government. But my work would not
begin till some two hundred miles farther on. So as soon as I could I
made a start for a place thirty miles higher up.

"I had my passage on a little sea-going steamer. Her captain was a
Swede, and knowing me for a seaman, invited me on the bridge. He
was a young man, lean, fair, and morose, with lanky hair and a shuffling
gait. As we left the miserable little wharf, he tossed his head contemptuously at the shore. 'Been living there?' he asked. I said, 'Yes.' 'Fine lot
these government chaps—are they not?' he went on, speaking English
with great precision and considerable bitterness. 'It is funny what some
people will do for a few francs a month. I wonder what becomes of that
kind when it goes up country?' I said to him I expected to see that soon.
'So-o-o!' he exclaimed. He shuffled athwart, keeping one eye ahead vig-
ilantly. 'Don't be too sure,' he continued. 'The other day I took up a
man who hanged himself on the road. He was a Swede, too.' 'Hanged
himself! Why, in God's name?' I cried. He kept on looking out watch-
fully. 'Who knows? The sun too much for him, or the country perhaps.'

"At last we opened a reach. A rocky cliff appeared, mounds of turnedup earth by the shore, houses on a hill, others with iron roofs, amongst
a waste of excavations, or hanging to the declivity. A continuous noise
of the rapids above hovered over this scene of inhabited devastation. A
lot of people, mostly black and naked, moved about like ants. A jetty
projected into the river. A blinding sunlight drowned all this at times in
a sudden recrudescence of glare. 'There's your Company's station,' said
the Swede, pointing to three wooden barrack-like structures on the rocky
slope. 'I will send your things up. Four boxes did you say? So. Farewell.'

"I came upon a boiler wallowing in the grass, then found a path leading up the hill. It turned aside for the boulders, and also for an under-
sized railway truck lying there on its back with its wheels in the air. One
was off. The thing looked as dead as the carcass of some animal. I came
upon more pieces of decaying machinery, a stack of rusty nails. To the
left a clump of trees made a shady spot, where dark things seemed to stir

feebly. I blinked, the path was steep. A horn tooted to the right, and I saw the black people run. A heavy and dull detonation shook the ground, a puff of smoke came out of the cliff, and that was all. No change appeared on the face of the rock. They were building a railway. The cliff was not in the way or anything; but this objectless blasting was all the work going on.

"A slight clinking behind me made me turn my head. Six black men advanced in a file, toiling up the path. They walked erect and slow, balancing small baskets full of earth on their heads, and the clink kept time with their footsteps. Black rags were wound round their loins, and the short ends behind waggled to and fro like tails. I could see every rib, the joints of their limbs were like knots in a rope; each had an iron collar on his neck, and all were connected together with a chain whose bights swung between them, rhythmically clinking. Another report from the cliff made me think suddenly of that ship of war I had seen firing into a continent. It was the same kind of ominous voice; but these men could by no stretch of imagination be called enemies. They were called criminals, and the outraged law, like the bursting shells, had come to them, an insoluble mystery from the sea. All their meagre breasts panted together, the violently dilated nostrils quivered, the eyes stared stonily uphill. They passed me within six inches, without a glance, with that complete, deathlike indifference of unhappy savages. Behind this raw matter one of the reclaimed, the product of the new forces at work, strolled despondently, carrying a rifle by its middle. He had a uniform jacket with one button off, and seeing a white man on the path, hoisted his weapon to his shoulder with alacrity. This was simple prudence, white men being so much alike at a distance that he could not tell who I might be. He was speedily reassured, and with a large, white, rascally grin, and a glance at his charge, seemed to take me into partnership in his exalted trust. After all, I also was a part of the great cause of these high and just proceedings.

"Instead of going up, I turned and descended to the left. My idea was to let that chain-gang get out of sight before I climbed the hill. You know I am not particularly tender; I've had to strike and to fend off. I've had to resist and to attack sometimes—that's only one way of resisting—without counting the exact cost, according to the demands of such sort of life as I had blundered into. I've seen the devil of violence, and the devil of greed, and the devil of hot desire; but, by all the stars! these were strong, lusty, red-eyed devils, that swayed and drove men—men, I tell you. But as I stood on this hillside, I foresaw that in the blinding sunshine of that land I would become acquainted with a flabby, pretending, weak-eyed devil of a rapacious and pitiless folly. How insidious he could be, too, I was only to find out several months later and a thousand miles farther. For a moment I stood appalled, as though by a warning. Finally I descended the hill, obliquely, towards the trees I had seen.

"I avoided a vast artificial hole somebody had been digging on the slope, the purpose of which I found it impossible to divine. It wasn't a quarry or a sandpit, anyhow. It was just a hole. It might have been connected with the philanthropic desire of giving the criminals something to do. I don't know. Then I nearly fell into a very narrow ravine, almost no more than a scar in the hillside. I discovered that a lot of imported drainage-pipes for the settlement had been tumbled in there. There wasn't one that was not broken. It was a wanton smash-up. At last I got under the trees. My purpose was to stroll into the shade for a moment; but no sooner within than it seemed to me I had stepped into the gloomy circle of some Inferno. The rapids were near, and an uninterrupted, uniform, headlong, rushing noise filled the mournful stillness of the grove, where not a breath stirred, not a leaf moved, with a mysterious sound—as though the tearing pace of the launched earth had suddenly become audible.

"Black shapes crouched, lay, sat between the trees, leaning against the trunks, clinging to the earth, half coming out, half effaced within the dim light, in all the attitudes of pain, abandonment, and despair. Another mine on the cliff went off, followed by a slight shudder of the soil under my feet. The work was going on. The work! And this was the place where some of the helpers had withdrawn to die.

"They were dying slowly—it was very clear. They were not enemies, they were not criminals, they were nothing earthly now—nothing but black shadows of disease and starvation, lying confusedly in the greenish gloom. Brought from all the recesses of the coast in all the legality of time contracts, lost in uncongenial surroundings, fed on unfamiliar food, they sickened, became inefficient, and were then allowed to crawl away and rest. These moribund shapes were free as air—and nearly as thin. I began to distinguish the gleam of eyes under the trees. Then, glancing down, I saw a face near my hand. The black bones reclined at full length with one shoulder against the tree, and slowly the eyelids rose and the sunken eyes looked up at me, enormous and vacant, a kind of blind, white flicker in the depths of the orbs, which died out slowly. The man seemed young—almost a boy—but you know with them it's hard to tell. I found nothing else to do but to offer him one of my good Swede's ship's biscuits I had in my pocket. The fingers closed slowly on it and held—there was no other movement and no other glance. He had tied a bit of white worsted round his neck—Why? Where did he get it? Was it a badge—an ornament—a charm—a propitiatory act? Was there any idea at all connected with it? It looked startling round his black neck, this bit of white thread from beyond the seas.

"Near the same tree two more bundles of acute angles sat with their legs drawn up. One, with his chin propped on his knees, stared at nothing, in an intolerable and appalling manner: his brother phantom rested its forehead, as if overcome with a great weariness; and all about others were scattered in every pose of contorted collapse, as in some picture of a massacre or a pestilence. While I stood horror-struck, one of these creatures rose to his hands and knees, and went off on all-fours towards the river to drink. He lapped out of his hand, then sat up in the sunlight, crossing his shins in front of him, and after a time let his woolly head fall on his breastbone.

"I didn't want any more loitering in the shade, and I made haste towards the station. When near the buildings I met a white man, in such an unexpected elegance of get-up that in the first moment I took him for a sort of vision. I saw a high starched collar, white cuffs, a light alpaca jacket, snowy trousers, a clear necktie, and varnished boots. No hat. Hair parted, brushed, oiled, under a green-lined parasol held in a big white hand. He was amazing, and had a penholder behind his ear.

"I shook hands with this miracle, and I learned he was the Company's chief accountant, and that all the book-keeping was done at this station. He had come out for a moment, he said, 'to get a breath of fresh air.' The expression sounded wonderfully odd, with its suggestion of sedentary desk-life. I wouldn't have mentioned the fellow to you at all, only it was from his lips that I first heard the name of the man who is so indissolubly connected with the memories of that time. Moreover, I respected the fellow. Yes; I respected his collars, his vast cuffs, his brushed hair. His appearance was certainly that of a hairdresser's dummy; but in the great demoralisation of the land he kept up his appearance. That's backbone. His starched collars and got-up shirt-fronts were achievements of character. He had been out nearly three years; and, later, I could not help asking him how he managed to sport such linen. He had just the faintest blush, and said modestly, 'I've been teaching one of the native women about the station. It was difficult. She had a distaste for the work.' Thus this man had verily accomplished something. And he was devoted to his books, which were in apple-pie order.

"Everything else in the station was in a muddle,—heads, things, buildings. Strings of dusty niggers with splay feet arrived and departed; a stream of manufactured goods, rubbishy cottons, beads, and brass-wire set into the depths of darkness, and in return came a precious trickle of ivory.

"I had to wait in the station for ten days—an eternity. I lived in a hut in the yard, but to be out of the chaos I would sometimes get into the accountant's office. It was built of horizontal planks, and so badly put together that, as he bent over his high desk, he was barred from neck to heels with narrow strips of sunlight. There was no need to open the big shutter to see. It was hot there too; big flies buzzed fiendishly, and did not sting, but stabbed. I sat generally on the floor, while, of faultless appearance (and even slightly scented), perching on a high stool, he wrote, he wrote. Sometimes he stood up for exercise. When a truckle-bed with a sick man (some invalided agent from up country) was put in there, he exhibited a gentle annoyance. 'The groans of this sick person' he said, 'distract my attention. And without that it is extremely difficult to guard against clerical errors in this climate.'

"One day he remarked, without lifting his head, 'In the interior you will no doubt meet Mr. Kurtz.' On my asking who Mr. Kurtz was, he said he was a first-class agent; and seeing my disappointment at this information, he added slowly, laying down his pen, 'He is a very remark-able person.' Further questions elicited from him that Mr. Kurtz was at present in charge of a trading-post, a very important one, in the true ivory-country, at 'the very bottom of there. Sends in as much ivory as all the others put together . . .' He began to write again. The sick man was too ill to groan. The flies buzzed in a great peace.

"Suddenly there was a growing murmur of voices and a great tramp-ing of feet. A caravan had come in. A violent babble of uncouth sounds burst out on the other side of the planks. All the carriers were speaking together, and in the midst of the uproar the lamentable voice of the chief agent was heard 'giving it up' tearfully for the twentieth time that day. . . . He rose slowly. 'What a frightful row,' he said. He crossed the room gently to look at the sick man, and returning, said to me, 'He does not hear.' 'What! Dead?' I asked, startled. 'No, not yet,' he answered, with great composure. Then, alluding with a toss of the head to the tumult in the station-yard, 'When one has got to make correct entries, one comes to hate those savages—hate them to the death.' He remained thoughtful for a moment. 'When you see Mr. Kurtz,' he went on, 'tell him from me that everything here'—he glanced at the desk—'is very satisfactory. I don't like to write to him—with those messengers of ours you never know who may get hold of your letter—at that Central Sta-tion.' He stared at me for a moment with his mild, bulging eyes. 'Oh, he will go far, very far,' he began again. 'He will be a somebody in the Administration before long. They, above—the Council in Europe, you know—mean him to be.'

"He turned to his work. The noise outside had ceased, and presently in going out I stopped at the door. In the steady buzz of flies the home-ward-bound agent was lying flushed and insensible; the other, bent over his books, was making correct entries of perfectly correct transactions; and fifty feet below the doorstep I could see the still tree-tops of the grove of death.

"Next day I left that station at last, with a caravan of sixty men, for a two-hundred-mile tramp.

"No use telling you much about that. Paths, paths, everywhere; a stamped-in network of paths spreading over the empty land, through long grass, through burnt grass, through thickets, down and up chilly ravines, up and down stony hills ablaze with heat; and a solitude, a solitude, nobody, not a hut. The population had cleared out a long time ago. Well, if a lot of mysterious niggers armed with all kinds of fearful weapons suddenly took to travelling on the road between Deal and Gravesend, catching the yokels right and left to carry heavy loads for them, I fancy every farm and cottage thereabouts would get empty very soon. Only here the dwellings were gone too. Still, I passed through several abandoned villages. There's something pathetically childish in the ruins of grass walls. Day after day, with the stamp and shuffle of sixty pair of bare feet behind me, each pair under a 60-lb. load. Camp, cook, sleep, strike camp, march. Now and then a carrier dead in harness, at rest in the long grass near the path, with an empty water-gourd and his long staff lying by his side. A great silence around and above. Perhaps on some quiet night the tremor of far-off drums, sinking, swelling, a tremor vast, faint; a sound weird, appealing, suggestive, and wild—and perhaps with as profound a meaning as the sound of bells in a Christian country. Once a white man in an unbuttoned uniform, camping on the path with an armed escort of lank Zanzibaris,[9] very hospitable and fes- tive—not to say drunk. Was looking after the upkeep of the road, he declared. Can't say I saw any road or any upkeep, unless the body of a middle-aged negro, with a bullet-hole in the forehead, upon which I absolutely stumbled three miles farther on, may be considered as a per- manent improvement. I had a white companion too, not a bad chap, but rather too fleshy and with the exasperating habit of fainting on the hot hillsides, miles away from the least bit of shade and water. Annoy- ing, you know, to hold your own coat like a parasol over a man's head while he is coming-to. I couldn't help asking him once what he meant by coming there at all. 'To make money, of course. What do you think?' he said scornfully. Then he got fever, and had to be carried in a ham- mock slung under a pole. As he weighed sixteen stone[1] I had no end of rows with the carriers. They jibbed, ran away, sneaked off with their loads in the night—quite a mutiny. So, one evening, I made a speech in English with gestures, not one of which was lost to the sixty pairs of eyes before me, and the next morning I started the hammock off in front all right. An hour afterwards I came upon the whole concern wrecked in a bush—man, hammock, groans, blankets, horrors. The heavy pole had skinned his poor nose. He was very anxious for me to kill somebody, but there wasn't the shadow of a carrier near. I remembered the old doctor—'It would be interesting for science to watch the mental changes of individuals, on the spot.' I felt I was becoming scientifically interest- ing. However, all that is to no purpose. On the fifteenth day I came in sight of the big river again, and hobbled into the Central Station. It was on a back water surrounded by scrub and forest, with a pretty border of smelly mud on one side, and on the three others enclosed by a crazy fence of rushes. A neglected gap was all the gate it had, and the first glance at the place was enough to let you see the flabby devil was run- ning that show. White men with long staves in their hands appeared languidly from amongst the buildings, strolling up to take a look at me, and then retired out of sight somewhere. One of them, a stout, excitable chap with black moustaches, informed me with great volubility and many digressions, as soon as I told him who I was, that my steamer was at the bottom of the river. I was thunderstruck. What, how, why? Oh, it was

---

9. Natives of Zanzibar, an island off the east coast of Africa, once part of the sultanate of Zanzibar and a British protectorate, now part of the inde- pendent state of Tanzania (made up of Zanzibar and Tanganyika). Natives of Zanzibar were used as mercenaries throughout Africa.
1. One stone equals 14 pounds. The man weighed 224 pounds.

'all right.' The 'manager himself' was there. All quite correct. 'Everybody had behaved splendidly! splendidly!'—'You must,' he said in agitation, 'go and see the general manager at once. He is waiting!'

"I did not see the real significance of that wreck at once. I fancy I see it now, but I am not sure—not at all. Certainly the affair was too stupid—when I think of it—to be altogether natural. Still . . . But at the moment it presented itself simply as a confounded nuisance. The steamer was sunk. They had started two days before in a sudden hurry up the river with the manager on board, in charge of some volunteer skipper, and before they had been out three hours they tore the bottom out of her on stones, and she sank near the south bank. I asked myself what I was to do there, now my boat was lost. As a matter of fact, I had plenty to do in fishing my command out of the river. I had to set about it the very next day. That, and the repairs when I brought the pieces to the station, took some months.

"My first interview with the manager was curious. He did not ask me to sit down after my twenty-mile walk that morning. He was commonplace in complexion, in feature, in manners, and in voice. He was of middle size and of ordinary build. His eyes, of the usual blue, were perhaps remarkably cold, and he certainly could make his glance fall on one as trenchant and heavy as an axe. But even at these times the rest of his person seemed to disclaim the intention. Otherwise there was only an indefinable, faint expression of his lips, something stealthy—a smile—not a smile—I remember it, but I can't explain. It was unconscious, this smile was, though just after he had said something it got intensified for an instant. It came at the end of his speeches like a seal applied on the words to make the meaning of the commonest phrase appear absolutely inscrutable. He was a common trader, from his youth up employed in these parts—nothing more. He was obeyed, yet he inspired neither love nor fear, nor even respect. He inspired uneasiness. That was it! Uneasiness. Not a definite mistrust—just uneasiness—nothing more. You have no idea how effective such a . . . a . . . faculty can be. He had no genius for organising, for initiative, or for order even. That was evident in such things as the deplorable state of the station. He had no learning, and no intelligence. His position had come to him—why? Perhaps because he was never ill. . . . He had served three terms of three years out there . . . Because triumphant health in the general rout of constitutions is a kind of power in itself. When he went home on leave he rioted on a large scale—pompously. Jack ashore—with a difference—in externals only. This one could gather from his casual talk. He originated nothing, he could keep the routine going—that's all. But he was great. He was great by this little thing that it was impossible to tell what could control such a man. He never gave that secret away. Perhaps there was nothing within him. Such a suspicion made one pause—for out there there were no external checks. Once when various tropical diseases had laid low almost every 'agent' in the station, he was heard to say, 'Men who come out here should have no entrails.' He sealed the utterance with that smile of his, as though it had been a door opening into a darkness he had in his keeping. You fancied you had seen things—but the seal was on. When annoyed at meal-times by the constant quarrels of the white men about precedence, he ordered an immense round table to be made, for which a special house had to be built. This was the station's mess-room. Where he sat was the first place—the rest were nowhere. One felt this to be his unalterable conviction. He was neither civil nor uncivil. He was quiet. He allowed his 'boy'—an overfed young negro from the coast—to treat the white men, under his very eyes, with provoking insolence.

"He began to speak as soon as he saw me. I had been very long on the road. He could not wait. Had to start without me. The up-river stations had to be relieved. There had been so many delays already that he did not know who was dead and who was alive, and how they got on—and so on, and so on. He paid no attention to my explanations, and, playing with a stick of sealing-wax, repeated several times that the situation was 'very grave, very grave.' There were rumors that a very important station was in jeopardy, and its chief, Mr. Kurtz, was ill. Hoped it was not true. Mr. Kurtz was . . . I felt weary and irritable. Hang Kurtz, I thought. I interrupted him by saying I had heard of Mr. Kurtz on the coast. 'Ah! So they talk of him down there,' he murmured to himself. Then he began again, assuring me Mr. Kurtz was the best agent he had, an exceptional man, of the greatest importance to the Company; therefore I could understand his anxiety. He was, he said, 'very, very uneasy.' Certainly he fidgeted on his chair a good deal, exclaimed, 'Ah, Mr. Kurtz!' broke the stick of sealing-wax and seemed dumbfounded by the accident. Next thing he wanted to know 'how long it would take to' . . . I interrupted him again. Being hungry, you know, and kept on my feet too, I was getting savage. 'How can I tell?' I said, 'I haven't even seen the wreck yet—some months, no doubt.' All this talk seemed to me so futile. 'Some months,' he said. 'Well, let us say three months before we can make a start. Yes. That ought to do the affair.' I flung out of his hut (he lived all alone in a clay hut with a sort of verandah) muttering to myself my opinion of him. He was a chattering idiot. Afterwards I took it back when it was borne in upon me startlingly with what extreme nicety he had estimated the time requisite for the 'affair.'

"I went to work the next day, turning, so to speak, my back on that station. In that way only it seemed to me I could keep my hold on the redeeming facts of life. Still, one must look about sometimes; and then I saw this station, these men strolling aimlessly about in the sunshine of the yard. I asked myself sometimes what it all meant. They wandered here and there with their absurd long staves in their hands, like a lot of faithless pilgrims bewitched inside a rotten fence. The word 'ivory' rang in the air, was whispered, was sighed. You would think they were pray-ing to it. A taint of imbecile rapacity blew through it all, like a whiff from some corpse. By Jove! I've never seen anything so unreal in my life. And outside, the silent wilderness surrounding this cleared speck on the earth struck me as something great and invincible, like evil or truth, waiting patiently for the passing away of this fantastic invasion.

"Oh, these months! Well, never mind. Various things happened. One evening a grass shed full of calico, cotton prints, beads, and I don't know what else, burst into a blaze so suddenly that you would have thought the earth had opened to let an avenging fire consume all that trash. I was smoking my pipe quietly by my dismantled steamer, and saw them all cutting capers in the light, with their arms lifted high, when the stout man with moustaches came tearing down to the river, a tin pail in his hand, assured me that everybody was 'behaving splendidly, splendidly,' dipped about a quart of water and tore back again. I noticed there was a hole in the bottom of his pail.

"I strolled up. There was no hurry. You see the thing had gone off like a box of matches. It had been hopeless from the very first. The flame had leaped high, driven everybody back, lighted up everything—and collapsed. The shed was already a heap of embers glowing fiercely. A nigger was being beaten near by. They said he had caused the fire in some way; be that as it may, he was screeching most horribly. I saw him, later, for several days, sitting in a bit of shade looking very sick and trying to recover himself: afterwards he arose and went out—and the wilderness without a sound took him into its bosom again. As I approached the glow from the dark I found myself at the back of two men, talking. I heard the name of Kurtz pronounced, then the words, 'take advantage of this unfortunate accident.' One of the men was the manager. I wished him a good evening. 'Did you ever see anything like it—eh? it is incredible,' he said, and walked off. The other man remained. He was a first-class agent, young, gentlemanly, a bit reserved, with a forked little beard and a hooked nose. He was standoffish with the other agents, and they on their side said he was the manager's spy upon them. As to me, I had hardly ever spoken to him before. We got into talk, and by and by we strolled away from the hissing ruins. Then he asked me to his room, which was in the main building of the station. He struck a match, and I perceived that this young aristocrat had not only a silver-mounted dressing-case but also a whole candle all to himself. Just at that time the manager was the only man supposed to have any right to candles. Native mats covered the clay walls; a collection of spears, assegais,[2] shields, knives, was hung up in trophies. The business entrusted to this fellow was the making of bricks—so I had been informed; but there wasn't a fragment of a brick anywhere in the station, and he had been there more than a year—waiting. It seems he could not make bricks without something, I don't know what—straw maybe. Anyway, it could not be found there, and as it was not likely to be sent from Europe, it did not appear clear to me what he was waiting for. An act of special creation perhaps. However, they were all waiting—all the sixteen or twenty pilgrims of

2. Slender iron-tipped spears.

them—for something; and upon my word it did not seem an uncongenial occupation, from the way they took it, though the only thing that ever came to them was disease—as far as I could see. They beguiled the time by backbiting and intriguing against each other in a foolish kind of way. There was an air of plotting about that station, but nothing came of it, of course. It was as unreal as everything else—as the philanthropic pretence of the whole concern, as their talk, as their government, as their show of work. The only real feeling was a desire to get appointed to a trading-post where ivory was to be had, so that they could earn percentages. They intrigued and slandered and hated each other only on that account—but as to effectually lifting a little finger—oh no. By heavens! there is something after all in the world allowing one man to steal a horse while another must not look at a halter. Steal a horse straight out. Very well. He has done it. Perhaps he can ride. But there is a way of looking at a halter that would provoke the most charitable of saints into a kick.

"I had no idea why he wanted to be sociable, but as we chatted in there it suddenly occurred to me the fellow was trying to get at something—in fact, pumping me. He alluded constantly to Europe, to the people I was supposed to know there—putting leading questions as to my acquaintances in the sepulchral city, and so on. His little eyes glittered like mica discs—with curiosity—though he tried to keep up a bit of superciliousness. At first I was astonished, but very soon I became awfully curious to see what he would find out from me. I couldn't possibly imagine what I had in me to make it worth his while. It was very pretty to see how he baffled himself, for in truth my body was full only of chills, and my head had nothing in it but that wretched steamboat business. It was evident he took me for a perfectly shameless prevaricator. At last he got angry, and, to conceal a movement of furious annoyance, he yawned. I rose. Then I noticed a small sketch in oils, on a panel, representing a woman, draped and blindfolded, carrying a lighted torch. The background was sombre—almost black. The movement of the woman was stately, and the effect of the torchlight on the face was sinister.

"It arrested me, and he stood by civilly, holding an empty half-pint champagne bottle (medical comforts) with the candle stuck in it. To my question he said Mr. Kurtz had painted this—in this very station more than a year ago—while waiting for means to go to his trading-post. 'Tell me, pray,' said I, 'who is this Mr. Kurtz?'

" 'The chief of the Inner Station,' he answered in a short tone, looking away. 'Much obliged,' I said, laughing. 'And you are the brickmaker of the Central Station. Every one knows that.' He was silent for a while. 'He is a prodigy,' he said at last. 'He is an emissary of pity, and science, and progress, and devil knows what else. We want,' he began to declaim suddenly, 'for the guidance of the cause entrusted to us by Europe, so to speak, higher intelligence, wide sympathies, a singleness of purpose.' 'Who says that?' I asked. 'Lots of them,' he replied. 'Some even write that; and so *he* comes here, a special being, as you ought to know.' 'Why ought I to know?' I interrupted, really surprised. He paid no attention. 'Yes. To-day he is chief of the best station, next year he will be assistant-manager, two years more and . . . but I daresay you know what he will be in two years' time. You are of the new gang—the gang of virtue. The same people who sent him specially also recommended you. Oh, don't say no. I've my own eyes to trust.' Light dawned upon me. My dear aunt's influential acquaintances were producing an unexpected effect upon that young man. I nearly burst into a laugh. 'Do you read the Company's confidential correspondence?' I asked. He hadn't a word to say. It was great fun. 'When Mr. Kurtz,' I continued severely, 'is General Manager, you won't have the opportunity.'

"He blew the candle out suddenly, and we went outside. The moon had risen. Black figures strolled about listlessly, pouring water on the glow, whence proceeded a sound of hissing; steam ascended in the moonlight; the beaten nigger groaned somewhere. 'What a row the brute makes!' said the indefatigable man with the moustaches, appearing near us. 'Serve him right. Transgression—punishment—bang! Pitiless, piti-less. That's the only way. This will prevent all conflagrations for the future. I was just telling the manager . . .' He noticed my companion, and became crestfallen all at once. 'Not in bed yet,' he said, with a kind of servile heartiness; 'it's so natural. Ha! Danger—agitation.' He van-ished. I went on to the river-side, and the other followed me. I heard a scathing murmur at my ear, 'Heap of muffs—go to.' The pilgrims could be seen in knots gesticulating, discussing. Several had still their staves in their hands. I verily believe they took these sticks to bed with them. Beyond the fence the forest stood up spectrally in the moonlight, and through the dim stir, through the faint sounds of that lamentable court-yard, the silence of the land went home to one's very heart—its mystery, its greatness, the amazing reality of its concealed life. The hurt nigger moaned feebly somewhere near by, and then fetched a deep sigh that made me mend my pace away from there. I felt a hand introducing itself under my arm. 'My dear sir,' said the fellow, 'I don't want to be mis-understood, and especially by you, who will see Mr. Kurtz long before I can have that pleasure. I wouldn't like him to get a false idea of my disposition. . . .'

"I let him run on, this papier-mâché Mephistopheles, and it seemed to me that if I tried I could poke my forefinger through him, and would find nothing inside but a little loose dirt, maybe. He, don't you see, had been planning to be assistant-manager by and by under the present man, and I could see that the coming of that Kurtz had upset them both not a little. He talked precipitately, and I did not try to stop him. I had my shoulders against the wreck of my steamer, hauled up on the slope like a carcass of some big river animal. The smell of mud, of primeval mud, by Jove! was in my nostrils, the high stillness of primeval forest was before my eyes; there were shiny patches on the black creek. The moon had spread over everything a thin layer of silver—over the rank grass, over the mud, upon the wall of matted vegetation standing higher than the wall of a temple, over the great river I could see through a sombre gap glittering, glittering, as it flowed broadly by without a murmur. All this was great, expectant, mute, while the man jabbered about himself. I wondered whether the stillness on the face of the immensity looking at us two were meant as an appeal or as a menace. What were we who had strayed in here? Could we handle that dumb thing, or would it handle us? I felt how big, how confoundedly big, was that thing that couldn't talk and perhaps was deaf as well. What was in there? I could see a little ivory coming out from there, and I had heard Mr. Kurtz was in there. I had heard enough about it too—God knows! Yet somehow it didn't bring any image with it—no more than if I had been told an angel or a fiend was in there. I believed it in the same way one of you might believe there are inhabitants in the planet Mars. I knew once a Scotch sailmaker who was certain, dead sure, there were people in Mars. If you asked him for some idea how they looked and behaved, he would get shy and mutter something about 'walking on all-fours.' If you as much as smiled, he would—though a man of sixty—offer to fight you. I would not have gone so far as to fight for Kurtz, but I went for him near enough to a lie. You know I hate, detest, and can't bear a lie, not because I am straighter than the rest of us, but simply because it appals me. There is a taint of death, a flavour of mortality in lies—which is exactly what I hate and detest in the world—what I want to forget. It makes me miserable and sick, like biting something rotten would do. Temperament, I suppose. Well, I went near enough to it by letting the young fool there believe anything he liked to imagine as to my influence in Europe. I became in an instant as much of a pretence as the rest of the bewitched pilgrims. This simply because I had a notion it somehow would be of help to that Kurtz whom at the time I did not see—you understand. He was just a word for me. I did not see the man in the name any more than you do. Do you see him? Do you see the story? Do you see anything? It seems to me I am trying to tell you a dream—making a vain attempt, because no relation of a dream can convey the dream-sensation, that commingling of absurdity, surprise, and bewilderment in a tremor of struggling revolt, that notion of being captured by the incredible which is of the very essence of dreams. . . ."

He was silent for a while.

". . . No, it is impossible; it is impossible to convey the life-sensation of any given epoch of one's existence—that which makes its truth, its meaning—its subtle and penetrating essence. It is impossible. We live, as we dream—alone. . . ."

He paused again as if reflecting, then added:

"Of course in this you fellows see more than I could then. You see me, whom you know. . . ."

It had become so pitch dark that we listeners could hardly see one another. For a long time already he, sitting apart, had been no more to us than a voice. There was not a word from anybody. The others might have been asleep, but I was awake. I listened, I listened on the watch for the sentence, for the word, that would give me the clue to the faint uneasiness inspired by this narrative that seemed to shape itself without human lips in the heavy night-air of the river.

". . . Yes—I let him run on," Marlow began again, "and think what he pleased about the powers that were behind me. I did! And there was nothing behind me! There was nothing but that wretched, old, mangled steamboat I was leaning against, while he talked fluently about 'the necessity for every man to get on.' 'And when one comes out here, you conceive, it is not to gaze at the moon.' Mr. Kurtz was a 'universal genius,' but even a genius would find it easier to work with 'adequate tools—intelligent men.' He did not make bricks—why, there was a physical impossibility in the way—as I was well aware; and if he did secretarial work for the manager, it was because 'no sensible man rejects wantonly the confidence of his superiors.' Did I see it? I saw it. What more did I want? What I really wanted was rivets, by heaven! Rivets. To get on with the work—to stop the hole. Rivets I wanted. There were cases of them down at the coast—cases—piled up—burst—split! You kicked a loose rivet at every second step in that station yard on the hillside. Rivets had rolled into the grove of death. You could fill your pockets with rivets for the trouble of stooping down—and there wasn't one rivet to be found where it was wanted. We had plates that would do, but nothing to fasten them with. And every week the messenger, a lone negro, letter-bag on shoulder and staff in hand, left our station for the coast. And several times a week a coast caravan came in with trade goods—ghastly glazed calico that made you shudder only to look at it, glass beads value about a penny a quart, confounded spotted cotton handkerchiefs. And no rivets. Three carriers could have brought all that was wanted to set that steamboat afloat.

"He was becoming confidential now, but I fancy my unresponsive attitude must have exasperated him at last, for he judged it necessary to inform me he feared neither God nor devil, let alone any mere man. I said I could see that very well, but what I wanted was a certain quantity of rivets—and rivets were what really Mr. Kurtz wanted, if he had only known it. Now letters went to the coast every week. . . . 'My dear sir,' he cried, 'I write from dictation.' I demanded rivets. There was a way—for an intelligent man. He changed his manner; became very cold, and suddenly began to talk about a hippopotamus; wondered whether sleeping on board the steamer (I stuck to my salvage night and day) I wasn't disturbed. There was an old hippo that had the bad habit of getting out on the bank and roaming at night over the station grounds. The pilgrims used to turn out in a body and empty every rifle they could lay hands on at him. Some even had sat up o' nights for him. All his energy was wasted, though. 'That animal has a charmed life,' he said; 'but you can say this only of brutes in this country. No man—you apprehend me?—no man here bears a charmed life.' He stood there for a moment in the moonlight with his delicate hooked nose set a little askew, and his mica eyes glittering without a wink, then, with a curt Good-night, he strode off. I could see he was disturbed and considerably puzzled, which made me feel more hopeful than I had been for days. It was a great comfort to turn from that chap to my influential friend, the battered, twisted, ruined, tinpot steamboat. I clambered on board. She rang under my feet like an empty Huntley & Palmer biscuit-tin kicked along a gutter; she was nothing so solid in make, and rather less pretty in shape, but I had expended enough hard work on her to make me love her. No influential friend would have served me better. She had given me a chance to come out a bit—to find out what I could do. No, I don't like work. I had rather laze about and think of all the fine things that can be done. I don't like work—no man does—but I like what is in the work—the chance to find yourself. Your own reality—for yourself, not for others—what no other man can ever know. They can only see the mere show, and never can tell what it really means.

"I was not surprised to see somebody sitting aft, on the deck, with his legs dangling over the mud. You see I rather chummed with the few mechanics there were in that station, whom the other pilgrims naturally despised—on account of their imperfect manners, I suppose. This was the foreman—a boiler-maker by trade—a good worker. He was a lank, bony, yellow-faced man, with big intense eyes. His aspect was worried, and his head was as bald as the palm of my hand; but his hair in falling seemed to have stuck to his chin, and had prospered in the new locality, for his beard hung down to his waist. He was a widower with six young children (he had left them in charge of a sister of his to come out there), and the passion of his life was pigeon-flying. He was an enthusiast and a connoisseur. He would rave about pigeons. After work hours he used sometimes to come over from his hut for a talk about his children and his pigeons; at work, when he had to crawl in the mud under the bottom of the steamboat, he would tie up that beard of his in a kind of white serviette[3] he brought for the purpose. It had loops to go over his ears. In the evening he could be seen squatted on the bank rinsing that wrapper in the creek with great care, then spreading it solemnly on a bush to dry.

"I slapped him on the back and shouted 'We shall have rivets!' He scrambled to his feet exclaiming 'No! Rivets!' as though he couldn't believe his ears. Then in a low voice, 'You . . . eh?' I don't know why we behaved like lunatics. I put my finger to the side of my nose and nodded mysteriously. 'Good for you!' he cried, snapped his fingers above his head, lifting one foot. I tried a jig. We capered on the iron deck. A frightful clatter came out of that hulk, and the virgin forest on the other bank of the creek sent it back in a thundering roll upon the sleeping station. It must have made some of the pilgrims sit up in their hovels. A dark figure obscured the lighted doorway of the manager's hut, vanished, then, a second or so after, the doorway itself vanished too. We stopped, and the silence driven away by the stamping of our feet flowed back

---

3. Table napkin.

again from the recesses of the land. The great wall of vegetation, an exuberant and entangled mass of trunks, branches, leaves, boughs, festoons, motionless in the moonlight, was like a rioting invasion of soundless life, a rolling wave of plants, piled up, crested, ready to topple over the creek, to sweep every little man of us out of his little existence. And it moved not. A deadened burst of mighty splashes and snorts reached us from afar, as though an ichthyosaurus had been taking a bath of glitter in the great river. 'After all,' said the boiler-maker in a reasonable tone, 'why shouldn't we get the rivets?' Why not, indeed! I did not know of any reason why we shouldn't. 'They'll come in three weeks,' I said confidently.

"But they didn't. Instead of rivets there came an invasion, an infliction, a visitation. It came in sections during the next three weeks, each section headed by a donkey carrying a white man in new clothes and tan shoes, bowing from that elevation right and left to the impressed pilgrims. A quarrelsome band of footsore sulky niggers trod on the heels of the donkey; a lot of tents, camp-stools, tin boxes, white cases, brown bales would be shot down in the courtyard, and the air of mystery would deepen a little over the muddle of the station. Five such instalments came, with their absurd air of disorderly flight with the loot of innumerable outfit shops and provision stores, that, one would think, they were lugging, after a raid, into the wilderness for equitable division. It was an inextricable mess of things decent in themselves but that human folly made look like the spoils of thieving.

"This devoted band called itself the Eldorado Exploring Expedition, and I believe they were sworn to secrecy. Their talk, however, was the talk of sordid buccaneers: it was reckless without hardihood, greedy without audacity, and cruel without courage; there was not an atom of foresight or of serious intention in the whole batch of them, and they did not seem aware these things are wanted for the work of the world. To tear treasure out of the bowels of the land was their desire, with no more moral purpose at the back of it than there is in burglars breaking into a safe. Who paid the expenses of the noble enterprise I don't know; but the uncle of our manager was leader of that lot.

"In exterior he resembled a butcher in a poor neighbourhood, and his eyes had a look of sleepy cunning. He carried his fat paunch with ostentation on his short legs, and during the time his gang infested the station spoke to no one but his nephew. You could see these two roaming about all day long with their heads close together in an everlasting confab.

"I had given up worrying myself about the rivets. One's capacity for that kind of folly is more limited than you would suppose. I said Hang!—and let things slide. I had plenty of time for meditation, and now and then I would give some thought to Kurtz. I wasn't very interested in him. No. Still, I was curious to see whether this man, who had come out equipped with moral ideas of some sort, would climb to the top after all, and how he would set about his work when there."

2

"One evening as I was lying flat on the deck of my steamboat, I heard voices approaching—and there were the nephew and the uncle strolling along the bank. I laid my head on my arm again, and had nearly lost myself in a doze, when somebody said in my ear, as it were: 'I am as harmless as a little child, but I don't like to be dictated to. Am I the manager—or am I not? I was ordered to send him there. It's incredible.' . . . I became aware that the two were standing on the shore alongside the forepart of the steamboat, just below my head. I did not move; it did not occur to me to move: I was sleepy. 'It *is* unpleasant,' grunted the uncle. 'He has asked the Administration to be sent there,' said the other, 'with the idea of showing what he could do; and I was instructed accordingly. Look at the influence that man must have. Is it not frightful?' They both agreed it was frightful, then made several bizarre remarks: 'Make rain and fine weather—one man—the Council—by the nose'— bits of absurd sentences that got the better of my drowsiness, so that I had pretty near the whole of my wits about me when the uncle said, 'The climate may do away with this difficulty for you. Is he alone there?' 'Yes,' answered the manager; 'he sent his assistant down the river with a note to me in these terms: "Clear this poor devil out of the country, and don't bother sending more of that sort. I had rather be alone than have the kind of men you can dispose of with me." It was more than a year ago. Can you imagine such impudence?' 'Anything since then?' asked the other hoarsely. 'Ivory,' jerked the nephew; 'lots of it—prime sort— lots—most annoying, from him.' 'And with that?' questioned the heavy rumble. 'Invoice,' was the reply fired out, so to speak. Then silence. They had been talking about Kurtz.

"I was broad awake by this time, but, lying perfectly at ease, remained still, having no inducement to change my position. 'How did that ivory come all this way?' growled the elder man, who seemed very vexed. The other explained that it had come with a fleet of canoes in charge of an English half-caste clerk Kurtz had with him; that Kurtz had apparently intended to return himself, the station being by that time bare of goods and stores, but after coming three hundred miles, had suddenly decided to go back, which he started to do alone in a small dugout with four paddlers, leaving the half-caste to continue down the river with the ivory. The two fellows there seemed astounded at anybody attempting such a thing. They were at a loss for an adequate motive. As for me, I seemed to see Kurtz for the first time. It was a distinct glimpse: the dugout, four paddling savages, and the lone white man turning his back suddenly on the headquarters, on relief, on thoughts of home—perhaps; setting his face towards the depths of the wilderness, towards his empty and desolate station. I did not know the motive. Perhaps he was just simply a fine fellow who stuck to his work for its own sake. His name, you understand, had not been pronounced once. He was 'that man.' The half-caste, who, as far as I could see, had conducted a difficult trip with great prudence and pluck, was invariably alluded to as 'that scoundrel.' The 'scoundrel' had reported that the 'man' had been very ill—had recovered imperfectly. . . . The two below me moved away then a few paces, and strolled back and forth at some little distance. I heard: 'Military post—doctor—two hundred miles—quite alone now—unavoidable delays—nine months—no news—strange rumours.' They approached again, just as the manager was saying, 'No one, as far as I know, unless a species of wandering trader—a pestilential fellow, snapping ivory from the natives.' Who was it they were talking about now? I gathered in snatches that this was some man supposed to be in Kurtz's district, and of whom the manager did not approve. 'We will not be free from unfair competition till one of these fellows is hanged for an example,' he said. 'Certainly,' grunted the other; 'get him hanged! Why not? Anything—anything can be done in this country. That's what I say; nobody here, you understand, *here*, can endanger your position. And why? You stand the climate—you outlast them all. The danger is in Europe; but there before I left I took care to—' They moved off and whispered, then their voices rose again. 'The extraordinary series of delays is not my fault. I did my possible.'[4] The fat man sighed, 'Very sad.' 'And the pestiferous absurdity of his talk,' continued the other; 'he bothered me enough when he was here. "Each station should be like a beacon on the road towards better things, a centre for trade of course, but also for humanising, improving, instructing." Conceive you—that ass! And he wants to be manager! No, it's—' Here he got choked by excessive indignation, and I lifted my head the least bit. I was surprised to see how near they were—right under me. I could have spat upon their hats. They were looking on the ground, absorbed in thought. The manager was switching his leg with a slender twig: his sagacious relative lifted his head. 'You have been well since you came out this time?' he asked. The other gave a start. 'Who? I? Oh! Like a charm—like a charm. But the rest—oh, my goodness! All sick. They die so quick, too, that I haven't the time to send them out of the country—it's incredible!' 'H'm. Just so,' grunted the uncle. 'Ah! my boy, trust to this—I say, trust to this.' I saw him extend his short flipper of an arm for a gesture that took in the forest, the creek, the mud, the river—seemed to beckon with a dishonouring flourish before the sunlit face of the land a treacherous appeal to the lurking death, to the hidden evil, to the profound darkness of its heart. It was so startling that I leaped to my feet and looked back at the edge of the forest, as though I had expected an answer of some sort to that black display of confidence. You know the foolish notions that come to one sometimes. The high stillness confronted these two figures with its ominous patience, waiting for the passing away of a fantastic invasion.

"They swore aloud together—out of sheer fright, I believe—then, pretending not to know anything of my existence, turned back to the sta-

4. Conrad, who wrote and spoke French perfectly, sometimes slipped into a French usage when writing English. This is one of his Gallicisms, a literal rendering of *J'ai fait mon possible*.

tion. The sun was low; and leaning forward side by side, they seemed to be tugging painfully uphill their two ridiculous shadows of unequal length, that trailed behind them slowly over the tall grass without bending a single blade.

"In a few days the Eldorado Expedition went into the patient wilderness, that closed upon it as the sea closes over a diver. Long afterwards the news came that all the donkeys were dead. I know nothing as to the fate of the less valuable animals. They, no doubt, like the rest of us, found what they deserved. I did not inquire. I was then rather excited at the prospect of meeting Kurtz very soon. When I say very soon I mean it comparatively. It was just two months from the day we left the creek when we came to the bank below Kurtz's station.

"Going up that river was like travelling back to the earliest beginnings of the world, when vegetation rioted on the earth and the big trees were kings. An empty stream, a great silence, an impenetrable forest. The air was warm, thick, heavy, sluggish. There was no joy in the brilliance of sunshine. The long stretches of the waterway ran on, deserted, into the gloom of overshadowed distances. On silvery sandbanks hippos and alligators sunned themselves side by side. The broadening waters flowed through a mob of wooded islands; you lost your way on that river as you would in a desert, and butted all day long against shoals, trying to find the channel, till you thought yourself bewitched and cut off for ever from everything you had known once—somewhere—far away—in another existence perhaps. There were moments when one's past came back to one, as it will sometimes when you have not a moment to spare to yourself; but it came in the shape of an unrestful and noisy dream, remembered with wonder amongst the overwhelming realities of this strange world of plants, and water, and silence. And this stillness of life did not in the least resemble a peace. It was the stillness of an implacable force brooding over an inscrutable intention. It looked at you with a vengeful aspect. I got used to it afterwards; I did not see it any more; I had no time. I had to keep guessing at the channel; I had to discern, mostly by inspiration, the signs of hidden banks; I watched for sunken stones; I was learning to clap my teeth smartly before my heart flew out, when I shaved by a fluke some infernal sly old snag that would have ripped the life out of the tin-pot steamboat and drowned all the pilgrims; I had to keep a look-out for the signs of dead wood we could cut up in the night for next day's steaming. When you have to attend to things of that sort, to the mere incidents of the surface, the reality—the reality, I tell you—fades. The inner truth is hidden—luckily, luckily. But I felt it all the same; I felt often its mysterious stillness watching me at my monkey tricks, just as it watches you fellows performing on your respective tight-ropes for—what is it? half a crown a tumble—"

"Try to be civil, Marlow," growled a voice, and I knew there was at least one listener awake besides myself.

"I beg your pardon. I forgot the heartache which makes up the rest of the price. And indeed what does the price matter, if the trick be well done? You do your tricks very well. And I didn't do badly either, since I managed not to sink that steamboat on my first trip. It's a wonder to me yet. Imagine a blindfolded man set to drive a van over a bad road. I sweated and shivered over that business considerably, I can tell you. After all, for a seaman, to scrape the bottom of the thing that's supposed to float all the time under his care is the unpardonable sin. No one may know of it, but you never forget the thump—eh? A blow on the very heart. You remember it, you dream of it, you wake up at night and think of it—years after—and go hot and cold all over. I don't pretend to say that steamboat floated all the time. More than once she had to wade for a bit, with twenty cannibals splashing around and pushing. We had enlisted some of these chaps on the way for a crew. Fine fellows—cannibals—in their place. They were men one could work with, and I am grateful to them. And, after all, they did not eat each other before my face: they had brought along a provision of hippo-meat which went rotten, and made the mystery of the wilderness stink in my nostrils. Phoo! I can sniff it now. I had the manager on board and three or four pilgrims with their staves—all complete. Sometimes we came upon a station close by the bank, clinging to the skirts of the unknown, and the white men rushing out of a tumble-down hovel, with great gestures of joy and surprise and welcome, seemed very strange—had the appearance of being held there captive by a spell. The word 'ivory' would ring in the air for a while—and on we went again into the silence, along empty reaches, round the still bends, between the high walls of our winding way, reverberating in hollow claps the ponderous beat of the stern-wheel. Trees, trees, millions of trees, massive, immense, running up high; and at their foot, hugging the bank against the stream, crept the little begrimed steamboat, like a sluggish beetle crawling on the floor of a lofty portico. It made you feel very small, very lost, and yet it was not altogether depressing, that feeling. After all, if you were small, the grimy beetle crawled on—which was just what you wanted it to do. Where the pilgrims imagined it crawled to I don't know. To some place where they expected to get something, I bet! For me it crawled towards Kurtz—exclusively; but when the steam-pipes started leaking we crawled very slow. The reaches opened before us and closed behind, as if the forest had stepped leisurely across the water to bar the way for our return. We penetrated deeper and deeper into the heart of darkness. It was very quiet there. At night sometimes the roll of drums behind the curtain of trees would run up the river and remain sustained faintly, as if hovering in the air high over our heads, till the first break of day. Whether it meant war, peace, or prayer we could not tell. The dawns were heralded by the descent of a chill stillness; the woodcutters slept, their fires burned low; the snapping of a twig would make you start. We were wanderers on a prehistoric earth, on an earth that wore the aspect of an unknown planet. We could have fancied ourselves the first of men taking possession of an accursed inheritance, to be subdued at the cost of profound anguish and of excessive toil. But suddenly, as we struggled round a bend, there would be a glimpse of rush walls, of peaked grass-roofs, a burst of yells, a whirl of black limbs, a mass of hands clapping, of feet stamping, of bodies swaying, of eyes rolling, under the droop of heavy and motionless foliage. The steamer toiled along slowly on the edge of a black and incomprehensible frenzy. The prehistoric man was cursing us, praying to us, welcoming us—who could tell? We were cut off from the comprehension of our surroundings; we glided past like phantoms, wondering and secretly appalled, as sane men would be before an enthusiastic outbreak in a madhouse. We could not understand because we were too far and could not remember, because we were travelling in the night of first ages, of those ages that are gone, leaving hardly a sign—and no memories.

"The earth seemed unearthly. We are accustomed to look upon the shackled form of a conquered monster, but there—there you could look at a thing monstrous and free. It was unearthly, and the men were— No, they were not inhuman. Well, you know, that was the worst of it— this suspicion of their not being inhuman. It would come slowly to one. They howled and leaped, and spun, and made horrid faces; but what thrilled you was just the thought of their humanity—like yours—the thought of your remote kinship with this wild and passionate uproar. Ugly. Yes, it was ugly enough; but if you were man enough you would admit to yourself that there was in you just the faintest trace of a response to the terrible frankness of that noise, a dim suspicion of there being a meaning in it which you—you so remote from the night of first ages— could comprehend. And why not? The mind of man is capable of anything—because everything is in it, all the past as well as all the future. What was there after all? Joy, fear, sorrow, devotion, valour, rage—who can tell?—but truth—truth stripped of its cloak of time. Let the fool gape and shudder—the man knows, and can look on without a wink. But he must at least be as much of a man as these on the shore. He must meet that truth with his own true stuff—with his own inborn strength. Principles? Principles won't do. Acquisitions, clothes, pretty rags—rags that would fly off at the first good shake. No; you want a deliberate belief. An appeal to me in this fiendish row—is there? Very well; I hear; I admit, but I have a voice too, and for good or evil mine is the speech that cannot be silenced. Of course, a fool, what with sheer fright and fine sentiments, is always safe. Who's that grunting? You wonder I didn't go ashore for a howl and a dance? Well, no—I didn't. Fine sentiments, you say? Fine sentiments be hanged! I had no time. I had to mess about with white-lead and strips of woollen blanket helping to put bandages on those leaky steam-pipes—I tell you. I had to watch the steering, and circumvent those snags, and get the tin-pot along by hook or by crook. There was surface-truth enough in these things to save a wiser man. And between whiles I had to look after the savage who was fireman. He was an improved specimen; he could fire up a vertical boiler. He was there below me, and, upon my word, to look at him was as edifying as seeing a dog in a parody of breeches and a feather hat, walking on his hind legs. A few months of training had done for that really fine chap. He squinted at the steam-gauge and at the water-gauge with an evident effort of intrepidity—and he had filed teeth too, the poor devil, and the wool of his pate shaved into queer patterns, and three ornamental scars on each of his cheeks. He ought to have been clapping his hands and stamping his feet on the bank, instead of which he was hard at work, a thrall to strange witchcraft, full of improving knowledge. He was useful because he had been instructed; and what he knew was this—that should the water in that transparent thing disappear, the evil spirit inside the boiler would get angry through the greatness of his thirst, and take a terrible vengeance. So he sweated and fired up and watched the glass fearfully (with an impromptu charm, made of rags, tied to his arm, and a piece of polished bone, as big as a watch, stuck flatways through his lower lip), while the wooded banks slipped past us slowly, the short noise was left behind, the interminable miles of silence—and we crept on, towards Kurtz. But the snags were thick, the water was treacherous and shallow, the boiler seemed indeed to have a sulky devil in it, and thus neither that fireman nor I had any time to peer into our creepy thoughts.

"Some fifty miles below the Inner Station we came upon a hut of reeds, an inclined and melancholy pole, with the unrecognisable tatters of what had been a flag of some sort flying from it, and a neatly stacked wood-pile. This was unexpected. We came to the bank, and on the stack of firewood found a flat piece of board with some faded pencil-writing on it. When deciphered it said: 'Wood for you. Hurry up. Approach cautiously.' There was a signature, but it was illegible—not Kurtz—a much longer word. Hurry up. Where? Up the river? 'Approach cautiously.' We had not done so. But the warning could not have been meant for the place where it could be only found after approach. Something was wrong above. But what—and how much? That was the question. We commented adversely upon the imbecility of that telegraphic style. The bush around said nothing, and would not let us look very far, either. A torn curtain of red twill hung in the doorway of the hut, and flapped sadly in our faces. The dwelling was dismantled; but we could see a white man had lived there not very long ago. There remained a rude table—a plank on two posts; a heap of rubbish reposed in a dark corner, and by the door I picked up a book. It had lost its covers, and the pages had been thumbed into a state of extremely dirty softness; but the back had been lovingly stitched afresh with white cotton thread, which looked clean yet. It was an extraordinary find. Its title was, *An Inquiry into some Points of Seamanship*, by a man Towser, Towson—some such name—Master in His Majesty's Navy. The matter looked dreary reading enough, with illustrative diagrams and repulsive tables of figures, and the copy was sixty years old. I handled this amazing antiquity with the greatest possible tenderness, lest it should dissolve in my hands. Within, Towson or Towser was inquiring earnestly into the breaking strain of ships' chains and tackle, and other such matters. Not a very enthralling book; but at the first glance you could see there a singleness of intention, an honest concern for the right way of going to work, which made these humble pages, thought out so many years ago, luminous with another than a professional light. The simple old sailor, with his talk of chains and purchases, made me forget the jungle and the pilgrims in a delicious sensation of having come upon something unmistakably real. Such a book being there was wonderful enough; but still more astounding were the notes pencilled in the margin, and plainly referring to the text. I couldn't believe my eyes! They were in cipher! Yes, it looked like cipher. Fancy a man lugging with him a book of that description into this nowhere and studying it—and making notes—in cipher at that! It was an extravagant mystery.

"I had been dimly aware for some time of a worrying noise, and when I lifted my eyes I saw the wood-pile was gone, and the manager, aided by all the pilgrims, was shouting at me from the river-side. I slipped the book into my pocket. I assure you to leave off reading was like tearing myself away from the shelter of an old and solid friendship.

"I started the lame engine ahead. 'It must be this miserable trader—this intruder,' exclaimed the manager, looking back malevolently at the place we had left. 'He must be English,' I said. 'It will not save him from getting into trouble if he is not careful,' muttered the manager darkly. I observed with assumed innocence that no man was safe from trouble in this world.

"The current was more rapid now, the steamer seemed at her last gasp, the stern-wheel flopped languidly, and I caught myself listening on tiptoe for the next beat of the float,[5] for in sober truth I expected the wretched thing to give up every moment. It was like watching the last flickers of a life. But still we crawled. Sometimes I would pick out a tree a little way ahead to measure our progress towards Kurtz by, but I lost it invariably before we got abreast. To keep the eyes so long on one thing was too much for human patience. The manager displayed a beautiful resignation. I fretted and fumed and took to arguing with myself whether or no I would talk openly with Kurtz; but before I could come to any conclusion it occurred to me that my speech or my silence, indeed any action of mine, would be a mere futility. What did it matter what any one knew or ignored? What did it matter who was manager? One gets sometimes such a flash of insight. The essentials of this affair lay deep under the surface, beyond my reach, and beyond my power of meddling.

"Towards the evening of the second day we judged ourselves about eight miles from Kurtz's station. I wanted to push on; but the manager looked grave, and told me the navigation up there was so dangerous that it would be advisable, the sun being very low already, to wait where we were till next morning. Moreover, he pointed out that if the warning to approach cautiously were to be followed, we must approach in daylight—not at dusk, or in the dark. This was sensible enough. Eight miles

---

5. Automatic water-level regulator opening and closing a water-supply valve.

meant nearly three hours' steaming for us, and I could also see suspicious ripples at the upper end of the reach. Nevertheless, I was annoyed beyond expression at the delay, and most unreasonably too, since one night more could not matter much after so many months. As we had plenty of wood, and caution was the word, I brought up in the middle of the stream. The reach was narrow, straight, with high sides like a railway cutting. The dusk came gliding into it long before the sun had set. The current ran smooth and swift, but a dumb immobility sat on the banks. The living trees, lashed together by the creepers and every living bush of the undergrowth, might have been changed into stone, even to the slenderest twig, to the lightest leaf. It was not sleep—it seemed unnatural, like a state of trance. Not the faintest sound of any kind could be heard. You looked on amazed, and began to suspect yourself of being deaf—then the night came suddenly, and struck you blind as well. About three in the morning some large fish leaped, and the loud splash made me jump as though a gun had been fired. When the sun rose there was a white fog, very warm and clammy, and more blinding than the night. It did not shift or drive; it was just there, standing all round you like something solid. At eight or nine, perhaps, it lifted as a shutter lifts. We had a glimpse of the towering multitude of trees, of the immense matted jungle, with the blazing little ball of the sun hanging over it—all perfectly still—and then the white shutter came down again, smoothly, as if sliding in greased grooves. I ordered the chain, which we had begun to heave in, to be paid out again. Before it stopped running with a muffled rattle, a cry, a very loud cry, as of infinite desolation, soared slowly in the opaque air. It ceased. A complaining clamour, modulated in savage discords, filled our ears. The sheer unexpectedness of it made my hair stir under my cap. I don't know how it struck the others: to me it seemed as though the mist itself had screamed, so suddenly, and apparently from all sides at once, did this tumultuous and mournful uproar arise. It culminated in a hurried outbreak of almost intolerably excessive shrieking, which stopped short, leaving us stiffened in a variety of silly attitudes, and obstinately listening to the nearly as appalling and excessive silence. 'Good God! What is the meaning—?' stammered at my elbow one of the pilgrims—a little fat man, with sandy hair and red whiskers, who wore side-spring boots, and pink pyjamas tucked into his socks. Two others remained open-mouthed a whole minute, then dashed into the little cabin, to rush out incontinently and stand darting scared glances, with Winchesters at 'ready' in their hands. What we could see was just the steamer we were on, her outlines blurred as though she had been on the point of dissolving, and a misty strip of water, perhaps two feet broad, around her—and that was all. The rest of the world was nowhere, as far as our eyes and ears were concerned. Just nowhere. Gone, disappeared; swept off without leaving a whisper or a shadow behind.

"I went forward, and ordered the chain to be hauled in short, so as to be ready to trip the anchor and move the steamboat at once if necessary.

'Will they attack?' whispered an awed voice. 'We will all be butchered in this fog,' murmured another. The faces twitched with the strain, the hands trembled slightly, the eyes forgot to wink. It was very curious to see the contrast of expressions of the white men and of the black fellows of our crew, who were as much strangers to that part of the river as we, though their homes were only eight hundred miles away. The whites, of course greatly discomposed, had besides a curious look of being painfully shocked by such an outrageous row. The others had an alert, naturally interested expression; but their faces were essentially quiet, even those of the one or two who grinned as they hauled at the chain. Several exchanged short, grunting phrases, which seemed to settle the matter to their satisfaction. Their headman, a young, broad-chested black, severely draped in dark-blue fringed cloths, with fierce nostrils and his hair all done up artfully in oily ringlets, stood near me. 'Aha!' I said, just for good fellowship's sake. 'Catch 'im,' he snapped, with a bloodshot widening of his eyes and a flash of sharp teeth—'catch 'im. Give 'im to us.' 'To you, eh?' I asked; 'what would you do with them?' 'Eat 'im!' he said curtly, and, leaning his elbow on the rail, looked out into the fog in a dignified and profoundly pensive attitude. I would no doubt have been properly horrified, had it not occurred to me that he and his chaps must be very hungry: that they must have been growing increasingly hungry for at least this month past. They had been engaged for six months (I don't think a single one of them had any clear idea of time, as we at the end of countless ages have. They still belonged to the beginnings of time—had no inherited experience to teach them, as it were), and of course, as long as there was a piece of paper written over in accordance with some farcical law or other made down the river, it didn't enter anybody's head to trouble how they would live. Certainly they had brought with them some rotten hippo-meat, which couldn't have lasted very long, anyway, even if the pilgrims hadn't, in the midst of a shocking hullabaloo, thrown a considerable quantity of it overboard. It looked like a highhanded proceeding; but it was really a case of legitimate self-defence. You can't breathe dead hippo waking, sleeping, and eating, and at the same time keep your precarious grip on existence. Besides that, they had given them every week three pieces of brass wire, each about nine inches long; and the theory was they were to buy their provisions with that currency in river-side villages. You can see how *that* worked. There were either no villages, or the people were hostile, or the director, who like the rest of us fed out of tins, with an occasional old he-goat thrown in, didn't want to stop the steamer for some more or less recondite reasons. So, unless they swallowed the wire itself, or made loops of it to snare the fishes with, I don't see what good their extravagant salary could be to them. I must say it was paid with a regularity worthy of a large and honourable trading company. For the rest, the only thing to eat—though it didn't look eatable in the least—I saw in their possession was a few lumps of some stuff like half-cooked dough, of a dirty lavender colour, they kept wrapped in leaves, and now and then swallowed a piece of, but so small that it seemed done more for the look of the thing than for any serious purpose of sustenance. Why in the name of all the gnawing devils of hunger they didn't go for us—they were thirty to five—and have a good tuck-in for once, amazes me now when I think of it. They were big powerful men, with not much capacity to weigh the consequences, with courage, with strength, even yet, though their skins were no longer glossy and their muscles no longer hard. And I saw that something restraining, one of those human secrets that baffle probability, had come into play there. I looked at them with a swift quickening of interest— not because it occurred to me I might be eaten by them before very long, though I own to you that just then I perceived—in a new light, as it were—how unwholesome the pilgrims looked, and I hoped, yes, I positively hoped, that my aspect was not so—what shall I say?—so—unappetising: a touch of fantastic vanity which fitted well with the dreamsensation that pervaded all my days at that time. Perhaps I had a little fever too. One can't live with one's finger everlastingly on one's pulse. I had often 'a little fever,' or a little touch of other things—the playful paw-strokes of the wilderness, the preliminary trifling before the more serious onslaught which came in due course. Yes; I looked at them as you would on any human being, with a curiosity of their impulses, motives, capacities, weaknesses, when brought to the test of an inexorable physical necessity. Restraint! What possible restraint? Was it superstition, disgust, patience, fear—or some kind of primitive honour? No fear can stand up to hunger, no patience can wear it out, disgust simply does not exist where hunger is; and as to superstition, beliefs, and what you may call principles, they are less than chaff in a breeze. Don't you know the devilry of lingering starvation, its exasperating torment, its black thoughts, its sombre and brooding ferocity? Well, I do. It takes a man all his inborn strength to fight hunger properly. It's really easier to face bereavement, dishonour, and the perdition of one's soul—than this kind of prolonged hunger. Sad, but true. And these chaps too had no earthly reason for any kind of scruple. Restraint! I would just as soon have expected restraint from a hyena prowling amongst the corpses of a battlefield. But there was the fact facing me—the fact dazzling, to be seen, like the foam on the depths of the sea, like a ripple on an unfathomable enigma, a mystery greater—when I thought of it—than the curious, inexplicable note of desperate grief in this savage clamour that had swept by us on the river-bank, behind the blind whiteness of the fog.

"Two pilgrims were quarrelling in hurried whispers as to which bank. 'Left.' 'No, no; how can you? Right, right, of course.' 'It is very serious,' said the manager's voice behind me; 'I would be desolated if anything should happen to Mr. Kurtz before we came up.' I looked at him, and had not the slightest doubt he was sincere. He was just the kind of man who would wish to preserve appearances. That was his restraint. But when he muttered something about going on at once, I did not even take the trouble to answer him. I knew, and he knew, that it was impossible. Were we to let go our hold of the bottom, we would be absolutely in the air—in space. We wouldn't be able to tell where we were going to—whether up or down stream, or across—till we fetched against one bank or the other—and then we wouldn't know at first which it was. Of course I made no move. I had no mind for a smash-up. You couldn't imagine a more deadly place for a shipwreck. Whether drowned at once or not, we were sure to perish speedily in one way or another. 'I authorise you to take all the risks,' he said, after a short silence. 'I refuse to take any,' I said shortly; which was just the answer he expected, though its tone might have surprised him. 'Well, I must defer to your judgment. You are captain,' he said, with marked civility. I turned my shoulder to him in sign of my appreciation, and looked into the fog. How long would it last? It was the most hopeless look-out. The approach to this Kurtz grubbing for ivory in the wretched bush was beset by as many dangers as though he had been an enchanted princess sleeping in a fabulous castle. 'Will they attack, do you think?' asked the manager, in a confidential tone.

"I did not think they would attack, for several obvious reasons. The thick fog was one. If they left the bank in their canoes they would get lost in it, as we would be if we attempted to move. Still, I had also judged the jungle of both banks quite impenetrable—and yet eyes were in it, eyes that had seen us. The river-side bushes were certainly very thick; but the undergrowth behind was evidently penetrable. However, during the short lift I had seen no canoes anywhere in the reach—certainly not abreast of the steamer. But what made the idea of attack inconceivable to me was the nature of the noise—of the cries we had heard. They had not the fierce character boding of immediate hostile intention. Unexpected, wild, and violent as they had been, they had given me an irresistible impression of sorrow. The glimpse of the steamboat had for some reason filled those savages with unrestrained grief. The danger, if any, I expounded, was from our proximity to a great human passion let loose. Even extreme grief may ultimately vent itself in violence—but more generally takes the form of apathy. . . .

"You should have seen the pilgrims stare! They had no heart to grin, or even to revile me; but I believe they thought me gone mad—with fright, maybe. I delivered a regular lecture. My dear boys, it was no good bothering. Keep a look-out? Well, you may guess I watched the fog for the signs of lifting as a cat watches a mouse; but for anything else our eyes were of no more use to us than if we had been buried miles deep in a heap of cotton-wool. It felt like it too—choking, warm, stifling. Besides, all I said, though it sounded extravagant, was absolutely true to fact. What we afterwards alluded to as an attack was really an attempt at repulse. The action was very far from being aggressive—it was not even defensive, in the usual sense: it was undertaken under the stress of desperation, and in its essence was purely protective.

"It developed itself, I should say, two hours after the fog lifted, and its commencement was at a spot, roughly speaking, about a mile and a half below Kurtz's station. We had just floundered and flopped round a bend, when I saw an islet, a mere grassy hummock of bright green, in the middle of the stream. It was the only thing of the kind; but as we opened the reach more, I perceived it was the head of a long sandbank, or rather of a chain of shallow patches stretching down the middle of the river. They were discoloured, just awash, and the whole lot was seen just under the water, exactly as a man's backbone is seen running down the middle of his back under the skin. Now, as far as I did see, I could go to the right or to the left of this. I didn't know either channel, of course. The banks looked pretty well alike, the depth appeared the same; but as I had been informed the station was on the west side, I naturally headed for the western passage.

"No sooner had we fairly entered it than I became aware it was much narrower than I had supposed. To the left of us there was the long uninterrupted shoal, and to the right a high steep bank heavily overgrown with bushes. Above the bush the trees stood in serried ranks. The twigs overhung the current thickly, and from distance to distance a large limb of some tree projected rigidly over the stream. It was then well on in the afternoon, the face of the forest was gloomy, and a broad strip of shadow had already fallen on the water. In this shadow we steamed up—very slowly, as you may imagine. I sheered her well inshore—the water being deepest near the bank, as the sounding-pole informed me.

"One of my hungry and forbearing friends was sounding in the bows just below me. This steamboat was exactly like a decked scow. On the deck there were two little teak-wood houses, with doors and windows. The boiler was in the fore-end, and the machinery right astern. Over the whole there was a light roof, supported on stanchions. The funnel projected through that roof, and in front of the funnel a small cabin built of light planks served for a pilot-house. It contained a couch, two camp-stools, a loaded Martini-Henry[6] leaning in one corner, a tiny table, and the steering-wheel. It had a wide door in front and a broad shutter at each side. All these were always thrown open, of course. I spent my days perched up there on the extreme fore-end of that roof, before the door. At night I slept, or tried to, on the couch. An athletic black belonging to some coast tribe, and educated by my poor predecessor, was the helmsman. He sported a pair of brass earrings, wore a blue cloth wrapper from the waist to the ankles, and thought all the world of himself. He was the most unstable kind of fool I had ever seen. He steered with no end of a swagger while you were by; but if he lost sight of you, he became instantly the prey of an abject funk, and would let that cripple of a steamboat get the upper hand of him in a minute.

"I was looking down at the sounding-pole, and feeling much annoyed to see at each try a little more of it stick out of that river, when I saw my poleman give up the business suddenly, and stretch himself flat on the deck, without even taking the trouble to haul his pole in. He kept hold on it though, and it trailed in the water. At the same time the fireman,

6. Rifle combining the 7-grooved barrel of the Scottish gunmaker A. Henry with the block-action breech mechanism introduced by the Swiss inventor F. Martini.

whom I could also see below me, sat down abruptly before his furnace and ducked his head. I was amazed. Then I had to look at the river mighty quick, because there was a snag in the fairway. Sticks, little sticks, were flying about—thick; they were whizzing before my nose, dropping below me, striking behind me against my pilot-house. All this time the river, the shore, the woods, were very quiet—perfectly quiet. I could only hear the heavy splashing thump of the stern-wheel and the patter of these things. We cleared the snag clumsily. Arrows, by Jove! We were being shot at! I stepped in quickly to close the shutter on the land-side. That fool-helmsman, his hands on the spokes, was lifting his knees high, stamping his feet, champing his mouth, like a reined-in horse. Confound him! And we were staggering within ten feet of the bank. I had to lean right out to swing the heavy shutter, and I saw a face amongst the leaves on the level with my own, looking at me very fierce and steady; and then suddenly, as though a veil had been removed from my eyes, I made out, deep in the tangled gloom, naked breasts, arms, legs, glaring eyes—the bush was swarming with human limbs in movement, glistening, of bronze colour. The twigs shook, swayed, and rustled, the arrows flew out of them, and then the shutter came to. 'Steer her straight,' I said to the helmsman. He held his head rigid, face forward; but his eyes rolled, he kept on lifting and setting down his feet gently, his mouth foamed a little. 'Keep quiet!' I said in a fury. I might just as well have ordered a tree not to sway in the wind. I darted out. Below me there was a great scuffle of feet on the iron deck; confused exclamations; a voice screamed, 'Can you turn back?' I caught sight of a V-shaped ripple on the water ahead. What? Another snag! A fusillade burst out under my feet. The pilgrims had opened with their Winchesters, and were simply squirting lead into that bush. A deuce of a lot of smoke came up and drove slowly forward. I swore at it. Now I couldn't see the ripple or the snag either. I stood in the doorway, peering, and the arrows came in swarms. They might have been poisoned, but they looked as though they wouldn't kill a cat. The bush began to howl. Our wood-cutters raised a warlike whoop; the report of a rifle just at my back deafened me. I glanced over my shoulder, and the pilot-house was yet full of noise and smoke when I made a dash at the wheel. The fool-nigger had dropped everything, to throw the shutter open and let off that Martini-Henry. He stood before the wide opening, glaring, and I yelled at him to come back, while I straightened the sudden twist out of that steamboat. There was no room to turn even if I had wanted to, the snag was somewhere very near ahead in that confounded smoke, there was no time to lose, so I just crowded her into the bank—right into the bank, where I knew the water was deep.

"We tore slowly along the overhanging bushes in a whirl of broken twigs and flying leaves. The fusillade below stopped short, as I had foreseen it would when the squirts got empty. I threw my head back to a glinting whizz that traversed the pilot-house, in at one shutter-hole and out at the other. Looking past that mad helmsman, who was shaking the empty rifle and yelling at the shore, I saw vague forms of men running bent double, leaping, gliding, distinct, incomplete, evanescent. Something big appeared in the air before the shutter, the rifle went overboard, and the man stepped back swiftly, looked at me over his shoulder in an extraordinary, profound, familiar manner, and fell upon my feet. The side of his head hit the wheel twice, and the end of what appeared a long cane clattered round and knocked over a little camp-stool. It looked as though after wrenching that thing from somebody ashore he had lost his balance in the effort. The thin smoke had blown away, we were clear of the snag, and looking ahead I could see that in another hundred yards or so I would be free to sheer off, away from the bank; but my feet felt so very warm and wet that I had to look down. The man had rolled on his back and stared straight up at me; both his hands clutched that cane. It was the shaft of a spear that, either thrown or lunged through the opening, had caught him in the side just below the ribs; the blade had gone in out of sight, after making a frightful gash; my shoes were full; a pool of blood lay very still, gleaming dark-red under the wheel; his eyes shone with an amazing lustre. The fusillade burst out again. He looked at me anxiously, gripping the spear like something precious, with an air of being afraid I would try to take it away from him. I had to make an effort to free my eyes from his gaze and attend to the steering. With one hand I felt above my head for the line of the steam whistle, and jerked out screech after screech hurriedly. The tumult of angry and warlike yells was checked instantly, and then from the depths of the woods went out such a tremulous and prolonged wail of mournful fear and utter despair as may be imagined to follow the flight of the last hope from the earth. There was a great commotion in the bush; the shower of arrows stopped, a few dropping shots rang out sharply—then silence, in which the languid beat of the stern-wheel came plainly to my ears. I put the helm hard a-starboard at the moment when the pilgrim in pink pyjamas, very hot and agitated, appeared in the doorway. 'The manager sends me—' he began in an official tone, and stopped short. 'Good God!' he said, glaring at the wounded man.

"We two whites stood over him, and his lustrous and inquiring glance enveloped us both. I declare it looked as though he would presently put to us some question in an understandable language; but he died without uttering a sound, without moving a limb, without twitching a muscle. Only in the very last moment, as though in response to some sign we could not see, to some whisper we could not hear, he frowned heavily, and that frown gave to his black death-mask an inconceivably sombre, brooding, and menacing expression. The lustre of inquiring glance faded swiftly into vacant glassiness. 'Can you steer?' I asked the agent eagerly. He looked very dubious; but I made a grab at his arm, and he understood at once I meant him to steer whether or no. To tell you the truth, I was morbidly anxious to change my shoes and socks. 'He is dead,' murmured the fellow, immensely impressed. 'No doubt about it,' said I, tugging like mad at the shoe-laces. 'And by the way, I suppose Mr. Kurtz is dead as well by this time.'

"For the moment that was the dominant thought. There was a sense of extreme disappointment, as though I had found out I had been striving after something altogether without a substance. I couldn't have been more disgusted if I had travelled all this way for the sole purpose of talking with Mr. Kurtz. Talking with . . . I flung one shoe overboard, and became aware that that was exactly what I had been looking forward to—a talk with Kurtz. I made the strange discovery that I had never imagined him as doing, you know, but as discoursing. I didn't say to myself, 'Now I will never see him,' or 'Now I will never shake him by the hand,' but, 'Now I will never hear him.' The man presented himself as a voice. Not of course that I did not connect him with some sort of action. Hadn't I been told in all the tones of jealousy and admiration that he had collected, bartered, swindled, or stolen more ivory than all the other agents together? That was not the point. The point was in his being a gifted creature, and that of all his gifts the one that stood out pre-eminently, that carried with it a sense of real presence, was his ability to talk, his words—the gift of expression, the bewildering, the illuminating, the most exalted and the most contemptible, the pulsating stream of light, or the deceitful flow from the heart of an impenetrable darkness.

"The other shoe went flying unto the devil-god of that river. I thought, By Jove! it's all over. We are too late; he has vanished—the gift has vanished, by means of some spear, arrow, or club. I will never hear that chap speak after all—and my sorrow had a startling extravagance of emotion, even such as I had noticed in the howling sorrow of these savages in the bush. I couldn't have felt more of lonely desolation somehow, had I been robbed of a belief or had missed my destiny in life. . . . Why do you sigh in this beastly way, somebody? Absurd? Well, absurd. Good Lord! mustn't a man ever—Here, give me some tobacco." . . .

There was a pause of profound stillness, then a match flared, and Marlow's lean face appeared, worn, hollow, with downward folds and dropped eyelids, with an aspect of concentrated attention; and as he took vigorous draws at his pipe, it seemed to retreat and advance out of the night in the regular flicker of the tiny flame. The match went out.

"Absurd!" he cried. "This is the worst of trying to tell . . . Here you all are, each moored with two good addresses, like a hulk with two anchors, a butcher round one corner, a policeman round another, excellent appetites, and temperature normal—you hear—normal from year's end to year's end. And you say, Absurd! Absurd be—exploded! Absurd! My dear boys, what can you expect from a man who out of sheer nervousness had just flung overboard a pair of new shoes? Now I think of it, it is amazing I did not shed tears. I am, upon the whole, proud of my fortitude. I was cut to the quick at the idea of having lost the inestimable privilege of listening to the gifted Kurtz. Of course I was wrong. The privilege was waiting for me. Oh yes, I heard more than enough. And I was right, too. A voice. He was very little more than a voice. And I heard—him—it—this voice—other voices—all of them were so little more than voices—and the memory of that time itself lingers around me, impalpable, like a dying vibration of one immense jabber, silly, atrocious, sordid, savage, or simply mean, without any kind of sense. Voices, voices—even the girl herself—now—"

He was silent for a long time.

"I laid the ghost of his gifts at last with a lie," he began suddenly. "Girl! What? Did I mention a girl? Oh, she is out of it—completely. They—the women I mean—are out of it—should be out of it. We must help them to stay in that beautiful world of their own, lest ours gets worse. Oh, she had to be out of it. You should have heard the disinterred body of Mr. Kurtz saying, 'My Intended.' You would have perceived directly then how completely she was out of it. And the lofty frontal bone of Mr. Kurtz! They say the hair goes on growing sometimes, but this—ah—specimen was impressively bald. The wilderness had patted him on the head, and, behold, it was like a ball—an ivory ball; it had caressed him, and—lo!—he had withered; it had taken him, loved him, embraced him, got into his veins, consumed his flesh, and sealed his soul to its own by the inconceivable ceremonies of some devilish initiation. He was its spoiled and pampered favourite. Ivory? I should think so. Heaps of it, stacks of it. The old mud shanty was bursting with it. You would think there was not a single tusk left either above or below the ground in the whole country. 'Mostly fossil,' the manager had remarked disparagingly. It was no more fossil than I am; but they call it fossil when it is dug up. It appears these niggers do bury the tusks sometimes—but evidently they couldn't bury this parcel deep enough to save the gifted Mr. Kurtz from his fate. We filled the steamboat with it, and had to pile a lot on the deck. Thus he could see and enjoy as long as he could see, because the appreciation of this favour had remained with him to the last. You should have heard him say, 'My ivory.' Oh yes, I heard him. 'My Intended, my ivory, my station, my river, my—' everything belonged to him. It made me hold my breath in expectation of hearing the wilderness burst into a prodigious peal of laughter that would shake the fixed stars in their places. Everything belonged to him—but that was a trifle. The thing was to know what he belonged to, how many powers of darkness claimed him for their own. That was the reflection that made you creepy all over. It was impossible—it was not good for one either—trying to imagine. He had taken a high seat amongst the devils of the land—I mean literally. You can't understand. How could you?—with solid pavement under your feet, surrounded by kind neighbours ready to cheer you or to fall on you, stepping delicately between the butcher and the policeman, in the holy terror of scandal and gallows and lunatic asylums—how can you imagine what particular region of the first ages a man's untrammelled feet may take him into by the way of solitude—utter solitude without a policeman—by the way of silence—

utter silence, where no warning voice of a kind neighbour can be heard whispering of public opinion? These little things make all the great difference. When they are gone you must fall back upon your own innate strength, upon your own capacity for faithfulness. Of course you may be too much of a fool to go wrong—too dull even to know you are being assaulted by the powers of darkness. I take it, no fool ever made a bargain for his soul with the devil: the fool is too much of a fool, or the devil too much of a devil—I don't know which. Or you may be such a thunderingly exalted creature as to be altogether deaf and blind to anything but heavenly sights and sounds. Then the earth for you is only a standing place—and whether to be like this is your loss or your gain I won't pretend to say. But most of us are neither one nor the other. The earth for us is a place to live in, where we must put up with sights, with sounds, with smells, too, by Jove!—breathe dead hippo, so to speak, and not be contaminated. And there, don't you see? your strength comes in, the faith in your ability for the digging of unostentatious holes to bury the stuff in—your power of devotion, not to yourself, but to an obscure, back-breaking business. And that's difficult enough. Mind, I am not trying to excuse or even explain—I am trying to account to myself for—for—Mr. Kurtz—for the shade of Mr. Kurtz. This initiated wraith from the back of Nowhere honoured me with its amazing confidence before it vanished altogether. This was because it could speak English to me. The original Kurtz had been educated partly in England, and—as he was good enough to say himself—his sympathies were in the right place. His mother was half-English, his father was half-French. All Europe contributed to the making of Kurtz; and by and by I learned that, most appropriately, the International Society for the Suppression of Savage Customs had entrusted him with the making of a report, for its future guidance. And he had written it too. I've seen it. I've read it. It was eloquent, vibrating with eloquence, but too high-strung, I think. Seventeen pages of close writing he had found time for! But this must have been before his—let us say—nerves went wrong, and caused him to preside at certain midnight dances ending with unspeakable rites, which—as far as I reluctantly gathered from what I heard at various times—were offered up to him—do you understand?—to Mr. Kurtz himself. But it was a beautiful piece of writing. The opening paragraph, however, in the light of later information, strikes me now as ominous. He began with the argument that we whites, from the point of development we had arrived at, 'must necessarily appear to them [savages] in the nature of supernatural beings—we approach them with the might as of a deity,' and so on, and so on. 'By the simple exercise of our will we can exert a power for good practically unbounded,' etc. etc. From that point he soared and took me with him. The peroration was magnificent, though difficult to remember, you know. It gave me the notion of an exotic Immensity ruled by an august Benevolence. It made me tingle with enthusiasm. This was the unbounded power of eloquence—of words—of burning noble words. There were no practical hints to interrupt the magic current of phrases, unless a kind of note at the foot of the last page, scrawled evidently much later, in an unsteady hand, may be regarded as the exposition of a method. It was very simple, and at the end of that moving appeal to every altruistic sentiment it blazed at you, luminous and terrifying, like a flash of lightning in a serene sky: 'Exterminate all the brutes!' The curious part was that he had apparently forgotten all about that valuable postscriptum, because, later on, when he in a sense came to himself, he repeatedly entreated me to take good care of 'my pamphlet' (he called it), as it was sure to have in the future a good influence upon his career. I had full information about all these things, and, besides, as it turned out, I was to have the care of his memory. I've done enough for it to give me the indisputable right to lay it, if I choose, for an everlasting rest in the dust-bin of progress, amongst all the sweepings and, figuratively speaking, all the dead cats of civilisation. But then, you see, I can't choose. He won't be forgotten. Whatever he was, he was not common. He had the power to charm or frighten rudimentary souls into an aggravated witchdance in his honour; he could also fill the small souls of the pilgrims with bitter misgivings: he had one devoted friend at least, and he had conquered one soul in the world that was neither rudimentary nor tainted with self-seeking. No; I can't forget him, though I am not prepared to affirm the fellow was exactly worth the life we lost in getting to him. I missed my late helmsman awfully—I missed him even while his body was still lying in the pilot-house. Perhaps you will think it passing strange this regret for a savage who was no more account than a grain of sand in a black Sahara. Well, don't you see, he had done something, he had steered; for months I had him at my back— a help—an instrument. It was a kind of partnership. He steered for me— I had to look after him, I worried about his deficiencies, and thus a subtle bond had been created, of which I only became aware when it was suddenly broken. And the intimate profundity of that look he gave me when he received his hurt remains to this day in my memory—like a claim of distant kinship affirmed in a supreme moment.

"Poor fool! If he had only left that shutter alone. He had no restraint, no restraint—just like Kurtz—a tree swayed by the wind. As soon as I had put on a dry pair of slippers, I dragged him out, after first jerking the spear out of his side, which operation I confess I performed with my eyes shut tight. His heels leaped together over the little doorstep; his shoulders were pressed to my breast; I hugged him from behind desperately. Oh! he was heavy, heavy; heavier than any man on earth, I should imagine. Then without more ado I tipped him overboard. The current snatched him as though he had been a wisp of grass, and I saw the body roll over twice before I lost sight of it for ever. All the pilgrims and the manager were then congregated on the awning-deck about the pilot-house, chattering at each other like a flock of excited magpies, and there was a scandalised murmur at my heartless promptitude. What they wanted to keep that body hanging about for I can't guess. Embalm it, maybe.

But I had also heard another, and a very ominous, murmur on the deck below. My friend the wood-cutters were likewise scandalised, and with a better show of reason—though I admit that the reason itself was quite inadmissible. Oh, quite! I had made up my mind that if my late helmsman was to be eaten, the fishes alone should have him. He had been a very second-rate helmsman while alive, but now he was dead he might have become a first-class temptation, and possibly cause some startling trouble. Besides, I was anxious to take the wheel, the man in pink pyjamas showing himself a hopeless duffer at the business.

"This I did directly the simple funeral was over. We were going half-speed, keeping right in the middle of the stream, and I listened to the talk about me. They had given up Kurtz, they had given up the station; Kurtz was dead, and the station had been burnt—and so on—and so on. The red-haired pilgrim was beside himself with the thought that at least this poor Kurtz had been properly revenged. 'Say! We must have made a glorious slaughter of them in the bush. Eh? What do you think? Say?' He positively danced, the bloodthirsty little gingery beggar.[7] And he had nearly fainted when he saw the wounded man! I could not help saying, 'You made a glorious lot of smoke, anyhow.' I had seen, from the way the tops of the bushes rustled and flew, that almost all the shots had gone too high. You can't hit anything unless you take aim and fire from the shoulder; but these chaps fired from the hip with their eyes shut. The retreat, I maintained—and I was right—was caused by the screeching of the steam-whistle. Upon this they forgot Kurtz, and began to howl at me with indignant protests.

"The manager stood by the wheel murmuring confidentially about the necessity of getting well away down the river before dark at all events, when I saw in the distance a clearing on the river-side and the outlines of some sort of building. 'What's this?' I asked. He clapped his hands in wonder. 'The station!' he cried. I edged in at once, still going half-speed.

"Through my glasses I saw the slope of a hill interspersed with rare trees and perfectly free from undergrowth. A long decaying building on the summit was half buried in the high grass; the large holes in the peaked roof gaped black from afar; the jungle and the woods made a background. There was no enclosure or fence of any kind; but there had been one apparently, for near the house half a dozen slim posts remained in a row, roughly trimmed, and with their upper ends ornamented with round carved balls. The rails, or whatever there had been between, had disappeared. Of course the forest surrounded all that. The river-bank was clear, and on the water side I saw a white man under a hat like a cart-wheel beckoning persistently with his whole arm. Examining the edge of the forest above and below, I was almost certain I could see movements—human forms gliding here and there. I steamed past prudently, then stopped the engines and let her drift down. The man on

7. Red-headed rascal.

the shore began to shout, urging us to land. 'We have been attacked,' screamed the manager. 'I know—I know. It's all right,' yelled back the other, as cheerful as you please. 'Come along. It's all right. I am glad.'

"His aspect reminded me of something I had seen—something funny I had seen somewhere. As I manœuvred to get alongside, I was asking myself, 'What does this fellow look like?' Suddenly I got it. He looked like a harlequin. His clothes had been made of some stuff that was brown holland probably, but it was covered with patches all over, with bright patches, blue, red, and yellow—patches on the back, patches on the front, patches on elbows, on knees; coloured binding round his jacket, scarlet edging at the bottom of his trousers; and the sunshine made him look extremely gay and wonderfully neat withal, because you could see how beautifully all this patching had been done. A beardless, boyish face, very fair, no features to speak of, nose peeling, little blue eyes, smiles and frowns chasing each other over that open countenance like sunshine and shadow on a wind-swept plain. 'Look out, captain!' he cried; 'there's a snag lodged in here last night.' What! Another snag? I confess I swore shamefully. I had nearly holed my cripple, to finish off that charming trip. The harlequin on the bank turned his little pug nose up to me. 'You English?' he asked, all smiles. 'Are you?' I shouted from the wheel. The smiles vanished, and he shook his head as if sorry for my disappointment. Then he brightened up. 'Never mind!' he cried encouragingly. 'Are we in time?' I asked. 'He is up there,' he replied, with a toss of the head up the hill, and becoming gloomy all of a sudden. His face was like the autumn sky, overcast one moment and bright the next.

"When the manager, escorted by the pilgrims, all of them armed to the teeth, had gone to the house, this chap came on board. 'I say, I don't like this. These natives are in the bush,' I said. He assured me earnestly it was all right. 'They are simple people,' he added; 'well, I am glad you came. It took me all my time to keep them off.' 'But you said it was all right,' I cried. 'Oh, they meant no harm,' he said; and as I stared he corrected himself, 'Not exactly.' Then vivaciously, 'My faith, your pilot-house wants a clean up!' In the next breath he advised me to keep enough steam on the boiler to blow the whistle in case of any trouble. 'One good screech will do more for you than all your rifles. They are simple people,' he repeated. He rattled away at such a rate he quite overwhelmed me. He seemed to be trying to make up for lots of silence, and actually hinted, laughing, that such was the case. 'Don't you talk with Mr. Kurtz?' I said. 'You don't talk with that man—you listen to him,' he exclaimed with severe exaltation. 'But now—' He waved his arm, and in the twinkling of an eye was in the uttermost depths of despondency. In a moment he came up again with a jump, possessed himself of both my hands, shook them continuously, while he gabbled: 'Brother sailor . . . honour . . . pleasure . . . delight . . . introduce myself . . . Russian . . . son of an arch-priest . . . Government of Tambov . . . What? Tobacco!

English tobacco; the excellent English tobacco! Now, that's brotherly. Smoke? Where's a sailor that does not smoke?'

"The pipe soothed him, and gradually I made out he had run away from school, had gone to sea in a Russian ship; ran away again; served some time in English ships; was now reconciled with the arch-priest. He made a point of that. 'But when one is young one must see things, gather experience, ideas; enlarge the mind.' 'Here!' I interrupted. 'You can never tell! Here I met Mr. Kurtz,' he said, youthfully solemn and reproachful. I held my tongue after that. It appears he had persuaded a Dutch trading-house on the coast to fit him out with stores and goods, and had started for the interior with a light heart, and no more idea of what would happen to him than a baby. He had been wandering about that river for nearly two years alone, cut off from everybody and everything. 'I am not so young as I look. I am twenty-five,' he said. 'At first old Van Shuyten would tell me to go to the devil,' he narrated with keen enjoyment; 'but I stuck to him, and talked and talked, till at last he got afraid I would talk the hind-leg off his favourite dog, so he gave me some cheap things and a few guns, and told me he hoped he would never see my face again. Good old Dutchman, Van Shuyten. I sent him one small lot of ivory a year ago, so that he can't call me a little thief when I get back. I hope he got it. And for the rest I don't care. I had some wood stacked for you. That was my old house. Did you see?'

"I gave him Towson's book. He made as though he would kiss me, but restrained himself. 'The only book I had left, and I thought I had lost it,' he said, looking at it ecstatically. 'So many accidents happen to a man going about alone, you know. Canoes get upset sometimes—and sometimes you've got to clear out so quick when the people get angry.' He thumbed the pages. 'You made notes in Russian?' I asked. He nodded. 'I thought they were written in cipher,' I said. He laughed, then became serious. 'I had lots of trouble to keep these people off,' he said. 'Did they want to kill you?' I asked. 'Oh no!' he cried, and checked himself. 'Why did they attack us?' I pursued. He hesitated, then said shamefacedly, 'They don't want him to go.' 'Don't they?' I said curiously. He nodded a nod full of mystery and wisdom. 'I tell you,' he cried, 'this man has enlarged my mind.' He opened his arms wide, staring at me with his little blue eyes that were perfectly round."

3

"I looked at him, lost in astonishment. There he was before me, in motley, as though he had absconded from a troupe of mimes, enthusiastic, fabulous. His very existence was improbable, inexplicable, and altogether bewildering. He was an insoluble problem. It was inconceivable how he had existed, how he had succeeded in getting so far, how he had managed to remain—why he did not instantly disappear. 'I went a little farther,' he said, 'then still a little farther—till I had gone so far that I don't know how I'll ever get back. Never mind. Plenty time. I can manage. You take Kurtz away quick—quick—I tell you.' The glamour of youth enveloped his particoloured rags, his destitution, his loneliness, the essential desolation of his futile wanderings. For months—for years—his life hadn't been worth a day's purchase; and there he was gallantly, thoughtlessly alive, to all appearance indestructible solely by the virtue of his few years and of his unreflecting audacity. I was seduced into something like admiration—like envy. Glamour urged him on, glamour kept him unscathed. He surely wanted nothing from the wilderness but space to breathe in and to push on through. His need was to exist, and to move onwards at the greatest possible risk, and with a maximum of privation. If the absolutely pure, uncalculating, unpractical spirit of adventure had ever ruled a human being, it ruled this be-patched youth. I almost envied him the possession of this modest and clear flame. It seemed to have consumed all thought of self so completely, that, even while he was talking to you, you forgot that it was he—the man before your eyes—who had gone through these things. I did not envy him his devotion to Kurtz, though. He had not meditated over it. It came to him, and he accepted it with a sort of eager fatalism. I must say that to me it appeared about the most dangerous thing in every way he had come upon so far.

"They had come together unavoidably, like two ships becalmed near each other, and lay rubbing sides at last. I suppose Kurtz wanted an audience, because on a certain occasion, when encamped in the forest, they had talked all night, or more probably Kurtz had talked. 'We talked of everything,' he said, quite transported at the recollection. 'I forgot there was such a thing as sleep. The night did not seem to last an hour. Everything! Everything! . . . Of love too.' 'Ah, he talked to you of love!' I said, much amused. 'It isn't what you think,' he cried, almost passion-ately. 'It was in general. He made me see things—things.'

"He threw his arms up. We were on deck at the time, and the head-man of my wood-cutters, lounging near by, turned upon him his heavy and glittering eyes. I looked around, and I don't know why, but I assure you that never, never before, did this land, this river, this jungle, the very arch of this blazing sky, appear to me so hopeless and so dark, so impenetrable to human thought, so pitiless to human weakness. 'And, ever since, you have been with him, of course?' I said.

"On the contrary. It appears their intercourse had been very much broken by various causes. He had, as he informed me proudly, managed to nurse Kurtz through two illnesses (he alluded to it as you would to some risky feat), but as a rule Kurtz wandered alone, far in the depths of the forest. 'Very often coming to this station, I had to wait days and days before he would turn up,' he said. 'Ah, it was worth waiting for!—some-times.' 'What was he doing? exploring or what?' I asked. 'Oh yes, of course'; he had discovered lots of villages, a lake too—he did not know exactly in what direction; it was dangerous to inquire too much—but mostly his expeditions had been for ivory. 'But he had no goods to trade with by that time,' I objected. 'There's a good lot of cartridges left even yet,' he answered, looking away. 'To speak plainly, he raided the country,' I said. He nodded. 'Not alone, surely!' He muttered something about the villages round that lake. 'Kurtz got the tribe to follow him, did he?' I suggested. He fidgeted a little. 'They adored him,' he said. The tone of these words was so extraordinary that I looked at him searchingly. It was curious to see his mingled eagerness and reluctance to speak of Kurtz. The man filled his life, occupied his thoughts, swayed his emotions. 'What can you expect?' he burst out; 'he came to them with thunder and lightning, you know—and they had never seen anything like it—and very terrible. He could be very terrible. You can't judge Mr. Kurtz as you would an ordinary man. No, no, no! Now—just to give you an idea—I don't mind telling you, he wanted to shoot me too one day—but I don't judge him.' 'Shoot you!' I cried. 'What for?' 'Well, I had a small lot of ivory the chief of that village near my house gave me. You see I used to shoot game for them. Well, he wanted it, and wouldn't hear reason. He declared he would shoot me unless I gave him the ivory and then cleared out of the country, because he could do so, and had a fancy for it, and there was nothing on earth to prevent him killing whom he jolly well pleased. And it was true too. I gave him the ivory. What did I care! But I didn't clear out. No, no. I couldn't leave him. I had to be careful, of course, till we got friendly again for a time. He had his second illness then. Afterwards I had to keep out of the way; but I didn't mind. He was living for the most part in those villages on the lake. When he came down to the river, sometimes he would take to me, and sometimes it was better for me to be careful. This man suffered too much. He hated all this, and somehow he couldn't get away. When I had a chance I begged him to try and leave while there was time; I offered to go back with him. And he would say yes, and then he would remain; go off on another ivory hunt; disappear for weeks; forget himself amongst these people—forget himself—you know.' 'Why! he's mad,' I said. He protested indignantly. Mr. Kurtz couldn't be mad. If I had heard him talk, only two days ago, I wouldn't dare hint at such a thing. . . . I had taken up my binoculars while we talked, and was looking at the shore, sweeping the limit of the forest at each side and at the back of the house. The consciousness of there being people in that bush, so silent, so quiet—as silent and quiet as the ruined house on the hill— made me uneasy. There was no sign on the face of nature of this amazing tale that was not so much told as suggested to me in desolate exclamations, completed by shrugs, in interrupted phrases, in hints ending in deep sighs. The woods were unmoved, like a mask—heavy, like the closed door of a prison—they looked with their air of hidden knowledge, of patient expectation, of unapproachable silence. The Russian was explaining to me that it was only lately that Mr. Kurtz had come down to the river, bringing along with him all the fighting men of that lake tribe. He had been absent for several months—getting himself adored, I suppose—and had come down unexpectedly, with the intention to all appearance of making a raid either across the river or down stream.

Evidently the appetite for more ivory had got the better of the—what shall I say?—less material aspirations. However, he had got much worse suddenly. 'I heard he was lying helpless, and so I came up—took my chance,' said the Russian. 'Oh, he is bad, very bad.' I directed my glass to the house. There were no signs of life, but there was the ruined roof, the long mud wall peeping above the grass, with three little square window-holes, no two of the same size; all this brought within reach of my hand, as it were. And then I made a brusque movement, and one of the remaining posts of that vanished fence leaped up in the field of my glass. You remember I told you I had been struck at the distance by certain attempts at ornamentation, rather remarkable in the ruinous aspect of the place. Now I had suddenly a nearer view, and its first result was to make me throw my head back as if before a blow. Then I went carefully from post to post with my glass, and I saw my mistake. These round knobs were not ornamental but symbolic; they were expressive and puzzling, striking and disturbing—food for thought and also for the vultures if there had been any looking down from the sky; but at all events for such ants as were industrious enough to ascend the pole. They would have been even more impressive, those heads on the stakes, if their faces had not been turned to the house. Only one, the first I had made out, was facing my way. I was not so shocked as you may think. The start back I had given was really nothing but a movement of surprise. I had expected to see a knob of wood there, you know. I returned deliberately to the first I had seen—and there it was, black, dried, sunken, with closed eyelids—a head that seemed to sleep at the top of that pole, and, with the shrunken dry lips showing a narrow white line of the teeth, was smiling too, smiling continuously at some endless and jocose dream of that eternal slumber.

"I am not disclosing any trade secrets. In fact the manager said afterwards that Mr. Kurtz's methods had ruined the district. I have no opinion on that point, but I want you clearly to understand that there was nothing exactly profitable in these heads being there. They only show that Mr. Kurtz lacked restraint in the gratification of his various lusts, that there was something wanting in him—some small matter which, when the pressing need arose, could not be found under his magnificent eloquence. Whether he knew of this deficiency himself I can't say. I think the knowledge came to him at last—only at the very last. But the wilderness had found him out early, and had taken on him a terrible vengeance for the fantastic invasion. I think it had whispered to him things about himself which he did not know, things of which he had no conception till he took counsel with this great solitude—and the whisper had proved irresistibly fascinating. It echoed loudly within him because he was hollow at the core. . . . I put down the glass, and the head that had appeared near enough to be spoken to seemed at once to have leaped away from me into inaccessible distance.

"The admirer of Mr. Kurtz was a bit crestfallen. In a hurried, indistinct voice he began to assure me he had not dared to take these—say, symbols—down. He was not afraid of the natives; they would not stir till Mr. Kurtz gave the word. His ascendancy was extraordinary. The camps of these people surrounded the place, and the chiefs came every day to see him. They would crawl . . . 'I don't want to know anything of the ceremonies used when approaching Mr. Kurtz,' I shouted. Curious, this feeling that came over me that such details would be more intolerable than those heads drying on the stakes under Mr. Kurtz's windows. After all, that was only a savage sight, while I seemed at one bound to have been transported into some lightless region of subtle horrors, where pure, uncomplicated savagery was a positive relief, being something that had a right to exist—obviously—in the sunshine. The young man looked at me with surprise. I suppose it did not occur to him that Mr. Kurtz was no idol of mine. He forgot I hadn't heard any of these splendid mono-logues on, what was it? on love, justice, conduct of life—or what not. If it had come to crawling before Mr. Kurtz, he crawled as much as the veriest savage of them all. I had no idea of the conditions, he said: these heads were the heads of rebels. I shocked him excessively by laughing. Rebels! What would be the next definition I was to hear? There had been enemies, criminals, workers—and these were rebels. Those rebel-lious heads looked very subdued to me on their sticks. 'You don't know how such a life tries a man like Kurtz,' cried Kurtz's last disciple. 'Well, and you?' I said. 'I! I! I am a simple man. I have no great thoughts. I want nothing from anybody. How can you compare me to . . . ?' His feelings were too much for speech, and suddenly he broke down. 'I don't understand,' he groaned. 'I've been doing my best to keep him alive, and that's enough. I had no hand in all this. I have no abilities. There hasn't been a drop of medicine or a mouthful of invalid food for months here. He was shamefully abandoned. A man like this, with such ideas. Shamefully! Shamefully! I—I—haven't slept for the last ten nights. . . .'

"His voice lost itself in the calm of the evening. The long shadows of the forest had slipped down hill while we talked, had gone far beyond the ruined hovel, beyond the symbolic row of stakes. All this was in the gloom, while we down there were yet in the sunshine, and the stretch of the river abreast of the clearing glittered in a still and dazzling splen-dour, with a murky and overshadowed bend above and below. Not a living soul was seen on the shore. The bushes did not rustle.

"Suddenly round the corner of the house a group of men appeared, as though they had come up from the ground. They waded waist-deep in the grass, in a compact body, bearing an improvised stretcher in their midst. Instantly, in the emptiness of the landscape, a cry arose whose shrillness pierced the still air like a sharp arrow flying straight to the very heart of the land; and, as if by enchantment, streams of human beings—of naked human beings—with spears in their hands, with bows, with shields, with wild glances and savage movements, were poured into the clearing by the dark-faced and pensive forest. The bushes shook, the grass swayed for a time, and then everything stood still in attentive immobility.

" 'Now, if he does not say the right thing to them we are all done for,' said the Russian at my elbow. The knot of men with the stretcher had stopped too, half-way to the steamer, as if petrified. I saw the man on the stretcher sit up, lank and with an uplifted arm, above the shoulders of the bearers. 'Let us hope that the man who can talk so well of love in general will find some particular reason to spare us this time,' I said. I resented bitterly the absurd danger of our situation, as if to be at the mercy of that atrocious phantom had been a dishonouring necessity. I could not hear a sound, but through my glasses I saw the thin arm extended commandingly, the lower jaw moving, the eyes of that apparition shining darkly far in its bony head that nodded with grotesque jerks. Kurtz—Kurtz—that means 'short' in German—don't it? Well, the name was as true as everything else in his life—and death. He looked at least seven feet long. His covering had fallen off, and his body emerged from it pitiful and appalling as from a winding-sheet. I could see the cage of his ribs all astir, the bones of his arm waving. It was as though an animated image of death carved out of old ivory had been shaking its hand with menaces at a motionless crowd of men made of dark and glittering bronze. I saw him open his mouth wide—it gave him a weirdly voracious aspect, as though he had wanted to swallow all the air, all the earth, all the men before him. A deep voice reached me faintly. He must have been shouting. He fell back suddenly. The stretcher shook as the bearers staggered forward again, and almost at the same time I noticed that the crowd of savages was vanishing without any perceptible movement of retreat, as if the forest that had ejected these beings so suddenly had drawn them in again as the breath is drawn in a long aspiration.

"Some of the pilgrims behind the stretcher carried his arms—two shotguns, a heavy rifle, and a light revolver-carbine—the thunderbolts of that pitiful Jupiter. The manager bent over him murmuring as he walked beside his head. They laid him down in one of the little cabins—just a room for a bedplace and a camp-stool or two, you know. We had brought his belated correspondence, and a lot of torn envelopes and open letters littered his bed. His hand roamed feebly amongst these papers. I was struck by the fire of his eyes and the composed languor of his expression. It was not so much the exhaustion of disease. He did not seem in pain. This shadow looked satiated and calm, as though for the moment it had had its fill of all the emotions.

"He rustled one of the letters, and looking straight in my face said, 'I am glad.' Somebody had been writing to him about me. These special recommendations were turning up again. The volume of tone he emitted without effort, almost without the trouble of moving his lips, amazed me. A voice! a voice! It was grave, profound, vibrating, while the man did not seem capable of a whisper. However, he had enough strength in him—factitious no doubt—to very nearly make an end of us, as you shall hear directly.

"The manager appeared silently in the doorway; I stepped out at once and he drew the curtain after me. The Russian, eyed curiously by the pilgrims, was staring at the shore. I followed the direction of his glance.

"Dark human shapes could be made out in the distance, flitting indistinctly against the gloomy border of the forest, and near the river two bronze figures, leaning on tall spears, stood in the sunlight under fantastic head-dresses of spotted skins, warlike and still in statuesque repose. And from right to left along the lighted shore moved a wild and gorgeous apparition of a woman.

"She walked with measured steps, draped in striped and fringed cloths, treading the earth proudly, with a slight jingle and flash of barbarous ornaments. She carried her head high; her hair was done in the shape of a helmet; she had brass leggings to the knee, brass wire gauntlets to the elbow, a crimson spot on her tawny cheek, innumerable necklaces of glass beads on her neck; bizarre things, charms, gifts of witch-men, that hung about her, glittered and trembled at every step. She must have had the value of several elephant tusks upon her. She was savage and superb, wild-eyed and magnificent; there was something ominous and stately in her deliberate progress. And in the hush that had fallen suddenly upon the whole sorrowful land, the immense wilderness, the colossal body of the fecund and mysterious life seemed to look at her, pensive, as though it had been looking at the image of its own tenebrous and passionate soul.

"She came abreast of the steamer, stood still, and faced us. Her long shadow fell to the water's edge. Her face had a tragic and fierce aspect of wild sorrow and of dumb pain mingled with the fear of some struggling, half-shaped resolve. She stood looking at us without a stir, and like the wilderness itself, with an air of brooding over an inscrutable purpose. A whole minute passed, and then she made a step forward. There was a low jingle, a glint of yellow metal, a sway of fringed draperies, and she stopped as if her heart had failed her. The young fellow by my side growled. The pilgrims murmured at my back. She looked at us all as if her life had depended upon the unswerving steadiness of her glance. Suddenly she opened her bared arms and threw them up rigid above her head, as though in an uncontrollable desire to touch the sky, and at the same time the swift shadows darted out on the earth, swept around on the river, gathering the steamer into a shadowy embrace. A formidable silence hung over the scene.

"She turned away slowly, walked on, following the bank, and passed into the bushes to the left. Once only her eyes gleamed back at us in the dusk of the thickets before she disappeared.

" 'If she had offered to come aboard I really think I would have tried to shoot her,' said the man of patches nervously. 'I had been risking my life every day for the last fortnight to keep her out of the house. She got in one day and kicked up a row about those miserable rags I picked up in the storeroom to mend my clothes with. I wasn't decent. At least it must have been that, for she talked like a fury to Kurtz for an hour, pointing at me now and then. I don't understand the dialect of this tribe. Luckily for me, I fancy Kurtz felt too ill that day to care, or there would have been mischief. I don't understand. . . . No—it's too much for me. Ah, well, it's all over now.'

"At this moment I heard Kurtz's deep voice behind the curtain: 'Save me!—save the ivory, you mean. Don't tell me. Save *me*! Why, I've had to save you. You are interrupting my plans now. Sick! Sick! Not so sick as you would like to believe. Never mind. I'll carry my ideas out yet—I will return. I'll show you what can be done. You with your little peddling notions—you are interfering with me. I will return. I . . .'

"The manager came out. He did me the honour to take me under the arm and lead me aside. 'He is very low, very low,' he said. He considered it necessary to sigh, but neglected to be consistently sorrowful. 'We have done all we could for him—haven't we? But there is no disguising the fact, Mr. Kurtz has done more harm than good to the Company. He did not see the time was not ripe for vigorous action. Cautiously, cautiously—that's my principle. We must be cautious yet. The district is closed to us for a time. Deplorable! Upon the whole, the trade will suffer. I don't deny there is a remarkable quantity of ivory—mostly fossil. We must save it, at all events—but look how precarious the position is— and why? Because the method is unsound.' 'Do you,' said I, looking at the shore, 'call it "unsound method"?' 'Without doubt,' he exclaimed hotly, 'Don't you?' . . . 'No method at all,' I murmured after a while. 'Exactly,' he exulted. 'I anticipated this. Shows a complete want of judgment. It is my duty to point it out in the proper quarter.' 'Oh,' said I, 'that fellow—what's his name?—the brickmaker, will make a readable report for you.' He appeared confounded for a moment. It seemed to me I had never breathed an atmosphere so vile, and I turned mentally to Kurtz for relief—positively for relief. 'Nevertheless, I think Mr. Kurtz is a remarkable man,' I said with emphasis. He started, dropped on me a cold heavy glance, said very quietly, 'He *was*,' and turned his back on me. My hour of favour was over; I found myself lumped along with Kurtz as a partisan of methods for which the time was not ripe: I was unsound! Ah! but it was something to have at least a choice of nightmares.

"I had turned to the wilderness really, not to Mr. Kurtz, who, I was ready to admit, was as good as buried. And for a moment it seemed to me as if I also were buried in a vast grave full of unspeakable secrets. I felt an intolerable weight oppressing my breast, the smell of the damp earth, the unseen presence of victorious corruption, the darkness of an impenetrable night. . . . The Russian tapped me on the shoulder. I heard him mumbling and stammering something about 'brother seaman—couldn't conceal—knowledge of matters that would affect Mr. Kurtz's reputation.' I waited. For him evidently Mr. Kurtz was not in his grave; I suspect that for him Mr. Kurtz was one of the immortals. 'Well!' said I at last, 'speak out. As it happens, I am Mr. Kurtz's friend— in a way.'

"He stated with a good deal of formality that had we not been 'of the same profession,' he would have kept the matter to himself without regard to consequences. He suspected 'there was an active ill-will towards him on the part of these white men that—' 'You are right,' I said, remembering a certain conversation I had overheard. 'The manager thinks you ought to be hanged.' He showed a concern at this intelligence which amused me at first. 'I had better get out of the way quietly,' he said earnestly. 'I can do no more for Kurtz now, and they would soon find some excuse. What's to stop them? There's a military post three hundred miles from here.' 'Well, upon my word,' said I, 'perhaps you had better go if you have any friends amongst the savages near by.' 'Plenty,' he said. 'They are simple people—and I want nothing, you know.' He stood biting his lip, then: 'I don't want any harm to happen to these whites here, but of course I was thinking of Mr. Kurtz's reputation—but you are a brother seaman and—' 'All right,' said I, after a time. 'Mr. Kurtz's reputation is safe with me.' I did not know how truly I spoke.

"He informed me, lowering his voice, that it was Kurtz who had ordered the attack to be made on the steamer. 'He hated sometimes the idea of being taken away—and then again . . . But I don't understand these matters. I am a simple man. He thought it would scare you away—that you would give it up, thinking him dead. I could not stop him. Oh, I had an awful time of it this last month.' 'Very well,' I said. 'He is all right now.' 'Ye-e-es,' he muttered, not very convinced apparently. 'Thanks,' said I; 'I shall keep my eyes open.' 'But quiet—eh?' he urged anxiously. 'It would be awful for his reputation if anybody here—' I promised a complete discretion with great gravity. 'I have a canoe and three black fellows waiting not very far. I am off. Could you give me a few Martini-Henry cartridges?' I could, and did, with proper secrecy. He helped himself, with a wink at me, to a handful of my tobacco. 'Between sailors—you know—good English tobacco.' At the door of the pilot-house he turned round—'I say, haven't you a pair of shoes you could spare?' He raised one leg. 'Look.' The soles were tied with knotted strings sandal-wise under his bare feet. I rooted out an old pair, at which he looked with admiration before tucking it under his left arm. One of his pockets (bright red) was bulging with cartridges, from the other (dark blue) peeped 'Towson's Inquiry,' etc. etc. He seemed to think himself excellently well equipped for a renewed encounter with the wilderness. 'Ah! I'll never, never meet such a man again. You ought to have heard him recite poetry—his own too it was, he told me. Poetry!' He rolled his eyes at the recollection of these delights. 'Oh, he enlarged my mind!' 'Good-bye,' said I. He shook hands and vanished in the night. Sometimes I ask myself whether I had ever really seen him—whether it was possible to meet such a phenomenon! . . .

"When I woke up shortly after midnight his warning came to my mind with its hint of danger that seemed, in the starred darkness, real enough to make me get up for the purpose of having a look round. On the hill a big fire burned, illuminating fitfully a crooked corner of the station-house. One of the agents with a picket of a few of our blacks, armed for the purpose, was keeping guard over the ivory; but deep within the forest, red gleams that wavered, that seemed to sink and rise from the ground amongst confused columnar shapes of intense blackness, showed the exact position of the camp where Mr. Kurtz's adorers were keeping their uneasy vigil. The monotonous beating of a big drum filled the air with muffled shocks and a lingering vibration. A steady droning sound of many men chanting each to himself some weird incantation came out from the black, flat wall of the woods as the humming of bees comes out of a hive, and had a strange narcotic effect upon my half-awake senses. I believe I dozed off leaning over the rail, till an abrupt burst of yells, an overwhelming outbreak of a pent-up and mysterious frenzy, woke me up in a bewildered wonder. It was cut short all at once, and the low droning went on with an effect of audible and soothing silence. I glanced casually into the little cabin. A light was burning within, but Mr. Kurtz was not there.

"I think I would have raised an outcry if I had believed my eyes. But I didn't believe them at first—the thing seemed so impossible. The fact is I was completely unnerved by a sheer blank fright, pure abstract terror, unconnected with any distinct shape of physical danger. What made this emotion so overpowering was—how shall I define it?—the moral shock I received, as if something altogether monstrous, intolerable to thought and odious to the soul, had been thrust upon me unexpectedly. This lasted of course the merest fraction of a second, and then the usual sense of commonplace, deadly danger, the possibility of a sudden onslaught and massacre, or something of the kind, which I saw impending, was positively welcome and composing. It pacified me, in fact, so much, that I did not raise an alarm.

"There was an agent buttoned up inside an ulster and sleeping on a chair on deck within three feet of me. The yells had not awakened him; he snored very slightly; I left him to his slumbers and leaped ashore. I did not betray Mr. Kurtz—it was ordered I should never betray him—it was written I should be loyal to the nightmare of my choice. I was anxious to deal with this shadow by myself alone—and to this day I don't know why I was so jealous of sharing with any one the peculiar blackness of that experience.

"As soon as I got on the bank I saw a trail—a broad trail through the grass. I remember the exultation with which I said to myself, 'He can't walk—he is crawling on all-fours—I've got him.' The grass was wet with dew. I strode rapidly with clenched fists. I fancy I had some vague notion of falling upon him and giving him a drubbing. I don't know. I had some imbecile thoughts. The knitting old woman with the cat obtruded herself upon my memory as a most improper person to be sitting at the other end of such an affair. I saw a row of pilgrims squirting lead in the air out of Winchesters held to the hip. I thought I would never get back to the steamer, and imagined myself living alone and unarmed in the woods to an advanced age. Such silly things—you know. And I remember I confounded the beat of the drum with the beating of my heart, and was pleased at its calm regularity.

"I kept to the track though—then stopped to listen. The night was very clear; a dark blue space, sparkling with dew and starlight, in which black things stood very still. I thought I could see a kind of motion ahead of me. I was strangely cocksure of everything that night. I actually left the track and ran in a wide semicircle (I verily believe chuckling to myself) so as to get in front of that stir, of that motion I had seen—if indeed I had seen anything. I was circumventing Kurtz as though it had been a boyish game.

"I came upon him, and, if he had not heard me coming, I would have fallen over him too, but he got up in time. He rose, unsteady, long, pale, indistinct, like a vapour exhaled by the earth, and swayed slightly, misty and silent before me; while at my back the fires loomed between the trees, and the murmur of many voices issued from the forest. I had cut him off cleverly; but when actually confronting him I seemed to come to my senses, I saw the danger in its right proportion. It was by no means over yet. Suppose he began to shout? Though he could hardly stand, there was still plenty of vigour in his voice. 'Go away—hide yourself,' he said, in that profound tone. It was very awful. I glanced back. We were within thirty yards of the nearest fire. A black figure stood up, strode on long black legs, waving long black arms, across the glow. It had horns—antelope horns, I think—on its head. Some sorcerer, some witch-man no doubt: it looked fiend-like enough. 'Do you know what you are doing?' I whispered. 'Perfectly,' he answered, raising his voice for that single word: it sounded to me far off and yet loud, like a hail through a speaking-trumpet. If he makes a row we are lost, I thought to myself. This clearly was not a case for fisticuffs, even apart from the very natural aversion I had to beat that Shadow—this wandering and tormented thing. 'You will be lost,' I said—'utterly lost.' One gets sometimes such a flash of inspiration, you know. I did say the right thing, though indeed he could not have been more irretrievably lost than he was at this very moment, when the foundations of our intimacy were being laid—to endure—to endure—even to the end—even beyond.

" 'I had immense plans,' he muttered irresolutely. 'Yes,' said I; 'but if you try to shout I'll smash your head with—' There was not a stick or a stone near. 'I will throttle you for good,' I corrected myself. 'I was on the threshold of great things,' he pleaded, in a voice of longing, with a wistfulness of tone that made my blood run cold. 'And now for this stupid scoundrel—' 'Your success in Europe is assured in any case,' I affirmed steadily. I did not want to have the throttling of him, you understand—and indeed it would have been very little use for any practical purpose. I tried to break the spell—the heavy, mute spell of the wilderness—that seemed to draw him to its pitiless breast by the awakening of forgotten and brutal instincts, by the memory of gratified and monstrous passions. This alone, I was convinced, had driven him out to the edge of the forest, to the bush, towards the gleam of fires, the throb of drums, the drone of weird incantations; this alone had beguiled his unlawful soul beyond the bounds of permitted aspirations. And, don't you see, the terror of the position was not in being knocked on the head—though I had a very lively sense of that danger too—but in this, that I had to deal with a being to whom I could not appeal in the name of anything high or low. I had, even like the niggers, to invoke him—himself—his own exalted and incredible degradation. There was nothing either above or below him, and I knew it. He had kicked himself loose of the earth. Confound the man! he had kicked the very earth to pieces. He was alone, and I before him did not know whether I stood on the ground or floated in the air. I've been telling you what we said—repeating the phrases we pronounced—but what's the good? They were common everyday words—the familiar, vague sounds exchanged on every waking day of life. But what of that? They had behind them, to my mind, the terrific suggestiveness of words heard in dreams, of phrases spoken in nightmares. Soul! If anybody had ever struggled with a soul, I am the man. And I wasn't arguing with a lunatic either. Believe me or not, his intelligence was perfectly clear—concentrated, it is true, upon himself with horrible intensity, yet clear; and therein was my only chance—barring, of course, the killing him there and then, which wasn't so good, on account of unavoidable noise. But his soul was mad. Being alone in the wilderness, it had looked within itself, and, by heavens! I tell you, it had gone mad. I had—for my sins, I suppose, to go through the ordeal of looking into it myself. No eloquence could have been so withering to one's belief in mankind as his final burst of sincerity. He struggled with himself too. I saw it—I heard it. I saw the inconceivable mystery of a soul that knew no restraint, no faith, and no fear, yet struggling blindly with itself. I kept my head pretty well; but when I had him at last stretched on the couch, I wiped my forehead, while my legs shook under me as though I had carried half a ton on my back down that hill. And yet I had only supported him, his bony arm clasped round my neck—and he was not much heavier than a child.

"When next day we left at noon, the crowd, of whose presence behind the curtain of trees I had been acutely conscious all the time, flowed out of the woods again, filled the clearing, covered the slope with a mass of naked, breathing, quivering, bronze bodies. I steamed up a bit, then swung down-stream, and two thousand eyes followed the evolutions of the splashing, thumping, fierce river-demon beating the water with its terrible tail and breathing black smoke into the air. In front of the first rank, along the river, three men, plastered with bright red earth from head to foot, strutted to and fro restlessly. When we came abreast again, they faced the river, stamped their feet, nodded their horned heads, swayed their scarlet bodies; they shook towards the fierce river-demon a bunch of black feathers, a mangy skin with a pendent tail—something that looked like a dried gourd; they shouted periodically together strings of amazing words that resembled no sounds of human language; and the deep murmurs of the crowd, interrupted suddenly, were like the responses of some satanic litany.

"We had carried Kurtz into the pilot-house: there was more air there. Lying on the couch, he stared through the open shutter. There was an eddy in the mass of human bodies, and the woman with helmeted head and tawny cheeks rushed out to the very brink of the stream. She put out her hands, shouted something, and all that wild mob took up the shout in a roaring chorus of articulated, rapid, breathless utterance.

" 'Do you understand this?' I asked.

"He kept on looking out past me with fiery, longing eyes, with a mingled expression of wistfulness and hate. He made no answer, but I saw a smile, a smile of indefinable meaning, appear on his colourless lips that a moment after twitched convulsively. 'Do I not?' he said slowly, gasping, as if the words had been torn out of him by a supernatural power.

"I pulled the string of the whistle, and I did this because I saw the pilgrims on deck getting out their rifles with an air of anticipating a jolly lark. At the sudden screech there was a movement of abject terror through that wedged mass of bodies. 'Don't! don't you frighten them away,' cried some one on deck disconsolately. I pulled the string time after time. They broke and ran, they leaped, they crouched, they swerved, they dodged the flying terror of the sound. The three red chaps had fallen flat, face down on the shore, as though they had been shot dead. Only the barbarous and superb woman did not so much as flinch, and stretched tragically her bare arms after us over the sombre and glittering river.

"And then that imbecile crowd down on the deck started their little fun, and I could see nothing more for smoke.

"The brown current ran swiftly out of the heart of darkness, bearing us down towards the sea with twice the speed of our upward progress; and Kurtz's life was running swiftly too, ebbing, ebbing out of his heart into the sea of inexorable time. The manager was very placid, he had no vital anxieties now, he took us both in with a comprehensive and satisfied glance: the 'affair' had come off as well as could be wished. I saw the time approaching when I would be left alone of the party of 'unsound method.' The pilgrims looked upon me with disfavour. I was, so to speak, numbered with the dead. It is strange how I accepted this unforeseen partnership, this choice of nightmares forced upon me in the tenebrous land invaded by these mean and greedy phantoms.

"Kurtz discoursed. A voice! a voice! It rang deep to the very last. It survived his strength to hide in the magnificent folds of eloquence the barren darkness of his heart. Oh, he struggled! he struggled! The wastes of his weary brain were haunted by shadowy images now—images of wealth and fame revolving obsequiously round his unextinguishable gift of noble and lofty expression. My Intended, my station, my career, my ideas—these were the subjects for the occasional utterances of elevated sentiments. The shade of the original Kurtz frequented the bedside of the hollow sham, whose fate it was to be buried presently in the mould of primeval earth. But both the diabolic love and the unearthly hate of the mysteries it had penetrated fought for the possession of that soul satiated with primitive emotions, avid of lying fame, of sham distinction, of all the appearances of success and power.

"Sometimes he was contemptibly childish. He desired to have kings meet him at railway stations on his return from some ghastly Nowhere, where he intended to accomplish great things. 'You show them you have in you something that is really profitable, and then there will be no limits to the recognition of your ability,' he would say. 'Of course you must take care of the motives—right motives—always.' The long reaches that were like one and the same reach, monotonous bends that were exactly alike, slipped past the steamer with their multitude of secular[8] trees looking patiently after this grimy fragment of another world, the forerunner of change, of conquest, of trade, of massacres, of blessings. I looked ahead—piloting. 'Close the shutter,' said Kurtz suddenly one day; 'I can't bear to look at this.' I did so. There was a silence. 'Oh, but I will wring your heart yet!' he cried at the invisible wilderness.

"We broke down—as I had expected—and had to lie up for repairs at the head of an island. This delay was the first thing that shook Kurtz's confidence. One morning he gave me a packet of papers and a photograph—the lot tied together with a shoe-string. 'Keep this for me,' he said. 'This noxious fool' (meaning the manager) 'is capable of prying into my boxes when I am not looking.' In the afternoon I saw him. He was lying on his back with closed eyes, and I withdrew quietly, but I heard him mutter, 'Live rightly, die, die . . .' I listened. There was nothing more. Was he rehearsing some speech in his sleep, or was it a fragment of a phrase from some newspaper article? He had been writing for the papers and meant to do so again, 'for the furthering of my ideas. It's a duty.'

"His was an impenetrable darkness. I looked at him as you peer down at a man who is lying at the bottom of a precipice where the sun never shines. But I had not much time to give him, because I was helping the engine-driver to take to pieces the leaky cylinders, to straighten a bent connecting-rod, and in other such matters. I lived in an infernal mess of rust, filings, nuts, bolts, spanners, hammers, ratchet-drills—things I abominate, because I don't get on with them. I tended the little forge we fortunately had aboard; I toiled wearily in a wretched scrap-heap—unless I had the shakes too bad to stand.

"One evening coming in with a candle I was startled to hear him say a little tremulously, 'I am lying here in the dark waiting for death.' The light was within a foot of his eyes. I forced myself to murmur, 'Oh, nonsense!' and stood over him as if transfixed.

"Anything approaching the change that came over his features I have never seen before, and hope never to see again. Oh, I wasn't touched. I

---

8. Centuries old.

was fascinated. It was as though a veil had been rent. I saw on that ivory face the expression of sombre pride, of ruthless power, of craven terror— of an intense and hopeless despair. Did he live his life again in every detail of desire, temptation, and surrender during that supreme moment of complete knowledge? He cried in a whisper at some image, at some vision—he cried out twice, a cry that was no more than a breath:

" 'The horror! The horror!'

"I blew the candle out and left the cabin. The pilgrims were dining in the mess-room, and I took my place opposite the manager, who lifted his eyes to give me a questioning glance, which I successfully ignored. He leaned back, serene, with that peculiar smile of his sealing the unex- pressed depths of his meanness. A continuous shower of small flies streamed upon the lamp, upon the cloth, upon our hands and faces. Suddenly the manager's boy put his insolent black head in the doorway, and said in a tone of scathing contempt:

" 'Mistah Kurtz—he dead.'

"All the pilgrims rushed out to see. I remained, and went on with my dinner. I believe I was considered brutally callous. However, I did not eat much. There was a lamp in there—light, don't you know—and out- side it was so beastly, beastly dark. I went no more near the remarkable man who had pronounced a judgment upon the adventures of his soul on this earth. The voice was gone. What else had been there? But I am of course aware that next day the pilgrims buried something in a muddy hole.

"And then they very nearly buried me.

"However, as you see, I did not go to join Kurtz there and then. I did not. I remained to dream the nightmare out to the end, and to show my loyalty to Kurtz once more. Destiny. My destiny! Droll thing life is— that mysterious arrangement of merciless logic for a futile purpose. The most you can hope from it is some knowledge of yourself—that comes too late—a crop of unextinguishable regrets. I have wrestled with death. It is the most unexciting contest you can imagine. It takes place in an impalpable greyness, with nothing underfoot, with nothing around, without spectators, without clamour, without glory, without the great desire of victory, without the great fear of defeat, in a sickly atmosphere of tepid scepticism, without much belief in your own right, and still less in that of your adversary. If such is the form of ultimate wisdom, then life is a greater riddle than some of us think it to be. I was within a hair's- breadth of the last opportunity for pronouncement, and I found with humiliation that probably I would have nothing to say. This is the rea- son why I affirm that Kurtz was a remarkable man. He had something to say. He said it. Since I had peeped over the edge myself, I understand better the meaning of his stare, that could not see the flame of the can- dle, but was wide enough to embrace the whole universe, piercing enough to penetrate all the hearts that beat in the darkness. He had summed up—he had judged. 'The horror!' He was a remarkable man. After all, this was the expression of some sort of belief; it had candour, it had conviction, it had a vibrating note of revolt in its whisper, it had the appalling face of a glimpsed truth—the strange commingling of desire and hate. And it is not my own extremity I remember best—a vision of greyness without form filled with physical pain, and a careless contempt for the evanescence of all things—even of this pain itself. No! It is his extremity that I seem to have lived through. True, he had made that last stride, he had stepped over the edge, while I had been permitted to draw back my hesitating foot. And perhaps in this is the whole difference; perhaps all the wisdom, and all truth, and all sincerity, are just compressed into that inappreciable moment of time in which we step over the threshold of the invisible. Perhaps! I like to think my summing-up would not have been a word of careless contempt. Better his cry—much better. It was an affirmation, a moral victory paid for by innumerable defeats, by abominable terrors, by adominable satisfactions. But it was a victory! That is why I have remained loyal to Kurtz to the last, and even beyond, when a long time after I heard once more, not his own voice, but the echo of his magnificent eloquence thrown to me from a soul as translucently pure as a cliff of crystal.

"No, they did not bury me, though there is a period of time which I remember mistily, with a shuddering wonder, like a passage through some inconceivable world that had no hope in it and no desire. I found myself back in the sepulchral city resenting the sight of people hurrying through the streets to filch a little money from each other, to devour their infamous cookery, to gulp their unwholesome beer, to dream their insignificant and silly dreams. They trespassed upon my thoughts. They were intruders whose knowledge of life was to me an irritating pretence, because I felt so sure they could not possibly know the things I knew. Their bearing, which was simply the bearing of commonplace individuals going about their business in the assurance of perfect safety, was offensive to me like the outrageous flauntings of folly in the face of a danger it is unable to comprehend. I had no particular desire to enlighten them, but I had some difficulty in restraining myself from laughing in their faces, so full of stupid importance. I daresay I was not very well at that time. I tottered about the streets—there were various affairs to settle—grinning bitterly at perfectly respectable persons. I admit my behaviour was inexcusable, but then my temperature was seldom normal in these days. My dear aunt's endeavours to 'nurse up my strength' seemed altogether beside the mark. It was not my strength that wanted nursing, it was my imagination that wanted soothing. I kept the bundle of papers given me by Kurtz, not knowing exactly what to do with it. His mother had died lately, watched over, as I was told, by his Intended. A clean-shaven man, with an official manner and wearing gold-rimmed spectacles, called on me one day and made inquiries, at first circuitous, afterwards suavely pressing, about what he was pleased to denominate certain 'documents.' I was not surprised, because I had had two rows with the manager on the subject out there. I had refused to give up the smallest scrap out of that package, and I took the same attitude with the spectacled man. He became darkly menacing at last, and with much heat argued that the Company had the right to every bit of information about its 'territories.' And, said he, 'Mr. Kurtz's knowledge of unexplored regions must have been necessarily extensive and peculiar—owing to his great abilities and to the deplorable circumstances in which he had been placed: therefore—' I assured him Mr. Kurtz's knowledge, however extensive, did not bear upon the problems of commerce or administration. He invoked then the name of science. 'It would be an incalculable loss if,' etc. etc. I offered him the report on the 'Suppression of Savage Customs,' with the postscriptum torn off. He took it up eagerly, but ended by sniffing at it with an air of contempt. 'This is not what we had a right to expect,' he remarked. 'Expect nothing else,' I said. 'There are only private letters.' He withdrew upon some threat of legal proceedings, and I saw him no more; but another fellow, calling himself Kurtz's cousin, appeared two days later, and was anxious to hear all the details about his dear relative's last moments. Incidentally he gave me to understand that Kurtz had been essentially a great musician. 'There was the making of an immense success,' said the man, who was an organist, I believe, with lank grey hair flowing over a greasy coat-collar. I had no reason to doubt his statement; and to this day I am unable to say what was Kurtz's profession, whether he ever had any—which was the greatest of his talents. I had taken him for a painter who wrote for the papers, or else for a journalist who could paint—but even the cousin (who took snuff during the interview) could not tell me what he had been—exactly. He was a universal genius—on that point I agreed with the old chap, who thereupon blew his nose noisily into a large cotton handkerchief and withdrew in senile agitation, bearing off some family letters and memoranda without importance. Ultimately a journalist anxious to know something of the fate of his 'dear colleague' turned up. This visitor informed me Kurtz's proper sphere ought to have been politics 'on the popular side.' He had furry straight eyebrows, bristly hair cropped short, an eyeglass on a broad ribbon, and, becoming expansive, confessed his opinion that Kurtz really couldn't write a bit—'but heavens! how that man could talk! He electrified large meetings. He had faith—don't you see?—he had the faith. He could get himself to believe anything—anything. He would have been a splendid leader of an extreme party.' 'What party?' I asked. 'Any party,' answered the other. 'He was an—an—extremist.' Did I not think so? I assented. Did I know, he asked, with a sudden flash of curiosity, 'what it was that had induced him to go out there?' 'Yes,' said I, and forthwith handed him the famous Report for publication, if he thought fit. He glanced through it hurriedly, mumbling all the time, judged 'it would do,' and took himself off with this plunder.

"Thus I was left at last with a slim packet of letters and the girl's portrait. She struck me as beautiful—I mean she had a beautiful expression. I know that the sunlight can be made to lie too, yet one felt that no manipulation of light and pose could have conveyed the delicate shade of truthfulness upon those features. She seemed ready to listen without mental reservation, without suspicion, without a thought for herself. I concluded I would go and give her back her portrait and those letters myself. Curiosity? Yes; and also some other feeling perhaps. All that had been Kurtz's had passed out of my hands: his soul, his body, his station, his plans, his ivory, his career. There remained only his memory and his Intended—and I wanted to give that up too to the past, in a way—to surrender personally all that remained of him with me to that oblivion which is the last word of our common fate. I don't defend myself. I had no clear perception of what it was I really wanted. Perhaps it was an impulse of unconscious loyalty, or the fulfilment of one of those ironic necessities that lurk in the facts of human existence. I don't know. I can't tell. But I went.

"I thought his memory was like the other memories of the dead that accumulate in every man's life—a vague impress on the brain of shadows that had fallen on it in their swift and final passage; but before the high and ponderous door, between the tall houses of a street as still and decorous as a well-kept alley in a cemetery, I had a vision of him on the stretcher, opening his mouth voraciously, as if to devour all the earth with all its mankind. He lived then before me; he lived as much as he had ever lived—a shadow insatiable of splendid appearances, of frightful realities; a shadow darker than the shadow of the night, and draped nobly in the folds of a gorgeous eloquence. The vision seemed to enter the house with me—the stretcher, the phantom-bearers, the wild crowd of obedient worshippers, the gloom of the forests, the glitter of the reach between the murky bends, the beat of the drum, regular and muffled like the beating of a heart—the heart of a conquering darkness. It was a moment of triumph for the wilderness, an invading and vengeful rush which, it seemed to me, I would have to keep back alone for the salvation of another soul. And the memory of what I had heard him say afar there, with the horned shapes stirring at my back, in the glow of fires, within the patient woods, those broken phrases came back to me, were heard again in their ominous and terrifying simplicity. I remembered his abject pleading, his abject threats, the colossal scale of his vile desires, the meanness, the torment, the tempestuous anguish of his soul. And later on I seemed to see his collected languid manner, when he said one day, 'This lot of ivory now is really mine. The Company did not pay for it. I collected it myself at a very great personal risk. I am afraid they will try to claim it as theirs though. H'm. It is a difficult case. What do you think I ought to do—resist? Eh? I want no more than justice.' . . . He wanted no more than justice—no more than justice. I rang the bell before a mahogany door on the first floor, and while I waited he seemed to stare at me out of the glossy panel—stare with that wide and immense stare embracing, condemning, loathing all the universe. I seemed to hear the whispered cry, 'The horror! The horror!'

"The dusk was falling. I had to wait in a lofty drawing-room with three long windows from floor to ceiling that were like three luminous and bedraped columns. The bent gilt legs and backs of the furniture shone in indistinct curves. The tall marble fireplace had a cold and monumental whiteness. A grand piano stood massively in a corner; with dark gleams on the flat surfaces like a sombre and polished sarcophagus. A high door opened—closed. I rose.

"She came forward, all in black, with a pale head, floating towards me in the dusk. She was in mourning. It was more than a year since his death, more than a year since the news came; she seemed as though she would remember and mourn for ever. She took both my hands in hers and murmured, 'I had heard you were coming.' I noticed she was not very young—I mean not girlish. She had a mature capacity for fidelity, for belief, for suffering. The room seemed to have grown darker, as if all the sad light of the cloudy evening had taken refuge on her forehead. This fair hair, this pale visage, this pure brow, seemed surrounded by an ashy halo from which the dark eyes looked out at me. Their glance was guileless, profound, confident, and trustful. She carried her sorrowful head as though she were proud of that sorrow, as though she would say, I—I alone know how to mourn for him as he deserves. But while we were still shaking hands, such a look of awful desolation came upon her face that I perceived she was one of those creatures that are not the playthings of Time. For her he had died only yesterday. And, by Jove! the impression was so powerful that for me too he seemed to have died only yesterday—nay, this very minute. I saw her and him in the same instant of time—his death and her sorrow—I saw her sorrow in the very moment of his death. Do you understand? I saw them together—I heard them together. She had said, with a deep catch of the breath, 'I have survived'; while my strained ears seemed to hear distinctly, mingled with her tone of despairing regret, the summing-up whisper of his eternal condemnation. I asked myself what I was doing there, with a sensation of panic in my heart as though I had blundered into a place of cruel and absurd mysteries not fit for a human being to behold. She motioned me to a chair. We sat down. I laid the packet gently on the little table, and she put her hand over it. . . . 'You knew him well,' she murmured, after a moment of mourning silence.

" 'Intimacy grows quickly out there,' I said. 'I knew him as well as it is possible for one man to know another.'

" 'And you admired him,' she said. 'It was impossible to know him and not to admire him. Was it?'

" 'He was a remarkable man,' I said unsteadily. Then before the appealing fixity of her gaze, that seemed to watch for more words on my lips, I went on, 'It was impossible not to—'

" 'Love him,' she finished eagerly, silencing me into an appalled dumbness. 'How true! how true! But when you think that no one knew him so well as I! I had all his noble confidence. I knew him best.'

" 'You knew him best,' I repeated. And perhaps she did. But with every word spoken the room was growing darker, and only her forehead, smooth and white, remained illumined by the unextinguishable light of belief and love.

" 'You were his friend,' she went on. 'His friend,' she repeated, a little louder. 'You must have been, if he had given you this, and sent you to me. I feel I can speak to you—and oh! I must speak. I want you—you who have heard his last words—to know I have been worthy of him. . . . It is not pride. . . . Yes! I am proud to know I understood him better than any one on earth—he told me so himself. And since his mother died I have had no one—no one—to—to—'

"I listened. The darkness deepened. I was not even sure whether he had given me the right bundle. I rather suspect he wanted me to take care of another batch of his papers which, after his death, I saw the manager examining under the lamp. And the girl talked, easing her pain in the certitude of my sympathy; she talked as thirsty men drink. I had heard that her engagement with Kurtz had been disapproved by her people. He wasn't rich enough or something. And indeed I don't know whether he had not been a pauper all his life. He had given me some reason to infer that it was his impatience of comparative poverty that drove him out there.

" ' . . . Who was not his friend who had heard him speak once?' she was saying. 'He drew men towards him by what was best in them.' She looked at me with intensity. 'It is the gift of the great,' she went on, and the sound of her low voice seemed to have the accompaniment of all the other sounds, full of mystery, desolation, and sorrow, I had ever heard—the ripple of the river, the soughing of the trees swayed by the wind, the murmurs of the crowds, the faint ring of incomprehensible words cried from afar, the whisper of a voice speaking from beyond the threshold of an eternal darkness. 'But you have heard him! You know!' she cried.

" 'Yes, I know,' I said with something like despair in my heart, but bowing my head before the faith that was in her, before that great and saving illusion that shone with an unearthly glow in the darkness, in the triumphant darkness from which I could not have defended her—from which I could not even defend myself.

" 'What a loss to me—to us!'—she corrected herself with beautiful generosity; then added in a murmur, 'To the world.' By the last gleams of twilight I could see the glitter of her eyes, full of tears—of tears that would not fall.

" 'I have been very happy—very fortunate—very proud,' she went on. 'Too fortunate. Too happy for a little while. And now I am unhappy for—for life.'

"She stood up; her fair hair seemed to catch all the remaining light in a glimmer of gold. I rose too.

" 'And of all this,' she went on mournfully, 'of all his promise, and of all his greatness, of his generous mind, of his noble heart, nothing remains—nothing but a memory. You and I—'

" 'We shall always remember him,' I said hastily.

" 'No!' she cried. 'It is impossible that all this should be lost—that such a life should be sacrificed to leave nothing—but sorrow. You know

what vast plans he had. I knew of them too—I could not perhaps understand—but others knew of them. Something must remain. His words,
at least, have not died.'

" 'His words will remain,' I said.

" 'And his example,' she whispered to herself. 'Men looked up to
him—his goodness shone in every act. His example—'

" 'True,' I said; 'his example too. Yes, his example. I forgot that.'

" 'But I do not. I cannot—I cannot believe—not yet. I cannot believe
that I shall never see him again, that nobody will see him again, never,
never, never.'

"She put out her arms as if after a retreating figure, stretching them
black and with clasped pale hands across the fading and narrow sheen of
the window. Never see him! I saw him clearly enough then. I shall see
this eloquent phantom as long as I live, and I shall see her too, a tragic
and familiar Shade, resembling in this gesture another one, tragic also,
and bedecked with powerless charms, stretching bare brown arms over
the glitter of the infernal stream, the stream of darkness. She said suddenly very low, 'He died as he lived.'

" 'His end,' said I, with dull anger stirring in me, 'was in every way
worthy of his life.'

" 'And I was not with him,' she murmured. My anger subsided before
a feeling of infinite pity.

" 'Everything that could be done—' I mumbled.

" 'Ah, but I believed in him more than any one on earth—more than
his own mother, more than—himself. He needed me! Me! I would have
treasured every sigh, every word, every sign, every glance.'

"I felt like a chill grip on my chest. 'Don't,' I said, in a muffled voice.

" 'Forgive me. I—I—have mourned so long in silence—in silence.
. . . You were with him—to the last? I think of his loneliness. Nobody
near to understand him as I would have understood. Perhaps no one to
hear. . . .'

" 'To the very end,' I said shakily. 'I heard his very last words. . . .' I
stopped in a fright.

" 'Repeat them,' she murmured in a heart-broken tone. 'I want—I
want—something—something—to—to live with.'

"I was on the point of crying at her, 'Don't you hear them?' The dusk
was repeating them in a persistent whisper all around us, in a whisper
that seemed to swell menacingly like the first whisper of a rising wind.
'The horror! The horror!'

" 'His last word—to live with,' she insisted. 'Don't you understand I
loved him—I loved him—I loved him!'

"I pulled myself together and spoke slowly.

" 'The last word he pronounced was—your name.'

"I heard a light sigh and then my heart stood still, stopped dead short
by an exulting and terrible cry, by the cry of inconceivable triumph and
of unspeakable pain. 'I knew it—I was sure!' . . . She knew. She was
sure. I heard her weeping; she had hidden her face in her hands. It

seemed to me that the house would collapse before I could escape, that
the heavens would fall upon my head. But nothing happened. The
heavens do not fall for such a trifle. Would they have fallen, I wonder,
if I had rendered Kurtz that justice which was his due? Hadn't he said
he wanted only justice? But I couldn't. I could not tell her. It would
have been too dark—too dark altogether. . . ."[9]

Marlow ceased, and sat apart, indistinct and silent, in the pose of a
meditating Buddha. Nobody moved for a time. "We have lost the first
of the ebb," said the Director suddenly. I raised my head. The offing
was barred by a black bank of clouds, and the tranquil waterway leading
to the uttermost ends of the earth flowed sombre under an overcast sky—
seemed to lead into the heart of an immense darkness.

1899   1902

9. Writing to William Blackwood (editor of *Black-*   view of a whole phase of life, and makes of that
wood's Magazine, where the story first appeared)   story something quite on another plane than an
in May 1902, Conrad referred to "the last pages of   anecdote of a man who went mad in the Centre of
Heart of Darkness where the interview of the man   Africa" (Joseph Conrad, *Letters to William Black-*
and the girl locks in—as it were—the whole 30,000   *wood and David S. Meldrum,* ed. William Black-
words of narrative description into one suggestive   burn, 1958).

WILLIAM BUTLER YEATS
1865–1939

    1891:   Organization of the Rhymers' Club.
    1899:   Launching of the Irish National Theatre.
    1914:   *Responsibilities.*
    1923:   Nobel Prize.
    1928:   *The Tower.*

William Butler Yeats was born in Sandymount, Dublin. His father's family,
of English stock, had been in Ireland for at least two hundred years; his
mother's, the Pollexfens, hailing originally from Devon, had been for some
generations in Sligo, in the west of Ireland. J. B. Yeats, his father, had
abandoned the law to take up painting, at which he made a somewhat precarious living. The Yeatses were in London from 1874 until 1883, when
they returned to Ireland—to Howth, a few miles from Dublin. On leaving
high school in Dublin in 1883 Yeats decided to be an artist, with poetry as
his avocation, and attended art school; but he soon left, to concentrate on
poetry. His first published poems appeared in the *Dublin University Review*
in 1885.

Yeats's father was a religious skeptic, but he believed in the "religion of
art." Yeats himself, religious by temperament but unable to believe in Christian
orthodoxy, sought all his life for traditions of esoteric thought that would
compensate for a lost religion. This search led him to various kinds of mysticism, to folklore, theosophy, spiritualism, and Neoplatonism—not in any
strict chronological order, for he kept returning to and reworking earlier

aspects of his thought. In middle life he elaborated a symbolic system of his own, based on a variety of sources, which enabled him to strengthen the pattern and coherence of his poetic imagery. The student of Yeats is constantly coming up against this willful and sometimes baffling estericism which he cultivated sometimes playfully, sometimes earnestly, sometimes treating it as though it were a body of truths and sometimes as though it were a convenient language of symbols. Modern scholarship has traced most of Yeats's mystical and quasi-mystical ideas to sources that were common to Blake and Shelley and which sometimes go far back into pre-Platonic beliefs and traditions. But his greatness as a poet lies in his ability to communicate the power and significance of his symbols, by the way he expresses and organizes them, even to readers who know nothing of his system.

Yeats's childhood and young manhood were spent between Dublin, London, and Sligo, and each of these places contributed something to his poetic development. In London in the 1890s he met the important poets of the day, and in 1891 was one of the founders of the Rhymers' Club, whose members included Lionel Johnson, Ernest Dowson, and many other characteristic figures of the nineties. Here he acquired ideas of poetry which were vaguely Pre-Raphaelite: he believed, in this early stage of his career, that a poet's language should be dreamy, evocative, and ethereal. From the countryside around Sligo he got something much more vigorous and earthy—a knowledge of the life of the peasantry and of their folklore. In Dublin he was influenced by the currents of Irish nationalism and, while often in disagreement with those who wished to use literature for crude political ends, he nevertheless learned to see his poetry as a contribution to a rejuvenated Irish culture. The three influences of Dublin, London, and Sligo did not develop in chronological order—he was going to and fro between these places throughout his early life—and we sometimes find a poem based on Sligo folklore in the midst of a group of dreamy poems written under the influence of the Rhymers' Club or an echo of Irish nationalist feeling in a lyric otherwise wholly Pre-Raphaelite in tone.

We can distinguish quite clearly, however, the main periods into which Yeats's poetic career falls. He began in the tradition of self-conscious romanticism which he learned from the London poets of the 1890s. Spenser and Shelley, and a little later Blake, were also important influences. One of his early verse plays ends with a song:

> The woods of Arcady are dead
> And over is their antique joy;
> Of old the world on dreaming fed;
> Grey Truth is now her painted toy.

About the same time he was writing poems (e.g., *The Stolen Child*) deriving from his Sligo experience, with a quiet precision of natural imagery, country place names, and themes from folklore. A little later—i.e., in the latter part of his first period—Dublin literary circles sent him to Standish O'Grady's *History of Ireland: Heroic Period*, where he found the great stories of the heroic age of Irish history, and to George Sigerson's and Douglas Hyde's translations of Gaelic poetry into "that dialect which gets from Gaelic its syntax and keeps its still partly Tudor vocabulary." Even when he plays with Neoplatonic ideas, as in *The Rose of the World* (also the product of the latter part of his early period), he can link them with Irish heroic themes and so give a dignity and a *style* to his imagery not normally associated with this sort of poetic dreaminess. Thus the heroic legends of old Ireland and the folk traditions of the modern Irish countryside provided Yeats with a stiffening for his early dreamlike imagery, which is why even his first, "nineties" phase is productive of interesting poems. *The Lake Isle of Innisfree*, spoiled for some by over-anthologizing, is nevertheless a fine poem of its kind: it is the clarity and control shown in the handling of the imagery which keeps all romantic fuzziness out of it and gives it its haunting quality. In *The Man Who Dreamed of Faeryland* he makes something peculiarly effective out of the contrast between human activities and the strangeness of nature. (Such contrasts are common in the early Yeats; in his later poetry he tries to resolve what he called these "antinomies" in inclusive symbols. See, for example, *Crazy Jane Talks to the Bishop*.)

It is important to realize that Yeats had a habit of revising his earlier poems in later printings, tightening up the language and getting rid of the more self-indulgent romantic imagery. The revised versions are found in his *Collected Poems*, which therefore present a somewhat muted picture of his poetic development. For the complete picture one should consult the Variorum Edition edited by Peter Allt and Russell K. Alspach, 1957.

It was Irish nationalism that first sent Yeats in search of a consistently simpler and more popular style. He tells in one of his autobiographical essays how he sought for a style in which to express the elemental facts about Irish life and aspirations. This led him to the concrete image, as did Hyde's translations from Gaelic folk songs, in which "nothing . . . was abstract, nothing worn-out." But other forces were also working on him. In 1902, a friend gave him the works of the German philosopher Friedrich Nietzsche, to which he responded with great excitement and it would seem that, in persuading Yeats, the passive love-poet, to get off his knees, Nietzsche's books prompted his search for a more active stance, a more masculine style. Looking back in 1906, he found that he had mistaken the poetic ideal. "Without knowing it, I had come to care for nothing but impersonal beauty. . . . We should ascend out of common interests, the thoughts of the newspapers, of the market place, but only so far as we can carry the normal, passionate, reasoning self, the personality as a whole." The result of the abandonment of "impersonal beauty," and of the desire to "carry the normal, passionate, reasoning self" into his poetry, is seen in the volumes of collected poems, *In the Seven Woods* (1903) and *The Green Helmet and Other Poems* (1910). *The Folly of Being Comforted* and *Adam's Curse* are from the former of these, and one can see immediately how Yeats here combines the colloquial with the formal. This is characteristic of his "second period."

By this time Yeats had met the beautiful actress and violent Irish nationalist Maud Gonne, with whom he was desperately in love for many years, but who persistently refused to marry him. The affair is reflected in many of the poems of his second period, notably *No Second Troy*, published in *The Green Helmet*. He had also met Lady Gregory, Irish writer and promoter of Irish literature, in 1896 and she invited him to spend the following summer at her country house, Coole Park, in Galway. Yeats spent many holidays with Lady Gregory and discovered the attractiveness of the "country house ideal," seeing in an aristocratic life of elegance and leisure in a great house a method of imposing order on chaos and a symbol of the Neoplatonic dance of life. He expresses this view many times in his poetry—e.g., at the end of *A Prayer for My Daughter*—and it became an important part of his complex of attitudes. The middle classes, with their Philistine money grubbing, he detested, and for his ideal characters he looked either below them, to peasants and beggars, or above them, to the aristocracy, for each of these had their own traditions and lived according to them.

It was under Lady Gregory's influence that Yeats became involved in the founding of the Irish National Theatre in 1899. This led to his active participation in problems of play production, which included political problems of censorship, economic problems of paying carpenters and actors, and other aspects of "theater business, management of men." All this had an effect on his style. The reactions of Dublin audiences did not encourage Yeats's trust in popular judgment, and his bitterness with the "Paudeens," middle-class shopkeepers—who seemed to him to be without any dignity, or understanding, or nobility of spirit—produced some of the most effective poems of his third or middle period. He was now becoming more and more of a national figure. Three public controversies had moved him to anger and to poetry; the first over the hounding of Parnell (see *To a Shade*), the second over Synge's play, *The Playboy of The Western World* in 1907, and the third over the Lane pictures (see *September 1913*). In each, the cause for which he fought was defeated by representatives of the Roman Catholic middle class, and at last, bitterly turning his back on Ireland, Yeats moved to England. Then came the Easter Rising (see *Easter 1916*), mounted by members of the class and religion that had so long opposed him. Persuaded by Maud Gonne (whose estranged husband was one of the executed leaders of the Rising) that "tragic dignity had returned to Ireland," Yeats himself returned. To mark his new commitment, he rented, refurbished, occupied, and renamed "Thoor Ballylee" the Norman tower on Lady Gregory's land that was to become one of the central symbols of his later poetry. In 1922 he was appointed a senator of the recently established Irish Free State and served until 1928, playing an active part not only in promoting the arts but also in general political affairs, in which he supported the views of the Protestant landed class.

Meanwhile Yeats was responding in his own way to the change in poetic taste represented in the poetry and criticism of Ezra Pound and T. S. Eliot immediately before World War I. A gift for epigram had already begun to emerge in his poetry: in the volume entitled *The Wild Swans at Coole* (1919) he has a poem citing Walter Savage Landor (the nineteenth-century poet who wrote some fine lapidary verse) and John Donne as masters. To the precision, and the combination of colloquial and formal, which he had achieved early in the century, he now added a "metaphysical" as well as an epigrammatic element, and this is seen in the later poems of his third period. He also continued his experiments with different kinds of rhythm. At the same time he was continuing his search for a language of symbols and pursuing his esoteric studies. Yeats married in 1917, and his wife proved so sympathetic to his imaginative needs that the automatic writing which for several years she produced (believed by Yeats to have been dictated by spirits) gave him the elements of a symbolic system which he later worked out in his book *A Vision* (1925, 1937) and which he used in all sorts of ways in much of his later poetry. The system was both a theory of the movements of history and a theory of the different types of personality, each movement and type being related in various complicated ways to a different phase of the moon. Some of Yeats's poetry is unintelligible without a knowledge of *A Vision*; but the better poems, such as the two on Byzantium, can be appreciated without such knowledge by the experienced reader who responds sensitively to the patterning of the imagery reinforced by the incantatory effect of the rhythms. Some criticism decries attempts by those who are not experts in the background of Yeats's esoteric thought to discuss his poetry and insists that only a detailed knowledge of Yeats's sources can yield his poetic meaning; but while it is true that some particular images do not yield all their significance to those who are ignorant of the background, it is also true that too literal a paraphrase of the symbolism in the light of the sources robs the poems of their power by reducing them to mere exercises in the use of a code.

The Tower (1928) and *The Winding Stair* (1933), from which the poems from *Sailing to Byzantium* through *After Long Silence* have been here selected, represent the mature Yeats at his very best—a realist-symbolist-metaphysical poet with an uncanny power over words. These volumes represent his fourth and greatest period. Here, in his poems of the 1920s and 1930s, winding stairs, spinning tops, "gyres," spirals of all kinds, are important symbols; not only are they connected with Yeats's philosophy of history and of personality, but they also serve as a means of resolving some of those contraries that had arrested him from the beginning. Life is a journey up a spiral staircase; as we grow older we cover the ground we have covered before, only higher up; as we look down the winding stair below us we measure our progress by the number of places where we were but no longer are. The journey is both repetitious and progressive; we go both round and upward. Through symbolic images of this kind Yeats explores the paradoxes of time and change, of growth and identity, of love and age, of life and art, of madness and wisdom.

The Byzantium poems show him trying to escape from the turbulence of life to the calm eternity of art. But in his fifth and final period he returned to the turbulence after (if only partly as a result of) undergoing the Steinach operation to increase his sexual potency in 1934, and his last poems have a controlled yet startling wildness. Yeats's return to life, to "the foul rag-and-bone shop of the heart," is one of the most impressive final phases of any poet's career. "I shall be a sinful man to the end, and think upon my death-bed of all the nights I wasted in my youth," he wrote in old age to a correspondent, and in one of his last letters he wrote: "When I try to put all into a phrase I say, 'Man can embody truth but he cannot know it.' . . . The abstract is not life and everywhere draws out its contradictions. You can refute Hegel but not the Saint or the Song of Sixpence." When he died in January 1939, he left a body of verse which, in variety and power, makes him beyond question the greatest twentieth-century poet of the English language.

The Stolen Child

Where dips the rocky highland
Of Sleuth Wood[1] in the lake,
There lies a leafy island
Where flapping herons wake
The drowsy water-rats;   5

---

1. This and other places mentioned in the poem are in County Sligo, in northwestern Ireland, where Yeats spent much of his childhood.

There we've hid our faery vats,
Full of berries
And of reddest stolen cherries.
Come away, O human child!
To the waters and the wild   10
With a faery, hand in hand,
For the world's more full of weeping than you can understand.

Where the wave of moonlight glosses
The dim grey sands with light,
Far off by furthest Rosses   15
We foot it all the night,
Weaving olden dances,
Mingling hands and mingling glances
Till the moon has taken flight;
To and fro we leap   20
And chase the frothy bubbles,
While the world is full of troubles
And is anxious in its sleep.
Come away, O human child!
To the waters and the wild   25
With a faery, hand in hand,
For the world's more full of weeping than you can understand.

Where the wandering water gushes
From the hills above Glen-Car,
In pools among the rushes   30
That scarce could bathe a star,
We seek for slumbering trout
And whispering in their ears
Give them unquiet dreams;
Leaning softly out   35
From ferns that drop their tears
Over the young streams.
Come away, O human child!
To the waters and the wild
With a faery, hand in hand,   40
For the world's more full of weeping than you can understand.

Away with us he's going,
The solemn-eyed:
He'll hear no more the lowing
Of the calves on the warm hillside   45
Or the kettle on the hob
Sing peace into his breast,
Or see the brown mice bob
Round and round the oatmeal-chest.
For he comes, the human child,   50
To the waters and the wild

With a faery, hand in hand,
From a world more full of weeping than he can understand.

1886, 1889

The Rose of the World[1]

Who dreamed that beauty passes like a dream?
For these red lips, with all their mournful pride,
Mournful that no new wonder may betide,
Troy passed away in one high funeral gleam,
And Usna's children died.[2]   5

We and the labouring world are passing by:
Amid men's souls, that waver and give place
Like the pale waters in their wintry race,
Under the passing stars, foam of the sky,
Lives on this lonely face.   10

Bow down, archangels, in your dim abode:
Before you were, or any hearts to beat,
Weary and kind one lingered by His seat;
He made the world to be a grassy road
Before her wandering feet.   15

1892

The Lake Isle of Innisfree[1]

I will arise and go now, and go to Innisfree,
And a small cabin build there, of clay and wattles[2] made;
Nine bean-rows will I have there, a hive for the honey-bee,
And live alone in the bee-loud glade.

And I shall have some peace there, for peace comes dropping slow,   5
Dropping from the veils of the morning to where the cricket sings;
There midnight's all a glimmer, and noon a purple glow,
And evening full of the linnet's wings.

1. The Platonic Idea of eternal Beauty. "I notice upon reading these poems for the first time for several years that the quality symbolized as The Rose differs from the Intellectual Beauty of Shelley and of Spenser in that I have imagined it as suffering with man and not as something pursued and seen from afar" (Yeats, in 1925).
2. In Old Irish legend, the Ulster warrior Naoise, son of Usna or Usnach (pronounced *Úskna*,) carried off the beautiful Deirdre, whom King Con-

chubar of Ulster had intended to marry, and with his two brothers took her to Scotland. Eventually Cochubar lured the four of them back to Ireland and killed the three brothers.
1. Island in Lough Gill, County Sligo. "My father had read to me some passage out of [Thoreau's] *Walden*, and I planned to live some day in a cottage on a little island called Innisfree. . . ."
2. Stakes interwoven with twigs or branches.

I will arise and go now, for always night and day
I hear lake water lapping with low sounds by the shore;   10
While I stand on the roadway, or on the pavements grey,
I hear it in the deep heart's core.

1890   1890, 1892

The Sorrow of Love

The brawling of a sparrow in the eaves,
The brilliant moon and all the milky sky,
And all that famous harmony of leaves,
Had blotted out man's image and his cry.

A girl arose that had red mournful lips   5
And seemed the greatness of the world in tears,
Doomed like Odysseus and the labouring ships
And proud as Priam murdered with his peers;[1]

Arose, and on the instant clamorous eaves,
A climbing moon upon an empty sky,   10
And all that lamentation of the leaves,
Could but compose man's image and his cry.

1891   1892, 1925

When You Are Old[1]

When you are old and grey and full of sleep,
And nodding by the fire, take down this book,
And slowly read, and dream of the soft look
Your eyes had once, and of their shadows deep;

How many loved your moments of glad grace,   5
And loved your beauty with love false or true,
But one man loved the pilgrim soul in you,
And loved the sorrows of your changing face;

And bending down beside the glowing bars,[2]
Murmur, a little sadly, how Love fled   10

---

1. Odysseus (whom the Romans called Ulysses), hero of Homer's *Odyssey*, which describes how, after having fought in the siege of Troy, he wandered for 10 years before reaching his home, the Greek island of Ithaca. Priam was king of Troy at the time of the siege and was killed when the Greeks captured the city.

1. A poem suggested by a sonnet of the 16th-century French poet Pierre de Ronsard; it begins *"Quand vous serez bien vieille, au soir, à la chandelle"* ("When you are old, sitting at evening by candle light"), but ends very differently from Yeats's poem.
2. I.e., of the grate.

And paced upon the mountains overhead
And hid his face amid a crowd of stars.

October 1891   1892

Who Goes with Fergus?[1]

Who will go drive with Fergus now,
And pierce the deep wood's woven shade,
And dance upon the level shore?
Young man, lift up your russet brow,
And lift your tender eyelids, maid,   5
And brood on hopes and fear no more.

And no more turn aside and brood
Upon love's bitter mystery;
For Fergus rules the brazen cars,
And rules the shadows of the wood,   10
And the white breast of the dim sea
And all dishevelled wandering stars.

1893

The Man Who Dreamed of Faeryland

He stood among a crowd at Dromahair;[1]
His heart hung all upon a silken dress,
And he had known at last some tenderness,
Before earth took him to her stony care;
But when a man poured fish into a pile,   5
It seemed they raised their little silver heads,
And sang what gold morning or evening sheds
Upon a woven world-forgotten isle
Where people love beside the ravelled[2] seas;
That Time can never mar a lover's vows   10
Under that woven changeless roof of boughs:
The singing shook him out of his new ease.

He wandered by the sands of Lissadell;
His mind ran all on money cares and fears,
And he had known at last some prudent years   15
Before they heaped his grave under the hill;
But while he passed before a plashy place,

---

1. In a late version of this Irish heroic legend, Fergus, "king of the proud Red Branch Kings," gave up his throne voluntarily to Conchubar to learn by dreaming and meditating the bitter wis- dom of the poet and philosopher.
1. This and other place names in the poem refer to places in County Sligo.
2. Tangled; hence here "turbulent."

A lug-worm with its grey and muddy mouth
Sang that somewhere to north or west or south
There dwelt a gay, exulting, gentle race   20
Under the golden or the silver skies;
That if a dancer stayed his hungry foot
It seemed the sun and moon were in the fruit:
And at that singing he was no more wise.

He mused beside the well of Scanavin,   25
He mused upon his mockers: without fail
His sudden vengeance were a country tale,
When earthy night had drunk his body in;
But one small knot-grass growing by the pool
Sang where—unnecessary cruel voice—   30
Old silence bids its chosen race rejoice,
Whatever ravelled waters rise and fall
Or stormy silver fret the gold of day,
And midnight there enfold them like a fleece
And lover there by lover be at peace.   35
The tale drove his fine angry mood away.

He slept under the hill of Lugnagall;
And might have known at last unhaunted sleep
Under that cold and vapour-turbaned steep,
Now that the earth had taken man and all: 40
Did not the worms that spired about his bones
Proclaim with that unwearied, reedy cry
That God has laid His fingers on the sky,
That from those fingers glittering summer runs
Upon the dancer by the dreamless wave.   45
Why should those lovers that no lovers miss
Dream, until God burn Nature with a kiss?
The man has found no comfort in the grave.

                                                    1891, 1892

The Secret Rose[1]

Far-off, most secret, and inviolate Rose,
Enfold me in my hour of hours; where those

---

1. The Rose is a symbol of beauty (see *The Rose of the World*, above). Yeats reveals how he used his sources in an interesting note: "I find that I have unintentionally changed the old story of Conchubar's death. He did not see the Crucifixion in a vision but was told of it. . . . I have imagined Cuchulain meeting Fand 'walking among the flaming dew,' because, I think, of something in Mr. Standish O'Grady's books. [See above, p. 2291.] I have founded the man 'who drove the gods out of their liss,' or fort, upon something I have read about Caoilte after the battle of Gabhra, when almost all his companions were killed, driving the gods out of their liss, . . . I have founded 'the proud dreaming kind' upon Fergus, the son of Rogh, but when I wrote my poem here, and in the song in my early book, 'Who will drive with Fergus now?' I only knew him in Mr. Standish O'Grady, . . . I have founded 'him who sold tillage, and house, and goods,' upon something in 'The Red Pony,' a

Who sought thee in the Holy Sepulchre,
Or in the wine-vat, dwell beyond the stir
And tumult of defeated dreams; and deep   5
Among pale eyelids, heavy with the sleep
Men have named beauty. Thy great leaves enfold
The ancient beards, the helms of ruby and gold
Of the crowned Magi;[2] and the king whose eyes
Saw the Pierced Hands and Rood of elder rise   10
In Druid vapour and make the torches dim;
Till vain frenzy awoke and he died;[3] and him
Who met Fand walking among flaming dew
By a grey shore where the wind never blew,
And lost the world and Emer for a kiss;[4]   15
And him who drove the gods out of their liss,[5]
And till a hundred morns had flowered red
Feasted, and wept the barrows of his dead;
And the proud dreaming king who flung the crown
And sorrow away, and calling bard and clown   20
Dwelt among wine-stained wanderers in deep woods;[6]
And him who sold tillage, and house, and goods,
And sought through lands and islands numberless years,
Until he found, with laughter and with tears,
A woman of so shining loveliness   25
That men threshed corn at midnight by a tress,
A little stolen tress.[7] I, too, await
The hour of thy great wind of love and hate.
When shall the stars be blown about the sky,
Like the sparks blown out of a smithy, and die?   30
Surely thine hour has come, thy great wind blows,
Far-off, most secret, and inviolate Rose?

                                                        1896, 1897

folktale in Mr. Larminie's *West Irish Folk Tales*. A young man 'saw a light before him on the high-road. When he came as far, there was an open box on the road, and a light coming up out of it. He took up the box. There was a lock of hair in it. Presently he had to go to become the servant of a king for his living. There were eleven boys. When they were going out into the stable at ten o'clock, each of them took a light but he. He took no candle at all with him. Each of them went into his own stable. When he went into his stable he opened the box. He left it in a hole in the wall. The light was great. It was twice as much as in the other stables.' The king hears of it, and makes him show him the box. The king says, 'You must go and bring me the woman to whom the hair belongs.' In the end the young man, and not the king, marries the woman."

2. The Magi are the "wise men" from the East who came to do homage to the infant Jesus.
3. King Conchubar, in early Christian legend, is said to have died on the day of Christ's crucifixion in a fit of rage at hearing the news. Yeats, as his note explains, makes Conchubar see the crucifixion in a vision raised by the magic of the ancient Celtic priests, or Druids. The "Pierced Hands" are, of course, Christ's, and the "Rood" is the Cross.
4. The ancient Irish hero Cuchulain was seduced by Fand away from his wife Emer.
5. Fort. This is Caoilte, legendary Irish hero and companion of Oisin, son of Finn, poet and warrior.
6. The "proud dreaming king" is Fergus. See Yeats's note.
7. Yeats describes this tale in his note.

The Folly of Being Comforted

One that is ever kind said yesterday:
"Your well-belovèd's hair has threads of grey,
And little shadows come about her eyes;
Time can but make it easier to be wise
Though now it seem impossible, and so   5
All that you need is patience."

                             Heart cries, "No,
I have not a crumb of comfort, not a grain.
Time can but make her beauty over again:
Because of that great nobleness of hers
The fire that stirs about her, when she stirs,   10
Burns but more clearly. O she had not these ways
When all the wild summer was in her gaze."

O heart! O heart! if she'd but turn her head,
You'd know the folly of being comforted.

                                 1902, 1903

Adam's Curse[1]

We sat together at one summer's end,
That beautiful mild woman, your close friend,
And you and I, and talked of poetry.
I said: "A line will take us hours maybe;
Yet if it does not seem a moment's thought,   5
Our stitching and unstitching has been naught.
Better go down upon your marrow-bones
And scrub a kitchen pavement, or break stones
Like an old pauper, in all kinds of weather;
For to articulate sweet sounds together   10
Is to work harder than all these, and yet
Be thought an idler by the noisy set
Of bankers, schoolmasters, and clergymen
The martyrs call the world."

                           And thereupon   15
That beautiful mild woman for whose sake
There's many a one shall find out all heartache
On finding that her voice is sweet and low
Replied: "To be born woman is to know—

1. To work for a living was the curse imposed by God upon Adam after the Fall (see Genesis 3.17–19). The poem reflects an incident in Yeats's pas-sionate but hopeless love for the beautiful revolu-tionary Maud Gonne (see A. N. Jeffares, W. B. Yeats: Man and Poet, 1949, pp. 128–29).

Although they do not talk of it at school—   20
That we must labour to be beautiful."

I said: "It's certain there is no fine thing
Since Adam's fall but needs much labouring.
There have been lovers who thought love should be
So much compounded of high courtesy   25
That they would sigh and quote with learned looks
Precedents out of beautiful old books;
Yet now it seems an idle trade enough."

We sat grown quiet at the name of love;
We saw the last embers of daylight die,   30
And in the trembling blue-green of the sky
A moon, worn as if it had been a shell
Washed by time's waters as they rose and fell
About the stars and broke in days and years.

I had a thought for no one's but your ears: 35
That you were beautiful, and that I strove
To love you in the old high way of love;
That it had all seemed happy, and yet we'd grown
As weary-hearted as that hollow moon.

November 1902   1902, 1903

No Second Troy

Why should I blame her[1] that she filled my days
With misery, or that she would of late
Have taught to ignorant men most violent ways,
Or hurled the little streets upon the great,
Had they but courage equal to desire?   5
What could have made her peaceful with a mind
That nobleness made simple as a fire,
With beauty like a tightened bow, a kind
That is not natural in an age like this,
Being high and solitary and most stern?   10
Why, what could she have done, being what she is?
Was there another Troy for her to burn?[2]

December 1908   1910

1. Maud Gonne.
2. Helen of Troy was, of course, the cause of the destruction of the "first" Troy.

The Fascination of What's Difficult[1]

The fascination of what's difficult
Has dried the sap out of my veins, and rent
Spontaneous joy and natural content
Out of my heart. There's something ails our colt
That must, as if it had not holy blood   5
Nor on Olympus leaped from cloud to cloud,
Shiver under the lash, strain, sweat and jolt
As though it dragged road-metal. My curse on plays
That have to be set up in fifty ways,
On the day's war with every knave and dolt,   10
Theatre business, management of men.
I swear before the dawn comes round again
I'll find the stable and pull out the bolt.

September 1909–March 1910   1910

September 1913[1]

What need you,[2] being come to sense,
But fumble in a greasy till
And add the halfpence to the pence
And prayer to shivering prayer, until
You have dried the marrow from the bone?   5
For men were born to pray and save:
Romantic Ireland's dead and gone,
It's with O'Leary[3] in the grave.

Yet they were of a different kind,
The names that stilled your childish play,   10
They have gone about the world like wind,
But little time had they to pray
For whom the hangman's rope was spun,

---

1. Written when Yeats was director-manager of the
Abbey Theatre. "Subject. To complain of the fascination of what's difficult. It spoils spontaneity and
pleasure, and wastes time. Repeat the line ending
difficult three times and rhyme on bolt, exalt, colt,
jolt" (Yeats's diary for September 1909).
1. Originally entitled *Romance in Ireland (On
Reading Much of the Correspondence against the
Art Gallery)* and published in the *Irish Times* of
Sept. 8, 1913. Sir Hugh Lane, Lady Gregory's
nephew, had offered his collection of French
Impressionist paintings to the city of Dublin, provided they were permanently housed in a suitable
gallery. Fierce abuse of the paintings and of the
proposed design of the gallery in the Dublin

nationalist press caused Lane to send the pictures
to the London National Gallery. (Lane was drowned
in the *Lusitania* in 1915; after years of bitter court
dispute over an unwitnessed codicil to his will
bequeathing the paintings to Dublin, an arrangement was reached in 1959 for the pictures to hang
first in Dublin and then in London, for 5 years at
a time.)
2. Members of the new and predominantly Roman
Catholic middle class.
3. John O'Leary (1830–1907), Irish nationalist of
great courage and integrity who, returning to Dublin in 1885 after 5 years' imprisonment and 15 years'
exile, drew Yeats and others to the nationalist cause.

And what, God help us, could they save?
Romantic Ireland's dead and gone,   15
It's with O'Leary in the grave.

Was it for this the wild geese[4] spread
The grey wing upon every tide;
For this that all that blood was shed,
For this Edward Fitzgerald died,   20
And Robert Emmet and Wolfe Tone,[5]
All that delirium of the brave?
Romantic Ireland's dead and gone,
It's with O'Leary in the grave.

Yet could we turn the years again,   25
And call those exiles as they were
In all their loneliness and pain,
You'd cry, "Some woman's yellow hair
Has maddened every mother's son":
They weighed so lightly what they gave.   30
But let them be, they're dead and gone,
They're with O'Leary in the grave.

September 1913   1913

To a Shade[1]

If you have revisited the town, thin Shade,
Whether to look upon your monument
(I wonder if the builder has been paid)
Or happier-thoughted when the day is spent
To drink of that salt breath out of the sea   5
When grey gulls flit about instead of men,
And the gaunt houses put on majesty:
Let these content you and be gone again;
For they are at their old tricks yet.
                                        A man[2]
Of your own passionate serving kind who had brought   10
In his full hands what, had they only known,
Had given their children's children loftier thought,
Sweeter emotion, working in their veins
Like gentle blood, has been driven from the place,

4. Popular name for the Irishmen who, because
of the penal laws against Catholics, were forced to
flee to the continent from 1691 until Catholic
Emancipation in 1829. 120,000 fought in the
armies of France, Spain, and Austria.
5. Lord Edward Fitzgerald (1763–1798), a British
officer who, after being dismissed from the army
for disloyal activities, joined the United Irishmen
(an Irish nationalist organization), was arrested, and

died in prison. Robert Emmet (1778–1803) was
also an Irish patriot, executed for treason after a
heroic career. Theobald Wolfe Tone (1763–1798),
one of the chief founders of the United Irishmen,
committed suicide in prison in Dublin.
1. The spirit of the great Irish nationalist leader,
Charles Stewart Parnell (1846–1891).
2. Sir Hugh Lane (see above).

And insult heaped upon him for his pains,   15
And for his open-handedness, disgrace;
Your enemy, an old foul mouth, had set
The pack upon him.[3]
                              Go, unquiet wanderer,
And gather the Glasnevin[4] coverlet
About your head till the dust stops your ear,   20
The time for you to taste of that salt breath
And listen at the corners has not come;
You had enough of sorrow before death—
Away, away! You are safer in the tomb.

September 1913   1913

A Coat

I made my song a coat
Covered with embroideries
Out of old mythologies[1]
From heel to throat;
But the fools caught it,[2]   5
Wore it in the world's eyes
As though they'd wrought it.
Song, let them take it,
For there's more enterprise
In walking naked.   10

1912   1914

The Wild Swans at Coole[1]

The trees are in their autumn beauty,
The woodland paths are dry,
Under the October twilight the water
Mirrors a still sky;
Upon the brimming water among the stones   5
Are nine-and-fifty swans.

The nineteenth autumn has come upon me
Since I first made my count;[2]

---

3. William Martin Murphy, proprietor of the *Irish Independent* and *Evening Herald*. He had opposed the Lane benefaction and had earlier supported those who led the attack on Parnell.
4. The cemetery where Parnell is buried.
1. Gaelic legends, which Yeats had read in such translations as those of Standish O'Grady and James Clarence Mangan.

2. Probably a reference to the protegés of Æ [George William Russell], among them "Seamus O'Sullivan." Cf. *To a poet who would have me Praise certain Bad Poets, Imitators of His and Mine.*
1. Coole Park, Lady Gregory's country estate, where Yeats was a frequent guest.
2. His first visit had been in 1897 (19 years earlier).

I saw, before I had well finished,
All suddenly mount   10
And scatter wheeling in great broken rings
Upon their clamorous wings.

I have looked upon those brilliant creatures,
And now my heart is sore.
All's changed since I, hearing at twilight,   15
The first time on this shore,
The bell-beat of their wings above my head,
Trod with a lighter tread.

Unwearied still, lover by lover,[3]
They paddle in the cold
Companionable streams or climb the air;   20
Their hearts have not grown old;
Passion or conquest, wander where they will,
Attend upon them still.

But now they drift on the still water,   25
Mysterious, beautiful;
Among what rushes will they build,
By what lake's edge or pool
Delight men's eyes when I awake some day
To find they have flown away?

October 1916   1917

Easter 1916[1]

I have met them at close of day
Coming with vivid faces
From counter or desk among grey
Eighteenth-century houses.
I have passed with a nod of the head   5
Or polite meaningless words,
Or have lingered awhile and said
Polite meaningless words,
And thought before I had done
Of a mocking tale or a gibe   10
To please a companion
Around the fire at the club,

3. In Irish legend, the lovers Baile and Aillinn had been changed into swans, the subject of Yeats's poem, *Baile and Aillinn* (1903).
1. This title, with its resemblance to *September 1913*, suggests that the poem is a palinode (one in which the author retracts something said in a former poem). On Easter Monday of 1916, Irish nationalists launched a heroic but unsuccessful revolt against the British government; the week of street fighting that followed is known as the Easter Rebellion. As a result, a number of the nationalists were executed: Britain, at war with Germany, was in no mood to tolerate Irish agitation for independence—which was supported, for obvious reasons, by Germany. Yeats knew the chief rebels personally.

Being certain that they and I
But lived where motley[2] is worn:
All changed, changed utterly: 15
A terrible beauty is born.

That woman's days were spent
In ignorant good-will,
Her nights in argument
Until her voice grew shrill.   20
What voice more sweet than hers
When, young and beautiful,
She rode to harriers?[3]
This man had kept a school
And rode our wingèd horse;[4]   25
This other his helper and friend
Was coming into his force;
He might have won fame in the end,
So sensitive his nature seemed,
So daring and sweet his thought.   30
This other man I had dreamed
A drunken, vainglorious lout.[5]
He had done most bitter wrong
To some who are near my heart,
Yet I number him in the song;   35
He, too, has resigned his part
In the casual comedy;
He, too, has been changed in his turn,
Transformed utterly:
A terrible beauty is born.   40

Hearts with one purpose alone
Through summer and winter seem
Enchanted to a stone
To trouble the living stream.
The horse that comes from the road,   45
The rider, the birds that range
From cloud to tumbling cloud,
Minute by minute they change;
A shadow of cloud on the stream
Changes minute by minute;   50
A horse-hoof slides on the brim,
And a horse plashes within it;
The long-legged moor-hens dive,

---

2. Jester's particolored costume.
3. Constance Gore-Booth (afterwards Countess Markiewicz), a member of the Sligo county aristocracy. A gay and beautiful girl, she had annoyed Yeats by becoming an embittered nationalist.
4. Patrick Pearse, who was a schoolmaster, a leader in the movement to restore the Gaelic language in Ireland, and a poet (hence the reference to "our wingèd horse"—Pegasus, the horse of the Muses). "His helper and friend" was Thomas MacDonagh.
5. Major John MacBride. Maud Gonne, to Yeats's great disgust, had married MacBride in 1903, only to be separated from him after 2 years.

And hens to moor-cocks call;
Minute by minute they live: 55
The stone's in the midst of all.

Too long a sacrifice
Can make a stone of the heart.
O when may it suffice?
That is Heaven's part, our part   60
To murmur name upon name,
As a mother names her child
When sleep at last has come
On limbs that had run wild.
What is it but nightfall?   65
No, no, not night but death;
Was it needless death after all?
For England may keep faith
For all that is done and said.
We know their dream; enough   70
To know they dreamed and are dead;
And what if excess of love
Bewildered them till they died?
I write it out in a verse—
MacDonagh and MacBride
And Connolly[6] and Pearse
Now and in time to be,
Wherever green is worn,
Are changed, changed utterly:
A terrible beauty is born.   80

May–September 1916   1916, 1920

The Second Coming[1]

Turning and turning in the widening gyre
The falcon cannot hear the falconer;
Things fall apart; the center cannot hold;
Mere anarchy is loosed upon the world,
The blood-dimmed tide is loosed, and everywhere   5
The ceremony of innocence is drowned;
The best lack all conviction, while the worst
Are full of passionate intensity.[2]

6. James Connolly, Pearse's partner in leading the insurrection. Like the other rebels named here, he was executed by firing squad.
1. This poem expresses Yeats's sense of the dissolution of the civilization of his time, the end of one cycle of history and the approach of another. He called each cycle of history a "gyre" (line 1)—literally a circular or spiral turn (Yeats pronounced it with a hard g). The birth of Christ brought to an end the cycle that had lasted from what Yeats called the "Babylonian mathematical starlight" (2000 B.C.) to the dissolution of Greco-Roman culture. "What if the irrational return?" Yeats asked in his prose work A Vision. "What if the circle begin again?" He speculates that "we may be about to accept the most implacable authority the world has known."
2. Lines 4–8 refer to the Russian Revolution of 1917. "The ceremony of innocence" suggests Yeats's view of ritual as the basis of civilized living. Cf. the last stanza of A Prayer for My Daughter.

Surely some revelation is at hand;   10
Surely the Second Coming is at hand.
The Second Coming! Hardly are those words out
When a vast image out of *Spiritus Mundi*[3]
Troubles my sight: somewhere in sands of the desert
A shape with lion body and the head of a man,
A gaze blank and pitiless as the sun,   15
Is moving its slow thighs, while all about it
Reel shadows of the indignant desert birds.
The darkness drops again; but now I know
That twenty centuries of stony sleep
Were vexed to nightmare by a rocking cradle,[4]   20
And what rough beast, its hour come round at last,
Slouches towards Bethlehem to be born?

January 1919   1920, 1921

A Prayer for My Daughter[1]

Once more the storm is howling, and half hid
Under this cradle-hood and coverlid
My child sleeps on. There is no obstacle
But Gregory's wood[2] and one bare hill
Whereby the haystack- and roof-levelling wind,   5
Bred on the Atlantic, can be stayed;
And for an hour I have walked and prayed
Because of the great gloom that is in my mind.

I have walked and prayed for this young child an hour
And heard the sea-wind scream upon the tower,   10
And under the arches of the bridge, and scream
In the elms above the flooded stream;
Imagining in excited reverie
That the future years had come,
Dancing to a frenzied drum,   15
Out of the murderous innocence of the sea.[3]

May she be granted beauty and yet not
Beauty to make a stranger's eye distraught,
Or hers before a looking-glass, for such,
Being made beautiful overmuch,   20
Consider beauty a sufficient end,

3. The Spirit or Soul of the Universe, with which all individual souls are connected through the "Great Memory," which Yeats held to be a universal subconscious in which the human race preserves its past memories. It is thus a source of symbolic images for the poet.
4. I.e., the cradle of the infant Christ.
1. Yeats's daughter, christened Anne Butler, was born on Feb. 26, 1919, in the refitted Norman tower of Thoor Ballylee (Ballylee Castle) in Galway, where Yeats lived: it is not far from Coole Park.
2. Originally part of the Gregory estate, which had once also included Thoor Ballylee.
3. A reference to Yeats's visions of the future (cf. *The Second Coming*).

Lose natural kindness and maybe
The heart-revealing intimacy
That chooses right, and never find a friend.

Helen being chosen found life flat and dull   25
And later had much trouble from a fool,[4]
While that great Queen, that rose out of the spray,[5]
Being fatherless could have her way
Yet chose a bandy-leggèd smith for man.
It's certain that fine women eat   30
A crazy salad with their meat
Whereby the Horn of Plenty is undone.

In courtesy I'd have her chiefly learned;
Hearts are not had as a gift but hearts are earned
By those that are not entirely beautiful;   35
Yet many, that have played the fool
For beauty's very self, has charm made wise,
And many a poor man that has roved,
Loved and thought himself beloved,
From a glad kindness cannot take his eyes.   40

May she become a flourishing hidden tree
That all her thoughts may like the linnet[6] be,
And have no business but dispensing round
Their magnanimities of sound,
Not but in merriment begin a chase,   45
Nor but in merriment a quarrel.
O may she live like some green laurel
Rooted in one dear perpetual place.

My mind, because the minds that I have loved,
The sort of beauty that I have approved,   50
Prosper but little, has dried up of late,
Yet knows that to be choked with hate
May well be of all evil chances chief.
If there's no hatred in a mind
Assault and battery of the wind   55
Can never tear the linnet from the leaf.

An intellectual hatred is the worst,
So let her think opinions are accursed.
Have I not seen the loveliest woman born[7]
Out of the mouth of Plenty's horn,   60
Because of her opinionated mind

---

4. Menelaus, the husband of Helen, whom she deserted in favor of Paris.
5. Venus, wife (in the *Odyssey* and later accounts) of Vulcan, "bandy-legged" god of fire and forge (line 29).
6. A small European songbird.
7. Maud Gonne.

Barter that horn and every good
By quiet natures understood
For an old bellows full of angry wind?

Considering that, all hatred driven hence,   65
The soul recovers radical innocence
And learns at last that it is self-delighting,
Self-appeasing, self-affrighting,
And that its own sweet will is Heaven's will;
She can, though every face should scowl   70
And every windy quarter howl
Or every bellows burst, be happy still.

And may her bridegroom bring her to a house
Where all's accustomed, ceremonious;
For arrogance and hatred are the wares   75
Peddled in the thoroughfares.
How but in custom and in ceremony
Are innocence and beauty born?
Ceremony's a name for the rich horn,
And custom for the spreading laurel tree.   80

February–June 1919   1919, 1921

Sailing to Byzantium[1]

1

That is no country for old men. The young
In one another's arms, birds in the trees
—Those dying generations—at their song,
The salmon-falls, the mackerel-crowded seas,
Fish, flesh, or fowl, commend all summer long   5
Whatever is begotten, born, and dies.
Caught in that sensual music all neglect
Monuments of unageing intellect.

2

An aged man is but a paltry thing,
A tattered coat upon a stick, unless   10
Soul clap its hands and sing, and louder sing
For every tatter in its mortal dress,
Nor is there singing school but studying
Monuments of its own magnificence;

1. Yeats wrote in *A Vision:* "I think that if I could be given a month of antiquity and leave to spend it where I chose, I would spend it in Byzantium [modern Istanbul] a little before Justinian opened St. Sophia and closed the Academy of Plato [i.e., ca. A.D. 535]. . . . I think that in early Byzantium, maybe never before or since in recorded history, religious, aesthetic, and practical life were one, that architects and artificers . . . spoke to the multitude in gold and silver. The painter, the mosaic worker, the worker in gold and silver, the illuminator of sacred books were almost impersonal, almost perhaps without the consciousness of individual design, absorbed in their subject matter and that the vision of a whole people."

And therefore I have sailed the seas and come   15
To the holy city of Byzantium.

                              3

O sages standing in God's holy fire
As in the gold mosaic of a wall,[2]
Come from the holy fire, perne in a gyre,[3]
And be the singing-masters of my soul.   20
Consume my heart away; sick with desire
And fastened to a dying animal
It knows not what it is; and gather me
Into the artifice of eternity.

                              4

Once out of nature I shall never take   25
My bodily form from any natural thing,
But such a form as Grecian goldsmiths make
Of hammered gold and gold enamelling
To keep a drowsy Emperor awake;[4]
Or set upon a golden bough to sing   30
To lords and ladies of Byzantium
Of what is past, or passing, or to come.

September 1926   1927

Leda and the Swan[1]

A sudden blow: the great wings beating still
Above the staggering girl, her thighs caressed
By the dark webs, her nape caught in his bill,
He holds her helpless breast upon his breast.

How can those terrified vague fingers push   5
The feathered glory from her loosening thighs?

2. Yeats had in mind the mosaic frieze of the holy martyrs in the church of San Apollinare Nuovo at Ravenna, which he had visited in 1907.
3. I.e., whirl round in a spiral motion. "Perne" (or "pirn") is literally a bobbin, reel, or spool, on which something is wound. It became a favorite word of Yeats's, used as a verb meaning "to spin round"; he associated the spinning with the spinning of fate.
4. "I have read somewhere," Yeats wrote, "that in the Emperor's palace at Byzantium was a tree made of gold and silver, and artificial birds that sang." Cf. also Hans Christian Andersen's *Emperor's Nightingale*, which may have been in Yeats's mind at the time.
1. In Greek mythology Zeus visited Leda in the form of a swan. As a result of the union Leda gave birth to Helen and to Clytemnestra (wife of Agamemnon). Yeats saw Zeus's visit to Leda as an "annunciation," marking the beginning of Greek civilization: "I imagine the annunciation that founded Greece as made to Leda, remembering

that they showed in a Spartan temple, strung up to the roof as a holy relic, an unhatched egg of hers, and that from one of her eggs came love and from the other war" (*A Vision*). In the original Cuala Press edition Yeats noted: "I wrote *Leda and the Swan* because the editor of a political review asked me for a poem. I thought, 'After the individualist, demagogic movement, founded by Hobbes and popularized by the Encyclopedists and the French Revolution, we have a soil so exhausted that it cannot grow that crop again for centuries.' Then I thought, 'Nothing is now possible but some movement from above preceded by some violent annunciation.' My fancy began to play with Leda and the Swan for metaphor, and I began this poem; but as I wrote, bird and lady took such possession of the scene that all politics went out of it, and my friend tells me that his 'conservative readers would misunderstand the poem.' "
For the author's revisions while composing this poem, see "Poems in Process," below.

And how can body, laid in that white rush,
But feel the strange heart beating where it lies?

A shudder in the loins engenders there
The broken wall, the burning roof and tower[2]   10
And Agamemnon dead.
                Being so caught up,
So mastered by the brute blood of the air,
Did she put on his knowledge with his power
Before the indifferent beak could let her drop?

September 1923   1924, 1928

Among School Children

1

I walk through the long schoolroom questioning;
A kind old nun in a white hood replies;
The children learn to cipher and to sing,
To study reading-books and history,
To cut and sew, be neat in everything   5
In the best modern way—the children's eyes
In momentary wonder stare upon
A sixty-year-old smiling public man.

2

I dream of a Ledaean body,[1] bent
Above a sinking fire, a tale that she   10
Told of a harsh reproof, or trivial event
That changed some childish day to tragedy—
Told, and it seemed that our two natures blent
Into a sphere from youthful sympathy,
Or else, to alter Plato's parable,   15
Into the yolk and white of the one shell.[2]

3

And thinking of that fit of grief or rage
I look upon one child or t'other there
And wonder if she stood so at that age—
For even daughters of the swan can share   20
Something of every paddler's heritage—
And had that colour upon cheek or hair,
And thereupon my heart is driven wild:
She stands before me as a living child.

2. I.e., the destruction of Troy, caused by Helen's elopement with the Trojan Paris. Agamemnon was murdered by his wife, Clytemnestra, the other daughter of Leda and the Swan.
1. "Ledaean"; adjective from "Leda," meaning "like Helen of Troy" (Leda's daughter). The reference is to Maud Gonne (as also in lines 19–28).
2. In Plato's *Symposium* Aristophanes explains Love by supposing that "the primeval man was round and had four hands and four feet, back and sides forming a circle, one head with two faces," and was subsequently divided into two. "After the division, the two parts of man, each desiring his other half, came together, and threw their arms about one another eager to grow into one." The fact that Helen was born from an egg (as the daughter of Leda and the Swan) suggests Yeats's image for such a union.

4

Her present image floats into the mind—   25
Did Quattrocento[3] finger fashion it
Hollow of cheek as though it drank the wind
And took a mess of shadows for its meat?
And I though never of Ledaean kind
Had pretty plumage once—enough of that,   30
Better to smile on all that smile, and show
There is a comfortable kind of old scarecrow.

5

What youthful mother, a shape upon her lap
Honey of generation had betrayed,
And that must sleep, shriek, struggle to escape   35
As recollection or the drug decide,[4]
Would think her son, did she but see that shape
With sixty or more winters on its head,
A compensation for the pang of his birth,
Or the uncertainty of his setting forth?   40

6

Plato thought nature but a spume that plays
Upon a ghostly paradigm of things;
Solider Aristotle played the taws
Upon the bottom of a king of kings;[5]
World-famous golden-thighed Pythagoras[6]   45
Fingered upon a fiddle-stick or strings
What a star sang and careless Muses heard:
Old clothes upon old sticks to scare a bird.[7]

7

Both nuns and mothers worship images,[8]
But those the candles light are not as those   50
That animate a mother's reveries,
But keep a marble or a bronze repose.
And yet they too break hearts—O Presences
That passion, piety or affection knows,

---

3. 15th-century; a reference to Italian painters of the period.

4. "I have taken the 'honey of generation' from Porphyry's essay on 'The Cave of the Nymphs,' but find no warrant in Porphyry for considering it the 'drug' that destroys the 'recollection' of pre-natal freedom" [Yeats's note]. Porphyry was a Neoplatonic philosopher of the 3rd century A.D. "Honey of generation," by blotting out the memory of prenatal happiness, "betrays" an infant to be born into this world. The infant will either "sleep" or "struggle to escape" (from this world) depending on whether the drug works or the recollection of blissful prenatal life overcomes the oblivion caused by the drug.

5. Plato thought nature was a mere appearance ("spume") veiling the ultimate spiritual and mathematical reality ("ghostly paradigm"); Aristotle was "solider" in that he believed that form really inhered in the matter of nature, and thus that nature itself had reality. Aristotle was tutor to Alexander the Great, and disciplined him by applying the "taws" or strap.

6. Greek philosopher (early 6th century B.C.), interested in mathematics and the mathematical study of acoustics and music; his disciples, the Pythagoreans, developed a mystical philosophy of numerical relations and united the notions of astronomical and mathematical relations in the theory of the music of the spheres. Pythagoreans regarded their master with veneration as a god with a golden thigh.

7. A contemptuous description of the philosophies of Plato, Aristotle, and Pythagoras.

8. Nuns worship images of Christ or the Virgin; mothers worship their own inward images of their children.

And that all heavenly glory symbolise—   55
O self-born mockers of man's enterprise;

8

Labour is blossoming or dancing where
The body is not bruised to pleasure soul,
Nor beauty born out of its own despair,
Nor blear-eyed wisdom out of midnight oil.   60
O chestnut tree, great-rooted blossomer,
Are you the leaf, the blossom, or the bole?
O body swayed to music, O brightening glance,
How can we know the dancer from the dance?

June 1926   1927

A Dialogue of Self and Soul[1]

1

MY SOUL. I summon to the winding ancient stair;
    Set all your mind upon the steep ascent,
    Upon the broken, crumbling battlement,
    Upon the breathless starlit air,
    Upon the star that marks the hidden pole;   5
    Fix every wandering thought upon
    That quarter where all thought is done:
    Who can distinguish darkness from the soul?

MY SELF. The consecrated blade upon my knees
    Is Sato's ancient blade, still as it was,   10
    Still razor-keen, still like a looking-glass
    Unspotted by the centuries;
    That flowering, silken, old embroidery, torn
    From some court-lady's dress and round
    The wooden scabbard bound and wound,   15
    Can, tattered, still protect, faded adorn.

MY SOUL. Why should the imagination of a man
    Long past his prime remember things that are
    Emblematical of love and war?
    Think of ancestral night that can,   20
    If but imagination scorn the earth
    And intellect its wandering
    To this and that and t'other thing,
    Deliver from the crime of death and birth.

MY SELF. Montashigi, third of his family, fashioned it   25
    Five hundred years ago, about it lie

---

1. In a letter of Oct. 2, 1923, Yeats wrote: "I am writing a new tower poem 'Sword and Tower,' which is a choice of rebirth rather than deliverance from birth. I make the Japanese sword and its silk covering my symbol of life. . . ." The sword was a present from a friend, Junzo Sato.

Flowers from I know not what embroidery—
Heart's purple—and all these I set
For emblems of the day against the tower
Emblematical of the night,   30
And claim as by a soldier's right
A charter to commit the crime once more.

MY SOUL. Such fullness in that quarter overflows
    And falls into the basin of the mind
    That man is stricken deaf and dumb and blind,   35
    For intellect no longer knows
    Is from *Ought*, or *Knower* from the *Known*—
    That is to say, ascends to Heaven;
    Only the dead can be forgiven;
    But when I think of that my tongue's a stone.   40

                            2
MY SELF. A living man is blind and drinks his drop.
    What matter if the ditches are impure?
    What matter if I live it all once more?
    Endure that toil of growing up;
    The ignominy of boyhood; the distress   45
    Of boyhood changing into man;
    The unfinished man and his pain
    Brought face to face with his own clumsiness;

    The finished man among his enemies?—
    How in the name of Heaven can he escape   50
    That defiling and disfigured shape
    The mirror of malicious eyes
    Casts upon his eyes until at last
    He thinks that shape must be his shape?
    And what's the good of an escape   55
    If honour find him in the wintry blast?

    I am content to live it all again
    And yet again, if it be life to pitch
    Into the frog-spawn of a blind man's ditch,
    A blind man battering blind men;   60
    Or into that most fecund ditch of all,
    The folly that man does
    Or must suffer, if he woos
    A proud woman not kindred of his soul.

    I am content to follow to its source   65
    Every event in action or in thought;
    Measure the lot; forgive myself the lot!
    When such as I cast our remorse
    So great a sweetness flows into the breast
    We must laugh and we must sing,   70

We are blest by everything,
Everything we look upon is blest.

July–December 1927   1929

For Anne Gregory

"Never shall a young man,
Thrown into despair
By those great honey-coloured
Ramparts at your ear,
Love you for yourself alone   5
And not your yellow hair."

"But I can get a hair-dye
And set such colour there,
Brown, or black, or carrot,
That young men in despair   10
May love me for myself alone
And not my yellow hair."

"I heard an old religious man
But yesternight declare
That he had found a text to prove   15
That only God, my dear,
Could love you for yourself alone
And not your yellow hair."

September 1930   1931, 1932

Byzantium[1]

The unpurged images of day recede;
The Emperor's drunken soldiery are abed;
Night resonance recedes, night-walkers' song
After great cathedral gong;
A starlit or a moonlit dome[2] disdains   5
All that man is,
All mere complexities,
The fury and the mire of human veins.

---

1. On Oct. 4, 1930, Yeats sent his friend Sturge Moore a copy of *Byzantium,* saying: "The poem originates from a criticism of yours. You objected to the last verse of 'Sailing to Byzantium' because a bird made by a goldsmith was just as natural as anything else. That showed me that the idea needed exposition." The previous April, Yeats had noted in his diary: "Subject for a poem / Describe Byzan- tium as it is in the system towards the end of the first Christian millennium. A walking mummy; flames at the street corners where the soul is puri- fied. Birds of hammered gold singing in the golden trees. In the harbour [dolphins] offering their backs to the wailing dead that they may carry them to paradise."
2. Of the great church of St. Sophia.

Before me floats an image, man or shade,
Shade more than man, more image than a shade;   10
For Hades' bobbin bound in mummy-cloth
May unwind the winding path;[3]
A mouth that has no moisture and no breath
Breathless mouths may summon;
I hail the superhuman;   15
I call it death-in-life and life-in-death.

Miracle, bird or golden handiwork,
More miracle than bird or handiwork,
Planted on the star-lit golden bough,[4]
Can like the cocks of Hades crow,   20
Or, by the moon embittered, scorn aloud
In glory of changeless metal
Common bird or petal
And all complexities of mire or blood.

At midnight on the Emperor's pavement flit   25
Flames that no faggot feeds, nor steel has lit,
Nor storm disturbs, flames begotten of flame,
Where blood-begotten spirits come
And all complexities of fury leave,
Dying into a dance,   30
An agony of trance,
An agony of flame[5] that cannot singe a sleeve.

Astraddle on the dolphin's mire and blood,[6]
Spirit after spirit! The smithies break the flood,
The golden smithies of the Emperor!   35
Marbles of the dancing floor
Break bitter furies of complexity,
Those images that yet
Fresh images beget,
That dolphin-torn, that gong-tormented sea.   40

September 1930   1932

---

3. The spool of people's fate, which spins their destiny and which is symbolized by the wrappings around a mummy, may lead people, as it unwinds, to the realm of pure spirit.

4. The "star-lit golden bough" is part of the death-world of artifice and eternity; it is opposed to a real, living bough, which would be lighted by the sun or the moon. Reminiscent of the golden bough that guides Aeneas through the Underworld, in Virgil's *Aeneid*, it is also associated with the mystical tree of the esoteric Hebrew doctrine of the cabala, in whose branches "the birds lodge and build their nests; that is, the souls or angels have their place." The cock, that crows at dawn, appears on Roman tombstones as a herald of rebirth.

5. The "agony of flame" was suggested to Yeats by a Japanese Nō play, *Motomezuka*, wherein a young girl suffers from perpetual burning, which is a sense of her own guilt. A priest tells her that the flames will cease if she no longer believes in their reality; she finds herself incapable of disbelief, however, and the play ends in "the dance of her agony."

6. The dolphin, in ancient art, was a symbol of the soul in transit from one state to another.

Crazy Jane Talks with the Bishop[1]

I met the Bishop on the road
And much said he and I.
"Those breasts are flat and fallen now,
Those veins must soon be dry;
Live in a heavenly mansion,   5
Not in some foul sty."

"Fair and foul are near of kin,
And fair needs foul," I cried.
"My friends are gone, but that's a truth
Nor grave nor bed denied,   10
Learned in bodily lowliness
And in the heart's pride.

"A woman can be proud and stiff
When on love intent;
But Love has pitched his mansion in   15
The place of excrement;
For nothing can be sole or whole
That has not been rent."

November 1931   1932

After Long Silence[1]

Speech after long silence; it is right,
All other lovers being estranged or dead,
Unfriendly lamplight hid under its shade,
The curtains drawn upon unfriendly night,
That we descant and yet again descant   5
Upon the supreme theme of Art and Song:
Bodily decrepitude is wisdom; young
We loved each other and were ignorant.

November 1929   1932

---

1. One of a series of poems dealing with the paradox that wisdom may reside with fools and beggars (such as Jane) rather than with the respectable
representatives of orthodoxy (such as the Bishop).
1. For the author's revisions while composing this
poem, see "Poems in Process," below.

Lapis Lazuli[1]

(For Harry Clifton)

I have heard that hysterical women say
They are sick of the palette and fiddle-bow,
Of poets that are always gay,
For everybody knows or else should know
That if nothing drastic is done   5
Aeroplane and Zeppelin will come out,
Pitch like King Billy[2] bomb-balls in
Until the town lie beaten flat.

All perform their tragic play,
There struts Hamlet, there is Lear,   10
That's Ophelia, that Cordelia;
Yet they, should the last scene be there,
The great stage curtain about to drop,
If worthy their prominent part in the play,
Do not break up their lines to weep.   15
They know that Hamlet and Lear are gay;
Gaiety transfiguring all that dread.
All men have aimed at, found and lost;
Black out; Heaven blazing into the head:
Tragedy wrought to its uttermost.   20
Though Hamlet rambles and Lear rages,
And all the drop-scenes drop at once
Upon a hundred thousand stages,
It cannot grow by an inch or an ounce.

On their own feet they came, or on shipboard,   25
Camel-back, horse-back, ass-back, mule-back,
Old civilisations put to the sword.
Then they and their wisdom went to rack:
No handiwork of Callimachus,[3]
Who handled marble as if it were bronze,   30
Made draperies that seemed to rise
When sea-wind swept the corner, stands;

---

1. A deep blue stone. "I notice that you have much lapis lazuli; someone has sent me a present of a great piece carved by some Chinese sculptor into the semblance of a mountain with temple, trees, paths, and an ascetic and pupil about to climb the mountain. Ascetic, pupil, hard stone, eternal theme of the sensual east. The heroic cry in the midst of despair. But no, I am wrong, the east has its solutions always and therefore knows nothing of tragedy. It is we, not the east, that must raise the heroic cry" (Yeats to Dorothy Wellesley, July 6, 1935).
2. King William III (William of Orange), who defeated the army of King James II at the Battle of the Boyne in 1690.
3. Greek sculptor (5th century B.C.), supposedly the originator of the Corinthian column and of the use of the running drill to imitate folds in drapery in statues. Yeats wrote of him: "With Callimachus pure Ionic revives again . . . and upon the only example of his work known to us, a marble chair, a Persian is represented, and may one not discover a Persian symbol in that bronze lamp, shaped like a palm . . . ? But he was an archaistic workman, and those who set him to work brought back public life to an older form" (A Vision).

His long lamp-chimney shaped like the stem
Of a slender palm, stood but a day;
All things fall and are built again, 35
And those that build them again are gay.

Two Chinamen, behind them a third,
Are carved in lapis lazuli,
Over them flies a long-legged bird,
A symbol of longevity; 40
The third, doubtless a serving-man,
Carries a musical instrument.

Every discolouration of the stone,
Every accidental crack or dent,
Seems a water-course or an avalanche, 45
Or lofty slope where it still snows
Though doubtless plum or cherry-branch
Sweetens the little half-way house
Those Chinamen climb towards, and I
Delight to imagine them seated there; 50
There, on the mountain and the sky,
On all the tragic scene they stare.
One asks for mournful melodies;
Accomplished fingers begin to play.
Their eyes mid many wrinkles, their eyes, 55
Their ancient, glittering eyes, are gay.

July 1936   1938

Long-Legged Fly

That civilisation may not sink,
Its great battle lost,
Quiet the dog, tether the pony
To a distant post;
Our master Caesar[1] is in the tent 5
Where the maps are spread,
His eye fixed upon nothing,
A hand under his head.
Like a long-legged fly upon the stream
His mind moves upon silence. 10

That the topless towers be burnt
And men recall that face,
Move most gently if move you must
In this lonely place.

1. Emperor of Rome.

She[2] thinks, part woman, three parts a child,   15
That nobody looks; her feet
Practice a tinker shuffle
Picked up on a street.
Like a long-legged fly upon the stream
Her mind moves upon silence.   20

That girls at puberty may find
The first Adam in their thought,
Shut the door of the Pope's chapel,
Keep those children out.
There on that scaffolding reclines   25
Michael Angelo.[3]
With no more sound than the mice make
His hand moves to and fro.
Like a long-legged fly upon the stream
His mind moves upon silence.   30

November 1937   1939

The Circus Animals' Desertion

1

I sought a theme and sought for it in vain,
I sought it daily for six weeks or so.
Maybe at last, being but a broken man,
I must be satisfied with my heart, although
Winter and summer till old age began   5
My circus animals were all on show,
Those stilted boys, that burnished chariot,
Lion and woman and the Lord knows what.[1]

2

What can I but enumerate old themes?
First that sea-rider Oisin[2] led by the nose   10
Through three enchanted islands, allegorical dreams,
Vain gaiety, vain battle, vain repose,
Themes of the embittered heart, or so it seems,
That might adorn old songs or courtly shows;
But what cared I that set him on to ride,   15
I, starved for the bosom of his faery bride?

2. Helen of Troy, who precipitated the Trojan War.
Cf. "Was this the face that launched a thousand
ships / And burnt the topless towers of Ilium?"
(Marlowe, *Dr. Faustus*).
3. Michaelangelo is painting *The Creation of Man*
on the Sistine Chapel ceiling in the Vatican. Cf.
Under Ben Bulben, p. 2323.
1. Yeats refers to the ancient Irish heroes of his
early work ("those stilted boys"), the gilded carriage of his play *The Unicorn from the Stars* (1908),
and "A Sphinx with woman breast and lion paw"
in his poem *The Double Vision of Michael Robartes*.
2. In the long title-poem of Yeats's first book, *The
Wanderings of Oisin and Other Poems* (1889), the
legendary poet-warrior Oisin (pronounced *Ushéén*)
is bewitched by the beautiful fairy woman Niamh.
He returns 150 years later to find his friends dead
and Ireland Christian.

And then a counter-truth filled out its play,
The Countess Cathleen was the name I gave it;[3]
She, pity-crazed, had given her soul away,
But masterful Heaven had intervened to save it.   20
I thought my dear must her own soul destroy,
So did fanaticism and hate enslave it,
And this brought forth a dream and soon enough
This dream itself had all my thought and love.

And when the Fool and Blind Man stole the bread   25
Cuchulain fought the ungovernable sea;[4]
Heart-mysteries there, and yet when all is said
It was the dream itself enchanted me:
Character isolated by a deed
To engross the present and dominate memory.   30
Players and painted stage took all my love,
And not those things that they were emblems of.

3

Those masterful images because complete
Grew in pure mind, but out of what began?
A mound of refuse or the sweepings of a street,   35
Old kettles, old bottles, and a broken can,
Old iron, old bones, old rags, that raving slut
Who keeps the till. Now that my ladder's gone,
I must lie down where all the ladders start,
In the foul rag-and-bone shop of the heart.   40

1939

Under Ben Bulben[1]

1

Swear by what the sages spoke
Round the Mareotic Lake[2]
That the Witch of Atlas knew,
Spoke and set the cocks a-crow.

---

3. This play (1892), about an Irish countess who sells her soul to the devil in order to buy food for the starving peasantry but is taken up to Heaven (for God "Looks always on the motive, not the deed"), was dedicated to Maud Gonne ("my dear") and inspired by her work on behalf of evicted peasants in the West of Ireland.
4. In Yeats's play *On Baile's Strand* (1904).
1. Mountain in Country Sligo, which Yeats had often climbed as a boy. Nine years after he died in the South of France, his body was brought home to Ireland and buried in Drumcliff churchyard at the foot of Ben Bulben.

2. Lake Mareotis, bordering the city of Alexandria where a school of Neo-Pythagorean philosophers flourished in the 1st century A.D. By Lake Mareotis also flourished (3rd century A.D.) the Christian Neoplatonists, in whom Yeats was much interested. The lake is mentioned in Shelley's poem *The Witch of Atlas*, a poem which Yeats admired and interpreted in his own way, seeing the Witch as a symbol of timeless, absolute beauty; hence what she "knew" and "spoke" and what "set the cocks a-crow" can be related to the "miracle" that "can like the cocks of Hades crow" in *Byzantium*.

Swear by those horsemen, by those women   5
Complexion and form prove superhuman,[3]
That pale, long-visaged company
That air in immortality
Completeness of their passions won;
Now they ride the wintry dawn   10
Where Ben Bulben sets the scene.

Here's the gist of what they mean.

2

Many times man lives and dies
Between his two eternities,
That of race and that of soul,   15
And ancient Ireland knew it all.
Whether man die in his bed
Or the rifle knocks him dead,
A brief parting from those dear
Is the worst man has to fear.   20
Though grave-diggers' toil is long,
Sharp their spades, their muscles strong,
They but thrust their buried men
Back in the human mind again.

3

You that Mitchel's prayer have heard,   25
"Send war in our time, O Lord!"[4]
Know that when all words are said
And a man is fighting mad,
Something drops from eyes long blind,
He completes his partial mind,   30
For an instant stands at ease,
Laughs aloud, his heart at peace.
Even the wisest man grows tense
With some sort of violence
Before he can accomplish fate,   35
Know his work or choose his mate.

4

Poet and sculptor, do the work,
Nor let the modish painter shirk
What his great forefathers did,
Bring the soul of man to God.   40
Make him fill the cradles right.

Measurement began our might:
Forms a stark Egyptian thought,

3. The *sidhe,* or fairy folk, who were believed to ride through the countryside near Ben Bulben.
4. John Mitchel (1815–1875), an Irish patriot imprisoned for his activities, wrote in his *Jail Journal:* "Give us war in our time, O Lord!"

Forms that gentler Phidias wrought[5]
Michael Angelo left a proof   45
On the Sistine Chapel roof,
Where but half-awakened Adam
Can disturb globe-trotting Madam
Till her bowels are in heat,[6]
Proof that there's a purpose set   50
Before the secret working mind:
Profane perfection of mankind.

Quattrocento[7] put in paint
On backgrounds for a God or Saint
Gardens where a soul's at ease;   55
Where everything that meets the eye,
Flowers and grass and cloudless sky,
Resemble forms that are or seem
When sleepers wake and yet still dream,
And when it's vanished still declare,   60
With only bed and bedstead there,
That heavens had opened.
                    Gyres run on;
When that greater dream had gone
Calvert and Wilson, Blake and Claude,[8]
Prepared a rest for the people of God,   65
Palmer's phrase, but after that
Confusion fell upon our thought.

5

Irish poets, learn your trade,
Sing whatever is well made,
Scorn the sort now growing up   70
All out of shape from toe to top,
Their unremembering hearts and heads
Base-born products of base beds.
Sing the peasantry, and then
Hard-riding country gentlemen,   75
The holiness of monks, and after
Porter-drinkers'[9] randy laughter;
Sing the lords and ladies gay
That were beaten into the clay

---

5. Greek sculptor (5th century B.C.), generally
thought to have raised the classical ideal in art to
its highest culmination. Yeats here itemizes steps
in his history of knowledge and the arts, beginning
with Babylonian mathematics ("measurement"),
through "stark Egyptian thought," to the Renaissance of Michelangelo. Each of these steps is related
to Yeats's cyclical theory of history.
6. Cf. *Long-Legged Fly*, above, stanza 3.
7. 15th-century Italian art.
8. Works by the five artists mentioned in lines 64–

66 all provided images for Yeats's poetry: Edward
Calvert, 19th-century wood-engraver; Richard
Wilson, 18th-century landscape painter; William
Blake, "one of the great mythmakers and mask-
makers"; Claude Lorrain, 17th-century landscape
painter; and (in line 66) Samuel Palmer, 19th-
century landscape painter and etcher, one of whose
works was "The Lonely Tower." Calvert, Blake,
and Palmer knew one another and shared a view
of the holiness of art.
9. Drinkers of dark-brown bitter beer.

Through seven heroic centuries;   80
Cast your mind on other days
That we in coming days may be
Still the indomitable Irishry.

6

Under bare Ben Bulben's head
In Drumcliff churchyard Yeats is laid.   85
An ancestor was rector there[1]
Long years ago, a church stands near,
By the road an ancient cross.
No marble, no conventional phrase;
On limestone quarried near the spot   90
By his command these words are cut:

    Cast a cold eye
    On life, on death.
    Horseman, pass by!

September 1938   1939

From Reveries over Childhood and Youth[1]

[*The Yeats Family*]

Some six miles off towards Ben Bulben and beyond the Channel,[2] as we call the tidal river between Sligo and the Rosses, and on top of a hill there was a little square two-storied house covered with creepers and looking out upon a garden where the box borders were larger than any I had ever seen, and where I saw for the first time the crimson streak of the gladiolus and awaited its blossom with excitement. Under one gable a dark thicket of small trees made a shut-in mysterious place, where one played and believed that something was going to happen. My great-aunt Micky lived there. Micky was not her right name for she was Mary Yeats and her father had been my great-grandfather, John Yeats, who had been Rector of Drumcliffe, a few miles further off, and died in 1847. She was a spare, high-coloured, elderly woman and had the oldest-looking cat I had ever seen, for its hair had grown into matted locks of yellowy white. She farmed and had one old man-servant, but could not have farmed at all, had not neighbouring farmers helped to gather in the crops, in return for the loan of her farm implements and "out of respect for the family," for as Johnny MacGurk, the Sligo barber said to me, "The Yeats's were always very respectable." She was full of family history; all her dinner-knives were pointed like daggers through much cleaning, and there was a little James the First cream-jug with the Yeats

1. The Rev. John Yeats (1774–1847) was rector of Drumcliff from 1805.
1. Yeats wrote a variety of autobiographical essays between 1914 and 1928; these were originally published separately and later collected as *The Auto-* *biography of W. B. Yeats* (1936, 1953). The selections given here are from *Reveries over Childhood and Youth*, first published in 1915.
2. Yeats's favorite County Sligo landscape. Cf. the places named in *The Stolen Child*.

motto and crest, and on her dining-room mantel-piece a beautiful silver cup that had belonged to my great-great-grandfather, who had married a certain Mary Butler. It had upon it the Butler crest and had been already old at the date 1534, when the initials of some bride and bridegroom were engraved under the lip. All its history for generations was rolled up inside it upon a piece of paper yellow with age, until some caller took the paper to light his pipe.

Another family of Yeats, a widow and her two children on whom I called sometimes with my grandmother, lived near in a long low cottage, and owned a very fierce turkey-cock that did battle with their visitors; and some miles away lived the secretary to the Grand Jury and Land Agent, my great-uncle Mat Yeats and his big family of boys and girls; but I think it was only in later years that I came to know them well. I do not think any of these liked the Pollexfens, who were well off and seemed to them purse-proud, whereas they themselves had come down in the world. I remember them as very well-bred and very religious in the Evangelical way and thinking a good deal of Aunt Micky's old histories. There had been among our ancestors a King's County soldier, one of Marlborough's[3] generals, and when his nephew came to dine he gave him boiled pork, and when the nephew said he disliked boiled pork he had asked him to dine again and promised him something he would like better. However, he gave him boiled pork again and the nephew took the hint in silence. The other day as I was coming home from America, I met one of his descendants whose family has not another discoverable link with ours, and he too knew the boiled pork story and nothing else. We have the General's portrait, and he looks very fine in his armour and his long curly wig, and underneath it, after his name, are many honours that have left no tradition among us. Were we country people, we could have summarised his life in a legend. Other ancestors or great-uncles bore a part in Irish history; one saved the life of Sarsfield[4] at the battle of Sedgmoor; another, taken prisoner by King James's army, owed his to Sarsfield's gratitude; another, a century later, roused the gentlemen of Meath[5] against some local Jacquère,[6] and was shot dead upon a country road, and yet another "chased the United Irishmen[7] for a fortnight, fell into their hands and was hanged." The notorious Major Sirr, who arrested Lord Edward Fitzgerald[8] and gave him the bullet wound he died of in the jail, was godfather to several of my great-great-grandfather's children; while to make a balance, my great-grandfather had

3. John Churchill, Duke of Marlborough (1650–1722), English general in the War of the Spanish Succession (1702–13).
4. Patrick Sarsfield (d. 1693), Irish Jacobite general who served in the battle of Sedgemoor (1685) when the Duke of Monmouth, illegitimate son of Charles II who was claiming the throne from his uncle James II, was defeated and captured.
5. Maritime county in province of Leinster, in the east of Ireland.
6. Peasant revolutionary. The "Jacquerie" was a

peasants' revolt (1358) against the nobles in northern France (the term derived from *Jacques Bonhomme*, the nobility's contemptuous name for a peasant).
7. Irish society founded 1791 by Theobald Wolfe Tone which later was influential in causing the Irish rebellion of 1798.
8. British officer (1763–98) who, after dismissal from the army for disloyal activities, joined the United Irishmen. Cf. *September 1913*, lines 19–22.

been Robert Emmett's[9] friend and was suspected and imprisoned though
but for a few hours. One great-uncle fell at New Orleans in 1813, while
another, who became Governor of Penang,[1] led the forlorn hope at the
taking of Rangoon, and even in the last generation of all there had been
lives of some power and pleasure. An old man who had entertained
many famous people, in his eighteenth-century house, where battle-
ment and tower showed the influence of Horace Walpole,[2] had but lately,
after losing all his money, drowned himself, first taking off his rings and
chain and watch as became a collector of many beautiful things; and
once to remind us of more passionate life, a gunboat put into Rosses,
commanded by the illegitimate son of some great-uncle or other. Now
that I can look at their miniatures, turning them over to find the name
of soldier, or lawyer, or Castle official,[3] and wondering if they cared for
good books or good music, I am delighted with all that joins my life to
those who had power in Ireland or with those anywhere that were good
servants and poor bargainers, but I cared nothing as a child for Micky's
tales. I could see my grandfather's ships come up the bay or the river,
and his sailors treated me with deference, and a ship's carpenter made
and mended my toy boats and I thought that nobody could be so important as my grandfather. Perhaps, too, it is only now that I can value
those more gentle natures so unlike his passion and violence. An old
Sligo priest has told me how my great-grandfather John Yeats always
went into his kitchen rattling the keys, so much did he fear finding some
one doing wrong, and of a speech of his when the agent of the great
landowner of his parish brought him from cottage to cottage to bid the
women send their children to the Protestant school. All promised till
they came to one who cried, "Child of mine will never darken your
door." "Thank you, my woman," he said, "you are the first honest woman
I have met to-day." My uncle, Mat Yeats, the Land Agent, had once
waited up every night for a week to catch some boys who stole his apples
and when he caught them had given them six-pence and told them not
to do it again. Perhaps it is only fancy or the softening touch of the
miniaturist that makes me discover in their faces some courtesy and
much gentleness. Two eighteenth-century faces interest me the most,
one that of a great-great-grandfather, for both have under their powdered
curling wigs a half-feminine charm, and as I look at them I discover a
something clumsy and heavy in myself. Yet it was a Yeats who spoke
the only eulogy that turns my head: "We have ideas and no passions,
but by marriage with a Pollexfen we have given a tongue to the sea
cliffs."

9. 1778–1803; Irish patriot, hanged at Dublin for
treason.
1. Island in Malaya. Rangoon, capital of Burma,
was taken by the British in 1824.
2. The 18th-century English author whose pseudo-
Gothic house, Strawberry Hill, much influenced

subsequent "Gothic" architecture in England and
elsewhere.
3. Official at Dublin Castle, where the Viceroy
(representing the British Crown) lived with his staff
before Irish independence was achieved in 1922.

Among the miniatures there is a larger picture, an admirable drawing by I know not what master, that is too harsh and merry for its company. He was a connection and close friend of my great-grandmother Corbet, and though we spoke of him as "Uncle Beattie" in our childhood, no blood relation. My great-grandmother who died at ninety-three had many memories of him. He was the friend of Goldsmith and was accustomed to boast, clergyman though he was, that he belonged to a hunt-club of which every member but himself had been hanged or transported for treason, and that it was not possible to ask him a question he could not reply to with a perfectly appropriate blasphemy or indecency.

[An Irish Literature]

From these debates, from O'Leary's[4] conversation, and from the Irish books he lent or gave me has come all I have set my hand to since. I had begun to know a great deal about the Irish poets who had written in English. I read with excitement books I should find unreadable to-day, and found romance in lives that had neither wit nor adventure. I did not deceive myself, I knew how often they wrote a cold and abstract language, and yet I who had never wanted to see the houses where Keats and Shelley lived would ask everybody what sort of place Inchedony was, because Callanan[5] had named after it a bad poem in the manner of *Childe Harold*. Walking home from a debate, I remember saying to some college student, "Ireland cannot put from her the habits learned from her old military civilisation and from a church that prays in Latin. Those popular poets have not touched her heart, her poetry when it comes will be distinguished and lonely." O'Leary had once said to me, "Neither Ireland nor England knows the good from the bad in any art, but Ireland unlike England does not hate the good when it is pointed out to her." I began to plot and scheme how one might seal with the right image the soft wax before it began to harden. I had noticed that Irish Catholics among whom had been born so many political martyrs had not the good taste, the household courtesy and decency of the Protestant Ireland I had known, yet Protestant Ireland seemed to think of nothing but getting on in the world. I thought we might bring the halves together if we had a national literature that made Ireland beautiful in the memory, and yet had been freed from provincialism by an exacting criticism, an European pose.

1915

---

4. John O'Leary (d. 1907), an Irish nationalist, for whom Yeats had great respect. Cf. *September 1913* ("Romantic Ireland's dead and gone, / It's with O'Leary in the grave").

5. Jeremiah John Callanan, Anglo-Irish poet, published *The Recluse of Inchedony and Other Poems* in 1830.

VIRGINIA WOOLF
1882–1941

1912:   Marries Leonard Woolf.
1921:   *Monday or Tuesday.*
1925:   *Mrs. Dalloway.*

Virginia Woolf was born in London, daughter of Leslie Stephen, the Victorian critic, philosopher, biographer, and scholar. She grew up as a member of a large and talented family, educating herself in her father's magnificent library, meeting in childhood many eminent Victorians, learning Greek from Walter Pater's sister. After her father's death in 1904 she settled with her sister and two brothers in Bloomsbury, that district of London which later was to become associated with her and the group among whom she moved. The "Bloomsbury group" included Lytton Strachey, the biographer; J. M. Keynes, the eminent economist; Roger Fry, an art critic; and E. M. Forster. When her sister Vanessa, a notable painter, married Clive Bell, an art critic, in 1907, she and her brother took together another house in Bloomsbury, and there they entertained their literary and artistic friends at evening gatherings where the conversation sparkled. Their intelligence was equaled by their frankness, notably on sexual topics, and the sexual life of "Bloomsbury" provided ample material for discussion. The painter Duncan Grant, for example, was at different times the lover of Maynard Keynes, Virginia Woolf's brother Adrian and her sister Vanessa, and he was the father of Vanessa's daughter, Angelica. Virginia was herself bisexual and, thirteen years after her marriage to the journalist and essayist Leonard Woolf, she fell passionately in love with the poet Vita [Victoria] Sackville-West, wife of the bisexual diplomat and author, Harold Nicolson. Woolf's relationship with this aristocratic lesbian was to produce the most light-hearted and scintillating of her books, *Orlando* (1928). She was fortunate to have a husband as supportive emotionally as he was intellectually, and their marriage withstood this and other strains. Together they founded the Hogarth Press in 1917—a press which published some of the most interesting literature of our time, including an early volume of Eliot's poems (1919) and his *Homage to John Dryden* (1924) as well as her own novels. Her suicide in March 1941, resulting from her dread of World War II and her fear that she was about to lose her mind and become a burden on her husband, first revealed to the public that she had been subject to periods of nervous depression, particularly after finishing a book, and that underneath the liveliness and wit so well known among the Bloomsbury group lay disturbing pyschological tensions.

Woolf came naturally into the profession of writing. Moving among writers and artists, her world was from the beginning the cultured world of the middle-class and upper-middle-class London intelligentsia. She rebelled against what she called the "materialism" of such novelists as Arnold Bennett and John Galsworthy, and sought a more delicate rendering of those aspects of consciousness in which she felt that the truth of human experience really lay. After two novels cast rather cumbersomely in traditional form, she developed her own style, which handled the "stream of consciousness" with a carefully modulated poetic flow and brought into prose fiction something of the rhythms and the imagery of lyric poetry. The sketches in which she explored the possibilities of moving between action and contemplation, between specific external events in time and delicate tracings of the flow of consciousness where the mind moves between retrospect and anticipation, were collected in *Monday or Tuesday* (1921). These were technical experiments, and they made possible those later novels where her characteristic method is fully developed—*Jacob's Room* (1922); *Mrs. Dalloway* (1925), the first completely successful novel in her "new" style; *To the Lighthouse* (1927); *The Waves* (1931), the most stylized of her novels; and *Between the Acts* (1941), published after her death. She was a skilled exponent of the "stream of consciousness" technique in her novels, exploring with great subtlety problems of personal identity and personal relationships as well as the significance of time, change, and memory for human personality.

Woolf was increasingly concerned with the position of women, especially professional women, and the constrictions they suffered under. She wrote several cogent essays on the subject, notably in *A Room of One's Own* (1929) and *Three Guineas* (1938). Her novel *The Years* (1937) was originally to have included reflections on the position of women interspersed amid the action, but she later decided to publish them as a separate book, which became *Three Guineas*.

She also wrote a great many reviews and critical essays, collected in *The Common Reader* (1925) and *The Second Common Reader* (1932); informal and personal in tone, her criticism is suggestive rather than authoritative and has an engaging air of spontaneity. She is equally concerned with her own craft as a writer and with what it was like to be a quite different person living in a different age. At once more informal and more revealing are the six volumes of her *Letters* (1975–1980) and five volumes of her *Diary* (1977–1984). These, with their running commentary on her life and work, resemble the sketchbooks of a great painter and serve as a reminder that her writings, for all their variety, have the coherence found only in the greatest writers.

The Mark on the Wall

Perhaps it was the middle of January in the present year that I first looked up and saw the mark on the wall. In order to fix a date it is necessary to remember what one saw. So now I think of the fire; the steady film of yellow light upon the page of my book; the three chrysanthemums in the round glass bowl on the mantelpiece. Yes, it must have been the winter time, and we had just finished our tea, for I remember that I was smoking a cigarette when I looked up and saw the mark on the wall for the first time. I looked up through the smoke of my cigarette and my eye lodged for a moment upon the burning coals, and that old fancy of the crimson flag flapping from the castle tower came into my mind, and I thought of the cavalcade of red knights riding up the side of the black rock. Rather to my relief the sight of the mark interrupted the fancy, for it is an old fancy, an automatic fancy, made as a child perhaps. The mark was a small round mark, black upon the white wall, about six or seven inches above the mantelpiece.

How readily our thoughts swarm upon a new object, lifting it a little way, as ants carry a blade of straw so feverishly, and then leave it. . . . If that mark was made by a nail, it can't have been for a picture, it must have been for a miniature—the miniature of a lady with white powdered curls, powder-dusted cheeks, and lips like red carnations. A fraud of course, for the people who had this house before us would have chosen pictures in that way—an old picture for an old room. That is the sort of people they were—very interesting people, and I think of them so often, in such queer places, because one will never see them again, never know what happened next. They wanted to leave this house because they wanted to change their style of furniture, so he said, and he was in process of saying that in his opinion art should have ideas behind it when we were torn asunder, as one is torn from the old lady about to pour out tea and the young man about to hit the tennis ball in the back garden of the suburban villa as one rushes past in the train.

But for that mark, I'm not sure about it; I don't believe it was made by a nail after all; it's too big, too round, for that. I might get up, but if I got up and looked at it, ten to one I shouldn't be able to say for certain; because once a thing's done, no one ever knows how it happened. Oh! dear me, the mystery of life; the inaccuracy of thought! The ignorance of humanity! To show how very little control of our possessions we have— what an accidental affair this living is after all our civilisation—let me just count over a few of the things lost in one lifetime, beginning, for that seems always the most mysterious of losses—what cat would gnaw, what rat would nibble—three pale blue canisters of book-binding tools? Then there were the bird cages, the iron hoops, the steel skates, the Queen Anne coal-scuttle, the bagatelle board, the hand organ—all gone, and jewels, too. Opals and emeralds, they lie about the roots of turnips. What a scraping paring affair it is to be sure! The wonder is that I've any clothes on my back, that I sit surrounded by solid furniture at this moment. Why, if one wants to compare life to anything, one must liken it to being blown through the Tube[1] at fifty miles an hour—landing at the other end without a single hairpin in one's hair! Shot out at the feet of God entirely naked! Tumbling head over heels in the asphodel meadows[2] like brown paper parcels pitched down a shoot in the post office! With one's hair flying back like the tail of a race-horse. Yes, that seems to express the rapidity of life, the perpetual waste and repair; all so casual, all so haphazard. . . .

But after life. The slow pulling down of thick green stalks so that the cup of the flower, as it turns over, deluges one with purple and red light. Why, after all, should one not be born there as one is born here, help-less, speechless, unable to focus one's eyesight, groping at the roots of the grass, at the toes of the Giants? As for saying which are trees, and

1. London underground railway, or subway.
2. I.e., heaven, the next world (in Greek mythology, asphodel flowers grow in the Elysian fields).

which are men and women, or whether there are such things, that one won't be in a condition to do for fifty years or so. There will be nothing but spaces of light and dark, intersected by thick stalks, and rather higher up perhaps, rose-shaped blots of an indistinct colour—dim pinks and blues—which will, as time goes on, become more definite, become—I don't know what. . . .

And yet that mark on the wall is not a hole at all. It may even be caused by some round black substance, such as a small rose leaf, left over from the summer, and I, not being a very vigilant housekeeper— look at the dust on the mantelpiece, for example, the dust which, so they say, buried Troy three times over, only fragments of pots utterly refusing annihilation, as one can believe.

The tree outside the window taps very gently on the pane. . . . I want to think quietly, calmly, spaciously, never to be interrupted, never to have to rise from my chair, to slip easily from one thing to another, without any sense of hostility, or obstacle. I want to sink deeper and deeper, away from the surface, with its hard separate facts. To steady myself, let me catch hold of the first idea that passes . . . Shakespeare. . . . Well, he will do as well as another. A man who sat himself solidly in an arm-chair, and looked into the fire, so— A shower of ideas fell perpetually from some very high Heaven down through his mind. He leant his forehead on his hand, and people, looking in through the open door—for this scene is supposed to take place on a summer's evening— But how dull this is, this historical fiction! It doesn't interest me at all. I wish I could hit upon a pleasant track of thought, a track indirectly reflecting credit upon myself, for those are the pleasantest thoughts, and very frequent even in the minds of modest mouse-coloured people, who believe genuinely that they dislike to hear their own praises. They are not thoughts directly praising oneself; that is the beauty of them; they are thoughts like this:

"And then I came into the room. They were discussing botany. I said how I'd seen a flower growing on a dust heap on the site of an old house in Kingsway.[3] The seed, I said, must have been sown in the reign of Charles the First. What flowers grew in the reign of Charles the First?" I asked— (But I don't remember the answer.) Tall flowers with purple tassels to them perhaps. And so it goes on. All the time I'm dressing up the figure of myself in my own mind, lovingly, stealthily, not openly adoring it, for if I did that, I should catch myself out, and stretch my hand at once for a book in self-protection. Indeed, it is curious how instinctively one protects the image of oneself from idolatry or any other handling that could make it ridiculous, or too unlike the original to be believed in any longer. Or is it not so very curious after all? It is a matter of great importance. Suppose the looking-glass smashes, the image disappears, and the romantic figure with the green of forest depths all about it is there no longer, but only that shell of a person which is seen by

3. Street in London.

other people—what an airless, shallow, bald, prominent world it becomes! A world not to be lived in. As we face each other in omnibuses and underground railways we are looking into the mirror; that accounts for the vagueness, the gleam of glassiness, in our eyes. And the novelists in future will realize more and more the importance of these reflections, for of course there is not one reflection but an almost infinite number; those are the depths they will explore, those the phantoms they will pursue, leaving the description of reality more and more out of their stories, taking a knowledge of it for granted, as the Greeks did and Shakespeare perhaps—but these generalizations are very worthless. The military sound of the word is enough. It recalls leading articles, cabinet ministers—a whole class of things indeed which, as a child, one thought the thing itself, the standard thing, the real thing, from which one could not depart save at the risk of nameless damnation. Generalizations bring back somehow Sunday in London, Sunday afternoon walks, Sunday luncheons, and also ways of speaking of the dead, clothes, and habits—like the habit of sitting all together in one room until a certain hour, although nobody liked it. There was a rule for everything. The rule for tablecloths at that particular period was that they should be made of tapestry with little yellow compartments marked upon them, such as you may see in photographs of the carpets in the corridors of the royal palaces. Tablecloths of a different kind were not real tablecloths. How shocking, and yet how wonderful it was to discover that these real things, Sunday luncheons, Sunday walks, country houses, and tablecloths were not entirely real, were indeed half phantoms, and the damnation which visited the disbeliever in them was only a sense of illegitimate freedom. What now takes the place of those things I wonder, those real standard things? Men perhaps, should you be a woman; the masculine point of view which governs our lives, which sets the standard, which establishes Whitaker's Table of Precedency,[4] which has become, I suppose, since the war, half a phantom to many men and women, which soon, one may hope, will be laughed into the dustbin where the phantoms go, the mahogany sideboards and the Landseer[5] prints, Gods and Devils, Hell and so forth, leaving us all with an intoxicating sense of illegitimate freedom—if freedom exists. . . .

In certain lights that mark on the wall seems actually to project from the wall. Nor is it entirely circular. I cannot be sure, but it seems to cast a perceptible shadow, suggesting that if I ran my finger down that strip of the wall it would, at a certain point, mount and descend a small tumulus, a smooth tumulus like those barrows[6] on the South Downs which are, they say, either tombs or camps. Of the two I should prefer

---

4. *Whitaker's Almanack*, an annual compendium of information, prints a "Table of Precedency," which shows the order in which the various ranks in public life and society proceed on formal occasions.
5. Edwin Henry Landseer, 19th-century animal painter, reproductions of whose *Stag at Bay*,

Monarch of the Glen, and similar paintings were often found in Victorian homes.
6. Mounds of earth or stones erected by prehistoric peoples, usually as burial places; the South Downs are a range of low hills in southeastern England.

them to be tombs, desiring melancholy like most English people, and
finding it natural at the end of a walk to think of the bones stretched
beneath the turf. . . . There must be some book about it. Some antiquary must have dug up those bones and given them a name. . . . What
sort of a man is an antiquary, I wonder? Retired Colonels for the most
part, I daresay, leading parties of aged labourers to the top here, examining clods of earth and stone, and getting into correspondence with the
neighbouring clergy, which, being opened at breakfast time, gives them
a feeling of importance, and the comparison of arrow-heads necessitates
cross-country journeys to the country towns, an agreeable necessity both
to them and to their elderly wives, who wish to make plum jam or to
clean out the study, and have every reason for keeping that great question of the camp or the tomb in perpetual suspension, while the Colonel
himself feels agreeably philosophic in accumulating evidence on both
sides of the question. It is true that he does finally incline to believe in
the camp; and, being opposed, indites a pamphlet which he is about to
read at the quarterly meeting of the local society when a stroke lays him
low, and his last conscious thoughts are not of wife or child, but of the
camp and that arrow-head there, which is now in the case at the local
museum, together with the foot of a Chinese murderess, a handful of
Elizabethan nails, a great many Tudor clay pipes, a piece of Roman
pottery, and the wineglass that Nelson drank out of—proving I really
don't know what.

   No, no, nothing is proved, nothing is known. And if I were to get up
at this very moment and ascertain that the mark on the wall is really—
what shall we say?—the head of a gigantic old nail, driven in two hundred
years ago, which has now, owing to the patient attrition of many generations of housemaids, revealed its head above the coat of paint, and is
taking its first view of modern life in the sight of a white-walled fire-lit
room, what should I gain?—Knowledge? Matter for further speculation?
I can think sitting still as well as standing up. And what is knowledge?
What are our learned men save the descendants of witches and hermits
who crouched in caves and in woods brewing herbs, interrogating shrew-
mice and writing down the language of the stars? And the less we honour
them as our superstitions dwindle and our respect for beauty and health
of mind increases. . . . Yes, one could imagine a very pleasant world.
A quiet, spacious world, with the flowers so red and blue in the open
fields. A world without professors or specialists or house-keepers with the
profiles of policemen, a world which one could slice with one's thought
as a fish slices the water with his fin, grazing the stems of the water-
lilies, hanging suspended over nests of white sea eggs. . . . How peaceful
it is down here, rooted in the centre of the world and gazing up through
the grey waters, with their sudden gleams of light, and their reflections—
if it were not for Whitaker's Almanack—if it were not for the Table of
Precedency!

   I must jump up and see for myself what that mark on the wall really
is—a nail, a rose-leaf, a crack in the wood?

Here is nature once more at her old game of self-preservation. This train of thought, she perceives, is threatening mere waste of energy, even some collision with reality, for who will ever be able to lift a finger against Whitaker's Table of Precedency? The Archbishop of Canterbury is followed by the Lord High Chancellor; the Lord High Chancellor is followed by the Archbishop of York. Everybody follows somebody, such is the philosophy of Whitaker; and the great thing is to know who follows whom. Whitaker knows, and let that, so Nature counsels, comfort you, instead of enraging you; and if you can't be comforted, if you must shatter this hour of peace, think of the mark on the wall.

I understand Nature's game—her prompting to take action as a way of ending any thought that threatens to excite or to pain. Hence, I suppose, comes our slight contempt for men of action—men, we assume, who don't think. Still, there's no harm in putting a full stop to one's disagreeable thoughts by looking at a mark on the wall.

Indeed, now that I have fixed my eyes upon it, I feel that I have grasped a plank in the sea; I feel a satisfying sense of reality which at once turns the two Archbishops and the Lord High Chancellor to the shadows of shades. Here is something definite, something real. Thus, waking from a midnight dream of horror, one hastily turns on the light and lies quiescent, worshipping the chest of drawers, worshipping solidity, worshipping reality, worshipping the impersonal world which is a proof of some existence other than ours. That is what one wants to be sure of. . . . Wood is a pleasant thing to think about. It comes from a tree; and trees grow, and we don't know how they grow. For years and years they grow, without paying any attention to us, in meadows, in forests, and by the side of rivers—all things one likes to think about. The cows swish their tails beneath them on hot afternoons; they paint rivers so green that when a moorhen dives one expects to see its feathers all green when it comes up again. I like to think of the fish balanced against the stream like flags blown out; and of water-beetles slowly raising domes of mud upon the bed of the river. I like to think of the tree itself: first of the close dry sensation of being wood; then the grinding of the storm; then the slow, delicious ooze of sap; I like to think of it, too, on winter's nights standing in the empty field with all leaves close-furled, nothing tender exposed to the iron bullets of the moon, a naked mast upon an earth that goes tumbling, tumbling, all night long. The song of birds must sound very loud and strange in June; and how cold the feet of insects must feel upon it, as they make laborious progresses up the creases of the bark, or sun themselves upon the thin green awning of the leaves, and look straight in front of them with diamond-cut red eyes. . . . One by one the fibres snap beneath the immense cold pressure of the earth, then the last storm comes and, falling, the highest branches drive deep into the ground again. Even so, life isn't done with; there are a million patient, watchful lives still for a tree, all over the world, in bedrooms, in ships, on the pavement, living rooms, where men and women sit after tea, smoking cigarettes. It is full of peaceful thoughts, happy thoughts, this tree. I should like to take each one separately—but something is getting in the way. . . . Where was I? What has it all been about? A tree? A river? The Downs? Whitaker's Almanack? The fields of asphodel? I can't remember a thing. Everything's moving, falling, slipping, vanishing. . . . There is a vast upheaval of matter. Someone is standing over me and saying:

"I'm going out to buy a newspaper."

"Yes?"

"Though it's no good buying newspapers. . . . Nothing ever happens. Curse this war; God damn this war! . . . All the same, I don't see why we should have a snail on our wall."

Ah, the mark on the wall! It was a snail.

1921

Modern Fiction

In making any survey, even the freest and loosest, of modern fiction, it is difficult not to take it for granted that the modern practice of the art is somehow an improvement upon the old. With their simple tools and primitive materials, it might be said, Fielding[1] did well and Jane Austen even better, but compare their opportunities with ours! Their masterpieces certainly have a strange air of simplicity. And yet the analogy between literature and the process, to choose an example, of making motor cars scarcely holds good beyond the first glance. It is doubtful whether in the course of the centuries, though we have learnt much about making machines, we have learnt anything about making literature. We do not come to write better; all that we can be said to do is to keep moving, now a little in this direction, now in that, but with a circular tendency should the whole course of the track be viewed from a sufficiently lofty pinnacle. It need scarcely be said that we make no claim to stand, even momentarily, upon that vantage-ground. On the flat, in the crowd, half blind with dust, we look back with envy to those happier warriors, whose battle is won and whose achievements wear so serene an air of accomplishment that we can scarcely refrain from whispering that the fight was not so fierce for them as for us. It is for the historian of literature to decide; for him to say if we are now beginning or ending or standing in the middle of a great period of prose fiction, for down in the plain little is visible. We only know that certain gratitudes and hostilities inspire us; that certain paths seem to lead to fertile land, others to the dust and the desert; and of this perhaps it may be worth while to attempt some account.

Our quarrel, then, is not with the classics, and if we speak of quarrelling with Mr. Wells, Mr. Bennett, and Mr. Galsworthy;[2] it is partly that by the mere fact of their existence in the flesh their work has a living,

1. The novelist Henry Fielding (1707–1754).
2. The novelists H. G. Wells (1866–1946), Arnold Bennett (1867–1931), and John Galsworthy (1867–1933).

breathing, everyday imperfection which bids us take what liberties with it we choose. But it is also true, that, while we thank them for a thousand gifts, we reserve our unconditional gratitude for Mr. Hardy, for Mr. Conrad, and in much lesser degree for the Mr. Hudson of *The Purple Land, Green Mansions,* and *Far Away and Long Ago.*[3] Mr. Wells, Mr. Bennett, and Mr. Galsworthy have excited so many hopes and disappointed them so persistently that our gratitude largely takes the form of thanking them for having shown us what they might have done but have not done; what we certainly could not do, but as certainly, perhaps, do not wish to do. No single phrase will sum up the charge or grievance which we have to bring against a mass of work so large in its volume and embodying so many qualities, both admirable and the reverse. If we tried to formulate our meaning in one word we should say that these three writers are materialists. It is because they are concerned not with the spirit but with the body that they have disappointed us, and left us with the feeling that the sooner English fiction turns its back upon them, as politely as may be, and marches, if only into the desert, the better for its soul. Naturally, no single word reaches the centre of three separate targets. In the case of Mr. Wells it falls notably wide of the mark. And yet even with him it indicates to our thinking the fatal alloy in his genius, the great clod of clay that has got itself mixed up with the purity of his inspiration. But Mr. Bennett is perhaps the worst culprit of the three, inasmuch as he is by far the best workman. He can make a book so well constructed and solid in its craftsmanship that it is difficult for the most exacting of critics to see through what chink or crevice decay can creep in. There is not so much as a draught between the frames of the windows, or a crack in the boards. And yet—if life should refuse to live there? That is a risk which the creator of *The Old Wives' Tale,* George Cannon, Edwin Clayhanger,[4] and hosts of other figures, may well claim to have surmounted. His characters live abundantly, even unexpectedly, but it remains to ask how do they live, and what do they live for? More and more they seem to us, deserting even the well-built villa in the Five Towns,[5] to spend their time in some softly padded first-class railway carriage, pressing bells and buttons innumerable; and the destiny to which they travel so luxuriously becomes more and more unquestionably an eternity of bliss spent in the very best hotel in Brighton.[6] It can scarcely be said of Mr. Wells that he is a materialist in the sense that he takes too much delight in the solidity of his fabric. His mind is too generous in its sympathies to allow him to spend much time in making things shipshape and substantial. He is a materialist from sheer goodness of heart, taking upon his shoulders the work that ought to have been discharged by Government officials, and in the plethora of his ideas and facts scarcely

---

3. W. H. Hudson (1841–1922), naturalist and writer, was born in Argentina, though he later lived in London. *The Purple Land* (1885) is about South America; *Green Mansions* (1904), a novel set in South America, was his first real success.
4. Characters in Arnold Bennett's novels; *The Old*

Wives' Tale (1908) is his best known novel.
5. The pottery towns of Staffordshire in which many of Bennett's novels and stories were set.
6. One-time fashionable seaside resort on southwest coast of England.

having leisure to realize, or forgetting to think important, the crudity and coarseness of his human beings. Yet what more damaging criticism can there be both of his earth and of his Heaven than that they are to be inhabited here and hereafter by his Joans and his Peters? Does not the inferiority of their natures tarnish whatever institutions and ideals may be provided for them by the generosity of their creator? Nor, profoundly though we respect the integrity and humanity of Mr. Galsworthy, shall we find what we seek in his pages.

If we fasten, then, one label on all these books, on which is one word, materialists, we mean by it that they write of unimportant things; that they spend immense skill and immense industry making the trivial and the transitory appear the true and the enduring.

We have to admit that we are exacting, and, further, that we find it difficult to justify our discontent by explaining what it is that we exact. We frame our question differently at different times. But it reappears most persistently as we drop the finished novel on the crest of a sigh—Is it worth while? What is the point of it all? Can it be that, owing to one of those little deviations which the human spirit seems to make from time to time, Mr. Bennett has come down with his magnificent apparatus for catching life just an inch or two on the wrong side? Life escapes; and perhaps without life nothing else is worth while. It is a confession of vagueness to have to make use of such a figure as this, but we scarcely better the matter by speaking, as critics are prone to do, of reality. Admitting the vagueness which afflicts all criticism of novels, let us hazard the opinion that for us at this moment the form of fiction most in vogue more often misses then secures the thing we seek. Whether we call it life or spirit, truth or reality, this, the essential thing, has moved off, or on, and refuses to be contained any longer in such ill-fitting vestments as we provide. Nevertheless, we go on perseveringly, conscientiously, constructing our two and thirty chapters after a design which more and more ceases to resemble the vision in our minds. So much of the enormous labour of proving the solidity, the likeness to life, of the story is not merely labour thrown away but labour misplaced to the extent of obscuring and blotting out the light of the conception. The writer seems constrained, not by his own free will but by some powerful and unscrupulous tyrant who has him in thrall, to provide a plot, to provide comedy, tragedy, love interest, and an air of probability embalming the whole so impeccable that if all his figures were to come to life they would find themselves dressed down to the last button of their coats in the fashion of the hour. The tyrant is obeyed; the novel is done to a turn. But sometimes, more and more often as time goes by, we suspect a momentary doubt, a spasm of rebellion, as the pages fill themselves in the customary way. Is life like this? Must novels be like this?

Look within and life, it seems, is very far from being "like this." Examine for a moment an ordinary mind on an ordinary day. The mind receives a myriad impressions—trivial, fantastic, evanescent, or engraved with the sharpness of steel. From all sides they come, an incessant shower of innumerable atoms; and as they fall, as they shape themselves into the life of Monday or Tuesday,[7] the accent falls differently from of old; the moment of importance came not here but there; so that, if a writer were a free man and not a slave, if he could write what he chose, not what he must, if he could base his work upon his own feeling and not upon convention, there would be no plot, no comedy, no tragedy, no love interest or catastrophe in the accepted style, and perhaps not a single button sewn on as the Bond Street[8] tailors would have it. Life is not a series of gig-lamps[9] symmetrically arranged; life is a luminous halo, a semi-transparent envelope surrounding us from the beginning of consciousness to the end. Is it not the task of the novelist to convey this varying, this unknown and uncircumscribed spirit, whatever aberration or complexity it may display, with as little mixture of the alien and external as possible? We are not pleading merely for courage and sincerity; we are suggesting that the proper stuff of fiction is a little other than custom would have us believe it.

It is, at any rate, in some such fashion as this that we seek to define the quality which distinguishes the work of several young writers, among whom Mr. James Joyce is the most notable, from that of their predecessors. They attempt to come closer to life, and to preserve more sincerely and exactly what interests and moves them, even if to do so they must discard most of the conventions which are commonly observed by the novelist. Let us record the atoms as they fall upon the mind in the order in which they fall, let us trace the pattern, however disconnected and incoherent in appearance, which each sight or incident scores upon the consciousness. Let us not take it for granted that life exists more fully in what is commonly thought big than in what is commonly thought small. Anyone who has read *The Portrait of the Artist as a Young Man* or, what promises to be a far more interesting work, *Ulysses*,[1] now appearing in the *Little Review*, will have hazarded some theory of this nature as to Mr. Joyce's intention. On our part, with such a fragment before us, it is hazarded rather than affirmed; but whatever the intention of the whole, there can be no question but that it is of the utmost sincerity and that the result, difficult or unpleasant as we may judge it, is undeniably important. In contrast with those whom we have called materialists, Mr. Joyce is spiritual; he is concerned at all costs to reveal the flickerings of that innermost flame which flashes its messages through the brain, and in order to preserve it he disregards with complete courage whatever seems to him adventitious, whether it be probability, or coherence, or any other of these signposts which for generations have served to support the imagination of a reader when called upon to imagine what he can neither touch nor see. The scene in the cemetery,[2] for instance, with its brilliancy, its sordidity, its incoherence, its sudden lightning flashes of

---

7. *Monday or Tuesday* was the title of the collection of experimental stories and sketches that Woolf brought out in 1921.
8. Fashionable shopping street in London.

9. Carriage lamps.
1. "Written April, 1919" [Woolf's note].
2. The sixth episode ("Hades") of *Ulysses*, where Bloom goes to Paddy Dignam's funeral.

significance, does undoubtedly come so close to the quick of the mind that, on a first reading at any rate, it is difficult not to acclaim a masterpiece. If we want life itself, here surely we have it. Indeed, we find ourselves fumbling rather awkwardly if we try to say what else we wish, and for what reason a work of such originality yet fails to compare, for we must take high examples, with *Youth* or *The Mayor of Casterbridge*.[3] It fails because of the comparative poverty of the writer's mind, we might say simply and have done with it. But it is possible to press a little further and wonder whether we may not refer our sense of being in a bright yet narrow room, confined and shut in, rather than enlarged and set free, to some limitation imposed by the method as well as by the mind. Is it the method that inhibits the creative power? Is it due to the method that we feel neither jovial nor magnanimous, but centred in a self which, in spite of its tremor of susceptibility, never embraces or creates what is outside itself and beyond? Does the emphasis laid, perhaps didactically, upon indecency contribute to the effect of something angular and isolated? Or is it merely that in any effort of such originality it is much easier, for contemporaries especially, to feel what it lacks than to name what it gives? In any case it is a mistake to stand outside examining "methods". Any method is right, every method is right, that expresses what we wish to express, if we are writers; that brings us closer to the novelist's intention if we are readers. This method has the merit of bringing us closer to what we were prepared to call life itself; did not the reading of *Ulysses* suggest how much of life is excluded or ignored, and did it not come with a shock to open *Tristram Shandy* or even *Pendennis*[4] and be by them convinced that there are not only other aspects of life, but more important ones into the bargain.

However this may be, the problem before the novelist at present, as we suppose it to have been in the past, is to contrive means of being free to set down what he chooses. He has to have the courage to say that what interests him is no longer "this" but "that": out of "that" alone must he construct his work. For the moderns "that", the point of interest, lies very likely in the dark places of psychology. At once, therefore, the accent falls a little differently; the emphasis is upon something hitherto ignored; at once a different outline of form becomes necessary, difficult for us to grasp, incomprehensible to our predecessors. No one but a modern, no one perhaps but a Russian, would have felt the interest of the situation which Tchekov[5] has made into the short story which he calls "Gusev." Some Russian soldiers lie ill on board a ship which is taking them back to Russia. We are given a few scraps of their talk and some of their thoughts; then one of them dies and is carried away; the talk goes on among the others for a time, until Gusev himself dies, and looking "like a carrot or a radish" is thrown overboard. The emphasis is laid upon such unexpected places that at first it seems as if there were

---

3. Stories by, respectively, Joseph Conrad and Thomas Hardy.
4. Novels by, respectively, Laurence Sterne (1713–

1768) and William Makepeace Thackeray (1811–1863).
5. Anton Pavlovich Chekhov (1860–1904).

no emphasis at all; and then, as the eyes accustom themselves to twilight and discern the shapes of things in a room we see how complete the story is, how profound, and how truly in obedience to his vision Tchekov has chosen this, that, and the other, and placed them together to compose something new. But it is impossible to say "this is comic," or "that is tragic," nor are we certain, since short stories, we have been taught, should be brief and conclusive, whether this, which is vague and inconclusive, should be called a short story at all.

The most elementary remarks upon modern English fiction can hardly avoid some mention of the Russian influence, and if the Russians are mentioned one runs the risk of feeling that to write of any fiction save theirs is waste of time. If we want understanding of the soul and heart where else shall we find it of comparable profundity? If we are sick of our own materialism the least considerable of their novelists has by right of birth a natural reverence for the human spirit. "Learn to make yourself akin to people. . . . But let this sympathy be not with the mind—for it is easy with the mind—but with the heart, with love towards them." In every great Russian writer we seem to discern the features of a saint, if sympathy for the sufferings of others, love towards them, endeavour to reach some goal worthy of the most exacting demands of the spirit constitute saintliness. It is the saint in them which confounds us with a feeling of our own irreligious triviality, and turns so many of our famous novels to tinsel and trickery. The conclusions of the Russian mind, thus comprehensive and compassionate, are inevitably, perhaps, of the utmost sadness. More accurately indeed we might speak of the inconclusiveness of the Russian mind. It is the sense that there is no answer, that if honestly examined life presents question after question which must be left to sound on and on after the story is over in hopeless interrogation that fills us with a deep, and finally it may be with a resentful, despair. They are right perhaps; unquestionably they see further than we do and without our gross impediments of vision. But perhaps we see something that escapes them, or why should this voice of protest mix itself with our gloom? The voice of protest is the voice of another and an ancient civilization which seems to have bred in us the instinct to enjoy and fight rather than to suffer and understand. English fiction from Sterne to Meredith[6] bears witness to our natural delight in humour and comedy, in the beauty of earth, in the activities of the intellect, and in the splendour of the body. But any deductions that we may draw from the comparison of two fictions so immeasurably far apart are futile save indeed as they flood us with a view of the infinite possibilities of the art and remind us that there is no limit to the horizon, and that nothing—no "method," no experiment, even of the wildest—is forbidden, but only falsity and pretence. "The proper stuff of fiction" does not exist; everything is the proper stuff of fiction, every feeling, every thought; every quality of brain and spirit is drawn upon; no perception comes amiss.

---

6. The novelist George Meredith (1828–1909).

And if we can imagine the art of fiction come alive and standing in our midst, she would undoubtedly bid us break her and bully her, as well as honour and love her, for so her youth is renewed and her sovereignty assured.

1925

From A Room of One's Own

[Shakespeare's Sister][1]

It was disappointing not to have brought back in the evening some important statement, some authentic fact. Women are poorer than men because—this or that. Perhaps now it would be better to give up seeking for the truth, and receiving on one's head an avalanche of opinion hot as lava, discoloured as dish-water. It would be better to draw the curtains; to shut out distractions; to light the lamp; to narrow the enquiry and to ask the historian, who records not opinions but facts, to describe under what conditions women lived, not throughout the ages, but in England, say in the time of Elizabeth.

For it is a perennial puzzle why no woman wrote a word of that extraordinary literature when every other man, it seemed, was capable of song or sonnet. What were the conditions in which women lived, I asked myself; for fiction, imaginative work that is, is not dropped like a pebble upon the ground, as science may be; fiction is like a spider's web, attached ever so lightly perhaps, but still attached to life at all four corners. Often the attachment is scarcely perceptible; Shakespeare's plays, for instance, seem to hang there complete by themselves. But when the web is pulled askew, hooked up at the edge, torn in the middle, one remembers that these webs are not spun in midair by incorporeal creatures, but are the work of suffering human beings, and are attached to grossly material things, like health and money and the houses we live in.

I went, therefore, to the shelf where the histories stand and took down one of the latest, Professor Trevelyan's *History of England*.[2] Once more I looked up Women, found "position of," and turned to the pages indicated. "Wife-beating," I read, "was a recognised right of man, and was practised without shame by high as well as low. . . . Similarly," the historian goes on, "the daughter who refused to marry the gentleman of her parents' choice was liable to be locked up, beaten and flung about the room, without any shock being inflicted on public opinion. Marriage was not an affair of personal affection, but of family avarice, particularly in the "chivalrous" upper classes. . . . Betrothal often took place

---

1. The selection is drawn from chap. 3 and from the conclusion to the final chapter. In chap. 2, she has been to the library of the British Museum, trying in vain to find answers to questions about the different fates of men and women.

2. G. M. Trevelyan's *History of England* (1926) long held its place as the standard one-volume history of the country.

while one or both of the parties was in the cradle, and marriage when they were scarcely out of the nurses' charge." That was about 1470, soon after Chaucer's time. The next reference to the position of women is some two hundred years later, in the time of the Stuarts. "It was still the exception for women of the upper and middle class to choose their own husbands, and when the husband had been assigned, he was lord and master, so far at least as law and custom could make him. Yet even so," Professor Trevelyan concludes, "neither Shakespeare's women nor those of authentic seventeenth-century memoirs, like the Verneys and the Hutchinsons,[3] seem wanting in personality and character." Certainly, if we consider it, Cleopatra must have had a way with her; Lady Macbeth, one would suppose, had a will of her own; Rosalind, one might conclude, was an attractive girl.[4] Professor Trevelyan is speaking no more than the truth when he remarks that Shakespeare's women do not seem wanting in personality and character. Not being a historian, one might go even further and say that women have burnt like beacons in all the works of all the poets from the beginning of time—Clytemnestra, Antigone, Cleopatra, Lady Macbeth, Phèdre, Cressida, Rosalind, Desdemona, the Duchess of Malfi, among the dramatists; then among the prose writers: Millamant, Clarissa, Becky Sharp, Anna Karenina, Emma Bovary, Madame de Guermantes[5]—the names flock to mind, nor do they recall women "lacking in personality and character." Indeed, if woman had no existence save in the fiction written by men, one would imagine her a person of the utmost importance; very various; heroic and mean; splendid and sordid; infinitely beautiful and hideous in the extreme; as great as a man, some think even greater.[6] But this is woman in fiction. In fact, as Professor Trevelyan points out, she was locked up, beaten and flung about the room.

A very queer, composite being thus emerges. Imaginatively she is of the highest importance; practically she is completely insignificant. She pervades poetry from cover to cover; she is all but absent from history.

3. "The ideal family life of the period [1640–50] that ended in such tragic political division has been recorded once for all in the *Memoirs of the Verney Family*" (Trevelyan, *History of England*). Lucy Hutchinson (b. 1628) wrote the biography of her husband, Col. John Hutchinson (1616–1684); it was first published in 1806.
4. These three Shakespearean heroines are, respectively, in *Antony and Cleopatra*, *Macbeth*, and *As You Like It*.
5. Characters in, respectively, Aeschylus's *Agamemnon*, Sophocles's *Antigone*, Shakespeare's *Antony and Cleopatra* and *Macbeth*, Racine's *Phèdre*, Shakespeare's *Troilus and Cressida*, *As You Like It* and *Othello*, Webster's *The Duchess of Malfi*, Congreve's *Way of the World*, Richardson's *Clarissa*, Thackeray's *Vanity Fair*, Tolstoy's *Anna Karenina*, Flaubert's *Madame Bovary*, and Proust's *À la Récherche du Temps Perdu*.
6. " 'It remains a strange and almost inexplicable fact that in Athena's city, where women were kept in almost Oriental suppression as odalisques or

drudges, the stage should yet have produced figures like Clytemnestra and Cassandra, Atossa and Antigone, Phèdre and Medea, and all the other heroines who dominate play after play of the "misogynist" Euripides. But the paradox of this world where in real life a respectable woman could hardly show her face alone in the street, and yet on the stage woman equals or surpasses man, has never been satisfactorily explained. In modern tragedy the same predominance exists. At all events, a very cursory survey of Shakespeare's work (similarly with Webster, though not with Marlowe or Jonson) suffices to reveal how this dominance, this initiative of women, persists from Rosalind to Lady Macbeth. So too in Racine; six of his tragedies bear their heroines' names; and what male characters of his shall we set against Hermione and Andromaque, Bérénice and Roxane, Phèdre and Athalie? So again with Ibsen; what men shall we match with Solveig and Nora, Hedda and Hilda Wangel and Rebecca West?'—F. L. Lucas, *Tragedy*, pp. 114–15" [Woolf's note].

She dominates the lives of kings and conquerors in fiction; in fact she was the slave of any boy whose parents forced a ring upon her finger. Some of the most inspired words, some of the most profound thoughts in literature fall from her lips; in real life she could hardly read, could scarcely spell, and was the property of her husband.

It was certainly an odd monster that one made up by reading the historians first and the poets afterwards—a worm winged like an eagle; the spirit of life and beauty in a kitchen chopping up suet. But these monsters, however amusing to the imagination, have no existence in fact. What one must do to bring her to life was to think poetically and prosaically at one and the same moment, thus keeping in touch with fact—that she is Mrs. Martin, aged thirty-six, dressed in blue, wearing a black hat and brown shoes; but not losing sight of fiction either—that she is a vessel in which all sorts of spirits and forces are coursing and flashing perpetually. The moment, however, that one tries this method with the Elizabethan woman, one branch of illumination fails; one is held up by the scarcity of facts. One knows nothing detailed, nothing perfectly true and substantial about her. History scarcely mentions her. And I turned to Professor Trevelyan again to see what history meant to him. I found by looking at his chapter headings that it meant—

"The Manor Court and the Methods of Open-field Agriculture . . . The Cistercians and Sheep-farming . . . The Crusades . . . The University . . . The House of Commons . . . The Hundred Years' War . . . The Wars of the Roses. . . The Renaissance Scholars . . . The Dissolution of the Monasteries . . . Agrarian and Religious Strife . . . The Origin of English Sea-power . . . The Armada . . ." and so on. Occasionally an individual woman is mentioned, an Elizabeth, or a Mary; a queen or a great lady. But by no possible means could middle-class women with nothing but brains and character at their command have taken part in any one of the great movements which, brought together, constitute the historian's view of the past. Nor shall we find her in any collection of anecdotes. Aubrey[7] hardly mentions her. She never writes her own life and scarcely keeps a diary; there are only a handful of her letters in existence. She left no plays or poems by which we can judge her. What one wants, I thought—and why does not some brilliant student at Newnham or Girton[8] supply it?—is a mass of information; at what age did she marry; how many children had she as a rule; what was her house like; had she a room to herself; did she do the cooking; would she be likely to have a servant? All these facts lie somewhere, presumably, in parish registers and account books; the life of the average Elizabethan woman must be scattered about somewhere, could one collect it and make a book of it. It would be ambitious beyond my daring, I thought, looking about the shelves for books that were not there, to suggest to the students of those famous colleges that they should re-write history, though I own that it often seems a little queer as it is, unreal,

---

7. The diarist John Aubrey (1626–1697).   8. The two women's colleges at Cambridge.

lop-sided; but why should they not add a supplement to history? calling it, of course, by some inconspicuous name so that women might figure there without impropriety? For one often catches a glimpse of them in the lives of the great, whisking away into the background, concealing, I sometimes think, a wink, a laugh, perhaps a tear. And, after all, we have lives enough of Jane Austen; it scarcely seems necessary to consider again the influence of the tragedies of Joanna Baillie[9] upon the poetry of Edgar Allan Poe; as for myself, I should not mind if the homes and haunts of Mary Russell Mitford[1] were closed to the public for a century at least. But what I find deplorable, I continued, looking about the book-shelves again, is that nothing is known about women before the eighteenth century. I have no model in my mind to turn about this way and that. Here am I asking why women did not write poetry in the Elizabethan age, and I am not sure how they were educated; whether they were taught to write; whether they had sitting-rooms to themselves; how many women had children before they were twenty-one; what, in short, they did from eight in the morning till eight at night. They had no money evidently; according to Professor Trevelyan they were married whether they liked it or not before they were out of the nursery, at fifteen or sixteen very likely. It would have been extremely odd, even upon this showing, had one of them suddenly written the plays of Shakespeare, I concluded, and I thought of that old gentleman, who is dead now, but was a bishop, I think, who declared that it was impossible for any woman, past, present, or to come, to have the genius of Shakespeare. He wrote to the papers about it. He also told a lady who applied to him for information that cats do not as a matter of fact go to heaven, though they have, he added, souls of a sort. How much thinking those old gentlemen used to save one! How the borders of ignorance shrank back at their approach! Cats do not go to heaven. Women cannot write the plays of Shakespeare.

Be that as it may, I could not help thinking, as I looked at the works of Shakespeare on the shelf, that the bishop was right at least in this; it would have been impossible, completely and entirely, for any woman to have written the plays of Shakespeare in the age of Shakespeare. Let me imagine, since facts are so hard to come by, what would have happened had Shakespeare had a wonderfully gifted sister, called Judith, let us say. Shakespeare himself went, very probably—his mother was an heiress—to the grammar school, where he may have learnt Latin—Ovid, Virgil and Horace—and the elements of grammar and logic. He was, it is well known, a wild boy who poached rabbits, perhaps shot a deer, and had, rather sooner than he should have done, to marry a woman in the neighbourhood, who bore him a child rather quicker than was right. That escapade sent him to seek his fortune in London. He had, it seemed, a taste for the theatre; he began by holding horses at the stage door. Very soon he got work in the theatre, became a successful actor, and lived at

9. Poet and dramatist (1762–1851) now forgotten, but admired by Walter Scott.

1. Poet and novelist (1787–1855) best known for her sketches of country life.

the hub of the universe, meeting everybody, knowing everybody, practising his art on the boards, exercising his wits in the streets, and even getting access to the palace of the queen. Meanwhile his extraordinarily gifted sister, let us suppose, remained at home. She was as adventurous, as imaginative, as agog to see the world as he was. But she was not sent to school. She had no chance of learning grammar and logic, let alone of reading Horace and Virgil. She picked up a book now and then, one of her brother's perhaps, and read a few pages. But then her parents came in and told her to mend the stockings or mind the stew and not moon about with books and papers. They would have spoken sharply but kindly, for they were substantial people who knew the conditions of life for a woman and loved their daughter—indeed, more likely than not she was the apple of her father's eye. Perhaps she scribbled some pages up in an apple loft on the sly, but was careful to hide them or set fire to them. Soon, however, before she was out of her teens, she was to be betrothed to the son of a neighbouring wool-stapler.[2] She cried out that marriage was hateful to her, and for that she was severely beaten by her father. Then he ceased to scold her. He begged her instead not to hurt him, not to shame him in this matter of her marriage. He would give her a chain of beads or a fine petticoat, he said; and there were tears in his eyes. How could she disobey him? How could she break his heart? The force of her own gift alone drove her to it. She made up a small parcel of her belongings, let herself down by a rope one summer's night and took the road to London. She was not seventeen. The birds that sang in the hedge were not more musical than she was. She had the quickest fancy, a gift like her brother's, for the tune of words. Like him, she had a taste for the theatre. She stood at the stage door; she wanted to act, she said. Men laughed in her face. The manager—a fat, loose-lipped man—guffawed. He bellowed something about poodles dancing and women acting—no woman, he said, could possibly be an actress. He hinted—you can imagine what. She could get no training in her craft. Could she even seek her dinner in a tavern or roam the streets at midnight? Yet her genius was for fiction and lusted to feed abundantly upon the lives of men and women and the study of their ways. At last— for she was very young, oddly like Shakespeare the poet in her face, with the same grey eyes and rounded brows—at last Nick Greene the actor-manager took pity on her; she found herself with child by that gentleman and so—who shall measure the heat and violence of the poet's heart when caught and tangled in a woman's body?—killed herself one winter's night and lies buried at some cross-roads where the omnibuses now stop outside the Elephant and Castle.[3]

That, more or less, is how the story would run, I think, if a woman in Shakespeare's day had had Shakespeare's genius. But for my part, I agree with the deceased bishop, if such he was—it is unthinkable that any woman in Shakespeare's day should have had Shakespeare's genius. For genius like Shakespeare's is not born among labouring, uneducated, servile people. It was not born in England among the Saxons and the Britons. It is not born today among the working classes. How, then, could it have been born among women whose work began, according to Professor Trevelyan, almost before they were out of the nursery, who were forced to it by their parents and held to it by all the power of law and custom? Yet genius of a sort must have existed among women as it must have existed among the working classes. Now and again an Emily Brontë or a Robert Burns blazes out and proves its presence. But certainly it never got itself on to paper. When, however, one reads of a witch being ducked, of a woman possessed by devils, of a wise woman selling herbs, or even of a very remarkable man who had a mother, then I think we are on the track of a lost novelist, a suppressed poet, of some mute and inglorious[4] Jane Austen, some Emily Brontë who dashed her brains out on the moor or mopped and mowed about the highways crazed with the torture that her gift had put her to. Indeed, I would venture to guess that Anon, who wrote so many poems without signing them, was often a woman. It was a woman Edward Fitzgerald,[5] I think, suggested who made the ballads and the folk-songs, crooning them to her children, beguiling her spinning with them, or the length of the winter's night.

This may be true or it may be false—who can say?—but what is true in it, so it seemed to me, reviewing the story of Shakespeare's sister as I had made it, is that any woman born with a great gift in the sixteenth century would certainly have gone crazed, shot herself, or ended her days in some lonely cottage outside the village, half witch, half wizard, feared and mocked at. For it needs little skill in psychology to be sure that a highly gifted girl who had tried to use her gift for poetry would have been so thwarted and hindered by other people, so tortured and pulled asunder by her own contrary instincts, that she must have lost her health and sanity to a certainty. No girl could have walked to London and stood at a stage door and forced her way into the presence of actor-managers without doing herself a violence and suffering an anguish which may have been irrational—for chastity may be a fetish invented by certain societies for unknown reasons—but were none the less inevitable. Chastity had then, it has even now, a religious importance in a woman's life, and has so wrapped itself round with nerves and instincts that to cut it free and bring it to the light of day demands courage of the rarest. To have lived a free life in London in the sixteenth century would have meant for a woman who was poet and playwright a nervous stress and dilemma which might well have killed her. Had she survived, whatever she had written would have been twisted and deformed, issuing from a strained and morbid imagination. And undoubtedly, I thought,

4. An echo of Thomas Gray's famous line about "some mute inglorious Milton" in *Elegy Written* *in a Country Churchyard* (1751), line 59.
5. Poet and translator (1809–1883).

looking at the shelf where there are no plays by women, her work would have gone unsigned. That refuge she would have sought certainly. It was the relic of the sense of chastity that dictated anonymity to women even so late as the nineteenth century. Currer Bell, George Eliot, George Sand,[6] all the victims of inner strife as their writings prove, sought ineffectively to veil themselves by using the name of a man. Thus they did homage to the convention, which if not implanted by the other sex was liberally encouraged by them (the chief glory of a woman is not to be talked of, said Pericles, himself a much-talked-of man), that publicity in women is detestable. Anonymity runs in their blood. The desire to be veiled still possesses them.

* * *

I told you in the course of this paper that Shakespeare had a sister; but do not look for her in Sir Sidney Lee's[7] life of the poet. She died young— alas, she never wrote a word. She lies buried where the omnibuses now stop, opposite the Elephant and Castle. Now my belief is that this poet who never wrote a word and was buried at the crossroads still lives. She lives in you and in me, and in many other women who are not here tonight, for they are washing up the dishes and putting the children to bed. But she lives; for great poets do not die; they are continuing presences; they need only the opportunity to walk among us in the flesh. This opportunity, as I think, it is now coming within your power to give her. For my belief is that if we live another century or so—I am talking of the common life which is the real life and not of the little separate lives which we live as individuals—and have five hundred a year each of us and rooms of our own; if we have the habit of freedom and the courage to write exactly what we think; if we escape a little from the common sitting-room and see human beings not always in their relation to each other but in relation to reality; and the sky, too, and the trees or whatever it may be in themselves; if we look past Milton's bogey,[8] for no human being should shut out the view; if we face the fact, for it is a fact, that there is no arm to cling to, but that we go alone and that our relation is to the world of reality and not only to the world of men and women, then the opportunity will come and the dead poet who was Shakespeare's sister will put on the body which she has so often laid down. Drawing her life from the lives of the unknown who were her forerunners, as her brother did before her, she will be born. As for her coming without that preparation, without that effort on our part, without that determination that when she is born again she shall find it possible to live and write her poetry, that we cannot expect, for that would be impossible. But I

6. Male pseudonyms, respectively, of Charlotte Brontë, Marian Evans, and Amandine-Aurore-Lucie Dupin.
7. Sir Sidney Lee (1859–1926), biographer and Shakespeare scholar, published his *Life of William Shakespeare* in 1898.

8. Milton, with his unhappy first marriage, his campaign for freedom of divorce, and his deliberate subordination of Eve to Adam in *Paradise Lost*, was and often still is held to be (not altogether accurately) an example of what the present age calls a "male chauvinist" attitude to women.

maintain that she would come if we worked for her, and that so to work, even in poverty and obscurity, is worth while.

1929

Moments of Being: "Slater's Pins Have No Points"[1]

"Slater's pins have no points—don't you always find that?" said Miss Craye, turning round as the rose fell out of Fanny Wilmot's dress, and Fanny stooped with her ears full of the music, to look for the pin on the floor.

The words gave her an extraordinary shock, as Miss Craye struck the last chord of the Bach fugue. Did Miss Craye actually go to Slater's and buy pins then, Fanny Wilmot asked herself, transfixed for a moment? Did she stand at the counter waiting like anybody else, and was she given a bill with coppers wrapped in it, and did she slip them into her purse and then, an hour later, stand by her dressing table and take out the pins? What need had she of pins? For she was not so much dressed as cased, like a beetle compactly in its sheath, blue in winter, green in summer. What need had she of pins—Julia Craye—who lived, it seemed, in the cool, glassy world of Bach fugues, playing to herself what she liked and only consenting to take one or two pupils at the Archer Street College of Music (so the Principal, Miss Kingston, said) as a special favour to herself, who had "the greatest admiration for her in every way." Miss Craye was left badly off, Miss Kingston was afraid, at her brother's death. Oh, they used to have such lovely things, when they lived at Salisbury and her brother Julius was, of course, a very well-known man: a famous archaeologist. It was a great privilege to stay with them, Miss Kingston said ("My family had always known them—they were regular Salisbury[2] people," Miss Kingston said), but a little frightening for a child; one had to be careful not to slam the door or bounce into the room unexpectedly. Miss Kingston, who gave little character sketches like this on the first day of term while she received cheques and wrote out receipts for them, smiled here. Yes, she had been rather a tomboy; she had bounced in and set all those green Roman glasses and things jumping in their case. The Crayes were none of them married. The Crayes were not used to children. They kept cats. The cats, one used to feel, knew as much about the Roman urns and things as anybody.

"Far more than I did!" said Miss Kingston brightly, writing her name across the stamp, in her dashing, cheerful, full-bodied hand, for she had always been practical.

Perhaps then, Fanny Wilmot thought, looking for the pin, Miss Craye said that about "Slater's pins having no points," at a venture. None of the Crayes had ever married. She knew nothing about pins—nothing

1. See Woolf's discussion of "moments of being   2. Cathedral town in the south of England.
and non-being" on pp. 2358–2366.

whatever. But she wanted to break the spell that had fallen on the house; to break the pane of glass which separated them from other people. When Polly Kingston, that merry little girl, had slammed the door and made the Roman vases jump, Julius, seeing that no harm was done (that would be his first instinct) looked, for the case was stood in the window, at Polly skipping home across the fields; looked with the look his sister often had, that lingering, desiring look.

"Stars, sun, moon," it seemed to say, "the daisy in the grass, fires, frost on the window pane, my heart goes out to you. But," it always seemed to add, "you break, you pass, you go." And simultaneously it covered the intensity of both these states of mind with "I can't reach you—I can't get at you," spoken wistfully, frustratedly. And the stars faded, and the child went.

That was the kind of spell, that was the glassy surface that Miss Craye wanted to break by showing, when she had played Bach beautifully as a reward to a favourite pupil (Fanny Wilmot knew that she was Miss Craye's favourite pupil) that she too felt as other people felt about pins. Slater's pins had no points.

Yes, the "famous archaeologist" had looked like that, too. "The famous archaeologist"—as she said that endorsing cheques, ascertaining the day of the month, speaking so brightly and frankly, there was in Miss Kingston's voice an indescribable tone which hinted at something odd, something queer, in Julius Craye. It was the very same thing that was odd perhaps in Julia too. One could have sworn, thought Fanny Wilmot, as she looked for the pin, that at parties, meetings (Miss Kingston's father was a clergyman) she had picked up some piece of gossip, or it might only have been a smile, or a tone when his name was mentioned, which had given her "a feeling" about Julius Craye. Needless to say, she had never spoken about it to anybody. Probably she scarcely knew what she meant by it. But whenever she spoke of Julius, or heard him mentioned, that was the first thought that came to mind: there was something odd about Julius Craye.

It was so that Julia looked too, as she sat half turned on the music stool, smiling. It's on the field, it's on the pane, it's in the sky—beauty; and I can't get at it; I can't have it—I, she seemed to add, with that little clutch of the hand which was so characteristic, who adore it so passionately, would give the whole world to possess it! And she picked up the carnation which had fallen on the floor, while Fanny searched for the pin. She crushed it, Fanny felt, voluptuously in her smooth, veined hands stuck about with water-coloured rings set in pearls. The pressure of her fingers seemed to increase all that was most brilliant in the flower; to set it off; to make it more frilled, fresh, immaculate. What was odd in her, and perhaps in her brother too, was that this crush and grasp of the fingers was combined with a perpetual frustration. So it was even now with the carnation. She had her hands on it; she pressed it; but she did not possess it, enjoy it, not altogether.

None of the Crayes had married, Fanny Wilmot remembered. She had in mind how one evening when the lesson had lasted longer than usual and it was dark, Julia Craye had said, "It's the use of men, surely, to protect us," smiling at her that same odd smile, as she stood fastening her cloak, which made her, like the flower, conscious to her finger tips of youth, and brilliance, but, like the flower too, Fanny suspected, inhibited.

"Oh, but I don't want protection," Fanny had laughed, and when Julia Craye, fixing on her that extraordinary look, had said she was not so sure of that, Fanny positively blushed under the admiration in her eyes.

It was the only use of men, she had said. Was it for that reason then, Fanny wondered, with her eyes on the floor, that she had never married? After all, she had not lived all her life in Salisbury. "Much the nicest part of London," she had said once, "(but I'm speaking of fifteen or twenty years ago) is Kensington.[3] One was in the Gardens in ten minutes—it was like the heart of the country. One could dine out in one's slippers without catching cold. Kensington—it was like a village then, you know," she had said.

Here she had broken off, to denounce acridly, the draughts in the Tubes.[4]

"It was the use of men," she had said, with a queer, wry acerbity. Did that throw any light on the problem why she had not married? One could imagine every sort of scene in her youth, when with her good, blue eyes, her straight, firm nose, her piano playing, her rose flowering with chaste passion in the bosom of her muslin dress, she had attracted first the young men to whom such things, and the china tea-cups and the silver candlesticks, and the inlaid tables (for the Crayes had such nice things) were wonderful; young men not sufficiently distinguished; young men of the Cathedral town with ambitions. She had attracted them first, and then her brother's friends from Oxford or Cambridge. They would come down in the summer, row her up the river, continue the argument about Browning by letter, and arrange perhaps on the rare occasions when she stayed in London to show her—Kensington Gardens?

"Much the nicest part of London—Kensington. I'm speaking of fifteen or twenty years ago," she had said once. "One was in the Gardens in ten minutes—in the heart of the country." One could make that yield what one liked, Fanny Wilmot thought, single out for instance, Mr Sherman, the painter, an old friend of hers; make him call for her by appointment one sunny day in June; take her to have tea under the trees. (They had met, too, at those parties to which one tripped in slippers without fear of catching a cold.) The aunt or other elderly relative was to wait there while they looked at the Serpentine. They looked at the Serpentine.[5] He may have rowed her across. They compared it with the

---

3. A fashionable London district with an elegant park—"the Gardens."

4. London subway.

5. Artificial body of water in London's Hyde Park.

Avon.[6] She would have considered the comparison very seriously, for views of rivers were important to her. She sat hunched a little, a little angular, though she was graceful then, steering. At the critical moment, for he had determined that she must speak now—it was his only chance of getting her alone—he was speaking with his head turned at an absurd angle, in his great nervousness, over his shoulder—at the very moment she interrupted fiercely. He would have them[7] into the Bridge, she cried. It was a moment of horror, of disillusionment, of revelation for both of them. I can't have it, I can't possess it, she thought. He could not see why she had come then. With a great splash of his oar he pulled the boat round. Merely to snub him? He rowed her back and said good-bye to her.

The setting of that scene could be varied as one chose, Fanny Wilmot reflected. (Where had that pin fallen?) It might be Ravenna—or Edinburgh, where she had kept house for her brother. The scene could be changed and the young man and the exact manner of it all; but one thing was constant—her refusal and her frown and her anger with herself afterwards and her argument, and her relief—yes, certainly her immense relief. The very next day perhaps she would get up at six, put on her cloak, and walk all the way from Kensington to the river. She was so thankful that she had not sacrificed her right to go and look at things when they are at their best—before people are up, that is to say. She could have her breakfast in bed if she liked. She had not sacrificed her independence.

Yes, Fanny Wilmot smiled, Julia had not endangered her habits. They remained safe, and her habits would have suffered if she had married. "They're ogres," she had said one evening, half laughing, when another pupil, a girl lately married, suddenly bethinking her that she would miss her husband, had rushed off in haste.

"They're ogres," she had said, laughing grimly. An ogre would have interfered perhaps with breakfast in bed; with walks at dawn down to the river. What would have happened (but one could hardly conceive this) had she had children? She took astonishing precautions against chills, fatigue, rich food, the wrong food, draughts, heated rooms, journeys in the Tube, for she could never determine which of these it was exactly that brought on those terrible headaches that gave her life the semblance of a battlefield. She was always engaged in outwitting the enemy, until it seemed as if the pursuit had its interest; could she have beaten the enemy finally she would have found life a little dull. As it was, the tug-of-war was perpetual—on one side the nightingale or the view which she loved with passion—yes, for views and birds she felt nothing less than passion; on the other, the damp path or the horrid long drag up a steep hill which would certainly make her good for nothing next day and bring on one of her headaches. When, therefore, from time to time, she man-

6. English river, near Shakespeare's birthplace.   7. I.e., run them.

aged her forces adroitly and brought off a visit to Hampton Court the week the crocuses (those glossy bright flowers were her favourites) were at their best, it was a victory. It was something that lasted; something that mattered for ever. She strung the afternoon on the necklace of memorable days, which was not too long for her to be able to recall this one or that one; this view, that city; to finger it, to feel it, to savour, sighing, the quality that made it unique.

"It was so beautiful last Friday," she said, "that I determined I must go there." So she had gone off to Waterloo on her great undertaking—to visit Hampton Court—alone. Naturally, but perhaps foolishly, one pitied her for the thing she never asked pity for (indeed she was reticent habitually, speaking of her health only as a warrior might speak of his foe)—one pitied her for always doing everything alone. Her brother was dead. Her sister was asthmatic. She found the climate of Edinburgh good for her. It was too bleak for Julia. Perhaps too she found the associations painful, for her brother, the famous archaeologist, had died there; and she had loved her brother. She lived in a little house off the Brompton Road entirely alone.

Fanny Wilmot saw the pin on the carpet; she picked it up. She looked at Miss Craye. Was Miss Craye so lonely? No, Miss Craye was steadily, blissfully, if only for a moment, a happy woman. Fanny had surprised her in a moment of ecstasy. She sat there, half turned away from the piano, with her hands clasped in her lap holding the carnation upright, while behind her was the sharp square of the window, uncurtained, purple in the evening, intensely purple after the brilliant electric lights which burnt unshaded in the bare music room. Julia Craye sitting hunched and compact holding her flower seemed to emerge out of the London night, seemed to fling it like a cloak behind her. It seemed in its bareness and intensity the effluence of her spirit, something she had made which surrounded her, which was her. Fanny stared.

All seemed transparent for a moment to the gaze of Fanny Wilmot, as if looking through Miss Craye, she saw the very fountain of her being spurt up in pure, silver drops. She saw back and back into the past behind her. She saw the green Roman vases stood in their case; heard the choristers playing cricket; saw Julia quietly descend the curving steps on to the lawn; saw her pour out tea beneath the cedar tree; softly enclose the old man's hand in hers; saw her going round and about the corridors of that ancient Cathedral dwelling place with towels in her hand to mark them;[8] lamenting as she went the pettiness of daily life; and slowly age-ing, and putting away clothes when summer came, because at her age they were too bright to wear; and tending her father's sickness; and cleav-ing her way ever more definitely as her will stiffened towards her solitary goal; travelling frugally; counting the cost and measuring out of her tight shut purse the sum needed for this journey, or for that old mirror; obsti-

8. I.e., mark them for the laundry.

nately adhering whatever people might say in choosing her pleasures for herself. She saw Julia—

She saw Julia open her arms; saw her blaze; saw her kindle. Out of the night she burnt like a dead white star. Julia kissed her. Julia possessed her.

"Slater's pins have no points," Miss Craye said, laughing queerly and relaxing her arms, as Fanny Wilmot pinned the flower to her breast with trembling fingers.

1944

The Searchlight

The mansion of the eighteenth century Earl had been changed in the twentieth century into a Club. And it was pleasant, after dining in the great room with the pillars and the chandeliers under a glare of light to go out on to the balcony overlooking the Park. The trees were in full leaf, and had there been a moon, one could have seen the pink and cream coloured cockades on the chestnut trees. But it was a moonless night; very warm, after a fine summer's day.

Mr and Mrs Ivimey's party were drinking coffee and smoking on the balcony. As if to relieve them from the need of talking, to entertain them without any effort on their part, rods of light wheeled across the sky. It was peace then; the air force was practising; searching for enemy aircraft in the sky. After pausing to prod some suspected spot, the light wheeled, like the wings of a windmill, or again like the antennae of some prodigious insect and revealed here a cadaverous stone front; here a chestnut tree with all its blossoms riding; and then suddenly the light struck straight at the balcony, and for a second a bright disc shone—perhaps it was a mirror in a lady's hand-bag.

"Look!" Mrs Ivimey exclaimed.

The light passed. They were in darkness again.

"You'll never guess what *that* made me see!" she added. Naturally, they guessed.

"No, no, no," she protested. Nobody could guess; only she knew; only she could know, because she was the great-grand-daughter of the man himself. He had told her the story. What story? If they liked, she would try to tell it. There was still time before the play.

"But where do I begin?" she pondered. "In the year 1820? . . . It must have been about then that my great-grandfather was a boy. I'm not young myself"—no, but she was very well set up and handsome—"and he was a very old man when I was a child—when he told me the story. A very handsome old man," she explained, "with a shock of white hair, and blue eyes. He must have been a beautiful boy. But queer. . . . That was only natural—seeing how they lived. The name was Comber. They'd come down in the world. They'd been gentlefolk; they'd owned land up in Yorkshire. But when he was a boy only the tower was left. The house was nothing but a little farmhouse, standing in the middle of the fields. We saw it ten years ago and went over it. We had to leave the car and walk across the fields. There isn't any road to the house. It stands all alone, the grass grows right up to the gate . . . there were chickens pecking about, running in and out of the rooms. All gone to rack and ruin. I remember a stone fell from the tower suddenly." She paused. "There they lived," she went on, "the old man, the woman and the boy. She wasn't his wife, or the boy's mother. She was just a farm hand, a girl the old man had taken to live with him when his wife died. Another reason perhaps why nobody visited them—why the whole place was gone to rack and ruin. But I remember a coat of arms over the door; and books, old books, gone mouldy. He taught himself all he knew from books. He read and read, he told me, old books, books with maps hanging out from the pages. He dragged them up to the top of the tower—the rope's still there and the broken steps. There's a chair still in the window with the bottom fallen out; and the window swinging open, and the panes broken, and a view for miles and miles across the moors."

She paused as if she were up in the tower looking from the window that swung open.

"But we couldn't," she said, "find the telescope." In the dining-room behind them the clatter of plates grew louder. But Mrs Ivimey, on the balcony, seemed puzzled, because she could not find the telescope.

"Why a telescope?" someone asked her.

"Why? Because if there hadn't been a telescope," she laughed, "I shouldn't be sitting here now!"

And certainly she was sitting there now, a well set-up, middle-aged woman, with something blue over her shoulders.

"It must have been there," she resumed, "because, he told me, every night when the old people had gone to bed he sat at the window looking through the telescope at the stars. Jupiter, Aldebaran, Cassiopeia." She waved her hand at the stars that were beginning to show over the trees. It was growing darker. And the searchlight seemed brighter, sweeping across the sky, pausing here and there to stare at the stars.

"There they were," she went on, "the stars. And he asked himself, my grandfather—the boy, 'What are they? why are they? And who am I?' as one does, sitting alone, with no one to talk to, looking at the stars."

She was silent. They all looked at the stars that were coming out in the darkness over the trees. The stars seemed very permanent, very unchanging. The roar of London sank away. A hundred years seemed nothing. They felt that the boy was looking at the stars with them. They seemed to be with him, in the tower, looking out over the moors at the stars.

Then a voice behind them said:

"Right you are. Friday."

They all turned, shifted, felt dropped down on to the balcony again.

"Ah, but there was nobody to say that to him," she murmured. The couple rose and walked away.

"*He* was alone," she resumed. "It was a fine summer's day. A June day. One of those perfect summer days when everything seems to stand still in the heat. There were the chickens pecking in the farm-yard; the old horse stamping in the stable; the old man dozing over his glass. The woman scouring pails in the scullery. Perhaps a stone fell from the tower. It seemed as if the day would never end. And he had no one to talk to— nothing whatever to do. The whole world stretched before him. The moor rising and falling; the sky meeting the moor; green and blue, green and blue, for ever and ever."

In the half light, they could see that Mrs Ivimey was leaning over the balcony, with her chin propped on her hands, as if she were looking out over the moors from the top of a tower.

"Nothing but moor and sky, moor and sky, for ever and ever," she murmured.

Then she made a movement, as if she swung something into position.

"But what did the earth look like through the telescope?" she asked.

She made another quick little movement with her fingers as if she were twirling something.

"He focussed it," she said. "He focussed it upon the earth. He focussed it upon a dark mass of wood upon the horizon. He focussed it so that he could see . . . each tree . . . each tree separate . . . and the birds . . . rising and falling . . . and a stem of smoke . . . there . . . in the mist of the trees. . . . And then . . . lower . . . lower . . . (she lowered her eyes) . . . there was a house . . . a house among the trees . . . a farm house . . . every brick showed . . . and the tubs on either side of the door . . . with flowers in them blue, pink, hydrangeas perhaps . . ." She paused . . . "And then a girl came out of the house . . . wearing something blue upon her head . . . and stood there . . . feeding birds . . . pigeons . . . they came fluttering round her. . . . And then . . . look. . . . A man. . . . A man! He came round the corner. He seized her in his arms! They kissed . . . they kissed!"

Mrs Ivimey opened her arms and closed them as if she were kissing someone.

"It was the first time he had seen a man kiss a woman—in his tele-scope—miles and miles away across the moors!"

She thrust something from her—the telescope presumably. She sat upright.

"So he ran down the stairs. He ran through the fields. He ran down lanes, out upon the high road, through woods. He ran for miles and miles, and just when the stars were showing above the trees he reached the house . . . covered with dust, streaming with sweat. . . ."

She stopped, as if she saw him.

"And then, and then . . . what did he do then? What did he say? And the girl . . ." they pressed her.

A shaft of light fell upon Mrs Ivimey as if someone had focussed the lens of a telescope upon her. (It was the air force, looking for enemy air craft.) She had risen. She had something blue on her head. She had raised her hand, as if she stood in a doorway, amazed.

"Oh the girl . . . She was my—" she hesitated, as if she were about to say "myself." But she remembered; and corrected herself. "She was my great-grandmother," she said.

She turned to look for her cloak. It was on a chair behind her.

"But tell us—what about the other man, the man who came round the corner?" they asked.

"That man? That man," Mrs Ivimey murmured, stooping to fumble with her cloak, (the searchlight had left the balcony), "he, I suppose, vanished."

"The light," she added, gathering her things about her, "only falls here and there."

The searchlight had passed on. It was now focussed on the plain expanse of Buckingham Palace. And it was time they went on to the play.

1944

From A Sketch of the Past[1]

[Moments of Being and Non-Being]

—I begin: the first memory.

This was of red and purple flowers on a black ground—my mother's dress; and she was sitting either in a train or in an omnibus, and I was on her lap. I therefore saw the flowers she was wearing very close; and can still see purple and red and blue, I think, against the black; they must have been anemones, I suppose. Perhaps we were going to St Ives; more probably, for from the light it must have been evening, we were coming back to London. But it is more convenient artistically to suppose that we were going to St Ives, for that will lead to my other memory, which also seems to be my first memory, and in fact it is the most important of all my memories. If life has a base that it stands upon, if it is a bowl that one fills and fills and fills—then my bowl without a doubt stands upon this memory. It is of lying half asleep, half awake, in bed in the nursery at St Ives. It is of hearing the waves breaking, one, two, one, two, and sending a splash of water over the beach; and then breaking, one, two, one, two, behind a yellow blind. It is of hearing the blind draw its little acorn[2] across the floor as the wind blew the blind out. It is of lying and hearing this splash and seeing this light, and feeling, it is almost impossible that I should be here; of feeling the purest ecstasy I can conceive.

1. The autobiographical essay from which this extract is taken was published in *Moments of Being*, ed. Jeanne Schulkind (1978). Woolf began it on April 18, 1939, as a relief from the labor of writing *Roger Fry: A Biography* (1940). The last date entered in the manuscript is Nov. 17, 1940, some 4 months before her death. Under the shadow of approach-ing war, she gropes back for the bright memories of childhood, especially those associated with Stephens' summer home, Talland House, at St. Ives in Cornwall, the setting for her novel *To the Lighthouse*.
2. I.e., the acorn-shaped button on the end of the blind cord.

I could spend hours trying to write that as it should be written, in order to give the feeling which is even at this moment very strong in me. But I should fail (unless I had some wonderful luck); I dare say I should only succeed in having the luck if I had begun by describing Virginia herself.

Here I come to one of the memoir writer's difficulties—one of the reasons why, though I read so many, so many are failures. They leave out the person to whom things happened. The reason is that it is so difficult to describe any human being. So they say: "This is what happened"; but they do not say what the person was like to whom it happened. And the events mean very little unless we know first to whom they happened. Who was I then? Adeline Virginia Stephen, the second daughter of Leslie and Julia Prinsep Stephen, born on 25th January 1882, descended from a great many people, some famous, others obscure; born into a large connection, born not of rich parents, but of well-to-do parents, born into a very communicative, literate, letter writing, visiting, articulate, late nineteenth century world; so that I could if I liked to take the trouble, write a great deal here not only about my mother and father but about uncles and aunts, cousins and friends. But I do not know how much of this, or what part of this, made me feel what I felt in the nursery at St Ives. I do not know how far I differ from other people. That is another memoir writer's difficulty. Yet to describe oneself truly one must have some standard of comparison; was I clever, stupid, good looking, ugly, passionate, cold—? Owing partly to the fact that I was never at school, never competed in any way with children of my own age, I have never been able to compare my gifts and defects with other people's. But of course there was one external reason for the intensity of this first impression: the impression of the waves and the acorn on the blind; the feeling, as I describe it sometimes to myself, of lying in a grape and seeing through a film of semi-transparent yellow—it was due partly to the many months we spent in London. The change of nursery was a great change. And there was the long train journey; and the excitement. I remember the dark; the lights; the stir of the going up to bed.

But to fix my mind upon the nursery—it had a balcony; there was a partition, but it joined the balcony of my father's and mother's bedroom. My mother would come out onto her balcony in a white dressing gown. There were passion flowers growing on the wall; they were great starry blossoms, with purple streaks, and large green buds, part empty, part full.

If I were a painter I should paint these first impressions in pale yellow, silver, and green. There was the pale yellow blind; the green sea; and the silver of the passion flowers. I should make a picture that was globular; semi-transparent. I should make a picture of curved petals; of shells; of things that were semi-transparent; I should make curved shapes, showing the light through, but not giving a clear outline. Everything would be large and dim; and what was seen would at the same time be heard; sounds would come through this petal or leaf—sounds indistinguishable from sights. Sound and sight seem to make equal parts of these first impressions. When I think of the early morning in bed I also hear the caw of rooks[3] falling from a great height. The sound seems to fall through an elastic, gummy air; which holds it up; which prevents it from being sharp and distinct. The quality of the air above Talland House seemed to suspend sound, to let it sink down slowly, as if it were caught in a blue gummy veil. The rooks cawing is part of the waves breaking—one, two, one, two—and the splash as the wave drew back and then it gathered again, and I lay there half awake, half asleep, drawing in such ecstasy as I cannot describe.

The next memory—all these colour-and-sound memories hang together at St Ives—was much more robust; it was highly sensual. It was later. It still makes me feel warm; as if everything were ripe; humming; sunny; smelling so many smells at once; and all making a whole that even now makes me stop—as I stopped then going down to the beach; I stopped at the top to look down at the gardens. They were sunk beneath the road. The apples were on a level with one's head. The gardens gave off a murmur of bees; the apples were red and gold; there were also pink flowers; and grey and silver leaves. The buzz, the croon, the smell, all seemed to press voluptuously against some membrane; not to burst it; but to hum round one such a complete rapture of pleasure that I stopped, smelt; looked. But again I cannot describe that rapture. It was rapture rather than ecstasy.

The strength of these pictures—but sight was always then so much mixed with sound that picture is not the right word—the strength anyhow of these impressions makes me again digress. Those moments—in the nursery, on the road to the beach—can still be more real than the present moment. This I have just tested. For I got up and crossed the garden. Percy was digging the asparagus bed; Louie was shaking a mat in front of the bedroom door.[4] But I was seeing them through the sight I saw here—the nursery and the road to the beach. At times I can go back to St Ives more completely than I can this morning. I can reach a state where I seem to be watching things happen as if I were there. That is, I suppose, that my memory supplies what I had forgotten, so that it seems as if it were happening independently, though I am really making it happen. In certain favourable moods, memories—what one has forgotten—come to the top. Now if this is so, is it not possible—I often wonder—that things we have felt with great intensity have an existence independent of our minds; are in fact still in existence? And if so, will it not be possible, in time, that some device will be invented by which we can tap them? I see it—the past—as an avenue lying behind; a long ribbon of scenes, emotions. There at the end of the avenue still, are the garden and the nursery. Instead of remembering here a scene and there a sound, I shall fit a plug into the wall;[5] and listen in to the past. I shall

3. Black crows.
4. The gardener and "daily help," respectively, at Monks House, the Woolfs' country home in Rod-
mell, Sussex.
5. I.e., as if plugging in a radio.

turn up August 1890. I feel that strong emotion must leave its trace; and it is only a question of discovering how we can get ourselves again attached to it, so that we shall be able to live our lives through from the start.

But the peculiarity of these two strong memories is that each was very simple. I am hardly aware of myself, but only of the sensation. I am only the container of the feeling of ecstasy, of the feeling of rapture. Perhaps this is characteristic of all childhood memories; perhaps it accounts for their strength. Later we add to feelings much that makes them more complex; and therefore less strong; or if not less strong, less isolated, less complete. But instead of analysing this, here is an instance of what I mean—my feeling about the looking-glass in the hall.

There was a small looking-glass in the hall at Talland House. It had, I remember, a ledge with a brush on it. By standing on tiptoe I could see my face in the glass. When I was six or seven perhaps, I got into the habit of looking at my face in the glass. But I only did this if I was sure that I was alone. I was ashamed of it. A strong feeling of guilt seemed naturally attached to it. But why was this so? One obvious reason occurs to me—Vanessa and I were both what was called tomboys; that is, we played cricket, scrambled over rocks, climbed trees, were said not to care for clothes and so on. Perhaps therefore to have been found looking in the glass would have been against our tomboy code. But I think that my feeling of shame went a great deal deeper. I am almost inclined to drag in my grandfather—Sir James, who once smoked a cigar, liked it, and so threw away his cigar and never smoked another. I am almost inclined to think that I inherited a streak of the puritan, of the Clapham Sect.[6] At any rate, the looking-glass shame has lasted all my life, long after the tomboy phase was over. I cannot now powder my nose in public. Everything to do with dress—to be fitted, to come into a room wearing a new dress—still frightens me; at least makes me shy, self-conscious, uncomfortable. "Oh to be able to run, like Julian Morrell,[7] all over the garden in a new dress", I thought not many years ago at Garsington; when Julian undid a parcel and put on a new dress and scampered round and round like a hare. Yet femininity was very strong in our family. We were famous for our beauty—my mother's beauty, Stella's beauty, gave me as early as I can remember, pride and pleasure. What then gave me this feeling of shame, unless it were that I inherited some opposite instinct? My father was spartan, ascetic, puritanical. He had I think no feeling for pictures; no ear for music; no sense of the sound of words. This leads me to think that my—I would say 'our' if I knew enough about Vanessa, Thoby and Adrian[8]—but how little we know even about brothers and sisters—this leads me to think that my natural love for beauty was checked

6. In marrying Jane Catherine Venn, Woolf's grandfather, James Stephen, had allied himself with the heart of the so-called Clapham Sect. John and Henry Venn, respectively rector and curate of Clapham in South London, were prominent members of this evangelical society which, in the early 19th century, was instrumental in bringing about the abolition of the slave trade.

7. Daughter of Philip Morrell, Member of Parliament, and his wife Ottoline, the celebrated literary hostess. Garsington Manor was their house in Oxfordshire.

8. Woolf's sister and brothers.

by some ancestral dread. Yet this did not prevent me from feeling ecstasies and raptures spontaneously and intensely and without any shame or the least sense of guilt, so long as they were disconnected with my own body. I thus detect another element in the shame which I had in being caught looking at myself in the glass in the hall. I must have been ashamed or afraid of my own body. Another memory, also of the hall, may help to explain this. There was a slab outside the dining room door for standing dishes upon. Once when I was very small Gerald Duckworth[9] lifted me onto this, and as I sat there he began to explore my body. I can remember the feel of his hand going under my clothes; going firmly and steadily lower and lower. I remember how I hoped that he would stop; how I stiffened and wriggled as his hand approached my private parts. But it did not stop. His hand explored my private parts too. I remember resenting, disliking it—what is the word for so dumb and mixed a feeling? It must have been strong, since I still recall it. This seems to show that a feeling about certain parts of the body; how they must not be touched; how it is wrong to allow them to be touched; must be instinctive. It proves that Virginia Stephen was not born on the 25th January 1882, but was born many thousands of years ago; and had from the very first to encounter instincts already acquired by thousands of ancestresses in the past.

And this throws light not merely on my own case, but upon the problem that I touched on the first page; why it is so difficult to give any account of the person to whom things happen. The person is evidently immensely complicated. Witness the incident of the looking-glass. Though I have done my best to explain why I was ashamed of looking at my own face I have only been able to discover some possible reasons; there may be others; I do not suppose that I have got at the truth; yet this is a simple incident; and it happened to me personally; and I have no motive for lying about it. In spite of all this, people write what they call "lives" of other people; that is, they collect a number of events, and leave the person to whom it happened unknown. Let me add a dream; for it may refer to the incident of the looking-glass. I dreamt that I was looking in a glass when a horrible face—the face of an animal—suddenly showed over my shoulder. I cannot be sure if this was a dream, or if it happened. Was I looking in the glass one day when something in the background moved, and seemed to me alive? I cannot be sure. But I have always remembered the other face in the glass, whether it was a dream or a fact, and that it frightened me.

These then are some of my first memories. But of course as an account of my life they are misleading, because the things one does not remember are as important; perhaps they are more important. If I could remember one whole day I should be able to describe, superficially at least, what life was like as a child. Unfortunately, one only remembers what is exceptional. And there seems to be no reason why one thing is excep-

9. Woolf's half-brother and the subject of her autobiographical essay, 22 Hyde Park Gate, writ-   ten in 1920 and published in *Moments of Being* (1978).

tional and another not. Why have I forgotten so many things that must have been, one would have thought, more memorable than what I do remember? Why remember the hum of bees in the garden going down to the beach, and forget completely being thrown naked by father into the sea? (Mrs Swanwick says she saw that happen.)[1]

This leads to a digression, which perhaps may explain a little of my own psychology; even of other people's. Often when I have been writing one of my so-called novels I have been baffled by this same problem; that is, how to describe what I call in my private shorthand—"non-being." Every day includes much more non-being than being. Yesterday for example, Tuesday the 18th of April, was [as] it happened a good day; above the average in "being." It was fine; I enjoyed writing these first pages; my head was relieved of the pressure of writing about Roger; I walked over Mount Misery[2] and along the river; and save that the tide was out, the country, which I notice very closely always, was coloured and shaded as I like—there were the willows, I remember, all plumy and soft green and purple against the blue. I also read Chaucer with pleasure; and began a book—the memoirs of Madame de la Fayette—which interested me. These separate moments of being were however embedded in many more moments of non-being. I have already forgotten what Leonard and I talked about at lunch; and at tea; although it was a good day the goodness was embedded in a kind of nondescript cotton wool. This is always so. A great part of every day is not lived consciously. One walks, eats, sees things, deals with what has to be done; the broken vacuum cleaner; ordering dinner; writing orders to Mabel;[3] washing; cooking dinner; bookbinding. When it is a bad day the proportion of non-being is much larger. I had a slight temperature last week; almost the whole day was non-being. The real novelist can somehow convey both sorts of being. I think Jane Austen can; and Trollope; perhaps Thackeray and Dickens and Tolstoy. I have never been able to do both. I tried—in *Night and Day*; and in *The Years*.[4] But I will leave the literary side alone for the moment.

As a child then, my days, just as they do now, contained a large proportion of this cotton wool, this non-being. Week after week passed at St Ives and nothing made any dint upon me. Then, for no reason that I know about, there was a sudden violent shock; something happened so violently that I have remembered it all my life. I will give a few instances. The first: I was fighting with Thoby on the lawn. We were pommelling each other with our fists. Just as I raised my fist to hit him, I felt: why hurt another person? I dropped my hand instantly, and stood there, and let him beat me. I remember the feeling. It was a feeling of hopeless sadness. It was as if I became aware of something terrible; and of my

---

1. In Mrs. Swanwick's autobiography, *I Have Been Young* (1935), she recalls having known Leslie Stephen at St. Ives: "We watched with delight his naked babies running about the beach or being towed into the sea between his legs, and their beautiful mother."

2. Two cottages on the hillside between South-ease and Piddinghoe known locally as Mount Misery.
3. Instructions to the Woolfs' maid.
4. Novels published in 1919 and 1938, respectively.

own powerlessness. I slunk off alone, feeling horribly depressed. The second instance was also in the garden at St Ives. I was looking at the flower bed by the front door; "That is the whole," I said. I was looking at a plant with a spread of leaves; and it seemed suddenly plain that the flower itself was a part of the earth; that a ring enclosed what was the flower; and that was the real flower; part earth; part flower. It was a thought I put away as being likely to be very useful to me later. The third case was also at St Ives. Some people called Valpy had been staying at St Ives, and had left. We were waiting at dinner one night, when somehow I overheard my father or my mother say that Mr Valpy had killed himself. The next thing I remember is being in the garden at night and walking on the path by the apple tree. It seemed to me that the apple tree was connected with the horror of Mr Valpy's suicide. I could not pass it. I stood there looking at the grey-green creases of the bark— it was a moonlit night—in a trance of horror. I seemed to be dragged down, hopelessly, into some pit of absolute despair from which I could not escape. My body seemed paralysed.

These are three instances of exceptional moments. I often tell them over, or rather they come to the surface unexpectedly. But now that for the first time I have written them down, I realise something that I have never realised before. Two of these moments ended in a state of despair. The other ended, on the contrary, in a state of satisfaction. When I said about the flower "That is the whole," I felt that I had made a discovery. I felt that I had put away in my mind something that I should go back [to], to turn over and explore. It strikes me now that this was a profound difference. It was the difference in the first place between despair and satisfaction. This difference I think arose from the fact that I was quite unable to deal with the pain of discovering that people hurt each other; that a man I had seen had killed himself. The sense of horror held me powerless. But in the case of the flower I found a reason; and was thus able to deal with the sensation. I was not powerless. I was conscious—if only at a distance—that I should in time explain it. I do not know if I was older when I saw the flower than I was when I had the other two experiences. I only know that many of these exceptional moments brought with them a peculiar horror and a physical collapse; they seemed dominant; myself passive. This suggests that as one gets older one has a greater power through reason to provide an explanation; and that this explanation blunts the sledge-hammer force of the blow. I think this is true, because though I still have the peculiarity that I receive these sudden shocks, they are now always welcome; after the first surprise, I always feel instantly that they are particularly valuable. And so I go on to suppose that the shock-receiving capacity is what makes me a writer. I hazard the explanation that a shock is at once in my case followed by the desire to explain it. I feel that I have had a blow; but it is not, as I thought as a child, simply a blow from an enemy hidden behind the cotton wool of daily life; it is or will become a revelation of some order; it is a token of some real thing behind appearances; and I make it real by putting it into words. It is only by putting it into words that I make it whole; this wholeness means that it has lost its power to hurt me; it gives me, perhaps because by doing so I take away the pain, a great delight to put the severed parts together. Perhaps this is the strongest pleasure known to me. It is the rapture I get when in writing I seem to be discovering what belongs to what; making a scene come right; making a character come together. From this I reach what I might call a philosophy; at any rate it is a constant idea of mine; that behind the cotton wool is hidden a pattern; that we—I mean all human beings—are connected with this; that the whole word is a work of art; that we are parts of the work of art. *Hamlet* or a Beethoven quartet is the truth about this vast mass that we call the world. But there is no Shakespeare, there is no Beethoven; certainly and emphatically there is no God; we are the words; we are the music; we are the thing itself. And I see this when I have a shock.

This intuition of mine—it is so instinctive that it seems given to me, not made by me—has certainly given its scale to my life ever since I saw the flower in the bed by the front door at St Ives. If I were painting myself I should have to find some—rod, shall I say—something that would stand for the conception. It proves that one's life is not confined to one's body and what one says and does; one is living all the time in relation to certain background rods or conceptions. Mine is that there is a pattern hid behind the cotton wool. And this conception affects me every day. I prove this, now, by spending the morning writing, when I might be walking, running a shop, or learning to do something that will be useful if war comes. I feel that by writing I am doing what is far more necessary than anything else.

All artists I suppose feel something like this. It is one of the obscure elements in life that has never been much discussed. It is left out in almost all biographies and autobiographies, even of artists. Why did Dickens spend his entire life writing stories? What was his conception? I bring in Dickens partly because I am reading *Nicholas Nickleby* at the moment; also partly because it struck me, on my walk yesterday, that these moments of being of mine were scaffolding in the background; were the invisible and silent part of my life as a child. But in the foreground there were of course people; and these people were very like characters in Dickens. They were caricatures; they were very simple; they were immensely alive. They could be made with three strokes of the pen, if I could do it. Dickens owes his astonishing power to make characters alive to the fact that he saw them as a child sees them; as I saw Mr Wolstenholme; C. B. Clarke, and Mr Gibbs.

I name these three people because they all died when I was a child. Therefore they have never been altered. I see them exactly as I saw them then. Mr Wolstenholme was a very old gentleman who came every summer to stay with us. He was brown; he had a beard and very small eyes in fat cheeks; and he fitted into a brown wicker beehive chair as if it had been his nest. He used to sit in this beehive chair smoking and reading. He had only one characteristic—that when he ate plum tart he spurted the juice through his nose so that it made a purple stain on his grey moustache. This seemed enough to cause us perpetual delight. We called him "The Woolly One." By way of shading him a little I remember that we had to be kind to him because he was not happy at home; that he was very poor, yet once gave Thoby half a crown; that he had a son who was drowned in Australia; and I know too that he was a great mathematician. He never said a word all the time I knew him. But he still seems to me a complete character; and whenever I think of him I begin to laugh.

Mr Gibbs was perhaps less simple. He wore a tie ring; had a bald, benevolent head; was dry; neat; precise; and had folds of skin under his chin. He made father groan—"why can't you go—why can't you go?" And he gave Vanessa and myself two ermine skins, with slits down the middle out of which poured endless wealth—streams of silver. I also remember him lying in bed, dying; husky; in a night shirt; and showing us drawings by Retzsch.[5] The character of Mr Gibbs also seems to me complete and amuses me very much.

As for C. B. Clarke, he was an old botanist; and he said to my father "All you young botanists like Osmunda."[6] He had an aunt aged eighty who went for a walking tour in the New Forest. That is all—that is all I have to say about these three old gentlemen. But how real they were! How we laughed at them! What an immense part they played in our lives!

One more caricature comes into my mind; though pity entered into this one. I am thinking of Justine Nonon. She was immensely old. Little hairs sprouted on her long bony chin. She was a hunchback; and walked like a spider, feeling her way with her long dry fingers from one chair to another. Most of the time she sat in the arm-chair beside the fire. I used to sit on her knee; and her knee jogged up and down; and she sang in a hoarse cracked voice "Ron ron ron—et plon plon plon—" and then her knee gave and I was tumbled onto the floor. She was French; she had been with the Thackerays. She only came to us on visits. She lived by herself at Shepherd's Bush; and used to bring Adrian a glass jar of honey. I got the notion that she was extremely poor; and it made me uncomfortable that she brought this honey, because I felt she did it by way of making her visit acceptable. She said too: "I have come in my carriage and pair"—which meant the red omnibus. For this too I pitied her; also because she began to wheeze; and the nurses said she would not live much longer; and soon she died. That is all I know about her; but I remember her as if she were a completely real person, with nothing left out, like the three old men.

April 1939–November 1940　　　　　　　　　1978

---

5. Friedrich Retzsch (1779–1857), German engraver.　　6. Flowering ferns.

JAMES JOYCE
1882–1941

1914:   *Dubliners.*
1916:   *A Portrait of the Artist as a Young Man.*
1922:   *Ulysses.*
1939:   *Finnegans Wake.*

James Joyce was born in Dublin, son of a talented but feckless father who is accurately described by Stephen Dedalus in *A Portrait of the Artist as a Young Man* as a man who had in his time been "a medical student, an oarsman, a tenor, an amateur actor, a shouting politician, a small landlord, a small investor, a drinker, a good fellow, a storyteller, somebody's secretary, something in a distillery, a tax-gatherer, a bankrupt, and at present a praiser of his own past." The elder Joyce drifted steadily down the financial and social scale, his family moving from house to house, each one less genteel and more shabby than the previous. James Joyce's whole education was Catholic, from the age of six to the age of nine at Clongowes Wood College, and from eleven to sixteen at Belvedere College, Dublin. Both were Jesuit institutions, and were normal roads to the priesthood. He then studied modern languages at University College, Dublin.

From a comparatively early age Joyce regarded himself as a rebel against the shabbiness and Philistinism of Dublin. In his early youth he was very religious, but in his last year at Belvedere he began to reject his Catholic faith in favor of a literary mission which he saw as involving rebellion and exile. He refused to play any part in the nationalist or other popular activities of his fellow students, and created some stir by his outspoken articles, one of which, on the Norwegian playwright Henrik Ibsen, appeared in the *Fortnightly Review* for April 1900. He taught himself Norwegian to be able to read Ibsen and to write to him. When an article by Joyce, significantly entitled *The Day of the Rabblement*, was refused, on instructions of the faculty adviser, by the student magazine that had commissioned it, he had it printed privately. By 1902, when he received his A.B. degree, he was already committed to a career as exile and writer. For Joyce, as for his character Stephen Dedalus, the latter implied the former. To preserve his integrity, to avoid involvement in popular sentimentalities and dishonesties, and above all to be able to re-create with both total understanding and total objectivity the Dublin life he knew so well, he felt that he had to go abroad.

Joyce went to Paris after graduation, was recalled to Dublin by his mother's fatal illness, had a short spell there as a schoolteacher, then returned to the Continent in 1904 to teach English at Trieste and then at Zurich. He took with him Nora Barnacle, an uneducated Galway girl with no interest in literature; her native vivacity and peasant wit charmed Joyce, and the two lived in devoted companionship until Joyce's death, though they were not married until 1931. In 1920 Joyce settled in Paris, where he lived until December 1940, when the war forced him to take refuge in Switzerland; he died in Zurich a few weeks later.

Proud, obstinate, absolutely convinced of his genius, given to fits of sudden gaiety and of sudden silence, Joyce was not always an easy person to get on with, yet he never lacked friends and throughout his thirty-six years on the Continent was always the center of a literary circle. Life was hard at first. At Trieste he had very little money, and he did not improve matters by drinking heavily, a habit checked somewhat by his brother Stanislaus who came out from Dublin to act (as Stanislaus put it much later) as his "brother's keeper." His financial position was much improved by the patronage of Mrs. Harold McCormick (Edith Rockefeller), who provided him with a monthly stipend from March 1917, until September 1919, when they quarreled, apparently because Joyce refused to submit to psychoanalysis by Carl Jung, who had been heavily endowed by Mrs. McCormick. The New York lawyer and art patron John Quinn, steered in Joyce's direction by Ezra Pound, also helped Joyce financially in 1917. A more permanent benefactor was the English feminist and editor Harriet Shaw Weaver, who not only subsidized Joyce generously from 1917 to the end of his life, but occupied herself indefatigably with arrangements for publishing his work.

Joyce's almost life-long exile from his native Ireland has something paradoxical about it. No writer has ever been more soaked in Dublin, its atmosphere, its history, its topography; in spite of doing most of his writing in Trieste, Zurich, and Paris, he wrote only and always about Dublin. He devised ways of expanding his accounts of Dublin, however, so that they became microcosms, small-scale models, of all human life, of all history and all geography. Indeed that was his life's work: to write about Dublin in such a way that he was writing about all of human experience.

Joyce began his career by writing a series of stories etching with extraordinary clarity aspects of Dublin life. But these stories—published as *Dubliners* in 1914—are more than sharp realistic sketches. In each, the detail is so chosen and organized that carefully interacting symbolic meanings are set up, and as a result *Dubliners* is a book about man's fate as well as a series of sketches of Dublin. Further, the stories are presented in a particular order so that new meanings arise from the relation between them.

The last story in Dubliners, *The Dead*, was not part of the original draft of the book, but was added later, at a time when Joyce was preoccupied with the nature of artistic objectivity. A series of jolting events frees the protagonist, Gabriel, from his possessiveness and egotism; the view he attains at the end is the mood of supreme neutrality that Joyce saw as the beginning of artistic awareness. It is the view of art developed by Stephen Dedalus in A *Portrait of the Artist as a Young Man*. *Dubliners* represents Joyce's first phase: he had to come directly to terms with the life he had rejected, to see it for what it was and for what it meant. Next, he had to come to terms with the meaning of his own development as a man dedicated to writing. He did this by weaving his autobiography into a novel so finely chiseled and carefully organized, so stripped of everything superfluous, that each word contributes to the presentation of the theme: the parallel movement toward art and toward exile. A part of Joyce's first draft has been posthumously published under the original title of *Stephen Hero* (1944): a comparison between it and the final version which Joyce gave to the world, A *Portrait of the Artist as a Young Man* (1916), will show how carefully Joyce reworked and compressed his material for maximum effect. The *Portrait* is not literally true as autobiography, though it has many autobiographical elements; but it is representatively true not only of Joyce but of the relation between the artist and society in the modern world.

In the *Portrait* Stephen worked out a theory of art which considers that art moves from the lyrical form—which is the simplest, the personal expression of an instant of emotion—through the narrative form—no longer purely personal—to the dramatic—the highest and most perfect form, where "the artist, like the God of creation, remains within or behind or beyond or above his handiwork, invisible, refined out of existence, indifferent, paring his fingernails." This view of art, which involves the objectivity, even the exile, of the artist (even though the artist uses only the materials provided for him by his own life) is related to that held by the poets of the nineties. More widely, it is related to the rejection by the artist of the ordinary world of middleclass values and activities which we see equally, though in different ways, in Matthew Arnold's war against the Philistines and in the concept (very un-Arnoldian) of the artist as bohemian. Joyce's career belongs to that long chapter in the history of the arts in Western civilization which begins with the artist's declaring his independence and ends with his feeling his inevitable "alienation." But if Joyce was alienated, as in certain ways he clearly was, he made his alienation serve his art: the kinds of writing represented by *Ulysses* and *Finnegans Wake* represent the most consummate craftsmanship put at the service of a humanely comic vision of all life. Some of Joyce's innovations in organization and style have been imitated by other writers, but these books are, and will probably remain, unique in our literature.

From the beginning Joyce had trouble with the Philistines. Publication of *Dubliners* was held up for many years while he fought with both English and Irish publishers about certain words and phrases which they wished to eliminate. (It was the former who finally published the book.) His masterpiece *Ulysses* was banned in both Britain and America on its first appearance in 1922, its earlier serialization in the *Little Review* (March 1918–December 1920) having had to stop abruptly when the U.S. Post Office brought a charge of obscenity against it. Fortunately, Judge Woolsey's history-making decision in favor of *Ulysses* in the United States District Court on December 6, 1933, resulted in the lifting of the ban and the free circulation of the work first in America and soon afterwards in Britain.

ULYSSES

Ulysses is an account of one day in the lives of citizens of Dublin in the year 1904: it is thus the description of a limited number of events involving a limited number of people in a limited environment. Yet Joyce's ambition—which took him seven years to realize—is to make his action into a microcosm of all human experience. The events are not therefore told on a single level; the story is presented in such a manner that depth and implication are given to them and they become symbolic of the activity of Man in the World. The most obvious of the devices which Joyce employs in order to make clear the microcosmic aspect of his story is the parallel with Homer's *Odyssey*: every episode in *Ulysses* corresponds in some way to an episode in the *Odyssey*. Joyce regarded Homer's Ulysses as the most "complete" man in literature, a man who is shown in all his aspects—both coward and hero, cautious and reckless, weak and strong, husband and lover, father and son, sublime and ridiculous; so he makes his hero, Leopold Bloom, an Irish Jew, into a modern Ulysses, and by so doing helps to make him Everyman and to make Dublin the world.

The book opens at eight o'clock on the morning of June 16, 1904. Stephen Dedalus (the same character we saw in the *Portrait*, but this is two years after our last glimpse of him there) had been summoned back to Dublin by his mother's fatal illness and now lives in an old military tower on the shore with Buck Mulligan, a rollicking medical student, and an Englishman called Haines. In the first three episodes of *Ulysses*, which concentrate on Stephen, he is built up as an aloof, uncompromising artist, rejecting all advances by representatives of the normal world, the incomplete man, to be contrasted later with the complete Leopold Bloom, who is much more "normal" and conciliatory. After tracing Stephen through his early-morning activities and learning the main currents of his mind, we go, in the fourth episode, to the home of Bloom. We follow closely his every activity: attending a funeral, transacting his business, eating his lunch, walking through the Dublin streets, worrying about his wife's infidelity with Blazes Boylan—and at each point the contents of his mind, including retrospect and anticipation, are presented to the reader, until all his past history is revealed. Finally, Bloom and Stephen, who have just been missing each other all day, get together. By this time it is late, and Stephen, who has been drinking with some medical students, is the worse for liquor. Bloom, moved by a paternal feeling towards Stephen (his own son had died in infancy and in a symbolic way Stephen takes his place), follows him during subsequent adventures in the role of protector. The climax of the book comes when Stephen, far gone in drink, and Bloom, worn out with fatigue, succumb to a series of hallucinations where their subconscious and unconscious come to the surface in dramatic form and their whole personalities are revealed with a completeness and a frankness unique in literature. Then Bloom takes the unresponsive Stephen home and gives him a meal. After Stephen's departure Bloom retires to bed—it is now 2 A.M. on June 17—while his wife Molly, representing the principles of sex and reproduction on which all human life is based, closes the book with a long monologue in which her experiences as woman are remembered.

On the level of realistic description, *Ulysses* pulses with life and can be enjoyed for its evocation of early twentieth-century Dublin. On the level of psychological exploration, it gives a profound and moving presentation of the personality and consciousness of Leopold Bloom and (to a lesser extent) Stephen Dedalus. On the level of style, it exhibits the most fascinating linguistic virtuosity. On a deeper symbolic level, the novel explores the paradoxes of human loneliness and sociability (for Bloom is both Jew and Dubliner, both exile and citizen, just as all of us are in a sense both exiles and citizens), and it explores the problems posed by the relations between parent and child, between the generations, and between the sexes. At the same time, through its use of themes from Homer, Dante, and Shakespeare, from literature, philosophy, and history, the book weaves a subtle pattern of allusion and suggestion which illuminates many aspects of human experience. The more one reads *Ulysses* the more one finds in it, but at the same time one does not need to probe into the symbolic meaning in order to relish both its literary artistry and its human feeling. At the forefront stands Leopold Bloom, from one point of view a frustrated and confused outsider in the society in which he moves, from another a champion of kindness and justice whose humane curiosity about his fellows redeems him from mere vulgarity and gives the book its positive human foundation.

Readers who come to *Ulysses* with expectations about the way the story is to be presented derived from their reading of Victorian novels or even of such 20th-century novelists as Conrad and Lawrence will find much that is at first puzzling. Joyce presents the consciousness of his characters directly, without any explanatory comment which tells the reader whose consciousness is being rendered (this is the "stream-of-consciousness" method). He may move, in the same paragraph and without any sign that he is making such a transition, from a description of a character's action—e.g., Stephen walking along the shore or Bloom entering a restaurant—to an evocation of the character's mental response to this action. That response is always multiple: it derives partly from the character's immediate situation and partly from the whole complex of attitudes which his past history has created in him. To suggest this multiplicity, Joyce may vary his style, from the flippant to the serious or from a realistic description to a suggestive set of images which indicate what might be called the general tone of the character's consciousness. Past and present mingle in the texture of the prose because they mingle in the texture of consciousness; and this mingling can be indicated by puns, by sudden breaks into a new kind of style or a new kind of subject matter, or by some other device for keeping the reader constantly in sight of the shifting, kaleidoscopic nature of human awareness. With a little experience, the reader learns to follow the implications of Joyce's shifts in manner and content—even to follow that at first sight bewildering passage in the "Proteus" episode where Stephen does not go to visit his uncle and aunt but, passing the road that leads to their house, imagines the kind of conversation that would take place in his home *if* he had gone to visit his uncle and had then returned home and reported that he had done so. *Ulysses* must not be approached as though it were a novel written in a traditional manner; all preconceptions must be set aside and we must follow wherever the author leads us and let the language tell us what it has to say without our troubling whether language is being used "properly" or not.

FINNEGANS WAKE

Joyce's last work, *Finnegans Wake*, was published in 1939; it took more than fourteen years to write, and Joyce considered it his masterpiece. In *Ulysses* he had made the symbolic aspect of the novel at least as important as the realistic aspect, but in *Finnegans Wake* he gave up realism altogether. This vast story of a symbolic Irishman's cosmic dream develops by enormous reverberating puns a continuous expansion of meaning, the elements in the puns deriving from every conceivable source in history, literature, mythology, and Joyce's personal experience. The whole book being (on one level at least) a dream, Joyce invents his own dream language in which words are combined, distorted, created by fitting together bits of other words, used with several different meanings at once, often drawn from several different languages at once, and fused in all sorts of ways to achieve whole clusters of meaning simultaneously. In fact, so many echoing suggestions can be found in every word or phrase that a full annotation of even a few pages would require a large book. It has taken the co-operative work of a number of devoted readers to make clear the complex interactions of the multiple puns and pun-clusters through which the ideas are projected, and every rereading

reveals new meanings. It is true that many readers find the efforts of explication demanded by *Finegans Wake* too arduous; some, indeed, feel that
the law of diminishing returns has now begun to operate, and that the effort
of both author and reader is disproportionate. Nevertheless, the book has
great beauty and fascination even for the casual reader. Students are advised
to read aloud—or to listen to the record of Joyce reading aloud—the extract
printed in this anthology, in order to appreciate the degree to which the
rhythms of the prose assist in conveying the meaning.

To an even greater extent than *Ulysses*, *Finnegans Wake* aims at embracing all of human history. The title is from an Irish-American ballad about
Tom Finnegan, a hod carrier who falls off a ladder when drunk and is
apparently killed, but who revives when during the "wake" (the watch by the
dead body) someone spills whiskey on him. The theme of death and resurrection, of cycles of change coming round in the course of history, is central
to *Finnegans Wake*, which derives one of its main principles of organization
from the cyclical theory of history put forward in 1725 by the Italian philosopher Giambattista Vico. Vico held that history passes through four phases:
the divine or theocratic, when people are governed by their awe of the supernatural; the aristocratic (the "heroic age" reflected in Homer and in *Beowulf*); the democratic and individualistic; and the final stage of chaos, a fall
into confusion which startles man back into supernatural reverence and starts
the process once again. Joyce, like Yeats, saw his own generation as in the
final stage awaiting the shock that will bring man back to the first.

A mere account of the narrative line of *Finnegans Wake* cannot, of course,
give any idea of the content of the work. If one explains that it opens with
Finnegan's fall, then introduces his successor Humphrey Chimpden Earwicker, who is Everyman, and whose dream constitutes the novel; that he is
presented as having guilt feelings about an indecency he committed (or may
have committed) in Phoenix Park, Dublin; that his wife Anna Livia Plurabelle or ALP (who is also Eve, Iseult, Ireland, the River Liffey) changes her
role just as he does; that he has two sons Shem and Shaun (or Jerry and
Kevin), who represent introvert and extrovert, artist and practical man, creator and popularizer, and symbolize this basic dichotomy in human nature
by all kinds of metamorphoses; and if one adds that, in the four books into
which *Finnegans Wake* is divided (after Vico's pattern), actions comic or
grotesque or sad or tender or desperate or passionate or terribly ordinary (and
very often several of these things at the same time) take place with all the
shifting meanings of a dream, so that characters change into others or into
inanimate objects and the setting keeps shifting—if we explain all this, we
still have said very little about what makes *Finnegans Wake* what it is. The
dreamer, whose initials HCE indicate his universality ("Here Comes Everybody"), is at the same time a particular person, who keeps a pub in Chapel-
izod, a Dublin suburb on the River Liffey near Phoenix Park. His mysterious
misdemeanor in Phoenix Park is in a sense Original Sin: Earwicker is Adam
as well as a primeval giant, the Hill of Howth, the Great Parent ("Haveth
Childers Everywhere" is another expansion of HCE), and Man in History.
Other characters who flit and change through the book, such as the Twelve
Customers (who are also twelve jurymen and public opinion) and the Four
Old Men (who are also judges, the authors of the four Gospels, and the four
elements), help to weave the texture of multiple significance so characteristic
of the work. But always it is the punning language, extending significance

downwards—rather than the plot, developing it lengthwise—that bears the main load of meaning.

The Dead

Lily, the caretaker's daughter, was literally run off her feet. Hardly had she brought one gentleman into the little pantry behind the office on the ground floor and helped him off with his overcoat than the wheezy hall-door bell clanged again and she had to scamper along the bare hall-way to let in another guest. It was well for her she had not to attend to the ladies also. But Miss Kate and Miss Julia had thought of that and had converted the bathroom upstairs into a ladies' dressing-room. Miss Kate and Miss Julia were there, gossiping and laughing and fussing, walking after each other to the head of the stairs, peering down over the banisters and calling down to Lily to ask her who had come.

It was always a great affair, the Misses Morkan's annual dance. Every-body who knew them came to it, members of the family, old friends of the family, the members of Julia's choir, any of Kate's pupils that were grown up enough and even some of Mary Jane's pupils too. Never once had it fallen flat. For years and years it had gone off in splendid style as long as anyone could remember; ever since Kate and Julia, after the death of their brother Pat, had left the house in Stoney Batter and taken Mary Jane, their only niece, to live with them in the dark gaunt house on Usher's Island, the upper part of which they had rented from Mr Fulham, the cornfactor[1] on the ground floor. That was a good thirty years ago if it was a day. Mary Jane, who was then a little girl in short clothes, was now the main prop of the household for she had the organ in Haddington Road. She had been through the Academy and gave a pupils' concert every year in the upper room of the Antient Concert Rooms.[2] Many of her pupils belonged to better-class families on the Kingstown and Dalkey line. Old as they were, her aunts also did their share. Julia, though she was quite grey, was still the leading soprano in Adam and Eve's, and Kate, being too feeble to go about much, gave music lessons to beginners on the old square piano in the back room. Lily, the caretaker's daughter, did housemaid's work for them. Though their life was modest they believed in eating well; the best of everything: diamond-bone sirloins, three-shilling tea and the best bottled stout.[3] But Lily seldom made a mistake in the orders so that she got on well with her three mistresses. They were fussy, that was all. But the only thing they would not stand was back answers.

Of course they had good reason to be fussy on such a night. And then it was long after ten o'clock and yet there was no sign of Gabriel and his

1. Grain merchant.
2. Concert hall in Dublin; the Academy was the Royal Irish Academy of Music.
3. A dark-brown malt liquor, akin to beer.

wife. Besides they were dreadfully afraid that Freddy Malins might turn up screwed. They would not wish for worlds that any of Mary Jane's pupils should see him under the influence; and when he was like that it was sometimes very hard to manage him. Freddy Malins always came late but they wondered what could be keeping Gabriel: and that was what brought them every two minutes to the banisters to ask Lily had Gabriel or Freddy come.

—O, Mr Conroy, said Lily to Gabriel when she opened the door for him, Miss Kate and Miss Julia thought you were never coming. Goodnight, Mrs Conroy.

—I'll engage they did, said Gabriel, but they forget that my wife here takes three mortal hours to dress herself.

He stood on the mat, scraping the snow from his goloshes, while Lily led his wife to the foot of the stairs and called out:

—Miss Kate, here's Mrs Conroy.

Kate and Julia came toddling down the dark stairs at once. Both of them kissed Gabriel's wife, said she must be perished alive and asked was Gabriel with her.

—Here I am as right as the mail, Aunt Kate! Go on up. I'll follow, called out Gabriel from the dark.

He continued scraping his feet vigorously while the three women went upstairs, laughing, to the ladies' dressing-room. A light fringe of snow lay like a cape on the shoulders of his overcoat and like toecaps on the toes of his goloshes; and, as the buttons of his overcoat slipped with a squeaking noise through the snow-stiffened frieze, a cold fragrant air from out-of-doors escaped from crevices and folds.

—Is it snowing again, Mr Conroy? asked Lily.

She had preceded him into the pantry to help him off with his overcoat. Gabriel smiled at the three syllables she had given his surname and glanced at her. She was a slim, growing girl, pale in complexion and with hay-coloured hair. The gas in the pantry made her look still paler. Gabriel had known her when she was a child and used to sit on the lowest step nursing a rag doll.

—Yes, Lily, he answered, and I think we're in for a night of it.

He looked up at the pantry ceiling, which was shaking with the stamping and shuffling of feet on the floor above, listened for a moment to the piano and then glanced at the girl, who was folding his overcoat carefully at the end of a shelf.

—Tell me, Lily, he said in a friendly tone, do you still go to school?

—O no, sir, she answered. I'm done schooling this year and more.

—O, then, said Gabriel gaily, I suppose we'll be going to your wedding one of these fine days with your young man, eh?

The girl glanced back at him over her shoulder and said with great bitterness:

—The men that is now is only all palaver and what they can get out of you.

Gabriel coloured as if he felt he had made a mistake and, without looking at her, kicked off his goloshes and flicked actively with his muffler at his patent-leather shoes.

He was a stout tallish young man. The high colour of his cheeks pushed upwards even to his forehead where it scattered itself in a few formless patches of pale red; and on his hairless face there scintillated restlessly the polished lenses and the bright gilt rims of the glasses which screened his delicate and restless eyes. His glossy black hair was parted in the middle and brushed in a long curve behind his ears where it curled slightly beneath the groove left by his hat.

When he had flicked lustre into his shoes he stood up and pulled his waistcoat down more tightly on his plump body. Then he took a coin rapidly from his pocket.

—O Lily, he said, thrusting it into her hands, it's Christmas-time, isn't it? Just . . . here's a little. . . .

He walked rapidly towards the door.

—O no, sir! cried the girl, following him. Really, sir, I wouldn't take it.

—Christmas-time! Christmas-time! said Gabriel, almost trotting to the stairs and waving his hand to her in deprecation.

The girl, seeing that he had gained the stairs, called out after him:

—Well, thank you, sir.

He waited outside the drawing-room door until the waltz should finish, listening to the skirts that swept against it and to the shuffling of feet. He was still discomposed by the girl's bitter and sudden retort. It had cast a gloom over him which he tried to dispel by arranging his cuffs and the bows of his tie. Then he took from his waistcoat pocket a little paper and glanced at the headings he had made for his speech. He was undecided about the lines from Robert Browning for he feared they would be above the heads of his hearers. Some quotation that they could recognise from Shakespeare or from the Melodies[4] would be better. The indelicate clacking of the men's heels and the shuffling of their soles reminded him that their grade of culture differed from his. He would only make himself ridiculous by quoting poetry to them which they could not understand. They would think that he was airing his superior education. He would fail with them just as he had failed with the girl in the pantry. He had taken up a wrong tone. His whole speech was a mistake from first to last, an utter failure.

Just then his aunts and his wife came out of the ladies' dressing-room. His aunts were two small plainly dressed old women. Aunt Julia was an inch or so taller. Her hair, drawn low over the tops of her ears, was grey; and grey also, with darker shadows, was her large flaccid face. Though she was stout in build and stood erect her slow eyes and parted lips gave her the appearance of a woman who did not know where she was or where she was going. Aunt Kate was more vivacious. Her face, healthier than her sister's, was all puckers and creases, like a shrivelled red apple,

---

4. *Irish Melodies* by Dublin-born Thomas Moore (1779–1852), a collection of songs—words and music—that was extremely popular in late 19th- and early 20th-century Ireland.

and her hair, braided in the same old-fashioned way, had not lost its ripe nut colour.

They both kissed Gabriel frankly. He was their favourite nephew, the son of their dead elder sister, Ellen, who had married T. J. Conroy of the Port and Docks.

—Gretta tells me you're not going to take a cab back to Monkstown to-night, Gabriel, said Aunt Kate.

—No, said Gabriel, turning to his wife, we had quite enough of that last year, hadn't we. Don't you remember, Aunt Kate, what a cold Gretta got out of it? Cab windows rattling all the way, and the east wind blowing in after we passed Merrion. Very jolly it was. Gretta caught a dreadful cold.

Aunt Kate frowned severely and nodded her head at every word.

—Quite right, Gabriel, quite right, she said. You can't be too careful.

—But as for Gretta there, said Gabriel, she'd walk home in the snow if she were let.

Mrs Conroy laughed.

—Don't mind him, Aunt Kate, she said. He's really an awful bother, what with green shades for Tom's eyes at night and making him do the dumb-bells, and forcing Eva to eat the stirabout.[5] The poor child! And she simply hates the sight of it! . . . O, but you'll never guess what he makes me wear now!

She broke out into a peal of laughter and glanced at her husband, whose admiring and happy eyes had been wandering from her dress to her face and hair. The two aunts laughed heartily too, for Gabriel's solicitude was a standing joke with them.

—Goloshes! said Mrs Conroy. That's the latest. Whenever it's wet underfoot I must put on my goloshes. To-night even he wanted me to put them on, but I wouldn't. The next thing he'll buy me will be a diving suit.

Gabriel laughed nervously and patted his tie reassuringly while Aunt Kate nearly doubled herself, so heartily did she enjoy the joke. The smile soon faded from Aunt Julia's face and her mirthless eyes were directed towards her nephew's face. After a pause she asked:

—And what are goloshes, Gabriel?

—Goloshes, Julia! exclaimed her sister. Goodness me, don't you know what goloshes are? You wear them over your . . . over your boots, Gretta, isn't it?

—Yes, said Mrs Conroy. Guttapercha things. We both have a pair now. Gabriel says everyone wears them on the continent.

—O, on the continent, murmured Aunt Julia, nodding her head slowly.

Gabriel knitted his brows and said, as if he were slightly angered:

—It's nothing very wonderful but Gretta thinks it very funny because she says the word reminds her of Christy Minstrels.[6]

5. Porridge made by stirring oatmeal in boiling milk or water.
6. Originally the name of a troupe of entertainers imitating Negroes, founded by George Christy of New York. By Joyce's time the meaning had become extended to any group with blackened faces

—But tell me, Gabriel, said Aunt Kate, with brisk tact. Of course, you've seen about the room. Gretta was saying . . .

—O, the room is all right, replied Gabriel. I've taken one in the Gresham.[7]

—To be sure, said Aunt Kate, by far the best thing to do. And the children, Gretta, you're not anxious about them?

—O, for one night, said Mrs Conroy. Besides, Bessie will look after them.

—To be sure, said Aunt Kate again. What a comfort it is to have a girl like that, one you can depend on! There's that Lily, I'm sure I don't know what has come over her lately. She's not the girl she was at all.

Gabriel was about to ask his aunt some questions on this point but she broke off suddenly to gaze after her sister who had wandered down the stairs and was craning her neck over the banisters.

—Now, I ask you, she said, almost testily, where is Julia going? Julia! Julia! Where are you going?

Julia, who had gone halfway down one flight, came back and announced blandly:

—Here's Freddy.

At the same moment a clapping of hands and a final flourish of the pianist told that the waltz had ended. The drawing-room door was opened from within and some couples came out. Aunt Kate drew Gabriel aside hurriedly and whispered into his ear:

—Slip down, Gabriel, like a good fellow and see if he's all right, and don't let him up if he's screwed. I'm sure he's screwed. I'm sure he is.

Gabriel went to the stairs and listened over the banisters. He could hear two persons talking in the pantry. Then he recognised Freddy Malins' laugh. He went down the stairs noisily.

—It's such a relief, said Aunt Kate to Mrs Conroy, that Gabriel is here. I always feel easier in my mind when he's here. . . . Julia, there's Miss Daly and Miss Power will take some refreshment. Thanks for your beautiful waltz, Miss Daly. It made lovely time.

A tall wizen-faced man, with a stiff grizzled moustache and swarthy skin, who was passing out with his partner said:

—And may we have some refreshment, too, Miss Morkan?

—Julia, said Aunt Kate summarily, and here's Mr Browne and Miss Furlong. Take them in, Julia, with Miss Daly and Miss Power.

—I'm the man for the ladies, said Mr Browne, pursing his lips until his moustache bristled and smiling in all his wrinkles. You know, Miss Morkan, the reason they are so fond of me is—

He did not finish his sentence, but, seeing that Aunt Kate was out of earshot, at once led the three young ladies into the back room. The middle of the room was occupied by two square tables placed end to end, and on these Aunt Julia and the caretaker were straightening and smoothing a large cloth. On the sideboard were arrayed dishes and plates,

who sang what were known as Negro melodies to banjo accompaniment, interspersed with jokes.

7. The Gresham Hotel, still one of the best hotels in Dublin.

and glasses and bundles of knives and forks and spoons. The top of the closed square piano served also as a sideboard for viands and sweets. At a smaller sideboard in one corner two young men were standing, drinking hop-bitters.

Mr Browne led his charges thither and invited them all, in jest, to some ladies' punch, hot, strong and sweet. As they said they never took anything strong he opened three bottles of lemonade for them. Then he asked one of the young men to move aside, and, taking hold of the decanter, filled out for himself a goodly measure of whisky. The young men eyed him respectfully while he took a trial sip.

—God help me, he said, smiling, it's the doctor's orders.

His wizened face broke into a broader smile, and the three young ladies laughed in musical echo to his pleasantry, swaying their bodies to and fro, with nervous jerks of their shoulders. The boldest said:

—O, now, Mr Browne, I'm sure the doctor never ordered anything of the kind.

Mr Browne took another sip of his whisky and said, with sidling mimicry:

—Well, you see, I'm like the famous Mrs Cassidy, who is reported to have said: *Now, Mary Grimes, if I don't take it, make me take it, for I feel I want it.*

His hot face had leaned forward a little too confidentially and he had assumed a very low Dublin accent so that the young ladies, with one instinct, received his speech in silence. Miss Furlong, who was one of Mary Jane's pupils, asked Miss Daly what was the name of the pretty waltz she had played; and Mr Browne, seeing that he was ignored, turned promptly to the two young men who were more appreciative.

A red-faced young woman, dressed in pansy, came into the room, excitedly clapping her hands and crying:

—Quadrilles! Quadrilles![8]

Close on her heels came Aunt Kate, crying:

—Two gentlemen and three ladies, Mary Jane!

—O, here's Mr Bergin and Mr Kerrigan, said Mary Jane. Mr Kerrigan, will you take Miss Power? Miss Furlong, may I get you a partner, Mr Bergin. O, that'll just do now.

—Three ladies, Mary Jane, said Aunt Kate.

The two young gentlemen asked the ladies if they might have the pleasure, and Mary Jane turned to Miss Daly.

—O, Miss Daly, you're really awfully good, after playing for the last two dances, but really we're so short of ladies to-night.

—I don't mind in the least, Miss Morkan.

—But I've a nice partner for you, Mr Bartell D'Arcy, the tenor. I'll get him to sing later on. All Dublin is raving about him.

—Lovely voice, lovely voice! said Aunt Kate.

---

8. The quadrille is a square dance usually performed by four couples.

   As the piano had twice begun the prelude to the first figure Mary Jane led her recruits quickly from the room. They had hardly gone when Aunt Julia wandered slowly into the room, looking behind her at something.

   —What is the matter, Julia? asked Aunt Kate anxiously. Who is it?

   Julia, who was carrying in a column of table-napkins, turned to her sister and said, simply, as if the question had surprised her:

   —It's only Freddy, Kate, and Gabriel with him.

   In fact right behind her Gabriel could be seen piloting Freddy Malins across the landing. The latter, a young man of about forty, was of Gabriel's size and build, with very round shoulders. His face was fleshy and pallid, touched with colour only at the thick hanging lobes of his ears and at the wide wings of his nose. He had coarse features, a blunt nose, a convex and receding brow, tumid and protruded lips. His heavy-lidded eyes and the disorder of his scanty hair made him look sleepy. He was laughing heartily in a high key at a story which he had been telling Gabriel on the stairs and at the same time rubbing the knuckles of his left fist backwards and forwards into his left eye.

   —Good-evening, Freddy, said Aunt Julia.

   Freddy Malins bade the Misses Morkan good-evening in what seemed an offhand fashion by reason of the habitual catch in his voice and then, seeing that Mr Browne was grinning at him from the sideboard, crossed the room on rather shaky legs and began to repeat in an undertone the story he had just told to Gabriel.

   —He's not so bad, is he? said Aunt Kate to Gabriel.

   Gabriel's brows were dark but he raised them quickly and answered:

   —O no, hardly noticeable.

   —Now, isn't he a terrible fellow! she said. And his poor mother made him take the pledge[9] on New Year's Eve. But come on, Gabriel, into the drawing-room.

   Before leaving the room with Gabriel she signalled to Mr Browne by frowning and shaking her forefinger in warning to and fro. Mr Browne nodded in answer and, when she had gone, said to Freddy Malins:

   —Now, then, Teddy, I'm going to fill you out a good glass of lemonade just to buck you up.

   Freddy Malins, who was nearing the climax of his story, waved the offer aside impatiently but Mr Browne, having first called Freddy Malins' attention to a disarray in his dress, filled out and handed him a full glass of lemonade. Freddy Malins' left hand accepted the glass mechanically, his right hand being engaged in the mechanical readjustment of his dress. Mr Browne, whose face was once more wrinkling with mirth, poured out for himself a glass of whisky while Freddy Malins exploded, before he had well reached the climax of his story, in a kink of high-pitched bronchitic laughter and, setting down his untasted and overflow-

9. Sign a solemn engagement not to drink alcohol.

ing glass, began to rub the knuckles of his left fist backwards and forwards
into his left eye, repeating words of his last phrase as well as his fit of
laughter would allow him.

. . .

Gabriel could not listen while Mary Jane was playing her Academy
piece, full of runs and difficult passages, to the hushed drawing-room.
He liked music but the piece she was playing had no melody for him
and he doubted whether it had any melody for the other listeners, though
they had begged Mary Jane to play something. Four young men, who
had come from the refreshment-room to stand in the door-way at the
sound of the piano, had gone away quietly in couples after a few minutes. The only persons who seemed to follow the music were Mary Jane
herself, her hands racing along the key-board or lifted from it at the
pauses like those of a priestess in momentary imprecation, and Aunt
Kate standing at her elbow to turn the page.

Gabriel's eyes, irritated by the floor, which glittered with beeswax under
the heavy chandelier, wandered to the wall above the piano. A picture
of the balcony scene in *Romeo and Juliet* hung there and beside it was a
picture of the two murdered princes in the Tower which Aunt Julia had
worked in red, blue and brown wools when she was a girl. Probably in
the school they had gone to as girls that kind of work had been taught,
for one year his mother had worked for him as a birthday present a
waistcoat of purple tabinet, with little foxes' heads upon it, lined with
brown satin and having round mulberry buttons. It was strange that his
mother had had no musical talent though Aunt Kate used to call her
the brains carrier of the Morkan family. Both she and Julia had always
seemed a little proud of their serious and matronly sister. Her photograph stood before the pierglass. She held an open book on her knees
and was pointing out something in it to Constantine who, dressed in a
man-o'-war suit,[1] lay at her feet. It was she who had chosen the names
for her sons for she was very sensible of the dignity of family life. Thanks
to her, Constantine was now senior curate[2] in Balbriggan and, thanks to
her, Gabriel himself had taken his degree in the Royal University. A
shadow passed over his face as he remembered her sullen opposition to
his marriage. Some slighting phrases she had used still rankled in his
memory; she had once spoken of Gretta as being country cute and that
was not true of Gretta at all. It was Gretta who had nursed her during
all her last long illness in their house at Monkstown.

He knew that Mary Jane must be near the end of her piece for she
was playing again the opening melody with runs of scales after every bar
and while he waited for the end the resentment died down in his heart.
The piece ended with a trill of octaves in the treble and a final deep
octave in the bass. Great applause greeted Mary Jane as, blushing and
rolling up her music nervously, she escaped from the room. The most

1. Sailor-suit, favorite wear for children of both   mirror.
sexes early in this century. "Pierglass": large tall   2. Clergyman appointed to assist a parish priest.

vigorous clapping came from the four young men in the doorway who had gone away to the refreshment-room at the beginning of the piece but had come back when the piano had stopped.

Lancers[3] were arranged. Gabriel found himself partnered with Miss Ivors. She was a frank-mannered talkative young lady, with a freckled face and prominent brown eyes. She did not wear a low-cut bodice and the large brooch which was fixed in the front of her collar bore on it an Irish device.

When they had taken their places she said abruptly:

—I have a crow to pluck with you.

—With me? said Gabriel.

She nodded her head gravely.

—What is it? asked Gabriel, smiling at her solemn manner.

—Who is G. C.? answered Miss Ivors, turning her eyes upon him.

Gabriel coloured and was about to knit his brows, as if he did not understand, when she said bluntly:

—O, innocent Amy! I have found out that you write for *The Daily Express*. Now, aren't you ashamed of yourself?

—Why should I be ashamed of myself? asked Gabriel, blinking his eyes and trying to smile.

—Well, I'm ashamed of you, said Miss Ivors frankly. To say you'd write for a rag like that. I didn't think you were a West Briton.[4]

A look of perplexity appeared on Gabriel's face. It was true that he wrote a literary column every Wednesday in *The Daily Express*, for which he was paid fifteen shillings. But that did not make him a West Briton surely. The books he received for review were almost more welcome than the paltry cheque. He loved to feel the covers and turn over the pages of newly printed books. Nearly every day when his teaching in the college was ended he used to wander down the quays to the second-hand booksellers, to Hickey's on Bachelor's Walk, to Webb's, or Massey's on Aston's Quay, or to O'Clohissey's in the by-street. He did not know how to meet her charge. He wanted to say that literature was above politics. But they were friends of many years' standing and their careers had been parallel, first at the University and then as teachers: he could not risk a grandiose phrase with her. He continued blinking his eyes and trying to smile and murmured lamely that he saw nothing political in writing reviews of books.

When their turn to cross had come he was still perplexed and inattentive. Miss Ivors promptly took his hand in a warm grasp and said in a soft friendly tone:

—Of course, I was only joking. Come, we cross now.

When they were together again she spoke of the University question and Gabriel felt more at ease. A friend of hers had shown her his review of Browning's poems. That was how she had found out the secret: but she liked the review immensely. Then she said suddenly:

3. A square dance for four or more couples.
4. One who denies a separate Irish nationality and sees Ireland as simply the western part of Great Britain.

—O, Mr Conroy, will you come for an excursion to the Aran Isles[5] this summer? We're going to stay there a whole month. It will be splendid out in the Atlantic. You ought to come. Mr Clancy is coming, and Mr Kilkelly and Kathleen Kearney. It would be splendid for Gretta too if she'd come. She's from Connacht,[6] isn't she?

—Her people are, said Gabriel shortly.

—But you will come, won't you? said Miss Ivors, laying her warm hand eagerly on his arm.

—The fact is, said Gabriel, I have already arranged to go—

—Go where? asked Miss Ivors.

—Well, you know, every year I go for a cycling tour with some fellows and so—

—But where? asked Miss Ivors.

—Well, we usually go to France or Belgium or perhaps Germany, said Gabriel awkwardly.

—And why do you go to France and Belgium, said Miss Ivors, instead of visiting your own land?

—Well, said Gabriel, it's partly to keep in touch with the languages and partly for a change.

—And haven't you your own language to keep in touch with—Irish? asked Miss Ivors.

—Well, said Gabriel, if it comes to that, you know, Irish is not my language.

Their neighbours had turned to listen to the cross-examination. Gabriel glanced right and left nervously and tried to keep his good humour under the ordeal which was making a blush invade his forehead.

—And haven't you your own land to visit, continued Miss Ivors, that you know nothing of, your own people, and your own country?

—O, to tell you the truth, retorted Gabriel suddenly, I'm sick of my own country, sick of it!

—Why? asked Miss Ivors.

Gabriel did not answer for his retort had heated him.

—Why? repeated Miss Ivors.

They had to go visiting together and, as he had not answered her, Miss Ivors said warmly:

—Of course, you've no answer.

Gabriel tried to cover his agitation by taking part in the dance with great energy. He avoided her eyes for he had seen a sour expression on her face. But when they met in the long chain he was surprised to feel his hand firmly pressed. She looked at him from under her brows for a moment quizzically until he smiled. Then, just as the chain was about to start again, she stood on tiptoe and whispered into his ear:

—West Briton!

---

5. Three small islands lying across the entrance to Galway Bay, on the west coast of Ireland.
6. Connacht (or Connaught) is a region in the west of Ireland containing largely a poor peasant population.

When the lancers were over Gabriel went away to a remote corner of the room where Freddy Malins' mother was sitting. She was a stout feeble old woman with white hair. Her voice had a catch in it like her son's and she stuttered slightly. She had been told that Freddy had come and that he was nearly all right. Gabriel asked her whether she had had a good crossing. She lived with her married daughter in Glasgow and came to Dublin on a visit once a year. She answered placidly that she had had a beautiful crossing and that the captain had been most attentive to her. She spoke also of the beautiful house her daughter kept in Glasgow, and of all the nice friends they had there. While her tongue rambled on Gabriel tried to banish from his mind all memory of the unpleasant incident with Miss Ivors. Of course the girl or woman, or whatever she was, was an enthusiast but there was a time for all things. Perhaps he ought not to have answered her like that. But she had no right to call him a West Briton before people, even in joke. She had tried to make him ridiculous before people, heckling him and staring at him with her rabbit's eyes.

He saw his wife making her way towards him through the waltzing couples. When she reached him she said into his ear:

—Gabriel, Aunt Kate wants to know won't you carve the goose as usual. Miss Daly will carve the ham and I'll do the pudding.

—All right, said Gabriel.

—She's sending in the younger ones first as soon as this waltz is over so that we'll have the table to ourselves.

—Were you dancing? asked Gabriel.

—Of course I was. Didn't you see me? What words had you with Molly Ivors?

—No words. Why? Did she say so?

—Something like that. I'm trying to get that Mr D'Arcy to sing. He's full of conceit, I think.

—There were no words, said Gabriel moodily, only she wanted me to go for a trip to the west of Ireland and I said I wouldn't.

His wife clasped her hands excitedly and gave a little jump.

—O, do go, Gabriel, she cried. I'd love to see Galway again.

—You can go if you like, said Gabriel coldly.

She looked at him for a moment, then turned to Mrs Malins and said:

—There's a nice husband for you, Mrs Malins.

While she was threading her way back across the room Mrs Malins, without adverting to the interruption, went on to tell Gabriel what beautiful places there were in Scotland and beautiful scenery. Her son-in-law brought them every year to the lakes and they used to go fishing. Her son-in-law was a splendid fisher. One day he caught a fish, a beautiful big big fish, and the man in the hotel boiled it for their dinner.

Gabriel hardly heard what she said. Now that supper was coming near he began to think again about his speech and about the quotation. When he saw Freddy Malins coming across the room to visit his mother Gabriel left the chair free for him and retired into the embrasure of the window. The room had already cleared and from the back room came the clatter of plates and knives. Those who still remained in the drawing-room seemed tired of dancing and were conversing quietly in little groups. Gabriel's warm trembling fingers tapped the cold pane of the window. How cool it must be outside! How pleasant it would be to walk out alone, first along by the river and then through the park! The snow would be lying on the branches of the trees and forming a bright cap on the top of the Wellington Monument. How much more pleasant it would be there than at the supper-table!

He ran over the headings of his speech: Irish hospitality, sad memories, the Three Graces,[7] Paris, the quotation from Browning. He repeated to himself a phrase he had written in his review: *One feels that one is listening to a thought-tormented music.* Miss Ivors had praised the review. Was she sincere? Had she really any life of her own behind all her propagandism? There had never been any ill-feeling between them until that night. It unnerved him to think that she would be at the supper-table, looking up at him while he spoke with her critical quizzing eyes. Perhaps she would not be sorry to see him fail in his speech. An idea came into his mind and gave him courage. He would say, alluding to Aunt Kate and Aunt Julia: *Ladies and Gentlemen, the generation which is now on the wane among us may have had its faults but for my part I think it had certain qualities of hospitality, of humour, of humanity, which the new and very serious and hypereducated generation that is growing up around us seems to me to lack.* Very good: that was one for Miss Ivors. What did he care that his aunts were only two ignorant old women?

A murmur in the room attracted his attention. Mr Browne was advancing from the door, gallantly escorting Aunt Julia, who leaned upon his arm, smiling and hanging her head. An irregular musketry of applause escorted her also as far as the piano and then, as Mary Jane seated herself on the stool, and Aunt Julia, no longer smiling, half turned so as to pitch her voice fairly into the room, gradually ceased. Gabriel recognised the prelude. It was that of an old song of Aunt Julia's—*Arrayed for the Bridal.*[8] Her voice, strong and clear in tone, attacked with great spirit the runs which embellish the air and though she sang very rapidly she did not miss even the smallest of the grace notes. To follow the voice, without looking at the singer's face, was to feel and share the excitement of swift and secure flight. Gabriel applauded loudly with all the others at the close of the song and loud applause was borne in from

---

7. In Greek mythology, three goddesses—Aglaia, splendor; Euphrosyne, festivity; and Thalia, rejoicing—who together represented loveliness and joy. Gabriel is making a mental note to refer to his two aunts and Mary Jane in this complimentary way.

8. This old song (beginning "Arrayed for the bridal,

in beauty behold her") "is replete with long and complicated runs, requiring a sophisticated and gifted singer" (Zack Bowen, *Musical Allusions in the Works of James Joyce* [Albany 1974]); the suggestion is that Aunt Julia was a really accomplished singer.

the invisible supper-table. It sounded so genuine that a little colour struggled into Aunt Julia's face as she bent to replace in the music-stand the old leather-bound songbook that had her initials on the cover. Freddy Malins, who had listened with his head perched sideways to hear her better, was still applauding when everyone else had ceased and talking animatedly to his mother who nodded her head gravely and slowly in acquiescence. At last, when he could clap no more, he stood up suddenly and hurried across the room to Aunt Julia whose hand he seized and held in both his hands, shaking it when words failed him or the catch in his voice proved too much for him.

—I was just telling my mother, he said, I never heard you sing so well, never. No, I never heard your voice so good as it is to-night. Now! Would you believe that now? That's the truth. Upon my word and honour that's the truth I never heard your voice sound so fresh and so . . . so clear and fresh, never.

Aunt Julia smiled broadly and murmured something about compliments as she released her hand from his grasp. Mr Browne extended his open hand towards her and said to those who were near him in the manner of a showman introducing a prodigy to an audience:

—Miss Julia Morkan, my latest discovery!

He was laughing very heartily at this himself when Freddy Malins turned to him and said:

—Well, Browne, if you're serious you might make a worse discovery. All I can say is I never heard her sing half so well as long as I am coming here. And that's the honest truth.

—Neither did I, said Mr Browne. I think her voice has greatly improved.

Aunt Julia shrugged her shoulders and said with meek pride:

—Thirty years ago I hadn't a bad voice as voices go.

—I often told Julia, said Aunt Kate emphatically, that she was simply thrown away in that choir. But she never would be said by me.

She turned as if to appeal to the good sense of the others against a refractory child while Aunt Julia gazed in front of her, a vague smile of reminiscence playing on her face.

—No, continued Aunt Kate, she wouldn't be said or led by anyone, slaving there in that choir night and day, night and day. Six o'clock on Christmas morning! And all for what?

—Well, isn't it for the honour of God, Aunt Kate? asked Mary Jane, twisting round on the piano-stool and smiling.

Aunt Kate turned fiercely on her niece and said:

—I know all about the honour of God, Mary Jane, but I think it's not at all honourable for the pope to turn out the women out of the choirs that have slaved there all their lives and put little whipper-snappers of boys over their heads. I suppose it is for the good of the Church if the pope does it. But it's not just, Mary Jane, and it's not right.

She had worked herself into a passion and would have continued in defence of her sister for it was a sore subject with her but Mary Jane, seeing that all the dancers had come back, intervened pacifically:

—Now, Aunt Kate, you're giving scandal to Mr Browne who is of the other persuasion.[9]

Aunt Kate turned to Mr Browne, who was grinning at this allusion to his religion, and said hastily:

—O, I don't question the pope's being right. I'm only a stupid old woman and I wouldn't presume to do such a thing. But there's such a thing as common everyday politeness and gratitude. And if I were in Julia's place I'd tell that Father Healy straight up to his face . . .

—And besides, Aunt Kate, said Mary Jane, we really are all hungry and when we are hungry we are all very quarrelsome.

—And when we are thirsty we are also quarrelsome, added Mr Browne.

—So that we had better go to supper, said Mary Jane, and finish the discussion afterwards.

On the landing outside the drawing-room Gabriel found his wife and Mary Jane trying to persuade Miss Ivors to stay for supper. But Miss Ivors, who had put on her hat and was buttoning her cloak, would not stay. She did not feel in the least hungry and she had already overstayed her time.

—But only for ten minutes, Molly, said Mrs Conroy. That won't delay you.

—To take a pick itself, said Mary Jane, after all your dancing.

—I really couldn't, said Miss Ivors.

—I am afraid you didn't enjoy yourself at all, said Mary Jane hopelessly.

—Ever so much, I assure you, said Miss Ivors, but you really must let me run off now.

—But how can you get home? asked Mrs Conroy.

—O, it's only two steps up the quay.

Gabriel hesitated a moment and said:

—If you will allow me, Miss Ivors, I'll see you home if you really are obliged to go.

But Miss Ivors broke away from them.

—I won't hear of it, she cried. For goodness sake go in to your suppers and don't mind me. I'm quite well able to take care of myself.

—Well, you're the comical girl, Molly, said Mrs Conroy frankly.

—*Beannacht libh*,[1] cried Miss Ivors, with a laugh, as she ran down the staircase.

Mary Jane gazed after her, a moody puzzled expression on her face, while Mrs Conroy leaned over the banisters to listen for the hall-door. Gabriel asked himself was he the cause of her abrupt departure. But she did not seem to be in ill humour: she had gone away laughing. He stared blankly down the staircase.

At that moment Aunt Kate came toddling out of the supper-room, almost wringing her hands in despair.

9. I.e., Protestant.
1. Gaelic for "good-bye" (literally "blessing on you").

—Where is Gabriel? she cried. Where on earth is Gabriel? There's everyone waiting in there, stage to let, and nobody to carve the goose!

—Here I am, Aunt Kate! cried Gabriel, with sudden animation, ready to carve a flock of geese, if necessary.

A fat brown goose lay at one end of the table and at the other end, on a bed of creased paper strewn with sprigs of parsley, lay a great ham, stripped of its outer skin and peppered over with crust crumbs, a neat paper frill round its shin and beside this was a round of spiced beef. Between these rival ends ran parallel lines of side-dishes: two little mins-ters of jelly, red and yellow; a shallow dish full of blocks of blancmange and red jam, a large green leaf-shaped dish with a stalk-shaped handle, on which lay bunches of purple raisins and peeled almonds, a compan-ion dish on which lay a solid rectangle of Smyrna figs, a dish of custard topped with grated nutmeg, a small bowl full of chocolates and sweets wrapped in gold and silver papers and a glass vase in which stood some tall celery stalks. In the centre of the table there stood, as sentries to a fruit-stand which upheld a pyramid of oranges and American apples, two squat old-fashioned decanters of cut glass, one containing port and the other dark sherry. On the closed square piano a pudding in a huge yellow dish lay in waiting and behind it were three squads of bottles of stout and ale and minerals, drawn up according to the colours of their uniforms, the first two black, with brown and red labels, the third and smallest squad white, with transverse green sashes.

Gabriel took his seat boldly at the head of the table and, having looked to the edge of the carver, plunged his fork firmly into the goose. He felt quite at ease now for he was an expert carver and liked nothing better than to find himself at the head of a well-laden table.

—Miss Furlong, what shall I send you? he asked. A wing or a slice of the breast?

—Just a small slice of the breast.

—Miss Higgins, what for you?

—O, anything at all, Mr Conroy.

While Gabriel and Miss Daly exchanged plates of goose and plates of ham and spiced beef Lily went from guest to guest with a dish of hot floury potatoes wrapped in a white napkin. This was Mary Jane's idea and she had also suggested apple sauce for the goose but Aunt Kate had said that plain roast goose without apple sauce had always been good enough for her and she hoped she might never eat worse. Mary Jane waited on her pupils and saw that they got the best slices and Aunt Kate and Aunt Julia opened and carried across from the piano bottles of stout and ale for the gentlemen and bottles of minerals for the ladies. There was a great deal of confusion and laughter and noise, the noise of orders and counter-orders, of knives and forks, of corks and glass-stoppers. Gabriel began to carve second helpings as soon as he had finished the first round without serving himself. Everyone protested loudly so that he compro-mised by taking a long draught of stout for he had found the carving hot

work. Mary Jane settled down quietly to her supper but Aunt Kate and
Aunt Julia were still toddling round the table, walking on each other's
heels, getting in each other's way and giving each other unheeded orders.
Mr Browne begged of them to sit down and eat their suppers and so did
Gabriel but they said there was time enough so that, at last, Freddy
Malins stood up and, capturing Aunt Kate, plumped her down on her
chair amid general laughter.

When everyone had been well served Gabriel said, smiling:

—Now, if anyone wants a little more of what vulgar people call stuffing let him or her speak.

A chorus of voices invited him to begin his own supper and Lily came
forward with three potatoes which she had reserved for him.

—Very well, said Gabriel amiably, as he took another preparatory
draught, kindly forget my existence, ladies and gentlemen, for a few
minutes.

He set to his supper and took no part in the conversation with which
the table covered Lily's removal of the plates. The subject of talk was
the opera company which was then at the Theatre Royal. Mr Bartell
D'Arcy, the tenor, a dark-complexioned young man with a smart moustache, praised very highly the leading contralto of the company but Miss
Furlong thought she had a rather vulgar style of production. Freddy
Malins said there was a negro chieftain singing in the second part of the
Gaiety pantomime who had one of the finest tenor voices he had every
heard.

—Have you heard him? he asked Mr Bartell D'Arcy across the table.

—No, answered Mr Bartell D'Arcy carelessly.

—Because, Freddy Malins explained, now I'd be curious to hear your
opinion of him. I think he has a grand voice.

—It takes Teddy to find out the really good things, said Mr Browne
familiarly to the table.

—And why couldn't he have a voice too? asked Freddy Malins sharply.
Is it because he's only a black?

Nobody answered this question and Mary Jane led the table back to
the legitimate opera. One of her pupils had given her a pass for *Mignon*.[2]
Of course it was very fine, she said, but it made her think of poor Geor-
gina Burns. Mr Browne could go back farther still, to the old Italian
companies that used to come to Dublin—Tietjens, Ilma de Murzka,
Campanini, the great Trebelli, Giuglini, Ravelli, Aramburo. Those were
the days, he said, when there was something like singing to be heard in
Dublin. He told too of how the top gallery of the old Royal used to be
packed night after night, of how one night an Italian tenor had sung five
encores to *Let Me Like a Soldier Fall*,[3] introducing a high C every time,

2. Opera by Ambroise Thomas first produced in
Paris in 1866, and in London in 1870.
3. This song, from the opera *Maritana* by W.
Wallace (it actually begins "Yes! let me like a soldier fall"), ends on middle C; it would be a piece
of exhibitionism to end on a high C, as Joyce's
father, who had a good voice, used to do. Joyce's
brother Stanislaus remembered the song as insufferable rubbish. Mr. Browne is not to be taken
seriously as a music critic.

and of how the gallery boys would sometimes in their enthusiasm unyoke the horses from the carriage of some great *prima donna* and pull her themselves through the streets to her hotel. Why did they never play the grand old operas now, he asked, *Dinorah, Lucrezia Borgia?*[4] Because they could not get the voices to sing them: that was why.

—O, well, said Mr Bartell D'Arcy, I presume there are as good singers to-day as there were then.

—Where are they? asked Mr Browne defiantly.

—In London, Paris, Milan, said Mr Bartell d'Arcy warmly. I suppose Caruso,[5] for example, is quite as good, if not better than any of the men you have mentioned.

—Maybe so, said Mr Browne. But I may tell you I doubt it strongly.

—O, I'd give anything to hear Caruso sing, said Mary Jane.

—For me, said Aunt Kate, who had been picking a bone, there was only one tenor. To please me, I mean. But I suppose none of you ever heard of him.

—Who was he, Miss Morkan? asked Mr Bartell D'Arcy politely.

—His name, said Aunt Kate, was Parkinson. I heard him when he was in his prime and I think he had then the purest tenor voice that was ever put into a man's throat.

—Strange, said Mr Bartell d'Arcy. I never even heard of him.

—Yes, yes, Miss Morkan is right, said Mr Browne. I remember hearing of old Parkinson but he's too far back for me.

—A beautiful pure sweet mellow English tenor, said Aunt Kate with enthusiasm.

Gabriel having finished, the huge pudding was transferred to the table. The clatter of forks and spoons began again. Gabriel's wife served out spoonfuls of the pudding and passed the plates down the table. Midway down they were held up by Mary Jane, who replenished them with raspberry or orange jelly or with blancmange and jam. The pudding was of Aunt Julia's making and she received praises for it from all quarters. She herself said that it was not quite brown enough.

—Well, I hope, Miss Morkan, said Mr Browne, that I'm brown enough for you because, you know, I'm all brown.

All the gentlemen, except Gabriel, ate some of the pudding out of compliment to Aunt Julia. As Gabriel never ate sweets the celery had been left for him. Freddy Malins also took a stalk of celery and ate it with his pudding. He had been told that celery was a capital thing for the blood and he was just then under doctor's care. Mrs Malins, who had been silent all through the supper, said that her son was going down to Mount Melleray in a week or so. The table then spoke of Mount Melleray, how bracing the air was down there, how hospitable the monks were and how they never asked for a penny-piece from their guests.

—And do you mean to say, asked Mr Browne incredulously, that a

---

4. *Lucrezia Borgia* is an opera by Donizetti, first produced at La Scala, Milan, in 1833; *Dinorah* is an opera by Meyerbeer, first produced in Paris in 1859.

5. Enrico Caruso, 1873–1921, the great Italian dramatic tenor.

chap can go down there and put up there as if it were a hotel and live on the fat of the land and then come away without paying a farthing?

—O, most people give some donation to the monastery when they leave, said Mary Jane.

—I wish we had an institution like that in our Church, said Mr Browne candidly.

He was astonished to hear that the monks never spoke, got up at two in the morning and slept in their coffins. He asked what they did it for.

—That's the rule of the order, said Aunt Kate firmly.

—Yes, but why? asked Mr Browne.

Aunt Kate repeated that it was the rule, that was all. Mr Browne still seemed not to understand. Freddy Malins explained to him, as best he could, that the monks were trying to make up for the sins committed by all the sinners in the outside world. The explanation was not very clear for Mr Browne grinned and said:

—I like that idea very much but wouldn't a comfortable spring bed do them as well as a coffin?

—The coffin, said Mary Jane, is to remind them of their last end.

As the subject had grown lugubrious it was buried in a silence of the table during which Mrs Malins could be heard saying to her neighbour in an indistinct undertone:

—They are very good men, the monks, very pious men.

The raisins and almonds and figs and apples and oranges and chocolates and sweets were now passed about the table and Aunt Julia invited all the guests to have either port or sherry. At first Mr Bartell D'Arcy refused to take either but one of his neighbours nudged him and whispered something to him upon which he allowed his glass to be filled. Gradually as the last glasses were being filled the conversation ceased. A pause followed, broken only by the noise of the wine and by unsettlings of chairs. The Misses Morkan, all three, looked down at the tablecloth. Someone coughed once or twice and then a few gentlemen patted the table gently as a signal for silence. The silence came and Gabriel pushed back his chair and stood up.

The patting at once grew louder in encouragement and then ceased altogether. Gabriel leaned his ten trembling fingers on the tablecloth and smiled nervously at the company. Meeting a row of upturned faces he raised his eyes to the chandelier. The piano was playing a waltz tune and he could hear the skirts sweeping against the drawing-room door. People, perhaps, were standing in the snow on the quay outside, gazing up at the lighted windows and listening to the waltz music. The air was pure there. In the distance lay the park where the trees were weighted with snow. The Wellington Monument wore a gleaming cap of snow that flashed westward over the white field of Fifteen Acres.

He began:

—Ladies and Gentlemen.

—It has fallen to my lot this evening, as in years past, to perform a very pleasing task but a task for which I am afraid my poor powers as a speaker are all too inadequate.

—No, no! said Mr Browne.

—But, however that may be, I can only ask you to-night to take the will for the deed and to lend me your attention for a few moments while I endeavour to express to you in words what my feelings are on this occasion.

—Ladies and Gentlemen. It is not the first time that we have gathered together under this hospitable roof, around this hospitable board. It is not the first time that we have been the recipients—or perhaps, I had better say, the victims—of the hospitality of certain good ladies.

He made a circle in the air with his arm and paused. Everyone laughed or smiled at Aunt Kate and Aunt Julia and Mary Jane who all turned crimson with pleasure. Gabriel went on more boldly:

—I feel more strongly with every recurring year that our country has no tradition which does it so much honour and which it should guard so jealously as that of its hospitality. It is a tradition that is unique as far as my experience goes (and I have visited not a few places abroad) among the modern nations. Some would say, perhaps, that with us it is rather a failing than anything to be boasted of. But granted even that, it is, to my mind, a princely failing, and one that I trust will long be cultivated among us. Of one thing, at least, I am sure. As long as this one roof shelters the good ladies aforesaid—and I wish from my heart it may do so for many and many a long year to come—the tradition of genuine warm-hearted courteous Irish hospitality, which our forefathers have handed down to us and which we in turn must hand down to our descendants, is still alive among us.

A hearty murmur of assent ran round the table. It shot through Gabriel's mind that Miss Ivors was not there and that she had gone away discourteously: and he said with confidence in himself:

—Ladies and Gentlemen.

—A new generation is growing up in our midst, a generation actuated by new ideas and new principles. It is serious and enthusiastic for these new ideas and its enthusiasm, even when it is misdirected, is, I believe, in the main sincere. But we are living in a sceptical and, if I may use the phrase, a thought-tormented age: and sometimes I fear that this new generation, educated or hypereducated as it is, will lack those qualities of humanity, of hospitality, of kindly humour which belonged to an older day. Listening to-night to the names of all those great singers of the past it seemed to me, I must confess, that we were living in a less spacious age. Those days might, without exaggeration, be called spacious days: and if they are gone beyond recall let us hope, at least, that in gatherings such as this we shall still speak of them with pride and affection, still cherish in our hearts the memory of those dead and gone great ones whose fame the world will not willingly let die.

—Hear, hear! said Mr Browne loudly.

—But yet, continued Gabriel, his voice falling into a softer inflection, there are always in gatherings such as this sadder thoughts that will recur to our minds: thoughts of the past, of youth, of changes, of absent faces that we miss here to-night. Our path through life is strewn with many such sad memories: and were we to brood upon them always we could not find the heart to go on bravely with our work among the living. We have all of us living duties and living affections which claim, and rightly claim, our strenuous endeavours.

—Therefore, I will not linger on the past. I will not let any gloomy moralising intrude upon us here to-night. Here we are gathered together for a brief moment from the bustle and rush of our everyday routine. We are met here as friends, in the spirit of good-fellowship, as colleagues, also to a certain extent, in the true spirit of *camaraderie*, and as the guests of—what shall I call them?—the Three Graces of the Dublin musical world.

The table burst into applause and laughter at this sally. Aunt Julia vainly asked each of her neighbours in turn to tell her what Gabriel had said.

—He says we are the Three Graces, Aunt Julia, said Mary Jane.

Aunt Julia did not understand but she looked up, smiling, at Gabriel, who continued in the same vein:

—Ladies and Gentlemen.

—I will not attempt to play to-night the part that Paris played on another occasion. I will not attempt to choose between them. The task would be an invidious one and one beyond my poor powers. For when I view them in turn, whether it be our chief hostess herself, whose good heart, whose too good heart, has become a byword with all who know her, or her sister, who seems to be gifted with perennial youth and whose singing must have been a surprise and a revelation to us all to-night, or, last but not least, when I consider our youngest hostess, talented, cheerful, hard-working and the best of nieces, I confess, Ladies and Gentlemen, that I do not know to which of them I should award the prize.

Gabriel glanced down at his aunts and, seeing the large smile on Aunt Julia's face and the tears which had risen to Aunt Kate's eyes, hastened to his close. He raised his glass of port gallantly, while every member of the company fingered a glass expectantly, and said loudly:

—Let us toast them all three together. Let us drink to their health, wealth, long life, happiness and prosperity and may they long continue to hold the proud and self-won position which they hold in their profession and the position of honour and affection which they hold in our hearts.

All the guests stood up, glass in hand, and, turning towards the three seated ladies, sang in unison, with Mr Browne as leader:

> For they are jolly gay fellows,
> For they are jolly gay fellows,
> For they are jolly gay fellows,
> Which nobody can deny.

Aunt Kate was making frank use of her handkerchief and even Aunt
Julia seemed moved. Freddy Malins beat time with his pudding-fork and
the singers turned towards one another, as if in melodious conference,
while they sang, with emphasis:

> *Unless he tells a lie,*
> *Unless he tells a lie.*

Then, turning once more towards their hostesses, they sang:

> *For they are jolly gay fellows,*
> *For they are jolly gay fellows,*
> *For they are jolly gay fellows,*
> *Which nobody can deny.*

The acclamation which followed was taken up beyond the door of the
supper-room by many of the other guests and renewed time after time,
Freddy Malins acting as officer with his fork on high.

· · ·

The piercing morning air came into the hall where they were standing
so that Aunt Kate said:

—Close the door, somebody. Mrs Malins will get her death of cold.

—Browne is out there, Aunt Kate, said Mary Jane.

—Browne is everywhere, said Aunt Kate, lowering her voice.

Mary Jane laughed at her tone.

—Really, she said archly, he is very attentive.

—He has been laid on here like the gas, said Aunt Kate in the same
tone, all during the Christmas.

She laughed herself this time good-humouredly and then added quickly:

—But tell him to come in, Mary Jane, and close the door. I hope to
goodness he didn't hear me.

At that moment the hall-door was opened and Mr Browne came in
from the doorstep, laughing as if his heart would break. He was dressed
in a long green overcoat with mock astrakhan cuffs and collar and wore
on his head an oval fur cap. He pointed down the snow-covered quay
from where the sound of shrill prolonged whistling was borne in.

—Teddy will have all the cabs in Dublin out, he said.

Gabriel advanced from the little pantry behind the office, struggling
into his overcoat and, looking round the hall, said:

—Gretta not down yet?

—She's getting on her things, Gabriel, said Aunt Kate.

—Who's playing up there? asked Gabriel.

—Nobody. They're all gone.

—O no, Aunt Kate, said Mary Jane. Bartell D'Arcy and Miss O'Callaghan aren't gone yet.

—Someone is strumming at the piano, anyhow, said Gabriel.

Mary Jane glanced at Gabriel and Mr Browne and said with a shiver:

—It makes me feel cold to look at you two gentlemen muffled up like
that. I wouldn't like to face your journey home at this hour.

—I'd like nothing better this minute, said Mr Browne stoutly, than a rattling fine walk in the country or a fast drive with a good spanking goer between the shafts.

—We used to have a very good horse and trap[6] at home, said Aunt Julia sadly.

—The never-to-be-forgotten Johnny, said Mary Jane, laughing.

Aunt Kate and Gabriel laughed too.

—Why, what was wonderful about Johnny? asked Mr Browne.

—The late lamented Patrick Morkan, our grandfather, that is, explained Gabriel, commonly known in his later years as the old gentleman, was a glue-boiler.

—O, now, Gabriel, said Aunt Kate, laughing, he had a starch mill.

—Well, glue or starch, said Gabriel, the old gentleman had a horse by the name of Johnny. And Johnny used to work in the old gentleman's mill, walking round and round in order to drive the mill. That was all very well; but now comes the tragic part about Johnny. One fine day the old gentleman thought he'd like to drive out with the quality[7] to a military review in the park.

—The Lord have mercy on his soul, said Aunt Kate compassionately.

—Amen, said Gabriel. So the old gentleman, as I said, harnessed Johnny and put on his very best tall hat and his very best stock collar and drive out in grand style from his ancestral mansion somewhere near Back Lane, I think.

Everyone laughed, even Mrs Malins, at Gabriel's manner and Aunt Kate said:

—O now, Gabriel, he didn't live in Back Lane, really. Only the mill was there.

—Out from the mansion of his forefathers, continued Gabriel, he drove with Johnny. And everything went on beautifully until Johnny came in sight of King Billy's statue: and whether he fell in love with the horse King Billy sits on or whether he thought he was back again in the mill, anyhow he began to walk round the statue.

Gabriel paced in a circle round the hall in his goloshes amid the laughter of the others.

—Round and round he went, said Gabriel, and the old gentleman, who was a very pompous old gentleman, was highly indignant. *Go on, sir! What do you mean, sir? Johnny! Johnny! Most extraordinary conduct! Can't understand the horse!*

The peals of laughter which followed Gabriel's imitation of the incident were interrupted by a resounding knock at the hall-door. Mary Jane ran to open it and let in Freddy Malins. Freddy Malins, with his hat well back on his head and his shoulders humped with cold, was puffing and steaming after his exertions.

—I could only get one cab, he said.

—O, we'll find another along the quay, said Gabriel.

6. A two-wheeled horse-drawn carriage on springs.   7. People of rank or high social position.

—Yes, said Aunt Kate. Better not keep Mrs Malins standing in the draught.

Mrs Malins was helped down the front steps by her son and Mr Browne and, after many manœuvres, hoisted into the cab. Freddy Malins clambered in after her and spent a long time settling her on the seat, Mr Browne helping him with advice. At last she was settled comfortably and Freddy Malins invited Mr Browne into the cab. There was a good deal of confused talk, and then Mr Browne got into the cab. The cabman settled his rug over his knees, and bent down for the address. The confusion grew greater and the cabman was directed differently by Freddy Malins and Mr Browne, each of whom had his head out through a window of the cab. The difficulty was to know where to drop Mr Browne along the route and Aunt Kate, Aunt Julia and Mary Jane helped the discussion from the doorstep with cross-directions and contradictions and abundance of laughter. As for Freddy Malins he was speechless with laughter. He popped his head in and out of the window every moment, to the great danger of his hat, and told his mother how the discussion was progressing till at last Mr Browne shouted to the bewildered cabman above the din of everybody's laughter:

—Do you know Trinity College?

—Yes, sir, said the cabman.

—Well, drive bang up against Trinity College gates, said Mr Browne, and then we'll tell you where to go. You understand now?

—Yes, sir, said the cabman.

—Make like a bird for Trinity College.

—Right, sir, cried the cabman.

The horse was whipped up and the cab rattled off along the quay amid a chorus of laughter and adieus.

Gabriel had not gone to the door with the others. He was in a dark part of the hall gazing up the staircase. A woman was standing near the top of the first flight, in the shadow also. He could not see her face but he could see the terracotta and salmonpink panels of her skirt which the shadow made appear black and white. It was his wife. She was leaning on the banisters, listening to something. Gabriel was surprised at her stillness and strained his ear to listen also. But he could hear little save the noise of laughter and dispute on the front steps, a few chords struck on the piano and a few notes of a man's voice singing.

He stood still in the gloom of the hall, trying to catch the air that the voice was singing and gazing up at his wife. There was grace and mystery in her attitude as if she were a symbol of something. He asked himself what is a woman standing on the stairs in the shadow, listening to distant music, a symbol of. If he were a painter he would paint her in that attitude. Her blue felt hat would show off the bronze of her hair against the darkness and the dark panels of her skirt would show off the light ones. *Distant Music* he would call the picture if he were a painter.

The hall-door was closed; and Aunt Kate, Aunt Julia and Mary Jane came down the hall, still laughing.

—Well, isn't Freddy terrible? said Mary Jane. He's really terrible.

Gabriel said nothing but pointed up the stairs towards where his wife was standing. Now that the hall-door was closed the voice and the piano could be heard more clearly. Gabriel held up his hand for them to be silent. The song seemed to be in the old Irish tonality and the singer seemed uncertain both of his words and of his voice. The voice, made plaintive by distance and by the singer's hoarseness, faintly illuminated the cadence of the air with words expressing grief:

> O, *the rain falls on my heavy locks*
> And *the dew wets my skin,*
> *My babe lies cold . . .*

—O, exclaimed Mary Jane. It's Bartell D'Arcy singing and he wouldn't sing all the night. O, I'll get him to sing a song before he goes.

—O do, Mary Jane, said Aunt Kate.

Mary Jane brushed past the others and ran to the staircase but before she reached it the singing stopped and the piano was closed abruptly.

—O, what a pity! she cried. Is he coming down, Gretta?

Gabriel heard his wife answer yes and saw her come down towards them. A few steps behind her were Mr Bartell D'Arcy and Miss O'Callaghan.

—O, Mr D'Arcy, cried Mary Jane, it's downright mean of you to break off like that when we were all in raptures listening to you.

—I have been at him all the evening, said Miss O'Callaghan, and Mrs Conroy too and he told us he had a dreadful cold and couldn't sing.

—O, Mr D'Arcy, said Aunt Kate, now that was a great fib to tell.

—Can't you see that I'm as hoarse as a crow? said Mr D'Arcy roughly.

He went into the pantry hastily and put on his overcoat. The others, taken aback by his rude speech, could find nothing to say. Aunt Kate wrinkled her brows and made signs to the others to drop the subject. Mr D'Arcy stood swathing his neck carefully and frowning.

—It's the weather, said Aunt Julia, after a pause.

—Yes, everybody has colds, said Aunt Kate readily, everybody.

—They say, said Mary Jane, we haven't had snow like it for thirty years; and I read this morning in the newspapers that the snow is general all over Ireland.

—I love the look of snow, said Aunt Julia sadly.

—So do I, said Miss O'Callaghan. I think Christmas is never really Christmas unless we have the snow on the ground.

—But poor Mr D'Arcy doesn't like the snow, said Aunt Kate, smiling.

Mr D'Arcy came from the pantry, full swathed and buttoned, and in a repentant tone told them the history of his cold. Everyone gave him advice and said it was a great pity and urged him to be very careful of his throat in the night air. Gabriel watched his wife who did not join in the conversation. She was standing right under the dusty fanlight and the flame of the gas lit up the rich bronze of her hair which he had seen her drying at the fire a few days before. She was in the same attitude and seemed unaware of the talk about her. At last she turned towards them and Gabriel saw that there was colour on her cheeks and that her eyes were shining. A sudden tide of joy went leaping out of his heart.

—Mr D'Arcy, she said, what is the name of that song you were singing?

—It's called *The Lass of Aughrim*,[8] said Mr D'Arcy, but I couldn't remember it properly. Why? Do you know it?

—*The Lass of Aughrim*, she repeated. I couldn't think of the name.

—It's a very nice air, said Mary Jane. I'm sorry you were not in voice to-night.

—Now, Mary Jane, said Aunt Kate, don't annoy Mr D'Arcy. I won't have him annoyed.

Seeing that all were ready to start she shepherded them to the door where good-night was said:

—Well, good-night, Aunt Kate, and thanks for the pleasant evening.

—Good-night, Gabriel. Good-night, Gretta!

—Good-night, Aunt Kate, and thanks ever so much. Good-night, Aunt Julia.

—O, good-night, Gretta, I didn't see you.

—Good-night, Mr D'Arcy. Good-night, Miss O'Callaghan.

—Good-night, Miss Morkan.

—Good-night, again.

—Good-night, all. Safe home.

—Good-night. Good-night.

The morning was still dark. A dull yellow light brooded over the houses and the river; and the sky seemed to be descending. It was slushy underfoot; and only streaks and patches of snow lay on the roofs, on the parapets of the quay and on the area railings. The lamps were still burning redly in the murky air and, across the river, the palace of the Four Courts stood out menacingly against the heavy sky.

She was walking on before him with Mr Bartell D'Arcy, her shoes in a brown parcel tucked under one arm and her hands holding her skirt up from the slush. She had no longer any grace of attitude but Gabriel's eyes were still bright with happiness. The blood went bounding along his veins; and the thoughts went rioting through his brain, proud, joyful, tender, valorous.

She was walking on before him so lightly and so erect that he longed to run after her noiselessly, catch her by the shoulders and say something foolish and affectionate into her ear. She seemed to him so frail that he longed to defend her against something and then to be alone with her. Moments of their secret life together burst like stars upon his memory. A heliotrope envelope was lying beside his breakfast-cup and he was caressing it with his hand. Birds were twittering in the ivy and the sunny web of the curtain was shimmering along the floor: he could not eat for

---

8. An Irish version of a ballad about a girl deserted by her lover whom she later tries to find, bringing the baby she had by him. Other versions are called *Love Gregory* and *Lord Gregory* (the name of the deserting lover), *The Lass of Lochryan*, and *The Lass of Ocram*.

happiness. They were standing on the crowded platform and he was placing a ticket inside the warm palm of her glove. He was standing with her in the cold, looking in through a grated window at a man making bottles in a roaring furnace. It was very cold. Her face, fragrant in the cold air, was quite close to his; and suddenly she called out to the man at the furnace:

—Is the fire hot, sir?

But the man could not hear her with the noise of the furnace. It was just as well. He might have answered rudely.

A wave of yet more tender joy escaped from his heart and went coursing in warm flood along his arteries. Like the tender fires of stars moments of their life together, that no one knew of or would ever know of, broke upon and illumined his memory. He longed to recall to her those moments, to make her forget the years of their dull existence together and remember only their moments of ecstasy. For the years, he felt, had not quenched his soul or hers. Their children, his writing, her household cares had not quenched all their souls' tender fire. In one letter that he had written to her then he had said: *Why is it that words like these seem to me so dull and cold? Is it because there is no word tender enough to be your name?*

Like distant music these words that he had written years before were borne towards him from the past. He longed to be alone with her. When the others had gone away, when he and she were in their room in the hotel, then they would be alone together. He would call her softly:

—Gretta!

Perhaps she would not hear at once: she would be undressing. Then something in his voice would strike her. She would turn and look at him. . . .

At the corner of Winetavern Street they met a cab. He was glad of its rattling noise as it saved him from conversation. She was looking out of the window and seemed tired. The others spoke only a few words, pointing out some building or street. The horse galloped along wearily under the murky morning sky, dragging his old rattling box after his heels, and Gabriel was again in a cab with her, galloping to catch the boat, galloping to their honeymoon.

As the cab drove across O'Connell Bridge[9] Miss O'Callaghan said:

—They say you never cross O'Connell Bridge without seeing a white horse.

—I see a white man this time, said Gabriel.

—Where? asked Mr Bartell D'Arcy.

Gabriel pointed to the statue, on which lay patches of snow. Then he nodded familiarly to it and waved his hand.

—Good-night, Dan, he said gaily.

When the cab drew up before the hotel Gabriel jumped out and, in

9. Daniel O'Connell, 1775–1847, Irish nationalist, statesman, and orator. His statue stands by O'Connell Bridge in Dublin.

spite of Mr Bartell D'Arcy's protest, paid the driver. He gave the man a shilling over his fare. The man saluted and said:

—A prosperous New Year to you, sir.

—The same to you, said Gabriel cordially.

She leaned for a moment on his arm in getting out of the cab and while standing at the curbstone, bidding the others good-night. She leaned lightly on his arm, as lightly as when she had danced with him a few hours before. He had felt proud and happy then, happy that she was his, proud of her grace and wifely carriage. But now, after the kindling again of so many memories, the first touch of her body, musical and strange and perfumed, sent through him a keen pang of lust. Under cover of her silence he pressed her arm closely to his side; and, as they stood at the hotel door, he felt that they had escaped from their lives and duties, escaped from home and friends and run away together with wild and radiant hearts to a new adventure.

An old man was dozing in a great hooded chair in the hall. He lit a candle in the office and went before them to the stairs. They followed him in silence, their feet falling in soft thuds on the thickly carpeted stairs. She mounted the stairs behind the porter, her head bowed in the ascent, her frail shoulders curved as with a burden, her skirt girt tightly about her. He could have flung his arms about her hips and held her still for his arms were trembling with desire to seize her and only the stress of his nails against the palms of his hands held the wild impulse of his body in check. The porter halted on the stairs to settle his guttering candle. They halted too on the steps below him. In the silence Gabriel could hear the falling of the molten wax into the tray and the thumping of his own heart against his ribs.

The porter led them along a corridor and opened a door. Then he set his unstable candle down on a toilet-table and asked at what hour they were to be called in the morning.

—Eight, said Gabriel.

The porter pointed to the tap of the electric-light and began a muttered apology but Gabriel cut him short.

—We don't want any light. We have light enough from the street. And I say, he added, pointing to the candle, you might remove that handsome article, like a good man.

The porter took up his candle again, but slowly for he was surprised by such a novel idea. Then he mumbled good-night and went out. Gabriel shot the lock to.

A ghostly light from the street lamp lay in a long shaft from one window to the door. Gabriel threw his overcoat and hat on a couch and crossed the room towards the window. He looked down into the street in order that his emotion might calm a little. Then he turned and leaned against a chest of drawers with his back to the light. She had taken off her hat and cloak and was standing before a large swinging mirror, unhooking her waist. Gabriel paused for a few moments, watching her, and then said:

—Gretta!

She turned away from the mirror slowly and walked along the shaft of light towards him. Her face looked so serious and weary that the words would not pass Gabriel's lips. No, it was not the moment yet.

—You looked tired, he said.

—I am a little, she answered.

—You don't feel ill or weak?

—No, tired: that's all.

She went on to the window and stood there, looking out. Gabriel waited again and then, fearing that diffidence was about to conquer him, he said abruptly:

—By the way, Gretta!

—What is it?

—You know that poor fellow Malins? he said quickly.

—Yes. What about him?

—Well, poor fellow, he's a decent sort of chap after all, continued Gabriel in a false voice. He gave me back that sovereign I lent him and I didn't expect it really. It's a pity he wouldn't keep away from that Browne, because he's not a bad fellow at heart.

He was trembling now with annoyance. Why did she seem so abstracted? He did not know how he could begin. Was she annoyed, too, about something? If she would only turn to him or come to him of her own accord! To take her as she was would be brutal. No, he must see some ardour in her eyes first. He longed to be master of her strange mood.

—When did you lend him the pound? she asked, after a pause.

Gabriel strove to restrain himself from breaking out into brutal language about the sottish Malins and his pound. He longed to cry to her from his soul, to crush her body against his, to overmaster her. But he said:

—O, at Christmas, when he opened that little Christmas-card shop in Henry Street.

He was in such a fever of rage and desire that he did not hear her come from the window. She stood before him for an instant, looking at him strangely. Then, suddenly raising herself on tiptoe and resting her hands lightly on his shoulders, she kissed him.

—You are a very generous person, Gabriel, she said.

Gabriel, trembling with delight at her sudden kiss and at the quaintness of her phrase, put his hands on her hair and began smoothing it back, scarcely touching it with his fingers. The washing had made it fine and brilliant. His heart was brimming over with happiness. Just when he was wishing for it she had come to him of her own accord. Perhaps her thoughts had been running with his. Perhaps she had felt the impetuous desire that was in him and then the yielding mood had come upon her. Now that she had fallen to him so easily he wondered why he had been so diffident.

He stood, holding her head between his hands. Then, slipping one arm swiftly about her body and drawing her towards him, he said softly:

—Gretta dear, what are you thinking about?

She did not answer nor yield wholly to his arm. He said again, softly:

—Tell me what it is, Gretta. I think I know what is the matter. Do I know?

She did not answer at once. Then she said in an outburst of tears:

—O, I am thinking about that song, *The Lass of Aughrim*.

She broke loose from him and ran to the bed and, throwing her arms across the bed-rail, hid her face. Gabriel stood stock-still for a moment in astonishment and then followed her. As he passed in the way of the cheval-glass he caught sight of himself in full length, his broad, well-filled shirt-front, the face whose expression always puzzled him when he saw it in a mirror and his glimmering gilt-rimmed eyeglasses. He halted a few paces from her and said:

—What about the song? Why does that make you cry?

She raised her head from her arms and dried her eyes with the back of her hand like a child. A kinder note than he had intended went into his voice.

—Why, Gretta? he asked.

—I am thinking about a person long ago who used to sing that song.

—And who was the person long ago? asked Gabriel, smiling.

—It was a person I used to know in Galway when I was living with my grandmother, she said.

The smile passed away from Gabriel's face. A dull anger began to gather again at the back of his mind and the dull fires of his lust began to glow angrily in his veins.

—Someone you were in love with? he asked ironically.

—It was a young boy I used to know, she answered, named Michael Furey. He used to sing that song, *The Lass of Aughrim*. He was very delicate.

Gabriel was silent. He did not wish her to think that he was interested in this delicate boy.

—I can see him so plainly, she said after a moment. Such eyes as he had: big dark eyes! And such an expression in them—an expression!

—O then, you were in love with him? said Gabriel.

—I used to go out walking with him, she said, when I was in Galway.

A thought flew across Gabriel's mind.

—Perhaps that was why you wanted to go to Galway with that Ivors girl? he said coldly.

She looked at him and asked in surprise:

—What for?

Her eyes made Gabriel feel awkward. He shrugged his shoulders and said.

—How do I know! To see him perhaps.

She looked away from him along the shaft of light towards the window in silence.

—He is dead, she said at length. He died when he was only seventeen. Isn't it a terrible thing to die so young as that?

—What was he? asked Gabriel, still ironically.

—He was in the gasworks, she said.

Gabriel felt humiliated by the failure of his irony and by the evocation
of this figure from the dead, a boy in the gasworks. While he had been
full of memories of their secret life together, full of tenderness and joy
and desire, she had been comparing him in her mind with another. A
shameful consciousness of his own person assailed him. He saw himself
as a ludicrous figure, acting as a pennyboy for his aunts, a nervous well-
meaning sentimentalist, orating to vulgarians and idealising his own
clownish lusts, the pitiable fatuous fellow he had caught a glimpse of in
the mirror. Instinctively he turned his back more to the light lest she
might see the shame that burned upon his forehead.

He tried to keep up his tone of cold interrogation but his voice when
he spoke was humble and indifferent.

—I suppose you were in love with this Michael Furey, Gretta, he
said.

—I was great with him at that time, she said.

Her voice was veiled and sad. Gabriel, feeling now how vain it would
be to try to lead her whither he had purposed, caressed one of her hands
and said, also sadly:

—And what did he die of so young, Gretta? Consumption, was it?

—I think he died for me, she answered.

A vague terror seized Gabriel at this answer as if, at that hour when
he had hoped to triumph, some impalpable and vindictive being was
coming against him, gathering forces against him in its vague world. But
he shook himself free of it with an effort of reason and continued to
caress her hand. He did not question her again for he felt that she would
tell him of herself. Her hand was warm and moist: it did not respond to
his touch but he continued to caress it just as he had caressed her first
letter to him that spring morning.

—It was in the winter, she said, about the beginning of the winter
when I was going to leave my grandmother's and come up here to the
convent. And he was ill at the time in his lodgings in Galway and wouldn't
be let out and his people in Oughterard were written to. He was in
decline, they said, or something like that. I never knew rightly.

She paused for a moment and sighed.

—Poor fellow, she said. He was very fond of me and he was such a
gentle boy. We used to go out together, walking, you know, Gabriel,
like the way they do in the country. He was going to study singing only
for his health. He had a very good voice, poor Michael Furey.

—Well; and then? asked Gabriel.

—And then when it came to the time for me to leave Galway and
come up to the convent he was much worse and I wouldn't be let see
him so I wrote a letter saying I was going up to Dublin and would be
back in the summer and hoping he would be better then.

She paused for a moment to get her voice under control and then went on:

—Then the night before I left I was in my grandmother's house in Nuns' Island, packing up, and I heard gravel thrown up against the window. The window was so wet I couldn't see so I ran downstairs as I was and slipped out the back into the garden and there was the poor fellow at the end of the garden, shivering.

—And did you not tell him to go back? asked Gabriel.

—I implored him to go home at once and told him he would get his death in the rain. But he said he did not want to live. I can see his eyes as well as well! He was standing at the end of the wall where there was a tree.

—And did he go home? asked Gabriel.

—Yes, he went home. And when I was only a week in the convent he died and he was buried in Oughterard where his people came from. O, the day I heard that, that he was dead!

She stopped, choking with sobs, and overcome by emotion, flung herself face downward on the bed, sobbing in the quilt. Gabriel held her hand for a moment longer, irresolutely, and then, shy of intruding on her grief, let it fall gently and walked quietly to the window.

She was fast asleep.

Gabriel, leaning on his elbow, looked for a few moments unresentfully on her tangled hair and half-open mouth, listening to her deep-drawn breath. So she had had that romance in her life: a man had died for her sake. It hardly pained him now to think how poor a part he, her husband, had played in her life. He watched her while she slept as though he and she had never lived together as man and wife. His curious eyes rested long upon her face and on her hair: and, as he thought of what she must have been then, in that time of her first girlish beauty, a strange friendly pity for her entered his soul. He did not like to say even to himself that her face was no longer beautiful but he knew that it was no longer the face for which Michael Furey had braved death.

Perhaps she had not told him all the story. His eyes moved to the chair over which she had thrown some of her clothes. A petticoat string dangled to the floor. One boot stood upright, its limp upper fallen down: the fellow of it lay upon its side. He wondered at his riot of emotions of an hour before. From what had it proceeded? From his aunt's supper, from his own foolish speech, from the wine and dancing, the merry-making when saying good-night in the hall, the pleasure of the walk along the river in the snow. Poor Aunt Julia! She, too, would soon be a shade with the shade of Patrick Morkan and his horse. He had caught that haggard look upon her face for a moment when she was singing *Arrayed for the Bridal*. Soon, perhaps, he would be sitting in that same drawing-room, dressed in black, his silk hat on his knees. The blinds would be drawn down and Aunt Kate would be sitting beside him, crying and blowing her nose and telling him how Julia had died. He would cast about in his mind for some words that might console her, and would find only lame and useless ones. Yes, yes: that would happen very soon.

The air of the room chilled his shoulders. He stretched himself cautiously along under the sheets and lay down beside his wife. One by one they were all becoming shades. Better pass boldly into that other world, in the full glory of some passion, than fade and wither dismally with age. He thought of how she who lay beside him had locked in her heart for so many years that image of her lover's eyes when he had told her that he did not wish to live.

Generous tears filled Gabriel's eyes. He had never felt like that himself towards any woman but he knew that such a feeling must be love. The tears gathered more thickly in his eyes and in the partial darkness he imagined he saw the form of a young man standing under a dripping tree. Other forms were near. His soul had approached that region where dwell the vast hosts of the dead. He was conscious of, but could not apprehend, their wayward and flickering existence. His own identity was fading out into a grey impalpable world: the solid world itself which these dead had one time reared and lived in was dissolving and dwindling.

A few light taps upon the pane made him turn to the window. It had begun to snow again. He watched sleepily the flakes, silver and dark, falling obliquely against the lamplight. The time had come for him to set out on his journey westward. Yes, the newspapers were right: snow was general all over Ireland. It was falling on every part of the dark central plain, on the treeless hills, falling softly upon the Bog of Allen[10] and, farther westward, softly falling into the dark mutinous Shannon waves. It was falling, too, upon every part of the lonely churchyard on the hill where Michael Furey lay buried. It lay thickly drifted on the crooked crosses and headstones, on the spears of the little gate, on the barren thorns. His soul swooned slowly as he heard the snow falling faintly through the universe and faintly falling, like the descent of their last end, upon all the living and the dead.

1914

---

10. The name given to many separate peat bogs between the rivers Liffey (which runs through Dublin) and Shannon (which runs through the central plain of Ireland).

From Ulysses[1]

[Proteus][2]

Ineluctable modality of the visible: at least that if no more, thought through my eyes.[3] Signatures of all things I am here to read, seaspawn and seawrack, the nearing tide, that rusty boot. Snotgreen, bluesilver, rust: coloured signs. Limits of the diaphane.[4] But he adds: in bodies. Then he was aware of them bodies before of them coloured. How? By knocking his sconce against them, sure. Go easy. Bald he was and a millionaire, *maestro di color che sanno.*[5] Limit of the diaphane in. Why in? Diaphane, adiaphane.[6] If you can put your five fingers through it, it is a gate, if not a door. Shut your eyes and see.

Stephen closed his eyes to hear his boots crush crackling wrack and shells. You are walking through it howsomever. I am, a stride at a time. A very short space of time through very short times of space. Five, six: the *Nacheinander.*[7] Exactly: and that is the ineluctable modality of the audible. Open your eyes. No. Jesus! If I fell over a cliff that beetles o'er

1. *Ulysses* was first published in book form on Feb. 2, 1922, Joyce's 40th birthday. The text given here has been collated with the 1932 Odyssey Press edition.

2. "Proteus" is so titled because of the deliberate analogies that exist between it and the description of Proteus in *Odyssey* 4 (Joyce did not title any of the episodes in *Ulysses*, but the names are his; he used them in correspondence and in talk with friends.)

In Homer's *Odyssey*, Proteus is the changing sea god who continually alters his shape: when Telemachus, the son of Ulysses, asks Menelaus for help in finding his father, Menelaus tells him that he encountered Proteus by the seashore on the island of Pharos "in front of Egypt," and that, by holding on to him while he changed from one shape to another, he was able to force him to tell what had happened to Ulysses and the other Greek heroes of the Trojan war. In Joyce's narrative, Stephen Dedalus (who, like Homer's Telemachus, is looking for a father, but not in the literal "consubstantial" sense) is walking in the Dublin shore alone, "along Sandymount strand," speculating on the shifting shapes of things and the possibility of knowing truth by mere appearances.

First Stephen meditates on the "modality of the visible" and on the mystical notion that God writes his signature on all His works; then on the "modality of the audible," closing his eyes and trying to know reality simply through the sense of hearing. As he continues his walk, the people and objects he sees mingle in his thoughts with memories of his past relations with his family, of his school-days, his residence in Paris whence he was recalled by his mother's fatal illness, his feeling of guilt about his mother's death (he had refused to kneel down

and pray at her bedside, since he considered it would be a betrayal of his integrity as an unbeliever), and a variety of speculations about life and reality often derived from mystical works he had read "in the stagnant bay of Marsh's library" (in Dublin). The highly theoretical, inquiring, musing, speculating mind of Stephen is in sharp contrast to the practical, humane, sensual, concrete imagination of the book's real hero, Leopold Bloom, but there are also significant parallels between the streams of consciousness of the two. Some of the more important themes which emerge in Stephen's reverie are pointed out in footnotes.

3. I.e., the sense of sight provides an unavoidable way ("ineluctable modality") of knowing reality, the knowledge thus provided being a kind of "thought through [the] eyes." The phrase "signature of all things" comes from the German mystic Jackob Böhme (1575–1624).

4. Transparency. Stephen is speculating on Aristotle's view of perception as developed in his *De Anima.*

5. There was a tradition that Aristotle was bald, with thin legs, small eyes, and a lisp. Aristotle is also traditionally supposed to have inherited considerable wealth and to have been presented with a fortune by his former pupil Alexander the Great. The Italian Phrase is Dante's description of Aristotle in the *Inferno,* and means "the master of them that know."

6. What is not transparent (opposite of "diaphane").

7. "After one another." Stephen, with eyes shut, is now sensing reality through the sense of sound only: unlike sight, sound falls on the sense of hearing in chronological sequence, one sound after another.

his base,[8] fell through the *Nebeneinander* ineluctably. I am getting on nicely in the dark. My ash sword hangs at my side. Tap with it: they do.[9] My two feet in his boots are at the ends of my legs, *nebeneinander*. Sounds solid: made by the mallet of *Los demiurgos*.[1] Am I walking into eternity along Sandymount strand? Crush, crack, crik, crick. Wild sea money. Dominie[2] Deasy kens them a'.

> *Won't you come to Sandymount,*
> *Madeline the mare?*

Rhythm begins, you see. I hear. A catalectic tetrameter[3] of iambs marching. No, agallop: *deline the mare*.

Open your eyes now. I will. One moment. Has all vanished since? If I open and am for ever in the black adiaphane. *Basta!*[4] I will see if I can see.

See now. There all the time without you: and ever shall be, world without end.

They came down the steps from Leahy's terrace prudently, *Frauenzimmer:*[5] and down the shelving shore flabbily, their splayed feet sinking in the silted sand. Like me, like Algy,[6] coming down to our mighty mother. Number one swung lourdily[7] her midwife's bag, the other's gamp poked in the beach. From the liberties, out for the day. Mrs Florence MacCabe, relict of the late Patk MacCabe,[8] deeply lamented, of Bride Street. One of her sisterhood lugged me squealing into life. Creation from nothing. What has she in the bag? A misbirth with a trailing navelcord, hushed in ruddy wool. The cords of all link back, strandentwining cable of all flesh. That is why mystic monks. Will you be as gods? Gaze in your *omphalos*. Hello. Kinch here. Put me on to Edenville. Aleph, alpha: nought, nought, one.[9]

8. "What if it tempt you toward the flood, my lord. / Or to the dreadful summit of the cliff / That beetles o'er his base into the sea . . ." (*Hamlet* 1.4.69–71). "*Nebeneinander*": beside one another.

9. Stephen is still walking with his eyes shut, tapping with his "ash sword" (the walking stick of ash wood he always carried), as "they" (i.e., blind people) do. "His boots": Buck Mulligan's. Stephen, lacking boots of his own, had borrowed a castoff pair of Mulligan's.

1. The Demiurge, supernatural being who made the world in subordination to God. The mystical notion of the Demiurge who created the world haunts Stephen's mind; it is the Demiurge who writes his signature on created objects and whose mallet fashioned them. The world, sensed by the ear only, "sounds solid," as though made by the Demiurge's hammer.

2. Schoolmaster, Mr. Deasy was the headmaster of the school where Stephen taught (the previous episode has shown Stephen teaching). "Kens them a' ": knows them all; Stephen is putting Deasy into a mock-Scottish folk song.

3. The first of the two lines of popular verse which have come into Stephen's head consists metrically of four iambic feet ("tetrameter") with the last foot unlike the first, not defective ("catalectic").

4. Italian, "Enough!"

5. Here "midwives"; Stephen sees them coming from Leahy's Terrace, which runs by the beach.

6. Algernon Charles Swinburne, who wrote: "I will go back to the great sweet mother, / Mother and lover of men, the sea. I will go down to her, I and none other . . ." (*The Triumph of Time*).

7. Heavily (coined by Stephen from the French *lourd*). Stephen, like Joyce, had studied modern languages at University College, Dublin, and his preoccupation with words and languages is part of his character as potential literary artist. "Gamp": umbrella; and perhaps reference to Mrs. Gamp, the nurse in Dickens' *Martin Chuzzlewit*.

8. Stephen imagines the first midwife is called Mrs. MacCabe. "Relict": widow.

9. Stephen is speculating on the mystical significance of the naval cord, seeing it as linking the generations, the combined navel cords stretching back to Adam and Eve. A mystic gazed in his *omphalos* (navel) to make contact with the first man. Stephen thinks of himself ("Kinch," his nickname) calling up Adam in "Edenville" through his navel, using the line of linked navel cords as a telephone line. Adam's telephone number, "Aleph, alpha: nought, nought, one," begins with the first letters of the Hebrew and of the Greek alphabet to suggest the great primeval number.

Spouse and helpmate of Adam Kadmon:[1] Heva, naked Eve. She had no navel. Gaze. Belly without blemish, bulging big, a buckler of taut vellum, no, whiteheaped corn, orient and immortal, standing from everlasting to everlasting.[2] Womb of sin.

Wombed in sin darkness I was too, made not begotten. By them, the man with my voice and my eyes and a ghostwoman with ashes on her breath.[3] They clasped and sundered, did the coupler's will. From before the ages He willed me and now may not will me away or ever. A *lex eterna*[4] stays about Him. Is that then the divine substance wherein Father and Son are consubstantial? Where is poor dear Arius[5] to try conclusions? Warring his life long on the contransmagnificandjewbangtantiality.[6] Illstarred heresiarch.[7] In a Greek watercloset he breathed his last: *euthanasia*. With beaded mitre and with crozier, stalled upon his throne, widower of a widowed see, with upstiffed omophorion, with clotted hinderparts.

Airs romped round him, nipping and eager airs. They are coming, waves. The whitemaned seahorses, champing, brightwindbridled, the steeds of Mananaan.[8]

I mustn't forget his letter for the press. And after? The Ship, half twelve. By the way go easy with that money like a good young imbecile. Yes, I must.[9]

His pace slackened. Here. Am I going to aunt Sara's or not? My consubstantial father's voice. Did you see anything of your artist brother Stephen lately? No? Sure he's not down in Strasburg terrace with his aunt Sally? Couldn't he fly a bit higher than that, eh? And and and and tell us Stephen, how is uncle Si? O weeping God, the things I married into. De boys up in de hayloft. The drunken little costdrawer and his

1. "Adam the Beginner," so called in Hebrew cabalistic literature of the Middle Ages; "Heva" is Hebrew for Eve. Because she was not born in the regular way, but created from Adam's rib, she had no navel.

2. Stephen is led, through reflection on Eve's navel-less "belly without blemish," to a recollection of the description of the original Eden (Paradise) by Thomas Traherne (ca. 1637–1674), from whose prose *Centuries of Meditation* he quotes: "The corn was orient and immortal wheat, which should never be reaped, nor was ever sown. I thought it had stood from everlasting to everlasting. . . ." But immediately afterwards Stephen reflects that such language is inappropriate to Eve's body, as hers was the "womb of sin"—i.e., she first ate the fatal apple and brought forth sin.

3. Stephen is haunted by thoughts of his mother in this guise.

4. Eternal law. God's eternal law, Stephen reflects, willed his birth from the beginning. He then goes on to speculate on the nature of the divine substance and whether God the Father and God the Son are of the same substance ("consubstantial").

5. 3rd-century theologian who "tried conclusions" on this matter, maintaining that Christ was less divine than God (Arius' views were condemned as

heretical by the Council of Nicaea in 325).

6. Ironic "portmanteau word" made up of terms connected with the Arian controversy—"consubstantial," "transubstantial" (of a substance that changes into another)—and with the facts of Christ's nature (e.g., "Jew"; Jesus was a Jew, as Leopold Bloom in a later episode reminds an anti-Semitic Irishman).

7. Arch-heretic. Arius died suddenly in Constantinople in 336. He was never a bishop, and Stephen's image of him at the moment of death in full episcopal attire seems to combine recollections of other early "heresiarchs." In an earlier reverie Stephen had conjured up in his mind "a horde of heresies fleeing with mitres awry." These heretics are connected in Stephen's mind with argument about the relation between God the Father and God the Son and so with the problem of the true nature of paternity, which haunts him constantly.

8. Mananaan MacLir, Celtic sea god; his steeds are the "white horses" (still the name in Britain for the white foam on top of waves).

9. Mr. Deasy had given Stephen a letter to the press to be taken to the newspaper office. After that he has an appointment with Mulligan at The Ship, a tavern. "That money" is Mr. Deasy's last payment to him.

brother, the cornet player. Highly respectable gondoliers. And skeweyed
Walter sirring his father, no less. Sir. Yes, sir. No, sir. Jesus wept: and
no wonder, by Christ.[1]

I pull the wheezy bell of their shuttered cottage: and wait. They take
me for a dun, peer out from a coign of vantage.[2]

—It's Stephen, sir.

—Let him in. Let Stephen in.

A bolt drawn back and Walter welcomes me.

—We thought you were someone else.

In his broad bed nuncle Richie, pillowed and blanketed, extends over
the hillock of his knees a sturdy forearm. Cleanchested. He has washed
the upper moiety.

—Morrow, nephew.

He lays aside the lapboard whereon he drafts his bills of costs for the
eyes of master Goff and master Shapland Tandy, filing consents and
common searches and a writ of *Duces Tecum.*[3] A bogoak frame over his
bald head: Wilde's *Requiescat.*[4] The drone of his misleading whistle brings
Walter back.

—Yes, sir?

—Malt[5] for Richie and Stephen, tell mother. Where is she?

—Bathing Crissie, sir.

Papa's little bedpal. Lump of love.

—No, uncle Richie. . .

—Call me Richie. Damn your lithia water. It lowers. Whusky!

—Uncle Richie, really. . . .

—Sit down or by the law Harry I'll knock you down.

Walter squints vainly for a chair.

—He has nothing to sit down on, sir.

—He has nowhere to put it, you mug. Bring in our chippendale chair.
Would you like a bite of something? None of your damned lawdeedaw
air here: the rich of a rasher fried with a herring? Sure? So much the
better. We have nothing in the house but backache pills.

All'erta![6]

He drones bars of Ferrando's *aria di sortita.* The grandest number,
Stephen, in the whole opera. Listen.

His tuneful whistle sounds again, finely shaded, with rushes of the
air, his fists bigdrumming on his padded knees.

This wind is sweeter.

1. Stephen has been wondering whether to call
on his uncle and aunt, Richie and Sara Goulding.
He imagines his father interrogating him about the
visit as if he had gone, and then pictures his cousins asking after his father, Simon Dedalus (his
cousins' "uncle Si"). Simon Dedalus is contemptuous of his wife's relations (Sara Goulding is his
wife's sister). Stephen knows that any mention of
them will bring on the familiar abuse of "the things
I married into"—at best "highly respectable gón-
doliers" (from Gilbert and Sullivan's opera *The
Gondoliers*). The scene that follows is also Ste-

phen's purely imaginary picture of what the visit
would be like.
2. Favorable corner.
3. "You shall take with you": opening words of
search warrant. Goulding was a law clerk with
Messrs. Goff and Tandy.
4. Poem by Oscar Wilde.
5. Whisky.
6. "Look out!" The first words of the *aria di sortita* (aria of a singer's entrance) sung by Ferrando,
captain of the guard, in Verdi's opera *Il Trovatore*.

Houses of decay, mine, his and all. You told the Clongowes gentry you had an uncle a judge and an uncle a general in the army.[7] Come out of them, Stephen. Beauty is not there. Nor in the stagnant bay of Marsh's library where you read the fading prophecies of Joachim Abbas.[8] For whom? The hundredheaded rabble of the cathedral close.[9] A hater of his kind ran from them to the wood of madness, his mane foaming in the moon, his eyeballs stars. Houyhnhnm, horsenostrilled.[1] The oval equine faces, Temple, Buck Mulligan, Foxy Campbell. Lantern jaws. Abbas father,[2] furious dean, what offence laid fire to their brains? Paff! *Descende, calve, ut nimium decalveris.*[3] A garland of grey hair on his comminated head see him me clambering down to the footpace (*descende*), clutching a monstrance, basiliskeyed. Get down, bald poll! A choir gives back menace and echo, assisting about the altar's horns, the snorted Latin of jackpriests moving burly in their albs, tonsured and oiled and gelded, fat with the fat of kidneys of wheat.

And at the same instant perhaps a priest round the corner is elevating it. Dringdring! And two streets off another locking it into a pyx.[4] Dringadring! And in a ladychapel another taking housel all to his own cheek. Dringdring! Down, up, forward, back. Dan Occam[5] thought of that, invincible doctor. A misty English morning the imp hypostasis tickled his brain. Bringing his host down and kneeling he heard twine with his second bell the first bell in the transept (he is lifting his) and, rising, heard (now I am lifting) their two bells (he is kneeling) twang in diphthong.

Cousin Stephen, you will never be a saint.[6] Isle of saints.[7] You were awfully holy, weren't you? You prayed to the Blessed Virgin that you might not have a red nose. You prayed to the devil in Serpentine avenue that the fubsy widow in front might lift her clothes still more from the wet street. O *si, certo!*[8] Sell your soul for that, do, dyed rags pinned round a squaw. More tell me, more still! On the top of the Howth tram alone crying to the rain: *Naked women!* What about that, eh?

---

7. Stephen, reflecting on the steady social decline of his family, is remembering that, while at school at Clongowes Wood College, he had pretended to have important relations.

8. Abbot Joachim of Floris (the monastery of San Giovanni in Fiore, Italy), 12th-century mystic and theologian, whose prophetic work *Expositio in Apocalypsin* Stephen (i.e., Joyce) had read in Marsha's Library.

9. I.e., the precinct of a cathedral (Marsh's Library is in the close of St. Patrick's Cathedral).

1. St. Patrick's Close has recalled Jonathan Swift (who was Dean of St. Patrick's). Stephen remembers Swift's misanthropy (he was "a hater of his kind") and his creation of the Houyhnhnms (noble horses) in Book 4 of *Gulliver's Travels*. Then he thinks of people he knew who have horse-faces.

2. "Abbas" means literally "father."

3. "Go down, bald-head, lest you become even balder." This sentence, from Joachim's *Concordia* of the Old and New Testaments, is based on the mocking cry of the children to the prophet Elisha

(2 Kings 2.23: "Go up, thou bald head"); Joachim saw Elisha as a forerunner of St. Benedict—both had shaven or baldish heads. Stephen imagines the "comminated" (i.e., threatened) head of Joachim descending, clutching a "monstrance" (receptacle in which the consecrated host is exposed for adoration), in the midst of a nightmare church service.

4. Vessel in which the Host (consecrated bread or wafer) is kept. Stephen is imagining such a service, with himself officiating (he almost became a priest).

5. William of Occam or Ockham ("Dan" means "master"), 14th-century English theologian, who held that the individual thing is the reality and its name, the universal, an abstraction; he was concerned with "hypostasis"—the essential part of a thing as distinct from its attributes.

6. A parody of the words of Dryden to his distant relative Swift: "Cousin, you will never make a poet."

7. Ireland was called "*insula sanctorum*," ("isle of saints") in the Middle Ages.

8. "Oh yes, certainly!"

What about what? What else were they invented for?

Reading two pages apiece of seven books every night, eh? I was young. You bowed to yourself in the mirror, stepping forward to applause earnestly, striking face. Hurray for the Goddamned idiot! Hray! No-one saw: tell no-one. Books you were going to write with letters for titles. Have you read his F? O yes, but I prefer Q. Yes, but W is wonderful. O yes, W. Remember your epiphanies[9] on green oval leaves, deeply deep, copies to be sent if you died to all the great libraries of the world, including Alexandria? Someone was to read them there after a few thousand years, a mahamanvantara.[1] Pico della Mirandola like. Ay, very like a whale.[2] When one reads these strange pages of one long gone one feels that one is at one with one who once. . .

The grainy sand had gone from under his feet. His boots trod again a damp crackling mast, razorshells, squeaking pebbles, that on the unnumbered pebbles beats, wood sieved by the shipworm, lost Armada. Unwholesome sandflats waited to suck his treading soles, breathing upward sewage breath. He coasted them, walking warily. A porterbottle stood up, stogged to its waist, in the cakey sand dough. A sentinel: isle of dreadful thirst.[3] Broken hoops on the shore; at the land a maze of dark cunning nets; farther away chalkscrawled backdoors and on the higher beach a dryingline with two crucified shirts. Ringsend: wigwams of brown steersmen and master mariners. Human shells.

He halted. I have passed the way to aunt Sara's. Am I not going there? Seems not. No-one about. He turned northeast and crossed the firmer sand towards the Pigeonhouse.[4]

—*Qui vous a mis dans cette fichue position?*

—*C'est le pigeon, Joseph.*

Patrice, home on furlough, lapped warm milk with me in the bar MacMahon. Son of the wild goose, Kevin Egan of Paris. My father's a bird, he lapped the sweet *lait chaud* with pink young tongue, plump bunny's face. Lap, *lapin*. He hopes to win in the *gros lots*. About the

---

9. Joyce's own term for the prose poems he wrote as a young man. An epiphany, he said, was the sudden "revelation of the whatness of a thing"—of a gesture, a phrase, or a thought which he had experienced; he attempted to express, in the writing, the moment at which "the soul of the commonest object . . . seems to us radiant." Stephen's recollection of early and exotic literary ambitions is drawn directly from Joyce's own ambitions at the same age.

1. Cycle of change and recurrence, in Indian mystical thought. It is connected in Stephen's mind with the constant ebb and flow of the sea by which he is walking. Pico della Mirandola was a 15th-century mystical philosopher; his *Heptaplus* is a mystical account of the creation, much influenced by Jewish cabalistic thought.

2. Polonius to Hamlet (*Hamlet* 3.2.399) with reference to the changing shape of a cloud. The Protean theme of constant change, of ebb and flow, and of metempsychosis (i.e., transmigration of souls:

a major theme in *Ulysses*), is working in Stephen's mind. The following sentence is a parody of an elegant, condescending modern essay on Pico or some other early mystic.

3. The atmosphere of the sandflats reminds Stephen of a desert island where men die of thirst. (The island of Pharos, where Menelaus found Proteus, was an "island of dreadful hunger.")

4. The Pigeon House in Ringsend, an old structure built on a breakwater in Dublin Bay and which in the course of time has served a great variety of purposes, suggests to Stephen the Dove which is the symbol of the Holy Spirit, and this in turn suggests an irreverent dialogue (supposedly between Joseph and Mary when Mary is found to be pregnant: "Who has got you into this wretched condition?" "It was the pigeon [i.e., the Holy Dove], Joseph"). This he had picked up in Paris from the blasphemous M. Léo Taxil, whose book *La Vie de Jésus* ("The Life of Jesus") is mentioned in the next paragraph.

nature of women he read in Michelet. But he must send me *La Vie de Jésus* by M. Léo Taxil. Lent it to his friend.[5]

—*C'est tordant, vous savez. Moi, je suis socialiste. Je ne crois pas en l'existence de Dieu. Faut pas le dire à mon père.*

—*Il croit?*

—*Mon père, oui.*

Schluss.[6] He laps.

My Latin quarter hat. God, we simply must dress the character. I want puce gloves. You were a student, weren't you? Of what in the other devil's name? Paysayenn. P. C. N., you know: *physiques, chimiques et naturelles.*[7] Aha. Eating your groatsworth of *mou en civet,* fleshpots of Egypt, elbowed by belching cabmen. Just say in the most natural tone: when I was in Paris, *boul'Mich',*[8] I used to. Yes, used to carry punched tickets to prove an alibi if they arrested you for murder somewhere. Justice. On the night of the seventeenth of February 1904 the prisoner was seen by two witnesses. Other fellow did it: other me. Hat, tie, overcoat, nose. *Lui, c'est moi.*[9] You seem to have enjoyed yourself.

Proudly walking. Whom were you trying to walk like? Forget: a dispossessed. With mother's money order, eight shillings, the banging door of the post office slammed in your face by the usher. Hunger toothache. *Encore deux minutes.* Look clock. Must get. *Fermé.* Hired dog! Shoot him to bloody bits with a bang shotgun, bits man spattered walls all brass buttons. Bits all khrrrrklak in place clack back. Not hurt? O, that's all right. Shake hands. See what I meant, see? O, that's all right. Shake a shake. O, that's all only all right.[1]

You were going to do wonders, what? Missionary to Europe after fiery Columbanus.[2] Fiacre and Scotus on their creepystools in heaven spilt from their pintpots, loudlatinlaughing: *Euge! Euge!*[3] Pretending to speak broken English as you dragged your valise, porter threepence, across the slimy pier at Newhaven. *Comment?* Rich booty you brought back; *Le*

---

5. Stephen had first met Léo Taxil through Patrice, the son of "Kevin Egan of Paris," who in real life was the exiled nationalist Joseph Casey. The phrase "my father's a bird" comes from *The Song of the Cheerful Jesus,* a blasphemous poem by Buck Mulligan (actually Oliver Gogarty, who really wrote the poem); Stephen recalls Patrice reciting it as he drank warm milk *("lait chaud"),* lapping it like a *"lapin"* ("rabbit"), and expressing the hope that he would win something substantial in the French national lottery *(gros lot:* "first prize"). Jules Michelet (1798–1874) was a French historian.

6. Conversation between Stephen and Patrice: "It's screamingly funny, you know. I'm a socialist myself. I don't believe in the existence of God. Mustn't tell my father." "He is a believer?" "My father, yes." *"Schluss":* end.

7. I.e., the faculty of physics, chemistry, and biology at the École de Médecine in Paris, where Stephen, like Joyce, took a premedical course for a short time. The faculty was popularly known as "P. C. N." (pronounced "Paysayenn"). *"Mou en*

civet": stew.

8. Popular Parisian abbreviation for the Boulevard Saint Michel.

9. "He is me"—a parody of Louis XIV's remark, *"L'état c'est moi"* ("I am the state").

1. A recollection of the occasion when, desperate for money, Stephen had received a money order for eight shillings from his mother. Afflicted with both hunger and toothache, he had gone to cash it at the post office—which was closed, even though, as he expostulated with the man at the door, there were still two minutes *("encore deux minutes")* until the official closing time. In his retrospective rage he imagines himself shooting the "hired dog" to bits, and then in a revulsion of feeling has a mental reconciliation with him.

2. 6th-century Irish missionary on the Continent. Fiacre was a 6th-century Irish saint. Duns Scotus (ca. 1265–1308): Scholastic theologian and philosopher. "Creepystools": low stools.

3. "Well done!"

Tutu, five tattered numbers of *Pantalon Blanc et Culotte Rouge,*[4] a blue French telegram, curiosity to show:

—Mother dying come home father.[5]

The aunt thinks you killed your mother. That's why she won't.[6]

> *Then here's a health to Mulligan's aunt*
> *And I'll tell you the reason why.*
> *She always kept things decent in*
> *The Hannigan famileye.*

His feet marched in sudden proud rhythm over the sand furrows, along by the boulders of the south wall. He stared at them proudly, piled stone mammoth skulls. Gold light on sea, on sand, on boulders. The sun is there, the slender trees, the lemon houses.

Paris rawly waking, crude sunlight on her lemon streets. Moist pith of farls[7] of bread, the froggreen wormwood, her matin incense, court the air. Belluomo rises from the bed of his wife's lover's wife, the kerchiefed housewife is astir, a saucer of acetic acid in her hand. In Rodot's Yvonne and Madeleine newmake their tumbled beauties, shattering with gold teeth *chaussons* of pastry, their mouths yellowed with the *pus* of *flan breton.*[8] Faces of Paris men go by, their wellpleased pleasers, curled *conquistadores.*[9]

Noon slumbers. Kevin Egan rolls gunpowder cigarettes through fingers smeared with printer's ink,[1] sipping his green fairy as Patrice his white. About us gobblers fork spiced beans down their gullets. *Un demi setier!*[2] A jet of coffee steam from the burnished caldron. She serves me at his beck. *Il est irlandais. Hollandais? Non fromage. Deux irlandais, nous, Irlande, vous savez? Ah, oui!*[3] She thought you wanted a cheese *hollandais.* Your postprandial, do you know that word? Postprandial. There was a fellow I knew once in Barcelona, queer fellow, used to call it his postprandial. Well: *slainte!*[4] Around the slabbed tables the tangle of wined breaths and grumbling gorges. His breath hangs over our saucestained plates, the green fairy's fang thrusting between his lips. Of Ireland, the Dalcassians, of hopes, conspiracies, of Arthur Griffith now.[5] To yoke me as his yokefellow, our crimes our common cause. You're your father's son. I know the voice. His fustian shirt, sanguineflowered,

4. Like the preceding name, name of French popular periodical.

5. This telegram was actually received by Joyce in Paris.

6. Stephen recalls Buck Mulligan's telling him that his (Mulligan's) aunt disapproved of Stephen because, by refusing to pray at his dying mother's bedside, he had hastened her death. Stephen then tries to laugh away his feeling of guilt by quoting mentally a (slightly parodied) verse of a popular song.

7. Thin circular cakes.

8. Memories of a restaurant in Paris: *"chaussons"* are pastry turnovers; *"flan breton"* is a pastry filled with custard.

9. Conquerors (Spanish).

1. Egan (i.e., Joseph Casey) became a typesetter for the Parisian edition of the *New York Herald.*

2. Abusive Parisian slang for a liquid measure (about one fourth of a liter)—here, presumably, of wine or beer.

3. "He is Irish. Dutch? Not cheese. We are two Irishmen, Ireland, you understand? Oh, yes!"

4. Gaelic, "Your health!"

5. Two extremes of Irish history: from the Dalcassian line came the early kings of Munster (from A.D. 300 on); Arthur Griffith (1872–1922) was an Irish revolutionary leader, founder of the Sinn Fein ("We Ourselves") movement.

trembles its Spanish tassels at his secrets. M. Drumont,[6] famous journalist, Drumont, know what he called queen Victoria? Old hag with the yellow teeth. *Vieille ogresse* with the *dents jaunes*. Maud Gonne, beautiful woman, *la Patrie*, M. Millevoye, Félix Faure,[7] know how he died? Licentious men. The *froeken, bonne à tout faire*,[8] who rubs male nakedness in the bath at Upsala. *Moi faire*, she said, *tous les messieurs*.[9] Not this *monsieur*, I said. Most licentious custom. Bath a most private thing. I wouldn't let my brother, not even my own brother, most lascivious thing. Green eyes, I see you. Fang, I feel. Lascivious people.

The blue fuse burns deadly between hands and burns clear. Loose tobacco shreds catch fire: a flame and acrid smoke light our corner. Raw facebones under his peep of day boy's hat. How the head centre got away, authentic version. Got up as a young bride, man, veil, orangeblossoms, drove out the road to Malahide. Did, faith. Of lost leaders, the betrayed, wild escapes. Disguises, clutched at, gone not here.[1]

Spurned lover. I was a strapping young gossoon[2] at that time, I tell you. I'll show you my likeness one day. I was, faith. Lover, for her love he prowled with colonel Richard Burke, tanist[3] of his sept, under the walls of Clerkenwell[4] and, crouching, saw a flame of vengeance hurl them upward in the fog. Shattered glass and toppling masonry. In gay Paree he hides, Egan of Paris, unsought by any save by me. Making his day's stations, the dingy printing-case, his three taverns, the Montmartre lair he sleeps short night in, *rue de la Goutte-d'Or*, damascened with flyblown faces of the gone. Loveless, landless, wifeless. She is quite nicey comfy without her outcast man,[5] madame in *rue Gît-le-Cœur*, canary and two buck lodgers. Peachy cheeks, a zebra skirt, frisky as a young thing's. Spurned and undespairing. Tell Pat[6] you saw me, won't you? I wanted to get poor Pat a job one time. *Mon fils*, soldier of France. I taught him to sing *The boys of Kilkenny are stout roaring blades*. Know that old lay? I taught Patrice that. Old Kilkenny:[7] saint Canice, Strongbow's castle on the Nore. Goes like this. O, O. He takes me, Napper Tandy,[8] by the hand.

O, O the boys of
Kilkenny. . .

6. Edouard Drumont (1844–1917), French politician and bitter anti-Semite.

7. Maud Gonne, the beautiful actress and violent Irish nationalist whom Yeats loved; "La Patrie": journal edited by Lucien Millevoye, French Nationalist Deputy and Maud Gonne's lover; Félix Faure, 19th-century French statesman.

8. Maid-of-all-work (French, translating the preceding Swedish word).

9. "I do all the gentlemen" (in broken French).

1. Another Protean theme of change. Egan had told Stephen of his cousin James Stephens' escape from prison disguised as a bride (Stephens was really the cousin of Casey, the original of Egan in this episode).

2. Boy.

3. Successor-apparent to a Celtic chief. "Sept":

clan.

4. District in east central London. Stephen is recalling Egan's conversation about the Fenian violence in London which necessitated his fleeing to France.

5. I.e., Egan's wife, who is "quite nicey comfy" in the metaphorical "rue Git-le-Coeur" (i.e., the street where the heart lies dead) back home in Ireland.

6. Patrice, Egan's son.

7. Kilkenny is called after the Irish St. Canice (its Irish name is Cill Chainnigh), on the river Nore, where Strongbow (the second Earl of Pembroke, who invaded Ireland in the 12th century), had his stronghold.

8. James Napper Tandy (1740–1803), Irish revolutionary hero of the song *The Wearing of the Green*.

Weak wasting hand on mine. They have forgotten Kevin Egan, not he them. Remembering thee, O Sion.[9]

He had come nearer the edge of the sea and wet sand slapped his boots. The new air greeted him, harping in wild nerves, wind of wild air of seeds of brightness. Here, I am not walking out to the Kish lightship, am I? He stood suddenly, his feet beginning to sink slowly in the quaking soil. Turn back.

Turning, he scanned the shore south, his feet sinking again slowly in new sockets. The cold domed room of the tower[1] waits. Through the barbicans[2] the shafts of light are moving ever, slowly ever as my feet are sinking, creeping duskward over the dial floor. Blue dusk, nightfall, deep blue night. In the darkness of the dome they wait, their pushedback chairs, my obelisk valise, around a board of abandoned platters. Who to clear it? He has the key.[3] I will not sleep there when this night comes. A shut door of a silent tower, entombing their blind bodies, the panthersahib and his pointer.[4] Call: no answer. He lifted his feet up from the suck and turned back by the mole of boulders. Take all, keep all. My soul walks with me, form of forms. So in the moon's midwatches I pace the path above the rocks, in sable silvered, hearing Elsinore's tempting flood.[5]

The flood is following me. I can watch it flow past from here. Get back then by the Poolbeg road to the strand there. He climbed over the sedge and eely oarweeds and sat on a stool of rock, resting his ashplant in a grike.

A bloated carcass of a dog lay lolled on bladderwrack. Before him the gunwale of a boat, sunk in sand. *Un coche ensablé*[6] Louis Veuillot called Gautier's prose. These heavy sands are language tide and wind have silted here. And there, the stoneheaps of dead builders, a warren of weasel rats. Hide gold there. Try it. You have some. Sands and stones. Heavy of the past. Sir Lout's toys. Mind you don't get one bang on the ear. I'm the bloody well gigant rolls all them bloody well boulders, bones for my steppingstones. Feefawfum. I zmellz de bloodz oldz an Iridzman.[7]

A point, live dog, grew into sight running across the sweep of sand. Lord, is he going to attack me? Respect his liberty. You will not be master of others or their slave. I have my stick. Sit tight. From farther

---

9. Cf. Psalm 137.1 (in the King James Bible): "we wept, when we remembered Zion." But "Zion" in the Douay (Roman Catholic) Bible, is spelled "Sion," and the Book of Common Prayer has "When we remembered thee, O Sion."

1. Where Stephen lived with Buck Mulligan.

2. Outworks of a castle.

3. In the preceding episode, Mulligan asked for and got the key of the tower from Stephen.

4. I.e., Mulligan and the Englishman Haines, who lived with Stephen in the tower. Stephen thinks of them as calling for him in vain, since he has decided not to return.

5. Cf. *Hamlet* 1.2.242, where the ghost of Hamlet's murdered father is described as having a beard of "sable silver'd." Allusions to *Hamlet* occur often in *Ulysses*; in a later episode Stephen expounds the theory that Shakespeare is to be identified, not with Hamlet himself, but with his betrayed father.

6. "A coach embedded in the sand." Louis Veuillot was a 19th-century French journalist; Théophile Gautier, a 19th-century French poet, novelist, and critic.

7. Stephen is thinking of the boulders on the shore as the work of a large but clumsy giant ("Sir Lout"). "They [Sir Lout and his family] were giants right enough . . . My Sir Lout has rocks in his mouth instead of teeth. He articulates badly" (Joyce to Frank Budgen, reported in Budgen's *James Joyce and the Making of Ulysses*, 1934).

away, walking shoreward across from the crested tide, figures, two. The two maries. They have tucked it safe mong the bulrushes. Peekaboo. I see you. No, the dog. He is running back to them. Who?

Galleys of the Lochlanns[8] ran here to beach, in quest of prey, their bloodbeaked prows riding low on a molten pewter surf. Dane vikings, torcs of tomahawks aglitter on their breasts when Malachi wore the collar of gold. A school of turlehide whales stranded in hot noon, spouting, hobbling in the shallows. Then from the starving cagework city a horde of jerkined dwarfs, my people, with flayers' knives, running, scaling, hacking in green blubbery whalemeat. Famine, plague and slaughters. Their blood is in me, their lusts my waves. I moved among them on the frozen Liffey, that I, a changeling, among the spluttering resin fires. I spoke to no-one: none to me.

The dog's bark ran towards him, stopped, ran back.[9] Dog of my enemy. I just simply stood pale, silent, bayed about. *Terribilia meditans.*[1] A primrose doublet, fortune's knave, smiled on my fear. For that are you pining, the bark of their applause? Pretenders: live their lives. The Bruce's brother, Thomas Fitzgerald, silken knight, Perkin Warbeck, York's false scion, in breeches of silk of whiterose ivory, wonder of a day, and Lambert Simnel, with a tail of nans and sutlers, a scullion crowned.[2] All kings' sons. Paradise of pretenders then and now. He saved men from drowning[3] and you shake at a cur's yelping. But the courtiers who mocked Guido in Or san Michele were in their own house. House of . . . We don't want any of your medieval abstrusiosities. Would you do what he did? A boat would be near, a lifebuoy. *Natürlich,*[4] put there for you. Would you or would you not? The man that was drowned nine days ago off Maiden's rock. They are waiting for him now. The truth, spit it out. I would want to. I would try. I am not a strong swimmer. Water cold soft. When I put my face into it in the basin at Clongowes. Can't see! Who's behind me? Out quickly, quickly! Do you see the tide flowing quickly in on all sides, sheeting the lows of sands quickly, shellcocoa-coloured? If I had land under my feet. I want his life still to be his, mine to be mine. A drowning man. His human eyes scream to me out of horror of his death. I . . . With him together down . . . I could not save her.[5] Waters: bitter death: lost.

A woman and a man. I see her skirties. Pinned up, I bet.

Their dog ambled about a bank of dwindling sand, trotting, sniffing on all sides. Looking for something lost in a past life. Suddenly he made off like a bounding hare, ears flung back, chasing the shadow of a low-skimming gull. The man's shrieked whistle struck his limp ears. He

8. Scandinavians (Gaelic). Stephen is meditating on the Vikings who settled Dublin; it was here that they came ashore, he thinks.

9. The dog in this and subsequent paragraphs keeps changing in appearance; he "is the mummer among beasts—the Protean animal" (Joyce to Budgen). Joyce himself was afraid of dogs.

1. "Meditating terrible things."

2. Stephen is meditating on pretenders (i.e., false

claimants): the names here are those of pretenders who have figured in English history. This is the Proteus theme again—disguises and changes.

3. Mulligan had saved a man from drowning.

4. Of course.

5. A man had been drowned off the coast, and his body had not yet been recovered. As Stephen thinks of the horror of drowning he recalls once again his mother's death.

turned, bounded back, came nearer, trotted on twinkling shanks. On a field tenney a buck, trippant, proper, unattired.[6] At the lacefringe of the tide he halted with stiff forehoofs, seawardpointed ears. His snout lifted barked at the wavenoise, herds of seamorse. They serpented towards his feet, curling, unfurling many crests, every ninth, breaking, plashing, from far, from farther out, waves and waves.

Cocklepickers.[7] They waded a little way in the water and, stooping, soused their bags, and, lifting them again, waded out. The dog yelped running to them, reared up and pawed them, dropping on all fours, again reared up at them with mute bearish fawning. Unheeded he kept by them as they came towards the drier sand, a rag of wolf's tongue redpanting from his jaws. His speckled body ambled ahead of them and then loped off at a calf's gallop. The carcass lay on his path. He stopped, sniffed, stalked round it, brother, nosing closer, went round it, sniffing rapidly like a dog all over the dead dog's bedraggled fell. Dogskull, dogsniff, eyes on the ground, moves to one great goal. Ah, poor dogsbody. Here lies poor dogsbody's body.

—Tatters! Outofthat, you mongrel.

The cry brought him skulking back to his master and a blunt bootless kick sent him unscathed across a spit of sand, crouched in flight. He slunk back in a curve. Doesn't see me. Along by the edge of the mole he lolloped, dawdled, smelt a rock and from under a cocked hindleg pissed against it. He trotted forward and, lifting his hindleg, pissed quick short at an unsmelt rock. The simple pleasures of the poor. His hindpaws then scattered sand: then his forepaws dabbled and delved. Something he buried there, his grandmother.[8] He rooted in the sand, dabbling, delving and stopped to listen to the air, scraped up the sand again with a fury of his claws, soon ceasing, a pard,[9] a panther, got in spousebreach,[1] vulturing the dead.

After he woke me last night same dream or was it? Wait. Open hallway. Street of harlots. Remember. Haroun al Raschid.[2] I am almosting it. That man led me, spoke. I was not afraid. The melon he had he held against my face. Smiled: creamfruit smell. That was the rule, said. In. Come. Red carpet spread. You will see who.

Shouldering their bags they trudged, the red Egyptians.[3] His blued

6. At this point in its constantly changing appearance the dog looks like a heraldic animal and is described in the language of heraldry; the sentence "On a field . . . unattired" means: "On an orange-brown (tawny) background, a buck, tripping, in natural colors, without horns."

7. Stephen recognizes the man and woman on the beach as gypsy cocklepickers (cockles are edible shellfish, like mussels).

8. Reference to a joke Stephen had made to his pupils in school that morning about "the fox burying his grandmother under a hollybush." This has many symbolic reverberations throughout *Ulysses.* The buried grandmother suggests Stephen's mother, the Church, and Ireland (the "Poor old Woman"), while the hollybush, evergreen tree of life, represents resurrection in which in spite of his religious disbelief, Stephen is much interested and about which (as about metempsychosis) he is continually brooding.

9. Leopard or panther.

1. I.e., begotten in adultery.

2. Stephen's dream of the famous Caliph of Baghdad, of the "street of harlots," and of his meeting a man with a melon, foreshadows his meeting later in the day with Leopold Bloom and his visit to the brothel area of Dublin.

3. I.e., gypsies. As Stephen watches the gypsy cockle-pickers with their dog he imagines their vagabond life and recalls fragments of gypsy speech and of thieves' slang.

feet out of turnedup trousers slapped the clammy sand, a dull brick muffler strangling his unshaven neck. With woman steps she followed: the
ruffian and his strolling mort.[4] Spoils slung at her back. Loose sand and
shellgrit crusted her bare feet. About her windraw face her hair trailed.
Behind her lord his helpmate, bing awast, to Romeville.[5] When night
hides her body's flaws calling under her brown shawl from an archway
where dogs have mired. Her fancyman is treating two Royal Dublins in
O'Loughlin's of Blackpitts. Buss her, wap in rogues' rum lingo, for, O,
my dimber wapping dell.[6] A shefiend's whiteness under her rancid rags.
Fumbally's lane that night: the tanyard smells.

> White thy fambles, red thy gan
> And thy quarrons dainty is.
> Couch a hogshead with me then.
> In the darkmans clip and kiss.[7]

Morose delectation Aquinas tunbelly calls this, *frate porcospino*.[8]
Unfallen Adam rode and not rutted. Call away let him:[9] *thy quarrons
dainty is*. Language no whit worse than his. Monkwords, marybeads
jabber on their girdles: roguewords, tough nuggets patter in their
pockets.

Passing now.

A side-eye at my Hamlet hat. If I were suddenly naked here as I sit? I
am not. Across the sands of all the world, followed by the sun's flaming
sword, to the west, trekking to evening lands. She trudges, schlepps,
trains, drags, trascines her load.[1] A tide westering, moondrawn, in her
wake. Tides, myriadislanded, within her, blood not mine, *oinopa pon-
ton*,[2] a winedark sea. Behold the handmaid of the moon. In sleep the
wet sign calls her hour, bids her rise. Bridebed, childbed, bed of death,
ghostcandled.[3] *Omnis caro ad te veniet*. He comes, pale vampire, through
storm his eyes, his bat sails bloodying the sea, mouth to her mouth's
kiss.[4]

Here. Put a pin in that chap, will you? My tablets.[5] Mouth to her
kiss. No. Must be two of em. Glue 'em well. Mouth to her mouth's kiss.

His lips lipped and mouthed fleshless lips of air: mouth to her womb.

---

4. Gypsies' "freewoman" (i.e., a harlot). "Spoils":
the association gypsy-Egyptian reminds Stephen of
the Israelites "spoiling the Egyptians" in Exodus
12.36.

5. Go away to London.

6. 17th-century thieves' slang—"buss": kiss; "wap":
copulate with; "rum": good; "dimber": pretty;
"wapping dell": whore.

7. More thieves' slang: "fambles": hands; "gan":
mouth; "quarrons": body; "couch a hogshead":
come to bed; "darkmans": night; "clip": kiss. These
four lines and some of the phrases in the preceding
paragraph are quoted from a song of the period,
The Rogue's Delight in Praise of His Strolling Mort
(cf. note 3).

8. "Brother porcupine" (Italian), a reference to the
fat ("tunbelly") but prickly philosopher, St. Thomas
Aquinas.

9. The gypsy is calling his dog.

1. All words suggesting moving or dragging. " 'I
like that crescendo of verbs,' he [Joyce] said. 'The
irresistible tug of the tides' " (Budgen).

2. "Winedark sea" (Homer).

3. He is thinking of his mother again. The Latin
(from the burial service) means: "All flesh will come
to thee."

4. Death comes like the Flying Dutchman in a
phantom ship to give the fatal kiss.

5. Cf. *Hamlet* 1.5.107: "My tablets!"

Oomb, allwombing tomb.[6] His mouth moulded issuing breath, unspeeched: ooeeehah: roar of cataractic planets, globed, blazing, roaring wayawayawayawayawayaway. Paper. The banknotes, blast them. Old Deasy's letter. Here. Thanking you for the hospitality tear the blank end off. Turning his back to the sun he bent over far to a table of rock and scribbled words.[7] That's twice I forgot to take slips from the library counter.

His shadow lay over the rocks as he bent, ending. Why not endless till the farthest star? Darkly they are there behind this light, darkness shining in the brightness, delta of Cassiopeia, worlds. Me sits there with his augur's rod of ash, in borrowed sandals, by day beside a livid sea, unbeheld, in violet night walking beneath a reign of uncouth stars.[8] I throw this ended shadow from me, manshape ineluctable, call it back. Endless, would it be mine, form of my form? Who watches me here? Who ever anywhere will read these written words? Signs on a white field. Somewhere to someone in your flutiest voice. The good bishop of Cloyne[9] took the veil of the temple out of his shovel hat: veil of space with coloured emblems hatched on its field. Hold hard. Coloured on a flat: yes, that's right. Flat I see, then think distance, near, far, flat I see, east, back. Ah, see now. Falls back suddenly, frozen in stereoscope. Click does the trick. You find my words dark. Darkness is in our souls, do you not think? Flutier. Our souls, shamewounded by our sins, cling to us yet more, a woman to her lover clinging, the more the more.

She trusts me, her hand gentle, the longlashed eyes. Now where the blue hell am I bringing her beyond the veil?[1] Into the ineluctable modality of the ineluctable visuality. She, she, she. What she? The virgin at Hodges Figgis' window on Monday looking in for one of the alphabet books you were going to write. Keen glance you gave her. Wrist through the braided jess of her sunshade. She lives in Leeson park with a grief and kickshaws, a lady of letters. Talk that to some else, Stevie: a pickmeup. Bet she wears those curse of God stays suspenders and yellow stockings, darned with lumpy wool. Talk about apple dumplings, *piuttosto*.[2] Where are your wits?

Touch me. Soft eyes. Soft soft soft hand. I am lonely here. O, touch me soon, now. What is that word known to all men? I am quiet here alone. Sad too. Touch, touch me.

He lay back at full stretch over the sharp rocks, cramming the scrib-

6. Our understanding of Stephen's consciousness here can be illuminated with reference to Blake's poem *The Gates of Paradise*, which concludes: "The door of death I open found / And the worm weaving in the ground: / Thou'rt my mother from the womb, / Wife, sister, daughter, to the tomb . . ." Cf. also "the earth that's nature's mother is her tomb. / What is her burying ground that is her womb . . ." (*Romeo and Juliet*, 2.3.9–10).

7. Stephen tears off the blank end of Mr. Deasy's letter to the press and writes a poem that will be quoted later in the novel.

8. He imagines himself as the constellation Cassiopeia, supposed to represent the wife of Cepheus (an Ethiopian king) seated in a chair and holding up her arms. His ash walking stick he thinks of as an "augur's [Roman soothsayer's] rod of ash."

9. George Berkeley, bishop of Cloyne (in Ireland), 1685–1753, who argued that the external world has no objective reality but exists only in the mind of the perceiver. Stephen (as at the opening of this episode) is experimenting again with ways of sensing reality.

1. "She" is Psyche, the soul, whom he is bringing from "beyond the veil." But from metaphysical speculations on reality and the soul Stephen is led (by the Psyche association) to think of "the virgin at Hodges Figgis' [a bookseller's] window."

2. Rather, sooner.

bled note and pencil into a pocket, his hat tilted down on his eyes. That
is Kevin Egan's movement I made, nodding for his nap, sabbath sleep.
Et vidit Deus. Et erant valde bona.[3] Alo! *Bonjour.* Welcome as the
flowers in May. Under its leaf he watched through peacocktwittering
lashes the southing sun. I am caught in this burning scene. Pan's hour,
the faunal noon. Among gumheavy serpentplants, milkoozing fruits,
where on the tawny waters leaves lie wide. Pain is far.

And no more turn aside and brood.[4]

His gaze brooded on his broadtoed boots, a buck's castoffs, *nebeneinander.* He counted the creases of rucked leather wherein another's foot
had nested warm. The foot that beat the ground in tripudium, foot I
dislove. But you were delighted when Esther Osvalt's shoe went on you:
girl I knew in Paris. *Tiens, quel petit pied!*[5] Staunch friend, a brother
soul: Wilde's love that dare not speak its name. He now will leave me.
And the blame? As I am. As I am. All or not at all.

In long lassoes from the Cock lake the water flowed full, covering
greengoldenly lagoons of sand, rising, flowing. My ashplant will float
away. I shall wait. No, they will pass on, passing chafing against the low
rocks, swirling, passing. Better get this job over quick. Listen: a four-
worded wavespeech: seesoo, hrss, rsseeiss ooos. Vehement breath of waters
amid seasnakes, rearing horses, rocks. In cups of rocks it slops: flop, slop,
slap: bounded in barrels. And, spent, its speech ceases. It flows purling,
widely flowing, floating foampool, flower unfurling.

Under the upswelling tide he saw the writhing weeds lift languidly
and sway reluctant arms, hising up their petticoats,[6] in whispering water
swaying and upturning coy silver fronds. Day by day: night by night:
lifted, flooded and let fall. Lord, they are weary: and, whispered to, they
sigh. Saint Ambrose heard it, sigh of leaves and waves, waiting, awaiting
the fullness of their times, *diebus ac noctibus iniurias patiens ingemis-
cit.*[7] To no end gathered; vainly then released, forthflowing, wending
back: loom of the moon. Weary too in sight of lovers, lascivious men, a
naked woman shining in her courts, she draws a toil of waters.

Five fathoms out there. Full fathom five thy father lies.[8] At one he
said. Found drowned. High water at Dublin bar. Driving before it a
loose drift of rubble, fanshoals of fishes, silly shells. A corpse rising salt-
white from the undertow, bobbing landward a pace a pace a porpoise.
There he is. Hook it quick. Sunk though he be beneath the watery floor.
We have him. Easy now.

Bag of corpsegas sopping in foul brine. A quiver of minnows, fat of a

3. Connecting two phrases from the Vulgate: "And
God saw" (Genesis 1.4) and "And they were very
good" (Genesis 1.31).

4. The first line of the second (and last) stanza of
Yeats's poem *Who Goes with Fergus?* which is often
in Stephen's mind. The line expresses for him the
mood of noontide stillness and of lotos-eating in a
lush oriental scene which overcomes him
momentarily when he realizes that it is 12 o'clock,
the hour of the Greek nature god Pan, "faunal
noon." This oriental lotos-eating theme, which is

associated also with Bloom, is important in the
Odyssey.

5. "Look, what a little foot!"

6. A phrase from a vulgar song sung by Mulligan
earlier that morning.

7. "Night and day he patiently groaned forth his
wrongs" (St. Ambrose).

8. The theme of the drowned man is important in
this episode (cf. the drowned sailor in Eliot's *Waste
Land*). This line is from Ariel's song in *The Tempest* (1.2.397).

spongy titbit, flash through the slits of his buttoned trouserfly. God becomes man becomes fish becomes barnacle goose becomes featherbed mountain. Dead breaths I living breathe, tread dead dust, devour a urinous offal from all dead. Hauled stark over the gunwhale he breathes upward the stench of his green grave, his leprous nosehole snoring to the sun.

A seachange this, brown eyes saltblue. Seadeath, mildest of all deaths known to man. Old Father Ocean. *Prix de Paris:*[9] beware of imitations. Just you give it a fair trial. We enjoyed ourselves immensely.

Come. I thirst. Clouding over. No black clouds anywhere, are there?[1] Thunderstorm. Allbright he falls, proud lightning of the intellect, *Lucifer, dico, qui nescit occasum.*[2] No. My cockle hat and staff and hismy sandal shoon.[3] Where? To evening lands. Evening will find itself.

He took the hilt of his ashplant, lunging with it softly, dallying still. Yes, evening will find itself in me, without me. All days make their end. By the way next when is it? Tuesday will be the longest day. Of all the glad new year, mother,[4] the rum tum tiddledy tum. Lawn Tennyson, gentleman poet. *Già.*[5] For the old hag with the yellow teeth. And Monsieur Drumont, gentleman journalist. *Già.* My teeth are very bad. Why, I wonder? Feel. That one is going too. Shells. Ought I go to a dentist, I wonder, with what money? That one. Toothless Kinch, the superman. Why is that, I wonder, or does it mean something perhaps?

My handkerchief. He threw it. I remember. Did I not take it up?

His hand groped vainly in his pockets. No, I didn't. Better buy one.

He laid the dry snot picked from his nostril on a ledge of rock, carefully. For the rest let look who will.

Behind. Perhaps there is someone.

He turned his face over a shoulder, rere regardant.[6] Moving through the air high spars of a threemaster, her sails brailed up on the crosstrees,[7] homing, upstream, silently moving, a silent ship.

---

9. "Prize of Paris"; the reference is probably to the Paris Exposition of 1889, where prizes were awarded in various categories of food, etc.: the prize-winning commodities bear the seal of the prize on the label (hence, "beware of imitations"). Stephen mentally awards the prize to death by drowning. "Seachange" is from Ariel's song, once more.
1. Stephen is looking up to make sure the sky does not threaten a thunderstorm; like Joyce, he hates thunder.
2. Thunder and lightning recall the Fall of Lucifer, "Lucifer, I say, who knows not his fall."
3. From Ophelia's mad song (*Hamlet*, 4.5.23–26): "How should I your true-love know / From another one? / By his cockle hat and staff / And his sandal shoon." Ophelia, too, was drowned.
4. "You must wake and call me early, call me early, mother dear; / Tomorrow 'ill be the happiest time

of all the glad New Year . . ." From *The May Queen* by Alfred, Lord Tennyson ("Lawn Tennyson").
5. Of course!
6. Looking behind him (heraldic terminology). Stephen, as we leave him sitting by the shore, is described in a highly stylized, heraldic language.
7. When Budgen pointed out to Joyce that "crosstrees" was not the proper nautical term for the spars to which the sails are bent, Joyce thanked him but added: "But the word 'crosstrees' is essential. It comes in later on and I can't change it. After all, a yard is also a crosstree for the onlooking landlubber." Joyce later uses "crosstree" in a reference to the crucifixion of Christ, so that the suggestion here is of Stephen as both artist and martyr (as his name implies). But the ship is also a real ship, which arrived in Dublin on June 16, 1904.

[Lestrygonians][1]

Pineapple rock, lemon platt, butter scotch. A sugarsticky girl shovelling scoopfuls of creams for a christian brother. Some school treat. Bad for their tummies. Lozenge and comfit manufacturer to His Majesty the King. God. Save. Our. Sitting on his throne sucking red jujubes white.

A sombre Y. M. C. A. young man, watchful among the warm sweet fumes of Graham Lemon's, placed a throwaway in a hand of Mr Bloom.

Heart to heart talks.

Bloo . . . Me? No.

Blood of the Lamb.[2]

His slow feet walked him riverward, reading. Are you saved? All are washed in the blood of the lamb. God wants blood victim. Birth, hymen, martyr, war, foundation of a building, sacrifice, kidney burntoffering, druids' altars. Elijah is coming. Dr John Alexander Dowie, restorer of the church in Zion, is coming.[3]

> *Is coming! Is coming!! Is coming!!!*
> *All heartily welcome.*

Paying game. Torry and Alexander last year. Polygamy. His wife will put the stopper on that. Where was that ad some Birmingham firm the luminous crucifix. Our Saviour. Wake up in the dead of night and see him on the wall, hanging. Pepper's ghost idea.[4] Iron Nails Ran In.

Phosphorus it must be done with. If you leave a bit of codfish for

---

1. It is lunch time in Dublin and Leopold Bloom, as he walks through the city in no great hurry (for he likes to linger and watch what goes on around him), thinks of food. The Lestrygonians in Book 10 of the *Odyssey* are cannibals, and throughout this episode there are suggestions of the slaughter of living creatures for food, or of food as something disgusting, which make somewhat tenuous contact with Homer's description of the cannibals spearing Ulysses' men for food; the parallel is not, however, profound or very important. What is most important about this episode is that it shows us Bloom's consciousness responding to the sights and sounds of Dublin. His humane curiosity, his desire to learn and to improve the human lot, his sympathetic concern for Mrs. Breen and Mrs. Purefoy, his feeding the gulls, his recollections of a happier time when his daughter was a baby and his relations with his wife Molly were thoroughly satisfactory, his interest in opera, his continuous shying away from thoughts of his wife's rendezvous with the dashing Blazes Boylan—all this helps to build up his character in depth and to differentiate him sharply from Stephen. Unlike Stephen, Bloom's interest in language is confined to simple puns and translations, his interest in poetry is obvious and sentimental; his interest in the nature of reality takes the form of half-forgotten fragments of science remaining in his mind from schooldays. Everything about him is concrete, practical, sensual, and middlebrow or lowbrow, as distinct from the abstract, theoretical, esoteric speculations of Stephen in the "Proteus" episode. For example, when Stephen saw seagulls, he speculated on Daedalus and on flying as a symbol of the artist going into exile; when Bloom sees them, he thinks they must be hungry and buys a bun to feed them. There are parallels between their two streams of consciousness. Bloom's thoughts, in a sense, include Stephen's but in a popularized and even vulgarized form.

2. Bloom has been handed a religious leaflet ("throwaway") containing the phrase "Blood of the Lamb." He at first mistakes "Blood" for "Bloom."

3. Dowie was a Scottish-American evangelist who established the "Christian Catholic Apostolic Church in Zion" (i.e., Zion City, Illinois) in 1901.

4. A dramatic troupe advertising themselves as "The original Pepper's Ghost! and Spectral Opera Company" was popular in the late 19th century; they seem to have specialized in ghostly special effects, possibly achieved through the use of phosphorescent material on their costumes.

instance. I could see the bluey silver over it. Night I went down to the
pantry in the kitchen. Don't like all the smells in it waiting to rush out.
What was it she wanted?[5] The Malaga raisins. Thinking of Spain. Before
Rudy[6] was born. The phosphorescence, that bluey greeny. Very good
for the brain.

From Butler's monument house corner he glanced along Bachelor's
walk. Dedalus' daughter there still outside Dillon's auctionrooms. Must
be selling off some old furniture. Knew her eyes at once from the father.
Lobbing about waiting for him. Home always breaks up when the mother
goes. Fifteen children he had. Birth every year almost. That's in their
theology or the priest won't give the poor woman the confession, the
absolution. Increase and multiply. Did you ever hear such an idea? Eat
you out of house and home. No families themselves to feed. Living on
the fat of the land. Their butteries and larders. I'd like to see them do
the black fast Yom Kippur.[7] Crossbuns. One meal and a collation for
fear he'd collapse on the altar. A housekeeper of one of those fellows if
you could pick it out of her. Never pick it out of her. Like getting L s.
d.[8] out of him. Does himself well. No guests. All for number one.
Watching his water. Bring your own bread and butter. His reverence.
Mum's the word.

Good Lord, that poor child's dress is in flitters. Underfed she looks
too. Potatoes and marge, marge and potatoes. It's after they feel it. Proof
of the pudding. Undermines the constitution.

As he set foot on O'Connell bridge a puffball of smoke plumed up
from the parapet. Brewery barge with export stout. England. Sea air
sours it, I heard. Be interesting some day get a pass through Hancock to
see the brewery. Regular world in itself. Vats of porter, wonderful. Rats
get in too. Drink themselves bloated as big as a collie floating. Dead
drunk on the porter. Drink till they puke again like christians. Imagine
drinking that! Rats: vats. Well of course if we knew all the things.

Looking down he saw flapping strongly, wheeling between the gaunt
quaywalls, gulls. Rough weather outside. If I threw myself down? Reuben J's son must have swallowed a good bellyful of that sewage.[9] One
and eightpence too much. Hhhhm. It's the droll way he comes out with
the things. Knows how to tell a story too.

They wheeled lower. Looking for grub. Wait.

He threw down among them a crumpled paper ball. Elijah thirtytwo
feet per sec is com.[1] Not a bit. The ball bobbed unheeded on the wake
of swells, floated under by the bridgepiers. Not such damn fools. Also

5. "She" is Bloom's wife Molly, born in Gibraltar.
6. Their son, who had died in infancy eleven years
before.
7. Jewish Day of Atonement.
8. I.e., cash: £, s., d. are the abbreviations,
respectively, for pounds, shillings, and pence.
9. Reuben J. Dodd, Dublin solicitor (lawyer),
whose son had been rescued from the Liffey River
by a man to whom Reuben J. had given two shill-

ings as a reward—"one and eightpence too much,"
as Simon Dedalus had remarked to Bloom earlier
that morning when they were discussing the incident. It is Dedalus' comment that Bloom is thinking of in the following sentences.
1. I.e., Elijah is coming, accelerating at the rate
of 32 feet per second per second, the acceleration
rate of falling bodies. ("Elijah is coming" is the
legend on the handbill Bloom is tossing away).

the day I threw that stale cake out of the Erin's King picked it up in the wake fifty yards astern. Live by their wits. They wheeled, flapping.

> The hungry famished gull
> Flaps o'er the waters dull.

That is how poets write, the similar sounds. But then Shakespeare has no rhymes: blank verse. The flow of the language it is. The thoughts. Solemn.

> Hamlet, I am thy father's spirit
> Doomed for a certain time to walk the earth.[2]

—Two apples a penny! Two for a penny!

His gaze passed over the glazed apples serried on her stand. Australians they must be this time of year. Shiny peels: polishes them up with a rag or a handkerchief.

Wait. Those poor birds.

He halted again and bought from the old applewoman two Banbury cakes for a penny and broke the brittle paste and threw its fragments down into the Liffey. See that? The gulls swooped silently two, then all from their heights, pouncing on prey. Gone. Every morsel.

Aware of their greed and cunning he shook the powdery crumb from his hands. They never expected that. Manna.[3] Live on fishy flesh they have to, all seabirds, gulls, seagoose. Swans from Anna Liffey[4] swim down here sometimes to preen themselves. No accounting for tastes. Wonder what kind is swanmeat. Robinson Crusoe had to live on them.

They wheeled, flapping weakly. I'm not going to throw any more. Penny quite enough. Lot of thanks I get. Not even a caw. They spread foot and mouth disease too. If you cram a turkey, say, on chestnutmeal it tastes like that. Eat pig like pig. But then why is it that saltwater fish are not salty? How is that?

His eyes sought answer from the river and saw a rowboat rock at anchor on the treacly swells lazily its plastered board.

Kino's

11 / -

Trousers[5]

Good idea that. Wonder if he pays rent to the corporation. How can you own water really? It's always flowing in a stream, never the same, which in the stream of life we trace. Because life is a stream. All kinds of places are good for ads. That quack doctor for the clap used to be stuck up in all the greenhouses. Never see it now. Strictly confidential. Dr Hy Franks. Didn't cost him a red like Maginni the dancing master self advertisement. Got fellows to stick them up or stick them up himself

---

2. *Hamlet* 1.5.9–10 (slightly misquoted).

3. The divine food (small, round, and white) which the children of Israel ate in the wilderness (Exodus 16.14–15).

4. The Liffey flows from the Wicklow Mountains northeast and east to Dublin Bay.

5. I.e., eleven shillings ("11 / -") for Kino's Trousers. Bloom is a canvasser for advertisements: he receives commissions from newspapers for getting tradesmen to place advertisements with them.

for that matter on the q.t. running in to loosen a button. Flybynight. Just the place too. POST NO BILLS. POST NO PILLS. Some chap with a dose burning him.

If he . . .

O!

Eh?

No. . . No.

No, no. I don't believe it. He wouldn't surely?

No, no.[6]

Mr Bloom moved forward, raising his troubled eyes. Think no more about that. After one. Timeball on the ballastoffice is down. Dunsink time. Fascinating little book that is of Sir Robert Ball's.[7] Parallax. I never exactly understood. There's a priest. Could ask him. Par it's Greek: parallel, parallax. Met him pike hoses[8] she called it till I told her about the transmigration. O rocks!

Mr Bloom smiled O rocks at two windows of the ballastoffice. She's right after all. Only big words for ordinary things on account of the sound. She's not exactly witty. Can be rude too. Blurt out what I was thinking. Still I don't know. She used to say Ben Dollard had a base barreltone voice. He has legs like barrels and you'd think he was singing into a barrel. Now isn't that wit? They used to call him big Ben. Not half as witty as calling him base barreltone. Appetite like an albatross. Get outside of a baron of beef. Powerful man he was at stowing away number one Bass.[9] Barrel of Bass. See? It all works out.

A procession of whitesmocked men marched slowly towards him along the gutter, scarlet sashes across their boards. Bargains. Like that priest they are this morning: we have sinned: we have suffered. He read the scarlet letters on their five tall white hats: H. E. L. Y. S. Wisdom Hely's. Y lagging behind drew a chunk of bread from under his foreboard, crammed it into his mouth and munched as he walked. Our staple food. Three bob a day, walking along the gutters, street after street. Just keep skin and bone together, bread and skilly. They are not Boyl: no: M'Glade's men. Doesn't bring in any business either. I suggested to him about a transparent showcart with two smart girls sitting inside writing letters, copybooks, envelopes, blottingpaper. I bet that would have caught on. Smart girls writing something catch the eye at once. Everyone dying to know what she's writing. Get twenty of them round you if you stare at nothing. Have a finger in the pie. Women too. Curiosity. Pillar of salt.

---

6. Blazes Boylan, flashy philanderer, is due to call on Molly Bloom that afternoon, to discuss the program of a concert which he is managing for her (Molly is a singer). Bloom knows that Boylan and his wife will commit adultery together. Here it suddenly occurs to him that Boylan might give Molly a "dose" of veneral disease, but he puts the thought from him as incredible.

7. The "timeball on the ballastoffice" registers the official time of the observatory at Dunsink. Noticing that the timeball is down, which means that it is after 1 o'clock, Bloom is reminded of the observatory, then of the Irish astronomer Sir Robert Ball's popular book on astronomy, *The Story of the Heavens* (1886), and of the astronomical term "parallax" he found in the book but which he "never exactly understood."

8. Molly's way of pronouncing "metempsychosis." When Bloom had explained metempsychosis to her that morning, she had exclaimed "O rocks" at the pretentious term. He now mentally repeats "O rocks!" at the thought of the word "parallax."

9. A popular British ale.

Wouldn't have it of course because he didn't think of it himself first. Or the inkbottle I suggested with a false stain of black celluloid. His ideas for ads like Plumtree's potted under the obituaries, cold meat department. You can't lick 'em. What? Our envelopes. Hello! Jones, where are you going? Can't stop, Robinson, I am hastening to purchase the only reliable inkeraser *Kansell*, sold by Hely's Ltd, 85 Dame street. Well out of that ruck I am. Devil of a job it was collecting accounts of those convents. Tranquilla convent. That was a nice nun there, really sweet face. Wimple suited her small head. Sister? Sister? I am sure she was crossed in love by her eyes. Very hard to bargain with that sort of a woman. I disturbed her at her devotions that morning. But glad to communicate with the outside world. Our great day, she said. Feast of Our Lady of Mount Carmel. Sweet name too: caramel. She knew, I think she knew by the way she. If she had married she would have changed. I suppose they really were short of money. Fried everything in the best butter all the same. No lard for them. My heart's broke eating dripping. They like buttering themselves in and out. Molly tasting it, her veil up. Sister? Pat Claffey, the pawnbroker's daughter. It was a nun they say invented barbed wire.

He crossed Westmoreland street when apostrophe S had plodded by. Rover cycleshop. Those races are on today. How long ago is that? Year Phil Gilligan died. We were in Lombard street west. Wait, was in Thom's. Got the job in Wisdom Hely's year we married. Six years. Ten years ago: ninetyfour he died, yes that's right the big fire at Arnott's. Val Dillon was lord mayor. The Glencree dinner. Alderman Robert O'Reilly emptying the port into his soup before the flag fell, Bobbob lapping it for the inner alderman. Couldn't hear what the band played. For what we have already received may the Lord make us. Milly[1] was a kiddy then. Molly had that elephantgrey dress with the braided frogs. Mantailored with selfcovered buttons. She didn't like it because I sprained my ankle first day she wore choir picnic at the Sugarloaf. As if that. Old Goodwin's tall hat done up with some sticky stuff. Flies' picnic too. Never put a dress on her back like it. Fitted her like a glove, shoulder and hips. Just beginning to plump it out well. Rabbitpie we had that day. People looking after her.

Happy. Happier then. Snug little room that was with the red wallpaper, Dockrell's, one and ninepence a dozen. Milly's tubbing night. American soap I bought: elderflower. Cosy smell of her bathwater. Funny she looked soaped all over. Shapely too. Now photography.[2] Poor papa's daguerreotype atelier he told me of. Hereditary taste.

He walked along the curbstone.

Stream of life. What was the name of that priestlylooking chap was always squinting in when he passed? Weak eyes, woman. Stopped in Citron's saint Kevin's parade. Pen something. Pendennis? My memory is getting. Pen . . . ? Of course it's years ago. Noise of the trams proba-

---

1. Bloom's 15-year-old daughter.   2. Milly is working at a photographer's.

bly. Well, if he couldn't remember the dayfather's name that he sees every day.

Bartell d'Arcy was the tenor, just coming out then. Seeing her home after practice. Conceited fellow with his waxedup moustache. Gave her that song *Winds that blow from the south*.

Windy night that was I went to fetch her there was that lodge meeting on about those lottery tickets after Goodwin's concert in the supperroom or oakroom of the Mansion house. He and I behind. Sheet of her music blew out of my hand against the High school railings. Lucky it didn't. Thing like that spoils the effect of a night for her. Professor Goodwin linking her in front. Shaky on his pins, poor old sot. His farewell concerts. Positively last appearance on any stage. May be for months and may be for never. Remember her laughing at the wind, her blizzard collar up. Corner of Harcourt road remember that gust. Brrfoo! Blew up all her skirts and her boa nearly smothered old Goodwin. She did get flushed in the wind. Remember when we got home raking up the fire and frying up those pieces of lap of mutton for her supper with the Chutney sauce she liked. And the mulled rum. Could see her in the bedroom from the hearth unclamping the busk of her stays: white.

Swish and soft flop her stays made on the bed. Always warm from her. Always liked to let her self out. Sitting there after till near two taking out her hairpins. Milly tucked up in beddyhouse. Happy. Happy. That was the night. . .

—O, Mr Bloom, how do you do?

—O, how do you do, Mrs Breen?[3]

—No use complaining. How is Molly those times? Haven't seen her for ages.

—In the pink, Mr Bloom said gaily, Milly has a position down in Mullingar, you know.

—Go away! Isn't that grand for her?

—Yes, in a photographer's there. Getting on like a house on fire. How are all your charges?

—All on the baker's list, Mrs Breen said.

How many has she? No other in sight.

—You're in black I see. You have no . . .

—No, Mr Bloom said. I have just come from a funeral.

Going to crop up all day, I foresee. Who's dead, when and what did he die of? Turn up like a bad penny.

—O dear me, Mrs Breen said, I hope it wasn't any near relation.

May as well get her sympathy.

—Dignam, Mr Bloom said. An old friend of mine. He died quite suddenly, poor fellow. Heart trouble, I believe. Funeral was this morning.

> *Your funeral's tomorrow*
> *While you're coming through the rye.*

3. Mrs. Breen had been an old sweetheart of Bloom's.

Diddlediddle dumdum
Diddlediddle . . .

—Sad to lose the old friends, Mrs Breen's womaneyes said melancholily.

Now that's quite enough about that. Just quietly: husband.

—And your lord and master?

Mrs Breen turned up her two large eyes. Hasn't lost them anyhow.

—O, don't be talking, she said. He's a caution to rattlesnakes. He's in there now with his lawbooks finding out the law of libel. He has me heartscalded. Wait till I show you.

Hot mockturtle vapour and steam of newbaked jampuffs rolypoly poured out from Harrison's. The heavy noonreek tickled the top of Mr Bloom's gullet. Want to make good pastry, butter, best flour, Demerara sugar, or they'd taste it with the hot tea. Or is it from her? A barefoot arab stood over the grating, breathing in the fumes. Deaden the gnaw of hunger that way. Pleasure or pain is it? Penny dinner. Knife and fork chained to the table.

Opening her handbag, chipped leather, hatpin: ought to have a guard on those things. Stick it in a chap's eye in the tram. Rummaging. Open. Money. Please take one. Devils if they lose sixpence. Raise Cain. Husband barging. Where's the ten shillings I gave you on Monday? Are you feeding your little brother's family? Soiled handkerchief: medicinebottle. Pastille that was fell. What is she? . . .

—There must be a new moon out, she said. He's always bad then.[4] Do you know what he did last night?

Her hand ceased to rummage. Her eyes fixed themselves on him, wide in alarm, yet smiling.

—What? Mr. Bloom asked.

Let her speak. Look straight in her eyes. I believe you. Trust me.

—Woke me up in the night, she said. Dream he had, a nightmare. Indiges.

—Said the ace of spades[5] was walking up the stairs.

—The ace of spades! Mr Bloom said.

She took a folded postcard from her handbag.

—Read that, she said. He got it this morning.

—What is it? Mr Bloom asked, taking the card. U. P.?

—U.p.: up, she said. Someone taking a rise out of him. It's a great shame for them whoever he is.

—Indeed it is, Mr Bloom said.

She took back the card, sighing.

—And now he's going round to Mr Menton's office. He's going to take an action for ten thousand pounds, he says.

She folded the card into her untidy bag and snapped the catch.

Same blue serge dress she had two years ago, the nap bleaching. Seen its best days. Wispish hair over her ears. And that dowdy toque: three

4. Mr. Breen is mentally disturbed.   5. Symbol of death.

old grapes to take the harm out of it. Shabby genteel. She used to be a tasty dresser. Lines round her mouth. Only a year or so older than Molly.

See the eye that woman gave her, passing. Cruel. The unfair sex.

He looked still at her, holding back behind his look his discontent. Pungent mockturtle oxtail mulligatawny. I'm hungry too. Flakes of pastry on the gusset of her dress: daub of sugary flour stuck to her cheek. Rhubarb tart with liberal fillings, rich fruit interior. Josie Powell that was. In Luke Doyle's long ago, Dolphin's Barn, the charades. U.p.: up.

Change the subject.

—Do you ever see anything of Mrs Beaufoy, Mr Bloom asked.

—Mina Purefoy? she said.

Philip Beaufoy I was thinking. Playgoers' Club[6] Matcham often thinks of the masterstroke. Did I pull the chain? Yes. The last act.

—Yes.

—I just called to ask on the way in is she over it. She's in the lying-in hospital in Holles street. Dr Horne got her in. She's three days bad now.

—O, Mr Bloom said. I'm sorry to hear that.

—Yes, Mrs Breen said. And a houseful of kids at home. It's a very stiff birth, the nurse told me.

—O, Mr Bloom said.

His heavy pitying gaze absorbed her news. His tongue clacked in compassion. Dth! Dth!

—I'm sorry to hear that, he said. Poor thing! Three days! That's terrible for her.

Mrs Breen nodded

—She was taken bad on the Tuesday . . .

Mr Bloom touched her funnybone gently, warning her.

—Mind! Let this man pass.

A bony form strode along the curbstone from the river, staring with a rapt gaze into the sunlight through a heavystringed glass. Tight as a skullpiece a tiny hat gripped his head. From his arm a folded dustcoat, a stick and an umbrella dangled to his stride.

—Watch him, Mr Bloom said. He always walks outside the lampposts. Watch!

—Who is he if it's a fair question? Mrs Breen asked. Is he dotty?

—His name is Cashel Boyle O'Connor Fitzmaurice Tisdall Farrell, Mr Bloom said smiling. Watch!

—He has enough of them, she said. Denis will be like that one of these days.

She broke off suddenly.

—There he is, she said. I must go after him. Goodbye. Remember me to Molly, won't you?

—I will, Mr Bloom said.

He watched her dodge through passers towards the shopfronts. Denis

---

6. Bloom is thinking of the story *Matcham's Masterstroke*, by "Mr. Philip Beaufoy, Playgoers' Club, London," which he had read in the toilet that morning. He then mentally quotes the opening sentence.

Breen in skimpy frockcoat and blue canvas shoes shuffled out of Harrison's hugging two heavy tomes to his ribs. Blown in from the bay. Like old times. He suffered her to overtake him without surprise and thrust his dull grey beard towards her, his loose jaw wagging as he spoke earnestly.

Meshuggah.[7] Off his chump.

Mr Bloom walked on again easily, seeing ahead of him in sunlight the tight skullpiece, the dangling stick, umbrella, dustcoat. Going the two days. Watch him! Out he goes again. One way of getting on in the world. And that other old mosey lunatic in those duds. Hard time she must have with him.

U.p.: up. I'll take my oath that's Alf Bergan or Richie Goulding. Wrote it for a lark in the Scotch house, I bet anything. Round to Menton's office. His oyster eyes staring at the postcard. Be a feast for the gods.

He passed the *Irish Times*. There might be other answers lying there. Like to answer them all. Good system for criminals. Code. At their lunch now. Clerk with the glasses there doesn't know me. O, leave them there to simmer. Enough bother wading through fortyfour of them. Wanted smart lady typist to aid gentleman in literary work. I called you naughty darling because I do not like that other world. Please tell me what is the meaning. Please tell me what perfume does your wife.[8] Tell me who made the world. The way they spring those questions on you. And the other one Lizzie Twigg. My literary efforts have had the good fortune to meet with the approval of the eminent poet A. E. (Mr Geo. Russell).[9] No time to do her hair drinking sloppy tea with a book of poetry.

Best paper by long chalks for a small ad. Got the provinces now. Cook and general, exc cuisine, housemaid kept. Wanted live man for spirit counter. Resp. girl (R. C.) wishes to hear of post in fruit or pork shop. James Carlisle made that. Six and a half per cent dividend. Made a big deal on Coates's shares. Ca' canny. Cunning old Scotch hunks. All the toady news. Our gracious and popular vicereine.[1] Bought the *Irish Field* now. Lady Mountcashel has quite recovered after her confinement and rode out with the Ward Union staghounds at the enlargement yesterday at Rathoath. Uneatable fox. Pothunters too. Fear injects juices make it tender enough for them. Riding astride. Sit her horse like a man. Weightcarrying huntress. No sidesaddle or pillion for her, not for Joe. First to the meet and in at the death. Strong as a broodmare some of those horsey women. Swagger around livery stables. Toss off a glass of

---

7. Yiddish, "mad."

8. Bloom is mentally quoting a letter written to him by the typist Martha Clifford, with whom he is carrying on a purely epistolary love affair (she had misspelled "word" as "world": "I do not like that other world"). Lizzie Twigg was one of the other typists who had answered his advertisement for a secretary "to aid gentleman in literary work" (Bloom's pretext for beginning such an affair).

9. Æ (George Russell, 1867–1935), the Irish poet mentioned as a reference by Lizzie Twigg when she answered Bloom's advertisement, is later encountered by Bloom with a woman who Bloom speculates might be Lizzie.

1. Wife of the Viceroy, who represented the British Crown in Ireland; Bloom is thinking of the society column in the *Irish Times*.

brandy neat while you'd say knife. That one at the Grosvenor this morning. Up with her on the car: wishswish. Stonewall or fivebarred gate put
her mount to it. Think that pugnosed driver did it out of spite. Who is
this she was like? O yes! Mrs Miriam Dandrade that sold me her old
wraps and black underclothes in the Shelbourne hotel. Divorced Spanish American. Didn't take a feather out of her my handling them. As if
I was her clotheshorse. Saw her in the viceregal party when Stubbs the
park ranger got me in with Whelan of the *Express*. Scavenging what the
quality left. High tea. Mayonnaise I poured on the plums thinking it
was custard. Her ears ought to have tingled for a few weeks after. Want
to be a bull for her. Born courtesan. No nursery work for her, thanks.

Poor Mrs Purefoy! Methodist husband. Method in his madness. Saffron bun and milk and soda lunch in the educational dairy. Eating with
a stopwatch, thirtytwo chews to the minute. Still his muttonchop whiskers grew. Supposed to be well connected. Theodore's cousin in Dublin
Castle. One tony relative in every family. Hardy annuals he presents her
with. Saw him out at the Three Jolly Topers marching along bareheaded
and his eldest boy carrying one in a marketnet. The squallers. Poor
thing! Then having to give the breast year after year all hours of the
night. Selfish those t.t's[2] are. Dog in the manger. Only one lump of
sugar in my tea, if you please.

He stood at Fleet street crossing. Luncheon interval a sixpenny at
Rowe's? Must look up that ad in the national library.[3] An eightpenny in
the Burton. Better. On my way.

He walked on past Bolton's Westmoreland house. Tea. Tea. Tea. I
forgot to tap Tom Kernan.[4]

Sss. Dth, dth, dth! Three days imagine groaning on a bed with a
vinegared handkerchief round her forehead, her belly swollen out!. Phew!
Dreadful simply! Child's head too big: forceps. Doubled up inside her
trying to butt its way out blindly, groping for the way out. Kill me that
would. Lucky Molly got over hers lightly. They ought to invent something to stop that. Life with hard labour. Twilightsleep idea: queen Victoria was given that. Nine she had. A good layer. Old woman that lived
in a shoe she had so many children. Suppose he was consumptive. Time
someone thought about it instead of gassing about the what was it the
pensive bosom of the silver effulgence. Flapdoddle to feed fools on. They
could easily have big establishments. Whole thing quite painless out of
all the taxes give every child born five quid at compound interest up to
twentyone, five per cent is a hundred shillings and five tiresome pounds,
multiply by twenty decimal system, encourage people to put by money
save hundred and ten and a bit twentyone years want to work it out on
paper come to a tidy sum, more than you think.

2. Abbreviation of "Teetotallers," total abstainers
from alcohol.
3. Bloom's goal, on his walk through Dublin, is
the National Library, where he wants to look up
an advertisement in a back number of the *Kilk-*

enny People.
4. A Dublin tea merchant and friend of Bloom's,
whom Bloom had earlier intended to ask ("tap")
for some tea.

Not stillborn of course. They are not even registered. Trouble for nothing.

Funny sight two of them together, their bellies out. Molly and Mrs Moisel. Mothers' meeting. Phthisis retires for the time being, then returns. How flat they look after all of a sudden! Peaceful eyes. Weight off their mind. Old Mrs Thornton was a jolly old soul. All my babies, she said. The spoon of pap in her mouth before she fed them. O, that's nyumyum. Got her hand crushed by old Tom Wall's son. His first bow to the public. Head like a prize pumpkin. Snuffy Dr Murren. People knocking them up at all hours. For God's sake doctor. Wife in her throes. Then keep them waiting months for their fee. To attendance on your wife. No gratitude in people. Humane doctors, most of them.

Before the huge high door of the Irish house of parliament a flock of pigeons flew. Their little frolic after meals. Who will we do it on? I pick the fellow in black. Here goes. Here's good luck. Must be thrilling from the air. Apjohn, myself and Owen Goldberg up in the trees near Goose green playing the monkeys. Mackerel they called me.

A squad of constables debouched from College street, marching in Indian file. Goosestep. Foodheated faces, sweating helmets, patting their truncheons. After their feed with a good load of fat soup under their belts. Policeman's lot is oft a happy one.[5] They split up into groups and scattered, saluting towards their beats. Let out to graze. Best moment to attack one in pudding time. A punch in his dinner. A squad of others, marching irregularly, rounded Trinity railings, making for the station. Bound for their troughs. Prepare to receive cavalry. Prepare to receive soup.

He crossed under Tommy Moore's roguish finger. They did right to put him up over a urinal: meeting of the waters.[6] Ought to be places for women. Running into cakeshops. Settle my hat straight. *There is not in this wide world a vallee.* Great song of Julia Morkan's. Kept her voice up to the very last. Pupil of Michael Balfe's wasn't she?

He gazed after the last broad tunic. Nasty customers to tackle. Jack Power could a tale unfold: father a G man. If a fellow gave them trouble being lagged they let him have it hot and heavy in the bridewell.[7] Can't blame them after all with the job they have especially the young hornies. That horsepoliceman the day Joe Chamberlain was given his degree in Trinity he got a run for his money.[8] My word he did! His horse's hoofs clattering after us down Abbey street. Luck I had the presence of mind to dive into Manning's or I was souped. He did come a wallop, by George. Must have cracked his skull on the cobblestones. I oughtn't to have got myself swept along with those medicals. And the Trinity jibs[9] in their mortarboards. Looking for trouble. Still I got to know that young Dixon

---

5. Cf. "The policeman's lot is not a happy one" (W. S. Gilbert, *Pirates of Penzance*).
6. *The Meeting of the Waters* was a famous poem by the much-loved Irish poet Thomas Moore (1779–1852) whose statue Bloom now passes.
7. Prison.

8. When Joseph Chamberlain, the British Colonial Secretary, came to Dublin to receive an honorary degree from Trinity College, a group of medical students rioted against him and against the Boer War.
9. Trinity College students.

who dressed that sting for me in the Mater and now he's in Holles street where Mrs Purefoy. Wheels within wheels. Police whistle in my ears still. All skedaddled. Why he fixed on me. Give me in charge. Right here it began.

—Up the Boers!

—Three cheers for De Wet![1]

—We'll hang Joe Chamberlain on a sourapple tree.

Silly billies: mob of young cubs yelling their guts out. Vinegar hill. The Butter exchange band. Few years' time half of them magistrates and civil servants. War comes on: into the army helterskelter: same fellows used to. Whether on the scaffold high.

Never know who you're talking to. Corny Kelleher he has Harvey Duff in his eye. Like that Peter or Denis or James Carey that blew the gaff on the invincibles. Member of the corporation too. Egging raw youths on to get in the know. All the time drawing secret service pay from the castle.[2] Drop him like a hot potato. Why those plainclothes men are always courting slaveys. Easily twig a man used to uniform. Squarepushing up against a backdoor. Maul her a bit. Then the next thing on the menu. And who is the gentleman does be visiting there? Was the young master saying anything? Peeping Tom through the keyhole. Decoy duck. Hotblooded young student fooling round her fat arms ironing.

—Are those yours, Mary?

—I don't wear such things. . . Stop or I'll tell the missus on you. Out half the night.

—There are great times coming, Mary. Wait till you see.

—Ah, get along with your great times coming.

Barmaids too. Tobaccoshopgirls.

James Stephens'[3] idea was the best. He knew them. Circles of ten so that a fellow couldn't round on more than his own ring. Sinn Fein.[4] Back out you get the knife. Hidden hand. Stay in. The firing squad. Turnkey's daughter got him out of Richmond, off from Lusk. Putting up in the Buckingham Palace hotel under their very noses. Garibaldi.[5]

You must have a certain fascination: Parnell.[6] Arthur Griffith is a squareheaded fellow but he has no go in him for the mob. Want to gas about our lovely land. Gammon and spinach. Dublin Bakery Company's tearoom. Debating societies. That republicanism is the best form of government. That the language question should take precedence of the economic question. Have your daughters inveigling them to your house. Stuff them up with meat and drink. Michaelmas goose. Here's a good lump of thyme seasoning under the apron for you. Have another quart of goosegrease before it gets too cold. Halffed enthusiasts. Penny roll and

1. Boer general.

2. I.e., from the British government, whose representative lived at Dublin Castle.

3. Irish nationalist revolutionary.

4. Irish revolutionary movement; the Gaelic words mean "We Ourselves."

5. Bloom is thinking of a variety of nationalist conspirators who escaped from danger, among them the 19th-century Italian patriot and general Giuseppe Garibaldi.

6. Charles Stewart Parnell (1846–1891), Irish nationalist political leader. Arthur Griffith was founder of the Sinn Fein.

a walk with the band. No grace for the carver. The thought that the other chap pays best sauce in the world. Make themselves thoroughly at home. Show us over those apricots, meaning peaches. The not far distant day. Home Rule sun rising up in the northwest.[7]

His smile faded as he walked, a heavy cloud hiding the sun slowly, shadowing Trinity's surly front. Trams passed one another, ingoing, outgoing, clanging. Useless words. Things go on same; day after day: squads of police marching out, back: trams in, out. Those two loonies mooching about. Dignam carted off. Mina Purefoy swollen belly on a bed groaning to have a child tugged out of her. One born every second somewhere. Other dying every second. Since I fed the birds five minutes. Three hundred kicked the bucket. Other three hundred born, washing the blood off, all are washed in the blood of the lamb, bawling maaaaaa.

Cityful passing away, other cityful coming, passing away too: other coming on, passing on. Houses, lines of houses, streets, miles of pavements, piledup bricks, stones. Changing hands. This owner, that. Landlord never dies they say. Other steps into his shoes when he gets his notice to quit. They buy the place up with gold and still they have all the gold. Swindle in it somewhere. Piled up in cities, worn away age after age. Pyramids in sand. Built on bread and onions. Slaves Chinese wall. Babylon. Big stones left. Round towers. Rest rubble, sprawling suburbs, jerrybuilt, Kerwan's mushroom houses built of breeze. Shelter for the night.

No-one is anything.

This is the very worst hour of the day. Vitality. Dull, gloomy: hate this hour. Feel as if I had been eaten and spewed.

Provost's house. The reverend Dr Salmon: tinned salmon. Well tinned in there. Wouldn't live in it if they paid me. Hope they have liver and bacon today. Nature abhors a vacuum.

The sun freed itself slowly and lit glints of light among the silverware in Walter Sexton's window opposite by which John Howard Parnell[8] passed, unseeing.

There he is: the brother. Image of him. Haunting face. Now that's a coincidence. Course hundreds of times you think of a person and don't meet him. Like a man walking in his sleep. No-one knows him. Must be a corporation meeting today. They say he never put on the city marshal's uniform since he got the job. Charley Beulger used to come out on his high horse, cocked hat, puffed, powdered and shaved. Look at the woebegone walk of him. Eaten a bad egg. Poached eyes on ghost. I have a pain. Great man's brother: his brother's brother. He'd look nice on the city charger. Drop into the D. B. C. probably for his coffee, play chess there. His brother used men as pawns. Let them all go to pot. Afraid to pass a remark on him. Freeze them up with that eye of his. That's the fascination: the name. All a bit touched. Mad Fanny and his

7. Reference to Arthur Griffith's comment on the *Freeman* masthead, which showed the sun rising in the northwest from behind the Bank of Ireland.

Bloom has a *Freeman* in his pocket.
8. C. S. Parnell's brother.

other sister Mrs Dickinson driving about with scarlet harness. Bolt upright like surgeon M'Ardle. Still David Sheehy beat him for south Meath. Apply for the Chiltern Hundreds[9] and retire into public life. The patriot's banquet. Eating orangepeels in the park. Simon Dedalus said when they put him in parliament that Parnell would come back from the grave and lead him out of the House of Commons by the arm.

—Of the twoheaded octopus, one of whose heads is the head upon which the ends of the world have forgotten to come while the other speaks with a Scotch accent. The tentacles . . .

They passed from behind Mr Bloom along the curbstone. Beard and bicycle. Young woman.

And there he is too. Now that's really a coincidence: second time. Coming events cast their shadows before. With the approval of the eminent poet, Mr Geo Russell.[1] That might be Lizzie Twigg with him. A. E.: what does that mean? Initials perhaps. Albert Edward, Arthur Edmund, Alphonsus Eb Ed El Esquire. What was he saying? The ends of the world with a Scotch accent. Tentacles: octopus. Something occult: symbolism. Holding forth. She's taking it all in. Not saying a word. To aid gentleman in literary work.

His eyes followed the high figure in homespun, beard and bicycle, a listening woman at his side. Coming from the vegetarian. Only wegge-bobbles and fruit. Don't eat a beefsteak. If you do the eyes of that cow will pursue you through all eternity. They say it's healthier. Wind and watery though. Tried it. Keep you on the run all day. Bad as a bloater. Dreams all night. Why do they call that thing they gave me nutsteak? Nutarians. Fruitarians. To give you the idea you are eating rumpsteak. Absurd. Salty too. They cook in soda. Keep you sitting by the tap all night.

Her stockings are loose over her ankles. I detest that: so tasteless. Those literary etherial people they are all. Dreamy, cloudy, symbolistic. Esthetes they are. I wouldn't be surprised if it was that kind of food you see produces the like waves of the brain the poetical. For example one of those policemen sweating Irish stew into their shirts; you couldn't squeeze a line of poetry out of him. Don't know what poetry is even. Must be in a certain mood.

> The dreamy cloudy gull
> Waves o'er the waters dull.

He crossed at Nassau street corner and stood before the window of Yeates and Son, pricing the fieldglasses. Or will I drop into old Harris's and have a chat with young Sinclair? Wellmannered fellow. Probably at

---

9. The Stewardship of the Chiltern Hundreds (a tract of land in central England owned by the British Crown) is by a legal figment held to be an office of profit under the Crown, and is conferred on any Member of Parliament wishing to resign his seat, which by law he cannot do, so long as he is duly qualified. A Member of Parliament who accepts an office of profit under the Crown must vacate his seat.

1. Bloom wonders whether the woman with Æ might be Lizzie Twigg and then goes on to speculate on the meaning of "Æ" and on Russell's mystical ideas.

his lunch. Must get those old glasses of mine set right. Gœrz lenses six guineas. Germans making their way everywhere. Sell on easy terms to capture trade. Undercutting. Might chance on a pair in the railway lost property office. Astonishing the things people leave behind them in trains and cloakrooms. What do they be thinking about? Women too. Incredible. Last year travelling to Ennis had to pick up that farmer's daughter's bag and hand it to her at Limerick junction. Unclaimed money too. There's a little watch up there on the roof of the bank to test those glasses by.

His lids came down on the lower rims of his irides. Can't see it. If you imagine it's there you can almost see it. Can't see it.

He faced about and, standing between the awnings, held out his right hand at arm's length towards the sun. Wanted to try that often. Yes: completely. The tip of his little finger blotted out the sun's disk. Must be the focus where the rays cross. If I had black glasses. Interesting. There was a lot of talk about those sunspots when we were in Lombard street west. Terrific explosions they are. There will be a total eclipse this year: autumn some time.

Now that I come to think of it, that ball falls at Greenwich time. It's the clock is worked by an electric wire from Dunsink. Must go out there some first Saturday of the month. If I could get an introduction to professor Joly or learn up something about his family. That would do to: man always feels complimented. Flattery where least expected. Nobleman proud to be descended from some king's mistress. His foremother. Lay it on with a trowel. Cap in hand goes through the land. Not go in and blurt out what you know you're not to: what's parallax? Show this gentleman the door.

Ah.

His hand fell again to his side.

Never know anything about it. Waste of time. Gasballs spinning about, crossing each other, passing. Same old dingdong always. Gas, then solid, then world, then cold, then dead shell drifting around, frozen rock like that pineapple rock. The moon. Must be a new moon out, she said. I believe there is.

He went on by la maison Claire.

Wait. The full moon was the night we were Sunday fortnight exactly there is a new moon. Walking down by the Tolka. Not bad for a Fairview moon. She was humming. The young May moon she's beaming, love. He other side of her. Elbow, arm. He. Glowworm's la-amp is gleaming, love. Touch. Fingers. Asking. Answer. Yes.

Stop. Stop. If it was it was.[2] Must.

Mr Bloom, quickbreathing, slowlier walking passed Adam court.

With deep quiet relief, his eyes took note: this is street here middle of the day Bob Doran's bottle shoulders. On his annual bend, M'Coy said. They drink in order to say or do something or *cherchez la femme*.[3] Up

---

2. Bloom is thinking again of his wife's infidelity.   3. "Look for the woman" (in the case).

in the Coombe with chummies and streetwalkers and then the rest of the year as sober as a judge.

Yes. Thought so. Sloping into the Empire. Gone. Plain soda would do him good. Where Pat Kinsella had his Harp theatre before Whitbread ran the Queen's.[4] Broth of a boy. Dion Boucicault business with his harvestmoon face in a poky bonnet. Three Purty Maids from School. How time flies eh? Showing long red pantaloons under his skirts. Drinkers, drinking, laughed spluttering, their drink against their breath. More power, Pat. Coarse red: fun for drunkards: guffaw and smoke. Take off that white hat. His parboiled eyes. Where is he now? Beggar somewhere. The harp that once did starve us all.[5]

I was happier then. Or was that I? Or am I now I? Twentyeight I was. She twentythree when we left Lombard street west something changed. Could never like it again after Rudy. Can't bring back time. Like holding water in your hand. Would you go back to then? Just beginning then. Would you? Are you not happy in your home, you poor little naughty boy? Wants to sew on buttons for me. I must answer. Write it in the library.

Grafton street gay with housed awnings lured his senses. Muslin prints silk, dames and dowagers, jingle of harnesses, hoofthuds lowringing in the baking causeway. Thick feet that woman has in the white stockings. Hope the rain mucks them up on her. Countrybred chawbacon. All the beef to the heels were in. Always gives a woman clumsy feet. Molly looks out of plumb.

He passed, dallying, the windows of Brown Thomas, silk mercers. Cascades of ribbons. Flimsy China silks. A tilted urn poured from its mouth a flood of bloodhued poplin: lustrous blood. The huguenots brought that here. *La causa è santa! Tara tara.*[6] Great chorus that. *Tara.* Must be washed in rainwater. Meyerbeer. *Tara: bom bom bom.*

Pincushions. I'm a long time threatening to buy one. Stick them all over the place. Needles in window curtains.

He bared slightly his left forearm. Scrape: nearly gone. Not today anyhow. Must go back for that lotion. For her birthday perhaps. Junejuly augseptember eighth. Nearly three months off. Then she mightn't like it. Women won't pick up pins. Say it cuts lo.

Gleaming silks, petticoats on slim brass rails, rays of flat silk stockings.

Useless to go back. Had to be. Tell me all.

High voices. Sunwarm silk. Jingling harnesses. All for a woman, home and houses, silkwebs, silver, rich fruits, spicy from Jaffa. Agendath Netaim.[7] Wealth of the world.

---

4. The Queen's Theatre. Dion Boucicault was an Irish-born American dramatist, manager, and actor.
5. A reference to the lack of financial success of the Harp Theatre through a punning reworking (almost worthy of Stephen Dedalus) of Tom Moore's famous *Harp That Once Through Tara's Halls.*
6. *La causa è santa,* "The cause is sacred," chorus from Meyerbeer's opera *Les Huguenots,* which

Bloom is recalling. The Huguenots were 16th- and 17th-century French Protestants, many of whom fled to Britain to escape persecution.
7. "Planters' Company" (Hebrew). Bloom recalls a leaflet advertising an early Zionist settlement which he had seen that morning and is still carrying in his pocket.

A warm human plumpness settled down on his brain. His brain yielded. Perfume of embraces all him assailed. With hungered flesh obscurely, he mutely craved to adore.

Duke street. Here we are. Must eat. The Burton. Feel better then.

He turned Combridge's corner, still pursued. Jingling hoofthuds. Perfumed bodies, warm, full. All kissed, yielded: in deep summer fields, tangled pressed grass, in trickling hallways of tenements, along sofas, creaking beds.

—Jack, love!

—Darling!

—Kiss me, Reggy!

—My boy!

—Love![8]

His heart astir he pushed in the door of the Burton restaurant. Stink gripped his trembling breath: pungent meatjuice, slop of greens. See the animals feed.

Men, men, men.

Perched on high stools by the bar, hats shoved back, at the tables calling for more bread no charge, swilling, wolfing gobfuls of sloppy food, their eyes bulging, wiping wetted moustaches. A pallid suetfaced young man polished his tumbler knife fork and spoon with his napkin. New set of microbes. A man with an infant's saucestained napkin tucked round him shovelled gurgling soup down his gullet. A man spitting back on his plate: halfmasticated gristle: no teeth to chewchewchew it. Chump chop from the grill. Bolting to get it over. Sad booser's eyes. Bitten off more than he can chew. Am I like that? See ourselves as others see us. Hungry man is an angry man. Working tooth and jaw. Don't! O! A bone! That last pagan king of Ireland Cormac in the schoolpoem choked himself at Sletty southward of the Boyne.[9] Wonder what he was eating. Something galoptious. Saint Patrick converted him to Christianity. Couldn't swallow it all however.

—Roast beef and cabbage.

—One stew.

Smells of men. His gorge rose. Spaton sawdust, sweetish warmish cigarettesmoke, reek of plug, spilt beer, men's beery piss, the stale of ferment.

Couldn't eat a morsel here. Fellow sharpening knife and fork, to eat all before him, old chap picking his tootles. Slight spasm, full, chewing the cud. Before and after. Grace after meals. Look on this picture then on that. Scoffing up stewgravy with sopping sippets of bread. Lick it off the plate, man! Get out of this.

He gazed round the stooled and tabled eaters, tightening the wings of his nose.

8. Sensual images are leading Bloom to imagine love scenes from a sentimental novel. The cannibal Lestrygonians had used "the handsome daughter of Lestrygonian Antiphates" as a decoy to lure Ulysses' men to her father, and Bloom is drawn by his sensual and sexual imagination to enter Burton's restaurant—only to be disgusted by the grossness of the atmosphere.

9. Bloom is recalling a "schoolpoem" about a legendary incident in Irish history.

—Two stouts here.

—One corned and cabbage.

That fellow ramming a knifeful of cabbage down as if his life depended on it. Good stroke. Give me the fidgets to look. Safer to eat from his three hands. Tear it limb from limb. Second nature to him. Born with a silver knife in his mouth. That's witty, I think. Or no. Silver means born rich. Born with a knife. But then the allusion is lost.

An illgirt server gathered sticky clattering plates. Rock, the bailiff, standing at the bar blew the foamy crown from his tankard. Well up: it splashed yellow near his boot. A diner, knife and fork upright, elbows on table, ready for a second helping stared towards the food-lift across his stained square of newspaper. Other chap telling him something with his mouth full. Sympathetic listener. Table talk. I munched hum un thu Unchster Bunk un Munchday. Ha? Did you, faith?

Mr Bloom raised two fingers doubtfully to his lips. His eyes said:

—Not here. Don't see him.[1]

Out. I hate dirty eaters.

He backed towards the door. Get a light snack in Davy Byrne's. Stop-gap. Keep me going. Had a good breakfast.

—Roast and mashed here.

—Pint of stout.

Every fellow for his own, tooth and nail. Gulp. Grub. Gulp. Gob-stuff.

He came out into clearer air and turned back towards Grafton street. Eat or be eaten. Kill! Kill!

Suppose that communal kitchen years to come perhaps. All trotting down with porringers and tommycans to be filled. Devour contents in the street. John Howard Parnell example the provost of Trinity every mother's son don't talk of your provosts and provost of Trinity women and children, cabmen, priests, parsons, fieldmarshals, archbishops. From Ailesbury road, Clyde road, artisans' dwellings north Dublin union, lord mayor in his gingerbread coach, old queen in a bathchair. My plate's empty. After you with our incorporated drinking cup. Like sir Philip Crampton's fountain. Rub off the microbes with your handkerchief. Next chap rubs on a new batch with his. Father O'Flynn would make hares of them all. Have rows all the same. All for number one. Children fighting for the scrapings of the pot. Want a souppot as big as the Phoenix park. Harpooning flitches and hindquarters out of it. Hate people all round you. City Arms hotel *table d'hôte* she called it. Soup, joint and sweet. Never know whose thoughts you're chewing. Then who'd wash up all the plates and forks? Might be all feeding on tabloids that time. Teeth getting worse and worse.

After all there's a lot in that vegetarian fine flavour of things from the earth garlic, of course, it stinks Italian organgrinders crisp of onions mushrooms truffles. Pain to animal too. Pluck and draw fowl. Wretched

1. He pretends he is looking for someone he cannot see, so that he has an excuse to leave without eating.

brutes there at the cattlemarket waiting for the poleaxe to split their skulls open. Moo. Poor trembling calves. Meh. Staggering bob. Bubble and squeak. Butchers' buckets wobble lights. Give us that brisket off the hook. Plup. Rawhead and bloody bones. Flayed glasseyed sheep hung from their haunches, sheepsnouts bloodypapered snivelling nosejam on sawdust. Top and lashers going out. Don't maul them pieces, young one.

Hot fresh blood they prescribe for decline. Blood always needed. Insidious. Lick it up smokinghot, thick sugary. Famished ghosts.

Ah, I'm hungry.

He entered Davy Byrne's. Moral pub. He doesn't chat. Stands a drink now and then. But in leapyear once in four. Cashed a cheque for me once.

What will I take now? He drew his watch. Let me see now. Shandygaff?

—Hello, Bloom, Nosey Flynn said from his nook.

—Hello, Flynn.

—How's things?

—Tiptop . . . Let me see. I'll take a glass of burgundy and . . . let me see.

Sardines on the shelves. Almost taste them by looking. Sandwich? Ham and his descendants mustered and bred there. Potted meats. What is home without Plumtree's potted meat? Incomplete. What a stupid ad! Under the obituary notices they stuck it. All up a plumtree. Dignam's potted mat. Cannibals would with lemon and rice. White missionary too salty. Like pickled pork. Expect the chief consumes the parts of honour. Ought to be tough from exercise. His wives in a row to watch the effect. *There was a right royal old nigger. Who ate or something the somethings of the reverend Mr MacTrigger.* With it an abode of bliss. Lord knows what concoction. Cauls mouldy tripes windpipes faked and minced up. Puzzle find the meat. Kosher. No meat and milk together. Hygiene that was what they call now, Yom Kippur fast spring cleaning of inside. Peace and war depend on some fellow's digestion. Religions. Christmas turkeys and geese. Slaughter of innocents. Eat, drink and be merry. Then casual wards full after. Heads bandaged. Cheese digests all but itself. Mighty cheese.

—Have you a cheese sandwich?

—Yes, sir.

Like a few olives too if they had them. Italian I prefer. Good glass of burgundy; take away that. Lubricate. A nice salad, cool as a cucumber. Tom Kernan can dress. Puts gusto into it. Pure olive oil. Milly served me that cutlet with a sprig of parsley. Take one Spanish onion. God made food, the devil the cooks. Devilled crab.

—Wife well?

—Quite well, thanks. . . A cheese sandwich, then. Gorgonzola, have you?

—Yes, sir.

Nosey Flynn sipped his grog.

—Doing any singing those times?

Look at his mouth. Could whistle in his own ear. Flap ears to match. Music. Knows as much about it as my coachman. Still better tell him. Does no harm. Free ad.

—She's engaged for a big tour end of this month. You may have heard perhaps.

—No. O, that's the style. Who's getting it up?

The curate[2] served.

—How much is that?

—Seven d., sir. . . Thank you, sir.

Mr Bloom cut his sandwich into slender strips. *Mr MacTrigger.* Easier than the dreamy creamy stuff. *His five hundred wives. Had the time of their lives.*

—Mustard, sir?

—Thank you.

He studded under each lifted strip yellow blobs. *Their lives.* I have it. *It grew bigger and bigger and bigger.*

—Getting it up? he said. Well, it's like a company idea, you see. Part shares and part profits.

—Ay, now I remember, Nosey Flynn said, putting his hand in his pocket to scratch his groin. Who is this was telling me? Isn't Blazes Boylan mixed up in it?

A warm shock of air heat of mustard hanched on Mr Bloom's heart. He raised his eyes and met the stare of a bilious clock. Two. Pub clock five minutes fast. Time going on. Hands moving. Two. Not yet.[3]

His midriff yearned then upward, sank within him, yearned more longly, longingly.

Wine.

He smellsipped the cordial juice and, bidding his throat strongly to speed it, set his wineglass delicately down.

—Yes, he said. He's the organiser in point of fact.

No fear: no brains.

Nosey Flynn snuffled and scratched. Flea having a good square meal.

—He had a good slice of luck, Jack Mooney was telling me, over that boxing match Myler Keogh won again that soldier in the Portobello barracks. By God, he had the little kipper down in the country Carlow he was telling me. . . .

Hope that dewdrop doesn't come down into his glass. No, snuffled it up.

—For near a month, man, before it came off. Sucking duck eggs by God till further orders. Keep him off the boose, see? O, by God, Blazes is a hairy chap.

Davy Byrne came forward from the hindbar in tuckstitched shirtsleeves, cleaning his lips with two wipes of his napkin. Herring's blush.

Whose smile upon each feature plays with such and such replete. Too much fat on the parsnips.

—And here's himself and pepper on him, Nosey Flynn said. Can you give us a good one for the Gold cup?

—I'm off that, Mr Flynn, Davy Byrne answered. I never put anything on a horse.

—You're right there, Nosey Flynn said.

Mr Bloom ate his strips of sandwich, fresh clean bread, with relish of disgust, pungent mustard, the feety savour of green cheese. Sips of his wine soothed his palate. Not logwood that. Tastes fuller this weather with the chill off.

Nice quiet bar. Nice piece of wood in that counter. Nicely planed. Like the way it curves there.

—I wouldn't do anything at all in that line, Davy Byrne said. It ruined many a man, the same horses.

Vintners' sweepstake. Licensed for the sale of beer, wine and spirits for consumption on the premises. Heads I win tails you lose.

—True for you, Nosey Flynn said. Unless you're in the know. There's no straight sport going now. Lenehan gets some good ones. He's giving Sceptre today. Zinfandel's the favourite, lord Howard de Walden's, won at Epsom. Morny Cannon is riding him. I could have got seven to one against Saint Amant a fortnight before.

—That so? Davy Byrne said. . . .

He went towards the window and, taking up the petty cash book, scanned its pages.

—I could, faith, Nosey Flynn said, snuffling. That was a rare bit of horseflesh. Saint Frusquin was her sire. She won in a thunderstorm, Rothschild's filly, with wadding in her ears. Blue jacket and yellow cap. Bad luck to big Ben Dollard and his John O'Gaunt. He put me off it. Ay.

He drank resignedly from his tumbler, running his fingers down the flutes.

—Ay, he said, sighing.

Mr Bloom, champing standing, looked upon his sigh. Nosey numb-skull. Will I tell him that horse Lenehan?[4] He knows already. Better let him forget. Go and lose more. Fool and his money. Dewdrop coming down again. Cold nose he'd have kissing a woman. Still they might like. Prickly beards they like. Dogs' cold noses. Old Mrs Riordan with the rumbling stomach's Skye terrier in the City Arms hotel. Molly fondling him in her lap. O, the big doggybowwowsywowsy!

Wine soaked and softened rolled pith of bread mustard a moment mawkish cheese. Nice wine it is. Taste it better because I'm not thirsty. Bath of course does that. Just a bite or two. Then about six o'clock I can. Six. Six. Time will be gone then. She. . .

---

4. Bloom is wondering whether to pass on a tip from Lenehan, who wrote for the racing paper *Sport*.

Mild fire of wine kindled his veins. I wanted that badly. Felt so off colour. His eyes unhungrily saw shelves of tins, sardines, gaudy lobsters' claws. All the odd things people pick up for food. Out of shells, periwinkles with a pin, off trees, snails out of the ground the French eat, out of the sea with bait on a hook. Silly fish learn nothing in a thousand years. If you didn't know risky putting anything into your mouth. Poisonous berries. Johnny Magories. Roundness you think good. Gaudy colour warns you off. One fellow told another and so on. Try it on the dog first. Led on by the smell or the look. Tempting fruit. Ice cones. Cream. Instinct. Orangegroves for instance. Need artificial irrigation. Bleibtreustrasse.[5] Yes but what about oysters. Unsightly like a clot of phlegm. Filthy shells. Devil to open them too. Who found them out? Garbage, sewage they feed on. Fizz and Red bank oysters. Effect on the sexual. Aphrodis. He was in the Red bank this morning. Was he oyster old fish at table. Perhaps he young flesh in bed. No. June has no ar no oysters. But there are people like tainted game. Jugged hare. First catch your hare. Chinese eating eggs fifty years old, blue and green again. Dinner of thirty courses. Each dish harmless might mix inside. Idea for a poison mystery. That archduke Leopold was it. No. Yes, or was it Otto one of those Habsburgs? Or who was it used to eat the scruff off his own head? Cheapest lunch in town. Of course, aristocrats, then the others copy to be in the fashion. Milly too rock oil and flour. Raw pastry I like myself. Half the catch of oysters they throw back in the sea to keep up the price. Cheap. No-one would buy. Caviare. Do the grand. Hock in green glasses. Swell blowout. Lady this. Powdered bosom pearls. The *élite*. *Crème de la crème*.[6] They want special dishes to pretend they're. Hermit with a platter of pulse keep down the stings of the flesh. Know me come eat with me. Royal sturgeon. High sheriff, Coffey, the butcher, right to venisons of the forest from his ex.[7] Send him back the half of a cow. Spread I saw down in the Master of the Rolls' kitchen area. Whitehatted *Chef* like a rabbi. Combustible duck. Curly cabbage *à la duchesse de Parme*. Just as well to write it on the bill of fare so you can know what you've eaten too many drugs spoil the broth. I know it myself. Dosing it with Edwards' desicated soup. Geese stuffed silly for them. Lobsters boiled alive. Do ptake some ptarmigan. Wouldn't mind being a waiter in a swell hotel. Tips, evening dress, halfnaked ladies. May I tempt you to a little more filleted lemon sole, miss Dubedat? Yes, do bedad. And she did bedad. Huguenot name I expect that. A miss Dubedat lived in Killiney, I remember. *Du, de la*, French. Still it's the same fish, perhaps old Micky Hanlon of Moore street ripped the guts out of making money, hand over fist, finger in fishes' gills, can't write his name on a cheque,

5. The Berlin street which contained the offices of the "Planters' Company."
6. "Cream of the cream" (i.e., the very best, socially).
7. All sturgeon caught in or off Britain were the property of the king, according to the ancient traditional rights to certain kinds of fish or game. Bloom goes on to imagine a Dublin butcher having a "right to venisons of the forest from his ex[cellency]"—i.e., the Viceroy.

think he was painting the landscape with his mouth twisted. Moooikill
A Aitcha Ha. Ignorant as a kish of brogues,[8] worth fifty thousand pounds.
    Stuck on the pane two flies buzzed, stuck.
    Glowing wine on his palate lingered swallowed. Crushing in the
winepress grapes of Burgundy. Sun's heat it is. Seems to a secret touch
telling me memory. Touched his sense moistened remembered. Hidden
under wild ferns on Howth. Below us bay sleeping sky. No sound. The
sky. The bay purple by the Lion's head. Green by Drumleck. Yel-
lowgreen towards Sutton. Fields of undersea, the lines faint brown in
grass, buried cities. Pillowed on my coat she had her hair, earwigs in
the heather scrub my hand under her nape, you'll toss me all. O wonder! Coolsoft with ointments her hand touched me, caressed: her eyes
upon me did not turn away. Ravished over her I lay, full lips full open,
kissed her mouth. Yum. Softly she gave me in my mouth the seedcake
warm and chewed. Mawkish pulp her mouth had mumbled sweet and
sour with spittle. Joy: I ate it: joy. Young life, her lips that gave me
pouting. Soft, warm, sticky gumjelly lips. Flowers her eyes were, take
me, willing eyes. Pebbles fell. She lay still. A goat. No-one. High on
Ben Howth rhododendrons a nannygoat walking surefooted, dropping
currants. Screened under ferns she laughed warmfolded. Wildly I lay
on her, kissed her, eyes, her lips, her stretched neck, beating, woman's
breasts full in her blouse of nun's veiling, fat nipples upright. Hot I
tongued her. She kissed me. I was kissed. All yielding she tossed my
hair. Kissed, she kissed me.[9]
    Me. And me now.
    Stuck, the flies buzzed.
    His downcast eyes followed the silent veining of the oaken slab. Beauty:
it curves: curves are beauty. Shapely goddesses, Venus, Juno: curves the
world admires. Can see them library museum standing in the round
hall, naked goddesses. Aids to digestion. They don't care what man looks.
All to see. Never speaking, I mean to say to fellows like Flynn. Suppose
she did Pygmalion and Galatea[1] what would she say first? Mortal! Put
you in your proper place. Quaffing nectar at mess with gods, golden
dishes, all ambrosial. Not like a tanner lunch we have, boiled mutton,
carrots and turnips, bottle of Allsop. Nectar, imagine it drinking electricity: god's food. Lovely forms of women sculped Junonian. Immortal
lovely. And we stuffing food in one hole and out behind: food, chyle,
blood, dung, earth, food: have to feed it like stoking an engine. They
have no. Never looked. I'll look today. Keeper won't see. Bend down let
something see if she.

8. A basket of shoes.
9. Bloom is remembering when he first proposed
to Molly, on the Hill of Howth, near Dublin, Molly
also recalls this in the final "Penelope" episodes,
which is her soliloquy: ". . . we were lying among
the rhododendrons on Howth head in the gray
tweed suit and his straw hat the day I got him to
propose to me yes . . . my God after that long kiss
I near lost my breath . . . I saw he understood or
felt what a woman is and I knew I could always get
round him and I gave him all the pleasure I could
leading him on . . ."
1. Pygmalion was the sculptor whose statue of
Galatea came alive.

Dribbling a quiet message from his bladder came to go to do not to do there to do. A man and ready he drained his glass to the lees and walked, to men too they gave themselves, manly conscious, lay with men lovers, a youth enjoyed her, to the yard.

When the sound of his boots had ceased Davy Byrne said from his book:

—What is this he is? Isn't he in the insurance line?

—He's out of that long ago, Nosey Flynn said. He does canvassing for the *Freeman*.

—I know him well to see, Davy Byrne said. Is he in trouble?

—Trouble? Nosey Flynn said. Not that I heard of. Why?

—I noticed he was in mourning.

—Was he? Nosey Flynn said. So he was, faith. I asked him how was all at home. You're right, by God. So he was.

—I never broach the subject, Davy Byrne said humanely, if I see a gentleman is in trouble that way. It only brings it up fresh in their minds.

—It's not the wife anyhow, Nosey Flynn said. I met him the day before yesterday and he coming out of that Irish farm dairy John Wyse Nolan's wife has in Henry street with a jar of cream in his hand taking it home to his better half. She's well nourished, I tell you. Plovers on toast.

—And is he doing for the *Freeman?* Davy Byrne said.

Nosey Flynn pursed his lips.

—He doesn't buy cream on the ads he picks up. You can make bacon of that.

—How so? Davy Byrne asked, coming from his book.

Nosey Flynn made swift passes in the air with juggling fingers. He winked.

—He's in the craft,[2] he said.

—Do you tell me so? Davy Byrne said.

—Very much so, Nosey Flynn said. Ancient free and accepted order. Light, life and love, by God. They give him a leg up. I was told that by a, well, I won't say who.

—Is that a fact?

—O, it's a fine order, Nosey Flynn said. They stick to you when you're down. I know a fellow was trying to get into it, but they're as close as damn it. By God they did right to keep the women out of it.

Davy Byrne smiledyawnednodded all in one:

—Iiiiiichaaaaaaach!

—There was one woman, Nosey Flynn said, hid herself in a clock to find out what they do be doing. But be damned but they smelt her out and swore her in on the spot a master mason. That was one of the Saint Legers of Doneraile.

Davy Byrne, sated after his yawn, said with tearwashed eyes:

2. I.e., in the "free and accepted order" of Free- masons, one of the oldest European secret socie- ties; it was not in good repute in predominantly Roman Catholic countries like Ireland.

—And is that a fact? Decent quiet man he is. I often saw him in here and I never once saw him, you know, over the line.

—God Almighty couldn't make him drunk, Nosey Flynn said firmly. Slips off when the fun gets too hot. Didn't you see him look at his watch? Ah, you weren't there. If you ask him to have a drink first thing he does he outs with the watch to see what he ought to imbibe. Declare to God he does.

—There are some like that, Davy Byrne said. He's a safe man, I'd say.

—He's not too bad, Nosey Flynn said, snuffling it up. He has been known to put his hand down too to help a fellow. Give the devil his due. O, Bloom has his good points. But there's one thing he'll never do.

His hand scrawled a dry pen signature beside his grog.

—I know, Davy Byrne said.

—Nothing in black and white, Nosey Flynn said.

Paddy Leonard and Bantam Lyons came in. Tom Rochford followed frowning, a plaining hand on his claret waistcoat.

—Day, Mr Byrne.

—Day, gentlemen.

They paused at the counter.

—Who's standing? Paddy Leonard asked.

—I'm sitting anyhow, Nosey Flynn answered.

—Well, what'll it be? Paddy Leonard asked.

—I'll take a stone ginger, Bantam Lyons said.

—How much? Paddy Leonard cried. Since when, for God's sake? What's yours, Tom?

—How is the main drainage? Nosey Flynn asked, sipping.

For answer Tom Rochford pressed his hand to his breastbone and hiccupped.

—Would I trouble you for a glass of fresh water, Mr Byrne? he said.

—Certainly, sir.

Paddy Leonard eyed his alemates.

—Lord love a duck, he said, look at what I'm standing drinks to! Cold water and gingerpop! Two fellows that would suck whisky off a sore leg. He has some bloody horse up his sleeve for the Gold cup. A dead snip.

—Zinfandel is it? Nosey Flynn asked.

Tom Rochford spilt powder from a twisted paper into the water set before him.

—That cursed dyspepsia, he said before drinking.

—Breadsoda is very good, Davy Byrne said.

Tom Rochford nodded and drank.

—Is it Zinfandel?

—Say nothing, Bantam Lyons winked. I'm going to plunge five bob on my own.

—Tell us if you're worth your salt and be damned to you, Paddy Leonard said. Who gave it to you?

Mr Bloom on his way out raised three fingers in greeting.

—So long, Nosey Flynn said.

The others turned.

—That's the man now that gave it to me, Bantam Lyons whispered.

—Prrwht! Paddy Leonard said with scorn. Mr Byrne, sir, we'll take two of your small Jamesons[3] after that and a . . .

—Stone ginger, Davy Byrne added civilly.

—Ay, Paddy Leonard said. A suckingbottle for the baby.

Mr Bloom walked towards Dawson street, his tongue brushing his teeth smooth. Something green it would have to be: spinach say. Then with those Röntgen rays searchlight you could.

At Duke lane a ravenous terrier choked up a sick knuckly cud on the cobblestones and lapped it with new zest. Surfeit. Returned with thanks having fully digested the contents. First sweet then savoury. Mr Bloom coasted warily. Ruminants. His second course. Their upper jaw they move. Wonder if Tom Rochford will do anything with that invention of his. Wasting time explaining it to Flynn's mouth. Lean people long mouths. Ought to be a hall or a place where inventors could go in and invent free. Course then you'd have all the cranks pestering.

He hummed, prolonging in solemn echo, the closes of the bars:

> Don Giovanni, a cenar teco
> M'invitasti.[4]

Feel better. Burgundy. Good pick me up. Who distilled first? Some chap in the blues. Dutch courage. That *Kilkenny People* in the national library now I must.

Bare clean closestools, waiting, in the window of William Miller, plumber, turned back his thoughts. They could: and watch it all the way down, swallow a pin sometimes come out of the ribs years after, tour round the body, changing biliary duct, spleen squirting liver, gastric juice coils of intestines like pipes. But the poor buffer would have to stand all the time with his insides entrails on show. Science.

—A *cenar teco*.

What does that *teco* mean? Tonight perhaps.

> Don Giovanni, thou haste me invited
> To come to supper tonight,
> The rum the rumdum.

3. Brand of Irish whiskey.

4. Since Molly is a singer, Bloom is familiar with opera. Here he recalls the song sung by the Commendatore's statue in Mozart's *Don Giovanni*, and translates accurately the Italian words he quotes, except for *"teco"* ("with you"). This opera supplies some of the key themes in *Ulysses*, and the famous duet between Don Giovanni and Zerlina. *"Là ci darèm la mano"* ("There we will join hands"), haunts Bloom's mind continually throughout the day. It is on the program of Molly's concert which she is discussing with Boylan that afternoon, and Bloom associates it with her adultery with Boylan.

Doesn't go properly.

Keyes: two months if I get Nannetti[5] to. That'll be two pounds ten, about two pounds eight. Three Hynes owes me. Two eleven. Prescott's ad. Two fifteen. Five guineas about. On the pig's back.

Could buy one of those silk petticoats for Molly, colour of her new garters.

Today. Today. Not think.[6]

Tour the south then. What about English wateringplaces? Brighton, Margate. Piers by moonlight. Her voice floating out. Those lovely sea-side girls. Against John Long's a drowsing loafer lounged in heavy thought, gnawing a crusted knuckle. Handy man wants job. Small wages. Will eat anything.

Mr Bloom turned at Gray's confectioner's window of unbought tarts and passed the reverend Thomas Connellan's bookstore. *Why I left the church of Rome? Birds' Nest.* Women run him. They say they used to give pauper children soup to change to protestants in the time of the potato blight. Society over the way papa went to for the conversion of poor jews. Same bait. *Why we left the church of Rome?*

A blind stripling stood tapping the curbstone with his slender cane. No tram in sight. Wants to cross.

—Do you want to cross? Mr Bloom asked.

The blind stripling did not answer. His wallface frowned weakly. He moved his head uncertainly.

—You're in Dawson street, Mr Bloom said. Molesworth street is opposite. Do you want to cross? There's nothing in the way.

The cane moved out trembling to the left. Mr Bloom's eye followed its line and saw again the dyeworks' van drawn up before Drago's. Where I saw his brillantined hair just when I was. Horse drooping. Driver in John Long's. Slaking his drouth.

—There's a van there, Mr Bloom said, but it's not moving. I'll see you across. Do you want to go to Molesworth street?

—Yes, the stripling answered. South Frederick street.

—Come, Mr Bloom said.

He touched the thin elbow gently: then took the limp seeing hand to guide it forward.

Say something to him. Better not do the condescending. They mistrust what you tell them. Pass a common remark.

—The rain kept off.

No answer.

Stains on his coat. Slobbers his food, I suppose. Tastes all different for him. Have to be spoonfed first. Like a child's hand, his hand. Like Milly's was. Sensitive. Sizing me up I daresay from my hand. Wonder if he has a name. Van. Keep his cane clear of the horse's legs tired

5. Proofreader and business manager of the *Freeman's Journal*, and in charge of the advertising Bloom is trying to get for the paper. If he will add a complimentary reference to Keyes, a grocer, in a gossip column, Keyes promises to renew his advertisement, which means a commission for Bloom.

6. I.e., of Molly and Boylan.

drudge get his doze. That's right. Clear. Behind a bull: in front of a horse.

—Thanks, sir.

Knows I'm a man. Voice.

—Right now? First turn to the left.

The blind stripling tapped the curbstone and went on his way, drawing his cane back, feeling again.

Mr Bloom walked behind the eyeless feet, a flatcut suit of herringbone tweed. Poor young fellow! How on earth did he know that van was there? Must have felt it. See things in their foreheads perhaps. Kind of sense of volume. Weight would he feel it if something was removed. Feel a gap. Queer idea of Dublin he must have, tapping his way round by the stones. Could he walk in a beeline if he hadn't that cane? Bloodless pious face like a fellow going in to be a priest.

Penrose! That was that chap's name.

Look at all the things they can learn to do. Read with their fingers. Tune pianos. Or we are surprised they have any brains. Why we think a deformed person or a hunchback clever if he says something we might say. Of course the other senses are more. Embroider. Plait baskets. People ought to help. Workbasket I could buy Molly's birthday. Hates sewing. Might take an objection. Dark men they call them.

Sense of smell must be stronger too. Smells on all sides bunched together. Each person too. Then the spring, the summer: smells. Tastes. They say you can't taste wines with your eyes shut or a cold in the head. Also smoke in the dark they say get no pleasure.

And with a woman, for instance. More shameless not seeing. That girl passing the Stewart institution, head in the air. Look at me. I have them all on. Must be strange not to see her. Kind of a form in his mind's eye. The voice temperature when he touches her with fingers must almost see the lines, the curves. His hands on her hair, for instance. Say it was black for instance. Good. We call it black. Then passing over her white skin. Different feel perhaps. Feeling of white.

Postoffice. Must answer.[7] Fag[8] today. Send her a postal order two shillings half a crown. Accept my little present. Stationer's just here too. Wait. Think over it.

With a gentle finger he felt ever so slowly the hair combed back above his ears. Again. Fibres of fine fine straw. Then gently his finger felt the skin of his right cheek. Downy hair there too. Not smooth enough. The belly is the smoothest. No-one about. There he goes into Frederick street. Perhaps to Levenston's dancing academy piano. Might be settling my braces.

Walking by Doran's public house he slid his hand between waistcoat and trousers and, pulling aside his shirt gently, felt a slack fold of his belly. But I know it's whitey yellow. Want to try in the dark to see.

He withdrew his hand and pulled his dress to.

---

7. Martha Clifford's letter.   8. Nuisance.

Poor fellow! Quite a boy. Terrible. Really terrible. What dreams would he have, not seeing. Life a dream for him. Where is the justice being born that way. All those women and children excursion beanfeast burned and drowned in New York.[9] Holocaust. Karma they call that transmigration for sins you did in a past life the reincarnation met him pike hoses.[1] Dear, dear, dear. Pity of course: but somehow you can't cotton on to them someway.

Sir Frederick Falkiner going into the freemasons' hall. Solemn as Troy. After his good lunch in Earlsfort terrace. Old legal cronies cracking a magnum. Tales of the bench and assizes and annals of the bluecoat school.[2] I sentenced him to ten years. I suppose he'd turn up his nose at that stuff I drank. Vintage wine for them, the year marked on a dusty bottle. Has his own ideas of justice in the recorder's court. Wellmeaning old man. Police charge sheets crammed with cases get their percentage manufacturing crime. Sends them to the rightabout. The devil on moneylenders. Gave Reuben J. a great strawcalling. Now he's really what they call a dirty jew. Power those judges have. Crusty old topers in wigs. Bear with a sore paw. And may the Lord have mercy on your soul.

Hello, placard. Mirus bazaar. His excellency the lord lieutenant. Sixteenth today it is. In aid of funds for Mercer's hospital. The *Messiah* was first given for that. Yes. Handel. What about going out there. Ballsbridge. Drop in on Keyes. No use sticking to him like a leech. Wear out my welcome. Sure to know someone on the gate.

Mr Bloom came to Kildare street. First I must. Library.

Straw hat in sunlight. Tan shoes. Turnedup trousers. It is. It is.[3]

His heart quopped softly. To the right. Museum. Goddesses. He swerved to the right.

Is it? Almost certain. Won't look. Wine in my face. Why did I? Too heady. Yes, it is. The walk. Not see. Not see. Get on.

Making for the museum gate with long windy strides he lifted his eyes. Handsome building. Sir Thomas Deane designed. Not following me?

Didn't see me perhaps. Light in his eyes.

The flutter of his breath came forth in short sighs. Quick. Cold statues: quiet there. Safe in a minute.

No, didn't see me. After two. Just at the gate.

My heart!

His eyes beating looked steadfastly at cream curves of stone. Sir Thomas Deane was the Greek architecture.

Look for something I.

His hasty hand went quick into a pocket, took out, read unfolded Agendath Netaim. Where did I?

Busy looking for.

9. This terrible disaster on an excursion steamer on the Hudson took place on June 15, 1904, and was reported in the Dublin papers on June 16.

1. I.e., metempsychosis: Bloom is remembering again their morning conversation on this subject, when Molly exclaimed "O rocks!"

2. Sir Frederick Falkiner wrote the history of the "bluecoat school" in Oxmantown, Dublin. The Dublin "bluecoat school" was founded by Charles II for poor children.

3. Bloom catches a glimpse of Boylan and tries to avoid an encounter.

He thrust back quickly Agendath.

Afternoon she said.

I am looking for that. Yes, that. Try all pockets. Handker. *Freeman.*
Where did I? Ah, yes. Trousers. Purse. Potato. Where did I?

Hurry. Walk quietly. Moment more. My heart.

His hand looking for the where did I put found in his hip pocket soap
lotion have to call tepid paper stuck. Ah, soap there! Yes. Gate.[4]

Safe!

1914–21   1922

From Finnegans Wake[1]

From *Anna Livia Plurabelle*

* * * Well, you know or don't you kennet[2] or haven't I told you
every telling has a taling and that's the he and the she of it. Look, look,
the dusk is growing! My branches lofty are taking root. And my cold
cher's[3] gone ashley. Fieluhr?[4] Filou! What age is at? It saon[5] is late. 'Tis

---

4. Anxious to avoid Boylan, Bloom pretends to admire the architecture of the Museum and National Library building, and then pretends to be looking for something in his pockets, where he finds the "Agendath Netaim" leaflet. He continues to search desperately in his pockets to avoid looking up and seeing Boylan, discovers the potato he carries as a remedy against rheumatism and a cake of soap he had bought that morning (the soap reminds him that he must call at the chemist's to collect a face lotion he had ordered for Molly). At last he goes through the National Library gate and feels safe.

1. Because the meanings in *Finnegans Wake* are developed not by action but by language—a great network of multiple puns that echo themes back and forth throughout the book—the careful reading of a single passage, even out of context, will convey more than any summary of the "plot" (some discussion of the general plan of the work is given in the Joyce introduction). The particular passage selected here was one of Joyce's favorites, and there exists a phonograph recording of it made by himself. It consists of the closing pages of the eighth chapter of Book 1; the chapter was published separately as *Anna Livia Plurabelle* in 1928 and 1930, although the finished book omits this title.

The entire chapter is a dialogue, and the scene is the river Liffey: two washerwomen are washing in public the dirty linen of HCE and ALP (the "hero" and "heroine"; see the Joyce introduction) and gossiping as they work. As this excerpt opens, it is growing dark; things become gradually less and less distinct, so that the washerwomen cannot be sure what the objects seen in the dusk really are. As it grows darker, the river becomes wider (we get nearer its mouth) and the wind rises, so that the women have more and more difficulty hearing each

other. At last, as night falls, they become part of the landscape, an elm tree and a stone on the river bank. Toward the end of the dialogue they ask to hear a tale of Shem and Shaun (HCE's two sons), and this question points the way to Book 2, which opens with the two boys (metamorphosed for the moment into Glugg and Chuff) playing in front of the tavern in the evening.

A complete annotation of even this brief passage is, of course, a physical impossibility in this anthology. The notes that are provided are intended to indicate the nature of what Joyce does with language and to enable the reader to see what is going on. But there are all sorts of suggestions built up in the language that are not referred to in the notes: all readers will find some for themselves.

2. Ken it ("know it") + Kennet (river in England). Rivers in *Finnegans Wake* symbolize the flow of life, and thousands of river names are suggested throughout the book in allusive pun-combinations, as here.

3. Cold cheer (i.e., cold comfort) + cold chair + (perhaps) culture. "Gone ashley": gone to ashes. Going to ashes suggests the fiery death and rebirth of the mythical phoenix: from the ashes of the dead phoenix rises a new one. Modern culture, which can provide only cold cheer, is in the state of decay, the "going to ashes," which precedes the stage of rebirth into a new cultural cycle (according to Giambattista Vico's cyclical theory of history, which is important to *Finnegans Wake*). "Gone ashley" also means "turned into an ash tree" (i.e., it is so cold that the speaker feels herself turning into a tree).

4. *Viel Uhr?* (German, "What's the time?") "Filou": pickpocket, thief (French). The question echoes so as to suggest that time is a thief.

5. Soon + Saône (river in France).

endless now senne[6] eye or erewone[7] last saw Waterhouse's clogh.[8] They took it asunder, I hurd thum sigh. When will they reassemble it? O, my back, my back, my bach![9] I'd want to go to Aches-les-Pains.[10] Pingpong! There's the Belle for Sexaloitez![11] And Concepta de Send-us-pray! Pang! Wring out the Clothes! Wring in the dew![12] Godavari,[13] vert the showers! And grant thaya grace! Aman. Will we spread them here now? Ay, we will. Flip! Spread on your bank and I'll spread mine on mine. Flep! It's what I'm doing. Spread! It's churning chill. Der went[14] is rising. I'll lay a few stones on the hostel sheets. A man and his bride embraced between them. Else I'd have sprinkled and folded them only. And I'll tie my butcher's apron here. It's suety yet. The strollers will pass it by. Six shifts, ten kerchiefs, nine to hold to the fire and this for the code,[15] the convent napkins, twelve, one baby's shawl. Good mother Jossiph[16] knows, she said. Whose head? Mutter snores? Deataceas![17] Wharnow are alle her childer, say? In kingdome gone or power to come or gloria be to them farther? Allalivial, allalluvial![18] Some here, more no more, more again lost alla stranger.[19] I've heard tell that same brooch of the Shannons[20] was married into a family in Spain. And all the Dunders de Dunnes[21] in Markland's[22] Vineland beyond the Brendan's herring pool[23] takes number nine in yangsee's[24] hats. And one of Biddy's[25] beads went bobbing till she rounded up lost histereve[26] with a marigold and a cobbler's candle in a side strain of a main drain of a manzinahurries[27] off

6. Since + Senne (river in Belgium).

7. E'er a one + *Erewhon* (novel by Samuel Butler—"Nowhere" spelled backwards).

8. Clock or bell (Irish) + the name of an Irish river.

9. Brook (German) + dear (Welsh).

10. Cf. Aix-les-Bains, France.

11. *Sex* (Latin, "six") + *laüten* (German, "to ring [the bells]"). The Angelus bell is rung every six hours.

12. Cf. "Ring out the old, ring in the new" (Tennyson, *In Memoriam*).

13. God of Eire; also the name of a river in India. "Vert": avert + *vert* (French, "green"), for "the showers" make grass green.

14. *Der Wind* (German, "the wind") + Derwent (river in England).

15. Cold + code (i.e., the code in which the book is written). The numbers in this sentence have special meanings indicated in other episodes.

16. Joseph + *joss* (pidgin English, "God") + gossip (which derives from *god-sib*, Middle English, "godparent").

17. Latin, "Goddess, may you be silent!" Dea Tacita, in Roman mythology, is the name sometimes given to Acca Laurentia, mistress of Hercules and foster-mother of Romulus and Remus.

18. Multiple punning—Anna Livia + all alive + *la lluvia* (Spanish, "rain") + alluvial—suggesting the mother-river-fertility associations of ALP. At least two other meanings are also present: All alive O! (street cry of shellfish vendors) + Alleluia (Vulgate Latin form of "Hallelujah").

19. Cf. *à l'étranger* (French, "abroad").

20. Ornament and branch of the Shannons (family and river).

21. The form of the name suggests an aristocratic Anglo-Norman family. "Dunder" suggests thunder; *dun* is an Irish word meaning "hill," "fort on a hill."

22. Borderland + land of the mark (i.e., land of money, or America; "Vineland" or Vinland was the Norse name for America). Both King Mark of Cornwall (a character in the Tristan and Iseult story) and Mark of the Gospels are primary symbolic characters in *Finnegans Wake*.

23. The Atlantic Ocean; St. Brendan was an Irish monk who sailed out into the Atlantic to find the terrestrial paradise.

24. Yankees' + Yangtze (river in China). The de Dunnes have swollen heads now that they have emigrated to America.

25. Diminutive form of the name Bridget; St. Brigid (or Bridget) is a patron saint of Ireland. "Biddy" is also a term for an Irish maidservant.

26. Yester eve (last night) + eve of history. The sentence may be paraphrased: "Irish history got lost when she went off in a side branch of the main Roman Catholic Church, and Biddy (i.e., Ireland) landed herself in the dirt." There are also Freudian implications here.

27. Man's in a hurry + Manzanares (river in Spain).

Bachelor's Walk. But all that's left to the last of the Meaghers[28] in the loup of the years prefixed and between is one kneebuckle and two hooks in the front. Do you tell me that now? I do in troth. Orara por Orbe and poor Las Animals![29] Ussa, Ulla, we're umbas[30] all! Mezha, didn't you hear it a deluge of times, ufer[31] and ufer, respund to spond?[32] You deed, you deed! I need, I need! It's that irrawaddyng[33] I've stoke in my aars. It all but husheth the lethest zswound. Oronoko![34] What's your trouble? Is that the great Finnleader[35] himself in his joakimono on his statue riding the high horse there forehengist?[36] Father of Otters,[37] it is himself! Yonne there! Isset that? On Fallareen Common? You're thinking of Astley's Amphitheayter where the bobby restrained you making sugarstuck pouts to the ghostwhite horse of the Peppers.[38] Throw the cobwebs from your eyes, woman, and spread your washing proper! It's well I know your sort of slop. Flap! Ireland sober is Ireland stiff. Lord help you, Maria, full of grease, the load is with me! Your prayers. I sonht zo![39] Madammangut! Were you lifting your elbow, tell us, glazy cheeks, in Conway's Carrigacurra canteen? Was I what, hobbledyhips?[40] Flop! Your rere gait's creakorheuman bitts your butts disagrees.[41] Amn't I up since the damp dawn, marthared mary allacook, with Corrigan's pulse and varicoarse veins, my pramaxle smashed, Alice Jane in decline and my oneeyed mongrel twice run over, soaking and bleaching boiler rags, and sweating cold, a widow like me, for to deck my tennis champion son, the laundryman with the lavandier flannels? You won your limpopo[42] limp from the husky[43] hussars when Collars and Cuffs was heir to the town and your slur gave the stink to Carlow.[44] Holy Scamander,[45] I sar it again!

---

28. Thomas Francis Meagher, Irish patriot and revolutionary, who was transported to Van Diemen's Land in 1849 and escaped to America in 1852. "Loup": loop + *loup* (French, "wolf" and also "solitary man"). Cf. Wolfe Tone, the ill-fated Irish revolutionist.

29. *Ora pro nobis* (Latin, "pray for us") + Orara (river in New South Wales) + *pro orbe* (Latin, "for the world") + Orbe (river in France). "Las Animas": souls (Spanish); also the name of a river in Colorado. The entire sentence may be read: "Pray for us and for all souls."

30. *Umbra* (Latin, "shade") + Umba (river in Africa). "Ussa," "Ulla," and "Mezha" are also river names; each contains a number of other meanings.

31. Bank (of river).

32. *Spund* (German, "bung").

33. A multiple pun: Irrawady (river in Burma) + irritating + wadding. This and the following sentence may be paraphrased: "It's that wadding I've stuck in my ears. It hushes the least sound."

34. *Oroonoko* (novel by Aphra Behn about a "noble savage," published ca. 1678). The Orinoco is a river in Venezuela.

35. Fionn mac Cumhail (Finn MacCool), legendary hero of ancient Ireland. "Joakimono": i.e., comic kimono; *joki* is the Finnish word for river; the name Joachim is perhaps also implied.

36. Hengist was the Jute invader of England (with Horsa), ca. 449; he founded the kingdom of Kent.

37. Father of Waters (i.e., the Mississippi) + Father of Orders (i.e., Saint Patrick).

38. Philip Astley's Royal Amphitheatre was a famous late 18th-century English circus, specializing in trained horses; "Pepper's Ghost" is a popular circus act. One of the washerwomen has been reproving the other, who thought she saw the great Finn himself riding his high horse, by telling her that once before she had to be restrained by a policeman for making "sugarstuck pouts" at a circus horse.

39. I thought so + Izontzo (river in Italy).

40. Hobbledehoy + wobbly hips.

41. The sentence is a punning discussion of her hard wear and ailments. The first four words may also be read: "Your rear get (i.e., your last child) is Greek or Roman."

42. Name of a river in south Africa.

43. Cf. *uisge* (Gaelic, "whisky," but literally, "water [of life]").

44. I.e., "You got a slur on your reputation carrying on with soldiers in the Age of Elegance, and the scandal was all over Ireland" (ALP is being addressed, and some of her many lovers are mentioned). "Carlow" is a county in Ireland.

45. River near Troy, famous in classical legend. "I sar": I saw + Isar (river in Germany).

Near the golden falls. Icis on us! Seints of light! Zezere![46] Subdue your noise, you hamble creature! What is it but a blackburry growth or the dwyergray ass them four old codgers[47] owns. Are you meanam[48] Tarpey and Lyons and Gregory? I meyne now, thank all, the four of them, and the roar of them, that draves[49] that stray in the mist and old Johnny MacDougal along with them. Is that the Poolbeg flasher beyant,[50] pharphar, or a fireboat coasting nyar[51] the Kishtna or a glow I behold within a hedge or my Garry come back from the Indes? Wait till the honeying of the lune,[52] love! Die eve, little eve, die![53] We see that wonder in your eye. We'll meet again, we'll part once more. The spot I'll seek if the hour you'll find. My chart shines high where the blue milk's upset. Forgivemequick. I'm going! Bubye! And you, pluck your watch, forgetmenot. Your evenlode.[54] So save to jurna's[55] end! My sights are swimming thicker on me by the shadows to this place. I sow[56] home slowly now by own way, moyvalley way. Towy[57] I too, rathmine.

Ah, but she was the queer old skeowsha anyhow, Anna Livia, trinkettoes! And sure he was the quare old buntz too, Dear Dirty Dumpling,[58] foostherfather of fingalls[59] and dotthergills. Gammer and gaffer we're all their gangsters. Hadn't he seven dams to wive him? And every dam had her seven crutches. And every crutch had its seven hues.[60] And each hue had a differing cry. Sudds[61] for me and supper for you and the doctor's bill for Joe John. Befor! Bifur![62] He married his markets, cheap by foul, I know, like any Etrurian Catholic Heathen, in their pinky limony creamy birnies[63] and their turkiss indienne mauves. But at milkidmass[64] who was the spouse? Then all that was was fair. Tys Elven-

---

46. See there + Zezere (river in Portugal).

47. The Four Old Men, who represent, among other things, the authors of the Gospels and the four elements.

48. Meaning + Menam (river in Thailand). The precise connotations of the three proper names that follow escape the present annotator.

49. Drives + Drave (river in Hungary).

50. I.e., the Poolbeg Lighthouse beyond (this lighthouse is in Dublin Bay); "pharphar": far far + Pharphar (river in Damascus) + *pharos* (Greek, "lighthouse").

51. Near + Nyar (river in India). "Kishtna": (city in ancient Mesopotamia, traditionally the ruling city after the Flood) + Krishna (Hindu god of joy) + Kistna (river in India) + the Kish lightship (in Dublin Bay).

52. Loon (Scottish, "boy") + *luna* (Latin, "moon"). "Honeying of the lune": honeymoon, etc.

53. This sentence suggests traditional lovers' prayers for the day to die and night to come, and it also recalls the death of "little Eva" in *Uncle Tom's Cabin*. The sentences that follow are echoes of popular songs.

54. Evening load + Evenlode (river in England).

55. Journey + Jurna (river in Brazil).

56. Sow (river in England).

57. Name of a river in Wales. Moy is the name

of an Irish river, and Moyvalley and Rathmine are names of Dublin suburbs.

58. "Dumpling" suggests Humpty Dumpty, whose fall is one of the many involved in the vastly symbolic fall of Finnegan. The phrase "Dear Dirty Dublin" occurs in *Ulysses*.

59. A pun-cluster: Fine Gael (the United Ireland Party) + fine Gaels + Fingal (river in Tasmania) + *Fingal* (the poem by James Macpherson, supposedly a translation from the Gaelic original of Ossian, an ancient Gaelic poet and son of Fingal—who is the same as Fionn mac Cumhail or Finn MacCool).

60. Colors of the rainbow (suggested a few lines later by "pinky limony creamy" and "turkiss indienne mauves"). In these sentences Joyce is punningly parodying the nursery rhyme, "As I was going to St. Ives / I met a man with seven wives . . ."

61. Suds (slang term for beer) + soapsuds + sudd (the floating vegetable matter which often obstructs navigation on the White Nile).

62. Bifurcated creature! This image of man as a forked being suggests HCE (cf. "Etrurian Catholic Heathen"). HCE's marital history, in his role as the Great Parent or generator, is one of the themes in this passage.

63. Coats of mail.

64. Milking time + Michaelmas (September 29).

land![65] Teems of times and happy returns. The seim anew.[66] Ordovico[67] or viricordo. Anna was, Livia is, Plurabelle's to be. Northmen's thing made southfolk's place but howmulty plurators made each one in person?[68] Latin me that, my trinity scholard, out of eure sanscreed into oure eryan![69] *Hircus Civis Eblanensis!*[70] He had buckgoat paps on him, soft ones for orphans. Ho,[71] Lord! Twins of his bosom. Lord save us! And ho! Hey? What all men. Hot? His tittering daughters of. Whawk?

Can't hear with the waters of. The chittering waters of. Flittering bats, fieldmice bawk talk. Ho! Are you not gone ahome? What Thom Malone? Can't hear with bawk of bats, all thim liffeying waters of. Ho, talk save us! My foos won't moos.[72] I feel as old as yonder elm. A tale told of Shaun or Shem? All Livia's daughter-sons. Dark hawks hear us. Night! Night! My ho head halls. I feel as heavy as yonder stone. Tell me of John or Shaun? Who were Shem and Shaun the living sons or daughters of? Night now! Tell me, tell me, tell me, elm! Night night! Telmetale of stem or stone.[73] Beside the rivering waters of, hitherandthithering waters of. Night!

1923–38   1939

65. 'Tis the land of Elves + Tys Elv (Norway).

66. The same again + Seim (river in Ireland).

67. The Ordovices were an ancient British tribe in northern Wales, and Ordovician is a term for a geological period. "Ordovico" is also a pun on Vico and his order of historical phases. Joyce is here suggesting the cyclical nature of things: the marital history of HCE is the history of ever-renewing life ("the seim anew"), and HCE's bride is Everywoman, past, present, and future ("Anna was, Livia is, Plurabelle's to be"). "Viricordo" is another verbal twist to Vico and his cycles, suggesting his *ricorso* ("recurrence," i.e., the 4th stage of the cycle which brings back the 1st), as well as overtones from the Latin *vir* (man) and *cor* (heart): the heart of man beats on, through all phases of civilization.

68. This sentence may be paraphrased: "The assembly of the Norsemen made the South-folk's place (i.e., as the Vikings settled Dublin), but how many marital pluralists (the word 'plurators' suggests men who had many wives or mistresses) went into the making of each of us?" The question is another link with the theme of HCE as the Great

Parent.

69. I.e., out of your Sanskrit into your Aryan. "Sanscreed" has further punning meanings: *sans* screed (without script) + *sans* creed (without faith). Thus the phrase can read: "out of your illiteracy or faithlessness into Irish" (Eire-an). The greatest skeptic must pause in reverence before the endless flow of life, represented by Irish history.

70. Latin, "The Goat-Citizen of Dublin!" The goat is the symbol of lust and so of fecundity; "*Eblanensis*" is the adjective form of Eblana, the name given by the 3rd-century Alexandrian geographer Ptolemy to what may have been the site of the modern Dublin.

71. Chinese, "river."

72. Move + *Moos* (German, "moss"). Her foot ("foos") won't move; it is also turning to moss.

73. Stone and elm tree are important symbols in *Finnegans Wake.* Signifying permanence and change, time and space, mercy and justice, they undergo many changes of symbolic meaning throughout the book.

D. H. LAWRENCE
1885–1930

1912:   Gives up schoolteaching for literature.

1915:   *The Rainbow*, first of the "new" novels.

David Herbert Lawrence was born in the Midland mining village of Eastwood, Nottinghamshire. His father was a miner; his mother, better educated than her husband and self-consciously genteel, fought all her married life to lift her children out of the working class. Lawrence was aware from an early age of the struggle between his parents; he was very much on his mother's side during his childhood, resenting his father's coarse and sometimes drunken behavior and allying himself with his mother's delicacy and refinement. After the death of an elder brother he became the center of his mother's emotional life and played in his own relation to her a loving and protective role. His mother's claims on him kept frustrating his relationships with women, and the personal problems and conflicts that resulted are presented in his first really distinguished novel, *Sons and Lovers* (1913), where, against a background of paternal coarseness and vitality conflicting with maternal refinement and gentility, he sets the theme of the demanding mother who has given up the prospect of achieving a true emotional life with her husband and turns to her sons with a stultifying and possessive love. Many years later Lawrence came to feel that he had misjudged his father, whose coarseness represented after all a genuine vitality and some wholeness of personality, even if these qualities were impoverished and distorted by the civilization in which he lived.

Spurred on by his mother, Lawrence escaped through education from the mining world of his father. He won a scholarship to Nottingham high school and later, after working first as a clerk and then as an elementary school teacher (1902–6), studied for two years at Nottingham University College, where he obtained his teacher's certificate in 1908. Meanwhile he was reading on his own a great deal of literature and some philosophy and was working on his first novel, encouraged (as he was in all his early writing) by Jessie Chambers, the "Miriam" of *Sons and Lovers*. His first published work was a group of poems which appeared in the *English Review* for November 1909. The following February the same periodical published his first short story. He was now regarded in London literary circles as a promising young writer; his first novel, *The White Peacock* (1910), was received with respect. From 1908 to 1912 he taught school in Croydon, a southern suburb of London, but he gave this up after falling in love with Frieda von Richthofen, the German wife of a professor of French at Nottingham. They went to Germany together and married in 1914, after Frieda had been divorced by her first husband.

Abroad with Frieda, Lawrence finished *Sons and Lovers*, the autobiographical novel at which he had been working off and on for years. The war brought them back to England, where Frieda's German origins and Lawrence's fierce objection to the war gave him trouble with the authorities. More and more—especially after the banning of his next novel, *The Rainbow*, in 1915—Lawrence came to feel that the forces of modern civilization were arrayed against him. As soon as he could leave England after the war he sought refuge in Italy, Australia, Mexico, then again in Italy, and finally in the south of France, often desperately ill, restlessly searching for an ideal, or at least a tolerable, community in which to live. He died of tuberculosis in the south of France on March 2, 1930, at the early age of forty-four.

Shortly before his death he had written:

> Give me the moon at my feet
> Put my feet upon the crescent, like a Lord!
> O let my ankles be bathed in moonlight, that I may go

sure and moon-shod, cool and bright-footed
towards my goal.

For the sun is hostile, now
his face is like the red lion . . .

In these elemental images he invoked his end, a gesture at once heroic and
desperate. It was typical of him to symbolize his passing with reference to
the sun and moon, for Lawrence was at home with such cosmic images as
no other English writer except Blake has ever been; he was at home, one
might say, with the universe, with all that is deep-rooted and elemental in
Man and Nature, and at constant war with the mechanical and artificial,
with the constraints and hypocrisies that civilization imposes on our fundamental selves. His most characteristic writings are essentially a record in
symbolic terms of his explorations of human individuality and of all that
hindered it and all that might fulfill it, whether in the natural world or in
the world of other individuals.

This is not what the English novel is generally supposed to do, and Lawrence, with new things to say and a new way of using the novel form, was
not easily or quickly appreciated. His early novels, *The White Peacock, The
Trespasser,* and even the original and impressive *Sons and Lovers,* were more
conventional in style and treatment; they aroused contemporary interest and
even acclaim, and it appeared that he might be on his way to becoming one
of the acknowledged and popular Georgian novelists. But with the publication of *The Rainbow* in 1915 the true, original Lawrence first emerged clearly,
and the critics turned away in bewilderment and condemnation. *The Rainbow* was suppressed as indecent a month after its publication, and the war
between Lawrence and the world of timid convention was on. The rest of
his life, during which he produced about a dozen more novels and many
poems, short stories, sketches, and miscellaneous articles, was, in his own
words, "a savage enough pilgrimage," marked by incessant struggle and by
moments of frustration and despair. Lawrence was one of those artists who
had to create the taste by which they could be appreciated. He had no gift
for explaining his attitude and literary technique in simple expository prose.
He could explain himself only by performing, by operating in his own way
as an artist, letting the work of art speak with its own voice and pulse with
its own life. When he tried to talk *about* his ideas, instead of projecting
them symbolically in art, he was often irritatingly and vaguely rhetorical.
"Sense of truth," "supreme impulse" are phrases characteristic of Lawrence's
belief in intuition, in the dark forces of the inner self, that must not be
allowed to be swamped by the rational faculties but must be brought into a
harmonious relation with them. It was a point of view—or rather, a perception, a passionate insight—which could not be convincingly expressed in
argument, but demanded direct projection in art.

The genteel culture of Lawrence's mother came more and more to represent death for Lawrence. In much of his later work, and especially in some
of his short stories, he sets the deadening restrictiveness of middle-class conventional living against the forces of liberation that are often represented by
an outsider—a peasant, a gypsy, a worker, a primitive of some kind, someone free by circumstance or personal effort. The recurring theme of his short
stories—which contain some of his best work—is the distortion of love by
possessiveness or gentility or a false romanticism or a false conception of the

life of the artists, and the achievement of a living relation between a man and a woman against the pressure of class-feeling or tradition or habit or prejudice.

His two masterpieces, *The Rainbow* and *Women in Love* (both of which developed out of what was originally conceived as a single novel to be called *The Sisters*), are to be read as symbolic and dramatic poems in prose. In these novels Lawrence probes with both subtlety and power into various aspects of relationship—the relationship between man and his environment, the relationship between the generations, the relationship between man and woman, the relationship between instinct and intellect, and above all the proper basis for the marriage relationship as he conceived it. Lawrence's view of marriage as a struggle derived from his own relationship with his strong-minded German-born wife Frieda. There are more and bitterer lovers' quarrels in Lawrence's novels than anywhere else in English literature. Lawrence's "crockery-throwing" view of love could become tedious, except that, as he presents it, it is bound up with the deepest rhythms and most profound instincts of the man-woman relationship.

In *The Rainbow* and *Women in Love* Lawrence is developing a radically new kind of novel in which he explores kinds of human relationships with a combination of uncanny psychological precision and intense poetic feeling. They have an acute surface realism, a sharp sense of time and place, and brilliant topographical detail, and at the same time their high poetic symbolism, both of the total pattern of action and of incidents and objects within it, establishes a rhythm of meaning that is missed by those who read the novels with the conventional categories of "plot" and "characters" in mind. His next novel, *Aaron's Rod* (1922), is more uneven; in it Lawrence, employing many of his own experiences, explores problems of human relations under the question of moral and political leadership, which for a time obsessed him. He was concerned with the struggle for leadership in marriage as well as in politics. Two other novels on the theme of leadership, *Kangaroo* (1923), set in Australia, and *The Plumed Serpent* (1926), set in Mexico, similarly uneven, show him trying to give symbolic fictional form to his own problems and preoccupations. But *Kangaroo* in particular has its moments of uncanny perceptiveness, and it is extraordinary how Lawrence, drawing on his experiences during a short stay in Australia, was able to get beneath the skin of the country and evoke so much of the essential reality of both place and people.

It is hard to think of another English novelist whose best and most characteristic work makes such a disquieting assault on our normal patterns of thought and feeling. It is not simply that Lawrence is a rebel against convention—many writers have been that—or that his views are startling, though they sometimes are. It is rather that the whole response to life, and in particular to the problems posed by human relationships, that emerges from his novels and stories seems to come so profoundly from the deepest recesses of his being and therefore assault the deepest recesses of *our* being, that the challenge seems to go beyond that which is normally asserted by a work of art. It is difficult to escape the challenge; to make any attempt to respond fully to what he is saying is to be drawn into his world, forced to share his vision.

Although there are complex critical reasons for the posthumous triumph of this writer who was so much reviled in his lifetime, there is also a simple and striking reason that must not be forgotten. Lawrence had vision; he had a poetic sense of life; he had a keen ear and a piercing eye for every kind of vitality and color and sound in the world, for landscape—be it of England or Italy or New Mexico—for the individuality and concreteness of things in nature, and for the individuality and concreteness of people. His travel sketches are as impressive in their way as his novels; he seizes both on the symbolic incident and on the concrete reality, and each is interpreted in terms of the other. He looked at the world freshly, with his own eyes, avoiding formulas and clichés; and he forged for himself a kind of utterance which, at his best, was able to convey powerfully and vividly what his fresh, original vision showed him. This kind of originality has its drawbacks; he was sometimes shrill, sometimes repetitive, sometimes almost hysterical; some scenes in his novels are murky with unachieved symbolism or splutter with unresolved passion. But the great Lawrence remains.

This restless pilgrim with his uncanny perceptions into the depths of physical things, with his uncompromising honesty and originality in his view of men and the world, cannot be dismissed as merely a great eccentric. Nor is he a great prophet. He is essentially an artist; it is his *rendering* of life in his art, not his preaching about life's meaning, that matters.

Odor of Chrysanthemums

1

The small locomotive engine, Number 4, came clanking, stumbling down from Selston with seven full wagons. It appeared round the corner with loud threats of speed, but the colt that it startled from among the gorse,[1] which still flickered indistinctly in the raw afternoon, out-distanced it at a canter. A woman, walking up the railway line to Underwood, drew back into the hedge, held her basket aside, and watched the footplate of the engine advancing. The trucks[2] thumped heavily past, one by one, with slow inevitable movement, as she stood insignificantly trapped between the jolting black wagons and the hedge; then they curved away towards the coppice[3] where the withered oak leaves dropped noiselessly, while the birds, pulling at the scarlet hips beside the track, made off into the dusk that had already crept into the spinney.[4] In the open, the smoke from the engine sank and cleaved to the rough grass. The fields were dreary and forsaken, and in the marshy strip that led to the whimsey,[5] a reedy pit pond, the fowls had already abandoned their run among the alders, to roost in the tarred fowl house. The pit bank loomed up beyond the pond, flames like red sores licking its ashy sides, in the afternoon's stagnant light. Just beyond rose the tapering chimneys and the clumsy black headstocks of Brinsley Colliery.[6] The two wheels were spinning fast up against the sky, and the winding engine rapped out its little spasms. The miners were being turned up.

1. Also known as furze or whin, a prickly bush with yellow flowers common on heaths, moors, and hillsides all over Britain.
2. Open freight cars.
3. A wood of small trees or shrubs.
4. Copse, thicket.
5. Machine for raising ore or water from a mine.
6. Coal mine; "headstocks" support revolving parts of a machine.

The engine whistled as it came into the wide bay of railway lines beside the colliery, where rows of trucks stood in harbor.

Miners, single, trailing, and in groups, passed like shadows diverging home. At the edge of the ribbed level of sidings squat a low cottage, three steps down from the cinder track. A large bony vine clutched at the house, as if to claw down the tiled roof. Round the bricked yard grew a few wintry primroses. Beyond, the long garden sloped down to a bush-covered brook course. There were some twiggy apple trees, winter-crack trees, and ragged cabbages. Beside the path hung disheveled pink chrysanthemums, like pink cloths hung on bushes. A woman came stooping out of the felt-covered fowl house, halfway down the garden. She closed and padlocked the door, then drew herself erect, having brushed some bits from her white apron.

She was a tall woman of imperious mien, handsome, with definite black eyebrows. Her smooth black hair was parted exactly. For a few moments she stood steadily watching the miners as they passed along the railway: then she turned towards the brook course. Her face was calm and set, her mouth was closed with disillusionment. After a moment she called:

"John!" There was no answer. She waited, and then said distinctly:
"Where are you?"

"Here!" replied a child's sulky voice from among the bushes. The woman looked piercingly through the dusk.

"Are you at that brook?" she asked sternly.

For answer the child showed himself before the raspberry canes that rose like whips. He was a small, sturdy boy of five. He stood quite still, defiantly.

"Oh!" said the mother, conciliated. "I thought you were down at that wet brook—and you remember what I told you——"

The boy did not move or answer.

"Come, come on in," she said more gently, "it's getting dark. There's your grandfather's engine coming down the line!"

The lad advanced slowly, with resentful, taciturn movement. He was dressed in trousers and waistcoat of cloth that was too thick and hard for the size of the garments. They were evidently cut down from a man's clothes.

As they went slowly towards the house he tore at the ragged wisps of chrysanthemums and dropped the petals in handfuls along the path.

"Don't do that—it does look nasty," said his mother. He refrained, and she, suddenly pitiful, broke off a twig with three or four wan flowers and held them against her face. When mother and son reached the yard her hand hesitated, and instead of laying the flower aside, she pushed it in her apron-band. The mother and son stood at the foot of the three steps looking across the bay of lines at the passing home of the miners. The trundle of the small train was imminent. Suddenly the engine loomed past the house and came to a stop opposite the gate.

The engine-driver, a short man with round gray beard, leaned out of the cab high above the woman.

"Have you got a cup of tea?" he said in a cheery, hearty fashion.

It was her father. She went in, saying she would mash.[7] Directly, she returned.

"I didn't come to see you on Sunday," began the little gray-bearded man.

"I didn't expect you," said his daughter.

The engine driver winced; then, reassuming his cheery, airy manner, he said:

"Oh, have you heard then? Well, and what do you think———?"

"I think it is soon enough," she replied.

At her brief censure the little man made an impatient gesture, and said coaxingly, yet with dangerous coldness:

"Well, what's a man to do? It's no sort of life for a man of my years, to sit at my own hearth like a stranger. And if I'm going to marry again it may as well be soon as late—what does it matter to anybody?"

The woman did not reply, but turned and went into the house. The man in the engine-cab stood assertive, till she returned with a cup of tea and a piece of bread and butter on a plate. She went up the steps and stood near the footplate of the hissing engine.

"You needn't 'a' brought me bread an' butter," said her father. "But a cup of tea"—he sipped appreciatively—"it's very nice." He sipped for a moment or two, then: "I hear as Walter's got another bout on," he said.

"When hasn't he?" said the woman bitterly.

"I heerd tell of him in the Lord Nelson braggin' as he was going to spend that b—— afore he went: half a sovereign[8] that was."

"When?" asked the woman.

"A' Sat'day night—I know that's true."

"Very likely," she laughed bitterly. "He gives me twenty-three shillings."

"Aye, it's a nice thing, when a man can do nothing with his money but make a beast of himself!" said the gray-whiskered man. The woman turned her head away. Her father swallowed the last of his tea and handed her the cup.

"Aye, he sighed, wiping his mouth. "It's a settler,[9] it is———"

He put his hand on the lever. The little engine strained and groaned, and the train rumbled towards the crossing. The woman again looked across the metals. Darkness was settling over the spaces of the railway and trucks: the miners, in gray somber groups, were still passing home. The winding engine pulsed hurriedly, with brief pauses. Elizabeth Bates looked at the dreary flow of men, then she went indoors. Her husband did not come.

---

7. Infuse the tea, i.e., let it stand after pouring boiling water over the tea leaves in order to gain strength.

8. Gold coin worth 20 shillings. Half a sovereign is worth 10.

9. Crushing (or final) blow.

The kitchen was small and full of firelight; red coals piled glowing up the chimney mouth. All the life of the room seemed in the white, warm hearth and the steel fender reflecting the red fire. The cloth was laid for tea; cups glinted in the shadows. At the back, where the lowest stairs protruded into the room, the boy sat struggling with a knife and a piece of white wood. He was almost hidden in the shadow. It was half-past four. They had but to await the father's coming to begin tea. As the mother watched her son's sullen little struggle with the wood, she saw herself in his silence and pertinacity; she saw the father in her child's indifference to all but himself. She seemed to be occupied by her husband. He had probably gone past his home, slunk past his own door, to drink before he came in, while his dinner spoiled and wasted in waiting. She glanced at the clock, then took the potatoes to strain them in the yard. The garden and fields beyond the brook were closed in uncertain darkness. When she rose with the saucepan, leaving the drain streaming into the night behind her, she saw the yellow lamps were lit along the high road that went up the hill away beyond the space of the railway lines and the field.

Then again she watched the men trooping home, fewer now and fewer.

Indoors the fire was sinking and the room was dark red. The woman put her saucepan on the hob, and set a batter pudding near the mouth of the oven. Then she stood unmoving. Directly, gratefully, came quick young steps to the door. Someone hung on the latch a moment, then a little girl entered and began pulling off her outdoor things, dragging a mass of curls, just ripening from gold to brown, over her eyes with her hat.

Her mother chid her for coming late from school, and said she would have to keep her at home the dark winter days.

"Why, mother, it's hardly a bit dark yet. The lamp's not lighted, and my father's not home."

"No, he isn't. But it's a quarter to five! Did you see anything of him?"

The child became serious. She looked at her mother with large, wistful blue eyes.

"No, mother, I've never seen him. Why? Has he come up an' gone past, to Old Brinsley? He hasn't, mother, 'cos I never saw him."

"He'd watch that," said the mother bitterly, "he'd take care as you didn't see him. But you may depend upon it, he's seated in the Prince o' Wales. He wouldn't be this late."

The girl looked at her mother piteously.

"Let's have our teas, mother, should we?" said she.

The mother called John to table. She opened the door once more and looked out across the darkness of the lines. All was deserted: she could not hear the winding-engines.

"Perhaps," she said to herself, "he's stopped to get some ripping[1] done."

They sat down to tea. John, at the end of the table near the door, was

---

1. Taking out or cutting away coal or stone (a mining and quarrying term).

almost lost in the darkness. Their faces were hidden from each other. The girl crouched against the fender slowly moving a thick piece of bread before the fire. The lad, his face a dusky mark on the shadow, sat watching her who was transfigured in the red glow.

"I do think it's beautiful to look in the fire," said the child.

"Do you?" said her mother. "Why?"

"It's so red, and full of little caves—and it feels so nice, and you can fair smell it."

"It'll want mending directly," replied her mother, "and then if your father comes he'll carry on and say there never is a fire when a man comes home sweating from the pit. A public house is always warm enough."

There was silence till the boy said complainingly: "Make haste, our Annie."

"Well, I am doing! I can't make the fire do it no faster, can I?"

"She keeps wafflin' it about so's to make 'er slow," grumbled the boy.

"Don't have such an evil imagination, child," replied the mother.

Soon the room was busy in the darkness with the crisp sound of crunching. The mother ate very little. She drank her tea determinedly, and sat thinking. When she rose her anger was evident in the stern unbending of her head. She looked at the pudding in the fender, and broke out:

"It *is* a scandalous thing as a man can't even come home to his dinner! If it's crozzled up to a cinder I don't see why I should care. Past his very door he goes to get to a public house, and here I sit with his dinner waiting for him——"

She went out. As she dropped piece after piece of coal on the red fire, the shadows fell on the walls, till the room was almost in total darkness.

"I canna see," grumbled the invisible John. In spite of herself, the mother laughed.

"You know the way to your mouth," she said. She set the dust pan outside the door. When she came again like a shadow on the hearth, the lad repeated, complaining sulkily:

"I canna see."

"Good gracious!" cried the mother irritably, "you're as bad as your father if it's a bit dusk!"

Nevertheless, she took a paper spill from a sheaf on the mantelpiece and proceeded to light the lamp that hung from the ceiling in the middle of the room. As she reached up, her figure displayed itself just rounding with maternity.

"Oh, mother——!" exclaimed the girl.

"What?" said the woman, suspended in the act of putting the lamp glass over the flame. The copper reflector shone handsomely on her, as she stood with uplifted arm, turning to face her daughter.

"You've got a flower in your apron!" said the child, in a little rapture at this unusual event.

"Goodness me!" exclaimed the woman, relieved. "One would think the house was afire." She replaced the glass and waited a moment before turning up the wick. A pale shadow was seen floating vaguely on the floor.

"Let me smell!" said the child, still rapturously, coming forward and putting her face to her mother's waist.

"Go along, silly!" said the mother, turning up the lamp. The light revealed their suspense so that the woman felt it almost unbearable. Annie was still bending at her waist. Irritably, the mother took the flowers out from her apron band.

"Oh, mother—don't take them out!" Annie cried, catching her hand and trying to replace the sprig.

"Such nonsense!" said the mother, turning away. The child put the pale chrysanthemums to her lips, murmuring:

"Don't they smell beautiful!"

Her mother gave a short laugh.

"No," she said, "not to me. It was chrysanthemums when I married him, and chrysanthemums when you were born, and the first time they ever brought him home drunk, he'd got brown chrysanthemums in his buttonhole."

She looked at the children. Their eyes and their parted lips were wondering. The mother sat rocking in silence for some time. Then she looked at the clock.

"Twenty minutes to six!" In a tone of fine bitter carelessness she continued: "Eh, he'll not come now till they bring him. There he'll stick! But he needn't come rolling in here in his pit dirt, for *I* won't wash him. He can lie on the floor——Eh, what a fool I've been, what a fool! And this is what I came here for, to this dirty hole, rats and all, for him to slink past his very door. Twice last week—he's begun now——"

She silenced herself and rose to clear the table.

While for an hour or more the children played, subduedly intent, fertile of imagination, united in fear of the mother's wrath, and in dread of their father's home-coming, Mrs. Bates sat in her rocking chair making a "singlet" of thick cream-colored flannel, which gave a dull wounded sound as she tore off the gray edge. She worked at her sewing with energy, listening to the children, and her anger wearied itself, lay down to rest, opening its eyes from time to time and steadily watching, its ears raised to listen. Sometimes even her anger quailed and shrank, and the mother suspended her sewing, tracing the footsteps that thudded along the sleepers outside; she would lift her head sharply to bid the children "hush," but she recovered herself in time, and the footsteps went past the gate, and the children were not flung out of their play-world.

But at last Annie sighed, and gave in. She glanced at her wagon of slippers, and loathed the game. She turned plaintively to her mother.

"Mother!"—but she was inarticulate.

John crept out like a frog from under the sofa. His mother glanced up.

"Yes," she said, "just look at those shirt-sleeves!"

The boy held them out to survey them, saying nothing. Then some-body called in a hoarse voice away down the line, and suspense bristled in the room, till two people had gone by outside, talking.

"It is time for bed," said the mother.

"My father hasn't come," wailed Annie plaintively. But her mother was primed with courage.

"Never mind. They'll bring him when he does come—like a log." She meant there would be no scene. "And he may sleep on the floor till he wakes himself. I know he'll not go to work tomorrow after this!"

The children had their hands and faces wiped with a flannel. They were very quiet. When they had put on their nightdresses, they said their prayers, the boy mumbling. The mother looked down at them, at the brown silken bush of intertwining curls in the nape of the girl's neck, at the little black head of the lad, and her heart burst with anger at their father, who caused all three such distress. The children hid their faces in her skirts for comfort.

When Mrs. Bates came down, the room was strangely empty, with a tension of expectancy. She took up her sewing and stitched for some time without raising her head. Meantime her anger was tinged with fear.

2

The clock struck eight and she rose suddenly, dropping her sewing on her chair. She went to the stair-foot door, opened it, listening. Then she went out, locking the door behind her.

Something scuffled in the yard, and she started, though she knew it was only the rats with which the place was over-run. The night was very dark. In the great bay of railway lines, bulked with trucks, there was no trace of light, only away back she could see a few yellow lamps at the pit top, and the red smear of the burning pit bank on the night. She hurried along the edge of the track, then, crossing the converging lines, came to the stile by the white gates, whence she emerged on the road. Then the fear which had led her shrank. People were walking up to New Brinsley; she saw the lights in the houses; twenty yards farther on were the broad windows of the Prince of Wales, very warm and bright, and the loud voices of men could be heard distinctly. What a fool she had been to imagine that anything had happened to him! He was merely drinking over there at the Prince of Wales. She faltered. She had never yet been to fetch him, and she never would go. So she continued her walk towards the long straggling line of houses, standing back on the highway. She entered a passage between the dwellings.

"Mr. Rigley?—Yes! Did you want him? No, he's not in at this min-ute."

The raw-boned woman leaned forward from her dark scullery and peered at the other, upon whom fell a dim light through the blind of the kitchen window.

"Is it Mrs. Bates?" she asked in a tone tinged with respect.

"Yes. I wondered if your Master was at home. Mine hasn't come yet."

" 'Asn't 'e! Oh, Jack's been 'ome an' 'ad 'is dinner an' gone out. 'E's just gone for 'alf an hour afore bedtime. Did you call at the Prince of Wales?"

"No——"

"No, you didn't like——! It's not very nice." The other woman was indulgent. There was an awkward pause. "Jack never said nothink about—about your Master," she said.

"No!—I expect he's stuck in there!"

Elizabeth Bates said this bitterly, and with recklessness. She knew that the woman across the yard was standing at her door listening, but she did not care. As she turned:

"Stop a minute! I'll just go an' ask Jack if 'e knows anythink," said Mrs. Rigley.

"Oh no—I wouldn't like to put——!"

"Yes, I will, if you'll just step inside an' see as th' childer doesn't come downstairs and set theirselves afire."

Elizabeth Bates, murmuring a remonstrance, stepped inside. The other woman apologized for the state of the room.

The kitchen needed apology. There were little frocks and trousers and childish undergarments on the squab[2] and on the floor, and a litter of playthings everywhere. On the black American cloth[3] of the table were pieces of bread and cake, crusts, slops, and a teapot with cold tea.

"Eh, ours is just as bad," said Elizabeth Bates, looking at the woman, not at the house. Mrs. Rigley put a shawl over her head and hurried out, saying:

"I shanna be a minute."

The other sat, noting with faint disapproval the general untidiness of the room. Then she fell to counting the shoes of various sizes scattered over the floor. There were twelve. She sighed and said to herself: "No wonder!"—glancing at the litter. There came the scratching of two pairs of feet on the yard, and the Rigleys entered. Elizabeth Bates rose. Rigley was a big man, with very large bones. His head looked particularly bony. Across his temple was a blue scar, caused by a wound got in the pit, a wound in which the coal dust remained blue like tattooing.

" 'Asna 'e come whoam yit?" asked the man, without any form of greeting, but with deference and sympathy. "I couldna say wheer he is—'e's non ower theer!"—he jerked his head to signify the Prince of Wales.

" 'E's 'appen gone up to th' Yew," said Mrs. Rigley.

There was another pause. Rigley had evidently something to get off his mind:

"Ah left 'im finishin' a stint," he began. "Loose-all[4] 'ad bin gone about ten minutes when we com'n away, an' I shouted: 'Are ter comin', Walt?' an' 'e said: 'Go on, Ah shanna be but a'ef a minnit,' so we com'n ter th' bottom, me an' Bowers, thinkin' as 'e wor just behint, an' 'ud come up i' th' next bantle[5]——"

2. Couch.
3. Oilcloth.

4. Signal for end of work.
5. Group.

He stood perplexed, as if answering a charge of deserting his mate. Elizabeth Bates, now again certain of disaster, hastened to reassure him:

"I expect 'e's gone up to th' Yew Tree, as you say. It's not the first time. I've fretted myself into a fever before now. He'll come home when they carry him."

"Ay, isn't it too bad!" deplored the other woman.

"I'll just step up to Dick's an' see if 'e *is* theer," offered the man, afraid of appearing alarmed, afraid of taking liberties.

"Oh, I wouldn't think of bothering you that far," said Elizabeth Bates, with emphasis, but he knew she was glad of his offer.

As they stumbled up the entry, Elizabeth Bates heard Rigley's wife run across the yard and open her neighbor's door. At this, suddenly all the blood in her body seemed to switch away from her heart.

"Mind!" warned Rigley. "Ah've said many a time as Ah'd fill up them ruts in this entry, sumb'dy 'll be breakin' their legs yit."

She recovered herself and walked quickly along with the miner.

"I don't like leaving the children in bed, and nobody in the house," she said.

"No, you dunna!" he replied courteously. They were soon at the gate of the cottage.

"Well, I shanna be many minnits. Dunna you be frettin' now, 'e'll be all right," said the butty.[6]

"Thank you very much, Mr. Rigley," she replied.

"You're welcome!" he stammered, moving away. "I shanna be many minnits."

The house was quiet. Elizabeth Bates took off her hat and shawl, and rolled back the rug. When she had finished, she sat down. It was a few minutes past nine. She was startled by the rapid chuff of the winding engine at the pit, and the sharp whirr of the brakes on the rope as it descended. Again she felt the painful sweep of her blood, and she put her hand to her side, saying aloud: "Good gracious!—it's only the nine o'clock deputy[7] going down," rebuking herself.

She sat still, listening. Half an hour of this, and she was wearied out.

"What am I working myself up like this for?" she said pitiably to herself, "I s'll only be doing myself some damage."

She took out her sewing again.

At a quarter to ten there were footsteps. One person! She watched for the door to open. It was an elderly woman, in a black bonnet and a black woolen shawl—his mother. She was about sixty years old, pale, with blue eyes, and her face all wrinkled and lamentable. She shut the door and turned to her daughter-in-law peevishly.

"Eh, Lizzie, whatever shall we do, whatever shall we do!" she cried.

Elizabeth drew back a little, sharply.

"What is it, mother?" she said.

The elder woman seated herself on the sofa.

6. Workmate (cf. "buddy"). Among English coal-miners it has the special meaning of "a supervisor intermediary between the employers and the men."
7. Minor coal-mine official.

"I don't know, child, I can't tell you!"—she shook her head slowly. Elizabeth sat watching her, anxious and vexed.

"I don't know," replied the grandmother, sighing very deeply. "There's no end to my troubles, there isn't. The things I've gone through, I'm sure it's enough——!" She wept without wiping her eyes, the tears running.

"But, mother," interrupted Elizabeth, "what do you mean? What is it?"

The grandmother slowly wiped her eyes. The fountains of her tears were stopped by Elizabeth's directness. She wiped her eyes slowly.

"Poor child! Eh, you poor thing!" she moaned. "I don't know what we're going to do, I don't—and you as you are—it's a thing, it is indeed!"

Elizabeth waited.

"Is he dead?" she asked, and at the words her heart swung violently, though she felt a slight flush of shame at the ultimate extravagance of the question. Her words sufficiently frightened the old lady, almost brought her to herself.

"Don't say so, Elizabeth! We'll hope it's not as bad as that; no, may the Lord spare us that, Elizabeth. Jack Rigley came just as I was sittin' down to a glass afore going to bed, an' 'e said: ' 'Appen you'll go down th' line, Mrs. Bates. Walt's had an accident. 'Appen you'll go an' sit wi' 'er till we can get him home.' I hadn't time to ask him a word afore he was gone. An' I put my bonnet on an' come straight down, Lizzie. I thought to myself: 'Eh, that poor blessed child, if anybody should come an' tell her of a sudden, there's no knowin' what'll 'appen to 'er.' You mustn't let it upset you, Lizzie—or you know what to expect. How long is it, six months—or is it five, Lizzie? Ay!"—the old woman shook her head—"time slips on, it slips on! Ay!"

Elizabeth's thoughts were busy elsewhere. If he was killed—would she be able to manage on the little pension and what she could earn?—she counted up rapidly. If he was hurt—they wouldn't take him to the hospital—how tiresome he would be to nurse!—but perhaps she'd be able to get him away from the drink and his hateful ways. She would—while he was ill. The tears offered to come to her eyes at the picture. But what sentimental luxury was this she was beginning? She turned to consider the children. At any rate she was absolutely necessary for them. They were her business.

"Ay!" repeated the old woman, "it seems but a week or two since he brought me his first wages. Ay—he was a good lad, Elizabeth, he was, in his way. I don't know why he got to be such a trouble, I don't. He was a happy lad at home, only full of spirits. But there's no mistake he's been a handful of trouble, he has! I hope the Lord'll spare him to mend his ways. I hope so, I hope so. You've had a sight o' trouble with him, Elizabeth, you have indeed. But he was a jolly enough lad wi' me, he was, I can assure you. I don't know how it is. . . ."

The old woman continued to muse aloud, a monotonous irritating sound, while Elizabeth thought concentratedly, startled once, when she heard the winding engine chuff quickly, and the brakes skirr with a shriek. Then she heard the engine more slowly, and the brakes made no sound. The old woman did not notice. Elizabeth waited in suspense. The mother-in-law talked, with lapses into silence.

"But he wasn't your son, Lizzie, an' it makes a difference. Whatever he was, I remember him when he was little, an' I learned to understand him and to make allowances. You've got to make allowances for them——"

It was half-past ten, and the old woman was saying: "But it's trouble from beginning to end; you're never too old for trouble, never too old for that——" when the gate banged back, and there were heavy feet on the steps.

"I'll go, Lizzie, let me go," cried the old woman, rising. But Elizabeth was at the door. It was a man in pit clothes.

"They're bringin' 'im, Missis," he said. Elizabeth's heart halted a moment. Then it surged on again, almost suffocating her.

"Is he—is it bad?" she asked.

The man turned away, looking at the darkness:

"The doctor says 'e'd been dead hours. 'E saw 'im i' th' lamp-cabin."

The old woman, who stood just behind Elizabeth, dropped into a chair, and folded her hands, crying: "Oh, my boy, my boy!"

"Hush!" said Elizabeth, with a sharp twitch of a frown. "Be still, mother, don't waken th' children: I wouldn't have them down for anything!"

The old woman moaned softly, rocking herself. The man was drawing away. Elizabeth took a step forward.

"How was it?" she asked.

"Well, I couldn't say for sure," the man replied, very ill at ease. "'E wor finishin' a stint an' th' butties 'ad gone, an' a lot o' stuff come down atop 'n 'im."

"And crushed him?" cried the widow, with a shudder.

"No," said the man, "it fell at th' back of 'im. 'E wor under th' face an' it niver touched 'im. It shut 'im in. It seems 'e wor smothered."

Elizabeth shrank back. She heard the old woman behind her cry:

"What?—what did 'e say it was?"

The man replied, more loudly: "'E wor smothered!"

Then the old woman wailed aloud, and this relieved Elizabeth.

"Oh, mother," she said, putting her hand on the old woman, "don't waken th' children, don't waken th' children."

She wept a little, unknowing, while the old mother rocked herself and moaned. Elizabeth remembered that they were bringing him home, and she must be ready. "They'll lay him in the parlor," she said to herself, standing a moment pale and perplexed.

Then she lighted a candle and went into the tiny room. The air was cold and damp, but she could not make a fire, there was no fireplace. She set down the candle and looked round. The candlelight glittered on the luster-glasses, on the two vases that held some of the pink chrysanthemums, and on the dark mahogany. There was a cold, deathly smell of chrysanthemums in the room. Elizabeth stood looking at the flowers. She turned away, and calculated whether there would be room to lay him on the floor, between the couch and the chiffonier. She pushed the chairs aside. There would be room to lay him down and to step round him. Then she fetched the old red tablecloth, and another old cloth, spreading them down to save her bit of carpet. She shivered on leaving the parlor; so, from the dresser drawer she took a clean shirt and put it at the fire to air. All the time her mother-in-law was rocking herself in the chair and moaning.

"You'll have to move from there, mother," said Elizabeth. "They'll be bringing him in. Come in the rocker."

The old mother rose mechanically, and seated herself by the fire, continuing to lament. Elizabeth went into the pantry for another candle, and there, in the little penthouse under the naked tiles, she heard them coming. She stood still in the pantry doorway, listening. She heard them pass the end of the house, and come awkwardly down the three steps, a jumble of shuffling footsteps and muttering voices. The old woman was silent. The men were in the yard.

Then Elizabeth heard Matthews, the manager of the pit, say: "You go in first, Jim. Mind!"

The door came open, and the two women saw a collier backing into the room, holding one end of a stretcher, on which they could see the nailed pit boots of the dead man. The two carriers halted, the man at the head stooping to the lintel of the door.

"Wheer will you have him?" asked the manager, a short, white-bearded man.

Elizabeth roused herself and came from the pantry carrying the unlighted candle.

"In the parlor," she said.

"In there, Jim!" pointed the manager, and the carriers backed round into the tiny room. The coat with which they had covered the body fell off as they awkwardly turned through the two doorways, and the women saw their man, naked to the waist, lying stripped for work. The old woman began to moan in a low voice of horror.

"Lay th' stretcher at th' side," snapped the manager, "an' put 'im on th' cloths. Mind now, mind! Look you now——!"

One of the men had knocked off a vase of chrysanthemums. He stared awkwardly, then they set down the stretcher. Elizabeth did not look at her husband. As soon as she could get in the room, she went and picked up the broken vase and the flowers.

"Wait a minute!" she said.

The three men waited in silence while she mopped up the water with a duster.

"Eh, what a job, what a job, to be sure!" the manager was saying, rubbing his brow with trouble and perplexity. "Never knew such a thing in my life, never! He'd no business to ha' been left. I never knew such a thing in my life! Fell over him clean as a whistle, an' shut him in. Not four foot of space, there wasn't—yet it scarce bruised him."

He looked down at the dead man, lying prone, half naked, all grimed with coal dust.

" ' 'Sphyxiated', the doctor said. It *is* the most terrible job I've ever known Seems as if it was done o' purpose. Clean over him, an' shut 'im in, like a mouse-trap"—he made a sharp, descending gesture with his hand.

The colliers standing by jerked aside their heads in hopeless comment.

The horror of the thing bristled upon them all.

Then they heard the girl's voice upstairs calling shrilly: "Mother, mother—who is it? Mother, who is it?"

Elizabeth hurried to the foot of the stairs and opened the door:

"Go to sleep!" she commanded sharply. "What are you shouting about? Go to sleep at once—there's nothing——"

Then she began to mount the stairs. They could hear her on the boards, and on the plaster floor of the little bedroom. They could hear her distinctly:

"What's the matter now?—what's the matter with you, silly thing?"— her voice was much agitated, with an unreal gentleness.

"I thought it was some men come," said the plaintive voice of the child. "Has he come?"

"Yes, they've brought him. There's nothing to make a fuss about. Go to sleep now, like a good child."

They could hear her voice in the bedroom, they waited whilst she covered the children under the bedclothes.

"Is he drunk?" asked the girl, timidly, faintly.

"No! No—he's not! He—he's asleep."

"Is he asleep downstairs?"

"Yes—and don't make a noise."

There was silence for a moment, then the men heard the frightened child again:

"What's that noise?"

"It's nothing, I tell you, what are you bothering for?"

The noise was the grandmother moaning. She was oblivious of everything, sitting on her chair rocking and moaning. The manager put his hand on her arm and bade her "Sh—sh! !"

The old woman opened her eyes and looked at him. She was shocked by this interruption, and seemed to wonder.

"What time is it?" the plaintive thin voice of the child, sinking back unhappily into sleep, asked this last question.

"Ten o'clock," answered the mother more softly. Then she must have bent down and kissed the children.

Matthews beckoned to the men to come away. They put on their caps and took up the stretcher. Stepping over the body, they tiptoed out of the house. None of them spoke till they were far from the wakeful children.

When Elizabeth came down she found her mother alone on the parlor floor, leaning over the dead man, the tears dropping on him.

"We must lay him out," the wife said. She put on the kettle, then returning knelt at the feet, and began to unfasten the knotted leather laces. The room was clammy and dim with only one candle, so that she had to bend her face almost to the floor. At last she got off the heavy boots and put them away.

"You must help me now," she whispered to the old woman. Together they stripped the man.

When they arose, saw him lying in the naïve dignity of death, the women stood arrested in fear and respect. For a few moments they remained still, looking down, the old mother whimpering. Elizabeth felt countermanded. She saw him, how utterly inviolable he lay in himself. She had nothing to do with him. She could not accept it. Stooping, she laid her hand on him, in claim. He was still warm, for the mine was hot where he had died. His mother had his face between her hands, and was murmuring incoherently. The old tears fell in succession as drops from wet leaves; the mother was not weeping, merely her tears flowed. Elizabeth embraced the body of her husband, with cheek and lips. She seemed to be listening, inquiring, trying to get some connection. But she could not. She was driven away. He was impregnable.

She rose, went into the kitchen where she poured warm water into a bowl, brought soap and flannel and a soft towel. "I must wash him," she said.

Then the old mother rose stiffy, and watched Elizabeth as she carefully washed his face, carefully brushing his big blond moustache from his mouth with the flannel. She was afraid with a bottomless fear, so she ministered to him. The old woman, jealous, said:

"Let me wipe him!"—and she kneeled on the other side drying slowly as Elizabeth washed, her big black bonnet sometimes brushing the dark head of her daughter-in-law. They worked thus in silence for a long time. They never forgot it was death, and the touch of the man's dead body gave them strange emotions, different in each of the women; a great dread possessed them both, the mother felt the lie was given to her womb, she was denied; the wife felt the utter isolation of the human soul, the child within her was a weight apart from her.

At last it was finished. He was a man of handsome body, and his face showed no traces of drink. He was blond, full fleshed, with fine limbs. But he was dead.

"Bless him," whispered his mother, looking always at his face, and speaking out of sheer terror. "Dear lad—bless him!" She spoke in a faint, sibilant ecstasy of fear and mother love.

Elizabeth sank down again to the floor, and put her face against his neck, and trembled and shuddered. But she had to draw away again. He was dead, and her living flesh had no place against his. A great dread and weariness held her: she was so unavailing. Her life was gone like this.

"White as milk he is, clear as a twelve-month baby, bless him, the darling!" the old mother murmured to herself. "Not a mark on him, clear and clean and white, beautiful as ever a child was made," she murmured with pride. Elizabeth kept her face hidden.

"He went peaceful, Lizzie—peaceful as sleep. Isn't he beautiful, the lamb? Ay—he must ha' made his peace, Lizzie. 'Appen he made it all right, Lizzie, shut in there. He'd have time. He wouldn't look like this if he hadn't made his peace. The lamb, the dear lamb. Eh, but he had a hearty laugh. I loved to hear it. He had the heartiest laugh, Lizzie, as a lad——"

Elizabeth looked up. The man's mouth was fallen back, slightly open under the cover of the moustache. The eyes, half shut, did not show glazed in the obscurity. Life with its smoky burning gone from him, had left him apart and utterly alien to her. And she knew what a stranger he was to her. In her womb was ice of fear, because of this separate stranger with whom she had been living as one flesh. Was this what it all meant—utter, intact separateness, obscured by heat of living? In dread she turned her face away. The fact was too deadly. There had been nothing between them, and yet they had come together, exchanging their nakedness repeatedly. Each time he had taken her, they had been two isolated beings, far apart as now. He was no more responsible than she. The child was like ice in her womb. For as she looked at the dead man, her mind, cold and detached, said clearly: "Who am I? What have I been doing? I have been fighting a husband who did not exist. *He* existed all the time. What wrong have I done? What was that I have been living with? There lies the reality, this man." And her soul died in her for fear: she knew she had never seen him, he had never seen her, they had met in the dark and had fought in the dark, not knowing whom they met or whom they fought. And now she saw, and turned silent in seeing. For she had been wrong. She had said he was something he was not; she had felt familiar with him. Whereas he was apart all the while, living as she never lived, feeling as she never felt.

In fear and shame she looked at his naked body, that she had known falsely. And he was the father of her children. Her soul was torn from her body and stood apart. She looked at his naked body and was ashamed, as if she had denied it. After all, it was itself. It seemed awful to her. She looked at his face, and she turned her own face to the wall. For his look was other than hers, his way was not her way. She had denied him what he was—she saw it now. She had refused him as himself. And this had been her life, and his life. She was grateful to death, which restored the truth. And she knew she was not dead.

And all the while her heart was bursting with grief and pity for him. What had he suffered? What stretch of horror for this helpless man! She was rigid with agony. She had not been able to help him. He had been cruelly injured, this naked man, this other being, and she could make no reparation. There were the children—but the children belonged to life. This dead man had nothing to do with them. He and she were only channels through which life had flowed to issue in the children. She was a mother—but how awful she knew it now to have been a wife. And he, dead now, how awful he must have felt it to be a husband. She felt that in the next world he would be a stranger to her. If they met there, in the beyond, they would only be ashamed of what had been before. The children had come, for some mysterious reason, out of both of them. But the children did not unite them. Now he was dead, she knew how eternally he was apart from her, how eternally he had nothing more to do with her. She saw this episode of her life closed. They had denied each other in life. Now he had withdrawn. An anguish came over her. It was finished then: it had become hopeless between them long before he died. Yet he had been her husband. But how little!

"Have you got his shirt, 'Lizabeth?"

Elizabeth turned without answering, though she strove to weep and behave as her mother-in-law expected. But she could not, she was silenced. She went into the kitchen and returned with the garment.

"It is aired," she said, grasping the cotton shirt here and there to try. She was almost ashamed to handle him; what right had she or anyone to lay hands on him; but her touch was humble on his body. It was hard work to clothe him. He was so heavy and inert. A terrible dread gripped her all the while: that he could be so heavy and utterly inert, unresponsive, apart. The horror of the distance between them was almost too much for her—it was so infinite a gap she must look across.

At last it was finished. They covered him with a sheet and left him lying, with his face bound. And she fastened the door of the little parlor, lest the children should see what was lying there. Then, with peace sunk heavy on her heart, she went about making tidy the kitchen. She knew she submitted to life, which was her immediate master. But from death, her ultimate master, she winced with fear and shame.

1911, 1914

The Horse-Dealer's Daughter

"Well, Mabel, and what are you going to do with yourself?" asked Joe, with foolish flippancy. He felt quite safe himself. Without listening for an answer, he turned aside, worked a grain of tobacco to the tip of his tongue, and spat it out. He did not care about anything, since he felt safe himself.

The three brothers and the sister sat round the desolate breakfast-table, attempting some sort of desultory consultation. The morning's post had given the final tap to the family fortunes, and all was over. The dreary dining-room itself, with its heavy mahogany furniture, looked as if it were waiting to be done away with.

But the consultation amounted to nothing. There was a strange air of ineffectuality about the three men, as they sprawled at table, smoking and reflecting vaguely on their own condition. The girl was alone, a rather short, sullen-looking young woman of twenty-seven. She did not share the same life as her brothers. She would have been good-looking, save for the impressive fixity of her face, "bull-dog," as her brothers called it.

There was a confused tramping of horses' feet outside. The three men all sprawled round in their chairs to watch. Beyond the dark holly bushes that separated the strip of lawn from the highroad, they could see a cavalcade of shire horses swinging out of their own yard, being taken for exercise. This was the last time. These were the last horses that would go through their hands. The young men watched with critical, callous look. They were all frightened at the collapse of their lives, and the sense of disaster in which they were involved left them no inner freedom.

Yet they were three fine, well-set fellows enough. Joe, the eldest, was a man of thirty-three, broad and handsome in a hot, flushed way. His face was red, he twisted his black moustache over a thick finger, his eyes were shallow and restless. He had a sensual way of uncovering his teeth when he laughed, and his bearing was stupid. Now he watched the horses with a glazed look of helplessness in his eyes, a certain stupor of downfall.

The great draught horses swung past. They were tied head to tail, four of them, and they heaved along to where a lane branched off from the highroad, planting their great hoofs floutingly in the fine black mud, swinging their great rounded haunches sumptuously, and trotting a few sudden steps as they were led into the lane, round the corner. Every movement showed a massive, slumbrous strength, and a stupidity which held them in subjection. The groom at the head looked back, jerking the leading rope. And the cavalcade moved out of sight up the lane, the tail of the last horse, bobbed up tight and stiff, held out taut from the swinging great haunches as they rocked behind the hedges in a motion-like sleep.

Joe watched with glazed hopeless eyes. The horses were almost like his own body to him. He felt he was done for now. Luckily he was engaged to a woman as old as himself, and therefore her father, who was steward of a neighboring estate, would provide him with a job. He would marry and go into harness. His life was over, he would be a subject animal now.

He turned uneasily aside, the retreating steps of the horses echoing in his ears. Then, with foolish restlessness, he reached for the scraps of bacon rind from the plates, and making a faint whistling sound, flung them to the terrier that lay against the fender. He watched the dog swallow them, and waited till the creature looked into his eyes. Then a faint grin came on his face, and in a high, foolish voice he said:

"You won't get much more bacon, shall you, you little b——?"

The dog faintly and dismally wagged its tail, then lowered its haunches, circled round, and lay down again.

There was another helpless silence at the table. Joe sprawled uneasily in his seat, not willing to go till the family conclave was dissolved. Fred Henry, the second brother, was erect, clean-limbed, alert. He had watched the passing of the horses with more *sang froid*. If he was an animal, like Joe, he was an animal which controls, not one which is controlled. He was master of any horse, and he carried himself with a well-tempered air of mastery. But he was not master of the situations of life. He pushed his coarse brown moustache upwards, off his lip, and glanced irritably at his sister, who sat impassive and inscrutable.

"You'll go and stop with Lucy for a bit, shan't you?" he asked. The girl did not answer.

"I don't see what else you can do," persisted Fred Henry.

"Go as a skivvy,"[1] Joe interpolated laconically.

The girl did not move a muscle.

"If I was her, I should go in for training for a nurse," said Malcolm, the youngest of them all. He was the baby of the family, a young man of twenty-two, with a fresh, jaunty *museau*.[2]

But Mabel did not take any notice of him. They had talked at her and round her for so many years, that she hardly heard them at all.

The marble clock on the mantelpiece softly chimed the half-hour, the dog rose uneasily from the hearth-rug and looked at the party at the breakfast-table. But still they sat in an ineffectual conclave.

"Oh, all right," said Joe suddenly, apropos of nothing. "I'll get a move on."

He pushed back his chair, straddled his knees with a downward jerk, to get them free, in horsey fashion, and went to the fire. Still he did not go out of the room; he was curious to know what the others would do or say. He began to charge his pipe, looking down at the dog and saying in a high, affected voice:

"Going wi' me? Going wi' me are ter? Tha'rt goin' further than tha counts on just now, dost hear?"

The dog faintly wagged his tail, the man stuck out his jaw and covered his pipe with his hands, and puffed intently, losing himself in the tobacco, looking down all the while at the dog with an absent brown eye. The dog looked up at him in mournful distrust. Joe stood with his knees stuck out, in real horsey fashion.

"Have you had a letter from Lucy?" Fred Henry asked of his sister.

"Last week," came the neutral reply.

"And what does she say?"

There was no answer.

"Does she *ask* you to go and stop there?" persisted Fred Henry.

"She says I can if I like."

---

1. Servant girl.   2. Face (French slang).

"Well, then, you'd better. Tell her you'll come on Monday."

This was received in silence.

"That's what you'll do then, is it?" said Fred Henry, in some exasperation.

But she made no answer. There was a silence of futility and irritation in the room. Malcolm grinned fatuously.

"You'll have to make up your mind between now and next Wednesday," said Joe loudly, "or else find yourself lodgings on the curbstone."

The face of the young woman darkened, but she sat on immutable.

"Here's Jack Ferguson!" exclaimed Malcolm, who was looking aimlessly out of the window.

"Where?" exclaimed Joe loudly.

"Just gone past."

"Coming in?"

Malcolm craned his neck to see the gate.

"Yes," he said.

There was a silence. Mabel sat on like one condemned, at the head of the table. Then a whistle was heard from the kitchen. The dog got up and barked sharply. Joe opened the door and shouted:

"Come on."

After a moment a young man entered. He was muffled up in overcoat and a purple woolen scarf, and his tweed cap, which he did not remove, was pulled down on his head. He was of medium height, his face was rather long and pale, his eyes looked tired.

"Hello, Jack! Well, Jack!" exclaimed Malcolm and Joe. Fred Henry merely said: "Jack."

"What's doing?" asked the newcomer, evidently addressing Fred Henry.

"Same. We've got to be out by Wednesday. Got a cold?"

"I have—got it bad, too."

"Why don't you stop in?"

"*Me* stop in? When I can't stand on my legs, perhaps I shall have a chance." The young man spoke huskily. He had a slight Scotch accent.

"It's a knockout, isn't it," said Joe, boisterously, "if a doctor goes round croaking with a cold. Looks bad for the patients, doesn't it?"

The young doctor looked at him slowly.

"Anything the matter with *you*, then?" he asked sarcastically.

"Not as I know of. Damn your eyes, I hope not. Why?"

"I thought you were very concerned about the patients, wondered if you might be one yourself."

"Damn it, no, I've never been patient to no flaming doctor, and hope I never shall be," returned Joe.

At this point Mabel rose from the table, and they all seemed to become aware of her existence. She began putting the dishes together. The young doctor looked at her, but did not address her. He had not greeted her. She went out of the room with the tray, her face impassive and unchanged.

"When are you off then, all of you?" asked the doctor.

"I'm catching the eleven-forty," replied Malcolm. "Are you goin' down wi' th' trap, Joe?"

"Yes, I've told you I'm going down wi' th' trap, haven't I?"

"We'd better be getting her in then. So long Jack, if I don't see you before I go," said Malcolm, shaking hands.

He went out, followed by Joe, who seemed to have his tail between his legs.

"Well, this is the devil's own," exclaimed the doctor, when he was left alone with Fred Henry. "Going before Wednesday, are you?"

"That's the orders," replied the other.

"Where, to Northampton?"

"That's it."

"The devil!" exclaimed Ferguson, with quiet chagrin.

And there was silence between the two.

"All settled up, are you?" asked Ferguson.

"About."

There was another pause.

"Well, I shall miss yer, Freddy, boy," said the young doctor.

"And I shall miss thee, Jack," returned the other.

"Miss you like hell," mused the doctor.

Fred Henry turned aside. There was nothing to say. Mabel came in again, to finish clearing the table.

"What are *you* going to do, then, Miss Pervin?" asked Ferguson. "Going to your sister's, are you?"

Mabel looked at him with her steady, dangerous eyes, that always made him uncomfortable, unsettling his superficial ease.

"No," she said.

"Well, what in the name of fortune *are* you going to do? Say what you mean to do," cried Fred Henry, with futile intensity.

But she only averted her head, and continued her work. She folded the white table cloth, and put on the chenille cloth.

"The sulkiest bitch that ever trod!" muttered her brother.

But she finished her task with perfectly impassive face, the young doctor watching her interestedly all the while. Then she went out.

Fred Henry stared after her, clenching his lips, his blue eyes fixing in sharp antagonism, as he made a grimace of sour exasperation.

"You could bray her into bits, and that's all you'd get out of her," he said, in a small, narrowed tone.

The doctor smiled faintly.

"What's she *going* to do, then?" he asked.

"Strike me if *I* know!" returned the other.

There was a pause. Then the doctor stirred.

"I'll be seeing you tonight, shall I?" he said to his friend.

"Ay—where's it to be? Are we going over to Jessdale?"

"I don't know. I've got such a cold on me. I'll come round to the Moon and Stars, anyway."

"Let Lizzie and May miss their night for once, eh?"

"That's it—if I feel as I do now."

"All's one——"

The two young men went through the passage and down to the back door together. The house was large, but it was servantless now, and desolate. At the back was a small bricked house yard and beyond that a big square, graveled fine and red, and having stables on two sides. Sloping, dank, winter-dark fields stretched away on the open sides.

But the stables were empty. Joseph Pervin, the father of the family, had been a man of no education, who had become a fairly large horse dealer. The stables had been full of horses, there was a great turmoil and come-and-go of horses and of dealers and grooms. Then the kitchen was full of servants. But of late things had declined. The old man had married a second time, to retrieve his fortunes. Now he was dead and everything was gone to the dogs, there was nothing but debt and threatening.

For months, Mabel had been servantless in the big house, keeping the home together in penury for her ineffectual brothers. She had kept house for ten years. But previously it was with unstinted means. Then, however brutal and coarse everything was, the sense of money had kept her proud, confident. The men might be foul-mouthed, the women in the kitchen might have had reputations, her brothers might have illegitimate children. But so long as there was money, the girl felt herself established, and brutally proud, reserved.

No company came to the house, save dealers and coarse men. Mabel had no associates of her own sex, after her sister went away. But she did not mind. She went regularly to church, she attended to her father. And she lived in the memory of her mother, who had died when she was fourteen, and whom she had loved. She had loved her father, too, in a different way, depending upon him, and feeling secure in him, until at the age of fifty-four, he married again. And then she had set hard against him. Now he had died and left them all hopelessly in debt.

She had suffered badly during the period of poverty. Nothing, however, could shake the curious, sullen, animal pride that dominated each member of the family. Now, for Mabel, the end had come. Still she would not cast about her. She would follow her own way just the same. She would always hold the keys of her own situation. Mindless and persistent, she endured from day to day. Why should she think? Why should she answer anybody? It was enough that this was the end, and there was no way out. She need not pass any more darkly along the main street of the small town, avoiding every eye. She need not demean herself any more, going into the shops and buying the cheapest food. This was at an end. She thought of nobody, not even of herself. Mindless and persistent, she seemed in a sort of ecstasy to be coming nearer to her fulfillment, her own glorification, approaching her dead mother, who was glorified.

In the afternoon, she took a little bag, with shears and sponge and a small scrubbing-brush, and went out. It was a gray, wintry day, with saddened, dark green fields and an atmosphere blackened by the smoke of foundries not far off. She went quickly, darkly along the causeway, heeding nobody, through the town to the churchyard.

There she always felt secure, as if no one could see her, although as a matter of fact she was exposed to the stare of everyone who passed along under the churchyard wall. Nevertheless, once under the shadow of the great looming church, among the graves, she felt immune from the world, reserved within the thick churchyard wall as in another country.

Carefully she clipped the grass from the grave, and arranged the pinky-white, small chrysanthemums in the tin cross. When this was done, she took an empty jar from a neighboring grave, brought water, and carefully, most scrupulously sponged the marble headstone and the coping-stone.

It gave her sincere satisfaction to do this. She felt in immediate contact with the world of her mother. She took minute pains, went through the park in a state bordering on pure happiness, as if in performing this task she came into a subtle, intimate connection with her mother. For the life she followed here in the world was far less real than the world of death she inherited from her mother.

The doctor's house was just by the church. Ferguson, being a mere hired assistant, was slave to the countryside. As he hurried now to attend to the out-patients in the surgery, glancing across the graveyard with his quick eye, he saw the girl at her task at the grave. She seemed so intent and remote, it was like looking into another world. Some mystical element was touched in him. He slowed down as he walked, watching her as if spellbound.

She lifted her eyes, feeling him looking. Their eyes met. And each looked again at once, each feeling, in some way, found out by the other. He lifted his cap and passed on down the road. There remained distinct in his consciousness, like a vision, the memory of her face, lifted from the tombstone in the churchyard, and looking at him with slow, large, portentous eyes. It *was* portentous, her face. It seemed to mesmerize him. There was a heavy power in her eyes which laid hold of his whole being, as if he had drunk some powerful drug. He had been feeling weak and done before. Now the life came back into him, he felt delivered from his own fretted, daily self.

He finished his duties at the surgery as quickly as might be, hastily filling up the bottles of the waiting people with cheap drugs. Then, in perpetual haste, he set off again to visit several cases in another part of his round, before tea-time. At all times he preferred to walk if he could, but particularly when he was not well. He fancied the motion restored him.

The afternoon was falling. It was gray, deadened, and wintry, with a slow, moist, heavy coldness sinking in and deadening all the faculties. But why should he think or notice? He hastily climbed the hill and turned across the dark green fields, following the black cinder-track. In the distance, across a shallow dip in the country, the small town was clustered like smouldering ash, a tower, a spire, a heap of low, raw, extinct houses. And on the nearest fringe of the town, sloping into the dip, was Oldmeadow, the Pervins' house. He could see the stables and the outbuildings distinctly, as they lay towards him on the slope. Well, he would not go there many more times! Another resource would be lost to him, another place gone: the only company he cared for in the alien, ugly little town he was losing. Nothing but work, drudgery, constant hastening from dwelling to dwelling among the colliers and the iron-workers. It wore him out, but at the same time he had a craving for it. It was a stimulant to him to be in the homes of the working people, moving, as it were, through the innermost body of their life. His nerves were excited and gratified. He could come so near, into the very lives of the rough, inarticulate, powerfully emotional men and women. He grumbled, he said he hated the hellish hole. But as a matter of fact it excited him, the contact with the rough, strongly-feeling people was a stimulant applied direct to his nerves.

Below Oldmeadow, in the green, shallow, soddened hollow of fields, lay a square, deep pond. Roving across the landscape, the doctor's quick eye detected a figure in black passing through the gate of the field, down towards the pond. He looked again. It would be Mabel Pervin. His mind suddenly became alive and attentive.

Why was she going down there? He pulled up on the path on the slope above, and stood staring. He could just make sure of the small black figure moving in the hollow of the failing day. He seemed to see her in the midst of such obscurity, that he was like a clairvoyant, seeing rather with the mind's eye than with ordinary sight. Yet he could see her positively enough, whilst he kept his eye attentive. He felt, if he looked away from her, in the thick, ugly falling dusk, he would lose her altogether.

He followed her minutely as she moved, direct and intent, like something transmitted rather than stirring in voluntary activity, straight down the field towards the pond. There she stood on the bank for a moment. She never raised her head. Then she waded slowly into the water.

He stood motionless as the small black figure walked slowly and deliberately towards the center of the pond, very slowly, gradually moving deeper into the motionless water, and still moving forward as the water got up to her breast. Then he could see her no more in the dusk of the dead afternoon.

"There!" he exclaimed. "Would you believe it?"

And he hastened straight down, running over the wet, soddened fields, pushing through the hedges, down into the depression of callous wintry obscurity. It took him several minutes to come to the pond. He stood on the bank, breathing heavily. He could see nothing. His eyes seemed to penetrate the dead water. Yes, perhaps that was the dark shadow of her black clothing beneath the surface of the water.

He slowly ventured into the pond. The bottom was deep, soft clay, he sank in, and the water clasped dead cold round his legs. As he stirred he could smell the cold, rotten clay that fouled up into the water. It was objectionable in his lungs. Still, repelled and yet not heeding, he moved deeper into the pond. The cold water rose over his thighs, over his loins, upon his abdomen. The lower part of his body was all sunk in the hideous cold element. And the bottom was so deeply soft and uncertain, he was afraid of pitching with his mouth underneath. He could not swim, and was afraid.

He crouched a little, spreading his hands under the water and moving them round, trying to feel for her. The dead cold pond swayed upon his chest. He moved again, a little deeper, and again, with his hands underneath, he felt all around under the water. And he touched her clothing. But it evaded his fingers. He made a desperate effort to grasp it.

And so doing he lost his balance and went under, horribly, suffocating in the foul earthy water, struggling madly for a few moments. At last, after what seemed an eternity, he got his footing, rose again into the air and looked around. He gasped, and knew he was in the world. Then he looked at the water. She had risen near him. He grasped her clothing, and drawing her nearer, turned to take his way to land again.

He went very slowly, carefully, absorbed in the slow progress. He rose higher, climbing out of the pond. The water was now only about his legs; he was thankful, full of relief to be out of the clutches of the pond. He lifted her and staggered on to the bank, out of the horror of wet, gray clay.

He laid her down on the bank. She was quite unconscious and running with water. He made the water come from her mouth, he worked to restore her. He did not have to work very long before he could feel the breathing begin again in her; she was breathing naturally. He worked a little longer. He could feel her live beneath his hands; she was coming back. He wiped her face, wrapped her in his overcoat, looked round into the dim, dark gray world, then lifted her and staggered down the bank and across the fields.

It seemed an unthinkably long way, and his burden so heavy he felt he would never get to the house. But at last he was in the stable yard, and then in the house yard. He opened the door and went into the house. In the kitchen he laid her down on the hearth-rug and called. The house was empty. But the fire was burning in the grate.

Then again he kneeled to attend to her. She was breathing regularly, her eyes were wide open and as if conscious, but there seemed something missing in her look. She was conscious in herself, but unconscious of her surroundings.

He ran upstairs, took blankets from a bed, and put them before the fire to warm. Then he removed her saturated, earthy-smelling clothing, rubbed her dry with a towel, and wrapped her naked in the blankets. Then he went into the dining room, to look for spirits. There was a little whisky. He drank a gulp himself, and put some into her mouth.

The effect was instantaneous. She looked full into his face, as if she had been seeing him for some time, and yet had only just become conscious of him.

"Dr. Ferguson?" she said.

"What?" he answered.

He was divesting himself of his coat, intending to find some dry clothing upstairs. He could not bear the smell of the dead, clayey water, and he was mortally afraid for his own health.

"What did I do?" she asked.

"Walked into the pond," he replied. He had begun to shudder like one sick, and could hardly attend to her. Her eyes remained full on him, he seemed to be going dark in his mind, looking back at her helplessly. The shuddering became quieter in him, his life came back to him, dark and unknowning, but strong again.

"Was I out of my mind?" she asked, while her eyes were fixed on him all the time.

"Maybe, for the moment," he replied. He felt quiet, because his strength had come back. The strange fretful strain had left him.

"Am I out of my mind now?" she asked.

"Are you?" he reflected a moment. "No," he answered truthfully. "I don't see that you are." He turned his face aside. He was afraid now, because he felt dazed, and felt dimly that her power was stronger than his, in this issue. And she continued to look at him fixedly all the time. "Can you tell me where I shall find some dry things to put on?" he asked.

"Did you dive into the pond for me?" she asked.

"No," he answered. "I walked in. But I went in overhead as well."

There was silence for a moment. He hesitated. He very much wanted to go upstairs to get into dry clothing. But there was another desire in him. And she seemed to hold him. His will seemed to have gone to sleep, and left him, standing there slack before her. But he felt warm inside himself. He did not shudder at all, though his clothes were sodden on him.

"Why did you?" she asked.

"Because I didn't want you to do such a foolish thing," he said.

"It wasn't foolish," she said, still gazing at him as she lay on the floor, with a sofa cushion under her head. "It was the right thing to do. I knew best, then."

"I'll go and shift these wet things," he said. But still he had not the power to move out of her presence, until she sent him. It was as if she had the life of his body in her hands, and he could not extricate himself. Or perhaps he did not want to.

Suddenly she sat up. Then she became aware of her own immediate condition. She felt the blankets about her, she knew her own limbs. For a moment it seemed as if her reason were going. She looked round, with wild eye, as if seeking something. He stood still with fear. She saw her clothing lying scattered.

"Who undressed me?" she asked, her eyes resting full and inevitable on his face.

"I did," he replied, "to bring you round."

For some moments she sat and gazed at him awfully, her lips parted.

"Do you love me, then?" she asked.

He only stood and stared at her, fascinated. His soul seemed to melt.

She shuffled forward on her knees, and put her arms round him, round his legs, as he stood there, pressing her breasts against his knees and thighs, clutching him with strange, convulsive certainty, pressing his thighs against her, drawing him to her face, her throat, as she looked up at him with flaring, humble eyes of transfiguration, triumphant in first possession.

"You love me," she murmured, in strange transport, yearning and triumphant and confident. "You love me. I know you love me, I know."

And she was passionately kissing his knees, through the wet clothing, passionately and indiscriminately kissing his knees, his legs, as if unaware of everything.

He looked down at the tangled wet hair, the wild, bare, animal shoulders. He was amazed, bewildered, and afraid. He had never thought of loving her. He had never wanted to love her. When he rescued her and restored her, he was a doctor, and she was a patient. He had had no single personal thought of her. Nay, this introduction of the personal element was very distasteful to him, a violation of his professional honor. It was horrible to have her there embracing his knees. It was horrible. He revolted from it, violently. And yet—and yet—he had not the power to break away.

She looked at him again, with the same supplication of powerful love, and that same transcendent, frightening light of triumph. In view of the delicate flame which seemed to come from her face like a light, he was powerless. And yet he had never intended to love her. He had never intended. And something stubborn in him could not give way.

"You love me," she repeated, in a murmur of deep, rhapsodic assurance. "You love me."

Her hands were drawing him, drawing him down to her. He was afraid, even a little horrified. For he had, really, no intention of loving her. Yet her hands were drawing him towards her. He put out his hand quickly to steady himself, and grasped her bare shoulder. A flame seemed to burn the hand that grasped her soft shoulder. He had no intention of loving her: his whole will was against his yielding. It was horrible. And yet wonderful was the touch of her shoulders, beautiful the shining of her face. Was she perhaps mad? He had a horror of yielding to her. Yet something in him ached also.

He had been staring away at the door, away from her. But his hand remained on her shoulder. She had gone suddenly very still. He looked down at her. Her eyes were now wide with fear, with doubt, the light was dying from her face, a shadow of terrible grayness was returning. He could not bear the touch of her eyes' question upon him, and the look of death behind the question.

With an inward groan he gave way, and let his heart yield towards her. A sudden gentle smile came on his face. And her eyes, which never left his face, slowly, slowly filled with tears. He watched the strange water rise in her eyes, like some slow fountain coming up. And his heart seemed to burn and melt away in his breast.

He could not bear to look at her any more. He dropped on his knees and caught her head with his arms and pressed her face against his throat. She was very still. His heart, which seemed to have broken, was burning with a kind of agony in his breast. And he felt her slow, hot tears wetting his throat. But he could not move.

He felt the hot tears wet his neck and the hollows of his neck, and he remained motionless, suspended through one of man's eternities. Only now it had become indispensable to him to have her face pressed close to him; he could never let her go again. He could never let her head go away from the close clutch of his arm. He wanted to remain like that for ever, with his heart hurting him in a pain that was also life to him. Without knowing, he was looking down on her damp, soft brown hair.

Then, as it were suddenly, he smelt the horrid stagnant smell of that water. And at the same moment she drew away from him and looked at him. Her eyes were wistful and unfathomable. He was afraid of them, and he fell to kissing her, not knowing what he was doing. He wanted her eyes not to have that terrible, wistful, unfathomable look.

When she turned her face to him again, a faint delicate flush was glowing, and there was again dawning that terrible shining of joy in her eyes, which really terrified him, and yet which he now wanted to see, because he feared the look of doubt still more.

"You love me?" she said, rather faltering.

"Yes." The word cost him a painful effort. Not because it wasn't true. But because it was too newly true, the *saying* seemed to tear open again his newly torn heart. And he hardly wanted it to be true, even now.

She lifted her face to him, and he bent forward and kissed her on the mouth, gently, with the one kiss that is an eternal pledge. And as he kissed her his heart strained again in his breast. He never intended to love her. But now it was over. He had crossed over the gulf to her, and all that he had left behind had shriveled and become void.

After the kiss, her eyes again slowly filled with tears. She sat still, away from him, with her face drooped aside, and her hands folded in her lap. The tears fell very slowly. There was complete silence. He too sat there motionless and silent on the hearth rug. The strange pain of his heart that was broken seemed to consume him. That he should love her? That this was love! That he should be ripped open in this way! Him, a doctor! How they would all jeer if they knew! It was agony to him to think they might know.

In the curious naked pain of the thought he looked again to her. She was sitting there drooped into a muse. He saw a tear fall, and his heart flared hot. He saw for the first time that one of her shoulders was quite uncovered, one arm bare, he could see one of her small breasts; dimly, because it had become almost dark in the room.

"Why are you crying?" he asked, in an altered voice.

She looked up at him, and behind her tears the consciousness of her situation for the first time brought a dark look of shame to her eyes.

"I'm not crying, really," she said, watching him, half frightened.

He reached his hand, and softly closed it on her bare arm.

"I love you! I love you!" he said in a soft, low vibrating voice, unlike himself.

She shrank, and dropped her head. The soft, penetrating grip of his hand on her arm distressed her. She looked up at him.

"I want to go," she said. "I want to go and get you some dry things."

"Why?" he said. "I'm all right."

"But I want to go," she said. "And I want you to change your things."

He released her arm, and she wrapped herself in the blanket, looking at him, rather frightened. And still she did not rise.

"Kiss me," she said wistfully.

He kissed her, but briefly, half in anger.

Then, after a second, she rose nervously, all mixed up in the blanket. He watched her in her confusion as she tried to extricate herself and wrap herself up so that she could walk. He watched her relentlessly, as she knew. And as she went, the blanket trailing, and as he saw a glimpse of her feet and her white leg, he tried to remember her as she was when he had wrapped her in the blanket. But then he didn't want to remember, because she had been nothing to him then, and his nature revolted from remembering her as she was when she was nothing to him.

A tumbling muffled noise from within the dark house startled him. Then he heard her voice: "There are clothes." He rose and went to the foot of the stairs, and gathered up the garments she had thrown down. Then he came back to the fire, to rub himself down and dress. He grinned at his own appearance when he had finished.

The fire was sinking, so he put on coal. The house was now quite dark, save for the light of a street-lamp that shone in faintly from beyond the holly trees. He lit the gas with matches he found on the mantelpiece. Then he emptied the pockets of his own clothes, and threw all his wet things in a heap into the scullery. After which he gathered up her sodden clothes, gently, and put them in a separate heap on the copper-top in the scullery.

It was six o'clock on the clock. His own watch had stopped. He ought to go back to the surgery. He waited, and still she did not come down. So he went to the foot of the stairs and called:

"I shall have to go."

Almost immediately he heard her coming down. She had on her best dress of black voile, and her hair was tidy, but still damp. She looked at him—and in spite of herself, smiled.

"I don't like you in those clothes," she said.

"Do I look a sight?" he answered.

They were shy of one another.

"I'll make you some tea," she said.

"No, I must go."

"Must you?" And she looked at him again with the wide, strained, doubtful eyes. And again, from the pain of his breast, he knew how he loved her. He went and bent to kiss her, gently, passionately, with his heart's painful kiss.

"And my hair smells so horrible," she murmured in distraction. "And I'm so awful, I'm so awful! Oh no, I'm too awful." And she broke into bitter, heart-broken sobbing. "You can't want to love me, I'm horrible."

"Don't be silly, don't be silly," he said, trying to comfort her, kissing her, holding her in his arms. "I want you, I want to marry you, we're going to be married, quickly, quickly—tomorrow if I can."

But she only sobbed terribly, and cried:

"I feel awful. I feel awful. I feel I'm horrible to you."

"No, I want you, I want you," was all he answered, blindly, with that terrible intonation which frightened her almost more than her horror lest he should *not* want her.

1922

Why the Novel Matters

We have curious ideas of ourselves. We think of ourselves as a body with a spirit in it, or a body with a soul in it, or a body with a mind in it. *Mens sana in corpore sano.*[1] The years drink up the wine, and at last throw the bottle away, the body, of course, being the bottle.

It is a funny sort of superstition. Why should I look at my hand, as it so cleverly writes these words, and decide that it is a mere nothing compared to the mind that directs it? Is there really any huge difference between my hand and my brain? Or my mind? My hand is alive, it flickers with a life of its own. It meets all the strange universe in touch, and learns a vast number of things, and knows a vast number of things. My hand, as it writes these words, slips gaily along, jumps like a grasshopper to dot an *i*, feels the table rather cold, gets a little bored if I write too long, has its own rudiments of thought, and is just as much *me* as is my brain, my mind, or my soul. Why should I imagine that there is a *me* which is more *me* than my hand is? Since my hand is absolutely alive, me alive.

Whereas, of course, as far as I am concerned, my pen isn't alive at all. My pen *isn't me* alive. Me alive ends at my finger tips.

Whatever is me alive is me. Every tiny bit of my hands is alive, every little freckle and hair and fold of skin. And whatever is me alive is me. Only my fingernails, those ten little weapons between me and an inan-

---

1. "A healthy mind in a healthy body."

imate universe, they cross the mysterious Rubicon[2] between me alive and things like my pen, which are not alive, in my own sense.

So, seeing my hand is all alive, and me alive, wherein is it just a bottle, or a jug, or a tin can, or a vessel of clay, or any of the rest of that nonsense? True, if I cut it it will bleed, like a can of cherries. But then the skin that is cut, and the veins that bleed, and the bones that should never be seen, they are all just as alive as the blood that flows. So the tin can business, or vessel of clay, is just bunk.

And that's what you learn, when you're a novelist. And that's what you are very liable *not* to know, if you're a parson, or a philosopher, or a scientist, or a stupid person. If you're a parson, you talk about souls in heaven. If you're a novelist, you know that paradise is in the palm of your hand, and on the end of your nose, because both are alive; and alive, and man alive, which is more than you can say, for certain, of paradise. Paradise is after life, and I for one am not keen on anything that is *after* life. If you are a philosopher, you talk about infinity, and the pure spirit which knows all things. But if you pick up a novel, you realize immediately that infinity is just a handle to this self-same jug of a body of mine; while as for knowing, if I find my finger in the fire, I know that fire burns, with a knowledge so emphatic and vital, it leaves Nirvana[3] merely a conjecture. Oh, yes, my body, me alive, *knows*, and knows intensely. And as for the sum of all knowledge, it can't be anything more than an accumulation of all the things I know in the body, and you, dear reader, know in the body.

These damned philosophers, they talk as if they suddenly went off in steam, and were then much more important than they are when they're in their shirts. It is nonsense. Every man, philosopher included, ends in his own finger tips. That's the end of his man alive. As for the words and thoughts and sighs and aspirations that fly from him, they are so many tremulations in the ether, and not alive at all. But if the tremulations reach another man alive, he may receive them into his life, and his life may take on a new color, like a chameleon creeping from a brown rock on to a green leaf. All very well and good. It still doesn't alter the fact that the so-called spirit, the message or teaching of the philosopher or the saint, isn't alive at all, but just a tremulation upon the ether, like a radio message. All this spirit stuff is just tremulations upon the ether. If you, as man alive, quiver from the tremulation of the ether into new life, that is because you are man alive, and you take sustenance and stimulation into your alive man in a myriad ways. But to say that the message, or the spirit which is communicated to you, is more important than your living body, is nonsense. You might as well say that the potato at dinner was more important.

2. When Julius Caesar crossed the River Rubicon (near Rimini, Italy) in 49 B.C., in defiance of the Senate's orders, this indicated his intention of advancing against Pompey and thus involving the country in civil war. Hence to "cross the Rubicon" means to take an important and irrevocable decision.
3. In Buddhist theology, the extinction of the self and its desires and the attainment of perfect beatitude.

Nothing is important but life. And for myself, I can absolutely see life nowhere but in the living. Life with a capital L is only man alive. Even a cabbage in the rain is cabbage alive. All things that are alive are amazing. And all things that are dead are subsidiary to the living. Better a live dog than a dead lion. But better a live lion than a live dog. *C'est la vie!*

It seems impossible to get a saint, or a philosopher, or a scientist, to stick to this simple truth. They are all, in a sense, renegades. The saint wishes to offer himself up as spiritual food for the multitude. Even Francis of Assisi turns himself into a sort of angel-cake, of which anyone may take a slice. But an angel-cake is rather less than man alive. And poor St. Francis might well apologize to his body, when he is dying: "Oh, pardon me, my body, the wrong I did you through the years!" It was no wafer, for others to eat.

The philosopher, on the other hand, because he can think, decides that nothing but thoughts matter. It is as if a rabbit, because he can make little pills, should decide that nothing but little pills matter. As for the scientist, he has absolutely no use for me so long as I am man alive. To the scientist, I am dead. He puts under the microscope a bit of dead me, and calls it me. He takes me to pieces, and says first one piece, and then another piece, is me. My heart, my liver, my stomach have all been scientifically me, according to the scientist; and nowadays I am either a brain, or nerves, or glands, or something more up-to-date in the tissue line.

Now I absolutely flatly deny that I am a soul, or a body, or a mind, or an intelligence, or a brain, or a nervous system, or a bunch of glands, or any of the rest of these bits of me. The whole is greater than the part. And therefore, I, who am man alive, am greater than my soul, or spirit, or body, or mind, or consciousness, or anything else that is merely a part of me. I am a man, and alive. I am man alive, and as long as I can, I intend to go on being man alive.

For this reason I am a novelist. And being a novelist, I consider myself superior to the saint, the scientist, the philosopher, and the poet, who are all great masters of different bits of man alive, but never get the whole hog.

The novel is the one bright book of life. Books are not life. They are only tremulations on the ether. But the novel as a tremulation can make the whole man alive tremble. Which is more than poetry, philosophy, science, or any other book-tremulation can do.

The novel is the book of life. In this sense, the Bible is a great confused novel. You may say, it is about God. But it is really about man alive. Adam, Eve, Sarai, Abraham, Isaac, Jacob, Samuel, David, Bath-Sheba, Ruth, Esther, Solomon, Job, Isaiah, Jesus, Mark, Judas, Paul, Peter: what is it but man alive, from start to finish? Man alive, not mere bits. Even the Lord is another man alive, in a burning bush, throwing the tablets of stone at Moses's head.

I do hope you begin to get my idea, why the novel is supremely important, as a tremulation on the ether. Plato makes the perfect ideal being tremble in me. But that's only a bit of me. Perfection is only a bit, in the strange make-up of man alive. The Sermon on the Mount makes the selfless spirit of me quiver. But that, too, is only a bit of me. The Ten Commandments set the old Adam shivering in me, warning me that I am a thief and a murderer, unless I watch it. But even the old Adam is only a bit of me.

I very much like all these bits of me to be set trembling with life and the wisdom of life. But I do ask that the whole of me shall tremble in its wholeness, some time or other.

And this, of course, must happen in me, living.

But as far as it can happen from a communication, it can only happen when a whole novel communicates itself to me. The Bible—but *all* the Bible—and Homer, and Shakespeare: these are the supreme old novels. These are all things to all men. Which means that in their wholeness they affect the whole man alive, which is the man himself, beyond any part of him. They set the whole tree trembling with a new access of life, they do not just stimulate growth in one direction.

I don't want to grow in any one direction any more. And, if I can help it, I don't want to stimulate anybody else into some particular direction. A particular direction ends in a *cul-de-sac*. We're in a *cul-de-sac* at present.

I don't believe in any dazzling revelation, or in any supreme Word. "The grass withereth, the flower fadeth, but the Word of the Lord shall stand for ever." That's the kind of stuff we've drugged ourselves with. As a matter of fact, the grass withereth, but comes up all the greener for that reason, after the rains. The flower fadeth, and therefore the bud opens. But the Word of the Lord, being man-uttered and a mere vibration on the ether, becomes staler and staler, more and more boring, till at last we turn a deaf ear and it ceases to exist, far more finally than any withered grass. It is grass that renews its youth like the eagle, not any Word.

We should ask for no absolutes, or absolute. Once and for all and for ever, let us have done with the ugly imperialism of any absolute. There is no absolute good, there is nothing absolutely right. All things flow and change, and even change is not absolute. The whole is a strange assembly of apparently incongruous parts, slipping past one another.

Me, man alive, I am a very curious assembly of incongruous parts. My yea! of today is oddly different from my yea! of yesterday. My tears of tomorrow will have nothing to do with my tears of a year ago. If the one I love remains unchanged and unchanging, I shall cease to love her. It is only because she changes and startles me into change and defies my inertia, and is herself staggered in her inertia by my changing, that I can continue to love her. If she stayed put, I might as well love the pepper pot.

In all this change, I maintain a certain integrity. But woe betide me if I try to put my finger on it. If I say of myself, I am this, I am that!— then, if I stick to it, I turn into a stupid fixed thing like a lamp-post. I shall never know wherein lies my integrity, my individuality, my me. I *can* never know it. It is useless to talk about my ego. That only means that I have made up an *idea* of myself, and that I am trying to cut myself out to pattern. Which is no good. You can cut your cloth to fit your coat, but you can't clip bits off your living body, to trim it down to your idea. True, you can put yourself into ideal corsets. But even in ideal corsets, fashions change.

Let us learn from the novel. In the novel, the characters can do nothing but *live*. If they keep on being good, according to pattern, or bad, according to pattern, or even volatile, according to pattern, they cease to live, and the novel falls dead. A character in a novel has got to live, or it is nothing.

We, likewise, in life have got to live, or we are nothing.

What we mean by living is, of course, just as indescribable as what we mean by *being*. Men get ideas into their heads, of what they mean by Life, and they proceed to cut life out to pattern. Sometimes they go into the desert to seek God, sometimes they go into the desert to seek cash, sometimes it is wine, woman, and song, and again it is water, political reform, and votes. You never know what it will be next: from killing your neighbor with hideous bombs and gas that tears the lungs, to supporting a Foundlings Home and preaching infinite Love, and being co-respondent in a divorce.

In all this wild welter, we need some sort of guide. It's no good inventing Thou Shalt Nots!

What then? Turn truly, honorably to the novel, and see wherein you are man alive, and wherein you are dead man in life. You may love a woman as man alive, and you may be making love to a woman as sheer dead man in life. You may eat your dinner as man alive, or as a mere masticating corpse. As man alive you may have shot at your enemy. But as a ghastly simulacrum of life you may be firing bombs into men who are neither your enemies nor your friends, but just things you are dead to. Which is criminal, when the things happen to be alive.

To be alive, to be man alive, to be whole man alive: that is the point. And at its best, the novel, and the novel supremely, can help you. It can help you not to be dead man in life. So much of a man walks about dead and a carcass in the street and house, today: so much of women is merely dead. Like a pianoforte with half the notes mute.

But the novel you can see, plainly, when the man goes dead, the woman goes inert. You can develop an instinct for life, if you will, instead of a theory of right and wrong, good and bad.

In life, there is right and wrong, good and bad, all the time. But what is right in one case is wrong in another. And in the novel you see one man becoming a corpse, because of his so-called goodness, another going dead because of his so-called wickedness. Right and wrong is an instinct: but an instinct of the whole consciousness in a man, bodily, mental, spiritual at once. And only in the novel are *all* things given full play, or at least, they may be given full play, when we realize that life itself, and not inert safety, is the reason for living. For out of the full play of all things emerges the only thing that is anything, the wholeness of a man, the wholeness of a woman, man live, and live woman.

1936

Love on the Farm[1]

What large, dark hands are those at the window
Grasping in the golden light
Which weaves its way through the evening wind
    At my heart's delight?

Ah, only the leaves! But in the west   5
I see a redness suddenly come
Into the evening's anxious breast—
    'Tis the wound of love goes home!

The woodbine creeps abroad
Calling low to her lover: 10
    The sunlit flirt who all the day
    Has poised above her lips in play
    And stolen kisses, shallow and gay
    Of pollen, now has gone away—
    She woos the moth with her sweet, low word;   15
And when above her his moth-wings hover
Then her bright breast she will uncover
And yield her honey-drop to her lover.

Into the yellow, evening glow
Saunters a man from the farm below;   20
Leans, and looks in at the low-built shed
Where the swallow has hung her marriage bed.
    The bird lies warm against the wall.
    She glances quick her startled eyes
    Towards him, then she turns away   25
    Her small head, making warm display
    Of red upon the throat. Her terrors sway
    Her out of the nest's warm, busy ball,
    Whose plaintive cry is heard as she flies
    In one blue stoop from out the sties   30
    Into the twilight's empty hall.
Oh, water-hen, beside the rushes
Hide your quaintly scarlet blushes,
Still your quick tail, lie still as dead,
Till the distance folds over his ominous tread!   35

1. Called *Cruelty and Love* when first published in 1913, and *Love on the Farm* when it appeared in *Collected Poems* (1928).

The rabbit presses back her ears,
Turns back her liquid, anguished eyes
And crouches low; then with wild spring
Spurts from the terror of *his* oncoming;
To be choked back, the wire ring   40
Her frantic effort throttling:
    Piteous brown ball of quivering fears!
Ah, soon in his large, hard hands she dies,
And swings all loose from the swing of his walk!
Yet calm and kindly are his eyes   45
And ready to open in brown surprise
Should I not answer to his talk
Or should he my tears surmise.

I hear his hand on the latch, and rise from my chair
Watching the door open; he flashes bare   50
His strong teeth in a smile, and flashes his eyes
In a smile like triumph upon me; then careless-wise
He flings the rabbit soft on the table board
And comes towards me: ah! the uplifted sword
Of his hand against my bosom! and oh, the broad   55
Blade of his glance that asks me to applaud
His coming! With his hand he turns my face to him
And caresses me with his fingers that still smell grim
Of the rabbit's fur! God, I am caught in a snare!
I know not what fine wire is round my throat;   60
I only know I let him finger there
My pulse of life, and let him nose like a stoat
Who sniffs with joy before he drinks the blood.

And down his mouth comes to my mouth! and down
His bright dark eyes come over me, like a hood   65
Upon my mind! his lips meet mine, and a flood
Of sweet fire sweeps across me, so I drown
Against him, die, and find death good.

                                                    1913, 1928

Piano[1]

Softly, in the dusk, a woman is singing to me;
Taking me back down the vista of years, till I see
A child sitting under the piano, in the boom of the tingling strings
And pressing the small, poised feet of a mother who smiles as she
    sings.

---

1. For an earlier version of this poem, see "Poems in Process," below.

In spite of myself, the insidious mastery of song 5
Betrays me back, till the heart of me weeps to belong
To the old Sunday evenings at home, with winter outside
And hymns in the cozy parlor, the tinkling piano our guide.

So now it is vain for the singer to burst into clamor
With the great black piano appassionato. The glamor 10
Of childish days is upon me, my manhood is cast
Down in the flood of remembrance, I weep like a child for the past.

1918

Bavarian Gentians[1]

Not every man has gentians in his house
in Soft September, at slow, Sad Michaelmas.

Bavarian gentians, big and dark, only dark
darkening the daytime torchlike with the smoking blueness of Pluto's
    gloom,[2]
ribbed and torchlike, with their blaze of darkness spread blue 5
down flattening into points, flattened under the sweep of white day
torch-flower of the blue-smoking darkness, Pluto's dark-blue daze,
black lamps from the halls of Dis, burning dark blue,
giving off darkness, blue darkness, as Demeter's pale lamps give off light,
lead me then, lead me the way. 10

Reach me a gentian, give me a torch
let me guide myself with the blue, forked torch of this flower
down the darker and darker stairs, where blue is darkened on blueness.
even where Persephone[3] goes, just now, from the frosted September
to the sightless realm where darkness was awake upon the dark 15
and Persephone herself is but a voice
or a darkness invisible enfolded in the deeper dark
of the arms Plutonic, and pierced with the passion of dense gloom,
among the splendor of torches of darkness, shedding darkness on the lost
    bride and her groom.

1923

---

1. Keith Sagar challenges the accepted view that this is the final version of the poem in "The Genesis of 'Bavarian Gentians,' " *The D. H. Lawrence Review*, Spring 1975, pp. 47–53. He prefers the longer version printed in *The Collected Poems of D. H. Lawrence* (1964), edited by Vivian de Sola Pinto and Warren Roberts, page 975.
2. Pluto was god of the underworld in classical mythology; he was also called "Dis" (line 8).

3. Bride of Pluto, who abducted her from the earth, and daughter of Demeter, goddess of the fruits of the earth (line 14). She was allowed to return to earth every spring but had to descend again to Hades in the autumn, "the frosted September." Demeter and Persephone were central figures in ancient fertility myths, where Persephone's annual descent and return were linked with the death and rebirth of vegetation.

Snake

A snake came to my water trough
On a hot, hot day, and I in pajamas for the heat,
To drink there.

In the deep, strange-scented shade of the great dark carob tree
I came down the steps with my pitcher   5
And must wait, must stand and wait, for there he was at the trough
 before me.

He reached down from a fissure in the earth-wall in the gloom
And trailed his yellow-brown slackness soft-bellied down, over the edge
 of the stone trough
And rested his throat upon the stone bottom,
And where the water had dripped from the tap, in a small clearness,   10
He sipped with his straight mouth,
Softly drank through his straight gums, into his slack long body,
Silently.

Someone was before me at my water trough,
And I, like a second-comer, waiting.   15

He lifted his head from his drinking, as cattle do,
And looked at me vaguely, as drinking cattle do,
And flickered his two-forked tongue from his lips, and mused a moment,
And stooped and drank a little more,
Being earth-brown, earth-golden from the burning bowels of the
 earth   20
On the day of Sicilian July, with Etna smoking.

The voice of my education said to me
He must be killed,
For in Sicily the black black snakes are innocent, the gold are venom-
 ous.

And voices in me said, If you were a man   25
You would take a stick and break him now, and finish him off.

But must I confess how I liked him,
How glad I was he had come like a guest in quiet, to drink at my water
 trough
And depart peaceful, pacified, and thankless
Into the burning bowels of this earth?   30

Was it cowardice, that I dared not kill him?
Was it perversity, that I longed to talk to him?

Was it humility, to feel so honored?
I felt so honored.

And yet those voices: 35
If you were not afraid, you would kill him!

And truly I was afraid, I was most afraid,
But even so, honored still more
That he should seek my hospitality
From out the dark door of the secret earth.   40

He drank enough
And lifted his head, dreamily, as one who has drunken,
And flickered his tongue like a forked night on the air, so black,
Seeming to lick his lips,
And looked around like a god, unseeing, into the air,   45
And slowly turned his head,
And slowly, very slowly, as if thrice adream
Proceeded to draw his slow length curving round
And climb the broken bank of my wall-face.

And as he put his head into that dreadful hole,   50
And as he slowly drew up, snake-easing his shoulders, and entered fur-
    ther,
A sort of horror, a sort of protest against his withdrawing into that horrid
    black hole,
Deliberately going into the blackness, and slowly drawing himself after,
Overcame me now his back was turned.

I looked round, I put down my pitcher,   55
I picked up a clumsy log
And threw it at the water trough with a clatter.

I think it did not hit him;
But suddenly that part of him that was left behind convulsed in undig-
    nified haste,
Writhed like lightning, and was gone   60
Into the black hole, the earth-lipped fissure in the wall-front
At which, in the intense still noon, I stared with fascination.

And immediately I regretted it.
I thought how paltry, how vulgar, what a mean act!
I despised myself and the voices of my accursed human education.   65

And I thought of the albatross,[1]
And I wished he would come back, my snake.

---

1. In Coleridge's *Ancient Mariner*.

For he seemed to me again like a king,
Like a king in exile, uncrowned in the underworld,
Now due to be crowned again.   70

And so, I missed my chance with one of the lords
Of life.
And I have something to expiate:
A pettiness.

                                                        1923

How Beastly the Bourgeois Is

How beastly the bourgeois is
especially the male of the species—

Presentable, eminently presentable—
shall I make you a present of him?

Isn't he handsome? Isn't he healthy? Isn't he a fine specimen?   5
Doesn't he look the fresh clean Englishman, outside?
Isn't it God's own image? tramping his thirty miles a day
after partridges, or a little rubber ball?
wouldn't you like to be like that, well off, and quite the thing?

Oh, but wait!   10
Let him meet a new emotion, let him be faced with another man's need,
let him come home to a bit of moral difficulty, let life face him with a
        new demand on his understanding
and then watch him go soggy, like a wet meringue.
Watch him turn into a mess, either a fool or a bully.   15
Just watch the display of him, confronted with a new demand on his
        intelligence,
a new life-demand.

How beastly the bourgeois is
especially the male of the species—   20

Nicely groomed, like a mushroom
standing there so sleek and erect and eyeable—
and like a fungus, living on the remains of bygone life
sucking his life out of the dead leaves of greater life than his own.

And even so, he's stale, he's been there too long.   25
Touch him, and you'll find he's all gone inside
just like an old mushroom, all wormy inside, and hollow
under a smooth skin and an upright appearance.

Full of seething, wormy, hollow feelings
rather nasty—   30
How beastly the bourgeois is!

Standing in their thousands, these appearances, in damp England
what a pity they can't all be kicked over
like sickening toadstools, and left to melt back, swiftly
into the soil of England.   35

1929

The Ship of Death

1

Now it is autumn and the falling fruit
and the long journey towards oblivion.

The apples falling like great drops of dew
to bruise themselves an exit from themselves.

And it is time to go, to bid farewell   5
to one's own self, and find an exit
from the fallen self.

2

Have you built your ship of death, O have you?
O build your ship of death, for you will need it.

The grim frost is at hand, when the apples will fall   10
thick, almost thundrous, on the hardened earth.

And death is on the air like a smell of ashes!
Ah! can't you smell it?

And in the bruised body, the frightened soul
finds itself shrinking, wincing from the cold   15
that blows upon it through the orifices.

3

And can a man his own quietus make
with a bare bodkin?[1]

With daggers, bodkins, bullets, man can make
a bruise or break of exit for his life;   20
but is that a quietus, O tell me, is it quietus?

Surely not so! for how could murder, even self-murder
ever a quietus make?

1. Cf. "For who would bear the whips and scorns of time, / . . . When he himself might his quietus make / With a bare bodkin?" (*Hamlet*, 3.1.74–75).

4

O let us talk of quiet that we know,
that we can know, the deep and lovely quiet   25
of a strong heart at peace!

How can we this, our own quietus, make?

5

Build then the ship of death, for you must take
the longest journey, to oblivion.

And die the death, the long and painful death   30
that lies between the old self and the new.

Already our bodies are fallen, bruised, badly bruised,
already our souls are oozing through the exit
of the cruel bruise.

Already the dark and endless ocean of the end   35
is washing in through the breaches of our wounds,
already the flood is upon us.

Oh build your ship of death, your little ark
and furnish it with food, with little cakes, and wine
for the dark flight down oblivion.   40

6

Piecemeal the body dies, and the timid soul
has her footing washed away, as the dark flood rises.

We are dying, we are dying, we are all of us dying
and nothing will stay the death-flood rising within us
and soon it will rise on the world, on the outside world.   45

We are dying, we are dying, piecemeal our bodies are dying
and our strength leaves us,
and our soul cowers naked in the dark rain over the flood,
cowering in the last branches of the tree of our life.

7

We are dying, we are dying, so all we can do   50
is now to be willing to die, and to build the ship
of death to carry the soul on the longest journey.

A little ship, with oars and food
and little dishes, and all accoutrements
fitting and ready for the departing soul.   55

Now launch the small ship, now as the body dies
and life departs, launch out, the fragile soul
in the fragile ship of courage, the ark of faith
with its store of food and little cooking pans

and change of clothes,   60
upon the flood's back waste
upon the waters of the end
upon the sea of death, where still we sail
darkly, for we cannot steer, and have no port.

There is no port, there is nowhere to go   65
only the deepening blackness darkening still
blacker upon the soundless, ungurgling flood
darkness at one with darkness, up and down
and sideways utterly dark, so there is no direction any more
and the little ship is there; yet she is gone.   70
She is not seen, for there is nothing to see her by.
She is gone! gone! and yet
somewhere she is there.
Nowhere!

8

And everything is gone, the body is gone   75
completely under, gone, entirely gone.
The upper darkness is heavy as the lower,
between them the little ship
is gone

It is the end, it is oblivion.

9

And yet out of eternity a thread   80
separates itself on the blackness,
a horizontal thread
that fumes a little with pallor upon the dark.

Is it illusion? or does the pallor fume
A little higher?
Ah wait, wait, for there's the dawn,   85
the cruel dawn of coming back to life
out of oblivion

Wait, wait, the little ship
drifting, beneath the deathly ashy gray
of a flood-dawn.   90

Wait, wait! even so, a flush of yellow
and strangely, O chilled wan soul, a flush of rose.

A flush of rose, and the whole thing starts again.

10

The flood subsides, and the body, like a worn sea-shell
emerges strange and lovely.   95
And the little ship wings home, faltering and lapsing
on the pink flood,

and the frail soul steps out, into her house again
filling the heart with peace.

Swings the heart renewed with peace   100
even of oblivion.

Oh build your ship of death, oh build it!
for you will need it.
For the voyage of oblivion awaits you.

1929–30   1933

T. S. ELIOT
1888–1965

1915:   Settles in London.
1917:   *Prufrock and Other Observations.*
1922:   *The Waste Land.*
1927:   Becomes British subject; confirmed in Anglican Church.
1944:   *Four Quartets.*

Thomas Stearns Eliot was born in St. Louis, Missouri, of New England stock. He entered Harvard in 1906, and was influenced there by the anti-Romanticism of Irving Babbitt and the philosophical and critical interests of George Santayana, as well as by the enthusiasm that prevailed in certain Harvard circles for Elizabethan and Jacobean literature, the Italian Renaissance, and Indian mystical philosophy. His philosophical studies included intensive work on the English idealist philosopher F. H. Bradley, on whom he eventually wrote his Harvard dissertation. (Bradley's emphasis on the private nature of individual experience, "a circle enclosed on the outside," had considerable influence on the private imagery of Eliot's poetry and on the view of the relation between the individual and other individuals reflected in much of his poetry.) Later Eliot studied literature and philosophy in France and Germany, before going to England shortly after the outbreak of World War I in 1914. He studied Greek philosophy at Oxford, taught school in London, and then obtained a position with Lloyd's Bank. In 1915 he married an English writer, Vivienne Haigh-Wood, but the marriage was not a success. She was highly neurotic and increasingly in bad health. The strain told on Eliot, too. By November 1921, distress and worry had brought him to the verge of a nervous breakdown and, on medical advice, he went to recuperate in a Swiss sanitorium. Two months later he returned, pausing in Paris long enough to give Ezra Pound the manuscript of *The Waste Land.* Eliot left his wife in 1933, and she was eventually committed to a mental home where she died in 1947. Ten years later he married again and, for the 8 years that remained to him, at last knew happiness.

Eliot started writing literary and philosophical reviews soon after settling in London. He wrote for the *Athenaeum* and the *Times Literary Supple-*

ment, among other periodicals, and was assistant editor of the *Egoist* from 1917 to 1919. In 1922 he founded the influential quarterly *Criterion*, which he edited until it ceased publication in 1939. His poetry first appeared in 1915, when *The Love Song of J. Alfred Prufrock* was printed in *Poetry* magazine (Chicago) and a few other short poems were published in the short-lived periodical, *Blast*. His first published collection of poems was *Prufrock and Other Observations*, 1917; two other small collections followed in 1919 and 1920; in 1922 *The Waste Land* appeared, first in the *Criterion* in October, then in the *Dial* (in America) in November, and finally in book form. *Poems 1909–25* (1925) collected these earlier poems. Meanwhile he was also publishing collections of his critical essays, notably *The Sacred Wood* in 1920 and *Homage to John Dryden* in 1924. *For Lancelot Andrewes* followed in 1928 and in 1932 he included most of these earlier essays with some new ones in *Selected Essays*. In 1925 he joined the London publishing firm of Faber and Gwyer, becoming a director when the firm became Faber and Faber. He became a British subject and joined the Church of England in 1927.

"Our civilization comprehends great variety and complexity, and this variety and complexity, playing upon a refined sensibility, must produce various and complex results. The poet must become more and more comprehensive, more allusive, more indirect, in order to force, to dislocate if necessary, language into his meaning." This remark, from Eliot's essay on *The Metaphysical Poets* (1921), gives one clue to his poetic method from *Prufrock* through *The Waste Land*. In the tradition of the Georgian poets who were active when he settled in London, he saw an exhausted poetic mode being employed, with no verbal excitement or original craftsmanship. He sought to make poetry more subtle, more suggestive, and at the same time more precise. He had learned from the Imagists the necessity of clear and precise images, and he learned, too, from the philosopher-poet T. E. Hulme and from his early supporter and adviser Ezra Pound to fear romantic softness and to regard the poetic medium rather than the poet's personality as the important factor. At the same time, the "hard dry" images advocated by Hulme were not enough for him; he wanted wit, allusiveness, irony. He saw in the metaphysical poets how wit and passion could be combined, and he saw in the French Symbolists how an image could be both absolutely precise in what it referred to physically and at the same time endlessly suggestive in the meanings it set up because of its relationship to other images. The combination of precision, symbolic suggestion, and ironic mockery in the poetry of the late nineteenth-century French poet Jules Laforgue attracted and influenced him, and he was influenced too by other nineteenth-century French poets: by Théophile Gautier's artful carving of impersonal shapes of meaning; by Charles Baudelaire's strangely evocative explorations of the symbolic suggestions of objects and images; by the Symbolists poets Paul Verlaine, Arthur Rimbaud, and Stéphane Mallarmé. He also found in the Jacobean dramatists a flexible blank verse with overtones of colloquial movement: Middleton, Tourneur, Webster, and others, taught him as much—in the way of verse movement, imagery, the counterpointing of the accent of conversation and the note of terror—as either the metaphysicals or the French Symbolists.

Hulme's protests against the romantic concept of poetry fitted in well enough with what Eliot had learned from Irving Babbitt at Harvard; yet for all his severity with such poets as Shelley, for all his conscious cultivation of a classical viewpoint and his insistence on order and discipline rather than on mere self-expression in art, one side of Eliot's poetic genius is, in one sense of the word, Romantic. The Symbolist influence on his imagery, his interest in the evocative and the suggestive, such lines as "And fiddled whisper music on those strings / And bats with baby faces in the violet light / Whistled, and beat their wings," and such recurring images as the hyacinth girl and the rose garden, all show what could be called a Romantic element in his poetry. But it is combined with a dry ironic allusiveness, a play of wit, and a collo-quial element, which are not normally found in poets of the romantic tra-dition.

Eliot's real novelty—and the cause of much bewilderment when his poems first appeared—was his deliberate elimination of all merely connective and transitional passages, his building up of the total pattern of meaning through the immediate juxtaposition of images without overt explanation of what they are doing, together with his use of oblique references to other works of literature (some of them quite obscure to most readers of his time). *Prufrock* presents a symbolic landscape where the meaning emerges from the mutual interaction of the images, and that meaning is enlarged by echoes, often ironic, of Hesiod and Dante and Shakespeare. *The Waste Land* is a series of scenes and images with no author's voice intervening to tell us where we are, but with the implications developed through multiple contrasts and through analogies with older literary works often referred to in a distorted quotation or half-concealed allusion. Further, the works referred to are not necessarily works which are central in the Western literary tradition: besides Dante and Shakespeare there are pre-Socratic philosophers, minor (as well as major) seventeenth-century poets and dramatists, works of anthropology, history, and philosophy, and other echoes of the poet's private reading. In a culture where there is no longer any assurance on the part of the poet that his public has a common cultural heritage, a common knowledge of works of the past, Eliot felt it necessary to build up his own body of references. It is this which marks the difference between Eliot's use of earlier literature and, say, Milton's. Both poets are difficult to the modern reader, who needs editorial assistance in recognizing and understanding many of the allu-sions—but Milton was drawing on a body of knowledge common to edu-cated people in his day. Nevertheless, this aspect of Eliot can be exaggerated: the fact remains that the nature of his imagery together with the movement of his verse generally succeed in setting the tone he requires, in establishing the area of meaning to be developed, so that even a reader ignorant of most of the literary allusions can often get the "feel" of the poem and achieve some understanding of what it says.

Eliot's early poetry, until at least the middle 1920s, is mostly concerned in one way or another with the Waste Land, with aspects of the decay of culture in the modern Western world. After his formal acceptance of Angli-can Christianity we find a penitential note in much of his verse, a note of quiet searching for spiritual peace, with considerable allusion to Biblical, liturgical, and mystical religious literature and to Dante. *Ash Wednesday* (1930), a poem in six parts, much less fiercely concentrated in style than the earlier poetry, explores with gentle insistence a mood both penitential and questioning. The so-called "Ariel" poems (the title has nothing to do with their form or content) present or explore aspects of religious doubt or discov-ery or revelation, sometimes, as in *Marina*, using a purely secular imagery and sometimes, as in *Journey of the Magi*, drawing on Biblical incident. In *Four Quartets* (of which the first, *Burnt Norton*, appeared in the *Collected Poems* of 1935, though all four were not completed until 1943, when they were published together) Eliot further explored essentially religious moods, dealing with the relation between time and eternity and the cultivation of that selfless passivity which can yield the moment of timeless revelation in the midst of time. The mocking irony, the savage humor, the deliberately startling juxtaposition of the sordid and the romantic, give way in these later poems to a quieter poetic idiom, often still complexly allusive but never deliberately shocking.

Eliot's criticism was the criticism of a practicing poet who worked out in relation to his reading of older literature what he needed to hold and to admire. He lent the growing weight of his authority to that shift in literary taste that replaced Milton by Donne as the great seventeenth-century English poet, and replaced Tennyson in the nineteenth century by Hopkins. His often-quoted description of the late seventeenth-century "dissociation of sensibility"—keeping wit and passion in separate compartments—which he saw as determining the course of English poetry throughout the eighteenth and nineteenth centuries, is both a contribution to the rewriting of English literary history and an explanation of what he was aiming at in his own poetry: the re-establishment of that *unified* sensibility he found in Donne and other early seventeenth-century poets and dramatists. His view of tradition, his dislike of the poetic exploitation of the author's own personality, his advocacy of what he called "orthodoxy," made him suspicious of what he considered eccentric geniuses such as Blake and D. H. Lawrence. On the other side, his dislike of the grandiloquent and his insistence on complexity and on the mingling of the formal with the conversational made him distrustful of the influence of Milton on English poetry. He considered himself "classicist in literature, royalist in politics, and Anglo-Catholic in religion" (*For Lancelot Andrewes*, 1928), in favor of order against chaos, tradition against eccentricity, authority against rampant individualism; yet his own poetry is in many respects untraditional and certainly highly individual in tone. His conservative and even authoritarian habit of mind alienated some who admire—and some whose own poetry has been much influenced by—his poetry.

Eliot's plays have all been, directly or indirectly, on religious themes. *Murder in the Cathedral* (1935) deals with the murder of Archbishop Thomas à Becket in an appropriately ritual manner, with much use of a chorus and with the central speech in the form of a sermon by the archbishop in his cathedral shortly before his murder. *The Family Reunion* (1939) deals with the problem of guilt and redemption in a modern upper-class English family; it makes a deliberate attempt to combine choric devices from Greek tragedy with a poetic idiom subdued to the accents of drawing-room conversation. In his three later plays, all written in the 1950s, *The Cocktail Party*, *The Confidential Clerk*, and *The Elder Statesman*, he achieved popular success by casting a serious religious theme in the form of a sophisticated modern social comedy, using a verse that is so conversational in movement that when spoken in the theater it does not sound like verse at all.

Critics differ on the degree to which Eliot succeeded in his last plays in combining box-office success with dramatic effectiveness. But there is no disagreement on his importance as one of the great renovators of the English poetic dialect, whose influence on a whole generation of poets, critics, and intellectuals generally was enormous. His range as a poet is limited, and his interest in the great middle ground of human experience (as distinct from the extremes of saint and sinner) deficient: but when in 1948 he was awarded the rare honor of the Order of Merit by King George VI and also gained the Nobel Prize in literature, his positive qualities were widely and fully recognized—his poetic cunning, his fine craftsmanship, his original accent, his historical and representative importance as *the* poet of the modern Symbolist-metaphysical tradition.

The Love Song of J. Alfred Prufrock[1]

> S'io credesse che mia risposta fosse
> A persona che mai tornasse al mondo,
> Questa fiamma staria senza piu scosse.
> Ma perciocche giammai di questo fondo
> Non torno vivo alcun, s'i'odo il vero,
> Senza tema d'infamia ti rispondo.[2]

Let us go then, you and I,
When the evening is spread out against the sky
Like a patient etherized upon a table;
Let us go, through certain half-deserted streets,
The muttering retreats   5
Of restless nights in one-night cheap hotels
And sawdust restaurants with oyster shells:
Streets that follow like a tedious argument
Of insidious intent
To lead you to an overwhelming question . . .   10
Oh, do not ask, "What is it?"
Let us go and make our visit.

In the room the women come and go
Talking of Michelangelo.

The yellow fog that rubs its back upon the windowpanes,   15
The yellow smoke that rubs its muzzle on the windowpanes
Licked its tongue into the corners of the evening,
Lingered upon the pools that stand in drains,
Let fall upon its back the soot that falls from chimneys,
Slipped by the terrace, made a sudden leap,   20
And seeing that it was a soft October night,
Curled once about the house, and fell asleep.

---

1. The title implies an ironic contrast between the romantic suggestions of "love song" and the dully prosaic name "J. Alfred Prufrock."
2. "If I thought that my reply would be to one who would ever return to the world, this flame would stay without further movement; but since none has ever returned alive from this depth, if what I hear is true, I answer you without fear of infamy." Dante, *Inferno* 27.61–66. Guido da Montefeltro, shut up in his flame (the punishment given to false counselors), tells the shame of his evil life to Dante because he believes Dante will never return to earth to report it.

And indeed there will be time[3]
For the yellow smoke that slides along the street,
Rubbing its back upon the windowpanes;   25
There will be time, there will be time
To prepare a face to meet the faces that you meet;
There will be time to murder and create,
And time for all the works and days of hands[4]
That lift and drop a question on your plate;   30
Time for you and time for me,
And time yet for a hundred indecisions,
And for a hundred visions and revisions,
Before the taking of a toast and tea.

    In the room the women come and go   35
Talking of Michelangelo.

    And indeed there will be time
To wonder, "Do I dare?" and, "Do I dare?"
Time to turn back and descend the stair,
With a bald spot in the middle of my hair—
(They will say: "How his hair is growing thin!")   40
My morning coat, my collar mounting firmly to the chin,
My necktie rich and modest, but asserted by a simple pin—
(They will say: "But how his arms and legs are thin!")
Do I dare   45
Disturb the universe?
In a minute there is time
For decisions and revisions which a minute will reverse.

    For I have known them all already, known them all—
Have known the evenings, mornings, afternoons,   50
I have measured out my life with coffee spoons;
I know the voices dying with a dying fall[5]
Beneath the music from a farther room.
    So how should I presume?

    And I have known the eyes already, known them all—   55
The eyes that fix you in a formulated phrase,
And when I am formulated, sprawling on a pin,
When I am pinned and wriggling on the wall,
Then how should I begin
To spit out all the butt-ends of my days and ways?   60
    And how should I presume?

---

3. Cf. Andrew Marvell's *To His Coy Mistress:* "Had we but world enough and time . . ."
4. *Works and Days* is a poem about the farming year by Hesiod, Greek poet of 8th century B.C. Eliot's contrast is between useful agricultural labor and the futile "works and days of hands" engaged in meaningless social gesturing.
5. Ironic recollection of Orsino's speech in *Twelfth Night* (1.1.4): "That strain again! It had a dying fall."

And I have known the arms already, known them all—
Arms that are braceleted and white and bare
(But in the lamplight, downed with light brown hair!)
Is it perfume from a dress   65
That makes me so digress?
Arms that lie along a table, or wrap about a shawl.
    And should I then presume?
    And how should I begin?

                              .   .   .

Shall I say, I have gone at dusk through narrow streets   70
And watched the smoke that rises from the pipes
Of lonely men in shirt-sleeves, leaning out of windows?   .   .   .

I should have been a pair of ragged claws
Scuttling across the floors of silent seas.[6]

                              .   .   .

And the afternoon, the evening, sleeps so peacefully!   75
Smoothed by long fingers,
Asleep . . . tired . . . or it malingers,
Stretched on the floor, here beside you and me.
Should I, after tea and cakes and ices,
Have the strength to force the moment to its crisis?   80
But though I have wept and fasted, wept and prayed,
Though I have seen my head (grown slightly bald) brought in upon a
        platter,[7]
I am no prophet—and here's no great matter;
I have seen the moment of my greatness flicker,
And I have seen the eternal Footman hold my coat, and snicker,   85
And in short, I was afraid.

And would it have been worth it, after all,
After the cups, the marmalade, the tea,
Among the porcelain, among some talk of you and me,
Would it have been worth while,   90
To have bitten off the matter with a smile,
To have squeezed the universe into a ball[8]
To roll it toward some overwhelming question,
To say: "I am Lazarus,[9] come from the dead,
Come back to tell you all, I shall tell you all"—   95
If one, settling a pillow by her head,
    Should say: "That is not what I meant at all.
    That is not it, at all."

6. I.e., he would have been better as a crab on
the ocean bed. Perhaps, too, the motion of a crab
suggests futility and growing old; cf. *Hamlet*
2.2.205–6: "for you yourself, sir, should be old as
I am, if, like a crab, you could go backward."
7. Like that of John the Baptist. See Mark 6.17–

28 and Matthew 14.3–11.
8. Cf., again Marvell's *To His Coy Mistress:* "Let
us roll all our strength and all / Our sweetness up
into a ball, / And tear our pleasures with rough
strife / Thorough the iron gates of life."
9. Cf. Luke 16.19–31 and John 11.1–44.

And would it have been worth it, after all,
Would it have been worth while,   100
After the sunsets and the dooryards and the sprinkled streets,
After the novels, after the teacups, after the skirts that trail along the
    floor—
And this, and so much more?—
It is impossible to say just what I mean!
But as if a magic lantern threw the nerves in patterns on a screen: 105
Would it have been worth while
If one, settling a pillow or throwing off a shawl,
And turning toward the window, should say:
    "That is not it at all,
    That is not what I meant, at all."   110

          . . .

    No! I am not Prince Hamlet, nor was meant to be;
Am an attendant lord, one that will do
To swell a progress[1] start a scene or two,
Advise the prince; no doubt, an easy tool,
Deferential, glad to be of use,   115
Politic, cautious, and meticulous;
Full of high sentence,[2] but a bit obtuse;
At times, indeed, almost ridiculous—
Almost, at times, the Fool.

    I grow old . . . I grow old . . .   120
I shall wear the bottoms of my trousers rolled.

    Shall I part my hair behind? Do I dare to eat a peach?
I shall wear white flannel trousers, and walk upon the beach.
I have heard the mermaids singing, each to each.

I do not think that they will sing to me.   125

I have seen them riding seaward on the waves
Combing the white hair of the waves blown back
When the wind blows the water white and black.

We have lingered in the chambers of the sea
By sea-girls wreathed with seaweed red and brown   130
Till human voices wake us, and we drown.

1910–11   1915, 1917

---

1. In the Elizabethan sense of a state journey made
by a royal or noble person. Elizabethan plays
sometimes showed such "progresses" crossing the
stage.
2. In its older meanings, "opinions," "senten-
tiousness."

Sweeney Among the Nightingales

ómoi, péplegmai kairían plegén éso.[1]

Apeneck Sweeney spreads his knees
Letting his arms hang down to laugh,
The zebra stripes along his jaw
Swelling to maculate[2] giraffe.

The circles of the stormy moon   5
Slide westward toward the River Plate,[3]
Death and the Raven drift above
And Sweeney guards the hornèd gate.[4]

Gloomy Orion and the Dog
Are veiled;[5] and hushed the shrunken seas;   10
The person in the Spanish cape
Tries to sit on Sweeney's knees

Slips and pulls the tablecloth
Overturns a coffee cup,
Reorganized upon the floor   15
She yawns and draws a stocking up;

The silent man in mocha brown
Sprawls at the window sill and gapes;
The waiter brings in oranges
Bananas figs and hothouse grapes;   20

The silent vertebrate in brown
Contracts and concentrates, withdraws;
Rachel *née* Rabinovitch
Tears at the grapes with murderous paws;

She and the lady in the cape   25
Are suspect, thought to be in league;
Therefore the man with heavy eyes
Declines the gambit, shows fatigue,

Leaves the room and reappears
Outside the window, leaning in,   30
Branches of wistaria
Circumscribe a golden grin;

1. "Alas, I am struck with a mortal blow within" (Aeschylus, *Agamemnon*, line 1343). The voice of Agamemnon heard crying out from the palace as he is murdered by his wife Clytemnestra.
2. Spotted, stained.
3. Estuary on South American coast between Argentina and Uruguay, formed by the Uruguay and Paraná rivers.
4. The gates of horn, in Hades, through which true dreams come to the upper world.
5. "Orion" and the "Dog" are the constellations. For Sweeney and his lady friend, the gate of vision is blocked and the great mythmaking constellations are "veiled."

The host with someone indistinct
Converses at the door apart,
The nightingales are singing near   35
The Convent of the Sacred Heart,

And sang within the bloody wood
When Agamemnon cried aloud,[6]
And let their liquid siftings fall
To stain the stiff dishonored shroud.   40

1918, 1919

The Hippopotamus

*And when this epistle is read among you, cause that
it be read also in the church of the Laodiceans.*[1]

The broad-backed hippopotamus
Rests on his belly in the mud;
Although he seems so firm to us
He is merely flesh and blood.

Flesh and blood is weak and frail,   5
Susceptible to nervous shock;
While the True Church can never fail
For it is based upon a rock.[2]

The hippo's feeble steps may err
In compassing material ends,   10
While the True Church need never stir
To gather in its dividends.

The 'potamus can never reach
The mango on the mango-tree;
But fruits of pomegranate and peach   15
Refresh the Church from over sea.

At mating time the hippo's voice
Betrays inflections hoarse and odd,
But every week we hear rejoice
The Church, at being one with God.[3]   20

6. Agamemnon was not murdered in a "bloody wood," but in his bath. Eliot is here telescoping Agamemnon's murder with the wood where Philomela, in Greek myth, was ravished by her sister's husband Terens (she was subsequently turned into a nightingale), and also with the "bloody wood" of Nemi, where, in ancient times, the old priest was slain by his successor (as described in the first chapter of Sir James Frazer's *Golden Bough*).

1. Colossians, 4.16. The inhabitants of Laodicea, a city in Asia Minor, were regarded by St John as "lukewarm, and neither cold nor hot" (Revelation 3.16).

2. Jesus said to his disciple: "And I also say unto thee, that thou art Peter [Greek, *Petros*], and upon this rock [Greek, *petra*] I will build my church" (Matthew 16.18).

3. The Biblical Song of Solomon is traditionally interpreted as depicting Christ's marriage with His Church.

The hippopotamus's day
Is passed in sleep; at night he hunts;
God works in a mysterious way—[4]
The Church can sleep and feed at once.

I saw the 'potamus take wing[5]   25
Ascending from the damp savannas,
And quiring angels round him sing
The praise of God, in loud hosannas.

Blood of the Lamb shall wash him clean
And him shall heavenly arms enfold,   30
Among the saints he shall be seen
Performing on a harp of gold.

He shall be washed as white as snow,
By all the martyr'd virgins kist,
While the True Church remains below   35
Wrapt in the old miasmal mist.

                                                            1920

The Waste Land   This is a poem about spiritual dryness, about the kind of existence in which no regenerating belief gives significance and value to men's daily activities, sex brings no fruitfulness, and death heralds no resurrection. Eliot himself gives one of the main clues to the theme and structure of the poem in a general note, in which he stated that "not only the title, but the plan and a good deal of the symbolism of the poem were suggested by Miss Jessie L. Weston's book on the Grail legend: *From Ritual to Romance*" (1920). He further acknowledged a general indebtedness to Sir James Frazer's *Golden Bough* (12 volumes, 1890–1915), "especially the two volumes *Adonis, Attis, Osiris*," in which Frazer deals with ancient vegetation myths and fertility ceremonies. Weston's study, drawing on material from Frazer and other anthropologists, traced the relationship of these myths and rituals to Christianity and most especially to the legend of the Holy Grail. She found an archetypal fertility myth in the story of the Fisher King whose death, infirmity, or impotence (there are many forms of the myth) brought drought and desolation to the land and failure of the power to reproduce themselves among both humans and beasts. This symbolic Waste Land can be revived only if a "questing knight" goes to the Chapel Perilous, situated in the heart of it, and there asks certain ritual questions about the Grail (or Cup) and the Lance—originally fertility symbols, female and male respectively. The proper asking of these questions revives the king and restores fertility to the land. The relation of this original Grail myth to fertility cults and rituals found in many different civilizations, and represented by stories of a dying god who is later resurrected (e.g., Tammuz, Adonis, Attis), shows their common origin in a response to the cyclical movement of the seasons, with vegetation dying in winter to be resurrected again in the spring. Chris-

4. Cf. William Cowper's *Olney Hymn* 35: "God moves in a mysterious way / His wonders to perform; / He plants his footsteps in the sea, / And rides upon the storm."
5. Cf. Revelation 20.1: "And I saw an angel coming down out of heaven . . ."

tianity, according to Weston, gave its own spiritual meaning to the myth; it "did not hesitate to utilize the already existing medium of instruction, but boldly identified the Deity of Vegetation, regarded as Life Principle, with the God of the Christian Faith." The Fisher King is related to the use of the fish symbol in early Christianity. Weston states "with certainty that the Fish is a Life symbol of immemorial antiquity, and that the title of Fisher has, from the earliest ages, been associated with the Deities who were held to be specially connected with the origin and preservation of Life." Eliot, following Weston, thus uses a great variety of mythological and religious material, both occidental and oriental, in order to paint a symbolic picture of the modern Waste Land and the need for regeneration. The terror of that life—its loneliness, emptiness, and irrational apprehensions—as well as its misuse of sexuality are vividly presented, but, paradoxically, the poem ends with a benediction. Another significant general source for the poem is the composer Richard Wagner, some of whose operas (*Götterdämmerung* ["Twilight of the Gods"], *Parsifal, Rheingold*, and *Tristan and Isolde*) are drawn on.

The poem as published owed a great deal to the severe pruning of Ezra Pound; the original manuscript, with Pound's excisions and comments, provides fascinating information about the genesis and development of the poem. It was reproduced in facsimile in 1971, edited by Eliot's widow Valerie Eliot, who also supplied notes supplementing those that Eliot himself added when the poem was first published in book form in 1922 and which are included with the present editors' footnotes to the poem.

The Waste Land

"Nam Sibyllam quidem Cumis ego ipse oculis meis vidi in ampulla pendere, et cum illi pueri dicerent: Σίβυλλα τί θέλεις; respondebat illa: ἀποθανεῖν θέλω."[1]

FOR EZRA POUND[2]
il miglior fabbro

1. *The Burial of the Dead*[3]

April is the cruelest month, breeding
Lilacs out of the dead land, mixing
Memory and desire, stirring
Dull roots with spring rain.
Winter kept us warm, covering   5

---

1. From the *Satyricon* of Petronius (1st century A.D.): "For once I myself saw with my own eyes the Sibyl at Cumae hanging in a cage, and when the boys said to her 'Sibyl, what do you want?' she replied, 'I want to die.' " (The Greek may be transliterated, "Síbylla tí théleis?" and "apothanéin thélo.") The Cumaean Sibyl was the most famous of the Sibyls, the prophetic old women of Greek mythology: she guided Aeneas through Hades in the *Aeneid*. She had been granted immortality by Apollo, but since she forgot to ask for perpetual youth, she shrank into withered old age and her authority declined.

2. Ezra Pound (1885–1972), the American expatriate poet who was a key figure in the modern movement in poetry, helped Eliot with the final revisions. "*Il miglior fabbro*" (i.e., the better craftsman) was a tribute originally paid to the Provençal poet Arnaut Daniel in Dante's *Purgatorio* 26.117.

3. The title comes from the Anglican burial service.

Earth in forgetful snow, feeding
A little life with dried tubers.
Summer surprised us, coming over the Starnbergersee[4]
With a shower of rain; we stopped in the colonnade,
And went on in sunlight, into the Hofgarten,[5]					10
And drank coffee, and talked for an hour.
Bin gar keine Russin, stamm' aus Litauen, echt deutsch.[6]
And when we were children, staying at the archduke's,
My cousin's, he took me out on a sled,
And I was frightened. He said, Marie,					15
Marie, hold on tight. And down we went.
In the mountains, there you feel free.
I read, much of the night, and go south in the winter.

    What are the roots that clutch, what branches grow
Out of this stony rubbish? Son of man,[7]					20
You cannot say, or guess, for you know only
A heap of broken images, where the sun beats,
And the dead tree gives no shelter, the cricket no relief,[8]
And the dry stone no sound of water. Only
There is shadow under this red rock,[9]					25
(Come in under the shadow of this red rock),
And I will show you something different from either
Your shadow at morning striding behind you
Or your shadow at evening rising to meet you;
I will show you fear in a handful of dust.					30
            Frisch weht der Wind
            Der Heimat zu
            Mein Irisch Kind,
            Wo weilest du?[1]
"You gave me hyacinths first a year ago;					35
They called me the hyacinth girl."
—Yet when we came back, late, from the Hyacinth garden,
Yours arms full, and your hair wet, I could not
Speak, and my eyes failed, I was neither
Living nor dead, and I knew nothing,					40

---

4. Lake near Munich. The scene in this and the following eight lines, which evokes European decadence before World War I, seems to have been suggested by an autobiographical work by Countess Marie Larisch. *My Past* (London, 1913), but Valerie Eliot says that Eliot had never read the book and got his information from the Countess directly, in conversations with her.
5. A small public park in Munich.
6. "I am not Russian at all; I come from Lithuania, a true German."
7. "Cf. Ezekiel 2.1" [Eliot's note]. Here God is addressing Ezekiel. "Son of man." God continues, "stand upon thy feet, and I will speak unto thee."

8. "Cf. Ecclesiastes 12.5" [Eliot's note]. The verse cited by Eliot is part of the Preacher's picture of the desolation of old age, "when they shall be afraid of that which is high, and fears shall be in the way, and the almond tree shall flourish, and the grasshopper shall be a burden, and desire shall fail . . ."
9. Cf. Isaiah 32.2: the "righteous king" "shall be . . . as rivers of water in a dry place, as the shadow of a great rock in a weary land."
1. "V. [see] *Tristan und Isolde*, 1, verses 5–8" [Eliot's note]. In Wagner's opera, a sailor recalls the girl he has left behind: "Fresh blows the wind to the homeland; my Irish child, where are you waiting?"

Looking into the heart of light, the silence.
Oed' und leer das Meer.[2]

Madame Sosostris,[3] famous clairvoyante,
Had a bad cold, nevertheless
Is known to be the wisest woman in Europe,   45
With a wicked pack of cards.[4] Here, said she,
Is your card, the drowned Phoenician Sailor,[5]
(Those are pearls that were his eyes. Look!)
Here is Belladonna, the Lady of the Rocks,[6]
The lady of situations.   50
Here is the man with three staves,[7] and here the Wheel,
And here is the one-eyed merchant,[8] and this card,
Which is blank, is something he carries on his back,
Which I am forbidden to see. I do not find
The Hanged Man.[9] Fear death by water.   55
I see crowds of people, walking round in a ring.
Thank you. If you see dear Mrs. Equitone,
Tell her I bring the horoscope myself:
One must be so careful these days.

2. "Id. [Ibid] 3, verse 24" [Eliot's note]. In act 3 of *Tristan und Isolde*, Tristan lies dying. He is waiting for Isolde to come to him from Cornwall, but a shepherd, appointed to watch for her sail, can only report, "Waste and empty is the sea."

3. A mock Egyptian name (suggested to Eliot by "Sesostris, the Sorceress of Ecbatana," the name assumed by a character in Aldous Huxley's novel *Crome Yellow* who dresses up as a gypsy to tell fortunes at a fair).

4. I.e., the Tarot deck of cards. The four suits of the Tarot pack, discussed by Jessie Weston in *From Ritual to Romance*, are the cup, lance, sword, and dish—the life symbols found in the Grail story. Weston noted that "today the Tarot has fallen somewhat into disrepute, being principally used for purposes of divination." Some of the cards mentioned in lines 46–56 are discussed by Eliot in his note to this passage: "I am not familiar with the exact constitution of the Tarot pack of cards, from which I have obviously departed to suit my own convenience. The Hanged Man, a member of the traditional pack, fits my purpose in two ways: because he is associated in my mind with the Hanged God of Frazer, and because I associate him with the hooded figure in the passage of the disciples to Emmaus in part 5. The Phoenician Sailor and the Merchant appear later; also the 'crowds of people,' and Death by Water is executed in part 4. The Man with Three Staves (an authentic member of the Tarot pack) I associate, quite arbitrarily, with the Fisher King himself."

5. See part 4. Phlebas the Phoenician and Mr. Eugenides, the Smyrna merchant—both of whom appear later in the poem—are different phases of the same symbolic character, here identified as the "Phoenician Sailor." Mr. Eugenides exports "currants" (line 210); the drowned Phlebas floats in the "current" (line 315). The line that follows is from Shakespeare's *Tempest* (1.2.398). Ariel's song to the shipwrecked Ferdinand, who was "sitting on a bank / Weeping again the King my father's wrack," when "this music crept by me on the waters." The song is about the supposed drowning of Ferdinand's father, Alonso. *The Waste Land* contains many references to *The Tempest*. Ferdinand is associated with Phlebas and Mr. Eugenides and therefore with the "drowned Phoenician Sailor."

6. "Belladonna": beautiful lady. The word also suggests Madonna (the Virgin Mary) and therefore the Madonna of the Rocks (as in Leonardo da Vinci's painting); the rocks symbolize the Church. Belladonna is also an eye cosmetic and a poison—the "deadly" nightshade. In the next line, the woman-figure of the Virgin becomes "the lady of situations," foreshadowing the neurasthenic lady of intrigue in Part 2.

7. Life-force symbol, associated by Eliot with the Fisher King. The "Wheel" is the wheel of fortune, whose turning represents the reversals of human life.

8. Mr. Eugenides, "one-eyed" because the figure is in profile on the card and also as a suggestion of evil or crookedness.

9. On his card in the Tarot pack he is shown hanging from one foot from a T-shaped cross. He symbolizes the self-sacrifice of the fertility god who is killed in order that his resurrection may bring fertility once again to land and people.

Unreal City,[1]   60
Under the brown fog of a winter dawn,
A crowd flowed over London Bridge, so many,[2]
I had not thought death had undone so many.
Sighs, short and infrequent, were exhaled,[3]
And each man fixed his eyes before his feet.   65
Flowed up the hill and down King William Street,
To where Saint Mary Woolnoth kept the hours
With a dead sound on the final stroke of nine.[4]
There I saw one I knew, and stopped him, crying: "Stetson![5]
You who were with me in the ships at Mylae![6]   70
That corpse you planted last year in your garden,
Has it begun to sprout?[7] Will it bloom this year?
Or has the sudden frost disturbed its bed?
Oh keep the Dog far hence, that's friend to men,
Or with his nails he'll dig it up again![8]   75
You! hypocrite lecteur!—mon semblable—mon frère!"[9]

2. A *Game of Chess*[1]

The Chair she sat in, like a burnished throne,[2]
Glowed on the marble, where the glass

---

1. "Cf. Baudelaire: '*Fourmillante cité, cité pleine de rêves, / Où le spectre en plein jour raccroche le passant*" [Eliot's note]. The lines are quoted from *Les Sept Vieillards* ("The Seven Old Men") by Charles Baudelaire (1821–1867); it is poem 93 of *Les Fleurs du Mal* ("The Flowers of Evil"). The lines may be translated: "Swarming city, city full of dreams, / Where the specter in broad daylight accosts the passerby."
2. "Cf. Inferno 3.55–57 . . ." [Eliot's note]. The note goes on to quote Dante's lines, which may be translated: "So long a train of people, / that I should never have believed / That death had undone so many." Dante, just outside the gate of Hell, has seen "the wretched souls of those who lived without disgrace and without praise." In his essay on Baudelaire Eliot argued that in a sense it was better to be positively evil than to be neither good nor evil.
3. "Cf. Inferno 4.25–27 . . ." [Eliot's note]. In Limbo, the first circle of Hell, Dante has found the virtuous heathen, who lived before Christianity and are therefore eternally unable to achieve their desire of seeing God. Dante's lines, cited by Eliot, mean: "Here, so far as I could tell by listening, / there was no lamentation except sighs, / which caused the eternal air to tremble."
4. "A phenomenon which I have often noticed" [Eliot's note]. St. Mary Woolnoth is a church in the "City" of London (the financial district); the crowd is flowing across London Bridge to work in the City.
5. Presumably representing the "average businessman."
6. The battle of Mylae (260 B.C.) in the First Punic War, which, like World War I, was fought for

economic reasons.
7. A distortion of the ritual death of the fertility god.
8. "Cf. the Dirge in Webster's *White Devil*" [Eliot's note]. In the play by John Webster (d. 1625), the dirge, sung by Cornelia, has the lines: "But keep the wolf far thence, that's foe to men, / For with his nails he'll dig them up again." Eliot makes the "wolf" into a "Dog," which is not a "foe" but a "friend" to man. There may be a reference to Sirius, the Dog Star, which is important in Egyptian mythology as heralding the fertilizing floods of the Nile (this is discussed by Miss Weston).
9. "V. Baudelaire, Preface to *Fleurs du Mal*" [Eliot's note]. The passage is the last line of the introductory poem *Au Lecteur* ("To the Reader") in Baudelaire's *Fleurs du Mal*; it may be translated: "Hypocrite reader!—my likeness—my brother!" *Au Lecteur* describes man as sunk in stupidity, sin, and evil; but the worst in "each man's foul menagerie of sin" is Boredom, the "*monstre délicat*"—"You know him, reader . . ."
1. The title suggests two plays by Thomas Middleton (1580–1627): *A Game at Chess* and, more significantly, *Women Beware Women*, which has a scene in which a mother-in-law is distracted by a game of chess while her daughter-in-law is seduced: every move in the chess game represents a move in the seduction.
2. "Cf. *Antony and Cleopatra*, 2.2.1.190" [Eliot's note]. In Shakespeare's play, Enobarbus's famous description of the first meeting of Antony and Cleopatra begins, "The barge she sat in, like a burnish'd throne, / Burn'd on the water . . ." Eliot's language in the opening lines of part 2 is full of ironic distortions of Enobarbus' speech.

Held up by standards wrought with fruited vines
From which a golden Cupidon peeped out   80
(Another hid his eyes behind his wing)
Doubled the flames of sevenbranched candelabra
Reflecting light upon the table as
The glitter of her jewels rose to meet it,
From satin cases poured in rich profusion.   85
In vials of ivory and colored glass
Unstoppered, lurked her strange synthetic perfumes,
Unguent, powdered, or liquid—troubled, confused
And drowned the sense in odors; stirred by the air
That freshened from the window, these ascended   90
In fattening the prolonged candle flames,
Flung their smoke into the laquearia,[3]
Stirring the pattern on the coffered ceiling.
Huge sea-wood fed with copper
Burned green and orange, framed by the colored stone,   95
In which sad light a carvèd dolphin swam.
Above the antique mantel was displayed
As though a window gave upon the sylvan scene[4]
The change of Philomel,[5] by the barbarous king
So rudely forced; yet there the nightingale   100
Filled all the desert with inviolable voice
And still she cried, and still the world pursues,
"Jug Jug"[6] to dirty ears.
And other withered stumps of time
Were told upon the walls; staring forms   105
Leaned out, leaning, hushing the room enclosed.
Footsteps shuffled on the stair.
Under the firelight, under the brush, her hair
Spread out in fiery points
Glowed into words, then would be savagely still.   110

   "My nerves are bad tonight. Yes, bad. Stay with me.
Speak to me. Why do you never speak. Speak.
   What are you thinking of? What thinking? What?
I never know what you are thinking. Think."

   I think we are in rats' alley[7]   115
Where the dead men lost their bones.

---

3. "Laquearia. V. *Aeneid*, 1. 726 . . ." [Eliot's note]. *Laquearia* means "a paneled ceiling," and Eliot's note quotes the passage in the *Aeneid* which was his source for the word. The passage may be translated: "Blazing torches hang from the gold-paneled ceiling [*laquearibus aureis*], and torches conquer the night with flames." Virgil is here describing the banquet given by Dido, queen of Carthage, for Aeneas, with whom she fell in love.
4. "Sylvan scene. V. Milton, *Paradise Lost*, 4.140" [Eliot's note]. The phrase is part of the first description of Eden, which we see through Satan's

eyes.
5. "V. Ovid, *Metamorphoses*, 6, Philomela" [Eliot's note]. The note is a reference to Ovid's version of the Greek myth of the rape of Philomela by "the barbarous king" Tereus, husband of her sister Procne. Philomela was transformed into a nightingale. Eliot's note for line 100 refers ahead to his elaboration of the nightingale's song.
6. Conventional representation of nightingale's song in Elizabethan poetry.
7. "Cf. part 3, line 195" [Eliot's note].

"What is that noise?"
                              The wind under the door.[8]
"What is that noise now? What is the wind doing?"
                              Nothing again nothing.   120
                                        "Do
You know nothing? Do you see nothing? Do you remember
Nothing?"

        I remember
Those are pearls that were his eyes.   125
"Are you alive, or not? Is there nothing in your head?"
                                        But

O O O O that Shakespeherian Rag—[9]
It's so elegant
So intelligent   130
"What shall I do now? What shall I do?"
"I shall rush out as I am, and walk the street
With my hair down, so. What shall we do tomorrow?
What shall we ever do?"
                              The hot water at ten.   135
And if it rains, a closed car at four.
And we shall play a game of chess,[1]
Pressing lidless eyes and waiting for a knock upon the door.

        When Lil's husband got demobbed,[2] I said—
I didn't mince my words, I said to her myself,   140
HURRY UP PLEASE ITS TIME[3]
Now Albert's coming back, make yourself a bit smart.
He'll want to know what you done with that money he gave you
To get yourself some teeth. He did, I was there.
You have them all out, Lil, and get a nice set,   145
He said, I swear, I can't bear to look at you.
And no more can't I, I said, and think of poor Albert,
He's been in the army four years, he wants a good time,
And if you don't give it him, there's others will, I said.
Oh is there, she said. Something o' that, I said.   150
Then I'll know who to thank, she said, and give me a straight look.
HURRY UP PLEASE ITS TIME
If you don't like it you can get on with it, I said.
Others can pick and choose if you can't.
But if Albert makes off, it won't be for lack of telling.   155
You ought to be ashamed, I said, to look so antique.
(And her only thirty-one.)

---

8. "Cf. Webster: 'Is the wind in that door still?' " [Eliot's note]. The line cited in the note is from John Webster's *The Devil's Law Case* (3.2.162).
9. American ragtime song, which was a hit of Ziegfeld's Follies in 1912.
1. "Cf. the game of chess in Middleton's *Women Beware Women*" [Eliot's note]. The significance of this chess game is discussed in note 1 for this section.
2. British slang for "demobilized" (discharged from the army).
3. The traditional call of the British bartender at closing time.

I can't help it, she said, pulling a long face,
It's them pills I took, to bring it off,[4] she said.
(She's had five already, and nearly died of young George.)   160
The chemist[5] said it would be all right, but I've never been the same.
You *are* a proper fool, I said.
Well, if Albert won't leave you alone, there it is, I said,
What you get married for if you don't want children?
HURRY UP PLEASE ITS TIME   165
Well, that Sunday Albert was home, they had a hot gammon,[6]
And they asked me in to dinner, to get the beauty of it hot—
HURRY UP PLEASE ITS TIME
HURRY UP PLEASE ITS TIME
Goonight Bill. Goonight Lou. Goonight May. Goonight.   170
Ta ta. Goonight. Goonight.
Good night, ladies, good night, sweet ladies, good night, good night.[7]

3. *The Fire Sermon*[8]

   The river's tent is broken: the last fingers of leaf
Clutch and sink into the wet bank. The wind
Crosses the brown land, unheard. The nymphs are departed.   175
Sweet Thames, run softly, till I end my song.[9]
The river bears no empty bottles, sandwich papers,
Silk handkerchiefs, cardboard boxes, cigarette ends
Or other testimony of summer nights. The nymphs are departed.
And their friends, the loitering heirs of city directors;   180
Departed, have left no addresses.
By the waters of Leman I sat down and wept . . .[1]
Sweet Thames, run softly till I end my song,
Sweet Thames, run softly, for I speak not loud or long.
But at my back in a cold blast I hear[2]   185
The rattle of the bones, and chuckle spread from ear to ear.

A rat crept softly through the vegetation
Dragging its slimy belly on the bank
While I was fishing in the dull canal
On a winter evening round behind the gashouse   190
Musing upon the king my brother's wreck[3]

---

4. To have an abortion.
5. Druggist.
6. Ham or bacon.
7. Cf. the mad Ophelia's departing words (*Hamlet* 4.5.72). Ophelia, too, met "death by water."
8. The Fire Sermon was preached by the Buddha against the fires of lust and other passions which destroy men and prevent their regeneration. See also note 1 on page 0000.
9. "V. Spenser, *Prothalamion*" [Eliot's note]. Eliot's line is the refrain from Spenser's marriage song, which is also set by the Thames in London—but a very different Thames from the modern littered river.

1. Cf. Psalms 137.1, in which the exiled Hebrews mourn for their homeland: "By the rivers of Babylon, there we sat down, yea, we wept, when we remembered Zion." Lake Leman is another name for Lake Geneva; Eliot wrote *The Waste Land* in Lausanne, by that lake. The common noun "leman" is an archaic word meaning, in the bad sense, an illicit sweetheart or mistress.
2. An ironic distortion of Andrew Marvell's *To His Coy Mistress*: "But at my back I always hear / Time's wingèd chariot hurrying near . . ." Cf. line 196.
3. "Cf. *The Tempest*, 1.2" [Eliot's note]. See line 48.

And on the king my father's death before him.
White bodies naked on the low damp ground
And bones cast in a little low dry garret,
Rattled by the rat's foot only, year to year.   195
But at my back from time to time I hear[4]
The sound of horns and motors, which shall bring
Sweeney to Mrs. Porter in the spring.[5]
O the moon shone bright on Mrs. Porter
And on her daughter   200
They wash their feet in soda water[6]
Et O ces voix d'enfants, chantant dans la coupole![7]

Twit twit twit
Jug jug jug jug jug jug
So rudely forc'd.   205
Tereu[8]

   Unreal City
Under the brown fog of a winter noon
Mr. Eugenides, the Smyrna[9] merchant
Unshaven, with a pocket full of currants   210
C.i.f.[1] London: documents at sight,
Asked me in demotic French[2]
To luncheon at the Cannon Street Hotel[3]
Followed by a weekend at the Metropole.

   At the violet hour, when the eyes and back   215
Turn upward from the desk, when the human engine waits
Like a taxi throbbing waiting,

---

4. "Cf. Marvell, *To His Coy Mistress*" [Eliot's note].

5. "Cf. Day, *Parliament of Bees*: 'When of the sudden, listening, you shall hear, / A noise of horns and hunting, which shall bring / Actaeon to Diana in the spring, / Where all shall see her naked skin . . .'" [Eliot's note]. Actaeon was changed to a stag and hunted to death after he saw Diana, the goddess of chastity, bathing with her nymphs.

6. "I do not know the origin of the ballad from which these lines are taken: it was reported to me from Sydney, Australia" [Eliot's note]. One of the less bawdy versions of the song, which was popular among Australian troops in World War I, went as follows: "O the moon shines bright on Mrs. Porter / And on the daughter / Of Mrs. Porter. / They wash their feet in soda water / And so they oughter / To keep them clean."

7. "V. Verlaine, *Parsifal*" [Eliot's note]. The line is translated, "And O those children's voices singing in the dome!" Verlaine's sonnet describes Parsifal, the questing knight, resisting all sensual temptations to keep himself pure for the Grail; Wagner's Parsifal had his feet washed before entering the castle of the Grail.

8. "Tereu" is a reference to Tereus, who "rudely forc'd" Philomela; it was also one of the conventional words for a nightingale's song in Elizabethan poetry. Cf. the song from John Lyly's *Alexander and Campaspe* (1564): "Oh, 'tis the ravished nightingale. / Jug, jug, jug, jug, *tereu!* she cries," and lines 100 ff.

9. Seaport in western Turkey; here associated with Carthage and the ancient Phoenician and Syrian merchants (unlike those of modern Smyrna), who spread the old mystery cults. The sort of cult spread by Mr. Eugenides is indicated by his suggestion of "a weekend at the Metropole" (a luxury hotel at Brighton).

1. "The currants were quoted at a price 'carriage and insurance free to London'; and the Bill of Lading etc. were to be handed to the buyer upon payment of the sight draft" [Eliot's note].

2. Popular French.

3. By the station which was then chief terminus for travelers to the continent; hence, a favorite meeting place for businessmen going or coming from abroad.

I Tiresias,[4] though blind, throbbing between two lives,
Old man with wrinkled female breasts, can see
At the violet hour, the evening hour that strives   220
Homeward, and brings the sailor home from sea,[5]
The typist home at teatime, clears her breakfast, lights
Her stove, and lays out food in tins.
Out of the window perilously spread
Her drying combinations touched by the sun's last rays,   225
On the divan are piled (at night her bed)
Stockings, slippers, camisoles, and stays.
I Tiresias, old man with wrinkled dugs
Perceived the scene, and foretold the rest—
I too awaited the expected guest.   230
He, the young man carbuncular,[6] arrives,
A small house agent's clerk, with one bold stare,
One of the low on whom assurance sits
As a silk hat on a Bradford[7] millionaire.
The time is now propitious, as he guesses,   235
The meal is ended, she is bored and tired,
Endeavors to engage her in caresses
Which still are unreproved, if undesired.
Flushed and decided, he assaults at once;
Exploring hands encounter no defense;   240
His vanity requires no response,
And makes a welcome of indifference.
(And I Tiresias have foresuffered all
Enacted on this same divan or bed;
I who have sat by Thebes[8] below the wall   245

---

4. "Tiresias, although a mere spectator and not indeed a 'character,' is yet the most important personage in the poem, uniting all the rest. Just as the one-eyed merchant, seller of currants, melts into the Phoenician Sailor, and the latter is not wholly distinct from Ferdinand Prince of Naples, so all the women are one woman, and the two sexes meet in Tiresias. What Tiresias *sees*, in fact, is the substance of the poem. The whole passage from Ovid is of great anthropological interest . . ." [Eliot's note.] The note then quotes the Latin text of Ovid's *Metamorphoses* which tells the story of Tiresias's change of sex. The Latin may be translated: "[The story goes that once Jove, having drunk a great deal,] jested with Juno. He said, 'Your pleasure in love is really greater than that enjoyed by men.' She denied it; so they decided to seek the opinion of the wise Tiresias, for he knew both aspects of love. For once, with a blow of his staff, he had committed violence on two huge snakes as they copulated in the green forest; and—wonderful to tell—was turned from a man into a woman and thus spent seven years. In the eighth year he saw the same snakes again and said: 'If a blow struck at you is so powerful that it changes the sex of the giver, I will now strike at you again.' With these words he struck the snakes, and his former shape was restored to him and he became as he had been born. So he

was appointed arbitrator in the playful quarrel, and supported Jove's statement. It is said that Saturnia [i.e., Juno] was quite disproportionately upset, and condemned the arbitrator to perpetual blindness. But the almighty father (for no god may undo what has been done by another god), in return for the sight that was taken away, gave him the power to know the future and so lightened the penalty paid by the honor."
5. "This may not appear as exact as Sappho's lines, but I had in mind the 'longshore' or 'dory' fisherman, who returns at nightfall" [Eliot's note]. Sappho's poem addressed Hesperus, the evening star, as the star that brings everyone home from work to evening rest; her poem is here distorted by Eliot. There is also an echo of Robert Louis Stevenson's *Requiem* in line 221 ("Home is the sailor, home from sea").
6. Pimply.
7. Either the Yorkshire woolen manufacturing town, where many fortunes were made in World War I, or the pioneer oil town of Bradford, Pennsylvania, the home of one of Eliot's wealthy Harvard contemporaries, T. E. Hanley.
8. Tiresias lived in Thebes for many generations, where he witnessed the tragic fates of Oedipus and Creon; he prophesied in the market place by the wall of Thebes.

And walked among the lowest of the dead.)
Bestows one final patronizing kiss,
And gropes his way, finding the stairs unlit . . .

    She turns and looks a moment in the glass,
Hardly aware of her departed lover;   250
Her brain allows one half-formed thought to pass:
"Well now that's done: and I'm glad it's over."
When lovely woman stoops to folly and
Paces about her room again, alone,
She smoothes her hair with automatic hand,   255
And puts a record on the gramophone.[9]

    "This music crept by me upon the waters"[1]
And along the Strand, up Queen Victoria Street.
O City city, I can sometimes hear
Beside a public bar in Lower Thames Street,   260
The pleasant whining of a mandolin
And a clatter and a chatter from within
Where fishmen lounge at noon: where the walls
Of Magnus Martyr hold
Inexplicable splendor of Ionian white and gold.[2]   265

        The river sweats[3]
        Oil and tar
        The barges drift
        With the turning tide
        Red sails   270
        Wide
        To leeward, swing on the heavy spar.
        The barges wash
        Drifting logs
        Down Greenwich reach   275
        Past the Isle of Dogs.[4]

9. "V. Goldsmith, the song in *The Vicar of Wakefield*" [Eliot's note]. Olivia, a character in Oliver Goldsmith's novel, sings the following song when she returns to the place where she was seduced: "When lovely woman stoops to folly / And finds too late that men betray / What charm can soothe her melancholy, / What art can wash her guilt away? / The only art her guilt to cover, / To hide her shame from every eye, / To give repentance to her lover / And wring his bosom—is to die."

1. "V. *The Tempest*, as above" [Eliot's note]. Cf. line 48. (The line is from Ferdinand's speech, continuing after "weeping again the King my father's wrack.")

2. "The interior of St. Magnus Martyr is to my mind one of the finest among [Sir Christopher] Wren's interiors." [Eliot's note]. In these lines, the "pleasant" music, the "fishmen" resting after labor, and the splendor of the church interior all suggest a world of true values, where work and relaxation are both real and take place in a context of religious meaning. It is but a momentary glimpse of an almost lost world.

3. "The Song of the (three) Thames-daughters begins here. From line 292 to 306 inclusive they speak in turn. V. *Götterdämmerung*, 3.1: the Rhine-daughters" [Eliot's note]. Eliot parallels the Thames-daughters with the Rhine-maidens in Wagner's opera *Die Götterdämmerung* ("The Twilight of the Gods") who lament that, with the gold of the Nibelungs stolen, the beauty of the river is gone. The refrain in lines 277–78 is borrowed from Wagner.

4. Greenwich is a borough in London on the south side of the Thames; opposite is the Isle of Dogs (a peninsula): Eliot presumably intends a reference to the earlier theme of the Dog.

Weialala leia
Wallala leialala

Elizabeth and Leicester[5]
Beating oars   280
The stern was formed
A gilded shell
Red and gold
The brisk swell
Rippled both shores   285
Southwest wind
Carried down stream
The peal of bells
White towers
                    Weialala leia   290
                    Wallala leialala

"Trams and dusty trees.
Highbury bore me. Richmond and Kew
Undid me.[6] By Richmond I raised my knees
Supine on the floor of a narrow canoe."   295

"My feet are at Moorgate,[7] and my heart
Under my feet. After the event
He wept. He promised 'a new start.'
I made no comment. What should I resent?"

"On Margate[8] Sands.   300
I can connect
Nothing with nothing.
The broken fingernails of dirty hands.
My people humble people who expect
Nothing."   305
            la la

To Carthage then I came[9]

---

5. The fruitless love of Queen Elizabeth and the
Earl of Leicester (Sir Robert Dudley) is recalled in
Eliot's note: "V. [J. A.] Froude, *Elizabeth*, Vol.
1, ch. 4, letter of De Quadra to Philip of Spain:
'In the afternoon we were in a barge, watching the
games on the river. (The queen) was alone with
Lord Robert and myself on the poop, when they
began to talk nonsense, and went so far that Lord
Robert at last said, as I was on the spot there was
no reason why they should not be married if the
queen pleased.' " (Queen Elizabeth was born in
the old Greenwich House, by the river, where
Greenwich Hospital now stands.)
6. "Cf. *Purgatorio*, 5.133 . . ." [Eliot's note]. The
Purgatorio lines, which Eliot here parodies, may

be translated: "Remember me, who am La Pia. /
Siena made me, Maremma undid me." Highbury
is a residential London suburb; Richmond is a
pleasant part of London westward up the Thames,
with boating and riverside hotels; Kew, adjoining
Richmond, has the famous Kew Gardens.
7. Slum area in east London.
8. Popular seaside resort on Thames estuary.
9. "V. St. Augustine's *Confessions*: 'to Carthage
then I came, where a caldron of unholy loves sang
all about mine ears' " [Eliot's note]. The passage
from the *Confessions* quoted here occurs in St.
Augustine's account of his youthful life of lust. Cf.
line 92 and its note.

Burning burning burning burning[1]
O Lord Thou pluckest me out[2]
O Lord Thou pluckest   310

burning

4. Death by Water[3]

Phlebas the Phoenician, a fortnight dead,
Forgot the cry of gulls, and the deep sea swell
And the profit and loss.
                    A current under sea   315
Picked his bones in whispers. As he rose and fell
He passed the stages of his age and youth
Entering the whirlpool.
                    Gentile or Jew
O you who turn the wheel and look to windward,   320
consider Phlebas, who was once handsome and tall as you.

5. What the Thunder Said[4]

After the torchlight red on sweaty faces
After the frosty silence in the gardens
After the agony in stony places
The shouting and the crying   325
Prison and palace and reverberation
Of thunder of spring over distant mountains
He who was living is now dead[5]
We who were living are now dying
With a little patience   330

1. "The complete text of the Buddha's Fire Sermon (which corresponds in importance to the Sermon on the Mount) from which these words are taken, will be found translated in the late Henry Clarke Warren's *Buddhism in Translation* (Harvard Oriental Series) . . ." [Eliot's note]. In the sermon, the Buddha instructs his priests that all things "are on fire . . . The eye . . . is on fire; forms are on fire; eye-consciousness is on fire; impressions received by the eye are on fire; and whatever sensation, pleasant, unpleasant, or indifferent, originates in dependence on impressions received by the eye, that also is on fire. And with what are these on fire? With the fire of passion, say I, with the fire of hatred, with the fire of infatuation . . ." For Christ's Sermon on the Mount see Matthew 5–7.

2. "From St. Augustine's *Confessions* again. The collocation of these two representatives of eastern and western asceticism, as the culmination of this part of the poem, is not an accident" [Eliot's note]. Cf. also Zechariah 3.2, where God, rebuking Satan, speaks of Joshua the high priest as "a brand plucked out of the fire."

3. This section has been interpreted in two ways: either it signifies death by water without resurrec-

tion (water *misused*), or it symbolizes the sacrificial death which precedes rebirth. It is true that Phlebas is purged of his commercial interests and vanities when he suffers a sea change, and Weston tells of the annual casting into the sea at Alexandria of an effigy of the head of Adonis—to be taken out after seven days by jubilant celebrators of the cult. The majority of interpreters, however, see Phlebas's drowning as a death by water which brings no resurrection, although there is a strange sense of peace in the death. Cf. line 47 and its note.

4. "In the first part of part 5 three themes are employed: the journey to Emmaus, the approach to the Chapel Perilous (see Miss Weston's book), and the present decay of eastern Europe" [Eliot's note]. The journey to Emmaus (see line 360 and its note) is a significant feature in the story of Christ, and in this section the Waste Land is more clearly related to that story. Christ is associated with the slain fertility god, but there is still no resurrection.

5. These lines, containing allusions to Christ's imprisonment and trial, and to Gethsemane and Golgotha, suggest the hopeless days between Good Friday and Easter, between the Crucifixion and the Resurrection—associated with the death of the Fisher King.

Here is no water but only rock
Rock and no water and the sandy road
The road winding above among the mountains
Which are mountains of rock without water
If there were water we should stop and drink   335
Amongst the rock one cannot stop or think
Sweat is dry and feet are in the sand
If there were only water amongst the rock
Dead mountain mouth of carious teeth that cannot spit
Here one can neither stand nor lie nor sit   340
There is not even silence in the mountains
But dry sterile thunder without rain
There is not even solitude in the mountains
But red sullen faces sneer and snarl
From doors of mudcracked houses   345
                                        If there were water
        And no rock
        If there were rock
        And also water
        And water   350
        A spring
        A pool among the rock
        If there were the sound of water only
        Not the cicada[6]
        And dry grass singing   355
        But sound of water over a rock
        Where the hermit thrush[7] sings in the pine trees
        Drip drop drip drop drop drop drop
        But there is no water

Who is the third who walks always beside you?[8]   360
When I count, there are only you and I together
But when I look ahead up the white road
There is always another one walking beside you
Gliding wrapped in a brown mantle, hooded
I do not know whether a man or a woman   365
—But who is that on the other side of you?

    What is that sound high in the air[9]
Murmur of maternal lamentation

---

6. Grasshopper. Cf. the prophecy of Ecclesiastes, "the grasshopper shall be a burden, and desire shall fail . . ." (and cf. also line 23 and its note).
7. "This is . . . the hermit thrush which I have heard in Quebec County . . . Its 'water-dripping song' is justly celebrated" [Eliot's note].
8. "The following lines were stimulated by the account of one of the Antarctic expeditions (I forget which, but I think one of Shackleton's): it was related that the party of explorers, at the extremity of their strength, had the constant delusion that

there was *one more member* than could actually be counted" [Eliot's note]. This reminiscence is associated with the journey of Christ's disciples to Emmaus given in Luke 24.13–16: "And it came to pass, that, while they communed together and reasoned, Jesus himself drew near, and went with them. But their eyes were holden that they should not know him."
9. Eliot's note for lines 367–77 is: "Cf. Herman Hesse, *Blick ins Chaos* ["A Glimpse into Chaos"] . . ." The note then quotes a passage from the

Who are those hooded hordes swarming
Over endless plains, stumbling in cracked earth   370
Ringed by the flat horizon only
What is the city over the mountains
Cracks and reforms and bursts in the violet air
Falling towers
Jerusalem Athens Alexandria   375
Vienna London
Unreal

   A woman drew her long black hair out tight
And fiddled whisper music on those strings
And bats with baby faces in the violet light   380
Whistled, and beat their wings
And crawled head downward down a blackened wall
And upside down in air were towers
Tolling reminiscent bells, that kept the hours
And voices singing out of empty cisterns and exhausted wells.   385

   In this decayed hole among the mountains
In the faint moonlight, the grass is singing
Over the tumbled graves, about the chapel
There is the empty chapel, only the wind's home.[1]
It has no windows, and the door swings,   390
Dry bones can harm no one.
Only a cock stood on the rooftree
Co co rico co co rico[2]
In a flash of lightning. Then a damp gust
Bringing rain   395

   Ganga[3] was sunken, and the limp leaves
Waited for rain, while the black clouds
Gathered far distant, over Himavant.[4]
The jungle crouched, humped in silence.
Then spoke the thunder   400
DA[5]

German text, which is translated: "Already half of Europe, already at least half of Eastern Europe, on the way to Chaos, drives drunk in sacred infatuation along the edge of the precipice, sings drunkenly, as though hymn singing, as Dmitri Karamazov [in Dostoyevski's *Brothers Karamazov*] sang. The offended bourgeois laughs at the songs; the saint and the seer hear them with tears."
1. Suggesting the moment of near despair before the Chapel Perilous, when the questing knight sees nothing there but decay. This illusion of nothingness is the knight's final test.
2. The crowing of the cock signals the departure of ghosts and evil spirits. Cf. *Hamlet* 1.1.157 ff.
3. The river Ganges.
4. I.e., snowy mountain; the name of a peak in the Himalayas.

5. " 'Datta, dayadhvam, damyata' (Give, sympathize, control). The fable of the meaning of the Thunder is found in the *Brihadaranyaka—Upanishad*, 5, 1 . . ." [Eliot's note]. The Hindu fable referred to is that of gods, men, and demons each in turn asking of their father Prajapati. "Speak to us, O Lord." To each he replied with the one syllable "DA," and each group interpreted it in a different way: "*Datta*," to give alms; "*Dayadhvam*," to have compassion; "*Damyata*," to practice self-control. The fable concludes, "This is what the divine voice, the Thunder, repeats when he says: DA, DA, DA: 'Control yourselves; give alms; be compassionate.' Therefore one should practice these three things: self-control, alms-giving, and compassion."

Datta: what have we given?
My friend, blood shaking my heart
The awful daring of a moment's surrender
Which an age of prudence can never retract   405
By this, and this only, we have existed
Which is not to be found in our obituaries
Or in memories draped by the beneficent spider[6]
Or under seals broken by the lean solicitor[7]
In our empty rooms   410
DA
Dayadhvam: I have heard the key[8]
Turn in the door once and turn once only
We think of the key, each in his prison
Thinking of the key, each confirms a prison   415
Only at nightfall, ethereal rumors
Revive for a moment a broken Coriolanus[9]
DA
Damyata: The boat responded
Gaily, to the hand expert with sail and oar   420
The sea was calm, your heart would have responded
Gaily, when invited, beating obedient
To controlling hands
                              I sat upon the shore
Fishing,[1] with the arid plain behind me   425
Shall I at least set my lands in order?[2]
London Bridge is falling down falling down falling down[3]
Poi s'ascose nel foco che gli affina[4]
Quando fiam uti chelidon[5]—O swallow swallow

---

6. "Cf. Webster, *The White Devil*, 5.6: '. . . they'll remarry / Ere the worm pierce your winding-sheet, ere the spider / Make a thin curtain for your epitaphs' " [Eliot's note].
7. Lawyer.
8. "Cf. *Inferno*, 33.46 . . ." [Eliot's note]. In this passage from the *Inferno* Ugolino recalls his imprisonment in the tower with his children, where they starved to death: "And I heard below the door of the horrible tower being locked up." Eliot implies that we cannot obey the command to sympathize because we are imprisoned within the circle of our own egotism. Eliot's note for this line goes on to quote F. H. Bradley, *Appearance and Reality*, p. 346, as follows: " 'My external sensations are no less private to myself than are my thoughts or my feelings. In either case my experience falls within my own circle, a circle closed on the outside; and, with all its elements alike, every sphere is opaque to the others which surround it. . . . In brief, regarded as an existence which appears in a soul, the whole world for each is peculiar and private to that soul.' "
9. Coriolanus, who acted out of pride rather than duty, is an obvious example of a man locked in the prison of his own self. He led the enemy against his native city out of injured pride (cf. Shake-speare's *Coriolanus*).
1. "V. Weston: *From Ritual to Romance*; chapter on the Fisher King" [Eliot's note].
2. Cf. Isaiah 38.1: "Thus saith the Lord, Set thine house in order; for thou shalt die, and not live." The inclusive "I," who sits in the symbolic act of fishing (seeking salvation, regeneration, eternity) with the Waste Land behind him, wonders how far he can order his affairs.
3. One of the later lines of this nursery rhyme is: "Take the key and lock her up, my fair lady."
4. "V. *Purgatorio*, 26.148 . . ." [Eliot's note]. The note goes on to quote lines 145–48 of the *Purgatorio*, in which Arnaut Daniel, the Provençal poet, addresses Dante: " 'Now I pray you, by that virtue which guides you to the summit of the stairway, be mindful in due time of my pain.' " Then (in the line Eliot quotes here) "he hid himself in the fire which refines them." The purgatorial vision of refining fire—as distinct from the fires of lust—represents one of the hopeful fragments shored up by the seeker for regeneration and order.
5. "V. *Pervigilium Veneris*. Cf. Philomela in parts 2 and 3" [Eliot's note]. The Latin phrase in the text means, "When shall I be as the swallow?" It comes from the *Pervigilium Veneris* ("Vigil of Venus"), an anonymous late Latin poem combin-

Le Prince d'Aquitaine à la tour abolie[6]   430
These fragments I have shored against my ruins[7]
Why then Ile fit you. Hieronymo's mad againe.[8]
Datta. Dayadhvam. Damyata.
            Shantih shantih shantih[9]

1921   1922

Journey of the Magi[1]

   "A cold coming we had of it,
Just the worst time of the year
For a journey, and such a long journey:
The ways deep and the weather sharp,
The very dead of winter."[2]   5
And the camels galled, sore-footed, refractory,
Lying down in the melting snow.
There were times we regretted
The summer palaces on slopes, the terraces,
And the silken girls bringing sherbet.   10
Then the camel men cursing and grumbling
And running away, and wanting their liquor and women,
And the night-fires going out, and the lack of shelters,
And the cities hostile and the towns unfriendly
And the villages dirty and charging high prices: 15
A hard time we had of it.
At the end we preferred to travel all night,

ing a hymn to Venus with a description of spring.
In the last two stanzas of the *Pervigilium* occurs a
recollection of the Tereus-Procne-Philomela myth
(except that in this version the swallow is identified
with Philomela); the anonymous poet's mood
changes to one of sadness, combined with hope for
renewal: "The maid of Tereus sings under the poplar
shade, so that you would think musical trills of
love came from her mouth and not a sister's complaint of a barbarous husband. . . . She sings, we
are silent. When will my spring come? When shall
I be as the swallow that I may cease to be silent? I
have lost the Muse in silence, and Apollo regards
me not . . ." For "O swallow swallow" cf. Swinburne's *Itylus*, which begins, "Swallow, my sister,
O sister swallow, / How can thine heart be full of
spring?" and Tennyson's lyric in *The Princess:* "O
Swallow, Swallow, flying, flying south . . ."
6. "V. Gerard de Nerval, Sonnet *El Desdichado*"
[Eliot's note]. The French line may be translated,
"The Prince of Aquitaine in the ruined tower."
One of the cards in the Tarot pack is "the tower
struck by lightning."
7. This may refer to the whole poem—fragments
assembled by the speaker in the attempt to come
to terms with his situation.
8. "V. Kyd's *Spanish Tragedy*" [Eliot's note].
Subtitled "Hieronymo's Mad Againe," Kyd's play

(1594) is an early example of the Elizabethan tragedy of revenge. Hieronymo, driven mad by the
murder of his son, has his revenge when he is asked
to write a court entertainment. He replies, "Why
then Ile fit you!" (i.e., accommodate you), and
assigns the parts in the entertainment so that, in
the course of the action, his son's murderers are
killed.
9. "Shantih. Repeated as here, a formal ending to
an Upanishad. 'The Peace which passeth understanding' is our equivalent to this word" [Eliot's
note]. The Upanishads are poetic dialogues on
Hindu metaphysics, written after the Vedas, the
ancient Hindu scriptures, and in part commenting
on them. The fact that the benediction is in a language so foreign to Western tradition may indicate
that the solution is willed, not achieved.
1. One of the three wise men who came from the
east to Jerusalem to do homage to the infant Jesus
(Matthew 2.1–12) is recalling in old age the meaning of the experience.
2. Adapted from a passage in a Nativity sermon by
the 17th-century divine, Lancelot Andrewes: "A
cold coming they had of it at this time of the year,
just the worst time of the year to take a journey,
and specially a long journey in. The ways deep,
the weather sharp, the days short, the sun farthest
off, *in solstitio brumali*, 'the very dead of winter.'"

Sleeping in snatches,
With the voices singing in our ears, saying
That this was all folly.   20

    Then at dawn we came down to a temperate valley,
Wet, below the snow line, smelling of vegetation;
With a running stream and a water mill beating the darkness,
And three trees on the low sky,
And an old white horse galloped away in the meadow.[3]   25
Then we came to a tavern with vine-leaves over the lintel,
Six hands at an open door dicing for pieces of silver,[4]
And feet kicking the empty wineskins.
But there was no information, and so we continued
And arrived at evening, not a moment too soon   30
Finding the place; it was (you may say) satisfactory.

    All this was a long time ago, I remember,
And I would do it again, but set down
This set down
This: were we led all that way for   35
Birth or Death? There was a Birth, certainly,
We had evidence and no doubt. I had seen birth and death,
But had thought they were different; this Birth was
Hard and bitter agony for us, like Death, our death.
We returned to our places, these Kingdoms,   40
But no longer at ease here, in the old dispensation,
With an alien people clutching their gods.
I should be glad of another death.

1927

Marina[1]

Quis hic locus, quae regio, quae mundi plaga?[2]

    What seas what shores what gray rocks and what islands
What water lapping the bow
And scent of pine and the woodthrush singing through the fog

---

3. The "three trees on the low sky" suggest the three crosses, with Christ crucified on the center one; the men dicing for pieces of silver suggest the soldiers dicing for Christ's garments and Judas' betrayal of him for thirty pieces of silver.
4. "Why, for all of us, out of all that we have heard, seen, felt, in a lifetime, do certain images recur, charged with emotion, rather than others? . . . six ruffians seen through an open window playing cards at night at a small French railway junction where there was a water mill" (Eliot, *The Use of Poetry and the Use of Criticism*).

1. Pericles' daughter in Shakespeare's play *Pericles Prince of Tyre*: she was born at sea, lost to her father, then as a young woman found by him again.
2. "What place is this, what country, what region of the world?" Spoken by Hercules on regaining sanity after having killed his children in his madness, in Seneca's play *Hercules Furens* ("The Mad Hercules"). This is a situation contrary to the one evoked in the poem. Eliot once wrote to a correspondent that he wished to achieve a "crisscross" between the scenes in the Senecan and the Shakespearean plays.

What images return
O my daughter.   5

   Those who sharpen the tooth of the dog, meaning
Death
Those who glitter with the glory of the hummingbird, meaning
Death
Those who sit in the sty of contentment, meaning   10
Death
Those who suffer the ecstasy of the animals, meaning
Death

   Are become unsubstantial, reduced by a wind,
A breath of pine, and the woodsong fog   15
By this grace dissolved in place

   What is this face, less clear and clearer
The pulse in the arm, less strong and stronger—
Given or lent? more distant than stars and nearer than the eye

   Whispers and small laughter between leaves and hurrying
feet   20
Under sleep, where all the waters meet.

   Bowsprit cracked with ice and paint cracked with heat.
I made this, I have forgotten
And remember.
The rigging weak and the canvas rotten   25
Between one June and another September.
Made this unknowing, half conscious, unknown, my own.
The garboard strake[3] leaks, the seams need calking.
This form, this face, this life
Living to live in a world of time beyond me; let me   30
Resign my life for this life, my speech for that unspoken,
The awakened, lips parted, the hope, the new ships.

   What seas what shores what granite islands towards my tim-
bers
And woodthrush calling through the fog
My daughter.   35

1930

---

3. The planking nearest to the boat's keel—hence its most vital spot.

From FOUR QUARTETS

Little Gidding[1]

1

Midwinter spring is its own season
Sempiternal[2] though sodden towards sundown,
Suspended in time, between pole and tropic,
When the short day is brightest, with frost and fire,
The brief sun flames the ice, on pond and ditches,   5
In windless cold that is the heart's heat,
Reflecting in a watery mirror
A glare that is blindness in the early afternoon.
And glow more intense than blaze of branch, or brazier,
Stirs the dumb spirit: no wind, but pentecostal fire[3]   10
In the dark time of the year. Between melting and freezing
The soul's sap quivers. There is no earth smell
Or smell of living thing. This is the springtime
But not in time's covenant. Now the hedgerow
Is blanched for an hour with transitory blossom   15
Of snow, a bloom more sudden
Than that of summer, neither budding nor fading,
Not in the scheme of generation.
Where is the summer, the unimaginable
Zero summer?
             If you came this way,   20
Taking the route you would be likely to take
From the place you would be likely to come from,
If you came this way in may time, you would find the hedges
White again, in May, with voluptuary sweetness.
It would be the same at the end of the journey,   25
If you came at night like a broken king,[4]
If you came by day not knowing what you came for,
It would be the same, when you leave the rough road
And turn behind the pigsty to the dull façade

---

1. This is the fourth of Eliot's *Four Quartets*, 4 related poems each divided into 5 "movements" in a manner reminiscent of the structure of a quartet or a sonata and each dealing with some aspect of the relation of time and eternity, the meaning of history, the achievement of the moment of timeless insight. Though the *Four Quartets* constitute a unified sequence, they were each written separately and can be read as individual poems. "*Little Gidding* can be understood by itself, without reference to the preceding poems, which it yet so beautifully completes" (Helen Gardner). Each of the 4 is named after a place. Little Gidding is a village in Huntingdonshire where in 1625 Nicholas Ferrar established an Anglican religious community; it was broken up in 1647, toward the end of the Civil War, by the victorious Puritans; the chapel, however, was rebuilt in the 19th century and still exists. Eliot wrote the poem in 1942, when he was taking his turn as a nighttime fire-watcher during the incendiary bombings of London in World War II, and he looks back at the history and meaning of Little Gidding from his own war experience in order to project its present significance.
2. Eternal, everlasting.
3. On the Pentecost day after the death and resurrection of Christ, there appeared to His apostles "cloven tongues like as of fire . . . And they were all filled with the Holy Ghost" (Acts 2).
4. King Charles I visited Ferrar's community more than once, and is said to have paid his last visit in secret after his final defeat at the battle of Naseby in the Civil War.

And the tombstone. And what you thought you came for   30
Is only a shell, a husk of meaning
From which the purpose breaks only when it is fulfilled
If at all. Either you had no purpose
Or the purpose is beyond the end you figured
And is altered in fulfillment. There are other places   35
Which also are the world's end, some at the sea jaws,
Or over a dark lake, in a desert or a city[5]—
But this is the nearest, in place and time,
Now and in England.
                              If you came this way,
Taking any route, starting from anywhere,   40
At any time or at any season,
It would always be the same: you would have to put off
Sense and notion. You are not here to verify,
Instruct yourself, or inform curiosity
Or carry report. You are here to kneel   45
Where prayer has been valid. And prayer is more
Than an order of words, the conscious occupation
Of the praying mind, or the sound of the voice praying.
And what the dead had no speech for, when living,
They can tell you, being dead: the communication   50
Of the dead is tongued with fire beyond the language of the living.
Here, the intersection of the timeless moment
Is England and nowhere. Never and always.

                                      2

Ash on an old man's sleeve
Is all the ash the burnt roses leave.   55
Dust in the air suspended
Marks the place where a story ended.[6]
Dust inbreathed was a house—
The wall, the wainscot, and the mouse.
The death of hope and despair,   60
        This is the death of air.[7]

There are flood and drouth
Over the eyes and in the mouth,
Dead water and dead sand
Contending for the upper hand.
The parched eviscerate soil   65
Gapes at the vanity of toil,

5. "The 'sea jaws' [Eliot] associated with Iona and
St. Columba and with Lindisfarne and St. Cuthbert: the 'dark lake' with the lake of Glendalough
and St. Kevin's hermitage in County Wicklow: the
desert with the hermits of the Thebaid and St.
Antony: the city with Padua and the other St.
Antony" (Helen Gardner, *The Composition of Four
Quartets*, 1978, p. 163).
6. Eliot wrote to a friend: "During the Blitz
[bombing] the accumulated debris was suspended

in the London air for hours after a bombing. Then
it would slowly descend and cover one's sleeves
and coat with a fine white ash."
7. "The death of air," like that of "earth" and of
"water and fire" in the succeeding stanzas, recalls
the theory of the creative strife of the four elements
propounded by Heraclitus (Greek philosopher of
4th and 5th centuries B.C.): "Fire lives in the death
of air; water lives in the death of earth; and earth
lives in the death of water."

Laughs without mirth.
    This is the death of earth.

Water and fire succeed 70
The town, the pasture, and the weed.
Water and fire deride
The sacrifice that we denied.
Water and fire shall rot
The marred foundations we forgot, 75
Of sanctuary and choir.
    This is the death of water and fire.

In the uncertain hour before the morning[8]
  Near the ending of interminable night
    At the recurrent end of the unending 80
After the dark dove with the flickering tongue[9]
  Had passed below the horizon of his homing
    While the dead leaves still rattled on like tin
Over the asphalt where no other sound was
  Between three districts whence the smoke arose 85
    I met one walking, loitering and hurried
As if blown towards me like the metal leaves
  Before the urban dawn wind unresisting.
    And as I fixed upon the down-turned face
That pointed scrutiny with which we challenge 90
  The first-met stranger in the waning dusk
    I caught the sudden look of some dead master
Whom I had known, forgotten, half recalled
  Both one and many; in the brown baked features
    The eyes of a familiar compound ghost[1] 95
Both intimate and unidentifiable.
  So I assumed a double part, and cried
    And heard another's voice cry: "What! are *you* here?"
Although we were not. I was still the same,
  Knowing myself yet being someone other— 100
    And he a face still forming; yet the words sufficed
To compel the recognition they preceded.
  And so, compliant to the common wind,
    Too strange to each other for misunderstanding,
In concord at this intersection time 105
  Of meeting nowhere, no before and after,
    We trod the pavement in a dead patrol.
I said: "The wonder that I feel is easy,

---

8. The pattern of indentation in the left-hand margin of lines 78–149, their movement and elevated diction, are meant to suggest the *terza rima* or Dante's *Inferno*.
9. The German dive-bomber.
1. This encounter with a ghost "compounded" of W. B. Yeats and his fellow Irishman, Jonathan Swift, is modeled on Dante's meeting with Brunetto Latini *(Inferno 15)*, closing with a direct translation of Dante's cry of horrified recognition: *"Siete voi qui, ser Brunetto?"* Cf. also Shakespeare's *Sonnet* 86, line 9: "that affable familiar ghost."

Yet ease is cause of wonder. Therefore speak:
  I may not comprehend, may not remember."   110
And he: "I am not eager to rehearse
  My thought and theory which you have forgotten.
  These things have served their purpose: let them be.
So with your own, and pray they be forgiven
  By others, as I pray you to forgive   115
  Both bad and good. Last season's fruit is eaten
And the fullfed beast shall kick the empty pail.
  For last year's words belong to last year's language
  And next year's words await another voice.
But, as the passage now presents no hindrance   120
  To the spirit unappeased and peregrine[2]
  Between two worlds become much like each other,
So I find words I never thought to speak
  In streets I never thought I should revisit
  When I left my body on a distant shore.[3]   125
Since our concern was speech, and speech impelled us
  To purify the dialect of the tribe[4]
  And urge the mind to aftersight and foresight,
Let me disclose the gifts reserved for age
  To set a crown upon your lifetime's effort.   130
  First, the cold friction of expiring sense
Without enchantment, offering no promise
  But bitter tastelessness of shadow fruit
  As body and soul begin to fall asunder.
Second, the conscious impotence of rage[5]   135
  At human folly, and the laceration
  Of laughter at what ceases to amuse.[6]
And last, the rending pain of re-enactment
  Of all that you have done, and been;[7] the shame
  Of motives late revealed, and the awareness   140
Of things ill done and done to other's harm
  Which once you took for exercise of virtue.
  Then fools's approval stings, and honor stains.
From wrong to wrong the exasperated spirit
  Proceeds, unless restored by that refining fire[8]   145
  Where you must move in measure, like a dancer."[9]
The day was breaking. In the disfigured street

---

2. Foreign, wandering.
3. Yeats died on Jan. 28, 1939, at Roquebrune in the South of France.
4. A rendering of the line *"Donner un sens plus pur aux mots de la tribu"* in Stéphane Mallarmé's sonnet *Le Tombeau d'Edgar Poe* ("The Tomb of Edgar Poe").
5. Cf. Yeats's *The Spur*: "You think it horrible that lust and rage / Should dance attention upon my old age."
6. Cf. Yeats's *Swift's Epitaph* (translated from Swift's own Latin): "Savage indignation there /

Cannot lacerate his breast."
7. Cf. Yeats's *The Man and the Echo*: "All that I have said and done, / Now that I am old and ill, / Turns into a question till / I lie awake night after night / And never get the answer right. / Did that play of mine send out / Certain men the English shot?"
8. Cf. *The Waste Land*, line 428 and its note; also the refining fire in Yeats's *Byzantium*, lines 25–32.
9. Cf. Yeats's *Among School Children*: "How can we know the dancer from the dance?"

He left me, with a kind of valediction,
And faded on the blowing of the horn.[1]

3

There are three conditions which often look alike   150
Yet differ completely, flourish in the same hedgerow:
Attachment to self and to things and to persons, detachment
From self and from things and from persons; and, growing between them,
  indifference
Which resembles the others as death resembles life,
Being between two lives—unflowering, between   155
The live and the dead nettle.[2] This is the use of memory:
For liberation—not less of love but expanding
Of love beyond desire, and so liberation
From the future as well as the past. Thus, love of a country
Begins as attachment to our own field of action   160
And comes to find that action of little importance
Though never indifferent. History may be servitude,
History may be freedom. See, now they vanish,
The faces and places, with the self which, as it could, loved them,
To become renewed, transfigured, in another pattern.   165

Sin is Behovely, but
All shall be well, and
All manner of thing shall be well.[3]
If I think, again, of this place,
And of people, not wholly commendable,   170
Of no immediate kin or kindness,
But some of peculiar genius,
All touched by a common genius,
United in the strife which divided them;
If I think of a king at nightfall,[4]   175
Of three men, and more, on the scaffold
And a few who died forgotten
In other places, here and abroad,
And of one who died blind and quiet[5]
Why should we celebrate   180
These dead men more than the dying?
It is not to ring the bell backward
Nor is it an incantation

1. Cf. *Hamlet*, 1.2.157. "It faded on the crowing
of the cock." The horn is the All Clear signal after
an air raid (the dialogue has taken place between
the dropping of the last bomb and the sounding of
the All Clear). Eliot called the section which ends
with this line "the nearest equivalent to a canto of
the *Inferno* or *Purgatorio*" that he could achieve,
and spoke of his intention to present "a parallel,
by means of contrast, between the *Inferno* and the
Purgatorio . . . and a hallucinated scene after an
air raid."
2. Eliot wrote to a friend: "The dead nettle is the
family of flowering plants of which the White

Archangel is one of the commonest and closely
resembles the stinging nettle and is found in its
company."
3. A quotation from the 14th-century English
mystic, Dame Julian of Norwich: "Sin is behova-
bil [inevitable], but all shall be well and all shall
be well and all manner of thing shall be well."
4. Charles I. He died "on the scaffold" in 1649,
while his principal advisers, Archbishop Laud and
Thomas Wentworth, earl of Strafford, were both
executed earlier by the victorious Parliamentary
forces.
5. Milton.

To summon the specter of a Rose.
We cannot revive old factions 185
We cannot restore old policies
Or follow an antique drum.
These men, and those who opposed them
And those whom they opposed
Accept the constitution of silence 190
And are folded in a single party.
Whatever we inherit from the fortunate
We have taken from the defeated
What they had to leave us—a symbol:
A symbol perfected in death. 195
And all shall be well and
All manner of thing shall be well
By the purification of the motive
In the ground of our beseeching.[6]

4

The dove descending breaks the air 200
With flame of incandescent terror
Of which the tongues declare
The one discharge from sin and error.
The only hope, or else despair
    Lies in the choice of pyre or pyre— 205
    To be redeemed from fire by fire.

Who then devised the torment? Love.
Love is the unfamiliar Name.
Behind the hands that wove
The intolerable shirt of flame[7] 210
Which human power cannot remove.
    We only live, only suspire
    Consumed by either fire or fire.

5

What we call the beginning is often the end
And to make an end is to make a beginning. 215
The end is where we start from. And every phrase
And sentence that is right (where every word is at home,
Taking its place to support the others,
The word neither diffident nor ostentatious,
And easy commerce of the old and the new, 220
The common word exact without vulgarity,
The formal word precise but not pedantic,
The complete consort[8] dancing together)
Every phrase and every sentence is an end and a beginning,

6. Dame Julian of Norwich was instructed in a vision that "the ground of our beseeching" is love.
7. Out of love for her husband Hercules, Deianira gave him the poisoned shirt of Nessus. She had been told that it would increase his love for her, but instead it so corroded his flesh that in his agony he mounted a funeral pyre and burned himself to death.
8. The word means both "company" and "harmony of sounds."

Every poem an epitaph. And any action   225
Is a step to the block, to the fire, down the sea's throat
Or to an illegible stone: and that is where we start.
We die with the dying:
See, they depart, and we go with them.
We are born with the dead: 230
See, they return, and bring us with them.
The moment of the rose and the moment of the yew tree
Are of equal duration. A people without history
Is not redeemed from time, for history is a pattern
Of timeless moments. So, while the light fails   235
On a winter's afternoon, in a secluded chapel
History is now and England.

With the drawing of this Love and the voice of this Calling[9]
We shall not cease from exploration
And the end of all our exploring   240
Will be to arrive where we started
And know the place for the first time.
Through the unknown, remembered gate
When the last of earth left to discover
Is that which was the beginning;   245
At the source of the longest river
The voice of the hidden waterfall
And the children in the apple tree
Not known, because not looked for
But heard, half-heard, in the stillness   250
Between two waves of the sea.[1]
Quick now, here, now, always—
A condition of complete simplicity
(Costing not less than everything)
And all shall be well and   255
All manner of thing shall be well
When the tongues of flame are in-folded
Into the crowned knot of fire
And the fire and the rose are one.

1942   1942, 1943

Tradition and the Individual Talent[1]

1

  In English writing we seldom speak of tradition, though we occasionally apply its name in deploring its absence. We cannot refer to "the

9. This line is from an anonymous 14th-century mystical work, the *Cloud of Unknowing*.
1. The voice of the children in the apple tree symbolizes the sudden moment of insight. Cf. the conclusion to *Burnt Norton* (the first of the *Four Quartets*), where the laughter of the children in

the garden has a like meaning: "Sudden in a shaft of sunlight / Even while the dust moves / There rises the hidden laughter / Of children in the foliage / Quick now, here, now, always . . ."
1. First published in the *Egoist* (1919) and later collected in *The Sacred Wood* (1920).

tradition" or to "a tradition"; at most, we employ the adjective in saying that the poetry of So-and-so is "traditional" or even "too traditional." Seldom, perhaps, does the word appear except in a phrase of censure. If otherwise, it is vaguely approbative, with the implication, as to the work approved, of some pleasing archaeological reconstruction. You can hardly make the word agreeable to English ears without this comfortable reference to the reassuring science of archaeology.

Certainly the word is not likely to appear in our appreciations of living or dead writers. Every nation, every race, has not only its own creative, but its own critical turn of mind; and is even more oblivious of the shortcomings and limitations of its critical habits than of those of its creative genius. We know, or think we know, from the enormous mass of critical writing that has appeared in the French language the critical method or habit of the French; we only conclude (we are such unconscious people) that the French are "more critical" than we, and sometimes even plume ourselves a little with the fact, as if the French were the less spontaneous. Perhaps they are; but we might remind ourselves that criticism is as inevitable as breathing, and that we should be none the worse for articulating what passes in our minds when we read a book and feel an emotion about it, for criticizing our own minds in their work of criticism. One of the facts that might come to light in this process is our tendency to insist, when we praise a poet, upon those aspects of his work in which he least resembles anyone else. In these aspects or parts of his work we pretend to find what is individual, what is the peculiar essence of the man. We dwell with satisfaction upon the poet's difference from his predecessors, especially his immediate predecessors; we endeavor to find something that can be isolated in order to be enjoyed. Whereas if we approach a poet without this prejudice we shall often find that not only the best, but the most individual parts of his work may be those in which the dead poets, his ancestors, assert their immortality most vigorously. And I do not mean the impressionable period of adolescence, but the period of full maturity.

Yet if the only form of tradition, of handing down, consisted in following the ways of the immediate generation before us in a blind or timid adherence to its successes, "tradition" should positively be discouraged. We have seen many such simple currents soon lost in the sand; and novelty is better than repetition. Tradition is a matter of much wider significance. It cannot be inherited, and if you want it you must obtain it by great labor. It involves, in the first place, the historical sense, which we may call nearly indispensable to any one who would continue to be a poet beyond his twenty-fifth year; and the historical sense involves a perception, not only of the pastness of the past, but of its presence; the historical sense compels a man to write not merely with his own generation in his bones, but with a feeling that the whole of the literature of Europe from Homer and within it the whole of the literature of his own country has a simultaneous existence and composes a simultaneous order. This historical sense, which is a sense of the timeless as well as of the temporal and of the timeless and of the temporal together, is what makes a writer traditional. And it is at the same time what makes a writer most acutely conscious of his place in time, of his own contemporaneity.

No poet, no artist of any art, has his complete meaning alone. His significance, his appreciation is the appreciation of his relation to the dead poets and artists. You cannot value him alone; you must set him, for contrast and comparison, among the dead. I mean this as a principle of aesthetic, not merely historical, criticism. The necessity that he shall conform, that he shall cohere, is not one-sided; what happens when a new work of art is created is something that happens simultaneously to all the works of art which preceded it. The existing monuments form an ideal order among themselves, which is modified by the introduction of the new (the really new) work of art among them. The existing order is complete before the new work arrives; for order to persist after the super-vention of novelty, the *whole* existing order must be, if ever so slightly, altered; and so the relations, proportions, values of each work of art toward the whole are readjusted; and this is conformity between the old and the new. Whoever has approved this idea of order, of the form of European, of English literature will not find it preposterous that the past should be altered by the present as much as the present is directed by the past. And the poet who is aware of this will be aware of great diffi-culties and responsibilities.

In a peculiar sense he will be aware also that he must inevitably be judged by the standards of the past. I say judged, not amputated, by them; not judged to be as good as, or worse or better than, the dead; and certainly not judged by the canons of dead critics. It is a judgment, a comparison, in which two things are measured by each other. To con-form merely would be for the new work not really to conform at all; it would not be new, and would therefore not be a work of art. And we do not quite say that the new is more valuable because it fits in; but its fitting in is a test of its value—a test, it is true, which can only be slowly and cautiously applied, for we are none of us infallible judges of con-formity. We say: it appears to conform, and is perhaps individual, or it appears individual, and may conform; but we are hardly likely to find that it is one and not the other.

To proceed to a more intelligible exposition of the relation of the poet to the past: he can neither take the past as a lump, an indiscriminate bolus,[2] nor can he form himself wholly on one or two private admira-tions, nor can he form himself wholly upon one preferred period. The first course is inadmissible, the second is an important experience of youth, and the third is a pleasant and highly desirable supplement. The poet must be very conscious of the main current, which does not at all flow invariably through the most distinguished reputations. He must be quite aware of the obvious fact that art never improves, but that the material of art is never quite the same. He must be aware that the mind

2. A round mass of anything: a large pill.

of Europe—the mind of his own country—a mind which he learns in time to be much more important than his own private mind—is a mind which changes, and that this change is a development which abandons nothing en route, which does not superannuate either Shakespeare, or Homer, or the rock drawing of the Magdalenian[3] draftsmen. That this development, refinement perhaps, complication certainly, is not, from the point of view of the artist, any improvement. Perhaps not even an improvement from the point of view of the psychologist or not to the extent which we imagine; perhaps only in the end based upon a complication in economics and machinery. But the difference between the present and the past is that the conscious present is an awareness of the past in a way and to an extent which the past's awareness of itself cannot show.

Someone said: "The dead writers are remote from us because we *know* so much more than they did." Precisely, and they are that which we know.

I am alive to a usual objection to what is clearly part of my program for the métier of poetry. The objection is that the doctrine requires a ridiculous amount of erudition (pedantry), a claim which can be rejected by appeal to the lives of poets in any pantheon. It will even be affirmed that much learning deadens or perverts poetic sensibility. While, however, we persist in believing that a poet ought to know as much as will not encroach upon his necessary receptivity and necessary laziness, it is not desirable to confine knowledge to whatever can be put into a useful shape for examinations, drawing rooms, or the still more pretentious modes of publicity. Some can absorb knowledge, the more tardy must sweat for it. Shakespeare acquired more essential history from Plutarch[4] than most men could from the whole British Museum. What is to be insisted upon is that the poet must develop or procure the consciousness of the past and that he should continue to develop this consciousness throughout his career.

What happens is a continual surrender of himself as he is at the moment to something which is more valuable. The progress of an artist is a continual self-sacrifice, a continual extinction of personality.

There remains to define this process of depersonalization and its relation to the sense of tradition. It is in this depersonalization that art may be said to approach the condition of science. I, therefore, invite you to consider, as a suggestive analogy, the action which takes place when a bit of finely filiated[5] platinum is introduced into a chamber containing oxygen and sulphur dioxide.

3. The most advanced culture of the European Paleolithic period (from discoveries at La Madeleine, France).
4. Greek biographer (1st century A.D.) of Greek and Roman celebrities, from whose work Shakespeare drew the plots of his Roman plays.
5. Drawn out like a thread.

2

Honest criticism and sensitive appreciation are directed not upon the poet but upon the poetry. If we attend to the confused cries of the newspaper critics and the *susurrus*[6] of popular repetition that follows, we shall hear the names of poets in great numbers; if we seek not Blue-book[7] knowledge but the enjoyment of poetry, and ask for a poem, we shall seldom find it. I have tried to point out the importance of the relation of the poem to other poems by other authors, and suggested the conception of poetry as a living whole of all the poetry that has ever been written. The other aspect of this Impersonal theory of poetry is the relation of the poem to its author. And I hinted, by an analogy, that the mind of the mature poet differs from that of the immature one not precisely in any valuation of "personality," not being necessarily more interesting, or having "more to say," but rather by being a more finely perfected medium in which special, or very varied, feelings are at liberty to enter into new combinations.

The analogy was that of the catalyst.[8] When the two gases previously mentioned are mixed in the presence of a filament of platinum, they form sulphurous acid. This combination takes place only if the platinum is present; nevertheless the newly formed acid contains no trace of platinum, and the platinum itself is apparently unaffected; has remained inert, neutral, and unchanged. The mind of the poet is the shred of platinum. It may partly or exclusively operate upon the experience of the man himself; but, the more perfect the artist, the more completely separate in him will be the man who suffers and the mind which creates; the more perfectly will the mind digest and transmute the passions which are its material.

The experience, you will notice, the elements which enter the presence of the transforming catalyst, are of two kinds: emotions and feelings. The effect of a work of art upon the person who enjoys it is an experience different in kind from any experience not of art. It may be formed out of one emotion, or may be a combination of several; and various feelings, inhering for the writer in particular words or phrases or images, may be added to compose the final result. Or great poetry may be made without the direct use of any emotion whatever: composed out of feelings solely. Canto XV of the *Inferno* (Brunetto Latini)[9] is a working up of the emotion evident in the situation; but the effect, though single as that of any work of art, is obtained by considerable complexity of detail. The last quatrain gives an image, a feeling attaching to an image, which "came," which did not develop simply out of what precedes, but which was probably in suspension in the poet's mind until

6. Murmuring, buzzing.
7. British official government publication.
8. Substance that triggers a chemical change without itself being affected by the reaction.
9. Dante meets in Hell his old master Brunetto Latini, suffering eternal punishment for unnatural lust, yet still loved and admired by Dante, who addresses him with affectionate courtesy. See note 1, below.

the proper combination arrived for it to add itself to.[1] The poet's mind is in fact a receptacle for seizing and storing up numberless feelings, phrases, images, which remain there until all the particles which can unite to form a new compound are present together.

If you compare several representative passages of the greatest poetry you see how great is the variety of types of combination, and also how completely any semi-ethical criterion of "sublimity" misses the mark. For it is not the "greatness," the intensity, of the emotions, the components, but the intensity of the artistic process, the pressure, so to speak, under which the fusion takes place, that counts. The episode of Paolo and Francesca[2] employs a definite emotion, but the intensity of the poetry is something quite different from whatever intensity in the supposed experience it may give the impression of. It is no more intense, furthermore, than Canto XXVI,[3] the voyage of Ulysses, which has not the direct dependence upon an emotion. Great variety is possible in the process of transmutation of emotion: the murder of Agamemnon,[4] or the agony of Othello, gives an artistic effect apparently closer to a possible original than the scenes from Dante. In the *Agamemnon*, the artistic emotion approximates to the emotion of an actual spectator; in *Othello* to the emotion of the protagonist himself. But the difference between art and the event is always absolute; the combination which is the murder of Agamemnon is probably as complex as that which is the voyage of Ulysses. In either case there has been a fusion of elements. The ode of Keats contains a number of feelings which have nothing particular to do with the nightingale, but which the nightingale, partly, perhaps, because of its attractive name, and partly because of its reputation, served to bring together.

The point of view which I am struggling to attack is perhaps related to the metaphysical theory of the substantial unity of the soul: for my meaning is, that the poet has, not a "personality" to express, but a particular medium, which is only a medium and not a personality, in which impressions and experiences combine in peculiar and unexpected ways. Impressions and experiences which are important for the man may take no place in the poetry, and those which become important in the poetry may play quite a negligible part in the man, the personality.

I will quote a passage which is unfamiliar enough to be regarded with fresh attention in the light—or darkness—of these observations:

> And now methinks I could e'en chide myself
> For doting on her beauty, though her death
> Shall be revenged after no common action.
> Does the silkworm expend her yellow labors

1. Dante's strange interview with Brunetto is over, and Brunetto moves off to continue his punishment: "Then he turned round, and seemed like one of those / Who run for the green cloth [in the footrace] at Verona / In the field; and he seemed among them / Not the loser but the winner."

2. Illicit lovers whom Dante meets in the second circle of Hell (*Inferno* 5) and at whose punishment and sorrows he swoons with pity.

3. Of the *Inferno*. Ulysses, suffering in Hell for "false counseling," tells Dante of his final voyage.

4. By his wife Clytemnestra; the central action of Aeschylus' play *Agamemnon*.

> For thee? For thee does she undo herself?
> Are lordships sold to maintain ladyships
> For the poor benefit of a bewildering minute?
> Why does yon fellow falsify highways,
> And put his life between the judge's lips,
> To refine such a thing—keeps horse and men
> To beat their valors for her? . . .[5]

In this passage (as is evident if it is taken in its context) there is a combination of positive and negative emotions: an intensely strong attraction toward beauty and an equally intense fascination by the ugliness which is contrasted with it and which destroys it. This balance of contrasted emotion is in the dramatic situation to which the speech is pertinent, but that situation alone is inadequate to it. This is, so to speak, the structural emotion, provided by the drama. But the whole effect, the dominant tone, is due to the fact that a number of floating feelings, having an affinity to this emotion by no means superficially evident, have combined with it to give us a new art emotion.

It is not in his personal emotions, the emotions provoked by particular events in his life, that the poet is in any way remarkable or interesting. His particular emotions may be simple, or crude, or flat. The emotion in his poetry will be a very complex thing, but not with the complexity of the emotions of people who have very complex or unusual emotions in life. One error, in fact, of eccentricity in poetry is to seek for new human emotions to express; and in this search for novelty in the wrong place it discovers the perverse. The business of the poet is not to find new emotions, but to use the ordinary ones and, in working them up into poetry, to express feelings which are not in actual emotions at all. And emotions which he has never experienced will serve his turn as well as those familiar to him. Consequently, we must believe that "emotion recollected in tranquility"[6] is an inexact formula. For it is neither emotion, nor recollection, nor, without distortion of meaning, tranquility. It is a concentration, and a new thing resulting from the concentration, of a very great number of experiences which to the practical and active person would not seem to be experiences at all; it is a concentration which does not happen consciously or of deliberation. These experiences are not "recollected," and they finally unite in an atmosphere which is "tranquil" only in that it is a passive attending upon the event. Of course this is not quite the whole story. There is a great deal, in the writing of poetry, which must be conscious and deliberate. In fact, the bad poet is usually unconscious where he ought to be conscious, and conscious where he ought to be unconscious. Both errors tend to make him "personal." Poetry is not a turning loose of emotion, but an escape from emotion; it is not the expression of personality, but an escape from

---

5. From Cyril Tourneur's *The Revenger's Tragedy* (1607), 3,4.
6. Wordsworth, Preface to *Lyrical Ballads*, 2nd edition (1800). Wordsworth said that poetry "takes its origin from emotion recollected in tranquility."

personality. But, of course, only those who have personality and emotions know what it means to want to escape from these things.

3

o dé noús ísos Theióterón ti chaí apathés estin.[7]

This essay proposes to halt at the frontier of metaphysics or mysticism, and confine itself to such practical conclusions as can be applied by the responsible person interested in poetry. To divert interest from the poet to the poetry is a laudable aim: for it would conduce to a juster estimation of actual poetry, good and bad. There are many people who appreciate the expression of sincere emotion in verse, and there is a smaller number of people who can appreciate technical excellence. But very few know when there is an expression of *significant* emotion, emotion which has its life in the poem and not in the history of the poet. The emotion of art is impersonal. And the poet cannot reach this impersonality without surrendering himself wholly to the work to be done. And he is not likely to know what is to be done unless he lives in what is not merely the present, but the present moment of the past, unless he is conscious, not of what is dead, but of what is already living.

1919, 1920

---

7. "The mind is doubtless something more divine and unimpressionable." Aristotle, *De Anima* ("On the Soul"), 1.4.

SAMUEL BECKETT

1906–

1937:	Moved to Paris.
1952:	*Waiting for Godot*.
1969:	Nobel Prize.

Samuel Beckett, born near Dublin, took a degree at Trinity College (Dublin's Protestant university), but then went abroad and settled for good in Paris in 1937. He has lived in Paris ever since, teaching in French *lycées*, and serving occasionally as Joyce's secretary, translator and critical defender— but mostly writing. Since the mid-1940s, he generally writes in French as a first tongue and then sometimes translates his French into an eloquent, Irish-tinged English. Shortly after the war, he published three interrelated novels, *Molloy, Malone Dies*, and *The Unnamable*. They may well be thought his masterpiece some day, but Beckett's first major public recognition came as a result of a somber, static, and hilarious stage-vaudeville titled *Waiting for Godot*. The play is simplicity itself. Vladimir and Estragon, a pair of derelicts, are waiting in a bleak place for Godot, who tantalizes them by promising to come but never doing so. They talk, they complain, they try to kill time; the play ends with them still waiting. It is a play without plot or intrigue, which uses brilliantly the idea of nothing happening on stage, the vacancy experienced when something is expected but never found. It is a despairing and funny play. In 1958, *Endgame*, even more despairing and just as funny, repeated the success of *Godot*; and despite wiseacre predictions that each grotesque, hilarious work would be his last, Beckett has remained vigorously active in fiction, in drama for stage and radio, in mime, and in film. In 1969 he received the Nobel Prize for Literature.

His work is always stripped, severe, grotesquely comic, and haunted by the theme of nonexistence. He seeks to represent the mind purified down to its last bitter, almost unbearably pure negation—and kept alive simply by the force of that negation. From René Descartes, the seventeenth-century French thinker, and his follower Arnold Geulincx, Beckett took over premises regarding the separation of body and mind which led him to represent, almost uniformly throughout his work, mind under the compulsion of questioning itself. Fastened to a dying animal, as Yeats said, the mind of a Beckett character seeks constantly to reassure itself of its own existence by developing a brilliant, sterile dialectic of its own. The old scarecrows and crones who animate what a clever undergraduate once called Beckett's "crucifictions" live in a disgusting world and are themselves disintegrating. They all have stories to tell, and as long as they can keep talking, can keep some sort of empty verbal game going, they need not despair of their being. But any sort of comfort or security beyond the absolute minimum eludes them. They take no action, they preach no doctrine, they know nothing save their own ignorance, they are kicked and cuffed by society, they stink, they sulk, they snarl at their own disgusting condition. And yet in some dark way, they represent mankind, "without the courage to end or the strength to go on"— as the narrator of *The End* describes himself. Whether clinging to hopelessness as their one hope or, like the heroine of *Happy Days*, to love in the grip of the grave, they bear witness, as more comfortable folk could not, to the essential holiness of existence.

Happy Days[1]

Act 1

Expanse of scorched grass rising centre to low mound. Gentle slopes down to front and either side of stage. Back an abrupter fall to stage level. Maximum of simplicity and symmetry.
Blazing light.
Very pompier trompe-l'oeil[2] backcloth to represent unbroken plain and sky receding to meet in far distance.
Imbedded up to above her waist in exact centre of mound, WINNIE. *About fifty, well preserved, blond for preference, plump, arms and shoulders bare, low bodice, big bosom, pearl necklet. She is discovered sleeping, her arms on the ground before her, her head on her arms. Beside her on ground*

1. *Happy Days* takes its English title from the song "Happy Days Are Here Again," the words of which were written by Jack Yellen, the music by Milton Ager (1929).
2. Conventionally realistic, literally "deceiving the eye" (French).

to her left a capacious black bag, shopping variety, and to her right a
collapsible collapsed parasol, beak of handle emerging from sheath.
To her right and rear, lying asleep on ground, hidden by mound, WILLIE.
Long pause. A bell rings piercingly, say ten seconds, stops. She does not
move. Pause. Bell more piercingly, say five seconds. Bell stops.
She raises her head, gazes front. Long pause. She straightens up, lays her
hands flat on ground, throws back her head and gazes at zenith.[3] Long
pause.

WINNIE [gazing at zenith]. Another heavenly day. [Pause. Head back
level, eyes front, pause. She clasps hands to breast, closes eyes. Lips
move in inaudible prayer, say ten seconds. Lips still. Hands remain
clasped. Low.] For Jesus Christ sake Amen. [Eyes open, hands unclasp,
return to mound. Pause. She clasps hands to breast again, closes eyes,
lips move again in inaudible addendum, say five seconds. Low.] World
without end Amen.[4] [Eyes open, hands unclasp, return to mound.
Pause.] Begin, Winnie. [Pause.] Begin your day, Winnie. [Pause. She
turns to bag, rummages in it without moving it from its place, brings
out toothbrush, rummages again, brings out flat tube of toothpaste,
turns back front, unscrews cap of tube, lays cap on ground, squeezes
with difficulty small blob of paste on brush, holds tube in one hand
and brushes teeth with other. She turns modestly aside and back to her
right to spit out behind mound. In this position her eyes rest on WILLIE.
She spits out. She cranes a little further back and down. Loud.] Hoo-
oo! [Pause. Louder.] Hoo-oo! [Pause. Tender smile as she turns back
front, lays down brush.] Poor Willie—[examines tube, smile off]—
running out—[looks for cap]—ah well—[finds cap]—can't be helped—
[screws on cap]—just one of those old things—[lays down tube]—another
of those old things—[turns towards bag]—just can't be cured—[rum-
mages in bag]—cannot be cured—[brings out small mirror, turns back
front]—ah yes—[inspects teeth in mirror]—poor dear Willie—[testing
upper front teeth with thumb, indistinctly]—good Lord! —[pulling
back upper lip to inspect gums, do.][5] —good God!—[pulling back corner of mouth, mouth open, do.]—ah well—[other corner, do.]—no
worse—[abandons inspection, normal speech]—no better, no worse—
[lays down mirror]—no change—[wipes fingers on grass]—no pain—
[looks for toothbrush]—hardly any—[takes up toothbrush]—great thing
that—[examines handle of brush]—nothing like it—[examines handle,
reads]—pure . . . what?—[pause]—what?—[lays down brush]—ah
yes—[turns towards bag]—poor Willie—[rummages in bag]—no zest—
[rummages]—for anything—[brings out spectacles in case]—no interest—[turns back front]—in life— [takes spectacles from case]—poor
dear Willie—[lays down case]—sleep for ever—[opens spectacles]—
marvellous gift—[puts on spectacles]—nothing to touch it—[looks for
toothbrush]—in my opinion—[takes up toothbrush]—always said so—
[examines handle of brush]—wish I had it—[examines handle, reads]—
genuine . . . pure . . . what?—[lays down brush]—blind next—[takes
off spectacles]—ah well—[lays down spectacles]—seen enough—[feels
in bodice for handkerchief]—I suppose—[takes out folded handker-

---

3. The sky directly overhead.　　　　　　Book of Common Prayer.
4. Conclusion of "The Gloria" in the Anglican　5. Abbreviation for "ditto."

chief]—by now—[*shakes out handkerchief*]—what are those wonderful lines—[*wipes one eye*]—woe woe is me—[*wipes the other*]—to see what I see[6]—[*looks for spectacles*]—ah yes—[*takes up spectacles*]— wouldn't miss it—[*starts polishing spectacles, breathing on lenses*]—or would I?—[*polishes*]—holy light—[*polishes*]—bob up out of dark— [*polishes*]—blaze of hellish light. [*Stops polishing, raises face to sky, pause, head back level, resumes polishing, stops polishing, cranes back to her right and down.*] Hoo-oo! [*Pause. Tender smile as she turns back front and resumes polishing. Smile off.*] Marvellous gift—[*stops polishing, lays down spectacles.*]—wish I had it—[*folds handkerchief*]—ah well—[*puts handkerchief back in bodice*]—can't complain—[*looks for spectacles*]—no no—[*takes up spectacles*]—mustn't complain—[*holds up spectacles, looks through lens*]—so much to be thankful for—[*looks through other lens*]—no pain—[*puts on spectacles*]—hardly any—[*looks for toothbrush*]—wonderful thing that—[*takes up toothbrush*]—nothing like it—[*examines handle of brush*]—slight headache sometimes— [*examines handle, reads*]—guaranteed . . . genuine . . . pure . . . what?—[*looks closer*]—genuine pure . . .—[*takes handkerchief from bodice*]—ah yes—[*shakes out handkerchief*]—occasional mild migraine—[*starts wiping handle of brush*]—it comes—[*wipes*]—then goes—[*wiping mechanically*]—ah yes—[*wiping*]—many mercies— [*wiping*]—great mercies—[*stops wiping, fixed lost gaze, brokenly*]— prayers perhaps not for naught—[*pause, do.*]—first thing—[*pause, do.*]—last thing—[*head down, resumes wiping, stops wiping, head up, calmed, wipes eyes, folds handkerchief, puts it back in bodice, examines handle of brush, reads*]—fully guaranteed . . . genuine pure . . . —[*looks closer*]—genuine pure . . . [*Takes off spectacles, lays them and brush down, gazes before her.*] Old things. [*Pause.*] Old eyes. [*Long pause.*] On, Winnie. [*She casts about her, sees parasol, considers it at length, takes it up and develops from sheath a handle of surprising length. Holding butt of parasol in right hand she cranes back and down to her right to hang over* WILLIE.] Hoo-oo! [*Pause.*] Willie! [*Pause.*] Wonderful gift. [*She strikes down at him with beak of parasol.*] Wish I had it. [*She strikes again. The parasol slips from her grasp and falls behind mound. It is immediately restored to her by* WILLIE's *invisible hand.*] Thank you, dear. [*She transfers parasol to left hand, turns back front and examines right palm.*] Damp. [*Returns parasol to right hand, examines left palm.*] Ah well, no worse. [*Head up, cheerfully.*] No better, no worse, no change. [*Pause. Do.*] No pain. [*Cranes back to look down at* WILLIE, *holding parasol by butt as before.*] Don't go off on me again now dear will you please, I may need you. [*Pause.*] No hurry, no hurry, just don't curl up on me again. [*Turns back front, lays down parasol, examines palms together, wipes them on grass.*] Perhaps a shade off colour just the same. [*Turns to bag, rummages in it, brings out revolver, holds it up, kisses it rapidly, puts it back, rummages, brings out almost empty bottle of red medicine, turns back front, looks for spectacles, puts them on, reads label.*] Loss of spirits . . . lack of keenness . . . want of appetite . . . infants . . . children . . . adults . . . six level . . . tablespoonfuls daily— [*head up, smile*]—the old style!—[*smile off, head down, reads*]—daily

6. Cf. *Hamlet*, 3.1: "O, woe is me, / T' have seen what I have seen, see what I see!"

. . . before and after . . . meals . . . instantaneous . . . [*looks closer*] . . . improvement. [*Takes off spectacles, lays them down, holds up bottle at arm's length to see level, unscrews cap, swigs it off head well back, tosses cap and bottle away in* WILLIE's *direction. Sound of breaking glass.*] Ah that's better! [*Turns to bag, rummages in it, brings out lipstick, turns back front, examines lipstick.*] Running out. [*Looks for spectacles.*] Ah well. [*Puts on spectacles, looks for mirror.*] Mustn't complain. [*Takes up mirror, starts doing lips.*] What is that wonderful line? [*Lips.*] Oh fleeting joys—[*lips*]—oh something lasting woe.[7] [*Lips. She is interrupted by disturbance from* WILLIE. *He is sitting up. She lowers lipstick and mirror and cranes back and down to look at him. Pause. Top back of* WILLIE's *bald head, trickling blood, rises to view above slope, comes to rest.* WINNIE *pushes up her spectacles. Pause. His hand appears with handkerchief, spreads it on skull, disappears. Pause. The hand appears with boater,[8] club ribbon, settles it on head, rakish angle, disappears. Pause.* WINNIE *cranes a little further back and down.*] Slip on your drawers, dear, before you get singed. [*Pause.*] No? [*Pause.*] Oh I see, you still have some of that stuff left. [*Pause.*] Work it well in, dear. [*Pause.*] Now the other. [*Pause. She turns back front, gazes before her. Happy expression.*] Oh this is going to be another happy day! [*Pause. Happy expression off. She pulls down spectacles and resumes lips.* WILLIE *opens newspaper, hands invisible. Tops of yellow sheets appear on either side of his head.* WINNIE *finishes lips, inspects them in mirror held a little further away.*] Ensign crimson. [WILLIE *turns page.* WINNIE *lays down lipstick and mirror, turns towards bag.*] Pale flag.[9]

> WILLIE *turns page.* WINNIE *rummages in bag, brings out small ornate brimless hat with crumpled feather, turns back front, straightens hat, smooths feather, raises it towards head, arrests gesture as* WILLIE *reads.*

WILLIE. His Grace and Most Reverend Father in God Dr Carolus Hunter dead in tub.

> *Pause.*

WINNIE [*gazing front, hat in hand, tone of fervent reminiscence.*] Charlie Hunter! [*Pause.*] I close my eyes—[*she takes off spectacles and does so, hat in one hand, spectacles in other,* WILLIE *turns page*]—and am sitting on his knees again, in the back garden at Borough Green, under the horse-beech. [*Pause. She opens eyes, puts on spectacles, fiddles with hat.*] Oh the happy memories!

> *Pause. She raises hat towards head, arrests gesture as* WILLIE *reads.*

WILLIE. Opening for smart youth.

> *Pause. She raises hat towards head, arrests gesture, takes off spectacles, gazes front, hat in one hand, spectacles in other.*

---

7. Cf. Milton's *Paradise Lost*, 10.741–42: "O fleeting joys / Of Paradise, dear bought with lasting woes!"

8. Hard straw hat, with a flat top, originally worn when boating.

9. Cf. *Romeo and Juliet*, 5.3: "beauty's ensign yet / Is crimson in thy lips and in thy cheeks, / And death's pale flag is not advancèd there."

WINNIE. My first ball! [*Long pause.*] My second ball! [*Long pause. Closes eyes.*] My first kiss! [*Pause.* WILLIE *turns page.* WINNIE *opens eyes.*] A Mr Johnson, or Johnston, or perhaps I should say Johnstone. Very bushy moustache, very tawny. [*Reverently.*] Almost ginger! [*Pause.*] Within a toolshed, though whose I cannot conceive. We had no toolshed and he most certainly had no toolshed. [*Closes eyes.*] I see the piles of pots. [*Pause.*] The tangles of bast.[1] [*Pause.*] The shadows deepening among the rafters.

> *Pause. She opens eyes, puts on spectacles, raises hat towards head, arrests gesture as* WILLIE *reads.*

WILLIE. Wanted bright boy.

> *Pause.* WINNIE *puts on hat hurriedly, looks for mirror.* WILLIE *turns page.* WINNIE *takes up mirror, inspects hat, lays down mirror, turns towards bag. Paper disappears.* WINNIE *rummages in bag, brings out magnifying-glass, turns back front, looks for toothbrush. Paper reappears, folded, and begins to fan* WILLIE's *face, hand invisible.* WINNIE *takes up toothbrush and examines handle through glass.*

WINNIE. Fully guaranteed . . . [WILLIE *stops fanning*] . . . genuine pure . . . [*Pause.* WILLIE *resumes fanning.* WINNIE *looks closer, reads.*] Fully guaranteed . . . [WILLIE *stops fanning*] . . . genuine pure . . . [*Pause.* WILLIE *resumes fanning.* WINNIE *lays down glass and brush, takes handkerchief from bodice, takes off and polishes spectacles, puts on spectacles, looks for glass, takes up and polishes glass, lays down glass, looks for brush, takes up brush and wipes handle, lays down brush, puts handkerchief back in bodice, looks for glass, takes up glass, looks for brush, takes up brush and examines handle through glass.*] Fully guaranteed . . . [WILLIE *stops fanning*] . . . genuine pure . . . [*pause,* WILLIE *resumes fanning*] . . . hog's [WILLIE *stops fanning, pause*] . . . setae.[2] [*Pause.* WINNIE *lays down glass and brush, paper disappears,* WINNIE *takes off spectacles, lays them down, gazes front.*] Hog's setae. [*Pause.*] That is what I find so wonderful, that not a day goes by— [*smile*]—to speak in the old style—[*smile off*]—hardly a day, without some addition to one's knowledge however trifling, the addition I mean, provided one takes the pains. [WILLIE's *hand reappears with a postcard which he examines close to eyes.*] And if for some strange reason no further pains are possible, why then just close the eyes—[*she does so*]—and wait for the day to come—[*opens eyes*]—the happy day to come when flesh melts at so many degrees and the night of the moon has so many hundred hours. [*Pause.*] That is what I find so comforting when I lose heart and envy the brute beast. [*Turning towards* WILLIE.] I hope you are taking in—[*She sees postcard, bends lower.*] What is that you have there, Willie, may I see? [*She reaches down with hand and* WILLIE *hands her card. The hairy forearm appears above slope, raised in gesture of giving, the hand open to take back, and remains in this position till card is returned.* WINNIE *turns back front and examines card.*] Heavens what are they up to! [*She looks for spec-*

---

1. Type of coarse string.   2. Bristles.

tacles, puts them on and examines card.] No but this is just genuine pure filth! [*Examines card.*] Make any nice-minded person want to vomit! [*Impatience of* WILLIE's *fingers. She looks for glass, takes it up and examines card through glass. Long pause.*] What does that creature in the background think he's doing? [*Looks closer.*] Oh no really! [*Impatience of fingers. Last long look. She lays down glass, takes edge of card between right forefinger and thumb, averts head, takes nose between left forefinger and thumb.*] Pah! [*Drops card.*] Take it away! [WILLIE's *arm disappears. His hand reappears immediately, holding card.* WINNIE *takes off spectacles, lays them down, gazes before her. During what follows* WILLIE *continues to relish card, varying angles and distance from his eyes.*] Hog's setae. [*Puzzled expression.*] What exactly is a hog? [*Pause. Do.*] A sow of course I know, but a hog . . . [*Puzzled expression off.*] Oh well what does it matter, that is what I always say, it will come back, that is what I find so wonderful, all comes back. [*Pause.*] All? [*Pause.*] No, not all. [*Smile.*] No no. [*Smile off.*] Not quite. [*Pause.*] A part. [*Pause.*] Floats up, one fine day, out of the blue. [*Pause.*] That is what I find so wonderful. [*Pause. She turns towards bag. Hand and card disappear. She makes to rummage in bag, arrests gesture.*] No. [*She turns back front. Smile.*] No no. [*Smile off.*] Gently Winnie. [*She gazes front.* WILLIE's *hand reappears, takes off hat, disappears with hat.*] What then? [*Hand reappears, takes handkerchief from skull, disappears with handkerchief. Sharply, as to one not paying attention.*] Winnie! [WILLIE *bows head out of sight.*] What *is* the alternative? [*Pause.*] What *is* the al—[WILLIE *blows nose loud and long, head and hands invisible. She turns to look at him. Pause. Head reappears. Pause. Hand reappears with handkerchief, spreads it on skull, disappears. Pause. Hand reappears with boater, settles it on head, rakish angle, disappears. Pause.*] Would I had let you sleep on. [*She turns back front. Intermittent plucking at grass, head up and down, to animate following.*] Ah yes, if only I could bear to be alone, I mean prattle away with not a soul to hear. [*Pause.*] Not that I flatter myself you hear much, no Willie, God forbid. [*Pause.*] Days perhaps when you hear nothing. [*Pause.*] But days too when you answer. [*Pause.*] So that I may say at all times, even when you do not answer and perhaps hear nothing, Something of this is being heard, I am not merely talking to myself, that is in the wilderness, a thing I could never bear to do—for any length of time. [*Pause.*] That is what enables me to go on, go on talking that is. [*Pause.*] Whereas if you were to die—[*smile*]—to speak in the old style—[*smile off*]—or go away and leave me, then what would I do, what *could* I do, all day long, I mean between the bell for waking and the bell for sleep? [*Pause.*] Simply gaze before me with compressed lips. [*Long pause while she does so. No more plucking.*] Not another word as long as I drew breath, nothing to break the silence of this place. [*Pause.*] Save possibly, now and then, every now and then, a sigh into my looking-glass. [*Pause.*] Or a brief . . . gale of laughter, should I happen to see the old joke again. [*Pause. Smile appears, broadens and seems about to culminate in laugh when suddenly replaced by expression of anxiety.*] My hair! [*Pause.*] Did I brush and comb my hair? [*Pause.*] I may have done. [*Pause.*] Normally I do. [*Pause.*] There is so little one *can* do. [*Pause.*] One does it all. [*Pause.*] All one can. [*Pause.*] 'Tis only human. [*Pause.*]

Human nature. [*She begins to inspect mound, looks up.*] Human weakness. [*She resumes inspection of mound, looks up.*] Natural weakness. [*She resumes inspection of mound.*] I see no comb. [*Inspects.*] Nor any hairbrush. [*Looks up. Puzzled expression. She turns to bag, rummages in it.*] The comb is here. [*Back front. Puzzled expression. Back to bag. Rummages.*] The brush is here. [*Back front. Puzzled expression.*] Perhaps I put them back, after use. [*Pause. Do.*] But normally I do not put things back, after use, no, I leave them lying about and put them back all together, at the end of the day. [*Smile.*] To speak in the old style. [*Pause.*] The sweet old style. [*Smile off.*] And yet . . . I seem . . . to remember . . . [*Suddenly careless.*] Oh well, what does it matter, that is what I always say, I shall simply brush and comb them later on, purely and simply, I have the whole—[*Pause. Puzzled.*] Them? [*Pause.*] Or it? [*Pause.*] Brush and comb it? [*Pause.*] Sounds improper somehow. [*Pause. Turning a little towards* WILLIE.] What would you say, Willie? [*Pause. Turning a little further.*] What would you say, Willie, speaking of your hair, them or it? [*Pause.*] The hair on your head, I mean. [*Pause. Turning a little further.*] The hair on your head, Willie, what would you say speaking of the hair on your head, them or it?

Long pause.

WILLIE. It.

WINNIE [*turning back front, joyful*]. Oh you are going to talk to me today, this is going to be a happy day! [*Pause. Joy off.*] Another happy day. [*Pause.*] Ah well, where was I, my hair, yes, later on, I shall be thankful for it later on. [*Pause.*] I have my—[*raises hands to hat*]—yes, on, my hat on—[*lowers hands*]—I cannot take it off now. [*Pause.*] To think there are times one cannot take off one's hat, not if one's life were at stake. Times one cannot put it on, times one cannot take it off. [*Pause.*] How often I have said, Put on your hat now, Winnie, there is nothing else for it, take off your hat now, Winnie, like a good girl, it will do you good, and did not. [*Pause.*] Could not. [*Pause. She raises hand, frees a strand of hair from under hat, draws it towards eye, squints at it, lets it go, hand down.*] Golden you called it, that day, when the last guest was gone—[*hand up in gesture of raising a glass*]—to your golden . . . may it never . . . [*Voice breaks*] . . . may it never . . . [*Hand down. Head down. Pause. Low.*] That day. [*Pause. Do.*] What day? [*Pause. Head up. Normal voice.*] What now? [*Pause.*] Words fail, there are times when even they fail. [*Turning a little towards* WILLIE.] Is that not so, Willie? [*Pause. Turning a little further.*] Is not that so, Willie, that even words fail, at times? [*Pause. Back front.*] What is one to do then, until they come again? Brush and comb the hair, if it has not been done, or if there is some doubt, trim the nails if they are in need of trimming, these things tide one over. [*Pause.*] That is what I mean. [*Pause.*] That is all I mean. [*Pause.*] That is what I find so wonderful, that not a day goes by—[*smile*]—to speak in the old style—[*smile off*]—without some blessing—[WILLIE *collapses behind slope, his head disappears,* WINNIE *turns towards event*]—in disguise. [*She cranes back and down.*] Go back into your hole now, Willie, you've exposed yourself enough. [*Pause.*] Do as I say, Willie, don't lie sprawling there in this hellish sun, go back into your hole.

[*Pause.*] Go on now, Willie. [WILLIE *invisible starts crawling left towards hole.*] That's the man. [*She follows his progress with her eyes.*] Not head first, stupid, how are you going to turn? [*Pause.*] That's it . . . right round . . . now . . . back in. [*Pause.*] Oh I know it is not easy, dear, crawling backwards, but it is rewarding in the end. [*Pause.*] You have left your vaseline behind. [*She watches as he crawls back for vaseline.*] The lid! [*She watches as he crawls back towards hole. Irritated.*] Not head first, I tell you! [*Pause.*] More to the right. [*Pause.*] The *right*, I said. [*Pause. Irritated.*] Keep your tail down, can't you! [*Pause.*] Now. [*Pause.*] There! [*All these directions loud. Now in her normal voice, still turned towards him.*] Can you hear me? [*Pause.*] I beseech you, Willie, just yes or no, can you hear me, just yes or nothing.

      Pause.

WILLIE. Yes.

WINNIE [*turning front, same voice*]. And now?

WILLIE [*irritated*]. Yes.

WINNIE [*less loud*]. And now?

WILLIE [*more irritated*]. Yes.

WINNIE [*still less loud*]. And now? [*A little louder.*] And now?

WILLIE [*violently*]. Yes!

WINNIE [*same voice*]. Fear no more the heat o' the sun.[3] [*Pause.*] Did you hear that?

WILLIE [*irritated*]. Yes.

WINNIE [*same voice*]. What? [*Pause.*] What?

WILLIE [*more irritated*]. Fear no more.

      Pause.

WINNIE [*same voice*]. No more what? [*Pause.*] Fear no more what?

WILLIE [*violently*]. Fear no more!

WINNIE [*normal voice, gabbled*]. Bless you Willie I do appreciate your goodness I know what an effort it costs you, now you may relax I shall not trouble you again unless I am obliged to, by that I mean unless I come to the end of my own resources which is most unlikely, just to know that in theory you can hear me even though in fact you don't is all I need, just to feel you there within earshot and conceivably on the qui vive[4] is all I ask, not to say anything I would not wish you to hear or liable to cause you pain, not to be just babbling away on trust as it is were not knowing and something gnawing at me. [*Pause for breath.*] Doubt. [*Places index and second finger on heart area, moves them about, brings them to rest.*] Here. [*Moves them slightly.*] Abouts. [*Hand away.*] Oh no doubt the time will come when before I can utter a word I must make sure you heard the one that went before and then no doubt another come another time when I must learn to talk to myself a thing I could never bear to do such wilderness. [*Pause.*] Or gaze before me with compressed lips. [*She does so.*] All day long. [*Gaze and lips again.*] No. [*Smile.*] No no. [*Smile off.*] There is of course the bag: [*Turns towards it.*] There will always be the bag. [*Back*

3. Cf. *Cymbeline,* 4.2.258.
4. Alert, literally "[long] live who?"—a French sentinel's challenge.

front.] Yes, I suppose so. [*Pause.*] Even when you are gone, Willie. [*She turns a little towards him.*] You *are* going, Willie, aren't you? [*Pause. Louder.*] You *will* be going soon, Willie, won't you? [*Pause. Louder.*] Willie! [*Pause. She cranes back and down to look at him.*] So you have taken off your straw, that is wise. [*Pause.*] You do look snug, I must say, with your chin on your hands and the old blue eyes like saucers in the shadows. [*Pause.*] Can you see me from there I wonder, I still wonder. [*Pause.*] No? [*Back front.*] Oh I know it does not follow when two are gathered together—[*faltering*]—in this way—[*normal*]—that because one sees the other the other sees the one, life has taught me that . . . too. [*Pause.*] Yes, life I suppose, there is no other word. [*She turns a little towards him.*] Could you see me, Willie, do you think, from where you are, if you were to raise your eyes in my direction? [*Turns a little further.*] Lift up your eyes to me, Willie, and tell me can you see me, do that for me, I'll lean back as far as I can. [*Does so. Pause.*] No? [*Pause.*] Well never mind. [*Turns back painfully front.*] The earth is very tight today, can it be I have put on flesh, I trust not. [*Pause. Absently, eyes lowered.*] The great heat possibly. [*Starts to pat and stroke ground.*] All things expanding, some more than others. [*Pause. Patting and stroking.*] Some less. [*Pause. Do.*] Oh I can well imagine what is passing through your mind, it is not enough to have to listen to the woman, now I must look at her as well. [*Pause. Do.*] Well it is very understandable. [*Pause. Do.*] Most understandable. [*Pause. Do.*] One does not appear to be asking a great deal, indeed at times it would seem hardly possible—[*voice breaks, falls to a murmur*]—to ask less—of a fellow-creature—to put it mildly—whereas actually—when you think about it—look into your heart—see the other—what he needs—peace—to be left in peace—then perhaps the moon—all this time—asking for the moon. [*Pause. Stroking hand suddenly still. Lively.*] Oh I say, what have we here? [*Bending head to ground, incredulous.*] Looks like life of some kind! [*Looks for spectacles, puts them on, bends closer. Pause.*] An emmet![5] [*Recoils. Shrill.*] Willie, an emmet, a live emmet! [*Seizes magnifying-glass, bends to ground again, inspects through glass.*] Where's it gone? [*Inspects.*] Ah! [*Follows its progress through grass.*] Has like a little white ball in its arms. [*Follows progress. Hand still. Pause.*] It's gone in. [*Continues a moment to gaze at spot through glass, then slowly straightens up, lays down glass, takes off spectacles and gazes before her, spectacles in hand. Finally.*] Like a little white ball.

     Long pause. Gesture to lay down spectacles.

WILLIE. Eggs.
WINNIE [*arresting gesture*]. What?

     Pause.

WILLIE. Eggs. [*Pause. Gesture to lay down glasses.*] Formication.[6]
WINNIE [*arresting gesture*]. What?

     Pause.

---

5. Ant.

6. Sensation as of ants crawling over the skin.

WILLIE. Formication.

Pause. She lays down spectacles, gazes before her. Finally.

WINNIE [*murmur*]. God. [*Pause.* WILLIE *laughs quietly. After a moment she joins in. They laugh quietly together.* WILLIE *stops. She laughs on a moment alone.* WILLIE *joins in. They laugh together. She stops.* WILLIE *laughs on a moment alone. He stops. Pause. Normal voice.*] Ah well what a joy in any case to hear you laugh again, Willie, I was convinced I never would, you never would. [*Pause.*] I suppose some people might think us a trifle irreverent, but I doubt it. [*Pause.*] How can one better magnify the Almighty than by sniggering with him at his little jokes, particularly the poorer ones? [*Pause.*] I think you would back me up there, Willie. [*Pause.*] Or were we perhaps diverted by two quite different things? [*Pause.*] Oh well, what does it matter, that is what I always say, so long as one . . . you know . . . what is that wonderful line . . . laughing wild . . . something something laughing wild amid severest woe.[7] [*Pause.*] And now? [*Long pause.*] Was I lovable once, Willie? [*Pause.*] Was I ever lovable? [*Pause.*] Do not misunderstand my question, I am not asking you if you loved me, we know all about that, I am asking you if you found me lovable—at one stage. [*Pause.*] No? [*Pause.*] You can't? [*Pause.*] Well I admit it is a teaser. And you have done more than your bit already, for the time being, just lie back now and relax, I shall not trouble you again unless I am compelled to, just to know you are there within hearing and conceivably on the semi-alert is . . . er. . . paradise enow.[8] [*Pause.*] The day is now well advanced. [*Smile.*] To speak in the old style. [*Smile off.*] And yet it is perhaps a little soon for my song. [*Pause.*] To sing too soon is a great mistake, I find. [*Turning towards bag.*] There is of course the bag. [*Looking at bag.*] The bag. [*Back front.*] Could I enumerate its contents? [*Pause.*] No. [*Pause.*] Could I, if some kind person were to come along and ask, What all have you got in that big black bag, Winnie? give an exhaustive answer? [*Pause.*] No. [*Pause.*] The depths in particular, who knows what treasures. [*Pause.*] What comforts. [*Turns to look at bag.*] Yes, there is the bag. [*Back front.*] But something tells me, Do not overdo the bag, Winnie, make use of it of course, let it help you . . . along, when stuck, by all means, but cast your mind forward, something tells me, cast your mind forward, Winnie, to the time when words must fail—[*she closes eyes, pause, opens eyes*]—and do not overdo the bag. [*Pause. She turns to look at bag.*] Perhaps just one quick dip. [*She turns back front, closes eyes, throws out left arm, plunges hand in bag and brings out revolver. Disgusted.*] You again! [*She opens eyes, brings revolver front and contemplates it. She weighs it in her palm.*] You'd think the weight of this thing would bring it down among the . . . last rounds. But no. It doesn't. Ever uppermost, like Browning.[9] [*Pause.*] Brownie . . .

7. Cf. Gray's *Ode on a Distant Prospect of Eton College*, lines 79–80: "And moody Madness laughing wild / Amid severest woe."
8. Cf. Fitzgerald's *The Rubáiyát of Omar Khayyám*, 12: "A Book of Verses underneath the Bough, / A Jug of Wine, a Loaf of Bread—and Thou / Beside me singing in the Wilderness—/ Oh, Wilderness were Paradise enow!"
9. Cf. Browning's *Paracelsus*, 3. lines 372–73: "I say confusedly what comes uppermost; / But there are times when patience proves a fault / As now: This morning's strange encounter—you / Beside me once again!"

[*Turning a little towards* WILLIE.] Remember Brownie, Willie? [*Pause.*] Remember how you used to keep on at me to take it away from you? Take it away, Winnie, take it away, before I put myself out of my misery. [*Back front. Derisive.*] Your misery! [*To revolver.*] Oh I suppose it's a comfort to know you're there, but I'm tired of you. [*Pause.*] I'll leave you out, that's what I'll do. [*She lays revolver on ground to her right.*] There, that's your home from this day out. [*Smile.*] The old style! [*Smile off.*] And now? [*Long pause.*] Is gravity what it was, Willie, I fancy not. [*Pause.*] Yes, the feeling more and more that if I were not held—[*gesture*]—in this way, I would simply float up into the blue. [*Pause.*] And that perhaps some day the earth will yield and let me go, the pull is so great, yes, crack all round me and let me out. [*Pause.*] Don't you ever have that feeling, Willie, of being sucked up? [*Pause.*] Don't you have to cling on sometimes, Willie? [*Pause. She turns a little towards him.*] Willie.

   Pause.

WILLIE. *Sucked* up?

WINNIE. Yes love, up into the blue, like gossamer. [*Pause.*] No? [*Pause.*] You don't? [*Pause.*] Ah well, natural laws, natural laws, I suppose it's like everything else, it all depends on the creature you happen to be. All I can say is for my part is that for me they are not what they were when I was young and . . . foolish and . . . [*faltering, head down*] . . . beautiful . . . possibly . . . lovely . . . in a way . . . to look at. [*Pause. Head up.*] Forgive me, Willie, sorrow keeps breaking in. [*Normal voice.*] Ah well what a joy in any case to know you are there, as usual, and perhaps awake, and perhaps taking all this in, some of all this, what a happy day for me . . . it will have been. [*Pause.*] So far. [*Pause.*] What a blessing nothing grows, imagine if all this stuff were to start growing. [*Pause.*] Imagine. [*Pause.*] Ah yes, great mercies. [*Long pause.*] I can say no more. [*Pause.*] For the moment. [*Pause. Turns to look at bag. Back front. Smile.*] No no. [*Smile off. Looks at parasol.*] I suppose I might—[*takes up parasol*]—yes, I suppose I might . . . hoist this thing now. [*Begins to unfurl it. Following punctuated by mechanical difficulties overcome.*] One keeps putting off—putting up—for fear of putting up—too soon—and the day goes by—quite by—without one's having put up—at all. [*Parasol now fully open. Turned to her right she twirls it idly this way and that.*] Ah yes, so little to say, so little to do, and the fear so great, certain days, of finding oneself . . . left, with hours still to run, before the bell for sleep, and nothing more to say, nothing more to do, that the days go by, certain days go by, quite by, the bell goes, and little or nothing said, little or nothing done. [*Raising parasol.*] That is the danger. [*Turning front.*] To be guarded against. [*She gazes front, holding up parasol with right hand. Maximum pause.*] I used to perspire freely. [*Pause.*] Now hardly at all. [*Pause.*] The heat is much greater. [*Pause.*] The perspiration much less. [*Pause.*] That is what I find so wonderful. [*Pause.*] The way man adapts himself. [*Pause.*] To changing conditions. [*She transfers parasol to left hand. Long pause.*] Holding up wearies the arm. [*Pause.*] Not if one is going along. [*Pause.*] Only if one is at rest. [*Pause.*] That is a curious observation. [*Pause.*] I hope you heard that, Willie, I should be grieved to think you had not heard that. [*She takes parasol in both hands. Long pause.*] I am weary, holding it up, and I cannot put it down. [*Pause.*] I am worse off with it up than with it down, and I cannot put it down. [*Pause.*] Reason says, Put it down, Winnie, it is not helping you, put the thing down and get on with something else. [*Pause.*] I cannot. [*Pause.*] I cannot move. [*Pause.*] No, something must happen, in the world, take place, some change, I cannot, if I am to move again. [*Pause.*] Willie. [*Mildly.*] Help. [*Pause.*] No? [*Pause.*] Bid me put this thing down, Willie, I would obey you instantly, as I have always done, honoured and obeyed. [*Pause.*] Please, Willie. [*Mildly.*] For pity's sake. [*Pause.*] No? [*Pause.*] You can't? [*Pause.*] Well I don't blame you, no, it would ill become me, who cannot move, to blame my Willie because he cannot speak. [*Pause.*] Fortunately I am in tongue again. [*Pause.*] That is what I find so wonderful, my two lamps, when one goes out the other burns brighter. [*Pause.*] Oh yes, great mercies. [*Maximum pause. The parasol goes on fire. Smoke, flames if feasible. She sniffs, looks up, throws parasol to her right behind mound, cranes back to watch it burning. Pause.*] Ah earth you old extinguisher. [*Back front.*] I presume this has occurred before, though I cannot recall it. [*Pause.*] Can you, Willy? [*Turns a little towards him.*] Can you recall this having occurred before? [*Pause. Cranes back to look at him.*] Do you know what has occurred, Willie? [*Pause.*] Have you gone off on me again? [*Pause.*] I do not ask if you are alive to all that is going on, I merely ask if you have not gone off on me again. [*Pause.*] Your eyes appear to be closed, but that has no particular significance we know. [*Pause.*] Raise a finger, dear, will you please, if you are not quite senseless. [*Pause.*] Do that for me, Willie please, just the little finger, if you are still conscious. [*Pause. Joyful.*] Oh all five, you are a darling today, now I may continue with an easy mind. [*Back front.*] Yes, what ever occurred that did not occur before and yet . . . I wonder, yes, I confess I wonder. [*Pause.*] With the sun blazing so much fiercer down, and hourly fiercer, is it not natural things should go on fire never known to do so, in this way I mean, spontaneous like. [*Pause.*] Shall I myself not melt perhaps in the end, or burn, oh I do not mean necessarily burst into flames, no, just little by little be charred to a black cinder, all this—[*ample gesture of arms*]—visible flesh. [*Pause.*] On the other hand, did I ever know a temperate time? [*Pause.*] No. [*Pause.*] I speak of temperate times and torrid times, they are empty words. [*Pause.*] I speak of when I was not yet caught—in this way—and had my legs and had the use of my legs, and could seek out a shady place, like you, when I was tired of the sun, or a sunny place when I was tired of the shade, like you, and they are all empty words. [*Pause.*] It is no hotter today than yesterday, it will be no hotter tomorrow than today, how could it, and so on back into the far past, forward into the far future. [*Pause.*] And should one day the earth cover my breasts, then I shall never have seen my breasts, no one ever seen my breasts. [*Pause.*] I hope you caught something of that, Willie, I should be sorry to think you had caught nothing of all that, it is not every day I rise to such heights. [*Pause.*] Yes, something seems to have occurred, something has seemed to occur, and nothing has occurred, nothing at all, you are quite right, Willie. [*Pause.*] The sunshade will be there again tomorrow, beside me on this mound, to help me through the day. [*Pause. She takes up mirror.*] I take up this little glass, I shiver it on a stone—[*does so*]—I throw it away—[*does so far behind her*]—it will be in the bag again tomorrow, without a scratch, to help me through the day. [*Pause.*] No, one can do nothing. [*Pause.*] That is what I find so wonderful, the way things . . . [*voice breaks, head down*] . . . things . . . so wonderful. [*Long pause, head down. Finally turns, still bowed, to bag, brings out unidentifiable odds and ends, stuffs them back, fumbles deeper, brings out finally musical-box, winds it up, turns it on, listens for a moment holding it in both hands, huddled over it, turns back front, straightens up and listens to tune, holding box to breast with both hands. It plays the Waltz Duet "I love you so" from* The Merry Widow.[1] *Gradually happy expression. She sways to the rhythm. Music stops. Pause. Brief burst of hoarse song without words—musical-box tune—from* WILLIE. *Increase of happy expression. She lays down box.*] Oh this will have been a happy day! [*She claps hands.*] Again, Willie, again! [*Claps.*] Encore, Willie, please! [*Pause. Happy expression off.*] No? You won't do that for me? [*Pause.*] Well it is very understandable, very understandable. One cannot sing just to please someone, however much one loves them, no, song must come from the heart, that is what I always say, pour out from the inmost, like a thrush. [*Pause.*] How often I have said, in evil hours, Sing now, Winnie, sing your song, there is nothing else for it, and did not. [*Pause.*] Could not. [*Pause.*] No, like the thrush, or the bird of dawning,[2] with no thought of benefit, to oneself or anyone else. [*Pause.*] And now? [*Long pause. Low.*] Strange feeling. [*Pause. Do.*][3] Strange feeling that someone is looking at me. I am clear, then dim, then gone, then dim again, then clear again, and so on, back and forth, in and out of someone's eye. [*Pause. Do.*] Strange? [*Pause. Do.*] No, here all is strange. [*Pause. Normal voice.*] Something says, Stop talking now, Winnie, for a minute, don't squander all your words for the day, stop talking and do something for a change, will you? [*She raises hands and holds them open before her eyes. Apostrophic.*][4] Do something! [*She closes hands.*] What claws! [*She turns to bag, rummages in it, brings out finally a nailfile, turns back front and begins to file nails. Files for a time in silence, then the following punctuated by filing.*] There floats up—into my thoughts—a Mr Shower—a Mr and perhaps a Mrs Shower—no—they are holding hands—his fiancée then more likely—or just some—loved one. [*Looks closer at nails.*] Very brittle today. [*Resumes filing.*] Shower—Shower—does the name mean anything—to you, Willie—evoke any reality, I mean—for you, Willie—don't answer if you don't—feel up to it—you have done more—

---

1. Opera (1905) by Franz Lehár (1870–1948).
2. Cf. *Hamlet*, 1.1: "Some say that ever 'gainst that season comes / Wherein our Saviour's birth is celebrated, / This bird of dawning singeth all night long."
3. Abbreviation for "ditto."
4. Exclamatory.

than your bit—already—Shower—Shower. [*Inspects filed nails.*] Bit
more like it. [*Raises head, gazes front.*] Keep yourself nice, Winnie,
that's what I always say, come what may, keep yourself nice. [*Pause.
Resumes filing.*] Yes—Shower—Shower—[*stops filing, raises head,
gazes front, pause*]—or Cooker, perhaps I should say Cooker. [*Turning a little towards* WILLIE.] Cooker, Willie, does Cooker strike a chord?
[*Pause. Turns a little further. Louder.*] Cooker, Willie, does Cooker
ring a bell, the name Cooker? [*Pause. She cranes back to look at him.
Pause.*] Oh really! [*Pause.*] Have you no handkerchief darling? [*Pause.*]
Have you no delicacy? [*Pause.*] Oh, Willie, you're not eating it! Spit
it out, dear, spit it out! [*Pause. Back front.*] Ah well, I suppose it's
only natural. [*Break in voice.*] Human. [*Pause. Do.*] What *is* one to
do? [*Head down. Do.*] All day long. [*Pause. Do.*] Day after day. [*Pause.
Head up. Smile. Calm.*] The old style! [*Smile off. Resumes nails.*] No,
done him. [*Passes on to next.*] Should have put on my glasses. [*Pauses.*]
Too late now. [*Finishes left hand, inspects it.*] Bit more human. [*Starts
right hand. Following punctuated as before.*] Well anyway—this man
Shower—or Cooker—no matter—and the woman—hand in hand—
in the other hands bags—kind of big brown grips—standing there gaping at me—and at last this man Shower—or Cooker—ends in er anyway—stake my life on that—What's she doing? he says—What's the
idea? he says—stuck up to her diddies[5] in the bleeding ground—coarse
fellow—What does it mean? he says—What's it meant to mean?—
and so on—lot more stuff like that—usual drivel—Do you hear me?
he says—I do, she says, God help me—What do you mean, he says,
God help you? [*Stops filing, raises head, gazes front.*] And you, she
says, what's the idea of you, she says, what are you meant to mean? It
is because you're still on your two flat feet, with your old ditty[6] full of
tinned muck and changes of underwear, dragging me up and down
this fornicating wilderness, coarse creature, fit mate—[*with sudden
violence*]—let go of my hand and drop for God's sake, she says, drop!
[*Pause. Resumes filing.*] Why doesn't he dig her out? he says—referring to you, my dear—What good is she to him like that?—What
good is he to her like that?—and so on—usual tosh—Good! she says,
have a heart for God's sake—Dig her out, he says, dig her out, no
sense in her like that—Dig her out with what? she says—I'd dig her
out with my bare hands, he says—must have been man and—wife.
[*Files in silence.*] Next thing they're away—hand in hand—and the
bags—dim—then gone—last human kind—to stray this way. [*Finishes right hand, inspects it, lays down file, gazes front.*] Strange thing,
time like this, drift up into the mind. [*Pause.*] Strange? [*Pause.*] No,
here all is strange. [*Pause.*] Thankful for it in any case. [*Voice breaks.*]
Most thankful. [*Head down. Pause. Head up. Calm.*] Bow and raise
the head, bow and raise, always that. [*Pause.*] And now? [*Long pause.
Starts putting things back in bag, toothbrush last. This operation,
interrupted by pauses as indicated, punctuates following.*] It is perhaps

5. Breasts.
6. Short for "ditty-bag," or "ditty-box," a sailor's or fisherman's receptacle for odds and ends.

a little soon—to make ready—for the night—[*stops tidying, head up, smile*]—the old style!—[*smile off, resumes tidying*]—and yet I do— make ready for the night—feeling it at hand—the bell for sleep— saying to myself—Winnie—it will not be long now, Winnie—until the bell for sleep. [*Stops tidying, head up.*] Sometimes I am wrong. [*Smile.*] But not often. [*Smile off.*] Sometimes all is over, for the day, all done, all said, all ready for the night, and the day not over, far from over, the night not ready, far, far from ready. [*Smile.*] But not often. [*Smile off.*] Yes, the bell for sleep, when I feel it at hand, and so make ready for the night—[*gesture*]—in this way, sometimes I am wrong—[*smile*]—but not often. [*Smile off. Resumes tidying.*] I used to think—I say I used to think—that all these things—put back into the bag—if too soon—put back too soon—could be taken out again—if necessary—if needed—and so on—indefinitely—back into the bag— back out of the bag—until the bell—went. [*Stops tidying, head up, smile.*] But no. [*Smile broader.*] No no. [*Smile off. Resumes tidying.*] I suppose this—might seem strange—this—what shall I say—this what I have said—yes—[*she takes up revolver*]—strange—[*she turns to put revolver in bag*]—were it not—[*about to put revolver in bag she arrests gesture and turns back front*]—were it not—[*she lays down revolver to her right, stops tidying, head up*]—that all seems strange. [*Pause.*] Most strange. [*Pause.*] Never any change. [*Pause.*] And more and more strange. [*Pause. She bends to mound again, takes up last object, i.e., toothbrush, and turns to put it in bag when her attention is drawn to disturbance from* WILLIE. *She cranes back and to her right to see. Pause.*] Weary of your hole, dear? [*Pause.*] Well I can understand that. [*Pause.*] Don't forget your straw. [*Pause.*] Not the crawler you were, poor darling. [*Pause.*] No, not the crawler I gave my heart to. [*Pause.*] The hands and knees, love, try the hands and knees. [*Pause.*] The knees! The knees! [*Pause.*] What a curse, mobility! [*She follows with eyes his progress towards her behind mound, i.e. towards place he occupied at beginning of act.*] Another foot, Willie, and you're home. [*Pause as she observes last foot.*] Ah! [*Turns back front laboriously, rubs neck.*] Crick in my neck admiring you. [*Rubs neck.*] But it's worth it, well worth it. [*Turning slightly towards him.*] Do you know what I dream sometimes? [*Pause.*] What I dream sometimes, Willie. [*Pause.*] That you'll come round and live this side where I could see you. [*Pause. Back front.*] I'd be a different woman. [*Pause.*] Unrecognizable. [*Turning slightly towards him.*] Or just now and then, come round this side just every now and then and let me feast on you. [*Back front.*] But you can't, I know. [*Head down.*] I know. [*Pause. Head up.*] Well anyway—[*looks at toothbrush in her hand*]—can't be long now—[*looks at brush*]—until the bell. [*Top back of* WILLIE'*s head appears above slope.* WINNIE *looks closer at brush.*] Fully guaranteed . . . [*head up*] . . . what's this it was? [WILLIE'*s hand appears with handkerchief, spreads it on skull, disappears.*] Genuine pure . . . fully guaranteed . . . [WIL-LIE'*s hand appears with boater, settles it on head, rakish angle, disappears*] . . . genuine pure . . . ah! hog's setae. [*Pause.*] What is a hog exactly? [*Pause. Turns slightly towards* WILLIE.] What exactly is a hog,

Willie, do you know, I can't remember. [*Pause. Turning a little further, pleading.*] What *is* a hog, Willie, please!

  Pause.

WILLIE. Castrated male swine. [*Happy expression appears on* WINNIE'*s face.*] Reared for slaughter.

  Happy expression increases. WILLIE *opens newspaper, hands invisible. Tops of yellow sheets appear on either side of his head.* WINNIE *gazes before her with happy expression.*

WINNIE. Oh this *is* a happy day! This will have been another happy day! [*Pause.*] After all. [*Pause.*] So far.

  Pause. Happy expression off. WILLIE *turns page. Pause. He turns another page. Pause.*

WILLIE. Opening for smart youth.

  Pause. WINNIE *takes off hat, turns to put it in bag, arrests gesture, turns back front. Smile.*

WINNIE. No. [*Smile broader.*] No no. [*Smile off. Puts on hat again, gazes front, pause.*] And now? [*Pause.*] Sing. [*Pause.*] Sing your song, Winnie. [*Pause.*] No? [*Pause.*] Then pray. [*Pause.*] Pray your prayer, Winnie.

  Pause. WILLIE *turns page. Pause.*

WILLIE. Wanted bright boy.

  Pause. WINNIE *gazes before her.* WILLIE *turns page. Pause. Newspaper disappears. Long pause.*

WINNIE. *Pray your old prayer, Winnie.*

  Long pause.

CURTAIN

Act 2

Scene as before.
WINNIE *imbedded up to neck, hat on head, eyes closed. Her head, which she can no longer turn, nor bow, nor raise, faces front motionless throughout act. Movements of eyes as indicated.*
Bag and parasol as before. Revolver conspicuous to her right on mound. Long pause.
Bell rings loudly. She opens eyes at once. Bell stops. She gazes front. Long pause.

WINNIE. Hail, holy light.[7] [*Long pause. She closes her eyes. Bell rings loudly. She opens eyes at once. Bell stops. She gazes front. Long smile. Smile off. Long pause.*] Someone is looking at me still. [*Pause.*] Caring for me still. [*Pause.*] That is what I find so wonderful. [*Pause.*]

---

7. Milton's *Paradise Lost*, 3.1.

Eyes on my eyes. [*Pause.*] What is that unforgettable line? [*Pause. Eyes right.*] Willie. [*Pause. Louder.*] Willie. [*Pause. Eyes front.*] May one still speak of time? [*Pause.*] Say it is a long time now, Willie, since I saw you. [*Pause.*] Since I heard you. [*Pause.*] May one? [*Pause.*] One does. [*Smile.*] The old style! [*Smile off.*] There is so little one can speak of. [*Pause.*] One speaks of it all. [*Pause.*] All one can. [*Pause.*] I used to think . . . [*pause*] . . . I say I used to think that I would learn to talk alone. [*Pause.*] By that I mean to myself, the wilderness. [*Smile.*] But no. [*Smile broader.*] No no. [*Smile off.*] Ergo[8] you are there. [*Pause.*] Oh no doubt you are dead, like the others, no doubt you have died, or gone away and left me, like the others, it doesn't matter, you are there. [*Pause. Eyes left.*] The bag too is there, the same as ever, I can see it. [*Pause. Eyes right. Louder.*] The bag is there, Willie, as good as ever, the one you gave me that day . . . to go to market. [*Pause. Eyes front.*] That day. [*Pause.*] What day? [*Pause.*] I used to pray. [*Pause.*] I say I used to pray. [*Pause.*] Yes, I must confess I did. [*Smile.*] Not now. [*Smile broader.*] No no. [*Smile off. Pause.*] Then . . . now . . . what difficulties here, for the mind. [*Pause.*] To have been always what I am—and so changed from what I was. [*Pause.*] I am the one, I say the one, then the other. [*Pause.*] Now the one, then the other. [*Pause.*] There is so little one can say, one says it all. [*Pause.*] All one can. [*Pause.*] And no truth in it anywhere. [*Pause.*] My arms. [*Pause.*] My breasts. [*Pause.*] What arms? [*Pause.*] What breasts? [*Pause.*] Willie. [*Pause.*] What Willie? [*Sudden vehement affirmation.*] My Willie! [*Eyes right, calling.*] Willie! [*Pause. Louder.*] Willie! [*Pause. Eyes front.*] Ah well, not to know, not to know for sure, great mercy, all I ask. [*Pause.*] Ah yes . . . then . . . now . . . beechen green[9] . . . this . . . Charlie . . . kisses . . . this . . . all that . . . deep trouble for the mind. [*Pause.*] But it does not trouble mine. [*Smile.*] Not now. [*Smile broader.*] No no. [*Smile off. Long pause. She closes eyes. Bell rings loudly. She opens eyes. Pause.*] Eyes float up that seem to close in peace . . . to see . . . in peace. [*Pause.*] Not mine. [*Smile.*] Not now. [*Smile broader.*] No no. [*Smile off. Long pause.*] Willie. [*Pause.*] Do you think the earth has lost its atmosphere, Willie? [*Pause.*] Do you, Willie? [*Pause.*] You have no opinion? [*Pause.*] Well that is like you, you never had any opinion about anything. [*Pause.*] It's understandable. [*Pause.*] Most. [*Pause.*] The earthball. [*Pause.*] I sometimes wonder. [*Pause.*] Perhaps not quite all. [*Pause.*] There always remains something. [*Pause.*] Of everything. [*Pause.*] Some remains. [*Pause.*] If the mind were to go. [*Pause.*] It won't of course. [*Pause.*] Not quite. [*Pause.*] Not mine. [*Smile*] Not now. [*Smile broader.*] No no. [*Smile off. Long pause.*] It might be the eternal cold. [*Pause.*] Everlasting perishing cold. [*Pause.*] Just chance, I take it, happy chance. [*Pause.*] Oh yes, great mercies, great mercies. [*Pause.*] And now? [*Long pause.*] The face. [*Pause.*] The nose. [*She squints down.*] I can see it . . . [*squinting down*] . . . the tip . . . the

8. Therefore (Latin).
9. Cf. Keats's *Ode to a Nightingale*, lines 7–10: "That thou, light-winged Dryad of the trees, / In some melodious plot / Of beechen green, and shadows numberless, / Singest of summer in full-throated ease."

nostrils . . . breath of life . . . that curve you so admired . . . [*pouts*] . . . a hint of lip . . . [*pouts again*] . . . if I pout them out . . . [*sticks out tongue*] . . . the tongue of course . . . you so admired . . . if I stick it out . . . [*sticks it out again*] . . . the tip . . . [*eyes up*] . . . suspicion of brow . . . eyebrow . . . imagination possibly . . . [*eyes left*] . . . cheek . . . no . . . [*eyes right*] . . . no . . . [*distends cheeks*] . . . even if I puff them out . . . [*eyes left, distends cheeks again*] . . . no . . . no damask.[1] [*Eyes front.*] That is all. [*Pause.*] The bag of course . . . [*eyes left*] . . . a little blurred perhaps . . . but the bag. [*Eyes front. Offhand.*] The earth of course and sky. [*Eyes right.*] The sunshade you gave me . . . that day . . . [*pause*] . . . that day . . . the lake . . . the reeds. [*Eyes front. Pause.*] What day? [*Pause.*] What reeds? [*Long pause. Eyes close. Bell rings loudly. Eyes open. Pause. Eyes right.*] Brownie of course. [*Pause.*] You remember Brownie, Willie, I can see him. [*Pause.*] Brownie is there, Willie, beside me. [*Pause. Loud.*] Brownie is there, Willie. [*Pause. Eyes front.*] That is all. [*Pause.*] What would I do without them? [*Pause.*] What would I do without them, when words fail? [*Pause.*] Gaze before me, with compressed lips. [*Long pause while she does so.*] I cannot. [*Pause.*] Ah yes, great mercies, great mercies. [*Long pause. Low.*] Sometimes I hear sounds. [*Listening expression. Normal voice.*] But not often. [*Pause.*] They are a boon, sounds are a boon, they help me . . . through the day. [*Smile*] The old style! [*Smile off.*] Yes, those are happy days, when there are sounds. [*Pause.*] When I hear sounds. [*Pause.*] I used to think . . . [*pause*] . . . I say I used to think they were in my head. [*Smile.*] But no. [*Smile broader.*] No no. [*Smile off.*] That was just logic. [*Pause.*] Reason. [*Pause.*] I have not lost my reason. [*Pause.*] Not yet. [*Pause.*] Not all. [*Pause.*] Some remains. [*Pause.*] Sounds. [*Pause.*] Like little . . . sunderings, little falls . . . apart. [*Pause. Low.*] It's things, Willie. [*Pause. Normal voice.*] In the bag, outside the bag. [*Pause.*] Ah yes, things have their life, that is what I always say, *things* have a life. [*Pause.*] Take my looking-glass, it doesn't need me. [*Pause.*] The bell. [*Pause.*] It hurts like a knife. [*Pause.*] A gouge. [*Pause.*] One cannot ignore it. [*Pause.*] How often . . . [*pause*] . . . I say how often I have said, Ignore it, Winnie, ignore the bell, pay no heed, just sleep and wake, sleep and wake, as you please, open and close the eyes, as you please, or in the way you find most helpful. [*Pause.*] Open and close the eyes, Winnie, open and close, always that. [*Pause.*] But no. [*Smile.*] Not now. [*Smile broader.*] No no. [*Smile off. Pause.*] What now? [*Pause.*] What now, Willie? [*Long pause.*] There is my story of course, when all else fails. [*Pause.*] A life. [*Smile*] A long life. [*Smile off.*] Beginning in the womb, where life used to begin, Mildred has memories, she will have memories, of the womb, before she dies, the mother's womb. [*Pause.*] She is now four or five already and has recently been given a big waxen dolly. [*Pause.*] Fully clothed, complete outfit. [*Pause.*] Shoes, socks, undies, complete set, frilly frock, gloves. [*Pause.*]

1. Cf. *Twelfth Night*, 2.4: "She never told her love, / But let concealment, like a worm i' the bud, / Feed on her damask cheek." Damask is a woven material (originally of silk) often used for white table linen.

White mesh. [*Pause.*] A little white straw hat with a chin elastic. [*Pause.*] Pearly necklet. [*Pause.*] A little picture-book with legends in real print to go under her arm when she takes her walk. [*Pause.*] China blue eyes that open and shut. [*Pause. Narrative.*] The sun was not well up when Milly rose, descended the steep . . . [*pause*] . . . slipped on her nightgown, descended all alone the steep wooden stairs, backwards on all fours, though she had been forbidden to do so, entered the . . . [*pause*] . . . tiptoed down the silent passage, entered the nursery and began to undress Dolly. [*Pause.*] Crept under the table and began to undress Dolly. [*Pause.*] Scolding her . . . the while. [*Pause.*] Suddenly a mouse—[*Long pause.*] Gently, Winnie. [*Long pause. Calling.*] Willie! [*Pause. Louder.*] Willie! [*Pause. Mild reproach.*] I sometimes find your attitude a little strange, Willie, all this time, it is not like you to be wantonly cruel. [*Pause.*] Strange? [*Pause.*] No. [*Smile.*] Not here. [*Smile broader.*] Not now. [*Smile off.*] And yet . . . [*Suddenly anxious.*] I do hope nothing is amiss. [*Eyes right, loud.*] Is all well, dear? [*Pause. Eyes front. To herself.*] God grant he did not go in head foremost! [*Eyes right, loud.*] You're not stuck, Willie? [*Pause. Do.*] You're not jammed, Willie? [*Eyes front, distressed.*] Perhaps he is crying out for help all this time and I do not hear him! [*Pause.*] I do of course hear cries. [*Pause.*] But they are in my head surely. [*Pause.*] Is it possible that . . . [*Pause. With finality.*] No no, my head was always full of cries. [*Pause.*] Faint confused cries. [*Pause.*] They come. [*Pause.*] Then go. [*Pause.*] As on a wind. [*Pause.*] That is what I find so wonderful. [*Pause.*] They cease. [*Pause.*] Ah yes, great mercies, great mercies. [*Pause.*] The day is now well advanced. [*Smile. Smile off.*] And yet it is perhaps a little soon for my song. [*Pause.*] To sing too soon is fatal, I always find. [*Pause.*] On the other hand it is possible to leave it too late. [*Pause.*] The bell goes for sleep and one has not sung. [*Pause.*] The whole day has flown—[*smile, smile off*]—flown by, quite by, and no song of any class, kind or description. [*Pause.*] There is a problem here. [*Pause.*] One cannot sing . . . just like that, no. [*Pause.*] It bubbles up, for some unknown reason, the time is ill chosen, one chokes it back. [*Pause.*] One says, Now is the time, it is now or never, and one cannot. [*Pause.*] Simply cannot sing. [*Pause.*] Not a note. [*Pause.*] Another thing, Willie, while we are on this subject. [*Pause.*] The sadness after song. [*Pause.*] Have you run across that, Willie? [*Pause.*] In the course of your experience. [*Pause.*] No? [*Pause.*] Sadness after intimate sexual intercourse one is familiar with of course. [*Pause.*] You would concur with Aristotle[2] there, Willie, I fancy. [*Pause.*] Yes, that one knows and is prepared to face. [*Pause.*] But after song . . . [*Pause.*] It does not last of course. [*Pause.*] That is what I find so wonderful. [*Pause.*] It wears away. [*Pause.*] What are those exquisite lines? [*Pause.*] Go forget me why should something o'er that something shadow fling . . . go forget me . . . why should sorrow . . . brightly smile . . . go forget me . . . never hear me . . .

2. Cf. the pseudo-Aristotelian *Problems*, 30.1. 955a 23: "After sexual intercourse the majority become more despondent."

sweetly smile . . . brightly sing . . .³ [*Pause. With a sigh.*] One loses one's classics. [*Pause.*] Oh not all. [*Pause.*] A part. [*Pause.*] A part remains. [*Pause.*] That is what I find so wonderful, a part remains, of one's classics, to help one through the day. [*Pause.*] Oh yes, many mercies, many mercies. [*Pause.*] And now? [*Pause.*] And now, Willie? [*Long pause.*] I call to the eye of the mind⁴ . . . Mr Shower—or Cooker. [*She closes her eyes. Bell rings loudly. She opens her eyes. Pause.*] Hand in hand, in the other hands bags. [*Pause.*] Getting on . . . in life. [*Pause.*] No longer young, not yet old. [*Pause.*] Standing there gaping at me. [*Pause.*] Can't have been a bad bosom, he says, in its day. [*Pause.*] Seen worse shoulders, he says, in my time. [*Pause.*] Does she feel her legs? he says. [*Pause.*] Is there any life in her legs? he says [*Pause.*] Has she anything on underneath? he says. [*Pause.*] Ask her, he says, I'm shy. [*Pause.*] Ask her what? she says. [*Pause.*] Is there any life in her legs. [*Pause.*] Has she anything on underneath. [*Pause.*] Ask her yourself, she says. [*Pause. With sudden violence.*] Let go of me for Christ sake and drop! [*Pause. Do.*] Drop dead! [*Smile.*] But no. [*Smile broader.*] No no. [*Smile off.*] I watch them recede. [*Pause.*] Hand in hand—and the bags. [*Pause.*] Dim. [*Pause.*] Then gone. [*Pause.*] Last human kind—to stray this way. [*Pause.*] Up to date. [*Pause.*] And now? [*Pause. Low.*] Help. [*Pause. Do.*] Help, Willie. [*Pause. Do.*] No? [*Long pause. Narrative.*] Suddenly a mouse . . . [*Pause.*] Suddenly a mouse ran up her little thigh and Mildred, dropping Dolly in her fright, began to scream—[WINNIE *gives a sudden piercing scream*]—and screamed and screamed—[WINNIE *screams twice*]—screamed and screamed and screamed and screamed till all came running, in their night attire, papa, mamma, Bibby and . . . old Annie, to see what was the matter . . . [*pause*] . . . what on earth could possibly be the matter. [*Pause.*] Too late. [*Pause.*] Too late. [*Long pause. Just audible.*] Willie. [*Pause. Normal voice.*] Ah well, not long now, Winnie, can't be long now, until the bell for sleep. [*Pause.*] Then you may close your eyes, then you *must* close your eyes—and keep them closed. [*Pause.*] Why say that again? [*Pause.*] I used to think . . . [*pause.*] . . . I say I used to think there was no difference between one fraction of a second and the next. [*Pause.*] I used to say . . . [*pause*] . . . I say I used to say, Winnie, you are changeless, there is never any difference between one fraction of a second and the next. [*Pause.*] Why bring that up again? [*Pause.*] There is so little one can bring up, one brings up all. [*Pause.*] All one can. [*Pause.*] My neck is hurting me. [*Pause. With sudden violence.*] My neck is hurting me! [*Pause.*] Ah that's better. [*With mild irritation.*] Everything within reason. [*Long pause.*] I can do no more. [*Pause.*] Say no more. [*Pause.*] But I must say more. [*Pause.*] Problem here. [*Pause.*] No, something must move, in the world, I can't any more. [*Pause.*] A zephyr.⁵ [*Pause.*] A breath. [*Pause.*] What are those immortal

3. Cf. Charles Wolfe's *Song*, lines 1–8: "Go, forget me—why should sorrow/O'er that brow a shadow fling?/Go, forget me—and to-morrow/Brightly smile and sweetly sing. / Smile—though I shall not be near thee;/Sing—though I shall never hear thee;/May thy soul with pleasure shine/Lasting as the gloom of mine!"

4. Yeats' *At the Hawk's Well*, line 1.

5. Wind.

lines? [*Pause.*] It might be the eternal dark. [*Pause.*] Black night without end. [*Pause.*] Just chance, I take it, happy chance. [*Pause.*] Oh yes, abounding mercies. [*Long pause.*] And now? [*Pause.*] And now, Willie? [*Long pause.*] That day. [*Pause.*] The pink fizz. [*Pause.*] The flute glasses. [*Pause.*] The last guest gone. [*Pause.*] The last bumper[6] with the bodies nearly touching. [*Pause.*] The look. [*Long pause.*] What day? [*Long pause.*] What look? [*Long pause.*] I hear cries. [*Pause.*] Sing. [*Pause.*] Sing your old song, Winnie. *Long pause. Suddenly alert expression. Eyes switch right.* WILLIE's *head appears to her right round corner of mound. He is on all fours, dressed to kill—top hat, morning coat, striped trousers, etc., white gloves in hand. Very long bushy white Battle of Britain moustache.*[7] *He halts, gazes front, smooths moustache. He emerges completely from behind mound, turns to his left, halts, looks up at* WINNIE. *He advances on all fours towards centre, halts, turns head front, gazes front, strokes moustache, straightens tie, adjusts hat, advances a little further, halts, takes off hat and looks up at* WINNIE. *He is now not far from centre and within her field of vision. Unable to sustain effort of looking up he sinks head to ground.*

WINNIE [*mondaine*].[8] Well this is an unexpected pleasure! [*Pause.*] Reminds me of the day you came whining for my hand. [*Pause.*] I worship you, Winnie, be mine. [*He looks up.*] Life a mockery without Win. [*She goes off into a giggle.*] What a get up, you do look a sight! [*Giggles.*] Where are the flowers?[9] [*Pause.*] That smile today. [WILLIE *sinks head.*] What's that on your neck, an anthrax?[1] [*Pause.*] Want to watch that, Willie, before it gets a hold on you. [*Pause.*] Where were you all this time? [*Pause.*] What were you doing all this time? [*Pause.*] Changing? [*Pause.*] Did you not hear me screaming for you? [*Pause.*] Did you get stuck in your hole? [*Pause. He looks up.*] That's right, Willie, look at me. [*Pause.*] Feast your old eyes, Willie. [*Pause.*] Does anything remain? [*Pause.*] Any remains? [*Pause.*] No? [*Pause.*] I haven't been able to look after it, you know. [*He sinks his head.*] You are still recognizable, in a way. [*Pause.*] Are you thinking of coming to live this side now . . . for a bit maybe? [*Pause.*] No? [*Pause.*] Just a brief call? [*Pause.*] Have you gone deaf, Willie? [*Pause.*] Dumb? [*Pause.*] Oh I know you were never one to talk, I worship you Winnie be mine and then nothing from that day forth only titbits from Reynolds' News.[2] [*Eyes front. Pause.*] Ah well, what matter, that's what I always say, it will have been a happy day, after all, another happy day. [*Pause.*] Not long now, Winnie. [*Pause.*] I hear cries. [*Pause.*] Do you ever hear cries, Willie? [*Pause.*] No? [*Eyes back on* WILLIE.] Willie. [*Pause.*] Look at me again, Willie. [*Pause.*] Once more, Willie. [*He looks up. Happily.*] Ah! [*Pause. Shocked.*] What ails you, Willie, I never saw such an expression! [*Pause.*] Put on your hat, dear, it's the sun, don't stand on ceremony, I won't mind. [*He drops hat and gloves and starts*

---

6. Glass filled to the brim for a toast. "Pink fizz": champagne.

7. As worn by the British fighter-pilot heroes of the Battle of Britain in World War II.

8. In a sophisticated manner.

9. Cf. Robert Herrick's *To the Virgins, To Make Much of Time*, line 1: "Gather ye rosebuds while ye may. . . ."

1. Carbuncle or malignant boil.

2. English newspaper.

to crawl up mound towards her. Gleeful.] Oh I say, this is terrific! [*He halts, clinging to mound with one hand, reaching up with the other.*] Come on, dear, put a bit of jizz into it, I'll cheer you on. [*Pause.*] Is it me you're after, Willie . . . or is it something else? [*Pause.*] Do you want to touch my face . . . again? [*Pause.*] Is it a kiss you're after, Willie . . . or is it something else? [*Pause.*] There was a time when I could have given you a hand. [*Pause.*] And then a time before that again when I did give you a hand. [*Pause.*] You were always in dire need of a hand, Willie. [*He slithers back to foot of mound and lies with face to ground.*] Brrum! [*Pause. He rises to hands and knees, raises his face towards her.*] Have another go, Willie, I'll cheer you on. [*Pause.*] Don't look at me like that! [*Pause. Vehement.*] Don't look at me like that! [*Pause. Low.*] Have you gone off your head, Willie? [*Pause. Do.*] Out of your poor old wits, Willie?

     Pause.

WILLIE [*just audible*]. Win.

     Pause. WINNIE'*s eyes front. Happy expression appears, grows.*

WINNIE. Win! [*Pause.*] Oh this *is* a happy day, this will have been another happy day! [*Pause.*] After all. [*Pause.*] So far.

     Pause. She hums tentatively beginning of song, then sings softly, musical-box tune.

> Though I say not
> What I may not
> Let you hear,
> Yet the swaying
> Dance is saying,
> Love me dear!
> Every touch of fingers
> Tells me what I know,
> Says for you,
> It's true, it's true,
> You love me so![3]

Pause. Happy expression off. She closes her eyes. Bell rings loudly. She opens her eyes. She smiles, gazing front. She turns her eyes, smiling, to WILLIE, *still on his hands and knees looking up at her. Smile off. They look at each other. Long pause.*

                         CURTAIN

                                          1961

---

3. The Waltz Duet, "I Love You So" (in Adrian Ross's English libretto) from Franz Lehár's opera *The Merry Widow* (1905). See p. 2555.

W. H. AUDEN

1907–1973

Wystan Hugh Auden was born in York and educated at Gresham's School, Holt, Norfolk, and Christ Church, Oxford. After leaving Oxford he taught school from 1930 to 1935 and later worked for a government film unit. His sympathies in the 1930s were with the Left, like those of most intellectuals of his age, and he went to Spain during the Civil War, intending to serve as an ambulance driver on the Left-wing Republican side. He found himself, to his surprise however, so disturbed by the sight of the many Roman Catholic churches gutted and looted by the Republicans that he returned to England without fulfilling his ambition. He traveled in Iceland and China before coming to America in 1939; in 1946 he became an American citizen. He taught at a number of American colleges, and was professor of poetry at Oxford from 1956 to 1960.

Auden was the most active of the group of young English poets who, in the late 1920s and early 1930s, saw themselves bringing new techniques and attitudes to English poetry. Stephen Spender and Cecil Day Lewis were at the time the most prominent of the other members of the new school, which soon afterward fell apart, each poet going his own separate way. Like all his generation, Auden learned poetic wit and irony from Eliot, and he also learned metrical and verbal techniques from Hopkins and from Wilfred Owen. His English studies at Oxford familiarized him with the rhythms and long alliterative line of Anglo-Saxon poetry as well as with the rapid and rollicking short lines (a sort of inspired doggerel) of the early sixteenth-century poet John Skelton: both influenced his own versification. He learned, too, from the songs of the English music hall and, later, from American blues singers.

The depression which upset America in 1929 hit England soon afterwards, and Auden and his contemporaries looked out at an England of industrial stagnation and mass unemployment, seeing not the metaphorical Waste Land of Eliot but a more literal Waste Land of poverty and "depressed areas." His early poetry is much concerned with a diagnosis of the ills of his country. This diagnosis, conducted in a verse which combined deliberate irreverence and sometimes even clowning with a cunning verbal craftsmanship, drew on both Freud and Marx to show England now as a nation of neurotic invalids who must learn to "throw away their rugs," and now as the victim of an antiquated economic system. The liveliness and nervous force of this early poetry of Auden's made a great impression, even though an uncertainty about his audience led him to introduce purely private symbols, intelligible only to a few friends, in some of his poems.

Gradually, Auden learned to clarify his imagery and control his desire to shock, and he produced, in the years around 1940, some poems (such as, in this anthology, *Lullaby*) of finely disciplined movement, pellucid clarity, and deep yet unsentimental feeling. At the same time he was developing a more complex view of the world, moving from his earlier diagnosis of modern ills in terms of Freud and Marx to a more religious view of personal responsibility and traditional value without, however, abandoning the ideas and terms he had learned from modern psychology. But he never lost his

ear for popular speech or his ability to combine elements from popular art
with an extreme technical formality. He was always the experimenter, particularly in ways of bringing together high artifice and a colloquial tone.

Some of Auden's most exciting work is found in his early volumes, *Poems*
(1930) and *On This Island* (1937). *Another Time* (1940) shows greater control and less violence. Of his later volumes, *Nones* (1951) shows most clearly
his characteristic ways of combining or alternating the grave and the flippant. For the first part of his career—the English and the early American
phase—Auden was very much the poet of his times, first of the Depression
and then of the Age of the Refugee. In the poems of this period he preferred
to confront modern problems directly rather than to filter them, as Eliot did,
through symbolic situations. The poems of the last phase of his career, notably those in *About the House* (1967) and *City without Walls* (1970), are
increasingly personal in tone and combine an apparent air of offhand informality with remarkable technical skill in versification. Auden grew increasingly hostile to the modern world and skeptical of all remedies offered for
modern ills: he took refuge in love and friendship, particularly the love and
friendship he shared with Chester Kallmann; emotions grounded in an ever
deepening but rarely obtrusive religious feeling. In the last year of his life he
returned to England to live in Oxford, feeling the need to be part of a university community as a protection against loneliness. An uneven poet, a poet
who in the opinion of some critics never quite fulfilled the enormous promise of his early work, Auden is nevertheless now generally recognized as one
of the masters of twentieth-century English poetry, a thoughtful, seriously
playful (if one may put it in this paradoxical way) poet whom more than one
critic has compared to Dryden in his combination of lively intelligence and
immense craftsmanship.

Petition

Sir, no man's enemy, forgiving all
But will his negative inversion, be prodigal:
Send to us power and light, a sovereign touch[1]
Curing the intolerable neural itch,
The exhaustion of weaning, the liar's quinsy,[2]   5
And the distortions of ingrown virginity.
Prohibit sharply the rehearsed response
And gradually correct the coward's stance;
Cover in time with beams those in retreat
That, spotted, they turn though the reverse were great;   10
Publish each healer that in city lives
Or country houses at the end of drives;
Harrow the house of the dead; look shining at
New styles of architecture, a change of heart.

October 1929   1930

---

1. The "king's touch" was often regarded as
miraculous cure for disease (cf. "sovereign" as an
adjective, meaning "the best").
2. Tonsillitis.

On This Island

Look, stranger, on this island now
The leaping light for your delight discovers,
Stand stable here
And silent be,
That through the channels of the ear   5
May wander like a river
The swaying sound of the sea.

Here at the small field's ending pause
When the chalk wall falls to the foam and its tall ledges
Oppose the pluck   10
And knock of the tide,
And the shingle scrambles after the suck-
-ing surf,
And the gull lodges
A moment on its sheer side.   15

Far off like floating seeds the ships
Diverge on urgent voluntary errands,
And the full view
Indeed may enter
And move in memory as now these clouds do,   20
That pass the harbour mirror
And all the summer through the water saunter.

1935   1936

Spain 1937[1]

Yesterday all the past. The language of size
Spreading to China along the trade routes; the diffusion
          Of the counting-frame and the cromlech;[2]
Yesterday the shadow-reckoning in the sunny climates.

Yesterday the assessment of insurance by cards,   5
The divination of water; yesterday the invention
          Of cart-wheels and clocks, the taming of
Horses; yesterday the bustling world of the navigators.

Yesterday the abolition of fairies and giants;
The fortress like a motionless eagle eyeing the valley,   10

1. Written when the Spanish Civil War was raging. The rebellion by General Franco's Right-wing
army against the Left-wing Spanish government,
which broke out in 1936 and provoked full-scale
civil war, was viewed by British liberal intellectuals
at the time as a testing struggle between fascism
and democracy. The poem first appeared separately in 1937, the proceeds of its sale going to
"Medical Aid for Spain." This is Auden's revised
version of 1940.
2. Ancient stone circle.

The chapel built in the forest;
Yesterday the carving of angels and of frightening gargoyles;

The trial of heretics among the columns of stone;
Yesterday the theological feuds in the taverns
                    And the miraculous cure at the fountain;   15
Yesterday the Sabbath of Witches.[3] But to-day the struggle.

Yesterday the installation of dynamos and turbines;
The construction of railways in the colonial desert;
                    Yesterday the classic lecture
On the origin of Mankind. But to-day the struggle.   20

Yesterday the belief in the absolute value of Greek;
The fall of the curtain upon the death of a hero;
                    Yesterday the prayer to the sunset,
And the adoration of madmen. But to-day the struggle.

As the poet whispers, startled among the pines   25
Or, where the loose waterfall sings, compact, or upright
                    On the crag by the leaning tower:
"O my vision. O send me the luck of the sailor."

And the investigator peers through his instruments
At the inhuman provinces, the virile bacillus   30
                    Or enormous Jupiter finished:
"But the lives of my friends. I inquire, I inquire."

And the poor in their fireless lodgings dropping the sheets
Of the evening paper: "Our day is our loss. O show us
                    History the operator, the   35
Organizer, Time the refreshing river."

And the nations combine each cry, invoking the life
That shapes the individual belly and orders
                    The private nocturnal terror:
"Did you not found once the city state of the sponge,   40

"Raise the vast military empires of the shark
And the tiger, establish the robin's plucky canton?[4]
                    Intervene. O descend as a dove or
A furious papa or a mild engineer: but descend."

And the life, if it answers at all, replies from the heart   45
And the eyes and the lungs, from the shops and squares of the city:
                    "O no, I am not the Mover,
Not to-day, not to you. To you I'm the

3. Convocation of witches in parody of Christian service.
4. District.

"Yes-man, the bar-companion, the easily-duped:
I am whatever you do; I am your vow to be   50
              Good, your humorous story;
I am your business voice; I am your marriage.

"What's your proposal? To build the Just City? I will.
I agree. Or is it the suicide pact, the romantic
              Death? Very well, I accept, for   55
I am your choice, your decision: yes, I am Spain."

Many have heard it on remote peninsulas,
On sleepy plains, in the aberrant fishermen's islands,
              In the corrupt heart of the city;
Have heard and migrated like gulls or the seeds of a flower.   60

They clung like burrs to the long expresses that lurch
Through the unjust lands, through the night, through the alpine tunnel;
              They floated over the oceans;
They walked the passes: they came to present their lives.

On that arid square, that fragment nipped off from hot   65
Africa, soldered so crudely to inventive Europe,
              On that tableland scored by rivers,
Our fever's menacing shapes are precise and alive.

To-morrow, perhaps, the future: the research on fatigue
And the movements of packers; the gradual exploring of all the   70
              Octaves of radiation;
To-morrow the enlarging of consciousness by diet and breathing.

To-morrow the rediscovery of romantic love;
The photographing of ravens; all the fun under
              Liberty's masterful shadow;   75
To-morrow the hour of the pageant-master and the musician.

To-morrow for the young the poets exploding like bombs,
The walks by the lake, the winter of perfect communion;
              To-morrow the bicycle races
Through the suburbs on summer evenings: but to-day the struggle.   80

To-day the inevitable increase in the chances of death;
The conscious acceptance of guilt in the fact of murder;
              To-day the expending of powers
On the flat ephemeral pamphlet and the boring meeting.

To-day the makeshift consolations; the shared cigarette;   85
The cards in the candle-lit barn and the scraping concert,
              The masculine jokes; to-day the
Fumbled and unsatisfactory embrace before hurting.

The stars are dead; the animals will not look:
We are left alone with our day, and the time is short and   90
               History to the defeated
May say Alas but cannot help or pardon.

1937   1937, 1940

Musée des Beaux Arts[1]

About suffering they were never wrong,
The Old Masters: how well they understood
Its human position; how it takes place
While someone else is eating or opening a window or just walking
     dully along;
How, when the aged are reverently, passionately waiting   5
For the miraculous birth, there always must be
Children who did not specially want it to happen, skating
On a pond at the edge of the wood:
They never forgot
That even the dreadful martyrdom must run its course   10
Anyhow in a corner, some untidy spot
Where the dogs go on with their doggy life and the torturer's horse
Scratches its innocent behind on a tree.

In Brueghel's *Icarus*,[2] for instance: how everything turns away
Quite leisurely from the disaster; the ploughman may   15
Have heard the splash, the forsaken cry,
But for him it was not an important failure; the sun shone
As it had to on the white legs disappearing into the green
Water; and the expensive delicate ship that must have seen
Something amazing, a boy falling out of the sky,   20
Had somewhere to get to and sailed calmly on.

December 1938   1940

Lullaby

Lay your sleeping head, my love,
Human on my faithless arm;
Time and fevers burn away
Individual beauty from
Thoughtful children, and the grave   5

---

1. "Museum of Fine Arts." The reference is to the Museum of Fine Arts in Brussels, which contains Brueghel's *Icarus*.
2. Icarus was the son of Daedalus, the cunning craftsman of ancient legend. Together they flew on artificial wings fastened to their shoulders with wax, but Icarus ventured too near the sun, which melted the wax, and so he fell and perished. The painting of the fall of Icarus is by the Flemish painter Pieter Brueghel (ca. 1520–1569): Icarus' legs are disappearing into the sea in one corner of the picture, the rest of which has nothing to do with him.

Proves the child ephemeral:
But in my arms till break of day
Let the living creature lie,
Mortal, guilty, but to me
The entirely beautiful.   10

Soul and body have no bounds:
To lovers as they lie upon
Her tolerant enchanted slope
In their ordinary swoon,
Grave the vision Venus sends   15
Of supernatural sympathy,
Universal love and hope;
While an abstract insight wakes
Among the glaciers and the rocks
The hermit's carnal ecstasy.   20

Certainty, fidelity
On the stroke of midnight pass
Like vibrations of a bell,
And fashionable madmen raise
Their pedantic boring cry: 25
Every farthing[1] of the cost,
All the dreaded cards foretell,
Shall be paid, but from this night
Not a whisper, not a thought,
Not a kiss nor look be lost.   30

Beauty, midnight, vision dies:
Let the winds of dawn that blow
Softly round your dreaming head
Such a day of sweetness show
Eye and knocking heart may bless,   35
Find the mortal world enough;
Noons of dryness see you fed
By the involuntary powers,
Nights of insult let you pass
Watched by every human love.   40

January 1937   1940

In Memory of W. B. Yeats

(d. Jan. 1939)

1

He disappeared in the dead of winter:
The brooks were frozen, the airports almost deserted,

1. At one time the smallest and least valuable British coin.

And snow disfigured the public statues;
The mercury sank in the mouth of the dying day.
What instruments we have agree   5
The day of his death was a dark cold day.

Far from his illness
The wolves ran on through the evergreen forests,
The peasant river was untempted by the fashionable quays;
By mourning tongues   10
The death of the poet was kept from his poems.

But for him it was his last afternoon as himself,
An afternoon of nurses and rumours;
The provinces of his body revolted,
The squares of his mind were empty,   15
Silence invaded the suburbs,
The current of his feeling failed: he became his admirers.

Now he is scattered among a hundred cities
And wholly given over to unfamiliar affections;
To find his happiness in another kind of wood[1]
And be punished under a foreign code of conscience.   20
The words of a dead man
Are modified in the guts of the living.

But in the importance and noise of to-morrow
When the brokers are roaring like beasts on the floor of the Bourse,[2]   25
And the poor have the sufferings to which they are fairly accustomed,
And each in the cell of himself is almost convinced of his freedom,
A few thousand will think of this day
As one thinks of a day when one did something slightly unusual.
What instruments we have agree   30
The day of his death was a dark cold day.

2

You were silly like us: your gift survived it all:
The parish of rich women, physical decay,
Yourself. Mad Ireland hurt you into poetry.
Now Ireland has her madness and her weather still,   35
For poetry makes nothing happen: it survives
In the valley of its making where executives
Would never want to tamper, flows on south
From ranches of isolation and the busy griefs,
Raw towns that we believe and die in; it survives,   40
A way of happening, a mouth.

3

Earth, receive an honoured guest:
William Yeats is laid to rest.

1. Cf. Dante's *Inferno*, 1.1–3 (translated): "In the   in a dark wood where the straight way was lost."
middle of the journey of our life I came to myself   2. Stock exchange.

Let the Irish vessel lie
Emptied of its poetry.[3]   45

In the nightmare of the dark
All the dogs of Europe bark,
And the living nations wait,
Each sequestered in its hate;

                                                            50

Intellectual disgrace
Stares from every human face,
And the seas of pity lie
Locked and frozen in each eye.

Follow, poet, follow right
To the bottom of the night,   55
With your unconstraining voice
Still persuade us to rejoice;

With the farming of a verse
Make a vineyard of the curse,
Sing of human unsuccess   60
In a rapture of distress;

In the deserts of the heart
Let the healing fountain start,
In the prison of his days
Teach the free man how to praise.   65

February 1939   1940, 1966

Their Lonely Betters

As I listened from a beach-chair in the shade
To all the noises that my garden made,
It seemed to me only proper that words
Should be withheld from vegetables and birds.

A robin with no Christian name ran through   5
The Robin-Anthem which was all it knew,
And rustling flowers for some third party waited
To say which pairs, if any, should get mated.

---

3. Three stanzas that originally followed this were omitted in the 1966 edition of Auden's *Collected Shorter Poems* and thereafter: "Time that is intolerant / Of the brave and innocent, / And indifferent in a week / To a beautiful physique, / / Worships language and forgives / Everyone by whom it lives; / Pardons cowardice, conceit, / Lays its honours at their feet. / / Time that with this strange excuse / Pardoned Kipling and his views, / And will pardon Paul Claudel, / Pardons him for writing well." Kipling's views were imperialistic and jingoistic; Paul Claudel (1868–1955), French poet, dramatist, and diplomat, was an extreme Right-winger in his political ideas. Yeats's own politics were at times antidemocratic and appeared to favor dictatorship.

Not one of them was capable of lying,
There was not one which knew that it was dying   10
Or could have with a rhythm or a rhyme
Assumed responsibility for time.

Let them leave language to their lonely betters
Who count some days and long for certain letters;
We, too, make noises when we laugh or weep,   15
Words are for those with promises to keep.

1950   1951

In Praise of Limestone[1]

If it form the one landscape that we the inconstant ones
    Are consistently homesick for, this is chiefly
Because it dissolves in water. Mark these rounded slopes
    With their surface fragrance of thyme and, beneath,
A secret system of caves and conduits; hear the springs   5
    That spurt out everywhere with a chuckle
Each filling a private pool for its fish and carving
    Its own little ravine whose cliffs entertain
The butterfly and the lizard; examine this region
    Of short distances and definite places: 10
What could be more like Mother or a fitter background
    For her son, for the flirtatious male who lounges
Against a rock in the sunlight, never doubting
    That for all his faults he is loved; whose works are but
Extensions of his power to charm? From weathered outcrop   15
    To hill-top temple, from appearing waters to
Conspicuous fountains, from a wild to a formal vineyard,
    Are ingenious but short steps that a child's wish
To receive more attention than his brothers, whether
    By pleasing or teasing, can easily take.   20

Watch, then, the band of rivals as they climb up and down
    Their steep stone gennels[2] in twos and threes, at times
Arm in arm, but never, thank God, in step; or engaged
    On the shady side of a square at midday in
Voluble discourse, knowing each other too well to think   25
    There are any important secrets, unable
To conceive a god whose temper-tantrums are moral
    And not to be pacified by a clever line
Or a good lay: for, accustomed to a stone that responds,

---

1. The landscape of this poem derives from Auden's
native Yorkshire. Cf. his New Year Letter: "I see
the nature of my kind / As a locality I love / Those
limestone moors that stretch from Brough / To
Hexham on the Roman Wall / That is my symbol

of us all."
2. A "gennel," in the dialect of Yorkshire and other
northern counties, is a long narrow passage between
houses. Here it is a passage between rocks.

They have never had to veil their faces in awe   30
Of a crater whose blazing fury could not be fixed;
    Adjusted to the local needs of valleys
Where everything can be touched or reached by walking,
    Their eyes have never looked into infinite space
Through the lattice-work of a nomad's comb;[3] born lucky,   35
    Their legs have never encountered the fungi
And insects of the jungle, the monstrous forms and lives
    With which we have nothing, we like to hope, in common.
So, when one of them goes to the bad, the way his mind works
    Remains comprehensible: to become a pimp   40
Or deal in fake jewelry or ruin a fine tenor voice
    For effects that bring down the house, could happen to all
But the best and the worst of us . . .
                                    That is why, I suppose,
The best and worst never stayed here long but sought   45
Immoderate soils where the beauty was not so external,
    The light less public and the meaning of life
Something more than a mad camp. "Come!" cried the granite wastes,
    "How evasive is your humour, how accidental
Your kindest kiss, how permanent is death." (Saints-to-be
    Slipped away sighing.) "Come!" purred the clays and gravels.   50
"On our plains there is room for armies to drill; rivers
    Wait to be tamed and slaves to construct you a tomb
In the grand manner: soft as the earth is mankind and both
    Need to be altered." (Intendant Caesars[4] rose and
Left, slamming the door.) But the really reckless were fetched   55
    By an older colder voice, the oceanic whisper:
"I am the solitude that asks and promises nothing;
    That is how I shall set you free. There is no love;
There are only the various envies, all of them sad."

They were right, my dear, all those voices were right   60
And still are; this land is not the sweet home that it looks,
    Nor its peace the historical calm of a site
Where something was settled once and for all: A backward
    And dilapidated province, connected
To the big busy world by a tunnel, with a certain   65
    Seedy appeal, is that all it is now? Not quite:
It has a worldly duty which in spite of itself
    It does not neglect, but calls into question
All the Great Powers assume; it disturbs our rights. The poet,
    Admired for his earnest habit of calling   70
The sun the sun, his mind Puzzle, is made uneasy
    By these marble statues which so obviously doubt

---

3. The context suggests that this might be a popular name for a plant or tree (cf. "traveler's joy"
and "traveler's palm"), but Auden is probably using
the phrase quite literally to suggest that these people have never led a nomad's (wanderer's) life. The

"nomad's comb" might be the fringe of unkempt
hair through which the nomad peers at wild landscapes.
4. Roman emperors.

His antimythological myth; and these gamins,[5]
  Pursuing the scientist down the tiled colonnade
With such lively offers, rebuke his concern for Nature's   75
  Remotest aspects: I, too, am reproached, for what
And how much you know. Not to lose time, not to get caught,
  Not to be left behind, not, please! to resemble
The beasts who repeat themselves, or a thing like water
  Or stone whose conduct can be predicted, these   80
Are our Common Prayer, whose greatest comfort is music
  Which can be made anywhere, is invisible,
And does not smell. In so far as we have to look forward
  To death as a fact, no doubt we are right: But if
Sins can be forgiven, if bodies rise from the dead,   85
  These modifications of matter into
Innocent athletes and gesticulating fountains,
  Made solely for pleasure, make a further point:
The blessed will not care what angle they are regarded from,
  Having nothing to hide. Dear, I know nothing of   90
Either, but when I try to imagine a faultless love
  Or the life to come, what I hear is the murmur
Of underground streams, what I see is a limestone landscape.

May 1948   1948, 1951

The Shield of Achilles[1]

    She looked over his shoulder
      For vines and olive trees,
    Marble well-governed cities
      And ships upon untamed seas,
    But there on the shining metal   5
      His hands had put instead
    An artificial wilderness
      And a sky like lead.

A plain without a feature, bare and brown,
  No blade of grass, no sign of neighborhood,   10
Nothing to eat and nowhere to sit down,
    Yet, congregated on its blankness, stood
      An unintelligible multitude,
A million eyes, a million boots in line,
  Without expression, waiting for a sign.   15

5. Urchins.
1. In books 16 and 17 of Homer's *Iliad*, Achilles, the chief Greek hero in the war against Troy, lends his armor to his friend Patroclus and loses it when Patroclus is killed by the Trojan hero Hector. While Achilles is mourning for his friend, his mother, the goddess Thetis, goes to Mount Olympus to beg Hephaestos, god of fire, to forge new armor for Achilles. The splendid shield that Hephaestos then makes him is described in Book 18 of the *Iliad* (lines 478–608). On it he depicts the heavens, the sea, and the earth represented by many scenes such as a city at peace and a city at war.

Out of the air a voice without a face
   Proved by statistics that some cause was just
In tones as dry and level as the place:
   No one was cheered and nothing was discussed;
   Column by column in a cloud of dust   20
They marched away enduring a belief
Whose logic brought them, somewhere else, to grief.

      She looked over his shoulder
         For ritual pieties,
      White flower-garlanded heifers,   25
         Libation and sacrifice,[2]
      But there on the shining metal
         Where the altar should have been,
      She saw by his flickering forge-light
         Quite another scene.   30

Barbed wire enclosed an arbitrary spot
   Where bored officials lounged (one cracked a joke)
And sentries sweated for the day was hot:
   A crowd of ordinary decent folk
   Watched from without and neither moved nor spoke   35
As three pale figures were led forth and bound
To three posts driven upright in the ground.

The mass and majesty of this world, all
   That carries weight and always weighs the same
Lay in the hands of others; they were small   40
   And could not hope for help and no help came:
   What their foes liked to do was done, their shame
Was all the worst could wish; they lost their pride
And died as men before their bodies died.

      She looked over his shoulder   45
         For athletes at their games,
      Men and women in a dance
         Moving their sweet limbs
      Quick, quick, to music,
         But there on the shining shield   50
      His hands had set no dancing-floor
         But a weed-choked field.

A ragged urchin, aimless and alone,
   Loitered about that vacancy; a bird
Flew up to safety from his well-aimed stone: 55
   That girls are raped, that two boys knife a third,

---

2. Cf. Keats's *Ode on a Grecian Urn*: "Who are these coming to the sacrifice? / To what green altar, O mysterious priest, / Lead'st thou that heifer low-ing at the skies, / And all her silken flanks with garlands dressed?"

Were axioms to him, who'd never heard
Of any world where promises were kept,
Or one could weep because another wept.

The thin-lipped armorer,   60
Hephaestos, hobbled away,
Thetis of the shining breasts
Cried out in dismay
At what the god had wrought
To please her son, the strong   65
Iron-hearted man-slaying Achilles
Who would not live long.

1952   1955

DYLAN THOMAS
1914–1953

Dylan Thomas was born in Swansea, Wales, and educated at Swansea
Grammar School. After working for a time as a newspaper reporter, he was
"discovered" as a poet in 1933 through a poetry contest in a popular newspaper. The following year his *Eighteen Poems* caused considerable excitement because of the strange violence of their imagery and their powerfully
suggestive obscurity. It looked as though a new kind of strength and romantic
picturesqueness had been restored to English poetry after the deliberately
muted tones of Eliot and his followers. Thomas did not, however, turn out
to be the founder of a neo-Romantic movement, though some early critics
took him to be so. As his poetry became better known, and after he had
clarified the somewhat clotted imagery of his early style in his later volumes—*The Map of Love* (1939), *Deaths and Entrances* (1946), *Collected
Poems* (1953)—it became clear that he was a master craftsman, and not the
shouting rhapsodist that some had taken him to be. His images were most
carefully ordered in a patterned sequence, and his major theme was the
unity of all life, the continuing *process* of life and death and new life which
linked the generations to each other. Thomas saw the workings of biology as
a magical transformation producing unity out of diversity, and again and
again in his poetry he sought a poetic ritual to celebrate this unity ("The
force that through the green fuse drives the flower / Drives my green age").
He saw men and women locked in a round of identities—with the beginning
of growth also the first movement toward death, the beginning of love leading to procreation, new growth, and so in turn to death again and to life
again, and because of this view he comforted himself with the unity of man
and nature, of past and present, of life and death, and so "refused to mourn
the death of a child." In his best poems the closely woven imagery (deriving
from the Bible, Welsh folklore and preaching, and Freud) is organized to
present aspects of this theme. His more open-worked poems of reminiscence
and autobiographical emotion, such as *Poem in October*, communicate more
immediately to the reader through their fine lyrical feeling and compelling

use of simple natural images. His autobiographical work *Portrait of the Artist as a Young Dog* and his radio play *Under Milk Wood* reveal a vividness of observation and a combination of violence and tenderness in expression that shows he could handle prose as excitingly as verse.

Thomas was a brilliant talker (when he felt like it), a considerable drinker, a reckless and impulsive man whose short life was packed with emotional ups and downs. His poetry readings in America between 1950 and 1953 were enormous successes, in spite of his sometimes reckless antics. He died suddenly in New York, in November 1953, of what was diagnosed as "an insult to the brain," precipitated by alcohol. He acted the wild bohemian poet as that role had not been played since the nineties; some thought this behavior wonderful, though others deplored it. He was a brilliant reader of his own and others' poems, and many people who do not normally read poetry were drawn to Thomas's by the magic of his own reading. After his premature death a reaction set in: some critics declared that he had been overrated as a poet because of the sensational role he had played in life. But a balanced view is now possible; it is clear that at his best he was an original poet of great power and beauty.

The Force That Through the Green Fuse Drives the Flower

The force that through the green fuse drives the flower
Drives my green age; that blasts the roots of trees
Is my destroyer.
And I am dumb to tell the crooked rose
My youth is bent by the same wintry fever.   5

The force that drives the water through the rocks
Drives my red blood; that dries the mouthing streams
Turns mine to wax.
And I am dumb to mouth unto my veins
How at the mountain spring the same mouth sucks.   10

The hand that whirls the water in the pool
Stirs the quicksand; that ropes the blowing wind
Hauls my shroud sail.
And I am dumb to tell the hanging man
How of my clay is made the hangman's lime.[1]   15

The lips of time leech to the fountain head;
Love drips and gathers, but the fallen blood
Shall calm her sores.
And I am dumb to tell a weather's wind
How time has ticked a heaven round the stars.   20

---

1. Quicklime was sometimes poured into the graves of victims of the public hangmen, to accelerate decomposition.

And I am dumb to tell the lover's tomb
How at my sheet goes the same crooked worm.

1933

After the Funeral[1]

(In Memory of Ann Jones)

After the funeral, mule praises, brays,
Windshake of sailshaped ears, muffle-toed tap
Tap happily of one peg in the thick
Grave's foot, blinds down the lids, the teeth in black,
The spittled eyes, the salt ponds in the sleeves,   5
Morning smack of the spade that wakes up sleep,
Shakes a desolate boy who slits his throat
In the dark of the coffin and sheds dry leaves,
That breaks one bone to light with a judgment clout,
After the feast of tear-stuffed time and thistles   10
In a room with a stuffed fox and a stale fern,
I stand, for this memorial's sake, alone
In the snivelling hours with dead, humped Ann
Whose hooded, fountain heart once fell in puddles
Round the parched worlds of Wales and drowned each sun   15
(Though this for her is a monstrous image blindly
Magnified out of praise; her death was a still drop;
She would not have me sinking in the holy
Flood of her heart's fame; she would lie dumb and deep
And need no druid[2] of her broken body).   20
But I, Ann's bard on a raised hearth, call all
The seas to service that her wood-tongued virtue
Babble like a bellbuoy over the hymning heads,
Bow down the walls of the ferned and foxy woods
That her love sing and swing through a brown chapel,   25
Bless her bent spirit with four, crossing birds.
Her flesh was meek as milk, but this skyward statue
With the wild breast and blessed and giant skull
Is carved from her in a room with a wet window
In a fiercely mourning house in a crooked year.   30
I know her scrubbed and sour humble hands
Lie with religion in their cramp, her threadbare
Whisper in a damp word, her wits drilled hollow,
Her fist of a face died clenched on a round pain;
And sculptured Ann is seventy years of stone.   35
These cloud-sopped, marble hands, this monumental

---

1. Ann Jones was Thomas's aunt; she lived at a   2. Priest of the ancient Celtic pagans (ancestors of
farmhouse called "Fern Hill" in the Welsh land-   the modern Welsh).
scape described in *Poem in October.*

Argument of the hewn voice, gesture and psalm,
Storm me forever over her grave until
The stuffed lung of the fox twitch and cry Love
And the strutting fern lay seeds on the black sill.   40

1938, 1939

There Was a Saviour

There was a saviour
    Rarer than radium,
Commoner than water, crueller than truth;
    Children kept from the sun
    Assembled at his tongue   5
To hear the golden note turn in a groove,
Prisoners of wishes locked their eyes
In the jails and studies of his keyless smiles.

    The voice of children says
    From a lost wilderness   10
There was calm to be done in his safe unrest,
    When hindering man hurt
    Man, animal, or bird
We hid our fears in that murdering breath,
Silence, silence to do, when earth grew loud,   15
In lairs and asylums of the tremendous shout.

    There was glory to hear
    In the churches of his tears,
Under his downy arm you sighed as he struck,
    O you who could not cry   20
    On to the ground when a man died
Put a tear for joy in the unearthly flood
And laid your cheek against a cloud-formed shell:
Now in the dark there is only yourself and myself.

    Two proud, blacked brothers cry,   25
    Winter-locked side by side,
To this inhospitable hollow year,
    O we who could not stir
    One lean sigh when we heard
Greed on man beating near and fire neighbour   30
But wailed and nested in the sky-blue wall
Now break a giant tear for the little known fall,

    For the drooping of homes
    That did not nurse our bones,
Brave deaths of only ones but never found,   35

Now see, alone in us,
    Our own true strangers' dust
Ride through the doors of our unentered house.
Exiled in us we arouse the soft,
Unclenched, armless, silk and rough love that breaks all rocks.   40

1940

The Hunchback in the Park

The hunchback in the park
A solitary mister
Propped between trees and water
From the opening of the garden lock
That lets the trees and water enter   5
Until the Sunday sombre bell at dark

Eating bread from a newspaper
Drinking water from the chained cup
That the children filled with gravel
In the fountain basin where I sailed my ship   10
Slept at night in a dog kennel
But nobody chained him up.

Like the park birds he came early
Like the water he sat down
And Mister they called Hey mister   15
The truant boys from the town
Running when he had heard them clearly
On out of sound

Past lake and rockery
Laughing when he shook his paper   20
Hunchbacked in mockery
Through the loud zoo of the willow groves
Dodging the park keeper
With his stick that picked up leaves.

And the old dog sleeper   25
Alone between nurses and swans
While the boys among willows
Made the tigers jump out of their eyes
To roar on the rockery stones
And the groves were blue with sailors   30

Made all day until bell time
A woman figure without fault
Straight as a young elm

Straight and tall from his crooked bones
That she might stand in the night   35
After the locks and chains

All night in the unmade park
After the railings and shrubberies
The birds the grass the trees the lake
And the wild boys innocent as strawberries   40
Had followed the hunchback
To his kennel in the dark.

1941

Poem in October

It was my thirtieth year to heaven
Woke to my hearing from harbour and neighbour wood
   And the mussel pooled and the heron
       Priested shore
     The morning beckon   5
With water praying and call of seagull and rook
And the knock of sailing boats on the net webbed wall
     Myself to set foot
       That second
In the still sleeping town and set forth.   10

My birthday began with the water-
Birds and the birds of the winged trees flying my name
   Above the farms and the white horses
      And I rose
     In rainy autumn   15
And walked abroad in a shower of all my days.
High tide and the heron dived when I took the road
     Over the border
      And the gates
Of the town closed as the town awoke.   20

A springful of larks in a rolling
Cloud and the roadside bushes brimming with whistling
   Blackbirds and the sun of October
      Summery
     On the hill's shoulder,   25
Here were fond climates and sweet singers suddenly
Come in the morning where I wandered and listened
     To the rain wringing
      Wind blow cold
In the wood faraway under me.   30

Pale rain over the dwindling harbour
And over the sea wet church the size of a snail
            With its horns through mist and the castle
                        Brown as owls
                        But all the gardens   35
Of spring and summer were blooming in the tall tales
Beyond the border and under the lark full cloud.
            There could I marvel
                        My birthday
Away but the weather turned around.   40

It turned away from the blithe country
And down the other air and the blue altered sky
            Streamed again a wonder of summer
                        With apples
                        Pears and red currants   45
And I saw in the turning so clearly a child's
Forgotten mornings when he walked with his mother
            Through the parables
                        Of sun light
And the legends of the green chapels   50

And the twice told fields of infancy
That his tears burned my cheeks and his heart moved in mine.
            These were the woods the river and sea
                        Where a boy
                        In the listening   55
Summertime of the dead whispered the truth of his joy
To the trees and the stones and the fish in the tide.
            And the mystery
                        Sang alive
Still in the water and singingbirds.   60

And there could I marvel my birthday
Away but the weather turned around. And the true
            Joy of the long dead child sang burning
                        In the sun.
                        It was my thirtieth   65
Year to heaven stood there then in the summer noon
Though the town below lay leaved with October blood.
            O may my heart's truth
                        Still be sung
On this high hill in a year's turning.   70

1945, 1946

Do Not Go Gentle into That Good Night

Do not go gentle into that good night,
Old age should burn and rave at close of day;
Rage, rage against the dying of the light.

Though wise men at their end know dark is right,
Because their words had forked no lightning they   5
Do not go gentle into that good night.

Good men, the last wave by, crying how bright
Their frail deeds might have danced in a green bay,
Rage, rage against the dying of the light.

Wild men who caught and sang the sun in flight,   10
And learn, too late, they grieved it on its way,
Do not go gentle into that good night.

Grave men, near death, who see with blinding sight
Blind eyes could blaze like meteors and be gay,
Rage, rage against the dying of the light.   15

And you, my father, there on the sad height,
Curse, bless, me now with your fierce tears, I pray.
Do not go gentle into that good night.
Rage, rage against the dying of the light.

                                        1951, 1952

Poems in Process

Poets in all ages have claimed that their poems were not willed but were inspired, whether by a muse, by divine visitation, or by sudden emergence from the author's unconscious mind. But as the poet Richard Aldington has remarked, "Genius is not enough; one must also work." The working manuscripts of the greatest writers show that, however involuntary the origin of a poem, vision was usually followed by laborious revision before the work achieved the seeming inevitability of its final form.

Milton is the first major English author for whom we possess drafts of poems indubitably written in his own hand; the excerpt from his manuscript of *Lycidas* shows him altering and expanding his initial efforts. We have increasing numbers of manuscripts written in the eighteenth century, such as those reproduced below from Pope and Johnson. In the early nineteenth century, the working drafts of many poets began to be carefully preserved, and so remain abundantly available.

The examples from major poets that are transcribed here represent various stages in the evolution of a poem, and a variety of procedures in the mode of composition by individual poets; some writers even continued to revise long after the original version had been committed to print. In all these instances we look on as the poets, no matter how rapidly they may have achieved a result they were willing to let stand, carried on their tentative efforts to meet the multiple requirements of meaning, syntax, meter, sound pattern, and the constraints imposed by a chosen stanza. And because these are all very good poets, the seeming conflict between the necessities of significance and form results not in the distortion but in the perfection of the poetic statement.

Our transcriptions from the poets' drafts attempt to reproduce, as accurately as the change from script to print will allow, the appearance of the manuscript page. A poet's first attempt at a line or phrase is reproduced in larger type, the revisions in smaller type. The line numbers which are used to identify an excerpt are those of the final form of the complete poem, as reprinted in this anthology. The marginal numbers beside the extract from *The Vanity of Human Wishes*, however, are Johnson's own additions in his manuscript.

SELECTED BIBLIOGRAPHY

Autograph Poetry in the English Language, 2 vols., 1973, compiled by P. J. Croft, reproduces and transcribes one or more pages of manuscript in the poet's own hand, from the 14th century to the present time. Books which discuss the process of composition and revision, with examples from the manuscripts and printed versions of poems, are:

Charles D. Abbott, ed., *Poets at Work*, 1948; Phyllis Bartlett, *Poems in Process*, 1951; A. F. Scott, *The Poet's Craft*, 1957. In *Word for Word: A Study of Authors' Alterations*, 1965, Wallace Hildick analyzes the composition of prose fiction as well as poems; a shorter version, *Word for Word: The Rewriting of Fiction*, 1965, discusses the revision of novels by George Eliot, Samuel Butler, Hardy, Lawrence, James, and Woolf. Byron's *"Don Juan,"* edited by T. G. Steffan and W. W. Pratt, 4 vols., 1957, transcribes the manuscript drafts; the Cornell Wordsworth, in process, reproduces, transcribes, and discusses various versions of Wordsworth's poems from the first manuscript drafts to the final publication in his lifetime. M. R. Ridley has written a study of the poet's manuscripts in *Keats' Craftsmanship*, 1933; and Jon Stallworthy, *Between the Lines: Yeats's Poetry in the Making*, 1963, reproduces and analyzes the sequential drafts of a number of Yeats's major poems. Valerie Eliot has edited T. S. Eliot's *The Waste Land: A Facsimile and Transcript of the Original Drafts Including the Annotations of Ezra Pound*, 1971, while Dame Helen Gardner has transcribed and analyzed the manuscript drafts of Eliot's *Four Quartets* in *The Composition of Four Quartets*, 1978.

JOHN MILTON
From Lycidas[1]

[*Lines* 1–14][2]

yet once more O ye laurells and once more

ye myrtl's browne wth Ivie never sere

I come to pluck yor berries harsh and crude

~~before the mellowing yeare~~ and wth forc't fingers rude

~~and crop yor young~~ shatter yor leaves before y^e mellowing yeare

bitter constraint, and sad occasion deare

compells me to disturbe yor season due

for ~~young~~ Lycidas is dead, dead ere his prime

young Lycidas and hath not left his peere

who would $\overset{\text{not}}{\wedge}$ sing for Lycidas he well knew

himselfe to sing & build the loftie rime

he must not flote upon his watrie beare

unwept, and welter to the parching wind

without the meed of some melodious teare

---

1. Transcribed from a manuscript of 50 pages in the library of Trinity College, Cambridge. Among the poems written in Milton's own hand are *Lycidas*, *Comus*, seven sonnets, and several other short poems. The manuscript has been photographically reproduced, with printed transcriptions, by W. Aldis Wright, *Facsimile of the Manuscript of Milton's Minor Poems* (Cambridge, England, 1899).

2. This draft is written on a separate page of the manuscript, which also contains drafts of the passages, "What could the muse her selfe" and "Bring the rathe primrose," transcribed below.

[*Lines 56–63*]

ay mee I fondly dreame
~~had yee~~ bin there, ~~for~~ what could that have don?
~~what could the golden hayrd Calliope~~
for her inchaunting son
~~when shee beheld   (the gods farre sighted bee)~~
~~his goarie scalpe rowle downe the Thracian lee~~

whome universal nature
might lament
~~and heaven and hel deplore~~
~~when his divine head downe~~
the streame was sent
downe the Swift Hebrus to the
    Lesbian shore.

[THE THIRD AND FOLLOWING LINES ARE REWRITTEN ON A SEPARATE PAGE]

what could the muse her selfe that Orpheus bore
the muse her selfe for her inchanting son
~~for her inchanting son~~

                            did
whome universal nature ~~might~~ lament
when by the rout that made the hideous roare
                    gorie
*goarie his ~~diving~~ visage down the streame was sent
downe the swift Hebrus to ye Lesbian shoare.

[*Lines 132–53*]

Returne Alpheus the dred voice is past
    that shrunk thy streams, returne Sicilian Muse
    and call the vales and bid them hither cast
    thire bells, and flowrets of a thousand hues
    yee vallies low where the mild wispers use

    of shades, and wanton winds, and g$\overset{u}{o}$shing brooks

    on whose fresh lap the swart starre sparely looks   sparely
                                                            ~~faintly~~
* ~~bring~~ hither all yor quaint enamel'd eyes   throw
    that on the greene terfe suck the honied showrs
    and purple all the ground wth vernal flowrs

                            ———— Bring the rathe &c.[3]
    to strew the laureat herse where Lycid' lies
    for so to interpose a little ease
           fraile
    let our ~~sad~~ thoughts dally wth false surmise   fraile

[LINES 142–50 ARE DRAFTED ON A SEPARATE PAGE, AS FOLLOWS]

    Bring the rathe primrose that unwedded dies
    ~~collu~~ colouring the pale cheeke of uninjoyd love
    and that sad floure that strove
    to write his owne woes on the vermeil graine
    next adde Narcissus that still weeps in vaine

---

3. I.e., Milton plans to insert here the passage that follows.

the woodbine and ye pancie freak't wth jet
the glowing violet
the cowslip wan that hangs his pensive head
and every bud that sorrows liverie weares

let Daffadillies fill thire cups^with teares
bid Amaranthus all his beautie shed
to strew the laureat herse &c.

Bring the rathe primrose that forsaken dies
the tufted crowtoe and pale Gessamin

the white pinke, and ^ye pansie freakt wth jet
the glowing violet
                    the well-attired woodbine
the muske rose and ~~the garish columbine~~
wth cowslips wan that hang the pensive head
                              weare   weares
and every flower that sad escutcheon ~~beares~~ imbroidric ~~beares~~
   &
2 ~~let~~ daffadillies fill thire cups wth teares
1 bid Amaranthus all his beauties shed
to strew &c.

ALEXANDER POPE
From An Essay on Man[1]

[*From the First Manuscript*]

            we ourselves
1. Learn ~~then thyself~~, not God presume to scan,
      But
   ~~And~~ know, the Study of Mankind is <u>Man</u>.
   Plac'd on this <u>Isthmus</u> of a Middle State,
   A Being <u>darkly wise</u>, & <u>rudely great</u>.
   With too much <u>knowledge</u> for the <u>Sceptic</u> side,
   And too much <u>Weakness</u> for a <u>Stoic's</u> Pride,
   He hangs between, uncertain where to rest;
   Whether to deem himself a <u>God</u> or <u>Beast</u>;
   Whether his <u>Mind</u> or <u>Body</u> to prefer,
   Born but to <u>die</u>, & reas'ning but to <u>err</u>;
              his
   Alike in <u>Ignorance</u>, (~~that~~ Reason such)
            Who   ~~who thinks~~
   Whether he thinks too <u>little</u> or too <u>much</u>:

---

1. Two of Pope's holograph manuscripts of *An Essay on Man* have survived. The earlier one is at the Pierpont Morgan Library in New York. The second one, at the Houghton Library, Harvard, was evidently intended as a fair copy for printing; but Pope, who was an inveterate reviser, intro-duced some last-minute improvements. The passage transcribed here from each of these manuscripts is Pope's famed description of man's "middle state" in the great chain of being; in the published version, it opens Epistle 2, lines 1–18.

Chaos of Thought & Passion, all confus'd,
Still by himself abus'd & dis-abus'd:
Created half to rise, & half to fall;
Great Lord of all things, yet a prey to all;
Sole Judge of Truth, in endless Error hurl'd;
The Glory, Jest, and Riddle of the World.

[*From the Second Manuscript*][2]

~~Incipit I~~   Know
~~Incipit III~~   ~~Learn~~ we ourselves, not God presume to scan,
The only Science   Convinc'd,
         ~~But know,~~ the Study of Mankind is Man;
    ⌈Plac'd on this Isthmus of a Middle State,
    A Being darkly wise, and rudely great;
    With too much Knowledge for the Sceptic side,
         With
    ~~And~~ too much Weakness for a Stoic's Pride,
                        in doubt to act or
    He hangs between, ~~uncertain where to~~ rest,
                   Part of
    Whether ~~To~~ deem himself a ͜ God or Beast;
       In doubt
    Whether his Mind, or Body to prefer.
       ~~This born~~   ~~that~~
    Born but to die, and reas'ning but to err;
    Alike in Ignorance, his Reason such,

         Whether he thinks   or too much.
    ~~Who thinks~~ too little, ~~or who thinks too much:~~
    Chaos of Thought and Passion, all confus'd,
    Still by himself abus'd and dis-abus'd:
    Created half to rise, and half to fall;
    Great Lord of all things, yet a prey to all;
    Sole Judge of Truth, in endless error hurl'd;
    The Glory, Jest, and Riddle of the World!

2. In this version of the manuscript, Pope inserted some marginal glosses. In the right-hand margin (next to the line beginning "Learn we ourselves . . ."), he wrote: "Of Man, as an Individual," while next to the line beginning "Plac'd on this Isthmus . . . ," he wrote "His Middle Nature." And in the left-hand margin, a little below the line beginning "With too much knowledge . . . ," he wrote "His Powers, and Imperfections."

SAMUEL JOHNSON

Johnson told Boswell in 1766 that when composing verses "I have generally had them in my mind, perhaps fifty at a time, walking up and down in my room; and then I have written them down, and often, from laziness, have written only half lines. . . . I remember I wrote a hundred lines of *The Vanity of Human Wishes* in a day." When the first manuscript draft of this poem turned up in the 1940s among Boswell's papers at Malahide Castle, it supported Johnson's account, for it had been written and corrected in haste, with only sparse punctuation; while the second half of each line had been filled out, obviously from memory, at some time after the writing of the first half, in a darker ink. In the transcriptions from this manuscript (which is in the collection of Mary Hyde, Somerville, New Jersey), the half-lines and emendations that Johnson added to his initial draft are printed in boldface type.

The draft was written on the right-hand pages of a small homemade pocket book; some words in the added half-line, impinging on the right margin of the page, had to be completed above or below the line. The two added lines, "See Nations slowly wise . . . the tardy Bust," were written on the blank left-hand page, at the place where they were to be inserted. The numeration of every tenth line was added by Johnson in the manuscript, and incorporates these two additional lines.

Johnson published the poem in 1749 and revised it for a second publication in 1755, when it achieved the final form printed in the selections from Johnson, above. It was in 1755 that Johnson introduced his most famous emendation when, after his disillusionment with Lord Chesterfield as literary patron, he substituted in line 162 the word "patron" for "garret": "Toil, envy, want, the patron, and the jail."

From The Vanity of Human Wishes

[*Lines* 135–64]

When first the College Rolls **receive his nam**^e
The young Enthusiast **quits his ease for fame**

Quick fires his breast
~~Each act betrays~~ **the fever of renown**
Caught from **the strong Contagion of the Gown**
On his banks he waves, **from noise withdrawn**
140 In sober state th' imaginary Lawn
O'er Bodley's Dome **his future Labours spread**
And Bacon's Mansion **trembles o'er his head.**
Are these thy views, **proceed illustrious Youth**
And Virtue guard **thee to the throne of Trut**^h
Yet should th~~y fate~~ Soul indulge the gen'rous
                                          Heat

Till Captive Science **yields her last Retreat**
Should Reason **guide thee with her brightest Ray**
And pour on misty Doubt **resistless day**
Should no false kindness **lure to loose delight**
150 Nor Praise relax, nor **difficulty fright**
Should tempting Novelty **thy cell refrain**
                                          vain
And Sloth's bland opiates **shed their fumes in**
sShould Beuty blunt **on fops her fatal dart**
Nor claim the **triumph of a letter'd heart**
~~S Nor~~ Should no Disease **thy torpid veins invade**
Nor Melancholys Spectres **haunt thy Shade**

>   hope
> Yet ~~dream~~ not Life **from Grief or Danger free**,
> Nor think the doom of **Man revers'd for thee**
>   Deign   passing   to
> ~~Turn~~ on the ˄world ~~awhile~~ **turn thine eyes**
> 160 And pause **awhile from Learning to be wise**
> There mark what **ill the Scholar's life assail**
>
>   the
> Toil envy Want ~~a~~ **Garret and the Jayl**
>   Dreams
> If ~~Hope~~ yet **flatter once again attend**
> Hear Lydiats life **and Galileo's End.**

See Nations slowly wise, and meanly just,
To buried merit raise the tardy Bust.

WILLIAM BLAKE
The Tyger[1]

[*First Draft*]

      The Tyger

1   Tyger Tyger burning bright
        In the forests of the night
        What immortal hand or eye
   ~~Dare~~ **Could** frame thy fearful symmetry

        Burnt in
2   ~~In what~~ distant deeps or skies
 ~~The cruel~~ **Burnt the** fire of thine eyes
        On what wings dare he aspire
        What the hand dare sieze the fire

3   And what shoulder & what art
        Could twist the sinews of thy heart
        And when thy heart began to beat
        What dread hand & what dread feet

        ~~Could fetch it from the furnace deep~~
        ~~And in thy horrid ribs dare steep~~
        ~~In the well of sanguine woe~~
        ~~In what clay & what mould~~
        ~~Were thy eyes of fury rolld~~

        ~~Where~~   ~~where~~
4   ~~What~~ the hammer ~~what~~ the chain
        In what furnace was thy brain

---

1. These drafts have been taken from a notebook used by William Blake, called the Rossetti MS because it was once owned by Dante Gabriel Rossetti, the Victorian poet and painter; David V. Erdman's edition of *The Notebook of William Blake* (1973) contains a photographic facsimile. The stanza and line numbers were written by Blake in the manuscript.

                              dread grasp
What the anvil what ~~the arm arm grasp clasp~~
Dare ~~Could~~ its deadly terrors ~~clasp grasp~~ clasp

6   Tyger Tyger burning bright
         In the forests of the night
         What immortal hand & eye
             frame
         Dare ~~form~~ thy fearful symmetry

[Trial Stanzas]

Burnt in distant deeps or skies
The cruel fire of thine eye,
Could heart descend or wings aspire
What the hand dare sieze the fire

          dare he ~~smile laugh~~
5   And ~~did he laugh~~ his work to see
        ankle
  ~~What the shoulder what the knee~~
     Dare
4 ~~Did~~ he who made the lamb make thee
1 When the stars threw down their spears
2 And waterd heaven with their tears

[Second Full Draft]

Tyger Tyger burning/bright
In the forests of the night
What Immortal hand & eye
Dare frame thy fearful symmetry

And what shoulder & what art
Could twist the sinews of thy heart
And when thy heart began to beat
What dread hand & what dread feet

When the stars threw down their spears
And waterd heaven with their tears
Did he smile his work to see
Did he who made the lamb make thee

Tyger Tyger burning bright
In the forests of the night
What immortal hand & eye
Dare frame thy fearful symmetry

[*Final Version, 1794*]²

The Tyger

Tyger Tyger, burning bright,
In the forests of the night;
What immortal hand or eye,
Could frame thy fearful symmetry?

In what distant deeps or skies
Burnt the fire of thine eyes!
On what wings dare he aspire?
What the hand, dare sieze the fire?

And what shoulder, & what art,
Could twist the sinews of thy heart?
And when thy heart began to beat,
What dread hand? & what dread feet?

What the hammer? what the chain,
In what furnace was thy brain?
What the anvil? what dread grasp,
Dare its deadly terrors clasp?

When the stars threw down their spears
And water'd heaven with their tears:
Did he smile his work to see?
Did he who made the Lamb make thee?

Tyger, Tyger burning bright,
In the forests of the night:
What immortal hand or eye,
Dare frame thy fearful symmetry?

WILLIAM WORDSWORTH
She Dwelt Among the Untrodden Ways

[*Version in a Letter to Coleridge,
December 1798 or January 1799*]¹

My hope was one, from cities far
    Nursed on a lonesome heath:
Her lips were red as roses are,
    Her hair a woodbine wreath.

2. As published in *Songs of Experience*.
1. Printed in Ernest de Selincourt's *Early Letters of William and Dorothy Wordsworth* (1935). Simply by deleting two weak stanzas from this draft, and making a few verbal changes, Wordsworth converted a rather conventional poem into one of the great dirges in the language.

She lived among the untrodden ways
    Beside the springs of Dove,
A maid whom there were none to praise,
    And very few to love;

A violet by a mossy stone
    Half-hidden from the eye!
Fair as a star when only one
    Is shining in the sky!

And she was graceful as the broom[2]
    That flowers by Carron's side;
But slow distemper checked her bloom,
    And on the Heath she died.

Long time before her head lay low
    Dead to the world was she:
But now she's in her grave, and Oh!
    The difference to me!

[Final Version, 1800][3]

Song

She dwelt among th' untrodden ways
    Beside the springs of Dove,
A Maid whom there were none to praise
    And very few to love.

A Violet by a mossy stone
    Half-hidden from the Eye!
—Fair, as a star when only one
    Is shining in the sky!

She *liv'd* unknown, and few could know
    When Lucy ceas'd to be;   10
But she is in her Grave, and Oh!
    The difference to me.

LORD BYRON
From Don Juan[1]

[First Draft: Canto 3, Stanza 9]

~~Life is a play and men~~
All tragedies are finished by a death,

---

2. A shrub with long slender branches and yellow flowers; the Carron is a river in northwestern Scotland.
3. As published in the second edition of *Lyrical Ballads*.

1. Reproduced from transcripts made of Byron's manuscripts in T. G. Steffan and W. W. Pratt, *Byron's "Don Juan"* (1957). The stanzas were published by Bryon in their emended form.

All Comedies are ended by a marriage,
~~For Life can go no further~~
~~These two form the last gasp of Passion's breath~~
~~All further is a blank—I won't disparage~~
~~That holy state—but certainly beneath~~
~~The Sun—of human things~~
~~These two are levellers, and human breath~~
~~So~~ ~~These point the epigram of human breath,~~
~~Or any~~ The future states of both are left to faith,
~~Though Life and love I like not to disparage~~
~~The~~ For authors ~~think~~ description might disparage
            fear
~~Tis strange that poets never try to wreathe~~ [sic?]
~~With eith~~ ~~Tis strange that poets of the Catholic faith~~
~~Neer go beyond—and~~ ~~but seem to dread miscarriage~~
~~So dramas close with death or settlement for life~~
~~Veiling~~ ~~Leaving the future states of Love and Life~~
~~The paradise beyond like that of life~~
~~And neer describing either~~
~~To more conjecture of a devil~~ ~~and~~ ~~or wife~~
~~And don't say much of paradise or wife~~
The worlds to come of both—~~&~~ or fall beneath,
And ~~all~~ ~~both the worlds would blame them for miscarriage~~
And then both worlds would punish their miscarriage—
~~So leaving both with priest & prayerbook ready~~
So leaving ~~Clerg both a~~ each their Priest and prayerbook ready,
They say no more of death or of the Lady.

[*First Draft: Canto 14, Stanza 95*]

                quote   seldom
Alas! ~~I speak by~~ Experience—~~never~~ yet
~~I had a paramour—and I've had many—~~
                        ~~some small~~
~~To whom I did not cause a deep~~ regret—
~~Whom I had not some reason to~~ regret
~~For Whom—I did not feel myself~~ a Zany—
Alas! by all experience, seldom yet
(I merely quote what I have heard from many)
Had lovers not some reason to regret
The passion which made Solomon a Zany.
~~I also had a wife~~—not to forget—
I've also seen some wives—not to forget—
The marriage state—the best or worst of any—
        were   paragons
Who ~~was~~ the very ~~paragon~~ of wives,
Yet made the misery of ~~both our~~ lives.
                    ~~many~~
                    ~~several~~
                    ~~of~~ at least two

PERCY BYSSHE SHELLEY

The three stages of this poem labeled "First Draft" are scattered through one of Shelley's notebooks, now in the Huntington Library, San Marino, California; these drafts have been transcribed and analyzed by Bennett Weaver, "Shelley Works Out the Rhythm of *A Lament*," *PMLA*, 47 (1932), 570–76. They show Shelley working with fragmentary words and phrases, and simultaneously with a wordless pattern of pulses which marked out the meter of the single lines and the shape of the lyric stanzas. Shelley left this draft unfinished.

Apparently at some later time, Shelley returned to the poem and wrote what is here called the "Second Draft"; from this he then made, on a second page, a revised fair copy which provided the text that Mary Shelley published in 1824, after the poet's death. These two manuscript pages are now in the Bodleian Library, Oxford; the first page is photographically reproduced and discussed by John Carter and John Sparrow, "Shelley, Swinburne, and Housman," *Times Literary Supplement* Nov. 21, 1968, pp. 1318–19.

O World, O Life, O Time

[*First Draft, Stage 1*]

Ah time, oh night, oh day
~~Ni nal ni na, na ni~~
~~Ni na ni na, ni na~~
Oh life O death, O time
    Time a di
~~Never Time~~
Ah time, a time O-time
    ~~Time!~~

[*First Draft, Stage 2*]

Oh time, oh night oh day
~~O day oh night, alas~~
  ~~O~~ Death time night ~~oh~~
Oh, Time
Oh time o night oh day

[*First Draft, Stage 3*]

Na na, na na ná na
Nă nă na na na—nă nă
  Nă nă nă nă nă nă
Na na nă nă nâ ă na

Na na na—nă nă—na na
  Na na na na—na na na na na
Na na na na na.
    Na na
Na na na na na
    Na na
Na na na na na ˇ na!

Oh time, oh night, o day
         alas
  O day ~~serenest,~~ o day
  O day alas the day
That thou shouldst sleep when we awake to say

  O time time—o death—o day
          for
    O day, o death life is far from thee
    O thou wert never free
    For death is now with thee
    ~~And life is far from~~
    O death, o day for life is far from thee

[Second Draft][1]

    Out of the day & night   I am
    A joy has taken flight   despair
  Fresh spring & summer   & winter hoar
    Fill my faint heart with grief, but with
                  delight
        No more—o never more!

~~Wo~~
    O World, o life, o time
    ~~Will ye~~ On whose last steps I climb
Trembling at those which I have trod[2] before
When will return the glory of yr prime
      No more   Oh never more

     Out of the day & night
     A joy has taken flight—
          autumn
~~From~~ Green spring, & ~~summer gra~~[3] & winter hoar

1. Shelley apparently wrote the first stanza of this draft low down on the page, and ran out of space after crowding in the third line of the second stanza; he then, in a lighter ink, wrote a revised form of the whole of the second stanza at the top of the page. In this revision, he left a space after "summer" in line 3, indicating that he planned an insertion that would fill out the four-foot meter of this line, and so make it match the five feet in the corresponding line of the first stanza.

In the upper right-hand corner of this manuscript page Shelley wrote "I am despair"—seemingly to express his bleak mood at the time he wrote the poem.

For this, and for the transcript of the fair copy that follows, the editor is indebted to Donald H. Reiman of The Pforzheimer Library.

2. Shelley at first wrote "trod," then overwrote that with "stood." In the following line, Shelley at first wrote "yr," then overwrote "thy."

3. Not clearly legible; it is either "gra" or "gre." A difference in the ink from the rest of the line indicates that Shelley, having left a blank space, later started to fill it in, but thought better of it and crossed out the fragmentary insertion.

[FAIR COPY]

O World   o Life   o Time
On whose last steps I climb
Trembling at that where I had stood before
   When will return the glory of yr prime?
      No more, o never more

            2

    Out of the day & night
    A joy has taken flight
Fresh spring & summer   ⁴ & winter hoar
   Move my faint heart with grief but with delight
      No more, o, never more

JOHN KEATS
From The Eve of St. Agnes[1]

[*Stanza 26*]

But soon his heart revives—her prayers said
  She ~~lays aside her veil~~

              pearled
     strips her hair of all its ⌃ wreathed ~~pearl~~
~~Unclasps her bosom jewels~~
~~And twists it in one knot upon her head~~

                 ~~soon~~
But soon his heart revives—her prayers (ing) done,
  Sh (Of)   all her (its) wreathed pearl she strips her hair
Unclasps her warmed jewels one by one

      her bursting
Loosens ~~her boddice from her~~
     ~~her Boddice lace string~~
      ~~her Boddice and her bosom bar~~
    her

[HERE KEATS BEGINS A NEW SHEET]

Loosens her fragrant ~~boddice~~ and doth bare
Her

    Anon
~~But soon~~ his heart revives—her praying done

---

4. This fair copy of the second draft retains, and even enlarges, the blank space, indicating that Shelley still hasn't made up his mind what to insert after the word "summer"; we may speculate, by reference to the fragmentary version of this stanza in the second draft, that he had in mind as possibilities either an adjective, "gray" or "green," or else the noun "autumn." Mary Shelley closed up this space when she published the poem in 1824, with the result that later editors, following her version, have until very recently printed this line as though Shelley had intended it to be one metric foot shorter than the corresponding line of stanza 1.

1. Transcribed from what is probably the best known of all manuscripts, that which contains Keats's first draft of all but the first seven stanzas of *The Eve of St. Agnes*; it is now in the Houghton Library, Harvard University. Keats's published version of the poem, above, contains some further changes in wording.

                 frees

Of all its wreathéd pearl her hair she ~~strips~~

Unclasps her warmed jewels one by one

                  by degrees

               ~~to her knees~~

Loosens her fragrant boddice: ~~and down slips~~

Her sweet attire ~~falls light creeps down by~~

           creeps rusteling to her knees

       Mermaid   in sea weed

Half hidden like a ~~Syren of the Sea~~

~~And more melodious~~

               dreaming

       She stands awhile in ∧ thought, and sees

In fancy fair Saint Agnes in her bed

But dares not look behind or all the charm is ~~fled~~ dead

              [Stanza 30]

~~But~~

~~And still she slept.~~

And still she slept an azure-lidded sleep

In blanched linen smooth and lavender'd;

While he from frorth the closet brought a heap

         fruits

Of candied ~~sweets sweets with~~ and plumb and gourd

     apple   Quince

With jellies soother than the ~~dairy~~ curd

         creamed

        tinct

And lucent syrups ~~smooth~~ with crannamon

~~And sugar'd dates from that o'er Euphrates fard~~

       ~~in Brigantine transferred~~

           ~~transferred~~

    Manna and daites in Bragine ~~wild transferrd~~

      ~~and Manna~~

~~And Manna wild and~~

           ~~Brigantine~~

          ~~sugar'd~~ dates transferrd

 argosy ~~In Brigantine from Fez~~

    From fez—and spiced danties every one

      ~~glutted~~

From ~~wealthy~~ Samarchand to cedard lebanon

   silken

GERARD MANLEY HOPKINS
[Thou Art Indeed Just, Lord][1]

*Justus quidem tu es, Domine, si disputem tecum; verumtamen justa
loquar ad te: quare via impiorum prosperatur? etc.—Jer. xii 1.*

March 17 1889

Thou art indeed just, ~~were I to~~ ^{Lord, if I} contend

With thee; but, ~~Lord,~~ ^{sir,} so what I ~~speak~~ ^{plead} is just.

Why do sinners' ways prosper? and why must

Disappointment all I endeavour end?
Wert thou my enemy, O thou my friend,
How wouldst thou worse, I wonder, than thou dost

Defeat, thwart me? ~~Ah! sots, revellers,~~ ^{O the sots and} thralls to lust

~~In~~ ^{Do in} spare hours ~~do~~ more thrive than I ~~who~~ ^{that} spend,

Sir, ~~my~~ ^{great} life on thy cause. ~~Look,~~ ^{see,} banks and brakes

~~Leavèd~~ ^{Now, leavèd} how thick! ~~broidered all~~ ^{lacèd they are} again

With fretty chervil, ~~now,~~ ^{look} and fresh winds shakes

Them; birds build—but not I build; no, but strain,
Time's eunuch, and not breed one work that wakes.

~~Then send,~~ ^{Mine, O} thou lord of life, ~~these~~ roots ~~their~~ ^{send my} rain.

WILLIAM BUTLER YEATS

Yeats usually composed very slowly and with painful effort. He tells us in
his *Autobiography* that "five or six lines in two or three laborious hours were
a day's work, and I longed for somebody to interrupt me." His manuscripts
show the slow evolution of his best poems, which sometimes began with a
prose sketch, were then versified, and underwent numerous revisions. Even
after many of his poems had been published, Yeats continued to revise them,
sometimes drastically, in later printings.

1. From a manuscript in the Bodleian Library,
Oxford University; it is a clean copy, made after
earlier drafts, which Hopkins goes on to revise fur-
ther. Differences in the ink show that the emen-
dation "lacèd they are" (line 10) was made during
the first writing, but that the other verbal changes
were made later. The interlinear markings are
Hopkins' metrical indicators; he explains their
significance in the "Author's Preface," included in
Poems of Gerard Manley Hopkins (1970), edited by
W. H. Gardner and N. H. MacKenzie.
   The epigraph is from the Vulgate translation of
Jeremiah 12.1; a literal translation of the Latin is:
"Thou art indeed just, Lord, [even] if I plead with
Thee; nevertheless I will speak what is just to Thee:
Why does the way of the wicked prosper? etc."

Leda and the Swan[1]

[*First Version*]

Annunciation

Now can the swooping Godhead have his will
Yet hovers, though her helpless thighs are pressed
By the webbed toes; and that all powerful bill
Has suddenly bowed her face upon his breast.
How can those terrified vague fingers push
The feathered glory from her loosening thighs?
All the stretched body's laid on that white rush

And feels the <s>strong</s> ^{strange} heart beating where it lies
A shudder in the loins engenders there
The broken wall, the burning roof and tower
And Agamemnon dead. . . .

                        Being so caught up
Did nothing pass before her in the air?
Did she put on his knowledge with his power
Before the indifferent beak could let her drop.
                  Sept 18 1923

The <s>trembl</s> ^{swooping} godhead is half hovering still,
Yet <s>climbs</s> ^{climbs} upon her trembling body pressed
By the ^{webbed} toes; & <s>through</s> that all powerful bill
Has suddenly <s>bowed</s> ^{thrown bowed} her face upon his breast.
How can those terrified vague fingers push
The feathered glory from her loosening thighs

All the stretched body <s>leans</s> ^{laid} on that white rush
             or
<s>Her falling body thrown on the white</s> white rush
Can feel etc
or Her body can but lean on the white rush

But mounts until her trembling thighs are pressed[2]

1. From Yeats's manuscript *Journal*, Sections 248
and 250. This *Journal*, including facsimiles and
transcriptions of the drafts of *Leda and the Swan*,
has been published in W. B. Yeats, *Memoirs*, edited
by Denis Donoghue (Macmillan, London, 1972).

The first version, entitled *Annunciation*, seems
to be a clean copy of earlier drafts; Yeats went on
to revise it further, especially the opening octave.
Neither of the other two complete drafts, each of
which Yeats labeled "Final Version," was in fact
final. Yeats himself crossed out the first draft. The
second, although Yeats published it in 1924, was

subjected to further revision before he published
the poem in *The Tower* (1928), in the final form
reprinted in the selections from Yeats, above.

Yeats's handwriting is hasty and very difficult to
decipher. The readings of some words, both in the
manuscripts of this poem and of *After Long Silence*,
below, are uncertain.

2. This passage is written across the blank page
opposite the first version; Yeats drew a line indicating that it was to replace the revised lines 2–4,
which he had written below the first version.

~~B~~
By the webbed toes; & that all powerful bill
Has suddenly bowed her head on his breast

Final Version

Can hold

Annunciation

The swooping godhead is half hovering still
But mounts, until her trembling thighs are pressed
By the webbed toes, & that all powerful bill
~~Has hung~~ her helpless body
~~Has suddenly bowed her head up~~on his breast.
How can those terrified vague fingers push
The feathered glory from her loosening thighs?
~~How   now its body leans on~~
~~With her body laid on the white rush~~
all the stretched body laid on the white rush
and ~~Can~~ feel the strange heart beating where it lies?
A shudder in the loins engenders there
The broken wall, the burning roof & tower
And Agamemnon dead . . .

Being mastered so
~~Being so caught up~~
So
~~And~~ mastered by the brute blood of the air
~~Being mastered so~~
~~Did nothing pass before her in the air?~~
Did she put on his knowledge with his power
Before the indifferent beak could let her drop.

WBY. Sept 18 1923

swoop
A ~~rush~~ upon great wings & hovering still
~~He sinks until~~
~~He has sunk on her down, & her hair~~
~~The great bird sinks, till~~
The bird descends, & her frail ~~thigh~~ thighs are pressed
By the webbed toes, & that all

that
Now ~~all~~ her body's laid on ~~that~~ white rush[3]
~~All the stretched body, laid on that white rush~~
~~Now that whole~~
~~Now that her body on the white rush~~
~~Can feel~~

Final Version

Leda & the Swan

A rush, a sudden wheel and
~~A swoop upon great wings &~~ hovering still
                    sinks down   *bare* *frail*
stet The bird ~~descends~~ & her ~~frail~~ thighs are pressed

---

3. Written on the blank page across from the complete version, with an arrow indicating that it was a revision of the seventh line.

By the ~~toes~~ webbed toes, & that all powerful bill
     laid
Has ~~driven~~ her helpless face upon his breast.
How can those terrified vague fingers push
The feathered glory from her loosening thighs?
        s laid
All the stretched body ~~laid~~ on that white rush
And ~~feel~~ feels the strange heart beating where it lies.
A shudder in the loins engenders there
The broken wall, the burning roof & tower
And Agamemnon dead.
                Being so caught up
So mastered by the ~~br~~ brute blood of the air
Did she put on his knowledge with his power
Before the indifferent beak could let her drop.

After Long Silence[4]

[Draft 1]

Subject

Your hair is white
My hair is white
Come let us talk of love
What other theme do we know
When we were young
We were in love with one another
~~A O~~ And therefore ignorant

[Draft 2]

Those
~~Your~~ other lover^s being dead & gone

        friendly light
        hair is white
   ~~on love descant~~   descant
Upon the ~~sole theme~~ supreme theme of art & song
Wherein there's theme so fitting for the aged. ;young
We loved each other & were ignorant

4. The drafts of *After Long Silence* are interspersed with other materials on seven pages of a manuscript book, begun in 1928, which includes a number of additional poems that were published in *The Winding Stair and Other Poems* (1933). It begins, like many of Yeats's poems, with a prose sketch, and is labeled simply "Subject." It then passes through a tentative versified stage (Draft 2) in which Yeats sets down four complete lines and a set of possible rhyme words; is subjected to various drafts and revisions; and concludes with the final text that Yeats published in 1933. Yeats did not add the title *After Long Silence* until he wrote out a fair copy for his typist at some time after August 14, 1931.

David R. Clark, "After 'Silence,' The 'Supreme Theme': Eight Lines of Yeats," includes photocopies and transcripts of the drafts of this poem, together with a discussion of its biographical occasion and its interpretation (in *Myth and Reality in Irish Literature*, edited by Joseph Ronsley, Waterloo, Canada, 1977, pp. 149–73).

[Draft 3]

~~I h~~

Once more I have kissed your hand & it is right—
All other lovers being estranged or dead
~~The heavy curtain drawn—the candle light~~
~~Waging a doubtful battle with the shade~~

                                                        distant,
~~We call our wisdom up upon our wisdom &~~ ~~descant~~
~~Upon the supreme theme of art & song—~~
Decrepitude increases wisdom—young
We loved each other & were ~~ignorant ignor~~   ignorant

[Draft 4]

Un
~~The~~ friendly lamplight hidden by its shade
~~And shutters clapped upon the deepening night~~
~~The candle hidden by its friendly shade~~
Those curtains drawn upon the deepening night—

                s
~~The curtain drawn on the unfriendly night~~
That we descant & yet again descant
                supreme theme
Upon the ~~supreme theme~~ of ~~art & song~~   art & song—
Bodily decrepitude is wisdom—young

[Final MS Version]

Speech after long silence; it is right—
                                    or
All other lovers being estranged ~~&~~ dead,
                            hid
Unfriendly lamp-light ~~hid~~ under its shade,
                            upon
The curtain's drawn ~~upon~~ unfriendly night—
That we descant & yet again descant
Upon the supreme theme of art & song,
Bodily decrepitude is wisdom; young
We loved each other & were ignorant

                                            Nov
                                            ~~Oct~~ 1929

D. H. LAWRENCE
The Piano[1]

Somewhere beneath that piano's superb sleek black

1. Transcribed from a notebook in which Lawrence at first entered various academic assignments while he was a student at the University College of Nottingham, 1906–8, but then used to write drafts of some of his early poems. These were probably composed in the period from 1906 to 1910.

Must hide my mother's piano, little and brown, with
      the back

    stood close to
That ~~was against~~ the wall, and the front's faded silk, both torn
And the keys with little hollows, that my mother's fingers
      had worn.

Softly, in the shadows, a woman is singing to me
Quietly, through the years I have crept back to see
A child sitting under the piano, in the boom of the
    shaking ~~tingling~~ strings
Pressing the little poised feet of the mother who smiles
      as she sings

The full throated woman has chosen a winning, living[2]
      song
And surely the heart that is in me must belong
To the old Sunday evenings, when darkness wandered
      outside
And hymns gleamed on our warm lips, as we watched
      mother's fingers glide

        is
Or ~~is~~ this my sister at home in the old front room
Singing love's first surprised gladness, alone in
      the gloom.
She will start when she sees me, and blushing,
      spread out her hands
To cover my mouth's raillery, till I'm bound in
       heart-spun
     her shame's ~~pleading~~ bands.

A woman is singing me a wild Hungarian
    air
And her arms, and her bosom and the whole
    of her soul is bare
And the great black piano is clamouring as my
    mother's never could clamour
 my mother's [   ][3] tunes are
And ~~the tunes of the past is~~ devoured of this music's
    ravaging glamour.

The text reproduced here was revised and published with the title *Piano* in Lawrence's *New Poems*, 1918. A comparison of this draft with *Piano*, reprinted above, will show that Lawrence eliminated the first and fourth stanzas (as well as the last two lines of the third stanza); revised the remaining three stanzas, sometimes radically; and most surprisingly, reversed his original conclusion. As Lawrence himself explained his revisions of some of his early poems, they "had to be altered, where sometimes the hand of commonplace youth had been laid on the mouth of the demon. It is not for technique that these poems are altered: it is to say the real say."

For transcriptions and discussions of this and other poems in Lawrence's early notebook, see Vivian de Sola Pinto, "D.H. Lawrence: Letter-Writer and Craftsman in Verse," in *Renaissance and Modern Studies*, vol. 1 (1957), pp. 5–34.

2. A conjectural reading; the word is not clearly legible.

3. An undecipherable word is crossed out here.

Selected Bibliographies

SUGGESTED GENERAL READINGS

Histories of England and of English Literature

George Macaulay Trevelyan's *History of England*, rev.,1945, is an excellent survey in one volume; for detailed studies of single periods, see *The Oxford History of England*, 15 vols., 1934 ff., by a variety of historians. Designed especially as a background for students of literature is Robert M. Adams, *The Land and Literature of England: A Historical Account*, 1983. A *Guide to English Literature*, ed. Boris Ford, 1954–63, is available in 7 paperback volumes. Useful one-volume histories of English literature are Albert C. Baugh and others, *A Literary History of England*, rev., 1967; Hardin Craig and others, *A History of English Literature*, 1950; and (less densely factual) David Daiches, *A Critical History of English Literature*, 2 vols., rev., 1970. Ellen Moers, *Literary Women*, 1976, is a history of the circumstances, interinfluences, and distinctive features of literature written by women; the editorial materials in Sandra M. Gilbert and Susan Gubar, *The Norton Anthology of Literature by Women*, 1985, serve as a concise history and collection of biographies of women authors since the Middle Ages.

Drama

Allardyce Nicoll, *British Drama*, rev., 1962, and *A History of English Drama, 1660–1900*, 6 vols., rev., 1952–59; Richard Courtney, *Outline History of British Drama*, 1982.

The Novel

The most detailed, although somewhat pedestrian, survey is Ernest A. Baker's *History of the English Novel*, 10 vols., 1924–39. Among the short histories are Arnold Kettle, *An Introduction to the English Novel*, 2 vols., 1951–53; Walter Allen, *The English Novel*, 1954; Ian Watt, *The Rise of the Novel*, 1957; and Lionel Stevenson, *The English Novel*, 1960.

Poetry

Douglas Bush, *English Poetry: The Main Currents from Chaucer to the Present*, rev., 1965; E. M. W. Tillyard, *The English Epic and Its Backgrounds*, 1954. For other useful works on the history of English poetry see A. E. Dyson, *English Poetry: Select Bibliographical Guides*, 1971.

Literary Criticism

Recent histories of English criticism are M. H. Abrams, *The Mirror and the Lamp: Romantic Theory and the Critical Tradition*, 1953; W. K. Wimsatt, Jr., and Cleanth Brooks, *Litearary Criticism: A Short History*, 1957; George Watson, *The Literary Critics*, 1962; René Wellek, *A History of Modern Criticism: 1750–1950*, 1955 ff; and Frank Lentricchia, *After the New Criticism*, 1980. René Wellek and Austin Warren, *Theory of Literature*, rev., 1970, is a useful introduction to the variety of scholarly and critical approaches up to the time of its publication. Convenient introductions to structuralist, poststructuralist, and other recent theories are Jonathan Culler, *Structuralist Poetics*, 1975, and *On Deconstruction*, 1982. Among recent collections of feminist criticism are Mary Jacobus, ed., *Women Writing and Writing about Women*, 1979, and Elaine Showalter, ed., *The New Feminist Criticism*, 1985.

Reference Works

The New Cambridge Bibliography of English Literature, ed. George Watson, 1969–77, lists all the books of the major and many minor British authors, together with a large selection from biographical, scholarly, and critical works written about these authors. Literary biographies and critical books published since that time can be found in the *MLA International Bibliography*. F. W. Bateson, ed., *A Guide to English Literature*, rev., 1968, is a selected list of editions, and of scholarly and critical treatments, of important English writers; for poetry only see

A. E. Dyson, ed., *English Poetry: Select Bibliographical Guides*, 1971. *Poetry Explication*, rev. Joseph M. Kuntz, 1962, lists close analyses of English poems, old and recent; and I. F. Bell and Donald Baird, *The English Novel, 1578–1956*, 1958, provides a useful list of 20th-century criticisms of fiction. Further bibliographical aids are described in Richard D. Altick and Andrew Wright, *Selective Bibliography for the Study of English and American Literature*, rev., 1979; and Margaret C. Patterson, *Literary Research Guide*, rev., 1983.

For compact biographies of English authors, see the multivolumed *Dictionary of National Biography*, ed. Leslie Stephen and Sidney Lee in 1885–1900, with supplements that carry the work to 1960; condensed biographies will be found in the *Concise Dictionary of National Biography*, part 1 (1953) and part 2 (1961). Handy reference books of authors, works, and various literary terms and allusions are *The Oxford Companion to English Literature*, ed. Margaret Drabble, rev., 1985; *The Oxford Companion to the Theatre*, Phyllis Hartnoll, rev., 1967; and *Encyclopedia of Poetry and Poetics*, ed. Alex Preminger and others, 1965. Low-priced handbooks that define and illustrate literary concepts and terms are: M. H. Abrams, *A Glossary of Literary Terms*, rev., 1981; and W. F. Thrall and Addison Hibbard, *A Handbook to Literature*, rev. C. Hugh Holman, 1960. On the Greek and Roman background, see *The Oxford Classical Dictionary*, rev., 1970.

Some useful treatments of English meters and stanza forms are: Karl Shapiro and Robert Beum, *A Prosody Handbook*, 1965; Paul Fussell, Jr., *Poetic Meter and Poetic Form*, 1966; and Derek Attridge, *Rhythms of English Poetry*, 1982.

Intellectual History and Criticism

Students interested in intellectual history as a background for English literature will profit from Arthur T. Lovejoy, *The Great Chain of Being*, 1936, and *Essays in the History of Ideas*, 1948; Marjorie Nicolson, *Science and Imagination*, 1956, and *Mountain Gloom and Mountain Glory*, 1959; Basil Willey, *The Seventeenth-Century Background*, 1934, *The Eighteenth-Century Background*, 1940, and *Nineteenth-Century Studies*, 1949; and M. H. Abrams, *Natural Supernaturalism: Tradition and Revolution in Romantic Literature*, 1971. In addition, the following is a selection of books in literary history and criticism that have been notably influential in shaping modern approaches to English literature and literary forms: I. A. Richards, *Practical Criticism*, 1930; Maud Bodkin, *Archetypal Patterns in Poetry*, 1934; Henry James, *The Art of the Novel: Critical Prefaces*, 1934; Edmund Wilson, *Axel's Castle: A Study in the Imaginative Literature of 1870–1930*, 1936, and *The Wound and the Bow*, 1941; C. S. Lewis, *The Allegory of Love*, rev., 1938; Cleanth Brooks, *The Well Wrought Urn*, 1947; Lionel Trilling, *The Liberal Imagination*, 1950, and *The Opposing Self*, 1955; T. S. Eliot, *Selected Essays*, 3rd ed., 1951, and *On Poetry and Poets*, 1957; Erich Auerbach, *Mimesis: The Representation of Reality in Western Literature*, 1953; Ronald Crane, *The Languages of Criticism and the Structure of Poetry*, 1953; William Empson, *Seven Types of Ambiguity*, 3rd ed., 1953; William K. Wimsatt, *The Verbal Icon*, 1954; Northrop Frye, *Anatomy of Criticism*, 1957; Wayne C. Booth, *The Rhetoric of Fiction*, 1961, and *A Rhetoric of Irony*, 1974; and Harold Bloom, *The Anxiety of Influence*, 1973.

Matthew Arnold

The standard modern edition of Arnold's poetry is *Poems of Arnold*, ed. Miriam Allott, 1979. R. H. Super has produced an authoritative edition of *The Complete Prose Works*, 11 vols., 1960–77. The most satisfactory biography is Park Honan's *Matthew Arnold: A Life*, 1981, but Lionel Trilling's excellent *Matthew Arnold*, 1949, remains a standard critical and biographical study. For a study of Arnold's prose works, see William Robbins's *The Ethical Idealism of Matthew*

Arnold, 1959, and Joseph Carroll's *The Cultural Theory of Matthew Arnold*, 1982. For a study of his poetry, see Dwight Culler's *Imaginative Reason*, 1966, and G. Robert Stange's *The Poet as Humanist*, 1967.

W. H. Auden

W. H. Auden: Collected Poems, ed. Edward Mendelson, 1976, contains all the poems that the author wished to preserve, in the texts that received his final approval. *The*

English Auden, Poems, Essays and Dramatic Writings 1927–1939, ed. Edward Mendelson, 1977, reprints in their original versions all the poems Auden published in book form during the 1930s, together with some previously unpublished and uncollected poems and a selection of Auden's early prose writings. *The Dyer's Hand and Other Essays*, 1968, brings together a selection of his stimulating literary-critical articles, lectures, and reviews. The best critical studies are *The Poetry of W. H. Auden*, by M. K. Spears, 1963; *Early Auden*, by Edward Mendelson, 1981; and *Auden: A Carnival of Intellect*, by Edward Callan, 1983. A *Reader's Guide to W. H. Auden*, by John Fuller, 1970, provides a commentary on Auden's poetry and drama in chronological order; while *The Auden Generation: Literature and Politics in England in the 1930s*, by Samuel Hynes, 1976, is an illuminating study of Auden and his contemporaries in their historical context. The most comprehensive biography is *W. H. Auden: A Biography*, by Humphrey Carpenter, 1981.

Samuel Beckett

Deirdre Bair's *Samuel Beckett: A Biography*, 1978, is a very useful but problematical study. Good introductions to the works are *Samuel Beckett: A Critical Study*, 1961, and *Reader's Guide to Samuel Beckett*, 1973, both by Hugh Kenner. Beckett's philosophical and religious ideas are well presented in *The Ship of Chaos*, by David T. Hesla, 1971; and *Beckett/Beckett*, by Vivian Mercier, 1977, shows that the Paris flowering grew from Dublin soil. Colin Duckworth's English introduction to his edition of *En attendant Godot*, 1966, is the classic essay on the classic play, *Waiting for Godot*.

Beowulf

The standard text is *Beowulf and the Fight at Finnsburg*, 3rd ed. by F. Klaeber, 1950; C. L. Wrenn's edition, *Beowulf, with the Finnsburg Fragment*, rev. W. F. Bolton, 1973, is very useful; H. D. Chickering, Jr.'s *Beowulf: A Dual-language Edition*, 1977, contains extensive commentary. For general background see Dorothy Whitelock's concise study, *The Beginnings of English Society*, 1952, and H. M. Chadwick's classic work on the culture of the primitive Germanic peoples, *The Heroic Age*, 1912. The best critical essay on *Beowulf* remains J.R.R.

Tolkien's Gollancz lecture, *Beowulf, the Monsters, and the Critics*, 1937, which is reprinted in useful collections of essays by L. E. Nicholson, *An Anthology of Beowulf Criticism*, 1963, and D. K. Fry, *The Beowulf Poet*, 1968. *Beowulf*, A Norton Critical Edition, ed. J. F. Tuso, 1975, also contains helpful materials, including an abridgement of Tolkien's essay. For excellent general criticism mixed with specialized discussion, see Dorothy Whitelock, *The Audience of Beowulf*, 1958, and E. B. Irving's *A Reading of Beowulf*, 1968, and *Introduction to Beowulf*, 1969.

William Blake

The standard scholarly edition is *The Poetry and Prose of William Blake*, ed. David Erdman and Harold Bloom, rev., 1982. Erdman has also prepared a modernized text of all Blake's verse, with copious explanatory notes by W. H. Stevenson, *The Poems of William Blake* (Longman-Norton Annotated English Poets), 1971; and a useful, annotated selection of *Blake's Poetry and Designs* has been edited by Mary Lynn Johnson and John E. Grant, 1979. For biography, see Mona Wilson's *Life of William Blake*, 1927, rev., 1948, and Raymond Lister's *William Blake: An Introduction to the Man and His Work*, 1968. Influential critical studies include Mark Schorer's *William Blake: The Politics of Vision*, 1946; Northrop Frye's *Fearful Symmetry*, 1947; and David V. Erdman's *Blake: Prophet against Empire*, rev., 1969. Modern critical essays are collected in *Blake*, ed. Northrop Frye, 1966, and in *Blake's Visionary Forms Dramatic*, ed. D. V. Erdman and J. E. Grant, 1970. The following concentrate on the shorter poems: Robert F. Gleckner, *The Piper and the Bard*, 1959; Hazard Adams, *William Blake: A Reading of the Shorter Poems*, 1963; and E. D. Hirsch, Jr., *Innocence and Experience: An Introduction to Blake*, 1964.

Elizabeth Barrett Browning

The standard *Complete Works* were edited by Charlotte Porter and Helen Clarke, 6 vols., 1900. Cora Kaplan's edition of *Aurora Leigh and Other Poems*, 1978, is a useful selection. A reasonable biography is Gardner B. Taplin's *The Life of Elizabeth Barrett Browning*, 1957. Ellen Moers in *Literary Women*, 1976, and Sandra Gilbert and

Susan Gubar in *Madwoman in the Attic*, 1979, write interestingly about Barrett Browning from a feminist perspective.

Robert Browning

A standard edition has been that edited by F. G. Kenyon, 10 vols., 1912. A convenient two-volume collection of the poems, edited by John Pettigrew and Thomas J. Collins, was published in 1981. The best biography is William Irvine's and Park Honan's *The Book, The Ring, and the Poet*, 1974. W. C. DeVane's *A Browning Handbook* is a model compilation of factual data concerning each of Browning's poems: sources, composition, and reputation. The critical assessments in G. K. Chesterton's *Robert Browning*, 1903, are colorfully expressed and often shrewd. Robert Langbaums's *The Poetry of Experience* (1957) is an admirable attempt to relate Browning's monologues to some of the main developments in modern literature. Many of the best discussions of Browning's achievement, especially of individual poems, have been conveniently assembled in two collections that rarely overlap each other: *Robert Browning: A Collection of Critical Essays*, ed. Philip Drew, 1966, and *The Browning Critics*, ed. Boyd Litzinger and K. L. Knickerbocker, 1965. See also *Robert Browning*, ed. Isabel Armstrong, 1974, and *Robert Browning: A Collection of Critical Essays*, ed. Harold Bloom and Adrienne Munich, 1979.

George Gordon, Lord Byron

The most reliable edition of the poetry is by Jerome J. McGann, *The Complete Poetical Works*, 1980 ff.; for the letters, Leslie A. Marchand's edition of *Byron's Letters and Journals*, 12 vols., 1973–82 (see also Marchand's one-volume *Selected Letters and Journals*, 1982). The standard biography is Marchand's *Byron: A Biography*, 3 vols., 1957 (condensed in one vol. as *Byron, A Portrait*, 1970). Among numerous book-length studies are G. Wilson Knight, *The Burning Oracle*, 1939; Andrew Rutherford, *Byron*, 1961; and Jerome J. McGann, *Fiery Dust: Byron's Poetic Development*, 1968. Works focusing on *Don Juan* include George M. Ridenour, *The Style of "Don Juan,"* 1960; J. J. McGann, *"Don Juan" in Context*, 1976; and E. E. Bostetter's collection of *Twentieth Century Interpretations of "Don Juan,"* 1969.

Geoffrey Chaucer

The standard edition of Chaucer's writing is F. N. Robinson's *The Complete Works of Chaucer*, 2nd ed., 1957, to be superseded in 1987 by a 3rd ed. by various hands. Editions especially helpful to the nonspecialist are E. T. Donaldson's *Chaucer's Poetry*, 2nd ed., 1975, from which the selections printed here are taken, A. C. Baugh's *Chaucer's Major Poetry*, 1963, and J. H. Fisher's *The Complete Poetry and Prose of Geoffrey Chaucer*, 1977. D. S. Brewer's *Chaucer and His World*, 1978, provides a vivid and beautifully illustrated introduction to the poet's life and work against the background of 14th-century England. Muriel Bowden, *A Commentary on the General Prologue to the Canterbury Tales*, 1948, and Jill Mann's *Chaucer and Medieval Estates Satire*, 1973, provide a wealth of background information on the pilgrims and the structure of the General Prologue. Stimulating general criticism of Chaucer and of particular Canterbury tales may be found in the commentary to the edition by Donaldson, cited above, and in the following works: Alfred David, *The Strumpet Muse*, 1976; E. T. Donaldson, *Speaking of Chaucer*, 1970; G. L. Kittredge, *Chaucer and His Poetry*, 1915; Charles Muscatine, *Chaucer and the French Tradition*, 1957; and D. A. Pearsall, *The Canterbury Tales*, 1985. The collection edited by R. J. Schoeck and J. Taylor, *Chaucer: Modern Essays in Criticism*, 1960, contains many basic articles. Perhaps the most reliable glossary is that edited by Norman Davis, *et al.*, 1979.

Samuel Taylor Coleridge

The still standard edition of the poetry (long out of date) is *The Complete Poetical Works*, ed. E. H. Coleridge, 2 vols., 1912. E. L. Griggs has edited the *Collected Letters*, 6 vols., 1956–71. The most fully annotated edition of *Biographia Literaria* is that by James Engell and W. J. Bate, 2 vols., 1983 (part of the Collected Edition of Coleridge's writings now in progress under the general editorship of Kathleen Coburn, 1968 ff.). The best short study of the life and works is by W. J. Bate, *Coleridge*, 1968. On the poetry see Humphry House, *Coleridge*, 1953; Max F. Schulz, *The Poetic Voices of Cole-*

ridge, 1963; Reeve Parker, *Coleridge's Meditative Art*, 1975; and M. H. Abrams, *The Correspondent Breeze*, 1984. On the criticism: M. H. Abrams, *The Mirror and the Lamp*, 1953; René Wellek, *A History of Modern Criticism 1750–1950*, vol. 2, 1955; and J. A. Appleyard, *Coleridge's Philosophy of Literature*, 1965. On Coleridge's philosophy: Richard Haven, *Patterns of Consciousness*, 1969; Thomas McFarland, *Coleridge and the Pantheist Tradition*, 1969; and Lawrence S. Lockridge, *Coleridge the Moralist*, 1977. Modern essays in criticism have been collected by Kathleen Coburn, *Coleridge*, 1977, and John Beer, *Coleridge's Variety*, 1974.

Joseph Conrad

Standard is *The Uniform Edition of the Works of Joseph Conrad*, 22 vols., 1923–38, reprinted in 1946–55 as *The Collected Edition of the Works of Joseph Conrad*. When completed, the Cambridge University Press's variorum edition will be the standard edition. Many of the novels are available with useful critical essays in individual paperbound editions; among the best are the Norton Critical Editions of *Heart of Darkness*, ed., Robert Kimbrough, rev., 1972; *Lord Jim*, ed. Thomas C. Moser, 1968; and *The Nigger of the "Narcissus,"* ed. Robert Kimbrough, 1979.

The Portable Conrad, ed. Morton D. Zabel, 1947, contains a good selection with a helpful introduction, and *Conrad in the Nineteenth Century*, 1981, by Ian Watt is the most notable critical study, although it only goes up to 1900. Excellent essays are that on *Lord Jim* in *The English Novel: Form and Function*, by Dorothy Van Ghent, 1953, and the introduction to the Modern Library edition of *Nostromo*, ed. Robert Penn Warren, 1951. *Paradise of Snakes*, by Claire Rosenfield, 1967; and *Conrad's Politics: Community and Anarchy in the Fiction of Joseph Conrad*, by Avrom Fleishman, 1967. Zdzislaw Najder's *Joseph Conrad: A Chronicle*, 1983, is now the standard biography. The first volume of the letters has recently appeared, *The Collected Letters of Joseph Conrad: Volume One, 1861–97*, ed. Frederick R. Karl and Lawrence Davies. Until this edition is completed *Joseph Conrad: Life and Letters*, ed. G. Jean-Aubry, 2 vols., 1927, will remain the standard if very incomplete edition. This should be supple-

mented by *Letters from Joseph Conrad*, ed. Edward Garnett, 1928, and *Joseph Conrad's Letters to R. B. Cunninghame Graham*, ed. C. T. Watts, 1969.

John Donne

For nearly 50 years the accepted edition of Donne's poems was that in 2 volumes edited by Sir Herbert J. C. Grierson, 1912. In 1952 Dame Helen Gardner re-edited the *Divine Poems*, rev., 1978, and in 1965 a volume containing *The Elegies and The Songs and Sonnets*. In 1967 W. Milgate added to this series the *Satires, Epigrams, and Verse Letters*, and in 1978 the *Epithalamions, Anniversaries, and Epicedes*. There are also several handy paperback editions, among which we note *John Donne's Poetry*, ed. A. L. Clements for Norton Critical Editions, 1966, and editions of the *Complete English Poems* by A. J. Smith, 1971, and C. A. Patrides, 1985. Anthony Raspa has edited the *Devotions Upon Emergent Occasions* (1975).

The best biographies are R. C. Bald, *John Donne, a Life*, 1970, and John Carey, *John Donne, Life, Mind, and Art*, 1981. Carey presents a rough, vigorous, and challenging view of Donne; his book could well be read in counterpoint with the first and most famous biography of the poet, Izaak Walton's much blander, much more "establishment" portrait (several editions, including Sir Geoffrey Keynes, *The Compleat Walton*, 1929).

Pierre Legouis's pioneering *Donne the Craftsman*, 1928, paved the way for close studies of Donne's poetry by J. B. Leishman, 1951, Clay Hunt, 1954, Arnold Stein, 1962, and Murray Roston, 1974. Donne's poetry is also treated in Barbara K. Lewalski's *Protestant Poetics and the Seventeenth-Century Religious Lyric*, 1979, and in Terry G. Sherwood's *Fulfilling the Circle: A Study of John Donne's Thought*, 1984. Hardly any of Donne's lyrics has not been the subject of several articles at least; but Cleanth Brooks's *The Well Wrought Urn*, 1947, contains in its discussion of *The Canonization* one of the most influential poetic explications of modern criticism. Collections of critical essays by different hands have been assembled by Helen Gardner and Frank Kermode, both 1962, and by A. J. Smith, 1972. Joan Webber has studied Donne's prose style in *Contrary Music*, 1963.

There are annotated bibliographies of

modern criticism by John R. Roberts—one for the period 1912–67, published 1973, and another for 1968–78, published 1982.

T. S. Eliot

The fullest one-volume collections of Eliot's poetry are *Collected Poems, 1909–1963*, 1963, and *The Complete Poems and Plays* (including *Poems Written in Early Youth*), 1969. Some of his critical essays are in *Selected Essays*, 3rd ed., 1972; *On Poetry and Poets*, 1957; and *Selected Prose of T. S. Eliot*, ed. Frank Kermode, 1975. T. S. Eliot, *The Waste Land: A Facsimile and Transcript of the Original Drafts including the Annotations of Ezra Pound*, ed. Valerie Eliot, 1971, is an indispensable tool for study of *The Waste Land*. *T. S. Eliot, The Waste Land*, by Helen Williams, 2nd rev. ed., 1973, is a critical study of the poem. *The Composition of Four Quartets*, by Helen Gardner, 1978, describes the growth of the poem from the drafts and includes new information on its sources. *The Art of T. S. Eliot*, by the same author, is a perceptive critical study of his poetry. There is no full-length biography; but see *T. S. Eliot: The Man and His Work*, a collection of memoirs, ed. Allen Tate, 1967; *Notes on Some Figures behind T. S. Eliot*, by Herbert Howarth, 1965; *Eliot's Early Years*, by Lyndall Gordon, 1977, and *T. S. Eliot: A Study in Character and Style*, by Ronald Bush, 1984. *T. S. Eliot: A Bibliography*, ed. Donald Gallup, rev., 1969, lists the extensive criticism on Eliot through 1967.

Thomas Hardy

The Collected Poems were issued in one volume in 1932; and *The Complete Poems*, ed. James Gibson, in 1976. There are several collected editions of Hardy's complete work, notably the Wessex Edition, 21 vols., 1912–14, and the Mellstock Edition, 37 vols., 1919–20. Many of the novels are in paperbound editions; among the most notable are the Norton Critical Editions of *Jude the Obscure*, ed. Norman Page, 1978; *The Mayor of Casterbridge*, ed. James K. Robinson, 1977; *The Return of the Native*, ed. James Gindin, 1969; and *Tess of the D'Urbervilles*, ed. Scott Elledge, rev., 1979.

The best biographies are *Young Thomas Hardy*, 1975, *Thomas Hardy's Later Years*, 1978, both by Robert Gittings, and *Thomas Hardy: A Biography*, by Michael Millgate,

1982. *Hardy: A Collection of Critical Essays*, ed. Albert Guerard, 1963, treats both the prose and the poetry, as do *Thomas Hardy: Distance and Desire*, by J. Hillis Miller, 1970; *An Essay on Hardy*, by John Bayley, 1978; and *Thomas Hardy: The Writer and His Background*, ed. Norman Page, 1980, which contains a useful bibliography. *The Great Web: The Form of Hardy's Major Fiction*, by Ian Gregor, 1974, and *Critical Approaches to the Fiction of Thomas Hardy*, ed. Dale Kramer, 1979, provide good discussions of Hardy's novels. *The Pattern of Hardy's Poetry*, by Samuel Hynes, 1956, remains sound and useful. *The Poetry of Thomas Hardy*, ed. Patricia Clements and Juliet Grindle, 1980, and *The Poetry of Thomas Hardy: A Study in Art and Ideas*, by William Earl Buckler, 1983, contain good recent criticism of the poetry; and *The Poetry of Thomas Hardy*, by J. O. Bailey, 1970, and *A Commentary on the Poems of Thomas Hardy*, by F. B. Pinion, 1976, are helpful on individual poems.

Gerard Manley Hopkins

The standard edition of Hopkins's poetry has been edited by W. H. Gardner and N. H. MacKenzie, 1967. The best biography is John Pick's *Gerard Manley Hopkins: Priest and Poet*, 2nd ed., 1966. A good critical study is Paul L. Mariani, *A Commentary on the Complete Poems of Gerard Manley Hopkins*, 1970. There are three good collections of critical essays: *Gerard Manley Hopkins* by the Kenyon Critics, 1945; *Immortal Diamond*, ed. Norman Weyand and Raymond Schoder, 1949; and the particularly fine *Hopkins*, ed. Geoffrey Hartman, 1966.

Ben Jonson

The standard edition of Jonson's plays and other works is that by C. H. Herford and Percy and Evelyn Simpson, 11 volumes, 1925–52. Three handy editions of the complete poetry are those by W. B. Hunter, 1963, Ian Donaldson, 1975, and George Parfitt, also 1975. Wesley Trimpi (1962) and Richard S. Peterson (1981) have written good critical accounts of the poetry, and notable responses to Jonson and his poetry from his time to ours are included in Hugh Maclean's Norton Critical Edition, *Ben Jonson and the Cavalier Poets*, 1974. The best biography is J. B. Bamborough, *Ben Jonson*, 1970. D. Heyward Brock, *A Ben Jonson Companion*,

1983, is a kind of Jonson encyclopedia, complete with bibliography.

James Joyce

The Viking Critical Editions of *Dubliners*, ed. R. Scholes and A. W. Litz, 1969, and *A Portrait of the Artist as a Young Man*, ed. C. Anderson, 1968, offer reliable texts and valuable supplementary materials. *The Portable James Joyce*, ed. H. Levin, 1968, is a useful collection, and Stuart Gilbert and Richard Ellmann have edited *The Letters of James Joyce* in 3 vols., 1957–66.

Good general accounts of Joyce's work will be found in *James Joyce*, by A. W. Litz, rev., 1972, and *James Joyce*, by A. Goldman, 1968. A useful critical work on *Dubliners* is *James Joyce's Dubliners: Critical Essays*, ed. Clive Hart, 1969. The most helpful of many critical studies of *Ulysses* are *Ulysses*, by Hugh Kenner, 1980; *James Joyce's Ulysses: Critical Essays*, ed. Clive Hart and David Hayman, 1974; *The Odyssey of Style in Ulysses*, by Karen Lawrence, 1981; *Allusions in Ulysses*, by Weldon Thornton, 1973; and *Notes for Joyce: An Annotation of James Joyce's Ulysses*, by Don Gifford and Robert Seidman, 1974. *Surface and Symbol*, by Robert M. Adams, 1963, studies the raw material of actual Dublin life in *Ulysses*. Illuminating books on *Finnegans Wake* include *Structure and Motif in Finnegans Wake*, by Clive Hart, 1962; *The Sigla of Finnegans Wake*, 1976, and *Annotations to Finnegans Wake*, 1980, both by Roland McHugh.

James Joyce, by Richard Ellmann, 2nd ed., 1982, is the standard biography; see also, *Ulysses on the Liffey*, 1973, and *The Consciousness of Joyce*, 1977.

John Keats

The standard edition of the poetry is Jack Stillinger's *The Poems of John Keats*, 1978. Miriam Allott's *The Poems of John Keats*, 1970, is copiously annotated. Hyder E. Rollins's edition of *The Letters of John Keats*, 2 vols., 1958, is definitive. The best biography is W. J. Bate's *John Keats*, 1963; see also Aileen Ward, *John Keats: The Making of a Poet*, 1963, and Robert Gittings, *John Keats*, 1968. General critical studies include Earl Wasserman, *The Finer Tone*, 1953; Walter Evert, *Aesthetic and Myth in the Poetry of Keats*, 1965; Morris Dickstein, *Keats and His Poetry*, 1971; Jack Stillinger, *The Hoodwinking of Madeline*, 1971; Stuart

Sperry, *Keats the Poet*, 1973; and Leon Waldoff, *Keats and the Silent Work of Imagination*, 1985. Specifically on the odes see Helen Vendler, *The Odes of John Keats*, 1983.

D. H. Lawrence

The definitive Cambridge Edition, in progress under the editorship of James T. Boulton, has to date issued several meticulously edited texts of the fiction and three volumes of a complete *Letters*. The poetry is collected in *The Complete Poems*, edited by V. de Sola Pinto and W. Roberts, 3rd ed., 1972.

Biographical information can be found in *D. H. Lawrence: A Composite Biography*, by Edward Nehls, 3 vols, 1957–59; *The Priest of Love*, by Harry T. Moore, 1974; and *D. H. Lawrence: A Calendar of His Works*, by Keith Sagar, 1979.

Pioneering critical studies include *D. H. Lawrence: Novelist*, by F. R. Leavis, 1956; *The Dark Sun*, by Graham Hough, 1957; and *Double Measure*, by George Ford, 1965. Among valuable recent analyses are *Acts of Attention: The Poems of D. H. Lawrence*, by Sandra Gilbert, 1972; *The Mysteries of Identity*, by Robert Langbaum, 1977; *Beyond Egotism*, by Robert Kiely, 1980; and *D. H. Lawrence and Feminism*, by Hilary Simpson, 1982. *D. H. Lawrence: A Centenary Consideration*, ed. P. Balbert and P. Marcus, 1985, is an attempt to assess Lawrence's current stature.

Christopher Marlowe

Fredson Bowers edited the *Complete Works* in 2 vols., 1973; and W. W. Greg edited parallel texts of the two versions in 1950. For Marlowe's biography, see John Bakeless, *The Tragicall History of Christopher Marlowe*, 2 vols., 1942. Useful critical studies include J. D. Jump, ed., *Marlowe: Dr. Faustus, A Casebook*, 1969, and Harry Levin, *The Overreacher*, 1952. "Recent Studies in Marlowe" are surveyed in *ELR* 7 (1977) 382–399.

John Milton

The Columbia edition, comprising the complete poetry and prose in 18 volumes (1931–38) with a 2-volume index (1940), remains standard for the text of Milton's works. But this edition is unannotated, and for most purposes several other authoritative editions are much preferable: these include

Merritt Y. Hughes's *Complete Poems and Major Prose*, 1957, and two other editions of the complete poems, by Douglas Bush, 1965, and John Carey and Alastair Fowler, 1968. There is also an 8-volume annotated edition of the complete prose (Latin works given only in translation), published by Yale, 1953–82.

The best life of Milton is W. R. Parker's 2-volume survey, 1968; and Christopher Hill has written a masterful account of *Milton and the English Revolution*, 1977. For a general orientation to Milton's works, see Douglas Bush's chapter on him in *English Literature in the Earlier Seventeenth Century*, rev., 1962, or either of two guidebooks: Marjorie Nicolson's *John Milton: A Reader's Guide to His Poetry*, 1963, and Lois Potter's *Preface to Milton*, 1971. Mary Ann Radzinowicz, *Toward Samson Agonistes: The Growth of Milton's Mind*, 1978, charts Milton's poetic development. B. Rajan studies his major poetry in *The Lofty Rhyme*, 1970.

A lively introduction to Milton's great epic that has proved its permanent value is C. S. Lewis's *Preface to Paradise Lost*, 1942; it is one-sided, in giving little weight to Milton's Puritanism, but stimulating nonetheless. Other suggestive books on *Paradise Lost* include Joseph Summers, *The Muse's Method*, 1962, Christopher Ricks, *Milton's Grand Style*, 1963, Helen Gardner, *A Reading of Paradise Lost*, 1965, William Empson, *Milton's God*, rev., 1965, Stanley Fish, *Surprised by Sin*, 1967, John M. Steadman, *Milton and the Renaissance Hero*, 1967, Thomas Wheeler, *Paradise Lost and the Modern Reader*, 1974, Robert Crosman, *Reading Paradise Lost*, 1980, and Barbara K. Lewalski, *Paradise Lost and the Rhetoric of Literary Forms*, 1985.

There is a concise bibliography of Milton by James H. Hanford and William A. McQueen, rev., 1979, in the Goldentree series.

William Shakespeare

Major editions of *1 Henry IV* are the *Variorum*, ed. S. B. Hemingway, 1936, with a supplement by G. B. Evans, 1956; the *New Arden*, ed. A. R. Humphries, 1960; and *The Riverside Shakespeare*, ed. G. B. Evans, 1974. For criticism see the Norton Critical Edition, ed. J. L. Sanderson, rev., 1969; Robert Ornstein, *A Kingdom for a Stage: The Achievment of Shakespeare's History*

Plays, 1972; and E. M. W. Tillyard, *Shakespeare's History Plays*, 1944.

The sonnets have been edited by Stephen Booth (1977), Hyder Rollins (The *Variorum* edition, 2 vols, 1944), and W. G. Ingram and T. Redpath (1965); there are many paperback editions. Significant criticism includes Stephen Booth, *An Essay on Shakespeare's Sonnets*, 1969; Hallett Smith, *The Tension of the Lyre: Poetry in Shakespeare's Sonnets*, 1981; *The Sonnets: A Casebook*, ed. Peter Jones, 1977.

Important biographical studies include E. K. Chambers, *William Shakespeare: A Study of Facts and Problems*, 2 vols. 1930; and S. Schoenbaum, *William Shakespeare: A Documentary Life*, 1975. A useful selective bibliography is the Goldentree *Shakespeare*, by David Bevington (1978).

Percy Bysshe Shelley

The most widely used complete edition of the poems has been *The Complete Poetical Works*, ed. Thomas Hutchinson and rev. G. M. Matthews, 1970. For selected poems the best texts are those in *The Lyrics of Shelley*, ed. Judith Chernaik, 1972, and *Shelley's Poetry and Prose*, A Norton Critical Edition, ed. Donald H. Reiman and Sharon B. Powers, 1977. *Shelley's Prose* has been collected by David Lee Clark, 1954, and *The Letters* have been edited by Frederick L. Jones, 2 vols., 1964. The classic life is Newman Ivey White's *Shelley*, 2 vols., 1940 (condensed in one volume as *Portrait of Shelley*, 1945). Important critical studies include Carlos Baker, *Shelley's Major Poetry*, 1948; C. E. Pulos, *The Deep Truth: A Study of Shelley's Scepticism*, 1954; Harold Bloom, *Shelley's Mythmaking*, 1959; Desmond King-Hele, *Shelley: His Thought and Work*, 1960; Donald Reiman, *Percy Bysshe Shelley*, 1969; Earl Wasserman, *Shelley: A Critical Reading* (1971); Stuart Curran, *Shelley's Annus Mirabilis: The Maturing Epic Vision*, 1975; Timothy Webb, *Shelley: A Voice Not Understood*, 1977; and William Keach, *Shelley's Style*, 1984.

Sir Gawain and the Green Knight

The standard Middle English text is that edited by J.R.R. Tolkien and E. V. Gordon, 1925, rev. by Norman Davis, 1967, although the edition by R. A. Waldron, 1970, rev. for *The Poems of the Pearl Manuscript*, 1978, is better suited to the needs of the general reader. Helpful criticism may be found in the chapters on the poem in A. C. Spearing's *Criticism and Medieval Poetry*, 2nd ed., 1972, and *The Gawain Poet*, 1971. The most comprehensive collection of essays is that edited by D. R. Howard and C. K. Zacher, *Critical Studies of Sir Gawain and the Green Knight*, 1968.

Edmund Spenser

The major scholarly edition is *The Works of Edmund Spenser, a Variorum Edition*, ed. Edwin A. Greenlaw et al., 10 vols., 1932–49; also important is A. C. Hamilton's annotated edition of *The Faerie Queene*, 1977. The chief biography is *The Life of Edmund Spenser* by Alexander Judson, 1945. Important critical studies include: Paul J. Alpers, *The Poetry of The Faerie Queene*, 1967; C. S. Lewis, *The Allegory of Love*, 1936; William Nelson, *The Poetry of Edmund Spenser*, 1963; Mark Rose, *Spenser's Art: A Companion to Book I of the Faerie Queene*, 1975; and the Norton Critical Edition, ed. Hugh Maclean, rev. 1982. A review of recent studies appears in *ELR* 2 (1971), 188–191.

Alfred Lord Tennyson

The standard modern edition of Tennyson's poetry has been edited by Christopher Ricks, 1969. The standard biography is Robert Martin, *Tennyson*, 1980. An excellent critical study is *The Poetry of Tennyson* by A. Dwight Culler, 1977. See also E. D. H. Johnson's *The Alien Vision of Victorian Poetry*, 1952; Jerome H. Buckley's *Tennyson: The Growth of a Poet*, 1961; *Critical Essays on the Poetry of Tennyson*, ed. John Killham, 1962; Christopher Rick's *Tennyson*, 1972; and James R. Kincaid's *Tennyson's Major Poems: The Comic and Ironic Patterns*, 1975.

Dylan Thomas

The Poems of Dylan Thomas, rev., 1974, is the fullest collection of Thomas's poetry. He also wrote the autobiographical prose *Portrait of the Artist as a Young Dog*, 1940; *Adventures in the Skin Trade*, 1955; a radio play, *Under Milk Wood*, 1954, which has proved a great popular success; and *Quite Early One Morning*, 1954, a collection of stories, essays, and minor pieces. In 1957 Vernon Watkins edited *Thomas's Letters to Vernon Watkins*, and *The Notebooks of Dylan Thomas* were edited by Ralph N.

Maud in 1967. Maud's *Entrances to Dylan Thomas's Poetry*, 1963, and *The Craft and Art of Dylan Thomas*, by William T. Moynahan, 1966, are useful introductions to the workings of the poet's mind. *The Life of Dylan Thomas*, by Constantine Fitzgibbon, 1965, and *Dylan Thomas: A Biography*, by Paul Ferris, 1977, are good biographies, while *The Days of Dylan Thomas*, by Bill Read, 1964, supplements a straightforward narrative with many photographs.

Virginia Woolf

All ten of her novels are available in paperback. The *Collected Essays*, 4 vols., 1966–67, are supplemented by *Books and Portraits*, ed. Mary Lyon, 1977. *The Diary of Virginia Woolf* has been edited in 5 vols. by Anne Olivier Bell and Andrew McNeillie, 1977–84, and *The Letters of Virginia Woolf* in 6 vols. by Nigel Nicholson and Joanne Trautmann, 1977–80.

The most detailed critical study of the novels and essays is *Virginia Woolf and Her Works*, by Jean Guiget (trans. Jean Stewart), 1965. *Virginia Woolf, the Inward Voyage*, by Harvena Richter, 1970, analyzes her use of the subjective mode in the development of her characters, and *Virginia Woolf: A Collection of Critical Essays*, ed. Thomas Lewis, 1975, contains useful studies of individual novels, as does *Virginia Woolf: Revaluation and Continuity*, by Ralph Freedman, 1980. Other critical works include *Virginia Woolf: Her Art as a Novelist*, by Joan Bennett, 2nd ed., 1964; and *Feminism and Art: A Study of Virginia Woolf*, by Herbert Marder, 1968, which emphasizes the social and feminist relevance of her novels, a topic illuminated by Woolf's own *A Room of One's Own*, 1929, and *Three Guineas*, 1938. More recent critical studies include *The Novels of Virginia Woolf*, by M. Leaska, 1977, and *The World Without a Self: Virginia Woolf and the Novel*, by J. Naremore, 1973.

Virginia Woolf, by Quentin Bell, 2 vols., 1972, offers the fullest and most balanced account of her life, while the most lively critical biography is *Virginia Woolf: A Writer's Life*, by Lyndall Gordon, 1984.

Moments of Being, ed. Jeanne Schulkind, 1976, contains satirical and hilarious autobiographical fragments, as well as a helpful introduction. See also *Bloomsbury*, by Quentin Bell, 1968, and *The Bloomsbury Group*, ed. S. P. Rosenbaum, 1975.

William Wordsworth

Ernest de Selincourt has edited *The Poetical Works* (with Helen Darbishire), 5 vols., 1940–49; the variorum edition of *The Prelude*, with the texts of 1805 and 1850 on facing pages, rev. Helen Darbishire, 1959; and *The Letters of William and Dorothy Wordsworth*, 6 vols., 1935–39 (now being revised by C. L. Shaver and others, 1967 ff.). Newly edited texts of the 1805 and 1850 *Preludes* on facing pages, together with the "Two-Part *Prelude*" of 1799, are available in *The Prelude: 1799, 1805, 1850*, A Norton Critical Edition, ed. Jonathan Wordsworth, M. H. Abrams, and Stephen Gill, 1979. A new multivolume series, the Cornell Wordsworth, 1975 ff., prints texts of poems and variant readings, along with photographs and transcriptions of manuscripts. W. J. B. Owen and Jane W. Smyser have edited *The Prose Works*, 3 vols., 1974. The standard biography is Mary Moorman's *William Wordsworth*, 2 vols., 1957 (rev. 1968) and 1965. General critical studies of the poetry include Geoffrey Hartman, *Wordsworth's Poetry, 1787–1814*, 1964; Carl Woodring, *Wordsworth*, 1965; James H. Averill, *Wordsworth and the Poetry of Human Suffering*, 1980; and Kenneth R. Johnston, *Wordsworth and "The Recluse,"* 1984. On the *Lyrical Ballads* see Stephen M. Parrish, *The Art of the "Lyrical Ballads,"* 1973; Mary Jacobus, *Tradition and Experiment in Wordsworth's "Lyrical Ballads,"* 1976; and John E. Jordan, *Why the "Lyrical Ballads"?* 1976. On *The Prelude*: Raymond D. Havens, *The Mind of a Poet*, 2 vols., 1941; Herbert Lindenberger, *On Wordsworth's "Prelude,"* 1963; Richard J. Onorato, *The Character of the Poet: Wordsworth in "The Prelude,"* 1971. On Wordsworth's concept of imagination: James A. W. Heffernan, *Wordsworth's Theory of Poetry: The Transforming Imagination*, 1969.

William Butler Yeats

The major editions of his poems and plays are *The Variorum Edition of the Poems*, edited by Peter Allt and Russell K. Alspach, 1957, corrected 3rd printing, 1966, and *The Variorum Edition of the Plays*, edited by Russell K. Alspach, 1966, corrected 2nd printing, 1966. *The Poems of W. B. Yeats*, ed. Richard J. Finneran, 1983, attempts to provide more accurate texts than those of the *Variorum*, with extensive annotation; and *Selected Poems and Two Plays of William Butler Yeats*, ed. M. L. Rosenthal, rev., 1966, is the best of several paperback selections. An edition of his voluminous correspondence, now in preparation is *The Letters of W. B. Yeats*, ed. Allan Wade, 1954. Yeats's mystical work *A Vision* was first published in 1925; a much revised edition appeared in 1937. His autobiographical writings are combined in *The Autobiography of W. B. Yeats*, 1938 ff. *Mythologies*, 1959, contains the bulk of Yeats's prose fiction; *Essays and Introductions*, 1961, the most important of his critical prose; and *Explorations*, 1962, miscellaneous prose pieces not readily available elsewhere.

The critical literature on Yeats is more extensive than that on any other 20th-century poet. *W. B. Yeats: A Critical Introduction*, by Balachandra Rajan, 2nd ed., 1969, is the most satisfactory of many short introductory studies, though less substantial than *The Identity of Yeats*, by Richard Ellmann, 2nd ed., 1964, and *The Lonely Tower: Studies in the Poetry of W. B. Yeats*, by T. R. Henn, 2nd ed., 1965. The most helpful commentaries are *A New Commentary on the Poems of W. B. Yeats*, 1984, and *A Commentary on The Collected Plays of W. B. Yeats*, 1975, both by A. N. Jeffares. Three specialist critical studies of important areas of Yeats's work are *W. B. Yeats Self Critic: A Study of His Early Verse*, by Thomas Parkinson, 1951, reprinted 1971 with *The Later Poetry* and a new foreword; *Between the Lines: W. B. Yeats's Poetry in the Making*, by Jon Stallworthy, 1963, corrected 2nd imp., 1965; and *Swan and Shadow: Yeats's Dialogue with History*, by Thomas R. Whitaker, 1964.

The best critical biography is *Yeats: The Man and the Masks*, by Richard Ellmann, 1948; and *Yeats*, by Frank Tuohy, 1976, supplements a straightforward narrative with many excellent illustrations.

A LONDON PLAYHOUSE OF SHAKESPEARE'S TIME

Building above stage known as the "Heavens". It contains a windlass for special effects (e.g. descent of enthroned "gods" from the "sky" to the stage).

Flag is flown every playing day.

Trumpet sounded to announce performance.

Ceiling under roof ornamentally painted as "sky".

Two penny Gallery

"Private Rooms (Boxes)

A. Privileged spectators seated on stage.
B. Upper stage and windows (see *Volpone* II i)
C. Curtained recess. (See *Dr Faustus* I and *Volpone* I i,)

D. Trapdoor to "Hell" area under the stage (traditionally used for appearances of ghosts, etc.)
E. One-penny audience ("groundlings") standing in yard.

Backstage area (called the "Tiring House.")

Staircases to galleries

C. Walter Hodges. 1978

THE UNIVERSE ACCORDING TO PTOLEMY

Ptolemy was a Roman astronomer of Greek descent, born in Egypt during the second century A.D.; after his death, for nearly 1500 years his account of the design of the universe was accepted as standard. During that long period, the basic pattern underwent many detailed modifications and was fitted out with many astrological and pseudo-scientific trappings. But in essence Ptolemy's followers agreed in portraying the earth as the center of the universe, with the sun, planets, and fixed stars set in transparent spheres orbiting around it. In this scheme of things, as modified for Christian usage, Hell was usually placed under the earth's surface at the center of the cosmic globe, while Heaven, the abode of the blessed spirits, was in the outermost, uppermost circle, the empyrean. But in 1543 the Polish astronomer Copernicus proposed an alternative hypothesis—that the earth rotates around the sun, not vice versa; and despite theological opposition, observations with the new telescope and careful mathematical calculations insured ultimate acceptance of the new view.

The map of the Ptolemaic universe represented here is a simplified version of a diagram in Peter Apian's *Cosmography* (1584). In such a diagram, the Firmament is the sphere which contained the fixed stars; the Crystalline Sphere, which contained no heavenly bodies, is a late innovation, included to explain certain anomalies in the observed movement of the heavenly

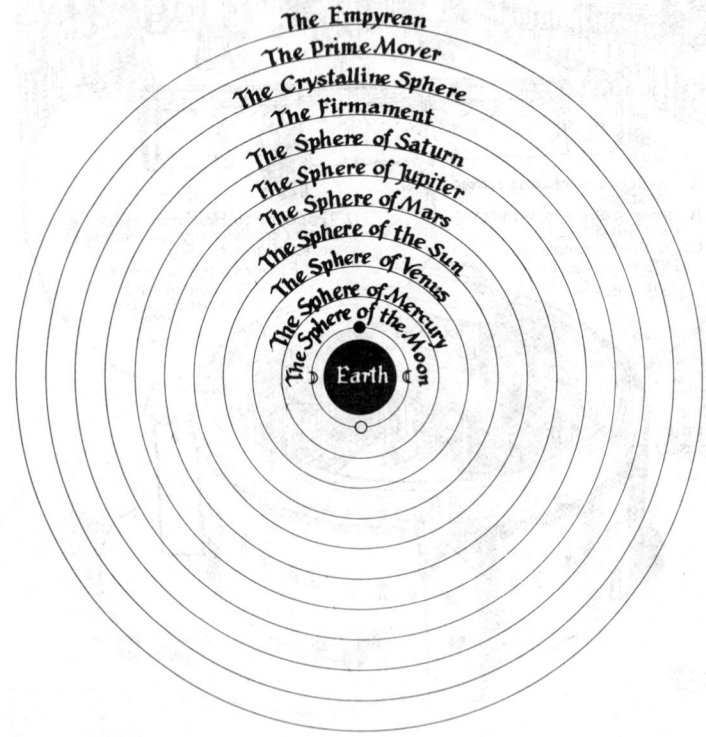

The Empyrean
The Prime Mover
The Crystalline Sphere
The Firmament
The Sphere of Saturn
The Sphere of Jupiter
The Sphere of Mars
The Sphere of the Sun
The Sphere of Venus
The Sphere of Mercury
The Sphere of the Moon
Earth

bodies; and the Prime Mover is the sphere which, itself put into motion by God, imparts rotation around the earth to all the other spheres.

Milton, writing in mid-seventeenth century, made use of two universes. The Copernican universe, though he alludes to it, was too large, formless, and unfamiliar to serve as the setting for the war between Heaven and Hell in *Paradise Lost*. He therefore adopted as his setting the Ptolemaic cosmos, but placed Heaven well outside this smaller earth-centered universe, Hell far beneath it, and assigned the vast middle space to Chaos.

British Money

Since 1971, British money has been calculated on the decimal system, with 100 pence to the pound; the pound has fluctuated from a bit more than 2 American dollars to virtual parity—whatever dollars may be worth. Before 1971, the pound consisted of 20 shillings, each containing 12 pence, thus 240 pence to the pound. In paper money the change has not been great; 1-, 5-, and 10-pound notes constitute the mass of the bills under both the old and the new systems; nowadays, in addition, 20- and 50-pound notes have been added. But in the smaller coinage the change has been considerable and the simplification remarkable. Most notable is abolition of the shilling, which goes into retirement now with the mark (worth in its day two-thirds of a pound or 13 shillings 4 pence) and the angel (once worth 10 shillings but replaced by the 10-shilling note, now in its turn abolished). The guinea, an oddity of the old currency, amounted to a pound and a shilling; though it has not been minted since 1813, quality products (a suit from a good tailor, a piece of fine silver, a rare book) are still generally priced in guineas. Colloquially, a pound used to be a quid, a shilling a bob, sixpence a tanner, a penny a copper. The common signs were £ for pound, s. for shilling, d. for a penny (from Latin *denarius*). A sum would normally be written £2.19.3, i.e., 2 pounds, 19 shillings, 3 pence. That is Bloom's budget for June 16, 1904. In new currency, it would be about £2.96d.

Old	New
1 pound note	1 pound note
10 shilling (half-pound) note	50 pence
5 shilling (crown)	
2 ½ shilling (half crown)	
2 shilling (florin)	10 pence
1 shilling	5 pence
6 pence	
3 pence	1 penny
2 pence	
1 penny	½ penny
½ penny	
¼ penny (farthing)	

What the pound was worth at any point in history is never easy to state. In the first part of the twentieth century, 1 pound equalled about 5 American dollars; but those dollars bought more than twice what 1985 dollars will buy. The value of the pound might be definable in terms of the goods and services it would purchase; but these too vary radically with special circumstances, wars, harvests, and the like. In a loose way, it's clear that money used to be worth much more than it is now. A Saxon penny was the biggest coin in general circulation; four of them would buy a sheep. Peasants before the Black Death made 2 or 3 pence a day—an annual income of £3 or £4. At the modern ratio that would be only $5 or so per annum. However incredibly low their standard of living, however much they supplemented their cash income with produce from their own fields, that figure is impossible: the pound must have been worth much more than it is now, perhaps by a factor of several hundred. Hugh Latimer reports that in his day (the early 1500s) it was a common saying, "Oh, he's a rich man, he's worth £500." Probably he means, not fabulously, just comfortably rich; still, it's clear that the pound was a solid sum of money, equal perhaps to 400 or 500 American dollars of the year 1983.

In Jonson's *Alchemist*, Subtle tells Face that as an honest servant he had been a mere "livery-three-pound thrum"— that is, he had his uniform, food, and lodging, plus £3 a year. By cheating on household expenses, he had built up over the years, "a pretty stock, some twenty marks," about £13. Of course, the comic point of all this is the miserable sums involved in the lives of such squalid rascals. Forty pounds a year in independent income (generally rents) was the minimum requirement for a justice of the peace; it was also the sum fixed by King James at which a man could be forced to accept knighthood. It marked the threshold of gentry, and we must multiply it by 150 or 200 to get an equivalent in dollars. In 1661 that good bourgeois Samuel Pepys, just after he began working for the navy, calculated his worth at a modest £650; five years later, he was worth more than £6,000 and his annual income was about £3,000—cause for complacency. Of course, he was working for most of this income. Pepys was a rising official and would become a very important one; but he never achieved a title or even knighthood because the smell of commerce had never been washed from his money by possession of land.

On a far humbler level, Joseph Andrews (in Fielding's novel, published 1742) worked as a footman in the house of Lady Booby for £8 a year; but he got his room, board, and livery in addition, plus the occasional tip. Among the comfortable classes again, Mr. Bennet of Jane Austen's *Pride and Prejudice* (1813) enjoyed an income of £2,000 a year (but he had a family of five nonearning females to support, and the income ceased at his death). Mr. Bingley had £4,000 per year of his own, Mr. Darcy close to £10,000; and this raises us close to the rarefied atmosphere of the aristocracy. In his deepest degradation David Copperfield (of Dickens's 1850 novel) worked in the warehouse of Murdstone & Grinby for 6 or 7 shillings a week (£15 to £18 a year). Mr. Murdstone paid extra for his lodging and laundry, but even so the boy was bitterly impoverished, though he had only himself to feed. When his father died, his mother was thought to be pretty well taken care of with £105 a year, a little less than £9 per month. Only a few years later, Dorothea Brooke of *Middlemarch* (1872) is more than easy with £700 per year of her own; if she marries and has a son, he may inherit from her uncle as much as £3,000 per year in addition. That is high plutocracy for the folk of Tipton parish; one may estimate that Miss Brooke's pound is now worth between 20 and 50 American dollars of 1985 vintage. When John Davidson at the end of the century wrote of the horrors of being a clerk with a family at 30 bob a week, that stipend wouldn't work out much better than $1,500 to $3,000 of modern money. We see what he means.

Across the centuries, it's evident that money diminished in value; it's equally apparent that in every era there's been a gap between the poor and the rich. What money was worth depended heavily on which of those classes you belonged to. It also depended on where you lived. London was always very dear, and in the provinces (as is traditional everywhere) a small income went further. Finally, the value of money depended on the current rate of taxation. In the days of the Danegeld (ancestor of the modern income tax), nobody was rich except the Danes. Pitt introduced the modern income tax in 1798 as a war measure, Peel in 1842 made it a routine part of government financing; and it is one reason why an income of £10,000, though it was glorious aristocratic luxury for Mr. Fitzwilliam Darcy and his Elizabeth, does not today represent much more than solid middle-class comfort. For now, in addition to being heavily taxed, it's worth only a bit more than the same number of current dollars.

The British Baronage

The English monarchy is hereditary, passing from father to elder son, to daughters in order of seniority if there is no son, to a brother if there are no children, and in default of direct descendants to collateral lines (cousins, nephews, nieces) in order of closeness. There have been breaks in the order of succession (1066, 1399, 1688), but so far as possible the usurpers always tried to paper over the break with a legitimate, i.e., a hereditary claim. When a queen succeeds to the throne and takes a husband, he does not become king unless he is in the line of blood succession; rather, he is named prince consort, as Albert was to Victoria and Philip is to Queen Elizabeth II. He may father kings, but is not one himself.

The original Saxon nobles were the king's thanes, ealdormen, or earls, who in return for booty, gifts, or landed estates provided the king with military service and counsel. William the Conqueror, arriving from France where feudalism was fully developed, added largely to this group. Archbishops and bishops, abbots and priors, who frequently held their land from the king though they might hold their office from the pope, served as counselors and very often in secular offices as well, as royal administrators. In addition, as the king distributed the lands of his new kingdom, he also distributed dignities to men who became known collectively as "the baronage." "Baron" in its root meaning signifies simply "man," and barons were the king's men. As the title was common, a distinction was early made between greater and lesser barons, the former gradually assuming loftier and more impressive titles. The king, no longer duke of Normandy, created the first English duke in 1337. "Marquess" or "marquis" was created in 1385 and "viscount" in 1440 (the former pronounced "markwis," the latter "vyekount"); though it's the oldest title of all, an "earl" now comes, in order of dignity and precedence, between a marquess and a viscount; only "baronets," created first in 1611, rank below barons in the scale of hereditary nobility.

Kings and queens are addressed as "Your Majesty," princes and princesses as "Your Highness," the other hereditary nobility as "My Lord" or "Your Lordship." When a commoner is created a peer (always by the monarch), he may select his own title; thus Disraeli became earl of Beaconsfield after the district where his house stood; modest Clement Attlee, prime minister from 1945 to 1951, became simply Earl Attlee. Byron was the sixth baron of that line, by birth; Tennyson was created first Baron Tennyson. Peerages (other than the recently created Life Peerages) descend by primogeniture; they are given to a man with right of succession, they are not incidental to tenure of land—though when a man is given a peerage, he is sometimes given a pension or an estate to sustain the dignity. On the other hand, the children, even of a duke, are commoners unless they are specifically granted some other title or inherit their father's title from him. (Sons may enjoy the courtesy title "the Honorable," as daughters are referred to as "Lady" So and So; but these carry no social rank.) A peerage can be forfeited by act of attainder, as for example when a lord is convicted of treason; and, when forfeited, or lapsed for lack of a successor, can be bestowed on another family. Thus Robert Cecil was made in 1605 first earl of Salisbury in the third creation, the first creation dating from 1149, the second from 1337, the title having been in abeyance since 1539.

Scottish peers sat in the Parliament of Scotland, as English peers did in the Parliament of England till at the Act of Union (1707) Scots peers were granted 16 seats in the English House of Lords, to be filled by election. Similarly, Irish peers, when the Irish Parliament was abolished in 1801, were granted the right to elect 28 of their number to the House of Lords in Westminister. (Now that Eire is a separate nation, of course, this no longer applies.) For a genealogical guide through the tangled thickets of the aristocracy, see the classic compilation of Sir John Burke, known for brevity's sake as *Burke's Peerage*. The same author's *Landed Gentry* is popularly known in county society as "the stud book."

Below the hereditary peerage the chief title of honor is knight. Knighthood is not hereditary; it is generally a reward for services rendered. Though the word itself comes from Anglo-Saxon *cniht*, there seems to be some doubt whether knighthood amounted to much before the arrival of the Normans. The feudal system required military service as a condition of land tenure, and a man who came to serve his king at the head of an army of tenants required a title of authority and badges of identity—hence the title of knighthood and the coat of arms. During the Crusades, when men were far removed from their land (or had even sold it in order to go on crusade), more elaborate forms of fealty sprang up which soon expanded into the orders of knighthood. The Templars, Hospitallers, Knights of the Teutonic Order, Knights of Malta, and Knights of the Golden Fleece were but a few of these companionships; their similarity to the monastic and itinerant orders of friars was often remarked.

Gradually, with the rise of centralized government and the decline of feudal tenures, military knighthood became obsolete, and the rank largely honorific—sometimes it even degenerated into a scheme of the royal government for making money. For hundreds of years after its establishment in the fourteenth century, the Order of the Garter was the only English order of knighthood, an exclusive courtly companionship. Then, during the late seventeenth, eighteenth, and nineteenth centuries, a number of additional orders were created—the Thistle, Saint Patrick, the Bath, Saint Michael and Saint George, plus a number of special Victorian and Indian orders. They retain the terminology, ceremony, and dignity of knighthood, but the military implications are all vestigial.

Knights are addressed using their first names, as "Sir John"; their wives are "Lady Eleanor"; their children are commoners. The female equivalent of a knight bears the title of "Dame." The Order of Merit, instituted by Edward VII, is an exclusive and very honorable order. The Distinguished Service Order and the Victoria Cross—DSO and VC—are high awards for military heroism, the VC the very highest. The OBE (Order of the British Empire) is awarded for services to the empire, either at home or abroad, by persons of either gender. It is but one of many special medals awarded for outstanding accomplishment in one form or another.

The king and queen   (These are all of the royal line.)
Prince and princess

Duke and duchess   (These may or may not be of the
Marquess and marchioness   royal line, but are ordinarily
Earl and countess   remote from the succession.)
Viscount and viscountess
Baron and baroness
Baronet and lady

Adapted from *The Land and Literature of England:
A Historical Account*, by Robert M. Adams (New
York: Norton, 1983).

Religious Sects in England

Religious distinctions and denominations are important in British social history, hence deeply woven into the nation's literature. The numerous (over 300) British churches and sects divide along a scale from high to low, depending on the amount of authority they give to the church or the amount of liberty they concede to the individual conscience. At one end of the scale is the Roman Catholic Church, asserting papal infallibility, universal jurisdiction, and the supreme importance of hierarchy as guide and intercessor. For political and social reasons, Catholicism struck deep roots in Ireland but was the object of prolonged, bitter hatred on the part of Protestants from the Reformation through the nineteenth century. The Established English (Anglican) Episcopal Church has been the official national church since the sixteenth century; it enjoys the support (once direct and exclusive, now indirect and peripheral) of the national government. Its creed is defined by Thirty-Nine Articles, but these are intentionally vague, so there are numerous ways of adhering to the Church of England. Roughly and intermittently, the chief classes of Anglicans have been known as High Church (with its highest portion calling itself Anglo-Catholic); Broad Church or Latitudinarian (when they get so broad that they admit anyone believing in God, they may be known as Deists, or some may leave the church altogether and be known as Unitarians); and Low Church, whose adherents may stay in the English church and yet come close to shaking hands with Presbyterians or Methodists. These various groups may be arranged, from the High down to the Low Church, in direct relation to the amount of ritual each prefers and in the degree of authority conceded to the upper clergy—and in inverse relation to the importance ascribed to a saving faith directly infused by God into an individual conscience.

All English Protestants who decline to subscribe to the English established church are classed as Dissenters or Nonconformists; for a time in the sixteenth and seventeenth centuries, they were also known as Puritans. (Nowadays, though Puritanism has less distinct theological meaning, it marks a distinct character type; because of his passionate emphasis on individual conscience and moral economy, George Bernard Shaw was a prototypical Puritan.) The Presbyterians model their church government on that established by John Calvin in the Swiss city of Geneva. It has no bishops, and therefore is more democratic for the clergy; but it gains energy by associating lay elders with clergymen in matters of social discipline, and tends to be strict with the ungodly. From its first reformation the Scottish Kirk was fixed on the Presbyterian model. During the civil wars of the seventeenth century, a great many sects sprang up on the left wing of the Presbyterians, most of them touched by Calvinism but some rebelling against it; a few of these still survive. The Independents became our modern Congregationalists; the Quakers are still Quakers, as Baptists are still Baptists, though multiply divided.

But many of the sects flourished and perished within the space of a few years. Among these now vanished groups were the Shakers (though a few groups still exist in America), the Seekers, the Ranters, the Anabaptists, the Muggletonians, the Fifth Monarchy Men, the Family of Love, the Sweet Singers of Israel, and many others, forgotten by all except scholars. During the eighteenth and nineteenth centuries, new sects arose, supplanting old ones; the Methodists, under John and Charles Wesley, became numerous and important, taking root particularly in Wales. (The three "subject" nationalities, Ireland, Scotland, and Wales, thus turned three different ways to avoid the Anglican church.) With the passage of time a small number of Swedenborgians sprang up, followers of the Swedish mystic Emanuel Swedenborg—to be followed by the Plymouth Brethren, Christian Scientists, Jehovah's Witnesses, and countless other nineteenth-century groups. All these sects constantly grow, shrink, split, and occasionally disappear as they succeed or fail in attracting new converts.

Within the various churches and sects, independent of them all but amazingly persistent, there has always survived a stream of esoteric or hermetic thought—a belief in occult powers, and sometimes in magic as well, exemplified by the pseudo-sciences of astrology and alchemy but taking many other forms. From the mythical Egyptian seer Hermes Trismegistus through Paracelsus, Cornelius Agrippa, Giordano Bruno, Jakob Boehme, the society of Rosicrucians, and a hundred other shadowy figures, the line can be traced to William Blake and William Butler Yeats, who both in their different ways brought hermetic Protestantism close to its ultimate goal, a mystic church of one single man, poised within his own mind-elaborated cosmos.

Poetic Forms and Literary Terminology

Verse is generally distinguished from prose as a more compressed and more regularly rhythmic form of statement. This approximate truth underlines the importance of **meter** in poetry, as the means by which rhythm is measured and described.

In the classical languages, meter was established on a **quantitative** basis, by the regular alternation of long and short syllables (that is, syllables classified according to the time taken to pronounce them). Outside of a few experiments (and the songs of Thomas Campion), this system has never proved congenial to English, which distinguishes, instead, between **stressed** and **unstressed,** or accented and unaccented syllables. Two varieties of accented stress may be distinguished. On the one hand, there is the natural stress pattern of words themselves; *sỳllable* is accented on the first syllable, *deplòrable* on the second, and so on. Then there is the sort of stress which indicates rhetorical emphasis. If the sentence "You went to Greece?" is given a pronounced accent on the last word, it implies "Greece (of all places)?" If the accent falls on the first word, it implies "you (of all people)?" The meter of poetry—that is, its rhythm—is ordinarily built up out of a regular recurrence of accents, whether established as **word accents** or **rhetorical accents**; once started in the reader's mind, it has (like all rhythm) a persistent effect of its own.

The unit which is repeated to give steady rhythm to a poem is called a **poetic foot**; in English it usually consists of accented and unaccented syllables in one of five fairly simple patterns:

The **iambic foot** (or **iamb**) consists of an unstressed followed by a stressed syllable, as in *unìte, repeàt,* or *insìst.* Most English verse falls naturally into the iambic pattern.

The **trochaic foot** (**trochee**) inverts this order; it is a stressed followed by an unstressed syllable—for example, *ùnit, rèaper,* or *ìnstant.*

The **anapestic foot** (**anapest**) consists of two unstressed syllables followed by a stressed syllable, as in *intercède, disarrànged,* or *Cameròon.*

The **dactylic foot** (**dactyl**) consists of a stressed syllable followed by two unstressed syllables, as in *Wàshington, Ècuador,* or *àpplejack.*

The **spondaic foot** (**spondee**) consists of two successive stressed syllables, as in *heartbreak, headline,* or *Kashmir.*

In all the examples above, word accent and the quality of the metrical foot coincide exactly. But the metrical foot may well consist of several words, or, on the other hand, one word may well consist of several metrical feet.

Photolithography consists of two excellent dactyls in a single word; *dàrk and with spòts on it,* though it consists of six words rather than one, is also two dactyls—not quite such good ones. When we read a piece of poetry with the intention of discovering its underlying metrical pattern, we are said to scan it—that is, we go through it line by line, indicating by conventional signs which are the accented and which the unaccented syllables within the feet (the ictus ˋ generally designates accented, the mora ˇ unaccented syllables). We also count the number of feet in each line, or, more properly, **verse**— since a single poetic line is generally called a "verse." Verse lengths are conventionally described in terms derived from the Greek:

Monometer: one foot (of rare occurrence)
Dimeter: two feet (also rare)
Trimeter: three feet
Tetrameter: four feet
Pentameter: five feet
Hexameter: six feet (six iambic feet make an **Alexandrine**)
Heptameter: seven feet (also rare)

Samuel Johnson's little parody of simpleminded poets would thus be scanned this way:

> Ĭ pùt m̆y hàt ŭpòn m̆y hèad
> Ăňd wàlked ĭntò thĕ Strànd,
> Ăňd thère Ĭ mèt ănòthĕr man
> Whŏse hàt wăs ĭn hĭs hànd.

The poem is iambic in rhythm, alternating tetrameter and trimeter in verse length. The fact that it scans so nicely is, however, no proof that it is good poetry. Quite the contrary. Many of poetry's most subtle effects are achieved by establishing an underlying rhythm and then varying it by means of a whole series of devices, some dramatic and expressive, others designed simply to lend variety and interest to the verse. A well-known sonnet of Shakespeare's (116) begins,

> Let me not to the marriage of true minds
> Admit impediments. Love is not love
> Which alters when it alteration finds,
> Or bends with the remover to remove.

It is perfectly possible, if one crushes all one's sensitivities, to read the first line of this poem as mechanical iambic pentameter:

> Lĕt mè nŏt tò thĕ màrriăge òf trūe mìnds.

But of course nobody ever reads it that way, except to make a point; read with normal English accent and some sense of what it is saying, the line would probably form a pattern something like this:

> Lèt mĕ nŏt tŏ thĕ màrriăge òf trùe mìnds,

which is neither pentameter nor in any way iambic. The second line is a little more iambic, but, read for expression, falls just as far short of pentameter:

Ădmĭt ĭmpèdĭmeňts. Lòve ĭs nŏt lòve.

Only in the third and fourth lines of the sonnet do we get verses which read as well as scan like five iambic feet.

The fact is that perfectly regular metrical verse is easy to write and dull to read. Among the devices in common use for varying too regular a pattern are, for instance, the insertion of a trochaic foot among iambics, especially at the opening of a line, where the soft first syllable of the iambic foot often needs stiffening (see line 1 above); the more or less free addition of extra unaccented syllables; and the use of **caesura**, or strong grammatical pause within a line (conventionally indicated, in scanning, by the sign ‖). The second line of the sonnet above is a good example of caesura:

Admit impediments. ‖ Love is not love.

The strength of the caesura, and its placing in the line, may be varied to produce striking variations of effect. More broadly, the whole relation between the poem's sound- and rhythm-patterns and its pattern as a sequence of assertions (phrases, clauses, sentences) may be manipulated by the poet. Sometimes his statements fit neatly within the lines, so that each line ends with a strong mark of punctuation; they are then known as **end-stopped lines**. Sometimes the sense flows over the ends of the lines, creating **run-on lines**; this process is also known, from the French, as **enjambment** (literally, "straddling").

End-stopped lines (Marlowe, *Hero and Leander*, lines 45–48):

So lovely fair was Hero, Venus' nun,
As Nature wept, thinking she was undone,
Because she took more from her than she left
And of such wondrous beauty her bereft.

Run-on lines (Keats, *Endymion* 1.89–93):

Full in the middle of this pleasantness
There stood a marble altar, with a tress
Of flowers budded newly; and the dew
Had taken fairy fantasies to strew
Daisies upon the sacred sward, . . .

Following the example of such poets as Blake, Rimbaud, and Whitman, many poets of the twentieth century have undertaken to write what is called **free verse**—that is, verse which has neither a fixed metrical foot, nor (consequently) a fixed number of feet in its lines, but which depends for its rhythm on a pattern of cadences, or the rise and fall of the voice in utterance. All freedom in art is of course relative; free verse, with its special aptitude for metrical variety and nervous, colloquial phrasing—its total responsiveness, in other words, to its subject matter—has so successfully established itself that it is now widely recognized as a new and rather demanding form of artistic discipline.

SENSE AND SOUND

The very words of which poetic lines—whether free or traditional—are composed cause them to have different sounds and produce different effects.

Polysyllables, being pronounced fast, often cause a line to move swiftly; monosyllables, especially when heavy and requiring distinct accents, may cause it to move heavily, as in Milton's famous line (*Paradise Lost* 2.621):

> Rocks, caves, lakes, fens, bogs, dens, and shades of death.

Poetic assertions are often dramatized and reinforced by means of **alliteration**—that is, the use of several nearby words or stressed syllables beginning with the same consonant. When Shakespeare writes (*Sonnet 64*),

> Ruin hath taught me thus to ruminate
> That Time will come and take my love away,

the rich, round, vague echoes of the first line contrast most effectively with the sharp anxiety and directness of the alliterative *t*'s in the second. When Dryden starts *Absalom and Achitophel* with that wicked couplet,

> In pious times, ere priestcraft did begin,
> Before polygamy was made a sin,

the satiric undercutting is strongly reinforced by the triple alliteration which links "*p*ious" with "*p*riestcraft" and "*p*olygamy."

Assonance, or repetition of the same or similar vowel sounds within a passage (usually in accented syllables), also serves to enrich it, as in two lines from Keats's *Ode on Melancholy*:

> For shade to shade will come too drowsily,
> And drown the wakeful anguish of the soul.

It is clear that the round, hollow tones of "drowsily," repeated in "drown" and darkening to the full *o*-sound of "soul," have much to do with the effect of the passage. A related device is **consonance,** or the repetition of a pattern of consonants with changes in the intervening vowels—for example: *linger, longer, languor; rider, reader, raider, ruder.*

Direct verbal imitation of natural sounds (known as **onomatopoeia**) has been much attempted, from Virgil's galloping horse—

> *Quadrupedante putrem sonitu quatit ungula campum—*

to Tennyson's account, in *The Princess*, of

> The moan of doves in immemorial elms,
> And murmuring of innumerable bees.

Often ingeniously exploited as a side effect, onomatopoeia is essentially a trick, with about the same value in poetry as it has in music.

RHYME AND STANZA

Rhyme consists of a repetition of accented sounds in words, usually those falling at the end of verse lines. If the rhyme sound is the very last syllable of the line (*rebound, sound*), the rhyme is called **masculine;** if the accented syllable is followed by an unaccented syllable (*hounding, bounding*), the rhyme is called **feminine.** Rhymes amounting to three or more syllables, like forced rhymes, generally have a comic effect in English, and have been freely used for this purpose, e.g., by Byron (*intellectual, henpecked-you-all*). Rhymes occurring within a single line are called **internal;** for instance, the Mother Goose rhyme, "Mary, Mary, quite contrary," or from Coleridge's *Ancient Mariner* ("We were the first that ever burst / Into that silent sea"). **Eye rhymes** are words used as rhymes which look alike but actually sound different (for example, *alone, done; remove, love*); **off rhymes** (sometimes called **partial, imperfect,** or **slant rhymes**) are occasionally the result of pressing exigencies or lack of skill, but are also, at times, used deliberately by modern poets for special effects. For instance, a poem by Wilfred Owen (*Strange Meeting*) contains such "rhymes" as *years / yours* or *tigress / progress*. Owen called these pairings "pararhymes;" they are varieties of assonance.

Blank verse is unrhymed iambic pentameter; until the recent advent of free verse, it was the only unrhymed measure to achieve general popularity in English. First used by the earl of Surrey, blank verse was during the sixteenth century largely dramatic in character; *Paradise Lost* was one of the first nondramatic poems in English to use it. But Milton's authority and his success were so great that during the eighteenth and nineteenth centuries blank verse came to be used for a great variety of discursive, descriptive, and philosophical poems—besides remaining the standard metrical form for epics. Thomson's *Seasons*, Cowper's *Task*, Wordsworth's *Prelude*, and Tennyson's *Idylls of the King* were all written in blank verse.

A **stanza** is a recurring unit of a poem, consisting of a number of verses. Certain poems (for example, Dryden's *Alexander's Feast*) have stanzas comprising a variable number of verses, of varying lengths. Others are more regular, hence easier to describe.

The simplest form of stanza is the **couplet;** it is two lines rhyming together. A single couplet considered in isolation is sometimes called a **distich;** when it expresses a complete thought, ending with a terminal mark of punctuation, it is called a **closed couplet.** The development of very regular end-stopped couplets in the mid-seventeenth century, their use in so-called heroic tragedies, and their consequent acquisition of the name **heroic couplets** are described in the introduction to The Early Seventeenth Century, volume 1. The heroic couplet was the principal form of English neoclassical style.

Another traditional and challenging form of couplet is the **tetrameter,** or **four-beat couplet.** All rhymed couplets are hard to manage without monotony; and since, in addition, a four-beat line is hard to divide by caesura without splitting it into two tick-tock dimeters, tetrameter couplets have posed a perpetual challenge to poets, and still provide an admirable finger-exercise for aspiring versifiers. A model of tetrameter couplets managed with marvelous variety, complexity, and expressiveness is Marvell's *To His Coy Mistress:*

> Thou by the Indian Ganges' side
> Shouldst rubies find; I by the tide
> Of Humber would complain. I would
> Love you ten years before the flood,
> And you should, if you please, refuse
> Till the conversion of the Jews.

English has not done much with rhymes grouped in threes, but has borrowed from Italian the form known as **terza rima**, in which Dante composed his *Divine Comedy*. This form consists of linked groups of three rhymes according to the following pattern: *aba bcb cdc ded*, etc. Shelley's *Ode to the West Wind* is composed in stanzas of *terza rima*, the poem as a whole ending with a couplet.

Quatrains are stanzas of four lines; the lines usually rhyme alternately, *abab*, or in the second and fourth lines, *abcb*. When they alternate tetrameter and trimeter lines, as in Johnson's little poem about men in hats (above), or as in *Sir Patrick Spens*, they are called **ballad stanza**. Dryden's *Annus Mirabilis* and Gray's *Elegy Written in a Country Churchyard* are in **heroic quatrains**; these rhyme alternately, and employ five-stress iambic verse throughout. Tennyson used for *In Memoriam* a tetrameter quatrain rhymed *abba*, and FitzGerald translated *The Rubáiyát of Omar Khayyám* into a pentameter quatrain rhymed *aaba*; but these forms have not been very generally adopted.

Chaucer's *Troilus and Criseyde* is an early example in English of **rime royal**, a seven-line iambic pentameter stanza consisting essentially of a quatrain dovetailed onto two couplets, according to the rhyme scheme *ababbcc* (the fourth line serves both as the final line of the quatrain and the first line of the first couplet). Closely akin to rime royal, but differentiated by an extra *a*-rhyme between the two *b*-rhymes, is **ottava rima**, that is, an eight-line stanza rhyming *abababcc*. As its name suggests, ottava rima is of Italian origin; it was first used in English by Wyatt. Its final couplet, being less prepared for than in rime royal, and usually set off as a separate verbal unit, has a special witty snap to it, for which Byron found good use in *Don Juan*.

The longest and most intricate stanza generally used for narrative purposes in English is that devised by Edmund Spenser for *The Faerie Queene*. The **Spenserian stanza** has nine lines rhyming *ababbcbcc*; the first eight lines are pentameter, the last line an Alexandrine. Slow-moving, intricate of pattern, and demanding in its rhyme scheme (the *b*-sound recurs four times, the *c*-sound three), the Spenserian stanza has nonetheless appealed widely to poets seeking a rich and complicated metrical form. Keats's *Eve of St. Agnes* and Shelley's *Adonais* are brilliantly successful nineteenth-century examples of its use.

The **sonnet**, originally a stanza of Italian origin which has developed into an independent lyric form, is usually defined nowadays as fourteen lines of iambic pentameter. None of the elements in this definition is absolute and in earlier centuries there were sonnets in hexameters (the first of Sidney's *Astrophil and Stella*), and sonnets of as many as twenty lines (Milton's *On the New Forcers of Conscience*). Most, however, come close to the definition. The different varieties—Petrarchan, Shakespearean, and Spenserian— are described in the introduction to the sixteenth-century section, 1.413. Most Elizabethan sonnets dealt with courtly love; and some poets, like Sidney, Spenser, and Shakespeare, imitated Petrarch in grouping together their sonnets dealing with a particular lady or situation. A neutral word for these gatherings is **sonnet sequences**; whether or not they tell a story is a matter of long-standing dispute. Since Elizabethan times, the sonnet has been applied to a wide range of subject matters—religious, political, satiric, moral and philosophic.

In blank verse or irregularly rhymed verse, where stanzaic divisions do not exist or are indistinct, the poetry sometimes falls into **verse paragraphs**, which are in effect divisions of sense like prose paragraphs. This division can be clearly seen in Milton's *Lycidas* or Spenser's *Epithalamion*. In the latter poem, it is reinforced by **a refrain,** which is simply a line repeated at the end of each stanza. Ballads also customarily have refrains; for example, the refrain of *Lord Randall* is

> mother, make my bed soon,
> For I'm weary wi' hunting, and fain wald lie down.

FIGURATIVE LANGUAGE

The act of bringing words together into rich and vigorous poetic lines is complex and demanding, chiefly because so many variables require control. There is the "thought" of the lines, their verbal texture, their emotional resonance, the developing perspective of the reader—all these to be managed at once. One of the poet's chief resources toward this end is figurative language. Here, as in matters of meter, one may distinguish a great variety of devices, some of which we use in everyday speech without special awareness of their names and natures. When we say someone eats "like a horse" or "like a bird," we are using a **simile,** that is, a comparison marked out by a specific word of likening—"like" or "as." When we omit the word of comparison but imply a likeness—as in the sentence, "That hog has guzzled all the champagne"—we are making use of **metaphor.** The **epic simile,** frequent in epic poetry, is an extended simile in which the thing compared is described as an object in its own right, beyond its point of likeness with the main subject. Milton starts to compare Satan to Leviathan, but concludes his simile with the story of a sailor who moored his ship by mistake, one night, to a whale (*Paradise Lost* 1.200–208). Metaphors and similes have been complexly but usefully distinguished according to their special effects; they may be, for instance, violent, comic, degrading, decorative, or ennobling.

When we speak of "forty head of cattle" or ask someone to "lend a hand" with a job, we are using **synecdoche,** a figure which substitutes the part for the whole. When we speak of a statement coming "from the White House," or a man much interested in "the turf," we are using **metonymy,** or the substitution of one term for another with which it is closely associated. **Antithesis** is a device for placing opposing ideas in grammatical parallel, as, for example, in the following passage from Pope's *Rape of the Lock* (5.25–30), where there are more examples of antithesis than there are lines:

> But since, alas! frail beauty must decay,
> Curled or uncurled, since locks will turn to gray;
> Since painted, or not painted, all shall fade,
> And she who scorns a man must die a maid;
> What then remains but well our power to use,
> And keep good humor still whate'er we lose?

Irony is a verbal device which implies an attitude quite different from (and often opposite to) that which is literally expressed. When Eliot writes, in *Whispers of Immortality*, that "Grishkin is nice," the adjective is carefully chosen to let an ironic grimace of distaste appear. And when Donne "proves," in *The Canonization*, that he and his mistress are going to found a new religion of love, he seems to be inviting us to take a subtly ironic attitude toward religion as well as love.

Because it is easy to see through, **hyperbole**, or willful exaggeration, is a favorite device of irony—which is not to say that it may not be "serious" as well. When she hears that a young man is "dying for love" of her, a sensible girl does not accept this statement literally, but it may convey a serious meaning to her nonetheless. The **pun**, or play on words (known to the learned, sometimes, as **paronomasia**), may also be serious or comic in intent; witness, for example, the famous series of puns in Donne's *Hymn to God the Father*. **Oxymoron** is a figure of flat contradiction—for instance, Milton's famous description of hell as containing "darkness visible" (*Paradise Lost* 1.63). A **paradox** is a statement which seems absurd but turns out to have rational meaning after all, usually in some unexpected sense; Donne speaks of fear being great courage and high valor (*Satire* 3, line 16), and turns out to mean that fear of God is greater courage than any earthly bravery. A **conceit** is a far-fetched and ingenious comparison. Writing in the fourteenth century, the Italian poet Francis Petrarch popularized a great number of conceits handy for use in love poetry, and readily adapted by his English imitators. Wyatt, for example, is using **Petrarchan conceits** when he compares love to a warrior, or the lover's state to that of a storm-tossed ship; and a hundred other sonneteers developed the themes of the lady's stony heart, incendiary glances, and so forth. On the other hand, the **metaphysical conceit** was a more intellectualized, many-leveled comparison, giving a strong sense of the poet's ingenuity in overcoming obstacles—for instance, Donne's comparison of separated lovers to the legs of a compass (*A Valediction: Forbidding Mourning*) or Herbert's comparison of devotion to a pulley, in the poem of that name.

Images are often described as "mental pictures"; it is more accurate to say that they are verbal representations of something capable of being visualized; some readers form such mental pictures, and respond to them, more than others. Images not only convey what things look like, but direct us, by their pattern of associated and involved feelings, in our reactions to what is being represented. Indeed, there may be such a weight of meaning or feeling behind the image that the verbal picture itself becomes transparent and its "meaning" becomes primary. Abstract ideas can get attached to specific images—water, snake, bird, sun, worm, lion, whatever—in a multitude of ways, of which the reader need sometimes only be reminded. Of course the poet can also be arbitrary about it, letting his reader know simply that Redcrosse "stands for" Holiness and Archimago "stands for" Hypocrisy. If that's as far as it goes, we have a primitive variety of **allegory**. But the relation between the tenor of the image (its abstract meaning) and the vehicle (the concrete picture) can be much more indefinite and insubstantial. If the poet mentions a peacock, he may or may not intend his reader to think of immortality, because the unfolding of the peacock's tail and the opening of its "eyes" has traditionally suggested the rebirth of the soul after death. If that is the way the image works, then it is a **symbol**. Or again, if the poet mentions a fish, he may well intend the reader to think of Christ. This isn't because of any similarity between the fish and Christ; the identification depends on a mildly esoteric bit of information, that the Greek word for fish, *ichthys*, forms an anagram of the Greek words for "Jesus Christ, Son of God, Savior." When the connection between tenor and vehicle is arbitrary, or involves the elements of a puzzle, the image may be referred to as an **emblem**. In the sixteenth and seventeenth centuries, emblems often took the form of puzzling little drawings, the meaning of which was explained in appended verses: for an example see the emblem prefixed to Crashaw's poem *To the Countess of Denbigh* (1.1361).

Personification is the attribution of human qualities to an inanimate object (for example, the Sea) or an abstract concept (Freedom); a special variety of it is called (in a term of John Ruskin's invention) the **pathetic fallacy.** When we speak of leaves "dancing" or a lake "smiling," we attribute human traits to nonhuman objects. Ruskin thought this was false and therefore "morbid"; modern criticism tends to view the practice as artistically and morally neutral. A more formal and abstract variety of personification is **allegory,** in which a narrative (such as *Pilgrim's Progress*) is constructed by representing general concepts (Faithfulness, Sin, Despair) as persons. A **fable** (like *The Nun's Priest's Tale*) represents beasts behaving like humans; a **parable** is a brief story, or simply an observation, with strong moral application; and an **exemplum** is a story told to illustrate a point in a sermon. A special series of devices, nearly obsolete today, used to be available to poets who could count on readers trained in the classics. These were the devices of **classical epithet** and **allusion.** In their simplest form, the classic myths used to provide a repertoire of agreeable stage properties, and a convenient shorthand for expressing emotional attitudes. Picturesque creatures like centaurs, satyrs, and sphinxes, heroes and heroines like Hector and Helen, and the whole pantheon of Olympic deities could be used to make ready reference to a great many aspects of human nature. One does not have to explain the problems of a man who is "cleaning the Augean stables"; if he is afflicted with an "Achilles' heel," or is assailing "Hydra-headed difficulties," his state is clear. These epithets, or descriptive phrases, making reference to mythological stories, suggest in a phrase situations that would normally require cumbersome explanations. Conceivably other mythologies might have served the same end in analogous ways. But because they could be taken for granted as the common possession of all educated readers, the classic myths entered into English literature as early as Chaucer, and are only now passing away as a viable system of allusions. In poets like Spenser and Milton, classical allusion becomes a kind of enormously learned game, in which the poet seeks to make his points as indirectly as possible. For instance, Spenser writes in the *Epithalamion*, lines 328–29:

> Lyke as when Jove with fayre Alcmena lay,
> When he begot the great Tirynthian groome.

The mere mention of Alcmena in the first line suggests, to the knowing reader, Hercules; Spenser's problem in the second line is to find a way of referring to him which is neither redundant nor heavy-handed. "Tirynthian" reminds us of his long connection with the city of Tiryns, stretching our minds (as it were) across his whole career; and "groome" compresses references to a man-child, a servant, and a bridegroom, all of which apply to different aspects of Hercules' history. Thus, far from simply avoiding redundancy, Spenser has enriched the whole texture of his verse, thought, and feeling by his gift for precise classical epithet.

Within the broad periods it is customary to group in **schools** writers who show common stylistic traits or thematic concerns. Whether they considered themselves a group doesn't much matter. None of the **Romantic poets** knew they were being romantic, although Hazlitt, Shelley, and other writers of the time recognized shared features that they called "the spirit of the age." The followers of Spenser are known as **Spenserians**; they knew they liked Spenser, but didn't realize that made them a group. **Cavalier** poets are set decisively apart from **Metaphysical** poets, though pretty surely none of the two-dozen-odd men involved knew that was what they were. And so with the **Gothic novelists**, and the so-called **Graveyard School** of the eighteenth century, so with the modern surrealists. These schools are generally grouped, defined, and named by scholars and critics after the event. Use of a common form or subject matter constitutes a more superficial similarity than use of a common style, common techniques, or common philosophical backgrounds. But literary history, being nothing if not pragmatic, makes use of all sorts of common denominators.

Intellectual affinities have led some writers to be classified under the names of the philosophical schools of Greece and Rome. These are chiefly the **Epicureans**, who specify that the aim of life and the source of value is pleasure; the **Stoics**, who emphasize stern virtue and the dignified endurance of what cannot be avoided; and the **Skeptics**, who doubt that anything can be known for sure. These categories are useful as capsule descriptions, but they aren't very tidy, as they overlap one another and cut across other categories. Dryden is an author strongly tinged with **skepticism**, but many of his poems suggest an unabashed **epicureanism**. *The Vanity of Human Wishes*, by Samuel Johnson, is the classic poem in English of **stoic** philosophy, but it also expresses a particularly strong coloring of **Christian humanism.**

Plato and **Aristotle**, as they summarized contrasting attitudes toward existence, are often used to define the outlook of writers. Both were prolific writers of enormous range and complexity, but in literary contexts their names most often define attitudes toward reality. Aristotle tended to find reality, not exclusively but primarily, in concrete and particular substances, which he brilliantly categorized and generalized. Plato tended to place reality in abstract ideal forms, of which the concrete things we experience in daily life are but partial and shadowy manifestations. During the Middle Ages, many Dominican friars, of whom St. Thomas Aquinas is best known, tended to be **Aristotelian** in their assumptions and in the structure of their logic; St. Bonaventura, among the Franciscans, was more strongly tinged with a **Platonism** that he derived largely from Saint Augustine. During the Renaissance Spenser, and during the Romantic period Shelley, were **Platonists** or **Neo-Platonists**. (A Neo-Platonist is a Platonist diluted with other worldviews—perhaps Pythagorean mysticism, perhaps Christian theology, perhaps Aristotelian thought itself. In a narrower sense, the term is applied to philosophers writing in the tradition of Plotinus [3rd century A.D.], who held that all things in the world, spiritual and material, "emanate," or flow out, from the "Absolute," or the "One"—the single source of all truth, goodness, and beauty.) **Aristotelianism**, as it is more commonsensical, had faded by Spenser's time to the common teaching of the schools, and by Shelley's time to the practical, pragmatic materialism of everyday life.

TERMS OF ART

The following section groups together various sets of frequently used and closely related literary terms in an effort to discriminate and define them.

Allegory, Symbol, Emblem, Type. Allegory is an extended metaphorical narrative in which a figure (say, Spenser's Redcrosse Knight) stands for a specific quality (Holiness). A **symbol** may have several different meanings, which typically grow out of its relation to other symbols, as in the twenty-odd poems of Yeats which allude to the rose. An **emblem,** in the sixteenth and seventeenth centuries, was an enigmatic picture with a motto and an explanatory verse attached. In modern usage, an emblem is a visible object representing an abstract quality, as a dove is the emblem of peace. A **type** is a historical figure who prefigures another and later figure as (in some Christian interpretations) Moses in liberating the children of Israel was thought to prefigure Christ in freeing men from Satan.

Baroque and **Mannerist** are terms imported into literary study from the history of art, and applied by analogy. Michelangelo is a **baroque** artist; he holds great masses in powerful dynamic tension, his style is heavily ornamented and restless. In these respects he is sometimes compared to Milton. El Greco is a **mannerist**, whose gaunt and distorted figures often seem to be laboring under great spiritual stress, whose light seems to be focused in spots against a dark background. He has been compared to Donne. Analogies of this sort are occasionally suggestive, but they must be carefully handled to avoid degenerating into parallels which are forced and nominal rather than substantial.

Bathos. See **Pathos, Bathos, and the Sublime.**

Burlesque and **Mock Heroic** differ in that the former makes its subject mean and absurd by directly cutting it down, the latter makes its subject ludicrous by inflating it. In Pope's mock-heroic *Dunciad*, the figure of Dulness (Colley Cibber) is given inappropriately heroic dimensions; in Butler's burlesque *Hudibras*, the knightly hero is characterized by low and vulgar attributes, and persistently engages in inappropriately low behavior. Burlesque contributed to the development of the English novel; and during the nineteenth century, when formal drama tended to be stagy and melodramatic, a vigorous burlesque stage flourished in England, making fun of the classics. See **Imitation and Parody.**

Classic and **Neo-Classic.** See **Gothic, Classic, Neo-Classic.**

Convention and **Tradition. Conventions** are agreed-upon artistic procedures peculiar to an art form. None of Shakespeare's contemporaries spoke blank verse in everyday life, but characters in his plays do, and the audience accepts it—as the audience at an opera accepts that characters will sing arias to express their feelings, something that few of us do in everyday life. A **tradition** is a particular way of viewing or representing things; it generally includes a great many conventions. Often thought of as a dead weight to be overcome by "originality," tradition (since an important essay by T. S. Eliot) is now more often recognized as an active energy, working to enrich an art form that makes knowing use of it by playing variations on it.

Didactic poetry teaches a lesson, generally practical. The eighteenth century, for example, produced didactic poetry on the wool trade, field sports, health practices, and the sexuality of plants.

Dramatic irony and **Dramatic monologue** are quite different devices. In dramatic irony a stage character says something which has one meaning for him and for the onstage person he is addressing, but quite another for the audience. The **dramatic monologue** is a poetic form associated with Robert Browning and discussed in the introduction to that poet's work (2.1229); it presents a character as revealed unintentionally by his own words.

Eclogue. See **Pastorals.**

Emblem. See **Allegory, Symbol, Emblem, Type.**

Eulogy and **Elegy.** The **eulogy** is a work of praise, in prose or poetry, for a person either very distinguished or recently dead; an **elegy** is a poem of lamentation for the dead. In Greek and Latin poetry, elegies were poems written in alternating pentameters and hexameters, called elegiac meter. They could deal with a broad variety of topics, and English elegies also tended to be discursive poems on meditative themes. Donne, following his Roman predecessors, wrote some elegies that are jocose, even bawdy.

Euphemism and **Euphuism. Euphemism,** or "fine speech" is a verbal device for avoiding an unpleasant concept or expression, as when, instead of saying a person "died," we say he "passed away." Euphues was the hero of a prose romance (published 1579–80) by John Lyly; his adventures are recounted in a mannered style full of puns, alliteration, and antithetical "points." Under the name of **Euphuism** this courtly style enjoyed a brief vogue.

Fancy and **Imagination.** The distinction between these two mental powers greatly exercised the early Romantic poets. **Fancy** (a word directly derived by contraction from "fantasy") was defined by Coleridge as essentially the power of combining several known properties into new combinations; **imagination,** on the other hand, was the faculty of using those known properties to create a whole that is entirely new.

Folios, Quartos, etc. are terms used to define the size of book pages. To make a **folio,** a sheet of paper (14″ x 20″ or larger) is folded just once (producing thereby four pages); **quartos** are folded twice (producing eight pages). Shakespeare's plays were first printed in quartos (often in several different editions) but when they were collected together, in 1623, they appeared as the First Folio.

Genre, Decorum. A **genre** is an established literary form, such as stage comedy, the picaresque novel, the epic, the sonnet. Being of a certain genre predisposes a work to represent certain characters and events and to seek certain effects. Its success in achieving these effects and avoiding incongruous ones can thus be judged; and this is one sort of **decorum** (fittingness), the decorum of genre. Satire was once considered a low, popular form, for which only low, popular speech was decorous (fitting). There are also decorums of character, of occasion, of rhetorical mode, etc.

Gothic, Classic, Neo-Classic. Gothic and **Classic** distinguish styles and tendencies in art and literature. **Gothic** implies vital, primitive, but irregular work, with the qualities of the barbarian North. **Classic** implies lucid, rational, and idealized work, as in the sunlit Southern civilizations of Greece and Rome. For Pope and his contemporaries "Gothic" was generally a word of contempt; for Ruskin, in the nineteenth century, it was a term of highest praise. "Gothic" novels, written in the period of transition between these two attitudes, and taking full advantage of dark medieval settings, were shockers and thrillers of the late eighteenth and early nineteenth centuries. **Neo-classicism** describes work which, while keeping one eye on a classical original, modifies it to comment on modern conditions: a literary example is Doctor Samuel Johnson's *Vanity of Human Wishes*, based on Juvenal's *Tenth Satire*.

Heroic poems, heroic couplets. Because they concentrate on the figure of a typical hero (Achilles, Aeneas), epic poems were frequently called "**heroic**." Trying to transfer epic grandeur to the stage, playwrights of the Restoration period generally achieved only grandiosity; but the stately couplets in which they made their characters speak became known as **heroic couplets**.

Humor. See **Wit and Humor.**

Humors and **Temperaments** are psychological terms used by Renaissance writers. The four basic humors of every constitution were the **choleric** (bile), the **sanguine** (blood), the **phlegmatic** (phlegm), and the **melancholy** (black bile). A man's **temperament** was determined by the mixture of these humors, the way in which they were "tempered." When a particular humor predominated, it pushed the character in that direction: choler = anger; sanguine = geniality; phlegm = cold torpor; and melancholy = gloomy self-absorption.

Imagination. See **Fancy** and **Imagination.**

Imitation and **Parody** are devices by which a literary work assumes an attitude toward its own predecessor. **Imitation** involves not simply copying, but transposing the different features of the earlier work into modern particulars, while retaining the same pattern and the same approximate tonal level. **Parody** generally lowers the level of its original; it is a device of ridicule, though sometimes of self-ridicule. When Joyce parodies ancient Irish legend (as in the "Cyclops" chapter of *Ulysses*), there is no separating ridicule of the past from contempt for the present. See also **Burlesque.**

Irony, Sarcasm. Irony and **sarcasm**, though both are ways of saying one thing and meaning another, go about the job differently. **Sarcasm** is broader and more deliberate in its reversal of meanings; **irony** may be, and in literature generally is, very fine. The patriarch Job is bitterly **sarcastic** when he replies to his comforters (12.2) "No doubt but ye are the people, and wisdom shall die with you." On the other hand, Jane Austen, in the first sentence of *Pride and Prejudice* overstates her case just enough to make it drily **ironic** when she writes, "It is a truth universally acknowledged, that a single man in possession of a good fortune, must be in want of a wife."

Legend. See **Myth and Legend.**

Logic. See **Rhetoric and Logic.**

Masque. For a discussion of the English **masque**, see the introduction to Jonson's *Pleasure Reconciled to Virtue* (1.1232).

Myth and **Legend** are stories that incorporate themselves into the instinctual thinking of humanity. **Myths** are narratives which purport to account, in supernatural terms, for why the world is as it is, why people act as they do. Myths often spring up to explain rituals, the original meanings of which have been forgotten; or they may be folk tales based on popular nightmares or fantasies. An ordinary or even inferior tale may take on mythic dimensions—witness Mary Wollstonecraft Shelley's *Frankenstein* or the wooden volumes of Horatio Alger, Jr. A **legend** is any old and popularly repeated story; the word usually implies, in addition, that the story is false. But a proper myth hardly pretends to be historically true—

it is a flowering of the mind into narrative. Three great bodies of mythical material are the Celtic, the Norse or Germanic, and the classical fables. A body of associated myths is **a mythology;** a student and collector of myths is **a mythographer.**

Naturalism. See **Realism and Naturalism.**

Neo-Classic. See **Gothic, Classic, Neo-Classic.**

Novel. See **Romance, Novel.**

Ode. See the discussions of English odes in the headnote to Jonson's *Ode to Cary and Morison* (1.1221), and Dryden's *Ode to the Memory of Mrs. Anne Killigrew* (1.1825).

Pastorals (from the Latin word for "shepherd," *pastor*) are poems set in idealized, often artificial, rural surroundings. They are sometimes called **eclogues.** Though low on the social scale and limited in his interests, the shepherd can be made to comment indirectly on large social issues. Virgil's shepherds regularly do so, and John Gay, by transferring his scene (in *The Beggar's Opera*) from the rural fields to Newgate prison, was able to make his whores and highwaymen reflect sardonically on the national politics of his day. Alice, the heroine of *Alice in Wonderland* has been seen, very perceptively as a pastoral figure. Clearly, the concept is very adaptable. **Pastoral elegies** (like *Lycidas* by Milton, *Adonais* by Shelley, and *Thyrsis* by Matthew Arnold) have been particulary successful, perhaps because a somber theme adds weight to a basically artificial form.

Pathos, Bathos, and the Sublime. Pathos is the feeling of sympathy—pity or sorrow particularly—aroused by a literary work; the word comes from the Greek term for "suffering." **Bathos,** a comic parallel from the Greek word for "deep," describes the anticlimax that comes when an author, striving for elevation, trips and falls on his face. The idea of loftiness as the most desirable of literary qualities goes back to the late-classical rhetorician Longinus, who wrote a treatise *On the Sublime*. An early publication by Edmund Burke distinguishes the **sublime** (with its mixture of pain and danger) from the merely beautiful.

Quarto. See **Folios, Quartos.**

Realism and **Naturalism** are both terms used to describe fiction which aims at minute fidelity to actual existence. **Realism** connotes an attempt to give the illusion of ordinary life, in which unexceptional people undergo everyday experiences. **Naturalism** is associated with the example of Émile Zola and the thesis that a novel should present a "slice of life," a cross-section of actual existence; the emphasis is usually on man's instinctual nature, especially the sexual and acquisitive instincts. This type flourished during the late nineteenth and early twentieth centuries. Harold Biffen, a character in George Gissing's novel *New Grub Street*, is devoting his life to a work of "absolute realism in the sphere of the ignobly decent"—and this can epitomize realism. A work of naturalism, on the other hand, might be said to devote itself to the ignobly indecent.

Rhetoric and Logic. During the Renaissance, **rhetoric,** which is the art of persuading an audience, assumed fresh importance by contrast with the **logic** traditionally used by scholastic philosophers. Cicero particularly exemplified the "open hand" of rhetoric as opposed to the "closed fist" of Aristotelian logic. Though mostly fought out in terms of Latin style, the controversy had its effect on an evolving ideal of English prose. Sidney's *Defense of Poesy* and Milton's *Areopagitica* are both structured along the lines of a classical oration. During the Renaissance, "figures of rhetoric," often culled from textbooks and anthologies, comprised the substance of many schoolboy themes, and then carried over into mature works of literary art, such as (most spectacularly) the euphuistic romances of John Lyly: see **Euphemism, Euphuism.**

Romance, Novel. Medieval **romances** are narratives of adventure, following a hero through the successive episodes of a quest toward his chosen or appointed goal. **Novels** are more or less realistic studies of social relationships, more tightly structured than romances, less given to the fabulous, and dealing generally with the middle strata of society. But these distinctions were far from airtight to begin with, and with the years have grown steadily vaguer. Is Kafka's *The Castle* a novel or a romance? It is always called the former, it looks much more like the latter, and it is actually more like an extended parable.

Sarcasm. See **Irony, Sarcasm.**

Satire comes from the Latin word for medley, *satura*; the impression that it has to do with the word "satyr" is a popular delusion. Under **satire** are included all the many literary ways for diminishing a subject by making it laughable or contemptible. For a discussion of the backgrounds of English satire, see the introduction to Donne's *Satire* 3 (1.1085).

Sensibility, as used in literary discussion, does not mean "sensitivity," but the entire complex of thoughts, feelings, and suppositions characteristic of an individual or an age. T. S. Eliot, borrowing the concept from Rémy de Gourmont, said the seventeenth century did not have, as people have had since, a sensibility divided between the world of rational thought and that of feeling. But this idea has not proved very applicable to studies of particular authors or periods.

Style in a minimal sense is the way anyone uses language; thus each of us possesses (for better or worse) an individual style. In the better sense of language endowed with point and force, language of special distinction which accomplishes its ends swiftly and clearly, it has been described by Swift as "proper words in proper places"—a definition on which there is no improving.

Sublime. See **Pathos, Bathos, and the Sublime.**

Symbol. See **Allegory, Symbol, Emblem, Type.**

Tradition. See **Convention and Tradition.**

Type. See **Allegory, Symbol, Emblem, Type.**

Wit and Humor. Wit is one of those words too useful ever to be exactly defined. As employed during the seventeenth and eighteenth centuries, it might mean general intelligence or the ability to say something funny, wisdom or ability, prudence, fantasy, vivacity of speech, quickness of repartee, a good command of sexual innuendo, and many other things including the current meaning of a verbal thrust or dig. **Humor** is a gentler, less intellectual quality; it is tinged with the feeling of "good humor," which is geniality.

Index